Choice's

Outstanding Academic Books
1992-1997

Reviews of Scholarly Titles That Every Library Should Own

Other titles in *Choice*'s bibliographic series

Environmental Studies Reviews

Choice *Reviews in Women's Studies, 1990-96*

Choice's

Outstanding Academic Books
1992-1997

Reviews of Scholarly Titles That Every Library Should Own

edited by

Rebecca Ann Bartlett
Choice Magazine

Association of College & Research Libraries
A division of the American Library Association
Chicago 1998

Choice Editorial Staff

Editor & Publisher
Irving Rockwood

Managing Editor
Francine Graf

Subject Editors
Robert Balay, *Reference*
Rebecca Ann Bartlett, *Humanities*
Susanne Bjørner, *Special Projects*
Judith A. Douville, *Science*
Helen MacLam, *Social Sciences*
Kenneth McLintock, *Humanities*

Copy Editor
David Durgin

Production Manager
Lisa M. Gross

Production Assistant
Barbara May

Promotion Coordinator
Vee Carrington

The paper used in this publication meets the minimum requirements of American National Standard for Information Sciences–Permanence of Paper for Printed Library Materials, ANSI Z39.48-1992. ∞

Library of Congress Cataloging-in-Publication Data
Choice's outstanding academic books, 1992–1997 : reviews of scholarly
    titles that every library should own / edited by Rebecca Ann
    Bartlett.
        p.   cm.
    Includes index.
    ISBN 0-8389-7929-7 (alk. paper)
    1. Academic libraries--United States--Book lists. 2. Research
libraries--United States--Book lists.   I. Bartlett, Rebecca Ann.
II. Choice (Chicago, Ill.)
Z1035.C55   1998
028.1'2--dc21   98-19856

Printed in the United States of America.

02 01 00 99 98   5 4 3 2 1

About

Choice: Current Reviews for Academic Libraries

C*hoice* is a publication of the ASSOCIATION OF COLLEGE & RESEARCH LIBRARIES, a division of the AMERICAN LIBRARY ASSOCIATION. Directed toward academic librarians and faculty, *Choice* publishes reviews of significant current titles—print and electronic—in more than 50 subdisciplines spanning the humanities, science and technology, and the social and behavioral sciences.

Focusing on materials suitable for undergraduate collections, *Choice* has reviewed more than 225,000 titles since it's founding in 1964 and has become the most widely used review source for selection in academic libraries.

Choice subject editors examine more than 22,000 scholarly and trade books annually; they assign for review materials that meet numerous criteria, which are fully articulated in "Choice's Selection Policy," published in the September 1997 issue of the magazine. *Choice* reviewers are teaching faculty from institutions across the United States and Canada, individuals selected for their subject expertise, their active involvement with undergraduate students and curricula, their diverse viewpoints and backgrounds, and their sensitivity to scholarly trends. Academic librarians, many of them subject specialists with advanced degrees, evaluate reference resources.

A review in *Choice* carries significant weight in the academic community, in part because of *Choice*'s commitment to excellent scholarship and in part because of the timeliness of the reviews, which are usually the first postpublication peer evaluation of scholarly titles.

Table of Contents

SCIENCE & TECHNOLOGY
239

SOCIAL & BEHAVIORAL SCIENCES
335

INDEXES
565

OABs: The Best of the Best in Published Scholarship

Choice's *Outstanding Academic Books 1992-1997* brings together reviews of materials selected by *Choice* editors as the best scholarship from the years 1992 to 1997. First awarded in April 1965 for titles in volume 1 of *Choice*, the OAB designation was originally conceived as a checklist of necessary acquisitions for collection development librarians—books "no college library should overlook." That first year, *Choice* honored 297 books. Over the years, inclusion in the OAB list has come to be one of the most sought-after distinctions in scholarly publishing; librarians anxiously await the annual January listing, which now numbers in the 600s and includeselectronic resources.

Choice's editors do not undertake the difficult task of identifying OAB finalists lightly. Editors base their initial selection on their knowledge of the field, the reviewer's evaluation of the work, and the reviewer's record. In addition, they apply several criteria:

- Overall excellence in presentation and scholarship
- Importance relative to other literature in the field
- Distinction as a first treatment of a given subject
- Originality or uniqueness of treatment
- Value to undergraduate students
- Importance in building undergraduate library collections

The editors balance these elements, always keeping in mind the undergraduate user.

Unlike the annual OAB feature (which includes only bibliographic citations and identifies the *Choice* issue in which the review appeared), this cumulation provides the entire review to assist users wishing detailed evaluations. Readers will quickly discover that not every OAB is flawless. Indeed, some of the most valuable titles merit inclusion solely for their unique treatment of new areas of scholarship, shortcomings notwithstanding.

The amount of material in this cumulation—3,112 reviews in all—created corresponding organizational headaches, as we strove for consistency throughout the sections. The format mirrors that of *Choice* itself, with subsections added as necessary to make the groupings of reviews more manageable. Early on we abandoned our initial notion that no section should include more than a set number of reviews, a restraint that proved no more logical than a numerical limit on a library's volumes on, say, Horace's *Odes*. Instead, we permitted the sections to run as long as necessary, with paramount consideration going to a logical arrangement that serves the purposes of collection development librarians. Works that are general, comparative, or interdisciplinary appear under the main heading in each discipline (e.g., Social and Behavioral Sciences, Language and Literature); titles that span chronological divisions are for the most part placed in the period in which they flourished. Efforts to divide all disciplines into parallel subsections were likewise abandoned in favor of discipline-specific divisions (see, e.g., under Philosophy). In general, reviews slipped in comfortably among their companions, only a few needing to be wrestled into place. Failing any other applicable rationale, titles have been placed according to Library of Congress classification number. To facilitate access to this material, we have included name and title indexes, and an extensive topical index, brought up to date for this volume. Reviews are numbered consecutively for easy access through the indexes. However, we have made no attempt to determine the in-print status of titles.

But the difficulties of arrangement fade in comparison to the pleasure of editing a volume such as this, because every review to be categorized represented a book or resource of singular scholarship—whether nestled or wrestled into the schema. Contained between the covers of this volume is a wealth of published riches, and rereading the evaluations of the past five years causes us to muse on the dire predictions of the death of print so prevalent as the century nears its end. Though we at *Choice* are not such troglodytes as to shy away from the electronic threshold at our feet—indeed, in 1997 for the first time we began reviewing Websites—we cannot but remark on the fact that many fine print publications continue to pour from scholarly and trade presses.

An unscientific analysis of the 611 imprints represented in this volume reveals that almost a quarter are university presses (accounting for just over half the titles), three percent are trade (six percent of titles), and the rest are academic and association publishers. These figures have remained remarkably consistent over the five-year span of these reviews—e.g., university presses produced 54 percent of OABs in 1993, 55 percent in 1997; trade press contributions hover in the four to seven percent. All these publishers merit recognition for their vital contribution to the scholarly endeavor. Their support for and nurturing of serious scholarship on so many diverse topics enrich the resources available to the library community and its users—both students and faculty.

In publishing this cumulation of Outstanding Academic Books, *Choice* acknowledges and honors in particular the authors and editors of these works. Scholarly publications—be they print, electronic, or virtual—demand an enormous commitment of time and energy, thousands of hours devoted to research, thinking, and writing. *Choice* applauds the accomplishment of these individuals.

REBECCA ANN BARTLETT
Humanities Editor
Choice

REFERENCE

■ General

OAB-0001   Z711   94-10861 CIP
The American Library Association guide to information access: a complete research handbook and directory, ed. by Sandy Whiteley. Random House, 1994. 533p index ISBN 0-679-43060-1, $35.00; ISBN 0-679-75075-4 pbk, $19.00

Whiteley (ed. of *Reference Books Bulletin*) has compiled varied information into a single reference volume aimed at the general reader and undergraduate researcher. She involved an impressive group of editorial advisors (Betsy Baker and James Rettig, to name two) and contributors from academic, public, and specialized information environments. Whiteley refers to this research handbook as a "directory" of subject-related resources. Arranged in 36 topical chapters, the resources cover "popular research areas" ranging from agriculture to parenting to writing. Each chapter presents relevant citation information and brief annotations in the following format: guides to the literature, electronic sources (if available), periodicals, government publications and agencies, nonprofit associations, special collections, LC subject headings, and research centers. The sources cited are current and varied in format. Also included are sources widely regarded as standard reference tools. Preceding the topical chapters are 17 chapters that introduce high school, undergraduate, and independent researchers to the research process in libraries and the electronic transformation of information tools. The inconsistencies are few and minor (e.g., the chapter on agriculture is the only chapter with margin notes of directory information set in gray boxes). Recommended as a tool for public, secondary school, and undergraduate libraries.—*K. Sendi, University of Toledo*

OAB-0002   G1021   92-14534 CIP
Atlas of the world. Oxford, 1992. 288p index ISBN 0-19-520955-9, $65.00

Oxford's new atlas presents new techniques, new information, and new maps of the explosive changes in Eastern Europe. It is divided into six sections: five pages on world statistics; a 46-page Introduction to World Geography; 66 city maps on 32 plates; a 15-page index to the city maps; 94 maps on 160 pages; and a 75,000-entry index. The index maps on the front endpapers are reasonably clear except for some overlap in Europe. Several features in this atlas are noteworthy. The list of maps includes a diagram of each area covered as well as its scale, the lengthy introduction includes 20 thematic maps, and the city maps, all at the same scale (1:200,000), are detailed enough to be useful. Not surprisingly, this atlas has a slightly European bias; more than a quarter of the maps depict all or a part of that continent. The cartography has been prepared by the noted European firm George Philip Ltd., and employs color to indicate elevation rather than shaded relief. A color bar on each map indicates height in both feet and meters. The resultant maps are visually attractive, but the use of color for relief prevents its use to indicate cultural features, which are absent from these maps. There are still some awkward country and state divisions, there has been no attempt to keep all maps viewable from the same direction. (This atlas does not have the same page size as *National Geographic Atlas of the World*, 6th ed., 1992, which is not only 4" taller, but bleeds its maps to the edge of the page and thus has an effective map height of 18+" vs. 12+" for Oxford.) The maps contain fewer place names than other atlases and thus have a less crowded look but afford identification of fewer places. The thin, faint lines used to mark national/state borders make these divisions hard to discern. Still, the Oxford atlas is excellent, if moderately expensive, meriting acquisition by large public and college/university libraries.—*B. McCorkle, Yale University*

OAB-0003   Orig
Ayto, John. **The Oxford dictionary of modern slang,** by John Ayto and John Simpson. Oxford, 1992. 299p ISBN 0-19-866181-9, $25.00

Defining more than 5,000 slang terms currently or recently in use in the English-speaking world, this dictionary (*ODMS*) is based on the *Oxford English Dictionary* (*OED*) (2nd ed., 1989), although the editors state that *ODMS* contains about 500 terms not defined in *OED*. They based their selection of terms on written use, hence most definitions are accompanied by illustrative quotations drawn from published sources. Despite its exclusion of slang terms that have not appeared in print, *ODMS* is reasonably up to date, including such terms as "tubular" (1982), "crack" (1986), and "outing" (1990). Entries give the date of earliest written use and include indicators that tell where or among what group a slang term originated or is used. Surprisingly, *ODMS* is divided evenly between US and UK-Commonwealth slang, making it a better-balanced source than the mostly British *Dictionary of Contemporary Slang* by Tony Thorne, published in UK as *Bloomsbury Dictionary of Contemporary Slang* (CH, Sep'92). Well bound and clearly printed; recommended for all reference collections.—*D. A. Barclay, New Mexico State University*

OAB-0004   [CD-ROM]
Black studies on disc. G.K. Hall, 1995. ISBN 0-8161-1653-9 $995.00. 1 disc; user manual. 1989-93. Updates: annual. System requirements: IBM-PC; 512K RAM; Microsoft Extensions 2.0 or higher.

Black Studies on Disc (BSD) is a bibliographic database of books, periodical articles, and other published materials on the peoples of Africa and the African diasporan populations of the Americas and other areas of the world. The contents are largely derived from the holdings of the Schomburg Center for Research in Black Culture, a division of the Research Libraries of the New York Public Library. There are about 120,000 records in the database, primarily materials from the 20th century, but including items from as far back as the 17th century. The Schomburg Center's collections are strongest for studies of the African American experiences of the post-Civil War period, yet they do endeavor to cover any aspect of African and diasporan history and culture.

The program can be utilized directly from the CD-ROM or installed on a hard disk. Running BSD from the disc is simplicity itself; one just inserts the disc and types RUN at the appropriate drive prompt. Thus, the program can be operated from virtually any PC-compatible computer with a CD-ROM drive. Potential users should note that this is a DOS-based, not Windows-based, program. However, if the disc will be used as part of a menu system or mounted on a network, then a full installation is necessary. The installation process is quite straightforward and takes only a few moments to complete. No installation problems were encountered after testing on three different machines. No matter which of the above options for operating the disc is utilized, the program runs the same. There are no additional charges for using this product on a LAN in one building.

There are two kinds of searching mechanisms available for locating desired information. The default mechanism is keyword searching, which includes some Boolean limiting capabilities (AND, OR, NOT), wildcard indicators for searching word variants, and the ability to modify past searches. Response time for keyword searches is quick, and the user is generally rewarded with an extensive list of hits depending on the input keywords. Search results can be tagged, sorted in a number of ways, or printed and/or saved. Alternatively, the user may search by browsing various indexes. Results can be viewed in one of three display formats. The brief display, the default, provides basic bibliographic information (author, title, source, date, etc.), while the full display shows all data fields. A third option allows users to select only certain fields for a custom display. BSD provides an invaluable reference resource for any library. With an easy-to-use searching mechanism and several options for modifying and outputting retrieved information, users from high school students through doctoral researchers can rely on this product for much of their research needs. Undergraduate through professional.—*E. C. Burt, Art Institute of Seattle*

OAB-0005   Can. CIP

Bond, Mary E. **Canadian reference sources: an annotated bibliography: general reference works, history, humanities,** comp. by Mary E. Bond and Martine M. Caron; ed. by Mary E. Bond. UBC Press/National Library of Canada, 1996. (Dist. by UBC Press, University of British Columbia, 6344 Memorial Rd., Vancouver, BC V6T 1Z2, Canada) 1,076p indexes English and French.   ISBN 0-7748-0565-X, $225.00

One of the most important Canadian reference works ever published, this splendid retrospective bibliography should not be confused with *Guide to Reference Materials for Canadian Libraries*, ed. by Kirsti Nilsen (8th ed., 1992), which contains many non-Canadian publications and serves largely as a student checklist of basic reference titles. In updating Dorothy Ryder's *Canadian Reference Sources: A Selective Guide* (CH, Sep'75; 2nd ed., 1981), Bond and Caron (National Library of Canada) have annotated more than 4,000 reference works about Canada. They include not only general reference sources (as well as some monographs) but also titles in history and the humanities up to July 1995; unfortunately, neither the social sciences nor science and technology are covered. Each entry furnishes a full bibliographical citation for the title's latest edition, ISBN or ISSN, a descriptive rather than critical annotation in English and French (including details on various editions and formats), and Dewey Decimal and Library of Congress classification numbers. Entries are arranged by subject, genre, document type, and geographical jurisdiction. Multidisciplinary works appear in several locations, and bilingual publications have two entries "in order to provide access and bibliographical description in both of Canada's official languages." Bilingual name, title, and subject indexes. Essential for all Canadiana, research, and large public collections.—*J. D. Blackwell, Algoma University College*

OAB-0006   [CD-ROM]

Britannica CD 2.0. Encyclopedia Britannica, 1995. $299.00. 1 disc; user manual; installation videotape. System requirements: IBM-PC, 386 or higher; 4MB RAM; 10MB free hard drive space; Windows 3.1; mouse. Macintosh, IIci or better; 8MB RAM; 15MB free hard drive space; mouse.

Britannica CD 2.0 is a marvelous package. Based in hypertext technology (where keywords are highlighted and act as links to other blocks of text on the CD), it merges traditional uses—e.g., topical overviews and research starting points—with the speed and ease of use of the personal computer. (This new package replaces the text-only Britannica CD 1.0, published in 1994.) Installation is very easy; the clear instructions make the accompanying installation videotape (VHS format) superfluous. The Netscape interface makes searching the database very intuitive.

The design is based on the Britannica Online information service on the World Wide Web; both that service and this CD version contain the complete printed version of the *Encyclopaedia Britannica*, with its more than 65,000 subjects, more than 400,000 citations cross-referenced and linked, more than a thousand additional articles over what is in the print version, and *Merriam-Webster's Collegiate Dictionary* (10th ed.). Illustrations include 2,000-plus maps, flags, photographs, and line illustrations. Even fairly obscure topics (e.g., the 15th-century Chinese explorer Cheng Ho) are discussed.

Searching is easy; one types in an ordinary question such as "Who was the first woman in space?" The result of this search is a list of articles, ranked according to their relevance to the query, with articles most likely to have the answer placed at the head of the list. The hypertext feature makes possible the linking of various subjects, often needing several passes in a conventional printed index. In this query, the program links the concepts "space" and "women," much more quickly than manual searching would accomplish. A question on "What causes earthquakes?" provides an illustrated explanation of seismic tremors, as well as articles on earthquake prediction, seismological differences between earthquakes and underground nuclear explosions, and phenomena related to earthquakes, such as aftershocks, foreshocks, and swarms. A mouse click will take the searcher from one article and concept to another related article and concept.

The product requires a hardware key (a physical piece of apparatus), inserted in the serial port of the computer, that limits its use to a single computer (it cannot be networked). Despite this possible limitation, Britannica CD sets a very high standard for comprehensive coverage and ease of use for online encyclopedias. General; undergraduates.—*E. J. Delaney, University of Colorado at Colorado Springs*

OAB-0007   E154   95-39038 CIP

Buttlar, Lois J. **Guide to information resources in ethnic museum, library, and archival collections in the United States,** comp. by Lois J. Buttlar and Lubomyr R. Wynar. Greenwood, 1996. 369p indexes afp (Bibliographies and indexes in ethnic studies, 7) ISBN 0-313-29846-7, $75.00

Increased recognition of cultural diversity in the US has piqued research interest. With the exception of *Ethnic Information Sources of the United States* (CH, Jan'77; 2nd ed., 1983), few reference guides have indexed ethnic resources at museums, libraries, archives, and educational institutions. Buttlar and Wynar intended to provide researchers a timely, comprehensive listing of ethnic resources in one volume. In 1993-95, the authors compiled information from a national survey of 2,340 ethnic organizations. Data from the survey was collated with pertinent material from *Official Museum Directory, Directory of Special Libraries and Information Centers*, Lee Ash's *Subject Collections*, and *Encyclopedia of Associations*. More than 70 ethnic groups are represented in the text; locations with multiethnic collections are included. Institutions are arranged alphabetically under ethnic group. Each entry includes type of institution, availability to the public, admission, publications, collections, and a brief comment about the organization. The table of contents serves as subject index, but there is also a geographical and institutional index. Researchers and general readers alike will find this guide invaluable for locating information on ethnic America.—*M. A. Lutes, University of Notre Dame*

OAB-0008   [CD-ROM]

Current biography, 1940-1996. H.W. Wilson, 1997. ISBN 0-8242-0910-9 1 to 4 users: $499.00 first year, annual renewals $149.00; networking rates available. 1 disc; user manual. Updates: annual. System requirements: IBM-PC, MS-DOS; Macintosh.

This CD-ROM reproduces the full text of the more than 15,000 biographies and obituaries that have appeared in all the *Current Biography Annuals* (1940-). The CD does not include the 1997 monthly issues or photographs, but does note printed versions that include photographs. The major advantage of the CD over the print, however, is the addition of a listing of recent biographical citations taken from Wilson's *Biography Index* (1946-). The CD runs on the WilsonDisc platform and comes complete with WilsonDisc 3.4 for DOS and Macintosh. The DOS version runs well in both Windows 3.x and 95 environments. Installation is straightforward; the disc includes a complete step-by-step guide. Some advanced setup options allow system administrators to change options for display and print, among others. Readers can search, with little help, the entire database using three basic modes. The first allows the user to search by name (e.g., "Adams, Douglas") or profession (e.g., "writer"). The second searches the database by key word in several predefined fields, including name, profession, place of origin, date of birth, or keyword. The third, an optional command search, permits advanced users to search using Boolean operators, basic commands such as "near" (WilsonDisc's "neighbor") or "expand," and data element qualifiers. A simple search for "Winston Churchill," for example, returns four entries: the yearbook profiles from 1940, 1942, and 1953, and the obituary from 1965. The profiles are exact reproductions of the respective yearbook texts (except where the date of death has been added), including the bibliography. The citations from *Biography Index*, however, are from the 1990s, and in Churchill's case ignore standard biographies that appeared in the 1960s and 1980s. Overall a wonderful resource for the researcher, compiling as it does the entire set on one easy-to-use CD-ROM. The price justifies the purchase, although libraries that wish to remain up-to-date will continue to subscribe to the monthly printed issues. All levels.—*J. J. Doherty, Montana State University—Bozeman*

OAB-0009   QC82   93-47005 CIP
Darton, Mike. **The Macmillan dictionary of measurement,** by Mike Darton and John Clark. Macmillan, 1994. 538p index ISBN 0-02-525750-1, $27.50

What are the dimensions of a soccer field? This new dictionary gives not only the overall dimensions but those of each part of the field. No more comprehensive dictionary on measurement is available. Its closest equivalent is H.G. Jerrarde and D.B. McNeill's *Dictionary of Scientific Units* (6th edition, 1992). The present volume successfully covers the broad spectrum of terms related to measurement and all the typical units of measurement. Examples of the breadth of this dictionary include military ranks, geological periods, historical epochs, weights and measurements of fencing weapons, and musical pitch. The definitions are concise and accurate; illustrations are included when helpful. An index of selected themes categorizes the entries under general topics. This dictionary's one fault is its lack of bibliographical references; but it is still well worth the modest price and should be purchased by all libraries.—*J. O. Christensen, Brigham Young University*

OAB-0010   E76   96-21411 CIP
Encyclopedia of North American Indians, ed. by Frederick E. Hoxie. Houghton Mifflin, 1996. 756p indexes ISBN 0-395-66921-9, $45.00

In an excellent and inexpensive addition to the burgeoning reference literature on native North America, Hoxie (*A Final Promise: The Campaign to Assimilate the Indians, 1880-1920*, CH, Sep'84) has assembled nearly 450 articles to provide a representative, if not comprehensive, coverage of people, tribes, and topics. Most entries have been written and are signed by prominent scholars in history, anthropology, Native American studies, or other fields, the remainder by graduate students. Most are well written and concise, ranging in length from two paragraphs ("cradleboards") to six pages ("contemporary arts"). Hoxie made a deliberate attempt to include many Native American authors; many entries on particular tribes, for example, were written by tribal members. Coverage is balanced from a variety of perspectives. A hundred entries each treat tribes or regions, prominent people, and broad topics; the remaining articles concern terms or events. Both events and the bibliographies that conclude articles are up-to-date. Topics include a mix of archaeological, historical, and contemporary issues; Canada is well represented. Separate entries concerning origins from Native American and anthropological perspectives are

included. Interspersed through the text are well-produced black-and-white photos and maps, and a decent index ties the volume together. The only minor distraction is the placement of page numbers near the gutter. A bargain, highly recommended for all libraries.—*J. C. Wanser, Hiram College*

OAB-0011   DS43   96-11800 CIP
Encyclopedia of the modern Middle East, ed. by Reeva S. Simon, Philip Mattar, and Richard W. Bulliet. Macmillan Reference USA/Simon & Schuster and Prentice Hall International, 1996. 4v. 2,182p bibl index afp ISBN 0-02-896011-4, $350.00

The editors provide a thorough compilation of biographies; descriptions of committees, groups, organizations, and other corporate bodies; descriptions of Middle Eastern countries; and short topical entries relating to the study of the modern culture, geography, politics, wars and treaties, economics, arts, and literature of the region spanning North Africa and western Asia from Morocco to Afghanistan. There are entries on all the region's major religious and ethnic groups. Over 4,000 articles prepared by Middle East scholars compose this broad survey of the history and affairs of the peoples of this region. An excellent reference source, easy to use and of great value to librarians and students alike.—*P. I. Nielson, Getty Research Institute*

OAB-0012   Orig
Fowler, H.W. **The new Fowler's modern English usage,** ed. by R.W. Burchfield. 3rd ed. Oxford, 1996. 864p afp ISBN 0-19-869126-2, $25.00

Burchfield has essentially created a new reference work using the historical approach similar to that in his *A Supplement to the Oxford English Dictionary* (CH, Feb'73). He dates the entrance of new usages when possible and gives examples of changes that have taken place throughout the words' history. He expands Fowler's database of the best fiction to include the best newspapers and magazines. Unlike Fowler, he does not consult traditional grammar books. With few modifications, Burchfield has maintained Fowler's prosodic and poetic terms, but has replaced Fowler's spelling system with the International Phonetic Alphabet. Significantly, Burchfield discusses sexist language and assails words such as "man" and "he" as generic pronouns. He maintains the discussion of the difference between traditional problem words such as "affect" and "effect," but expands the discussion of words such as "disinterest" to include both "impartial" and "lack of interest." Essential for all libraries.—*M. D. Linn, University of Minnesota-Duluth*

OAB-0013   HA155   93-29316 CIP
Gale book of averages, ed. by Kathleen Droste and Jennifer Dye. Gale, 1994. 617p index afp ISBN 0-8103-9138-4, $49.95

An excellent compilation of statistical, tabular, and textual data, international in scope, culled from a wide variety of sources, including government publications, books, newspapers, and magazines. Approximately 1,100 entries are arranged by broad subject categories (e.g., pollution and recycling, consumption, vital statistics, weather and nature) and include thousands of specific average values. The data are presented in large, easy-to-read type, with two or three entries per page. Each entry includes a source, although most are secondary sources; primary sources are cited only occasionally. The source is followed by remarks about it, such as any additional statistical information it may contain. Two indexes are included: a detailed subject index and a very useful "Selective Numerical Values Locator" arranged by category (e.g., money, percentage, temperature), then by numerical value. For example, under "Money" and then under $1000, one may note that in 1988, this amount was the average cost for testing a school's radon level and for a cellular telephone. This reference work has gathered all sorts of statistical information in one handy resource and would be extremely useful in any type of library, public or academic. Highly recommended.—*J. M. Jaguszewski, University of Minnesota*

OAB-0014   LC1023   95-39225 CIP
Greening the college curriculum: a guide to environmental teaching in the liberal arts, ed. by Jonathan Collett and Stephen Karakashian. Island Press, 1996. 328p bibl afp ISBN 1-55963-421-9, $40.00; ISBN 1-55963-422-7 pbk, $22.00

Intending to foster the mainstreaming of teaching about the environment in higher education, this effective and unique curriculum guide demonstrates connections between environmental education and many academic disciplines. The editors and contributors find urgent the need for "environmental literacy" and have designed this guide with separate chapters presenting environmental educational opportunities, techniques, course objectives, class projects, and teaching strategies for the disciplines of anthropology, biology, economics, geography, history, literature, media and journalism, philosophy, political science, and religion. Despite this chapter format, the editors promote interdisciplinary inquiry and teaching, perhaps most effectively by frequent insertion of cross-references to other chapters where similar topics are treated from a different perspective. Each disciplinary chapter includes four elements: a rationale for including material on the environment in teaching the basic concepts of the discipline; curricular guidelines for introductory units or full courses using environmental components; course plans for upper-division courses; and an annotated list of selected resources. Contributors have had experience in teaching and publishing and include such well-known environmental educators as Karl Grossman, John Opie, David Orr, Steven Rockefeller, and Holmes Rolston. This guide provides diverse areas of curricular focus and multifaceted teaching techniques, including the role of zoos, uses of computer Geographic Information Systems, interfaith dialogue, etc. Essential to support environmental studies programs; should be acquired by all academic libraries, community colleges to research institutions.—*J. A. Adams, SUNY at Buffalo*

OAB-0015   CS3010   91-46313 CIP
Guggenheimer, Heinrich W. **Jewish family names and their origins: an etymological dictionary,** by Heinrich W. Guggenheimer and Eva H. Guggenheimer. Ktav, 1992. 882p ISBN 0-88125-297-2, $99.50

Although Jewish names have a history thousands of years old, involving many countries and cultures, very little has been written on this fascinating subject. Only one book has appeared in English, Benzion Kaganoff's brief but interesting *Dictionary of Jewish Names and their History* (CH, Jun'78). Perhaps the necessary fluency in many languages, including historical derivations of earlier dialects, proved too daunting an obstacle. Even a cursory glance at this book reveals a mastery of at least a dozen languages, Arabic to Yiddish, all given in their original form. The sheer number of names, approximately 65,000 out of an estimated 75,000 ever used by Jews the world over, is one indication of the thoroughness of this work. Not every name receives a separate entry; related names are found under the primary, usually shorter term, which is given a brief historical-linguistic derivation in the original languages. The likelihood is good that Jewish browsers, scholar or general reader alike, would find their name in this work. An excellent, detailed introduction provides a good historical survey of the entire subject. The only defect is the surprising omission of Kaganoff's book from the detailed bibliography. This superb work is essential for every library.—*D. Kranzler, Queensborough Community College, CUNY*

OAB-0016   HQ1115   94 48253 CIP
Humm, Maggie. **The dictionary of feminist theory.** 2nd ed. Ohio State, 1995. 354p bibl ISBN 0-8142-0666-2, $59.50; ISBN 0-8142-0667-0 pbk, $20.00

After flourishing in the eighties, the publication of feminist dictionaries has come almost to a standstill. This second edition continues the excellence while expanding the scope of the first edition (CH, Sep'90). The average length of entries is two paragraphs, although some (e.g., abortion, essentialism, language, marriage, postcolonialism, sexuality, womanculture) are given a full page. Humm assumes common beliefs among feminists but does not attempt to homogenize them. She gives general overviews of concepts and explains differences and distinctions within feminism. This edition's 354 pages compares with the first edition's 278. Terms added include "Autobiography," "Backlash," "Binary," "Rey Chow," and "Citizenship." Some entries have been expanded (e.g., "Helen Cixous"), others shortened (e.g., "Consciousness-raising"). In the preface to the first edition, Humm explained that she excluded terms in critical theory such as "Deconstruction" and "Postmodernism" because she believed they received enough attention elsewhere. Without retracting that statement, she has added both "Deconstruction" and "Postmodernism," as well as theorists Ann Kaplan, Sandra Gilbert and Susan Gubar, and Trinh Minh-ha (look under Minh-ha). Cross-referencing is uneven: Gilbert and Gubar share a single entry, but there is no reference from one to the other. Catherine MacKinnon lacks her own entry, although she is referred to many times throughout the book. Birth and death dates are not included in personal name entries. Books or articles from which theories are derived are identified by publication date to enable readers to refer to those works in the bibliography. This is sometimes confusing: none of Melanie Klein's works are referenced in her entry, so readers do not know the time period in which she lived and worked. Small criticisms aside, this book is probably the best scholarly source for defining French and Anglo-American theory.—*P. N. Arnold, Central Michigan University*

OAB-0017   PA91   95-52209 CIP
Jenkins, Fred W. **Classical studies: a guide to the reference literature.** Libraries Unlimited, 1996. 263p indexes ISBN 1-56308-110-5, $43.00

Jenkins (Univ. of Dayton) divides his introduction to 667 reference sources for classical languages and literature, history, archaeology, and allied disciplines into three parts. The first, "Bibliographical Resources," lists general guides to the literature, indexes and abstracts, review journals, topical bibliographies, bibliographies of individuals, and library catalogs. The second and longest section, "Information Resources," covers general and specialized dictionaries, encyclopedias and handbooks, biographical and geographical sources, lexica and grammars, primary sources in translation, core periodicals, directories, and Internet resources. A brief final section, "Organizations," lists research centers and professional associations and societies. Each section is introduced by an informative headnote, and each entry includes full bibliographic information, usually with pagination, along with detailed descriptive and critical comments and cross-references to related works as appropriate. Citing mostly works in English, the author intends his guide for beginning classicists, reference librarians, and general readers, but he has not neglected major reference works in French, German, Italian, and Spanish. For this reason, practicing classicists, "when venturing beyond their specialities," are likely to find it a handy source. The book ends with a complete author/title index and an adequate subject index. Coverage is through 1994, with a few works from 1995. Overall, an outstanding piece of work, well balanced and carefully arranged, that belongs in every college and university library. Highly recommended for all levels.—*J. H. Kaimowitz, Trinity College (CT)*

OAB-0018   E185   92-11493 CIP
The Kaiser index to black resources, 1948-1986. Carlson Publishing, 1992. 5v afp ISBN 0-926019-60-0, $995.00

Researchers and reference librarians will find the *Kaiser Index*, sponsored by the New York Public Library's Schomburg Center for Research in Black Culture and named for Ernest Kaiser, a Schomburg staff member, a veritable gold mine, especially since it covers a period when there were very few reference books that treated blacks. A file of handwritten slips maintained at the Center as a finding aid for librarians and readers, consisting of citations to books, articles, newspaper and vertical file clippings, scrapbooks, etc., was used as the basis for this 174,000-item printed index. This monumental and enviable work may be "the most comprehensive bibliographical resource ever published on the Black experience in the third quarter of the twentieth century." Subject headings are arranged alphabetically, then by date beginning with the most recent, then alphabetically by first word. Most entries give annotation, author, title, medium (newspaper, periodical, etc.), date, page. Although only materials at the Schomburg Center are indexed, the Center will supply photocopies of indexed materials. Recommended for academic and large public libraries, especially those with respectable holdings in black studies.—*G. T. Johnson, Central State University (OH)*

OAB-0019   F1436   94-10359 CIP
Leonard, Thomas M. **A guide to Central American collections in the United States.** Greenwood, 1994. 186p index afp (Reference guides to archival and manuscript sources in world history, 3) ISBN 0-313-28689-2, $65.00

This is the third in a series of excellent reference guides to archival and manuscript sources worldwide. Previous volumes in the series are Louis A. Perez's *A Guide to Cuban collections in the United States* (CH, Nov'91) and John F. Riddick's *A Guide to Indian Manuscripts* (CH, Mar'94). The volume is arranged alphabetically by state. Leonard (history, Univ. of North Florida) lists 747 numbered collections, ranging from a few papers or a diary to major holdings. Among the largest collections included are those at the Bancroft Library, the Newberry Library, Tulane's Latin American Library, and the Columbus Memorial Library in Washington, DC. The Genealogical Society of Utah owns 3,600 microfilm rolls from Guatemala's Archivo General de Centroámerica focusing on the Colonial period and the 19th century. A unique feature of this guide is its extensive coverage of American religious archives, e.g., the Billy Graham Center in Wheaton, Illinois, and the Archives of the Mennonite Church at Goshen, Indiana. A detailed index allows the searcher to locate materials easily: e.g., manuscript collections about Ephraim G. Squier, a 19th-century traveler and diplomat, can be found at the universities of Florida, Michigan, and Tulane; at the Bancroft and Huntington Libraries; at the Indiana and New York Historical Societies; and at the Columbus Memorial Library. For each repository Leonard provides a complete mailing address but no phone numbers or other information about hours or accessibility. Nonetheless, this very helpful guide, which illustrates the vast archival and manuscript sources available on an often turbulent part of the world, will be immensely valuable to researchers, upper-division undergraduates and above.—*B. E. Coutts, Western Kentucky University*

OAB-0020   PE2832   93-31878 CIP
Lutz, William D. **The Cambridge thesaurus of American English.** Cambridge, 1994. 515p ISBN 0-521-41427-X, $16.95

At last—a current thesaurus of American English that is both easy to use and appropriate for all levels. While this title competes with another favorite, *Merriam-Webster's Collegiate Thesaurus* (1993), libraries should make room for both titles on their reference shelves. Lutz (Rutgers Univ.) has done a fine job choosing some 200,000 synonyms and antonyms (for selected words) for approximately 1,500 entries. Although a classified arrangement has its uses, this work combines the more accessible dictionary arrangement with a clean typeface and uncluttered pages. The result is an excellent tool for quick reference. Commonly used words prevail over fad words or technical jargon. Highly recommended for all libraries.—*P. S. Thomas, Sangamon State University*

OAB-0021   G1200   96-10494 CIP
Mattson, Mark T. **Macmillan color atlas of the states.** Macmillan Library Reference USA/Prentice Hall International, 1996. 377p afp ISBN 0-02-864659-2, $100.00

"Encyclopedia" would be a better name than "Color Atlas" for this nicely packaged reference work. There are maps, a dozen for each state, but the atlas gives much more space to text, statistics, graphs, and tables. Arranged alphabetically by state, the atlas presents information for each state in seven categories: basic facts, cultural features, climate and environment, history, popu-

lation and government, ethnicity and education, and economy and resources, with each category being the same length for every state. Among the text, tables, and illustrations are maps that show each state's regional setting, physical features, population/ethnic characteristics (in seven maps), and economic status. A well-drawn principal state map, which appears under the category "Cultural Features," shows the state's counties, highways, major cities, and other themes such as state parks and important colleges and universities. The cartographer fits each main map to one page, to avoid discontinuities when maps fall across two pages. The atlas concludes with a useful statistical appendix. It complements the author's thematic *Contemporary Atlas of the United States* (CH, May'91) and is more useful to college and university audiences than *National Geographic Picture Atlas of Our Fifty States* (1991). Well designed, informative, and accomplished though this atlas may be, the price paid for the uniform presentation of data is a sameness state after state, in contrast to the National Geographic atlas, which celebrates the unique qualities of each state within its regional context. Despite a few mistakes (California's Admission Day is September 9, not April 9), a few proofreading errors, and the high price, this important atlas is recommended for all college and university libraries.—*P. L. Stark, University of Oregon*

OAB-0022   E184   96-27392 CIP
Meier, Matt S. **Notable Latino Americans: a biographical dictionary,** by Matt S. Meier with Conchita Franco Serri and Richard A. Garcia. Greenwood, 1997. 431p bibl index afp ISBN 0-313-29105-5, $65.00

Since several biographical dictionaries on US Latinos are already available, one may doubt the need for yet another. In fact, works already published exhibit problems: *Dictionary of Hispanic Biography* (1996) and *Notable Hispanic American Women* (CH, Jul'93) contain obvious errors, fail adequately to define "Hispanic American," and profile Latin Americans, peninsular Spaniards, US Latinos, and even an Italian or two. *Hispanic American Almanac* (CH, Jul'93) fares better, but biographical entries are scattered and lack bibliographies. This new publication profiles 127 Mexican Americans, Puerto Ricans, Cuban Americans, and other Latinos who have made important and varied contributions in the US and internationally. Entries are informative, lively, carefully prepared, and include bibliographies for further reading. Historical and cultural information in the introduction demonstrates the authors' understanding of Latino populations in the US; Meier's previous publications include well-regarded reference works on Mexican Americans. The only negative aspect of this work is its awkward use of "Latino Americans" in the title—evidently not the choice of the authors, who use the term "U.S. Latino" consistently. Why complicate Latino identity by inventing yet another name? Nonetheless, this authoritative book is highly recommended for all libraries and levels.—*S. A. Vega Garcia, Iowa State University*

OAB-0023   PE1628   93-20206 CIP
Merriam-Webster's collegiate dictionary. 10th ed. Merriam-Webster, 1993. 1,559p index ISBN 0-87779-709-9, $21.95

The evolution of Merriam's collegiate dictionary series continues, this edition entitled for the first time *Merriam-Webster's Collegiate Dictionary*, rather than *Webster's Collegiate Dictionary*, to accentuate the ownership and provenance of the database and to make the point that anyone can use the name "Webster," but not "Merriam-Webster." This is still an abridged dictionary; we are not told how many words it contains, but through the use of uncomfortably small type, it probably includes most of the words in the unabridged grandparent, *Webster's Third New International Dictionary* (1961), and of course it has added many new words, illustrative quotations (the entry for "ain't" includes quotations from Nixon, Mike Royko, and Andy Rooney), and illustrations. On the other hand, some terms and illustrations in previous editions have been dropped, for no apparent reason. This edition adds dates for almost every word helping place the words in much clearer historical context. The treatment of slang and obscene words and phrases is improved over both the unabridged dictionary, and over recent abridged editions, arguing not only great courage and a refusal to pander to ignorance, but also serious, conscientious lexicography. In general, the dictionary is nonprescriptive in spelling and usage, although it points out what is accepted and usual practice in every case. One could wish for more editorial background and rationale on changes from previous editions, but this dictionary compares favorably with other abridged and unabridged dictionaries published in the last several years, at a price that is reasonable. A worthy scion of the Merriam family, it will be wanted by all libraries and many individuals.—*W. Miller, Florida Atlantic University*

OAB-0024   PN6081   91-25960 CIP
The New quotable woman, comp. and ed. by Elaine Partnow. Completely rev. and updated. Facts on File, 1992. 714p indexes afp ISBN 0-8160-2134-1, $40.00

Speakers, writers, and librarians will welcome these two new collections of quotations by women which, taken together, provide solid if not comprehensive coverage. Partnow has combined two previous volumes (*The Quotable Woman: From Eve to 1799*, 1985, and *The Quotable Woman: 1800-1981*, 1982), completely revising and updating her coverage into one handy compendium. While eliminating a third of the quotations from earlier editions ("less relevant stuff of the sixties and seventies"), she adds approximately 2,000 new quotations, updates material on about 150 contemporary women, and includes 450 new contributors. Following a short section of quotations from the Bible, the main section of the volume is arranged numerically by contributor in chronological order by year of birth. Quotations indicate source with copyright or publication date and, when possible, the location of the quotation within the source; they often are footnoted as well, generally providing informative context about persons of note or the quotation itself. To biographical and subject indexes have been added two new indexes, "Career and Occupation" and "Ethnicity and Nationality," that uniquely facilitate the synergistic use of indexes to identify, for instance, humorous quotations on a particular topic or remarks about the environment by Native American women. Although it includes just over half the number of contributors, *The Beacon Book of Quotations by Women* has a helpful topical arrangement that encourages browsing as well as quick thematic reference. The quotations (more than 5,000) cover more than 800 subjects including the expected (friendship, love, work) and the refreshingly uncommon (differences, insomnia, secrets, "they"). Somewhat less scholarly than Partnow, Maggio simply cites sources with date of first publication, but also provides occasional cross-references to related subjects, and name and subject indexes. Both collections include familiar and unfamiliar quotations from famous and lesser-known but notable women; each provides unique coverage of certain women and often selects different quotations from contributors included in both. While regrettable omissions and inevitable biases in selection occur in each, the differences combine with the distinctive arrangements of each to support a strong recommendation that academic and public libraries obtain both.—*J. Ariel, University of California, Irvine*

OAB-0025   PE1421   93-33255 CIP
The New York Public Library writer's guide to style and usage. HarperCollins, 1994. 838p bibl index ISBN 0-06-270064-2, $35.00

This comprehensive guide represents the work of 18 writers and editors commissioned by Stonesong Press and the New York Public Library to develop an additional volume for their reference series, which includes the well-known *The New York Public Library Desk Reference* (2nd ed., CH, May'94). Its purpose is to guide writers and editors across the spectrum of publishing know-how from a command of usage, grammar, and style to the technical aspects of manuscript preparation, production, and printing. The guide is divided into five parts. The first three are aimed at the "careful writer" who seeks a clear understanding of bias-free usage, spelling choices, misused and easily confused words, and difficult points of grammar. The approach is usually prescriptive where practitioners agree on a rule or tradition and descriptive when there is disagreement. The last two parts serve as introductions to principles and processes inherent in both commercial and desktop publishing. Although comparable in general purpose and scope to *The Chicago Manual of Style* (14th ed., CH,

Jan'94), this guide may attract a wider audience with its particular focus on the needs of writers and editors who have become directly involved in layout and production through computing technologies. Notable in this regard is chapter 29, "Computers in the Editorial and Production Process," which includes overviews of 11 different types of production-process software. Numerous examples illustrate the text and provide quick solutions to real-life problems. Starting points that do not appear in the table of contents can be found easily in the topical index. An annotated bibliography lists up-to-date and authoritative reference works for those who want to study writing and publishing in more depth. Citations appear within the text as well. An attractive layout and typeface make this work very easy to read. Highly recommended for all reference collections, large and small.—*J. W. Reit, University of Vermont*

OAB-0026   DE5   96-5352 CIP
The Oxford classical dictionary, ed. by Simon Hornblower and Antony Spawforth. 3rd ed. Oxford, 1997 (c1996). 1,640p afp ISBN 0-19-866172-X, $75.00

First published in 1949, the *OCD* is itself a classic. The first edition offered a uniquely comprehensive, English-language reference for general readers and scholars, with articles on the persons, places, works, and institutions of ancient Greece and Rome by authors whose names still grace required reading lists (e.g., Highet, Momigliano, Nilsson, and Tarn). The second edition (1970) attempted to update the original by incorporating scholarship and archaeological discoveries from the intervening decades. For this third edition, editors Hornblower (Oriel College, Oxford) and Spawforth (Univ. of Newcastle upon Tyne) have led an international team of 364 scholars in an effort to revise older entries while expanding coverage of previously neglected regions (e.g., the Near East and North Africa), periods (late antiquity), and topics (ecology, suicide, motherhood).

The result is a hefty tome of more than 6,000 entries, with more than 800 new articles and bibliographies updated through 1994/95, 30 percent larger than the previous edition. In addition to this thematic, interdisciplinary approach, the editors have tried to emphasize ease of use and eliminate academic arcana. Untranslated Greek and Latin terms have been kept to a minimum, and most Greek proper names have been romanized to their more familiar Latinate forms, with *see* references from variant transliterations (e.g., "Kronos" *see* "Cronus"). The volume is rich with cross-references, since the less useful name index from the second edition has been replaced with much more helpful *see* and *see also* references in the main alphabetical list of the *Dictionary* itself. Readers will need those cross-references to find many a noble or ignoble Roman, since they are listed under *nomen* (family name) rather than *cognomen* (hence, Tullius Cicero, not Cicero; Iunius Brutus, not Brutus). Unfortunately, this edition has also dropped the useful practice of providing Greek spellings for most proper Greek names; given the volume's preference for Latinate transliterations, this may make it more difficult for students with little Greek to find the correct spellings for names in lexica and gazetteers.

This *OCD* is a highly readable and browseable delight, from one-paragraph gems, such as "keys and locks" or "cotton," to lengthier surprises, such as "breast-feeding" or "careers," to expansive explorations on topics such as "constellations and named stars" or "sacrifice." Many of the articles are by leading authorities in the field, including David Halperin ("homosexuality") and Martha Nussbaum ("Aristotle"). A very few entries are marred by inadequate editing, and some provide only a bibliographic citation in place of any text (e.g., "supplication, Greek"). Many entries, such as "literacy," are carefully written to cover current scholarly contentions, although, as with any work by so many hands, one finds occasional unevenness of tone or coverage. For example, Martin Bernal's controversial *Black Athena* (CH, Jan'92) is cited in the article on Hellenism but is not mentioned even dismissively in the entries for "race," "ethnicity," "linguistics," "Africa," "Egypt," or "Ethiopia." These small quibbles do not diminish the overall achievement of this edition. Matthew Bunson's *Encyclopedia of the Roman Empire* (CH, Oct'94), Lesley and Roy Adkins's *Handbook to Life in Ancient Rome* (CH, Oct'94), Robert E. Bell's *Dictionary of Classical Mythology* (CH, Dec'82), and Bell's *Women of Classical Mythology*

(CH, Apr'92) do not approach *OCD* in comprehensiveness or scholarly sophistication. *Civilization of the Ancient Mediterranean: Greece and Rome*, ed. by Michael Grant and Rachel Kitzinger (CH, Jan'89), treats much of the same information, but in narrative form; Graham Speake's excellent *Dictionary of Ancient History* (1994) does not cover mythology or literature. *OCD* is the one work on the ancient world that should be in every reference collection.—*B. Juhl, University of Arkansas, Fayetteville*

OAB-0027   G103   95-22546 MARC
The Oxford dictionary of the world, [ed.] by David Munro. Oxford, 1996 (c1995). 704p afp ISBN 0-19-866184-3, $39.95

Since the classic *Columbia Lippincott Gazetteer of the World* (1952, 1961 supplement) set the standard for gazetteers by providing compass direction and distance from place-name entries to other places or major physical features, as well as their economic and historical significance, there have been worthy successors. Among them are *Webster's New Geographical Dictionary* (CH, Feb'73; later editions in 1984, 1988), *Statesmen's Year-Book World Gazetteer* (1991), both concise, and *Chambers World Gazetteer* (CH, Mar'89, printed in the US as *Cambridge World Gazetteer* in 1990), with distinctly longer entries. Munro (Univ. of Edinburgh, also editor of Chambers/Cambridge) focuses more on political than physical features in this volume, thereby guaranteeing its success as an update of earlier works. Entries are current (Eritrea, independent in 1993); place-name changes are noted (Yekaterinburg replaced Sverdlovsk in 1992). Place-name etymology also is well served (Macedonia receives three definitions). Political subunits are set off in shaded sections clearly and effectively, e.g., Russia's 76 internal regions. Other terms with geographic foundation appear, e.g., Esperanto. Flaws are few and minor; e.g., Debrecen and Miskolc both are described as the third-largest city in Hungary. Twenty-three charts in the appendixes make this more than a gazetteer; e.g., highest and lowest elevations, countries with highest and lowest life expectancy 1990, and members of the UN. Concluding this sturdy, beautifully printed book are 16 pages of political/physical maps in color. Essential for all academic libraries.—*T. R. Zogg, University of Minnesota—Duluth*

OAB-0028   CD-ROM
The Oxford English dictionary on compact disc. 2nd ed. Oxford, 1992. ISBN 0-19-861260-5 $895.00. Updates: (Macintosh version to be published in 1993.). System requirements: High Sierra format; 3.5" and/or 5.25" diskette with retrieval software; IBM-PC or compatible with 80386 processor; DOS 3.0 or higher; 1 Mb free RAM (minimum); CD-ROM drive with Microsoft extensions 2.0 or higher; 1 Mb free hard-disk space, Windows 3.0 or higher; EGA/VGA monitor.

The single CD-ROM (OED2-CD) produced from the 20-volume print edition of the second edition or the OED contains more than a half million searchable "headwords," and a single workstation license is roughly one third the cost of the print edition. Software installation procedures are explained clearly in the manual. Although experience in using Windows and a mouse is an advantage, a novice can install and use the software with ease. Unlike the first edition of the OED CD-ROM (CH, Dec'88) this edition allows a user to search the complete text of the dictionary. In addition to searching for words as in a printed book, a user can seek more indirectly the words and phrases wherever they occur. Searches may be limited to a particular section of the entry such as etymology, quotations, part of speech, or date. During a word search the screen is divided into three portions. One portion shows the word typed, the kind of search performed, and options within the search; another shows the list of adjacent words or phrases that result from a search; the largest shows the results of the search with up to 19 lines of text printed on screen. Quotation searches may be executed as part of a word search or as stand-alone searches. Each instance of an author who is quoted in the OED2-CD may be viewed. The use of Windows software has allowed this CD-ROM to become an exciting and powerful tool for the researcher. Under the OED2 screen heading are listed the basic commands; each screen portion in every search shows additional options

available. Reading and knowing the printed manual is not essential for beginners wishing to use this resource; however, the manual explains precisely how to manipulate the system to perform more advanced searches. For example, the default setting for a word search is "exact mode," that is, only those characters typed are located. If "phobia" is typed, the definition entry shows only "fear, horror or aversion" and is without etymology because the etymological information is included with the suffix "-phobia." If a user examines the preceding word (double click on (double click on {word) "-phobia" is displayed in its complete form. If the settings menu is changed to"extended string," both instances of the word will be retrieved and the results displayed. Users may also use"wildcard" characters to retrieve words when the exact spelling is not known or when variant forms of the word are desired. The results of queries can be saved to a field and then redisplayed during the same session or at a future one. Comments may also be associated with results files, although they do not become part of the results. These files are, unfortunately for the user, not text files and may not be edited or printed out since they are not really"text" files: "They are held in a format meaningful only to the software." The help files are extensive and easy to use. The response time for word searches is very good; understandably, the response time for quotation searches is longer. The OED2-CD belongs not only in reference departments in academic and public libraries but in office and home workstations as well. Highly recommended.— *R. Hanson, Muskingum College*

OAB-0029   CIP
The Oxford-Hachette French dictionary: French-English/English-French, ed. by Marie-Hélène Corréard and Valerie Grundy. Hachette Livre/Oxford, 1994. 1,943p ISBN 0-19-864519-8, $35.00

This new dictionary is unique in being the "first ever French and English dictionary to be based on the evidence of electronic databases of current language." It was compiled from a corpus of electronic texts that contained over 10 million words of the two languages. Access to this large number of texts provides a full range of idiomatic uses of both languages and ensures the authenticity and accuracy of each entry. The dictionary contains more than 350,000 words and "over 530,000 translations" of general, scientific, literary, and technical usage. Numerous current words and expressions are included. Many of the entries are lengthy and stress idiomatic variations and meanings in special phrases. There are frequent cross-references to lexical usage notes. The dictionary includes an introduction, a section on pronunciation, a list of abbreviations, and examples of French correspondence and French advertisements. An original dictionary; highly recommended for all libraries, including those that already own more than one French dictionary.—*J. C. Jurgens, St. Cloud State University*

OAB-0030   PE2846   94-9721 CIP
Random House historical dictionary of American slang: v.1: A-G, ed. by J.E. Lighter. Random House, 1994. 1,006p ISBN 0-394-54427-7, $50.00

This is not the first dictionary of American slang, but it is the first to take a comprehensive, linguistically sound approach to the subject. As such it takes its place as first among all other American slang dictionaries. Scrupulously researched, the first volume of this monumental work bases all of its definitions on accurately quoted and dated examples of slang collected from sources ranging from books and periodicals to television programs, rap lyrics, and personal interviews. The editor has used primary sources almost exclusively, a practice that prevents the work from reprinting errors found in many earlier slang dictionaries. Besides the excellent definitions, three features add immensely to the book's value: first, Lighter's excellent introduction, a lengthy discourse on the history and meaning of slang; second, the selected annotated bibliography, a piece of scholarship that will be of use to students of slang and to librarians who tend reference collections; and, third, the forthcoming bibliography of the 8,000 sources from which the dictionary's entries were collected. This reviewer's only complaint is that volumes 2 and 3 will not appear until 1996 and 1997. They should be worth the wait, however, and if they are priced anything like volume 1, *RHHDAS* will be one of the reference-book bargains of the century. Librarians should do whatever they must to make room in their budgets and on their shelves for this landmark reference book. Recommended for all libraries where English is spoken.—*D. A. Barclay, New Mexico State University*

OAB-0031 PE1628 94-29143 CIP
Random House Webster's college dictionary. [Newly rev. and updated ed.]. Random House, 1996. 1,568p ISBN 0-679-43886-6, $23.95

The new *Random House Webster's* has many features that are comparable, if not superior, to *Merriam Webster's Collegiate Dictionary* (10th ed., CH, Oct'93) and *Webster's New World Dictionary of American English* (3rd college ed., CH, Mar'94). All three dictionaries have bright red covers, red-sprinkled edges, and thumb indexes. Among the notable features that distinguish *Random House Webster's* are its much simplified introductory sections; "Using This Dictionary," for example, is a model of clarity. A section of new words at the front contains more than 600 words apparently too new for inclusion in the main word list, a nice feature for those who think to look there for entries such as "drive-by," "netiquette," or "urban legend." Some 180,000 entries contain the wealth of descriptive information one expects in a good dictionary: accented syllables, syllabifications, parts of speech, pronunciations, spellings for other tenses, variant spellings, British spellings, archaic or obsolete definitions, and capitalized senses. This dictionary has good encyclopedic features: more than 7,000 geographical and 4,000 biographical entries. Many illustrations are more useful than those in its rivals. The maps are clear and the time zone map of the US and Canada easy to decipher. College students will find the "Guide for Writers" section at the end helpful, especially the sample citation forms. The final section, "Avoiding Sexist Language," should prove useful for all who wish to avoid gender blunders. A very fine dictionary, highly recommended for all libraries.—*P. S. Thomas, Illinois State University*

OAB-0032 HQ1587 92-13451 CIP
Snyder, Paula. **The European women's almanac.** Columbia, 1992. 399p afp ISBN 0-231-08064-6, $35.00

Crammed with facts and multidisciplinary in content, this sourcebook will be a friend to researchers, librarians, and students. A snapshot of women's status and condition in 26 countries, it covers the map of Europe—Iceland south to Malta and Ireland east to Romania. The chapters, arranged alphabetically by country, begin with a map and a description of political and cultural status. Statistics are abundant and cover vital issues—e.g., equal rights, health care, parental leave, lesbian rights, employment, education. Snyder attempts to be comprehensive despite inconsistent information from some Eastern European countries. Statistics are current 1987-91, making the almanac particularly useful to scholars of contemporary international issues. Comparative tables list each country under such headings as women's life expectancy, number of TV sets per 1,000 people, date of women's suffrage (Finland was first, 1906, and Portugal last, 1976). The page format makes the book easy to use for reference or browsing. Other books offering similar information employ essay format or are not specific to women's issues, hence are not as comprehensive or easily consulted. Advanced undergraduate; graduate; faculty.—*P. A. Wand, American University*

OAB-0033 [CD-ROM]
Sternberg, Martin L.A. **The American sign language dictionary on CD-ROM.** HarperCollins Interactive, 1994. ISBN 0-06-279015-3 $69.95. 1 CD-ROM disc; user manual. System requirements: IBM-PC, 386 or better; Windows 3.1 or higher; 4MB RAM; color monitor; mouse.

There is no shortage of dictionaries of American Sign Language (ASL) currently available; indeed, the last few years have witnessed the publication of a

number of quite good works of this sort. However, all of the dictionaries of ASL have been faced with the same set of problems, which are related to the nature of signed language. In essence, the trouble is that neither a photograph, a drawing, nor even a narrative description of a sign is fully satisfactory for the user of the dictionary who is trying to determine how to produce a sign that he or she has never actually seen produced before. *The American Sign Language Dictionary on CD-ROM* not only solves this problem but provides a most encouraging indication of how emergent technologies may further aid both the learner and user of ASL in the years ahead.

Containing some 2200 separate video clips, the *Dictionary* allows the user to actually watch a signer produce the target sign and also offers the more traditional description of the sign, clues for remembering the sign, and a line drawing of the sign. This product is actually considerably more than just a dictionary, however; it includes a dictionary and multilingual index (allowing one to locate signs using English, French, German, Italian, or Spanish as a base language), a program designed to facilitate the learning of finger spelling, a skills development program, and an overview of the history and nature of ASL as a modern language, which also contains a valuable bibliography. Further, the dictionary itself allows one either to look up a particular sign or to browse—either alphabetically or by category. This latter feature is one which is common to many ASL and sign language textbooks as well, and many individuals with at least some signing skills will feel quite at home with it.

This CD-ROM is remarkably easy to use and will be especially valuable for beginning students of ASL. Indeed, one could easily imagine someone using this product to begin self-study of ASL, though of course it cannot take the place of real interaction with a deaf person in a natural communicative environment. This is, in short, a very high quality product, and one that demonstrates quite clearly some of the benefits that can be attained from such technology. General; lower-division undergraduate; professional.—*T. Reagan, University of Connecticut*

OAB-0034 PN6429 93-27296 MARC
Strauss, Emanuel. **Dictionary of European proverbs.** Routledge, 1995 (c1994). 3v. 1,232p; 789p bibl index afp ISBN 0-415-09624-3, $550.00

One of the primary difficulties in researching proverbs has always been the failure of existing reference works to provide access to various forms of the same saying in more than one language. This three-volume work fills this need admirably for 1,804 semantic groups, beginning with the earliest known form of a particular proverb in English. Subsequent versions are presented in chronological sequence, followed by equivalents in more than 60 languages written in the Roman alphabet. Organization is by language family (Germanic, Romance, Slavonic, and Finno-Ugric) with specific dialect differences noted. This reflects the linguistic training of the compiler and his familiarity with the masterworks of the Russian folklorist Vladimir Dal. The data set from which the contents of this dictionary are drawn represents more than 40 years of collection and is unparalleled in any other reference work currently available. The third volume comprises a brief unannotated bibliography of sources used and an alphabetic index by letter. Libraries that own Wolfgang Mieder's *International Proverb Scholarship* (1982) or his *Prentice-Hall Encyclopedia of World Proverbs* (CH, Jul'86) will find this an essential purchase. Most suitable for large public, college, and university libraries.—*R. B. M. Ridinger, Northern Illinois University*

OAB-0035 PE2832 91-3938 CIP
Urdang, Laurence. **The Oxford thesaurus.** American ed. Oxford, 1992. 1,005p afp ISBN 0-19-507354-1, $19.95

Originally announced as the *Oxford Thesaurus of American English*, this excellent tome is now more suitably titled, since there is plenty of British flavor in the text. There are even a few instances of excessive British influence; for example, the word "duff" is given only British definitions in its main entry, although the more common American usage (as in "get off your duff") is honored under synonyms for "bottom." Such examples underline an important rule for using this thesaurus: first, look up the term in the index, and only then go to the relevant main entry. This means that the dictionary arrangement is not quite as convenient as one might wish, but the richness of index references plus the built-in safeguard of classification by "sense" of use justify the extra step. One apparent oddity: synonyms, even vulgar ones, for the human posterior and for the putatively feminine bosom appear, but there seem to be no entries for primary sexual organs. A famous female lament that women are reduced to "tits and ass" seems here to have been applied to both sexes. However, the work is splendidly comprehensive in most other areas, and is easy to use. Highly recommended.—*N. F. George, Kenyon College*

OAB-0036 [CD-ROM]
Victorian database on CD-ROM, 1970-1995, comp. and ed. by Brahma Chandhuri, James Mulvihill, and Fred Radford. LITIR Database, c/o Dept. of English, University of Alberta, Edmonton, Alberta T6G 2E5, Canada, 1996. $995.00. 1 disc. Updates: annual; 2,500 records per update. System requirements: IBM-PC 386 or higher; Windows 3.1 or Windows 95; 2MB RAM or higher.

Representing 25 years' research and information compiled from *Cumulative Bibliographies of Victorian Studies*, this CD-ROM version of the LITIR Database comprises approximately 60,000 items from books, articles, and research documents (including abstracts of dissertations) drawn from more than 500 journals. Updates will enlarge the database by an estimated 2,500 entries yearly. The primary strength of this research tool is its interdisciplinary scope, containing entries in English on the following topics in the Victorian period: painting, architecture, and music; philosophy and religion; histories of England, Scotland, Wales, Ireland, and the British Empire; military and naval history; politics, commerce, and economics; sociology, women's studies, law, and education; science, technology, and medicine; and literature—drama, poetry, prose, and fiction. Undergraduate students will find immediate value in this resource, since it is straightforward and easy to use. Initial screens are uncluttered, a function key guide as well as searching tips appear at the bottom of each screen, and help screens are easy to understand and truly useful. Users may construct searches for words or subjects, authors, and titles, singly or in combination. Boolean operators may be used but are not necessary; advanced searching with wildcard letters is possible. Search results are clearly identified by author, title, journal or book, date, collation, area, type, and descriptor. Words used in the search are highlighted in each entry, and the search can be modified to broaden or narrow desired results with a few keystrokes. Results are presented in chronological order, a drawback which this reviewer hopes future cumulations will change to the reverse system preferred by most researchers. Like other standard databases, results may be printed; up to 200 entries at a time may be marked for printing. However, saving results to a diskette for later use is not an obvious choice and may be difficult to do. Currently, the list of sources used to compile the database is not available to view or search. These minor faults do not diminish the value and importance of this source. Highly recommended for undergraduates and above.—*R. Hanson, Muskingum College*

OAB-0037 AG5 91-43020 CIP
Webster's new world encyclopedia. Prentice Hall, 1992. 1,230p ISBN 0-13-947482-X, $75.00

This excellent one-volume desk encyclopedia for library or home reference meets the criteria for a successful encyclopedia set out in its own introduction: that it be useful for general readers rather than experts, include up-to-date facts and figures, be accurate, and provide helpful illustrations as relevant. Arranged alphabetically and including charts and chronologies, *Webster's* is a revision of the 9th edition of the British *Hutchinson Encyclopedia* (1990), but can be judged on its own since few US libraries own *Hutchinson* and the revision has Americanized the text. Portraits of US presidents are larger than those for British prime ministers, American spellings are used throughout,

and such entries as "robin" or "constitution" have an American emphasis. In comparison with *The Cambridge Encyclopedia* (1990) and *The Random House Encyclopedia* (CH, Mar'91), *Webster's* is more current and better reflects recent world changes. It reports events of 1991 and in some cases 1992, while *Cambridge* extends only to the 1960s (Japan) or 1970s (Egypt), while *Random House* covers 1989 (Japan) or the "late 1980s" (Egypt). All three claim 25,000 entries (*Random House* in its "Alphapedia"), but a random comparison shows *Webster's* has the best coverage and largest number of unique entries. For several substantial reasons, *Webster's* is the most useful one-volume desk encyclopedia currently available.—*J. E. Sheets, Baylor University*

OAB-0038 G63 94-29086 Orig
World geographical encyclopedia: v.1: Africa; v.2: Americas; v.3: Asia; v.4: Europe; v.5: Oceania, polar regions, general geography, [ed. by Sybil P. Parker]. [English ed.]. McGraw-Hill, 1995. 5v. 350-357p bibl index ISBN 0-07-911496-2, $500.00

This set stands as an exalted affirmation of the beauty and utility of the book. Its principal multivolume rival, *Worldmark Encyclopedia of the Nations* (CH, Jun'95), has similar volume titles but pales by comparison with the five volumes of *WGE*, whose profuse illustrations place it in a very special niche. Its color photographs are eclectic, stunning, even awe-inspiring. There is no comparison with single-volume atlases, either those that are text-rich (e.g., *Encyclopedic World Atlas*, CH, Mar'95) or those having abundant color graphics and surface and satellite photos (e.g., *The Great World Atlas*, c1989, and *National Geographic Atlas of the World*, 6th ed., 1995). Each volume is arranged by country within multinational regions. Each multinational region is followed by a section of photographs in color, beginning with a detailed introduction to the numbered photos. Color also effectively highlights four data sets for each entry: geopolitical, climate, administration structure, and socioeconomic. Historical and scholarly passages embellish the text, e.g., von Humboldt describing Venezuela. A translation of the original Italian-language *Enciclopedia Geografica Universale* (1994), the set possesses both generality and specificity. Its scientific consultants were academics from a variety of European, South Asian, Australasian, and Canadian institutions. Data are as recent as the late 1980s to 1990/91. The set possesses both generality and specificity. Each region within a continent receives an introductory essay. Twelve of the 15 former Soviet republics are treated as one region, called North Central Eurasia; Estonia, Latvia, and Lithuania appropriately form part of the Scandinavia and Baltic region. A historical section entitled "Great Routes and Voyages of Discovery" concludes the multinational regions description in each volume. In Volume 5, a "General Geography" section provides an outstanding physical, demographic, and economic overview of the planet. This final volume also has an extensive "World Statistics" section, a brief lexicon, and an accurate index of names. This photographic panorama of the world deserves a place in every academic library.—*T. R. Zogg, University of Minnesota—Duluth*

OAB-0039 DT19 97-5671 CIP
Zell, Hans M. **The African studies companion: a resource guide & directory,** by Hans M. Zell and Cecile Lomer. 2nd rev. ed. H. Zell, 1997. 276p bibl index afp ISBN 1-873836-41-4, $75.00

General libraries should not assume *The African Studies Companion* is too specialized for their collections. Zell, noted for his thorough, accurate, and totally dependable reference works, has produced a volume that scholars and reference librarians will turn to as a first step for every Africa-related question, even if the collection holds no other sources on Africa. Larger than the first edition (CH, Jul'90), this one fulfills its promise to "provide quick and easy access for a wide range of information" for Africa studies. Bibliographic references include 159 general reference resources, 17 current bibliographies, and titles of 158 journals. Full descriptions of Africana collections and services are listed for 140 major libraries and documentation centers worldwide. Names, addresses, and descriptions of Africana offerings are given for 164 publishers, along with addresses for 139 Africana vendors worldwide. Contact information is given for 65 of the major Africa-related organizations, 18 African studies associations, and 155 foundations and donor agencies. Information on awards for Africana publications, with citations for winners, and a list of abbreviations and acronyms round out the volume, which is thoroughly indexed. Highly recommended for all libraries.—*G. Walsh, Boston University*

■ Humanities

OAB-0040   AZ221   CIP
Blazek, Ron. **The humanities: a selective guide to information sources,** by Ron Blazek and Elizabeth Aversa. 4th ed. Libraries Unlimited, 1994. 504p indexes ISBN 1-56308-167-9, $45.00; ISBN 1-56308-168-7 pbk, $35.00

The fourth edition of this important guide updates and expands the third edition (CH, Sep'88), increasing coverage from 973 to 1,250 major entries with a corresponding increase in the number of minor entries in notes. (A more comprehensive guide on computer disk is planned for the near future.) New emphases on the influence of women and multiculturalism and on the impact of electronic information make this guide even more valuable. The purpose of this book remains the same—to provide a guide for library science students and teachers and for librarians and scholars "who have information needs in the broad discipline." The format is also the same, with "accessing information" and "sources" chapters for philosophy, religion, visual arts, performing arts, and language and literature. Whereas the third edition included only databases accessible through Dialog, BRS, and Wilsonline, this edition includes all formats. The access chapters highlight useful Internet resources; the sources chapters integrate electronic resources in the major listings, indicating those available in multiple formats. A section on additional helpful resources has been added to each access chapter for students and general readers with limited backgrounds in the discipline. As in the previous editions, the sources chapters were completed with input from bibliographic specialists, and the annotations are thorough and informative. New to this edition is the inclusion of ISBN and ISSN numbers for the major entries. Though the primary emphasis is still English-language materials, some foreign literature sections, notably Spanish/Latin American literature, have been greatly expanded. Subject and author/title indexes are provided. Though individual Internet sources are not fully indexed, this is a minor flaw in a work of great value. Recommended for all libraries.—*L. O. Rein, George Mason University*

OAB-0041   PN3433   95-8083 CIP
Clute, John. **Science fiction: the illustrated encyclopedia.** Dorling Kindersley, 1995. 312p index ISBN 0-7894-0185-1, $39.95

Clute's handsome volume offers not only a reference source but an esthetic object that will please scholars and fans alike. Profuse illustrations depict the history of science fiction in all its dimensions. Timelines situate the genre in a historical continuum, charting books, key themes, and media developments. Photographs accompany chapters on influential magazines, classic titles, and graphic works. Coverage is international, with sections on European television and Japanese comics. Other sections, such as "Gender Roles" and "The Red Planet," reflect current scholarly concerns. Clute coedited the definitive *The Encyclopedia of Science Fiction* (CH, Oct'93) and has written about the genre for 30 years. His commentary is at once incisive and provocative. Dickens's London and Dostoevsky's Moscow are identified as "Cyberpunk cities," for example, and Iain Banks is proclaimed "the most important British writer in decades to do SF." If this volume proves a tenth as influential as *The Encyclopedia of Science Fiction*—and it assuredly will—it represents a mandatory purchase for most libraries. Clute not only examines the history of science fiction but sets the shape of future critical debate. All levels.—*N. A. Baker, Dickinson College*

OAB-0042   PN3435   96-37472 CIP
The Encyclopedia of fantasy, ed. by John Clute and John Grant et al. St. Martin's, 1997. 1,049p ISBN 0-312-15897-1, $75.00

A sibling of the recent *Encyclopedia of Science Fiction*, ed. by Clute and Peter Nicholls (CH, Oct'93), Clute and Grant's monumental work, the first comprehensive encyclopedia on fantasy, covers literature, films, television, opera, art, and comics in more than 4,000 entries, angels to zombies. An outgrowth of the earlier work, this one stems from the realization by the editorial team of the need to cover the field of fantasy in a similar manner. Extensive cross-references and current author bibliographies are found in most entries. The editors drafted a list of themes and used that to shape a structure for the field of fantasy, which is decidedly more difficult to define than science fiction. The interrelationship of themes and place in fantasy adds continuity. The large group of contributors and the experience and reputation of the editors are demonstrated in the breadth, depth, and outstanding quality of this work. Previous attempts have resulted in collections of biobibliographies. The contribution this work makes is to structure the field by defining its themes and creating a "map of fantasy." All levels.—*J. O. Christensen, Brigham Young University*

OAB-0043   PE1704   91-45575 CIP
Grote, David. **British English for American readers: a dictionary of the language, customs, and places of British life and literature.** Greenwood, 1992. 709p bibl afp ISBN 0-313-27851-2, $85.00

This work deserves its full title; it is much more than a dictionary of British English. Grote, an American and author of *Common Knowledge: A Reader's Guide to Literary Allusions* (CH, Apr'88), has collected and explained an impressive array of terms for Americans who read British literature or view British television and film. His goal is to help us grasp what is essentially a foreign culture, despite years of BBC programs and the US's kinship with the UK. A mix of gazetteer, historical guidebook, almanac, and socio/political/cultural dictionary, the work includes places, events, foods, flora and fauna, social and legal practices, organizations, and everyday words. The result is a handy, one-stop dictionary of definitions and connotations of terms that can puzzle: Bank holidays, haha, Giro, tripos, bubble and squeak, pantomime, parish, ITV, OBE, cookers, the Booker, the gentleman, Wormwood Scrubs, Fleet Street, etc. A work that will serve students of British literature, television, and film well and delight Anglophiles in general. Strongly recommended for circulating and reference collection in all academic and public libraries.—*M. H. Loe, SUNY College at Oswego*

OAB-0044   NX650   92-35374 CIP
Reid, Jane Davidson. **The Oxford guide to classical mythology in the arts, 1300-1990s,** by Jane Davidson Reid with Chris Rohmann. Oxford, 1993. 2v. 1,310p afp ISBN 0-19-504998-5, $195.00

This addition to the Oxford guide series represents a truly innovative approach to bibliography. It includes references to the treatment of classical Greek and Roman mythological figures and stories from the 14th to 20th centuries in most media of the arts, including drama and dance, throughout the Western world. More than 30,000 works of art are cited under 205 main subdivisions in alphabetical order by Greek name. Entries for figures with a complex history are subdivided thematically. For each figure, a brief narrative introduction is followed by a listing of classical sources. The references are then arranged chronologically; the dates 1300 to 1990 are interpreted loosely, entries actually ranging from 1165 to 1987. The form of individual entries varies according to the medium but always includes reference to a catalog or learned publication. Additional explanatory text accompanies some entries. Other encyclopedias dealing with mythology may include references to treatment in the artistic tradition but none as systematically or extensively as these two volumes. This work responds to the need for a new generation of sources that cross the boundaries of individual disciplines. This guide belongs in every reference collection.—*M. Nilsen, University of Pennsylvania*

■ Art & Architecture

OAB-0045 GN645 96-19439 CIP
Biebuyck, Daniel P. **African ethnonyms: index to art-producing peoples of Africa,** by Daniel P. Biebuyck, Susan Kelliher, and Linda McRae. G.K. Hall, NY/Prentice Hall International, 1996. 378p bibl indexes afp ISBN 0-7838-1532-8, $95.00

Sub-Saharan Africa has been the home for hundreds, if not thousands, of distinct traditional cultures. Anyone doing research on Africa has faced the difficulty of identifying the most appropriate name for any of those cultures. This confusing diversity of "ethnonyms" can result from many factors: alternative spellings or even misspellings, differing concepts of cultural self-identity within African communities, and the way that early Euro-Americans recorded (or simply assigned) names to the peoples they met. The compilers have combined and organized as many of these culture name variations as they could find in the research literature (their bibliography exceeds 1,000 titles) into a single alphabetically arranged, cross-referenced resource. The use of the qualifier "art-producing people" in the subtitle is something of a misnomer, since the book appears to include all known African peoples. Biebuyck, Kelliher, and McRae have rendered the African studies research community a valuable service by compiling this work, which will immediately become a standard reference resource. Upper-division undergraduates and higher.—*E. C. Burt, Art Institute of Seattle*

OAB-0046 ND548 94-2848 CIP
Clement, Russell T. **Les fauves: a sourcebook.** Greenwood, 1994. 683p indexes afp (Art reference collection, 17) ISBN 0-313-28333-8, $115.00

The Fauve movement in art began with the 1905 scandal of Salle VII of the annual Salon d'Automne in the Paris Grand Palais. Paintings with ravishing colors and clashing harmonies led art critic Louis Vauxcelles to claim that they were "fauves," or wild beasts. By 1907 Fauvism was replaced by Cubism. This annotated bibliography's organization will prove particularly useful to art historians. A section on each Fauve artist presents a biographical sketch, a chronology, and a primary and secondary bibliography on the artist. The primary bibliography consists of the artist's own writings and interviews; the secondary bibliography includes books and articles about the artist's life, work, and influence. The secondary bibliography is easily accessible by the categories listed in the table of contents and by a citation number through the indexes. Citations are alphabetical by author and numbered consecutively throughout. This user-friendly sourcebook will be an invaluable asset to scholars researching the Fauve movement. No college or university reference department should be without it.—*R. T. Ivey, University of Memphis*

OAB-0047 TT505 95-23329 Orig
Contemporary fashion, ed. by Richard Martin. St. James Press, 1995. 575p bibl indexes afp ISBN 1-55862-173-3, $135.00

Focusing on architectural, sculptural, and painterly characteristics of designs, 50 fashion and costume historians bring fashion to fruition as an art form in this monumental scholarly work edited by Martin (Curator, Metropolitan Museum of Art Costume Institute). International in scope, it is in dictionary format and includes designers, design houses, and corporations, 1945 to the present. With a latitude made possible because Martin links art, culture, and fashion, the designs embody the diversity and virtual reality of contemporary fashion, and range from haute couture to fashions inspired by popular culture, high technology, futurism, and folk or ethnic dress. The book follows the format of the "Contemporary Arts Series." Each entry consists of a biography; bibliographical citations; where possible, statements about styles and design philosophy supplied by design houses and designers themselves, many of whom (e.g., Balmain, Cardin) profess affinities for or training in certain art forms; and a critical essay by a scholar or critic of fashion and costume history. Essays describe principles of design, signature styles, and colors and fabrics used. Inexplicably, the essay on Dior omits mention of his bent for architecture and his penchant for constructing designs like buildings. Illustrations consist of photographs; more

would have been welcome. Includes notes on contributors and a geographical list of designers representing 27 countries. The work is a godsend in a field that has had scant attention. Essential for comprehensive fashion and art collections. All levels.—*M. F. Morris, East Carolina University*

OAB-0048 NA31 92-43562 MARC
Dictionary of architecture & construction, ed. by Cyril M. Harris. 2nd ed. McGraw-Hill, 1993. 924p ISBN 0-07-026888-6, $59.50

The 1975 edition of this dictionary is accepted as authoritative on architectural terminology. This second edition updates and incorporates new definitions in building services, materials, systems, trades, and architectural styles and history. Again, contributors are experts from widely different backgrounds including architects, engineers, manufacturers, architecture faculty, art historians, specification writers, craftsmen, contractors, and safety and legal specialists. The list of contributors also defines the scope of the work: the editor strives for comprehensive and accurate coverage with a wide applicability. The format of this edition is modified: the print is larger, and illustrations are incorporated into the two columns of the text instead of in the margins. This dictionary remains the most comprehensive one-volume reference tool on architecture and construction. More extensive or more specialized dictionaries exist, but this volume will nonetheless remain a first step in defining terminology. A staple in the library of practitioners in architecture and related trades or professions, it should be available in architecture and general reference collections.—*M. Nilsen, University of Pennsylvania*

OAB-0049 N31 96-13628 Orig
The Dictionary of art, ed. by Jane Turner. Grove's Dictionaries, 1996. 34v. bibl index ISBN 1-884446-00-0, $8,000.00

Webster's Third New International Dictionary defines an "encyclopedia" as "a work that treats comprehensively all the various branches of knowledge, and that is usually composed of individual articles arranged alphabetically," while a "dictionary" is a "reference book containing words usually alphabetically arranged, along with information about their forms, pronunciations, functions, etymologies, meaning, and syntactical and idiomatic uses." Setting aside the misnaming of *The Dictionary of Art*, this monumental multivolume reference work is, in every other way, an extraordinary achievement.

The *Dictionary* is the largest and most comprehensive reference tool on the visual arts that has ever been published. Unlike earlier art dictionaries and encyclopedias, such as *Encyclopedia of World Art* (CH, Mar'69) or *McGraw-Hill Dictionary of Art* (CH, Mar'70), the *Dictionary* places equal emphasis on Western and non-Western cultures, the decorative arts, and contemporary art and artists. Since the task of reviewing such a work was considered too large for an individual reviewer, a small team (consisting of Ross Day, Linda Seckelson, Kenneth Soehner, and Doralynn Pines, all of the Metropolitan Museum of Art) was assembled to offer critiques of specific articles and of the overall organization of the *Dictionary*. The reviewers read related articles and followed cross-references to other topics, including biographies, cities, cultures, and artistic terms and concepts, noting the quality and clarity of the writing, the choice of photographs, and bibliographic citations. The team found articles to be well written, accessible to specialists and nonspecialists alike, but with a British preference for authors and spellings. Longer articles use a consistent pattern of outlining from broader to narrower topics.

The 34 volumes contain 45,000 signed articles written by 6,700 scholars from more than 120 countries. Individual articles cover cities, countries, and artistic terms, but the greatest number consists of biographies totaling slightly less than half the entries. More than 300,000 bibliographic citations are appended to the ends of articles, or to sections of longer entries. Among the 15,000 images are black-and-white reproductions set within the articles, and sections of color plates interspersed within the appropriate volume. The images, of good quality, are perfectly acceptable for identification purposes. Numerous maps accompany articles on archaeological sites, cities, countries, and other geographical locations.

The index, which fills the last volume, provides approximately 750,000 entries and is preceded by a lengthy introduction that describes its coverage, choice of headings, and alphabetization. Place-names follow UN conventions for modern country names. Names of groups (such as societies and architectural partnerships) and abstract concepts are also indexed.

The first volume begins with a preface and an introduction. Although it is unlikely that anyone other than a reviewer would read straight through these pages, they are worth skimming, if only to understand how a reference work of this magnitude was created. The preface outlines when, how, and why the *Dictionary* was begun. The introduction includes explanations of alphabetization and terminology. Especially fascinating is a section outlining calendars and dates, noting the adoption of the Gregorian calendar and its exceptions. The arrangement of bibliographic citations is also clearly outlined. The acknowledgments that follow include not only the standard thanks, but also the names of the editorial advisory board, the area advisors, and other scholars who defined cultures and civilizations, regional surveys, art forms, and general issues. The scholars on the advisory board are identified by their institutional affiliations, but other authors are not, nor do affiliations appear in the extensive list of contributors in the appendix. The reviewers found this a serious lacuna.

The appendixes in volume 33 are extraordinarily useful tools. Appendix A (p. 750-888) lists locations, with abbreviations and full forms, of the museums, galleries, and other institutions that own or display works of art. Appendix B (p. 889-960) includes the abbreviated and full forms of periodical titles cited in the bibliographies. Lists of standard reference books and series appear in appendix C. Volume 34 ends with another helpful appendix, listing non-Western dynasties and peoples.

Charles Avery's article on Donatello (volume 9), is an excellent example of a longer biography, beginning with a table of contents, followed by the sections "Life and Work," "Working Methods and Techniques," "Character and Personality," and "Critical Reception and Posthumous Reception." The bibliographic citations are well chosen, and are broken into four groups: general, monographs, exhibition catalogues and congresses, and "Specialist Studies," including important articles.

The introduction in volume 1 provides a lengthy explanation of cross-referencing, but the system is not as seamless as one would expect. Readers are told that the names of artists will appear in small capitals within an article to indicate the existence of another entry, but this signage is not always consistent. Readers are asked to assume that biographies exist for well-known artists, such as Michelangelo, even if their names are not capitalized. Unfortunately, this method can be frustrating when trying to determine if an artist is famous enough not to be listed in caps. Help can sometimes be found in the index. The headings under Donatello, for example, occupy 1 1/4 columns, and are useful in overcoming some of this confusion. When all else fails, it is fun to hunt around in the *Dictionary* and its index, which is, after all, the preferred method for most researchers using similar reference tools.

Turning to the decorative arts, the reviewers found a noticeable inconsistency in terminology that reiterated some of the cross-reference problems. Articles were found under "Glass" but not under "Furniture," and there is no entry for "Craft." The reviewers wonder why the article for "Native North American Art" was considerably longer than for "United States of America." Entries for American painters were well done by predictable authors, such as Gail Levin on Edward Hopper. Readers will be pleased to read Elizabeth Johns on Albert Pinkham Ryder and Thomas Eakins, and John I.H. Baur on Luminism. The article "Africa" fills more than 200 pages in volume 1, with 163 illustrations and 10 maps, and serves as a paradigm for the coverage of non-Western arts. This and other country or culture articles should, in future, be republished as stand-alone publications.

The *Dictionary* has been in preparation for more than 15 years. The present price of almost $260.00 per volume is high, but prepublication prices for the set started as low as $6,000.00, and installment plans are available. The *Dictionary* has been in use in the Metropolitan Museum library for several weeks and has proved an extremely valuable resource, especially for researchers and lecturers requesting information outside their immediate areas of specialization. A

substantial portion of a typical library's budget will need to be spent to purchase the *Dictionary*, but is should find its way into every museum and university art library. College and public libraries, particularly those without significant art collections, should consider purchase, in this way acquiring a mini-art library in 34 volumes.

When planning for the *Dictionary* was begun in the early 1980s, electronic publications were barely a glimmer in the editor's eye. The publishers appear to have no plans at this writing to issue the *Dictionary* in electronic format. The ease of use of an electronic version would certainly alleviate some of the cross-reference difficulties, and the small size of CD-ROMs would appeal to space-starved libraries. Reviewers and libraries around the world can only hope to see Macmillan move in this direction before the end of the millennium.—*D. S. Pines, The Metropolitan Museum of Art*

OAB-0050   Orig
Encyclopedia of interior design, ed. by Joanna Banham. Fitzroy Dearborn, 1997. 2v. 1,450p bibl index ISBN 1-884964-19-2, $250.00

Essential and much needed, this encyclopedia meets its goal of providing a source that combines the disparate elements of interior design into one comprehensive reference work. Two main categories of entries are included: individual entries covering architects, critics, designers, and patrons; and topical entries describing room types, decoration, and types of furniture. Longer survey articles relating to individual countries, periods, and styles are also included. The work is limited in focus to 19th- and 20th-century American and European secular design. Each entry includes a signed critical essay, a list of collections where representative examples of the works can be viewed, cross-references, and a bibliography of major writings. The impressive list of contributors consists of professors, curators, and professionals working in interior design. Excellent black-and-white illustrations. Enthusiastically recommended for all undergraduate library collections.—*M. Fusich, California State University, Fresno*

OAB-0051   TR9   92-44267 CIP
The Focal encyclopedia of photography, ed. by Leslie Stroebel and Richard Zakia. 3rd ed. Focal Press, 1993. 914p afp ISBN 0-240-80059-1, $125.00

A revised version of the 1969 edition, but *greatly* expanded and updated, this comprehensive encyclopedia should become the standard work in photography. Some 90 expert contributors have written articles on definitions, "abrasions and scratches" to "zooming." Some articles are highly technical while others may benefit the amateur photographer. "Advances in Photographic Technology" gives readers a time line from the 1200s, when glass lenses were introduced, to 1991, with Kodak's XL 7700 Digital Continuous Tone Printer. Numerous biographical articles portray key people in the field. Such diverse topics as aesthetics, business practices, chemistry, light and light measurement, optics, and physics are covered. The work is generously illustrated with charts, graphs, photographs, and diagrams. Appendixes include a chart of photographic effects, charts and tables of film and paper reciprocity data, logarithmic notations and arithmetic equivalents, a temperature conversion scale, and much more. It would be hard to imagine a more complete one-volume work. An essential purchase.—*C. Larry, Northern Illinois University*

OAB-0052   NA727   93-25433 CIP
An Illustrated glossary of early southern architecture and landscape, ed. by Carl R. Lounsbury. Oxford, 1994. 430p bibl afp ISBN 0-19-507992-2, $75.00

There are many glossaries of architectural terms, but even the briefest comparison shows that Lounsbury's work far surpasses the others in quality and fills a large gap in the literature by addressing the first two centuries of building in the southern US. More than simply providing a definition and, in many cases, an illustration of the term, each entry places the term in the context of the period and region. Thus, one is given insight into why a word was commonly used in Delaware, but labeled vulgar by British builders of the same period. The entries in many cases are more comprehensive than in other glossaries. Excerpts from primary sources that document the term's usage through two centuries complete each entry. Nearly 1,500 terms used from the 1610s through 1820s, from Delaware to Georgia and as far west as Kentucky and Tennessee, are included. Entries are limited to English-language terms except for foreign terms that were adopted by southern residents. Lounsbury's preface and introduction provide a concise overview of changes in design and construction that took place during this period, rendering his book invaluable to researchers. Given changes between historical usage and the language of modern architectural analysis, it should be in the reference collection of every library supporting the study of architecture or American history.—*S. M. Klos, University of Oregon*

OAB-0053　　　　　N7830　　　　　96-17840 CIP
Murray, Peter. **The Oxford companion to Christian art and architecture,** by Peter and Linda Murray. Oxford, 1997 (c1996). 596p bibl afp ISBN 0-19-866165-7, $45.00

The latest addition to the "Oxford Companion" series addresses the need created by increasingly secular and diverse readers for a tool to help understand and interpret the predominant religious tradition in Western art. The authors have solid art historical credentials, primarily for their writings on the Renaissance. The alphabetical listing includes artists, religious figures, terminology, symbols, geographic names, and media, as well as longer sections (e.g., "Gothic Art and Architecture"). Cross-references and alternate spellings are included in alphabetical sequence. Many entries include references to significant interpretations as expressed in painting or sculpture. Small black-and-white and some full-page color illustrations are used selectively. A glossary of architectural terms supplements the text. The short bibliography is organized by subject but is neither annotated nor comprehensive. Even relatively obscure topics are treated in a concise manner that allows further research in more detailed and specialized works. A good road map for the uninitiated and a firm stepping stone for specialists, this source belongs in all collections with holdings in art or religion.—*M. Nilsen, University of Pennsylvania*

OAB-0054　　　　　N6503　　　　　94-49710 CIP
North American women artists of the twentieth century: a biographical dictionary, ed. by Jules Heller and Nancy G. Heller. Garland, 1995. 612p bibl index afp (Garland reference library of the humanities, 1219) ISBN 0-8240-6049-0, $125.00

The Hellers have compiled an extensive biographical dictionary of 20th-century women artists born prior to 1960 who worked primarily in the US, Canada, and Mexico. Their book does much to remedy the paucity of basic biographical information about women artists. More than 100 contributors, including academics, curators, and artists, wrote the 1,500 entries; no major omissions were detected. Artists were selected if they demonstrated a serious commitment to the visual arts by participating in specific types of exhibitions, and by paper trails of reviews, articles, or monographs. Accounts of individual artists, averaging 330 words, describe general artistic characterizations, media of choice, biographical and professional backgrounds, representative exhibitions and awards (including dates), and include brief bibliographies. This information will satisfy basic information needs as well as provide avenues for further research about Canadian, Mexican, and American women artists. Although color photographs would have been preferable, some 100 glossy black-and-white photographs are of high quality and illustrate the varied styles and media used by these artists. This valuable reference book should be in every art, academic, and large public library collection.—*P. Keeran, University of Denver*

OAB-0055　　　　　NA705　　　　　94-13941 CIP
Packard, Robert T. **Encyclopedia of American architecture.** 2nd ed. McGraw-Hill, 1995. 724p index ISBN 0-07-048010-9, $89.50

The first edition of this work (1980) appeared to high acclaim. The 1980s, however, saw many changes in the American architectural landscape. Most older architects trained in Europe passed from the scene, and were replaced by younger American-trained architects with new philosophies and aesthetic approaches. The use of computers and other technological advances have added to the mix. Packard, architect, writer, and associate editor of the five-volume *Encyclopedia of Architecture* (CH, Nov'88; Jul'90), has prepared this new edition. New facts, biographies, and histories of architectural firms, as well as new essays on earthquake protection, computer applications, environmental protection, post-modernism, and facilities for the handicapped, have been added. Most notable, however, is the inclusion of more than 500 full-color photographs by the eminent architectural photographer Balthazar Korab, which virtually take over the book with their excitement and dynamism. Because of the amount of material the book covers and the diversity of its intended audience, it is nontechnical in nature, although new ideas, technical advances, and designs are reviewed. The 18-page, three-column index and the list of further readings at the end of each essay add to this exciting new architectural reference book. General; professional.—*R. J. Havlik, emeritus, University of Notre Dame*

OAB-0056　　　　　SB470　　　　　96-34507 MARC
Vogelsong, Diana. **Landscape architecture sourcebook: a guide to resources on the history and practice of landscape architecture in the United States.** Omnigraphics, 1997. 382p indexes afp (Design reference series, 1) ISBN 0-7808-0196-2, $45.00

In this first volume of a new series, Vogelsong provides a key to the major resources for the study and practice of landscape architecture, creating an indispensable reference source for those seeking either to build a collection or conduct research in landscape and architecture. A brief introduction precedes the bibliography, which has ten chapters, each subdivided topically. Entries provide complete bibliographic citations with concise annotations. Publications the editor considers to be core works essential for a basic collection are marked by an asterisk. Chapter 6 is made up entirely of core works organized under the headings "Gardens," "Parks and Public Lands," "City Planning - Urban Landscape Design," "Landscape Preservation and Restoration," and "Special Projects and Sites." Other chapters provide extensive information on reference works, histories, handbooks, professionals and firms, plant materials, environmental concerns, institutional resources such as libraries and government agencies, and computer and media resources. Occasional minor inaccuracies and typographic errors do not diminish the book's value. Well edited by an academic librarian, this is an important acquisition for both academic researchers and professionals.—*S. M. Klos, University of Oregon*

OAB-0057　　　　　Orig
Wood, Christopher. **Victorian painters: [v.] 1: The text; [v.] 2: Historical survey and plates.** [3rd ed., rev. and updated]. Antique Collectors' Club, 1995. 2v. 595, 475p (Dictionary of British art, IV) ISBN 1-85149-171-6, v.1; ISBN 1-85149-172-4, v.2; $69.50 ea.

This is a welcome, greatly enlarged third edition of a standard reference work (*Dictionary of Victorian Painters*) by the former director of 19th-century paintings at Christie's, who since 1977 has had his own London dealership in Victorian art and is arguably the world's leading expert on the endless range and variety of Victorian painting. The first and second editions (1971 and 1978) have been frequently reprinted, so there is proven demand for this new edition, with its 11,000 biographical entries (some new, some revised and updated), a new 104-page introductory essay that is witty, literate, and scholarly, and 750 excellent black-and-white illustrations and 47 color plates. Christopher Newall and Margaret Richardson are acknowledged for research assistance. Wood's introduction is kept lively by many informal phrases. He recognizes artists of genius as well as "extremely minor figures, or mediocrities"; Herkomer's portraiture "is worthy but dull"; while Wood's love of the Pre-Raphaelite movement is revealed when he speaks of "the mystical reverence for the minutiae of nature." Wood discusses more than 35 subcategories of Victorian painters, some of whom he suggests rank with the masters of painting. This startling concept may be enough to make this edition worth consideration; but Wood emphasizes that "Victorian art was, in truth, popular art." Highly recommended for general and academic collections, especially those that lack the earlier editions.—*M. Hamel-Schwulst, Towson State University*

■Language & Literature

OAB-0058 PL8010 96-16128 CIP
African writers, ed. by C. Brian Cox. Scribner/Simon & Schuster Prentice Hall International, 1997. 2v. 936p bibl index afp ISBN 0-684-19651-4, $220.00

Handsome and well crafted, this work will make African literature, a genre not yet in the mainstream, accessible to the broad readership it deserves. Essays by international literary scholars discuss the life and work of 65 authors "who were born or spent a good deal of their lives in Africa." Some names will be familiar, while others, despite sizable bodies of writing, may seem obscure. The list includes four Nobel laureates—Wole Soyinka, Najib Mahfouz, Nadine Gordimer, and Albert Camus (the latter included because of his Algerian birthplace). The insightful introduction describes the criteria for selection of authors and discusses major issues in the study of African literature, including colonialism, identity, and choice of language. A list of authors by country and a detailed chronology of political as well as literary events help to put the work in perspective. Each entry includes a selected bibliography of literary titles by the author and critical studies of the author's work. The essays are an excellent introduction, sure to whet readers' appetites for the books themselves. *African Writers* should be on the shelves of all libraries with literature collections.—*G. Walsh, Boston University*

OAB-0059 PS221 91-30603 CIP
American literary magazines: the twentieth century, ed. by Edward E. Chielens. Greenwood, 1992. 474p index afp ISBN 0-313-23986-X, $89.50

Chielens (English, Henry Ford Community College), has edited numerous excellent publications on literary journals including the companion volume, *American Literary Magazines: The Eighteenth and Nineteenth Centuries* (CH, Feb'87). There are many indexes, directories, and bibliographies devoted to American literary magazines, but fewer evaluative histories like Chielens's. This follows the format of the earlier volume, offering signed essays on the major journals of the period that "most influenced the development of American literature" either through primary publication or "promoting groups of writers and new schools of literature." Scholarly journals, single author newsletters, etc. are excluded. Titles treated include defunct publications such as *Broom, Double Dealer,* and *Twice a Year,* and very active publications such as *American Poetry Review, Paris Review,* and *Sulfur.* The essays describe the founding and editorial history of each journal, examine its reputation and influence, note significant contributions, and compare it to similar journals. The current work supersedes previous histories such as *The Little Magazine in America* (CH, May'79), whose evaluations it cites in the bibliographies of articles and books that conclude each essay. A "Publication History" follows the bibliographies, providing, e.g., title changes, years of publication, frequency, and names of editors. Appendix A, "Minor Literary Magazines," lists briefly journals not given full profiles, including titles that deserve major essays, e.g., *Georgia Review.* Appendix B is a chronology of social and literary events, that occurred the year the journal was founded. Appendix C provides data on 28 little magazine collections in the US and Canada. Useful general index of authors, titles, and subjects. Highly recommended.—*R. R. Centing, Ohio State University*

OAB-0060 B905 95-45187 CIP
Biographical dictionary of transcendentalism, ed. by Wesley T. Mott. Greenwood, 1996. 315p bibl index afp ISBN 0-313-28836-4, $79.50

Covering American transcendentalism between 1830 and the Civil War, mainly in New England, this source makes several contributions to existing reference literature on this movement. First, it aims to cover the movement more broadly than has been done before. The 204 biographical entries include minor and international figures of transcendentalism, and those involved with the movement but not themselves transcendentalists. Other biographical sources on the movement, such as *The American Renaissance in New England,* ed. by Joel Myerson (CH, Jul'79), and Myerson's *The New England Transcenden-*

talists and the Dial (CH, Apr'81) cover less than half as many figures. Mott takes into account recent biographies and critical works about the persons his book covers, hence its biographical sketches and bibliographies are more up-to-date than the earlier sources. The sketches are well written and focus on details about each subject's transcendentalism. The cross-references to other entries and to definitions of terms are like those in another publication edited by Mott, *Encyclopedia of Transcendentalism* (1996). The index and brief bibliographic essay are both helpful. An alphabetical list of all persons covered would be a useful addition. The source lacks some features of Myerson: portraits and autographs of each person, and information on how each was viewed in periods after their deaths. The contributors are mostly academics in English; Mott is professor of English at Worcester Polytechnic Institute, secretary and founder of the Ralph Waldo Emerson Society, and managing editor of *Emerson Society Papers.* Highly recommended for academic libraries.—*N. G. Stewart, Library of Congress*

OAB-0061 PN471 92-10415 CIP
The Bloomsbury guide to women's literature, ed. by Claire Buck. Prentice Hall General Reference, 1992. 1,171p ISBN 0-13-689621-9, $40.00; ISBN 0-13-089665-9 pbk, $20.00

A companion to *Bloomsbury Guide to English Literature* (1989), this work provides more than 5,000 biographical, bibliographical, and critical entries for women authors and fiction by women, from all time periods and nationalities. Thirty-six brief but fascinating essays, organized by countries or regions, treat the historical and cultural contexts for authors, and the differences and similarities in women's literature. An extensive brief-entry section, arranged alphabetically, contains name, work, and thematic entries, and includes brief bibliographies and synopses of works. Frequent cross-references strengthen the sense of commonality and connectivity in women's writing. Prose, poetry, and a range of popular fiction genres are included, but nonfiction is excluded. Lesser-known figures and non-Western writers are emphasized. An important criterion for inclusion is the availability of works in English translation, but some authors for whom few or no translations are available are included to represent all nationalities and periods. Closely resembling *Feminist Companion to Literature in English* by Virginia Blain et al. (CH, Feb'91), *Bloomsbury's* narrower focus on fiction eliminates some well-known writers, but its emphasis on lesser-known figures is commendable. Although other sources provide considerably more detail (e.g., *Modern American Women Writers,* ed. by Elaine Showalter, 1991, or *Biographical Dictionary of English Women Writers,* ed. by Maureen Bell, George Parfitt, and Simon Shepherd, CH, Jan'91), *Bloomsbury* stands out both for its emphasis on lesser-known writers and works and its illumination of the contextual links of women writers across boundaries of history, region, and culture. It is gratifying that extensive resources now exist to support research on women writers (particularly Western writers) and that works like *Bloomsbury* venture beyond the mainstream to introduce, however briefly, many new faces. Advanced undergraduate; graduate; faculty.—*E. Patterson, Emory University*

OAB-0062 PQ401 92-22129 CIP
Coleman, Kathleen. **Guide to French poetry explication.** G.K. Hall, 1993. 594p index afp ISBN 0-8161-9075-5, $55.00

Since few works that provide access to criticism of French poetry exist, this guide fills a need. To keep the guide from becoming unwieldy, the editor limits its scope to explications published between 1960 and 1990 in English and French, and to poets that appeared in editions published in the 19th and 20th centuries. The largest section (Checklist of Interpretation) is an alphabetical listing of poets ranging from 12th-century Marie de France to Yves Bonnefoy. For each poet, individual poems are listed alphabetically, followed by critical writings about that poem. A shorter section (Main Sources Consulted) lists critics for whom five or more explications are listed. The critics belong to many literary schools of thought. In the guide's simplicity lies its strength; its user-friendly format will aid scholars and will lead students to insightful criticism of French poetry. Recommended for all college and university collections.—*R. T. Ivey, Memphis State University*

OAB-0063 PS3509 95-4884 CIP

A Concordance to the complete poems and plays of T.S. Eliot, ed. by J.L. Dawson, P.D. Holland, and D.J. McKitterick. Cornell, 1995. 1,240p indexes afp ISBN 0-8014-1561-6, $85.00

The compiler's labors have the approval of Valerie Eliot, the copyright holder. The copy text for the concordance is *The Complete Poems and Plays of T.S. Eliot* (London, 1969). As Holland indicates in his preface, "in the slowly developing field of Eliot textual studies, a concordance such as this one is bound to be provisional." Eliot's poems published after the 1969 edition are excluded. In an age of electronic texts "book-form publication of a concordance may seem outdated." A clear "Technical Introduction" is followed by a "Short Title Index," a "Speaker Abbreviation Index," and a "List of Omitted Words." The concordance itself is followed by "Reverse Index of Word Forms," "Statistical Ranking List of Word Forms," "Lines Containing Numbers," and "Index of Words Containing Hyphen or Apostrophe." Until a variorum Eliot appears, this computer-generated keyword-in-context work will remain the definitive hard-copy concordance. The binding seems strong enough to withstand constant use, and the computer typeface is not too displeasing. An indispensable purchase for all graduate and research libraries and for larger general reference collections.—*W. Baker, Northern Illinois University*

OAB-0064 Orig

A Critical bibliography of French literature: v.5: The nineteenth century in two parts, ed. by David Baguley. Syracuse, 1994. 2v. 1,488p index afp ISBN 0-8156-2566-9, $225.00

Since the 1950s, students and researchers in French literature have been awaiting these promised 19th-century volumes in this distinguished bibliographic series. From the vast amount of criticism published about the literature of this period until 1989, Baguley and his team of scholars have culled the most significant works and arranged them in chronological order, with individual chapters devoted to major authors, groups of writers, and genres. The sections for major authors follow the traditional arrangement: bibliographical studies, critical editions, correspondence, biography, and works of criticism. Most of the entries are annotated and some list book reviews. A very useful appendix lists reference works dealing with literary criticism of the works of 19th-century authors from Belgium, Africa, the Caribbean, French Canada, the Maghreb, Switzerland, and other Francophone areas. In an age that aspires to the anonymous comprehensiveness of computerized listings, Baguley's work reminds us of the importance of the intellectual filter provided by the specialist. Indispensable for all college and research libraries; upper-division undergraduates and above.—*E. Sartori, University of Nebraska-Lincoln*

OAB-0065 PR149 92-30648 CIP

A dictionary of biblical tradition in English literature, ed. by David Lyle Jeffrey. Eerdmans, 1992. 960p ISBN 0-8028-3634-8, $79.99

The purpose of this monumental work—to help modern readers understand how biblical motifs have been used in English literature from the Middle Ages to the present—is amply met in more than 750 essays ranging from one paragraph to several pages. Jeffrey has attempted to compile a book that is accessible to general readers, and that uses a "readable gender-inclusive prose." The 160 contributors are drawn from theology, biblical studies, and literature. Each essay, insofar as possible, follows the same form, and describes the aspects of the word or phrase being defined as it occurs in the Bible, in the exegetical tradition, and in English literature. Lengthy signed entries conclude with bibliographies, and provide numerous cross-references and "see also" references. Three exhaustive bibliographies follow the text, totaling more than 100 pages: "Biblical Studies," "The History of Biblical Interpretation," and "Biblical Tradition in English Literature." Each subsumes more specific bibliographies (e.g., "A Guide to Biblical Studies for the Student of Literature," "Historical Studies in Biblical Hermeneutics"). This exhaustive reference work will be welcome in all academic library reference departments, as well as on the shelves of interested readers.—*J. M. Parker, St. Olaf College*

OAB-0066 PQ4006 95-33077 CIP

Dictionary of Italian literature, ed. by Peter Bondanella, Julia Conaway Bondanella, and Jody Robin Shiffman. Greenwood, 1996. 716p bibl index afp ISBN 0-313-27745-1, $99.50

Coming 15 years after the first, this second edition adds 38 new entries and updates others. New material covers not just contemporary poets, screenwriters, and journalists but also authors from the 12th to 20th centuries whose importance has become more apparent. A few entries have been dropped. Like its predecessor, this edition provides clear, concise bibliographies that attempt to place major and minor Italian authors within a broad cultural context. The editors assume that many general readers will turn to this work for an introduction to Italian literature, and therefore they have included literary movements and terminology. Each entry concludes with a brief bibliography of primary works, including English translations, and selected works of criticism; particular attention has been given to updating these bibliographies. Most entries are written by the editors; others are written and signed by experts whose credentials are fully described. Useful appendixes provide chronological tables that correlate Italian literature with world literature and with political, cultural, and scientific events; a listing of entries grouped by topic or period; and a comprehensive index. Recommended for all academic and larger public libraries.—*J. G. Bryan, University of Pennsylvania*

OAB-0067 PM155 94-3811 CIP

Dictionary of Native American literature, ed. by Andrew Wiget. Garland, 1994. 598p bibl index afp (Garland reference library of the humanities, 1815) ISBN 0-8153-1560-0, $95.00

Since the appearance of overviews such as Wiget's *Critical Essays on Native American Literature* (CH, Sep'85) and A. LaVonne Brown Ruoff's *American Indian Literatures: An Introduction, Bibliographic Review, and Selected Bibliography* (CH, Jun'91), the field of Native American literature and criticism has grown considerably. Wiget (New Mexico State Univ.) offers 73 essays, written by experts and arranged by subject and by period in three parts. The first, "Native American Oral Literatures," has an overview by Wiget and nine chapters on the oral literature of different geographic areas of Native America, followed by chapters on themes such as oratory, the trickster, dreams and songs, and revitalization movements. The second section, "The Historical Emergence of Native American Writing," with an introduction by Ruoff, is followed by chapters on topics such as federal Indian policy, autobiography, women's autobiography, and humor, as a backdrop to descriptions of the major native writers of the period. The third section, "A Native American Renaissance: 1967 to the Present," presents an overview by Joseph Bruchac followed by chapters on critical responses to Native American literature, teaching American Indian literature, the literature of Canada, fiction, theater, and Indians in Anglo-American literature. Descriptions of prominent contemporary native writers follow. All essays are accompanied by bibliographies of primary and secondary sources. The volume concludes with a name/title/subject index. Excluded are film, journalism, children's literature, and song. This volume complements *Native North American Literature* (CH, Jun'95), which profiles 78 authors and includes newer voices (e.g., Sherman Alexie, Luci Tapahonso). Wiget's book has essays on 43 authors but gives a better historical and critical picture of this field. Both books should be acquired for all library collections serving programs in Native American and comparative literatures.—*C. E. Carter, University of New Mexico*

OAB-0068 PK2902 87-901256 MARC

Encyclopaedia of Indian literature: v. 1-5, v. 1-3 ed. by Amaresh Datta; v. 4-5 ed. by Mohan Lal. Sahitya Akademi, 1987-1992.(Dist. by South Asia Books) 5v. $44.00 ea.

Not only scholarly and authoritative, this encyclopedia (issued by the Sahitya Akademi, India's National Academy of Letters, founded 1954) testifies to the range and vitality of the Indian languages (classical and modern) and their literatures. As described by the editor, the work intends "to give a fairly clear and comprehensive idea about the growth and development of Indian literature in

22 languages recognised by the Sahitya Akademi. The entries. . .in alphabetical order cover practically all the important aspects of Indian literature. . .with general historical surveys of genres and movement and adequate notes on established authors born in or before 1947 and on significant books in each of these 22. . .languages." Headwords are in boldface. Each of the five volumes (4,650 pages in all) has introductory material, names of the contributors (many of them well-known literary figures), and a transliteration table for Devanagari characters. Volume 1 has a language map of India based on the 1971 census. The entries are signed, and some have short bibliographies, but there are no illustrations, portraits, or drawings. Entries treat authors, individual works, genres, and movements, and are arranged in alphabetical order, but there are no cross-references. Perhaps understandably in a work of this scope, the treatment is uneven. Some entries are quite elaborate (e.g., "Biography"); but "Associations and Institutes" is treated only under the Marathi language, implying that no other associations or institutes exist for other Indian languages. To cover the major Indian literatures in a multitude of languages, some going back to ancient times, is a large task requiring careful selection. Many headings treated in *An Encyclopaedia of Indian Literature*, by Ganga Ram Garg (CH, Dec'83) that deserve inclusion here are missing. A work of lasting value such as this should have been printed on the best quality paper. Volume 6, consisting of indexes and cross-references, will be released soon. Despite these minor irritations, this is a great contribution to scholarship and a very useful addition to college/university or large public libraries that support South Asian studies.—*O. P. Sharma, University of Michigan*

OAB-0069   Can. CIP
Encyclopedia of contemporary literary theory: approaches, scholars, terms, ed. and comp. by Irena R. Makaryk. Toronto, 1993. 656p index afp ISBN 0-8020-5914-7, $150.00; ISBN 0-8020-6860-X pbk, $39.95

Contemporary Anglo-US literary theory began about 50 years ago with New Criticism and today looks back through strong social science and continental philosophical influences to Freud, Marx, and Nietzsche. Makaryk's *Encyclopedia* maps this terrain with "Approaches," critical essays that run from hundreds to thousands of words on 49 critical methods; "Scholars," biographical-critical articles on 133 theorists; and "Terms," 130 entries (some of them *see* references and others occupying several pages) selected for their difficulty, frequency of use, and centrality to discussion. Entries are exclusively European or North American and are accompanied by good bibliographies. The 170 contributors, mostly Canadians, do a commendable job of providing the summary one wants from an encyclopedia while attending to the complexity and controversy that characterize the field. The target audience is post-graduate, for whom the *Encyclopedia* is much superior to Wendel Harris's *Dictionary of Concepts in Literary Criticism and Theory* (CII, Oct'92) or Leonard Orr's *Dictionary of Critical Theory* (CH, May'92). Although M.H. Abrams's *Glossary of Literary Terms* (6th ed., CH, Sep'93) and Jeremy Hawthorn's *A Glossary of Contemporary Literary Theory* (CH, Oct'92) are preferable for most students, the *Encyclopedia* should be used with Abrams and Hawthorn because, unlike them, it offers articles on individual theorists. A welcome addition to any literary studies collection despite its price.—*R. H. Kieft, Haverford College*

OAB-0070   P29   93-37778 CIP
The Encyclopedia of language and linguistics, ed. by R.E. Asher and J.M.Y. Simpson. Pergamon, 1994. 10v. 5,644p indexes afp ISBN 0-08-035943-4, $2,400.00

The editors intend their work simply to be the most authoritative, up-to-date, comprehensive, international reference source in the field. There can be little doubt of its having achieved that goal. It owes its authority to its distinguished editorial boards and the 1,000 specialists who contributed articles. That it is as current as possible in a rapidly changing field is due in part to a policy of recruiting specialists "working at the frontiers of their particular discipline." Although comprehensiveness is difficult to achieve in a field as fundamental as language, the editors have succeeded not only in treating thoroughly the standard "core" areas of linguisitics (e.g., morphology, phonology, semantics) but in

attempting to include more "peripheral" areas as well (e.g., speech pathology, speech technology). A distinguishing feature of the work is its interdisciplinary nature; significant space is devoted to aspects of anthropology, psychology, sociology, and philosophy that impinge on language. The encyclopedia reveals its international character both in its attempt to cover the contributions of all civilizations (though with a pronounced emphasis on the West) and in the fact that the authors come from 75 countries. The intended audience is academic and professional, though the style is accessible to general readers. Articles range in length from a few sentences to a dozen double-columned pages and cover academic fields, linguistic topics, languages, countries, and individual scholars. Examples and illustrations are numerous, there are cross-references, and each article concludes with a short bibliography. A superb subject index is accompanied by a name index, glossary, list of the world's languages, and many other useful lists and appendixes. Although there is substantial overlap with *International Encyclopedia of Linguistics*, ed. by William Bright (CH, Sep'92), this monumental reference work is noticeably broader in scope. Enthusiastically recommended for academic and larger public libraries.—*J. R. Luttrell, Princeton University*

OAB-0071   Orig
Encyclopedia of post-colonial literatures in English, ed. by Eugene Benson and L.W. Conolly. Routledge, 1994. 2v. 1,874p index ISBN 0-415-05199-1, $225.00

Benson and Conolly build on the success of their *Oxford Companion to Canadian Theatre* (CH, Jul'90) with this alphabetically arranged encyclopedia of worldwide literatures in English. It is a literary and organizational achievement that will support curricular trends at most campuses. Earlier titles, like *International Literature in English*, ed. by Robert L. Ross (CH, Jan'92), do not have the scope and informed, systematic coverage of this new work, which involved regional editors and 574 contributors, most from the countries covered. The editors' goal was to introduce authors and writing from the Philippines and countries influenced by British imperialism—i.e., regions where postcolonial writing in English occurs—and to focus on works that have not received much critical attention. Some authors, for example Margaret Atwood and Salman Rushdie, are certainly well known, but the vast majority will be new to North American readers. The wide-ranging topics and historical surveys are especially useful; genres reach beyond traditional ones to include prison writing and exploration literature, for example. The more than 50 countries represented range from Australia to Hong Kong and Zimbabwe; literary topics include censorship, aborigines in literature, and broadcasting. The 1,600 entries are introductory but often well developed and evaluative, with important contextual information and brief reading lists. Cross-references and a full, text-generated index are a user's delight. Strongly recommended for all libraries with literature collections.—*M. H. Loe, SUNY College at Oswego*

OAB-0072   PS377   92-32466 CIP
Facts on File bibliography of American fiction, 1866-1918, ed. by James Nagel and Gwen L. Nagel. Facts on File, 1993. 412p bibl index afp ISBN 0-8160-2116-3, $95.00

An independent part of a four-volume set, this book lists about 150 authors whose earliest significant work was published between the Civil War and WW I. Less ambitious than Lyle Wright's *American Fiction, 1774-1990* (3 v., 1965-69), which lists 11,000 novels, more inclusive than Donna Gerstenberger's *The American Novel, 1789-1959* (1961), which lists only secondary works, and more extensive than David Kirby's *American Fiction to 1900* (CH, Oct'76) which covers works by and about only 41 writers, this new work is intended "to serve the purposes of literary history and research." Alphabetically arranged author entries, compiled by "scholar-specialists," begin with brief headnotes. Each entry is followed by bibliographies, catalogs, and chronological listings of primary works (books, diaries, letters, notebooks, translations [by the author], editions, archives and their location) and secondary works (concordances, biographies, interviews, and critical studies) in complete bibliographic citations. The front matter includes "Author Entries," general bibliographies, works specific to American fiction 1866-1918, and a list of electronic databases.

"Chronology of American Fiction and Authors," a list of acronyms and journals, and a comprehensive index complete the volume. Highly recommended for college and research libraries.—*P. Kujoory, University of the District of Columbia*

OAB-0073   PN451   96-25679 CIP
Feminist writers, ed. by Pamela Kester-Shelton. St. James Press, 1996. 641p bibl indexes afp ISBN 1-55862-217-9, $130.00

A selective encyclopedia of 300 feminist authors of fiction and nonfiction, *Feminist Writers* is international in scope, focusing on 20th-century authors writing in English. Introductory material provides a definition of feminist writing and its historical grounding. Similar in format to *Gay and Lesbian Literature* (CH, Sep'94), each entry contains a biographical sketch of the author, a list of primary and secondary sources, and an original critical essay on the life and work of the writer. This resource contains nationality, subject, genre, and title indexes as well as lists of sources for additional information. Highly recommended for all academic libraries.—*J. C. Jurgens, St. Cloud State University*

OAB-0074   PN56   93-47362 MARC
Gay & lesbian literature, ed. by Sharon Malinowski. St. James Press, 1994. 488p indexes afp ISBN 1-55862-174-1, $85.00

The vitality and increasing recognition of the field of gay and lesbian literature finds another reflection in this impressive compilation of biographical, bibliographical, and critical information tracing the accomplishments of prominent writers since 1900. This work covers more than 200 novelists, poets, short story writers, dramatists, journalists, editors, and writers of nonfiction whose work has contributed significantly to the lesbian and gay literary, social, and political landscape. Two introductory essays on gay male literature and lesbian literature precede and frame the alphabetical entries. International in scope and featuring authors selected for the lesbian or gay thematic content of their work rather than their sexual identity, this volume serves as a useful companion to the recent bio-bibliographical sourcebooks *Contemporary Lesbian Writers of the United States* (CH, Mar'94) and *Contemporary Gay American Novelists* (CH, Jul'93). Informative and well-organized, each entry provides biographical information and lists of writings by and about the author, followed by a signed critical essay focusing on the importance of the author's work "to his/her own literary canon specifically and to the gay and lesbian literary or historical world generally." In addition to a general index to the featured entries, indexes provide multiple access by nationality, gender, subject, genre, and recipients of gay and lesbian literary awards. Lists of additional authors of gay and lesbian literature and of important published anthologies round out the volume and serve as useful guides for further investigation. Highly recommended for both academic and public libraries.—*J. Ariel, University of California, Irvine*

OAB-0075   PR9340x   Brit. CIP
Lindfors, Bernth. **Black African literature in English, 1987-1991.** H. Zell, 1995. 682p indexes (Bibliographical research in African literatures, 3) ISBN 1-873836-16-3, $125.00

The first *Black African Literature in English* (CH, Mar'80) contained citations as early as the late 1930s but focused primarily on the 1960s and 70s. The two previous supplements covered 1977-81 (1986) and 1982-86 (1989). This important new supplement offers about 8,800 citations published 1987-91 relating to black African literature in English. The entries cite monographs, individual chapters in monographs, and articles in scholarly journals, popular and news magazines, and newspapers. The breadth of sources used in compilation is enormous, including about 1,000 serial titles published worldwide. Although most entries cite English-language sources, other languages are included as well. The main body of the bibliography has two parts: "Genre and Topical Studies and Reference Sources," with 26 subdivisions including such diverse headings as bibliographies, drama, and censorship; and an author-specific section, with four subdivisions (bibliography, biography and autobiography, interviews, and criticism). As interest in African literature increases among both undergraduates and graduate students, Lindfors's compilations

become increasingly essential. This supplement and its predecessors are invaluable reference tools that belong in collections supporting work in African or world literature.—*D. L. Easterbrook, Northwestern University*

OAB-0076   PN81   92-33515 CIP
Marshall, Donald G. **Contemporary critical theory: a selective bibliography.** Modern Language Association of America, 1993. 201p index ISBN 0-87352-963-4, $32.00; ISBN 0-87352-964-2 pbk, $15.50

In the US we like our theory, like our orchestra conductors, to come from Europe, and the entries in Marshall's superb, long-promised bibliography amply attest that we tend not to think in grand ways for ourselves. Anchored in the New Criticism and moving through to the current vogue for various cultural criticisms, the bibliography covers the post-'60s theoretical transformation of US literature studies. Marshall lists in 14 topical sections 1,690 English-language reference books, collections, and monographs ranging from survey and synthetic works to books by and studies of individual theorists. Brief, clear, cogent introductory notes head each section; to say that the entries are inconsistently annotated is perhaps only to say that other compilers would have chosen to annotate them differently. Cross-references and duplicated listings help map the complex set of relationships among these theories. A list of journals specializing in theory and an author index are also provided. Marshall's book has no effective competition; it is one of the few reference works all academic libraries should have for literature studies.—*R. H. Kieft, Haverford College*

OAB-0077   90-49129 CIP
Martinez, Nancy C. **Guide to British poetry explication: v.4: Victorian-contemporary,** by Nancy C. Martinez, Joseph G.R. Martinez, and Erland Anderson. G.K. Hall, NY/Prentice Hall International, 1995. 720p bibl afp ISBN 0-8161-8988-9, $60.00

With this volume, the authors complete their revision and expansion of Kuntz's *Poetry Explication: A Checklist of Interpretation* (3rd ed., CH, May'81), begun in 1991 (for reviews of earlier volumes, see CH, Jul'91 and Jan'94). This final installment indexes more than 5,000 additional explications and increases coverage to include both longer poems by well-known authors (e.g., Tennyson's *Idylls of the King*) and poets not addressed in earlier editions (Seamus Heaney and Stevie Smith). Taken with the compilers' two companion volumes devoted to American verse (*Guides to American Poetry Explication*, CH, May'90), the two series constitute a must purchase for college libraries supporting undergraduate research in literature.—*B. Juhl, University of Arkansas, Fayetteville*

OAB-0078   PS3513   94-41266 CIP
Morgan, Bill. **The works of Allen Ginsberg, 1941-1994: a descriptive bibliography.** Greenwood, 1995. 456p indexes afp (Bibliographies and indexes in American literature, 19) ISBN 0-313-29389-9, $75.00

Fifteen years in the making, Morgan's monumental bibliography contains more than 10,000 entries documenting the work of one of America's most prolific poets. It covers Allen Ginberg's poetry and his other writings on a wide range of topics including, but not limited to, drugs, politics, music, photography, and religion. Translations of Ginsberg's works, excluded here, will appear in a secondary bibliography to be published next year. Prepared with the poet's full cooperation, the bibliography provides a comprehensive and accurate history of Ginsberg's work. Entries are organized in eight sections: English-language books and pamphlets; broadsides; books by other authors and editors that contain first book appearances of Ginsberg's works; first appearances of Ginsberg's works; first appearances of works in periodicals; publications that reproduce photographs by Ginsberg; miscellaneous publications such as dust jacket blurbs, printed post cards, and other ephemera; commercial recordings; and film, radio, and television appearances. Within each section, items are arranged chronologically. There is a general index as well as a separate index of titles and first lines of Ginsberg's writings. Indispensable for scholars doing work on Ginsberg and the Beat generation, Morgan's bibliography is an essential purchase for all libraries supporting literary research.—*W. M. Gargan, Brooklyn College, CUNY*

OAB-0079 Orig
The New Oxford companion to literature in French, ed. by Peter France. Oxford, 1995. 865p afp ISBN 0-19-866125-8, $49.95

This *New Oxford Companion* reflects a change in focus from its predecessors, *The Oxford Companion to French Literature*, ed. by Paul Harvey (1959), and *The Concise Oxford Dictionary of French Literature* (CH, May'77). The words "literature in French" in the title signal this change: the companion includes 200 new entries on francophone literature (writing in French outside France in former French possessions), as well as entries on Provençal (or Occitan) and Breton literature (literature in other languages native to France). The work also updates recent research on literary, cultural, and political history with entries on versification, *fin'amor*, libraries, and occupation and resistance. It includes entries on new developments and shifts in French literature such as music hall, detective fiction, *photo-roman*, and the *bande dessinée*. At the book's beginning the editor helpfully provides a chronology, which lists, alongside "reigning monarch, or regime," corresponding historical and cultural events and prominent authors of each period. The editor also includes maps of France at different periods and a map of central Paris. Asterisks beside a title or author indicate separate entries in the book. A fine, up-to-date reference book for French literature, highly recommended for all college and university reference collections.—*R. T. Ivey, University of Memphis*

OAB-0080 PN1021 92-41887 CIP
The New Princeton encyclopedia of poetry and poetics, ed. by Alex Preminger and T.V.F. Brogan. Princeton, 1993. 1,383p afp ISBN 0-691-03271-8, $125.00; ISBN 0-691-02123-6 pbk, $29.95

Certain works are so comprehensive and trustworthy it is difficult to imagine a reference department without them. Since 1965, readers and librarians have turned to the *Princeton Encyclopedia* for thorough scholarly treatment of the forms, genres, and styles of and critical approaches to practically every variety and period of written or oral verse. Unfortunately, even with the awkward 100-page supplement and update included in the "enlarged edition" of 1975 (CH, Oct'75) the work's authoritativeness has been progressively compromised as its contents age by newer, if less exhaustive, poetry handbooks and dictionaries. With almost all the original entries revised, bibliographies and cross-references significantly expanded, and 162 entirely new entries, this *New Princeton Encyclopedia* should restore the title to a premier place on the reference shelf. This revision, begun in 1984, aims to "address new topics and approaches," to "survey new work on old topics," and to increase "coverage of emergent and non-Western entries." New articles treat multicultural and international subjects such as "Feminist Poetics" or "Chicano Poetry" as well as drawing together material previously scattered throughout the volume, as in "Love Poetry" and "Hermeneutics." Individual authors are still not covered and, despite the addition of several hundred cross-references, a personal names index would have been helpful in locating the poets and critics covered in topical articles. In all other respects, this volume should delight browsers and scholars alike. A must for all libraries.—*B. Juhl, University of Arkansas*

OAB-0081 PR4589 95-2453 CIP
Newlin, George, comp. **Everyone in Dickens: v.1: Plots, people and publishing particulars in the complete works, 1833-1849; v.2: Plots, people and publishing particulars in the complete works, 1850-1870; v.3: Characteristics and commentaries, tables and tabulations: a taxonomy.** Greenwood, 1995. 3v. 1,725, 704p indexes afp ISBN 0-313-29580-8, $275.00

Newlin provides a gold mine of information about the 13,143 people mentioned by Dickens in the 588 works that constitute his literary output. This number includes both fictional characters and historical figures, including references to Shakespeare or to figures such as Oliver Cromwell. The set includes a two-volume chronological analysis of all characters beginning with *Sketches by Boz* and concluding with *The Mystery of Edwin Drood*. For the Dickens lover, these two volumes would be the most enjoyable. Extracting directly from the text, Newlin presents characters in Dickens's own words, describing not only the characters but their typical traits. All the favorite Dickens characters are here, often accompanied by the earliest illustrations (in most cases, approved by Dickens himself). Newlin presents the characters using typical stage terminology (something Dickens would probably have approved)—principals, supporting roles, others, walk-ons, and spear-carriers. Volume 3 contains 12 subject indexes to the earlier volumes, where one learns, e.g., that exactly 11 wine merchants and six wine merchant employees are mentioned in Dickens works, each listed with exact location. The ultimate source for "anyone" in Dickens, highly recommended for both scholarly research and Dickens lovers.—*R. B. Meeker, Chicago State University*

OAB-0082 PS217 96-35351 CIP
Nineteenth-century American women writers: a bio-bibliographical critical sourcebook, ed. by Denise D. Knight with Emmanuel S. Nelson. Greenwood, 1997. 534p bibl index afp ISBN 0-313-29713-4, $99.50

Until recently, the Western literary canon was dominated by male authors, with only a few representative females. However, the canon has recently undergone considerable discussion and revision, with an eye to including non-European cultures and female voices. Several 19th-century women writers who had fallen into obscurity are now being celebrated, hence the growing popularity of Kate Chopin, Harriet Beecher Stowe, Charlotte Perkins Gilman, and others. The present book attempts to bring together representative US women writers whose best-known works were written or published during the 19th century. A variety of authors make up the 77 entries—children's authors, novelists, poets, abolitionists, former slaves—and they provide an understanding of women's issues of that day. Each entry features a short biography, discussion of the author's major themes, critical studies, and a bibliography of works by and about the author. A comprehensive bibliography is also provided. A few minor authors are omitted, but the editor (English, SUNY-Cortland) points out this volume can only be representative of the period, so enough authors remain to make up a second volume. A volume on 20th-century US women authors would be appropriate, as would a comprehensive index to the series. Highly recommended for all public and academic libraries.—*S. R. Moore, University of Southwestern Louisiana*

OAB-0083 PR8706 95-44943 MARC
The Oxford companion to Irish literature, ed. by Robert Welch with Bruce Stewart. Oxford, 1996. 614p bibl afp ISBN 0-19-866158-4 pbk, $49.95

Reference works in Irish studies have appeared fairly regularly in recent years. For this *Oxford Companion*, Welch (Univ. of Ulster, Coleraine) has assembled a strong body of contributors to survey the Irish literary landscape in some 2,000 entries. Not restricted to writers, the entries include historical figures and events that provide background for the literature. One of the strengths of the work is its demonstration of the cross-fertilization and continuity between the Gaelic and Anglo traditions. Some omissions are surprising—e.g., Marina Carr (dramatist), Denis Donoghue (writer and critic)—as well as factual errors that are inevitable and should be corrected in future editions. The work includes a chronology and a select bibliography. Comparisons will be made with *Dictionary of Irish Literature*, ed. by Robert Hogan et al. (CH, Apr'80); however one would have to come down on the side of the present work for its currency alone. This work belongs in all academic and large public libraries.—*M. J. Durkan, Swarthmore College*

OAB-0084 Orig
The Oxford companion to the English language, ed. by Tom McArthur. Oxford, 1992. 1,184p index afp ISBN 0-19-214183-X, $45.00

This invaluable work has no competitor; the real problem will be trying to keep it on reference shelves, since it is as delightful to browse as it is useful for specific questions about any and all forms of the English language. There is an informative essay on the organization of the work, a usable if hardly definitive map of "English throughout the world," and a splendidly detailed presentation of the values of the phonetic symbols used. Cross-referencing is generous, with the inevitable occasional dropped ball as a result; try the "IGBO" entries for one example of incomplete information. Articles are signed and sources supplied in most cases. Essential for any library with even a moderate interest in the English language, this title is especially valuable in the present climate of concern for a variety of creoles, vernaculars, etc. Enthusiastically recommended.—*N. F. George, Kenyon College*

OAB-0085   PR471   96-26699 MARC
The Oxford companion to twentieth-century literature in English, ed. by Jenny Stringer. Oxford, 1996. 751p afp ISBN 0-19-212271-1, $45.00

Stringer's compilation follows the established format of Oxford companions—short entries devoted mostly to biographies but including works, genres, critical terms, periodicals (a particular strength of the volume), and literary groups. Yet it is forced to deal with issues of scope that stretch the neat compartmentalization that is the series hallmark. Geographically, it includes all areas of the Anglophone world, with roughly a third devoted to Britain, a third to the US, and a third to the rest. This definition leads to uncomfortable decisions—Vladimir Nabokov is in, but not Czeslaw Milosz. Conceptually, the book includes not only writers of fiction and poetry (including authors of genre fiction and bestsellers) but also historians, philosophers, critics, and others in related fields. Chronologically, it includes those who wrote in the 20th century (including many living authors) but omits individual entries for their 19th-century works. The biographies are all appropriately concise, including not only facts, enumerations of major works, and achievements, but pithy critical commentary. There is some overlap with other sources, but this is wide-ranging enough to be of particular value to academic readers, upper-division undergraduate through faculty.—*W. S. Brockman, University of Illinois at Urbana-Champaign*

OAB-0086   PR601   93-1436 CIP
The Oxford companion to twentieth-century poetry in English, ed. by Ian Hamilton. Oxford, 1994. 602p afp ISBN 0-19-866147-9, $35.00

Reference works with "Oxford Companion" in the title commonly become standards, and this magisterial work is certain to achieve that status among librarians. The criteria for inclusion are quite specific: the poet must have lived (however briefly) in this century, must have written in English, must be at least 30 years old, and must have published one "substantial" work of poetry. Hamilton, the author of the exceptional biography *Robert Lowell* (CH, Mar'83) and the subject of a lawsuit by J.D. Salinger, considers this work "a map of modern poetry in English" in 1994. That is entirely accurate. The poets, movements, magazines, and hoaxes are in alphabetical order with numerous cross-references. The text is on the whole decently written and browsable. Poets currently in favor tend to have longer entries, but there are also generous references to poets as disparate as Robinson Jeffers and Dylan Thomas. All libraries will find this worthy addition to the Oxford Companion line an invaluable source. All levels.— *R. S. Bravard, Lock Haven University of Pennsylvania*

OAB-0087   PS153   92-12897 MARC
Peck, David R. **American ethnic literatures: native American, African American, Chicano/Latino, and Asian American writers and their backgrounds: an annotated bibliography.** Salem Press, 1992. 218p index afp ISBN 0-89356-684-5, $40.00

Peck's valuable, timely bibliography is aimed at teachers, librarians, and students interested in identifying, reading, and understanding Native American, African American, Chicano/Latino, and Asian American literature. The recent growth in primary and secondary sources on American ethnic literature has involved a wide range of publishers and produced a confusing array of reference works. This bibliography will make the search for material to use in teaching or studying authors like Jamaica Kinkaid or Leslie Silko far more efficient and successful. Peck briefly introduces the four ethnic literatures; pulls together and annotates secondary sources, important background studies, reference works, journals, teaching guides, and comparative literature studies; and lists full-length

primary works by their authors. The author index is very useful, connecting material that can be scattered in the many sections needed to classify ethnic literature, e.g., Native American speeches and memoirs; collections of plays, poetry, etc.; collections of Latina writings. Coverage is limited to works in English, including some bilingual texts. Very highly recommended for all libraries. Useful to students, from beginning undergraduates up, and faculty alike.—*M. H. Loe, SUNY College at Oswego*

OAB-0088   PR581   94-4657 CIP
Reilly, Catherine W. **Late Victorian poetry, 1880-1899: an annotated biobibliography.** Mansell, 1994. 577p index ISBN 0-7201-2001-2, $120.00

The first of three volumes to include both major and minor Victorian poets, this biobibliography lists 2,964 poets and volumes of their verse published 1880-99. Reilly provides brief biographical information, where available, about her subjects, followed by entries for individual volumes found in the UK's national libraries, older public libraries and private subscription libraries, and the library of the University of California-Davis, which houses the Kohler collection of minor British poets, 1789-1918. Following the cross-referenced alphabetical listing by poet is an index of all distinctive titles; an index of publishers' series would have been welcome as well. The biobibliography excludes books with poems by more than two poets; volumes consisting exclusively of verse drama, dialect poetry, or hymns or songs with music; most volumes of children's verse; and pamphlets. Yeats and other members of the Rhymers' Club can be found here, as can Elisha Walton (commercial traveler) and Sarah Dale (Lancashire millworker). Reilly has assembled a fascinating list of poets and their works in what promises to be a unique resource for students of Victorian poetry in all its variety.—*A. L. Ronchetti, University of Pittsburgh*

OAB-0089   Aust. CIP
Simkin, John E., comp. **The whole story: 3000 years of sequels and sequences.** Thorpe, 1996.(Dist. by Reed Reference Publishing) 1,198p ISBN 1-875589-26-0, $135.00

The definitive work to date in English covering sequels and novel sequences, *Whole Story* quite simply eclipses all previous efforts. It is a crown jewel of bibliographic scholarship. Librarians everywhere will find it an invaluable source of information. The scope runs from Greek drama through dime novels to contemporary "men's action" sequences. Any author who wrote a sequence or created a character that survived into a sequence is almost certain to be here. The only sequences this reviewer did not find were Simon Raven's second novel sequence, *The First-Born of Egypt,* and the "Cabin" series of John Faulkner (and recent numbers of many sequences like "Star Trek" that increase monthly). The main section, "Sequels and Sequences," is arranged by sequel or sequence title, and there are title and author indexes. Cross-references and notes are numerous and helpful. Clearly, as the introduction indicates, this is a labor of love and has resulted in a reference work that is a pleasure to use and fun to browse. Simkin on sequels and sequences joins that select list of reference works known forever by an individual's name. An essential reference purchase for all but the smallest libraries.—*R. S. Bravard, Lock Haven University of Pennsylvania*

OAB-0090   PS374   94-37400 CIP
Simone, Roberta. **The immigrant experience in American fiction: an annotated bibliography.** Scarecrow, 1995. 203p bibl indexes afp ISBN 0-8108-2962-2, $39.50

Simone, a professor of English, has produced an erudite bibliography of fiction and major criticism with a precise focus: English-language fiction concerning immigrants and their descendants that "tells the story of becoming American"—the tensions, exploitation, persecution, experiences, work, and rewards of becoming part of American culture. Besides novels and short fiction, the bibliography also cites selected influential criticism. The fiction of English and Scots immigrants is excluded, since the compiler considers they set the dominant culture in America to which all others had to adapt. African American literature is also excluded because this group came to America as slaves—involuntary immigrants—and because many bibliographies already exist for this literature. The generously annotated bibliography is arranged alphabetically by more than 40 immigrant groups, e.g., Armenian, Chinese, German, Hungarian, Japanese, Slovakian, Swedish, and West Indian. The largest sections cover Irish, Italian, Jewish, and Mexican groups. Although descriptive, the annotations are well written and are helpful in identifying appropriate fiction for classroom use, research, or personal interest. In addition to author and title indexes, Simone provides a theme and genre index that has such entries as "Conflicts between Generations," "Factories," "Inter-Ethnic Relations," and many geographic locations. She mentions only six other useful bibliographies, but some others should have been cited, e.g., *Dickinson's American Historical Fiction* (5th ed., by Virginia Brokaw Gerhardstein, 1986), and Donald Hartman and Jerome Drost's *Themes and Settings in Fiction* (CH, May'89). Because of its tight focus, this volume does not duplicate information available elsewhere. It can be paired with Vicki Anderson's *Immigrants in the United States in Fiction* (1994), a guide for K-9 teachers and librarians. Simone's bibliography is an impressive source for college-level studies of immigrant fiction, cultural and sociological history of the US, immigrant publishing history, and trends in ethnic/cultural criticism. A necessary acquisition for public and academic libraries.—*J. A. Adams, SUNY at Buffalo*

OAB-0091 PN841 95-36733 MARC

Valade, Roger M. **The Schomburg Center Guide to black literature from the eighteenth century to the present,** ed. by Roger M. Valade with Denise Kasinec. Gale, 1996. 545p index afp ISBN 0-7876-0289-2, $75.00

This valuable handbook will be extremely useful in approaching the field of black literature. It covers fiction and nonfiction written by blacks in the US and abroad, published in or translated into English. There are five types of entries: writer's name, name of work, theme/movement, literary term, and character name cross-reference. None of the entries is signed. Biographical essays treat novelists, short story writers, poets, dramatists, critics, essayists, journalists, screenwriters, and children's writers; and each lists references for further reading (e.g., entries in "Dictionary of Literary Biography"). The writer's nationality, occupation (e.g., poet), and birth/death dates are listed under each entry. Entries for works supply the author, type of work, and date of publication as well as a brief plot synopsis. There are many photographs of authors and book jackets. The volume concludes with a chronology and a carefully crafted subject index that identifies numerous terms that otherwise would not be found. This book is a treasure that should be highly useful to most libraries.—*C. A. Larson, University of Nebraska at Omaha*

OAB-0092 [CD-ROM]

The World Shakespeare bibliography on CD-ROM, 1990-1993, ed. by James L. Harner. Cambridge/Folger Shakespeare Library, 1996. ISBN 0-521-55627-9, $240.00. 1 disc; user manual. System requirements: Windows 3.1 or higher; Macintosh.

Probably the most useful and certainly the most comprehensive tool for Shakespearean study, *World Shakespeare Bibliography*, edited by James L. Harner and formerly by Harrison T. Meserole, has appeared annually since 1950 in the fifth number of *Shakespeare Quarterly*. It is now available on CD-ROM for 1990-93, a period whose restricted coverage might persuade some purchasers to wait until greater yearly coverage becomes available. The manual (prepared by Harner) is well designed, well illustrated with useful diagrams, and easy to use. On a laptop computer with Windows 95, the CD was simple to install and proved user-friendly. The CD-ROM version contains an extensive subject and name index, the latter incorporating the paperbound indexes for actors, actresses, authors, editors, and dramatists, among a host of other rubrics. The CD-ROM version has more options than the printed version, offering the facility for cross-referencing and access to several years (in this case, four) in place of the bulky, single-year printed versions. The screen is multicolored, and there are various points of access and the capability for hypertext navigation—e.g., through the help menu—which allows users to create a search history for

their research interests. The content of the CD-ROM is somewhat different from the printed version; entries have been modified in a number of cases to provide greater clarity. Keywords and points of reference allow users to access related entries. Although individual purchasers and some institutions might legitimately balk at the electronic package's price, this already powerful research tool is even better in its CD-ROM version. It is essential for all undergraduate, graduate, and research libraries, as well as general reference collections.—*W. Baker, Northern Illinois University*

■ Performing Arts & Communication

OAB-0093 PN2035 95-1011 CIP

Banham, Martin. **The Cambridge guide to theatre.** [New ed.]. Cambridge, 1995. 1,233p ISBN 0-521-434378, $49.95

The new edition improves on the excellent first edition (*The Cambridge Guide to World Theatre*, CH, Jun'89). It "contains over two hundred entirely new entries, and major reworkings of many other substantial entries." The worldwide list of scholarly contributors, expanded by 50 percent, now numbers more than 160; all entries are signed. Significant events that changed or expanded theater practice or understanding since the first edition are not appended to the original article, but are interwoven within articles. The original intention of the first edition is reiterated: to offer "a comprehensive view of the history and present practice of theatre in all parts of the world, thus pointing to the dynamic interaction of performance traditions from all cultures in present day theatre." This edition is encyclopedic in scope and international in coverage. The articles have a depth one might not expect in a volume as comprehensive as this. To be sure, there are short, pithy entries (e.g., "Stainless Stephen" or "Pepper's ghost"). The "Less Obvious Entries" list in the first edition has been expanded from 37 to more than 100; these entries help define the extent of topics covered and their various categories ("claque," "inns as playhouses,"; "nudity," "waxworks," etc.). At the same time, the work covers in fine detail many national theater traditions, dramatic theory, criticism and censorship, as well as stage lighting, sound and design, and hundreds of theater personages. The editor aims "to offer both students of the theatre and the general theatregoer information, assessment and entertainment, and a base from which they may explore particular interests." Enthusiastically recommended for serious students and general theatergoers.—*R. G. Stephen, emeritus, Rider University*

OAB-0094 TK6540X 71-649524 Orig

Broadcasting & cable market place, 1992: the industry source for radio, television and cable. R.R. Bowker, 1992. various pagings indexes ISBN 0-8352-3178-X pbk, $159.95

Broadcasting Yearbook, long the reference bible of the radio, television, and cable industries, reflects in this title change its greater coverage of cable information. Now doubled in size due to the addition of a yellow pages section containing names of industry personnel and stations, it also contains new information on the top 38 cable MSOs (Multiple Systems Operators), a handy subject index providing the whereabouts of, e.g., "Hindi" or "jazz" or "nostalgia" programming in the country, and the expanded book and periodical section including videos, more industry statistics, and increased company information. While continuing to provide the basics (e.g., listings of radio, television, and cable stations, lists of producers of programming services, satellite services, broadcasting associations, FCC regulations), it includes a new list of trade shows and a valuable chronology of broadcasting and cable events since 1931. New tabs and sectional tables of contents improve the book's ease of use. This is a one-stop-shop for broadcasting information and no reference collection should be without it.—*S. G. Williamson, University of Pennsylvania*

OAB-0095 ML102 93-4742 CIP

Encyclopedia of keyboard instruments: v.1: The piano, ed. by Robert Palmieri. Garland, 1994. 521p index afp (Garland reference library of the humanities, 1131) ISBN 0-8240-5685-X, $95.00

The first volume of a projected three-volume encyclopedia devoted to keyboard instruments, this timely work has been published just prior to the 300th anniversary of the invention of the piano. Palmieri (emeritus, Kent State Univ.) has also published *Piano Information Guide: An Aid to Research* (CH, Jul'89), a very useful companion volume. The signed articles in this new work, although arranged in the usual A to Z format, vary in length, some being concise definitions, while others explore the topic in depth. Comprehensive in scope, the work emphasizes the historical evolution of the piano, including articles on the most important piano makers in various countries, builders, companies, and those composers most directly influencing the development of the instrument. Technical terms ranging from "acoustical block" to "wrest plank" are explained with an excellent system of cross-references and numerous illustrations. Selected bibliographies follow many of the articles, and a detailed index leads the user to articles that mention the people or terms listed. Beautifully printed and bound, this should be considered an essential purchase for all academic and for large public libraries.—*L. Smith, University of Western Ontario*

OAB-0096 PN1992x Orig
Encyclopedia of television, by the Museum of Broadcast Communications; ed. by Horace Newcomb. Fitzroy Dearborn, 1997. 3v. 1,948p bibl index ISBN 1-884964-26-5, $300.00

Newcomb (radio, television and film, Univ. of Texas at Austin) is to be commended for compiling this large collaborative work. It goes beyond existing encyclopedias by providing substantive commentary by academic writers, not only on a large selection of famous English-language shows but about topics (e.g., high definition television, Vietnam on television, experimental video), genres (science programs, westerns), networks (Univision), personalities (actors, producers, journalists), and institutions (European Broadcasting Union). Essays on actors contain biographical and critical commentaries followed by filmographies and screen/stage appearances. Television show descriptions include programming histories. Famous documentaries (e.g., *Victory at Sea*) are also included. Most of the 1,000 lengthy essays contain bibliographies and superb photographs. These bibliographies and the length and academic nature of the essays distinguish this encyclopedia from Les Brown's *Encyclopedia of Television*, (CH, Nov'92) and Jeff Evan's *The Guiness Television Encyclopedia* (Enfield, UK, 1995). The list of contributors reads like a who's who of television pundits. Although the emphasis is clearly on the US, the encyclopedia also provides overview essays on the history, institutional development, programming, and policies for television in Canada, Britain, and Australia. Given its size and scope, the price is reasonable. Highly recommended for reference collections at all academic levels.—*S. G. Williamson, University of Pennsylvania*

OAB-0097 ML102 93-48237 CIP
Gänzl, Kurt. **The encyclopedia of the musical theatre.** Schirmer Books, 1994. 2v. 1,610p afp ISBN 0-02-871445-8, $150.00

Gänzl's experience in the musical theater and his years of research and writing on the subject make him uniquely qualified to produce this magnificent two-volume reference work. To treat American or British musical stage productions would be a daunting task, but the author capably expands his coverage to include Germany, France, Hungary, and Australia. This treatment includes operettas, musical revues, and musical plays. Gänzl is no newcomer to producing reference works on musical theater. His earlier efforts include *The British Musical Theatre* (CH, Oct'87), *The Blackwell Guide to Musical Theatre on Record* (CH, Mar'91), and, in collaboration with Andrew Lamb, *Gänzl's Book of the Musical Theatre* (CH, Jun'89). This new set comprehensively covers the history, people, and plots of over 2,000 works from the 19th century to the present. For each play the author provides an introduction listing the titles, credits as they appeared on the original playbill, and place of the first production. The body of the entry summarizes the plot, including important musical numbers. Entries are enriched by Gänzl's insightful commentary. He places each play in its historical context, relates it to other works, and highlights salient features in a highly readable prose style. As evidence of Gänzl's attention to detail, every mention of a character in a play is followed by the name of the actor who created that role. Each play entry closes with a supplemen-

tary section tracing the work's appearance in major cities other than that of its premier. Discographic data is also supplied in this section. The entries on people provide a refreshing wealth of detail for persons outside of the Broadway and West End enclaves. In fact, one of the most striking features of this set is its evenhanded treatment of the genre: the reader gains a comprehensive view of Western musical theatre around the world. Gänzl's painstaking dedication to examining as much primary source material as possible gives him an intimacy with the subject unparalleled in most reference works. One gets the impression that Gänzl has watched each production and met each performer personally. The work is attractively presented in a two-column format with legible type. Sharp, clear black-and-white illustrations are liberally spread throughout. For a work with such popular appeal a sturdier binding is certainly warranted for library use. An index to persons would be a nice addition to future editions, since not all the individuals mentioned in the text have their own entries. These small failings notwithstanding, this is a monumental achievement in the field of music scholarship and a delight to read. Highly recommended for all libraries and a must for music collections.—*G. S. Geary, University of Hawaii*

OAB-0098 ML128 94-28796 CIP
Griscom, Richard. **The recorder: a guide to writings about the instrument for players and researchers,** by Richard Griscom and David Lasocki. Garland, 1994. 504p index afp (Music research and information guides, 19) ISBN 0-8240-2945-3, $70.00

The scope and quality of this book quickly identify it as a labor of love. The authors' obvious joy in preparing this unique reference tool for the recorder shines throughout and imparts confidence to the user. Unlike many annotated bibliographies, *The Recorder* can actually be read for its informative text. The annotations are not merely descriptive but offer critical observations, often referring to published reviews of the cited work. Coverage is uniquely comprehensive for the US; the only other current specialized bibliography of literature on the recorder is Hugo Alker's two-volume *Blockflöten-Bibliographie* (1984), which is devoted largely to German publications difficult or impossible to obtain in the US. The annotated bibliography of periodicals on the recorder is an excellent tool for collection development. An index of authors, titles, and subjects provides thorough and varied access to subjects mentioned in the annotations. In spite of its price, *The Recorder* is an indispensable addition to large music collections and highly recommended for smaller collections as well. Upper-division undergraduate level and above.—*H. J. Diamond, Herbert H. Lehman College, CUNY*

OAB-0099 Orig
The Guinness encyclopedia of popular music, ed. by Colin Larkin. [2nd ed.]. Guinness Publishing, 1995.(Dist. by Stockton) 6v. 4,991p bibl index ISBN 1-56159-176-9, $495.00

To the first edition (CH, Mar'93), issued only three years ago, this edition adds two volumes. More than 70 percent of the original entries have been revised by 30 contributors (reduced from the first edition's 82), making style more consistent across the entries. Many discographies now include record labels, but the British label is often the only one listed (e.g., the William Orbit entry gives the N-Gram label, but neither the UK Virgin distributor nor the US Discovery label). Some birth and death dates have been added, as have selected videos, and emphasis added for reggae, Latin, and African pop artists. About half the errors this reviewer found in the first edition have been corrected, but entries for Stealin' Horses, Three Dog Night drummer Floyd Sneed, and KGB are still incorrect. Several significant artists are still omitted (David Baerwald, Luna, Poi Dog Pondering, Letters to Cleo); Larkin's preface points out that about 26,000 artists' entries are not yet prepared. This is very much a work in progress, with expected new and expensive editions adding new information (Larkin projects a 20-volume 4th edition). Nonetheless, no other work approaches *Guinness*'s coverage. Most entries are excellent surveys, and volume 6 has useful artist and subject bibliographies. Supplemental volumes would have been more awkward to use but less expensive. Essential for any serious collection of popular music.—*R. A. Aken, University of Kentucky*

OAB-0100   ML105   96-16456 CIP
The Harvard biographical dictionary of music, ed. by Don Michael Randel. Belknap, Harvard, 1996. 1,013p ISBN 0-674-37299-9, $39.95

For more than 50 years, *Harvard Dictionary of Music* (1969) has been a mainstay of all reference collections, but the entries have been restricted to musical topics, omitting biographical articles. Therefore, this source is a natural companion to its venerable ancestor. International in scope and covering all eras of music from the ancient to the present, this important new reference source has information concerning 5,500 individuals. Most are associated with classical concert music, although prominent jazz, rock, folk, and popular personalities are also represented: Madonna, Mozart, Zoot Sims, Mick Jagger, and Dolly Parton are included. Musicologists, educators, teachers, and reviewers, no matter how influential, are excluded. Entries consist of brief to long paragraphs that may include a bibliography or a list of compositions. Major composers such as J.S. Bach rate many pages. One may quibble over inclusions or exclusions and the volume is not perfect (Vincent Persichetti did not die on August 15), but this is an authoritative and significant new reference work which all libraries must purchase. Highest recommendation.—*J. L. Patterson, University of Wisconsin—Eau Claire*

OAB-0101   ML102   94-40853 CIP
Hischak, Thomas S. **The American musical theatre song encyclopedia.** Greenwood, 1995. 543p bibl index afp ISBN 0-313-29407-0, $59.95

Hischak (SUNY-Cortland) follows his superb *Stage It with Music: An Encyclopedic Guide to the American Musical Theatre* (CH, Dec'95) with this excellent guide that ventures to explain the context of some 1,800 songs representing all major shows, genres, authors, and eras of the American stage, from *The Black Crook* (1866) to Sondheim's *Passion* (1993). What separates this work from earlier useful editions, such as Richard Lewine and Alfred Simon's *Songs of the American Theatre* (CH, Oct'73) and *Lissauer's Encyclopedia of Popular Music in America* (1991), is the quality of each individual entry, which not only puts each song in context but also verifies the original performer (most of the time), provides a brief recording history (including noncast album covers), and explains the song's uniqueness in theater history. The arrangement, alphabetical by song, is supplemented by a brief list of alternate titles of songs and a personnel/show title index. For its breadth, scope, and pure readability, this volume is highly recommended for all theater collections, large or small.—*A. J. Adam, Prairie View Agricultural and Mechanical University*

OAB-0102   GV1585   93-25051 CIP
International dictionary of ballet, ed. by Martha Bremser and Larraine Nicholas. St. James, 1993. 2v. 1,600p indexes afp ISBN 1-55862-084-2, $230.00

Bremser and Nicholas provide 750 entries on dancers, choreographers, ballets, composers, librettists, and ballet companies from the Renaissance to the present. The work's scope is international, although it emphasizes Russia, Europe, and the US. All the entries are signed and many are illustrated, including lavish full-page black-and-white photographs, lithographs, and paintings. The entries are a model of thoroughness and organization, making this an important reference source. For dancers, a brief biographical summary is followed by a complete list of roles, articles by and about the dancer, and a critical essay. Entries on ballets include complete information on the premiere, a chronological list of other important productions of the ballet, and a bibliography of major publications about it. Also included are a listing of dancers by country, an index of professions and institutions, and notes on the contributors. Future editions would benefit by the addition of entries for major ballet critics and historians, a listing of major reviews of individual productions, citations to obituaries, and Russian-language titles in addition to English translated titles in bibliographical notes. Highly recommended for public, college, and research libraries.—*S. C. Summer, Columbia University*

OAB-0103   PN2035   92-215736 Orig
International dictionary of theatre: v.1: Plays, ed. by Mark Hawkins-Dady; picture editor, Leanda Shrimpton. St. James Press, 1993 (c1992). 954p ISBN 1-55862-095-8, $120.00

An encyclopedic guide to more than 600 notable plays, ancient Greece to the present. Entries, by distinguished international scholars, are signed and arranged alphabetically by title, *Absurd Person Singular* to *Zoo Story*. The work focuses on drama "as distinct from the other performing arts such as opera, dance, mime, the musical, performance art, and folk, ritual, and community theatre." The entries, a page or more in length, provide facts (e.g., first production dates, published texts, bibliography of secondary sources), but the bulk of the entry consists of a plot summary combined with an assessment of the play's importance. There are no character lists. The number, size, detail, and quality of the illustrations (all black-and-white) are excellent. Illustrations are often drawn from British productions, even for American plays—an advantage, since the pictures offer views not available in American sources—but in many illustrations, actors are not identified. *Plays* complements other works (e.g., J.T. Shipley's *Crown Guide to the World's Great Plays*, rev. ed., CH, Jun'85; Steve Fletcher's *The Book of 1000 Plays*, CH, Dec'89). *Plays* is the first of a projected three-volume set that will also cover playwrights (v.2) and actors, directors, and designers (v.3). Recommended as a perfect addition to undergraduate collections in the humanities.—*R. R. Centing, Ohio State University*

OAB-0104   PN1993   93-43318 CIP
Katz, Ephraim. **The film encyclopedia.** [2nd ed.]. Harper Perennial, 1994. 1,496p ISBN 0-06-273089-4 pbk, $25.00

Truly a monumental reference work, containing over 7,000 well-researched entries in its 1,496 pages, this title is the best single-volume film encyclopedia in the English language. The enormous task of updating the first edition (CH, May'80) was carried out with admirable thoroughness and was completed after Katz's death in 1992. Many new topics were added, and essays on active persons and ongoing topics were brought up to date through 1993. Articles on film personalities whose careers had changed dramatically since the first edition were thoroughly rewritten. For example, the entry on Sean Connery was completely revised to reflect the stature the actor gained late in his career with many fine dramatic performances and an Academy Award. Alternatively, the article on Michael Cimino was rewritten in view of his reversal of fortunes after a promising beginning in the 1970s. Katz's work contains no illustrations and no entries for individual films. This information can be supplied by *Halliwell's Film Guide* (CH, Jul'78; Jun'80), which contains brief descriptions of thousands of feature films. *The Film Encyclopedia* is strongly recommended for all libraries. The book is a tremendous value, affordable for libraries of all sizes and for individuals.—*W. P. Hogan, Eastern Michigan University*

OAB-0105   ML102   92-36276 MARC
The New Grove dictionary of opera, ed. by Stanley Sadie; managing editor, Christina Bashford. Macmillan, UK/Grove's Dictionaries of Music, 1992. 4v. ISBN 0-935859-92-6, $850.00

Editor Sadie's latest *New Grove* title is a treasure trove of opera information that can be endlessly mined by scholars and interested students. It concentrates on opera of the Western World from the inception of opera to the present. Conceived as an offspring of the *New Grove Dictionary of Music and Musicians* (CH, Feb'81), it has emerged as an essentially new work. With contributions by more than 1,300 specialists, it provides entries for composers, librettists, conductors, singers, stage designers, opera houses (listed by location), and titles (with plot summaries), as well as thorough reviews of all manner of topics. Lesser-known operas and performers of the 17th and 19th centuries are particularly well represented. Everything is here from film and filming and videotaping to costumes, publishing, voice types, and travesty roles and breeches parts (the British terms for the American "trouser" roles). Major articles are remarkably well written and include substantial bibliographies. There is even an appendix of roles. Has anything been left out? Probably, but who could quibble over the lack of entries on women's or African American contributions, which would be of most interest, perhaps, to Americans. We can only wish for more. Expensive, but well worth the price for any library with the funds and patron interest. Another such magnificent endeavor will not soon be produced. Undergraduate; graduate; faculty.—*J. S. Sauer, SUNY College at New Paltz*

OAB-0106   ML158   93-28491 MARC

Opera mediagraphy: videorecordings and motion pictures, comp. by Sharon G. Almquist. Greenwood, 1993. 269p index afp (Music reference collection, 40) ISBN 0-313-28490-3, $55.00

A useful, well-executed selection aid for a type of material not systematically dealt with elsewhere. Almquist (media library, Univ. of North Texas) presents a title list of 156 operas that have appeared in videocassette or motion picture versions (movie adaptations are covered as well as filmed stage productions). All in-print, and some out-of-print, videos in US format are listed for each opera, as are all available motion pictures and laser disks. For each entry the cast is given, with timing, distributor, and review citations. The citations—from 22 journals in the library or opera fields—have rating symbols that reflect the appraisals of the reviewers, in the mode of the *Media Review Digest*, for which this volume is an admirable partner. There are indexes to singers, conductors, composers, opera companies, and media used. Recommended for all academic library reference sections.—*G. A. Marco, Rosary College*

OAB-0107   ML128   92-46475 CIP

Rabson, Carolyn. **Orchestral excerpts: a comprehensive index.** Fallen Leaf, CA, 1993. 221p bibl afp (Fallen Leaf reference books in music, 25) ISBN 0-914913-26-3, $35.00

This long-needed index began as a database developed at the Oberlin College Conservatory Library; the print version, revised and expanded by a retired Oberlin music reference librarian, makes the information available to a wider audience. As the title indicates, the volume indexes published orchestral excerpts; it excludes arranged solo pieces based on symphonic or operatic melodies. The main part of the book is the index of compositions, arranged alphabetically by composer, then title. Under each entry, each instrument is listed with the abbreviations of the excerpt book, volume, and beginning page number, as appropriate. The length of the excerpts is indicated in the bibliographic entry of the excerpt book in the "Sources" section, which is arranged alphabetically by instrument, then by main entry. Excerpt books that cover more than one instrument are cross-listed under the appropriate instruments. A general bibliography on instruments rounds out the volume. The index is well conceived with much attention to detail; the length indication of excerpts and the clear layout of the book make quick reference easy. The comprehensive coverage, logical layout, and ease of use make this a book that every music library (community college onward) and instrument teacher should own.—*J. Tsou, University of California, Berkeley*

OAB-0108   Orig

Rajadhyaksha, Ashish. **Encyclopaedia of Indian cinema,** by Ashish Rajadhyaksha and Paul Willemen. BFI/Oxford, New Delhi, 1995 (c1994). (Dist. by Indiana) 568p bibl index ISBN 0-85170-455-7, $49.95

This massive reference work encompasses the history of Indian cinema writ large, as is just and necessary. Although India lays claim to the world's largest film industry, it is, with the significant exception of Satyajit Ray, virtually unknown and unappreciated outside the subcontinent or those communities with direct ties to it. Defining "India" as a sociocultural process rather than a political or geographical entity, the authors organize their work around two large sections entitled "Dictionary" and "Films," supplemented by an extensive multilingual bibliography and a vast and detailed index. The latter includes references to translated titles and to films mentioned in the filmographies appended to the "Dictionary" entries but not entered independently in the "Films" section. "Dictionary" entries are restricted to directors, actors, composers, scenarists, and lyric writers, with entries for studios, genres, and art movements. Entries in the "Films" section are necessarily, and probably mercifully, limited to

films the authors judge to be important in the development of the Indian cinema. As a reference book, this encyclopedia is indispensable for college and university libraries. For the reader with an interest in film history, it is a wonderful gift.—*Xia Li, University of Vermont*

OAB-0109   PN1993   92-40226 CIP

Shale, Richard. **The Academy Awards index: the complete categorical and chronological record.** Greenwood, 1993. 785p bibl index afp ISBN 0-313-27738-9, $75.00

It is easy to find lists of the winners of major Academy Awards—*The World Almanac* lists the winners of the four to six best-known categories from the first awards in 1928 to the present, plus last year's winners in every category, all in about three pages. So why a 785-page book on the subject? As the subtitle indicates, Shale's work is *complete*. To begin with, his *Index* covers all nominees, not just the winners, of Academy Awards through 1992. *Every* award category is covered, including technical, special, and discontinued awards. The material is arranged both chronologically and by award category. With a full index to persons and films cited, essays on the Academy and on the history of each award category, and several useful appendixes, *The Academy Awards Index* is a truly comprehensive reference source. The book is essentially an updating of Shale's previous work, *Academy Awards: An Ungar Reference Index* (CH, Sep'79; 2nd ed., 1982). Highly recommended for all collections.—*W. P. Hogan, Eastern Michigan University*

OAB-0110   Orig

Silvester, Robert. **United States theatre: a bibliography from the beginning to 1990.** Motley Press, 1993.(Dist. by G.K. Hall Library Reference, 18 Pine St., Weston, MA 02193) 400p indexes ISBN 0-900281-03-0, $150.00

The second in a series intended to encompass all the world's theatrical publication, this volume excludes dance, mime, circus, opera, film, television, and puppetry, and covers English-language theater only. US theater in other languages will be covered in future volumes. Included are books, pamphlets, and theses; excluded are journal articles, programs, souvenirs, or play texts (unless they include significant critical information). In most cases items have been physically examined, and a location is noted; there are occasional annotations, rarely more than one line long. Within its defined parameters, this is a very fine bibliography, offering extensive coverage not only of individual dramatists but also of reference items, theater history, theater by geographic region, theater companies, biography, and criticism, among many other categories. Musical theater receives particularly full treatment. A serious and important work of scholarship, and little that is here can be found in other bibliographies. Recommended for all major reference collections.—*W. Miller, Florida Atlantic University*

OAB-0111   PN1968   93-8632 CIP

Slide, Anthony. **The encyclopedia of vaudeville.** Greenwood, 1994. 605p bibl index afp ISBN 0-313-28027-4, $75.00

This encyclopedia offers a delightful glimpse of a bygone era. Slide includes all the elements of vaudeville, from persons long forgotten to vaudeville theaters, buildings, fires, ballads, and touring circuits. Some vaudeville personalities—e.g., George Burns and Gracie Allen, Jack Benny, Milton Berle, Martha Raye, and Ed Wynn—achieved later fame in radio and television. But it is surprising to find here also Sarah Bernhardt, Ethel Barrymore, Cary Grant, opera star Rosa Ponselle, and even Carrie Nation, all of whom at one time performed in vaudeville. The more than 500 entries range from one paragraph to several pages and cover the period from the 1800s to the 1930s. Entries are spiked with hilarious dialogue from vaudeville routines and popular songs. Some include trade paper reviews of particular shows. The helpful index lists all persons mentioned in every entry; bibliographies appear at the end of some entries. A valuable and entertaining reference book for those interested in a lost art form; recommended for all libraries.—*R. T. Ivey, Memphis State University*

■ Philosophy & Religion

OAB-0112 G2230 92-27895 CIP
Aharoni, Yohanan. **The Macmillan Bible atlas,** by Yohanan Aharoni and Michael Avi-Yonah; rev. by Anson F. Rainey and Ze'ev Safrai. Completely rev. 3rd ed. Macmillan, 1993. 215p index ISBN 0-02-500605-3, $35.00

One of the outstanding Bible atlases of our time. The texts accompanying the maps in the Old Testament section have been thoroughly rewritten as have many of the New Testament sections, especially those concerning Jerusalem in Herodian times. New achievements in the study of ancient documents on which the maps are based, greater emphasis on the ecology of the land of the Bible, and extensive archeological discoveries since the 2nd edition (1977) are all reflected in this revision. While the land of the Bible is always the focus, biblical history is set in the context of the Ancient Near East and the Greco-Roman world. The coverage, 3000 BCE-200 CE, includes such diverse topics as the settlements and migrations of populations, conquests and battles, economic developments, the movement of biblical characters in various areas, and the growth of the church. The combination of maps, text, and drawings of various artifacts facilitates use and understanding and makes this one of the most helpful volumes for biblical study. The lighter shade of green used in the maps improves clarity over the second edition. Although the type size of the chronological charts at the end is too small for easy reading, the charts themselves are very useful. Highly recommended for every library needing background material to biblical study.—*D. Bourquin, California State University, San Bernardino*

OAB-0113 BS440 91-8385 CIP
The Anchor Bible dictionary, ed. by David Noel Freedman et al. Doubleday, 1992. 6v. ISBN 0-385-19351-3, v.1; ISBN 0-385-19360-2, v.2; ISBN 0-385-19361-0, v.3; ISBN 0-385-19362-9, v.4; ISBN 0-385-19363-7

ABD is this generation's long-awaited successor to *Interpreter's Dictionary of the Bible* (4 v., 1960; supplementary volume, 1976). Its 7,035 pages (44% more text than *IDB*) make it the largest modern Bible dictionary in English. Although it includes entries on all the standard topics, *ABD* also has extensive articles on all relevant aspects of the biblical world, amounting to a virtual encyclopedia of the ancient Near East (e.g., Egyptian history, literature, and religion [90p. versus *IDB*'s 28p.], Mesopotamian history and culture [62p.], Judaism [52p.], biblical theology [56p.], Sociology [19p.]). Archaeological sites and extracanonical writings receive special attention: coverage of the Dead Sea Scrolls and Nag Hammadi codices is extensive. Most articles include substantial bibliographies; about 12% of *ABD* is devoted to bibliographic citations. Two weaknesses must be noted: cross-references are used inconsistently and generally too infrequently (e.g., "Biblical Criticism" lacks cross-references to articles on individual types of criticism), and the size and comprehensiveness of bibliographies varies widely even among similar topics ("Flora" has 28 citations, "Zoology [Fauna]" has 433). Although libraries should keep *IDB* for its more complete coverage of biblical words, *ABD* is essential for all academic and large public libraries.—*K. Moll, Rolvaag Memorial Library, St. Olaf College*

OAB-0114 BS440 96-13033 CIP
Browning, W.R.F. **A dictionary of the Bible.** Oxford, 1997 (c1996). 413p bibl afp ISBN 0-19-211691-6, $25.00

Browning, author of several books on the Bible and honorary canon of Christ Church Cathedral, has produced an excellent dictionary of the Christian Bible whose purpose is to explain its main ideas and give information about its principal people and places. It is intended for general readers and students of secondary school or university level. It assumes use of the Revised Standard or other modern translation of the Bible. The author cautions that some names or terms may not be historical and that territorial names attached to the land do not necessarily represent current political or geographical areas. There are lists of abbreviations, books of the Bible in various editions, measures and weights, lists of important dates in biblical history, and a few maps. In the text, cross-

references to main entries are indicated by asterisks. Names mentioned only once in the Bible are excluded. This dictionary is less detailed than *The Harper-Collins Bible Dictionary* (1996). Definitions are not signed but include biblical citations. Highly recommended for all levels of readers.—*D. D. Siles, Elmhurst College*

OAB-0115 BL31 93-36623 CIP
Continuum dictionary of religion, ed. by Michael Pye. Continuum, 1994. 319p bibl ISBN 0-8264-0639-4, $34.95

Pye (Lancaster) has edited more than 5,000 entries written by 43 international scholars that cover topics from all major world religions, including Native American, African, and Eastern. Both new and ancient religions are covered, as well as related fields such as social anthropology. The only other recent religion dictionary with coverage this broad is *The Facts on File Dictionary of Religions*, ed. by John Hinnells (CH, Dec'84). A comparison of the two found less than 50 percent overlap, partly because of the many entries in the *Continuum Dictionary* related to religions of the Far East and Africa. The book ends with a substantial bibliography. Arrangement is alphabetical with ample cross-references. Recommended, especially for smaller reference collections that do not have specialized dictionaries for individual religions, mythology, or cults, and as a supplementary volume to Hinnells.—*E. Peterson, Montana State University*

OAB-0116 BS680 95-11503 MARC
Dictionary of deities and demons in the Bible (DDD), ed. by Karel van der Toorn, Bob Becking, and Pieter W. van der Horst. E.J. Brill, 1995. various pagings index afp ISBN 90-04-10313-9, $128.75

Van der Toorn (Leiden) and Becking and van der Horst (both Utrecht) have edited a scholarly work that gives background and cultural context information on deities and demons in the Bible. The words "in the Bible" refer to four groups explained in the introduction: (1) deities and demons whose names are actually mentioned in the Bible (e.g., Baal or Zeus); (2) those not named independently but as an " ... element in personal names or place names"; (3) those mentioned in the Bible but not in their "capacity" as a god (e.g., the Hebrew word *yareah* means moon but is an etymological equivalent of " ... Yarikh, the moon-god known from Ugaritic texts"); (4) gods whose presence in the Bible or whose divinity is questionable. The canon of the Bible chosen for use by the editors is that of the Orthodox Churches: the Septuagint and the Greek New Testament. The dictionary's almost 600 entries are arranged alphabetically and range in length from one to four or five pages. Each entry has four parts. Part 1 includes the name of the god, its etymology, "its occurrence in the various ancient civilisations surrounding Israel and Judah," and a survey of the biblical evidence. Part 2 deals with the role of the deity or demon in its culture of origin. Part 3 discusses the extrabiblical references, and part 4 is a bibliography in which asterisks precede the name of any author whose work is especially important for the topic. Many of the bibliographical entries are in German, although a substantial amount of English-language material is included. A list of the 101 scholars who contributed is arranged alphabetically by last name and the city where they teach. Most contributors are European, though several prominent US scholars are included, e.g., Hans-Dieter Betz (Chicago) and George Nickelsburg (Iowa City). The lists of abbreviations include biblical books, pseudepigraphical and early patristic works, the Dead Sea Scrolls, Targumic material, and a nine-page list of periodicals, reference works, and series. The index prints page numbers for the main entry in boldface but also lists all other occurrences of the term. This unique source is a grand scholarly achievement whose depth, breadth, and contemporaneity will make it useful to scholars and graduate students in religion and ancient cultures. Highly recommended for any library supporting programs in religion.—*D. Bourquin, California State University, San Bernardino*

OAB-0117 BM50 95-31543 CIP
Dictionary of Judaism in the biblical period: 450 B.C.E. to 600 C.E, ed. by Jacob Neusner and William Scott Green. Macmillan Library

Reference USA/Simon & Schuster and Prentice Hall International, 1996. 2v. 693p afp ISBN 0-02-897292-9, $175.00

This superb new work is a classic in the making, delivering more than its title indicates. "Biblical period" refers not to the time of which the Bible speaks, but to the era during which both Judaism and Christianity were established and canonized—from before 450 BCE when the Pentateuch was formulated to the close of the Babylonian Talmud around 600 CE. It also covers a wide range of subjects not found in similar works, including the composition of the Dead Sea Scrolls; the writings of Philo and Josephus; the New Testament as well as the classic writings of Judaism beyond the Scriptures, such as the Mishnah, Tosephta, the two Talmuds, and Midrashic collections. The work includes words, terms, rituals, customs, and theological categories found not only in those works but also in those written about the Jews in many languages. Even difficult concepts are presented in a uniformly lucid manner. Although many are brief, most subjects receive a third of a column, while two or more pages are devoted to major categories. Numerous cross-references present terms in a transliteration of the original language or its contemporary translation. A good introduction provides a concise explanation of a very rational transliteration scheme necessary for an array of highly complicated subjects. Nine good maps add a graphic portrait of more than a millennium of Near Eastern history. Although the articles are not signed, the internationally renowned contributing scholars are listed, including Protestants and Catholics as well as Jews. The work is handsomely produced and printed in large, clear type. Very highly recommended for all libraries.—*D. Kranzler, Queensborough Community College, CUNY*

OAB-0118   B41   95-47988 CIP
The Encyclopedia of philosophy. Supplement, ed. by Donald M. Borchert. Macmillan Reference USA/Simon & Schuster and Prentice Hall International, 1996. 775p bibl index afp ISBN 0-02-864629-0, $125.00

Since its publication in 1967, *The Encyclopedia of Philosophy* has been the cornerstone of any reference collection in philosophy and related fields. In this volume, produced nearly three decades later, certain of the entries are updated. A more important aspect of the project is its coverage of topics given little attention before (like "Women" and "Feminism") or of recent vintage (the various postmodern intellectual currents). The editors are to be commended for the breadth of coverage to which they have aspired and for their efforts to integrate these several entries into the older volumes by means of cross-references in the text and the index. (The index covers both the original volumes and the supplement.) The book opens with an explanatory preface. There follow "List of Articles," "List of Contributors," and "Outline of Contents," which groups the articles under larger headings. The body of the book consists of articles arranged alphabetically, each signed and followed by a bibliography. Some individuals, including such neglected women as Anne Conway, receive separate treatment. This reviewer noted that some deserving individuals (e.g., Richard Rorty) were not accorded their own entries, but they are mentioned in the index. The bibliographies deserve special mention. Some entries, like that for Heidegger, provide guidance to the philosopher's own works, as well as to literature about him. One can only repeat for the supplement what *Choice* (Jun'67) said about the original: "integral for all adult libraries."—*T. M. Izbicki, Johns Hopkins University*

OAB-0119   BL31   95-37024 CIP
The HarperCollins dictionary of religion, ed. by Jonathan Z. Smith et al. Harper San Francisco, 1995. 1,154p ISBN 0-06-067515-2, $45.00

HarperCollins and 327 scholars (members of the American Academy of Religion) have produced an important reference source for religion that covers "significant religious formations of mankind from every geographical area and from the Paleolithic era to the present day," adding in magnificent understatement that it is therefore selective. Under large subject areas (e.g., Buddhism) contributors are listed alphabetically together with the institutions where they teach. Individual articles are not signed and there are no bibliographies. The work's 3,200 entries are arranged alphabetically; most consist of a brief

paragraph, often including cross-references, but some cover several pages. All the entries fall into one of 11 categories, which are described in long (12- to 16-page) essays covering major religions of the world (Buddhism, Christianity, Hinduism, Islam, Judaism), "Religions of Antiquity," "Chinese Religion," "Japanese Religion," "New Religions" (defined as "independent groups that have arisen from the encounter of existing religious traditions"), "Religions of Traditional Peoples," and "The Study of Religion." A number of these longer articles have time lines that give important events and persons in the tradition as well as maps that locate adherents. Such a vast array of topics requires that entries often be brief, but this rich and extensive resource treats subjects in an evenhanded and scholarly way. A few entries are so brief they provide no context for the information nor an explanation of how the topic fits the religious tradition. The entry for Aaron, for example, reads, "In the Hebrew Bible, the brother of Moses and the first Israelite priest," without indicating Aaron's own importance or the role Israelite priests played in the religion. Biases are not always acknowledged; in the subsection "Early Christologies" under the entry "Jesus Christ," the contributor writes, "In his Person the divine and human have been joined, so much that it is possible to say that Mary, Jesus' mother, was not simply the mother of Christ, but the mother of God." This passage, written from a Roman Catholic perspective, is not so identified, and those unfamiliar with Christianity might think this language is used by all Christians. These concerns aside, this book offers an excellent, thorough, scholarly, current introduction to religion, especially for those not acquainted with the terms and concepts of a specific religion. Highly recommended for any library supporting study of religion.—*D. Bourquin, California State University, San Bernardino*

OAB-0120   BM50   95-3203 CIP
Jacobs, Louis. **The Jewish religion: a companion.** Oxford, 1995. 641p bibl afp ISBN 0-19-826463-1, $39.95

Although there is no dearth of good one-volume reference books on Jewish culture, Jewish history, Jewish biography, and the like, Judaism itself—the religion that defines the whole enterprise—has not been as well served. The more welcome, then, Jacobs's fine dictionary. A well-known British rabbi and writer, Jacobs, an outspoken advocate of what in the US would be called "conservative" Judaism, has been a controversial figure in contemporary, orthodox-dominated English Jewish life. Nonetheless, by US standards, his perspective (about which he is explicit) is solidly in the mainstream. The book is enormously useful, with articles of varying length on the wide spectrum of ethical, doctrinal, and ritual issues encountered in the practice of Judaism (two paragraphs on "beard," more than eight columns on "dietary laws"). Included are subjects such as abortion, conversion, miracles, women; numerous common Hebrew terms (*bimah, mikveh, tefillin*); important figures in the development of Judaism (Buber, Heschel, Hirsch, Kaplan). The presentation of facts and issues is invariably clear and to the point. An indispensable resource for all libraries.—*S. Lehmann, University of Pennsylvania*

OAB-0121   BX7260   94-31540 CIP
Jonathan Edwards: an annotated bibliography, 1979-1993, comp. by M.X. Lesser. Greenwood, 1994. 189p index afp (Bibliographies and indexes in religious studies, 30) ISBN 0-313-29237-X, $65.00

Lesser (American literature, Northeastern Univ.), an Edwards scholar, here follows the format of his *Jonathan Edwards : A Reference Guide* (CH, Oct'81) in bringing his record of research on Edwards up through 1993. International in scope, the bibliography includes books, parts of books, articles, dissertations, reviews, and reprints. An excellent introduction places current research on this 18th-century theologian in perspective and apprises scholars and researchers of the publications of the past two decades. There is an index of authors, titles, and subjects. Although many of the works cited can be accessed by means of machine-readable databases, Lesser's introduction and annotations make this volume a necessary addition for upper-division and research libraries. Highly recommended for upper-division undergraduates, graduate students, researchers, and faculty.—*D. D. Siles, Wells College*

OAB-0122 Orig
Longman guide to living religions, by Ian Harris et al. Stockton, 1995 (c1994). 278p ISBN 1-56159-089-4 pbk, $29.95

Longman's distinctive guide, written by 45 contributors (chiefly representing British institutions of higher education) includes "Introductory Classification of Groups and Movements," an introductory essay, "Guide to Living Religions," by Ninian Smart, and 268 pages of entries. The source enables one to research the variety and complexity of current religious groups and movements, underscoring those in the modern world, including religious groups and movements that are mainly political. The range of entries ("Adat Israel" to "Zoroastrians") is considerable. In the introductory essay, Smart (Univ. of California, Santa Barbara) provides a global contextualization of living religions in modern times. Highly recommended for honors students, scholars, and researchers with an interest in religious groups and movements active in today's world.—*F. A. Hall, Virginia Commonwealth University*

OAB-0123 Aust. CIP
McIntosh, Lawrence D. **Religion & theology: a guide to current reference resources.** Centre for Information Studies, Charles Sturt University, Locked Bag 660, Wagga Wagga, NSW 2678, Australia, 1997. 251p indexes ISBN 0-949060-37-2 pbk, $50.00

McIntosh annotates 655 recent (1980-96), authoritative, mostly US- and UK-published reference sources reflecting mainline scholarship. Selective and well written, this guide updates similar works such as John Bollier's *The Literature of Theology* (CH, Nov'79) and features Australian and New Zealand resources. Mirroring the state of the literature, works on Christianity predominate. Substantial sections cover Judaism as well as general and comprehensive religion sources. Islam and the religions of Australia figure prominently in the "Religions of the World" section. MacIntosh's comments are descriptive and insightful, pointing out uses, cautions, and historical development of and relationships between resources. Offering twice the number of citations as historian William M. Johnston's *Recent Reference Books in Religion* (1996), *R&T* is more succinct and less opinionated. *R&T*'s pithy notes, inviting layout, and clear organization should enhance its appeal for undergraduates. It is adequately indexed and concludes with an unannotated core list of 100 periodicals that highlights Australasian-edited titles. Unfortunately, the paper binding will withstand only light use. McIntosh weaves wisdom and library experience into this excellent, practical guide for students, scholars, and bibliographers.—*D. R. Rodgers, Baylor University*

OAB-0124 B51 94-36914 CIP
The Oxford companion to philosophy, ed. by Ted Honderich. Oxford, 1995. 1,009p index afp ISBN 0-19-866132-0, $49.95

Honderich assembled for this project a team of scholars that includes Isaiah Berlin and W.V. Quine. They provide brief entries on a wide range of persons, ideas, and schools, including such entries as "Brain in a Vat" and "Law, Feminist Philosophy of." The entries are arranged alphabetically, and each is followed by one or more bibliographic citations and/or cross-references. Although the editor admits to a bias toward the English-speaking world, in this reviewer's own field, medieval and Renaissance thought, which is characterized by sources, topics, and key persons from many regions and languages, all entries searched for were found. Portraits of many famous philosophers and appendixes ("Logical Symbols," "Maps of Philosophy" and "A Chronological Table of Philosophy") are included. "Maps of Philosophy" provides schematic guidance to the relationships of topics and concepts in philosophy. The volume closes with an extensive index and a list of entries, the latter useful for relating individuals to their contributions. For example, Peirce is mentioned in a dozen places, including under "Sign and Symbol." General readers may find some entries difficult since they presume some knowledge of the particular topic, but informed readers will find this volume useful for almost any aspect of philosophical study. Highly recommended for all academic and research libraries.—*T. M. Izbicki, Johns Hopkins University*

OAB-0125 BS440 93-19315 CIP
The Oxford companion to the Bible, ed. by Bruce M. Metzger and Michael D. Coogan. Oxford, 1993. 874p bibl index afp ISBN 0-19-504645-5, $45.00

More than 700 signed entries alphabetically arranged provide information on the development of the Bible, its transmission and circulation, the Biblical world, Biblical concepts, and the interpretation of the Bible through history from Christian, Jewish, and Muslim perspectives. What sets this volume apart is the attention given to the influence of the Bible in Western culture. For example, there are articles on such subjects as Marx and the Bible, women and the Bible, and the influence of the Bible on literature, dance, law, music, and science. More than 250 renowned scholars from 20 countries contributed interesting, readable entries that range in length from a quarter of a page to several pages. The editors have allowed contributors to present their own judgments without imposing an artificial consensus. A separate entry for any Biblical book or part of a book recognized as canonical by a community is included. "See also" references are starred; 14 color maps and an index of place names make the volume even more useful. Highly recommended for general and academic libraries needing a one-volume source presenting the results of recent scholarly Biblical study.—*D. Bourquin, California State University, San Bernardino*

OAB-0126 BM50 96-45517 CIP
The Oxford dictionary of the Jewish religion, ed. by R.J. Zwi Werblowsky and Geoffrey Wigoder. Oxford, 1997. 764p afp ISBN 0-19-508605-8, $95.00

Technically a revision of R.J.Z. Werblowsky's *Encyclopedia of the Jewish Religion* (CH, Mar'67; rev. ed., 1986), this important work includes changes so extensive that it is in effect an entirely new publication. Since it is more comprehensive than Louis Jacobs's similarly conceived *The Jewish Religion: A Companion* (CH, May'96) and has been written by a large and distinguished team of scholars from Israel, North America, and the UK, it can safely be designated as authoritative. Jacobs's work, by contrast, carries an appealing personal stamp that gives it a consistently articulated point of view without sacrificing seriousness, and its more selective coverage notwithstanding, includes entries on topics absent from *Oxford* (e.g., "Games and Sport": is it permitted for a Jew to be a "professional pugilist"?). Both are distinctive in concerning themselves solely with Judaism *as a religion.* They cover doctrinal issues, religious concepts and controversies, formative thinkers, rituals, symbols, etc. They do not list Jewish Nobel Prize winners or baseball players, and always deal with historical topics (e.g., Zionism) in the context of the Jewish religion. The bibliographies that conclude each *Oxford* entry are fuller and list more scholarly, less popular sources than Jacobs, who often omits bibliographic references entirely. *Oxford* is essential for all libraries, although Jacobs remains a useful, necessary source.—*S. Lehmann, University of Pennsylvania*

OAB-0127 Orig
The Oxford dictionary of world religions, ed. by John Bowker. Oxford, 1997. 1,111p indexes afp ISBN 0-19-213965-7, $45.00

World religions here include Christianity, Judaism, Islam, Buddhism, Hinduism, Sikhism, Zoroastrianism, various Chinese and Japanese religions, and what are defined as "other" religions. The 8,200 entries focus on ideas, people, and texts important for each religion and are arranged alphabetically. The contributors list contains 78 international scholars and their affiliations; most are from Great Britain. Editor Bowker (Gresham College, London), with some help from his wife Margaret (Emeritus Reader, Univ. of Lancaster, UK), is responsible for half the entries. The quality of scholarship is consistently high, but the brevity of many entries is a problem for two reasons. First, although some items can be defined clearly in the brief space allowed (e.g., Cheese Sunday: "Amongst Greek Orthodox Christians, the last Sunday before Lent on which cheese and eggs may be eaten"), others, such as the attempt to define Buddhist scriptures in half a column, suffer from inadequacy. Second, terms included in the dictionary are preceded by an asterisk when they occur in other entries, but they are defined only at their main entry; readers unfamiliar with the

Choice's Outstanding Academic Books

terms will need to look them up, which can be distracting when there are many of them. Bibliographies at the end of entries are brief, and though well chosen, many seem dated. Nevertheless, the amount of material covered and the depth and breadth of accurate, evenhanded scholarship make this work truly outstanding. Despite limitations, highly recommended for libraries serving undergraduate and graduate students in religion.—*D. Bourquin, California State University, San Bernardino*

OAB-0128   BR302   95-24520 CIP
The Oxford encyclopedia of the Reformation, ed. by Hans J. Hillerbrand. Oxford, 1996. 4v. 484-506p ea. bibl index afp ISBN 0-19-506493-3, $450.00

The editor of this volume has chosen the widest possible definition of "Reformation," including all countries, cultures, and theological viewpoints. Entries are provided for background issues like alchemy, as well as for doctrinal issues like faith. The editor's introduction, which emphasizes "the rich diversity of all religious life," is followed by four volumes of articles by a strong team of experts. Each entry concludes with a bibliography, and cross-references are provided. The fourth volume concludes with an appendix of maps, a directory of contributors, a "Synoptic Outline of Contents," and an alphabetical index. The scope of the project is impressive; for example, coverage of the roles of women includes not only marriage and witchcraft but also nuns and sexuality. Most of the entries are very good. There is little to criticize and much to praise in the entries on the papacy and the Dominican order, two of this reviewer's own research areas. Occasionally, however, the bibliographies fall short. The entry on Francisco de Vitoria, for example, fails to list Jeremy Lawrence's translation of that theologian's political works. Small lapses will occur in large projects, and omissions of this sort do not adversely affect the whole encyclopedia. Students interested in any aspect of the Reformation era can start here for reliable guidance to a wide range of subjects. Highly recommended for all academic and research libraries.—*T. M. Izbicki, Johns Hopkins University*

OAB-0129   BL2525   96-2487 CIP
Queen, Edward L. **The encyclopedia of American religious history,** by Edward L. Queen, Stephen R. Prothero, and Gardiner H. Shattuck. Facts on File, 1996. 2v. 800p bibl indexes afp ISBN 0-8160-2406-5, $99.00

The role of religion in US history is often overlooked in history texts, and students and scholars of this discipline have long needed a good encyclopedia, a requirement this work fills capably. The well-written entries are arranged alphabetically, include persons, concepts, denominations, and places, and end with brief bibliographies. The three principal authors and the contributors are all noted scholars in the field. All religions that have contributed to religious development in the US are included. Historical terms are redefined in the context of religion; e.g., "manifest destiny," usually considered the moral basis for the US's territorial expansion, is here shown to have religious significance as well. The only comparable work is *Encyclopedia of the American Religious Experience*, ed. by C.H. Lippy and P.W. Williams (CH, May'88), still useful but dated. The present book, useful for any library, will be essential for college and university libraries.—*R. Dyson, Wabash College*

OAB-0130   BR526   95-44344 CIP
Utter, Glenn H. **The religious right: a reference handbook,** by Glenn H. Utter and John W. Storey. ABC-Clio, 1995. 298p index afp ISBN 0-87436-778-6, $39.50

As the religious right becomes increasingly prominent in the news and increasingly influential in politics, the need for an authoritative, comprehensive, and unbiased source of information on the who, what, where, when, and how of this group becomes urgent. Utter and Storey's work attempts to meet this need; it provides an overview and chronology of the religious right together with biographical sketches of its leaders. Also included is a survey of conservative Christian attitudes towards social and moral issues, political preferences of the right, and policy issues of ongoing concern. Beliefs of the religious right (e.g., on the US, communism, education, the Bible, evolution, abortion) are given through a series of quotations and documented through an annotated bibliography of print and nonprint resources both about and by the religious right. Also included is a directory of organizations; radio and television programs; CD-ROMs, databases, e-mail addresses; and a glossary. Extremely valuable for students and general readers, this source is recommended for public, college, and university libraries and for special collections in theology and politics.—*N. L. Powell, Catholic University of America*

■ Science & Technology

OAB-0131   GE123   95-38571 CIP
Cooper, André R., comp. **Cooper's comprehensive environmental desk reference.** Van Nostrand Reinhold, 1996. 1,039p index disk (IBM-PC) ISBN 0-442-02159-3, $99.95

Two unique features of this excellent handbook are a 40-page environmental "jargon finder" that can also be used as a topical thesaurus, and a 32-page sample Phase I Site Assessment. The latter section can be used as a companion to *Cooper's Pocket Environmental Compliance Dictionary* (1995), which contains a detailed Environmental Assessment (EA) outline and a comprehensive Phase I inspection checklist. The other features, standard but complete, include a 762-page environmental dictionary, 168 pages of acronyms and abbreviations, a chemical elements table, data conversion tables, EPA Agency data, and a Hazardous Air Pollutants (HAPs) list with CAS numbers. Highly recommended for academic libraries.—*B. K. Delzell, New Mexico State University*

OAB-0132   QH332   94-38743 CIP
Encyclopedia of bioethics, ed. by Warren Thomas Reich. Rev. ed. Macmillan, 1995. 5v. 2,950p bibl index afp ISBN 0-02-897355-0, $425.00

The original edition of this encyclopedia (CH, Nov'79) was the first work to synthesize, analyze, and compare the major positions of a complex field still in its infancy. Received with great enthusiasm at its publication, it set the standard for discussion and study of challenging issues relating to life, death, health, and basic human values. When the editor began in the 1980s to contemplate a new edition, he solicited input from hundreds of scholars regarding the need for and extent of revision that would be required. He concluded that an updated version was not simply desirable but would be crucial to the future of the field: scarcely a single topic in the first edition had been unaffected by profound changes not only in science, technology, and ethics but in the ways in which moral problems are perceived. The resulting revision is a "fresh, new work" that surpasses the extraordinary model of its predecessor. Lengthy entries (many extend to dozens of pages) are arranged alphabetically in five volumes. To provide an interdisciplinary viewpoint, most entries consist of several articles, each an original, signed contribution. In comparison to the first edition, the contents have increased from 315 articles by 285 contributors to 464 articles by 437 contributors. These scholars represent every continent and many disciplines: ethics, biology, health professions, theology, sociology, feminist scholarship, demography, anthropology, language, literature, policy science, etc. The intent is to provide a broad historical and international base while also examining current developments. For example, the articles in the entry "Death and Dying: Euthanasia and Sustaining Life" discuss religious, philosophical, and public policy considerations from antiquity through the 20th century, and mention 1994 jury decisions involving Dr. Jack Kevorkian. More than 100 entries are totally new to this edition, including "DNA Typing," "Adoption," "Sustainable Development," "African Religion," "Hazardous Wastes and Toxic Substances," "Disability," "AIDS," "Endangered Species and Biodiversity," and "Abuse, Interpersonal." Some topics whose emphasis is expanded from the first edition include animal welfare and rights, environmental issues, organ and tissue transplantation, sexuality and gender, fertility and human reproduction, and population ethics. Throughout the encyclopedia, the extensive bibliographies for each article include citations as recent as 1994, as well as many older works; the bibliographies, like the articles themselves, have been completely revised. Also entirely revised is the appendix, on "Codes, Oaths, and Directives Related to Bioethics," which offers documentation with brief commentaries. Many directives have been added, including topics not previously covered (e.g., Rio Declaration on Environment and Development). As in the first edition, the language of the text is accessible for educated readers. Numerous *see* and *see also* references, plus an excellent subject index, enhance the work's usability. Even if they own the first edition, academic and large public libraries should definitely purchase the revised *Encyclopedia of Bioethics*. Like its predecessor, it will retain its research value for many years to come.— *L. N. Pander, Bowdoin College*

OAB-0133 [CD-ROM]
Environment Abstracts: also including 1975-1993 Energyline Abstracts. Congressional Information Service, 1994. $1,295.00; other purchasing plans available. 1 disc. Covers 1975-Feb. 1994. User manual. Updates: Updated quarterly. System requirements: IBM-PC, 286 or higher; DOS 5.0 or later; 4MB hard disk space; 640K RAM.

Finding information on environmental issues can be arduous and tedious, as researchers have to employ an interdisciplinary approach to searching the literature. This CD-ROM makes it much easier to track such information, with more than 800 English-language journals indexed along with conference papers, proceedings, and selected reports of international agencies, nongovernmental agencies, associations, and private corporations. Some selected monographs are also included. Topics include climatic change and global warming, waste management, solid and toxic wastes, population, toxicological effects, risk management, wildlife habitat and management, and radiological contamination. Coverage in *Environment Abstracts* begins in 1975; included is *Energy Information Abstracts* (1975-93) and *Acid Rain Precipitation Abstracts* (1984-90).

The databases can be searched simultaneously or individually. The product is easy to load and learn; the manuals are simple and easy to understand. Searches can be performed at a simple browse level, or at a more sophisticated level utilizing Boolean operators. Abstracts are lengthy and informative. A toll-free number is also provided for additional help. Congressional Information Service also provides an article delivery service and tape licensing of the database.

This major research tool, much easier to use than the print version, will be extremely valuable to any library supporting environmental studies of science programs. Smaller libraries will need to carefully weigh the cost of purchasing this product since they may only hold a fraction of the materials indexed. The advantage of having access to information of this caliber without having the documents on site will impact on interlibrary loan and document delivery departments. A collection containing a majority of the documents on microfiche may be purchased separately. Suitable for undergraduates, graduates, faculty, professionals, and two-year technical program students.—*J. C. Stachacz, Dickinson College*

OAB-0134 Orig
Environmental encyclopedia, ed. by William P. Cunningham et al. Gale, 1994. 981p index afp ISBN 0-8103-8856-1, $195.00

A recent addition and supplement to the "Gale Environmental Library" series, this is an important source for information on virtually every aspect of the environment and environmental sciences. Contributors have been selected from both academia and the environmental field. In addition, the publisher solicited comments on the work from the ALA Task Force on the Environment. Entries are arranged alphabetically; bold-faced terms within each entry direct the user to related entries. Contact information is provided for organizations profiled, and each entry concludes with a helpful and relevant reading list. Two appendixes— "Historical Chronology," which outlines important dates in environmental history, and "Environmental Legislation in the United States," which lists environmentally related legislation back to 1962—may be helpful in ready reference. A minor criticism is the omission of the public law number for legislation in appendix 2. All libraries.—*S. Maret, University of Colorado at Denver*

OAB-0135 Orig
International directory of bioethics organizations, ed. by Anita L. Nolen and Mary Carrington Coutts. National Reference Center for Bioethics Literature, Kennedy Institute of Ethics, Georgetown University 1993, Washington, DC 20057-1065. 371p indexes ISBN 1-883913-11-X pbk, $35.00

Representing more than 40 countries, the nearly 350 organizations listed here are engaged in the study, teaching, research, or practice of bioethics or health care ethics. Groups focusing only on a subfield of bioethics (such as euthanasia or human experimentation) are excluded. Arrangement is alphabetical by country name, or by state in the US section. In large, clear type, the entries (one per page) give the organization's name, address, director and other staff, phone and fax numbers, followed by brief descriptions of the group's purpose, educational programs, publications, and other information as available. More than half the entries are US organizations; a check of these against *Research Centers Directory* (1994) reveals a comprehensive list. In addition to an alphabetical index are indexes of organizations that grant academic degrees, provide consulting services, or have an international focus. The Kennedy Institute of Ethics produces the database *BIOETHICSLINE* and its print companion, the annual *Bibliography of Bioethics* (1975-). Eminently qualified to publish the first directory of bioethics organizations, the Institute has created a quality reference work at a reasonable price. Recommended for academic and public libraries.—*L. N. Pander, Bowdoin College*

OAB-0136 GE1 92-41800 CIP
Katz, Linda Sobel. **Environmental profiles: a global guide to projects and people,** by Linda Sobel Katz, Sarah Orrick, and Robert Honig. Garland, 1993. 1,083p index afp (Garland reference library of social science, 736) ISBN 0-8153-0063-8, $125.00

One of the most comprehensive directories of environmental agencies yet produced, citing agencies from 115 countries. Alphabetic by country, each listing has extensive information including addresses, telephone numbers, activities, organizational structure, projects, personnel, resources, and publications. Federal, state and province, and private organizations are cited. All summaries are thorough and informative, including the history and mission of the organization. US organizations predominate, but researchers looking for worldwide agencies will find this a wonderful tool. An appendix lists all organizations by topic—e.g., air quality, biodiversity, recycling/waste management, sustainable development, global warming, health, deforestation, energy, population, transportation, and water quality. A thorough subject index and a helpful table of abbreviations and acronyms are included. An important research tool for anyone looking for information on environmental organizations. Recommended for all libraries.—*J. C. Stachacz, Dickinson College*

OAB-0137 94-73123 Orig
Larousse dictionary of science and technology, ed. by Peter M.B. Walker. Larousse, 1995. 1,236p ISBN 0-7523-0010-5, $45.00

Formerly known as *Chambers Science and Technology Dictionary* (CH, Mar'89), this revised edition offers several major changes. Most noticeable is the inclusion of more than 500 fine sketches and illustrations and the addition of a new category, "Food Science." Despite the new name the work maintains the same scope and intention, to provide both general readers and professionals with scientific and technical vocabulary beyond the basics. Appendixes include a classification of the animal and plant kingdoms, a list of the subdivisions of geological time, properties of the elements, and a chronology of discoveries and inventions. Compared to two other works in the same category, the 5th edition of *McGraw-Hill Dictionary of Scientific and Technical Terms* (1994), ed. by Sybil Parker, and *Academic Press Dictionary of Science and Technology* (1992), Larousse has fewer entries but is comprehensive and convenient in size, making it attractive as a desk dictionary. Essential for libraries serving general through professional readers.—*H. T. Ton-Nu, University of Virginia*

OAB-0138   GF41   92-18613 CIP
Merideth, Robert. **The environmentalist's bookshelf: a guide to the best books.** G.K. Hall, 1993. 272p indexes afp ISBN 0-8161-7359-1, $40.00

This is a "guide to the best books. . .on nature and the environment, as determined by a questionnaire. . .sent to environmental leaders and experts around the world. The guide describes the 500 most recommended books, based on a tally of the responses, and provides selected quotes indicating why the respondents think a particular book is important or meaningful." Meridith's excellent annotated bibliography has six sections (Introduction, Top 40 Books, Core Books, Strongly Recommended Books, Other Recommended Books, Respondents to the Questionnaire), an appendix (Sources for Further Reference), and author, title, and subject indexes. Like most G.K. Hall bibliographies, this one has practical organization, clear page formatting, and indexing that is excellent and accurate. Indispensable for collection development and highly recommended for reference collections in college and university libraries.— *T. C. Trawick, Troy State University*

OAB-0139   [CD-ROM]
Science navigator. McGraw-Hill, 1995. ISBN 0-07-852717-1 $149.95, single-user; $295.00, network version. 1 disc; user manual. System requirements: IBM-PC, 386 or later; 1MB RAM; DOS 3.0 or later; hard drive. Windows 3.1; 4MB RAM. Macintosh IIsi or higher, System 7 or higher; 2MB RAM. Mouse recommended.

This CD-ROM combines all 8,200 articles from the *McGraw-Hill Concise Encyclopedia of Science & Technology* (3rd ed., CH, Jan'95) with all 104,300 entries from the *McGraw-Hill Dictionary of Scientific and Technical Terms* (5th ed., CH, May'94). Furthermore, the product includes a biographical dictionary listing of more than 1,100 scientists and engineers, 750 graphic images, and a category browsing navigator of 75 major fields of science and engineering. Although optional, the use of a mouse enhances the convenience of the product. Installation of the product is handled from the Windows program manager.

Searching with AND, OR, and NOT boolean operators is supported, and searches may also be nested. Two wild card searches are possible: "*" for zero or more characters or "?" for exactly one character. Either wild card can be used anywhere in a search term. In addition, proximity operators can be used, case sensitivity can be (de)selected, and entries or text can be searched. While viewing the results, the terms used in the search are highlighted. Any word can be searched by selecting it; this allows the user to cross-reference the dictionary, encyclopedia, or biographical dictionary with any term. An unknown term from an encyclopedia article can easily be searched in the dictionary. History buttons then allow returning to the article. Extensive help screens are provided, and the help is application sensitive. If help is chosen from the search dialog box, the help is related to performing searches.

Like most Windows products, commands can be chosen by three different methods: tool bar, pull-down menu, or shortcut keys. It is possible to print the complete entry or a selected portion including illustrations. Saving text to a file can be done through the Windows clipboard. Overall, an excellent, quick reference tool, well worth the price for an undergraduate science library. General; undergraduate; two-year technical program students.— *W. M. Baer, Brigham Young University*

OAB-0140   Database
World Resources, 1992-93: a guide to the global environment, by the World Resources Institute. Oxford, 1992. $119.95. Updates: 3.5" or 5.25" high-density diskettes. System requirements: IBM PC-AT or equivalent; 512K RAM; hard disk; CGA, EGA, VGA; or Hercules monitor

Several fundamental changes have occurred in this reference work since its last review (CH, Jun'89). Foremost is the theme of this year's publication,

the management of the natural resources essential for a country to achieve sustainable economic development. New topic areas include regional problems of development and population, food and agriculture, forests, wildlife, energy, water, climate, and policies. The tables found in Section 4 are once again the heart of the work. However, the most significant addition is the inclusion of the *Data Base Diskette*, the subject of this review. The data included on the computer diskette are expanded from the data in Section 4 of *World Resources* and cover 483 variables for 176 countries, including population, economic indicators, land cover and settlements, food and agriculture, forests, wildlife, energy, and water resources. The time series of the variables range from 2- to 75-year periods, but many variables lack data for more than a few years; in some cases, no data exist. This a common problem with international statistics. The data can be depicted in either statistical, graphic, or tabular form. The program requires a hard disk with 1.7 megabytes of free space and additional space to create worksheets and export data. The program is easy to load and learn; users will be able to create worksheets by topic or by country, making the available data very useful for comparative studies. For example, the diskette allows readers to create, for one country, several countries, or large regional and economic groups, worksheets using any number or combination of the 483 variables. Worksheets can also be created using the economic variable tables along with the geographic variables. An index to the data on the diskette is located at the back of the main work. Although the printed version can stand alone as a reference tool, the diskette adds a broader dimension by allowing researchers to track and manipulate large amounts of data in an easy, flexible manner. Highly recommended for all academic libraries.—*J. C. Stachacz, Dickinson College*

■ Natural & Biological Sciences

OAB-0141   [CD-ROM]
Beacham's international threatened, endangered, and extinct species. Beacham Publishing, Inc., P.O. Box 830, Osprey, FL 34229-0830, 1995. $395.00; new releases through 1996: $95.00. 1 disc; user manual. Updates: annual. System requirements: IBM-PC, 386/33 or higher; Windows 3.1 or higher; 4MB RAM. Macintosh, System 7+; 8MB RAM.

Beacham offers a comprehensive, full-text database, updating the well-known and highly regarded Beacham's four-volume set, *The Oxford World Wildlife Fund Guide to Endangered Species of North America* (1989-94; v.3, CH, Jan'93; v.4, CH, Mar'95). The purchase price includes networking on up to four stations. Revisions are expected as warranted by changes in species status. The CD-ROM can run in a DOS, Windows, or MAC environment, takes up no space on the hard drive (except for possible icon or menuing options), and requires no installation, since the search engine runs off the CD. Proprietary software provides multimedia (text, images, and audio) and interactive (linked questions, answers, and explanations) capabilities for more than 1,300 threatened, endangered, or extinct species worldwide. Current up to the date of publication, each entry ranges from 20 to 60 pages in length and is written by professionals in the field. Technical support is available via a toll phone number or fax during ZCI business hours, or on COMPUSERVE's ROM Vendor's Forum.

Upon starting the program, a large snow leopard graphic, dramatic music, and button options appear on the opening screen. Choices include the Main Index, an introduction to the operating system, and a multimedia presentation narrated by Walton Beacham that highlights coverage of the CD. Clicking on the Main Index button permits access to data. The index combines different categories of data and allows searching by common name and US, international, extinct, and delisted species categories. A keyword search on "gibbon" in the common name index resulted in 357 occurrences in 15 documents. Choosing "Kloss' Gibbon" resulted in the following options: large photo; locator map of the species range; pronunciation (sound capabilities are necessary for this choice); a report that includes status, biology, ecology, and laws affecting the species; and a report index that allows a jump directly to a particular section of the article. The report on Kloss' Gibbon consisted of 22 pages of text and was compiled by two primatologists. The Main Index also provides a habitats index, a listing for conventions on prohibiting or restricting trade on endangered species, environmental organization phonebooks, legislation affecting endangered species, and an extensive, annotated bibliography. Additional features available on a limited number of entries include questions and answers, habitat articles, and species vocalization. Speed keys that offer searching shortcuts are provided. On-line help is offered on the Main Index menu under "Getting the Most Out of This Encyclopedia." Unfortunately, printing an article or a portion of it (not including photos) is the only means of producing a copy; articles cannot be saved or copied to disk at this time. In addition to networking capabilities, on-line advantages include rapid data access, keyword searching capabilities, hypertext links to maps and definitions, and audible common and scientific name pronunciations. The search software is intuitive and will require little librarian mediation. Suitable for reference or electronic text centers; highly recommended for undergraduates through professionals.—*P. M. Beile, Louisiana State University*

OAB-0142   Orig
The Birds of North America: life histories for the 21st century, v.1, ed. by Alan F. Poole, Peter Stettenheim, and Frank B. Gill. American Ornithologists' Union/Academy of Natural Sciences of Philadelphia, 1992-. 18v. $1,875.00; $175.00 ea. ISSN 1061-5466

This first comprehensive compendium of life histories of North American birds since A. C. Bent's *Life Histories of North American Birds* (21 v., 1919-68) is superb. *Birds of North America* (*BNA*) will consist of 720 fascicles, each 8.5 x 11 inches in size, 12-32 pages in length, issued 40 at a time in slipcases, due for completion in about the year 2000. Written by some 300 experts, many of them professional ornithologists, and laid out attractively with maps, photographs, charts, diagrams, and an authoritative, fully referenced text, *BONA* should become indispensable for biologists, ecologists, land managers, and others, just as Bent was. The excellent text provides for each bird sections on distinguishing characteristics, distribution, systematics, migration, habitat, food habits, sounds, behavior, breeding, demography and populations, conservation and management, appearance, measurements, acknowledgements, references, and a page-long introductory essay with a color photo and detailed map. One of *BNA*'s virtues is that by indicating what is *not* known, it points to potential areas for research. Since *BNA*'s species accounts are being serially produced, they are freed from the constraint that plagued some compendia—production in phylogenetic sequence. Libraries can treat them as serials and bind them in numerical order, since there will be cumulative indexes. Bent will be worth retaining, since it contains a wealth of details (sometimes overwhelming readers) and far more photographs, but *BNA* is much more accessible, authoritative, and current. Despite its excellence, *BNA*, at about $2.50 per fascicle, is not expensive. A landmark publication, most highly recommended for libraries at all levels.—*H. T. Armistead, Thomas Jefferson University*

OAB-0143   QL696   93-5101 CIP
Clement, Peter. **Finches & sparrows: an identification guide.** Princeton, 1993. 500p bibl index ISBN 0-691-03424-9, $49.50

Here is an excellent addition to an unofficial, unnamed series of identification guides on bird groups, others being *Gulls*, by P.J. Grant (CH, Oct'82), *Seabirds*, by P. Harrison (CH, Jan'84), *Shorebirds*, by P. Hayman (1986), *Waterfowl*, by S. Madge (CH, Oct'88) and *Swallows & Martins*, by A. Turner (1989). All world surveys by UK writers, these guides are similar in dimensions and format. They feature extensive if not exhaustive species accounts with fine detail, good range maps, and copious, well-executed illustrations, usually in color. *Finches & Sparrows* treats 290 species of "true" finches in the families Fringillidae, Estrildidae, and Passeridae. This is important to note since many birds commonly thought of as finches or sparrows are therefore excluded (e.g., Darwin's finches of the Galapagos and North American sparrows such as the song sparrow). The 73 color plates by Alan Harris and John Davis are excellent, showing many morphs (950 total) for each species. Opposite each plate are range maps plus a written range description, short descriptions of each species' morphs, and the habitats each prefers. The maps would have been more useful had they shown political boundaries. The superb species accounts include extensive sections on

identification (including similar species), description, geographical variation, voice, status, habitat and behavior, distribution, movements, measurements, and references. Thoroughly referenced throughout, this is a fine bird family monograph. Highly recommended.—*H. T. Armistead, Thomas Jefferson University*

OAB-0144   QH303   95-11639 CIP
Davis, Elisabeth B. **Using the biological literature: a practical guide,** by Elisabeth B. Davis and Diane Schmidt. 2nd ed., rev. and expanded. Dekker, 1995. 421p bibl afp (Books in library and information science, 57) ISBN 0-8247-9477-X, $85.00

Because of its broad scope and recent coverage, this bibliography in its second edition will be useful for collection development and for teaching biological literature. The introductory chapter summarizes the history, characteristics, and electronic delivery of biological literature, and is followed by a succinct overview of subject searching. Most chapters emphasize bibliography; one of general sources is followed by others on biochemistry and biophysics, molecular and cellular biology, genetics, microbiology and immunology, ecology, plant biology, anatomy and physiology, entomology, and zoology. Subdivisions within chapters include English-language reference sources, periodicals, reviews, societies, and textbooks. A sampling of citations shows most to be accurate. Descriptive annotations include price and ISBN or ISSN. The *Choice* review of the first edition (Jan'82) commented that subject headings at the beginning of chapters were of "little use because of their general nature," that there was "no information on library research," and that annotations were too short. In the second edition, subject headings and research strategies are treated briefly in the chapter on subject access but are not emphasized, and annotations remain brief, as one may expect in a book of such large scope. A review of the first edition in *American Reference Books Annual* 14 (1983): 613 suggested addition of LC call numbers, but they are still omitted. Highly recommended for academic libraries.—*T. C. Trawick, Troy State University*

OAB-0145   Can. CIP
Dunster, Julian. **Dictionary of natural resource management,** by Julian Dunster and Katherine Dunster. UBC Press, University of British Columbia, 6344 Memorial Rd., Vancouver, BC V6T 1Z2, Canada, 1996. 363p afp ISBN 0-7748-0503-X, $74.95

Many environmental and ecological dictionaries do not adequately cover natural resource terms or concepts in areas such as forestry, sustainability, and biodiversity. This valuable addition to the literature of natural resources has bridged that gap. Terms were selected from a myriad of sources that were once available only as journal articles ("Conservation for Sustainable Development of Forests Worldwide: A Compendium of Concepts and Terms," which originally appeared in *Forestry Chronicle*, or from private organizations (American Fisheries Society). In addition, the authors took pains to have many of the technical terms in the *Dictionary* reviewed by specialists in ecology, wildlife, silviculture, and geomorphology "... in order to ensure the widest possible review of terms and definitions." Encompassing traditional components of the field of natural resources, the *Dictionary* includes natural resource terms from forestry, soil science, and botany, and branches out to include terms from fields usually considered outside the realm of natural resources, such as dispute resolution and environmental philosophy. Three very helpful appendixes, "Classification of Organisms," "Geological Time Scales," and "Conversion Tables and Other Measurements" supplement the dictionary proper. Highly recommended for undergraduate and graduate collections in the sciences and in natural resources.—*S. Maret, University of Colorado at Denver*

OAB-0146   S411   94-3143 CIP
Encyclopedia of agricultural science, ed. by Charles J. Arntzen and Ellen M. Ritter. Academic Press, 1994. 4v. 634-778p ea. bibl indexes afp ISBN 0-12-226670-6, $499.00

This encyclopedia is intended to serve "as a compendium of current knowledge about specific topics within agriculture." Articles, arranged alphabetically by subject, begin with a table of contents, a glossary of terms, and a short definition or description of the subject. *See* references are scattered throughout each article. Articles "average ten pages in length" (preface), end with bibliographies, and have been peer reviewed. At the end of volume 4 are two appendixes, (A) "United States Colleges and Universities Offering Academic Programs in Agriculture" and (B) "United Nations Agricultural and Other Related Organizations," and an excellent subject index. The listings of academic programs in Appendix A appear to be incomplete; under New York, at least two two-year agricultural colleges are not listed, including Morrisville College, which has a very strong agricultural program. Apart from that problem, the encyclopedia is an excellent work that should be in every library supporting an interest in agriculture. Highly recommended for all libraries and reading levels, researchers to farmers to general readers.—*W. E. Drew Jr., SUNY Agricultural and Technical College at Morrisville*

OAB-0147   Orig
Encyclopedia of endangered species, ed. by Mary Emanoil in association with IUCN-The World Conservation Union. Gale, 1994. 1,230p bibl indexes afp ISBN 0-8103-8857-X, $95.00

The *Encyclopedia of Endangered Species* "describes over 700 animals and plants worldwide that are currently threatened with extinction." Though similar in many ways to *The Official World Wildlife Fund Guide to Endangered Species of North America* (CH, Mar'95), it takes a global perspective. Species are grouped according to class for animals and insects. Plants are in one section. Each entry is under the common name (if one is known), with the scientific name listed below. In many cases a shaded box includes phylum, class, order, and family information along with current status and range. Each entry also includes description and biology, habitat and current distribution, and history and conservation measures. Photographs are included if available. The encyclopedia also includes an appendix titled "Species Watch," a directory of wildlife and conservation organizations, a bibliography organized by major groups (mammals, birds, etc.), maps, a geographic index, and a combined scientific and common-name species index with cross-references. This excellent work is highly recommended for all libraries.—*W. E. Drew Jr., SUNY Agricultural and Technical College at Morrisville*

OAB-0148   QH540   94-24917 CIP
Encyclopedia of environmental biology, ed. by William A. Nierenberg. Academic Press, 1995. 3v. 767, 654, 693p bibl indexes afp ISBN 0-12-226730-3, $395.00

Comprehensively covering all environmental subjects in great detail—ranging from "Acid Rain" and "Fishing" to "Packrat Middens" and "Seed Banks"—this encyclopedia's 154 articles cover all aspects of ecology, including oceans, wetlands, desertification, and limnology as well as current problems such as oil spills and endangered species. The well-written articles range from 3 to 38 pages, the majority ten pages or more. Technical vocabulary predominates, but glossaries at the ends of articles define only a few major terms. Tables, charts, and figures abound and are very informative but may occasionally be too small or too low in contrast to be clear. Black-and-white photographs are included sporadically. Cross-references appear in the text, with a complete list at the end. The full table of contents and instructions for use are reprinted in the front of each volume. A list of contributors can be found at the end of volume 3, as well as a detailed index. The quality of scholarship is very high and all articles contain current bibliographies, but the vocabulary employed demands knowledgeable readers. Contributors are practicing scientists, hence the terminology can be abstruse and nonscientists could find many subjects difficult to understand. For college students and professionals in environmentally related fields, the encyclopedia is very thorough and needed. An excellent specialized encyclopedia, useful for all college libraries and for professionals.—*M. S. Muskiewicz, University of Massachusetts at Lowell*

OAB-0149   QR9   92-4429 CIP
Encyclopedia of microbiology, ed. by Joshua Lederberg.

Academic Press, 1992. 4v. 582-648p ea. indexes afp ISBN 0-12-226890-3, $595.00

This survey of microbiology, consisting of 204 articles that vary in length from 6 to 30 pages, is well organized and well written. The contributors emphasize basic science, but some articles also include aspects of agriculture, technology, disease, public health, and medicine. The material complements both undergraduate and graduate study. All the articles end with small but timely bibliographies that include review articles, recent books, and chapters from books. Illustrations are helpful and enhance the articles they accompany. The scope is broad enough to include viruses, bacteria, protozoa, and the unicellular fungi and algae. Appendixes include linkage maps and a list of the 293 contributors, and there are indexes of subjects and related titles. Although the bibliographies cite the titles of books and chapters, the titles of journal articles are unaccountably omitted. There is no comparable work. Highly recommended for libraries that support study, teaching, or research in microbiology.—*E. Williams, Vassar College*

OAB-0150   QK110   92-30459 CIP
Flora of North America north of Mexico: v.1: Introduction; v.2: Pteridophytes and gymnosperms, ed. by Flora of North America Editorial Committee. Oxford, 1993. 2v. 372, 475p bibl index afp ISBN 0-19-505713-9, v.1; ISBN 0-19-508242-7, v.2; $75.00 ea.

Clear, well-organized, and thoroughly referenced, this project (conceived nearly 30 years ago!) intends "to serve both as a means of identifying plants within the region and as a systematic conspectus" and is "designed to draw on the expertise of the entire systmatic botany community." The results to this point are exceptional (the set is projected for completion in 14 volumes by 2002). Volume 1, a set of readable, introductory essays by recognized authorities, covers plants in their physical, ecological, systematic, historical, and prehistoric settings. Volume 2 provides detailed treatments by experts who have critically reviewed the literature and examined herbarium and living (when possible) specimens for the pteridophytes and gymnosperms. All native plants (including recently extinct ones) as well as well-established waifs, cultivated plants, and hybrids are examined. Each treatment incorporates keys for families, genera and species, synonymies, descriptions, geographic ranges and species maps, habitat summaries, and other biological information such as chromosome numbers and phenologies. Each volume has a bibliography and index to taxa. Taxa are listed in taxonomic sequence, or if classifications are unresolved, alphabetically with problem discussions; all classifications are supported by other literature as no unpublished nomenclatural innovations are introduced in this set. One minor disappointment is that only about a third of the species is illustrated. A glossary would also be useful, especially for nonbotanists. A unique and important aspect of this work is a permanently maintained and continuously updated database (taxonomy at the Missouri Botanical Garden and bibliography at the Hunt Institute) to make current data accessible on demand and revisions of the printed volumes expeditious. While it cannot replace extensive local floras (C.L. Hitchcock and A. Cronquist, *Flora of the Pacific Northwest*, CH, Mar'74 or M.L. Fernald's *Gray's Manual of Botany*, 8th ed., 1987) the first two volumes promise that the full set will be an invaluable regional reference. Highly recommended for public and academic institutions with botanical reference responsibilities.—*C. Rinaldo, Dartmouth College*

OAB-0151   QL708   92-22703 CIP
Mammal species of the world: a taxonomic and geographic reference, ed. by Don E. Wilson and DeeAnn M. Reeder. 2nd ed. Smithsonian Institution Press, 1993. 1,206p bibl index afp ISBN 1-56098-217-9, $75.00

An authoritative taxonomy written by 20 specialists that delineates to a fine and current degree each recognized species of living mammal. In updating the 1st edition (1982), 171 species have been added. Three of the newly added species, chosen at random, are not found in either *Walker's Mammals of the World* (5th ed., 1991) or *Grzimek's Encyclopedia of Mammal.* (CH, Jun'90) suggesting more complete coverage in the present work. Maximum content for each entry consists of: species Latin name; namer with source and year of publication for the original description; place where the specimen was found; geographical range and status of the species; synonymous names (a feature useful for tracking literature over time); and comments on taxonomic history. This source is not as well known as Walker or Grzimek, possibly due in part to its lack of common (English) names or illustrations. Incorporation of common names into the index and entries would greatly expand the usefulness of this source as a reference tool. Nonetheless, a valuable and unique compilation, necessary for in-depth reference collections.—*L. Bronars, Yale University*

OAB-0152   95-81456 Orig
Whitaker, John O. **National Audubon Society field guide to North American mammals.** Rev. ed. Knopf, 1996. 937p index ISBN 0-679-44631-1 sc, $19.00

This second edition of a deservedly popular field guide contains a greater number of beautiful photographs and clear descriptions than the first. Although its groupings of photographs of unrelated animals are somewhat confusing (pikas with voles, for instance), it is a reasonable attempt to make field identification easier for novices by using shape. The silhouette shapes may have been enough to serve this goal. Tracks are also grouped in an intuitive way. The introductory text is helpful in describing habitat and providing examples of how to use the different sections to identify mammals. Species descriptions and the more general introductions at the family level are rich in information, including range maps. R.P. Grossenheider's drawings in W.H. Burt's *Field Guide to the Mammals* (CH, Feb'77) present key field characteristics in a better way for comparing similar species and also include some photographs of skulls. The larger number of species covered, vivid photographs, and thorough, professional descriptions in Whitaker's guide make it a necessary purchase for academic or public library collections in natural history.—*C. Rinaldo, Dartmouth College*

■ Physical Sciences

OAB-0153   [Database, CD-ROM]
Albers, Josef. **Interaction of color: interactive CD-ROM edition, Version 1, for Macintosh computers.** Yale, 1994. ISBN 0-300-05995-7 $125.00. User manual. System requirements: Macintosh, 2 MB RAM; color monitor; System 7.0 or later.

This experimental, interactive CD-ROM holds great promise as a model for cooperative publishing and educational enterprise. It is a highly valuable electronic demonstration of the color principles practiced by one of the most distinguished artist/teachers of the modern period, the German-born artist Josef Albers (1888-1976). Albers taught generations of art students first at the Bauhaus, then at Black Mountain College, and, from 1950 to 1958, at Yale University while chair of the Department of Design. Produced in conjunction with the Josef Albers Foundation, this electronic product is a high achievement and a worthy successor to Albers's magnificent but rare, delicate yet cumbersome *Interaction of Color* (1963), a combination folio- and book-form guide and teaching aid for artists, instructors, and students. (The Yale University Press 22-pound boxed original contained 80 color studies, a bound *Interaction of Color: Commentary*, and a separately bound *Interaction of Color: Text*. It appeared after eight years of planning with color compositions made by the master-teacher himself, as well as many studies contributed by Albers's now-famous students, e.g., Eva Hesse and William Bailey. Subsequent versions were issued worldwide in numerous languages, although most were pocket editions with few illustrations.) Now Albers's color teaching reaches into the realm of the computer, offering electronic imaging as a new and effective tool to explore the behavior of color. The reader already familiar with the original folio version will find here—after much searching and lost time—the equivalent of all that is contained in that 1963 version, plus an immense interactive capability through use of the added electronic tools. Perhaps the sole criticism of the basic presentation lies with the difficulty of completely exploring the navigation system. The installation disk provided works easily enough, but the program documentation and technical support are inadequate for the demands of the software. Editorial notes addressing the difference between

silkscreen prints of the 1963 edition and computer-generated colors are useful. There is print screen capability. The illuminated palette with its 256 color choices is augmented by a color wheel tied to a pool of colors totaling "16.7 million shades [sic] to be exact." Facile replacement of colors, shapes, etc., promotes freedom to experiment, observe, and learn. Finally and most importantly, color interactions are demonstrated to be as phenomenal on the computer as in the printed version devised by Albers. Highly recommended for library, classroom, and individual use. All levels.—*M. Hamel-Schwulst, Towson State University*

OAB-0154   Orig
Chambers nuclear energy and radiation dictionary, ed. by P.M.B. Walker. Chambers, 1992. 260p ISBN 0-550-13246-5, $40.00

In the first half of this extensive guide, 11 chapters treat the concepts and history of nuclear energy and radiation (e.g., Atoms and Neutrons, The Reactor Problem, Energy from Fusion, Fission and Fusion Bombs, Photons and Electrons, Biological Effects). Each chapter provides figures or line drawings. The front matter also includes a chronology of nuclear power and a brief two-page glossary of nuclear terms. The dictionary proper—the second half of the book—was drawn from the publisher's proprietary *Chambers Science and Technology Dictionary Database*, with a number of a new and revised entries covering nuclear energy and radiation. When applicable, dictionary entries include cross-references to the opening chapters. An invaluable reference work, highly recommended for nuclear energy, nuclear radiation, nuclear industry, and high-school honors collections, as well as college and university libraries.—*F. A. Hall, Virginia Commonwealth University*

OAB-0155   QC854   95-31019 CIP
Encyclopedia of climate and weather, ed. by Stephen H. Schneider [et al.]. Oxford, 1996. 2v. 929p bibl index afp ISBN 0-19-509485-9, $195.00

The second major encyclopedia devoted to the study of weather and climate, this work is very similar to *Encyclopedia of Climatology*, ed. by John E. Oliver and Rhodes W. Fairbridge (CH, Apr'87). The information in Schneider's work is more current, both in the text and in the bibliographies that accompany the entries. The editors also incorporated sections concerning the effects of weather on people. Included are biographies of those who have helped advance the study of weather and climate and entries on the influence of weather on religion and literature. Schneider provides an extensive glossary. This work encompasses a more diverse range of weather-related topics than Oliver and Fairbridge's encyclopedia and will benefit a wider audience. Highly recommended for all libraries.—*J. C. Stachacz, Dickinson College*

OAB-0156   TJ163   94-44119 CIP
Encyclopedia of energy technology and the environment, ed. by Attilio Bisio and Sharon Boots. Wiley-Interscience, 1995. 4v. 2,964p bibl index afp ISBN 0-471-54458-2, $750.00

For this definitive encyclopedia on energy technology, the editors attempted to gather as much relevant information as possible on all aspects of energy technology, as well as its effect on the environment. A large and impressive group of authors was assembled for this work. Articles are extensive, some running as long as 30 pages. All articles are signed and thoroughly cross-referenced, and all contain extensive bibliographies. All aspects of energy technology are covered; the sections pertaining to environmental law are especially timely and helpful. Statistics, charts, and graphs are plentiful and up-to-date. Although the high cost of this work may place it out of reach for many libraries, it is highly recommended for all upper-division undergraduate and graduate students, as well as scholars and professionals in environmental studies and the energy field.—*J. C. Stachacz, Dickinson College*

OAB-0157   QB14   94-26275 CIP
The Facts on File dictionary of astronomy, ed. by Valerie Illingworth. 3rd ed. Facts on File, 1994. 520p afp ISBN 0-8160-3184-3, $27.95

This useful and authoritative reference work has expanded its list of contributors and added 1,200 entries, an increase of 34 percent in definitions over the second edition (CH, Jul'86). Unlike the previous edition, the third has been substantially revised, increasing the length of the work by nearly 100 pages. This reviewer randomly sampled 30 entries retained from the earlier edition, selecting topics likely to have changed since 1985. Two-thirds of these entries had been substantially revised. Some entries on current "hot topics," e.g., quasars and dark matter, had been not only updated but greatly expanded. The cramped two-column format of the earlier editions, a poor design for right-justified text, has been eliminated, and the increased line length makes the text much more readable. Libraries already owning either previous edition should consider replacing it with this greatly revised and improved third edition. Highly recommended for all college and university libraries, as well as large public libraries. All levels.—*B. E. Fleury, Tulane University*

OAB-0158 QC5 96-30977 CIP
Macmillan encyclopedia of physics, ed. by John S. Rigden. Macmillan Reference USA/Simon & Schuster and Prentice Hall International, 1996. 4v. 1,881p bibl index afp ISBN 0-02-897359-3, $400.00

Macmillan's encyclopedia provides excellent treatment of historical topics, biography, and everyday phenomena and is written in language accessible to most readers. Credentials of the authors are superb. In the first volume, a "Reader's Guide" cross-references related articles. The last volume has a glossary and useful index. Each volume contains a list of abbreviations and symbols. Some entries omit mathematical language, even though the nature of the subject requires it. This work compares favorably with similar reference works, e.g., *McGraw-Hill Encyclopedia of Physics*, ed. by Sybil P. Parker (CH, Oct'93), and *Encyclopedia of Physics*, ed. by R.G. Lerner and G.L. Trigg (2nd ed., 1991). Since the former is a subset of the 7th edition of *McGraw-Hill Encyclopedia of Science and Technology* (1992), some libraries may choose *MEP* as their physics encyclopedia, but limited funds may compel purchase of one of the alternatives. The most recently published *MEP* reflects current developments more accurately, but a third edition of *Encyclopedia of Physics* is expected within the next four years. Recommended for physical science collections and for general and academic readers, all levels.—*C. Shaffer, University of Wisconsin-Madison*

OAB-0159 QC981 92-19059 CIP
Maunder, W. John, comp. **Dictionary of global climate change.** Chapman & Hall, 1992. 240p ISBN 0-412-03901-X, $45.00

One of the first dictionaries devoted to climate change. Originally compiled for participants at the second World Climate Conference (1990), the dictionary has been expanded to make it useful to anyone studying ecology, earth science, environmental science, or geography. It is therefore broader in scope than climatological encyclopedias such as *Encyclopedia of Climatology* ed. by J.E. Oliver and R.W. Fairbridge (CH, Apr'87), and will be widely consulted, particularly by nonspecialists. Entries are concise, informative, and easy to understand. Among the most useful features are the descriptions of international organizations and an extensive list of abbreviations and acronyms. Helpful to anyone interested in global warming and climate change; essential for all libraries.—*J. C. Stachacz, Dickinson College*

OAB-0160 TJ163 93-30307 CIP
Miller, E. Willard. **Energy and American society: a reference handbook,** by E. Willard Miller and Ruby M. Miller. ABC-Clio, 1993. 418p bibl index afp ISBN 0-87436-689-5, $39.50

The Millers' new volume in the "Contemporary World Issues" series sets out to be a "one-stop information source and a guide to in-depth research" for investigation of the role of energy in American society in six chapters and an index. Chapter 1, "Energy: A Perspective," examines the history of energy, consumption, energy sources, and trends in national energy policy. Chapter 2,

"Chronologies and Statistics," has chronologies for each type of energy source and statistical information covering all aspects of energy use and production. Statistics are presented in easy-to-read tables and charts; sources are cited. Chapter 3, "Laws and Regulations," lists and summarizes federal laws and regulations and offers some analysis of their effects. Chapter 4, "Directory of Organizations," lists five types of organizations: US government, US intergovernmental advisory committees, private US organizations, individual energy organizations, and international organizations. For librarians, the most interesting and useful section will be Chapter 5, "Bibliography," which contains lists of reference materials, books, articles, and government publications, and an extensive list of journal titles. Machine-readable databases are omitted, as are sources available over the Internet. Chapter 6, "Films and Videocassettes," lists films and videocassettes with short abstracts. The book is well indexed with many cross-references. It belongs in every public and academic library and in every research and corporate library that deals with energy issues.—*W. E. Drew Jr., SUNY Agricultural and Technical College at Morrisville*

OAB-0161 [Database, CD-ROM]
Properties of organic compounds, Version 3.1. CRC Press, 1993. $2,795.00. About 27,000 records. System requirements: IBM-PC compatibles, 80386 or above; 2 MB RAM; DOS 3.1 or higher; Windows 3.1; MS Word for Windows, 2.0; high-density disk drive; CD-ROM drive with Microsoft Extensions. Software on 3.5" and 5.25" diskettes. User manual.

A handy software package that runs on Windows 3.1, and an important resource for all chemistry collections. Installation and operating directions are clearly stated and follow normal Microsoft 3.1 conventions. The program includes information on more than 27,000 organic compounds, approximately the same number as in its printed counterpart, the *Handbook of Data on Organic Compounds*, ed. by Robert C. Weast and Jeanette G. Grasselli (2nd ed., 1989). A major advantage over the *Handbook* is the program's searchability by Chemical Abstracts Service Registry Numbers. Boolean and range searching are also available. In addition to the Registry Numbers, molecular formula, names, synonyms, spectral peaks, and physical properties are all searchable. Types of spectra include infrared, Raman, ultraviolet, H NMR, C NMR, and mass, with up to 25 peaks allowed for each type of spectrum. Melting point, boiling point, density, and molecular weight are among the searchable properties. In addition to the searchable fields, entries include information such as Beilstein references, refractive index, color, specific rotation, density, spectral references, and solubility. Data and chemical structures can easily be sent to an attached printer, a file on hard disc, or a floppy, or copied to a Windows clipboard and imported into a word processing document. The help screens and written documentation are explicit and include useful examples. Highly recommended for all undergraduate, graduate, and professional chemistry collections.—*M. A. Manion, University of Massachusetts—Lowell*

■ Health, Sports & Physical Education

OAB-0162 HV5804 95-2321 MARC
Encyclopedia of drugs and alcohol, ed. by Jerome H. Jaffe. Macmillan Library Reference USA/Simon & Schuster and Prentice Hall International, 1995. 4v. 1,861p bibl index afp ISBN 0-02-897185-X, $340.00

This comprehensive encyclopedia on drug use and abuse and society's response to it offers long articles that provide overviews of general subjects and briefer articles on specific topics, all written by experts from various disciplines. The editorial board is composed of internationally recognized experts. Broader in coverage than comparable works (e.g., Richard R. Lingeman's *Drugs From A-Z*, 2nd ed., 1974), the set brings together history and pharmacology of drugs, treatment of addiction, and social issues, and is not limited to the US but is international. Volumes 1-3 include an alphabetical list of topics, a list of contributors with credentials, and entries arranged alphabetically by topic. Sample entries include "Brain Structures and Drugs," "Drunk Driving," "Industry and Workplace Drug Use," "Women and Substance Abuse," "Abuse Liability of Drugs," "Ethnic Issues and Cultural Relevance in Treatment," and "Causes of Substance Abuse." Each entry ends with a bibliography. Volume 4 consists of five appendixes: "List of Poison Control Centers," "US and State Government Drug Resources Directory," "Drug Abuse and Alcoholism Treatment and Preventions Programs" by state (more than 400 pages), Bureau of Justice statistics, and "Schedules of Controlled Substances—Illicit and Licit Drugs of Abuse." This one-stop, easy to use source contains a wealth of information. Highly recommended for undergraduates, graduate students, faculty.—*M. E. Leverence, Governors State University*

OAB-0163 Orig
HIV/AIDS resources: the national directory of resources on HIV infection/AIDS: the professionals' reference. National Directory of Children, Youth & Families Services, P.O. Box 1837, Longmont, CO 80502, 1994. 624p pbk $110.00

With the proliferation of the number of people providing AIDS-related services, there has come the concomitant problem of locating the most appropriate provider or peer. This directory provides federal government and state information; state chapters are subdivided to provide county and local information. A wide variety of services and institutions are listed (including support centers that are not specifically AIDS related), e.g., hospitals, counseling centers, substance abuse departments, governmental agencies, People with AIDS Coalitions. Most listings include individual names. Comprehensive in scope and clear in presentation, this directory will be essential for AIDS professionals and a valuable resource in all libraries.—*D. S. Azzolina, University of Pennsylvania*

OAB-0164 95-92096 Orig
Plunkett, Jack W. **Plunkett's health care industry almanac,** editors and publishers, Jack W. Plunkett and Michelle LeGate Plunkett. Corporate Jobs Outlook, 1995. 699p ISBN 0-9638268-1-6 pbk, $125.00

True to the publisher's claim, this is the only complete guide to the health care industry in the US. The book has two primary sections. The first presents five important topics: major trends affecting the health care industry, an overview of the nation's health care, industry-by-industry outlook for the '90s, outlook for technology, and careers in health care. The abundant graphics and charts illustrate five-ten-year changes in such areas as medicare expenditures, inflation rate for medical care and items, hospital occupancy rates, source of funds for personal health care expenditures, and HIV infection mortality. The second addresses "the health care 500," and provides profile information concerning the most successful and largest companies from all health care-related industry segments, e.g., insurance companies, manufacturers and distributors of health care products, pharmaceutical firms, clinics, hospitals, nursing homes, medical record information management companies, and even medical waste disposal firms. All companies selected are publicly held, are nongovernment, and have no less than $10 million in annual sales. Unlike other health care sources (e.g., American Medical Association's *Healthcare Resource and Reference Guide,* CH, Dec'93, and Gale's *Medical and Health Information Directory,* CH, Jun'78), this almanac gives overviews of the present and projects the future of the health care and related industries, summarizing and organizing the findings from government sources. It gives a very comprehensive presentation of the state of the US health care industry. As with other printed sources, some of the data are outdated at the time of printing; most information is dated 1992 or earlier. Highly recommended for public and academic library users.—*E. L. Yang, University of Colorado at Denver*

OAB-0165 GV865 94-138 CIP
Riley, James A. **The biographical encyclopedia of the Negro baseball leagues.** Carroll & Graf, 1994. (Dist. by Publishers Group West) 926p index ISBN 0-7867-0065-3, $29.95

Black Americans have participated in organized baseball from its early years

but were barred from the major leagues until Jackie Robinson took the field with the Brooklyn Dodgers in 1947. For decades the Negro leagues and independent teams provided a crucial forum for the development of African American players, but these organizations declined rapidly after Robinson's major league debut. Riley, author of numerous baseball books including *The Baseball Encyclopedia,* 9th ed. rev. (CH, Sep'93), has compiled an alphabetical compendium of some 4,000 biographical entries and team histories from the Negro leagues and independent teams "of major-league quality." Ranging in length from one line to two and a half pages, the biographies include dates, teams (Negro and major league), height, weight, batting average, won/lost record, and more. Photographs, a "Brief History of the Negro Leagues," and a foreword by Monte Irvin, a Negro league alumnus, complement and enhance the biographies. The bibliography includes interviews, newspaper accounts, periodicals, team histories, books, and pamphlets. Although there are a number of monographs on the Negro leagues and *The Baseball Encyclopedia* includes a brief section (130 players), the current title is the most ambitious effort to date. In summary, this is a solid achievement and a significant contribution to the literature of the Negro leagues. Recommended for all academic and public libraries.—*H. E. Whitmore, emritus, University of Maine at Augusta*

OAB-0166 GV863 92-45555 CIP
Total baseball, ed. by John Thorn and Pete Palmer with Michael Gershman. 3rd ed. Harper Perennial, 1993. 2,362p ISBN 0-06-273189-0 pbk, $35.00

A remarkable compilation of essays, statistics, and rosters. The book presents an impressive array of player and team statistics as well as records and lists of players, umpires, managers, owners, and officials. Most of the statistical and roster information focuses on major league baseball, but there is a roster of Negro Leagues players too. What sets *Total Baseball* apart from other statistical sources is its collection of more than 40 essays written by experts. Essay titles suggest the variety of topics, such as "Ballparks," "Japanese Baseball," "Baseball in the Caribbean," "Women in Baseball," and "The Business of Baseball." Inevitably, *Total Baseball* will be compared to the MacMillan *Baseball Encyclopedia* (9th ed., 1993; 3rd ed., CH, Jan'77). In terms of statistical and roster information, *Total Baseball* matches or exceeds that encyclopedia in most categories. *Total Baseball,* however, does not include information on baseball trades or season-by-season comparisons of home-game versus road-game performances of teams. On balance, though, *Total Baseball* offers a wider range of information than *The Baseball Encyclopedia* and probably will prove more useful to reference librarians. Highly recommended.—*W. Wilson, Amateur Athletic Foundation of Los Angeles*

OAB-0167 RA981 94 37062 CIP
Wright, John W. **The best hospitals in America,** by John W. Wright and Linda Sunshine. 2nd ed. Gale, 1995. 609p indexes afp ISBN 0-8103-9874-5, $34.95

The only comprehensive guide to services offered at medical institutions in the US and Canada, this book intends to identify special programs and areas of expertise of top-ranked hospitals and medical centers, based on information drawn from government sources, professional and popular publications, and surveys and interviews conducted at many hospitals. Criteria for selection and ranking include reputation of the physicians, use of up-to-date medical technologies, quality of facilities and nursing staff, patient satisfaction, commitment to quality assurance, and reputation as referral centers. Many of these best medical institutions are teaching hospitals attached to well-known medical schools, and many are leading recipients of research grants from the National Institutes of Health. The combination of teaching and clinical practice has resulted in exceptional medical innovations, and many of the "best" physicians are associated with these hospitals. The entry for each hospital describes special facilities and programs, and lists both well-known specialists and recent or current research projects. A section called "Patient Satisfaction," new to this edition, reports results of patient surveys. Useful information concerning admission policy includes hospital practice concerning insurance coverage and alternate financial arrangements. Appendixes include lists of hospitals by state or province and by specialty, a description of the National Cancer Institute, and a list of the best cancer centers in the US. There are subject, general, and specialist indexes. Constant change in the health care field and in the quality and specialization of individual hospitals will require frequent revision of this source. Highly recommended for general readers and academic libraries.—*E. L. Yang, University of Colorado at Denver*

■ Social & Behavioral Sciences

OAB-0168   Orig
The 1995 information please women's sourcebook, ed. by Lisa DiMona and Constance Herndon. Houghton Mifflin, 1994. 591p indexes ISBN 0-395-70067-1 pbk, $13.95

A compendium of statistics, resources, guidelines, and advice for women concerning education, work, child care, health, well-being, fertility, sexuality and relationships, divorce and custody, retirement, politics, violence, and activism, this makes a handy desk reference. The statistics alone justify the price. Short essays and articles scattered throughout are an added bonus and make this more than just a dull gathering of statistics. Appendixes list important judicial and legislative decisions; documents, newsletters, and publications; and book and periodical resources. The organization and subject indexes provide additional access. Highly recommended for college, university, and public libraries as well as any organization that serves women or families.—*J. E. Peelle, Kenyon College*

OAB-0169   HQ1090   94-32454 CIP
August, Eugene R. **The new men's studies: a selected and annotated interdisciplinary bibliography.** Libraries Unlimited, 1995 (c1994). 440p indexes ISBN 1-56308-084-2, $45.00

Recognizing the exponential growth in courses and books for men's studies, August has compiled a new edition of his groundbreaking bibliography *Men's Studies* (CH, Nov'85). Like the previous volume, this one includes only books written in English or available in English translation. The first edition contained nearly all men's studies books available in 1985, but a rigorous selection process was instituted with the new version. Materials chosen were those deemed significant or noteworthy in the field, those which illustrate a wide range of philosophical or political viewpoints, and those which cover numerous academic disciplines. Many entries from the previous bibliography have been retained. Twenty-four topical chapters of fully annotated scholarly and popular entries cover a gamut of subjects—e.g., male midlife transition, sexuality, relationships. Each chapter includes a section of cross-references to related chapters and entries. A subject index with headings and subheadings and an author/title index provide uncomplicated access. *New Men's Studies* is an invaluable resource for scholars seeking literature from a male perspective. An excellent selection for all libraries with interests in gender studies.—*M. A. Lutes, University of Notre Dame*

OAB-0170   G116   96-6097 CIP
Companion encyclopedia of geography: the environment and humankind, ed. by Ian Douglas et al. Routledge, 1996. 1,021p bibl index afp ISBN 0-415-07417-7, $150.00

Each of the prominent contributors to this 1,000 page, 45-chapter tome was directed to address the interrelationships between the human species and its habitat in a style "more personal than discursive." Essays are grouped in six parts. Part 1 (seven chapters) treats the evolution of the physical environment and the impact of cultural systems. Part 2 (eight chapters) considers the last three centuries of modification of the ecosphere by human activities. Part 3 (seven chapters) examines the complexity of new environmental and social forces that have had an impact on the human habitat since WW II. Part 4 (13 chapters) concen-

trates on the contemporary problems of ecological degradation and socioeconomic inequities. Part 5 (six chapters) presents interpretations of recent theoretical developments in geography. Finally, part 6 (four chapters) appraises the future of the discipline. Each essay is an authoritative statement, accompanied by tables, diagrams, maps, and up-to-date lists of references. Despite the price, this is an indispensable item for any library that wishes to strengthen its reference section, and for the professional geographer who wants to keep abreast of developments in the field.—*B. Osborne, Queen's University at Kingston*

OAB-0171   LB15   92-12654 MARC
The Encyclopedia of higher education: v.1: National systems of higher education; v.2-3: Analytical perspectives; v.4: Academic disciplines and indexes, ed. by Burton R. Clark and Guy R. Neave. Pergamon, 1992. 4v. 2,530p afp ISBN 0-08-037251-1, $1,500.00

In the last half of the 20th century, higher education has become a critical institution in the development of societies and nations and the university, wherever it has risen, has shown itself a uniquely durable institution. The study of higher education long has needed an integrative and comprehensive encyclopedia. This work is a monumental achievement that goes well beyond both the parent work, *International Encyclopedia of Education* (CH, Sep'86), and *The International Encyclopedia of Higher Education*, ed. by Asa Knowles (CH, Jul'78; now out of print and in many areas obsolete). Arguably, this new effort is one of the most important reference tools in higher education since the Knowles work. Volume 1 contains analyses of more than 135 national systems of higher education. Volumes 2 and 3 present analytical papers on an extensive range of issues and problems within the field, while Voluume 4 offers a unique and comprehensive review of the development of core academic disciplines. Volume 4 is heavily contextual and portrays disciplines as ongoing concerns that reach across institutions and nations. This important section permits readers to grasp readily the patterns of thought in the major disciplines, the traditional symbols and identities associated with those disciplines, and the distinctive disciplinary practices that condition the academic lives of faculty and students. An impressive work, organized to render it invaluable to scholars in many disciplines. The price can be justified even if that means not purchasing a few other new reference works in higher education.—*E. Garten, University of Dayton*

OAB-0172   E184   93-23405 CIP
Encyclopedia of multiculturalism, ed. by Susan Auerbach. M. Cavendish, 1994. 6v. 1,835p bibl index afp ISBN 1-85435-670-4, $449.95

Concepts of US pluralism (social sciences), multiculturalism, ethnology, and ethnic and race relations form the framework for this valuable, inclusive encyclopedic reference set "devoted to 'minority groups' that have suffered discrimination and exclusion—African-Americans, American Indians, Asian/Pacific Americans, Latinos and women." Sources on interdisciplinary multiculturalism are widely dispersed and often too specialized for general readers and others doing introductory research. Focusing on multicultural perspectives that unite and divide diverse Americans, this work examines American society and history through the experiences of culturally diverse groups whose contributions and issues have often been ignored. The list of contributors is impressive; their goal of presenting controversial and previously ill-documented information with objectivity and clarity has been met. Volume 6 includes additional research aids; a unique time line (43,000 BCE to 1993); a resource list; a filmography; a bibliography of recent multicultural studies; an accessible, useful subject list; and a comprehensive index. Two searches quickly uncovered topics recently researched by undergraduate students in this reviewer's library: "gays in the military" and "Japanese American internment camps." One is a brief identification of key terms and individuals, the other an overview essay; both concluded with pertinent recommended readings. Useful for middle and high school students, college undergraduate students, and general readers in the initial reference overview and background portion of their library research. Recommended to all libraries.—*N. S. Osborne, SUNY College at Oswego*

OAB-0173 HQ1883 93-13702 MARC

Encyclopedia of women's associations worldwide: a guide to over 3,400 national and multinational nonprofit women's and women-related organizations, ed. by Jacqueline K. Barrett; Jane A. Malonis, associate editor. Gale, 1993. 471p indexes afp ISBN 1-873477-25-2, $80.00

The editors of *EWAW*, which lists emerging and established women's organizations worldwide, intend that their book be used to promote communication and networking. For example, this new affordable directory includes 95 women's groups in the Russian section, all founded since 1989. The recent formation of such groups and the sketchiness of other entries, illustrate the fragility of these budding societies and their need for support and representation. The plurality of groups are from the US (1,027 out of 3,435) while some countries have only a single entry (Lithuania, Algeria, Bhutan) and others none at all (particularly countries of the Commonwealth of Independent States). Those interested in women's issues will be able to locate regional contacts or associations involved in particular activities. The directory arrangement is geographic, with alphabetic and "activities" indexes (e.g., arts, politics, peace, health, economics, sports). Entries compiled from *Encyclopedia of Associations, Encyclopedia of Associations: International Organizations* and from questionnaires, contain, when available, address, phone, fax, year founded, description, and publications. Highly recommended.—*P. Keeran, University of Denver*

OAB-0174 HV640 94-8747 CIP

Gorman, Robert F. **Historical dictionary of refugee and disaster relief organizations.** Scarecrow, 1994. 263p bibl afp (International organizations series, 7) ISBN 0-8108-2876-6, $32.50

Gorman (Southwest Texas State Univ.) has written the seventh title in this series of directories of international organizations. This volume "focuses primarily on the dozens of international organizations and hundreds of nongovernmental agencies that have emerged mainly in the twentieth century to cope with disasters and humanitarian emergencies." Opening this dictionary is a list of acronyms and abbreviations for the organizations profiled, followed by a chronology of notable refugee and disaster relief events in this century. Following an excellent historical introduction is a glossary of terms used in discussion of refugee issues. Then come the dictionary entries: alphabetical lists of intergovernmental organizations (IGOs), nongovernmental or private voluntary organizations (NGOs or PVOs), and a section on legal instruments, conferences, programs, and peacekeeping forces. Each organizational entry gives founding date, purpose, and an address. There is also an alphabetical list of 20th-century humanitarian relief events that take the reader from the Balkan wars of 1912-13 through the Somali civil war and famine of 1989-93. An annotated bibliography of major resources on relief followed by a listing of other historical and literary sources will be invaluable to researchers and librarians. Nine appendixes detail important individuals, statistics, budgetary figures, and major disasters. Organizational charts for notable international agencies (e.g., UN High Commissioner for Refugees) round out this work. A subject index of exiled populations (e.g., Afghans, Cambodians, Palestinians, etc.) would have been a useful addition. Highly recommended. General readers; undergraduate through faculty.—*C. E. Carter, University of New Mexico*

OAB-0175 HD30 94-540 CIP

Graham, John W. **Mission statements: a guide to the corporate and nonprofit sectors,** by John W. Graham and Wendy C. Havlick. Garland, 1994. 551p indexes afp (Garland reference library of social science, 900) ISBN 0-8153-1297-0, $90.00

Reference books are seldom timely and well organized. This one is! The authors, both librarians, compiled this book because mission statements are generally unpublished and thus not available in libraries. This book makes available mission statements for 622 corporations, government agencies, nonprofit organizations, and charitable foundations in the US and Canada. Aside from the statements per se, the strengths of the book are its organization, clarity, precision of methodology, and conciseness in discussing the purpose, creation, and function of mission statements. The foreword is written by a known expert on strategic management. In the introduction, the authors suggest areas for possible mission-statement research and present a 64-item bibliography. The mission statements were solicited by mail from over 2,900 organizations, and participation was voluntary. Entries are arranged alphabetically, each including organization name, address, and telephone number, and at least one industry code obtained from the *Standard Industrial Classification Manual* (1987). The mission statements follow with appropriate credit, acknowledgment, copyright notice, or date if available. The work ends with geographic and industry indexes. Students, researchers, or job hunters will find this resource useful in determining the "culture" of an organization. Highly recommended for academic libraries, upper-division undergraduate and above.—*P. P. Philbin, University of Vermont*

OAB-0176 Z699 92-32899 CIP

Knapp, Sara D., comp. **The contemporary thesaurus of social science terms and synonyms:** a guide for natural language computer searching. Oryx, 1993. 400p bibl afp ISBN 0-89774-595-7, $95.00

The soundest test of a reference work's value, presumably, is how often it is used. If that is so, this work passes with flying colors. Only hours after the volume was received it helped this reviewer find the precise phrase needed for a computer search in child psychology, a phrase that the American Psychological Association's *Thesaurus of Psychological Index Terms* had failed to uncover. And just such cases of helping "users find meaningful words for natural language computer searching" will be the primary use of this work. It does so by listing synonyms and related terms for more than 6,000 concepts and terms in the social sciences and by listing them logically, clearly, and thoroughly with an incredible number of *see* and *see also* references, making it almost impossible to fail in one's search for a useful term. The few pages headed "Basics of Computer Searching" and "Natural Language Searching" are well done; and along with an appendix on search features used in most online and CD-ROM systems, these sections could provide reference and BI librarians with material for handouts. Knapp (SUNY-Albany), who has written extensively about online database searching, has produced a work that librarians and other searchers will turn to again and again. Some may quibble over minor omissions, but the volume should be available, even pointed out, in any reference area where there is computer searching in the social sciences; in areas containing many such work stations, there perhaps ought to be more than one copy. Undergraduate; graduate; pre-professional; professional.—*E. I. Farber, Earlham College*

OAB-0177 Orig

Schlachter, Gail Ann. **College student's guide to merit and other no-need funding, 1996-1998,** by Gail Ann Schlachter and R. David Weber. Reference Service, 1996. 364p indexes ISBN 0-918276-30-6, $29.95

Although there is no shortage of college financial aid resource books, this guide distinguishes itself in a number of ways. Schlachter, who has collaborated with Weber on several other financial aid guides, focuses on more than 1,000 programs that offer merit or no-need funding to currently enrolled college students. Entries include the program title, contact information, purpose, eligibility requirements, financial data, duration, number awarded, special features, and deadline date. Furthermore, Schlachter goes beyond the typical financial aid book by providing six different indexes: program title, sponsoring organization, residency limitations, geographic limitations, subject, and deadline date. These indexes allow one to focus very quickly and efficiently on entries relevant to personal need. An annotated listing of additional financial aid resources and contact information for sources of financial aid offered by each state complete the volume. No comparable guide exists. Highly recommended for undergraduate collections.—*D. L. Miller, Lebanon Valley College*

OAB-0178 Orig

Statistical abstract of the world, ed. by Marlita A. Reddy. Gale, 1994. 1,111p index afp ISBN 0-8103-9199-6, $49.95

Statistical Abstract of the World (*SAW*) provides comparative statistics for each of 185 countries in a compact format. Derived from standard international and US statistical compendia, this abstract devotes between five and six pages to each of eight major areas: geography (map, land use, terrain), human factors (demographics, religion, etc.), education, science and technology, government and law, the labor force, production sectors, manufacturing sectors, and finance, economics, and trade. Designed in a panel or "windows" format, the abstract leaves panels blank when reliable information is unavailable, an approach that could lead to misinterpretation by unsophisticated users. The editors combine the presentations into one panel, "Energy" or "Industrial Summary," for countries for which statistics are lacking in either of those areas. Each table's legend clearly indicates how values are to be interpreted. The "Annotated Source Appendix" with each topical area provides both footnotes and citations to the published sources from which *SAW* is compiled. An exceptionally uncluttered presentation adds to *SAW*'s value for the price. Ending with a keyword index, *SAW* is the place to start for statistical information about countries of the world. Recommended for all libraries for its presentation and timeliness.—*H. H. Ives, American University*

OAB-0179   93-78367 Orig
Statistical record of Hispanic Americans, ed. by Marlita A. Reddy. Gale, 1993. 1,173p index afp ISBN 0-8103-8962-2, $89.50

Gale's massive data compilations continue to find a ready market among libraries because they bring together in one place information otherwise difficult to find. Census data continues to be difficult and time-consuming to use and understand, even for skilled researchers. This *Statistical Record* fills a niche that will exist until the information is compiled uniformly and made accessible for any student or researcher. The summary at the beginning of the volume provides a useful overview, since it both lists the sources of the data for each chapter and states the major points of each chapter. Subject chapters provide a clear division of the statistical information, with related data grouped under one heading (e.g., "Population Trends" and "Immigration" are joined in Chapter 1, Demographics). A commendable work, recommended for advanced undergraduates, graduate students, faculty, and practitioners.—*D. R. Brown, DePaul University*

OAB-0180   E98   93-14164 MARC
Statistical record of Native North Americans, ed. by Marlita A. Reddy. Gale, 1993. 1,661p index afp ISBN 0-8103-8963-0, $89.50

A hefty compilation that presents statistical information from federal agencies (primarily the Bureau of Indian Affairs and the Census Bureau) as well as state agencies, tribal governments, associations, and other organizations. While some of the data is available in other sources, much has never been published; it has never before been collected in one convenient volume. Acknowledging controversies over the accuracy of some information and the difficulties of comparing data from different sources, the work offers both historical and current statistical tables, ranging from 20th-century estimates of pre-1942 populations to the 1980 census. Figures from the 1990 census are not included since detailed information on Native Americans has not yet been released. Twelve broad subject chapters (e.g., Demographics, Business and Industry, Education) are subdived by topic. One chapter treats Native Canadians. The source for each table is cited; often, both primary and secondary sources are given. A keyword index of more than 3,000 items includes individuals, tribes, organizations, and places. A source list is useful but does not include all sources cited in the tables. Although heavy and difficult to handle, the book will be very useful for both ready reference and research.—*J. Drueke, University of Nebraska-Lincoln*

OAB-0181   CD3026   96-1113 MARC
United States. National Archives and Records Administration. **Guide to federal records in the National Archives of the United States,** comp. by Robert B. Matchette with Anne B. Eales et al.; index comp. by Jan Shelton Danis. National Archives and Records Administration, 1996 (c1995).(Forsale by U.S. GPO) 3v. index afp ISBN 0-16-048312-3, $95.00

Superseding in all respects the 1974 *Guide to the National Archives of the United States*, this magisterial reference work provides an introduction to more than 1.7 million cubic feet of textual records, 300,000 rolls of microfilm, 2.3 million maps and charts, 9.2 million aerial photographs, 7.4 million still pictures, 178,000 sound recordings, 123,000 motion picture reels, and 7,000 computer data sets located in National Archives depositories in Washington; College Park, MD;, regional branches; presidential libraries; and affiliated archives. It describes NARA's holdings as of September 1, 1994. The *Guide* is organized into descriptions of nearly 500 record groups, some dating from the prefederal period, that document the executive, legislative, and judicial branches of government. Separately published finding aids noted in some record group descriptions supplement *Guide* entries. The third volume is a comprehensive index. A brief review of so important and thorough a guide to our nation's public records does not do justice to its complexity and its utility. Suffice it to note here that the *Guide* should be found in all academic libraries.—*N. C. Burckel, Marquette University*

OAB-0182   HA17   93-728 CIP
Vogt, W. Paul. **Dictionary of statistics and methodology: a nontechnical guide for the social sciences.** Sage, 1993. 253p ISBN 0-8039-5276-7, $38.95; ISBN 0-8039-5277-5 pbk, $18.95

Social scientists use statistics to try to validate answers to questions in their field. These statistical data are often found in articles and books with a broad reading audience. Statistics is a relatively small discipline, and the proportion of readers who understand statistics is understandably small. This dictionary helps nonspecialist readers understand the statistics encountered in their reading. Definitions are written in lay terms where possible, sometimes include examples, and are very understandable. Many definitions, of necessity, include other statistical terms; those defined in the dictionary are cross-referenced. Vogt emphasizes understanding the concept rather than explaining the mathematics involved. A short bibliography of additional readings is included. The book should be part of every reference collection, and some scholars may want to purchase a personal copy.—*J. O. Christensen, Brigham Young University*

■ Anthropology

OAB-0183   GR101   95-53734 CIP
American folklore: an encyclopedia, ed. by Jan Harold Brunvand. Garland, 1996. 794p bibl index afp (Garland reference library of the humanities, 1551) ISBN 0-8153-0751-9, $95.00

An excellent resource for the study of American folklore, this encyclopedia provides extensive coverage of folk traditions and folklore scholarship in the US and Canada. Native American subjects have been intentionally excluded, since they will be covered in a separate encyclopedia. Folklorist Brunvand has compiled a collection of informative essays written by a distinguished group of academic folklore specialists. Subjects range from traditional folk genres such as ballads and quilt making to more modern studies such as computer folklore and urban traditions. Folklore of various regions and ethnic populations is treated in general survey entries as well as specifically by group. Particular attention is given to approaches to folklore studies and scholarship issues. Biographies of prominent folk performers are included, but significant folklore scholars were added only if their "life work has been completed." Each signed entry contains a concise definition, general background information, discussion of significant developments, and a short bibliography of sources for further study. Ample cross-references increase the volume's usefulness. Photographs and illustrations throughout the work enhance its appeal. Scholarly in its approach, this unique reference source is highly recommended for researchers as well as general readers with an interest in folklore studies.—*E. R. Hitchcock, University of the South*

OAB-0184   DS57   95-1712 CIP
Civilizations of the ancient Near East, ed. by Jack M. Sasson et al. Scribner, 1995. 4v. 2,966p bibl index afp ISBN 0-684-19279-9, $449.00

In the recent flurry of reference publishing focused on the ancient world, this four-volume set is distinguished by its rich, comprehensive approach, solid scholarship, and accessibility to students, scholars, and interested general readers. As the first major compendium of its kind, it fills an important gap in the current scholarly literature of the ancient Near East. Drawing on both archaeological and textual sources, a large international team of the most respected scholars from numerous disciplines have contributed 189 essays on a wide range of topics. The nearly 3,000 pages of text spanning more than 4,000 years of history are divided into 11 broad subjects, which include the ancient Near East in Western thought; the environment; population; social institutions; history and culture; economy and trade; technology and artistic production; religion and science; language, writing, and literature; visual and performing arts; and retrospective essays. Included also are 46 maps, 612 photographs and line drawings, time lines comparing ancient Near Eastern civilizations, and a very useful index. Essential for all libraries supporting this topic.—*M. R. Dittemore, Smithsonian Institution Libraries*

OAB-0185   GN307   95-37237 Orig
Encyclopedia of cultural anthropology, ed. by David Levinson and Melvin Ember. H. Holt, 1996. 4v. bibl index ISBN 0-8050-2877-3, $395.00

Among the notable one-volume encyclopedias of anthropology are *Dictionary of Anthropology*, ed. by Charlotte Seymour-Smith (CH, Jul'87), John Joseph Honigmann's *Handbook of Social and Cultural Anthropology* (1973), *Encyclopedia of Anthropology*, ed. by David E. Hunter and Phillip Whitten (CH, Sep'76), and *Companion Encyclopedia of Anthropology* (1994). There are also reference works that concentrate on peoples of the world. This much larger work is sponsored by Human Relations Area Files, one of the major research centers in cultural anthropology, which has emphasized collecting data to facilitate cultural comparisons. Its editors are associated with HRAF but have not been limited by their organization's orientation. They emphasize major topics in the discipline, from historic concerns (e.g., field work) to recent theoretical issues (feminist anthropology). The 300 contributors range from major figures such as George Marcus through recent graduates. The articles themselves are good summaries of contemporary views in the field and include bibliographies that would have been enhanced had they been annotated, since many of the encyclopedia's users will be novices who could profit from guidance in reading. An appendix that lists anthropological journals is useful in a discipline whose bibliographic control is difficult. The index (not available for this review) will, it is hoped, refer to the various peoples discussed in the articles, since there are no articles on individual groups. There are, however, many articles on cultural regions. Regrettably, there are no illustrations, but including them would probably have greatly increased the cost of the set. These comments are meant to be suggestive; the encyclopedia fills an enormous gap in anthropological reference and belongs in every college and university library, even those where anthropology is not taught.—*D. S. Azzolina, University of Pennsylvania*

OAB-0186   Orig
Encyclopedia of social and cultural anthropology, ed. by Alan Barnard and Jonathan Spencer. Routledge, 1996. 658p bibl indexes ISBN 0-415-09996-X, $120.00

Two hundred thirty-one substantial entries, arranged alphabetically, form the bulk of this encyclopedia. Entries are followed by selective reading lists and by cross-references. The editors have attempted to balance coverage of this "pluralistic and occasionally fractious discipline" by choosing a variety of contributors and asking them to write from their own points of view. An analytical table of contents indicates five categories of entries: ethnographic surveys, history of anthropology, subdisciplines and neighboring disciplines, anthropological concepts and methods, and anthropological objects. Entries on abstract topics are liberally illustrated with ethnographic detail. Although only five people (Franz Boas, Claude Levi-Strauss, B.K. Malinowski, L.H. Morgan, and A.R.

Radcliffe-Brown) are given separate substantial entries, a biographical appendix gives brief biographies of 238 other figures who have been important in the development of anthropology. A glossary of technical terms supplements the more extensive entries. Name, subject, and peoples and places indexes are detailed enough to offset what the editors call the "inevitably rather arbitrary" choice of headings. The result is an intelligent, informative, and entertaining addition to the deplorably small number of reference works in the field. Academic readers, all levels.—*J. Drueke, University of Nebraska—Lincoln*

OAB-0187   GN307   90-49123 CIP
Encyclopedia of world cultures: v.7: South America, ed. by Johannes Wilbert. G.K. Hall, 1994. 426p bibl index afp ISBN 0-8161-1813-2, $100.00

Tropical forest and savanna cultures of South America prevail among 93 detailed profiles and 58 shorter articles treating indigenous South Americans in this seventh volume of the series (v.1, *North America*, ed. by Timothy J. O'Leary and David Levinson, CH, Oct'91; v. 2, *Oceania*, by Terrence E. Hays, CH, Apr'92; v. 3, *South Asia*, ed. by Paul Hickings, CH, Dec'92). Signed articles written by specialists, mostly anthropologists, and unsigned accounts researched by Human Relations Area Files personnel are included, all with bibliographic references. An ethnym-indexed list of 187 additional cultures appears as an appendix. Articles show recent ethnographic interest in cosmology and cultural ecology and documentation of language groups by the Summer Institute of Linguistics. The volume is enhanced by the indexed filmography, glossary, and general ethnym index with boldface indicating culture names used for titles. The work lacks a general index. Articles are alphabetically ordered by culture name. There is some helpful cross-referencing, as in the short Quechua article, which refers the reader to seven other entries. A separate profile treats the large Aymara group of the Titicaca region. This volume redresses an unintended imbalance in treatment of indigenous populations in the previous master reference of its kind, *Handbook of South American Indians* (1946-59), ed. by the late Julian Steward, which focuses on culture areas (summarized in the introduction and maps of the current volume) and trait constellations related to technology, and is organized according to an evolutionary scheme contrasting "marginal" hunting or fishing tribes with Andean "civilization." Steward's categories were actually directed toward cultural ecology and marked an important paradigm shift in anthropological theory at the time; the diversity of tropical forest cultures, although actually greater at that time, was then less documented by anthropologists. Extinct cultures should be searched in the *Handbook*. Those interested in highland indigenous cultures will find updated bibliography and general synthesis rather than details of Quechua or Aymara diversity in the current volume. Populations resulting from Iberian colonization, African slavery, and all subsequent immigration are peripheral to the intent of the series, although these groups are, along with the Quechua and Aymara, numerically important in South America today. Six articles treat Afro-South Americans, mostly by region; Asian, European, Jewish, and Mennonite immigrants are covered with one article per group. A must for large public and all academic and research libraries; libraries owning the *Handbook* will want this welcome complement.—*K. M. Cleland, Swarthmore College*

OAB-0188   GN307   90-49123 CIP
Encyclopedia of world cultures: v.8: Middle America and the Caribbean; v.9: Africa and the Middle East; v.10: Indexes, ed. by James W. Dow with Robert Van Kemper (v.8); John Middleton and Amal Rassam et al. (v.9); David Levinson (v.10). G.K. Hall, NY, 1995. 3v. 329, 447, 322p bibl filmography index afp ISBN 0-8161-1816-7, v.8; ISBN 0-8161-1815-9, v.9; ISBN 0-8161-1817-5, v.10; $110.00 ea.

These volumes complete the set (for vols. 1-3 and 7, see CH, Oct'91, Apr'92, Dec'92, Feb'95). Regional volumes begin with an alphabetical list of contributors noting their articles. Levinson's preface defines selection criteria, emphasizing indigenous peoples and unassimilated immigrants, and the format recommended to contributors for comparability. Signed articles in both volumes often follow this format, but shorter summaries by HRAF staff (unsigned in vol. 8 and sometimes longer and signed in vol. 9) generally do not. Nearly all entries end with bibliographic references. Introductions by the volume editors orient readers to the region. Volume 8 offers 28 entries on Caribbean island peoples and 93 on Middle American continental groups. Volume 9 features 40 Middle Eastern, eight continental North African Middle Eastern, and 93 African peoples. About one-fifth of the volume 8 contributors are based in Mexico or Central America, while most contributors to volume 9 are based in North America or Europe, regardless of varied national origin. Dow's introduction to volume 8 is generally good and very comprehensive, despite unqualified reference to evidence for "transoceanic" contact before the Spanish invasion. Textual redundancy, typos, and consistent misspelling of Elizabeth Brumfiel's name detract from a quality work. Middleton's "Introduction to Africa" gives a helpful history of anthropological classifications of African peoples that builds on George P. Murdock's *Africa: Its Peoples and Their Culture History* (1959). Middleton's dated reference to "Bushmen" is surprising; the entry on San-speaking groups notes correct usage. Rassam's separate "Introduction to the Middle East" clarifies ways in which language, culture, and religion dominate or interact in self-definition of groups. Both volumes include helpful maps, but number codes for culture names are inconsistent from map to map within each volume, and in volume 8 some Middle American cultures that lack entries appear on the maps. Volume 9 includes a section listing and locating about 500 more African cultures. Essential volume-specific glossaries are included before the filmography in each volume (45 items in vol. 8 and 136 in vol. 9). Each regional volume ends with an "Ethonym Index." Murdock serves a similar purpose for African cultures, while Louise Elizabeth Sweet's *Peoples and Cultures of the Middle East: An Anthropological Reader* (2v., 1970) is analogous for that region. The *Indexes* (vol. 10) to the entire set are a welcome addition, because the regional volumes are unindexed. Its access points are by country, ethonym (culture name), and subject. Its second section, the "Ethonym Index," is the principal access point. It is unfortunate that "List of Cultures by Country" comes first for two reasons: one must know where a group lives to use it and users may be misled into thinking this is a comprehensive cultural reference by country—it is not. The "List" is limited to groups treated in *Encyclopedia of World Cultures*. The "Subject Index" is very detailed, but somewhat inconsistent; Maasai are listed under "cattle herding," while Gusii appear under "cattle raising." More entries treat iron metallurgy or metalworking in Africa than the related headings indicate. Users are advised to try multiple headings. *The Encyclopedia of the Peoples of the World*, ed. by Amiram Gonen (CH, Apr'94), includes more cultures in less detail. *Encyclopedia of World Cultures* remains the master work for current encyclopedia articles about living cultures for undergraduate and research libraries.—*K. M. Cleland, Swarthmore College*

OAB-0189   E98   92-27053 CIP
Gill, Sam D. **Dictionary of Native American mythology,** by Sam D. Gill and Irene F. Sullivan. ABC-CLIO, 1992. 425p bibl index afp ISBN 0-87436-621-6, $65.00

Gill and Sullivan (Univ. of Colorado, Boulder) have gathered a unique dictionary of more than 1,300 stories, characters, themes, symbols, and motifs from cultures throughout Native North America. Entries vary in length, but all have cross-references to related entries and cite items for further reading that are listed in full at the back of the book in an excellent bibliography of well-known scholarship in the field (most of them, however, written by non-Native ethnographers and folklorists). Entries are preceded by 11 maps delineating culture areas and are complemented by 45 captioned illustrations. An index by tribe is also keyed to sources in the bibliography. One shortcoming is the use in many cases of the European appellation instead of a group's own name (e.g., "Papago" instead of the Native term "Tohono O'odham"), showing the dictionary's dependence on non-Native textual representations of myths and legends. Nevertheless, this is an important new work that will facilitate study. Recommended for all Native American, religion, and folklore collections.—*C. E. Carter, California State University, Fresno*

OAB-0190   E184   93-13348 CIP
Handbook of Hispanic cultures in the United States: literature and art, ed. by Francisco Lomelí. Arte Publico, 1994 (1993). 413p index afp ISBN 1-55885-074-0, $60.00

Rather than discuss any potential shortcomings of these publications (e.g., only Cubans, Mexicans, and Puerto Ricans are included in "Part Four: The Recent Past" in the history volume), this reviewer enthusiastically recommends this two-volume set to every library in the US. It presents such a concise, easy-to-read yet scholarly approach to Hispanic culture in the US that it should be readily available to readers on all levels and with any degree of interest. The two-volume division into "Literature and Art" and "History" provides a simple separation for students or general readers wanting basic information on a topic in either area. The introduction implies an expansion into coverage of other areas, and the format provides a good model for coverage of other ethnic groups in the US multicultural society. Currency is a problem with this handbook, as with any printed text, because of the time delay in production (e.g., "Latino Cinema" is not up to date), but the reader learns a lot about the overall topic and then can use periodicals for more current information. For a work of this magnitude, the price should not be an impediment for a library to purchase the text.—*D. R. Brown, DePaul University*

OAB-0191   GN50   96-34389 Orig
History of physical anthropology, ed. by Frank Spencer. Garland, 1997. 2v. 1,195p bibl indexes afp (Garland reference library of social science, 677) ISBN 0-8153-0490-0, $175.00

The reference literature of physical anthropology has long needed a clear and comprehensive synthesis of historical aspects of this complex science. The present work fills this gap admirably. Building on experience gained by overseeing the collection *A History of American Physical Anthropology, 1930-1980* (1982) and subsequently compiling *Ecce Homo: An Annotated Bibliographic History of Physical Anthropology* (1986), the editor has assembled articles "dealing with the development of specific areas of scientific inquiry and theory ... the discipline's intellectual and institutional development in specific countries," to which are added 303 biographical sketches of both major and minor figures. Of the latter, approximately one-fifth (64) are also included in *International Dictionary of Anthropologists* (CH, Apr'92). Contributors to this truly international project include 169 scholars from more than 30 nations. Clear and readable entries are followed by listings of primary and secondary resources and a select bibliography. Illustrations are high-quality black-and-white photographs and tables. A solid work that will remain basic for any reference collection in the biological or social sciences well into the next century.—*R. B. M. Ridinger, Northern Illinois University*

OAB-0192   CC70   96-30792 CIP
The Oxford companion to archaeology, ed. by Brian M. Fagan et al. Oxford, 1997 (c1996). 844p index afp ISBN 0-19-507618-4, $55.00

Nearly 700 signed, alphabetically arranged entries, multiparagraph to multipage, by more than 370 writers who are specialists or who teach in a related area, treat world regions, artifactual analysis, field methods, Western theory, and archaeology's history and future. Most include cross-references and end with bibliographies that cite recent materials. Formats vary from solo articles to nearly 60 umbrella collections on major topics that begin with overviews. The only graphics are small maps (which show few sites) and time lines at the end of the volume. *Oxford* might appear to update and expand on the general, well-illustrated *Cambridge Encyclopedia of Archaeology* (CH, Oct'80); it does in content, but words cannot fully replace illustrations of artifacts, architectural forms, and ancient artistic expression. *Oxford* attempts too much for the world's regions to be represented evenly. Well-known sites and cultures predominate, Austronesia and sub-Saharan Africa are better represented than in most reference works, while the "westernness" of archaeology itself is acknowledged. Canada, Pacific North America, northern Mexico, non-Mayan Central America, non-Andean South America, most of central Europe and western Asia, the Maghreb, and Saudi Arabia are treated only generally. Forty percent of the mostly brief biographies were written by the editor; they make up three percent of the entries. Historically important archaeologists are mentioned in passing throughout the volume.

There are some errors; a troubling one dates the apogee of Aksum to the 11th century BCE, well before Christianity came to Ethiopia. Time line and index users will no doubt discover others. Since there is no table of contents, the index provides the principal access point. Most index terms simply repeat article title and heading words, except for some proper names. Some basics are omitted from the index; for example, rice, wheat, maize, cattle, sheep, goats. There are leads under "domestication," but that assumes prior knowledge. The situation is worse with regard to common metals; index entries are limited to "Bronze Age" and "Iron Age," with *see also* references to area and site names. Users must already know or suspect which areas or sites had bronze or iron in order to find them. *Cambridge* has ample listings under the plants, animals, and metals *Oxford* uses as examples. Novice users will benefit by consulting *Oxford* jointly with other works that have better indexing, maps, and illustrations, or more biographies (e.g., for maps and illustrations *World Atlas of Archaeology*, CH, Mar'86, and *Past Worlds: The Times Atlas of Archaeology*, CH, Mar'89; for illustrations, the brief, specialized *Dictionary of Terms and Techniques in Archaeology*, CH, Apr'81, or *Collins Dictionary of Archaeology*, CH, Mar'94; and for biographies of anthropological archaeologists born before 1920, *International Dictionary of Anthropologists*, CH, Apr'92). Although more accessible to readers with some background in archaeology, *Oxford* is unlike any reference work since 1980 in the depth and currency of its treatment. Highly recommended for academic, research, large public, or museum libraries, or for interested individuals with background in archaeology.—*K. M. Cleland, Swarthmore College*

OAB-0193   Aust. CIP
The Oxford companion to Australian folklore, ed. by Gwenda Beed Davey and Graham Seal. Oxford, 1993. 381p ISBN 0-19-553057-8, $49.95

The rationale for this first Oxford companion in folklore is the opposite of all the other Oxford companions. Here, Davey and Seal, authors of definitive works on Australian folklore, acknowledge the lack of a scholarly foundation for their work; instead, they provide the basis for one to be laid. As they indicate in their preface, the companion attempts "to draw together the various threads of what is known [about Australian folklore] and to present these to the reader in an informed and accessible manner." They are far too modest in their claims. Not only do they cover the major genres and ethnic groups, they also include biographical entries on scholars and performers, and descriptions of institutions and publications. Entries were written by more than 25 contributors; longer articles are signed and many include bibliographies. Some illustrations are included, but for a collection of texts, readers need to consult one of the many collections available. An appendix covering bibliographic topics in Australian folklore makes a fine addition. One hopes Oxford will continue to publish such excellent reference works in folklore. All libraries.—*D. S. Azzolina, University of Pennsylvania*

OAB-0194   DS56   96-17152 CIP
The Oxford encyclopedia of archaeology in the Near East, prep. under the auspices of the American Schools of Oriental Research; ed. by Eric M. Meyers. Oxford, 1997. 5v. 488-553p ea. bibl index afp ISBN 0-19-506512-3, $575.00

The latest in a series of important reference works on the ancient Near East, this encyclopedia is distinguished by its comprehensive approach, solid scholarship, highly respected contributors, and usefulness not only to scholars but to general readers. Published under the auspices of the American Schools of Oriental Research (ASOR), it will be a major authoritative source in this field for some time to come. It includes 1,125 alphabetically arranged entries written by more than 550 leading international scholars. The entries cover more than 450 archaeological sites as well as many regional overviews, languages, aspects of material culture, important organizations, institutions and individuals, discussions of archaeological method and theory, etc. Geographically, coverage extends from the eastern Mediterranean to Iran and from Anatolia to the Arab Peninsula with Egypt, Cyprus, and parts of North and East Africa also included. Chronologically, it runs from prehistoric times generally through the rise of Islam and the Crusades. Generously illustrated, the encyclopedia includes 650 drawings, plans, and photographs, and a separate series of regional maps and chrono-logical charts. A synoptic outline of contents and an index with many cross-references complete the set.

In an impressively integrated approach, archaeological and textual information are brought together in dialogue, as are scholars from all countries of the region (no small task in the Near East when this effort began in 1988). As a result, entries range from largely descriptive (e.g., site reports) or more technical (ceramic technology) to regional syntheses (Palestine) and interpretations (formulation of languages). The history of archaeology in the Near East is especially well covered, including the multipart entry, "History of the Field," in which individual countries and regions are represented.

The encyclopedia follows on the heels of several other major reference works, including the Israel Exploration Society's *Encyclopedia of Archaeological Excavations in the Holy Land* (CH, Jul'76, Jun'78, May'79) and *Civilizations of the Ancient Near East* (4v., CH, Jun'96), which includes some 200 topical essays divided into 11 broad subject areas. Despite similar sounding titles, all three resources complement one another very well and together form a sorely needed reference base in this important field of study. Essential for all libraries supporting ancient history, archaeology, and Holy Land and Middle Eastern studies as well as world civilizations and the history of art.—*M. R. Dittemore, Smithsonian Institution Libraries*

OAB-0195   E98   93-39337 CIP
Paterek, Josephine. **Encyclopedia of American Indian costume.** ABC-Clio, 1994. 516p bibl index afp ISBN 0-87436-685-2, $75.00

This impressive reference work took ten years to write, and the waiting was well worth it. Nothing of this scope and magnitude on this subject has been done before. Paterek (emerita, speech and theater, Univ. of Wisconsin) focuses on traditional (non-European) and early transition materials of Native Americans and Inuits (the author chose to use the less-favored terms "American Indian" and "Eskimo" in this work). In addition to basic dress, the author describes footwear, hairstyles, accessories, armor, decoration, and masks. An introduction explains the organization and contents: North America is divided into ten cultural regions, and each section begins with a description of the area and an overview of the individual tribes in alphabetical order. An appendix on clothing arts is especially informative, giving details of the clothing and how it was constructed, with a section of diagrams. The 150 black-and-white illustrations are attractive and well chosen. The photographs come from a large number of museums. A glossary of terms, a comprehensive bibliography, and a detailed and accurate index complete this well-written work. Paterek's one other book, *Costuming for the Theatre* (1959), a handbook for amateur theatrical groups, is much used to this day. Highly recommended for all libraries.—*P. Brauch, Brooklyn College, CUNY*

OAB-0196   GN66   92-13594 CIP
Steinfirst, Susan. **Folklore and folklife: a guide to English-language reference sources.** Garland, 1992. 2v. 1,208p indexes afp (Garland folklore bibliographies, 16) ISBN 0-8153-0068-9, $120.00

With eight major sections and more than a dozen subsections listing more than 1,400 titles, this guide begins to give novices an understanding of the breadth of folklore studies. Steinfirst rightly aims at inclusiveness, defining neither folklore/folklife nor reference work narrowly. Many titles included are at the margins of the academic study of folklore, a good thing given its porous borders. The whole array of topics is covered, from the long-studied folktale to more recently investigated folk belief systems. Annotations are substantial, often carefully evaluative. The work's best feature is the bibliographic essays that introduce the sections. These refer to major studies on each topic and help set the intellectual context for the reference materials in the listings that follow. There has long been a need for this work in libraries of all types to update and expand J.H. Brunvand's *Folklore: a Study and Research Guide* (CH, Jan'77). The price might make its purchase difficult for some libraries, but it will prove continually useful. Since most graduate students in the field will need their own copy, a less expensive edition is perhaps in order.—*D. S. Azzolina, University of Pennsylvania*

■ Business & Economics

OAB-0197 Orig
Business statistics of the United States, ed. by Courtenay M. Slater. 1995 ed. Bernan, 1996. 391p index afp ISBN 0-89059-040-0 pbk, $49.00

This reliable compilation from numerous government and a few private sources reactivates the US Commerce Department's discontinued "blue pages" of *Business Statistics.* Comprehensive in scope, it has two sections, the US economy and industry profiles, and is packed with valuable historical economic information. Topics covered include gross domestic product; consumer income and spending; employment, hours and earnings; international comparisons; and employment costs, productivity, and profits. Approximately 2,000 economic data series offer annual statistics 1966-94 and monthly updates 1991-94. The industry profiles, following the structure of the Standard Industrial Classification (SIC), provide snapshots of enterprises in construction and housing; mining, oil and gas; manufacturing; transportation; communications and utilities; retail and wholesale trade; services; and government. The editor, former chief economist of the Commerce Department, has added interesting features: an introductory article surveys patterns of economic activity 1966-94, a special section reviews changes in federal statistical programs, and summary charts and text highlight trends in the data of the two principal sections. In addition, two new appendixes furnish selected per capita data from the national income and product accounts and annual income and employment information for each state and region, 1959-94. Essential for business collections.—*M. Rosenthal, Nassau Community College*

OAB-0198 HD9710 93-35797 CIP
Chao, Sheau-yueh J., comp. **The Japanese automobile industry: an annotated bibliography.** Greenwood, 1994. 188p indexes afp (Bibliographies and indexes in economics and economic history, 15) ISBN 0-313-286787, $65.00

Japan, making dramatic progress in automobile production, especially since 1980, has become the biggest automaker in the world, while the US imports the world's largest number of automobiles, most of them from Japan. The Japanese auto industry, largely responsible for a trade surplus with the US of tens of billions of dollars, has drawn increasing interest among academics and the public, creating an enormous amount of literature on the subject. The author, a professional librarian, has compiled an annotated bibliography of 601 works in English chiefly from the period 1980-92. Entries cover such topics as the relationship between Japanese auto manufacturers and their US counterparts, joint ventures between the two countries, management of Japanese auto plants in Japan and the US, and government trade. Included are general and reference books, government documents, monographs, periodicals, audiovisual materials, and articles from scholarly journals and selected newspapers. There is a chronology and indexes. The first core bibliography in this field, Chao's work is highly recommended to libraries supporting study of the automobile industry and its administration, marketing, and trade.—*K. S. Kim, Queensborough Community College, CUNY*

OAB-0199 HF1001 95-23813 CIP
Cross, Wilbur. **Prentice Hall encyclopedic dictionary of business terms.** Prentice Hall, 1995. 472p ISBN 0-13-026221-8, $29.95

This unique dictionary provides not only short and long definitions of business terms but also an "Essay Section" on five important issues: (1) management—management techniques for all types of business, public and private; (2) resources—the historical forces that have made organizations viable competitors in business (manpower, capital, communications, inventory, etc.); (3) regulations and procedures—the regulatory procedures that formalize the working operations of organizations; (4) money—e.g., cash flow, commodities, credit rating, securities, and taxation factors; and (5) communications—the use of available technology that makes it possible for organizations to communicate more quickly and effectively. At the end of each essay, the author refers to entries in the dictionary (located at the front of the book) that elaborate on the terms and phrases used in the

essays. An appendix lists foreign currencies, computer terms and phrases, government systems of the world, roman numerals, etc. The Internet is defined, as it should be, but the term "wholesale price index" is used instead of the more current "producer price index." GATT is defined, but there is no entry for "Uruguay Round." The binding and graphics are good. Because of this dictionary's "Essay Section," there is no comparable title. Recommended for all business collections.—*L. Page, California Polytechnic State University, San Luis Obispo*

OAB-0200 HF1001 95-33676 CIP
Encyclopedia of business, [ed.] by John G. Maurer et al. Gale, 1996 (c1995). 2v. 1,584p bibl indexes afp ISBN 0-8103-9187-2, $395.00

According to the preface, this encyclopedia combines the practical and the theoretical, covering both current and classical areas of interest, and defining concepts, issues, and terms. The contributors were selected by a team of editors (four business academicians), who reviewed and critiqued each essay for accuracy, relevance, and comprehensiveness. The essays, arranged alphabetically, have an average length of 2,500 words. Charts, graphs, tables, and formulas are used, and many entries include bibliographies. Topics were selected by advisors chosen by the publisher. The major issues addressed are entrepreneurship, small business, globalization, quality, and diversity; other areas of concern are external factors affecting business (the economy, government, and financial institutions) and internal functions of business (accounting, business ethics, decision making, research and development). More than 60 entries treat international marketing, including several on doing business in such locations as China, Japan, Korea, and Eastern Europe. Subtopics deal with such concepts as gender roles and nonverbal communication. Included are a few brief industry surveys like those once found in *U.S. Industrial Outlook* (1960-79). Included are an index to 31 disciplinary areas (e.g., computers and technology, business and society) and a general index to important or unusual terms mentioned in the entries. There is no comparable source; for example, the term "exit strategies" (related to abandoning products or industries) does not appear in any other reference book. The closest rival is *Handbook for Professional Managers,* ed. by L.R. Bittel and J.E. Ramsey (CH, Oct'85), which covers fewer topics and is becoming dated. A valuable source, highly recommended for academic or public libraries.—*J. G. Packer, Central Connecticut State University*

OAB-0201 Orig
Handbook of U.S. labor statistics: employment, earnings, prices, productivity, and other labor data, ed. by Eva E. Jacobs. Bernan, 1997. 316p index afp ISBN 0-89059-062-1 pbk, $59.00

This compendium fills the void created when the Bureau of Labor Statistics (BLS) ceased publishing its *Handbook of Labor Statistics* in 1989. Jacobs (former chief of the Division of Consumer Expenditure Surveys of BLS) has gathered BLS data into a well-formatted, well-indexed resource essential for all libraries. The tables represent the wealth of historical data collected by the federal government (e.g., consumer and producer price information back to 1913 and payroll employment figures to 1919). Organized by subject in nine chapters, the handbook includes more than 100 tables of comprehensive statistics profiling a wide range of labor market topics. Each chapter begins with a helpful graph representing the trends supported by that section's data, along with explanations of concepts and definitions, descriptions of data series, and other information designed to facilitate use of the data. The section detailing BLS projections of future employment by industry and occupation is of practical value to undergraduate students. Also noteworthy is the chapter containing comparisons of US and foreign labor and price statistics. Highly recommended for all libraries.—*J. H. Pollitz, St. Ambrose University*

OAB-0202 HF3010 CIP
Hoover's handbook of American business, 1993, ed. by Gary Hoover, Alta Campbell, and Patrick J. Spain. Reference Press, 1992. 646p indexes ISBN 1-878753-05-3, $34.95; ISBN 1-878753-03-7 pbk, $24.95

Is yet another directory of companies really needed? Yes, if it is *Hoover's Hand-*

book of American Business. Published annually, this one-volume guide to 500 American businesses packs a lot of information into a very compact package, including much hard-to-find information on operating results for private companies and partnerships. Although in direct competition with such standards as *Moody's Handbook of Common Stocks* (1965-), Standard and Poor's *Stock Reports* (1990-), *International Directory of Company Histories* (CH, May'89), *Hoover's* merits purchase based on its inclusion of privately held enterprises and its low price. The highly readable, concise company summaries include business description with major product lines, key financial data for the last ten years (most recent covered is 1991), officers, subsidiaries and affiliates, and major competitors. For publicly held companies, the stock exchange and symbol for the company is given; for other types of enterprise, the form of ownership is indicated (private company, partnership, etc.). Introductory sections explain the use of financial data to evaluate or compare businesses, list other sources of business information, and contain 63 lists and rankings of companies by size, profit, growth, and various other measures. The editors have achieved their mission of providing high quality, accurate, and readable business information. The price makes it affordable for even the smallest library. Recommended for all libraries with any need for information about major US businesses.—*K. M. Weir, Illinois State University*

OAB-0203 Orig
International bibliography of business history, ed. by Francis Goodall, Terry Gourvish, and Steven Tolliday. Routledge, 1997. 668p indexes ISBN 0-415-08641-8, $125.00

Library shelves are not sagging under the weight of good business history bibliographies. The better titles, such as *Handbook of American Business History,* ed. by David O. and Bessie E. Whitten (1990), or *British Business History,* ed. by Stephanie Zarach (1994), are limited to one country, era, industry, or firm. This new bibliography lists primarily monographs, embraces the globe, is not restricted by era, and emphasizes the UK, the US, and Japan. The editors stretch beyond traditional business bibliographies to include social and economic histories, but there are some omissions: no Veblen, only one J.K. Galbraith work, and no T.C. Cochran's *Age of Enterprise* (1942). Good industry and firm histories are included. Publication dates range from 1898 to 1994, and biographical entries from Moses to Ted Turner. The material is arranged in broad topical sections (e.g., "Trade and Distribution," "Banking and Finance") with appropriate geographic subsections. Bibliographic entries carry excellent critical annotations, and works are often cross-listed. Indexes are provided for firm names and authors. A helpful addition would be a limited keyword index to locate quickly works on topics such as "capitalism" or "AFL-CIO." The editors plan future revisions, which should make this work a classic. Highly recommended for academic collections.—*C. Le Beau, Creighton University*

OAB-0204 HF1001 96-12245 CIP
International encyclopedia of business and management, ed. by Malcolm Warner. Routledge, 1996. (Dist. by International Thomson Publishing) 6v. 5,523p bibl index afp ISBN 0-415-07399-5, $999.95

IEBM provides articles, international in scope, ranging in length from 2,000 to 10,000 words on more than 500 topics in accounting, operations research, marketing, finance, human resources, and virtually every other area that might be treated in a typical business school. Lists of contributors and subject headings are also provided. Although the volumes reveal a slight European bias, the editors cover trends in the US, the European community, Japan, and other parts of the world as appropriate. The authors and editors constitute an eminent group of scholars representing a cross-section of universities worldwide. The topics are well chosen, and the well-researched and readable articles provide solid introductions to their subjects. Good graphics appear throughout, and very current annotated bibliographies follow each article. The set is handsomely produced, with sturdy bindings befitting a reference tool designed to stand up to frequent use.

Although *IEBM* can be recommended highly, some features in its organization are unfortunate. First, phrases are alphabetized unconventionally. Con-

necting words like "and," "in," and "the" in the middle of phrases are ignored, hence "Management research" appears between "Management in the Philippines" and "Management in Russia." The headings assigned to articles are not used consistently: there is no obvious pattern in personal names; related articles are not consistently given headings that group them together; cross-references are provided too infrequently; similar subject headings are assigned to dissimilar treatments of topics; and headings used do not always accurately describe the content of articles. Although these problems do not affect the value of individual articles, they indicate an unfortunate lack of care in editing. Despite these shortcomings, because of the universality of its coverage and the quality of its articles, this excellent set will become a staple of business collections in colleges and universities. It occupies well the ground between short-entry dictionaries of management and handbooks that offer extended treatment of broad topics.—*D. E. Williams, University of Akron*

OAB-0205 G2306 93-31441 CIP
The National economic atlas of China, comp. and ed. by the Institute of Geography, Chinese Academy of Sciences and State Planning Committee, the State Economic Information Center, and the Institute of Statistics, State Statistical Bureau. Oxford, 1994. 314p ISBN 0-19-585736-4, $375.00

This is another fine atlas coming out of China, and another, like *The Population Atlas of China* (CH, Jun'88), published in cooperation with Oxford University Press. Data are derived from national industrial and population censuses (1982-90) and from a variety of special internal reports and ministry surveys. Most of the 265 maps are arranged under nine major categories: "Resources," "Population," "General Economy," "Agriculture," "Industry," "Transportation, Post, and Telecommunicatons," "Building, Urban Construction, and Environmental Protection," "Commerce, Foreign Trade, Tourism, and Finance," and "Education, Science, Sports, Culture, and Public Health." The final section, "Regional Comprehensive Economy," provides economic overviews of provinces, major municipalities, and autonomous regions. The production quality is excellent, with large maps (some are half page, and a few are smaller, but most are full page or two pages), brilliant and clear color distinctions, and an appealing variation of graphic representations. The textual materials consist of introductory comments about the collection, compilation, and accuracy of the data, and four booklets, designed to be used alongside the open atlas, that provide detailed information about sections and specific maps. It would have been helpful to have this textual material printed in the volume as well, maintaining usefulness if the booklets are misplaced. A valuable addition to collections serving those interested in contemporary China. China plans to publish additional volumes in this series. Public and academic libraries.—*K. W. Berger, Duke University*

OAB-0206 HG151 92-28016 MARC
The New Palgrave dictionary of money & finance, ed. by Peter Newman, Murray Milgate, and John Eatwell. Macmillan, UK/Stockton, 1992. 3v. 865, 834, 860p ISBN 1-56159-041-X, $595.00

Numerous changes in the monetary and financial environment in recent years have created information needs for those practitioners and policymakers who "should be aware of modern theoretical advances" and those academic researchers who "should know more about how modern capital markets and credit institutions actually work." Aimed at that audience, this unique collection of information shares editors with *The New Palgrave: A Dictionary of Economics* (CH, Nov'88) and has an international advisory board of economists from universities, financial institutions, etc. Of the 1,008 essays and 70 short glossarial entries, written by more than 800 experts, 80% are new and all but one of the remaining essays, some revised, are drawn from *The New Palgrave.* The essays range in length from a column to 15 pages and their bibliographies from three citations to more than 80. Essays on related topics are linked by cross-references. International in coverage, the encyclopedia treats the national monetary and financial systems of 29 countries (the US and UK are each covered in several essays) and 8 stock exchanges. Many essays were written by economists who were major developers or contributors to the topics they discuss. Contributors are listed at the end of Vol. 3 with their affiliations and the essays they prepared. There is a guide, "Using the Dictionary," and appendixes that include a "List of

Entries A-Z," a subject classification, and a list of 104 subheadings. Recommended for all academic and corporate libraries supporting research at advanced undergraduate or graduate level in money and finance, theoretical or institutional.—*J. A. Aufdenkamp, Northern Illinois University*

OAB-0207 Orig
Wholesale and retail trade USA: industry analyses, statistics, and leading organizations, ed. by Arsen J. Darnay and Gary Alampi. Gale, 1995. 993p indexes afp ISBN 0-7876-0865-3, $195.00

This new compendium (*WRTUSA*) intends to provide a comprehensive statistical picture of 69 wholesale and 64 retail industries, including information about some 5,000 public and private companies employing people in nearly 100 occupational specialties. The volume has two parts. Part 1 lists industries by Standard Industrial Classification and provides national and state data about each, including general statistics profiling the industry, indexes of change, selected ratios, occupational titles, names and addresses of leading companies, state-by-state comparisons of activity for that industry, and graphs that show the main concentrations of the industries. Part 2 provides an alphabetical listing of 591 cities and metropolitan areas showing cumulative statistics for wholesale and retail trade in those cities. The statistics are drawn from the 1982, 1987, and 1992 *Economic Census* of the US Department of Commerce and from *County Business Patterns* for 1983-86 and 1988-91. Projections are also provided to 1996 in most cases. Indexes are provided for SIC, subject, company name, city and metropolitan area, and occupation. *WRTUSA* provides an excellent thumbnail sketch of retail and wholesale activity in the US and in its states and cities. It complements *American Wholesalers and Distributors Directory* and is likely to join that source as a standard in virtually every business reference collection. Its value for market research, employment analysis, locational analysis, and the like easily justifies its cost. Recommended for all academic or research library collections.—*D. E. Williams, University of Akron*

OAB-0208 Orig
World development indicators. World Bank, 1997. 339p bibl ISBN 0-8213-3701-7 pbk, $60.00

World Development Indicators, formerly published as part of the World Bank's *World Development Report*, has been greatly expanded and issued as a stand-alone publication. It contains much of the data previously published in the Bank's *World Tables* (1976-) and *Social Indicators of Development* (1987- , CH, Nov'93). Data have been supplied by the World Bank and at least 24 international, governmental, and private bodies. These partners include agencies of the UN, the Organization for Economic Cooperation and Development, International Monetary Fund, World Trade Organization, Euromoney Publications, Inc., Political Risk Services, and Price Waterhouse. Topical sections provide statistics on demographics, the environment, economy, national finances, markets, trade, and commodities. Each section includes an introductory essay, often with charts; tables of country data; and information about the data, definitions of terms, and data source lists. Although currency varies, it is always clearly indicated; most data are from 1994 or 1995. As is usual with World Bank publications, this new source provides a wealth of information in a convenient package at a reasonable price. For many smaller collections, this may be the only source needed for international social and economic data. A CD-ROM version is also available. Highly recommended for public, college, and university libraries.—*K. M. Weir, Illinois State University*

OAB-0209 [CD-ROM]
World marketing data and statistics 1995 on CD-ROM. Euromonitor, 1995. ISBN 0-86638-558-3 $1,190.00. 1 disc; user manual. System requirements: IBM-PC, 386 or better; 4MB RAM; 4MB free hard drive space; MSCDEX 2.2 or higher; Windows 3.0 or later.

This up-to-date electronic product combines data with a display/graphing spreadsheet system. The data, compiled from Euromonitor's hardcopy editions of the annual *European Marketing Data and Statistics* and the annual *International Marketing Data And Statistics* (1993 ed., CH, Jun'93), cover a wide range of topics suitable for studies of marketing geography. This product could be useful in a variety of teaching/research situations outside those suggested by the title. Data include demographic, population health, economic, defense, environmental, infrastructure, and cultural indicators. The scope of this data set is global, employing a variety of sources to provide coverage. Data are used from 1977 to 1994, using earlier information and/or estimates where contemporary data are unavailable. The hardcopy documentation is largely example-based. The on-line help system is more useful than the documentation but did not discuss all functions (e.g., "export").

The package requires Windows and is very easy to install. It allows easy transfer of data to other Windows applications through cut-and-paste operations. Searching is menu driven, by subject keyword, region, or country. Searches using Boolean operations are supported. Searches by keyword are confounded for users of American English through the use of terms like "holiday" for "vacation" without cross-referencing between similar terms. A search of "holiday" for the region "Europe" results in references to 66 records concerning hotel accommodations for European countries. "Vacation" turns up another six. It is very easy to move into spreadsheet mode to view the data and to chart them. Chart options are limited to histograms and pie charts, but the easy transfer of data to other Windows applications (like Excel) allow more sophisticated processing.

World Marketing Data and Statistics 1995 appears to be an extremely useful package. Students and faculty should find this useful in virtually any class with a global or major-region focus. Undergraduate through professional.—*E. J. Delaney, University of Colorado at Colorado Springs*

■ History

OAB-0210 D20 94-36720 CIP
The American Historical Association's guide to historical literature, ed. by Mary Beth Norton and Pamela Gerardi. 3rd ed. Oxford, 1995. 2v. 2,027p indexes afp ISBN 0-19-505727-9, $150.00

Norton and Gerardi, working with more than 400 contributors, have produced a monumental work of historical bibliography. It is composed of 26,926 annotated entries in 48 sections that cite books, articles, and chapters in books primarily in English published from 1961, the date of the last edition, through 1992. The 1st edition appeared in 1931. More than a decade in the making, this project, funded by the National Endowment for the Humanities with support from the Rockefeller, Mellon, and Luce foundations, sets out to identify "the finest and most useful books and articles in every field of historical scholarship" and "combines qualitative selectivity, inclusive breadth, and intellectual integration." The editorial board identified three user needs that governed the selection of items: "the need for reliable syntheses and reference works that provided entry into a historical field, the need to know the most highly esteemed works that set the standard of excellence ... and the need to explore major alternative interpretations represented in current scholarly debate." Although most sections relate to geographical areas, some are subject-oriented (e.g., "Science, Technology, and Medicine," "International Relations"), still others relate to such specialized topics as "Theory and Practice in Historical Study" or "Native Peoples in the Americas." Each section begins with an introductory essay followed by a guide to the arrangement of that section. Within a section, reference works and general studies precede entries arranged to suit the materials in that field. Citation to a given work generally appears only once, and the most recent American edition is preferred. In addition to standard bibliographical information, entries include series titles associated with scholarly institutes, societies, and associations, and ISBN or ISSN. Annotations average 30 words and are signed. Some sections have *see also* references at the end. Following the last section is a list of journals grouped by section name. The second volume concludes with a 118-page author index and an extremely detailed, useful, and accurate subject index of nearly 300 pages. The set is worth much more than its price and deserves to be in all but the smallest libraries.—*J. D. Haskell Jr., College of William and Mary*

OAB-0211 GN370 94-20640 CIP
Chaliand, Gérard. **The Penguin atlas of diasporas,** by Gérard Chaliand and Jean-Pierre Rageau; tr. by A.M. Berrett. Viking, 1995. 183p afp ISBN 0-670-85439-5, $34.95

This translation of *Atlas des diaspora* (Paris, 1991) offers a geohistorical overview of the three classical diasporas (Jewish, Greek, and Armenian) and of the most important new ones, e.g., African (called "Black" here), Chinese, and Palestinian. Some of the latter are hardly "new" (the African is 400 years old), but they have only recently begun to consider themselves "diasporas" rather than "overseas" populations. The maps are numerous and superb, the illustrations many and helpful. There are neglected areas: e.g., Greek Alexandria, a cradle of diasporan Hellenism, is dealt with almost dismissively; distinctions between "diaspora" and other terms that share the same semantic domain (e.g., "ethnics," "refugees," "exiles," "migrants") do not receive the detailed consideration they deserve. Nevertheless, the core geographical and historical material is rich, expertly condensed, and lucidly presented. The study of all variants of multiculturalism, including diasporas, is a rapidly growing cross-disciplinary field, as evidenced by the journal *Diaspora* (Oxford, 1991-) and by this volume. Essential for all college and university libraries.—*K. Tölölyan, Wesleyan University*

OAB-0212 D839 92-30496 MARC
The Cold War, 1945-1991: [v.1:] Leaders and other important figures in the United States and Western Europe, ed. by Benjamin Frankel. Gale, 1992. 3v. (v.1, 535p) index afp ISBN 0-8103-8926-6, $250.00 set

Destined to be a major reference source, this is a unique compilation of lengthy analytical biographies of 283 important world political and military leaders from the last half of the 20th century. Volume 1 focuses on the US and Europe; Volume 2 will cover the USSR, China, communist East Europe and Asia, and the Third World; and Volume 3 will include a 120-page narrative history of the Cold War, a chronology, a glossary, a list of manuscript and oral history collections, and a bibliography of additional research sources. The signed essays in Volume 1, each two to six pages in length, "concentrate on the individuals' participation in and contribution to the events of the Cold War" and include a photograph and bibliography. A list of contributors that gives affiliations and credentials is absent from Volume 1, but it is hoped will be included in future volumes. Both historical and contemporary figures are included; other sources (e.g., *Columbia Dictionary of Political Biography*, CH, Nov'91, or *Who's Who in International Affairs*, CH, Jan'91) cover only contemporary individuals and provide less information about each. Warren Kuehl's *Biographical Dictionary of Internationalists* (CH, May'84) and *McGraw-Hill Encyclopedia of World Biography* (CH, Apr'74) treat only historical figures. *The Cold War* deserves a place in any library that can afford it.—*L. Stwalley, University of Colorado at Denver*

OAB-0213 D419 96-45597 CIP
Cook, Chris. **What happened where: a guide to places and events in twentieth-century history,** by Chris Cook and Diccon Bewes. St. Martin's, 1997. 310p afp ISBN 0-312-17278-8 pbk, $30.00

With geography as the linchpin, Cook's guide demonstrates his forte—distilling world events in compact volumes. His formidable record of publications includes monographs, encyclopedias, atlases, guides to papers and archives, almanacs, and handbooks. Based on the premise that historical events are linked to their location, the guide contains hundreds of places of historical significance in the 20th century, 1900 to mid-1900s. A few entries prior to 1900 are included when their significance spills over into the 20th century. Worldwide in scope, entries cover geopolitics, modern history, politics, international affairs, economic and social history, environmental issues, trade unionism, and religion. Individual countries are not included unless they are important for one major event—e.g., the missile crisis in Cuba. Cook omits many US places synonymous with landmark events: e.g., New York (UN); Long Island (Lindbergh's flight); Hopewell, NJ (the Lindbergh kidnapping); Levittown; South Braintree, MA (Sacco-Vanzetti); Mount St. Helens; Valdez, AK; and Brooklyn (Margaret Sanger). The entry for Cape Canaveral omits the explosion of the

Challenger; that for Greensboro, NC omits the first black sit-in at a lunch counter. Perhaps the next edition will be more cognizant of the US as a major player on Cook's world stage. Entries reflect contemporary forces of decolonization, nationalism, new nation-states, boundary conflicts, and ethnic tensions. A list of abbreviations and acronyms is included, and two appendixes list name changes of nations and give a summary of the major wars with a chronology. Invaluable for the study of modern history and a guide to the passing of old orders and the maze of new nations; recommended for academic libraries at all levels.—*M. F. Morris, East Carolina University*

OAB-0214 Z675 92-8833 CIP
D'Aniello, Charles A. **Teaching bibliographic skills in history: a sourcebook for historians and librarians.** Greenwood, 1993. 385p index afp ISBN 0-313-25266-1, $65.00

Intended for "historians and librarians who teach history students how to use the library and do bibliographic research," this work is in four parts. The first, "The Study of History," includes two chapters, on the evolution of historical study and on interdisciplinary history. Part 2, "Bibliographic Instruction in History," has a brief chapter on historians' approaches to research and the kinds of materials beginning and advanced students need, with a much longer chapter on approaches and methods of BI, with examples of exercises. Part 3, "Special Topics," includes a variety of chapters: on using traditional and electronic catalogs and indexes; the kinds of reference sources and ways of teaching them; sources for interdisciplinary research; the nature and use of electronic data bases; the uses and means of access to archival and manuscript materials. Part 4 contains a superbly annotated bibliography on all aspects of teaching the methods and materials of historical research. D'Aniello, history bibliographer at SUNY-Buffalo, not only served as editor, but wrote three of the ten chapters. The volume could be used as a text for historiography courses, but is also useful to reference librarians, especially to BI librarians who work with history classes. For them it provides ideas about material to include in presentations and handouts, suggestions for assignments, and one of the most useful bibliographies on BI in general. The volume belongs in all academic libraries.—*E. I. Farber, Earlham College*

OAB-0215 HN28 93-29230 CIP
Encyclopedia of social history, ed. by Peter N. Stearns. Garland, 1994. 856p index afp (Garland reference library of social science, 780) ISBN 0-8153-0342-4, $95.00

Stearns, a scholar of European social history and editor-in-chief of *Journal of Social History*, here offers a major work that gathers, organizes, and synthesizes scholarship from the many threads of social history. Its broad scope includes the earliest civilizations, while its geographical reach extends to all continents. Since social history examines groups, behaviors, and ideas, little will be found on notable people and significant events. The introduction gives a fine, brief overview of the nature of social history, and refers readers to the entry on "Social History." The "List of Entries" includes 457 articles and 20 *see* references. Also in the front matter is a "Topical Contents," which lists each article under one or more of 24 subjects, including six regions (of which one is Classical Civilizations), where articles germane to each region are recorded. Among the list of contributors are 285 historians and social scientists. The signed articles range in length from half a page to more than five pages. Each article has a list of references, and many articles have additional references in the text. Cross-references are used frequently. An index includes general concepts, people, events, and institutions. Highly recommended for public and academic libraries.—*P. A. Frisch, University of Illinois at Chicago*

OAB-0216 92-55094 Orig
Explorers and discoverers of the world, ed. by Daniel B. Baker. Gale, 1993. 637p index afp ISBN 0-8103-5421-7, $59.95

One of the first things one notices about this book is its decided departure from the accustomed roll call of Western European, male explorers. There are 322 fairly well-chosen and balanced accounts ranging from traveling scholars of the classical period to underwater and space explorers. The exploits of both men and women from all parts of the globe are presented. The editor has done a fine job putting a great deal of information into a relatively small package. Within a few pages, the introduction describes the differences between "exploration" and "discovery," and puts the act of exploration into its personal, historical, and societal context. Each of the entries is brief (2-3 pages) but authoritative and includes a few annotated references to key primary and secondary sources. Besides the entries arranged by explorer, there is a chronology of exploration arranged by geographical area, a list of explorers by area explored and by country of birth, and a general subject index. It is difficult to imagine a library, public or academic, where this book would not be a welcome and useful addition.—*B. K. Wycoff, University of Oregon*

OAB-0217 DS117 92-53169 Orig
A Historical atlas of the Jewish people: from the time of the patriarchs to the present, ed. by Eli Barnavi; English edition ed. by Miriam Eliav-Feldon. Knopf, 1992. 299p index ISBN 0-679-40332-9, $50.00

This is at least the sixth Jewish atlas to appear in the past ten years. Some, such as Evyatar Friesel's excellent *Atlas of Modern Jewish History* (CH, Dec'90) and Haim Beinart's *Atlas of Medieval Jewish History* (CH, Jan'93) are more focused in coverage and do not extend, as this newest atlas does, from Biblical times to the present. Martin Gilbert's *Illustrated Atlas of Jewish Civilization* (CH, Jul'91), his *Atlas of Jewish History* (1993), and N.R.M. De Lange's *Atlas of the Jewish World* (1984) are roughly comparable to the new work, which has, however, a clear edge in the quality of its graphics. An enormous amount of information is conveyed through charts, maps, photos, drawings, and graphs designed for maximum visual impact—from a satellite photo showing the different routes of the Exodus to an outline of Europe with colored bars over each country representing the number of Jews before the war and the number exterminated by the Germans. Is difficult to imagine how the scale of the Holocaust might be illustrated more dramatically, especially for Poland. Text and a timeline accompany each set of illustrations in more than 130 double-page spreads presented more or less chronologically. Highly recommended for general readers and undergraduate collections.—*S. Lehmann, University of Pennsylvania*

OAB-0218 Orig
The Hutchinson dictionary of world history. ABC-Clio, 1994 (c1993). 699p ISBN 0-87436-765-4, $49.50

Any attempt to produce a dictionary or encyclopedia of high quality that treats world history is a daunting task. Can one imagine a broader range of knowledge to organize, summarize, present? These editors have nevertheless realized success. Unexpected depth of coverage is shown by the inclusion of entries for topics of lesser significance—colonial governors, social reformers, small countries no longer in existence, etc.—along with the expected entries for wars, emperors, and countries. International and chronological coverage is balanced. Finally, the currentness of reporting will be very useful in libraries; important historical events through 1992 are incorporated. These factors alone would make the work a valuable source for most libraries. However, the contributors also offer longer analytical articles for many issues of significance, illuminating quotations from major historical sources, and interesting special features such as chronologies, thematic maps, rankings, etc. All this frosting is left out of many dictionaries. A valuable addition to reference collections.—*T. L. Wesley, Northern Kentucky University*

OAB-0219 Orig
The Oxford companion to World War II, ed. by I.C.B. Dear and M.R.D. Foot. Oxford, 1995. 1,343p afp ISBN 0-19-866225-4, $49.95

Of the many fine encyclopedic works about WW II to appear since the 1970s, this is among the best. The editors have written extensively and compiled reference works on military history. Contributors include such scholars as Ian Hogg (author with Bryan Perrett of *Encyclopedia of the Second World War*, 1989). The other 150 contributors, representing expertise in all theaters, provide some 1,700 entries that range from brief identification to in-depth articles. Coverage is comprehensive, including military campaigns, battles, biographies of leading figures, diplomacy, the home front, and of particular note, the effect of the war on noncombatants. Economic and social experiences of the participants are discussed at length (e.g., "African Americans at War," "Women at War"). Entries are alphabetically arranged, include cross-references, and in the case of more substantial entries are followed by bibliographies. Maps, charts, graphs, and photographs are found throughout, and there is a set of maps in color. Small libraries that hold the Hogg dictionary, Elizabeth-Anne Wheal's *A Dictionary of the Second World War* (CH, Jan'91), L.L. Snyder's *Historical Guide to World War II* (CH, Jun'83), or *Historical Encyclopedia of World War II*, ed. by Marcel Baudot (CH, Mar'81), will not need this book, but those holding only earlier publications should add it as a supplement. It will become the standard one-volume encyclopedia of WW II. Public libraries and medium-sized or larger college libraries.—*M. J. Haeuser, Gustavus Adolphus College*

OAB-0220 DG68 91-45046 CIP
Richardson, L. **A new topographical dictionary of ancient Rome.** Johns Hopkins, 1992. 459p afp ISBN 0-8018-4300-6, $65.00

In this massive compilation treating the monuments and topography of ancient Rome, Richardson, a leading specialist on Roman architecture, brings up to date S.B. Platner's great *Topographical Dictionary of Ancient Rome* (1929, completed by T. Ashby, hence called *PA*). Like *PA*, Richardson excludes Rome's early Christian monuments, and in general follows the titling and structure of *PA*, but all entries have been rewritten. Richardson makes his dictionary more accessible to undergraduates by including a helpful essay on documentary sources, by quoting less Latin and no Greek, and by introducing general accounts of a broad range of architectural forms. But this is no book for beginners. A basic knowledge of Latin and of Roman civilization is required, and Richardson does not seem entirely certain of his audience. Some entries will be cryptic for those not expert on Roman typography or who lack access to *PA*. Richardson assumes readers will have both *PA* and Ernest Nash's *Pictorial Dictionary of Ancient Rome* (2 v., 1961-62), for he refers readers to their bibliographies and cites only the most significant and recent studies. The book is provided with a useful series of textual plans and drawings, but one misses a detailed map of Rome. Even with these drawbacks, an essential purchase.—*J. H. Kaimowitz, Trinity College (CT)*

AFRICA, MIDDLE EAST, ASIA & OCEANIA

OAB-0221 DS805 92-8167 MARC
The Cambridge encyclopedia of Japan, ed. by Richard Bowring and Peter Kornicki. Cambridge, 1993. 400p index ISBN 0-521-40352-9, $49.95

Bowring and Kornicki (both Cambridge) have brought together 54 international scholars, representing some of the best in US and UK Japanese scholarship (with additional representation from Japan, Australia, Austria, Germany, Canada, and Italy) to compile what is unquestionably the best single-volume work on Japan. The eight broad, topical chapter essays, illustrated with numerous color maps and photographs, are uniformly well written. Each chapter (covering geography, language and literature, arts and crafts, politics, history, thought and religion, society, and economy) is divided into subtopics that can be viewed as succinct independent essays; colored boxes scattered throughout present special topics. The index is adequate, but could be improved; it does not, for example, index the highlighted special topics. The glossary is probably superfluous and the guide to further reading thin but adequate for the needs of most undergraduates. This title stands up very well with and complements the larger, alphabetically arranged *Kodansha Encyclopedia of Japan* (CH, Jun'89) and should also complement *Japan: An Illustrated Encyclopedia* (CH, Nov'93), also published by Kodansha (unseen by this reviewer). Bowring and Kornicki fulfill the preface's promise "to be the first port-of-call for anyone who wishes to know more about Japan and its history." An extraordinary resource for students, scholars, travelers, and casual readers alike; it could easily serve as a text for survey courses. It deserves to be on the shelves, both reference and circulating, of almost all libraries.—*M. K. Ewing, St. Cloud State University*

OAB-0222   DS405x   Orig
Encyclopaedia of India, ed. by P.N. Chopra. Rima Publishing House, 1992. (Dist. by South Asia Books) 32v. bibl indexes $1,550.00

A vast and disparate country, India is home to many religions (Hinduism, Buddhism, Christianity, Jainism, Islam, Parsiism, Sikhism) and to 860 million people who occupy 2.4% of the world's land area and speak many languages, of which no fewer than 15 have been recognized as official, including Bengali, Gujarati, Hindi, Punjabi, Sanskrit, Tamil Telugu, and Urdu (English is used widely in communication, education, and literature). Until now, there has been no detailed encyclopedia of India. Of the projected 32 volumes, each devoted to one of the 25 states or union territories, five have so far appeared. Each volume has been written by a prominent Indian scholar and is arranged in nine chapters that treat history, people, agriculture and irrigation, government, education and culture, languages and literature, economic life, and places of interest in the state or union territory. Each volume also considers physical, religious, and social aspects, and such topics as festivals and political parties, and contains a bibliography, chronology, and index. Some volumes also have a glossary. The information is recent and the style scholarly, although some volumes written in simple English lack bibliographies. The set shows the achievements and progress made by India, especially since independence in 1947. Authoritative and up-to-date (although expensive), this set is highly recommended for all libraries supporting Indian studies.—*R. N. Sharma, University of Evansville*

OAB-0223   DS114   93-17295 MARC
Gribetz, Judah. **The timetables of Jewish history: a chronology of the most important people and events in Jewish history,** by Judah Gribetz, Edward L. Greenstein, and Regina Stein. Simon & Schuster, 1994 (c1993). 808p index ISBN 0-671-64007-0, $35.00; ISBN 0-671-88577-4 pbk, $20.00

Gribetz's volume is a welcome addition to the already large collection of Judaic reference material. Although there is a large body of work in Judaica, there are very few chronologies with the scope of this volume, and none presenting Jewish history in the tabular format that Gribetz employs. Coverage is from 9000 BCE to December 1991. Depending on the specific historical period, there are three, four, or five columns with such headings as "General History," "Jewish History," "Jewish Culture," and "Jews in the Middle East," "Jews in Europe," and "Jews in North and South America." Span of dates depends on the historical period covered: during the fifth and sixth centuries, there are entries for every three to five years; for the Judaically fascinating 1940s, there are several entries for each month of the decade. Illustrations, photographs, tables, and charts are sprinkled throughout. An exceptionally complete index and rather minimal glossary complete the work. No other works compare with this volume. Several chronologies of Jewish history exist, but they detail only a short span of Jewish experience. For instance, Hershel Edelheit and Abraham Edelheit's *A World in Turmoil: An Integrated Chronology* (CH, Apr'92) does a good job of outlining important events concerning the Holocaust, but does so in a narrative form, for a limited span of years. Gribetz's work is an important and valuable resource and is strongly recommended for inclusion in academic and public libraries at all levels.—*T. Koppel, Colorado Alliance of Research Libraries*

OAB-0224   UF500   95-38945 CIP
Grossman, Mark. **Encyclopedia of the Persian Gulf War.** ABC-Clio, 1995. 522p bibl index afp ISBN 0-87436-684-4, $75.00

Grossman's excellent encyclopedia has several hundred entries and reveals his extensive research concerning the topic. The book is well written and peppered with many helpful and clear illustrations. The articles, four detailed appendixes, and the bibliography contain thorough references to assist further

investigation, and there is a useful chronology of events. The author includes helpful background information that explains how the world was overtaken by Desert Storm. There is a definite US bias: the book contains a complete list of US POWs and casualties, but similar lists for other countries are missing. *See* references are unevenly applied. There are subentries for each country that fought Iraq under the main entry, "Coalition Nations." The major partners then rate individual entries, but only some of the minor partners have *see* references from their names to the coalition entry. The maps are the book's biggest weakness; the bibliography, the illustrations of weapons, and the documents appendix its greatest assets. Highly recommended for every library.—*S. J. Stillwell Jr., University of North Texas*

OAB-0225   DS43   96-4395 CIP
Hiro, Dilip. **Dictionary of the Middle East.** St. Martin's, 1996. 367p index ISBN 0-312-12554-2, $30.00

This resource is well researched and well written. The straightforward transliteration system uses forms generally understandable by both Middle Eastern scholars and general readers. The index is complete and useful. The maps included, particularly eight on the Arab-Israeli disputes (covering 1947-95) are clear, concise, and helpful. The author limits the scope of the work to the 20th century. The definition of "Middle East" has always been nebulous. Under the entry for that term, Hiro explains the options for setting the geographic boundaries and defines the region for this source to include Egypt, the Arabian peninsula, the Fertile Crescent, and Iran. Omitting Turkey is problematic because that nation, at least nominally, ruled much of the area for the first 20 years of this century. There are several other problems: the complicated ethnic and religious divisions of Lebanon are not shown in the maps; no photographs are included of the people discussed; there are no illustrations other than the few maps; there are several blind cross- or *see* references; only four of the seven states within the United Arab Emirates rate their own entries. Even with these problems, highly recommended for undergraduate collections.—*S. J. Stillwell Jr., University of North Texas*

OAB-0226   Orig
Marr, David G. **Vietnam,** comp. by David G. Marr with Kristine Alilunas-Rodgers. Clio, 1993 (c1992). (Dist. by ABC-Clio) 393p bibl indexes (World bibliographical series, 147) ISBN 1-85109-092-4, $110.00

A selected and fully annotated bibliography of 1,038 books and articles concerning the culture and history of Vietnam. References are chiefly to English or French-language sources; Vietnamese-language works, with a few exceptions, are not included. The compiler, an American now living in Australia, and author of *Vietnamese Anticolonialism, 1885-1925* (CH, Jan'72) and other works on Vietnam, begins with a brief historical essay, followed by a detailed 30-page national chronology. The bibliography emphasizes the Vietnamese and their culture, rather than military or foreign policy issues. The compiler cites publications in a broad array of topics ranging from folkways to the natural sciences, travel, and children's books. Historical topics are well represented. The extensive literature on the first and second Vietnamese wars is only briefly mentioned; several bibliographies on those topics (e.g., Christopher L. Sugnet and John T. Hickey's *Vietnam War Bibliography*, CH, Feb'84) are available. Marr's annotations are informative, thoughtful, and occasionally critical, and enhance the value of a bibliography that is well organized and fully indexed. Michael Cotter's *Vietnam: A Guide to Reference Sources* (CH, Jul'78) (now out of print) continues to be essential for research collections. Highly recommended; a necessary resource for most college and university libraries, small or large.—*L. S. Dutton, Northern Illinois University*

OAB-0227   DT3   92-38578 CIP
McIlwaine, John. **Africa: a guide to reference material.** H. Zell, 1993. 507p index afp (Regional reference guides, 1) ISBN 0-905450-43-4, $145.00

The high level of scholarship and clarity of organization of this excellent work will make it a benchmark for years to come, and underscore the reference and bibliographic need it fills. The preface, clearly describes the scope of the work, gives cogent definitions for the types of works included and excluded, and touches on the serious issue of how and where reference books are reviewed. "Reference material" here excludes bibliographies, which are well served elsewhere, and concentrates on factual data arranged for rapid consultation. The work is arranged geographically—Africa in general, then regions subdivided by individual countries. Each subsection is divided by genre: handbooks, yearbooks, statistics, directories, biographical sources, atlases, and gazetteers. Entries within each subdivision are arranged chronologically. The result is a high degree of utility—readers searching for information can pinpoint the place and time period sought. The book also provides a fascinating and intellectually valuable overview of the way information about Africa has been compiled and presented. The goal has clearly been to provide a full guide to resources, whatever their source, although many works cited are published in Africa. While this work provides a real service to researchers and librarians concerned with Africa, its cost may cause generalist libraries to pass it by. Libraries with any clientele interested in Africa should consider it seriously; it will be useful for collection development as well as reference.—*G. Walsh, Boston University*

OAB-0228   Brit. CIP
Nordby, Judith, comp. **Mongolia.** Clio, 1993. (Dist. by ABC-Clio) 192p index (World bibliographical series, 156) ISBN 1-85109-129-7, $73.00

Nordby's contribution to this series, which is gradually covering all the countries of the world, is similar to the others: primarily directed at more general, English-language users, and unfortunately, featuring poor quality binding and a high price. As with other volumes, subject coverage is broad: geography, history, sociology, politics, language and literature, economics, science and technology, the arts, religion, agriculture, sports and recreation, etc. A few sections (e.g., "Encyclopedias and Directories," "Bibliographies") are helpful guides to other reference works. The series is particularly important, however, when treating lesser-known and more bibliographically esoteric countries, a category into which Mongolia certainly falls. The paucity of the usual series staple (English-language monographs) is pronounced, and *Mongolia* includes an atypically high number of journal articles and non-English language materials. Nearly 500 entries range in date from the 19th century (e.g., travelers' accounts) through 1992, each with full bibliographical citations and informative annotations. The work concludes with an author-title-subject index and a simple map. Nordby has ably filled a significant void in Central Asian studies. Highly recommended for subject area, academic, and larger public libraries.—*K. W. Berger, Duke University*

OAB-0229   DT351   94-34482 CIP
Scheven, Yvette. **Bibliographies for African studies, 1987-1993,** comp. by Phyllis Bischof et al; ed. by Yvette Scheven. H. Zell, 1994. 176p indexes afp ISBN 1-873836-51-1, $70.00

Scheven's *Bibliographies for African Studies, 1970-1986* (1988) is such a tough act to follow she had to interrupt retirement to edit the current work herself. A compromise solution to the lack of a successor, perhaps, but the information world would be a better place with more compromises like this. This 1987-1993 successor cumulates the annual lists of Africana reference works (bibliographic articles as well as books) that have appeared in *African Book Publishing Record* (1975-). The introduction defines the scope, lists the sources, and describes the arrangement and format of the entries. There is a list of abbreviations. The bibliography is arranged by Library of Congress subject headings, including names of persons, places, and ethnic groups, as well as subject terms subdivided by country or region. Each entry has a detailed descriptive annotation. The few works not examined are duly noted, with reference to the source of information. This excellent work renders accessible a large body of unusual and useful information. All African studies libraries need it, and many general libraries will find it of use.—*G. Walsh, Boston University*

OAB-0230   DS135   94-18554 CIP
The **"Jewish question" in German-speaking countries, 1848-1914:** a bibliography, ed. by Rena R. Auerbach. Garland, 1994. 385p indexes afp (Garland reference library of the humanities, 1571) ISBN 0-8153-0812-4, $62.00

By the mid-19th century, after decades of emancipation and assimilation of Jews in western Europe, there erupted among non-Jews and Jews heated discussions focusing on the desirability, degree, and level of acceptance and integration of Jews into general society. This was labeled the "Jewish question." In their most extreme form, these discussions emerged as fanatical, secular, racist antisemitism; the Jewish versions appeared as apologetics and religious reform. This excellent, comprehensive tool includes more than 3,700 entries primarily of published material in German, Hebrew, French, and other European languages, with the location of the materials cited at the end of the entry. Only the Hebrew titles are translated. There are some useful explanatory annotations. The work is arranged by broad categories such as literature and the arts, antisemitism, and apologetics; within each category, the entries are listed alphabetically by author. Among the many issues covered in this title are tolerance, emancipation, demography, economics, ideologies, law, and the "solution to the Jewish question." Lists of periodicals, collections, newspapers, and pamphlets and detailed subject and author indexes tie everything together. Highly recommended for upper-division undergraduates and above, although users without knowledge of foreign languages—particularly German—will be at a disadvantage.—*D. Kranzler, Queensborough Community College, CUNY*

OAB-0231   DK14   94-24668 Orig
The **Cambridge encyclopedia of Russia and the former Soviet Union,** ed. by Archie Brown, Michael Kaser, and Gerald S. Smith. [2nd ed.]. Cambridge, 1994. 604p bibl index ISBN 0-521-35593-1, $49.95

This revised and enlarged edition of *The Cambridge Encyclopedia of Russia and the Soviet Union* (CH, Sep'82) includes a considerable amount of new textual material and numerous new illustrations and updated maps. The list of contributors has grown, the thematic coverage has expanded, and the focus is now on the last ten years of Communist rule and the post-Soviet period. Despite the second part of the title ("the Former Soviet Union"), the work deals only cursorily with the non-Russian Soviet republics and the new independent states. The volume is divided into 13 major subject fields, each subdivided further either topically or chronologically. A glossary and an index facilitate the use of this encyclopedia. The bibliography has also been substantially updated. What is lacking, however, is an up-to-date general map of the new political configurations. The two maps prominently placed inside the front and back covers display Russia in 1913 and the Soviet Union in 1989. Considering the scale of changes in Russia/USSR since 1982, the low price, and the attractive appearance of this encyclopedia, no academic or public library should be without it, for it will serve well the needs of both general readers and undergraduates.—*L. Siegelbaum, Michigan State University*

OAB-0232   DA34   96-23774 Orig
The **Columbia companion to British history,** ed. by Juliet Gardiner and Neil Wenborn. Columbia, 1997. 840p afp ISBN 0-231-10792-7, $40.00

British history is served by a number of excellent reference works, but their ranks should definitely make room for this fine new volume. It consists of 4,500 alphabetically arranged entries covering the era from the Roman invasion to 1979. Individual entries range widely, dealing with people (Boudicca), institutions (Parliament), battles (Homildon Hill), places (Gwynedd), groups (Plaid Cymru), laws (Six Articles, Act of), legal cases (Bate's Case), broad subjects (Education), specialized subjects) (Eugenics), politics (Home Rule), economics (Chambers of Commerce), religion (Savoy Conference), literature (War Poets), and art (Pre-Raphaelites). Cross-references are supplied generously throughout the work. Nine maps are included in the text, and lists of monarchs and prime ministers are supplied. Six respected historians (David Bates, John Gillingham, Diarmaid MacCulloch, Joanna Innes, David Englander, and John Stevenson) wrote many of the unsigned entries with the assistance of nine other scholars. First published in England as *History Today Companion to British History* (1995), this new work supersedes *A Dictionary of British History*, ed. by J.P. Kenyon (1983), as the best one-volume dictionary of British history. All libraries and individuals with an interest in British history will want this reasonably priced reference book.—*R. Fritze, Lamar University*

OAB-0233   Orig
Day, Alan, comp. **England.** Clio, 1993. (Dist. by ABC-Clio) 591p index (World bibliographical series, 160) ISBN 1-85109-040-1, $134.75

One of the most daunting tasks a series editor could assign would be to compile a bibliography of books in English on England. In the 160th volume of this series, Day tries to do that. While many items are not included, the 2,364 entries in this annotated bibliography certainly make an excellent first attempt. Subdivided into 34 broad categories (some of which are divided further), this work has excellent cross- and *see* references and a thorough author-title-subject index. The annotations are short, concise, and helpful. The compiler omits works that concentrate on Scotland and Wales but includes many that are technically about Great Britain or the UK, as well as those specifically on England. Collection development for books on England just got a whole lot easier. Highly recommended for all libraries and individual Anglophiles.—*S. J. Stillwell Jr., formerly, Harvard University*

OAB-0234   DK265   95-2463 CIP
Frame, Murray, comp. **The Russian Revolution, 1905-1921: a bibliographic guide to works in English.** Greenwood, 1995. 308p indexes afp (Bibliographies and indexes in world history, 40) ISBN 0-313-29559-X, $79.50

Frame (Slavonic Studies, Cambridge Univ.) has compiled this fine-tuned reference tool. The preface explains the dates covered, the categories selected, and which works are excluded (mere mention of the revolution does not merit inclusion). Chapters or categories range from (A) "Reference, Documents and General," to (X) "Place and Significance of the Revolution in Russian and World History." These broad subject areas (of which there are 24) are divided into subcategories, often both by subject and chronology. "Society" (D) is divided by groups (workers, peasants, etc.) and under each group by date (1905-07, 1907-14, etc.). Each citation within a lettered chapter is assigned a number preceded by the letter. This is extremely helpful when searching for entries in author and subject indexes. The compiler limits entries in the literature section, since he found enough references for another book. Otherwise, the bibliography aims at inclusiveness for works in English, including monographs, articles, and doctoral theses. Entries are not annotated, but this is compensated for by the detailed classification. This is a gem for researchers and students at all levels.—*R. P. Sasscer, Catholic University of America*

OAB-0235   Orig
A Guide to historiography in Slovakia, ed. by Elena Mannová and David Paul Daniel. Bratislava, 1995. (Dist. by Interpress Ltd., 206 Blythe Rd., London W14 OHH, UK) 209p (Studia historica Slovaca, 20) ISBN 80-967150-8-9 pbk, $25.00

Well-organized and useful, this guide to basic literature on Slovak history and historiography emphasizes research carried out during the last 50 years and includes many recently published works. The essays in the history section are genre-based, with sections for encyclopedias, bibliographies, regional sources, periodicals, and atlases. Each essay places the works in context with full annotations and bibliographic citations. The authors discuss the ideological limitations of many publications, giving where possible references to current or forthcoming publications aimed at filling the gaps. The literature on historiography is organized chronologically, beginning with the pre-Hungarian period (1st to 9th centuries) and moving to the present time.

The essays summarize the main trends in historiography of the period and include a wealth of bibliographic detail in the footnotes. As in the earlier section, the essays frequently refer to the fall of the totalitarian system and the removal of the ideological barriers to scholarship. The third section, "Organization of Historical Work," provides a thorough guide to Slovak research institutions, universities, libraries, archives, and museums, with up-to-date listings that include, in many cases, contact names, telephone numbers, e-mail addresses, available finding aids, and inventories. Future editions would benefit from author and subject indexes as well as access information for the libraries and research collections listed. Highly recommended for college and research libraries.—*S. C. Summer, Columbia University*

OAB-0236   G2081   96-35560 CIP
Hupchick, Dennis P. **A concise historical atlas of Eastern Europe,** by Dennis P. Hupchick and Harold E. Cox. St. Martin's, 1996. 120p bibl index ISBN 0-312-15893-9, $49.95

Compiled as a companion to introductory courses in East European history, this atlas is a well organized, easy-to-use set of 50 maps providing a visual aid for studying the basic geopolitical history of Eastern Europe from the early medieval period through 1991. Four introductory maps cover the political situation in 1996, the basic physical region, demographics, and the cultural forces of the area. The rest of the maps are arranged chronologically and by topic, such as "The Barbarian Migrations, 4th-6th Centuries," "The Rise of the Ottoman Empire, 13th-15th Centuries," "The Partitions of Poland, 1772-1795," "The Macedonian Question," and "Eastern Europe, 1948-1991." Opposite each map is a well-written, succinct summary of the topic, including the main political events, dates, places, and figures, with key names and concepts highlighted, making the atlas itself a basic textbook. In addition to the maps, the volume includes a substantial bibliography of general studies and commonly available atlases, and a thorough index. A welcome publication, highly recommended for undergraduate and public libraries.—*S. C. Summer, Columbia University*

OAB-0237   DK4123   94-46940 CIP
Lerski, George J. **Historical dictionary of Poland, 966-1945,** with special editing and emendations by Piotr Wróbel and Richard J. Kozicki. Greenwood, 1996. 750p bibl index afp ISBN 0-313-26007-9, $125.00

A worthy memorial, this important posthumous work (Lerski died in September 1992) is dedicated to Pope John Paul II. It was prepared for publication by Lerski's widow in close cooperation wit Wróbel and Kozicki, and will become one of the most important reference works treating Poland. In some 2,000 entries, it covers meticulously the history of Poland from its beginnings to 1945. Each entry gives full references to sources and uses asterisks to cross-reference separate entries. With a penetrating foreword by Aleksander Gieysztor (president, Polish Academy of Science and Learning) and crowned by a scholarly bibliography and helpful index, this work is essential for college or university libraries that support study of east central European history.—*G. J. Maciuszko, Baldwin-Wallace College*

OAB-0238   G2081   93-13783 CIP
Magocsi, Paul Robert. **Historical atlas of East Central Europe.** Washington, 1993. 218p bibl index afp (A history of East Central Europe, 1) ISBN 0-295-97248-3, $75.00

An attractive scholarly atlas that is part of a ten-volume series and is the first comprehensive history of the region in English. It is a fascinating cartographic chronicle of political and cultural layering from the late 5th century through 1992 in the lands limited by "the eastern linguistic frontier of German- and Italian-speaking peoples on the west, and the political borders of Russia/the former USSR on the east." Treated in depth are Poles, Czechs, Slovaks, Hungarians, Romanians, Yugoslav peoples, Albanians, Bulgarians, and Greeks. Text, tables, charts, bibliography, and index support 89 detailed color maps illustrating political and administrative boundaries (including internal subdivisions), the economy, education and culture, religion, demography, and ethnicity. Coverage of the medieval and early modern periods is particularly good; 20th-century thematic maps are comparatively few in number. A unique resource that provides more regional focus and depth than *Times Atlas of World History* (4th ed., CH, Apr'94), this atlas can be used for reference and would also make an excellent supplementary text in this age of visual learning.—*J. M. Alexander, Northwestern University*

OAB-0239　　　DC33　　　95-2617 CIP
Medieval France: an encyclopedia, ed. by William W. Kibler et al. Garland, 1995. 1,047p bibl index afp (Garland encyclopedias of the Middle Ages, 2) ISBN 0-8240-4444-4, $95.00

This excellent work provides introductions to the political, economic, social, religious, economic, intellectual, literary, and artistic history of medieval France. Intended primarily for students and general readers, it will prove useful for scholars seeking general orientation, bibliography, and interpretation in areas beyond their field of expertise. Coverage extends from the 5th to the late 15th century in the region where the French court emerged and flourished. Some 200 hundred scholars, many with distinguished reputations, have contributed more than 2,400 well-written articles. Shorter pieces summarize biographies, events, cities, monuments, works of art, literature, theology, and more, accompanied by basic bibliographies. Longer essays explain and often interpret major institutions, writers, works, and movements. Although the long article on pilgrimages, for example, is descriptive, that on Gothic architecture reinterprets the field. The articles are cross-referenced and accompanied by useful lists of kings, counts, and dukes with regnal dates; architectural terms with diagrams of Gothic, Romanesque, and military structures; musical terms; and abbreviations. Numerous maps and pictures illustrate the text, and page layout is pleasing. An index enhances both the cross-reference structure and the volume's cross-disciplinary focus. Highly recommended for all libraries.—*S. F. Roberts, Yale University*

THE AMERICAS

OAB-0240　　　E456　　　95-53132 CIP
The American Civil War: a handbook of literature and research, ed. by Steven E. Woodworth. Greenwood, 1996. 754p bibl index afp ISBN 0-313-29019-9, $99.50

Someone has estimated that Civil War titles exceed 60,000 volumes, and additional titles (scholarly and popular) are published annually at a frightening rate. Woodworth's handbook is an excellent guide through the immense bibliography of America's greatest conflict. More than 45 specialists provide bibliographic essays on a wide range of topics including slavery, international relations, strategy and tactics, prisons, economics, ordnance, state and local politics, social conditions, and the various elements of Reconstruction. Many of the topics, such as Harris Riley Jr.'s 13-page essay on medical activities, are surprisingly detailed. Even fictional works and film and television productions are covered. Many of the substantial essays are important not only for their bibliographic content, but for their analysis of the changing themes and trends of Civil War scholarship. Each essay concludes with a strong bibliography that is usually arranged thematically. The volume also contains a useful listing of Civil War publishers and vendors. The book concludes with a combined subject, name, and title index. Scope and quality make this an ideal reference text for students, bibliographers, scholars, and curators of Civil War materials. Highly recommended.—*D. E. Richards, Southwest Missouri State University*

OAB-0241　　　E208　　　92-42541 CIP
The American Revolution, 1775-1783: an encyclopedia, ed. by Richard L. Blanco with Paul J. Sanborn. Garland, 1993. 2v. 1,857p index afp ISBN 0-8240-5623-X, $175.00

The most recent (and unfortunately pricey) reference book on the American Revolution. Narrower in scope but greater in depth than *Encyclopedia of Colonial and Revolutionary America*, ed. by J. M. Faragher (CH, Jul'90) and more traditional than *Blackwell Encyclopedia of the American Revolution*, ed. by J. P. Greene and J. R. Pole (CH, Jul'92), this work updates and broadens the scope of such standards as M. M. Boatner's *Encyclopedia of the American Revolution* (CH, Dec'74) or those entries in *Dictionary of American History* (1976) that treat the Revolution. This set covers in depth all military and naval aspects of the war, and places the Revolution in global context, with many entries on worldwide conquest and on European, Mexican, Caribbean, and East Indian diplomacy. For major battles or minor skirmishes alike, the book provides pertinent data and up-to-date bibliography. Biographies of people from many ethnic backgrounds, well known or obscure, are included. Much valuable information on military history is provided: military medicine, supply, equipment, tactics, music, strategy, chaplains, uniforms, camp followers. There is an excellent glossary of military terms, many maps, and an index of major entries. These volumes augment and enhance standard reference sources. Highly recommended.—*D. D. Siles, Wells College*

OAB-0242　　　E184　　　94-33003 CIP
The Asian American encyclopedia, ed. by Franklin Ng and John D. Wilson. M. Cavendish, 1995. 6v. 1,837p bibl index afp ISBN 1-85435-677-1, $449.95

The work of hundreds of scholars from a variety of academic and cultural backgrounds, this first large-scale reference book devoted to Asian Americans reflects a need to understand this diverse, historically neglected group. The volumes emphasize the experiences of Asian immigrants and their communities, and provide essential background information concerning the history, language, and culture of the countries of origin of various Asian American groups. Some 2,000 entries, ranging from brief definitions to 4,000-word essays, treat important individuals, organizations, laws, and landmark court cases. The text is enhanced by many charts, tables, lists, maps, and more than 1,000 vivid historical photographs. The set offers as well a comprehensive bibliography, a general index, and a subject list arranged by population groups and by subject headings. Highly recommended for college and university libraries.—*M. Meng, St. John's University*

OAB-0243　　　E185　　　92-39947 CIP
Black women in America: an historical encyclopedia, ed. by Darlene Clark Hine. Carlson, 1993. 2v. 1,530p bibl index afp ISBN 0-926019-61-9, $195.00

The unique viewpoint of the African-American woman's experience permeates every aspect of the 804 essays in this encyclopedia, from the topics of the entries to the strength of language in each description. The signed essays range in length from two paragraphs to 25 pages, and accompanying bibliographies indicate that many are based on rare or unpublished sources of information. Although Jesse Carney Smith's *Notable Black American Women* (CH, Jun'92) contained material on a number of the 641 figures included, many are not covered in any standard reference source. In addition, this encyclopedia contains 163 topical articles, including general discussions of slavery and free black women during the Civil War, historical accounts of black women's organizations, and articles on stereotypes such as Aunt Jemima and Mammy. Some 450 black-and-white photos scattered through the text are striking; while sources such as *The Negro Almanac* (5th ed., 1989) include similar photographs, this is the first to exhibit so many archival photos of black women. The entries are followed by a chronology of black women in the US, beginning with the first three women put ashore at Jamestown in 1619, then tracing famous firsts and important events through 1992. Following the chronology is an excellent annotated bibliography of basic resources in the field. The index is detailed and accurate, with fine cross-references, and the list of biographical entries by profession is useful and clearly defined. Hine, editor of *Black Women in United States History: From Colonial Times to the Present* (16v., 1990) and author of books on African-American history (e.g., *Black Women in White: Racial Conflict and Cooperation in the Nursing Profession* CH,

Mar'90), has produced a sound work that will be a standard reference source for years to come. Highly recommended for all libraries.—*M. F. Jones, Muskingum College*

OAB-0244   E178   93-41174 CIP
Blazek, Ron. **United States history: a selective guide to information sources,** by Ron Blazek and Anna H. Perrault. Libraries Unlimited, 1994. 411p indexes ISBN 0-87287-984-4, $55.00

Blazek and Perrault successfuly span the chasm between traditional listings of sources in American history and the burgeoning literature of the "new" history's attention to social and economic history of minorities, urban areas, science and technology, and popular culture during the last 30 years. Arranged by broad topic areas (general, politics and government, diplomacy, military, regional history, economics) the guide balances its focus by devoting 420 of its 947 main entries to the section on social, cultural, and intellectual history. Content coverage ends in 1975, but sources were published as late as 1993. Many main entries offer, besides lucid evaluative annotations, cross-references to "minor entries." There is an author-title-subject index. Entries are subdivided somewhat artificially in each subject category into sections entitled "library resources," "bibliographic sources," "information sources," and "biographical sources," and annotations spotlight strong points for the source, such as biographies, for particular groups of users. An essay prefacing each topic describes: publishing and research trends in that area; related associations and their publications; data sets such as census and those of Inter-University Consortium for Political and Social Research, and the usefulness of indexes available in electronic format. Designed for students and reference/bibliographic instruction librarians, this guide is valuable as well for collection development. Highly recommended for academic and large public libraries.— *H. H. Ives, American University Library*

OAB-0245   PE2970   92-4336 CIP
Blevins, Winfred. **Dictionary of the American West.** Facts on File, 1993. 400p afp ISBN 0-8160-2031-0, $35.00

Blevins, western novelist and Wyoming resident, has created an updated dictionary of the West that attempts to correct the "Anglo-centric, Texas-centric, male-centric and cowboy-centric" biases of earlier dictionaries of the West. "A large part of the purpose of this book is to give their rightful place back to the disenfranchised"—women, Native Americans, Mormons, Hispanics, African Americans, French Canadians, mountain men, and half-breeds. Blevins covers everyday words, both contemporary and historical, while purposely giving minimal attention to technical vocabulary on activities such as mining, logging, and stock raising. He defines the geographical range of the West as the Rocky Mountains, the Great Plains, the Great Basin, and the Southwest. Where pronunciation is provided, it conforms to the "customary pronunciation of educated Americans," not the correct foreign pronunciation. Cross-references are used frequently, and 80 illustrations, both drawings and photographs, are scattered among the more than 5,000 terms and expressions. For currency, inclusiveness, and rich definitions, Blevins's work surpasses other dictionaries of the West, including Ramon F. Adams's *Western Words: A Dictionary of the American West* (CH, Sep'69), and Peter Watts's *A Dictionary of the Old West, 1850-1900* (CH, Sep'77). Highly recommended for public libraries with western fiction collections and academic libraries that support courses in literature of the American West.—*P. A. Frisch, University of Illinois at Chicago*

OAB-0246   Can. CIP
Canadian history: a reader's guide. v.1: Beginnings to Con-federation; v.2: Confederation to the present, v.1 ed. by M. Brook Taylor; v.2 ed. by Doug Owram. Toronto, 1994. 2v. 506, 417p indexes ISBN 0-8020-5016-6, v.1, $55.00; ISBN 0-8020-6826-X pbk, v.1, $19.95; ISBN 0-8020-2801-2, v.2, $47.50; ISBN 0-8020-7676-9 pbk, v.2, $19.95

The first edition of this indispensable scholarly reference work, entitled *A Reader's Guide to Canadian History* (CH, Jan'83), met a serious need among students of Canadian history. The long-awaited second edition updates, but does not wholly supersede, its predecessor. Completely rewritten by a younger generation of Canadian historians (alas, few contributors are women), the 22 bibliographical essays in these two volumes direct the reader to select works, including articles, on traditional and avant-garde themes relating to various geographical regions, historical periods, and recent specialties (e.g., labor and native history). The essays are carefully crafted and read surprisingly well, despite the profusion of titles mentioned. Unfortunately, even though the second edition is almost twice the size of the first, such essential sources as unpublished theses are not systematically covered. Each volume contains a separate author and subject index, but the latter is not thorough enough for quick reference. Nevertheless, scholars, researchers, undergraduate and graduate students, general readers, and librarians will value this wide-ranging revision of the standard guide to Canadian historiography. One only regrets the use of low-quality paper.— *J. D. Blackwell, formerly, St. Francis Xavier University*

OAB-0247   E179   92-23520 CIP
Conzen, Michael P. **A scholar's guide to geographical writing on the American and Canadian past,** by Michael P. Conzen, Thomas A. Rumney, and Graeme Wynn. Chicago, 1993. 741p index afp ISBN 0-226-11569-0 pbk, $29.95

Three leading historical geographers have collaborated to produce an exceptionally complete guide to the discipline in their bibliography of more than 10,000 books, dissertations, and articles, 1850-1990. The *Guide's* purpose, which the editors expertly meet, is to provide a comprehensive and cumulative survey of the literature. Conzen presents a benchmark review essay describing more than a century of historical-geographical scholarship in the US; Wynn does the same for Canada. The bibliography follows a simple geographic arrangement in which chapters are divided into broad topical subheadings (e.g., environmental change, land use, urban structure). Citations under each topic are arranged chronologically. Missing topics imply gaps in existing research; the arrangement by date points to the direction research has taken in that topic. This work goes far beyond the more modest scope and purpose found in Ronald E. Grim's *Historical Geography of the United States: A Guide to Information Sources* (CH, Apr'83) and reflects the coming of age of historical geography in North America. Truly a landmark work that should be in all academic libraries whether or not they support a geography program.—*P. L. Stark, University of Oregon*

OAB-0248   E159   95-5788 CIP
Curtis, Nancy C. **Black heritage sites: an African American odyssey and finder's guide.** American Library Association, 1996. 677p bibl index afp ISBN 0-8389-0643-5, $55.00

For many years the American Oil Company's *American Traveler's Guide to Negro Monuments* (1963) was recognized as the best guidebook for locating African American monuments. Since its appearance, at least three other guidebooks have been published: George Cantor's *Historic Landmarks of Black America* (CH, Nov'91), Marcella Thum's *Hippocrene U.S.A. Guide to Black America: A Directory of Historic and Cultural Sites Relating to Black America* (CH, Jun'92), and the National Register of Historic Places' *African American Historic Places*, ed. by Beth L. Savage (CH, May'95). Curtis's superb compilation, which "honors the humble as well as the famous," is a welcome complement. The guidebook is arranged according to five geographical regions: South, Northeast, Midwest, Southwest, and the West and noncontiguous states. Some Canadian sites are included as special features. Each section includes an introduction, a brief description of the states in the region, and such highlights as existing churches, schools, buildings, battlefields, cemeteries, etc. A 12-page essay on African Americans precedes the section on the South, the first region in the guidebook. A works consulted list follows each section. The table of contents provides detailed access by geographic region, type of structure, theme, subject, etc. Entries, ranging in length from six lines to one and one-half pages, are arranged alphabetically under state, and include a description of the site, date established, address/telephone, visiting hours, and fees. Highly recommended as a first purchase for most libraries.—*G. T. Johnson, Central State University (OH)*

OAB-0249   E185   95-33607 CIP

Encyclopedia of African-American culture and history, ed. by Jack Salzman, David Lionel Smith, and Cornel West. Macmillan Library Reference USA/Simon & Schuster and Prentice Hall International, 1996. 5v. 3,203p bibl index afp ISBN 0-02-897345-3, $425.00

Undergraduates and graduate students may use this set as a starting point for researching the cultural, social, political, economic, and intellectual history of African Americans, especially for the later 19th and 20th centuries. It includes brief biographical sketches of 1,188 men and 382 women representing education, medicine, politics, religion, sports, the social sciences, and especially the creative arts. It also offers 500 short- to medium-length topical entries covering historical events; organizations; social, political, and cultural movements; business enterprises; the professions; and other subjects relating to the African American experience. The 50 states, major American cities, Mexico, and Canada each have separate entries. Most useful are about 40 broad thematic essays, eight to 24 pages in length with extensive bibliographies, that survey African American contributions to business, drama, education, music, painting, religion, sports, television, and other areas of US life. The articles report recent developments on the person or topic when that is essential. The writing style generally is clear and succinct. More than 1,000 illustrations from the Schomburg Center, Howard University, Library of Congress, and other sources add interest. The appendix provides statistical tables showing historical trends and lists of persons and organizations for different categories of achievement. The detailed index and the many cross-references within the articles provide excellent access points and link persons, events, facts, and concepts. The introduction does not adequately explain the encyclopedia's scope and focus, nor does it give enough details about the selection of biographical and topical entries or the credentials of the contributors. The volumes are well bound and the page layout is attractive. The 600 contributors represent professors and freelance writers, including some well-known authorities in the field. Although all the essays are signed and include bibliographies, most summarize existing knowledge rather than present new research findings, and many short entries list only a few secondary references. A separate subject bibliography of the most significant works on the African American experience would have enhanced this work. *African-American Encyclopedia,* ed. by Michael W. Williams (6 v., CH, Nov'93) overlaps with the present work to some degree, but deals more with contemporary popular culture and social issues and includes more entertainers, military officers, government officials, rock groups, films, and television shows. *The African-American Almanac* (6th ed., 1994) remains a solid resource for homes and for libraries with limited budgets. Researchers interested in more specialized and scholarly treatment of additional biographical or historical subjects may consult a growing list of related sources, such as John N. Ingham and Lynne B. Feldman's *African-American Business Leaders* (1994); *Black Women in America,* ed. by Darlene Clark Hine (2 v., CH, Jun'93); Eric Ledell Smith's *Blacks in Opera* (CH, Apr'96); *Encyclopedia of African-American Civil Rights* (CH, Dec'92); *Encyclopedia of African American Religions,* ed. by Larry G. Murphy et al. (CH, Mar'94); and *Notable Black American Women* (CH, Jun'92). All college and university libraries will want this set for its breadth of coverage of general biographical and historical data concerning the African American experience. (The reviewer gratefully acknowledges the cooperation of his colleagues Winifred Dean and Alice Reviere Smith in appraising this source and writing the review).—*G. B. Thompson, Cleveland State University*

OAB-0250   HN57   92-10577 CIP

Encyclopedia of American social history, ed. by Mary Kupiec Cayton, Elliott J. Gorn, and Peter W. Williams. Scribner, 1993. 3v. 2,653p index afp ISBN 0-684-19246-2, $350.00

The editors, with nearly 200 contributors, have produced a monumental and extremely useful synthesis of American social history. They note that "the range of subjects and approaches is daunting," to which 14 thematic sections and 180 essays attest. Contributions by historians and scholars from ethnology, geography, literature, religion, anthropology, and sociology discuss the major issues such as gender, race, ethnicity, religion, social class, and sexual and political orientation that have dominated historical inquiry since the late 1960s. The section titles—Periods of Social Change; Methods and Context; The Construction of Social Identity; Processes of Social Change; Ethnic and Racial Subcultures; Regionalism and Regional Subcultures; Space and Place; Patterns of Everyday Life; Work and Labor; Popular Culture and Recreation; Family History; Social Problems, Social Control, and Social Protest; Science, Medicine and Technology; and Education and Literacy—convey the breadth of coverage. The longest section, reflecting the considerable interest in popular culture, includes essays ranging from sports, travel, and amusement parks to rock music, humor, and journalism. Other sections include essays on such theoretical matters as modernization theory, quantification, and poststructural theory. The typical essay runs 13 double-column pages and is followed by an extensive bibliography of books and articles as well as *see also* references to other essays. Maps, graphs, and tables enhance the text, and the essays on architecture and housing are accompanied by photographs. The 92-page index, in Volume 3, refers to both page number and column. It is extremely detailed, with extensive subheadings, and includes not only subjects, people, and place-names but also organizations and institutions and titles of songs, films, and books. The vast range of this work is revealed by a glance at the first column, where one finds entries for abolitionism, abortion, acid rain, acid rock, Acoma Indians, ACT-UP (Aids Coalition to Unleash Power), and Roy Acuff. A useful feature of the index is a footer on each page indicating the inclusive pagination of each volume. The 8.5-by-11 page size and sheer bulk and weight of each volume, one of which exceeds 1,000 pages, makes the set somewhat cumbersome to use. Perhaps four volumes would have been a handier format. The sixth title in the "Scribner American Civilization Series," this will undoubtedly take its place among the classic reference works in American history and should be acquired by all libraries.—*J. D. Haskell Jr., College of William and Mary*

OAB-0251   F1406   95-31042 CIP

Encyclopedia of Latin American history and culture, ed. by Barbara A. Tenenbaum et al. Scribner/Simon & Schuster and Prentice Hall International, 1996. 5v. 590-696p ea. index afp ISBN 0-684-19253-5, $449.00

This encyclopedia, which focuses on Latin American history and culture including the contemporary scene, meets a longstanding need for comprehensive, up-to-date information in English based on recent scholarship. In dictionary format, its 5,287 entries include both short but thorough identifications/definitions/descriptions and long essays about countries and general topics ("Theater," "Income Distribution," "Textile Industry"). More than half the entries (about 3,000) are biographical, while others cover places, events, groups such as indigenous peoples, and other topics. The encyclopedia has the broadest possible geographic scope, including the Spanish borderlands that are now a part of the US, Mexico, Central America, South America (including Brazil, often excluded from reference works that are limited to Spanish Latin America), and the Caribbean area. Its signed entries, which include bibliographies and cross-references to related entries, were prepared by 832 scholars. Black-and-white maps and illustrations enhance the text. An appendix provides a useful classification of biographical entries according to occupation or field of activity, and lists women in a separate category. The index is thorough. The work builds upon, updates, and expands three earlier one-volume encyclopedias. Michael Rheta Martin and Gabriel H. Lovett's *An Encyclopedia of Latin-American History* (1956) emphasizes the political and legal aspects of history. *Encyclopedia of Latin America,* ed. by Helen Delpar (CH, May'75), an excellent tool, similar in subject coverage to the present encyclopedia, is more limited in geographic scope with less coverage of the Caribbean islands, contains fewer entries overall, and, of course, is out-of-date with regard to contemporary Latin America. *The Cambridge Encyclopedia of Latin America and the Caribbean* (2nd ed., 1992) takes a topical approach in detail-packed essays that survey six major subjects: "Physical Environment," "The Economy," "The Peoples," "History," "Politics and Society," and "Culture." Its thorough index provides access to information about individuals, events, and other topics mentioned in the essays, but it lacks the ease of use of a dictionary format for quick reference purposes, and the biographical information it supplies is limited. All libraries with clientele seeking information about Latin America will want to acquire *The Encyclopedia of Latin American History and Culture* as the source to rely on for dependable and recent information.—*A. Hartness, University of Texas at Austin*

OAB-0252   E487   93-4133 CIP
Encyclopedia of the Confederacy, ed. by Richard N. Current et al.
Simon & Schuster, 1993. 4v. 1,916p index afp ISBN 0-13-275991-8,
$355.00

A marvelous reference source. Prominent Civil War historian Current has
assembled in four attractive volumes more than 1,400 alphabetically arranged
articles ranging from 250 to 17,250 words by more than 300 leading scholars,
which treat the Confederacy as a nation unto itself. The encyclopedia is
broad in scope, covering all aspects of Confederate life. Articles trace the various features of its government and politics, military campaigns, and biographical sketches of the famous and obscure. Significant space has been
devoted to social and cultural issues in an effort to cover nontraditional and
often neglected topics. Each article is signed and has a bibliography citing
from two to fifteen sources. The volumes contain more than 600 illustrations including contemporary photographs and etchings, maps, and specially
commissioned photographs of a number of military arms and accoutrements.
Of particular aid to the reader are numerous cross-references throughout the
text, a detailed index, and a synoptic outline at the end of the set which
groups all entries pertaining to major subject areas. Occasionally articles treating similar subjects have been grouped in composite entries; for example, four
articles on battle injuries are under the heading "Health and medicine." In the
preface, Current states "those curious about the Confederacy have hitherto had
no comprehensive reference work to which to turn as a convenient and reliable source of information on all aspects of the subject." They do now.
Highly recommended for both academic and public libraries.—*C. C. Hay III,
Eastern Kentucky University*

OAB-0253   E45   93-7609 CIP
Encyclopedia of the North American colonies, ed. by Jacob Ernest
Cooke et al. Scribner, 1993. 3v. 745, 787, 865p index afp ISBN 0-684-
19269-1, $300.00

Cooke, working with contributors of stature in history, anthropology, sociology, and folklore drawn from the US, Canada, Great Britain, and Western
Europe, has produced a unique publication. It fulfills its aim "to provide a fuller
understanding of our colonial heritage by incorporating recent literature on previously neglected areas of colonial history." Materials on the Spanish borderlands, information from the New Netherlands Project at the New York State
Library, and topics such as Native American worship, detribalized and manu-
mitted Indians, interracial societies, Native American aesthetics, gender relations, childhood and adolescence, and free blacks all demonstrate inclusion of
the latest research. Although emphasis rests on the four major imperial powers (France, Great Britain, Holland, and Spain) in colonization, the Norse,
Russians, and Swedes are also included. The 274 signed essays cover the
period 900-1860 and range in length from 1,000 to 15,000 words, with bibliographies and related cross-references. There are excellent maps, a chronology
of events, and an index in Volume 3. For most topics, coverage is comprehensive and comparative. An excellent starting place for research, this set has
greater depth and is more up-to-date than *Dictionary of American History* or
Encyclopedia of Colonial and Revolutionary History, ed. by J.M. Faragher (CH,
Jul'90). Very highly recommended.—*D. D. Siles, Wells College*

OAB-0254   E740   95-22696 CIP
Encyclopedia of the United States in the twentieth century, ed.
by Stanley I. Kutler et al. Scribner/Simon & Schuster and Prentice Hall
International, 1996. 4v. (4v. plus index) 1,941p; 89p bibl index afp ISBN
0-13-210535-7, $385.00

Historian Kutler (Univ. of Wisconsin-Madison), noting social scientist Peter
F. Drucker's observation that "no century in recorded history has experienced
so many social transformations and such radical ones as the twentieth century," has produced a masterly edited publication that captures the essence of
many political, social, cultural, and technological developments and trends
that have occurred in the US during this century. In six broad topical sections
("The American People"; "Politics"; "Global America"; "Science, Technology,

and Medicine"; "The Economy"; and "Culture"), 80 prominent academic historians provide 74 interpretative essays based on current scholarship that analyze major topics and themes of the century. The lengthy essays, accompanied by judiciously selected photographs and illustrations, cover such traditional
and emerging subjects as regionalism, gender issues, Congress, limited wars,
health and disease, the infrastructure, and sports; they are followed by informative and thorough bibliographical essays. A unique chronology organized in
six columns that correspond to the encyclopedia's topical arrangement can be
used to compare noteworthy annual accomplishments and events, 1898-1995.
An excellent index appears in a separate softbound volume. Kutler and his
colleagues have produced a significant reference work that skillfully and accurately analyzes the complexity of the 20th-century US. Highly recommended
for all academic libraries.—*C. C. Hay III, Eastern Kentucky University*

OAB-0255   G1201   94-29084 CIP
Fast, Timothy H. **The women's atlas of the United States,** by
Timothy H. Fast and Cathy Carroll Fast. rev ed. Facts on File, 1995. 246p
bibl index afp ISBN 0-8160-2970-9, $75.00

Based on the 1990 census and other data up through 1993, this edition
updates the first, which drew on the 1980 census and other data prior to 1990.
Text and maps have been added to illuminate 1990s issues such as homelessness and AIDS, and computer graphics have made the maps more attractive and
easy to read. The organization of the first edition has been retained, beginning with a general section on demographics followed by six topical sections.
Sections on politics, education, and health have been expanded, but maps
showing particular occupations have been dropped. New to this edition are multiracial data and maps in some topical sections. The introduction and text for
each section have been rewritten, and the index expanded and made easier to
use. The "Bibliography for Maps" gives the data sources. Timothy Fast, geographer and coauthor of the first edition, and Cathy Carroll Fast, AutoCAD
specialist, present a wealth of information in a very accessible format. This is
an important reference work. Highly recommended for undergraduates and general readers.—*B. K. Lacks, California State University, Fresno*

OAB-0256   HQ1410   94-9355 CIP
Frost-Knappman, Elizabeth. **The ABC-CLIO companion to women's
progress in America,** by Elizabeth Frost-Knappman with Sarah Kurian.
ABC-Clio, 1994. 389p bibl index afp ISBN 0-87436-667-4, $55.00

While researching her book *Women's Suffrage in America*, written under the
name Elizabeth Frost (CH, Feb'93), which focused on the 19th century, Frost-
Knappman became curious about "women's public achievements since the founding of the colonies." This book, covering the years 1619-1993, is the result. The
bulk of the book is devoted to an alphabetical listing of topics, organizations,
individuals, laws, and court cases that illuminate women's progress. The text
is accompanied by contemporary illustrations. Articles are succinct and authoritative, and written with admirable clarity. It is unfortunate that two worthwhile
reference books on American women's history have come out at the same
time. Dorothy Weatherford's *American Women's History* (1994) is similar in
content and format, covers many more topics, but lacks an index. Weatherford's
articles tend to emphasize different aspects of the same topics, so that the two
books complement one another. Academic libraries should have both titles, but
if a choice has to be made, this reviewer recommends the Frost-Knappman
because of its unique chronology, excellent bibliography, and detailed subject
matter.—*B. K. Lacks, California State University, Fresno*

OAB-0257   E184   95-23341 CIP
Gale encyclopedia of multicultural America, ed. by Judy Galens,
Anna Sheets, and Robyn V. Young. Gale, 1995. 2v. 1,477p bibl index
afp ISBN 0-8103-9163-5, $125.00

Harvard Encyclopedia of American Ethnic Groups (CH, Jan'81) provides a
good starting point for research on minorities, ethnicity, and ethnic relations,
and *Encyclopedia of Multiculturalism*, ed. by Susan Auerbach (CH, Jul'94),

is additionally useful for research on pluralism, ethnology, and multicultural-ism. Endorsed by the Ethnic Materials Information Exchange Round Table of the American Library Association, this new set, with more than 100 signed original essays, recognizes not only more established ethnic groups but also newer ones like Hmong Americans and Guatemalan Americans. Ethnoreligious groups such as the Amish are included, as are over 12 Native American groups. Each group's experiences are described in the areas of acculturation/assimila-tion, family/community dynamics, language, religion, employment/economic traditions, politics/government, and significant contributions. Additional sources for further study, periodicals, radio and television stations, organizations and associations, and museums and research centers are included, as is a general bib-liography of some 100 books and periodicals. The text is highlighted by 171 photographs, and a general subject index provides access to terms, people, places, movements, events, and organizations. Most of the articles were written by scholars with knowledge and special interest in the ethnic groups about which they write; additional scholars completed final reviews. Highly recommended for academic, public, school, and specialized libraries.—*N. S. Osborne, SUNY College at Oswego*

OAB-0258   E99   94-4415 CIP

Haas, Marilyn L. **The Seneca and Tuscarora Indians: an annotated bibliography.** Scarecrow, 1994. 450p indexes afp (Native American bibliography series, 17) ISBN 0-8108-2740-9, $55.00

Haas, author of one of the standard general reference sources on Native Americans, *Indians of North America* (CH, Jul'84), has compiled this first major bibliography on two of the six tribes of the Haudenosaunee (the Peo-ple of the Longhouse) or the League of the Iroquois, as they were called by the French. Haas has divided the 1,229 mostly English-language entries—arranged alphabetically by main entry—among 24 topical categories, ranging from archaeology and artifacts to fiction and poetry to treaties. Particularly detailed sections are those covering biographies, land, and social life and customs. Reflecting the coverage in the literature, 85 percent of entries cover the Seneca, ten percent cover the Tuscarora, and five percent cover both, with a time period of 1792-1992. Books, book chapters, pamphlets, periodical arti-cles, dissertations, master's theses, ERIC documents, juvenile fiction and non-fiction, government publications, and tribal periodicals are described. Anno-tations are descriptive rather than evaluative. The section on treaties includes a descriptive essay that precedes the list of references; similar essays would have been nice for each of the other sections. This is an extremely valuable compilation that all users interested in the Seneca and Tuscarora, the Iroquois peoples, or American Indians in general will welcome. Recommended for all regional and large collections on Native Americans. Public and academic libraries.—*C. E. Carter, University of New Mexico*

OAB-0259   E77   93-1057 CIP

Hirschfelder, Arlene. **The Native American almanac: a portrait of Native America today,** by Arlene Hirschfelder and Martha Kreipe de Montaño. Prentice Hall General Reference & Travel, 1993. 341p bibl index ISBN 0-671-85012-1, $25.00

A handy one-volume reference work that serves as an excellent introduction to Native Americans and covers all areas of Native American experience and present-day activities. It is arranged by subject and includes education, religion, law, health, employment, arts, and sports. An excellent 35-page historical overview provides an informative introduction. Appendixes provide lists of books by state, reservations, treaties, landmarks, and a chronology. Charts and maps are clear and most helpful, and photographs and line drawings delight-ful. The bibliography is good and the index accurate. Hirschfelder has compiled reference books and bibliographies on Native Americans, including *Encyclo-pedia of Native American Religion: An Introduction* with Paulette Molin (CH, Oct'92). Kreipe de Montaño, from the Potawatomi nation, is manager at the Smithsonian National Museum of the America Indian. No other reference book on this subject is quite like this one, or has the information so readily avail-able and up-to-date. Recommended for general readers and all college libraries.—*P. Brauch, Brooklyn College, CUNY*

OAB-0260   E342   94-12322 CIP

James Madison and the American nation, 1751-1836: an ency-clopedia, ed. by Robert A. Rutland. Simon & Schuster, 1995 (c1994). 509p index afp ISBN 0-13-508425-3, $95.00

For this first-rate reference work on Madison's life, times, and influence, Rutland, one of the premier Madison historians, has assembled an impressive group of 88 expert contributors. Their 400 signed articles sustain a high stan-dard of scholarship and balanced historical analysis. The entries include bio-graphical articles on important Madison contemporaries. Each article ends with a bibliography, and there are valuable cross-references throughout. The book's research utility is augmented by appendixes including important doc-uments, a chronology, and a conceptual outline of contents. The index is detailed enough to be genuinely utilitarian. This will be the standard refer-ence work on the Madisonian era and a model for others to follow. Many handsome illustrations. Academic collections.—*C. V. Stanley, Washington & Lee University*

OAB-0261   E184   92-35753 CIP

Japanese American history: an A-to-Z reference from 1868 to the present, ed. by Brian Niiya. Facts On File, 1993. 386p bibl index afp ISBN 0-8160-2680-7, $45.00

The first encyclopedic work to provide an overview of the Japanese Amer-ican experience. Its editor stresses its intention to reflect the "current state of knowledge" in the field of Japanese American studies. The work focuses on the thoughts and actions of Japanese Americans themselves rather than on an external image of them or on what was done to them. Thus the materials uti-lized include many Japanese-language sources, oral histories, and other previ-ously neglected source materials. However, the strength of the book is not in its original research, but in its synthesis of existing studies. The book is set in an easily accessible and comprehensive reference format. It consists of an illu-minating historical overview by a leading scholar in the field, dictionary entries pertaining to Japanese American history, a detailed chronology providing dates and glimpses of important issues, and a bibliography including all major works on the topic. An excellent choice for all academic reference collections.—*M. Meng, St. John's University*

OAB-0262   G1281   93-46478 CIP

Martis, Kenneth C. **The historical atlas of the Congresses of the Confederate States of America, 1861-1865.** Simon & Schuster, 1994. 157p bibl index afp ISBN 0-13-389115-1, $60.00

In this landmark work, noted historical political cartographer Martis (West Virginia Univ.) closely examines the organization, proceedings, and actions of the Confederate Congress. The atlas concentrates on the civilian politi-cal geography of the South as seen through the Provisional Congress of 1861 and the First and Second Permanent Congresses (1862-65). Orga-nized into six chapters and five appendixes, the volume contains 45 full-page maps (all but two in color) along with 48 statistical tables that provide details and analysis on congressional districts, election patterns, and signif-icant regional differences in roll-call voting behavior. In fact, the 106 rep-resentatives and 26 senators had no political party affiliations and thus had a freedom of roll-call voting unprecedented in American legislative his-tory. A variety of topics—e.g., the significant role that Union occupation had on the laws and politics established by the Confederate government, the con-gressional history of the 13 states officially admitted to the Confederacy, and major issues confronting the Confederate Congress (including foreign affairs, military operations, and conscription)—are thoroughly presented in the atlas. All but the concluding chapter begin with a footnoted analytical essay followed by meticulously drawn maps. The appendixes and other appara-tus enhance this excellent reference work. This scholarly volume is path-breaking since it is the first political atlas ever produced on the American Civil War. Upper-division undergraduate and graduate students and research faculty.—*C. C. Hay III, Eastern Kentucky University*

OAB-0263 Orig

Merriam, Louise A. **United States history: a bibliography of the new writings on American history,** comp. by Louise A. Merriam and James W. Oberly. Manchester, 1996 (c1995). (Dist. by St. Martin's) 227p indexes ISBN 0-7190-3688-7, $60.00

This bibliography provides convenient, well-organized access to more than 4,000 carefully selected "important and useful" English-language publications of the 1980s and very early 1990s on American social and political history. Two-thirds of the listings cite books. A special effort was made to include new syntheses and approaches to topics and periods. Most of the journal entries are review articles, or articles not suitable for monographic presentation. Section 1 contains general historiographic and methodological items. Sections 2-8 cover conventional chronological periods, e.g., "The New Nation." Each chronological section is subdivided into the same ten topical subheadings, e.g., "Social History." These subheadings are frequently subdivided, e.g., "Gender Relations," "Class and Community," enabling easy comparison of topics in all the chronological sections. Each entry is numbered, and many include brief annotations. An author index and a subject index with more then 1,300 entries are included. This book will be a useful first stop for undergraduates, graduate students, and higher education teachers. Highly recommended for all academic libraries.—*L. Kincaid, Boise State University*

OAB-0264 F1502 93-49521 CIP

Meyer, Harvey K. **Historical dictionary of Honduras,** by Harvey K. Meyer and Jessie H. Meyer. 2nd ed., rev., enlarged, and updated. Scarecrow, 1994. 708p bibl afp (Latin American historical dictionaries, 25) ISBN 0-8108-2845-6, $77.50

Historical dictionaries are best written by local experts or by outsiders who have immersed themselves in the local culture over an extended period of time. The Meyers, he a retired professor (Univ. of Florida) and she a retired school teacher, have been traveling the roads, airways, lagoons, lakes, and trails of Honduras for more than 40 years. The first fruit of these travels was the first edition of this dictionary, ed. by Harvey Meyer alone (CH, Feb'77). The second edition is a vastly superior dictionary, almost double the size of the original, with 4,276 alphabetically arranged entries. There are new entries for every *municipio,* a detailed list of the colonial governors, a list of intendants from 1787 to 1821, and a complete list of heads of state since 1821. The dictionary defines terms such as "acuerdo" and "banana republic," gives a history of the Bay Islands and the Mosquito Shore, discusses agriculture under such terms as "bananas" and "coffee," and addresses poverty under entries ranging from "Agrarian Reform" to "Tegucigalpa." Largely ignored by the North American press, save for oddities such as the Soccer War of 1969, the region became a staging ground for the Reagan Administration's support of the Nicaraguan contras in the 1980s. This support is described in entries for Elliot Abrams, Oliver North, contras, and Big Pine. Likewise, US involvement in the Honduran economy appears in entries for Standard Fruit and United Brands. There is a historical chronology (250 CE to 1994) and a detailed, topically arranged, annotated bibliography. Numerous black-and-white line-drawn maps and illustrations complement the other information. Overall, this is an outstanding volume, perhaps the best yet published in Scarecrow's historical dictionary series. Academic and public collections at all levels.—*B. E. Coutts, Western Kentucky University*

OAB-0265 E98 92-19990 CIP

Native American women: a biographical dictionary, ed. by Gretchen M. Bataille. Garland, 1993. 333p index afp (Biographical dictionaries of minority women, 1) ISBN 0-8240-5267-6, $40.00

This first in a new series of volumes of biographical sketches of minority women includes brief descriptions of 240 Native American women past and present, ably edited by Bataille (Arizona State Univ.), a specialist in this field, who with Kathleen M. Sands also produced the recent *American Indian Women: A Guide to Research* (CH, Nov'91). A good introductory overview is followed by a selected bibliography of other works on Native American women.

The entries, arranged alphabetically, vary in length because they were written by 62 contributors. Each entry concludes with a list of references on the woman described. Several indexes follow the entries: one by broad and somewhat arbitrary "areas of specialization" (e.g., "activism," "cultural interpretation"); one by decades of birth; one by state/province of birth; one by tribal affiliation; and finally, a general index of subjects and names. The indexes will help facilitate comparative research. Recommended for all Native American and women's studies collections and all larger academic reference collections.—*C. E. Carter, California State University, Fresno*

OAB-0266 E185 CIP

Notable black American women, book II, ed. by Jessie Carney Smith. Gale, 1996. 775p bibl indexes afp ISBN 0-8103-9177-5, $75.00

This second book in the set, like the first, contains narrative biographical essays, personal statements, and photographs of black American women notable for their achievements in many arenas. *Book I* (CH, Jun'92) had 500 entries treating historical and contemporary women; *Book II* has 300, and there is no overlap in coverage. The birth dates of women covered range from 1686 to 1970, and occupations include abolitionists, educators, physicians, journalists, and photographers, among others. Entries are arranged alphabetically, cite sources for further reading, give addresses for living subjects, where possible provide quotations obtained by interviewing the subjects, and often include photographs, which lend the work a welcome personal touch. No ranking by importance is attempted. The indexes, which make this book invaluable and easy to use, include an occupation index, a geographic index (by birthplace and place of residence), and a subject index that covers both volumes in the set. Highly recommended for all levels of readers.—*M. E. Leverence, Governors State University*

OAB-0267 E89 94-36202 CIP

Notable Native Americans, ed. by Sharon Malinowski with George H.J. Abrams. Gale, 1995. 492p bibl index afp ISBN 0-8103-9638-6, $65.00

The recent surge in reference works devoted to Native Americans has yet to subside. This latest offering, a biographical dictionary of Native North Americans, concentrates on prominent living or 20th-century individuals. The signed entries (there are more than 250) range in length from one to four pages, each with a list of sources for further reading and many with accompanying photos or illustrations. Most entries are well written, with general readers in mind, but there are a few exceptions. Typographical errors appear occasionally. Choice of individuals for inclusion was made by an advisory board, but no rationale is provided to explain the presence or absence of particular people. A comparison of several sections with other recent works reveals considerable overlap with the same publisher's *Native North American Almanac* (CH, May'94), although each has unique entries. The current work has essays that are longer and in greater depth, and includes a larger proportion of women. The authors belong to many disciplines and include many younger Native American scholars and writers. Other features include an introductory essay on the nature of Indian identity by consulting editor Abrams, which, while fascinating, has little to do with the work; lists of individuals by tribal affiliation and occupation; and a subject index. Despite minor flaws, this excellent biographical dictionary is highly recommended for all libraries, even those possessing the *Native North American Almanac* or other works.—*J. C. Wanser, Hiram College*

OAB-0268 E668 96-46616 CIP

Richter, William L. **The ABC-CLIO companion to American Reconstruction, 1862-1877.** ABC-Clio, 1996. 504p bibl index afp ISBN 0-87436-851-0, $60.00

Many historians have argued that while the Union won the Civil War, the South won the peace. Reconstruction represented the US's first attempt at social engineering, and by most measures it failed. The fierce historiographical debate over Reconstruction has been waged since that era ended in 1877. Until now, librarians lacked a reference book on this epoch of US history. Richter's book has a historiographical essay and a chronology, but the bulk of it contains descriptive essays on important events, personages, organizations, legislation, and ideas relating to Reconstruction. Each essay not only offers definitions but also puts its subjects in perspective in relation to Reconstruction as well as the historiographical debate. Richter (history, Univ. of Arizona) has done an outstanding job; his book belongs in every college reference collection.—*R. Dyson, Kutztown University of Pennsylvania*

OAB-0269   U52   93-46408 Orig

Schubert, Frank N., comp. **On the trail of the buffalo soldier: biographies of African Americans in the U.S. Army, 1866-1917.** Scholarly Resources, 1995. 519p bibl afp ISBN 0-8420-2482-4, $125.00

Schubert's introduction to the literature and basic sources for biographical information concerning nearly 8,000 soldiers constitutes a collective biography of African American soldiers who served the US during the 50 years between the Civil War and WW I. The bibliography cites monographs, articles, periodicals, newspapers, US government publications and documents, unpublished manuscripts and documents, archival collections, military records, and Veterans Administration pension files. An 11-page appendix includes sections on black enlisted men in the regular Army, 1867-1916; buffalo soldiers killed in action, 1867-1916; buffalo soldier recipients of the Medal of Honor; etc. This compilation and the author's more than 25 years of biographical research on buffalo soldiers (a group of soldiers that contributed substantially to US development) help ensure that buffalo soldiers are not neglected in American history. A commendable, valuable reference, highly recommended for academic libraries.—*F. A. Hall, Virginia Commonwealth University*

OAB-0270   Z1361   95-38637 CIP

Weinberg, Meyer, comp. **Racism in contemporary America.** Greenwood, 1996. 838p bibl indexes afp ISBN 0-313-29659-6, $125.00

Weinberg's comprehensive bibliography cites a wealth of research on myriad topics relating to racism in contemporary America. It is the third in a series from Greenwood (following *Racism in the United States*, CH, Oct'90, and *World Racism and Related Inhumanities*, CH, Nov'92). It contains 14,671 entries and offers 110 pages of indispensable indexing. The contents are arranged under 87 subject headings (e.g., affirmative action, concentration camps, economics of racism, IQ and race, Ku Klux Klan, multiculturalism, racist groups, slavery, women of color). The editor bases his selection on the premise that "racism is an ideology or system of ideas that allocates superiority and inferiority to separate sections of people so as to award privileges to the former and deprivations to the latter." This top-notch, timely bibliography, with numerous citations to pertinent research, will be essential for academic and large public libraries and for researchers.—*M. E. Leverence, Governors State University*

OAB-0271   E77   94-24345 CIP

White, Phillip M. **American Indian studies: a bibliographic guide.** Libraries Unlimited, 1995. 163p indexes ISBN 1-56308-243-8, $29.00

Among many recent publications on Native Americans, this guide stands out as a simple, useful introduction to sources published primarily between 1970 and 1993. Intended for college students, librarians, and selected researchers, it focuses principally on Indians of North America, touching on many aspects of their history and life. Organized by type of publication, the volume includes guides, directories, encyclopedias, bibliographies, biographical sources, theses, newsletters, government publications, microform collections, and computer databases. Periodicals and newspapers, together with indexes for both, are also included. Sources range from specific (e.g., A.E. Hippler's *The Subarctic Athabascans*, 1974) to general (*Abstracts in Anthropology*, 1970-). Most entries are amply annotated. An initial four-page section that describes how to locate books by topic within the Library of Congress (LC) classification and an appendix on LC subject headings complete the volume. Author/title and subject indexes provide access to the listings. More up-to-date than similar

1980s guides (M.L. Haas's *Indians of North America: Methods and Sources for Library Research*, CH Jul'84, and A.B. Hirschfelder's *Guide to Research on North American Indians*, CH, Apr'84), the present volume also includes longer bibliographies than other recent directories and encyclopedias.—*M. R. Dittemore, Smithsonian Institution Libraries*

■ Political Science

OAB-0272   U162   93-17707 CIP

Booth, Ken. **Keyguide to information sources in strategic studies,** by Ken Booth and Eric Herring. Mansell, 1994. 242p index ISBN 0-7201-1960-X, $95.00

A burgeoning interdisciplinary field in universities across the globe, strategic studies encompasses history; political science; economic, peace, and conflict studies; sociology; and psychology. Into this vast wilderness of information step the two authors of this fine reference book. This work most definitely does not suffer from the sin of parochialism, a common problem with many reference works on topics with an international scope. The book is divided into three sections: lucid discussions on the history, structure, contours, and "channels of communication" of strategic studies; a very useful listing of secondary materials for conducting research; and listings of international organizations concerned with strategic studies. The authors, who plan to update this work periodically, have given birth to a wonderful book on a complicated topic. Undergraduate and graduate students.—*R. Dyson, Wabash College*

OAB-0273   F1235   95-840 CIP

Camp, Roderic Ai. **Mexican political biographies, 1935-1993.** 3rd ed. Texas, 1995. 985p bibl afp ISBN 0-292-71174-3, $55.00; ISBN 0-292-71181-6 pbk, $24.95

Few English-language reference works on foreign countries provide the breadth of coverage of this one. It is not a traditional biographical dictionary providing essays and commentary on prominent Mexican politicians of the last half century, but an exhaustive list of 1,950 Mexican politicians prominent since 1935. Earlier editions appeared in 1976 and 1982 (CH, May'83). The 1995 edition, with 50 percent more entries than the second edition, updates information to the end of the Carlos Salinas de Gortari administration. The present president, Ernesto Zedillo, is listed as the PRI candidate for president. Coverage has been broadened to include rectors of the two major Mexico City universities (UNAM and IPN) and third-ranking officials in cabinet departments. There is additional coverage of opposition leaders. Entries provide 12 categories of information from birth to death, including education, elective positions, and family connections. Additional sources of information are listed at the end of the book. Ten appendixes (218 p.) provide valuable lists by term and year for Supreme Court justices, senators, federal deputies, cabinet officials, governors, key party officials of PRI, and selected opposition. Camp (Tulane), a distinguished Mexicanist, is author of other reference works on Mexico (e.g., *Who's Who in Mexico Today*, 2nd ed., 1993, and *Mexican Political Biographies 1884-1935*, CH, Dec'91) and of numerous monographs (including *Political Recruitment across Two Centuries: Mexico, 1984-1991*, 1995). This edition adds Spanish diacritical marks and is crisply printed in larger type on whiter pages. Essential for all academic libraries with an interest in Mexico.—*B. E. Coutts, Western Kentucky University*

UNITED STATES

OAB-0274   E839   96-26176 CIP

Clucas, Richard A. **Encyclopedia of American political reform.** ABC-Clio, 1996. 346p bibl index afp ISBN 0-87436-855-3, $60.00

Clucas correctly assesses the need for a reference source on political reform, especially since public demand for political reform has accelerated in recent years, spurred by Watergate and other scandals. He wisely limits his scope to reforms occurring after 1960 but defines "reform" loosely to include reform proposals, innovations, counterreforms, etc., in four areas: economic reform, increased political participation, more effective government, and government ethics. This helpful book contains entries for actors, issues, and concepts that fostered reform. Entries include investigations like the FBI's "Abscam," reforms ("New Federalism"), law suits that triggered reform (*Serrano* v. *Priest, Buckley* v. *Valeo*), and individuals associated with reform or political change (Betty Friedan, Geraldine Ferraro). A useful chronology follows, which begins in 1960 and lists noteworthy events and reforms each year thereafter. Highly recommended for all college and university reference collections, and particularly for college undergraduates.—*R. T. Ivey, University of Memphis*

OAB-0275 JK1341 93-34324 CIP
Congressional districts in the 1990s: a portrait of America. Congressional Quarterly, 1993. 1,016p indexes ISBN 0-87187-722-8, $150.00

This successor to the highly acclaimed *Congressional Districts in the 1980s* (1983) presents a demographic and economic profile of each US Congressional district, 435 newly redrawn. Profiles are again arranged by state: each state section starts with an overview of the state's redistricting following the 1990 census, a map of the districts, and basic state and district demographic data (population, ethnic and age composition of the voting-age population, income, occupation, education, and residential ownership patterns). District sections begin with a text description of economic and political trends. The statistical portion, now in easier-to-read columnar format, adds to the state overview with election returns from 1986 to 1992 (reconfigured to show political party affiliations of the residents of the new districts) and additional demographic data from the 1990 census (county and city population, land area, race, and ancestry). The rest of the data is like that in the 1980s edition, but is also easier to read: local universities and colleges and their enrollments; major newspapers, television stations and, new to this edition, cable television systems with numbers of subscribers; military installations and population; and the district's major employers, indicating what they do and the number employed. New to this edition is a separate appendix section for the District of Columbia, which has only a nonvoting delegate in the House. "Reapportionment and Redistricting," a theoretical and historical discussion with a historical apportionment table, has moved to the front of the volume. The "Redistricting for the 1990s" prefatory section, like the essay "Redistricting for the 1980s" in the earlier edition, draws a picture of the results of redistricting after the 1990 census, showing the states' gains and losses, the richest and poorest districts, and the 25 districts with the highest percentage of African American and Hispanic residents. The largest and smallest districts and population deviation from the "ideal" size have been dropped. "Sources and Explanations" still describes the scope and criteria of the information gathered. The appendix material has been expanded to include national census tables comparing population, income, education, and housing patterns for the states and a new table of Zip codes by Congressional district, very useful and hard to find elsewhere. The House membership has been updated to include the 100th through the 103rd Congress. The earlier volume had no index; this one has six: city, county, university and college, cable television, military installation, and business name (especially useful). Although the 1990 census volumes for the Congressional districts of the 103rd Congress give far more detail in demographic and housing characteristics, this new work adds other information to the basic statistics to present a descriptive "snapshot" of each district that will be used by political science students, sociologists, and marketers, to name a few. It is an essential reference work for almost any (but the smallest and poorest) college or public library, worth every penny, and no doubt destined to be "an outstanding reference source" just as the 1980s volume was.—*L. Treff, University of Colorado at Denver*

OAB-0276 JK1967 94-19015 CIP
Congressional Quarterly's guide to U.S. elections. 3rd ed. Congressional Quarterly, 1994. 1,543p indexes ISBN 0-87187-996-4, $220.00

The third edition of CQ's *Guide to U.S. Elections* is bigger and better than ever. The extra 238 pages over the previous edition are devoted to the 1988 and 1992 presidential election returns and the 1985-93 congressional/gubernatorial election results. New features include a narrative chronology of 1789-1992 US presidential elections, a "Politics and Issues" narrative for 1945-92 that helps put national and state politics into some semblance of proper context, and a number of other useful ready-reference type sections. The body of the work has three main parts, "Political Parties," "Presidential Elections," and "Gubernatorial and Congressional Elections," all broken down into various subdivisions. The table of contents differs somewhat from that of earlier editions (2nd ed., CH, May '86) to reflect minor changes in the work's organization. There are ten appendixes and seven indexes, including the general index. This magnificent volume continues to be the most comprehensive and authoritative source for reference and background information on the history of US elections. With its invaluable charts, tables, election maps, narratives, etc., this is an absolutely essential purchase for any library that can afford the price.—*S. W. Green, University of Colorado at Denver*

OAB-0277 JX1974 92-36167 CIP
Encyclopedia of arms control and disarmament, ed. by Richard Dean Burns. Scribner, 1993. 3v. 1,692p index afp ISBN 0-684-19281-0, $280.00

A massive work by an editor who is the doyen of arms control bibliography. The contributors include many recognized scholars as well as up-and-coming stars in the field. The 76 articles in the first two volumes are well written and contain excellent bibliographies with some annotations. The third volume changes the approach slightly and includes discussions (with some excerpts and some full texts) of 141 treaties from ancient times to the present that deal with the issues of arms control, disarmament, and neutrality. This set is highly recommended for all libraries, since it will serve either as ready reference for advanced scholars or a strong starting point for beginning scholars or general readers.—*S. J. Stillwell Jr., Harvard University*

OAB-0278 JF501 93-35874 CIP
Encyclopedia of the American legislative system: studies of the principal structures, processes, and policies of Congress and the state legislatures since the Colonial era, ed. by Joel H. Silbey. Scribner, 1994. 3v. 1,738p index afp ISBN 0-684-19243-8, $300.00

This impressive three-volume set covers federal, state, and to a limited degree local legislative structures from Colonial times to the present. The 91 original essays (10-20 pages) are divided into six subject areas: history; recruitment, personnel, and elections (who gets elected and how); structures and processes; behavior (party allegiance, ethics, role of individual committees); specific policy issues; and relationships with nonlegislative entities. Among the authors are David W. Brady, Heinz Eulau, Morris Fiorina, David R. Mayhew, Garrison Nelson, David Rohde, and Barbara Sinclair. Each essay has a short bibliography. "See" references are given to other essays of interest; these would be more useful if they included volume and page numbers. There is no overall index. The clearly written essays are generally more analytical but less fact filled than those in *Congressional Quarterly's Guide to Congress* (2nd ed., CH, May '77). Recommended. General; lower-division undergraduate through graduate.—*C. Teague, Michigan State University*

OAB-0279 UA23 93-49621 CIP
Encyclopedia of the American military: studies of the history, traditions, policies, institutions, and roles of the armed forces in war and peace, ed. by John E. Jessup and Louise B. Ketz. Scribner, 1994. 3v. 2,255p index afp ISBN 0-684-19255-1, $320.00

This three-volume encyclopedia is an important contribution to a field that has spawned a rebirth of scholarship in the last decade. There is no equivalent encyclopedia in print, namely a collection of expertly written, substantive essays by well-known authorities in the field of military affairs. Subjects range from the topical ("Sexual Orientation and the Military") to the broadly historical ("The War of the Revolution"). The work provides overviews of the major military engagements of the US and also treats issues that have transformed the armed forces: the role of women in the modern military, personnel management, education and training, and the military-industrial complex. The more than 65 individual essays range in length from 20 to 50 pages, and most conclude with an excellent bibliography. Jessup and Ketz provide a wealth of information that can be difficult for researchers to find outside of Department of Defense publications, and the treatment and organization should be suitable for all levels of academe. One noticeable drawback is the index. Lesser personages mentioned in the text are not indexed, leading one to conclude initially that coverage is incomplete. These omissions are forgivable, however, in a reference work intended to serve as an introduction to military themes. Recommended for all academic and larger public libraries.—*P. Heller, Norwich University*

OAB-0280 JK511 93-13574 CIP
Encyclopedia of the American presidency, ed. by Leonard W. Levy and Louis Fisher. Simon & Schuster, 1994. 4v. 1,827p indexes afp ISBN 0-13-275983-7 $295.00

The most comprehensive, detailed, and multidisciplinary one-stop resource available on the American presidency. The encyclopedia contains 1,011 essays by 335 contributors covering all aspects of the executive branch of government. A complete list of contributors is provided in the first volume. The articles vary in length depending on the complexity of the issue discussed, but all are well written and end with bibliographies. In commissioning the articles, the editors created a balance of views among the contributors. This is important because the editors encouraged the contributors not only to provide facts, but also to express "opinions and judgements." The encyclopedia is extensively cross-referenced. Particularly helpful is the quick reference table of the presidential cabinets, the table of other key presidential appointed officials, and the synoptic outline of contents. Also included is an index to legal cases and a keyword index. Although expensive, the unbiased and comprehensive coverage of the American presidency that this encyclopedia provides makes it an important investment for all libraries.—*R. V. Labaree, American University*

OAB-0281 JK1067 94-21203 CIP
The Encyclopedia of the United States Congress, ed. by Donald C. Bacon, Roger H. Davidson, and Morton Keller. Simon & Schuster, 1995. 4v. 2,359p bibl index afp ISBN 0-13-276361-3, $355.00

In this set aimed at both specialists and general readers, more than 1,000 entries by 550 faculty, historians, and other authorities on Congress (including the historians of the House and Senate and scholars from the Congressional Research Service) describe and explain the history, functions, and relationships of Congress. First proposed by the late D.B. Hardeman (authority on American politics and former aide and biographer of Speaker Sam Rayburn), the work was supported by the Lyndon B. Johnson Foundation, the University of Texas, and the US Commission on the Bicentennial of the US Constitution. The alphabetically arranged entries cover such topics as "History of Congress"; "Congress" with several subheadings; committees; biographies of former members whose impact has been significant; the ethnic and gender composition of Congress throughout its history; Congress's record in important public policy areas such as civil rights, the environment, social welfare, and taxation; landmark laws; lobbying; women's issues; the 50 states; the Capitol building; and unique subjects such as the portrayal of Congress in literature, the movies, and comedy. Entries include useful tables of related legislation, individuals, etc., as well as illustrations and photographs, and each concludes with a short bibliography. A bibliographical guide, one of the subentries under "Congress," includes printed indexes, journals, books, CD-ROMS, on-line databases, and broadcast media such as C-SPAN but none of the new Internet sites such as GPO Access or Thomas. Finding aids include cross-references to related articles, a subject outline of the contents (but without page numbers), and a detailed index. The Constitution and a glossary of terms which do not have full-length entries are also appended. Coverage is more comprehensive than either *Encyclopedia of the American Legislative System* (CH, Nov'94) or *Congressional Quarterly's Guide to Congress* (4th ed, 1991). The former contains 91 longer analytical essays, also by academicians and historians (some of whom wrote portions of *Encyclopedia of the U.S. Congress*), on

similar aspects of Congress as well as state legislatures. CQ's guide is drawn from staff reports in its *Almanac* and *Weekly Report*, is topically arranged, has only one volume, and generally takes a more factual approach. The alphabetical arrangement of more than 1,000 articles in *Encyclopedia of the U.S. Congress* can facilitate quick reference but requires frequent referral to cross-referenced entries in the other volumes and to the index. The topical outline in the last volume does not have page numbers, so one must use the index to locate articles. Although there is overlap among these three works, each contains unique material with different approaches. All will be staples in academic and public library collections for many years to come. Highly recommended.—*L. Treff, University of Colorado at Denver*

OAB-0282 E183 96-8159 CIP
Encyclopedia of U.S. foreign relations, ed. by Bruce W. Jentleson and Thomas G. Paterson. Oxford, 1997. 4v. 422-490p ea. bibl index afp ISBN 0-19-511055-2, $450.00

As late as 1950, diplomat and historian George F. Kennan noted that foreign policy caused "utter confusion in the public mind." This set attempts to clear up some of that confusion, with extraordinary results. Editors Jentleson and Paterson commissioned 373 scholars and foreign policy analysts to write 1,024 articles on an enormous range of subjects. The majority of articles are brief (less than 1,000 words), but there are also 217 articles that range up to 5,000 words and 51 that run to 10,000. The selection of topics is not without flaws; notable for their omission, for example, are the Tonkin Gulf Resolution, Julius and Ethel Rosenberg, the American Relief Administration, and Owen Lattimore. The volumes are enhanced by a clear and concise introduction that explains key ways of understanding foreign relations, defines eight distinct periods in US diplomatic history, and articulates five core goals that have been the foundation of US foreign policy. Minor flaws aside, this is a masterful achievement that belongs in every library in the US.—*T. Walch, Hoover Presidential Library*

OAB-0283 KF8742 93-23845 CIP
Epstein, Lee. **The Supreme Court compendium: data, decisions, and developments,** by Lee Epstein et al. Congressional Quarterly, 1994. 741p bibl index ISBN 0-87187-771-6, $54.95; ISBN 0-87187-770-8 pbk, $34.95

This compilation of Supreme Court data goes a long way in alleviating the sometimes arduous task of researching the high court. The 160 tables cover such information as the history of the Supreme Court, caseloads and landmark decisions (organized by subject), facts about the Justices, the Court in politics and public opinion, and other courts in the judicial system. Explanatory notes following the tables identify sources, explain data inclusion decisions, and define the legal or technical terms used. Tables such as "Formally Decided Cases by Issue Area, 1953-1991," "Appointment Anomalies," and "Classic Statements from the Bench" (organized by subject) make hard-to-find information readily accessible. This outstanding and much-needed source should prove useful in answering both in-depth and ready-reference questions. Recommended for all libraries.—*M. E. Wall, Carnegie Library of Pittsburgh*

OAB-0284 JX1226 92-4117 MARC
Fox, James R. **Dictionary of international & comparative law.** Oceana, 1992. 495p afp ISBN 0-379-20430-4, $65.00

An excellent beginner's or general reader's dictionary for international and comparative law. Several thousand entries are described briefly, and nearly 100 leading journals were used to provide most entries with annotations. Terms in French, German, Italian, and Latin are included. Cross-references and "see" references are excellent and the treatment of acronyms is clear and helpful. There could be a few more cross-references, e.g., linking the various treaties that ended WW I. Some of the information has gone out of date with the tremendous changes in the international arena; but this is a problem with books in many fields. Recommended wholeheartedly for all libraries, since it will help students who have questions as well as seasoned scholars who need quick citations.—*S. J. Stillwell Jr., Harvard University*

OAB-0285   KF156   95-3863 CIP
Garner, Bryan A. **A dictionary of modern legal usage.** 2nd ed. Oxford, 1995. 953p bibl afp ISBN 0-19-507769-5, $65.00

The second edition is an impressive enhancement of the original edition (CH, Apr'88), although the book jacket's claim that the work is "more than double the length and coverage of the original" is not quite met. The average length of definitions in the first and second editions is remarkably similar (92 and 94 words respectively). The first edition defines approximately 4,200 terms, the second about 7,230. Nevertheless, the work has clearly been improved. The entry for "habeas corpus" can serve as a fine example; in the first edition the term was dispatched in four lines, whereas the second edition provides 27 lines, including historical background. Many other terms have been similarly enhanced. Puzzling is the omission of "sexual harassment"; the first edition includes an entry under "harass" but omits a separate entry for "harassment," while in the second edition under "sex," readers are referred to "sexual," but again there is no "sexual harassment." The second edition provides an entry under "harassment," referring to the Senate hearings on the appointment of Justice Clarence Thomas. In a new feature, the second edition includes thousands of quotes as examples (all with full citations) selected from cases, books, and "other sources." A substantial number of *see* references are incorporated. Some terms receive extended coverage. Garner writes in the preface that he has chosen the "conservative side of usage and grammar," which he calls "informed conservatism." Garner's approach to legal language makes this resource essential to law and social science collections and to all levels of readers, including lawyers.—*G. R. Walden, Ohio State University*

OAB-0286   JK1061   94-47925 CIP
Goehlert, Robert U. **The United States Congress: an annotated bibliography, 1980-1993,** by Robert U. Goehlert and Fenton S. Martin. Congressional Quarterly, 1995. 640p indexes afp ISBN 0-87187-810-0, $185.00

For this update of his *The United States Congress: A Bibliography* (1982), which had 5,620 unannotated entries and covered Congress's first 200 years, Goehlert has added descriptive annotations. Some abstracts for the 3,200 entries were written for this book, some are reprinted or edited from their original form. This edition resembles the earlier one in scope (scholarly books, articles, dissertations, essays in books, and research reports that are for sale and are available in libraries are included, but popular literature, speeches, editorials, and primarily biographical articles are excluded) and in arrangement (by topical sections for history, process, reform powers, investigations, foreign affairs, committees, legislative analysis, leadership, pressures, relations with the electorate, members, and support). A new introduction describes reference sources for researching Congress: almanacs, collective biographies, dictionaries, indexes, bibliographies, atlases, CD-ROM and on-line databases, etc. The bibliography is indexed by author and subject. The only comprehensive bibliography to cover all aspects of Congress, this definitely belongs with the 1982 work in academic and public libraries.—*L. Treff, University of Colorado at Denver*

OAB-0287   DT30   93-42579 CIP
Harris, Gordon, comp. **Organization of African unity.** Transaction, 1994. 139p indexes (International organizations series, 7) ISBN 1-56000-153-4, $51.95

The Organization of African Unity (OAU) was founded in 1963 just as the nations of Africa were becoming independent of colonial powers. Based on the ideal of pan-Africanism, the OAU has managed to survive the end of colonialism, wars of independence, civil wars, ethnic clashes, drought, famine, hopeful periods of economic development, dispiriting years of structural adjustment, apartheid, aggression, military coups, and dictators. The organization has not been notably effective in dealing with crises and longterm problems, but its continued existence provides at least a forum for discussion and a framework for progress. The OAU is not well known or understood outside of Africa, and Harris's useful and well-constructed book provides considerable enlightenment. A thoughtful introduction sets the tone, including valuable information about the lack of official OAU documentation. Other helpful sections include a detailed chronology and lists of acronyms, annual assemblies and meetings of its Council of Ministers, secretaries-general and chairpersons, OAU agencies, and member nations (with a map). The bibliography includes sections on OAU's ideological basis in pan-Africanism, OAU's structure and general assessments of its accomplishments, and commentary on specific issues and events in African and world politics. Clear descriptive annotations add significantly to the ease with which researchers can use this work. Highly recommended.—*G. Walsh, Boston University*

OAB-0288   K3236x   Orig
Human rights bibliography: United Nations documents and publications, 1980-1990, comp. by the United Nations Library, Geneva, in cooperation with the Centre for Human Rights. United Nations, 1993. 5v. 2,048p indexes ISBN 92-1-100377-6 pbk, $95.00

Published on the occasion of the World Conference on Human Rights in June 1993, this bibliography contains approximately 9,000 entries from the UN Bibliographic Information System database. They constitute "the essential references to the most significant documents" on human rights produced by the UN over the ten-year period. The five paperback volumes will be augmented by annual updates and, eventually, by a CD-ROM product. A future companion set will cover a variety of publishers worldwide. Volume 1 is a "Main List By Category," including sections on "violations and threats to the enjoyment of human rights" and "self-determination of peoples." Subcategories include "Namibia question," "disabled persons," and "terrorism and hostage taking." Volumes 2-5 are author indexes listing personal names, agencies and countries, and alphabetical subject indexes. All indexes give the full title and the UN document number. Anything that provides better access to UN documents is welcome. The current world focus on human rights and the increased activities of the UN makes this a valuable addition to all library collections.—*J. Drueke, University of Nebraska-Lincoln*

OAB-0289   U24   92-33750 CIP
International military and defense encyclopedia, ed. by Trevor N. Dupuy et al. Brassey's (US), 1993. 6v. 3,132p index ISBN 0-02-881011-2, $1,250.00

In an effort to provide a single all-encompassing, reliable, multicultural source for international military and defense information, this work provides 785 articles (including 129 for regions or countries complete with historical data) ranging in length from 100 to 10,000 words. Under Dupuy's editorship, more than 400 authors from around the globe have written entries in 17 major subject areas, from "Aerospace Forces and Warfare" to "General Military." Much of the emphasis is on current events, theories, etc., but numerous historical and biographical articles are also provided. Nations are cited under their latest identities (e.g., Belarus, formerly Byelorussia); much of the background information for country entries is based on data from (and may presumably be updated by) *Military Balance* (1963/67-), the *Statesman's Year-Book*, and the C.I.A.'s *World Factbook* (annual, 1984-). Each article is signed, provides "see also" references, and closes with a bibliography. Volume 1 lists all the authors and articles; each volume includes a list of its acronyms and abbreviations. More than 25,000 index terms are employed, an editorially-estimated 7-10 per encyclopedia page. Comprehensive and useful for a wide audience from specialists to general readers; recommended for all reference collections.—*M. J. Smith Jr, Tusculum College*

OAB-0290   JK2352   96-12187 MARC
Kurian, George Thomas. **The encyclopedia of the Republican Party, v.1 & 2; The encyclopedia of the Democratic Party, v.3 & 4,** ed. by George Thomas Kurian with Jeffrey D. Schultz. Sharpe Reference, 1997. 4v. 906, 918p bibl indexes afp ISBN 1-56324-729-1, $399.00

"There can be but two great political parties in this country"—Stephen A. Douglas, 1858 (preface). So at the bicentennial of the birth of political parties in the US, it is fitting to publish a comprehensive encyclopedia that devotes two volumes to each of the two major political parties today. The first volume begins with a history (about 65 p.) of the development of the party through various presidents, political events, and movements, ending with a two-page bibliography of books. Next, almost 50 well-written and interesting signed essays, three to four pages each, give an overview of party position on a wide variety of topics, from abortion to women, and provide cross-references to related articles and a short bibliography. The contributors are mostly university scholars, but a few are well-known authors (e.g., Jessamyn West). The essays include such recent topics as Newt Gingrich and the Contract with America. The first volume concludes with 200 pages of signed biographies, three to four pages each, for the party's presidents, vice presidents, losing presidential candidates, speakers of the House, and other notable party members, together with lists of that party's members of Congress and governors. The second volume consists of brief accounts of each presidential nominating convention and election, but 80 percent of the volume reprints the election platforms. Appendixes document the rules or charter of the party, House and Senate party leaders for each Congress, party defections, convention sites, chairs of the national committees, addresses of the state party headquarters, congressional election statistics, and party affiliations by Congress. Several indexes—general, biographical, geographical, and minorities and women—conclude the set for each party.

These volumes update Arthur M. Schlesinger's *History of U.S. Political Parties* (4v., 1973), which includes many speeches, convention documents, platforms, editorials, magazine articles, and other documents. George Mayer's *Republican Party 1854-1964* (CH, Nov'64) does not include the platform texts. Also similar is William N. Chambers' *The Democrats 1789-1964* (1964). Several recent reference works (*Encyclopedia of the United States Congress*, ed. by D.C. Bacon, R.H. Davidson, and M. Keller, 4v., CH, Sep'95; *Encyclopedia of the American Presidency*, ed. by L.W. Levy and L. Fisher, 4v., CH, Feb'94; and *Political Parties & Elections in the U.S.: An Encyclopedia*, ed. by L.S. Maisel, 2v., CH, Dec'91) include essays on major legislation, policies, issues, biographies, election results, and short histories of the parties, but no texts of platforms. *Congressional Quarterly's Guide to U.S. Elections* (3rd ed., CH, Jan'95) covers national conventions and includes brief histories of the parties and election results. D.B. Johnson and K.H. Porter's *National Party Platforms, 1840-1972* (5th ed., CH, Oct'74) contains the full text of platforms. The original essays in these new volumes on a wide range of topics from the viewpoints of each party set them apart from previous works. Highly recommended for political science reference collections.—*L. Treff-Gangler, University of Colorado at Denver*

OAB-0291 HN59 93-31603 CIP
Leaders from the 1960s: a biographical sourcebook of American activism, ed. by David DeLeon. Greenwood, 1994. 601p index afp ISBN 0-313-27414-2, $75.00

In the 1960s America underwent profound social changes. It was also a time of forceful leaders. This book attempts to identify leaders and their significance. DeLeon (history, Howard Univ.) has divided the book into six parts: "Racial Democracy," "Peace and Freedom," "Sexuality and Gender," "For a Safe Environment," "Radical Culture," and "Visions of Alternative Societies." Each section is introduced by a topical essay that includes a select bibliography of primary and secondary sources. Within each section individual leaders are treated in signed articles of varying length that explain the biographees' background and significance and include a bibliography of works by and about them. The list of contributors, most of them teaching faculty, is impressive. The best feature of this work is its breadth of coverage, which encompasses well-known leaders and individuals who are often forgotten. This is a valuable compendium and sourcebook for all students of the sixties; general and undergraduate collections.—*R. Dyson, Wabash College*

OAB-0292 D412 94-13310 CIP
Lentz, Harris M. **Heads of states and governments: a worldwide encyclopedia of over 2,300 leaders, 1945 through 1992.** McFarland, 1994. 912p index afp ISBN 0-89950-926-6, $95.00

Whether in power for a day or for more than half a century, famous or unknown, the leaders of 190 independent countries each have a substantial biography in this new cumulation. The information is taken from more than 200 sources (listed in the bibliography) on individual countries. The arrangement is by country; then the heads of state, most often presidents, are listed in chronological order followed by the heads of government, most often prime ministers. Individual names, countries, and international organizations can be found through the index. The biographies vary in length (up to one page), but even the shorter entries for lesser-known politicians give quite detailed biographical information that would be difficult to find elsewhere. No other directory covers these lesser-known individuals as well as prominent leaders for almost a 50-year period. Most comprehensive annual political directories that include biographical information for foreign heads of state and government officials—e.g., *The International Year Book and Statesmen's Who's Who*—only cover the current year, and such sources as Jay Shafritz's *The Dictionary of 20th-Century World Politics* (CH, Jan'94) include only selected biographies of the most well-known figures (De Gaulle, Yeltsin, Mao Zedong, Pieter Botha). *Heads of State and Governments* is a unique and valuable reference source for historical biographies of the heads of government worldwide. Highly recommended for academic and public libraries.—*L. Treff, University of Colorado at Denver*

OAB-0293 [CD-ROM]
Local government in Europe, in association with Newmedia Publishing Ltd. Mansell Electronic, 1996. ISBN 0-7201-2299-6 $590.00. 1 disc; user manual. Updates: annual. System requirements: IBM compatible PC 386 or higher; 16-color monitor; 4MB RAM; hard disc with 8MB free space; MS-DOS 3.31 or higher; Windows 3.1 or higher; CD-ROM drive with controller card supporting CD-ROM version 2.2 or higher.

This CD-ROM will prove invaluable for reference librarians and scholars who require a convenient and thorough database on local government in Western Europe; it can also be useful for journalists and professionals who need databases of government personnel there. Finally, it is an excellent research source for undergraduate and graduate students studying European democracies. Installation is simple, using Windows 95 and requiring a password obtained from the publisher on purchase. The CD-ROM holds details of more than 12,500 agencies of local government, nearly 44,000 names, across 16 Western European countries. These data are drawn primarily from *European Municipal Directory* (1995) and *What's What and Who's Who in Europe* (1995). For students and scholars, it contains valuable though brief descriptions of each country's local government administration, taxation, political authority, history, economy, and demography, and a host of other useful information pertaining to each country's units of local government. Maps of individual countries and subnational divisions are basic and plentiful, but too general; the geographical locations of local governmental units are not identified on detailed maps. Nonetheless, users may easily search the databases for personnel by country and subnational geographical region, as well as government unit. Bonus features include the ability to print address labels and send faxes. This easy-to-use reference tool should be a standard addition to research libraries.—*J. D. Robertson, Texas A&M University*

OAB-0294 Orig
Longman biographical directory of decision-makers in Russia and the successor states, ed. by Martin McCauley. Longman Current Affairs, 1994 (c1993). (Dist. by Gale) 726p index ISBN 0-582-20999-4, $152.00

The continuing upheavals in the former Soviet Union took many Western observers by complete surprise. As new states sprout from the ruins of that vast Eurasian empire, new elites will achieve eminence within them. The West has been too used to the dubious idea that a "Who's Who in the Soviet Union" means one thing: Russians. McCauley's new biographical dictionary dispels that notion. This is the most up-to-date biographical guide to the new leaders of the Russian federation and the successor states to the former Soviet empire. In the directory, leadership and membership in the new elite classes is cross-societal. Orthographical changes are given (e.g., Kirgizia is now Kyrgystan), as are city name changes. Confusing as this might be, it is helpful that McCauley provides a current list of the bewildering new national subdivisions like the Republic of Komi and the North Ossetian Republic. A glossary is sprinkled with numerous Russian terms with English explanations. The biographical entries are alphabetical; however, there are appended helpful lists of those entries by national state and topic (for example, dissidents in Russia and writers in Georgia). The entries themselves are remarkably detailed and sometimes include addresses and telephone numbers. Although most of the subjects are either Russian, Ukrainian, or Belorussian, the other successor nations are far from neglected. Strongly recommended for all libraries.—*A. N. Vinh, Yale University*

OAB-0295 HV6431 92-46525 CIP
Mickolus, Edward F. **Terrorism, 1988-1991: a chronology of events and a selectively annotated bibliography.** Greenwood, 1993. 916p afp (Bibliographies and indexes in military studies, 6) ISBN 0-313-28970-0, $125.00

The fourth volume of a series that unfortunately must continue, there being still a need to write, publish, review, and discuss books on international terrorism. The book is in three parts, the first an update on various terrorist incidents that occurred between 1960 and 1987. The second section (the bulk of the book) is a review of terrorist incidents 1988-91, ranging from bombings that break a few windows to those that bring down airliners, as well as assassinations, hijackings and kidnappings, and the rest of the litany of violence. Names of perpetrators and victims are included where possible. The final piece is an excellent bibliography on terrorism. Some of the entries are annotated, and occasionally an author is noted as an authority on the subject. The bibliography includes books and journal articles in many languages. Works of fiction and other bibliographies are also included. Highly recommended, all levels.—*S. J. Stillwell Jr., Harvard University*

OAB-0296 E185 92-34223 CIP
Murray, Paul T. **The civil rights movement: references and resources.** G.K. Hall, 1993. 265p indexes afp ISBN 0-8161-1837-X, $40.00

The civil rights movement has engendered countless publications, but attempts to deal with the subject as a whole have been few. Thus, it is some relief to find in Murray's effort more than a bibliography, but a bibliographic guide to what is probably the most significant social upheaval in the US in the 20th century. Following an introductory essay reviewing the trends of the literature, some 1,389 entries covering English-language materials through 1991 are divided among 41 headings. Left out are the innumerable news articles from contemporary papers and magazines, as well as subjects already covered elsewhere (e.g., Martin Luther King, school integration, and employment discrimination). Murray also excluded black nationalism as a subject in its own right, although the debate that it caused within the civil rights movement is discussed, as are the organizations of reaction: White Citizens Councils, Ku Klux Klan, and the like. A particular strength is the well-crafted annotations for each item, and the comprehensive index also deserves praise. An important book and one required for all academic libraries.—*P. L. Holmer, Southern Connecticut State University*

OAB-0297 DT352 91-39641 CIP
Political leaders of contemporary Africa south of the Sahara: a biographical dictionary, ed. by Harvey Glickman. Greenwood, 1992. 361p index afp ISBN 0-313-26781-2, $65.00

In-depth analytical entries for 54 political leaders who have most shaped political events in sub-Saharan Africa since 1945. Social scientists who are authorities on African politics selected the subjects and wrote the entries. Each entry includes information on the leader's personal life; education, including formal schooling and informal training; leadership skills; political goals, means mobilized to carry them out, and extent to which they were accomplished; an assessment of the leader's impact on his country, within and outside Africa; and a short bibliography of works by and about the leader. The entries

are well written, authoritative, and easy to compare, even though the styles differ. An appendix lists leaders by country and a chronology from 1892 to 1991 includes major events from the leaders' lives and selected political events of significance for the subcontinent. Themes in sub-Saharan Africa are discussed in an introduction. There is a select bibliography on politics and political elites in sub-Saharan Africa since 1945 and an index of personal and corporate names and countries. For the 54 persons covered, the entries are more detailed and authoritative than those in Alan Rake's *Who's Who in Africa: Leaders for the 1990s* (CH, Oct'92). Leaders from Sudan and North Africa are included in *Political Leaders of the Contemporary Middle East and North Africa*, ed. by Bernard Reich (CH, Jul'90). An important reference work for academic libraries at all levels.—*N. J. Schmidt, Indiana University-Bloomington*

OAB-0298 Orig
Political parties of Eastern Europe, Russia and the successor states, ed. by Bogdan Szajkowski. Stockton, 1994. 735p bibl index ISBN 1-56159-079-7, $195.00

This extensive, annotated listing of political parties and movements in 27 countries is well organized, clearly written, and highly informative. The directory is arranged by country; each section begins with a brief essay on recent political history and provides, where available, substantial information about election results. The selection of parties and movements is broad, including former communist parties, parties that grew out of "dissident" groups, nationalist parties, and groups devoted to particular ethnic or religious affiliation as well as those with topical platforms such as the environment or feminism. Individual entries range in length from very brief (four lines) to several pages long (with footnotes where applicable) and include information such as address, telephone/fax, leadership, membership, history, program, and publications. The volume includes a general bibliography, helpful cross-references, and an index. Future editions would benefit from expanded coverage of the Russian Federation and more subject headings in the index, and the history sections would be more useful if they included both translated and original-language names of the corporate bodies cited. Highly recommended for college and research libraries.—*S. C. Summer, Columbia University*

OAB-0299 JQ1758 93-25067 CIP
Political parties of the Middle East and North Africa, ed. by Frank Tachau. Greenwood, 1994. 711p index afp ISBN 0-313-26649-2, $125.00

This is an excellent work, one that can be highly recommended for all college libraries whose students or faculty have any interest in Middle Eastern history or politics—or current world events. Each country of the region—and the Palestinians—has an introductory chapter, a bibliography, and a dictionary of political parties past and present. The book is worth the price for the bibliographies alone. If the nation does not have any party structure, the country's political system is still reviewed. The political party lists are cross-referenced using acronyms, which is always helpful. There are more than two dozen tables, including complete Knesset election results, and many helpful notes to each chapter. The two appendixes could have been broken down and included in the individual chapters. One appendix, "Genealogy of Parties," shows the merging, splintering, and re-merging of parties, which is so prevalent in this region. The index is excellent and the contributor list is an impressive one, including many distinguished scholars of Middle Eastern studies in American academic institutions. All academic collections.—*S. J. Stillwell Jr., formerly, Harvard University*

OAB-0300 JK518 95-33031 CIP
Ragsdale, Lyn. **Vital statistics on the presidency: Washington to Clinton.** Congressional Quarterly, 1996. 455p bibl index afp ISBN 1-56802-050-3, $46.95; ISBN 1-56802-049-X pbk, $32.95

A revision of Gary King's *The Elusive Executive* (CH, Mar'89), this book can best be described as akin to a statistical abstract of the American presidency, but more valuable because descriptive analyses accompany the data. The book is meant to reflect the American presidency as an institution rather than "emphasizing the uniqueness of individual presidents." It begins with an introductory chapter that outlines the content and examines current research trends associated with the presidency. Nine chapters follow that present data under broad topics reflecting the institution of the presidency. Chapter 1 gives data about the individual presidents; chapters 2-3 cover election data and the nominating process; chapters 4-5 provide statistics that reflect institutional behavior, by examining public appearances by the presidents and presenting public opinion data; chapters 6-7 look at the organizational structure of the presidency; chapters 8-9 examine data that illustrate the relation between the White House and other institutions in government. As with most statistical compilations, no data are presented here that are not available in other sources. The book intends to collect statistics from many sources in a single easy-to-use resource. However, its greatest value lies in the introductory essays before each chapter. Each is well written, places the data in historical context, shows how a quantitative analysis of the American presidency can broaden and enhance our understanding of institutional behavior, and explains how the statistics may highlight trends and issues regarding the executive office. Each of the approximately 150 statistical charts and tables is clearly presented and always lists the source of the data. An essential source for all libraries.—*R. V. Labaree, University of Southern California*

OAB-0301 D843 96-38573 CIP
Schwartz, Richard Alan. **The Cold War reference guide: a general history and annotated chronology, with selected biographies.** McFarland, 1997. 321p bibl index afp ISBN 0-7864-0173-7, $55.00

Schwartz offers a US perspective on the Cold War that focuses on the US and the former Soviet Union and presents a greater number of detailed sketches of US figures than of leaders from other major powers. Liberal and conservative views on important issues are included to ensure objectivity. Section 1 provides background on the entire postwar period and is especially useful for identifying changes in US policy. Ensuing chapters expand on shifts in policy: containment (1947-54), massive retaliation (1954-69), mutually assured destruction (1969-79), and winnable nuclear war (1980-90). Section 2 covers McCarthyism, the Korean conflict, the Cuban missile crisis, the Vietnam War and protest activities, and more. Section 3 is an annotated chronology of important events, while section 4 contains biographies of prominent Cold War figures. These sketches vary in length from one to nine pages. Heads of state and cabinet officials receive the most attention (e.g., Dean Acheson, Henry Kissinger, John Foster Dulles, and presidents Truman, Eisenhower, Nixon, and Reagan). World leaders, treated separately, include Konrad Adenauer, Leonid Brezhnev, Nikita Khruschev, Mikhail Gorbachev, and Deng Xiaoping. A topical bibliography and subject index complete this useful volume, which provides lower-division undergraduates with an excellent introduction to the field and is highly recommended for all academic libraries.—*G. D. Barber, SUNY College at Fredonia*

OAB-0302 JA61 93-15204 CIP
Shafritz, Jay M. **The dictionary of 20th-century world politics,** by Jay M. Shafritz, Phil Williams, and Ronald S. Calinger. H. Holt, 1993. 756p afp ISBN 0-8050-1976-6, $60.00

An excellent and resourceful reference tool for information about the language, terminology, and personalities of modern world history and politics. Shafritz, Williams, and Calinger have created a superior source that provides informed, concise, up-to-the-minute definitions as well as informative (and often entertaining) biographical sketches. The diversity of terms defined is striking. There are nearly five pages of definitions for some variation of "diplomat," "diplomacy," or "diplomatic"; many buzz words (e.g., "skinheads") are cited that do not appear in Walter Raymond's *Dictionary of Politics* (CH, Jan'93) or *Oxford Companion to Politics of the World* (CH, Sep'93). The latter two, surprisingly, do not contain a definition for Secretary of State, but Shafritz et al. give an excellent, balanced definition with biographical sketches for each American Secretary of State in the century. The book's strongest points are its biographical notes, which often offer quotes and asides that range from solemn

to irreverent. Although biographical sketches of the most familiar figures of the century are excellent, the authors give equal attention to major figures often neglected in dictionary-style reference sources. A wide range of terms and personalities from the developing world, and consistent use of cross-references, quotes, and tables are included. First-rate, well conceived, and wittily written. Highly recommended for academic, college, school and personal libraries.—*M. Whichard, University of North Carolina at Chapel Hill*

OAB-0303 Orig
Stern, Peter A. **Sendero Luminoso: an annotated bibliography of the Shining Path Guerrilla Movement, 1980-1993.** SALALM Secretariat, General Library, University of New Mexico, 1995. (Dist. by SALALM Secretariat, Benson Latin American Collection, Sid Richardson Hall 1.109, University of Texas at Austin, Austin, TX 78713) 363p indexes ISBN 0-917617-43-6 pbk, $56.95

From the beginning of the last decade until the early part of this one, *Sendero Luminoso* (Shining Path), a Peruvian Marxist guerilla movement, seemed poised, with singular violence and slaughter, to take over the government of Peru. Stern has compiled the first thorough, but admittedly not comprehensive, annotated bibliography of books and periodical articles published in Peru and the US on this pivotal movement. For 1,185 entries, organized in chapters by year of publication, Stern's critical annotations, generally of at least 200 words, provide both a sense of the history and development of *Sendero Luminoso* and a thoughtful overview of it. The work is well indexed (author and subject), facilitating its use for both reference and research, as one would expect from this publisher. Use is enhanced by a list of acronyms and terms, a chronology, and a note on sources allowing one to track future Shining Path developments. This last, given the vicissitudes of Latin American politics, may prove the most timely, reinforcing the ongoing relevance of Stern's work. Highly recommended for academic collections.—*E. A. Riedinger, Ohio State University*

OAB-0304 JC319 91-57956 CIP
Sukhwal, B.L. **Political geography: a comprehensive systematic bibliography,** by B.L. Sukhwal and Lilawati Sukhwal. AMS Press, 1996. 715p index afp (AMS international studies, 1) ISBN 0-404-63151-7, $159.50

For the most comprehensive bibliography on political geography ever compiled, the editors thoroughly scoured the geographical literature for citations. Seventeen chapters, which include 17,382 entries, are each divided into general and theoretical sections for the topic and for regional works. Along with the standard works on general and historical political geography, the editors include chapters on the organization of political territory; categories of nation states; frontiers, boundaries, and buffer zones; civilizations and cultures; electoral geography; the geography of international relations; colonialism, geopolitics and geostrategy; and the political geography of the oceans. Most of the entries cite English-language publications, but citations to non-English publications are included. Both books and journal articles are included. The bibliography's only drawback is its lack of annotations, but the work's comprehensiveness more than compensates for this deficiency. Highly recommended for all institutions supporting programs at any level in geography, political science, and international studies.—*J. C. Stachacz, Dickinson College*

OAB-0305 KF8744 93-1446 CIP
The Supreme Court justices: illustrated biographies, 1789-1993, ed. by Clare Cushman. Congressional Quarterly, 1993. 576p bibl index ISBN 0-87187-723-6, $39.95

Developed by The Supreme Court Historical Society, this is the first one-volume reference work presenting biographical sketches of all 106 justices from John Jay to Clarence Thomas. Entries are arranged chronologically by date of appointment. Coverage spans the justices' lives, including their families, educational backgrounds, and pre-Supreme Court careers. Contributions to the Supreme Court are discussed in relation to their philosophies and to the major cases and opinions that shaped their unique roles on the Court. This work helps to humanize the image of the justices and lends insight into the different personalities that made up each Court. A primary strength is the recognition the work gives to the many justices that have received little or no attention from the general public. Illustrations include a portrait of each justice, photographs, and political cartoons. A handy chart of the justices is included that lists important dates, the states each represented, the president who appointed them, whom they replaced, and their years of service. The volume concludes with an extensive bibliography and index. Given the outstanding content and affordable price, no general reference collection should be without this handsome and impressive new work. Strongly recommended for general and academic collections.—*M. E. Wall, Carnegie Library of Pittsburgh*

OAB-0306   KF8742   93-2979 CIP
The Supreme Court A to Z: a ready reference encyclopedia, ed. by Elder Witt. Congressional Quarterly, 1993. 528p bibl index (CQ's encyclopedia of American government, 3) ISBN 0-87187-777-5, $110.00

The final volume in this series, this work follows the same ready-reference format as the two previous volumes, *Congress A to Z* (CH, Mar'89) and *The Presidency A to Z* (CH, May'93). The easy-to-use arrangement of essays and shorter entries sets this source apart from other works on the Supreme Court. Much of the content is drawn from Witt's *Guide to the US Supreme Court* (2nd ed., 1990). Entries treat abortion to zoning and provide background on important cases and decisions, procedures of the Court, short biographies of the justices, the history of almost all the constitutional amendments, and the meanings behind legal terms and phrases such as "stare decisis" and "due process." Appendixes include the Supreme Court nominations, 1789-1992; a seating chart for the justices; and a US government organizational chart. The index and extensive cross-references make this single volume especially useful and convenient for supplying quick answers to frequently-asked questions. An outstanding encyclopedia, recommended for all libraries.—*M. E. Wall, Carnegie Library of Pittsburgh*

OAB-0307   JC423   96-44880 CIP
Van Wyk, J.J. **Contemporary democracy: a bibliography of periodical literature, 1974-1994,** by J.J. van Wyk and Mary C. Custy. Congressional Quarterly, 1997. 449p index ISBN 1-56802-244-1, $120.00

Political scientist van Wyk and librarian Custy have produced a first-rate multidisciplinary bibliography of scholarly journal citations on democracy, the first known to this reviewer. Inspired by the global resurgence of democracy in the late 1970s, this ambitious undertaking, a boon to students and scholars, conveniently synthesizes the burgeoning periodical literature on the subject. Its expansive approach, including "any article" from some 1,400 journals "that dealt with democracy in one form or another," ensures thoroughness, if not total comprehensiveness. The meticulously prepared, 116-page subject index is the principal access point to the bibliographic section of several thousand entries. Primary and occasional secondary subdivisions of principal terms are drawn from geographic names, institutions, individuals, important events, or major concepts, and are divided into subcategories such as "Islam" and into subtopics ("democratization," "fundamentalism"). Although English-language sources predominate, this is a minor shortcoming of this useful work, recommended for all college and university political science research collections.—*D. Ettinger, George Washington University*

OAB-0308   Orig
Vital statistics on Congress, 1993-1994, ed. by Norman J. Ornstein, Thomas E. Mann, and Michael J. Malbin. Congressional Quarterly, 1994. 279p index ISBN 0-87187-778-3, $42.95; ISBN 0-87187-779-1 pbk, $28.95

A relatively slim volume that contains a wealth of information on Congress. More than 100 tables detail facts on the members of Congress and their work. The chapters on the members, elections, campaign finance, committees, staff and operating expenses, workload, budgeting, and voting alignments provide historical and current figures. Published biennially, the 1993-94 edition updates

the tables variously through 1991, 1992, or 1993. A brief introduction to each chapter provides an overview of the topic and trends. Eighteen charts and graphs supplement the statisstical tables, and the 57-page appendix presents information on individual members of the 103rd and 102nd Congresses, such as years of service, age, election results, and voting ratings by various groups such as Americans for Democratic Action. Various public and private sources are used for all data. This is the only source available for such extensive statistical data on Congress. *Congress A to Z* (CH, Mar'89) and the *Guide to Congress*, (4th ed., 1991) contain fewer than 18 statistical tables each, concentrating on such basics as workload, pay, campaign expenditures, ethnic composition, and votes. No library serving a political science curriculum should be without *Vital Statistics*.—*L. Stwalley, University of Colorado at Denver*

OAB-0309   KF478   95-46893 CIP
Women's legal guide, ed. by Barbara R. Hauser with Julie A. Tigges. Fulcrum, 1996. 526p bibl index ISBN 1-55591-913-8, $39.95; ISBN 1-55591-303-2 pbk, $22.95

A handy, well-organized, comprehensive compendium, *Women's Legal Guide* aims to help women make informed decisions by providing information and guidance in negotiating both straightforward and complex legal questions. Beginning with a chapter on selecting and working with a lawyer, this handbook is arranged in five broad sections: personal/body issues, family law, women's rights at school and in the workplace, business law, and life planning. Twenty-nine female attorneys contribute chapters focusing on a wide range of expected legal issues of particular concern to women including health care, marriage and divorce, spousal and family violence, sexual harassment, and retirement and estate planning. Of particular note, however, are chapters dealing with timely and relevant issues such as child care planning for seriously ill mothers, sports, legal rights of lesbian women, disabilities, and legal issues for refugee women. Chapters are enhanced by bibliographies and organizational resources for further information and assistance. A glossary and comprehensive index round out the volume. Priced reasonably enough for personal collections, and essential for academic and public libraries.—*J. Ariel, University of California, Irvine*

■ Psychology

OAB-0310   Orig
Companion encyclopedia to psychology, ed. by Andrew M. Colman. Routledge, 1994. 2v. 1,356 index afp ISBN 0-415-06446-5, $199.95

Defining psychology as the science of the nature, functions, and phenomena of behavior, Colman (Univ. of Leicester) presents an impressive array of self-contained essays grouped thematically under 13 broad headings such as sensation and perception, cognition, emotion and motivation, and abnormal psychology. A concise introduction before each essay outlines the contents, indicates cross-references, and discusses technical terms and concepts. Numerous illustrations and the glossary of technical terms serve as aids in visualizing and comprehending difficult discussions. Each essay concludes with a list of further readings and references. The detailed index allows easy access to topics. An update of the first edition published a decade ago, this in-depth reference covers all major branches of psychological research and professional practice. Contributors include J. Allan Hobson, Leonard Hamilton, Harvey Schiffman, Donald Baer, and K. Anders Ericsson. For those interested in additional reference works, the *Encyclopedia of Psychology* (2nd ed., 1994) offers a different approach to similar information. Scholarly, well researched, and authoritative, Colman's work will be a welcome addition to any public, academic, or health science center reference collection. Highly recommended.—*J. M. Coggan, University of Florida*

OAB-0311   BF31   93-34371 CIP
Encyclopedia of human behavior, ed. by V.S. Ramachandran. Academic Press, 1994. 4v. 651-728p ea. index afp ISBN 0-12-226920-9, $499.00

This encyclopedia fills a 20-year need for a comprehensive reference source in this area of study. Though there have been major advances in our understanding of human behavior, particularly in the fields of neuroscience and psychology, and though there are very fine encyclopedias and handbooks for psychology, psychiatry, and medicine, until now no interdisciplinary or encyclopedic source has updated Robert Goldenson's *Encyclopedia of Human Behavior* (1970). The encyclopedia is organized alphabetically by subject. Essays are written by experts in the field and contain an outline of contents, a glossary, and a comprehensive discussion that includes history, theories, theorists, implications, interventions, treatments, and conclusions. Articles are cross-referenced and a bibliography is included for each entry. A very good index provides a complete listing of where and in what context a topic is covered within the broad subject areas. Volume 4 includes a list of all contributors and their credentials. A "must have" acquisition for university, health science, and special libraries.—*N. L. Powell, Catholic University of America*

OAB-0312   BF431   93-46975 CIP
Encyclopedia of human intelligence, ed. by Robert J. Sternberg. Macmillan, 1994. 2v. 1,235p bibl index afp ISBN 0-02-897407-7, $175.00

Sternberg (Yale Univ.) has edited a remarkable two-volume encyclopedia on human intelligence. More than 250 alphabetically arranged entries cover a variety of topics in articles with titles ranging from "Birth Order, Spacing, and Family Size" and "Bias in Testing" to "Latent Trait Theory" and "Artificial Intelligence." Historical perspectives are also discussed under "Galton, Francis," "Piagetian Theory of Intellectual Development," and "Evolution of Human Intelligence." Entries are cross-referenced and signed. Top scholars from the field have contributed to this work, including Hans Eysenck, Lloyd Humphreys, and Arthur Jensen. This unique reference tool is of exceptional quality from the standpoint of both variety of coverage and continuity of content. A superb encyclopedia that is highly recommended for all libraries.—*K. Condic, Oakland University*

OAB-0313   RC437   95-41116 CIP
The Encyclopedia of psychiatry, psychology, and psychoanalysis, ed. by Benjamin B. Wolman. H. Holt, 1996. 649p bibl index afp ISBN 0-8050-2234-1, $135.00

Jean Piaget's foreword to *International Encyclopedia of Psychiatry, Psychology, Psychoanalysis, and Neurology* (CH, Apr'78) described it as an "ambitious but infinitely useful ... great work." The primary drawback to this impressive reference source was its price. Twenty years later its editor-in-chief Wolman has assembled a single-volume synthesis that contains the "best of the best" from the original set in an abridged, revised, and updated version. It has new entries, a new bibliography, the original easy-to-use alphabetical arrangement, and coverage of the most significant advances in the field since 1977. This reference source both updates the original publication and makes it affordable to researchers, students, and practitioners in the mental health field. Wolman decided that neurology warranted a separate volume, omitted descriptions of developments in other countries, and shortened the biographical entries, but he reviewed every entry from the original publication. More than 680 authors are represented in the hundreds of entries. Although no single volume can contain knowledge of all the fields of psychology, this encyclopedia will serve as an excellent starting place for research. Very highly recommended for general readers and upper-division undergraduates through faculty.—*J. M. Coggan, University of Florida*

OAB-0314   BF31   93-22638 CIP
Encyclopedia of psychology, ed. by Raymond J. Corsini. 2nd ed. Wiley-Interscience, 1994. 4v. 533-668p ea. bibl indexes afp ISBN 0-471-55819-2, $475.00

For those libraries that missed the first edition (CH, Dec'84) and those that can update their holdings, the second edition of this unmatched encyclopedia retains about 90 percent of the material in the first edition while adding about 2,000 pages to the subject and bibliographical entries. More than 500

experts from around the world have contributed essays in all fields of psychology. The first three volumes contain subject entries, cross-references, and additional readings. Volume 4 contains biographies, bibliographies, a subject and name index, an appendix titled "Ethical Principles of Psychologists and Code of Conduct," and sample "Contracts for Practicing Psychologists." This work walks the user through the entire field of psychology, guided by a who's who of today's psychologists. Recommended for all libraries.—*N. L. Powell, Catholic University of America*

■ Sociology

OAB-0315   HV5138   94-41371 CIP
Alcoholism and aging: an annotated bibliography and review, comp. by Nancy J. Osgood, Helen E. Wood, and Iris A. Parham. Greenwood, 1995. 250p indexes afp (Bibliographies and indexes in gerontology, 24) ISBN 0-313-28398-2, $65.00

Although the percentage of older people in the population is increasing, other age groups are better covered than the elderly in alcoholism research. The compilers offer an excellent and thorough attempt to identify research that focuses on alcoholism in the elderly. The book has five chapters: literature review, overview of articles, books and book chapters, empirical studies, and miscellaneous works. First comes a valuable literature review covering diagnostic tools, stress factors and alcoholism, early versus late onset, etc. In the other sections, cited titles have annotations written for this book which are lengthy, informative, detailed, and invaluable. The book deals with the need for detection, treatment, and prevention of alcoholism in older adults. It is a toss-up as to which part of the book is better—the 50-page literature overview or the annotated lists. Highly recommended for health care providers, ministers, social workers, service agencies, addictions professionals, and students of these disciplines, as well as for friends and families of alcoholics.—*M. E. Leverence, Governors State University*

OAB-0316   HN60   95-5648 CIP
Andrews, Alice C. **The atlas of American society,** by Alice C. Andrews and James W. Fonseca. New York University, 1995. 303p bibl index afp ISBN 0-8147-2626-7, $40.00

This atlas covers a variety of social issues in a clear and concise format by presenting for each topic a map, explanatory text, and, in some cases, additional charts as illustrations. Readers at a glance can identify local, state, and national trends in each of the following areas: affluence versus poverty, crime and violence, demographics (birth, marriage, and divorce rates among others), education, ethnic and cultural diversity, health, disease and other medical issues, migration, politics and religion, rural/urban population, and the status of women, children, and older adults. The authors cover areas of topical interest to students as well as researchers by including data and maps on homelessness, crime rates, and poverty rates, to name but a few. Reference librarians will find this an invaluable source for answering questions on many social issues. For each topic, an appendix lists each state's rank, which is very helpful in comparing trends by state and by region. A national summary is also included. Highly recommended for all collections.—*G. A. Schultis, Park College*

OAB-0317   GN480   94-38979 CIP
Broude, Gwen J. **Marriage, family, and relationships: a cross-cultural encyclopedia.** ABC-Clio, 1995 (c1994). 372p bibl index afp ISBN 0-87436-736-0, $49.50

Broude treats major topics relevant to human relationships from a cross-cultural perspective. For more than 560 cultures, the book discusses beliefs, customs, taboos, etc. It also provides excellent historical bases and present-day norms for cultural activities such as double standards in sexual behavior, adolescent male-female interaction, attitudes towards sex, marriage customs, spouse beating, and the incest taboo. This wealth of sociological information features fascinating differences and similarities among cultures. In an age of multiculturalism, it is an essential reference tool. Entries, in alphabetical order, include cross-references, bibliographic citations, a beneficial subject index, and 30 illustrations. Social science research on many societies of the world is summarized; e.g., the Igbo of Nigeria, the Kapauku of New Guinea, the Taiwanese, and Native American cultures. Unique discussions of US customs are contrasted with social practices of other cultures. A timely, well-organized reference source. Highly recommended for academic or public libraries.—*M. E. Leverence, Governors State University*

OAB-0318 Orig

The Complete directory for people with learning disabilities: products, resources, books, services: a one-stop sourcebook for individuals and professionals. 1993/94 ed. Grey House, 1993. 539p indexes ISBN 0-939300-24-9 pbk, $125.00

An excellent, timely, one-stop resource both for people with learning disabilities and those who live or work with the learning disabled. It is packed with 5,900 entries about schools, learning centers, colleges (arranged by state), screening/testing resources, government agencies, transition skills and employment programs, associations, newsletters, and support services for the learning disabled. Multifaceted, it includes more than 160 videos, 1,525 computer software packages, assistive devices, testing centers, toys, games, books, camps, and summer programs all geared to those with learning disabilities. Classroom materials and computer sections are arranged by subject. The 50-page detailed index makes information very accessible. A computerized version is also available. Other disability reference books by this publisher are *The Complete Directory for People with Disabilities* (CH, Jul'92) and *The National Housing Directory for People with Disabilities* (CH, Apr'93). In this age, characterized by the American Disabilities Act and the desire to serve the special learner, this book is highly recommended for all libraries; it will be vital to people with learning disabilities and the libraries that serve them.—*M. E. Leverence, Governors State University*

OAB-0319 Orig

Crime in America's top-rated cities: a statistical profile, ed. by Rhoda Garoogian and Andrew Garoogian. 1995-1996 ed. Universal Reference Publications, 1995. 759p ISBN 1-881220-28-1 pbk, $75.00

The Garoogians' massive compendium provides statistics for the past 20 years in all major crime areas (murder, rape, robbery, etc.) for some 75 US cities included in their *America's Top-Rated Cities: A Statistical Handbook* (CH, Feb'93, 3rd ed., 1995). The editors have neatly repackaged information drawn from numerous government sources (most notably the FBI's *Uniform Crime Reports for the United States*) to present multiyear tables and graphs under uniform subject headings. Entries are alphabetically arranged by city with statistical data and graphs prefaced by an overview of the city's crime problem, 1975-94, its anticrime programs, and the statistical risk individuals have of becoming victims. The source also includes statistics on illegal drugs, correctional facilities, inmates and HIV/AIDS, the death penalty, and gun laws. Although this information is accessible through a variety of government sources, this statistical profile of several cities (judged in various magazine surveys to be among the best places for business and living) presents these data in a clear and concise manner. Highly recommended for large public, college, and university libraries.—*D. K. Frasier, Indiana University-Bloomington*

OAB-0320 HV9471 95-41593 CIP

Encyclopedia of American prisons, ed. by Marilyn D. McShane and Frank P. Williams. Garland, 1996. 532p bibl index afp (Garland reference library of the humanities, 1748) ISBN 0-8153-1350-0, $95.00

The editors provide more than 150 signed articles, two to 20 pages in length, on all aspects of prisons, including AIDS, crowding, correctional officers,

history, legal issues, and prison industries. Articles treat specific prisons (Alcatraz, Attica, Sing Sing) and important people (Dorthea Dix, Benjamin Rush). Up-to-date bibliographies (articles, books, and relevant cases) follow most articles. Excellent for overviews of prison life, history, management, and procedures, the book is less helpful for specific facts. One must dig through the article on executions to learn when the last woman was executed; there is no table by state of the number of inmates on death row. Housekeeping inconsistencies include entries in two forms: "sentences, excessive" and "indeterminate sentences." The index could be much improved: some major subheadings (e.g., "career opportunities" under "Correctional Officers") are omitted, as are specific gangs (e.g., Aryan Brotherhood, the Mexican Mafia), although they receive a lengthy paragraph under "Gangs." However, this lack of depth in indexing does not seriously detract from an otherwise very valuable work. Essential for academic libraries supporting criminal justice programs.—*K. F. Muther, California State University, Sacramento*

OAB-0321 HV1568 95-24454 CIP

Encyclopedia of disability and rehabilitation, ed. by Arthur E. Dell Orto and Robert P. Marinelli. Macmillan Library Reference USA/Simon & Schuster and Prentice Hall International, 1995. 820p bibl index afp ISBN 0-02-897297-X, $105.00

This superb encyclopedia, in a format that makes it easy to use, focuses on disability and rehabilitation, and is intended both for those with disabilities and for their families, friends, and health care professionals. It treats a wide range of disabilities (physical, mental, organic, and traumatic) from the viewpoints of consumers, clients, and patients. It covers a wide range of topics, e.g., disability law, credentials and licensure, hospices, music therapy, life care planning, wheelchairs. The articles, three to six pages in length, are alphabetically arranged and include cross-references. An invaluable 16-page list of resources, organizations, and foundations is included. Highly recommended for general readers, undergraduates through faculty, and professionals.—*M. E. Leverence, Governors State University*

OAB-0322 HV35 CIP

Encyclopedia of social work, ed. by Richard L. Edwards et al. National Association of Social Workers/NASW Press, 1995. 3v. 2,746p bibl index ISBN 0-87101-255-3, $150.00; ISBN 0-87101-256-1 pbk, $120.00

Although all topics were reviewed for relevance, the most significant changes in the first new edition of this title since 1987 (17th ed., CH, Jan'78) reflect recent social shifts. Particular attention, according to the editor, is given to "diversity and the ugliness of racism." Longer overview entries were written for major areas (e.g., "HIV/AIDS," "Racial and Ethnic Groups," "Sexual Orientation.") The work was thoroughly edited to eliminate "language that might inappropriately label people." Rather than grouping people under the heading "minorities," separate entries are devoted to people of different national origins. The number of biographies was expanded to 99, with more entries on women and people of color. Authors of greater diversity were recruited. In addition, the work was made more usable by dividing it into three continuously paged volumes with a complete table of contents in each, ordering the 290 entries alphabetically, adding numerous cross-references, using 80 "Reader's Guide" boxes listing all entries on major topics, describing each entry with two to five keywords supplied by the author, and listing both a bibliography and suggestions for further reading. The thorough index includes people, organizations, places, and legislation. One complaint: the index and tables of contents indicate page but not volume numbers, and the binding does not indicate which pages are included in each volume. Appendixes include the NASW Code of Ethics, distinctive dates in social welfare history, and acronyms. The set is supplemented by the simultaneous publication of the 2nd edition of *Social Work Almanac* (1995), which provides statistical tables, charts, and graphs. The first edition to be published on CD-ROM, this set will, like its predecessors, be the core of any social work collection. As a group, the 19 editions provide a fascinating view of changes in society and the profession since 1929. Undergraduates through faculty.—*J. Drueke, University of Nebraska—Lincoln*

OAB-0323   HD6223   93-38803 MARC
Ghorayshi, Parvin, comp. **Women and work in developing countries: an annotated bibliography.** Greenwood, 1994. 223p indexes afp ISBN 0-313-28834-8, $59.95

This is a welcome contribution to the growing literature on women in the Third World. The introduction covers general works, organizing them into such categories as "The Developing World and the Global Economy," "Theoretical Considerations," and "Gender and Work." The main body of the bibliography is organized by geographical region—Africa, Asia, Latin American and the Caribbean, and the Middle East—and subdivided into sections, e.g., "Social Construction of Gender" and "Women's Experience of Wage-Work." A final chapter lists audiovisual resources. The numbered entries, covering books, articles, reports, and dissertations, are two to three sentences long and contain cross-references by entry number. A preface draws the material together conceptually and outlines the overall organization of the bibliography. The work also contains an appendix of women's organizations and research centers and indexes by author, country and region, and subject. Well-conceived and well-written, this bibliography should prove useful to those interested in women's issues and international development. There is no current comparable resource. Recommended for upper-division undergraduate and graduate collections.— *G. M. Herrmann, SUNY College at Cortland*

OAB-0324   HV4493   92-41254 CIP
Henslin, James M. **Homelessness: an annotated bibliography.** Garland, 1993. 2v. 1,076p index afp (Garland reference library of social science, 534) ISBN 0-8240-4115-1, $125.00

An exhaustive bibliography that meets the needs of researchers on homelessness who have long awaited a comprehensive literature resource. Volume 1 is a list of works arranged alphabetically by author, followed by those written anonymously. Each entry includes an annotation providing a succinct overview of the piece's findings, issues, research relevance, and theme. In lieu of a subject index, Volume 2 consists of 41 topical sub-bibliographies derived from the main volume, in which all items are unannotated; readers must refer back to Volume 1 for annotations. Sources cited include books, major newspapers, academic and nonacademic journals, government publications, and conference proceedings. Henslin provides a thorough review of the literature of homelessness from preindustrial America to the present, going far beyond Joan Nordquist's *The Homeless in America: A Bibliography* (1988). The dearth of current bibliographic guides on homelessness makes Henslin's book invaluable for all academic institutions supporting social science programs.— *M. A. Lutes, University of Notre Dame*

OAB-0325   HM136   94-38978 CIP
Levinson, David. **Aggression and conflict: a cross-cultural encyclopedia.** ABC-Clio, 1994. 234p bibl index afp ISBN 0-87436-728-X, $49.50

Levinson here discusses 90 terms pertaining to how people hurt each other physically, emotionally, and socially. Each form of behavior or custom is defined, variant forms in different cultures are described, distribution of the phenomenon is specified, and possible explanations for the behavior are discussed. The emphasis and examples are taken almost exclusively from the non-Western world, and the data are drawn from approximately 100 ethnographic and numerous cross-cultural surveys. Entries are alphabetically arranged, and each is followed by *see also* references and a bibliography. These references are merged at the end of the volume into a 13-page bibliography. There is an excellent and extensive index. The author, editor of the new series "Encyclopedias of the Human Experience," of which this book is a part, is vice president of Human Relations Area Files, Inc., one of the world's leading institutions for cross-cultural research. Levinson's research and publishing in the areas of ethnicity, social relations, and comparative studies is reflected in the extremely well crafted entries that constitute this title. Highly recommended for larger public libraries and all undergraduate and graduate collections.—*C. J. Busick, University of Colorado at Boulder*

OAB-0326   HQ1064   94-9305 CIP
Older Americans almanac: a reference work on seniors in the United States, ed. by Ronald J. Manheimer with North Carolina Center for Creative Retirement, University of North Carolina at Asheville. Gale, 1994. 881p bibl index afp ISBN 0-8103-8348-9, $99.50

If you can afford only one reference on aging, plan to purchase this almanac. The 38 chapters, beginning with aging viewed in early America and ending with "Productive Aging in the 1990's and Beyond," cover all aspects of aging—demographics, politics, health care, volunteerism, and more. The list of contributors is impressive and distinguished. Lawyers, researchers, writers, and practitioners from many fields are represented. Each chapter provides lucid explanations of the issues; integrated disucssions of past and present views; suggestions for further research; and a substantial list of additional references. Two mini-series are interspersed throughout: "Voices of Creative Aging" by Connie Goldman consists of excerpts of radio interviews with senior individuals who exhibit diverse/creative attitudes toward aging; "Profiles of Productive Aging" presents many renowned, older citizens who have remained active or created new careers in later life. Isaac Asimov, Julia Child, John Forsythe, and John Gardner are just a few of the individuals profiled. Each chapter begins with a list of topics covered. The typography is clear and rather large. There is a precise, uncluttered table of contents and an extensive, well-done index. Tables, graphs, and photography are attractively presented. Although it looks like a textbook, this is not a volume to be dismissed. It will be of value to all libraries.—*C. Snelling, Chicago State University*

OAB-0327   Orig
Researching the family: a guide to survey and statistical data on U.S. families, ed. by Nicholas Zill and Margaret Daly. Child Trends, 1993. 460p ISBN 0-932359-03-5 pbk, $30.00

This guide arrives at an opportune time. Increased mention of "family values," "putting family first," and "family violence" in the press and in everyday conversations is likely to spark greater interest in research on the family by academic researchers and policy analysts. The guide intends to assist such activity by familiarizing the research community with the resources in more than 60 national survey and statistical databases, which the editors think have been greatly underutilized because of access obstacles and lack of knowledge of their contents. Many of these data sets are now available on CD-ROM, facilitating their access. Surveys include data on health, education, poverty, crime, employment and unemployment, family formation and dissolution, child development, and substance abuse. Most are derived from large national survey projects using samples of the population. The guide includes details on each database's purpose, sponsorship, design, periodicity, content, limitations, availability, use by publications, and a three-page checklist of its characteristics at the family, adult, and child levels. The checklists should help reseachers determine if the data are pertinent to their research question. An essential purchase for academic libraries.—*C. Hagle, University of Dallas*

GENERAL

OAB-0328   Z989   95-10396 CIP
Dickinson, Donald C. **Henry E. Huntington's library of libraries.** Huntington Library, 1995. 286p bibl index ISBN 0-87328-153-5, $24.95

Sumptuously illustrated in black and white, attractively bound with decorated endpapers, with a dust jacket worth preserving, this is a finely printed, wide margined, well-written study of the book-buying activities of the magnate Henry Edwards Huntington (1850-1927). Between 1911 and his death he accumulated a great library. Dickinson's account of Huntington's motives for collecting and his analysis of the patterns, changes, and developments in Huntington's book and manuscript acquisition draw on unpublished primary materials. Huntington's collecting is placed in the context of the book trade and its personalities during the first three decades of this century. Larger than life figures such as George D. Smith (the New York dealer) and A.S.W. Rosenbach (the Philadelphia dealer and scholar whose purchases for Huntington between 1923 and 1925 averaged one million dollars per year) bestride Dickinson's canvas. The bibliography and index augment an important study complementing James Thorpe's *Henry Edwards Huntington: A Biography* (CH, Dec'94), which concentrates on its subject's life and business activities rather than on the construction of a great rare book and manuscript library. Dickinson's book is indispensable for all libraries with materials on the history of the book, the study of cultural artifacts, collecting, and cultural and library history.—*W. Baker, Northern Illinois University*

OAB-0329   P106   94-29141 CIP
Eco, Umberto. **The search for the perfect language,** tr. by James Fentress. Blackwell, 1995. 385p bibl index afp ISBN 0-631-17465-6, $24.95

Written by a world-class semioticist, *The Search for the Perfect Language* details, with large brush strokes, the principle episodes of the search for the language before Babel. However, this book does not belong with semiotics or the history of linguistics, but with the history of ideas. Eco relates how until the Renaissance, when Greek and Latin were rediscovered, scholars believed that Adam's first language was Hebrew. Since the Renaissance and with the rise of nationalism, the search for the perfect language has been primarily nationalistic. Eco describes how philosophers and scholars devised their own "perfect languages," and he discusses kabbalism, Egyptology, polygraphies, and the language of images and magic. Using the readable but scholarly style he perfected in *The Name of the Rose* (1983), Eco has again written a masterful work with an air of mystery. The book is well bound with a comprehensive bibliography and excellent index. Highly recommended for both general readers and academic libraries.—*M. D. Linn, University of Minnesota-Duluth*

OAB-0330   Z1003   92-41688 CIP
Gerrig, Richard J. **Experiencing narrative worlds: on the psychological activities of reading.** Yale, 1993. 274p bibl index afp ISBN 0-300-05434-3, $30.00

A psychologist's well-written account of how readers extract meaning from narratives. The approach is interdisciplinary, drawing from cognitive psychology, literary criticism, and philosophy. Gerrig examines the ways readers infer causality from narrative passages and come to be "side participants" in the story. He reviews recent research to show how general cognitive processes bring about these effects with minimal effort on the part of the reader. Interesting features of narratives, such as suspense, are explained in terms of these basic processes, and Gerrig discusses the active role that readers play in constructing narrative experiences. He illustrates his points with a variety of engaging examples. A significant contribution that integrates contemporary research in cognitive psychology with important ideas from literary criticism. Recommended to libraries serving upper-division undergraduates, graduate students, and faculty in psychology, literary criticism, and philosophy.—*R. Madigan, University of Alaska, Anchorage*

OAB-0331   E185   94-32738 CIP
Holloway, Karla F.C. **Codes of conduct: race, ethics, and the color of our character.** Rutgers, 1995. 225p index ISBN 0-8135-2155-6, $24.95

This work combines literary analysis, political commentary, and autobiographical meditations in a manner that makes a major contribution to the understanding of the cultural significance of race and gender. Drawing on her experience as a black woman teaching at a prestigious mainstream university, Holloway (Duke Univ.) addresses issues with public policy implications much more directly than she has done in the writing that established her reputation in African American literary studies (e.g., *The Character of the Word*, CH, Sep'87; *New Dimensions of Spirituality*, CH, Feb'88). Her central thesis is deceptively clear: the reality of racism in the US makes it impossible to separate ethical conduct from ethnic identity. *Codes of Conduct* makes its real contribution, however, in presenting case studies of African American women, language, and children. Holloway's chapter on how black women's bodies determine political dynamics contains an excellent comparison of the experiences of Anita Hill, Phyllis Wheatley, and Zora Neale Hurston. The one problem with this frequently lyrical book is Holloway's occasional lapses into an arcane academic vocabulary that adds little to her analysis and may alienate some potential readers. Nonetheless, this title adds an important voice to the ongoing discussions of the importance of race and gender in American cultural life. Upper-division undergraduates and above.—*C. Werner, University of Wisconsin—Madison*

OAB-0332   Z282   94-10027 CIP
International book publishing: an encyclopedia, ed. by Philip G. Altbach and Edith S. Hoshino. Garland, 1995. 736p index afp (Garland reference library of the humanities, 1562) ISBN 0-8153-0786-1, $95.00

Rather than an encyclopedia, this is a collection of 64 very good essays on many aspects of publishing; moreover, it has about as much on US practices and experiences as on international aspects. The 34 topical essays (several of which appeared elsewhere) range from the specific (e.g., feminist publishing, scholarly book publishing in the 1990s) to the general (e.g., the societal context of book publishing). The 30 geographical essays treat regions (e.g., Francophone Africa, Central and Eastern Europe) or individual countries. The contributors include scholars and practitioners, all of whom "were given considerable latitude to express their own views." The essays vary from somewhat personal (particularly about publishing in developing nations) to first-rate historical summations and expert analyses of recent developments. Altbach, who has published widely on international publishing and higher education, contributed several of the essays. The volume, which could serve as a text for a course on book publishing, should be in all academic libraries, but probably in the circulating collection. Its usefulness lies not in the occasional compilations of statistics, most of which are available elsewhere, but in the very readable and informative essays, all enhanced by an excellent index.— *E. I. Farber, Earlham College*

OAB-0333   Z286   91-41669 CIP
Lafollette, Marcel C. **Stealing into print: fraud, plagiarism, and misconduct in scientific publishing.** California, 1992. 293p bibl index afp ISBN 0-520-07831-4, $30.00

This book offers considerably more than its title might lead readers to expect. Although the author does detail a number of the recent incidents of scientific fraud familiar to anyone attentive to the news media, she also provides substantive background on scientific publishing practices and informed, and well-documented, discussion of the key issues. The book is organized logically, beginning with an overview of the problem and following with an analysis of the common types of scientific fraud and plagiarism. Subsequent chapters discuss the nature of authorship and editorial decision making, including the role of referees. LaFollette appears to understand the variety of policies and practices across scientific disciplines; she quotes knowledgeable sources ranging from Robert Merton and Diana Crane to Dorothy Sayers's Lord Peter Wimsey. The book outlines possible courses of action when fraud is suspected and offers suggestions for resolution after intent to defraud has been determined. This is a readable and thoughtful presentation of a timely topic. The work is recommended for science libraries and other collections with holdings on scholarly publishing. Undergraduate; graduate; faculty; pre-professional; professional.—*J. M. Hurd, University of Illinois at Chicago*

OAB-0334   Z658   92-826 CIP
Ohles, Frederik. **Germany's rude awakening: censorship in the land of the Brothers Grimm.** Kent State, 1992. 227p bibl index ISBN 0-87338-460-1, $35.00

Ohles's remarkable book gives a detailed description of the development, evolution, and eventual unravelling of the state censorship mechanism in the Hesse-Kassel Electorate in the first half of the 19th century. In addition to providing a superbly documented history of the Electorate's censorship practices, it also supplies an interesting narrative of the social and politcal conditions that characterized this period and region in Germany and that gave rise to the practice of a rigid yet surprisingly inept censorship. Perhaps most important, it gives insights into the mentalities both of the censors themselves—including Jacob Grimm—and of their supposed adversaries, the producers and purveyors of materials that came under the censors' scrutiny. Written in an engaging and elegant style, it is one of the rare recent works of historical research that will find a ready readership among nonacademics and scholars alike. It includes a useful and fascinating appendix listing all the works banned in Hesse-Kassel from 1831 to 1848. Recommended for all collections with an interest or strength in modern German history.—*J. H. Spohrer, University of California, Berkeley*

OAB-0335   PA8030   95-9739 CIP
Remer, Gary. **Humanism and the rhetoric of toleration.** Pennsylvania State, 1996. 318p bibl index afp ISBN 0-271-01480-6, $45.00

Remer (Tulane Univ.) has written an exceptionally lucid account of the intellectual and political tradition underlying the idea of religious toleration and the implications of that tradition for contemporary policy on free speech. He traces the idea of toleration to the Renaissance humanists and their commitment to the precepts of classical rhetoric on debating both sides of an issue, decorum in expressing one's views, preference for dialogue (*sermo*), and prudent reasoning. In a detailed study of the works of Erasmus, Acontius, William Chillingworth, and Jean Bodin, Remer traces the vicissitudes of the fortunes of both rhetoric and toleration. Thomas Hobbes issued the first serious threat to the humanists' rhetoric-based toleration, but with John Locke their principles were incorporated into liberalism, especially in the theory of an individual's right to conscience. Modern debate about free speech, and the truth claims implied by the "marketplace of ideas" reasoning, continues the discussion in terms that still resemble those used in the Renaissance. This wide-ranging, thoroughly researched, and systematically argued book makes an important contribution to the history of rhetoric, political theory, and Western intellectual history. Highly recommended. Upper-division undergraduate through professional.— *R. W. Cape Jr., Austin College*

HUMANITIES

■ General

OAB-0336   N6797   94-4251 CIP
Alexander, Christine. **The art of the Brontës,** by Christine Alexander and Jane Sellars. Cambridge, 1995. 484p bibl indexes ISBN 0-521-43248-0, $79.95; ISBN 0-521-43841-1 pbk, $34.95

This thorough interdisciplinary study focuses on Anne, Charlotte, Emily, and Bramwell Brontë and the significance of their training in the visual arts. The book's 370 black-and-white illustrations and 32 beautiful color plates reveal that the Brontës relied on the visual arts in mining relationships and connections beyond the isolation of Haworth and frequently referred to the idioms and perspectives of the world of art in the creation of fiction. A discussion of the interesting mix of visual influences—Thomas Bewick, John Martin, and Byron—is the most compelling segment of five scholarly essays, which, though more biographical than analytical, comprise an informative and lucid art history of the Brontës. This work, with commentary for each image, will be a revelation for literary and art critics of the Romantic age. The appendixes, excellent bibliography, and well-organized index reveal the authors' impressive scholarship. Upper-division undergraduate and above.—*W. C. Snyder, St. Vincent College and Seminary*

OAB-0337   PS261   94-43049 CIP
Brooks, Cleanth. **Community, religion, and literature: essays.** Missouri, 1995. 334p index afp ISBN 0-8262-0993-9, $34.95

It is not uncommon for an essayist to publish a retrospective collection in his or her later years, but this volume is truly unique in this category. It is remarkable for its thematic unity and for the close collaboration between the author and the publisher. Readers should be sure to read the publisher's note. Likewise of special note is the final and crowning piece, "The Real Importance of the Humanities." Delivered as a lecture just two months before Brooks died, this essay is a confirmation of his mind. In his younger years, he had claimed an internal unity for *Modern Poetry and the Tradition* (CH, Apr'66) and *The Well Wrought Urn* (1947), even though each was compiled from previously published essays. Here, however, he has out-Brooksed himself, this collection confirming what he stood for. All who seek to understand and maintain the quality of the humanities will want to enhance their shelves with this gem. All academic libraries.—*A. G. Tassin, University of New Orleans*

OAB-0338   PN98   92-33742 CIP
The Digital word: text-based computing in the humanities, ed. by George P. Landow and Paul Delany. MIT, 1993. 362p index ISBN 0-262-12176-X, $39.95

The rapidly increasing national and international networking of computers makes possible, if not mandatory, a new conceptualization of what constitutes a "text." It also necessitates new technological approaches to the ways in which texts can be addressed or studied, particularly as this concerns humanities scholarship. This highly informative collection of 16 essays, written by leaders in the field, does a thorough job of treating these and related issues. Should

there, for example, be some central authority that oversees the storage of electronic documents in a specifiable format, like what is done at the Bibliothèque de France? What software products are available for distributed text management? What new kinds of questions can be asked of texts through the use of this software? What are the implications for joint scholarship of the fact that a "text" can now actually be a database consisting of hundreds or thousands of text segments stored individually across many different computers? Highly recommended for humanities undergraduate, community college, and graduate students; faculty; and the informed general reader.—*C. Koch, Oberlin College*

OAB-0339   PR535   94-13794 CIP
Estrin, Barbara L. **Laura: uncovering gender and genre in Wyatt, Donne, and Marvell.** Duke University, 1995 (c1994). 345p index afp ISBN 0-8223-1500-9, $49.95; ISBN 0-8223-1499-1 pbk, $18.95

This bold and provocative study presents a systematic and wholesale revaluation of Petrarch's love poetry and of the movement called Petrarchism, especially with reference to selected lyric poems in 16th- and 17th-century England. By focusing on the interplay of gender and genre in selected poetry by Petrarch, Thomas Wyatt, John Donne, and Andrew Marvell, Estrin (Stonehill College) amalgamates traditional literary interpretation and postmodern theoretical perspectives. What results is a sensitive and subtle analysis of the many faces of Petrarch's Laura in the *Canzoniere* and of their permutations thereafter. Enriching the argument is simultaneous consideration of the visual arts, so that aesthetics and poetics are most effectively integrated. As Estrin's argument progresses, it becomes more complicated and nuanced, though it remains unified and cohesive across the several chapters. Though this book will be invaluable to traditionalists and postmodern critics alike, not to mention art historians and aestheticians, it serves the double function of theorizing understandably and persuasively and of engaging in first-rate practical criticism. Rarely has the alignment between postmodern theory and textual analysis been so well enacted. There are three black-and-white plates and extensive references to other well-known visualizations. Very highly recommended for upper-division undergraduates, graduate students, faculty, and researchers.—*A. C. Labriola, Duquesne University*

OAB-0340   B804   96-44334 CIP
Everdell, William R. **The first moderns: profiles in the origins of twentieth-century thought.** Chicago, 1997. 501p bibl index afp ISBN 0-226-22480-5, $29.95

Everdell (St. Ann's School, Brooklyn, NY) looks to a number of fields and persons in the few decades before and after the turn of the 20th century to discover the birth of modernism in the growing awareness that the world is discontinuous and discrete instead of continuous and whole. With an animated, erudite narrative he elucidates crucial shifts in mathematics, physics, painting, literature, logical philosophy, psychology, and the culture of cities away from continuity and tradition toward a pervasive atomism—discrete numbers, disconnected neurons, specks of color, peoples isolated in concentration camps, still frames in moving pictures, multiple perspectives in cubist art, or tones without melodic lines to hold them. He masterfully interweaves accounts of the personal lives of figures as diverse as Cantor, Bolzman, Seurat, Rimbaud, Cajal (discoverer of the neuron), Weyler (inventor of the concentration camp), Bertrand Russell, Einstein, Freud, Schoenberg, Joyce, and Kandinsky with their discoveries that helped launch modernity. He gives us intimate sketches of city life in Vienna, Paris, St. Louis, and St. Petersburg, revealing how modernity was both resisted and produced in these cities. In short, this is a wonderfully crafted work delineating the rise of modernity through the analysis of its key founding figures. Highly recommended for all libraries and for any individual who delights in intellectual history. General; undergraduate; graduate; faculty.—*J. H. Riker, Colorado College*

OAB-0341 GR305 95-50444 CIP
Flueckiger, Joyce Burkhalter. **Gender and genre in the folklore of Middle India.** Cornell, 1996. 351p bibl index afp ISBN 0-8014-3206-5, $49.95

In this superbly crafted, absorbing book, Flueckiger (religion, Emory Univ.) explores the relationships among folklore genres in the Chattisgarh region of north India, achieving a pioneering model of the study of a "folklore system" in its entirety. She deploys the very process of distinguishing between scholarly analytical categories and indigenous understandings of genre to illuminate the latter. By exploring the ways in which performance, "folklore regions," and "folklore communities" define genre, she shows the multidimensionality of genre itself, conceptualized as verbal text, performance, and ritual or festival context. The reader is initiated into the worlds of diverse genres, ranging from women's ritual dance-songs to local epics and adventure tales. Pan-Indian motifs (dice games, women disguised as men) are seen in a new light, and the Chattisgarhi folklore world emerges as remarkably female-centered. Each genre is beautifully visualized and carefully delineated, creating a vivid sense of contexts, performers, and audiences, and ultimately, of a dynamic intertextuality of genres. This is ethnographic scholarship at its best. The multigenre approach is a major contribution, and this rich book should be read by all students of folklore, literature, performance, and South Asia. Upper-division undergraduates through faculty; general audiences.—*I. V. Peterson, Mount Holyoke College*

OAB-0342 PR830 95-948 CIP
Halberstam, Judith. **Skin shows: Gothic horror and the technology of monsters.** Duke University, 1995. 215p bibl index afp ISBN 0-8223-1651-X, $45.95; ISBN 0-8223-1663-3 pbk, $15.95

The eight chapters of this work attend to familiar fictions by Shelley, Stevenson, Stoker, and Wilde, and individual films of Hitchcock, Hooper, and Demme. In earlier Gothic stories, Halberstam suggests, "monstrosity" is a complex of national, sexual, racial, gender, and class signifiers, within textual systems that disrupted realism. The forms taken by flesh and narrative became hybrid: "the text as monster that must be identified, decoded, captured, and consumed." Halberstam frequently repeats certain dramatic, fascinating topics associated with the creature: foreignness, perversity, antisemitism, "buried" sexual secrets, the "profound entanglement of identities and genres," and the categories of fear. The secondary references are provocative, because horror stories create "all kinds of gothicizations across disciplinary and ideological boundaries." Only the discussion of contemporary films—female paranoia, "gender with an edge," the "postmodern monster"—seems somewhat tendentious. This intense, closely argued revisioning and replacement of Gothic convention is sophisticated, sometimes mordant, and often startling. Its cool intelligence and careful presentation recommend it for any Gothic-cum-Romantic collection and among histories of the novel. Upper-division undergraduates and above.—*L. K. MacKendrick, University of Windsor*

OAB-0343 E184 93-13348 CIP
Handbook of Hispanic cultures in the United States: history, ed. by Alfredo Jiménez. Arte Publico, 1994. 339p index afp ISBN 1-55885-100-3, $60.00

Rather than discuss any potential shortcomings of these publications (e.g., only Cubans, Mexicans, and Puerto Ricans are included in "Part Four: The Recent

Past" in the history volume), this reviewer enthusiastically recommends this two-volume set to every library in the US. It presents such a concise, easy-to-read yet scholarly approach to Hispanic culture in the US that it should be readily available to readers on all levels and with any degree of interest. The two-volume division into "Literature and Art" and "History" provides a simple separation for students or general readers wanting basic information on a topic in either area. The introduction implies an expansion into coverage of other areas, and the format provides a good model for coverage of other ethnic groups in the US multicultural society. Currency is a problem with this handbook, as with any printed text, because of the time delay in production (e.g., "Latino Cinema" is not up to date), but the reader learns a lot about the overall topic and then can use periodicals for more current information. For a work of this magnitude, the price should not be an impediment for a library to purchase the text.—*D. R. Brown, DePaul University*

OAB-0344 PR6003 95-1324 CIP
Hatcher, John. **Laurence Binyon: poet, scholar of East and West.** Oxford, 1995. 345p bibl index afp ISBN 0-19-812296-9, $72.00

Binyon is a formidable subject, and now for the first time justice is done to his whole remarkable career. His prodigious poetic output, which began to impress his school contemporaries in the 1880s, includes meditative verse once much valued and poems on public themes (his 1914 elegy "For the Fallen" provided lines for countless memorials after both world wars). His Oxford years brought friendships that later gave him access to fin de siècle artistic and literary London; and at the British Museum from 1892 to 1933 his studies led to important books on English landscape, Blake, and the Oriental art (Japanese, Chinese, Persian, and Indian) he was instrumental in gaining appreciation for in the West. Countless well-known names from the 1880s to the 1940s take on new resonance in these pages, and Binyon emerges as gifted, modest, reserved, and generous with his great learning. Photographs of him and his family, and of Japanese and Chinese artworks discussed in the text, enhance this fine book, and the bibliography adds to its scholarly value. A prizewinner for the serious student. All academic collections.—*M. S. Vogeler, emeritus, California State University, Fullerton*

OAB-0345 PR5295 91-45198 CIP
Jones, Dorothy Richardson. **King of critics: George Saintsbury, 1845-1933, critic, journalist, historian, professor.** Michigan, 1992. 386p bibl index afp ISBN 0-472-10316-4, $42.50

Who reads George Saintsbury now? Jones appears to have read him, every word, as well as everything ever written about him. She has revealed details of his personal life heretofore obscured, including his fascinating epistolary affair with the great medievalist, Helen Waddell. Jones is thus able to relate Saintsbury's personality to his work in the various roles listed in her title. In each, she provides us with the context in which he worked; thus she describes the ungentlemanly rows amongst Victorian academic journalists, as in the Churton Collins/Edmund Gosse duel; places Saintsbury's role as professor of English at Edinburgh in the history of English studies in British universities; and displays his criticism in relation to other Victorian critics. She persuades us that some of Saintsbury is still worth reading, but she is by no means uncritical: the crown on the "King of Critics" is often awry. Her style is competent if not brilliant, varying from the pedestrian to the vivid; her research is thorough as evident from her extensive bibliography and careful documentation. The index is reliable. Appropriate for upper-level undergraduate and graduate students as well as Victorian scholars.—*J. W. Bicknell, emeritus, Drew University*

OAB-0346 NX180 95-34639 CIP
Kistenberg, Cindy J. **Aids, social change, and theater: performance as protest.** Garland, 1995. 208p bibl index afp ISBN 0-8153-2159-7, $35.00

This clearly written, valuable, and interesting addition to the fast-growing body of criticism on AIDS and the media explores how the AIDS crisis has been politically and linguistically constructed by the mass media. Kistenberg analyzes conventional theatrical performances such as Larry Kramer's *The Normal Heart* (1985) and William Hoffman's *As Is* (1993), the work of performance artists Karen Finley and Tim Miller, and cultural performances sponsored by ACT-UP and The NAMES Project to determine "whether performance can be used to intervene discursively in the dominant construction of AIDS." In her attempt to show how performance can contribute to social change, Kistenberg is balanced and wise, never claiming more for art than it can accomplish in the short term. With its full and helpful bibliography, this work would make a wonderful textbook in a course on drama or on the artistic response to HIV/AIDS. A superb addition to a literature that includes *Fluid Exchanges*, ed. by James Miller (1992); Alexandra Juhasz's *AIDS TV* (CH, May'96); *A Leap in the Dark*, ed. by Allan Klusacek and Ken Morrison (1992); *Ecstatic Antibodies*, ed. by Tessa Boffin and Sunil Gupta (1990); *AIDS: Cultural Analysis, Cultural Activism*, ed. by Douglas Crimp (1988); and Steven C. Dubin's *Arresting Images* (CH, Mar'93). Upper-division undergraduate and up.—*L. Winters, College of Saint Elizabeth*

OAB-0347 PR478 95-4350 CIP
Koritz, Amy. **Gendering bodies/performing art: dance and literature in early twentieth-century British culture.** Michigan, 1995. 218p bibl index afp ISBN 0-472-10616-3, $37.50

Approaching literature figures in the context of dance, Koritz (Tulane Univ.) reveals significant connections between literature and dance; she positions dance as central in shaping aesthetics and ideology in British culture between 1890 and the 1920s. She traces dance of the music hall, Maud Allan, Isadora Duncan, and Ballets Russes de Diaghilev (as experienced by Oscar Wilde, W.B. Yeats, George Bernard Shaw, T.S. Eliot, Edward Gordon Craig, and Arthur Symons) as catalysts in the development of aesthetic theory—a theory that in turn shaped critical evaluations of dance and exerted powerful influences on it. The author is knowledgeable about interdisciplinary content and methodology; her well-researched and stimulating discussion embraces dance history and gender and cultural studies. Her themes include the devaluation of the dancer, which occurred simultaneously with the increased acceptance of women on the British stage, and the separation of the work of art from the creative artist (which denied the dancer status as artist, and reserved that elite designation for composers, directors, and choreographers). This thematic ideology characterized aestheticism, symbolism, and modernism and affected dance artists at the time. The author argues that although the definition of dance as an elite art required the separation between dancer and creative artist (as exemplified by Ballets Russes de Diaghilev), it stymied the careers of early female modern dancers such as Maud Allan and Isadora Duncan. Upper-division undergraduate and above.—*C. T. Bond, Goucher College*

OAB-0348 NX454 93-24555 CIP
Leonard, George J. **Into the light of things: the art of the commonplace from Wordsworth to John Cage.** Chicago, 1994. 249p index afp ISBN 0-226-47252-3, $24.95

To many who are serious about art, so-called avant-garde works often appear meaningless or absurd in some way. This book is about the ideas that inform and link together many compositions by avant-garde artists. One important theme developed is that the ideas are not really new; indeed, they are expressed by many earlier and more widely appreciated figures—e.g., Carlyle, Emerson, and Thoreau. What binds these historically diverse figures together is opposition to a certain way of regarding works of art, viz., a conception of them as unique sources of knowledge and value, essentially different and distinct from ordinary objects and everyday life. Leonard (San Francisco State Univ.) discusses the form this opposition takes in different artists and in different historical settings, and he suggests that it is part of an essentially religious set of attitudes and beliefs. This is a rich and rewarding study written in a clear and accessible style with excellent references and a very useful index. Highly recommended for all collections. Undergraduate; graduate; faculty.—*J. White, University of Maine*

OAB-0349 PN51 95-18076 CIP
Nussbaum, Martha C. **Poetic justice: the literary imagination and public life.** Beacon Press, 1996 (c1995). 143p index ISBN 0-8070-4108-4, $20.00

Contending that contemporary public discourse is too often restricted by the narrow bounds of pseudoscientific theorizing and the rhetoric of rationalism, Nussbaum (ethics, Univ. of Chicago) issues a clarion call for the introduction of the literary imagination into discourses of public life like law and economics. Weaving colorful readings of Dickens's *Hard Times*, Wright's *Native Son*, and Forster's *Maurice* into a brilliant textual tapestry, the author argues that reading novels creates in readers an imaginative sympathy for the lives of others. Such sympathy transcends the utilitarian view of humanity that focuses on the ends to which humans might be used without ever considering how their individual lives contribute to the richness of society. As she does in *Love's Knowledge* (1990), Nussbaum demonstrates the ways in which reading imaginative literature is an ethical act and reinvigorates the life of culture. Nussbaum's book will be best read in dialogue with Wayne Booth's *The Company We Keep* (CH, May'89), Stanley Fish's *Doing What Comes Naturally* (CH, Nov'89), and Andrew Delbanco's *The Death of Satan* (CH, Jul'96), because each of these works emphasizes reading as the recovery of the humanistic values so often buried in the mire of factuality that marks the modern world. All academic collections.—*H. L. Carrigan, Jr., Otterbein College*

OAB-0350 PN751 94-26406 CIP
Peckham, Morse. **The romantic virtuoso.** Wesleyan/University Press of New England, 1995. 246p bibl index afp ISBN 0-8195-5280-1, $39.95

With the publication of *Beyond the Tragic Vision: The Quest for Identity in the Nineteenth Century* (1962), Peckham at once established himself as a leading historian, critic, and theoretician of the New Critical era. At his death in 1993, he left behind not only a vast body of important books and articles but also the completed manuscript now published. Peckham was a scholar of breathtaking range and virtuosity, virtues here on dazzling display. Two-thirds of the volume deals with a mere ten years of the 19th century (1815-25) and consists of a series of brief, immensely learned, sometimes idiosyncratic, but always original and absorbing reflections on European novelists, poets, musicians, and philosophers. Faculty as well as freshmen will find here a broad spectrum of intellectual and aesthetic concerns to engage their interest. The final chapter, "Meditations on the Consequences of Romanticism," is "must" reading for students of literature, especially seniors and graduate students. Leo Daugherty's introduction and H.W. Matalene's "Biographical Afterword" frame this highly recommended volume.—*N. Fruman, University of Minnesota*

OAB-0351 BH301 96-28088 CIP
Rapaport, Herman. **Is there truth in art?** Cornell, 1997. 221p index afp ISBN 0-8014-3275-8, $45.00; ISBN 0-8014-8353-0 pbk, $17.95

This refreshing and intriguing book is a pleasant change from the exculpating and finger-pointing that seem to have consumed Heidegger studies in recent years. Rapaport calmly and thoroughly engages the relation between Heidegger and art. This is an area that deserves further study, and Rapaport's book is an innovative contribution to it. One of the great merits of this book is that it does not just add to the discussion of obvious topics such as Heidegger's understanding of Hölderlin or Celan, but addresses a wide range of specific works of art. It explores songs by Anton von Webern, environmental art by Richard Long, fiction by Julian Gracq and Maurice Blanchot, and films and texts by Marquerite Duras. These are all original and unusual connections that illuminate Heidegger's thought in new and provocative ways. Each essay in this volume stands on its own as a rigorous interpretation of its topic. Yet the essays also work together to make a powerful and original argument. This volume also has a substantial introduction that should be read by anyone with an interest in the philosophy of art. Highly recommended. Upper-division undergraduate; graduate; faculty.—*S. Barnett, Central Connecticut State University*

OAB-0352   PN175   94-34983 CIP
Rummel, Erika. **The humanist-scholastic debate in the Renaissance & Reformation.** Harvard, 1995. 249p bibl index afp (Harvard historical studies, 120) ISBN 0-674-42250-3, $45.00

The distinguishing quality of this study is its thorough investigation of primary sources, many of them unfamiliar to the reader of Renaissance intellectual history. Rummel (Wilfred Laurier Univ.) has delved diligently into manuscripts and early printed books in libraries throughout the West, bringing to light texts on both sides of the debate between humanists and scholastics over philology and dialectic. The scholastics strove for logic and orderliness of thought, whereas the humanists favored a more general and universal interpretation. Rummel begins her history of the debate with two exemplary figures, Petrarch for the humanists, and Jean Gerson, chancellor of the University of Paris, for the scholastics. She pursues the argument into the universities, where theologians disputed the right of the humanists to interpret the Bible and change the text of the Vulgate. The treatment of this struggle in the German and Spanish universities is particularly good. Inevitably the humanist cause, in its challenging of church authority, became identified with that of the reformers, an association that Erasmus sought vainly to refute. Rummel concludes that neither side won: the humanists succeeded in reshaping the curriculum while the scholastics experienced a certain renewal, but their dispute was overshadowed by the rise of the Scientific Age. The book is a pleasure to read; it is written in a clear and straightforward style and is free of any tendentious parti pris. Upper-division undergraduates and above.—*C. Fantazzi, University of Windsor*

OAB-0353   P116   94-29938 CIP
Thomas, Downing A. **Music and the origins of language: theories from the French Enlightenment.** Cambridge, 1995. 195p bibl index ISBN 0-521-47307-1, $49.95

In this volume in the "New Perspectives in Music History and Criticism" series, Thomas (Univ. of Iowa) examines the epistemological role of music in the mosaic of cultural, social, linguistic, and scientific phenomena as seen and analyzed by Rameau, Rousseau, Diderot, Condillac, and other Enlightenment figures. The identification of music as the vocal expression of passion, emotion, or need leading eventually to speech and systematized language fits nicely into theories on the origin of language while raising further questions on music's function in culture. Rameau, the outstanding French musician and theorist of his age, described and promoted a theory of harmonics in opposition to Rousseau's postulation of melody as the foundation of a semiotic and aesthetic value. Reacting to, among other works, Catherine Kintzler's *Jean-Philippe Rameau* (1983, in French), Thomas points to the richness of associations between music on the one hand and anthropology, law, social bonding, passions, sensations, and thought. He throws valuable light on the extent to which music preoccupied the philosophes, not just as a pleasurable activity but as a medium with its own rhetoric linking sensation and language, sensibility and knowledge, and creativity and social revitalization. A penetrating monograph recommended for upper-division undergraduates upward.—*D. A. Collins, Kalamazoo College*

OAB-0354   GN470   93-37644 CIP
Torrance, Robert M. **The spiritual quest: transcendence in myth, religion, and science.** California, 1994. 367p bibl index afp ISBN 0-520-08132-3, $35.00

This brilliantly written (and perfectly edited), important work by Robert Torrance (U. of California, Davis) displays a dazzling array of knowledge from contemporary philosophy, literary theory, and anthropology to myth, religion, and science. Torrance rescues the major humanistic endeavor, the dynamic spiritual quest, from the "closed" system of modern structuralists, poststructuralists, deconstructionists, positivists, and determinists of all stripes, and from the seemingly-closed traditional, tribal societies where ritualists seek the return to a static past. Illustrating that the quest to transcend is grounded in human nature and expresses itself everywhere, Torrance explores first the preconditions of the quest, then considers collective rituals that, while affirming society's stability, also allow for individual transformation and the incorporation of the "unknow-

able beyond" into human experience. He then moves to the individual quest of the shaman, from Australia to northern Eurasia, and finally discusses the dialogue of ritualism and shamanism in Native America, emphasizing the dynamic, active shaman freely creating the future. Extraordinarily thorough bibliography. Excellent index. For upper-division humanities students and general readers.—*N. B. Palmer, Western Maryland College*

OAB-0355   Orig
Virilio, Paul. **The vision machine.** Indiana/BFI, 1994. 81p index ISBN 0-253-32574-9, $35.00; ISBN 0-253-20901-3 pbk, $14.95

We live in an age dominated by the "visual," but we have little understanding of what this means. The past two centuries have witnessed the development of photography, film, video, and holography, yet scant attention has been paid to the social and philosophic implications of a culture that is now devoted to the generally uncritical consumption of processed images. In this slim but amazingly provocative book, Virilio (architecture, Ecole Speciale d'Architecture, Paris) attempts to outline the intellectual ramifications of technological development upon visual perception. He traces an elusive yet freewheeling path from the Renaissance to the computer age and pursues his quest in a manner that challenges many basic assumptions about perception and social structure. For Virilio, the visual image is not simply a construct of a predetermined ideology. Instead, the perceptual process is a two-way street in which the social structure is being overrun by various new visual technologies. He subtly debunks the democratic myths about the new technologies and strongly suggests that the very concept of being human is threatened by the advent of digital images. Virilio brings to this thesis a unique perspective that virtually transcends traditional theoretical lines. But he has produced a book that is an essential text for all scholars of mass media. Virilio offers a cool, precise look at an impending future in which reality shall simply cease to exist. Highly recommended. General; upper-division undergraduate and above.—*D. Toth, formerly, Columbus Museum of Art*

OAB-0356   HM101   94-29007 CIP
Walters, Suzanna Danuta. **Material girls: making sense of feminist cultural theory.** California, 1995. 221p bibl index afp ISBN 0-520-08977-4, $40.00; ISBN 0-520-08978-2 pbk, $14.00

Walters has written an excellent monograph explaining and summarizing the scholarly literature in the field of feminist cultural studies, no mean task. Her accomplishment is even greater in that she writes in an accessible style that makes her ideas understandable to an audience larger than the academy. Indeed, she notes that a major problem of cultural, literary, and film criticism in the last two decades is that it has been laden with the jargon of semiotics and psychoanalysis. Walters offers a readable analysis of the liberal feminist literature on images of women in film as well as on the later scholarship, which has largely ignored this material and has explored the subject within a Marxist, Freudian, or Lacanian perspective. She also looks at communications research and then offers her own intertextual, contextual framework, which devotes a great deal of attention to spectators, the audience who absorbs, responds to, and integrates the visual, aural, and oral messages sent. Highly recommended for all levels.—*J. Sochen, Northeastern Illinois University*

OAB-0357   NX650   92-50571 CIP
Williams, Robert I. **Comic practice/comic response.** Delaware, 1993. (Dist. by Associated University Presses) 199p bibl index afp ISBN 0-87413-463-3, $35.00

This lively, illuminating study investigates how comedy works. Williams declares that comedy has two ways to express meaning: "by play between comic and serious judgment and with perception." Comedy works when its audience accepts its "trickery"; "meaning is what comedy plays *with*." The author locates the essence of comedy not in the work itself but in its interaction with the audience. "There is finally only the interplay of meanings, the tantalizing dialectic of play which becomes the 'meaning' of the comic experience .... It is a question of how two kinds of meaning—signification through perceptual play alone and implications accruing in the emotional and judgmental underside of our response—work together." To apply his thesis, Williams rounds up the usual suspects: Beckett, Synge, Shakespeare, Neil Simon, Twain, Swift, Jonson, Wilde, Shaw, American TV sitcoms. But he ranges more widely. He parallels *Winnie-the-Pooh* and *Catch-22*. Instead of reducing comedy to a literary form, he acknowledges all the arts: Hogarth, trompe l'oeil painting, Klee, a Richard Wilbur poem, the Bloom County comic strip, John Cage, dance, Mozart, Monty Python, Calder. The illuminating discussion of specific examples keeps Williams's theoretical discussion both accessible and fascinating. Undergraduates; graduates; faculty.—*M. Yacowar, Emily Carr College of Art and Design*

■ Art & Architecture

OAB-0358 NX512 91-13823 CIP
Allston, Washington. **The correspondence of Washington Allston,** ed. by Nathalia Wright. University Press of Kentucky, 1993. 682p bibl index afp ISBN 0-8131-1708-9, $75.00

This massive compilation, by a professor emerita at the University of Tennessee who is perhaps best known as the biographer of Horatio Greenough, will be the last word on Allston for many years to come. In its nearly 700 pages, we get an even more detailed picture of Allston's life and friendships than what emerged from the monograph and exhibition catalog by William Gerdts and Theodore Stebbins, Jr., *"A Man of Genius": The Art of Washington Allston* (1979). In her editorial notes, Wright gives remarkably complete biographical details about all of Allston's correspondents, and she makes the first serious attempt to clarify the relationship between Allston's paintings and his literary pieces. In addition, she gives us the texts of three previously unpublished satires by the painter. She also includes excerpts from many hard-to-find contemporary reviews of Allston's work. The book contains only 16 black-and-white illustrations, but devoted students of Allston will already have consulted Gerdts and Stebbins's book, which illustrates most of Allston's paintings in color. Highly recommended, as a model of meticulous scholarship. Advanced undergraduate; graduate; faculty.—*M. W. Sullivan, Villanova University*

OAB-0359 N8210 91-36280 CIP
Amishai-Maisels, Ziva. **Depiction and interpretation: the influence of the Holocaust on the visual arts.** Pergamon, 1993. 567p bibl index ISBN 0-08-040656-4, $190.00

A relatively large body of popular and scholarly literature deals directly or indirectly with visual artists' responses to German military, social, and other inhumane aggression before and during WW II, and a significant body of material deals specifically with the Holocaust iconographically. Amishai-Maisels's book, however, is the first to so comprehensively attempt to deal with this essentially overwhelming and universally sobering subject. The result is approachable and scholarly. Furthermore, the book is well produced: a double-columned layout of 366 pages of text, 140 plus pages of endnotes, 35 pages of general and artist-specific bibliographic references, a 20-page index, a 3-page introduction and a 1-page preface, and 560 black-and-white and 99 color plates. This book is the result of 20 years' work and related articles published since the early 1980s on artists such as Lipchitz and Shahn, and on themes such as biblical imagery and Christological symbolism. Problems faced by artists attempting to wrestle with the Holocaust theme(s) and conceptual and organizational problems faced by the author which is considered a beginning and not a final statement, are lucidly discussed in the introduction and the preface. Scholarly notes have been separated from the text to allow easy access to the latter by general readers. Rather than attempt inclusiveness, the author concentrates on a smaller, yet still impressively large, number of artists. A very important and manageable study of a daunting subject. Recommended for general and academic readers.—*J. Weidman, Oberlin College*

OAB-0360 91-51144 Orig
Bayón, Damián. **History of South American colonial art and architecture: Spanish South America and Brazil,** by Damián Bayón and Murillo Marx. Rizzoli, 1992 (c1989). 442p bibl indexes ISBN 0-8478-1555-2, $85.00

This faithful English translation of the monumental work originally published in Spanish (Barcelona, 1989) supersedes Leopoldo Castedo's very sketchy *A History of Latin American Art and Architecture from Pre-Columbian Times to the Present* (1969), providing a comprehensive overview of colonial South American architecture, painting, and sculpture from Panama to Chile, including Brazil. The organization of the text is strictly chronological and by modern country, however, not necessarily reflecting the reality of artistic geography during the colonial period. Despite the opening statement by one of the authors indicating that "[p]art of the difficulty involved in presenting a cultural overview of the colonies lies in recognizing the geographical, climatic and human differences which the new colonists found with each new step," the discussion focuses almost exclusively on description and factual information drawn from secondary sources. The documentation presented is thus far from complete; and major omissions can be noted in the general bibliographies. Nevertheless, useful catalogs of principal monuments including additional historical data and individual bibliographical references follow Parts 1 and 2 by Damián Bayón; and Part 3 by Murillo Marx. Most importantly, the 891 excellent illustrations—many in stunning color—permit a true appreciation of the special qualities of the rich artistic and architectural heritage of colonial South America. This impressive visual corpus will be invaluable for future studies. Recommended for all levels.—*H. Rodriguez-Camilloni, Virginia Polytechnic Institute and State University*

OAB-0361 N6260 93-49561 CIP
Blair, Sheila S. **The art and architecture of Islam, 1250-1800,** by Sheila S. Blair and Jonathan M. Bloom. Yale, 1994. 348p bibl index ISBN 0-300-05888-8, $65.00

This is a worthy sequel to *The Art and Architecture of Islam, 650-1250* (1987) by the eminent scholars Richard Ettinghausen and Oleg Grabar in the series "The Pelican History of Art." Produced in a remarkably short time for a book of its breadth and scholarship, the work under review is up-to-date in the current research on Islamic art, and the text is informative as well as lucid. The authors investigate the vast artistic material of the Muslim world succinctly, explaining subjects such as patronage and the role of the artist and workshops and raising questions regarding the function, purpose, and meaning of the work of art in regional and imperial Islamic lands. The survey begins with the era of the Mongol invasion of the Near East and ends around 1800, with the expansion of European political and artistic influences into the Muslim world, and its consequences for the arts. The choice and quality of illustrations are quite satisfactory in most cases. The plans provided for architecture are adequate. The bibliography, including the references in the endnotes, is extremely useful to the student of Islamic art. This book, together with the first volume, is the best, if not the only text to be recommended for college-level courses, and a useful reference book for scholars.—*U. U. Bates, CUNY Hunter College*

OAB-0362 N5340 94-16269 CIP
Boardman, John. **The diffusion of classical art in antiquity.** Princeton, 1995 (c1994). 352p index afp (Bollingen series, 42) ISBN 0-691-03680-2, $49.50

Boardman, a distinguished scholar of Classical art, has achieved a magisterial exposition of the diffusion of Greek fifth- and fourth-century BCE art, first to the limits of Alexander's conquests and finally to the boundaries of the Roman Empire. He traces the intrusion of Greek art into Persia, India, and Central Asia, into Egypt and North Africa, along the Black Sea, and into the Punic West, Italy, and Western Europe. Boardman concentrates on the successes and failures of Greek art in penetrating into the artistic cultures of non-Greeks; his book is primarily about the foreigners' reception, often without much understanding of that art; and he emphasizes the importance of media, packed with images, motifs, and representative conventions rather than their meaning, asserting, as well, the opacity of the Greek artists' intentions. He also takes pains to record the foreigners' responses to the elements he considers essentially Greek: nudity and the naturalistic representation of the human body and its ambient space; expressive modes of emotional or ethical states; narrative; and ornamental repertories derived from vegetal forms—all features of a descriptive realism, associated in his mind with Greek art. He has, thus, redefined Greek art in terms of its strangeness and desirability in the eyes of "others." Undergraduate; graduate; faculty.—*R. Brilliant, Columbia University*

OAB-0363 N7428 92-29047 CIP
Braun, Barbara. **Pre-Columbian art and the post-Columbian world: ancient American sources of modern art.** Abrams, 1993. 339p bibl index ISBN 0-8109-3723-9, $75.00

In contrast to previous studies, which focused principally on the effects of African and Oceanic "primitivism" on 20th-century art, this book explores the significance of Pre-Columbian artistic forms and ideas, "influences [the author informs us] that have been generally overlooked." Following a decade of meticulous research, Braun (curator and lecturer in art history and archaeology) examines various characteristics of Mesoamerica (Mexico and Guatemala) and the Peruvian-Bolivian area that significantly influenced the works of five eminent modern artists: Paul Gauguin, Henry Moore, Frank Lloyd Wright, Diego Rivera, and Joaquin Torres-Garcia. Discussions note the affinities of Gauguin's ceramics and Moche stirrup-spout jars; Moore's monumental sculpture and Toltec-Maya stone figures; Wright's innovative architecture and Maya Revival buildings and decorative symbolism; Rivera's vast public murals rooted in pre-Hispanic themes; and Torres-Garcia's Constructivist grids and the pictographic motifs found in Paracas textiles, Nazca ceramics, and at Tiwanaku. Superbly illustrated with more than 100 colored plates and 200 black-and-white photographs. An illustrated time chart designates major regional developments for Mexican, Mayan, and Andean areas, and detailed maps locate relevant sites within contemporary national boundaries. Extensive notes and references. Invaluable for art historians, anthropologists, and other scholars of Pre-Columbian art and culture.—*H. H. Schuster, emerita, Iowa State University*

OAB-0364 N6510 96-5929 CIP
Burns, Sarah. **Inventing the modern artist: art and culture in Gilded Age America.** Yale, 1997 (c1996). 380p index afp ISBN 0-300-06445-4, $50.00

The most interesting work being done today in art history is that which explores art in its social and historical context. Burns (Indiana Univ.) has produced a consummate example of this kind of scholarship. Her book is deeply researched, thoughtful, and wonderfully well written. Her time is the last two decades of the 19th century and the early years of the 20th. The principal artists involved are Whistler, Sargent, Homer, Ryder, Inness, William Merritt Chase, Charles Dana Gibson, Cecilia Beaux, and Thomas Hovenden. The argument, a cluster of essays really, is the cultural construction of the artist, the relationship among image making, the marketplace, gender, politics, and the formation of American artistic identity, a formidable task that is brilliantly accomplished. Upper-division undergraduate; graduate; faculty; general.—*J. T. Frazer, Wesleyan University*

OAB-0365 N6510 93-9784 CIP
Cooper, Wendy A. **Classical taste in America, 1800-1840.** Baltimore Museum of Art/Abbeville, 1993. 308p bibl index ISBN 1-55859-385-3, $55.00

With splendid pictures in lavish color, this book forms the catalog/explication for an exhibition in 1993-94 in Baltimore, Charlotte, and Houston. An introduction by Richard L. Bushman (Columbia) offers context for the period, indicating how Americans were "mesmerized by the classical world." Not a catalog per se, this book is rather five essays with objects as examples, in which Cooper (curator, Decorative Arts, Baltimore Museum of Art) shows how the objects indicate new—for Americans—classical ideas and ideals. Though Americans bor-

rowed from classical Antiquity, and occasionally from Egypt, contemporary France, and England, they always made "American" interpretations. This is the theme through which Cooper's research and all the objects discussed are integrated. Most of the material culture of the period is covered, with the exception of architecture, but furniture and furnishings are the major focus. Excellent information about dissemination of ideas, consumer demand, technology, marketing, trade practices, collections, and collectors. Extensive notes, definitive bibliography, and checklist for the objects in the three exhibitions. This book is now *the* authority on this period's material culture and on the some 200 specific objects discussed. Highly recommended.—*W. L. Whitwell, Hollins College*

OAB-0366 Orig
Cox-Rearick, Janet. **The collection of Francis I: royal treasures.** Fonds Mercator/Abrams, 1995. 493p bibl index ISBN 0-8109-4038-8, $145.00

This lavish book documents the royal collection of Italian Renaissance and Mannerist painting and sculpture formed by Francis I, king of France between 1515 and 1547. Although not the first study of this collection, this work is unparalleled in depth and breadth of research material. The text, written in a clear, straightforward manner, consists of a discussion of the patronage, goals, and taste of the king, as traced through the creation of his collection. Although Cox-Rearick (Hunter College) focuses on painting and sculpture, Francis I made no distinction between the arts. Images and objects were integrated into the setting at Fontainebleau to create an environment that demonstrated royal power and taste. Francis I was the first French king to collect art in a systematic way. His precocious development is traced through documents, which describe how, at age ten, he requested a work by Mantegna. As king, he surrounded himself with Italian, French, and Flemish court artists, creating a vibrant art culture worthy of study. The text concludes with a complete catalog of the collection that includes beautiful illustrations and extensive documentary research. Upper-division undergraduate; graduate; faculty.—*A. L. Palmer, University of Oklahoma*

OAB-0367 N8214 95-7051 CIP
Davis, John. **The landscape of belief: encountering the Holy Land in nineteenth-century American art and culture.** Princeton, 1996. 264p bibl index afp ISBN 0-691-04373-6, $65.00

The high-flown praise in the dust jacket blurb is almost unnecessary. The book is clearly a major contribution to American cultural studies. It is an outgrowth of an article Davis (Smith College) wrote for *Smithsonian Studies in American Art* in 1987, entitled "Frederic Church's 'Sacred Geography.'" In that article, Davis explored Church's motives for going to what used to be called the Near East. In the present work Davis casts his net wider and asks why 19th-century Americans in general visited, wrote about, and depicted the Holy Land. He demonstrates clearly that Americans could find corroboration, in the Holy Land, of just about any ideological or aesthetic viewpoint they chose to maintain. This book is to be lauded for its interdisciplinary approach and for the way in which equal attention is paid to major and minor artists (Miner Kellogg, Edward Troye, and James Fairman get as much respect and coverage as the more famous Frederic Church). The book is written in a light and engaging style, with little of the jargon so often found in art-historical texts today. Seven color plates and 100 black-and-white illustrations. Highly recommended. General; undergraduate; graduate; faculty.—*M. W. Sullivan, Villanova University*

OAB-0368 N6520 96-9373 CIP
Delehanty, Randolph. **Art in the American South: works from the Ogden collection.** Louisiana State, 1996. 292p bibl indexes afp ISBN 0-8071-2100-2, $59.95

In his first chapter, Delehanty states that "the visual arts in the South are beginning to get the attention they deserve. The last frontier of American art is at last being explored." His book is an exemplary survey of Southern art selected from the collection of New Orleans attorney Roger Houston Ogden. Delehanty, former curator of the collection, focuses on 237 pieces from more than 1,100.

He includes works by both self-taught artists and artists from academic schools and provides an eclectic mix of paintings, drawings, watercolors, pastels, engraving, lithographs, photography, ceramics, and sculpture. The works are arranged thematically—landscapes; marine paintings; representations of southern flora and fauna; and works in clay; still lifes; rural and urban scenes; and portraits of southerners—but also, within each section, chronologically. Thus Delehanty's expert commentary enables the readers to trace the complex history of the region's art. Delehanty points out that many, if not most, of the artists are not well known and little research is available on them; therefore he tells the basics: who, what, when, and where of the artists and the works selected. An excellent and significant contribution to the emerging study of Southern art. Highly recommended for all academic libraries with art collections. General; undergraduate through professional.—*N. M. Lambert, University of South Carolina at Spartanburg*

OAB-0369 N71 93-3468 CIP
Freeman, Mark. **Finding the muse: a sociopsychological inquiry into the conditions of artistic creativity.** Cambridge, 1994 (c1993). 330p bibl index ISBN 0-521-39218-7, $44.95

An outstanding work, this book provides novel and profound insights into the complex of factors underpinning artistic creativity. Focusing on the lives of a number of aspiring artists working during the turbulent period of the 1960s to 1980s, Freeman examines specific economic, political, cultural, and ideological factors that both allow for, and militate against, artistic creativity in the contemporary world. Rejecting essentialist and reified conceptions of creativity and of the artist as transcending his or her life conditions, Freeman seeks to demonstrate that aspiring artists are impacted in their work by all of the conditions that beset any who strive to be productive and innovative in a radically changing world. Engaging, critically, a variety of "individualist" views focusing on the encapsulation of the artist, the author makes a strong case for the socio-historical-cultural constitution both of artists and works of art. An exceptionally well written book, accessible both to professional scholars and to intelligent general readers. A "find." General; upper-division undergraduate through faculty.—*B. Kaplan, Clark University*

OAB-0370 N6250 96-45584 CIP
The Glory of Byzantium: art and culture of the Middle Byzantine era, A.D. 843-1261, ed. by Helen C. Evans and William D. Wixom. Metropolitan Museum of Art, 1997. (Dist. by Abrams) 574p bibl index ISBN 0-8109-6507-0, $85.00

This catalog of the stupendous exhibition of Byzantine art that closed in July 1997 is by far the most lavish example of the genre yet produced. Weighing nearly seven pounds and recording more than 400 objects (clusters of similar pieces are sometimes grouped in a single entry), it automatically becomes for scholars a standard reference work, even while students, unaccustomed to the presence of conflicting opinions within the pages of a single work, will be puzzled by radical differences in modes of description, chronology, and conceptions of relative significance. The great triumph of the show was the assemblage of icons and other objects from Sinai and the monasteries of Mount Athos, but scarcely less important is the host of little-known objects in a great variety of media, from Ukraine, Bulgaria, Georgia, and Egypt. Almost every piece is superbly reproduced in color, often for the first time. It is this documentation, rather than the 17 short and sometimes quite pedestrian introductory essays, that constitutes the book's enduring value. General; upper-division undergraduate; graduate; faculty.—*A. Cutler, Pennsylvania State University, University Park Campus*

OAB-0371 94-61010 Orig
The Glory of Venice: art in the eighteenth century, ed. by Jane Martineau and Andrew Robison. Yale, 1994. 528p bibl index ISBN 0-300-06185-4, $55.00

This superb book is the catalog of the exhibition shown at the Royal Academy,

London, from September through December 1994 and being shown at the National Gallery of Art, Washington, from January through April 1995. It includes 292 paintings, drawings, prints, books, and sculpture, most of which are illustrated in color. The plates are distributed throughout the volume, appearing as illustrations for the essays, which are written by English, American, and Italian authorities and are devoted to such subjects as the international taste for Venetian art and cultural politics, and to such major artists as the Tiepolos, Canaletto, Piazzetta, the Riccis, the Guardis, Bellotto, Piranesi, and Canova. There are also essays on such subjects as Rococo artists and religious, genre, townscape, and landscape painting. The individual catalog entries of the works are listed by the artist and preceded by excellent brief biographies and bibliography. These are all by specialists. The book has a thorough bibliography and an excellent index. Naturally limited to works that could be borrowed (although it includes illustrations of others such as wall paintings and architecture), the catalog is a major contribution to the subject and invites comparison with *Painting in 18th Century Venice* (3rd ed., 1994; 2nd ed., CH,Feb'81), by Sir Michael Levey, who incidentally, is one of the contributors to the present volume. Highly recommended. Upper-division undergraduate; graduate; faculty; general.—*T. J. McCormick, emeritus, Wheaton College (MA)*

OAB-0372 N6921 92-36349 CIP
Humfrey, Peter. **The altarpiece in Renaissance Venice.** Yale, 1993. 382p bibl index ISBN 0-300-05358-4, $60.00

As art historians turn their attention away from stylistic development and ask new questions of works of art, the issue of genres of artistic production becomes increasingly important. This book is the most comprehensive treatment of the altarpiece to date. It provides a wealth of information regarding the production, function, development, and major practitioners of the altarpiece in Venice, focusing on the period 1450-1530. Particularly welcome is the attention to the sculpted altarpiece, a specialty of the Venetian art market. The first half of the book emphasizes production, including illuminating discussions of matters such as altar patronage—*jus patronatus*—and design and construction of frames. The second half highlights the contributions of individual artists to the genre, placing well-known works by Giovanni Bellini and Titian in a broad perspective that includes many lesser workshops. Useful features are the numerous tables, which provide instant surveys of the material, and the appendix of 100 selected altarpieces, which gives a cross-section of the book's contents. The author's scrupulous attention to detail combined with an encyclopedic knowledge of the subject make this a study that will set the standard for all future work in the field. Lavishly illustrated with good color plates and numerous views of altarpieces in their settings. General; graduate; undergraduate; faculty.—*D. Pincus, University of British Columbia*

OAB-0373 N6537 95-35800 CIP
Icons of American Protestantism: the art of Warner Sallman, ed. by David Morgan. Yale, 1996. 246p index afp ISBN 0-300-06342-3, $35.00

At first glance, this book's small format (about 9" x 6") and title could lead one to think that it is a modest monograph on a lesser-known American religious artist. But *Icons*, which grew out of an article on Sallman's *Head of Christ* that Morgan wrote for *The Christian Century* in 1992, is much more than a study of Sallman's life and work. Some of the country's leading historians of American culture here test out their latest theories on the development of culture, using Sallman as a case study. There is a foreword by Neil Harris, whose *The Artist in American Society* (CH, Jul'67) was one of the first attempts to "contextualize" the American work of art; and essays by Morgan, Erika Doss, Colleen McDannell, Betty A. DeBerg, and Sally M. Promey, all of whom are already noted for their belief that one can learn as much by studying commercial art as by studying "fine" art. This book, along with Michele Bogart's *Artists, Advertising, and the Borders of Art* (1995), will guarantee that commercial art will never again be treated lightly by scholars. Highly recommended; a great example of the recent trend toward interdisciplinary approaches as well. Upper-division undergraduate; graduate; faculty.—*M. W. Sullivan, Villanova University*

OAB-0374   N6537   95-2520 CIP
John Singleton Copley in America, by Carrie Rebora et al. Metropolitan Museum of Art, 1995. (Dist. by Abrams) 348p bibl index ISBN 0-8109-6492-9, $65.00

With 364 illustrations, 117 in superb color, this book now defines Copley. There are eight essays by seven well-known scholars, an 81-item catalog with pictures, detailed notes, and a comprehensive bibliography—all offering new scholarship about Copley's American work (c. 1765-74). Art, social history, structural analysis, genealogy, economics, patronage, and iconography are used to place the artist in the context of 18th-century Boston. Many new theories are put foward about colonial American conspicuous consumption and class expression, along with Copley's patronage and marketing. How Copley created identity and class definition for his sitters by settings, body language, and costumes is a revelation. Insights into 18th-century life continue in extensive sources from many disciplines. Jules David Prown's two-volume *John Singleton Copley* (CH, Oct'66) remains important; but this work goes far beyond, into the artist's contribution to Amerian culture before the Revolution. The work covers paintings, pastels, prints, miniatures, and the original frames. A valuable purchase for its survey of Copley's American work, his images and their social content, and for many new understandings of 18th-century culture. General; upper-division undergraduate through professional.—*W. L. Whitwell, Hollins College*

OAB-0375   N6490   92-1733 CIP
Kuspit, Donald. **The cult of the avant-garde artist.** Cambridge, 1993. 175p index ISBN 0-521-41345-1, $40.00

A profoundly intelligent and provocative psychological discussion of the changing role of the avant-garde artist and art object within the paradigmatic shift from modernism to postmodernism. Beginning with a compelling description of the modern heroicization of the avant-garde artist into an artist-healer, Kuspit then segues neatly into his theory of modernism's therapeutic intent. Various attempts at healing are traced in chapters that focus on distortion (Picasso, Duchamp), geometry (Mondrian, Malevich), and expression (Kandinsky, Surrealism). Though problematic, all appear favorable when compared to the disillusionment, narcissism, and irony that characterize postmodernism and its societal values, as exemplified in chapters on Warhol, Beuys, and appropriation artists. This complex, sometimes difficult book offers a new treatment on modern art, and it should also prove worthwhile to graduate and advanced undergraduate students interested in the relationship between modernism and postmodernism, the application of a psychological methodology, and the author's thought-provoking perspectives on the above-mentioned artists. Kuspit (Cornell and SUNY, Stony Brook) has produced an impressive text consistent with his prolific contribution to contemporary art history.—*S. L. Jenkins, University of Southern California*

OAB-0376   N6853   96-21441 CIP
Laughton, Bruce. **Honoré Daumier.** Yale, 1997 (c1996). 200p bibl index ISBN 0-300-06945-6, $55.00

Earlier, Yale published Laughton's lovely book *The Drawings of Daumier and Millet* (CH, Dec'91). This new volume on the life and art of Daumier is an even finer work, a deeply researched, carefully detailed analysis of all areas of Daumier's work. This will be the catalogue raisonné on Daumier in the English language. The work looks at not only the familiar political lithographs but also the watercolors and, most interestingly, the much less studied oils and sculptures. Throughout the book, Laughton (emeritus, Queen's Univ., Canada) emphasizes the interrelatedness of the several media and the connections between Daumier's work and his life. This is an exemplary volume with many excellent reproductions. General; undergraduate through professional.—*J. T. Frazer, Wesleyan University*

OAB-0377   N5970   92-6252 CIP
Mellinkoff, Ruth. **Outcasts: signs of otherness in northern European art of the late Middle Ages. v.1: Text; v.2: Illustrations.** California, 1994 (c1993). 2v. 360p; v.2 unpaged bibl index (California studies in the history of art, 32) ISBN 0-520-07815-2, $195.00

This study widens our interpretive horizon of 14th- and 15th-century Netherlandish and German society and its mentality. Most of the arguments in the *Text* volume revolve around a framing analysis of imagery, in particular the often neglected and less researched signs of the "other" and the unfamiliar. Throughout, the author weaves a net of meaning with emphasis on the negative. Mellinkoff argues quite convincingly that society's most profound views are expressed in these. The book has an unusual subdivision, but this helps the reader who wants to approach all the material at once. There are two distinct sections, consisting of four chapters and seven chapters respectively. Mellinkoff, in the first part, analyzes elements of costume via a decoding frame of context. She proceeds with her contextual analysis in four distinct chapters: artists' use of patterns; the use of color; headgear; and special meaning and the use of Hebrew and pseudo-Hebrew lettering. The second part is entirely devoted to physical features and the body; the principles of unusual physical features; use of distortions and deformations; the meaning of colored hair and hairstyles; vulgar gestures; and, finally, social rank and moral character suggested by location, position, and stance. Most arguments are well crafted and thematically focused, with minute attention to contemporary mentality and prejudice. This allows any reader to access the chapters independently and in no particular order, which is one of the many attractive features of this book.

Equally appropriate and thoughtful is a second volume entirely devoted to high-quality illustrations, providing an impressive and very necessary visual archive for further detailed study. Mellinkoff's study offers a unique and at times very imaginative interpretation that moves away from the rather traditional frame of art historical interpretation. It is a most valuable introduction to imagery and referential sign systems in the Late Middle Ages and a critical reminder of the latent presence of societal prejudice in all its hidden constructs. General; undergraduate through professional.—*H. J. Van Miegroet, Duke University*

OAB-0378   DU125   91-15544 MARC
Morphy, Howard. **Ancestral connections: art and an aboriginal system of knowledge.** Chicago, 1992 (c1991). 329p bibl index afp ISBN 0-226-53865-6, $47.50; ISBN 0-226-53866-4 pbk, $19.95

The Yolngu peoples of Australia's Northeast Arnhem Land have been the focus of anthropological inquiry since the 1930s, documenting a culture rich in aesthetic, religious, and social life. Morphy (Oxford) makes a major contribution with this analysis of Yolngu art as a communication system. Drawing on fieldwork at Yirrkala in the 1970s and 1980s, he uses a semiotic frame to detail how art (specifically, bark paintings) encodes the multiple meanings of the larger sociocultural system. His view is holistic, the subject complex, the presentation admirable clear: (1) the historical and social context; (2) the structural components and types of paintings; and (3) the iconography of the Manggalili clan art of Narritjin Maymuru. The art codes "inside" and "outside" knowledge, validates clan rights, ties the ancestral past to the present, and structures adaptation. Line drawings; photographs; extensive bibliography; orthography note. This reviewer (who worked at Yirrkala in the 1950s) highly recommends Morphy's book to students (and buyers) of art, communication systems, culture, and culture change as well as to Australianists. General; undergraduate through faculty.—*P. Waterman, University of South Florida*

OAB-0379   N5633   91-23831 CIP
Morris, Sarah P. **Daidalos and the origins of Greek art.** Princeton, 1992. 411p, 62 plates bibl index afp ISBN 0-691-03599-7, $69.50

No brief review can do justice to the originality and breadth of this major work of revisionist scholarship that uses the pivotal role of Daidalos, the magical artificer of ancient Crete, to characterize fundamental changes in Greek culture, myth, and art over a millenium. Gathering an imposing array of linguistic, literary, archaeological, and historical sources from around the Mediterranean, the author has demonstrated the profound, appreciative dependence of the

Greeks on the Levantine "East", beginning in the Late Bronze Age. Morris claims that Greek culture took shape largely in response to Levantine models of economic and social organization, cult, metal-working crafts, and verbal and visual imagery, and then transformed them. With the Greek triumph over the Persians and their Phoenician allies in the fifth century BCE., the thought of this cultural dependence was no longer acceptable. In Athens the Greek debt to the East was intentionally suppressed and even replaced by an inventive mythology that affirmed Greek cultural independence and its superiority over the barbarian "other." Thus, the Athenian hero Theseus would bring Daidalos to Athens, contemporary historical events were given an indigenous mythological pedigree, and a doctrine of negative Orientalism was confected, not by modern scholars but by the ancient Greeks to assert an uncontaminated Hellensim. Advanced undergraduate; graduate.—*R. Brilliant, Columbia University*

OAB-0380   N7355   94-4557 CIP
Munroe, Alexandra. **Japanese art after 1945: scream against the sky.** Abrams, 1994. 416p bibl index ISBN 0-8109-3512-0, $65.00

It is incredible that an English-language book on this subject has only now appeared. This explains, perhaps, why this catalog, written to accompany a major exhibition (being shown at the SoHo Guggenheim in New York City and at the San Francisco Museum of Modern Art), seems stuffed to the bursting point with ideas, personalities, aesthetic concepts, cultural and political attitudes, and everything else touched by the contemporary arts of Japan in the past 50 years. There are 15 essays by or concerning such figures as Isozaki Arata, Nam June Paik, the Gutai Group, Butoh performance art, painting, sculpture, theater, film, video, metaphysics, and on and on. The book has many superb reproductions and concludes with a fine critical anthology. In short, this is the essential book about an important sector of contemporary art, an area too often neglected until now. General; undergraduate through professional.—*J. T. Frazer, Wesleyan University*

OAB-0381   N6915   96-18459 CIP
Paoletti, John T. **Art in Renaissance Italy,** by John T. Paoletti and Gary M. Radke. Abrams, 1997. 480p bibl index ISBN 0-8109-1978-8, $60.00

For almost 30 years, the best-known, comprehensive textbook on Italian Renaissance art has been Frederick Hartt's *History of Italian Renaissance Art* (CH, May'70; 4th ed., 1994), although its traditional, somewhat narrow emphasis on style and artistic biography has made it increasingly problematic. The impressively erudite volume under review can be seen as an alternative to Hartt that is based on more contemporary methodological approaches. Paoletti and Radke stress above all the importance of patron and context and the ways in which the milieu can influence form and content. The text is organized by cities and types of commissions, not by artists. In addition, this new book redresses the overwhelmingly Tuscan bias of most Renaissance texts, giving substantial coverage to other centers such as Naples, Milan, Venice, and Rome; it is especially effective in treating courtly art, including its manifestation in 16th-century Mannerism. Richly illustrated, the text contains useful supplements such as excerpts from contemporary writings, city maps, capsule artist biographies, and a glossary. Although there are surprising omissions of certain "canonical" works, this is an obvious and necessary addition for any library, and will serve as a sound reference for all readers. General; undergraduate; graduate; faculty.—*J. I. Miller, California State University, Long Beach*

OAB-0382   NX556   92-20814 CIP
Parton, Anthony. **Mikhail Larionov and the Russian avant-garde.** Princeton, 1993. 254p bibl index afp ISBN 0-691-03603-9, $49.50

Parton's study sets a new standard for scholarly books on Russian art. Although he gives few detailed explications of the lavishly reproduced paintings (30 in color, 216 paintings and photographs in black and white), he discusses as no one before has done the intellectual setting of Larionov's work. Parton explains in lucid prose what Larionov knew of such diverse phenom-

ena as shamans and X rays, where he acquired this knowledge, and what he made of it. Parton also takes seriously the phrase "and the Russian Avante Garde" in his title. Drawing on the Larionov archive at the Victoria and Albert Museum as well as other sources, he describes the various people—some famous, some obscure—with whom Larionov collaborated, what he learned from them, and how they affected his work. In doing so, Parton also gives us some idea of how one might organize a synthetic, well-informed history of modern Russian culture. All in all, a most impressive achievement. Advanced undergraduate; graduate; faculty.—*J. M. Curtis, University of Missouri—Columbia*

OAB-0383   N6797   91-40344 CIP
Patten, Robert L. **George Cruikshank's life, times, and art: v.1: 1792-1835.** Rutgers, 1992. 495p indexes ISBN 0-8135-1813-X, $50.00

Patten, a noted scholar of English literature whose publications include *Charles Dickens and His Publishers* (1978), presents a closely argued yet readable biography of George Cruikshank. Chronologically organized, the text illuminates the sociopolitical and cultural fabric of this first phase of the caricaturist's career while also evoking his personality and artistic practice. Particularly commendable are Patten's deft analyses of Cruikshank's more significant etchings, adequately rather than well reproduced, to describe his interpretation of current iconographic conventions and historical events. Moreover, these are used to reconstruct the London print trade and discuss audience reaction, taking full account of the ambivalent attitude of sovereign and grandees. The book is crammed with information and much insight on the Regency era. In support are a useful prefatory chronology, abbreviated list of archival sources, full endnotes—of no little fascination—and genealogies; a bibliography will doubtless accompany the second volume. Of interest to the general reader but most appropriate for professional scholars, this will become a standard work of reference, greatly extending the Victorian accounts and more recent exhibitions at the J.B. Speed Art Museum, Louisville, 1968, and Victoria and Albert Museum, London, 1974, as well as such general studies as E. Lucie-Smith, *The Art of Caricature* (CH, Feb'82).—*R. W. Liscombe, University of British Columbia*

OAB-0384   Orig
Piranesi, Giambattista. **Giovanni Battista Piranesi: the complete etchings,** by John Wilton-Ely. A. Wofsy Fine Arts, 1994. 2v. 1,264p bibl indexes ISBN 1-55660-150-6, $350.00

Piranesi's more than 1,000 etchings of real and imaginary ancient and modern Rome, including antiquities, archaeological sites, maps, and illustrations for theoretical works, were the greatest single force in the reawakening interest in Antiquity, that began in the second half of the 18th century. Their tremendous influence on taste and scholarship continued through the 19th century and into the 20th.

Although Piranesi's work has been extensively studied and cataloged, this major publication is the first to reproduce all the known works—including one rediscovered in the 1960s and several begun by him and completed by his son Francesco. Henri Focillon's basic catalog of 1918 listed nearly all of the etchings but was unillustrated. Arthur Hind's 1922 study was limited to the *Vedute di Roma* and the *Carceri*, and Andrew Robison's book of 1986 discussed only the early architectural fantasies, although both these books were fully illustrated.

Wilton-Ely, the leading Piranesi scholar and author of *Piranesi as Architect and Designer* (CH, Feb'94), now offers this superb two-volume production, which includes the etchings, arranged chronologically and topically grouped as they originally appeared—i.e., as Piranesi had published them. Wilton-Ely has supplied an excellent general introduction, a good description and history preceding each group of etchings, excellent appendixes, four indexes, a concordance to the various catalogs of prints, and a very complete bibliography, all of which make this a superb reference work. A major contribution, highly recommended. General; upper-division undergraduate through professional.—*T. J. McCormick, emeritus, Wheaton College (MA)*

OAB-0385   N7321   92-8272 CIP
Poshyananda, Apinan. **Modern art in Thailand.** Oxford, 1992. 259p bibl index ISBN 0-19-588562-7, $59.00

The first book to extensively examine the development of art in modern Thailand proves to be excellent. A broad range of influences—European and American as well as Buddhist and traditional—make for an intrinsically interesting subject. The 64 color plates of first-rate quality and 150 black-and-white plates reveal this fascinating variety of styles. For example, color plate 53 shows two realistically rendered happy young Thai children playing in the sun, surrounded by darker areas, which reveal tanks and money, and starving youngsters. Plate 54 shows Thai palace buildings with royal rowboats, done in traditional style. Abstract expressionism, folk-style realism, photo realism, emotional paintings with antiwar themes, Western-style portraits, surrealistic scenes and mixed media are some (but not all) of the varieties of approach. Poshyananda, a professor at a Thai university, has the breadth of knowledge and objectivity to write intelligently about all facets of what could be a bewildering eclecticism. He manages to exclude subjective reactions in his admirable discussions of the widely differing art works. Highly recommended. Advanced undergraduate, graduate, faculty, general.—*T. B. Hoffman, University of South Florida*

OAB-0386   N3750   95-49102 Orig
Possessing the past: treasures from the National Palace Museum, by Wen C. Fong and James C.Y. Watt. Metropolitan Museum of Art/National Palace Museum, 1996. (Dist. by Abrams) 648p bibl index ISBN 0-8109-6494-5, $85.00

This hefty volume accompanies an exhibition (currently being seen in major US museums) selected from what had been the Imperial treasures of China—specifically, the personal collection of the emperor Ch'ien-lung, who ruled from 1736 to 1795. It is much more than a catalog of that exhibition. Conceived as a grand cultural history of Imperial China and written by major scholars of Chinese art, through an ingenious collaborative effort, it tells the story of Chinese art from its beginnings until the dawn of the modern era. Drawing on an extraordinary Palace collection passed on from dynasty to dynasty and continuously augmented, it demonstrates, as well, the comprehensive character of the collection of treasures it celebrates. The major theme is the cultural significance of the visual arts—as this is understood from a Chinese vantage point—and the evolution, over a long stretch of time, of highly specified views of the social functions of art. Another major theme informs the commentary and gives the book its title: the traditions of defining and shaping change through inventive reconstitutions of the past. The authors, individually and together, synthesize the best scholarship of the past three decades on the subject and reexamine the cultural dynamics of China's history, providing new bases for understanding it. Sumptuous color photographs; chronologies; charts; extensive bibliography. Indispensable for the study of Chinese art for years to come. General; undergraduate through professional.—*D. K. Dohanian, University of Rochester*

OAB-0387   N6512   95-17096 CIP
Sandler, Irving. **Art of the postmodern era: from the late 1960s to the early 1990s.** Icon Editions, 1996. 636p bibl index ISBN 0-06-438509-4, $65.00

This very hefty book (with 200 black-and-white and eight color plates) is a continuation of Sandler's previous publications on American art of the modern period. It will undoubtedly and deservedly become as much of a classic and frequently thumbed text (and textbook) as the earlier volumes. The book presents an astonishing variety of material in a lucid and generally chronological manner, although openly privileging painting and sculpture over the other arts. The very real and rare strength of this book is that Sandler consistently presents multiple and often conflicting interpretations of the art, thus leading the reader to active engagement of the issues it represents. The bibliography is impressive (60 pages) and very useful, as are the notes for each chapter. There will be criticisms of Sandler's interpretations; his slighting of conceptual art and—despite a chapter on Italian and German art—his implicit assertion of the lead-

ership and hegemony of American art in the international artistic community are but two possible areas for controversy. On the whole, however, the book is a splendid compendium of the art and ideas of the last 30 years of American art. General; undergraduate (including two-year technical program); graduate.—*J. T. Paoletti, Wesleyan University*

OAB-0388   N6915   91-27246 CIP
Shearman, John. **Only connect: art and the spectator in the Italian Renaissance.** Princeton, 1992. 281p index afp (Bollingen series, 37) ISBN 0-691-09972-3, $49.50

Combining the directness and informality of their delivery as lectures with an extraordinary array of scholarly footnotes, Shearman's essays on Italian Renaissance sculpture, altarpieces, portraits, domes, and history painting should be read by all art historians and anyone interested in the Renaissance. Not since medieval manuscript painting, perhaps, have lower margins been so much fun; the footnotes (authentic footnotes still live!) introduce archival findings, literary references, an exceptionally wide range of historiographical information, ruminations on other parts of art history, asides that enhance the book's intellectual liveliness, and basic gallantry. The thesis that unifies this series of newly revealing, thorough analyses of familiar monuments is that Renaissance artists from Donatello through Titian developed a "transitive mode" by which a more engaged spectator was posited as the image's necessary complement. Pace medievalists, this entails no disparagement of earlier art; indeed, much respect is paid to Byzantine domes. It does offer an alternative axis to the old talk about progressive naturalism. A summation of decades of study, this text is due to become a classic, as have many of its predecessors deriving from the prestigious Mellon lecture series at the National Gallery.—*P. Emison, University of New Hampshire*

OAB-0389   N7399   92-47387 MARC
Steiner, Christopher B. **African art in transit.** Cambridge, 1994. 220p bibl index ISBN 0-521-43447-5, $54.95; ISBN 0-521-45752-1 pbk, $19.95

Expanding on Sally Price's challenging study, *Primitive Art in Civilized Places* (1989), Steiner raises further disquieting questions in his important research on the "commodification or commercial aspects" of African art trading activities in the international art market, including trade in cultural information and the mediation of knowledge as well as objects. The book is based on the Harvard-trained author's dissertation, a product of his study of African art markets in Côte d'Ivoire (Ivory Coast) in 1987-88 and 1990-91. Steiner describes the art markets and other commodity outlets, the various kinds of art traders who serve as mediators and "cultural brokers" between art producers and art consumers, and the transit and transition of African Art objects and their meanings through local, national, and transnational economies. The work is written in a clear, creative style, with eloquent descriptive phrases, making this important theoretical as well as factual and analytic study a reading delight. The bibliography and index are very complete; the references are meticulous in providing solid field documentation and other sources; and a 30-page section of notes contributes a wealth of additional, related information. Several maps and more than 40 black-and-white photographs provide visual details of Côte d'Ivoire and its markets and market traders. This study fills a critical gap in the fields of anthropology and art history; it also contributes valuable cross-cultural materials to political economy and sociology.—*H. H. Schuster, emerita, Iowa State University*

OAB-0390   N6505   91-3264 CIP
Strazdes, Diana. **American paintings and sculpture to 1945 in the Carnegie Museum of Art.** Hudson Hills/Carnegie Museum of Art, 1992. 511p index ISBN 1-55595-055-8, $95.00

This substantial catalogue raisonné from the Carnegie Art Museum is the lastest in a distinguished group, which includes, e.g., *American Figurative Sculpture in the Museum of Fine Arts Boston* (1986), *The American Collections: Columbus Museum of Art* (1988), and *The American Canvas: Paintings from* the Collection of the Fine Arts Museums of San Francisco (1989). It also serves as an important complement to *American Drawings and Watercolors in the Museum of Art, Carnegie Institute* (1985). Strazdes and her excellent staff have presented a wealth of material on a broad spectrum in the history of American art and within an exemplary format and a well-bound support. Arranged alphabetically by artist's last name, the catalogue documents more than 270 works by some 230 artists, with 20 of the artists/works listed as "Unidentified," after the Ws. Besides the high quality catalogue entries, each work is accompanied by a small black-and-white photograph. More than 100 entries for more than ten artists concern the work of Pittsburgh-area painters, and all of the Pittsburgh-area artists have three or more. Artists represented include the best-known John Kane and David Gilmour Blythe. Other well-known artists include Chase, Eakins, Hassam, Manship, Roesen, Saint-Gaudens, and Sully. With 36 color plates, an essay on the collection's development by Strazdes, and a good index, this is a model of comprehensive scholarship and accessibility. Highly recommended for all collections of American art.— *J. Weidman, Oberlin College*

OAB-0391   N7343   94-49679 MARC
Watson, William. **The arts of China to AD 900.** Yale, 1996 (c1995). 276p bibl index ISBN 0-300-05989-2, $65.00

The first of three volumes ("The Pelican History of Art") that will survey the arts of China from prehistoric times through the 20th century, this lavishly illustrated book investigates the beginnings of the production of art in China—multiple in character, mode, and technique—and of the traditions that have shaped it and on which it is based. The discourse extends chronologically until the end of the era of the T'ang Dynasty. Watson (Univ. of London) offers a broad and varied sample: metalwork, jade, pottery and porcelain, lacquerwork, architecture, sculpture, and the distinguished arts of painting. These are presented side by side and in technological and chronological groupings. Religious and secular themes are carefully examined and, where pertinent, discussed in relation to each other. Color and black-and-white illustrations inform the text at every stage and relieve the somewhat stilted writing. The text is full of useful information culled from the best scholarly research, to which both notes and bibliography generously refer. Poor editing mars the discussion here and there but does not diminish the high authority of both author and text. When complete, the three-volume set will prove indispensable to all libraries. Lower-division undergraduate; general.—*D. K. Dohanian, University of Rochester*

OAB-0392   N7343   94-18434 CIP
Wu, Hung. **Monumentality in early Chinese art and architecture.** Stanford, 1995. 376p bibl index ISBN 0-8047-2428-8, $75.00

With this book, Wu (Univ. of Chicago) has clearly cemented his leading position among a very small group of scholars of early Chinese art, broadly defined. Its scope (about 3,000 years from the Neolithic through the Northern and Southern Dynasties) is breathtaking and its insights are simply unmatched in depth by any other book. The "organizing concept" of "monumentality" here has nothing to do with size; rather it refers to objects of greatest cultural, political, ethical, or religious significance in their time—objects that "reminded the public of what it should believe and how it should act." The five chapters are in one sense a rich synthesis (with more than 400 well-chosen figures), but Wu so consistently and effectively challenges "conventional wisdom" that virtually every page contains a stunning new insight. For example, no one would have imagined that "temple," "palace," and "tomb" changed as concepts over some 2,000 years so that "Important signifiers of monumentality thus shifted from within to without—from objects to architecture, depth to surface, concealment to exhibition." If one is going to have only one book on early Chinese art, this is it. Undergraduate; graduate; faculty; general.—*J. O. Caswell, University of British Columbia*

■ Architecture

OAB-0393   NA2707   93-25102 CIP
The architectural drawings of Antonio da Sangallo the Younger and his circle: v.1: Fortifications, machines, and festival architecture, ed. by Christoph L. Frommel and Nicholas Adams. Architectural History Foundation/MIT, 1994. 522p bibl indexes ISBN 0-262-06155-4, $95.00

When completed, this set will be a monument and the benchmark against which all similar architectural studies must be measured. In his masterful introductory essay, Frommel asserts that Antonio da SanGallo the younger is pivotal in a study of 16th-century Italian architecture. He was formed by 15th-century architectural practice and especially by the work of his uncles, Bramante, Raphael, and antiquity. From the pontificates of Leo X through Paul III he was involved in major projects—St. Peter's, palaces, churches, and fortifications—and directly or indirectly influenced architects of the late 16th century. Clearly he deserves a study of such depth and breadth. The set will eventually include more than 1,000 drawings in at least three volumes. The introductory essay could stand alone as a succinct but complete study of Sangallo. It puts him in his historical context, details his own accomplishments, and identifies the host of relatives and associates who collaborated in his many projects. Each drawing in this volume is illustrated and accompanied by a full catalog entry that describes the physical state of the sheet and provides a discussion of its contents. Although catalog and illustrations are separated, it is easy to move from one to the other. Indexes of architectural terms and proper names and a bibliography make the volume even more useful. Upper-division undergraduate through professional—*J. R. Spencer, emeritus, Duke University*

OAB-0394   NA1123   92-38117 CIP
Argan, Giulio Carlo. **Michelangelo architect,** by Giulio Carlo Argan and Bruno Contardi; tr. by Marion L. Grayson. Abrams, 1993. 388p bibl index ISBN 0-8109-3638-0, $125.00

The Italian edition of this book (Milan, 1990) was the last crowning achievement of the late doyen in the study of Renaissance architecture. It is a magnificent volume, with 522 photographs and visual documents, and the most complete monograph on the subject since J.S. Ackerman's seminal *The Architecture of Michelangelo* (1961; 2nd ed., 1986) and the massive *Michelangiolo architetto,* ed. by P. Portoghesi and B. Zevi (1964). Contardi's catalogue raisonné, comprising 31 items, is a readable compilation providing convenient historical/documentary summaries. These are arranged in four groups: painted and sculpted works, Florentine designs, the Campidoglio and the Farnese Palace, and St. Peter's and after. Argan provided the prologue, four critical essays introducing the four sections, and the epilogue. Argan's elegant prose, with its layered phrasing and cadences, does not translate well, and this translation is often awkward; his penetrating critical mind is nevertheless evident: analytical acumen, incisive descriptions, and breadth of historical perspective. His analogy between architecture and poetics is unsurpassed. The bibliography, carried up to 1990, somewhat slights American scholarship. Essential for all libraries.—*T. K. Kitao, Swarthmore College*

OAB-0395   NA1510   95-35280 CIP
Bernier, Ronald M. **Himalayan architecture.** Fairleigh Dickinson, 1997. (Dist. by Associated University Presses) 196p bibl index afp ISBN 0-8386-3602-0, $55.00

This study of Himalayan architecture is a valuable first of its kind in the field of Asian art. Bernier investigates a cultural area comprising Nepal, Sikkim, Bhutan, Assam, the Darjeeling area of India, Northern Pakistan, and Himachal Pradesh, which is tied by materials of construction as well as design. The organization of the work is geographical and moves from the east in Assam to the west in Northern Pakistan following the Karakoram mountain range. Images from "animism," Buddhism, Islam, and Hinduism are shown in relationship. The focus is on temples and mosques with some discussion of palaces and houses.

The related arts within the complexes are well documented and receive much-needed concentration. The photographs and illustrations are what truly make this a solid contribution to the field. Much of the material is presented so scholars can draw their own conclusions. This book is a resource for Asian studies as well as a tool for the general reader to investigate the region. In a rapidly changing world, as the foreword by the Dalai Lama states, the recording of this heritage is crucial to its continued survival. General; upper-division undergraduate; graduate; faculty.—*L. L. Lam-Easton, California State University, Northridge*

OAB-0396   NA1123   93-3120 CIP
Boucher, Bruce. **Andrea Palladio: the architect in his time.** Abbeville, 1994. 336p bibl index ISBN 1-55859-381-0, $95.00

Architectural historians as well as general readers will welcome this lavishly produced monograph on the architecture of Andrea Palladio (1508-80). Boucher began working on Palladio nearly 20 years ago as one of the organizers of the 1975 Palladio exhibition, and his recent two-volume work on the sculpture of Jacopo Sansovino (1991) has been very well received. The text is well organized and clearly written, and the author's avowed intention to provide a "synthesis of Palladio's ... achievements as an architect and theoretician" is fully realized. The extensive endnotes and the bibliography of more than 250 items will provide the specialist with the current state of a number of complex problems of building history, interpretation, and patronage. Photographer Paolo Marton has done a superb job of capturing the beauty of Palladio's work. The nearly 290 illustrations, most of them in color and 58 of them reproduced as full pages, provide the best visual introduction available to Palladio's work. There is no better book on Palladio available in English, and all college and university libraries will want to add this book to their collections. Lower-division undergraduate through professional.—*E. Van Schaack, Colgate University*

OAB-0397   NA1181   92-29554 CIP
Brumfield, William Craft. **A history of Russian architecture.** Cambridge, 1993. 644p bibl index ISBN 0-521-40333-2, $95.00

Once in a great while, a book appears that both defines a scholarly discipline and sets a research agenda for the foreseeable future. Such a book is Brumfield's present work, which incorporates some text and photographs from his *Gold in Azure* (CH, Feb'84) but includes so much additional material as to amount to a new work altogether. Encyclopedic in length and exhaustive in its treatment, it features many ravishing color photographs as well as hundreds of black-and-white photographs, plans, and elevations. And Brumfield, who took all the photographs in the book himself, matches this visual record with meticulous documentation for the buildings, their architects, and their owners. He has an exceptional gift for helping readers to understand a building. By verbalizing its constituent parts and their interrelationships, he explicates a structure as if it were a poem. Both a reference work and a tool for the serious scholar, this book belongs in the collection of every library.—*J. M. Curtis, University of Missouri—Columbia*

OAB-0398   NA1181   94-23065 CIP
Brumfield, William Craft. **Lost Russia: photographing the ruins of Russian architecture.** Duke University, 1995. 132p bibl index afp ISBN 0-8223-1557-2, $59.95; ISBN 0-8223-1568-8 pbk, $27.95

This book is a delight to hold, to look at, and to read. Unlike Brumfield's previous major works (*The Origins of Modernism in Russian Architecture*, CH, Oct'91; *A History of Russian Architecture*, CH, Jun'94), it ranges far off the beaten track into the provinces around Moscow and presents the abandoned churches and estate buildings (mostly from the 16th and 17th centuries) that still serve as reminders of Russia's complex and diverse past. Brumfield, a seemingly indefatigable explorer of that past, takes us along as he makes forays into the countryside over bumpy, inadequate roads. Drawing on his vast erudition, he explains who built each structure and what happened to it over the course of the centuries. A proper appreciation of this book must also acknowl-

edge designer Cherie Westmoreland's work, such as the double-spaced text, the wonderful paper, and the extraordinary duotone printing of the 66 black-and-white photographs. A beautiful, satisfying, thoughtful, and thought-provoking book. General; undergraduate; graduate; faculty.—*J. M. Curtis, University of Missouri—Columbia*

OAB-0399   NA5471   95-17386 CIP
Campbell, Louise. **Coventry Cathedral: art and architecture in post-war Britain.** Oxford, 1996. 287p bibl index afp ISBN 0-19-817519-1, $140.00

This is the fullest and most scholarly study of the rebuilding of Coventry Cathedral following its destruction by German bombing in 1940. Although the story has been told before in general works, such as the one by the cathedral's architect, Sir Basil Spence, *Phoenix at Coventry; The Building of a Cathedral* (1962), the present book is more detailed in every way and also provides a perspective from the 1990s. Campbell (Univ. of Warwick) begins with the architectural and political background in the 1940s and with various projects for a new or rebuilt cathedral on the site, moving on to the 1950s competition and Spence's winning design and its modifications. Designs by such other leading modern architects as Alison and Peter Smithson and Colin St. John Wilson are also discussed. Throughout her study, Campbell carefully relates the project to its time and to other works in Europe. Perhaps most interesting is the detailed story of the integration of works of art by such major artists as Sir Jacob Epstein, Graham Sutherland, and John Piper, which can be seen as a continuation of the Arts and Crafts tradition. The 20 color plates and 198 black-and-white illustrations, far richer than those in Spence's pioneering study, are invaluable and contribute nearly as much as Campbell's superb text. Her complete mastery of all the material and the breadth of her vision make this a major work. Comprehensive bibliography; appendix of donation of works of art. Highly recommended. Upper-division undergraduate; graduate; faculty; general.—*T. J. McCormick, emeritus, Wheaton College (MA)*

OAB-0400   NA737   94-20789 CIP
Clausen, Meredith L. **Pietro Belluschi: modern American architect.** MIT, 1995 (c1994). 469p bibl index ISBN 0-262-03220-1, $60.00

This work transcends the limited horizons of most monographic studies to provide a provocative account of the rise and decline of modern architecture in the US. In this outstanding study, architectural historian Clausen (Univ. of Washington) argues persuasively that Pietro Belluschi (1899-1994) was one of the most influential architects in the US during the 1950s and 1960s. In addition to his design for seminal examples of modern architecture such as the Equitable Building in Portland, Oregon (1948), Belluschi exerted his influence through his position as Dean of Architecture and Urban Planning at MIT (1951-1965), his role as a design advisor to government, university, and corporate leaders, and his service as a juror for design competitions. The author's account of Belluschi's career is based on original archival research, interviews with participants, and a critical review of existing literature. The admirably clear text is accompanied by detailed notes and includes an extensive bibliography. The selection and quality of the illustrations are excellent. Anyone interested in the history of post-WW II American architecture and the critical reception of modernism in American culture will find this model study invaluable. Lower-division undergraduate through professional.—*D. P. Doordan, University of Notre Dame*

OAB-0401   NA2542   94-45594 CIP
Crowe, Norman. **Nature and the idea of a man-made world: an investigation into the evolutionary roots of form and order in the built environment.** MIT, 1995. 270p bibl index ISBN 0-262-03222-8, $29.95

Crowe (Notre Dame) explores and explains the ways in which ideas about nature have influenced and determined the forms of our buildings and cities. Both architectural theory and urban theory are addressed. Coverage begins in Neolithic times and is worldwide, but emphasis is on Europe since the Middle

Ages. The special virtue of the book lies in the marvelous lucidity of Crowe's writing. As he untangles the complexities and ambiguities of his subject matter, he clarifies masterfully its meanings and implications. The book's common sense is especially welcome, given today's academic obscurantism. In fact, this book may well become a classic—one of those slender volumes that gets read and reread, printed and reprinted, translated and retranslated—because it makes so much sense for both students and experts and because it distills so much knowledge and good judgment. Beautifully produced, the book is timely in its argument for more nature in architecture today and timeless in the clarity and balance of its treatment of the subject. General; upper-division undergraduate through professional.—*P. Kaufman, Boston Architectural Center*

OAB-0402 NA6165 93-12099 CIP
Driskel, Michael Paul. **As befits a legend: building a tomb for Napoleon, 1840-1861.** Kent State, 1994. 251p bibl index afp ISBN 0-87338-484-9, $32.00

The decision in 1840 to translate the remains of Napoleon from the island of St. Helena to Paris and the political, sociological, symbolic, and aesthetic repercussions that resulted are the subjects of Driskel's study. At every level politics was all. The author explains the labyrinthine avenues of political self-interest, compromise, and promotion that the installation of the Emperor's body represented to various factions of government (monarchist, republican, socialist, bonapartist, ultramontane), beginning with its location at the Hotel des Invalides. A fascinating chapter is devoted to the competition for the design of the sepulchral monument, the architectural and iconographic complexities of the many submissions, and the artistic rivalries exhibited. The study concludes with a chapter on the meaning of artistic authorship, ritual, and the political power of heroic sepulchral monuments, bringing the discussion well into the 20th century. The quality of scholarship is impeccable, and the author's judgments and speculations are balanced. The book's layout is exemplary: no image—it is profusely illustrated—is less than a page from its reference, and the clarity of the plates is excellent. Recommended for advanced undergraduate and above, especially graduate level.—*L. R. Matteson, University of Southern California*

OAB-0403 NA7756 91-34435 CIP
Goy, Richard J. **The house of gold: building a palace in medieval Venice.** Cambridge, 1993 (c1992). 304p bibl index ISBN 0-521-40513-0, $95.00

Goy has written an exemplary architectural study of a major urban dwelling, which not only presents a careful analysis of the physical aspects of the house itself, but also fuses this with a thorough and intelligent study of the archival sources. This material, in turn, is combined with an excellent description of the particularities of Venetian social, economic, topographical, and cultural history, so that the *Ca'Doro* is presented to the reader on the one hand as a structure integral to Venetian society, and yet on the other as a building that reflects the special circumstances of its patrons and builders. Written with commanding control of both architecture and historical sources, the book fully integrates this remarkable palace into the society that produced it. Goy's study of the masons and sculptors, and the intricacies of the building workshop, as well as his sensitive portrayal of the patron, presents the reader with a full sense of the process of constructing a magnificent residence in Venice. General; undergraduate and up.—*C. Bruzelius, Duke University*

OAB-0404 MA7572 91-51109 CIP
Hinchcliffe, Tanis. **North Oxford.** Yale, 1992. 261p bibl index ISBN 0-300-05184-0, $45.00

In recent years architectural history has become broader and less exclusive in its interest and coverage. The pioneering work of John Summerson and Donald Olson on the building estates in London and those concerned with the provinces by David Cannadine and H.J. Dyos are major examples of this new architectural and urban history. Related to this has been the flourishing of social history. Hinchcliffe's study of North Oxford from the early 19th century (particu-

larly after 1850) as it was developed by St. John's College for the middle classes, is the latest and one of the very best of these studies. An architectural historian, Hinchcliffe sensitively discusses and illustrates (in excellent color photographs and drawings as well as old and new black-and-white ones) the wide range of houses and churches erected by such architects as J. J. Stevenson and R. W. Edis, relating them to works by the more famous of the time. Equally as valuable is her discussion of the developers, builders, and financiers who made all this possible. One of the most fascinating chapters is on the view of the inhabitants, which adds a new dimension to architectural and social history. An excellent appendix lists every building by address, date, leaseholder, architect, and occupation of leaseholder. The footnotes and bibliography are equally as complete. This is an ideal study in every way. Highly recommended to a wide variety of readers.—*T. J. McCormick, emeritus, Wheaton College (MA)*

OAB-0405 NA737 95-32307 CIP
Levine, Neil. **The architecture of Frank Lloyd Wright.** Princeton, 1996. 524p bibl index afp ISBN 0-691-03371-4, $85.00

This first full-length, scholarly study of the life and work of America's (and probably the world's) greatest architect is a major publication, a benchmark study not only of Wright's career but of architectural history as well. It has been written over the past 20 years as a magnum opus by the Gleason Professor of Fine Arts at Harvard University, one of the most highly regarded architectural historians of our day. The bibliography on Wright is enormous but contains only one other full-length study, William Allin Storrer's *Frank Lloyd Wright Companion* (CH, May'94), a catalogue raisonné of Wright's built work, which does not address his importance as an artist. The standard study of Wright, Henry-Russell Hitchcock's *In the Nature of Materials* (1942), was published too early to consider Wright's important, late work of the 1940s and 1950s. Arthur Drexler, former curator of architecture at The Museum of Modern Art in New York, used to say that if one put all of the works of Mies van der Rohe, Walter Gropius, and Le Corbusier on one side of a scale, Wright's would outweigh them in both quantity and quality. What is most rewarding and refreshing in this book is the fact that Levine has approached his subject matter relatively free of the historicist determinism that has affected most 20th-century architectural writing. Thus, he does not augment or diminish Wright's reputation as part of any tendentious ideological agenda such as modernism, nationalism, or conservatism. General; upper-division undergraduate; graduate; professional.—*P. Kaufman, Boston Architectural Center*

OAB-0406 NA1353 95-47561 CIP
Mallgrave, Harry Francis. **Gottfried Semper: architect of the nineteenth century.** Yale, 1996. 443p bibl index afp ISBN 0-300-06624-4, $50.00

Semper had a profound impact on 19th-century European architecture, on the history of art (especially through Alois Riegl), and on classical archaeology. Rivaled only by Ruskin and Viollet-le-Duc, he transformed European architectural thought and had a substantial impact, as well, on a generation of early modernists such as Sullivan, Wright, and Berlage. Mallgrave's monograph deftly weaves together aspects of Semper's intriguing biography with his achievements as an architect and theoretician, placing them against the larger picture of architectural and political thought in 19th-century Europe. Seldom is such a complex subject so engagingly presented. Copiously illustrated with black-and-white photographs and drawings, and with a few illustrations in color, the study, a "must" for students of the history of architecture, concludes with an extensive bibliography of writings by and about Semper. Upper-division undergraduate through professional.—*J. Quinan, SUNY at Buffalo*

OAB-0407 DS554 96-4368 CIP
Mannikka, Eleanor. **Angkor Wat: time, space, and kingship.** Hawaii, 1996. 341p bibl index afp ISBN 0-8248-1720-6, $55.00

Magnificently illustrated and richly detailed, this book describes the art and architecture of the 12th-century Buddhist temple complex of Angkor Wat in Cambodia. By themselves, the elaborate descriptions, elegant drawings, and beautiful black-and-white and color photographs of architectural features and Khmer art make this book an invaluable reference work for specialists in Asian art history, archaeology, architecture, and religion. The introductory chapter provides the most coherent treatment of the historical and cultural setting of Angkor Wat found in English-language publications, but the author goes beyond material description and historical synthesis to offer a fascinating interpretation of Angkor Wat as a precisely constructed "sacred environment," built according to certain Indian- and Chinese-influenced but uniquely Khmer philosophical and religious principles. Transforming Western metric measurements into what are likely to have been indigenous spatial units, the author demonstrates that in temple architecture, orientation and spatial relationships reflect sophisticated knowledge of astronomical phenomena and complex cosmological notions. Historians and anthropologists should find Mannikka's analysis of considerable appeal in examining the ideological underpinnings of kingship in Southeast Asia. Upper-division undergraduates through faculty.—*L. L. Junker, Vanderbilt University*

OAB-0408   NA2707   94-39125 CIP
Meyer, Esther da Costa. **The work of Antonio Sant'Elia: retreat into the future.** Yale, 1995. 249p bibl index afp ISBN 0-300-04309-0, $45.00

The brief but tumultuous career of the Italian architect and futurist Antonio Sant'Elia (1888-1916) left an indelible impression on the history of 20th-century European architecture. The sources for his provocative skyscraper designs and his contribution to the development of the Italian futurist movement have long been the subject of scholarly controversy. Meyer (art history, Yale) has produced an admirably thorough and well-written study, which clearly surpasses the existing Italian and English literature on the subject. The quality of the many black-and-white and color illustrations is excellent, although the most complete publication of Sant'Elia drawings (in terms of the number of drawings illustrated) remains Luciano Caramel and Alberto Longatti's *Antonio Sant'Elia, the Complete Works* (1988). Thanks to the author's insightful discussion of early 20th century political and aesthetic ideologies and the extensive supporting notes and bibliography, students of modern Italian culture and history as well as scholars interested in architecture and urbanism will find this a valuable addition to the literature. This promises to be the definitive work on Sant'Elia and his cultural milieu and should appeal to a wide audience. Undergraduate; graduate; faculty; general.—*D. P. Doordan, University of Notre Dame*

OAB-0409   NA2706   95-14621 CIP
Necipoglu, Gülru. **The Topkapi scroll: geometry and ornament in Islamic architecture: Topkapi Palace Museum Library MS H. 1956.** Getty Center for the History of Art and the Humanities, 1996 (c1995). 395p bibl index ISBN 0-89236-335-5, $160.00

This is a remarkable and accomplished study of a late-15th- or early-16th-century pattern scroll of planar and spatial geometric designs used in Islamic architecture. The book is a groundbreaking study in several ways: for the first time an entire scroll of drawings is published, and the patterns are explained through overlays and supplementary drawings. In a series of computer-generated modulations, an addendum demonstrates the transformation of drawings into three-dimensional architectural elements, thus suggesting a possible manipulation for the patterns in the scroll. There is a brief but critical section on Western studies of Islamic ornamentation, followed by Necipoglu's innovative analysis of patterns utilizing the current theoretical and critical discourses. The author expands the parameters of such studies by offering convincing interpretations of the Islamic geometric patterns, which had been previously perused, as largely disengaged and noninformative decorative designs. These patterns, while decorative, may inform the viewer of the historical circumstances when they occur. Necipoglu's analysis of the patterns is in terms of the changing ideological, intellectual, and aesthetic concepts of the Muslims regarding architectural decoration in a constantly shifting religious and political context. A creative investigation of an Islamic visual idiom, and a model for further inquiries into Islamic art and architecture. Upper-division undergraduate through professional—*U. U. Bates, CUNY Hunter College*

OAB-0410   TH1301   92-24191 CIP
Plumridge, Andrew. **Brickwork: architecture and design,** by Andrew Plumridge and Wim Meulenkamp. Abrams, 1993. 224p bibl index ISBN 0-8109-3123-0, $39.95

This is a wonderful book on an important subject for architects and connoisseurs of architecture. It traces the history of brickwork, some fundamentals of design, and construction methods. Written by a British architect and a Dutch art historian, it is by no means provincial, but it does concentrate on English examples of this almost ubiquitous building material. Well written, well researched, and well illustrated, it seems to be unique; no other book covers brickwork quite so comprehensively with so many sumptuous color illustrations. Ronald V. Brunskill's *Brick Building in Britain* (1990) is geographically limited, and Karl Gurcke's fascinating *Bricks and Brickmaking* (CH, Apr'88) concentrates on American subject matter. General; advanced undergraduate; professional.—*P. Kaufman, Boston College*

OAB-0411   NA4287   94-10254 CIP
Port, M.H. **Imperial London: civil government building in London, 1850-1915.** Yale, 1995. 344p bibl index ISBN 0-300-05977-9, $60.00

This splendid examination of government building in London during Britain's Victorian and Edwardian eras represents architectural history at its best. Port, author of the standard book on the 19th-century houses of Parliament, focuses on structures for the great ministries, law courts, and national museums during the apogee of British power, wealth, and responsibility. Architects and their plans receive expected attention, as does the issue of public financing and the character of the state bureaucracy responsible for receiving, developing, and, ultimately, occupying the new buildings. But this book is as much social history as it is architectural history. More than 300 photographs of plans, elevations, maps, and period scenes range from adequate to excellent. The dozen or so color plates are mostly superb. The extensive endnotes, bibliography, and appendixes add the final touches to this admirable and indispensable work of scholarship. Recommended for research and most college libraries and for public libraries interested in architecture and government planning. Upper-division undergraduate through professional.—*W. S. Rodner, Tidewater Community College*

OAB-0412   NA1123   92-46535 Orig
Saalman, Howard. **Filippo Brunelleschi: the buildings.** Pennsylvania State, 1993. 470p bibl index ISBN 0-271-01067-3, $175.00

Like "classic," the term "definitive study" has been so overused as to have become a cliché; yet, on occasion, no other accolade is appropriate. For more than 30 years, Saalman has been the commanding voice in the study of 15th-century Florentine architecture. His many writings on Michelozzo, Alberti, and especially Brunelleschi form an imposing body of work, including the major study on Florence's most visible monument, the cathedral dome (*Filippo Brunelleschi: The Cupola of Santa Maria del Fiore*, CH, Apr'81). This richly illustrated tome covers Brunelleschi's other Florentine projects, carefully articulating their complex and often tortuous programs of construction and modification, and grounding each commission within its particular familial, social, and historical contexts revealed through a wealth of documentary evidence. Although certain aspects in the reconstruction of building campaigns, changes in design, and the artist's original intention involve speculation, Saalman's conclusions truly emerge as "definitive." This is a masterful book, and it belongs in every academic library.—*J. I. Miller, California State University, Long Beach*

OAB-0413   NA7332   94-36805 CIP
Schofield, John. **Medieval London houses.** Yale, 1995. 272p bibl index ISBN 0-300-05578-1, $60.00

This is an amazing book and an amazing achievement. Drawing on surviving remains, old photographs and drawings, descriptions, surveys, and plans of all sorts, Schofield provides a comprehensive view of vernacular architecture in London from c. 1200 up to the destruction of much of the city in the fire of 1666. The focus is especially on houses, ranging from dwellings of the rich and powerful aristocrats to tradesmen, but also treated are commercial buildings such as taverns, shops, and guild halls. Organized according to topics such as sources, topography, planning of interior and exterior spaces, furnishings, and construction materials and techniques, this book will be of great interest not only to architectural and social historians concerned with the late medieval and modern period, but to anyone interested in life in London into the 20th century. Richly illustrated, with full scholarly apparatus of footnotes and bibliography, it also has a detailed review of 201 different London sites and structures. Upper-division undergraduate through professional.—*L. Nees, University of Delaware*

OAB-0414   NA737   93-30127 CIP
Storrer, William Allin. **The Frank Lloyd Wright companion.** Chicago, 1994 (c1993). 492p index afp ISBN 0-226-77624-7, $75.00

For 20 years Storrer has been writing guides to Frank Lloyd Wright's architecture. The first effort, *The Architecture of Frank Lloyd Wright: A Complete Catalog* (CH, Nov'74; 2nd ed., CH, Jun'79) listed almost all of Wright's built work in North America. It has been indispensable for students and tourists as a travel guide to Wright's work. The *Companion* represents a quantum leap beyond and above these earlier publications, comprising a scholarly catalog of Wright's built work worldwide. What Köchel was to Mozart, Storrer is to Wright. Paging through the voluminous black-and-white illustrations of excellent quality; the clear expository text, which summarizes the circumstances and layout of each commision; and the detailed, computerized plans of each building, one is inclined to believe that now, and only now, almost half a century after his death can we begin to encompass, measure, and analyze the staggering output and achievement of this man who could be arguably, the greatest architect of all time. Much of this analysis will flow from this book, which illustrates commissions heretofore unseen, unknown, or unillustrated. The book contains almost 1,000 photos and more than 700 floor plans illustrating more than 500 built works, one fifth of which have been destroyed. If a library owned just five books on Wright, this should be one of them. General; advanced udergraduate and above.—*P. Kaufman, Boston Architectural Center*

OAB-0415   NA1123   93-25274 CIP
Wallace, William E. **Michelangelo at San Lorenzo: the genius as entrepreneur.** Cambridge, 1994. 266p bibl index ISBN 0-521-41021-5, $60.00

Whoever the architect, no great building gets to be built without a reliable and well-supervised crew, and Michelangelo was no exception. What is remarkable, as Wallace convinces us in this equally remarkable book, is that Michelangelo cultivated his entrepreneurial skill basically in one decade—from 1516 to 1526—while he worked successively on the three Florentine projects for the Medici: the facade of San Lorenzo, the Medici Chapel, and the Laurentian Library. The author combed through, and interpreted with magisterial skill, heretofore unexplored bank documents in Pisa as well as vast published records and letters and forged a narrative, at once intelligible and intriguing, of the artist's activities as he searched for and opened new quarries, oversaw their excavations, arranged for the moving and delivery of marble blocks, inspected them on arrival in Florence, recruited artisans as needed, kept books on the weekly wages of his crew, and, of course, supervised the work on the site and corresponded tirelessly with everyone. The book adds little to our knowledge of Michelangelo's art, but it fleshes out as never before the artist at daily work as a contractor and the network of those who worked for and with him. This is a history of business, technology, and Florentine life in one package. The study is amply illustrated and impeccably documented with more than 1,000 endnotes and an expert bibliography. Indispensable for all academic libraries. Lower-division undergraduate through graduate.—*T. K. Kitao, Swarthmore College*

■ Decorative Arts, Print, Drawing & Design

OAB-0416   NK1412   94-13536 CIP
Abercrombie, Stanley. **George Nelson: the design of modern design.** MIT, 1995. 353p bibl index ISBN 0-262-01142-5, $55.00

Nelson, one of America's pioneering modernists, created some of industrial design's classic works. This book is a definitive biography and a well-researched reference for those readers fascinated by the development of the design profession after WW II. What is particularly pleasurable about reading this book is the inclusion of a profuse number of quotes from the man. His comment about the "absurd" architectural projects he was assigned while studying at Yale, where he was given the problem of designing a diplomat's residence on the outskirts of Peking, is classic: "What a bunch of nineteen-year-old kids from small towns in America with mostly middle-class parents knew about an ambassador's establishment—this was a little difficult to figure out." Nelson's ability to self-analyze is also refreshing: "As a designer I have contributed my mite to the modern look over the past two decades, and since modern is a mass style essentially, it is sometimes refreshing to walk back into an older world where the individual is more visible, particularly since it is disintegrating at a high rate of speed." Venice was one of his favorite subjects for photography, and some of these images are reproduced in the book. Overall, this is a joy to read and is an important document for all art historians and designers. Upper-division undergraduate through professional.—*J. Mendenhall, California Polytechnic State University, San Luis Obispo*

OAB-0417   Orig
Amico, Leonard N. **Bernard Palissy: in search of earthly paradise.** Flammarion, 1996. 256p bibl index ISBN 2-08013-614-3, $75.00

This is a remarkable book about a remarkable man. Palissy, a member of the rural artisan class in 16th-century France, is today best known as a potter who created distinctive ceramic wares decorated with three-dimensional illusionistic plants, animals, and seashells. But his work as an artist included designs for gardens, grottoes, and an ideal city plan; in addition he was a writer, something of a scientist, and a contentious intellectual and religious reformer. He has, not without reason, been called a French Leonardo da Vinci. This lucid, thoroughly documented, and beautifully illustrated book is focused on Palissy's activity as a ceramist and sheds new light on his art's variety, character, techniques, and sources, as well as on the revival and imitation of the Palissy style in the 19th century. But Amico has also made a detailed exploration of the context of the artist's work. The book will interest anyone concerned with the art and culture of the Renaissance, for, in documenting Palissy's "search for earthly paradise," it opens a window onto the religious and philosophical meanings that contemporaries saw in the structure of nature and in the products of human artifice. General; upper-division undergraduate through professional.—*D. Posner, New York University*

OAB-0418   NK8298x   92-90938 Orig
Andrews, Jack. **Samuel Yellin, metalworker.** Skipjack, 1992. 127p index ISBN 1-879535-05-X, $40.00

Spanning the years 1909-1940, Yellin's work in iron is the culmination of classical 19th-century wrought iron design. In this tradition, Yellin's workshops in Philadelphia created lasting examples of art in iron for private residences, corporate clients, churches, and universities throughout this country. This book is the only attempt to record carefully the evolution of this artistic giant. Andrews, who is himself a blacksmith, has lovingly collected excellent photographs of Yellin's major, as well as less ambitious, works. The reader is also treated to numerous views of the workshops with works in progress. A record of Yellin's works in the form of workshop job cards will help other researchers in locating existing samples of this master's work. Because much of this work is in public places and is not being cared for, there is a real danger that this country will lose these unique manifestations of a craftsman's love affair with his challenging medium. We are indebted to Andrews for undertaking this project to help preserve Yellin's works for future generations.—*S. Lechtzin, Temple University*

OAB-0419   E78   91-50994 MARC

Burnham, Dorothy K. **To please the caribou: painted caribou-skin coats worn by the Naskapi, Montagnais, and Cree hunters of the Quebec-Labrador Peninsula.** Washington, 1992. 314p bibl index ISBN 0-295-97177-0, $60.00; ISBN 0-295-97178-9 pbk, $35.00

Burnham's book continues the University of Washington Press's tradition of publishing analytical, beautifully illustrated studies of North American Indian art. This time the subject is the elaborately painted caribou hide coats worn by hunters of the Quebec-Labrador region to attract the caribou. Since the coats are no longer being made, the author utilizes museum collections, historic records, ethnographic accounts, scientific analyses, and the coats as sources of information. Descriptions of the research methods and the results are presented in the first part of the book. Burnham demonstrates a correlation between European coat styles and the Native American versions, but also points out that the coats continue to fit into the belief systems of the tribes. Even when the coat styles change, certain design elements can be traced through 200 years of use. Most of the book is a catalog of 60 of the most significant coats. This book not only contributes important new knowledge about the coats, but also illustrates the value of museum collections. By describing the research methods employed in this study the author establishes a model for other researchers to follow. Advanced undergraduate; graduate.—*M. J. Schneider, University of North Dakota*

OAB-0420   NE1321   93-6382 CIP

Clark, Timothy T. **The actor's image: print makers of the Katsukawa School,** by Timothy T. Clark and Osamu Ueda with Donald Jenkins; ed. by Naomi Noble Richard. Art Institute of Chicago/Princeton, 1994. 503p bibl index ISBN 0-691-03627-6, $125.00

This magnificent work by Clark (Curator of Japanese Prints, British Museum) and Ueda (former Keeper of the collection) is the third volume of the Buckingham Collection of Japanese Prints in the Chicago Art Institute. Based on Ueda's 20 years' research, it is a study of a late 18th and early 19th century Edo school of *ukiyo-e*, the Katsukawa school, which concentrated on Kabuki actors and their plays. Most significant here are the illuminating details ferreted out by Ueda and Clark—technical, sociological, cultural—generously interwoven with an acute regard for playbills to authenticate individual prints and place them in their historical context. Jenkins's introductory essay discusses actor prints of the period and the development of the Katsukawa school; Clark's essay on Edo Kabuki in the 1780s puts the reader in intimate contact with the world of Kabuki, giving details surrounding the performance of a single play in 1784. The bulk of the book, Clark's detailed analyses of 136 prints, includes information on both the actors and plays in addition to the prints with their publishing histories, often with a comparative study of other impressions or related images in other collections. The remaining 745 prints are illustrated in black and white and cataloged by Ueda. Biographical data on all actors represented and of each printmaker; chronological listing of actor critiques and Kabuki playbills and programs. Highly recommended. Undergraduate; graduate; faculty.—*D. K. Haworth, Carleton College*

OAB-0421   NK5872   93-14332 CIP

Cutler, Anthony. **The hand of the master: craftsmanship, ivory, and society in Byzantium (9th-11th centuries).** Princeton, 1994. 293p bibl index afp ISBN 0-691-03366-8, $69.50

Cutler has written a remarkable book, both more detailed and more comprehensive than anything previously written about the art and craft of carving ivory in medieval Byzantium. Many of the objects studied are well known to scholars, but no one has considered their physical nature and manufacture to

such an extent, or provided photographs (often of backs or sides, or at oblique angles) that permit the reader to at least imagine the experience of intimately handling the ivories, as Cutler shows they were meant to be and often were handled. The book is beautifully written, pointed without being argumentative, and brilliantly covers a wide span of topics within a short space by using salient examples rather than exhaustive surveys. All scholars and students interested in any form or period of ivory carving will find this book indispensable, yet at the same time it should appeal to sophisticated lay persons, who will enjoy sharing the experience of learning from and handling, as it were, great works of art in the company of a distinguished connoisseur and critical thinker. Upper-division undergraduate; graduate; professional.—*L. Nees, University of Delaware*

OAB-0422   NC998   95-21550 Orig

Fraser, James. **Japanese modern: graphic design between the wars,** by James Fraser, Steven Heller, and Seymour Chwast. Chronicle Books, 1996. 131p bibl ISBN 0-8118-0509-3 pbk, $16.95

Continuing the publisher's excellent series on design history, this outstanding volume, which should be included on every designer's bookshelf, is a thorough compilation of an overlooked area of graphic design: the posters, trademarks, labels, and printed ephemera emanating from Japan during the era between the two world wars. The hundreds of color examples included show the influence of Constructivism and Art Deco, as well as Modernism. Yet the Japanese designers of this period display a uniquely non-Western interpretation of space in their work. Images almost explode across the surface of the page; typography is emphatic and dynamic. There is a richness to these designs, though at first it may go unnoticed. On closer examination, however, the viewer is intrigued by the diversity (and surrealism) of many of the graphics. The book is well researched, especially in its detailing of how photography influenced a generation of young designers. By introducing Asian graphic design history to a profession that tends to be biased towards European movements, the authors have produced not only a beautiful book but one that reminds us of the truly global nature of visual communication. Undergraduate; graduate; faculty; professional.—*J. Mendenhall, California Polytechnic State University, San Luis Obispo*

OAB-0423   NK1052   93-33770 CIP

Fraser-Lu, Sylvia. **Burmese crafts: past and present.** Oxford, 1994. 371p bibl index ISBN 0-19-588608-9, $150.00

One sentence sets this book apart from most books that "survey" a nation's art: "The Burmese do not make a distinction between the 'fine arts' and the decorative or 'applied arts'"; "crafts" in the title is thus slightly misleading. Where so many surveys focus on the so-called high arts, this sumptuous volume, with almost 300 excellent color and monochrome illustrations, makes its comprehensive focus clear. Everything from major monuments to everyday utensils in a great array of media are included here and reflect the richness of the civilization they represent. More information is richly provided in the appendix, which includes a chronology and a trilingual glossary, and in the extensive bibliography. Strictly speaking, this is not a book on "art history," for, in fact, what is represented here is a study of the whole culture, ancient and modern—a culture all too little known in the West and one that, although related to its neighbors in South and Southeast Asia, has its own distinct characteristics that are worth notice. If a library could have but one book on Burma (now called Myanmar), this would be it. Undergraduate; graduate; faculty; general.—*J. O. Caswell, University of British Columbia*

OAB-0424   PN6710   93-45937 CIP

Harvey, Robert C. **The art of the funnies: an aesthetic history.** University Press of Mississippi, 1994. 252p index ISBN 0-87805-612-2, $42.50; ISBN 0-87805-674-2 pbk, $19.95

This book has substance. This may seem like a wimpish accolade in a field so glutted with chroniclers, critics, and culture analysts; one would expect substance to be a given. The sagging shelves of bookstores testify otherwise, with their many hastily slapped-together anthologies, threadbare, recycled histories, and seemingly résumé-based biographies of cartoonists. Harvey's work is an exception, with its meticulous and comprehensive scholarly research, instructive but readable style, and critical analysis. His preamble chapter so thoroughly, yet succinctly, articulates what critical analysis is that it deserves to be used as a supplement to the jargon-heavy textbooks on this research technique. The other ten chapters provide new insights into the visual and verbal aspects of various genres of the funnies, as represented by cartoonists who shaped the medium—Winsor McCay, Bud Fisher, George McManus, Sidney Smith, Roy Crane, Chester Gould, Hal Foster, Harold Gray, Dick Calkins, Alex Raymond, Milton Caniff, George Herriman, Mort Walker, Charles Schulz, and others. One chapter discusses the vital, but normally unnoticed, role that publisher Joseph Patterson played in the development of the comic strip. Profusely illustrated and delightfully told, this is a milestone in comic-art scholarship, in the tradition of the strips it documents. All libraries.—*J. A. Lent, Temple University*

OAB-0425   94-70768 Orig
Herter Brothers: furniture and interiors for a gilded age, by Katherine S. Howe et al. Abrams/Museum of Fine Arts, Houston, 1994. 272p bibl index ISBN 0-8109-3426-4, $60.00

At last we have a definitive book on the Herter brothers, foremost tastemakers of 19th-century New York City. Published for an exhibition in 1994-95 in Houston, Atlanta, and New York (the Metropolitan), it is the work of eight well-known decorative arts scholars. Gustav (1830-92) and Christian (1839-83) Herter's highly decorative furniture and interior decoration based on European prototypes are carefully explored up to 1883. Context of European and New York City cabinetmaking is emphasized, as is their role as interior decorators for newly wealthy clients. Social history makes this book much more than a description of furniture and design. The detailed examination of nineteenth century New York furniture design, production, trade practices, and patronage will be sources for future research. The book is organized into introduction, five articles, and 42-piece catalog in standard museum form. The catalog has descriptions of the furniture and pictures of the houses for which many pieces were made. Many show the pieces in situ. There are four appendixes of furniture details and a chronology from 1830 (birth of Gustav) to 1907 (the last Herter entry in New York directories). Excellent pictures, especially those in color; period photographs of the spectacular environments designed for their rich clients; fine details; period documents. Notes enable the reader to follow the detailed research in papers of patrons and public records. Selected bibliography. Highly recommended. General: upper-division undergraduate through professional.—*W. L. Whitwell, Hollins College*

OAB-0426   94-67907 Orig
Hiesinger, Kathryn B. **Japanese design: a survey since 1950,** by Kathryn B. Hiesinger and Felice Fischer. Philadelphia Museum of Art/Abrams, 1994. 236p bibl index ISBN 0-8109-3509-0, $60.00

This first comprehensive presentation of modern design in Japan provides extraordinary documentation of the forms and aesthetics of products made for everyday use. Encompassing the fields of furniture, fashion, textile design, housewares, consumer electronics, graphics, and crafts, this book explores the development of more than 250 objects and the quality that makes them uniquely Japanese. Published in conjunction with an exhibition in 1994 at the Philadelphia Museum of Art, this book is a richly rewarding experience to read and behold. Its impeccably researched text is accompanied by beautifully reproduced plates of a wide variety of products. The extensive bibliography contains valuable information on designers and makers, including interesting insights on a number of popular companies. For example, Canon is anglicized "Kwanon," which is Japanese for export; the Sharp Corporation derives its name from one of its earliest products, the Ever-Sharp mechanical pencil. Without question, this volume will make an outstanding addition to any library. General; lower-division undergraduate and up.—*J. Mendenhall, California Polytechnic State University, San Luis Obispo*

OAB-0427   NE400   95-7231 CIP
Hults, Linda C. **The print in the western world: an introductory history.** Wisconsin, 1996. 948p bibl index ISBN 0-299-13700-7, $65.00

The history of prints is a vital complement to the standard history of painting, sculpture, and architecture; and anyone tackling this great chronicle should come away convinced of it. Profusely illustrated and equipped with basic bibliographic apparatus (updated but not indexed in the concluding "Note"), this provides the long-wished-for replacement for A. Hyatt Mayor's pleasant but unpaginated and generally casual *Prints & People* (CH, Jun '72). More thoughtful and provocative than some of its sister surveys of the "finer arts," Hults's tome is enlivened by its reference to recent research literature, and it is qua subject unencumbered by canon. The author describes Dürer, Rembrandt, Goya, Picasso, and Johns as forming the "spine" of the book, but there is no cult of personality here. At the fore instead are issues of collecting and taste, propaganda, and pornography. Reproductive prints are granted a chapter, mercifully undefensive. Expert and novice alike will happen upon new and wonderful images, as well as variously appealing interpretative cruxes. Although the author is known for her work on Baldung's witch imagery, modern and American art are extensively treated (six out of 13 chapters), which likely will increase the book's usefulness to the general and collecting public. Essential for all libraries. General; lower-division undergraduate (including two-year technical) through professional.—*P. Emison, University of New Hampshire*

OAB-0428   NK4568   95-37747 CIP
Impey, Oliver. **The early porcelain kilns of Japan: Arita in the first half of the seventeenth century.** Oxford, 1996. 156p bibl index afp ISBN 0-19-826370-8, $160.00

Impey (Ashmolean Museum, Oxford) has written a scholarly work covering a subject little known to English-speaking readers. It deals with domestic porcelain production in southern Japan during the first half of the 17th century prior to the export trade of this ceramic ware, to both Europe and the near East in the second half of the 17th century. The present volume is a comprehensive study as well as an amalgamation of a large bibliographic source of information. Of great interest to both ceramic historians and potters are the reconstructions of the practices in the various workshops during this period. Impey includes an assessment of individual kiln sites at Arita, the community where the kilns were located, and examines the contemporary workshop environment to better understand the conditions and practices of the early-17th-century potters. An abundance of superb colored plates and black-and-white photographs enhance the text. An inclusive bibliography not only of English but of Japanese and European sources greatly enhances the worth of this book. A valuable addition to holdings in ceramics. Upper-division undergraduate through professional.—*A. C. Garzio, emeritus, Kansas State University*

OAB-0429   N7353   96-17758 CIP
Japan's golden age: Momoyama, by Money L. Hickman et al. Yale/Sun & Star 1996/Dallas Museum of Art, 1996. 320p bibl index afp ISBN 0-300-06897-2, $60.00

As part of a three-month festival on Japanese culture ("Sun and Star 1996"), the Dallas Museum of Art mounted an exhibition of astonishing breadth on the art of the Momoyama Period (1573-1615) selected from 68 lenders—temples, shrines, museums, the Imperial Household Agency, and private collections; this is not only its handsome catalog but a superb treatment of that glorious period. Although very brief, the Momoyama is a significant period when Japan was first consolidated politically. There is a striking emphasis on the secular arts at this time, ranging from the austere in some tea ceremony ware to the lavish, exquisite, and at times ostentatious in the traditional crafts and architecture. Hickman (former Senior Curator, MFA Boston) introduces this catalog with a 48-page historical essay placing the Momoyama in the context of 16th- and 17th-century Japan. The catalog proper follows in nine sections by different scholars, each of whom writes a brief overview of his or her material and discusses the 162 individual objects in the following categories: on portraiture, sculpture, painting, calligraphy, tea ceremony utensils and ceramics, lacquer and metalwork, arms and armor, textiles, and Noh masks. The inclusion of many major pieces of art elevates this above other recent exhibition catalogs on Japanese art: more than one-third are either National treasures, Important Cultural Properties, or Important Objects. Excellent color reproductions, glossary, comparative (with the West) chronological table. This is a crucial "must-buy" acquisition for all libraries having anything to do with Japan. General; undergraduate; graduate; faculty.—*D. K. Haworth, emeritus, Carleton College*

OAB-0430 NK4210x Orig
Jones, Joan. **Minton: the first two hundred years of design & production.** Swan Hill, 1993. (Dist. by Antique Collectors' Club) 391p bibl index ISBN 1-85310-283-0, $140.00

This volume, a definitive work on the history of Minton Pottery in England (begun in 1793) is a work of art in itself. Jones, curator of the Minton Museum since 1979, has written a knowledgeable, sympathetic, and inclusive catalog of the ceramic artistic output of the factory, one of the oldest bone china institutions in Europe. Its astounding contents cover such areas as techniques and innovations associated with Minton wares—e.g., majolica glazes, excaustic tiles, L. Solon's pâte-sur-pâte, and acid gold. Jones's writing style is easily read, and supplementing the text are superb color plates. There are five appendixes, cataloging and classifying various production items; the Minton marks, etc. and a bibliographic listing of books, catalogs, newspapers, and periodicals, round out this awesome volume.—*A. C. Garzio, Kansas State University*

OAB-0431 Orig
Lightbown, Ronald W. **Mediaeval European jewellery: with a catalogue of the collection in the Victoria & Albert Museum.** Victoria & Albert Museum, 1992. (Dist. by Trafalgar Square) 589p bibl index ISBN 0-948107-87-1, $175.00

The first in-depth study of medieval jewelry, this encyclopedic volume covers the period c.800 to c.1520 (thus omitting the earlier well-studied migration period), concentrating on the years after 1200. Geographically, discussion is limited to Western Europe (including Hungary and Poland), thus excluding the Byzantine East. The book is divided into two major parts, the first consisting of chapters on types of gems, the history of gemcutting, styles of jewelry, its sale, and the use of jewels in magic. The second, longer portion then looks at individual forms of jewelry including coronets, brooches, badges, pendants, chains, collars, and rosaries. Rings are excluded. It is densely packed with information from a wide variety of primary sources, among them inventories, chronicles, literature, and law. The author is currently Curator of Metalwork at the Victoria and Albert Museum and hence began his study with the collection there, which is accorded a separate catalog (at the end of the book) of 92 entries. Beautifully illustrated with 208 black-and-white and 152 color photos of high quality, this is a fundamental reference work and may be profitably dipped into at almost any point.—*J. Oliver, Colgate University*

OAB-0432 NE647 95-50606 CIP
Melot, Michel. **The impressionist print,** tr. by Caroline Beamish. Yale, 1997 (c1996). 296p bibl index ISBN 0-300-06792-5, $65.00

This beautifully written and produced book is most worthy of its subject, prints by artists associated with the Impressionists, from 1850 to 1900. This topic has received much attention in recent years, often in the form of monographs on single artists or exhibition catalogs; these include the author's own well-respected publications and his seminal 1974 Bibliothèque Nationale catalogue, *L'estampe impressioniste*. The present volume surveys thoroughly the artists involved and the means by which printmaking thrived as both market- and aesthetic-driven media. The author examines the collaborative nature of printmaking, the public and private meaning of the various media, and the interaction among artists and publishers. One measure of the overall prosperity of Parisian printmaking is the Society of Etchers, which, guided by Cadart, promoted original prints in folio volumes from 1861 to 1867. Other astute deal-

ers, critics, and artists who contributed to the wider flourishing of print publishing include Delâtre, Corot, Baudelaire, Burty, Degas, Buhot, Manet, Pissarro, Morisot, Cezanne, Vollard, and Forain. Without being overly technical, the author clarifies the various techniques and stages in making prints and demonstrates how commercial success could develop from artistic endeavors that cultivated spontaneity, expressiveness, uniqueness, and invention. Highly recommended. General; undergraduate (including two-year technical program) through professional.—*A. Golahny, Lycoming College*

OAB-0433 NK1355 92-28364 CIP
Morley, John. **Regency design, 1790-1840: gardens, buildings, interiors, furniture.** Abrams, 1993. 473p index ISBN 0-8109-3768-9, $150.00

Politically the English Regency is the period 1811-20, but in terms of the arts it extends from 1790 to 1840. In this superb survey, Morley (former Director of the Brighton Pavilion and Museum and Keeper of Furniture and Interior Design at the Victoria and Albert Museum) presents and describes the style and its major manifestations—garden design, architecture, interior design, and furniture. An excellent, wide-ranging introduction is followed by sections dedicated to each of these. The sections on architecture, interior design, and furniture are similar in arrangement, dealing with formative influences, or antecedents, and various styles—classical, gothic, and exotic. The section devoted to gardens is somewhat different as it includes chapters on association, eclecticism, and, most fascinating of all, town and village planning. The text is scholarly, and the excellent notes, which are very complete, are, in effect, the bibliography. Perhaps the most valuable feature—and certainly the most striking—consists of the rich variety of the well-produced illustrations that form the heart of the book: 471 plates, of which 132 are in color. This is the most comprehensive scholarly work on the subject and should be an invaluable source for a wide audience, from advanced undergraduates on. Highly recommended.—*T. J. McCormick, emeritus, Wheaton College (MA)*

OAB-0434 Orig
Neich, Roger. **Painted histories: early Maori figurative painting.** Auckland, 1994 (c1993). (Dist. by Oxford) 330p bibl indexes ISBN 1-86940-087-9, $75.00

Neich's book is the first written on this subject and promises to stand as the definitive work for years to come. Maori art in other media has long been admired in the Western world. Neich has given attention to technique, symbolism, and historical context. Painting is carried out in highly conventionalized geometric styles, with careful respect for the "powers" thought to be vested in various colors, etc. For about 50 years, beginning around 1870, old media were used in wholly new ways to represent people, places, and things important in the history (both mythological and "factual") of local populations, and these representations were incorporated in the community meeting houses. Such figurative painting rapidly spread, rapidly evolved (with few practitioners), and then rapidly disappeared when the government sponsored a revival of more traditional arts and crafts. Neich's study chronicles this strange, short-lived, and excitingly varied art. With meticulous detail, Neich describes individual artists. He demonstrates an understanding of cultural process and sensitivity to Maori beliefs and behavior, and provides remarkably full documentation. A fascinating window on a heretofore virtually unknown genre of art, and a genuine tour de force of scholarship. Graduate, faculty, professional.—*D. B. Heath, Brown University*

OAB-0435 E78 96-5517 CIP
Plains Indian drawings, 1865-1935: pages from a visual history, ed. by Janet Catherine Berlo. Abrams/American Federation of Arts/ Drawing Center, 1996. 240p bibl index ISBN 0-8109-3742-5, $60.00

Since its introduction in the 1960s with seminal works by notables such as Adamson Hoebel, Karen Petersen, Dorothy Dunn, and Joyce Szabo, "ledger art" has received accelerated attention into the 1990s, leading to an increasing number of publications. This authoritative, highly readable, informed book presents one of the best of this tradition—a comprehensive catalog to accompany a touring exhibition of mainly 19th-century drawings in ledger books and on other available paper, which features works by Kiowa, Arapaho Cheyenne, and Lakota native artists. Instead of treating the drawings strictly as pictorial, visual history or as ethnographic documents, editor Berlo (art history, Univ. of Missouri, St. Louis) and her knowledgeable, multidisciplinary research collaborators explore them from expanded perspectives, providing a comprehensive overview along with an analytic and interpretive approach to the complexity of these works of art, described by Berlo as "encyclopedias of experience." Innovative contributions also include artistic statements by four notable contemporary Plains artists. The detailed catalog essays for more than 150 colored plates and 39 black-and-white figures promote a solid base for appreciating and understanding the origin, diversity, and influences of ledger drawings as pictorial systems of communication by 19th-century native artists/warriors/historians still living within an oral tradition, one "commemorated" in hide paintings in the past. Extensive bibliography and index. General; undergraduate through professional.—*H. H. Schuster, emeritus, Iowa State University*

OAB-0436   Z161   92-3878 CIP
Purvis, Alston W. **Dutch graphic design, 1918-1945.** Van Nostrand Reinhold, 1992. 234p bibl index ISBN 0-442-00444-3, $39.95

The recent influx of books on contemporary design history has made a tremendous impact on the teaching of design and has served to define the role and function of graphic design in our society. *Dutch Graphic Design: 1918-1945* is a 27-year chronology of one of the most exciting periods in design history. Purvis describes it as an "overview" but one that is crafted and written with a keen sensitivity and love of the work and the country. More than 200 black-and-white illustrations are spread over 8 chapters illuminating the lives of some of the most innovative and creative designers of the 20th century. The publisher's decision to separate and insert 20 pages of color reproductions in the middle of the book is problematic. To eliminate color would minimize the scholarship of an historical examination such as this; however, these images are not keyed to the text and may come as a surprise to the reader. The color reproductions are great; the halftone black-and-whites are gray and somewhat muddy. Format aside, the narrative is clear and well written, the notes extensive and the bibliography comprehensive. Purvis, who has spent more than a decade in the Netherlands teaching design, brings experience and expertise to an important subject long neglected. His book will become the definitive book on the subject and an important reference for historians, collectors, professional designers, and students.—*D. Ichiyama, Purdue University*

OAB-0437   NK2049   95-11085 CIP
Scott, Katie. **The Rococo interior: decoration and social spaces in early eighteenth-century Paris.** Yale, 1995. 342p bibl index ISBN 0-300-04582-4, $65.00

Fiske Kimball's *The Creation of the Rococo* (1943) was the first detailed study of the development that led from the *style Louis XIV* to the *genre pittoresque* in French interior design in the first half of the 18th century. Some of Kimball's ideas have been superseded, but his book remains a pioneering work on the subject. The same can be said of Michel Gallet's *Paris: Domestic Architecture of the Eighteenth Century* (London, 1972), which covers the Louis XVI style as well. Both works are concerned primarily with style and biography. Scott (Courtauld Institute of Art, London) builds on these as well as others, but she is equally concerned with the technological, political, social, and economic concerns and movements as they relate to the architecture—the actual creation and building, the functions, and the symbolism of the buildings as well as their stylistic development. Her excellent introduction describes a typical noble house; then follow the book's three (rather unsatisfactorily titled) parts. The first—and one of the most fascinating— is devoted to the production and technical creation of the interiors, including woodwork, tapestries, mirrors, and paintings as well as with organizations—workshops, academies, and guilds and their roles. The second deals with the imagery and meanings of the interi-

ors and their relationship to the patron and his status. The final part discusses ideological positions and the various types of subject matter and their relationship to the changing state. This carefully balanced, first-rate study never loses sight of the work of art. Superb black-and-white and color illustrations; very complete notes and bibliography. Upper-division undergraduate; graduate; faculty; general.—*T. J. McCormick, emeritus, Wheaton College (MA)*

OAB-0438   NC242   94-18473 CIP
Snodgrass, Chris. **Aubrey Beardsley, dandy of the grotesque.** Oxford, 1995. 338p bibl index afp ISBN 0-19-509062-4, $45.00

Beardsley was the epitome of the Decadence, an aesthetic movement that flourished in the 1890s and encompassed such intriguing concepts as "art for art's sake," "beauty in ugliness," and "ambiguity of gender." The art of the "Fra Angelico of Satanism," as Beardsley was once rather unfairly labeled, is indispensable to an understanding of fin-de-siècle Victorian culture. This latest addition to a growing number of explorations of his life and art is more than just another critical approach to his drawings. What this perceptive volume attempts primarily is an examination of the details of Beardsley's works and, within the personal and historical contexts of Beardsley's life, an extrapolation of the thematic structures that inform those works. Specifically, Snodgrass (Univ. of Florida) deals with the larger pattern that underlies the various styles and tropes of Beardsley's drawings. Six tightly reasoned chapters, well illustrated with reproductions of Beardsley's works, delve into the "visions" in his oeuvre and then situate their formulations within a spirited framework. In fine, this comprehensive examination resolves many of the questions and paradoxes that surround the "Dandy of the Grotesque" and should become the standard work on Beardsley for years to come. Essential for all academic collections.—*G. A. Cevasco, St. John's University (NY)*

OAB-0439   E99   93-39709 CIP
Torrence, Gaylord. **The American Indian Parfleche: a tradition of abstract painting.** Washington/Des Moines Art Center, 1994. 272p bibl index afp ISBN 0-295-97332-3, $60.00; ISBN 0-295-97333-1 pbk, $35.00

This book accompanies an exhibition at the Des Moines Art Center, the "first major presentation" focused exclusively on rawhide parfleches, the principal means for storage and transport of food and possessions for nomadic Western tribes. The superb text presents a comprehensive overview and analyses of the expressive qualities of the parfleche tradition as "significant works of art" utilizing abstract painting, a tribute to the skills of Native American women from more than 40 tribes. Torrence (Drake Univ.) surveyed more than 100 collections in the US, Canada, and Europe. Chapters cover the origin and chronological history of parfleches, materials used, techniques of painting and construction, types of containers, aesthetic as well as practical functions, formal characteristics, and the symbolism and associative meanings of the abstract painted images that decorated parfleches. A major contribution identifies attributes that define six major regional/tribal styles: Eastern Plains, Central Plains, Southern Plains and Southwest, North Plains, Transmontane, and Western Plateau. The articulate text combines clear, direct, factual information with vivid expressive descriptions. References are meticulously cited; 127 superb color plates accompany the text, as well as black-and-white historic photographs. Extensive bibliography. An invaluable reference for scholars of Native American studies, historians, and anthropologists alike, as well as museologists and art historians. Undergraduate (all levels) through professional.—*H. H. Schuster, emerita, Iowa State University*

OAB-0440   N5760   93-49464 CIP
Virginia Museum of Fine Arts. **Art of Late Rome and Byzantium in the Virginia Museum of Fine Arts,** by Anna Gonosová and Christine Kondoleon. Virginia Museum of Fine Arts, 1994. 451p bibl index ISBN 0-917046-36-6 pbk, $45.00

Rarely can the catalog of all or part of a permanent collection serve as both a useful introduction to undergraduates and a scholarly record for specialists. This long-awaited account of the holdings at Richmond meets these needs and, in so doing, will serve as a model for other institutions. This is achieved by "wrapping" entries on the 136 items—mostly jewelry, metalwork, bone and ivory, ceramics and textiles—in unaffected language; many are accompanied by the sort of technical study still too rare in this field. Research in these areas is advancing so fast that the bibliographies ("essentially completed by 1991") are occasionally out-of-date. But this is compensated for by essential revisions to our understanding of objects not only in this museum but also many at Dumbarton Oaks, both collections initially assembled and published by M.C. Ross in the 1950s and '60s. All classes of user will delight in the illustrations, often to scale and from multiple points of view. The color pictures, in which, for example, gold does not assume the nasty red hues sometimes imposed on it by photography, are an especial joy. General; undergraduate; graduate; faculty.—*A. Cutler, Pennsylvania State University, University Park Campus*

OAB-0441   NE642   92-4261 CIP

Viscomi, Joseph. **Blake and the idea of the book.** Princeton, 1994 (c1993). 453p bibl index afp ISBN 0-691-06962-X, $49.50

This perceptive study of Blake's illuminated printing draws on Viscomi's unique accomplishments as both scholar and printmaker. In initial chapters Viscomi essentially recounts efforts to demonstrate Blake's processes by recreating them in a modern workshop with the tools, materials, and techniques then available to Blake. Remaining chapters recount the technical evidence and arguments for dating Blake's individual works from 1787 to 1827. The volume is heavily illustrated, including 312 black-and-white photos of Blake's illuminations and Viscomi's reproductions and technical demonstrations, as well as 13 color plates. Shedding new light on all previous accounts of Blake's printing processes—including G.E. Bentley Jr.'s *Blake Records* (1969) and its *Supplement* (1988); David V. Erdman's revised edition of *The Complete Poetry and Prose of William Blake* (1988); and Robert N. Essick's *The Separate Plates of William Blake* (CH, Oct'83), among others—Viscomi's work must be regarded as benchmark in Blake scholarship. Graduate; faculty.—*J. K. Bracken, Ohio State University*

■ Painting

OAB-0442   96-60714 Orig

Ahl, Diane Cole. **Benozzo Gozzoli.** Yale, 1996. 340p bibl index ISBN 0-300-06699-6, $60.00

This monograph on Benozzo Gozzoli is a long-overdue account in English of the life of this underappreciated Florentine Renaissance artist. Benozzo enjoyed a long career, and among his patrons were the Medici, a variety of different religious orders, and even the most humble patrons in Florence and in smaller communities. Ahl (Lafayette College) has written a book impressive for its tight prose, extensive documentation, and excellent color illustrations. She has organized the monograph chronologically, establishing Benozzo's early work in Fra Angelico's shop, then detailing his stylistic development and examining the needs and goals of his patrons. For example, Ahl's discussion of Benozzo's *Journey of the Magi*, painted in 1459 for the Medici palace private chapel in Florence, comes alive with her sensitive formal analysis of the newly cleaned murals, her presentation of documents that reveal Benozzo's repeatedly patient and diplomatic requests for finances and materials from the temperamental Cosimo de' Medici, and finally her examination of the Medici devotion to the cult of the Magi and how Benozzo's murals respond to Medici spiritual and political needs. One wonders only if we will ever know more about Benozzo's ideas, his philosophy of art, and his own needs. Recommended acquisition for lower-division undergraduates (for the plates) and for upper-division undergraduates, graduate students, and faculty.—*A. L. Palmer, University of Oklahoma*

OAB-0443   Orig

Barnett, Vivian Endicott. **Vasily Kandinsky: a colorful life: the collection of the Lenbachhaus, Munich,** ed. by Helmut Friedel. Dumont/Abrams, 1996 (c1995). 664p bibl ISBN 0-8109-6319-1, $95.00

Among recent books on Kandinsky, this title must rank among the most impressive, from both an aesthetic and a scholarly point of view. Its content is defined by the unsurpassed collection of works by Kandinsky in the Munich Lenbachhaus museum. Every sketch, watercolor, and painting, as well as ancillary material, is reproduced (usually in color plates of excellent quality) and annotated. These items include works that he produced in Munich and Murnau between 1896 and 1914 and left behind in his sudden departure from Germany at the outbreak of WW I. The text explains the provenance of this wealth as the result of a rancorous legal dispute when Kandinsky tried after the war to reclaim the works from his former lover, the artist Gabriele Münter. She retained most of them, preserved them from harm during the Nazi era, and lived to see their installation in the Städtische Galerie im Lenbachhaus. The book presents all of the art, from sketches to finished painting, in 15 sections arranged in chronological order. Each of the sections is prefaced with an extensively annotated biographical sketch. The book concludes with an essay on Kandinsky's painting technique and a complete catalog. Undergraduates; graduate; faculty.—*W. C. Brumfield, Tulane University*

OAB-0444   ND2068   95-32972 CIP

Bickford, Maggie. **Ink plum: the making of a Chinese scholar-painting genre.** Cambridge, 1996. 295p; 40 plates bibl index ISBN 0-521-39152-0, $85.00

Bickford (humanities and history of art, Brown Univ.) has produced a brilliantly researched and intrinsically interesting book, which traces the development of an artistic genre, *momei*, from Northern Sung through Yuan (primarily), including literary, historical, and political, as well as artistic considerations. The breadth and depth of Bickford's scholarship allows her to write in a most welcome, free-flowing style, far removed from the stilted, even timid manner of many younger scholars. On page 183, to cite one of many available examples, she writes of "the basic pitfall of literati painting practice: sloppiness masquerading as spontaneity; ignorance and inadequacy posing as the inspired transcendence of small-minded constraints." It is difficult to imagine how this could be put any better. The book is illustrated by 51 smaller figures of paintings, 40 larger plates, and a photograph of plum blossoms. It is an almost unforgivable drawback of the book, considering the splendid quality of the text, that the publisher did not include any color prints. Just three or four representative prints in color might have sufficed. Nevertheless, an outstanding contribution. Upper-division undergraduate through professional.—*T. B. Hoffman, University of South Florida*

OAB-0445   E99   96-50100 MARC

Brody, J.J. **Pueblo Indian painting: tradition and modernism in New Mexico, 1900-1930.** School of American Research, 1997. 225p bibl index ISBN 0-933452-45-4, $60.00; ISBN 0-933452-46-2 pbk, $30.00

This study is an outstanding example of scholarly maturity in the study of Native American art. Brody (emeritus, Univ. of New Mexico), a distinguished and established researcher and author, provides a work that substantially enlarges the understanding of a critical phase of the early development of modern Native American painting. The study focuses on the new tradition of Pueblo fine art painting formed in the first three decades of the 20th century from a merger of ancient influences with aesthetic principles of Euro-American modernism. The publication can be justifiably characterized as the first comprehensive history of this new tradition. Based on research in the collections of the School of American Research in Santa Fe, NM, it traces the lives and explores the accomplishments of seven key artists: Fred Kabotie, Otis Polelonema, Velino Shije Herrera, Awa Tsireh, Crescencio Martinez, Oqua Pi, and Tonita Peña. In addition, the author investigates the artists' interaction with the vital Euro-American community of collectors who helped define the new tradition. Masterfully written, the text is organized chronologically into six chapters charting the development of Pueblo fine art painting from 1900 to 1920. Two appendixes catalogue early Pueblo watercolor painting and related works on paper from the redoubtable collections of the School of American Research at the Indian Arts Research Center and at the Laboratory of Anthropology/Museum of Indian Arts and Culture. There are 99 high-quality plates and 49 figures. Certain to become a standard in the literature on Native American art history; a "must" for all libraries with an interest in Native American art and culture. General; undergraduate; graduate; faculty.—*J. A. Day, University of South Dakota*

OAB-0446   ND1043   93-8790 CIP
Cahill, James. **The painter's practice: how artists lived and worked in traditional China.** Columbia, 1994. 187p bibl index afp (Bampton lectures in America, 29) ISBN 0-231-08180-4, $32.50

This book amends some of the time-honored assumptions about Chinese painters' relationship to their art, particularly professionalism and the notion that the scholar-artist always rose above everyday concerns. Among the most rewarding of the many carefully documented observations are commentaries on ghost painting, how painters gained their livelihoods, and production studios wherein specialists combined their talents. But the vital contribution by Cahill (Univ. of California, Berkeley) is to challenge such myths as the aloofness of scholar-painters, to bring down to earth unnecessarily romanticized versions of a great tradition. Cahill, an internationally respected authority, indicates that this type of social knowlege will enrich our appreciation of the art works. Although some—including this reviewer—may feel that the importance of social and historic factors in understanding a work of art can be overemphasized, there is no doubt that Cahill has produced a brilliant example of creative scholarship. This could well be the most important commentary on Chinese painting in decades. Includes notes and 119 black-and-white plates of good quality. Upper-division undergraduate; graduate; faculty.—*T. B. Hoffman, University of South Florida*

OAB-0447   N6537   91-46222 CIP
Carr, Gerald L. **Frederic Edwin Church: catalogue raisonné of works of art at Olana State Historic Site. v.1: Text; v.2: Plates.** Cambridge, 1994. 2v. 565p; various plates indexes ISBN 0-521-38540-7, $350.00

It seems nearly impossible to think of the American landscape painter Church (1826-1900) without thinking about the late Church scholar David C. Huntington (1922-1990). His writings (including the 1966 monograph *The Landscapes of Frederic Edwin Church*) and fervor for Church's works that he instilled in his Smith and University of Michigan students gave impetus to a Church resurgence that otherwise would have had to wait several more decades. Of several notable younger Church scholars, including Katherine Manthorne and Franklin Kelly, Carr seems the fitting Huntington successor. Before the appearance of the magnificent critical catalogue raisonné on Church's works at Olana, Carr's significant published works on Church included a 1980 study of Church's *The Icebergs* at the Dallas Museum of Fine Arts and the monograph *Olana Landscapes* (1989). His present work, a two-volume magnum opus, is a model of scholarship infused with spirit and good writing. The heart of volume 1 is the critical catalogue, consisting of individual entries for the 701 works by Church at Olana and the 62 prints after Church's work, which are arranged within chronological chapters, each with an introduction. Amplifying material consists of Carr's introduction; an essay by Huntington (which represents the latter's final written statement on Church); a conservative essay; a general index; an index of titles of works at Olana; and concordances of accession numbers for works at Olana, at the Cooper-Hewitt Museum, and at the Detroit Institute of Arts. There are 157 illustrations. Volume 2 consists of 47 color and nearly 1,000 black-and-white plates for Church's works at Olana as well as a detailed list of these plates. This study is unequivocally worth its hefty price, but its specialized nature recommends it to collections emphasizing 19th-century American art. Upper-division undergraduate; graduate; faculty.—*J. Weidman, Oberlin College*

OAB-0448   N6537   95-19025 CIP
Cikovsky, Nicolai. **Winslow Homer,** by Nicolai Cikovsky and Franklin Kelly. National Gallery of Art, Washington/Yale, 1995. 420p bibl index ISBN 0-300-06555-8, $60.00

The richness and variety of publications on this important artist are clearly apparent in the bibliography of the present volume. Even so, this well-produced and reasonably priced catalog of the current comprehensive exhibition at the National Gallery in Washington, DC, which will travel in 1996 to the Museum of Fine Arts, Boston, and then to the Metropolitan Museum of Art, is one of the most impressive in recent years, albeit resting upon the scholarship of many others fully credited in the lengthy acknowledgments section. Cikovsky and Kelly, perhaps best known, respectively, for work on Inness and on Church, and both curators of American Art at the Gallery, have collaborated on a wonderful publication. Cikovsky, the senior curator, contributes five chapters and Kelly two. An additional chapter by conservator Judith Walsh describes innovations in Homer's late watercolors, and Charles Brock adds a detailed chronology and an equally impressive listing of exhibitions in Homer's lifetime. Each chapter consists of a scholarly essay with endnotes, followed by detailed catalog entries for each work discussed in the chapter. Each of the 235 works in the show/catalog is represented by at least one high-quality color reproduction—some of details—and these are amplified by more than 250 smaller black-and-white images. Highly recommended for all levels.—*J. Weidman, Oberlin College*

OAB-0449   ND553   95-5243 CIP
Cropper, Elizabeth. **Nicolas Poussin: friendship and the love of painting,** by Elizabeth Cropper and Charles Dempsey. Princeton, 1996. 374p bibl index afp ISBN 0-691-04449-X, $95.00

Cropper and Dempsey (both of Johns Hopkins Univ.) have written an important book that is a significant step forward in understanding the intellectual milieu and assumptions of one of the major figures of 17th-century art. It is not an introductory volume for those coming to Poussin for the first time, or a catalogue raisonné of his works, but rather an exploration of the intellectual and social context of this highly literate, sophisticated artist. It is replete with references to and comparisons with contemporary artists, such as Rubens, and extended discussion of 17th-century poets and collectors friendly with Poussin, as well as a careful evocation of his attitudes toward ancient Greek and Roman literature and sculpture and his place within various iconographic traditions. The text even touches on such matters as sex in Virgil, hunting in the 17th century, and the theory of lighting geometrical solids. Cropper and Dempsey are widely recognized authorities in Italian art, and they write in an easy, accessible style. The book includes 165 good black-and-white and 12 full color reproductions, and full scholarly apparatus, including endnotes. Upper-division undergraduate through professional.—*F. W. Robinson, Cornell University*

OAB-0450   N6853   90-55530 CIP
Daix, Pierre. **Picasso: life and art,** tr. by Olivia Emmet. Icon Editions, 1993. 450p indexes ISBN 0-06-430976-2, $30.00

Originally published in France in 1987 as *Picasso Créateur* and now expanded, updated, and translated, this is an excellent monographic study of Picasso's life and art by a major French scholar, author of the best two catalogue raisonnés of Picasso's work—with Georges Boudaille, *Picasso: The Blue and Pink Period* (CH, Jun'68) and with Joan Rosselet, *Picasso: The Cubist Years, 1907-1916* (CH, May'80). Among biographers of Picasso, most of whom knew the artist himself, Daix is the most open-minded and the least burdened by a limiting interpretive agenda; consequently, his book considers a broader range of issues (many "controversial") than any other one-volume artistic biography of this crucial artist. Daix has brought more accurate detail to bear on an interpretation of Picasso's life than ever before, and he has uniquely incorporated and responded to recent specialized research on various aspects of the artist, including political history. Using this increased knowledge and information generally responsibly in his interpretations of the artist's paintings and other works, this is as close as anyone has yet come to a scholarly biography of Picasso. With 49 black-and-white illustrations, extensive (though unfortunately not thorough) notes on sources, and an appendix, this book is highly recommended for graduate and undergraduate students and any interested general reader.—*P. Leighten, University of Delaware*

OAB-0451 ND3362 94-36661 CIP
Deshman, Robert. **The Benedictional of Æthelwold.** Princeton, 1995. 287p; 213 plates bibl index afp (Studies in manuscript illumination, 9) ISBN 0-691-04386-8, $99.50

This is a profound study of the most richly decorated and renowned illuminated manuscript produced in Anglo-Saxon England, a collection of blessings made for Bishop (St.) Æthelwold of Winchester (the royal capital), the leader of ecclesiastical reform. Written by the preeminent scholar of this artistic tradition, the book is richly illustrated with color plates of all the major decoration in the manuscript, and has a penetrating and detailed commentary. Deshman (Univ. of Toronto) treats each miniature in turn, revealing its pictorial and literary sources, and then discusses in several very important chapters the structure of the cycle of illustrations as a whole. He considers the many layers of symbolic and liturgical significance in the illustrations, and their context within both the monastic milieu and the royal milieu. The work is full of new insights and challenging interpretative suggestions (such as the rich symbolic significance seen in many of the clouds depicted) and interpretative strategies (such as the notion of entire cycles endowed with symbolic meaning). Anyone interested in early medieval art and culture will want to read this major contribution to the field. Upper-division undergraduate; graduate; professional.—*L. Nees, University of Delaware*

OAB-0452 E99 96-49341 MARC
Dobkins, Rebecca J. **Memory and imagination: the legacy of Maidu Indian artist Frank Day,** by Rebecca J. Dobkins with Carey T. Caldwell and Frank R. LaPena. Oakland Museum of California, 1997. (Dist. by Washington) 106p bibl afp ISBN 0-295-97612-8 pbk, $24.95

This catalog supporting a touring exhibition by the same title organized by the Oakland Museum of California is the first in-depth scholarly evaluation of Day's art and impact. Day (1902-76) was a Konkow Maidu self-taught painter whose life and art contributed to the revitalization of Native American dance and art in California in the 1960s and '70s. Day blended his memory of traditional Indian beliefs with a highly personal perspective to produce paintings rich in symbolism yet evasive of exact interpretation. Dobkins (anthropology, Willamette Univ.) wrote her doctoral dissertation on Maidu art. Her essay "The Life and Art of Frank Day" admirably contextualizes the artist in terms of the Maidu and larger Native American communities. The text is supplemented by a remembrance of Day by Frank R. LaPena, a Wintu artist. Three contemporary Maidu artists, Dolbert Castro, Harry Fonseca, and Judith Lowry, provide personal testimonials to Day's influence on contemporary California Indian artists. The book also offers a substantive catalogue of the works in the exhibit with interpretations of the paintings by the artist. The text is readable and well integrated. Chronology of Day's life and work. Illustrated with 24 black-and-white figures of historical significance and 58 high-quality color plates, of which 53 feature Day's paintings. Likely to be the definitive work on Day; should be acquired by all libraries with an interest in Native American art. General; undergraduate through professional.—*J. A. Day, University of South Dakota*

OAB-0453 Orig
Eldredge, Charles C. **Georgia O'Keeffe: American and modern.** Yale/InterCultura/Georgia O'Keeffe Foundation, 1993. 226p bibl ISBN 0-300-05576-5, $45.00

This handsome publication is more than just a catalog to travel along with the international Georgia O'Keeffe exhibition tour to Japan, London, and Mexico City. Rather, it is a long-overdue and eminently deserved tribute to one of the greatest 20th-century US artists. Eldredge, formerly the director of the National Museum of Art, Washington, DC, and now Hall Distinguished Professor at the University of Kansas, spells out what makes O'Keeffe's work

uniquely modern and specifically American. Called surrealist, precisionist, existentialist, or regionalist, O'Keeffe rejected all these labels and asked to be remembered "as a painter, just as a painter." Eldredge's significant and valuable essay focuses on the formal aspects of Modernism in her work. (Like the Modernists, she chose to work in series.) Eldredge comments on O'Keeffe's connection to the perception of nature by the American transcendentalists. This work fits in with the contemporary need to define an American tradition and to find the roots of the American experience. A series of photographs of O'Keeffe from her student days to her last days in New Mexico parallels a detailed chronology. There are superb reproductions of her works spanning her active career from 1915 to 1963. A major contribution to American art and American cultural history.—*M. Kren, Kansas State University*

OAB-0454 Orig
Finaldi, Gabriele. **Discovering the Italian Baroque: the Denis Mahon collection,** by Gabriele Finaldi and Michael Kitson. National Gallery Publications, London, 1997. (Dist. by Yale) 192p bibl index ISBN 0-300-07141-8, $55.00

The 79 color plates cataloged to a T, plus 30 drawings (five in color) cataloged and reproduced small-scale, a rich bibliography plus a bibliography of Sir Denis Mahon's art historical writings through 1997—all these make this catalog of an exhibition at the National Gallery, London, both pleasurable and useful. The elderly Mahon, heir to the Guiness Mahon Group, willed his private collection, acquired during the 1930s-60s, to several public institutions throughout the UK. Therefore much exhibited and often cataloged works here receive their most polished and coherent treatment to date, following Mahon's own researches and conclusions. The drawings are actually cataloged by Mahon; the paintings primarily by Kitson and Finaldi. Kitson's concise and clear essay compares Mahon to Poussin's intellectual companion Cassiano dal Pozzo for his combination of roles as collector, familiar in places of political power, and writer about art. Moreover, the essay brilliantly surveys the study of Italian Baroque painting from Winckelman and Wöfflin, assessing Mahon's not inconsequential place in it as rehabilitator and polemicist for the purely visual distinction of the style. The potentially sticky job of saluting a major donor and documenting a collection, before its limited dispersal, has been done with panache. General; undergraduate; faculty.—*P. Emison, University of New Hampshire*

OAB-0455 N6923 93-47989 CIP
Franklin, David. **Rosso in Italy: the Italian career of Rosso Fiorentino.** Yale, 1994. 326p bibl indexes ISBN 0-300-05893-4, $55.00

This is the first monograph in English on the highly original artist Rosso Fiorentino, a crucial figure among the so-called Mannerists of the early 16th century. Franklin has written an excellent account of Rosso's Italian years, from his birth in 1494 to his departure for France in 1530. Using new archival information—much of it unearthed by the author and included in an appendix—Franklin charts the unsteady course of Rosso's early career with particular attention to the artist's patronage, an aspect virtually ignored by previous scholarship. Franklin writes lucidly about Rosso's technique and the unique stylistic qualities of his paintings and drawings. The author successfully interweaves biography, patronage, and style and demonstrates how each affects the others. The beautiful, large-format volume is lavishly illustrated with more than 200 excellent photographs (49 in color and many details). Anybody who thinks the art historical monograph is an antiquated genre should read this book: it is an important, well-written, multifaceted contextual study of a fascinating Renaissance artist. A valuable book for scholars and graduate students; accessible to undergraduates and informed readers.—*W. E. Wallace, Washington University*

OAB-0456 N6537 95-38383 CIP
Gerdts, William H. **William Glackens,** text by William H. Gerdts; essay by Jorge H. Santis. Museum of Art, Fort Lauderdale/Abbeville, 1996. 279p bibl index ISBN 1-55859-868-5, $85.00

From several points of view this is an important book. It is the first major monograph on Glackens, being far more comprehensive than any previous texts dealing with his work (some good examples of which include the Delaware Art Museum's 1985 *William Glackens: Illustrator in New York, 1897-1919* and Ira Glackens's *William Glackens and the Ashcan Group*, 1957). It is also important in that it contains the first complete catalog of the Glackens Collection, a group of more than 400 works of art just acquired from the Glackens family by the Fort Lauderdale Museum of Art. This catalog, and the introductory essay by Santis, add significantly to our understanding of Glackens and the Ashcan School. The book is painstakingly researched and documented, yet written with a light touch. Gerdts (Graduate School, CUNY) concentrates on how Glackens interacted with his world, rather than (as other writers might have done) trying to cast Glackens as a larger-than-life figure. Attractive square quarto format that makes for easier handling and reading; numerous color and black-and-white illustrations. Highly recommended. General; undergraduate through professional.—*M. W. Sullivan, Villanova University*

OAB-0457 N7113X 93-83944 Orig
Gimferrer, Pere. **The roots of Miró.** Ediciones Pol'igrafa/Rizzoli, 1993. 435p bibl ISBN 0-8478-1768-7, $150.00

Very rarely does one encounter such an extraordinarily detailed and scholarly analysis of works of art as Gimferrer's *The Roots of Miró.* The book traces, in depth, the process of synthesization, mutation, and reduction of elements in Miró's rich oeuvre, according to an internal need. Gimferrer explains the reworkings of Miró's themes chronologically, stressing the ever-innovative and surprising exposition of a single theme that exists beyond the imitative stage, and he analyzes Miró's transfigurations that bring forth the poetic impact and dream-like quality. This is a large book with superb illustrations, many reproducing works previously unpublished. The author does capture, albeit a bit repetitively and pedantically, the very vastness of Miró's creative process. He stresses the importance of variations, evolution, metamorphosis, and ideograms in each of Miró's compositional spaces, as they are reworked many times. The author also honors the uniqueness of this Catalan master, celebrating and paying attention to Miró's smallest detail, line, and mark; pointing out the relevance of each genesis. The book includes many preparatory sketches, a long appendix, Miró's sculpture, ceramics, ballets, graphic collages, murals, and monuments. Gimferrer acknowledges Dupin's earlier cataloging. A sumptuous, meticulous, fascinating inspection of Miró's creative process. Recommended. Graduate; faculty; professional.—*I. Spalatin, East Texas State University*

OAB-0458 Orig
Goswamy, B.N. **Pahari masters: court painters of northern India,** by B.N. Goswamy and Eberhard Fischer. Oxford, 1997. 391p bibl ISBN 0-19-564014-4 pbk, $95.00

Two gifted scholars have combined their broad and penetrating talents to produce what may well be the most thoroughgoing and satisfactory book available concerning Pahari (north Indian hill country) painting. Good quality color plates of 170 well-chosen paintings cover the history of the most significant Pahari painters (from c. 1552, an apparent folk style, to c. 1830, much more sophisticated but still basically folk art). Paintings were selected from the museums of five countries and numerous collectors around the world. The detailed and well written commentary relates the paintings to the magnificent legends of Hinduism; considers stylistic, historical, and social aspects; includes biographical information concerning the painters and displays, always, great sensibility (not at all inevitable in art books). This reviewer has long favored the *Gita Govinda* paintings (prints 130 to 137), so brilliantly reproduced in 1965 (M.S. Randhawa, *Kangra Paintings of the Gita Govinda*, CH, Mar'66), but this excellent volume reveals many other types of superb Pahari accomplishments of equal stature. Included are 120 black-and-white plates. Highly recommended.—*T. B. Hoffman, University of South Florida*

OAB-0459 91-52769 Orig
Hahl-Koch, Jelena. **Kandinsky.** Rizzoli, 1993. 431p bibl indexes ISBN 0-8478-1404-1, $150.00

With 420 illustrations (220 in color), 400 pages of text, including important previously unpublished letters, poems, and newspaper articles, and a 12-page bibliography, *Kandinsky* is a blockbuster, even by the standards of the 1990s. Its scope invites comparison with the huge catalog of the recent Russian avant-garde show, *The Great Utopia.* Yet this volume celebrates the work of only one artist and culminates decades of research by the author, who has the requisite linguistic and cultural background to investigate all of Kandinsky's sources and artistic connections. Hahl-Koch adduces important new documents that help us to understand Kandinsky in the context of his family, friends, and wives. However, she quite properly devotes most of her attention to the paintings themselves. In the course of her detailed discussions of the artist's complex evolution she criticizes most recent Kandinsky scholars, and thus will surely provoke considerable controversy. Nevertheless, Hahl-Koch has written the definitive book on Kandinsky for our lifetime; it will stand the test of time. All levels.—*J. M. Curtis, University of Missouri—Columbia*

OAB-0460 ND673 93-34947 CIP
Hall, Edwin. **The Arnolfini betrothal: medieval marriage and the enigma of Van Eyck's double portrait.** California, 1994. 180p bibl index afp (Discovery series, 3) ISBN 0-520-08251-6, $45.00

The publication of this monograph on Jan van Eyck's Arnolfini double portrait in the National Gallery in London follows by only a year Linda Seidel's *Jan van Eyck's Arnolfini Portrait* (CH, Jun'94). Despite the fact that both books are about a single painting and that both take Erwin Panofsky's interpretation of that painting as their point of departure, these are two distinctly different studies. Far be it from superfluous to acquire this book, too. A historian already known for his excellent contributions to Eyckian studies, Hall concludes that the painting is a representation of the couple's betrothal and is not a document of their matrimony. The visual and historical evidence assembled by the author in arriving at this distinction makes his book not only an important study on the painting but also a valuable account of medieval marriage practices in Italy and the Netherlands. In a concluding chapter, Hall presents a strong opposing argument in the ongoing art historical debate about "disguised symbolism" in early Netherlandish painting. For its information, method, clarity, and insight, this well-illustrated book is to be recommended to all libraries that support historical and art historical studies.—*C. W. Talbot, Trinity University*

OAB-0461 ND853 95-19298 MARC
Hauptman, William. **Charles Gleyre, 1806-1874: v.1: Life and works; v.2: Catalogue raisonné.** Swiss Institute for Art Research/Princeton/Wiese Publishing Ltd., 1997 (c1996). 2v. 396, 591p bibl index ISBN 0-691-04448-1, $160.00

To students and scholars familiar with 19th-century French art, the legacy of Charles Gleyre, the Swiss academic, Romantic artist, and Parisian teacher of such well-known and important artists as Bazille, Sisley, Renoir, and Monet, is well known. Despite the existence of Charles Clément's 1878 critical biography of Gleyre, the life and art of this important artist have remained elusive and certainly not well documented until Hauptman's magnificent study and catalogue. The publishers are to be commended for bringing out such an important and well-produced title at such a reasonable price, for comparable catalogues raisonnés often cost twice or more the price of this superb publication. Replete with high-quality scholarly entries and reproductions of Gleyre's more than 1,100 paintings, drawings, and watercolors, and examining for the first time material in 17 rediscovered sketchbooks, Hauptman's comprehensive monograph and catalogue are models of thorough scholarship. Recommended for all comprehensive collections of modern art.—*J. Weidman, Oberlin College*

OAB-0462 Orig
Hiesinger, Ulrich W. **Childe Hassam: American impressionist.** Prestel, 1994. 191p bibl index ISBN 3-7913-1364-9, $65.00

A model monograph, this work is definitive art history without political correctness or current interpretations of Hassam's milieu. After a short introduction, which profiles the artist's personality, Hassam's oeuvre is traced chronologically in the places in which he lived and worked. The book provides outstanding insights into Hassam's subject matter, influences, interpretation of French impressionism, involvement in art affairs of his day, and exhibitions and sales. Changes of style and subject matter during the artist's life and his extensive travel are among the surprises. Hiesinger, an independent scholar, has made extensive use of the artist's notebooks and correspondence and of the writings of contemporary critics, and throughout, he makes perceptive judgments on the paintings and on Hassam's attitudes. Wonderful color plates match the verve of the paintings; there are only a few etchings, however. Period photographs of cities, particularly New York, match sites painted. Appendixes: letters from Paris, 1888-89; selected writings and interviews; chronology, 1881-1935. Extensive notes; selected bibliography; list of works by title; index of names. A much-needed, comprehensive study of this important American impressionist. Upper-division undergraduate; graduate; faculty; general.— *W. L. Whitwell, Hollins College*

OAB-0463   N6537   92-10163 CIP
Homer, William Innes. **Thomas Eakins: his life and art.** Abbeville, 1992. 276p bibl index ISBN 1-55859-281-4, $95.00

Eakins has been the subject of scores of books and articles in the last few years, and Abbeville's concern for a novel approach (the dust jacket calls Homer's book a "revisionist study") is understandable. But this book does not need much justification. It is a masterful combination of well-known data with information that became available only very recently. Homer (Univ. of Delaware) draws upon the untapped riches of the Bregler Collection at the Pennsylvania Academy of Fine Arts; the Gordon Hendricks papers at the Archives of American Art; the Eakins archive at the Philadelphia Museum of Art; and the Eakins collection of Mr. and Mrs. Daniel W. Dietrich II (once the property of Seymour Adelman). Homer's book, with its 270 full-color and 110 black-and-white illustrations, is more than revisionist. It has an immediacy and a vividness that are rare in scholarly publications, and it makes the reader feel that he or she has actually met the painter and watched him at work. Highly recommended.—*M. W. Sullivan, Villanova University*

OAB-0464   ND623   92-14504 CIP
Hood, William. **Fra Angelico at San Marco.** Yale, 1993. 338p bibl index ISBN 0-300-05734-2, $60.00

Although Fra Angelico's famous complex of works made for the Florentine Dominican monastery of San Marco have been studied in a number of Italian publications over the past 30 years, the English-reading public has been largely limited to John Pope-Hennessy's useful though somewhat outdated monograph on the artist (2nd ed., 1974). Hood's ambitious new book synthesizes years of careful and original study on the artist and rewards the reader with a sophisticated understanding of the various parts of the monastery's decoration, from the more "worldly" altarpiece made for the church choir to the austere, simplified frescoes painted in the friars' dormitory cells. Beyond addressing stylistic and technical concerns, Hood focuses on the religious function of the works: how ritual prayer, liturgical practices, and theological ideas particular to the Observant branch of the Dominican order affected the form and content of Angelico's paintings. Richly illustrated with excellent color plates. Informed general readers; advanced undergraduate and above.—*J. I. Miller, California State University, Long Beach*

OAB-0465   ND621   94-35348 CIP
Humfrey, Peter. **Painting in Renaissance Venice.** Yale, 1995. 320p bibl index ISBN 0-300-06247-8, $35.00

This is a handy volume, aimed at the nonspecialist, into which a great deal of specialist information has been gracefully inserted. The approach is chronological, following the traditional schema of Early, High, and Late Renaissance. But within these categories there is much rethinking and an up-to-the-minute absorption of the scholarly literature. The Venetian facility for narrative

painting has been emphasized, and there is serious attention to genres of painting (in the first instance, portraiture) as well as consistent attention to the demands of patronage and site. The Venetian High Renaissance is treated as a very particular phenomenon produced by the knitting together of diverse influences, including the powerful contribution of Albrecht Dürer. The apparatus includes a short but excellent bibliography, an informative introduction, and an appendix of lively artist biographies. Care has gone into the choice of illustrations, which include numerous lesser-known images as well as the old warhorses, and good details. An ideal entry into the subject. Undergraduate; graduate; faculty; general.—*D. Pincus, University of British Columbia*

OAB-0466   ND653   95-23917 CIP
Johannes Vermeer. National Gallery of Art/Royal Cabinet of Paintings Mauritshuis/Yale, 1995. 229p bibl index ISBN 0-300-06558-2, $45.00

Although this book is actually the catalog of an exhibition of 22 of the 35 accepted paintings by Vermeer at the National Gallery of Art, Washington (Nov. 12, 1995 - Feb. 11, 1996) and the Royal Cabinet of Paintings Mauritshuis, The Hague (March 1 - June 2, 1996), it is the best and most up-to-date work on the artist's career and oeuvre. The authors of two of the essays, Arthur K. Wheelock Jr. (National Gallery of Art) and Albert Blankert (Utrecht Univ.), are already well known for their monographs on Vermeer (Wheelock, 1981, 1988; Blankert, 1988). The two other essays are by Mauritshuis staff members Ben Broos and Jørgen Wadum. The catalog of the exhibited paintings is by Wheelock and Broos, with each work illustrated in color, often with details. There are elaborate technical descriptions of the paintings by Nicola Costaras. Perhaps of the greatest interest is the cleaned *View of Delft*. Other works by Vermeer not in the exhibition are discussed and illustrated in the catalog and in the four essays; thus the book is, in effect, a complete study of the artist's works. In keeping with the increasing interest in context and collecting, portraits of major previous owners are included. Exhaustive bibliography of books, articles, and exhibitions; invaluable chronology of the few known facts based on documents; maps. A first-rate publication, which should have a wide appeal. Upper-division undergraduate; graduate; faculty; general.—*T. J. McCormick, emeritus, Wheaton College (MA)*

OAB-0467   94-73938 Orig
Jordan, William B. **Spanish still life: from Velázquez to Goya,** by William B. Jordan and Peter Cherry. National Gallery Publications, London, 1995. (Dist. by Yale) 224p bibl index ISBN 0-300-06356-3, $45.00

This first-rate study accompanied the exhibition of Spanish still life painting, from the 17th to the early 19th century, held at the National Gallery, London, Feb.-May 1995. In effect, it is the catalog of that superb and groundbreaking exhibition, the first in England to be devoted to the subject. In addition to excellent essays on such subjects as the origins of Spanish still life, there are essays on the major 17th-century artists—Sánchez Cotán (one of the stars of the exhibition), Diego Velázquez, Juan van der Hamen, Juan de Valdés Leal, and, in the 18th century, Luis Melendez and Goya. Besides the discussion of minor artists, who vary greatly in quality, there are chapters on still life painting in the major cities and areas of Spain. Illustrating all of these are excellent color and black-and-white plates of the works included in the exhibition as well as related ones. Therefore this is a complete study of the subject, far surpassing anything published before in English. Comparable American catalogs, such as William Jordan's of the exhibition held at the Kimball Art Museum in 1985 and two earlier ones held in Nottingham in 1981 and in Newark, NJ, in 1964, were limited to paintings of the Golden Age (part or all of the 17th century). The complete bibliography and a most useful map make this superb book even more valuable. Highly recommended. Upper-division undergraduate; graduate; general.— *T. J. McCormick, emeritus, Wheaton College (MA)*

OAB-0468   94-75917 Orig
Kanter, Laurence B. **Italian paintings in the Museum of Fine Arts, Boston: v.1: 13th-15th century.** Museum of Fine Arts, Boston, 1994. (Dist. by Northeastern University) 248p indexes ISBN 0-87846-420-4, $60.00

Somewhat misleadingly titled, this scholarly and well-illustrated catalog omits early Venetian paintings, which will be included in a later volume. The Museum of Fine Arts has been laggard in documenting its collection but now makes up for lost time with this admirable volume, the work of the director of the Lehman Collection of the Metropolitan Museum, New York, and formerly at the MFA. Entries are arranged by century, then town (the bulk are Florentine or Sienese), then chronologically by artist. Approximately 40 color illustrations, supplemented with some in black and white, accompany the entries, an arrangement that facilitates browsing. Unusually complete information on condition and measurements are provided, along with bibliography and two indexes, one for collectors and dealers. An appealing essay on Bostonian collecting of early Italian art by the associate curator of European painting, Eric Zafran, extends up to the year 1992 and includes the embarrassing incident of the purchase of a fake Piero della Francesca in 1940 (not illustrated). An essential acquisition, this volume both summarizes and contributes to the state of knowledge about these paintings, and it sets a standard for the anticipated complementary catalogs. It combines the virtues of a catalog with the appeal of a keepsake book for the general public. Undergraduate; graduate; faculty; general.—*P. Emison, University of New Hampshire*

OAB-0469   ND1839   92-21542 CIP
Ketner, Joseph D. **The emergence of the African-American artist: Robert S. Duncanson, 1821-1872.** Missouri, 1993. 235p bibl indexes afp ISBN 0-8262-0880-0, $39.95

Since 1980, when Ketner, now director of the Washington University Gallery of Art in St. Louis, wrote his MA thesis (Indiana Univ.) on Robert Duncanson's late literary landscape paintings, Duncanson scholarship has deservedly been increasing in both breadth and depth. The culmination of more than a decade of research, Ketner's study is the most thorough and valuable to appear on this important African American artist, whose travels and reputation not only were concentrated in Cincinnati but extended also to Canada, to Europe, and throughout the US. The author treats Duncanson and his art within the context of his own times as well as within the tradition of former, current, and subsequent 19th-century African American artists, such as Edmonia Lewis and Henry Ossawa Tanner. Supporting the excellent text are a fine section of endnotes, a most welcome catalog of Duncanson's 163 known works, 115 black-and-white illustrations of his and others' works, 20 high-quality color plates of his work, a list of illustrations, and a good index. Minor detractions include the lack of a list of works arranged by collection and the use of the somewhat quirky double-column arrangement of the text. On the whole, an important contribution to American and African American studies and art history. Recommended for all collections.—*J. Weidman, Oberlin College*

OAB-0470   ND212   92-32992 CIP
Leja, Michael. **Reframing abstract expressionism: subjectivity and painting in the 1940s.** Yale, 1993. 392p bibl index afp ISBN 0-300-04461-5, $50.00

A paradigmatic product of the "new art history," this study strives to position Abstract Expressionism within modernist discourses of self-representation. As such, the post-WW II American self is largely understood as a conflicted primordial and preconscious identity constituting the deeper meaning of action painting. Through careful interrogation of a number of recent monographs on the art of Jackson Pollock—e.g., Ellen Landau's *Jackson Pollock* (CH, Feb'90) and Claude Cernuschi's *Jackson Pollock's "Psychoanalytic Drawings"* (CH, Jul'93)—the author provides the best and fullest account to date of the content of New York School painting and its intense subjectivity. Informed and insightful readings of major works afford provisional solutions to the broader Pollock problematic together with the welcome acknowledgment that there can be no fixed, lasting, or stable understanding of the painter's artistic intention and reception. This is a brilliant book, informed by a powerful critical intelligence as well as sensitivity and imagination. It eclipses all previous publications and opens new vistas for future interpretations. Highly recommended. Advanced undergraduate; graduate; faculty.—*R. L. McGrath, Dartmouth College*

OAB-0471   ND2757   91-12980 MARC
Lewine, Carol F. **The Sistine Chapel walls and the Roman liturgy.** Pennsylvania State, 1993. 134p bibl index afp ISBN 0-271-00792-3, $45.00

That much-discussed and many-layered interior, the Sistine Chapel, turns out to have still another reference system embedded in its decorative program—the calendar of the Roman liturgical year. The focus here is on the Christ and Moses fresco cycle on the lower walls of the chapel, executed during the Sixtus IV campaign of the 1480s. It has generally been recognized that the cycle functions to assert papal primacy, using the time-honored typological schema as the vehicle. Now we have Lewine's convincing argument that embedded in the narratives, is, as well, a dense pattern of references to the liturgical themes of the weeks between Advent and Pentecost, with particular emphasis on the Lenten season. The bulk of the text is given over to a fresco-by-fresco demonstration of the liturgical subtext. Opening and closing chapters give the context and reasons for the liturgical reference system, the most important being the stance of Sixtus IV as champion of the venerable liturgy of the early Church and the ideals of early Christianity. Restrained in its presentation, the book stands as a major contribution to our understanding of one of Christendom's major monuments. Advanced undergraduate; graduate; faculty.—*D. Pincus, University of British Columbia*

OAB-0472   ND614   93-12237 CIP
Lloyd, Christopher. **Italian paintings before 1600 in the Art Institute of Chicago: a catalogue of the collection**, ed. by Martha Wolff. Art Institute of Chicago/Princeton, 1993. 312p ISBN 0-691-03351-X, $90.00

The Art Institute of Chicago has inaugurated a series of projected catalogs of its permanent collection with this exemplary volume, covering a group of more than 90 paintings dating from the mid-13th century to just before 1600. The catalog is carefully researched and provides full bibliography, provenance, and condition reports for each work in addition to a well-argued essay discussing attribution, date, iconography, and function. The text is also a model for honest and responsible scholarship, not hesitating to designate a work "after" or "workshop of" a major artist instead of defending a questionable attribution, and even admits to the accession of a forgery. Every work is illustrated (some in color), with comparative illustrations when relevant. Although Chicago's collection of Italian paintings contains few works of outstanding importance (the Giovanni di Paolo *St. John the Baptist* paintings are among the most notable), the catalog provides much useful information for scholars. Recommended for libraries that serve specialized programs in art history; future catalogs covering the areas of the museum's greatest strengths, especially 19th- and 20th-century art, should have a broader appeal to general readers. Advanced undergraduate; graduate; faculty.—*J. I. Miller, California State University, Long Beach*

OAB-0473   92-81515 Orig
Matisse, Henri. **Henri Matisse: a retrospective,** catalogue by John Elderfield. Museum of Modern Art, New York, 1992. (Dist. by Abrams) 480p bibl index ISBN 0-8109-6116-4, $75.00

This impressive volume accompanies the Museum of Modern Art's 1992 mammoth retrospective exhibition. The color plates of this comprehensive selection of Matisse's paintings (as excellently reproduced as they are extensive), the chronology of his career (compiled by Judith Cousins), and the annotated bibliography would alone justify its publication. But it also includes an elegantly literate and perceptive essay on Matisse's artistic intention and interpretation by the show's curator, John Elderfield. Director of the Museum's Department of Drawing, Elderfield is a distinguished scholar of modern art, having already catalogued the Matisse Collection at the Museum (1978) and published the discerning *The Cut-Outs of Henri Matisse* (1978). The catalog, completed with his colleague Beatrice Kernan, is arranged by the major eras in Matisse's career, and, reflecting Elderfield's aim of re-examining the work afresh, bereft of all but brief factual information and a prefatory summary. The book joins the admirable literature initiated by Alfred Barr's *Matisse: His Art and Public* (1951),

Lawrence Gowing's *Matisse* (CH, Jul'80) and the studies of J. D. Flam, notably *Matisse, The Man and his Art 1869-1918* (CH, Apr'87).—*R. W. Liscombe, University of British Columbia*

OAB-0474   ND547   94-15426 CIP
Meixner, Laura L. **French realist painting and the critique of American society, 1865-1900.** Cambridge, 1995. 322p index ISBN 0-521-46103-0, $100.00

In four essays, Meixner (Cornell Univ.) analyzes American society's response to French art during the post-Civil War period. Her thesis is that, through the meaning and interpretation that Americans gave to French art, they connected "French realism to the preoccupations that defined their particular American realities." The four essays, "Peasant Images as Critique and Capital," "Peasant Icons for the Conflicted Middle Class," "Courbet, Corot, and Democratic Poetics," and "Impressionism, Pathology, and Progress," describe popular responses (1865 to the 1890s) recorded in the press and radical journals to paintings by Jean-François Millet, Gustave Courbet, Edouard Manet, and Claude Monet. Meixner refers to the writings of Ralph Waldo Emerson and Walt Whitman as she discusses Americans' evolving definitions of democracy and equality. Though this work is very scholarly and assumes a grasp of art history criticism and the even more complex reception theory in literary criticism, it could be appreciated by audiences not fully versed in these theories of criticism but able to appreciate how visual images shaped American thought. A valuable addition to undergraduate and graduate collections in art history, government, and sociology.—*N. M. Lambert, University of South Carolina at Spartanburg*

OAB-0475   N6537   95-1223 CIP
Nemerov, Alexander. **Frederic Remington and turn-of-the-century America.** Yale, 1995. 244p bibl index afp ISBN 0-300-05566-8, $40.00

Remington was among the most popular and talented of the artists who portrayed life in the American West in the last decades of the 19th century and the first decade of the 20th century. His paintings and sculptures have been often praised for their nostalgic realism but seldom subjected to sustained modern, critical analysis. This provocative and carefully crafted work seeks to understand the symbiotic relationship of Remington's art to turn-of-the-century American culture and how his art was informed, knowingly and unknowingly, by the intellectual, literary, artistic, and cultural discourses of that era. Examples of Remington's art are examined in great detail as Nemerov attempts to reveal the assumptions and metaphors that are both present in his work and inform them. Although Remington has been frequently praised as a literal interpreter of western life, the author suggests that even in Remington's most literal works there may be found strong metaphors and suggestive themes. Intimately familiar with the works of Remington and contemporary theories of criticism in art, Nemerov has written an exceptionally significant work for understanding the art of an individual who thought he was documenting the transitory life of the old West. Upper-division undergraduate; graduate; faculty.—*P. D. Thomas, Wichita State University*

OAB-0476   ND1001   93-317 CIP
Pal, Pratapaditya. **Indian painting: a catalogue of the Los Angeles County Museum of Art Collection. v.1: 1000-1700.** Los Angeles County Museum of Art, 1993. (Dist. by Abrams) 384p bibl index ISBN 0-8109-3465-5, $65.00

Dealing with Buddhist manuscript illuminations (1000-1300), Jain, Hindu, Mughal, and Deccan paintings (1300-1700) and Islamic and Deccani calligraphy (1400-1700), Pal, its curator, writes clearly, extensively, and intensively about the Indian collection of the Los Angeles County Museum of Art. His overall descriptions of these distinctive periods of Indian art are excellent; even more rewarding are his comments on individual art works, often including fascinating commentary concerning minute details. Of the 200 illustrations, more than 70 are in remarkably sensitive color. Frequently an enlarged black-and-

white detail appears just prior to a color print (e.g., p. 267, p. 269), a most effective way of giving the reader greater insight into the painting. Calligraphy examples sometimes prove to be the aesthetic equal of even the most superb of the paintings (see page 278). An outstanding catalog, raising hopes that a future volume will include 20th-century Indian painting, an area too long neglected. Highly recommended. Advanced undergraduate; graduate; faculty; general.—*T. B. Hoffman, University of South Florida*

OAB-0477   [Multimedia]
A Passion for art: Renoir, Cézanne, Matisse, and Dr. Barnes. Corbis Publishing, 15395 SE 30th Place, Suite 300, Bellevue, WA 98007, 1995. ISBN 1-886802-00-9 $49.95. 1 disc; user manual. System requirements: IBM-PC, 486 or better; 8MB RAM; Windows 3.1; double-speed CD-ROM drive; mouse; color display.

This highly significant CD-ROM, deserving of many accolades, covers a 336-plus selection of artworks from one of the greatest private art collections of paintings of the early 20th century. It definitely supersedes the prior catalog *Great French Paintings from the Barnes Foundation: Impressionist, Post-Impressionist, and Early Modern* (CH, Oct'93). Albert C. Barnes (1872-1951) was a controversial but brilliant Philadelphian who amassed an astonishing collection of major European early 20th century paintings. His legacy, The Barnes Foundation, includes 180 works by Renoir, the largest group in the world, and an amazing 51 compositions by Cézanne. The collection also includes some old master paintings and African sculptures, as well as decorative arts including furniture and ironwork not treated in this publication. With monetary success in the field of medical chemistry marketing the antiseptic eye product Argyrol, Barnes became a self-made specialist in contemporary art. He believed in the value of scientific method for practical forms of education for everyday people. He specialized in promoting contemporary art: Impressionism, Postimpressionism, Neo-Impressionism, Cubism, Fauvism, fantasy art, and even surrealist figure in his collections.

More than 336 artworks were selected from the full Barnes collection for an audience that will include the general public as well as the most serious of scholars. Innumerable close ups of single works, added to overviews throughout the gallery, plus the erudite and interesting commentaries from luminary historians and museum directors make this CD-ROM one of the top five currently available treating the history of art. There are 12 audio presentations in the Archives Section, and more than 45 minutes of introductory audio tours given by experts including Joseph J. Rischel, J. Carter Brown, and Jack Flam. Biographical material and commentaries were contributed by 13 other essay authors. There is a timeline section, an alphabetical index of individual artists, and an important "slide show" section that could be used for teaching purposes since the ROM is especially user-friendly. Highly recommended. General; upper division undergraduate through professional.—*M. Hamel-Schwulst, Towson State University*

OAB-0478   ND1329   94-42682 MARC
Saunders, Richard H. **John Smibert: colonial America's first portrait painter.** Yale, 1996 (c1995). 280p bibl index afp ISBN 0-300-04258-2, $45.00

The notable literature (including the bibliography) on John Smibert (1688-1751) is relatively thin compared to that on other important American painters as well as on other American Colonial portrait painters. The most important recent work has been done by Saunders, primarily in his 1979 Yale dissertation and his contributions to the 1987 National Portrait Gallery exhibition catalog, *American Colonial Portraits, 1700-1776*. His current monograph with catalogue raisonné is the culmination of 20 years' work on Smibert and is the most important study of the artist to date. Saunders's long familiarity with, and study of, a single artist, his work, and his milieu are eminently clear in this study, in which primary and secondary sources have been thoroughly integrated into a scholarly and readable text. The invaluable catalogue, with its five sections on types of works (accepted, disputed, unlocated, misattributed and fake, and copied); the valuable appendixes, bibliography, and index;

unobtrusive notes; and large number of excellent black-and-white and color plates render Saunders's study of interest to the student and scholar of American art and American studies, as well as to the general reader interested in American culture. Undergraduate; graduate; faculty; general.—*J. Weidman, Oberlin College*

OAB-0479   92-50137 Orig
Spate, Virginia. **Claude Monet: life and work.** Rizzoli, 1992. 348p bibl index ISBN 0-8478-1571-4, $75.00

A monumental three-part study of Monet and his work, comprehensive in scope, generous in detail, and rich in insight. It begins with Monet's emergence as an artist in the ethos of the Second Empire and then explores his early involvement with the "suburban" River Seine, with its now familiar locales in Paris and Argenteuil. In Part 2 attention shifts to Monet's mature efforts of the years 1878-1904. Centering first on the paintings done at Vétheuil and along the coast of Normandy (1878-1883), the discussion proceeds to consider Monet's subsequent involvement with "domestic landscapes" and his "tourist painting trips" of 1883-89, as the newly famous avant-garde artist converted favorite architectural monuments into icons of a newly emergent bourgeois fashion for tourism. A third chapter, "Concentration and Fragmentation," explores the challenging phenomena realized in the various series that preoccupied Monet in the years 1890-1904. In those haystacks, poplars, views of the River Epte and of Rouen Cathedral, his splendid and persistent originality of purpose and vision was fully revealed. Finally, in Part 3 Monet's heroic, culminating struggles with the *Nympheas* are presented, with all their majestic yet baffling depth. Spate offers a comprehensive image of a great artist whom she reveals as far more complex than usually supposed, and she enframes her portrait within a lucidly wrought but unobtrusive discussion of the social, historical, and technical contexts that pertain. Fully documented and highly recommended.—*F. A. Trapp, Amherst College*

OAB-0480   ND623   96-51128 Orig
Spike, John T. **Fra Angelico.** Abbeville, 1996. 280p bibl index ISBN 0-7892-0322-7, $95.00

Fra Angelico has recently received a good deal of attention, but Spike's beautifully illustrated monograph on this early Renaissance Florentine painter presents the clearest interpretation of his career to date. Spike's sensitive formal analysis of Angelico's lyrical work and his convincing reconfiguration of Angelico's chronology and early sources reveal an innovative, sophisticated artist who masterfully blended his humanistic ideals with his religious calling. This contradicts the traditional image of Angelico as a simple priest-painter who merely continued a lingering Gothic style. Spike gives the first cogent explanation of the iconography of Angelico's Dominican fresco cycle in the monastery of San Marco in Florence by discussing his influence within the milieu of the Dominican Observant reform order and contemporary Florentine humanism. The author demonstrates that Angelico's "dreamlike" images in San Marco cannot be interpreted as historical narratives, but draw from *The Ecclesiastical Hierarchy* by Pseudo-Dionysius the Areopagite. Angelico presents three ascending levels of imagery, toward greater elaboration both spiritually and visually using the themes of purification, illumination, and perfection, that parallel the three levels of the clergy outlined by Pseudo-Dionysius. Upper-division undergraduate; graduate; faculty.—*A. L. Palmer, University of Oklahoma*

OAB-0481   Orig
Stuckey, Charles F. **Claude Monet, 1840-1926,** by Charles F. Stuckey with Sophia Shaw. Thames & Hudson/Art Institute of Chicago, 1995. 282p bibl index ISBN 0-500-09246-X, $50.00

This highly important, impeccable, and scholarly Art Institute of Chicago museum catalog records the largest retrospective of Monet's works ever held—from July 22 through November 26, 1995. Of great historical interest, the show includes approximately 160 of Monet's masterpieces, assembled from collections throughout the world. This large-format volume is an exemplary record of the show. Practically all exhibited works are well reproduced, with excellent color, one per page. (There are 278 illustrations, 226 in color.) Stuckey, curator and specialist on Monet, provides a truly monumental addition to Monet scholarship, especially in the 82 archival-style small-print pages of Monet's chronology, treating the artist's life on a month-by-month basis. Stuckey's essay identifies several new issues in Monet studies, but the intention is "before all else to be a reader's guide Wildenstein's complex, expensive publication in French" (Daniel Wildenstein's five-volume *Claude Monet: Biographie et catalogue raisonné*, Lausanne, 1974, the classic resource on Monet). With all due restraint Stuckey carefully documents but also *interprets* Monet's family situations, habits, and complex personality. Thus Stuckey's admirable volume *must* be read in light of still another new monograph: Paul Hayes Tucker's *Claude Monet: Life and Art* (CH, Oct'95). Highest recommendation. Upper-division undergraduate; graduate; professional; general.—*M. Hamel-Schwulst, Towson State University*

OAB-0482   N6537   93-10439 CIP
Zilczer, Judith. **Willem de Kooning from the Hirshhorn Museum collection.** Hirshhorn Museum and Sculpture Garden, Smithsonian Institution/Rizzoli, 1993. 218p bibl ISBN 0-8478-1769-5, $60.00

More than a collection inventory, this beautifully produced and exceptionally well written catalog makes a valuble contribution to existing De Kooning literature. Hirshhorn curator Zilczer's thoughtful essay views his first 60 years' work through his experience of urban America, relating it to the Western caricature tradition as well as modern expressionism. Lynne Cooke (curator, Dia Center for the Arts) places his late works (after his move from city to country) firmly within the pastoral mode, linking this to the sweeping social changes of the 1960s. She pays particular attention to the nuances and tensions within De Kooning's images of women—images that still provoke controversy. Hitherto-unpublished correspondence between de Kooning and his patron, Joseph Hirshhorn, provides a glimpse into an oft-overlooked relationship. The "Documentation" section includes provenance and exhibition histories for each artwork helpful to graduate students and scholars. Likewise, the pioneering examination of his works with infrared reflectography provides insight into De Kooning's working methods and the in-progress states of several important paintings. This is an outstanding complement to Diane Waldman's 1988 monograph. Advanced undergraduate through professional.—*A. Pappas, University of Southern California*

■ Photography

OAB-0483   F590   95-25999 CIP
Castleberry, May. **Perpetual mirage: photographic narratives of the desert West.** Whitney Museum of American Art, 1996. (Dist. by Abrams) 240p bibl ISBN 0-8109-6820-7, $49.50

Prepared to accompany the similarly titled Whitney Museum of American Art's exhibition, this volume of essays provides not only an excellent introduction to those bound photographic books that portrayed, interpreted, and shaped the image of the desert lands of the American West but also to a more general examination of the role of photography and photographers in its history. The focus of the exhibition is on printed and bound photographic books that contain photographs of the desert regions of Arizona, New Mexico, Utah, Nevada, and eastern California and the arid regions of Oregon, Wyoming, Texas, Kansas, and Nebraska from the mid-19th century to the last decade of this century; thus the reader is presented with a complete history of the chronicling of this region by photographers. Inherent in this history is an examination of the changes in printing, book production, and the reproduction of photographic images that occurred and that allowed the books to be produced less expensively and for larger audiences. Beautifully illustrated and meticulously documented, the essays in this volume constitute a significant contribution to the history of this region and of the development of photography in America. General; undergraduate through professional.—*P. D. Thomas, Wichita State University*

OAB-0484 TR187 94-18753 CIP

Eisinger, Joel. **Trace and transformation: American criticism of photography in the modernist period.** New Mexico, 1995. 314p bibl index ISBN 0-8263-1623-9, $45.00

This book surveys American theory and criticism of art photography from the development of pictorialism in the late 19th century through the formalism of the 1970s; it is the first study of this depth and with this breadth of coverage. Eisinger (humanities, Univ. of Minnesota, Morris Campus) is thoroughly familiar with his subject and has written a balanced, jargon-free account that readers holding a variety of critical persuasions will find informative and without prejudice. This is particularly the case with the treatment of current postmodernist issues, which are taken up at the conclusion of the book to differentiate the tenets of modernism (his main focus). An important aspect of this book is the author's concern for the art of photography rather than for the ontology of photography itself, which gets so much attention today. A second important feature is his examination of those key figures within the field who are responsible for setting the dialogue between photographers, and between historians, curators, critics, and scholars, and not so much of those outside the medium and looking in. The author surveys all of the essential literature, including the important small-edition journals, and offers analyses of many critics and writers who are not widely known except within the art photography field. Extensive notes and bibliography; only nine reproductions. Highly recommended—a unique and outstanding contribution to the literature of photography. Undergraduate; graduate; faculty; general.—*P. C. Bunnell, Princeton University*

OAB-0485 TR681 92-5020 CIP

Ellenzweig, Allen. **The homoerotic photograph: male images from Durieu/Delacroix to Mapplethorpe.** Columbia, 1992. 230p index afp ISBN 0-231-07536-7, $44.95

An important contribution to the understanding of contemporary gay expression and sexual politics, this book is from a scholarly series on lesbian and gay studies. Ellenzweig, an art and photography critic, cultural journalist, and freelance curator in New York, has written extensively on gay images in photography. Building on the now-notorious confrontation in the courts, in the Senate, and within the National Endowment for the Arts over photographs by Robert Mapplethorpe, he sets the controversy and the artist's work in the context of the history of photography and the complex and varied images of the homoerotic in pictures made since the 1850s. Without sensationalism, the focus is on art photography and popular illustration. Beginning with academic studies made in the circle of the French painter Delacroix, Ellenzweig traces the development and changes in photographs of the male nude through a sequence of chapters based on a pairing of selected European and American photographers: Frank Sutcliffe and Thomas Eakins, Wilhelm von Gloeden and Holland Day, Herbert List and George Platt Lynes, and he concludes with the most sustantial chapter titled, "Mapplethorpe/Tress/Michals/Weber: American Photography after Stonewall." A final chapter surveys current imagery. Each artist featured is placed in context with biographical and cultural background; individual images are analyzed. Reproductions (a total of 127) vividly depict the gamut of erotic fantasies, types of photographs, and pictorial artistry employed over the years. Introduction by George Stambolian, extensive notes, and capsule artists' biographies. A seriously researched and broadly conceived study of the subject. Highly recommended.—*P. C. Bunnell, Princeton University*

OAB-0486 Brit. CIP

Hamber, Anthony J. **"A higher branch of the art": photographing the fine arts in England, 1839-1880.** Gordon & Breach, 1996. 578p bibl index (Documenting the image, 4) ISBN 2-88449-143-0, $95.00

A major addition to the literature of art and photographic history, this pioneering book analyzes photography in relation to the fine arts in England from 1839 (the date of its introduction) to 1880, when most of its characteristics were formed. Hamber has converted his doctoral thesis for the University of London

into a book of rare originality, in which he examines the use of photography to record the fine and decorative arts, and how these images shaped the modern study of art history. The subject of commercial reproduction photography has largely been ignored in most studies of the medium, which have focused on issues of aesthetics or techniques. Hamber is concerned with how photography played a role in changing not only the commerce of picture dissemination and publication (engraving, lithography, etc.) but the entire visual culture of Victorian Britain. Through case studies, he examines in detail the use of photography in three London public art collections: the British Museum, the National Gallery, and the South Kensington Museum. In so doing, he illuminates a vast array of subjects ranging from commercial entrepreneurship, technical issues with regard to processes, public taste and education, notions of truth, and facsimile and the concept of copyright, to the idea of photography as an art in its own right. Richly illustrated in color and black and white, with extensive notes, appendixes, and bibliography; a work of exceptional scholarly achievement. Highly recommended. Upper-division undergraduate; graduate; faculty.—*P. C. Bunnell, Princeton University*

OAB-0487 TR485 95-22821 CIP

Henisch, Heinz K. **The painted photograph, 1839-1914: origins, techniques, aspirations,** by Heinz K. Henisch and Bridget A. Henisch. Pennsylvania State, 1996. 242p bibl index afp ISBN 0-271-01507-1, $75.00

Henisch's book exhaustively and explicitly investigates the practice of painting on photographs, which began soon after the invention of photography in 1839. Woven throughout are ongoing discussions of the art critic's disapproval of these techniques, the painter's dislike and suspicion of photography, and the public's love and demand for this unique genre. Painting on photographs prevented photography from becoming a mechanical multiple by allowing the photograph to transcend to the status of handmade work of art, the authors trace the history of this practice worldwide. The most intriguing part of the book is the detailing of its international appeal and application in such places as South Africa, Russia, Latin America, Turkey, and New Zealand, to name a few. Also presented are a wealth of techniques, materials, and processes, with some fascinating examples of painting and retouching on magic lantern slides, imprinted porcelain, milk glass, and enamel. This volume contributes a tremendous amount of knowledge to the history of the altered photograph. Richly illustrated with 131 black-and-white and color illustrations; chapter references and notes. Two-year technical program; upper-division undergraduate through professional.—*J. Natal, Nazareth College of Rochester*

OAB-0488 TR25 92-9852 CIP

Livingston, Jane. **The New York School: photographs, 1936-1963.** Stewart, Tabori & Chang/Professional Imaging, Eastman Kodak Company, 1992. 403p bibl index ISBN 1-55670-239-6, $75.00

Written by the former Chief Curator of the Corcoran Gallery of Art, this magnificent work represents portfolios of 12 images of each of 16 photographers. The New York School defined an artistic movement or photographic tradition. Its practitioners' style was to often break the obvious rules of composition and lighting. Documentary and candid by design the photographs were spontaneous and creative, involving no subject intervention or darkroom manipulation. Represented is the work of Arbus, Avedon, Brodovitch, Croner, Davidson, Donaghy, Faurer, Frank, Grossman, Klein, Leiter, Livingston, Levitt, Model, Vestal, and Weegie. The strength of the book is that it goes well beyond the obvious portfolios. Livingston includes an insightful article on the work, style, and contribution that each photographer made to the medium. There is also a one-page biography on each at the end of the book. The vast cultural climate of New York that shaped the school is particularly interesting. The role of galleries, books, and pictorial magazines is also discussed thoroughly as is the impact of the movies as cultural milieu. The factors that shaped and molded the school are as interesting as the school itself. Overall this is a very powerful work. The portfolios are well presented and interesting, but Livingston's scholarly approach to explaining the movement, how it was influenced, and what grew out of it really make this an outstanding success.—*W. A. McIntyre, New Hampshire Technical College*

OAB-0489   TR140   93-67 CIP

Lorenz, Richard. **Imogen Cunningham: ideas without end: a life in photographs.** Chronicle Books, 1993. 180p bibl index ISBN 0-8118-0390-2, $35.00; ISBN 0-8118-0357-0 pbk, $22.95

Cunningham first earned widespread popularity with her portraiture and botanical studies in the heyday of the photo magazine. In her 80s she reemerged as a star beloved for her tenacity and eccentricity. Much has been written about her, but Judy Date's *Imogen Cunningham: A Portrait* (CH, Mar'80) is now out of print. The present work, therefore, is a most welcome publication, filling an information gap on one of America's premiere photographers and providing a thorough retrospective review of the artist's work. Lorenz has written extensively about Cunningham and curated exhibitions of her photographs. In preparing the book, Lorenz used the rich resources of the Imogen Cunningham Trust with excellent results. His carefully researched and highly readable biocritical essay captures the personality of the artist. Authoritative and sensitive, this essay is the most extensive and well-documented rendering of Cunningham's life to date. The text is immeasurably enhanced by an excellent selection of 120 high-quality duotone plates surveying Cunningham's work, including many previously unpublished images. In addition, the book contains 76 smaller duotone figures, which illustrate Lorenz's essay. This graceful and dignified book does much to confirm Imogen Cunningham's accomplishments and sets the standard for future research on the artist. A "must" for all libraries with an interest in photography and American art.—*J. A. Day, University of South Dakota*

OAB-0490   TR647   95-889 CIP

Lowe, Sarah M. **Tina Modotti: photographs.** Abrams/Philadelphia Museum of Art, 1995. 160p bibl index ISBN 0-8109-4280-1, $45.00

Lowe, an art historian who specializes in photography and Latin American art, describes Modotti as the "best-known unknown photographer of the twentieth century"—an assessment based on Modotti's notoriety, earned through an eventful and complex life. Italian-born Modotti was a model, movie star, and revolutionary communist as well as a photographer. The brevity of her seven-year career as a photographer, her political activism, and her relationship with Edward Weston each in its own way contributed to suppressing awareness of Modotti's artistic accomplishments. In the past 15 years, there has been a resurgence of interest in her photography, and more critical attention has been paid to her rich cultural context, especially the period 1923-30 spent in postrevolutionary Mexico as a member of an international modernist community. This catalog for a touring exhibition by the same title, curated by Lowe and organized by the Alfred Stieglitz Center of the Philadelphia Museum of Art, is the first in-depth, art-historical study of the artist's work. Lowe demonstrates an acute aesthetic sensitivity to Modotti's photographs and a zeal for reconstructing the artist's cultural biography. Her substantial biocritical essay on Modotti is clearly organized, readable, and precisely researched. The text is supported by 140 excellent duotone illustrations, which present the full range of Modotti's photographic vision. A significant contribution to the history of photography; recommended to all libraries with a commitment to modern art and women's studies. Undergraduate; graduate; faculty; general.—*J. A. Day, University of South Dakota*

OAB-0491   TA1632   92-14462 CIP

Mitchell, William J. **The reconfigured eye: visual truth in the post-photographic era.** MIT, 1992. 273p bibl index ISBN 0-262-13286-9, $39.95

With significant originality and authority Mitchell writes about the new photography that is rapidly becoming standard practice. By "new photography" one means the technology of digital image manipulation and synthesis that is replacing the traditional form of chemical/optical photography. Radical and dramatic changes in visual communication and creative practice are occurring daily in image processing, and these are the author's primary concerns. Mitchell, dean of the School of Architecture and Planning at MIT, has written books on computer graphics and digital design media, and the present work, while devel-

oped out of seminars taught at the Harvard Graduate School of Design, is not a technical how-to-do-it book. Rather, Mitchell explains and analyzes the many complicated repercussions caused by the new techniques in areas that include concepts of truth and originality, of ethics, of transmission and accessibility; synthetic creation; and how pictures will function in our culture in future years. Writing in an accessible style with a minimum of jargon, the author explores the new techniques through reference to past methods, traditions, and guiding assumptions. The illustrations, most in color, are brilliantly illustrative of the ideas developed in the text. Notes, extensive bibliography. Highly recommended.—*P. C. Bunnell, Princeton University*

OAB-0492   TR820   91-26835 CIP

Nesbit, Molly. **Atget's seven albums.** Yale, 1993 (c1992). 428p bibl index afp ISBN 0-300-03580-2, $55.00

This publication of the work of Atget will shed new light on this already well known and respected photographer. "Seven Albums" was a book project that was never published. In this project Atget explored Paris at its height, presenting a view of the thinking process employed by Atget. Here we are given a fresh and new prespective on not only Atget the photographer, but also the human being as well. Presenting the albums in the order intended by Atget, Nesbit takes the reader on a journey through life in Paris in the early part of the 20th century, from the wealthiest parts of the city to the poorest. Nesbit has done a superb job in presenting a detailed view of Atget, and she provides fresh insight into the photographic thinking of Atget. The reproductions are excellent, and the text is thorough, insightful, and complete—a very exceptional book in every regard. All academic levels; general readers.—*H. Branch, Oregon State University*

OAB-0493   TR139   94-6713 CIP

Rosenblum, Naomi. **A history of women photographers.** Abbeville, 1994. 356p bibl index ISBN 1-55859-761-1, $60.00

Given the proliferation of books on the history of photography, a work surveying the contributions of women to this art form was perhaps inevitable. One is encouraged that the author is Naomi Rosenblum, a well-respected scholar whose *A World History of Photography* (CH, Apr'85) is a standard text. Beginning with the proposition that women's role in the development of photography is understudied and undervalued, Rosenblum produces a broad-ranging survey of the contributions of 233 women photographers between 1835 and 1950. The book's nine chapters are organized chronologically and culminate with the chapter "The Feminist Vision." The author effectively relates women photographers to the dominant social values of the time, and she writes clearly and concisely, using specific examples to elucidate broad general trends and features of the time. With 263 illustrations, including 35 color plates, the book offers an excellent visual survey of its subject. The section of biographies of the artists considered in the text is valuable; for, although succinct and formal, they include new information on a number of previously obscure women photographers. Other publications explore women's contributions to photography, most notably *Women Photographers*, edited by Constance Sullivan (CH, Dec'90), but Rosenblum is the first to do it so extensively and comprehensively. This will be a standard work in its area, and it provides a firm foundation for additional scholarship on the role of women in photography. A "must" acquisition for all libraries committed to photography and art history. General; undergraduate; graduate; faculty.—*J. A. Day, University of South Dakota*

OAB-0494   TR57   91-51108 CIP

Schaaf, Larry J. **Out of the shadows: Herschel, Talbot, & the invention of photography.** Yale, 1992. 188p index ISBN 0-300-05705-9, $50.00

Schaaf's book breathes new life into photographic history by illuminating and closely examining the relationship between the prominent scientist Sir John Herschel and the artist/scientist William Henry Fox Talbot. These two Englishmen—long considered to be responsible for the invention of photography—also played key roles in the formative early years of the new art of photography.

Based upon exhaustive research culled from hundreds of letters, diaries, and notebooks, the book explores the "pre-history" of photography until 1844, five years past the monumental events leading up to the birth announcement of photography in 1839. Delving into these unique personalities through careful reconstruction of events in this historic period, Schaaf has truly brought out of the shadows and into the light questions that have puzzled photo historians concerning the who, what, why, where, and when of the history of photography. Extensive notes and more than 100 reproductions (in full color and multi-colored duotones) of some of the earliest photographs ever made enrich this volume, a significant contribution to the literature on the history of photography.—*J. Natal, Nazareth College*

■ Sculpture

OAB-0495   95-60538 CIP
Bindman, David. **Roubiliac and the eighteenth-century monument: sculpture as theatre,** by David Bindman and Malcolm Baker. Yale, 1995. 409p bibl index ISBN 0-300-06333-4, $65.00

This is the first monograph since 1928 devoted to the sculptor Louis François Roubiliac, arguably the finest sculptor working in 18th-century England. Although it is limited to his funerary works (a volume on his statues and portraits will follow), it is a major contribution. Until its appearance, our chief source, besides Katharine Esdaile's *The Life and Works of Louis François Roubiliac* (1928), has been Margaret Whinney's "Pelican History of Art" volume *Sculpture in Britain, 1530-1830* (1964; rev. by John Physick, 1988). This new work is divided into three parts. The first, by Bindman (Univ. College London), discusses the social world of the monument, the sculptor's career, and the imagery of the monuments. The second, by Baker (Victoria and Albert Museum, London), covers designing, models, construction, and patrons. The third part is a catalog of the funerary monuments by Baker, Bindman, and Tessa Murdoch. These texts provide a detailed and scholarly discussion, complete with notes, of the works. Equally valuable are the excellent plates, including 16 in color, which will convince even the nonbeliever of Roubiliac's genius and inventiveness. Appendixes consist of an account of the Monument to the Duchess of Montagu and the sales catalog of works sold after Roubiliac's death; complete bibliography. It is hard to imagine how this superb work could be improved. Highly recommended. Upper-division undergraduate; graduate; faculty; general.—*T. J. McCormick, emeritus, Wheaton College (MA)*

OAB-0496   NB553   92-43552 CIP
Butler, Ruth. **Rodin: the shape of genius.** Yale, 1993. 591p bibl index afp ISBN 0-300-05400-9, $35.00

Unquestionably the 20th century's most significant sculptor, Auguste Rodin has been the subject of numerous biographies since as early as 1903. Many works of criticism about the artist are also heavy on biographical detail and speculation. Any new entry into this crowded field clearly must have something new to offer. Butler (Univ. of Massachusetts, Boston) provides not only new information but also fresh interpretations of the artist's character and personality. Exhibiting an authoritative knowledge of 19th-century France, this biography springs from the extensive correspondence received by Rodin throughout his life. Utilizing many unpublished letters and documents, largely from the archives of the Musée Rodin, the author, a well-established Rodin scholar, achieves a level of intimacy and subtlety missing in other biographies. Begun in 1981, apparently with the author's clear understanding of what was required to produce a significant new biography, this extensive, well-written book is based on careful research and insightful analysis. Organized chronologically between 1860 and 1917, the text is intelligently illustrated with more than 200 black-and-white photographs. This book should enjoy a preeminence among biographies on the artist: it effectively synthesizes previous scholarship and it substantially adds to the understanding of Rodin's personality. Extensive and useful bibliography and chapter notes. A must for libraries with an interest in Rodin or in modern sculpture.—*J. A. Day, University of South Dakota*

OAB-0497   NB133   96-41830 CIP
Conlin, Diane Atnally. **The artists of the Ara Pacis: the process of Hellenization in Roman relief sculpture.** North Carolina, 1997. 145p bibl index afp ISBN 0-8078-2343-0, $65.00

The examination of Augustan art has recently assumed new vigor, beginning with the great Berlin exhibition of 1988, complemented by the far-reaching, thematic studies of Paul Zanker (1988), Ann Kuttner, and David Castriota (both in 1995). Conlin's meticulous analysis of how the *Ara Pacis Augustae*, dedicated in Rome in 9 BCE, was sculpted offers a different but significant contribution to the field. Unlike its predecessors, her book concentrates on the details of artistic production, on the craft traditions and workshop practices of the unknown Italian sculptors responsible for the monument's relief decoration. By the close observation of distinguishing features of design and execution, documented by numerous, superb illustrations, Conlin has separated the original Augustan carving from later reworking and/or restoration. With a connoisseur's subtlety, she has defined the progressive Hellenization of Roman sculpture in its slow, still incomplete transition from a dependence on line and contour toward the more plastic qualities of volume and mass. Conlin has also shown that the *Ara Pacis* is no passive adaptation of Greek, especially Athenian or Pergamene, models but the product, at the most fundamental level of artistic creation, of a particular Roman sensibility for form, despite its Greek polish. Upper-division undergraduate through professional.—*R. Brilliant, Columbia University*

OAB-0498   NB135   95-36843 CIP
Mattusch, Carol C. **Classical bronzes: the art and craft of Greek and Roman statuary.** Cornell, 1996. 241p index afp ISBN 0-8014-3182-4, $47.95

Mattusch (George Mason Univ.), a recognized expert, has produced an informative, perceptive study of Greco-Roman bronze statuary. She describes the artistry and craft of bronze sculpture from clay model to mould to cast to finished work, establishing thereby criteria for dating, or not dating, individual pieces, based largely on technical matters, contextualized within the range of Greek stylistic evolution and the persistence of prestigious or popular types. Mattusch also exposes modern restorations and fakes, eliminating them from the ancient repertory; indicates the importance of serial production in the foundries; and deals, at length, with the alleged "original," an issue of great interest to historians, collectors, and all those concerned with the aesthetic character of reproductions. Because the ancient original is almost always a lost clay model, the surviving bronze cast exists at some distance from its artistic conception; even further removed, not the least by the alteration of medium, are marble copies of ancient bronzes, traditionally used to invoke the lost works of Greek masters. All this, and much more, has been soberly laid out in this excellent, definitive, yet accessible work of technical and visual analysis that combines general and particular observations. Undergraduate; graduate; faculty; general.—*R. Brilliant, Columbia University*

OAB-0499   NB454   92-21820 CIP
Penny, Nicholas. **Catalogue of European sculpture in the Ashmolean Museum, 1540 to the present day: v.1: Italian; v.2: French and other European sculpture (excluding Italian and British); v.3: British.** Oxford, 1993 (c1992). 3v. 329, 230, 261p indexes ISBN 0-19-951356-2, $525.00

Geared to the serious scholar, this permanent collection catalog shares the best reproductions and an enormous amount of object-centered detail with scholars worldwide. Even with a commercial copublisher, such an opus represents a tremendous investment in staff time, research, and photography. Introductory essays deal with the evolution of Ashmolean collections. The nearly 800 catalog entries are filled with facts from curatorial and registrar's files: comparisons to fully identified objects in other museums, physical description, brief provenance, sales catalog citations, mentions in other monographs and Ashmolean's own publications, and descriptions and paraphrases of correspondence (invaluable scholarly information). Concessions to the casual reader are biographical details and an attempt to place the work within the artist's oeuvre. The reader should expect minimal indexing; logical organization matters more. The sequence is always artist, anonymous artist by period, and decorative arts with sculptural characteristics (in one volume whimsically labled "trifles and rubbish reluctantly received.") Bibliographic references, although complete, occur only within the text of the entries. Drawing on the memories of colleagues, former Ashmolean Curator Penny (now with the National Gallery, London) has included "curatorial oral history" in the entries. Consequently, some informality got past the copy editor (i.e., references to "me"). Entry length varies from a paragraph to pages. Strongly recommended to libraries supporting a graduate art history program and to undergraduate collections with an interest in sculpture.—*M. M. Doherty, University of South Florida*

OAB-0500   NB623   93-19726 MARC
Pope-Hennessy, John. **Donatello: sculptor.** Abbeville, 1993. 376p bibl index ISBN 1-55859-645-3, $95.00

In the preface the author states, "This is a monograph, but it is also, in embryo, a biography." In fact, this book represents the epitomy of scholarship, monumental research, and perspicaciously analyzed conclusions, that divulges not only an artistic personality but also an individual, Donatello (1386-1466), in context with his era and society. Even more impressive is the vast number of primary sources, some being tangential, that Pope-Hennessy cites, not only to confirm and verify the sculptor's production but also to deal with those artists, associates, apprentices, employees, patrons, etc., with whom Donatello had contact. In part, this accounts for the exhaustive bibliography as well as the copious and erudite endnotes elucidating the text, often soliciting divergent ideas. Substantiating all of Donatello's innovations and techniques, the text elaborates meticuously the many influences (ancient, medieval, contemporary) that are observed in Donatello's work, while noting the present condition or recent restorations of his works. Of the 313 excellent illustrations accompanying the text, the majority are of superlative color, quality, and detail. Pope-Hennessy establishes with this book the definitive work on Donatello, not to be eclipsed for years to come.—*R. R. Henry, Pine Manor College*

OAB-0501   NB237   94-4369 CIP
Stewart, Rick. **Charles M. Russell, sculptor.** Amon Carter Museum, 1994. (Dist. by Abrams) 400p index ISBN 0-8109-3772-7, $95.00

Generally celebrated or maligned (depending on one's level of political correctness) as a painter of cowboys and Indians, Charles Marion Russell was also a prolific sculptor. Until the publication of this exhaustively researched catalog, however, the artist's three-dimensional work, largely confined to a few western museums, was not widely known outside of Texas and Montana. With this wonderfully illustrated volume, Russell takes his rightful place alongside Frederick Remington as a major bronze caster and a foundational figure in the construction of the myth of the West. Less daring and innovative than his great rival, Russell was, nonetheless, more versatile, working in wax, plaster, and wood, as well as modeling in clay. As interested in the representation of wild fauna as in the depiction of gunslingers, Russell also emerges from this study as one of the great animal sculptors around the turn of the last century. Among the many insights offered here is a new awareness of the primacy of sculpture in the artist's imagination. Many of Russell's paintings are based on earlier bronzes; from the comparison he emerges, arguably, a better sculptor than painter. Given the proliferation of Russell forgeries shortly after his death, this catalog provides a useful means of discriminating between the authentic and the spurious. The catalog entries themselves are especially informative; there are abundant color photographs of each object, taken from multiple vantages. Altogether, a new paradigm for the study and appreciation of the most spatial of the visual arts. Highly recommended for graduate and undergraduate libraries.—*R. L. McGrath, Dartmouth College*

■ Mass Communication & Journalism

OAB-0502   E836   92-35615 CIP
Allen, Craig. **Eisenhower and the mass media: peace, prosperity, & prime-time TV.** North Carolina, 1993. 259p bibl index afp ISBN 0-8078-2080-6, $39.95; ISBN 0-8078-4409-8 pbk, $14.95

Claiming that Eisenhower was "a master user of the US mass media," Allen traces the history of the 34th US President, focusing on the role that television played in his consensus-building style of political leadership. Beginning with Eisenhower's use of the media during the war, the author follows the President from roughly 1953 until his death in 1969, highlighting the many television "firsts" attributed to him, including the first televised presidential press conference and cabinet meeting. Other topics covered include television's growing importance in political campaigning and its role in transforming political conventions into campaign tools. In addition, Richard Nixon, John Kennedy, and Nikita Khrushchev are discussed. Sputnik, the U-2/Gary Powers debacle, the Bay of Pigs invasion, and the Vietnam conflict are also examined within the context of the rising importance of television. In essence, the book is an early history of television's initial role in presidential politics and of Eisenhower's mastery over this infant medium. This is a very readable and interestingly written book. Allen obviously knows his subject well and communicates a restrained, scholarly enthusiasm throughout. Extensive notes and workable bibliography. Highly recommended to both public and academic libraries at all levels for its media, political, and historical insights.—*W. E. Coleman, Mount Union College*

OAB-0503   P56   96-526 CIP
Alwood, Edward. **Straight news: gays, lesbians, and the news media.** Columbia, 1996. 386p index afp ISBN 0-231-08436-6, $29.95

Alwood addresses the changing news coverage of lesbians and gay men from immediately after WW II to the mid-1990s: "This book is an attempt to understand how and why the news media perpetuated antigay stereotypes through much of this century." Comparable to Rodger Streitmatter's *Unspeakable: The Rise of the Gay and Lesbian Press in America* (CH, May'96), Alwood's book explores how the media have perpetuated gay stereotypes and also worked to destroy the very same stereotypes they helped create. *Straight News* has many notable strengths. For example, the author provides a thought-provoking discussion about how gays and lesbians have used the media in order to organize and gain public visibility. Also notable is the book's thorough coverage of how the AIDS epidemic has impacted news coverage of homosexuality. This engaging, well-written book will make readers reevaluate their perception of the media as unbiased and recognize the important role the media play in representing minority groups to a mainstream audience. All students and professors of journalism should read Alwood's study to obtain a better understanding of how the press has presented a skewed portrait of gays and lesbians. All academic and public collections.—*S. A. Inness, Miami University*

OAB-0504   PN5359   94-9482 CIP
Ayalon, Ami. **The press in the Arab Middle East: a history.** Oxford, 1995. 300p bibl index afp ISBN 0-19-508780-1, $49.95

Although presented by its author as "no more than an introduction to the history of [the Arabic Press]" and "not a comprehensive study," this book contains a wealth of information on the nature, development, and progress of this rarefied topic in historical scholarship. Moreover, this competently researched, very well written, and elegantly produced study throws bright light on its subject matter, not only as a particular item in the inventory of Arab culture, but also an institution that exists within overall sociopolitical and economic systems of varied though closely related polities. Ayalon intelligently and objectively exam-

Humanities

ines the relationship of the native Arabic press to the different regimes under which it must live, serve, and prosper. With its predecessors—e.g., Tom McFadden's *Daily Journalism in the Arab States* (1954) and William Rugh's *The Arab Press* (CH, Feb'80; 2nd ed., 1987)—the English-speaking student of Arabic and international journalism now has available the major sources on this important subject. Wholeheartedly recommended, upper-division undergraduate and above.—*K. I. Semaan, emeritus, SUNY at Binghamton*

OAB-0505 PN4888 92-41011 MARC
Beasley, Maurine H. **Taking their place: a documentary history of women and journalism,** by Maurine H. Beasley and Sheila J. Gibbons. American University, in cooperation with Women's Institute for Freedom of the Press, 1993. 359p bibl index afp ISBN 1-879383-09-8, $51.00; ISBN 1-879383-01-1 pbk, $14.95

A first-of-its-kind presentation of material on the historical development of women in journalism, from 1790 to the present. Extensive original documents, all written by women journalists, make an outstanding contribution to a field that so far has had only three book-length overviews of American women journalists: Ishbel Ross, *Ladies of the Press* (1936), Marion Marzolf, *Up from the Footnote*, (CH, Mar'78), and Kay Mills, *A Place in the News* (1988). The materials included by Beasley and Gibbons, not generally available, give fascinating insight into the American experience of women journalists: a 1790 petition to the US Senate; editorials by early women editors; autobiographical data; letters to newspapers; magazine articles; Civil War writings; columns; early work of African American women; work of war correspondents, journalists, and sob sisters; and articles by present-day, groundbreaking women journalists in print and in broadcasting. Extensive bibliographies supporting each historical era further enhance the usefulness of this work, as does a valuable overview of the women's movement and parallel developments of women's participation in journalism. Highly recommended for undergraduate and graduate collections supporting courses on women and mass communication, journalism history, and the women's movement.—*M. R. Grant, Wheaton Graduate School (IL)*

OAB-0506 P90 95-11882 CIP
Berger, Arthur Asa. **Essentials of mass communication theory.** Sage Publications, CA, 1995. 208p bibl indexes afp ISBN 0-8039-7356-X, $38.00; ISBN 0-8039-7357-8 pbk, $15.95

Berger (San Francisco State Univ.) provides a succinct, accurate, and enjoyable introduction to the mass communications field. Although the book covers most of the same topics as other introductory works—communication models; differences between mass media; the concept of audiences; systems of mass communication and the influence of media practitioners on content—Berger's writing and organization make the material seem like a light repast rather than an overbearing meal. A series of line drawings that might appear out-of-place in most texts adds to the breezy tone and invites students to read and think about the materials. The surprise is that the organization and style do not impinge on the book's substance. Berger introduces most of the core ideas in mass communication and analyzes aesthetic media theories that most texts overlook. An extraordinary chapter explains how different narrative analytic frameworks (Marxist, feminist, semiotic, etc.) interpret *Rashomon*. Berger limits discussion of how professional conventions, standards, and mores influence the content of news and entertainment, which is one of the book's few debatable editorial decisions. Essential for all undergraduate collections in mass communication theory and mass media studies.—*R. A. Logan, University of Missouri—Columbia*

OAB-0507 P92 94-27829 CIP
Bourgault, Louise M. **Mass media in sub-Saharan Africa.** Indiana, 1995. 294p bibl index afp ISBN 0-253-31250-7, $35.00; ISBN 0-253-20938-2 pbk, $14.95

Bourgault's work differs from previous treatments of African mass com-

munications in that it covers all mass media in a representative cross section of sub-Saharan countries and draws on important ethnographic, historical, descriptive, and critical approaches. It is further enhanced by Bourgault's personal observations and accounts of experiences in at least 14 countries, vital discussions of African cultural traits that mix with communication patterns, and theoretical arguments on germane universal concerns (news flow, colonialism, dependency, media/cultural imperialism). The author (Northern Michigan Univ., Marquette) moves beyond outmoded Western concepts, adding numerous Asian and African experiences and theories. Occasional detailed case studies do not sacrifice more comprehensive and generalizable approaches. There are a few errors in this otherwise excellent volume: the author misspells Roy Thomson's name and confuses the Asian-conceived development journalism concept with development communication that emanated from Washington and Washington-financed academic think tanks. This volume is a significant contribution to the literature on Africa because of its intricate organization, up-to-date information, comprehensiveness, multicultural and multidisciplinary approaches, and story-like relating of both historical and contemporary phenomena. All collections.—*J. A. Lent, Temple University*

OAB-0508 Orig
Briggs, Asa. **The history of broadcasting in the United Kingdom: v.5: Competition.** Oxford, 1995. 1,133p index afp ISBN 0-19-215964-X, $72.00

With this volume Briggs completes his magisterial study of broadcasting in the UK (v.1: *The Birth of Broadcasting*, 1961; v.2: *The Golden Age of Wireless*, 1965; v.3: *The War of Words*, CH, Jul'71; v.4: *Sound and Vision*, CH, Oct'79). The author acknowledges that this volume can tell only part of the story, but this does not diminish its value as the capstone of the finest history of any country's broadcasting organization published thus far. Briggs, a respected British social historian, combed the extensive archives of the BBC, its published record, secondary resources, and arcane Parliamentary materials, but despite full cooperation from the BBC, this is not a "house" history. Briggs focuses on how the BBC faced competition from the newly developed Independent Television Authority and its expanding regional programming companies. Chapters discuss, among other topics, BBC decisions concerning its new competition; coverage of the Suez Crisis; audiences and programs in the late 1950s; the Pilkington Committee's study of the BBC; director-general Hugh Greene and his critics; politicians and educators at the BBC; pirate broadcasters; BBC local/regional/national/world services; and new technologies (including satellites and color). Appendixes offer statistics and documents, a detailed 65-page chronology, and a useful bibliographical note. This is detailed, articulate, and important reading for anyone who wishes to understand the current debate over the future of public-service broadcasting. The publisher has also reissued the previous four volumes—long out of print—at comparable prices. Upper-division undergraduate and up.—*C. Sterling, George Washington University*

OAB-0509 PN1992 94-39017 CIP
Caldwell, John Thornton. **Televisuality: style, crisis, and authority in American television.** Rutgers, 1995. 437p bibl index ISBN 0-8135-2163-7, $55.00; ISBN 0-8135-2164-5 pbk, $20.00

This may be the most sophisticated study of the American television medium, industry, and aesthetic to date. Caldwell (California State Univ., Long Beach) ranges through industry bumf and the academic bibliography to rescue the medium from theoretical simplifications. He provides sharp analyses of TV shows from the 1940s on. His most extensive analyses feature the television premiere of Oliver Stone's movie *Salvador* (1983), the *War and Remembrance* series (1988), *Pee-Wee's Playhouse* (1986-91), *Northern Exposure* (1992), *American Chronicles* (1990-91), and the Rodney King videos, trial, and riot coverage (1991). He demonstrates how industrial-based televisuality is a new and emerging mode of communication accessible even to the marginalized. Today television has moved from being primarily "word-based rhetoric and transmission" to "a visually based mythology, framework, and aesthetic based on an extreme self-consciousness of style." "Excessive visuality and formal radicality are now legitimate properties of the dominant media, even in trash variants, not the avant-garde."

Tables and stills enhance the argument in this dense, insightful, and allusive text that leaves virtually no familiar generalization unchallenged. Upper-division undergraduate and up.—*M. Yacowar, University of Calgary*

OAB-0510 PN4738 95-18582 CIP
Carpenter, Ted Galen. **The captive press: foreign policy crises and the First Amendment.** Cato Institute, 1995. 315p index ISBN 1-882577-22-1, $24.95; ISBN 1-882577-23-X pbk, $14.95

This much-needed and long-awaited follow-up to Phillip Knightley's *The First Casualty* (CH, Feb'76) traces the history of the US government's relations with the news media from 1798 to 1994 (in Haiti). Carpenter carefully documents what he considers the government's efforts to intimidate, co-opt, and censor the media and undermine the First Amendment. He points to the expansionist foreign-policy mentality of US political leadership, particularly over the last six decades, as the fundamental impetus for efforts to control information. He suggests that complacent, lazy, incompetent, and sometimes grossly irresponsible news reporters and editors contribute substantially to the too-frequent success of these attempts. Carpenter claims that the outcome is an American public poorly served, poorly informed about international affairs and foreign policy, and lacking needed accurate information. Journalists, both present and prospective, need to study and learn from the excellent and highly recommended critical analysis in this book published by the conservative Cato Institute. The result could be a better-informed public. General and academic libraries.—*P. E. Kane, emeritus, SUNY College at Brockport*

OAB-0511 P94 94-490 CIP
Douglas, Susan J. **Where the girls are: growing up female with the mass media.** Times Books/Random House, 1994. 340p index ISBN 0-8129-2206-9, $23.00

This well-written and extensively documented work offers a fresh, significant analysis of the confusing and contradictory media images of the girls and women of America's postwar era. Douglas reclaims a span of cultural history frequently ignored: from the girl group music of the mid-1950s and '60s, to the sitcom heroines of television shows like *Bewitched* and *The Flying Nun*, to network news departments' trivialization of the ERA, to the narcissistic advertisements of the Reagan era. In a witty and often humorous style, Douglas shows how the very ambiguity of the media messages flooding the increasingly important female teen and young-adult market accelerated the media-denigrated feminist movement. This book convincingly argues that in order to understand these ironic dynamics, scholars and students must move beyond the standard feminist political histories and explore the cultural histories of the millions of women consuming popular culture who become feminists. Even the young feminists of the 1990s who, for reasons explained in the book, preface their remarks with "I'm not a feminist, but—" are included. For feminist, media, and popular culture studies, sociology, and psychology. All levels.—*M. R. Grant, Wheaton Graduate School (IL)*

OAB-0512 PN1992 96-5604 CIP
Dow, Bonnie J. **Prime-time feminism: television, media culture, and the women's movement since 1970.** Pennsylvania, 1996. 240p bibl index afp ISBN 0-8122-3315-8, $39.95; ISBN 0-8122-1554-0 pbk, $17.50

This important book is concerned with how television programming has contributed to the cultural conversation about feminism. There is no lack of books that examine the synergism of feminism and the media, but Dow (North Dakota State Univ.) analyzes the progression of feminism and postfeminism in the US from the vantage point of public-address studies. She considers the intersection of the textual strategies of several prime-time series and discourses produced by and about feminism in the time period in which the series were originally broadcast. This type of contextualized analysis of television has become common among feminist media scholars in recent years, and like them, Dow emphasizes television's role in mediating social change and in reproducing assumptions about women's "appropriate roles." The author offers surprising

connections and comparisons in the book (she favors *Dr. Quinn* over *Murphy Brown* as an example of a feminist discourse), and she provides a solid overview of the women's movement in America to the present. The book concludes that media have been sophisticated in understanding the strategies that create mediated visions of feminism for their own purposes. Feminist analysis must be equally sophisticated in understanding those strategies. Highly recommended for upper-division and graduate media, cultural, and feminist studies collections.—*M. R. Grant, Wheaton College (IL)*

OAB-0513 HM263 96-2243 CIP
Ewen, Stuart. **PR!: a social history of spin.** Basic Books, 1996. 480p bibl index ISBN 0-465-06168-0, $30.00

A December 1996 *Esquire* article describes Ewen's books as a "magisterial new chronicle"—a good description of this account of public relations (PR) and its role in 20th-century American life. Although it is clearly written and readable, few will read this tome of 400-plus pages for entertainment or a quick lesson in cultural history. Rather, it is a book to be consulted for its exhaustive coverage and documentation—one that may (and should) become required reading in communications, journalism, and media studies programs. The closing chapter, "The Public and Its Problems: Some Notes for the New Millennium," could stand on its own as a fine essay; some readers will see it as important as the 16 historical chapters that precede it. Here Ewen summarizes public relations from its genesis (between 1900 and WW I) "as a reply to widespread public indignation at ... big business" to the fragmented concentration on targeted "lifestyles" or "subcultures" that characterizes much of today's public relations practice. Throughout this summary and in his closing thoughts, Ewen raises important questions and warnings about "current inequities regarding *who has a say? who gets to be heard?*" Those who consult this excellent volume for its historical documentation should also make time to read and reflect on the issues raised in this closing chapter. As Ewen observes, they deserve a book of their own; this reviewer hopes that will be his next project. Public and academic library collections.—*M. S. Myers, Carnegie-Mellon University*

OAB-0514 PN5404 93-31941 CIP
Feldman, Ofer. **Politics and the news media in Japan.** Michigan, 1993. 221p bibl index afp ISBN 0-472-10451-9, $39.50

Mutually beneficial relationships between Japanese reporters and Diet members are highlighted in this methodological, exhaustive study. From questionnaires returned by 402 Diet members (57.6 percent of the body) and interviews with 70 Diet members and 45 reporters, Feldman (Univ. of Tsubuka) has fashioned a fascinating and insightful report on topics such as reporters' work patterns and their formal/informal interaction with political news sources; objectives reporters and politicians have vis-à-vis one another; cultural factors affecting reporting; the unique demographics of the Japanese press; the *kisha kurabu* (press clubs) and consensus reporting; staffing overkill in coverage of events; subtle tactics used to obtain stories; keen competition among reporters; the elaborate reportorial reward system; and the uses politicians make of journalists. The insertion of tables, figures, and interview excerpts, and the skillful blending of otherwise dull survey results into the text, make for informative and interesting reading. Among the book's weaknesses: some data are old (the survey was administered in 1983 and 1984-86); the bibliography misses many sources on Japanese mass media; and the editing is poor. But, overall, this creative, pioneering analysis of Japanese political communication is a model for similar treatments of other countries. Upper-division undergraduate and above.—*J. A. Lent, Temple University*

OAB-0515 PN1992 93-38700 CIP
Hamamoto, Darrell Y. **Monitored peril: Asian Americans and the politics of TV representation.** Minnesota, 1994. 311p bibl index afp ISBN 0-8166-2368-6, $49.95; ISBN 0-8166-2369-4 pbk, $18.95

The author's contentions are that deep-seated racism, hatred, and fear of Asians and Asian Americans permeate American society and that these feelings are reflected in television news and programming. Tearing apart scores of series, documentaries, docu-dramas, and news, analysis, and "trash TV" shows, Hamamoto concludes that the medium negatively stereotypes the Asian American, twists Asian history (especially when US involvement is portrayed), and discriminates against Asian American actors and actresses in casting assignments. The book is packed with data, vignettes, and opinion on the history of US-Asia relations; textual analyses of individual television shows and series; and biographical sketches of Asian American performers. Hamamoto takes an appropriately critical stance, at times allows his anger to surface, and spares no institution or individual (Tom Dooley, Sun Myung Moon, and Walter Cronkite are all here) that has been unfair to Asians or Asian Americans. The book is well researched, interestingly written, and fully documented, although the editing leaves much to be desired. It is a "must" read for academicians, broadcasting practitioners, and the general public.—*J. A. Lent, Temple University*

OAB-0516   PN4882   92-19424 CIP
Hutton, Frankie. **The early black press in America, 1827 to 1860.** Greenwood, 1993. 182p bibl index afp (Contributions in Afro-American and African studies, 157) ISBN 0-313-28696-5, $45.00

The author of this scholarly, valuable book has plowed new ground. No other source describes the black press of the pre-Civil War era in such depth, and with such thoroughness and candor. These black journalists aimed their messages at the black middle class, a group small in number but significant in that it supplied the role models for brethren still enslaved. Despite the harshest of social conditions, these writers and editors published uplifting, idealistic news and features. They were given little or no assistance by the mainstream press of the era. The journals were short-lived for the most part. Their readers were rarely people of wealth; indeed, most were nearly destitute. Circulation figures are few and vague, but the author makes the plausible point that the pass-along rate was high. The book also contains the only thorough list of these journals, the years of their births and deaths. Writing is lucid if not sprightly; documentation is excellent; the bibliography is useful and thorough; but the several illustrations are of little value. Hutton (Lehigh Univ.) is a teacher of journalism and African American studies.—*R. Halverson, Arizona State University*

OAB-0517   PN5474   92-38861 CIP
Jackson, Gordon S. **Breaking story: the South African press.** Westview, 1993. 308p bibl index afp ISBN 0-8133-8453-2, $34.95

The way the press shaped and reflected apartheid and its subsequent demise is the major theme of this book. Choosing the daily and weekly press and the period from 1976 (year of the Soweto riots) through 1990, Jackson deals with the social/political climate and media environment in which the press found itself, as well as with alternative newspapers and with economic and legislative constraints upon newspapers. The last topic receives a rather detailed description of the various press acts under which South African media have operated. The treatment is comprehensive, dealing with many facets of the press. It is academically sound, using European, US, and African sources, and well written, often employing a literary style. Besides library research, Jackson, a South African who worked three years as a journalist in Johannesburg, interviews "some" 60 journalists, media scholars, and "other academics." Editors of nearly all daily and weekly newspapers were in his sample. Abbreviations, a glossary, an appendix of media emergency regulations, and a bibliography are provided. A shortcoming of the bibliography is the omission of some standard, or otherwise useful, works on African media by Ainslie, Head, Ugboajah, and Wilcox. Documentation would have been aided by a list of the interviewees. *Breaking Story* belongs in libraries supporting undergraduate or graduate journalism programs as well as on the shelves of researchers into international communication and foreign media.—*J. A. Lent, Temple University*

OAB-0518   PN4738   92-34828 CIP
Lawson, Linda. **Truth in publishing: federal regulation of the press's business practices, 1880-1920.** Southern Illinois, 1993. 229p bibl index afp ISBN 0-8093-1829-6, $29.95

This study centers on the Newspaper Publicity Act of 1912, which, Lawson notes, was the first regulation of the press since the Sedition Act of 1798. The act, which was attached to a postal service appropriations bill and made conformity to the regulations a condition for continued receipt of second-class mailing subsidies, addressed the three common press abuses: concealed ownership, paid advertising presented as news stories, and inflated circulation figures. As might be expected the newspaper industry challenged the law as a violation of the guarantees of the First Amendment, but a unanimous Supreme Court rejected this claim on the grounds that Congress could attach conditions to the press for the special privilege of second-class mail. Lawson (Indiana Univ.) presents a detailed study that makes a real contribution toward filling the gap in First Amendment history from 1800 to 1920. The volume, with its good index, excellent bibliography, and easy-to-use extensive documentation, is recommended for upper-division undergraduates, graduate students, faculty, and professionals.—*P. E. Kane, SUNY College at Brockport*

OAB-0519   PN4855   94-43251 CIP
Leonard, Thomas C. **News for all: America's coming-of-age with the press.** Oxford, 1995. 288p index afp ISBN 0-19-506454-2, $30.00

In this detailed history of news in print and its relation to people's lives, Leonard (Univ. of California, Berkeley) traces how Americans have gotten their news from colonial times (in taverns and via the US mail) to the present (electronic neighborhoods). Sections discuss how in the 19th century the US was a nation of readers and how the news-reading habit took hold, how readers chose what they read, how journalists have pulled away from readers today, and the social implications of the technology that makes news today universal. The book discusses how to rebuild America's love of the press by sustaining the sense of community that made American nationalism possible. Chapters cover antislavery publications and civil rights movements, circulation drives and marketing, the depiction of newspapers and journalists in art and the movies. The emphasis is on readers and the relation between them and publishers, editors, and reporters. Impressively documented, with charts, illustrations, and 60 pages of notes and further readings. All collections.—*C. M. Leder, emeritus, Mott Community College*

OAB-0520   PN1992   94-48616 CIP
Marc, David. **Bonfire of the humanities: television, subliteracy, and long-term memory loss.** Syracuse, 1995. 174p bibl index afp ISBN 0-8156-0321-5, $24.95

Channel-surfing academic Marc launches "The Television Series" with a zippy jeremiad that berates the humanities for snobbishly failing to attend to society's most symptomatic medium. Though focused in America, the argument applies beyond. The deconstructionists are "bastards" because their "freeing the text from history" turned "the study of culture into a kind of mental aerobics session." With its tangents, autobiographical anecdotes, energy, indecorum, and voice, this book is for, as well as about, the TV age. Pith abounds. Marc observes that "a reverence for literacy is outlasting a love for it"; scholarship and pedagogy, especially in the humanities, must acknowledge that very few people read print very much. "Mass culture, with its endless barrage of styles, suggestions, moral codes, and so on, has become the context for all our thinking." Television is not an alternative to literacy but another form of communication. Marc shrewdly explains the helplessness behind political correctness but opposes its censoriousness, especially in academia. He includes a sensible pointer to current TV scholarship and an homage to the neglected pioneer of TV criticism, Gilbert Seldes, who engaged thoughtfully with individual programs and series: "the first critic who would discuss matters of taste in television viewing without questioning a taste for television itself." Marc is a provocative, worthy scion of Seldes and McLuhan. All collections.—*M. Yacowar, University of Calgary*

OAB-0521   KF2840   95-1113 CIP
Minow, Newton N. **Abandoned in the wasteland: children, television, and the First Amendment,** by Newton N. Minow and Craig

L. LaMay. Hill & Wang, 1996 (c1995). 237p index ISBN 0-8090-1589-7 pbk, $11.00

As FCC chair in 1961, Minow (Northwestern Univ.) delivered the famous "vast wasteland" speech to the National Association of Broadcasters. The present title revisits the issue of television and children some 30 years later and argues vigorously for fundamental reform based on two guiding principles: that the public interest should determine the future of telecommunications and that this interest is best realized by putting children first. Minow and LaMay (Public-Service Television Project) develop their thesis in five chapters, first providing a concise history of children's programming and of the development of broadcast law. Arguing that competition in children's programming does not benefit children and that First Amendment exclusions can be used to protect children—as a special population—from rapacious commercial programmers, the authors outline broad public policy goals and offer a series of specific recommendations. "A Bill for Children's Telecommunications" is appendixed, as are the original "wasteland" speech and an updated 1991 version. The writing is excellent and accessible, making the book appropriate for all academic levels and even general collections. Highly recommended for upper-division undergraduates and above as a brilliantly reasoned and indispensable aid in navigating the immense changes taking place in telecommunications law.— T. Gleeson, Neumann College

OAB-0522   PN1991   92-50313 CIP
Mott, Robert L. **Radio sound effects: who did it, and how, in the era of live broadcasting.** McFarland, 1993. 295p index ISBN 0-89950-747-6, $39.95

Seldom does one have the good fortune to be able to state in a review that the work under consideration is not only sound and scholarly, but enjoyable to read. Such is the case with Mott's work, a delightful mixture of amusing anecdotes with serious documentation of a little-known, but vital, aspect of early radio history. Archival photographs are, alone, worth the time spent with this work, but the text is itself alternately amusing and informative. For instance, Mott writes about what he terms "horror stories" when radio sound staff failed to check their equipment before airtime, resulting in cascading ping-pong balls flooding the studio unexpectedly. The details included on the operation of now archaic mechanisms like the "gravel box," "thunderscreen," and "portable splash tank" both reveal another age in broadcasting and, simultaneously, enable us to understand their proper place in the development of modern sound effects techniques. In fact, in many ways, this work functions as a highly readable history of the entire medium of radio. Its dedication is "to the men and women of live broadcasting who made this book such a joy to write." It is also a joy to read.—A. J. Silvia Jr., University of Rhode Island

OAB-0523   PN1990   92-9389 CIP
Munson, Wayne. **All talk: the talkshow in media culture.** Temple University, 1993. 216p index afp ISBN 0-87722-995-3, $34.95

This slim volume packs a scholarly application of postmodernism into its rigorous analysis of contemporary radio and television talk shows. In just three engaging chapters the author offers a compelling case for talk shows as the prime example of a postmodern media practice that offers us a thing to think with, a way to both destruct and construct knowledge, reality, culture, politics, and the self. This much-maligned media form is dissected and revealed with surgical skill. Munson meaningfully explores its appeal as a people's forum, a political and social leveler, a voyeur's paradise, a commodifier of knowledge, and an ideal commodity for a postmodern market economy. Eschewing long and confusing quotes from the postmodern gurus, the author plunges into his own explication of the development of the talk show, its production and syndication, its myriad forms, its leading characters (Geraldo, Donahue, Oprah, Larry King), its proponents and opponents. He even offers a fascinating analysis of two films, Talk Radio and King of Comedy, in an act that itself demonstrates how media boundaries are effectively collapsed in the postmodern. Though dense and detailed the book is eminently readable. Even the chapter notes are interesting, revealing the depth and breadth of the research underlying this volume. No

matter how one feels about the absurdities and ethics of talk shows, Munson's book makes it impossible to ignore their significance in contemporary America.—R. Cathcart, Queens College, CUNY

OAB-0524   P96   96-10051 CIP
Neuzil, Mark. **Mass media & environmental conflict: America's green crusades,** by Mark Neuzil [and William Kovarik]. Sage Publications, CA, 1996. 243p bibl indexes afp ISBN 0-7619-0332-1, $45.95; ISBN 0-7619-0333-X pbk, $21.95

Using seven case studies presented chronologically from the mid-19th century to the 1960s, Neuzil and Kovarik highlight interactions of mass media, environmentalists, government, large corporations, and various lobbying groups to effect or hinder change relative to environmental issues. They examine battles over workplace toxins, ethyl gasoline, industrial pollution, species depletion and hunting laws, and destruction of public lands. Their selection of historical incidents, use of original documentation, and interesting narrative make this work scholarly, lively, and relevant. Some editors, reporters, and media are deservedly elevated from footnote status, among them Charles Hallock, George B. Grinnell, Walter Lippmann, Horace Greeley, Norman Hapgood, Lyman Abbott, Collier's, The New York World, and Field & Stream. Others, particularly William R. Hearst, Carr Van Anda, and The New York Times, merit the brickbats tossed at them. In some cases, the authors seem to hold back in their condemnations of media that supported corporate expediency over human life; at other times, they do not pay enough attention to the media as they discuss specific environmental causes. True to the times, grammatical errors mar this otherwise excellent work. Overall, however, it is a superb, scholarly treatment of a subject rarely looked at and deserving more attention. All collections.—J. A. Lent, Temple University

OAB-0525   P96   96-20329 CIP
Reeves, Byron. **The media equation: how people treat computers, television, and new media like real people and places,** by Byron Reeves and Clifford Nass. Cambridge/CSLI Publications, 1996. 305p bibl index ISBN 1-57586-052-X, $27.95

This interesting, breezy, trend-setting book makes sweeping theoretical and conceptual claims without burdening the reader with data, statistical analysis, tables, or other evidence. The authors (both Stanford) set out to establish that media equal real life: their research has proven, they claim, that all human interactions with TV, film, computers, the Internet, etc., are fundamentally as social and natural as interpersonal interactions. More than the widely practiced anthropomorphizing of mechanical and physical objects, this is a process by which all people make media full participants in their social and natural world. The authors' research involved examining responses to flattery, movement, and so on that emanated from media. They tested 22 interpersonal rules about manners, personality, emotion, social roles, and forms, and in every case found subjects responded to computers, TV, and film exactly as if they were real persons in the real world. The authors offer no data from the experiments and no caveats. In some cases the experimental methods were very creative, but since no data are presented, readers cannot check interpretations or claims. In other cases the methods used limited responses to a very narrow range that tended to predetermine the outcomes. Readers not particularly interested in how data are collected and interpreted can skip to the last chapter, which clearly and succinctly summarizes the authors' premises and conclusions. All collections.—R. Cathcart, Queens College, CUNY

OAB-0526   PN4874   94-45939 CIP
Silk, Mark. **Unsecular media: making news of religion in America.** Illinois, 1995. 181p index afp ISBN 0-252-01904-0, $19.95

Silk, a historian of religion and a working journalist, challenges the accepted wisdom that the news media in the US are implacably secular and hostile to religion. On the contrary, the author argues that the media reflect many religion-based values in America—e.g., good works, tolerance, repudiation of hypocrisy, and concern for "new" religious groups that are affronts to the social order. He uses historical analysis and his own experiences to explore the ideas and attitudes that inform the news media's approach to religious subject matter. The study focuses primarily on daily newspapers and news weeklies, although television news and movies are lightly addressed. This timely work, the first to provide an overview of how the American news media cover religion, comes at a point when news organizations are increasingly recognizing religion and moral values as areas of significant importance to a majority of people in America. Silk provides a framework for a less judgmental and more pluralistic approach to the coverage of religion in the US. Particularly helpful is the appendix of actual religion news stories written by the author, which illustrate the issues discussed in the book. Highly recommended for undergraduate and graduate collections in journalism, religious studies, and communications.—*M. R. Grant, Wheaton College (IL)*

OAB-0527   PN4855   94-4777 CIP
Sloan, Wm. David. **The early American press, 1690-1783,** by Wm. David Sloan and Julie Hedgepeth Williams. Greenwood, 1994. 233p bibl index afp (The history of American journalism, 1) ISBN 0-313-27525-4, $59.95

This excellent book describes the American press's first 93 years within the cultural context of the era. The authors (Univ. of Alabama) find that many newspaper publishers were more motivated by religious faith than by profit or political ideology: some significant early newspapers were published by Puritan dissidents who rebelled against the perceived dogma of the Anglican church. This work concludes that during the last 50 years of the period discussed the press was multifaceted, unpredictable, and inconsistent. The authors find only partial support for the romantic, historical view that publishers were pro- or anti-British. They critique historical perspectives that publishers (with the exception of Benjamin Franklin) wished to establish a new, business-oriented professional class. The authors reveal a mosaic of influences and discuss the parallel between the press in the American colonies and Great Britain after about 1750. The authors' viewpoint contrasts with most previous interpretations of the period, but their work is undergirded by meticulous scholarship. They provide both a bibliographic essay and a conclusion that contrasts their findings with those of previous historians. The book is the first volume in what looks to be a promising new series on the American press. Very highly recommended for all journalism and American history collections, upper-division undergraduates and above.—*R. A. Logan, University of Missouri—Columbia*

OAB-0528   PN5117   95-50042 CIP
Tunstall, Jeremy. **Newspaper power: the new national press in Britain.** Oxford, 1996. 441p bibl index afp ISBN 0-19-871132-8, $65.00; ISBN 0-19-871133-6 pbk, $24.95

Those who worry about the future of newspapers may take heart in this sweeping, insightful study of the British national (as opposed to regional) press. According to Tunstall (City Univ., London), not only have newspapers been the "most potent" of Britain's mass media, but their dominant role in shaping public policy, influencing public life, and setting the nation's news agenda is likely to continue. The British news world is unusual in the degree to which it is driven by newspapers, from the upright *Financial Times* to the rascally *Sun*—newspapers with a national scope and a competitive hunger that offer "a bewildering array of choices." How different from the monopolistic mentality of newspaper ownership in the US. Tunstall's chapter "Hacking Down the Monarchy" brilliantly analyzes the "interactive soap opera" that the press, the public, and the royals themselves have made of the likes of Charles and Fergie, with down-market tabloids in the vanguard and the up-market "prestige" papers traipsing behind (against their will, of course). This chapter alone justifies reading this book. Fortunately, Tunstall gives much more. Rarely is a work of such scope and sweep so rich in precision and detail. All academic collections serving upper-division undergraduates and above.—*A. R. Cannella, Central Connecticut State University*

OAB-0529   92-82780 Orig
Voices from the underground: v.1: Insider histories of the Vietnam era underground press; v.2: A directory of sources and resources on the Vietnam era underground press, ed. by Ken Wachsberger. Mica Press, Box 25544 - Library Lane, Tempe, AZ 85285, 1993. 2v. 608, 128p index afp ISBN 1-87946-103-X pbk, $74.50

Alternative newspapers of the late 1960s and early 1970s were rowdy, raunchy, brave, inspired, and foolish. No one called them respectable. Nevertheless, this two-volume appreciation looks so handsome, so tasteful, so serene that one might marvel (in the words of James Agee): "How far we all come away from ourselves." But prospective readers should not be fooled. Between the slick covers are plenty of fireworks, even hand grenades. Among the publications sampled in the first volume are *Fifth Estate, Great Speckled Bird, Muhammad Speaks, off our backs, Guardian,* and *Fag Rag*. Retrospective essays that are carefully edited, if occasionally too long, accompany the unruly prose of selections from the papers themselves. This juxtaposition can be jarring. In toto, however, the first volume is an enlightening journalistic romp through the period, in all its folly and glory. The second volume contains a helpful annotated bibliography and a thorough guide to archival materials. As a set, these volumes are both exhaustive and exhausting—much in the spirit of the originals. They may not be must-reads for many, but they certainly are must-haves for any student of alternative journalism. Academic libraries at all levels.—*A. R. Cannella, Central Connecticut State University*

OAB-0530   HM258   93-48986 CIP
Wark, McKenzie. **Virtual geography: living with global media events.** Indiana, 1994. 252p index afp ISBN 0-253-36349-7, $29.95; ISBN 0-253-20894-7 pbk, $14.95

Wark describes and critiques the global media information flow that made the Persian Gulf War, the fall of the Berlin Wall, the Tiananmen Square massacre, and the Black Monday stock market crash of 1987 part of everyday experience. She calls this phenomenon "telethesia." This is a new geography: we are everywhere in the world at once, a place constructed entirely by the convergence of mediated flows of information—virtual geography. She does not condemn this "third reality," but instead establishes the grounds for a new form of cultural studies that follows the contours of the media event and does not force the event into existing disciplines. The author's capacity to grasp and interpret these events is astounding, and her ability to provide insights into a world where unbounded information is circling the earth with the speed of light is startling. Her language at first seems forced and contrived as she pours out abstract and speculative explanations of vectors, nature, telethesia, etc. However, in the end she comes close to making the linearity of print project a world of global electronic information in which traditional modes of rationality are inadequate to explain what happens when information passes out of the orbit of one community into another. She demonstrates that the unstoppable rush of electronic information not only makes everything in the world knowable, but also carries with it the possibility of disinformation and discontrol. Recommended for upper-division undergraduate, graduate, and research collections.—*R. Cathcart, Queens College, CUNY*

OAB-0531   Orig
Wood, James. **History of international broadcasting.** P. Peregrinus/Science Museum, London, 1992. (Dist. by IEE Dept., IEEE Service Center, 445 Hoes Lane, Piscataway, NJ 08855) 258p index (IEE history of technology series, 19) ISBN 0-86341-281-5, $59.00

To describe the history of international broadcasting is a formidable task, a fact not lost on the author of this volume. Hard decisions must be made in selecting from among the world's 160 broadcasting authorities. Wood chose to concentrate on the Voice of America, BBC World Service, Deutsche Welle, and Radio France International, although he includes sections on Scandinavian, Soviet, and Japanese (wartime) international broadcasts. He writes virtually nothing about other Asian or African or Latin American attempts at international broadcasting, save for a chapter "Super Power in the Arab World." What is contained here, however, is very valuable and worthwhile—historically, technically, and diplomatically analyzed in a clear and usually interesting manner. Wood knows of what he writes, being an amateur radio operator from the 1930s and a transmitter designer most of his career. As would be expected, he emphasizs the transmission, rather than studio, aspect of international broadcasting, a topic that authors generally ignore or confuse with their "technicalese." Wood mixes the technical with historical and anecdotal accounts that make for fascinating reading. The first half of the book is especially enlightening with its differing accounts of who actually invented radio, and its appraisal of radio's role during the world wars and the Cold War. Highly recommended. Advanced undergraduate; graduate; faculty.—*J. A. Lent, Temple University*

■ Rhetoric & Discourse

OAB-0532   P302   94-31901 CIP
Benoit, William L. **Accounts, excuses, and apologies: a theory of image restoration strategies.** State University of New York, 1995. 197p bibl indexes ISBN 0-7914-2185-6, $44.50

Discourse to avoid or repair damaged reputations "from perceived wrongdoing" is a common and important area of interpersonal, forensic, and public communication. Since image (or reputation) is a "valuable commodity," how individuals and institutions seek to preserve or restore it deserves study. This well-structured text focuses on the public arena. Benoit (Univ. of Missouri) first explains that the activity of formulating and responding to image restoration discourse will always be necessary given an imperfect world and imperfect people. He then reviews the 20th-century history of the development of strategies for examining discourse aimed at image restoration and formulates his own strategy theory, which he applies to case studies in the fields of advertising, government, politics, and corporate business. Finally, he suggests what "more effective image repair efforts" might be, and what the future might offer for a more complete understanding of this kind of discourse. Benoit provides extensive analysis and evaluation of image restoration discourse in a Coca-Cola/Pepsi-Cola controversy, the *Exxon Valdez* oil spill case, Union Carbide and the Bhopal tragedy defense, and President Nixon's Cambodia address. Recommended for libraries that serve undergraduate and graduate classes in advanced rhetoric, communication, political science, and business.—*T. B. Dykeman, Fairfield University*

OAB-0533   PN203   94-18749 CIP
Carpenter, Ronald H. **History as rhetoric: style, narrative, and persuasion.** South Carolina, 1995. 350p bibl index ISBN 1-57003-032-4, $39.95

Refreshing in this age of rhetorical poverty, this impeccably researched book makes meaningfully clear that "the rhetoric of discourse approached and appreciated as history is persuasive." The explication of history as rhetoric and the investigation into its effect on subsequent actualities demonstrates the power of style. Particularly informative are the chapters on Alfred Thayer Mahan's *The Influence of Sea Power upon History, 1660-1783* (1890), interpreted differently by Franklin D. Roosevelt and by the Japanese yet of great influence on the decisions each made during WW II. Unique contributions of other histories include Frederick Jackson Turner's to the rhetoric of the frontier thesis, Carl Becker's to the propaganda of WW I, and Barbara Tuchman's to John F. Kennedy's Cuban Crisis. In view of its reception by the reading public, Frank L. Owsley's unsuccessful rhetoric is seen as being as necessary to analyze as is successful rhetoric. Relationships between these histories and subsequent actual events, fictive motion pictures, and television productions are well documented. Once he points out how the frontier metaphor expresses and shapes the American experience from the Boston Harbor to the Persian Gulf, Carpenter (Univ. of Florida) suggests that "in the American 'stream of time'" this metaphor might be redirected. All collections.—*T. B. Dykeman, Fairfield University*

OAB-0534   P301   93-16229 CIP
Farrell, Thomas B. **Norms of rhetorical culture.** Yale, 1993. 374p bibl index afp ISBN 0-300-05385-1, $35.00

Few readers unschooled in philosophy and classical rhetoric will benefit from this book—or be likely to complete it; those who do read it will gain immensely. Its strengths are an admirable depth of knowledge and modesty of presentation that support argumentation of impressive subtlety and speech analyses of both penetration and lucidity. In the past 20 years or more, speech communication studies have become divorced from their Aristotelian origins in rhetoric and dialectic; this study contributes largely to a rehabilitation of the field. Defining rhetoric as "a particularistic language in which meaning is redeemed not through the analytic justification of validity claims, but through their collaborative performance," the author makes generous use of Jurgen Habermas's theory of discourse ethics in examining several recent speeches, among which are Mario Cuomo's Notre Dame speech on abortion and Philipp Jenninger's speech at the Kristallnacht commemoration—which, Farrell concludes, was "an attempt to combine heroic style with a gesture of atonement," a major speech that was neither understood by its audience nor correctly reported by its detractors. It was, in Farrell's terms, "a spacious rhetoric of eloquence" rather than its antithesis, "an overblown rhetoric of bombast"; for true rhetoric restores the "power and wish in the thought and expression of our civic life." A major new study. Advanced undergraduate; graduate; faculty.—*M. B. McLeod, Trenton State College*

OAB-0535   PN4193   94-37392 CIP
Felton, Keith Spencer. **Warriors' words: a consideration of language and leadership.** Praeger, 1995. 196p bibl index afp ISBN 0-275-94992-3, $55.00

This book about how an elevated use of language can magnify meaning and the persuasive impact of oratory is one of the most impressive works in the excellent "Praeger Series in Political Communication," now numbering almost 40 volumes. Felton's previous work includes a prize-winning play, internationally syndicated articles, and an award-winning novel. *Warrior's Words* demonstrates his expertise in rhetoric and communication. Felton has divided his work into four parts—"Prophets of the New Century," "Voices of the Second World War," "Postwar Panic," and "The Modern Epoch"—each beginning with a prefatory "assay" (he borrows from the metallurgical meaning of the word *assay* to show how a historian gains a qualitative assessment of which elements of his subject's efforts are precious and which are base) that sets the scene and perspective. He analyzes the oral and written communications of 15 remarkable individuals at critical periods in the world's history. Although not all the oratory represented here strives for ennoblement (he includes Hitler and Joseph McCarthy), it meets the qualifications of motivating people and changing the course of ideas. His approach is to "reach inside [each subject] and free from its whale-mass the ambergris of its essence." One of the tasks of an orator is to create a poetic plane in which the orator's words convey the "colors of the feeling of us all." Felton has given the reader ambergris and poetry. Others who write about rhetoric and communication would do well to read this book and learn from a true artist. All collections.—*R. L. Fischer, University of North Dakota*

■ Language & Literature

OAB-0536   P116   95-47738 CIP
Aitchison, Jean. **The seeds of speech: language origin and evolution.** Cambridge, 1996. 281p bibl index ISBN 0-521-46246-0, $49.95; ISBN 0-521-46793-4 pbk, $17.95

Aitchison's latest book is very much in keeping with her previous works on language in terms of style, audience, and content. Her lavish use of witty metaphors, allusions, and quotations from a wide range of sources makes her writing lively and appropriate for a broad audience—simultaneously available to educated nonspecialists and informative for readers who are already familiar with many concepts in the field of linguistics. Beginning with basic questions like "What is language for?" Aitchison (Oxford Univ.) takes the reader on a fascinating journey through topics such as the possible origins of language in humans, comparisons between language and nonhuman communications, differences between languages, and language changes and how they spread. Although she covers much basic material that will be familiar to specialists, she also has innovative ideas about language evolution. She is careful to explain specialized terminology and employs numerous language examples and illustrations. Highly recommended both for general readers and undergraduate students; graduate students in fields such as anthropology and psychology will also find the book useful.—*L. Bebout, University of Windsor*

OAB-0537 PN3433 93-34821 CIP
Alkon, Paul K. **Science fiction before 1900: imagination discovers technology.** Twayne, 1994. 176p index afp (Studies in literary themes and genres, 3) ISBN 0-8057-0952-5, $22.95

This may be a model of compact critical attention to a literary genre. Unable to cover every work published before 1900 with claims to be science fiction, and not wanting to slight any, Alkon has been deliberately selective. He presents an overview of his subject, its themes, and some representative examples, followed by a close look at selected writers in England, France, and America. Some are obvious (Mary Shelley's *Frankenstein*; Jules Verne's *Twenty Thousand Leagues Under the Sea*; Edgar Allan Poe's "The Balloon Hoax"); some might not come readily to mind (Jonathan Swift's *Gulliver's Travels*; Mark Twain's *A Connecticut Yankee in King Arthur's Court*). Without seeming to be rushed, he manages to touch on the blurring of lines between science fiction and fantasy, the new perspectives which science can bring to fiction, and the role of technology. He knows his subject, his presentation is clear, and he allows the reader to test his choices and explore others with an excellent bibliographical essay discussing secondary sources and a list of recommended titles of works of fiction. General and academic audiences.—*J. R. Cox, St. Olaf College*

OAB-0538 PN56 95-35356 CIP
Alpers, Paul. **What is pastoral?** Chicago, 1996. 429p index afp ISBN 0-226-01516-5, $34.95

This is a long-awaited study, and the wait has been largely worth it. However, one must be prepared to disregard its grandiose ambition, which is nothing less than to define pastoral. Few are likely to agree with Alpers's central, conservative insistence that "we will have a far truer idea of pastoral if we take its representative anecdote to be herdsmen and their lives"; the effort to limit the term "pastoral" is refreshing but this is too restrictive. Moreover, the book is much too limited in the range of pastoral it examines to answer its titular question. Poussin is on the book's jacket, but Alpers (Univ. of California, Berkeley) says almost nothing about pastoral as a visual or musical phenomenon. The core of his work is Virgil and the pastoral of the English Renaissance, with attention in the later chapters to Wordsworth and more recent writers. Fair enough—if the reader can be persuaded that the chosen pastoralists are representative of what has been omitted. But Alpers does not do this. What he *does* do, and beautifully, is provide a series of brilliant, lucid readings of individual works. These will serve especially students of Virgil, Spenser, Shakespeare, Marvell, and Wordsworth. To have written so well on these authors is no small achievement, and whatever shortcomings the book may have, it is a major study by anyone's account.—*P. Cullen, CUNY Graduate Center and College of Staten Island*

OAB-0539 PN4500 91-42648 CIP
Atkins, G. Douglas. **Estranging the familiar: toward a revitalized critical writing.** Georgia, 1992. 203p index afp ISBN 0-8203-1452-8, $30.00; ISBN 0-8203-1453-6 pbk, $15.00

A brilliant, daring, and important book, *Estranging the Familiar* is a call for a return to the personal in writing literary criticism as well as a demonstration of its power. Atkins explores the nature of the essay as a literary form, tracing its European and American roots. He shows how critical theory (mostly European, but also American) has inevitably led the best critics away from the "scientific" article to the essay form and to the celebration of an aesthetic response

to an aesthetic object. The book demonstrates Atkin's broad reading in contemporary and older writers of poetry, fiction, and the essay (including the literary, scientific, and religious), which he uses not to show off his reading but to advance his view of how personal reading and critical writing operate at their best. The book concludes with a demonstration of the critical essay and a discussion of the voice of the writer, a combination of the deeply personal and the contemplative. Atkins emerges through his book as an engaging and thoughtful writer, one who should be read by every graduate student in the humanities. This book is destined to become a classic.—*A. C. Purves, SUNY at Albany*

OAB-0540 PN1241 95-9868 CIP
Burwick, Frederick. **Poetic madness and the Romantic imagination.** Pennsylvania State, 1996. 307p bibl index afp ISBN 0-271-01488-1, $49.50

This thoroughly researched and very learned book explores the ancient notions that creativity derives from inspiration and that, to the extent they are inspired, poets are "out of their minds." Burwick focuses his discussion on English and European literature of the late 18th and early 19th centuries. He devotes several chapters to Romantic theorizing of the notion of inspired madness and several others to the theme of the mad poet as it appeared in literature. Particularly significant is the chapter "Paradoxes of Rationality and Representation." Finally, the author looks at rhetorical strategies adopted by "mad poets"—Friedrich Hölderlin, Gérald de Nerval, and John Clare—to represent their visionary experiences. This is a difficult but important study of a pervasive concept in an age that valued literature more for its expressive than its mimetic qualities. Extensive bibliography and several illustrations in the chapter on Blake. Upper-division undergraduate through faculty.—*J. L. Culross, Eastern Kentucky University*

OAB-0541 PN151 94-8007 CIP
Cain, Mary Ann. **Revisioning writers' talk: gender and culture in acts of composing.** State University of New York Press, 1995. 215p bibl index afp ISBN 0-7914-2075-2, $49.50

A better title for this book would be "An Epistemology of Writers' Talk." Cain (Indiana Univ.) first establishes the terrain of inquiry: how gender and myth are written into personal and professional identities, and, hence, how lived and professional identities are related and transformed through the process of interpreting narrative texts. This phenomenological approach leads to a way of knowing that leads to new truths. The actual inquiry comes in the fascinating chapters that creatively present knowledge as it develops in writers groups, both academic and self-directed. In probing several short stories, Cain confronts literary, psychological, sociological, and (in getting at the "reality" of the text) feminist philosophical issues. This analytical process clarifies inherent problems often obscured by assumptions taken from stances heretofore insufficiently questioned in the context of "writing the subject." The reader learns not to skim the "shallows" and miss the "depths" of writer-reader, teacher-student, oneself-Other connections and to take into account that *how* one knows what one knows influences interpretation of what it is that is "narrated" in the experience/text. Highly recommended for anyone involved in serious creative writing: writers, teachers, upper-division undergraduate and graduate students, and community writers groups.—*T. B. Dykeman, Fairfield University*

OAB-0542 PN3355 94-39574 CIP
Doody, Margaret Anne. **The true story of the novel.** Rutgers, 1996. 580p bibl index ISBN 0-8135-2168-8, $44.95

The title of this extraordinary book promises an exposé: European culture has suppressed the "true story" of the novel—what it is, where it came from. The Novel (Doody's subject is much larger than the hundreds of lowercase novels she refers to) is *not* the product of a secularizing age; if it has no moment of origin, however, it does have a "matrix" ("the religion of the Goddess"—Demeter, Isis, et al.) and its earliest examples—multiracial and multilingual—are "mixed Mediterranean," the earliest, perhaps, being Chariton's *Chaereas and Callirhoe*. Moreover, for Doody (Vanderbilt Univ.) the novel has its own "true story" to tell—a life-affirming significance, essentially religious and feminine, encoded as "fictional tropes" in all novels, ancient and modern. Part 1 of Doody's book familiarizes readers with the themes, techniques, and plots of ten ancient novels; part 2 treats the survival of these works in manuscript copies and early printed versions from the Middle Ages to the 18th century; and part 3 examines the tropes, the attention-directing figures that act in the manner of moments in a liturgy. Doody's prose is clear, untechnical, friendly; documentation is relegated to extensive endnotes, where the originals of translated quotations are provided. This is a major contribution, recommended for all academic libraries.—*G. R. Wasserman, Russell Sage College*

OAB-0543   PN81   94-27021 CIP
Edmundson, Mark. **Literature against philosophy, Plato to Derrida: a defence of poetry.** Cambridge, 1995. 243p index ISBN 0-521-41093-2, $59.95; ISBN 0-521-48532-0 pbk, $17.95

In late 20th-century America, golden terms like "episteme," "intertexuality," and "differance" roll smoothly off the well-oiled tongues of literary critics intoxicated by deep and frequent draughts from the heady ferment of postmodern theoretical discourse about literature. Moreover, such critics are more likely to extol the virtues of Derrida rather than Dante, Bloom rather than the Bible, and Cixous rather than Shakespeare. What are the consequences of privileging theory over literature? Edmundson's deftly and tightly woven tapestry traces the threads of the contemporary struggle between literature and theory to Plato's banishment of the poets from the Republic. In a series of brilliantly argued reflections on critical terms like presence and blindness and insight, the author (Univ. of Virginia) demonstrates the various ways that poetry, here a synecdoche for any creative cultural experience, defends itself against the life-draining powers of critical theory. In particular, Edmundson uses Romantic poetry to challenge the reductionist readings of deconstruction, feminism, psychoanalysis, and new historicism. Edmundson's elegant essay sounds a clarion call for a conversation between theory and poetry in which the voice of poetry both challenges theory and sustains itself. Masterful cultural criticism in the tradition of Leavis and Trilling; recommended for upper-division undergraduates, graduates, and faculty.—*H. L. Carrigan, Jr., Otterbein College*

OAB-0544   PN1059   95-30608 CIP
Ferry, Ann. **The title to the poem.** Stanford, 1996. 312p indexes afp ISBN 0-8047-2610-8, $39.50

No other text makes such a bold, embracing attempt to say what there is to say about the titles of English lyric poems from 1475 to the present, and this will prove an exceptionally fine reference text. Organized into four parts, Ferry's discussion begins with the pre-17th-century practice of editorial (rather than authorial) naming, most forcefully subverted by Jonson. It then moves on to explore "who says" the poem and "who hears" it, as those fictions are construed through the title. Part 3 looks at the relationship between genre and title, and part 4 examines how poets have attempted to undermine the "authority" of the title in the 20th century through the use of allusive quotations within and epigraphs beneath. Ferry returns again and again to certain poets, including Jonson (whom she exhibits as especially important in affecting the possibilities of titling), Wordsworth, Browning, Whitman, Hardy, Frost, Williams, Stevens, Auden, Ashbery. (Her three-page discussion of Frost's naming of *A Boy's Will* is an exquisite piece of focused, provocative history combined with critique.) This subtle, well-informed, multilayered discussion belongs in every college library.—*D. Garrison, Spalding University*

OAB-0545   PQ431   95-10585 CIP
Frey, Hans-Jost. **Studies in poetic discourse: Mallarmé, Baudelaire, Rimbaud, Hölderlin,** tr. by William Whobrey; translations from the French and Latin by Bridget McDonald. Stanford, 1996. 198p bibl afp ISBN 0-8047-2469-5, $39.50; ISBN 0-8047-2600-0 pbk, $14.95

In his introduction Frey (Univ. of Zurich) offers a profound and complex analysis of poetic discourse as the creation of something permanent from the fleeting and impermanent. He insists that the power of discourse lies not in what

it expresses but in its speaking. Like music after it is played, once a discourse is spoken it no longer exists. Literature is a manner of speaking that is concerned uniquely with itself. Only occasionally does Frey's preoccupation with his involved subject lapse into tautology: "The word *expressing*, which I am constantly using, means the expressing that is expressed." Frey uses his introductory remarks in splendid analyses of poems or texts by three great symbolist French poets, Stéphane Mallarmé, Charles Baudelaire, and Arthur Rimbaud. He concludes with a fascinating analysis of a poem by the German Romantic poet Friedrich Hölderlin, who was born 50 years before Baudelaire. He notes that Hölderlin mentions the 18th-century Swiss-born writer Jean-Jacques Rousseau. In attempting to determine the meaning of the reference, he investigates one of Rousseau's texts at length and then considers the philosopher Martin Heidegger's interpretation of Hölderlin. In short, Frey succeeds admirably in his enormous task of explicating discourse. Upper-division undergraduates and above.—*F. C. St. Aubyn, emeritus, University of Pittsburgh*

OAB-0546   PN865   92-16810 CIP
Guillén, Claudio. **The challenge of comparative literature,** tr. by Cola Franzen. Harvard, 1993. 450p bibl index afp (Harvard studies in comparative literature, 42) ISBN 0-674-10687-3, $49.95; ISBN 0-674-10688-1 pbk, $19.95

Finding many traditional approaches to comparative literature limited either by a lack of historical consciousness or by a "cultural nationalism" that uses literature for "ideological ends," Guillén (Harvard) sets out to demonstrate that "the major task of comparative literature is the investigation, explanation, and ordering of diachronic and supranational structures." After a first section in which he examines the positive and negative ways in which various movements (romanticism, positivism), various theorists (Wellek, Jakobson), and various concepts (Goethe's *Weltliteratur, Littérature générale*) have contributed to the rise of comparative literature studies, Guillén proposes that the study of world literatures in terms of genres, themes, and forms must be revised by turning attention to the "literary relations" (supranationality) and the "historical configurations" (diachronic structures) of such literatures. The value of Guillén's work lies in its dialogue with contemporary literary theory, its balanced readings of hundreds of primary sources, and its examination of non-Western as well as Western literatures. An extremely important book on the future of comparative literature studies, Guillén's text is a valuable companion to René Wellek's *A History of Modern Criticism* (1955-93). Excellent bibliography. Highly recommended for graduate students and faculty.—*H. L. Carrigan, Jr., Otterbein College*

OAB-0547   PN56   91-43353 CIP
Hagstrum, Jean H. **Esteem enlivened by desire: the couple from Homer to Shakespeare.** Chicago, 1992. 518p index afp ISBN 0-226-31287-9, $36.00

The literary works of all cultures abound in writings about love, but few authors (if any) have made love a specialty or equaled the number and coverage of Jean Hagstrum's studies. His ten earlier books concentrated on a single author (e.g., Johnson, Blake) or period (e.g., 18th century). The present work spans the centuries from classical to Elizabethan times and searches with earnest analysis into the meaning of *eros*, *agape*, *amor*, *charis*, *philia*. This book may well be regarded as the capstone of Hagstrum's canon. The critiques proceed in chronological order and the types of love portrayed in each period are interpreted in terms of the culture of the period. This monumental work is nothing short of an encyclopedia of love as depicted in literature. Rich in detail and sensitivity to the varieties of love, the book is highly recommended for both academic and public libraries.—*A. G. Tassin, University of New Orleans*

OAB-0548   PN3499   94-36032 CIP
Hanne, Michael. **The power of the story: fiction and political change.** Berghahn Books, 1995 (c1994). (Dist. by Continuum) 262p bibl index ISBN 0-8264-0784-6, $29.95

Hanne (Auckland Univ.) has produced a spirited, well-researched volume that stakes out a relatively unvisited intersection: narrative fiction and political change. To this end, he dispatches Turgenev's *A Sportsman's Notebook*, Stowe's *Uncle Tom's Cabin*, Silone's *Fontamara*, Solzhenitsyn's *One Day in the Life of Ivan Denisovich*, and Rushdie's *The Satanic Verses*. An introductory chapter provides several apposite definitions and qualifications, along with the hybrid theoretical origins of Hanne's critical methods. The discussion in each of the following five chapters adroitly makes its way through a distinct tangle of historical, political, cultural, and literary factors, as it suggests the nature and scope of influence—intriguingly, on readers and nonreaders of the text—ascribed to the text under consideration. Especially intricate and compelling is the piece on *The Satanic Verses*. Although the aggregate effect of Hanne's discrete "case studies" would have been strengthened by a concluding chapter discussing the influence of the selected texts in comparative terms, this highly readable study is an impressive work of contemporary criticism, richly deserving its intended general and academic audiences. Upper-division undergraduate and above.—*J. Leondopoulos, CUNY City College*

OAB-0549 PN56 95-51818 CIP
Horowitz, Sara R. **Voicing the void: muteness and memory in Holocaust fiction.** State University of New York, 1997. 276p bibl index afp ISBN 0-7914-3129-0, $54.50

With this book Horowitz (Univ. of Delaware) assures her position as an important figure in Holocaust discourse. She demonstrates comprehensive familiarity with genres from testimony to imaginative literature and extensive knowledge of critical theory. Complementing the insightful commentary in her contributions to numerous collections, this volume turns to "the pivotal presence of mute characters in Holocaust fiction and the related motif of the untold or truncated story." It judiciously explores and explicates the trope of muteness designating the plight of *Shoah* victims in works by Wiesel, Kosinski, and Spiegelman; the adoption of voluntary muteness in the German tongue by Lind and Améry, and Celan's trope of lost language registering Jewish disenfranchisement in the Nazi universe. To contrast victims' muteness, Horowitz poses articulate, "hyperfluent" characters in novels about collaboration by Tournier and Grass. This study provides enormous range in analysis of national and stylistic Holocaust narratives, a lucid account of current critical discourse on Holocaust representability, and a discussion of the psychiatric literature on the trauma of loss and survival. It will be one of the central texts influencing reading of Holocaust literature. Highly recommended; upper-division undergraduate through faculty.—*S. L. Kremer, Kansas State University*

OAB-0550 PA3071 94-41498 CIP
Leontis, Artemis. **Topographies of Hellenism: mapping the homeland.** Cornell, 1995. 257p bibl index afp ISBN 0-8014-3057-7, $29.95

Leontis (Ohio State Univ.) investigates the relationship between the landscape and archeological "sites" of ancient Greece and the "cites" (citations, textual representations) that differently shaped both modern Greece and a "modernist" West that sought its cultural origins in Hellas. Starting with Virginia Woolf's "A Dialogue Upon Mount Pentelicus," Leontis contests prevailing views of "Western" literary modernisms, offering an analysis of Greek modernism as an aesthetic nationalism that, unlike its West European counterparts, often embraced the physical world instead of excluding it from the "autonomous semiotic system" of art. Leontis's account of the ways in which literature and other social practices "inscribe identities in places" also shows how, in the hands of a diverse group of Greek writers, such practices responded to geopolitical changes in the homeland (the end of Ottoman Turkish colonialism) and diaspora. Though related to Gregory Jusdanis's work on Greece (*Belated Modernity and Aesthetic Culture*, 1991) and Richard Helgerson's on England (*Forms of Nationhood*, 1992), this book explores genuinely new territory. A major contribution to studies of Greek literature, modernism, nationalism, postcolonialism, and cultural history. Essential for college and research libraries, at the upper-division undergraduate level and above.—*K. Tölölyan, Wesleyan University*

OAB-0551 PN56 95-19545 CIP
Lloyd, Rosemary. **Closer & closer apart: jealousy in literature.** Cornell, 1995. 205p bibl index afp ISBN 0-8014-3151-4, $32.50

Sexual jealousy as a literary device provides a vehicle for the exploration of self, Other, roles, society, and gender in this mature and elegantly written study. Lloyd (Indiana Univ.) explores sexual jealousy as a vehicle of control and explains the postsentimental reality of the 19th century, which replaced loyalty to family name or feudal possession by a husband with new obsessions about individual importance. Not a thematic or psychological study, this inquiry into the early modern presentation of sexual jealousy builds on recent critical precepts, rejecting current phallocentric theories, which refuse to account for female desire (e.g., those in Denis de Rougemont's *Love in the Western World*, 1956, and Toril Moi's *Sexual/Textual Politics: Feminist Literary Theory*, 1985). Using an eclectic choice of texts but grounded in French fiction, this study presents a series of jealous protagonists who provide readers with techniques of decoding, interpreting, and assessing information in texts. They are paradigms of the writer and suggest differences in spatial and temporal images associated with men's and women's sense of betrayal. Contains a useful bibliography and index. Highly recommended for all upper-division collections in fiction and gender studies.—*S. A. Parker, Hiram College*

OAB-0552 QA76 97-9187 CIP
Murray, Janet H. **Hamlet on the holodeck: the future of narrative in cyberspace.** Free Press, 1997. 324p bibl index afp ISBN 0-684-82723-9, $25.00

Murray (MIT) admirably avoids the trap of most celebrations of the new creative possibilities opened up by electronic media. Typically, digital technologies and environments are imagined in terms of *how* they will change the ways in which individuals communicate and create, rather than in terms of *what* they will alter at the level of content. Murray's superb guide to the shift into the digital takes into account the dramatic transformations in the "content" of human expression. The news of the death of narrative storytelling has been greatly exaggerated. Indeed, as Murray shows, the pleasures and enduring human truths of cybernarratives are fully continuous with those of more traditional literary forms. In its examinations of new media for storytelling, especially its discussion of the aesthetic theory and authorial practice of these media, this book distinguishes itself. Readers at all levels will be rewarded by Murray's intervention into the ongoing and crucial project concerning the future of fiction.—*M. Uebel, University of Kentucky*

OAB-0553 PN56 94-20498 CIP
Murrin, Michael. **History and warfare in Renaissance epic.** Chicago, 1995 (c1994). 371 bibl index afp ISBN 0-226-55403-1, $32.50

Murrin (Univ. of Chicago) explores the interaction of literature, politics, and technology. His subject is how warfare—the epic theme par excellence, and thus the most "exalted" narrative material—came to be regarded as an inappropriate vehicle for creative literature; "a profound change," Murrin notes, "and we still live with its consequences." His analysis commands assent, and the reader gains much by focusing so sharply on the epic genre in this period. In particular, the book raises questions about the place of warfare in the overall literary and cultural economy. If the decline of epic and the exceptional status of war novelists like Hemingway and Mailer are matters of fact, warfare has remained an enduring theme in popular history writing, filmmaking, and the festival reenactment of important battles. Murrin's thorough, convincing analysis of the literary and social crisis of 16th-century Europe will necessitate and make possible a more searching investigation of later periods. His command of the historical record and of the literary material is extensive and sure, and he writes beautifully. The book is an utter pleasure to read, and everyone can learn from it. Upper-division undergraduate and above.—*J. A. Farrell Jr., University of Pennsylvania*

OAB-0554 PS228 93-636 CIP

Nealon, Jeffrey T. **Double reading: postmodernism after decon-struction.** Cornell, 1993. 200p bibl index afp ISBN 0-8014-2853-X, $27.50

Nealon's study is a much-needed contribution to contemporary literary theory. The great strength of this book is the clarity with which it addresses both the current situation of theory and the real issues that tend to get obscured by fashionable critical discourse. Drawing on the important work of Rodolphe Gasché, Nealon argues that much that has passed for deconstruction has, in fact, been a misguided appropriation of the writings of Derrida. He argues instead for a notion of double reading, an extension of deconstruction beyond the mere fascination with reflexivity. He expands his argument into a thought-provoking analysis of the relation between deconstruction and New Historicism and, refreshingly, does not descend into either invective or journalism. Nealon then applies his arguments to an analysis of Pynchon's *Gravity's Rainbow* and the work of the Language poets. This is the type of book literary criticism sorely needs: careful, balanced, and rigorous. It will make us all re-think issues we assumed were long settled. Highly recommended. Advanced undergraduate; graduate; faculty.—*S. Barnett, Central Connecticut State University*

OAB-0555 P211 93-26382 CIP

Olson, David R. **The world on paper: the conceptual and cogni-tive implications of writing and reading.** Cambridge, 1994. 318p bibl indexes ISBN 0-521-44311-3, $24.95

In this important book, Olson addresses a series of fundamental questions about the nature of literacy, culture, and consciousness—questions that have preoccupied all sorts of scholars for a very long time: What is literacy? How does it differ from culture to culture? And what role has it played in shaping the way people think about themselves and the world? Olson's answers to these questions are tentative, yet bold. He is careful to point out that researchers have "done little more than begin to map out" the areas of knowledge that might lead to a full understanding of literacy. But he also draws upon an impressive array of sources to formulate a highly provocative theory: Speech is not a model for writing, Olson argues. Instead, the opposite is true. Writing "provides a model for speech; we introspect language in terms laid down by our scripts." With statements like this, Olson methodically goes about refuting Aristotle, Saussure, and two thousand years of traditional wisdom. The comprehensive bibliography alone makes this book valuable. But the intriguing insights and care-fully reasoned arguments make it a pleasure. Academic and general audiences.—*J. Aber, College of Mount St. Joseph*

OAB-0556 PN3352 96-27423 CIP

Overton, Bill. **The novel of female adultery: love and gender in continental European fiction, 1830-1900.** Macmillan (UK)/St. Martin's, 1996. 284p bibl index ISBN 0-312-16500-5, $65.00

Overton (Longborough Univ., UK) has written a truly prodigious study that concentrates on France but also includes Russia, Denmark, Portugal, and Spain. A flagrant double standard about adultery prevailed in these countries, with women given little attention and few, if any, rights. The author emphasizes that no classic novel is founded on *male* adultery. Overton first looks at Balzac, then discusses Chateaubriand, Constant, Musset, and Merimee. His thorough analyses provide details about the principal characters, their social status, and family involvements, and comparisons with other contemporary writers. Over-ton points out that only a few novels of this period about female adultery end *without* the heroine's death. Then, in 1857, Flaubert's *Madame Bovary* came out and the adulterous wife became the model for other French novels of adul-tery. Tolstoy's *Anna Karenina* is the lone classic in this period in Russia where an author describes the heroine as pitiful but not guilty, and also highlights the humor and moral dilemmas involved in adultery. Overton is exception-ally diligent in his specific details and research. Superior notes, index, and bibliography. All academic collections.—*G. O. Carey, emeritus, Eastern Kentucky University*

OAB-0557 PR508 93-28442 CIP

Pratt, Annis. **Dancing with goddesses: archetypes, poetry, and empowerment.** Indiana, 1994. 408p bibl index afp ISBN 0-253-34586-3, $39.95; ISBN 0-253-20865-3 pbk, $17.95

Pratt offers here an excellent and thorough study of Medusa, Aphrodite, and Artemis. After exploring in detail the myths and archetypes associated with these goddesses (all images of the Great Mother), Pratt discusses their repre-sentations in 19th- and 20th-century poetry—by men and by women. Although many of the poems come from the US and Great Britain, particularly illumi-nating are Pratt's discussions of Canadian poems influenced by landscape and environment in ways that American and British poetry usually is not. Moreover, Pratt distinguishes the angles, approaches, and tones in poems by men and those by women, men more likely to view Medusa, Aphrodite, and Artemis in tra-ditional, partriarchal, fearful, or unpleasant ways, whereas women poets (often, though not always) view the three goddesses as sources of empowerment. On the whole, Pratt rejects Jung's notion of fixed archetypes and allows the many-sided goddesses to find expression in extraordinary images and forms. An excel-lent study for students of myth, of modern literature, and of criticism (especially psychological, archetypal, and biographical criticism). Substantial bibliogra-phy. Upper-division undergraduate and up.—*S. B. Darrell, University of Southern Indiana*

OAB-0558 BS535 95-21587 CIP

Prickett, Stephen. **Origins of narrative: the romantic appropria-tion of the Bible.** Cambridge, 1996. 288p bibl index afp ISBN 0-521-44543-4, $54.95

The Bible has long been considered the foundation text of Western civi-lization. For believers it is the necessary document testifying to the divine pres-ence in human history, a transcription of the human quest for meaning. For crit-ics of culture such as Prickett (Univ. of Glasgow, UK), the Bible is the most important single book in the history of the world, a distinction that derives less from the Bible's religious significance than from its serving as metatype— the kind of book that helped to establish the very idea of what a book is and the interpretive method required to read it. Prickett demonstrates convinc-ingly that it was the English and continental Romantics who conceived the Bible as the essential work informing literary and cultural discourse; thus, at the very time that religious observance was seriously declining, the Bible gained enormous prestige as the book that shaped the conception of narrative art. From it one learned that a single volume could comprise diverse and seem-ingly unrelated tales, and that the core of meaning resides in the relationship among disparate parts; that the history of the Bible, a history of the appropria-tion of scenes and events from earlier traditions or the fables of surrounding peo-ples, pointed toward a theory of literature based on layers of appropriation. Prichett presents a detailed exposition of the ideas of writers, theologians, and philosophers—Coleridge, Austen, Chateaubriand, Goethe, Kant, Schlegel. He concludes with an impressive examination of Thomas Mann's fiction. An original and erudite contribution to cultural studies, which will occupy a posi-tion of equal importance to the author's previous work.—*M. Butovsky, Con-cordia University*

OAB-0559 PN241 93-20439 CIP

Raffel, Burton. **The art of translating prose.** Pennsylvania, 1994. 169p index afp ISBN 0-271-01080-0, $29.95

This genial demonstration continues Raffel's successfully delicate bal-ance between the claims of the source language literature and the target language audience. His earlier comments on his own practice in *The Forked Tongue* (1971) and *The Art of Translating Poetry* (CH, Apr'89) showed the same convincing conceptualizing of personal practice. Raffel, noted for his translations of canon-ical works (e.g., *Gargantua and Pantagruel*, *Père Goriot*, and a forthcoming *Don Quixote*), believes that many translators of literary prose err in assuming that semantic equivalence will suffice, when the author's syntax may well be more important than his lexicon. (Raffel considers no women authors, although he does cite women translators.) His chapters on "Famous and Infamous Translations" take up the attempts to get *Madame Bovary*, the *Decameron, Dona Perfecta*, St. Augustine's *Confessions, La Cousine Bette, Illusions perdues, Germinal*, and *À la recherche du temps perdu* into English. As he indicates in many a witty aside, it is impossible for a translation not to go awry somewhere. He devotes the second half of his book to his own decision making in translating Rabelais and Cervantes and admits that anyone offering a retranslation is making an "egocentric" claim. If it is egocentrism, it is firmly grounded on erudition and talent. Upper-division undergraduate through professional.—*M. Gaddis Rose, Binghamton State University*

OAB-0560   PN721   94-34553 CIP
Rebhorn, Wayne A. **The emperor of men's minds: literature and the Renaissance discourse of rhetoric.** Cornell, 1995. 276p bibl index afp ISBN 0-8014-2562-X, $35.00

Rebhorn (Univ. of Texas) here examines treatises on rhetoric in at least five languages from the 15th to the 17th centuries with a view to determining the self-image of the Renaissance rhetorician. The conclusion he reaches is not surprising in the mid-1990s: "Renaissance rhetoricians conceive their art in political terms as a matter of power and control, not debate and dialogue ... they identify orators as absolute kings and emperors." Rebhorn interprets this exalted self-image as a compensatory fantasy for the authors, the vast majority of whom came from middling social positions. The great service Rebhorn provides comes not in his New Historicist thesis but in the details of its presentation. He offers wonderfully useful analytic catalogs of the words, images, and allusions the rhetoric texts employ to characterize their art and provides an abundance of rich, inadequately known material for literary critics, historians, and indeed for all students of early modern England and Europe. Rebhorn's welcome study is likely to be much consulted, much cited for years to come. Definitely recommended for upper-division undergraduate and graduate collections.—*E. D. Hill, Mount Holyoke College*

OAB-0561   PN56   94-49531 CIP
Rennie, Neil. **Far-fetched facts: the literature of travel and the idea of the South Seas.** Oxford, 1996 (c1995). 330p bibl index afp ISBN 0-19-811975-5, $55.00

A work of exhaustive scholarship, this comprehensive account of the history of Western travel literature is a required holding for every humanities library. Through close readings of travel accounts—factual and imaginary—from biblical times to the early 20th century, Rennie (University College of London) advances the idea that Western civilization has clung immemorially to the theme of a lost Elysian paradise, an isolated reality existing somewhere in the physical world. Further, the author contends that from the time of Marco Polo's journeys, published accounts of real geographic discovery began reflecting popular assumptions of such "blessed isles." Rennie demonstrates that the reports of Columbus and other New World explorers support the argument that one discovers what one has been conditioned to discover within conventional parameters of myth and experience. The West's intoxication with the South Seas came a result of voluptuous tales brought back from Tahiti in 1769 by James Cook and Joseph Banks. Their sensational accounts of life "lived in a state of nature" appealed to the deepest romantic strains of European civilization, and Rennie cites the many literary works that have since reflected the infatuation with and puritanical gorging of this unearthly paradise, so quickly found and lost again. Highly recommended.—*T. Carolan, Kingston College*

OAB-0562   PN49   95-50366 CIP
Turner, Mark. **The literary mind.** Oxford, 1996. 187p bibl index afp ISBN 0-19-510411-0, $25.00

A literary scholar trained also in theoretical linguistics and cognitive science, Turner (Univ. of Maryland) provides a deeply thoughtful meditation on the impulse "to story" and "to parable"—i.e., to find meaning in experience by narrating it. Similar arguments have been mounted by "dra-

maturgical sociologists" such as Erving Goffman, and by historically minded philosophers like Alasdair MacIntyre; Turner goes beyond these thinkers in arguing that "narrativization" is fundamental to rationality itself, indeed that it precedes and shapes (rather than, as linguists such as Chomsky argue, being shaped by) grammar and the impulse to language. Among this book's greatest strengths are its detailed discussions of both visual and verbal examples, drawn from Proust and the *Thousand and One Nights*; news articles; familiar iconology (such as pictures of the Grim Reaper); and of how narrative processes that might be thought merely "literary" are essential to ordinary processes of constructing a sense of location in space and time. Throughout, Turner manages his complex argument in clear, fluent prose entirely accessible to undergraduate as well as more advanced readers.—*D. L. Patey, Smith College*

OAB-0563   PN56   95-31562 CIP
Watt, Ian. **Myths of modern individualism: Faust, Don Quixote, Don Juan, Robinson Crusoe.** Cambridge, 1996. 293p index ISBN 0-521-48011-6, $27.95

Watt, author of one of the classic studies of English fiction, *The Rise of the Novel* (1957), examines four literary characters who have attained mythic status in Western culture. Three of the figures—Faust, Don Juan, and Don Quixote—appeared during the Reformation and Counter-Reformation, and their restless, searching individualism is punished—by mockery and failure for Quixote and by death and damnation for Faust and Don Juan. Yet despite their defiance of societal codes and their seemingly definitive punishment, the energy and appeal of their individualism transcended their condemnation by conventional morality and gave them an enduring fascination. In the case of Robinson Crusoe, a century later, the tension between code and the powerful appeal of the transgressor is even more marked: Crusoe's exile is explicitly portrayed as his punishment (for defying his father and abandoning his station in society), but readers have also found it to be his triumph. Watt notes that he is writing for a general audience rather than specialists, but his erudition and breadth of mind are fully evident as he traces these four figures from their origins through their transformations in the Romantic era to their most recent literary incarnations. (The Faust legend, for example, is followed from the earliest accounts through Marlowe and Goethe to Thomas Mann.) This is intellectual and literary history at its best. Recommended for all collections.—*K. P. Mulcahy, Rutgers, The State University of New Jersey, New Brunswick*

OAB-0564   PE1617   94-11247 CIP
Willinsky, John. **Empire of words: the reign of the OED.** Princeton, 1994. 258p bibl index afp ISBN 0-691-03719-1, $22.95

Alas—in these revisionist days even the almighty *OED* must submit itself to iconoclastic scrutiny. Yet why not? So vast an undertaking as the *OED* could not help being a product of its own culture and that culture's assumptions about language and (among other things) nationhood. But Willinsky (Univ. of British Columbia) is surely right to insist that "the principal reference work in the English language" should not "[move] into the 21st century while continuing to reflect Victorian standards in scholarship." Author of *The Well-Tempered Tongue* (CH, Jul'85) and *The Triumph of Literature/The Fate of Literacy* (1991), Willinsky clearly reveres the dictionary and the scholars who produced it, beginning with James Murray, its first editor; but that does not keep him from pointing out, thoughtfully and in impressively researched detail, its inevitable inconsistencies and omissions. He traces the dictionary's history from its inception in 1857 through the release of the first fascicle of definitions in 1884, its completion in 1928, the preparation of the *Supplement* from 1957 to 1986, and the issuing of the second edition in 1989. He closes as the dictionary's editors prepare to undertake the first real revision and urges that they reformulate the dictionary's Victorian editorial philosophy and continue recent trends that include fuller representation of world English and of women writers. All colleges and universities should have this book, and they should shelve it right beside their copy of the *OED*.—*C. B. Dodson, University of North Carolina at Wilmington*

OAB-0565   PS374   94-48821 CIP
Wirth-Nesher, Hana. **City codes: reading the modern urban novel.**
Cambridge, 1996. 244p bibl index ISBN 0-521-47314-4, $49.95

This informative study of the modern urban novel devotes a chapter each to representative texts by Isaac B. Singer, Amos Oz, Theodore Dreiser, Ralph Ellison, Henry James, Henry Roth, James Joyce, and Virginia Woolf. Wirth-Nesher (Tel-Aviv Univ.) argues against a monolithic view of this genre and shows how factors such as nationality, gender, class, and race produce different representations of the city in fiction. The book emphasizes the diversity of urban settings rather than more traditional considerations of character, plot, and theme. For Wirth-Nesher the historical, religious, artistic, and political differences between (to use one example) Singer's Warsaw and Joyce's Dublin account for the variety of narratives in urban fiction. She provides an excellent comparative analysis of various cityscapes, showing how they vary as they are experienced by expatriates, tourists, provincials, immigrants, women, and African Americans. Moreover, the author makes good use of other disciplines, especially the visual arts, to illustrate key aspects of the fiction. Necessary reading for anyone interested in the modern novel.—*T. P. Riggio, University of Connecticut*

OAB-0566   PN56   94-24666 CIP
Wu, Qingyun. **Female rule in Chinese and English literary utopias.**
Syracuse, 1995. 225p bibl index afp ISBN 0-8156-2623-1, $34.95

This cross-cultural study seeks "to transcend Eurocentrism in feminist utopian study" by engaging both Western and Eastern literary traditions. By "feminist," Wu does not necessarily mean something written by a woman: four of the eight texts considered are by men who situate strong female figures in utopian idylls (in two cases, with a "pre-feminist" slant). The texts best known to Western readers—Spenser's *The Faerie Queene*, Charlotte Perkins Gilman's *Herland* (1979), Ursula Le Guin's *The Dispossessed* (1974)—are thoughtfully discussed. However, it is their pairing with comparable Chinese utopias that provides a fresh reading of each. Of the four Chinese utopias considered, only one has an adequate recent English translation—Bai Hua's *Remote Country of Women* (1988; cotranslated by Wu and Thomas O. Beebee, CH, Jan'95)—and two have no English translation. However, Wu's jargon-free discussion makes all the books accessible to the attentive reader. A return to the matrilineal prehistory of Chinese culture recovers the goddess myths that led to figures like the women warrior, countering the stereotype that China has always and only oppressed its women with customs like foot binding. Wu's demonstration that feminist utopias dramatize the liberation of both genders from hierarchies of domination is a provocative contribution to gender studies. Recommended at the upper-division undergraduate level and above.—*M. J. Emery, Cottey College*

■ African & Middle Eastern

OAB-0567   PL8014   95-15523 CIP
Chapman, Michael. **Southern African literatures.** Longman, 1996. 533p bibl index ISBN 0-582-05307-2 pbk, $28.95

This deeply impressive book represents an ideal marriage of love and scholarship. During the 30 years Chapman (Univ. of Natal) has been studying the political history and literatures of southern Africa, he has acquired an unequaled body of knowledge. This study is marked by temperate judgment and respect for all cultures. More the social-political historian than the literary critic, the author is ideally suited to his undertaking, one in which the colonial past has constantly to be reinterpreted. Despite the vast scope of the book—literatures in a number of African languages as well as in English, Afrikaans, and Portuguese are analyzed—the scholarship is consistently thorough. The 30-page chronological table of literature and historical-cultural events in southern Africa provides invaluable background for Chapman's analyses. A general bibliography focuses on southern African languages and literatures, and another cites biographies and chief works of individual authors. An indispensable volume recommended for all academic collections.—*J. B. Beston, Nazareth College of Rochester*

OAB-0568   PN23448   96-11601 CIP
Cooke, Miriam. **Women and the war story.** California, 1996. 367p bibl index afp ISBN 0-520-20612-6, $50.00; ISBN 0-520-20613-4 pbk, $18.95

Taking up where her *War's Other Voices: Women Writers on the Lebanese Civil War* (CH, Jul'88) left off, Cooke (Duke Univ.) expands on her thesis that women tell The War Story (as she nominalizes the concept) differently than men, and that by their very presence in the process of war, women have completely changed the understanding of what war means. Her approach is cultural and narrative; she discusses how the world should view what she contends are now only postcolonial wars and how one must move beyond narrowly defined masculine pursuits and read war and the telling of war as a gendered concept. The literary focus is on the writings of Algerian, Lebanese, Palestinian, and Iraqi women, populations traditionally silent and often mythically portrayed by male writers as having nothing to do with war. By writing as they do, creating a new space for women's voices, these women work toward social transformation, toward the "possibility of constructing a discourse that unsettles identities." Like Cooke's earlier book, this is a radical study, opening up a new field and a new perspective in war literature. Highly recommended for upper-division and higher; essential for women's studies collections.—*B. Adler, Valdosta State University*

OAB-0569   PJ5030   95-2681 CIP
Domb, Risa. **Home thoughts from abroad: distant visions of Israel in contemporary Hebrew fiction.** Vallentine Mitchell, 1995. 125p bibl index ISBN 0-85303-303-X, $29.50

The establishment of the State of Israel in 1948 was the culmination of waves of European Jewish immigrants who for more than a century had determined that only a revitalized existence in their own land could promise national survival. The first generation of Israeli writers was concerned mainly with nation building—military conflicts, class and ethnic tensions, social organization. In recent decades, writers have increasingly explored the complex relationship between Israel and Europe, conceiving Europe as a source of Jewish identity, a distant yet integral part of the Israeli self. In this illuminating study, Domb (Univ. of Cambridge) examines the fiction of six writers who (in a striking revision of Henry James's "international theme") dramatize the action of Israeli protagonists whose travels abroad result in a radical understanding of themselves and their world. Leaving home, they cross boundaries into other places that reflexively insist on the inescapability of home. Domb elaborates on the metaphor of travel within the Israeli context in her lucid introduction, then proceeds to a close reading of fictions by her selected leading novelists: Yaakov Shabtai, A.B. Yehoshua, Ruth Almog, Benjamin Tammuz, Shlomo Nizan, and Yehuda Amichai. Her explications are insightful and convincing. Nuanced readings avoid a dogmatic insistence on the underlying thesis. A valuable discourse for students of contemporary literature, Jewish studies, and Middle East studies, upper-division undergraduate and above.—*M. Butovsky, Concordia University*

OAB-0570   PJ7846   92-28677 CIP
El-Enany, Rasheed. **Naguib Mahfouz: the pursuit of meaning.**
Routledge, 1993. 271p index ISBN 0-415-02286-X, $62.50; ISBN 0-415-07395-2 pbk, $16.95

Competently researched, logically organized, and elegantly written, this book is a comprehensive presentation of the artistic development of Naguib Mahfouz and of his oeuvre. This volume is one in the series "Arabic Thought and Culture" and the first to deal with belles lettres. Among similar works, it shines brilliantly, being written by a specialist who reads, understands, and feels the ideas he experiences, analyzes them, and renders his opinion of them in a clear, precise, expressive, and elegant English. The book contains eight essays on Mahfouz's early social, political, and intellectual development and on the totality of his creative writings, from *The Game of Fate* (1939) to *The False Dawn* (1989). Although the first Arab novelist to be recognized by the Nobel Committee, Mahfouz is one of a few Arab artists whose work is being slowly integrated in the universal world of arts. Both the author and the publishers are to be congratulated for giving the general reader, the student, and the teacher of literature this indispensable tool for the understanding and enjoyment of Mahfouz's admirable writings.—*K. I. H. Semaan, SUNY at Binghamton*

OAB-0571   PL8010   94-16121 CIP
The gong and the flute: African literary development and celebration, ed. by Kalu Ogbaa. Greenwood, 1994. 203p index afp (Contributions in Afro-American and African studies, 173) ISBN 0-313-29281-7, $49.95

This book is a collection of essays by 11 prominent Nigerian literary scholars, including Ernest Emenyonu and Isidore Okpesho, concerning the works of a wide range of Nigerian authors. It includes well-known writers such as Chinua Achebe and Wole Soyinka, as well as a number of lesser-known writers, including several who write only in Nigerian languages. Its articles emphasize contemporary prose and drama, and introduce the reader to a number of important issues reaching beyond Nigeria to embrace much of African literature today. It offers insights into such diverse themes as the connections between oral literature (orature) and written literature, Yoruba symbolism in Soyinka's poetry, the portrayal of the theme of victimization in African novels and plays, and the development of African language writing. In separate articles it suggests, among other things, how European colonial manners and values are reflected in Joyce Cary's *Mister Johnson* (1939), the parallels between the "absurd" works of Soyinka, Rotimi, Ionesco, and Beckett, the need to give direction and definition to Igbo-language writing, and the cultural continuity of Achebe's novels. This book has more than a little for anyone with some background in African literature, and a lot for those with considerable background. General; undergraduate and up.—*C. Pike, University of Minnesota*

OAB-0572   PJ5129   96-28593 CIP
Hadda, Janet. **Isaac Bashevis Singer: a life.** Oxford, 1997. 243p index afp ISBN 0-19-508420-9, $27.50

Hadda's biography differs in two important ways from previous accounts, including Paul Kresh's *Isaac Bashevis Singer: The Magician of West 86th Street* (CH, Mar'80). First, as an expert in Yiddish literature, Hadda (UCLA) can place Singer's writing in its full literary context. For instance, she shows the difference in manner and substance between his writing for an American audience and his work for readers of *Forverts* (1919-51). Second, she is able to speculate on Singer's psychology in a way that was not possible while he lived. Singer emerges as a more complex man than the kindly, comically naive figure he invented. Hadda deftly explores the literary implications of Singer's major life crises, including his disturbed relationship to his parents and siblings, particularly his brother Israel Joshua Singer; his early, often depressing struggles to write; his ambivalent relations with women; his response to the Holocaust. Hadda manages to treat such issues honestly without losing sympathy for her subject. This is a model of interpretive biography, a study that probes the underside of the immigrant Nobel laureate, who re-created himself as the genial Jewish grandfather of American letters. All collections.—*T. P. Riggio, University of Connecticut*

OAB-0573   PJ7694   94-49178 CIP
Modern Arabic drama: an anthology, ed. by Salma Khadra Jayyusi and Roger Allen. Indiana, 1995. 416p afp ISBN 0-253-32897-7, $57.50; ISBN 0-253-20973-0 pbk, $24.95

This anthology of English translations of modern Arabic drama maintains the consistently high scholarly and literary standards set by previous volumes

in the "Indiana Series in Arab and Islamic Studies." As the editors' preface and M.M. Badawi's introduction point out, modern Arabic drama has both a long tradition within related historical Arab forms and an immediate relationship to contemporary European influences in the late-19th and early-20th centuries. The 12 plays presented here, in exemplary translations, exhibit the ways in which those several contexts have contributed to the genre. The editors acknowledge the significance of Egypt as a dramatic center, but they include plays and unpublished scenarios from across the Arab world—Syria, Lebanon, Palestine, Iraq, and Kuwait. And the work of playwrights and theatrical companies, from the now canonical Salah 'Abd al-Sabur to the Palestinian troupe Balalin, are included in the collection. A dynamically important asset for the study of theater and drama, modern literature, the Middle East, and comparative literature, this volume is recommended for all academic libraries.—*B. Harlow, University of Texas at Austin*

OAB-0574   PR9387   95-26721 CIP
Richards, Sandra L. **Ancient songs set ablaze: the theatre of Femi Osofisan.** Howard University, 1996. 210p bibl index afp ISBN 0-88258-109-0, $29.95

Much current literature in English addresses as primary audience a society in which other languages predominate. Therefore, Richards's multifaceted approach to the works of Osofisan, "the Bertholt Brecht of Nigeria," has general implications for literature, especially theater in social context. Osofisan's plays and essays are particularly revealing because of his erudition, his panoply of dramatic strategies, his protean styles and abiding popularity, and his commitment to "progressive social change." In these respects he requires more attention than his Nobel laureate countryman, Wole Soyinka. Richards (Northwestern Univ.)—actor, director, and scholar with extensive experience in Nigeria—considers every aspect of theatrical meaning, including adaptation of traditional and competing theatrical forms in other Nigerian languages, especially Yoruba; use of traditional genres such as the dilemma tale; the inevitable and the deliberate modulations between Yoruba and Western cosmologies (with, for example, their implication for characterization, plot developments, and audiences' construction of meaning); the nexus of political belief, moral intent, and theatrical form with the variable roles of audience; and even theatrical production for alien audiences. Her conclusions are invaluable for anyone interested in contemporary theater, African literature, or postmodern literary theory. General readers, graduate students, and up.—*D. F. Dorsey, Clark Atlanta University*

OAB-0575   PJ5124   94-45963 CIP
Roskies, David G. **A bridge of longing: the lost art of Yiddish storytelling.** Harvard, 1995. 419p index ISBN 0-674-08139-0, $37.50

As teacher, scholar, editor, and writer, Roskies (Jewish Theological Seminary of America) has gained a reputation as a central figure among those at work in the field of modern Yiddish culture. That reputation will be enhanced with the publication of this excellent study of the cultural dynamics that determined the shape of Yiddish literature. Roskies's main thesis is that Yiddish writers of the 19th and 20th centuries reinvented "folk" art in order to express the complex relationship between their modernistic impulses and the traditional societies that served as their subject and audience. These writers practiced a form of "creative betrayal": they had already distanced themselves from the life of the folk yet recast themselves (or their narrators) in order to communicate in the grammar of the traditional life they had abandoned. Their works—novels, stories, lullabies, love songs, workers' and soldiers' songs—became immensely popular and were looked on as authentically historical instead of as the creations of sophisticated modernists. Roskies traces this self-conscious artistic determination from the pietistic narratives of Nahman of Bratslav and includes incisive chapters on I.M. Dik, I.L. Peretz, Sholem Aleichem, Der Nister, Itzik Manger, and Isaac Bashevis Singer. This thoroughly rewarding study, written with grace and wit, will enrich studies in Jewish and ethnic literature, comparative literature, narratology, and cultural criticism. Upper-division undergraduate and above.—*M. Butovsky, Concordia University*

OAB-0576   PJ4545   93-20367 CIP
Sáenz-Badillos, Angel. **A history of the Hebrew language,** by Angel Sáenz-Badillos; tr. by John Elwolde. Cambridge, 1994 (c1993). 371p bibl index ISBN 0-521-43157-3, $39.95

The revival of the Hebrew language is one of the great linguistic achievements of modern times. Sáenz-Badillos's chapters, eloquently translated from the original Spanish by John Elwolde (Univ. of Sheffield) help explain why. There is a lot to praise about this volume. The eight chapters and 37 subdivisions overflow with information, mostly on linguistic topics such as phonology, morphology, syntax, and vocabulary. But there are sections as well on the epochs of Hebrew language and literature on and off the land of Israel, key shakers and brokers, and the effect on Hebrew from other languages. It is a one-stop, educated source for learning about the classification, unity, and diversity of Hebrew throughout its biblical and rabbinic history; comparative semitics; features of medieval belles lettres; contemporary Israeli Hebrew; and, in general, the interweaving of Hebrew in the diverse cultural history of the Jewish people. Another highlight is the author's respectful consultation and dialogue with the gamut of scholarship (there are 67 pages of bibliography) on special problems bearing on Hebrew language and literature. As testimony to his impeccable scholarship, Sáenz-Badillos's understanding of Hebrew is accurate and true. A thoughtful work, deceptively compact; an engrossing pacemaker all the way. Upper-division undergraduate; graduate; faculty.—*Z. Garber, Los Angeles Valley College*

OAB-0577   PJ5113   96-39172 CIP
Seidman, Naomi. **A marriage made in heaven: the sexual politics of Hebrew and Yiddish.** California, 1997. 160p index afp (Contra-versions, 7) ISBN 0-520-20193-0, $40.00

This intriguing analysis of the two languages of Ashkenazic Jewry—Hebrew and Yiddish—takes the reader through three disciplines: linguistics, cultural studies, and literary criticism. But at every turn the reader is educated in feminist theory uniquely applicable to this two-language culture. For centuries, these two languages have struggled for the attention of the Jewish people: Yiddish, "the mother's tongue" (*Mama-loschen*), spoken and read by women, a language without religious authority or respect for hundreds of years before it exploded late in the 19th century to produce a literature with a world standing and an eventual Nobel prize winner in I.B. Singer; and Hebrew, the holy tongue, spoken and written by men. This struggle gives Seidman's analysis of sexual politics and language its credibility. In chapter 1, the author traces the linguistic and sexual struggle of the two languages; in the middle two chapters she follows the gendering of Hebrew and Yiddish in the works of two bilingual writers, Mendele Mocher Sforim and Dvora Baron. In the final chapter she takes this linguistic "marriage" to the stage of "divorce," as the two languages dissolve their symbiosis at the end of the 20th century. Upper-division undergraduates through faculty.—*S. Gittleman, Tufts University*

OAB-0578   BL1685   96-12390 CIP
Stetkevych, Jaroslav. **Muḥammad and the golden bough: reconstructing Arabian myth.** Indiana, 1996. 169p bibl index afp ISBN 0-253-33208-7, $39.95

Until now Arabian myth has been ignored at the same time that other ancient Near Eastern myths have been studied at length. Stetkevych (Univ. of Chicago) succeeds brilliantly in reconstructing the myth of the destruction of the Thamud, an ancient people of north Arabia. His key to this myth is a canonical story of the discovery by the prophet Muhammad of a golden bough at the very site where the Thamud are thought to have been destroyed by a scourge from God. Through careful philological, historical, and literary analysis he sets the story of this golden bough in an ever-widening context of myth and legend, reaching back to *Gilgamesh*, the Bible, the *Odyssey*, and the *Aeneid*. James Frazer's *The Golden Bough* (1890-1915) is examined and reevaluated in the light of the other "golden bough" myths. Stetkevych's argument for the existence of an autochthonous Arabian myth is entirely convincing, and this book will add a new dimension to the study of Near East-

ern and Mediterranean myth and legend. Highly recommended for collections in folklore and mythology, ancient Near Eastern studies, and Islam.—*W. L. Hanaway, emeritus, University of Pennsylvania*

OAB-0579   PJ7525   94-1007 CIP
Zeidan, Joseph T. **Arab women novelists: the formative years and beyond.** State University of New York, 1995. 363p bibl index afp ISBN 0-7914-2171-6, $74.50

This invaluable book presents for the first time, in any language, the variety and energy of Arab women novelists. Zeidan (Ohio State Univ.) builds on his Arabic-language bibliography (1986) of almost 500 Arab women writers who have published during the 20th century. Though touching on the writings of dozens of novelists, the author has summarized and analyzed at length the work of 11 novelists. He divides progress in the development of Arab women's literary interests into three stages: members of the Pioneering Generation, active until the late 1940s, whose "apologetic and hesitant" novels dealt with historical themes or described social problems outside their cultures; the "Quest for Personal Identity" stage (the 1950s and 1960s) encompasses women who wrote about their frustrated searches for self-fulfillment in a harsh society; and, last, novelists in search of national identity. Zeidan highlights the Palestinian question and the Lebanese civil war. The book ends with a chronological listing of Arab women's journals. Despite some misgivings about the totalizing framework, this reviewer applauds the scope of Zeidan's book and his clear commitment. A must for all libraries with Middle Eastern, women's studies, and non-Western literature collections.—*M. Cooke, Duke University*

■ Asian & Oceanian

OAB-0580   PL4378   94-22390 CIP
Bao Ninh. **The sorrow of war: a novel of North Vietnam,** by Bao Ninh; tr. by Phan Thanh Hao; ed. by Frank Palmos. Pantheon Books, 1995 (c1993). 233p ISBN 0-679-43961-7, $21.00

This novel joins a very small group of works of literature about the Vietnam War: those written from the perspective of the North, the side of the Other. The author's note says Bao Ninh "served with the Glorious 27th Youth Brigade. Of the five hundred who went to war with the Brigade ... he is one of ten who survived." This is the compelling story of Kien, as he negotiates the war and its aftermath, viewing the wreckage of 30 years of brutality on his people, his loves, and himself. The novel's progress repeatedly corkscrews back to April 30, 1975, the day the war officially ended, with the author's insights into the burdens and the hauntings victory brings. Kien says, "Since returning to Hanoi, I've had to live with this parade of horrific memories, day after day, long night after long night. For how many years now?" The novel has the force and realism of Remarque's writing while displaying metafictional characteristics similar to Tim O'Brien's works. Sensitive, dramatic, and revealing, full of poetry, pathos, and a deep sense of tragedy and loss, this war novel will, in this reviewer's opinion, be seen in time as a classic. Highly recommended for all levels.—*B. Adler, Valdosta State College*

OAB-0581   PL788   96-25663 CIP
Bargen, Doris G. **A woman's weapon: spirit possession in *The tale of Genji*.** Hawaii, 1997. 379p bibl index afp ISBN 0-8248-1801-6, $50.00

Bargen (Univ. of Massachusetts) provocatively argues that five cases of spirit possession in this famous classical narrative are manipulative efforts orchestrated by the possessed, in which possessing spirits are summoned to function as allies. In a culture in which women were relatively powerless, spirit possession was one way they might forcefully and safely air their grievances. This radically new view contrasts starkly with traditional assessments that treat the possessed women as passive, innocent victims of malicious mischief wreaked by the possessing spirit. Unfortunately for the women resorting to this extreme measure, not only scholars through the centuries have mistaken these

Humanities

voices, the work's other characters also failed to heed their cries. Spirit possession may have been an ineffectual weapon, but Bargen makes a powerful argument nevertheless. A significant addition to the still-small body of English-language scholarship dedicated to *The Tale of Genji*. Upper-division undergraduate and up.—*M. H. Childs, University of Kansas*

OAB-0582   PL2658   93-48174 CIP
The Columbia anthology of traditional Chinese literature, ed. by Victor H. Mair. Columbia, 1995 (c1994). 1,335p bibl afp ISBN 0-231-07428-X, $65.00

Like its recently published companion, *The Columbia Anthology of Modern Chinese Literature*, ed. by Joseph S.M. Lau and Howard Goldblatt (CH, Nov'95), this work sets a new standard in comprehensive coverage of all major genres, with translations by 109 of the best-known and most competent Chinese literature translators of the 20th century. Its historical reach covers all periods from the 12th century BCE to the 19th century CE, with works included from the well-known authors and anonymous folk of each era. One of the many strengths of this anthology is that it covers not only the standard literary genres of poetry, essays, drama, and fiction but several others less known in the West, yet very important for a fuller understanding of what literature has meant to Chinese people over the millennia: divinations and inscriptions; literary criticism and theory; moral lessons; prefaces and postfaces; sketches and travelogues; biographies and autobiographies; oral and performing arts. Together with *The Indiana Companion to Traditional Chinese Literature*, comp. and ed. by William H. Nienhauser (CH, Jul'86), it is a work of fundamental importance in its field. All academic collections.—*J. W. Walls, Simon Fraser University*

OAB-0583   PK5416   95-20938 CIP
Handbook of twentieth-century literatures of India, ed. by Nalini Natarajan. Greenwood, 1996. 440p bibl index afp ISBN 0-313-28778-3, $85.00

The Indian press played a vital role in colonial India, and by the close of the 19th century it was virtually an irresistible force. Indian literature comprises the religious and secular; epic, dramatic, and didactic poetry; narrative; and scientific prose. India's National Academy of Letters recognizes some 22 major languages. Natarajan has collected papers that discuss literature in selected languages (Assamese, Bengali, English, Gujarati, Hindi, Kannada, Malayalam, Marathi, Panjabi, Tamil, Telugu, and Urdu); in addition he devotes individual chapters to Dalit literature in Marathi, Parsi literature in English, Sanskrit poetics, and Bengali film and literature. Each essay contains a short, useful bibliography. A very well-written and researched introduction provides a bird's-eye view of the whole scene. Contributors represent a variety of disciplines—language, translation, creative writing, political science, philosophy, film, and sociology—and the essays a variety of ideological approaches, both analytical and empirical in nature. This volume joins a number of publications on Indian literature in various languages, including the authoritative six-volume *Encyclopaedia of Indian literature*, ed. by Amaresh Datta (1987- ; v.1, CH, Apr'89, v.2, Nov'89). Beautifully printed and bound, though costly, this will be a valuable addition to the collections of college and university libraries supporting South Asian studies and of large public libraries.—*O. P. Sharma, University of Michigan*

OAB-0584   PL2698   92-45054 Orig
Hsiao-hsiao-sheng. **The plum in the golden vase, or, Chin P'ing Mei: v.1: The gathering,** tr. by David Tod Roy. Princeton, 1993. 610p bibl index afp ISBN 0-691-06932-8, $39.95

The first of five projected volumes of David Tod Roy's long-awaited translation of the famous 16th-century erotic novel *Chin P'ing Mei*. Certainly best known for the graphic portrayal of its protagonist Hsi-men Ch'ing's seemingly inexhaustible sexual appetite and adventures, *The Plum in the Golden Vase* plays a landmark role in the development of the Chinese novel, not only because of its (anonymous) author's innovative narrative style and

use of surprisingly modern rhetorical devices, but also because *Chin P'ing Mei* inspired and served as a model for China's greatest work, *Dream of the Red Chamber* (or *Story of the Stone*). Since all previous European-language translations of *The Plum in the Golden Vase* (now out of print) either are abridged or follow an incomplete version of the text, this effort by Roy (Univ. of Chicago) to produce a complete translation of *Chin P'ing Mei* (based on the earliest, most complete text available) deserves special commendation. Moreover, the high scholarly quality, exceptional degree of faithfulness to the original language, and overall readability of the translator's first volume make this and subsequent installments essential reading for all students of Chinese literature. Highly recommended. Undergraduate; graduate; faculty; general.—*J. M. Hargett, SUNY at Albany*

OAB-0585   PL2271   96-42978 CIP
Idema, Wilt. **A guide to Chinese literature,** by Wilt Idema and Lloyd Haft. University of Michigan, Center for Chinese Studies, 1997. 473p bibl index afp (Michigan monographs in Chinese studies, 74) ISBN 0-89264-099-5, $50.00; ISBN 0-89264-123-1 pbk, $25.00

This volume's introductory chapters, a chronological overview of traditions, genres, and authors, comprise an invaluable organizing tool for the student of Chinese literature. Part 1, which discusses the emphasis in Chinese literature on historical "records" exemplifying virtuous actions and correct behavior in an ordered society, is a useful foundation for the bibliographic material that follows. Part 2 elucidates Chinese literary genres, which do not correspond precisely to those of Western literature. The book's comprehensive coverage of China's vast body of literature, divided by genre and historical period, and the accompanying bibliographies for each section, are indispensable for any institution teaching courses on China. The genres—history, philosophy, poetry, ancient prose, drama, the novel, the novella, and modern literature—are subdivided by author and contain critical summaries of major pieces. The annotated bibliographies for each genre (located somewhat inconveniently at the end of the volume) include translations, background reading, and critical studies. This volume admirably fulfills its stated purpose of guiding both the casual and more scholarly reader through thousands of years of Chinese letters. Consulting it will save hours of random searching even for the more advanced researcher in the field. All collections.—*J. Gregg, CUNY, New York City Technical College*

OAB-0586   PL4328   95-20959 CIP
Jacob, Judith M. **The traditional literature of Cambodia: a preliminary guide.** Oxford, 1996. 282p bibl index afp (London Oriental series, 40) ISBN 0-19-713612-5, $52.00

Oxford's "London Oriental Series" has long represented the summa cum laude of Asian studies in philology, classical literatures, history, and religion. Its exotic, esoteric, and worthy titles have been quintessentially academic. Happily, this pathbreaking study of the traditional literature of Cambodia is proof that sound scholarship need not be dreary. In simple declarative sentences, Jacob (Univ. of London) walks the reader through the history of this little-known literature, introducing its ten classical genres and their historical and religious roots. Rules of versification and poetics are economically presented, and a scholarly index to authors and works is provided. Similar to J. Thomas Rimer's excellent *A Reader's Guide to Japanese Literature* (CH, Mar'89), this book also offers insightful summaries of the folktales and narrative poems, chiefly Buddhist in origin, that form the canon of Cambodian letters. An impressively humble guide certain to prove invaluable as Western experience with Asia grows exponentially, this is a must addition to every serious Asian literary collection. It is a template for what should become a series of guides to Asia's national literatures.—*T. Carolan, Kingston College*

OAB-0587   PL726   93-1082 CIP
Keene, Donald. **Seeds in the heart: Japanese literature from earliest times to the late sixteenth century.** H. Holt, 1993. 1,265p index afp ISBN 0-8050-1999-5, $50.00

Distinguished as translator, interpreter, and teacher, Keene (Columbia) is widely considered foremost among scholars of Japanese literature in the West. This volume completes his massive history of Japanese literature. (Previously published: *World Within Walls*, CH, Nov'77, on the period 1600-1867, and *Dawn to the West*, CH, Jul'84, on the modern era.) As with the other volumes, its approach is extremely comprehensive; along with the more usual works and genres, it examines, for example, such lesser-known topics as "Late-Heian Poetry and Prose in Chinese" and "Courtly Fiction of the Kamakura Period." Particularly valuable are Keene's accounts of a variety of theories and opinions in Japanese secondary sources in regard to works under discussion. As always, his writing is clear and agreeable, so that the book is accessible to the general reader as well as the specialist, unlike Jin'ichi Konishi's similar multivolume history of Japanese literature (still in progress), which is difficult reading even for scholars. Where Konishi labors to open new theoretical paths, Keene assumes the existence of such identifiable, universally acknowledged qualities as "literary interest" and "literary value." Copious, but still incomplete, bibliographies; informative notes; index. A "must" for all academic libraries; also recommended for large public libraries.—*M. Ury, University of California, Davis*

OAB-0588 PL787 93-10237 CIP
Kim, Yung-Hee. **Songs to make the dust dance: the Ryōjin hishō of twelfth-century Japan.** California, 1994. 222p bibl indexes afp ISBN 0-520-08066-1, $37.50

There are very few resources for the study of popular culture in the Heian period, 794-1185. Thus, this study of *imayo*, songs of plebeian female entertainers, commands our attention. It offers a new vista into Heian society. Yung-Hee Kim's introductory chapters provide a historical context for the collection's compiler, Emperor Go Shirakawa, and the tradition of female entertainers in Japan. The selected translations are embedded in chapters describing poetic forms and techniques, religion, and Heian society as revealed in the songs. The translations are accurate and poetic, but it is the author's commentary that really makes the texts come alive. Since these texts were meant to be sung, the commentaries are essential to help the reader reconstruct something of the original performance experience and to point out subtleties and hidden meanings that are easily overlooked. Kim's commentaries are deft and to the point. The notes and bibliography are of the high standard one would expect. This well-balanced and engagingly written volume will be an asset as a supplementary text for survey courses in Japanese literature or history. Anyone interested in popular culture in the ancient world will find this text informative.—*S. Arntzen, University of Alberta*

OAB-0589 PL2665 94-39652 CIP
Kwong, Charles Yim-tze. **Tao Qian and the Chinese poetic tradition: the quest for cultural identity.** University of Michigan, Center for Chinese Studies, 1995 (c1994). 281p bibl index afp (Michigan monographs in Chinese studies, 66) ISBN 0-89264-108-8, $40.00; ISBN 0-89264-109-6 pbk, $20.00

Tao Qian (CE 365-427) is one of the best known poets of medieval China and one of the greatest poets of the post-Han, pre-Tang period. Kwong (Tufts Univ.) has previously published articles in the periodical *Chinese Literature: Essays, Articles, Reviews.* The current study (with its 37 pages of notes) opens with the observation that poetry is art embedded in history and culture. The ensuing 11 chapters and epilogue go on to examine the historical background and qualities of Tao's poetry that have caused him to be regarded as the founder of "farmstead poetry" in China. Kwong considers Tao's worldview and lifestyle ideals in the context of the Daoist and Confucianist value systems, and he examines the political and economic realities that characterized Tao's era. He goes on to show how Tao achieved admirable, elegantly unified verse style, lifestyle, and worldview. Kwong's many enlightening comparisons and contrasts between Chinese and Western visions of pastoral life make this a very important, interesting, solid piece of socioliterary criticism. Upper-division undergraduate and above.—*J. W. Walls, Simon Fraser University*

OAB-0590 HQ18 94-33072 CIP
McMahon, Keith. **Misers, shrews, and polygamists: sexuality and male-female relations in eighteenth-century Chinese fiction.** Duke University, 1995. 378p bibl index afp ISBN 0-8223-1555-6, $49.95; ISBN 0-8223-1566-1 pbk, $19.95·

It is a pleasant surprise to find a literary study from this press that closely analyzes primary source materials rather than soaring in an ethereal theoretical realm. A continuation of his *Causality and Containment in Seventeenth-Century Fiction* (1988), McMahon's book opens a new field of study through its investigation of how the issues of polygamy and sexuality are treated in Chinese fiction. The book also introduces to the English reader many lesser-known novels from the mid-17th to the mid-19th centuries. After examining the representation of male and female sexual capacities in the *ars erotica*, McMahon (Univ. of Kansas) discusses important character types on the spectrum of sexual economy—misers, shrews, polygamists, and wastrels—revealing them as either conforming or subversive to the patriarchal system. The author analyzes the novels from the angle of whether they are constructed for or against polygamy, dividing them into the categories of erotic or nonerotic, and further according to depictions of relations as discordant or harmonious. He contrasts chaste scholar-beauty romances with erotic fiction, and goes on to examine literati novels in more detailed separate chapters. This original and insightful book is highly recommended for upper-division undergraduates, graduates, and faculty.—*Y. Wu, University of California, Riverside*

OAB-0591 PL2302 95-1269 CIP
Modern Chinese literary thought: writings on literature, 1893-1945, ed. by Kirk A. Denton. Stanford, 1996. 554p bibl index afp ISBN 0-8047-2558-6, $75.00; ISBN 0-8047-2559-4 pbk, $24.95

Most English-language books on modern Chinese literary criticism must be recommended with caution, if at all, since they often reflect the views and concerns of a single critic, a single school of thought, or a single set of priorities. They fail to reflect the full range of social, philosophical, and literary issues that characterize the rich discourse of the time. By contrast, this volume may be recommended as a comprehensive collection that helps readers understand the important cultural context of the literary texts produced in China in the first half of the 20th century. The 32 translators have produced smooth and accurate renderings of 55 essays, most of which are here anthologized for the first time in English. The editor contributes a major (61-page) general introduction to the entire historical period; shorter introductions to each of the five subsections; a very thorough and helpful glossary of names of Chinese historical figures, organizations, movements, journals, etc.; a comprehensive bibliography of English and Chinese resources; and a fairly thorough index. This is a fundamental reference work for the study of modern Chinese literature.—*J. W. Walls, Simon Fraser University*

OAB-0592 PL728 95-30185 MARC
Mostow, Joshua S. **Pictures of the heart: the *Hyakunin isshu* in word and image.** Hawaii, 1996. 522p bibl indexes afp English and Japanese. ISBN 0-8248-1705-2, $45.00

For the uninitiated, most Japanese poetry seems trivial or nonsensical. Even those acquainted with its general principles and conventions find much of it obscure. This book provides, for the first time in English, the kind of information that allows an accurate appreciation of the meanings and quality of Japanese poems. The poems in *Hyakunin Isshu* (*One Hundred Poets, One Poem Each*), a collection by Fujiwara Teika (1162-1241), are not easy for Westerners to appreciate, but they are widely known in Japan and are an excellent example of how poetry was integrated with politics, romance, folklore, history, and other fine arts including kimono design. Teika is shown to have considered the history of poetry, politics, family ties, and local allusions in choosing this set of poems first intended to decorate the walls of a villa. Mostow's reception-oriented approach in this poem-by-poem discussion inspires an excellent essay on the history of English translations of this collection, the first of which was done in 1866. He covers the work's almost

750-year history in Japan, using pictorializations of the poems to demonstrate varying interpretations. All academic and general collections of Asian literature.—*M. H. Childs, University of Kansas*

OAB-0593 PL5139 94-28337 MARC
Muhammad Haji Salleh. **Beyond the archipelago: selected poems.** Ohio University Center for International Studies, 1995. 243p afp (Monographs in international studies. Southeast Asia series, 93) English and Malaysian. ISBN 0-89680-181-0 pbk, $20.00

One of Asia's most consistently interesting poets, Haji Salleh is at last available to North American readers in this excellent bilingual edition of selected work. The poet himself has crafted these fine translations, which hold up well in English and offer much insight into the evolution of his own poetic voice and into the "shadow play" mystery of the Malay world. Overlaid with rich strands drawn from the region's archipelago culture, ancient Ramayana tales, Islamic refinement, and English and European lyric models, these taut, disciplined poems reveal Haji Salleh's own wide reading in addition to his mastery of traditional Malay literary forms. In the past, this poet has acknowledged the influence of Shakespeare and Auden, and it shows in the collection's tightest, most absorbing section, "Sejarah Melayu." A linked series of meditative reflections on a 16th-century Malayan epic, these poems meld the best of both Western and classic Malay literary skills in creating an impressive poetic tapestry of values, custom, and history that is at once uniquely Southeast Asian and genuinely international as literature. An essential addition to modern Asian and literary collections at all levels.—*T. Carolan, Kingston College*

OAB-0594 95-73165 Orig
Night, again: contemporary fiction from Vietnam, ed. by Linh Dinh. 7 Stories Press, 632 Broadway, 7th Floor, New York, NY 10012, 1996. 157p ISBN 1-888363-02-9, $25.00; ISBN 1-888363-07-X pbk, $12.95

With the exception of Bao Ninh's brilliant novel *The Sorrow of War* (English trans., CH, Jul'95) and *To Be Made Over*, Huynh Sanh Thông's anthology of social realist tales from Vietnam (1988), little translated contemporary literature has been available for many years from this once-flourishing literary nation. Linh Dinh shatters this stagnancy with this stunning collection. A dozen post-Indochina War stories that plumb everyday reality, *Night, Again* presents accounts of life in Vietnam's present rough-and-tumble period of economic liberalization, revealing a society's single-minded attempt to reroot itself in something like dignity and justice. As the celebrated international case of novelist Duong Thu Huong (whose work also appears here) has shown, the writer's lot in North and subsequently unified Vietnam has been Kafkaesque. This collecton laudably reveals the extent to which writers have been willing to criticize and experiment stylistically in the face of brutal authority. Not everything here ranks as first-rate: far from it. But several pieces demonstrate such unexpected power that they rank as world-class contributions. Nguyen Huy Thiep's "Without a King" in a strong translation is a complex modern family portrait with deep social and political reverberations. Duong Thu Huong's "Reflections of Spring" looks at the emotional cost of a successful bureaucrat's career. Pham Thi Hoai, now an emigré in Berlin, offers "Nine Down Makes Ten," an exquisite woman's meditation on romantic experience. A forceful and stunning compendium by a talented editor, *Night, Again* is unquestionably one of the finest literary entries in years from the new Asia and is essential for all modern Asia-Pacific collections.—*T. Carolan, Kingston College*

OAB-0595 PL5531 95-47191 CIP
San Juan, E. **The Philippine temptation: dialectics of Philippines-U.S. literary relations.** Temple University, 1996. 305p bibl index afp ISBN 1-56639-417-1, $54.95; ISBN 1-56639-418-X pbk, $19.95

English is one of the languages of literature and criticism in the multilingual Philippines and its diaspora. Filipino scholarship is considerable but has had little impact on American perceptions. Working from within American academia, San Juan (Bowling Green State Univ.) is one of the few Filipino scholars whose work has long challenged both conservative scholarship (whose euphemisms describe the century-old relationship between the Philippines and the US as a vexed tutelage followed by a troubled alliance) and liberal scholarship (which deploys a blissfully evasive vocabulary of postcolonial hybridity). In this book, the author discusses imperialism, wars of national liberation, decolonization, and the current transnational domination within which the texts he discusses emerged. His readings of Filipino writers—Carlos Bulosan, Philip Vera Cruz, and especially José García Villa—are an important contribution to the understanding of the transnational and diasporic features of Filipino writing, features that are not incidental to but constitutive of it. His discussion of Third World modernism joins Gregory Jusdanis' study of Greece, *Belated Modernity and Aesthetic Culture* (1991), as an important corrective to the narrow but academically dominant view of modernism as a transatlantic anglophone phenomenon. Strongly recommended for college libraries; essential for university libraries.—*K. Tölölyan, Wesleyan University*

OAB-0596 PL817 93-20845 CIP
Torrance, Richard. **The fiction of Tokuda Shūsei and the emergence of Japan's new middle class.** Washington, 1994. 268p bibl index afp ISBN 0-295-97296-3, $40.00

Torrance has done a great service to American readers by introducing them to Tokuda Shūsei, one of the many fine writers of Japan who has virtually no exposure in the US. Torrance's biocritical approach, verging at times on the conventional, is grounded in thorough research and careful intellectual argument. He presents a slice of Japanese history in its most tumultuous period, from the beginning of Japan's modernization/Westernization through the middle of the Pacific War, paralleling Tokuda's life as he strived to depict the ordinary life of common citizens. Rather than emphasize the exotic, unique, unusual elements of Japanese literature, Torrance presents the life and work of a writer whose passionate concerns were to set down on paper what he saw and witnessed in everyday life: typically his central metaphor was a woman struggling with her newly found social freedom. It is remarkable that Shūsei never romanticized the image of woman the way, for example, his contemporaries Tanizaki Junichiro or Kawabata Yasunari did, nor exploited it for his own therapeutic ends like Yukio Mishima. Torrance portrays a man whom Marxist writers accused of passivity and apoliticality, yet a man who treated women with respect, sympathy, and a generous dosage of equality—both in fiction and life—which we know was not quite the practice among Japanese Marxist intellectuals of Tokuda's days. Strongly recommended for undergraduate and graduate literature, sociology, and psychology courses, as well as to the general public.—*M. N. Wilson, University of Virginia*

OAB-0597 PL782 91-48074 MARC
A Waka anthology: v.1: The gem-glistening cup, tr., with a commentary and notes by Edwin A. Cranston. Stanford, 1993. 988p indexes afp ISBN 0-8047-1922-5, $95.00

Monumental in size and extraordinary in quality, this is the first volume of a projected four-volume anthology of Japanese *waka* (poems in the classical tradition) through the 16th century. The contents consist of about a third of the approximately 4,500 poems collected in *Man'yōshū* (751 CE), arguably not only the greatest Japanese anthology but the one with the broadest appeal, plus the entire corpus of early (pre-*Man'yōshū*) poetry. As a translator, Cranston (Harvard) is unexcelled, both in the uncompromising accuracy of his readings and in his sense of the weight and music of English words. His commentary, less unsystematic than may seem at first glance, is generous in every sense. Specialists and scholars will appreciate the inclusion of romanized originals of the poems, as well as translations of the prose that provides context for them, but the book offers treasures for poetry lovers at almost every level. (Unsophisticated readers, however, may have difficulty distinguishing Cranston's own comments from the translated ones.) A must for larger and academic libraries, although *Traditional Japanese Poetry*, tr. by Steven D. Carter (1991), can still be recommended, especially where budgets are very limited. Notes; extensive indexes. Advanced undergraduate; graduate.—*M. Ury, University of California, Davis*

OAB-0598   PL2722   92-9764 CIP
Zeitlin, Judith T. **Historian of the strange: Pu Songling and the Chinese classical tale.** Stanford, 1993. 332p bibl index afp ISBN 0-8047-2085-1, $39.50

This is the first major study in English of the *Liaozhai zhiyi*, a famous 17th-century collection of tales that chronicle "strange" or "unusual" events. Its title derives from a literary name sometimes used by the author of the collection, Pu Songling (1640-1715). Pu's sobriquet also suggests the critical approach used here: Zeitlin (Harvard) argues that the relationship between historical and fictional readings of the *Liaozhai* is essential to understanding its author's concept of the "strange." Furthermore, once understood, this concept can help readers and critics to understand the *Liaozhai* collection as a whole. After outlining the interpretive history of the text and Pu Songling's self-introduction (in his preface) as "Historian of the Strange" in Part 1, Zeitlin devotes individual chapters in Part 2 to three fascinating areas of human experience that play prominent roles in the *Liaozhai*: (1) obsession; (2) dislocations of gender (that it, sexual transformations); and (3) dreams (illusion versus reality, etc.). An appendix provides translations of four of the stories discussed in the book. Zeitlin's study is the most informed, original piece of criticism on *Liaozhai* written in a Western language to date. Highly recommended. Advanced undergraduate; graduate; faculty.—*J. M. Hargett, SUNY at Albany*

■ Classical

OAB-0599   PA4037   96-31979 CIP
Bakker, Egbert J. **Poetry in speech: orality and Homeric discourse.** Cornell, 1997. 237p bibl indexes afp ISBN 0-8014-3295-2, $49.95

Bakker (Univ. of Montreal) skillfully applies to Homeric poetry the linguistic theory of discourse, and in particular the findings of linguist W. Chafe in his work on ordinary language. In so doing, the author challenges the concepts of orality and literacy as they have been commonly understood since the seminal work of M. Parry and A. Lord. Spoken discourse, whether ordinary speech or poetry, occurs as a series of brief temporal units (two to three seconds), characterized by a coherent intonation contour. Bakker presents a new definition of formulas as "stylised intonation units," a new way of reading the hexameter that treats it as a result, not only a constraint, of Homeric language, and, finally, a new way of looking at Homeric syntax and style. The book also offers interesting insights into the construction of larger mythological and narrative patterns. In spite of some attempts to deal with diachronic problems concerning the Homeric language, Bakker's analysis remains essentially a synchronic one: he shows more how Homeric language works than how it became what it is. A very important contribution to Homeric studies; recommended for upper-division undergraduates and above.—*P. Nieto, Brown University*

OAB-0600   PA3945   95-2674 CIP
Cameron, Alan. **Callimachus and his critics.** Princeton, 1995. 534p bibl index afp ISBN 0-691-04367-1, $49.50

No ancient poet is more important and difficult than the Alexandrian Callimachus. The erudite author and polemical critic meets his equal in Cameron (Columbia Univ.), author of *The Greek Anthology* (1993). Eighteen exuberant chapters explore Hellenistic social and literary history. Callimachus, not a pedant cloistered from the public, participated in Ptolemaic festivals and panegyrics. He did not direct his caustic wit at contemporary epic because such poems hardly existed. His vituperative poetry addressed the nature of elegiac narrative and style. Like Jasper Griffin on Callimachus's Roman successors (*Latin Poets and Roman Life*, CH, Jul'86), Cameron finds the contemporary world pervasive in the fastidious poet's fragmented remains. Cameron's omnivorous, up-to-date reading leaves few scholars or dogmas unbloodied. The beauty of the study appears in its detailed readings. Cameron notices relevant historical events and recondite poetic parallels to develop what lacunose literary history we can salvage. His mandarin academic style and his assumption of

equally initiated audiences float his book beyond startled undergraduates. No library can dispense with it, however, if it aspires to house the masters of literature. Cameron provides the only comprehensive study of a great, pugnacious poet.—*D. Lateiner, Ohio Wesleyan University*

OAB-0601   PA6281   95-1196 CIP
Cicero, Marcus Tullius. **Cicero: pro P. Sulla oratio,** ed., introd., and commentary by D.H. Berry. Cambridge, 1996. 335p index (Cambridge classical texts and commentaries, 30) ISBN 0-521-48174-0, $64.95

Cicero's orations provide the best guides to the public maneuverings of Roman politicians in the last decades of the Republic, yet the 20th century has seen scholarly commentaries in English on only a handful of the 58 extant speeches. Berry's new text, introduction, and commentary on *Pro Sulla* is a welcome and impressive addition to this small group of distinguished books. Berry (Leeds Univ., UK) bases the text on a thorough reexamination of the principal manuscripts and new materials he has discovered. The introduction is superb, placing the speech in historical and rhetorical context and refuting previous unfounded, yet still prevalent, interpretations. Since the speech was delivered in the aftermath of the Catilinarian conspiracy and says as much about Cicero as about Sulla, it is an important document for interpretations of both the conspiracy and Cicero's subsequent career. Berry offers a wealth of details about these matters and balances linguistic, historical, political, and rhetorical materials more effectively than any other English commentary on a Ciceronian speech. This masterly, magisterial treatment is destined to become the standard commentary on *Pro Sulla* until well into the 21st century. Essential for upper-division undergraduates through faculty.—*R. W. Cape Jr., Austin College*

OAB-0602   PA6008   93-20985 CIP
Conte, Gian Biagio. **Latin literature: a history,** tr. by Joseph B. Solodow; rev. by Don Fowler and Glenn W. Most. Johns Hopkins, 1994. 827p index afp ISBN 0-8018-4638-2, $65.00

A more congenial, instructive, and stimulating history of Latin literature than this text, supplemented by features intended for American and British readers, could hardly be hoped for. At once a reference work, a bibliographic guide, a literary study, and a readers handbook, it covers a thousand years of Latin letters from the origin of Latin to the dawn of the Middle Ages. In his critical approach, Conte gives much emphasis to intertextuality, including the relations of the extant texts to those that have been lost. He strives to reintegrate works within their historical context and sees every text as an interlocutor of some other text. Conte stresses the cultural otherness of these texts, to which we must accede by attempting to reconstruct the expectations of their audiences. This very different, engaging kind of literary history involves the reader in quite a sophisticated manner. Besides brief discussions of the literary success of individual authors in later times, Conte provides preliminary historical discussions to each new section. The design of the book is very spacious with descriptive headings in the margins and updated bibliographies at the end of each chapter; in the supplementary material are found chronological tables of both Greek and Roman history and culture, definitions of key Roman concepts such as *fides* and *gravitas*, and a glossary of rhetorical terms. This excellent volume should easily eclipse any of the standard histories of Latin literature now in print. Upper-division undergraduate and up.—*C. Fantazzi, University of Windsor*

OAB-0603   PA4167   95-9557 CIP
Cook, Erwin F. **The *Odyssey* in Athens: myths of cultural origins.** Cornell, 1995. 218p bibl index afp ISBN 0-8014-3121-2, $35.00

In a work of perceptive and persuasive scholarship, lucidly written and argued, Cook (Univ. of Texas at Austin) provides an intellectually satisfying guide to the thematic and structural unity of the *Odyssey*. He correctly perceives that the central unifying theme of the poem as a whole is an ongoing struggle between the forces of *metis* ("cunning intelligence") and *bie* ("violent might"). That struggle is embodied in Odysseus's conflicts with such antagonists as Polyphemus in the "enchanted realm" of Books 9-12, a narrative sequence that forms a thematic parallel to his climactic struggle against the suitors. This polarity of intelligence and might is also seen to operate at the divine level, with Zeus and Athena representing intellect and Poseidon force. Cook makes some interesting suggestions about the role that Athena and Poseidon play in actual Athenian cults, a role that parallels their symbolic one in the *Odyssey*. The text of this study is accompanied by two appendixes, "Homer and the Analysts"—in which the author defends further his view of a consistent authorial perspective concerning the theological perspective of Zeus and Athena—and "Poseidon and Athene in Myth and Cult." There is much in this fine study that can be read with profit by both general readers and advanced scholars, upper-division undergraduate and above.—*L. Golden, Florida State University*

OAB-0604   PA6003   95-37599 CIP
Fantham, Elaine. **Roman literary culture: from Cicero to Apuleius.** Johns Hopkins, 1996. 326p bibl index afp ISBN 0-8018-5204-8, $39.95

True to her prefatory promise, Fantham (Princeton Univ.) has produced the perfect companion volume to the much-praised English version of Gian Biagio Conte's *Latin literature: A History* (CH, Nov'94). Fantham herself wrote the foreword to Conte's volume, and here she follows the Italian critic in her emphasis on the historical and cultural context, the audience, the medium, the method of literary production, and the uses of genre. Unlike Conte she confines her investigation to a limited period, from the last years of the Roman Republic (50-43 BCE) to the time of strong reassertion of Greek influence in the second century, ending with Apuleius's exuberant *The Golden Ass*. In a short introduction she gives a lucid explanation of what she means by a social history of Latin literature, which she develops chronologically rather than thematically. New perspectives, new connections, and new insights into both major and minor writers fill every page, and all are woven together in a brilliant manner. The study is a culmination of her previous work and a harbinger of things to come. Fantham is surely one of the foremost interpreters of Latin literature in the English-speaking world. The book is a delight to read and peruse, for students of other literary periods as well as for students of Latin letters. All collections.—*C. Fantazzi, University of Windsor*

OAB-0605   BL782   92-26010 CIP
Gantz, Timothy. **Early Greek myth: a guide to literary and artistic sources.** Johns Hopkins, 1993. 909p bibl index afp ISBN 0-8018-4410-X, $60.00

The first of its kind in English, this is a comprehensive, chronologically organized handbook of early Greek myth. The author locates in literary and artistic sources the first appearance of virtually all myths encountered in reading ancient Greek texts (roughly from Homer to Bakhylides) and traces their subsequent appearances through the Roman period. What he does not do, given the voluminousness of his material, is treat systematically any myth's development in later times for its own sake, or engage in subjective evaluation of his sources. He also leaves the complete compilation of artistic sources to the now nearly completed *Lexicon Iconographicum Mythologiae Classicae* (1992-). Appendixes on ancient texts cited, catalog of artistic representations, genealogical tables, bibliography, and full index complete this invaluable source reference.—*M. Dobson, Colorado College*

OAB-0606   PA3825   91-42829 Orig
Goldhill, Simon. **Aeschylus, the *Oresteia*.** Cambridge, 1992. 102p ISBN 0-521-40293-X, $27.95; ISBN 0-521-40853-9 pbk, $10.95

Informed by meticulous scholarship, respect for tradition, and a refreshingly modern sensibility, this is an excellent introduction, not only to one of the most popular, widely read, and often taught of the ancient Greek tragedies, but also to the institutions of the ancient *polis* and the dramatic festivals. In the first of three chapters, "Drama and the City of Athens," Goldhill summarizes, explains, and analyzes the major features of the ancient city-state (*polis*) and Great Dionysia (at which the dramas were performed). Drawing on a

wealth of recent scholarship (including his own), he discusses the communitarian, privatistic, and agonistic aspects of ancient Greek society and explains how they functioned together to both define and embody a particular sociocultural formation. The second and longest chapter, "The Oresteia," discusses the language, themes, sociopolitical implications, and dramatic form of the play, analyzing, in 11 subsections, such issues as plot structure, justice and revenge, gender roles and the patriarchal order, the Homeric paradigm, persuasion and linguistic usage, prophecy and the relation of past to present, the imagery of hunting and sacrifice, divine authority and control, lyric poetry and its relation to dramatic dialogue, and the function of political rhetoric. Greek terms and concepts are translated and explained clearly and concisely. Throughout, the discussion is informative and stimulating, the judgments invariably sound. A final chapter surveys briefly the influence of the trilogy, focusing on three instances of reuse and reinterpretaiton. Undergraduate; advanced undergraduate; faculty.—*M. A. Katz, Wesleyan University*

OAB-0607   PA6276   92-43064 CIP
Janan, Micaela. **"When the lamp is shattered": desire and narrative in Catullus.** Southern Illinois, 1994. 204p bibl index afp ISBN 0-8093-1765-6, $34.95

Few readers of Catullus would now dismiss his work as the object of more critical attention than it deserves. To the contrary, most modern scholars agree that Catullus, a discordant, self-contradictory, and not easily assimilable voice of his time, must be taken very seriously. Among other features, it is this discord, this resistance to external constraint, that attracts the modern reader to the complexities of Catullus's art. Janan explores many of the poems by applying a rich, dynamic critical method, one that is quite in keeping with contemporary preoccupations with selfhood, gender, and reader response. Her method reflects a combination of Callimachean aesthetics and Platonic psychology, as the latter is elaborated by Freud and Jacques Lacan. The method works admirably in the elucidation of Catullus's celebrated affair with Lesbia and of other instances of his sensitive, ambivalent personality. Janan's vocabulary is highly literate, gender-conscious, and psychoanalytical; she evinces an intense engagement with the text. Her book will appeal primarily to kindred spirits, but probably to only the few undergraduates who share her understanding of Hellenistic poetry and Freudian psychoanalysis. This limitation is regrettable, since the book is well conceived and its conclusions well grounded, in literary theory as well as in the text of Catullus. In all, a welcome, challenging addition to the growing body of contemporary Catullan criticism. Graduate; faculty.—*E. R. Mix, Elmira College*

OAB-0608   PA4037   95-1704 CIP
Lateiner, Donald. **Sardonic smile: nonverbal behavior in Homeric epic.** Michigan, 1995. 340p bibl indexes afp ISBN 0-472-10598-1, $47.50

The purpose of this book is, in the words of its author, to examine "reported non-verbal acts, purposely performed or uncontrollably leaked, that enhance, devalue, or disguise verbal messages" in the *Iliad* and *Odyssey*. In other words, this work investigates body language and the ways in which it communicates character and influences others. To pursue this fascinating study, classicist Lateiner (Ohio Wesleyan Univ.) uses the perspectives of the social sciences, notably anthropology and psychology. The book has three major sections: the first part offers a general introduction to the subject of nonverbal behavior and a detailed presentation of the variety of nonverbal communication in the *Iliad*, Book 24; the second focuses more specifically on bodily expressions of respect and disrespect in the *Odyssey*; the final part considers the character and social status, according to specific body language, of four personalities in the *Odyssey*. Lateiner includes a glossary of technical terms, an extensive bibliography, and several indexes. Written in scholarly yet frequently witty prose, this book is a thoughtful and absorbing piece of interdisciplinary research about a universal aspect of human communication and its manifestation in Homer. An important contribution to Homeric studies. Recommended for college and university libraries at the upper-division undergraduate level and above.—*J. C. Brown, Hartwick College*

OAB-0609 PA78 96-36021 CIP
McManus, Barbara F. **Classics & feminism: gendering the classics.**
Twayne/Prentice Hall International, 1997. 201p bibl index afp ISBN 0-8057-9757-2, $28.95

In this important study, McManus (Univ. of New Rochelle) surveys changes in the conceptual construction of the discipline (chapter 1), profession (chapter 2), and scholarship (chapter 3) of American classics in the wake of feminism. McManus has brought together a great deal of data, tabulating it carefully in both statistical (ten tables and ten figures) and narrative form, to show that in the last 30 years second-wave feminism has completely changed the way the cultures of Greco-Roman antiquity are studied and taught in the US. Two final chapters exemplify current trends in feminist theory and practice: chapter 4 offers an interpretation of Vergil's *Aeneid* informed by feminist theory; chapter 5 opens the discussion to the views of various individual classicists (female and male, professor and student, young and old) concerning the impact of feminism on teaching, scholarship, and the profession. This invaluable study should be required reading, particularly for classics faculty and chairs.—*A. M. Keith, University of Toronto*

OAB-0610 PA4037 95-39353 CIP
Nagy, Gregory. **Homeric questions.** Texas, 1996. 180p bibl index afp ISBN 0-292-75561-9, $30.00; ISBN 0-292-75562-7 pbk, $12.95

In this book, the latest in his series of brilliant and provocative works that open up new vistas in Homeric studies (e.g., *The Best of the Achaeans*, 1979, and *Poetry as Performance*, CH, Feb'97), Nagy (Harvard Univ.) at one point distills several points into one: "The essence of performing song and poetry" is "the primary question." Drawing on the disciplinary perspectives of linguistics and anthropology as well as the groundbreaking work of Milman Parry and Albert Lord, the author examines the performative aspect of oral traditional poetry. The body of the work consists of four chapters: the first defines important terms and clarifies common, but misleading, usages; the second uses comparative data from the living traditions of other cultures to develop an evolutionary model for Homeric poetry; the third part seeks to explain the evolution of the Homeric text; the last chapter considers mythological exempla in the context of tradition and change. The introduction and epilogue include passionate appeals to classicists for tolerance and respect of other perspectives in philological investigations. An extensive bibliography and general index complete the work. Informed and creative, wide-ranging and profound, this book stands at the cutting edge of Homeric scholarship and reminds readers why its author is one of the foremost classical scholars in the world today. Recommended for all college and university libraries.—*J. C. Brown, Hartwick College*

OAB-0611 PA6522 92-5682 MARC
Ovid. **Sorrows of an exile:** *Tristia*, tr. by A.D. Melville. Oxford, 1992. 173p index ISBN 0-19-814792-9, $55.00

Melville has added another excellent translation of Ovid's poetry to his two earlier renditions—of the *Metamorphoses* (CH, Sep'86) and *Love Poems* (CH, Dec'90). He has used the same elegiac rhythm that he employed in *Love Poems* and has rendered Ovid's elegiac couplets into graceful and flowing English. Preserving the mythological allusions, so marked a feature of all Ovid's writing, and eschewing both the jarring modernisms of D. Slavitt (CH, Jan'87) and the ponderous rendition of L.R. Lind (CH, Jul'75), he has given the reader of whatever background a real taste of the Ovid who has delighted generations of readers. An informative historical introduction by the eminent classicist E.J. Kenney and an explanation of the classical elegiac couplet by Melville precede the text. Also included are a select bibliography, helpful notes, and two maps—one of the lo ale of the poet's exile and one of the walk through Rome. This translation is an unqualified desideratum for anyone who wants to enjoy Ovid's poetry and his frame of mind in his last unhappy years of exile.—*B. N. Quinn, Mount Holyoke College*

OAB-0612 PA409 95-20124 CIP
Williamson, Margaret. **Sappho's immortal daughters.** Harvard, 1995. 196p index afp ISBN 0-674-78912-1, $24.95

Williamson's lucid and absorbing study successfully presents what can be known about the cultural context of Sappho's life and work. Using social, political, and literary materials that influenced and reflect Sappho's experience, the author (Univ. of Surrey) reconstructs the atmosphere in which Sappho lived, breathed, and worked. References abound, providing readers with reproductions of relevant vase paintings, fragments of contemporary poetry, and a brief annotated bibliography for further research. It is of particular note that this interpretation of Sappho locates her within her culture in the broadest sense, not as an anachronism or a marginal figure but instead deriving much of the intensity of her lyrics from the tradition in which Williamson sees them embedded. The many strands of investigation come together, finally, in the analysis of the songs locating Sappho in the religion, society, and culture of the Homeric tradition. Aphrodite emerges as not simply Sappho's "patron goddess" but as the carrier of her sense of self: Sappho transforms the identity of Aphrodite as she transforms the conventions of the love relationship itself. This study insists on both reflective and integrative reading. Understanding Sappho in such a variety of contexts enriches both the fragmentary texts and their readers. General; upper-division undergraduate through faculty.—*R. Nadelhaft, University of Maine*

■ English & American

UNITED KINGDOM & IRELAND — Medieval & Renaissance

OAB-0613 PR2674 92-45865 CIP
Bartels, Emily C. **Spectacles of strangeness: imperialism, alienation, and Marlowe.** Pennsylvania, 1993. 221p bibl index afp ISBN 0-8122-3193-7, $29.95

Bartels's well-researched, well-written study of Marlowe's drama contains lessons for those interested in how art and society interact. The author maintains that Marlowe stylizes place to achieve dramatic purpose, rendering foreign places English and English places foreign. Amelioration of differences between the alien and the familiar reveal themselves even more in Marlowe's treatment of character, with *Tamburlaine* offering a clear example of Marlowe's strategy: the shifting settings of conquest illustrate that one empire is much like another; the hero's interactions with secondary characters emphasize that they construct their images of him to fit their own agendas. Marlowe's dramas are seen as subverting the Elizabethan establishment's aim of emphasizing the otherness of the alien in order to promote imperial action. Marlowe's discourse of domination, whether in Africa, the East, or in England, is "part of a continuum." In addition to offering an excellent command of critics such as Bevington, Dessen, and Greenblatt, Bartels has added greatly to the critical discussion of Marlowe's dramaturgy. Well edited with helpful notes and adequate bibliography and index, this study is a "must" for any library seeking an adequate collection of Marlowe criticism. Undergraduate; graduate; general.—*R. H. Peake, Clinch Valley College of the University of Virginia*

OAB-0614 Can. CIP
Calin, William. **The French tradition and the literature of medieval England.** Toronto, 1994. 587p bibl index afp ISBN 0-8020-0565-9, $75.00; ISBN 0-8020-7202-X pbk, $25.95

Not since the work of Charles Muscatine (*Chaucer and the French Traditions*, 1957) and James Wimsatt (*Chaucer and His French Contemporaries*, CH, Jul'92) has the French background to medieval English literature received such attention, but Calin's study is far broader in scope. Calin (Univ. of Florida) widens his examination to include 12th-century Anglo-Norman romance, hagiographic writings, and Continental French works of the 13th to the 15th centuries. Finally, he takes up specific authors (from Chaucer to Malory) and the Middle English romance, paying close attention to the French contribution to their literary production. He concludes that the English reading public was attracted to two French modes of imaginative literature—the romance with its stories of heroism, love, and adventure; and allegory, which provided English authors with the model for psychological insights expressed through personifications. Calin observes that these two genres extend over much of the most mature period of Middle English literature. This important study by an outstanding specialist of French literature sheds new light on the contact between the literatures of these two cultures. It will surely be regarded for years to come as the standard study of French literature written in England and of French-inspired English literature. A must for any college or university library.—*R. O'Gorman, University of Iowa*

OAB-0615   PR3069   95-37296 CIP
Carroll, William C. **Fat king, lean beggar: representations of poverty in the age of Shakespeare.** Cornell, 1996. 237p bibl index afp ISBN 0-8014-3185-9, $37.50

Carroll (Boston Univ.) devotes more than half of this exhaustive study to almost every available document (and illustration) of the period; the remainder focuses on Shakespearean figures like Jack Cade, Christopher Sly, Autolycus, and Edgar's Mad Tom persona. The culmination of a decade's work, the study is influenced by new historicism, but it employs a variety of scholarly approaches. Shakespeare's contemporaries consistently disposed of the problems of dispossession, poverty, vagrancy, and beggary by denial—outlawing and marginalizing the symptoms, but not treating the cause. Since tinkers, peddlers, and beggars were legal nonentities, the only literary alternative was the romanticized beggar. Shakespeare and his contemporaries were not as deeply versed in the lore and cant of beggary as Thomas Dekker, but Shakespeare's depictions of Autolycus and, particularly, Mad Tom show the emptiness of Tudor-Stuart class categories and "the necessary political and social bond between high and low, fat king and lean beggar—two dishes, but to one table." Edgar's Mad Tom experience shows him how it feels to be Edmund and perhaps prepares him to be the kind of king that Lear did not survive to be. Highly recommended for all students of Shakespeare and Tudor-Elizabeth-Stuart drama, upper-division undergraduates and up.—*D. O. Dickerson, Judson College*

OAB-0616   PR2991   96-2686 CIP
Dash, Irene G. **Women's worlds in Shakespeare's plays.** Delaware, 1997. (Dist. by Associated University Presses) 304p bibl index afp ISBN 0-87413-599-0, $45.00

Building on Dash's *Wooing, Wedding, and Power* (CH, Apr'82), this book is informed by comprehensive study of promptbooks and the widely used stage versions of plays developed by such theatrical leaders as David Garrick, John Philip Kemble, Henry Irving, and Augustin Daly. Dash (Hunter College, CUNY) traces a two-century tradition of oversimplified and diminished feminine characters as depicted on the English and American stage. She has selected plays in which women seek self-sovereignty, examining the enigmatic responses a dominantly patriarchal culture gives them, even in the uncut texts, and suggesting how cultural biases have guided cuts, rearrangements, and rewrites of feminine parts, and of male interactions with key female characters. Proceeding systematically through the plays chosen for study (*AWW, MND, HAM, MAC,* and *TN*), Dash progressively contrasts the characters Shakespeare created with the caricatures theatrical performances have often presented. Though not everyone will agree with every allegation of cultural bias and sexual politics behind every textual cut, all will admire the overwhelming evidence Dash has pulled together from comprehensive study of the promptbooks, and appreciate the restoration of Shakespeare's heroines to their original complexity. Recommended for all collections.—*D. O. Dickerson, Judson College*

OAB-0617   PR1882   92-21191 CIP
Delany, Sheila. **The naked text: Chaucer's *Legend of good women*.** California, 1994. 259p bibl index afp ISBN 0-520-08119-6, $42.00

Original in scope and provocative in its findings, this informed and accessible study considers the oft-maligned *Legend* in relation to both late 14th century cultural contexts and Chaucer's own aesthetic and literary development. Delany (Simon Fraser Univ.) rejects long-held beliefs that the *Legend* is inferior to Chaucer's other works, asserting that such opinion suggests an "erudite philistinism." She instead argues that it is important as a transitional work in the development of the Chaucerian narrator, as an ideological manifestation of orthodox Augustinianism, and as a self-reflexive expression of verbal production and interpretation. The five chapters explore in detail such topics as reading, writing, and intertextuality; relationships between gender, language, and culture; epistemology and its metaphors; expressions of difference; and ambivalence in representation. The chapters are framed by an introduction that assesses the *Legend's* critical reception and a conclusion that considers questions of readership. Indispensable for Chaucerians, this is an important study for all teachers and students of Chaucer and medieval culture. Recommended for all academic libraries.—*C. S. Cox, University of Pittsburgh—Johnstown*

OAB-0618   PR658   94-41169 CIP
Diehl, Huston. **Staging reform, reforming the stage: Protestantism and popular theater in early modern England.** Cornell, 1997. 238p bibl index afp ISBN 0-8014-3303-7, $39.95

Identifying John Foxe's *Actes and Monuments* as one of the most influential works of Renaissance England, Diehl (Univ. of Iowa) shows that Foxe used the same rhetorical strategies that later appeared in the theater, strategies that emphasize iconoclastic Protestant responses to the iconophilia of the traditional church. The author convincingly shows how Elizabethan and Jacobean dramatists subverted traditional theater even as they created a new Protestant aesthetic. She contends that the theater of the time did not exist in an antagonistic relationship to the efforts of the reformers; instead, it was actually a product of Reformation culture. Placing *Dr. Faustus, Hamlet, Women Beware Women,* and *The Spanish Tragedy* within the context of religious controversies, Diehl explores the way Protestant understanding of the Lord's Supper shaped the play-within-a-play convention. Her reading of *Othello* emphasizes what the reformers would interpret as a fallible human need for visible proof (the handkerchief) over faith, and in *The Duchess of Malfi* she finds John Webster employing a Protestant rhetoric of witnessing. A provocative and engaging addition to recent work (e.g., Paul White's *Theatre and Reformation,* 1992; Bryan Crockett's *The Play of Paradox,* CH, Jun'96; and Donna Hamilton's *Shakespeare and the Politics of Protestant England,* CH, Jan'93). Upper-division undergraduate through faculty—*J. P. Baumgaertner, Wheaton College (IL)*

OAB-0619   PR2968   92-12096 CIP
Dobson, Michael. **The making of the national poet: Shakespeare, adaptation and authorship, 1660-1769.** Oxford, 1992. 266p bibl index ISBN 0-19-811233-5, $52.00

In this seminal study, Dobson describes how Shakespeare, generally disregarded by the time of the Restoration, came to occupy by the 1760s the position of England's preeminent writer. He argues that this elevation of Shakespeare constitutes "one of the central cultural expressions of England's own transition from the aristocratic regime of the Stuarts to the commercial empire presided over by the Hanoverians," and that certain political and social characteristics of the English were preeminent in the plays; thus the English—particularly playwrights and directors—were able to adapt radically these plays to reflect changing emphases and fresh developments in commerce, politics, and society generally. In the process of elevating Shakespeare almost to a god the English wildly revised his plays—frequently creating new plays out of portions of Shakespeare's work. Although this process served the nation, it paradoxically served to raise Shakespeare's reputation—and encouraged the English to see in him, for example, a national father figure analogous to heroic father figures in his plays and as emblematic of the power and enduring qualities of the

English people. For persons interested in how Shakespeare became the national poet, this volume is "must" reading. Reader-friendly notes (located at the bottoms of pages); extensive and valuable bibliography; reproductions of selected frontispieces from Shakespearean editions. Required for British intellectual history, Shakespearean criticism, and drama collections generally.—*C. B. Darrell, Kentucky Wesleyan College*

OAB-0620   PR2825   92-35672 CIP
Gross, John. **Shylock: a legend and its legacy.** Simon & Schuster, 1993 (c1992). 386p index ISBN 0-671-70707-8, $25.00

After analyzing the elements included in the original character, Gross studies interpretations of Shylock for the past 400 years, showing how Shylock has developed a life independent of *The Merchant of Venice* and has become a figure in world mythology. He reviews transmutations of the ethnic stereotype in Shakespearean productions (ranging from those attempting to embody the author's "intentions" to the wildest reinterpretations), and in all other literary genres as well. Without intending to, he comes close to proving that the Holocaust prevents us from understanding Shakespeare's play, and he often assumes that empathy for Shylock as a Jew is touchstone for the seriousness of a production, adaptation, allusion, or literary redaction. Though it may or may not illuminate our reading of *Merchant*, this is likely to be the definitive work on Shylock in world culture for some time to come. Recommended. Advanced undergraduates and beyond.—*D. O. Dickerson, Judson College*

OAB-0621   PR1933   95-50230 CIP
Grudin, Michaela Paasche. **Chaucer and the politics of discourse.** South Carolina, 1996. 200p bibl index afp ISBN 1-57003-102-9, $29.95

In this insightful and original study, Grudin (Lewis and Clark College) explores the significance of speech in Chaucer's works. She looks at the spoken word and the relationships between speakers and audiences. Her analyses of specific texts offer a fresh perspective of a Chaucer who, alone of the early humanists, recognizes the limitations of discourse. Seven chapters provide close readings of significant texts: the dynamics of reciprocity in the early dream-visions; misperceptions in connection with communicative transactions in *Troilus and Criseyde*; and, from the *Canterbury Tales*, the political considerations of dialogue and authority in the *Knight's Tale*, the social implications of discursive freedom in the *Wife of Bath's Prologue*, distinctions between uses and misuses of speech in the *Squire's Tale* and the *Franklin's Tale*, and the political implications of speech and truth in the *Manciple's Tale*. A concluding chapter focuses on the dynamics of discourse in relation to social conventions and poetic closure. This engaging volume has much to offer scholars, teachers, and upper-division undergraduate students of medieval English literature and culture.—*C. S. Cox, University of Pittsburgh*

OAB-0622   PR129   94-45082 CIP
Hamlin, William M. **The image of America in Montaigne, Spenser, and Shakespeare: Renaissance ethnography and literary reflection.** St. Martin's, 1995. 234p bibl index ISBN 0-312-12506-2, $39.95

Hamlin (Idaho State Univ.) examines the ways in which early modern ethnological descriptions of the inhabitants of the New World influenced Montaigne's, Spenser's, and Shakespeare's explorations of savagery and civility. He focuses primarily on "Of Cannibals"; pastoralism, the Wild Man, the satyrs, and the Salvage Man in *The Faerie Queene*; "unaccommodated man" in *King Lear*; and Caliban and the island in *The Tempest*. That these three authors achieve a complex, nonreductive, and questioning view of culture is, of course, not a new idea. This work's importance lies in the fullness of Hamlin's description of the authors' ethnographic context, and his conclusions are finely nuanced. Anyone interested in the way in which the Old World came to see itself through its images of the New World will find this a necessary book. In the current fashion, Hamlin is much concerned with theory, and a full quarter of his book is devoted to analyzing the theoretical implications and lim-

itations of his project. He provides 56 pages of notes and a 32-page bibliography. Upper-division undergraduates and above.—*B. E. Brandt, South Dakota State University*

OAB-0623   PR2997   95-36472 CIP
Parker, Patricia. **Shakespeare from the margins: language, culture, context.** Chicago, 1996. 392p index afp ISBN 0-226-64584-3, $52.00; ISBN 0-226-64585-1 pbk, $19.95

In a study informed by materialist feminist criticism and by the conviction that all of Shakespeare's discourse is inseparable from the social and political, Parker (Stanford Univ.) extensively analyzes what has been marginalized or overlooked in Shakespearean wordplay. Although Johnson dismissed much wordplay as mere "quibbles," Parker finds significant meaning clusters through reading Shakespeare's language with a full awareness of its crucial historical resonances; this greatly expands the reader's sense of the plays' linkages with their contemporary culture and contributes to understanding early modern cultures. The readings range from the sexual (the meanings of preposterous and dilation/delation from *LLL* to *WT*) to the theological (the importance of Paul's epistle to the Ephesians in demarginalizing *ERR*), and much more. Massively documented (581 footnotes filling 100-plus pages), this work significantly extends such studies as Keir Elam's *Shakespeare's Universe of Discourse* (CH, Jul'85), M. M. Mahood's *Shakespeare's Wordplay* (1968), and Catherine Belsey's *Critical Practice* (1980). Highly recommended for upper-division students and beyond.—*D. O. Dickerson, Judson College*

OAB-0624   PR428   94-35106 CIP
Strier, Richard. **Resistant structures: particularity, radicalism, and Renaissance texts.** California, 1995. 239p index afp (The new historian, 34) ISBN 0-520-08915-4, $38.00

In this triumphant combination of common sense and careful close reading, Strier (Univ. of Chicago) takes Wittgenstein's statement "Don't think, but look" as his credo: "This book means to defend the importance of the obvious, the surface, and the literal as well as the particular." The author is particularly interested in those moments when "texts resist even very brilliant, illuminating, and well-founded hypotheses," times when criticism dismisses the obvious ("'This seems to be doing or saying X, but it is really doing or saying Y'"). Strier aims to "encourage a certain modesty in the scope that is claimed for critical or historical insights." Part 1 impartially impales all stripes of English Renaissance scholarship and criticism. Part 2 treats specific instances of how ideas have worked against the "seeing or reading particular texts" in the Renaissance: the saintliness of authors St. François de Sales (*Introduction to the Devout Life*, 1608) and George Herbert ("The Church-Porch"); the idea of "unthinkability" in older texts, specifically Donne's third Satire and the *King Lear*s of Shakespeare and Nahum Tate. Well written and well argued, this gem in what Paul Alpers calls "the emerging genre of corrective studies" belongs in libraries serving upper-division undergraduates and above.—*A. F. Erlebach, Michigan Technological University*

OAB-0625   PR421   95-45465 CIP
Tricomi, Albert H. **Reading Tudor-Stuart texts through cultural historicism.** University Press of Florida, 1996. 201p bibl index afp ISBN 0-8130-1435-2, $39.95

In an effort to go beyond new historicist methodologies, Tricomi (SUNY at Binghamton) argues convincingly for a "new cultural historicism." Whether his term sticks or not, he offers one of the best critiques of new historicism currently available. In part 1, he presents an excellent theoretical analysis of "surveillance" as verified in literary tropes (particularly evident in the power of conscience as an internal spy or "informer"), a powerful addition to the cultural dialogue about subjectivity. Unfortunately, part 2 is not as strong, despite a convincing critique of the work of Lawrence Stone. When Tricome applies his interest in surveillance to the control of the "sexual female body" in selected plays by George Chapman, John Marston, John Webster, and Thomas Drue, his prose becomes jargon-laden, and his analysis, at times mired in textual detail, is not supported (as it is part 1) by clear and constant contextual grounding. As he focuses on the dichotomy between "respectable" wives and the libertine allowances made for relationships with whores, Tricomi might have used the mediating influence of Stephen Orgel (*Impersonations: The Performance of Gender in Shakespeare's England*, 1996), who analyzes the households established for mistresses like Elizabeth, Countess of Shrewsbury. Overall, however, this book is highly recommended; its bibliography is excellent, its notes careful and suggestive. The intelligent, focused, and specific critique of new historicism alone is worth the price of the book. Upper-level undergraduates, graduate students, and scholars.—*M. C. Riggio, Trinity College (CT)*

OAB-0626   PR2367   94-33643 CIP
Watkins, John. **The specter of Dido: Spenser and Virgilian epic.** Yale, 1995. 208p index afp ISBN 0-300-05883-7, $20.00

The last decade has witnessed a genuinely extraordinary production of distinguished studies of the epic, among them Mihoko Suzuki's *Metamorphoses of Helen* (CH, Mar'90), Theresa Krier's *Gazing on Secret Sights* (CH, Nov'90), Barbara Pavlock's *Eros, Imitation, and the Epic Tradition* (1990), Susanne Wofford's *The Choice of Achilles* (CH, Nov'92), and David Quint's *Epic and Empire* (1993). It is probably not too much to say that we are in a "golden age" of epic studies, and it is no small compliment to John Watkins's slender but dense new volume that it loses no lustre in this eminent company. The most groundbreaking and exciting chapter of this excellent work may be the first, on the *Aeneid*; Watkins (Univ. of Minnesota—Twin Cities) sees in Aeneas's abandonment of Dido for his heroic destiny a reflexive trope for Virgil's own heroic project and its repudiation (in part) of his precursor's, Homer's, project. The next chapter, on medieval and Renaissance transformations of Virgil's Dido, seems a bit perfunctory, its scholarship often secondhand; but the remaining four chapters of the book, on Spenser's *Shepheardes Calender* and *The Faerie Queene*, are all top-notch. This is an elegantly argued, well-written, and deeply reflective book, indispensable to specialists in the epic and Spenser but also highly recommended to undergraduate readers.—*P. Cullen, CUNY Graduate Center and College of Staten Island*

OAB-0627   Orig
Wilson, Richard. **Will power: essays on Shakespearean authority.** Wayne State, 1993. 289p index ISBN 0-8143-2491-6, $45.00; ISBN 0-8143-2492-4 pbk, $15.00

A notable event in the history of Shakespeare scholarship. The great theme of these essays is Shakespeare's role in the historical construction of modern subjectivity, and it particularizes that role in a series of readings that concretely link *Julius Caesar, Coriolanus, As You Like It, The Winter's Tale,* and *King Lear* to the economic forces at work in the social struggles of Shakespeare's time. Wilson is as adept in his arguments as he is indefatigable in his labors in the archives, and he succeeds in depicting a historical Shakespeare whose writing is at every crucial instance expressive of clearly defined class interests. Shakespeare's writing appears to be relentlessly organized around the effort to legitimize the power of capital and the will of the individual to overtake the community's most intimate sense of its collective identity. Writing from the Midlands, Wilson is particularly concerned with Shakespeare's analysis of the transformation of English rural society. By unpacking the complex interrelations of *Coriolanus* to Warwickshire politics, by revealing the effect of physician John Hall's marriage to Susanna Shakespeare on her father's last plays, and by uncovering the connection between Shakespeare's last will and testament, the origins of *King Lear*, and the poet's understanding of the destiny of his life's work, Wilson takes the "cultural materialist" reading of Shakespeare to new heights. Undergraduate; graduate; faculty; general.—*N. Lukacher, University of Illinois at Chicago*

OAB-0628   PR2342   96-1813 CIP
Worden, Blair. **The sound of virtue: Philip Sidney's *Arcadia* and**

Elizabethan politics. Yale, 1996. 406p bibl index ISBN 0-300-06693-7, $50.00

Worden has produced an intensive and persuasive study of the relationships of the three versions of the *Arcadia* and their philosophical, historical, and religious backgrounds. Through a mass of detail he draws parallels between Elizabethan England and the realm of King Basilius, using the various failures of Elizabeth that brought her kingdom close to rebellion. Obvious parallels exist with the *Arcadia*: the volatility and inconsistency of the monarch; the unpredictability of foreign policy in dealing with France, Spain, and the Netherlands; Elizabeth's dealings with Mary Stuart; her willingness to consider marriage to the Catholic Duke of Anjou and the consequent internal and external threats to the loyalty of political and religious groups. Worden also studies the influence of the *Arcadia* on later Elizabethan writings and the influence of sources on Sidney, both literary or philosophical. Discussions of stoicism, Machiavelli, Castiglione, and Tacitus are particularly enlightening. A long analysis of Philisides's fable nicely illustrates a number of major political themes. Not an easy read, but essential to an understanding of Sidney's work. Bibliography and index are very well done. Upper-division undergraduates and above.—*J. R. Buchert, emeritus, University of North Carolina at Greensboro*

United Kingdom & Ireland — 17th & 18th Centuries

OAB-0629   PR438   94-46922 CIP
Anselment, Raymond A. **The realms of Apollo: literature and healing in seventeenth-century England.** Delaware, 1995. (Dist. by Associated University Presses) 316p bibl index afp ISBN 0-87413-553-2, $47.50

Anselment (Univ. of Connecticut and author of *Betwixt Jest and Earnest*, CH, Apr'80, and *Loyalist Resolve*, 1988) examines attempts of victims and mourners to describe and to understand the various medical catastrophes that swept through the populace during the 17th century. Separate chapters discuss infant mortality, plague, syphilis, and smallpox; Anselment describes the nature, extent, and medical understanding of each affliction and then shows in detail how writers responded to it in prose (medical treatises, diaries, journals, broadsides, correspondence), verse, and occasionally drama. His syntheses and analyses of the poetry are especially perceptive, and some of his findings are a bit surprising. For example, poetry describing the plague tended to be generalized or restrained; syphilis, though often responded to with irony and wit, was by no means treated lightly. The seeming randomness of smallpox visitations was particularly unnerving. Many passages are quite moving, such as John Evelyn's anguished diary entry on the death from smallpox of his favorite child, but the anguish of less articulate victims and mourners has its own poignancy too. Anselment's research ranges far beyond the familiar writings of Evelyn and Pepys: his bibliography of primary sources alone extends for 22 pages. A well-written study, sympathetic yet restrained in tone and almost encyclopedic in its coverage. Literary scholars, historians, anthropologists, and students of the history of medicine will find it useful. Highly recommended for upper-level undergraduate collections and above.—*C. B. Dodson, University of North Carolina at Wilmington*

OAB-0630   PR545   95-53219 CIP
Barash, Carol. **English women's poetry, 1649-1714: politics, community, and linguistic authority.** Oxford, 1997 (c1996). 345p bibl index afp ISBN 0-19-811973-9, $55.00

This is a clearly written, well-argued, and informative book about the political and private poems of women in the period following the Restoration. Barash (Seton Hall Univ.) has previously contributed essays to *Women, Writing, History, 1640-1740*, ed. by Isobel Grundy and Susan Wiseman (1992), and *Gulliver's Travels*, ed. by Christopher Fox (1995). Here she argues that women poets began as political and/or court writers and that, like their male counterparts, they assumed personas. The distinctive voices these women eventually developed are illustrated by careful examination of manuscript copies and of first editions. Detailed accounts of Mary of Modena as a "model of women's artists," of Katherine Philips as a political writer, and of the literary careers of Jane Barker and Anne Finch strengthen a book that concentrates on writers and contexts without falling victim to theory. Recommended for upper-division undergraduates through faculty.—*J. Wilkinson, emeritus, Youngstown State University*

OAB-0631   PR778   95-43861 CIP
Bohls, Elizabeth A. **Women travel writers and the language of aesthetics, 1716-1818.** Cambridge, 1995. 309p bibl index (Cambridge studies in Romanticism, 13) ISBN 0-521-47458-2, $49.95

Without new historicist readings of travel literature, scholars might wrongly assume that privileged British women of the 18th and early 19th centuries were restricted to the narrow province of a polite and amateurish appreciation of aesthetic experience. Bohls (Univ. of Illinois at Urbana-Champagne) presents women writers who "broke out of masculine tutelage" and made significant contributions to modern aesthetic theory during its formative period. Bohls's introduction charts essential developments in aesthetic theory and practice in the 18th century. Bohls analyzes Lady Mary Wortley Montagu's difficulty in taking up the role of power spectator in her famous accounts of Turkish harems and Janet Shaw's account of colonial slaves in the West Indies in the 1770s. The author describes the gathering momentum of scenic tourism and landscape gardening and explains the dominant theories of Burke, Kant, William Kent, William Gilpin, and others. She reads Dorothy Wordsworth's journals as examples of making an aesthetic of the commonplace and works by Mary Wollstonecraft and Ann Radcliffe as creative redefinitions of the picturesque and the beautiful. A final chapter on Mary Shelley's *Frankenstein* is stunning in its judgments on the profound meaning of the aesthetic experience of the creature. Essential for collections on aesthetic theory and the history of romanticism. Upper-division undergraduate and up.—*S. Pathak, Johns Hopkins University*

OAB-0632   Orig
Bowers, Toni. **The politics of motherhood: British writing and culture, 1680-1760.** Cambridge, 1996. 262p bibl index ISBN 0-521-55174-9, $54.95

In this thoroughly researched and well-written book, Bowers explores representations of motherhood in Augustan literature and culture. She points out that although maternity, particularly examples of faulty and failed motherhood, is a frequent theme in 18th-century novels and conduct books, it has received little critical attention. The author begins by reviewing Queen Anne's reign and the Queen's ultimately unsuccessful attempt to foster political authority through maternal representation. Moving from political and historical precedent to literature, Bowers shows how representations of motherhood in the works of Defoe, Haywood, and Richardson illustrate the cruel dissonance experienced by women caught between cultural expectations of virtuous motherhood and the economic, social, and patriarchal inevitabilities of their lives. She concludes with Lady Sarah Pennington's *An Unfortunate Mother's Advice to Her Absent Daughters*, which, within the context of a conventional conduct book, offers the possibility for maternal virtue's representation in acts of resistance, choice, and legitimate self-representation. This book's interesting and convincing exploration of maternity as an important theme in Augustan life and literature makes it a good choice for students of social history and feminist theory as well as literature. All academic collections.—*H. Benoist, Our Lady of the Lake University of San Antonio*

OAB-0633   PR541   93-44508 CIP
The Cambridge companion to English poetry, Donne to Marvell,

ed. by Thomas N. Corns. Cambridge, 1993. 306p index ISBN 0-521-41147-5, $64.95; ISBN 0-521-42309-0 pbk, $17.95

Like other volumes of similar titles, this one is superbly envisioned and carried out in fresh, important, useful essays. In the opening set of contextual studies, the topics—pressures on the verse of religion and politics, of gender politics, the social circumstances of manuscript and print dissemination, matters of genre theory and of rhetoric—are handled by scholars who have done substantial and groundbreaking work. D. Loewenstein, E. Hobby, A. Marotti, A. Fowler, and B. Vickers—write accessibly and clearly about issues that are being opened or reexamined in current scholarship. These essays explore questions that vibrantly matter in 17th-century verse; that all closely discuss specific poems as well as large-scale issues makes them especially useful and credible. Similar praise is due the essays on individual poets (Donne, Jonson, Herrick, Herbert, Carew-Suckling-Lovelace, early Milton, Crashaw, Vaughan, Marvell). There is no bad work here: All the individual studies have value as "companions" to new readers of the poetry, yet are sophisticated and critically shrewd inquiries. (There *are* problems: many lapses in proofreading, and some plain boners, as in Cromwell's "refusal not to be crowned," or attribution of Satan's first words in *Paradise Lost* to Beelzebub; a second printing ought to deal with these). The bibliographies are particularly good. No other current volume does the work of this one: essential; highly recommended. Upper-division undergraduate through faculty.—*R. Boston, California State University, Fullerton*

OAB-0634   PR3458   94-33011 CIP
Campbell, Jill. **Natural masques: gender and identity in Fielding's plays and novels.** Stanford, 1995. 324p bibl index afp ISBN 0-8047-2391-5, $45.00; ISBN 0-8047-2520-9 pbk, $16.95

This excellent study of Fielding's works takes as its central metaphor the masque (or mask), which, Campbell (Yale) convincingly argues, Fielding used throughout his career to explore the often complicated relationships among biological sex, gender, sexuality, and identity. The author is impressive both in her scope (she surveys all the major works—especially the plays, *Joseph Andrews*, *Tom Jones*, and *Amelia*—and traces Fielding's changing opinions over time) and in her incisiveness, for she reads closely and has something important to say in nearly every sentence. She deftly relates Fielding's concerns about gender and identity to such larger questions as the development of the early novel, Milton's Eve, 18th-century theories of motherhood, the role of gender and sexuality in contemporary politics, and the relationship between gender and genre (novel, epic, satire, etc.). Deeply learned but never obscure, thoroughly up-to-date but never merely trendy, this is a major work: essential reading not only for Fielding scholars but also for upper-division undergraduate and graduate students.—*J. T. Lynch, University of Pennsylvania*

OAB-0635   PR698   96-48626 CIP
Canfield, J. Douglas. **Tricksters & estates: on the ideology of restoration comedy.** University Press of Kentucky, 1997. 315p bibl index afp ISBN 0-8131-2012-8, $44.95

While recognizing the importance of generic classifications and formal criticism of the drama, Canfield (Univ. of Arizona) develops another perspective, one based in cultural history. Informed by the cultural history of the Restoration, this study innovatively proposes a threefold classification of comedy, derived in large measure from its function: social comedy, which supports the Stuart ideology; subversive comedy, which undercuts it; and comical satire, which attacks it as immoral or amoral. This taxonomy allows the author to integrate analytical and comparative discussion of better-known (Behn, Wycherley, Dryden) and lesser-known (Orrery, Lacy, Rawlins) dramatists in ways heretofore unrecognized. By not relying on generic and formalist perspectives, Canfield enriches understanding of social, economic, political, and religious currents and countercurrents of cultural history and their presence in drama. A model of interdisciplinary interpretation, in which drama becomes a lively document not only shaped by cultural forces but also enacting cultural conflicts. Highly recommended for upper-division undergraduates and above.—*A. C. Labriola, Duquesne University*

OAB-0636   Can. CIP
Comensoli, Viviana. **'Household business': domestic plays of early modern England.** Toronto, 1996. 238p bibl index afp ISBN 0-8020-0733-3, $50.00

Comensoli's study of both tragic and comic domestic plays is essential for an understanding of the subject. Comensoli (Wilfrid Laurier Univ., Canada) combines a careful review of previous scholarship on the origin of the drama with thorough analyses of individual plays, using the most recent studies of 16th- and early 17th-century England. By analyzing treatments of older stories such as those of Noah, Griselda, and Sophonisba, as well as 17th-century English plots such as Thomas Heywood's *A Woman Killed with Kindness*, the author shows how the plays treat the themes of marriage codes, the roles of women and the source of their power, and order in society as well as in the home. This is an excellent job, well done, on a significant subject that has suffered from narrow treatment in the past. Full notes and bibliography; clear and readable style. Upper-division undergraduate and above.—*J. R. Buchert, emeritus, University of North Carolina at Greensboro*

OAB-0637   PR858   92-30851 CIP
Craft-Fairchild, Catherine. **Masquerade and gender: disguise and female identity in eighteenth-century fictions by women.** Pennsylvania State, 1993. 190p bibl index afp ISBN 0-271-00918-7, $30.00; ISBN 0-271-00919-5 pbk, $14.95

Craft-Fairchild sets out "to analyze the relationship of masquerade to the construction of femininity in eighteenth-century fiction by women" (introduction); her analysis of the novels discussed is clear and to the point. In five novels from the late Restoration and early 18th century—Aphra Behn's *The Dumb Virgin*, Mary Davys's *The Accomplished Rake*, and Eliza Haywood's *The Masqueraders*, *Fantominia*, and *The City Jilt*—she finds "the female protagonists ... effect role reversals ... that leave the fundamental terms of representation intact." In two novels of a later period—Elizabeth Inchbald's *A Simple Story* and Frances Burney's *The Wanderer*—she finds "the dissolving of gender difference between lovers is coupled with an increased emphasis on the savagery of rivals and, more important, on the patriarchal tyranny of fathers." *A Simple Story* is "subversive" in that "it probes the psychological underpinnings of patriarchal authority"; in *The Wanderer* both female characters "fail to escape the masquerade of femininity." Illustrations supporting Craft-Fairchild's thesis are carefully chosen; her arguments are persuasive. She cites a wide range of scholars who have written about masquerade—e.g., Terry Castle (*Masquerade and Civilization*, CH, Feb'87), Jane Spencer (*The Rise of the Woman Novelist*, CH, May'87), Mary Anne Scholfield (*Masking and Unmasking the Female Mind*, CH, Dec'90). An important contribution. Advanced undergraduate; graduate; faculty.—*A. Jenkins, Georgia Institute of Technology*

OAB-0638   PR935   95-4362 CIP
Cutting edges: postmodern critical essays on eighteenth-century satire, ed. by James E. Gill. Tennessee, 1996 (c1995). 438p bibl index afp (Tennessee studies in literature, 37) ISBN 0-87049-892-4, $38.00

There is much to recommend in this new collection of essays on 18th century satire. Assuming that both satire and the new methods of postmodern criticism are essentially "skeptical" and with the understanding "that language is always ironic," Gill (Univ. of Tennessee, Knoxville) justifies including diverse approaches that present fresh insights into and assessments of major and minor satires. Every postmodern perspective seems to be included: deconstruction (one of the best essays examines part 4 of *Gulliver's Travels*), Marxism, reader-reception theory, new historicism, feminist critical methods, structuralism, Foucaultian discourse analysis, etc. The satires of Butler, Lord Rochester, Swift, Pope, Gay, Fielding, Sterne, and Johnson are reexamined and rethought in interesting and provocative ways; Jonathan Lamb's insightful and exploratory discussion of the special use of satire in Dr. Johnson's *The Vanity of Human Wishes* is especially noteworthy. Several minor writers are also considered: Thomas Shadwell, Mrs. Manley, Fanny Burney, Mary Davys, and Elizabeth Hamilton. This thoughtful volume allows even a traditionalist to see that these new meth-

ods have something to offer, even if it is simply the awareness of a new relationship between language and reality. Notes and works cited are provided after each essay, and there is a substantial index. Highly recommended to anyone interested in 18th-century satire or postmodern criticism. Upper-division undergraduate and above.—*R. G. Brown, Ball State University*

OAB-0639   PR3334   96-24313 CIP
De Bruyn, Frans. **The literary genres of Edmund Burke: the political uses of literary form.** Oxford, 1996. 318p bibl index afp ISBN 0-19-812182-2, $72.00

Many 18th-century British figures notable in their own day as historians, philosophers, or politicians have come to be appreciated for their way with language. Edward Gibbon is now read for his caustic irony, David Hume for his Ciceronian economy, and Edmund Burke for his passionately figurative style. The century also gave birth to several lasting literary genres, most notably the novel, and for a time sustained many others, from the philosophical dialogue to the great ode. Some of these forms are lost to literary history, others enjoy a readerly afterlife even today, and still others remain embedded in a wide variety of period works not primarily literary. The central argument of this elegant study is that while Burke is now most often read as political philosopher and literary stylist, he should be also appreciated for his sophisticated understanding of genre—for example, *Letter to a Noble Lord* draws inspiration from the verse epistles of Alexander Pope, and *Reflections on the Revolution in France* deploys metaphors of tragic theater to find a subtle path through local political discourses. These discerning, intricate, and densely contextual readings of the major works are highly recommended for upper-division undergraduates through faculty.—*T. Erwin, University of Nevada, Las Vegas*

OAB-0640   PR448   95-22803 CIP
Donoghue, Frank. **The fame machine: book reviewing and eighteenth-century literary careers.** Stanford, 1996. 213p bibl index afp ISBN 0-8047-2563-2, $37.50

Donoghue (Ohio State Univ.) posits that during the period between the decline of aristocratic patronage and the emergence of the open literary market in the Victorian age, the literary reviews—specifically *The Monthly Review* and *The Critical Review*—"made possible" literary careers. (In developing his argument he also challenges accepted notions about the expansion of printing in the 18th century and contributes to current discussion of the relationship between biography and criticism.) After a preliminary chapter on how both reviews attempted to define and institutionalize the role of criticism, Donoghue scrutinizes the careers of Sterne, Goldsmith, and Smollett. Sterne, for example, though indifferent to the reviews of the early volumes of *Tristram Shandy*, ultimately "complied with his critics by composing *A Sentimental Journey*"; Goldsmith, on the other hand, deftly manipulated critics; and Smollett, on becoming the editor of the *The Critical Review*, changed his mind-set from author to critic, maintaining the latter point of view even after leaving the editorship to write *Travels through France and Italy* and *The Expedition of Humphrey Clinker*. A final chapter shows how the reviews patronized women authors by subjecting them to less exacting standards, with the result that, try as they might, women were unable to achieve the level of success that prominent male authors did. Impressively researched, closely argued, and gracefully written. A welcome addition to upper-division undergraduate, graduate, and research collections.—*C. B. Dodson, University of North Carolina at Wilmington*

OAB-0641   PR3698   95-1786 CIP
Douglas, Aileen. **Uneasy sensations: Smollett and the body.** Chicago, 1995. 201p index afp ISBN 0-226-16051-3, $29.95

This well-thought-out commentary on the novels of Tobias Smollett, whose works have been often criticized for referring to the body in crude and distasteful ways, offers a most interesting and convincing reading, which claims that each novel contributes a different view of how bodies acquire meaning. Douglas (Trinity College, Dublin) brings to bear on her cogent argument an understanding of the feminist approach to literature as well as other appropriate critical tools. In the first chapter she carefully presents—with copious references to Descartes, Robert Whytt, and Locke—a philosophical basis for viewing human bodies as "cultural constructs"; she next discusses Smollett's nonfiction work *Travels through France and Italy* as his obvious recognition of the importance of human materiality. Douglas then explores how each of Smollett's novels (*The Adventures of Roderick Random*, *The Adventures of Peregrine Pickle*, *The Adventures of Ferdinand Count Fathom*, *The Life and Adventures of Sir Launcelot Greaves*, *The Adventures of an Atom*, and *The Expedition of Humphry Clinker*) uses in its own special way the theme of sentience, with much emphasis on physical suffering and pain, indicating quite significantly how the body relates to society and politics. With its solid footnotes and excellent index, this volume is highly recommended to anyone interested in 18th-century fiction. Upper-division undergraduate and up.—*R. G. Brown, Ball State University*

OAB-0642   PR769   93-48138 CIP
Edwards, Philip. **The story of the voyage: sea-narratives in eighteenth-century England.** Cambridge, 1995 (c1994). 244p bibl index (Cambridge studies in eighteenth-century English literature and thought, 24) ISBN 0-521-41301-X, $54.95

Beginning with William Dampier's *New Voyage Round the World* (1697), which influenced Defoe, Swift, and Coleridge, narratives of sea voyages were extremely popular and involved a wide social spread of readers. Never before has this aspect of British literature, long an accepted donnée, been treated with such clear and insightful focus. This comprehensive work is divided into three parts. The first and most interesting section deals with Dampier and those associated with him. The second, most painstakingly researched section centers on narratives of Anson's, Cook's, and Bligh's Pacific voyages (1726-98). The last part, the least unified, includes separate narratives on slave trade, accounts of passengers (e.g., Henry Fielding and Mary Wollstonecraft), and autobiographical narratives by seamen, with some attention given to stories of transported convicts, indentured servants, and shipwrecked sailors. This fascinating study not only presents accurate assessments of individual accomplishments of the various sea narratives but also explores the motives and impulses behind such writings and the reasons for their popularity. Illustrated, with an excellent bibliography and index, this title is highly recommended for all public and academic collections.—*R. G. Brown, Ball State University*

OAB-0643   PR3592   94-41636 CIP
Fallon, Robert Thomas. **Divided empire: Milton's political imagery.** Pennsylvania State, 1995. 190p bibl index afp ISBN 0-271-01460-1, $40.00

Fallon (LaSalle Univ.) continues work begun in his *Milton in Government* (CH, Dec'93) by examining the government-related diction and imagery in Milton's major poems. Although he devotes most of his study to *Paradise Lost*, he includes a final chapter dealing with *Paradise Regained* and *Samson Agonistes*. Assuming that Milton's experience in Cromwell's government influenced his poetic assumptions and expressions about governance, Fallon explores the treatment of polity in all realms of Milton's poetic creation: heaven, unfallen and fallen earth, chaos, and hell. Each realm is shown to have something in common with the others, usually rule by two or three individuals with one of them dominant. Fallon cites numerous parallels between passages in Milton's poetry and actual rulers, political structures, and public events that the poet would have known. He makes the case that knowledge gained from firsthand experience shaped Milton's poetic imagery and diction. Although he ignores other possibilities that might account for some of Milton's concepts (e.g., the monarchical imagery of the Bible and classical poetry), he reveals a highly original direction for study of the major poems and provides a fresh perspective on Milton's poetic. Upper-division undergraduate and above.—*S. Archer, Texas A&M University*

OAB-0644   PR555   95-7156 CIP
Goodridge, John. **Rural life in eighteenth-century English poetry.** Cambridge, 1996. 227p bibl index ISBN 0-521-43381-9, $59.95

Few scholars bring to the study of rural poetry a working knowledge of modern as well as 18th-century agricultural life. Goodridge writes about his subject as if he knows his sheep and understands the seasons and rhythms of country life. Even such historical cruxes as the difficulty of identifying breeds that lived before the improvements of Robert Bakewell have been accounted for. But Goodridge is far from being the kind of literal-minded critic who attempts to extract the raw materials of social history from literature. Theoretically alert to the complexities of poetic convention, he cautions readers against assuming that they will hear authentic testimony from laborers like Stephen Duck but get only artificial pastoralism from the more elite James Thomson. There are indeed experiential differences to be deduced from their poetry, he argues, but one must not therefore ignore the literariness of Collier and Duck or Thomson's engagement with the problem of rural labor. Goodridge also miraculously resuscitates John Dyer's neglected georgic *The Fleece* (1757). The best book on 18th-century poetry in years. Rigorous enough for period specialists and historians, but accessible to all.—*D. Landry, Wayne State University*

OAB-0645   PR428   95-36592 CIP
Hall, Kim F. **Things of darkness: economies of race and gender in early modern England.** Cornell, 1995. 319p bibl index afp ISBN 0-8014-3117-4, $45.00

Not until very recently has research into race and racial consciousness in early-modern English literature been recognized as a subject. In the late 1980s and the 1990s scattered studies began appearing, but Hall's eagerly awaited volume is the first book-length study of the subject. Hall examines race in a wide range of materials and issues: travel literature; sonnets as a subtext for English colonialism; drama and its cultural anxieties over England's imperial expansion; the writings of women, principally Lady Mary Wroth and Elizabeth Carey; and the visual arts, especially portraiture and cameos. The author does not claim that the book is comprehensive, but this genuinely and remarkably trailblazing work covers more territory than any study before it. The book has its problems; it is too quick to generalize and like other new historicist studies too confidently locates the general in a few particulars. But the limits of the book pale beside its signal accomplishment, which is to undo the erasure of race from early-modern literary study. A major study recommended for all academic collections at the upper-division undergraduate level and above.—*P. Cullen, CUNY Graduate Center and College of Staten Island*

OAB-0646   PR3427   92-27140 CIP
Harth, Phillip. **Pen for a party: Dryden's Tory propaganda in its contexts.** Princeton, 1993. 341p index afp ISBN 0-691-06972-7, $45.00

Twenty-five years ago, in *Contexts of Dryden's Thought* (CH, Mar'69), Harth revolutionized our way of reading John Dryden and Restoration religious and philosophical poetry; in his first book since then, Harth now revises our understanding of the last years of Charles II's reign and the growth of Tory propaganda, 1675-85. Drawing on his unparalleled knowledge of the age's pamphlets, newspapers, and documentary sources, Harth relates in magisterially simple and engrossing fashion the tangled wars of opinion that divided England from the Popish Plot to the Rye House Plot, and the process by which Charles's government learned to manage public sentiment. This history in turn serves as context for detailed rereadings of John Dryden's classic contributions to the cause, *Absalom and Achitophel* and *The Medall*, as well as less well known works such as *The Duke of Guise*, *The History of the League*, and *Albion and Albanius*, all of which emerge crucially changed—their meaning and purpose clarified and sharpened—in light of Harth's splendid scholarship. Undergraduate and up.—*D. L. Patey, Smith College*

OAB-0647   PR3533   90-8806 CIP
Johnson, Samuel. **The letters of Samuel Johnson: v.4: 1782-1784; v.5: Appendices and comprehensive index,** ed. by Bruce Redford. Princeton, 1994. 2v. 462, 174p index afp ISBN 0-691-06977-8, v.4; ISBN 0-691-06978-6, v.5; $29.95 ea.

These volumes complete the magisterial edition whose first three volumes were enthusiastically reviewed in *Choice* (Jul'92). The letters of the last three years of Johnson's life make for poignant reading. These are the missives of an extraordinary man, enduring bodily afflictions and certain death with unflagging courage, beset by the deaths of longtime companions, and tormented by the collapse of his loving friendship with Hester Thrale. Professor Redford's notes are a model of learning and unobtrusive scholarship. The magnificent 100-page analytical index in volume 5 deserves the highest praise. The set as a whole is an obligatory purchase for all university libraries supporting graduate work in English literature. Graduate; faculty.—*N. Fruman, University of Minnesota*

OAB-0648   PR3592   93-23007 CIP
Knoppers, Laura Lunger. **Historicizing Milton: spectacle, power, and poetry in Restoration England.** Georgia, 1994. 209p bibl index afp ISBN 0-8203-1594-X, $45.00

This book is the first sustained study of Milton's major poems—*Paradise Lost* (1667), *Paradise Regained* (1671), *Samson Agonistes* (1671)—in the context of Restoration political history. Typically interpreted as a humanist poet, on the one hand, or a puritan, on the other, Milton becomes for Knoppers (Penn. State Univ.) a poet of the Restoration, who engages the political implications of the royalist spectacles that strive to validate and virtually divinize royal power. In large measure Milton's poems participate in an oppositional discourse, questioning earthly spectacle and promoting an iconoclastic art that features a heroism of inner witness. From these perspectives, Knoppers develops innovative and, at times, brilliant interpretations of characters such as the Son in *Paradise Lost*, the Christ of *Paradise Regained*, and Samson. In the process, Knoppers explains Milton's revisionist understanding and presentation of crucial concepts, including martyrdom, glory, and conquest. Highly recommended. Upper-division undergraduate and up.—*A. C. Labriola, Duquesne University*

OAB-0649   PR448   93-27263 CIP
Nicholson, Colin. **Writing and the rise of finance: capital satires of the early eighteenth century.** Cambridge, 1994. 219p bibl index ISBN 0-521-45323-2, $54.95

The 21st addition to the "Cambridge Studies in 18th-century English Literature and Thought" series, this most original study centers on the effects that the financial revolution in English society (the establishment of the capitalist financial systems) had on some of the major writers of the period; it is well grounded in the historical and economical analyses of the period, with special emphasis given to the essays of Mandeville and Defoe, which act as a primary basis for a "capitalist" reading of major works by Swift (*Gulliver's Travels*), Pope (*Dunciad*), and John Gay (*The Beggar's Opera*). Despite the fact that they themselves invested in stocks and shares, they used their satires as vehicles for attacking the deleterious effects of this new financial world of promissory notes of credit, money as the "arbiter of value," and the market morality. The author's approach to these works from this specialized political-economical point of view is consistent, resourceful, elucidating, and convincing; Nicholson (Univ. of Edinburgh) has presented a very valuable argument for viewing these 18th-century writers "in terms of a developing political economy that was permanently changing their world as they wrote." Illustrations and footnotes; excellent bibliography and index. Highly recommended to those interested in 18th-century history and literature. Upper-division undergraduate and up.—*R. G. Brown, Ball State University*

OAB-0650   PR2308   93-37277 CIP
Raylor, Timothy. **Cavaliers, clubs, and literary culture: Sir John Mennes, James Smith, and the Order of the Fancy.** Delaware, 1994. (Dist. by Associated University Presses) 335p bibl index afp ISBN 0-87413-523-0, $48.50

Because of its focus on two fairly minor writers of Stuart and interregnum England, this original and substantial study may not get the attention it deserves. The exactness of its focus is in fact the source of its strength, for Raylor's careful research into Mennes and Smith is constantly feeding into an account of

the world in which they operated, and it is his account of this larger picture that makes his book a genuinely revelatory and potentially revolutionary contribution to the cultural and literary history of 17th-century England. There is scarcely a page of this book that does not reward the reader with either new information (e.g., on the clubs of Caroline England) or new perspectives (e.g., on the continuity of Caroline and Restoration literary forms). For many readers, the most compelling and controversial material will be Raylor's discussion of the role of popular culture in the burlesque literary productions of the clubs and his portrayal of the relation between court and club culture. Both are hot properties these days in early-modern studies; but Raylor's exploration is much less agenda-directed and more carefully historical, with original archival research, than most work in these areas. This superb study establishes Raylor as one of his generation's leading early-modern scholars. Upper-division undergraduate and up.—*P. Cullen, CUNY Graduate Center and College of Staten Island*

OAB-0651   PR435   96-3856 CIP
Rogers, John. **The matter of revolution: science, poetry, and politics in the age of Milton.** Cornell, 1996. 257p bibl index afp ISBN 0-8014-3238-3, $39.95

This is one of the most original and prospectively seminal studies to date of a particular era, the brief period between 1649 and 1666, the so-called "Vitalist Moment," which encompasses the English civil wars, the interregnum, and the onset of the Stuart Restoration. In the cultural interplay of science, poetry, and politics, an intellectual paradigm prevailed, a form of philosophical idealism that correlated animist materialism with the new political philosophy of popular sovereignty. The former manifests the view that matter is imbued with motion, spirit, and energy; the latter, that government would and should change by liberalism, self-termination, and consensus. Examining this intellectual paradigm in the writings of John Milton, Andrew Marvell, Gerrard Winstanley, William Harvey, and Margaret Cavendish, Rogers (Yale Univ.) distinguishes his viewpoint from those articulated in other political, historical, and religious studies of the same era. In doing so, he is always decorous, deeply insightful, cogent, and lucid. The deeper value of this book, which is admirable simply for the interpretations of the authors cited above, derives from its astute analysis of an intellectual climate. Intellectual history at its best. Most highly recommended. Upper-division undergraduate through faculty.—*A. C. Labriola, Duquesne University*

OAB-0652   PR3581   92-22037 CIP
Shawcross, John T. **John Milton: the self and the world.** The University Press of Kentucky, 1993. 358p index afp ISBN 0-8131-1808-5, $35.00

"The trend of this biography is psychological—Milton as anal personality, Milton conditioned by oedipal influences, and Milton as one caught between his self and his world." Shawcross thus makes plain at the outset his interests and angle of vision. Three events give Milton's career its shape: the identity crisis of 1629-30 and the manifestation of a "homoerotic personality" in the friendship with Charles Diodati; the formation of a new attitude toward his father in the aftermath of his mother's death (1637-38); and his acceptance of mortality and the limitations of the human condition following the deaths of his first wife and only son and his descent into utter darkness (1655). Gender roles, what it means to be male or female, masculine or feminine, in Milton's life and works are a central concern. Despite a sometimes craggy style, this is a major work by one of the great Miltonists of our era. It should be acquired by every academic library.—*D. Littlefield, Middlebury College*

OAB-0653   PR3698   93-49538 CIP
Spector, Robert D. **Smollett's women: a study in an eighteenth-century masculine sensibility.** Greenwood, 1994. 196p bibl index afp (Contributors to the study of world literature, 56) ISBN 0-313-28790-2, $55.00

In this superbly argued study, Spector, the undisputed expert on Smollett and his works, has emphasized the thesis that Smollett's fiction essentially represents the "male-dominated world of 18th-century England" and therefore primarily appeals to the masculine mind. Spector concentrates on suggesting some of the shaping forces behind the development of Smollett's special masculine approach such as his marital relationship with Anne, his insistence on heroic, manly conduct, and his disdain of homosexual behavior. Spector applies this analysis in great detail to Smollett's heroines, who represent the best that 18th-century society could produce and whose duty it was to uphold the highest ideals of womanhood despite the fact that they were essentially asexual. His Hogarthian view of the often harmful effect of a woman's vanity and his typical 18th-century notions of a woman's sexuality can be seen in Smollett's treatment of fallen women and women as victims. The last chapter is devoted to the matter of Smollett's comic and grotesque female characters, who served his satiric and humorous purposes exceedingly well, given his tendency to create memorable caricatures and stereotypes; indeed, Smollett's choice of the epistolary technique provided him with the opportunity to create a convincing structure and to develop a remarkable variety of female characters, some of whom go beyond the limitation of stereotype and caricature. Highly recommended. Upper-division undergraduate and up.—*R. G. Brown, Ball State University*

OAB-0654   PR3330   91-44385 CIP
Swaim, Kathleen M. *Pilgrim's progress*, puritan progress: discourses and contexts. Illinois, 1993. 368p bibl index afp ISBN 0-252-01894-X, $44.95

This is the most comprehensive and thorough study of *Pilgrim's Progress* as a manifestation of 17th-century Puritan culture, rather than as a work that transcends the historical moment in which it was written and that formulates universal truths. Viewed as a microcosm of theological, political, and intellectual history, *Pilgrim's Progress* is richly and insightfully studied also in relation to Bunyan's numerous other works. Bunyan's theology, strategies of interpreting Scripture, and objectives as an author are all clearly and systematically examined. Moreover, comparative study of the two parts of *Pilgrim's Progress* (1678, 1684) cogently highlights their different worldviews—the earlier part glancing backward toward the Middle Ages and Reformation, the later ahead to the uncertainties of the modern era. More than any other analysis of *Pilgrim's Progress* (published in more than 1,300 editions and translated into 200 languages), this study interprets the relationship of so-called popular fiction to the particular contexts in which it was written. As such, this study exemplifies the New Historicist scholarly and critical methodology at its finest. Excellent. Advanced undergraduate; graduate; faculty.—*A. C. Labriola, Duquesne University*

OAB-0655   PR3669   92-34379 CIP
Thormählen, Marianne. **Rochester: the poems in context.** Cambridge, 1993. 383p bibl index ISBN 0-521-44042-4, $44.95

This is the third and longest critical study of Rochester's poems. Generally speaking, Dustin H. Griffin's *Satires Against Man* (CH, Jul'74) is psychologically and philosophically oriented; David Farley-Hill's *Rochester's Poetry* (CH, Jun'79) considers the poems within the large literary traditions of love poetry, satire, and burlesque. For Thormälen, "context" is much more varied—any field of reference, in fact, that allows her to enlarge upon the significance of one of Rochester's poems: the modern critical tradition itself; parallel passages in the writings of Rochester's contemporaries; items of political, social, and intellectual history culled from the writings of an older generation of scholars and from her own research in continental sources. There is, therefore, much in this book that will be familiar to Rochester scholars; but nowhere has it been brought together more clearly, cogently, and interestingly for the non-specialist reader. This is not to scant the book's value for professional scholars. Unburdened by ideological commitments and totalizing views of the poet, Thormählen's discussions are guided by careful adjustments of more extreme readings of Rochester. Each of the major poems is treated in a separate chapter, the *Satyr* in two chapters (more than 70 pages). The book has a useful bibliography and a detailed index; the notes (properly located at the foot of pages) are a generous bonus, rewarding and often amusing. Recommended for all levels.—*G. R. Wasserman, Russell Sage College*

OAB-0656   PR8749   93-37453 CIP
Thuente, Mary Helen. **The harp restrung: the United Irishmen and the rise of Irish literary nationalism.** Syracuse, 1994. 286p bibl indexes afp ISBN 0-8156-2616-9, $45.00

Thuente's study of the literary expressions of the United Irishmen's movement has a few prominent antecedents—Rosamond Jacobs's *The Rise of the United Irishmen, 1791-94* (1937), R.B. McDowell's *Ireland in the Age of Imperialism and Revolution, 1760-1801* (CH, Jul'80), Joseph Leerssen's *Mere Irish & Fior-ghael* (1986), and John Hutchinson's *The Dynamics of Cultural Nationalism* (CH, Jul'88). However, Thuente's book differs markedly from these by rejecting the commonly held notion that the United Irishmen were a political movement unconcerned with literature and culture. Thuente unearths some revealing documents—songbooks, collections of poetry, and prose satires (a number of which were previously unpublished—to demonstrate the literary dimensions of this nationalist movement. Furthermore, she clarifies the pivotal role the United Irishmen played in the evolution of 18th- and 19th-century thought and literature and establishes a line of development from them to Thomas Moore. She writes with precision and clarity, and the breadth and depth of her research are evident throughout. There is no question that this will become a premier book on its subject, and the three appendixes of songs, poems, and other publications are themselves significant contributions to a coherent assessment of the movement. General and academic audiences.—*D. W. Madden, California State University, Sacramento*

OAB-0657   PR113   95-51404 CIP
Women and literature in Britain, 1500-1700, ed. by Helen Wilcox. Cambridge, 1996. 307p bibl index ISBN 0-521-46219-3, $54.95; ISBN 0-521-46777-2 pbk, $18.95

This splendid collection provides uniformly excellent coverage of women writers and their contexts (e.g., humanist education, religion, literacy, the stage). The book's multiple authorship offers the signal advantage of exposing the beginning student to a range of approaches and a variety of feminisms. Happily, Wilcox made no effort to create the illusion of intellectual and political uniformity, and that is wonderfully liberating. What she did do was insist that everyone write well, so there is not an essay in the book, no matter how theoretical, that an intelligent undergraduate cannot grasp. A wealth of references in the ample notes to each essay supplements the short general bibliography. One final bonus is an invaluable chronology. Wilcox deserves hearty thanks from general and undergraduate readers and from early modern specialists. Her book deserves the widest possible circulation and is without doubt the first work to recommend to anyone interested in this comparatively new but enormously important field. All collections.—*P. Cullen, CUNY Graduate Center and College of Staten Island*

OAB-0658   PR3316   96-42178 CIP
Zonitch, Barbara. **Familiar violence: gender and social upheaval in the novels of Frances Burney.** Delaware, 1997. (Dist. by Associated University Presses) 167p bibl index afp ISBN 0-87413-618-0, $31.50

From the outset Zonitch (Rutgers Univ.) places this feminist study in the context of numerous other studies of Burney, many of them also feminist, but she quickly establishes her unique perspective. The introduction provides an excellent overview of the conditions of social change in the late 18th century while arguing that "Burney's preoccupation with violence originates in the fear that the death of aristocratic social domination subjects women to the escalating violence of the modern world.... [T]he choice for women is an untenable one ... between the harsh and even violent restraints of aristocratic rule and the alternative forms of violence created by newer versions of social control." Zonitch's definition of "violence" is broad, ranging from "sexual and physical abuse" to "emotional violation." Devoting one chapter to each of Burney's four novels, she not only demonstrates the interrelation among them, but also analyzes each in terms of the "progression" of Burney's major themes. Throughout, the discussion is mercifully free of current critical jargon, which makes this volume suitable for upper-division undergraduates as well as researchers and faculty.—*J. E. Steiner, Drew University*

OAB-0659   PR468   95-11320 CIP
Adams, James Eli. **Dandies and desert saints: styles of Victorian masculinity.** Cornell, 1995. 249p bibl index afp ISBN 0-8014-3017-8, $39.95

Adam provides a fascinating exploration of how Victorian intellectuals fashion masculinity according to an ascetic regimen. He begins with Carlyle's vision of the "hero as a man of letters" and demonstrates the double life inherent in this prophetic styling. Carlyle's cultivation of a solitary hero or "wildness" depends on the dandy, a figure craving public attention, as a shadow self. The force binding the prophet to the dandy is a "charismatic subjectivity," which appears throughout Victorian discourse. The aesthetic hero refashions traditional signs of masculinity—"virility," "martial strength," and "wealth"—into a dialectical play between depth (intellectual vocation) and surface (the spectacle of manhood). Adams traces this tension across a spectrum of Victorian culture that ranges from the rise of secret societies and the public school system to Charles Kingsley's novels of "Muscular Christianity" and Tennyson's poetics of renunciation. The author reads "The Lotus-Eaters" as an ambivalent exemplification of dramatic tension between the duty of imperial manhood and the desire for erotic surrender to a tropical woman or extravagant emotion. Adams concludes with a stimulating analysis of Walter Pater's writing, applying Pater's essay on Leonardo da Vinci to Oscar Wilde's *The Picture of Dorian Gray* to demonstrate the play between visibility and its dangerous shadow (often homophobia, but also political subversion). Recommended to all students of literature, men's studies, and Victorian culture.—*D. Seelow, SUNY College at Old Westbury*

OAB-0660   PR4023   95-50448 CIP
Arnold, Matthew. **The letters of Matthew Arnold,** ed. by Cecil Y. Lang. v.1: 1829-1859. University Press of Virginia, 1996. 549p index afp ISBN 0-8139-1651-8, $60.00

Lang (Univ. of Virginia) was designated by A. Dwight Culler "the prince of editors among Victorians." Lang built that reputation in part on his fine editions of Swinburne's letters and of Tennyson's, and now he offers the first volume of what will be the definitive critical edition of all the known letters of Matthew Arnold. When the six volumes are complete the edition will include almost 4,000 letters (approximately five times the number in the two-volume *Letters of Matthew Arnold 1848-1888*, compiled by G.W.E. Russell, 1895). Many of the letters appear in their entirety in print for the first time. In his 60-page introduction, Lang discusses previous editions of Arnold's letters and acclaims the letters as "perhaps the finest portrait of an age and of a person, representing the main movements of mind and of events of nearly half a century and at the same time revealing the actual intimate life of the participant-observer, in any collection of English letters in the nineteenth century, possibly in existence." Volume 1 includes both letters and diaries written by Arnold and some letters written to/about him. Detailed notes and appendixes. This scholarly achievement merits applause. Highly recommended.—*L. M. Tenbusch, emeritus, Immaculata College*

OAB-0661   PR4681   94-10513 CIP
Bodenheimer, Rosemarie. **The real life of Mary Ann Evans: George Eliot, her letters and fiction.** Cornell, 1994. 295p index afp ISBN 0-8014-2988-9, $33.95

We should all write letters to Bodenheimer and thank her for this book. Here we have the first full-scale study of George Eliot's correspondence (as collected in nine volumes by Gordon Height, Yale Univ. Press, 1954-74), helpfully organized by topic, and connected thematically to both life and fiction. Every paragraph is filled with information and insight, as issues both familiar (public and private) and not so familiar (Eliots's stepsons) are treated with immense and quiet sophistication. Unlike so much contemporary criticism, which spends half its time ostentatiously arm wrestling with theory or theorists, Bodenheimer shows clear awareness of contemporary accounts of biographical or epis-

tolary subject construction (and there are substantial bibliographical guides in these areas), yet for the most part allows Eliot and her contemporaries to provide their own best contexts. Both the fictive nature of letters and the autobiographical "reality" of fiction are well discussed in this very welcome book. General and academic audiences.—*S. C. Dillon, Bates College*

OAB-0662   PR4426   91-33937 CIP
Carlyle, Thomas. **On heroes, hero-worship, & the heroic in history,** text established by Michael K. Goldberg, Joel J. Brattin, and Mark Engel. California, 1993. 519p index afp ISBN 0-520-07515-3, $45.00

An exceptionally fine critical edition is an academic reviewer's delight. Here is such a book. The editors of the Strouse Carlyle Edition (to include all Carlyle's major works in eight volumes of accurate texts edited for the first time according to the standards of contemporary scholarship) succeed in giving Carlyle new life and in offering scholars new directions. Carlyle's powerful *On Heroes, Hero-worship, and the Heroic in History* has needed reworking. Until now, reliable editions of *Heroes* and Carlyle's other works have not been available. In contrast to the Centenary Edition (1896-99), described as the "most respectfully and generally used [and] textually the worst" (ciii), the present edition is a triumph of scholarship and technology, a remarkable advance in editing, whose "inspiration, base of operation and invaluable resource" was the Norman and Charlotte Strouse Collection of Thomas Carlyle (housed at the University of California, Santa Cruz). The Preface creates enthusiasm for the project by explaining its beginning then tracing it to its scholarly end—publication of the definitive edition of *Heroes*. The editors devised an integrated system for the computer-assisted production of an accurate text and used electronic technology in every stage of the editorial process, leaving to the scholars all decisions requiring editorial judgment. Includes an 80-page historical introduction, a valuable 25-page list of works cited, 163 pages of notes, 11 plates, a 30-page index, and much more. A feast, every page of which deserves pondering and praise. General; undergraduate and beyond.—*L. M. Tenbusch, Immaculata College*

OAB-0663   PR4612   95-2663 CIP
Cohen, Morton N. **Lewis Carroll: a biography.** Knopf, 1995. 577p index ISBN 0-679-42298-6, $35.00

Cohen (CUNY), editor of *The Letters of Lewis Carroll* (1979) and, with Anita Gandolfo, *Lewis Carroll and the House of Macmillan* (CH, Oct'87), has written the best and most scholarly biography of Lewis Carroll to date. His approach is mainly chronological, but a number of the chapters are thematic—e.g., "The Child," about Carroll's love for small girls, a love without (conscious) eroticism; "The *Alice* Books," with a commonsense autobiographical reading; "The Fire Within," about Carroll's guilt feelings, as revealed in his diary entries, and their probable causes; and "The Man's Faith," about Carroll's Broad Church position, in contrast to his father's High Church beliefs. Cohen looks at Carroll in the context of the Victorian age (e.g., see the treatment of the Romantic idealization of children), which is one of the reasons this book is twice as long as Anne Clark's similarly titled *Lewis Carroll: A Biography* (CH, Mar'80). Highly recommended for undergraduate and graduate academic libraries and large public libraries.—*J. R. Christopher, Tarleton State University*

OAB-0664   PR4038   94-2050 Orig
Collins, Irene. **Jane Austen and the clergy.** Hambledon, 1994. 242p bibl index afp ISBN 1-85285-114-7, $40.00

In this superbly readable book Collins fills two genuine needs: she has managed at once an important historical study of the condition of England's lesser clergy at the turn of the 19th century (too often simply assumed to be moribund or corrupt) and a marvelously revealing guide to Jane Austen's fiction. She begins with a review of Austen's own multifarious clerical connections; then, in chapters on such matters as "Patronage," "The Parson's Income," "The Parson's Parish," "The Clergy and the Neighbourhood," "The Parson's Wife," and "Worship and Belief," Collins brings fresh historical evidence to bear in readings of hundreds of passages from Austen's novels and letters. Beginners can learn much here (about

128

the difference between a rectory and a vicarage, or the good qualities of the preposterous Mr. Collins in *Pride and Prejudice*); those who have read the novels many times will benefit even more. This is a book that every college library will want to have; Collins writes so engagingly that public libraries will also find it a good investment.—*D. L. Patey, Smith College*

OAB-0665   PR868   94-10269 CIP
Copeland, Edward. **Women writing about money: women's fiction in England, 1790-1820.** Cambridge, 1995. 291p bibl index ISBN 0-521-45461-1, $49.95

Meticulously researched and solidly written, this study makes a valuable contribution to the understanding of women's literature. Copeland (Pomona College) takes as his subject "the consumer agenda of women's fiction, 1790-1820." The author provides discussions of fiction of the 1790s (including gothic), in which women were usually depicted as victims of imposed impoverishment; fiction after 1800, which recognizes the empowerment of women through their control of domestic economy; and Jane Austen's use of money and rank "to convey social meaning and power." He also offers a provocative analysis of 19 illustrations from *The Lady's Magazine* and readings of several novels dealing with women's employment, including the profession of writing. Copeland's strength is close textual analysis, informed by the perspectives of economic history and cultural studies. He makes nodding references to Bakhtin, Derrida, Jameson, Poovey, and others. He provides one particularly useful tool: a scale that enables readers to calculate costs, competencies, and worth (e.g., if a character is described as having an annual income of a thousand pounds, what does that mean in terms of rank and consumer power?). The exhaustive and useful bibliography includes both primary sources (many of them obscure) and secondary sources. Highly recommended for upper-division undergraduates and above.—*E. R. Baer, Gustavus Adolphus College*

OAB-0666   PR468   95-32733 CIP
David, Deirdre. **Rule Britannia: women, empire, and Victorian writing.** Cornell, 1995. 234p bibl index afp ISBN 0-8014-3170-0, $29.50

"Women, empire, and Victorian writing," David declares, "form a rich ideological cluster and a compelling subject for cultural analysis." Her objective is to find in Victorian writing the dominating attitudes toward empire, with particular emphasis on women writers, on women as represented in the texts, and on women as objects of sacrifice in the imperial world. For source material the author turns to "significant cultural documents" such as political essays, parliamentary reports and speeches, missionary literature, and travel writing, in addition to traditional fiction. The six chapters consider Wilkie Collins's *The Moonstone*, Thomas Macaulay's parliamentary speeches, and letters written home from India by Emily Eden; Charles Dickens's *The Old Curiosity Shop* and *Dombey and Son*; Charlotte Bronte's *Jane Eyre* combined with travel writing about Jamaica and literature about the Indian practice of suttee; education of the native Indian population and a legal case in Calcutta in the mid-1880s in which a female missionary was accused of loose behavior; assertive women in the imperial metropolis, the new imperialism, adventure fiction of H. Rider Haggard, and Tennyson's empire poetry; and Emilia Gould in Conrad's *Nostromo* and gender differences in constructing empire. This is a relatively new area of scholarly investigation, begun only as recently as 25 years ago, but David's excellent, detailed bibliography indicates that much progress has been made. This highly original and provocative book is recommended for upper-division undergraduates and above and for the general reader.—*R. T. Van Arsdel, emerita, University of Puget Sound*

OAB-0667   PR468   93-32781 CIP
Dowling, Linda. **Hellenism and homosexuality in Victorian Oxford.** Cornell, 1994. 173p bibl index afp ISBN 0-8014-2960-9, $25.95

Dowling's study is an exceptionally clear-headed and far-reaching analysis of "the way Greek studies operated as a 'homosexual code' during the great age of English university reform." By establishing the context within which the "spiritual procreancy" delineated in Plato's *Symposium* came to transform the intellectual and cultural climate of 19th-century Oxford, Dowling offers a fresh perspective on the social impact of such figures as Pater, Symonds, Wilde, and Jowett. But more importantly, Dowling shows how the development of homosexuality as a "normality unencumbered by norms ... originally entered Anglo-American consciousness through ... the ideal of Oxford Hellenism." Beautifully written and argued with subtlety, the book is indispensable for students of Victorian literature, culture, gender studies, and the nature of social change. Upper-division undergraduate and up.—*D. A. Barton, California State University, Long Beach*

OAB-0668   PR468   95-314 CIP
Dowling, Linda. **The vulgarization of art: the Victorians and aesthetic democracy.** University Press of Virginia, 1996. 133p bibl index afp ISBN 0-8139-1634-8, $32.50

As a title, *The Vulgarization of Art* is literally correct, yet misleading; the subtitle accurately describes this theoretical study in aesthetics. Dowling (Rutgers Univ.) seeks a philosophical matrix for the democratic aesthetics of Ruskin, William Morris, Walter Pater, and Oscar Wilde. She finds it in some early 18th-century writings of Anthony Ashley Cooper, Earl of Shaftesbury, whose exaggerated reputation (Montesquieu included him with Plato among the four great poets of the world) did not survive his century. His faith in the innate goodness of the general public and its receptivity to beauty and shared good taste was more durable. His democratic position influenced Matthew Arnold's concept of culture and, less obviously, the aesthetics of Dowling's chosen figures. Ruskin, while his religious faith remained unimpaired, shared Shaftesbury's confidence in the universal accessibility of good taste. Morris, until souring on disengaged beauty as redemption, was similarly influenced, as were Pater with his doctrine of individual experience and Wilde, whose reconciliation of beauty and socialism owed much to Morris. Dowling buttresses her integrated, well-crafted explication of a challenging thesis with exhaustive notes that anticipate the questions an intellectually engaged reader might raise. Upper-division undergraduate through faculty.—*D. Rutenberg, emeritus, University of South Florida*

OAB-0669   PR468   94-20629 CIP
Elfenbein, Andrew. **Byron and the Victorians.** Cambridge, 1995. 285p index (Cambridge studies in nineteenth-century literature and culture, 4) ISBN 0-521-45452-2, $54.95

This wide-ranging and complex study demonstrates the tremendous staying power that Byron had for the Victorians, both as a writer and as a cultural and historical phenomenon. After defining "influence" from several perspectives in the introduction, Elfenbein (Univ. of Minnesota) proceeds to discuss various facets of the Byronic hero and numerous circumstances that led to the creation of "Byronism" (not the least of which was the proliferation of periodicals during the 19th century). The remainder of the book looks at Byron's influence on other writers: Carlyle's rejection of all things Byronic, especially in *Sartor Resartus*; Emily Bronte's heavy reliance on Byron in the Gondal poems, followed by her striking originality and self-effacement in *Wuthering Heights*; and Tennyson's complicated combination of borrowing from yet rejecting Byron in a number of his poems. The author also explores the novels of Bulwer Lytton and Disraeli and a number of works by Wilde, demonstrating, among other things, a variety of responses to Byron's putative homosexuality. An important contribution to 19th-century studies. Upper-division undergraduate and above.—*J. E. Steiner, Drew University*

OAB-0670   PR858   95-22758 CIP
Ellis, Markman. **The politics of sensibility: race, gender and commerce in the sentimental novel.** Cambridge, 1996. 264p index (Cambridge studies in Romanticism, 18) ISBN 0-521-55221-4, $54.95

This very learned study usefully analyzes the place of sentimentality in the literature and politics of late-18th- and early-19th-century England. Ellis

(Univ. of London) takes the literature of sensibility more seriously on its own terms than previous studies of this subject in British literature (for instance, Janet Todd's *Sensibility*, CH, Feb'87). He traces the role of sentiment in the moral philosophy of the period by supplementing familiar philosophical sources (such as Hume and Locke) with readings of conduct manuals and noncanonical novels. He then subjects specific sentimental novels to analyses that are "text-focussed, historicist, and materialist" in approach, scrutinizing not only their representation of domestic sensibilities, but also their interventions in such overtly political matters as the slave trade, the commercial reform of "British industry, agriculture, and financial services" through the building of canals, and the establishment of institutions for the rehabilitation of prostitutes. Resisting the temptation to say that sentimental novels matter just because they address public issues, Ellis acknowledges the importance of the literature of sensibility in the private lives of its middle-class, largely female readership. A valuable addition to the literary history of sensibility. Upper-division undergraduates and up.—*R. R. Warhol, University of Vermont*

OAB-0671   PR451   95-17054 CIP
Erickson, Lee. **The economy of literary form: English literature and the industrialization of publishing, 1800-1850.** Johns Hopkins, 1996. 219p bibl index afp ISBN 0-8018-5145-9, $35.00

Thanks to this book and studies such as Peter Shillingsburg's *Pegasus in Harness: Victorian Publishing and W. M. Thackeray* (CH, Feb'93) and John Klancher's *The Making of English Reading Audiences* (CH, Jul'87)—all complementing classic works like Richard Altick's *English Common Reader* (1957) and studies of individual publishing houses and periodicals—a comprehensive picture of publishing and authorship in 19th-century Britain is emerging. Erickson explores in convincing detail the relations among technology, economics, and literary tastes. Literature written during these decades was dictated as much by mundane factors like printing technology and the price of paper as by the literary imagination. The market for poetry essentially disappeared and the periodical became the dominant form. What was most profitable to author and publisher alike—the periodical essay and the serialized novel—appealed to a less sophisticated readership. Erickson's analysis is sometimes subtle, e.g., when he explains why at one point the price of novels went up even as the cost of book production and paper fell. Readers may question a few of his assertions (e.g., that the dramatic monologue was an expression of poets' alienation as the market for poetry disappeared), but overall Erickson's study is solidly researched, carefully argued, and gracefully written. Highly recommended for all upper-level undergraduate and graduate collections.—*C. B. Dodson, University of North Carolina at Wilmington*

OAB-0672   PR778   92-55127 CIP
Frawley, Maria H. **A wider range: travel writing by women in Victorian England.** Fairleigh Dickinson, 1994. (Dist. by Associated University Presses) 237p bibl index afp ISBN 0-8386-3544-X, $38.50

Victorian women travel writers were an intrepid group, and a comprehensive study of their exploits is certainly welcome. This author, however, also develops an ancillary modern cultural theme: that women used their travel writing to prepare themselves for further professional development and writing in other areas. It is a fresh approach and one that suggests many new interpretations of travel writing. Frawley succeeds in demonstrating the ways in which women's minds were opened during and after their travel. She also analyzes the work not only of the well-known names, but also the myriad of less well-known women who traveled to the four corners of the earth. The book is well written, meticulously researched, rich with evocative material, and valuable for its definitive bibliography. Academic and general audiences.—*R. T. Van Arsdel, emerita, University of Puget Sound*

OAB-0673   PR4169   92-22716 CIP
Gezari, Janet. **Charlotte Brontë and defensive conduct: the author and the body at risk.** Pennsylvania, 1992. 201p bibl index ISBN 0-8122-3162-7, $28.95

This elegantly written critical study seeks to reassess Charlotte Brontë's achievement by examining her representation of "the body—its organs, senses, and appendages—as the site of social conflict and constraint." Gezari believes that Brontë's "concern with self-defense and self-vindication" and her "representation of the body as the site of emotional, psychological, and social struggle—are interdependent." Gezari's inquiry is informed and substantiated by reference to a broad range of critical and psychoanalytic investigations and 19th- and 20th-century fiction. Each chapter has a primary focus on a specific attribute of the body—"the master's hand," for instance, in *The Professor*, "vision" in *Jane Eyre*, and the "mental stomach" in *Shirley*—but also contains a wealth of cross-references to other fictional and scholarly works. To get full benefit from this topical, refreshingly articulate, thorough, and convincingly argued book, one needs some familiarity with such works. The Brontë that emerges from this interpretation is far more resilient than the familiar version. Extensive notes and a valuable bibliography. Advanced undergraduate; graduate; faculty. Highly recommended.—*T. Loe, SUNY College at Oswego*

OAB-0674   PR4754   95-3706 CIP
Hands, Timothy. **Thomas Hardy.** St. Martin's, 1995. 209p bibl index ISBN 0-312-12643-3, $39.95

Part of the "Writers in Their Times" series, this volume seeks to ground Hardy in his contemporary milieu. Despite the staggering amount of information on this accomplished, multifaceted, and long-lived writer, Hands charts a remarkably clear course through this material. In the first four chapters he provides carefully documented biographical, literary, social, and intellectual contexts for Hardy, his fiction, and his poetry. Chapters 5 and 6 are more ambitious still: they attempt, in 25-30 pages each, to locate the relationship of Hardy to other arts and to formulate the critical response to Hardy over the last century. Obviously some broad strokes are called for. Hands's convincing generalizations and critical judgments are based on solid references from wide-ranging sources. If Hardy and his work can be grasped through a 200-page introduction, this is it. The book is best approached as a whole, but readers researching specific works, events, or individuals will appreciate the full notes, generous select bibliography, and detailed index. Highly recommended for all academic collections—and all aficionados.—*T. Loe, SUNY College at Oswego*

OAB-0675   PS2642   95-21686 CIP
Hansen, Thomas S. **The German face of Edgar Allan Poe: a study of literary references in his works,** by Thomas S. Hansen with Burton R. Pollin. Camden House, 1995. 140p bibl index afp ISBN 1-57113-069-1, $44.95

Because Poe scholars have often looked for sources in German tales and attributed to Poe a sophisticated understanding of post-Kantian thought, Hansen (Wellesley College) set out to establish how well Poe knew the language and its literature. The answer, in short: not at all. Poe culled phrases from the pieces he encountered as a magazine editor, blithely incorporating typographical errors and grammatical absurdities, in his effort to seem as cosmopolitan and authoritative as possible during a time when German intellectual culture provided the underpinnings for the Romantic revolution. However, when Poe's own *Tales of the Grotesque and Arabesque* (1839) came under fire for "excessive Germanism," he abandoned German models and developed "a mode of rendering horror with more complex psychological dimensions." Hansen's study was assisted by Burton R. Pollin (CUNY), who set the standard for Poe scholarship with his careful research into the backgrounds of Poe's work (*Dictionary of Names and Titles in Poe's Collected Works*, 1968; *Discoveries in Poe*, CH, Oct'71; *Poe, Creator of Words*, CH, Feb'75; *Images of Poe's Works*, CH, May'90). This swift, narrowly defined study has broad implications for Poe's peculiar place in American culture. Upper-division undergraduate and above.—*J. D. Wallace, Boston College*

OAB-0676   PR4742   91-36082 MARC
Hardy, Thomas. **Thomas Hardy: the excluded and collaborative**

stories, ed. by Pamela Dalziel. Oxford, 1992. 443p ISBN 0-19-812245-4, $105.00

Based on Dalziel's doctoral dissertation (Oxford, 1989), this volume presents seven Hardy short stories that collections during his lifetime did not include, plus three stories he supposedly collaborated on, one with Florence Henniker and two with Florence Dugdale. One of the latter, "The Unconquerable," appears here in print for the first time. Dalziel introduces each story with a complete composition and publication history, and she provides a full apparatus of bibliographical descriptions, explanatory notes, and textual notes. Aiming to produce "as far as possible, Hardy's own 'intentions' for each text," she has examined all known holographs, typescripts, printed texts, etc., and she offers many pages of punctuation and styling variants in addition to numerous terminology variants. Certainly textual correctness counts, but this book's main virtue resides in its bringing together a group of Hardy's stories that heretofore Hardy scholars have virtually ignored and that bear their own historic and—generally—intrinsic interest. In effect, it can help most university libraries complete their Hardy canons. Advanced undergraduate; graduate; faculty.—*J. Combs, Kentucky Wesleyan College*

OAB-0677   PR457   95-50637 CIP
Hoagwood, Terence Allan. **Politics, philosophy, and the production of romantic texts.** Northern Illinois, 1996. 222p bibl index afp ISBN 0-87580-206-0, $29.50

In this ambitious and mostly successful attempt to move the discussion of Romantic literature in a new direction (a direction anticipated by recent developments in cultural criticism), Hoagwood (Texas A&M Univ.) argues that even recent revisionary criticism persists in believing the myth that the "meaning" of a work resides primarily in the mental ideas that critics assume the author "intended." Hoagwood ranges over familiar and unfamiliar works—the poetry of Wordsworth, Blake, and Byron; the novels of Mary Hays; the poetry of Samuel Rogers and Charlotte Smith—to establish two points: that the physical details of book publication are as crucial as authorial intention in establishing meaning; and that interpretations of the first generation of Romantics as apostates in their mature years to their earlier faith in the French Revolution fail to see that conservatives and radicals alike used the same techniques of metaphorical displacement in treating political topics from the 1790s to the 1820s. The author builds on and revises the work of such critics as Jerome McGann (*The Romantic Ideology*, CH, Nov'83), David Simpson (*Wordsworth's Historical Imagination*, CH, Dec'87), and Tilottama Rajan (*The Supplement of Reading*, 1990). Although he is at times content to state that a new meaning has emerged when he should also be explaining what that meaning is, Hoagwood's arguments are at the cutting edge of current Romantic criticism. Extensive notes and bibliography help make this a book that all academic libraries keeping up on recent Romantic criticism will want to purchase.—*M. Minor, Morehead State University*

OAB-0678   PR691   95-40292 CIP
Hughes, Derek. **English drama, 1660-1700.** Oxford, 1996. 503p bibl indexes afp ISBN 0-19-811974-7, $105.00

No one planning to write papers or books on Restoration drama will ignore this work. Developed from a series of articles, and complementing and expanding Robert Hume's *The Development of English Drama in the Late Seventeenth Century* (CH, Sep'76), it is an admirably detailed study of "all surviving plays" of the period. Hughes's very economical and considered critiques (up to five pages for major plays) concisely place each play in the context of influence, genre, history (theatrical, political, and social), religion, and philosophy, yet he also offers acute comments on language structures. This close attention to chronology and to shifting and contrary tastes and influences makes Hughes's survey authoritative and persuasive. The dozen chapters alternate comedy and tragedy; a conclusion regales the reader with deft and fascinating observations. An extensive bibliography of nondramatic texts precedes an index of all mentioned plays and a general index. This masterful work is in many ways the culmination of the careful research in this period by many scholars over the last two decades.—*B. E. McCarthy, College of the Holy Cross*

OAB-0679   Orig
Lane, Maggie. **Jane Austen and food.** Hambledon, 1995. 184p bibl index afp ISBN 1-85285-124-4, $35.00

Every so often, an author publishes a book simple in concept yet fresh, witty, and insightful. The reader marvels at the ingenuity and ponders why no one thought of this before. Such is the case with Lane's study of Austen's attitudes toward eating, food preparation, housekeeping, hospitality, social class, and gender. Admitting the topic of food is "merely background," Lane delivers substantive analysis of characters and describes how Austen's evaluation of their moral worth is based on how they eat, keep house, and entertain. Austen's own feelings about food appear ambiguous because most of her protagonists (with the exception of Emma) disregard it; however, in her letters, Austen thoroughly enjoyed writing about food. Author of *Jane Austen's Family* (1984) and *Jane Austen's England* (CH, Mar'87), Lane uses a sociological approach in bringing together letters, novels, family papers, 18th-century cookbooks, and histories. Most interesting is the chapter "Gender and Greed," in which Lane employs a feminist approach to food and writes that "Austen is quite clear that both sexes must be allowed the full play of their moral autonomy and that a healthy society values equally the contributions each can make." Recommended for general readers and scholars.—*J. L. Thorndike, Lakeland College*

OAB-0680   PR468   93-45568 CIP
MacDonald, Robert H. **The language of empire: myths and metaphors of popular imperialism, 1880-1918.** Manchester, 1994. (Dist. by St. Martin's) 268p bibl index ISBN 0-7190-3749-2, $79.95

Imperialism may be buried deep in the hearts of Englishmen, but between 1880 and 1918 imperialist fantasies were absolutely and nakedly crucial in the making of the British imagination, both at home and abroad. This clear, systematic, and gracefully written study investigates how the peculiarly adventurous destinies shaped by empire were marketed and absorbed not only by literary elites but by readers of popular fiction, memoirs, and journalistic accounts. Particular chapters are devoted to very readable expositions of the use of semiotics, ideology critique, and discourse theory for an analysis of popular notions of imperialism, followed by studies of exemplary narratives and the construction of certain historical events as cultural texts. Ranging with judicious care from the invention of Rhodesia in the popular press, to Kipling's verse, the memoirs of adventurers and soldiers of fortune, and the fiction of Cutcliffe Hyne and Edgar Wallace, this study never claims too much, noting the masculine bias of the poetics of war and conquest upon which it is focused, while pointing towards areas of future work on gender and imperialism, and on voices of opposition and protest. MacDonald addresses many fascinating topics throughout, such as connections between war and sport, and foxhunting and colonial military exploits, and he cites invitingly a number of other books in the same series, "Studies in Imperialism," from Manchester Univ. Press, evidence that an exciting collective project is underway. Academic and general audiences.—*D. Landry, Wayne State University*

OAB-0681   PR468   95-10929 CIP
Mitchell, Sally. **The new girl: girls' culture in England, 1880-1915.** Columbia, 1995. 258p bibl index afp ISBN 0-231-10247-X pbk, $17.50

Mitchell's provocative study joins the growing number of books that revise understanding of girls and their literature at the turn of the century (see also Shirley Marchalonis's *College Girls: A Century in Fiction* and Shirley Foster and Judy Simons's *What Katy Read: Feminist Re-readings of "Classic" Stories for Girls*, both CH, Nov'95). Mitchell (Temple Univ.) proposes that around the turn of the century working- and middle-class girls "increasingly occupied a separate culture." Turning to books, magazines, clothing styles, clubs, sports, schools, and memoirs for evidence, Mitchell defines this culture as a "provisional free space" where girls were no longer children but not yet gendered or sexualized. She pays special attention to the writer L.T. Meade, the literature of girls' schools and pioneering experiences at Cambridge and Oxford, and the culture surrounding scouting; the approach is largely descriptive, leaving the field open for further analysis. In the most innovative chapter, "Reading Feelings," Mitchell attempts to move from an understanding of the fiction most often cited by girls as "addictive" to some understanding of their interior world and the connections between the act of reading and daydreaming and fantasy. Mitchell's conclusion traces the demographic and political influences (including WW I) that restricted the culture after 1920. An excellent bibliography and 30 illustrations enhance the text. Recommended for collections in women's studies, children's literature, and British history at all levels.—*E. R. Baer, Gustavus Adolphus College*

OAB-0682 PN5124 94-18033 CIP
Nelson, Claudia. **Invisible men: fatherhood in Victorian periodicals, 1850-1910.** Georgia, 1995. 332p bibl index afp ISBN 0-8203-1699-7, $45.00

Using Victorian periodicals—essentially the titles in *The Wellesley Index to Victorian Periodicals* plus a handful of others—Nelson (Southwest Texas State Univ.) traces the deterioration of the father's domestic role. Many commentators became increasingly distrustful of fatherhood, seeing men as programmed only for aggression and authority while women were viewed as supplying an indispensable moral influence. Progressively shut out of home and family life, the Victorian father became an "invisible man" in periodical literature and had significance only as financial provider. The author traces these developments in science, education, and law. This study has been carefully researched, encompassing thousands of articles in 19th-century magazines, and is beautifully presented. It is a vital source for anyone wanting a fuller view of the Victorian social order. All collections.—*J. D. Vann, University of North Texas*

OAB-0683 PR868 96-38211 CIP
O'Farrell, Mary Ann. **Telling complexions: the nineteenth-century English novel and the blush.** Duke University, 1997. 182p index afp ISBN 0-8223-1903-9, $49.95; ISBN 0-8223-1895-4 pbk, $16.95

This exquisitely subtle book brings together deconstruction and the body to focus on a previously neglected figure in the 19th-century novel: the blush. Combining meticulously argued close readings of Austen's *Pride and Prejudice* and *Persuasion*, Gaskell's *North and South*, and Dickens's *David Copperfield* with pertinent glimpses at blushes in novels by Braddon, Trollope, Eliot, and James—and in such popular texts as *Clueless* (1995), print advertisements, and Helen Wells's *Cherry Ames, Student Nurse* (1943)—O'Farrell (Texas A&M Univ.) traces the literary and cultural history of the blush since Jane Austen's time. Her argument shows how the blush has always teetered between the realms of manners and of erotics, and how the novel of manners has deployed images of the blush as one of its generic means for "teach[ing] the body to behave itself in public." Whereas the 19th-century blush functioned as an indicator of character, in 20th-century texts the blush is more often self-consciously announced (as in "you're making me blush") than represented or perceived. O'Farrell's insightful readings contribute significantly to the history of representations of the body in literature. Highly recommended for upper-division undergraduates through specialists.—*R. R. Warhol, University of Vermont*

OAB-0684 PR5892 93-34121 CIP
Page, Judith W. **Wordsworth and the cultivation of women.** California, 1994. 200p bibl index afp ISBN 0-520-08493-4, $35.00

Feminist critics have been known to dismiss Wordsworth as a poet of egotistical sublimity, an exploiter of women limited by gender stereotypes of his age. While there is truth in such charges that he forsook his natural daughter Caroline Vallon, purloined from his sister Dorothy's journals, and demanded subservience from his wife Mary and sister-in-law Sara Hutchinson, the author of this provocative volume questions accepted, even formulaic, ways in which the poet has been viewed and interpreted. She scrutinizes his life and work from the point of view of the women themselves. Obviously, it is simplistic to regard the women as slaves to male poetic genius. Instead of censuring Wordsworth for depreciating the women in his household, Page inquires into the value they placed on their own contributions to his creativity. Making use of Wordsworth's

journals, letters, published and unpublished materials, Page explores the tension between masculinity/solitude and affinity with feminine nurturing/community through an explication of popular as well as usually neglected works in the Wordsworth canon. The result: an informative study that sheds new light on the great poet's achievements in its critique of assumptions about women upon which Wordsworth's life and work were founded. Undergraduate and up.—*G. A. Cevasco, St. John's University (NY)*

OAB-0685 PR4496 93-15824 CIP
Peters, Catherine. **The king of inventors: a life of Wilkie Collins.** Princeton, 1993 (c1991). 502p bibl index afp ISBN 0-691-03392-7, $29.95

This eminently readable biography engages immediately through a wealth of detail, yet its distinguishing feature is its cohesiveness. Peters draws on her experience as an editor of three of Collins's novels and on exhaustive research (including some new sources) to create a lively, but also balanced and highly focused account of this kindly, hospitable, companionable writer. Collins, who suffered from an addiction to opium (taken for rheumatic pain) and who supported two common-law wives and their households, is shown to have helped form the Victorian reading public with his drama and fiction, especially his hugely popular *The Woman in White* and *The Moonstone*. Peters documents how Collins refused to pay homage to Victorian orthodoxy, but in spite of his unconventional behavior managed to maintain an important social position and a vast number of friends—just as he maintained his audience. Deftly written, and offering an informed but never obtrusive perspective, this book provides an elegant example of responsible scholarly writing at its best. Sound bibliography and index. Highly recommended. General; undergraduate and up.—*T. Loe, SUNY College at Oswego*

OAB-0686 PR457 94-27188 CIP
Re-visioning romanticism: British women writers, 1776-1837, ed. by Carol Shiner Wilson and Joel Haefner. Pennsylvania, 1994. 329p bibl index afp ISBN 0-8122-3231-3, $39.95; ISBN 0-8122-1421-8 pbk, $16.95

Aptly titled and enterprising, this collection of 14 essays mixes commentary by established Romantic critics with that of newer voices in the field. The volume maintains a sense of coherence even though it does not privilege any singular critical mode and ranges from autobiography, dissent, and domesticity to religion and gender in Welsh writers, botanical themes in poetry, "literary anti-history," and theater theory. Writers Felicia Hemans, Mary Robinson, Charlotte Smith, and Anna Laetitia Barbauld are given voice in a number of the articles, whereas writers such as Hannah More, Joanna Baillie, Maria Edgeworth, Mary Lamb, and Jane Taylor are placed in more limited critical contexts. Every article is focused, well directed, crisply written, threaded with grace or humor or passion. The scholars reveal themselves as long-standing investigators of a topic about which they care and which they want readers to discover, respect, or understand. Interesting points of view, important contributions by all critics, superb job by the editors. Bibliography separates primary and secondary works, is careful and current with a fast-moving field. Exemplary scholarship. Upper-division undergraduate and up.—*W. C. Snyder, St. Vincent College & Seminary*

OAB-0687 PR4231 92-30729 CIP
Ryals, Clyde de L. **The life of Robert Browning: a critical biography.** Blackwell, 1993. 291p bibl index afp (Blackwell critical biographies, 3) ISBN 1-55786-149-8, $29.95

Only a handful of scholars could have written this book, and it is surely now the best introduction to the entirety of Browning's career. Ryals, the author of important works on early Browning (*Becoming Browning*, CH, Jan'84) and the particularly difficult late Browning (*Browning's Later Poetry, 1871-1889*, CH, Apr'76), now casts his gaze over the whole opus, and sets the writing economically into a wide range of Victorian context. The most significant aspects of life, writing, theme, development, contemporary reception, and 20th-century criticism are presented with great clarity and efficiency. Ryals's mastery of his subject and period is both unrivaled and also somewhat disconcerting;

there is an absence of driving *questions* throughout the book. Thus the book is mainly retrospective in stance—what we know about Browning—rather than pointed towards a more experimental, speculative future. But there are many different kinds of books in the world; Ryals's work is to be recommended as the best first book to read on Browning, with his earlier books to follow. General; undergraduate and up.—*S. C. Dillon, Bates College*

OAB-0688 PR878 94-49074 CIP
Sutherland, John. **Victorian fiction: writers, publishers, readers.** St. Martin's, 1995. 191p index ISBN 0-312-12614-X, $39.95

Sutherland (Univ. College, London) must know more about Victorian fiction and its background than almost anyone currently writing about it, and this book amply demonstrates his virtuosity. His premise is that there is a difference between "reading" Victorian novels and "knowing" them, and that to achieve the latter one must recapture "what these works of literature meant to their contemporaries." His approach is not unlike that of Richard Altick in his massive study *The Presence of the Present* (CH, Sep'91). In an early chapter, Sutherland explores the relationship between the 1857 Matrimonial Clauses Act and the contemporaneous rise of the detective novel. His brilliant analysis in chapter 3 of the "delicately poised balance of forces between author, editor, publisher and reading public"—which ranges over the interrelationship of Bulwer Lytton, Thackeray, Dickens, Reade, mad wives, treatment of the insane, and professional skulduggery—reads like a spellbinding novel itself. Sutherland also takes up the subjects of Dickens and serialization; Trollope's work habits; the master/apprenticeship relationship of beginning novelists; and finally, the "infrastructure of Victorian fiction." The concluding chapter poses the question "Victorian Novelists: Who were they?" and offers statistical analysis based in part on information from his *Stanford Companion to Victorian Fiction* (CH, Jul'89). Sutherland asks interesting questions about the Victorian novel and offers practical good sense in his answers. Highly recommended for general audiences, upper-division undergraduates, graduate students, and faculty.—*R. T. Van Arsdel, emerita, University of Puget Sound*

OAB-0689 PR5642 92-43257 CIP
Thomas, Deborah A. **Thackeray and slavery.** Ohio University, 1993. 245p bibl index afp ISBN 0-8214-1038-5, $45.00

William Makepeace Thackeray started life in India and became fascinated by literal slavery (whether Oriental, penal, or New World) and metaphorical slavery (as in his mid-life discovery of one's inevitable bondage to work, marriage, and convention). Between these two poles, Thackerary's seven principal novels all build upon his concerns with exploitation, domination, and dehumanization. In fact, Thackeray recurrently described the human condition in terms of one's being doomed to labor at the oar. For Victorian society, slavery was a major political issue. Thackeray was no polemicist, but as his letters, writings, and novels show, the theme continued a lifelong preoccupation, interestingly, most powerfully exploited in his fiction that preceded two visits to America (in 1852-53 and 1855-56). Somehow real-life slavery visits reduced Thackeray's reliance upon it as a source of fictional metaphor, though *Vanity Fair*, *Pendennis*, *Henry Esmond*, and *The Newcomes* are significantly enriched by the theme. Thomas has written the first study to focus upon the broad effects of slavery on Victorian society as a background to mining this motif in Thackeray's thinking. Drawing upon history, sociology, and literary criticism, this wide-ranging and thoughtful study is meticulously researched and well written. Recommended to students of Victorian literature and fiction. General; undergraduate and beyond.—*S. A. Parker, Hiram College*

OAB-0690 PR878 94-5352 CIP
Vrettos, Athena. **Somatic fictions: imagining illness in Victorian culture.** Stanford, 1995. 250p bibl index afp ISBN 0-8047-2424-5, $39.50; ISBN 0-8047-2533-0 pbk, $14.95

Vrettos's purpose in this thoroughly researched and extensively documented study is "to analyze the complex interaction between nineteenth-

century medical theory and narrative discourse," showing how Victorian fiction "both challeng[ed] and reinforc[ed] stereotypes of gender, class, and race." In doing so, Vrettos (Univ. of Michigan) investigates such topics as the supposed linkages between women's emotional lives and physical illness; the belief that nervous diseases could be spread by empathic observation (through reading, personal contact, even viewing simulated disease in a theatrical performance) and that such susceptibility was especially inherent in women; and the interrelationships between Victorian concepts of personal health, empire, gender, and race. The author examines representative medical, literary, and other cultural texts (e.g., advice manuals). Novelists discussed include Charlotte Brontë, Eliot, Stowe, James, Meredith, Stoker, and Haggard, but Vrettos's reading includes a wide range of materials (particularly nonliterary texts). This impressive work of both scholarship and criticism is recommended for all upper-division and graduate collections. Notes, bibliography, index are extensive.—*C. B. Dodson, University of North Carolina at Wilmington*

UNITED KINGDOM & IRELAND — 20th Century

OAB-0691 PR6001 92-18681 CIP
Auden, W.H. **W.H. Auden and Chester Kallman: libretti and other dramatic writings by W.H. Auden, 1939-1973,** ed. by Edward Mendelson. Princeton, 1993. 758p index afp ISBN 0-691-03301-3, $49.50

Mendelson's efforts to organize Auden's papers as well as place his extensive published works into a context that is both accessible and enlightening (see Mendelson's *Early Auden*, CH, Nov'81) have gone a long way toward establishing Auden as the premier poet in English in the second half of the 20th century. In the volume under review, he has superbly edited all the scenarios, scenes, opera libretti, and other dramatic works that were crucial to Auden's career. Film narratives, liturgical dramas, adaptations of Euripides and Shakespeare, as well as such well-known works as *The Rake's Progress* demonstrate just how extensive and successful Auden was at writing poetic drama. Mendelson's 200 pages of notes make virtually all the references and textual problems clear. A necessary addition to every research library.—*D. A. Barton, California State University, Long Beach*

OAB-0692 PR6045 92-1305 MARC
Beaty, Frederick L. **The ironic world of Evelyn Waugh: a study of eight novels.** Northern Illinois, 1992. 209p bibl index afp ISBN 0-87580-171-4, $27.00

Beaty is especially effective in his discussion of *Decline and Fall, Vile Bodies, Handful of Dust, Brideshead Revisited,* and Waugh's incomplete novel, *Work Suspended,* which has often been misconstrued. Beaty calls attention to a vast number of ironic details, implications, and innuendos that have not previously been observed. He demonstrates that irony not only gives Waugh's work added dimension, but also is more in tune with our contemporary society, which finds "irony's indirect approach more persuasive than satire's frontal attack." Although there have been some articles and books dealing with aspects of Waugh's use of irony, this is the first full-scale, comprehensive study—a work of impressive proportions. Unlike some other recent critics, Beaty really understands Waugh's approach, motivations, and techniques. This is a "must" for all college and university libraries—very, very highly recommended.—*P. A. Doyle, Nassau Community College*

OAB-0693 PR6019 94-30319 CIP
Cheng, Vincent J. **Joyce, race, and empire.** Cambridge, 1995. 329p bibl index ISBN 0-521-43118-2, $59.95; ISBN 0-521-47859-6 pbk, $17.95

Although traditionally James Joyce has been regarded as apolitical, Cheng (USC) argues most persuasively in this first book-length consideration of Joyce's attitudes toward race and colonialism that, in fact, Joyce "consistently and repeatedly" took strong stances on matters such as "nationalism ... internationalism and multicultural politics; cultural stereotypes and racism; [and] essentialism, whether racial, cultural, or linguistic." Less persuasively, but still beguilingly, Cheng contends that Joyce's "socialistically democratic ideas" and his "ideological subversiveness" have had an indirect political impact through the agency of more populist writers who have been influenced by him, through teachers of literature, and through critics (like Cheng). Aside from its excessive reliance on the jargon of deconstruction, Cheng's book is well written: clear, balanced, and gracefully expressive. He uses to great effect the ideas of such social and literary critics as Benedict Anderson (*Imagined Communities*, CH, Mar'84), Homi K. Bhabha (editor of *Nation and Narration*, 1990), and Edward W. Said (*Orientalism*, CH, Apr'79). The book includes popular 19th-century cartoons depicting stereotypical lampoons of the Irish and other racist attitudes. Upper-division undergraduates and above.— *P. D. O'Connor, St. Thomas Aquinas College*

OAB-0694   PR5908   92-37636 CIP
Cullingford, Elizabeth Butler. **Gender and history in Yeats's love poetry.** Cambridge, 1993. 334p bibl index ISBN 0-521-43148-4, $54.95

Cullingford examines dozens of Yeats's lyric poems by reading them in the context of the following: Irish myth and history; gender definitions and relations in 19th- and 20th-century Ireland and England; Yeats's female friends and loves, particularly these women's activities in the suffragist and Republican movements; his interest in the occult; the influence of pre-Raphaelite writers and painters on Yeats; his work as a Protestant, a senator, and an artist opposing the patriarchy and sexual politics of Ireland's Catholic Church and of the de Valera government—as well as much recent Yeats scholarship and Cullingford's own feminist approach to these love poems and their contexts. This study offers new, important readings of Yeats and his development as thinker and poet, focusing on Yeats's ambivalent and changing attitudes toward women and Woman and Mother Ireland. Of special note are her readings of "Leda and the Swan," "Among School Children," the Crazy Jane poems, "A Woman Young and Old," and "The Wild Old Wicked Man." Some readers will find much to quarrel with here, but clearly Cullingford has raised the level of interpretive quarrels through her careful research and argument. Good notes, exceptional bibliography. Highly recommended for undergraduate and graduate libraries and for scholars of modern poetry, Irish history, and women's studies.—*S. B. Darrell, University of Southern Indiana*

OAB-0695   PR6023   91-34369 CIP
Downing, David C. **Planets in peril: a critical study of C.S. Lewis's ransom trilogy.** Massachusetts, 1992. 186p bibl index ISBN 0-87023-774-8, $25.00

This thorough study of the Lewis trilogy (*Out of the Silent Planet, Perelandra,* and *That Hideous Strength*) has gestated in Downing's mind for more than 15 years as he has studied and taught Lewis at Westmont College. It is not only the first book-length analysis of Lewis's three romances but also one of the best studies of Lewis to date. Lewis was a formidable polymath, and Downing develops his argument not only through specific internal analysis of the three texts but also by incorporation of Lewis's life (especially as described in *Surprised by Joy*), his literary scholarship, and his Christian apologetics into a rich web of analogies, echoes, and correspondences within the trilogy. Seven chapters present an extensive range of perspectives on each romance, including an excellent discussion of Dante's influence in *That Hideous Strength*. Lewis commentators, like his own romance characters, tend to divide into extremes of defense or vituperation, yet Downing is wondrously balanced, judicious, and open-minded. An excellent book for undergraduates and their instructors. Substantial bibliographical data, thorough indexing. Vigorously recommended.—*C. Rees, University of Connecticut*

OAB-0696   PR5906   96-31671 MARC
Foster, R.F. **W.B. Yeats: a life. [v.]1: The apprentice mage, 1865-1914.** Oxford, 1997. 640p index ISBN 0-19-211735-1, $35.00

This magisterial first authorized biography of Yeats in more than 50 years takes advantage of numerous significant materials unavailable to previous biographers. Foster examines Yeats's life into his 50th year and the beginning of WW I (Foster is working on the second volume to complete the biography). Although not a study of Yeats's works, the book uses many previously unavailable sources so sensitively that it will enable readers and scholars to discover new insights and interpretations in poems, plays, and philosophical prose. Foster focuses on Yeats's work as a constant search for supernatural knowledge and for understanding Maud Gonne's influence on Yeats's life. Readers also come to understand more fully how Yeats's friends and enemies fired his creative imagination into productivity. A pleasure to read, the study contains more than 30 photographic plates; almost 20 text illustrations; family trees; detailed chapter notes; detailed index; and Yeats's revealing interview with Ashton Stevens (originally published in the US). A must for all collections.—*C. B. Darrell, Kentucky Wesleyan College*

OAB-0697   PR6023   94-33418 CIP
Greene, Gayle. **Doris Lessing: the poetics of change.** Michigan, 1994. 285p bibl index afp ISBN 0-472-10568-X, $39.50

Most recent books on Lessing have been novel-by-novel primers expounding familiar themes and concepts. Greene's astute, well-informed book is a welcome exception, at once both analytical and personal. The "change" in the title applies to Lessing's evolution as a writer, to her reluctance to be identified too closely with causes such as feminism, and to her profound consciousness-raising influence in her readers' lives. Especially important are Greene's fresh look at *The Four-Gated City* (1969); her discussion of *The Memoirs of a Survivor* (1975); her balanced treatment of Lessing's mysticism; her sensitive discussion of *The Good Terrorist* (1985); and her consideration of Lessing's "reluctance" to create endings that might lead her to write series of books even though "few writers are so fixated on the End" as Lessing. Greene (Scripps College) does not discuss all of Lessing's writings, just those "where Lessing uses the writing as a 'growing point' and a probe, as an 'instrument of change.'" Hence, in addition to the novels cited above, Greene treats only two each of the "Children of Violence" and "Canopus" sequences, *The Golden Notebook* (1962), *The Summer Before the Dark* (1973), and *Diaries of Jane Somers* (1984). This highly recommended book, which is certain to have a major impact on Lessing studies, should be owned by all academic libraries.— *P. Schlueter, Warren County Community College*

OAB-0698   PR6005   94-45316 CIP
Griffith, John W. **Joseph Conrad and the anthropological dilemma: 'Bewildered traveller.'** Oxford, 1995. 248p bibl index afp ISBN 0-19-818300-3, $49.95

This clearly written monograph places in historical context Conrad's treatment in his early fiction of "the anthropological dilemma"—the fate of the European who travels to the so-called primitive societies of Africa and the Far East. Much of this ground has already been covered in such major works as Frederick Karl's *Joseph Conrad: The Three Lives* (CH, Jun'79) and Ian Watt's *Conrad in the Nineteenth Century* (CH, Jul'80), but Griffith makes a useful contribution to the massive body of Conrad criticism by the comprehensiveness of his study. Drawing on the work of scores of writers—including anthropologists, biologists, travel writers, novelists, philosophers, colonial administrators, and missionaries—the author shows how fully Conrad participated in the debates about progress, imperialism, altruism, race, evolution, and the nature of civilization that made the late Victorian era an "age of cultural crisis." Each chapter centers on *Heart of Darkness* and shows that practically every image, idea, and character in the novella has its counterpart in writings by Conrad's contemporaries. Griffith does not define the uniqueness of Conrad's work, but he deals sensibly with such controversial subjects as Conrad's alleged racism and his attitude toward cultural and ethical relativism.

This wide-ranging, well-documented survey is recommended to both specialists and upper-division undergraduate students.—*E. Nettels, College of William and Mary*

OAB-0699   PR8733   95-33075 CIP
Haberstroh, Patricia Boyle. **Women creating women: contemporary Irish women poets.** Syracuse, 1996. 250p bibl index afp ISBN 0-8156-2671-1, $39.95; ISBN 0-8156-0357-6 pbk, $16.95

This close examination of the works of Eithne Strong, Eavan Boland, Eiléan Ní Chuilleanáin, Medbh McGuckian, and Nuala Ni Dhomhnaill challenges the patriarchal view of modern Irish poetry as dominated by Yeats, Kavanagh, and now Heaney. Through a study of the themes, image patterns, and lyric voices that develop within and between these poets' works (along with a more cursory discussion of poetry written since the 1980s), Haberstroh (La Salle Univ.) shows how Irish women poets have created "alternatives to [the] stereotypical and idealized images" generated by traditional male representations. Impressive in her command of feminist literary theory and comprehensive in her knowledge of the poets and their works, Haberstroh never allows theory to displace the texts she explicates. This volume is a much-needed complement to Robert Garratt's exclusively male *Modern Irish Poetry: Tradition and Continuity from Yeats to Heaney* (CH, Apr'87). However, though her readings are often gender-comparative and sensitive to the tensions between nationalism and gender in many of the poets, Haberstroh contributes to the construction of separate if not separatist traditions, a phenomenon that any nationalist, gender-based criticism must address eventually. Undergraduate; graduate; faculty; general.—*D. R. McCarthy, Huron College*

OAB-0700   PR808   95-4572 CIP
Harris, Janice Hubbard. **Edwardian stories of divorce.** Rutgers, 1996. 214p bibl index afp ISBN 0-8135-2246-3, $42.00; ISBN 0-8135-2247-1 pbk, $18.00

Readers may be misled by the title of this book. It is not an anthology of Edwardian short fiction but a stylishly written and amply documented discussion of the issues raised during the Edwardian campaign for divorce reform. Harris means her book to complement existing studies (e.g., Roderick Phillips's *Putting Assunder*, CH, Jun'80, and Lawrence Stone's *Broken Lives*, CH, Mar'94, among others). She distinguishes between the "stock story," embodying conservative attitudes—which was heard in the divorce courts and reported with commentary in the tabloid press—and the "counterstory," which was offered by advocates of divorce reform and individuals seeking relief from troubled marriages. Many such challenges to the status quo were heard by the Royal Commission on Divorce and Matrimonial Causes. That commission's 1912 report is the subject of an especially informative chapter. Harris discusses Edwardian divorce novels, which she calls a neglected subgenre of the period's fiction. She cogently argues that such novels presented ambiguities and complexities of marital discord not found in court testimony, newspapers, or the evidence presented to the Royal Commission. Harris concludes with a summary of the commission's recommendations and their fate, and a discussion of Edwardian surveys on women's attitudes toward divorce. Upper-division undergraduate, graduate, and research collections; general readers.—*M. S. Vogeler, emeritus, California State University, Fullerton*

OAB-0701   PR6045   94-45396 CIP
Hastings, Selina. **Evelyn Waugh: a biography.** Houghton Mifflin, 1995 (c1994). 724p index ISBN 0-395-71821-X, $40.00

Those who do not have previous Waugh biographies fresh in mind—especially Martin Stannard's two-volume *Evelyn Waugh* (CH, Jan'88, Jan'93)—may not grasp, as they read this very entertaining book, what a superb scholarly achievement it really is. Hastings has uncovered masses of important material previously unknown; those interviewed were willing to tell her more than they had told anyone else. The result is not only the most persuasive and human portrait of Waugh to date, but also the first to give a convincing account of such tangled matters as the collapse of his first marriage and, avoiding the political partisanship that led Stannard to belittle his subject, Waugh's wartime experience. The book is disappointing only in that Hastings is resolutely the biographer, not the critic: she does not move beyond her (excellent) discussions of the ways Waugh's novels parallel real experience to full-scale critical examination. But this defect, if it is one, is small compared with Hasting's achievement: she has produced the first really satisfactory life of one of our century's major writers. And Hastings is so modest and graceful a writer herself that there will be equally long waiting lists for this book in public libraries and graduate research institutions. All collections—*D. L. Patey, Smith College*

OAB-0702   PR503   95-19556 CIP
Heaney, Seamus. **The redress of poetry.** Farrar, Straus & Giroux, 1995. 212p ISBN 0-374-24853-2, $22.00

The publication of any Heaney book is a literary event, and this collection of ten of his 15 Oxford lectures (1989-94), coming so soon after his Nobel prize, is unusually important. Corrective rather than revisionist, these lectures/essays provide a discussion of Marlowe, a look at an underappreciated Irish comic masterwork, a new reading of John Clare, a fresh approach to Wilde's *Reading Goal*, a generous appreciation of Hugh MacDiarmid, a sad reappreciation of fading Dylan Thomas, a strange and illuminating pairing of Yeats and gloomy Larkin, and an assessment of Elizabeth Bishop. General essays open and close the volume. Heaney frames all of the poets/works in richly textured readings of the works, thereby revealing, between the lines, his own ideals, standards, and practices. Heany has become a Virgilian humanitarian of prosody—wise, understanding, urbane, concerned. These pieces send the reader back to the poets and their works with new understanding and enthusiasm. All collections.—*J. N. Igo Jr., San Antonio College*

OAB-0703   PR6019   95-4398 CIP
Heller, Vivian. **Joyce, decadence, and emancipation.** Illinois, 1996 (c1995). 191p bibl index afp ISBN 0-252-02189-4, $29.95; ISBN 0-252-06485-2 pbk, $12.95

Heller's study reacts to attacks on the supposed subjectivism of modernism by Marxists like Georg Lukács and by poststructuralist critics in general. She describes Joyce as a writer who is at once a chronicler of decadence and an artist who points the way toward emancipation from such social degeneration. Heller is very good at weaving theoretical positions together with specific aspects of Joyce's work. In particular, she identifies the Joycean epiphany as key to Joyce's thematic progression, defines it, locates it, and comments on its evolution. Specifically, epiphany accomplishes "a synthesis of decadence of subject and emancipation of mind." The epiphanies of *Dubliners* are negative, as they shed light on social paralysis, but those of *Portrait* are positive but unlinked, so that they ultimately cancel each other out. The epiphanies of *Ulysses* relate to texts and to the art of narration, and they remind the reader of the need to refine the nature of reality by means of the circular journey through a work of art. This sophisticated treatment of the dance between decadence and emancipation will reward any student of Joyce and modern literature. Upper-division undergraduate and above.—*M. H. Begnal, Pennsylvania State University, University Park Campus*

OAB-0704   PR808   94-34792 MARC
Joannou, Maroula. **'Ladies, please don't smash these windows': women's writing, feminist consciousness and social change, 1918-38.** Berg, 1995. 236p bibl index ISBN 1-85973-022-1 pbk, $19.95

This is an important feminist survey of English women novelists between the two World Wars. Joannou is evenhanded in her treatment of the writers, from the less known, like Leonora Eyles, to the well known, like Virginia Woolf. She also touches on a wide variety of topics—e.g., spinsterhood, the history of feminism, patriarchialism, and factionalism within the feminist cause itself. Lesbianism, which is only narrowly dealt with by the writers she surveys, is seen simply as one issue among many. Since Joannou writes from what she calls a "socialist-feminism" viewpoint, she insists on a close relationship between feminism and political ideology. There is no similar work of American origin. A British study, Nicola Beaumann's *A Very Great Profession: The Woman's Novel 1914-39* (1983), deals with many of the same authors and ideas but without the political overtones and Joannou's advanced feminist perspective. A valuable addition to feminist literary criticism, recommended for upper-division and graduate levels.—*J. J. Patton, Atlantic Community College*

OAB-0705   PR6019   91-22324 MARC
Johnston, Denis. **The old lady says "no!"**, ed. with introd. by Christine St. Peter. Catholic University of America/Colin Smythe, 1992. 131p afp ISBN 0-8132-0751-7, $24.95

This thorough edition of Johnston's 1929 choral dream-play comes as close to the ideal as any drama-loving Hibernophile is likely to find. Although the stage fantasia focuses on Robert Emmet's beloved but abortive rising of 1803, Johnston shaped the play less according to history and more according to the Gaelic *aisling*, for the "Old Lady" of Johnston's title is the Sean Bhean Bhocht rather than patient Lady Gregory, as Abbey apocrypha would have it. Originally titled *Shadowdance*, and often mistaken as an instance of Weimar expressionism, the play proved a favorite with Dublin audiences and, frequently, a mystery for audiences elsewhere. As a dream-play for a chorus of sometimes impolitic and impolite Dublin voices, the text rather improves on Joyce's "nighttown" episode in the Calypso chapter of *Ulysses*. Indeed, the closest analogue for a single voice may well be Thomas MacGreevy's poem *Crón Tráth na nDéithe* (1923). Prepared in 1976 by Johnston himself, this edition of the play's text benefits hugely from St. Peter's interesting, jargon-free introduction and from her 246 annotations most of which *do* enlighten Johnston's many sometimes arcane allusions to Dublin's popular culture under the Free State. Chronology and bibliography of sources are awkwardly placed in front. The definitive and standard edition for years to come, a must for any college or university library professing a serious interest in Irish drama.—*T. D. Redshaw, University of St. Thomas*

OAB-0706   PR6063   96-12982 CIP
Kendall, Tim. **Paul Muldoon.** Dufour Editions, 1996. 258p bibl index ISBN 0-8023-1312-4, $29.95; ISBN 0-8023-13130-2 pbk, $14.95

The first book on a difficult but important contemporary Irish poet, this accessible, detailed, and comprehensive study will be a benchmark for future Muldoon criticism. Although heavily indebted to treatments of Muldoon by Edna Longley (in *Poetry in the Wars*, CH, Nov'87, and *The Living Stream*, 1994) and Clair Wills (*Improprieties*, 1993), Kendall (Univ. of Newcastle, UK) does more than repeat their insights about the themes of personal identity, the politics of Northern Ireland, and the linking of sex and violence in Muldoon's work. He relates the details of poems to their biographical, political, and, in particular, literary-political contexts (for example, Muldoon's indebtedness to Frost and his increasingly ambiguous attitude about Heaney) and argues cogently for neglected works like Muldoon's libretto for Daron Hagen's *Shining Brow* (1991) and for the poems he deems Muldoon's masterpieces: "The More a Man Has the More a Man Wants," in *Quoof* (1983), and "Yarrow," in *The Annals of Chile* (1994). Kendall's solid grasp of poetic forms leads him to reveal Muldoon's intricate play with sestina and sonnet in the longer narrative works. Kendall's thorough work covers every collection and poem of note up to *The Annals of Chile* and provides a comprehensive bibliography. Undergraduate; graduate; faculty.—*D. R. McCarthy, Huron College*

OAB-0707   PR6053   90-26185 CIP
Kritzer, Amelia Howe. **The plays of Caryl Churchill: theatre of empowerment.** St. Martin's, 1992 (c1991). 217p index ISBN 0-312-06091-2, $39.95

Kritzer's comprehensive study of Caryl Churchill's plays, though the first to appear, will surely remain a standard. In chapter after chapter, from the radio plays of the 1960s to the television plays of the 1970s to the most recent stage plays, Kritzer sustains a level of analysis that is both admirable and revealing. Her portrait of Churchill, a materialist-feminist acutely alert to the potential of drama, is gleaned almost exclusively from the plays, which collectively offer a social analysis of oppression and a political agenda of empowerment. Kritzer's readings of the little-known plays, often the first, are intelligent and perceptive. But it is her readings of the familiar plays—*Cloud Nine, Top Girls, Serious Money*—that are bound to attract attention. For here she focuses on the materials of oppression—on sex and gender, for example, and on labor and capital—with startling acuity. Her concluding chapter offers an excellent overview of Churchill's work, rehearsing the issues, techniques, and challenges her plays engage. One wishes only that Kritzer had not reviewed the theoretical positions of others in her introduction, which yields to a vocabulary she herself does not employ. This is a feminist analysis of the first rank, a book that opens up the possibility for a broader understanding of Britains foremost female playwright. Undergraduate; graduate; faculty.—*J. Schlueter, Lafayette College*

OAB-0708   97-71155 Orig
Lee, Hermione. **Virginia Woolf.** Knopf, 1997 (c1996). 893p bibl index ISBN 0-679-44707-5, $39.95

The best biography of Virginia Woolf since Lyndall Gordan's *Virginia Woolf: A Writer's Life* (CH, May'85), Lee's volume creates an integrated portrait of a life of writing without reducing the writing to the life. The author's extensive use of Woolf's autobiographical writings, *Moments of Being*, ed. by J. Schulkind (CH, May'77), diaries, letters, and essays makes for an expansive view of Woolf as an experimental writer—exploring the boundaries of biography, fiction, and poetry—and an iconoclastic individual synthesizing political, social, and aesthetic thought. Lee describes Woolf as plagued by both physical and emotional trauma as she maintains a complex, interdependent web of relationships with husband and coworker Leonard, the Bloomsbury family, and the numerous women who shaped her life, beginning with her mother, Julia Stephen. Lee captures the "many selves" that Woolf claimed the biographer often missed, leaving the reader with the sense that further exploration of the fiction and other writings will result in discovering the "many thousand" selves yet unexplored. Suitable for all academic libraries, undergraduate and graduate, and general readers interested in an aesthetic, literary, political, and historical perspective on 20th-century Britain.—*N. Allen, Beaver College*

OAB-0709   PR5906   94-19006 CIP
Murphy, William M. **Family secrets: William Butler Yeats and his relatives.** Syracuse, 1995. 534p bibl index afp ISBN 0-8156-0301-0, $39.95

Murphy's fourth volume about the Yeatses (after *Prodigal Father*, CH, Nov'78; *The Yeats Family and the Pollexfens of Sligo*, 1971; and *Letters to W.B. Yeats*, edited with Richard Finneran and George Harper, CH, Sep'78) is an illuminating, wonderfully written addition to Yeats studies. It draws on letters, diaries, scrapbooks, and other documents only recently available. Early chapters focus on the extended families and home lives of the Yeats family: John Butler Yeats (JBY); his wife, Susan Pollexfen Yeats; their four children—Willie, Lily, Lollie, and Jack. Offering much new material, chapters 3-6 concern the two sisters, Lily and Lollie, and their work first at Dun Emer and later at Cuala Industries, where Lily headed the embroidery department and Lollie the press. Chapter 7 addresses Jack—painter, writer, quiet rebel against his father. The last chapter concerns the 20-year Platonic love affair and correspondence between JBY and Rosa Butt. Murphy (Union College) discusses the Pollexfen and Yeats tendency to depression, even madness; family interest in the occult; Lollie's constant difficulties getting along with family and outsiders; Jack's separation from the family; the Yeatses' chronic financial difficulties; and the two sons' ultimate successes—Willie's in writing and Jack's in painting—and their generosity in paying business debts and living expenses for their father and two sisters. This first-rate biography is a gift to Yeats students. All collections.—*S. B. Darrell, University of Southern Indiana*

OAB-0710   PR888   94-48939 CIP
Parkes, Adam. **Modernism and the theater of censorship.** Oxford, 1996. 242p bibl index afp ISBN 0-19-509702-5, $45.00

Parkes observes several 20th-century British novels through the prism of the censorship battles they encountered in the 1920s and 1930s. He begins with an introductory chapter on obscenity trials as "reception studies" of a sort and theatrical events wherein "the culture of censorship itself was implicitly put on trial." His reading of Wilde's conviction for homosexuality crosses swords with recent queer readings of the same event. He goes on to consider Lawrence's *The Rainbow*, Joyce's *Ulysses* (including its initial magazine publication in *The Little Review*), Lawrence's *Lady Chatterley's Lover*, and Hall's *The Well of Loneliness* (read in tandem with Woolf's *Orlando*, the final form of which, Parkes suggests, was affected by the obscenity trial over Hall's book). The author's observation that "experimental modernism" contested the values of its time is a truism. However, his detailed reconstructions of the actual trials and their effects on authorship are brilliantly researched, particularly in regard to Lawrence and Woolf. As a whole, this book is as significant a contribution to the literature of modern censorship as Leonard Leff and Jerold Simmons's *The Dame in the Kimono* (CH, Jun'90). And, like Leff and Simmons, Parkes makes the censors as vivid and interesting as the censored. Recommended at the upper-division undergraduate level and above.—*M. J. Emery, Cottey College*

OAB-0711   PR5366   95-37248 CIP
Peters, Sally. **Bernard Shaw: the ascent of the superman.** Yale, 1996. 328p bibl index afp ISBN 0-300-06097-1, $28.50

What "secret spheres" lie embedded in "the labyrinthian psyche of the great creative artist"? This is the tantalizing question Peters answers so brilliantly in this searching inquiry into the innermost recesses of that towering but conflicted iconoclast Bernard Shaw. The author discusses how the beleaguered Shaw, racked by lifelong feelings of sexual anxiety, gender confusion, and ineluctable alienation, constructed formidable psychic defenses against a variety of perceived threats to his fragile sense of self. Always the outsider, the would-be superman perpetually sought the heights so he would not have to confront the "abyss" within his own riven spirit. In this ascent toward the heavens, emblematic of the attempt to realize a "cerebral" earthly paradise free of the unmerited suffering that often suffuses otherness and difference, Shaw was haunted by the subterranean knowledge that he bore the characteristic marks of the "noble invert": the coalescence of native genius, artistic prowess, and homoerotic tendencies in the same mortal frame. Inordinately rich in insight, this superb study provides the perfect antidote for those suffering from the illusion that nothing new and instructive can be said about Shaw. Highly recommended for all college and university libraries.—*H. I. Einsohn, Middlesex Community-Technical College*

OAB-0712   PR6045   95-26568 CIP
Reid, Panthea. **Art and affection: a life of Virginia Woolf.** Oxford, 1996. 570p bibl index afp ISBN 0-19-510195-2, $35.00

This is an insightful, readable, and innovative addition to Woolf criticism. Reid's exhaustive research, including reference to some heretofore unpublished original documents, contributes to the growing understanding of Woolf's creative process and the emotional influences that shaped her work: "the twin desires to write and to be loved." Rejecting what she considers exaggerated interpretations of sexual abuse by her half brothers, Reid focuses on Woolf's response to her mother's neglect and to the painful relationship with her sister Vanessa, "a sibling rivalry that also became a rivalry between these siblings' arts." This concentration on women's friendship and influence is surely an addition to feminist scholarship, and Reid's assertions may lead to interesting new readings of the major novels, particularly *To the Lighthouse* and *Mrs. Dalloway*. At moments Reid's thesis and minute detailing works against a balanced approach that takes in all evidence, certainly a danger for Woolf critics, who must digest a mountain of previous biographical speculation. Wonderful companion to Quentin Bell's *Virginia Woolf: A Biography* (CH, Feb'73), James King's *Vir-*

ginia Woolf (1994), and Phyllis Rose's *Woman of Letters: A Life of Virginia Woolf* (CH, Dec'78). Upper-division undergraduates through faculty.—*L. Winters, College of Saint Elizabeth*

OAB-0713   PR6029   91-58168 CIP
Shea, Thomas F. **Flann O'Brien's exorbitant novels.** Bucknell, 1992. (Dist. by Associated University Presses) 183p bibl index afp ISBN 0-8387-5220-9, $32.50

In five chapters Shea considers O'Brien's university writings as well as his four novels in English; *At Swim-Two-Birds* engages two of these, including one on the writer's earlier experiments to that splendid end. The presentation of unpublished manuscripts and letters suggests the completeness of this study on its own terms. Instances are often hilarious; Shea's commentary is persuasive, often invoking instructive analogies. In varying degrees, among the continuing topics are O'Brien's literary parodies, his "subversive" strategies, the foregrounding of language as performance ("self-conscious verbal posturings"), his texts as "palimpsests" with "competing fields of discourse," and his challenges to linear order and traditional forms of coherence. All this is served up with a disciplined enthusiasm. Shea's style often has its own exorbitancy within the parameters of his argument, a puckishness never completely dominated by the seriousness and insights of this study. Here are telling and well-turned phrases, delightful sentences, and a persistently trenchant linguistic analysis with nothing obscure or precious about it. This completely original criticism, with notes and a select bibliography, is recommended for its range, its depth, and its good humor. Advanced undergraduate; graduate; faculty.—*L. K. MacKendrick, University of Windsor*

OAB-0714   PR6093   92-56606 CIP
Swigg, Richard. **Charles Tomlinson and the objective tradition.** Bucknell, 1994. (Dist. by Associated University Presses) 271p bibl index afp ISBN 0-8387-5249-7, $41.50

This reading of the contemporary British poet's work from the 1940s to the present takes into account the imaginative fertilization Tomlinson received from Blake, Ruskin, and Wordsworth, and his debt to the great American modernists Wallace Stevens and Marianne Moore, and later, the larger inspirations of William Carlos Williams, whom Swigg credits with opening Tomlinson's poems to the deeper importance of particulars and a new sense of the possibilities of the poetic line. Tomlinson's poetry is compared to that of Philip Larkin and Auden in order to assess his grounding in the enriching textures of British history and mythology as opposed to their reductive, end-of-empire negations. Swigg has an educated ear for the nuances of language in Tomlinson's poems, and this book is a solid argument for Tomlinson's elevation among the handful of best contemporary British poets, as well as a vivid picture of the issues at stake in British poetry since WW II. Highest recommendation. Undergraduate (all levels); graduate; faculty; general.—*B. Galvin, Central Connecticut State University*

UNITED KINGDOM & IRELAND — Colonial & Postcolonial

OAB-0715   PR9272   91-42237 CIP
C.L.R. James's Caribbean, ed. by Paget Henry and Paul Buhle. Duke University, 1992. 287p index afp ISBN 0-8223-1231-X, $45.00; ISBN 0-8223-1244-1 pbk, $16.95

C.L.R. James is universally regarded as the principal political and social theoretician of the Caribbean. He is also highly regarded as a fictionist and pan-Africanist, and his indefatigable writing, speaking, and working for social change for more than a half century have left indelible marks on the whole region. This compendium of letters, interviews, excerpts from writings, and analytical articles is an important introduction to this major figure for those unacquainted with him and his philosophy—and a necessary text for those who are familiar with them. Long and challenging articles by the editors (both recognized scholars in James's work) and such other well-regarded academics as Sylvia Wynter, Selwyn Cudjoe, and Neil Lazarus provide erudite studies of James's theories of social transformation at the center and at the periphery, of the significance of folk creativity, and of economic and cultural interdependence. James's adage that the Caribbean peoples have "no native civilization at all" and that they invite permanent international marginality are critically examined and explicated. The style is free of jargon yet scholarly; the several parts are logical and cogent; the typeface is eminently readable. Highly recommended. Advanced undergraduate; graduate.—*A. L. McLeod, Rider College*

OAB-0716 PR9369 96-36020 CIP
Clayton, Cherry. **Olive Schreiner.** Twayne/Prentice Hall International, 1997. 140p bibl index afp (TWAS, 865. African literature) ISBN 0-8057-8287-7, $26.95

This is an important scholarly study of the works of a major 19th-century writer—and the first novelist to emerge from colonial South Africa. Schreiner offered insights into the position of women within the European colonial world and was perhaps the first writer to suggest how colonial social structures marginalized European women. Clayton suggests that Schreiner's growing understanding of the relationship between gender and imperialism led to her anticolonial activities. She analyzes both Schreiner's fiction and her nonfiction, examining such major works as *From Man to Man, The Story of an African Farm,* and *Women and Labour,* and her pamphlets and political writings. In the year of her death (1923), Schreiner asked how "from our political states and discordant races, can a great, a healthy, a united, and organized nation be formed?" This thorough analysis of Schreiner's work builds on earlier scholarship by Kathleen Blake, Karel Schoeman, Marion Friedmann, Ruth First, Ann Scott, Rachel Blau Du Plessis, among others. It is well written—with excellent notes, bibliography, and historical outline—and offers readers a wonderful story of a heroic artist whose life and writings chronicle an important period of African colonial history. General; upper-division undergraduates; graduates; faculty.—*C. Pike, University of Minnesota*

OAB-0717 PR9369 92-27675 CIP
Ettin, Andrew Vogel. **Betrayals of the body politic: the literary commitments of Nadine Gordimer.** University Press of Virginia, 1993 (c1992). 150p index ISBN 0-8139-1430-2, $26.50

No one should be put off this fine little study by its obfuscatory title. It is written for the (best) common reader, who will find it as good a book on Nadine Gordimer as anything we have seen so far, and maybe, given its intense brevity, a better one. Working apparently from published sources only, including a number of interviews and autobiographical statements, but with unusual skills of imaginative sympathy, Ettin puts us inside Gordimer's life's work. He takes it (arguable on her own terms) as a single entity, effectively re-creating it as a space—a theater of historical simultaneity—within which we may freely, if circumspectly, move, learning the "springs" of her creativity and following the vectors of her development over the course of her writing career. Important, too, as a new introduction to Gordimer as Nobel laureate, Ettin's readings may perhaps draw more Americans into her work. Here she is accessible; the stories one may not have read are recounted clearly in subtle but jargon-free prose, plain speech escorting close analytical readings sustained by a clearly sophisticated critical mind and an informed and acute political as well as moral sensibility. Ettin's strength, in fact, is to make us feel the common ground shared by history, politics, art, and morality—no small matter for a writer for whom such common ground is home. Spare but useful notes, index of names. For good college libraries and up.—*F. Alaya, Ramapo College of New Jersey*

OAB-0718 PR9084 91-28482 CIP
Harris, Michael. **Outsiders and insiders: perspectives of Third**

World culture in British and post-colonial fiction. P. Lang, 1992. 203p bibl index afp (Studies of world literature in English, 1) ISBN 0-8204-1668-1, $47.95

Long interpreted by writers from Britain, the "mother country," a number of Third World countries have recently found their own voice in fiction of their own creation. The "outsiders" of British fiction, that is, have become the "insiders" of fiction written by postcolonial nationals—a fundamental difference in viewpoint that is the central theme of this study. Harris discusses in separate chapters the fiction of India, southern Africa, West and East Africa (Nigeria and Kenya), and the West Indies, a roughly chronological sequence that serves to reveal changes in the writers' attitudes to the Empire and its colonies. Both British outsiders and indigenous insiders tend to focus primarily on relationships between colonizers and colonized. Harris's discussion proceeds by juxtaposing paradigmatic novels by a British and a postcolonial writer (for instance, by Joyce Cary and Chinua Achebe in the west African section). The method is a sound one, but the individual chapters are less incisive and less involving than the clear and cogent conclusion. The first in the series "Studies of World Literature in English," this work sets an impressive standard. It is, in fact, one of the very best studies of postcolonial fiction. Highly recommended for all libraries.—*J. B. Beston, Nazareth College of Rochester*

OAB-0719 PR9272 92-21012 CIP
King, Bruce. **V.S. Naipaul.** St. Martin's, 1993. 170p bibl index ISBN 0-312-08646-6, $35.00

The introduction to this volume is perhaps the best 15-page essay on Naipaul and his art; and the subsequent eight chapters are written with the authority that King is known to possess on post-colonial literature and in a style that is both crisp and admirably textured. Apart from the deft synopses of the plots of the works under discussion, the insightful and analytical evaluations that are presented, one distinct asset of this study is the first-hand acquaintance that the author has with the West Indies, India, and the other areas that Naipaul himself writes about. And King does not clutter his prose with the jargon of some one school of literary criticism: rather, he writes from an eclectic viewpoint and yet draws on a number of contemporary approaches to elucidate his readings. It might be said of King as he says of Naipaul: "He has one of the most analytical perspectives in the post-colonial world." Perhaps the only weak chapter is that on *Guerrillas*; however, the account of the etiology of that work is itself of interest and value. As King points out, Naipaul (in fiction) and Walcott (in poetry) have given new depth and seriousness to West Indian literature; in Naipaul "the European perspective dominates, but the Indian world view contests it and has its attractions." No beginning student should fail to read this work; no scholar will want to miss it.—*A. L. McLeod, Rider College*

OAB-0720 Can. CIP
Letters of love and duty: the correspondence of Susanna and John Moodie, ed. by Carl Ballstadt, Elizabeth Hopkins, and Michael Peterman. Toronto, 1993. 360p index afp ISBN 0-8020-5708-X, $35.00

The 1988 announcement of a cache of previously unknown Moodie papers has necessitated this sequel to the excellent *Letters of a Lifetime*, ed. by Carl Ballstadt et al. (1985). Arranged chronologically in six sections are 18 letters by Susanna and 64 by her husband: courtship, marriage, migration to Canada (1830-37); the Upper Canada rebellion (1838); John's Belleville political life and Susanna's backwoods hardships (1838-49); the reunited Moodies in Belleville (1840-9); encounters with spiritualism (1850-60); and retirement (1861-85). Full of love, courage, and mutual support, the 30 letters between husband and wife complement 12 to family and another 40 business, political, literary, or social letters as sources on their private lives and careers and conditions in 19th-century Canada. Highly readable, the letters demonstrate wide interests, social consciousness and conscience, philosophical and moral concerns, public ambitions, family loyalty, humor, meticulous detail, and descriptive flair. Seven meaty prefaces, useful notes, 15 illustrations, a list of sources, and an index complete a volume of great value to scholars of 19th-century Canadian literature, history, politics, culture, spiritualism, and Susanna Moodie; it is suitable to all levels of university and to an informed public readership.—*L. B. Thompson, University of Vermont*

OAB-0721   JV51   97-9259 Orig
Moore-Gilbert, Bart. **Postcolonial theory: contexts, practices, politics.** Verso, 1997. (Dist. by W.W. Norton) 243p index ISBN 1-85984-034-5 pbk, $19.00

Moore-Gilbert provides a timely and comprehensive account of the emergence of postcolonial theory and criticism from Commonwealth literary studies. Although he devotes three long chapters to Edward Said, Gayatri Spivak, and Homi Bhabha, the author demonstrates that such earlier writers as Frantz Fanon, Chinua Achebe, and Wilson Harris anticipated these influential theorists. The outstanding chapter on Spivak provides a lucid rationale for Spivak's deliberate difficulties, while admitting that she is sometimes inconsistent, "even equivocal." Here and elsewhere, Moore-Gilbert gives resourceful and thorough syntheses of previous debates, to which he always has something to add. His larger argument is that the tensions between postcolonial theory and criticism are productive, and that "the most significant problems each subfield now faces are to a large extent shared by the other." The historical perspective enables Moore-Gilbert to maintain that "some of the current enthusiasm for and antagonism towards postcolonial theory are equally misguided." He largely succeeds in his attempt to write an accessible survey, and the bibliographical range of his notes is immense. Highly recommended for upper-division undergraduates through faculty.—*T. Ware, Queen's University at Kingston*

OAB-0722   PR9369   90-5906 CIP
Schreiner, Olive. **"My other self": the letters of Olive Schreiner and Havelock Ellis, 1884-1920,** ed. by Yaffa Claire Draznin. P. Lang, 1993 (c1992). 583p index afp ISBN 0-8204-1360-7, $79.95

No previously published collections of Olive Schreiner's letters have focused exclusively on her correspondence with Havelock Ellis. Yet, what an amazing slice it is, capturing in many ways the entire multilayered sexual consciousness of the late 19th century. More than half of the 607 notes and letters included here are Schreiner's (367). Nevertheless we see—intensely in the rapidly exchanged early correspondence, more discontinuously later on—two brilliant, vanguard writers, both vigorous feminists, bold political activists, and pioneers in the rearticulation of the psychological and social implications of sexuality, writing themselves into, and nearly out of, sexual existence over the course of 36 years. They explored their own emotions, psychosomatically, relentlessly, vividly, sighting a new horizon of freedom, but too burdened with history and pain, and in some sense too shackled to science, ever to experience it. Editor Draznin has done a service to specialists and nonspecialists alike because there exist no other collected Ellis letters. This work supplements, rather than supplants, two earlier Schreiner collections, but it also defines a higher standard of editorial rigor, printing from holographs exclusively. Comprehensive introduction (a primer in editing), good notes, extensive index. All levels.—*F. Alaya, Ramapo College of New Jersey*

OAB-0723   PR916   92-29033 CIP
Williams, Mark. **Patrick White.** St. Martin's, 1993. 185p bibl index ISBN 0-312-08990-2, $35.00

Williams (Univ. of Canterbury, New Zealand) does himself a disservice in not providing a defining subtitle to his book: it is, in fact, a quite specific and highly original study. Williams looks at White's novels and the rather sparse information that White has provided on their genesis in order to examine White's relation to Australia after he returned there in 1948. In "The Prodigal Son" White spoke out against the low value placed on art and love and religion in Australian life. Williams first considers White's relation to the material aspects of Australian life and then focuses on the function of religious thought in White's work, understanding with considerable perception that that is connected to White's sense of what it means for him to be an *Australian* novelist. Williams is the first

to look at White's novels thoroughly and dispassionately in order to determine whether there is any discernible consistency in the various religious positions of his characters. He warns us to be careful about identifying White's own point of view with that of any of his characters or with any overall vision that can be wrung from the novels. Williams's study represents an extremely important contribution towards an understanding of the thinking of an elusive literary giant. Highly recommended for all libraries.—*J. B. Beston, Nazareth College of Rochester*

UNITED STATES

OAB-0724   PS153   94-11782 CIP
American realism and the canon, ed. by Tom Quirk and Gary Scharnhorst. Delaware, 1994. (Dist. by Associated University Presses) 227p index afp ISBN 0-87413-524-9, $37.50

In this provocative new study, Quirk (Univ. of Missouri—Columbia) and Scharnhorst (Univ. of New Mexico) challenge several of the long-standing assumptions about American literary realism. Featuring essays by 12 prominent scholars, this collection offers compelling arguments that, contrary to some of the more traditional perceptions of American realism represented by only a handful of writers and texts, the realist era was, in actuality, "one of unprecedented literary diversity." The contributors to this volume demonstrate that realism "was flexible enough and of sufficient range" and the era "hospitable enough" to accommodate a multitude of women and minority writers who produced texts that "gave voice to the most urgent concerns of race and ethnicity, gender, class, section, and region." Among the topics examined here are a reevaluation of texts by writers of color, the assimilation into the canon of rediscovered texts, the double consciousness of the Jewish American realist writer, the political correctness of *Huckleberry Finn*, and the decanonization of the once-prominent American writer Bret Harte. This volume is a superb addition to the ongoing debate over issues of canonicity and periodicity. Strongly recommended for all libraries.—*D. D. Knight, SUNY College at Cortland*

OAB-0725   PS267   92-42846 CIP
Bryan, Violet Harrington. **The myth of New Orleans in literature: dialogues of race and gender.** Tennessee, 1993. 222p bibl index afp ISBN 0-87049-789-8, $31.95

A bibliography of about 600 items testifies to the thoroughness of Bryan's research into literary documents of New Orleans race and gender, reaching back more than 100 years. The book that she composed from this treasury is unique in three ways: the scope of the chronological survey; the comparative notes voiced by the very authors whose writings in turn become the study of succeeding generations; and Bryan's own insights and interpretations of the rituals, attitudes, and language of New Orleans. The text flows well, with appropriate citations. The reader's attention will be held by well-framed questions and an accurately sketched social panorama. Best of all is the overall ring of authenticity. Highly recommended for academic and public libraries interested in the history and ethnic studies of New Orleans and Louisiana at large.—*A. G. Tassin, University of New Orleans*

OAB-0726   GR111   93-31848 CIP
Cajun and Creole folktales: the French oral tradition of South Louisiana, coll. and ann. by Barry Jean Ancelet. Garland, 1994. 224p bibl indexes afp (World folktale library, 1) ISBN 0-8153-1498-1, $40.00

One would be hard put to exaggerate the quality and unique character of this study. It is destined to be a classic, a quotable source from here on out. In scope and thoroughness this book exceeds James F. Brossard's *The Louisiana Creole Dialect* (1942). Ancelet has brought together a solid and rich compilation of bilingual Cajun and Creole folktales, the fruit of his own experience and research. They are grouped under seven headings: animal tales, magic, jokes, tall tales, paschal stories, legends, and historical tales. The collection represents over two decades of collecting and organizing. To set this lore in context are two prefaces (Carl Lindahl and Ancelet) and several introductory essays about the context, the evolution of the study, the repertoire, the language, and the storytellers. Three topical indexes follow the 12-page bibliography. All told, the work records folklore in the best academic form. An indispensable item for public and academic libraries and collectors of folklore, Louisiana studies, and French/English studies in the US.—*A. G. Tassin, University of New Orleans*

OAB-0727   PR830   96-19804 CIP
Clark, Beverly Lyon. **Regendering the school story: sassy sissies and tattling tomboys.** Garland, 1996. 297p bibl index afp (Children's literature and culture, 3) ISBN 0-8153-2116-3, $45.00

Claiming that such texts "can reshape and reclaim a genre" due to their transgressive nature, Clark (Wheaton College) focuses on boys' school stories written by women and girls' school stories written by men. By analyzing what she calls the "crossgendering of school stories," Clark examines how the gender of the authors influenced their work. In particular, she is concerned with what gendered ideologies the writers brought to bear. The author discusses the writings of Charles Lamb, Dorothy Kilner, Mary Martha Sherwood, Louisa May Alcott, and others, looking at how these writers created uniquely gendered stories that combined values commonly ascribed to males or females. This work benefits from the meticulous scholarship that has made Clark a leading expert in children's literature. Her carefully researched study of the school story's beginnings will interest anyone curious about the historical development of children's literature. Her thoughtful analysis of the cross-gendered school story demonstrates the importance of the genre from the early-19th to the mid-20th century. Without a doubt, Clark's book is an important addition to children's literature criticism and should be acquired by all libraries collecting in that area.—*S. A. Inness, Miami University*

OAB-0728   PM197   94-13457 CIP
Coming to light: contemporary translations of the native literatures of North America, ed. with introd. by Brian Swann. Random House, 1995 (c1994). 801p bibl index ISBN 0-679-41816-4, $30.00

This is by far the best anthology of translations from Native American oral traditions ever published. It represents the work of a group of university-based scholars and community-based Native American intellectuals who for the past 20 years devoted themselves to producing new translations of the considerable oral literatures that Native American communities throughout the Americas continue to preserve. Among the leaders in this work were linguist Dell Hymes, anthropologist Dennis Tedlock, and community based educators Nora and Richard Dauenhauer. Their exemplary work is well represented in this collection, along with a generous and representative selection of the work of the North American translators they inspired. Truly continental in scope, this collection includes thoughtfully introduced and carefully contextualized stories and songs from Native American communities all over the continent, from Alaska to Sonora, from California to Maine. In his introduction Swann (Cooper Univ.) provides a rich history of the translation and an appreciation of Native American oral literature. His deft editorial touch maintains the rich and challenging cultural distances represented in these lively stories and songs while making them all accessible enough to engage a very wide American reading audience. Every public and academic library in North America should own this book.—*L. Evers, University of Arizona*

OAB-0729   PS430   96-43457 CIP
Covici, Pascal. **Humor and revelation in American literature: the Puritan connection.** Missouri, 1997. 226p bibl index afp ISBN 0-8262-1095-3, $39.95

Covici (Southern Methodist Univ.) relates religious beliefs about revelation to concepts of political and religious "truth" in the writings of Franklin, Emer-

son, Thoreau, Hawthorne, Melville, Twain, and others. This solid, imaginative study examines underlying assumptions of possessing "inside information" about God's intentions and the nature of the universe. The author uncovers surprising parallels between Puritan beliefs and the humor of the Southwest, and even in the rebellions against genteel propriety in such diverse works as Emerson's *Nature* and Hemingway's and Fitzgerald's novels. The heart of Covici's argument is that much of American literature uses the technique of surprising readers into an epiphany of insights. This concept, developed in Covici's earlier *Mark Twain's Humor: The Image of a World* (1962) and in D.H. Monro's notion of "universe changing" in *Argument of Laughter* (1951), allows an effective investigation of the religious, social, and political assumptions that writers explode to develop meaning. Covici's knowledge of American literary history and its British religious roots is impressive; his sense of humor and ability to select the revealing incident or relevant allusion make for a lively and engaging study. Recommended for anyone interested in American humor or literature. All academic collections.—*D. R. Stoddard, Anne Arundel Community College*

OAB-0730   PS169   91-21347 CIP
Fender, Stephen. **Sea changes: British emigration & American literature.** Cambridge, 1992. 400p index ISBN 0-521-41175-0, $44.95

Fender's demanding cultural history has an unexpected epic quality, an intensifying force, and an enormous cast, including Jamestown's Captain John Smith, the Puritan divines, major 19th-century authors, 20th-century modernist writers, and even characters in WW II and Vietnam war novels. The effects of British emigration may be seen in four aspects of American literature. First, there is the heroic element: both Britain's 17th-century America-bound emigrants and their Americanized descendants, biological and cultural, described as the "collective singular" (We the People, the American character). Second is the view of their destination as the Promised Land, America biblically imagined, or, paradoxically, as a wilderness to be tamed, possibly rejected if found unlivable. Third, a common root of conflict is whether to forsake cultural security (Mother England), risking failure or disaster in contending with raw nature, the Indians, and debilitating self-doubts. Fourth, characters' courses of action following emigration may be read as the initiation of the individual, a testing process involving "lighting out for the territory," or as another mode of basic self-redefinition. Though omitting Emma Lazarus's poem "The New Colossus" (1883) and Thomas Bailey Aldrich's anti-immigrant poem "The Unguarded Gates" (1892), and a few other items, *Sea Changes* is a major work, highly recommended to libraries and readers at all levels.—*S. I. Bellman, California State Polytechnic University, Pomona*

OAB-0731   PS303   94-24157 CIP
Golding, Alan. **From outlaw to classic: canons in American poetry.** Wisconsin, 1995. 243p bibl index ISBN 0-299-14600-6, $52.00; ISBN 0-299-14604-9 pbk, $19.95

Golding's is the best study of canon formation available; it is rare because it focuses on American poetry. Its only rival is Cary Nelson's *Repression and Recovery: Modern American Poetry and the Politics of Cultural Memory, 1910-1945* (CH, Jun'90), which is concerned with what has been left out of the canon. Golding looks at who decided what should be in the canon and how the decisions were made and implemented. She looks at both "radical" critics' tendency to reread canonical texts and canonical scholars' preference for treating fiction. Especially valuable is the detailed and brilliant history of American poetry anthologies, through which canon formation can be followed in detail. Golding offers good treatments of poets' roles in establishing canonical status for older poets; the New Critics' role in setting poetry's place in the academy; the role of little magazines in creating canon; and the recent role of "language writing" in resisting the academy's conformist power over poetry writing (and, subsequently, language poets' efforts to wield that degree of power themselves). There are 38 pages of excellent and useful notes. All libraries should own this book.—*Q. Grigg, Hamline University*

OAB-0732   PS374   91-31115 CIP

Griswold, Jerry. **Audacious kids: coming of age in America's classic children's books.** Oxford, 1992. 285p index afp ISBN 0-19-505888-7, $25.00

Griswold explores the golden age of children's books in America (1865-1914) with penetrating analyses of 12 classics: *Little Women, The Wizard of Oz, Little Lord Fauntleroy, The Secret Garden, Tarzan of the Apes, Hans Brinker, Toby Tyler, Pollyanna, The Prince and the Pauper, Tom Sawyer, Huckleberry Finn,* and *Rebecca of Sunnybrook Farm.* The discussions of individual books are pointed and insightful, but Griswold's contextual frameworks are even more illuminating: each book repeats the characteristically American story of an orphan child's rebellious growth toward maturity, while celebrating American values of natural nobility (and the need for legitimacy), emotional control, and optimism and positive thinking. Of course there are numerous studies of individual works and authors such as Alcott and Twain, and *Narratives of Love and Loss* by M. and M. Rustin (CH, Nov'88) points to a similar core narrative structure of psychological growth in children's books, but Griswold's focus on American themes is both original and persuasive. Moreover, he writes with flair and provides extensive notes and numerous echoes, transitions, and analogies that help to interrelate the separate narratives. This engaging book will quickly become an essential authority for students of children's literature and should reach a wide audience among librarians, parents, and scholars of American literature.—*C. Rees, University of Connecticut*

OAB-0733   PS153   94-9968 CIP

Hubbard, Dolan. **The sermon and the African American literary imagination.** Missouri, 1994. 176p bibl index afp ISBN 0-8262-0961-0, $29.95

This is a compelling and much-needed study of the impact of the sermon on the aesthetic consciousness of selected African American literary artists. Hubbard begins by defining the African American sermon as a folk narrative grounded in the ethos of the Southern slave communities in which it originated in response to an array of personal, political, and spiritual exigencies. He then proceeds to demonstrate—cogently and convincingly—how the sermonic rhetoric and the moral vision embodied in the traditional African American pulpit oratory inform the themes and structures of selected works by Frederick Douglass, Zora Neale Hurston, Ralph Ellison, James Baldwin, and Toni Morrison. Theoretically sophisticated and exceptionally well-written, *The Sermon and the African American Literary Imagination* makes a singular contribution to contemporary literary and cultural studies. Highly recommended to all libraries as well as to general readers.—*E. S. Nelson, SUNY College at Cortland*

OAB-0734   PS374   96-38809 CIP

Jablon, Madelyn. **Black metafiction: self-consciousness in African American literature.** Iowa, 1997. 209p bibl index afp ISBN 0-87745-560-0, $27.95

Surveying literary theories currently applied to African American fiction, Jablon identifies "inductive" theories arising from the corpus and "extrinsic" theories applied to it. "Metafiction" "draws attention to itself as artifact to pose questions about the relationship between fiction and reality." Noting that traditional African American critics' positioning of formal against political precluded interest in the political significance of formal structures, the author demonstrates that formal innovation is integral to this literature and metafictional techniques are used to explore philosophic and political agendas. Although Jablon adduces evidence from the breadth of African American fiction and autobiography, she provides extended analyses of contemporary works. Rejecting rigid classifications, she describes various techniques and objectives in black metafiction: texts that imitate the creative process; those in which the artistic protagonists are circumscribed by their medium, audience, or environment; those where "voice" (and dialects) define the multiplicity and politicism of selfhood; those that exploit intertextuality; and those that infuse popular genres with political commentary and prescription. This excellent, cogent, erudite book has profound implications for narratology, African American literature, popular fiction, and metafiction. General readers; upper-division undergraduates and up.—*D. F. Dorsey, Clark Atlanta University*

OAB-0735   PS193   95-29993 CIP

Looby, Christopher. **Voicing America: language, literary form, and the origins of the United States.** Chicago, 1996. 287p index afp ISBN 0-226-49282-6, $29.95

Early American print culture has received much sophisticated attention in recent years: Kenneth Lockridge's *Literacy in Colonial New England* (1974); William J. Gilmore's *Reading Becomes a Necessity of Life* (CH, Mar'90); Richard D. Brown's *The Strength of a People* (1996). Looby (Univ. of Chicago) examines a countertradition of the *living* voice, "vocal utterance as a deeply politically invested phenomenon of the social world." Beginning with the intriguing claim that "the United States was actually 'spoken into being,'" the author analyzes the history of "the difference between the abstract, alienated, rational polis of print culture and the more passionately attached, quasi-somatically experienced nation for which many Americans longed." The first chapter, "Logocracy in America," weaves historical material from Dr. Johnson, Adams, Benjamin Rush, Jefferson, and Irving with language theory from Gramsci, Wittgenstein, Derrida, and Habermas. Three more chapters treat Franklin's *Autobiography,* Charles Brockden Brown's *Wieland,* and Brackenridge's *Modern Chivalry* with similar deep learning and eclecticism. A "coda" meditates on the tradition of the "living voice" of Patrick Henry: "In the phenomenological integrity of the speaking voice, its imaginary conjunction of intention and expression ... its lack of discord, its seeming autonomy ... a divided and contentious nation found its preferred image of its origins." This highly original and important study of culture in the early Republic is recommended for upper-division undergraduates and above.—*J. D. Wallace, Boston College*

OAB-0736   PS25   94-17486 CIP

Martin, Terence. **Parables of possibility: the American need for beginnings.** Columbia, 1995. 263p index afp ISBN 0-231-07050-0, $27.50

Like an energetic explorer, Martin (Indiana Univ.) sets sail on the murky waters of history and literature to explore this enormous interdisciplinary thesis: "The protean importance of a sense of beginning in American literature and culture." He charts his course by examining attempts to fix the nation's beginning as 1492 and to use negation to clear away European baggage and thus establish a national identity. Thomas Paine, Ralph Waldo Emerson, and Charlotte Perkins Gilman serve him here. The author then sails into a sophisticated examination of how beginnings "affect characterization, evoke certain kinds of description, and serve to organize experience." Mark Twain, William Faulkner, and Willa Cather serve him here. Martin's most difficult task, however, lies in demonstrating his theory that now an exhaustion of resources and frontiers leaves America without a vision of the future. Although the issue of national identity caught the attention of writers from Washington Irving to Robert Penn Warren, Martin's meticulous exploration of a new destination of community deserves serious study by American literature scholars. Particularly engaging are his observations on the role of negation in America's national psyche, the notion that Europe invented America, and the works of Willa Cather. Upper-division undergraduates; graduates; researchers; faculty.—*R. F. Cayton, emeritus, Marietta College*

OAB-0737   PS303   94-12411 CIP

Morris, Timothy. **Becoming canonical in American poetry.** Illinois, 1995. 173p index afp ISBN 0-252-02136-3, $34.95; ISBN 0-252-06428-3 pbk, $12.95

Morris (Univ. of Texas at Arlington) gives to a reader seeking a liberal reading of poetry a respite from the pseudo-objective norms of the New Criticism and the pseudophilosophy of deconstruction. His approach is the poetics of presence, to see our American poetry and poets as "now," but coming to that view via the history of acceptance/nonacceptance of their works. His study focuses on Whitman, Emily Dickinson, Marianne Moore, and Elizabeth Bishop. His method is not primarily historical but rather proposes a stream of appreciations in various periods. "The basic guarantee of the poetics of presence," says Morris, "is a unity that implies the author's—and the critic's—ability to

Humanities

control them." The poet is present with originality and style, a speaker not a reciter. Morris's is a highly original presentation in clear, readable prose. He may be forgiven his tendency to pretentious vocabulary, such as: "A truly present American poet ... would provide an Adamic beginning for an autochthonous American culture, freeing it from its umbilical connection to England." Highly recommended for academic collections serving upper-division undergraduates and above, this title will be of special interest to classes in literary criticism of poetry.—*A. G. Tassin, University of New Orleans*

OAB-0738   PN6426   95-53818 CIP
Prahlad, Sw. Anand. **African-American proverbs in context.** University Press of Mississippi, 1996. 292p bibl index afp ISBN 0-87805-889-3, $45.00; ISBN 0-87805-890-7 pbk, $20.00

This is the first extensive study to examine the many meanings and functions of a wide variety of proverbs—98 in all—used by African Americans from the time of slavery to the late 20th century. Prahlad (Univ. of Wisconsin—Columbia) views proverbs within a variety of interrelated contexts, including linguistic, social and cultural, and symbolic. The author is well versed in the literature of folklore and anthropology and shows a keen understanding of the profound influence of African speech patterns on African American oral culture. He draws on a rich variety of sources, from WPA interviews with former slaves to blues lyrics and everyday speech. The book is divided into two sections: the first is largely historical, discussing proverbs used within a broad American context; the second focuses on the large number of proverbs that adults recite to children. Each section is imbued with rich examples and is carefully annotated. A clear, well-organized appendix lists proverbs alphabetically by keyword. Excellent reference section. All collections.—*C. Pike, University of Minnesota*

OAB-0739   PS153   94-18740 CIP
Rebolledo, Tey Diana. **Women singing in the snow: a cultural analysis of Chicana literature.** Arizona, 1995. 250p bibl index afp ISBN 0-8165-1520-4, $35.00; ISBN 0-8165-1546-8 pbk, $16.95

Rebolledo provides a literary history of Chicana writers. Oral histories document the creative, imaginative world of the pioneer Chicana. The discussion of three New Mexican writers—Nina Otero-Warren, Cleofas Jaramillo, and Fabiola Cabeza de Baca—illustrates how these writers embedded in their texts the ideology of resistance. This work studies how Chicana writers choose, define, and integrate traditional myths and archetypes into their texts. The study of *Coatlicue, La Llorona,* and *La Virgen de Guadalupe,* archetypes entrenched in the psyche of Chicanas, are significant for the student of the Chicana. Rebolledo's inclusion of a variety of literary pieces provides insight into the revisionary process that the Chicana writer has embarked on. As the author states, "To become ourselves, in the fullest way possible, one must integrate the serpents, the 'negative,' and accept the power of self-knowledge and self-expression that comes with it." Finally, Rebolledo illustrates that as Chicanas remember their past and write their narratives, they construct and reconstruct their own identity and acquire an "understanding of their historical role in families and communities." An excellent companion to *Infinite Divisions: An Anthology of Chicana Literature* (CH, Jan'94), this book includes an extensive bibliography on Chicana literature and criticism. Strongly recommended for all collections, particularly those serving students of women's literature.—*J. Luna Lawhn, San Antonio College*

OAB-0740   PS217   96-24554 CIP
Rowe, John Carlos. **At Emerson's tomb: the politics of classic American literature.** Columbia, 1997. 302p index afp ISBN 0-231-05894-2, $49.50; ISBN 0-231-05895-0 pbk, $16.50

Rowe (Univ. of California, Irvine) offers a pioneer series of studies of key works by nine American authors (Emerson, Poe, Melville, Douglas, Whitman, Twain, James, Chopin, and Faulkner). He challenges "the text-bound myopia" of standard literary judgments to relate his authors to changing views of race relations and the position of women in the social, psychological, and

political developments in American history and culture. He decries the tendency of conventional literary criticism "to trivialize biographical and historical facts," which frequently provide real understanding of literary accomplishment and are relevant to defining the canon of American literary studies (a problem that has occasioned so much recent attention). Rowe's is a difficult, provocative, but important contribution both to literary history's methodology and to understanding the individual writers and the works he examines and discusses in detail. Upper-division undergraduates through faculty.—*A. E. Jones Jr., emeritus, Drew University*

OAB-0741   PS163   96-2399 CIP
Scheese, Don. **Nature writing: the pastoral impulse in America.** Twayne/Prentice Hall International, 1996. 227p bibl index afp (Twayne's literary themes and genres, 7) ISBN 0-8057-0964-9, $24.95

To borrow a common trope of ecocriticism, Sheese's volume is a fine field guide to American nature writing. A cogent introduction to an important species of contemporary literature, the volume provides a primer on the relation of "the word and the world" and stands as a reference guide to primary and secondary literatures of the environment. The "natural history essay" or "nature writing" is not a neat classification, but this deeply personal book imposes order on a rich and diverse tradition. The body of the text consists of insightful essays on Thoreau, John Muir, Mary Austin, Aldo Leopold, Edward Abbey, and Annie Dillard. Scheese (Gustavus Adolphus College) sets American nature writing in the broader context of Western pastoral and concludes that by "combining the place-consciousness of pastoralism and the scientific curiosity of natural history, the religious quest of spiritual autobiography and the peregrinations of travel writing ... nature writing as a cultural activity is more vital than ever." The chronological bibliographic essay allows Scheese to highlight diagnostic features of the genre as he interprets the changing cultural milieu of nature writers. Like the writers he discusses, Scheese draws his inspiration from personal involvement with both land *and* literature, and his book is a valuable contribution to the practice of narrative scholarship. All collections.—*W. R. Stott III, University of North Carolina at Chapel Hill*

OAB-0742   PS374   96-21998 CIP
Thomson, Rosemarie Garland. **Extraordinary bodies: figuring physical disability in American culture and literature.** Columbia, 1997. 200p bibl index afp ISBN 0-231-10516-9, $45.00; ISBN 0-231-10517-7 pbk, $16.50

This short but important book is the first literary-critical work to address "disability" as a category of identity in American literature and culture. Rejecting the dominant notion of disability as disease or misfortune, Thomson (Howard Univ.) shows how disability is "not so much a property of bodies as a product of cultural rules about what bodies should be or do." The author draws on feminist theory as well as sociological and anthropological work on stigma and aberrance to argue that disability—like race, gender, nationality, and sexuality—is a socially constructed category that defines the "normal" by embodying its opposite. A theoretical introduction precedes three chapters: a helpful, illustrated historical account of "freak shows" in Victorian American culture; an analysis of conventions used in sentimental novels by Harriet Beecher Stowe, Rebecca Harding Davis, and Elizabeth Stuart Phelps to enlist sympathy and reform on behalf of disabled persons; and an explication of more "liberatory" representations of disability in texts by Ann Petry, Toni Morrison, and Audre Lorde. This is a well written and provocative beginning to a conversation about disability that is long overdue among scholars in literary and cultural studies. All academic collections.—*R. R. Warhol, University of Vermont*

OAB-0743   PS169   95-13288 CIP
True, Michael. **An energy field more intense than war: the nonviolent tradition and American literature.** Syracuse, 1995. 169p bibl index afp ISBN 0-8156-2679-7, $34.95; ISBN 0-8156-0367-3 pbk, $16.95

True's study is a much-needed counterpart to Richard Slotkin's influential

Regeneration Through Violence: The Mythology of the American Frontier (CH, Jun'73). Like Slotkin, True (Assumption College) traces his subject to early America, but True brings the study on to the present. He thus provides a context for Thoreau, conscientious objection, Robert Bly, and Martin Luther King. The context centers around Quakers and Whitman, placing new light on their roles in US culture as well on the numerous poets who have kept the nonviolent tradition alive. Slotkin and True together provide a center for studies of American culture. True's index reveals that he is also writing a history of American poetry; few narrative writers figure in this work. True's excellent study is supplemented by a preface, an introduction, full notes, and an extensive bibliographical essay—all very useful to any scholar or student of American culture and its poets. All collections.—*Q. Grigg, Hamline University*

OAB-0744   PM168   94-42708 CIP
Zolbrod, Paul G. **Reading the voice: Native American oral poetry on the page.** Utah, 1995. 146p bibl afp ISBN 0-87480-457-4, $25.00

Today many students are being exposed to oral literature in a printed form. Teachers in secondary and postsecondary institutions may not be well prepared in this area, so this excellent work appears at an opportune moment. After many years of study, Zolbrod has created an understandable and comprehensive classification of oral material designed to aid comparison and analysis. He broadens the use of the term "poetry" to include all cultural expression based on the human voice. Using the accessible concepts of colloquial and lyrical voice and narrative and dramatic mode, he creates a useful structural paradigm. However, he also wishes to show how such a paradigm can revitalize discussions of Western poetry and electronically transmitted poetic structures. Because he believes poetry evolved from vocal attempts to unite an individual with community and a greater-than-human reality, Zolbrod's discussions of sample texts also explore the ways in which they engage creation stories. This is first-rate scholarship with practical application for any discussion of literature and verbal expression. It is essential reading for anyone who has tried to find the oral voice behind the printed page. All academic collections.—*J. Ruppert, University of Alaska Fairbanks*

UNITED STATES — 18th & 19th Centuries

OAB-0745   PS374   94-11283 CIP
Baym, Nina. **American women writers and the work of history, 1790-1860.** Rutgers, 1995. 307p bibl index ISBN 0-8135-2142-4, $48.00; ISBN 0-8135-2143-2 pbk, $17.95

This is a comprehensive study of historical writing by American women before the Civil War; and as Baym (Univ. of Illinois at Urbana-Champaigne) notes in her introduction, "there is so much more of it than one could have imagined." Her research led to more than 350 titles by more than 150 authors, in various genres. Textual illustrations are frequent, yet this volume is not an anthology but a scholarly study referring readers to extensive primary and secondary sources. Some writers' names will be familiar—Margaret Fuller, Catharine Beecher, the Grimké sisters—but scores will be new to readers of both traditional and feminist-oriented American studies. These authors used the public sphere of publishing to uphold and promulgate ideas within the private spheres of home libraries, reading circles, and schools, and most upheld the status quo. Though a few composed poems of protest, others supported popular prejudices. The literary genres and subjects these women chose may have been diverse, but their ideologies often were not, reflecting the prevailing Anglo-Protestant culture. But Baym's main picture is "a view of American women participating with gusto in the work of writing history"—participating in dynamic literary activity to such an extent that they exerted great control over popular reading habits and therefore over the way Americans perceived history. Upper-division undergraduate and above.—*J. S. Gabin, University of North Carolina at Chapel Hill*

OAB-0746   PS3231   92-5311 CIP
Callow, Philip. **From noon to starry night: a life of Walt Whitman.** I.R. Dee, 1992. 394p bibl index afp ISBN 0-929587-95-2, $28.50

Timely, indeed, that an outstanding biography of Whitman should appear in 1992, the centennial of the poet's death. The author of biographies of Vincent Van Gogh and D.H. Lawrence as well as of 12 novels, Callow brings to his work the imagination and artistry of a master storyteller. The result is a life of Whitman that exhibits assurance, verve, and craftsmanship. Callow's focus, however, is less on the known or legendary Whitman than on the actual man. He offers no new and startling revelations, nor does he solve the riddles of Whitman's furtiveness, mercurial sexuality, or miraculous transformation from buccaneer journalist to world-class poet, but he nevertheless marshals and interprets the known facts exceedingly well, sometimes penetrating the poet's "thicket of identities." Perhaps above all else, Whitman emerges in this book as democracy's poet, and "the message of his democracy is that modern life has not even begun. Modern man waits in the wings." Rich in historical detail, liberally illustrated with quotes from the poetry, and studded with characters memorably drawn, Callow's book ranks with the best of earlier lives of Whitman: Paul Zweig's *Walt Whitman* (CH, Sep'84), Justin Kaplan's *Walt Whitman* (1980), and Gay Wilson Allen's *The Solitary Singer* (rev. ed., 1967). Strongly recommended for all academic and public libraries.—*D. D. Kummings, University of Wisconsin-Parkside*

OAB-0747   PS2124   92-1129 CIP
A companion to Henry James studies, ed. by Daniel Mark Fogel. Greenwood, 1993. 545p bibl index afp ISBN 0-313-25792-2, $79.95

This monumental collection of essays by established critics of modern literature embraces all the forms in which James wrote. Nine essays are devoted to the fiction, five to the literary criticism, and one each to the letters, notebooks, autobiographies, travel writings, and plays. Most of the essays are accessible to the general reader; several assume a specialist's knowledge of contemporary theory. All are substantial works of criticism, packed with information and detailed analysis of individual texts. At their best, as in the essays by Jean Frantz Blackall, Charles Caramello, James W. Gargano, and Philip M. Weinstein, original insight into James's work accompanies succinct notation of important trends in recent criticism. Other distinguished critics represented include Lyall H. Powers, John Carlos Rowe, Daniel R. Schwarz, Adeline Tintner, and James Tuttleton. A narrative history of James criticism by Richard Hocks and annotated chronologies of James's works and of the major critical studies from 1905 to 1991 enhance the value of this unique book, a landmark of James criticism and scholarship, which students and teachers will find as valuable as any single volume on James's work.—*E. Nettels, College of William and Mary*

OAB-0748   PS1294   93-4664 CIP
Dyer, Joyce. *The awakening: a novel of beginnings.* Twayne, 1993. 147p bibl index afp (Twayne's masterwork studies, 130) ISBN 0-8057-8382-2, $22.95; ISBN 0-8057-8383-0 pbk, $7.95

Kate Chopin's *The Awakening* (1899), after startling audiences upon publication, remained obscure until the last two decades. Now it is a staple of courses in American literature, women's literature, and southern literature. Dyer (Hiram College) has endeavored to present to readers a primer on the novel, introducing us, in concise and lucid prose, to its literary and historical contexts, its signficance, and its critical reception. In this, she succeeds admirably. She also includes substantial readings of several key aspects of Chopin's novel: bird imagery, concepts of women's space, mythic scenes and references, depiction of the female artist, and various interpretations of Edna's suicide. Some of this interpretive material Dyer has previously published. All of it will be helpful to both teachers and students of the work. The volume is enriched by a careful chronology of Chopin's life, a substantial bibliography of Chopin's work and critical materials, and several photographs. Strongly recommended for all collections.—*E. R. Baer, Gustavus Adolphus College*

OAB-0749   PS1305   92-31228 CIP
Fishkin, Shelley Fisher. **Was Huck black? Mark Twain and African-American voices.** Oxford, 1993. 270p bibl index afp ISBN 0-19-508214-1, $25.00

Fishkin exhaustively reviews various theories concerning the sources of Twain's unique use of language in *Huckleberry Finn*, a book that helped scores of subsequent American writers to shape their dialogue. Scholars have conjectured that Twain's language was based on that of southwestern humorists, northeastern literary comedians, his brother's speech patterns, and other white sources. Fishkin contends that Twain fashioned Huck Finn's language from black sources—notably a black boy Twain met named Jimmy—and shows how another black, Jerry, taught Twain about black dialect and storytelling, particularly about signifying (using black satire). She shows how the Fisk Jubilee Singers influenced Twain and notes that in 1970, Ralph Ellison pointed out black influences in Huck's speech patterns. She credits David Sewell's *Mark Twain's Language* (CH, Dec'87) with providing important insights into black prototypes in Huck's language. Fishkin's balance between text and documentation—145 pages of text, 100 pages of notes and bibliography—makes the text accessible to general readers while gracefully providing extensive scholarly apparatus for readers who need it. A uniquely important cross-disciplinary study. Advanced undergraduate; graduate; faculty; general.—*R. B. Shuman, University of Illinois at Urbana-Champaign*

OAB-0750   PS3242   93-29689 CIP
Folsom, Ed. **Walt Whitman's native representations.** Cambridge, 1994. 194p bibl index ISBN 0-521-45357-7, $54.95

Folsom returns to 19th-century America, revitalizing there some disparate, surprising, even unlikely, cultural contexts: the growth of American dictionaries, development of baseball, history of American Indians, and evolution of photography. His primary focus is on Walt Whitman's lifelong interest in and poetic uses of these four contexts. This focus, though, entails looking at many other fascinating individuals, for example, Noah Webster, Joseph Worcester, Albert Spalding, Harry Wright, Lou Sockalexis, Osceola, Mathew Brady, and Alexander Gardner. It also entails revisiting widely resonating social developments, such as the "war of the dictionaries," the formation of the New York Knickerbocker baseball club (1845), the "Trail of Tears" (1838) and Indian massacre at Wounded Knee, South Dakota (1890), and the impact of Civil War photographs. Such individuals, such events, Folsom insists, helped Whitman "define democratic poetry and ultimately democracy itself." Most important, they gave him ample provision, consisting less of subject matter for poems than of a lexicon of "American words." Ultimately a book about language, *Native Representations* is impressive scholarship, one of the best studies ever published on Whitman. If any reader, academic or nonacademic, has been wondering if there exists a thoroughly accessible, richly informative, and profoundly stimulating book on the poet regarded by many as America's greatest—well, here it is.—*D. D. Kummings, University of Wisconsin-Parkside*

OAB-0751   PS2384   93-640 CIP
Garner, Stanton. **The Civil War world of Herman Melville.** University Press of Kansas, 1993. 544p bibl index afp ISBN 0-7006-0602-5, $29.95

This remarkable study examines Melville's biography during the Civil War to uncover the background against which *Battle-Pieces* was written, to understand Melville's intentions and achievement in that book of war poetry. The writing is lucid and pleasing, the research in letters, archives, reminiscences, and journals noteworthy. The study draws not only from Melville's life (the period 1859-66) but also from the lives of his circle of family and friends. Opinions of contemporary writers—Emerson, Thoreau, Hawthorne, Whittier, Whitman, Dickinson, Lowell, Holmes—are related to those of Melville. This chronological study analyzes the poems in *Battle-Pieces* in relation to the events they describe, showing that the poems developed out of relationships, trips, and scenes from Melville's life. It evaluates and summarizes *Battle-Pieces*, analyzing Melville's achievement and making a case for Melville as a major 19th-century American poet, pointing out that Melville's rough verse has

been denigrated in terms of 19th-century conventions in a way that Whitman's and Dickinson's poetry has not. This book is recommended for all libraries.—*M. S. Stephenson, The University of Texas at Brownsville*

OAB-0752   PS2123   94-32510 CIP
Graham, Kenneth. **Henry James: a literary life.** St. Martin's, 1995. 207p bibl index ISBN 0-312-12504-6, $35.00

This "introduction" to James is arguably the best study of his work to appear in years, and it gives the lie to the notion that real scholarship has to be narrow and hermetic in nature. At the core of Graham's argument is an image of the mature James in the garden room of Lamb House, dictating his finest work to a typist, "the mind's voice filling out a loved room." But the road to that room was long and hazardous as James proceeded from Romanticism (*Roderick Hudson*) through Victorianism (*The Tragic Muse*) to a period of crisis followed by an experimental period (*The Spoils of Poynton, What Maisie Knew, The Awkward Age, The Sacred Fount*) that amounts to the most "razor-edged performance ... in the *oeuvre* of any major novelist in English, before or since." James's new focus on "the forms of consciousness" rather than direct contact with reality became one of the keys to Modernism. In the aggregate, his works amount to a short course in the history of the novel, and Graham's lively comments make for indispensable new lessons in that field of study. All collections.—*D. Kirby, Florida State University*

OAB-0753   PS2853   91-35919 CIP
Guilds, John Caldwell. **Simms: a literary life.** Arkansas, 1992. 426p index afp ISBN 1-55728-245-5, $35.00

An outstanding book, this critical biography of William Gilmore Simms is the harvest of three decades of research. It should do much in boosting Simms to a higher place among American writers, for Guilds is quite convincing in crediting Simms as the only 19th-century American writer who conceived, created, and sustained an epic portrayal of the US. The author of 82 books during periods of fluctuation between high and low creativity and intermittent tragedy and despondency, Simms was at his best when dealing with American themes and topics; everything he did was for the betterment of his region and nation. This book, stylistically fluent and even graceful (except for the overuse of "perhaps"), is strong in meticulous detail supported by lengthy footnoting. Following upon Mary Ann Wimsatt's *The Major Fiction of William Gilmore Simms* (CH, Sep'89) and James E. Kibler Jr.'s edition of Simms's *Selected Poetry* (1990), Guilds's study is well timed. The volume includes photographs, several appendixes, a chart of Simms's "Four Periods of American History," and extensive footnotes but no bibliography. Strongly recommended for community college and traditional academic libraries.—*S. W. Whyte, Montgomery County Community College*

OAB-0754   PS2127   93-10066 CIP
Jolly, Roslyn. **Henry James: history, narrative, fiction.** Oxford, 1993. 239p bibl index afp ISBN 0-19-811985-2, $41.00

Historiography became more "scientific" in the mid-19th century, and novelists appropriated the new methods as a way of distancing themselves from critics who thought fiction immoral—claiming, for example, that their characters evolved as their own histories dictated and without reference to readerly expectations, authorial biases, or critical censoriousness. James was one such novelist, though as early as 1884 in "The Art of Fiction" he was making contradictory claims for fiction, describing it as both a representational discourse, which reproduced life exactly, and an oppositional discourse, which offered new experiences. The permutations of this idea define James's career, from the "defeat of plot by history" in such early novels as *The Portrait of a Lady* to the displacement of the novelist-as-historian in such mid-career works as *The Turn of the Screw* and the eventual declaration of immunity from history in *The Sense of the Past*, an unfinished work about time travel. Comprehensive, succinct, and clearly written, this is one of the best books on James to appear in recent years as well as an essential study for anyone interested in the evolution of the novel. Graduate; faculty.—*D. Kirby, Florida State University*

OAB-0755   PS1541   93-786 CIP
Juhasz, Suzanne. **Comic power in Emily Dickinson,** by Suzanne Juhasz, Cristanne Miller, and Martha Nell Smith. Texas, 1993. 173p bibl indexes afp ISBN 0-292-740298-8, $27.50

Although this solid critical study of an essential ingredient of Dickinson's poetry is the work of three authors, it reads more like a seamless monograph than just a collection or symposium. In the process of demonstrating the force and meaning that derive from the sense of the comic and the use of literary comedy through much of her poetry, the authors do battle to alter the dominant perception of a pathetic New England spinster-nun, which colored the early (and prefeminist) biographies. Surely all students can benefit from the authors' demonstrations of the way the comic functions in particular poems to control form, force, and final effect (power?). The book is such a significant and closely argued contribution to the reading of this great American woman poet (and to an aspect of literary theory) that one might enter a small objection to the authors' method of citation employed in its extensive footnoting, or an occasionally belligerent view of less modern scholars. But this book should certainly prove useful in a college library. Advanced undergraduate; graduate; faculty; general.—*A. E. Jones Jr., emeritus, Drew University*

OAB-0756   PS3238   92-46142 CIP
Killingsworth, M. Jimmie. **The growth of *Leaves of grass*: the organic tradition in Whitman studies.** Camden House, 1993. 153p bibl index afp ISBN 1-879751-44-5, $49.50

This is an important and useful history of, and commentary on, the scholarship written about Walt Whitman's *Leaves of Grass*, which has been based upon the theory of organicism. According to Killingsworth, "the theory of organicism informs not only Whitman's best work but also the sturdiest line of descent in the critical tradition." Discussions of literature and life reflecting "organic" values emphasize "growth, process, holism, and fluidity," as opposed to values that emphasize the mechanistic and the rational. It seems very appropriate that scholars would discuss the poet who spoke continually of life's passages from birth to death to rebirth in terms that match his evolutionary and cyclical set of ideas. Killingsworth gives excellent summaries of primarily book-length studies written on Whitman's life, career, social and political ideas, and language. Every student and scholar of literature will want to consult this valuable reference tool for a necessary orientation to the poet and criticism about him. More than providing a mere listing, "Literary Criticism in Perspective," the series of which this volume is a part, serves the important function of tracing the development over time in the criticism of a particular author, work, or movement. This provides the reader with the opportunity of seeing the forces of society and history at work in the establishment of critical judgments. Undergraduate and beyond.—*P. J. Ferlazzo, Northern Arizona University*

OAB-0757   PS366   96-9614 CIP
Levine, Robert S. **Martin Delany, Frederick Douglass, and the politics of representative identity.** North Carolina, 1997. 314p index afp ISBN 0-8078-2323-6, $45.00; ISBN 0-8078-4633-3 pbk, $18.95

During the antislavery struggles of the 1850s, Delany was Douglass's chief rival for the title of "black Moses," and Lincoln chose Delany over Douglass as the first African American major in 1865. This fascinating book emphasizes the "overlapping and shared concerns" of the two leaders, challenging the "reductive binarisms that lead to Delany and Douglass being regarded as unequivocal opponents on the subjects of race and nation." Levine (Univ. of Maryland) nevertheless acknowledges their many contrasts. Whereas the mulatto ex-slave Douglass stressed his roots in America and demanded US citizenship for African Americans, Delany boasted of his "unadulterated" African heritage and proposed that 600,000 free Northern blacks should carry the "regenerative" forces of Christianity and commerce to Africa. Extended readings of neglected texts show how Delany, Douglass, and also Harriet Beecher Stowe shaped each other's bold labors in pursuit of "black elevation." Through careful research, Levine restores Delany to his hard-won rank

as a "representative man" for the African American race. Highly recommended for all academic libraries serving upper-division undergraduates and above.—*J. W. Hall, University of Mississippi*

OAB-0758   Can. CIP
Martin, W.R. **Henry James's apprenticeship: the tales, 1864-1882,** by W.R. Martin and Warren U. Ober. P.D. Meany, 1994. 213p bibl index afp ISBN 0-88835-034-1, $38.00

Leon Edel's monument leaves little shelfroom for new writing on James; it is refreshing therefore to see several recent works defying the overshadowing, not to say smothering, effect of the monolith, even to the point of challenging some of Edel's conclusions. This book, by two Canadian scholars, is a fine exploration of the work James was doing while becoming a master. Between the ages of 19 and 35, James published a series of "tales," culminating in *Daisy Miller* (his first real success), as well as novels. Each of these is examined chronologically as to theme, technique, and probable sources in James's imagination. The authors argue that these early tales, rather than the early novels, were James's real workshop, where he experimented and refined his craft in preparction for the great novels of his mature years. They refer, of course, to Edel and to Adeline Tintner's two excellent works on "the book world" and "the museum world" of Henry James, but they rely most heavily on James's own words—in the autobiography, the letters, and the great prefaces. There is a serviceable summary of James's life and principal artistic concerns, as well as a wide-ranging bibliography and full notes, continuing the scholarly debate. Clear, jargon-free language makes this extensively researched work readable, and above all, interesting. Appropriate for graduate students and faculty, but also an excellent introduction to James for the serious undergraduate, a level where James is too often neglected.—*S. Donovan, St. Thomas University*

OAB-0759   92-85490 Orig
Melville, Herman. **Correspondence,** ed. and annot. by Lynn Horth. Northwestern University/Newberry Library, 1993. 923p index (The writings of Herman Melville, 14) ISBN 0-8101-0981-6, $89.95; ISBN 0-8101-0995-6 pbk, $29.95

Building on the previous editions of Melville's correspondence, particularly the work of Merrell Davis and William Gilman and both the older and forthcoming editions of Jay Leyda's *The Melville Log* (CH,Jul'70), Lynn Horth, the editor of this 14th volume in the Northwestern Newberry Edition of Melville's writings, has produced an indispensable book for Melville students and a model for all editorial publication of the correspondence of authors important for literary study. All available manuscript letters to and from Melville have been reexamined and accurately transcribed. Unlocated manuscripts of previously printed letters have been copied from available sources. Unlocated letters whose existence can be established or reasonably conjectured have been described or contents noted. All of this is with full biographical and textual descriptions, relationships, and full annotations. Possibly this volume provides Melville with the most adequately edited correspondence of any American author, although its comprehensiveness and specificity may also have the effect of bringing more Melville letters to light than we now have. Horth's volume, in this master edition, is, of course, a required part of any sizable collection supporting academic study of American literature, even if it were not so splendidly done. General; advanced undergraduate through professional.—*A. E. Jones Jr., emeritus, Drew University*

OAB-0760   PS1342   94-37579 CIP
Michelson, Bruce. **Mark Twain on the loose: a comic writer and the American self.** Massachusetts, 1995. 269p bibl index ISBN 0-87023-966-X, $45.00; ISBN 0-87023-967-8 pbk, $16.95

Since Samuel Clemens became the focus of academic attention in the 1920s, critics and biographers have explored the dichotomies of his persona and his writing: his image as funny man against his dark musings, his roots in Western humor against his aspirations to gentility, his power to engage readers against the structural weaknesses of his books, and his stature as a moralist against his often anarchic, nihilistic visions. Michelson (Univ. of Illinois at Urbana-Champaign) discusses Clemens's art without trying to resolve these dualisms or taking sides. Rather, he finds that contradictions arise because at the heart of the sketches, travel books, and novels is anarchy that rises out of a central concern with being "on the loose," escaping and subverting social definitions and categories. This radical approach has positive results. For one, the reader is reminded that the writings of Mark Twain are funny, something often missed by scholars. For another, the complex images of death and transformation found throughout the works are analyzed on their own terms, without recourse to polemics or biographical pleading. This overview, from the early sketches to the nightmarish later fragments, is especially effective in its treatment of the travel books, especially *Innocents Abroad*, and of *Huckleberry Finn*, which embraces Huck's multiplicity in escaping definition rather than condemns him for moral inconsistency. A stimulating and civil critical exercise that is recommended for all collections.—*H. J. Lindborg, Marian College of Fond du Lac*

OAB-0761   PS373   91-40827 CIP
Moss, Elizabeth. **Domestic novelists in the Old South: defenders of Southern culture.** Louisiana State, 1992. 249p bibl index ISBN 0-8071-1730-7, $27.50

A significant milestone in our growing understanding of the uniqueness of antebellum southern womanhood and the literature and history thereof. Historian Moss (Advisory Council on Historic Preservation in Washington, DC), brings to bear that discipline's insights on her study of five 19th-century southern women writers: Caroline Gilman, Caroline Hentz, Maria McIntosh, Mary Virginia Terhune, and Augusta Evans. Moss consulted not only all the major historical and literary studies written about the South in the past two decades, but also collections of unpublished materials in almost two dozen libraries, archives, and historical societies. She endeavors to correct what she views as two errors made in earlier critiques of domestic fiction: the failure by scholars to recognize regional differences; and the disparagement of domestic fiction as either narrowly focused and conservative or the praise of these writers as profoundly radical. Moss presents an alternative interpretation of "the defiance of southern domestic heroines," in their attempting "not to subvert authority but simply to assert their moral autonomy." Moss accomplishes her task in crisp, elegant prose. Of particular interest is her chapter that traces the responses of Hentz and McIntosh in their own fiction to Harriet Beecher Stowe's *Uncle Tom's Cabin*. Extensive bibliography of primary and secondary sources. Strongly recommended for all undergraduate and graduate collections.—*E. R. Baer, Gustavus Adolphus College*

OAB-0762   PS3231   94-12841 CIP
Reynolds, David S. **Walt Whitman's America: a cultural biography.** Knopf, 1995. 671p index ISBN 0-394-58023-0, $35.00

Here is contextualization with a vengeance. Reynolds (CUNY Bernard M. Baruch College) reconstructs Whitman's life and times in massive detail, clarifying the dynamic and often complex interaction between the poet and the carnivalized social, political, and cultural contexts of 19th-century America. With amplitude surpassing that of previous biographers, Reynolds reveals the extent to which *Leaves of Grass* was indebted to the "wildest players" of American life: sensational novelists and journalists, street toughs, vehement actors, slang-whanging orators, native humorists, Italian divas, singing families, blackface minstrels, daguerreotypists, luminists, genre painters, Emersonian transcendentalists, reformers, physiologists, phrenologists, mesmerists, spirit-rappers, free lovers, and trance poets, to mention some of the more prominent. Reynolds also exhumes figures in the Whitman biography who have been either underappreciated or ignored altogether, for example, Ralph Smith, McDonald Clarke, George Lippard, Junius Brutus Booth, Justus Liebig, Alexander von Humboldt, Emanuel Swedenborg, and Thomas Lake Harris. One finishes this book persuaded that *Leaves of Grass* was, as the poet himself said, "the age transfigured." Like Reynolds's previous book, *Beneath the American Renaissance* (CH, Sep'88), *Walt Whitman's America* is an inspired synthesis of biographical

and historical data, a truly Whitman size contribution to the study of American literature, and an indispensable acquisition for libraries at all levels.— *D. D. Kummings, University of Wisconsin—Parkside*

OAB-0763   PS1631   94-36008 CIP
Richardson, Robert D. **Emerson: the mind on fire: a biography.** California, 1995. 671p bibl index afp ISBN 0-520-08808-5, $35.00

A knowledge of the principal writings of Emerson is critical to understanding all of American literature and thought. His insightful statements about nature, individualism, the role of the poet, and the place of science, scholarship, and faith in the world are as vital at the end of the 20th century as they were to his contemporaries in the 19th century. Richardson's biography not only brings to life Emerson's day-to-day activities, concerns, and relationships but also gives the reader a real sense of the germination and articulation of much of Emerson's philosophy. Richardson (Wesleyan Univ.) achieves something very rare and special among biographers of American authors: he makes his reader experience the life of his subject as a contemporary might have actually witnessed it being lived. Richardson's writing style creates a graceful, seamless web among all the original journals, notebooks, letters, and other documents quoted throughout the book. Here Emerson is not an icy remote image but a living, thinking, passionate, and suffering human trying to make a contribution to the life and world he deeply loved. This should become the new standard biography for Emerson. All collections.—*P. J. Ferlazzo, Northern Arizona University*

OAB-0764   PS2798   CIP
Sedgwick, Catharine Maria. **The power of her sympathy: the autobiography and journal of Catharine Maria Sedgwick,** ed. with introd. by Mary Kelley. Massachusetts Historical Society, 1993. 165p index ISBN 0-934909-35-0, $25.00; ISBN 0-934909-36-9 pbk, $8.95

Kelley (Dartmouth College) has performed an invaluable service to students of 19th-century American literature by editing and publishing the autobiography and journals of Catharine Maria Sedgwick, one of the country's first women fiction writers. The author of six novels and close to 100 tales published between 1822-1857, Sedgwick was a literary pioneer whose works and reputation helped open the field to other women writers in the 19th century. Some of her most important works have been reprinted in recent years, and now the publication of her autobiography and journals will make available in her own words Sedgwick's view on such topics as her childhood experiences, family relationships, educational background, and her ambivalence about her celebrated public career. Kelley's lucidly written and well-documented critical introduction is informative, and it places Sedgwick's writing in the social, political, and historical contexts of the years spanning the American Revolution and the Civil War. Moreover, Kelley traces the means by which Sedgwick negotiates the gender conventions of antebellum America in order to define a persona that was uniquely her own. An indispensable resource for any library.— *D. D. Knight, SUNY College at Cortland*

OAB-0765   PS1332   94-19712 CIP
Skandera-Trombley, Laura E. **Mark Twain in the company of women.** Pennsylvania, 1994. 219p bibl index afp ISBN 0-8122-3218-6, $29.95

This study is of genuine interest to Twain specialists and American studies scholars. Skandera-Trombley (SUNY-Potsdam) successfully presents and supports her significant interpretation that Twain was highly influenced by the women in his life, principally Olivia Langdon and her family of Elmira, NY. The Langdons and their friends, along with many citizens of Elmira, were actively involved in reform movements such as women's suffrage and slave abolition. The author closely examines the long-accepted criticism of Van Wyck Brooks and Bernard DeVoto and convincingly modifies or refutes their conclusions on the social and cultural practices of the Langdon family, especially how they influenced Twain's personal and literary beliefs. Skandera-Trombley indisputably establishes Twain's acceptance of and reliance on the advanced thinking of his wife. Also, of unusual background interest are the two chapters on the city of Elmira (including Elmira College and Elmira Reformatory), abolition, feminism, and cultural advancements. Because it is trailblazing in its thesis, painstaking in its extensive research, and resolutely efficacious in its presentation, this monograph deserves full recognition and sincere accolades for its author. Bibliography and index are both superior in their thoroughness and reliability. Undergraduate and up.—*G. O. Carey, emeritus, Eastern Kentucky University*

OAB-0766   PS1541   95-12591 CIP
Smith, Robert McClure. **The seductions of Emily Dickinson.** Alabama, 1996. 222p bibl index afp ISBN 0-8173-0806-7, $34.95

Dickinson has been well served by a number of critics over the years: Charles Anderson (*Emily Dickinson's Poetry: Stairway of Surprise*, 1960), Margaret Homans (*Women Writers and Poetic Identity: Dorothy Wordsworth, Emily Brontë and Emily Dickinson*, CH, Apr'81), E. Miller Budick (*Emily Dickinson and the Life of Language*, 1985), and Christopher Benfey (*Emily Dickinson and the Problem of Others*, 1984), to name only a few of the most insightful. Smith (George Washington Univ.) now joins this company. One of the very best readings of this enigmatic poet ever, demonstrating some of Dickinson's own talent for compression, this study covers a remarkable variety of material. The author offers not only close and persuasive readings of selected poems from a number of critical stances—historical, psychoanalytical, feminist, reader-response—but close and brilliant readings of some of the poet's most influential critics as well. This volume will prove a landmark in Dickinson criticism, addressing with wit, penetrating insight, and a refreshing lack of critical hubris the relationship between poet, poem, and reader that has always been at the heart of Dickinson's aesthetic. Highly recommended for all academic collections.—*S. R. Graham, emerita, Nazareth College of Rochester*

OAB-0767   PS153   92-34164 CIP
Sundquist, Eric J. **To wake the nations: race in the making of American literature.** Harvard, 1993. 705p index afp ISBN 0-674-89330-1, $29.95

This impressive study is a major work of American literary criticism. Comparable in importance to Henry Nash Smith's *Virgin Land* and Leo Marx's *The Machine in the Garden* (CH, Feb'65), Sundquist's study focuses on the significance of race in American literature of the 19th and early 20th centuries. Effectively balancing historical contexts and detailed textual readings, Sundquist addresses central issues such as the use of revolutionary ideology by abolitionist writers; the relationship between vernacular culture and formal literature; and the interaction of legal and literary discourses. Like David S. Reynolds's *Beneath the American Renaissance* (CH, Sep'88) and Jane Tompkins's *Sensational Designs* (CH, Nov'85), the present volume expands the boundaries of the American canon by creating a dialogue between the texts of established masters (Twain, Douglass, Melville) and less known writers (Chesnutt, Delany, DuBois). Clearly written and jargon-free, Sundquist's extended discussions of Melville's *Benito Cereno*, Chesnutt's *The Marrow of Tradition*, and the problematic "Confessions of Nat Turner" are among the highlights of a book that should command the attention of all students of American literary culture.—*C. Werner, University of Wisconsin—Madison*

OAB-0768   PS2127   95-30683 CIP
Teahan, Sheila. **The rhetorical logic of Henry James.** Louisiana State, 1995. 176p bibl index afp ISBN 0-8071-2005-7, $30.00

"As soon as I begin to appreciate simplification is imperilled," wrote James, which is hardly news to anyone who has ever tangled with one of his heavily embroidered texts. The critical industry has spent decades drawing out one Jamesian thread or another, but Teahan (Michigan State Univ.) goes to the very core of James's creation, the so-called center of consciousness by means of which the author narrates his major fictions. Whereas earlier critics have discussed this narrative device from the viewpoint of perception, psychology, or ethics, Teahan examines it as a rhetorical device that is programmed for self-destruction,

a "containing vessel" that eventually will "rupture from within by a natural growth or fruition." Thus, seemingly realistic works like *The Princess Casamassima* come across as little more than elaborate rhetorical apparatuses, for "though the Jamesian center of consciousness may appear the ultimate vehicle of psychological realism, it finally dismantles its central assumptions, such as the idea of a narrative as a mimetic presentation of consciousness." This book is a refreshing addendum to such classics as Philip Weinstein's *Henry James and the Requirements of the Imagination* (CH, Mar'72), though its shrewdness is dulled occasionally by stylistic opacity. Upper-division undergraduate and above.—*D. Kirby, Florida State University*

OAB-0769   PS374   96-3719 CIP
Thomas, Brook. **American literary realism and the failed promise of contract.** California, 1997. 359p index afp ISBN 0-520-20647-9, $35.00

This authoritative, wide-ranging study of late 19th-century fiction and law develops a new definition of literary realism and creates a new perspective for the study of influential novelists, e.g., Howells, Twain, James, Charles Chesnutt, and Elizabeth Stuart Phelps. Through extended analysis of more than 15 novels, Thomas (Univ. of California, Irvine) shows how racism, gender and class bias, and the structures of corporate capitalism subverted the realists' vision of an equitable social order based on contract, not status. Dealing with such contracts as slavery, segregation, marriage, copyright, and business, the author explores human interconnections. The integration of legal theory and literary criticism yields important insights into such canonical works as *The Rise of Silas Lapham, Pudd'nhead Wilson, The Bostonians,* and *The Awakening,* and into less familiar novels by David Graham Phillips, Albion Tourgée, and Francis Lynde. By placing fiction in the context of US constitutional and cultural history, Thomas also illuminates complex and controversial issues of current and historical importance—e.g., free speech, privacy, and the relation of morality to economics. His book has the depth and scope of a major work of scholarship. Upper-division undergraduate and advanced scholars of American literature and legal and intellectual history.—*E. Nettels, formerly, College of William and Mary*

OAB-0770   PS2127   92-15495 CIP
Tintner, Adeline R. **Henry James and the lust of the eyes: thirteen artists in his work.** Louisiana State, 1993. 265p index afp ISBN 0-8071-1752-8, $39.95

Each of the 12 chapters of Tintner's book develops analogies between the work of a painter or sculptor and a novel or story by James. Extending the scope of her *The Museum World of Henry James* (1986), Tintner, the foremost authority on James and the arts, shows how a work of art functions in the narrative to control the plot and create a subtext that illuminates the author's attitude and the actions and relationships of the characters. Each chapter moves beyond the single work to link characters and settings to the culture of an entire period, including historical associations of characters' names. As in her previous books, Tintner enlarges the reader's appreciation of the immense web of associations—historical, literary, mythic—that informs James's fiction. Her work thus reveals both the processes of James's imagination and the meanings of his fiction. All the chapters—five of them published for the first time—give new insight into James's work, including several major novels as well as half a dozen stories and nouvelles. The value of the book, notable for Tintner's meticulous scholarship and comprehensive analysis, is enhanced by 98 plates of the works of art treated in the chapters. Highly recommended to all specialists and students of James and the interrelationships of literature and the visual arts.—*E. Nettels, College of William and Mary*

OAB-0771   PS1300   93-23042 CIP
Twain, Mark. **Roughing it,** ed. by Harriet Elinor Smith et al. California, 1994 (c1993). 1,072p bibl afp (The works of Mark Twain, 2) ISBN 0-520-08498-5, $65.00

This edition supersedes the 1972 edition. The text, although it remains essentially the same, is more nearly what Twain intended and includes the pictures in the first American edition. Smith's introduction is more thorough than the brief earlier introduction (122 pages compared with 25 pages) and gives students much more information about Twain's difficulties in completing *Roughing It*. Making use of all available information, Smith painstakingly traces Twain's work on the book from the time he signed the contract with Elisha Bliss in July 1871, to its publication in February 1872. The expanded explanatory notes, description of the texts, textual notes, more detailed maps, the emendations and rejected substantives, and the addition of a bibliography of references used in establishing this text—all add greatly to our understanding of the text and of Twain's life and methods of composition. A meticulous and herculean effort, this edition belongs in every university and college library.—*E. Suderman, Gustavus Adolphus College*

OAB-0772   PS2388   91-7325 CIP
Wallace, Robert K. **Melville & Turner: spheres of love and fright.** Georgia, 1992. 643p bibl index afp ISBN 0-8203-1366-1, $75.00

Wallace's study of Herman Melville's literary debt to painter J.M.W. Turner is ambitious and exhaustive, and though it lacks the collective breadth of the essays edited by Christopher Sten in *Savage Eye: Melville and the Visual Arts* (CH, Sep'92), it is a superb example of interdisciplinary scholarship. Wallace believes that Melville's greatest debt is to the "powerful aesthetic of the indistinct" found in Turner's mature works, and he examines the means whereby, borrowing painterly effects from Turner, Melville evolved, from *Typee* to *Moby-Dick*, a prose style capable of profound philosophical inquiry and emotional intensity. Although there is no evidence Melville ever met Turner, much of the excitement of this book comes from Wallace's conviction that the two men were "soulmates." Examples of similarity and influence abound, and even when Wallace occasionally overruns the scent, his intuitive speculations argue convincingly for a perceptual understanding at the heart of Melville's aesthetic. The handsome, hefty volume is copiously illustrated with black-and-white reproductions and 12 color plates. The notes, bibliography, and index are thorough, and there is a useful appendix itemizing Melville's collection of engravings after Turner. Recommended for upper-level undergraduate and graduate students, and essential for Melville and interdisciplinary arts collections.—*J. J. Wydeven, Bellevue College*

OAB-0773   PS1449   93-8872 CIP
Wertheim, Stanley. **The Crane log: a documentary life of Stephen Crane, 1871-1900,** by Stanley Wertheim and Paul Sorrentino. G.K. Hall, 1994. 500p bibl index afp ISBN 0-8161-7292-7, $75.00

This volume, following a well-established pattern of biographical research on famous authors, is arguably the best available source of information on the life and background of Crane, whose brief, prodigious career (he died at 28 in 1900) remains an intriguing puzzle to serious students of American literature. The author of *Maggie*, *Red Badge*, a host of action-packed tales and journalistic dispatches, and a number of darkly ruminative poems is presented here in far more meaningful detail (short "takes," to use the contemporary term) than a full-length biography or lenthy personal account could provide. The authors begin by explaining the inadequacy or unreliability of Crane's major biographers, and they seek to remedy matters by utilizing dozens of reference sources including, but not limited to, journalistic reports, personal accounts, scholarly articles (literary criticism is not the point here), and Crane family archival materials. One of the most useful editorial features, aside from the index, photographic illustrations, and list of references, is the series of biographical notes on persons mentioned in the text, particularly Crane's mistress Cora Howarth. An unforgettable portrait of the artist as the eternal young man: frail, precocious, death-defying, crudely articulate, and drawn irresistibly to society's lower depths. Very enthusiastically recommended. Undergraduate; graduate; faculty; general.—*S. I. Bellman, California State Polytechnic University, Pomona*

OAB-0774   PS152   91-32103 CIP
Winter, Kari J. **Subjects of slavery, agents of change: women and**

power in Gothic novels and slave narratives, 1790-1865. Georgia, 1992. 172p bibl index afp ISBN 0-8203-1420-X, $30.00

A study that yokes Gothic novels and slave narratives seems at first improbable. Winter (Univ. of Vermont) has, however, illuminated both genres by this comparative study. Starting with Aristotle's views of slavery as informing the foundation of the Western social order, Winter asserts that "the oppression of women and male slaves can be understood fully only when the ideology of male domination is examined in conjunction with the ideology of slavery." She is careful, though, not to equate the status of slave and female. Reading "both genres as sites of ideological struggle," Winter states that her primary concern is "to examine how female Gothic novels and slave narratives engaged the dominant classist, racist, patriarchal discourse and created possibilities for new, feminist ways of thinking." Her sweep is sometimes dizzying, as she moves between Ann Radcliffe and Toni Morrison, Frederick Douglass and Charlotte Brontë. In addition, the book's organizational structure is rather idosyncratic, being based on the movement of an Emily Dickinson poem which first represents the horrors of patriarchy, traces attempts at resistance and escape, and ends with images of enclosure again. Nonetheless, those readers already familiar with texts in both genres will find Winter's analysis often startingly innovative and persuasive. Her prose is fluid and deft, informed but not burdened by theory. Strongly recommended for undergraduate and graduate collections.—*E. R. Baer, Gustavus Adolphus College*

OAB-0775   PS2508   94-32185 CIP
Zwarg, Christina. **Feminist conversations: Fuller, Emerson, and the play of reading.** Cornell, 1995. 302p index afp ISBN 0-8014-2872-6, $39.95; ISBN 0-8014-8110-4 pbk, $16.95

This theoretically dense, well-researched book focuses on the relationship between two great 19th-century intellectuals: Ralph Waldo Emerson and Margaret Fuller. Relying on the extensive correspondence between Emerson and Fuller, Zwarg (Haverford College) discusses how this epistolary exchange, which continued for nearly 14 years, furthered the intellectual growth of both individuals. She also sheds new light on how Emerson and Fuller were influenced by the work of the French utopian Charles Fourier. Her commentary on Emerson is graceful and succinct, but Zwarg is at her best when she is analyzing the work of Fuller, breaking new ground by examining Fuller's work as a translator and exploring the connections between feminism and translating. Zwarg also examines other elements of Fuller's oeuvre, e.g., journalism writing for the *New-York Daily Tribune*, which deserve further research. Because of its originality and excellent research, this book will be mandatory reading for Fuller and Emerson scholars and those interested in the development of 19th-century women's writing. Recommended for upper-division undergraduate collections and university and college libraries that serve professors and graduate students.—*S. A. Inness, Miami University*

UNITED STATES —
20th Century to 1950

OAB-0776   PS310   96-7639 CIP
Albright, Daniel. **Quantum poetics: Yeats, Pound, Eliot, and the science of modernism.** Cambridge, 1997. 307p bibl index ISBN 0-521-57305-X, $59.95

Albright (Univ. of Rochester) presents an insightful and delightful study of the relationship between physics and poetry (and other arts) in the first half of the 20th century. For him, developments in scientific theory become metaphors for a poetics of modernism. He proposes a dialectic of wave/particle theory as a ground for reading the works of Yeats, Pound, Eliot, and their contemporaries. He then integrates this theory into a reading of the poets own treatises on poetics: Yeats's *A Vision*, Pound's articulation of imagism and vorticism, and

Eliot's PhD dissertation (on F.H. Bradley) and his essays. Throughout, Albright is generous in providing samples of these writers' poetry along with the work of Lawrence, Woolf, and Joyce, among others. Albright's argument centers on the modernist attempt to redefine poetics in terms analogous to the wave theory or the particle theory in quantum physics. According to Albright, the result is a dialectic of the wave and the particle within the aesthetics of modernism. Like all good studies, this one stimulates a desire to reread familiar material with new energy. Upper-division undergraduates through faculty.—*R. T. Prus, Southeastern Oklahoma State University*

OAB-0777   PS3523   96-14682 CIP
Auerbach, Jonathan. **Male call: becoming Jack London.** Duke University, 1996. 289p index afp ISBN 0-8223-1827-X, $49.95; ISBN 0-8223-1820-2 pbk, $17.95

This full-length study of London employs the critical methodology and insights of contemporary writers on American literary naturalism, including Christopher Gair, June Howard, Walter Benn Michaels, Mark Seltzer, Lee Clark Mitchell, and Christopher Wilson. Auerbach (Univ. of Maryland, College Park) devotes chapters to London's major early fiction, including the "Malemute Kid" series of Yukon stories, *The Call of the Wild, The People of the Abyss, The Kempton-Wace Letters*, and *The Sea-Wolf*, all written and published between 1898 and 1904. These are framed by chapters that trace the trajectory of London's conscious efforts to manufacture a trademark "self" to satisfy the demand of the new popular magazine and book industry for authenticity, celebrity, power, and personality. Auerbach employs these concepts along with that of masculinity to analyze London's writings as the expression of a self made in public. In providing a thoroughly new reading of London's early works, this book makes a fine contribution to both contemporary literary criticism and London research. Destined to influence future studies of this great American writer and of professional writing of the period, it belongs in every library.—*S. M. Nuernberg, University of Wisconsin—Oshkosh*

OAB-0778   PS228   94-16668 CIP
Barnard, Rita. **The Great Depression and the culture of abundance: Kenneth Fearing, Nathanael West, and mass culture in the 1930s.** Cambridge, 1995. 273p index (Cambridge studies in American literature and culture, 87) ISBN 0-521-45034-9, $49.95

Barnard (Univ. of Pennsylvania) begins her study by probing the relationship between two apparently contradictory sets of terms: Depression/abundance and literature/mass culture. She argues that in the midst of the Depression one could already see the emergence of a consumer society. During this period the sharp distinction between "high art" and "mass culture" was sharply contested at many levels, and many writers incorporated the discourse of the mass media in their works. Barnard sees Fearing and West as key figures whose works both illuminate and anticipate many of the political and cultural forces at work in postmodern America. This is a major contribution to the rich body of recent scholarship dedicated to the recovery of the dynamic culture of the Left in the US, including Cary Nelson's *Repression and Recovery: Modern American Poetry and the Politics of Cultural Memory, 1910-1945* (CH, Jun'90), Barbara Foley's *Radical Representations: Politics and Form in U.S. Proletarian Fiction, 1929-1941* (CH, May'94), and Michael Staub's *Voices of Persuasion: Politics of Representation in 1930s America* (CH, Jan'95). Meticulously researched, theoretically sophisticated, and elegantly written, this title should appeal to academic specialists and general readers alike.—*J. A. Miller, Trinity College (CT)*

OAB-0779   PS3505   91-31149 CIP
Cather, Willa. **O pioneers!,** ed. by Susan J. Rosowski and Charles W. Mignon with Kathleen Danker. Nebraska, 1993 (c1992). 391p ISBN 0-8032-1457-X, $45.00

Labeled "Scholarly Edition" and carrying the Modern Language Association of America's seal of approval, this edition of *O Pioneers!* certainly lives up to expectations. It is a generous edition, to be sure. This early novel is now held

to be a very crucial and pivotal one in the whole development of the novelist, and this new scholarly edition provides a large selection of meaningful tools for the scholars, as well as a fine printing for the readers. A 20-page historical essay on the coming into being of *O Pioneers!* is supported by ten black-and-white background photos, which are helpful in demonstrating how much this novel is really rooted in the Nebraska plains. Other specifically textual apparatus (also generous) consists of five sections: textual commentary, emendations; notes on emendations, rejected substantives, and word division. Editors Rosowski and Mignon, along with Kathleen Danker and David Stouck, deserve a full measure of praise for their work. Advanced undergraduate; graduate; faculty; general.—*J. P. Lovering, Canisius College*

OAB-0780   PS3509   96-24155 CIP
Childs, Donald J. **T.S. Eliot: mystic, son and lover.** St. Martin's, 1997. 255p index ISBN 0-312-16417-3, $45.00

Childs (Univ. of Ottawa) makes a number of original observations in this exploration of Eliot's attitudes toward and treatment of Theosophy, spiritualism, occultism, and mysticism in its various forms. The author examines Eliot's lifelong interest in mysticism by analyzing his Harvard doctoral dissertation (*Knowledge and Experience in the Philosophy of F.H. Bradley*, submitted in 1916, published in 1964), criticism, lectures, and literary output, some of which is uncollected. Building on the material available in the newer biographies of Eliot—Peter Ackroyd's *T.S. Eliot: A Life* (CH, Feb'85), Lyndall Gordon's *Eliot's Early Years* (CH, Jul'77), and *Eliot's New Life* (1988)—Childs profitably discusses Eliot's relationship with his mother and first wife, Viviennne, vis-à-vis Shakespeare's play *Coriolanus* and selected works of D.H. Lawrence (thus, the "son and lover" of the title). The focus of this book makes it fairly unique, with the only other comparable treatment being Paul Murray's *T.S. Eliot and Mysticism: The Secret History of Four Quartets* (CH, Dec'91). But Child's considerations are far broader than Eliot's poetry. Recommended for upper-division undergraduates and up.—*A. R. Nourie, Illinois State University*

OAB-0781   PS374   93-41004 CIP
Civello, Paul. **American literary naturalism and its twentieth-century transformations: Frank Norris, Ernest Hemingway, Don DeLillo.** Georgia, 1994. 191p bibl index afp ISBN 0-8203-1649-0, $35.00

Civello's fine new book defines and illustrates the protean nature of American literary naturalism and the criticism that surrounds it. The author (San Jose State Univ.) corrects the popular assumption that naturalism in American fiction was a static form "largely confined to the nineteenth century or as a literary anachronism in the twentieth." He analyzes representative texts by Norris, Hemingway, and DeLillo, tracing transformations in the literary naturalism of each and demonstrating that the narrative reality of naturalism presented by these authors "is grounded in contemporary constructions of 'reality'—particularly scientific and philosophical constructions." This method provides impressive insights into the fictional universes of the authors studied. Opening chapters provide lucid and logically developed summations of Darwinism and determinism. When Civello then turns to two key works for each author, his coupling of zeitgeists and the fiction's themes amply demonstrates his method's potential and richness. This reviewer found the Hemingway and DeLillo chapters among the most perceptive studies of these authors to date. Highly recommended for all undergraduate and graduate libraries.—*D. R. Stoddard, Anne Arundel Community College*

OAB-0782   Can. CIP
Cobley, Evelyn. **Representing war: form and ideology in First World War narratives.** Toronto, 1993. 261p bibl index afp ISBN 0-8020-0537-3, $45.00

In extensively using critical theory of structuralist and poststructuralist narratologists (de Lauretis in particular), as well as deconstructive theory primarily of Derrida, Barthes, and White, the author has created a critically sophisticated study of WW I literature that will do much to set the theoretical standards and issues of debate in the field. Cobley offers probing and subtle analyses of Barbusse's *Le Feu* (1916), Dos Passos's *Three Soldiers* (1921), Mottram's *The Spanish Farm Trilogy* (1927), Aldington's *Death of a Hero* (1929), Hemingway's *A Farewell to Arms* (1929), and David Jones's *In Parenthesis* (1937), demonstrating the deconstructive perspective that no work can escape complicity with the values it seeks to subvert. The author demonstrates how each one of these works adapts formal strategies that are ideologically significant in their subversion of the ostensible critiques of the experience. Cobley also examines Herr's *Dispatches* (1977) and O'Brien's *Going After Cacciato* (1978), works that obviously demonstrate how narrative devices problematize sense-making with contradictory inscriptions that challenge an author's desire to represent experience in particular ways. This is a work of high critical reflection, fully informed in its multiple theoretical perspectives and forceful in its conclusions. Graduate; faculty.—*B. Adler, Valdosta State University*

OAB-0783   PS3515   93-49752 CIP
Comley, Nancy R. **Hemingway's genders: rereading the Hemingway text,** by Nancy R. Comley and Robert Scholes. Yale, 1994. 154p bibl index afp ISBN 0-300-05967-1, $23.00

This intelligent study of the complex issue of gender in Hemingway's works is a fine addition to Hemingway scholarship and a pleasure to read. Not only do Scholes and Comley deal incisively and comprehensively with the Hemingway text (comprising both published and unpublished material) as well as with the burgeoning mass of Hemingway biography, they do so with clever good humor. One character, for example, "frees himself ... from the Mummy's curse." The publication of a heavily edited version of Hemingway's unfinished novel *The Garden of Eden* (CH, Sep'86) presented scholars with a new vision of Hemingway's fascination with androgyny and lesbianism. Scholes and Comley, in exploring this and other works, extend their analysis to include Hemingway's interest in male homosexuality and miscegenation: "These motifs— sex across racial boundaries and sex that violates cultural taboos—are the warp and woof of sexuality in the Hemingway Text." Much fine criticism and biography of Hemingway, such as Carlos Baker's *Ernest Hemingway: A Life Story* (CH, Sep'69) and Bernice Kert's *The Hemingway Women* (CH, Nov'83) have dealt with this complex author's attitude toward the women in his life and his books. This volume carries the analysis to a new level of sophistication. Academic and general audiences.—*B. H. Leeds, Central Connecticut State University*

OAB-0784   PS3503   95-43105 CIP
Conn, Peter. **Pearl S. Buck: a cultural biography.** Cambridge, 1996. 468p index ISBN 0-521-56080-2, $29.95

This biography is the best available scholarly discussion of a remarkably popular author and Nobel laureate who has been neglected by most literary historians. Like Paul A. Doyle (*Pearl S. Buck*, CH, Nov'65; rev. ed., 1980) and Nora Stirling (*Pearl Buck: A Woman in Conflict*, 1983), Conn (Univ. of Pennsylvania) provides a sympathetic but balanced overview of Buck's nonfiction and fiction, including *The Good Earth* (1931), a best-selling novel that won the Pulitzer Prize. Conn surpasses these earlier biographers, however, in so thoroughly exploring the author's lifelong relationship with China. A daughter and wife of missionaries, the bilingual Buck spent the first half of her life in Asia. Her experience as an outsider had a great impact on her books and on the many causes she championed— from birth control to civil rights—in the face of criticism from both liberals and conservatives. "Never before or since has one writer so personally shaped the imaginative terms in which America addresses a foreign culture," Conn persuasively argues. The father of a child adopted through Buck's Welcome House agency, Conn brings a personal interest to this absorbing and carefully documented study. Highly recommended as a valuable addition to all public and academic library collections.—*J. W. Hall, University of Mississippi*

OAB-0785   DK27   96-20778 CIP
Dreiser, Theodore. **Dreiser's Russian diary,** ed. by Thomas P. Riggio and James L.W. West. Pennsylvania, 1996. 297p index afp ISBN 0-8122-8091-1, $38.50

This firsthand record of Dreiser's experiences in and observations of Russia is a landmark in American literature. The diary also includes his itinerary, both en route to Russia (Paris, Berlin and Warsaw) and in Russia—Moscow, Leningrad, and the port cities along the Black Sea, with a Russian guide and secretary as companions. Along the way Dreiser met Sinclair Lewis, Dorothy Thompson, Ernest Hemingway, Diego Rivera. In Moscow he was an observant spectator of the ten-day celebration of the tenth anniversary of the revolution. Dreiser's descriptions are superior, including those of workers' housing, model prisons, lecture halls, gymnasia. Dreiser is highly accurate and his reportage historically valuable. Bibliographic apparatus are excellent. All collections of American literature and Russian and Soviet history.—*G. O. Carey, emeritus, Eastern Kentucky University*

OAB-0786   PS3507   92-20462 CIP
Dreiser, Theodore. **Jennie Gerhardt,** ed. by James L.W. West. Pennsylvania, 1992. 577p afp ISBN 0-8122-8164-0, $39.95; ISBN 0-8122-1284-3 pbk, $19.95

Dreiser's *Jennie Gerhardt* (1911), considered one of his three major novels, was published by Harper's after extensive revisions and cuttings that deprived the pathetic heroine of certain original endowments: force of personality and spiritual breadth. Editor West, assisted by numerous scholars and support-staff members, and utilizing manuscripts at the University of Pennsylvania and the University of Virginia's Barrett Collection, has produced a text representing substantially what Dreiser had first submitted to Harper's—i.e., first, a far more honest work of social criticism with disturbingly unconventional views on the institution of marriage and institutionalized religion; and second, a more realistically rendered portrait of a lady, essentially a "loser" because she lacked the ingenuity of the "grand design" to overcome her social and economic handicaps (but in today's terms, not the "fallen woman" as seen by a constricted, hypocritical society in the early 1900s). Elaborate editorial apparatus detailing how the present text has been assembled and related textual matters enhance this superb edition, a must for all important library collections.— *S. I. Bellman, California State Polytechnic University, Pomona*

OAB-0787   PS3511   93-8423 CIP
Fitzgerald, F. Scott. **The love of *The last tycoon*: a western,** ed. by Matthew J. Bruccoli. Cambridge, 1993. 352p ISBN 0-521-40231-X, $34.95

This new *Last Tycoon*, issued as part of the Cambridge edition of F. Scott Fitzgerald's works and expertly edited, is freshly minted in many ways, some suggested by the revised title. Until now, readers and literary scholars have known Fitzgerald's last novel (far from finished at his death in 1940) only in the posthumous version published by Edmund Wilson and Scribner. Wilson aimed to produce a readable novel, as complete as a competent editor-writer-critic-friend could manage out of presumably finished episodes and evidence from documents, conversations, and conjecture. Now the Bruccoli version adds new, valuable, and important information regarding Fitzgerald's artistry, his knowledge of the film industry, and the accomplishment represented by what still must be regarded as work in progress. It includes the history of the author's composition, facsimiles, and a full explanation of the editorial methods employed by Bruccoli. It contains notes that will prove helpful to undergraduate students in aiding comprehension. This book, essential for the support of detailed study of Fitzgerald and the American novel, may well replace the older Wilson version. All levels.—*A. E. Jones Jr., emeritus, Drew University*

OAB-0788   PS3515   93-13245 CIP
Fleming, Robert E. **The face in the mirror: Hemingway's writers.** Alabama, 1994. 195p bibl index afp ISBN 0-8173-0703-6, $34.95

It is, in retrospect, rather astounding that a concerted study on this subject has not been made before. Hemingway's focus on the role and the responsibilities—and the perils—of the authorial state may well exceed that of even Henry James. Yet the critic, in concentrating on the appearance of characters who are also "writers" in Hemingway's fiction—a category that enables him to include *A Moveable Feast* by way of finale and grace note—is understandably and commendably unabashed in leaving out consideration of some major works while including others that are patently more germane. Thus we are given consideration of "Banal Story" and "A Sea Change" while a couple of the major novels are intelligently ignored. But Fleming is also majestic in the area of the posthumous works, including *Islands in the Stream*; and his treatment of *The Garden of Eden* is, quite simply, superb. Here the "mirror" metaphor of the title is given full play, and to great effect; again, Hemingway's psychological hangups seem to come to final focus in this work we will probably never quite bottom, but which seems rich in evocations of crises of both gender and art. The text is smooth and eminently readable, and the only (few) problems involve the index. Highly recommended. Undergraduate; graduate; faculty; general.—*J. M. Ditsky, University of Windsor*

OAB-0789   PS374   93-18687 CIP
Foley, Barbara. **Radical representations: politics and form in U.S. proleterian fiction, 1929-1941.** Duke University, 1994 (c1993). 459p index afp ISBN 0-8223-1361-8, $55.00; ISBN 0-8223-1394-4 pbk, $19.95

This monumental study of the proletarian literary movement in the US examines the debates over modernism and experimentation, the definition of proletarian literature, over the relation of art to propaganda, which engaged radical writers in the 1930s and set the tone for all subsequent criticism of this movement. Citing recent scholarship on race, class, and the "Negro question," Foley investigates ways that black and white leftists of the 1930s formulated the relation of race to class. The chapter on women writers and the left only briefly addresses the complex and ongoing debate on the relation of sex to class. More thoroughly developed is Foley's discussion of the four major genres of proletarian fiction—the fictional autobiography, the bildungsroman, the social novel, and the collective novel—and her analyses of ways in which many proletarian writers did and did not transcend these genres' limitations. Exhaustively researched and documented, this book rescues proletarian literature from undeserved neglect and offers a serious reconsideration and positive reassessment of 1930s literary radicalism. All levels.—*S. M. Nuernberg, University of Wisconsin-Oshkosh*

OAB-0790   PS173   95-36520 CIP
Gunning, Sandra. **Race, rape, and lynching: the red record of American literature, 1890-1912.** Oxford, 1996. 195p bibl index afp ISBN 0-19-509990-7, $35.00

In this challenging and comprehensive study, Gunning (Univ. of Michigan) analyzes representations of racial violence in the works of more than a dozen writers, black and white, male and female. Focusing on the stereotype of the Negro man as sexual brute, she shows how the idea of the "black rapist" enabled white supremacists to justify their violence against blacks and also to confine the white woman to the status of powerless victim. Juxtaposing influential black writers (e.g., Charles Chesnutt, Pauline Hopkins, Ida B. Wells) and their white contemporaries (including Mark Twain, Thomas Dixon, and Kate Chopin), the book effectively demonstrates the conflicting impulses within the individual writer, the range of attitudes among writers of the same race, and the differences generated by the complex interaction of desires based on gender, class, and region, as well as race. The analyses of the fiction are sound, illuminating, and rigorously argued, alert to the ways novels both subvert and reinforce racist ideology. The author draws on autobiographies, newspapers, scientific treatises, and essays to connect the fiction to historical events such as Supreme Court cases, race riots, the Ku Klux Klan, women's suffrage, the Clarence Thomas hearings, and the O.J. Simpson trial. Gunning's dense style assumes a sophisticated reader, but she sustains a balanced and powerful argument. Detailed notes and an extensive bibliography. Upper-division and graduate students in American, African American, and women's studies.—*E. Nettels, College of William and Mary*

OAB-0791   PS374   94-40316 CIP
Hapke, Laura. **Daughters of the Great Depression: women, work, and fiction in the American 1930s.** Georgia, 1995. 286p index afp ISBN 0-8203-1718-7, $45.00

In a masterful integration of history and literature, Hapke (Pace Univ.) incisively analyzes the many ways that fiction in the 1930s reflected and reinforced the widespread hostility and exploitation suffered by women in the work force during the Depression. Notable for its comprehensiveness, the book draws material from letters, autobiographies, photographs, newspapers, government surveys, New Deal legislation and reports, and the careers of writers and other professional women such as Dorothy Thompson and Frances Perkins. Hapke thus creates a rich historical context for the study of scores of novels about female workers in a variety of settings, including factories, textile mills, offices, farms, labor unions, and domestic service. The author compares prominent mainstream male writers (e.g., Sherwood Anderson, Sinclair Lewis, John Steinbeck, and James Farrell) with influential black writers (e.g., Langston Hughes, Richard Wright) and with lesser-known "militant" women writers (e.g., Agnes Smedley, Muriel LeSueur) whose "female revisions of male ideology" undermined but failed to subvert the conventional view of woman's proper role as mother and helpmeet. Like the author's *Tales of the Working Girl: Wage-Earning Women in American Literature, 1890-1925* (CH, Jan'93), this is a groundbreaking work, outstanding for its clarity, scope, exemplary scholarship, and wealth of fact and insight. Highly recommended to all students of American literature and history and women's studies.—*E. Nettels, College of William and Mary*

OAB-0792   PS374   92-10568 CIP
Hapke, Laura. **Tales of the working girl: wage-earning women in American literature, 1890-1925.** Twayne, 1992. 167p bibl index afp (Twayne's literature & society series, 2) ISBN 0-8057-8855-7, $26.95; ISBN 0-8057-8860-3 pbk, $13.95

The first comprehensive scholarly study to trace the changing representations of the working woman in American literature of the post-Civil War era. Drawing on the fiction and essays of more than 100 writers, Hapke defines the differing attitudes and goals of authors and their characters expressed in successive depictions of the female worker—as sexually exploited victim, as fallen woman, as aspirant to the middle class, and as militant protester. Muckraking journalism, autobiography, and stories and novels of women in factories, sweatshops, stores, and offices are all analyzed in relation to prevailing ideologies of gender and class and to the impact of such institutions as the settlement house, clubs for working girls, and women's trade unions. The integration of literary criticism and social history yields fresh insights into well-known works by Dreiser, Edith Wharton, and Stephen Crane, among others, as well as scores of novels and stories by writers who have received little if any critical attention. Clear and concise in style, enhanced by a wide-ranging annotated bibliography, this book is highly recommended to all specialists and to students, undergraduate onward, of American studies and women's history.—*E. Nettels, College of William and Mary*

OAB-0793   PS3505   92-16093 CIP
Harrell, David. **From Mesa Verde to *The professor's house*.** New Mexico, 1992. 302p bibl index ISBN 0-8263-1386-8, $29.95

Cather biographer James Woodress has written that, more than most writers, "Cather presents readers with the chance to compare biographical data with its transmutation into art." Harrell's lucid and well-organized work, an engaging combination of history and literary criticism, is an enlightening resource for critics of *The Professor's House*, as he gathers source material and photographs on the Wetherill brothers and the development of Mesa Verde National Park in order to shed light on Cather's process of composition. He documents the ways in which she was, since her childhood, both haunted and teased by the ancient cliff dwellings until she wrote *The Professor's House*, what Harrell calls a "historically inspired narrative to articualte a long-standing personal myth." Certainly the novel will be seen anew as a result of the compilation of the background material and Harrell's analysis of the structure of "Tom Outland's

Story." He is convincing in his assertion that the novel "took shape over a period of years rather than months and that, of the many influences upon it, those related directly to Mesa Verde account for more of the novel's final form and meaning than any other." An interesting addition to Merrill Skaggs's *After the World Broke in Two* (CH, Apr'91), JoAnn Middleton's *Willa Cather's Modernism* (1990), and James Woodress's *Willa Cather: A Literary Life* (CH, Jun'88).—*L. Winters, College of Saint Elizabeth*

OAB-0794   PS3503   95-7630 CIP
Herring, Phillip. **Djuna: the life and work of Djuna Barnes.** Viking, 1995. 386p bibl index afp ISBN 0-670-84969-3, $27.95

This engaging, readable study details the painful life of Djuna Barnes, a master wit, a woman of beauty and style, and an elusive near genius. Barnes seemed to know everyone in the 1920s, but she never made it fully into the high modernist canon. Her personal and professional life was kept from full tragedy by the intervention of key figures, particularly T.S. Eliot, who championed the publication of her best work, the novel *Nightwood.* Herring unfolds a fascinating tale of painful sexual initiation, bisexuality, alcoholism, and debilitating illness. Particularly good is his analysis of the mixed motives and complex emotional ties in Barnes's most significant relationship, her intense love for Thelma Wood, who would betray her. This biography should encourage closer study of Barnes's work and will be enormously useful in women's studies and gay and lesbian studies classrooms, where it might be used with James Woodress's *Willa Cather: A Literary Life* (CH, Jun'88) and Gary Fountain and Peter Brazeau's *Remembering Elizabeth Bishop* (1994) to reveal the pressures on women artists who do not fit conventional categories. General; upperdivision undergraduate and above.—*L. Winters, College of Saint Elizabeth*

OAB-0795   PS3545   95-8519 CIP
Killoran, Helen. **Edith Wharton: art and allusion.** Alabama, 1996. 223p bibl index afp ISBN 0-8173-0766-4, $39.95

Killoran (Ohio Univ.—Lancaster) makes an important contribution in her exhaustive study of literary allusions in Wharton's fiction. In detailed analysis of ten novels, she shows for the first time how different types of allusions (e.g., structural, thematic, layered) function as "messages" or "pieces of an encoded puzzle." These messages link Wharton's novels; expose hidden themes, such as incest and insanity, that could not be directly stated; and reveal a "personal mythology" in which myths of the Sphinx and the Furies assume primary importance. Identifying scores of literary works embedded in Wharton's texts, Killoran illuminates the significance of the books characters read, the plays they see, and the poems they quote, as well as the origin and meaning of place names, key phrases, titles of the novels, and names of characters. The complex patterns of allusions demonstrate Wharton's artistry and extraordinary knowledge, and Killoran's exploration yields new insights into both the intensively analyzed novels (*The House of Mirth* and *The Age of Innocence*) and reveals unexpected depths in the less-studied novels (*The Children* and *Twilight Sleep*). Comprehensive, sound in its scholarship, clear and concise in style, this book is highly recommended as a valuable resource to all students and specialists in American literature and narrative art. Upper-division undergraduate and up.—*E. Nettels, College of William and Mary*

OAB-0796   PS309   96-4457 CIP
Kirby-Smith, H.T. **The origins of free verse.** Michigan, 1996. 304p bibl index afp ISBN 0-472-10698-8, $49.50

Kirby-Smith (Univ. of North Carolina, Greensboro) presents a witty and polemical account of the emergence and development of free verse. He declares at the outset that good free verse achieves its idiosyncratic effects by playing against the expectations of well-established metrical traditions. Though conceding that free verse is largely a 20th-century phenomenon, the author nevertheless finds significant instances of the genre much earlier—for example, in the writings of Milton, Blake, Arnold, W.H. Henley, and the *vers libre* poets of France. He acknowledges Whitman's pioneering achievement and massive influence but finally seems to have reservations about his poetry, for he noticeably excludes Whitman from his list of the "best writers of free verse, such as H.D., Eliot, Pound, Williams, and Levertov." In the course of this literary history, Kirby-Smith hurls maledictions against both organicists and neoclassicists, against writers of the prose poem, against language poets, and against the prosodically vacuous free verse that fills so many of today's poetry journals. Almost every reader of this book will find, at some point, hackles-raising arguments. At the same time, almost every reader will encounter fresh and fertile ideas, for instance, Kirby-Smith's taxonomy for classifying free verse and his insights into the increasing importance of its typographical dimension of free verse. A necessary acquisition for college and university libraries serving upper-division undergraduates and up.—*D. D. Kummings, University of Wisconsin—Parkside*

OAB-0797   PS310   94-25159 CIP
Korg, Jacob. **Ritual and experiment in modern poetry.** St. Martin's, 1995. 244p bibl index ISBN 0-312-12453-8, $39.95

As he did in his discussions of authors (*George Gissing*, 1963; *Dylan Thomas*, 1965), Korg (Univ. of Washington) begins this study with an explanatory background and a key to the analysis to follow. He presents two chapters preparatory to his analysis of Yeats, Eliot, Pound, H.D., and David Jones. "Ritual" is seen both as a source and as a matrix for thought and rhythm. "Experiment" refers to the poet allowing innovations to burgeon from ritual without obscuring it. Korg traces the respective sources: Theosophy and Cabalism for Yeats; Christianity for Eliot; Confucianism and Eleusinian Mysteries for Pound; Moravian and Greek traditions for H.D.; and Cassirer's aesthetics and Catholicism as seen in Maritain for David Jones. Korg sheds new light on the modern poets and provides abundant examples of ritual in each poet's work. This fine contribution to the appreciation of early 20th century poetry is recommended for undergraduate and graduate study alike, particularly for students seeking the roots of modern poetry.—*A. G. Tassin, University of New Orleans*

OAB-0798   PS3523   92-44856 CIP
London, Jack. **The complete short stories of Jack London,** ed. by Earle Labor, Robert C. Leitz, and I. Milo Shepard. Stanford, 1993. 3v. 2,557p index afp ISBN 0-8047-2058-4, $180.00

The London scholar and enthusiast will find this collection of Jack London's short fiction invaluable for the five previously unpublished stories it contains and for the 28 others it collects for the first time since their original publication in magazines. This is the first comprehensive collection of London's stories to appear in the US. It signals the long-overdue establishment of London's place as a great story writer in the history of American letters. Superbly edited by the trio who prepared *The Letters of Jack London* (CH, Mar'89), this collection deserves to call itself "complete." Volume 1 includes an introduction, "About This Edition," which identifies the copy text for 161 of the 197 stories as the text of the collected stories which were typeset from carbon copies of his original typescripts, a chronology of Jack London's life, and stories from 1893 to 1902 arranged in order of composition. Volume 2 contains stories from 1902 to 1910. Volume 3 includes stories from 1910 to 1916; a publication history (Appendix A) which is an annotated version of London's "Magazine Sales" notebooks; textual emendations (Appendix B); and an index of titles. It is destined to become the definitive text for London's short stories.—*S. M. Nuernberg, University of Wisconsin-Oshkosh*

OAB-0799   PS3545   93-38636 CIP
Marzán, Julio. **The Spanish American roots of William Carlos Williams.** Texas, 1994. 288p bibl index afp ISBN 0-292-75160-5, $30.00

Any serious work on William Carlos Williams hereafter will have to take into account Marzán's new study of his Caribbean roots. Essentially, Marzán shows that Williams carefully crafted his literary persona to assert both "William" and "Carlos" but then allowed Anglo-poet "Bill" to dominate and suppress the "Carlos" persona until late in his life. One of Marzán's successes is in show-

Choice's Outstanding Academic Books

ing that "Carlos" asserted himself all along. He developed the Anglo identity more fully because his audience clearly preferred it, but the Puerto Rican mother and the Caribbean father (who from the age of five lived in Spanish-speaking Caribbean areas) produced undercurrents of the Spanish American in Williams's work from the beginning. Marzán traces those undercurrents and shows their emergence to the surface in the later work. Looking from this fresh angle permits Marzán to make breakthroughs. For instance, the Hispanic connection between Williams and Picasso lets him make more sense than has been made of the ties between Williams and cubism. Close reading of many poems will let readers view well-known poems freshly. Undergraduate and graduate academic libraries certainly should own this book. The multicultural material will interest a broad span of academic and general readers. Notes and bibliography will assist scholars.—*Q. Grigg, Hamline University*

OAB-0800   PS3525   91-16968 CIP
Masters, Edgar Lee. **Spoon River anthology: an annotated edition,** ed. and introd. by John E. Hallwas. Illinois, 1993 (c1992). 436p ISBN 0-252-01561-4 pbk, $14.95

For students and scholars this is now the definitive edition. The real-life persons, or composites of them, who are the subjects of the poems are thoroughly identified. Allusions in the poems, often classical and historical, are annotated. In the interest of completeness the "Spooniad," an attempt at the mock-heroic style, and the "Epilogue," a kind of verse drama, are also included. In his lengthy and highly informative introduction, Hallwas sheds new light on the mythic and autobiographical elements in the *Anthology*. Masters's relationship to other literary figures of the time—e.g., Dreiser, Sandburg—is also explored. It is the best brief study of Masters to appear, surpassing Lois Hartley's monograph, *Spoon River Revisited* (1963), both in breadth and depth of treatment. This volume provides a sound basis for a new appreciation of Masters's critically underrated achievement and is indispensable to the study of early 20th century American poetry and to the small body of scholarship on Masters. Undergraduate; graduate; faculty.—*J. J. Patton, Atlantic Community College*

OAB-0801   PS3505   95-40624 CIP
Peck, Demaree C. **The imaginative claims of the artist in Willa Cather's fiction: "possession granted by a different lease."** Susquehanna, 1996. (Dist. by Associated University Presses) 342p bibl indexes afp ISBN 0-945636-87-3, $48.50

This outstanding study is a discreet combination of psychobiography and historical overview—although Peck observes that "the power that Cather has exerted over her readers is profoundly ahistorical, undictated by gender." The source of Cather's power and of the enduring appeal of her novels is, to use her own words, something "for which language has no name." That something, Peck argues, is imaginative possession, the projection of Cather's own romantic ego, "the childhood fantasy of power" to which readers unconsciously respond. He claims Cather dismisses "all externals as no more than superficial illusions next to man's sole spiritual responsibility to himself." However, *The Professor's House* (1925) brought a major change—a movement from self-absorption ("the individual's precious possession of self") to friendship. Peck's overall argument is strong, but her particular interpretations will be disputed (e.g., her discussion of Cather's relationship with Isabelle McClung, and whether or not it was intimate). An exceptionally well researched study. Notes, general index, and index of correspondents. Highly recommended for all public, college, and university libraries.—*W. J. Martz, Ripon College*

OAB-0802   PS3529   94-26336 CIP
Pfister, Joel. **Staging depth: Eugene O'Neill and the politics of psychological discourse.** North Carolina, 1995. 327p bibl index afp ISBN 0-8078-2186-1, $45.00; ISBN 0-8078-4496-9 pbk, $17.95

Pfister (Wesleyan Univ.) restores a much-needed cultural breadth to a field of scholarship now dominated by formal, biographical, and thematic approaches

to O'Neill's work. In a nuanced, lucid, and wide-ranging argument, the author shows how the psychological depth for which O'Neill is famous is both a deliberately staged and an unconsciously determined effect of an emerging *category* of the psychological, one that met the subjective needs of an emerging professional-managerial class at a particular historical moment. As a form of cultural capital, psychological depth was both exploited and at times resisted by O'Neill. Pfister makes good use of cultural material ranging from rare photographs and production reviews, to racist cartoons and advertising, to quotations from feminist-anarchist literature. His discussion of the effect of pop psychology on biographical criticism, his critical consideration of O'Neill's "race plays," and his acknowledgment of the influence on O'Neill's thinking of Emma Goldman and Susan Glaspell are especially useful. The extensive bibliography, detailed footnotes, and careful index take up the last 90 pages, making this text a significant contribution to the study of American cultural history. Recommended for all libraries.—*J. S. Spencer, University of Massachusetts at Amherst*

OAB-0803   PS3531   92-44730 CIP
Pound, Ezra. **Ezra Pound and James Laughlin: selected letters,** ed. by David M. Gordon. W.W. Norton, 1994. 313p index ISBN 0-393-03540-9, $30.00

Long-awaited, these letters between poet and publisher live up to expectations. The uncompromising poet as mentor influenced a publisher who would not bend his principles. From the beginning in 1934, Laughlin was never intimidated by Pound's willfulness. Pound, in turn, was totally secure in Laughlin's support, even when Laughlin overruled him. For example, only profound mutual respect could survive Letter 125, an unflinching repudiation of everything about Pound, except his poetry. Theirs was a match made in literary heaven to provide a new basic document of the modernist movement. Only the *Pound/The Little Review* letters (CH, Jul'89) rival these for access to the poet's mind, craft, art, stance, and career, and only his lifelong friend, William Carlos Williams, outdoes Laughlin for directness. In addition to the EP/JL letters, the book contains correspondence with Dorothy Pound, editors, lawyers, translators, all dealing with the publication of Pound's work, especially by New Directions, Laughlin's company. These letters, some in brief excerpts, have succinct annotations. For continuity, the editor, who is a poet and a translator, provides brief summaries of the correspondence between Pound and Dorothy. He includes Humphries's long-unused introduction to the *Selected Poems*, from 1949. Indispensable to all collections dealing, however remotely, with 20th-century poetry, poetics, and poets, this work is a gold mine. All levels.—*J. N. Igo Jr., San Antonio College*

OAB-0804   PS3535   92-42324 MARC
Rolfe, Edwin. **Collected poems,** ed. by Cary Nelson and Jefferson Hendricks. Illinois, 1993. 337p bibl afp ISBN 0-252-02026-X, $34.95

Like most Leftist writing from the 1930s, Rolfe's verse has suffered from critical and political repression. As Nelson's detailed introduction reveals, Rolfe (1909-54) suffered blacklisting from both the political Right and the political Left. This bias and revisionist view of history has denied several generations one of America's finest poets. Forced to make his living as a journalist for the *Daily Worker* and for a newspaper in fascist Spain, Rolfe nevertheless achieved a poetry of lyricism and history. Though his work is impassioned by a collective sense of brotherhood and justice, it never sacrifices poetic form for political rhetoric or bluntness. Rather, it blends meter and meaning to sing clearly a lived history. His is a gentle strength that takes us from the topical to the universal in a shared witness to the world. Rolfe's three published books—*To My Contemporaries* (1936), *First Love and Other Poems* (1951), and *Permit Me Refuge* (1955)—are joined by his uncollected and unpublished poems from each of the decades of his writing. Editors Nelson and Hendricks have done a thorough job of preserving and revealing these works by their notes and bibliography. Such classic poems as "Definition," "First Love," "Elegy for Our Dead," and "To My Contemporaries" prove essential artistic records. This is the definitive collection of Rolfe's verse; all libraries should have it.—*L. Smith, Bowling Green State University, Firelands College*

OAB-0805 PS648 95-43872 CIP
Soitos, Stephen F. **The blues detective: a study of African American detective fiction.** Massachusetts, 1996. 260p bibl index afp ISBN 0-87023-995-3, $40.00; ISBN 0-87023-996-1 pbk, $15.95

This is not intended as a comprehensive survey of all black authors of detective fiction who wrote about black detectives, only some of the earliest examples. Soitos is concerned with the perspectives on race, class, and gender that early African American writers brought to the traditions of the genre. In his introduction, the author demonstrates his thorough grounding in the history and theory of African American literature and criticism. He analyzes what he calls the "tropes of black detection": figures of speech and thought that are expressed through the detective persona, double consciousness of detection, black vernaculars, and examples of hoodoo in the stories. He concentrates on works by six writers: Pauline Hopkins's *Hagar's Daughter* (the first black detective novel, originally published in *Colored Magazine*, 1901-02, and reissued in *The Magazine Novels of Pauline Hopkins*, 1988), J.E. Bruce's *Black Sleuth* (published as a serial in *McGirt's Magazine*, 1907-09), Rudolph Fisher's *The Conjure-Man Dies* (1932), the novels and short stories of Chester Himes, Ishmael Reed's *Mumbo Jumbo* (CH, Mar'73), and Clarence Major's *Reflex and Bone Structure* (CH, Mar'76). Soitos concludes with some comments on how writers like Barbara Neely and Walter Mosely continue the tradition today. Thoughtfully executed and well written with a good bibliography, this book is recommended for college, university, and large public libraries.— *J. R. Cox, St. Olaf College*

OAB-0806 PS3531 94-42285 CIP
Stout, Janis P. **Katherine Anne Porter: a sense of the times.** University Press of Virginia, 1995. 381p bibl index ISBN 0-8139-1568-6, $34.95

"Coherence is not the appropriate model for Porter's political and social views," says Stout (Texas A&M Univ.) in this highly recommended account of Porter's cultural context. Joan Givner accomplished much of the biographical groundwork in *Katherine Anne Porter: A Life* (CH, Apr'83, revised 1991), and Robert H. Brinkmeyer emphasized the changing focus of Porter's writing in *Katherine Anne Porter's Artistic Development: Primitivism, Traditionalism, and Totalitarianism* (CH, Nov'93), but Stout, more completely than her predecessors, places Porter against the shifting national and international backdrop of her times (1890-1980). Stout depicts the "noisy radicalism" of turn-of-the-century Texas, the socialist intellectual circles of Mexico and New York in the 1920s, the conservative agrarianism of the 1930s, the patriotism of the WW II years, and other movements that influenced Porter's life and work. She praises Porter's "consummate artistry," especially in the short stories, but does not ignore her "sexual adventurism" and racism. Porter's chronic restlessness, her writer's block, her hostility to feminists, and all her "troubled complexity" make more sense to the reader of Stout's well-documented, fascinating, essential study. Recommended for all academic and public libraries.— *J. W. Hall, University of Mississippi*

OAB-0807 PS3507 95-14447 CIP
Theodore Dreiser: beyond naturalism, ed. by Miriam Gogol. New York University, 1995. 269p bibl index afp ISBN 0-8147-3073-6, $45.00; ISBN 0-8147-3074-4 pbk, $18.95

This is the finest collection of essays on Dreiser since *Critical Essays on Theodore Dreiser*, compiled by Donald Pizer (CH, Sep'81). Gogol has wisely selected the work of a new generation of critics, who take the study of Dreiser's fiction beyond the timeworn issue of his "naturalism" and who also raise questions dealing with biography and autobiography. This has, of course, been done before, as early as Ellen Moers's *Two Dreisers* (CH, Jan'70). The importance of the present collection, however, is that it explores the subject in ways that engage contemporary interests: among others, class and gender, psychoanalysis, the philosophy of Martin Heidegger, popular culture, the relationship between novels and their film adaptations. Contributors invoke Freud, Foucault, Lacan, the new historicists, and so-called postmodern ideas. The degree of insight

and readability of any given essay depends on the talents of the individual author, which vary here as in any collection; but even in the few weak articles new methodologies stimulate fresh ways of thinking about old problems in this most protean of writers. Anyone interested in Dreiser and modern American literature should read this book. Upper-division undergraduates and above.— *T. P. Riggio, University of Connecticut*

OAB-0808 PS3509 94-17435 CIP
Timmerman, John H. **T.S. Eliot's Ariel poems: the poetics of recovery.** Bucknell, 1994. (Dist. by Associated University Presses) 203p bibl index afp ISBN 0-8387-5286-1, $35.00

"Ariel Poems" refers to a series of pamphlet poems published from the 1920s through the 1950s by Geoffrey Faber, head of the British firm that bears his name. Over the years, several of Eliot's poems appeared in the Ariel series, including "Journey of the Magi," "A Song for Simeon," "Animula," "Triumphal March," "Marina," and "The Cultivation of Christmas Trees." The author also includes a discussion of two sections of *Ash-Wednesday*, even though technically it is not one of the Ariel poems. Timmerman considers these poems as transitional between the dissociated, "horrific poetic landscapes" of the early poetry (*The Waste Land*, *Prufrock*," "The Hollow Men," "Gerontion") and the poetry that focuses on historical events and spiritual life: in particular, the advent of the Christ. Much information is provided on the various literary influences, such as St. John of the Cross, Lancelot Andrews, and Dante, and pertinent historical and religious background. Entire chapters are devoted to discussions of the individual poems—discussions that are lucid and appropriate for the entire spectrum of readers. There is some first-rate explication here; and the book itself is unique in its focus, so there really is nothing comparable. It is well indexed and contains an excellent bibliography. Highly recommended for general and academic collections.— *A. R. Nourie, Illinois State University*

OAB-0809 PS3531 93-3361 CIP
Uncollected early prose of Katherine Anne Porter, ed. by Ruth M. Alvarez and Thomas F. Walsh. Texas, 1994. 282p afp ISBN 0-292-76544-4, $35.00

An excellent companion to Thomas F. Walsh's *Katherine Anne Porter and Mexico* (CH, Feb'93). According to the introduction, all but five of the 29 stories, literary sketches, book reviews, and essays collected here for the first time "focus on Mexico, the country where Porter first began to realize her creative potential." Walsh and Alvarez (assistant curator of the University of Maryland's Manuscripts Division) reprint pieces from many obscure sources dating from 1920 to 1932, including the children's magazine *Everyland* and the *Magazine of Mexico*. Their very fine headnotes and "Notes on Texts" provide biographical and bibliographical information and relate these works to more familiar writings by Porter, including the stories "María Concepción" and "Flowering Judas." The six previously unpublished stories and the few unpublished pieces of nonfiction (all from the University of Maryland's Katherine Anne Porter Collection) are of special interest. Also fascinating is Porter's enthusiastic *Outline of Mexican Popular Arts and Crafts*, commissioned for an exhibit in Mexico City in 1922 and here corrected, emended, and accompanied by photographs from the original monograph. Essential for students of Porter and a crucial addition to all libraries with Porter holdings.— *J. W. Hall, University of Mississippi*

OAB-0810 PS310 93-15653 CIP
Van Wienen, Mark W. **Partisans and poets: the political work of American poetry in the Great War.** Cambridge, 1997. 311p index ISBN 0-521-56396-8, $59.95

Focusing on political poetry that was produced by various groups in response to rising militarism and the US's ensuing involvement in WW I, Van Wienen (Augustana College) examines important historical and social movements, offering a rich and scholarly view of the time period. A highly readable example of new historicism informed by the theories of Althusser and Gramsci, the work focuses chiefly on poetry sponsored and published by the Women's Peace Party (WPP), the Industrial Workers of the World (IWW), and the National Association for the Advancement of Colored People (NAACP), whose journal, *The Crisis*, was edited by W.E.B. DuBois. The poetry itself (all of it genteel and much of it bad, as Van Wienen acknowledges) is indicative of much larger issues and developments, acting as signposts of ideological production and formation. The author uses the poetry to delineate the change that occurred from 1914 to 1918, as the US moved from isolationism to intervention. Other important issues covered here are the evolving definition of modernism and the definition of the war text in general. A rich and full view of a period that combines important social critique and historical perspective, this volume also rescues a sizable body of poetry from obscurity. Highly recommended for upper-division undergraduates through faculty.—*B. Adler, Valdosta State University*

OAB-0811 [CD-ROM]

Virginia Woolf, ed. by Mark Hussey. Primary Source Media, 1997. ISBN 1-57803-049-8 $1,995.00 research edition; $995.00 student edition. 1 disc; user guide. System requirements: Windows 3.1 or higher.

Using a tool such as this to study literary texts quickly persuades one that this is the future. This extraordinary resource contains a seemingly unlimited set of materials: the printout of the table of contents alone is 13 densely packed pages. Hussey (Pace Univ.), editor of *Woolf Studies Annual*, selected for inclusion all of Woolf's fiction (23 volumes, some in both the British and American versions); her diaries, including early journals (1897-1909), 25 volumes of diaries (1915-41), and her *A Writer's Diary* (1953), which is extracts of the above; her autobiography, *Moments of Being*, ed. by J. Schulkind (CH, May '77); a biography, Roger Fry's *Virginia Woolf* (1940); drama; essays; introductions; and letters. But that is just the beginning. The CD-ROM also contains literally hundreds of items previously inaccessible to most scholars. For example, the reader will find dozens of manuscripts, postcards Woolf wrote to Vanessa Bell, a scrap book of quotations and press clippings Woolf kept toward the volume that ultimately became *Three Guineas*, and reading notes. In addition, the collection includes the photographs originally published in the Hogarth Press editions of *Orlando* and *Three Guineas* (dropped from modern American editions), galley proofs, typescripts, and Hussey's *Virginia Woolf A to Z* (CH, Jan '96). The pièce de résistance for Woolf fans is the eight minute audio segment, the only extant recording of Woolf's voice, taped during a BBC broadcast in 1937 on a radio series called "Words Fail Me."

The disk is remarkably easy to navigate. The opening screen will look familiar to anyone who has used point-and-click technology, with toolbar buttons for the table of contents (searchable by type, author, date, or title), search commands, index, print, and help. The user can choose from among several browsing capabilities. Detailed search tips are available to guide the user in a standard search, advanced search, or natural language search. A bookmark function enables one to mark items for quick return. Hypertext links have been established from terms in Woolf's texts; a click on the colored word brings up a citation that provides contextual information. The print command includes an option to print the helpful "Guide to Citing This Material." A magnification function allows the user to enlarge a portion of a photograph or handwritten manuscript for closer study. Two windows can be displayed on the screen simultaneously. Many of the items are summarized in a brief descriptive caption, which appears at the bottom of the screen and can be scrolled. In summary, this remarkable resource will not require librarian intermediation and is highly recommended for both undergraduates and Woolf scholars.—*E. R. Baer, Gustavus Adolphus College*

OAB-0812 PS3531 91-24381 CIP

Walsh, Thomas F. **Katherine Anne Porter and Mexico: the illusion of Eden.** Texas, 1992. 269p bibl index afp ISBN 0-292-74311-4, $37.50

The combined memories of Katherine Anne Porter, recorded by Walsh from interviews with her in 1977, and the papers of Porter's Mexican friend Mary Louise Doherty are the materials out of which this important work developed.

Walsh attempts a full account of Porter's experience in Mexico and an interpretation of her works in the light of her experiences there. New dimensions of Porter's Edenic (hopeful) world emerge as Walsh examines nine published stories and sketches, three unpublished stories, numerous essays and book reviews, and the opening section of *Ship of Fools*. The careful consideration given by Walsh to Porter's four trips to Mexico during the period 1920-1931 dwarfs all previous studies of Mexico's influence on her, including Joan Givner's *Katherine Anne Porter: A Life* (CH, Apr '83), which gives only slight attention to the subject. This work is pivotal to an understanding of Porter's works.—*R. L. Brooks, Baylor University*

OAB-0813 PS3511 92-22780 CIP

Williamson, Joel. **William Faulkner and southern history.** Oxford, 1993. 509p index afp ISBN 0-19-507404-1, $35.00

In celebration of Faulkner's birthday, Oxford has published this massive study of William Faulkner, his family, his region, and his work. Williamson, a prize-winning historian, divides the book into three sections—the ancestry, the biography, and the writing. The first two are particularly important. Williamson traces a host of relatives through a century of southern history to place Faulkner and his ancestors in historical context. The colorful people and events foreshadow much of Faulkner's fiction. We discover the names, the relationships, the incidents, almost as Faulkner later recorded them—shaped by his epic imagination. The biographer explores the baroque mythology that Faulkner and his family accumulated through the years, the peculiar development of Mississippi historical perspective, sources for plot and characters, the actual writing and publishing, critical responses to the books, financial problems, love interests, and his major themes. Along the way he opens up fresh parallels and explodes old errors. Using the extensive array of tools available to the historian, including not only the letters, earlier scholarship, and published interviews, but also the new books, new interviews, and unpublished manuscripts, Williamson is able to explain earlier misconceptions and deceptions. With its genealogies, extensive notes, and excellent index, this book should long prove an essential resource for any Faulkner scholar. Undergraduate through professional.—*N. Tischler, Pennsylvania State University, University Park Campus*

OAB-0814 PS3537 96-17019 CIP

Yannella, Philip R. **The other Carl Sandburg.** University Press of Mississippi, 1996. 186p bibl index afp ISBN 0-87805-941-5, $27.00

This book adds significantly to Penelope Niven's authoritative biography *Carl Sandburg* (CH, Jan '92). Where Niven treats Sandburg's whole life and work, putting them into a large national and human perspective, Yannella (Temple Univ.) focuses on Sandburg's young manhood and his attachment to radical political and social theories during the period 1915-20. This is "the other Sandburg" of the title—an unfortunate title, perhaps, since it seems to suggest there are only two Sandburgs, the young radical and the popular literary/folk hero. Closer inspection of the poet's life may yet reveal several "other Sandburgs" worthy of such detailed study. Yannella's important book brings before the reader some 200 magazine and newspaper articles Sandburg wrote during his leftist phase, many of them not previously available, giving early and vigorous, though extreme, versions of his lifelong faith in the common workingman and -woman, and bone-deep distrust of the elitist, moneyed class. Yannella also recaptures some of the dynamism of Sandburg's early poems, a dynamism lost over the years in the elementary and secondary schoolroom, by placing them back in the context of radical political thought. Interesting, too, is his uncovering of the US military's intelligence files on Sandburg's political behavior during this period. All academic collections.—*P. J. Ferlazzo, Northern Arizona University*

OAB-0815 PS3507 93-16138 CIP

Zanine, Louis J. **Mechanism and mysticism: the influence of science on the thought and work of Theodore Dreiser.** Pennsylvania, 1993. 249p bibl index ISBN 0-8122-3171-6, $34.95

In examining the impact of science on Dreiser's thought and fiction, Zanine extends the pioneer work of Ellen Moers in *Two Dreisers* (CH, Jan'70) and Ronald Martin in *American Literature and the Universe of Force* (CH, Apr'82). Zanine's story is intriguing and complicated, and it does not lend itself easily to summary. It begins with Dreiser's absorption of 19th-century evolutionary theory in the writing of, among others, Thomas Huxley and Herbert Spencer; moves in the 1910s and 1920s to his "mechanistic" phase as a disciple of Jacques Loeb; along the way it is complicated by such influences as Elmer Gates, Freud, and Charles Fort; it ends in the last decade of his life with a peculiar mixture of intense scientific inquiry and philosophical speculation that includes the mystical beliefs of American transcendentalism, Quakerism, and Hinduism. Zanine does a fine job of making sense of all this, showing how Dreiser's scientific investigations influenced the themes of his fiction. He is correct in his assumption that Dreiser's quest for scientific truth was part of a larger search for spiritual meaning in his life. This is clearly the definitive work on the subject. Advanced undergraduate; graduate; faculty.—*T. P. Riggio, University of Connecticut*

UNITED STATES —
20th Century after 1950

OAB-0816   PS153   95-13362 CIP
Aarons, Victoria. **A measure of memory: storytelling and identity in American Jewish fiction.** Georgia, 1996. 218p bibl index afp ISBN 0-8203-1773-X, $35.00

The value of this impressive study lies in its departure from preoccupations with acculturation to focus on the process of storytelling as the most revealing act of authorial identity. By examining the narrative method in a wide range of short fictions, Aarons (Trinity Univ.) demonstrates that the typical first-person voice in Jewish storytelling provides for dramatic interplay between individual choice and historic compulsions. She begins with Scripture and extends to the great Yiddish modernists, particularly Sholom Aleichem, who relied on stories to bear witness to history and to the human need for both belonging and individuation. Separate chapters treat the fiction of Delmore Schwartz, Jerome Weidman and Gilbert Rogin, Bernard Malamud, and Grace Paley, and each of these major discussions includes briefer comparative readings of many more authors (e.g., Philip Roth, Herbert Gold, Cynthia Ozick, Lynne Sharon Schwartz, Salinger, Art Spiegelman, Lesléa Newman, Susan Fromburg Schaeffer, and Francine Prose). The author does not attempt to trim individual talents into a neat thesis; rather she sees the short stories as part of a larger pattern of generational conflict and changing cultural roles whereby the children of immigrants seek to define themselves in terms of loyalty to an inescapable past and to invent themselves according to personal desires. Storytelling confronts and helps bridge the gap between these needs. Useful notes supplement this intelligent study. Upper-division undergraduates and above.— *M. Butovsky, Concordia University*

OAB-0817   PS350   91-34056 CIP
Bigsby, C.W.E. **Modern American drama, 1945-1990.** Cambridge, 1992. 362p index ISBN 0-521-41649-3, $59.95; ISBN 0-521-42667-7 pbk, $17.95

"Redefining the Center: Politics, Race, Gender," the final, 87-page chapter of this thorough, intriguing book, explains trends in American drama from 1965 to the present better than anything yet in print. In this chapter, Bigsby brings to fruition social ruminations he wrestled with in several of his earlier books—*Confrontation and Commitment* (1968), *The Black American Writer* (1969), *The Second Black Renaissance* (CH, Feb'81), and his renowned three-volume study, *Critical Introduction to Twentieth-Century American Drama* (v.1, CH, Dec'82; v.2, CH, Sep'85; v.3, 1985). This book, the first single-volume history of American drama during the nearly half century following WW II, traces and amplifies the major redefinitions of the canon, from the early post-

O'Neill days through the period of the Vietnam War, the divisive conflict that caused notable social readjustments directly affecting literary production and interpretation. Bigsby's earlier books are important. This one is his capstone, representing the coalescence of the various strands of his complex thinking about American drama. A significant book, strongly recommended for public, college, and university libraries. Index, bibliographical notes.—*R. B. Shuman, University of Illinois at Urbana-Champaign*

OAB-0818   PS3525   92-7180 CIP
Brightman, Carol. **Writing dangerously: Mary McCarthy and her world.** C. Potter, 1992. 714p index ISBN 0-517-56400-9, $30.00

This definitive biography of Mary McCarthy (1912-89), America's "First Lady of Letters," covers three areas—personal, political, and literary. Brightman details the upbringing of McCarthy and her brothers by relatives after their parents' deaths; her Jewish and Catholic ancestry and her Catholic schooling; her four marriages, the second of which to Edmund Wilson produced her only son, Reuel; and her large circle of friends, among them Hannah Arendt, Nicola Chiaromonte, Philip Rahv, Robert Lowell, Dwight Macdonald, and Elizabeth Hardwick. Among her enemies were Lillian Hellman and Simone de Beauvoir. Her leftist-leaning political life involved her in such issues as the Moscow trials, McCarthyism and the Cold War, the Waldorf Conference for World Peace, and Vietnam. Brightman discusses McCarthy's use of her life in such works as her novels *The Group* (1963), which was made into a movie; *The Company She Keeps* (1942), and *The Birds of America* (1971); and her nonfiction books such as *Memories of a Catholic Girlhood* (1957) and *Venice Observed* (1956). Brightman states that McCarthy's "respect for words and their mysteries. . .makes her literary example worth pondering." This complex, contradictory woman and writer lives again in this sympathetic, intelligent, coolly probing study. Essential for women's studies and literature collections.—*J. Overmyer, Ohio State University*

OAB-0819   PS3552   92-50403 CIP
Burroughs, William S. **The letters of William S. Burroughs: 1945-1959,** ed. with introd. by Oliver Harris. Viking, 1993. 472p index ISBN 0-670-81348-6, $25.00

Burroughs's early letters, mostly to Allen Ginsberg, chronicle the prime years of the Beat Generation—1945 to 1959—and exist paradoxically because he was far from the Beat scene during most of this period. Laying low in Texas and Louisiana in the early days, then settling in Mexico City and exploring for exotic drugs in South America, and finally establishing his home base in Tangiers and finally Paris, Burroughs founded what became a literary correspondence school between himself and Ginsberg. The value of these letters is not the gossip of the Beat years, although there is plenty of this, but they record the gradual development of Burroughs from a writer of traditional narrative fiction (*Junkie*, 1953) to his sensational anti-narrative landmark (*Naked Lunch*, 1959). This well-edited and introduced volume supersedes Burroughs's own more limited 1982 selection and should be added to any collection of Beat and avant-garde literature.—*K. N. Richwine, Western Maryland College*

OAB-0820   PS379   95-38105 CIP
Chénetier, Marc. **Beyond suspicion: new American fiction since 1960,** tr. by Elizabeth A. Houlding. Pennsylvania, 1996. 321p index afp ISBN 0-8122-3059-0, $38.95

This substantial volume by a leading French critic of American literature references the work of many major authors and an extraordinarily large number of others who are not often discussed. Among American critics, only Frederick Karl has attempted to write this sort of encyclopedic work in recent years; his useful *American Fictions, 1940-1980* (CH, Apr'84) has many of the qualities of a reference book. By contrast, Chénetier, very much a formalist critic and occasionally a cultural and intellectual historian, underscores his preferences at the cost of his encyclopedic impulses. Thus, Jonathan Baumbach gets as much space as John Updike, and Robert Coover more than Toni Morrison. Coover is, of course, a major American writer, but the comparisons reveal a consistent neglect of American women writers and an occasional inflation of the reputation of experimental formalists. The first four general chapters, which provide overview, main themes, and perspective, will be useful to undergraduates. The remaining 10 chapters will appeal to specialists.—*K. Tölölyan, Wesleyan University*

OAB-0821   PS228   93-16129 CIP
Clayton, Jay. **The pleasures of Babel: contemporary American literature and theory.** Oxford, 1993. 209p bibl indexes afp ISBN 0-19-508372-5, $35.00

In this slim volume of clear, easily readable, vigorous prose, Clayton presents a concise overview of poststructuralist concern with language and textuality. He then moves through psychoanalytic theory and feminism into theoretical issues of multiculturalism. Clayton's presentation of theory travels through "metacritical reflection" into "those activities that elaborate the links between culture and society," and from "established masterpieces" of hegemonic culture to diverse literary works that represent an exciting "Babel of competing culture." He includes overviews of such current interests as "narrative and law" and draws examples from a broad range of contemporary novels. He is at his best in presenting "The Story of Deconstruction"; however, the presentation of cultural literary theory and the competing definitions of community and their relationships to feminism and multiculturalism are also noteworthy. The book is a model of scholarship and editing. The notes are pertinent, the references broad and useful, and the index directed toward searching theories (although a name index would have been nice, too.) Highly recommended. All levels.—*S. Hoover, Alfred University*

OAB-0822   PS3563   94-18767 CIP
Denniston, Dorothy Hamer. **The fiction of Paule Marshall: reconstructions of history, culture, and gender.** Tennessee, 1995. 187p bibl index afp ISBN 0-87049-838-X, $32.00; ISBN 0-87049-839-8 pbk, $15.00

Denniston's book joins the growing body of criticism on Marshall's oeuvre that examines the possibilities for spiritual wholeness among African diasporic peoples within "a racist, sexist, and materialistic society." She targets the "African cultural survivals" (oral narrative, the proverb tradition, ornate and highly performative language, nonlinear and nondualistic cosmologies) as they provide not only subject matter but "the essential framework for [Marshall's] artistry." Her chapter on *Brown Girl, Brownstones* (1959) best exemplifies the Barbadian cultural vernacular through which Marshall reveals her characters' mores and beliefs, via a wonderfully detailed reading of the sounds and figures of language of *Poets in the Kitchen* (1984). Denniston focuses as well on gender paradigms and interactions—notably, in her critical readings of "The Valley Between" (1954), Marshall's first published short story, and all of the novellas of *Soul Clap Hands and Sing* (1961). Lengthy citations and commentary and frequent emphasis on autobiographical connections substantiate Denniston's arguments, which, though wide-ranging conceptually and textually, cohere into an informative critique. All academic collections.—*S. Bryant, Alfred University*

OAB-0823   PS374   95-41735 CIP
Detweiler, Robert. **Uncivil rites: American fiction, religion, and the public sphere.** Illinois, 1996. 250p index afp ISBN 0-252-01932-6, $29.95; ISBN 0-252-06580-8 pbk, $17.95

Part of the "Public Expressions of Religion in America" series, this engaging sequel to Detweiler's award-winning *Breaking the Fall* (CH, Mar'90) adds to his impressive corpus of critical works on the intersections of religion and literature. Acknowledging that his study is more exploratory than definitive (because good literature "unsettles more than it comforts"), Detweiler (Emory Univ.) sets out to show how fiction with religious concerns can help shape three "bodies"— the body politic, the body erotic, and the body apocalyptic—and how fiction

"makes these bodies real as communal projections ... of who we are and what we live for." In the chapters dealing with the "body politic," Detweiler looks at three works that form part of the public discourse about the Rosenberg affair and the McCarthyism that made it possible. The "body erotic" seeks, among other things, to restore a sense of fleshiness to spirituality despite public and institutional traditions that would quell it, and the chapters dealing with the "body apocalyptic" reveal deep interconnections between literature (and film) about the Vietnam War and Native American literature. Literary expression of religious concerns, Detweiler concludes, shows our bodies ill, but not irremediably so. A first-rate critic at the top of his form. Upper-division undergraduate and above.—*E. J. Dupuy, St. Joseph Seminary College*

OAB-0824   PS3565   92-32128 CIP
Di Renzo, Anthony. **American gargoyles: Flannery O'Connor and the medieval grotesque.** Southern Illinois, 1993. 250p bibl index afp ISBN 0-8093-1848-2, $34.95

O'Connor's freaks jostle with Rabelais and Chaucer, the danse macabre, and the Christianized Saturnalia of the "Laughter of December" in Di Renzo's excellent tour-guide to "that strange passageway between the sacred and the profane, heaven and hell." Robert Brinkmeyer's *The Art and Vision of Flannery O'Connor* (CH, Jun'90) draws on Bakhtin's theory of the dialogic imagination, but to Di Renzo (Ithaca College and Syracuse Univ.) Bakhtin's discussion of carnival is crucial. "For Flannery O'Connor," says Di Renzo, "Judgement Day is a cosmic Mardi Gras"—a "renewal in destruction." Juggling medieval folklore with kindred representations of the "hideously beautiful, beautifully hideous" in Pirandello, Fellini, Monty Python, and Umberto Eco, this study vigorously responds to critics who have been "unsmiling" toward O'Connor. Di Renzo insists on "the hilarity of her comedy," exuberantly defending her "medievalism" and the Middle Ages too from "gloomy" readings. Mystery plays, fabliaux, northern Renaissance paintings, dream visions, and gargoyles are all prelude to O'Connor's "hapless grotesques," who manifest Christ in the "sufferings and occasional victories" of their own divine bodies. Index and extensive list of "works consulted." Enthusiastically recommended for all academic libraries and for any reader of O'Connor.—*J. W. Hall, University of Mississippi*

OAB-0825   PS3552   96-21425 CIP
Ferrari, Rita. **Innocence, power, and the novels of John Hawkes.** Pennsylvania, 1996. 220p bibl index afp ISBN 0-8122-3341-7, $34.95

For more than four decades Hawkes has been genuinely American in holding up the tradition of novelistic innovator and avant-garde experimenter in the vein of such writers as Kafka, Celine, and Hesse. Ferrari (St. Louis Univ.) provides the most up-to-date survey of Hawkes's works thus far; in its comprehensiveness and clarity the study will be valuable to a range of students, from upper-level undergraduate through the postgraduate scholar. Ferrari's purpose is "to explore the ways in which the broad ideas of innocence and power disperse into a multitude of thematic and textual concerns." In attempting "to find the essential human experiences when we are unhinged or alienated from familiar, secure life," Hawkes explores such topics as violence, misogyny, sexuality, mastery, and transcendence in a style that is self-reflexive, parodic, unique, and consummately imaginative. Ferrari's critical journey takes readers from Hawkes's first work, *The Cannibal* (1949), through his novels and ending with *Sweet William: A Memoir of Old Horse* (1993), which she describes "as a prism through which all of Hawkes' work is refracted." The study is well-documented; Ferrari examines Hawkes's work in relationship to other writers and to critics—Poe, Hawthorne, Sade, Freud, Sontag, Kristeva, Barthes, and Foucault.—*W. B. Warde Jr., University of North Texas*

OAB-0826   PS3565   94-49320 CIP
Frye, Joanne S. **Tillie Olsen: a study of the short fiction.** Twayne/Prentice Hall International, 1995. 232p bibl index afp (Twayne's studies in short fiction, 60) ISBN 0-8057-0863-4, $20.95

This study offers a close analysis of Olsen's short stories, an invaluable interview with Olsen, and a short section of critical responses. Frey (College of Wooster) focuses on Olsen's commitment to writing about "life comprehensions," ordinary human experiences, especially those of women and working-class people. Olsen's intensely felt and expressed stories, told in "transformative" language, have caused many readers to empathize strongly with her characters. The interview with Olsen reveals the connections between the actual people and events of her life and her nonautobiographical stories. The critics' section discusses comments both apt and inapt. Invaluable for English department libraries, this work complements Constance Coiner's *Better Red: The Writing and Resistance of Tillie Olsen and Meridel Le Sueur* (CH, Oct'95), which focuses on the authors' relationship to the Communist Party; Mickey Pearlman and Abby Werlock's *Tillie Olsen* (CH, Dec'91), with its interview of Olsen and comments on her *Silences* and *Yonnondio*; Abigail Martin's briefer *Tillie Olsen* (CH, Jan'85); and Elaine Neil Orr's *Tillie Olsen and a Feminist Spiritual Vision* (CH, Dec'87), which gives a religious interpretation of Olsen's work. All collections.—*J. Overmyer, emerita, Ohio State University*

OAB-0827   PS153   96-18577 CIP
Furman, Andrew. **Israel through the Jewish-American imagination: a survey of Jewish-American literature on Israel, 1928-1995.** State University of New York, 1997. 223p bibl index afp ISBN 0-7914-3251-3, $59.50

Furman's timely, insightful survey of the way ruminations about the State of Israel have shaped aspects of Jewish American imagination is a welcome addition to Jewish studies in general and to Jewish American literature in particular. Focusing on eight writers—Meyer Levin, Leon Uris, Saul Bellow, Hugh Nissenson, Chaim Potok, Philip Roth, Anne Roiphe, and Tova Reich—Furman combines attention to cultural context with savvy close readings, but manages to do both in a clear, engaging style. For far too long, *Exodus* (1958), Leon Uris's potboiler, has seemed the quintessential novel about Israel written by an American Jew. By considering the best work currently being done by serious Jewish American fictionists, Furman extends—and complicates—the understanding of what the possibilities for such fiction might be, just as his study (the first of its kind) raises questions about the inevitable tensions separating the individual writer from the tribe, spirituality from secularism, and militarism from dreams of peace. If the Middle East is simultaneously volatile and perplexing, the same thing might be said of the Jewish American fiction it inspires. Furman captures both sides of this increasingly important equation with acumen and balance. Highly recommended for all libraries.—*S. Pinsker, Franklin & Marshall College*

OAB-0828   PS153   96-40678 CIP
Gardaphé, Fred L. **Italian signs, American streets: the evolution of Italian American narrative.** Duke University, 1996. 241p bibl index afp ISBN 0-8223-1730-3, $39.95; ISBN 0-8223-1739-7 pbk, $16.95

There is much gnashing of teeth among Italian American scholars about why their ethnic group has not produced a greater literature in the US. Over the past 80 years American writers of Italian descent have created significant literary texts that receive little, if any, critical attention. Inspired by W.E.B. Dubois's argument that critical activity is a certain indicator of a tradition's sophistication, Gardaphé (Columbia College, Chicago) sets out to demonstrate that there is an Italian American literature beyond Mafia stories. Mindful of the distinctive "signs" generated through codes specific to Italian American culture, he examines the works of 15 authors (including Helen Barolini, Mary Caponegro, Tina DeRosa, and Carole Maso), beginning with the strongest of the immigrant narratives (Marie Hall Ets's *Rosa, the Life of an Italian Immigrant*, which, though dating from 1918, was not published until 1970) and ending with the subtler ethnicism of Don DeLillo. Gardaphé omits such important writers as Robert Ferro, Rocco Fumento, Len Giovannitti, and Joe Papaleo but this, according to Gardaphé, is no oversight; his goal is not to catalog the writers of an entire ethnic group but to present a new perspective by which its literature can be read and interpreted generally. This is truly a pioneering effort, since the papers of some of the authors he assesses (John Fante, Pietro di Donato) remain

in private collections, unprocessed and unavailable to scholars. All academic libraries serving upper-division undergraduates and up; also useful in feminist collections.—*J. Shreve, Allegany College of Maryland*

OAB-0829   PS352   93-30132 CIP
Geis, Deborah R. **Postmodern theatric(k)s: monologue in contemporary American drama.** Michigan, 1993. 205p index afp ISBN 0-472-10467-5, $34.50

This book is the first study of monologue from a current literary perspective. Geis (City Univ. of New York) offers an impressive discussion of the changing uses of monologue. Tracing the critical comments of Brecht, Artaud, Lyotard, and others, she successfully demonstrates the effective use of monologue by such skilled authors as Shepard, Finley, Fornes, Gray, and Mamet. Furthermore, her work follows the development of monolgoue from a vehicle for character development in the works of Williams to its more contemporary use as parody, con, sales, and narrative. Particularly gratifying is her inclusion of the effectiveness of monologue in many recent African American and feminist dramas. Excellent research, solid chapter notes, and an easy-to-follow index make this a book that will appeal to those interested in dramatic theory and to the more casual reader. Recommended for upper-division undergraduate and graduate collections and major research libraries.—*M. D. Whitlatch, Buena Vista College*

OAB-0830   PS374   96-13716 CIP
Hansen, Elaine Tuttle. **Mother without child: contemporary fiction and the crisis of motherhood.** California, 1997. 283p index afp ISBN 0-520-20577-4, $45.00; ISBN 0-520-20578-2 pbk, $16.95

Over the years feminists have had an ambivalent relationship with motherhood, the source of both power and entrapment. In this tightly argued discussion of "mothers and not-mothers," Hansen (Haverford College) considers child abandonment, infanticide, abortion, and "Othermothering." Also author of *Chaucer and the Fictions of Gender* (CH, Sep'92), Hansen uses traditional genre considerations and literary analysis to explore a cluster of writers—Jane Rule, Alice Walker, Louise Erdrich, Marge Piercy, Margaret Atwood, and Fay Weldon. She is particularly interested in "deviant" or marginalized women—lesbians, African Americans, Native Americans, and those of mixed color. Tracing the vast array of feminist arguments about mothers, daughters, the nature of the "good" and "bad" mother, Hansen seeks to "look, listen, and learn." This openly political study, with its host of annotations and close analyses of favorite feminist texts, targets academic literary feminists, many of whom have praised it as the necessary next step in understanding of this "new space." Upper-division undergraduates through faculty. *N. Tischler, emeritus, Pennsylvania State University, University Park Campus*

OAB-0831   PS3523   94-38430 CIP
Hart, Henry. **Robert Lowell and the sublime.** Syracuse, 1995. 168p bibl index afp ISBN 0-8156-2610-X, $34.95; ISBN 0-8156-2658-4 pbk, $17.95

Often, the essential ideas that American poets use have a way of echoing the philosophic ambivalence of Emerson. Hart (College of William and Mary) argues in this work that "Although their iconoclastic rebellions appeared in different forms and intensities, Emerson and Lowell could play American Lucifers bent on wrestling power from traditional authorities just as easily as they could play the authorities bent on bridling those Lucifers." The author confronts this authority by deconstructing both the formal element of verse and those means by which poets have traditionally used the lofty or the sublime to transcend the here and now. Hart's study is a clear and precisely written account of Lowell's relationship to the politics, psychopathology, and religious attributes of the sublime. More than any other recent study of the poet, this book demonstrates both the unity and the greatness of Lowell's work. A worthwhile study for undergraduates and graduates alike.—*D. A. Barton, California State University, Long Beach*

OAB-0832   PS228   96-53173 CIP
Inness, Sherrie A. **The lesbian menace: ideology, identity, and the representation of lesbian life.** Massachusetts, 1997. 256p bibl index afp ISBN 1-55849-090-6, $40.00; ISBN 1-55849-091-4 pbk, $14.95

This well-written, provocative analysis addresses the construction of lesbian identity in literature and popular culture from the 1920s to the present. Inness (Miami Univ., Ohio) is particularly interested in "how popular texts help constitute an image of the lesbian that is aimed primarily at heterosexual consumers, although homosexual readers can also read these texts and carry away very different messages than those intended." To this end, the author analyzes the depiction of lesbians in children's literature and in contemporary women's magazines, as well as in Radclyffe Hall's *The Well of Loneliness* and Edouard Bourdet's *The Captive*. Particularly insightful are two chapters, one on the ways in which popular fiction between the two world wars established a presumed linkage between women's colleges and lesbianism and another on the marginalization of butch identity. The major strength of this work is Inness's attempt to bring the same level of critical analysis to lesbian culture's depiction of itself as she does to popular culture's representation of lesbian experience. A fine addition to Eve Kosofsky Sedgwick's *The Epistemology of the Closet* (1990), Julia Penelope's *Call Me Lesbian: Lesbian Lives, Lesbian Theory* (1992), and renée hoogland's *Lesbian Configurations* (CH, Oct'97). All academic libraries serving upper-division undergraduates and above.—*L. Winters, College of Saint Elizabeth*

OAB-0833   PS3545   96-41770 CIP
Johnston, Carol Ann. **Eudora Welty: a study of the short fiction.** Twayne/Prentice Hall International, 1997. 259p bibl index afp (Twayne's studies in short fiction, 67) ISBN 0-8057-7936-1, $24.95

Sometimes volumes in a standardized series like this are perfunctory overviews, usable for quick reference but void of anything new. Johnston (Dickinson College) soars above the usual expectations. She succinctly synthesizes what Welty criticism has already accomplished (and judiciously illustrates this accomplishment in reprints of seven important essays); she offers for reexamination three key pieces in which Welty reflects on her own work; and she charts new ground in four brilliant chapters analyzing a significant sample of Welty's 43 collected stories. Johnston focuses on Welty's intertwined use of visual and lyrical experimental techniques and the two springs—"one bright, one dark"—that feed her themes. As she looks beneath the sheltered writer's bright celebration of harmonies, the author reveals the dark daring of the "conflicts beneath the smooth surface." Some stories that have been given such short shrift by other critics that they seemed minor rise to new prominence under Johnston's prodding. Perhaps better than anyone so far, Johnston elucidates Welty's often mystifying use of myth—especially Milton's Adam and Eve and Yeats's Wandering Aengus. A chronology, well-selected bibliography, and lucid style make this volume valuable for beginners; its deliciously provocative new readings recommend it to professionals as well.—*A. J. Griffith, Our Lady of the Lake University*

OAB-0834   PS3565   92-19603 CIP
Kauvar, Elaine M. **Cynthia Ozick's fiction: tradition & invention.** Indiana, 1993. 264p bibl index afp ISBN 0-253-33129-3, $29.95

Superb novelists deserve first-rate literary analysis. Cynthia Ozick has found such critics in Joseph Lowin, Victor Strandberg, and most recently in Elaine Kauvar, whose present work is simultaneously a profound contribution to Ozick interpretation and an astonishingly readable account of the novelist's ideas and artistic manner. Kauvar accounts for Ozick's views antithetical to those of T.S. Eliot; yet she observes Ozick's "allegiance to the judgements of history, her concept of tradition as itself innovation" and advances current conjecture that Cynthia Ozick "may eventually be judged our T.S. Eliot." Unlike some contemporary critics, who decontextualize literature, Kauvar offers a contextual examination of Ozick's recurrent themes, demonstrates Ozick's relationship to her artistic predecessors, and illuminates patterns and textual interconnections to reveal the substructure and doubling of the texts and establish the author's place in contemporary American letters. Although Kauvar echoes established

critical studies in her emphasis on the conflict between Hebraism and Hellenism, the perils of art, and the consequences of assimilation, she propels some of these concepts to surprising ends such as her interpretation of the Holocaust novella, *Rosa*, in light of the *Aeneid*, her perception of "the overarching concern with the father" in the fiction, and her attention to flower and color imagery. Kauvar faults critics who focus on the Jewishness of Ozick's work, arguing that such a view "cannot illuminate any of the intricacies of the fiction;" few critics, however, do exhibit the exclusivity she attributes to them. Kauvar herself places Ozick centrally in Hebraic, Hellenic, and American literary traditions. Highly recommended.—*S. L. Kremer, Kansas State University*

OAB-0835   PS151   95-39871 CIP
Keating, AnaLouise. **Women reading, women writing: self-invention in Paula Gunn Allen, Gloria Anzaldúa, and Audre Lorde.** Temple University, 1996. 240p bibl index afp ISBN 1-56639-419-8, $49.95; ISBN 1-56639-420-1 pbk, $18.95

Despite its misleading, trendy title this is a thoroughly useful study. Keating (Eastern New Mexico Univ.) grounds her readings on feminist, queer studies, performative, and identity-politics frameworks, achieving the rare feat (these days) of using theory to make the authors urgent, available, and seductive (rather than using the texts to display theory). The author establishes her overarching theme in chapter 3, "Transformational Identity Politics." She follows with a chapter focused on each of the three authors, but at every point she also reads each against the other two. Thus, she offers readers several valid and useful ways to enter the three authors' works. Keating makes this particular grouping seem inevitable and necessary, never coincidental, while never losing sight of the autonomous integrity of each author. The final chapter somewhat belatedly attempts to make good on the book's title as Keating shares autobiographically her own "transformational" experience as a reader; this material is interesting, but in the nature of an afterword. Readers seeking more than a cursory reading of each or all of these important current writers will be well served by Keating's nuanced and probing study. All academic collections.—*D. N. Mager, Johnson C. Smith University*

OAB-0836   PS3561   92-44011 CIP
Kushner, Tony. **Angels in America: a gay fantasia on national themes. Pt. 2: Perestroika.** Theatre Communications Group, 1994. 158p ISBN 1-55936-072-0, $21.95; ISBN 1-55936-073-9 pbk, $10.95

If it seems unlikely—given its thicket of accompanying blurbs—that any gay male reviewer could be dispassionate about Tony Kushner's two *Angels in America* plays, then what about the rest of reviewerkind? Truth to tell, the use of the angel motif in these dramas about living and dying with AIDS is both stunning and beautiful, while the presence of the late and unlamented Roy Cohn is as impressive as it is distracting. The dialogue throughout is deft, off-puttingly light, and slangy; the tone established is one of dark humor, whistling past the graveyard. What the reader must supply is a visual dimension merely adumbrated by the text—though that is hardly any fault of the text. Staged, this play and its predecessor (winners of 1993 and 1994 Tony Awards) prove masterfully arresting and engaging. Current politically correct norms make objectivity about these plays difficult for the moment, but for that moment, these are necessary acquisitions for libraries of every sort. The text has been well printed, introduced, and generally outfitted. Most highly recommended.—*J. M. Ditsky, University of Windsor*

OAB-0837   PS3545   95-6038 CIP
Leverich, Lyle. **Tom: the unknown Tennessee Williams.** Crown, 1995. 644p index ISBN 0-517-70225-8, $35.00

Since his death in 1983, Tennessee Williams has been the subject of more than 30 scholarly books. This authoritative, comprehensive, meticulously researched and annotated study of Williams's early years is the one readers have been waiting for. It is soon to be followed by volume 2, *Tennessee*, which will cover Williams's life after *The Glass Menagerie* (1944). In 1978, Williams

Humanities

named Leverich, a respected veteran of the theater world, his biographer. The playwright provided access to journals and letters, which are essential in discovering the story of the private man behind the antic facade. As chronicled in *The New Yorker* last year, Leverich was blocked from publication until now. Here, for the first time, we have the real story of the Williams family, especially Rose Williams, whose tragic life haunted her brother; insights into Tom's discovery of his sexual identity and his strategies for dealing with homosexuality in a hostile environment; and his incredible productivity despite many false starts. *Tom* is a treasure for Williams scholars and the layperson.— *N. Tischler, Pennsylvania State University, University Park Campus*

OAB-0838　　　　PS374　　　　94-29265 CIP
Lupack, Barbara Tepa. **Insanity as redemption in contemporary American fiction: inmates running the asylum.** University Press of Florida, 1995. 246p bibl index afp ISBN 0-8130-1331-3, $39.95

This incisive treatment of five major contemporary novels by five of the most significant US writers represents an important addition to the body of literary and cultural criticism, providing a new focus and innumerable original perceptions about these works and the development of American literature and society since WW II. Lupack devotes long chapters to Heller's *Catch-22* (1961), Kesey's *One Flew over the Cuckoo's Nest* (1962), Vonnegut's *Slaughterhouse-Five* (1969), Kosinski's *Being There* (1971), and Styron's *Sophie's Choice* (1979), but she consistently links them to her cohesive theme of insanity as redemption in a politically and ethically problematic society, making this a single forceful work rather than a simple collection of loosely connected essays. Demonstrating exhaustive research into earlier scholarship and the lives and public statements of these novelists, Lupack provides a clear overview of the existing knowledge and proceeds beyond it to present a forceful indictment of the paradoxes and hypocrisies in postwar American society. This is literary and cultural criticism at its best, sophisticated enough for academic specialists but presented with a clarity and accessibility that will make it useful for undergraduate and graduate students and interesting to any intelligent reader. With its comprehensive notes, bibliography, and index, this work is highly recommended for all libraries.—*B. H. Leeds, Central Connecticut State University*

OAB-0839　　　　PS3529　　　　94-44403 CIP
Maud, Ralph. **Charles Olson's reading: a biography.** Southern Illinois, 1996. 372p index afp ISBN 0-8093-1995-0, $44.95

Maud (Simon Fraser Univ.) has produced an important contribution to Charles Olson scholarship and to the study of 20th-century poetics. In tracing the reading that informs Olson's projective poetics, he continues the work begun by George Butterick in the journal *Olson* (1974-77). The present "biography" complements Tom Clark's biography *Charles Olson: The Allegory of a Poet's Life* (CH, Sep'91). Maud covers Olson's intellectual life from his young adulthood until his death, taking the tack that Olson himself first proposed to Merton Sealts in Herman Melville scholarship—to follow the author's reading. Maud studiously details the texts read by Olson with copious notes and an extensive bibliography, and he reveals Olson's intense desire to break down rigid boundaries of knowledge. Olson read not only poetry but also history, geography, psychology, and anthropology, and this reading was the context for his poetry and poetic theory. This study reveals to the reader the habits of mind of a poet whose work has had a profound effect on the poetry of the last half of the 20th century. Upper-division undergraduate and above.—*R. T. Prus, Southeastern Oklahoma State University*

OAB-0840　　　　PS374　　　　94-10663 CIP
McDowell, Deborah E. **"The changing same": black women's literature, criticism, and theory.** Indiana, 1995. 222p index afp ISBN 0-253-33629-5, $29.95; ISBN 0-253-20926-9 pbk, $12.95

Any scholar, beginning or seasoned, looking for an introduction to black feminist criticism and theory would be well advised to pick up McDowell's collection of essays. Written over the last 15 years, they document many of the cen-

tral critical issues to emerge from black feminist criticism—literary tradition, identity politics, shifting literary conventions, reader/reception politics, the construction of historical knowledge, and black feminists' relationships to the age of theory. Rather than provide a linear, chronological record of her changing ideas, McDowell (Univ. of Virginia) groups her essays thematically, with contemporary commentary on many of her earlier works. The result is a delightful dialogue with both herself and a rich variety of African American writers, critics, and theorists—Hazel Carby, Hortense Spillers, bell hooks, and Henry Louis Gates Jr., to name several. Her examinations of major contemporary novelists Alice Walker and Toni Morrison and of Harlem Renaissance writers Jessie Fauset and Nella Larsen provide important insights. Written with wit and style, this book is the mature work of an impressive scholar.—*J. Tharp, University of Wisconsin—Marshfield-Wood County*

OAB-0841　　　　PS3535　　　　93-5786 CIP
A Muriel Rukeyser reader, ed. by Jan Heller Levi. W.W. Norton, 1994. 294p index ISBN 0-393-03566-2, $25.00

This book is a treasure. Unlike other selections of Rukeyser's work, this reader includes large selections from her prose: part of her biography of the scientist Willard Gibbs (*Willard Gibbs*, 1942), her long essay "The Life of Poetry" (1949), and her lecture "The Education of a Poet" (1976). Levi's introductions to each publication, arranged chronologically, are written with tact and insight. Adrienne Rich's introduction adds to the understanding of this remarkable and inspired poet, who was a source of inspiration for Rich. Filled with moral and political passion, Rukeyser's engagement with public events from the two World Wars to the Vietnam war informed her poetry. Ignored and despised as a "she-poet" in her early years, Rukeyser has become a beacon for many contemporary poets today. Her daring, her compassion, and her immense intelligence have always stood in contrast to timid academic fashion in poetry. I count myself among the poets of her generation who fell in love with her poems from the early "Effort at Speech Between Two People" (*Theory of Flight*, 1935) to the affirmation of her last book, *The Gates* (1976). All levels.—*R. Whitman, Massachusetts Institute of Technology*

OAB-0842　　　　PS153　　　　91-28471 CIP
Nelson, Robert M. **Place and vision: the function of landscape in Native American fiction.** P. Lang, 1993. 189p bibl index afp (American Indian studies, 1) ISBN 0-8204-1720-3, $39.95

A very thorough study of three important Native American novels: Leslie Silko's *Ceremony* (CH, Jul'77), N. Scott Momaday's *House Made of Dawn* (1968), and James Welch's *The Death of Jim Loney* (1979). Nelson is editor of *The North American Indian Quarterly* and knows Native American writing and its issues well. His thesis is that the identification with the land attained by the protagonists of the novels is a fundamental experience that precedes cultural ideas about the landscape. It is a thesis that he thinks may be controversial, but one that explains why these novels of a marginalized minority have become currents in the mainstream, novels that readers who are not natives can understand. His readings of the novels are dogged rather than inspired, and far too much of the argument is conducted in elaborate footnotes. Nelson's work is thesis-ridden; nevertheless, his knowledge of the works and their backgrounds is deep, and future critics will need to have a look at what he says. The book is, therefore, an important acquisition. Lengthy bibliography, thorough index, including place names. Undergraduate; graduate; faculty.—*B. Almon, University of Alberta*

OAB-0843　　　　PS3537　　　　94-21893 CIP
Parini, Jay. **John Steinbeck: a biography.** H. Holt, 1995. 536p bibl index afp ISBN 0-8050-1673-2, $30.00

Jackson J. Benson, author of the previous definitive Steinbeck biography (*The True Adventures of John Steinbeck, Writer*, 1984), spent ten years at the task and was apparently so rattled by estate demands for cuts at the end of the process that he even left out the fact of Steinbeck's birth. Parini, poet and critic, had the cooperation of Steinbeck's widow, Elaine, and also made use of unpublished letters from the Stanford collection. The lengthy result (which for mysterious reasons was first published in England) is tight, smooth reading and admirably balanced, considering the fact that it attempts to be something of a traditional life-and-works volume. Though the author gives little space to elucidation of his evaluations, he is never unfair and seems quite open to unprejudiced readings of Steinbeck's later works—something earlier critics were seldom able or willing to do. Parini is especially good at fleshing out the middle and later periods of Steinbeck's life—WW II and after—and he includes an account of Steinbeck's late-life practice of placing new irons in a fire incapable of accommodating all it had already received. Steinbeck's struggle with his own fame—living it down, maintaining it, dealing with its perquisites—is especially well handled, as are his often stormy domestic relations. Illustrated with photos, this book is a necessary acquisition for all libraries.—*J. M. Ditsky, University of Windsor*

OAB-0844   PS3525   92-7616 CIP
Parker, Dorothy R. **Singing an Indian song: a biography of D'Arcy McNickle.** Nebraska, 1992. 316p bibl index afp ISBN 0-8032-3687-5, $35.00

In this, the first book-length study of D'Arcy McNickle's life, Parker makes accessible a wealth of information previously available only to researchers. As a modern Native American novelist, ethno-historian, Bureau of Indian Affairs (BIA) official, community organizer, Indian rights advocate, and university professor, McNickle has lived at the center of much federal Indian policy and significant activity in the social sciences. Parker's biography is a careful study of the public life of a very private man. Her work illuminates McNickle's mixed cultural background, his career, and his publications as it closely chronicles McNickle's years with John Collier and the BIA. Parker seeks to establish the way in which McNickle's Euro-American cultural heritage, combined with a conscious construction of a Pan-Indian perspective, created a "compound identity." Her biography challenges simple notions of ethnic identity and provides readers with the groundwork to develop their own insights into the transactions and negotiations of identity formation. Although at times McNickle the individual is backgrounded to McNickle the public official, Parker's biography is solid scholarship. She also makes a valuable contribution to the history of applied anthropology and of federal/Indian policy. Recommended. Undergraduate; advanced undergraduate; graduate; faculty.—*J. Ruppert, University of Alaska Fairbanks*

OAB-0845   PS153   94-22380 CIP
Pérez-Torres, Rafael. **Movements in Chicano poetry: against myths, against margins.** Cambridge, 1995. 334p bibl index (Cambridge studies in American literature and culture, 88) ISBN 0-521-47019-6, $59.95; ISBN 0-521-47803-0 pbk, $17.95

Pérez-Torres knows Chicano/a poetry very well and has mastered the growing body of scholarship, as his comprehensive bibliography (running to 20 pages) makes clear. He applies the terminology of postmodernism and postcolonialism to the writing brilliantly, though the reader may feel that the proliferation of terminology tends to overwhelm the poetry: is there an Occam's razor of taxonomy? He makes good use of Juan Bruce-Novoa's characterization of Chicano/a poetry as "interlingual" rather than "bilingual." He points to an important problem that arises from postmodernist assumptions about the fallacy of essentialism: Chicano/a poetry stresses ethnic identity and often uses myths and archetypes—and such tendencies assume or even assert fixed identities. The theory at times overwhelms the poetry, especially when a very minor poet is being discussed, but all in all this is a valuable contribution to the understanding of Chicano/a writing. Upper-division undergraduate collections and above.—*B. Almon, University of Alberta*

OAB-0846   PS3563   94-48916 CIP
Pettis, Joyce. **Toward wholeness in Paule Marshall's fiction.** University Press of Virginia, 1995. 173p bibl index ISBN 0-8139-1614-3, $29.50

Pettis (North Carolina State Univ.) situates Marshall's work preeminently in the growing body of African American literature and criticism that privileges the quests and possibilities for spiritual wholeness. She reads Marshall's canon (four novels, one collection of novellas, and one of short stories) within a matrix of black feminist critical theory (Patricia Hill Collins, Paula Giddings, Deborah McDowell, Barbara Christian) and Afrocentric psychological perspectives (Joseph A. Baldwin, Linda James Myers). Chapter 1, "Generative Spaces," argues intriguingly, though insufficiently, for the uniqueness of Marshall's literary vision of "resolution" to cultural, historical "psychic fracturing" for all peoples of the African diaspora. (Sustained comparative readings of Marshall's contemporaries—e.g., Toni Morrison, Gloria Naylor, Alice Walker—would complicate and substantiate Pettis's theory.) Organized topically rather than chronologically, chapters examine the importance of literal and psychological communities to diasporic quests and the "pernicious" dynamics of race, class, and gender: *Praisesong for the Widow* (1983) represents "satisfactory closure" to Marshall's quest for "psychic equilibrium"; *Daughters* (1991) depicts a viable, postquest community of spiritually whole, self-enabled women. This excellent introduction and critical analysis is recommended for upper-division undergraduates and above.—*S. Bryant, Alfred University*

OAB-0847   PS3537   92-39379 CIP
Schwarz, Daniel R. **Narrative and representation in the poetry of Wallace Stevens: a tune beyond us, yet ourselves.** Macmillan, UK/St. Martin's, 1993. 242p bibl index ISBN 0-312-09488-4, $39.95; ISBN 0-312-09594-5 pbk, $16.95

Most critical interpretations of Stevens's poetry primarily involve studies of his imagery and rhetoric, but Schwarz detects in both the lyrics and longer poems an implied narrative, spoken by a character, and emanating from an experience, all of which it is possible for the sensitive reader to unearth. In chapters built around such exemplary Stevens works as "Thirteen Ways of Looking at a Blackbird," "The Idea of Order at Key West," "Anecdote of the Prince of Peacocks," *The Man with the Blue Guitar, Notes Toward a Supreme Fiction* and others, Schwarz ably and clearly demonstrates his thesis while providing new and valuable readings of these much-discussed poems. Stevens is placed in American and modernist literary contexts as well, and the effects of his interest in modern painting are brought into focus. The result is a refreshing approach, outstanding among the current spate of books devoted to Stevens. Recommended. Undergraduate; graduate; faculty; general.—*B. Galvin, Central Connecticut State University*

OAB-0848   PS323   92-27648 CIP
Scott, Nathan A. **Visions of presence in modern American poetry.** Johns Hopkins, 1993. 298p index afp ISBN 0-8018-4537-8, $34.95

Essays on the poetry of Wallace Stevens, W.H. Auden, Theodore Roethke, Elizabeth Bishop, Robert Penn Warren, Richard Wilbur, A.R. Ammons, James Wright, and Howard Nemerov. Scott regards these nine poets as being on intimate terms with the "dimension of presence," which for him means to be involved with things as they are, that "rich density of the quotidian" in which American poets have usually found "the chief source of the sublime." Whether he is discussing "the splendor of mere being" as beheld by Wilbur, or Warren's arrival at a "guessed-at glory" derived from events in the natural world, or Bishop's sacramental view of things, Scott is surely the kind of generous reader poets must hope for, and particularly so when he opposes himself to current academic doctrines that claim poems are merely language constructs without outside referents. These essays embody the clearest kind of refutation of such exercises, and are brilliant critical assessments of the aims of these poets as well. Highly recommended. Undergraduate (all levels); graduate; faculty; general.—*B. Galvin, Central Connecticut State University*

OAB-0849   PS374   92-30830 CIP
Scruggs, Charles. **Sweet home: invisible cities in the Afro-American novel.** Johns Hopkins, 1993. 296p index afp ISBN 0-8018-4502-5, $37.50

An impressive and thoroughly engaging contribution to 20th-century African American literary studies, and to cultural studies as well. Scruggs begins by tracking the origins of African American urban fiction. Rather than offer a comprehensive but superficial survey of black urban literature, he judiciously focuses on the role of the city both real and imagined in the representative texts of Richard Wright, Ralph Ellison, James Baldwin, and Toni Morrison. The result is a meticulous, thoughtful, and scholarly work that not only widens our understanding of the canonical texts that he carefully analyzes but also delivers a compelling cultural narrative of the black urban experience in the US from the Great Migration to the 1980s. Though American urban fiction has received considerable critical attention, this volume by Scruggs is the first book-length study of the city, both visible and invisible, in representative African American novels. This sophisticated yet accessible book is recommended for all graduate, undergraduate, and large public libraries.—*E. S. Nelson, SUNY College at Cortland*

OAB-0850   PS3501   94-25956 CIP
Shoptaw, John. **On the outside looking out: John Ashbery's poetry.** Harvard, 1994. 386p index ISBN 0-674-63612-0, $49.95; ISBN 0-674-63613-9 pbk, $24.00

Beginning with his thesis that Ashbery should not be seen as the poetic "representative" of our confusing and disjointed age, but that he is best understood as the great "misrepresentative" of the world in which he lives, Shoptaw opens a discussion of the poet that combines history, biography, and criticism into a provocative and enlightening analysis. According to the author, at the root of Ashbery's "aesthetic of misrepresentation" is his homosexuality. Ashbery developed his poetics during the late 1940s and early 1950s, when homosexuals were the target of harassment and were excluded from the benefits available to mainstream American society. The need to "misrepresent" himself became at that time a survival tactic that, according to Shoptaw, gave his poetry a "homotextual dimension." Beginning his study of Ashbery with the poet's *Some Trees* (1956) and working chronologically to *Flow Chart* (1991), Shoptaw devotes a chapter to each of Ashbery's 12 books. Shoptaw is the first scholar to have full access to all of Ashbery's manuscripts and personal, unpublished papers. He also had access to the poet himself to answer questions and to check the accuracy of this book when it was in manuscript. Because of its deeply informed nature, Shoptaw's study must constitute the foundation of all future studies of Ashbery. Upper-division undergraduate; graduate; faculty.—*P. J. Ferlazzo, Northern Arizona University*

OAB-0851   PS261   93-8699 CIP
Simpson, Lewis P. **The fable of the southern writer.** Louisiana State, 1994. 249p index afp ISBN 0-8071-1871-0, $24.95

Based on an overview of previous writing, this book brings a new vision to the southernness of Jefferson, Tate, Faulkner, Robert Penn Warren, and Walker Percy. This collection of essays written over the past decade may prove to be the masterpiece of Lewis Simpson's literary career and could serve as the capstone of the Southern Renascence. Those who know Simpson know that he transcends all clichés regarding the subject of the South, southern writing, and the relevance of the Civil War. He is tenacious of the premise that regardless of social and economic changes, including the grim specter of industrial "progress," the Civil War is still here. In his "Prologue" Simpson notes that the literary criticism of the mid-century—characterized by men like Ransom, Tate, Brooks, and Warren—has been superseded by the "carnival" of critics who specialize in esoteric niceties that have little bearing on literature or its analysis. Suitable for undergraduate and graduate students in history and literature, this book is a fine addition to public as well as academic libraries and a boon to collectors of southern writing.—*A. G. Tassin, University of New Orleans*

OAB-0852   PR9199   95-50457 CIP
Sullivan, Robert. **A matter of faith: the fiction of Brian Moore.**

Greenwood, 1996. 137p bibl index afp (Contributions to the study of world literature, 69) ISBN 0-313-29871-8, $49.95

Sullivan offers the most useful single-volume study to date of the 19 novels produced by Moore over the last 40 years. He convincingly spotlights the "stylistic ingenuity [and] experimentation with narrative voice" of a true modern master. In five chapters Sullivan surveys Moore's overall themes; his three Belfast novels on the theme of thwarted desire; his five novels featuring escapees to the New World and their resultant internal conflicts; the five stellar novels on transcendental themes (*The Temptation of Eileen Hughes, Cold Heaven, Catholics, Black Robe,* and *The Color of Blood*); and what the author calls Moore's "masterplot," *The Great Victorian Collection* (CH, Oct'75). Except for an occasional dip into jargon ("... as a cultural poetics, the conflictual value systems [*sic*] which *Black Robe* emplots is one between individualistic ideology ... and a collective dream") and a failure to see Moore's striking resemblance as a globe-trotting moralist to Graham Greene, Sullivan's effort admirably distills Moore's technique and worth. This book takes a valuable place beside the established Moore commentaries of Hallvard Dahlie, John Wilson Foster, and Jeanne Flood. All academic collections.—*R. J. Thompson, Canisius College*

OAB-0853   PN3426   96-54875 CIP
Trites, Roberta Seelinger. **Waking Sleeping Beauty: feminist voices in children's novels.** Iowa, 1997. 170p bibl index afp ISBN 0-87745-590-2, $24.95; ISBN 0-87745-591-0 pbk, $12.95

Trites (Illinois State Univ.) explores the connections between children's literature and feminism, examining how the feminist movement has had a lasting influence on contemporary children's literature. The author is particularly interested in showing educators this connection and in demonstrating its importance: "The effect of feminism on children's literature is to create a corpus of literature that can speak to readers of all races and both genders." Trites's thoughtful, broad-reaching analysis addresses a wide range of books, including Jean George's *Julie of the Wolves* (1972), Janet Lunn's *The Root Cellar* (1983), Patricia MacLachlan's *Sarah, Plain and Tall* (1985), and Nancy Garden's *Annie on My Mind* (1982). She shows that understanding feminism and its philosophies is essential to understanding children's literature. This is an important and thought-provoking book, one that will interest a variety of readers—e.g., education students concerned about gender roles and stereotypes—in addition to students and scholars of children's literature. All collections.—*S. A. Inness, Miami University*

OAB-0854   PS3566   92-31233 CIP
Van Dyne, Susan R. **Revising life: Sylvia Plath's Ariel poems.** North Carolina, 1993. 206p index bibl afp ISBN 0-8078-2102-0, $27.50

A critical study becomes a pleasure when the writer sets about defining her subject in precise, realistic terms. This is exactly what Van Dyne does as she explores and explicates Plath's poems in the Ariel collection. As Van Dyne studies the poems she sees her task evolving. She has to put together in her own mind how "they [poems] suggest her culture's powerful shaping influence on the imagination, yet [are] strategic in that they represent Plath's efforts to rewrite experience in a poetics of survival." In order for Van Dyne to accomplish her way of looking at Plath's poems she has to cull other critical studies of Plath, Plath's own journals, letters, and the many early drafts of the poems that make up the group. By juxtaposing these various materials against the poems, Van Dyne provides a compelling argument for Plath's revision of the painful parts of her life—the failed marriage, her anxiety for success, and her ambivalence towards her mother, Aurelia Plath. Van Dyne does not gloss over Plath's excessive ambition, her "rituals," or her rages against Ted Hughes. The reader will feel the tension in the poetry and the life. What emerges in the end, though, is a better understanding of the effort Plath put forward in seeking completion and fulfillment. Here is a study that goes far beyond the earlier studies filled with psychoanalytic digressions about the brilliant tragic poet. The new portrait is of a poet who became empowered through her art. Graduate; faculty; general.—*H. Susskind, Monroe Community College*

OAB-0855 PS338 94-38076 CIP
Vorlicky, Robert. **Act like a man: challenging masculinities in American drama.** Michigan, 1995. 373p bibl index afp ISBN 0-472-09572-2, $49.50

It would take an especially hard-hearted feminist critic to object to having males learn something about themselves from the insights of recent feminist criticism, so the reader of this study can only be grateful for Vorlicky's volume. In fact, the author engagingly stands some traditional gender assumptions on their figurative heads in order to deal convincingly with plays on which his clever title proves to be a salient angle of view: "In spite of its place in realist tradition," the author states in his introduction, "most variations of American male-cast drama resist the diversity of American male experience and its challenge to traditional masculinities; rather, they aggressively limit themselves to perpetuating a rigid, antihistorical account of male identity." Guys often just do not "get it" is the implication, at least while the women are also onstage, and so this study is particularly rich in men-only instances in which issues not merely of gender but also of race and sexual orientation can be candidly examined. Lightly illustrated and heavily annotated, this book can easily be recommended as a source text for critical studies of a promisingly refreshing sort.—*J. M. Ditsky, University of Windsor*

■ Germanic

OAB-0856 PT289 92-46530 CIP
Bennett, Benjamin. **Beyond theory: eighteenth-century German literature and the poetics of irony.** Cornell, 1993. 354p index afp ISBN 0-8014-2841-6, $41.50

Carefully crafted and brilliantly and convincingly argued, this study is an erudite, provocative, and stimulating rereading and reexamination of 18th-century German texts with the goal of contemporizing the 18th century. Working with three main ideas—radical irony, the enactment of origins, and the reading function—the author seeks out the deeper meaning and applicability of the poetics of the age. Along with the chapter-length readings of Goethe's *Wilhelm Meisters Wanderjahre,* Hölderlin's "An die Parzen," and Lessing's *Laokoon* there are in-depth reevaluations of Herder, Kleist, Schiller, Nietsche, and Kant, to name only the most prominent. Their ideas, in turn, are scrutinized and applied under the lens of 20th-century theory and philosophy, in particular that of Foucault. Moreover, in his treatment of poetic irony Bennett adds a dimension by associating the locus of this irony in two historical entities, namely the theater and the Jews. The breadth, depth, and wealth of innovative ideas make this a challenging study that will not only lead to agreement, but will also undoubtedly provide discussion—and even disagreement—while stimulating further debate. At all times though the arguments are logically reasoned and admirably presented in this virtuoso tour de force through 18th-century German poetics.—*J. K. Fugate, Kalamazoo College*

OAB-0857 Orig
Brecht, Bertolt. **Bertolt Brecht journals,** tr. by Hugh Rorrison; ed. by John Willett. Routledge, 1993. 556p bibl index ISBN 0-415-90837-X, $39.95

When Brecht's *Arbeitsjournal 1938-1955* appeared in three volumes in 1973 (two volumes of entries and one of notes by Werner Hecht), it was a sensation among Brecht scholars because of its candid observations about life, colleagues, friends, literature, his plays, poetry, theories, and politics and for its silence about such things as the East German uprising of 1953. Now this important work—expanded slightly by a few entries from the *Tagebücher* (1975)—is available in English. Willett provides notes and an introduction helpful to both the general and the informed reader. Nevertheless, these notes of 1993 do not completely replace Hecht's. Willett updates and corrects Hecht on occasion but also omits some of his important material. However, no English reader seriously interested in Brecht can afford to neglect this book. These entries define Brecht better than his famous essays: his comments are filled with penetrating definitions, in simple direct language, of Brechtian terms. Also Brecht's own

analyses of his plays are more insightful than any critic's. Furthermore, Brecht's attitudes toward the Soviet Union, the war, Germany, socialist realism, modernism, Lukács, and the Frankfort School are more understandable here than in his other writings. Translating material of this sort is difficult, but Rorrison captures admirably Brecht's brilliant dialectical mind. Undergraduate; graduate; faculty; general.—*R. C. Conard, University of Dayton*

OAB-0858 PT2189 91-38308 CIP
Burgard, Peter J. **Idioms of uncertainty: Goethe and the essay.** Pennsylvania State, 1993 (c1992). 250p index afp ISBN 0-271-00845-8, $35.00

An unusually thorough analysis of Goethe as an essayist. Using, for example, the relatively unknown essay "The Collector and his Circle," Burgard illustrates how careful analysis of text and supporting documents, both from Goethe's oeuvre and from the philosophical context of the times, reveals the principle of dialogue that informed Goethe's writing and relationships with contemporaries. For example, after discussing Goethe's own essays, Burgard provides an absorbing discussion of Lessing's *Laocoön,* considering first how Lessing's correspondence with Nicolai and, to a larger extent, with Mendelssohn helped to create his text. He then shows how Goethe enters into a dialogue with that text in his own later works. Burgard makes an addition to criticism and gives a textured, contemporary understanding of several authors through this methodology. Using modern criticism (including Bakhtin, Kristeva, and other current theorists), while also referring to the tradition of the essay as practiced by Montaigne and others, Burgard suggests a new importance of the essay in Goethe's work. Translations of German texts are uniformly outstanding. References to literature of the age of Goethe are extensive and thought provoking. A well-researched, original book, Burgard's text is of interest to advanced students and specialists.—*E. Glass, Rosemont College*

OAB-0859 ND793 95-35409 CIP
Carlson, Harry G. **Out of inferno: Strindberg's reawakening as an artist.** Washington, 1996. 390p bibl index afp ISBN 0-295-97503-2, $45.00; ISBN 0-295-97564-4 pbk, $24.95

Imaginatively conceived, brilliantly executed, engagingly composed, effectively illustrated, thoroughly documented, eminently accessible—these are among the many virtues of Carlson's incisive inquiry into the life and work of a celebrated Swedish genius who, despite a series of debilitating psychic dislocations, "reawakened" from an encumbering dormancy. As Carlson (theater, Queens College, CUNY) perceptively elaborates, for Strindberg artistic and spiritual resurrection sprang from an energizing rediscovery of the imagination's revelatory potency, a potency that enables the gifted seer not merely to rearrange memories in aesthetically pleasing configurations but to generate new and striking images that provide privileged insights into the hidden correspondences that link the sacred and the profane. Once unleashed, the regenerated Strindbergian imagination encounters little difficulty coalescing time and space, past and present, conscious and unconscious, natural and supernatural, and religious and sociopolitical in a host of "post-Inferno" works that are still spellbinding for contemporary audiences. For its unsurpassed breadth, depth, and clarity, this volume is highly recommended for all college and university collections.—*H. I. Einsohn, Middlesex Community-Technical College*

OAB-0860 PT2685 93-17439 CIP
Cohen, Robert. **Understanding Peter Weiss.** South Carolina, 1993. 206p bibl index afp ISBN 0-87249-898-0, $39.95

Cohen has recently published two related books on Peter Weiss: *Versuch über Weiss' "Ästhetik des Widerstands"* (1989) and *Bio-bibliographisches Handbuch zu Weiss' "Ästhetik des Widerstands"* (Hamburg, 1989). With this new monograph in the series "Understanding Modern European and Latin American Literature," translated beautifully by Martha Humphreys, Cohen's immense knowledge of Weiss's oeuvre—including Weiss's work as filmmaker and painter—is available in English. The book is what the title promises: an in-depth understanding of one of postwar Germany's most important figures.

As is appropriate, Cohen is at his best in the chapters on the famous plays, *Marat/Sade*, *The Investigation*, and the monumental novel, *The Aesthetics of Resistance*. Cohen's approach is best labeled critical Marxism, and it yields extremely valuable insights when it confronts Weiss's own literary Marxism, as in the analyses of the plays about revolution—*Song of the Lusitanian Bogey*, *Viet Nam Discourse*, *Trotsky in Exile*, and *Hölderlin*—and especially in the discussion of Weiss's two dramatic versions of Kafka's *The Trial*. This book should serve the American public for a long time as a standard reference work on Weiss's oeuvre. Thorough index; excellent bibliographies of the secondary literature and of Weiss's work in German and English translation.— *R. C. Conard, University of Dayton*

OAB-0861   PT91   92-17763 CIP
A Concise history of German literature to 1900, ed. by Kim Vivian. Camden House, 1992. 345p index afp ISBN 1-879751-29-1, $59.95; ISBN 1-879751-30-5 pbk, $26.95

Oriented especially to the English-speaking reader, this history by 12 authors offers thorough coverage with up-to-date supportive information and interpretation. All chapters are by experts according to periods; beginning with the early Middle Ages, and concluding with Naturalism (1900). Each chapter is in an outline form. A section on "further reading" (about 80% in English) supplies about 15 to 20 books for each chapter, while a unified index accesses all parts of the volume. Good editing renders the book uniform, with a common structure, and a standard ideological or theoretical slant. There are a few illustrations scattered throughout. Undoubtedly space considerations prevented the authors from continuing through to the present. For the periods covered, however, the book ranks among the very best in English, comparable to John G. Robertson (*A History of German Literature*, 6th ed., 1970), and would make an ideal course text if supported by, say, the *Oxford Companion to German Literature*. A useful purchase for the general reader and an excellent addition for undergraduate college collections.—*L. J. Rippley, St. Olaf College*

OAB-0862   PT149   96-22248 CIP
Erspamer, Peter R. **The elusiveness of tolerance: the "Jewish question" from Lessing to the Napoleonic wars.** North Carolina, 1997. 189p bibl index afp (University of North Carolina studies in the Germanic languages and literatures, 117) ISBN 0-8078-8117-1, $34.95

In this interesting, well-conceived study, Erspamer considers the tolerance debate in Germany and Austria from the publication of Gotthold Ephraim Lessing's *Nathan the Wise* (1779) to the end of the Napoleonic era. Erspamer makes excellent use of sources, presenting a balance of documents for and against the Enlightenment ideal promulgated by Lessing and influenced by the leading figure of the Haskalah: Moses Mendelssohn. He discusses both authors in fresh, insightful ways, while providing a balanced view of historical criticism. He analyzes pamphlets engendered by Lessing's book from writers like Pfranger, Dohm, Ascher, and Diez, and dramas with Jewish themes by writers like Reinicke, Bischof, Lotich, and Ziegelhauser. In such chapters as "Emancipatory Drama after Lessing" and "Myths of Homogeneity: Anti-Semitic Literature after 1800," he traces the devastating effects of nationalistic sentiments inspired by the wars of liberation. He illuminates the polemics of antisemitic Romantics like Achim von Arnim and Fichte, using well-chosen quotations in German. Despite quirks of style, Erspamer provides an integrated view of a seminal era for German-Jewish relations, needed materials, and valuable insights. Extensive bibliography, notes, and index. Recommended for all collections.— *E. G. Wickersham, Rosemont College*

OAB-0863   PT2605   93-7654 CIP
Falk, Thomas H. **Elias Canetti.** Twayne, 1993. 185p bibl index afp (TWAS, 843) ISBN 0-8057-8276-1, $22.95

Often neglected, usually misinterpreted, and generally ignored by most American critics, the 88-year-old, Bulgarian-born Canetti presents numerous diffi-

culties for adequate and accurate critical discussions. Here Falk penetrates earlier cloudy considerations with his admirable study of Canetti—the writer and his writings—and resolves a large number of the perplexities encountered in Canetti's fiction, essays, dramas, and biographical pieces. Because of Falk's expertise in German (the language in which Canetti writes), he is well qualified to interpret/discuss Canetti's works and to explain Canetti's theory of the "acoustic masks" that make up each individual. Canetti abhorred war, and his life and work, as Falk makes clear, reflect his strong remonstrances against war. Falk believes that central to comprehending Canetti is his major book, *Crowds and Power* (1962), in which Canetti incorporates myth, religion, history, anthropology, biography, and psychology in order to understand the strength of crowds and power, mass behavior, and mass psychology. Falk's well-researched study of Canetti's writing is, to this reviewer, the best explication to date, and it should be required reading for all those intrigued by this enigmatic literary figure, winner of the 1981 Nobel prize for literature.—*G. O. Carey, emeritus, Eastern Kentucky University*

OAB-0864   PT2605   94-33942 CIP
Felstiner, John. **Paul Celan: poet, survivor, Jew.** Yale, 1995. 344p index afp ISBN 0-300-06068-8, $30.00

Felstiner's critical biography of Celan is a literary event of the first order. It not only establishes itself as the most definitive account of Celan in any language but goes far toward recognizing that Celan's effort to win back the German language and the language of poetry from both a global antisemitism and an uncritical aesthetic modernism remains the defining struggle for both poetry and thought in our time. The author (Stanford Univ.) sheds new light on virtually every aspect of Celan's life and work and has identified so profoundly with his subject that the reader throughout feels the impossible weight of Celan's effort to speak poetically for the victims of the Holocaust. But above and beyond all the extraordinary close readings of the poems and the deepened understanding of Celan's life, what Felstiner has alarmingly, fatefully grasped here is the insurmountable impasse between the German and the Jewish sense of the world. Felstiner unveils a monstrous break in Celan between the poetics of the most intimately German experience of language from Hölderlin to Rilke and Celan's own poetic conscience as a German Jewish survivor of the Holocaust. Celan's life and work reenact the catastrophe that will *not* allow Germanness and Jewishness to coexist and appear as the tragically inevitable results of a certain failure to separate the German language from an irreducibly antisemitic violence. The reader glimpses the terrifying possibility that Celan's tragedy may be the obituary of our time. Upper-division undergraduates; graduate students; researchers; faculty.—*N. Lukacher, University of Illinois at Chicago*

OAB-0865   PN5219   95-37608 CIP
Fritzsche, Peter. **Reading Berlin 1900.** Harvard, 1996. 308p index ISBN 0-674-74881-6, $39.95

This title looks at how Berlin newspapers mapped the city and captivated the citizenry during their heyday (1900-10). Fritzsche (Univ. of Illinois) bases his study on outstanding German sources. These include not only histories of Berlin and other cities, but insights from social commentators like Georg Simmel and Walter Benjamin and from authors and artists like Alfred Döblin, Robert Walser, and several Expressionists. Among Fritzsche's topics are the kinds of newspaper editions, content, distribution, readership, and influence on the rhythms of the emerging metropolis. He also considers the depiction of neighborhoods in the press, urban growth, architecture, changing economic realities, evolving modes of transportation, social classes, flaneurs, urban night life, crowds and their identity, spectacle, the relationship of the monarchy and police to the city, the contribution of the press to the definition of modern life, the role played by sensationalism, and the development of popular, versus high, culture. Although some of the seven chapters are repetitive, the author provides mature philosophical reflections, excellent notes, and unusually apposite illustrations. A good choice for students who have little access to the original sources. All collections.—*E. Glass, Rosemont College*

OAB-0866 PF3087 94-22023 CIP

The German language and the real world: sociolinguistic, cultural, and pragmatic perspectives on contemporary German, ed. by Patrick Stevenson. Oxford, 1995. 406p bibl index afp ISBN 0-19-824054-6, $70.00

This book delivers what its title promises. The 14 essays provide historical, sociopolitical, cultural, descriptive, theoretical, and analytical discussions along with forms and functions of modern German, extending insights into current interests of German linguists. What makes this collection so exciting is its demonstration of the linguistic dichotomy created by a unified Germany and the sociolinguistic ferment it generates. Articles address social change and linguistic variation in Berlin after the fall of the wall; the political language of the Right and Left; the speech of subcultures; language and gender; language and television; and language in intercultural communication. Many of these specially commissioned essays present findings from empirical studies with samples of worksheets and responses in their original German form appended. This volume fills a void in up-to-date English-language information on German linguistics. Highly recommended for all college and university collections, as well as public libraries.—*S. Van Ness, SUNY at Albany*

OAB-0867 PT671 95-50130 CIP

Hart, Gail K. **Tragedy in paradise: family and gender politics in German bourgeois tragedy, 1750-1850.** Camden House, 1996. 136p bibl index afp ISBN 1-57113-037-3, $52.95

Analyzing German bourgeois tragedy, Hart (Univ. of California, Irvine) discovers something new: "the ritual removal of women." She locates the source for the genre's image of woman in an English play, George Lillo's "Image of Woe," in which the character Sarah Millwood's aggressive sexuality destroys the lives of the male characters. Gotthold Lessing consciously draws on Lillo's drama in the classic bourgeois tragedy *Miss Sarah Sampson* (1789), in which all women disappear, leaving two men to raise a family together. Proceeding to analyze Goethe, Klinger, Heinreich Leopole Wagner, Kleist, Schiller, and Hebel, Hart sees men constantly encroaching on turf traditionally assigned to women. For example, Lessing's man of sensibility rendered the feminine unnecessary for the family, while Kleist turns "grace," a conventionally feminine attribute, into an exclusively masculine affair. Hart's well-written analysis judiciously and deftly alludes to Eve Kosofsky Sedgwick's ideas on homosociality in British literature. Hart argues, however, that the German tradition is about the sheer expulsion of women, rather than the use of women as items of exchange. Her work makes a nice addition to a genre thought to be well known and performs the service of bringing German studies in contact with American gender studies. Upper-division undergraduate; graduate; faculty.—*R. D. Tobin, Whitman College*

OAB-0868 PT2625 94-32467 CIP

Hayman, Ronald. **Thomas Mann: a biography.** Scribner, 1995. 672p bibl index ISBN 0-684-19319-1, $35.00

Hayman's biography will make all readers reassess their view of Germany's greatest novelist, whose works present their author as "dignified, elegant" and "somewhat aloof." Unlike previous biographers, Hayman read diaries, which exist only in proof. These offer a different picture of Mann, showing that the novels are concerned as much with his own "representative life" as with anything else, especially with his attraction to "beautiful men and boys," which he repressed in his respectable bourgeois life but developed fully in the novels, particularly *Death in Venice* (1912) and *Felix Krull* (1954). However, Hayman's book is not idle gossip about Mann's repressed homosexuality and troubled family life; it also treats in depth the essays and the novels. Hayman demonstrates vividly Mann's ambivalent attitude toward Nazi Germany, the Jews, the Cold War, and what he saw as the "crisis" of modern art: "collectivism" and the disappearance of a "bourgeois elite" (hence his need for parody and irony). A great book, indispensable for anyone interested in German literature. Upper-division undergraduates and up.—*H. D. Dickerson, Georgia State University*

OAB-0869 PT2352 90-34986 MARC

Herder, Johann Gottfried. **Johann Gottfried Herder: selected early works, 1764-1767: addresses, essays, and drafts; fragments on recent German literature,** ed. by Ernest A. Menze and Karl Menges; tr. by Ernest A. Menze with Michael Palma. Pennsylvania State, 1993 (c1992). 352p bibl index afp ISBN 0-271-00712-5, $35.00

A central figure in 18th-century German intellectual history, Herder (1744-1803) is a seminal thinker in such varied fields as philosophy, history, literary criticism, education, and translation. His influence beyond the borders of his homeland in these and other areas is widely acknowledged, even though for the most part his writings have been available only in the original German. This volume presents, for the first time in English, some of the early addresses, essays, and drafts (1764-66), as well as selections from the first three collections of the *Fragments*, all of which served to establish his reputation as a literary critic. The translators have admirably accomplished the daunting task of transferring Herder's language into accurate and readable English. In addition to the succinct and informative introduction to Herder's life and work, there are detailed commentaries on the translations, a select bibliography, and a very helpful index of names and works. Frankly, the excellent quality of the commentaries recommends acquisition of this volume even if one knows German. The inaccurate claim (p. 24) that there are only five English translations of various works available, the omission (p. 253) of the original text source for one translation, and the misspelling on the inside rear jacket flap constitute minor oversights in an otherwise splendid volume. One can only hope for the speedy appearance of further additions to the planned multivolume edition. Undergraduate and up.—*J. K. Fugate, Kalamazoo College*

OAB-0870 Orig

Heym, Georg. **The thief and other stories,** tr. by Susan Bennett. Libris, 1994. (Dist. by Paul & Company) 105p ISBN 1-870352-68-8, $29.95; ISBN 1-870352-48-3 pbk, $9.95

Heym was only 24 years old when he drowned, while ice skating, in the Havel river in Berlin on January 16, 1912. By that time, he had already emerged as one of the most gifted poets within his generation of young German Expressionist writers. His poems—many of which depict the demonic spectre of the modern metropolis—are still ranked among the finest of the epoch. At the time of his death, Heym left only a small oeuvre, which included the seven stories translated in this volume. They were first posthumously published in 1913 (Leipzig). In typical Expressionist fashion, all texts portray humans in extremis: these are studies in madness, isolation, and depravity ("The Thief," "The Madman") as well as essays in sickness, pestilence, and destruction ("The Autopsy," "Jonathan," "The Ship"). "The Fifth of October" captures the starving masses of Paris on the brink of revolution in 1789. In "An Afternoon," an adolescent boy experiences the first turmoil of jealousy and unrequited love. The unifying theme is ecstasy. All this is presented in Heym's inimitable style, which combines cool observation with the most striking, lurid imagery. The translation is superb throughout. After more than 80 years, these texts are now available to an English-speaking readership. Recommended to all libraries.—*G. P. Knapp, University of Utah*

OAB-0871 PT2291 94-11094 CIP

Mahoney, Dennis F. **The critical fortunes of a romantic novel: Novalis's** *Heinrich von Ofterdingen*. Camden House, 1994. 159p bibl index afp ISBN 1-879751-58-5, $54.95

At the risk of leaving himself open to the charge that he lacks an appropriate critical stand, this reviewer wants to state at the outset that he considers this study exemplary in its organization, sovereign in the mastery of the material, and exceptional in the lucidity of presentation. This gold mine of information is written in a clear and understandable style that makes it a pleasure to read. Its topic is a critical investigation of the reception history of *Heinrich von Ofterdingen* from its publication to the present. Proceeding chronologically, the author examines a variety of points, such as Novalis as *the* representative of German Romanticism, the relationship of Romanticism to the Enlightenment and Classicism, Heinrich as an archetypal figure, the novel's fate during National Socialism, the Cold War climate in East German criticism, and the renaissance of German Romanticism in East German literature and scholarship of the 1970s. Not only are the contributions of German and Anglo-Saxon scholars highlighted, but also those of Francophone critics. Of particular interest is the discussion of the role of Carlyle and Emerson in introducing Novalis to the American reading public. The comprehensive bibliography, arranged by date of publication, includes editions containing *Heinrich von Ofterdingen* and the critical works consulted. This study provides both a well-documented overview of criticism of *Heinrich von Ofterdingen* and an insightful look at German Romanticism in general. Its breadth and depth make it indispensable for any serious student of the novel. Undergraduate and up.—*J. K. Fugate, Kalamazoo College*

OAB-0872 PT2492 95-47381 CIP
Martinson, Steven D. **Harmonious tensions: the writings of Friedrich Schiller.** Delaware, 1996. (Dist. by Associated University Presses) 448p bibl index afp ISBN 0-87413-568-0, $55.00

In this ambitious, exhaustively researched study of selected writings from Schiller's entire corpus—natural-scientific and literary—Martinson demonstrates that Schiller "brought all his multidisciplinary activities to bear on the act of writing." Using the central metaphors of stringed instruments and "rupture" as well as new interpretations of historical and aesthetic theory, Martinson argues for multiple corrections to traditional assumptions in Schiller scholarship. He works from documents at the Schiller Museum and Literary Archives in Marbach an der Neckar—such as Schiller's annotated copy of the work of Kant—and seeks to correct omissions that affect scholarly interpretations. Throughout he attempts to compare Schiller's thought to contemporary philosophy, and he reports on Schiller's conversations with Gadamer and Habermas in an appendix that treats Schiller's reception in the 20th century. Because of its many suggestions for new understandings, use of sources, close textual analysis, and redirection of scholarly attention to hitherto neglected elements of interdependence between Schiller's publications—and despite any exception readers may take to individual arguments—this book is a necessary addition to the bookshelves of all students of Schiller, casual and expert alike.—*E. Glass, Rosemont College*

OAB-0873 Orig
Münsterer, Hanns Otto. **The young Brecht,** tr. with introd. by Tom Kuhn and Karen J. Leeder. Libris, 1992. 195p bibl index ISBN 1-870352-73-4, $35.00

Münsterer's book first appeared in 1963 was *Bert Brecht: Erinnerungen aus den Jahren 1917-22*. The title of this translation suggests the expansion of material that the translators are making available to the English reader. Not only have they translated Münsterer's memoirs, but have compiled a thorough biography for Brecht to about 1924, the time Brecht began to establish himself in the literary life of Berlin. They have accomplished this by translating and summarizing passages from about 30 other works dealing with Brecht's early years. Münsterer's 1963 book was important for the light it shed on Brecht's formative period in Augsburg, but this present volume with the latest available information unknown in 1963 is more valuable than the original. Münsterer's intention to show the development of Brecht's personality in the turbulent times during and after WW I, when Brecht was trying to define himself as a writer, is more completely realized in this new book. Kuhn and Leeder's translations are excellent and their research, manifested in notes and appendixes, extremely informative. Valuable bibliography and index. Undergraduate; graduate; researchers; general.—*R. C. Conard, University of Dayton*

OAB-0874 PT2625 94-44522 CIP
Prater, Donald. **Thomas Mann: a life.** Oxford, 1995. 554p bibl indexes afp ISBN 0-19-815861-0, $35.00

This new biography by the author of the acclaimed *A Ringing Glass: The*

Life of Rainer Maria Rilke (CH, Dec'86) will interest not only Mann scholars but all who are interested in intellectual and literary history. Mann is the best that 20th-century German literature (considered separately from the Austrian world of Kafka and Musil) has to offer. His stature—both as the creator of *Buddenbrooks, The Magic Mountain*, and *Doctor Faustus*, novels that have enormously influenced non-Germans' understanding of the German character, and as a cultural symbol comparable in the 20th century to Goethe in the 19th—overshadows the achievements of all his literary countrymen. A Nobel prize winner, Mann was a courageous opponent of the Nazi regime and was forced into exile because of his views. Precisely because Mann was in effect a cultural icon, an intellectual and moral force, it is important that scholars now have a painstaking and thorough depiction of his life and of those around him, in particular of his family members, all of whom in various ways basked in his glory but also suffered his notorious self-centeredness. The children (Michael, Klaus, Erika, Golo) also clearly suffered from his artistic sensibility, his analytical, cool, yet also highly vulnerable psyche. Prater's portrayal is detailed but limited in that he does not analyze the relationship of the life to the works as much as one might expect and desire. This reviewer admires his fairly strict adherence to this plan, but still misses treatment of the works themselves. All college and university libraries.—*J. Hardin, University of South Carolina*

OAB-0875 PT2617 95-52417 CIP
Richards, David G. **Exploring the divided self: Hermann Hesse's** *Steppenwolf* and its critics. Camden House, 1996. 169p bibl index afp ISBN 1-879751-77-1, $54.95

Richards (SUNY College at Buffalo), whose intimacy with the voluminous Hesse inquests and erudite criticism is impressive, offers an authoritative overview of scholarship on Hesse's best-known novel in the US. His third and central chapter, "Hesse Scholarship in America," explains Hesse's high popularity in America, as first recognized especially by Joseph Mileck (*Hermann Hesse and His Critics*, 1958; *Hermann Hesse: Biography and Bibliography*, CH, Nov'77; *Hermann Hesse: Life and Art*, CH, Oct'78) and as deepened by prominent American Germanists like Theodore Ziolkowski, who wrote manifold critical treatises on Hesse during the 1960s. In chapter 4, "Development and Consolidation," Richards guides assimilation of Hesse criticism through the 1970s and 1980s, leading the reader to his correct observations in chapter 5 ("Metaphors, Symbols, and "Archtypes")") that the popular lay reader of Hesse was vastly better connected to the Jungian and oriental infrastructure of Hesse's thought than initially were critics and scholars. Though focused specifically on *Steppenwolf*, and in no sense a breakthrough in Hesse criticism, Richards's volume, with chapter endnotes and an appended list of Hesse works, clearly and concisely summarizes and accurately pinpoints the salient features of Hesse for contemporary students and scholars. It is suitable for involved Hesse enthusiasts at the upper-division undergraduate level and above.—*L. J. Rippley, St. Olaf College*

OAB-0876 PT2681 96-22223 CIP
Sebald, W.G. **The emigrants,** tr. by Michael Hulse. New Directions, 1996. 237p afp ISBN 0-8112-1338-2, $22.95

This may be the best piece of fiction writing to appear in Germany since unification. Originally published as *Die Ausgewanderten* (1993), the book immediately received several awards. German reviewers praised Sebald's style and sensitivity to history. Born in 1944 in Bavaria, Sebald has lived since 1970 in England. Because of the similarity between himself and his narrator, he is both author and subject of his stories. These four accounts/reports/reminiscences tell of extraordinary, ordinary people who left Germany in the 20th century. Three are about Jews who went to England or Switzerland—either in the 1930s or before WW I—die or commit suicide long after WW II, but who, nonetheless, are victims of the Holocaust. One is about the narrator's non-Jewish great uncle, who went to America at the turn of the century, led an adventuresome life, and died a horrible death in the 1950s. With delicate, refined prose, Sebald describes exterior and interior realities with such subtlety—and here one cannot praise the translator highly enough—that the reader is transported to new worlds of compassion and visual experience. The genre of this kind of writing does not yet have a name: it is a combination of fiction, biography, autobiography, history, diary, personal journal, and photo album with commentary—each story is replete with photos of the characters, their friends and relatives, their houses, and landscapes—all brought together in an effective modern-postmodern montage that leaves the reader stunned. Horace surely had writing like this in mind when he said literature should delight and educate. All collections.—*R. C. Conard, University of Dayton*

OAB-0877   PT3826   92-24804 CIP
The Vienna coffeehouse wits, 1890-1938, tr., ed., and introd. by Harold B. Segel. Purdue, 1993. 390p index afp ISBN 1-55753-033-5, $40.00

In a series of brilliant translations Segal (Columbia) makes one of the most important cultural institutions of prewar Europe, the Vienna coffeehouse, accessible to anglophone readers. Selections from major figures like Bahr, Kraus, Altenberg, Salten, and others enable the reader to grasp the social and literary issues (and gossip) that were hotly discussed by these predominately Jewish intellectuals. Both the failure of positivist liberalism and the appearance of literary modernism conspired to put turn-of-the-century Vienna in the vanguard of the modern era, bringing about what Segal calls the dismantling of larger bourgeois structures, which found expression in the impressionistic miniature, the so-called "small style" unique to these "coffeehouse wits" of which Peter Altenberg is the prime example. An informative introduction sketches the Turkish origins of the coffeehouse and describes in detail the more famous of them (Griensteidl, Central, etc.). Plentiful notes and bibliography. A must for anyone interested in European culture. Undergraduate; graduate; faculty.—*H. D. Dickerson, Georgia State University*

OAB-0878   Orig
Wedekind, Frank. **Plays: one: *Spring awakening: a children's tragedy; Lulu: a monster tragedy,*** tr. and introd. by Edward Bond and Elisabeth Bond-Pablé. Methuen Drama, 1993. (Dist. by Heinemann) 212p bibl ISBN 0-413-67540-8 pbk, $15.95

This is a very attractive new translation of Frank Wedekind's most important plays, with an elegant introduction by Elisabeth Bond-Pablé. The translations are by the British Marxist dramatist Edward Bond, who takes some liberties in making certain that Wedekind was not only the first *modern* dramatist, but also the most committed anti-capitalist. But, no amount of strident ideology can detract from the power of the translations. Wedekind's plays are grotesque, brutal, comedic, and in the best traditions of German Expressionism. The end of *Lulu: A Monster Tragedy* may be one of the most horrible moments in all of theater literature. Bond took the original manuscript, which eventually Wedekind divided into two plays, *Earth Spirit* and *Pandora's Box*. In this modern version the two works are joined into one five-act mega-play. It is a delight to have these masterpieces once again available in the paperback edition in English. Drama departments and German general education classes will rejoice. *Spring Awakening* remains Wedekind's most powerful theatrical work.—*S. Gittleman, Tufts University*

■ Romance

FRENCH

OAB-0879   PQ2543   91-26749 CIP
Berg, William J. **The visual novel: Emile Zola and the art of his times.** Pennsylvania State, 1993 (c1992). 308p bibl index afp ISBN 0-271-00826-1, $39.50

An in-depth study of the visual content of Zola's 20-volume *Les Rougon-Macquart* novels. One normally associates Zola almost exclusively with nat-

uralism, determinism, cause-and-effect, the experimental novel, and the Dreyfus Affair. The originality of this book is that it adds an extra, subtle dimension to Zola studies by focusing on vision and description. Berg cleverly details a link between the methods and theories of Zola and the techniques of such Impressionist painters as Manet, Renoir, and Pissarro. And he relates Zola's writings to those of other novelists of his time. This book is carefully documented and has a full bibliography of works by and about Zola and studies in the visual arts. It is of solid interest to students and researchers of art history, experimental psychology, and French literature of the late 19th century.—*J. C. McLaren, University of Delaware*

OAB-0880   PQ2603   96-34860 CIP
Bruns, Gerald L. **Maurice Blanchot: the refusal of philosophy.** Johns Hopkins, 1997. 339p indexes afp ISBN 0-8018-5471-7, $39.95

Bruns's landmark study illuminates not only Blanchot's complex oeuvre but the entire intellectual horizon of French thought during the last half of the 20th century. Bruns's greatest achievement is enabling readers to grasp the contemporaneity of Blanchot and to recognize the extent to which Blanchot's terms and issues have determined the thought of Derrida and Deleuze and have influenced contemporary transformations of the ideas of Nietzsche and Heidegger. Bruns (Univ. of Notre Dame) is particularly adept at explicating Blanchot's anarchic dimension, which unveils in the midst of everyday life the uncanny enigma of the origins of time and being, without—and this is the key to Blanchot—ever satisfying one's desire for a concrete image or a phenomenal expression of the ground of existence itself. Unlike Nietzsche, Blanchot steps cautiously back from the extravagance of rhetorical invention to an absolutely rigorous resistance of thinking what cannot be thought. Bruns's notion that "Blanchot is a thinker of painful discretion" is perfectly Blanchotian in expressing the tensed exactitude to which thinking is constrained in this post-Nietzschean, postmetaphysical epoch that Bruns calls (using an expression by Levinas) the epoch of the *entre-temps*, the in-between time. Bruns's book will certainly be a help to readers of Blanchot for many years to come. Upper-division undergraduate and up.—*N. Lukacher, University of Illinois at Chicago*

OAB-0881   PQ2625   96-27987 CIP
Cate, Curtis. **André Malraux: a biography.** Fromm International, 1997 (c1995). 451p bibl index ISBN 0-88064-171-1, $29.95

All lives have their mysteries, but the life of André Malraux has more than most. Many of the enigmas have been resolved in the pages of scholarly journals and books and in memoirs of Malraux's contemporaries, but until now no one has brought this material together. Cate has added to it numerous interviews with the people who knew the writer well, and produced a thoroughly engaging biography. One can easily point to Malraux the exhibitionist, the mythomane, the fraud who was qualified for few of the positions he talked himself into. But the author never allows the reader to forget that Malraux played these roles magnificently while making important contributions to the life and history of France, and that he had a significant impact on art criticism and wrote several masterpieces of fiction. Cate's biography leaves readers with the understanding that Malraux was not only a brilliant speaker, writer, soldier, and politician but also an entrancing human being. General readers, students, and specialists alike will find this an excellent book.—*A. H. Pasco, University of Kansas*

OAB-0882   PQ2047   96-12922 CIP
Cranston, Maurice. **The solitary self: Jean-Jacques Rousseau in exile and adversity.** Chicago, 1997. 247p index afp ISBN 0-226-11865-7, $29.95

This third and concluding installment of Rousseau's biography (v. 1, *Jean-Jacques Rousseau: The Early Life*, CH, Sep'93; v.2, *The Noble Savage: Jean-Jacques Rousseau*, CH, Dec'91) appears three years after Cranston's death. Cranston had completed all but one chapter and a few pages, which Sanford Lakoff assembled from Cranston's notes. A meticulous account of the years

1762 to 1778 (when Rousseau died), this nearly day-by-day reconstruction of his flight from Montmorency and life and tribulations in Môtiers and the Isle de St.-Pierre highlights his involvement in Genevan religious politics. The disfavor he attracted for his *Lettre à Christophe de Beaumont*, 1763, and *Lettres écrites de la montagne*, 1764, led to his renunciation of Genevan citizenship and expulsion from Switzerland. Of the competing invitations to offer him protection, David Hume's prevailed. After several months in England, Rousseau returned to France, where he lived mostly as a recluse composing his *Rèveries* and *Confessions*. Cranston's painstaking archival research and lucid style yield the most detailed and thoroughly documented biography of Rousseau written in English. His epilogue masterfully sums up Rousseau's importance as political philosopher and initiator of Romantic sensibilities. Appendixes provide a chronology, principal abbreviations, and copious notes. Upper-division undergraduates and up.—*D. A. Collins, Kalamazoo College*

OAB-0883   PQ2683   94-8400 CIP
Davis, Colin. **Elie Wiesel's secretive texts.** University Press of Florida, 1994. 201p bibl index afp ISBN 0-8130-1303-8, $34.95

This is a searching and searing analysis of Wiesel's works from the perspective of the paradox at the center of Holocaust literature: how to explore and explain an event that is beyond human articulation and human understanding. The focus of this analysis is on how narrative not only breaks down, but how, in its structure, it embodies the process of the breakdown, refusing narrative closure by emphasizing the inability to achieve it. Making use of narrative theory primarily based on Frank Kermode, this study looks at textual hesitations and indeterminacies found in the fiction in order to support the thesis that writings on the Holocaust must embody narrative destruction in order paradoxically to convey some meaning of an event that lies beyond meaning. Davis takes issue with those critics who find narrative cohesion and moral development flowing through the still expanding body of Wiesel's work, especially his fiction. Instead he sees only a presumption of order in the early work, replaced by more recent writings that foreground lacunae as part of the experience being narratively conveyed. As a French scholar, Davis adds a rich stylistic criticism, useful, as is the entire study, for many of us who read Weisel always in translation. In the words of Shoshana Felman, Wiesel's task is to "let madness speak, to restore its language" (*La Folie et la chose littéraire*, 1978). A powerful reading of Wiesel's oeuvre: highly recommended to upper-division undergraduates and up.—*B. Adler, Valdosta State University*

OAB-0884   PQ1483   93-1095 CIP
Guillaume, de Machaut. **The fountain of love (La fonteinne amoureuse) and two other love vision poems,** ed. and tr. by R. Barton Palmer. Garland, 1993. 251p afp (Garland library of medieval literature, 54A) English and French (Old French). ISBN 0-8240-8781-X, $52.00

This work is concerned with two love vision poems of Guillaume de Machaut: *Story of the Orchard (Dit dou vergier)* and *The Book of the Fountain of Love (Livre de la fonteinne amoureuse)*, and the *Prologue*. Palmer provides a useful summary of Guillaume's life and work. The important roles played in Guillaume's life by Jean de Luxembourg and Jean de Berri are shown. In turn, Guillaume's influence on Deschamps, Christine de Pisan, and Chaucer is pointed out. Importantly, the editing of Guillaume's verses is entirely appropriate, giving us a clear reading of the text as close to the original as possible. Palmer's translation into English appearing on facing pages is faithful to the original, reads very well, and is excellent in all respects. The work is not burdened with unncessary notes and variants. The bibliography is extensive and most useful. This presentation of text and translation constitutes a model for medieval texts. The printing and paper are of excellent quality; the binding less so. Upper-division undergraduate and up.—*J. E. Parker Jr., Wake Forest University*

OAB-0885   PQ3919   92-28961 CIP
Hesse, M.G. **Yves Thériault, master storyteller.** P. Lang, 1993. 182p bibl index afp (American university studies. Series II, romance languages and literature, 145) ISBN 0-8204-1322-4, $39.95

This study is "an analytical and critical introduction to Thériault's major works" (preface) and is the first such study of this versatile "giant of Québecois literature," whose body of work embraces short stories, plays, novels, radio-TV drama, and articles. Hesse has drawn both his work and the writer himself into a unified whole, producing this basic, well-organized, scholarly, and comprehensive study. A biography and a chapter on "tradition and milieu" place Thériault in the context of his time—political, social, literary—and lead into a chapter on Thériault and his critics, preparation for the following chapters constituting a study of his major works. Grouping these according to themes (the "outsider," the struggle between two cultures, and a vision of Canada's native peoples, the Inuits and the Indians) and incorporating essential narrative details, Hesse skillfully analyzes themes, characters, and relationship to Thériault's own approach and primary talent as *conteur*. Her clear, readable style and substantial documentation enhance the value of her study. Chronological table, bibliography of primary and secondary sources, helpful notes and references for each chapter. A "must" for college and university libraries and those public libraries with Canadian literature holdings. Advanced undergraduate; graduate; faculty; general.—*M. H. Nachtsheim, emeritus, The College of St. Catherine*

OAB-0886   PN1995   95-15226 CIP
Higgins, Lynn A. **New novel, new wave, new politics: fiction and the representation of history in postwar France.** Nebraska, 1996. 259p index afp ISBN 0-8032-2377-3, $40.00

Higgins (Dartmouth College), author of *Parables of Theory: Jean Ricardou's Metafiction* (1984), has written an important book. With its perceptive analysis of works by Duras, Malle, Robbe-Grillet, Simon, and Truffaut, the volume will serve as an excellent resource for courses in literature and film; it should, however, also be read by those interested in contemporary French society. Higgins posits that, beyond their "shared écriture," the "new novel" and New Wave have in common an interest in the workings of historiography. She shows how the "retreat into formalism" may be attributed to the censorship of the early 1960s, when France was fighting its war of decolonization in Algeria. Higgins analyzes the May '68 crisis in France for "what it made it possible to say." Finally, she tackles the discourse on WW II, emphasizing the issue of personal responsibility. She looks at France's "murky role" in the war and the obstacle to reflection posed by the "official myth of the Resistance." Her extensive notes reveal that Higgins has read widely in politics, psychoanalysis, and history as well as in literature and film theory. Her prose remains, nonetheless, thoroughly accessible through the use of concrete examples and the avoidance of jargon. No comparable study exists. A must for all academic collections.—*A. M. Rea, Occidental College*

OAB-0887   PQ2605   92-28589 CIP
Huffer, Lynne. **Another Colette: the question of gendered writing.** Michigan, 1992. 194p bibl index ISBN 0-472-10307-5, $37.50

Other recent volumes on Colette (at least ten over the past ten years) have covered some of the same topics: maternal and paternal models, sexuality, and the sewing trope. Nicole Ward Jouve, in her 1987 *Colette* (CH, Feb'88), used some of the same theoretical sources. No other study, however, compares in the prodigious scope of research on Colette, feminism, and poststructuralist theory. Huffer (Yale), like her subject, is "hyperbolically intertextual," as revealed by her notes and bibliography, which constitute more than one fifth of the text. The extensive notes allow Huffer to expand on her revisionary reading of Colette's "subjectivity as gendered textual form," to suggest future projects, and, at times, to disagree with prominent critical figures. The book also includes in its dense analysis of Colette's narrative strategies some sensitive explications of well-chosen passages. The metaphorical point of view adopted by Huffer proves Colette a far more conscious and complex artist than generally thought. Advanced undergraduates with a grounding in literary theory will discover in this book, which only rarely succumbs to jargon, a model of analysis and research, and a stellar example of dissertation revision, sharply focused, benefiting from the maturity brought by reading and reflection beyond the PhD. A must for Colette scholars. Highly recommended.—*A. M. Rea, Occidental College*

OAB-0888 PQ1860 95-32324 CIP

Lalande, Roxanne Decker. **Intruders in the play world: the dynamics of gender in Molière's comedies.** Fairleigh Dickinson, 1996. (Dist. by Associated University Presses) 231p bibl index afp ISBN 0-8386-3592-X, $37.50

In this seminal study, Lalande (Lafayette College) promises to address a pressing need: an interpretation of Molière from a feminist perspective. Inspired by the work of Johan Huizinga, the author frames gender issues within a theory of comedy as ludic activity. Here comedy becomes the site of a "play world," a retreat from social and ethical reality. Lalande argues convincingly that this play world, like its empirical correlate, is patriarchal and based on the marginalization of threatening feminine Otherness. These observations ground the most impressive insights of the study. Lalande's discussion of the stakes and dynamics of gender persuasively establish models of feminine exclusion/empowerment and a typology of feminine Otherness in Molière's comedy. She draws from currents in contemporary feminist thought that have resulted from an interrogation and displacement of major concepts of psychoanalytic theory. Regrettably, many of these are not explicitly presented, contextualized, and problematized: for example, some discussion of the imaginary, the symbolic, and the real—concepts central to most of Lalande's work—would have helped situate and elucidate her argument. (Surprisingly, there is no bibliographic entry for Lacan.) But this is one minor flaw in a remarkable performance. Lalande's study will undoubtedly find its place among the important works on feminine alterity in Molière and in the comic sphere.—*E. R. Koch, Tulane University*

OAB-0889 PQ1877 95-18795 CIP

Lewis, Philip. **Seeing through the Mother Goose tales: visual turns in the writings of Charles Perrault.** Stanford, 1996. 300p bibl index afp ISBN 0-8047-2410-5, $39.50

This pathbreaking work tackles the challenging thought of Charles Perrault and discovers the important underlying unity of the works of this prominent 17th-century intellectual, propagandist of monarchy, advocate of the moderns, and author of the *Contes*. The first part of the study examines Perrault's compendious writings on thought, aesthetics, and language. Lewis traces Perrault's resistances, appropriations, and displacements of the concepts of such writers as Descartes, Boileau, and Racine and establishes in Perrault a practice of compromise grounded in the priority accorded to visual representation. The second part of the study is made up of rich interpretations of Perrault's tales through the optic established in part 1; that is, the troping of ideas and language into images and visualizations. This remarkable and important study reclaims Perrault from folklorists and formalists for 17th century studies. It is a landmark work that presents both a new vision of 17th-century intellectual history and also important new readings of Perrault's tales. Upper-division undergraduates and above.—*E. R. Koch, Tulane University*

OAB-0890 PQ145 95-9627 CIP

Marks, Elaine. **Marrano as metaphor: the Jewish presence in French writing.** Columbia, 1996. 187p bibl index afp ISBN 0-231-10308-5, $24.50

In this provocative and timely book, Marks (Univ. of Wisconsin) uses history, literary theory, and psychoanalysis to "take note of a Jewish presence without establishing a rigid Jewish difference." She examines a wide range of authors—from Garnier and Racine to Cohen and Derrida—to demonstrate the inevitability of intertexuality and assimilation in literary texts. Marks views this "contamination" as a positive condition, for it opens up the space of the "Marrano," the metaphor she has chosen to express the value of multiple identities. (Marrano is the name Christians gave to Jews in Medieval Spain who converted to Christianity in order to escape persecution, but who remained faithful to Judaism.) Commenting on "the acceptance of being Jewish and being assimilated, of being Jewish and ... being other(s) at the same time," she provides intelligent and meticulous readings that deftly illustrate the links between antisemitism, misogyny, homophobia, and the "death of God." At the same time, the book is a passionate and persuasive attempt to complicate simplistic notions of identity politics. For example, in a fas-

cinating chapter on the critical reception of Renée Vivien, Marks shows how Charles Maurras's fear of lesbianism and Gayle Rubin's welcoming of it both betray an essentializing and exclusionary vision. The book is beautifully written and compelling. Marks's arguments will likely be controversial, but no one can deny their power to captivate and challenge the reader. Upper-division undergraduate and up.—*G. Moskos, Swarthmore College*

OAB-0891 PQ307 95-48082 CIP

Mehlman, Jeffrey. **Genealogies of the text: literature, psychoanalysis, and politics in modern France.** Cambridge, 1995. 262p index (Cambridge studies in French, 54) ISBN 0-521-42713-X, $59.95

This dazzling exercise in political and ideological criticism combines recondite scholarship and an esoteric style in pursuit of a polemical and controversial argument. Mehlman's central concern is with the structure of repetition as it relates to the clandestine survival of antisemitism and fascism in contemporary French thought. His ultimate goal is to undermine the cultural currency of French theory in America, specifically Derridian deconstruction, by unearthing its covert historical debt to the reactionary tradition in French letters from Sainte-Beuve and Edouard Drumont to Léon Bloy, Paul Morand, Jean Paulhan, and, especially, Maurice Blanchot and Paul de Man. For Mehlman, those who fail to denounce the fascists are as pernicious as the fascists themselves. This book puts some very remarkable scholarship in the service of a very mistaken thesis, for Mehlman can denounce deconstruction only by presuming to collapse its philosophical issues into the singular historical referent of Nazism. Despite its somewhat paranoid anxiety about the underlying menace of deconstruction, this book offers numerous valuable insights into the historical horizon of French modernism. Although the argument is reductive, Mehlman's illumination of a wide range of texts and issues—from Sainte-Beuve's politics to Blanchot's secret political mythography and the hidden agenda of de Man's readings of Hugo—makes this book an authoritative and indispensable contribution to the study of modern French culture.—*N. Lukacher, University of Illinois at Chicago*

OAB-0892 Can. CIP

Paterson, Janet M. **Postmodernism and the Quebec novel,** tr. by David Homel and Charles Phillips. Toronto, 1994. 167p bibl index afp ISBN 0-8020-0530-6, $35.00; ISBN 0-8020-6968-1 pbk, $14.95

Paterson (Univ. of Toronto), author of the excellent *Anne Hébert: architexture romanesque* (in French, 1985) and articles on French and Quebec writers, has written another important book. This smooth English translation of her *Moments postmodernes dans le roman québécois* (1990, rev. 1993) makes the analysis available to a deservedly wider readership. The first two chapters present introductory materials on postmodernism. Eminently readable because of their clarity of expression, subdivisions with subject headings, and use of thought-provoking questions, these two chapters should be recommended reading for all students (and faculty) confused by the jargon-filled profusion of commentary on postmodernism. Paterson surveys the major theorists and their divergent positions, acknowledging special indebtedness to Jean-François Lyotard. For detailed analysis, she has chosen six texts published by male and female authors (Aquin, Bessette, Brossard, Godbout, Ouellette-Michalska, and Villemaire) between 1968 and 1987. Paterson stresses a different postmodern strategy in each chapter, including intertextuality, self-representation, and the legitimation of history. From time to time, she suggests topics to explore further. Although she concludes that "the word 'postmodern' remains vague, ambiguous, and often problematic," her study is a model of lucidity. No comparable volume exists. A must for understanding recent Quebecois fiction and, because of the first two chapters, for all good undergraduate humanities collections.—*A. M. Rea, Occidental College*

OAB-0893 PQ2178 94-18614 CIP

Robb, Graham. **Balzac: a life.** W.W. Norton, 1994. 521p bibl indexes ISBN 0-393-03679-0, $35.00

In this superb new biography of Honoré de Balzac (1799-1850), the great

French novelist's life appears as irrepressible and electric as that of any of his characters. The familiar tale, told here with sympathy, frankness, and admirable insight, gains in dramatic impact and psychological veracity. The emotional and intellectual growth of the sensitive child in Tours and Vendôme; the maturing writer's exhilarating discovery of the building-block structure of his *Human Comedy*; the ceaseless stream of predicaments faced by the son, lover, father, debtor, public figure, and artist in an era of profound social, economic, and political change—all of these elements in Balzac's biography are evoked by means of telling detail and with due attention to ambiguities. The story inexorably leads to the final trip in 1848 to the Ukraine, Eveline Hanska's decision to marry an ill and debt-ridden man, and their return to Paris and Balzac's gruesome death, unflinchingly related, from what was diagnosed as cardiac hypertrophy. Robb writes throughout with incisiveness and flair; his is a most judicious use of painstaking research. Anyone interested in Balzac will relish this book. Indeed, its publication makes a compelling case for a needed new English translation of Balzac's complete works. Academic and general audiences.—*J. Dargan, St. Lawrence University*

OAB-0894   PQ471   92-44197 CIP
Scott, Clive. **Reading the rhythm: the poetics of French free verse, 1910-1930.** Oxford, 1993. 290p bibl index afp ISBN 0-19-815882-3, $52.00

American students of modern French literature generally prefer to study the novel or theater, rather than poetry. This is especially true of undergraduates. Since the triumph of modernism, poetry (like art and music) is often seen as difficult to understand, and therefore to appreciate. The present study is a powerful, useful, and effective antidote to this condition, for it uses several linguistic concepts, combined with close readings and explications, to explain what free verse is, how it came to be developed, and how it functions. It focuses on works from the period 1910-30 but reaches back to the origins of free verse in the late 19th century to make its case. It is especially useful in resurrecting and making accessible the poetry of Blaise Cendrars, who is not as widely read in the English-speaking world as the other poets studied here—Saint-John Perse, Apollinaire, Supervielle, and Reverdy. In a day when university presses still largely shy away from publishing books that can be read by non-specialists, this study is a delightful surprise. Rigorously intelligent and clearly argued, it is a work that every college library should own.—*D. O'Connell, Georgia State University*

OAB-0895   PQ245   95-52449 CIP
Stone, Harriet. **The classical model: literature and knowledge in seventeenth-century France.** Cornell, 1996. 234p bibl index afp ISBN 0-8014-3212-X, $39.95

Simply(-istically) stated, this study deals with "lies" that reveal, if not truth, then an enriched version of knowledge exceeding what science and history, however objective, can deliver. Fiction and other forms of literature have long fought for their place within epistemological respectability. With Michel Foucault's *Les mots et les choses* (1st American ed., *The Order of Things*, 1971) as her point of departure, Stone (Washington University in St. Louis) seeks to demonstrate the enlarging effect of framing, ordering, patterning, and representing in Rotrou's *Saint Genest*, Corneille's *Horace*, Racine's *Phèdre, Andromaque*, and *Bérénice*, Molière's *Amphitryon*, La Rochefoucauld's *Maximes*, Madame de Lafayette's *Princesse de Clèves*, Descartes's *Discours de la méthode*, and Pascal's *Pensées*. The ostensible content of several of these works—while often reinforcing an authoritarian image of the monarch, Louis XIV—is nonetheless challenged, in *Phècre* for example, by the complete discomfiture of the authority figure, Thésée, even as he preserves his power. The "classical model" of the title valorizes the role of the literature of this period as both an encoding and decoding influence on the implicit messages of the texts and thus establishes literature as a vital part of an epistemological evolution. A brilliantly argued study. Upper-division undergraduate and above.—*D. A. Collins, Kalamazoo College*

OAB-0896   PQ2613   93-18234 CIP
White, Edmund. **Genet: a biography.** Knopf, 1993. 728p index ISBN 0-394-57171-1, $35.00

This will probably remain for a long time the definitive English-language biography of the French writer Jean Genet. White traces out in meticulous detail a life that began as an abandoned child, was spent in wandering about Europe and in numerous incarcerations for petty crimes, was then given over to writing novels and plays, and ended with Genet's eccentric identification with the cause of the Palestinians. Underscoring Genet's homosexuality, White gives a detailed record of the writer's encounters and affairs, as well as account of his usually troubled relations with the world of French letters. This is not a brilliant work like Jean-Paul Sartre's *Saint Genet* (1963), but it is an accurate and complete account of the details of the life of a criminal who was also one of the most interesting writers that 20th-century France has produced. White has undertaken the task of correcting both Sartre's tale of Genet's "choice" to be a criminal and a homosexual, and Genet's own autobiographical presentations in his poeticized fictions of himself. The scholar of modern French fiction will find this useful, and the general reader may well be fascinated by this story of the latest of French *poètes maudits*. Moreover, enthusiasts of modern theater will find interest in the story of the creation of such now modern classics for the stage as *The Maids* or *The Blacks*; and for readers wishing to see Genet's work in context, White's work also offers a fair amount of social history. Recommended for all libraries.—*A. Thiher, University of Missouri—Columbia*

ITALIAN

OAB-0897   PQ4315   95-12740 CIP
Dante Alighieri. **The *Divine comedy* of Dante Alighieri: v.1: Inferno,** ed. and tr. by Robert M. Durling; introd. and notes by Ronald L. Martinez and Robert M. Durling. Oxford, 1996. 654p bibl indexes afp ISBN 0-19-508740-2, $39.95

This outstanding parallel-text edition of Dante's masterpiece (*Purgatorio* and *Paradiso* will appear shortly) jumps straight to the head of a crowded field. Durling (Univ. of California, Santa Cruz) and Martinez (Univ. of Minnesota) provide Giorgio Petrocchi's standard text, an accurate and readable English prose translation carefully keyed to the terzine of the Italian original, a concise but thorough introduction to Dante's life and work, and remarkably comprehensive and up-to-date footnotes to individual cantos. Together with the more detailed "Additional Notes," which conclude the volume, this annotative material forms by far the most substantial help currently available to English-speaking readers of Dante. Although, being in prose, the translation itself does not aim to compete with recent versions by practicing poets such as John Ciardi, C.H. Sisson, Allen Mandelbaum, and Robert Pinsky, it is of consistently high quality; and the coverage of this modern edition as a whole should definitely replace not only J.D. Sinclair's fondly remembered but antiquated version (1961) but even the idiosyncratic and generally overrated contribution of Charles S. Singleton (1970-75). Enthusiastically recommended for all general and academic collections.—*S. Botterill, University of California, Berkeley*

OAB-0898   PQ4174   94-16037 CIP
Dombroski, Robert S. **Properties of writing: ideological discourse in modern Italian fiction.** Johns Hopkins, 1995 (c1994). 204p index afp ISBN 0-8018-4919-5, $32.50

Dombroski's critical volume is an elegantly written, engrossing exploration of milestones in the history of Italian prose fiction. Each of the nine chronologically ordered essays focuses on a major writer and fundamental text(s), analyzing authorial strategies and siting these within a sociohistorical context. Theoretically, Dombroski is applying the concepts of ideological criticism, stressing the importance of history and belief systems informing a writer's literary perceptions and values. His goal is to demonstrate the interrelationship of sociohistorical forces, rhetorical models and conventions, and individual literary strategies in producing a fictional text. The aesthetic properties of writing are called on, Dombroski suggests, to render an ideological discourse or to engage in the construction of reality for the reader. Whether discussing Lampedusa's metaliterary dimension or Svevo's reified capitalist world, each of Dombroski's essays is thought-provoking, lucid, well documented, and richly textured. An excellent contribution to literary studies for upper-division undergraduates and above.—*F. A. Bassanese, University of Massachusetts at Boston*

OAB-0899 PQ4295 95-43882 CIP
Forni, Pier Massimo. **Adventures in speech: rhetoric and narration in Boccaccio's *Decameron*.** Pennsylvania, 1996. 155p bibl index afp ISBN 0-8122-3338-7, $29.95

This deceptively slim but substantial volume is an outstanding contribution to an area of *Decameron* criticism that, in English at least, remains comparatively undernourished: the rhetorical. Forni (Johns Hopkins Univ.) has already achieved distinction with studies of Boccaccian narrative and rhetoric published in Italian (most notably *Forme complesse nel Decameron*, 1992). This book both introduces the important medievalist critic to monoglot English speakers and extends his earlier analysis in a number of interesting directions. It is divided into three sections: "The Rhetoric of Selection and Response"; "The Rhetoric of Beginnings"; and "Rhetoric and Imagination." A two-page afterword and a slightly tangential appendix, "Horror of Incest and Seduction of Literature in Boccaccio's *Decameron*," conclude the volume. Forni's book is distinguished throughout by its sensitive attention to Boccaccio's text, the clarity of its argument, and the ease and efficacy with which the author moves among a wide range of primary and secondary writings, from Boccaccio's classical and medieval sources to contemporary literary and rhetorical theory. A notable achievement, recommended for collections in Italian literature and medieval studies serving upper-division undergraduates and up.—*S. Botterill, University of California, Berkeley*

OAB-0900 PQ4809 91-33692 CIP
Hume, Kathryn. **Calvino's fictions: cogito and cosmos.** Oxford, 1992. 212p bibl index ISBN 0-19-815184-5, $49.95

This very handsomely produced study offers a comprehensive reading of Calvino's literary universe. Hume, a professor of English, comes to her view of Calvino in part as a result of her dissatisfaction with the dominant lines established by Italian criticism, in part because of direct encouragement from Calvino himself. The book proceeds nonchronologically through a number of early and later works, seeking always to bring out three fundamental assumptions: that fantasy is a legitimate mode for exploring ideas; that fantasy does not preclude moral seriousness; and that realism and fantasy are not competing or clashing forces in Calvino's fiction, but rather work together—in different balances—throughout his career. Two other basic elements are Calvino's concern with the Cartesian *cogito* and his love for pattern and form or what might be called his "cosmic" impulse. Very well researched and eloquently expounded, this study is an excellent synthesis of other critical views and a valuable new contribution to the understanding of one of this century's most important writers. Hume makes useful connections between critical and theoretical work of a general nature and the specific contours of Calvino's writing, as well as maintaining a productive dialogue with Calvino scholarship. Recommended to academic libraries as an important addition to Calvino studies.—*R. West, University of Chicago*

OAB-0901 PQ4050 94-21998 CIP
Kirkpatrick, Robin. **English and Italian literature from Dante to Shakespeare: a study of source, analogue and divergence.** Longman, 1995. 328p bibl index ISBN 0-582-06558-5 pbk, $25.95

The history of the literary affiliation between England and Italy is surely one of the most interesting in all of literary history. This volume in the new "Longman Medieval and Renaissance Library" series covers the early and richest phase of this history brilliantly. For the most part the Italian example predominates, but by the end of the 16th century English writers were increasingly conscious

of their own abilities. Kirkpatrick (Univ. of Cambridge) chronicles the response of English intellectuals to the Italian experience of civic life and carefully describes the transformation of Italian originals into their new English guise. Both major and minor writers are discussed, and all the important genres—lyric, epic, comedy, pastoral—are viewed in their historical and cultural context. The author presents not only the fact of Italian history but the myth of Italy as it seized and colored the imaginations of English writers. New and provoking aperçus abound, both literary and linguistic, on such disparate matters as Wyatt's poetic imitation of Ariosto's prose *Penitential Psalms* and the connection of Desdemona in Shakespeare's *Othello* with Dante's Beatrice. This is an excellent, accessible account of this period, designed for university students, upper-division undergraduates and above, and the general reader.—*C. Fantazzi, University of Windsor*

OAB-0902 PQ4392 92-5839 CIP
Mazzotta, Giuseppe. **Dante's vision and the circle of knowledge.** Princeton, 1993. 328p bibl index afp ISBN 0-691-06966-2, $37.50

This erudite and demanding study of the epistemological vision of Dante's *Divine Comedy* is conceived as a "companion volume" to its author's earlier *Dante, Poet of the Desert* (CH, Feb'80) but requires no detailed knowledge of its predecessor. Mazzotta (Yale Univ.) sets out, by means of close readings of individual cantos and by pursuing key themes—sacrifice, justice, logic, power, imagination, language, vision, poetry, exile, order—across the whole poem (especially *Paradiso*), "to explore Dante's radical claims about poetry as nothing less than the foundation of all possible knowledge." His audacious argument, though inevitably open to challenge on some points of detail, is ultimately compelling, and the book is unquestionably among the most significant readings of the *Comedy* to appear in recent years. Because of the vast range of Mazzotta's learning and his occasionally idiosyncratic style, this is a book that requires much of its readers; but it will be indispensable for serious collections in Italian literature and medieval studies. For faculty, graduate students, and—perhaps—adventurous undergraduates.—*S. Botterill, University of California at Berkeley*

OAB-0903 PQ4829 92-41153 CIP
Montale, Eugenio. **Cuttlefish bones: (1920-1927),** tr. by William Arrowsmith. W.W. Norton, 1993 (c1992). 269p English and Italian. ISBN 0-393-02803-8, $25.00

With the publication of Arrowsmith's translation of Montale's first book of poetry, *Cuttlefish Bones*, English-language readers now have the opportunity to enjoy the greatness of the Montalian "trilogy" (the second volume, *The Occasions*, CH, Dec'88, and the third, *The Storm and Other Things*, CH, Jun'86, appeared in Arrowsmith's renderings before his premature death in 1992). As is true of all of Arrowsmith's translations, this is a distillation and a recombination of the essence of Montale's difficult voice in a language that is quite congenial to his "anti-musicality," his willful "harshness," and his search, like Eliot, for objective correlatives rather than lyrical effusion. The translations are themselves important interpretations and commentaries on the originals, accompanied as well by copious and thoughtful critical notes that open out the complexities, challenges, and beauties of this verse. Although directed primarily to nonspecialist readers (and therefore not fitted out with bibliographical, philological, or historical information), this volume nonetheless holds great value for scholars of Montale as well, for it makes one hear again and anew the poems that by now have become part of a cultural "collective unconscious," so deeply and widely do they permeate subsequent Italian lyric. A major achievement, indispensable for academic libraries and for the private libraries of all readers for whom poetry continues to matter.—*R. West, University of Chicago*

OAB-0904 PN56 96-18284 CIP
Pike, David L. **Passage through hell: modernist descents, medieval underworlds.** Cornell, 1997. 292p bibl index afp ISBN 0-8014-3163-8, $37.50

A new approach to Dante's epic poem is always welcome, especially when (as the author admits in the preface) it is an "attempt to escape from the morass of competing claims to formalism on the one hand and historical relevance on the other." Pike (American Univ.) reviews Dante's poem in the light of both earlier works and modern literary texts. The footnotes reflect the author's wide sweep of interests. Chapter headings mirror his special approach to the subject: e.g., "'The Bataille du Styx': Céline's Allegory of Conversion"; "... Descent into Modernity: Peter Weiss's *Welttheater*"; "The Gender of Descent ... Christine de Pizan and the Topoi of Descent"; "'Romps of Fancy': Virginia Woolf, Turf Battles, and the Metaphorics of Descent"; "... Benjamin's Descent into the City of Light"; "... Beyond a Modernism of Reading: Heaney and Walcott." A useful bibliography and index add to this compelling study of the first great epic in the Italian vernacular. Some scholars may find Pike's handling of the subject arbitrary, personal even; but in its rich sampling of modern texts, this volume in fact provides fresh insights that can only add to the reader's appreciation of Dante's great poem. All academic collections.—*A. Paolucci, formerly, St. John's University (NY)*

SPANISH

OAB-0905   PQ6176   92-12099 CIP
Barnstone, Willis. **Six masters of the Spanish sonnet: Francisco De Quevedo, Sor Juana Inés De La Cruz, Antonio Machado, Federico García Lorca, Jorge Luis Borges, Miguel Hernández: essays and translations.** Southern Illinois, 1993. 311p bibl index afp ISBN 0-8093-1772-9, $24.95

Barnstone is justly renowned for his excellent translations, and he offers here some of his very best work. Focusing on his "obsession with a persistent anachronism," he traces in lively fashion the fate of the sonnet from the 17th to the 20th century in the Hispanic world. The elegant essays that precede the translations are a pleasure to read, from the scholarly introduction that leads the reader from Dante and Petrarch to the Marquess of Santillana and on, by way of Garcilaso, Fray Luis de León and Góngora, to Quevedo's raw and bawdy satire, Sor Juana Inés de la Cruz's articulate feminism, Antonio Machado's meditative austerity, García Lorca's poems of "dark love," Miguel Hernández's visceral surrealism, and Jorge Luis Borges's wry and cultivated eloquence. Erudite but never pedantic, Barnstone shows an enthusiasm that is as infectious as his style is engaging. Perhaps Quevedo and Borges are best served, but all are treated with admirable lucidity and genuine appreciation. The translations are pure magic: texture, diction, rhyme, and meter conspire to captivate the English reader as the Spanish originals have enchanted their primary audiences. General; advanced undergraduate; graduate; faculty.—*K. M. Sibbald, McGill University*

OAB-0906   PQ7797   91-45154 CIP
Barnstone, Willis. **With Borges on an ordinary evening in Buenos Aires: a memoir.** Illinois, 1993. 198p bibl index afp ISBN 0-252-01888-5, $27.50

Borges emerges alive from the pages of this book, written by a man who had the privilege of being his close friend and of sharing with him interesting experiences during difficult moments of Argentine politics. Barnstone's reminiscences begin in 1968 when he first met Borges in New York; but the bulk of the book deals with their conversations from 1975 to 1977, when he was a Fulbright professor in Buenos Aires, and continues later with their many days together—in the company of M. Kodame—in New York, Chicago, Bloomington, Cambridge, up to 1983. The last chapter is devoted to JLB's close working relation and friendship with María Kodama and—through A. Kerrigan's and A. Cara-Walker's accounts—to Borges's final months and his marriage to María. The product of mature scholarship and a thorough knowledge of JLB's works, this memoir includes conversations, biographical anecdotes, translations of JLB's poetry, literary analysis, and descriptions of places important in JLB's life. Barnstone's sensitive presentation of JLB's public and private persona provides valuable insights into the writer's aesthetics, philosophy, political views, linguistic interests, sense of humor, and devotion to friendship. Among the large number of books about Borges, this is really an outstanding one. Highly recommended for all libraries.—*J. A. Hernandez, Hood College*

OAB-0907   PQ7081   93-37750 CIP
The Cambridge history of Latin American literature: v.1: Discovery to modernism; v.2: The twentieth century; v.3: Brazilian literature; bibliographies, ed. by Roberto González Echevarría and Enrique Pupo-Walker. Cambridge, 1996. 3v. 670, 619, 864p bibl index ISBN 0-521-34069-1, v.1; ISBN 0-521-34070-5, v.2; ISBN 0-521-41035-5, v.3; $90.00 ea.

Most literary histories are at best adequate to their commitments. Not so this exceptional three-volume history of Latin American literature, which in fact surpasses its goals. The "General Preface" (helpfully included in each volume) sets forth the scope, methodology, and scholarly precepts that guided this long-overdue work. More than 40 scholars on three continents collaborated on what is without doubt the most comprehensive treatment to date of this subject. Its more than 2,000 pages cover topics ranging from the pre-Columbian era to the late 20th century. Chapters deal with matters as current as the Spanish American novel (1975-90) and include subjects not usually encountered in a history of Latin American literature (e.g., literary criticism, the autobiographical narrative, Chicano literature, and the novel of the Mexican revolution). The editors have added an interdisciplinary dimension to their work by incorporating the materials and methodologies proper to history. One notes some unevenness in the individual chapters both in quality and length; essays range from seven pages to more than 60. The inclusion of Brazilian literature here, not as a literature apart but as a legitimate component of the greater corpus of the continent's letters, in an indisputable contribution. Despite some inconsistency in its format, the 450-page bibliography is a definite plus. Congratulations to contributors, editors, and publishers on what will become a classic in the field. All academic libraries serving upper-division undergraduates and above.—*F. Colecchia, Duquesne University*

OAB-0908   PQ6085   93-36928 CIP
Debicki, Andrew P. **Spanish poetry of the twentieth century: modernity and beyond.** University Press of Kentucky, 1994. 261p bibl index afp (Studies in Romance languages, 37) ISBN 0-8131-1869-7, $29.95

Debicki succeeds admirably in his ambitious attempt to trace the evolution of Spanish poetry from 1915 to 1990. The major voices, their principal publications, and the salient Spanish language poetry magazines that appeared within that time frame are viewed in the context of the European poetic experience, and examined with lucid and compelling scholarship. This is a complex subject, and Debicki's achievement in presenting the most complete history under one cover of 20th-century Spanish poetry—written in the English language, including translated lines of verse—will enable his fellow scholars to clarify poetic trends, stylistic features, and avant-garde aesthetic currents prevalent during the 85-year period that his study covers. Debicki's thorough examination of the sweep of modern Spanish verse from the symbolist tradition to the postmodernists reaffirms the publisher's claim that this book "will be essential reading for specialists in modern Spanish letters, for advanced students, and for readers interested in comparative literature."—*D. R. McKay, University of Colorado at Colorado Springs*

OAB-0909   PQ7655   94-47196 CIP
Foster, David William. **Violence in Argentine literature: cultural responses to tyranny.** Missouri, 1995. 208p bibl index afp ISBN 0-8262-0991-2, $37.50

The bloody political and cultural repression that blighted Argentine society from 1976 to 1983—a period known as both the "Dirty War" and the "Process of National Reorganization"—forced writers who fled into exile and those who remained behind to come to literary terms with the turmoil. Foster's new book studies the prose fiction and drama produced during the full explosion of that national crisis and the few years leading up to and away from it. Foster's analytical approach is quite specific and elaborated in the precise terminology of a contemporary critical framework: author, narrator/metacharacter, character, addressee, and reader/viewer observe the tyranny as processed, "artified" experience. Because events treated in the book are so recent and his critical intent is so plainly on the side of postmodern literature as a display of the marginal and the synthesized, Foster (Arizona State Univ.) successfully balances the measured pace of academic exposition with breathless exposé: journalistic inquiry crowds into analytical discourse. Finally, Foster's explanation of "far-fetchedness" may offer a critical key for understanding Latin American texts that previously baffled readers with clumsy inconsistencies. Upper-division undergraduates; graduates; researchers.—*B. L. Lewis, Lyon College*

OAB-0910   PQ6356   95-16577 CIP

Gerli, E. Michael. **Refiguring authority: reading, writing, and rewriting in Cervantes.** University Press of Kentucky, 1995. 137p bibl index afp (Studies in Renaissance languages, 39) ISBN 0-8131-1922-7, $22.95

The guiding theme of Gerli's six essays is Cervantes's confrontation with the intertext. Looking at how Cervantes reads and then rewrites tradition, the author (Georgetown Univ.) focuses on *Don Quijote, El licenciado Vidriera, La gitanilla, El gallardo español,* and *El retablo de las maravillas.* Four of the chapters revise previously published work, but the grouping is effective and the transitions smooth. Gerli is an impressive close reader, and he presents the dialectics of established modes of writing and creative modifications with force and subtlety. His feeling that a text may offer "its own explicit instructions regarding its purpose and meaning" seems to undermine the inevitable inscription of recent critics, who tend to view explicitness as increasingly elusive. This is hardly a problem, however, since the reader will be interested in Gerli's particular conception of the picaresque, romance, verisimilitude, Renaissance theory, and narrative structure, among other topics, as they relate to Cervantes's writings. This is an engaging blend of literary critique and sociocultural observations. The style is politely polemical, and the arguments are formulated with care. Each essay sets forth a clearly defined thesis while leaving room for alternate visions. Gerli's critical sophistication is obvious and praiseworthy, and the study represents a major contribution to Cervantes criticism. Recommended for all academic libraries, upper-division undergraduate and up.—*E. H. Friedman, Indiana University-Bloomington*

OAB-0911   PQ7263   93-11609 CIP

Light from a nearby window: contemporary Mexican poetry, ed. by Juvenal Acosta. City Lights, 1994 (c1993). 231p English and Spanish. ISBN 0-87286-281-X pbk, $12.95

This bilingual anthology has translations of very high quality on facing pages. It is an outstanding collection of works by 21 writers born since 1945, who represent different regions of Mexico. The poets have all achieved national and international recognition; many have received literary awards. The editor has done a fine job of selecting works which are evocative of Mexico. Some of the poems reveal intensely personal experiences of universal human emotions. Others explore Mexican history, traditions, and modern life, displaying a profound sense of place and a deep feeling for the nation through descriptions of the landscape, natural beauty, ancient ruins, people, cities, and countryside. Since it makes recent Mexican literature accessible to the general public, this volume should bring much-deserved increased respect and recognition for Mexican poetry to English-speaking readers. The text is suitable for courses in comparative or Latin American literature and translation techniques, although a brief glossary of some lexical items might have been helpful. We see Mexican literature evolving beyond Octavio Paz and Carlos Fuentes. Highly recommended for all libraries and all levels of readership.—*M. V. Ekstrom, St. John Fisher College*

OAB-0912   PQ6066   93-4559 CIP

Navarrete, Ignacio. **Orphans of Petrarch: poetry and theory in the Spanish Renaissance.** California, 1994. 297p bibl index afp ISBN 0-520-08373-3, $40.00

Navarrete's dense but delightful study draws on Renaissance theory but also on the more modern theories and typologies of Harold Bloom in order to situate the Spanish poets who followed Petrarch—in the several senses of that word—with regard to their "belatedness," "displacedness," and other alterities, at different removes from the master; that is, within differing degrees of orphanhood with respect to the strong father figure who is Petrarch. For most of them, Petrarch is mediated by Garcilaso. The "anxiety of influence" is ubiquitous, nevertheless. Fortunately, the author himself does not suffer from such anxiety and is, in fact, generous to a fault in acknowledging some previous contributions in the area. Despite the complex and nuanced argument, the book reads well. It is, in this reviewer's estimation, a model of scholarly writing on the poetry of the 16th and 17th centuries in Spain. While many debts are acknowledged—such studies do not spring full-blown from the head of anyone—the marshaling of previous commentary and the synthesis of that commentary within itself and with Navarrete's own "misreadings" are valuable and compelling. No one should now venture into this challenging arena without first consulting Navarrete's book. For Spanish majors, graduate students, faculty, and others interested in the historical and theoretical dimensions of poetry.—*J. A. Parr, University of California, Riverside*

OAB-0913   PQ7297   95-3795 CIP

O'Connell, Joanna. **Prospero's daughter: the prose of Rosario Castellanos.** Texas, 1995. 263p bibl index afp ISBN 0-292-76041-8, $35.00; ISBN 0-292-76042-6 pbk, $17.95

As the years go by since Castellanos's tragic death in 1974, it becomes more and more apparent that Spanish American letters has lost one of its most gifted narrative, poetic, and journalistic voices; that voice is now being reclaimed by feminists on both sides of the Rio Grande. O'Connell's book is an important addition to the excellent work already done—*A Rosario Castellanos Reader,* ed. by Maureen Ahern (1988); Perla Schwartz's *Rosario Castellanos: mujer que supo latín* (1984); *Homenaje a Rosario Castellanos,* ed. by Ahern and Mary Seale Vasquez (1980); and Germaine Calderón's *El universo poético de Rosario Castellanos* (1979). In a highly lucid and accessible prose, O'Connell (Univ. of Minnesota) begins her study of the Mexican author by examining the evolution of the *Tempest* anthology traditionally used to symbolize the relations between colonizer and colonized. She analyzes the figure of Prospero's daughter Miranda as the embodiment of the difficult situation of many women intellectuals: because of their social status and race, they are automatically identified with the power of the colonizer, but as women living in a male-dominated world, they are in fact condemned to a role of subordination. O'Connell's insightful reading convincingly demonstrates how Castellanos uses writing to subvert the limitations that society imposed on her as just another of Prospero's daughters. Upper-division undergraduate upward.—*J. J. Hassett, Swarthmore College*

OAB-0914   PQ7082   94-17119 CIP

Reinterpreting the Spanish American essay: women writers of the 19th and 20th centuries, ed. by Doris Meyer. Texas, 1995. 246p bibl afp ISBN 0-292-75167-2, $25.00

This is a very important and wholeheartedly welcome contribution to the study of the essay in Latin America. The essay, a genre that "covers a literary terrain that is vast and remarkably varied," as Meyer (Connecticut College) puts it, has generally had a low status in most histories of Latin American literature. This regrettable situation is even more serious in the case of essays by women, which to a large extent have been absent from most other studies of the genre, e.g., Martin S. Stabb's *In Quest of Identity* (1967) and John Skirius's *El Ensayo hispano americano del siglo xx* (1981). Meyer's volume is a definite corrective to this situation: it looks at the Latin American essay in all its richness and diversity and reveals the contribution of women writers to the important traditions of the genre, restituting visibility to what she ironically calls the "literary disappeared." Individual chapters cover authors ranging from Flora Tristán (born 1803) to contemporary writers such as Carmen Naranjo and Margo Glantz. Recommended for all levels and academic and public libraries.—*G. Gómez Ocampo, Wabash College*

Humanities

OAB-0915   PQ7087   95-3564 CIP
Rereading the Spanish American essay: translations of 19th and 20th century women's essays, ed. by Doris Meyer. Texas, 1995. 324p afp ISBN 0-292-75179-6, $40.00; ISBN 0-292-75182-6 pbk, $19.95

This volume, companion to *Reinterpreting the Spanish American Essay: Women Writers of the 19th and 20th Centuries*, also ed. by Doris Meyer (CH, Jan'96), is essential to any Latin American collection. The editor has done a superb job of collecting some of the most important writings by women about women ever to come from that region. From works by relatively obscure writers (Eduarda Mansilla, Peru; Nellie Campobello, Mexico) to those by better known individuals such as Victoria Ocampo and Cristina Peri Rossi, every selection in this anthology is an eye-opener to the status of women in Latin American societies. A multiplicity of voices examine issues that run the gamut from the social to the personal and shed light on the constructs of power as they relate to gender, religion, morality, politics, and economics. It is surprising that many of these essays are hard to find in their Spanish-language originals, and it boggles the mind that most of them have never before been translated into English. Happily, these able translations now make them available to a much wider readership. The essays are preceded by short, useful introductions. This reviewer is pleased that footnotes are kept to a minimum, but an index of names and places would have been very useful. Recommended for all levels.— *G. Gómez Ocampo, Wabash College*

OAB-0916   PQ6555   92-41137 CIP
Ribbans, Geoffrey. **History and fiction in Galdós's narratives.** Oxford, 1993. 310p bibl index afp ISBN 0-19-815881-5, $52.00

Ribbans (Brown Univ.) is an outstanding authority on the 19th-century Spanish novelist Benito Pérez Galdós. This volume is an excellent example of a critical study that deals with the relations between history and fiction. Following "Introduction: The Novel and History" are seven chapters that deal with Spanish history as seen in Galdós's novels. The period covered is roughly 1843-74. Ribbans shows an almost complete mastery of material that deals with literary theory, history of 19th-century Spain, and the vast literature concerning Galdós. In his preface he rejects both the deconstructionist and the semiotic schools of criticism, stating his personal conviction: "... that only by a pluralistic use of appropriate criteria, both extrinsic and intrinsic, can a reasonably balanced and productive view of the literature of the past, including nineteenth-century narrative be achieved." References are worked into the text; the useful footnotes are often used to identify historical events and persons. Nine-section bibliography; very useful index.—*H. C. Woodbridge, emeritus, Southern Illinois University-Carbondale*

OAB-0917   PQ7797   93-22940 Orig
Sarlo, Beatriz. **Jorge Luis Borges: a writer on the edge,** ed. by John King. Verso, 1993. 148p bibl index ISBN 0-86091-440-2, $59.95; ISBN 0-86091-635-9 pbk, $18.95

One of the most original examinations of Borges's works, this is a reappraisal of Borges in the context of Argentine history and literary tradition. It addresses the patricidal tendencies and ambivalent attitudes toward Borges among Argentine younger writers, with the result, as the editor asserts, of a "thoughtful rethinking and rewriting of a tradition." Sarlo analyzes the forces at play in Argentine history and society from the late 19th century to the 1920s and 1930s, when Borges returned to Argentina. The heterogeneous character of that country, as compared to what it was in Borges's childhood, created a tension among political, aesthetic, and cultural ideologies. The writer's response was the creation of an "imaginary past" working "with all the meanings of the term *orilla* (edge, shore, margin, limit) to create a powerful ideologeme" that would characterize many of his poems and fictions. But the book goes beyond this imaginary territory; it explores Borges's inclination for marginal writers, and explains how his literature consciously "belongs to a frontier between Europe and America ..." in a marginal country. For Sarlo, Borges's fantastic literature is "another strategy for establishing order for a society whose old orders were vanishing," and through his involvement with

the avant-garde magazines, his "literary imagination ... redefined the space in Argentine letters." Sarlo is a brilliant critic. Recommended for all libraries.— *J. A. Hernandez, Hood College*

OAB-0918   PQ6055   94-21028 CIP
Scarlett, Elizabeth A. **Under construction: the body in Spanish novels.** University Press of Virginia, 1995 (c1994). 232p bibl index ISBN 0-8139-1532-5, $37.50

Looking at what she calls the intersections of textuality and physicality, Scarlett traces prominent women's and men's writing in Spain from the late 19th century through the 1980s. Beginning with the body as text in Emilio Pardo Bazán's *Insolación* (1892) and working through to Adelaida García Morales's *El silencio de las sirenas* (1985), Julio Llamazares's *Lund de lobos* (1985), Soledad Puértolas's *Queda la noche* (1989), and Antonio Muñoz Molina's *Beltenebros* (1989), she shows that over time, bodily flexibility between the genders increases as rapprochement in writing continues. Noteworthy discussions relate to Rosa Chacel, José Ortega y Gasset, and bodily disguises; disguises and codification of the female body in Mercè Rodoreda's novels; body politics in novels of Franco's Spain (Camilo José's *La familia de Pascual Duarte*, 1945); Carmen Martín Gaite's *Entre visillos* (1958); and Luis Martín-Santos's *Tiempo de silencio* (1962); and nomads and "schizos" as representative of postmodern trends in writing. Concluding that the body can never be constructed at total liberty from social norms, Scarlett sets new parameters for future investigations of other writings. A solid addition to gender studies in Spanish literature in upper-level undergraduate and graduate courses.—*C. E. Klein, Beaver College*

OAB-0919   PQ6613   95-32239 CIP
Soufas, C. Christopher. **Audience and authority in the modernist theater of Federico García Lorca.** Alabama, 1996. 190p bibl index afp ISBN 0-8173-0817-2, $42.95

The author's comprehensive awareness of Lorca scholarship manifests itself in this brilliant and innovative study of Lorca's theater. Soufas (Tulane Univ.) finds the traditional posture of criticism of the Spanish playwright's drama limited and insufficient. He decries the thematic focus characteristic of prior studies that have "rendered invisible the fuller dimension of an extended dialectical struggle for stage authority." Dismissing the emphasis on conventional realism and social message, Soufas argues for a reading of Lorca's plays that incorporates the Spanish writer's aesthetic concerns with authority in the theater. The issue of authority is twofold: retaking authority from the audience/entrepreneur and allowing the dramatist to speak openly and freely— actions that would result in the renovation of the Spanish theater and bring it into the European mainstream. Soufas insists that Lorca's theater be assessed in a performance context in light of modernist aesthetics and within a European framework. This focus uncovers a new dimension in Lorca's plays, and this thoroughly engrossing volume offers the reader fresh, incisive readings of well-known works. Upper-division undergraduate and up.—*F. Colecchia, Duquesne University*

OAB-0920   PQ7011   95-41931 CIP
Ugarte, Michael. **Madrid 1900: the capital as cradle of literature and culture.** Pennsylvania State, 1996. 203p bibl index afp ISBN 0-271-01559-4, $32.50

Ugarte examines the various conceptions of Madrid as a physical, political, and social entity, and the ways it influenced the lives and the texts of writers at the turn of the century. The author begins with a lucid and intelligent overview of the theoretical underpinnings of his analysis (the work of Williams, Jameson, Bakhtin, and Benjamin, along with feminist theorists such as Kolodny, Sizemore, and Squier). The first chapter discusses 19th-century Madrid in Larra, Mesonero Romanos, Galdós, and Pardo Bazán. Ugarte then devotes a chapter each to Baroja, Carmen de Burgos, Ginez de la Serna, Valle-Inclán, and Azorin. He highlights voices that denounce Madrid's rigid social organization (especially those of women), although others reject its chaos and uncleanliness, and still others revel in its excesses. What emerges is a multifarious, organic image of the city as a space built on institutionalized discourses, which at the same time allows for bohemia and challenges to the status quo. This work includes the necessary background to engage the general reader, and sophisticated insights that will appeal to specialists in Spanish literature and culture and to feminist critics. General readers; upper-division undergraduates through faculty.—*G. Pozzi, Grand Valley State University*

OAB-0921 PQ6055 96-9948 CIP
Wilcox, John C. **Women poets of Spain, 1860-1990: toward a gynocentric vision.** Illinois, 1997. 366p bibl index afp ISBN 0-252-02260-2, $49.95; ISBN 0-252-06559-X pbk, $19.95

Wilcox's superb essays seek out what the poets consider central to their own selves and then interpret those experiences from a feminist perspective, adopting Elaine Showalter's stages of "feminine, feminist, and female." The schema is essentially historical, covering poets such as Rosalía de Castro, Ernestina de Champourcin, Carmen Conde, Concha Zardoya, Gloria Fuertes, and the most significant women poets in the post-Franco era. An excellent introduction covers Wilcox's concept of "gynocentric vision," "gynocritical vision," "gynocentric style," and women poets in Spain prior to 1860, and briefly treats women poets in various national literatures. Wilcox (Univ. of Illinois at Urbana-Champaign) breaks much new ground, particularly in his chapters on contemporary poets. Examples appear in both Spanish and Wilcox's exceptional English translations. The 16-page works cited list is itself worth the modest price of the book. Unique, well written, highly readable; truly meticulous scholarship; a first-rate volume that no undergraduate or graduate library interested in Hispanism or feminism should be without.—*R. B. Klein, University of Mississippi*

■ Slavic

OAB-0922 PG3476 91-15190 CIP
Akhmatova, Anna. **My half century: selected prose,** ed. by Ronald Meyer. Ardis, 1992. 439p index afp ISBN 0-87501-063-6, $39.95

Akhmatova was one of Russia's truly magnificent poets. Her early poetic voice—restrained, subdued, given to exploring a limited personal world defined by repeated, inevitable failures in love—gave no hint of the majestic dignity she would achieve in her later years as *the* poet-chronicler of Russia's 20th-century miseries. Akhmatova survived the Stalinist era, emerging as a magisterial poet whose two major long poems—*Requiem* and *Poem Without a Hero*—bear witness, respectively, to the sufferings of ordinary citizens during the Great Terror and to the spiritual and artistic roots of her own doomed generation. Akhmatova never attempted to produce a prose record or indictment of her age, nor even a more conventional personal autobiography. She did, however, toy with the idea of publishing a book of memoirs about the many important artists she had known. *My Half Century* includes the sketches of nine writers and the painter Modigliani that would have been included in such a volume, as well as a number of autobiographical notes, Akhmatova's important critical studies of Pushkin, and a selection of public addresses and letters that together open a window into Russian intellectual life. This is an important, accessible volume; it is highly recommended. General readers; undergraduate; graduate.—*M. G. Levine, University of North Carolina at Chapel Hill*

OAB-0923 PG3326 Orig
Dostoyevsky, Fyodor. **A writer's diary: v.1: 1873-1876,** by Fyodor Dostoevsky; tr. and annot. by Kenneth Lantz; introductory study by Gary Saul Morson. Northwestern University, 1993. 805p afp ISBN 0-8101-1094-6, $49.95

Dostoevsky's interest and craftsmanship extended beyond novelistic imagination to more immediate concerns: commentaries on current events, polemics

with leading intellectuals of the time, reports on sensational crimes, reflections on historic happenings, and plans for future writing. Initially published as a special column in the conservative periodical *The Citizen*, the Diary became a monthly publication written, edited, and published solely by Dostoevsky. Not only is it a curious book in which to examine Dostoevsky's political and cultural biases; it represents a much larger problem—the writer's search for an alternative kind of writing that would depart from the already chiseled polyphonic novel and brilliantly mastered discourse of representation. In the context of literary evolution, it marks a beginning of disintegration of the traditional novel initiated by the writer who contributed most to its heyday. It is a heterogeneous assemblage of various generic forms and of authorial and narrative voices each of which deserves a special attention. Lantz's translation captures the idiosyncrasy of Dostoevsky's writing without sacrificing the clarity of meaning in English. His extensive annotations help the reader to contextualize many of Dostoevsky's historical and cultural references. Morson's extensive introductory essay offers the reader a fresh and interesting interpretation of Dostoevsky's work: Undergraduate; graduate; general.—*S. Roll, McGill University*

OAB-0924 PG3458 95-10913 CIP
Gilman, Richard. **Chekhov's plays: an opening into eternity.** Yale, 1995. 261p index afp ISBN 0-300-06461-6, $30.00

Gilman (Yale) has written a new and insightful work that is a welcome addition to such studies as David Magarshack's *The Real Chekhov* (CH, Apr'74), *Chekhov's Great Plays*, ed. by Jean-Pierre Barricelli (CH, Mar'82), and Richard Peace's *Chekhov, a Study of the Four Major Plays* (CH, Dec'83). An expert on drama, not Russian literature (made clear by his failure to include Eugene Onegin in a list of superfluous men and ignoring Gogol's tie to "laughter through tears"), the author brings a fresh and broad perspective to an interpretation of Chekhov's great plays. Gilman frequently connects themes, situations, and characters from Chekhov's short stories to his thoughtful and creative discussions of the individual plays; however, he is most original when he analyzes the ties among the major plays. Although the study lacks a bibliography, works cited are footnoted. Highly recommended for all libraries.—*E. Yarwood, Eastern Washington University*

OAB-0925 PG3213 93-22986 CIP
Lives in transit: a collection of recent Russian women's writing, ed. by Helena Goscilo. Ardis, 1995. 327p afp ISBN 0-87501-100-4, $39.95

Goscilo (Univ. of Pittsburg) here collects 23 short stories and roughly ten pages of lyric poetry by 20th-century Russian women writers, most of them still living. In both the lengthy introduction and in the choice of works itself, the editor emerges once again as the introducer and explicator of a new wave in women's writing in Russia. Though feminism per se remains an elusive term for political and artistic analysis alike, the more so in Russia, this collection testifies to a growing discomfort with and need for revision of previous or conventional views on women's writing. Although many of the stories are not at all politically oriented, Goscilo has masterfully selected writing that involves a feminine opinion—whether in the normative or social sense or as an experience evolving into the conflict in the story. The book may be read as a whole—producing a concentrated if kaleidoscopic view of women's artistic views; or, any single story can stand on its own merit, each one written with energy and translated effectively. This book should be read by everyone interested in Russia today. All collections.—*C. Tomei, Columbia University*

OAB-0926 PG2975 94-39054 CIP
Marsh, Rosalind. **History and literature in contemporary Russia.** New York University, 1995. 289p bibl index ISBN 0-8147-5527-5, $42.50

The study of historical revisionism, social coercion, and artistic control during the various periods of communist government in the former Soviet Union is developing as a new post-Soviet field. Within historical literary works, the function of history as either fact or fabrication is gaining in importance. In this burgeoning field, Marsh's work stands out in many respects. As a Briton,

Marsh (Univ. of Bath) does not have the ideological baggage of either of the main Cold War contenders; the result is a well-balanced analysis of literature, history, and their dialectic development in the Soviet regime. Her work is a historical document itself, chronicling the trends revisionism exhibited during this period. She concentrates mainly on the period 1987-92 and produces an excellent survey of the perception of history during this turbulent time. Her examples are singularly well chosen and excellently demonstrate her points about such issues as the extent of cultural ignorance in the former Soviet Union and the heaves and starts of lifting Soviet taboos. She also focuses on the more sociological issue of public reaction to new revelations of the past. Everyone interested either in glasnost or Soviet history should read this book.— *C. Tomei, Columbia University*

writers including novelists (Tolstoy, Dostoyevsky, Solzhenitsyn), poets (Joseph Brodsky and Mikhail Gendelev), and philosophers (Pavel Florensky and Lev Shestov). This original, thought-provoking study throws new light on some old classics (e.g., Tolstoy's *The Death of Ivan Illich* and *Resurrection*) and introduces the reader to personalities with whom he/she has probably not had much contact. As the author himself points out, it is not important whether the arguments presented in the book are convincing. Nor that the reader accept the personal task that Patterson prescribes in his final paragraph. What does matter is that this study compels the reader to look at the texts in a new way, that it breaks new ground in literary interpretation. For these reasons, it is highly recommended. Upper-division undergraduate; graduate; faculty.—*E. Yarwood, Eastern Washington University*

OAB-0927   PG3415   92-37860 CIP
Orwin, Donna Tussing. **Tolstoy's art and thought, 1847-1880.** Princeton, 1993. 269p bibl index afp ISBN 0-691-06991-3, $35.00

Orwin's is an outstanding study of Leo Tolstoy's changing philosophical views as they developed during the writing of his greatest works of literature, viz. *War and Peace* and *Anna Karenina*. This work is a thorough, perceptive, and profound analysis of how Tolstoy's readings of Hegel, Rousseau, Schopenhauer, Kant and Goethe, among others, from the 1850s through the 1870s coupled with his intense search for meaning in life, were reflected in and helped to shape his two major novels. In addition, Orwin also delves into some of Tolstoy's shorter prose works—e.g., *The Cossacks*—and examines the influences of several of Tolstoy's Russian contemporaries, especially Nikolai N. Strakhov. A challenging, thought-provoking study of the changing art and intellectual development of one of the world's greatest novelists by a scholar who is well versed in philosophy as well as in Russian literature and who offers new insights into the literary workings of a great artist. Copious footnotes. Graduate; faculty.—*E. Yarwood, Eastern Washington University*

OAB-0928   GR154   96-28121 CIP
Palkó, Zsuzsanna. **Hungarian folktales: the art of Zsuzsanna Palkó,** collected, transcribed, annot. and introd. by Linda Dégh; tr. by Vera Kalm. University Press of Mississippi, 1996 (c1995). 382p index afp ISBN 0-87805-912-1 pbk, $20.00

In *Folktales and Society* (CH, Mar'70; revised, 1989) Dégh analyzed the art of the great Hungarian storyteller Zsuzsanna Palkó. Now 35 of Palkó's fairy tales are finally available, in racy, idiomatic translations. Awarded the title Master of Folk Art by the Hungarian Minister of Culture in 1954, Palkó elaborates European folktales in the traditional manner: her versions are rich in detail, dialogue, personal comment, and even such anachronisms as telephones, revolvers, and 20-story buildings. Many—such as "I Don't Know," "Prince Gagyi," and "The Twelve Robbers"—are unusually long and full examples of this tradition. The selections, transcribed from performances taped, usually, in the storyteller's own kitchen, include "women's tales, hero tales, jokes, legends, pious tales, and realistic tales," with emphasis on variety and distinctiveness. Many feature strong female characters. Dégh (Indiana Univ.) demonstrates her mastery of fieldwork technique and of folktale scholarship in tale introductions that relate the stories to other Hungarian versions, to the European folktale tradition, and to experiences in Palkó's own life. An outstanding, unusual, and accessible folktale collection recommended for all types of libraries.— *W. B. McCarthy, Pennsylvania State University, DuBois Campus*

OAB-0929   PG3515   94-16230 CIP
Patterson, David. **Exile: the sense of alienation in modern Russian letters.** University Press of Kentucky, 1995. 204p bibl index afp ISBN 0-8131-1888-3, $29.95

"One of the distinguishing features of Russian thought over the last century and a half is the motif of exile." Patterson (Oklahoma State Univ.) begins with this provocative statement and then goes on to develop this theme in the works of a variety of well known and less well known Russian (or Russian-born)

OAB-0930   PG3098   96-52563 Orig
Peterson, Nadya L. **Subversive imaginations: fantastic prose and the end of Soviet literature, 1970s-1990s.** Westview, 1997. 216p bibl index afp ISBN 0-8133-8920-8, $19.95

Peterson (Univ. of Connecticut) provides a well-informed and well-organized survey of the preglasnost decade (approximately 1975-85) and of the subsequent quinquennium. She focuses on "fantastic prose," which afforded a mode for detachment from the official "socialist realism" and a bridge to the "alternative prose" of the postglasnost period. "Fantasy" pervades many literary genres, such as "village" or "urban" prose. Accordingly, Peterson retains such categories (with special emphasis on "women's writing") and treats the use of fantasy in each. The author probes representative works of more than 20 authors to demonstrate persuasively her "evolutionary" thesis. She directs due attention to the ideological context provided by Russian government and society. Although one might question the exclusion of emigré writers, this is an excellent study. Its thesis is somewhat similar to Edith Clowes's *Russian Experimental Fiction* (CH, Jan'94), but Peterson covers a wider and mostly different range of writers. There is little overlap with Deming Brown's excellent *The Last Years of Soviet Russian Literature* (CH, May'94) and virtually none with N.N. Shneidman's useful, if pedestrian, *Soviet Literature in the 1980s* (CH, Jan'90). Upper-division undergraduate through faculty.—*D. B. Johnson, emeritus, University of California, Santa Barbara*

OAB-0931   Can. CIP
Petro, Peter. **A history of Slovak literature.** McGill-Queen's, 1995. 164p bibl index afp ISBN 0-7735-1311-6, $44.95

Petro (Univ. of British Columbia) provides a detailed introduction to the thousand-year history of Slovak literature. Beginning with the mission of Cyril and Methodius to the Great Moravian Empire in the 9th century CE, the book analyzes each successive literary trend in light of the region's complex political and sociolinguistic development. Along with translations of short passages from key works, many appearing in English for the first time, the author provides a wealth of detail about each writer's life and aspirations. No significant Slovak writer or literary event escapes mention in this highly readable narrative. A few other books in English provide information about select aspects in Slovak literature, notably Norma Rudinsky's *Incipient Feminists: Women Writers in the Slovak National Revival* (1991), *An Anthology of Slovak Poetry*, ed. by I. Kramoris (1947), and *Modern Slovak Prose: Fiction Since 1954*, ed. by R. Pynsent (1990). The present title acquaints English readers for the first time with the full richness of a creative tradition that Petro aptly terms the "perennial Cinderella of central European literature." All collections.—*E. J. Vajda, Western Washington University*

OAB-0932   PS3527   93-16140 CIP
Rampton, David. **Vladimir Nabokov.** St. Martin's, 1993. 143p bibl index ISBN 0-312-09629-1, $29.95

Rampton (Univ. of Ottawa), author of the well-received *Vladimir Nabokov: A Critical Study of the Novels* (CH, Mar'85), offers a survey volume in St. Martin's "Modern Novelists" series. Intended as an introduction, his work is restricted by the series format to Nabokov's novels, leaving aside the poetry, stories, plays, translations, critical writings, and the autobiography. Even three novels—*King, Queen, Knave, Pnin,* and *Transparent Things*—have also been omitted for lack of space. Within these limitations, however, Rampton has done a fine job in providing concise, sophisticated critiques. Especially attractive is the grouping of the novels into bildungsromans; novels of obsession; the modernist; and "metafictions." *Lolita* receives its own chapter. Rampton, an erudite and eclectic critic, draws upon a variety of theoretical frameworks. Nabokov is a major figure, and this is the ninth such series survey. Rampton's nearest competitor is Stephen Jan Parker's *Understanding Vladimir Nabokov* (CH, Feb'88). Although Parker's much shorter volume better meets the needs of the "general reader," sophisticated users will find Rampton's work superior. It also has the advantage of a more current bibliography. Advanced undergraduate; graduate; faculty; general.—*D. B. Johnson, University of California, Santa Barbara*

OAB-0933   PG25   95-17853 CIP
Schenker, Alexander M. **The dawn of Slavic: an introduction to Slavic philology.** Yale, 1995. 346p bibl index afp ISBN 0-300-05846-2, $45.00

This unique book treats the historical and linguistic aspects of early written Slavic civilization. Other works have dealt with these aspects separately: the linguistic in W.J. Entwistle & W.A. Morison's *Russian and the Slavonic Languages* (1949, reprinted 1964), and in *The Slavonic Languages,* ed. by Bernard Comrie and Greville Corbett (1993) which are short on historical and cultural information; Slavic civilization in, for example, Francis Dvornik's *The Slavs: Their Early History and Civilization* (1956) and Marija Gimbutas's *The Slavs* (1971), which lack detailed linguistic information. Schenker's book is especially valuable since it summarizes and updates the above books and supplements them with a wealth of archaeological, textological, topological, paleographical, and liturgical data from a large variety of hard-to-find scholarly works and sources. The author (Yale) provides an extensive section on Proto-Slavic, a section on the isoglosses distinguishing the Slavic languages, and a very clear summary of Slavic accentology. The book has few, if any, misprints, unusual for a work of such linguistic diversity. The maps are clear, as are the photographs of early Slavic writings. Recommended for all libraries collecting in Slavic, Balkan, and Indo-European studies.—*B. K. Beynen, Des Moines Area Community College*

OAB-0934   PG3335   91-47505 CIP
Shapiro, Gavriel. **Nikolai Gogol and the baroque cultural heritage.** Pennsylvania State, 1993. 259p bibl index afp ISBN 0-271-00861-X, $40.00

With thoroughness and erudition Shapiro explores a fresh angle to a familiar subject. His method, rigorously observed throughout, is simple. He first defines a pertinent aspect of the baroque syndrome (a form, a *topos,* a figure of speech), then traces its genealogy from its beginnings (often in classical antiquity) to the 18th century, and then shows how Gogol's—mainly fictional—writings exemplify the feature in question. Among the various baroque, or baroque-related, forms that he examines are the puppet show (*vertep*), the cheap print (*lubok*), and the emblem; among the topoi—carpe diem, memento mori, and "life is a dream"; and among the figures of speech—anaphora, oxymoron, and antithesis. Because he leaves few stones unturned and seldom departs from his chosen method, the study sometimes partakes of a fact-crowded catalogue raisonné. But this may be a necessary (and small) defect among this monograph's many virtues. Clearly written, meticulously researched, and abundantly illustrated, this original study will be required reading for all Gogol specialists. Recommended for four-year colleges and universities with Russian departments.—*R. Gregg, Vassar College*

OAB-0935   PG2991   96-3154 CIP
Shentalinsky, Vitaly. **Arrested voices: resurrecting the disappeared writers of the Soviet regime,** tr. by John Crowfoot. Martin Kessler Books, Free Press, 1996. 322p index ISBN 0-684-82776-X, $25.00

Invited to submit suggestions to an "open meeting" of the USSR Writers' Union in 1988, poet Vitaly Shentalinsky proposed a commission to open the secret Stalinist police files on writers. This presentation of those documents from the files bears stunning witness to a nation's systematic purge of its cultural vanguard and to the brutal, conformist mentality of its functionaries. The chapters on Babel and Bulgakov underscore the testimony in Isaac Babel's *1920 Diary* (CH, Sep'95) and J.A.E. Curtis's *Manuscripts Don't Burn: Mikhail Bulgakov, A Life in Letters and Diaries* (CH, Apr'93). Readers of Nadezhda Mandelstam's memoirs will learn with fresh horror of the uncompromising poet's final days. Between chapters on arrests, interrogations, and incarcerations of literary persons are accounts of Shentalinsky's struggle to unearth and publish files and lost manuscripts. Particularly poignant are public reactions to his findings, from the resistance of former agents to the emotional outpouring of victim's relatives. In addition to reclaiming and preserving Russia's buried cultural wealth—an ongoing process—this volume contributes immeasurably to the understanding of Russia's present cultural state. Essential background is afforded by Robert Conquest's introduction, Crowfoot's concluding essay ("The Literary-Political Context"), and an exhaustive collection of biographical sketches. General readers, students, and scholars of the era will find an irreplaceable resource in Shentalinsky's truth-seeking crusade.—*N. Tittler, SUNY at Binghamton*

OAB-0936   P147   94-17845 CIP
Toman, Jindrich. **The magic of a common language: Jakobson, Mathesius, Trubetzkoy, and the Prague linguistic circle.** MIT, 1995. 355p bibl index (Current studies in linguistics, 26) ISBN 0-262-20096-1, $40.00

This is a reader-friendly, impeccably scholarly study of the sociocultural frame of the Prague Circle, a group of Czech, Russian, and Ukranian linguists who banded together in the interest of creating a new basis for the study of language. Fearing a Dostoyevskian thicket of Slavic names encapsulating turgid apologetics for the group's views, this reviewer was delighted to find instead a series of urbane essays in which the author expresses concern for his reader and assumes the intimate tone of high-table recall of significant persons and events past. Toman (Univ. of Michigan) reassuringly guides his reader through the biographies of major and important minor figures and their peripheral writings for insight into recurrent themes, and then moves on to their interaction in Prague and the positions they held on linguistics and culture during the 1920s and '30s. He does not retrace linguistic arguments covered by other scholars; rather, he presents the detailed story of a moment in the history of ideas. Chapters are headed by helpful abstracts; notes are copious and cross-referenced; the bibliography is thorough and current. Toman's introduction even suggests shortcuts for readers seeking specific information. Would that most scholarly works were as accessible. General readers; upper-division undergraduates and above.—*G. M. O'Brien, University of Minnesota—Duluth*

OAB-0937   PG2997   93-21143 CIP
Women writers in Russian literature, ed. by Toby W. Clyman and Diana Greene. Greenwood, 1994. 273p index afp (Contributions to the study of world literature, 53) ISBN 0-313-27521-1, $65.00

Faced with a tremendous undertaking both with respect to gender studies in Russia—which generally lags far behind the West—and evaluating Russian literature as a whole, Clyman and Greene achieve an unprecedented success in the conception and execution of their task. Each of the 14 essays, classified by period and genre, attempts to express the long-muted position of women in a literary milieu, spanning the time from the first writing in Russia about a millennium ago to the present and including literature written during glasnost and in emigration by Russian women authors. Each essay represents a new synthesis without involving the too-frequent bias of a contemporary cultural or feminist ideology. Thus feminists have the raw material to aid them in their understanding of Russian women writers, but the general reader with a different background will profit equally. For all readers interested in the fabric of women's literature and women in a literary society, this book represents the highest achievement to date in Russian studies. All levels.—*C. Tomei, American University*

■ Performing Arts

OAB-0938 GV1803 95-2792 CIP
Albrecht, Ernest. **The new American circus.** University Press of Florida, 1995. 258p bibl index afp ISBN 0-8130-1364-X, $29.95

Since the 1970s the American circus, especially the small, one-ring variety, has undergone fundamental changes. Ringling Brothers and Barnum & Bailey may still be dominant in popular perception as the epitome of American circus, yet the formula of the "Big One" has been challenged, often successfully, by circuses attempting to reinvent the circus as a form of art, often through radical experimentation. Albrecht (English, Middlesex County College) focuses on four examples: the Pickle Family Circus (San Francisco), the Big Apple (New York), Circus Flora (St. Louis), and Cirque du Soleil (Montreal and Las Vegas). Primarily through interviews Albrecht explores influences, key performances, circus economics, touring, training, various controversies facing the circus today (such as animal rights), and even the meaning of circus as envisioned by operations such as Cirque du Soleil; a final chapter offers an essentially optimistic picture of the circus of tomorrow. Despite some repetition and routine prose, as the first detailed overview of this unique movement, Albrecht's book is of seminal importance in providing the context and analysis of the "new American circus." Superb illustrations (including 16 in color), a chronology, notes, and sources add to the value of the book. Recommended for most libraries.—*D. B. Wilmeth, Brown University*

OAB-0939 GV1785 92-56797 CIP
Baker, Jean-Claude. **Josephine: the hungry heart,** by Jean-Claude Baker and Chris Chase. Random House, 1994 (c1993). 532p bibl index afp ISBN 0-679-40915-7, $27.50

Josephine Baker took Paris by storm as the exotic dancing star of *La Revue Nègre* in 1925. Fifty years, several husbands, hundreds of lovers, 11 adopted children, and many awards (including the French Legion of Honor) later, she wowed her adoring Parisian fans in a retrospective show that proved to be her final curtain. Jean-Claude Baker, who came to love and hate this woman he called "Mother," for whom he worked and whose surname he took, tells Josephine's story in absorbing, disquieting detail, from impoverished childhood in St. Louis through glittering international celebrity to wartime espionage for the French government and financially inept management of her chateau and its conglomerate ménage. Grounding his examination in 20 years of research and thousands of interviews, Baker pushes relentlessly (but not viciously) beyond the glamour and scandal to reveal a woman all the more remarkable and sympathetic for such triumphant perseverance despite her undeniable character flaws. A genuinely fabulous and scholarly book, enhanced by numerous photographs, for those interested in the life of an original talent who helped shape popular culture in the 20th century. All levels.—*J. Ellis, formerly, Mount Holyoke College*

OAB-0940 NX180 94-15703 CIP
Baker, Rob. **The art of AIDS.** Continuum, 1994. 255p index afp ISBN 0-8264-0653-X, $24.95

In this fascinating and often moving study, the author does a remarkable job of dealing with this new and devastating phenomena. He succeeds in demystifying AIDS by looking at the lives and works of artists afflicted with HIV. The study focuses on film, dance, and performance art, debunking the fallacies and misconceptions generated by the disease. Among the myths that the author overturns is the idea that AIDS is a judgment against the disenfranchised individuals who are the most frequent victims. Though Baker does not ignore the social, moral, and political implications, he makes it clear that looking at the human cost is more important than abstract philosophizing. Accordingly, the author provides readable, brief portraits of significant performers, musicians, dancers, filmmakers, and others whose work expresses a profound response to AIDS. Although the author was inspired to undertake this study after his lover died of AIDS, the tone never becomes excessively sentimental or elegiac. In fact, some of the descriptions indicate that the performances, dances, and films are often noteworthy for the energy, defiance, and, occasionally, humor with which the HIV artists have confronted the tragedy and hopelessness of their condition. The author's accumulated anecdotal evidence combined with his minimal analysis lends immediacy to the disease and its representation in art, with the result that it becomes understandable in human terms. This valuable work honestly presents a new performance genre that is becoming an inescapable element of the artistic community. All levels.—*E. Watson, Davenport College of Business*

OAB-0941 ML2075 93-46924 CIP
Brown, Royal S. **Overtones and undertones: reading film music.** California, 1994. 396p bibl disc index afp ISBN 0-520-08320-2, $50.00; ISBN 0-520-08544-2 pbk, $20.00

Although music is an essential element in most narrative film, relatively few theoretical studies examine the relationship between film music and the cinematic image. What distinguishes this groundbreaking work is the thoroughness with which Brown (Queens College) develops his philosophical and theoretical framework to explain the effectiveness of music in film. In its general approach, it is similar to Claudia Gorbman's *Unheard Melodies* (CH, Oct'88), which also discusses the theoretical underpinnings of the film score. However, Brown goes into significantly more detail when he situates film music theory in the context of semiotics, Marxism, psychoanalysis, and other sociopolitical factors that have redefined film criticism and film music theory. The author, mostly using analyses of film scores, demonstrates that though soundtrack music serves as effective backing for the images on screen, a powerful nonreferential musical text not composed for the film can also heighten and maximize the cinematic reality. His discussion of Bernard Herrmann's evocative and often innovative scoring of seven Hitchcock films is especially illuminating. The value of these analyses derives not just from the immediate and specific insights they provide but also from the access point they offer into this new and uncharted field. All academic collections.—*E. Watson, Davenport College of Business*

OAB-0942 PS3511 91-52779 CIP
Foote, Horton. **Horton Foote's three trips to Bountiful,** ed. by Barbara Moore and David G. Yellin. Southern Methodist, 1993. 259p bibl ISBN 0-87074-326-0, $22.50; ISBN 0-87074-327-9 pbk, $10.95

The transforming of literary material across different genres and media can cast great light on the nature of artistic choice, but the record of such transformations is not easy to come by. In 1985 David G. Yellin and Marie Connors gave us a valuable record in *Tomorrow and Tomorrow and Tomorrow*, which presented a Faulkner short story and the Horton Foote teleplay and film script based on it. Now Yellin (this time in collaboration with Barbara Moore) gives us Foote's original teleplay, stageplay, and screenplay of *The Trip to Bountiful*, supported by an informative general introduction, introductions to each separate version, interviews with Foote and the film's producer, director, and supporting actress, a scene-by-scene comparative chart of the three scripts, an afterword by Foote, and a bibliography. As a result, we are, as it were, invited into the writer's workshop to appreciate the opportunities and constraints that influence the adaptation of the same material to different forms, and we learn not only a lot about various dramatic media but about the very process of art itself. Like its predecessor, this book will fill an important niche in every library's mixed media collection and be an invaluable resource for courses at various levels in several disciplines.—*A. J. Griffith, Our Lady of the Lake University*

OAB-0943 E169 96-31522 CIP
Marshall, P. David. **Celebrity and power: fame in contemporary culture.** Minnesota, 1997. 290p index afp ISBN 0-8166-2724-X, $49.95; ISBN 0-8166-2725-8 pbk, $19.95

Contemporary celebrities, especially those in the entertainment industry, often wield significant power outside their areas of talent and expertise. How they derive and exercise their status and power is the subject of this intriguing study. Marshall (Univ. of Queensland) deserves high praise for his skillful handling of the topic from the viewpoints of a wide variety of scholarly disciplines—sociology, political science, psychology, semiotics, linguistics, cinema studies, and cultural studies—and for the minimum of academic jargon. Particularly astute are his three central chapters on representative celebrities: Tom Cruise from the movies, where distance from the public and control over one's aura are essential; Oprah Winfrey from television, where celebrities must be more sympathetic and familiar figures with their fans; and New Kids on the Block in the realm of popular music, where status is determined by authenticity and solidarity with one's audience. Intriguing also is Marshall's claim that contemporary politicians are using these three modes of celebrity status to construct their own political identities. Recommended for both public and academic libraries collecting in media and cultural studies.—*J. I. Deutsch, George Washington University*

OAB-0944   PN1995   94-2205 CIP
Nichols, Bill. **Blurred boundaries: questions of meaning in contemporary culture.** Indiana, 1995 (c1994). 187p index afp ISBN 0-253-34064-0, $29.95; ISBN 0-253-20900-5 pbk, $12.95

This trenchant, provocative study dealing with the boundaries between fiction and nonfiction film/video examines how contemporary forms of documentary expression force a reconsideration of "realism and its successors." In seven linked essays, Nichols (San Francisco State Univ.) examines several questions of meaning prompted by contemporary culture. He provides a rigorous evaluation of reality television; a discussion of the current trials and tribulations of modern ethnographic films and filmmakers; a stunning reclamation of Eisenstein's *Strike* (1925) as a "true" documentary; a brilliant exposition of the Rodney King video clip's contextual use in the trials of the accused police officers; and an unveiling of performing documentary (a fifth mode of documentary form, which he adds to expository, interactive, observational, and reflexive). The final essay deals with "retrospection," a complex analysis of how our models of the future, past, and present impinge on our "understanding" of four film/video texts (Oliver Stone's *JFK*; *Who Killed Vincent Chin*; *Dear America: Letters Home from Vietnam*; and a collective Gulf War text composed of recorded footage from ABC, CBS, NBC, and CNN). A demanding but extremely valuable work, recommended for upper-division undergraduate, graduate, and research collections.—*R. E. Sutton, American University*

OAB-0945   PN2286   92-18349 CIP
Tanner, Jo A. **Dusky maidens: the odyssey of the early black dramatic actress.** Greenwood, 1992. 171p bibl index afp (Contributions in Afro-American and African studies, 156) ISBN 0-313-27717-6, $45.00

An excellent introduction to early African American female performers, their route from minstrel shows and vaudeville to musical comedies and drama. Until Tanner's study they have not received such specific and deserved attention. As singers and dancers these women were prized for their light skins, but as actresses they were often forced to blacken up to play servant/mammy roles. The richest chapters are those about three outstanding singers and dancers—Dora Dean, Sissieretta Jones ("Black Patti"), and Ida Forsyne—and those about early dramatic actresses Inez Clough, Lottie Grady, Anita Bush, Laura Bowman, and Abbie Mitchell. Most of them had careers abroad as well as in the US, e.g., Ida Forsyne, who was too dark for the Harlem clubs of the 1920s, spent ten years in Russia. Bush, Bowman, and Mitchell all organized acting troupes and founded acting schools. Tanner makes good use of a variety of sources. One could wish for more photographs, but the ten included are excellent. The bibliography is adequate. This is a much needed reference source for academic readers, beginning undergraduates and up, and it should appeal to general readers as well.—*D. E. Abramson, emerita, University of Massachusetts at Amherst*

OAB-0946   PN2924   96-24498 CIP
Thornbury, Barbara E. **The folk performing arts: traditional cul-**

ture in contemporary Japan. State University of New York, 1997. 203p bibl index afp ISBN 0-7914-3255-6, $54.50

Traditional culture and folk performing arts in Japan are amazingly diverse, complex, and popular. Few Western writers have attempted even a definition or description, much less an evaluation. Thornbury (Temple Univ.) has undertaken this ambitious project and has accomplished much. She observes that the many forms of folk performance are forever being mixed, mutated, reborn, and enjoyed. Performances include dance, drama, music, properties, scenery, costumes, and lights; performers are amateur and professional, children and adult, real and puppets. The performances are presented in both elaborate and simple buildings, at expensive and exclusive show places, and in found space or make-do areas. According to the author, the repertories include historical and contemporary subject matter and themes. Despite the great popularity of the folk performing arts and the revised national heritage protection laws, Japan still has no national center for the folk arts. Thornbury went from area to area to get a clear idea of the diversity and impact of these cultural traditions. Her final chapter affirms the future of folk performing arts in Japan. Upper-division undergraduates; graduates; professionals; general audiences.—*C. C. Harbour, University of Montevallo*

■ Film

Biography & History

OAB-0947   PN1993   93-20640 CIP
Abel, Richard. **The ciné goes to town: French cinema, 1896-1914.** California, 1994. 568p bibl index afp ISBN 0-520-07935-3, $55.00

Abel has once again sailed into scholarly terra incognita—this time the first two decades of French cinema—and has returned with a richly detailed map and tales of unknown cinematic treasure. Several French film scholars first explored the area years ago, and a recent American study, Donald Crafton's *Emile Cohl, Caricature, and Film* (CH, Dec'90), began to inventory the many prominent landmarks. But Abel has now written a significantly more vivid, three-dimensional historical account of this formative period of world cinema. He skillfully reconstructs the systems of representation and narration developed in France, chronicles the growth of the film industry, describes typical genres and production methods, and highlights the careers of many pioneers (including Louis Feuillade, Alice Guy, Charles Pathé, and Leon Gaumont). Many important films—some entirely forgotten, all helpfully listed in an excellent filmography—are carefully described, and the footnotes and bibliography will be superb resources for future researchers. The study is capped by interesting reflections on the place of cinema in fin de siècle French culture and thoughtful comparisons to the soon-to-become-dominant American cinema. In sum, a magisterial contribution deserving a place in every serious film library, upper-division undergraduate and above.—*S. Liebman, CUNY Graduate School and University Center*

OAB-0948   NC1765   94-29075 CIP
Bendazzi, Giannalberto. **Cartoons: one hundred years of cinema animation.** Indiana, 1995 (c1994). 514p bibl indexes ISBN 0-253-31168-3, $89.95; ISBN 0-253-20937-4 pbk, $39.95

Few works have been so anticipated as Anna Taraboletti-Segre's splendid translation of Bendazzi's comprehensive history of animation cinema. This work reviews the decades of development in animation, from individuals like Emile Reynaud and Emile Cohl through the studios of Disney and the National Film Board of Canada into the revolutionary realm of computer animation. The thoroughness of *Cartoons* is evident in its international scope, for example, its inclusion of the exciting and neglected work produced in Latin America and Asia. This marvelous encyclopedia is brilliantly illustrated with dazzling color plates. Its scholarly breadth, richness, and attention to detail, along with its amazingly readable and engaging narrative, make this the most indispensable text on world animation history. Enthusiastically recommended as both a fascinating story and an incredible reference resource for both scholars and aficionados of the art of film.—*T. Lindvall, Regent University*

OAB-0949 PN1993 96-16839 CIP
Burns, Bryan. **World cinema: Hungary.** Fairleigh Dickinson/Flicks Books, 1996. (Dist. by Associated University Presses) 234p bibl filmography index afp ISBN 0-8386-3722-1, $38.50

Hungarian films of the past decade are nothing special. As a result Lia Somogyi's *Hungarian Film Directors, 1948-1983* (Budapest, 1984) is still useful, though hard to find in the US. However, two other hard-to-find books, Istvan Nemeskurty's *Word and Image: History of the Hungarian Cinema*, 2nd ed. (Budapest, 1974), and Graham Petrie's *History Must Answer to Man: The Contemporary Hungarian Cinema* (CH, Apr'81) need updating, and the present title is the full and welcome solution. Burns (Univ. of Sheffield, UK) surveys three areas: "Early Days" gives compact accounts of beginnings and the 1930s (with 3-4 page discussions of five directors) and the period 1939-47 (discussions of eight directors); "The Great Generation" covers 1956-72, a period of revolution and reformation (the seven directors here include giants Mikóos Jancsó and István Szabó, treated brilliantly); "Our Contemporaries" explores the "achievement and uncertainty" of 1972-95 (29 directors). Observations— whether factual, sociological, political, or personal—are always clear ("Both Jancso and Kovacs are cerebral and demanding; Szabo likes to tell stories"; "Humour is not common in the Hungarian cinema; irony is"). Everything is judicious, thoughtful, solidly supported. This book both informs and evaluates, and the reader emerges with a firm grasp of the rich, important, and sometimes astonishing body of Hungarian films, and the wish to see the films Burns so enthusiastically praises. All film titles are given in English.—*P. H. Stacy, emeritus, University of Hartford*

OAB-0950 PN1998 95-37138 CIP
Callow, Simon. **Orson Welles: the road to Xanadu.** Viking, 1996 (c1995). 640p bibl index afp ISBN 0-670-86722-5, $32.95

Eleven years after his death at the age of 70, Welles remains a prodigious force in American cultural mythology. In this ambitious, riveting first volume of a planned two-part biography, Callow develops "a synthesis and a deconstruction" of the Welles story until the release of *Citizen Kane* (1941). He confirms what has been long surmised: Welles himself single-mindedly orchestrated the Welles legend, "eagerly abetted ... by legions of interviewers, profile-writers and biographers, all, like him, unable to resist a good story." A significant portion of the massive collection of Wellesiana belongs in that legend-abetting category, and some of it (e.g., Peter Bogdanovich's interviews of Welles in *This Is Orson Welles*, ed. by Jonathan Rosenbaum, CH, Jun'93) remains invaluable to any Welles study. But Callow criticizes two influential biographers: Barbara Leaming (*Orson Welles*, CH, Apr'86)—for permitting Welles to use her "to pass on to posterity his side of the story"—and Frank Brady (*Citizen Welles*, CH, Oct'89), "one of the most diligent promulgators of Wellesian myth." Callow's thoroughly researched chronicle is laced with style and wit, energized particularly by his unique ability to bond with the multitalented Welles, whether acclaiming him for his dazzling inventiveness and Falstaffian chutzpah or angrily scolding him for his monumental ego and failure of promise. Welles would have loathed most of this book's messages, but he would have loved the messenger. Recommended for all collections.—*M. W. Estrin, Rhode Island College*

OAB-0951 D522 96-45979 CIP
DeBauche, Leslie Midkiff. **Reel patriotism: the movies and World War I.** Wisconsin, 1997. 244p bibl index afp ISBN 0-299-15400-9, $50.00; ISBN 0-299-15404-1 pbk, $15.95

While WW I was being waged in Europe, a powerful oligopoly was forming in Hollywood, as the US film industry rapidly expanded and consolidated its control over the production, distribution, and exhibition of motion pictures. How the Hollywood studios were able to practice "practical patriotism"—making films that enhanced not only the Allied war effort but also their own profits—is the subject of this admirable study by DeBauche (Univ. of Wisconsin—Stevens Point). Because previous books on WW I, such as Michael T. Isenberg's *War on Film* (1981) and Craig W. Campbell's *Reel America and World War I* (CH, Sep'85), have already covered the history of films dealing specifically with the war, *Reel Patriotism* looks instead at the broader social and cultural context, using representative case studies— films like *Joan the Woman* (1916), stars like Mary Pickford, and cities like Milwaukee—to detail significant developments within the movie industry from 1914 to 1929. To this end, DeBauche has dug deeply into the most relevant archives, trade papers, and other periodical literature. Recommended for both public and academic libraries collecting in film studies.— *J. I. Deutsch, George Washington University*

OAB-0952 Orig
Eisenstein, S.M. **Beyond the stars: the memoirs of Sergei Eisenstein: selected works, IV,** ed. by Richard Taylor; tr. by William Powell. BFI Publishing/Seagull Books, 1996 (c1995). (Dist. by Indiana) 889p index ISBN 0-85170-460-3, $75.00

Few film buffs and no serious scholars of cinema will be able to resist this most complete version yet of the great Russian director's autobiography. The editors admit that the arrangement of the text—actually a compendium of dozens of manuscripts—is speculative, since Eisenstein died before completing it. This edition, however, closely follows the authoritative Russian version (1979) and is twice as long as the previous English version, *Immortal Memories*, translated by Herbert Marshall (CH, Mar'84). Eisenstein's writing is elliptical, allusive, rambling, and cryptic, and Powell captures the notorious awkwardness of Eisenstein's style far better than Marshall did. Eisenstein was curiously proud of the digressive disorder of his manuscript, which mimicked the wayward course of his free associations. He expands on his relationships with his parents and his teacher, the great stage director and theorist Meyerhold. Surprisingly, he devotes little space to his many illustrious friends and coworkers and makes no effort to situate his work in the treacherous political circumstances surrounding his career. Taylor's useful notes clarify when each chapter was written and identify the hundreds of persons and art works cited. Copiously illustrated with sketches, production stills, frame enlargements, and personal snapshots, though the images are unfortunately often gray and grainy. Recommended for all serious film collections.—*S. Liebman, CUNY Graduate School and University Center*

OAB-0953 PN1993 96-10110 CIP
Hershfield, Joanne. **Mexican cinema/Mexican woman, 1940-1950.** Arizona, 1996. 159p bibl index afp ISBN 0-8165-1636-7, $39.95; ISBN 0-8165-1637-5 pbk, $16.95

Discussion of Mexico's extensive cinema tradition, long documented in the Spanish language, has only recently become available to English-language readers in such works as Charles Ramírez Berg's *Cinema of Solitude* (1992), Carl J. Mora's *Mexican Cinema: Reflections of a Society* (CH, Oct'82), and *Mexican Cinema*, ed. by Paulo Antonio Paranagua (CH, Nov'96). Hershfield (Univ. of North Carolina at Chapel Hill) contributes an important analysis of this impressive national cinema. She examines the cinematic construction of women in six woman-centered melodramas: *Maria Candelaria, Rio Escondido, Distinto Amanecer, Salón México, Doña Bárbara,* and *Susana*. By drawing on feminist and postcolonial theory, cultural studies, and film criticism, she provides a rigorous and insightful critique of these works; and by locating the filmic texts within their corresponding historical, economic, and social contexts, she proffers a model for the critique of expressive culture. Relevant notes, a comprehensive index, and photo reproductions complement the polished prose and convincing argument. Essential reading not only for film students and scholars but for practitioners of feminist theory, Latin American studies, and cultural studies. Highly recommended for upper-division undergraduates, graduate students, and faculty.— *A. M. Stock, College of William and Mary*

OAB-0954　　　PN1993　　　94-30577 CIP
Higson, Andrew. **Waving the flag: constructing a national cinema in Britain.** Oxford, 1995. 322p bibl index afp ISBN 0-19-812369-8, $65.00

Almost from its inception the British film industry has labored in the shadow of Hollywood. Higson (Univ. of East Anglia) endeavors to show how British filmmakers tried either to emulate the American product or to differentiate British film from Hollywood by emphasizing—often at the expense of narrative flow—British landscape, heritage, and character. Concentrating on five films—*Comin' Thro' the Rye* (1923), *Evergreen* (1934), *Sing as We Go* (1934), *Millions like Us* (1943), *This Happy Breed* (1944)—he discusses in great depth the concepts of the "nation" that were constructed, especially by the documentary "realism" of the later films. Covering some of the same ground as Sue Harper's *Picturing the Past* (CH, Jun'95), but far better, this book is carefully researched, closely reasoned, elegantly written, and highly thought-provoking. This reviewer hopes that Higson will follow up with an equally penetrating treatment of more recent British film. In short, this is by far the best book about British film yet published.—*W. A. Vincent, Michigan State University*

OAB-0955　　　PN1993　　　92-7033 CIP
Hirano, Kyoko. **Mr. Smith goes to Tokyo: Japanese cinema under the American occupation, 1945-1952.** Smithsonian Institution Press, 1992. 365p bibl indexes afp ISBN 1-56098-157-1, $34.95

Hirano's important book treats the clash of two very different cultures. It is a well-researched and clearly written work drawing on both English-language and Japanese sources about Japanese film during the American occupation of Japan (1945 to 1952). The author makes a detailed study of the period when the Japanese film industry survived strikes and rebuilt itself, and she provides valuable background for Japan's "golden age" of the 1950s, when by courageously facing the nation's identity crisis, confusion, and guilt, Japanese filmmakers made some of the finest films of the world. She is also thorough about the contradictions of American policy, including censorship and propaganda in a democracy, and Cold War politics—pulling Japan first to the left, away from fascism and militarism, and then pulling it back to the right again, out of fear that it would become communist. Highly recommended. Advanced undergraduate; graduate; faculty.—*J. J. Jorgens, American University*

OAB-0956　　　PN1995　　　92-22094 CIP
Jenkins, Henry. **What made pistachio nuts?: early sound comedy and the vaudeville aesthetic.** Columbia, 1992. 336p index afp ISBN 0-231-07854-4, $32.50

Rarely is a work of such thorough historical research and sterling scholarship expressed in such an engaging, even entertaining, writing style. Jenkins's persuasive and original investigation of the anarchistic films of the early sound period both instructs and delights. Grounded in the paradigm of the classical Hollywood narrative, this study explores how the comedian-centered comedy of vaudeville invaded and altered standard Hollywood practices. Integrating a complex array of topics (from Victorian comic theory to ethnicity), case studies (of performers, Eddie Cantor, and films, *Diplomaniacs*), rarely seen photographs (including vaudeville sequences), and snippets from fascinating primary sources, *What Made Pistachio Nuts?* is the best work on popular culture this year. It situates a neglected aesthetic tradition, its comic actors, and their vaudeville shtick in a cultural context that makes sense of the production and reception of the zany comedy of the early sound films. It reconstructs the sounds (and sites) of forgotten laughter, and subsequently celebrates their distinctiveness and vitality. Enthusiastically and exuberantly recommended.—*T. Lindvall, Regent University*

OAB-0957　　　PN1995　　　96-26745 CIP
Kirby, Lynne. **Parallel tracks: the railroad and silent cinema.** Duke University, 1997. 338p bibl index afp ISBN 0-8223-1833-4, $49.95; ISBN 0-8223-1839-3 pbk, $17.95

Kirby's analogy connecting the railroad and the silent cinema is both brilliant and resilient. Both innovations provided technological windows on the world, the wonders of visual tourism, progressive narrative journeys, potential shocks to a stabilized subject, the containing of action, and paradigmatic challenges to the status quo. With the skill of an engineer Kirby routes readers toward a destination where the intertextuality of trains and silent movies seems both obvious and novel. Departing from the stations of invention and social uncertainty, she tracks the crossing paths of these two mechanical marvels from Hale's Tours (which used stationary train cars as panoramic amusements) with the themes of romance, urbanity, and national identity connecting the two. This adapted dissertation stretches understanding across an international landscape, riding rail/reel/real insights from the Lumière Brothers' actualities and Edwin S. Porter's *The Great Train Robbery* (1903) through Abel Gance's *La Roue* (1921), Buster Keaton's *The General* (1926), and John Ford's *The Iron Horse* (1924). Kirby derails slightly in creating ideological ties to contemporary academic concerns such as psychoanalytic gender readings; sometimes a train is just a train. But this a quibble. Kirby's lucid and entertaining study is a model to train readers in how to see, think, and understand. Like the railroad and silent cinema, this work is indeed a splendid marvel. All collections.—*T. Lindvall, Regent University*

OAB-0958　　　PN1998　　　96-49075 CIP
McCarthy, Todd. **Howard Hawks: the grey fox of Hollywood.** Grove Press, 1997. 756p bibl filmography index ISBN 0-8021-1598-5, $35.00

Through countless interviews, Hawks provided an account of his career that has, until now, stood in for a critical biography. McCarthy has reached behind that self-serving facade to construct a fascinating view of Hawks's life, his films, and the conditions under which he made them. McCarthy offers a thoughtful and well-researched account of the intersections between the director's personal life and his films, arguing, for example, that his second marriage was a catalyst for the most productive period of his career and for a substantially more positive filmic view of heterosexual love (from *Only Angels Have Wings*, 1939, through the 1940s). The author also unearths unrealized projects that resonate tantalizingly with themes of the completed films, like Hawks's idea for an RKO version of *Cinderella* in drag with Cary Grant as the mother, James Stewart and Danny Kaye as the daughters, and Ginger Rogers as Prince Charming. McCarthy remains loyal to his subjects, but the story he tells of a strong personality confronting the multiple demands of the studio system implicitly reengages the fascinating old debates over authorship. Though academics will wish it were footnoted, McCarthy's book is an essential purchase for all serious film collections.—*K. S. Nolley, Willamette University*

OAB-0959　　　Orig
Merritt, Russell. **Walt in Wonderland: the silent films of Walt Disney,** by Russell Merritt and J.B. Kaufman. [Rev. English language ed.]. Le Giornate del Cinema Muto, 1994 (c1993). (Dist. by Johns Hopkins) 164p bibl index ISBN 0-8018-4907-1, $39.95

Scholarship has rarely been so engaging and charming as in Merritt and Kaufman's detailed study of the silent film animation of Walt Disney. The work is, simply, wonderful. With thorough research ferreting out such previously uncollected materials as publicity stills, frame enlargements, cartoon story panels, articles from *Universal Weekly* (1922-36), and sundry archival correspondence, the authors have fleshed out the image of Disney the undeterred artist/entrepreneur. They showcase the sketchy characters of the Alice cartoon comedies and Oswald the Lucky Rabbit, demonstrating that Mickey did not spring into existence like Minerva, but enjoyed a genealogical tradition of film technique and comic gags. The study both details the economic and political vicissitudes of young Disney and sheds light on friends and collaborators like Ub Iwerks, who shared his vision. The impressive annotated filmography of Disney silent cartoons from 1921 to 1928 and the exquisite artwork enhance the critical analysis and make this work one of the most significant, scintillating, and pleasurable texts to be published this year. Knowledge and delight have rarely been so wedded so well. Recommended with animated enthusiasm.—*T. Lindvall, Regent University*

OAB-0960   PN1995   92-33720 CIP
Palmer, William J. **The films of the eighties: a social history.**
Southern Illinois, 1993. 335p index afp ISBN 0-8093-1837-7, $39.95

Carrying forward Palmer's *The Films of the Seventies* (CH, Jul'87), this work involves a substantial advance in theory, methodology, and analysis. Utilizing a new historicist approach influenced by Hayden White and Dominick LaCapra, Palmer (English, Purdue) discusses popular films as part of the "holograph" of writing and making social history. He argues persuasively that 1980s films often functioned as more than a "reactive analytic text" that mirrored or co-opted established social facts. Palmer contends that films can and do function as simultaneous participants in creating texts of social history. He resourcefully examines the cultural/historical overtexts, film texts, and subtexts and metatexts of films, and he produces startling and fascinating observations. He shows that 1980s films dealt with serious international and domestic issues, and that below the layer of Reagan-era conservatism and complacent materialism, films expressed society's confusions and anxieties in complex ways. This is an absolute "must read" for all interested in film and its relationship to culture and society.— *D. A. Noverr, Michigan State University*

OAB-0961   PN19995   96-11731 CIP
Rentschler, Eric. **The ministry of illusion: Nazi cinema and its afterlife.** Harvard, 1996. 456p bibl index afp ISBN 0-674-57639-X, $60.00; ISBN 0-674-57640-3 pbk, $25.00

Nazi cinema has not lacked for exegetes in English-speaking countries— notable volumes are David Stewart Hull's *Film in the Third Reich* (1969), Erwin Leiser's *Nazi Cinema* (CH, May'76), and Julian Petley's *Capital and Culture* (1979). A host of more narrowly focused studies and sensational memoirs (such as Leni Riefenstahl's autobiography, *Leni Riefenstahl*, CH, Oct'94) have contributed to an understanding of a film industry carefully administered by Goebbels's cultural apparatus to maintain, in Rentschler's thoughtful formulation, a "discipline of distraction" over the German *Volk*. Rentschler's readable, superbly researched, and meticulously documented study does not attempt to engage all of the nearly 1,100 films made during the Third Reich. Rather, the author (Univ. of California, Irvine) provides measured, elegantly written assessments of several key films—such as the "movement film" *Hitler Youth Quex*, the breezy, American-style *Lucky Kids*, Sirk's *La Habanera*, the notorious *Jew Süss*, and the fantastic, still much beloved *Münchhausen*—to explore recent claims of their alleged resistance to the Nazi regime and to examine reasons for their enduring popularity, at least in Germany. Rentschler avoids both pitfalls often associated with discussions of these films—reductive ideological critique and evasive "aesthetic" appreciation. He enhances readers' awareness of the ways Nazi filmmakers used the "Jewish" Hollywood conventions Goebbels simultaneously feared and admired and their complex relationship with Weimar film culture. An immensely useful chronology of key events, the most extensive general bibliography of the subject ever compiled in English, and helpful filmographies of and bibliographies about the leading Nazi cineastes make this an essential acquisition for college libraries.— *S. Liebman, CUNY Graduate School and University Center*

OAB-0962   PN1993   95-19014 CIP
Robinson, David. **From peep show to palace: the birth of American film.** Columbia/Library of Congress, 1996. 213p bibl index afp ISBN 0-231-10338-7, $29.50

Robinson's history of the first 20 years in the development of film includes all the significant dates, technical innovations, and battling inventors such an account must contain. A book that perforce discusses phantasmascopes, Latham's loops, and Kinemacolor might be expected to be tedious or even baffling. Far from it! Robinson's history is orderly, precise, authoritative, and fun to read. His details are judiciously chosen; his style is clear and witty; and his theories of film development are delineated without fuss, certainly without the usual obfuscation associated with film theory. Even the most familiar aspects of movies from 1893 to 1913 emerge with fresh interest and significance. Robinson sees 1913 as a watershed year in film history, the time when all influences, tech-

nologies, and concepts had been assembled for the monumental evolution of a vaudeville novelty into the defining art form of the 20th century. In addition to its other merits this is a handsome book with extremely well chosen, copious illustrations, many of which are not the ones usually reproduced. Recommended for all libraries.— *R. D. Sears, Berea College*

OAB-0963   PN1995   96-17882 CIP
Schulte-Sasse, Linda. **Entertaining the Third Reich: illusions of wholeness in Nazi cinema.** Duke University, 1996. 347p bibl filmography index afp ISBN 0-8223-1830-X, $54.95; ISBN 0-8223-1824-5 pbk, $18.95

Here the serious reader will find a rare book that renders accessible many of the theories of so-called postmodern literary criticism. The author's successfully accomplished goal was to analyze movies of the Third Reich not as intentional propaganda (as in David Stewart Hull's *Film in the Third Reich*, 1969) but as the means by which German literary traditions provided the bedrock on which popular movies that happened to contain propaganda were constructed. For example, Schulte-Sasse (Macalaster College) studies *Jud Süss* (1940) not for its antisemitism but for the ease with which it marshaled 18th-century Wurttemburg history to slander Jews. In effect, a historically fragmented Germany readily embraced movies in which a foreign "Other" seemed to threaten the community of harmonious German folk. This fantasy-history was readily invoked in the service of Nazism, she argues, in several movie biographies of Frederick the Great, in a cycle of "genius" films about Schiller, Rudolf Diesel, and other German culture heroes, and in more lighthearted fare such as *Request Concert* (1940) and *The Great Love* (1942). Her achievement is remarkable not only for providing access to meanings in seemingly apolitical material, but also for providing new theoretical modeling for overt, conventionally Nazi films such as *Hans Westmar* and *S.A. Mann Brand*. Her work is well served by small frame enlargements. Upper-division undergraduates and up.— *T. Cripps, Morgan State University*

OAB-0964   PN1993   93-12309 CIP
Shlapentokh, Dmitry. **Soviet cinematography, 1918-1991: ideological conflict and social reality,** by Dmitry Shlapentokh and Vladimir Shlapentokh. Aldine de Gruyter, 1993. 278p bibl index afp ISBN 0-202-30461-2, $36.95; ISBN 0-202-30462-0 pbk, $21.95

The Shlapentokhs proceed simply. They make a statement about the Soviet Union (or even post Soviet Union), a statement of sociology, politics, religion, or psychology (like xenophobia or crime); then they support the statement (or contradict it with exceptions) by examining a handful of movies. The result, however, is far from simple; it is a superlative, rich, advanced course in the conflict between the real Soviet world and "the fictional reality created by directors attempting to obey the injunctions of the ideological apparatus." The authors use about 400 movies, a sample no one could argue as insufficient or nonrepresentational. Nor could anyone argue the solid intelligence of the interpretations of these films (particularly since aesthetics is never, never the point). Oddly enough, all the good books on Soviet cinema are now 20 years old; this new book concentrates on these 20 years. The best parts concern Stalin. Whenever a movie is about Stalin, directly or indirectly, positively or negatively, the book becomes vital, dramatic, unique. Alas, the index is foolish, listing vast topics—"historical figures" or "happy life" or "negative heroes"— but completely ignoring places, directors, titles. With a decent index, this would be one of the most useful books ever written on Soviet film. Even without, it is the most fascinating and up to date.— *P. H. Stacy, emeritus, University of Hartford*

OAB-0965   PN1993   93-12279 CIP
Sklar, Robert. **Film: an international history of the medium.** Abrams, 1993. 560p index ISBN 0-8109-3321-7, $49.50

Writing an "international history of the medium" may seem like an impossible task, but Sklar (New York Univ.) comes as close as anyone has to balancing the need for basic information about film technology, social and artistic evolution, and the growth of the industry with the need for making a selection of directors and titles. He offers critical evaluations from several different perspectives, including theoretical ones. Though the prose style is not as entertaining as that of some film histories, Sklar's writing does have the virtue of clarity and accuracy. He spares the reader cuteness, gossip, and the barbs of recent critical writing while by no means neglecting new ideas and approaches. Best of all, Sklar does not limit himself to the standard Great Films and Great Directors, but goes out of his way to give attention to neglected films and to little-known independents and national cinemas. This elegantly designed work offers hundreds of the clearest and most interesting illustrations this reviewer has ever seen in a work of this kind. Highly recommended for all libraries.—*J. J. Jorgens, American University*

OAB-0966   PN1998   91-47886 CIP
Thomson, David. **Showman: the life of David O. Selznick.** Knopf, 1992. 792p bibl index ISBN 0-394-56833-8, $35.00

"The Selznicks were larger than life," Thomson concludes at the end of the grand and ambitious biography which dramatizes that claim so vividly. "They were their own creation," particularly the tragic Selznick at the story's center: producer David O. A prodigious force of nature fueled further by Benzedrine, Selznick produced close to 100 films, among them *King Kong, Dinner at 8, David Copperfield, Rebecca, Duel in the Sun,* and, his monument, *Gone With the Wind,* the making of which emerges in Thomson's fresh retelling as a project of Machiavellian chaos. Encouraged by Selznick's two sons and (after a fashion) his first wife, Irene Mayer Selznick, Thomson thus gained access to private papers and three key perspectives. *Showman* is scrupulously researched and documented, its pages populated by an imposing cast of featured players (including the daunting Irene and her father, Louis B. Mayer; second wife Jennifer Jones; Hitchcock; Welles; Leigh and Olivier; Hepburn). Thomson adroitly views Selznick's career through the wider lens of Hollywood's golden age, an approach enhanced by the excellent photos and appended apparatus (genealogies, filmography, bibliography, and notes). The writing indulges in occasional Selznickian hyperbole but movie lovers will enjoy Thomson's stylistic reliance on film metaphor and allusion. An outstanding biography. Readers at all levels.—*M. W. Estrin, Rhode Island College*

CRITICISM

OAB-0967   PN1995   91-33706 Orig
Aesthetics of film, by Jacques Aumont et al.; tr. and rev. by Richard Neupert. Texas, 1992. 269p bibl index afp ISBN 0-292-70428-3, $40.00; ISBN 0-292-70437-2 pbk, $17.95

For the past 30 years, the French have dominated the field of film theory. It is appropriate, therefore, that they have finally produced the single most comprehensive survey of the subject yet written. This masterful book provides a critical and concise introduction to nearly 100 years of philosophic inquiry into the cinema, from the early German idealism of Hugo Munsterberg to the modern period of semiology, deconstructionism, and Lacanian psychoanalysis. Despite the book's wide-ranging subject matter, it offers a successfully balanced and well-reasoned discourse that not only clarifies many issues but also correctly places the work of various theorists into the greater, evolving history of the field. Though the book will inevitably cause a few controversies, especially with its concluding statements on the "death" of contemporary film theory, its merits far outweigh its possible faults. *Aesthetics of Film* is likely to become an essential text for the classroom and will provide an excellent backbone to the collegiate syllabus. Advanced undergraduate; graduate.—*D. Toth, formerly, Columbus Museum of Art*

OAB-0968   PN1995   92-35884 CIP
Babington, Bruce. **Biblical epics: sacred narrative in the Hollywood cinema,** by Bruce Babington and Peter William Evans. Manchester,

1993. (Dist. by St. Martin's) 248p index ISBN 0-7190-3268-7, $49.95; ISBN 0-7190-4030-2 pbk, $17.95

The sorely neglected and seemingly moribund genre of the biblical epic is revived, even resurrected, in this fascinating study. Where others have found only grist for the mills of their condescending mockery, these authors have discovered pearls of great insight in their massive reassessment of the scholarly significance of these Hollywood spectaculars. Their work provides a refreshingly text-centered analysis that eschews the reductionism of most ideological criticism; although several psychoanalytic concepts slip into their examination of sacred narratives. The study of the three subgenres of biblical epics (the Old Testament epic, the Christ film, and the Roman/Christian epic) are aptly placed in the unique contexts of American religion and culture. The work intersects critical questions regarding such topics as narrative, representations of Jews, film noir, romantic love, and secularism with detailed analyses of key films such as *The Robe*. Relevant photographic stills enhance this densely provocative study. Highly recommended for advanced studies in film and theology.—*T. Lindvall, Regent University*

OAB-0969   PN1995   93-48340 CIP
Black, Gregory D. **Hollywood censored: morality codes, Catholics, and the movies.** Cambridge, 1994. 336p bibl filmography index ISBN 0-521-45299-6, $27.95

This excellent study explains how Hollywood movies came—in Ben Hecht's words—to slip "into the American mind more misinformation in one evening than the Dark Ages could muster in a decade." Black (communications, Univ. of Missouri—Kansas City) uses studio and Legion of Decency records to demonstrate how in the 1930s film, the most democratic art, became America's most censored. Film censorship began in 1907, but the Roaring '20s provoked the conviction that films should promote the simplest idealism at whatever cost of realism and principle. Films veered toward one of two puerilities, the naive or the sanctimoniously tawdry. Black's documented case studies establish the political conservatism and fear behind the censorship forces' "morality." The author roots the movement in the Catholic church's institutional interests and in anti-semitism. The censors stifled the ur-feminism of Mae West; eviscerated literary and dramatic adaptations; obscured the problematic realities of domestic, political, and economic life and ethics; and inhibited thoughtful treatment of the Depression, the country's political issues, and the rise of fascism. Even Fritz Lang's classic antilynching drama *Fury* (1936) was hobbled by the studio's racism and timidity. This particular censorship movement ended with WW II. Black's study is most welcome now, when serious artists quail before the revived charges of being "liberal" or even "humanist" in the face of family and patriotic values. Ideas remain an endangered, because feared, species. All levels.—*M. Yacowar, Emily Carr College of Art and Design*

OAB-0970   PN1998   92-45678 CIP
Bordwell, David. **The cinema of Eisenstein.** Harvard, 1993. 316p bibl index afp ISBN 0-674-13137-1, $65.00; ISBN 0-674-13138-X pbk, $29.95

The last two decades have witnessed a glorious renaissance of the Russian filmmaker who must rank among the greatest ever to have taken up cinema's cause. More than eight volumes of Eisenstein's writings have been published in English, and many other texts have also been translated into the major European languages. Countless articles and longer critical monographs have explored in detail many fascinating aspects of his prodigious career as a theatrical director, teacher, political intellectual, and, of course, director of celebrated but still too little understood films. What has been needed is a volume summarizing and synthesizing what is now known. But Bordwell has provided much more than the "straightforward introduction to [Eisenstein's] accomplishments" he too modestly states as his book's purpose. He sketches Eisenstein's life in the artistic and political context in which he worked. He patiently traces the complex roots of Eisentein's film theory and pedagogy in often arcane currents of Russian and European intellectual history. Finally, Bordwell offers compelling close readings of all the major films in a way that substantially enhances our understanding of the master's methods and accomplishments. Effectively illustrated and containing a superb bibliography, this lucid and persuasive account is a model of economy and insight from which future research will proceed. Everyone from the serious general reader to the old Eisenstein hand can read it profitably.—*S. Liebman, CUNY Graduate School and University Center*

OAB-0971   PN1998   96-38444 MARC
Burke, Frank. **Fellini's films: from postwar to postmodern.** Twayne/Prentice Hall International, 1996. 398p bibl filmography index afp ISBN 0-8057-3893-2, $28.95; ISBN 0-8057-3894-0 pbk, $16.95

This may the best English-language study of the neglected maestro's work. Burke (Queen's Univ., Canada) expands his *Federico Fellini*: Variety Lights *to* La Dolce Vita (CH, Apr'85) to include all films through *Voices of the Moon* (1990), and he takes the opportunity to eliminate his "reverential auteurism" and to "situate Fellini's individualist emphasis culturally and historically." He gives each Fellini film a close, insightful analysis that demonstrates exemplary application of postmodern and deconstructivist theory. Burke's Fellini is divided between a godlike figure and an "increasingly disempowered artist-in-the-flesh." When Fellini turned to adaptations he moved away from relative realism and toward "representation and meaning." From *Fellini's Casanova* (1976) on, "Fellini's films are almost all explicitly about systems of signification lacking an 'outside.'" His last films both exemplify and dispute postmodernity. In this radically new reading of that most individualistic and indulgent of artists, Burke finds Fellini's postmodernity presaged in *La Dolce Vita* (1960). Indeed he gives the films multiple readings because "Fellini's later work is itself an implicit rereading of the earlier." Burke concludes with a shrewd analysis of Fellini's decline in critical respectability and a balanced critical summary of his place in current film theory. This book compels Fellini's return to the curricular pantheon. Upper-division undergraduate through faculty.—*M. Yacowar, University of Calgary*

OAB-0972   Orig
Cherchi Usai, Paolo. **Burning passions: an introduction to the study of silent cinema,** tr. by Emma Sansone Rittle. British Film Institute, 1994. 119p bibl ISBN 0-85170-407-7, $39.95; ISBN 0-85170-408-5 pbk, $19.95

Despite his bland subtitle Paola Cherchi Usai offers a set of systematic principles that guides the reader into the dark woods of silent film research. He sets a shining lamp before the reader's feet for exploring the dimly lit and distant, enchanted world of the early movies. He transforms the pedantic tasks of film historiography into an odyssey of the mind, an intellectual adventure through the labyrinths of institutional archives, which rewards those who diligently obey the rules of silent-film research. This work is an indisputable gem, a tightly constructed, succinct, and piercingly clear map for finding resource material and identifying films and facts. The reader will find both an urgent apologetic for silent-film scholarship and practical advice in finding, viewing, and analyzing the rare resources. The appendixes (especially one listing reference works recommended by film scholars such as Kevin Brownlow) and illustrated plates ignite this challenge. Every professional, scholar, technician, and fan of silent film should pick up this combustible bit of intellectual kindling and benefit from its light and wisdom. Upper-division undergraduates; graduates; researchers; professionals.—*T. Lindvall, Regent University*

OAB-0973   PN1998   93-9506 CIP
Cohen, Hubert I. **Ingmar Bergman: the art of confession.** Twayne, 1993. 507p bibl index afp ISBN 0-8057-9312-7, $26.95; ISBN 0-8057-9331-3 pbk, $14.95

Probably the best critical study of Bergman in English. It is the product of a 15-year exploration of the author/director through his plays, interviews, writings, and most of all his 50-odd films. The first 120 pages provide the expectedly dramatic, often lurid, biography. Then follow a chapter on Bergman's apprentice work on stage and screen and a chapter on his early comedies. Then come 300 pages of close analysis of each of the films Bergman directed

or wrote. Cohen's critical style is dangerous but successful. He recounts each scene in close detail. The danger is that such writing might drift into merely replaying the film, sans celluloid; but Cohen's detailing is so evocative of the full sensory, intellectual, and emotional experience of the film that the book works brilliantly on the level of re-creation. In addition, Cohen constantly deepens his evocation of the film with critical analysis. The effect is as if one were watching the films with a brilliant commentator murmuring a sensitive, illuminating overlay with none of the annoyance that real commentators practice. Cohen's reflections continually refer across to Bergman's life and other Bergman works and utterances, confirming the central thesis that his films are an intensely personal confession. (One wonders whether any other major artist has ever spun such a large and varied canon out of his most personal obsessions.) So comprehensive is the study that even Bergman's TV soap commercials are given an appropriately brief critical reflection. Both general and academic readers at all levels.—*M. Yacowar, Emily Carr College of Art and Design*

OAB-0974   PN1995   93-17016 CIP
Colombat, André Pierre. **The Holocaust in French film.** Scarecrow, 1993. 435p bibl index afp (Filmmakers, 33) ISBN 0-8108-2668-2, $47.50

This well-researched, hard-hitting study brings valuable insights to how the Holocaust remained a taboo subject in France—and worldwide until Steven Spielberg's *Schindler's List* (1993), which is outside the present study. Colombat (French literature, Loyola) finds French cinema perpetuating the "myth of a unified country resisting the invader" throughout the 1946-61 period, ignoring the Holocaust entirely. Even Alain Resnais's *Nuit et Brouillard* ("Night and Fog," 1955), a heroic breakthrough, lumped Jewish victims in with all the others and was censored for an image of a French guard at a camp. The author provides detailed descriptions of unavailable films and cogent analyses of the key works that have confronted the subject: *Nuit et Brouillard*, Marcel Ophuls's trilogy, Louis Malle's *Lacombe Lucien* (1975) and *Au Revoir, les Enfants* (1987), Joseph Losey's *Mr. Klein* (1976), Pierre Sauvage's *Weapons of the Spirit* (1988), and—towering over all—Claude Lanzmann's *Shoah* (1985). There is also an interview with Sauvage. The investigation is thorough, the study well crafted and discriminating, and the conclusions quite devastating: that a culture of such depth and richness excluded an embarassing reality completely. All the more impressive then the dissenting mission of such assertive individualists as Ophuls, Lanzmann, Sauvage—and even Spielberg. All levels.—*M. Yacowar, Emily Carr College of Art and Design*

OAB-0975   PN1993   95-22747 CIP
Davis, Darrell William. **Picturing Japaneseness: monumental style, national identity, Japanese film.** Columbia, 1996. 304p bibl filmography index afp ISBN 0-231-10230-5, $49.50; ISBN 0-231-10231-3 pbk, $17.50

Davis (USC) is an exciting scholar of Japanese film: he relates films, especially those of the 1930s and 1940s, to the Japanese identity—"Japan's vision of itself as it materialized at a certain time, in a certain medium." True, when he looks at an individual film, he may not dazzle (though he is consistently sharp, detailed, thoughtful); but when he stands back to ponder and generalize—exactly where most critics are weak—he is superior. He presents ideas (on nationalism, honor, suicide, emperor, family, war, nature, architecture) that are big and daring. Above all, this is a book about "monumentalism," a style or "aesthetic of totalitarianism permeating the Japanese empire." The didactic function of the 1930s films was to awaken cosmopolitan Japanese "to the glories of their own culture." Davis sees these films as paternalistic, thus anti-West, or anti-Westernization (Western values being excessive individualism, merriment, frivolity, insincerity, indecency, disrespect). Their stories aim to re-Confucianize the nation; their monumentalism sings a hymn to the Japanese feudal heritage. Observations on the Samurai and censorship, on camera work and editing, are not detours, since they are factors that are as exhilarating as they are essential. Whenever Davis turns anthropologist, he distinguishes himself. Beautifully. The excellent bibliography includes three pages on historiography, six on Japanese history and culture, and about 25 books on Japanese films and filmmakers.—*P. H. Stacy, emeritus, University of Hartford*

OAB-0976   PQ4835   96-26835 MARC
Gordon, Robert S.C. **Pasolini: forms of subjectivity.** Oxford, 1996.
324p bibl index afp ISBN 0-19-815905-6, $72.00

Pasolini's multifaceted literary, critical, journalistic, and cinematic production has been studied both in his native Italy and in the English-speaking context, but most critics have concentrated on a specific mode. In the US, his
film work has received the most critical attention, although David Ward's *A
Poetics of Resistance* (1995), a study of his prose writings, is an important exception. The biographical studies do not provide analyses of his work. Thus, Gordon's book is a welcome addition, since it aims at an all-encompassing assessment of Pasolini's oeuvre, from his essays to his poetry and prose, from his film
theory and practice to his last posthumously published prose project, *Petrolio*.
The unifying critical thread of Gordon's interpretation is what he calls the "work
of subjectivity." Pasolini deploys and experiences forms of expression and discourse as both active and subjective signifying practices rather than as objective
systems. According to Gordon, Pasolini's art is best explicated by highlighting the complex ways in which the "I" of the artist and writer is at the center
of his search for meaning and communication. This extremely well-researched
book includes an extensive bibliography and succeeds in providing an analytically astute and unifying reading of Pasolini's immensely diverse production. Highly recommended for upper-division undergraduates through professionals.—*R. West, University of Chicago*

OAB-0977   PN1995   93-33042 CIP
Grindon, Leger. **Shadows on the past: studies in the historical fiction film.** Temple University, 1994. 250p index afp ISBN 1-56639-181-
4, $44.95; ISBN 1-56639-182-2 pbk, $18.95

This solidly researched book deals with a topic of increasing importance
in the academy, yet one that film scholars have yet to address adequately:
social memory as embodied in the representation of historical events. Grindon
(Middlebury College) looks closely at several historical films from different
countries and different time periods: *La Marseillaise* (1938); Hollywood
treatments of the French Revolution; *Senso* (1953); *The Rise of Louis XIV*
(1966); and *Reds* (1981). On the basis of close and detailed formal analyses, the
author argues that the historical film constitutes a cinematic genre in that these
otherwise widely divergent films are all predicated upon similar notions of
historical causality rooted in their depictions of romance and historical spectacle. Yet the book is also sensitive to textual difference, as Grindon grounds
his interpretations through detailing the production circumstances and historical conditions that gave rise to each text. Discussion of contemporary historiographical and political trends connects the films to their particular historical
moments, and discussion of the conditions of production illustrates the ways
in which economic requirements inflect textual signification. The book thus
constitutes an important step toward a fuller reconsideration of what Grindon
terms "this often neglected genre." Upper-division undergraduate and above.—
R. E. Pearson, University of Pennsylvania

OAB-0978   PN1993   91-47875 CIP
Horton, Andrew. **The zero hour: glasnost and Soviet cinema in
transition,** by Andrew Horton and Michael Brashinsky. Princeton, 1992.
287p bibl index afp ISBN 0-691-06937-9, $49.50; ISBN 0-691-01920-7
pbk, $14.95

What a delight it is to read this informative, insightful book! Horton and
Brashinsky seem to have seen every important movie, attended every important
screening, and interviewed every important director in the final years of the
Soviet Union. They discuss everything that one would want such a book to discuss: gender roles; borrowings from Western models (as well as well-chosen
contrasts with Hollywood movies that usefully contextualize the material
under discussion); the exceptional importance of documentaries; controversial topics such as the polluted environment and the war in Afghanistan; the significance (and limitations) of film genres; and the achievements of the various Soviet nationalities. As their thoughtful, restrained use of the currently
fashionable terminology of Russian critic Mikhail Bakhtin shows, "postmod-

ern" does not necessarily mean "pretentious." In fact, this well-written study
will probably be used as a textbook. The appearance of this superb book so soon
after *Inside the Film Factory*, ed. by Richard Taylor and Ian Christie (CH, Mar'92),
may mean that a renaissance of Russian film studies has begun. Highly recommended for all libraries.—*J. M. Curtis, University of Missouri—Columbia*

OAB-0979   PN1995   95-15279 MARC
Jowett, Garth S. **Children and the movies: media influence and
the Payne Fund controversy,** by Garth S. Jowett, Ian C. Jarvie, and
Kathryn H. Fuller. Cambridge, 1996. 414p bibl indexes ISBN 0-521-
48292-5, $54.95

This book rescues from disdain and oblivion the eight-volume "Payne
Fund Studies" (1933-35), which explored the effects of motion pictures on youth.
Jowett traces the histories and ideologies behind the research, and he shows how
the more balanced efforts of the individual academic researchers were affected
by the director, Rev. William Short. The goal was to "subordinate the movies
to the traditional mechanisms of social control" by provoking public opinion
and action, but the researchers' desire for value-neutral science was overwhelmed by the zeal of antimovie activists on one side and the wrath of anti-
censorship forces on the other. The PFS were victims of a paradigm shift:
"Abandoned by their makers, their approach superseded by a theoretically
new and more professionalized social science and their ideas (attitude studies,
adult discount) borrowed without proper acknowledgment, they took on a
dusty and old-fashioned air" that is both "a myth and a distortion." The last 171
pages of Jowett's book provide a wealth of unpublished Payne Fund material.
Apart from the persistent currency of the issues they deal with, the Payne studies represent pioneering efforts in the development of the social sciences. This
excellent, timely study is meticulously researched and clearly written. Upper-
division undergraduate through faculty.—*M. Yacowar, University of Calgary*

OAB-0980   PN1995   92-3311 CIP
Lewis, Jon. **The road to romance and ruin: teen films and youth
culture.** Routledge, 1992. 173p index ISBN 0-415-90426-9, $45.00; ISBN
0-415-90427-7 pbk, $14.95

Lewis's investigation of teen films (films about teenagers rather than films
aimed at teenagers) covers a broad spectrum of critical theory to probe the
phenomenon of youth culture, a culture that exists as a mass market and mass
movement. He argues, convincingly, that teen films focus on the breakdown of
traditional forms of authority; and rather than being inherently progressive,
the films stress reassurance and nostalgia. Teen films essentially function as
signposts for the consuming and self-constructing generations of teenagers who
follow cinematic roads to romance and ruin. Lewis's incorporation of sociological research and postmodern trends is remarkably insightful and relevant.
And considering the potential obtuseness of some of his sources, Lewis writes
lucidly and cogently of the apocalyptic, apolitical, romantic, and self-reflexive dimensions of youth culture. This fascinating scholarly work is highly
recommended for its thoroughness, accessibility, and salience.—*T. Lindvall,
Regent University*

OAB-0981   PN1995   92-17446 CIP
MacDonald, Scott. **Avant-garde film: motion studies.** Cambridge, 1993.
199p index ISBN 0-521-38129-0, $44.95; ISBN 0-521-38821-X pbk, $13.95

At last! A work on avant-garde film that is not as confounding as the films.
Where most books in the field are either historical or abstrusely theoretical, this
one successfully undertakes to explicate 15 avant-garde films in a clear, accessible manner. Moreover, MacDonald's purpose is to demonstrate how the avant-
garde cinema critiques the pervasive context of mainstream narrative/com-
mercial film. He succeeds in his aim to show how this challenging and unfamiliar
cinema can enliven even conventional film viewing. As a result, this is the
perfect text for an undergraduate course in the area and for the general reader,
who in some utopian miracle might find access to these particular films. In Part
1 MacDonald demonstrates how five filmmakers (Yoko Ono, Michael Snow,

Ernie Gehr, J.J. Murphy, and Morgan Fisher) refute the assumption that the cinema is a neutral technology that requires unquestioning enjoyment. Part 2 presents five critiques of how commercial film narrowly fetishizes narrative procedures; contributors are Hollis Frampton, Laura Mulvey and Peter Wollen, James Benning, Su Friedrich, and Yervant Gianikian and Angela Ricci Lucchi. In Part 3 Warren Sonbert, Godfrey Reggio, Trinh T. Minh-ha, Yvonne Rainier, and Peter Watkins reject the assumptions of a national and nationalistic imperative in cinema. The climactic study of Watkins's 14.5-hour *The Journey* (1987) pulls together all MacDonald's themes and would alone be worth the price of admission.—*M. Yacowar, Emily Carr College of Art and Design*

OAB-0982   PN1993   92-18884 CIP
Marcus, Millicent. **Filmmaking by the book: Italian cinema and literary adaptation.** Johns Hopkins, 1993. 313p index afp ISBN 0-8018-4454-1, $48.50; ISBN 0-8018-4455-X pbk, $15.95

This may be the most sophisticated study of literary film adaptations. Marcus prefers multiple critical schools over any one reductive orthodoxy, and in mobilizing a wide range of critical approaches, she brilliantly transcends the tradition of fidelity analysis. She reads Visconti's *La terra trema* (1948) as a Resistance-based critique of the Verga source and *The Leopard* (1963) as a polemic response to the debate about Lampedusa's novel, rooted in Gramsci. A feminist analysis of De Sica's *Two Women* (1960) finds Moravia's gendered discourse reversed. His film of Bassani's *Garden of the Finzi-Continis* (1971) provokes a study in the film medium's forms of intertextuality. In *The Gospel According to St. Matthew* (1964) Pasolini uses the subjective camera to express the apostle's personal witness to divine truth. But in his *Decameron* (1971) Pasolini's transgressive strategy is to translate an elitist medieval text into the vernacular of mass media entertainment. The Taviani brothers' *Padre Padrone* (1977), from the book by Gavino Ledda, invites a psychoanalytic critique of patriarchy; and their *Kaos* (1984), combining stories by Pirandello, demonstrates how poetic cinema may free a work from the limitations of prose. Fellini's strongly personal cinema calls for lively auteurist analysis of his *Casanova* (1974) and *La voce della luna* (1989), from Ermanno Cavazzoni's *Poema dei lunatici*. In its grasp of a wide range of current theory and in its sensitive, practical application, this is an exemplary work. Advanced undergraduate through faculty.—*M. Yacowar, Emily Carr College of Art and Design*

OAB-0983   ML2075   93-25082 CIP
Marks, Martin Miller. **Music and the silent film: contexts and case studies, 1895-1924.** Oxford, 1997. 303p index afp ISBN 0-19-506891-2, $45.00

Out of the silent darkness, Marks (music and theater arts, MIT) brings sound and light to his seminal study of this neglected aesthetic duo. In this detailed scholarly treatment of the nature and function of silent-film music, Marks surveys literature about film music collections, cue sheets, editorial columns, and compilation manuals. Although structured like a polished academic dissertation, the work reads easily, even melodically. Building on the forerunners of film music, Marks conducts readers through several stages that provide historical and critical contexts. Particularly illuminating are the case studies of individual films—e.g., Kalem Studio's blockbuster *From the Manger to the Cross* (1912); D.W. Griffith's controversial classic *Birth of a Nation* (1915), scored by pioneer Joseph Carl Breil; and the frantically comic, avant-garde French film by René Clair and Erik Satie, *Entr'acte* (1924). Marks orchestrates a symphony of relevant materials (including actual scores, appendixes, and footnotes) into a harmonious and compelling composition. This is integrated scholarship at its best. Highly recommended for large public collections and academic libraries serving upper-division undergraduates and above.—*T. Lindvall, Regent University*

OAB-0984   PN1995   95-24927 CIP
Miles, Margaret R. **Seeing and believing: religion and values in the movies.** Beacon Press, 1996. 254p index ISBN 0-8070-1030-8, $25.00

In framing an apologetic for a religious and axiological study of popular film—a multimillennial descendent of Greek tragedies—Miles (Harvard Divin-

ity School) makes scholarship and critical thinking profoundly relevant for contemporary society. She discerns the rhetorical significance of what many view as "harmless entertainment," probing the emotional images and social values of films depicting and dealing with religion, films that suggest answers to the question "How should we live?" Miles examines key box-office films (1983-93)—e.g., *Chariots of Fire* (1981), *Jungle Fever* (1991), and *The Last Temptation of Christ* (1988)—to assess how Hollywood treats religion as a social phenomenon and to identify the values circulated through this pervasive popular medium. She considers Islam and Judaism alongside varieties of Christianity. The strength of Miles's study is her lucid analysis of the cultural context of film, and of the pleasures of film as a mode of communication. In her discussion of postmodern concerns of race, gender, sexual orientation, and violence, however, Miles advances some polemics and lists her desiderata; but she ultimately opts for understanding. *Seeing and Believing* is a splendidly readable, intelligent, and compelling volume in which reading *is* seeing. Upper-division undergraduates and above.—*T. Lindvall, Regent University*

OAB-0985   PN1995   93-27388 CIP
Paul, William. **Laughing, screaming: modern Hollywood horror and comedy.** Columbia, 1994. 510p index afp ISBN 0-231-08464-1, $29.50

As a scholarly apologetic for comic and horrific vulgarity in the film products of the 1970s and 1980s, Paul's provocative book is oddly effective and persuasive. He showcases the Dionysian sexuality and violence of what he calls gross-out films and argues for a revaluation of these base, disreputable entertainment forms. He finds in these exploitative, subversive films (e.g., *Animal House, Carrie, Porky's*) the legacy of Aristophanes, Rabelais, the Grand Guignol, and the exuberant carnival spirit articulated by Mikhail Bakhtin. A communal mood, festivity, and an aggressive celebration of the lower human body mark these genres with an aesthetic ignored by elitist critics. Paul's lucid and compelling study situates these phenomena of laughter and screams in the cultural and historical context of modern America, and does so in a remarkably readable and astute manner. With footnotes alone worth the price of the book, this substantial work is highly recommended for all intelligent audiences.—*T. Lindvall, Regent University*

OAB-0986   PN1995   93-73 CIP
Pick, Zuzana M. **The new Latin American cinema: a continental project.** Texas, 1993. 251p bibl index afp ISBN 0-292-76545-2, $37.50; ISBN 0-292-76549-5 pbk, $16.95

By positing "nation-oriented practices" within "a unified continental project" in her discussion of new Latin American cinema, Pick has produced a study essential for understanding not only the movement but contemporary critical theories as well. Six areas of inquiry structure the work: history, authorship, gender, popular cinema, exile, and ethnicity, each illustrated with in-depth analyses of three or four films. Analyses of works completed during the past decade, like *Mujer transparente* (1990) and *Tangos, l'exil de Gardel* (1985), accompany analyses of films associated with the early years of the movement—*La hora de los hornos* (1968, The hour of the furnaces), *Chircales* (1972, The brickmakers), and *De cierta manera* (1977, One way or another). Rather than merely listing "classic" films associated with the movement, Pick carefully examines the geopolitical configuration of cinema. This volume expands the discussion of new Latin American cinema begun by Julianne Burton, John King, and others, reflecting as it does upon the role of criticism in naming and shaping the movement. An important model for future scholarship. Both undergraduate and graduate collections.—*A. M. Stock, College of William and Mary in Virginia*

OAB-0987   PN1995   93-48900 CIP
Sikov, Ed. **Laughing hysterically: American screen comedy of the 1950s.** Columbia, 1994. 282p bibl index afp ISBN 0-231-07982-6, $29.50

Sikov's work is an engaging, slightly quirky exploration of the comedy of the 1950s through the work of four directors—Howard Hawks, Billy Wilder, Alfred Hitchcock, and Frank Tashlin. The book takes a traditionally *auteurist* approach, with little apology for its unfashionable formal assumptions. But Sikov's analysis is neither passé nor trite; an openly gay critic, he grounds his analysis in the representation of gender and sexuality, buttressing his own insights with particular reference to Gaylyn Studlar's study of masochism in the cinema, *In the Realm of Pleasure* (CH, Mar'89). At his best, Sikov is both provocative and delightfully funny, particularly in his consideration of Hawks's *Gentlemen Prefer Blondes* (1953), Hitchcock's "Lamb to the Slaughter" *Hitchcock Presents* episode (1958), Wilder's *Some Like It Hot* (1959), and Tashlin's films with Jerry Lewis. At other times, especially in his discussions of *Monkey Business* (1952) and *The Trouble with Harry* (1955), one wishes that his focus would allow the discussion of other films more suited to his approach. But overall, this is an excellent addition to a neglected area of study. Recommended for all academic libraries.—*K. S. Nolley, Willamette University*

OAB-0988   PN1993   92-26076 CIP
Ukadike, Nwachukwu Frank. **Black African cinema.** California, 1994. 371p bibl index afp ISBN 0-520-07747-4, $50.00; ISBN 0-520-07748-2 pbk, $17.00

Ukadike presents a detailed, vastly well informed historical analysis of black African filmmaking, a subject virtually untouched in film studies until now. Without overgeneralizing "African culture," the author keeps the subject matter firmly rooted in cultural contexts; he differentiates between countries, regions, linguistic traditions, and peoples, giving a sense of multifaceted, complex developments of African film. The motion picture industry arrived in Africa decades after it was already firmly established on other continents, bringing with it many "colonizing" assumptions, even to countries that were no longer colonies. How could Africans make movies without using Western equipment, without making Hollywood assumptions, without using film artistry already familiar around the world? Even though basic film styles and vocabularies had been globalized in Western terms, Ukadike argues that indigenous black African filmmakers have contributed to the techniques and artistry of world cinema; he convincingly maintains that oral traditions especially have shaped a new narrative form in the movies of sub-Saharan Africa, and he clearly believes that black African contributions in film will become increasingly significant in the 21st century. Highly recommended for all libraries.—*R. D. Sears, Berea College*

■ Music

OAB-0989   ML3845   92-32210 CIP
Berman, Laurence. **The musical image: a theory of content.** Greenwood, 1993. 391p bibl indexes afp (Contributions to the study of music and dance, 30) ISBN 0-313-28434-2, $55.00

Berman (Univ. of Massachusetts at Boston) here approaches the history of Western music from a refreshingly different stance: while following the customary chronology from Plato to the present day, he presents "a history of ideas which happen to express themselves in music." Berman sets forth a view of music as reflection of its Zeitgeist; he considers music to have content above and beyond its formal structure. The title of the first chapter, "Archetypal Criticism, or an Alternate Poetics of Music," indicates that the author ambitiously intends to take on the Modernists' formalism, as exemplified in Stravinsky's 1939 Harvard lectures published as *Poétique musicale* (1942; tr. as *Poetics of Music*, 1942). By and large, Berman succeeds. His archetypal model, consisting of five pairs of opposites (comic/tragic, romantic/ironic, mythic/humanistic, hieratic/demotic, and Apollonian/Dionysian), is a valuable tool that can greatly enhance one's understanding of music from all historical periods. This book is a very impressive achievement. Highly recommended.—*E. Gaub, Villa Maria College*

OAB-0990   ML82   93-18463 CIP
Cecilia reclaimed: feminist perspectives on gender and music, ed. by Susan C. Cook and Judy S. Tsou. Illinois, 1994. 241p index afp ISBN 0-252-02036-7, $34.95; ISBN 0-252-06341-4 pbk, $12.95

This work sets itself a fascinating task, which it accomplishes with distinction and interest. Ten essays—ranging from a discussion of the philosophy of feminist music criticism and musicology (Marcia J. Citron), through the psychology of rearing a child prodigy (Adrienne Fried Block on Amy Beach) and how the politics of representation influenced musical activities throughout history, to a tale of gender and power in American balladry (Susan C. Cook)—revisit some familiar musical paths with new maps. Cook and Tsou promise in their introduction to "add untold dimensions to our previous understanding of music history and musical activity" and they do. They present the reader with "an attempt to right the inequities of male-female relations by rewriting aspects of our musical past ... ask[ing] new questions ... examin[ing] neglected source materials...." This collection traverses the tale of women in music from the English Renaissance, 17th-century France, 18th-century Italy, 19th-century American magazine (popular) music, arriving at a discussion of female images in current rap music. The distinguished essayists are joined in the common cause of rethinking and reviewing the history of music, a cause that will be taken all the more seriously because of the excellence of their contributions. This volume is a must for any music history shelf in any library serving undergraduates, graduates, and the general musical public. It will also be a valuable addition to the literature of women's studies, sociology, and ethnomusicology. The excellent bibliographic references attached to each article will serve future scholars as a springboard for research for years to come.—*S. Glickman, formerly, Franklin and Marshall College*

OAB-0991   ML3795   94-19901 CIP
Chanan, Michael. **Musica practica: the social practice of Western music from Gregorian chant to postmodernism.** Verso, 1994. 302p index ISBN 1-85984-005-1 pbk, $18.95

One of the most exciting recent developments in music scholarship is the attempt to view music in larger contexts—social, political, economic, and technological—rather than focusing on its internal structure. Chanan, a filmmaker, writer, and teacher, here offers an engaging, well-written survey of this vast terrain, which manages to touch on many important issues. After a delightful introduction, the book is organized in four sections. The first, "The Shaping Forces of Music," includes a discussion of the central importance of musical notation in Western music. The second, "The Political Economy of Music," addresses music printing and publishing, and the development of the concert. "Musical Engineering" traces the evolution of musical instruments from antiquity to the present, with special emphasis on the piano. The final section, "Music in the Age of Electro-Acoustics," states that "modernism in music coincides with the emergence of recording" and goes on to describe the huge transformation in musical life brought about by the development of the gramophone, radio, and tape recorder, and later by the electric guitar and synthesizer. This book adds a fresh dimension to the standard view of music history; insights abound on virtually every page. Highly recommended for all collections.—*E. Gaub, Villa Maria College of Buffalo*

OAB-0992   ML200   92-11237 MARC
Crawford, Richard. **The American musical landscape.** California, 1993. 381p bibl index afp ISBN 0-520-07764-4, $45.00

This book consummates over 30 years of research in the history and criticism of American music, during which time the author has become a senior scholar in the field. Crawford has looked at much music, from early psalmody to rock, and at an impressive amount of previous writing (107 pages of densely packed backnotes and a 14-page bibliography support and augment the text). He arrives at some fresh conclusions about the vitality and character of American music and suggests new avenues for investigation. The text is divided into four parts: a critical review of American music histories; an examination of teaching, composing, and performing as they have interacted and developed over the past two centuries; assessments of three composers as exemplars of their musical cultures (William Billings and 18th-century religious music, George Root and 19th-century popular song, Duke Ellington and 20th-century jazz); and the evolution of Gershwin's "I Got Rhythm" along many different paths. Using some basic themes to draw together these various topics, Crawford develops an inclusive view which differs from previous, more exclusive, attempts at explaining the uniqueness of American music; and he finds that the US economic system, rather than being antithetical to music, has supported a diversity of types, from popular to elite. The importance of his ideas and the clarity of his prose make this an important book for all readers interested in any aspect of American music.—*W. K. Kearns, University of Colorado at Boulder*

OAB-0993   ML3845   91-47076 CIP
Lippman, Edward. **A history of Western musical aesthetics.** Nebraska, 1992. 551p bibl index afp ISBN 0-8032-2863-5, $70.00

To any serious music lover the ultimate in musical understanding is musical aesthetics, which comes closer than any other philosophical endeavor to explaining the extraordinarily powerful impact of art upon sensitive human beings. Lippman's book is a most welcome contribution, a veritable treasure trove of insight into what is usually regarded as a very recondite subject. So pervasive has been the fascination of aesthetics for critics and literary figures through the ages that the sheer number of their writings challenges the imagination. Lippman has organized the subject in a logical chronology starting with Plato and Aristotle and culminating in such figures as T.W. Adorno and Georg Lukács. This comprehensive, encyclopedic treatment of writers includes trenchant analyses of their writings and assessments of their contributions and of their relationships to their cultural and historical eras. Lippman writes in a clear and readable style, avoiding the prolixity and obscurantism so often encountered in scholarly publications. All the sections are top-notch; perhaps the best are those dealing with opera. Most highly recommended both as general reading and as a resource book at the undergraduate, graduate, and faculty/professional musician levels. A major addition to the bibliography of musical aesthetics.— *G. Muns, emeritus, Eastern Kentucky University*

OAB-0994   ML1700   93-24898 CIP
The Oxford illustrated history of opera, ed. by Roger Parker. Oxford, 1995 (c1994). 541p bibl index afp ISBN 0-19-816282-0, $35.00

This historical survey skillfully combines illustrations and narrative text, thereby achieving a dimension of opera analysis normally eschewed in scholarly studies. From 17th-century Florence to the 1990s, the visual aspects of opera are presented in nearly 300 illustrations, many in color, to form a splendid compendium of visual information. Individual chapters deal with opera from the 17th century; 18th-century serious opera; 18th-century comic opera; 19th-century French, Italian, and German opera; Russian, Czech, Polish, and Hungarian opera to 1900; 20th-century opera to 1945; and 20th-century opera from 1945 to the present. The staging of opera, opera singers, and opera as a social occasion are treated in separate chapters. The union of the arts that produces the operatic genre is engagingly examined. Suggested readings, an opera chronology, and a thorough index are included. General readers and scholars will take delight in this sturdily bound, excellently designed, reasonably priced publication. Highly recommended, it belongs in every collection.— *R. Miller, Oberlin College*

OAB-0995   ML196   92-10566 CIP
Ratner, Leonard G. **Romantic music: sound and syntax.** Schirmer Books, 1992. 348p bibl indexes afp ISBN 0-02-872065-2, $45.00

Ratner looks at familiar 19th-century pieces from a new perspective. He explores the nature of the 19th-century sound palette, how composers use it as a distinctive compositional element, and how these aspects of sound contrast with classical usage. He includes quotes from relevant contemporary theorists and composers to support his points. Part 1 studies 19th-century orchestration. The perspective is fresh and engaging, although Ratner does

not break new ground here. In Part 2 he describes his system of "rhetorical reduction" designed to capture the important elements of the music. Parts 3 and 4 apply these principles of reduction to 19th-century period structures and forms. Ratner compares pieces of Schubert, Chopin, Schumann, Liszt, Brahms, Mahler, and others with their rhetorical reductions. These comparisons highlight how the composers obscure, distort, and interrupt the syntax with elements of sound. Yet, the composers never entirely lose traditional, 18th-century syntax. The analyses are wide-ranging, penetrating, and convincing. Easily readable, with basic introductions to each section and many accessible examples, this book should be a welcome addition to all libraries.—*C. Cai, Kenyon College*

OAB-0996   ML3195   91-39456 CIP
Shiloah, Amnon. **Jewish musical traditions.** Wayne State, 1992. 274p bibl index ISBN 0-8143-2234-4, $39.95

In possibly the most important synthesis of knowledge regarding Jewish music since A.Z. Idelsohn's frequently reprinted *Jewish Music in Its Historical Development* (1929), Shiloah (Hebrew Univ. of Jerusalem) attempts to unravel the enormous complexities of this subject. Shiloah's familiarity with the vast repertory and scholarship on Middle Eastern art and on folk and liturgical music endows this work with important authoritative new insights. Unlike Idelsohn, Shiloah cannot comfortably structure this study around a single organic theme such as historical continuity. Instead, he presents a wide range of topics, utilizing the perspectives of ethnomusicology to look at Jewish music in its cultural context. While probably more appropriately reflecting that discipline's contemporary broad outlook, this book fails to totally integrate the encyclopedic information in a form readily assimilated by the reader. Shiloah also rejects a number of broadly held interpretations of Idelsohn and others, offering his own ideas in their place. These are not always well supported. Nevertheless, this is a must acquisition for anyone interested in Jewish history, culture, and music and their interrelationship in the broader context of the societies with which Jewish communities coexisted. A useful index and good bibliography make this an important research tool. Undergraduate; graduate; faculty; pre-professional and professional musicians.—*L. D. Loeb, University of Utah*

BIOGRAPHY

OAB-0997   ML410   92-21844 CIP
Anderson, Donna K. **Charles T. Griffes: a life in music.** Smithsonian Institution Press, 1993. 131p index afp ISBN 1-56098-191-1, $49.00

Anderson, author of *The Works of Charles T. Griffes: A Descriptive Catalogue* (CH, Feb'84) and of *Charles T. Griffes: An Annotated Bibliography-Discography* (CH, May'78), has now written what is certain to be the definitive biography of this important American composer. The book combines Anderson's meticulous research with her felicitous writing style to create a first-rate study of Griffes, who died in 1920 at the age of 35. Anderson traces Griffes's life and career from Elmira, New York, to his study in Berlin, to his teaching at the Hackley School in Tarrytown, New York, to his growing reputation as a composer. A large section of the book is given over to analyses of his music— detailed analyses that are delights for their lucidity. Photographs and music examples amply support Anderson's prose, and an updated discography and bibliography are welcome additions for the reader. This is *the* major book on Griffes and would be a valuable addition to any library.—*C. W. Henderson, Saint Mary's College (IN)*

OAB-0998   ML410   95-13537 CIP
Burkholder, J. Peter. **All made of tunes: Charles Ives and the uses of musical borrowing.** Yale, 1995. 554p bibl indexes afp ISBN 0-300-05642-7, $35.00

This major contribution to the literature on Ives builds on previous studies, especially the catalogs of John Kirkpatrick and James Sinclair and this reviewer's *The Charles Ives Tunebook* (CH, Apr'91). Burkholder (Indiana Univ.) carefully dissects Ives's musical borrowing, separating the composer's methods of using preexisting music into 14 categories: modeling, variations, paraphrase, setting (of a tune with an accompaniment different from its original form), cantus firmus treatment, use in a medley, use in a quodlibet, allusion to a general style or type of music, transcription, programmatic purpose, cumulative, collage, patchwork, and extended paraphrase. Although these categories *can* be discrete, one can find many instances where Ives uses more than one technique, in juxtaposition and simultaneously. Burkholder's main contribution to the Ives literature is in illustrating how the composer's different methods of quotation work within the context of the music and how his musical ideas frequently grew out of the preexistent music to which he was attracted. Additionally, Burkholder compares Ives's quotation techniques with those used by his European contemporaries and antecedents. Excellent notes and a comprehensive bibliography enhance this valuable study. One caveat: one must be careful not to attribute too much in Ives to quotation, for there is much originality in his music. Recommended for academic libraries, upper-division undergraduate upward.— *C. W. Henderson, Saint Mary's College (IN)*

OAB-0999 ML410 96-23177 CIP
Daverio, John. **Robert Schumann: herald of a "new poetic Age".** Oxford, 1997. 607p bibl index afp ISBN 0-19-509180-9, $45.00

This excellent and comprehensive book is masterfully written. Especially notable is its subtle interweaving of life and works. Daverio (Boston Univ.) reexamines common assumptions—for example, Schumann's allegedly uninspired use of four-bar phrasing and his supposed lack of inspiration in late works. The author suggests new interpretations at every turn through his sensitive handling of newly available primary sources, the marriage diaries, and other material. His approach enriches and redirects the reader's understanding of Schumann. Daverio gives particular attention to Schumann's little-known works, for example, *Genoveva, Manfred,* and *Faust,* with a view to rebalancing Schumann's current image as primarily a song and piano composer. Daverio's breadth of knowledge is especially apparent in his explorations of the relationship between Schumann's love of literature and Schumann's own literary and musical work. Daverio describes Schumann as a multitalented person and argues effectively that Schumann creates in his music a "coherence ... with the same intellectual substance as literature." Highly recommended for undergraduate, graduate, and public libraries.—*C. Cai, Kenyon College*

OAB-1000 ML410 92-43829 CIP
Frisch, Walter. **The early works of Arnold Schoenberg, 1893-1908.** California, 1993. 328p bibl indexes afp ISBN 0-520-07819-5, $48.00

This is as fine and thorough a coverage of Schoenberg's early tonal music as we are ever likely to have. In tracing Schoenberg's compositional development, Frisch divides the early works into three periods: the Brahmsian influence, 1893-97; expanded tonality using Wagnerian techniques, 1899-1903; and the move toward individualism, 1904-08. This is not a new view, but Frisch makes it persuasive and attributes Schoenberg's new direction in 1899 to the crucial influence of Dehmel's poetry. The book contains comprehensive analyses that take account of formal design, thematic structure, motivic variants, harmony, tonality, and metrics. Many lesser-known works are discussed and analyzed as well as the more familiar ones, such as *Verklärte Nacht, Gurrelieder, Pelléas und Mélisande,* Quartets 1 and 2, and the Chamber Symphonies. Frisch's expertise on Brahms and his close examination of the manuscript sources allow many useful comparisons and thoughtful insights. Examples are numerous, but readers will still need scores for the major works. Essential reading for anyone interested in Schoenberg; highly recommended for advanced undergraduate and graduate students and for faculty.—*C. Adams, Franklin and Marshall College*

OAB-1001 ML402 94-34560 CIP
Handy, D. Antoinette. **Black conductors.** Scarecrow, 1995. 557p bibl index afp ISBN 0-8108-2930-4, $69.50

This long-awaited publication is the most welcome addition to the field since Eileen Southern's *Biological Dictionary of Afro-American and African Musicians* (CH, Jan'83). Handy's rich and diverse background (she retired as music director of the National Endowment for the Arts in 1993) makes her the ideal person to compile this study. She traces the careers of 114 important figures, providing insights and many details never before available. These are stories of victories great and small: Handy includes such figures as Dean Dixon as well as internationally respected conductors (e.g., James DePreist and Paul Freeman). The work is carefully and accurately documented. The introductory material on the evolution and education of a conductor should be required reading for all music students, and acquisition librarians will want to examine the excellent bibliography. All collections.—*D.-R. de Lerma, Lawrence University*

OAB-1002 ML410 91-2454 CIP
Heyman, Barbara B. **Samuel Barber: the composer and his music.** Oxford, 1992. 586p bibl index afp ISBN 0-19-506650-2, $45.00

Would that every American composer might be as well served as is Samuel Barber by Barbara Heyman, whose book will, as critic Michael Steinberg observed, "be the foundation of all Barber scholarship forever." A bold claim, but one borne out by a careful reading of Heyman's text. Clearly and engagingly written, thorough yet never pedantic, sympathetic but not hagiographical, Heyman's study provides a painstaking consideration of every aspect of the composer's life, drawing frequently upon a rich trove of letters both to and from Barber. (One wonders what will happen to biography when people no longer write letters, even if few artists and fewer composers can boast Barber's literary skill.) Heyman does not pretend to deal exhaustively with Barber's music, although the many musical examples and her pointed commentary considerably enhance her book. Others may delve more deeply into the technicalities of Barber's art, but it is unlikely that anyone will add much to a consideration of his life, his family, his background, his education, his associates, or the curve of his career. Barber occupies a secure position in the small group of truly important American composers. Heyman's study goes far to explain why. The book includes a list of works, a bibliography, extensive notes, and an index. All libraries.—*F. Goossen, University of Alabama*

OAB-1003 ML410 92-46591 CIP
Knepler, Georg. **Wolfgang Amadé Mozart,** tr. by J. Bradford Robinson. Cambridge, 1994. 374p bibl index ISBN 0-521-41972-7, $49.95

Traditional biography has cast Mozart as a perpetual wunderkind, inhabiting a world only of music, remaining unaware of the larger world. Recently, a revisionist wind has been blowing. A few scholars have asked how Mozart's life, all of his life, affected his work. Now Knepler steps brazenly into the breach, examining Mozart's creative development with respect to all sorts of extramusical influences. Family, personal circumstance, and even biology are considered, although the argument centers on Mozart as Freemason and as child of the Enlightenment. Could the composer, who lived to see the French Revolution, have been immune to revolutionary thought? Emphatically not, Knepler says. Evidence appears through careful reading of Mozart's letters and from impressive analysis of several musical works, particularly parts of the operas. The book, translated brilliantly from the German by Robinson, includes notes, index, illustrations, musical examples, and a large bibliography; an appendix offers several texts that "played a role in Mozart's intellectual development." The final chapter displays Knepler's Marxist outlook rather too blatantly, but this provocative, original book is highly recommended to students of Mozart and to anyone interested in the cultural life of the late 18th century. Upper-division undergraduates and above.—*B. J. Murray, University of Alabama*

OAB-1004 ML410 92-37841 CIP
Phillips-Matz, Mary Jane. **Verdi: a biography.** Oxford, 1993. 941p bibl index ISBN 0-19-313204-4, $45.00

Andrew Porter, author of perhaps the best concise "life and works" of Verdi (his entry for the composer in the *New Grove*), wrote in his foreword to

Phillips-Matz's magnificent new study that it is the "latest, longest, and most thoroughly informed of the many Verdi biographies in English." One can only agree. The result of some 30 years of research, this achievement is very impressive. It also wears its enormous scholarship (120 pages of endnotes) lightly; the book is a pleasure to read. The Verdi who emerges is considerably more complex than hitherto known, almost Wagnerian in his egotism and capacity for repaying kindness with cruelty. The details of how *Rigoletto* came to be written and performed, for instance, form a case study in shrewd negotiating and salesmanship on the composer's part. Focusing exclusively on Verdi's life, this book pointedly excludes any musical examples or analysis from its purview, complementing Julian Budden's three-volume *The Operas of Verdi* (rev. ed., 1992; 1st ed., CH, Apr'79, Dec'81). This should be the definitive Verdi biography for some time. Highly recommended for most collections, both public and academic libraries.—*E. Gaub, Villa Maria College*

OAB-1005 ML410 95-22549 CIP
Swafford, Jan. **Charles Ives: a life with music.** W.W. Norton, 1996. 525p bibl index ISBN 0-393-03893-9, $30.00

By searching for consistencies within the paradoxes of Ives's life and music and setting it all in historical context, Swafford has written a superlative book for both academic and general readers. Introductory chapters about Danbury, Connecticut (where the composer was born), and the Ives clan teach history and consider the nonconformity of a New England family of "originals." Civil War music, Yale and New York City at the turn of the century, and the early years of the insurance business during the "Great War" are all settings for the romantic/experimental music of a justly admired hereditary eccentric. Most other recent works on Ives have been limited—treating Ives's relationship with his father, his musical style, his place in musical history (see Stuart Feder's *Charles Ives, "My Father's Song": A Psychoanalytic Biography*, CH, Nov'92; Larry Starr's *A Union of Diversities: Style in the Music of Charles Ives*, CH, Nov'92; *Charles Ives and the Classical Tradition*, ed. by Geoffrey Block and Peter Burkholder, CH, Nov'96). Swafford covers all of this and more. If inclined, the reader can find additional material in the excellent endnotes. A prize-winning book, certainly, for fans of history, biography, music, Americana, and general good writing. All collections.—*J. P. Ambrose, University of Vermont*

OAB-1006 ML300 96-41182 CIP
Taruskin, Richard. **Defining Russia musically: historical and hermeneutical essays.** Princeton, 1997. 561p index afp ISBN 0-691-01156-7, $49.50

The prolific Taruskin (Univ. of California, Berkeley) has produced another provocative, polemical, revisionist work. Explicitly hermeneutic, the book considers the entire landscape of Russian art music, from the 18th century to the late 20th. It is a bit of a patchwork; portions were composed originally for a variety of purposes, and some sections have appeared in print before. However, Taruskin has been mostly successful in pulling the pieces together, and the resulting shape seems oddly congruent to Russian music itself. The book has three parts. The seven essays in part 1 provide a history of Russian music. In part 2 Taruskin attempts to define what is "self" in Russian music and what is "other" and argues for the centrality of these concepts. Part 3, longer than the first two parts together, discusses four composers the author views as seminal: Tchaikovsky, Scriabin, Stravinsky, Shostakovich. Taruskin's hallmarks are evident throughout: research of almost astonishing breadth, impatience with facile views and those who propound them, and contempt for formalist modes of analysis that ignore the extramusical. This is an important, challenging book; no other book in English covers this ground with equal depth or brilliance. Highly recommended for upper-division undergraduates and above.—*B. J. Murray, University of Alabama*

OAB-1007 ML410 93-28500 MARC
Taruskin, Richard. **Stravinsky and the Russian traditions: a biography of the works through Mavra.** California, 1996. 2v. 1,757p bibl index afp ISBN 0-520-07099-2, $125.00

Taruskin (Univ. of California, Berkeley), the leading American scholar of Russian music, has written a study of Russian culture preceding and concurrent with Stravinsky's early career. It is monumental in size, content, and method. An introduction, 19 lengthy chapters, and an epilogue cover approximately one-fourth of the composer's creative life. Taruskin's introduction presents five theses of "the new image of Stravinsky": the composer played the traditions of Russian folk music against those of Russian art music; his knowledge of folklore came from visual artists; he combined Russian musical training with stylistic elements of Russian folklore to "excrete" anything "European"; this style "formed him as a composer"; and he is "the most completely Russian composer of art music that ever was and ... will be." Armed with a vast knowledge of Russian literature and intimate familiarity with many Russian and non-Russian composers, Taruskin convincingly proves his case. Biographical details are minimal; instead, the author provides the social, cultural, and political contexts in which the works were produced. He examines pieces both large and small, from Stravinsky's amateur beginnings in part 1 through the failed "Mavra" in part 4. The epilogue shows the continuing "Russianness" of Stravinsky's compositions. Beautifully printed and bound, the volumes include true footnotes, clear music examples, tables, figures, photographs, a glossary of Russian names and terms, a pronunciation guide, substantial bibliography, and extensive index. This landmark book will affect the writing of histories of Western music in the future. Primarily of interest to musicologists and music theorists, it will attract many others and is highly recommended for virtually all libraries.—*R. Stahura, Ripon College*

OAB-1008 ML410 92-19340 CIP
Taylor, Ronald. **Kurt Weill: composer in a divided world.** Northeastern University, 1992. 358p bibl index afp ISBN 1-55553-147-4, $29.95

This is the first full-length biography of Weill to benefit from the unexpected release of family letters in the early '80s. Largely avoiding technical language, Taylor manages to characterize Weill's early compositions (lacking in earlier biographies) as well as the better-known Americanized works of later years. The composer's development is traced against the background of his Jewish roots and Germany's troubled interwar years in more detail than in Ronald Sanders's popular biography *The Days Grow Short* (CH, Oct'80), but with less analysis of music and fewer musical examples than in Douglas Jarman's *Kurt Weill* (CH, Jun'83). Extensive accounts from those who knew Weill, as well as a fair number of photographs (Jarman has more), are interwoven with insightful sociological perspective. Although Taylor's study contains a useful, partially annotated select bibliography, it is not intended as a detailed reference work. There is no list of works or discography, and Taylor directs the reader to David Drew's *Kurt Weill: A Handbook* (CH, Feb'88), which contains both and remains the best single reference book. The tone of Taylor's biography is more scholarly than is usual in biographies intended for the nonmusician, and the author's description of the cultural and social factors that contributed to Weill's metamorphoses as a composer make this account of his life more compelling than any previous one. Strongly recommended for all libraries.—*J. J. Carbon, Franklin and Marshall College*

OAB-1009 ML410 95-19069 CIP
Youens, Susan. **Schubert's poets and the making of lieder.** Cambridge, 1996. 384p bibl index ISBN 0-521-55257-5, $64.95

This reviewer welcomes another Schubert book from Youens (Univ. of Notre Dame), whose previous writings (*Retracing a Winter's Journey: Schubert's Winterreise*, CH, Jun'92; *Schubert: Die schöne Müllerin*, CH, May'93; and *Hugo Wolf: The Vocal Music*, CH, Apr'93) have set the standard for musicological attention to Austrian lieder. Having already dealt intensively with Schubert's masterworks, she now moves on to another extremely productive level. She kills several birds with one stone: turning her attention to (mostly) early Schubert, she focuses on his poetic choices and the evolution of his adult "voice"; she examines these lieder from the perspective of four neglected poets, Gabriele von Baumberg, Theodor Körner, Johann Mayrhofer, and Ernst Schulze; she digs deeply into the relationship between selected poems and some of the songs they inspired; and eschewing current literary and critical systems she clarifies the psychological, social, and political context of these issues. A big bonus is that the author's delight in her material flows out like good scholarly conversation. Simply stated, the book is *interesting* from beginning to end. Abundant examples from both poetry and music are included along with copious, information-laden endnotes and a substantial bibliography. This very important book is recommended for comparative literature and German language studies as well as music. Upper-division undergraduate through faculty; general.—*M. S. Roy, Pennsylvania State University, University Park Campus*

HISTORY

OAB-1010   ML1711   96-4494 CIP
Ahlquist, Karen. **Democracy at the opera: music, theater, and culture in New York City, 1815-60.** Illinois, 1997. 248p bibl index afp ISBN 0-252-02272-6, $29.95

This thoroughly researched study traces the emergence and success of opera in 19th-century New York. This reviewer had trouble deciding which aspect of the book is most impressive: its detailed factual information or its evaluation of opera's progress as a social, economic, and musical phenomenon. Ahlquist (George Washington Univ.) documents all New York theatrical venues in which opera was performed, noting as well the extramusical reasons why certain works or performers succeeded or failed. She thus clarifies the connection between stage and audience. Nor is this connection faceless, for Ahlquist offers insights into the effectiveness of key players, the most interesting of whom is the young Maria Malibran. Ahlquist's prose is dense, and she often repeats the same points in different words. She is also too quick to attribute large audiences to increases in opera's democratic appeal and too slow to acknowledge the place of the city's intellectual elite (not necessarily synonymous with its economic elite) in opera's successes. Detailed musical analyses seem to have wandered in from another book, but there are only occasional errors of fact (e.g., only the third act of Rossini's *Otello* conforms to Shakespeare). All in all, a fine study that deserves a place in every general, undergraduate, and graduate music collection.—*K. Pendle, University of Cincinnati*

OAB-1011   ML169   94-28507 CIP
Anderson, Warren D. **Music and musicians in ancient Greece.** Cornell, 1995 (c1994). 248p bibl index afp ISBN 0-8014-3083-6, $35.00

Music making in Greek life, rather than the theory or philosophy of Greek music, is Anderson's emphasis in this excellent work on music from the Stone Age through the 5th century BCE. His ethnomusicological study begins 10,000 years ago with a bowed harp in the Dordogne caves and surveys harps, lyres, auloi, syrinxes, and their hybrids. Anderson (Univ. of Massachusetts at Amherst) reviews nonmusical sources; discusses performance practice (frequently in comparison with non-Greek cultures); studies the "major players"—Orpheus, Hermes, and Apollo—poets, and genres; and provides music references in Plato and Aristotle. The stunning chapter on the 5th century emphasizes the place of music in Greek drama. Extensive appendixes add material on instrumental resources (through lists and beautifully annotated plates), scale systems and notation, and illuminating commentary on the three major extant Greek compositions—the Leiden and Orestes fragments and the Song of Seikilos. A judicious bibliography follows. Anderson joins M.L. West (*Ancient Greek Music*, CH, Oct'93) on the short shelf of exemplary texts for the nonspecialist. All collections.—*J. P. Ambrose, University of Vermont*

OAB-1012   ML290   CIP
Baldauf-Berdes, Jane L. **Women musicians of Venice: musical foundations 1525-1855.** Oxford, 1993. 305p bibl index afp ISBN 0-19-816236-7, $55.00

Far from being the quasi-orphanages described in writings about Vivaldi's

violin concertos, the Venetian *ospedali grandi* were for over 350 years musical institutions of wealth and grandeur where patrons supported more than 300 external masters to teach more than 850 women the skills required of virtuosity. The works written for the *cori* or musicians of the *ospedali*, still uncataloged, number more than 4,000. The ecclesiastical independence of Venice from Rome allowed these grand charitable enterprises to permit females to become church musicians, and students ranging from orphans to such famous performers as Faustina Bordoni took advantage of the opportunity to receive the best training from European musicians of several countries. Although Venice itself has long been considered a center for the other arts, knowledge of music has been centered at San Marco. Baldauf-Berdes has opened a whole new and exciting area for research. Her extensive bibliography should provide the incentive for revelations about the history of women in Italian music and for the publication of "new" Venetian music. A major contribution to women's studies and to the history of music. Highly recommended to advanced undergraduate and graduate collections.—*J. P. Ambrose, University of Vermont*

OAB-1013   ML200   92-12422 CIP
Broyles, Michael. **Music of the highest class: elitism and populism in antebellum Boston.** Yale, 1992. 392p bibl index afp ISBN 0-300-05495-5, $37.50

Broyles's thesis is that, in 1840s Boston, abstract instrumental music and its principal agent, the symphony orchestra, became the symbol of the high culture and concomitant great moral value, a condition that extended to the entire US and persists, at the cost, however, of the division of music into elite and popular, high brow and low brow. Three Bostonians play key roles: Lowell Mason, who culminated the work of the "Presbyterian-Congregational" reformers by giving church music classically oriented ideals; Samuel Eliot, the mayor of Boston, who enlarged the scope of Mason's work in the Boston Academy of Music to include symphonic music; and John Sullivan Dwight, whose romantic-transcendentalist principles elevated purely instrumental music to a "sacralized" art. The story is quite complex, and Broyles follows each thread in some detail, reaching far back into the 18th century and encompassing activities throughout the country as well as in Boston. He also examines the roles of opera, the virtuosi, bands, and private music making in the shaping of the elitist aesthetic used to justify government appropriations for the arts. Broyles's research is extensive and his work on Samuel Eliot, who plays a pivotal role in the change from vocal to instrumental music as an aesthetic and ethical ideal, is new. A major contribution to the social and aesthetic history of American music and its cultural role.—*W. K. Kearns, University of Colorado at Boulder*

OAB-1014   ML2633   94-31376 CIP
Feldman, Martha. **City culture and the madrigal at Venice.** California, 1995. 473p bibl index afp ISBN 0-520-08314-8, $60.00

The story of musical life in the Italian peninsula of the 16th century is in many ways the story of its political and cultural geography, a terrain dominated by centers of aristocratic patronage on the one hand and the sponsorship of music and musicians by ecclesiastical authorities on the other. Feldman's book concerns a particular time and place (in this case mid-century Venice) and its influence on musical life, but this study is hardly confined to a particular institution or aristocratic family. Instead, the reader will find richly detailed explorations of Venetian academies and their patrician leaders, men like Domenico Venier, whose activities Feldman (Univ. of Chicago) finds remarkably revealing of the close connection between the obligations of civic harmony and the sorts of literary and rhetorical production those obligations help to engender. According to Feldman, these same ideals of literary restraint and euphonious expression were applied to music, notably in the mid-century madrigal books of Cipriano de Rore and Adrian Willaert and in the treatises of Willaert's pupil Gioseffo Zarlino. Feldman has undertaken an entirely new sort of enterprise, remarkable both in the variety of the academic and musical circles whose activities she circumscribes and in her profound critical insight. Upper-division undergraduates, graduate students; researchers, faculty; professionals.—*R. Freedman, Haverford College*

OAB-1015 ML2829 92-37138 CIP
Gorrell, Lorraine. **The nineteenth-century German Lied.** Amadeus Press, 1993. (Dist. by Timber) 398p bibl indexes ISBN 0-931340-59-4, $39.95

Gorrell (Winthrop Univ.) has written a book of considerable importance to those who teach the history and literature of song. We have needed a work such as this which would deal clearly and generously with the literary, cultural, and political environment that contributed to the development of the Lied and to the development of the piano, and would also deal more than superficially with individual composers and their works. These accomplishments alone would be enough for Gorrell's book to be considered as a possible resource for undergraduate song literature classes. But Gorrell has done more: without calling particular attention to it and without slighting the commonly acknowledged master composers, she has included an introduction to the major women composers of the century, a well-proportioned look at their compositions, a description of the societally assigned roles they played, and an evaluation of the part they played in the rise of song as an important genre. This is a first in the field. Until now, the work of women Lied composers has been treated only in journal articles, biographies, or biobibliographic books. Indeed, a few of Gorrell's chapters began as periodical articles. This is an important new tool for undergraduate teaching. Appendixes (chronology, performance editions, and program planning), endnotes, bibliography, song indexes listing titles and composers. Both general and academic readers at all levels.—*M. S. Roy, Pennsylvania State University, University Park Campus*

OAB-1016 ML345 94-42448 CIP
Hirshberg, Jehoash. **Music in the Jewish community of Palestine, 1880-1948: a social history.** Oxford, 1995. 297p bibl index afp ISBN 0-19-816242-1, $55.00

This tome is a very important undertaking, representing the first English-language effort to examine comprehensively the development of Jewish musical life in Palestine. Hirshberg chronicles the emergence of professional music making, research efforts in musicology, folk music and ethnomusicology, the effort to construct institutions for study and musical performance, the interplay of personalities and cultural experience, and the growth of innovative composition that led to "Israel" music. This effort is too brief to be considered comprehensive—there is nothing on liturgical music, little on the results of research into ethnic and folk music, and no serious discussion of "popular" music. The philosophic and academic issues of the period are well presented, and issues surrounding, for example, German-Jewish contributions to Palestinian art music (Philip Bohlman's *The Land Where Two Streams Flow*, CH, Feb'90, and *The World Centre for Jewish Music in Palestine, 1936-1940*, 1992)are brief. Despite these shortcomings, this is an easily read, remarkably interesting, and very important synthesis of pre-Israel music life. The author is to be especially commended for successfully avoiding too many technical terms. All collections.—*L. D. Loeb, University of Utah*

OAB-1017 ML270 94-6492 CIP
Johnson, James H. **Listening in Paris: a cultural history.** California, 1995. 384p bibl index afp (Studies on the history of society and culture, 21) ISBN 0-520-08564-7, $35.00

This fine book explores the experiences of musical audiences in 18th- and 19th-century Paris, detailing the shifting attitudes that spectators and listeners brought to the opera house and concert hall during that vibrant age of French culture. But this volume is neither a history of musical style nor a history of musical institutions as such. Rather, *Listening in Paris* attempts a history of musical experience itself, that curious meeting place for private aesthetic sensibilities and the protocols of public behavior. Johnson (Boston Univ.) artfully draws on an immense range of source materials: archival documents, memoirs and private correspondence, music journals, and public criticism. He also brings to bear an eclectic array of intellectual tools designed to illuminate the various attitudes and mentalities that elite and urban bourgeois audiences brought to their hearing of operas and symphonic music by composers

such as Rameau, Gluck, Mozart, and Beethoven. Tracing the gradual shift of audience behavior from an opportunity for social interaction to a kind of enraptured silence, this title manifests a growing concern on the part of cultural historians (and some musicologists, too) for a kind of reception history that illuminates the central role of audience in the history of artistic expression. Recommended for all academic libraries.—*R. Freedman, Haverford College*

OAB-1018 ML549 95-10439 CIP
Keyboard music before 1700, ed. by Alexander Silbiger. Schirmer Books/Prentice Hall International, 1995. 373p bibl index afp ISBN 0-02-872391-0, $42.00

Although music has been written for keyboard instruments since the late 14th century, the literature for organ, harpsichord, and clavichord composed before 1700 is relatively unknown to present-day audiences. This is in part due to the pervasive Bach centrism among scholars, performers, and audiences, most of whom until recently regarded the earlier music as merely precursive to the culminating works of the great Johann Sebastian. With the present volume, Silbiger (Duke Univ.) takes some first steps toward forming a canon of pre-Bach keyboard music. The book's five sections, each written by a specialist in the music of a particular region (Alan Brown on England, Bruce Gustafson on France, John Butt on Germany, Robert Judd on Italy, and Robert Parkins on Spain and Portugal) focus on a selection of "the composers and pieces that we believe still have most to offer in terms of artistic interest and value." Silbiger avoids direct comparison with Willi Apel's monumental but somewhat dated survey *The History of Keyboard Music to 1700* (1972), which Silbiger complements but does not replace. The more user-friendly Apel is better organized for quick reference—its table of contents is a model of clarity. Silbiger, however, is an essential purchase because its state-of-the-art scholarship approaches this wonderful music entirely on its own terms. All collections.—*E. Gaub, Grinnell College*

OAB-1019 ML430 92-5083 CIP
Lester, Joel. **Compositional theory in the eighteenth century.** Harvard, 1992. 355p bibl index afp ISBN 0-674-15522-X, $49.95

Because the influence of Zarlino was still being felt by musicians two centuries later, Lester employs Zarlino's legacy as a springboard into the 18th century. The close of the 18th century (and of Lester's book) is represented by Heinrich Christoph Koch, whose comprehensive works substantially synthesize the compositional practices of the era. The synthesist par excellence, however, is Lester. He surveys, analyzes, links, and interrelates the works of more than 100 theorists of the 17th and 18th centuries while focusing on the period from about 1720 to 1790. This period comprises a unique and engrossing mix of species counterpoint, harmonic theory, thoroughbass, and melodic studies that reflect the central works of (among others) Fux, Heinichen, Rameau, Mattheson, Marpurg, Kirnberger, and Riepel. This book offers the most (only!) objective and comprehensive presentation to date of 18th-century thought on compositional theory as taught and practiced by the leading musicians of the Enlightenment. Recommended for anyone interested in 18th-century music, and especially for musicologists, theorists, and libraries.—*B. A. Thompson, Winthrop University*

OAB-1020 ML275 93-5860 CIP
Levi, Erik. **Music in the Third Reich.** St. Martin's, 1994. 303p bibl index ISBN 0-312-10381-6, $39.95

Levi (Univ. of London) offers a carefully researched study of the impact of serious music on the Third Reich and vice-versa with a discussion of organization and structures that includes everything from folk music to *The Ring*. The reader is constantly aware that the time was so brief—from about 1932 to 1945. The author notes that the period was barren of works concerned with music. His work is cautious, but thorough and comprehensive. Chapter after chapter recounts the appalling reality; the "cast" (Hitler, Goering, Goebbels, Karajan, Bruno Walter, Fritz Busch, Béla Bartók, and dozens of others) are, at the very least, certain of their roles. The insanity of a regime approving Strauss's *Salome* and *Elektra* while refusing productions of Berg's *Lulu*, for example, is as unreal as the account of the entire period. Levi also gives space to discussions of the Third Reich's hatred of jazz, the importance of music technology (especially radio and recordings), *entartete* ("degenerate") music, music publishing, opera houses, symphony orchestras and repertories, and the musical press. This is a very important book for all libraries.—*J. Rayburn, Mercy College*

OAB-1021   ML196   94-46239 CIP
Rosen, Charles. **The romantic generation.** Harvard, 1995. 723p index afp CD ISBN 0-674-77933-9, $39.95

Rosen's expertise as a concert pianist and musicologist (*The Classical Style*, CH, May'73; *Sonata Forms*, CH, Dec'80) and in mathematics, French literature, philosophy, and modern languages provides an unusually rich background for the interdisciplinary approach taken here. Rosen focuses on composers whose styles were defined in the late 1820s and early 1830s because "the music of the 1830s was explicitly entangled with art, literature, politics, and personal life." Since this book originated as the Charles Eliot Norton lectures that Rosen gave in 1980-81 at Harvard and subsequently expanded, the individual chapters deal with discrete subjects, but all embody the concept of an interlinked cultural fabric. This is more than a discussion of music. For example, concepts discussed in "The Fragment as Romantic Form" are viewed in their literary and philosophic guises as well as in music; the chapter "Landscape and Music" shows the relationship of landscape painting and poetry to music, and demonstrates how musical devices such as horn calls evoke the image of the hunt and the feeling of nature. Always the reader is left with the character and thought of the period. Rosen's writing is concise, clear, and readable. A compact disk accompanies the book, providing readers with Rosen's performances of some of the musical examples. Highly recommended for all academic and general libraries.—*H. J. Diamond, CUNY Herbert H. Lehman College*

OAB-1022   ML189   95-38537 CIP
Shehadi, Fadlou. **Philosophies of music in medieval Islam.** E.J. Brill, 1996 (c1995). 175p bibl index afp (Brill's studies in intellectual history, 67) ISBN 90-04-10128-4, $80.75

The attitude toward music in Middle Eastern Islamic culture is essential to the understanding of Arabic, Turkish, and Persian music, past and present. Shehadi's accounting of the writings of the principal philosophers is both erudite and accessible. Dealing first with the relationship of the Arabic writers to ancient Greek musical thought and, in the second half, with the issues of acceptability of music, the book's basis of organization is the individual philosopher and his works. There are chapters on 12 figures, the most famous of them al-Kindi, al-Farabi, Ibn Sina (Avicenna), al-Ghazali, and Ibn Khaldūn, all philosophers in the broad sense (rather than specialist musical theorists), whose writings included discussions of music. The discussions of what kinds of music may be safely listened to by the devout provide background for the study of modern Middle Eastern culture and of medieval European musical thought. Written in a lively style, this work brings an obscure aspect of intellectual history closer to the contemporary reader. For college and university libraries supporting undergraduate and graduate collections in the fields of music and Middle Eastern studies.—*B. Nettl, University of Illinois at Urbana-Champaign*

OAB-1023   ML410   93-36805 CIP
Spotts, Frederic. **Bayreuth: a history of the Wagner festival.** Yale, 1994. 334p bibl index ISBN 0-300-05777-6, $35.00

From its inception in 1876, the Wagner festival in the small Bavarian town of Bayreuth has been sui generis. Site of the Festspielhaus, still considered the world's most perfect venue for opera, and for many years the only place one could hear *Parsifal*, Bayreuth has taken on the aura of a musical Mecca. Spotts (Center for European Studies, Harvard) has produced not only an exemplary history of the festival, but also an indispensable book about Wagner and his

legacy. The Wagner family has always controlled the festival. Leadership passed dynastically from the composer to his widow, Cosima; then to their son Siegfried; to Siegfried's widow, Winifrid; then to their son, Wieland, and his younger brother, Wolfgang (who became director on Wieland's death in 1966). Although Spotts is evenhanded in addressing each of the directors' virtues and flaws, heroes emerge, particularly Wieland, whose postwar series of revolutionary productions introduced a revisionist view of Wagner's oeuvre in universal, rather than German nationalistic, terms. Ironically, the other period of outstanding artistic achievement was the 1930s: Siegfried's British-born wife, Winifrid, was an early and ardent supporter of Hitler. An intimate friendship developed between them, which may have been more than Platonic in light of Siegfried's homosexuality. When Winifrid became director upon Siegfried's death in 1931, the Nazis gave her a unique degree of artistic freedom, which resulted in the intelligent choice of Heinz Tietjen as general manager and Wilhelm Furtwängler as conductor. Spotts's mastery of this fascinating material is complete and his writing is an unalloyed pleasure. Highly recommended for all collections.—*E. Gaub, Villa Maria College*

OAB-1024   ML240   92-2736 CIP
Strohm, Reinhard. **The rise of European music, 1380-1500.** Cambridge, 1994 (c1993). 720p bibl index ISBN 0-521-41745-7, $95.00

Not since the postwar years has a single author attempted a monograph of such scope and detail on the 15th century, arguably one of the most enigmatic and rich periods in the history of European music. Elegantly written and bristling with close discussions of musical works, the textual traditions upon which they rely, and the contexts in which they were first heard, Strohm draws heavily on some of the best musical scholarship of the last three decades (scholars will be grateful for the comprehensive lists of musical sources and of musicological studies). His passion for the many transformations that took place during this pivotal era in musical history is apparent at every turn: the musical implications of the papal schisms of the late 14th century, the fertile musical dialogue among written and oral traditions, the emergence and dissemination of central repertories, and the advent of expert composers (Dufay, Ockeghem, Obrecht, and Josquin among them) whose compositions still enjoy considerable audiences. Indeed, the author traces the very notion of the autonomous musical masterwork (and, by implication, the autonomous composer) to the middle years of the century, when there emerged a new compositional ethic of conscious emulation that privileged aesthetic perfection over immediate social purpose. Upper-division undergraduate and above.—*R. Freedman, Haverford College*

OAB-1025   ML169   91-5170 CIP
West, M.L. **Ancient Greek music.** Oxford, 1993 (c1992). 410p bibl index ISBN 0-19-814897-6, $98.00

It is hard to overestimate the value of this first book to present Greek music accessibly both to classicists and to musicologists whose specialty is not in this period. The history of complexity in musical theory is cyclical rather than progressive. Greek music is among the most complex even though its general melodic nature is monophonic. West, a classicist at Oxford, explains the theory, structure, and notation; transcribes and analyzes the 30 extant fragments; puts it all in historical context from the Bronze Age to the Roman period; and adds the ethnomusicological perspective that has become so important to musicological studies in the last few years. His choice of language is sophisticated yet nontechnical. An excellent bibliography, arranged by subject and then by date of publication rather than by alphabet, completes this important addition to a large collection of books about the ancient world for nonspecialists, many less comprehensible than West's volume. This book should become a model for a kind of scholarly writing that illuminates rather than obfuscates and teaches rather than confounds. Both general and academic readers at all levels.—*J. P. Ambrose, University of Vermont*

PERFORMANCE

OAB-1026   ML1255   96-28053 CIP
Bonds, Mark Evan. **After Beethoven: imperatives of originality in the symphony.** Harvard, 1996. 212p bibl index afp ISBN 0-674-00855-3, $35.00

Bonds (Univ. of North Carolina) packs a lot of information into relatively few pages, and yet the book is surprisingly easygoing—filled with references to art and literature, anecdotal (even chatty at times), clear, and accessible to any reader who is comfortable with music notation and familiar with the musical works discussed. *After Beethoven* provides a stimulating short course in 19th-century symphonic repertory, although from a deliberately limited perspective. Bonds has chosen a limited repertory, to be sure (works by Berlioz, Mendelssohn, Schumann, Brahms, and Mahler), and a feature that they all share—indebtedness to, and/or fear of, the Beethoven Ninth Symphony. His arguments are cogent, his musical examples persuasive. The latter are not only well chosen but sensitively transcribed in short-score reductions to be played at the piano. One might quibble at the overly Germanic focus—where is the Saint-Saëns Organ Symphony, or the Ives Fourth?—but what Bonds has chosen to do he does very well indeed. Highly recommended for general and academic collections or for textbook use.—*E. Schwartz, Bowdoin College*

OAB-1027   ML437   94-3878 CIP
Epstein, David. **Shaping time: music, the brain, and performance.** Schirmer Books/Prentice Hall International, 1995. 598p bibl index afp ISBN 0-02-873320-7, $47.00

A continuation of the studies first published in his *Beyond Orpheus* (CH, Nov'79), the present formidable volume is really two books within one cover: the first deals with philosophical-anthropological-psychophysical aspects of time; the second applies the author's conclusions and methods to examples of Western art music. Among the temporal topics discussed are rhythmic/metric structures, proportional tempos, rubato, and accelerando/ritardando. Epstein applies his findings to the music of more than a dozen composers from Haydn and Mozart to Scriabin and Stravinsky. Further, to show the universality of proportional tempos, he presents evidence of their existence in six distinct non-Western cultures. Among musicians, this volume should be of greatest interest to performers (especially conductors), theorists, and musicologists. Scholars from scientific disciplines should be interested in the way the author has applied findings and methods from their areas to music. Both the scholarship and production of this study are unsurpassed. Charts, graphs, musical examples—several on foldout pages—are clearly laid out, endnotes form almost a separate volume by themselves, all beautifully printed and bound. Highly recommended for all upper-division undergraduate and graduate libraries, as well as for personal collections.—*R. Stahura, Ripon College*

OAB-1028   ML410   96-1829 CIP
Holman, J.K. **Wagner's Ring: a listener's companion & concordance.** Amadeus Press, 1996. (Dist. by Timber) 440p bibl disc index ISBN 1-57467-014-X, $34.95

Holman weaves several interlocking paths of analysis and correspondences, both textual and musical, through Richard Wagner's tetralogy. An informed musical amateur, avid Wagnerite, and devoted patron of the arts, the author has compiled the first ever English-language concordance for the *Ring* cycle. Included are background chapters on Wagner's mythological sources, plot summaries for *Rheingold, Valkyrie, Siegfried*, and *Twilight*, and an evaluation of the various translations of the librettos. A chapter on characters is usefully laid out: all the major and minor figures are traced, including mythological sources, relationships with other characters, and a description of accompanying music. The musical discussions aim more at tune identification—a listing and naming of the motives, where they are first heard, and what characters or ideas they represent—drawing on the work of Deryck Cooke and Ernest Newman (who, in turn, owe much to the earliest commentators like Hans von Wolzogen in the *Bayreuther Blätter*, 1878-1938). The concordance chapter is the core

and the gem. Persons, places, emotions, and ideas are cross-listed, showing every occurrence in all four operas. Missing, unfortunately, is the original German word or phrase. Holman's work will be a lasting guide for all seeking entry into the world of the *Ring*. Upper-division undergraduate through professional.—*J. Peel, Willamette University*

OAB-1029   ML457   94-36842 CIP
Kivy, Peter. **Authenticities: philosophical reflections on musical performance.** Cornell, 1995. 299p bibl index afp ISBN 0-8014-3046-1, $35.00

In the past three decades a quiet revolution has occurred in the performance of old music. Now there are "mainstream" performers and "authentic" performers; the authenticists continue to move to the fore. Kivy (Rutgers, the State Univ. of New Jersey) explores the precarious aesthetic scaffold that supports the "authentic" movement. He finds five different meanings for "authentic" that might be applied to musical performance, and he examines the how and why of each. (Some practitioners prefer the term "historically informed" to "authentic," but Kivy insists that "authentic" is quite all right.) What are the performer's ethical responsibilities with respect to a composer's text? What does listening have to do with performance? These are very basic questions, and Kivy handles them brilliantly. In the process he touches on all sorts of general issues pertinent to the performance of music. Zealots may disagree with the conclusions, and philosophers may find some of the arguments lacking in rigor. Nevertheless, Kivy has provided a sorely needed framework for all future discussion of the authenticity matter. This is his best book, a major contribution to performance studies and to musical aesthetics; likely it will be studied and cited for generations. Recommended to all libraries.—*B. J. Murray, University of Alabama*

OAB-1030   ML410   94-29785 CIP
Levy, David Benjamin. **Beethoven: the Ninth Symphony.** Schirmer Books/Prentice Hall International, 1995. 226p bibl index afp ISBN 0-02-871363-X, $35.00

No Western musical work has assumed greater cultural significance than Beethoven's last symphony. The Ninth was performed for Hitler's birthday in 1942, and it was performed to celebrate the end of the Berlin Wall in 1989. Today it is played more in Japan than anywhere else. Levy operates from many perspectives—social, cultural, historical, and theoretical. The symphony's long gestation, its publication, and its early performances are described in detail. The center of the book is a long analysis; closer in spirit to Donald Tovey and Heinrich Schenker, it will be accessible to most musicians and others with even modest score-reading skills. A section on the work's performance history examines various "improvements" inflicted by Wagner, Mahler, and others. The elaborately annotated discography is limited to recordings of genuine importance, e.g., recordings that exemplify particular performing traditions. Levy's scholarship is formidable and absolutely current, and he shows admirable temperance when confronting the symphony's critics. Moreover, he has ordered information of strongly disparate types into a structure that is both useful and readable. The book, the first volume in Schirmer's "Monuments of Western Music" series, is recommended to all. This reviewer eagerly awaits further volumes in the series.—*B. J. Murray, University of Alabama*

OAB-1031   ML1263   93-11565 CIP
Norris, Jeremy. **The Russian piano concerto: v.1: The nineteenth century.** Indiana, 1994. 227p bibl disc index afp ISBN 0-253-34112-4, $35.00

This monograph, the first volume in the new series "Russian Music Studies," delves into the origins and development of the Russian piano concerto. The text is scholarly but a joy to read. Norris is highly analytical, diligently comparing and contrasting the concertos of Anton Rubinstein, Tchaikovsky, Balakirev, Mussorgsky, Taneyev et al. with those of their European progenitors. Interestingly, among the elements that gave the genre its particularly unique and colorful flavor was the introduction of materials extracted from Slavic folk songs and orthodox chant of the Slavic race (Rimsky-Korsakov and Balakirev in particular). The author includes copious musical examples and interesting charts, including one that skillfully delineates the importance and pedagogical influence of Irish pianist and composer John Field (who lived in Russian from 1803 to 1837) on Russian musicians and composers. David Griffioen's discography is invaluable for those interested in comparing renditions and tracing performance history. No less than 105 recordings of Tchaikovsky's First are given. Considering the significance of this well-written work, this reviewer hopes the publisher pursues additional volumes in the series. For all substantial music collections, academic and public.—*J. R. Belanger, San Diego Public Library*

OAB-1032   MT170   92-17854 CIP
Read, Gardner. **Compendium of modern instrumental techniques.** Greenwood, 1993. 276p bibl indexes afp ISBN 0-313-28512-8, $55.00

About 17 years ago in these pages this reviewer commented on the impressive scope and quality of Read's *Contemporary Instrumental Techniques* (CH, Jul'76). Obviously, the author's work habits have not changed in the intervening years; in his new book he has cataloged examples of "modern" techniques gleaned from hundreds of contemporary scores. The new work is considerably expanded, both in techniques discussed and examples cited. Although choosing to replace his earlier work with a new volume rather than a second edition, he has retained the two-part format: generalized techniques (extended ranges, muting, etc.) and idiomatic techniques common to the various families of instruments. Almost as important as the text itself is the thoroughness with which examples of individual techniques are documented and indexed, making the book an easy-to-use reference tool. Composers may well wish to study the entire volume, as they seek to determine which techniques will endure in compositional practice; but for most readers the book will serve as an excellent resource for exploring individual interests or needs. A debt of gratitude is owed the author for making so much information available in a concise and accessible form. Recommended for upper-division undergraduates and above.—*W. M. Bigham, emeritus, Morehead State University*

OAB-1033   ML1460   91-40160 CIP
Rosselli, John. **Singers of Italian opera: the history of a profession.** Cambridge, 1992. 272p index ISBN 0-521-41683-3, $44.95

To a San Francisco woman who gushed at a party "Oh, Mr. Gigli, aren't you thrilled when you hear all that applause?" the tenor replied "Signora, I'm happy when I get the money." In his fact-filled and meticulously documented study of the economic history of those who sang Italian opera from its beginnings until the recent past, Rosselli, a retired historian (Univ. of Sussex, UK) and passionate opera lover, traces the reality of the patronage system; the rise of a market for singers; the relative ascendencies of castrati, women singers, and tenors; the entry into the scene of agents; the changing nature of audiences; and the generally precarious process of supporting oneself as a singer. "How-they-got-the-money" is a fascinating story, one which strips away some of the glamour of the profession while, at the same time, it causes us to marvel at the fortitude of those who chose to make their living as opera singers. A marvelous cultural study and this reviewer's favorite new opera book in recent years. Copious notes, illustrations, and an ample guide to further reading. Of interest to both generalists and specialists.—*M. S. Roy, Pennsylvania State University, University Park Campus*

OAB-1034   MT145   91-39348 CIP
Schulenberg, David. **The keyboard music of J.S. Bach.** Schirmer Books, 1992. 475p bibl indexes afp ISBN 0-02-873275-8, $50.00

Schulenberg's coverage of Bach's keyboard music (here excluding music for the organ) will be a source of enlightenment and fascination to a wide range of readers. Listeners as well as performers and teachers will benefit particularly from chapter 2, which covers such subjects as preferred instruments,

"authentic" editions, and various performance practices. There is also a great deal of valuable analysis and criticism of individual works, mostly of concern to scholars, though often interlaced with historical background information of more general interest. Also included are two appendixes covering doubtful works and the *Clavier-Büchlein für Anna Magdalena Bach* (1722). This volume is particularly valuable in view of the continuing Bach research. The only previous guides to his complete keyboard works (by Hermann Keller and Erwin Bodky) are quite outdated. Schulenberg (Univ. of North Carolina at Chapel Hill) displays impressive scholarship; equally commendable is the general clarity of his prose and his "common sense" approach to some of the thornier questions of performance. This is not to suggest that the topic has been popularized or trivialized; this is unmistakably a serious book but more accessible than many of its genre. Public and academic libraries at all levels.—*J. E. Tucker, Northland College*

OAB-1035   MT110   95-5398 CIP
Stein, Deborah. **Poetry into song: performance and analysis of lieder,** by Deborah Stein and Robert Spillman. Oxford, 1996. 413p index ISBN 0-19-509328-3, $35.00

At last! A comprehensive, systematic text about lieder that is couched in analytical poetic and musical language! Theoretician Stein (New England Conservatory of Music) and pianist/accompanist Spillman (University of Colorado at Boulder) provide a thorough, serious study of song in a single volume; heretofore, such information had to be gleaned from a number of different sources. The authors provide an amazingly comprehensive (though brief) survey of German Romanticism, an analytical approach to poetry on its own terms, a discussion of the elements of interpretation, the basics of theory illustrated entirely with examples from lieder, and a chapter on settings by different composers of the same texts. Each chapter ends with thought-provoking questions. The authors also include questions in the body of the text, questions that will certainly challenge those hoping to become deeply acquainted with the masterworks of German 19th-century song. This is an important, carefully notated book; text translations, a glossary, an excellent bibliography, and scores of songs not readily available are included in appendixes. Of interest to singers, teachers, theorists, and those interested in the relationship between music and literature. Upper-division undergraduate and up.—*M. S. Roy, Pennsylvania State University, University Park Campus*

OAB-1036   ML52   95-16156 CIP
Walls, Peter. **Music in the English courtly masque, 1604-1640.** Oxford, 1996. 372p bibl index afp ISBN 0-19-816141-7, $70.00

This reviewer is tempted to call this book "definitive," so comprehensive is its coverage and research, so full of commonsense, so devoid of padding and puffery. Walls (Victoria Univ., NZ) seems to have read everything published on the problematic courtly masque and its music. Since he has also worked in manuscript collections and edited music for use in modern masque reconstructions, he speaks with confidence about the coming together of "poetry, music, and visual spectacle ... projecting a coherent ideology for the Stuart court," which, alas, many contemporary revelers probably thought of "as purely social occasions ... an incidental framework for dancing." Walls discusses composers, songs, and dance music; "choreography," staging, and visual effects; performers; instruments—and evidence that has survived for all of this. He analyzes the contributions of Ferrabosco, Lanier, Dowland, Campion, Lupo, Robert Johnson, Ben Jonson, and Inigo Jones; the various types of songs (polyphonic, simple tuneful, and declamatory) and dances used; the influences of Italian monody and French dancing-masters and the *ballet de cour*. Readers learn of the difficulty of attributing dances to specific masques, of the large musical forces employed, and of the wonderfully varied sounds they made (as many as 42 played "violins," lutes, hautboys, flutes, cornets, sackbuts, percussion and trumpets), of the still-open question of when English recitative began (1617? 1628?). Rich in detail, convincing in argument, pleasing in prose style, perfectly splendid! Upper-division undergraduate and up.—*W. Metcalfe, University of Vermont*

OAB-1037   ML3506   93-34660 CIP
Berliner, Paul F. **Thinking in jazz: the infinite art of improvisation.**
Chicago, 1994. 883p bibl disc index afp ISBN 0-226-04380-0, $85.00;
ISBN 0-226-04381-9 pbk, $29.95

Berliner (Northwestern Univ.), a noted ethnomusicologist, has attempted the
most in-depth study ever of how jazz is created. It ranges from the environment
in which one begins to study jazz through various ways in which one learns
its musical vocabulary to group interaction, both musical and personal. Some
of the topics discussed are routinely addressed in jazz method books, but never
before has there been a work of this breadth and scholarship. Berliner interviewed
more than 50 distinguished jazz musicians in collecting the very specific information that fills this text. Though this group represents an admirable mix of
generations and styles, the focus of the investigation is primarily on bop and hard
bop styles as practiced by such popular bands as those led by Charlie Parker,
Miles Davis, Max Roach, and John Coltrane. As influential as these groups
were, in so comprehensive a work this reviewer would have liked to see more
evidence of how both more traditional and more radical musicians affect jazz
today. The scope of the work presents at least one other problem: some of
the information is strictly for those just beginning their study of jazz, but other
material will be useful only to the most advanced students. Selective reading
will also be required for the extensive (approximately 250 pages) and carefully produced "musical texts." Their usefulness will vary widely from reader
to reader; their format in this large clothbound book makes them less accessible
to players than they are in ubiquitous jazz transcription books. Berliner provides
copious notes, a lengthy bibliography, a discography, and a videography.
Whatever the work's drawbacks, this is a milestone in the literature of jazz
and should be in all serious public, academic, and professional jazz collections.—
K. R. Dietrich, Ripon College

OAB-1038   ML3551   95-20951 CIP
Cantwell, Robert. **When we were good: the folk revival.** Harvard,
1996. 412p index afp ISBN 0-674-95132-8, $24.95

Essayist, literary scholar, and author of *Bluegrass Breakdown* (CH, Dec'84)
and *Ethnomimesis: Folklife and the Representation of Culture* (1993), Cantwell
(Univ. of North Carolina at Chapel Hill) presents an engaging, complex, wide-
ranging personal introduction to the folk revival of the 1950s and 1960s. Drawing on a variety of primary but mostly secondary sources, he begins with an
inspection of the Kingston Trio's "Tom Dooley," then proceeds through a discussion of minstrelsy, John Lomax, left-wing musical culture, Woody Guthrie
and the Weavers, the Folkways *Anthology of American Folk Music*, Pete Seeger,
summer camps and the Greenwich Village folk scene, Joan Baez, and Bob Dylan,
to name only a few topics. However, this is not a narrative history but a somewhat discursive exploration of myriad threads and themes. It is often difficult
to follow but usually insightful, rewarding, and informative. Well versed in most
of the secondary literature, Cantwell draws heavily on David Dunaway's *How
Can I Keep from Singing?: Pete Seeger* (CH, Nov'81), Joe Klein's *Woody Guthrie*
(CH, Jul'81), and Norm Cohen's *Folk Song America: A 20th Century Revival*
(1990). There is no comparable study. Strongly recommended for academic and
general libraries.—*R. D. Cohen, Indiana University Northwest*

OAB-1039   ML3545   93-26432 CIP
Cleveland, Les. **Dark laughter: war in song and popular culture.**
Praeger, 1994. 178p bibl indexes afp ISBN 0-275-94764-5, $49.95

M.A.S.H.'s "Hawkeye" said: "Joking is the only way of opening my mouth
without screaming." Cleveland's excellent and well-written book is a remarkable summary of that response to military life, song here being "a kind of dark
laughter in which the long and deadly saga of endurance of the ordinary combat soldier is memorialized." Cleveland surveys the vast wealth of wartime song
(primarily from WW II, Korea, and Vietnam), focusing on the warrior's experience as happy, reluctant, bawdy, hungry, and mortal. The introduction discusses the overall significance of popular culture in wartime, citing its useful-

ness in filling free time and supplying some sense of "domestic normality." But
throughout, the emphasis is on song's function as a militarily accepted way of
protest in an institution that cannot otherwise tolerate dissent. Clearly the product of thorough research and personal experience, this book is also the first comprehensive survey of its kind and deserves a prominent place in the burgeoning field of popular culture studies. Copious examples of song texts (some of
which are profane and sexually explicit) are included. There are excellent photographs, endnotes, a brief appendix of several especially significant songs, a
substantial bibliography, and indexes of subjects, song titles, and first lines. Recommended for all public and academic collections.—*M. S. Roy, Pennsylvania
State University, University Park Campus*

OAB-1040   ML3508   92-43644 MARC
Collier, James Lincoln. **Jazz: the American theme song.** Oxford,
1993. 326p index afp ISBN 0-19-507943-4, $25.00

Unlike the author's excellent and well-known biographical and historical
jazz studies, this is a book of provocative essays on a variety of topics. All
are researched carefully and provide the reader with insights that are tangential to the author's earlier monographs. Some of the viewpoints substantiated
within are controversial: particularly, those expressed in essays that question
whether jazz is "black music," or point out the limits of the sometimes sterile
academic jazz taught in higher education, or criticize jazz critics for being
uneducated and uninformed fans instead of critics. The ten essays are arranged
in roughly chronological order, from a discussion of the origins of jazz seen from
new perspectives to an exploration of the importance of local jazz. Collier breaks
new ground by crediting the rise of feminism and its clash with Victorianism
against the framework of an emerging immigrant nation as a sociological
influence in the emergence of jazz. Other essays touch on the influences jazz
has had on American popular music, the emergence of the jazz soloist, and
the interface between show business and jazz. This well-indexed book, with
careful bibliographical notes, will be an important addition to all libraries.—
J. J. Carbon, Franklin and Marshall College

OAB-1041   ML3534   95-1541 CIP
Cushman, Thomas. **Notes from underground: rock music counterculture in Russia.** State University of New York, 1995. 403p bibl
index ISBN 0-7914-2543-6, $59.50

Based on interviews and participant observation within St. Petersburg's
community of rock musicians and fans, this theoretically informed and ethnographically grounded study portrays the transition of this "counter-culture" from
the preglasnost era through the fall of communism. Cushman (sociology, Wellesley College) investigates the nature of Russian rock music culture, the "role, meaning, and function" of rock music in Russian society, and the nature of musical culture in times of transition. Although fascinating in its portrayal of contemporary
musical life, it neglects the problematic historical context of cultural imports to
Russia since the time of Catherine the Great, especially in the city that provided
Russia's "window to the West" (treated, for example, in Richard Stites's *Russian Popular Culture*, CH, Jun'93). Nonetheless, this study is a valuable contribution to the growing body of literature on rock music in Russia, supplementing *Rocking the State*, ed. by Sabrina Petra Ramet (CH, Jul'94), and Artemy
Troitsky's insider view, *Back in the USSR* (1988). Two appendixes describe
the methodology of sociological research in Russia, and a Soviet sociologist's
comparison of the lyric content of state-supported and independent rock groups.
A glossary of Russian rock music terminology is also included. Upper-division
undergraduates and above.—*M. Forry, University of California, Santa Cruz*

OAB-1042   ML3524   96-34682 CIP
Dawidoff, Nicholas. **In the country of country: people and places
in American music.** Pantheon Books, 1997. 371p bibl disc index ISBN
0-679-41567-X, $25.00

In his epilogue Dawidoff writes, "The country that will last uses deceptively
simple details to say profound things about the American experience." The same

could be said of this book. The author manages to combine simple, well-told stories about many legendary country musicians (among them Jimmy Rogers, Harlan Howard, Chet Atkins, Kitty Wells, Patsy Cline, Bill Monroe, the Stanley Brothers, Earl Scruggs, Doc Watson, Johnny Cash, George Jones, Merle Haggard, Iris Dement) with complex revelations about the places and times that shaped them. This is a fine combination of clear writing, passion for subject, and solid scholarship. The seven chapters offer multiple perspectives that come from a combination of the author's insights, interviews, and, whenever possible, the musicians' own words. Included are excellent black-and-white photographs; a useful bibliography of interviews, books, and articles; and a limited but helpful discography. Although some important musicians are not included, Dawidoff's selectivity does not diminish the value of this picture of American music that provided a "means of solidarity for people who felt marginalized by American society." All general and academic collections.—*D. Gordon, Christopher Newport University*

OAB-1043   ML3534   92-53859 CIP
Ennis, Philip H. **The seventh stream: the emergence of rocknroll in American popular music.** Wesleyan/University Press of New England, 1993 (c1992). 445p bibl index afp ISBN 0-8195-5238-0, $50.00; ISBN 0-8195-6257-2 pbk, $29.95

For anyone interested in how "rocknroll" (the author's spelling) entered the mainstream of American popular music, *The Seventh Stream* is an excellent starting point. Ennis's first book, by his own words "long in the making," exhibits a level of scholarship too rarely encountered in the popular culture field. His research covers 20th-century American music's six distinct streams; "Pop, Black Pop, Country Pop, Jazz, Folk and Gospel," noting how each contributed to rock. The book is much more than a typical music history, however. It also tracks nonmusical influences, from technological innovations to payola, from shifting demographics to bitter fights between ASCAP (American Society of Composers, Authors, and Publishers) and BMI (Broadcast Music, Inc.) and shows their impact on the musical end product. It is remarkable how much information Ennis has packed into the 380 pages of text and 47 pages of notes, bibliography, and index. The result is an exceptionally well documented book that has no current peers. An essential addition to academic libraries, *The Seventh Stream* should be required reading for students seriously studying American popular music at any academic level, beginning undergraduate and up.—*H. A. Keesing, University of Maryland at College Park*

OAB-1044   ML422   92-9485 CIP
Firestone, Ross. **Swing, swing, swing: the life & times of Benny Goodman.** W.W. Norton, 1993. 522p bibl index ISBN 0-393-03371-6, $29.95

Firestone has been successful in capturing, in words, the many sides of Benny Goodman—from the gentle and charming Goodman to the clarinetist who was at home in both classical and jazz idioms to the irascible Goodman who could wilt, with his wrathful "Goodman Ray," any musician who displeased him. A biography of this versatile musician could, in the hands of an ordinary writer, read like a superficial "Who's Who in 20th-century American Music." Firestone, however, has succeeded in weaving the many figures with whom Goodman was associated into a rich tapestry that reflects the richness of American culture in this century. Photographs were chosen carefully to support the text and the index is what one hopes for. A very important book about one of the seminal figures in American swing music in particular, and in the larger world of jazz in general, this volume belongs in any library and in the hands of all fans of Benny Goodman.—*C. W. Henderson, Saint Mary's College (IN)*

OAB-1045   ML3556   94-21 CIP
Floyd, Samuel A. **The power of black music: interpreting its history from Africa to the United States.** Oxford, 1995. 316p bibl disc index afp ISBN 0-19-508235-4, $30.00

Floyd (director of research, Center for Black Music Research, Columbia College, Chicago) presents a sweeping, selective overview of black music in the

US, beginning with the role of music in African society. Incorporating the latest scholarship, he agrees "that the aim of African music has always been to translate the experiences of life and of the spiritual world into sound," a connection carried over to the New World. Nineteenth-century spirituals, children's game songs, dance, and instruments and the more recent musical forms—gospel, ragtime, blues, marching bands, jazz, black classical compositions, rhythm and blues, and rock 'n' roll—all demonstrate African to African American musical continuity. Floyd stresses the importance of cool jazz, hard bop, and gospel in the 1950s and 60s and the development of soul by the 1970s. He focuses on continuity of traditional African religious and song expressions rather than on European musical influences, drawing heavily on recent black literary and musical criticism. He includes a detailed bibliography. Highly recommended for academic libraries, but probably difficult going for lower-division undergraduates.—*R. D. Cohen, Indiana University Northwest*

OAB-1046   PN1992   92-13861 CIP
Goodwin, Andrew. **Dancing in the distraction factory: music television and popular culture.** Minnesota, 1992. 237p bibl index ISBN 0-8166-2062-8, $44.95; ISBN 0-8166-2063-6 pbk, $16.95

Elvis, Chuck Berry, and Little Richard are but three of rock and roll's pioneers who understood that they were also part of a visual medium. Their fans wanted to see, as well as hear, them perform. Until the late 1960s, however, neither movies nor television seemed capable of capturing rock's dual essence. Movies changed with *Monterey Pop* and *Woodstock*, to name but two films. After a number of false starts such as *Shindig* and *Midnight Special*, television and rock found symbiosis with the advent of music television (MTV) in 1981. Goodwin's first solo book (he previously coedited *On Record* with Simon Frith, 1990), analyzes how music television is produced and consumed. More scholarly than Michael Shore's *The Rolling Stone Book of Rock Video* (CH, Mar'85), *Dancing in the Distraction Factory* extends and updates the research of E. Ann Kaplan's *Rocking Around the Clock* (CH, Dec'87). A music television "time line," extensive endnotes, and a superlative bibliography distinguish this important contribution to understanding one aspect of contemporary popular culture. Highly recommended for cultural studies courses at advanced undergraduate and graduate level.—*H. A. Keesing, University of Maryland at College Park*

OAB-1047   ML3554   95-18803 CIP
Grimes, Robert R. **How shall we sing in a foreign land?: music of Irish Catholic immigrants in the antebellum United States.** Notre Dame, 1996. 237p bibl index afp ISBN 0-268-01110-9, $32.95

Grimes (Fordham Univ.) skillfully weaves together several strands of American history to produce a unified, revealing study of a neglected subject. This volume will certainly have an impact on the larger issues of ethnicity, religion, culture, and social class, particularly as they relate to music in the antebellum US. The opening two chapters deal with the role of the Catholic church in providing spiritual, cultural, and social nourishment to the large Irish immigrant population of eastern cities and the equivocal reaction of the largely Protestant press to the flourishing musical practice in many of the large Catholic churches. On one hand, the press admired the quality of religious music performed (Haydn, Mozart, Beethoven, Rossini, Mercadante) and on the other it wrestled with Catholic doctrine. Chapter 3 follows the growth of musical activity in the Catholic parishes of Boston, and chapters 4-6 examine in detail the ritual and popular music used in the church and its auxiliary organizations and Irish music of the community itself. The repertory is extensive, from mass settings to popular religious song, and Grimes represents several American composers. The volume is amply illustrated with musical examples, and an appendix lists American Catholic music collections up to 1860. Highly recommended to musicians, scholars, and general readers.—*W. K. Kearns, University of Colorado at Boulder*

OAB-1048   ML3477   94-16949 CIP
Hyland, William G. **The song is ended: songwriters and American**

music, 1900-1950. Oxford, 1995. 336p indexes afp ISBN 0-19-508611-2, $25.00

Hyland (Georgetown Univ.) brings to this work passion for the music, mastery of the literature, and a critical sensibility. Divided into three sections—"Tin Pan Alley," "The Jazz Age," and "Hollywood and Beyond"—the work focuses on the major composers and lyricists (occasionally the same person), particularly Irving Berlin, Jerome Kern, George and Ira Gershwin, Richard Rodgers, Lorenz Hart, Oscar Hammerstein, and Cole Porter. In weaving together the story of their fascinating experiences, on Broadway and in Hollywood, Hyland touches on songs, musicals, movies, and much more. He provides little technical information but many colorful anecdotes. This book will be the first stop for those seeking to understand the colorful lives of modern popular songwriters. It can be supplemented by Allen Forte's *The American Popular Ballad of the Golden Era, 1924-1950* (CH, Apr'96), a technical discussion of selected songs. The few photos and useful endnotes add to the text. Highly recommended for all libraries.—*R. D. Cohen, Indiana University Northwest*

OAB-1049   ML3521   91-52627 CIP
Lomax, Alan. **The land where the blues began.** Pantheon Books, 1993. 539p bibl disc index ISBN 0-679-40424-4, $25.00

Lomax quotes legendary blues artist Big Bill Broonzy in a 1940s interview as saying, "You can't put no feelings down on paper." If Lomax has not captured the feelings of the blues on paper, it is difficult to imagine how anyone could come closer. This is not a work of academic scholarship, but it is the most revealing account possible of the emotional environment that produced and maintained the blues. Lomax began searching for the blues in the 1930s with his musicologist father, John, and has produced one of the most important bodies of knowledge on the subject. He reviews more than 50 years of field work, peeling back layers of protective coverings maintained by African Americans. Despite years of positive and successful relations with some of the most important blues artists in history, it took decades for certain subjects to be even mentioned to this white Southerner, who exposed himself to physical danger and hostility as he traveled the back roads of Mississippi in his quest for the blues. Lomax includes background on the historic recordings of black prison songs, the first recording of Muddy Waters, and the Broonzy story. Any serious exploration of this magnificent American music must now include Lomax's revelatory book as well as his recordings. Both public and academic libraries.—*C. M. Weisenberg, University of California, Los Angeles*

OAB-1050   ML3558   91-35181 CIP
Loza, Steven. **Barrio rhythm: Mexican American music in Los Angeles.** Illinois, 1993. 320p bibl index afp ISBN 0-252-01902-4, $42.50; ISBN 0-252-06288-4 pbk, $16.95

This is a welcome addition to the literature of urban musicology in general, especially to the study of Chicanos' musical activities in inner-city Los Angeles. Writing from an emic perspective, the author analyzes the social and musical history of Mexican Los Angeles starting with the foundation of the Pueblo (1781) to the present. This time span is scrutinized historically, ethnographically, and contextually. Discussion of these aspects is divided into seven chapters, which delve into a variety of specifics indicated by titles ranging from "Society and Music in Mexican Los Angeles" to "Reflections of a Homeboy." Throughout this book Loza points out the conflict between social classes and ethnic groups—Anglo-Americans and Chicanos—in the inner city of Los Angeles. To ethnomusicologists this work provides an excellent application of the reflective analysis highlighting the impact of intercultural conflict on Chicano musical vocabulary, forms, and content. This contextual analysis will certainly become one of the most cited models of urban ethnomusicology. It is a must for both humanists and social scientists. Upper-division undergraduate and graduate collections.—*Kazadi wa Mukuna, Kent State University*

OAB-1051   ML3565   95-3152 CIP
Manuel, Peter. **Caribbean currents: Caribbean music from rumba to reggae,** by Peter Manuel with Kenneth Bilby and Michael Largey. Temple University, 1995. 272p bibl index afp ISBN 1-56639-338-8, $49.95; ISBN 1-56639-339-6 pbk, $18.95

Caribbean musics have influenced North American music deeply, but they remain little known. Since they are considered "popular," they are routinely ignored by the (classical) music establishment, and until recently, when ethnomusicology turned to popular traditions, even that field ignored them. Manuel's book is just what scholars have needed. It was written as a "readable guide to Caribbean music" in response to the author's experience teaching a Caribbean survey for which reading lists were a nightmare. Manuel (John Jay College) aims at general readers and students and includes lists of further reading, audio recordings, and films. Importantly, this book is intended to be read in conjunction with a new double compact disc, *Caribbean Currents: A Panorama of Caribbean Music* (Rounder Records, not included). The book expands Manuel's earlier *Popular Musics of the Non-Western World* (CH, Jul'89): in addition to the Caribbean, it covers Guyana and Suriname (which Manuel argues are overwhelmingly Caribbean in orientation) but not coastal Venezuela, Central America, or Mexico. The author discusses both major genres (e.g., reggae and calypso) and minor ones (e.g., Haitian *rara* and Dominican *bachata*), in addition to tangential traditions (e.g., East Indian music). Manuel's approach is historical and cultural, with little musical analysis, but he offers much valuable contextual information. All collections.—*T. E. Miller, Kent State University*

OAB-1052   ML82   94-30683 CIP
Reynolds, Simon. **The sex revolts: gender, rebellion, and rock' n'roll,** by Simon Reynolds and Joy Press. Harvard, 1995. 410p bibl index afp ISBN 0-674-80272-1, $24.95

Controversial lyrics sung by artists living "deviant" lifestyles are not new. The alleged role of music in the perceived debasement of youthful morals and values has been argued for decades. In 1995, it is not only making headlines again but promises to become a Presidential election issue. Reynolds and Press's provocative and insightful *The Sex Revolts* should be read by everyone concerned with rock culture's impact. What differentiates this book from previous efforts, for example, Steven Simels's *Gender Chameleons* (1985), is its serious treatment of the central theme—the complex relationships among gender, rebellion, and rock music. Not an excuse to print photos selected mainly for their shock value, the book contains no illustrations. As with Reynolds's *Blissed Out* (CH, Apr'91), it is the confluence of carefully considered text, numerous footnotes, and a broad-ranging bibliography that shape and support the critical analysis. This timely volume adds reasoned understanding to a high-profile issue. It is strongly recommended for students at all levels and across a range of disciplines, as well as for general audiences.—*H. A. Keesing, University of Maryland College Park*

OAB-1053   ML3556   96-25273 CIP
Spencer, Jon Michael. **The new Negroes and their music: the success of the Harlem Renaissance.** Tennessee, 1997. 171p bibl index afp ISBN 0-87049-967-X pbk, $20.00

Perhaps the first major artistic flourishing in the US, the Harlem Renaissance of the 1920s was, as Dvořák had anticipated 30 years earlier, a highly significant blossoming of African American talents—not only in Harlem and the US but in Europe. Novels, poetry, and plays came first, with music soon to follow. The elevation of the folkloric may have culminated in William Grant Still's *Afro-American Symphony* (1930), but the era saw the popular rise of jazz in recordings, broadcasts, and club performances and a growing and geographically diverse recognition of the blues. Eubie Blake's musical *Shuffle Along* (1921) was a milestone. A virtuoso scholar, Spencer (Univ. of Richmond) shows that pessimistic evaluators of the period have erred: the energy of the Harlem Renaissance had roots in the century's start, and that impetus survived the Great Depression, only fading with the neoclassical and nondiscriminatory years after WW II. The author covers not only history, and not only music: he defines a national cultural aesthetic while reflecting on James Weldon Johnson's *Autobiography of an Ex-Coloured Man* (1912), fearlessly securing his argument's evidence from artifacts of arts and philosophic stances. Anyone working with 20th-century American history and music should consult this volume. All collections.—*D.-R. de Lerma, Lawrence University*

OAB-1054   PN1341   94-13608 CIP
Toelken, Barre. **Morning dew and roses: nuance, metaphor, and meaning in folksongs.** Illinois, 1995. 189p bibl index afp ISBN 0-252-02134-7, $32.95

Previous critics have regularly called attention to the haunting and evocative ambiguity of traditional ballad diction and imagery, but have been unable to do more than admire their surface charm. Now at last Toelken (Utah State Univ.) demonstrates the essential role in traditional song of constellations of images that bring into focus a specific range of interpretive possibilities and provide "intensification of plot, identification of moral themes, and depth of culture-based responses for the ballad and folksong audience." Stressing the ambiguous intertwined metaphors of sexuality and death ubiquitous in traditional Anglophone folksong (and northern European folksong generally), the author provides fresh and startling readings of "The Wife at Usher's Well," "The Cambric Shirt" ("Lady Isabel and the Elf Knight"), "I Gave My Love a Cherry," and more than a score of other classic ballads and lyrics, and clarifies such vexing issues as the validity of fragmentary versions and the relationship of riddle ballads to the rest of the ballad corpus. Toelken's extensive field experience gives weight and depth to his interpretations. This essential study of traditional poetics takes its place alongside Flemming Andersen's *Commonplace and Creativity* (1985), Roger Renwick's *English Folk Poetry, Structure and Meaning* (CH, Jan'81), and John Miles Foley's *Immanent Art* (CH, May'92). All academic and public collections.—*W. B. McCarthy, Pennsylvania State University, DuBois Campus*

OAB-1055   ML3534   92-56911 CIP
Walser, Robert. **Running with the devil: power, gender, and madness in heavy metal music.** Wesleyan/University Press of New England, 1993. 222p bibl index afp ISBN 0-8195-5252-6, $39.50; ISBN 0-8195-6260-2 pbk, $15.95

If heavy metal's history is traced back to late 1960s albums by Jimi Hendrix and Led Zeppelin, it has taken a quarter century for the genre to be meaningfully addressed. Walser's book (his first) is essential reading for anyone wishing to understand why this widely vilified music became the most popular and commercially successful style of the 1980s. It is not intended as a history; Philip Bashe's *Heavy Metal Thunder* (1985), though dated, is a better choice. Rather, it is a scholarly, provocative, copiously footnoted treatise in which Walser addresses issues (often myths) that have given heavy metal its notoriety. While covering the gamut from artists' misogyny and fans' nihilism to allegations of Satanism and lyrics suggesting "suicide solutions," Walser concludes that it is the music's power and its ability to empower listeners that must be understood. This ground-breaking book will force many readers to confront their prejudices about heavy metal, its performers, its audience, and its meanings. Indispensable for academic libraries both undergraduate and graduate level and highly recommended for general readership.—*H. A. Keesing, University of Maryland at College Park*

■ Theater & Dance

OAB-1056   Can. CIP
Bessai, Diane. **Playwrights of collective creation.** Simon & Pierre, P.O. Box 280, Adelaide Street Postal Station, Toronto, Ont. M5C 2J4 Canada, 1992. 292p index (The Canadian dramatist, 2) ISBN 0-88924-227-5 pbk, $29.95

Bessai (Univ. of Alberta) is one of the acknowledged authorities on collective creations in Canada. She provides a clear overview of the most important work of Theatre Passe Muraille and the influence of artistic director and animateur Paul Thompson on "play-makers" Rick Salutin, John Gray, and Linda Griffiths. She gives full descriptive accounts of the process and productions of well-known plays like *The Farm Show, 1837, Les Canadiens, Maggie and Pierre, Billy Bishop Goes to War, Rock and Roll*, and *Jessica* as well as less well documented plays like *Doukobors, Buffalo Jump, Them Donnellys, The West Show, Nathan Cohen: A Review*, and *O.D. On Paradise*. She places Canadian collective creation in the context of British and European traditions. She is particularly good on textual analysis and the interplay of the text in process, the play as performed, and the text as revised and published. Many of her sharp insights about the plays and the development of the playwrights complement those contained in Alan D. Filewod's *Collective Encounters* (1987). Instructors and libraries at all levels should have both. Quite accessible to undergraduates.—*M. J. Miller, Brock University*

OAB-1057   PN1590   93-40780 CIP
Dudden, Faye E. **Women in the American theatre: actresses & audiences, 1790-1870.** Yale, 1994. 260p bibl index afp ISBN 0-300-05636-2, $27.50

Well-known 19th-century female actresses Fanny Kemble and Charlotte Cushman are the centerpiece of this study. Dudden (history, Union College) documents their successes as a backdrop against which she portrays a theater environment unfavorable to a multitude of other talented actresses. Thomas Hamblin's cultivation of mass audiences at his Bowery Theatre in New York depended on his exploitation of women's talent—playwrights and performers who were either his mistresses or whose contracts provided only living expenses. English-born Laura Keene, managing her own companies, wavered between her goals of making the theater more respectable and cashing in on the demand for spectacle. Commercial interests tended to sensationalize the physical appearance of increasingly bare-legged and cross-dressed women. That Kemble refashioned her girlhood romantic image after enduring a bitter divorce trial and that Cushman defied many standards of a female star's image seem exceptions to the ways in which the American stage objectified women. Dudden's impressive historical documentation reinforces her uses of feminist performance theory. She provides new and personal ways to expose the questionable star status of women performers in these decades. The book provides ample scholarly annotations; high quality reproductions allow Dudden to comment on the way in which popularity was promoted through engravings, photographs, and illustrative souvenirs. Upper-division undergraduate and above.—*J. E. Gates, Jacksonville State University*

OAB-1058   PR2971   92-47235 CIP
Foreign Shakespeare: contemporary performance, ed. by Dennis Kennedy. Cambridge, 1994. 311p index ISBN 0-521-42025-3, $54.95

Following the recent publication of his discerning examination of visual dynamics in 20th-century Shakespearean performance *(Looking at Shakespeare,* CH, Jan'94), Kennedy here selects 14 diverse essays that look analytically at how Shakespeare's works are represented in productions and received by audiences in various parts of the non-English-speaking contemporary world. International scholars address a range of concerns including translation, transformations of text into nonverbal stage language, appropriation of Shakespeare's scripts as means of affirming cultural identity or asserting political ideology, the effect of native performance practices on the works, and implications drawn from notable acting and directing strategies. European models dominate, but one essay focuses on "Shakespeare and the Japanese Stage" and another on "intercultural" experiments by Peter Brook, Robert Wilson, and Peter Zadek. Collectively the studies offer lucid and richly detailed assessments of foreign production during recent decades. Kennedy's introduction and afterword provide an embracing critical framework and compel the reader to reexamine proprietary attachment to Shakespeare's English text by noting the eloquence of the works performed in other languages. This handsomely produced volume is valuable for academic and professional libraries at all levels.—*P. D. Nelsen, Marlboro College*

Humanities

OAB-1059   GV1649   96-2237 CIP
Foster, Susan Leigh. **Choreography narrative: ballet's staging of story and desire.** Indiana, 1996. 372p bibl index afp ISBN 0-253-33081-5, $59.95

This complex and beautifully written investigation of ballet's development in France from the early 18th through the late 19th century extends Foster's earlier efforts to link dance theory and practice (see *Reading Dancing: Bodies and Subjects in Contemporary American Dance*, CH, Apr'87; *Choreographing History*, 1995; and *Corporealities*, CH, Jun'96). Foster (Univ. of California at Riverside) has become increasingly adept at presenting historical, physical, and theoretical dancing bodies in relation to one another via written texts. This volume situates ballet as a cultural practice and analyzes its progress in relation to economic, political, and social developments—tracing its evolution through specific danced narratives and emphasizing class, gender, and racial identities. Each of the five chapters focuses on an issue relevant to choreography and training. These are augmented by "interludes," which contextualize the theoretical issues. Foster's word images awaken the reader to his/her own physicality and to the connections between an individual's lived experience and history. In previous works Foster has moved in this direction; here she negotiates the gap between theory and the actual body with increasing ease and depth. Illustrations are ample and well chosen throughout; the text is supported and enlarged by numerous notes and an extensive bibliography. This work is a landmark in the field and belongs in all libraries serving undergraduate, graduate, and faculty researchers in dance.—*S. E. Friedler, Swarthmore College*

OAB-1060   PN2193   95-22915 CIP
Fuchs, Elinor. **The death of character: perspectives on theater after modernism.** Indiana, 1996. 224p index afp ISBN 0-253-33038-6, $39.95; ISBN 0-253-21008-9 pbk, $17.95

Treating theater as "a crucial mediating term between the heterogeneous fullness of life and the clarifying abstractions of theory" and as a "grounding principle in a period of conflicting or dissolving truths," Fuchs (Yale and Columbia) demonstrates in this sage and sane examination of postmodern theater (especially in the US) why she is one of the most astute observers of the contemporary scene. As a critic she brings to this perceptive, dense study not only insights of sheer brilliance but historical perspective (including samplings of her own reviews and articles, 1979-93) and contextual overview rare in contemporary critical writing. Although clearly supportive of trends challenging more traditional approaches in theater, she remains objective and balanced throughout. She provides illuminating analyses of work by such artists as Richard Foreman, Robert Wilson, Meredith Monk, Reza Abdoh, Elizabeth LeCompte, and Suzan-Lori Parks, among others, and such influential theorists as Jacques Derrida. Arguably the most accessible yet learned road map to what remains for many impenetrable territory, Fuchs' book, heavily theoretical but constantly anchored to specific performances, is an obligatory addition to all academic libraries serving upper-division undergraduates and above.—*D. B. Wilmeth, Brown University*

OAB-1061   PN2061   91-40570 CIP
Harrop, John. **Acting.** Routledge, 1992. 135p bibl index ISBN 0-415-05961-5, $45.00; ISBN 0-415-05962-3 pbk, $13.95

Harrop, author of useful acting and directing texts (*Acting With Style*, CH, Jul'82, and, with Robert Cohen, *Creative Play Direction*, 2nd ed., 1984; 1st ed., CH, Oct'74), now presents intellectual speculations about the nature of acting and the spiritual and moral purposes of acting within society. Not just another "how-to" text, this book examines how we think and speak about acting, attempting to identify problems, examine them in various areas of acting experience, and provide the structure and fuel for future discussion. Deeply rooted in phenomenology and semiotics, Harrop ultimately sees acting as "a ritual testing of the soul," and he devotes his 12 brief chapters to developing this idea from a variety of perspectives. He includes a detailed examination of the actor's process and what he calls "the cybernetics of acting." As the first volume in a new series titled "Theatre Concepts," edited by John Russell Brown, this book begins the process of filling a wide and deep gap in the theoretical underpinnings of theatrical art.—*D. Stevens, Southern Illinois University-Carbondale*

OAB-1062   PA3238   94-48016 CIP
Hartigan, Karelisa V. **Greek tragedy on the American stage: ancient drama in the commercial theater, 1882-1994.** Greenwood, 1995. 161p bibl index afp (Contributions in drama and theatre studies, 60) ISBN 0-313-29283-3, $49.95

Hartigan surveys professional restagings of Greek tragedy in America from an 1882 rendering of *Oedipus Tyrannus* to Diana Rigg's triumphant portrayal of Medea in 1994. The author emphasizes the sociopolitical relevancy of these productions—how ancient themes found in the classical canon resonate with timely and changing concerns felt by successive generations of audiences. Chapters focus on chronological periods and selected "key performances" of Greek dramas that surfaced in American commercial theatrical repertoire within each time frame. Trained in classics, Hartigan demonstrates discerning knowledge of theater. She provides informative background discussion of performance history and a concise record of the critical reception of particular productions. She also supplies insightful commentary on hermeneutic cruxes found in each of the chosen scripts and examines such production challenges as communicating "the beauty and power of the classical text" in a world where visual action is more aesthetically valued than poetic eloquence. Lucidly written and handsomely produced, this book will appeal to all readers interested in interpretation of classical drama and in the theater as a mirror of social and intellectual history. All collections.—*P. D. Nelsen, Marlboro College*

OAB-1063   PN2270   93-2322 CIP
Hay, Samuel A. **African American theatre: a historical and critical analysis.** Cambridge, 1994. 287p bibl index ISBN 0-521-44522-1, $54.95; ISBN 0-521-46585-0 pbk, $18.95

This is another valuable addition to the "Cambridge Studies in American Theatre and Drama" series, under the excellent editorship of Don Wilmeth. Hay analyzes the origin and development of forms of expression that stem from indigenous African theater and their transformation by the American environment. The text revolves around the question of what means can be used today to insure growth of dramatic expression about the African American experience. The author examines two distinct schools of drama: "Black Arts," a strictly political and protest school focused on teaching African Americans the meanings of their background, and "Black Experience," expressing the real life of the people as collaborators and participants in American civilization. Both schools inform modern African American drama, and neither appears more correct or more modern. Hay's concern, however, is to secure the continuation of this theatrical tradition. Valuable appendixes provide outlines of viable strategies for organizational structuring and funding. Recommended for generalists interested in cultural studies and American theater, and for community and professional practitioners. All levels.—*E. C. Ramirez, University of Oregon*

OAB-1064   PN2055   93-4418 Orig
Hemmings, F.W.J. **Theatre and state in France, 1760-1905.** Cambridge, 1994. 285p bibl index ISBN 0-521-45088-8, $59.95

"It was the best of times; it was the worst of times." Dickens's most famous phrases precisely describe the theatrical circumstances discussed in this excellent study. Every condition here has its yin and yang: government protection and funding paired with onerous intervention and censorship; entrepreneurial freedom coupled with popular pandering; and so it goes. In the current era, theater has become a veritable weakling among the mass media: Goliath now plays David, and with an empty sling to boot. Following Frederick Brown's *Theater and Revolution: The Culture of the French State* (CH, Jan'81) by more than a decade, Hemmings's work provides an engrossing and (dare it be said of a scholarly book?) entertaining account of a complex era in theater history. She describes governments reacting in fear to the power wielded by playwrights and actors; theaters packed with parti-color political zealots; and, unfortunately, the beginnings of performance as product that has, it seems likely, bled dry and extricated the stage's vibrant heart. Despite this title's high price tag, everyone with an interest in theater, politics, sociology, and history in general should own and read this book. A writer of Hemmings's ability deserves encouragement!—*T. A. Pallen, Austin Peay State University*

OAB-1065 PR8789 90-50841 CIP

Hogan, Robert. **The years of O'Casey, 1921-1926: a documentary history,** by Robert Hogan and Richard Burnham. Delaware/C. Smythe, 1992. 437p index afp ISBN 0-87413-421-8, $55.00

This documentary history of the Irish theater from 1921 to 1926 includes incidental information on Irish locales other than Dublin and on art forms other than stage drama. But at the heart of the book stands Dublin's Abbey Theatre and the culminating struggle of its intrepid directors, playwrights, and performers to give the Irish nation its crowning cultural establishment. This volume is a worthy sequel to *The Modern Irish Drama*, published in five volumes between 1975 and 1984 by Ireland's Dolmen Press (Robert Hogan was also a coeditor of that series), which documents the Irish theater movement from its inception in 1899 to 1921. Hogan and Burnham have here produced a first-rate "climax" to the series. Their research not only brings together a treasure-trove of sharply focused snippets from contemporary playbills, newspaper reviews, journals, diaries, notes, letters, lectures, and general scuttlebutt that scholars will long be grateful to have, but furnishes a highly readable account of passionately involved men and women at a defining moment of Irish social, political, and artistic development—a moment that declined into discord with the mounting of O'Casey's *The Plough and the Stars* in early 1926. This packed assemblage will be a standard for good-sized undergraduate and all research collections. It concludes with an appendix of cast lists and production dates. Highly recommended.—*R. J. Thompson, Canisius College*

OAB-1066 GV1782 78-67320 Orig

Humphrey, Doris. **Doris Humphrey, the collected works, v.2.** Dance Notation Bureau, 1992. 217p ISBN 0-932583-29-X, $125.00

More than a decade has passed since the Dance Notation Bureau published its first volume of *Doris Humphrey: The Collected Works* (CH, Sep'79), which included *Water Study, Shakers*, and *Partita V, Op. 1 in G major*. The new volume comprises *Air for the G String, Two Ecstatic Themes*, and *Day on Earth* and represents the collaborative work of some of the most distinguished notators and dancers familiar with Humphrey's work including Jane Marriett, Muriel Topaz, Lucy Venalbe, Ernestine Stodelle, Letitia Ide, and Ruth Currier. It is a landmark publication. Each dance is provided movement analysis and historical background which would be enlightening for a broad readership. More than half of the book is devoted to the actual notated scores for each dance which could be "translated" only by serious scholars with professional expertise in Laban Notation, or in an academic environment where that expertise is being taught and developed. In such a context, it is an invaluable resource which clearly reflects the years of concerned scholarship devoted to its publication. The book is beautifully printed and spaced on fine quality paper—a tribute to the enduring work of Doris Humphrey, one of this century's most significant choreographers.—*C. W. Sherman, College of William and Mary*

OAB-1067 PN2596 92-52760 CIP

Ingram, William. **The business of playing: the beginnings of the adult professional theater in Elizabethan London.** Cornell, 1992. 255p index afp ISBN 0-8014-2671-5, $38.50

This engrossing study of professionalism in mid-16th century English theater skillfully attends to both ground and figure. Ingram provides a detailed, fresh look at professional playing and places the professional actor and the theater-owner in their social and economic contexts. Extending this process to theater history itself, Ingram begins with a thorough and well-reasoned discussion of theater historiography, a subject rarely encountered. These 11 pages alone make this book important reading, and Ingram continues to weave historiography into the rest of his text, constantly and candidly reminding the reader that good historians ply both fact and technique. In other hands, this rich mulligan of certitude and conjecture, content and commentary might have stewed away to dryness, but Ingram serves up the whole in a savory broth of artful narrative. Cornell University Press deserves compliments for placing Ingram's astute and helpful notes where they belong, at the foot of each page. Libraries at all academic levels.—*T. A. Pallen, Austin Peay State University*

OAB-1068 PN1968 93-16096 CIP

Jelavich, Peter. **Berlin cabaret.** Harvard, 1993. 322p index afp ISBN 0-674-06761-4, $39.95

Jelavich traces Berlin cabaret from its beginnings in vaudeville to its Imperial age heyday, through Weimar era inventiveness, and to the final degeneration back into a vapid variety under the National Socialists (cabaret entertainers were more often than not liberal, leftist, or Jewish). As the author illustrates, Berlin cabarets, through parody and satire, "cast an ironic eye on the goings-on of Berliners and other Germans." This superb study, ending with a brief look at concentration camp cabaret, is a masterful, erudite complement and addition to three standard studies in English: Lisa Appignanesi, *The Cabaret* (CH, Feb'77), Harold B. Segel, *Turn-of-the-Century Cabaret* (1987), and *Cabaret Performance: v.1, Europe 1890-1920*, ed. by Laurence Senelick (CH, May'90), the last not mentioned by Jelavich. Unlike these other studies, this one is more focused and limited in scope, yet it is definitive in its coverage, with impressive scholarship and text that is written in clear and elegant prose, without any impediments. Not only providing the necessary historical perspective and cultural context, this study goes a long way toward recreating as clearly as possible in words the actual performative aspect of cabaret, no small acccomplishment. Extensive notes, index, and illustrations. Recommended for all academic libraries, upper-division undergraduate and above.—*D. B. Wilmeth, Brown University*

OAB-1069 PN2969 95-10210 CIP

Kerr, David. **African popular theatre: from pre-colonial times to the present day.** J. Currey/Heinemann/EAEP/D. Philip/Baobab, 1995. 278p bibl index ISBN 0-435-08967-6, $60.00; ISBN 0-435-08969-2 pbk, $24.95

In the growing new research on African theater, such as John Conteh-Morgan's *Theatre and Drama in Francophone Africa* (CH, Sep'95), this study makes another important scholarly contribution. This comprehensive survey begins in the 15th century, investigating precolonial theater in relation to indigenous economic and social systems, class formation, and historical change. Kerr (English, Univ. of Botswana) discusses the evidence of a theatrical tradition of resistance that emerged in the colonial period; other topics include the populist theater and national ideology in modern Africa and the impact of performance in the struggle for liberation in Southern Africa to the present day. In an attempt to broaden the framework for understanding the popular theater in Africa, the author studies both literary and nonliterary forms. With its unusual attention to production details, this text is perhaps most valuable for its extensive translated firsthand accounts, unique illustrations of productions, and textual translations. Recommended for scholars in cultural, ethnic, and theater history studies and for professional theater practitioners interested in African performance, drama, and history. Upper-division undergraduates and up.—*E. C. Ramirez, University of Oregon*

OAB-1070 PR4622 92-31013 CIP

King, W.D. **Henry Irving's *Waterloo*: theatrical engagements ... late-Victorian culture ... and history.** California, 1993. 303p bibl index afp ISBN 0-520-08072-6, $40.00

Using what would seem to be insignificant primary "texts"—Arthur Conan Doyle's long-forgotten one-act play *A Story of Waterloo*, Henry Irving's acclaimed performance in it as Corporal Brewster, and George Bernard Shaw's damning criticism of it—King (Univ. of California, Santa Barbara) daringly and persuasively assesses the great tectonic shift from romantic to realistic in the theater, drama, and culture generally of the 1890s. King reads Irving's portrayal of an aged survivor of Waterloo reliving his heroic deed at the transcendent moment of his death as a parallel to the demise of the old actor's ideal style of theater. While never losing sight of his principal combatants, the "inspired actor" and the "supreme critic," King moves laterally into related efforts by the two (Irving's Louis XI; Shaw's responding Napoleonic drama *The Man of Destiny*) as well as back in time to the Battle of Waterloo itself and forward to the death of Irving. This is theater history as it ought to be written but seldom is—broad, contextualized, philosophic, yet simultaneously detailed, factual, tightly focused, without either the pretentious diction of many recent theoreticians or the tedious litany of names and dates from traditional scholars. May it prove a model for future theater historians. Highly recommended for anyone interested in the development of modern cultural and aesthetic sensibilities. Both general and academic readers—undergraduates, pre-professionals, and up.—*J. Ellis, formerly, Mount Holyoke College*

OAB-1071 PR739 94-44677 MARC

Lacey, Stephen. **British realist theatre: the new wave in its context, 1956-1965.** Routledge, 1995. 206p bibl index ISBN 0-415-07782-6, $49.95; ISBN 0-415-12311-9 pbk, $16.95

This fine volume demonstrates the complexity of the relationship between theater and the society in which it is created; it also shows how time changes critical perceptions. Lacey sees John Osborne's *Look Back in Anger* (1957) as more misogynistic than political and its apparent realism the result of contextual factors. The examination of film adaptations of plays probes the differences between the media as well as definitions of realism. The author further develops the concept of realism in analysis of Joan Littelwood's Theatre Workshop, George Devine's English Stage Company, and the work of playwrights Harold Pinter, John Arden, and Edward Bond. With its excellent bibliography and index, this is an important work for any theater collection serving upper-division undergraduates and above.—*R. Sugarman, emeritus, Southern Vermont College*

OAB-1072 PN2266 95-23422 CIP

Magnuson, Landis K. **Circle stock theater: touring American small towns, 1900-1960.** McFarland, 1996 (c1995). 258p bibl index afp ISBN 0-7864-0101-X, $32.50

Magnuson (Saint Anselm College) has produced the first detailed examination of circle stock touring in the US, an important first step in what might prove to be an exciting area for research. Circle troupes toured a limited number of communities usually surrounding a slightly larger home base. Circle rep companies existed throughout the country (150 troupes were active at times), and Magnuson focuses on the area of their greatest concentration—the Midwest. The author makes extensive use of the business records of the Chick Boyes Players and a trade publication, *Bill Bruno's Bulletin*. The interests of patrons, finances, the quality of the acting, technical aspects of production, and the ultimate demise of circle rep are covered. Interviews with surviving performers help make the study an incredibly personal one. A slightly stronger editorial hand might have helped eliminate some redundancies in the text. Nonetheless, this important study is strongly recommended for all college, university, and public libraries with strong theater history or popular culture collections.—*M. D. Whitlatch, Buena Vista University*

OAB-1073 GV1624 95-4413 CIP

Malone, Jacqui. **Steppin' on the blues: the visible rhythms of African American dance.** Illinois, 1996. 272p index afp ISBN 0-252-02211-4, $44.95; ISBN 0-252-06508-5 pbk, $16.95

This book takes on the interesting subject of how the African American culture has made a difference to art in America—what this difference is and how it is manifest. Malone (CUNY Queens College) is not so much interested in African influences as in the history and processes of African American creativity. She gives her readers eight well-researched chapters on the history of vernacular dance, followed by three chapters on vernacular dance in three contemporary African American institutions: vocal-harmony groups, black college and university marching bands, and black sororities and fraternities. From music and dance in Africa to step-dancing on college campuses, Malone's discussion of the celebratory, rhythmic, cultural, and artistic intricacies of African American vernacular dance is praiseworthy for its documentation of dance as well as for its analysis of complex cultural processes. Malone's eminently readable book revises one's understanding of both African American and European American vernacular dance. A welcome addition to a burgeoning literature on African American performance. Recommended for all academic collections.—*C. Martin, New York University*

OAB-1074 PN2287 94-22375 CIP

Menta, Ed. **The magic world behind the curtain: Andrei Serban in the American theatre.** P. Lang, 1995. 208p bibl index afp (Artists and issues in the theatre, 5) ISBN 0-8204-2640-7, $39.95

Since his work at New York's La Mama E.T.C. in the 1970s, Romanian-born director Andrei Serban has enriched American theater with visually stunning productions that reexamine classic texts. Serban draws on perspectives provided by Konstantin Stanislavski's contemporary Vsevolod Meyerhold; the 18th-century Italian Carlo Gozzi; traditional Eastern theater; and English director Peter Brook, with whom Serban worked before coming to the US. Menta interviewed Serban and many of his colleagues and provides a remarkable account of the final rehearsals of Serban's 1989 American Repertory Theatre production of *Twelfth Night.* The book also provides insight into Serban's unique work as professor of theater arts and director of the Oscar Hammerstein II Center for Theatre Studies at Columbia University. This thoroughly researched, well-written volume is indispensable for anyone who wishes to understand the forces animating serious contemporary theater. Even if one does not agree with all his answers, one can only admire the questions about texts and performance Serban raises and the passion with which he pursues them. Excellent notes, production history, bibliography, and photographs.—*R. Sugarman, emeritus, Southern Vermont College*

OAB-1075 PR3095 95-35335 CIP

Montrose, Louis. **The purpose of playing: Shakespeare and the cultural politics of the Elizabethan theatre.** Chicago, 1996. 227p index afp ISBN 0-226-53482-0, $45.00; ISBN 0-226-53483-9 pbk, $15.95

Montrose's stature among the illuminati of new historicist Shakespeareans should be noted. His overarching scholarly purpose here is to address "the politics of representation in the discursive and performative culture of later Elizabethan England"—a scope of ambition achieved through elegant mediation of selected representative details. The work is divided into two complementary parts. In part 1, Montrose examines how theatrical "play" holds a mirror up to the complex of culture, reflecting an abstract chronicle of the time. Throughout the first seven chapters, the author develops an astute discursive analysis, supported by diverse evidentiary sources, that illustrates dynamics of the "Elizabethan theatre's unstable articulation of socio-political domination and/or resistance." Part 2 focuses on the "dialectical character of ... cultural representations" indicated in the "dramatistic" construction of roles and rivalries in *A Midsummer Night's Dream*, especially those related to gender politics. Although a bibliography is not included, Montrose provides substantial annotation throughout and a useful index keyed to critical subject headings. The sophistication and perspicacity of Montrose's commentary will appeal to advanced readers; this volume should be included in all academic collections.—*P. D. Nelsen, Marlboro College*

OAB-1076 GV1786 93-27793 CIP

Nagrin, Daniel. **Dance and the specific image: improvisation.** Pittsburgh, 1994. 223p indexes afp ISBN 0-8229-3776-X, $49.95; ISBN 0-8229-5520-2 pbk, $19.95

The honesty, energy, and directness that have characterized the author's distinguished performing, teaching, and directing career are apparent throughout this new book. In contrast to his earlier *How to Dance Forever* (1988), which shares invaluable insights on extending a career in dance, Nagrin now provides a dynamic overview of the development of his Workgroup in the early 1970s. Part 1 outlines many structures that served as catalysts for the improvisational approach characteristic of the Workgroup. Nagrin's candid discussion of concepts resulting in cliché and banality—and the means to avoid them—is especially illuminating. Also valuable are his insights on teaching, directing, and preparing improvisation for performance, which are provided in part 2. Much shorter than part 1, this section includes useful diagrams for an in-the-round seating plan and light plot. The appendix includes an animated discussion, extracted from a tape transcription of guest teaching in Hawaii, on experiencing raw emotion in the context of performing. Several sections of photographs illuminate part 1. Unfortunately, the acid-free paper is translucent and allows print to show through—a feature common in newspapers, but surprising in a book of this cost. There is virtually no available writing on improvisation, and this book, together with Deborah Hay's *Lamb at the Altar: The Story of a Dance* (1994), makes a valuable contribution.—*C. W. Sherman, College of William and Mary*

OAB-1077   PN2309   94-27647 CIP
Negotiating performance: gender, sexuality, and theatricality in Latin/o America, ed. by Diana Taylor and Juan Villegas. Duke University, 1995 (c1994). 356p bibl index afp ISBN 0-8223-1504-1, $54.95; ISBN 0-8223-1515-7 pbk, $18.95

This much-needed and long-awaited volume on Latina/o and Latin American performance should be required reading for the many professional and university-based theater programs that profess diversity and multiculturalism in both training and performance. Issues of performance are examined historically, socially, and politically in 17 essays that blend informal prose with provocative critical discourse and on-site chronicling of events. Contributors include contemporary performers Guillermo Gómez-Peña and Cherrie Moraga; the leading scholar and critic on feminism and theater, Sue-Ellen Case; and the most noted historian of Chicano/a theater, Jorge Huerta (who provides a valuable clarification of the distinction between the contributions of that group and those of the many Latina/o groups in the US). Huerta boldly confronts the problems and pitfalls in producing ethno-specific plays, challenging non-Chicano/a theaters to educate themselves in understanding culture and community. Juan Villegas's contribution, "Closing Remarks," is probably most helpful if read at the onset, as an introduction; it provides important definitions and contexts and raises issues and ideas relevant to the entire collection. Recommended for all readers and researchers interested in performance and culture.—*E. C. Ramirez, University of Oregon*

OAB-1078   PN2053   95-45987 MARC
The Production notebooks, ed. with introd. by Mark Bly. Theatre Communications Group, 1996. 238p bibl (Theatre in process, 1) ISBN 1-55936-110-7 pbk, $16.95

Many leading theaters employ dramaturges as literary managers and researchers. This remarkable volume chronicles the work of four dramaturges on particular productions, and it records in a unique way the collaborative process of creating theater. One of the greatest contributions of dramaturges may be recording the ephemeral nature of theatrical creation. The book reminds those theaters and directors who do not have the luxury of a dramaturge's services of the value of sound research and preparation to the creation of daring theatrical work. The productions examined are *The Clytemnestra Project* at the Guthrie Theatre, developed from plays by Aeschylus, Sophocles, and Euripides; Robert Wilson's version of Georg Büchner's *Danton's Death* at the Alley Theatre in Houston; *The Love Space Demands*, created by Ntozaka Shange and Crossroads Theatre in New Jersey from her poetry; *Children of Paradise: Shooting a Dream*, by Theatre de la Jeune Lune in Minneapolis based on the making of Marcel Carné's film *Children of Paradise*. Each production stretched theatrical boundaries in exciting ways, and the dramaturges' diaries should inspire all who work in theater. This reviewer welcomes future volumes in this series. Good black-and-white photographs, useful bibliography for each production. Highly recommended for all theater collections.—*R. Sugarman, emeritus, Southern Vermont College*

OAB-1079   PN1647   94-3828 CIP
Rayner, Alice. **To act, to do, to perform: drama and the phenomenology of action.** Michigan, 1994. 165p bibl index afp ISBN 0-472-10537-X, $32.50

Rayner's elegant study examines the nature and complexity of dramatic action

from diverse critical perspectives. The triangle of infinitives configured in the book's title are drawn from the First Gravedigger's contemplation of Ophelia's death in *Hamlet*. Rayner (Stanford Univ.) adopts the tripartite delineation of types of action as a theoretical framework not only for interrogating aspects of drama but also as a paradigm for addressing ontological concerns. In sophisticated and carefully documented analysis, she defines distinctions between concepts of behavior, action, and performance and mediates such contingent issues as intent, materiality, passivity, and the dynamics of meaning. Points of reference are drawn from philosophy, semiotics, and psychology as well as from literary theory and performance methodology. Despite the scope of her inquiry, Rayner keeps matters in focus by applying theoretical constructs to illustrative instances in selected plays, particularly Shakespeare's *Macbeth* and *Hamlet*, Chekhov's *Three Sisters*, and Beckett's *Waiting for Godot*. Twenty-four pages of discursive endnotes expand understanding of the interplay of influences that shaped this author's significant contribution to works of dramatic theory. Upper-division undergraduates, graduate students, faculty, and scholarly professionals.—*P. D. Nelsen, Marlboro College*

OAB-1080   PR3034   93-17317 CIP
Skura, Meredith Anne. **Shakespeare the actor and the purposes of playing.** Chicago, 1993. 325p index afp ISBN 0-226-76179-7, $49.95; ISBN 0-226-76180-0 pbk, $17.95

Skura builds on Shakespearean performance criticism, which focuses on modern staging and actor/audience interrelationships, to address the particular Elizabethan conditions of, and attitudes toward, the stage and the acting profession. She argues that the actor, whether Elizabethan or modern, is trapped by an uneasy dependence on the audience for either applause and celebrity or rejection and victimization. When the Elizabethan acting troupe relies on patronage such ambivalence increases, and the actor may view himself as a proud beggar, a flattering dog, a childlike and foolish clown. Skura masterfully traces such image motifs throughout the entire canon (including the Sonnets), with particular emphasis on Richard III, Falstaff, Bottom, Christopher Sly, and King Lear. This book is impressively rich in its details and range of references (more than 78 pages of notes, and full indexing), including questions of Shakespeare's life as an actor, the mythic resonance of the deer hunt, the myth of Actaeon, bearbaiting, and Christ's martyrdom. The analyses are intelligent, incisive, and wondrously eclectic: modern acting practices and cultural analogues coexist with Renaissance allusions. No other study matches Skura's critical perceptiveness and daring. Strongly recommended for both literary and theater collections. Advanced undergraduate; graduate; faculty.—*C. Rees, University of Connecticut*

OAB-1081   PN2581   95-40921 CIP
Styan, J.L. **The English stage: a history of drama and performance.** Cambridge, 1996. 432p index ISBN 0-521-55398-9, $54.95; ISBN 0-521-55636-8 pbk, $11.95

Since writing *The Elements of Drama* (1960), Styan has been a strong advocate for a stage-centered approach to dramatic criticism. In theoretical works like *Drama, Stage, and Audience* (CH, Oct'75) and in studies of individual playwrights, e.g., *Chekhov in Performance* (1971), he has consistently sought to understand how a play creates meaning for an audience. In addition, he has argued that the performance perspective is the most valid basis for understanding not only what the play meant within its original historical context but what it can be understood to mean today. *The English Stage* demonstrates convincingly the truth of Styan's argument that theater history and the history of dramatic literature must go hand in hand. In this excellent survey of English drama and its performance from the medieval period to the modern era, Styan provides repeated insights into the complex process that occurs when the audience, the physical medium, the actors' performance, and the written text come together in the creation of the theater experience. However, the inclusion of a bibliography or a list of works cited would have added significantly to the book's considerable value. All collections.—*W. M. Tate, Portland State University*

OAB-1082   PN2581   94-25635 MARC
Trussler, Simon. **The Cambridge illustrated history of British the-atre.** Cambridge, 1994. 404p bibl indexes ISBN 0-521-41913-1, $39.95

This lavish, provocative survey of British theater from Roman times to the present complements and overshadows the only comparable previous publication, Alec Clunes's *The British Theatre* (1965). Surprisingly few of the well-selected, finely reproduced 232 illustrations (many in color) duplicate Clunes's 184. The congenial format, with topical essays scattered through the narrative and detailed captions appended to the plates, makes this history an informative delight whether dipped into or read from start to finish. The author's radical predisposition toward innovation creates a stimulating tension when focused on a topic so laden with tradition and continuity as the English stage. Best known as a Shakespearean scholar and critic, Trussler is particularly deft in assessing changes in Shakespearean production from age to age, but he ranges well and widely to other authors and performers and to modes of popular entertainment from trope to mumming to jig to music hall to improvisation. Women—from Hrotsvitha to Aphra Behn to Elizabeth Robins to Caryl Churchill—get their overdue share of attention. Handsome, important, astonishingly inexpensive, and replete with useful chronology, glossary, and who's who, this book belongs in every public and institutional library.—*J. Ellis, formerly, Mount Holyoke College*

OAB-1083   PN2266   96-31372 CIP
Wainscott, Ronald H. **The emergence of the modern American the-ater, 1914-1929.** Yale, 1997. 260p bibl index afp ISBN 0-300-06776-3, $30.00

Stemming from his earlier important work *Staging O'Neill: The Experimental Years, 1920-1934* (CH, Feb'89), this book adds a wealth of information about a period in American theater Wainscott (Indiana Univ.) describes as "Broadway's most prolific and influential." Through an examination of plays and productions, the reader witnesses the impact of American theater during critical periods including WW I and the postwar era, which witnessed the emerging role of women in popular sex farces, censorship battles, and the impact of expressionism. The author assesses both commercial and experimental productions within a political and social context. Eugene O'Neill serves as a springboard for comparison and evaluation of the work of other notable figures, including Maxwell Anderson, Susan Glaspell, Sophie Treadwell, Arthur Hopkins, Robert Edmund Jones, Lee Simonson, and Philip Barry. Included are 16 production photographs and an appendix of the sex farces (1915-21), a genre reflecting social assumptions, values, and artistic views of playwrights, producers, and audiences and clearly indicating the almost unequaled fascination with this Broadway entertainment. The bibliography provides an extensive compilation of unpublished materials, published plays, reviews, and articles. Recommended for general readers, undergraduates, and researchers in American theater history and cultural studies.—*E. C. Ramirez, University of Oregon*

OAB-1084   PN2266   92-10068 CIP
Weinberg, Mark S. **Challenging the hierarchy: collective theatre in the United States.** Greenwood, 1992. 267p bibl index afp (Contributions in drama and theatre studies, 48) ISBN 0-313-27219-0, $49.95

Weinberg makes a significant contribution to our understanding of the diverse forces that are part of US contemporary theater. Well outside the mainstream, the groups studied dramatize issues and ideas, often in unusual ways. Their collective methods of preparation receive as much attention as the performances. Introductory chapters examine the process and history of collective theater. Four chapters are then devoted to collectives whose work has been observed by the author and whose members he has interviewed. The groups are El Teatro de la Esperanza, a Chicano theater; the Dakota Theatre Caravan, which created works from research done with its audiences; United Mime Workers, which developed new ways of seeing and doing; and Split Britches, which "challenged audiences with its gender-bending, lesbio-centered, celebratory, and frequently hilarious productions." Weinberg documents how difficult sustaining such groups is. He also notes the continuing impulse they rep-

resent to question economic, social, and theatrical hierarchies. Excellent notes and bibliography. Recommended for all theater collections.—*R. Sugarman, emeritus, Southern Vermont College*

OAB-1085   PN2616   95-42994 CIP
Yates, W.E. **Theatre in Vienna: a critical history, 1776-1995.** Cambridge, 1996. 328p bibl index afp ISBN 0-521-42100-4, $59.95

Choosing 1776 as a starting point, Yates chronicles Vienna's varied and colorful theatrical history, putting particular emphasis on 19th- and 20th-century events. Of special note is Yates's attempt to include all of Vienna's theatrical enterprises—commercial, court, and state. The result is a rich work of depth and insight that not only paints in broad strokes the external events, but also includes the intellectual, social, and political backgrounds against which Viennese theater was formed and still thrives. The author gives an entire chapter to censorship, the active control by the government of everything that was to be staged. "Anything directed against the ruling house, anything that might threaten law and order ... anything offensive to religion or morality" was subject to the rigor of the censor's pen. The many black-and-white pictures, drawings, and sketches illustrate the variety and scope of the Viennese theater. Extensive posttextual notes include an appendix of documents that require a knowledge of German, an appendix of research resources in Austria, the usual scholarly notes, and a copious bibliography. A useful index provides separate listings of theaters and plays. An important book for theater scholars at the upper-division undergraduate level and above and for general readers.—*R. F. Falk, Lycoming College*

■ Philosophy

OAB-1086   B3317   94-31510 CIP
Ahern, Daniel R. **Nietzsche as cultural physician.** Pennsylvania State, 1995. 212p bibl index afp ISBN 0-271-01425-3, $35.00

Ahern's book is a welcome and interesting addition to the ever-increasing corpus of commentaries on Nietzsche's thought. Ahern proposes an understanding of Nietzsche's critique of traditional metaphysics—a tradition Nietzsche believes began with Socrates—by placing it in the context of the physiological concepts of health and sickness. Through exhaustive use of quotations, Ahern demonstrates the persistence and importance of physiology, not just as a metaphor for Nietzsche, but also as the conceptual framework within which his most fundamental critiques are formulated. Ahern focuses primarily on Nietzsche's critiques of Socrates (i.e., traditional metaphysics and philosophy) and Christianity, but he argues that the physiological framework applies elsewhere as well (e.g., Nietzsche's critique of Wagner). Such an emphasis is understandable, considering the amount Nietzsche wrote on just these two topics; but Ahern lays the basis for taking an interesting and illuminating approach to other areas of Nietzsche's thought. In short, Ahern makes a solid case for taking seriously Nietzsche's view of himself as a cultural physician, diagnosing and curing the ills of society. Well written and thoroughly documented, this book is highly recommended to anyone interested in Nietzsche, whether undergraduate or Nietzsche scholar. Undergraduate; graduate; general.—*J. A. Bell, Southeastern Louisiana University*

OAB-1087   B2693   93-39401 CIP
Arkush, Allan. **Moses Mendelssohn and the Enlightenment.** State University of New York, 1994. 304p bibl index ISBN 0-7914-2071-X, $59.50

Mendelssohn (1729-86) was a philosopher of the German Enlightenment and an observant Jew. Arkush's study situates Mendelssohn's thought in its late 18th century context: the metaphysics and natural theology of Leibniz and Wolff, and the political liberalism of Spinoza and Locke. Despite a broad compatibility of Mendelssohn's refashioned Judaism with natural theology, Arkush shows how Mendelssohn himself sensed the inadequacy of his synthesis. Furthermore,

Mendelssohn could not ultimately defend aspects of Judaism against a contemporary critique in part born of the very philosophical movement to which Mendelssohn belonged. Some of his writing, therefore, must be understood as strategic and evasive. An esoteric Mendelssohn, a Deist-oriented liberal who prudentially presented himself as a Jew of traditional commitments, emerges in Arkush's reading. Given Alexander Altmann's definitive biographical and social historical work *Moses Mendelssohn* (CH, Dec'73), this study focuses almost entirely on Mendelssohn's philosophical argumentation. Here Arkush distinguishes himself as a thorough scholar. His grasp of the entire Mendelssohn corpus and his ability to view problems in light of the whole gives him an advantage over some other recent scholars. This work, recommended for all academic libraries, will be a benchmark in the study of Mendelssohn for years to come. Upper-division undergraduate; graduate; faculty.—*A. L. Mittleman, Muhlenberg College*

OAB-1088   B3148   94-18811 CIP
Atwell, John E. **Schopenhauer on the character of the world: the metaphysics of will.** California, 1995. 224p index afp ISBN 0-520-08770-4, $35.00

Atwell (Temple Univ.) sympathetically examines the philosophy of Arthur Schopenhauer (1788-1860) as contained in the latter's main work, *The World as Will and Representation*. The focus of the study is on the nature and role of the will in Schopenhauer. Atwell examines in detail Schopenhauer's central claim of a close relation between human volition and the wider significance of the will as the principle of all reality. In particular, Atwell takes seriously Schopenhauer's statement that his entire philosophical system consists in the unfolding of a "single thought," viz., that the world is the will coming to self-knowledge. Atwell employs the "single thought" as a guiding thread through the epistemology, philosophy of nature, aesthetics, and ethics of Schopenhauer's main work, arguing for the consistency of Schopenhauer's system. The book is well written and well argued, forms a nice sequel to Atwell's own earlier study, *Schopenhauer: The Human Character* (1990), and may well be the best English-language study of Schopenhauer's metaphysics to date. Highly recommended. Upper-division undergraduate; graduate faculty.—*G. Zoeller, University of Iowa*

OAB-1089   B4238   94-34209 CIP
Boobbyer, Philip. **S. L. Frank: The life and work of a Russian philosopher, 1877-1950.** Ohio University, 1995. 292p bibl index afp ISBN 0-8214-1110-1, $45.00

The life and work of Simeon Frank have not received the kind of attention by scholars that has been devoted to many of his fellow contributors to the famous *Landmarks* (*Vekhi*) collection. With this monograph based on personal interviews, US and Russian archives, Frank's own material, and numerous secondary sources, Boobbyer has rescued Frank and his work from an undeserved obscurity. Beginning with his early Marxist phase, the author traces Frank's transition to "Legal Marxism" and then what he himself called a "religious humanism." This political-intellectual transition was also accompanied by a religious conversion from Judaism to Russian Orthodoxy, so that after his exile from the Soviet Union in 1922, Frank's major contribution was as a Christian philosopher and teacher. All this receives an extended and enlightening discussion to which no brief review can do full justice. A first-rate piece of biography, Boobbyer's study deserves to be read by history and philosophy undergraduates and graduates alike.—*G. E. Snow, Shippensburg University of Pennsylvania*

OAB-1090   B945   92-19888 CIP
Brent, Joseph. **Charles Sanders Peirce: a life.** Indiana, 1993. 388p bibl index afp ISBN 0-253-31267-1, $35.00

Peirce (1839-1914) is America's most creative, dominant, and original philosopher. Yet the first book-length biography of the founder of pragmatism was not published until 75 years after his death: Elisabeth Walther's *Charles Sanders Peirce: Leben und Werk* (Baden-Baden, 1989). Now we have the first

American biography, and a superb book it is. The 35 years Brent expended in making this biography have seasoned and enriched his definitive production. (The telling of Peirce's story, like his life, has been fraught with malversation. Someday the story of telling his story will be told.) Here, the facts of Peirce's life are integrated into the systematization that he hoped would "for a long time to come [influence] the entire work of human reason." From fields as diverse and powerful as semiotics, metaphysics, epistemology, aesthetics, ethics, psychology, linguistics, geology, philosophy of science, mathematics, and religion, these effects are being acknowledged. The role of Peirce's life in the chronological development of his ideas structures this narrative and gives an expositional argument for a solid interpretation of his philosophy as a single architectonic system. Five chapters of the biography cover in chronological order 75 years of Peirce's life. The sixth and last, a brilliant essay "The Wasp in the Bottle," could alone make this work a masterpiece. Indiana University Press is also publishing a complete edition, *Writings of Charles S. Peirce* (1982- ; v.1, CH, Feb'83). Six volumes are published of 30 expected. (The project, this year, is in a struggle for continued support from the National Endowment for the Humanities.) From the published volumes, IUP has now issued the first of a projected two-volume sampler: *The Essential Peirce*, containing 25 well-edited, important works written by Peirce from 1867 to 1893, with an excellent introduction by Nathan Houser, associate editor of the Peirce Edition project. From Harvard University Press comes Peirce's Cambridge Conference Lectures of 1898, *Reasoning and the Logic of Things*. The text, taken from the Houghton Library collections for the purpose of a study edition, is without the critical editorial work of the IUP editions. The 50 pages of comment by Hilary Putnam are of interest in themselves; the 160 pages of Peirce's eight lectures are demonstrations of the authority and originality of his thought. Here is a generally accessible and complete account of Peirce's mature work constructed by Peirce himself in order to introduce his philosophy to nonspecialists. This book in an undergraduate library would make Peirce's philosophy intelligible independently of philosophy courses and philosophy teachers. Each of these books is well published and contains effective notes and an adequate index. This reviewer's highest recommendation is for Brent's biography, which should be in every college and university library in America. The next priority is *Reasoning and the Logic of Things*, a new and valuable addition to Peirce primary sources presently available. Libraries not subscribing to the complete *Writings*. . .should certainly order *The Essential Peirce*.—*K. J. Dykeman, Fairfield University*

OAB-1091   B791   94-11683 CIP
Cahoone, Lawrence E. **The ends of philosophy.** State University of New York, 1995. 418p bibl index afp ISBN 0-7914-2321-2, $59.50

Cahoone (Boston Univ.), author of *The Dilemma of Modernity* (1988), has written an extraordinarily good work in which he meticulously examines the current philosophical and antiphilosophical scene. He addresses the question, "Is characteristically philosophical knowledge possible?" That is, can philosophical inquiry yield knowledge about such matters as the existence of God, the meaning of human life, whether science is true, whether morality is solely conventional, whether democracy is right. The aim of Cahoone's study is to accept and not avoid the blows of antiphilosophy, the philosophical undermining of philosophy, and then to "carefully assess the damage." He does this through a detailed examination of such thinkers as Peirce, Nietzsche, Wittgenstein, Buchler, Derrida, and Rorty. In particular, he offers to examine systematically and comparatively the metaphilosophical strategies of antiphilosophy. The work is extremely valuable for the light it throws, not only on the question of the validity of philosophy but also on the thought of the people whose work Cahoone examines. Highly recommended for graduate libraries. Well bound with useful index.—*R. L. Greenwood, University of South Alabama*

OAB-1092   B1297   93-33190 CIP
The Cambridge companion to Locke, ed. by Vere Chappell. Cambridge, 1994. 329p bibl indexes ISBN 0-521-38371-4, $59.95; ISBN 0-521-38772-8 pbk, $17.95

Between a beginning chapter on Locke's life and a concluding chapter on

Humanities

his influence are eight chapters on his philosophy. Five are on epistemology, metaphysics, and language and three are on religion, ethics, and political theory. All clearly written, they cover fundamentals of Locke's positions as well as discussions of recent scholarly disputes. Chappell's chapter on Locke's theory of ideas, McCann's on bodies, substance, and the issues surrounding Locke's atomism, and Schneewind's discussion of the moral philosophy are just outstanding. The book is an exceptional research tool. In addition to the essays it has a bibliography on Locke's influence, a bibliography citing the original works and dates of publication of Locke's works as well as a separate list of later editions and collections, and a very useful list of secondary sources. There is also a good name and subject index, plus an index to all passages in Locke that are cited. This is a model for books of this kind, and should be in the libraries of all four-year institutions. The paperback editions in this series are of very good quality and, given the price difference, may be preferable to the hardcover editions.—*R. H. Evans, University of Minnesota—Duluth*

OAB-1093   B945   95-1492 CIP
Campbell, James. **Understanding John Dewey: nature and cooperative intelligence.** Open Court, 1995. 310p bibl index ISBN 0-8126-9284-5, $43.95; ISBN 0-8126-9285-3 pbk, $17.95

Campbell does not spend much time on Dewey's life; however, he does relate Dewey's philosophy to the American experience and to the social and political scene. The style is clear and fresh, and the book's sensible organization makes it easy to focus on important topics. The author begins with the Darwinian and biological background, the importance of inquiry and process, and the root idea of the social nature of the individual. These issues serve as the background for chapters on metaphysics and experience, the good, and Dewey's social and political thought. The final chapter integrates these themes into Dewey's views on the communal religious life. If there is a weakness, it is the short shrift given to aesthetics and the aesthetic experience—an aspect treated in Thomas Alexander's *John Dewey's Theory of Art, Experience and Nature* (CH, Dec'87). Nevertheless, this superb book should be in all academic libraries and, given the importance of Dewey to American education and social life, in most public libraries. It is well produced with good readable type. Campbell has set a good precedent for future writers by deriving all references from the 37-volume critical edition of *The Works of John Dewey*. General; undergraduate; graduate; faculty.—*R. H. Evans, University of Minnesota—Duluth*

OAB-1094   B775   91-39554 CIP
Copenhaver, Brian P. **Renaissance philosophy,** by Brian P. Copenhaver and Charles B. Schmitt. Oxford, 1992. 450p bibl index (A History of Western philosophy, 3) ISBN 0-19-219203-5, $65.00; ISBN 0-19-289184-7 pbk, $18.95

The eminent Renaissance scholar C.B. Schmitt initiated this work; on his death, Copenhaver (Univ. of California-Riverside) wrote the bulk of it. He provides a unified and well-balanced presentation of the philosophical developments of an era that today's textbooks still largely ignore. The first chapter presents a rich tapestry of the historical context out of which and in which Renaissance philosophy developed. The next four chapters consider its main movements and figures. The final chapter discusses various links of Renaissance philosophy with modern and contemporary thought. The first and last chapters will be the more useful (and easier) for undergraduates while the middle chapters will give them and graduate students a fine introduction to this period. Thus, this work and *The Cambridge History of Renaissance Philosophy*, ed. by C.B. Schmitt et al. (CH, Dec.'88), which is more detailed and research-oriented, supplement one another nicely. Extensive bibliography and index. Recommended for all college and larger public libraries.—*G. J. Dalcourt, Seton Hall University*

OAB-1095   B809   96-45189 CIP
Deconstruction in a nutshell: a conversation with Jacques Derrida, ed. by John D. Caputo. Fordham University, 1997. 215p bibl indexes afp (Perspectives in continental philosophy, 1) ISBN 0-8232-1754-X, $25.00; ISBN 0-8232-1755-8 pbk, $17.95

In a nutshell, this is a wonderfully helpful and stimulating book. It contains a 25-page roundtable interview with Derrida, in which he answers a wide range of questions about his own work in a manner that is both concise and direct. The bulk of the book is taken up with John Caputo's commentary. While Caputo bills it as simply a commentary on the interview, it is really much more than that. It is a cogent, witty, and always accessible discussion of Derrida's work of the past ten to 20 years. There are many guides to Derrida's work, from *Of Grammatology* to *Glas*. There is, however, very little to help the student or researcher get an overview of Derrida's recent work. Along with Derrida's own *Points ...: Interviews, 1974-1994* (CH, Sep'95), this is one of the best guides available to his recent work. It is particularly stimulating on the question of the theological within Derrida—which, as Caputo suggests, is a relatively neglected topic that is worthy of further exploration. This book will no doubt be useful in courses dealing with Continental philosophy and literary theory and criticism. Highly recommended. Upper-division undergraduate; graduate; faculty.—*S. Barnett, Central Connecticut State University*

OAB-1096   E169   93-11686 CIP
Diggins, John Patrick. **The promise of pragmatism: modernism and the crisis of knowledge and authority.** Chicago, 1994. 515p index afp ISBN 0-226-14878-5, $29.95

In *The American Left in the Twentieth Century* (CH, Dec'73), Diggins made clear his preference for American-inspired leftist thought over its European counterpart. A revised version of that work (*The Rise and Fall of the American Left*, 1992) again illuminated Diggins's frustration with European intellectual imports, particularly poststructuralism and deconstructionism. It is in this context that his present work should be viewed. Although the subject is pragmatism, Diggins's target is poststructuralism. His thoughtful analysis of key thinkers "use[s] one author to interrogate another so that ideas speak to our condition as well as theirs." The approach renders the complex comprehensible. The author's conclusions certainly suggest that although pragmatism has not always lived up to its promise, the poststructuralist notion of knowledge as power is mired in hopelessness and offers nothing constructive. One curious paradox of this study is Diggins's effort to undermine the philosophical foundations of the poststructuralist/deconstructionist/postmodernist mindset while questioning its originality by highlighting the intellectual contributions of such Americans as theologian Reinhold Niebuhr and "cultural economist" Thorstein Veblen. In this outstanding work, Diggins succeeds in demonstrating the costliness of the pragmatists' derision of history and the prematureness of the neopragmatists' abandonment of philosophy. Upper-division undergraduates and above.—*D. M. Wrobel, Hartwick College*

OAB-1097   B3279   94-34 CIP
Fink, Eugen. **Sixth Cartesian meditation: the idea of transcendental theory of method,** tr. with introd. by Ronald Bruzina. Indiana, 1995. 207p index afp ISBN 0-253-32273-1, $35.00

Fink's study of Descartes's sixth *Meditation* is an invaluable addition to the corpus of Husserl scholarship. More than simply a scholarly treatise, however, it is the result of Fink's collaboration with Husserl during the last ten years of Husserl's life. The textual notations and appendixes by Husserl, which are included in this book, demonstrate the close work between the two thinkers, and indeed they also show Husserl's endorsement of Fink's project. Bruzina, whose lengthy introduction sets forth the historical circumstances and context from which this work emerged, does a fine job illustrating the rightful importance of this work. This truly essential work in phenomenology should find a prominent place alongside Husserl's own works. For readers interested in phenomenology—and in Husserl in particular—it cannot be recommended highly enough.—*J. A. Bell, Southeastern Louisiana University*

OAB-1098   B3248   96-48164 CIP
Gadamer, Hans-Georg. **The philosophy of Hans-Georg Gadamer,** ed. by Lewis Edwin Hahn. Open Court, 1997. 619p bibl index afp (The

library of living philosophers, 24) ISBN 0-8126-9341-8, $56.95; ISBN 0-8126-9342-6 pbk, $29.95

This volume fully lives up to the high standard of its predecessors. It begins with a 60-page autobiographical reflection by Gadamer on his philosophical development, including his years teaching and lecturing in America after 1968. Appearing here for the first time in English, this essay represents an irreplaceably valuable effort at self-critique and comment. Following this are 29 "critical essays" by such well-known contemporary philosophers as Donald Davidson, Roderick Chisholm, Karl-Otto Apel, Stanley Rosen, Robert Sokolowski, Don Verene, Joan Stambaugh, and John Sallis, as well as by leading Gadamer scholars P. Christopher Smith, David Hoy, Dennis Schmidt, Jean Grondin, and others. Each essay is followed by a reply from Gadamer. These replies, taken together, are a treasure house of statements by him on the main issues of his philosophy. A 30-page bibliography of his major books and articles in German and in English, plus a brief three-page list of secondary sources (books only), concludes the volume. Valuable in the bibliography and specially compiled for this volume is a list of archival audiotapes and videotapes of Gadamer's lectures in Germany from 1949 to 1996, obtainable from various radio and television archives in Germany. Comprehensive, and meticulously edited, this book is an indispensable resource for any scholar or student working with the philosophy of Gadamer. Undergraduate; graduate; faculty.— *R. E. Palmer, MacMurray College*

OAB-1099 B741 95-6053 MARC
History of Islamic philosophy, ed. by Seyyed Hossein Nasr and Oliver Leaman. Routledge, 1996. 2v. 1,211p bibl indexes (Routledge history of world philosophies, 1) ISBN 0-415-15667-5, $185.00

These volumes are the first installments in the "Routledge History of World Philosophies," the series now appearing in tandem with the "Routledge History of Philosophy," which scans philosophy from the Greeks to the present. Islamic philosophers are known to nonspecialists primarily as transmitters of Greek philosophy or as influences on Medieval European thinkers. *History of Islamic Philosophy* makes available, as never before, the full sweep of this rich and complex philosophical tradition. Part 1 surveys the religious and intellectual background. Parts 2 and 3 offer portraits of classical philosophers like Ibn Sîna and Ibn Rushd. Parts 4 and 5 focus on important mystical philosophers like Ibn 'Araî and Mullā Sadrā. Part 6 surveys Jewish philosophers in the Islamic context. Part 7 examines 11 systematic areas, from metaphysics to law. The last two parts address philosophy in the contemporary Islamic world and modern Western interpretations of Islamic philosophy. Each of the 71 chapters includes an up-to-date bibliography, an especially valuable resource in a rapidly expanding field. The editors deserve praise for assembling an outstanding team of 50 scholars and compiling the single most useful history of this rich tradition. Strongly recommended for academic and public libraries. General; undergraduate; graduate; faculty.—*J. Bussanich, University of New Mexico*

OAB-1100 B3199 95-3048 CIP
Hohendahl, Peter Uwe. **Prismatic thought: Theodor W. Adorno.** Nebraska, 1995. 287p index afp ISBN 0-8032-2378-1, $40.00

Adorno was the most prolific representative of the Frankfurt School from the 1950s until his death in 1969, and his writings still have an enormous impact on the Western world and beyond. Hohendahl, the author of previous studies on Adorno, ranks among the leading experts on critical theory in the US. His present work is one of the few truly ambitious assessments of Adorno's oeuvre published in English to date. Hohendahl rightly argues that a "comprehensive analysis" of this oeuvre is not feasible, given the unsystematic, non-traditional character of Adorno's thought. Instead, he opts for a multidirectional critique of particular areas with the goal of illuminating strengths and weaknesses, a methodology well adapted to Adorno's multifaceted ("prismatic") discourse. In this three-part study, which contains some previously printed materials, the first three chapters are devoted to the recent reception of Adorno in the US, the shift in his sociophilosophical position during his American exile, and the years after the Institute for Social Research returned to Germany.

Hohendahl next turns to Adorno's studies on literature and popular culture. Chapters 4 and 5 deal with his literary criticism—a sadly underresearched area in this country. The lecture on Heine ("Heine the Wound") serves as a demonstration piece for his fluid, "protean" essayistic method. Chapters 6 and 7 reexamine Adorno's cultural elitism and the greater issue of his dialectical approach to art within the social context, as well as his revisionist application of Marxist theory. Perhaps least conclusive is part 3, which focuses on a new reading of *Aesthetic Theory* and Adorno's positions on philosophy and language. An epilogue discusses critical theory after Adorno. Copious notes; generally viable translations. A highly original, important contribution to the present debate on critical theory. Undergraduate; graduate; faculty; general.— *G. P. Knapp, University of Utah*

OAB-1101 B1198 92-27259 CIP
Lampert, Laurence. **Nietzsche and modern times: a study of Bacon, Descartes, and Nietzsche.** Yale, 1993. 475p bibl index afp ISBN 0-300-05675-3, $35.00

In this scholarly, ambitious, and incisive endeavor, Lampert (Indiana Univ.) digs—following the lead of Leo Strauss and Stanley Rosen—patiently and deeply beneath the surface of the writings of Francis Bacon and René Descartes to uncover their "esoteric" teachings, their subtle and indirect efforts to displace a culture dominated by the dogmas and righteous violence of religion and establish the basis for a "philanthropic" culture of science. With remarkable care and close reading, he uncovers Bacon's "holy war" against religious fanaticism and for the advancement of science and sees Descartes' major writings as esoterically proposing a mathematical physics and a naturalism disguised by metaphysical meditations that Descartes signals are not worth considering. While both Bacon and Descartes follow Plato's "politic" advice concerning the importance of the "noble lie," Nietzsche, appearing in a different socio-historical period, dispenses "deadly truths" about cultural history within a philosophy of culture designated "Dionysian pessimism." Lampert's detailed (and bold) account of two giants of early "modernity" and his portrait of Nietzsche's project (the posthumanist, unlimited openness of a "joyous science" that sheds the once necessary cloak of esoteric communication) constitute a demanding, relentless defense of the subtlety of and importance of philosophy in history. Highly recommended. Advanced undergraduate; graduate; faculty.— *G. J. Stack, SUNY College at Brockport*

OAB-1102 B3279 94-48411 CIP
Löwith, Karl. **Martin Heidegger and European nihilism,** ed. by Richard Wolin; tr. by Gary Steiner. Columbia, 1995. 304p index afp ISBN 0-231-08406-4, $36.00

Since the publication of Victor Faris's *Heidegger and Nazism* (1989), a flurry of books has appeared on Heidegger's seduction by Nazism, two of these edited by Wolin—*The Politics of Being* (CH, Apr'91) and *The Heidegger Controversy* (CH, Jun'92). But Löwith's work has a very special claim, and its publication in English is an event of major significance. Löwith (d. 1973) is well known to English readers as a cultural historian (vide his *Meaning in History*, 1949). His posthumously translated works include *Max Weber and Karl Marx* (CH, Nov'82), *From Hegel to Nietzsche* (1964), and *My Life in Germany Before and After 1933* (1994). For the student of Heidegger, however, the present volume is unique as an indispensable, insightful, philosophical account of why Heidegger decided for National Socialism. As a devoted student and intimate friend of Heidegger in Freiburg already in the early 1920s, Löwith understands Heidegger minutely and sympathetically, and his interpretations of Heidegger's works are wide-ranging and unerring. Part 1 of the volume translates Löwith's *Heidegger: Denker in dürftiger Zeit* (Franfurt, 1953), which should have been translated long ago. In this essay, Löwith's analysis of Heidegger's Nietzschean interpretation is perceptive with regard to nihilism and is also hermeneutically significant. Part 2 discusses the decisionism of Carl Schmitt, identifying it with Heidegger's decisionism. Part 3 focuses on European nihilism as a major factor in Heidegger's vulnerability to National Socialism. In an appendix, two lengthy letters from Heidegger to Löwith give a very personal glimpse of the philosopher. Good translation; helpful introduction; extremely useful translator's notes. Lively, absorbing reading; indispensable reference on Heidegger and Nazism. Upper-division undergraduate through professional.—*R. E. Palmer, MacMurray College*

OAB-1103 B131 91-23781 CIP
Mohanty, Jitendra Nath. **Reason and tradition in Indian thought: an essay on the nature of Indian philosophical thinking.** Oxford, 1993 (c1992). 306p index ISBN 0-19-823960-2, $65.00

These two books are very much worth acquiring. Smart's is a revised edition of one of his best books (1st ed., CH Jul'65); Mohanty's is a ground-breaking effort by one of the foremost living authorities on Indian philosophy. Smart's textbook surveys the major orthodox and heterodox schools of Indian philosophy in Part 1. In Part 2 Smart does philosophy within Indian frames of reference, devoting chapters to arguments for and against the existence of God, arguments about rebirth and soul, epistemological questions, causation, and induction and inference. An interesting feature of the volume is the use throughout the exposition of English equivalents to Sanskrit terms (given in the glossary). This contributes to an even flow of reading for the beginning student. In the second revised edition the asterisks formerly used to indicate these technical Sanskrit terms and their English translations have been dropped both in the text and in the glossary, making for easier reading. Besides this there does not seem to be any substantial revision. Mohanty's very readable book is addressed more to intermediate and advanced students. In detailed chapters he examines with care the topics of tradition and modernity, consciousness and knowledge, language and meaning, the nature of Indian logic, theories of truth, the concept of being and ontologies, time, history, man and nature, theories of valid knowing, and the nature of Indian philosophical thinking. Both Smart and Mohanty have published a substantial number of books (about 20 each), and both have developed international careers. Both works are "musts" for collections in philosophy and religion—Smart especially for libraries serving lower-division undergraduates; Mohanty for those serving advanced undergraduates and up.—*F. J. Hoffman, West Chester University of Pennsylvania*

OAB-1104 B945 96-5509 CIP
Nagel, Thomas. **The last word.** Oxford, 1997. 147p index afp ISBN 0-19-510834-5, $19.95

Philosophy in the postmodernist age has been in a state of crisis, brought about by pervasive denial of the universality of reason through skepticism, relativism, and subjectivism. There are only a few philosophers who still hold that reason is universal and there are objective truths—truths independent of one's point of view. Nagel (New York Univ.) is one of these philosophers, and he has taken on the task of refuting skepticism, relativism, and subjectivism by demonstrating the universality of reason and defending not only the possibility but the actuality of objective truth. His fundamental insight is that reason cannot be consistently denied from outside. Thus, for example, one who is committed to the view that logic is futile has to employ logic to demonstrate its futility. Armed with this insight, Nagel systematically examines language, logic, science, and ethics, and persuasively demonstrates that universality of reason reigns supreme in all these areas and that skepticism, relativism, and subjectivism are self-stultifying. His most timely and richly rewarding book contributes to the restoration of rationality to public discourse. All students and teachers of philosophy will find it thought-provoking. Analytical clarity, stylistic elegance, and useful notes and index enhance the value of the work. Highly recommended. Upper-division undergraduate; graduate; faculty.—*R. Puligandla, University of Toledo*

OAB-1105 B3279 95-44553 CIP
Pöggeler, Otto. **The paths of Heidegger's life and thought,** tr. by John Bailiff. Humanities, 1997. 363p bibl index ISBN 0-391-03964-4, $60.00

Since Victor Farías's *Heidegger and Nazism* (CH, Apr'90) and Hugo Ott's *Martin Heidegger: A Political Life* (1993), students of Heidegger have struggled to rearticulate the contours of his thought in relation to the damaging rev-

elations concerning his personal fascination with Hitler and political link to Nazism. Heidegger's defenders have tended to insist on a radical separation between his life and thought; his detractors have treated them as a seamless whole. Avoiding both of these extremes, Pöggeler's synthesis of Heidegger's life and thought is fully sensitive to both his philosophical achievement and his ideological affiliations. He provides the most lucid and authoritative account available (at least in the scholarship in English, German, and French) of the ideological and intellectual issues at stake in Heidegger's transformation of hermeneutics and phenomenology. At the heart of Pöggeler's account is his brilliant assessment of the significance of Heidegger's still-untranslated magnum opus, the *Beiträge zur Philosophie (Vom Ereignis)*, which Heidegger wrote during 1936-38 and which was not published until 1989. Pöggeler reveals that the depth of Heidegger's alienation from all German ideologies and the radicality of his post-Christian ethos can be fully grasped only vis à-vis the *Beiträge*. Bailiff's translation is splendid; and his rendering of *Ereignis*, the keyword in Heidegger's thinking as "emergence" should prove definitive for all future work in English. Essential to all humanities collections. Upper-division undergraduate; graduate; faculty.—*N. Lukacher, University of Illinois at Chicago*

OAB-1106 B2430 95-52099 CIP
Reagan, Charles E. **Paul Ricoeur: his life and his work.** Chicago, 1996. 151p bibl index afp ISBN 0-226-70602-8, $24.95

Can the life and work of a preeminent and prolific philosopher be instructively encompassed within the pages of one slender volume? Occasionally, the answer is a resounding yes, as displayed in this happy conjunction of Ricoeur and Reagan. Justly renowned for his hermeneutic phenomenology and philosophical anthropology, Paul Ricoeur is among the world's most distinguished thinkers and teachers. And Charles Reagan (Kansas State Univ.), his student, colleague, and friend for more than three decades, succeeds admirably in introducing Ricoeur's overarching philosophical project: the carving out of a niche for human flourishing in an intermediate region bounded by Cartesian certainty at one unsustainable extreme and Nietzschean skepticism at the other. The structure of Reagan's work is unorthodox but uncommonly effective. It combines biographical and philosophical essays with a more personal memoir that makes Ricoeur's humane and magnanimous nature abundantly evident. Four revealing interviews, coupled with photographs, and an extensive bibliography of primary and secondary sources, complete this illuminating study. Interested readers should also consult *The Philosophy of Paul Ricoeur*, ed. by Lewis Edwin Hahn (CH, Jul'95), which includes, among other things, a substantial "intellectual autobiography." Highly recommended for all college and university libraries that support degree programs in philosophy. Upper-division undergraduate; graduate; faculty.—*H. I. Einsohn, Middlesex Community-Technical College*

OAB-1107 B2430 94-33870 CIP
Smith, Robert. **Derrida and autobiography.** Cambridge, 1995. 194p index ISBN 0-521-46005-0, $54.95; ISBN 0-521-46581-8 pbk, $17.95

Smith's spirited, allusive, and inventive survey of Jacques Derrida's work moves with swift deliberation and focus through Derrida's extensive oeuvre with a view toward reassembling, in one brief volume, many of Derrida's most illuminating accounts of the ways in which philosophy's quest for a realm of universality has been disrupted by an always untheorizable autobiographical contingency—a contingency that invariably, in one way or another, spills indecorously onto the text. And this exigency applies as well to Derrida's own exercises in autobiography. The real achievement of Smith's book is his recognition that the autobiographical impulse in Derrida is always ultimately the impulse of the other, of that which lies beyond the limits of the human while nevertheless remaining bound to human experience. Autobiography is therefore always the story of the expropriation of human subjectivity by the insurmountable contingency of the other. Smith's style tends toward the virtuoso, but he is always saved from excess by his supple grasp of the diverse modes of Derridean writing; more important, despite the density of allusion, the book is accessible and will prove very helpful for students who have read some Derrida and are looking for a lively and authoritative guide to the broad range of his writing and the issues involved. Specialists and advanced students will find it a mine of Derridean intertexts and a stimulating contribution to the always double task that is the ethics of deconstruction and the deconstruction of ethics. Upper-division undergraduate; graduate; faculty.—*N. Lukacher, University of Illinois at Chicago*

OAB-1108   B945   93-1275 CIP
Sprigge, T.L.S. **James and Bradley: American truth and British reality.** Open Court, 1993. 630p bibl index ISBN 0-8126-9226-8, $66.95; ISBN 0-8126-9227-6 pbk, $29.95

Sprigge is one of the few British philosophers to write accurately and sympathetically about American philosophy in the golden age (see *Santayana: An Examination of His Philosophy*, CH, Nov'74, and other papers). The present work is really two books in one, and it is broader than the title might indicate. The author begins by clearly stating eight themes he finds in James, seeing James's views on belief and truth as central. But he goes on to show, persuasively, the relevance of his work in psychology and radical empiricism to the central themes of James's pragmatism and pluralism. Especially useful throughout is Sprigge's ability to relate themes to present discussions without distorting the views of James and Bradley in their historical context. The clarity of Sprigge's writing even makes Bradley come alive, and a chapter that sketches Bradley's metaphysics will be especially useful to those unwilling to swallow Bradley whole. Scholarly, judicious, and balanced, this is a book worth owning and is essential reading for anyone interested in late 19th century British or American philosophy. Footnotes, a splendid bibliography and chronology, a 20-page index, and overall quality make this a model of a well-produced book. Recommended for upper-division undergraduates and for acquisition by all graduate libraries.—*R. H. Evans, University of Minnesota—Duluth*

OAB-1109   B3317   93-18455 CIP
Stambaugh, Joan. **The other Nietzsche.** State University of New York, 1994. 160p index ISBN 0-7914-1699-2, $44.50

Stambaugh's wise, spare, and perspicuous volume on Nietzsche is a delight on every page. Wide-ranging yet clear and direct, the book brings the insight of a fastidious translator and scholar to many difficult and disputed issues in Nietzsche. The author, a well-known interpreter and translator of Heidegger, has clearly spent decades wrestling with the texts of Nietzsche, is aware of other scholarship, and brings to each issue a judicious yet independent understanding. Among the many topics she addresses are the relevance of Nietzsche today; Nietzsche on creativity, music, pity, and revenge; the "highest feeling"; the true and the apparent world; *amor fati*; the innocence of becoming; and Nietzsche's nihilism. The final chapter, "The Other Nietzsche," furnishes the book's title. Originally presented at a conference of philosophy East and West, it explicates four passages from *Thus Spoke Zarathustra* and puts forward a Nietzsche who is poet of high noon and mystic lover of eternity. Existentialist, poet, philosopher-mystic, Nietzsche haunts the 20th century, and Stambaugh makes him intelligible, credible, indispensable. Enthusiastically recommended for libraries and for courses as a required text. Lower-division undergraduate and above.—*R. E. Palmer, MacMurray College*

OAB-1110   T49   92-3440 CIP
Street, John. **Politics and technology.** Guilford, 1992. 212p bibl index afp ISBN 0-89862-087-2, $40.00; ISBN 0-89862-019-8 pbk, $14.95

Street explores the relationship between technology and democratic politics with admirable lucidity, intelligence, and balance. He criticizes both autonomous technology (J. Ellul, *The Technological Society*, CH, Nov'64) and technological determinism, for instance, as distortions. This requires him to examine how political choices and structures affect technology and the converse. After looking at the different effects technology can have on politics specifically and culture more generally, Street discusses risk, accountability, technological assessment, questions of control, and how different models of democracy might best address the problems raised. He rejects "Green" politics, for example, as incoherent because it draws an untenable distinction between the natu-

ral and the artificial. Simultaneously Street objects to the "technical fix" mentality. Street's own recommendations stem from his conviction that technology and political processes cannot be separated. He advocates a "cultural approach" seeking the integration of political argument and technological assessment. Feminist writings on technology (M. Schwarz and M. Thompson, *Divided We Stand*, 1990, and *Machina Ex Dea*, ed. by J. Rothschild, CH, Apr'84) and the work of Langdon Winner (*The Whale and the Reactor*, CH, Oct'86) exemplify Street's approach. Indeed, Street's book is an excellent introduction for anyone looking for a clear, balanced introduction to a wide range of topics, issues, and authors on politics, technology, and philosophy. It does not delve deeply into specific areas discussed, but its comprehensiveness more than compensates. Highly recommended for general readers and undergraduates.—*H. Oberdiek, Swarthmore College*

OAB-1111   B105   96-30785 CIP
Waldenfels, Bernhard. **Order in the twilight,** tr. by David J. Parent. Oxford, 1996. 181p bibl index afp (Series in continental thought, 24) ISBN 0-8214-1168-3, $36.95

This translation of *Ordnung im Zwielicht* should help raise the visibility of Waldenfels's work among English-language readers, and that is a very good thing. Waldenfels offers a true development of phenomenology as a counterpoint to postmodernism, rather than an abandonment of the phenomenological stance and method. He operates in boundary zones between traditional philosophical distinctions and dichotomies, eliminating what some would regard as the key ontological weaknesses of Husserlian phenomenology while maintaining a vigorous notion of the subject (in an "agonal dialogue" with the other) as the active, transformative starting point. In a sense, Waldenfels is an essential figure in one of the most significant trialogues in contemporary European philosophy, with Levinas and Merleau-Ponty constituting the other two sides of the conversation. The primacy of the embodied subject in an always-value-imbued and shared world makes Waldenfels's work philosophically rigorous, sophisticated, and at the same time humane. The order that might be found "in the twilight" (*entre chien et loup*) is not the reason championed by Habermas, not a return to the old traditions, but also not the *pensée sauvage* of some postmodernism. As Waldenfels writes, "Whoever distrusts the barking of watchdogs, however, does not immediately have to begin howling with the wolves." Quite so. Highly recommended for advanced upper-division undergraduates, graduate students, and faculty.—*J. H. Barker, Albright College*

■ Aesthetics

OAB-1112   B3199   97-7729 CIP
Adorno, Theodor W. **Aesthetic theory,** ed. by Gretel Adorno and Rolf Tiedemann; newly translated and ed. by Robert Hullot-Kentor. Minnesota, 1997. 383p index afp (Theory and history of literature, 88) ISBN 0-8166-1799-6, $39.95

This volume, together with Paul de Man's *Aesthetic Ideology* (1996), constitutes the poignant farewell of a series that helped to change the nature of literary criticism. In this new and crisp translation Hullot-Kentor has accomplished a herculean feat in rendering Adorno into English. This is perhaps as close as one can get to Adorno's hypnotic and enigmatic style. Simply put, *Aesthetic Theory* is one of the most important philosophical works—and perhaps the most important study of aesthetics—of the 20th century. This fresh and rigorous translation is particularly welcome because Adorno has never been fully understood in America. *Aesthetic Theory* is perhaps the necessary challenge to the critical moment we inhabit. So much of the so-called political criticism of the arts discloses in the final analysis simply the naiveté of early Marxist criticism in a new, fashionable guise. Adorno is unique in that he does not pine for a lost realism in art but, rather, affirms and accounts for the development of art in the 20th century. He presents an examination of the social dimension of art that combines a comprehensive grasp of aesthetics as a discipline with an astonishingly intimate knowledge of a wide range of works of art. This is a book one returns to again and again. Highly recommended. General; upper-division undergraduate; graduate; faculty.—*S. Barnett, Central Connecticut State University*

OAB-1113   BH191   92-19307 CIP
Krukowski, Lucian. **Aesthetic legacies.** Temple University, 1993 (c1992). 245p index afp ISBN 0-87722-972-4, $44.95

The argument in *Aesthetic Legacies* is based upon a narrative of thematic development in which the philosophies of art of Kant, Schopenhauer, and Hegel are seen as central to an understanding of both modernist and postmodernist aesthetics. Krukowski's thesis is clearly and elegantly developed. Presenting each of these earlier views through a pivotal category—"taste" in Kant, "expression" in Schopenhauer, and "progress" in Hegel—Krukowski then traces the detachment of these concepts from their more systematic context and exhibits their transformation into the autonomous categories of 20th-century aesthetic discussion: "taste" is recast as "form," "expression" as "intention," and "progress" as "criticism." Although this neatly documented thematic development may be a bit too tidy, the overall direction of the book's narrative adds much depth and conceptual clarity to contemporary aesthetic debate. By focusing attention on "form," "intention," and "progress" as the three "dogmas" of modernism, Krukowski is able to provide conceptual contours for understanding the more amorphous phenomena of postmodernist thought and art. An important and very accessible work in contemporary aesthetics. Highly recommended for all four-year college and university libraries.—*M. Feder-Marcus, SUNY College at Old Westbury*

OAB-1114   BH151   92-35025 CIP
Taminiaux, Jacques. **Poetics, speculation, and judgement: the shadow of the work of art from Kant to phenomenology,** tr. and ed. by Michael Gendre. State University of New York, 1993. 191p index afp ISBN 0-7914-1547-3, $59.50

These lectures, delivered during more than two decades of teaching at the Université de Louvain and at Boston College, cohere into a very fine book, a polished achievement in terms of both scholarship and original interpretations of texts. Taminiaux opens up a fresh perpective on fundamental issues in aesthetics by situating thinking about art within the context of the history of philosophy understood as a tension between the Platonic emphasis on speculation as a totalizing project and the Aristotelian emphasis on judgment which preserves the phenomenal world in its finitude and plurality. This thematic juxtaposition leads to rich insights into the philosophies of art of the major Continental thinkers, in particular Kant, Hegel, the German idealists, Schopenhauer, and Nietzsche. Taminiaux ends with equally sensitive and nuanced readings of Heidegger and Merleau-Ponty from this same thematic perpsective. This book is not only a first-rate study in the history of aesthetics; it illustrates the strength of the phenomenological approach for generating distinctions of interpretive range and power. An important addition to all four-year academic libraries for its contribution to both contemporary aesthetic theory and the phenomenological tradition. Advanced undergraduate; graduate; faculty.—*M. Feder-Marcus, SUNY College at Old Westbury*

OAB-1115   B4378   93-38703 CIP
Walsh, Sylvia. **Living poetically: Kierkegaard's existential aesthetics.** Pennsylvania State, 1994. 294p bibl index afp ISBN 0-271-01328-1, $39.50

Walsh (Stetson Univ.) offers a lucid jewel of Kierkegaardian scholarship. Her work on the importance of Kierkegaard's aesthetics may be a perfect book. It is at once both a detailed exposition on the role that Kierkegaard's sense of the poetic plays as an axis for the integration of an aesthetic, ethical, and religious life, and a clearheaded and practical critique of postmodernism. It is an enjoyable and scholarly discussion, as well as an invaluable research tool and sourcebook. Even the footnotes are perfect. They are filled with delicious side dishes (that will satisfy the needs of the most demanding research) but in

no way interrupt the well-paced and effortless flow of her prose. In short, this may well be the new standard text for the role aesthetics plays in Kierkegaard's thought. It is easily accessible to upper-division undergraduate and graduate students, and should be considered indispensable for any professional scholar working in Kierkegaard's relation to philosophy, religious studies, or literature.—*M. C. E. Peterson, University of Wisconsin Centers*

OAB-1116   BH39   91-44410 CIP
Wegener, Charles. **The discipline of taste and feeling.** Chicago, 1992. 224p index afp ISBN 0-226-87893-7, $24.95

Using the analysis of aesthetic experience found in Kant's *Critique of Judgement* as a point of departure, Wegener has written a remarkably intelligent book which presents meaningful encounter with art as the "discipline of taste and feeling." The book reads not simply as an exposition but as a conversation in which the author thoughtfully and meticulously explores with the reader those norms that structure and define aesthetic experience. Wegener speaks from and refreshes a position that has sustained much criticism: not only is there a phenomenon that we call "cultivated taste," we have an obligation to discipline taste and sensibility if we take the notion of human development seriously. Wegener presents the norms of aesthetic experience as a series of juxtaposed concepts: freedom/engagement, austerity/objectivity, communicability/catholicity, authority/docility. His analysis of these categories provides a rich and coherent phenomenology of aesthetic experience as well as a compelling premise for the further argument of a moral obligation to undertake the cultivation of feeling and imagination if we are to participate in the ongoing human project of creating and realizing systematic order and purpose in the world. The book occupies an important place in contemporary aesthetic discussion. It combines rigorous philosophical analysis with a lifetime of personal reflection and is appropriate for both the professional philosopher and the student. All four-year college libraries.—*M. Feder-Marcus, SUNY College at Old Westbury*

OAB-1117   B2784   91-32390 CIP
Zammito, John H. **The genesis of Kant's *Critique of judgment*.** Chicago, 1992. 479p bibl index afp ISBN 0-226-97854-0, $65.00; ISBN 0-226-97855-9 pbk, $18.95

This is the best book on Kant's *Critique of Judgment* known to this reviewer. It should remain a classic resource for many years because of its erudition and its ability to clearly discuss the complexities of the text. Often these two important characteristics intimately relate; Zammito shows the development of Kant's thought, with its hesitancy, changes, and final formulations. Beyond the discussion of the text, the book also suggests the direction of Kant's thought at the final stages of his life. Again, this is a truly excellent book of great value to the Kant scholar. Advanced undergraduate; graduate; faculty.—*M. A. Bertman, formerly, SUNY at Potsdam*

■ Ancient & Medieval

OAB-1118   B317   92-38865 CIP
Brickhouse, Thomas C. **Plato's Socrates,** by Thomas C. Brickhouse and Nicholas D. Smith. Oxford, 1994. 240p bibl indexes afp ISBN 0-19-508175-7, $35.00

This excellent book on Socrates employs a broader perspective than the authors' *Socrates on Trial* (1989), the definitive study of the *Apology*. Comprehensive treatment of Socratic philosophy as presented in the early dialogues of Plato is framed in six chapters on these central topics: method, epistemology, psychology, ethics, politics, and religion. The book has numerous virtues: clear, detailed examination of the texts, which enables the reader to wrestle firsthand with the questions in context; wide-ranging, fair consideration of the secondary literature; strong arguments for original interpretations of important problems; and the uncanny capacity to educate the beginner and stimulate the scholar. Brickhouse and Smith vigorously advance their own new readings. Especially noteworthy are the attribution to Socrates of certain knowledge that still falls short of the wisdom he disavows; the claims that Socrates is not subject to the "Socratic fallacy" and that virtue is neither necessary nor sufficient for happiness; and the controversial view that Socrates' execution did not result from partisan politics. Certainly the best book on Socratic philosophy. Strongly recommended for all college and university libraries. Undergraduate; graduate; faculty; general.—*J. Bussanich, University of New Mexico*

OAB-1119   B187   95-33454 CIP
Detienne, Marcel. **The masters of truth in archaic Greece,** tr. by Janet Lloyd. Zone Books, 1996. 231p bibl index afp ISBN 0-942299-85-X, $22.50

As a cultural historian of ancient Greece, Detienne has exercised a deep and wide-ranging influence on classicists for 30 years; it is reason to be grateful, therefore, that *Ruses de l'intelligence*, Paris, 1974) his early, stimulating book on truth in the archaic period, is now finally available in an excellent English translation by Janet Lloyd. This edition contains, along with the original text, a valuable foreword by Detienne's sometime collaborator, Pierre Vidal-Naquet (*Cunning Intelligence in Greek Culture and Society*, 1991) and his own new 20-page preface, which offers a valuable retrospective on his work. Detienne studies the transitions from myth to reason and from religious to philosophical thought that occurred in the seventh through fifth centuries BCE in the Greek world. Through these broad cultural transformations Detienne tracks the concept of truth and the dispensers of truth (poets, diviners, philosophers), the changing functions of speech and language amidst the process of secularization, and the tension between truth and deception in poets, rhetoricians, and philosophers. Richly suggestive and written with verve and wit, this important study is highly recommended for all students of early Greek thought. Upper-division undergraduate; graduate; faculty.—*J. Bussanich, University of New Mexico*

OAB-1120   B667   94-24499 CIP
Dzielska, Maria. **Hypatia of Alexandria,** tr. by F. Lyra. Harvard, 1995. 157p index afp (Revealing antiquity, 8) ISBN 0-674-43775-6, $29.95

Dzielska, described on the jacket as "an internationally recognized authority on the cultural life of the Roman empire," provides here an exemplary "retrieval" of the life and achievements of Hypatia of Alexandria (c.335-415). Dzielska traces in detail the modern literary legend of Hypatia—from the Enlightenment authors who claimed her as the last of the great pagan neoplatonists, through Victorian novelist Charles Kingsley, to today's feminists (as in *Hypatia: Journal of the Society for Women in Philosophy*). The author portrays the close circle of her students and provides the context for her public lectures; she concludes with 35 sober pages on the "life and death of Hypatia," interpreting her death as a kind of witch-burning in the transition from pagan Empire to Christian state. Dzielska is meticulous in her pursuit of facts from the widely scattered sources, and she provides a concise 10-page essay on the sources, thorough notes, and index of names. The translation is clear and readable; the book as a whole is a model of feminist scholarship in its sorting out of legend from facts. Given Hypatia's importance for the history of neoplatonic philosophy and for her work in mathematics and astronomy, every strong collection in women's studies needs this book. Upper-division undergraduate through professional.—*H. J. John, Trinity College (DC)*

OAB-1121   B721   92-14375 Orig
Evans, G.R. **Philosophy and theology in the Middle Ages.** Routledge, 1993. 139p index ISBN 0-415-08908-5, $49.95; ISBN 0-415-08909-3 pbk, $14.95

A noteworthy feature of this study is the amount of detail encompassed in so short a survey. All the major issues and all the major thinkers receive attention. In spite of its size, this book gives a remarkably accurate picture of the liveliness, coherence, diversity, and depth of medieval intellectual life. Part 1 provides an account of the classical sources available to medieval thinkers

and an analysis of the medieval problems of language, logic, and rhetoric, as well as a discussion of the relationship between theology and philosophy. Part 2 is devoted to the major theological topics: the existence of God, the Trinity, the creation of the world, the soul, the sacraments, ethics, and politics. Extremely well written, this book is a valuable resource for upper-level undergraduates and graduate students in medieval studies. Gillian Rosemary Evans (history, Univ. of Cambridge) has written extensively on medieval philosophy and theology. Among her writings are *Anselm* (1989), *The Thought of Gregory the Great* (CH, Feb'87), *Augustine on Evil* (CH, Nov'83), and *Alan of Lille* (1983).—*P. L. Urban Jr., Swarthmore College*

OAB-1122   B751   91-40142 CIP
Goodman, Lenn E. **Avicenna.** Routledge, 1992. 240p index ISBN 0-415-01929-X, $72.50; ISBN 0-415-07409-6 pbk, $15.95

Goodman's splendid new book should be welcomed by all historians of philosophy as the best detailed introduction to the thought of the eminent Islamic philosopher Avicenna (980-1037). Part 1 crisply surveys the historical and intellectual context. Part 2, "Metaphysics," shows Avicenna's creative use of the doctrines of Greek Platonists and Aristotelians, Islamic philosophers, and the *mutakallimūm*, (Muslim dialectical theologians) in developing his own influential insights. Especially fine is Goodman's lucid account of Avicenna's synthesis of the metaphysics of necessity and of contingency, by which the philosopher's search for necessary, scientific truth is reconciled with the theologian's claim that everything depends on God (Goodman notes difficulties with Avicenna's abandoning the doctrine of creation). He also explains lucidly Avicenna's important distinction between essence and existence. Part 3 addresses epistemological and psychological problems, with special attention to Avicenna's arguments for the soul's immortality. Part 4 covers his original contributions to propositional logic and literary theory. Detailed problems are analyzed in extensive notes, but there is no bibliography. Highly recommended for all college and university libraries.—*J. Bussanich, University of New Mexico*

OAB-1123   B441   91-36774 CIP
McKirahan, Richard D. **Principles and proofs: Aristotle's theory of demonstrative science.** Princeton, 1992. 340p bibl indexes afp ISBN 0-691-07363-5, $47.50

This study of the *Posterior Analytics* is a rarity. It is an attempt to reconstruct and at times to construct Aristotle's theory of science. Its goal is a "synthetic and sympathetic" interpretation that recaptures "Aristotle's vision of the nature of science and scientific knowledge" by "making sense of each passage" in its own context and by "fitting all the passages together" in "a coherent whole." The topics discussed include the general nature of demonstrative science, the criteria for scientific principles, the kinds of scientific principles, the kinds of demonstrations, and the nature of scientific explanation. To supplement Aristotle's terse text, the author makes good use of passages from the *Prior Analytics*, the *Topics*, and the *Psychology* as well as from Euclid's *Elements*. He provides his own excellent translations, accompanied with judicious translation notes and detailed discussions of difficult passages. The workmanship is solid, and the work successfully ties together the essential strands of Aristotle's conception of science. Footnotes are brief and to the point, and the bibliography is quite good. The book will undoubtedly prove very useful for graduate students and faculty alike without being inaccessible to undergraduates. Highly recommended for all academic libraries.—*P. Schollmeier, University of Nevada, Las Vegas*

OAB-1124   B395   95-5879 CIP
Nightingale, Andrea Wilson. **Genres in dialogue: Plato and the construct of philosophy.** Cambridge, 1995. 222p bibl indexes ISBN 0-521-48264-X, $49.95

This fascinating study sheds new light on the old puzzle: despite his notorious attack on poetry, Plato was a literary genius. Nightingale (Stanford Univ.) does not simply explore literary aspects of Plato's writings, however; she articulates deep structural and thematic relations between the dialogues and the alien literary genres of tragedy, lyric, and comedy. This intertextual dialogue is more complex than many believe, Nightingale argues, in that Plato's opposition conceals extensive borrowing. She meticulously unravels a complex web of critique and appropriation, parody and reformulation that is informed by mastery of Greek history and literature and contemporary theorists like Mikhail Bakhtin. Beginning with a fine discussion of Plato's critique of sophists, poets, and politicians for their "trafficking in wisdom," i.e., selling their intellectual wares for money and fame, she brilliantly develops the idea that the philosopher as disinterested outsider emerges as the countertype to these more familiar creatures. She employs this dialectical model to explicate Plato's use of Euripides' *Antiope* as subtext for *Gorgias*, of the rhetoric of praise in *Symposium*, of lyric love poetry in the *Phaedrus*, and of the parodic resources of Old Comedy. Strongly recommended for college and university libraries. Upper-division undergraduate; graduate; faculty.—*J. Bussanich, University of New Mexico*

OAB-1125 Orig
Plato. **Republic 5,** with an introd., tr., and commentary by S. Halliwell. Aris & Phillips, UK, 1993. (Dist. by D. Brown Book Company) 228p index ISBN 0-85668-535-6, $49.95; ISBN 0-85668-536-4 pbk, $24.95

This is the first English commentary on Book 5 of Plato's *Republic*. There are several reasons for the previous lack: the text addresses a bewildering variety of topics, requiring a commentator with wide-ranging philological, philosophical, and historical knowledge. Halliwell succeeds admirably at introducing the student to Plato's remarkable proposals concerning the abolition of the family, eugenics, the training of a ruling elite (including philosopher-queens), a warrior code, and, finally, the philosophical distinctions between Being and Becoming, and between knowledge and belief. Following the "Classical Texts" series format, the volume contains a substantial introduction (with summaries of the main arguments), Greek text with excellent English translation, 100 pages of detailed exegetical notes, bibliography, and index. The commentary achieves just the right balance in providing, e.g., sociocultural background on the family and the state in the first part and basic philosophical analysis of the difficult section 476-80 at the end. Highly recommended for all four-year college and university libraries.—*J. Bussanich, University of New Mexico*

■ Ethics

OAB-1126 B2430 93-23370 CIP
Anderson, Thomas C. **Sartre's two ethics: from authenticity to integral humanity.** Open Court, 1993. 215p bibl index ISBN 0-8126-9232-2, $36.95; ISBN 0-8126-9233-0 pbk, $17.95

Anderson's text is one of the clearest discussions of Sartre's ethics available. He does an admirable job of explaining Sartre's "first" ethics, a topic covered in many other works. Where Anderson really shines is in his analysis of the "second" ethics that emerged from Sartre's unfinished *Notebooks for an Ethics* and from unpublished manuscripts, especially those from public lectures Sartre gave in Rome in 1964. Anderson includes a brief appendix on what he sees as Sartre's third ethics, a fragmentary but fascinating discussion of power and freedom. It is in explaining and comparing the idealistic, existentialist ethics of the 1940s and the realistic, materialistic ethics of the 1960s that Anderson breaks new ground in Sartre scholarship. Familiarity with Sartre's most important works, especially *Being and Nothingness* and the first volume of the *Critique of Dialectical Reason*, would be helpful in appreciating Anderson's arguments; but his explanations are so clear and careful that students with minimal exposure to Sartre will benefit from reading this book. Highly recommended. Upper-division undergraduate; graduate.—*J. H. Barker, Albright College*

OAB-1127 BJ171 92-37003 CIP
Annas, Julia. **The morality of happiness.** Oxford, 1993. 502p bibl indexes afp ISBN 0-19-507999-X, $55.00

Do ancient and modern ethical theories have anything to teach each other? Annas boldly answers in the affirmative—and wisely avoids endorsing one group's superiority over the other. She argues that the ancient concept of virtue "occupies the conceptual area we assign to the moral," so long as we do not limit "morality" to maximizing outcomes or the notion of obligation. The book is mostly a richly nuanced and exceptionally clear historical study of the ethical theories of Aristotle, Stoics, Skeptics, Epicurus, and later Aristotelians, with focus on the relative importance ascribed to virtue, concern for others, and external goods in their accounts of happiness. Key modern concepts like "egoism" and "altruism" are shown to be anachronistic. Ancient ethics, Annas argues, is no more intrinsically egoistic than modern morality; and rather than morally conservative, it is profoundly revisionary. These are controversial claims but they are defended with strong arguments and evenhanded treatment of scholarly opinion. This is a learned, provocative study that will redefine current debates about "virtue-ethics" and its differences from moral theory. Strongly recommended for all college and university libraries, lower-division undergraduate and up.—*J. Bussanich, University of New Mexico*

OAB-1128 B2799 95-9555 CIP
Baron, Marcia W. **Kantian ethics almost without apology.** Cornell, 1995. 244p bibl index afp ISBN 0-8014-2829-7, $29.95

Baron (Univ. of Illinois, Urbana-Champaign) has written a careful, diligent defense of Kant's deontological conception of ethics. She focuses on two main charges often raised against Kant's ethics: that Kant tries to subsume too much under duty, not leaving enough room for actions beyond the call of duty or supererogatory acts; and that he places too much value on impartial acting from duty, thereby disqualifying partiality in one's regard for others from the sphere of morality. Although Baron is sympathetic to the concerns behind those objections, she argues that Kant's ethics can be successfully defended against the objections themselves. The first of the book's two parts examines the alleged neglect of supererogation; the second examines the alleged coldness of Kant's ethics. Of particular interest are the discussion of latitude in imperfect duties and the notion of acting from duty as a second-order motive in Kant. Throughout the work Baron relates the specifics of Kant's ethics to current debates and issues in moral theory. In its combination of exemplary scholarship, philosophical sophistication, and sensitivity to moral concerns the book is on a par with Barbara Herman's *The Practice of Moral Judgment* (CH, Jul'93). Highly recommended. Upper-division undergraduate; graduate; faculty.—*G. Zoeller, University of Iowa*

OAB-1129 BJ1395 93-2697 CIP
Bell, Linda A. **Rethinking ethics in the midst of violence: a feminist approach to freedom.** Rowman & Littlefield, 1993. 296p bibl index afp ISBN 0-8476-7844-X, $64.00; ISBN 0-8476-7845-8 pbk, $22.95

An excellent book (with a terrible title) which reviews the ethical dilemmas faced by contemporary feminist philosophers. It is more than that, however. It is also a very good review of many of the dilemmas of contemporary ethics. Bell's thesis is that the feminist ethic of caring—first discussed by Carol Gilligan (*In a Different Voice*, CH, Oct'82) and advocated by Nell Noddings (*Caring*, CH, Nov'84) and others—is inadequate in a world of violence and oppression. Feminist ethics, Bell argues, must include a political consciousness that will enable feminists to avoid affirming the dominant political structures and may, at times, require the use of violence to fight violence. Her model for feminists is Sartre (and de Beauvoir), an ethics of authenticity and ambiguity. In developing her thesis Bell exposes the failure of traditional ethical theories, such as utilitarianism and Kantian ethics, to give satisfactory answers to those who are oppressed. Although ostensibly for feminists, her arguments are applicable to ethical debate generally and shed light on such difficult issues as the relationship between ends and means and the conflict between ethical ideals and violence. Bell's conclusion is somewhat disheartening or disappointing, but it is at least honest and should not detract from the depth and scope of her discussion. This book is a must for feminists and almost a must for ethics generally. Both general and academic readers at all levels.—*S. C. Schwarze, Cabrini College*

OAB-1130   B105   91-20166 CIP
Davis, Grady Scott. **Warcraft and the fragility of virtue: an essay in Aristotelian ethics.** Idaho, 1993 (c1992). 196p bibl index ISBN 0-89301-154-1 pbk, $12.95

This is an invaluable book for its powerful defense of both Aristotelian ethics and just war theory. Davis establishes his Aristotelian war-ethics of virtue by fairly testing it against challenges from utilitarianism, a secular deontologism of rights and obligations, and a Christian deontologism. Those subjected to his withering criticisms include Michael Walzer, the American Catholic bishops, Karl Marx, Mario Couomo, Dean Acheson, James Childress, and John Rawls. Those Davis first corrects, then critically appropriates to his argument and compliments, include Wittgenstein, Von Clausewitz, Jefferson, Aquinas, John Howard Yoder, Paul Ramsey, and Nelson Mandela. Davis forcefully rejects pacifism, the Crusades, total war, all nuclear weapons, national loyalty, conscription, and the reconstitution of the vanquished government in the victor's way. He boldly defends provincial loyalties, military disobedience, revolution, selective conscientious objection, and the all-volunteer army. Because Davis's book is an extended argument that it is "better to surrender than win unfairly" (p. 176), the book will sorely try the patience of most Americans, but this reviewer thinks most Americans badly need to read the book because of their chauvinism. A "must have" book for every library and a "must read" book for advanced students of the ethics of war.—*J. M. Betz, Villanova University*

OAB-1131   BJ1461   93-51073 CIP
Fischer, John Martin. **The metaphysics of free will: an essay on control.** Blackwell, 1994. 273p bibl index afp (Aristotelian Society series, 14) ISBN 1-557-86155-2, $49.95

Fischer (Univ. of California—Riverside) provides a thorough statement of the major grounds for skepticism about the reality of free will and moral responsibility and develops a detailed, plausible rebuttal. The traditional debate on these issues features conflicting claims about control; and the notion of control lies at the heart of Fischer's book. He distinguishes between two species of control—regulative control and guidance control. Having regulative control over our behavior requires that we have "alternative possibilities," that more than one future is open to us. Guidance control, exhibited when our actions appropriately issue from our responsiveness to reasons, does not require this. Fischer offers detailed accounts of both sorts of control and argues that guidance control, but not regulative control, is necessary for freedom and moral responsibility. He argues persuasively that control of the former sort is compatible both with determinism and with the existence of a God possessed of perfect foreknowledge. This is an excellent book, a first-rate contribution to the literature. Its combination of thoroughness and accessibility is rare in the literature on free will. The arguments are skillfully crafted and sometimes stunningly ingenious. Highly recommended. Upper-division undergraduate; graduate; faculty.—*A. R. Mele, Davidson College*

OAB-1132   BJ1533   92-460 CIP
Fletcher, George P. **Loyalty: an essay on the morality of relationships.** Oxford, 1993. 211p index afp ISBN 0-19-507026-7, $21.00

An interesting, much needed initial foray into the conflicting relationships of loyalty in contemporary life. From the conceptual classification of minimal loyalty based on nonbetrayal (Chapter 3) to maximum loyalty grounded in stronger ties of devotion (Chapter 4), the virtue and duty of loyalty are explicated through an analysis of examples drawn from the changing social and political landscape. The value of the "historical self," acting in harmony with the actual loyalty relations defining this "self," is negatively contrasted to the "utopian" classical "Englightenment" approach to moral relations in the tradition of Kant, Bentham, and Rawls. Although Fletcher frequently refers to the "permanent moral danger" that loyalty relations present to morality, the dangers of "relativism" and "subjectivism" remain underdetermined. Useful discussions of contemporary moral/political issues like surrogate motherhood, religious/patriotic dissension, and the teaching of patriotism in schools are certain to foster further debate on the emotional and moral bonds of loyalty. It is to be hoped that these debates

will involve comparisons between the Eastern/Asian approaches to loyalty and the Western tradition. Recommended for all undergraduate libraries.—*J. Gough, Red Deer College*

OAB-1133   BJ1431   91-46331 CIP
Fotion, Nick. **Toleration,** by Nick Fotion and Gerard Elfstrom. Alabama, 1992. 204p bibl index afp ISBN 0-8173-0581-5, $26.95

An extremely stimulating and readable monograph by two philosophers best known for their work in military ethics. Fotion and Elfstrom begin by analyzing the concept of tolerance and some allied notions. Tolerating turns out to be having a "negative attitude toward something with the restraint from acting in accordance with that attitude" (p. 10) or, more simply, "being permissive in a disapproving fashion" (p. 17). Not tolerating is either being intolerant—i.e., disapproving and not being permissive—or giving acceptance—i.e., approving and being permissive. The second third of the book is an interesting overview of the history of toleration in the West. Fotion and Elfstrom argue that the focus of debate over toleration has gradually shifted from belief to speech to action. They conclude with a critical evaluation of some of the main arguments for toleration and a discussion of the role of toleration in a liberal state. The writing is clear and unencumbered by philosophical jargon. Highly recommended for all libraries.—*R. B. Scott Jr., William Woods College*

OAB-1134   B2430   96-31819 CIP
Foucault, Michel. **Ethics: subjectivity and truth,** ed. by Paul Rabinow; tr. by Robert Hurley et al. New Press, NY, 1997. 334p index (Essential works of Michel Foucault, 1954-1984, 1) ISBN 1-56584-352-5, $27.50

In 1994, Foucault's French publisher Gallimard issued *Dits et écrits*, a four-volume complete edition of all Foucault's publications outside his texts. Edited by Paul Rabinow, this is the first of three volumes that will present the most important of the works of the four French volumes. The highlight of this volume is the first English translation of the 11 course summaries Foucault submitted to the Collège de France from 1970 to 1982, which provide concise overviews of his analyses of, among others, the will to knowledge, penal institutions, biopolitics, and the hermeneutic of the subject. Also included are several important essays and interviews from Foucault's last years, when his work turned explicitly toward questions of ethics and the care of the self. Although most of these appear in translation elsewhere, having them collected in a single volume will be helpful to those without access to major research libraries. Ably introduced by Rabinow and followed by a comprehensive index, this collection of writings by one of the leading intellectuals of the past 50 years belongs in every academic and public library. It will be profitably consulted by undergraduates and general readers looking for an introduction to the work of this important philosopher; professionals interested in Foucault will want it as part of their personal libraries.—*A. D. Schrift, Grinnell College*

OAB-1135   BJ319   93-18648 CIP
Hannaford, Robert V. **Moral anatomy and moral reasoning.** University Press of Kansas, 1993. 197p index afp ISBN 0-7006-0607-6, $29.95

Hannaford's wide-ranging philosophical investigation of "moral anatomy"—i.e., the interplay of motives, reasons, and responsiveness in judging and acting—shows how sound, objective moral reasoning involves generalizing, yet can take place only when rooted in particular, moral communities. He rejects the kind of sophisticated Hobbesian egoism developed by David Gauthier (*Morals by Agreement*, CH, Dec'86) and Bernard Gert (*The Moral Rules*, 1970) because mutual concern is a precondition for reaching moral agreement, not a consequence. And, although we must pay attention to the network of community attitudes and practices, Hannaford shows that this does not lead to vulgar relativism. For in framing moral judgments, we must take persons as embedded in their circumstances and relationships to others. Because of our relationships, we come to want to do what is morally demanded of us. This is compatible with a version of the Golden Rule, for applications of this universal rule yield judgments based on particularities of abilities, expectations, and relationships, not universally applicable laws of nature. In reaching this conclusion, Hannaford skillfully weaves together strands drawn both from philosophers, classical and contemporary, and from psychologists. His original yet accessible inquiry deserves careful attention, not only for its incisive argumentation, but also for its clear vision, common sense, and humanity. Highly recommended for all libraries.—*H. Oberdiek, Swarthmore College*

OAB-1136   BJ1012   95-12472 CIP
Harman, Gilbert. **Moral relativism and moral objectivity,** by Gilbert Harman and Judith Jarvis Thomson. Blackwell, 1996. 225p bibl index afp ISBN 0-631-19211-5 pbk, $21.95

This fine book features a debate over the relative merits/demerits of moral relativism and moral objectivism. Harman (Princeton Univ.), whose *The Nature of Morality* (CH, Sep'77) continues to influence American "realists" who react to his "anti-realism," defends relativism. Thomson (MIT), whose analysis of moral dilemmas in *Rights, Restitution, and Risk* (CH, Jan'87) and of rights in *The Realm of Rights* (CH, May'91) are widely read, defends objectivism. Each presents his or her respective case, and then each has "a go" at the other. Both offer clear, subtle versions of their positions, show great respect for each other, and write so that the argument is accessible to professional philosophers and upper-division undergraduates alike. The book could easily serve as the centerpiece for a course or seminar on contemporary metaethics, because it addresses most of the major issues. What makes the book especially unusual is that it actually advances the argument in an open-ended, illuminating way. It will, this reviewer believes, have an influence similar to that of J.J.C. Smart and Bernard Williams's *Utilitarianism: For and Against* (CH, Apr'74), which for many years framed the debate about utilitarianism. Highly recommended for all undergraduate and graduate collections and for larger public libraries.—*H. Oberdiek, Swarthmore College*

OAB-1137   BJ1012   96-26432 CIP
Hauerwas, Stanley. **Christians among the virtues: theological conversations with ancient and modern ethics,** by Stanley Hauerwas and Charles Pinches. Notre Dame, 1997. 230p indexes afp ISBN 0-268-00817-5, $29.95; ISBN 0-268-00819-1 pbk, $16.95

A revival of interest in the virtues has been stimulated by Alasdair MacIntyre's influential critique of ethical theories that attempt to discover purely formal moral principles that will create just societies without commitments to any particular vision of the good. In this joint study, Hauerwas (Divinity School, Duke Univ.) and Pinches (Univ. of Scranton) make an important contribution to an analysis of the place of the virtues in Christian ethics. The study is particularly timely in that it enters into dialogue, not only with MacIntyre, but also with recent champions of ethics of virtue like John Milbank, John Casey, and Martha Nussbaum, as well as classical thinkers like Aristotle and St. Thomas Aquinas. Conversations with these authors reveal how context-dependent the notion of the good life is and how virtues like prudence, courage, patience, and obedience take strikingly different forms when molded by Christian versus secular presuppositions. Unlike many jointly authored books, this one is a genuinely collaborative effort, each chapter being thoroughly worked over by both contributors. Highly recommended. Upper-division undergraduate; graduate; faculty.—*P. L. Urban Jr., emeritus, Swarthmore College*

OAB-1138   B2799   92-20915 CIP
Herman, Barbara. **The practice of moral judgment. Harvard, 1993.** 252p index afp ISBN 0-674-69717-0, $29.95

Herman, (philosophy and law, Univ. of Southern California) offers a new interpretation of Kantian ethics—no longer as paradigm of deontology, but as centered on the value of practical rationality, richly understood, as the final end of willing. From this perspective, "The principles of practical rationality introduce a complex, ordered set of conditions of goodness or choice-worthiness." The versions of the Categorical Imperative provide the basis of the

practice of moral judgment in a casuistry that can deal effectively with hard choices. By her convincing argument that Kant's formal principles are not empty of content, but present rational agency itself as its own grounding value, Herman moves ethical discussion beyond the divide of deontological and teleological ethics. She writes with clarity, cogency, and sensitivity to experience. Every scholar and student concerned with Kant and/or ethics should have access to her book. No bibliography, but reference footnotes and a fine index. Undergraduate; graduate; faculty.—*H. J. John, Trinity College (DC)*

OAB-1139   91-65826 Orig
Kofman, Sarah. **Nietzsche and metaphor,** tr. by Duncan Large. Stanford, 1994 (c1993). 239p bibl indexes afp ISBN 0-8047-1975-6, $37.50; ISBN 0-8047-2186-6 pbk, $12.95

Kofman's original and seminal interpretation of Nietzsche's mode of philosophizing and his conception of, and use of, metaphor is one of the earliest postmodern approaches to his thought and texts. It is a scintillating work that already has been often cited (and mined) by others in its original French. Large's translation is excellent (especially given Kofman's linguistic self-consciousness and subtle use of terms), and his introduction places it in historical context. Although she is within the penumbra of Derrida, Kofman has her own distinctive voice and is a sophisticated literary/philosophical analyst. Moving through Nietzsche's earlier writings and picking and choosing from published works and notations, she reveals Nietzsche's "deconstruction" of symbolic systems and his "privileging" of metaphorical language, and shows the link between deliberate metaphoric language and the presence of a "noble will." A remarkable interpreter of Nietzsche's texts, Kofman captures nuances and indirect communications and sees Nietzsche's style as aristocratic, distancing, designed for what is conveyed for the few. Her sophisticated analysis of the nature, use, and function of metaphor in Nietzsche's writings clearly anticipates and is influencing the postmodernist approach to his thought; but she hesititates to follow the implications of her disclosure of a plurality of metaphors and identify it as metaphorical. Highly recommended. Upper-division undergraduate; graduate; faculty.—*G. J. Stack, SUNY College at Brockport*

OAB-1140   BJ1458   95-12848 CIP
Korsgaard, Christine M. **The sources of normativity,** by Christine M. Korsgaard with G.A. Cohen et al.; ed. by Onora O'Neill. Cambridge, 1996. 273p bibl index ISBN 0-521-55059-9, $49.95; ISBN 0-521-55960-X pbk, $17.95

"It is the most striking fact about human life that we have values." Thus begins Korsgaard's examination of an exceedingly difficult task—the sources of normativity. In this brilliantly researched, argued, and written text, Korsgaard (Harvard Univ.) finds normativity to be rooted in the fact that "we are self-conscious rational animals, capable of reflection about what we ought to believe and do." Her main argument is Kantian in flavor, but goes well beyond Kant. In a clear and cogent way that is more than mere exegesis, Korsgaard buttresses her argument by exploring the history of normative ethical theories, including those of Aristotle, Hobbes, Hume, Mill, Moore, Williams, Nagle, and a myriad of other philosophers past and present. Korsgaard's four lectures are followed by comments by G.A. Cohen, Raymond Geuss, Thomas Nagle, and Bernard Williams. The final chapter is Korsgaard's reply. This book is destined to replace Kant as the ultimate formulation of Kantian ethics. It should be required reading for any philosopher and should be in every library. Undergraduate through professional.—*W. F. Desmond, Black Hawk College*

OAB-1141   BJ1212   93-10226 CIP
Meeks, Wayne A. **The origins of Christian morality: the first two centuries.** Yale, 1994 (c1993). 275p bibl index afp ISBN 0-300-05640-0, $30.00

An absorbing and groundbreaking study of early Christian moral discourse. Meeks (Yale, and author of *The First Urban Christians*, CH, Jun'93) not only places the ancient texts in their specific cultural and religious settings but also calls on contemporary philosophical discussion to illuminate features of the emerging Christian moral vision. Since early Christians did not produce a systematic discussion of their ethical perspective, its contours must be discerned in its legacies—letters, testaments, moral stories, rituals—and in its charitable institutions and its attitudes toward celibacy, sex, and female roles. Meeks frames his discussion with two additional considerations. Conversion to Christianity meant radically separating from one's past life and taking seriously the prospect of the end of the world. These viewpoints heightened Christians' sense of being members of "an alien nation." In addition, Meeks assesses the contributions from Jewish and Greco-Roman sources, as well as their similarities and contrasts to Christian ideas. This fine, comprehensive study should be a standard for many years. Upper-level undergraduate and above.—*P. L. Urban Jr., Swarthmore College*

OAB-1142 BJ1451 95-54001 CIP
Moran, Gabriel. **A grammar of responsibility.** Crossroad, NY, 1996. 253p index ISBN 0-8245-1554-4, $24.95

This is a timely and insightful book for an educated general readership. Moran (culture and communications, NYU) excavates our much-used but little-understood idiom of responsibility in which, for example, politicians and bureaucrats are admired for "taking responsibility for" the mistakes of their subordinates, with little or no consequences to themselves, and in which unwed teenage mothers on welfare are urged to "take responsibility for" their lives. Moran grounds responsibility in the ability to respond ("response-ability") and locates our confused attributions of "responsibility for" in a neglected and forgotten sense of "responsibility to." His discussion is neither jargon-laden nor technical, and yet Moran engages not only current events and personalities in the news but also a wide range of scholarly literature in various fields. The book's title suggests an ethical inquiry in the spirit of George Lindbeck's cultural-linguistic model of the meaning and function of church doctrine in *The Nature of Doctrine* (CH, Oct'84), but Moran approaches his task with more historical than anthropological focus. In the process he discusses intrapersonal, interpersonal, and collective responsibility, responsibility to and for nonhumans, and responsibility with respect to the past, the future, and peoples in other societies and cultures. This is a book of insight and wisdom, recommended for a wide audience. General; undergraduate through professional.—*D. R. C. Reed, Wittenberg University*

OAB-1143 BJ1421 92-20637 CIP
Nyberg, David. **The varnished truth: truth telling and deceiving in ordinary life.** Chicago, 1993. 244p bibl index afp ISBN 0-226-61051-9, $22.50

In this philosophical exploration of the ethics of deception, Nyberg argues strongly against the conventional wisdom that deception is presumptively wrong—the view articulated by, for example, Sissela Bok in *Lying: Moral Choice in Public and Private Life* (CH, Nov'78). It is Nyberg's contention that not only has truth-telling been highly overrated, but that "some deception and self-deception are necessary both to social stability and to individual mental health." After a short introductory chapter surveying various "theories of truth," which this reviewer found to be so grossly oversimplified as to be almost useless, Nyberg makes an interesting and rigorous case. Overall the book is well organized and clearly written, completely free of philosophical jargon. The breadth of references is very impressive and is reflected in good footnotes and bibliography. Accessible and appealing to a wide group of readers. Highly recommended.—*R. B. Scott Jr., William Woods College*

OAB-1144 B430 92-3648 CIP
Reeve, C.D.C. **Practices of reason: Aristotle's Nicomachean ethics.** Oxford, 1992. 229p bibl indexes ISBN 0-19-823984-X, $49.95

Reeve (Reed College) offers an important and compelling interpretation of Aristotle's conception of ethical reasoning, exploring related discussions throughout the Aristotelian corpus. Reeve carefully and meticulously reconstructs Aristotle's idiom, displaying the relations among *episteme* ("scientific

knowledge"), dialectic, *nous* ("intuitive intellect"), *phronesis* ("practical wisdom"), and *eudaimonia* ("happiness" or "flourishing"). His thesis is that *phronesis* is only one of the practices of ethical reason. The other involves *nous* and *episteme*, such that *eudaimonia* is the "quintessentially ethical [but not only] first principle of ethics." Primary *eudaimonia* is *theoria* ("study"), or activity expressing *nous* and *episteme*, and secondary *eudaimonia* is activity expressing *phronesis*, which presupposes *episteme* and is for the sake of primary *eudaimonia*. In its coverage of Aristotle's ethics, Reeve's book is most like John M. Cooper's *Reason and the Human Good in Aristotle* (CH, May'76) and Richard Kraut's *Aristotle on the Human Good* (CH, May'90), though it explores Aristotle's epistemology more broadly than these and is in this way comparable to Terence Irwin's *Aristotle's First Principles* (CH, Jan'90) and J. D. G. Evans's *Aristotle's Concept of Dialectic* (CH, Oct'77). Reeve's Aristotle "is wilder and less commonsensical than we have often been urged to believe" and is more or less that of Thomas Aquinas, of whom Reeve curiously makes no mention. Detailed "Index Locorum Aristotelis." Advanced undergraduates and up. An absolute must for any collection in ancient philosophy.—*D. R. C. Reed, Wittenberg University*

OAB-1145 B1887 96-18279 CIP
Sarasohn, Lisa T. **Gassendi's ethics: freedom in a mechanistic universe.** Cornell, 1996. 236p bibl index afp ISBN 0-8014-2947-1, $45.00

Sarasohn gives a top-notch demonstration of how the history of ideas informs philosophical studies in the history of science and history of ethics. She sets forth the philosophical thought of Pierre Gassendi, a 17th-century philosopher and priest whose intellectual project of reforming Epicureanism within a Christian and mechanistic framework serves as a bridge between Aristotelian, Epicurean, and Stoic views of nature and 17th-century scientific, ethical, and political thought. In tracing the origin of Gassendi's view of freedom through ancient, medieval, and 17th-century influences, Sarasohn reveals a unified philosophical system. She explores Gassendi's personal history, his intellectual and personal relationships with René Descartes, Marin Mersenne, and Thomas Hobbes, and his influence on the ethical and political writings of John Locke. The result is a wonderfully constructed narrative about freedom and its connection to Gassendi's ethical thought and philosophy of science. This book complements well Dennis Des Chene's *Physiologia: Natural Philosophy in Late Aristotelian and Cartesian Thought* (CH, Oct'96) and Margaret J. Osler's *Divine Will and the Mechanical Philosophy: Gassendi and Descartes on Contingency and Necessity in the Created World* (1994). Highly recommended for all collections, although most usable by upper-division undergraduates and above.—*S. Martinelli-Fernandez, Western Illinois University*

OAB-1146 BJ1451 95-45193 CIP
Schweiker, William. **Responsibility and Christian ethics.** Cambridge, 1995. 255p bibl index ISBN 0-521-47527-9, $54.95

In this impressively rigorous study, Schweiker (Univ. of Chicago) sets out to delineate an ethics of responsibility that explains the meaning and significance of Christian faith within the context of contemporary moral philosophy. Drawing on classical and contemporary sources of ethical insight, he argues that the profound extension of human power—brought on by the myriad technological innovations of the late 20th century—calls for sober reevaluation of concepts of responsibility. Schweiker limns an ethical theory based upon individual and corporate responsibility that has genuine moral integrity as its goal. It is here in his discussions of integrity that the powerful originality of Schweiker's theory unfolds. He maintains that Christian faith can make a distinctive contribution to present moral discourse by directing our attention beyond the constant temptation of the will to power and instead toward a humanizing realization that a person's or community's life has a purpose beyond its own quest for fulfillment. The scope of this book is challengingly broad, yet Schweiker's ability to smoothly integrate ethics and social theory renders it an erudite and crisply coherent work, worthy of sustained and careful reflection. Upper-division undergraduate; graduate; researchers/faculty.—*B. Stetson, The David Institute*

OAB-1147   BJ1031   95-53713 CIP
Scott, Charles E. **On the advantages and disadvantages of ethics and politics.** Indiana, 1996. 216p index afp ISBN 0-253-33073-4, $39.95; ISBN 0-253-21076-3 pbk, $15.95

Scott (Pennsylvania State Univ.), a leading author in the field of American Continental philosophy, writes from a vantage point beyond ethics, though the essence of "beyond" here is neither hostile to ethics nor standing above the ethical domain. He claims that Nietzsche and such contemporary philosophers as Heidegger, Levinas, Foucault, and Derrida argue persuasively that we no longer can think and justify our acts within the traditional framework of transcendence. Nevertheless, this does not imply an absence of ethics or renunciation of the legitimacy of ethical concerns. In fact Scott celebrates this apparent loss of transcendence as what frees ethics from its excess. This remarkable account of the impact of postmodern philosophy on the question of ethics and politics is particularly insightful in discussing the genealogical approach to practical philosophy that characterizes the work of Nietzsche and Foucault. The work is commendable also for its balanced view of Heidegger's relationship to politics and ethics. Scott offers an excellent account of Heidegger's philosophical understanding of technology, seeing evidence there of both of a lingering moral asceticism and a mode of temporally rooted questioning that overcomes ethical subjectivity and its notion of responsibility. Upper-division undergraduate; graduate; faculty.—*W. A. Brogan, Villanova University*

OAB-1148   B187   93-25811 CIP
Sorabji, Richard. **Animal minds and human morals: the origins of the Western debate.** Cornell, 1994 (c1993). 267p bibl indexes ISBN 0-8014-2948-X, $39.95

In this extraordinary, scholarly book, Sorabji (Univ. of London) traces the historical development of philosophers' attitudes about the mental capacities of (nonhuman) animals and the related issue of the appropriateness of ascribing moral rights to them. The study surveys a vast array of Greek texts and a few early Latin texts dealing with animal psychology. The overall weight of evidence reinforces the prevalent Western idea that animals do not have higher rational capacities and that it is therefore morally acceptable to use them for human ends. Sorabji duly notes the few exceptions to this conclusion, for example, the followers of Plotinus. A trained classicist, the author supplies copious documentation of his claims and interpretations. In the last sections he addresses the contemporary philosophic debates about animal rights found in the writings of Peter Singer, Tom Regan, and others; these brief parts are insightful and worthy of close study. Employing some "deconstructionist" methods, Sorabji criticizes "moral theorizing" and suggests studying the morally relevant ways in which animal minds differ from human minds with a view toward deciding the appropriateness of including them in the community of moral subjects. Sorabji's study is an historical prolegomenon to this further investigation. This work should interest any inquiring mind. All levels.—*P. A. Streveler, West Chester University*

OAB-1149   Can. CIP
Sparshott, Francis. **Taking life seriously: a study of the argument of the Nicomachean ethics.** Toronto, 1994. 461p bibl index afp ISBN 0-8020-2953-1, $60.00

This exceptional book deserves to replace W.F.R. Hardie's *Aristotle's Ethical Theory* (1968) as the standard one-volume companion to Aristotle's *Nicomachean Ethics* (*EN*). Sparshott (emeritus, Univ. of Toronto), like Hardie and too few other recent authors on Aristotle, offers a reading of the entire *EN*. But, unlike Hardie and other recent commentators, Sparshott intends "to show by paraphrase and comment how it might have seemed sensible to write just this text in just this order." Aristotle started from the fact that individuals with a sense of time and situated in concrete circumstances can conceive and thus plan a whole life, beginning or early middle to end. Being able to think of themselves as living "a life" (hence Sparshott's title), such individuals who are reflective pose to themselves the question, How should I organize my life? On Sparshott's reading, the argument of *EN* is "the unfolding of a single sequence of implications from [this] single

inescapable starting-point." Few will agree with this detailed reading at every point, but it repays careful consideration. Glossary of transliterated Greek terms. Interesting quasi-ethnographic appendix, "Aristotle's World," which is not about fourth-century Athens but about the world of Aristotle's theoretical construction. Highly recommended. Upper-division undergraduate; graduate; faculty.—*D. R. C. Reed, Wittenberg University*

OAB-1150   B2799   93-40557 CIP
Sullivan, Roger J. **An introduction to Kant's ethics.** Cambridge, 1994. 183p bibl index ISBN 0-521-46208-8, $49.95; ISBN 0-521-46769-1 pbk, $10.95

Sullivan takes up the challenge of presenting an introductory account of Kant's ethical theory that does not sacrifice any of the depth or subtlety of that theory; the result is an unqualified success. Sullivan's point of entry to Kant's moral theory is his political philosophy, which he discusses in the opening chapter. He then proceeds to explain key Kantian ideas, such as the Categorical Imperative and its various formulations, and the idea of moral character, and he shows how these hang together to produce a unified ethical theory. In another chapter Sullivan discusses some of the shortcomings of Kant's work. This book makes Kant comprehensible to any undergraduate willing to put a reasonable amount of effort into it, and will also profit graduate students and faculty members looking for a basic understanding of Kant's ethical thought. There are very few books that provide so lucid an account of Kant in such an accessible manner; consequently this volume is an especially valuable addition to college and university libraries.—*M. A. Michael, University of Nevada, Las Vegas*

■ Speculative

OAB-1151   BD171   95-31251 CIP
Alston, William P. **A realist conception of truth.** Cornell, 1996. 274p bibl index afp ISBN 0-8014-3187-5, $35.00

From the standpoint of both general readers and professionals in the field this may be one of the best philosophical books to come along in some time. Alston (emeritus, Syracuse Univ.) argues effectively for a conception of truth—he calls it "minimal realism"—currently out of fashion. His claims are presented through a remarkably clear and accurate history of recent epistemology and metaphysics as these bear on a philosophical account of truth. Most impressive in this history is a discerning treatment of the most influential recent arguments against a realist conception of truth—arguments developed by Michael Dummett and Hilary Putnam, for example. The depth, the scope, and the clarity of Alston's analysis is matched only by that of the great philosophers with whom he contends. Highest recommendation for all collections. General; upper-division undergraduate through professional.—*J. White, University of Maine*

OAB-1152   BD182   92-37597 CIP
Amico, Robert P. **The problem of the criterion.** Rowman & Littlefield, 1993. 156p bibl index afp ISBN 0-8476-7817-2, $39.50

We need a criterion to know which beliefs count as knowledge and which do not. To insure the criterion is a good one, we must check it against actual cases of knowledge. It seems we must already know what counts as knowledge in order to apply the criterion. This is the problem of the criterion. In a clearly written exposition and analysis of historical and contemporary texts, Amico (St. Bonaventure Univ.) identifies an ancient and modern version of this problem. Arguments by Sextus Empiricus, Michel de Montaigne, and Cardinal D.J. Mercier are presented and evaluated. Solutions to the modern problem by Nicholas Rescher and Roderick Chisholm are criticized. Amico concludes that the problem of the criterion is a meta-epistemological one and argues that the ancient and modern versions of it are dissolved. Chapter six details how modern skepticism is "epistemically self-refuting." Amico's writing style is succinct—arguments are precisely stated and explained. This substantive contribution to epistemology will revitalize interest in the problem of the criterion. Highly recommended for advanced undergraduates, graduate students, and faculty in philosophy.—*B. A. Dixon, SUNY College at Plattsburgh*

OAB-1153 BD161 92-8704 CIP
Cohen, L. Jonathan. **An essay on belief and acceptance.** Oxford, 1992. 163p index ISBN 0-19-824294-8, $29.95

Cohen carefully distinguishes belief from acceptance and instructively applies that distinction to a variety of important philosophical issues. To believe that *p* is to be disposed "normally to feel it true that *p* and false that *not-p*" under certain conditions. To accept that *p* is "to have or adopt a policy of. . .including [*p*] among one's premises for deciding what to do or think in a particular context, whether or not one feels it to be true that *p*" (p.4). Many topics are addressed in a lively discussion of the fruitfulness of the distinction between belief and acceptance. Cohen considers the scope of responsibility and of the voluntary, reasons for belief, demands for subjective consistency, whether (and when) reasons are causes, purposive explanation and distinctively human behavior, whether animals have beliefs, the viability of folk psychology, epistemic warrant, cognitive attitudes involved in speech acts and in intentions, and the conceptual possibility of self-deception and of action that manifests *akrasia* or weakness of will. An important, wide-ranging, and remarkably accessible book; highly recommended for all academic libraries.—*A. R. Mele, Davidson College*

OAB-1154 BD215 91-31795 CIP
Crimmins, Mark. **Talk about beliefs.** MIT, 1992. 214p bibl index ISBN 0-262-03185-X, $25.00

An ambitious and impressive attempt to provide a unified representationalist treatment of beliefs and the sentences we use to report them. Crimmins argues that a familiar range of puzzles that beset certain "naive"-Russellian semantics for belief reports can be avoided once we appreciate that the *propositions* we express when reporting beliefs standardly contain "constituents" that are "unarticulated" in the *sentences* we use to express those propositions. Crimmins makes four claims: first, in reporting a person's beliefs, we make claims not only about the (Russellian) propositional content of the beliefs but also about the ways the agent thinks about the propositions; second, these are best discriminated in terms of the ways the agent thinks about the objects, properties, and relations the propositions are about; third, these are best thought of not as shareable abstract objects like intensions or Fregean senses, but in terms of particular, concrete, unshareable, agent-specific representations; fourth, these are the relevant unarticulated constituents in our belief reports. Anyone interested in these issues will need to take seriously Crimmins's discussion and his defense of each claim. The implications of his proposal are wide ranging and will be of interest to philosophers of language and mind, to cognitive scientists, linguists, and cognitive psychologists. Recommended to advanced undergraduate and graduate collections.—*W. Taschek, Ohio State University*

OAB-1155 BD436 96-28841 CIP
D'Aragona, Tullia. **Dialogue on the infinity of love,** ed. and tr. by Rinaldina Russell and Bruce Merry; introd. and notes by Rinaldina Russell. Chicago, 1997. 114p bibl index afp ISBN 0-226-13638-8, $26.00; ISBN 0-226-13639-6 pbk, $12.95

During the Renaissance, vernacular popularizations of Neoplatonic thought were intended for an educated if not scholarly audience that included women. However, Tullia D'Aragona was the only female author to actually publish her own dialogue on love, which concurrently mirrored and modified the very fashionable genre. This slim volume in the University of Chicago's new series "The Other Voice" serves a multiple function: it makes available a previously untranslated work while serving as a window into the sophisticated world of the 16th-century salon culture, where courtesans like D'Aragona mingled freely with intellectuals and gentlemen to wittily debate philosophical and aesthetic issues. Russell's straightforward and clearly written introduction presents a brief biography, a discussion of the popular genre, and an analysis of the text. Rus-

sell convincingly argues that D'Aragona's discussion of love and sex is quite modern in its treatment of gender bias, the relationship of love and sexuality, self-representation, and in the suggestion of female equality. The *Dialogue* itself is a short work—some 50 pages including footnotes. The translation reads well, capturing the original's cosmopolitan tone without ignoring its historical genesis. General; undergraduate; graduate; faculty.—*F. A. Bassanese, University of Massachusetts at Boston*

OAB-1156 B2430 93-41815 CIP
Deleuze, Gilles. **Difference and repetition,** tr. by Paul Patton. Columbia, 1994. 350p bibl index afp ISBN 0-231-08158-8, $37.50

This is a long-overdue, and skillful, translation of one of Deleuze's most important and original works, which was first published in 1968. It occupies an important place in Deleuze's oeuvre as the first text, following a series of historical commentaries, in which he philosophizes on his own behalf. It occupies an equally important place in the evolution of French philosophy in the 20th century, as it articulates a profound critique of the philosophy of representation while constructing a metaphysics of difference freed from subordination to a logic of identity. While charting the development through the history of philosophy of the concepts "pure difference" and "complex repetition," Deleuze proposes a new image of thought, which readers familiar with his later works will recognize. A difficult and challenging text that has done as much as any to initiate the philosophy of difference that characterizes much recent French thought, this book is one of the classics of recent European philosophy. It belongs in any library with holdings in philosophy. Upper-division undergraduate; graduate; faculty.—*A. D. Schrift, Grinnell College*

OAB-1157 B808 92-10057 CIP
Flanagan, Owen. **Consciousness reconsidered.** MIT, 1992. 234p bibl index ISBN 0-262-06148-1, $24.95

Flanagan (Wellesley College and author of *The Science of Mind*, CH, Nov'84, and *Varieties of Moral Personality*, CH, Nov'91) has written an easily accessible look at the current state-of-the-art in the vexed subject of consciousness. While doing justice to the positions of others working in philosophy of mind, Flanagan offers fresh arguments for his own position, constructive naturalism. In particular, Flanagan challenges the view that consciousness does not exist and that the concept of consciousness should be abandoned. He defends qualia and claims they can be naturalized. He attacks the position of the "new mysterians": that the brain is the cause of consciousness but that we will never be able to achieve an understanding of the relation between the brain and consciousness. The epiphenomenalist suspicion is examined and dismissed. In his discussion of the phenomenology of consciousness, Flanagan calls upon the work of William James and the stream of consciousness. A well-bound book with useful index and bibliography, this is an excellent read and is absolutely essential to any collection devoted to philosophy of mind and cognitive science. Advanced undergraduate; graduate; faculty.—*R. L. Greenwood, University of South Alabama*

OAB-1158 BD241 94-12360 CIP
Grondin, Jean. **Introduction to philosophical hermeneutics,** tr. by Joel Weinsheimer. Yale, 1995 (c1994). 231p bibl index afp ISBN 0-300-05969-8, $25.00

In this excellent introduction, philosophical hermeneutics is traced back to Greek antiquity, keying on the issue of universality. Gerald Bruns, in *Inventions* (CH, Dec'82) and in *Hermeneutics: Ancient and Modern* (CH, Sep'93), had, of course, already extended the horizon of present hermeneutical discussion back to Jewish and Greek antiquity and the early Christian tradition; but Grondin (Univ. of Montreal) here offers a coherent, brief history of philosophical hermeneutics from antiquity through the Middle Ages, Reformation, and Enlightenment to the present discussion by Habermas and Derrida. Particularly helpful is the excellent 60-page, historically arranged bibliography, previously unavailable in English. The volume also has a foreword by Hans-Georg Gadamer, which the original work, *Einführung in die philosophische Hermeneutik* (Darmstadt, 1991), lacked. Gadamer is also the subject of Grondin's *Hermeneutische Wahrheit?* (Königstein, 1982). A much more extensive collection of Grondin's writings on hermeneutics is announced as forthcoming from SUNY Press, but they only supplement in greater depth this valuable introduction. The book under review is a major new step forward in the availability of hermeneutics to English-speaking readers. Highly recommended for both general readers and scholars. Upper-division undergraduate; graduate; faculty.—*R. E. Palmer, MacMurray College*

OAB-1159 B3279 93-18085 CIP
Haar, Michel. **Heidegger and the essence of man.** State University of New York, 1993. 195p bibl index afp ISBN 0-7914-1555-4, $49.50

First published in France (1990), this valuable and penetrating study by a prominent Sorbonne professor of philosophy and expert in Heidegger and Nietzsche traces the topic of the "essence of man" from the early through the later Heidegger. Necessarily, this involves Haar in themes that are central to understanding Heidegger: time, truth, language, history, animality, and technology, which he illuminatingly discusses. Haar's erudite readings range the increasingly voluminous Heideggerian corpus. They are both analytical and critical, appreciative and questioning. In his introduction to the book Hubert Dreyfus correctly characterizes it as "a dedicated and subtle attempt to experience the place from which Heidegger is speaking and to place him in our contemporary world." As in his parallel volume, *The Song of the Earth: Heidegger and the Grounds of the History of Being* (1993; tr. of *Chant de la terre*, Paris, 1987), Haar finds limitations in Heidegger's thinking of the priority of being over man especially with regard to nature, animality, and the fleshly embodiment of human existence. The volume is impeccable in scholarship, well translated, and an important contribution to the interpretive literature on Heidegger available in English. Advanced undergraduate; graduate; faculty.—*R. E. Palmer, MacMurray College*

OAB-1160 B3279 92-46633 CIP
Heidegger, Martin. **Basic concepts,** tr. by Gary E. Aylesworth. Indiana, 1993. 110p afp ISBN 0-253-32767-9, $20.00

This translation is an excellent and accessible introduction to the later Heidegger. Published posthumously in 1981 as *Grundbegriffe*, this 1941 lecture series is an important marker in Heidegger's thinking and gives us access to his respelling out of the question of being and time. Here he sets forth eight "guidewords" that seem to be irresolvably contradictory assertions about being. The fact that being eludes modern reflection leads Heidegger to return to the "beginnings" of Western philosophical thought in search of the fateful decision about how being was to be thought—and by extension, how human being was to be defined. He asks, "What if all previous answers to the questions of who we are were merely the repeated application of a [fatefully wrong] answer given long ago?" While Heidegger spells out more fully his critique of humanist definitions of man in *Letter on Humanism* (1947), the present text shows us how his view there arises out of the quest for the "meaning of being" in the face of our modern forgetfulness of the ontological difference. In the second part of this work, Heidegger turns to two fragments from Anaximander, which, taken together in his interpretation, articulate at the very dawn of Western philosophy an initial saying of being and time together as timely emergence. Aylesworth's well-translated edition is essential for undergraduate libraries, recommended also for general readers, graduate students, faculty.—*R. E. Palmer, MacMurray College*

OAB-1161 BD161 95-40996 CIP
Hetherington, Stephen Cade. **Knowledge puzzles: an introduction to epistemology.** Westview, 1996. 193p bibl index afp ISBN 0-8133-2486-6, $49.95; ISBN 0-8133-2487-4 pbk, $15.95

Hetherington has written an excellent introduction to epistemology. He makes all the major positions in contemporary epistemology comprehensible without oversimplifying them. This is the best book of its kind that has come out for quite some time. It is divided into short chapters: the topics of truth, belief, and justification each get a chapter, followed by one on the Gettier problem and then a chapter for just about every position that has been developed in recent epistemology. Each chapter begins with a puzzle from everyday life that pertains to an issue in epistemology. Hetherington helps motivate an understanding for epistemology by moving from these puzzles to the complex nuances of rival theories of justification. After going into most theories that have arisen as a response to the Gettier problem, Hetherington turns to a survey of the different kinds of skepticism. This book deserves to become the most used undergraduate introduction to epistemology, and graduate students and professionals will find it a handy reference work to keep in the office.—*S. M. Downes, University of Utah*

OAB-1162 Orig
Kim, Jaegwon. **Philosophy of mind.** Westview, 1996. 258p bibl index afp ISBN 0-8133-0775-9, $59.00; ISBN 0-8133-0776-7 pbk, $20.00

An introductory survey to philosophy of mind, this work is impressive equally for its clarity and depth as an overview and its forcefulness as an original contribution to its subject. Kim (Brown Univ.) is uncompromisingly honest and acute; he consequently makes complex issues approachable without sacrificing subtlety. For nonspecialist readers who have found discussions in analytic philosophy of mind arcane or otherwise off-putting, Kim's book will provide welcome relief. He explains what matters to contemporary philosophers and why it matters to them. (He is especially good on issues of externalism, supervenience, and mental causation.) At the same time, he is critical without being unduly polemical. As a sympathetic exposition of the most important trends in recent philosophy of mind, Kim's sustained treatment surpasses all other available options. It is both more unified than standard, good quality anthologies such as David M. Rosenthal's *The Nature of Mind*, (1991) and more accessible than the many works intended primarily for professional philosophers. This work should be purchased by public and academic libraries alike. Undergraduate; graduate; faculty; general.—*C. J. Shields, University of Colorado at Boulder*

OAB-1163 B3279 92-33888 CIP
Kisiel, Theodore. **The genesis of Heidegger's *Being and time*.** California, 1993. 608p bibl indexes afp ISBN 0-520-08150-1, $60.00

Ten years in the writing, Kisiel's book is nothing less than a mine of factual, historical, methodological, and philosophical materials previously unknown to the English-speaking world. In other words, the background to Heidegger's masterpiece is now revealed. Kisiel (Northern Illinois Univ.) accounts for Heidegger's early development and progress by reference to private correspondence, European archives, and personal experiences (including his experiences in WW I, his relation to Husserl after the war, and his religious "conversion"). The author also treats Heidegger's little-known interpretation of Aristotole, Aristotle's relation to hermeneutics, and the philosophy of culture. A work in both the history of ideas and interpretation theory, Kisiel's book cannot be praised too highly. Upper-level undergraduates and above.—*H. N. Tuttle, University of New Mexico*

OAB-1164 B72 92-53533 CIP
Murdoch, Iris. **Metaphysics as a guide to morals.** A. Lane, Penguin, 1993 (c1992). 520p index ISBN 0-7139-9100-3, $35.00

Whereas Heidegger said that metaphysics (i.e., Platonism) was at an end, Murdoch defends it here as a study of ideas necessary for any coherent moral reflection, indeed of any recognizably human life whatever: the ideas of goodness, reality, and truth. From Plato's allegory of the cave she takes her understanding of philosophy as a progressive destruction (but also a reinterpretation and redemption) of images, e.g., a personal God elsewhere, who was always only a dream of Good, which is not a thing existing among other things but a reality present everywhere. She discusses language and individuality, tragedy, the link between love and knowledge, the dimensions of morality and moral reflection (truthfulness "demands and effects an exercise of virtues and a purification of desires"), the relations of philosophy to literature, religion, morality, politics, and science. She refers constantly to Plato and Kant ("religious philosophers [whose] real world is the moral world"), as well as to Simone Weil, Wittgenstein, Heidegger, and Schopenhauer, with many helpful remarks on the Bible and on many other philosophers in the Western tradition. Lucid, dense, provocative, this book is essential for all collections in philosophy, perhaps with her *The Sovereignty of Good* (London, 1970), and *The Fire and the Sun: Why Plato Banished the Artists* (CH, Mar'78).—*M. Andic, University of Massachusetts at Boston*

OAB-1165   BD450   96-7018 CIP
Olson, Eric T. **The human animal: personal identity without psychology.** Oxford, 1997. 189p bibl index afp ISBN 0-19-510506-0, $29.95

For 20 years, philosophers have followed the lead of Derek Parfit, John Perry, and Sidney Shoemaker in formulating and fine-tuning psychological accounts of personal identity. Such accounts maintain that a person at an earlier time is identical to (or survives as) a person at a later time via overlapping chains of psychological connections. Olson provides an astounding contribution to current discussions of identity—one that will undoubtedly resonate for years to come. In a carefully defined and thoroughly argued manner, Olson defends the following thesis: "no sort of psychological continuity, with or without further physical qualifications, is either necessary or sufficient for us to persist through time." He proceeds to develop a "biological approach," which holds that "one survives just in case one's purely animal functions—metabolism, the capacity to breathe and circulate one's blood, and the like—continue." Olson's approach has considerable plausibility because he distinguishes it from several common formulations of bodily and physicalistic criteria and, surprisingly, suggests that his own account fits more comfortably with Locke's view of personhood and personal identity than do the rival psychological accounts. This text is highly recommended for those dissatisfied with current discussions of personal identity. Endnotes. Upper-division undergraduate; graduate; faculty.— *H. Storl, Augustana College (IL)*

OAB-1166   BD175   92-22750 CIP
Sassower, Raphael. **Knowledge without expertise: on the status of scientists.** State University of New York, 1993. 158p bibl indexes afp ISBN 0-7914-1481-7, $44.95

Sassower (philosophy, Univ. of Colorado at Colorado Springs) brings the implications of Lyotard's postmodernism down to the level of applied epistemology. The book revolves around the attempt in the 1870s by some leaders of the British Association for the Advancement of Science to expel economists because they lacked "truly scientific" expertise. However, an examination of the original documents reveals that the calls for expulsion were motivated by fears of a rapidly growing field, economics, whose members were drawn from many walks of life and were actively engaged in the political debates of the day. All of this threatened the elitism that many in the BAAS thought was necessary to maintain the public authority of science. Sassower argues that this case is typical of ones that the public must face today in evaluating the claims of rival experts. Denying that compromise among experts is an adequate surrogate for democratic decision making, Sassower believes that the public must learn to accept the risks involved in making its own decisions, as it takes to heart the political character of expertise. It is a strategy that allows experts a say, but never the final say. Strongly recommended for its readability, even for readers unfamiliar with postmodernism and contemporary epistemology. All levels.—*S. Fuller, Virginia Polytechnic Institute and State University*

OAB-1167   Orig
Schmitt, Frederick F. **Truth: a primer.** Westview, 1995. 251p bibl index afp ISBN 0-8133-2000-3, $49.95; ISBN 0-8133-2001-1 pbk, $16.95

Schmitt uses the philosophical disputes of realism versus idealism and absolutism versus relativism to frame his appraisal of four classic theories of truth:

the pragmatic, coherence, deflationary, and correspondence. He skillfully sketches the various positions and objections in relation to what he sees as the fundamental issue of contention, namely, how truth relates to believers. His analysis is evenly paced but leans throughout toward realism and absolutism. His odyssey concludes with an endorsement of Hartry Field's correspondence theory of truth. A number of advanced works on truth have appeared in recent years; the most notable comprehensive account is Richard L. Kirkham's *Theories of Truth* (CH, Feb'93). Schmitt's effort does not directly compete with these; instead he eschews ancillary issues and lays out intuitively significant threads of argument without exhaustive contextual detail. Nevertheless, the survey is precise and philosophically responsible. In sum, the book is an outstanding primer with an adequate bibliography and a modest index; it is remarkable as much for its skillful organization of essential themes as for its clarity of expression. Undergraduate; graduate; faculty.—*L. C. Archie, Lander University*

OAB-1168   B3318   93-40385 CIP
Sleinis, E.E. **Nietzsche's revaluation of values: a study in strategies.** Illinois, 1994. 238p bibl index afp ISBN 0-252-02090-1, $37.50; ISBN 0-252-06383-X pbk, $19.95

The critique of values, the analysis of moral, religious, and aesthetic values, and the ambitious attempt to inaugurate a "transvaluation of values" lie at the core of Nietzsche's philosophical enterprise. Surprisingly, Sleinis (Univ. of Tasmania) is one of the few interpreters of Nietzsche to deal with his general theory of values and his argumental strategies in a detailed, illuminating, and critically objective way. Sleinis focuses with unusual clarity on the problem of "transvaluing" values and does so in an appealing way that avoids either the typical inflammatory attacks or the totally supportive, "cult-like" adoration of the radical Dionysian thinker. Step by step the reader is guided by a lucid and fair interpreter through the analysis of cognitive, moral, aesthetic, and religious values. Though dealing with emotionally charged critiques of Christian metaphysics and the questioning of the origin and meaning of morality in general (and Christian morality in particular), the author's clarity of thought, ingenious arguments, and straightforward language neutralize reactive excess and show, in a favorable and rationally sound light, Nietzsche's praise of maximal life-affirmation and the richness of his analyses of values he opposed. By taking seriously (and with a rare sanguinity) Nietzsche's sometimes dramatic, sometimes visionary arguments, Sleinis has produced a valuable, interesting, and appealing study of Nietzsche's central cognitive and passionate concerns. Highly recommended. Upper-division undergraduate; graduate; faculty.— *G. J. Stack, SUNY College at Brockport*

OAB-1169   BD581   94-46739 CIP
Soper, Kate. **What is nature?: culture, politics and the non-human.** Blackwell, 1995. 289p index afp ISBN 0-631-18889-4, $54.95; ISBN 0-631-18891-6 pbk, $18.95

This is an impressive interdisciplinary synthesis and exploration of the many, often conflicting, cultural and political uses played by our ideas about nature. Soper (Univ. of North London) draws on the work of historians, feminists, environmentalists, cultural critics, and philosophers. As an environmentalist, she wishes to preserve "nature." However, Soper also rejects institutions (e.g., slavery and male domination) that for centuries were said to be justified by "nature." Soper makes a strong case in arguing that environmentalists should be more aware of the many misuses of various ideas about nature and that cultural critics, including many feminists, should be cautious about dismissing ideas about nature as "socially constructed." Appreciative of Ted Benton's *Natural Relations: Ecology, Animal Rights & Social Justice* (1993), Soper has a keen eye for tensions and contradictions. For example, one cannot simultaneously claim that nature has "inherent value" independently of humans and that magnificence and beauty, as judged by humans, is evidence of this inherent value. Further, a concern with future generations in the abstract is hypocritical if it is isolated from concern with the billions of people who are currently underfed. General; upper-division undergraduate through professional.—*D. Christie, University of New Hampshire*

OAB-1170 BD111 92-28613 CIP
Van Inwagen, Peter. **Metaphysics.** Westview, 1993. 222p bibl index afp ISBN 0-8133-0634-5, $44.00; ISBN 0-8133-0635-3 pbk, $16.95

An exceptionally lucid account of traditional metaphysical issues. Van Inwagen's approach is systematic rather than historical, although historical material is introduced, usually whenever Van Inwagen needs a foil or an example of some issue under discussion. The book is divided into three parts, in which Van Inwagen examines metaphysical problems relating to the world, God, and human beings. These sections contain discussions of the monism-pluralism debate, of the reality of the external world, of the necessary existence of God, and of the mind-body problem, among other topics. In discussing these issues Van Inwagen steers a course between dogmatism and the uncritical relativism that holds all metaphysical theories to be equally adequate and acceptable. The discussions never degenerate into obscurantism, and the book should be extremely useful to undergraduates, graduate students, and general readers who want to get a feel for the issues that trouble metaphysicians. This is one of the best overviews of metaphysics this reviewer has ever come across. A strong case could be made that if a college library collection could contain only one book on this subject, it should be Van Inwagen's *Metaphysics.*— *M. A. Michael, University of Nevada, Las Vegas*

OAB-1171 B2430 93-40293 CIP
Vetö, Miklos. **The religious metaphysics of Simone Weil,** tr. by Joan Dargan. State University of New York, 1994. 219p bibl indexes afp ISBN 0-7914-2077-9, $49.50

This is a translation of Vetö's *La Métaphysique religieuse de Simone Weil* (Paris, 1971), itself a revision of a doctoral dissertation written in English in the early 1960s at Oxford under the direction of Iris Murdoch. It was the first, and is still the best, systematic account of Weil's thought, and it presents her not as an antimetaphysical explorer of the meaning, implications, and presuppositions of religious and moral experience and life, but precisely as a religious and moral metaphysician, in the tradition of Plato and Kant, though influenced also by Descartes and Rousseau. It deals with the key ideas of decreation; attention and desire; motives and the void; affliction; beauty, time, and the self; and nonactive action—thus dealing methodically with the metaphysics of perfection, which is to say surrender and obedience. The work draws mainly on her notebooks rather than her finished essay, and so on her later, religious thought as opposed to earlier social and political studies. References are given to both French and English versions of her writings; there are endnotes and a chronology. Indispensable for all collections on Weil, along with Simone Pétrement's *Simone Weil: A Life* (CH, Jul'77) and Gabriela Fiori's *Simone Weil: An Intellectual Biography* (CH, Apr'90), works that combine analysis with biography. Upper-division undergraduate; graduate; faculty.—*M. Andic, University of Massachusetts at Boston*

OAB-1172 B785 96-16616 CIP
Weeks, Andrew. **Paracelsus: speculative theory and the crisis of the early Reformation.** State University of New York, 1997. 238p bibl index afp ISBN 0-7914-3147-9, $65.50

In this volume in the series "Western Esoteric Traditions," Weeks affirms that the 16th-century speculative thinker and man of medicine Paracelsus is indeed within the "esoteric tradition," insisting also, however, that his thought can best be understood and appreciated if we do not attempt to make it relevant to contemporary concerns. Weeks's basic thesis is that Paracelsus can be understood only within the conditions of life and knowledge of his own century, one of great complexity and confusion. He argues for a "text-centered historicism" that attempts to "let his writings speak for themselves" and evoke their own historical context. This approach is refreshing and valuable in the attempt to understand the thought of a figure who defies categorization and whose writings float freely among the disciplines of medicine, philosophy, theology, and science. Weeks is aware, of course, that the writings of Paracelsus do not simply "speak for themselves" but require in-depth analysis of both historical and philosophical vantage points. These latter Weeks supplies very well. Despite the

esoteric nature of the subject, his well-written and engaging book succeeds on many levels in making an important contribution to the scholarship of 16th-century German literature that is a genuine pleasure to read. All quotations from Paracelsus are given in English and German. Extensive footnotes and bibliography; adequate index. Recommended not only for scholars but also for curious readers. Upper-division undergraduates; graduates; researchers and faculty.— *P. A. Streveler, West Chester University of Pennsylvania*

OAB-1173 BD418 94-36307 CIP
Wilson, Robert A. **Cartesian psychology and physical minds: individualism and the sciences of the mind.** Cambridge, 1995. 273p bibl index ISBN 0-521-47402-7, $49.95

The viability of individualism is a central question in the philosophy of mind. Individualism is the view that the nature of mental states is "narrow"—that is, a study of mental states need not concern itself with considerations external to the individual. Thus, the individuation or classification of mental states does not "presuppose anything in particular about the external world of the individual who has those states." The present work is a powerful addition to the debate concerning individualism. Its value lies in its clear presentation and much-needed critical summary of recent developments in individualism. Wilson (Queen's Univ., Ont.) approaches individualism by uncovering its motivating intuitions and probing its plausibility vis-à-vis the philosophy of science. He begins with a careful examination of three arguments in favor of individualism: a priori, empirical, methodological. Next, Wilson argues that individualism relies on a problematic analysis of mental causation and psychological explanation. He concludes with a defense of "wide" explanations of behavior on grounds that such explanations are causally deeper and theoretically more appropriate. This text is highly recommended for philosophers, psychologists, cognitive scientists, and others who have taken seriously the arguments presented in Jerry Fodor's *Psychosemantics* (CH, Jan'88) or *A Theory of Content* (CH, May'91); Steven Stich's *From Folk Psychology to Cognitive Science* (CH, May'84); Lynne Rudder Baker's *Saving Belief* (CH, Jun'88); or Paul Churchland's *A Neurocomputational Perspective* (1989).—*H. Storl, Augustana College (IL)*

OAB-1174 BD161 95-49162 CIP
Yolton, John W. **Perception & reality: a history from Descartes to Kant.** Cornell, 1996. 240p bibl index afp ISBN 0-8014-3227-8, $39.95

In this book Yolton (emeritus, Rutgers Univ.) reconfirms his reputation as perhaps the best current scholar on 17th- and 18th-century philosophy; it builds upon his *Perceptual Acquaintance from Descartes to Reid* (1984). Everyone interested in the problem of perception needs to study this work; it covers not just the major and minor philosophers from Descartes to Kant but has penetrating critiques of such contemporaries as J.J. Gibson, J.J. Valberg, Richard Rorty, and Colin McGinn. Yolton's aim is not just historical; he is looking for the clearest statements of direct realism, the position he finds most adequate. In this regard he makes the epistemologies of such philosophers as Berkeley and Hume more plausible, although he is clearly at odds with standard interpretations. This is not easy stuff, but the writing is superbly clear, and the quotations and references to current scholarship clarify both the context and the importance of the contemporary debate. Recommended for all philosophers and psychologists interested in perception and the idealism-realism debates in the 17th and 18th centuries. Excellent footnotes.—*R. H. Evans, University of Minnesota—Duluth*

■ Religion

OAB-1175 BR128 93-17291 CIP
Berthrong, John H. **All under heaven: transforming paradigms in Confucian-Christian dialogue.** State University of New York, 1994. 273p bibl index afp ISBN 0-7914-1857-X, $65.50

This work of scholarship is of outstanding importance for interreligious dialogue between Christianity and Asian religions (since such dialogue is always in need of new models) and especially, says the author, when it becomes "complicated by the process of dialogue as conversation seeking conceptual cross-cultural clarity." Berthrong focuses entirely on Christian-Confucian dialogue from the perspective of a process theologian influenced by the works of Whitehead and Hartshorne (the latter's idea of "dual transcendence"), with a corresponding appreciation for the Southern Sung Neo-Confucian thinker Chu Hsi and "two key representatives of the New Confucian movement," i.e., Mou Tsung-san and Tu Wei-ming. Berthrong delves with exceptional clarity into dialogical issues (e.g., theism, creativity, ethics, community, "dual religious citizenship," even the element of *hope*); but he also argues convincingly that the resolution of the "key question of the relationship of transcendence and immanence" as categories common to both Confucianism and Christianity may somehow act as a paradigm for other religions in dialogue. This is a work of systematic skill and imaginative interpretation. Appendix with source-overview, scholarly notes, Chinese glossary. Graduate; faculty.—*W. C. Beane, University of Wisconsin—Oshkosh*

OAB-1176   BL48   95-44787 CIP
Burkert, Walter. **Creation of the sacred: tracks of biology in early religions.** Harvard, 1996. 255p bibl index ISBN 0-674-17569-7, $29.95

Burkert (classics, Univ. of Zurich) seeks to account for two traits of religion, its ubiquity and its persistence. The argument begins with sacrifice as both social and biological—an instinctive program activated during conditions of danger or anxiety that allows one member of a group to be sacrificed for the sake of the whole. It continues with narrative—the story of the quest for food to insure the survival of a species or a group. Then Burkert moves to hierarchy—the sense of higher and lower that orders societies. The next premise concerns exchange of gifts and the reciprocity it assumes—a rational strategy for ordering society that is supported by religious traditions. The final step concerns communication—the capacity of societies to make sense to and for themselves. The conclusion is that religion is a "tradition of serious communication with powers that cannot be seen," offering "coherence, stability, and control within this world." This book is a brilliant comparative account of the social and biological functions of religion throughout human history; philosophically, scientifically, and historically interesting, it is a book for libraries, scholars, and all students of religion. General; undergraduate through professional.—*L. J. Alderink, Concordia College*

OAB-1177   BV4466   94-31786 CIP
Cunningham, Hilary. **God and Caesar at the Rio Grande: sanctuary and the politics of religion.** Minnesota, 1995. 264p bibl index afp ISBN 0-8166-2457-7 pbk, $19.95

The product of eight years of anthropological research, this study of the sanctuary movement in Tucson, Arizona, is outstanding social science and a fascinating human chronicle of what it means to act on one's religious and personal convictions when these conflict with the laws of the state. Tucson's sanctuary movement and the subsequent arrest and trial of eight sanctuary workers forced participants and observers alike "to ponder the proper relation of religion to politics." As an interdenominational "community of believers," the movement redefined the meaning and reasserted the cultural power of "church" in "a political context that recognized the importance and relevance of 'religion' for 'politics.'" By dissecting the sanctuary network and refugee underground experience from the perspectives of the predominantly Anglo "rescuers" and the dependent Central Americans (largely from El Salvador and Guatemala) who sought asylum, the study reveals the clash between personal and moral commitments and the structures of sexism, racism, ideology, and politics that divided this community. This seemingly particular study broadly explores the role of "faith" in American culture and society. It is most readable, insightful, and highly recommended for all general and specialized audiences.—*W. Q. Morales, University of Central Florida*

OAB-1178   BL625   93-3928 CIP
Eller, Cynthia. **Living in the lap of the goddess: the feminist spirituality movement in America.** Crossroad, NY, 1993. 276p index ISBN 0-8245-1245-6, $24.95

Drawing from many sources of modern feminist spirituality, including its literature, workshops, retreats, rituals, and personal interviews, Eller has produced a superb empirical and phenomenological rendering of this diverse and complex religious movement. She defines a spiritual feminist as an individual who seriously believes herself to be one and/or adheres to at least three of the five following characteristics: "valuing women's empowerment, practicing ritual and/or magic, revering nature, using the feminine or gender as a primary mode of religious analysis, and espousing the revisionist version of Western history favored by the movement." She analyzes feminist spirituality in terms of its organization and structure, demographics, conversion experiences of its adherents, origin, rituals, magic, understanding of the Goddess, and view of history. Additionally, she explicates the historical and modern movements that influenced it as well as the startling differences between it and feminist politics. This is an essential work for all libraries since no other book parallels this one in its scope, accuracy, vividness, and scholarship.—*A. McDowell, Ithaca College*

OAB-1179   BL238   93-36094 Orig
Kepel, Gilles. **The revenge of God: the resurgence of Islam, Christianity and Judaism in the modern world,** tr. by Alan Braley. Pennsylvania State, 1994. 215p index afp ISBN 0-271-01313-3, $35.00; ISBN 0-271-01314-1 pbk, $14.95

Translated into lapidary English from the original French, this book merits the label "pioneering." Its author is the first European scholar to examine the major revivalist movements in three Abrahamic traditions—Islam, Christianity (Catholic as well as Protestant), and Judaism. He rejects both *integrisme* and fundamentalism as useful comparative categories. Instead, he maps out the re-Islamization of Middle Eastern politics (principally Egypt and Iran), the re-Christianzation of not only North America but also Europe (Eastern as well as Western), and finally the re-Judaization of Israel. While the new terminology may limit large-scale comparison, the analysis is deft, the insights multiple and rewarding. Each movement is examined from below as well as from above, disclosing its social appeal, but also the limits of that appeal. No movement is seen as monolithic or even majoritarian, though radically different minority groups within the same tradition may "cooperate" towards a common end as the Gush Emunim and the ultra-orthodox Haredim appear to do in Israel. A splendidly researched and narratively engaging book recommended for all levels of readers.—*B. B. Lawrence, Duke University*

OAB-1180   BL625   91-33777 CIP
Kraemer, Ross Shepard. **Her share of the blessings: women's religions among Pagans, Jews, and Christians in the Greco-Roman world.** Oxford, 1992. 275p bibl index afp ISBN 0-19-506686-3, $24.95

Kraemer attempts to reconstruct women's religious experience in the ancient world by applying a modified version of the anthropologist Mary Douglas's "group/grid" model to the scattered bits of information we possess. In 13 chapters treating Greek, Roman, Jewish, and Christian women in antiquity, and women as religious leaders in each culture, Kramer surveys a wealth of both primary and secondary source material. Her syntheses and reconstructions are necessarily speculative, but she provides good grounds for defending her major contention, which is that women's religious experience in antiquity was a coherent and distinct social/psychological phenomenon, and that women's religious practices served both to reinforce traditional gender distinctions, and to offer alternative and even subversive opportunities for self-expression and self-definition. Kraemer applies the Douglas model creatively and judiciously, and brings to bear a prodigious amount of knowledge and scholarship in four separate fields. Hers is one of a very few books that discuss women and religion from a historical rather than a theological perspective, and the only such that treats women in the entire ancient Mediterranean world except for Egypt. This useful, informative, and enlightening compendium and analysis will be of interest to students and scholars alike, as well as to the general reader.—*M. A. Katz, Wesleyan University*

OAB-1181   BT985   94-14396 CIP
McGinn, Bernard. **Antichrist: two thousand years of the human fascination with evil.** Harper San Francisco, 1994. 369p index afp ISBN 0-06-065543-7, $35.00

McGinn (historical theology, Chicago) invites readers into a splendid historical survey of images of Antichrist in the Western religious traditions. From examination of notions of evil in Second Temple Judaism to references to the Antichrist in biblical texts, from views of Antichrist as internalized evil to mystical reality, from fundamentalist efforts to identify Antichrist with particular historical figures to popular literature and film in the 20th century, McGinn brings the most thorough and erudite research to this study. As a new millennium approaches, fascination with evil and the Antichrist will mushroom; McGinn's comprehensive examination and analysis of virtually every dimension of thinking about such phenomena will undergird contemporary millennial speculation. He deftly shows how positing Antichrist as a fundamental source of evil is necessary to human efforts to give meaning to existence. At the same time, McGinn writes with a grace and style that will appeal to the general reader. He carefully explains the meaning of technical theological terms so that laypersons are drawn into his story. This book should be in all collections. Its topic is timely, its scholarship impeccable, and its presentation masterful. General; undergraduate through professional.—*C. H. Lippy, University of Tennessee at Chattanooga*

OAB-1182   BL2490   93-3929 CIP
Murphy, Joseph M. **Working the spirit: ceremonies of the African diaspora.** Beacon Press, 1994. 263p bibl index ISBN 0-8070-1220-3, $25.00

Murphy has succeeded in producing a brilliant comparative study of the workings of the Spirit among the practitioners of African-derived religions in the Western hemisphere, including Haitian Vaudou, Brazilian Candomble, Cuban and Cuban American Santeria, Jamaican Revivalism, and African American Christianity. Relying on an ethnographic approach, he focuses on the observed effects and personal interpretations of the work of the Spirit(s) on human beings. By examining the symbolic actions of participants in ceremonies, Murphy has deftly avoided the theological controversies of the one or many Spirits and provided a deeper look at the influence of the African background of these religions in their dances, rituals, and worship experiences. Murphy chose these five African-derived, Spirit-based religions from his own field experiences with them. Each chapter includes new field material and ethnographic descriptions. Readers will be fascinated by the summaries of the personal experiences of several Americans including Katherine Dunham, Maya Deren, and Zora Neale Hurston in their encounters with the world of the Spirit. A major contribution and a "must read" for students of African, Caribbean, Brazilian, and African American religions. The book contains a glossary of terms from African-derived religions and a selected bibliography.—*L. H. Mamiya, Vassar College*

OAB-1183   BT82   92-32233 CIP
Riesebrodt, Martin. **Pious passion: the emergence of modern fundamentalism in the United States and Iran,** tr. by Don Reneau. California, 1993. 262p bibl index afp (Comparative studies in religion and society, 6) ISBN 0-520-07463-7, $40.00

Riesebrodt provides a brilliant second-order investigation of the two most familiar cases of modern fundamentalism. The first is drawn from the American Protestant protest against biblical criticism and evolutionism; its formative phase was 1910-28. The second recapitualtes the Iranian Shi'ite revolt against the moral laxity, anti-clericalism, and foreign collusion of the Pahlavi regime. Its formative phase was 1961-79. From the perspective of historical sociology, the author provides an in-depth comparison of the genesis of each movement. By discounting their temporal and cultural differences, he can trace

a structural symmetry that is at once elegant and complex. He attributes a very large role to religion in facilitating social mobilization: fundamentalist leaders succeeded largely because they crystalized, and then redirected, patriarchal protest not merely against the tenets of scriptural or ecclesisastical liberalism but also against modern notions of family, labor, and education. Despite sometimes technical language, the translation from the German is fluent, at once lucid and lapidary, making a pivotal study accessible and therefore highly recommended for all advanced undergraduates, graduate students, and faculty.—*B. B. Lawrence, Duke University*

OAB-1184   BL2015   93-28079 CIP
Veer, Peter van der. **Religious nationalism: Hindus and Muslims in India.** California, 1994. 247p bibl index afp ISBN 0-520-08220-6, $40.00; ISBN 0-520-08256-7 pbk, $14.00

A masterful essay in which recent events in India serve as a basis for a much wider ranging inquiry into ways that religious discourse and ritual practice continue to constitute (or construct) social identities in the late 20th century. It builds on years of field research and reflection as well as on several earlier works by this estimable author, most notably his *Gods on Earth* (London, 1988), a study of the Ayodhya pilgrimage center, and *Orientalism and the Post-Colonial Predicament* (1993), which he coedited with Carol A. Breckenridge. In six thematic chapters (religious nationalism, religious formations, ritual communication, peregrinations, conceptions of time, and words and gestures) he offers arguments, interpretive proposals, and conceptual resources for a better understanding of highly publicized dilemmas, such as the ongoing mosque-temple dispute in Ayodhya and the threat hanging over Salman Rushdie for writing *The Satanic Verses*, and more generally for thinking about the roles of religion and politics in forming human identities in late modernity. He augments and corrects attempts by the previous generation of scholars to assess the same issues—e.g., Harold R. Isaacs, *Idols of the Tribe* (CH, Nov'75) and G.R. Thursby, *Hindu-Muslim Relations in British India* (Leiden, 1975). Highest recommendation.—*G. R. Thursby, University of Florida*

■ Buddhism & Hinduism

OAB-1185   BQ5125   96-35056 CIP
Brauen, Martin. **The mandala: sacred circle in Tibetan Buddhism,** tr. by Martin Willson; photographs by Peter Nebel and Doro Röthlisberger. Shambhala, 1997. 151p bibl index ISBN 1-57062-296-5, $45.00

Where such earlier works as Giuseppe Tucci's *The Theory and Practice of the Mandala* (London, 1961) and José and Miriam Argüelles's *Mandala* (CH, May'73) attempt to be universal in their treatment of mandalas, Brauen, of the Ethnographic Museum of the University of Zurich, concentrates more narrowly on a single mandala ritual, the Tibetan Buddhist Kālacakra Mandala ritual. TheKālacakra Mandala is analyzed in its simple diagrammatic form, as well as in the more elaborate patterns of cloth and sand paintings, and three-dimensional castings and structures. Brauen describes the different types of mandalas and their ritual use, explaining the underlying aspects of the Buddhist path in the process. The text is clear and detailed. What makes this work such a treasure, however, is the wealth of diagrams, charts, black-and-white photographs and, especially, gorgeous color plates depicting the mandalas and the ritual itself. Further visual clarification of the mandalas is provided by unique computerized, three-dimensional modelings. Specialists and devotees alike will find much of value, while the neophyte will learn a great deal simply by looking at the plates. This book is a real pleasure. Highly recommended. General; undergraduate through professional.—*J. P. McDermott, Canisius College*

OAB-1186   BL1351   92-237 CIP
Dundas, Paul. **The Jains.** Routledge, 1992. 276p bibl indexes ISBN 0-415-05183-5, $82.50; ISBN 0-415-05184-3 pbk, $19.95

Marking a new level of accomplishment in study of the Jains, this book introduces, surveys, and summarizes international scholarship on a religious tradition that originated in India and today has six million followers there. Jainism is similar to Buddhism but did not expand beyond India in the same way. Dundas offers lively and wise interpretations, descriptive detail, and apt references. He skillfully relates ancient texts to history and contemporary religious concerns. His book awakens curiosity about seemingly esoteric and enigmatic topics, then develops it into appreciation of their significance in relation to more familiar areas of knowledge. The most useful single work on the subject written in English to date, it is recommended to orient the beginner to study of the Jains, and as a reliable handbook for the advanced student and specialist. It would be complemented by E. Fischer and J. Jain's two-volume *Jaina Iconography* (Leiden, 1978), *The Assembly of Listeners: Jains in Society*, ed. by M. Carrithers and C. Humphrey (CH, Apr'92), and P. Jaini's *Gender and Salvation* (1991).—*G. R. Thursby, University of Florida*

OAB-1187   Orig
Fowler, Jeaneane. **Hinduism: beliefs and practices.** Sussex Academic, 1997.<avl> (Dist. by International Specialized Book Services) 162p bibl index afp ISBN 1-898723-60-5 pbk, $19.95

Beginning study of Hinduism is likely to generate perplexities and puzzlements on a scale greater than those generated by studies of most religions. Recent books, in fact, question whether the term "Hinduism" refers to a single religion, several, or none in the sense of "religion" that is familiar to Jews, Christians, or Muslims. Fowler addresses the problem in the first few pages, then develops a clearly stated model of Hinduism that she builds up on the basis of a judicious selection of key terms, dividing the book into two main parts—"The Hindu Way of Life" and "History and Tradition." Although hers is a particular reading or construction, it is a quite plausible one of what it can mean to be Hindu. In fact, no other strategy is likely to work as a way to enlist beginners in the study and appreciation of the various Hinduisms that have coexisted, for the most part peacefully, in India and, nowadays, overseas. Written mainly for British students, Fowler's book compares well to those prepared for North American students—e.g., David R. Kinsley's *Hinduism: A Cultural Perspective* (CH, Feb'82) and David M. Knipe's *Hinduism* (1991). It would prepare students to understand C.J. Fuller's more difficult and detailed anthropological study *The Camphor Flame* (CH, Dec'92), and to undertake exploration of some of the rather dense but important analyses of modern Hinduism and politics, such as Peter van der Veer's *Religious Nationalism* (CH, Jul'94) or Gerald James Larson's *India's Agony over Religion* (CH, Jun'95). In short, a commendable contribution to an excellent series of basic studies. Undergraduate; graduate.—*G. R. Thursby, University of Florida*

OAB-1188   BQ4570   92-9133 CIP
Gross, Rita M. **Buddhism after patriarchy: a feminist history, analysis, and reconstruction of Buddhism.** State University of New York, 1993. 365p bibl index ISBN 0-7914-1403-5, $44.50; ISBN 0-7914-1404-3 pbk, $14.95

Gross gives a feminist "revalorization" of Buddhism. Noting that the Buddhist treatment of women is problematic, but not irreparably so, the author provides what in many ways is a manual for rethinking Buddhism from a feminist perspective. Her concern is to work through a fourfold layering of androcentrism (creation of the canon, use of the canon, Western scholarship on the canon, and contemporary Buddhism itself) to find an "accurate and usable past." Gotama's reluctance to allow women to go forth, for example, must be placed within the context of the times, more serious consideration should be given to the *Therigatha*, the many Mahayana methods for dealing with liabilities against women (e.g., avoiding female rebirth, magical sex changes, gender-inclusive language) need to be rethought, and stories of Vajrayana *yoginis* like Yeshe Tsogyel need to be given due place. Moreover, because "the dharma is neither male nor female," key concepts in Buddhism that highlight its intersection with feminism (e.g., the ethics of nonviolence and the Bodhisattva path) need to be reemphasized. Gross then calls upon the modern Buddhist community to mandate and institutionalize gender equality through an androgynous vision that

would take seriously, for example, issues of child care among laywomen and greater economic support for orders of nuns. A significant book deserving a prominent place in every collection of Buddhist hermeneutics.—*E. Findly, Trinity College (CT)*

OAB-1189   BL2001   93-12492 CIP
Hardy, Friedhelm. **The religious culture of India: power, love and wisdom.** Cambridge, 1994. 613p index (Cambridge studies in religious traditions, 4) ISBN 0-521-44181-1, $74.95

Most books on the religions of India are either too facile or overburdened with Sanskrit jargon. This one is a welcome exception. Rarely has there been such a comprehensive and thoroughly scholarly volume on the religions of India. Hardy has managed to bring together an excellent and much-needed synthesis that provides insights at multiple layers of Indian religion and culture. This volume has been arranged around the themes of power, love, and wisdom. A thematic approach like this helps to reveal underlying threads that run through the whole fabric of Indian civilization. Hardy employs a unified and comprehensive methodology that includes both textual and contextual views of the South Asian cultural traditions. Particularly valuable are the many references to Jainism, Sikhism, Buddhism, and Islamic dimensions of Indian civilization. Frequently religion in the subcontinent is too heavily oriented around Hinduism alone. This volume is brilliantly written and deeply conceived. Not since Richard Lannoy's *The Speaking Tree* (CH, Mar'72) has there been such an accessible source for understanding the religions of India. It is highly recommended for both the general educated reader and advanced students of Indology. Undergraduate; graduate; faculty.—*J. J. Preston, SUNY College at Oneonta*

OAB-1190   BQ7981   95-30452 CIP
Kvaerne, Per. **The Bon religion of Tibet: the iconography of a living tradition.** Shambhala, 1995. 155p bibl index ISBN 1-57062-186-1, $55.00

The Bon religion is Tibet's other major tradition, tracing its origins back to the period before the introduction of Buddhism in the seventh century. It nonetheless shares many affinities with Tibetan Buddhism, as is evidenced by this beautifully produced work on Bon art. Kvaerne (Univ. of Oslo) is the leading Western scholar of Bon, and this volume brings together the results of the best and most up-to-date research on Bon, dispelling many myths and misconceptions by outlining the history, doctrines, ritual practices, and institutions of Bon. The major part of the book is devoted to the description of the major genres of Bon art, where many of the styles will be familiar to students of Tibetan Buddhist art, although the pantheon is quite different. The paintings, miniatures, and bronzes (dating from the 14th to the present century), beautifully reproduced in 60 color plates, are described in detail, with the deities (both peaceful and wrathful) and historical figures identified and contextualized. In many cases, prayers and invocations to the deities are provided in translation. This book is required reading for anyone interested in Asian art or religion. Undergraduate; graduate; faculty; general.—*D. S. Lopez Jr., University of Michigan*

OAB-1191   BL1325   95-20277 CIP
Laidlaw, James. **Riches and renunciation: religion, economy, and society among the Jains.** Oxford, 1996 (c1995). 436p bibl index afp ISBN 0-19-828031-9, $89.00; ISBN 0-19-828042-4 pbk, $29.95

This superb account of a contemporary urban community in India offers a well-conceived and clearly written description of "lived-reality" among people who follow what is arguably the least understood of the great religions. Jainism dates to the time of the Buddha or before; but, unlike Buddhism, it was prevented by its closely regulated lifestyle from spreading very far beyond India. It flourished more locally, largely because of support from industrious lay followers who attained notable worldly success in India—and, more recently, in other countries, too. The book, based on a study conducted at intervals over a seven-year period in the desert city of Jaipur, succeeds in resolving a seeming paradox: how one of the most austere of the world's religions continues to provide a major component of the social and personal identity of members of a prosperous business and professional community. A distinctive feature of the book is its discerning use of the work of Foucault to develop notions of "moral topographies" and "embodied ontologies" in ways that freshly illumine Jain reality. In short, this study is historically and culturally well grounded, replete with comparative insights, and above all very enjoyable to read. Laidlow's work is another indicator that Jain studies have been undergoing a remarkable development in recent years, and it richly complements even the best textbook treatments of the subject, such as *The Jains*, by Paul Dundas (CH, Apr'93). Photos; diagrams; glossary. Undergraduate through professional.—*G. R. Thursby, University of Florida*

OAB-1192   BQ7464   94-953 CIP
Liu, Ming-Wood. **Madhyamaka thought in China.** E.J. Brill, 1994. 288p bibl index afp (Sinica Leidensia, 30) ISBN 90-04-09984-0, $100.00

This is an exceptionally fine work of scholarship in the history of ideas. Liu (philosophy, Univ. of Hong Kong) has written a masterly study of Chinese Madhyamaka comparable, in authoritative presentation, to Richard H. Robinson's *Early Madhyamika in India and China* (1967), but supplementing the latter work with more attention to Chi-tsang. The Liu volume's strengths are clarity of exposition, crispness of definitions, and rigor of critical thought. Schemas and distinctions are set forth clearly in exposition, and the principal ones appear in charts throughout the volume. The author works his material from all angles, as is evident throughout and in the fine bibliography of Chinese, Japanese, and Western sources. There is a helpful list of Chinese and Japanese words (in both Chinese characters and romanization) and a detailed index. The volume contains very few typographical errors, but this reviewer did notice some (e.g., "we weeps" instead of "he weeps" and "Suartra" instead of "Sutra"). The volume is expensive but worth every penny. Most highly recommended for all libraries with holdings on Asian thought. Upper-division undergraduate; graduate; faculty.—*F. J. Hoffman, West Chester University of Pennsylvania*

OAB-1193   BQ1312   94-37636 Orig
The Middle length discourses of the Buddha: a new translation of the Majjhima Nikāya, orig. translation by Bhikkhu Ñāṇamoli; translation ed. and rev. by Bhikkhu Bodhi. Wisdom, MA, 1995. 1,412p bibl indexes afp ISBN 0-86171-072-X, $75.00

This new translation of the Majjhima Nikāya from the Pali, produced in association with the Barre Center for Buddhist Studies, joins the preeminent older translation done by I.B. Horner for the Pali Text Society in 1954, 1957, and 1959. Much of the work for the new translation was done by Bhikkhu Ñāṇamoli before his untimely death, and then extensively revised by Bhikkhu Bodhi. The "Middle Length Discourses" of the Pali canon are some of the oldest texts of Theravāda Buddhism; thus they are part of an invaluable record of early Buddhist thought and culture. Included in this collection are *suttas* dealing with central aspects of the Buddhist Dhammma (e.g., on *dukkha* "suffering" and on *suññata* "voidness"), *suttas* outlining important aspects of Buddhist practice (e.g., the *Satipatthāna Sutta* on foundations of mindfulness), and *suttas* delivered to various groups of renunciants and householders, including "advice" given to major donor/supporters of the Saṅgha, such as Anāthapindika. The text of the translation is eminently readable, often more so than in Horner's version, and is correlated by page number to the Pali Text Society's roman-script edition of the Majjhima Nikāya. The volume includes a good introduction with helpful discussions of a number of key terms, a brief summary of each of the 152 *suttas*, and explanatory notes at the end. An indispensable addition to any collection on Buddhist studies. Upper-division undergraduate; graduate; faculty.—*E. Findly, Trinity College (CT)*

OAB-1194   BL2017   94-13624 CIP
Oberoi, Harjot. **The construction of religious boundaries: culture, identity, and diversity in the Sikh tradition.** Chicago, 1994. 494p bibl index afp ISBN 0-226-61592-8, $49.95; ISBN 0-226-61593-6 pbk, $17.95

This is the most important reconsideration of the received history of India's Sikhs since W.H. McLeod's *The Evolution of the Sikh Community* (CH, Nov'76). In Oberoi's model, four major constituencies in recent Sikh tradition take their proper place: the Khalsa, established in the 18th century and made up of initiates who followed their own set of regulations; the followers of a more inclusive or Sanatan form of Sikh religious life who were primarily drawn from a social elite; the participants in folk or popular religion, for whom boundary lines between "Sikh" and other traditions were particularly blurred or irrelevant; and the still-powerful 19th-century Tat Khalsa orientation that provided the rationale for a separate Sikh religion based on newly developed rituals and an elaboration of the institutions of the older Khalsa order. Oberoi's work effectively corrects interpretations that give too much credit to the British colonial bureaucracy for "reviving" Sikh practice, such as in Richard G. Fox's *Lions of the Punjab* (1985), and to those that presume that current descendants of the Tat Khalsa determine "orthodoxy" in Sikh tradition, such as G.R. Thursby's *The Sikhs* (1992). Oberoi writes well and argues convincingly. His book will yield the added benefit of making W.H. McLeod's excellent but brief *Who Is a Sikh?* (CH, Feb'90) understandable to a wider range of readers. Glossary, maps, and tables. General; undergraduate through professional.—*G. R. Thursby, University of Florida*

OAB-1195   BL1237   95-39811 CIP
Pearson, Anne Mackenzie. **"Because it gives me peace of mind": ritual fasts in the religious lives of Hindu women.** State University of New York, 1996. 315p bibl index afp ISBN 0-7914-3037-5, $68.50

This welcome new book examines a tradition of women's domestic rituals in South Asia known as *vratas*. Drawing on classical practices as described in the Sanskrit *Dharmaśāstras*, Pearson details the relation of contemporary *vratas* or *vrats* to older expressions of the Hindu tradition, to the seasonal and festival life of the calendar, and to the life cycle stages of Hindu women as played out in communities of the north Indian city of Banaras. As rituals normally of and by women, *vratas* have as their beneficiaries all the members of the household, and the performance of these votive fasting rites are, in part, a way of meeting the obligations of women as wives, their *strīdharma*. As the author shows, however, knowledge of how to perform the rites is passed on by the women of each generation and their practice functions in important ways to bind women together as they pursue not only blessings for family members but also profound spiritual ends. The practice of *vratas* differ in each locality, but Pearson's discussion, based on extensive interviews, observations of domestic and public practice, and textual support from several periods highlights common thematic elements and shows that, indeed, the true beneficiaries are the women themselves. This contribution is a "must" for all undergraduates, graduates, and faculty.—*E. Findly, Trinity College (CT)*

OAB-1196   BQ8749   91-43551 CIP
Rogers, Minor. **Rennyo: the second founder of Shin Buddhism: with a translation of his letters,** by Minor and Ann Rogers. Asian Humanities, 1992 (c1991). 434p bibl index (Nanzan studies in Asian religions, 3) ISBN 0-89581-929-5, $75.00; ISBN 0-89581-930-9 pbk, $25.00

Two hundred years after Shinran founded the Jodo Shinshu, Rennyo (1415-99) led the Shinshu to new heights of influence and power. Of the many studies of Rennyo in English, none is as comprehensive as this joint work. Using sources in both Japanese and Western languages, the Rogers's study elucidates the nuances of important Japanese concepts used by Shinran and Rennyo, especially the relation between Shinran's faith (*shinjin*) and Rennyo's settled mind (*anjin*). A lengthy introduction surveys contemporary academic studies of Rennyo. The main three-part study begins with careful documentation of Rennyo's life, portraying him as a charismatic preacher and a determined administrator of Honganji. Part 2 is Ann Rogers's meticulous translation of Rennyo's letters into clear, understandable English that surpasses all earlier translations. Although filled with precise analysis of Japanese terms, these technical details do not interrupt the flow of the translation. Finally, the third part traces the history of Honganji after Rennyo. Copious footnotes and a large bibliography provide plenty of resources for further study. This research wil be the standard source on Rennyo for years to come.—*W. M. Smith, Marietta College*

OAB-1197 BL1280 96-29425 CIP
Sil, Narasingha P. **Swami Vivekananda: a reassessment.**
Susquehanna, 1997.<avl> (Dist. by Associated University Presses) 250p
bibl index afp ISBN 0-945636-97-0, $41.50

Sil (Western Oregon State College) provides a critical reassessment of the
life, career, and reputation of a figure who is nearly as central to the formation of
modern India as Mohandas K. Gandhi. The author is from Bengal and has a PhD
in history; thus he is well qualified for this kind of study. His subject is Bengal native Narendranath Datta (1863-1902), who became internationally known
as Swami Vivekananda in consequence of a lecture tour of the US following
his highly successful speech at the 1893 World's Parliament of Religions. Sil
reviews the extensive textual record, compares Bengali originals with English
translations, and offers a more accurate interpretation of the human strengths and
weaknesses of Vivekananda than previously has been available. He has performed a real service in retrieving the human complexity of Vivekananda from
hagiographical traditions that have obscured both his frailties and his genius. Sil
makes a convincing case that Vivekananda was a "worldly monk" who achieved
a "conquest of the West" and thereby gained a special quality of fame in his
own homeland. As a work of retrieval, this book belongs on a shelf with Jeffrey Kipal's *Kali's Child* (CH, Jan'96), which is a remarkable reinterpretation of
Vivekananda's master, Shri Ramakrishna. Sil's work also benefits from comparison with more conservative and laudatory treatments of Vivekananda, e.g.,
Tapan Raychaudhuri's *Europe Reconsidered: Perceptions of the West in Nineteenth Century Bengal* (1988). Photographs, glossary, notes. Undergraduate;
graduate; faculty.—*G. R. Thursby, University of Florida*

■ Christianity

OAB-1198 BT832 93-40008 CIP
Almond, Philip C. **Heaven and hell in Enlightenment England.**
Cambridge, 1994. 218p bibl index ISBN 0-521-45371-2, $49.95

Almond (Univ. of Queensland) has followed a succession of fine works in
world religions with this elegant historical presentation of Christian eschatology of the English Enlightenment. Meticulously researched, the book successfully weaves a remarkable mélange of views on the journey of the human
body/soul/person complex into a coherent and highly readable narrative. Almond
adopts the plan of Daniel Pickering Walker's *The Decline of Hell* (London, 1964)
to construct his own map of the soul's journey from its creation at the world's
beginning to its final destiny, and, in between, to describe views on the soul's
"life" between death and reunion with the body on the last day; the contours of
heaven and hell; and the last day and resurrection of the body as influenced by
"the new science." On the way, one traverses an unusual and sometimes bizarre
perceptual landscape of particular interest to cultural historians, philosophers
of history, and historical theologians. This work is particularly valuable for its
wealth of quotation from primary sources and its attempt (though all too occasional) to connect the views described with their social contexts. When Almond
does advert to social context, one learns a great deal about how theological or
philosophical images arise from, and so illuminate, their social matrix. One sees,
e.g., how images of eternal retribution developed in tandem with England's penal
system and how fantastical descriptions of suffering in the hereafter paralleled
current social conditions. A carefully edited, well-bound book containing striking illustrations. End notes. Warmly recommended. Upper-division undergraduate; graduate; faculty.—*D. G. Schultenover, Creighton University*

OAB-1199 BV4639 95-12866 CIP
Arendt, Hannah. **Love and Saint Augustine,** ed. and with an inter-
pretive essay by Joanna Vecchiarelli Scott and Judith Chelius Stark.
Chicago, 1996. 233p bibl index afp ISBN 0-226-02596-9, $22.50

Scott and Stark's publication of the corrected and revised English translation of Arendt's 1929 Heidelberg dissertation, *Der Liebesbegriff bei Augustin*,
is a scrupulous scholarly accomplishment. The editors show how Arendt

revised both the manuscript and its themes after her departure from Germany in
1933, and how the English translation was prepared in the early 1960s when
Arendt had contracted for publication of the work. Thus, the Augustinian
influence on Arendt's major works, including *Origins of Totalitarianism, On
Revolution*, and *Eichmann in Jerusalem*, is brought into focus by the publication of her dissertation and the accompanying interpretive text. As a work on
Augustine, however, the dissertation is dense, and, as the editors point out,
"the dissertation is far more revelatory about Arendt herself than it is as a
piece of scholarship on Augustine of Hippo." This is no small achievement,
though, since the guiding theme of the dissertation—the meaning and importance of *caritas*, or neighborly love—is central to Arendt's later work, and the
dissertation reveals new dimensions of her use of the concept. The editors'
admirably clear, extensive interpretive essay helps situate the dissertation
within Arendt's thought and life, with special attention to Arendt and Martin
Heidegger, and to Arendt and Karl Jaspers. Recommended for upper-division
undergraduates and graduate students.—*J. H. Barker, Albright College*

OAB-1200 Can. CIP
Bowen, Kurt. **Evangelism and apostasy: the evolution and impact
of Evangelicals in modern Mexico.** McGill-Queen's, 1996. 270p bibl
index afp ISBN 0-7735-1379-5, $39.95

Bowen (sociology, Acadia University, Canada) offers an instructive analysis of the progress and potential of Evangelical, particularly Pentecostal,
development in Mexico. He bases his work on sample surveys he conducted
of pastors and members, and on participant observation, between 1987 and 1993.
His work solidly builds on the literature in the field and related areas of research,
making for an especially valuable contribution. The book is well written,
carefully examining, in a well-organized fashion, virtually every major theory
or commonly held view regarding Evangelicals in Latin America. The general conclusion is that apostasy, or the falling away of once-committed converts,
has a dramatic effect on the long-term prospects of Evangelical Christianity
in Mexico and, by extension, in all of Latin America. "If the experience of Mexican Evangelicals is our guide, then the prospects of Latin America's turning
Protestant are slim and remote." The Evangelical community, vibrant as it is,
has an "inability to retain the many new members it has attracted." Bowen's
work will stimulate much debate and be of great interest to graduate students,
faculty, and researchers concerned with issues of religion and social change
in Latin America, but it could be read with great profit by scholars of religion
(particularly Evangelical or Pentecostal Christianity) in the US or other contexts.
General readers will find the style inviting. The book is likely to quickly
become one of the great classics in the field. Highest possible recommendation.—*B. T. Froehle, Georgetown University*

OAB-1201 BX8643 93-37366 CIP
Brooke, John L. **The refiner's fire: the making of Mormon cosmology, 1644-1844.** Cambridge, 1994. 421p bibl index ISBN 0-521-
34545-6, $34.95

In this provocative, intelligent, and well-researched book, Brooke argues
that Mormon cosmology derives from hermetic, millennial, and restorationist
themes originating in the Anabaptist Reformation, redefined by the sects of
the Puritan revolution, and preserved in Pennsylvania and the fringes of New
England. In a tour de force Brooke uses genealogies, town records, church
archives, and histories of counterfeiting to prove that there was a predisposition
to radical sectarian and hermetic ideas and practices in the families and villages that furnished many of the early converts of Joseph Smith. Mormonism
now becomes not just a reaction to social dislocation in the Burned Over District, but a creative response to an ancient religious heritage. Joseph Smith
espoused and redefined Freemasonry, Swedenborgianism, magic, alchemy, celestial marriage, deification of humanity, and mutuality of spirit and matter.
Brooke demonstrates that so-called popular religion is also intellectual history. The second half of the book shows the impact of the hermetic tradition
in the evolution of Joseph Smith's thought. In Kirtland, Ohio, and in Nau-
voo, Illinois, Smith changed fundamental tenets of the *Book of Mormon* in
creating a theocratic and revolutionary faith. In Utah, Brigham Young and

his successors toned down and then repudiated much of Smith's hermetic legacy. A "must" for all serious students of early American religion and Mormonism, highly recommended for upper-division undergraduates, graduate students, and faculty.—*J. W. Frost, Swarthmore College*

OAB-1202　　　　BS2665　　　　96-4727 CIP
Brooten, Bernadette J. **Love between women: early Christian responses to female homoeroticism.** Chicago, 1996. 412p bibl indexes afp ISBN 0-226-07591-5, $34.95

Through detailed analyses of magical spells, gynecological treatises, artistic representations, astrological castings, dream interpretations, and biblical, rabbinic, and patristic texts, Brooten (Brandeis Univ.) demonstrates widespread awareness in antiquity of love between women. The volume's insights are numerous, original, and frequently striking in their logic; these include critiques of Boswell, Foucault, and others; corrections to previously published translations of primary sources as well as original translations of others; elaborations on natural theology and impurity; and a verse-by-verse commentary on Romans 1:18-32. Situating her data within the conceptualizations of sexual relations in Hellenistic and Roman culture, Brooten concludes that violations of strict social distinctions between active and passive in female homoeroticism led to its condemnation as unnatural, licentious, lawless, and sick. Explicitly written both to provide a basis for interpreting Pauline teachings on homoeroticism and to bring "that interpretation into church and public policy debates about lesbians, gay men, and bisexuals," the volume is indispensable for anyone who values historically rigorous, intellectually honest debate on these issues. Very highly recommended. Upper-division undergraduate; graduate; faculty.—*A.-J. Levine, Vanderbilt University*

OAB-1203　　　　BV648　　　　91-36390 CIP
Burtchaell, James Tunstead. **From synagogue to church: public services and offices in the earliest Christian communities.** Cambridge, 1992. 375p indexes ISBN 0-521-41892-5, $59.95

It has been common—and all too popular—in NT and Patristic studies to assume that early Christianity underwent a process of evolution from a highly charismatic sect (Jesus and his earliest followers) to a structured organization (the Pastoral letters and the church of the second and third centuries). In this thoroughly researched and carefully argued volume, Burtchaell challenges the majority opinion. He does so by exhaustively tracing, in Chapters 1-4, the development of the received tradition from the Reformation forward. Chapter 5 turns the corner and offers a new hypothesis: that the pattern for offices in early Christianity was provided by the synagogue structure of a president, elders, and assistants; that the offices were filled from the earliest days and coexisted with gifted pneumatics, who were the earliest and most influential leaders of the church; and that only later did the officers become the authority for the church. Burtchaell documents this thesis in Chapters 6-8 before drawing some conclusions. This work is important for several reasons: it summarizes the positions of some 40 different church historians, theologians, and New Testament scholars on the origin and shape of early church offices; it offers a fresh, carefully nuanced revision of an often unexamined assumption; and it models the task of historical research. An appropriate resource in an advanced undergraduate course or as a text in graduate seminar; a must for all graduate work in the area of early church history.—*C. C. Newman, Palm Beach Atlantic College*

OAB-1204　　　　BT872　　　　94-17299 CIP
Bynum, Caroline Walker. **The resurrection of the body in western Christianity, 200-1336.** Columbia, 1995. 368p indexes afp (Lectures on the history of religions, new series, 15) ISBN 0-231-08126-X, $29.95

Bynum's new book is an enormous undertaking, which crosses almost every aspect of life in the Middle Ages for more than 1,000 years. In the past, scholars have almost exclusively concentrated on the fate of the soul at death, ignoring the physical body and its fate at resurrection. Thus Bynum provides

a long-neglected chapter in the intellectual history of medieval Europe and the Christian faith. The author amasses an impressive array of primary sources, which she proceeds to interpret by the language of the ancient writers themselves, letting the text follow its own metaphorical connections rather than imposing modern constructs of what those connections might be. What Bynum concludes is that physical resurrection of the body was a central belief throughout the time period studied regardless of attempts by prominent theologians to spiritualize the process. This book should be on the shelf of every university and public library as well as in the collection of all intellectual historians and students of Christian history. Upper-division undergraduate; graduate; faculty; general.—*D. C. West Jr., Northern Arizona University*

OAB-1205　　　　BR520　　　　94-12292 CIP
Conkin, Paul K. **The uneasy center: reformed Christianity in antebellum America.** North Carolina, 1995. 326p index afp ISBN 0-8078-2180-2, $39.95; ISBN 0-8078-4492-6 pbk, $16.95

Vanderbilt intellectual historian Conkin, author of *Puritans and Pragmatists* (CH, Sep'69) and *Cane Ridge* (CH, Sep'91), here examines central developments in American Protestantism to 1865. Conkin's usual splendid organization and narrative strength are apparent in this broad synthesis. He analyzes American theologians by focusing on differences in their understandings of salvation. His expositions of Samuel Hopkins, Nathaniel Taylor, Charles Hodge, and Horace Bushnell are particularly illuminating. His discussion of worship practices helps redress one of the most seriously neglected aspects of Protestant history. The author gives the reader a clear impression of variety in American denominationalism and of the relative significance of each group. His use of "Reformed" is unconventional—going beyond "Calvinist" to include Arminian Episcopalians and Methodists, while excluding Lutherans. His story thereby includes all of the major Protestant players—such as Congregationalists and Presbyterians—who excelled in higher education, benevolence, and serious theology and also the Methodists, who attracted the largest following. As a historian of ideas, Conkin has a superb grasp of the impact of both critical Biblical scholarship and geology, discoveries that precipitated crises for Protestantism. He is attentive to regional, gender, and especially racial dimensions of the story. Highly recommended. Undergraduate; general.—*W. L. Pitts Jr., Baylor University*

OAB-1206　　　　BV4490　　　　94-8854 CIP
Constable, Giles. **Three studies in medieval religious and social thought: The interpretation of Mary and Martha; The ideal of the imitation of Christ; The orders of society.** Cambridge, 1995. 423p bibl indexes ISBN 0-521-30515-2, $59.95

Constable's "three studies" constitute a far more organic and integrated book than the modest title implies. The subjects of these studies have several important things in common: each is a theme that attracted interpretation, discussion, and teaching from very early origins (two, and possibly three, of them biblical) until well into the modern period; each underwent a turning point in interpretation and relevance during the 12th century; each found visual as well as textual representation (amply and intelligently discussed here); each contributed genuinely and profoundly to social and political as well as religious thought. This book is an elegant complement to Constable's forthcoming book on the Reformation in the 12th century, a central time in the the history of these topics, which were some of the keys to the 12th century. But Constable's coverage of them ranges far beyond that century, back to early scriptural exegesis and forward to the 18th century. The book also casts important light on the active and contemplative lives, the individual Christian's appropriate behavior in the light of Christ's life, and the changing structures of medieval society, as does the rest of the rich recent literature on these topics—the work of Chenu, Baldwin, Duby, and others. The appendix really constitutes a fourth study, more specific to the Middle Ages but no less informative and provocative than the other three. The author's learning and eloquence are expected—but the topics and their treatment are original, fresh, and valuable. Upper-division undergraduate; graduate; faculty; general.—*E. Peters, University of Pennsylvania*

OAB-1207 BR560 91-39181 CIP

Demerath, N.J. **A bridging of faiths: religion and politics in a New England city,** by N.J. Demerath and Rhys H. Williams. Princeton, 1992. 358p bibl index afp ISBN 0-691-07413-5, $29.95

Using a wide range of methods, Demerath and Williams analyze the changing social organization of Springfield, Massachusetts, over a 300-year period. Their particular focus is on the decline in prominence and power of the Congregational Church and the rise of the Catholic Church after WW II as the major religious force in Springfield. The core of the book is an examination of the influence of religious institutions on the political process and the civic culture of Springfield. Although most citizens subscribe to the doctrine of separation of church and state, Demerath and Williams demonstrate that a much closer relationship exists than the formal governmental structure suggests. Perhaps more important, they reveal that Springfield residents consider this relationship appropriate. The authors use three case studies to examine in detail the dynamics of the relationship between church and state. Demerath and Williams are obviously familiar with the Springfield community study and other relevant literature, but they are sparing with footnotes and references, which contributes to the enjoyment of reading their book. This work belongs in the grand tradition of community studies and should be included in any collection on contemporary urban social organization. General, undergraduate; graduate; faculty.—*J. R. Hudson, Pennsylvania State University, Harrisburg*

OAB-1208 BX6065 93-2305 CIP

Guelzo, Allen C. **For the union of Evangelical Christendom: the irony of the Reformed Episcopalians.** Pennsylvania State, 1994. 404p bibl index afp ISBN 0-271-01002-9, $45.00

"Few Episcopalians," writes Guelzo, "and fewer Americans today are seriously troubled with much knowledge of the Reformed Episcopal Church." The author here proceeds to remedy this ignorance in a highly persuasive manner. This study of the one long-lasting schism in American Episcopalianism is elegantly written, is based on extensive original scholarship, and ably sets the issues in social, intellectual, and cultural context. Guelzo also puts extensive photographs to good use. In addition to discussing thoroughly the personalities and issues involved that led radical Evangelicals to break from the main body of the Episcopal Church, this work also brings to light the attraction of the Reformed Episcopal Church for African Americans otherwise denied Anglican ordination in the US. The author tends to exaggerate both the importance of his subject and the domination of the Episcopal Church by the Reformed Episcopalians' opponents, the Anglo-Catholics, and he grinds a few theological axes as well. On the whole, though, this is a highly impressive piece of scholarship that belongs in every serious collection of American religious history. Upper-division undergraduate; graduate; faculty.—*P. W. Williams, Miami University (OH)*

OAB-1209 BX2347 95-5122 CIP

Guider, Margaret Eletta. **Daughters of Rahab: prostitution and the church of liberation in Brazil.** Fortress, 1995. 235p index afp (Harvard theological studies, 40) ISBN 0-8006-7093-0 pbk, $16.00

Guider has made an important contribution to the documentation and analysis of current issues in the Catholic Church, particularly the portion of the Latin American church committed to Liberation Theology. Using outreach to prostitutes in Brazil as her case study, she marshals an array of materials and well-considered analysis to demonstrate not only a theological reflection on the issue but also social analysis of the changing role of the church. Her analysis of the church and changing times covers the period of official pastoral outreach to marginalized women (prostitutes) and shows an appreciation of broader historical developments. Thus, the reader is treated to a helpful synthesis of Brazilian church developments over the centuries and provided with the kind of contextual understanding necessary for a holistic approach to the church of liberation. Few other issues are so potent at revealing current conflicts and undercurrents within church debates and developments, and the author's work will therefore serve many audiences. The book contains an impressive and valuable documentation of the issue but is written in an approachable, scholarly tone. Suited for many levels of read-

ers, from general and lower-division undergraduate to faculty and researchers. Recommended to all who seek to understand the Catholic Church in Latin America over the past two decades, particularly those interested in women's issues within the church—*B. T. Froehle, Georgetown University*

OAB-1210 BR1360 94-5677 CIP

Hastings, Adrian. **The Church in Africa, 1450-1950.** Oxford, 1995 (c1994). 706p bibl index afp ISBN 0-19-826921-8, $110.00

In this first major study of the historical development of the Christian Church in the whole continent of Africa, Hastings (Univ. of Leeds) has produced a classic and masterful work. Bringing together the historical traditions of Ethiopian Orthodoxy, Roman Catholicism, Protestantism, and a variety of Africanized independent church movements, he focuses sensitively on the role of conversion, the development of church life and its relationship to traditional African religious values, and the impact of political power. Although the book concentrates on the 500 years of the European colonial period in Africa from 1450 until 1950, Hastings correctly begins his study with the development of Coptic Christianity in Egypt during the third century and the rise of the Ethiopian Orthodox Church. He counters the past scholarly attempts to divorce Egypt from Africa by showing the significant influence of the great Alexandrian theologians such as Athanasius, Cyril, and Augustine upon the doctrines and history of Christianity. Moving from region to region across the vast continent and including the work of former African American slaves in Liberia and Sierra Leone, Hastings has produced a balanced account of the positive and negative roles of Christian missionary activity and their political and economic linkages to colonial political power. His historical assessments of the role of Islam in Africa constitute a major contribution. Appendix of historical maps, extensive bibliography. Highly recommended for scholars and advanced graduate students. A major library resource on Africa and the history of Christianity.—*L. H. Mamiya, Vassar College*

OAB-1211 BX6447 92-19345 CIP

Higginbotham, Evelyn Brooks. **Righteous discontent: the women's movement in the Black Baptist Church, 1880-1920.** Harvard, 1993. 306p index afp ISBN 0-674-76977-5, $34.95

This landmark contribution to American religious history is the first full-scale study of the religious ideas and activities of a large cohort of African American women. Previous books on the religious activities of African Americans, such as *The Black Church in the African American Experience* by C. Eric Lincoln and Lawrence H. Mamiya (CH, Jul'91), tend to pay little attention to women. The few books that have studied the religious work of African American women, such as *Sisters of the Spirit*, ed. by William L. Andrews (CH, Oct'86), have focused on singular women prophets. Higginbotham's book is the first to study the religious work of a generation or more of African American Christian women. Higginbotham argues that women in African American Baptist churches between 1880 and 1920 worked against both racial and gender discrimination. Women figured importantly in the efforts of the National Baptist Convention to combat racism and to improve the conditions under which African Americans lived, while at the same time working toward greater equality and leadership as women within the Convention. This fine book is recommended for all libraries.—*A. Porterfield, Syracuse University*

OAB-1212 BT819 91-30765 CIP

Hill, Charles E. **Regnum caelorum: patterns of future hope in early Christianity.** Oxford, 1992. 236p bibl indexes ISBN 0-19-826738-X, $59.00

Hill (Northwestern College) examines the various patterns of early Christian belief regarding the anticipated second coming of Christ. More particularly he is concerned with identifying and defining the impact of chiliasm/millennialism ("the ancient belief in a thousand-year reign of Christ and his saints on earth between his second coming and the last judgement") and nonchiliasm in the Church of the first two centuries. In so doing he raises serious and well-founded objections to a long-accepted and widely held view among scholars:

namely, that chiliasm represented the dominant stream of Christian thought on this question until the time of the great Alexandrian theologians of the third century. Hill convincingly demonstrates that there existed alongside the chiliasts in the Church a substantial *and* orthodox opposition of nonchiliasts. Literary sources, ranging from the New Testament to the writings of Dionysius of Alexandria, are the primary focus of the author's attentions. A major contribution to the field of early Christian studies. Highly recommended for advanced undergraduates and above.—*C. L. Hanson, Muskingum College*

OAB-1213　　　　BX830　　　　95-42334 CIP
History of Vatican II: v.1: Announcing and preparing Vatican Council II toward a new era in Catholicism, ed. by Giuseppe Alberigo; English version ed. by Joseph A. Komonchak. Orbis/Peeters, 1996 (c1995). 527p indexes ISBN 1-57075-049-1, $80.00

It will be impossible for any serious student of Vatican II to dismiss this work, now in an English version. It is a landmark study of one of the half-dozen key events in the church history of our century. The contributing scholars self-consciously express their responsibility to future generations, who will not have experienced the council. Their goal—30 years later—is both to reconstruct the course of Vatican II and to delineate its significance. The range of their history is comprehensive; and the international specialists who contribute use a vast array of sources. The authors raised the question of whether a legitimate history can be produced so close to the event. They concluded not only that it could, but also that the reconstruction could still benefit from the testimonies of participants. The present volume, first of a projected five, is concerned with events leading to the actual meeting of the Vatican Council: the calling of the council, resistance to and support for a council, external and internal factors, and the efforts of pastoral and doctrinal commissions. The leadership of Pope John XXIII remained important throughout. This volume ends with the gathering of the council participants in Rome. This study should be acquired by every library with serious intent to hold the finest titles in current history and contemporary religious studies. Highly recommended. Undergraduate through professional.—*W. L. Pitts Jr., Baylor University*

OAB-1214　　　　BV5083　　　　94-44562 CIP
Jantzen, Grace M. **Power, gender and Christian mysticism.** Cambridge, 1995. 384p bibl index (Cambridge studies in ideology and religion, 8) ISBN 0-521-47376-4, $64.95; ISBN 0-521-47926-6 pbk, $18.95

Both historically and philosophically, this compelling, massively documented study is a superlative contribution to medieval, religious, and feminist studies. It is fueled by Jantzen's discontent with the concept of mysticism set forth by William James and the many philosophers who have followed in his wake. In a twofold indictment, she faults James for (1) shoddy documentation and (2) the notion that the primary characteristic of mysticism is an intense, subjective, private, ineffable, psychological experience. To deal with the first, Jantzen undertakes close readings of major medieval writings (e.g., those of Dionysius, Eckhart, Hadewijk, Hildegard, et al.). To deal with the second, she offers as a corrective the view that Christian mysticism has important sociopolitical dimensions. Among the fruits of her overall analysis is the recognition that there have been distinguishable male and female traditions of Christian spirituality. Allowing for diversities within each, one notes the contrasts between them: the male tradition elevates the intellect, favors a body-soul dualism, and is misogynistic, whereas the female one exalts direct visionary experience, is holistic, and esteems womanhood and the feminine. Contained here are important lessons in regard to the just empowerment of women today. An essential acquisition. Upper-division undergraduate; graduate; faculty.—*C. MacCormick, emeritus, Wells College*

OAB-1215　　　　BR1720　　　　95-1444 CIP
Kelly, J.N.D. **Golden mouth: the story of John Chrysostom— ascetic, preacher, bishop.** Cornell, 1995. 310p index afp ISBN 0-8014-3189-1, $47.50

Few figures in the history of Christendom have lived more eventful lives than

John Chrysostom, or John the "Golden Mouth" (c. 349-407). Famous ascetic, beloved teacher, brilliant orator, profound theologian, popular preacher, controversial patriarch—each of these descriptive titles can only hint at the complex personality of the man and his impact on late fourth century society in the East. The book under review is one of the few original, comprehensive biographies of Chrysostom published since C. Baur's magisterial work of 1929-30, and Kelly has done justice to this remarkable figure. Readers and admirers of Kelly's earlier biographical study of St. Jerome (CH, Nov'76) will once again delight in the author's profound knowledge of late antique Roman society and Christianity, masterful use of primary and secondary source material, provocative rethinking of issues long thought decided, and wonderful literary style. This is a book to be savored by all. A model of historical research methodology and presentation. Highly recommended for general readers, undergraduate students, and professional scholars.—*C. L. Hanson, Muskingum College*

OAB-1216　　　　BR305　　　　95-22971 CIP
Lindberg, Carter. **The European reformations.** Blackwell, 1996. 444p bibl index afp ISBN 1-55786-575-2 pbk, $22.95

Lindberg (Boston Univ.) has produced a splendid introduction to the Reformation. The range of the book is impressive: he employs the plural "Reformations" in his title and surveys the standard movements—Lutheran, Reformed, Radical, Anglican and Catholic—but also devotes full chapters to neglected issues, including social and educational implications and Protestant developments in the Netherlands and France. The book provides excellent orientation to the period. Lindberg begins with an informative survey of Reformation historiography and returns to this issue throughout his text. Reformation studies have made enormous strides, and this work accounts for interpretations devoted to the study of the Middle Ages (including conciliarism, anticlericalism, and theology), the cities, the press, money economy, and social and political transformations. Thus the book introduces both diverse theological positions and the social contexts that made them attractive. In short, Lindberg makes the reader aware of leading strands of Reformation research developed during the past generation. The author displays superb narrative style and provides useful aids to research, including an impressive current bibliography. This general study has grown out of years of teaching and will be a superb choice for classroom text as well as a desirable library acquisition. Undergraduate; graduate; faculty; general.—*W. L. Pitts Jr., Baylor University*

OAB-1217　　　　BT83　　　　96-12017 CIP
Löwy, Michael. **The war of gods: religion and politics in Latin America.** Verso, 1996. 163p index ISBN 1-85984-002-7, pbk $17.95

Löwy (Research Director of Sociology, Centre National de la Recherche Scientifique, Paris) has written a reflection on religious trends in Latin America that is useful to both beginning and established scholars alike. It presents a social theoretical background to understanding the rise of liberationist religion, with case studies of two of the most important experiences of liberationist Catholicism, Brazil and Central America, peppered with a consideration of the new Protestant movements, liberationist and conservative. Löwy's political preferences are clearly with liberationist Christianity (although he himself is an unbeliever of Brazilian Jewish origin); but the book presents so many interesting theoretical connections in such a striking way, and offers such an original review of the literature, that the quality of the scholarship is superb. It will be especially helpful for those with an interest in social theory, particularly Marx and Weber, or in theoretical analysis of the Catholic Church. Löwy's convincing argument—that liberation theology, although likely to continue to evolve, is here to stay—will also be a welcome antidote to the greatly exaggerated accounts of its demise in the face of Vatican threats on the one hand, and the rise of conservative Protestant groups on the other. Recommended to the theoretically inclined generalist, upper-division undergraduates, and graduate students.—*B. T. Froehle, Georgetown University*

OAB-1218　　　　BR828　　　　95-4836 CIP
Marnef, Guido. **Antwerp in the age of Reformation: underground**

Protestantism in a commercial metropolis, 1550-1577, tr. by J.C. Grayson. Johns Hopkins, 1996. 304p bibl index afp (Johns Hopkins University studies in historical and political science; 114th ser., 1) ISBN 0-8018-5169-6, $48.50

Marnef, Senior Researcher, National Fund for Scientific Research at the University of Antwerp, analyzes the process of personal religious change in the context of the political, socioeconomic, and cultural structures of Antwerp. The in-depth focus on Antwerp significantly contributes to Marnef's goal of "a better knowledge of the Reformation as one of the most innovative forces in early modern Europe." A major strength of this study is the perceptive relating of concrete social contexts and religion without slighting the importance of either. This is social history at its best because it is not reductionist. The reader is constantly reminded that the search for salvation, "one of the cornerstones for understanding the thought and actions of the religiously minded person of the sixteenth century," occurred "in a concrete social context." The book sketches the urban context of early Protestantism in Antwerp, its relative success from 1550 to 1567, and its forced underground existence from 1567 to 1577. The analysis of the Calvinist, Anabaptist, and Lutheran communities in Antwerp utilizes a prosopographical database of more than 1100 persons. Much of this material is presented in 26 tables, eight graphs, and six maps. Upper-division undergraduate; graduate; faculty; general.—*C. Lindberg, Boston University*

OAB-1219   BV5075   94-21508 CIP
McGinn, Bernard. **The growth of mysticism.** Crossroad, NY, 1995 (c1994). 630p bibl indexes (The presence of God: a history of Western Christian mysticism, 2) ISBN 0-8245-1450-5, $49.50

This volume covers the period 500-1200 CE. McGinn continues his superlative history of the *traditio* of *contemplatio* in Christian life and thought as an *element* in religious communities and as a *process* or way of life. His heuristic model of mysticism begins with an excellent description of the making of Christendom and then summarizes the contributions of Gregory the Great and John Scotus Erigena to the mystical tradition. Part 1 then concludes with a survey of the heritage of *contemplatio* as understood by monastic writers from 800 to 1100 CE. Part 2 takes up the mysticism of the 12th century as viewed through the works of Bernard of Clairvaux, William of St. Thierry, minor voices of Citeaux, visionaries and contemplatives, and finally the Victorines with their "scientific ordering of wisdom." Keenly aware of the wider context of Western Christianity, McGinn deftly sets forth the complex reactions produced by the encounter of *traditio* and developing culture, correctly acknowledging that all the writers "testify to the ambiguity and difficulty of talking about this ultimate mystery." Continuing the excellence of volume 1, *The Presence of God* (CH, Jun'92), this volume more deeply establishes the reputation of McGinn as the world's greatest interpreter of Western mysticism. The scholarship is staggering in its comprehensiveness, and the interpretations are unique and fresh. Completed, this series will doubtless become the preeminent available history of Christian mysticism in the West. Upper-division undergraduate; graduate; faculty.—*G. H. Shriver, Georgia Southern University*

OAB-1220   BX4200   96-3645 CIP
McNamara, Jo Ann Kay. **Sisters in arms: Catholic nuns through two millennia.** Harvard, 1996. 751p bibl index afp ISBN 0-674-80984-X, $35.00

McNamara's is the first comprehensive work on a scholarly level to treat organized religious life for women in the Catholic tradition as a unified whole. Arguably the oldest of human institutions—the way of life created by groups of widows and virgins in the early Christian era; by female ascetics in later classical times; by the women who formed monastic and cloistered contemplative communities in the Middle Ages, and the convents of later centuries—here finds a sympathetic and perceptive historian. Sections on women religious in the Roman Empire, in the medieval Reformation and early modern European periods, and in the 19th and 20th centuries, develop the subject from a feminist vantage point with careful respect for sources. The author's expertise in the classics and hagiographical literature is evident here. A work of

lesser scope but comparable purpose is Penelope D. Johnson's *Equal in Monastic Procession* (CH, Dec'91). Several essay collections, notably *Soldiers of Christ*, ed. by Thomas F.X. Noble and Thomas Head (1995) and *Medieval Religious Women* v.1, ed. by John A. Nichols and Lillian T. Shank (1984), anticipate themes in the broader subject. Although written for a "broadly educated public," *Sisters in Arms* will please the scholar with its command of original and secondary sources, amply documented in endnotes and chapter-by-chapter bibliographies. Recommended for all readership levels.—*K. Kennelly, Mount St. Mary's College*

OAB-1221   BX1795   91-16814 CIP
McNeal, Patricia. **Harder than war: Catholic peacemaking in twentieth- century America.** Rutgers, 1992. 316p index ISBN 0-8135-1739-7, $40.00; ISBN 0-8135-1740-0 pbk, $15.00

The Catholic Church's acceptance of the just war doctrine as normative and American Catholics' often uneasy immigrant status, which led them to emphasize patriotism, made "peacemaking harder than war," McNeal asserts. However, Dorothy Day's peace agitation of the 1930s added the concepts of pacifism, conscientious objection, and nuclear pacifism to the American Catholic agenda by the end of WW II. Thomas Merton would later articulate a theological rationale for those positions. Gandhian nonviolence was incorporated into Catholic pacifism starting in the 1950s and provided a new way to posit actions for peace as well as to address public policy issues although Cold War era Catholics did not widely support such activities. During the Vietnam War years (1963-1975), a sort of double turbulence affected American Catholics who had to adjust to church reforms mandated by Vatican II as well as to face up to civil rights and antiwar agitation. Out of this disruption arose the largest Catholic peace movement in US history, although pacifists are still a minority among American Catholics. McNeal's major conclusion is that Catholic peacemakers had the greatest impact not on their government but on their church. This well-documented and cogently written volume should become the standard treatment of these important topics. Highly recommended for all academic and general libraries.—*J. C. Scott, St. Martin's College*

OAB-1222   BX4700   92-1270 CIP
Meissner, W.W. **Ignatius of Loyola: the psychology of a saint.** Yale, 1992. 480p bibl index afp ISBN 0-300-05156-5, $35.00

Meissner's biographical and pyschoanalytic study of Ignatius of Loyola, mystic, saint, and founder of the Jesuits, is a masterful work that succeeds on several levels. First, it is a lively, detailed and very readable account of St. Ignatius's life. Second, it shows the hidden motivations and drives of this man as seen through psychoanalytic (Freudian) eyes. Although Meissner, who is both a Jesuit and psychoanalyst, interprets Ignatius's deeds and mystical experiences in terms of pyschoanalysis, he does not fall into the trap of reductionism. His own deep understanding of spirituality balances his psychoanalytic perspective. The reader begins to understand how psychological woundings can in fact be a spur to enduring and heroic accomplishments. At the same time the reader clearly understands some of the psychological causes of certain religious attitudes and experiences. The work helps to elucidate the distinction between quasi-mystical experiences, which are primarily psychological in origin, and more authentic ones. Similarly, it displays how authentic mystical experiences can become colored through the mystic's psyche. Highly recommended for both graduate and upper-level undergraduate students.—*A. McDowell, Ithaca College*

OAB-1223   BX1547   92-54971 CIP
Miller, Maureen C. **The formation of a medieval church: ecclesiastical change in Verona, 950-1150.** Cornell, 1993. 216p bibl index afp ISBN 0-8014-2837-8, $35.00

Dedicated to the memory of David Herlihy, this study of one northern Italian diocese in the two centuries of its strongest growth represents a new kind of church history in many ways. Neither pious nor contemptuous of religious motivations in the original actors or in their subsequent historians, Miller can explain novel institutional developments as ecclesiastical answers to social developments. Her economic explorations are thorough and convincing, not directed by any deterministic theoretical structure. Her technique is a modern variation on the traditional cogitation of charters and annals: she made databases of the masses of charters, of the religious institutions, and of the rural place-names, then queried those files statistically and compared her statistical maps with the narrative sources, tapping, for example, the underused Ratherius of Verona. The result compels attention and respect and invites a new assessment of the local forms taken by such cataclysms as the Gregorian age. This book belongs in any college library and should be considered for the reading list of any advanced course in medieval or church history.—*D. Williman, SUNY at Binghamton*

OAB-1224   BR563   92-21041 CIP
Montgomery, William E. **Under their own vine and fig tree: the African-American church in the South, 1865-1900.** Louisiana State, 1993. 358p index afp ISBN 0-8071-1745-5, $29.95

Montgomery's comprehensive study of African American churches during the Reconstruction period and its aftermath in the South is one of the few excellent and judicious works available. By focusing on their holistic dimensions, he has shown how the roles of African American churches were critically significant to the development of black communities in politics, economics, education, music, and worship. Montgomery's unique work fills in some of the historical details that were missing in Carter G. Woodson's treatment of the same period in *History of the Negro Church* (1921). He has succeeded in creating a readable historical narrative of one of the truly heroic periods in the history of black churches. The strengths of Montgomery's study include his sensitive treatment of the new synthesis of African survivals in African American worship, his inclusion of the complex interactions between blacks and whites as African Americans separated to form their own churches, and his detailed elaboration of the political role of black clergy in local, state, and national politics. The only lacuna is in Montgomery's failure to examine the collapse of the Freedman's Savings and Trust Company in 1874 and the subsequent efforts of African American churches, fraternal lodges, and mutual aid groups to establish black-owned banks and, later, life insurance companies, which were the major examples of black economic development in the late 19th century. This book, which contains photographs of black churches and their leaders, is recommended for college undergraduates (all levels), graduate students, faculty, and professionals.—*L. H. Mamiya, Vassar College*

OAB-1225   BT693   95-26017 CIP
Orsi, Robert A. **Thank you, St. Jude: women's devotion to the patron saint of hopeless causes.** Yale, 1996. 303p bibl index afp ISBN 0-300-06476-4, $30.00

Orsi (Indiana Univ.) revisits the territory he first made familiar in *The Madonna of 115th Street* (CH, May'86): the world of 20th-century urban Catholics, the children and grandchildren of immigrants. He examines the dynamics of Catholic devotionalism and provides a balanced perspective, grounded in the experiences of believers themselves. Anyone inclined to dismiss this study of American Catholic women's devotion to St. Jude, the patron saint of hopeless cases, as too narrow or "Catholic" for serious students of 20th-century American religion or women's studies should suspend disbelief and read the book first. It illuminates the experiences of working-class Catholic women of Irish and southern and eastern European immigrant backgrounds from the Depression to the recent past, drawing heavily on their own published letters in *The Voice of St. Jude*, and on wide-ranging interviews. The voices of Jude's devout female followers ring through in Orsi's narrative, and, together with Orsi's own measured observations, they leave us with a far richer understanding of the relationship between piety and the cultivation of female agency and identities. In this engaging and accessible volume, Orsi has raised questions that will occupy students and scholars in American history, women's history, and religious studies for years to come. General; undergraduate; graduate; faculty.—*D. Campbell, Colby College*

OAB-1226   BR759   92-26730 CIP
Paz, D.G. **Popular anti-Catholicism in Mid-Victorian England.** Stanford, 1992. 332p bibl index afp ISBN 0-8047-1984-5, $42.50

In the four middle decades of the 19th century, England experienced more intense religious controversy than at any time since the Puritan revolution. One great theme was Protestant fear and hatred of Catholicism, expressed through anti-Catholic organizations, oratory, literature, petitions, demonstrations, and violent acts. The phenomenon has been studied in recent years by Edward Norman, Derek Holmes, G.I.T. Machin, John Wolffe, and others; but Paz has written the most comprehensive and analytical book thus far. Its strengths lie in its massive research, displayed in about 1,450 footnotes and 23 pages of bibliography; its multiple perspectives, which supplant simplistic explanations of what produced and sustained anti-Catholicism; and its methodological resourcefulness in deploying documentary, literary, and statistical materials that not only illustrate but provide cross-confirming evidence of anti-Catholic attitudes. Paz painstakingly analyzes the relation of anti-Irish to anti-Catholic antagonism, emphasizes the differences among Nonconformist denominations in the styles of their anti-Catholicism; assesses the Tractarians' uncomfortable position between Roman and Protestant militants; acknowledges Catholic provocations as a factor in their vilification and victimization; and explains the rapid decline of anti-Catholicism in later Victorian England. Paz claims much for the book, and students of Victorian religion will probably agree with him. Highly recommended. Graduate and upper-division undergraduate.—*A. R. Vogeler, California State University, Fullerton*

OAB-1227   BX1446   96-367 CIP
Peterson, Anna L. **Martyrdom and the politics of religion: progressive Catholicism in El Salvador's civil war.** State University of New York, 1997. 211p bibl index afp ISBN 0-7914-3181-9, $54.50

Peterson (religious studies, Univ. of Florida) analyzes martyrdom in El Salvador during the 1970s and '80s, and shows how religion changes history as well as people's lives and how people respond to extraordinarily brutal and extreme conditions. Her qualitative approach convincingly blends life histories with personal experience and participant observation, giving readers an understanding of how religion works—and why religious teaching and experiences cannot be analyzed as simply so many "products" in a "marketplace." Moreover, Peterson demonstrates clear mastery of religious definitions and the nuances of the Catholic tradition. Her analysis of the place of murdered—"martyred"—Archbishop Oscar Romero is also helpful, and her theoretical analysis in this area alone is an important contribution. Clearly passionate about her topic, she nevertheless presents the reasoned, careful arguments one would expect of a seasoned scholar. Her focus on a particular aspect of a single country's recent history may make the work less appealing to generalists or undergraduates, but her work has a certain universality in the questions it raises, in the scope of its references to world historical experience, and even in its theological sophistication. Recommended for all interested in religion and social change in Latin America, particularly progressive Catholicism, or in the theoretical analysis of religion and social action in general. A provocative interdisciplinary treat for scholars in such fields as ethics, philosophy, religious studies, theology, sociology, political science, and Latin American studies. Upper-division undergraduate; graduate; faculty.—*B. T. Froehle, Georgetown University*

OAB-1228   BX6443   92-15256 CIP
Pitts, Walter F. **Old ship of Zion: the Afro-Baptist ritual in the African diaspora.** Oxford, 1993. 199p bibl index afp ISBN 0-19-507509-9, $29.95

Pitts, an anthropologist, linguist, and ethnomusicologist, has produced a marvelous groundbreaking study of African American ritual practices in rural churches in Texas. Based on extensive fieldwork in Baptist churches, where he also played the piano during services, Pitts in demonstrates the binary ritual structure that underlies both African and African American rituals. Siding with Melville Herskovits's view of the retention of aspects of African culture in the enduring debate between Herskovits and E. Franklin Frazier on African survivals in black American culture (Frazier, *The Negro Church in America*, 1964; Herskovits, *The Myth of the Negro Past*, 1941), Pitts convincingly argues that two dialectical frames appear in the worship experiences of Africans and their descendants in the US, the Caribbean, and Latin America. The first ritual frame is somber and melancholy; the second is joyful and ultimately results in an ecstatic trance. Pitts's major contribution lies in his extensive cross-cultural comparisons between the Afro-Baptist rituals in Texas with those of traditional African religions in Central and Western Africa, including some of the African-derived religions such as Jamaican Cumina, Haitian Vodun, and Brazilian Candomble. He also has a creative chapter on the linguistic analysis of black vernacular English. However, it is Pitts's background in music that makes *Old Ship of Zion* a delight to read. Highly recommended for advanced undergraduates, graduate students, and scholars of religious studies, cultural anthropology, ethnomusicology, and African American studies.—*L. H. Mamiya, Vassar College*

OAB-1229   BR563   94-4922 CIP
Sawyer, Mary R. **Black ecumenism: implementing the demands of justice.** Trinity Press International, 1994. 251p index ISBN 1-56338-092-7 pbk, $18.00

This is a first-class study of both national and local attempts at providing unity among black Christians. Using historical documents and sociological concepts, Sawyer argues that the various black ecumenical movements of the 20th century were directed towards implementing justice in American society and were led by politically progressive black preachers. Chapters include detailed examination of the goals, projects, institutional structure, and leaders of such black-led ecumenical efforts as the Fraternal Council of Churches, the Southern Christian Leadership Conference, the National Conference of Black Christians, local models of ecumenism in different cities, the National Black Evangelical Association, the Black Theology Project, Partners in Ecumenism, and the Congress of National Black Churches. The book concludes with reflections on the themes and social sources of black ecumenism. As the most comprehensive examination of black ecumenical movements, Sawyer's study uses a dialectical model of black churches to locate the position of each group on a series of issues, including their views on integration, governance, economics, women, lay participation, etc. By providing helpful charts of their positions, Sawyer shows how each group can change its position over time, thus escaping the rigidity of sociological typologies. Contained in the footnotes is the most extensive bibliography of documents on black ecumenical groups. Well-written and a major contribution to the field, this book is recommended for collections supporting undergraduate- and graduate-level courses on religion and social change.—*L. H. Mamiya, Vassar College*

OAB-1230   BR166   95-44197 CIP
Stark, Rodney. **The rise of Christianity: a sociologist reconsiders history.** Princeton, 1996. 246p bibl index afp ISBN 0-691-02749-8, $24.95

This book is an exciting and important addition to the literature on early Christianity. Stark (sociology and comparative literature, Univ. of Washington) analyzes the rapid rise and development of Christianity in the initial five centuries of its history from a sociological perspective. He combines this sociological methodology with broad familiarity with both classical and contemporary biblical and church historians. He begins with this focus: "Finally, all questions concerning the rise of Christianity are one: How was it done?" Through a very readable, analytical discussion one feels as though one has been part of an interdisciplinary experience. In the process, issues such as conversion, epidemics, gender, and geography are addressed—often quantitatively—to demonstrate Christianity's expansion through the Roman Empire. It is a book of fascinating detail, yet its broad sociological assumptions will intrigue any person interested in church growth. It will challenge common theological assumptions. But, its creative and persuasive insights also will engage the thoughtful person. It is a very significant book. Rich bibliography; helpful index. Upper-division undergraduate through professional.—*A. L. Kolp, Earlham College*

OAB-1231   BX1406   95-12644 CIP
Tropman, John E. **The Catholic ethic in American society: an exploration of values.** Jossey-Bass, 1995. 230p bibl index afp ISBN 0-7879-0123-7, $24.95

Max Weber's notion of a "Protestant ethic" has defined the American ethos and given rise to individualistic capitalism. Tropman (social policy, Univ. of Michigan) contends that there is a parallel, subdominant "Catholic Ethic" that might lead American society to treat the poor differently. The core values of the Protestant ethic are achievement and individualism. Work gives the self identity, and wealth confirms the soul's redemption. Needing help implies that one has not worked hard enough. The core values of the Catholic ethic are sharing and communalism. There is a sense in which all are in this pilgrimage together. Whether one is up or down, the resources produced by work are meant to be shared among the community. This ethic tends to see the poor as "us," not "them." Clearly these social constructs, rooted in religion, guide culture and public policy in very different directions. Tropman's conceptual explorations seem almost self-evident once they are put forth, and they yield understanding and commitment regarding the debate about welfare reform. This is an important book for professors, professionals, and citizens alike, and it is accessible to educated general readers. It should be in every library. General; undergraduate through professional.—*J. M. Thompson, Saint Joseph College*

■ Judaism & Islam

OAB-1232   [CD-ROM]
Alim: version 4.5. ISL Software Corporation, 2037 Featherwood St., Silver Spring, MD 20904, 1996. $169.00. 1 disc; 2 disks; user manual. System requirements: MS-DOS; Windows 3.1 or higher; sound card necessary for spoken parts.

This CD is a marvelous reference and teaching program. It provides an Arabic Qur'an text with a beautiful recitation, a transliteration, two translations popular among English-speaking Muslims, and Maududi's introduction to each sura. It has—in translation only—Hadith texts from al-Bukhari, Malik, and a selection from Muslim; a chronology, biographies of Muhammad's Companions, material on prayers, weddings, food, and more. After a few minutes, users can easily maneuver back and forth from each feature to explore points of Islamic law and practice, pronouncements on ethical, ritual, and spiritual issues from Qur'an and Hadith, and Islamic history. Ease of access will make this a delight both for Muslims and for non-Muslim students of Islam. The Qur'an recitation can be set to continue regardless of whatever else is running, although it might be useful for some to be able to hear the recitation and display Arabic text, transliteration, and translation simultaneously. Searches are easy, and results can be printed or copied into a word processor. Scholars and professionals may want to check references in the original Arabic, not provided except for the Qur'an. This program can be profitably used by beginning and advanced students. General; undergraduate through professional.—*S. Ward, University of Denver*

OAB-1233   BP163   94-2485 CIP
Arkoun, Mohammed. **Rethinking Islam: common questions, uncommon answers,** tr. and ed. by Robert D. Lee. Westview, 1994. 139p afp ISBN 0-8133-8474-5, $59.95; ISBN 0-8133-2294-4 pbk, $19.95

This is a translation of the second edition of Arkoun's carefully argued work *Ouvertures sur l'Islam* (1992), a series of critical reflections on Islam by one of the Muslim world's leading thinkers. Among the themes discussed are revelation, tradition, mysticism, theology, law, the status of women, human rights, and nationalism. Aiming to challenge both traditional Muslim and standard Western interpretations of Islam, Arkoun argues throughout that if non-Muslims and Muslims are to break out of the various forms of "dogmatic closure" to which they have fallen victim, and if the task of rethinking and reinterpretation is to achieve constructive results, both must draw on the full range of intellectual and cultural resources available. Although a critic of Western culture, Arkoun, holder of an important chair at the Sorbonne for many years, is also an admirer of Western intellectual achievements and liberal institutions. As a Muslim, however, Arkoun is also convinced that Islam has much to contribute to contemporary thought and culture. Impressive for its nondogmatic character, its openness to multiple disciplinary perspectives, and its insistence on approaching Islam from a comparative perspective, this brilliant and profound work deserves the attention of all those genuinely interested in the future of Islam. Lee's English version is accurate and readable; his preface will serve as both a useful introduction to the book and a sketch of Arkoun's thought. Glossary of technical terms; list of Arkoun's publications; short biographical notice. Highly recommended to all academic libraries and to those public libraries concerned with contemporary religion and culture in a global context. Undergraduate; graduate; general.—*M. Swartz, Boston University*

OAB-1234   BM535   93-42865 CIP
Cohen, Mark R. **Under crescent and cross: the Jews in the Middle Ages.** Princeton, 1994. 280p index afp ISBN 0-691-03378-1, $29.95

This book focuses on what may be the central issue in medieval Jewish history: the status of Jews within Islamic and Christian society. Regarding Jewish life under Islam, the author's area of expertise, Cohen strikes a firm balance between the myth of an interfaith utopia and the "neo-lachrymose counter-myth" of never-ending persecution. Cohen describes and contrasts Jewish status in both realms, displaying a deep familiarity with both modern and medieval sources in European languages, Hebrew, and Arabic. Beyond a reexamination of the legal status, he discusses economic integration and such social concerns as hierarchy, marginality, ethnicity, and sociability. Polemics and the historiography of persecutions occasion a balanced evaluation of intellectual historians' views of collective memory and identity, antisemitism, and Jewish attitudes towards the authorities in the many lands of their dispersion. Cohen probes deeply into a fundamental concern of Jewish life in the Middle Ages and provides comprehensive discussion of both primary sources and historiography, but maintains readability. This book should quickly become a fixture in undergraduate and graduate curricula, an important research tool, and a major contribution to our evaluation of this crucial issue.—*S. Ward, University of Denver*

OAB-1235   BP63   93-18488 CIP
DeWeese, Devin. **Islamization and native religion in the Golden Horde: Baba Tükles and conversion to Islam in historical and epic tradition.** Pennsylvania State, 1994. 638p bibl index afp ISBN 0-271-01072-X, $85.00; ISBN 0-271-01073-8 pbk, $25.00

This fascinating study of the Islamization of the Golden Horde (one of the more important Mongol successor states to emerge in the early 13th century), though limited in scope, manages to raise a series of important larger questions regarding the traditional Western understanding of conversion to Islam. Although his principal source is Ötemish Ḥajjî's account of the conversion of the Mongol sultan Özbek Khan through the heroic efforts of a certain Baba Tükles, DeWeese draws on a wide range of other sources (principally in Arabic, Persian, and Turkic, but also Russian and Latin) to provide a broader context within which to examine the conversion of the Golden Horde and the significance of that development. DeWeese's aim in this study, however, is not so much to reconstruct the historical process of Islamization itself as to examine how conversion was understood by the Islamized peoples of Inner Asia themselves. The author's analysis of the sources and the elaboration of his arguments are presented in seven substantive chapters. The text of Ötemish Ḥajjî's conversion narrative (in Chaghatay Turkic), along with a translation and detailed philological analysis of the text, is presented in a series of appendixes. One of the merits of this seminal work is that, despite its heavy reliance on a variety of sources in a number of Islamic languages, the study itself is readable, presenting little difficulty to the nonspecialist. No serious scholar of Islamization can afford to ignore it. Useful index of names and terms; 40-page bibliography. Highly recommended to all college and university collections in Islamic studies and the history of religion. Upper-division undergraduate; graduate; faculty.—*M. Swartz, Boston University*

OAB-1236   BM660   93-18401 CIP
Elbogen, Ismar. **Jewish liturgy: a comprehensive history,** tr. by Raymond P. Scheindlin. Jewish Publication Society/Jewish Theological Seminary of America, 1993. 501p bibl indexes ISBN 0-8276-0445-9, $55.00

The return to religion among the Jews, which is part of the present cultural scene, has resulted in a renewed interest in the origin and development of the liturgy. The amount of material available on Jewish prayer is incredibly meager. The translation into English of Elbogen's classic is enormously important. Included in the first section of this book is a description of the origin and development of the individual prayers for the weekday, Sabbath, and festivals. The second section offers a comprehensive history of the liturgy and the synagogue from biblical times to the present. Best understood as a reference work, the first section is comprehensible to the non-Hebrew reader though it has some Hebrew words. Elbogen's is the only scientific treatment available, but he has no interest in theology or in a reinterpretation of the prayers. For such matters, all readers—liberals and non-Jews included—will find the traditional *Hirsch Siddur* to be very useful; the exposition by B.S. Jacobson, *Sabbath Service* (Sinai, 1981) is a more comprehensive treatment. But neither of these works is "scientific." Elbogen is still the standard work in this field. Advanced undergraduate through faculty.—*M. Scult, Brooklyn College, CUNY*

OAB-1237   BM534   92-11952 CIP
Feldman, Louis H. **Jew and Gentile in the ancient world: attitudes and interactions from Alexander to Justinian.** Princeton, 1993. 679p bibl indexes afp ISBN 0-691-07416-X, $59.50

This volume revolves around the question of "how to explain the apparent success of Judaism in the Hellenistic-Roman period in winning so many converts and 'sympathizers' at a time when, apparently, Jews were hated by the Gentile masses." In keeping with this formulation, the author adopts a rather polarized approach to the data, sorting out evidence that certain people liked Jews while others disliked them, that certain considerations won respect for the Jews and others resentment, and so on. This approach resembles the self-obsessed tendency of some modern people to ask of any current event whether it is "good for the Jews," but the author has undoubtedly assembled a magisterial survey of data relating to his theme. His stance toward Jewish and especially rabbinic tradition is rather more defensive and less critical in method than this reviewer would have liked, but all students of Jewish history and of Judaism in late antiquity will be in his debt. Useful indexes; excellent bibliography and annotation. All libraries interested in the field must have this book. Advanced undergraduate; graduate; faculty; general.—*R. Goldenberg, SUNY at Stony Brook*

OAB-1238   BM198   92-47504 CIP
Idel, Moshe. **Hasidism: between ecstasy and magic.** State University of New York, 1995. 438p bibl indexes afp ISBN 0-7914-1733-6, $74.50

This is a major new study by the leading contemporary student of Jewish mysticism. Idel (Hebrew Univ.), well known for his earlier detailed studies of Abraham Abulafia (1987 and 1988) and his wide ranging volume *Kabbalah: New Perspectives* (1988), has written what promises to be a highly influential volume dealing with certain central aspects of Hasidic theology. In particular, Idel engages in an extended, many-sided investigation and analysis of the role of the *zaddik* (the charismatic leader at the center of Hasidic life) both as a seeker after mystical ecstasy—for himself and his disciples—and as a magician (Idel's term), meaning "the drawing down of the divine effluence for the benefit of the community." In the course of his review, after paying close attention to what he refers to as the "mystico-magical model" of the activity of the *zaddik*, Idel also deciphers the meaning of mystical and magical prayer and mystical and magical study in Hasidism. He does all this with methodological sophistication, a deep and wide-ranging erudition, and a developed critical sensibility that is different from his most illustrious predecessors in the field of Hasidic studies, Martin Buber and Gershom Scholem. In sum, this is a very significant contribution. All libraries serving religion and Judaica programs will want to add it to their collection. Upper-division undergraduate; graduate; faculty.—*S. T. Katz, Cornell University*

OAB-1239   95-72624 Orig
Kepel, Gilles. **Allah in the West: Islamic movements in America and Europe,** tr. by Susan Milner. Stanford, 1997. 273p index afp ISBN 0-8047-2751-1, $39.50; ISBN 0-8047-2753-8 pbk, $15.95

Comparative sociology at its best, this monograph conjoins three national contexts and provides a benchmark for assessing Muslim identity in the post-Cold War era. The three contexts are the US, England, and France; the three principal groups are African-American converts, Indo-Pakistanis, and Maghribis, or North Africans. The thesis is stark: modernity has gone awry for each group. Instead of being empowered as citizens in modern postindustrial states, these Muslims—whether converts or recent arrivals—perceive themselves as a new underclass, denied the rights and jobs that other, non-Muslims enjoy. Both dark-skinned and Muslim, they have become doubly marginalized. They respond to the appeal of Muslim communitarian forces because, in Kepel's words, they "transpose their demands for social and political recognition onto a religious register," advocating Islam as not only an alternative but also a counterweight to cultural Christianity. Not all Muslims can be subsumed within Kepel's thesis, and some will object to his searing analysis of race relations in all three societies; yet no other scholar has compared such disparate contexts, nor has any argued so passionately for sustained attention to the domestic dimension of contemporary Muslim identity in the West. A book to be commended for all levels of readers, especially since the English translation of the French original is lapidary. Undergraduate through professional.—*B. B. Lawrence, Duke University*

OAB-1240   BM525   91-36469 CIP
Liebes, Yehuda. **Studies in the Zohar,** tr. by Arnold Schwartz, Stephanie Nakache, and Penina Peli. State University of New York, 1993. 262p bibl indexes ISBN 0-7914-1189-3, $59.50; ISBN 0-7914-1190-7 pbk, $19.95

The *Zohar*, the great work of Jewish mysticism, is more referred to than read, and even when read is little understood. Liebes (Hebrew Univ.), in a series of essays expertly translated from the Hebrew, provides truly informed and scholarly guidance on three basic aspects of the theology of the *Zohar* and its world. Three issues are analyzed in detail under the headings: "The Messiah of the *Zohar*: On R. Simeon Bar Yohai as a Messianic Figure," "How the *Zohar* Was Written," and "Christian Influences on the *Zohar*." On all three topics Liebes has interesting, even provocative things to say, especially on the putative Christian influences on the *Zohar*. Liebes's claims on this issue have already aroused extensive, often critical, discussion in Israel and will almost certainly continue to do so in this new English-language context. Alternatively, his rich reworking of the manner of the composition of the *Zohar* is persuasive and a significant contribution beyond Gershom Scholem's basic researches on the subject. In sum, a valuable addition to the growing literature on *Kabala* in English that libraries serving upper-level Judaica and religion programs will want to purchase.—*S. T. Katz, Cornell University*

OAB-1241   Orig
Moussalli, Ahmad S. **Radical Islamic fundamentalism: the ideological and political discourse of Sayyid Qutb.** American University of Beirut, 1993 (c1992). 262p bibl index pbk, $20.00

A brilliantly conceived study of the major Egyptian political ideologue of the 20th-century, this book goes a long way toward exposing many extant fallacies about fundamentalism: it is intellectual as well as political; it transforms conservative rhetoric into progressive goals; it engages rather than ignores modern science, especially scientific truth claims. All these moves, carefully researched and exposited by the author, might suggest that he is an apologist for, not an analyst of, Islamic fundamentalism generally and Sayyid Qutb, in particular. However, in the conclusion he underscores how the strengths of fundamentalism are also its weaknesses: it sacrifices philosophical coherence for ideological expediency, or rather it forces political philosophy to shoulder the role of metaphysics, with the result that "God's relevance can only be seen in a political context." Fundamentalism is here represented as a powerful Islamic

ideology that is also ahistorical and nonsystematic. No one else has written such a powerful exposé. It deserves a wide reading especially among undergraduate, graduate students, and faculty.—*B. B. Lawrence, Duke University*

OAB-1242   BP187   93-47292 CIP
Peters, F.E. **The hajj: the Muslim pilgrimage to Mecca and the holy places.** Princeton, 1994. 399p bibl index afp ISBN 0-691-02120-1, $29.95

Among the duties incumbent on every able-bodied Muslim is that of making the hajj, or the pilgrimage to Mecca, once in a lifetime. In Islam, however, as Peters points out in the introduction, pilgrimage is not only a ritual filled with deep religious meaning but also a cultural, social, and commercial phenomenon. Peters draws on travelers' firsthand accounts and, by weaving these accounts into a connected narrative, provides a literary history of this central Islamic institution, from its inception in the pre-Islamic era to the modern period. The texts forming the bulk of this work have been selected with care and organized into a richly detailed narrative that highlights the characteristic features of the pilgrims' experience over time. The author makes no claim to be exhaustive or comprehensive in his treatment. Although some readers will need to read the work in conjunction with more specialized treatments of the hajj, it provides an overall perspective that is both unique and compelling, and its does so gracefully and with a sense of respect for those who have been the actors in the history here recounted. Essential reading for those who wish to view the institution in historical perspective; detailed notes and an extended bibliography for those who wish to delve further. Maps and drawings; a large number of photographs. Highly recommended to all academic libraries supporting Islamic studies, anthropology, and the history of religion. General; lower-division undergraduate through graduate.—*M. Swartz, Boston University*

OAB-1243   BP161   95-45130 CIP
Renard, John. **Seven doors to Islam: spirituality and the religious life of Muslims.** California, 1996. 333p index afp ISBN 0-520-20095-0, $45.00; ISBN 0-520-20417-4 pbk, $16.95

This book will open more than seven doors for most readers who come to it—or to the class where it is an assigned text—with only a bare introduction to Islam, especially its literary and aesthetic heritage, its reflective and spiritual legacy. Above all, the present survey displays the virtue of a single controlling hand that guides the reader through multiple cultural traditions and complex linguistic developments. One goal is paramount: to make evident not only the importance and difficulty of Islamic idioms but also their beauty and vitality. Like a house with seven floors, this textbook moves from the basement of prophetic revelation to the attic of personal experience; and, since every ascent presupposes a descent, it also provides a lucid reprise through the Qur'anic story of Joseph, a story that becomes, in the author's words, "a return journey through the (same) seven doors" that make the initial journey. The pictures, almost 40 black-and-white half plates, are chosen with the same deft attention to detail and nuance as the texts that they accompany. The book as a whole sets a new, very high standard for introductory surveys that attempt to combine primary source citations with cogent secondary analysis. Enthusiastically recommended. Upper-division undergraduate; graduate; faculty.—*B. B. Lawrence, Duke University*

OAB-1244   BP55   95-50616 CIP
Sonn, Tamara. **Interpreting Islam: Bandali Jawzi's Islamic intellectual history.** Oxford, 1996. 206p index afp ISBN 0-19-510051-4, $39.95

One of the first, if not the first, to attempt a critical analysis of Islamic history from a Marxist perspective was the Palestinian intellectual Bandali Jawzi (1875-1942) who in 1928 published his celebrated *Min Ta'rikh al-Harakat al-Fikriyyah fi'l-Islam* ("A History of Intellectual Movements in Islam"). Important both for the light it sheds on a critical period in the development of modern Arab thought (especially the early 20th century) and for its impact on modern Arab historical thinking since its publication, Jawzi's work has largely

Humanities

been overlooked by Western scholarship. Sonn's book represents a serious effort to compensate for this unfortunate neglect by providing a complete English translation of the work. Sonn's volume is more than a translation, however. In an introduction and lengthy commentary, Sonn attempts to place the work in historical context as well as to show the rather striking ways in which its views anticipate the "neohistoricist," postmodernist perspective of more recent authors, among them E. Said, F. Rahman, A.K. Khatibi, and M. Arkoun. It is a provocative and carefully crafted thesis that merits careful attention. Written in a clear, readable style, it is accompanied by a set of detailed notes and a short index. This translation, the first ever in English, is a welcome addition to the literature on modern Arab thought and is highly recommended to all academic and public libraries concerned with the modern Middle East and Islam. Upper-division undergraduate; graduate; faculty.—*M. Swartz, Boston University*

OAB-1245   BP134   94-3968 CIP
Stowasser, Barbara Freyer. **Women in the Qur'an, traditions, and interpretation.** Oxford, 1994. 206p bibl index afp ISBN 0-19-508480-2, $29.95

This is both an analytical study of the first order and a vade mecum of information on women in the faith, the law, and the imagination of Sunni Muslims. Stowasser's extensive use of Arabic texts, whether fully translated or merely summarized, is at once rare and welcome. In part 1 she tells the story of sacred heroines, from Eve to Mary, who are renowned in Abrahamic scriptures prior to the Qur'an; in part 2 she examines Qur'anic references to the Prophet's wives, together with Hadith (traditions attributed to the Prophet Muhammad himself) on these same paragons of virtue. The author also surveys some modern Muslim interpretations of the Prophet's wives, including the egalitarian message of feminist interpreters such as the Moroccan sociologist Fatima Mernissi. One misses the Shi'i viewpoint, but that gap is due to the author's decision to focus on the Prophet's wives rather than on his daughters, since it is Muhammad's daughter and Ali's wife, Fatima, whose role for Shi'i Muslims exceeds that of all other women. See, for example, Ali Shariati's *Fatima is Fatima*, tr. by Lateh Bakhtiar (Tehran, 1981). Recommended for general readers, upper-division undergraduate and graduate students, and faculty at all levels.—*B. B. Lawrence, Duke University*

OAB-1246   BM755   95-10952 CIP
Sussman, Lance J. **Isaac Leeser and the making of American Judaism.** Wayne State, 1996 (c1995). 311p bibl index afp ISBN 0-8143-1996-3, $39.95

Sussman (SUNY at Binghamton) has produced a first biography of one of the most important American Jewish leaders of the late Jacksonian and Antebellum eras, who envisioned and helped create in the US a major center of Jewish religion and culture. Arriving in the US in 1824, Isaac Leeser (1806-68) found no organized Jewish community and met Jews who had no concern for protecting Jewish rights or expanding the Jewish social position in America. He responded by working to unite the older generation of American-born Jews with the new immigrants of the 1830s-50s, by laying the foundation of the American Jewish press, by helping professionalize the American rabbinate, and by working to improve Jewish-Christian relations. Through the example of Leeser's life, Sussman's book shows how American Judaism emerged from, and is defined by, the tension between tradition and the creation of a new religion that speaks to thoroughly Americanized Jews. An excellent and comprehensive biography of an important individual, Sussman's book thus is also an important contribution to our understanding of the ideals and tensions that stand at the foundation of American Judaism as a whole. Undergraduate; graduate; faculty; general.—*A. J. Avery-Peck, College of The Holy Cross*

OAB-1247   BM205   92-54514 CIP
Wertheimer, Jack. **A people divided: Judaism in contemporary America.** Basic Books, 1993. 267p bibl index ISBN 0-465-00165-3, $25.00

Wertheimer asks: "What...is the condition of American Judaism? What

do we know about the vitality and meaning of religion for American Jews?" The problem is to explain the bipolar data provided by the American Jewish community: the growth of orthodoxy and the reappropriation by secularized Jews of long-abandoned religious rituals and symbols, on the one hand, and the steady increase in intermarriage, estrangement from Israel, and even the conversion of Jews away from Judaism, on the other. Wertheimer's historical and sociological evaluation yields a balanced perspective on the diversity of contemporary Jewish expression and its sources in Judaism and Americanism. The profundity of the analysis is reflected in the author's refusal to predict in all but the most general way the future of the American Jewish community or to offer solutions to its problems (an attitude that distinguishes this book from most others that plow similar territory). Wertheimer shows that, in the very nature of contemporary religious experience, such predictions and proposals are bound to fail. Contemporary Judaism is too complex, multifaceted, and relentlessly changing for its future to be either accurately predicted or shaped. This volume is a must for all students of contemporary Judaism, religion, and American culture. Advanced undergraduate; graduate; faculty; general.—*A. J. Avery-Peck, College of The Holy Cross*

OAB-1248   BM526   94-18186 CIP
Wolfson, Elliot R. **Through a speculum that shines: vision and imagination in medieval Jewish mysticism.** Princeton, 1995 (c1994). 452p bibl index afp ISBN 0-691-07343-0, $49.50

With the publication of this major study, Wolfson has confirmed his position as one of the leading students of medieval Jewish mysticism (Kabala) of this generation. The essence of Wolfson's argument is that kabalistic experience is first and foremost a visual rather than an aural experience as Gershom Scholem had contended. Yet, this visual experience is highly complex because of the necessary theological insistence of traditional Judaism that God cannot be seen. The sorts of experiential and literary consequences that this paradox generates provide the substance of this work. In separate chapters Wolfson traces the subject in rich detail, from its biblical origins through the mystical sources of the talmudic and posttalmudic era (Hekhalot literature), as the issue appears in early medieval kabalistic materials, in the works produced by the Hasidei Ashkenaz (German pietists), and as this type of experience culminates in what Wolfson calls the "Visionary Gnosis" of the Zohar. Though his argument for the sexual nature of much of this experience is not fully convincing, it is always thoughtful and provocative and could well be the most discussed and contested aspect of the book. The detailed discussion is supported by a full, learned, scholarly apparatus and bibliography. This important study should be in every library of any size serving religion or Judaica programs. Upper-division undergraduate through professional.—*S. T. Katz, Cornell University*

■ Theology & the Bible

OAB-1249   BL410   95-3202 MARC
Bracken, Joseph A. **The divine matrix: creativity as link between East and West.** Orbis Books/Gracewing, 1995. 179p bibl index ISBN 1-57075-004-1 pbk, $21.00

This is a brilliant and refreshing contribution to comparative theology. Bracken examines the nature of the infinite in a wide range of traditions, and he provides an important analytical frame for the comparative analysis of the major world religions. Through a discussion of creativity and the infinite in the philosophy of Aristotle and the theology of Thomas Aquinas, a bridge is built between East and West. Bracken grounds his discussion in the work of Alfred North Whitehead, then extends it in a splendid discussion of Advaita Vedanta. This is further explored in the Buddhist doctrine of "dependent co-arising" and in the Taoist notion of "pure movement." Unlike most other volumes on comparative religion, this one provides important hermeneutical tools for comparing different understandings of ultimate reality in a variety of world religions. Bracken has written a terse and concise volume that deserves special attention. It represents a truly sophisticated and unique contribution to the comparative study of religion. Highly recommended for upper-division undergraduates, graduate students, and the general educated reader.—*J. J. Preston, SUNY College at Oneonta*

OAB-1250 BS2555 93-9241 CIP
Brown, Raymond E. **The death of the Messiah: from Gethsemane to the grave: a commentary on the Passion narratives in the four Gospels.** Doubleday, 1994. 2v. 1,608p indexes ISBN 0-385-47177-7, $75.00

This is an extraordinary book. It is similar in format and approach to the author's widely read *The Birth of the Messiah* (1993), but it is even more thorough. It is not a history of the events concerning Jesus' death, nor is it a systematic theology of the significance of that death, although both of these topics are discussed. It is rather an extended commentary on the narratives told by the four evangelists to their respective audiences. In each section there is a fresh literal translation and an extended comment on the four texts, a supplemental analysis, and a valuable extensive bibliography. There are also illustrative tables, nine long appendixes, and thorough indexes. The scholarship can be described as both exhaustive and moderate. Those who know the field will not be surprised; those who do not will not be misled. No library with holdings in Biblical studies can afford to be without this book. Upper-division undergraduate through professional.—*L. Gaston, Vancouver School of Theology*

OAB-1251 BX4827 93-41759 CIP
Burrow, Rufus. **James H. Cone and black liberation theology.** McFarland, 1994. 256p bibl index afp ISBN 0-89950-900-2, $29.95

Burrow's splendid, sagacious, and systematic survey of the writings of James Cone, "the godfather of the development of black theology," is the first full-length book to be published on black theology's premier guru. The author pays special attention to four major transitions on Cone's theological pilgrimage: writing and doing theology for his own people; social analysis during the early period of his maturation; broadening his perspective on the full meaning of oppression; and his evolving encounter with the black church. Using as the book's theme his conviction that "all black theology is a footnote to James Cone," Burrow persuasively portrays the sweeping majesty in Cone's theological odyssey, beginning with his "word to Whitey" and continuing especially in his creative conversations with leading black theologians. Burrow highlights Cone's "courage to change," in particular his emerging openness to women, Marxism, the Third World, and other major living religions. This book is *must* reading for anyone who wants to appreciate the length, breadth, and depth of black theology. Excellent bibliography. Undergraduate; graduate; faculty; general.—*D. W. Ferm, Colby College*

OAB-1252 BS1235 95-46693 CIP
Carr, David M. **Reading the fractures of Genesis: historical and literary approaches.** Westminster John Knox, 1996. 388p bibl indexes afp ISBN 0-664-22071-1, $39.00

This study brings together the methodologies of both diachronic and synchronic approaches to biblical text. Carr (Methodist Theological School, OH) is interested in the ways in which our understanding of the history of the formation of the text can contribute to our understanding of its present shape. He presents a cogent analysis of the previous scholarship on the formation of the text of Genesis as well as breaking new ground. He displays an impressive mastery of scholarship, including both the classical literature on the formation of the Pentateuch and modern studies. In this judicious and balanced treatment, the author himself distinguishes between different levels of plausibility in his analysis. Carr's interest in the history of the formation of the text is in contrast to Robert Alter's primary focus on the literary coherence of Genesis in its present form (*Genesis: Translation and Commentary*, 1996). Because of its depth and focus, Carr's work complements other recent and broader studies such as Richard Elliott Friedman's *Who Wrote the Bible?* (1987) and *The*

Exile and Biblical Narrative (1991). This is a major work; it will command the attention of all scholars and students interested in Genesis. Undergraduate; graduate; faculty.—*H. O. Forshey, Miami University*

OAB-1253 BS646 95-23148 CIP
Cook, Stephen L. **Prophecy & apocalypticism: the postexilic social setting.** Fortress, 1996 (c1995). 246p bibl indexes afp ISBN 0-8006-2839-X pbk, $21.00

In this study, Cook (Union Theological Seminary, NY) provides a substantial critique of the currently held consensus on the origins of apocalypticism in the Hebrew Bible. Recent scholarship has been dominated by Paul D. Hanson's view that the roots of apocalypticism are to be found in a disenfranchised group excluded from power in the restored Jerusalem temple (*The Dawn of Apocalyptic*, rev. ed., 1979). Cook first provides a detailed analysis of the sociology of apocalyptic groups, rejecting the view that the apocalyptic worldview consistently develops from the experience of deprivation or relative deprivation. This analysis is followed by a detailed reinterpretation of the proto-apocalyptic texts of Ezekiel 38 and 39, Zechariah 1-8, and Joel, which leads to the conclusion that biblical apocalypticism stems from the writing and thinking of priestly groups in power rather than from despairing and marginalized groups within the postexilic community. This is an important study and one that will play a significant role in the ongoing scholarly discussion of prophecy and apocalypticism. Upper-division undergraduate; graduate; faculty.—*H. O. Forshey, Miami University*

OAB-1254 BS2455 93-27796 CIP
Culpepper, R. Alan. **John, the son of Zebedee: the life of a legend.** South Carolina, 1994. 376p bibl indexes afp ISBN 0-87249-962-6, $49.95

Culpepper (Baylor) has also written *The Johannine School* (1975), *Anatomy of the Fourth Gospel* (CH, Apr'84), and *1 John, 2 John, 3 John* (1985). Although the present book is concerned with both the life of the apostle John and the biography of the legend that formed around him, it is more the biography the latter than the former. Culpepper's intention was to collect and assess the development of the legends about John rather than to propose a novel solution to the issues related to the development of the traditions. Never has so much of the tradition about John been collected and made available in English. One of the great strengths of this volume is that primary sources are cited, and, where possible, reproduced in English. Beginning with the New Testament, Culpepper traces the legends about John through the Church Fathers, the apocryphal acts of John, medieval sources, Victorian poets, and 19th- and 20th-century historians of early Christianity. Historical tradition and legend are powerful: fisherman, apostle, beloved disciple, elder, seer, hero, saint, and icon. This well-documented book may be read with profit by the scholar, but it is also written in a style that makes it suitable for the general reader. Indexes of Scripture, ancient sources, and modern authors. This book will likely serve for many years to come as a sourcebook for anyone interested in the legends about John. Upper-division undergraduate; graduate; faculty; general.—*J. W. McCant, Point Loma Nazarene College*

OAB-1255 BT771 96-17346 CIP
Fries, Heinrich. **Fundamental theology,** tr. by Robert J. Daly. Catholic University of America, 1996. 682p indexes ISBN 0-8132-0862-9, $44.95; ISBN 0-8132-0863-7 pbk, $29.95

Fries's work is a major contribution to contemporary Roman Catholic theology and ecumenical dialogue, both ecclesiological and cultural. With the decline of Neo-Thomism after Vatican II, it is taking time for a new theological consensus to mature. A book such as this reveals the outlines of the future. At nearly 700 pages it is encyclopedic in nature but still bears the stamp of a single author's well thought out principled positions. To arbitrarily select three issues of interest: (1) Fries's strong stand that theology today must be stated in the plural despite some nostalgia in Catholic circles for "one" theology, which in many ways never really existed historically; (2) his insistence that secularization as opposed to secularism is a positive modern development that flows out of Christian faith in God's good creation; (3) his full repudiation of the outrageous injustice of anti-Semitism, as well as his support for the movement from missionizing to dialogue between Christians and Jews. Robert Daly's translation (an edition as much as a translation) is excellent, accurate, and readable. A "must" work for any library or reader seriously interested in recent developments in Roman Catholic theology. General; upper-division undergraduate through professional.—*R. W. Rousseau, University of Scranton*

OAB-1256   BS579   93-28112 CIP
Greenspahn, Frederick E. **When brothers dwell together: the pre-eminence of younger siblings in the Hebrew Bible.** Oxford, 1994. 193p bibl indexes afp ISBN 0-19-508253-2, $29.95

This provocative and wide-ranging study provides a long-overdue systematic treatment of the hitherto unexplained preference for younger siblings in biblical stories. After a careful review of the evidence, Greenspahn concludes that neither primogeniture, as is widely assumed, nor ultimogeniture were ever the norm in ancient Israel. Rather, he concludes that within the Israelite context fathers were free to choose their heirs. The preference for younger offspring in the biblical traditions in part derives from the belief in the innocence and vulnerability of the younger sibling, a belief widespread in folklore. This theme underscores God's role in choosing unlikely heroes for his purposes and mirrors God's relationship to Israel. Greenspahn is eclectic in his approach to these traditions, drawing on law, anthropology, folklore, and comparative material from the ancient Near East. This is a seminal work by an established biblical scholar and belongs in every library with an interest in biblical scholarship. Lower-division undergraduate through professional.—*H. O. Forshey, Miami University (OH)*

OAB-1257   BT83   92-4178 CIP
Johnson, Elizabeth A. **She who is: the mystery of God in feminist theological discourse.** Crossroad, NY, 1992. 316p indexes ISBN 0-8245-1162-X, $24.95

"What is the right way to speak about God in the face of women's newly cherished human dignity and equality? This is the crucial theological question." Johnson's response is to range far and wide from the early church all the way to the present day to unearth God as the She Who Is, the "creative, relational power of being who enlivens, suffers with, sustains, and enfolds the universe." The author's rich rhetoric is replete with nifty phrases: "mothering the universe," "sheer exuberant relational aliveness," "sacramental anticipatory moments," "the dark radiance of love in solidarity," and so on. The crowning achievement of Johnson's remarkably effortless writing style is that she engages in a gentle, nonconfrontational conversation with many of today's leading feminist theologians, among them Carol Christ and Judith Plaskow (*Weaving the Visions*, 1989), Anne E. Carr (*Transforming Grace*, 1988), Rebecca Chopp (*The Power to Speak*, CH, May'90), and Susan Brooks Thistlethwaite (*Sex, Race, and God*, 1989). Readers will find this incisive survey to be the finest yet written in the area of feminist theological discourse.—*D. W. Ferm, Colby College*

OAB-1258   BT65   92-9059 CIP
Kaufman, Gordon D. **In face of mystery: a constructive theology.** Harvard, 1993. 509p indexes afp ISBN 0-674-44575-9, $39.95

Kaufman's imaginative construction of Christian theology is a creative attempt to rethink the meaning of Christian faith in a modern world. Hence, it takes seriously our scientific and social knowings. In his constructive theology he begins with the issue of "God" and proceeds to examine the "world," "humanity," and "Christ." For instance, Kaufman develops the symbol "God" "in terms of the evolutionary-historical trajectory which has in fact brought human life into being and continues to sustain it." This is an exciting and provocative book. It is critically in touch with the history of Christian theology but also creatively in dialogue with the larger, contemporary intellectual world. It will be dismissed out of hand by fundamentalists. However, it will be very useful for people of faith trying to figure out how to be "faith-ful" in a complex world. It is well written, with helpful notes and indexes. Advanced undergraduate and up.—*A. L. Kolp, Earlham College*

OAB-1259   BX4827   94-19487 CIP
McCormack, Bruce L. **Karl Barth's critically realistic dialectical theology: its genesis and development, 1909-1936.** Oxford, 1995. 499p bibl indexes afp ISBN 0-19-826337-6, $65.00

Theologians love to tell the story of how Karl Barth first rebelled against liberalism (with the dialectics of the *Romans* commentary) and then embraced a new orthodoxy (with the analogy of faith of the *Church Dogmatics*). In this study, which is the best intellectual biography of Barth now available, McCormack (Princeton Theological Seminary) rejects this plot line. His work, which is as brilliant and comprehensive as it is meticulous and unorthodox, strives to demonstrate the continuity in Barth's development from 1915 on, showing, for example, how analogy is present in the dialectical Barth. He calls Barth's mature method critical realism, arguing that the objectivity of the *Church Dogmatics* continues the thrust of the dialectics. If there is a second conversion (away from dialectics), it is found in the *Göttingen Dogmatics* of 1924-25, not the book on Anselm. Moreover, McCormack argues that material theological decisions (mainly concerning eschatology) rather than methodological or cultural reflections motivate Barth's changes. Relying on recent German scholarship and dismissing nearly everything else (including Barth's own autobiographical reflections), McCormack's new preiodization will be required reading for every subsequent discussion of Barth. Upper-division undergraduate through professional.—*S. H. Webb, Wabash College*

OAB-1260   BS2506   95-49173 CIP
Murphy-O'Connor, Jerome. **Paul: a critical life.** Oxford, 1996. 416p bibl indexes afp ISBN 0-19-826749-5, $35.00

This work is the mature culmination of a lifetime of Pauline studies by a distinguished scholar (École Biblique, Jerusalem). While the book is primarily devoted to chronology, travel plans, and letter writing, theology is by no means neglected. It can be read with profit by most undergraduates and their professors. The discussion is clear and thorough, and there is much that can be learned, but there are also ample possibilities for disagreement in future discussions. In general, what is presented could be called the consensus view of much modern critical scholarship, but the author's unique solutions to some issues deserve further attention. This is likely to become the standard work on Paul's life for the next generation and is warmly recommended as such. Undergraduate; graduate; faculty.—*L. Gaston, Vancouver School of Theology*

OAB-1261   BT695   96-13022 CIP
Northcott, Michael S. **The environment and Christian ethics.** Cambridge, 1996. 379p index afp ISBN 0-521-44481-0, $59.95; ISBN 0-521-57631-8 pbk, $21.95

Northcott (Univ. of Edinburgh) provides a lucid and thoughtful assessment of the ecological crisis and its origins. The crisis originated not in Christianity, as is often supposed, but in a series of changes (including the development of a market economy and the enclosure of common lands by the rich) that occurred at the beginning of the modern era. A new individualistic morality became the secular warrant for the human use and abuse of nature and its creatures. After reviewing current philosophical and religious responses to the ecological crisis, Northcott provides a reassessment of the Hebrew Bible's perspective on creation, which compares favorably to other earth-friendly perspectives. The Hebrew Bible emphasizes the relatedness of divine, human, and nonhuman life, which contradicts the isolated individualism of the modern perspective. Finally, Northcott demonstrates how Christian natural law ethics extends the Hebrew ecology and provides the basis for a critical response to technological society. This is a well-written book, nuanced in its arguments and comparable, this reviewer believes, to Carolyn Merchant's *The Death of Nature*

(1980) in its rehabilitation of the past. Highly recommended for upper-division undergraduates, graduate students, researchers, and religious professionals.—*R. Severson, Marylhurst College for Lifelong Learning*

OAB-1262 BT610 96-24726 CIP
Pelikan, Jaroslav. **Mary through the centuries: her place in the history of culture.** Yale, 1996. 267p bibl indexes afp ISBN 0-300-06951-0, $25.00

Although volumes have been written about the Virgin Mary from a wide variety of perspectives, it is rare to find a scholarly work that is easily accessible to the general, educated reader. Pelikan has given us a brilliant and very well written history of Marian devotion. He discusses the biblical portrait of Mary and traces the complex Marian theology that has developed over the years. This is a sophisticated study of the image of Mary through various historical periods. Particularly interesting are chapters on the "second Eve," her role as "mother of God" (theotokos) and as "Heroine of the *Qur'an*." Also thoroughly explored is the symbol of Mary as a paragon of chastity, a model of faith, and the source of enormous devotion and miraculous experiences. As Queen of Heaven, the Virgin Mary represents powerful divine symbolism. Particularly strong is an analysis of Mary's place in literature, politics, and social history. According to Pelikan, Mary remains an important source of hope and solace. This volume is highly recommended for college-level students and the general reader.—*J. J. Preston, SUNY College at Oneonta*

OAB-1263 BS2515 93-5983 CIP
Perkins, Pheme. **Peter: apostle for the whole church.** South Carolina, 1994. 209p bibl indexes afp ISBN 0-87249-974-X, $34.95

Perkins introduces this excellent study by reviewing the contrasting ways in which the roles of Peter and Paul have been viewed both in the New Testament itself, and in later Christian interpretation. Opposing the "Tübingen" notion that Peter's legalistic Christianity and Paul's law-free Christianity were antithetical, Perkins insists that Peter reflected a "Centrist" position between these two poles, a view she then traces in Acts, the Gospels, and the canonical "Petrine" letters themselves. In the chapters that follow, the author reconstructs a life of Peter from the NT traditions, which she supplements with brief though important information drawn from archaeology and the work of Eusebius; reflects on Peter in comparison with the other apostles in Mark and Matthew and comments on the role of Peter found in the canonical Pauline and Petrine Epistles and in apocryphal NT materials; describes ways in which Peter was used by the second-century "authentic" Christian tradition; and finally, addresses issues of episcopacy and authority as these connect with Peter's role in the Roman church. Not since Oscar Cullmann's *Peter, Disciple, Apostle, Martyr* (1953; 2nd ed., 1962) has there been a study of this range and stature dealing historically and analytically with the "chief" of the Apostles. Documentation is meticulous and extensive; the bibliography superb. A major contribution both to NT studies and to ecumenical theology and ecclesiology. Indispensable to all undergraduate, graduate, and theological school libraries.—*R. F. Berkey, Mount Holyoke College*

OAB-1264 BT660 94-18724 CIP
Poole, Stafford. **Our Lady of Guadalupe: the origins and sources of a Mexican national symbol, 1531-1797.** Arizona, 1995. 325p bibl index afp ISBN 0-8165-1526-3, $40.00

The most complete and thorough study of the Guadalupan tradition to date, this is also an outstanding representative of the historian's art. It sensitively probes every available reference to the devotion and apparition stories related to the Lady of Guadalupe shrine near Mexico City. The evidence leads to the author's thesis that "the devotion ... prior to 1648 and the apparition devotion after that year are two distinct entities." That is, although the image of Our Lady of Guadalupe existed and had a devotion attached to it from perhaps the mid-1500s, it was not until much later that the apparition stories developed. Poole concludes that the "most powerful religious and national symbol in Mexico

today" has no "objective historical basis." Perhaps what makes this work most interesting to a wide audience of Latin Americanists and scholars in general is Poole's analysis of how the stories got interpreted and used by different groups over time. His work is very suggestive at this level, and it may inspire further scholarship in the interaction of religion and politics at the level of discourse and symbolism. The sources and references are exhaustive. Highly recommended for every sort of library. General; upper-division undergraduate through professional.—*B. T. Froehle, University of South Carolina—Spartanburg*

OAB-1265 BT846 96-41002 CIP
Russell, Jeffrey Burton. **A history of heaven: the singing silence.** Princeton, 1997. 220p bibl index afp ISBN 0-691-01161-3, $24.95

Russell (Univ. of California, Santa Barbara), author of 15 other books, offers a fascinating historical analysis of the concept of heaven. Acknowledging that "heaven" is logic-defying and literal language-resistant, Russell explores how heaven was presented by the ancient Jews, Greeks, and Romans, by early and medieval Eastern and Western Christianity, by the Christian mystics, and finally by Dante's *Paradiso*, which he considers the supreme expression. In the midst of addressing the intellectual problems posed by the concept(s) of heaven, Russell provides an insightful and creative study of the visionary, symbolic, poetic, and paradoxical modes of expression. Exploring the human longing for unity expressed in the concept of a blessed otherworld, Russell argues that the concept of heaven is as exciting and interesting as the historic concepts of hell, evil, and the Devil, some of the subjects of his earlier books. The scope, suggestiveness, and research base of this work make it a significant, even a landmark, study of heaven. The 20-page bibliography is a useful gateway to scholarship on heaven; the 18 illustrations supplement his interpretations visually. Not for novices, this is an important book for graduate and research libraries in religious studies and theology and for those scholars exploring the poetry of heaven. Upper-division undergraduate; graduate; faculty.—*R. L. Massanari, Alma College*

OAB-1266 BS680 CIP
Schüssler Fiorenza, Elisabeth. **But she said: feminist practices of biblical interpretation.** Beacon Press, 1992. 261p index ISBN 0-8070-1214-9, $24.00

This study takes its title from Mark 7:28. Mark's account of how a Syro-Phoenician women's wit transforms Jesus's rejection in order to benefit her daughter is the paradigm for Schüssler Fiorenza's critical rhetorical model of feminist biblical interpretation. This model, which Schüssler Fiorenza distinguishes from nine other feminist approaches to the Bible, is conceived as a strategy, envisioned as a dance, incorporating a variety of theoretical insights and methods. She sees it as a means to identify the rhetoric of patriarchy that interlocks androcentrism, racism, classicism, colonialism, and sexism within Second (New) Testament texts. She insists that the recognition of social and political oppression and injustice in texts is a necessary prelude to any reconceptualization of the Bible that might transform master-centered texts into prototypes for justice and liberation. The work is enhanced by her applications of this method to several gospel passages, most often from Luke. This is a landmark study. It should be as important to feminist biblical studies in the 1990s as her work, *In Memory of Her* (CH, Nov '83) was to the 1980s. Essential for libraries supporting upper-level undergraduate and graduate biblical, ministerial, and women's studies programs.—*R. A. Boisclair, University of San Diego*

OAB-1267 BD241 91-40572 CIP
Thiselton, Anthony C. **New horizons in hermeneutics.** Zondervan, 1992. 703p bibl indexes ISBN 0-310-51590-4, $29.95

Thiselton (Univ. of Nottingham), who has taught at Calvin College, intends this as a textbook. It is an exhaustive study of the hermeneutic debate focused on, but not limited to, biblical interpretation. It greatly expands his earlier work, *The Two Horizons*. His own position follows Wittgenstein, Austin, and Searle.

The text traces a short history of Early Church and Reformation hermeneutics and then develops in detail the theoretical models in the debate beginning with Schleiermacher. Thiselton does an exceptional job of classifying and clarifying the many dimensions of the present philosophical, theological, literary, and sociological debates. He weaves into his narrative an incredible number of proponents and critics of each model. The bibliography is extensive and useful. Criticisms that come to mind are few. The late Middle Ages and Renaissance are passed over too lightly. Thiselton's slight polemical bent toward "realism" leads him to a one-sided interepretation of Karl Barth and Richard Rorty. Some individual thinkers need treatment in more depth; but the breadth and organization of the material is comprehensive. This massive work of scholarship in hermeneutics is an excellent source for theologians and biblical scholars; highly recommended for upper-level undergraduates, graduate students, and faculty.—*J. H. Ware, Austin College*

OAB-1268   BS1171   94-40788 CIP
Wills, Lawrence M. **The Jewish novel in the ancient world.** Cornell, 1995. 279p bibl indexes afp ISBN 0-8014-3075-5, $37.50

Readers of the Bible and the Apochrypha are often puzzled by the character of certain narratives that appear to test the boundaries of scripture. Typically, such stories represent dramatic human incidents with only tangential reference to divine history, leaving the reader to question the inclusion of such works in a collection that serves as the foundation text of the three dominant Western religions. This important study defines a number of such Biblical stories as novels—fictional entertainments—and proceeds to analyze the form and content of these narrations in terms of the literary context of Hellenic culture, i.e., between about 200 BCE. and 100 CE. The result is a lucid critical account of the stories of Daniel/Susanna, Tobit, Esther, Judith, and Joseph and Aseneth. Wills (biblical studies, Episcopal Divinity School) notes the generic similarity between these Jewish texts and their literary counterparts in the Hellenic and Roman Diaspora where the majority of Jews lived. These "fictions"—like all great imaginative writing—compel the reader's attention not by imparting an already determined moral lesson, but because they represent human destiny in terms of uncertainty and mystery. This outstanding work will be of interest to literary/historical Bible students, as well as students of Judaism and Hellenism.—*M. Butovsky, Concordia University*

SCIENCE & TECHNOLOGY

■ General

OAB-1269   Q175   92-31286 CIP
The "Racial" economy of science: toward a democratic future, ed. by Sandra Harding. Indiana, 1993. 526p index afp ISBN 0-253-32693-1, $39.95; ISBN 0-253-20810-6 pbk, $18.95

By "racial economy" Harding means "those institutions, assumptions, and practices that are responsible for disproportionately distributing along 'racial' lines the benefits of Western science to the haves and the bad consequences to the have-nots, thereby enlarging the gap between them." Challenging traditional views of Western science as a progressive force and "pure" intellectual endeavor, she instead locates it as a Eurocentric institution shaped by the racist, sexist, and imperialist character of the dominant social order (from which ranks its practitioners are still largely drawn), and disserving the needs and interests of the peoples of the Third World and minorities in Western society. She further suggests that science itself has suffered as a creative force by neglecting the potential of non-Western contributions. An impressively broad array of scholarship has been assembled to explore these issues, drawn from scientists and historians of science, activists, and public policy analysts. The essays address themes of non-Western scientific traditions, scientific views of race, "who gets to do science," regressive effects of technology on peoples of non-European origin, the supposed value neutrality of science, and the possibilities for a different relationship between science and society. A rich lode of readily accessible thought on the nature and practice of science in society. Highly recommended. General; undergraduate; graduate.—*L. W. Moore, formerly, University of Kentucky*

OAB-1270   Q175   94-47940 CIP
Aronson, Jerrold L. **Realism rescued: how scientific progress is possible,** by Jerrold L. Aronson, Rom Harré, and Eileen Cornell Way. Open Court, 1995. 213p bibl indexes ISBN 0-8126-9288-8, $42.95; ISBN 0-8126-9289-6 pbk, $18.95

For more than two decades, Harré has been one of the principal architects of a realist philosophy of science, as has Aronson. This book is a tightly reasoned presentation of a new approach towards understanding the meaning of scientific knowledge in terms that reflect the actual practice of science since the 17th century. Analysis of the role of models in scientific discourse and understanding provides an approach less dependent on formal logical analysis, avoiding the paradoxes that make scientific realism difficult in more traditional approaches to the philosophy of science. The topic is very complex and has long been a matter of philosophical debate. As a result, this is not a simple textbook but an extended essay rich in detail requiring careful reading. In an era in which the possibility of scientific objectivity/truth is often questioned, *Realism Rescued* provides a basis for an alternative view in which scientific realism is philosophically acceptable. An essential resource for college and university libraries. Upper-division undergraduate through faculty.—*J. L. McKnight, College of William and Mary*

OAB-1271   Q141   95-31823 CIP
Brian, Denis. **Genius talk: conversations with Nobel scientists and other luminaries.** Plenum, 1995. 423p bibl index ISBN 0-306-45089-5, $28.95

Readers may approach these candid interviews with 22 of the greatest minds of the 20th century with expectations of sweeping revelations about the great scientific questions of our time. After all, nearly all are Nobel prize winners in their respective disciplines and acknowledged leaders in their fields. Insightful answers are offered for questions ranging from the big bang to the nature of human consciousness, but what strikes the reader is the human qualities one somehow forgets are associated with genius. From the flamboyant extrovert Richard Feynman to the painfully reclusive P.A.M. Dirac, we see people with the same needs, desires, and frustrations that drive us all. Linus Pauling's joking confession that his wife's activism led him into the peace movement and a second Nobel prize, Feynman's poignant letter to his young bride on the anniversary of her death, and Arno Penzias's recollections of what it is was like to be a Jewish child in prewar Germany are but a few of the stories that will keep the reader engrossed. Equally fascinating are the casual references to friendships and working relationships with those destined to become legends, such as Einstein, Bohr, Freud, and Jung. Several comment on whether the government's prosecution of Oppenheimer as a possible communist sympathizer was justified; who was the greatest physicist, Einstein or Bohr; and the origins of Freud's revolutionary ideas about psychoanalysis. The comments have the added weight of coming from those who knew and worked with these giants. Anyone interested in the beliefs, foibles, and thought processes of the extremely gifted will want to read this informative and entertaining book. Highly recommended! All levels.—*C. G. Wood, Eastern Maine Technical College*

OAB-1272   Q125   CIP
Collins, Harry. **The golem: what everyone should know about science,** by Harry Collins and Trevor Pinch. Cambridge, 1993. 164p bibl index ISBN 0-521-35601-6, $19.95

The golem is a human-made creature of Jewish mythology, obedient yet powerful, and capable of destroying its masters with its clumsiness when uncontrolled. It seems a fitting analog for modern science as a whole, but Collins and Pinch focus instead on scientific investigations themselves as golem-like beasts with lives of their own. Entirely independent chapters examine studies of chemical transfer of memory, proofs of relativity, cold fusion, spontaneous generation, gravity waves, and lizard sex lives, and raise interesting questions. What can scientists do when experimental results do not support even the strongest theories? How much does faith in our theories depend on those results? When is an experiment done well enough? The final chapter offers focused advice for modern society: It is more important for the public to know how science is done than to know science itself. The writing style is fluid and uncomplicated by superfluous detail, and simple illustrations appear as needed. A list for further reading is appended, along with a comprehensive index. A real pleasure to read; highly recommended. All levels.—*D. Carmichael, Pittsburg State University*

OAB-1273 [CD-ROM]
Earth summit: United Nations Conference on Environment and Development. United Nations Publications, 1993. $495.00. User manual. System requirements: IBM-PC or compatible, 386 or later; 2 MB RAM; 1.5 MB hard disk space; VGA monitor; Microsoft Windows 3.0 or higher; DOS 3.3 or higher; Microsoft extensions 2.0 or higher; Microsoft mouse.

The *Earth Summit* CD-ROM gathers all of the documents submitted to the 1992 Rio Earth Summit in one, relatively easy-to-use location. This disc includes all the preparatory documents from the various planning conferences, working documents addressed by the conference, and all of the conference documents. Virtually all the conference materials are available in English; in addition, many have been entered in their original language. Users may select from program menus written in English, French, or Spanish. Installation was trouble-free; however, this program really runs best with at least 4 megabytes of RAM. This Windows 3.1 program requires CD-ROM extensions 2.21. Users who are accustomed to Windows-style programs should find little difficulty using the pull-down menus. *Earth Summit* has sophisticated text retrieval features that allow access to all or parts of documents, based on keyword searches. An additional strength is the ability to call up any of the tables, images, or graphs for screen display or printing. Both forms of data, textual and graphic, can be copied to the clipboard for inclusion in other documents. The user is advised that some text searches can be slow, but the software also allows for faster index searches and for combinations of the two types of searches. Researchers seeking to compare different documents can simultaneously display multiple documents on the screen. This CD-ROM can be installed on a network for multiple access. Although the search and query features are worthwhile, the real utility of this collection lies in the documents themselves. This single disc stores the best collection of assessments and analyses of the Earth's environment yet compiled. A good introductory overview to the conference can be found in *AGENDA 21: the Earth Summit Strategy to Save Our Planet* (CH, Nov'93), ed. by Daniel Sitarz. *Earth Summit* CD-ROM provides an extensive library of original materials for researchers or policy analysts in a format that is far easier to use than *The Earth Summit*, introduction and commentary by Stanley P. Johnson (CH, Nov'93); moreover, it contains vastly more information. Recommended for research collections. Graduate; faculty.—*P. J. Pizor, Northwest College*

OAB-1274 GE195 96-34249 MARC
Ehrlich, Paul R. **Betrayal of science and reason: how anti-environmental rhetoric threatens our future,** by Paul R. Ehrlich and Anne H. Ehrlich. Island Press, 1996. 335p index afp ISBN 1-55963-483-9, $24.95

In this thought-provoking and extremely timely book, the Ehrlichs provide a disturbing insight into the rising antipathy toward environmentalism. Effectively stated "brownlash" efforts undermine and misinterpret environmental data and prolong the difficult search for solutions. This disturbing trend is well illustrated and explained in 13 chapters that outline environmental anti-science rhetoric; atmosphere and climate; toxic substances; and economics and the environment. Also included are biological diversity and the Endangered Species Act. The concluding chapter, "One Plant, One Experiment," shares compelling statements of the impact and assault of brownlash on natural ecosystems such as land degradation, deforestation, ecosystem toxification, depletion of the ozone shield, and others. This reviewer was impressed with Appendix A, which documents the brownlash literature, and Appendix B, which outlines the scientific consensus of 56 of the world's scientific academies and lists signatures of more than 1,670 concerned scientists. Helpful chapter notes and index. Highly recommended. Upper-division undergraduates through professionals.—*J. H. Hunter, William Marsh Rice University*

OAB-1275 BL240 95-19181 CIP
Ferguson, Kitty. **The fire in the equations: science, religion, and the search for God.** Eerdmans, 1995 (c1994). 308p bibl index afp ISBN 0-8028-3805-7, $25.00

During the past few decades, several things have been happening in the world of science as a human endeavor: major advances in our knowledge, major breakthroughs in our understanding, and quite a few new insights into what science is all about. Inevitably, the fundamental questions as to the scope and limitations of the human mind have also breathed new life into the age-old interactions between science and religion. In this beautifully and intelligently written book, Ferguson not only reports on some of the intellectual tremors jolting the world of thinking women and men, but also considers the basic questions with penetrating analysis, yet at a very readable level. For one who seems to have had no formal training in science (for years she was a professional singer and conductor) Ferguson displays remarkable familiarity with the issues and key concepts of current science, though her discussions would have been even more interesting if she had familiarized herself with Upanishadic worldviews. There are only two juxtaposed statements in the book that are not logically connected, but presented as such. "One of the assumptions of science and religion, that there is such a thing as objective truth, means that I might be dead wrong" (true). "Of what possible worth, then, in this quest, is my private view of the universe?" This reviewer believes it is of every worth, because (as Ferguson herself has rightly recognized) that is all that is ultimately meaningful, and of which one can speak with any confidence. An excellent book. Heartily recommended. All levels.—*V. V. Raman, Rochester Institute of Technology*

OAB-1276 Q180 94-35048 CIP
Friedlander, Michael W. **At the fringes of science.** Westview, 1995. 196p bibl index afp ISBN 0-8133-2200-6, $24.95

This book should very quickly make its way into syllabi of history of science courses as a worthy companion and successor to Martin Gardner's classic *Fads and Fallacies in the Name of Science* (1957). But it deserves an attentive reading by the public at large for its concise analysis of the reasons for, and the hazards attendant upon, the noncritical acceptance of pseudoscience. As his title suggests, physicist Friedlander (Washington Univ., St. Louis) focuses his attention on the borderland between what clearly is and what clearly is not science, in the process revealing that the boundary is not necessarily always fixed and distinct. He explicates the formal conduct of science as a means of setting it apart from pseudoscience, in which context, for example, the initial rejection but ultimate triumph of plate tectonics clearly contrasts with the speculations of Immanuel Velikovsky. He extends his examination across the spectrum from "respectable maverick ideas" such as the impact theory of dinosaur extinction, through the sloppy science of polywater and cold fusion, to the "tabloid science" of astrology and UFO abductions, with excursions along the way to consider research fraud and "political pseudoscience" such as Lysenkoism and creation science. The central theme that emerges is that the public must better understand how science is done if science is to serve the public interest, and Friedlander closes with prescriptions for how scientists themselves can assist this process. General through graduate.—*L. W. Moore, formerly, University of Kentucky*

OAB-1277 Orig
Greenwood, Addison. **Science at the frontier, v.1.** National Academy Press, 1992. 277p index ISBN 0-309-04592-4, $24.95

Greenwood provides a wider, not necessarily scientific, audience with insight into the frontiers of contemporary science. A group of science writers have translated the proceedings of the Second Frontiers of Science Symposia, organized by the National Academy of Sciences in 1990, into a volume which can be understood by readers with limited scientific backgrounds. Participants in the Second Symposia were young scientists on the verge of assuming leadership in US science and who had already distinguished themselves in their respective fields. The topics covered are at the cutting edge of scientific endeavors and will give both scientists and nonscientists an excellent summary of the state of the exciting developments in the major fields of scientific endeavor as well as in applied areas of science. The volume has been carefully written, documented, and illustrated. The National Academy of Sciences is to be commended for making such an excellent volume available to a larger public. The first volume of a continuing series, it should be in all undergraduate and public libraries. Required reading for all scientists and those who wish to be appraised of the frontiers of contemporary science. Highly recommended.—*D. A. Johnson, Spring Arbor College*

OAB-1278 Orig

Holdgate, Martin. **From care to action: making a sustainable world.** IUCN/Taylor & Francis, 1996. 346p bibl index ISBN 1-56032-560-7, $59.95; ISBN 1-56032-559-3 pbk, $24.95

In his admirable outline for a difficult task, Holdgate provides statements of position, useful ideas, and a plan of action for people confronting problems at the heart of the global environmental crisis. The book is well organized and begins with a concise review of development and conservation. After updating the reader on the current state of the environment, the author finishes setting the stage by identifying the barriers to success. Holdgate's contribution to the field is in chapters 5 through 11, which outline methods to develop new values, educate and inform people, understand nature, use nature sustainably, empower communities, build new alliances, and most importantly, move forward. Cumbersome issues such as sustainability, development, population growth, empowerment, and personal action are clearly addressed with excellent suggestions for further work. This outstanding work is well referenced, ideal for undergraduate classes or as a forum for discussion in graduate seminars, and also recommended for people in the field, professional policy analysts, faculty, and researchers.—*D. Ostergren, West Virginia University*

OAB-1279 Q175 93-272 CIP

Holton, Gerald. **Science and anti-science.** Harvard, 1993. 203p bibl index afp ISBN 0-674-79298-X, $24.95

This collection of essays by eminent scholar Holton embodies many thoughtful reflections on several aspects of the scientific enterprise as case studies from various historical perspectives. The chapters reveal the complexity of science as well as the subtle and often unrecognized factors that influence the evolution of science. Reflecting Holton's erudition and insights, this slender volume discusses Ernst Mach's influence on 20th-century thinkers, the *rhetorical* aspects of theory-presentations, as well as the "Jeffersonian Research Program." The essay "Controversy Over the End of Science" contains a very timely analysis of Spengler's prediction of the decline of the West. Perhaps the most important essay is the concluding "Anti-Science Phenomenon," and it deserves to be more widely disseminated. We live in an age in which even some serious thinkers (some of them "scientific") tend to be lured by the plethora of medieval pseudo-scientific worldviews that have been surfacing and strutting in the public arena with modernistic phraseology, creating the illusion of being rational and experimental. On the other hand, blatantly anti-scientific forces have also been raising their heads. It is important that thinkers and the educated public at large recognize the dangers implicit in such movements. They are injurious not only to the scientific spirit and enterprise, but are wrought with potential danger to society at large. Holton's book is one of the few powerful and well-informed statements on this matter. Advanced undergraduate through professional.—*V. V. Raman, Rochester Institute of Technology*

OAB-1280 GE42 96-26920 CIP

Katz, Eric. **Nature as subject: human obligation and natural community.** Rowman & Littlefield, 1997. 257p bibl index afp ISBN 0-8476-8303-6, $62.50; ISBN 0-8476-8304-4 pbk, $23.95

This is a unique, fine, and needed volume. Though there are literally hundreds, perhaps even thousands, of books documenting critical needs to preserve environments, some identifying the loss of many species and others presenting apocalyptic warnings about the world's ecosystems, there are too few devoted to environmental ethics and philosophy topics. Katz's educational background and scholarship are excellent preparation for these 16 philosophical essays, written over a 17-year period, 1979-1996. Integral to the essays, the introductory chapter is an intellectual history relevant to environmental ethics, the concept of moral concerns for nature's world systems, and nature's autonomy. The essays are clustered into four areas: the moral concerns of nature; restoration and domination; justice, genocide, and the environment; and history and tradition. Katz is deeply committed to nonanthropocentric, holistic concepts; he offers a moral approach to all natures, perhaps even a sanctity transcending any utilitarian, economic, or humanly beneficial purpose. The reader will

be moved well beyond the ordinarily repetitively treated environmental issues of saving a particular organism, recycling, or saving a river or a rain forest. Readers will need some background in philosophy and/or ethics. Upper-division undergraduates through professionals.—*J. N. Muzio, CUNY Kingsborough Community College*

OAB-1281 Orig

Kaye, Brian H. **Science and the detective: selected reading in forensic science.** VCH, 1995. 388p bibl indexes afp ISBN 3-527-29251-9, $90.00; ISBN 3-527-29252-7 sc, $39.95

This excellent quick resource should be read by everyone—from the law student who does not have time for an in-depth study of forensic science to the "average" citizen continually exposed to forensics from the limited viewpoint of the media handling of sensational crime cases. Kaye's style of writing makes this very complicated field both interesting and understandable in a nonmathematical presentation. He covers a surprising amount of material on each subject, with the objective of increasing the reader's understanding of the range of applications and limitations of forensic science. The book emphasizes the application of physical sciences to forensic problems, leaving the biological sciences to other works, but its treatment is excellent and includes case histories to illustrate applications of the principles discussed together with diagrams and photographs inserted to help understanding. Discussions range through such subjects as electronic imaging, fingerprinting, document analysis, genetic fingerprinting, etc. To increase its value as a reference, it contains an excellent word finder, author and subject indexes, chapter references, and new terms in bold type with definitions included in the text. All levels.—*P. R. Douville, emeritus, Central Connecticut State University*

OAB-1282 Q175 96-32555 Orig

Laszlo, Ervin. **The whispering pond: a personal guide to the emerging vision of science.** Element, MA, 1996. 242p bibl index ISBN 1-85230-899-0, $24.95

The Whispering Pond, like earlier books by Laszlo (e.g., *Vision 2020*, CH, Sep'94), is difficult to classify and review. The best that the reviewer can do is to provide the reader with a sketchy overview of the work. Laszlo offers a panoramic and breathtaking view of science by examining current perspectives in cosmology, physics, biology, and psychology as well as presenting his views on how these sciences are developing. Though the work is hardly a textbook, a gifted and enthusiastic teacher might make good use of it for supplementary reading in an integrated science course for nonscientists. If nothing else, students will learn of the exciting, open ended nature of the sciences examined and of their practitioners' concerns and quests. Readers will learn, as well, of the implications science provides for the educated layperson concerning our understanding of the universe. If the reviewer will be allowed a metaphor, *The Whispering Pond* is really one wild roller coaster of a read. General readers; undergraduate students.—*M. Levinson, University of Washington*

OAB-1283 Q175 95-40997 CIP

Laudan, Larry. **Beyond positivism and relativism: theory, method, and evidence.** Westview, 1996. 277p bibl index afp ISBN 0-8133-2468-8, $59.95; ISBN 0-8133-2469-6 pbk, $22.95

Laudan stakes his epistemological position not *between* the familiar polarities of positivism and relativism (were we not taught that the two spanned the field?) but, as his title explicitly states, *beyond them*—it being very much his argument that, far from being antipodal, positivism and relativism are sisters under the skin, the sterility of the latter deriving from the slavish formalism of the former. So he is eager to move the explanation of the scientific enterprise, in which he strongly believes, to ground where it does not get waylaid by the too-rigorous postulations of a Popper or a Carnap, and so be subject to the anarchistic snipings of a Kuhn or a Feyerabend, for whom no world picture is superior to any other. Clearly Laudan has one foot solidly planted in reality— and he is ready, along with Samuel Johnson, to kick the nearest pebble, refuting the extremists "thus!" He writes lucidly and provides convincing, original arguments to defend science against those too eager to find loopholes in its basically empirical and progressively cumulative process. This is a wise, beautifully written book that commands attention and respect, even as the author takes on both narrow and radical theories that collectively produce ironies enough, he laments, "to make grown men weep." General; upper-division undergraduates through faculty.—*M. Schiff, College of Staten Island, CUNY*

OAB-1284 Q175 96-3910 CIP
McAllister, James W. **Beauty & revolution in science.** Cornell, 1996. 231p bibl index afp ISBN 0-8014-3240-5, $29.95

The persistent, dense intellectual fog laid down by Thomas A. Kuhn's *Structure of Scientific Revolutions* (1962) is somewhat dissipated by McAllister's lucid contribution to the rationalist theory of scientific practice. Resurrecting some concepts of the 18th-century English aesthetician Francis Hutcheson, McAllister brilliantly answers two of the prevailing counterarguments to the rationalist view—that science is driven by culturally determined considerations of "beauty," and that (according to Kuhn) when the scientific paradigm changes, the objective criteria of science are so radically altered that no consistent notion of scientific "truth" survives. McAllister rather demonstrates that the empirical success of a given theory—its bringing uniformity to a great number of diverse events—triggers an aesthetic response, a response subservient *to* the empirical success. Moreover, though so-called scientific revolutions constitute a "rupture" in the scientific community's "aesthetic canon"—necessitated by new empirical information—the criteria for theory choice may nevertheless remain largely unchanged. In short, McAllister shows that there "may be a rational justification both for choosing theories on established aesthetic criteria and for abandoning those criteria in revolutions." In support of this thesis, McAllister discusses how in the 19th century the availability of new construction materials shaped a new architectural aesthetic. He then addresses the rise of Copernicus's and Kepler's theories of astronomy, and the discoveries of relativity and quantum mechanics in the 20th century. A valuable, important, persuasively argued book. Highly recommended. General; upper-division undergraduate through professional.—*M. Schiff, College of Staten Island, CUNY*

OAB-1285 BS651 92-34549 CIP
McKown, Delos B. **The mythmaker's magic: behind the illusion of "Creation Science."** Prometheus Books, 1993. 180p index afp ISBN 0-87975-770-1, $23.95

A rather harsh and/or bitter collection of ten essays that examine every facet of the controversy between evolution and creationism. McKown (philosophy, Auburn Univ.) uncovers the rather enigmatic standing of "creation science" in public education and, among other things, the clever ploys that the "scientific creationists," who believe the Bible is essentially and substantially true in its many particulars relating to science, use to obscure the real truth and to impose a pure myth upon public schools in the guise of respectable science. The book is "aimed at the kind of intelligent, reasonably open-minded, public-spirited people who serve on the nation's school boards; also at the nation's science teachers, particularly in the public schools; and, last but not least, at scientists in general, whether engaged in education or not." Should be read by all interested in combatting the dangerous spread of "scientific creationism" in the education of the public. Advanced undergraduate through professional.—*J. M. Carpenter, University of Kentucky*

OAB-1286 T174 93-9447 CIP
Morgall, Janine Marie. **Technology assessment: a feminist perspective.** Temple University, 1993. 249p bibl index afp ISBN 1-56639-090-7, $39.95; ISBN 1-56639-091-5 pbk, $18.95

Morgall has written an important book that provides an analysis of how technology assessment relates to women's lives. The subject matter is, therefore, the process of identifying and evaluating the impact of technological change on

women—in the workplace and in reproductive roles and, to a lesser extent, on their lifestyles. The author begins with a discussion of the evolution, organization, methods, and problems of technology assessment, and then proceeds to review the feminist literature on women and technology and the feminist scholarship already existing on technology assessment. She concludes with two examples: technology assessment of women in the clerical sector, and her own research on family planning, abortion, and technology assessment. Her style is straightforward; the writing is clear, concrete, and direct. A work to read with profit by scholars of women's studies, technology assessment, sociology, history of technology and culture, and labor. Fine bibliography; helpful index. All levels.—*M. H. Chaplin, Wellesley College*

OAB-1287 Q172 94-30622 CIP
Rosen, Joe. **Symmetry in science: an introduction to the general theory.** Springer-Verlag, 1995. 213p bibl index afp ISBN 0-387-94375-7, $49.00

Except for books by Rosen, the concept of symmetry has been largely ignored and is usually found buried within the presentations of other fundamental ideas. Nature loves symmetries, and so does the author, who has promoted their importance ever since his excellent earlier book *A Symmetry Primer for Scientists* (CH, Sep'83). This expanded and revised edition of that book includes three new chapters along with numerous modifications and additions throughout. Starting from scratch, symmetry concepts are presented in an orderly manner that requires familiarity with geometrical concepts, linear algebra, and some quantum theory. All the principles related to symmetry in their full generality within a coherent framework are gathered together for the first time: equivalence, initial and final states, group theory, symmetry evolution, approximate symmetry, and the foundations of science—reduction, reproducibility, and predictability. One also learns how to apply the rule that the symmetry of the effect is at least as symmetric as the cause. The numerous abstract and concrete examples significantly enhance a precise prose writing style. The index, an extensive bibliography, and lucid drawings help make this exposé a marvelous resource book. Upper-division undergraduate through faculty.—*F. Potter, University of California, Irvine*

OAB-1288 HQ1154 92-36338 CIP
Rosser, Sue V. **Biology & feminism: a dynamic interaction.** Twayne, 1992. 191p index afp ISBN 0-8057-9770-X, $26.95; ISBN 0-8057-9755-6 pbk, $14.95

Rosser's excellent overview of the current status of women in science is a comprehensive review of feminist theories and of critiques of science as it has developed since the 19th century. The book, clearly written and readily accessible to anyone, provides much data to support Rosser's claim that the modern scientific method, purported to be objective and value free, is rooted in male values. These assumptions will come as no surprise to anyone who has been following recent discussions by Sandra G. Harding (*The Science Question in Feminism*, CH, Dec'86), Ruth Bleier, (*Science and Gender: A Critique of Biology and its Theories on Women*, CH, Oct'84), and Ruth Hubbard (in *Women Look at Biology Looking at Women*, ed. by R. Hubbard et al., CH, Mar'80) to mention only a few. Rosser is thoughtful and original in her essay on transforming the biology curriculum, and she has provided an extremely useful bibliographic essay by Faye Chadwell that speaks to science in general, not just to biology. A helpful, informed, and valuable book, of particular interest to those wanting to teach less gender-biased biology. Undergraduate through professional.—*M. H. Chaplin, Wellesley College*

OAB-1289 Q173 96-52730 CIP
Sagan, Carl. **Billions and billions: thoughts on life and death at the brink of the millennium.** Random House, 1997. 241p bibl index afp ISBN 0-679-41160-7, $24.00

Sagan became an international celebrity after the smashing success of his TV series (and the accompanying book) *Cosmos* (1980). He was an astronomer and space scientist, but even more so a passionate lover of science, an ardent champion of the scientific worldview, and a merciless opponent of superstition and obscurantism. He was equally a gifted writer and a scientific mystic who held communion with all the subtleties of the universe, waxing poetic when it came to extolling the beauty and wonders of the world as revealed by the scientific enterprise, and admitting that he was not persuaded by anything beyond what scientific methodology reveals of the experienced universe. This precious collection of some of his previously published essays and speeches (recast in many instances) on a variety of themes of interest to the scientifically inclined bears witness to all these aspects of an exceptionally articulate, deeply sensitive, and brilliantly intelligent scientist and thinker who, through his writings and talks, has done perhaps more for the cause of the scientific spirit than have most scientific academies. Between the humor in the beginning essay on the book's title, for which (thanks to Johnny Carson) Sagan became famous, to the moving pathos in the concluding essay, in which he reflects on his imminent death, these essays are rich in thoughts and insights on many matters: from chess to extraterrestrial life, from the environment to the abortion issue. Highly recommended to all intelligent readers. All levels.—*V. V. Raman, Rochester Institute of Technology*

OAB-1290   Q183   94-41057 CIP
Shamos, Morris H. **The myth of scientific literacy.** Rutgers, 1995. 261p index ISBN 0-8135-2196-3, $27.95

Shamos (physics, New York Univ., emeritus) urges a critical review of mass education in science. He argues that literacy in science has not been defined adequately, especially as the term might be applied to the general adult population, and that universal *retained* competence in science is unachievable. He challenges the view, articulated by Dewey and still popular among many educators and scientists in the US, that society is well served if all citizens are introduced to disciplined "scientific" habits of mind. He advocates, instead, an understanding of technology, an *awareness of process* in science as a social/cultural enterprise, an ability to assess experts and use their advice wisely, and less emphasis on mathematics, theories, or a detailed body of information. There is a constructive critique of the Science/Technology/Society movement, an excellent brief discussion of the "two cultures" debate, a stinging indictment of antiscience fringe groups, and some provocative reflections on academic motives. For a wide audience—general readers, graduate students through "science educators" and administrators in K-12 systems. Recommended strongly for scientists, engineers, academics, and others who may be concerned with the threat of technological paralysis in the US.—*D. W. Larson, University of Regina*

OAB-1291   Q175   91-50577 CIP
The Social dimensions of science, ed. by Ernan McMullin. Notre Dame, 1992. 299p index (Studies in science and the humanities from the Reilly Center for Science, Technology, and Values, 3) ISBN 0-268-01741-7, $37.95; ISBN 0-268-01742-5 pbk, $19.95

An important collection, originally delivered as papers at a 1989 conference at the University of Notre Dame. It is thus an excellent reflection of some of the current thinking about the practice of science and its epistemological claims, and also an extremely diverse collection with contributions from philosophers, sociologists, historians of science, and specialists within these categories. Accordingly, it is a philosophical and social study of science (derived, with minor changes, from *A Mind of One's Own*, ed. by Louise Antony and Charlotte Witt, 1992) and a provocative case-history study of experiment and narrative in the (un)making of cold fusion. A very helpful introduction and valuable overview of the papers as a whole is provided by McMullin. Although many of the articles will be difficult for nonspecialists, this is a first-rate collection and belongs in every college and university library.—*M. H. Chaplin, Wellesley College*

OAB-1292   Q149   94-25219 CIP
Sonnert, Gerhard. **Gender differences in science careers: the Project Access study,** by Gerhard Sonnert with Gerald Holton. Rutgers, 1995. 187p bibl index ISBN 0-8135-2174-2, $50.00

Sonnert and Holton have prepared an important and informative book among the many in recent years that have tried to explain why there are fewer women than men in scientific careers, and why among the few who persist in science, even fewer attain the highest ranks. This monograph is a product of a large-scale research project organized to investigate the career paths of the men and women identified as promising scientists, mathematicians, and engineers by virtue of having been awarded a postdoctoral fellowship from the National Science Foundation, the National Research Council, or the Bunting Institute of Radcliffe College. The study was both quantitative and qualitative, so that the book includes a great deal of empirical data as well as some of the findings of open-ended interviews. As such, it is an indispensable contribution to the sociological literature and of immense value to those interested in the sociology of gender, women in science, and the sociology of science. The conclusions of this study tend to confirm other similar ones, but this book makes a real contribution by its wealth of information and the wide variety of its data. Undergraduate through professional.—*M. H. Chaplin, Wellesley College*

OAB-1293   GE105   95-30198 CIP
Southwick, Charles H. **Global ecology in human perspective.** Oxford, 1996. 392p bibl index afp ISBN 0-19-509867-6 pbk, $21.95

Southwick makes a significant contribution to the growing corpus of environmental literature. He examines fundamental ecological principles on a global scale, including the environmental impacts of human activity, especially its economic and social dimensions. His evenhanded examination of a complex set of interrelated and interacting issues offers a rational assessment of the immediate problem and the quality-of-life prospects of future generations of both human and nonhuman life. Most books of this ilk suffer from the professional parochialism and biased ideology of their authors. Southwick, a practicing ecologist of long standing who has lived in the US and India, provides a deep, realistic assessment of the issues, firmly grounded in basic ecological axioms. What is most impressive is that he has incorporated both breadth and depth in the coverage of these topics, a most notable achievement. The 26 chapters are arranged into four major sections: "Introduction to Global Ecology," "Basic Ecosystem Ecology," "Human Impacts on Planet Earth," and "Human Prospects and the Quality of Life." Chapter topics include the biosphere; ecosystems; energy flow and trophic structure; land degradation; human populations; the crisis of biodiversity; economics, demography, and health; the ecology of war; and sustainability. Glossary of important scientific terms; pertinent bibliography. Highly recommended. Undergraduates through professionals; two-year technical program students.—*P. R. Pinet, Colgate University*

OAB-1294   Q180   96-8131 CIP
Stuster, Jack. **Bold endeavors: lessons from polar and space exploration.** Naval Institute, 1996. 377p bibl index afp ISBN 1-55750-749-X, $32.95

Stuster's book is a fascinating search of Polar expedition literature for application to future space mission planning. He has examined accounts of expeditions involving such outstanding figures as Nansen, Amundsen, Scott, Shackleton, Cook, and Byrd, who provide vital insights on the styles of leadership, group interface, food, cramped quarters, darkness, and extreme hardship, in terms of mission success and survival. These accounts are the closest analogs available for planning future NASA space missions. The study extends to POWs, shipwreck and disaster survivors, astronauts, and aquanauts. Stuster is superbly experienced to undertake this first-of-its-kind analysis. His writing style is lucid and, beyond the serious results, the myriad mininarratives of human response to extreme conditions present an intriguing body of literature for the general readership. The implied condemnation of Peary, by simple exclusion save for a single criticism, should rouse the reader's inquisitiveness. There are many historical photographs, good references, and a competent index. The challenge for the future generation of bold endeavors into space can be set by Scott's own immortality: "To strive, to seek, to find, and not to yield." General readers; upper-division undergraduates through professionals.—*J. D. Ives, Carleton University*

Science & Tecnology

OAB-1295   BD581   96-11226 CIP
Wilson, Edward O. **In search of nature.** Island Press/Shearwater Books, 1996. 214p bibl index afp ISBN 1-55963-215-1, $19.95

In this delightful collection of 12 essays, Wilson, a very prolific and insightful writer, discusses two primal and elusive principles: wild nature and human nature. He has chosen to examine each closely and then together as products of evolution; he has done a masterful job of integrating information in both domains. He draws upon familiar animals (ants, serpents, sharks, hyenas) as examples of nature and extrapolates them into human nature. He explores altruism, aggression, culture, and evolution as windows on human nature. An especially poignant essay on biophilia and the environmental ethic decries the loss of biodiversity, extols the innate rights of species, and indicates that the future of humanity is predicated upon protecting biodiversity. Wilson concludes with an essay on the suicidal nature of humanity based on the plethora of environmental damages we are inflicting on nature. He writes in a lyrical and perceptive style, and his prose is engrossing and meaningful. A must for everyone, but especially for biologists, environmentalists, nature lovers, and futurists. General; undergraduates through professionals.—*P. E. Lutz, University of North Carolina at Greensboro*

OAB-1296   Q162   95-5006 CIP
Zimmerman, Michael. **Science, nonscience, and nonsense: approaching environmental literacy.** Johns Hopkins, 1995. 220p index afp ISBN 0-8018-5090-8, $25.95

Books and essays by scientists despairing over the scientific naiveté of the general public are almost as old as modern science itself. The times have never been more appropriate than now, though, for well-written explanations of the basic methodology of science. We all face increasingly complex environmental, economic, and political problems, and at the same time we are inundated with virtually unlimited and unconstrained information. Zimmerman's book is an excellent introduction to science and scientific literacy because it maintains throughout a firm connection to the practical considerations of people's lives. He develops the model of how science works by contrasting it to pseudoscience, especially "creation science" and other question practices clothed in scientific garb (such as homeopathy, graphology, and "biodynamic agriculture"). The author pulls no punches as he moves from this subtle but well-crafted introduction to scientific philosophy into the politics of science. He reveals the fallacies behind many corporate public relations campaigns that attempt to defend useless, dangerous, or destructive products and practices with "scientific" evidence, and he is most eloquent when decrying the damage we have done to the environment when we have ignored clear scientific evidence testifying to our harmful ways. Appropriate reading for any citizen. General; undergraduate; faculty; professional.—*M. A. Wilson, College of Wooster*

■ History of Science & Technology

OAB-1297   Q125   93-41784 CIP
Cohen, H. Floris. **The scientific revolution: a historiographical inquiry.** Chicago, 1994. 662p bibl index afp ISBN 0-226-11279-9, $75.00; ISBN 0-226-11280-2 pbk, $26.95

Where and when did modern science begin? This large and vague question has challenged the erudition and analytical ability of many historians of science during the past 60 years or so, and they have come up with a multitude of answers, most of them involving a concept called the "Scientific Revolution." Virtually all would agree on Western Europe (including Italy, France, the Low Countries, Germany, and England) as the geographical locus of this "revolution" and on the early 17th century as its time frame. Beyond that, however—and particularly when it comes to the identification of causes—the answers diverge dramatically and confusingly. Cohen has set out to chart the history of these answers. His goal is not to find a new and definitive answer to a question (which, after all, may not admit of such an answer) but rather to confront the diverse available answers with one another and with some critical historical data, in an effort to prepare the way for improved historical research in this area. Since Cohen deals with the views of more than sixty historians and appeals to historical data on the development of science in ancient Greece, medieval Europe (both Arabic and Latin), and China—as well as, of course, Western Europe—his task is a most demanding one. He succeeds admirably, with an expository style that is always patient, lucid, and absorbing. The conclusion of the book is a 20-page chapter, "The structure of the Scientific Revolution," in which all that has gone before is sifted and organized into a coherent—if "highly provisional"— sketch. Cohen hopes to fill out this sketch in another book. It will be well worth waiting for. Upper-division undergraduate through professional.—*R. Palter, emeritus, Trinity College (CT)*

OAB-1298   T21   94-4913 CIP
Early American technology: making and doing things from the Colonial era to 1850, ed. by Judith A. McGaw. North Carolina, 1994. 482p bibl index afp ISBN 0-8078-2173-X, $49.95; ISBN 0-8078-4484-5 pbk, $19.95

This excellent collection of essays in early American technological history honors Brooke Hindle for his pioneering work, demonstrates the importance of the field for general historians, and provides a benchmark for current researchers. Eschewing the histories of large enterprises, complex mechanisms, and famous firsts, McGaw focuses the collection on such commonplace activities of early Americans as household technologies, road building, and craft manufacturing; and on hitherto neglected themes, including women's reproductive health, food supply, and land use patterns. Robert Post's historiographical essay, subtitled "A View from the 1990s," and the works he cites should be read by every serious student of technology, as should Hindle's classic essay on the exhilaration of early American technology, reprinted here. The volume ends with more than a hundred pages of bibliography: Hindle's, first published in 1966, and a long essay by Nina Lerman covering books written between 1966 and 1991. Highly recommended. General; undergraduate through professional.—*J. R. Fleming, Colby College*

OAB-1299   Q143   94-35338 CIP
Geison, Gerald L. **The private science of Louis Pasteur.** Princeton, 1995. 378p bibl index afp ISBN 0-691-03442-7, $29.95

In 1878, Pasteur told his family never to show anyone his private laboratory notebooks. Only recently have they become available; Geison (history, Princeton) has taken excellent advantage of this invaluable resource. Geison uses Pasteur's laboratory notebooks and private papers to shed light on some of his most important research   the work on optical isomers, spontaneous generation, and the vaccines for anthrax and rabies. He analyzes both Pasteur's motivations and the way he actually conducted research (which sometimes differed markedly from public accounts). The portrait that emerges is of a great and innovative scientist who also was an ambitious, skilled, combative publicist and politician. Geison carefully documents both Pasteur's flaws and his strengths and exposes the discrepancies between the real Pasteur and the carefully nurtured Pasteurian legend. These discoveries lead Geison to reflect on the nature of science and biomedical ethics. Although not a complete biography like René Dubos's *Louis Pasteur: Free Lance of Science* (1951), this marvelous and fascinating scientific biography is indispensable in understanding Pasteur's life and research. Very highly recommended. Upper-division undergraduate through professional.—*L. M. Prescott, Augustana College (SD)*

OAB-1300   T21   92-17396 CIP
Gordon, Robert B. **The texture of industry: an archaeological view of the industrialization of North America,** by Robert B. Gordon and Patrick M. Malone. Oxford, 1994. 442p bibl indexes afp ISBN 0-19-505885-2, $49.95

Gordon and Malone, eminent industrial archaeologists with expertise in several other areas, write with broad sweep. Their book is as much a cultural, social, and economic history as it is a history of technology, of industrial architecture, and of the impact of industrialization upon the landscape, with sidelong glances at ecological issues. After an introduction to the methods of industrial archaeology and to the human and material components of industry, two main sections deal with the industrial landscape and with workplaces. The distinction is not easy to make, and is not made rigidly. Aspects of mining, milling, and railroading are covered in both sections. The book is very well written and beautifully produced, with more than 150 well-chosen photographs and line drawings. The end-of-chapter notes contain more than 600 literature references, all of which are also listed by author in a separate bibliography. There is a subject index as well as one of place and site names. This splendid example of interdisciplinary scholarship at its best will be valuable to readers at all levels and in many fields.—*C. W. Beck, emeritus, Vassar College*

OAB-1301   TA140   93-1119 CIP
Graham, Loren R. **The ghost of the executed engineer: technology and the fall of the Soviet Union.** Harvard, 1993. 128p index afp (Russian Research Center studies, 87) ISBN 0-674-35436-2, $22.95

It was a great pleasure to read the life story of Peter Akimovitch Palchinsky, a remarkable, radical, and visionary Russian engineer who protested the corruption of the system and the silencing of those who courageously spoke out and tried unsuccessfully to correct unacceptable errors made at the beginning of Soviet industrialization. Palchinsky predicted the failure of the Soviet Union to become a modern industrialized country and steadily criticized industrial inefficiency, the misuse of technology, and the waste of human resources that eventually contributed to its collapse at the end of 1991. Graham, an expert on Russian and Soviet science and engineering, stoically suffered without yielding to the frustrations of an extensive search of archives for information, in a constant tête-à-tête with the Soviet bureaucracy and its secrecy. The introductory prologue is followed by "The Radical Engineer," "From Political Prisoner to Soviet Consultant," "Early Soviet Industrialization," "Technology, Soviet Style," "Contemporary Engineering Failures," and the epilogue, "The Ghost of Peter Palchinsky." Notes, acknowledgments, informative illustrations, and comprehensive index. Those interested in the history of science and technology or in political science will benefit enormously from this very well written book. An excellent acquisition for all libraries.—*T. Z. Kattamis, University of Connecticut*

OAB-1302   Q127   92-5087 CIP
Graham, Loren R. **Science in Russia and the Soviet Union: a short history.** Cambridge, 1993. 321p index ISBN 0-521-24566-4, $29.95

A general history of the sciences and mathematics that covers the period from the arrival of Euler (1727) and the opening of Lomonosov's chemical laboratory (1748) through the Soviet years to the breakup of the Soviet state. Graham (history of science, MIT and Harvard) emphasizes the impact first of the Tsarist state and society, then of the Soviet state, on the development of each of the sciences as well as mathematics and technology. The chapters "The Role of Dialectical Materialism: The Authentic Phase," "Stalinist Ideology and the Lysenko Affair," and "Knowledge and Power in Russian and Soviet Society" serve to account for the mixed record of Soviet science despite strong support by a state strongly committed to scientific development. Two appendixes summarize the strengths and weaknesses of Russian and Soviet science, mathematics, medicine, and technology, and give brief accounts of the principal investigators. Highly recommended as a short, very readable history that emphasizes influences external to science. A "bibliographic essay" of English-language books and articles and a full index add to its usefulness. General; advanced undergraduate through professional.—*A. B. Stewart, Wright State University*

OAB-1303   TL789   96-35311 CIP
Harford, James. **Korolev: how one man masterminded the Soviet drive to beat America to the moon.** Wiley, 1997. 392p bibl index afp ISBN 0-471-14853-9, $30.00

Based on extensive interviews with family and friends, scientists, and engineers who worked with the founder of the Soviet space program (who remained officially anonymous from the 1930s until his death in early 1966), this excellent, in-depth biography and chronology of the life of S.P. Korolev is obligatory reading for everyone interested in the space race with the USSR and in the roots of US competition with the Soviets. Korolev made compromises, yet worked 15- to 16-hour days within the bureaucracy with a consuming passion. He cajoled and led his fellow workers by creating a results-oriented atmosphere. A victim of Stalin's purges in 1938, Korolev was banished to Siberia, then worked for the state while in confinement during WW II. He emerged to become the architect of the Soviet space program. His story is spelled out in a powerfully compelling way by talented author Harford, who did his homework well, although he never met Korolev. He provides a fascinating explanation of why the Soviets built their own space shuttle, "mirror imaging" their perception that our shuttle was militarily motivated. Fifteen-page chronology of the moon race, 30 pages of detailed notes on the text, a three-page bibliography, a two-page list of the people interviewed, 16 pages of (small) photographs and drawings, and a very detailed 16-page index. Highly recommended for all levels of readers.—*W. E. Howard III, Universities Space Research Association*

OAB-1304   TL515   94-26006 CIP
International Conference on the History of Civil and Commercial Aviation (1992: Lucerne, Switzerland). **From airships to airbus: the history of civil and commercial aviation. v.1: Infrastructure and environment; v.2: Pioneers and operations,** ed. by [v.1] William M. Leary and [v.2] by William F. Trimble. Smithsonian Institution Press, 1995. 2v. 203, 296p afp (Proceedings of the International Conference on the History of Civil and Commercial Aviation, 1 & 2) ISBN 1-56098-467-8, v.1, $33.00; ISBN 1-56098-468-6, v.2, $34.95

Although focused on the US and Europe, the essays in these two volumes have an international flavor and include Australia and Japan. Volume 1 deals mainly with technical development such as airports and air traffic control, along with case studies on jet engines, the SST, Airbus Industrie, and so on. Volume 2 covers economic and social issues, touching on social trends in US airline travel, a cultural analysis of cabin attendants, and the role of individuals and/or national interests in the evolution of flag carriers on several continents. The chronological span covered in the two books is comprehensive, ranging from airships and their operational issues to airport design of the midcentury, to recent controversies concerning airline competition and economics. The eclectic approach in these volumes presents a multitude of insights through fascinating studies of events in Switzerland, Sweden, Russia, France, Holland, and other regions not often presented in English. This collection of historical studies is an outstanding and stimulating source of aviation history. Recommended. General; undergraduate through professional.—*R. E. Bilstein, United States Air University*

OAB-1305   Q180   93-19919 CIP
Macrakis, Kristie. **Surviving the swastika: scientific research in Nazi Germany.** Oxford, 1993. 280p bibl index afp ISBN 0-19-507010-0, $39.95

Using newly available archival sources and interviews with scientists, Macrakis portrays the totalitarian regime of Nazi Germany as a collection of rival power blocs that, by default, allowed basic scientific research to survive intact at the prestigious Kaiser Wilhelm Society institutes. Most of the book describes the administrative details pertinent to the institutes, but some scientific research is discussed. Of major concern is the nuclear physics and chemistry research under the direction of Werner Heisenberg, Otto Hahn, and others, which could have produced an atomic bomb for Hitler's military. Fortunately for the Allied powers, several personal, political, and scientific factors delayed atomic bomb research in favor of controlled nuclear energy production. The complete index and an enormous list of references on science during the Third Reich are a researcher's dream. Advanced undergraduate through faculty.—*F. Potter, University of California, Irvine*

OAB-1306 QL799 95-3227 CIP

Nyhart, Lynn K. **Biology takes form: animal morphology and the German universities, 1800-1900.** Chicago, 1995. 414p bibl index afp ISBN 0-226-61086-1, $75.00; ISBN 0-226-61088-8 pbk, $27.50

This truly magnificent book should be required reading for anyone interested in the history of the biological sciences. Nyhart discusses that complex of subjects, animal morphology, that Darwin called the "very soul" of natural history, and one of biology's main streams in the 19th century. But, although rooted in the German universities, there were no professorships in the subject; instead, morphological research was carried out primarily in departments of zoology within philosophical faculties, and in departments of anatomy within medical schools. The author examines the numerous and changing "orientations" of morphology within the fluctuating institutional framework of German universities and through the work of six age-cohorts of professors—such men as von Baer, Kölliker, Leuckart, Gegenbauer, Haeckel, Weismann, the Hertwigs, Roux, Driesch, among others. Through these age-cohorts and departmental structures, she reexamines and presents new and more subtle interpretations of those phases of morphology well known to biological historians: the idealistic phase, the post-Darwinian phase of evolutionary morphology, and the final experimental phase. This book is a real gem, packed full of revealing and fascinating details; it is the finest this reviewer has read in some time. No library that covers the history of science should be without it. Enthusiastically recommended. Upper-division undergraduate through faculty.—*J. Farley, emeritus, Dalhousie University*

OAB-1307 Q127 95-22010 CIP

Rezun, Miron. **Science, technology, and ecopolitics in the USSR.** Praeger, 1996. 228p bibl index afp ISBN 0-275-95383-1, $57.95

Rezun identifies four dominant themes in the history of Soviet science and technology. First, science has always been the domain of the central government; second, the Communist Party strove to bring Soviet science into a tighter orbit around the party; third, emphasis has swung back and forth, from pure science to applied science; and fourth, Soviet science was almost entirely a reaction to the achievements of Western science. The author does an excellent job of demonstrating the historical role of these four themes and then illustrating the few positive results and numerous negative consequences of the Soviet government's control of technology. Rezun establishes the importance of science in Soviet society; reveals the great role that covert gathering of technology from the West (reverse engineering) played in Soviet research; and explores the missed opportunities and advances in computers, strategic minerals, and space technology. The final chapters on the economic and ecological fallout clearly demonstrate that Soviet control of science failed its society as well as the scientific community. A well-written, excellent analysis of the role of technology in the Soviet Union. Recommended for upper-division undergraduates, graduate students, faculty, and professionals.—*D. Ostergren, West Virginia University*

OAB-1308 TL540 93-14785 CIP

Rich, Doris L. **Queen Bess: daredevil aviator.** Smithsonian Institution Press, 1993. 153p bibl index afp ISBN 1-56098-265-9, $18.95

Despite her being one of the most fascinating figures in US aviation during the 1920s, the full story of Bessie Coleman's life and flying career has remained tantalizingly vague. In this short but pleasantly written and informative biography, Rich has performed an admirable service by preparing what is sure to be the definitive study of a remarkable young African American woman. Born in 1892 in Atlanta, Texas, Coleman came from a family that was poor in income and education, but rich in ambition. She eventually moved to Chicago, an attractive, ambitious, and free-spirited person keen on making a mark in life. She managed to get to France, earned a pilot's license there in 1921, returned to the US, and became a well-known figure in the air-show circuit until a fatal flying accident in 1926. Rich has done an outstanding job of tracking down will-of-the-wisp sources, including interviews and African American journals of the era, correcting the misinformation and rumors about an exceptional woman's unusual career.—*R. E. Bilstein, University of Houston—Clear Lake*

OAB-1309 Q175 95-34076 CIP

Sagan, Carl. **The demon-haunted world: science as a candle in the dark.** Random House, 1996 (c1995). 457p bibl index ISBN 0-394-53512-X, $25.95

One of the ironies of the last quarter century is the steady revival of beliefs of ages past. Dark-age worldviews are making a comeback. In this (as usual) beautifully written book, Sagan laments this dismal state in which the general public has not been touched by science. He talks about intelligent people believing in Atlantis and Nostradamus and of tabloids spreading canards such as the discovery of temple ruins on Mars, and bemoans the periodic reports on aliens and UFOs. He objects to assertions about spirits and mystery-mongering about the Bermuda Triangle, Big Foot, and the Loch Ness monster. He warns about the antiscience forces that are becoming more and more assertive. Though many people hear about spectacular discoveries in science, there is widespread illiteracy as to the nature and goals of science, and its framework and methodology. Surveys show that although science has imparted benefits through medicine and technology and has added to our creature comforts, its potentials for elevating the human spirit, endowing us with intellectual joys, and ridding the mind of stifling superstitions have not reached most people. This is Sagan's theme and message. There is a vast body of pseudoscientific literature that is appealing, understandable, and cheap, that entertains and deludes. People need some excitement, and the massive output of pseudoscience is out there to satisfy. Pseudoscience not only titillates but makes everything easy and understandable. Unless we explain to the young the framework of science—reasoned analysis, respect for meticulously gathered data from careful observations, and a readiness to correct itself in the face of appropriate evidence—our civilization will slide into the depths of darkness, to a "demon-haunted world." All levels.—*V. V. Raman, Rochester Institute of Technology*

OAB-1310 HD9660 91-60412 CIP

Travis, Anthony S. **The rainbow makers: the origins of the synthetic dyestuffs industry in western Europe.** Lehigh University, 1993. (Dist. by Associated University Presses) 335p bibl indexes afp ISBN 0-934223-18-1, $49.50

In the last half of the 19th century, synthetic dyes revolutionized industry in England and in Europe, especially Germany. Dyes were industrial high-tech a century ago in much the same way as the first synthetic textile fibers were a century later. *Rainbow Makers* is that 19th-century story, told in fascinating detail; with both historical accuracy and a sense of the economic and social implications of these chemical inventions and discoveries. The human dimension is not lost either. In fact, the panoply of great chemists is breathtaking, for here, between the endpapers, are Hofmann, Perkin, Baeyer, and the legendary chemists who introduced a revolution in synthetic organic chemistry that literally determined the wealth of the industrialized European nations. The presentation of what could easily have been deadly dull reading of archival historical material is as colorful as the splash made by Perkin's dyes when they hit the textile markets in 1859; and the chemistry Travis includes is equally accurate and lively reading—stylish, literary, and well worth the effort—for this is probably the penultimate, if not the ultimate, resource on the subject, with some 60 pages of detailed appendixes, notes, and annotated bibliographies. The main text begins on the English side of the channel with mauve and magenta, and then moves over to the spectacular, yet uniquely German successes with the chemistry and manufacture of alizarin and indigo. This reviewer can write only in superlatives about this outstanding, definitive work; all that is missing are a few color plates, like those on the dust jacket. (How could the publishers have missed that opportunity?) Librarians—get this book for your readers! Organic chemists and historians of science—get a copy for yourselves! Less than 50 bucks for this pot of 19th-century gold. All levels.—*L. W. Fine, Columbia University*

OAB-1311 VK549 92-8456 CIP

Williams, J.E.D. **From sails to satellites: the origin and development of navigational science.** Oxford, 1993 (c1992). 310p bibl index ISBN 0-19-856387-6, $35.00

Williams has been chief navigator of two major international airlines, president of the Royal Institute of Navigation, and is a lifelong student of navigation and its history. His wide-ranging book describes the interaction between the science and technology of navigation from Classical times, emphasizing the practical consequences (or lack of them) of each development. Neither a how-to book nor light reading for weekend sailors: explanations assume a reader comfortable with spherical trigonometry, differential and integral calculus, applied probability, and the physics of gyroscopes. But for those who persevere, it is a gold mine of insightful information. Roughly half is devoted to celestial and magnetic-compass navigation, and about a third to the recent development of gyrocompass and radio/radar/Doppler techniques. Global positioning systems, using orbiting satellites, are covered only briefly, ending with a caution against overdependence on them, despite their low consumer cost and amazing accuracy. Although in no way intrusive, the author's practical experience and sense of humor are present throughout. Highly recommended for collections in applied mathematics, navigation, or history of science and technology. Advanced undergraduate through faculty.—*G. E. Herrick, Maine Maritime Academy*

■ Agriculture

OAB-1312 SB388 91-28776 CIP
Biology of the grapevine, ed. by Michael G. Mullins, Alain Bouquet, and Larry E. Williams. Cambridge, 1992. 239p index ISBN 0-521-30507-1, $59.95

A welcome addition to viticultural literature. Various authors comprehensively provide a wealth of information on grapevine evolution, taxonomy, morphology, anatomy, physiology, and genetics. In this reviewer's experience, the book stands alone in the breadth of material covered, and would make an excellent text for introductory courses in viticulture. Chapters 3 and 4, which deal with morphology and anatomy, and vegetative growth, respectively, are especially good. The writers move from principles to practices in a seamless manner, showing continuity of generality as well as understanding of specifics. Since the authors' backgrounds are weighted in favor of irrigated deserts, three times as much space is allocated to water relations and irrigation as is to the physiology of winter kill, frost damage, and cold hardiness, which are, arguably, more limiting to viticulture in the English-speaking world than is water stress. The restatement that direct producer cultivars produce wines that are "coarse and have unfamiliar flavors" has become a self-fulfilling prophecy, for such cultivars are seldom, if ever, given superior cellar treatment. (This is an economic, not a scientific, issue and should have been noted as such or omitted.) Still, these are minor concerns, given the fine quality of the writing and clarity of the presentation. A joy to read; recommended to all advanced undergraduate and graduate students and colleagues.—*G. S. Howell, Michigan State University*

OAB-1313 SB433 92-42918 CIP
Bormann, F. Herbert. **Redesigning the American lawn: a search for environmental harmony,** by F. Herbert Bormann, Diana Balmori, and Gordon T. Geballe. Yale, 1993. 166p index afp ISBN 0-300-05401-7, $19.95

Three members of the Yale faculty—ecologist, land architect, forest biologist—and their graduate students combine talents to produce what should be a best-seller, to be read by everyone who has a lawn—some 58 million US households. In five chapters the authors present the basics of why we have lawns, why we should question the lawn, the high economic and environmental costs of intensive lawn care, and finally they propose a new US lawn or alternatives to the energy-intensive lawn management practices now promoted to the detriment of the local and global environment. Relevant tables, figures, and photographs make this book a gem. Every library in the US, from college to community, should have a copy. All levels.—*W. A. Niering, Connecticut College*

OAB-1314 SD418 94-5681 CIP
Dean, Warren. **With broadax and firebrand: the destruction of the Brazilian Atlantic forest.** California, 1995. 482p index afp ISBN 0-520-08775-5, $38.00

Dean has prepared an outstanding, scientifically researched, historical account of human intrusions into the Brazilian Atlantic forest, the most endangered in the world. A rather large percent of the book is devoted to notes that explain and reference the documents and resources the author utilized. Beginning with the first human inhabitants, the hunter-gatherers, and the subsequent European invasions of colonists including prospectors for gold and diamonds, slash and burn agriculturists, coffee planters, and finally the industrialists and developers, Dean examines the social and cultural factors that lead to the wanton waste and degradation of this once lush and diverse forest. He clearly describes the characteristics of the forest that made it ripe for exploitation as well as the inadequate attempts at conservation. His description of this shameful and deplorable time in history is very readable. If individuals and government officials heed the forewarnings detailed here, one can hope that the Amazon forest will be spared a similar fate. Its excellent index will be most helpful to individuals seeking specific information on the losses associated with the destruction of this tropical forest and its corresponding environmental movement. General; undergraduate; graduate; professional.—*C. S. Dunn, University of North Carolina at Wilmington*

OAB-1315 SD144 95-6583 CIP
Dobbs, David. **The northern forest,** by David Dobbs and Richard Ober. Chelsea Green, 1995. 356p bibl index ISBN 0-930031-72-5, $23.00

Dobbs and Ober provide a refreshingly open and honest look at the closely interconnected, but extremely fragile, web of people and forests in the vast woodland extending from Maine's coast to New York's Adirondack Mountains. Nearly 26 million acres in size, this great forest is under increasingly complex pressures for harvesting and development. The authors present a simple but elegant argument for wise management of this working forest. The statement "As the most consumptive society in the history of the world, we cannot in good conscience set this forest aside and satisfy our appetite in other parts of the world" shows the excellent understanding of the need and moral responsibility for working forests. In reading the stories of the people living in this great forest, this reviewer could not help but think of personal experiences growing up in northern Wisconsin's working forest. Highly recommended for environmentalists and foresters alike. General; undergraduate through professional.—*D. F. Karnosky, Michigan Technological University*

OAB-1316 SB433 93-28003 CIP
Jenkins, Virginia Scott. **The lawn: a history of an American obsession.** Smithsonian Institution Press, 1994. 246p bibl index afp ISBN 1-56098-406-6 pbk, $14.95

Jenkins, a cultural historian (Catholic Univ. of America), presents a comprehensive overview of how the lawn has evolved as a multibillion dollar business and as a US obsession and documents the major role of three groups—garden clubs, golf enthusiasts, and the US Department of Agriculture—in this evolution. Advertising also played an important part in the movement. A symbol of human control over nature, there are now 45 million lawns covering 30 million acres in the US. Jenkins highlights the war between people and nature in the use of pesticides, fertilizers, and excessive water usage, especially in arid regions unsuited for the traditional lawn. The age of high-tech horticulture during the 1970s and 1980s has resulted in many individuals and organizations, including the EPA (in terms of air pollution), questioning this obsession as the author asks, will we become more compatible with nature once again with such alternatives as "a meadow, wetland, vegetable garden and apple orchard?" Excellent illustrations trace the evolution of the lawn from Europe to the American present. For a wide audience. General.—*W. A. Niering, Connecticut College*

OAB-1317 S589 91-29201 CIP
Loomis, R.S. **Crop ecology: productivity and management in agricultural systems,** by R.S. Loomis and D.J. Connor. Cambridge, 1992. 538p bibl index ISBN 0-521-38379-X, $100.00; ISBN 0-521-38776-0 pbk, $39.95

Loomis and Connor explore four basic themes: farming systems and their biological components, physical and chemical environments, production processes, and resource management. Coverage is very thorough; the topics in the 18 chapters are all tied together by an exploration of two major case studies and a final chapter looking toward the future. The authors based this book on their courses in crop ecology. This reviewer's only complaint is minor: sustainable agriculture appears as a vaguely defined concept; considering that a professional journal on sustainable agriculture has existed for more than two years and that the concept is well defined within its pages, this reviewer disagrees with the authors' conclusions. This book promises to become a leading work; highly recommended for libraries maintaining agricultural and ecological collections. Advanced undergraduate through professional.—*R. P. Poincelot, Fairfield University*

OAB-1318 SB608 96-46954 CIP
Powell, Charles C. **Ball pest & disease manual: disease, insect, and mite control on flower and foliage crops,** by Charles C. Powell and Richard K. Lindquist. Ball Publishing, 1997. 426p bibl index ISBN 1-883052-13-0, $65.00

This holistic approach to pest management from the perspectives of plant pathology and entomology will be useful to the trade as well as academic and research areas involving flower and foliage plants; the "all new, updated pesticide, cultural, and environmental control information" is an indispensable part of any good reference library. Excellent black-and-white photographs and an expanded color section provide visual identification of pests for seasoned growers and beginning students. The text is divided into five sections: "Plant Health Management and Problem Diagnosis of Flower and Foliage Crops"; "Common Diseases of Flower and Foliage Crops and Their Management"; "Insect and Mite Pests of Flower and Foliage Crops"; "Insect and Disease Controls for Flower and Foliage Crops"; and "Putting It All Together" (which offers instruction in the preparation of plant protection programs designed to keep plants healthy). This easily read compendium of useful, up-to-date information and instructions for the production of healthy plant materials incorporates new safety regulations, new products, and more information about pesticides. Informative appendixes offer lists of organizations, math and conversion tables, a glossary, and an index to host plants, diseases, and insect and mite pests. A suggested readings list includes the URL for each of a dozen World Wide Web sites. An excellent choice for professionals in horticultural and botanical fields and a very suitable addition for libraries with comprehensive horticultural collections and degree programs in flower and foliage crops. Undergraduates through professionals; two-year technical programs students.—*K. T. Settlemyer, emeritus, Lock Haven University of Pennsylvania*

OAB-1319 SB170 94-25814 CIP
Tree management in farmer strategies: responses to agricultural intensification, ed. by J.E. Michael Arnold and Peter A. Dewees. Oxford, 1995. 292p bibl index ISBN 0-19-858414-8, $95.00

Within the last decade the scope of forestry in developing nations has expanded to include a broad social and economic context. This excellent book describes and illustrates why foresters must design projects as more than technical tree planting exercises. Apparently, good projects fail when planners misinterpret the incentives and constraints faced by farmers responding to changing agricultural patterns. The authors illustrate how farmers incorporate trees in their farms and environment rather than plant stand-alone investments. This perspective explains the sometimes counterintuitive impacts of forestry projects. Examples are drawn from Asia and Africa and cover a variety of topics, including tenure, labor scarcity, grazing patterns, and gender differences. Respected authorities such as D.A. Gilmour provide syntheses of their previous

work that do not require the reader to have an extensive background in the field. Separate chapters do not read as separate essays but develop a central theme. For economists, anthropologists, political scientists, and planners in addition to foresters and agronomists. Highly recommended. Upper-division undergraduate through professional.—*B. D. Orr, Michigan Technological University*

OAB-1320 S594 94-10959 CIP
Wolt, Jeffrey D. **Soil solution chemistry: applications to environmental science and agriculture.** Wiley, 1994. 345p bibl index afp ISBN 0-471-58554-8, $79.95

Wolt's book is a well-organized, in-depth reference on the soil-water, aqueous or soil-solution phase, of soil chemistry and its application to the interpretation of soil-solution research. This work differs from conventional soil chemistry books by not emphasizing the solid phase of the soil and its implication with soil-solution chemistry. The book's organization is excellent with respect to chapter subject matter; Wolt guides the reader through the development of soil-solution chemistry and constraints with laboratory and field methods, to chapters dealing with the interpretation of research results as they relate to environmental or agricultural concerns. Wolt has a sound grasp on soil-solution chemistry, and the approach in his book is necessary and refreshing. This reviewer finds the style of writing to be good, with excellent coverage of the subject matter and an excellent bibliography. The author has used terms students and researchers trained in soil chemistry would understand. Suitable for upper-division undergraduates, graduate students, and researchers and professionals in environmental and agricultural research.—*S. G. Shetron, Michigan Technological University*

■ Astronautics & Astronomy

OAB-1321 QB843 95-42959 CIP
Begelman, Mitchell. **Gravity's fatal attraction: black holes in the universe,** by Mitchell Begelman and Martin Rees. Scientific American Library, 1996. (Dist. by W. H. Freeman) 246p bibl index (Scientific American Library series, 58) ISBN 0-7167-5074-0, $32.95

Black holes have been of considerable interest to the general public in the last few years, and many books have been written about them. Begelman and Rees's lavishly illustrated book on many aspects of black holes has beautiful color pictures throughout, and the writing style and level are easily accessible to the layperson. The book begins with a review of the basic history of black holes, how they arise, and the evidence we now have for their existence. There is, in fact, a detailed discussion of whether black holes actually exist. The major thrust of the book is toward observation rather than theory. Evidence for black holes in active galaxies, quasars, and nearby galaxies is presented and, since the authors are both active researchers in the area, the book is extremely up-to-date. Topics related to black holes, such as gravitational waves, the big bang, and Hawking radiation, are also discussed. A good addition to any science library collection. Highly recommended. General; undergraduate.—*B. R. Parker, Idaho State University*

OAB-1322 QB36 92-33736 CIP
Biagioli, Mario. **Galileo, courtier: the practice of science in the culture of absolutism.** Chicago, 1993. 402p bibl index afp ISBN 0-226-04559-5, $29.95

Biagioli takes a refreshingly new look at Galileo's career, seen as critically influenced from beginning to end by considerations of patronage. Galileo's first employment, at the Universities of Pisa and Padua, stemmed directly from the influence of his patron, Guidobaldo del Monte, whose younger brother was a cardinal. In this book, devoted primarily to the more mature Galileo's career at the Medici court in his native Tuscany, Biagioli maintains, "the court contributed to the cognitive legitimation of the new science by providing venues for the social legitimation of its practitioners, and this, in turn, boosted the epistemological status of their discipline." More specifically, Galileo was seeking to raise the socioprofessional status of mathematicians relative to (Aristotelian) natural philosophers by enlisting the (sometimes grudgingly rendered) prestige of his noble patron. After elaborate analysis of the dynamics of patronage in the court of a 17th-century absolute ruler, accompanied by a brilliant excursus on the significance of the "Medicean stars" (the four moons of Jupiter), Biagioli supports his main thesis by meticulous—and, too often, unduly repetitious—attention to the context and content of two of Galileo's lesser known writings: the *Discourse on Bodies in Water* (1612) and *The Assayer* (1623). Well written and thoroughly documented from both manuscript and printed sources. Highly recommended. General; advanced undergraduate through faculty.—*R. Palter, emeritus, Trinity College (CT)*

OAB-1323 TL799 92-31849 CIP
Breuer, William B. **Race to the moon: America's duel with the Soviets.** Praeger, 1993. 222p bibl index afp ISBN 0-275-94481-6, $24.95

Breuer, who served in the US Army during WW II, writes with familiarity about events starting with John Kennedy's second State of the Union address in 1961, when he proposed putting an American on the moon before 1970. Based on his interviews with 112 persons involved, and review of Army and NASA documents, Breuer recounts the dramatic story of the race, involving the German development and use of the V-2 rocket on London, and the US and Soviet efforts to capture German rocket experts, and ends with Neil Armstrong's and Buzz Aldrin's sojourn on the moon in 1969. The hero in all this is Werner von Braun, rocket expert brought to the US where he succeeded against severe odds in winning the race. There is a full account of cosmonaut and astronaut training; 28 photos of people, scenes, and equipment; 11 pages of detailed footnotes; a 40-item bibliography; and a good, eight-column index. No mathematics are used. Highly recommended. General; community college; undergraduate; pre-professional.—*T. Page, NASA Johnson Space Center*

OAB-1324 Orig
The Cambridge atlas of astronomy, ed. by Jean Audouze and Guy Israël. 3rd ed. Cambridge, 1994. 470p bibl index ISBN 0-521-43438-6, $75.00

This new edition (the third within ten years) of the successful voluminous, encyclopedic, and exhaustive treatment of all of astronomy is a worthy successor to previous editions (2nd ed., CH, May'89) and arguably the best and most complete available collection of astronomical photographs and graphic illustrations. The 30 authors (all French professional astronomers) have written the terse and information-packed text to accompany the superb pictorial material, and the editors have succeeded in making it surprisingly uniform. This is one of the very few books that will be enjoyed by all lovers of astronomy, from the casually interested (for whom it is a wonderful addition to the coffee-table picture-book library) to the professionals who want reasonably reliable and quite detailed, up-to-date information on areas outside their specialties. A highly recommended bargain! All levels.—*H. K. Eichhorn, University of Florida*

OAB-1325 QB15 95-40923 CIP
The Cambridge illustrated history of astronomy, ed. by Michael Hoskin. Cambridge, 1997. 392p bibl index ISBN 0-521-41158-0, $39.95

This excellent overview of astronomy from prehistoric times to the present belongs in every library. Although written by six different experts, the text has a remarkably consistent and engaging style. Throughout, the authors thoughtfully discuss the intellectual passion that drove the development of astronomical concepts and are unusually sensitive to the influence of culture and politics. The most memorable sections are those on the astronomical significance of ancient ruins such as Stonehenge (which authors Clive Ruggles and Michael Hoskin treat with refreshing skepticism), Newton and his times (by Hoskin), and the rise of astrophysics (by David Dewhirst and Hoskin, who do an outstanding job of explaining a complex subject that many histories of astronomy cover inadequately). The superb illustrations (many of which are

hard to find elsewhere) and unusual conceptual insight will make this resource valuable to researchers in the field, but the writing level is appropriate for general readers. Strongly recommended. General, undergraduates through faculty.—*T. Barker, Wheaton College (MA)*

OAB-1326 TL789 93-48680 CIP
Chaikin, Andrew. **A man on the moon: the voyages of the Apollo astronauts.** Viking, 1994. 670p bibl index ISBN 0-670-81446-6, $27.95

A well-known writer on space exploration, Chaikin has gathered together everything about the Apollo Program in this book, which took him more than ten years to prepare. In that time he interviewed all 23 surviving Apollo astronauts as well as scores of others involved on the ground. He is able to describe accurately what went on in people's minds at various times, and records the sometimes vicious politics of astronauts eager to get on Moon flights. His six years on the staff of *Sky and Telescope* prepared him for clear, precise writing, starting with Neil Armstrong's "small step for (a) man, one giant leap for mankind" on July 20, 1969. Apparently he made close friends among the astronauts; Gene Cernan, *Apollo 17*, says: "I've been there. Chaikin took me back." The US public stopped watching, and NASA canceled the last two Apollo missions, but, along with Arthur C. Clark, Chaikin believes that the Apollo success will be "remembered a thousand years from now." The book is divided into 13 chapters and illustrated by 47 glossy plates; these include some of the most dramatic shots taken on the Moon. In a long epilogue, Chaikin describes many encounters of astronauts with unusual audiences, both in the US and overseas. Three appendixes treat astronaut biographical information (birth date, education, etc.); persons interviewed (astronauts, astronaut wives, children, engineers, scientists, etc.); and Apollo mission data (*Apollo 7* through *Apollo 17*; dates, crew, purpose, duration.) In the bibliography, Chaikin lists 60 books he found useful. There are 42 pages of author's notes, and a good, 42-column index. The best yet on the Apollo Program. Highly recommended for academic use at all levels above junior high school, and for general readers.—*T. Page, NASA Johnson Space Center*

OAB-1327 QB472 92-34641 CIP
Charles, Philip A. **Exploring the X-ray universe,** by Philip A. Charles and Frederick D. Seward. Cambridge, 1995. 398p bibl index ISBN 0-521-26182-1, $79.95; ISBN 0-521-43712-1 pbk, $39.95

This comprehensive, well-illustrated, and well-documented survey of the current state of X-ray astronomy provides extensive but elementary technical descriptions of the fundamental principles and physics of the observational techniques and instrumentation. Observations of the X-ray region of the spectrum require the use of satellites or high altitude rockets, and impose severe constraints on the design and construction of the instruments required. Charles and Seward integrate developments in X-ray astronomy with current knowledge in other areas in observational and theoretical astronomy. Profusely illustrated with color illustrations and graphs of observational data. For more advanced readers, there are special sections containing more technical descriptions, with equations when needed. Highly recommended for readers with an interest and curiosity in astronomy and space science who are comfortable reading about science at the level of *Scientific American* articles (and above). Well suited also for curious laypersons, undergraduates, graduate students, scientific workers in other fields, and professionals.—*C. A. Hein, Radex, Incorporated*

OAB-1328 QB63 92-43572 CIP
Davidson, Norman. **Sky phenomena: a guide to naked-eye observation of the stars: with sections on poetry in astronomy, constellation mythology, and the southern hemisphere sky.** Lindisfarne, 1993. 208p index ISBN 0-940262-56-8 pbk, $19.95

An excellent nontechnical introduction to naked-eye astronomy. Ten chapters and seven appendixes describe the motions we see in the sky and how early astronomers understood those motions, and how modern readers can appreciate those events. Separate chapters cover phases of the moon, eclipses, and telling time and location by the stars. Along the way, the reader gets a painless introduction to the history of astronomy. Davidson includes material on star lore and a chapter on the southern sky, material difficult to find in other sources. He has included a small anthology of poetry with astronomical motifs. That alone is worth the price of the book. This reviewer enjoyed it thoroughly. General; lower-division undergraduate.—*T. T. Arny, University of Massachusetts at Amherst*

OAB-1329   QB54   95-2499 CIP
Davies, Paul. **Are we alone?: philosophical implications of the discovery of extraterrestrial life.** Basic Books, 1995. 160p bibl index ISBN 0-465-00418-0, $20.00

Davies discusses the probability of communicating with intelligent extraterrestrial life and both the philosophical and religious implications of such an event. Specifically, he asks what assumptions must be made about the laws of physics, the nature of the universe, and the nature of life and intelligence in order for there to be a reasonable probability of finding intelligent extraterrestrial beings. And, what consequences would such a discovery have for science, religion, and philosophy? How would it affect the mind-body problem, the nature of life and consciousness, and the place of humankind in the universe? This book is broad and far-reaching; it is highly informative, extremely well written, and lucid. All levels.—*C. H. McGruder III, Western Kentucky University*

OAB-1330   QB362   96-108 CIP
Diacu, Florin. **Celestial encounters: the origins of chaos and stability,** by Florin Diacu and Philip Holmes. Princeton, 1996. 233p bibl index afp ISBN 0-691-02743-9, $24.95

The discoveries of Bruns and Poincaré, that the three- (and higher) body problems in dynamics are unsolvable in the sense that formulas giving the coordinates as functions of time cannot be established, have spawned new approaches to celestial mechanics. These approaches investigate the qualitative properties (range, stability, etc.) of the solutions that exist, yet cannot be found, rather than the quantitative details of the solutions themselves. These ideas started with Poincaré's efforts to explore the topology of the phase space of the solutions. Up until now, when Diacu and Holmes—active contributors to this area, one of the most abstract and, for the nonspecialist, most inaccessible fields of mathematics—collaborated to produce the present volume, there was no available comprehensive, descriptive, and semitechnical overview for this genuinely new approach to celestial mechanics. The authors have admirably succeeded in elucidating the ideas that pervade these various modern investigations. This book, which should be required reading for every nonspecialist astronomer, may well be headed toward becoming a classic. Upper-division undergraduates through faculty.—*H. K. Eichhorn, University of Florida*

OAB-1331   QB991   93-48580 CIP
Dressler, Alan. **Voyage to the Great Attractor: exploring intergalactic space.** Knopf, 1994. 355p index ISBN 0-394-58899-1, $25.00

This personalized story of the author-astronomer Dressler's own research tells how he and his six other collaborators—dubbed the "Seven Samurai"—approached the problem of how the universe has expanded and attempted to explain its evolution since the "big bang," which began the universe as we know it. The book is well written and entertaining, with an excellent sense of how science is really conducted and how good scientists interact while on the trail of truth. The reader is treated to excellent biographies of the principal participants through the author's simple, straightforward, engaging style. One gets a good "feel" for what astronomical research is all about, and there are many intriguing insights into how good astronomers think and how they approach their subject. The reader will share their elation of discovery. Readable figures; four-page glossary; good, 11-page index. For general readers, high-school level and above.—*W. E. Howard III, Advanced Concepts and Space, U.S. Army*

OAB-1332   QB65   93-8204 CIP
Garfinkle, Robert A. **Star-hopping: your visa to viewing the universe.** Cambridge, 1994. 329p bibl indexes ISBN 0-521-41590-X, $24.95

Garfinkle (freelance astronomy writer) has crafted the ultimate observing guide that belongs in every library—public, university, and the individual star-gazer's. Forsaking the equatorial coordinate system and setting circles for the universally accessible method of "star-hopping," Garfinkle's book can open up new observing horizons for the beginner and even show the seasoned observer a few new tricks. This self-contained guide to observing the night sky also includes a discussion on telescopes and basic observing tips, and an impressive glossary and bibliography. Even the armchair observer will enjoy the poetry and mythology as well as the information about each celestial object. The book concludes with an excellent discussion of the yearly ritual of the Messier Marathon—the attempt to view all one hundred-odd celestial objects in Messier's Catalog in a single night. Most enthusiastically recommended. All levels.—*K. Larsen, Central Connecticut State University*

OAB-1333   TL790   91-43590 CIP
Gibson, Roy. **Space.** Oxford, 1992. 153p index (Science, technology, and society, 7) ISBN 0-19-858343-5, $36.00

Gibson has a very complete knowledge of spacecraft and space missions from all countries, primarily the US, USSR, and France. He gives an illuminating history, starting with the ideas of Ptolemy, Copernicus, and Kepler, and noting the "science fiction" stories of trips to the Moon centuries before they happened. More recent scientific analysis by Konstantin Tsiolkovsky, J. D. Bernal, and Arthur C. Clarke helped develop the engineering technology of rocketry. This book is a primer on space science, well illustrated with 38 diagrams and photos, ranging from the Ariane rocket design to NASA Shuttle launches, ESA's Spacelab, and the Hubble Space Telescope. Gibson deals accurately with orbits, the Solar System's planets and comets, communications satellites, Earth observations, and military uses and commercial possibilities of space. The text is logical and easy to read, with no mathematics, a useful table of acronyms, and a good, 14-column index. Highly recommended for undergraduate science students and general readers.—*T. Page, NASA Johnson Space Center*

OAB-1334   QB15   91-26227 CIP
Gingerich, Owen. **The eye of heaven: Ptolemy, Copernicus, Kepler.** American Institute of Physics, 1993. 442p index ISBN 0-88318-863-5, $24.95

This outstanding volume collects 25 lightly edited papers on the history of astronomy, written by a well-known and highly respected astronomer/science historian. The papers, which focus primarily on Ptolemy, Copernicus, or Kepler, were originally published over the period 1964-89. They are presented here not chronologically, but in sections devoted to each of the three astronomers and within sections in a logical order. The papers are tied together with an excellent introduction by Gingerich, specially prepared for this volume and rounded out with a brief epilogue; they are uniformly well written and most contain graphs, charts, and photographs to amplify the text. In addition, each paper contains its own notes and references section, and the overall volume has an index. Collectively, these papers deal in depth with an extremely important period in the history of astronomy and are presented at a level understandable to a broad range of readers. Every college library should have this book. Highly recommended. Undergraduate through professional.—*H. E. Wylen, National Science Foundation*

OAB-1335   QB981   95-14762 CIP
Goldsmith, Donald. **Einstein's greatest blunder?: the cosmological constant and other fudge factors in the physics of the universe.** Harvard, 1995. 216p index ISBN 0-674-24241-6, $22.95

This aptly named book is a witty and succinct work on the problems of modern cosmology for the general reader and undergraduate student. In order to examine the "fudge factors" that scientists employ to make their pet theories fit with observations, Goldsmith provides clear explanations of both the theories and the relevant observations. Background information on the nature of gravity, the ages of stars, the use of the Doppler effect to map out the structure of the universe, curved space—all allow the reader without a deep scientific background to approach the major problems of modern cosmology. The reader needs curiosity and an open mind rather than mathematics. Among the problems discussed are these: How can stars be older than the universe in which they are contained? Is there missing mass, and is it in the form of "dark matter"? What is the future of the universe? The figures and diagrams are exceptionally well done and are vital to reader understanding. Recent color photographs from the Hubble Space Telescope enhance the work. In a rapidly changing field, this book captures the excitement and uncertainty of the science. Recommended. General; undergraduate.—*M.-K. Hemenway, University of Texas at Austin*

OAB-1336 QB808 91-27498 CIP
Hansen, C.J. **Stellar interiors: physical principles, structure, and evolution,** by C.J. Hansen and S.D. Kawaler. Springer-Verlag, 1994. 445p bibl index afp disk (any system compatible with FORTRAN Compiler ISBN 0-387-94138-X, $49.95

Two active and well-informed young researchers have written what may well become a classic in the field of stellar interiors and stellar evolution. This book will be invaluable not only for the audience targeted by the authors (i.e., students at the undergraduate-graduate boundary) but also for the nonspecialist astronomer (and physicist) who is looking for a complete and up-to-date presentation of this fascinating and fundamentally important field. The explanations are lucid, the mathematical developments are given with just the right amount of detail, the validity of the various models and their physical meaning is always clearly outlined, and the nearly impeccable language manages never to be boring. Hansen and Kawaler document their knowledge by extensive and annotated citations. Exercises help those who study the subject on their own. This will no doubt become the reference of choice in any course on the subject, considering that the existing monographic literature is largely either too extensive or obsolete. Upper-division undergraduate through professional.—*H. K. Eichhorn, University of Florida*

OAB-1337 QB815 95-34046 CIP
Hearnshaw, J.B. **The measurement of starlight: two centuries of astronomical photometry.** Cambridge, 1996. 511p bibl indexes ISBN 0-521-40393-6, $89.95

The flux from celestial objects is one of the measurable parameters and is indispensable as input for checking astrophysical theories. Hearnshaw, an extremely well-informed, respected, and accomplished photometrist in his own right, presents the history of measuring the brightness of the stars, starting with the ancients and continuing to the very present. For the first time, the interested scholar will find here a comprehensive (and rather complete) account of the various approaches (visual, photographic, and electronic) to measuring starlight and learn who did what, when, where, and why. The author also explains how these photometric measurements have advanced our knowledge of the universe; he succeeds very well in illuminating the importance of photometry for astronomy and astrophysics as a whole. The book cites several thousand articles and contains dozens of photographs (and drawings) of astronomers and instruments. Several tables provide a good overview of the more involved details. Extensive indexes. This is first-rate scholarship, a "must" for every science library.—*H. K. Eichhorn, University of Florida*

OAB-1338 QB981 95-41438 CIP
Kolb, Rocky. **Blind watchers of the sky: the people and ideas that shaped our view of the universe.** Addison-Wesley, 1996. 338p bibl index ISBN 0-201-48992-9, $25.00

This engaging and often whimsical story of the development of our current knowledge of the universe is divided into three sections: the development of mankind's view of the universe when our vistas were confined to the solar system (16th and 17th centuries); the extension of these views to the stars and the Milky Way (18th and 19th centuries); and the development of the modern 20th-century model. Intended for the layperson curious about the universe, the work explores the human side of discovery from Tycho Brahe through Hubble to the modern era and the big bang theory, developing an appreciation of what we know and how we got to know it in a style that succeeds in providing enjoyment without the need to know the technical details of the field. Contains a full and complete bibliography, plentiful and often humorous footnotes, a splendid section of definition of terms, eight-page index, and four pages of credits, with adequate photographs, tables, and diagrams. All levels.—*W. E. Howard III, Universities Space Research Association*

OAB-1339 QB355 92-56863 CIP
Kozhamthadam, Job. **The discovery of Kepler's laws: the interaction of science, philosophy, and religion.** Notre Dame, 1994. 315p bibl index afp ISBN 0-268-00868-X, $39.95

This is a remarkably readable monograph. The amount of careful and sympathetic scholarship is impressive and is so well integrated into the story line that one almost feels a sense of inevitability about the results being the right ones. Kozhamthadam is successful in creating an almost "you were there" feeling for the climate of opinion in which Kepler worked. One understands the role of belief in God, and Christ his son, and its connection with nature, his handiwork. One understands the role of mathematics as an expression of an image of God where rationality was central and as the language in which to understand nature; one also sees the "correcting" role played by experimental data. The bulk of the book is a detailed exposition of how Kepler arrived at the first and second laws. Like Kepler, the reader feels the tensions, worries about the possible solutions, and then sees the light. The connection among the roles of "science, philosophy, and religion" is made to appear almost seamless. Kepler emerges as a creative and introspective person with a strong sense of his ability to ask the right questions and to solve them. His place as one of the key links in the development of modern science is clear. He set the tone for Newton with his search for the causes of motion and the forces needed in explaining them, and so helped to determine the subsequent development of the picture of the universe as being mechanical. This book belongs in every library. All levels.—*K. L. Schick, Union College (NY)*

OAB-1340 QB981 96-5612 CIP
Kragh, Helge. **Cosmology and controversy: the historical development of two theories of the universe.** Princeton, 1996. 500p bibl index afp ISBN 0-691-02623-8, $35.00

This is a quite wonderful book: Kragh manages the trick of simultaneously being scholarly and eminently readable. The author has taken the trouble not only to do a careful study of the available historical literature, but to supplement the considerable written record he has personally contacted those major contributors who are still alive. Most of the book can be read by an educated nonscientist, but there are sections either sufficiently mathematical or sufficiently sophisticated in physics to require considerable technical background. Even in those places, the basic ideas, if not the details, should be understandable to the nonscientist. Kragh traces the evolution of cosmology from a speculative, not really respectable, edge of modern science to an observationally and theoretically rich discipline with ripple effects in both philosophy and religion. One of the most fascinating aspects of the book is the examination of scientists as people. The author is not averse to making value judgments and tries to set the record straight with regard to the virtual omission, in some histories, of the contributions of George Gamow, Ralph Alpher, and George Herman in the development of much of the apparatus of the big bang theory. This rich book belongs in every college library. All levels.—*K. L. Schick, Union College (NY)*

OAB-1341 QB991 96-10781 CIP
Mather, John C. **The very first light: the true inside story of the**

scientific journey back to the dawn of the universe, by John C. Mather and John Boslough. Basic Books, 1996. 328p bibl index ISBN 0-465-01575-1, $27.50

Mather and Boslough's book is must reading for those interested in astronomy, the sociology of science, big science, the philosophy of science, and science in general. They relate the story of the Cosmic Background Explorer (COBE)—a NASA spacecraft—whose purpose was to explore the beginning of the universe (the big bang). Apart from a history of COBE the book contains a clear, concise introduction into the history of astronomy, including some ancient astronomical sites, an excellent description of the history of the discovery of the cosmic background radiation, and a lucid introduction to the history of our ideas on cosmology, especially the history of Hubble's discovery of the expansion of the universe—it is almost unbelievable how clearly cosmology is explained. An extremely rich book that discusses such diverse topics as science, religion, and life in general, especially human life and its relation to the cosmos and Earth. An absolutely exciting book that one can hardly put down. All levels.— *C. H. McGruder III, Western Kentucky University*

OAB-1342 QB15x Orig
North, John. **The Norton history of astronomy and cosmology.** W.W. Norton, 1995. 697p bibl index ISBN 0-393-03656-1, $35.00; ISBN 0-393-31193-7 pbk, $18.95

North (Univ. of Groningen) has created a valuable reference for students and others interested in the development of cosmology. This volume covers 5,000 years of astronomy, beginning with a thorough discussion of the worldwide contributions of ancient astronomers and leading the reader through the Copernican Revolution, discovery of other galaxies, and the development of the big bang theory. Unlike other books, it also discusses improvements in technology such as radio astronomy and telescopes in space. The references are presented in an informative bibliographical essay. The black-and-white line drawings are spartan but adequate. The brief biographical sketches of famous astronomers contain some interesting sidelines not covered elsewhere. This book is not a trivial read but a valuable reference tool exploding with information. Recommended for all libraries. General; undergraduate through faculty.—*K. Larsen, Central Connecticut State University*

OAB-1343 QB82 96-25450 CIP
Osterbrock, Donald E. **Yerkes Observatory, 1892-1950: the birth, near death, and resurrection of a scientific research institute.** Chicago, 1997. 384p bibl index afp ISBN 0-226-63945-2, $40.00

This is an important book; the subtitle suggests that it reviews the history of a research institution. But the institution is the Yerkes Observatory, the wellspring of innovation in astrophysics during the quarter century that preceded Sputnik, and thus the book reflects the development of astrophysics in the US as well. The founding and early development of Yerkes is described in satisfactory detail, but Osterbrock concentrates on the era when Otto Struve was the force behind the research, and shows how a gifted individual, given strong support, can raise an institution to a position of dominance. An epilogue allows Osterbrock to discuss the lessons that might be drawn from this story. The material is well documented, with extensive footnotes; in addition, the author provides a critical evaluation of the actions of the principal figures. Because of his own distinguished research career, his recent experience as a historian of astronomy, and his personal association with Yerkes, Osterbrock is uniquely qualified to offer this review. The result—a book both authoritative and beautifully written. Highly recommended. General readers; undergraduates through professionals.—*D. E. Hogg, National Radio Astronomy Observatory*

OAB-1344 QB43 96-1482 CIP
Parker, Barry. **Chaos in the cosmos: the stunning complexity of the universe.** Plenum, 1996. 307p bibl index afp ISBN 0-306-45261-8, $28.95

There have been a large number of popular and semipopular books on

chaos and fractals published over the last several years. Parker's is distinctive. The first half is devoted to chaos and fractals. Many physical examples are used, and every attempt is made to define all of the new terms that are introduced and to give the reader a real sense of the nature of the problems. The kinds of connections that exist among chaos, fractals, and nonlinearity are explored in a way that should be accessible to a serious reader. A collection of minibiographies of the main players in the recent explosion in the field dot the book, making pleasant reading and also providing nonscientists a nice feel for the ways in which careers in the sciences develop. The latter half of the book treats the cosmos (e.g., the solar system, stars and galaxies, cosmology, and the early universe) as a giant laboratory for the ideas of chaos and fractals. A variety of intriguing insights relating to current research personally engage the reader with the real manner in which scientific ideas evolve. Every attempt is made to exhibit the provisional and tentative nature of the ongoing scientific enterprise. Belongs in all college libraries. General; lower-division undergraduates; two-year technical program students.—*K. L. Schick, Union College (NY)*

OAB-1345 QB981 92-43948 CIP
Parker, Barry. **The vindication of the Big Bang: breakthroughs and barriers.** Plenum, 1993. 361p bibl index ISBN 0-306-44469-0, $24.95

A very thorough book written by a prize-winning science writer who knows his field well. After a comprehensive introduction, Parker introduces the history of the discovery of the expansion of the universe, shows how the Big Bang model was formulated, describes it, discusses the cosmic background and the related observations, and reviews the difficulties with the Big Bang model. He describes what is known of the structure of the observable universe and the problems connected with our understanding of its origin and evolution and the strengths and weaknesses of competing cosmologies, and gives a good assessment of where we are in our understanding of the universe. The content is largely nontechnical and the style is chatty and in the first person. The 17 chapters hold the reader's attention; Parker personalizes the researchers well. Photographs are excellent; figures are adequate; there are no tables. There is a 7-page glossary, a 6-page bibliography, and a 6-page index. Recommended for the intelligent general reader who wants to find it all in one place. All levels.—*W. E. Howard III, Advanced Concepts and Space, U.S. Army*

OAB-1346 QC971 94-1458 CIP
Savage, Candace. **Aurora: the mysterious northern lights.** Sierra Club Books, 1994. 144p bibl index ISBN 0-87156-419-X, $25.00

A large segment of the earth's population has never experienced the polar lights because, as the author of this informative book states so nicely, "... the aurora spends most of its time around the ends of the earth, where it dances mainly for the pleasure of penguins and bears." With the publication of this volume everyone can experience the aurora vicariously through the magnificent photographs and prose contained within, and can also learn about the history, mythology, and science of the polar lights. Savage, who has previously written eight books of natural history, carefully researched the material for the book. In addition to the regular text, a number of stand-alone sidebars are included on interesting topics such as finding predictions of auroral activity, an auroral dictionary, and Inuit space flight. The photographs are supplemented with reproductions of plates from older texts and other graphics. The book is oversized and looks like it belongs on the coffee table, but the scholarly content qualifies this outstanding volume for inclusion in all college libraries. Extensive chapter notes. Highly recommended. General; undergraduate; two-year technical program students.—*H. E. Wylen, formerly, National Science Foundation*

OAB-1347 QB601 91-39398 CIP
Sheehan, William. **Worlds in the sky: planetary discovery from earliest times through Voyager and Magellan.** Arizona, 1992. 243p bibl index afp ISBN 0-8165-1290-6, $35.00; ISBN 0-8165-1308-2 pbk, $17.95

A splendid introduction to the descriptive aspects of the Moon, the planets, comets, and meteors of the Solar System. Well written by a knowledgeable amateur who describes them from the first primitive observations to modern planetary fly-bys with earth probes, the text is educational, free-flowing, and entertaining, and contains many anecdotes that will be new even to astronomers. Following a three-chapter introduction is a superb history of lunar mapping, including good drawings of the Moon and the planets. Sheehan includes interesting vignettes that make each chapter stimulating and entertaining. Details of the discovery of Neptune are presented in an exceptionally informative and often amusing way! There are appendixes with statistics on the major planets and the satellites of the Solar System; an excellent 7-page list of notes; a good 8-page bibliography; and a useful 13-page index. Good quality photographs and drawings. Highly recommended to any reader above age 10 curious about the planets and their satellites and as good recreation for professionals.—*W. E. Howard III, Space and Strategic Technology, U.S. Army*

OAB-1348   QB225   95-17402 CIP
Sobel, Dava. **Longitude: the true story of a lone genius who solved the greatest scientific problem of his time.** Walker & Company, 1995. 184p bibl index ISBN 0-8027-1312-2, $19.00

Throughout history, untold numbers of mariners died because they had no idea of just where they were located on Earth's oceans. Latitude, the position of a ship north or south of the equator, was well established by astronomical means. The determination of longitude, the hypothetical lines crossing the planet from north to south pole, was beyond the skills of early mariners, and the loss of countless ships was the tragic consequence. In 1707, five ships of the British navy smashed into the Scilly Isles with a loss of 2,000 lives; as a result, Parliament established the Longitude Board in 1714. Its mission was to find a true means of establishing longitude and a princely reward was offered, amounting to the present-day equivalent of several million dollars. John Harrison, a self-taught clockmaker, set out in 1721 to make a clock or chronometer that would keep exact time at sea no matter what the weather. Harrison realized that if his clock would tell a ship's navigator the exact time in Greenwich, England, comparison to local time would give the ship's position east or west. His 1759 device weighed only three pounds and kept an unheard-of accuracy of two minutes on a voyage to Jamaica lasting many months. Despite this achievement, Harrison was denied the prize for years because of rivalry and opposition from the head of the Greenwich observatory, who wanted the longitude solution to be found in the motions of the Moon and stars. Sobel's absorbing history is fascinating, well worth reading. General.—*C. G. Wood, Eastern Maine Technical College*

OAB-1349   QB501   92-25784 CIP
Taylor, Stuart Ross. **Solar system evolution: a new perspective: an inquiry into the chemical composition, origin, and evolution of the solar system.** Cambridge, 1992. 307p indexes ISBN 0-521-37212-7, $49.95

This splendid book provides a very broad commentary on the problems of the origin and evolution of the solar system. It is equation-free but does not avoid technical detail, much of which can be passed over by nontechnical readers who will still gain from the presentation. There are seven well-written chapters on a historical perspective of planetary formation, the solar nebula, meteorite evidence, the role of impacts, the planets, rings and satellites, and a summary chapter on "the new Solar System" that contains a fascinating two-page summary of how the Solar System was formed. The author notes the recognition of the emerging importance of large collisions during the accretion stage of planetary formation. Each chapter ends with excellent, extensive notes. There are good, readable tables, but the figures are sometimes too small. Adequate subject and name indexes. Overall, a good way to learn about how the Earth, Sun, and planets were formed. Highly recommended. All levels.—*W. E. Howard III, Advanced Concepts and Space, U.S. Army*

■ Biology

OAB-1350   QH541   95-9533 CIP
Agosta, William. **Bombardier beetles and fever trees: a close-up look at chemical warfare and signals in animals and plants.** Helix Books/Addison-Wesley, 1996. 224p index ISBN 0-201-62658-6, $25.00

For the uninitiated, this is a "believe it or not" type of book: mites that manufacture glycerol, an antifreeze enabling their survival at -28C; DOPA-containing proteins in the adhesive produced by sandcastle-building worms; chemicals from the female emperor moth that lure males from miles away; a spray used by certain ants to promote dissension and civil war in another species, enabling the former to capture and enslave the latter! Organic chemist Agosta introduces the wonders of chemical ecology, the study of the use of chemicals (mostly sui generis) by organisms interacting with others and with their physical surroundings. In a highly readable, jargon-free style, he details nature's storehouse of chemicals and their use by a wide range of organisms in activities ranging from defense and warfare to lovemaking. Among much else are fascinating accounts of opiums and other hallucinogens that affect life styles (like the pheromones that synchronize menstruation in baboon troops), the penicillin story, and that of other plant-derived medicines. Instead of the ponderous prose of a pedant, this is a brisk, accessible treat for a wide public audience as well as for professional scientists. All levels.—*E. J. Kormondy, emeritus, University of Hawaii at Hilo*

OAB-1351   QH501   94-49675 CIP
Angier, Natalie. **The beauty of the beastly: new views on the nature of life.** Houghton Mifflin, 1995. 278p index ISBN 0-395-71816-3, $21.95

As Angier notes, this book contains "new views on the nature of life" and makes the point that "the beauty of the natural world lies in its details, and most of these details are not the stuff of calendar art." The author makes it a point to write about organisms that most people find repugnant, such as worms, spiders, parasites, scorpions, rattlesnakes, dung beetles, or hyenas. She further hopes to "inspire in the readers an appreciation for diversity, for imagination, for the twisted, webbed, infinite possibility of the natural world. Every single story that nature tells is gorgeous." According to acclaimed author Timothy Ferris, Angier is considered "one of the strongest and wittiest science writers in the world today." She has learned science from the molecule up and has found everything from the supple structure of DNA to the erratic ways of many different animals to be most poignant in the complexities and necessary sadness of death. Few writers have covered so many facets of biology so well. All levels.—*J. M. Carpenter, University of Kentucky*

OAB-1352   QH604   90-26732 MARC
Barritt, Greg J. **Communication within animal cells.** Oxford, 1992. 343p index ISBN 0-19-854727-7, $95.00; ISBN 0-19-854726-9 pbk, $49.95

Although there are many fine reviews devoted to individual cellular control systems, few books deal with intracellular regulatory and communication systems as a whole. Barritt describes both the transfer of information within cells and how they receive information from their surroundings. He begins with a general introduction to intracellular communication and a discussion of the relationship between cell structure and regulation. Then are described in detail the major components of intracellular signaling systems, including topics such as plasma membrane receptors and G proteins, protein kinases, cyclic nucleotides, inositol polyphosphates, calcium, arachidonic metabolites, and nuclear DNA binding proteins. The book concludes with a chapter on oncogenes and a discussion of the interactions between various communication systems. Each chapter has a good summary and a carefully selected set of references, many of them as recent as 1990 or 1991. The index is extensive; tables and illustrations are plentiful and helpful. Barritt successfully provides a framework for understanding intracellular communication. An excellent introduction; highly recommended. Advanced undergraduate; graduate; faculty.—*L. M. Prescott, Augustana College (SD)*

OAB-1353 QH545 93-43804 CIP
Before and after an oil spill: the Arthur Kill, ed. by Joanna Burger. Rutgers, 1994. 305p index ISBN 0-8135-2095-9, $50.00

This excellent book contains 18 chapters prepared by 13 contributors. Each chapter is devoted to a discrete aspect of the release, in 1990, of 565,000 gallons of no. 2 fuel oil (a distillate resembling home-heating oil) into Arthur Kill, a tidal strait that separates Staten Island, New York, from New Jersey and connects with Newark Bay (north end) and Raritan Bay (south end). Chapters are devoted to spill effects on the major classes of biota (i.e., plant communities, crabs, fish and shrimp, and birds). The book's unique aspects include chapters on governmental cooperation (three federal agencies, two states, and two cities), legal concerns, conservation groups, and the mass media. It provides an outstanding concise protocol for preparedness for an environmental catastrophe. Lacking is any discussion of the chemistry of either the petroleum released or residue remaining in following years. A stunning feature of the book is its depiction of the tenacious and resilient character of a natural ecosystem in the face of mammoth human perturbation. Adequate illustrations. An excellent resource for libraries serving programs in biology, environmental sciences, mass communication, wildlife management, and community emergency response. Upper-division undergraduate through faculty.—*L. H. Stevenson, McNeese State University*

OAB-1354 QH31 92-41540 CIP
Bonner, John Tyler. **Life cycles: reflections of an evolutionary biologist.** Princeton, 1993. 209p index afp ISBN 0-691-03319-6, $19.95

Bonner has been an influential biologist, making his mark in the study of slime mold development; the book's subtitle fits almost perfectly. This work is not a tell-all history of Bonner, nor a summary of his scientific work. Although he writes that he does not like philosophy, the book is nevertheless a philosophical, reflective, splendid work. The philosophy is enlivened by frequent (apparently true) anecdotes, such as the one about the lady who was working with moth sex attractant, or Einstein's reaction to a movie about slime molds. Bonner considers living beings from the standpoint of life cycles, and writes about questions that biologists do not think about very often: "why" questions, such as why did multicellularity, larger sizes, sociality, and intelligence evolve, and "how" questions, such as how evolution works, not on a static organism, but on an organism throughout its life cycle. These are the sort of questions to which all biologists, and all students in biology courses, should be exposed. Brief index; few references. Easy reading for generalists and scientists alike, and should be in all college libraries. All levels.—*M. LaBar, Central Wesleyan College*

OAB-1355 QH84 92-10583 CIP
Campbell, David G. **The crystal desert: summers in Antarctica.** Houghton Mifflin, 1992. 308p bibl index ISBN 0-395-58969-X, $21.95

A magnificent natural history of the "other" Antarctica, the relatively small area outside the grip of Earth's greatest ice sheet. This involves, principally, the Antarctic Peninsula that juts north toward Tierra del Fuego, and a group of remarkable offshore islands, the South Shetlands. Campbell writes in personal narrative style; an outstanding writer, he has produced a highly scientific treatment of animal and plant life, both terrestrial and marine, for the general reader. He also gives an account of early explorers and present-day scientists. Passages of the text, while fully scientific, achieve the level of poetic prose, and the whole is beautifully readable. The subject, in its broadest sense, is about life on Earth and its prospects for continuity. The book is well bound and produced; there is a 20-page section of notes, valuable references, and index. A few good photographs of these fascinating landscapes would have added some icing to a marvelous cake. General through professional.—*J. D. Ives, University of California, Davis*

OAB-1356 QH75 95-1616 CIP
Caughley, Graeme. **Conservation biology in theory and practice,** by Graeme Caughley and Anne Gunn. Blackwell Science, 1996. 459p bibl index ISBN 0-86542-431-4 pbk, $44.95

According to a recent report, since the year 1600, some 486 animal and 600 plant species have become extinct, and another 3,565 animals and 22,137 plants are presently threatened with extinction. One of the newest disciplines to emerge during the past decade is conservation biology, which offers an interdisciplinary approach to why species are driven into decline and how these declines can be reversed. This authoritative book with a global perspective is intended for ecologists, field biologists, and wildlife managers. Caughley and Gunn discuss the merits and shortcomings of explanations for historic extinctions as well as for those species listed as endangered. They examine and evaluate the credibility of diagnosis and recovery treatments using specific case history approaches; establish theoretical concepts for metapopulation dynamics, small population demography, loss of genetic variation, and island biogeography; and provide new insights as well as practical guidelines on the design of reserves as a treatment for declining species. They critique established reserves as not meeting ecological requirements of endangered species and not demonstrating an appreciation of community dynamics, and they discuss paleontology, population dynamics, and people's economic aspirations. Examples are drawn mainly from mammalian and bird species but include amphibians, fish, and invertebrates. Excellent compilation of current literature along with ample illustrations, diagrams, maps, and box essays. An original contribution by two gifted scientists. Strongly recommended. Upper-division undergraduate through professional.—*S. M. Paracer, Worcester State College*

OAB-1357 QH186 92-14891 CIP
Cubitt, Gerald. **Wild Indonesia: the wildlife and scenery of the Indonesian archipelago,** photographs by Gerald Cubitt; text by Tony and Jane Whitten. MIT, 1992. 208p bibl index ISBN 0-262-23165-4, $39.95

An awesome book. The Indonesian archipelago displays perhaps the greatest biodiversity of any country in the world. Since the early studies of Alfred Russel Wallace focused on this exotic area, naturalists have marveled at the incredible variety of flora and fauna to be found here. To describe accurately and precisely the myriad ecosystems in this geographical region would seem difficult if not impossible. Yet the authors, Indonesia scholars, have produced a magnificent summary of this seldom-remarked area. Emphasis is given to its many national parks and reserves, including the relatively recent developments in Irian Jaya, which purists might still catalog along with New Guinea. There are supposedly almost 14,000 islands (at least at low tide) in Indonesia and just about all the significant ones are herein described. As is to be expected in a volume sponsored by the World Wide Fund for Nature, there is a strong conservation theme; because many of the taxa described are in danger of extinction, this emphasis is understandable. But the preservation of the whole environment, whether volcanic, coral reefs, cave, rain forest, wetland, is stressed. All of the articulate descriptions are neatly supplemented by Cubitt's superb and exquisite photography. For serious students there is a lengthy bibliography. The best natural history of Indonesia currently available. General; advanced undergraduate; graduate; professional.—*G. Nicholas, Manhattan College*

OAB-1358 QH375 94-49158 CIP
Dennett, Daniel C. **Darwin's dangerous idea: evolution and the meanings of life.** Simon & Schuster, 1995. 586p bibl index ISBN 0-684-80290-2, $30.00

Distinguished philosopher Dennett serves up an intellectual feast that happens perhaps once in a decade, if that often. This work is intelligible for those nonspecialists interested in such "big" topics as evolution in the biological and social spheres, yet it remains simultaneously a gold mine for philosophers, cognitive scientists, and evolutionary biologists concerned with evolutionary theory. The meticulously crafted arguments are laid out in three parts and 17 chapters. Part 1 is a novel and detailed account of the heart of the Darwinian algorithm approach to evolution; the second part examines head-on the current controversies in evolutionary theory; the third is a detailed examination of mind, meaning, mathematics, and morality. Dennett's two metaphors of "cranes" and "skyhooks" used to get at the understanding of causalities in science make accessible details of his seminal analysis. Although not a kneejerk

Darwinist, Dennett shows intellectual appreciation of the rigor and utility of Darwinian thinking on a level that overshadows that of many (lesser) theorists in biology. The book has been called "surpassingly brilliant" by professional evolutionary biologists, but it is also a methodological beacon for dealing with issues of evolutionary theory. Very highly recommended. All levels.—*F. S. Szalay, CUNY Hunter College*

OAB-1359   HT166   92-43261 CIP
Ecology of greenways: design and function of linear conservation areas, ed. by Daniel S. Smith and Paul Cawood Hellmund. Minnesota, 1993. 222p index afp ISBN 0-8166-2157-8, $39.95

Greenways are naturally vegetated, linear, open-space corridors that function as connections for networks of traditional open spaces such as natural areas, parks, and recreation areas. When sited and maintained properly, they help to maintain ecological balances in human-dominated landscapes, especially by enhancing biological diversity and protecting water quality. *Ecology of Greenways* offers an analysis of the benefits of these corridors and an applied, practical approach to creating and maintaining them. The book's utility is greatly enhanced by an interdisciplinary approach to content and an impressive selection of specialist authors for each chapter. Seven chapters, plus introduction and epilogue, cover the following subjects: history, ecology, and functions of greenways; overview of landscape ecology; wildlife corridors; riparian greenways and water resources; minimizing conflicts between recreation and nature conservation; and a method of ecological greenway design. The final chapter presents a series of insightful case studies from all over the US. References after each chapter allow entry into the primary literature of the appropriate fields. Edited by an ecological planner and a landscape architect, this unique volume will prove very useful to land planning professionals everywhere, and will help teach ecology to landscape designers and design to ecologists. Highly recommended. All levels.—*G. D. Dreyer, Connecticut College*

OAB-1360   92-10531 CIP
Ecosystem health: new goals for environmental management, ed. by Robert Costanza, Bryan G. Norton, and Benjamin D. Haskell. Island Press, 1992. 269p index afp ISBN 1-55963-141-4, $40.00; ISBN 1-55963-140-6 pbk, $22.00

This outstanding collection of papers, edited by Costanza (Maryland), Norton (Georgia Tech) and Haskell (Maryland), is the best single-volume treatment of the concept of ecosystem health. This book is important because in some circles ecosystem health is regarded as the goal of ecological management, yet it is a very difficult concept to define and to understand. This volume brings together the perspectives of philosophers, economists, biologists, and geographers who address such issues as whether nature has a good of its own, clinical ecology, ecological integrity, and alternative models of ecosystem restoration. For the most part the contributors are committed to the usefulness of the idea of ecosystem health, so skepticism about this concept is not well represented; and as in all edited collections, the quality is uneven and the contributors do not always stick to the point. Still there are many first-rate essays including those by Callicott, Ehrenfeld, and Rapport. This volume will become the first stop for those who are interested in ecosystem health. Highly recommended for all academic and professional libraries.—*D. Jamieson, University of Colorado at Boulder*

OAB-1361   QH325   91-22349 CIP
Eigen, Manfred. **Steps towards life: a perspective on evolution,** by Manfred Eigen with Ruthild Winkler-Oswatitsch; tr. by Paul Woolley. Oxford, 1992. 173p index ISBN 0-19-854751-X, $29.95

Eigen considers the origin of life from the viewpoint of molecular biology, and presents the case for modifying the Darwinian concept of selection. Evolution at the molecular level acts upon quasi-species ("the weighted distribution of mutants centered around one or several master [molecular] sequences") in a sequence space ("a multidimensional representation of all possible variants of

a sequence"). Evolution is likened to a series of phase transitions, resulting from the selection of superior mutants at the peaks or "mountain regions" in the sequence space. Selection can be expressed not only through competition, but also through cooperation via coupled cycles. Higher levels of evolution (procytes, eucytes, and complex eukaryotic organisms) then arise. The basic argument is developed in the compact first part of the book (52 pages). Technical details are presented in the second part, supplemented by helpful color diagrams. Part 3 consists of a short resumé, provocatively entitled "Darwin is dead—long live Darwin," along with bibliographical notes and a glossary of technical terms. A conceptually intriguing and well-documented book, highly recommended for undergraduate libraries.—*D. Blitz, Central Connecticut State University*

OAB-1362   TP248   94-6959 CIP
Glick, Bernard R. **Molecular biotechnology: principles and applications of recombinant DNA,** by Bernard R. Glick and Jack J. Pasternak. American Society for Microbiology, 1994. 500p bibl index ISBN 1-55581-071-3 pbk, $39.95

Captivatingly clear and written in a casual style, this moderate-sized book of 19 chapters should be in the hands of scientists interested in the field of biotechnology. The authors convey their pure enthusiasm for the subject, providing information for both the newcomer and the more experienced student of biotechnology and its applications. This book would be an excellent course supplement in biotechnology and/or bioanalysis, as well as advanced biochemistry or molecular biology, where course texts often cover a broader range of topics in lieu of the depth of this work. It should not be overlooked by any library with a serious interest in the sciences. Although it is not a methods book per se, the descriptions and definitions are written clearly enough that the reader is provided sufficiently detailed information to subsequently glean methodology from the primary literature. In addition to theoretical, practical, and applied information, the book also contains a comprehensive glossary and a treatise on the aspects of regulating new technologies and obtaining patents for new inventions. Upper-division undergraduate through professional.—*J. N. Granger, Sweet Briar College*

OAB-1363   QH541   95-26734 CIP
Gotelli, Nicholas J. **Null models in ecology,** by Nicholas J. Gotelli and Gary R. Graves. Smithsonian Institution Press, 1996. 368p bibl index afp ISBN 1-56098-657-3, $65.00; ISBN 1-56098-645-X pbk, $30.00

To what extent do sampling artifacts and random taxonomic associations limit our ability to infer community-level biological interactions from patterns of species abundance and distribution? As comprehensively described by Gotelli and Graves, null models address this question by providing powerful analytical tools for (1) delineating expected species associations within non-interactive communities, (2) describing random patterns in niche overlap, diversity indices, and species-area relationships, and (3) examining community complexity and stability as reflected by food webs. Each of ten chapters details hypotheses, assumptions, and predictions in community ecology to which historical and contemporary null models have been applied, describes the strengths and weaknesses of these models, and ends with specific recommendations for their application. Long-standing controversies surrounding character displacement and community assembly rules are given detailed coverage. Complementing a balanced and detailed overview, the book's epilogue provides constructive criticism of null models and suggestions for their improvement, particularly with respect to data quality and source pool construction. Well written, exhaustively referenced, and objectively presented, this first review of null models is a landmark contribution to the historical development and study of community ecology. Upper-division undergraduates through faculty.—*J. A. Hutchings, Dalhousie University*

OAB-1364   QH45   92-18737 CIP
Gould, Stephen Jay. **Eight little piggies: reflections in natural history.** W.W. Norton, 1993. 479p bibl index ISBN 0-393-03416-X, $22.95

Gould's interesting title derives from the probability that we, with our five fingers and toes, evolved from ancestors that had six or perhaps eight fingers and toes. The book is considered by some to be the most personal and thoughtful of all Gould's writings, since it speaks quite often of the importance of the solid connection between our lives and those of our ancestors, a theme of very great interest to evolutionists who realize that extinction is the final fate of all, and prolonged existence is the only successful measure of personal success. This measure of personal success leads Gould rather naturally to an area that has become for him one of major importance—the deterioration of the environment and the "massive" extinction of species on Earth. All the 31 essays appearing in the book's eight chapters originally appeared as columns in Gould's monthly series "This View of Life" in *Natural History* magazine, where they were widely read and enjoyed. A must for everyone interested in natural history. General; advanced undergraduate; graduate; pre-professional; faculty.— *J. M. Carpenter, University of Kentucky*

OAB-1365 QH441 95-23314 CIP
Harris, Henry. **The cells of the body: a history of somatic cell genetics.** Cold Spring Harbor Laboratory, 1995. 263p bibl indexes afp ISBN 0-87969-460-2, $55.00

Harris's historical review is a welcome companion for his previous work *Nucleus and Cytoplasm* (3rd ed., 1974), a classic on the technology of somatic cell genetics. The current volume elegantly sums up the field, which has now been largely subsumed (along with many other fields) by the application of molecular techniques. Harris rightly points out that modern molecular biology, with its attendant advances in basic and applied medicine, owes a large debt to somatic cell genetics. Additionally, a historical appreciation of this field, especially when written by one of its history makers, should lead to a deeper understanding of the genetic mechanisms involved in cancer, which are still very mysterious. In particular, the discussion of failed ideas and approaches, rarely included in a more technical review, adds immeasurably to the worth of this book. Both students and long-time researchers will benefit from reading this exhaustively researched history. The cogent style, sparkling prose, and abundant portraits of seldom-viewed somatic cell geneticists also add a lot to this small book, which rightly belongs in college, university, and research libraries. Undergraduate through professionals.—*D. A. Rintoul, Kansas State University*

OAB-1366 QL776 95-52290 CIP
Hauser, Marc D. **The evolution of communication.** MIT, 1996. 760p bibl index ISBN 0-262-08250-0, $55.00

In this broad, comprehensive, and integrative analysis of the evolution of communication, Hauser outlines the general argument and provides background information on the study of communication and the comparative method. He presents a historical overview and the conceptual issues surrounding the study of communication. He then examines comparative communication in a modified version of Tinbergen's four causal questions focusing on neurobiological, ontogenetic, adaptive, and psychological design. In the final chapter, Hauser synthesizes the material from earlier chapters and suggests future avenues for the study of comparative communication. This book represents a milestone in the study of comparative communication as it focuses on a variety of species, from insects to humans, and surveys the unique design features of these various communication systems in light of origin, current function, and future evolution. Hauser articulates difficult points clearly and provides numerous visual aids to further enhance the quality of his prose. Recommended for neurobiologists, ethologists, comparative and developmental psychologists, linguists, anthropologists, and evolutionary biologists. A valuable addition for all college and university libraries, and an excellent bibliographic source for public libraries. Extensive bibliography and index. Upper-division undergraduates through professionals.—*N. Krusko, Beloit College*

OAB-1367 GE140 94-27799 CIP
Johnson, Douglas L. **Land degradation: creation and destruction,** by Douglas L. Johnson and Laurence A. Lewis. Blackwell, 1995. 335p bibl index afp ISBN 0-631-17997-6, $74.95

When human interactions with the environment substantially decrease an area's biological productivity and/or usefulness, land degradation occurs. Johnson and Lewis delineate two opposing principles related to land degradation: "creative destruction" refers to changes that are useful and sustainable, whereas "destructive creation" refers to human-nature interactions that lead to ecological deterioration and collapse. Approaching the topic from a resource-management perspective, the authors first provide a brief overview of natural physical factors. They then discuss the negative (destructive creation) impacts of agriculture, animal husbandry, water demands, energy, transportation, and urbanization. After analyzing beneficial and sustainable changes (creative destruction), Johnson and Lewis state that a successful ecotechnology must involve the identification of critical zones necessary for sustainable use, application of sacrifice zones that are degraded in the interests of enhancing critical zones, and proper management. Well written, illustrated with numerous examples from around the globe, and filled with diverse biological, geological, and political information, *Land Degradation* provides an excellent overview of a compelling problem. General; upper-division undergraduate through professional.—*D. J. Campagna, College of William and Mary*

OAB-1368 QH541 92-39069 CIP
Jumars, Peter A. **Concepts in biological oceanography: an interdisciplinary primer.** Oxford, 1993. 348p index afp ISBN 0-19-506732-0, $49.95

Jumars's explicit purpose in writing this book was to make biological concepts more accessible to physical oceanographers in the hope of stimulating greater levels of collaboration between these two disciplines. The three main sections of the book gradually build the framework to achieve this goal by emphasizing the quantitative aspects of biology and avoiding the kinds of specific examples and nomenclature that nonbiologists often find intimidating. The first section introduces ecological principles (using marine examples), while the second focuses on the more important issues in biological oceanography. The final part completes the link of biological and physical elements, discussing the effects of organisms on sound, light, and sediment deposition and chemistry. Particularly valuable are the annotated reference lists at the end of each chapter that have been selected for their readability by nonspecialists. Although intended for physical oceanographers, there is much here for the biologist as well, and the volume is written in a lively and humorous style that is all too often lacking in scientific textbooks. An excellent book, highly recommended for advanced undergraduate and graduate students.—*G.C. Jensen, University of Washington*

OAB-1369 QH428 94-44222 CIP
Keller, Evelyn Fox. **Refiguring life: metaphors of twentieth-century biology.** Columbia, 1995. 134p bibl index afp ISBN 0-231-10204-6, $20.00

The subtitle of Keller's book is a succinct description of these three essays, originally given at the University of California, Irvine, as part of the Wellek Library Lecture Series. These lectures address the biological discourse of gene action, the gene as the shaper and mover of life, and, finally, the transformation of the concept of the body itself by machines (most notably but not exclusively the computer). Throughout Keller emphasizes that the guiding metaphors are both derived from and contribute to the biological processes being studied and the tools with which they are studied. It is not just that language shapes thought and research; the research and the creation of new technologies also shape and create new language and, in so doing, new ways to experience and understand the body. This book does an excellent job of making manifest the close interaction between science and humanities and showing that the one is not embedded in the other, but that they are mutually interactive forces. Fine index. Recommended for all college and university libraries. Upper-division undergraduate through professional.—*M. H. Chaplin, Wellesley College*

OAB-1370 QH431 95-41523 CIP
Kitcher, Philip. **The lives to come: the genetic revolution and**

human possibilities. Simon & Schuster, 1996. 381p index ISBN 0-684-80055-1, $25.00

DNA sequencing, DNA fingerprinting, transcription, translation, restriction enzymes, introns, restriction fragment length polymorphisms (RFLPs), variable number tandem repeats (VNTRs), positional cloning: Can a professional philosopher make all these buzzwords and acronyms of molecular biology and molecular genetics accessible and relevant to the general public, in 100,000 words or less, in a style that is lively, easy to read, and attractively packaged? Judging from *The Lives to Come*, the answer is a resounding yes. Kitcher does all this and more. His book is a guide to the current status of DNA technology, a primer in its esoteric techniques, a glimpse at its history, an evaluation of its ability to improve (but change) our lives, and a caution on the price such improvement/change will entail. Kitcher does a masterly job of laying out the science underlying DNA testing, DNA fingerprinting, and genetic screening—the here and now—and of pointing toward gene replacement and national databases containing every individual's DNA profile—the near now and future. It really is, as he says in chapter 5, "mice today, humans tomorrow." He integrates the ethical, political, economic, social, philosophical, medical, and scientific dimensions of our newfound ability to reconstruct ourselves in our own images, to repair damage, and to cure our genetic diseases. Excellent glossary. General; undergraduates through professionals.—*B. K. Hall, Dalhousie University*

OAB-1371   QH95   93-28273 CIP
Knox, George A. **The biology of the Southern Ocean.** Cambridge, 1995 (c1994). 444p bibl index ISBN 0-521-32211-1, $130.00

Over the past two decades, research conducted in the Antarctic has radically changed the understanding of the most basic ecological processes at work there. In particular, studies of primary production along the edges of the sea ice and the importance of bacteria, protozoa, and nano- and picophytoplankton have made obsolete much of what was previously "known" about the Southern Ocean. Knox provides a very timely and readable summary of the literature to date in a valuable basic reference that cites more than 2,000 sources. The 18 chapters cover all aspects of aquatic biology in the Antarctic region, from microbial, ice shelf, planktonic, and benthic communities to krill, seals, seabirds, and whales; in addition, resource exploitation and its effects and management are also discussed. An epilogue summarizes the changing views and highlights those additional needs and directions for future research not already covered in previous chapters. An extremely well-written and comprehensive book, suitable for upper-division undergraduates through professionals, highly recommended as a standard reference for all natural science libraries.—*G.C. Jensen, University of Washington*

OAB-1372   QP406   92-31167 CIP
Macphail, Euan M. **The neuroscience of animal intelligence: from the seahare to the seahorse.** Columbia, 1993. 506p bibl indexes afp ISBN 0-231-06144-7, $65.00

Recently, numerous books have been written surveying current work on the neurobiology of learning and memory. Many are quite good; for instance, Yadin Dudai's *The Neurobiology of Memory: Concepts, Findings, Trends* (CH, May '90) and Larry R. Squire's *Memory and Brain* (CH, Sep '87) both provide excellent overviews of this field. But as good as these books are, Macphail's is better. This intelligent, well-written, savvy book covers most major topics in the field, such as learning in simple systems: habituation, sensitization, and associative learning; the roles of the cerebellum and hippocampus in associative learning; long-term potentiation; spatial (contextual) learning; the concept of multiple memory processes; and the contribution of computational neuroscience. The book has many strengths: one is that Macphail has a solid, wide-ranging grasp of the learning and memory literature and, as a result, is able to integrate the historical literature on learning and memory with recent findings. Another strength is that he is a gifted interpreter of the literature and has a flair for explaining difficult concepts in a lucid fashion. A textbook of choice for advanced courses, and a mandatory addition for academic libraries. Advanced undergraduate through professional.—*D. A. Smith, Oberlin College*

OAB-1373   QH326   CIP
Margulis, Lynn. **What is life?,** by Lynn Margulis and Dorion Sagan. Simon & Schuster, 1995. 207p index ISBN 0-684-81087-5, $40.00

Margulis is a world-renowned life scientist; Sagan is a gifted writer. Together they have produced a beautifully written, profusely illustrated book that deals with life and death. Continuing Margulis's contention that organelles within cells, such as mitochondria, were originally free-living organisms that fused with others to form complex cells and bodies, the authors extend this concept to the Earth as a superorganism. Although following traditional evolutionary pathways, the authors argue that life has played a role in its own evolution. Designed for the general reader, this book could be used to interest students who are less than excited by standard biology textbooks, as well as by teachers who may derive new approaches. Because of the high quality of the photographs and line drawings, the lyrical writing, the thought-provoking approach to the question of what life is, and the excellent index, librarians will probably want to order more than one copy. General; undergraduate; two-year technical program students.—*W. Lener, Nassau Community College*

OAB-1374   QH352   96-28242 CIP
Metapopulation biology: ecology, genetics, and evolution, ed. by Ilkka Hanski and Michael E. Gilpin. Academic Press, 1997. 512p bibl index afp ISBN 0-12-323445-X, $89.95

Metapopulation is the latest paradigm in ecology, rapidly supplanting the concept of island biogeography in conservation biology and wildlife conservation. The number of papers, theoretical and applied, is increasing rapidly. Two new books have appeared within a year: *Metapopulations and Wildlife Conservation*, ed. by D. McCullough (1996), and the book under review. For these reasons it behooves all ecologists to understand the concept and its applications. This book provides the means to do so. It supersedes *Metapopulation Dynamics: Empirical and Theoretical Investigation*, ed. by Michael Gilpin and Ilkka Hanski (1991). There are 14 chapters, written by an international group of 30 contributors all active in metapopulation research. The three chapters of part 1 provide a solid introduction to the metapopulation concept, its evolution, and its relation to landscape ecology; part 2 reviews much of the existing theory, including evolution and genetics. Part 3 provides a detailed examination of metapopulation processes of local extinction, immigration, and colonization, and part 4 discusses four case studies of metapopulation dynamics. This important compendium belongs in the working library of ecologists and conservation and wildlife biologists and is a necessary acquisition for ecology reference libraries. Upper-division undergraduates through professionals.—*R. L. Smith, emeritus, West Virginia University*

OAB-1375   QH506   95-9063 CIP
Molecular biology and biotechnology: a comprehensive desk reference, ed. by Robert A. Meyers. VCH, 1995. 1,034p bibl index afp ISBN 1-56081-569-8, $149.95; ISBN 1-56081-925-1 pbk, $59.95

This excellent resource provides professional-level comprehensive coverage of modern molecular biology and biotechnology, or as stated in the preface, "the molecular basis of life and the application of that knowledge in genetics, medicine, and agriculture." Each of the 250-plus articles is written by a leading researcher, is arranged alphabetically by subject, and is a self-contained, complete treatment of an individual topic. Articles are cross-referenced and all provide additional citations; they include core articles that give basic information in a discipline, satellite articles that focus on active areas of research in that discipline, and specific subject articles that describe the specific application of recent findings. Every article is well illustrated with both black-and-white and color photos, diagrams, structures, charts, and tables. As a help to the reader, there is also a glossary of basic terms, instructions on the use of the book as a reference, and an excellent index. This fascinating collection will interest students at all levels, researchers, teachers, clinical physicians, and perhaps the press.—*J. L. Ninnemann, Adams State College*

OAB-1376   QH605   93-10477 CIP
Murray, Andrew. **The cell cycle: an introduction,** by Andrew Murray and Tim Hunt. W.H. Freeman, 1993. (Dist. by Oxford) 251p index ISBN 0-7167-7044-X, $45.00; ISBN 0-7167-7046-6 pbk, $22.95

Murray and Hunt have produced a marvelous introduction to the cell cycle and its control, one needed especially in view of the recent remarkable advances in this area. Both authors have contributed to this field and are well qualified to summarize its status. The first four chapters introduce the cell cycle and discuss the critical experiments leading to our current knowledge. The next four chapters are devoted to the details of the cycle: mitosis, the G1-to-S transition, the control of DNA replication, and checkpoints and feedback controls. Throughout, the authors describe the experiments and reasoning that support current knowledge, with particular emphasis on the cycle in embryonic cells, yeasts, and mammalian cells. The final three chapters deal with cancer, meiosis, and the bacterial cell cycle. There are carefully selected references at the end of each chapter, many very useful line drawings, and an excellent appendix describing 418 genes that affect the cell cycle. Highly recommended. Advanced undergraduate through faculty.—*L. M. Prescott, Augustana College (SD)*

OAB-1377   GE195   95-22324 MARC
Pepper, David. **Modern environmentalism: an introduction.** Routledge, 1996. 376p bibl index ISBN 0-415-05744-2, $65.00; ISBN 0-415-05745-0 pbk, $22.95

Pepper's overview of environmentalism is a superbly crafted synthesis of a complex, still-evolving field of inquiry. Rather than providing a mere documentation of pedantic facts about environmental movements, Pepper attempts and succeeds at critically examining the interwoven texture of important philosophical, ecological, economic, social, and political ideologies that underpin various green movements, such as biocentrism and ecocentrism. He aptly elucidates the main theses and suppositions of various conceptual perspectives (e.g., anarchism, ecologism, holism, materialism, postmodernism, structuralism) that attempt to reconcile human existence with the natural world. The book is divided into six chapters ("Defining Environmentalism," "Issues in Radical Environmentalism," "Roots of Technocentrism," "Roots of Ecocentrism," "Postmodern Science and Ecocentrism," "Ways Ahead"), a useful glossary of relevant terms and concepts, and an extensive (more than 500 citations) and an up-to-date reference list. Pepper's commentary and analysis are evenhanded, as he assesses the strengths and internal contradictions of each green view. Although the book introduces past and present-day environmental thought and action championed in North America and Europe, it brings the reader deep below the surface of these critically important ideas. Highly recommended. All levels.—*P. R. Pinet, Colgate University*

OAB-1378   QR100   93-11579 CIP
Postgate, John. **The outer reaches of life.** Cambridge, 1994. 276p index ISBN 0-521-44010-6, $22.95

In this easily read and understood book, Postgate describes various harsh environments in which some forms of microbial life not only live but also thrive. Such environments as those that are very cold or hot, highly acidic, or alkaline are described in detail along with the microorganisms that have adapted to these inhospitable places. One of the chief strengths of this book is the clear manner in which the chemical aspects of these environments are explained to the reader. Also covered are the mechanisms and theories as to how certain forms of microbial life have been able to adapt to fringe habitats. In a broader context, Postgate uses these bizarre microbes as clues to the origin and evolution of life on earth. Postgate considers that they might also be models for the establishment of life elsewhere in the universe. The author touches on the more profound questions as to what constitutes life and the possibility of immortality amongst bacteria. Informative and entertaining. Highly recommended. General.—*P. C. Radich, University of Indianapolis*

OAB-1379   QH390   95-49224 CIP
Raff, Rudolf A. **The shape of life: genes, development, and the evolution of animal form.** Chicago, 1996. 520p bibl index afp ISBN 0-226-70265-0, $55.00; ISBN 0-226-70266-9 pbk, $29.95

In this book, Raff updates and expands many of the ideas he initially proposed with Thomas C. Kaufman in *Embryos, Genes, and Evolution* (1983). Here he combines a rich history of the studies that support our current philosophy of evolution with his personal experience in an informative and entertaining fashion, laying the foundation for future questions challenging our thinking on evolution, cladistics, and phylogeny. Clear descriptions and examples from recent advances in molecular biology combine with discussions of model systems and less well-studied organisms to interweave the relationship among development, molecular biology, and evolution. The power, promise, and pitfalls of searching for genetic evidence linked to evolution in the fossil record, using recent advances in molecular biology, are discussed, in addition to genomic comparisons between extant and extinct organisms. Clear illustrations and tables are well placed throughout and truly enhance the ideas presented. The reference section alone makes this work an essential resource for developmental biologists, paleontologists, zoologists, morphologists, molecular biologists, and geneticists. A cornerstone and standard reference for all science libraries. Upper-division undergraduates, graduate students, and faculty.—*K. Crawford, St. Mary's College of Maryland*

OAB-1380   QH605   95-37443 CIP
Rappaport, R. **Cytokinesis in animal cells.** Cambridge, 1996. 386p bibl index (Developmental and cell biology series, 32) ISBN 0-521-40173-9, $84.95

Rappaport's beautifully written book is an extraordinary piece of scholarship and an appropriate culmination to more than 30 years of work on cytokinesis by the author and his wife. The process of cytokinesis in egg cells of vertebrates and invertebrates, as well as in cultured cells, is described with exceptional clarity, and the text is supplemented by many excellent photomicrographs and line drawings. The first chapter describes normal cell division, and the second provides a historical account of the diverse theories put forward to explain the phenomenon. Subsequent chapters examine the role of the surface or cortex of the cell in cytokinesis, coordination of cytokinesis and mitosis, and the importance of microsurgical techniques and fluorescent probes in studies of the process. Chapter 7 describes the stimulus-response system linking the mitotic apparatus to the cell surface, and chapters 8 and 9 examine the consequences of the division mechanism and variants, such as polar lobe formation, of the normal process. A final chapter summarizes the current state of the art and prospects for future research. References to more than 550 papers up to 1994 are provided, along with subject and author indexes. Upper-division undergraduates through faculty.—*M. J. O'Donnell, McMaster University*

OAB-1381   QH331   95-1443 CIP
Reinventing biology: respect for life and the creation of knowledge, ed. by Lynda Birke and Ruth Hubbard. Indiana, 1995. 291p index afp ISBN 0-253-32909-4, $35.00; ISBN 0-253-20981-1 pbk, $15.95

In many ways an exploration of human-other boundaries, *Reinventing Biology* explores the paradox of animals being similar enough to humans to serve as models but different enough to justify using and killing them. Much more than a book about animal welfare, it explores how the scientific questions and answers would be different if biology operated from a paradigm of respect for the objects of study. Thirteen contributions are arranged in four distinct sections; individual topics vary extensively but each is first-rate. The consequences of the distancing of objectivity are explored in the first section. The biographical accounts in the second section provide a refreshing contrast to much scientific writing and encourage readers to explore their own relationships to other organisms. The practice of biology is reviewed with authors asking what is really learned from some research, and is the knowledge worth the pain and suffering. The last section explores how boundaries between humans and others are being breached. A welcome addition to the literature critiquing science and an excellent resource for courses on the conceptual framework of science or objectivity in science. All levels.—*G. E. Stratton, Rhodes College*

OAB-1382   QH31   92-6897 MARC
Rivinus, E.F. **Spencer Baird of the Smithsonian,** by E.F. Rivinus and E.M. Youssef. Smithsonian Institution Press, 1992. 228p bibl index afp ISBN 1-56098-155-5, $29.95

Baird, a 19th-century naturalist, left us a great heritage: enormous collections of flora and fauna purchased by him for the Smithsonian Institution; the native North American anthropological collections in the National Museum of Natural History; and the Woods Hole Oceanographic Institute that evolved from his initial fish studies for scientific and commercial benefit. Rivinus and Youssef's concise biography tells about an honest man who paid careful attention to detail in all endeavors—scientific, managerial, and administrative. Baird completely dedicated himself to his goals, often at the cost of losing personal relationships; he achieved what led to his enormous legacy while attending his wife, who suffered ill health most of her life. An excellent reference book with bibliography, notes, pictures, and quotations that add color. Undergraduate through professional.—*F. Potter, University of California, Irvine*

OAB-1383   QH541   94-43391 CIP
Simon, Noel. **Nature in danger: threatened habitats and species,** by Noel Simon with the World Conservation Monitoring Centre. Oxford, 1996 (c1995). 240p bibl index ISBN 0-19-521152-9, $35.00

Simon highlights the current conditions and conservation efforts in the primary habitats of the world. His book is well laid out and divided into chapters on rain forests, grasslands, wetlands, islands, deserts, mountains, and Antarctica. An additional chapter on endangered species features familiar and unfamiliar plant and animal species facing the challenge to survive. Exceptional photographs, maps, and illustrations reveal the ecological richness in many of the world's principal natural areas. Each is outlined and supplies enough information to interest and inform the reader of threats to the region while encouraging further study. Sidebars throughout the book emphasize particular aspects of each area by supplying interesting stories and facts. The author describes proposed and active solutions to threats such as pollution, overpopulation, mismanagement, and careless development. An excellent book for all readers interested in global conservation.—*D. Ostergren, West Virginia University*

OAB-1384   QH361   96-5605 CIP
Smocovitis, Vassiliki Betty. **Unifying biology: the evolutionary synthesis and evolutionary biology.** Princeton, 1996. 230p bibl index afp ISBN 0-691-03343-9, $29.95

Smocovitis discusses the synthesis that irrevocably changed the shape of biology in the 1930s and 1940s. William Blake's watercolor *Fall of Man*—depicting forces pulling the world apart—is used to describe the historical and philosophical background of the union of evolution and modern genetics. The unification of modern biology is examined from every possible angle, including the role of many prominent evolutionary biologists, geneticists, and mathematicians who were active in its construction. The author visualizes this development as part of the 50-year effort to unify knowledge, a laudable goal in an age of specialization and fragmentation. She describes the differences between sociobiologists and biologists who oppose the reductionism of those genetic determinists. At the same time, she discovers that unifying science sometimes has an unfortunate price; e.g., the decline of organismic biology and the disproportionate attention given to molecular biology. This development has led many to reaffirm the importance of teaching evolution-centered biology despite the risk of taking such action today. An important book, indispensable for biologists, historians, and philosophers of science as well as social scientists. General readers; undergraduate students through professionals.—*J. S. Schwartz, CUNY College of Staten Island*

OAB-1385   Orig
Soper, Tony. **Antarctica: a guide to the wildlife.** Bradt/Globe Pequot, 1994. 144p bibl index ISBN 1-56440-533-8, $19.95

This little gem will be welcomed by anyone with an interest in the Antarctic and sub-Antarctic, especially anyone contemplating a visit there. Soper includes short chapters on discovery and exploitation; terrestrial plants and insects; and invertebrates and fish of the Antarctic. However, it focuses clearly on birds and mammals of the continent. Each is shown in an attractive color painting and its appearance, life cycle, and habitat are described in one or two pages that include a map of its distribution. The book closes with suggestions for further reading, a glossary of terms pertaining to ice, a code of conduct for visitors, a list of Antarctic tour operators, and a good index. The result is a most attractive volume, presented clearly and simply and well produced: truly an illustration that good things come in small packages. General.—*N. Caine, University of Colorado at Boulder*

OAB-1386   [CD-ROM]
Species information library. National Information Services Corp. (NISC), 1995. $495.00. 1 disc; user manual. System requirements: IBM-PC.

This CD-ROM in DOS makes accessible federal and ten state databases in the archives of the Fish and Wildlife Information Exchange at Virginia Polytechnic Institute and State University. The database describes 7,200 animal species, 1000 of them in detail, and endangered plant species. Major headings include taxonomy, food habits, management practices, habitat association, life history, environmental associations, and references, with many subheadings. Each full-text record is devoted to one vertebrate or selected invertebrate species or subspecies, or selected endangered plants; these records are very valuable because the information they contain is drawn not only from published literature but from "grey" literature and compiled internal agency reports.

Searching can be carried out in Novice, Advanced, and Expert Modes. All three modes are easy to use, although the Expert mode, a refined search, is more complex. However, it has a printable searching guide available by pressing the F1 key. The novice opening has three fields for search: Species, Basic Search, and Database (Region or Province). Typing the species name in the species field and pressing Enter brings up the Auto-index. To select an entry, one presses Insert and then Enter. The first page of the record for that species will scroll into view. Pressing on the spacebar for "Alternate Format" brings up the citations or reference list for the species. In the second field one may carry on a plural search by using the Boolean AND; e.g., ruffed grouse AND forest. One may then type in a habitat (such as grassland, bog, or desert) in the Basic field for a list of endangered species found in those habitats. Typing the species name in the Species field and the state name in the Database field brings up the state database for that species. The Advanced mode, offering ten fields, allows a more restricted search by typing in a combination of fields; e.g., a combination of species, habitat, and management practices for ruffed grouse (species), forest (habitat), and clearings (management practices) brings up the Pennsylvania database that holds such information. The Expert Mode involving set searching provides more flexibility in the focus of the search.

The user guide accompanying the product is the standard manual accompanying all NISC programs. On-screen, printable Help instructions are clear and quite adequate, an important consideration given that undergraduate users probably will be using it via a network, with no access to the manual. With a little experimentation the user can quickly discover how to navigate the pathways and efficiently make use of the tremendous amount of information available. Although the database was established for federal, state, and environmental consulting agencies, it is an indispensable, easily accessible source of information for students and researchers in wildlife, conservation biology, and ecology. Undergraduate students will find it particularly helpful as a data source for reports and papers, saving hours of library time searching through books and journals. Like other NISC discs, this one is designed for networking (LANs). This onetime purchase is essential for undergraduate through professional users.—*R. L. Smith, emeritus, West Virginia University*

OAB-1387 QH437 94-6076 CIP
Tudge, Colin. **The engineer in the garden: genes and genetics: from the idea of heredity to the creation of life.** Hill & Wang, 1995 (c1993). 388p index ISBN 0-8090-4259-2, $25.00

As genetics enters the realm of high-tech with genetic engineering, the need becomes crucial to understand this powerful technology in order to exercise "sensible control" over its future application. Tudge reviews classical genetics, and tells of the history and the scientists behind the greatest discoveries in the field. Present research and application of genetics are detailed, including the Human Genome Project, DNA analysis, and plant and animal breeding. Tudge's explanation of captive breeding programs is exceptional, and he references his book *Last Animals at the Zoo* (CH, Oct'92) for additional reading. The book finishes with potential future applications of genetic engineering, which he believes holds promise to feed Earth's ever increasing population while conserving animals and plants, and to improve modern medicine by conquering most infections. Although some of his futuristic ideas are wildly imaginative, the concepts suggested for genetically engineered agriculture are exciting. The book closes with the admonishment that science must become fully integrated into our culture so that such powerful technology can remain under our control. Highest recommendation as supplemental reading for undergraduates in genetics and medical ethics courses. Excellent reading for general science audiences.—*C. A. Zakzewski, University of Scranton*

OAB-1388 QH313 92-9018 CIP
Wilson, Edward O. **The diversity of life.** Harvard, 1992. 424p index afp ISBN 0-674-21298-3, $29.95

One of the most engaging and interesting books that this reviewer has seen recently. Wilson, internationally recognized as one of the leading experts in this field, leads the reader through the often-difficult subject of biodiversity. Written in a nontechnical and almost lyrical style, he explores the broad subjects of extinction, speciation, evolution, and adaptive radiation. He also treats the potential of another mass extinction caused by humankind, which may be the most serious and destructive force ever experienced by life. Wilson appeals for specific actions that can ameliorate the impending environmental crisis and that will preserve and enhance biodiversity. Richly illustrated with numerous full-color photographs, line drawings, and maps, its usefulness is further enhanced by a list of notes for each chapter and a glossary and index. Highly recommended for any student of biology or for the general reader intrigued by biodiversity, as one of the more important books written on this subject.—*P. E. Lutz, University of North Carolina at Greensboro*

OAB-1389 QH31 94-13111 CIP
Wilson, Edward O. **Naturalist.** Island Press/Shearwater Books, 1994. 380p index afp ISBN 1-55963-288-7, $24.95

Most autobiographies of scientists chronicle the chance meetings, important events, and intellectual avenues that directed a life. Instead, Wilson lets the reader listen in on his attempt to clarify for himself how he came to be. It is not a summation of a life but rather how his life's context has changed as his worldview has expanded. One might imagine that Wilson could write another autobiography once he looks back again from a new vantage point. This is not a chronology; this is a study of why alternative histories did not arise. As such, it is valuable as a background reference for recent advances in entomology, biogeography, sociobiology, and conservation biology. It is inspirational without being syrupy, candid without being boastful. An excellent example of science writing for a nontechnical audience that will be avidly read by scientists. All levels.—*G. Stevens, University of New Mexico*

OAB-1390 GN365 94-7486 CIP
Wright, Robert. **The moral animal: the new science of evolutionary psychology.** Pantheon Books, 1994. 467p bibl index ISBN 0-679-40773-1, $27.50

Wright's book provides a discussion of a wide array of issues important for understanding human behavior and social interaction—specifically, the evolutionary bases for social behaviors. Wright takes an interesting tack in the book, highlighting Darwin's ideas on topics such as sex, love, social relations, and morality, and then delving into current research literature that speaks to these topics. The writing style is a welcome relief from traditional academic prose; the author has written about technically demanding subjects in simple, understandable prose, yet has not lost accuracy in portraying positions. Indeed, academic researchers would learn a great deal about clear communication on technical issues from this book. Wright may not be well known to academic researchers, but he has a wealth of experience in writing on science and technology, having won or been nominated for a number of prestigious awards. All in all, this book is a joy to read, with its informed portrayal of issues of current debate about the behavioral sciences. For a broad audience. General; undergraduate through professional.—*K. F. Widaman, University of California, Riverside*

■ Botany

OAB-1391 QK122 95-51144 CIP
Adams, Kevin. **Wildflowers of the southern Appalachians: how to photograph and identify them,** by Kevin Adams and Marty Casstevens. John F. Blair, 1996. 257p bibl index afp ISBN 0-89587-143-2 pbk, $26.95

Adams and Casstevens have prepared an outstanding, comprehensive, affordable guide for learning more about identifying and photographing wildflowers. More than 300 of the 2,500 plant species found in the southern Appalachians are represented with full-color photographs and detailed descriptions, and most importantly, the photographic techniques utilized to record each specimen are provided. A description of the equipment and general techniques peculiar to photographing wildflowers is followed by chapters treating the natural setting, the botanical exploration of the southern Appalachians, environmental concerns, and the format of the text. A glossary of selected botanical terms is inserted between these and the section describing and picturing individual wildflowers. The easily read text and individual photographs are exceptionally well done. An appendix with photography sources, wildflower events, state agencies, botanical gardens, wildflower and conservation organizations, and national parks is followed by a short bibliography and index. An excellent choice for those interested in plants and photography as well as professionals in the botanical and horticultural fields. A very suitable addition for every library. All levels.—*K. T. Settlemyer, Lock Haven University of Pennsylvania*

OAB-1392 QK112 92-22135 CIP
Andrews, Jean. **American wildflower florilegium.** North Texas, 1992. 125p index ISBN 0-929398-43-2, $50.00

Andrews's botanical art and accurate, informative text combine aesthetics and science to produce a gathering of flowers (a florilegium) that will appeal to a wide circle of readers interested in the diverse flora of the US, both native and introduced, that can be viewed easily along the highways. Frequently recognized as the most beautiful of botanical works, florilegia had their beginnings in the 1500s; unlike floras that catalog a collection of plants in a particular area, a florilegium is a gathering together of a collection of plants designed to show their beauty through the eyes of the artist. Each of the 52 species, illustrated in color from nature, is described in detail by scientific name, family, life history, origin, range, description of the plant, bloom period, pollinators, habitat requirements, propagation, assorted remarks, and etymology; the number of related species found in the US is included as well, and each species is referenced to specific scientific literature. The botanical art portrays the plants in a way that reveals those characteristics of importance to the taxonomist and, at the same time, produces a work with aesthetic appeal to those involved in the arts, from practitioners to admirers. Beautiful, well organized, enjoyable, and easy to read and understand. All levels.—*K. T. Settlemyer, Lock Haven University of Pennsylvania*

OAB-1393   QK495   91-32733 CIP
Arditti, Joseph. **Fundamentals of orchid biology.** Wiley, 1992. 691p indexes ISBN 0-471-54906-1, $95.00

This authoritative work presents a large amount of information gleaned by the well-known author over many years and from many references, including material from the excellent five-volume series *Orchid Biology: Reviews and Perspectives*, ed. by Arditti (v. 1, CH, Jan'78; v. 2, CH, Apr'83; v. 5, CH, Jul'91). The scope of this large volume is evident from its chapter list. Chapter 1 consists of a history of orchids based on areas of the world and a section on orchid reproduction. Chapter 2's 50-page presentation treats the classification and naming of orchids. The next chapter discusses orchid evolution, followed by a chapter on cytology. Physiology and phytochemistry constitute topics for the next two chapters; chapters follow on morphology, anatomy, mycorrhiza, pollination, embryology, reproductive strategies, heredity and breeding, ecology, and commercial and ethnobotanical uses. Each chapter has a separate bibliography and there are three extensive indexes, names of individuals whose work is cited, organisms, and subjects. Copious illustrations (line drawings and black-and-white photographs) as well as many tables reproduced from various journals and the *Orchid Biology* series, illuminate the text. In this single reference volume, Arditti has brought together scientific material from a variety of sources, making it possible for interested readers to savor a wide gamut of topics in the biology of orchids. Every academic library should acquire this book.—*L. G. Kavaljian, California State University, Sacramento*

OAB-1394   QK50   95-17514 Orig
Attenborough, David. **The private life of plants: a natural history of plant behaviour.** Princeton, 1995. 320p index ISBN 0-691-00639-3, $26.95

Neither a text nor a reference work, this beautifully written, strikingly illustrated book is intended for the general public. Its utility in the college environment comes from its inspirational value. Attenborough's book, based on his BBC program of the same name, is packed with fascinating, generally accurate anecdotes about the plant world and especially about plant/animal interactions. The chapters have titles such as "Travelling," which covers mainly seed dispersal, and "Feeding and Growing," which discusses photosynthesis at a grade-school level but gives many nontechnical examples of herbivory, plant defenses, and carnivorous plants. Attenborough uses common names for plants and there are no references to the primary literature, but the scientific names appear in the index and the book may well stimulate nonscience majors or beginning botany students to explore further on their own. Arthur Galston's *Life Processes of Plants* (CH, Jun'94) is also intended for the general public, but it focuses on plant physiology, contains more scientific evidence, and includes brief bibliographies with each chapter.—*H. L. Gorton, St. Mary's College of Maryland*

OAB-1395   QK604   CIP
Cooke, R.C. **Ecophysiology of fungi,** by R.C. Cooke and J.M. Whipps. Blackwell Scientific, 1993. 337p bibl index ISBN 0-632-02168-3, $99.95

An examination of the physiology of fungi and its relationship to their distribution in nature. Cooke begins with an introduction that briefly outlines the origin and phylogeny of fungi and discusses strategy theory and niche determinants. Later sections, of several chapters each, include growth and development, reproduction and establishment, and interactions with other heterotrophs. This new book represents a contrasting view to Cooke's older work *Fungi, Man, and His Environment* (CH, Sep'78), and is primarily concerned with the physiological characteristics of fungi that allow them to occupy specific ecological niches, rather than about their economic aspects. Although there are a limited number of illustrations, they are outstanding and serve to illustrate the text well. A remarkably easy-to-read book that presents topics in a readily accessible form, even to beginning students, although some exposure to biochemistry would be helpful for the fullest understanding. An excellent work for advanced undergraduate and beginning graduate students.—*J. Dawson, Pittsburg State University*

OAB-1396   QH104   95-327 CIP
The Desert grassland, ed. by Mitchel P. McClaran and Thomas R. Van Devender. Arizona, 1995. 346p bibl index afp ISBN 0-8165-1580-8, $40.00

Desert grasslands extend throughout southwestern North America, reaching down from Texas, New Mexico, and Arizona deep into Mexico. This book describes these grasslands and the current state of knowledge about them. Topics covered include the transition from ice-age forests to modern, dry grasslands due to climate change; the role of fire on contemporary grasslands in the area; biotic and geomorphic processes that shape desert grasslands; and human impact on grassland ecology. Much of the information compiled here comes directly from long-term ecological research projects, undertaken by teams of investigators and funded by the National Science Foundation. As a result, it is an integrated, comprehensive, and thought-provoking overview of this endangered natural area. This book deserves a place on the shelves of libraries not only throughout the region as a guide to the natural history of the area but also outside the region as a reference for researchers interested in keeping up with the scientific literature associated with the biome. The index is logical and well developed and the literature current and extensive (more than 500 citations). A handsome, well-illustrated, well-written book. Upper-division undergraduate through professional; two-year technical program students.—*G. Stevens, University of New Mexico*

OAB-1397   94-72667 CIP
Dix, Neville J. **Fungal ecology,** by Neville J. Dix and John Webster. Chapman & Hall, 1995. 549p bibl index afp ISBN 0-412-64130-5 pbk, $44.95

Dix and Webster's excellent introduction to fungal ecology begins with a discussion of life strategies, including various selective forces. The book considers the growth and development of fungi, followed by an introduction to the structure of fungal communities. The real meat of this book is found in chapters devoted to the ecology of fungi on different substrates, and to the occurrence of fungi on leaves, stems and grasses, and wood. The chapter on leaves is the most complete treatment found in the book. Later chapters include fungi of the soil and roots, fungi of dung, and an excellent chapter on aquatic fungi. Final chapters treat nematode-destroying fungi and their potential use as biological control agents, and fungi found after fires and fungi of extreme environments, such as high temperatures and little water. A final chapter explores the ecology of the larger fungi, i.e., those that are commonly seen and collected. A well-illustrated and well-written book, with numerous illustrations and 99 pages of references. Upper-division undergraduate; graduate; professional.—*J. Dawson, Pittsburg State University*

OAB-1398   Orig
Elliott, Brent. **Treasures of the Royal Horticultural Society.** Sagapress/Timber/Royal Horticultural Society, 1994. 160p indexes ISBN 0-88192-297-8, $39.95

A visual feast! That comment sums up this reviewer's initial reaction to this book, which portrays the Royal Horticultural Society's remarkable collection of botanical art. Sadly, few public or private viewings of the drawings are allowed because of their fragile nature. Elliot, the Society's librarian, has assembled 70 paintings and drawings that span the years 1630 to the present. Works of the masters are heavily represented. A plus is that these color plates are reproduced from the original drawings and not from subsequent engravings. Here one can follow changing art techniques, such as from flower art to botanical illustration. The book's introduction covers art techniques, botanical nomenclature, and the Royal Horticultural Society's history. Each plate carries a discussion of the artist and other interesting information. More drawings are to be publicized in the future. Highly recommended for libraries maintaining botanical, horticultural, and art collections. General through faculty.—*R. P. Poincelot, Fairfield University*

OAB-1399　　　　QK110　　　　95-22678 MARC
Farrar, John Laird. **Trees of the northern United States and Canada.** Iowa State, 1996 (c1995). 502p bibl indexes afp ISBN 0-8138-2740-X, $39.95

This beautifully illustrated, highly functional, and very informative guide to trees of Canada and the northern US is an outgrowth of the old *Native Trees of Canada*, first published 1917. However, Farrar has substantially reworked the original format into a real masterpiece. The photos are fantastic, and the drawings and range map are very nicely done (although this reviewer would have liked to see complete ranges of the species shown). The last fifth of the book contains very useful botanical keys, hardiness maps, and two wonderful, compelling sections. First, there is a description of the botanical authors from which the abbreviated authority names are derived. Having used scientific names for 30 years, this reviewer found these extremely fascinating. Second, there is a wonderful section on the meaning of scientific names for trees. Great stuff! In summary, a classy work. All levels.—*D. F. Karnosky, Michigan Technological University*

OAB-1400　　　　QE980　　　　95-14824 CIP
Flowering plant origin, evolution & phylogeny, ed. by David Winship Taylor and Leo J. Hickey. Chapman & Hall, 1996. (Dist. by International Thomson Publishing) 403p bibl index afp ISBN 0-412-05341-1, $75.00

The chapters in this up-to-date, clearly presented work on the origin, early evolution, and phylogeny of flowering plants are written by recognized experts on paleobotany, comparative morphology, development, and structural and molecular phylogeny, and edited by two solid authorities on the origin and early evolution of angiosperms. Although heavily oriented towards paleobotany and morphological evidence, it is probably the best summary of the field to come out in the last ten to 15 years. Several other excellent works are still available on angiosperm evolution: *Origin and Early Evolution of Angiosperms*, ed. by Charles B. Beck (CH, Nov'76); *Historical Perspectives of Angiosperm Evolution*, by D.L. Dilcher and W.L. Crepet (1984); and *The Origins of Angiosperms and Their Biological Consequences*, ed. by E.M. Friis et al. (CH, Sep'88); but there has been sufficient new information generated to warrant preparation of the book under review. Although a compilation of different writing styles, this book is well edited for consistency of content, and all the authors follow a similar overall format. For anyone interested in the evolution of angiosperms, including systematists, morphologists, and paleobotanists. Upper-division undergraduates through faculty.—*F. G. Dennis Jr., Michigan State University*

OAB-1401　　　　QH109　　　　95-50299 CIP
The Food web of a tropical rain forest, ed. by Douglas P. Reagan and Robert B. Waide. Chicago, 1996. 616p bibl index afp ISBN 0-226-70599-4, $110.00; ISBN 0-226-70600-1 pbk, $39.95

Food Web treats one major subject at a single tropical rain forest site (El Verde, Puerto Rico). This approach uses the food web to integrate information on the biology of the organisms of a lowland forest community. The utilization of numerous experts writing separate chapters on various organisms (plants, microorganisms, termites, litter invertebrates, arboreal invertebrates, arboreal arachnids, amphibians, anoline lizards, nonanoline reptiles, birds, mammals, and the stream community) makes this book a rare, detailed look at a single locale in the tropics. One conclusion is that the island setting is likely much less complicated than a tropical setting on the continental mainland. It is suggested that one might expect a food web matrix with 100 times as many possible interconnections on the tropical mainland. The writing is clear, readable, and informative. There are 77 pages of bibliography, a ten-page glossary, numerous useful black-and-white photos, and tables and diagrams. A major contribution in a field where books are "rolling off" the press almost monthly. Recommended. Upper-division undergraduates through faculty.—*K. L. Williams, Northwestern State University*

OAB-1402　　　　QK711　　　　93-31986 CIP
Galston, Arthur W. **Life processes of plants.** Scientific American Library, 1994. (Dist. by W.H. Freeman) 246p index ISBN 0-7167-5044-9, $32.95

A work that is a plant physiology text "for the intelligent lay public," according to its preface. Galston (emeritus, Yale Univ.) has more than 50 years of experience in plant physiology and has previously written (with Peter J. Davies and Ruth L. Satter) a somewhat similar book, *The Life of the Green Plant* (3rd ed., 1980). The current work is much shorter, somewhat less detailed, and more direct and conversational in style, with good discussions of recent discoveries in such areas as nitrogen fixation, genetics, and stress physiology. The plentiful illustrations are helpful and beautiful, the index is excellent, and brief bibliographies are provided for each chapter. An extremely valuable book for anyone involved with plants. General; community college; undergraduate; pre-professional; professional.—*W. E. Williams, St. Mary's College of Maryland*

OAB-1403　　　　QK86　　　　93-5240 CIP
Given, David R. **Principles and practice of plant conservation.** Timber, 1994. 292p bibl index ISBN 0-88192-249-8, $39.95

At last, here is a balanced, thoughtful overview of plant conservation biology. It is not overly pessimistic and does not rely on scare tactics to develop a sense of the need for conservation efforts. Given provides such a well-reasoned and broad overview that his book is likely to become a standard reference work for both botanists and zoologists. Concepts are presented in a non-patronizing but simplified manner so that even those with a weak background in biology can grasp such complex issues as gene flow, metapopulation dynamics, minimum viable population sizes, and the demography of rare species. The text is printed on thick paper and the book itself is well made. Clearly, the intended audience is the library user and professional interested in a long-lasting reference work. The index is logically constructed and appropriately tuned to the browser. Nearly 600 citations are listed in the bibliography. Short "case studies" are provided throughout. In short, a must buy, to be heavily used by undergraduate through professional biologists.—*G. Stevens, University of New Mexico*

OAB-1404　　　　94-72015　　　　Orig
The growing fungus, ed. by Neil A.R. Gow and Geoffrey M. Gadd. Chapman & Hall, 1995. 473p bibl index afp ISBN 0-412-46600-7 pbk, $44.50

The Growing Fungus is divided in five parts of two to six chapters each. The first part, "The Growing Fungus," discusses the concept of unitary and modular organisms. The second, "The Architecture of Fungal Cells," includes excellent discussions of cell walls, the cytoskeleton, and cellular organelles. Part 3, "Metabolism and Genetic Regulation," includes outstanding chapters on fungal exoenzymes, including those excreted into the environment and those that are important industrially; and on intermediary metabolism including carbon, nitrogen, and sulfur metabolism. Other chapters treat fungal genetics and their molecular biology, including extrachromosomal inheritance. Part 4, "Coordination of Growth and Division," treats growth and polarity, kinetics of filamentous growth and branching, and mathematical modeling of fungal growth. The final part, "Differentiation," in five chapters, discusses asexual and sexual reproduction. The last two chapters, on yeast-hyphal dimorphism and tissue formation, are both outstanding introductions to these complex but very important processes. A well-written, closely edited, excellent book. Upper-division undergraduate through faculty.—*J. Dawson, Pittsburg State University*

OAB-1405　　　　QK9　　　　94-65026 CIP
Harris, James G. **Plant identification terminology: an illustrated glossary,** by James G. Harris and Melinda Woolf Harris. Spring Lake Publishing, P.O. Box 266 Payson, UT 84651, 1994. 197p afp ISBN 0-9640221-5-X pbk, $17.95

This is one of the most useful little books produced in a long time. It compares favorably with John Lindley's *A Glossary of Technical Terms Used in Botany* (1848). Benjamin Daydon Jackson's *A Glossary of Botanic Terms*

(4th ed., rev. and enl., 1949) and Camillo Karl Schneider's *Illustriertes Handwörterbuch der Botanik* (1905) are more comprehensive, but for the practicing taxonomist the Harris book has greater day-to-day utility. More than 2,400 terms are accounted for. Wherever possible the term is illustrated with a small line drawing. The text is divided into two parts: the first, p. 3-118, is an alphabetical listing of the terms; the second gathers related terms together in categories. This reviewer can think of no layperson, student, or practicing taxonomist who can afford to not have this book available for ready reference. All levels.—*G. P. DeWolf Jr., emeritus, Massachusetts Bay Community College*

OAB-1406   Orig
Jaarsveld, Ernst J. van. **Gasterias of South Africa: a new revision of a major succulent group.** Fernwood/National Botanical Institute, 1994. (Dist. by Timber) 96p bibl index ISBN 1-874950-01-6, $39.95

Van Jaarsveld has produced a beautifully illustrated, oversize monograph on a South African group of succulents in the genus *Gasteria*. Typical of coastal and semiarid regions, they closely resemble the aloes, with which they were often confused by early botanists. Since many are drought resistant and shade tolerant, they are well adapted to indoor use in the northern hemisphere. This taxonomic revision results in 16 species and several varieties; each is illustrated, life-size, in exquisite watercolors by an acclaimed botanical artist. The text, most readable, begins with a historical overview of the many botanists who studied or collected these succulents. This account is followed by the taxonomy, morphology, ecology, cultivation, and conservation of the genus. A two-page key to the species is followed by color plates and descriptions of specific taxa. This volume should be in all the botanical libraries of the world, and in libraries featuring succulents for cultivation. All levels.—*W. A. Niering, Connecticut College*

OAB-1407   RS164   93-49736 CIP
Joyce, Christopher. **Earthly goods: medicine-hunting in the rainforest.** Little, Brown, 1994. 304p index ISBN 0-316-47408-8, $23.95

The interaction among the pursuits of ethnobotanists, conservationists, AIDS and cancer researchers, and the executives of the world's largest drug companies is described in this book in a most fascinating way. The 16 chapters present many well-told, firsthand stories of exotic adventures in remote locales and encounters with native healers and their ceremonies. The details of the author's experiences are unified by referring to the complex of issues involved as a "pharmacological experiment" in which the preservation of the world's great forests is the goal. The experiment has led to a new pharmacological industry and renaissance in plant hunting. Joyce states that if it can be shown to all who look only for financial gain that the forests are worth more standing than cut or burned, then there is a chance for humans to retain and be nurtured by what he calls "our species' innate attachment to nature, our 'biophilia.'" Having been the founder and editor of the US bureau of *New Scientist*, he comes to this subject well prepared. That readers of this book will find it hard to put down should promote its message far and wide. Extensive list of references and chapter commentaries. Highly recommended for all libraries with readers in anthropology, plant usage, medicine, and ecology. General; undergraduate; faculty.—*L. G. Kavaljian, California State University, Sacramento*

OAB-1408   QK525   91-40920 CIP
Montgomery, James D. **New Jersey ferns and fern-allies,** by James D. Montgomery and David E. Fairbrothers. Rutgers, 1993 (c1992). 293p bibl index ISBN 0-8135-1817-2, $45.00

The 83 species, 10 subspecies, and 32 hybrids of New Jersey ferns and fern allies (clubmosses, horsetails, quillworts, and spikemosses) are described by environmental consultant Montgomery and Fairbrothers (emeritus, Rutgers Univ.). A fascinating historical introduction to ferns and New Jersey fern study is followed by solid background information on fern structure, classification, and hybrids; a key to New Jersey ferns and fern-allies; and a chapter on ecology and distribution. Most of the book is devoted to descriptions of New Jersey ferns and fern-allies. Information for each species includes common and scientific names, botanical description, habitat, geographic range, a map of New Jersey distribution, a detailed line drawing, its chromosome number, and whether or not it is endangered. A species checklist, more than 150 references, and an index are also included. Excellent for all levels as a field guide and authoritative reference.—*D. R. Hershey, University of Maryland at College Park*

OAB-1409   QK751   95-42780 CIP
Plant response to air pollution, ed. by Mohammad Yunus and Muhammad Iqbal. Wiley, 1996. 545p bibl indexes ISBN 0-471-96061-6, $105.00

As an air pollution researcher of some 25 years, this reviewer was somewhat skeptical about this air pollution book by Yunus and Iqbal, two unknowns in this field. However, after examining over their book from cover to cover, this reader was really impressed with these two editors. Their book is well written, well organized, timely in topics chosen for coverage, and includes original works from many eminent air pollution scientists from around the world. The book opens with a fine global overview of air pollution and closes with a short but worthy chapter on research needs. In between are separate chapters on crop growth, soil and weather effects, carbon dioxide, cuticle interactions, stomatal behavior, resistance mechanisms, root physiology, reproduction, and diagnosis. In addition, separate chapters are focused on sulfur and ozone. Finally, an honest and concise summary of the role of air pollutants in forest decline is presented. All in all, an excellent synthesis of plant responses to air pollution. Highly recommended for anyone in this field. General; undergraduates through professionals.—*D. F. Karnosky, Michigan Technological University*

OAB-1410   Orig
Proctor, Michael. **The natural history of pollination,** by Michael Proctor, Peter Yeo, and Andrew Lack. Timber, 1996. 479p bibl index ISBN 0-88192-352-4, $42.95; ISBN 0-88192-353-2 pbk, $24.95

This is the most complete introduction to the biology of pollination now available. Beautifully illustrated by precise, close-up photographs of flowers and their visitors, the book will be the standard reference for understanding mechanisms of pollination, functional significance of flower shape and color, and evolution of flowers. Separate chapters clearly summarize behavior of important classes of pollinators, such as beetles, flies, butterflies, moths, as well as bees on flowers. Pollination by vertebrates (bats, birds, and other curious groups) and by wind and water have caused different evolutionary responses in plants, and remarkable examples in the book show the elegance of these interactions. Many other plant species deceive flower visitors into moving pollen by offering mimics of food, of egg-laying sites, or even of females waiting for mating. These less-known initiators of pollination success show the subtle and intricate outcomes of evolutionary processes. Floral visits also determine breeding systems and movement of genes through the population. A modern and lucid overview of these genetic aspects of pollination is included, which will expand the reader's understanding of the processes that underlie floral diversity. General; upper-division undergraduates through faculty.—*S. N. Handel, Rutgers, The State University of New Jersey, New Brunswick*

OAB-1411   QK21   92-19205 CIP
Reveal, James L. **Gentle conquest: the botanical discovery of North America with illustrations from the Library of Congress.** Starwood, 1992. 160p bibl index ISBN 1-56373-002-2, $39.95

"This book brings to life the richness, variety, and importance of the discovery of North American flora from the time of the Columbus voyages to the end of the American frontier." Coupled with exquisite black-and-white and color plates from its art collection, this third in the "Library of Congress Classics" series is a fascinating account of the botanical discovery of North America covering the past 500 years. "This is a story of great adventures, of remarkable discoveries, of brave and daring men and women, and in some cases of bitter disputes. It is also the story of our own maturation, as people and nations, resulting in an increasing appreciation of the value of plants in their natural settings." It describes the collaboration of naturalists and artists merging their talents to produce the rare and beautiful botanical illustrations found in the Library of Congress and here made accessible to all. The text reveals the author's knowledge of the subject, and holds the interest of the reader. *Gentle Conquest* will appeal to a wide range of readers, including those interested in the flora as well as the art and history of the US and temperate North America; a valuable acquisition for every library collection. All levels.—*K. T. Settlemyer, Lock Haven University of Pennsylvania*

OAB-1412 QK938 93-49019 CIP

Richards, P.W. **The tropical rain forest: an ecological study,** by P.W. Richards with R.P.D. Walsh et al. 2nd ed. Cambridge, 1996. 575p bibl indexes ISBN 0-521-42054-7, $125.00; ISBN 0-521-42194-2 pbk, $49.95

This new edition (1st ed., 1952) is greatly expanded and updated. It includes important contributions by R.P.D. Walsh, I.C. Baillie, and P. Greig-Smith. In this most comprehensive and valuable reference relating to general concepts of tropical biology, Richards provides an excellent overview of the structure, physical environment, phenology, floristic composition, and ecological succession of tropical deciduous forests and savannas, and the past and present impact humans have had on tropical rainforests. This reference brings together much tropical rainforest data and the field experiences and research of the authors. The 19 chapters represent five major sections, in addition to a much-expanded reference section, an index to plant names, and a general index. A number of chapters and subheadings have been added or renamed to reflect current knowledge of tropical biology. Two appendixes also have been added; one provides a good overview of tree recognition in the field, and the other (contributed by Greig-Smith) discusses the application of numerical methods of analyzing floristic compositions of rainforests. There are 233 figures and 62 tables in this new edition. A wealth of information has been incorporated into this edition. An essential resource for all students of tropical biology. Upper-division undergraduates through faculty.—*S. L. Timme, Pittsburg State University*

OAB-1413 QK648 92-19569 MARC

Sandved, Kjell B. **Bark: the formation, characteristics, and uses of bark around the world,** photographs by Kjell B. Sandved; text by Ghillean Tolmie Prance and Anne E. Prance. Timber, 1993. 174p indexes ISBN 0-88192-262-5, $49.95

Sandved and the Prances have combined talents to produce an outstanding book that treats a plant part in a unique manner. (A previous work by G. Prance on leaves, CH, Jul'85, was named a 1985 *Choice* Outstanding Academic Book.) *Bark* will interest the same wide audience—botanists and others interested in the plant sciences, those involved in horticulture and gardening, nature lovers, and those interested in photography and art. The aesthetic appeal of the subject is enhanced by the exceptional photographic treatment that captures the beauty of form that exists in bark. The style is informative and delightful to read. Bark-related topics covered include photography; structure and function; field identification; photosynthetic bark; bark ecology; bark latexes, resins, medicines, and poisons; hallucinogenic bark; bark flavors and tannins; cork; cloth, canoe, fiber, fuel, mulch, and other uses of bark; bark as camouflage and food; and bark flora and dwellers. Many superb photographs demonstrate the diversity of pattern, color, and texture found in bark. Selections for further reading are included at the end of each chapter. An index of scientific names is included in addition to a general index. A beautiful, high quality book for every library.—*K. T. Settlemyer, Lock Haven University of Pennsylvania*

OAB-1414 SB433 96-9357 CIP

Schenk, George. **Moss gardening: including lichens, liverworts, and other miniatures.** Timber, 1997. 261p bibl index ISBN 0-88192-370-2, $34.95

An experienced gardener, nurseryman, and landscaper, entertaining and informing author Schenk provides an exhilarating book, perhaps only the sec-

ond of its kind in English, on gardening with mosses and other suitable cryptogams. The text and especially the many color photographs make it abundantly clear that these small plants, though nuisances to some, should captivate many gardeners into using them as garden friends. The 15 chapters cover topics such as the use of mosses in the gardens of Japan, in the public gardens of the West, in alpine gardens, in association with bonsai, and in containers. The longest chapter, "Portraits," provides an alphabetically arranged compilation of useful species, listing extensive characteristics and growing requirements. To the author's credit, botanical rather than common names are used throughout. He acknowledges that identification of species is often difficult; but no matter, the thrust here is in the visual joy provided by gardening with these primitive miniatures. A short reading list and an index of moss and other bryophyte names completes the book. Full of interesting and practical information, this exuberant book deserves to be in every library's gardening section. All levels.—*L. G. Kavaljian, California State University, Sacramento*

OAB-1415 QK495 93-49569 CIP

Sheehan, Tom. **An illustrated survey of orchid genera,** by Tom and Marion Sheehan. Timber, 1995 (c1994). 421p bibl index ISBN 0-88192-288-9, $99.95

Sheehan and Sheehan's expansion of a similar, earlier book, *Orchid Genera Illustrated* (1979), has led to this valuable addition to the orchid literature for growers and enthusiasts. Color reproductions of Marion Sheehan's beautiful and exact illustrations of fresh plants are the heart of the book. Thoughtful and helpful introductory chapters that define orchids and provide orchid classification and a family outline preface the alphabetically arranged discussion of 158 of mostly the best known genera in the family. Each genus is given coverage by means of habitat and floral drawings, a thorough description of identification characteristics, a list of the more popular species, a map of the approximate native habitat, culture suggestions, and flowering season. Another indication of the attention these very experienced authors have brought to this work are the front endpapers showing on a world map the approximate native locales of 51 epiphytic orchids; the back end papers do the same for a similar number of terrestrial orchids. Extensive, illustrated glossary. Very highly recommended for all libraries.—*L. G. Kavaljian, California State University, Sacramento*

OAB-1416 G1107 94-18723 CIP

Turner, Raymond M. **Sonoran desert plants: an ecological atlas,** by Raymond M. Turner, Janice E. Bowers, and Tony L. Burgess. Arizona, 1995. 504p bibl index afp ISBN 0-8165-1532-8, $70.00

Natural history is difficult to package. On the one hand, there are many books dealing with the interesting organisms of a region. These often are abridged and place most of their emphasis on a few easily recognized species. On the other hand, there are technical works that are complete floras or faunas of a region but are so densely written that they are inaccessible to the novice. Turner and colleagues have produced a useful compromise. Their book covers 331 species of woody and succulent plants with heavy emphasis on Cactaceae, Agavaceae, and legumes. It is comprehensive (but not exhaustive) and detailed (but not exhausting). Its bibliography overflows with more 1,100 citations, most of them recent and available in the US. The authors include a detailed glossary (337 entries) even though the text is not filled with jargon. Most enlightening, however, are the detailed distribution maps showing both the location and elevation of sightings and collecting areas for each species. This book should be in any library servicing biologists interested in the desert Southwest. Its summaries of rural history information are found nowhere else. All levels.—*G. Stevens, University of New Mexico*

■ Chemistry

OAB-1417   QD601   92-29544 CIP
Adloff, Jean-Pierre. **Fundamentals of radiochemistry,** by Jean-Pierre Adloff and Robert Guillaumont. CRC Press, 1993. 414p index afp ISBN 0-8493-4244-9, $95.00

Addressing a wide range of radiochemistry usually not a part of most chemists' backgrounds, this text runs the gamut from the early history of radioactive elements to positron emission tomography (PET) to "chemistry with a few atoms" (Chapter 9). The authors' qualifications span the full range of the text. They provide links in the appendixes of Chapters 5-9 to kinetics, statistical methods, analytical techniques, and calculations. However, they do not intend to provide information on methods of measuring radioactivity but rather assume these are known by the sophisticated reader or can be found elsewhere. The focus is on trace-level chemistry as present geochemically or in nuclear wastes; the inherent challenges in oxidation state determinations, partition and transport methods, and the chemistry of the actinide and postactinide elements are described clearly. Theirs is a presentation that will require paper and pencil to check derivations in the appendixes—which will turn up in later chapters—and statistical problems inherent in chemistry based on 100 or fewer atoms. A book suitable for advanced undergraduates that will provide real insight into radiochemistry for analytical, inorganic, and physical chemists who teach those undergraduates. It deserves a place in the college library and on the shelves of faculty in both undergraduate and graduate institutions: there is nothing like it.—*M. E. Thompson, College of St. Catherine*

OAB-1418   QD181   95-12422 CIP
Aldersey-Williams, Hugh. **The most beautiful molecule: the discovery of the buckyball.** Wiley, 1995. 340p bibl index afp ISBN 0-471-10938-X, $24.95

Aldersey-Williams offers an excellent, well-written account of the ideas and people behind the discovery of Buckminsterfullerene that will be enjoyable reading for a wide audience. He details the process and personal interactions among the principals behind the 1985 discovery of this third form of carbon. But the book offers much more than a delightful recounting of this discovery, as the author also spends entire chapters describing important background information necessary for understanding it. For example, a chapter on R. Buckminster Fuller provides a brief biography of this innovative thinker for whom the molecule is named. Another chapter gives a concise but complete account of different types of spectroscopy that were important in identifying C60 as a unique and novel species. A further chapter discusses symmetry and mathematical properties of the truncated icosahedron (the C60 soccer-ball structure). These chapters are written at a level understandable to beginning students, offering a history lesson as a bonus. An excellent introduction to scientific research, well worth the price. Undergraduate through faculty.—*M. Rossi, Vassar College*

OAB-1419   QD1   94-41862 CIP
Aquatic chemistry: interfacial and interspecies processes, ed. by Chin Pao Huang, Charles R. O'Melia, and James J. Morgan. American Chemical Society, 1995. 412p bibl indexes afp (Advances in chemistry series, 244) ISBN 0-8412-2921-X, $124.95

Distilled from a symposium honoring Werner Stumm for his pioneering development of the science of aquatic chemistry, this book is an excellent example of the utility and timeliness of ACS's "Advances in Chemistry" series. By selectively choosing chapters elucidating the mechanisms controlling the chemical composition of natural waters, the editors successfully provide examples of current research and avoid an encyclopedic rehash of all progress made since Stumm wrote the first book on aquatic chemistry in 1967. The first chapter uses Stumm's unifying description of the concept of functional groups on the aqueous interface of natural minerals and other particles to explain the mechanism of surface-controlled processes as diverse as nucleation, crystal growth, and photochemical reactions. Successive chapters focus on five key topics—

surface chemistry, earth sciences, biology, redox, and photochemistry—to illustrate the multidisciplinary applications of aquatic chemistry while emphasizing the importance of interfacial processes. There is much to recommend this volume to aquatic chemists, environmental engineers, and researchers looking for new frontiers. Upper-division undergraduate through professional.—*R. M. Ferguson, Eastern Connecticut State University*

OAB-1420   QD466   95-7362 CIP
Atkins, P.W. **The periodic kingdom: a journey into the land of the chemical elements.** Basic Books, 1995. 161p bibl index ISBN 0-465-07265-8, $20.00

This delightful book uncovers the richness and centrality of the periodic table for the nontechnical reader, but even the expert will find new and enjoyable insights into the table, or in the author's allegory, the "periodic kingdom." Although addressed to the scientifically uninitiated, this is a book for the well-educated. For example, Cavaliers and Roundheads are used to stand for those who would label the alkali metals Group IA and those who use Group IB, respectively. Some of the author's positions may be difficult, such as equating the better use of weapons "... for killing, subjugation and survival ..." with more opportunity for scholarship. Likewise, although helping to show the often-ignored human side of scientists, it is not clear what is added by introducing Mendeleev as "the bigamist and chemist." Nevertheless, such potential lapses in the details of this book should not be allowed to detract from the imaginative, serious, but sometimes whimsical, journey through the heart of chemistry, whether it be the chart on the wall of every chemistry classroom or an allegorical kingdom. All levels.—*M. D. Marshall, Amherst College*

OAB-1421   GB855   92-42114 CIP
Brezonik, Patrick L. **Chemical kinetics and process dynamics in aquatic systems.** Lewis Publishers, 1994. 754p bibl index afp ISBN 0-87371-431-8, $75.00

Brezonik's book is terrific in the breadth and depth of information provided about kinetics in general, and about aquatic kinetics in particular. Numerous references are provided, and the material is clearly presented in appropriate detail. Mathematical derivations are explained sufficiently to allow a reader with one year of calculus to follow and understand, yet the book does not bog down in details of mathematical solution. The book is divided into chapters as follows: (1) general overview, (2) rate expressions, (3) effects of physical conditions on rates, (4) overview of kinetics including reaction mechanisms, (5) practical applications of reactors and process models, (6) biochemical and microbial kinetics, (7) influence of compound structure and reactivity on reaction rates, and (8) photochemical kinetics. There is an incredible amount of information here: no major class of reactions or conditions is left out. The author has compiled numerous useful and clearly explained examples of kinetic applications in aqueous systems. Appropriate for any student or professional studying or working in the field of aquatic chemistry. An excellent reference. Upper-division undergraduates through professionals; two-year technical program students.—*N. W. Hinman, University of Montana*

OAB-1422   RA1270   92-7024 CIP
Briggs, Shirley A. **Basic guide to pesticides: their characteristics and hazards,** by Shirley A. Briggs and the staff of Rachel Carson Council. Hemisphere Publishing, 1992. 283p afp ISBN 1-56032-253-5, $39.50

Ever since Rachel Carson's *Silent Spring* was published in 1962, there has been growing concern about the use of pesticides. The situation is confusing for the nonspecialist, since the person who wishes to go beyond the information on the pesticide label will often find further data to be neither readily available nor easy to understand. To fill that need, this book provides more than 700 listings for pesticides and their known transformation products. In each case, a tabular presentation summarizes the available information on principal application, persistence in the environment, acute and chronic mammalian toxicity, and toxicity to other organisms. Access to the main table is facilitated by the excellent index, which is cross referenced by common name, chemical name, and Chemical Abstracts Service Registry Number. Finally, an informative set of appendixes discusses various aspects of pesticide use. An excellent resource. Highly recommended. All levels.—*H. E. Pence, SUNY College at Oneonta*

OAB-1423 QD11 93-19054 MARC
Brock, William H. **The Norton history of chemistry.** 1st American ed. W.W. Norton, 1993 (c1992). 744p bibl index ISBN 0-393-03536-0, $35.00; ISBN 0-393-31043-4 pbk, $15.95

This substantial one-volume history joins Aaron J. Ihde's *The Development of Modern Chemistry* (CH, Jun'65) as an authoritative and complete guide. Writing in an enjoyable style, Brock, well known for major contributions to the history of science, concisely covers early chemistry, up to the end of the 18th century, in his first two chapters. The following two chapters discuss the Lavoisier revolution and Dalton's work. The next six chapters give a beautifully clear account of the progress of chemistry in the 19th century including the complex process of unravelling organic structures; the growth of scientific industrial chemistry; the emergence of the Periodic Law; and the beginnings of physical chemistry. Chapters on chemical education and early periodicals are followed by the history of modern chemical bond theory, organic structure and mechanism, the rebirth of inorganic chemistry, and the modern chemical industry. The bibliographic essay is exceptionally valuable; there is a brief appendix on museums and collections, and a full index. A book to be read and re-read, and an excellent addition to the literature of the subject. All levels.—*H. Goldwhite, California State University, Los Angeles*

OAB-1424 QD11 95-24804 MARC
Cobb, Cathy. **Creations of fire: chemistry's lively history from alchemy to the atomic age,** by Cathy Cobb and Harold Goldwhite. Plenum, 1995. 475p bibl index ISBN 0-306-45087-9, $28.95

It has been said that history is a glorious entertainment and, without question, chemists (or those interested in chemistry) will be gloriously entertained by *Creations of Fire*, a work of large ambition and small proportion. Perhaps those who profess history will take umbrage with the authors (who were chemists first) for the license taken in the interests of brevity—430 pages takes one from the early alchemists to the Woodward-Hoffmann rules on orbital symmetry. But the selection of materials and the threads weaving ideas, people, and things together make for a delicious composite in two parts: from the beginnings to the year 1700 and the phlogiston nonsense; and from Lavoisier and the French Revolution to the superheavy elements. Almost an anecdotal history, it is excellently written and reads like a novel. Sadly, the selection of pictorial illustrations is idiosyncratic and Spartan—a lost opportunity to enrich an otherwise unblemished work. The 20 pages of detailed chapter notes will serve to introduce the reader to the primary and secondary literature in the history of chemistry with many of the basic references. Highly recommended for all who seek enlightenment and glorious entertainment. All levels.—*L. W. Fine, Columbia University*

OAB-1425 QD325 94-26989 CIP
Collins, Peter M. **Monosaccharides: their chemistry and their roles in natural products,** by Peter M. Collins and Robert J. Ferrier. Wiley, 1995. 574p bibl indexes ISBN 0-471-95342-3, $89.95; ISBN 0-471-95343-1 pbk, $39.95

As a result of the extraordinary growth of carbohydrate chemistry over the past 20 years, this once obscure branch of chemistry now forms a significant part of modern organic chemistry. A comprehensive but concise presentation of the current state of the field, this book is long overdue. The two chapters that deal with structures, shapes, sources, and syntheses of monosaccharides, along with the two chapters that cover related compounds either synthesized from or containing monosaccharides, are excellent general reading. The three chapters that discuss reactions and products are an outstanding resource. The book is well referenced, but the references do not include authors' names. The only

drawback to the book's general excellence is that figures and diagrams are often placed inconveniently in relation to the text. This book is, without doubt, the best this reviewer has seen. Must reading for all, from novice to expert, who are dealing with carbohydrate chemistry. Upper-division undergraduate through faculty.—*L. J. Liotta, Stonehill College*

OAB-1426 QD945 92-7886 MARC
Crystal structure analysis for chemists and biologists, by Jenny P. Glusker with Mitchell Lewis and Miriam Rossi. VCH, 1994. 854p bibl index afp ISBN 0-89573-273-4, $95.00

This book will be a classic! It was written "for those chemists and biochemists who may never themselves do X-ray diffraction analyses of crystals, but who need to be able to understand the results of such studies" and has two declared purposes: to acquaint readers with the general principles of crystal-structure analysis so they can critically appraise articles in the crystallographic literature, and to instruct them how to access the vast amount of structural information found in existing databases. The senior author, a respected research scientist, has coauthored a well-known introductory work with Kenneth N. Trueblood (*Crystal Structure Analysis: A Primer*, 2nd ed., 1985; 1st ed., CH, Mar'73). There are 18 authoritative chapters (basic crystallography; instrumentation; data collection, analysis and refinement; presentation and interpretation of structural results; and crystallographic databases), each containing many figures and tables, and ending with a summary, glossary of new terms, and an extensive list of references to the primary and secondary literature. Good subject separate index; index of terms defined in the glossaries. This book is quite versatile: an excellent introductory text; a useful reference text; a thorough introduction to the advanced literature; and a source of comprehensive reviews of specific structure-oriented topics. Highly recommended for chemists, molecular biologists, and materials scientists. Undergraduate through faculty.—*R. Rudman, Adelphi University*

OAB-1427 QD415 91-29378 CIP
Fruton, Joseph S. **A skeptical biochemist.** Harvard, 1992. 330p bibl indexes afp ISBN 0-674-81077-5, $29.95

Fruton is a truly eminent scientist, whose textbook, (written with S. Simmons) *General Biochemistry* (1953), served to painlessly introduce many to the wonders of biochemistry. Fruton took his title from Robert Boyle's *The Sceptical Chymist* (1661) and Joseph Needham's *The Sceptical Biologist* (1930), and he raises some fundamental questions about how biology and chemistry have come together to form biochemistry. He begins with his own skeptical thoughts on the process of the scientific method, drawing from the ideas of Peter Medawar, Claude Bernard, and Francis Bacon, among others. Readers interested in the history of science will thoroughly enjoy Fruton's analyses, with respect to the search for simplicity when formulating a hypothesis or the focus involved when biology and chemistry blended. Fruton also tackles the biochemical literature, reflecting on the C.P. Snow-Aldous Huxley debates and moving on to the issue of chemical classification and the development of a rational nomenclature. Extensive bibliography, detailed index of personal names. A delightful primer for scientists still searching for roots. All levels.—*D. Malamud, University of Pennsylvania*

OAB-1428 TP187 93-28653 CIP
Hall, Stephen K. **Chemical safety in the laboratory.** Lewis Publishers, 1994. 242p bibl index afp ISBN 0-87371-896-8, $59.95

Comprehensive safety and health programs are vital to all workplaces, but chemical laboratories are particularly challenging. The diversification and dispersal of chemical laboratories in recent decades parallels the range of substances processed, consumed, or measured at industrial locations. Hall's guidebook for implementing and managing a chemical hygiene program begins with the Occupational Safety and Health Act of 1970, pilots the reader through federal and state safety regulations, and outlines the responsibilities of workers, managers, safety instructors, and laboratory users. With more than 20 years as a corporate consultant on chemical safety, industrial hygiene, and toxicology, the author encourages academic, industrial, and hospital laboratory personnel to develop a common base of understanding in preparation for any complexities resulting from a chemical mishap. Hall casts a clear beam of light through the sometimes murky jungle of regulations pertaining to chemical handling procedures, inventory control, labeling systems, safety equipment, monitoring of chemical exposure, emergency response planning, and even record keeping. Highly recommended for enhancing strong safety awareness programs. Undergraduate; technical/two year; graduate through professional.—*R. M. Ferguson, Eastern Connecticut State University*

OAB-1429 93-85291 Orig
Hegedus, Louis S. **Transition metals in the synthesis of complex organic molecules.** University Science Books, 1994. 358p index ISBN 0-935702-28-8 pbk, $38.00

Hegedus's excellent book covers a very important area of organic synthesis, that involving organometallic transition metal complexes as intermediates. Useful in an advanced undergraduate course or a first-year graduate course in organometallic chemistry, the book is based on the second edition of James P. Collman and Hegedus's *Principles and Applications of Organotransition Metal Chemistry* (1988). Chapters 1 and 2 are gems, presenting excellent introductions to electron counting in organometallic compounds and reaction mechanisms of these compounds, respectively. The remaining eight chapters treat synthetic applications of organic compounds through various transition metal complexes. Each of these chapters categorizes specific types of complexes such as metal hydrids; metal carbon sigma-bonds; metal carbonyls; and metal carbene, alkene, alkyne, allyl, and arene compounds. Hegedus's writing style is clear and concise, and illustrative figures and equations are complete and easy to follow. A very thorough book, with references up through early 1993. Recommended. Upper-division undergraduate; graduate; faculty; professional.— *W. H. Hohman, Marietta College*

OAB-1430 QD11 91-47598 CIP
Knight, David. **Ideas in chemistry: a history of the science.** Rutgers, 1992. 213p index ISBN 0-8135-1835-0, $47.00; ISBN 0-8135-1836-9 pbk, $18.00

Knight's subtitle does not fairly describe his valuable and entertaining little book: it is not a history of chemistry, but rather a collection of essays written "to pick instructive episodes in a more or less chronological order." The sameness of the essay titles overshoots the book's presumed aim of being provocative and becomes slightly irritating: "an occult science" is a fair description of alchemy, but "a useful science" and "a teachable science" are mere tautologies, and neither chemists nor historians and philosophers of science will agree that chemistry ever has been, is now, or is soon likely to be "a deductive science," or that its latest phases are those of "a reduced science" or "a service science." The author's idiosyncratic temperament is evident throughout, but more often than not adds interest and readability. Here a distinguished historian of science has distilled a wealth of information and thought, documented by 460 notes and references, into a work that is profound but never ponderous. It will add to the knowledge of the adept and inspire the novice. It will give pleasure to both. Strongly recommended for all academic libraries.— *C. W. Beck, Vassar College*

OAB-1431 QD921 93-21864 CIP
Kosuge, Koji. **Chemistry of non-stoichiometric compounds.** Oxford, 1994 (c1993). 262p indexes ISBN 0-19-855555-5, $75.00

Kosuge describes the chemistry of nonstoichiometric compounds, based on statistical thermodynamics and structural inorganic chemistry. The use of inorganic materials in electric, magnetic, and optical devices as well as in mechanical ones has increased dramatically in recent years. Continued progress in materials science and ceramics requires clear understanding of the chemical and physical properties of inorganic compounds. This book is an impor-

tant contribution to the literature of solid-state chemistry. It is unique in that it provides an excellent theoretical and experimental base for understanding inorganic properties and gives examples of the practical use of selected inorganics. Kosuge has published extensively in solid-state chemistry and here gives the scientific community a reference book, well written and clearly documented. A basic background in chemical thermodynamics and structural inorganic chemistry is required for understanding. Excellent writing and illustrations; subject and formula indexes. Excellent resource for researchers, faculty, graduate students, and upper-division undergraduates.—*D. A. Johnson, Spring Arbor College*

OAB-1432 TD899 93-45546 CIP
Laboratory waste management: a guidebook, by the ACS Task Force on Laboratory Waste Management. American Chemical Society, 1994. 211p bibl index afp ISBN 0-8412-2735-7, $24.95; ISBN 0-8412-2849-3 pbk, $16.95

In fewer than 200 large-type pages, with ample margin annotations, the ACS has produced an easily accessible resource for the purpose of developing effective strategies for managing laboratory wastes—from the laboratory perspective. Chapters include laws and regulations, organizational responsibilities, worker training, identification and characterization of wastes, waste reduction and handling, monitoring and control, and thoughts on how to operate reasonably with the regulatory community. A useful glossary of about 100 terms (and acronyms) is included, along with appendixes that provide a considerable number of useful items and examples, reports, sources, and resources. It is a practical compendium that should be on the desks of laboratory managers and administrators and in the back pockets of health and safety professionals in the chemical industry. (If only it had been designed with that in mind, and printed on half as many pages in a narrower trim size. But no matter; it is quite good just as it is.) Buy this book! Community college; upper-division undergraduate through professional.—*L. W. Fine, Columbia University*

OAB-1433 QD452 92-41635 CIP
Laidler, Keith J. **The world of physical chemistry.** Oxford, 1993. 476p bibl index ISBN 0-19-855597-0, $85.00

The title of a scientific treatise must be both attractive and correct, not vague and misleading, as this reviewer found with Laidler's choice. The author's own uncertainty is given away in the preface's opening line where he refers to his text as a "history of physical chemistry." Well, it isn't that, either. What is it, then, beyond a book in search of a better title? A book every professor should own for its wealth of information on the human dimensions of the subject. At the same time, it provides some sense of the flow of the history of chemistry in the major areas of kinetic and quantum theories, colloid and surface science, thermodynamics, spectroscopy, and electrochemistry. This must be the distillation of what makes Laidler's lectures great fun and entertainment, and at the same time, a simply marvelous presentation of the science. And if every professor should own a copy, so should every chemistry major. Laidler's references and annotations are largely drawn from *Journal of Chemical Education* and the more easily accessible historical studies, and his forays into history are accurate and well chosen, though frustratingly short on substance. The springboard to understanding of physical chemistry. Advanced undergraduate through professional.—*L. W. Fine, Columbia University*

OAB-1434 QH545 94-22460 CIP
Neilson, Alasdair H. **Organic chemicals in the aquatic environment: distribution, persistence, and toxicity.** Lewis Publishers, 1994. 438p bibl index afp ISBN 0-87371-597-7, $79.95

Neilson compiles information on most aspects related to the behavior of organic chemicals in the aquatic environment. The book includes chapters on analytical techniques, partitioning, persistence, biodegradation and biotransformation, toxicology, and environmental hazard assessment. Emphasis is placed on biological processes controlling xenobiotic distributions. Throughout, complete discussions, analytical techniques, and partitioning of organic chemicals in aqueous and sedimentary environments are provided. Modeling is not addressed. The subject matter of each chapter is carefully presented and fully referenced. Neilson's style of presenting pertinent information and examples in lists provides the reader easy access to the material, with the option of delving further into references or additional information. References to other chapters ensure that the reader gets all related material for each topic in the book. The information is current, well presented, and carefully indexed. Controversial conclusions or methods are clearly identified. An excellent resource for upper-division undergraduates through professionals and researchers.—*N. W. Hinman, University of Montana*

OAB-1435   QD262   93-2193 CIP
Organometallics in synthesis: a manual, ed. by M. Schlosser. Wiley, 1994. 603p bibl indexes ISBN 0-471-93637-5, $100.00

Chemists (and all scientists) have always been dependent upon the quality of the publications that constitute the scientific literature for the progress of the field and the advancement of their own work. Nowhere is that more in evidence than in the experimental sections of those publications. From time to time, volumes such as the classic works of Gilman, Elderfield, House, Jolly, and others have been published, along with annual series such as the volumes of *Organic Reactions.* These compendia of tried and true (and carefully tested) recipes for important standard procedures have proved to be invaluable. Thank heavens for all of that, and for a most welcome newcomer in the area of organometallics in organic synthesis. Now we have a one-volume treatise that, although restricted to only a few metals, promises to serve a diversity of synthetic interests. Beginning with the most comprehensive of the eight chapters, the editor's own contribution (on organoalkali reagents) sets the style for the entire work: an overview, structures, reactivity and selectivity, preparation of intermediates, and handling of reagents. Other contributions, though generally shorter, are similarly conceived and executed: "Organolithium Compounds—Industrial Applications and Handling"; "Titanium in Organic Synthesis"; "Synthetic Procedures Involving Organocopper Reagents"; "Palladium in Organic Synthesis"; "Organoboron Chemistry"; "Organoaluminum Chemistry"; and "Organotin Chemistry." All are outstanding; the production gives the reader clear and easy-to-read recipes, and there is an effective subject index and a formula index. Each of the eight chapters is accompanied by hundreds of literature references. Simply, an outstanding contribution to the practicing chemist. Highly recommended. Upper-division undergraduate through professional.—*L. W. Fine, Columbia University*

OAB-1436   QD475   93-29740 CIP
The Physical basis of chemistry, [ed.] by Warren S. Warren. Academic Press, 1994. 168p bibl index afp ISBN 0-12-735850-1 pbk, $19.95

Warren has developed a highly lucid book on the mathematical basis of chemistry by using both historical as well as philosophical approaches to the understanding of how mathematics relates to the present paradigms of modern chemistry. He moves the student efficiently through the maze of statistics, all the time showing the rationale behind seemingly unrelated pieces of data, formulas, and concepts. From the statistical approach, the student is led to thermodynamics, kinetics, and quantum mechanics with enough rigor, but the material is not unduly difficult for a well-prepared first- or second-year college student. This book would be an ideal supplement for an honors course or as a seminar text for students who have taken a general chemistry course and desire deeper insight into the field from mathematical, philosophical, and historical perspectives. The bibliography, completed example problems, and homework problems are adequate without being voluminous. The calculus is presented to the student in a clear but elegant manner with immediate application to physical phenomena. Highly recommended for any college library.—*K. Bennett, Kalamazoo Valley Community College*

OAB-1437   QD502   94-46221 MARC
Pilling, Michael J. **Reaction kinetics,** by Michael J. Pilling and Paul

W. Seakins. Oxford, 1996 (c1995). 305p bibl index ISBN 0-19-855528-8, $69.95; ISBN 0-19-855527-X pbk, $29.95

This book is intended for students and others interested in modern methods of carrying out kinetics experiments. It ranges through experimental methods in gas phase, at metal surfaces, and in solutions. Theoretical models are developed from many perspectives: transition-state theory, collision theory, the Lindemann unimolecular reaction theory, and RKK-M modifications. Especially interesting and helpful is the compilation and presentation of modern methods of measurement of kinetics—from laser-induced reactions, reactions in the atmosphere, and enzyme kinetics to the field of reaction dynamics. Pilling and Seakins are generous with diagrams, the references are complete, and they provide a series of problems to test the reader on the material in each chapter. This book will fill a real need for students of kinetics, be they formally enrolled in a course or just interested in how measurements, mathematics, and dynamics come together in experimental design; they will be able to access this material through its thorough development. The book replaces other kinetics works (even that of John W. Moore and Ralph G. Pearson, *Kinetics and Mechanism,* 3rd ed., CH, May '82) because it truly covers modern kinetics logically, carefully, mathematically, and succinctly. Undergraduates through practitioners.—*M. E. Thompson, College of St. Catherine*

OAB-1438   QD305   96-13456 CIP
Preparation of alkenes: a practical approach, ed. by Jonathan M.J. Williams. Oxford, 1996. 253p bibl index ISBN 0-19-855794-9 pbk, $55.00

Alkenes are a common class of organic compounds for which a large number of preparative methods are known. Although compendia of these methods abound, this one has many features making it ideal for college library collections. Each chapter, written in accessible style by an expert in a subspecialty of alkene chemistry, includes detailed step-by-step instructions for every procedure discussed, along with full lists of equipment, chemicals needed, and safety precautions for each. Though literature references are included, the researcher will be able to use this book on its own—a positive feature for a college library without ready access to the full range of chemical literature. Other useful features, especially for a novice researcher, include an excellent introductory chapter describing general laboratory techniques, a list of chemical suppliers in the US and abroad, and a list of abbreviations. A summary chapter and chart aid in finding a needed procedure, though the book's clear organization may obviate them. Particularly appropriate for undergraduates and graduate students starting out in chemical research, as well as for their faculty advisers.—*S. M. Adamus, Providence College*

OAB-1439   QD22   94-4351/ CIP
Quinn, Susan. **Marie Curie: a life.** Simon & Schuster, 1995. 509p bibl index ISBN 0-671-67542-7, $30.00

Quinn has written the first biography of Marie Curie's that is able to draw upon her own journal, written during the year after her husband died, and only opened to researchers in 1990. By virtue of this journal, as well as personal correspondence and conversations with family members and others who knew her intimately, Quinn presents a picture of Marie Curie that emphasizes scientific rigor, her exceptional abilities, and her dedication to work noted in other biographies of her. In addition, Quinn was able to portray how that same passionate attachment to knowledge also manifested itself in passionate attachments to people. A significant section of the book describes her affair with a married colleague, a relationship that clearly helped her to recover from the devastating effect of her husband's premature death but also reveals her complexity and emotional needs. This fine and important biography does an excellent job of explaining both the significance of Marie Curie's scientific work and how she experienced herself, her husband, her colleagues, and the larger scientific community. For all levels of readers.—*M. H. Chaplin, Wellesley College*

OAB-1440   QD151   97-1552 CIP
Swaddle, T.W. **Inorganic chemistry: an industrial and environ-**

mental perspective. Academic Press, 1997. 482p bibl index afp ISBN 0-12-678550-3, $65.00

This book should be in every library that serves anyone even remotely connected with chemistry. Although nominally offering a text for second-year chemistry students, Swaddle provides a unique array of topics not available in any other single volume. Interspersed throughout are discussions of the theory and practical applications of inorganic chemistry, covering an exceptional range of industrial and environmental topics. An excellent introductory discussion of thermodynamics and kinetics, along with a quite adequate introduction to the solid state, serves as the background for detailed descriptions of the chemistry of inorganic polymers, semiconductors, metallurgy, catalysis, ion-exchange materials, glasses, atmospheric chemistry and pollution control, agriculture, cement, water conditioning, fuel cells, corrosion of metals, and some of the latest in solid-state chemistry (gels, electronic materials, superconductive materials, and fullerenes). The chemical background of many topics with current political and environmental overtones are presented in a technical, unbiased manner, e.g., use of ammonium compounds as fertilizers (and terrorist bombs); paper production and recycling (and the use of sulfite and chlorine bleaching compounds); water treatment (and sewage control); and processes for extracting metals from their ores (and the environmental consequences of these processes). The writing is clear, the production quality first-rate, and the references as current as is practically feasible in a printed book. Most of the references are to recent review articles in readily available journals, so that further research on a given topic is facilitated. As Swaddle states: "The central purpose of this book is to explain the role of inorganic chemistry in the modern world and to provide a sourcebook of readable proportions for scientists and the interested public." He has clearly succeeded. Undergraduates through professionals; two-year technical program students.—*R. Rudman, Adelphi University*

OAB-1441 GB855 94-13929 CIP
Trace elements in natural waters, ed. by Brit Salbu and Eiliv Steinnes. CRC Press, 1995. 302p bibl index afp ISBN 0-8493-6304-7, $189.95

The study of trace elements presents special challenges. Low concentrations make accurate sampling difficult, and chemical reactivity is often modified by interactions with colloidal particles or other phase boundaries. Despite these problems, the potential toxicity of some trace elements makes essential a better understanding of how they behave in solution. There have been relatively few recent books on this topic, so this discussion is timely and valuable. The editors have done an excellent job of coordinating the individual contributions from a panel of international experts to create comprehensive coverage. Most of the chapters deal with trace elements in the various components of the hydrologic cycle, but there are also sections on sampling and data analysis. In conclusion, the editors summarize the important issues in the field. Each article includes extensive references and a good index is provided. Recommended especially for libraries that support environmental programs. Upper-division undergraduate through professional.—*H. E. Pence, SUNY College at Oneonta*

■ Computer Science

OAB-1442 QA76 96-17756 CIP
Abelson, Harold. **Structure and interpretation of computer programs,** by Harold Abelson and Gerald Jay Sussman with Julie Sussman. 2nd ed. MIT/McGraw-Hill, 1996. 657p bibl index ISBN 0-262-01153-0, $55.00

This book is a revision (1st ed., CH, Dec'84) of one of the great classic texts in computer science, used in MIT's entry-level computer science course since the 1980s. Programming is examined, but through the wide range of subjects used as examples in the programs, the book touches on almost every part of computer science. The language used is Scheme, a modern dialect of LISP; its advantage is its great flexibility and power—the programs developed in the text

cover an enormous range of applications. The exercises vary from straightforward applications to subtle and challenging problems. This new edition includes many clarifications, and most of the major programs have been redesigned; new material in concurrency and nondeterminism has been added. Like its predecessor, the book is written in a lively, clear, stimulating style. Combining that style with the great richness of content yields a book hard to put down: open it anywhere and you are "hooked" in a matter of moments. This book should be in every library, and on every computer scientist's bookshelf. Undergraduate through professional.—*H. D. Warner, Western New England College*

OAB-1443 QA76 94-19295 CIP
Abiteboul, Serge. **Foundations of databases,** by Serge Abiteboul, Richard Hull, and Victor Vianu. Addison-Wesley, 1995. 685p bibl index ISBN 0-201-53771-0, $54.95

Through the years, database theory has evolved into an elegant and sophisticated field that has been continuously propelled into its significant niche within the sphere of computer science. This book makes an admirable contribution to that evolution and will clearly find an appropriately highly regarded slot within the echelon of its counterparts. The presentation is rigorous and precise, providing an abundance of theorems and proofs. It dwells primarily on the mathematical view of databases and presents many concepts and techniques that have not yet found their place in practical systems. The major portion of the book is devoted to the study of the relational model, while also providing a framework for analyzing a broad range of abstract query languages. A substantial focus is on conjunctive queries. There are many references to both classical material and advanced topics. If it could be said that this book has two purposes—one, to explain the underlying principles and characteristics of databases systems and two, to arouse the curiosity of theoreticians—then it is a resounding success. An excellent resource for researchers in database theory as well as for practitioners. Upper-division undergraduate through professional.—*E. Hook, formerly, Gettysburg College*

OAB-1444 QA76 94-1199 CIP
Bharath, Ramachandran. **Neural network computing,** by Ramachandran Bharath and James Drosen. Windcrest/McGraw-Hill, 1994. 188p bibl index disk (IBM-PC) ISBN 0-8306-4523-3 pbk, $29.95

The concept of artificial neural networks is a novel and exciting idea in this present information age. This manuscript provides a gentle introduction to the field of artificial neural networks that have been applied to a wide area of scientific disciplines. Aiming toward a general audience, the authors provide a clear explanation of the basic and important ideas of artificial networks in use today, including multilayer perceptrons, Hopfield networks, Boltzmann machines, and many more. The presentation is nontechnical. Only basic mathematical skills are required to understand the materials and the style of writing is extremely easy to follow. To foster further exploration of the subject area, well-documented software written in the C language is also supplied with the book to give readers hands-on experience. An annotated reference guides the conscientious reader to further reading. Ideal for a beginning student who wants to gain working experience in this exciting field. Highly recommended. General; two-year technical.—*J. Y. Cheung, University of Oklahoma*

OAB-1445 QA76 94-36653 MARC
Brooks, Frederick P. **The mythical man-month: essays on software engineering.** Anniversary ed. Addison-Wesley, 1995. 322p bibl index ISBN 0-201-83595-9 pbk, $24.69

This exciting and vital work is as valuable today as it was 20 years ago. Advances in the computer software industry, made possible by the increase in memory capacity and CPU power, make some of the original text sound old-fashioned, but the crux of the solution of the problem of software creation remains: a successful method of tackling large software development tasks is founded on the creative talent of one or two design leaders, the project management skills of a facilitator, and the fostering of a team atmosphere. The new chapters examine previous criticisms in an evenhanded manner and underscore the correctness of the earlier edition's conclusion that modular programming is essential to reducing development time. The controversial principle—that the designer of a module should be in ignorance of the other modules—is discussed, and the admission by Brooks that he has been persuaded to change his mind on this issue is an indication of his flexibility. Perhaps it is this generosity of spirit that makes this book such a fine learning experience. Undergraduate through professional.—*D. A. Dobbin, Maine Maritime Academy*

OAB-1446 QA76 96-2098 CIP
Campbell-Kelly, Martin. **Computer: a history of the information machine,** by Martin Campbell-Kelly and William Aspray. Basic Books, 1996. 342p bibl index ISBN 0-465-02989-2, $28.00

Campbell-Kelly's and Aspray's fascinating history of large-scale computation ranges from the teams of human computers of tables in the early 19th century to the present. Written in an easy-to-read, expository style, the book is a well-documented account of the development of modern computers. The authors chronicle what is now a dynamic industry, and the material covered through 1995 will be of continuing interest to a wide range of readers. The book will serve equally well as resource for students of the history of science, or light reading for anyone interested in history and technology. Highly recommended for all libraries, academic to public. In fact, many libraries will want more than one copy for their collections.—*D. Z. Spicer, Vanderbilt University*

OAB-1447 QA76 94-20994 CIP
Communication in the age of virtual reality, ed. by Frank Biocca and Mark R. Levy. L. Erlbaum, 1995. 401p bibl indexes afp ISBN 0-8058-1549-X, $79.95

The authors represented in this book explore the premise that communication in the age of virtual reality (VR) is about the transmission of experience. They describe overcoming the limitations of spatial separation in the experiencing of objects and transcending the limitations of the physical body in the kinds of electronic experience now possible. This is a particularly thorough and well-organized collection of essays on subjects ranging from the vision and philosophy of VR to specific VR technologies and the meaning of the cyberpunk culture. It explores VR as communication medium, environmental design, and social reality. It emphasizes the notion of VR as interface to cyberspace and the Internet; it describes various educational, entertainment, and business applications of VR; and it points out the growing tendency to represent information with concrete physical images rather than abstract categories. It also includes insightful treatments of dramatic narrative presented through VR and of VR and interpersonal communication. Not a surface, glitzy treatment of the hot topic of VR, but a solid, comprehensive overview of the domain and its possibilities in the context of communication. Highly recommended. All levels.—*C. Koch, Oberlin College*

OAB-1448 HV1569 94-21251 CIP
Computer resources for people with disabilities: a guide to exploring today's assistive technology, by the Alliance for Technology Access. Hunter House, 1994. 284p index ISBN 0-89793-111-4, $24.95; ISBN 0-89793-112-2 pbk, $14.95

This work is not just a reference book (although it is that in part) but one to empower people with disabilities to use computers to help realize their dreams, and it provides a comprehensive set of tools for fulfilling them. Guidance is provided on all major matters involving computers and the disabled, from conceptualizing goals and understanding legislation for the disabled, to finding sources of funding for assistive devices and presenting detailed, up-to-date information about the availability of computer hardware and software. The book is divided into three main parts: "The Search for Solutions" (the motivating, conceptualizing section), "The Technology Toolbox" (an extremely useful presentation of products to help achieve particular ends), and "Helpful Resources and References" (other important information such as on-line databases,

national conferences, and state and federal legislation). The Alliance for Technology Access is a network of resource centers, based in San Rafael, California, that helps people with disabilities realize the benefits of today's high-tech world. Highly recommended for all those concerned with assistive technology. All levels.—*C. Koch, Oberlin College*

OAB-1449 Q335 91-55461 CIP
Crevier, Daniel. **AI: the tumultuous history of the search for artificial intelligence.** Basic Books, 1993. 386p index ISBN 0-465-02997-3, $27.50

An extremely well-written book about artificial intelligence (AI) and an engrossing mix of history, speculation, and philosophy. The first four chapters give a concise history of AI up until 1970, with many interesting anecdotes—some classic, some new. The next four are an analytical account of the successes and the difficulties in the next two decades. The last section of the book is a balanced critique of the problems and promises of the field, with discussions of connectionist computing and of the philosophical, psychological, and social aspects of AI. Crevier, once a student at MIT, is now a researcher in AI. His personal knowledge of many leaders in AI, and his interviews with numerous AI superstars, including Herbert Simon and Marvin Minsky, make the book both interesting and authoritative. Extremely rewarding reading for anyone interested in computers at any level that will provide as much pleasure and knowledge to the reader as did that earlier classic, Pamela McCorduck's *Machines Who Think* (1979). All levels.—*R. Bharath, Northern Michigan University*

OAB-1450 QA76 95-32935 CIP
Eck, David J. **The most complex machine: a survey of computers and computing.** A.K. Peters, 289 Linden St., Wellesley, MA 02181, 1995. 445p bibl index ISBN 1-56881-054-7, $49.95

Eck has written a course text, but it is so much more than that. He presents a unique perspective on computers and computing, neither a standard introduction to programming nor a computing literacy work. The book begins with an introduction to computers and how they function. Chapter 1 discusses bits and bytes; other chapters treat circuits, logic, and arithmetic, and there is a clear presentation of how computers work at the most basic level. The book takes some unique twists and turns in introducing readers to the many facets of computer science. The next nine chapters are an unusual and refreshing introduction to the discipline: there is a clear nontechnical presentation of computer science theory leading to Turing machines and the halting problem, as well as an encouraging presentation of the basics of programming; Eck does not get bogged down in programming language details. Remaining chapters investigate the areas of analysis of algorithms, multiprocessing and networks, graphics, and artificial intelligence. Chapter exercises; answers at the end of the book. Excellent annotated bibliography; World Wide Web site with material to support the text. Strongly recommended as a foundation for guided self-study for gifted high school students as well as noncomputing majors. General; lower-division undergraduate; two-year technical program students.—*J. Beidler, University of Scranton*

OAB-1451 QA76 95-50560 CIP
Englander, Irv. **The architecture of computer hardware systems software: an information technology approach.** Wiley, 1996. 750p bibl index afp ISBN 0-471-31037-9, $67.95

Englander (information systems, Bentley College) provides students, especially those in information systems curricula, with a broad background in the architecture—hardware and software—of computer systems. He effectively blends material from several areas—data representation (found in introductory hardware or assembly language courses), computer architecture, and operating systems—using a descriptive rather than an analytical approach, appropriate from the user's point of view. The book is well organized and clearly written, substantially complete within itself. The coverage of topics is quite extensive and quite current (as of spring '96), with much material on the currently most widely used microprocessors, such as the Intel Pentium and the Power PC, and operating systems, including Windows 95, issued August 1995. The technical material is presented in a clear and accessible manner. Because of its breadth of coverage, accessibility, and completeness, this book will be an excellent resource. Highly recommended. General; undergraduates through faculty; two-year technical program students.—*H. D. Warner, Western New England College*

OAB-1452   QA76   CIP
Heim, Michael. **The metaphysics of virtual reality.** Oxford, 1993. 175p bibl index afp ISBN 0-19-508178-1, $21.00

A thought-provoking book examining the technology of virtual reality from a philosophical point of view, written by Heim, a leading philosopher and expert on virtual reality. He raises the basic question of how this technology will impact the human experience and our perception of ourselves and the real world around us. The discussion is organized into ten chapters: "Informania," "Logic and Intuition," "Hypertext Heaven," "Thought Processing," "Heidegger and McLuhan: The Computer as Component," "From Interface to Cyberspace," "The Erotic Ontology of Cyberspace," "The Essence of VR," "Virtual-Reality Check," and "The Electronic Cafe Lecture." The book is intended for general readers and does not require any technical background. The reader is taken on a journey beginning with the ideas of well-known philosophers and terminating with the modern era of information. While on this excursion, Heim relates the various developments and projects into the future. Comprehensive list of references, arranged alphabetically; adequate index. An excellent acquisition. General; advanced undergraduate; faculty.—*A. Aziz, Gonzaga University*

OAB-1453   HE7631   93-8259 CIP
Heldman, Robert K. **Information telecommunications: networks, products, & services.** McGraw-Hill, 1994. 393p index ISBN 0-07-028040-1, $45.00

While similar to one of Heldman's recent books (*Global Telecommunications: Layered Networks' Layered Services*, CH, Oct'92), this volume represents a further development of Heldman's thinking about the future of global telecommunications. Whereas in the earlier book the topic of ISDN (integrated services digital network) was treated at length in an appendix, here ISDN is integrated throughout the book. It is seen as the basis for the future provision of all types of information communications services (voice, data, image, video) over high-capacity integrated networks spanning the globe. The book is intended for both marketing and technical planners and thinkers. It does not attempt to shelter the reader from the myriad details of telecommunications technology but rather to integrate technical aspects with marketing aspects. Highly recommended for upper-division undergraduate and graduate students, researchers and faculty, and telecommunications professionals.—*E. J. Szewczak, Canisius College*

OAB-1454   QA76   95-50054 CIP
Kasabov, Nikola K. **Foundations of neural networks, fuzzy systems, and knowledge engineering.** MIT, 1996. 550p bibl index afp ISBN 0-262-11212-4, $60.00

Kasabov explains the principles of neural networks and fuzzy systems and demonstrates how they can be applied to building knowledge-based systems for problem solving. Chapter 1 gives a clear introduction to the problems of classical artificial intelligence, the basics of neural networks and fuzzy systems, and their complementary relationships. Chapter 2 comprehensively overviews the field of knowledge engineering, and chapters 3 and 4 cover fuzzy systems and their applications to major problems and the principles of neural networks. Chapter 5 reviews the use of neural networks for knowledge engineering, and chapter 6 discusses hybrids of symbolic, fuzzy, and connectionist systems. Chapter 7 explains chaos theory, its relationship to neural networks and fuzzy systems, and newer developments arising from them. An appendix offers educational software available by ftp. The breadth of coverage and the integrated per-

spective and clarity make this most definitely a must for libraries of all institutions. Highly recommended for self-study. All levels.—*R. Bharath, Northern Michigan University*

OAB-1455   QA76   93-25428 CIP
Kidwell, Peggy A. **Landmarks in digital computing: a Smithsonian pictorial history,** by Peggy A. Kidwell and Paul E. Ceruzzi. Smithsonian Institution Press, 1994. 148p bibl index afp ISBN 1-56098-311-6 pbk, $15.95

This expertly written and totally captivating book recounts the history of computing devices dating back to such computing aids as quipus and abacuses. In this information age, it is good to realize that the roots of the present information explosion were made possible by the technological advances and revolution of computing devices. Written in nontechnical terms and with special emphasis on dates and names, the authors (Smithsonian Institution) have painstakingly traced and documented the major events, devices, and people in the history of computing devices (which include calculators and computers). Pictures of these monstrosities of past times help the reader to appreciate the technological advances of the last half century. Of special interest is the detailed chronology of major events, a glossary, an index to referenced persons, and a general index. Highly recommended. General; two-year technical.—*J. Y. Cheung, University of Oklahoma*

OAB-1456   QA76   94-48745 CIP
Landauer, Thomas K. **The trouble with computers: usefulness, usability, and productivity.** MIT, 1995. 425p bibl index afp ISBN 0-262-12186-7, $27.50

The Trouble With Computers speaks from the heart but appeals to the head. Landauer has tried to prove in concrete terms that computers help people to be more productive. He treats two topics: (1) the things people cannot do without computers, and (2) the things that computers are supposed to help people do better. The problem is not with the first benefit: there are many examples where computers enable humans to do things not possible without them. The problem comes in integrating computers into activities that people have been doing for some time, for which computers are supposed to be a help. The early chapters of the book deal entirely with questions surrounding productivity of computers: the cases for and against. However, Landauer takes an interesting turn and sets the blame for productivity failings squarely on issues in software development, and goes on to say what software engineering practitioners should do to correct the situation. This book now has a place of honor on this reviewer's shelf right next to Donald A. Norman's *The Psychology of Everyday Things* (CH, Oct'88). Every computer science student, undergraduate and graduate alike, should read this book and take its message to heart.—*F. H. Wild III, University of Rhode Island*

OAB-1457   QA76   94-44629 CIP
Marchionini, Gary. **Information seeking in electronic environments.** Cambridge, 1995. 224p bibl index (Cambridge series on human-computer interaction, 9) ISBN 0-521-44372-5, $49.95

Marchionini's very timely book looks at the state of the art of information seeking in digital environments. The book is intended not for the casual reader but for those studying the field. In a very compact nine chapters and 200 pages, the author takes the reader from the basics to an understanding of possible future areas of development in this important field. The first two chapters are very brief but sufficient for establishing the terminology and foundation for the remainder of the book. The next three chapters overview the traditional research efforts in information-seeking efforts and strategies. Chapters 6 and 7 are the keystone; they describe browsing strategies and systems that support them. The final two chapters describe the author's very realistic views of trends and strategies for the future development of this discipline. The book also includes an exhaustive 14-page set of references, an excellent index, and chapter notes at the end of the book. A requirement for every undergraduate computer science and information science library. Upper-division undergraduate through professional.—*J. Beidler, University of Scranton*

OAB-1458   QA76   96-27609 CIP
Menezes, Alfred J. **Handbook of applied cryptography,** by Alfred J. Menezes, Paul C. van Oorschot, and Scott A. Vanstone. CRC Press, 1997. 780p bibl index afp ISBN 0-8493-8523-7, $79.95

Over the last two decades, the discipline of cryptography has witnessed explosive growth both in its diversity of techniques and its range of concerns. Mathematical methods replaced the ad hoc, and the construction of (and attack against) novel protocols such as zero-knowledge proofs, digital signatures, and secret sharing schemes now occupies the cryptographer as much as the age-old activities of making and breaking secret codes. This volume, addressed equally to the industrial practitioner, academic researcher, and student, does nothing less than provide a detailed and comprehensive overview of all these activities. Aiming the book at a wide audience and keeping it to a manageable size (if 780 pages can be called manageable) required two compromises of the authors: omitting language-specific source code (while providing detailed informal algorithm specifications), and omitting most rigorous argumentation (while providing adequate references). Thus the book forms a nice pair with more theoretical treatments, like Douglas R. Stinson's *Cryptography: Theory and Practice* (1995), to pick a recent example. Designed for reference and browsing, the authors still intend that a front-to-back read have "some merit." One hopes for their sake that the authors found a labor of love in compiling this enormous wealth of useful and fascinating information. Highly recommended for all academic library collections, undergraduate through faculty.—*D. V. Feldman, University of New Hampshire*

OAB-1459   QA76   95-45243 CIP
Mitchell, John C. **Foundations for programming languages.** MIT, 1996. 846p bibl index afp ISBN 0-262-13321-0, $60.00

Mitchell's prodigiously comprehensive work presents a theoretical view of programming languages using lambda calculus as its primary means of conveyance for all associated concepts. It teems with the mathematical components of theories, propositions, proofs, corollaries, and algorithms as it strives to expound on the various elements of programming language theory. There is an abundance of exercises, with many positioned following significant topics as well as at the close of chapters. The book is replete with vibrant representational formulas and examples. Use is made of a less-than-full-blown, easily analyzed lambda calculus-based language to study the properties and techniques applicable to other languages. The author suggests that the book can be appropriately segmented to support either an introductory course, a course on semantics and typed lambda calculus, or a course on type theory. The excellent extensive bibliography should be exceptionally rewarding to those desiring additional perspectives on this significant subject matter. Upper-division undergraduates, graduate students, or faculty exploring the theoretical aspects of computer programming languages will find this an ideally relevant and challenging choice.—*E. Hook, formerly, Gettysburg College*

OAB-1460   T57   89-17804 MARC
Nering, Evar D. **Linear programs and related problems,** by Evar D. Nering and Albert W. Tucker. Academic Press, 1993. 584p bibl index afp disk (IBM-PC) ISBN 0-12-515440-2, $59.95

Linear programming is of enormous practical importance in economics, business, and industry and of theoretical importance in combinatorics and computer science. Its basics are the standard stuff of finite mathematics courses for nonmajors, while its advanced manifestations fill research monographs. Tucker, one of the pioneers of the field, and collaborator Nering present an exposition at once sophisticated and broadly accessible. The merest background in linear algebra should suffice for a reading. The first half deals with duality theory and much detail on the simplex algorithm, and includes the most elementary presentation of the landmark 1984 Karmarkar algorithm yet in print. Concrete examples are discussed throughout. The second half includes connections to game theory, transportation, network flow, and trans-shipment problems, and a final chapter on nonlinear programming. This beautifully produced, richly

illustrated volume should become a classic. Detailed answers are offered for all exercises and software is included. Highly recommended for all libraries.—*D. V. Feldman, University of New Hampshire*

OAB-1461   Orig
Ojeda, Oscar Riera. **Hyper-realistic: computer generated architectural renderings,** by Oscar Riera Ojeda and Lucas H. Guerra. McGraw-Hill, 1996. 191p CD-ROM ISBN 0-07-856635-5, $79.95

Ojeda and Guerra explore the application of advanced digital imaging technology for dazzling presentations of architectural design. The layout of the book is itself as exciting and aesthetically pleasing as the computer-generated architectural renderings that it presents. The book is suitable for a wide range of readership levels, and the accompanying CD-ROM provides the opportunity for a fun departure from traditional print media. The CD-ROM is very appropriate for the topic, providing archives of architectural elevations and working drawings, slide shows of existing structures, models, more than 200 digital renderings, and walk-through "virtual" excursions into the computer-generated design projects. It is well organized with reasonably smooth transitions from one segment of the quasi-interactive presentation to another. Like the book, the CD-ROM is tastefully produced and an example of good design in the relatively new sphere of CD-ROM publishing. Although the publication form may captivate the reader, the content is yet another strength of the publication—offering a sampler of outstanding architectural designs from internationally acclaimed architects and illustrators. Overall, an excellent resource. All levels.—*M. Snyder, Pennsylvania College of Technology*

OAB-1462   Orig
Paul, Gregory S. **Beyond humanity: cyberevolution and future minds,** by Gregory S. Paul and Earl Cox. Charles River Media, 1996. 487p bibl index afp ISBN 1-886801-21-5 pbk, $20.95

This fascinating book by two well-known scientists, one in biology and the other in computers, is a preview of the computer technology of the 21st century resulting from the so-called "CyberEvolution." Based on futuristic thinking of the authors, it is in many respects in agreement with the views of a number of famous scientists and philosophers. The authors argue that computing power, neuroscience, and nanotechnologies are advancing so rapidly that they will continue to produce the most significant evolutionary developments since the origin of life itself. The authors hypothesize that although a computer cannot be designed to fully replicate a human brain, in the 21st century it will come quite close to this ideal. They discuss in detail the process of "CyberEvolution," which will make this a reality, and they hypothesize that such computers will be more efficient than humans. Associated with the advent of such powerful thinking machines are some of the most interesting sociological, technological, and scientific dilemmas humankind will ever face. The book is written lucidly, and anyone with some background in science and computers will find it very interesting. Useful list of related books. A must for academic as well as public libraries. All levels.—*P. K. Basu, Vanderbilt University*

OAB-1463   HD62   95-45550 CIP
Reed, Kenneth. **Data network handbook: an interactive guide to network architecture and operations.** Van Nostrand Reinhold, 1996. 391p index disc (IBM-PC) ISBN 0-442-02299-9, $49.95

Although computer data networking as a profession dates to the mid-1960s, it took until the early '90s, with the rapid commercialization of the Internet, for this field to develop a shortage of knowledgeable practitioners. Employment opportunities for students and retrained professionals are numerous and pay very well. Reed offers an excellent introduction to this field of work. The book's first section covers basic network concepts and the classic OSI (open systems interconnection) model used to describe data networks. The second discusses local area network technologies and architectures, including the client/server model, and the third introduces wide area protocols and architectural variations; among those described is TCP/IP, used by the Internet. The final section presents related telecommunication technologies and integrates the concepts of earlier sections. Each easy-to-read chapter begins with a list of objectives, features numerous helpful figures and examples, has a summary of what was covered, and points to additional information available on the accompanying CD-ROM. Extensive glossary; very helpful list of acronyms; appendix explaining the CD-ROM's use. An excellent addition to the data network learning and reference literature. Lower-division undergraduates; two-year technical program students; professionals.—*E. M. Aupperle, University of Michigan*

OAB-1464   QA76   96-41003 CIP
Rochlin, Gene I. **Trapped in the net: the unanticipated consequences of computerization.** Princeton, 1997. 293p bibl index afp ISBN 0-691-01080-3, $29.95

An important contribution to the discussion of the "unanticipated consequences [and] direct and indirect costs of increased dependence on computers," this book is written with a stylistic grace that is rare in this genre. Rochlin's beautiful, concise history of personal computers and networks is followed by an analysis of the consequent "emergence of new modes of organizational control." Two lucid and insightful chapters on the computerization of the financial markets focus on the deepening loss of human control it has engendered. This theme is further pursued in the chapter on automation of airplane cockpits and of air traffic control rooms. Four chapters trace the evolution of the military, from the Civil War to the Gulf War, to a fully computerized "command, control, communications, and intelligence" operation with the resultant increase in cost and decrease in robustness against errors and surprises. The often fascinating endnotes and an extensive, eclectic bibliography cover 70 pages. This book is such a thoughtful, informative, and evenhanded "exploration of [the] longer-term systemic and societal implications" of the use of computer systems that it should be studied by everyone who uses them or controls their use. All levels.—*J. Mayer, formerly, Lebanon Valley College*

OAB-1465   Q335   94-36444 CIP
Russell, Stuart J. **Artificial intelligence: a modern approach,** by Stuart J. Russell and Peter Norvig. Prentice Hall, 1995. 932p bibl index ISBN 0-13-103805-2, $61.33

Russell and Norvig, acknowledged experts in the field, have produced a marvelously clear, exciting, and coherent book on artificial intelligence (AI). Perhaps for the first time, AI is presented as a unified field with the concept of intelligent agents that receive percepts from the environment and perform actions as the unifying theme. All the usual areas of AI are covered, such as reasoning under uncertainty, learning, neural networks, natural language, vision, robotics, and philosophical foundations, as well as the more recent ideas of simulated annealing, memory-bound search, global ontologies, dynamic and adaptive probabilistic networks, computational learning theory, and reinforcement learning. The book gives equal emphasis to theory and practice, includes more than 100 algorithms and 300 exercises, and contains extensive notes and references to the research literature. Overall, an excellent work. Highly recommended. General; upper-division undergraduate through professional.—*C. Tappert, United States Military Academy*

OAB-1466   QA76   95-2537 CIP
Stoll, Clifford. **Silicon snake oil: second thoughts on the information highway.** Doubleday, 1995. 247p index ISBN 0-385-41993-7, $22.00

In spite of being an optimist about computers and the data superhighway helping the world in many ways, this reviewer thoroughly enjoyed Stoll's book. His observations about the false assumptions, overselling, and limitations of the Internet are astute and extremely important. Stoll (an astronomer and long-time user of computers and the Internet) reminds us that the real world, and not virtual worlds, should receive most of our attention, and he describes how shallow many of the information bases, news group postings, and "friendships" made on the net typically are. He argues that library book and staff budgets should not be cut in order to buy equipment that will age quickly and expensive electronic services that tend

to limit, rather than enhance, users' access to literature. This book is written so clearly and vividly that anyone from junior-high-school age on up can appreciate it. Any current or potential user of the Internet should be aware of Stoll's main point—that the Internet cannot live up to all the expectations being generated about it. Every library should have at least one copy of this book. All levels.—*S. L. Tanimoto, University of Washington*

OAB-1467   Orig
Talbott, Stephen L. **The future does not compute: transcending the machines in our midst.** O'Reilly & Associates, 1995. 481p bibl index afp ISBN 1-56592-085-6, $22.95

Talbott's important, seminal work should be read by everyone working with computers. Teachers of computer science and use at all educational levels would especially gain from pondering the author's thoughts and the questions he poses. He raises serious philosophical issues that deserve the attention of everyone who wrestles with the deep cultural crisis engendered by "the computer [that] brings to a perfect conclusion the primary 'drift' of our civilization over the past few hundred years." Talbott attempts to fathom the essence of this machine that is at once the image of the human mind qua its creator and its distortion via its user. Deeply influenced by Owen Barfield, he asserts that "human life can only be sustained within a sea of meaning," while a computer deals only in information without "meaning," be it on the Internet or in the classroom. His penetrating discussions of works by H. Rheingold, G. Gilder, and S. Papert are models of dispassionate analysis. This short review cannot do justice to the scope and depth of this first critical study of computers since J. Weizenbaum's *Computer Power and Human Reason* (CH, Jun'76). General; upper-division undergraduate through professional; two-year technical program students.—*J. Mayer, Lebanon Valley College*

OAB-1468   QA76   93-43289 CIP
Van de Velde, Eric F. **Concurrent scientific computing.** Springer-Verlag, 1994. 328p bibl index afp (Texts in applied mathematics, 16) ISBN 0-387-94195-9, $39.95

In university courses, there has been a gap between computer science (CS) and scientific applications. Graduates of CS programs are often poorly prepared to write programs that efficiently implement numerical algorithms on state-of-the-art parallel computers. This book, intended primarily as a text for seniors and graduate students in computer science or applied mathematics, covers both the numerical algorithms and the computer programming approach needed to take advantage of "parallel" computers for scientific and engineering applications. In order to profit from the book, a reader needs a grounding in numerical linear algebra, numerical analysis, and conventional computer programming. Algorithms are presented in a version of the UNITY notation system of Chandy and Misra; these are not runnable programs, but would need to be coded in a language such as a parallel FORTRAN or a dialect of C with support for multiple threads. The book appears to be unique in its integration of wisdom regarding the mathematical, numerical, and parallel programming aspects of scientific computation. Care has been given to clear presentation of mathematical and algorithmic formalisms. The diagrams and charts are effective. Highly recommended. Undergraduate through professional.—*S. L. Tanimoto, University of Washington*

■ Earth Science

OAB-1469   QE515   95-23040 CIP
Anderson, G.M. **Thermodynamics of natural systems.** Wiley, 1996. 382p bibl index afp ISBN 0-471-10943-6 pbk, $25.95

In writing this book, Anderson did not cater to the typical audience of a thermodynamics text. Instead, he aimed his book at undergraduates in fields such as forestry, soil science, or other disciplines where the thermodynamics of natural systems is important. The application of thermodynamics is a focus throughout: Anderson carefully introduces the fundamental laws of thermodynamics as they apply to chemical reactions by stating the problems that these laws address; i.e., why do reactions proceed the way they do and what makes a reaction reversible or irreversible? Many familiar examples are cited, and helpful analogies to mechanical systems are used in exploring these questions. Anderson's approach is more than adequate to help readers apply thermodynamic principles in later chapters, which cover topics from calorimetry to statistical thermodynamics. There are problems at the end of the chapters and answers in an appendix. Another particularly helpful appendix reviews some principles of calculus and shows their application to thermodynamics. An excellent book. Undergraduate.—*L. M. Lawson, Providence College*

OAB-1470   QE79   95-4344 CIP
Baars, Donald L. **Navajo country: a geology and natural history of the Four Corners region.** New Mexico, 1995. 255p bibl index ISBN 0-8263-1587-9 pbk, $19.95

Baars discusses the geology, natural history, and Native American history of southeastern Utah, northeastern Arizona, northwestern New Mexico, and southwestern Colorado. Major sections include the geological story that unfolded over about four billion years as delineated by unexcelled exposures of incredibly beautiful rock strata; Indian history over the last 500 years mainly as revealed in their words and legends usually based on natural settings; and Anglo history over the last 200 years with emphasis on oil, uranium, and coal developments. Baars, a well-known geologist with a long career in the Four Corners region, skillfully weaves the geological story into human history and influence, making the book essential for any traveler or explorer in the region. Many sections describe roads into back country and what one can see along them geologically and historically—excellent for the real as well as the vicarious traveler! Illustrations are very well chosen in relation to the text, i.e., numerous oblique airphotos (that show view direction—rarely done in most books), geologic maps, cross sections, stratigraphic charts, and other useful sections. Especially helpful and interesting is the glossary of place names. Many general and selected geologic references round out the book. An excellent introduction to geology with reference to the world-famous Colorado Plateau region. Such an educational and notably enjoyable book will interest every inhabitant in the region. All levels.—*T. L. T. Grose, Colorado School of Mines*

OAB-1471   QE534   93-12636 CIP
Bolt, Bruce A. **Earthquakes and geological discovery.** Scientific American Library, 1993. (Dist. by W.H. Freeman) 229p index ISBN 0-7167-5040-6, $32.95

A compact and handsome volume, written by an internationally renowned seismologist and geologist, combining the most interesting and important aspects of earthquakes to capture the attention of all concerned with natural phenomena and the environment. The book's major focus centers on the origin and history of seismology and how they provide insights into geological understanding, and how both together are underpinning advancements in earthquake prediction and risk reduction. Some chapter topics include seismic waves, instrumental surveillance, earthquake sources, Earth's tectonic plates, Earth's interior, ground shaking, forecasting earthquakes, and reducing seismic risk. An outstanding attribute of the book is the carefully chosen, informative, and colorful photos, charts, and maps. The excitement and spirit of scientific discovery, utilizing particularly seismology and geology together to mitigate hazards to humanity, is a first-rate chronicle dynamically presented in semi-technical language in this attractive book. All levels.—*T. L. T. Grose, Colorado School of Mines*

OAB-1472   G70   94-28315 CIP
Bonham-Carter, Graeme F. **Geographic information systems for geoscientists: modelling with GIS.** Pergamon, 1995 (c1994). 398p bibl index (Computer methods in the geosciences, 13) ISBN 0-08-041867-8, $110.00; ISBN 0-08-042420-1 pbk, $43.00

This essential reference is for all who use, interpret, and apply geoscience

data in map and spatial contexts. The recent literature on geographic information systems (GIS) has been mainly directed to cartographers, geographers, and others who work with thematic maps; Bonham-Carter (Geological Survey of Canada) addresses geologists, particularly those involved in mineral exploration, natural resources, and the environment. Well-organized and clearly written, the entire book is a thorough and practical treatment of the subject, with specific illustrations and case studies of GIS applications to geologic projects in every chapter. The first few chapters explain the purpose, meaning, and functions of GIS. Further chapters deal with data models and data structures, input, and visualization. Final chapters treat geologic map analysis and quantification and discuss the models and methods of mineral potential mapping. Appendixes provide guides to the related mathematical syntax, GIS acronyms, a Fortran example, and an especially helpful and detailed glossary of GIS terms. The book is abundantly and very effectively illustrated with drawings, graphs, and maps. References accompany each chapter, and there is an ample index. Highly recommended for college libraries serving students in earth science, civil engineering, and geography. Upper-division undergraduate through professional.—*W. C. Peters, University of Arizona*

OAB-1473   QE841   96-44161 CIP
Carroll, Robert L. **Patterns and processes of vertebrate evolution.** Cambridge, 1997. 448p bibl index (Cambridge paleobiology series, 2) ISBN 0-521-47232-6, $85.00; ISBN 0-521-47809-X pbk, $39.95

Carroll's volume is one of a half dozen most significant books on evolutionary patterns and their explanations since George Gaylord Simpson's 1944 epoch-making *Tempo and Mode in Evolution*. It is a thorough and modern inquiry into the forces and various causes responsible for the evolutionary patterns of fossil and living organisms (not only vertebrates, either) and the processes responsible for them. It is also a sober and painstakingly argued rebuttal of the recasting and "reinvention" of Darwin and Simpson by Eldredge, Gould, Stanley, and Vrba. Carroll's resounding conclusion is that while macroevolutionary patterns reflect unique and fascinating historical events channeled by ancestral and physical constraints, natural selection, and geographical contingencies, there are no law-like macroevolutionary explanations beyond the forces of developmental and population level dynamics. Yet the volume faithfully reflects the excitement and challenge to understand the macroevolutionary patterns of organisms. Though microevolution and macroevolution are conceptually inseparable, the extremes of inquiry in evolutionary studies continue to inspire different, albeit interconnected, approaches. Profusely illustrated, the book is an exemplar of style and brevity, given the vast and complex subject matter covered. This book is a milestone and is highly recommended. General readers; undergraduates through faculty.—*F. S. Szalay, CUNY Hunter College*

OAB-1474   GB5014   92-73848 MARC
The Citizen's guide to geologic hazards: a guide to understanding geologic hazards—including asbestos, radon, swelling soils, earthquakes, volcanoes, landslides, subsidence, floods and coastal hazards, prep. by the American Institute of Professional Geologists; authors, Edward B. Nuhfer, Richard J. Proctor, and Paul H. Moser. American Institute of Professional Geologists, 7828 Vance Drive, Suite 103, Arvada, CO 80003, 1994 (c1993). 134p index ISBN 0-933637-10-1 pbk, $19.95

The primary authors of this book, commissioned by the American Institute of Professional Geologists, are not only well qualified but have diverse expertise in the geosciences that adds credence to the work. The book's essential goal is to provide for the public a guide to geologic hazards and their understanding. Topics cover not only the obvious dangers of earthquakes, volcanoes, floods, and landslides, but the more subtle ones such as radon, asbestos, swelling soils, coastal hazards, and subsidence. Easy to read and profusely illustrated with many color photographs and drawings, this book also contains a geologic hazards checklist for home owners/buyers and a list of help sources from geology and insurance professionals. Highly recommended for all general readers; should be included in the collections of all public libraries. General; community college; lower-division undergraduate.—*B. D. Dod, Mercer University*

OAB-1475   QE501   94-7763 CIP

Coastal evolution: Late Quaternary shoreline morphodynamics, ed. by R.W.G. Carter and C.D. Woodroffe. Cambridge, 1995 (c1994). 517p bibl index ISBN 0-521-41976-X, $79.95

This collection of 13 chapters in the form of review articles concentrates on the various dynamic processes involved in the evolution and modification of shorelines. The chapters are written by 22 experts from all over the world. After two chapters that cover general processes, the remaining ones deal with specific types of coastal regions such as those dominated by deltas, coral reefs, lagoons, etc. Each article is self-contained and has an extensive list of references together with many fine line drawings, photographs, and/or maps. The overall quality of the writing and editing is very good. In fact, the whole book is excellent in concept and in execution. It will serve as the latest and the last word on the subject for years to come. Highly recommended for all geologists and other environmental scientists, together with engineers, planners, and others involved in any way with coastal processes. All levels.—*C. J. Casella, Northern Illinois University*

OAB-1476   GB451   93-25452 CIP

Davis, Richard A. **The evolving coast.** Scientific American Library, 1994. (Dist. by W.H. Freeman) 231p bibl index ISBN 0-7167-5042-2, $32.95

An outstanding addition to the literature on the geology of coastlines and the physical processes that shape them. Davis devotes three chapters to factors and processes that shape coastlines; there are four chapters on different types of coastlines. The very high quality photographs of coastal landforms are an outstanding feature; these photographs provide excellent illustrations of a large number of coastal landforms and conditions. Davis (Univ. of South Florida, Tampa) specializes in coastal processes. Highly recommended for all college and university libraries serving geology and coastal engineering programs. General; undergraduate through faculty; professional.—*D. B. Stafford, Clemson University*

OAB-1477   QE881   96-11747 CIP

The Evolution of Western Eurasian Neogene mammal faunas, ed. by Raymond L. Bernor, Volker Fahlbusch, and Hans-Walter Mittmann. Columbia, 1997 (c1996). 487p bibl indexes afp ISBN 0-231-08246-0, $92.00

There are no dimensions of time as important for a genuinely contextual and causal understanding of the origin and evolution of humankind than the Neogene period (Miocene and Pliocene epochs, from about 23.5 to 1.6 million years ago). The outcome of a definitive symposium that unites the contributions of more than 60 specialists, this book is an exceptional achievement. The contributors are geochronologists, sedimentologists, vertebrate and invertebrate paleontologists, and paleobotanists—the very scholars that will find this volume indispensable. The major subdivisions of this tome, "Geological Background" (part 1), "Mammalian Systematics, Biogeography, and Biochronology" (part 2), and "Paleobotany, Paleobiogeography, and Paleoecology" (part 3) give an indication of the breadth and density of information and analysis that is brought together. Numerous figures, tables, summaries, and thorough locality and taxonomic indexes make this symposium volume an exemplar of its genre. The book rates the highest recommendation for upper-division undergraduates through professionals.—*F. S. Szalay, CUNY Hunter College*

OAB-1478   QE515   93-233054 MARC

Fletcher, Philip. **Chemical thermodynamics for earth scientists.** Longman Scientific & Technical/Wiley, 1993. 464p index ISBN 0-470-22072-4 pbk, $44.95

Fletcher provides an excellent outline of general thermodynamic principles and their application to chemical reactions in geological environments. Three major topic areas are covered: the physical properties of geological materials, the principles of thermodynamics, and methods for the application of thermodynamic principles. Chapters 1-6 are devoted to the composition, struc-

ture, and reactivity of geological materials. Chapters 7-12 deal with the basic principles of thermodynamcis along with discussions of energy and related properties. Chapters 13-19 concentrate on more specific properties of geochemical materials (solids, liquids, and vapors); demonstrate how thermodynamic properties reflect changes in T and P; and discuss various graphical and computer-based methods that can be utilized in the application of thermodynamic data. The work is well illustrated and has an extensive index, a comprehensive list of references, and useful lists of books recommended for supplemental reading. Although well suited for chemical thermodynamics courses, this book will provide excellent support material for both advanced undergraduate and graduate courses in geochemistry, petrology, soil science, environmental science, and chemistry, as well as a valuable reference for faculty and professionals.—*M. E. McCallum, Colorado State University*

OAB-1479   QE522   92-29756 CIP

Francis, Peter. **Volcanoes: a planetary perspective.** Oxford, 1993. 443p index ISBN 0-19-854452-9, $85.00; ISBN 0-19-854033-7 pbk, $42.95

This lively book on volcanoes and volcanism is a landmark contribution to a science that, just a few years ago, was of interest to only a very limited number of people and was portrayed in few publications. Francis's book is remarkable for the breadth of appeal to general readership, to anyone interested in natural phenomena, and to geologists as well as volcanologists. Major topics include (1) volcanoes in the planetary scheme of things, (2) four classic eruptions, (3) types of eruptions, (4) volcanic rocks and how they formed, (5) submarine volcanism, (6) extraterrestrial volcanism, and (7) others, e.g., landforms, structures. Especially instructive and attractive are the many illustrations—photos, maps, charts, schematics—obviously chosen to inform and to spark wonder. Also very valuable are the carefully selected seminal references to specific and general topics listed at the end of each chapter. No earth science and environmental library should be without this book. All levels.—*T. L. T. Grose, Colorado School of Mines*

OAB-1480   QE390   96-34529 CIP

Geochemistry of hydrothermal ore deposits, ed. by Hubert Lloyd Barnes. 3rd ed. Wiley, 1997. 972p bibl index afp ISBN 0-471-57144-X, $115.00

Here is an expanded and thoroughly revised new edition of the most widely recognized and cited reference work on geochemistry in mineral deposits. Although the organization is similar to that of the second edition (CH, Jun'80), it is essentially a new book that emphasizes the knowledge of the last two decades in the principles and theories of ore genesis. Chapters progress from a fundamental treatment of the sources and flow paths of hydrothermal solutions to a detailed consideration of the complex conditions of ore mineral deposition. As in previous editions, some important chapters deal with wall-rock hydrothermal alteration, isotope and fluid inclusion studies, and currently active hydrothermal systems. Significant new chapters deal with the role of organic matter in hydrothermal ore deposits, with submarine hydrothermal systems, and ore-forming brines in active continental rifts. An appendix of chemical and physical data is supplemented by the inclusion of a computer disk with files to support the graphs and charts. Well written, and very effectively illustrated, the book has a comprehensive index, and ample references at chapter ends. Highly recommended for all college libraries serving programs in geoscience. Upper-division undergraduates through faculty.—*W. C. Peters, University of Arizona*

OAB-1481   QE391   95-651 CIP

Grimaldi, David A. **Amber: window to the past.** Abrams/American Museum of Natural History, 1996. 216p bibl index ISBN 0-8109-1966-4, $49.50

This book might have been more aptly titled "Amber: The Coffee-Table Book," for that is just what it is. But what a coffee-table book! The illustrations, especially the photographs of animal inclusions in amber, range from good to spectacular. Line drawings by the author, one of the leading figures in the scientific study of insects found in amber, are also top notch, and the text is up-to-date, scientifically accurate, and nicely written. Two-thirds of the book is devoted to the natural history of amber, including the fantastic menageries of insects and other animals found entombed in this golden material; the remaining third discusses amber in art. A selected bibliography at the end of the book can serve as an entry into the literature on amber. This work complements the recent work of George O. Poinar, especially *Life in Amber* (CH, Jun'93). In academic institutions the book will introduce amber; advanced students can pore over the color photographs that, because of cost limitations, will not likely be in the scientific literature. The book coincides with an American Museum of Natural History exhibit on amber. All levels.—*J. Hannibal, Cleveland Museum of Natural History*

OAB-1482   TS752   93-28348 Orig
Hall, Cally. **Gemstones.** Dorling Kindersley, 1994. 160p index ISBN 1-56458-499-2, $29.95; ISBN 1-56458-498-4 pbk, $17.95

Hall's volume is truly a gem among numerous books on gems. Its outstanding features include superb choice and quality of more than 800 photographs, organization and coverage of the entire subject of gemology through human history, and information and format style with authority and excitement for the subject. A concise photo-encyclopedic approach to more than 130 gem varieties highlights the ease of using this book. Contents include how gemstones form, crystal and optical properties, mining and processing, history and folklore, synthetics, precious metals, cut stones, organics, table of gem properties, glossary, and index. The book is eminently useful as a field guide to gem occurrences, as a guide to specimen identification, and as a source of critical information on each specific gem type. The amateur and professional alike will welcome this book. All levels.—*T. L. T. Grose, Colorado School of Mines*

OAB-1483   QE851   95-26847 CIP
Janvier, Philippe. **Early vertebrates.** Oxford, 1996. 393p bibl indexes (Oxford monographs on geology and geophysics, 33) ISBN 0-19-854047-7, $135.00

There are few books that we can confidently note upon publication will be "classics," but this is one. Janvier provides a thoroughly modern analysis of the relationships and evolution of early vertebrates (primarily fishes), with clear text, recent anatomical and paleontological evidence, and superb line drawings. The key to this book's success, however, transcends its technical beauty—it is the first systematic and comprehensible book-length application of cladistic methodology to these complex and fascinating organisms. Janvier states that he wished to keep his approach simple so that the ideas presented could be at least theoretically refuted by additional evidence. He invites the reader to think of other explanations for the patterns he describes, and the necessary information to begin an independent analysis is often readily at hand in the same chapter. Janvier has been very careful to separate speculations from the physical evidence, so there is not the confusion between the two so often found in older works. As a bonus, he has added a chapter on techniques of fossil preparation and analysis (including a lucid introduction to cladistics), and a chapter describing the history of research on early vertebrates. A critical addition to the literature on organic evolution, which should be in every academic library. Upper-division undergraduates through professionals.—*M. A. Wilson, College of Wooster*

OAB-1484   HT393   91-41261 CIP
Living with the Georgia shore, by Tonya D. Clayton et al. Duke University, 1992. 188p index afp ISBN 0-8223-1215-8, $42.50; ISBN 0-8223-1219-0 pbk, $17.95

An excellent book that brings together in one guide some of what is known about the Georgia coastline. It is especially for those working with that shore in various capacities—as residents, visitors, planners, and real estate agents. Major topics include understanding the coastal perspectives, such as the geol-

ogy of the different barrier islands, beach maintenance, and helpful guidance to coastal developers; and how to cope with climatic hazards, such as hurricanes and the accompanying wind, waves, and flood. In other words, it makes an outstanding effort to alert readers about risky consequences of unplanned development on the shore. The book is well written and quite informative. The splendid illustrations relate well to the topics they cover. For those interested in coastal residence, recreation, and any scientific information regarding the Georgian coastline, there are sufficient references. Highly recommended for general and academic readers.—*R. N. Khan, Armstrong State College*

OAB-1485   QE538   93-40909 CIP
Lomnitz, Cinna. **Fundamentals of earthquake prediction.** Wiley, 1994. 326p bibl index afp ISBN 0-471-57419-8, $89.95

This is the best book this reviewer has ever read on this important and timely subject. Lomnitz deals with all the sense and nonsense that make this topic fascinating to anyone who is at all concerned with earthquakes. It is a somewhat technical book with some mathematics, but can easily be read by anyone who is sufficiently diligent. The book is written in a breezy style that is almost iconoclastic in the sense that it destroys the cherished concept that all we need is faith in the regularity or predictability of nature and we will someday be easily able to predict when, where, and how strong an earthquake will be. This important, unique book should be carefully studied by all who have the responsibility for public safety. It is also a "must read" for all geoscientists and others who are responsible for attempting to predict earthquakes. There is a most useful set of appendixes that list earthquake data. All in all, a most attractive volume for all libraries. All levels.—*C. J. Casella, Northern Illinois University*

OAB-1486   QE851   96-6907 MARC
Maisey, John G. **Discovering fossil fishes.** H. Holt, 1996. 223p index ISBN 0-8050-4366-7, $40.00

Fish are spectacular organisms for studying evolutionary dynamics and history. They have a long and detailed fossil record dating back at least 500 million years, and they have made an astonishing range of adaptations to aquatic environments. Maisey presents a superb introduction to the history of fishes. There are many attractive coffee-table picture books of fossil fish, and this one looks superficially like numerous others, but do not be misled. This is a thorough evolutionary analysis of the fossil record and of recent anatomy of fishes. The author has carefully outlined the major hypotheses of fish evolution, and he is one of the few paleontologists to discuss modern genetic evidence (including an excellent discussion of Hox genes). The description of most groups includes simple and useful cladograms, sometimes with alternative interpretations. The photographs are of the highest quality, as are the reconstruction diagrams (which are usually matched with photographs of the fossils from which they were derived). There are a few minor errors (e.g., *Pikaia* is sometimes spelled "*Pikaea*"), and the occasional cheerleading about fish and their "mastery of the oceans" can be a bit annoying. Nonetheless, anyone with an interest in fish or paleontology will enjoy this book. Undergraduates through faculty.—*M. A. Wilson, College of Wooster*

OAB-1487   QE721   93-26195 CIP
The Mass-extinction debates: how science works in a crisis, ed. by William Glen. Stanford, 1994. 370p bibl index afp ISBN 0-8047-2285-4, $49.50; ISBN 0-8047-2286-2 pbk, $17.95

This is a wonderful volume, highly recommended for all libraries and everyone in science or the philosophy of science. Glen edited this book as part of a larger project documenting the history of the "Impact Hypothesis" as an explanation for the Cretaceous mass extinction. His genius has been to record interviews and collect papers, preprints, and referee reports on the issue "as it has unfolded" since 1980. He can thus provide an extraordinary view of how scientists work during a conceptual "crisis." The analysis of the social dynamics affecting how disciplines and subdisciplines receive new ideas is fascinating, and the revelation of the levels of ignorance some scientists have as they state strong opinions on the issue is disturbing. Glen is a geologist, so he knows the subject and the main characters well, and he expresses complex concepts in clear language. The book has many contributions, but those by Glen are the most interesting. An analysis of the Impact Hypothesis and "popular science" by Elisabeth Clemens is also well done. Many primary proponents and opponents of the hypothesis contributed separate chapters or were interviewed for the book. There are even contributions from scientists who deny that there ever were mass extinctions. An excellent book for upper-division undergraduates or graduate students. All levels.—*M. A. Wilson, College of Wooster*

OAB-1488   QE721   95-38419 CIP
McGhee, George R. **The Late Devonian mass extinction: the Frasnian/Famennian crisis.** Columbia, 1996. 303p bibl index afp ISBN 0-231-07505-7 pbk, $20.00

Mass extinction in the history of life has become a prominent issue in evolutionary theory and historical geology. The concept that the Cretaceous extinctions were caused by a collision between Earth and an extraterrestrial object opened new avenues of inquiry into the mechanisms behind other mass extinctions, provoking in turn questions about methods and underlying philosophies that geologists and biologists continue to debate. McGhee thoroughly assesses knowledge about the Late Devonian mass extinction, during which at least 70 percent of species vanished. The text is so comprehensive and well written, though, that it could serve as a basic resource for thinking about *all* extinctions, mass or otherwise. The author begins with an extended discussion about the severity of the extinction, its duration, the various organisms affected, and likely causes. His approach is based first on a description of the evidence, and then on an analysis of the hypotheses. He ends each chapter with a summary and his own conclusions, helpful after such complete documentation of competing ideas. The objectivity of the book is enhanced by the author's willingness to even disagree with his own previous work, and he urges the reader to keep a pencil handy to update the data he presents. Anyone interested in extinctions should have this book. General; undergraduate through professionals.—*M. A. Wilson, College of Wooster*

OAB-1489   QE471   96-139242 MARC
Miall, Andrew D. **The geology of fluvial deposits: sedimentary facies, basin analysis, and petroleum geology.** Springer, 1996. 582p bibl indexes afp ISBN 3-540-59186-9, $69.00

A rapid and overwhelming flood of literature on a topic calls for a pause, reflection, and a synthesis of the current state of knowledge on that topic. Such is this welcome book on the geology of river systems, written and compiled masterfully by an expert of international renown. All geological aspects of fluvial systems are incorporated in this encyclopedic volume. Major subjects include historical development, concepts of scale, architectural analysis and methods, lithofacies, fluvial styles and models, autogenic sedimentary controls, regional fluvial stratigraphy, tectonic controls, climatic influence, sequence stratigraphy, and oil and gas in fluvial rocks, with case studies. One of the most valuable attributes of this book is the exceptional high quality of the hundreds of illustrations—photos, maps, charts, drawings, and especially the three-dimensional interpretations. Captions are full and exceptionally explanatory. References cited number close to 1400! Professionals and advanced students of petroleum geology, hydrogeology, and geology in general will find this volume an indispensable addition to their libraries—a wonderful source of data, references, and ideas. Upper-division undergraduates and above.—*T. L. T. Grose, Colorado School of Mines*

OAB-1490   Orig
Middleton, Nick. **The global casino: an introduction to environmental issues.** E. Arnold/Halsted, 1995. 332p bibl index ISBN 0-470-23532-2 pbk, $26.95

Interest in environmental issues has certainly grown since Rachel Carson first published *Silent Spring* in the early 1960s. Today, countless books detailing environmental problems and their solutions abound. Since data on such things as population growth, food production, and fertilizer and pesticide utilization are continually being updated, the half-life of books dealing with environmental issues must, by necessity, be short. *Global Casino* represents the most recent information on what has become a rather standard subject. Included are 18 chapters on such familiar topics as deforestation, threatened species, waste management, energy production, and soil erosion. In addition, introductory chapters treat the physical and human environment, and there is a concluding chapter on conservation and sustainable development. Most tables and graphs reflect current information from the late 1980s and early 1990s, and numerous case studies provide specific examples that illustrate general statements. In all, an excellent book. General; lower-division undergraduate.—*F. T. Kuserk, Moravian College*

OAB-1491   QE391   92-33970 Orig
Natural zeolites, by G.V. Tsitsishvili et al.; tr. by I.B. Potashnikov; translation editor, P.A. Williams. E. Horwood, 1992. (Dist. by Prentice Hall) 295p index ISBN 0-13-612037-7, $85.00

Natural zeolites have exceptionally important commercial uses, both in industry and in agriculture. Consequently, much research has been done on the isolation, structure determination, and physical properties of naturally occurring zeolites. In contrast to Rudy W. Tschernich's recent detailed field guide to zeolite locations (*Zeolites of the World*, CH, Oct'92), *Natural Zeolites* concentrates on the theory and applications of the naturally occurring zeolites. In this excellent introductory work, mineralogy and structure, physical properties, and applications each occupy approximately a third of the book. There are many useful figures and photographs, references as recent as 1988 (remarkable for a translated book), and an acceptable subject index. The many references, placed at the ends of each of the five chapters, are listed in order of appearance; there is no alphabetical listing of authors. While Tschernich's guide tells you where to find naturally occuring zeolites, this book tells you what they are and what to do with them. The two books complement one another, but this volume should have a wider appeal due to its more fundamental approach. Highly recommended for industrial and nonindustrial chemistry, mineralogy, and geology libraries. Advanced undergraduates through professional.—*R. Rudman, Adelphi University*

OAB-1492   QE862   94-46225 CIP
Norell, Mark A. **Discovering dinosaurs in the Museum of Natural History**, by Mark A. Norell, Eugene S. Gaffney, and Lowell Dingus. Knopf, 1995. 204p index ISBN 0-679-43386-4, $35.00

The 1995 opening of the revamped American Museum of Natural History (AMNH) dinosaur exhibit halls prompted the publication of this book, but it also comes amid a more than decade-long flood of publications on these extinct animals. The authors, all associated with AMNH, are specialists in reptilian and/or dinosaurian paleontology and biology. Because the collection is huge and diversified and was assembled over more than a century, its history and study have been critical to our knowledge of dinosaurs. Since understanding dinosaurian relationships may be key to interpretation of their biology, there is a short introduction to the cladistic relationships of dinosaurs. Approximately 40 percent of the book covers the dinosaurs seen in the AMNH; information on the characteristics, discovery, and significant "tidbits" of their biology are provided. Nearly half the book is organized around 50 well-posed and controversial questions about dinosaurs and the authors are especially circumspect in their answers. Cross-referencing to other questions helps to integrate and expand the responses. A short section examines several sites from which dinosaur eggs and tracks have been obtained. Finally, five of the most productive localities in North America and Asia that produced the AMNH fossils are described. An excellent source; authoritative rather than authoritarian. Photographs of skeletons are superb. This is one dinosaur book that all libraries should have. General; undergraduate through professional.—*D. Bardack, University of Illinois at Chicago*

OAB-1493 QE742 94-3043 CIP
Poinar, George. **The quest for life in amber,** by George and Roberta Poinar. Addison-Wesley, 1994. 219p bibl index ISBN 0-201-62660-8, $25.00

The Quest is one of those books that educates the general reader about a scientific topic without requiring very much scientific background. Although educational, it is also highly entertaining and should be read for pleasure as much as for knowledge. Both George and Roberta Poinar (husband and wife) appear on the title page of this book, but it is written primarily from George's perspective and is loaded with anecdotal detail of his search for amber in all parts of the world, including a few dangerous encounters. The Poinars have spent more than 20 years together working on amber samples, identifying and analyzing the life forms embedded in them and, in later years, successfully extracting ancient DNA from preserved tissue. An article about this achievement was published in *Science* in 1982 and strongly influenced Michael Crichton in writing his novel *Jurassic Park* (1990), later made into a very popular movie. Recommended. General; lower-division undergraduate.—*C. W. Dimmick, Central Connecticut State University*

OAB-1494 QE692 93-44535 CIP
Prothero, Donald R. **The Eocene-Oligocene transition: paradise lost.** Columbia, 1994. 291p bibl index afp ISBN 0-231-08090-5, $65.00; ISBN 0-231-08091-3 pbk, $24.00

The Eocene and Oligocene are two successive epochs (intervals of earth history) lasting from roughly 55 to 25 million years ago, nearly half the time since the extinction of the dinosaurs. The boundary between them is marked by a time of major climatic disruption, when the generally warm (paradisiacal) environments of the Eocene gave way to the colder Oligocene. This interval saw extinctions of a variety of animals and plants, both terrestrial and aquatic. In this engagingly written essay-style book, Prothero tells the story of the changing pattern of fauna and flora, explains the geological reasons for the change, and introduces the scientists who traced out the riddles. This book is essentially a popularization of *Eocene-Oligocene Climatic and Biotic Evolution*, ed. by Prothero and William A. Berggren (CH, Apr'93). Prothero is an expert on fossil mammals, their environments, and the means to date them, but he has enlarged that perspective to include discussions of such topics as extinctions in general, especially those potentially caused by asteroid impacts; means of reconstructing climate from the shape of leaves or the oxygen isotopic content of deep-sea microshells; and the history of the recovery of mammalian and other fossils. Well suited as a case study in paleontology courses or to introduce the modern study of evolution. Highly recommended. General, undergraduate; graduate.—*E. Delson, Herbert H. Lehman College, CUNY*

OAB-1495 QE48 96-34516 CIP
Ritter, Michael E. **Earth online: an Internet guide for Earth science.** Wadsworth Publishing, 1997. 264p bibl index afp ISBN 0-534-51707-2 pbk, $12.00

Earth Online is a marvelous guide to Internet use. Despite its subtitle, it will have useful applications far beyond the earth sciences. Biologists, sociologists, economists, and other members of the academic community should have a look at it. Ritter takes the reader from "basics" to "web page" creation, and he offers very good explanations of Internet fundamentals through a well-written text, diagrams, and examples. Contents include chapters on definitions and navigation, Gopher and WWW use, electronic mail and bulletin boards, file transfers, and the use of Internet-specific software. The chapter on educational and professional uses of the Internet will be helpful to teachers and students alike. Each chapter ends with a chapter review and suggestions for applications. The reference section at the end of the book contains lists of Internet sites, a very useful Internet glossary, and a brief guide to hypertext markup language (HTML). Despite the rapid change inherent in the Internet, this book should retain its value as a teaching guide and reference for a considerable time. Even old hands are likely to benefit from it. All levels.—*E. J. Delaney, Northern Michigan University*

OAB-1496 QE366 91-42362 CIP
Schumann, Walter. **Minerals of the world.** Sterling, 1992. 224p index ISBN 0-8069-8570-4, $19.95

An absolute bargain. This small, ruggedly constructed field guide covers about 500 mineral species commonly found around the world. The first pages describe the various characteristics by which minerals are classified. This, together with a good glossary, serves as an introduction to beginners and a refresher to the more advanced. Almost half the book is a series of hundreds of magnificent color photographs of representative specimens, printed on high-quality paper. The other half is a series of systematic descriptions of the specific characteristics of each mineral, accompanied by line drawings of the crystal forms of the minerals. Together, these all allow for the identification of most of the many minerals a field collector is apt to find. This book would also be an excellent explanatory guide to bring on trips to museum collections. However, its visual orientation makes the book enjoyable by anyone who has an eye for the exquisite beauty of natural materials. Highly recommended to all libraries, and is, indeed, a must.—*C. J. Casella, Northern Illinois University*

OAB-1497 QE39x Orig
Seibold, E. **The sea floor: an introduction to marine geology,** by E. Seibold and W.H. Berger. 3rd ed. Springer, 1996. 356p bibl indexes afp ISBN 3-540-60191-0, $54.50

Seibold and Berger's well-referenced and well-written book treats all aspects of the sea floor and the history of the world's oceans. A wide range of subjects are included, from chapter 1, "Origin and Morphology of Ocean Basins," to chapter 9, "Paleoceanography—The Deep-Sea Record." The tenth and final chapter, "Resources from the Ocean Floor," also includes a discussion of waste disposal and pollution. As the book covers virtually all aspects of marine geology, it includes elements of geophysics, geochemistry, sedimentology, stratigraphy, paleontology, and geochronology. An excellent resource for undergraduates studying marine geology; however, the interested public will benefit from reading this comprehensive and well-illustrated treatise. Series of indexes, including an index of geographic names and a thorough subject index. All levels.—*J. T. Andrews, University of Colorado at Boulder*

OAB-1498 QE364 92-20179 CIP
The Stability of minerals, ed. by Geoffrey D. Price and Nancy L. Ross. Chapman & Hall, 1992. 368p index (Mineralogical society series, 3) ISBN 0-412-44150-0, $149.95

A compilation of papers from a two-day meeting in 1989 at University College London, England, organized to review and address the problems of mineral stability. Although all aspects of this diverse subject cannot be covered within the framework of such a format, the nine very well qualified contributors have provided an excellent overview of many important topics of mineral behavior and crystal chemistry. Structural stability of minerals is evaluated on both an atomic and quantum mechanical basis. Several mineral systems are assessed thermodynamically, and abundant thermodynamic and thermochemical data are presented for a number of minerals and mineral assemblages. Timing of this book is particularly appropriate, considering the importance of the topic to solid state chemists and physicists as well as to mineralogists and crystallographers. The volume is well illustrated, and has reference lists at the end of each topic section. An excellent source that will be useful to advanced science students as well as geological and solid state scientists.—*M. E. McCallum, Colorado State University*

OAB-1499 Aust. CIP
Sutherland, Lin. **The volcanic Earth: volcanoes and plate tectonics past, present & future.** UNSW Press, 1995. (Dist. by International Specialized Book Services) 248p bibl index ISBN 0-86840-071-8, $49.95

Outstanding books on volcanoes have appeared during the last 15 years. This most recent one by Sutherland deals with volcanoes in the Australian and southwestern Pacific region; however, it is enormously instructive and applicable to all other volcanic regions of the world and, hence, has value to all readers on an international scale. Subject coverage is comprehensive, skillfully striking a rich balance among levels of presentation for children, general readers, and advanced students and professionals. Descriptions of volcanoes, eruptive styles and dynamics, history, occurrences, associated commodities of use to humans including gemstones, volcanic impact on human history, present time, future predictions, and guides to volcanic field trips in Australia—to name some major topics addressed—characterize this remarkable book. Extensive maps loaded with essential volcanic information from Australia and New Zealand reinforce the text. An excellent select bibliography grades the literature for beginning to advanced readers. But the most attractive, useful, and outstanding features are the maps and photos of natural volcanic phenomena and products at all scales, interpretive drawings—all obviously selected with great care and understanding of the subject. Browsers or readers at any level will learn and will be captivated.—*T. L. T. Grose, Colorado School of Mines*

OAB-1500   QE33   91-27970 CIP
Turcotte, Donald L. **Fractals and chaos in geology and geophysics.** Cambridge, 1992. 221p bibl index ISBN 0-521-41270-6, $54.95

Turcotte's excellent introductory work is aimed at scientists in the wide spectrum of the earth sciences. It is well written and remarkably unencumbered by either jargon or abstruse mathematics. The first eight chapters stress fractals and cover scale invariance, fractal sets, problems of fragmentation, fractals in seismicity and tectonics, estimation of mineral (and petroleum) deposit grade and tonnage, fractal clustering, self-affine fractals, and geomorphological analyses. All concepts are developed with good examples. Chapters 9 through 15 study chaos; coverage includes dynamical systems, logistic maps, slider-block models, the Lorenz equations, mantle convection, and the Rikitake dynamo. These complex subjects are clearly explained and the applications of chaotic theory to problems of turbulence are stressed. The volume concludes with chapters on renormalization group methods and self-organized criticality, and a final chapter ponders the long-term significance of fractals and chaos in explaining the characteristics of the Earth. The figures are clear, the mathematics simple, and the references give the opportunity to further delve into these fascinating subjects. An excellent starter book. Advanced undergraduate through professional.—*J. M. Sharp Jr., University of Texas at Austin*

OAB-1501   GB5014   96-37794 CIP
Zebrowski, Ernest. **Perils of a restless planet: scientific perspectives on natural disasters.** Cambridge, 1997. 306p index ISBN 0-521-57374-2, $24.95

Perils is physicist Zebrowski's personal exploration of the major unpredictable and violent manifestations of nature that have wrought death and destruction throughout human history. He describes earthquakes, tsunamis, volcanic eruptions, floods, hurricanes, and asteroid impacts. There is a fascinating section on epidemics, ranging from the Plague of Justinian (CE 540) to AIDS, the microbe's development of resistance to antibiotics, and the growing future threat of pandemic in a world with a rapidly expanding human population. The author, displaying a rare combination of literary skill, wit, and new and provocative insights into the progress and nature of science, has produced a masterpiece that should be obligatory reading for all university students and thinking adults. The relationship between the development of science from Pythagoras to Newton, Einstein, and the postmodern theory of chaos, and explanations of major historic and recent natural tragedies make for not only the gripping reading experience of a first-class mystery novel, but also provide a compelling account of the status of the species *Homo Sapiens* on the threshold of a new and very uncertain millennium. All levels.—*J. D. Ives, Carleton University*

■ Engineering

OAB-1502   TA15   95-43653 CIP
Billington, David P. **The innovators: the engineering pioneers who made America modern.** Wiley, 1996. 245p bibl index afp ISBN 0-471-14026-0, $24.95

Woven into this delightful history of America's 19th-century engineering geniuses are the four essentials of engineering in a modern industrial society: structures, machines, networks, and processes. The names are famous—Fulton, Morse, Edison—and the approach involves an informative analysis of the early blast furnaces, steamboats, railroads, textile looms, power grids, engines, bridges, turbines, the telegraph, and lighting systems. The insertion of a few of the key engineering formulas significantly enhances one's appreciation of these innovators. Numerous pictures, drawings, and sidebar explanations combine with an abundance of references, notes, and a complete index to bring special insight on engineering to the general reader. All levels.—*F. Potter, University of California, Irvine*

OAB-1503   TA15   92-30615 MARC
The Builders: marvels of engineering, prep. by the Book Division, National Geographic Society. National Geographic Society, 1992. 288p index ISBN 0-87044-836-6, $35.20

The Builders presents, in a very unique way, some of the most ambitious projects created by civil engineers. Some of the structures discussed in this easy-to-read book include the Pan American Highway, the Trans-Alaska Pipeline, the George Washington Bridge, the Golden Gate Bridge, the Panama Canal, the Leaning Tower of Pisa, the Eiffel Tower, the CN Tower, the Channel Tunnel, and others. The book is divided into several sections, including roads, canals, pipelines, bridges, towers, skyscrapers, sports arenas, domes, and many other interesting civil engineering topics. Each section contains examples, with graphs and pictures, related to these topics. One of the most interesting of reading materials for any engineer, and an excellent source of references. Recommended for the libraries of all engineering schools.—*S. N. Amirkhanian, Clemson University*

OAB-1504   TA151   94-45572 CIP
The Civil engineering handbook, ed. by W.F. Chen. CRC Press, 1995. 2,609p bibl index afp ISBN 0-8493-8953-4, $99.95

This handbook contains sections on the eight traditional areas of civil engineering: construction, environmental, geotechnical, hydraulic, materials, structural, surveying, and transportation. Each section treats many specific topics related to the area, has a separate contents listing, defines terms, and contains an extensive list of references. There are many useful tables placed in a separate section at the end of the volume. This handbook is an excellent initial reference for finding and learning material in these eight areas of civil engineering. A work written with the practitioner in mind, it should be purchased as a reference book for every engineering school's library. Upper-division undergraduate through professional; two-year technical program students.—*H. I. Epstein, University of Connecticut*

OAB-1505   TK9014   93-42697 CIP
Crowley-Milling, Michael C. **John Bertram Adams: engineer extraordinary: a tribute.** Gordon & Breach, 1993. 194p index ISBN 2-88124-875-6, $48.00; ISBN 2-88124-876-4 pbk, $28.00

Written by Adams's long-time close friend about an extraordinary man with a bare minimum of formal education, mostly self-taught, who went on to become very prominent in the world's largest high-energy physics research facility in Europe. Crowley-Milling traces the life of this remarkable man, from his roots in England, his early life, his early achievements in wartime radar research and his leadership in post-WW II research at Harwell, to the establishment of the first European research center, CERN, and the immediate construction of the first 600 MeV synchro-cyclotron. Adams's administrative skills are superbly illustrated by the author with personal notes, supplemented with those of Adams's wife and close friends. The success of CERN owes a great deal to the genius of this man: Adams sought the right people for the success of this research center that eventually built the world's largest high-energy particle accelerator. The efficient management and operation of CERN are the fruits of Adams's many skills. Excellent illustrations; two excellent short appendixes on accelerators and particle physics. Highly recommended. All levels.—*H. Shwe, East Stroudsburg University of Pennsylvania*

OAB-1506   TA151   95-32292 CIP
The Engineering handbook, ed. by Richard C. Dorf. CRC Press/IEEE Press, 1996. 2,298p bibl indexes afp ISBN 0-8493-8344-7, $99.95

This handbook will become an important addition to the library of practicing, academic, and student engineers. It is well organized with 30 sections and 211 subsections, a clear table of contents, excellent cross-referencing, and useful appendixes and indexes. Most importantly, it will guide readers into new areas and, on occasion, specialists will find it an efficient way to refresh their memories. Although it contains a vast amount of information, it would be too much to expect that everything a reader wishes to know could be contained in o: e single volume (cf. *Kirk-Othmer Encyclopedia of Chemical Technology*, 4th ed., 1991- , 27 volumes projected and $295 per volume; v.1, 2, 4, CH, Mar'93; v.12, CH, Apr'95). This reviewer would hope that future editions of this excellent handbook will include a section on areas where traditional engineering disciplines and biology are both pertinent. This, the reviewer believes, would go well beyond the fashionable area referred to as "biotechnology." The engineering community owes thanks to the publisher, whose venerable *Handbook of Chemistry and Physics* (71st ed., CH, Sep'91; 75th ed., Mar'95) has long graced the shelves of many engineers, for this excellent reference work that belongs in all engineering libraries as well as on the shelves of most engineers. It is good value for the money. Upper-division undergraduate through professional.—*M. Levinson, University of Washington*

OAB-1507   TP184   94-45872 CIP
Hanna, Owen T. **Computational methods in chemical engineering,** by Owen T. Hanna and Orville C. Sandall. Prentice Hall PTR, 1995. 456p bibl index disk (IBM-PC) ISBN 0-13-307398-X, $65.00

Hanna and Sandall's excellent reference source for the chemical engineer is quite user-friendly, well laid out, and supported by computer software. The topics they cover, too numerous to mention, include solution of differential equations, matrix equations, expansions, series, least squares and regression analyses, integrals, and various numerical methods. The software is provided in both FORTRAN 77 and True BASIC. It is tempting to compare the software with commercial software available elsewhere; however, commercial packages seldom describe the methods and applications of the solutions. The connection between theory, application, and computer solution is a major strength of the book. The authors state that knowledge of calculus is sufficient to use this book, but this may not be true with respect to the chapter on linear algebra. Virtually all of the examples are processes familiar to the chemical engineer, and each chapter contains several unsolved practice problems. Although intended as an undergraduate text, the usually crowded chemical engineering curriculum may make it more appropriate as a resource. Very useful to undergraduates, graduate students, faculty, and practicing professionals.—*K. I. Mumme, University of Maine*

OAB-1508   T58   94-46915 CIP
Lesurf, J.C.G. **Information and measurement.** IOP (Institute of Physics), 1995. 243p index ISBN 0-7503-0308-5, $99.00

According to the preface, Lesurf wanted to make the book different from others by integrating the mathematical concepts of information theory, the physics of instrumentation and measurement techniques, and information technology engineering into one undergraduate-level introduction giving a balanced picture of

how the three fit together. He has superbly achieved his goal. The continuing example of how information is encoded in and recovered from an audio CD player is a very happy choice for illustrating all these aspects of the subject. The concise chapters have clear explanations, examples, and diagrams. The careful summaries at the end of each chapter will help readers to monitor their understanding and refresh what has been learned, or to conveniently identify what has been missed and needs to be reviewed. The numerical problems with solutions, and programs in BASIC and C in the appendix, are additional features of value. Recommended as a *must* for the libraries of all institutions where there are undergraduate courses in information theory, computer science, computer engineering, or information technology. Undergraduate through professional; two-year technical program students.—*R. Bharath, Northern Michigan University*

OAB-1509   TS183   96-149120 MARC
Waters, T.F. **Fundamentals of manufacturing for engineers.** UCL Press, 1996. 321p bibl index ISBN 1-85728-338-4 pbk, $34.95

Waters writes with authority from both industrial and teaching experience. The book is refreshingly short, with about 300 very worthwhile figures. The author has immensely succeeded in his goal of writing a book for beginners, "to present the basic essentials for manufacturing that all engineering students should grasp by the time they begin their industrial career." This paperback costs less than $35.00, a welcome contrast to most books in this field. The book is concise but not at the cost of essentials. Preparation in mathematics for the reader is minimal. There are not many chapter-end numerical problems, a common trend; such problems may serve some pedagogical purpose but are not essential in the real life of most manufacturing engineers—a merit of the book. Recommended for lower-division undergraduates and two-year technical program students in a first course in manufacturing, and also as an excellent guide for self-study by manufacturing engineers.—*K. Srinagesh, University of Massachusetts Dartmouth*

■ Electrical

OAB-1510   TK140   94-27984 CIP
Baldwin, Neil. **Edison: inventing the century.** Hyperion, NY, 1995. 531p index ISBN 0-7868-6041-3, $27.95

This richly textured biography of an American icon provides a picture of Edison that both humanizes him and explains the basis for his larger-than-life image, which remains engraved on our national psyche. We learn of his forbears as well as his early life, both as a boy and as a young man. But nothing ever quite explains the emergence of singular genius so that readers will form their own explanations of the rise of the greatest of American inventors just after the Civil War. He claimed, or at least tried to claim, that he was only a practical man who worked mostly on his own. In fact, Edison's greatest invention probably was the industrial research and development laboratory employing a staff of highly competent specialists. Moreover, as Charles Proteus Steinmetz, a genius in his own right, shrewdly observed before the turn of the century, although Edison had never gone to college, he knew more theory than many college-educated persons. Using the best recent Edison scholarship, Baldwin has written an unusually good popular study of the man and his times that displays the inevitable warts as well as the accomplishments in context. More than a hundred pages of notes for readers inclined to scholarship. A book well worth reading. General; undergraduate; two-year technical program students.—*M. Levinson, University of Washington*

OAB-1511   TK5105   94-10084 CIP
Boisseau, M. **High-speed networks,** by M. Boisseau, M. Demange, and J.-M. Munier. Wiley, 1995 (c1994). 192p bibl index ISBN 0-471-95109-9 pbk, $34.95

Boisseau and colleagues have prepared an extremely timely work on high

Choice's Outstanding Academic Books

speed networks, particularly their transmission protocols. With the explosion of telecommunications taking place throughout the world, it is a welcome addition to the materials available. It presents in clear terms all the ideas playing important roles in this rapidly evolving field and, with the aid of many excellent diagrams, describes the current and evolving standards and various transmission media. Coverage ranges from local area (LAN) to wide area (WAN) networks, and topics include circuit- and packet-switched as well as frame and cell (ATM) relay networks. Descriptions are clear and practical. An excellent addition to libraries of institutions offering computer science and engineering degrees. Upper-division undergraduate through professional.—*B. Krinsky, California State University, Dominguez Hills*

OAB-1512   Orig
E Source technology atlas series: v.1: Lighting; v.2: Commercial space cooling and air handling; v.3: Space heating; v.4: Drivepower; v.5: Residential appliances, [ed. by Jeanne Travisono]. E Source, Inc., 1033 Walnut St., Boulder, CO 80302-5114, 1996 (c1993-1996). 5v. bibl indexes CD-ROM (Windows and Macintosh), pbk $950.00 set; 5v. pbk $750.00; CD-ROM $750.00

For those interested in any and all facets of the current state of energy technology and energy efficiency, look no further; this collection of oversized volumes covers the subject impressively in highly readable fashion. It will be easily comprehended by readers at all levels, and yet remain highly respected and useful to professionals and general practitioners in the energy field. Though the price may seem impressive, the information collected and presented here has no peer—either in terms of completeness of detail or clarity of presentation. The illustrations are wonderfully drawn and add to, or explain, the text beautifully. And though there are multiple authors and contributors (different groups for each of the five volumes), the editors have managed to draw this immense amount of information into a seamless and highly understandable work. The entire undertaking is so well prepared that neophytes, students at all levels, and energy experts will find valuable information, clearly presented. In addition, numerous references are provided so that readers can have more detailed information if desired. In sum, there is no truly comparable work in this area, and it is doubly impressive that such a singular work is so outstandingly excellent. Perhaps that is to be expected, for this compendium was prepared in association with the Rocky Mountain Institute, headed by Amory Lovins, an outstanding expert and highly articulate expositor on energy technology. A CD-ROM is provided so that readers can readily research and retrieve data via computer. Truly a "must have" for any good library. All levels.—*L. Crane, formerly, University of Maryland*

OAB-1513   TK145   92-35356 CIP
The Electrical engineering handbook, ed. by Richard C. Dorf. CRC Press, 1993. 2,661p indexes afp ISBN 0-8493-0185-8, $89.95

An excellent and useful reference for practicing engineers, students, and teachers in electrical engineering. Its 12 sections cover all the major branches of electrical engineering, including circuits, signals, electromagnetic fields, energy systems, communications, computers, and biomedical fields. Data on physical constants for materials, symbols, and mathematical formulas are provided at the end. There are several indexes that make it easy to look up information on any topic. Each section deals with several major topics that are each authored by a well-known expert in that field. There is a uniform style of presentation in every section, in the following order: an important device photo, historical background, concepts and applications, definition of terms, and references. A very large group of well-known professionals from many universities and industrial organizations have contributed to this up-to-date, well-organized handbook that presents each subject with sufficient depth and clarity. Community college through professional.—*K. K. Surti, University of New Haven*

OAB-1514   Orig
Electrical resistivity handbook, ed. by G.T. Dyos and T. Farrell. P. Peregrinus Ltd./IEE, IEEE Service Center, 445 Hoes Lane, Piscataway, NJ

08855, 1992. 735p (IEE materials and devices series, 10) ISBN 0-86341-266-1, $175.00

This British import provides a comprehensive compilation of experimental data, in graphical form, of electrical resistivity versus temperature for a wide range of solid materials. These include pure metals, metallic alloys (both dilute and concentrated), and semiconductors (both pure and with impurities). Alphabetically arranged resistivity-temperature graphs occupy the major portion (92%) of the work, beginning with a theoretical introduction to resistivity and electrical conduction in solids and the practical techniques used to determine temperature variation of resistivity, followed by an explanation of the graphs and how to use them. An alphabetical index of materials and a list of 344 international references to pertinent texts and periodical research literature are included. Highly recommended for both graduate and advanced technical/industrial libraries serving scientists and engineers.—*I. L. Kosow, emeritus, City University of New York*

OAB-1515   Orig
Engen, Glenn F. **Microwave circuit theory and foundations of microwave metrology.** P. Peregrinus Ltd./IEE, IEEE Service Center, 445 Hoes Lane, Piscataway, NJ 08855, 1992. 240p index (IEE electrical measurement series, 9) ISBN 0-86341-287-4, $49.00

A concise but definitive British import divided into two major parts: microwave theory (Chapters 1-9) and microwave measurement (Chapters 10-21). The first part (primarily Chapter 2, foundations of microwave circuit theory) is intended as a simplified outline (vis-à-vis conventional low frequency theory). The second part describes the different basic methods designed to measure the various parameters associated with the microwave model developed in the first part. The author freely admits that some of the measurement methods described are now "obsolete" with the advent of the automated network analyzer (Chapter 16). But he justifies the inclusion of basic measurement methods because they enhance understanding of the microwave circuit model and "operation of other measurement techniques." The work is somewhat limited by lack of worked examples and end-of-chapter problems; nor is there a bibliography for further reading. But as a concise summary, it is a refreshing and timely addition. Highly recommended. Advanced undergraduate through professional.—*I. L. Kosow, emeritus, City University of New York*

OAB-1516   TK7868   94-32727 CIP
Lenk, John D. **Simplified design of switching power supplies.** Butterworth-Heinemann, 1995. 224p index afp ISBN 0-7506-9507-2, $29.95

Lenk's how-to book is designed for beginners building switching power supplies. Over half of it is devoted to descriptions of how to build regulated, constant voltage supplies using integrated circuits available from several manufacturers. The 11 examples given include detailed circuit diagrams and methods for choosing external components to meet given specifications. Although this information is available from the manufacturers, Lenk compiles it into a single convenient source and adds many practical hints. Early chapters describe the basic theory of switching regulators, the use of heat sinks, and troubleshooting the supplies. Lenk, a prolific writer on the practical aspects of electrical engineering, has more than 35 books in print. A similar book is Irving M. Gottlieb's *Power Supplies, Switching Regulators, Inverters, and Converters* (2nd ed., 1994; 1st ed., CH, Oct'84). A more theoretical treatment that nevertheless retains the practical examples is Otmar Kilgenstein's *Switched-Mode Power Supplies in Practice* (1989). Lenk has written an excellent book for undergraduates, bridging the gap between classroom theory and the practical knowledge required to build a working power supply. General; undergraduate; two-year technical program students.—*L. J. Bohmann, Michigan Technological University*

OAB-1517   TK7867   93-51084 CIP
Newby, Bruce. **Electronic signal conditioning.** Butterworth-Heinemann, 1994. 304p index ISBN 0-7506-1844-2 pbk, $29.95

Newby intends his book for undergraduate electronics engineering students taking courses in instrumentation, control, signal conditioning, and/or operational amplifiers. He is coauthor, with G.B. Clayton, of *Operational Amplifiers* (3rd ed., 1992). Chapters treat dc and ac bridges; operational amplifiers; basic linear scaling circuits; integrators and differentiators; switching and waveform generation; analog processing applications; noise; analog signal filters; modulation and demodulation; analog and digital conversions; and digital conditioning techniques. Each chapter concludes with relevant exercises for student solution, although few worked examples are provided in the body of the text. Appended are the Texas Instruments operational amplifier and logarithmic amplifier data sheets and answers to exercises. This authoritative, informative, well-written, and extremely compact work is highly recommended for libraries serving engineering technology and/or undergraduate engineering college students as well as practicing professionals and two-year technical program students.—*I. L. Kosow, emeritus, City University of New York*

OAB-1518   TK5103   94-22900 CIP
Pahlavan, Kaveh. **Wireless information networks,** by Kaveh Pahlavan and Allen H. Levesque. Wiley-Interscience, 1995. 572p bibl index afp ISBN 0-471-10607-0, $74.95

The telecommunications industry is currently evolving from wired to wireless ("tetherless") networks, providing a wide variety of new products, systems, and services. The 21st century will undoubtedly witness the widespread use of wireless information networks integrating voice, data, and even video signals (including new spectrally efficient digital cellular mobile radio, personal communication services, wireless local area networks, alpha numeric message paging, mobile data services, and spread-spectrum cordless telephones). Pahlavan and Levesque present, from a systems perspective, all the major components of wireless technology necessary to design such systems, including standards and descriptions of wireless systems and products, detailed and extensive discussions of measurement and modeling of radio and optical wave propagation (with special emphasis on indoor communication channels), wireless transmission and signal processing techniques, wireless multiple access techniques, network architecture issues, and an overview of major wireless services and commercial products currently available. Each chapter concludes with a section of questions to provide a check on basic issues discussed, as well as traditional problem sets. An excellent work, well referenced and illustrated. Upper-division undergraduate through professional.—*F. A. Cassara, Polytechnic University*

OAB-1519   TK7876   92-16863 CIP
Scott, Allan W. **Understanding microwaves.** Wiley-Interscience, 1993. 545p index afp ISBN 0-471-57567-4, $54.95

Scott presents clearly and understandably the range of topics encompassing the entire field of microwaves. He introduces microwave terminology, details of devices, and their integration into systems encountered in communications, navigation, and radar. Part 1 (five chapters) overviews microwave systems and components, electromagnetic fields, transmission lines, power, loss, s-parameters, Smith charting, and matching. Part 2 (eight chapters) provides a clear description of the whole range of microwave devices, their theory, operation, and construction. Some of the devices are waveguides and striplines, semiconductor devices, oscillators, antennas, and so forth. Part 3 (six chapters) treats microwave systems, including satellite communications, radar, electronic warfare, and navigation systems. The book is profusely illustrated with diagrams, photographs, graphs, and other data. Each chapter ends with a bibliography and exercises for self testing, with answers to exercises included. An excellent book for obtaining an overview or gaining broad knowledge of microwave theory and practice. Advanced undergraduates; professional.—*K. K. Surti, University of New Haven*

OAB-1520   TA340   93-5851 CIP
Vardeman, Stephen B. **Statistics for engineering problem solving.** PWS Publishing, 1994. 811p index ISBN 0-534-92871-4, $59.95

An interesting, useful, and well-written book with a practical, rather than

theoretical, orientation. An appealing feature is the introduction of statistical concepts for engineering problems exclusively through examples involving real data and/or real scenarios. No formal background in statistics is required of the reader. There are 11 chapters in all, of which the first three are on data collection and descriptive statistics. Other chapters deal with fitting curves and surfaces by the principle of least squares; material on random variables and their distributions and the Central Limit Theorem; statistical inferences concerning means, proportions, and variances for one and two populations; analysis of variance and Shewhart Control Charts; inferences concerning statistical designs with factorial structure; inference techniques concerning curves and surfaces fitted to a set of data by the principle of least squares; and fractional factorial designs, latin squares, and other orthogonal designs. The last chapter discusses a real industrial case study undertaken at the Dow Chemical Company on the effectiveness of various statistical tools. Useful index; chapter exercises; numerous statistical tables; appendixes. A very suitable and appealing book for all interested in the applications of statistical methodology for solving engineering problems. Highly recommended. Advanced undergraduate through faculty.—*D. V. Chopra, Wichita State University*

■ Environmental

OAB-1521   TD791   92-23977 CIP
Alexander, Judd H. **In defense of garbage.** Praeger, 1993. 239p bibl index afp ISBN 0-275-93627-9, $22.95

A second book of monumental proportions published in a year's time "in defense of garbage"; the first, William Rathje's widely acclaimed *Rubbish* (CH, Feb'93). Both now serve to raise individual and collective societal and scientific consciousness to garbage, as an expression of who we are (or were) and what we do (or did), as an article of waste to be disposed of, or as a resource to be recovered and recycled. Each book in its own way is outstanding—Rathje's in a somewhat more popular and journalistic style, Alexander's in a more traditional academic format. They complement each other and both are eminently readable, entertaining, and very important statements about what garbage is, why it is important, who should care about it, and what is likely to happen in profligate societies (such as the Western nations of the world, particularly the US). The 13 fact-filled chapters begin with a few pages of historical perspective. Then Alexander's industrial and academic experience together with his sprightly literary style informs, educates, and instructs the reader on the nature of waste, the disposal problem, the value of garbage, the impact of packaging in a throw-away society, the benefits of source reduction, the promise and problems of reclaiming and recycling, the illusion of simple solutions based on biodegradability, the politics of garbage, and a host of other issues. But surprise, surprise! All is not lost. As did Rathje, Alexander sounds an optimistic note. Complete and accessible bibliography; essentially flawless editing. The only other thing one could ask for is an affordable price, and the publisher has given that. All levels.—*L. W. Fine, Columbia University*

OAB-1522   TD883   96-27515 MARC
Baumbach, Günter. **Air quality control: formation and sources, dispersion, characteristics and impact of air pollutants: measuring methods, techniques for reduction of emissions and regulations for air quality control,** by Günter Baumbach with K. Baumann et al. Springer, 1996. 490p bibl index afp ISBN 3-540-57992-3, $99.95

Air quality is a problem of international concern, not only because most of the developed countries of the world use technologies that produce similar pollutants but also because the resulting emissions can readily cross national boundaries to become a problem for neighboring countries. Because Baumbach wrote for German students, the original text has been revised, adding a number of references to situations and regulations in the US. As a result, the book offers an unusual international perspective in addition to being an excellent reference for readers in this country. The translation is very readable; the selection of topics is thorough and the presentation excellent. A fine book especially useful for practitioners and a good source of information for students with some scientific background. Strongly recommended. Upper-division undergraduates through professionals.—*H. E. Pence, SUNY College at Oneonta*

OAB-1523 TD899 92-12251 CIP
Dorfman, Mark H. **Environmental dividends: cutting more chemical wastes,** by Mark H. Dorfman, Warren R. Muir, and Catherine G. Miller. INFORM, 1992. 271p bibl index ISBN 0-918780-50-0 pbk, $75.00

A sequel to INFORM's 1985 report on the tenth anniversary of their initial study, *Cutting Chemical Wastes* (1982). Whereas their first report focused on disposal, this report focuses on source reduction; the optimistic conclusion is that great progress has been made. Reading the book's list of advances in federal and state legislation and the reports on 29 chemical companies, one has to agree with the conclusions, although clearly, this is only the tip of the iceberg; the companies studied are the biggest, most visible, and most likely to be squeaky clean or as close to that state as necessary. The first part of the book (two chapters) covers the background and nature of the study, including the economic climate, methodology, and scope, and findings and conclusions. The second part reports on the 29 companies. Reports on Merck and Monsanto are typical, ranging up to ten pages and covering products and operations, environmental policies, internal methods of materials data collection (where insufficient or incomplete data were offered by the company, INFORM acquired data supplied to government agencies to fill in the blanks), and source reduction activities. An easily accessible compendium of useful information and data of the most important kind by a group whose work has been made all the more credible by their success at winning the confidence and cooperation of the members of their target group. Appendixes include a glossary of about 50 key terms and a manageable list of key references. A report that should be part of every industrial chemical library, every college and university library, and in every public library.—*L. W. Fine, Columbia University*

OAB-1524 TJ808 92-13963 CIP
Golob, Richard. **The almanac of renewable energy,** by Richard Golob and Eric Brus. H. Holt, 1993. 348p bibl index afp ISBN 0-8050-1948-0, $50.00

A short primer on the renewable energy situation worldwide. Ten major topics are covered in 227 pages; an appendix has an extensive set of more than 50 tables that condenses data on everything from energy intensities of passenger modes (by BTU per passenger mile—965 BTU/mile for intercity buses versus 12,000 BTU/mile for general aviation) to operational tidal power projects and potential tidal power sites (operational: 240 megawatt plant at La Rance, France versus potential: 25,000 megawatt plant in Okhotsk, Russia). Chapters include energy from hydroelectric, biomass, geothermal, solar, photovoltaic, wind, and ocean sources, one on nonrenewable energy (read: conventional), plus one each on energy storage and energy efficiency. Although the treatments in general are brief, the book is not superficial. Facts and figures abound and a reader can discern easily from where each piece of data is derived. A second appendix lists dozens of books, periodicals, and organizations and agencies in the field. A major plus is the general readability of the book in contrast to the usual jumble of styles in omnibus collections. An excellent starting point for new students of energy problems or for the general reader with specific questions. General; community college through pre-professional.—*J. C. Comer, emeritus, Northern Illinois University*

OAB-1525 TD427 92-20758 CIP
Groundwater contamination and analysis at hazardous waste sites, ed. by Suzanne Lesage and Richard E. Jackson. Dekker, 1992. 548p index afp ISBN 0-8247-8720-X, $175.00

A discussion of the monitoring, analysis, and interpretation of groundwater contaminants from waste facilities. Topics include site investigation procedures, monitoring protocols, contaminant chemistry, fate and mobility of con-

taminants, and statistical interpretation. Hydrogeologic concepts and siting criteria are not specifically addressed, although several case studies are given. A significant feature is its detailed, practical account of how to optimize monitoring strategy by avoiding redundant or inconsequential procedures. This book is a compendium of work by an international group of 32 authors, with each chapter conceived as part of the whole. The result is well integrated, highly readable, and presented at a uniform technical level. Illustrations are clear and well integrated with the text. Highly recommended for undergraduate and graduate students and professionals in water quality and related fields.—*A. N. Palmer, SUNY College at Oneonta*

OAB-1526 TD191 92-35451 CIP
Holmes, Gwendolyn. **Handbook of environmental management and technology,** by Gwendolyn Holmes, Ben Ramnarine Singh, and Louis Theodore. Wiley-Interscience, 1993. 651p index afp ISBN 0-471-58584-X, $74.95

Primarily written for engineers, health officials, and managers, this comprehensive handbook reviews the history and significance of all major pollution problems and their solution. Regulatory approaches, monitoring, remediation, risk assessment, and pollution prevention are presented in nonmathematical language suitable for lawyers, reporters, and environmental advocates. Beginning with the premise that environmental regulations represent advances in the face of internationally ranked disasters, the authors then point to global warming and stratospheric ozone depletion as issues best dealt with through environmental diplomacy and international agreements. Subsequent sections of this book deal with air and water pollution; solid and hazardous waste management; miscellaneous environmental concerns; and management considerations. Appendixes list the national and state offices to call for assistance with hazardous waste control. Well organized and user friendly. Recommended for public and academic libraries. General; advanced undergraduate through professional.—*R. M. Ferguson, Eastern Connecticut State University*

OAB-1527 TD194 95-7979 MARC
Industrial pollution prevention handbook, [ed.] by Harry M. Freeman. McGraw-Hill, 1995. 935p bibl index afp ISBN 0-07-022148-0, $94.50

Pollution prevention, succinctly termed "P2," generally refers to any in-plant practice that reduces or eliminates waste prior to end-of-pipe recovery, treatment, and disposal. Drawing on the expertise of 78 contributing authors, Freeman has successfully blended elements of total quality management, sustainable industrial development, and pollution aversion into a valuable P2 handbook. From a logical and disarming "ounce of prevention" in chapter 1 to the listing of sources for P2 information in chapter 53, this essential guide blazes a trail through processes and technologies from design to implementation. The detailed table of contents allows managers and engineers rapid access to the full spectrum of current P2 strategies as well as access to the P2 techniques and experiences of 16 specific industries ranging from biotechnology to textiles and chemicals. Federal laws and executive orders directing P2 advances are clearly separated from voluntary programs, while key state-specific components are addressed in a separate chapter. The acid-free, 50 percent recycled paper used in this book serves as a final reminder of the move toward environmental sustainability. Upper-division undergraduate through professional.—*R. M. Ferguson, Eastern Connecticut State University*

OAB-1528 TC547 95-2355 CIP
Jackson, Donald C. **Building the ultimate dam: John S. Eastwood and the control of water in the West.** University Press of Kansas, 1995. 336p index afp ISBN 0-7006-0716-1, $45.00

This book is more than a historical treatise on dam design and construction in the early 20th-century American West. Jackson dexterously weaves the engineering technology of dam building with the professional career of Eastwood, a hydraulic engineer responsible for introducing a new multiple-arch dam design. The reader is made aware that capturing and redirecting water supplies for irrigation and power during the New Deal involved many economic, political, technical, and personal controversies. The influence of nongovernmental cooperative funding and private capital investment for many of these water development projects permeates the text and offers an insight into some of today's issues surrounding western rivers and water supplies. The book is profusely illustrated with photographs and drawings that allow the reader to quickly grasp the concepts of dam design. A well-written, enjoyable book containing extensive notes, references, and a glossary of terms used in dam design and construction. The historical orientation will appeal to a wide group of biographers, political scientists, and economists, while architects and engineers will value the technical aspects of dam design and construction. Strongly recommended for all readership levels.—*M. J. Zwolinski, University of Arizona*

OAB-1529   TD755   95-9492 CIP
Kadlec, Robert H. **Treatment wetlands,** by Robert H. Kadlec and Robert L. Knight. Lewis Publishers, 1996. 893p bibl index afp ISBN 0-87371-930-1, $79.95

This weighty tome (four pounds!) was written by two professionals—a chemical engineer and a wetland ecologist—who have extensive experience in creating treatment wetlands. As Kadlec and Knight indicate, the purpose of the book is "technology transfer," which in essence presents the state of the art in using or creating wetlands to treat or remove a diversity of pollutants, such as sewage effluent, suspended solids, and heavy metals. A total of 27 chapters are divided into six sections that discuss topics such as wetland structure and function, effects on water quality, planning and designing treatment wetlands, establishing and operating wetlands, and case histories. There is an amazing amount of basic background information about wetlands in addition to the applied aspects of using wetlands for pollution filtration. Figures and tables, including photographs, greatly enhance the volume; excellent references, more than 800 cited. An indispensable resource for both academic libraries and professional consultants. Upper-division undergraduates through professionals.—*W. A. Niering, Connecticut College*

OAB-1530   T174   93-48100 CIP
Learning from disaster: risk management after Bhopal, ed. by Sheila Jasanoff. Pennsylvania, 1994. 291p bibl index afp ISBN 0-8122-3250-X, $36.95; ISBN 0-8122-1532-X pbk, $17.95

The staggering and inadequately documented toll from Union Carbide's Bhopal disaster opened a fresh page in environmental regulation, both in the US and internationally. This collection is replete with examples of legal and fiscal settlements, not just from Bhopal but from many other case studies, some of which were settled expeditiously while others (e.g., asbestos litigation) have lingered in the courts for years. The book is not about Bhopal, but about the impact of Bhopal. The first third of the book deals in detail with that accident's impact on Union Carbide and on India. Wil Lepkowski suggests that the Bhopal disaster was responsible for the company's severe downsizing. Other studies are drawn from North America, Europe, and developing nations. Susan G. Hadden examines how in the US SARA Title III attempted to involve citizens in setting environmental policy. In both the US and India, she argues, the public has the right to toxics and pollution information. Marc Galanter demonstrates that victims of mass workplace tragedies receive less compensation on average than those killed individually, using as examples the "acute" Triangle Shirtwaist disaster and the "chronic" Hawk's Nest Disaster. An excellent resource. Undergraduate through faculty; technical/professional.—*J. Burger, Rutgers, The State University of New Jersey*

OAB-1531   TD195   96-25439 MARC
McCully, Patrick. **Silenced rivers: the ecology and politics of large dams.** Zed Books, 1996. 350p index ISBN 1-85649-435-7, $60.00

McCully presents a powerful, comprehensive argument against the construction of large dams and offers scientific, environmental, social, and eco-

nomic evidence, with case studies from every continent, that building large structures across rivers is not justified. The expected benefits of dam construction are identified, carefully analyzed, and refuted. A short history of rivers and damming from a global perspective is followed by chapters focusing on the environmental and human impacts of large dams, geologic and hydrologic problems, elusive benefits, irrigation efficiency, energy production, and economic realities. Alternative solutions to damming are offered. *Silenced Rivers* will precipitate discussion with proponents of dam building, particularly by international funding organizations trying to improve living standards in less-developed regions of the world. Well written and extensively documented, with substantial supporting data and reference notes. Strongly recommended for all readership levels, both the general public and all academic readers, as well as professionals in engineering, hydrology, watershed management, environmental science, and economics.—*M. J. Zwolinski, University of Arizona*

OAB-1532   TD794   92-18267 CIP
The McGraw-Hill recycling handbook, ed. by Herbert F. Lund. McGraw-Hill, 1993. various pagings index afp ISBN 0-07-039096-7, $84.50

This hefty handbook provides an in-depth look at all elements of recycling—process, policy, materials, education, economics, and case studies. Although written by and for practitioners, it is still quite useful as an authoritative, up-to-date reference to recycling for undergraduates—this reviewer has used it twice in the past week to answer undergraduate reference questions. It is arranged in 35 topical chapters filled with clear explanations, background, charts, graphs, photos, and drawings, and access is enhanced by a 65-page index. Appendixes include a good glossary, conversion tables, and sample worksheets. The writing is technical but not garbled by obtuse professional verbiage. *Recycling Sourcebook*, ed. by Thomas Cichonski and Karen Hill (CH, Apr'93), although superior as a directory, lacks the depth, graphics, and practitioner focus of the work under review. Highly recommended for all college and university libraries. Undergraduate through faculty.—*T. Link, Michigan State University Library*

OAB-1533   TD794   92-10099 CIP
Powelson, David R. **The recycler's manual for business, government, and the environmental community,** by David R. Powelson and Melinda A. Powelson. Van Nostrand Reinhold, 1992. 512p bibl index ISBN 0-442-01190-3, $64.95

In a volume described as the recycler's manual for business, government, and the environmental community, Powelson presents the essence of his long experience in the recycling industry. The use of an efficient organizational design makes the information in each of the 32 chapters (in 4 sections) particularly easy to access. Readers will never be bored with the fast-paced journalistic style. Here is what one needs to know, not what might be nice to know. It is an excellent introduction to recycling that includes chapters on solid waste and the history of recycling in the US, a select list of important commodity materials from aluminum to zinc, and glass, motor oil, paper, plastics, tires, steel, wooden pallets; each is set off by an "overview-benefits-outlook" capsule. There is a section on recycling influences that touches on theory, practice, and legislative stimulation and constraint; there are "how to" chapters having to do with raising money, improving business, manufacturing and recycling programs, and finally, a set of appendixes called "Technical Assistance" that puts one in touch with experts. This book is going to be so useful and used that one hopes the authors are already planning the next edition to keep the material current. Vote "yes" for this volume. For all industrial, academic, and public libraries.—*L. W. Fine, Columbia University*

OAB-1534   94-60645 Orig
Qasim, Syed R. **Sanitary landfill leachate: generation, control and treatment,** by Syed R. Qasim and Walter Chiang. Technomic, 1994. 339p bibl index ISBN 1-56676-129-8 pbk, $49.00

A well-written, lucid description of the various topics in sanitary landfill leachate, this joint effort by Qasim and Chiang offers an excellent and thorough literature review of "various methodologies that have been developed for prediction, generation, characterization, containment, control, and treatment of leachate from sanitary landfills." There are nine chapters, each self-contained, so that the reader can easily focus on a particular aspect of the subject. Appendixes include "Soil Moisture Retention Tables Used for Calculation of Leachate Generation from Sanitary Landfills" and a list of useful acronyms. Intended as a design manual for consulting engineers and as a guidebook for technical personnel in governmental organizations, the book is well integrated and highly recommended for use in industrial, academic, and public libraries. Undergraduate through professional; two-year technical program students.—*P. C. Chan, New Jersey Institute of Technology*

OAB-1535   TD793   91-50452 CIP
Rathje, William. **Rubbish!: the archaeology of garbage,** by William Rathje and Cullen Murphy. HarperCollins, 1992. 250p ISBN 0-06-016603-7, $23.00

"Rubbish!" A wonderful title, but hardly appropriate. This much-heralded, oft-quoted, and widely acclaimed work deserves all the accolades it has received. It is at once an intellectual achievement, a scientific contribution, and a literary event for bringing us this crisp, fast-paced, highly readable summary of the 20-year-old Garbage Project led by anthropologist Rathje (Univ. of Arizona). It is filled with facts and figures that are already being used by the *Congressional Record* and the press and contains a treasure trove of information and ideas. It reads like a novel, but stands up to the scrutiny of peer review even though it is probably twice-removed from the primary scientific literature in its present form. But in this form it will have its greatest impact for audiences. Within its 4 parts and 11 chapters through 250 honest pages, the reader can expect to find out about what our garbage is, how it is generated—and was generated—what we do with it, what it tells us about ourselves, and where conventional wisdom has gone astray on important issues like biodegradabilty, siting of landfills and their future, and lively controversies such as fast-food restaurant use of paper and plastic and the controversy over disposable/reuseable diapers. Everyone should read this book.—*L. W. Fine, Columbia University*

OAB-1536   Orig
Rowe, R. Kerry. **Clayey barrier systems for waste disposal facilities,** by R. Kerry Rowe, Robert M. Quigley, and John R. Booker. E & FN Spon, 1995. 390p bibl indexes afp ISBN 0-419-19320-0, $159.95

Rowe and colleagues, internationally known authors who have done extensive research in the area of waste containment and groundwater pollution, treat the design and performance of barrier systems for waste disposal facilities, a very appropriate subject for these times. No other book deals with this subject matter with such depth and clarity. The primary emphasis is on clay barriers where advection and diffusion are the two predominant mechanisms for pollutant transport. Methods are presented for determining the appropriate design parameters, and the validity of underlying theory is substantiated with case studies. Several chapters conclude with summaries. Numerous excellent examples are presented throughout. Quality of illustrations is very good. Author and subject indexes. An excellent book. Upper-division undergraduate; graduate; faculty; professional.—*R. P. Khera, New Jersey Institute of Technology*

OAB-1537   GB656   95-35668 CIP
Singh, Vijay P. **Kinematic wave modeling in water resources: surface-water hydrology.** Wiley-Interscience, 1996. 1,399p bibl index afp ISBN 0-471-10945-2, $125.00

Kinematic wave theory is an accepted analytical tool for modeling a variety of hydrologic and environmental processes. A number of noted contributors have made important strides in applications, including Henderson, Wooding, Ponce, etc. Singh "intends to provide a unified treatment of the theory ... and to describe its application to a range of hydrologic and water resources problems." The book itself is divided into five parts. Following an overview of

the subject, the first five chapters (300 pages) present the fundamentals of water resources and modeling. Continuity and momentum equations are derived from both differential and integral forms. The shallow water wave theories (kinematic and dynamic) are presented in part 3 (300 pages). The applications of kinematic wave theory on overland flow are given in part 4 (450 pages). The book concludes with channel flow routing (part 5, 200 pages). Numerous examples and results are presented throughout. Overall, an impressive monograph summarizing the results of extensive research during the past 40 years. Extensive bibliography. Highly recommended for academic and professional libraries. Upper-division undergraduates through professionals.—*P. C. Chan, New Jersey Institute of Technology*

OAB-1538   TD1052   96-38473 CIP
Soesilo, J. Andy. **Site remediation: planning and management,** by J. Andy Soesilo and Stephanie R. Wilson. Lewis Publishers, 1997. 409p bibl index afp ISBN 1-56670-207-0, $59.95

Soesilo and Wilson offer an excellent introduction to site remediation planning and management. The laws related to remediation, Superfund, Resource Conservation and Recovery Act (RCRA), and underground storage tank regulations are considered. The authors' balanced coverage includes statutory and regulatory provisions, remediation standards, environmental sampling, site characterization, risk assessment, cleanup criteria, issues in site remediation, and public participation. Although there is introductory information on remediation technologies, the strength of the book is its attention to the planning and management of the site remediation process. There are many references to the earlier work of others, and an appropriate number of figures and tables. The material selected to be included in the tables is one of the strengths of the book. Most parts of the book are very readable. It can be used for public education as well as for professional development. All levels of readers.—*L. E. Erickson, Kansas State University*

OAB-1539   TD180   96-38383 CIP
Tarr, Joel A. **The search for the ultimate sink: urban pollution in historical perspective.** University of Akron, 1996. 419p indexes afp ISBN 1-884836-05-4, $49.95; ISBN 1-884836-06-2 pbk, $24.95

Tarr has prepared one of the premier books on environmental history, a relatively new discipline. The subtitle reflects the book's mission: to describe the impact of technology on the environment, with particular focus on American cities. Tarr begins with an overview of environmental quality and then progresses through water, air, and land pollution. The development of municipal water works, starting with Philadelphia in the early 1800s, and the ensuing increase in water consumption per person per day spreading from city to city are traced in impressive detail. The resulting problem of wastewater treatment and handling, and the link with technological development and industrialization are emphasized, as well as the impact this had on the three major northeastern rivers and their common basin or estuary. Smoke generated from railroad trains and coke ovens in Pittsburgh, the first sources of air pollution, are viewed as signs of important urban activity and technological progress for the entire country. Land as a filter for wastewater as well as a disposal ground for hazardous wastes is also discussed. Reading this kind of accounting of environmental history gives one a greater awareness of the punishment environmental resources have sustained so far, and raises the obvious question as to how much more they can take. General readers; undergraduates; faculty.—*A. S. Casparian, Wentworth Institute of Technology*

OAB-1540   Orig
Wetlands regulation: a complete guide to federal and California programs, by Paul D. Cylinder et al. Solano, 1995. 363p bibl index ISBN 0-923956-20-4 pbk, $40.00

This excellent guide treats the Federal regulations concerning the protection of US wetlands. Although there is an emphasis on California in the book, it is one of the states that has suffered the greatest loss of wetlands. Written by ecologists and environmental planners, the book covers a diversity of topics, i.e., wetlands, ecology, jurisdictional limits of wetlands, federal and California regulations, and mitigation (including mitigation banking). The extensive appendixes offer basic regulations from various agencies. This will be an invaluable volume for a great variety of groups, such as land use planners, developers, lawyers, public officials, and many others devoted to protecting wetlands. The glossary, detailed index, and excellent illustrations make this a most practical and useful book that should be readily available in libraries throughout the country. All levels.—*W. A. Niering, Connecticut College*

OAB-1541   TC1050   92-41873 CIP
Wise, Marian. **Preventing industrial toxic hazards: a guide for communities,** by Marian Wise and Lauren Kenworthy. Rev. ed. INFORM, 1993. 199p ISBN 0-918780-60-8 pbk, $25.00

INFORM is a nonprofit research organization that reports on environmental and health issues. This comprehensive update of their work by Lauren Kenworthy, *A Citizen's Guide to Promoting Toxic Waste Reduction* (CH, Apr'91), in its simple, straightforward style and large format, offers readers the opportunity to learn how to use the EPA's inventories of toxic substances and mount a personal or public campaign directed at industrial source reduction. The update contains everything anyone needs to know about RCRA hazardous waste reports, occupational health and safety information, data on accidents and spills, and much more. The half dozen chapters cover the need for reducing toxic chemical wastes at the source, options and strategies, how to create reduction programs, how to effectively survey local plants, and government policies that encourage source reduction. Indexes provide every kind of information, from the inventory of toxic substances to important state and federal contacts to useful questionnaires and forms. An easily accessible compendium by a credible group whose work has been made all the more worthy by their success at winning the confidence and cooperation of the members of their target group. Excellent glossary of key terms; manageable list of key references; nicely printed on good quality, recycled paper (of course). This report should be part of every industrial chemical library, every academic library, and every public library.—*L. W. Fine, Columbia University*

■ Materials, Building & Mechanical

OAB-1542   TA403   96-37051 CIP
Amato, Ivan. **Stuff: the materials the world is made of.** Basic Books, 1997. 294p index ISBN 0-465-08328-5, $25.00

Amato, a well-known science writer, provides an exciting account of the evolution of materials and their processing from prehistory and historic antiquity through the Industrial Revolution to the present. Stone chipping and tool making, ore smelting, nonferrous metal production and working, cast iron and steel production, ceramics and polymers, composites and thin coatings, electronic materials, nanomaterials, biomimetic materials, synthetic diamonds, new analytical tools for microstructural investigation, smart materials, atom-by-atom building of materials with tailor-made properties, microstructural effects on properties, and the economic and societal impact of materials are in this fascinating procession through the millennia. A very well written and illustrated book, very affordably priced. An excellent acquisition for academic and public libraries. For general readers, students at all levels, and faculty interested in the history of materials and technology.—*T. Z. Kattamis, University of Connecticut*

OAB-1543   QC320   92-25535 CIP
Bejan, Adrian. **Heat transfer.** Wiley, 1993. 675p indexes afp ISBN 0-471-50290-1, $75.95

There are numerous books on introductory heat transfer available; Bejan's is yet another that must compete. However, it has several unique features that would attract the attention of educators and engineering professionals; these

include an interdisciplinary approach; emphasis on the close link between heat transfer, fluid mechanics, and thermodynamics; applications of scale analysis; and a wide variety of design and project problems. The book covers all the traditional topics that normally appear in undergraduate books on heat transfer. The writing style is clear, crisp, and delightful. Bejan, author of four other books, has established an excellent reputation as a writer, teacher, and researcher. Bibliography, index, printing, and binding are all of good quality. As remarked by the author, the book "reflects the changes currently taking place in the engineering profession and in engineering education," and as such is highly recommended for upper-division undergraduates and graduate students. An excellent buy for engineering libraries.—*A. Aziz, Gonzaga University*

OAB-1544   TG300   93-9747 CIP
Brown, David J. **Bridges.** Macmillan, 1993. 176p bibl index ISBN 0-02-517455-X, $30.00

Brown, publications coordinator for one of the UK's most prestigious engineering firms, traces the art of bridge construction from its origins, with tree trunk, rope, or vines, through the modern cable-stayed and suspension bridges. Developments are organized in four time frames, starting in the medieval era, with its many stone and masonry arches; the Industrial Revolution with iron and steel trusses and suspension spans; the 20th century with new materials and long-span cantilever, suspension, and cable-stayed bridges; and closing with a view of the future from projects yet on the drawing board. The salient features of most of the world's important bridges, constructed at various times, are described. Not all the discussion centers around successful projects; some of the news-making failures are also noted. Illustrations are excellent, well chosen, and nicely reproduced. Very helpful glossary and index; modest bibliography. The American Society of Civil Engineers has recently published a similar book restricted to North American bridges, *Landmark American Bridges*, ed. by Eric DeLony (1993). The two books complement each other. *Bridges* does have a much broader scope and wider appeal to general readers. The technical content is sufficient for structural engineers interested in bridges. Both technical and public libraries should have this one for their bridge fans. General; undergraduate through professional.—*W. C. Schnobrich, University of Illinois at Urbana—Champaign*

OAB-1545   TJ625   94-44850 CIP
Brown, John K. **The Baldwin Locomotive Works, 1831-1915.** Johns Hopkins, 1995. 328p bibl index afp (Studies in industry and society, 8) ISBN 0-8018-5047-9, $35.95

Historical study of US capital equipment/heavy machinery industries in recent decades has fallen behind the study of the mass production industries that developed from "armory practice" and the "American system of manufactures." Brown has made a major contribution to the correction of that imbalance with his engaging study of the Baldwin Locomotive Works, the largest firm producing capital equipment in the US during the 19th century. Professional scholars, diligent lay readers, and railroad enthusiasts all will be indebted to him for providing insights into how customer-specified, batch-produced capital equipment was produced then and how that production influenced the development of the US as the premier industrial giant by the end of the last century. Brown's study is the result of extensive, original research into various, mostly archival, sources. Brown was most fortunate in that many original Baldwin records have survived, and he has made good use of them. He incorporated industrial/labor, economic, business, technological, and social history into his virtually seamless narrative; even the notes are good reading. Many well-chosen and informative illustrations; useful charts and graphs. Highly recommended. General; undergraduate through faculty; two-year technical program students.—*M. Levinson, University of Washington*

OAB-1546   TJ211   91-42524 CIP
Caudill, Maureen. **In our own image: building an artificial person.** Oxford, 1992. 242p index afp ISBN 0-19-507338-X, $23.00

Although the field of robotics has grown to embrace many aspects of industrial automation, the greatest enthusiasm has been reserved for human-like robots, or "androids." Caudill considers many of the technical questions (but at a general reader's level) that must be solved in order for androids to become a reality. Two technologies are given particular emphasis: artificial intelligence and neural networks. The strengths of the book are Caudill's engaging writing style and the clarity of her examples. It is not technically deep and is certainly not a substitute for a textbook on either robotics, artificial intelligence, psychology, or neural networks, but it does a good job of filling in the gap between science fiction and currently available technology. Several diagrams and photographs help to illustrate the text. A bibliography is provided for each chapter. Highly recommended for libraries of undergraduate institutions. General; undergraduate; graduate.—*S. L. Tanimoto, University of Washington*

OAB-1547   TA405   95-34726 CIP
Craig, Roy R. **Mechanics of materials.** Wiley, 1996. various pagings bibl index afp ISBN 0-471-50284-7, $92.95

Mechanics of materials is a fundamentally important part of engineering and material science. Craig covers a broad range of topics in a superbly structured work. He stresses the fundamental concepts along with applications necessary for developing strong analytical and systematic problem-solving skills in this area. His book is indispensable as a standard reference for any engineering library and can serve as a course resource. Twelve chapters treat stress and strain; axial deformation; torsion; beam equilibrium, stresses, and deflection; transformation of stress and shear; Mohr's circle; stresses due to combined loading; pressure vessels; buckling columns; energy methods; and special topics related to design. In addition, there is an excellent list of references and six useful appendixes including information on numerical accuracy and approximation, material properties, and computational mechanics (MechSOLID computer software). The general layout of the book makes it a pleasure to use. Highly recommended. Upper-division undergraduates through professionals.—*P. C. Chan, New Jersey Institute of Technology*

OAB-1548   93-74475 Orig
Cummins, C. Lyle. **Diesel's engine: v.1: From conception to 1918.** Carnot Press, P.O. Box 1544, Lake Oswego, OR 97035, 1993. 746p bibl index ISBN 0-917308-03-4, $55.00

The diesel was the first engine developed from scientific theory rather than from utilizing technology. Cummins uses Diesel's own design and test notebooks, original sources in the archives of early manufacturers, and the personal records of many of the engine's innovators to interweave Rudolf Diesel's life and ideas with the people and events contributing to the early development of his engine. (There is no comparable work available in English.) Cummins describes three overlapping phases: development and tests up to 1897 when efficient operation was first achieved; further development by licensees and competitors (in both Europe and the US) centered around the expiration of Diesel's original patent in 1907; and applications to ships, submarines, and locomotives through 1918. The book's emphasis is on technology rather than social impact. The evidence, including excellent chapter notes and hundreds of contemporary drawings and photographs of early engines, supports Diesel's controversial claim as the true inventor of the engine. Because of the complexity of the material, some sections may be too technical for general readers. Highly recommended for library collections in the history of technology, mechanical engineering design, and operating engineering/mechanical engineering technology. Community college; upper-division undergraduate; faculty; preprofessional; professional.—*G. E. Herrick, Maine Maritime Academy*

OAB-1549   Orig
Degobert, Paul. **Automobiles and pollution,** tr. by Nissim Marshall and reviewed by Frank Carr. Society of Automotive Engineers/Technip, 1995. 491p bibl index ISBN 1-56091-563-3, $110.00

This is THE definitive analysis of the problems of automotive pollution. Coverage is exhaustive and the detailed treatment of each topic is impressive.

Although Degobert is French and many of the cited sources are from Europe, the text is not the awkward pastiche that often results from less-gifted translators. The style is straightforward and unobtrusive except for a few overspecialized terms like anthropogenic (for human-made) and of course, a large number of chemical terms describing the myriad reactions that follow combustion in engines. Chapters treat characterization of air pollution; inventory of air pollutants; air pollution and health; air pollution and the environment; laws and regulations; characterization and analysis methods; analysis of pollutants, including carbon and nitrogen compounds; mechanisms of pollutant formation in engines; influence of fuel properties; postcombustion treatments; and economic challenges. Many charts, tables, and illustrations are provided, and each chapter is followed by a bibliography. As an example of the depth of this book, the chapter on pollutant formation in engines cites not just typical automotive engines but diesel engines, two-stroke engines, jet engines, supercharged engines, and experimental engines designed to minimize pollutants. Highly recommended for all serious students of this technology. All levels.—*J. C. Comer, emeritus, Northern Illinois University*

OAB-1550   Orig
The Development of plastics, ed. by S.T.I. Mossman and P.J.T. Morris. Royal Society of Chemistry, 1994. 120p bibl index (Special publication, 141) ISBN 0-85186-575-5, $65.00

The Development of Plastics is a truly enjoyable reading experience. Individual chapters are concise, informative, and well written; each details the development of a specific plastic material or industry in terms of world events and historical forces driving the industries; some chapters even give the geographical locations of the manufacturing sites. Often, chapter narrators were personally involved in the early development of these materials and industries. Thus they were able to provide firsthand knowledge regarding the research and development of a material and, in effect, the evolution of modern materials science. One can easily employ this book to put the modern plastics industry into historical perspective. A valuable aid to science historians and an absorbing narrative for any individual with an interest in plastics. General; undergraduate; graduate; two-year technical program students.—*P. G. Heiden, Michigan Technological University*

OAB-1551   TP1122   92-27130 CIP
Emerging technologies in plastics recycling, ed. by Gerald D. Andrews and Pallatheri M. Subramanian. American Chemical Society, 1992. 322p indexes afp (ACS symposium series, 513) ISBN 0-8412-2499-4, $79.95

Emerging technologies in recycling plastics are hot topics these days and deserve the fast attention given in this ACS series. Here is exciting stuff in a rapidly evolving technology-based field of great current interest; thus, this publication, available less than a year after the topic's public presentation, is timely and will be greatly appreciated by workers in the field. Beginning with the essential theme of recycling plastics from municipal solid wastes, topics include environmental compatibility of polymers, automotive recycling, characterization problems, recovery, blends, additives, and general applications. Having sat through what was then an excellent set of presentations, this reviewer is happy to add an excellent print record of that important collection to his library, and any interested individuals and professional libraries would be well advised to do the same. It is an obviously specialized collection of papers but of special importance. Kudos to the ACS for expediency without sacrifice of scientific integrity or literary quality. There is even a useful index. Surprise, surprise!—*L. W. Fine, Columbia University*

OAB-1552   TH441   96-33425 CIP
Feld, Jacob. **Construction failure,** by Jacob Feld and Kenneth L. Carper. 2nd ed. Wiley-Interscience, 1997. 512p bibl index afp ISBN 0-471-57477-5, $69.95

The original edition of this classic work (1968) by the late Jacob Feld was among the first to openly discuss failure investigations in the construction indus-

Science & Tecnology

try. Carper's current edition presents new and updated material with substantial references to recent case studies. He first classifies failures, then presents examples from specific structural types (bridges, buildings, foundations, etc.) and materials (steel, poured and precast concrete, wood, etc.); and then discusses legal aspects and lessons learned from failures. There are even chapters on "nonstructural" failures such as in roofs and facades and in other components, including those associated with a building's mechanical systems. Failures during construction as well as construction safety are also addressed. This work could be used as an excellent textbook in architectural as well as structural programs and would be a valuable reference for any library serving these disciplines, even for two-year technology programs. Extensive chapter reference lists. Upper-division undergraduates through professionals; two-year technical program students.—*H. I. Epstein, University of Connecticut*

OAB-1553   TJ820   94-36564 CIP
Gipe, Paul. **Wind energy comes of age.** Wiley, 1995. 536p index afp ISBN 0-471-10924-X, $64.95

This is the definitive word on wind energy. Gipe is very knowledgeable and writes in a clear unambiguous style. The literature in this field is often either very sketchy or suspect because of commercial bias. The actual technology has been replete with failures, some due to the extreme vagaries of the wind itself and others because designers and their backers failed to comprehend how difficult it is to achieve a viable project when the machine must survive with minimal maintenance over thousands of hours of use. A major mistake was entrusting the designs to aerospace engineers who built massive projects that then failed in massive and spectacular ways. Too often, these episodes are unreported or glossed over, but Gipe chronicles them all. There is even a nationalistic twist: Denmark builds the most durable and successful machines, while Sweden, Germany, and the US have built the giants that failed. California has most of the presently operating units (because of past tax credits), and most of them are Danish. The future is bright; most of what does not work has been discovered, and there are excellent sites in the Third World, where the demand for electricity is growing but an infrastructure of powerline grids simply does not exist. A clever new parlay is the installation of both a wind generator and a photovoltaic array as a unit; either wind or sunshine makes the system productive. The book is both broad in scope and rich in detail. Bibliographies follow each section; extensive charts, tables, and illustrations. Recommended. Undergraduate through professional; two-year technical program students.—*J. C. Comer, emeritus, Northern Illinois University*

OAB-1554   TC409   93-11165 CIP
Haan, C.T. **Design hydrology and sedimentology for small catchments,** by C.T. Haan, B.J. Barfield, and J.C. Hayes. Academic Press, 1994. 588p index afp ISBN 0-12-312340-2, $89.95

This is a unique and excellent book on small catchment engineering. Drawing from extensive experience in both academic and practicing arenas, Haan, Barfield, and Hayes provide a thorough overview with great depth. In 14 chapters and nine appendixes, this book covers three different areas—hydrology (four chapters), open channel (four chapters), and sedimentation (three chapters) for small catchments. Filled with useful tables and graphs, the book emphasizes engineering design and analysis. Practicing engineers should find the book useful and informative; likewise, there is sufficient theoretical treatment for readers interested in the analytical aspects of the subject. With its pedagogical structure, ample illustrative examples, and end of chapter problems, this book could be used as a text for advanced undergraduate and graduate courses in agricultural, civil, and environmental engineering. In addition, there is an up-to-date bibliography in each chapter for further detailed study. Overall, a well-written and well-organized book, with outstanding presentation, printing, and illustrations. Highly recommended. Upper-division undergraduate through professional.—*P. C. Chan, New Jersey Institute of Technology*

OAB-1555   QD381   92-10169 CIP
Handbook of polymer degradation, ed. by S. Halim Hamid, Mohamed B. Amin, and Ali G. Maadhah. Dekker, 1992. 649p index (Environmental science and pollution control, 2) ISBN 0-8247-8671-8, $175.00

An excellent review of available information on polymer degradation technology, at the leading edge of possible solutions to some of the world's pressing problems, such as pollution, solid waste disposal, and product disintegration. The handbook discusses thoroughly photodegradation, thermodegradation, biodegradation, and the effects of chemical reactions such as acid rain, and offers a very complete description of techniques used to determine the rate of degradation of a wide range of polymers under various conditions. Numerous very useful charts and graphs increase the handbook's effectiveness as do complete bibliographies on each topic. Chemical mechanisms are described clearly and elegantly as far as present knowledge allows. Concise descriptions of various instrumentation techniques, such as infrared spectrophotometry and degradation monitoring, are provided to aid readers unfamiliar with them. An excellent acquisition for libraries serving chemistry or chemical engineering students at the advanced undergraduate level.—*K. Bennett, Kalamazoo Valley Community College*

OAB-1556   TA676   94-34084 CIP
Heyman, Jacques. **The stone skeleton: structural engineering of masonry architecture.** Cambridge, 1995. 160p bibl index ISBN 0-521-47270-9, $59.95

This is one of the most fascinating books on structural engineering that this reviewer has read in recent years. Heyman provides answers to many questions: What is the time scale for the settlement and cracking of an old stone building? How do the elegant flying buttresses of a Gothic cathedral safely transfer thrust to the foundations? What is the effect of wind on a stone spire, or bell-ringing on a church tower? With a firm scientific bias, but without the use of complex mathematics, the author provides a thorough and intuitive understanding of masonry structures. The basis of masonry analysis is introduced in the first two chapters, after which individual elements—including piers, pinnacles, towers, vaults, and domes—are considered in more detail. Heyman, retired head of the Department of Engineering, University of Cambridge, is a fellow of the Institution of Civil Engineers and the Royal Academy of Engineering, and also consults for a number of English cathedrals. This informative book will be of particular interest to structural engineers, practicing architects, and others involved in the renovation and care of old stone buildings. Upper-division undergraduate through professional.—*S. C. Anand, Clemson University*

OAB-1557   TF847   93-11169 CIP
Hood, Clifton. **722 miles: the building of the subways and how they transformed New York.** Simon & Schuster, 1993. 335p index ISBN 0-671-67756-X, $25.00

Hood provides an interesting and informative history of the New York City subway system, the longest urban rail transit system in the world. He covers in detail the political and financial background behind the development of the subway system. A unique aspect is the description of the impact of the subway system on the development of New York City. The engineering of the subway system and the construction difficulties encountered are also discussed. The ability of the subway system to overcome the geographical limitations of the New York City area and the complex geology of Manhattan are described. Highly recommended for college and university libraries serving urban planning, civil engineering, and political science programs. General; undergraduate through faculty.—*D. B. Stafford, Clemson University*

OAB-1558   TS533   96-24139 CIP
Hosley, William. **Colt: the making of an American legend.** Massachusetts, 1996. 254p afp ISBN 1-55849-042-6, $49.95; ISBN 1-55849-043-4 pbk, $29.95

Hosley tells the story of the legendary Samuel Colt, his wife Elizabeth—The

First Lady of Connecticut—and their gun manufacturing empire. Colt's successes and failures, the Colt revolver and armories, the unprecedented development of the Connecticut Valley in Victorian times, Colt's premature death, the endurance of the Colt legacy, the destruction by fire of the Hartford Armory and its rebuilding by Elizabeth—are all vividly described and illustrated, as are Elizabeth's patronage of the arts and her endowment of parks, museums, and memorials. Hosley, Curator of American Decorative Arts at the Wadsworth Atheneum in Hartford, Connecticut, is undoubtedly the most qualified person to write this book, which is very well written and presented with black-and-white photographs and superb color illustrations. Following a preface, there are ten chapters on such topics as the Colts, the revolution in machine-based manufacturing, guns and gun culture, Coltsville, the Charter Oak and the dreamhouse Armsmear, and the Colts as the patrons of the arts. All those interested in the history of American culture and technology will greatly benefit from the book. Comprehensive notes. An excellent acquisition by public as well as academic libraries. General readers; upper-division undergraduate and graduate students.— *T. Z. Kattamis, University of Connecticut*

OAB-1559   TG71   96-13570 CIP
Kranakis, Eda. **Constructing a bridge: an exploration of engineering culture, design, and research in nineteenth-century France and America.** MIT, 1997. 453p bibl index ISBN 0-262-11217-5, $45.00

Kranakis explores the role that social and class systems have on the shaping of technology, research, and knowledge within a given or particular environment. This finely researched study documents the achievements in the development, design, and construction of suspension bridges by James Finley in the US and Claude Louis Marie Henri Navier in France. Their markedly different approaches to the suspension bridge problem are related to social, economic, and educational differences that existed between these two countries in the 1800s. Finley's empirical approach is contrasted with Navier's mathematical approach by examining the environments in which these two engineers worked. Kranakis compares, in a scholarly yet lively fashion, these contrasting approaches. She pays particular attention to the educational, institutional, and professional social structures of the two countries. The scholarly nature of the book is evident in the 75 pages of notes and the 45 pages of bibliography that document the author's thesis. Illustrations are excellent; many are reproductions from library and institutional manuscripts. This book will delight the general public interested in the history of technology as well as the specialist focusing on bridges. An absolute must for any library collecting in the history of technology. General readers; upper-division undergraduates; professionals.—*W. C. Schnobrich, University of Illinois at Urbana-Champaign*

OAB-1560   TJ23   96-31573 MARC
Landmarks in mechanical engineering, by ASME International History and Heritage. Purdue, 1997. 364p bibl index afp ISBN 1-55753-093-9, $39.95

This fascinating collection of 135 brief essays on (almost exclusively) American "industrial archaeology" discusses still-existing artifacts ranging from the Saugus Ironworks (1640s) to the Saturn V rocket, one of which propelled the *Apollo 11* spacecraft to a first moon landing in 1969. The book is more than just a gee-whiz celebration of technology in that it provides satisfying sketches of the social contexts of technological artifacts and the people involved. In a short review of this well-illustrated presentation, all one can do is list the areas considered, which include pumping, mechanical and electrical power, power transmission, minerals extraction and refining, manufacturing, food processing, materials handling, environmental control, water transportation through space transportation, research, communications and processing, and biomedical engineering. Each section contains an introductory essay, and each article suggests additional readings as well as information on location and access. The ASME History and Heritage Committee has been well served by its literary voice, Carol Poh Miller; she has done an excellent job. The book belongs in all general libraries, public and institutional, as well as in appropriate specialized libraries. All levels.—*M. Levinson, University of Washington*

OAB-1561   TJ260   94-11638 CIP
Lock, G.S.H. **Latent heat transfer: an introduction to fundamentals.** Oxford, 1994. 288p bibl index afp (Oxford engineering science series, 43) ISBN 0-19-856285-3, $85.00

Lock's unique and comprehensive exposition of latent heat transfer covers a variety of phase change processes: freezing, melting, evaporation, condensation, sublimation, and deposition. The material is organized into eight chapters; the last chapter is a collection of worked examples. The first three chapters introduce the reader to the history and importance of thermodynamics and fluid dynamics as they relate to latent heat transfer problems. Individual chapters follow on solidification and fluidification, condensation, and evaporation. A final chapter is devoted to direct contact condensation, evaporation, crystallization, and combustion of condensed phases. Lock is exceptionally well qualified in the area of heat transfer and writes in a clear, crisp style. Each chapter has its own bibliography. Must reading for upper-division undergraduates, graduate students, and faculty specializing in thermal sciences. An excellent buy.—*A. Aziz, Gonzaga University*

OAB-1562   Orig
Maxwell, James. **Plastics in the automotive industry.** Society of Automotive Engineers/Woodhead, 1994. 189p bibl index ISBN 1-56091-527-7, $69.00

Maxwell has made a nontechnical survey of the application of plastics in the automotive industry. He carefully explains the advantages and shortcomings of various polymers and polymer systems in a variety of automotive applications. The book is well written in an attractive format with appropriate figures, tables, and photographs. This quote will serve to convey the character of this work: "In the days when plastics were first being considered for exterior panels, it was often said that these new materials foretold the end of the automotive paint shop, with all its problems. With plastics there was no corrosion and therefore no need for protection; unlimited pigmentation possibilities would provide in-depth solid colour across the complete spectrum, and high lustre surfaces could be achieved through high quality tooling. These arguments proved to be fallacious." Highly recommended for engineering and technology collections. General; lower-division undergraduate; two-year technical program students; professional.—*A. M. Strauss, Vanderbilt University*

OAB-1563   TP1117   95-15187 CIP
Meikle, Jeffrey L. **American plastic: a cultural history.** Rutgers, 1995. 403p index afp ISBN 0-8135-2234-X, $49.95

The signature of the ages of humanity is materials: Stone Age, Iron Age, Bronze Age, etc. And our own age? The Age of Plastics, chronicled here in a sweeping cultural history that will satisfy the scientist and technologist as much as the reader seeking the seeds of the social and historical dimensions of American plastic (not plastics), a carefully (and well) chosen title. From this truly outstanding work, polymer chemists and physicists and plastics engineers will glean special benefits from chapters dedicated to celluloid, Bakelite, and nylon, as well as the treatment of other major classes of synthetic polymers and plastics scattered throughout. Titles and topics of other chapters can only be described as beguiling in their simplicity and subtlety, for here is a work of intellectual strength written with great literary style. The "notes" at the end of the work are copious, annotated, up-to-date, and appear to be accurate to a fault. In 300 pages, Meikle provides a definitive resource for scholarly research in the history and sociology of this most important and characterizing science of our century, a cultural history of plastic's presence in American life. No matter what one may call these materials, this significant work is likely to be widely cited in academic circles, defining the field for a generation of readers. Don't let it pass you by! An extraordinary contribution, for all levels of readers, in the sciences and engineering, and in the arts and humanities.—*L. W. Fine, Columbia University*

OAB-1564   Brit. CIP
Minsker, Karl S. **Fast polymerization processes,** by Karl S. Minsker and Alexandre Al. Berlin. Gordon & Breach, 1996. 146p bibl index (Polymer science and engineering monographs: a state-of-the-art tutorial series, 1) ISBN 2-88449-149-X, $65.50; ISBN 2-88449-191-0 pbk, $32.50

Minsker and Berlin have prepared an excellent first volume in this new publisher series. They clearly describe the characteristics of fast polymerization processes (polymerizations where reaction rates are equal to or greater than the rate of reactant mixing), the problems associated with engineering fast polymerizations, and methods of gaining control over fast polymerizations. Topics discussed include polymerizations with and without heat removal, the effect of the method of catalyst introduction, reagent mixing in turbulent flow regimes, how to optimize molecular mass, and how reactor design affects reagent mixing and the polymerization process. A final chapter describes the development and evaluation of new-generation small tubular turbulent reactors designed for fast polymerization processes, e.g., for polyisobutylene. A clearly written and economically priced work, of special interest to chemists, chemical engineers, and chemistry and engineering students. Upper-division undergraduates through professionals.—*P. G. Heiden, Michigan Technological University*

OAB-1565   TA357   92-34111 CIP
Papanastasiou, Tasos C. **Applied fluid mechanics.** PTR Prentice Hall, 1994. 520p index ISBN 0-13-060799-1, $70.00

Several unique features distinguish this book from many others on fluid mechanics in an overcrowded market; these include chapters on lubrication, non-Newtonian fluids and rheology, linear stability analysis, and a large number of application-oriented examples and problems. The book covers all the traditional topics that one normally finds in undergraduate-level works in fluid mechanics. The writing style is clear and appealing. Each chapter has its own adequate and up-to-date bibliography. The eight-page index is comprehensive and easy to use. Papanastasiou has combined his industrial and academic experience to produce a book that will appeal to lower-division undergraduates through researchers and faculty. An excellent buy for engineering libraries, particularly those with chemical engineering collections.—*A. Aziz, Gonzaga University*

OAB-1566   TG23   94-48893 CIP
Petroski, Henry. **Engineers of dreams: great bridge builders and the spanning of America.** Knopf, 1995. 479p bibl index ISBN 0-679-43939-0, $30.00

Petroski is a prominent figure in civil engineering education, whose research into the history and heritage of the engineering profession has been recognized through many awards. This book concentrates on that group of individuals whose foresight and ambitions drove US bridge building in the late 19th and early 20th centuries. A chapter is devoted to each of several engineers who played major roles in the building of a number of landmark bridges from 1870 to 1940: James B. Eads, Peter Cooper, Gustav Lindenthal, Othmar H. Amman, and David B. Steinman. Although each chapter focuses on one particular engineer, others practicing around the same time and involved in or contributing to major bridge projects are mentioned. The presentation is very scholarly, with notes identifying information sources, an excellent bibliography, and a listing of illustration sources. The illustrations (sketches and photographs) of completed and proposed bridges are very good reproductions, well suited to the nature of the book. A somewhat similar book, *Bridges and Their Builders* (1941) by D.B. Steinman and S.R. Watson, has a broader scope, looking at all bridges, but it also concentrates on the same group of bridges as major contributions to the infrastructure of this country. An excellent addition to any library. General; upper-division undergraduate.—*W. C. Schnobrich, University of Illinois at Urbana-Champaign*

OAB-1567   Orig
Postel, Sandra. **Last oasis: facing water scarcity.** W.W. Norton,

1992. 239p index ISBN 0-393-03428-3, $21.95; ISBN 0-393-30961-4 pbk, $9.95

A general reader's introduction to current and future problems of water supply. Postel describes the rapid convergence between accelerating demands for water and the finite nature of the resource. She covers the limitations of engineering solutions, hydro-political problems, and the prediction of chronic water shortages for many parts of the world. Recommendations are given for improving efficiency of water use through improved irrigation practices, small-scale projects, wastewater recycling, economic strategies, and promoting a more realistic ethic of water use. Postel, vice president for research, Worldwatch Institute, presents a well-balanced global view of the subject. Except for a map and a few graphs, the book has no illustrations. It can be readily understood by general readers as young as junior high-school level, but is also worthwhile for more advanced readers. Highly recommended for any public or academic library.—*A. N. Palmer, SUNY College at Oneonta*

OAB-1568   TA418   94-25647 CIP
Ragone, David V. **Thermodynamics of materials.** Wiley, 1995. 2v. 311, 242p bibl indexes afp ISBN 0-471-30885-4, v.1, $75.95; ISBN 0-471-30886-2, v.2, $72.95

The first volume in this set focuses on the study of energy and its transformations as applied to different classes of materials generally encountered in materials science and engineering. Polymers, ceramics, and semiconductors are growing in importance, both economically and technologically, making these volumes timely and important. Ragone treats macroscopic thermodynamics from a classical perspective. He then applies thermodynamic principles to various classes of materials. Ragone has had a distinguished career as scientist and educator, and does an admirable job in presenting technical material in a readable and understandable way. He introduces statistical thermodynamics to provide a background for understanding differences in the classes of materials. Diagrams are clear and readable. References and problem sets are provided, and there is an appendix covering units and mathematical techniques. The second volume assumes of the reader a background in chemistry, physics, and calculus, together with the principles and materials treated in volume 1. Ragone's excellent resource provides good discussions and a very fine bibliography. Problems are very helpful for student practice. The topics are excellently covered, including defects in solids, surfaces, diffusion, and reaction kinetics. A final chapter on nonequilibrium thermodynamics will be most helpful for those who work with applications in which the materials do not exist in an equilibrium state. Libraries supporting undergraduate and graduate programs in engineering, chemistry, physics, and materials science will be well advised to add these volumes to their collections. Upper-division undergraduate through professional.—*D. A. Johnson, Spring Arbor College*

OAB-1569   TS1890   93-8796 CIP
Science and technology of rubber, ed. by James E. Mark, Burak Erman, and Frederick R. Eirich. 2nd ed. Academic Press, 1994. 751p index afp ISBN 0-12-472525-2, $85.00

How can one improve on a good thing? By providing more of it, and that's what the editors of this simply marvelous treatise on the science and technology of rubber have done. The format maintains the integrity of the original (1st ed., CH, Apr'79) 14-chapter layout and design while expanding the work by twenty-five percent and updating the bibliography to the present. Although rubber is the subject, it never escaped the attention of the original users (including this reviewer) that the elegant early chapters were generally applicable to any general introduction to polymer chemistry. Later chapters were generally applicable to any general introduction to engineering properties, composites, materials science, and applications ("Tire Engineering"—a special delight). If professors often turned to it, students were the ultimate beneficiaries of the uniformly readable work and simplified illustrations. And it should come as no surprise that the first edition became something of a constant companion to the industrial chemist and chemical engineer working in the field. This new edition is more of the same and better still. Originally conceived as a graduate-level work, the writing is so smoothly done and the organization so well conceived that it should serve advanced undergraduate chemistry and engineering students too. Excellent! Go for it. A lower-priced paperback version would be nice.—*L. W. Fine, Columbia University*

OAB-1570   Brit. CIP
Simons, Geoff. **Robots: the quest for living machines.** Cassell, 1993 (c1992). (Dist. by Sterling Publishing Company) 224p bibl index ISBN 0-304-34086-3, $29.95

A fascinating book on robotics written in an informal and delightful style. Not a traditional text on robotics for engineering or technology students, but rather a journey that covers the field of robotics in all its aspects. There are eight chapters: In Mythology, Early Automata, Modern Robotics, Intelligent Machines, The Applications Spectrum, Surrogate People, and The Impact on Our Attitudes. The book does not require any background in mathematics or engineering and is written primarily for general readers wishing a quick overview of the history of robotics and modern developments. Simons has written several lucid and interesting books on computing, artificial intelligence, and robotics, and is eminently qualified to write on these subjects. He provides an excellent list of references, cited by chapter. All pictures in the book are reproduced on art paper and are of good quality. An excellent acquisition for college and university libraries. General through professional.—*A. Aziz, Gonzaga University*

OAB-1571   TN671   90-2106 CIP
Smithells metals reference book, ed. by E.A. Brandes and G.B. Brook. 7th ed. Butterworth-Heinemann, 1992. various p index ISBN 0-7506-1020-4, $250.00

Smithells has been a valuable, unparalleled source of information for metallurgists all over the world for more than 40 years. This reviewer welcomes this thoroughly revised new edition (6th ed., CH, Oct'83), which includes information and data in such novel areas as metal-matrix composites as well as updated and substantially expanded sections on equilibrium phase diagrams. Most sections have been rewritten and include very recent developments in areas such as welding, soldering and brazing, vapor deposition, laser processing, superplasticity, electroplating, sintering, metal casting, heat treatment, X-ray analysis, shape memory alloys, magnetic materials, engineering ceramics, tribology and lubrication, and general physical, electrical, thermoelectric, radiating, and mechanical properties. The book is well written and consists of 37 sections that are placed in a logical order and are accompanied by a comprehensive list of references. There is a good index and illustrations are of high quality and most informative. Unfortunately, unlike previous clothbound editions, this one is paper; the binding will probably rupture and tear after very short usage. An indispensable acquisition for metallurgists and professionals dealing with metals and materials in academia, government, and industry, and for all academic and industrial libraries.—*T. Z. Kattamis, University of Connecticut*

OAB-1572   TA418   93-25572 CIP
Speyer, Robert F. **Thermal analysis of materials.** M. Dekker, 1994. 285p index afp (Materials engineering, 5) ISBN 0-8247-8963-6, $99.75

Speyer's background and research interests are in materials (ceramics) science and engineering, and so he extends their analyses from the "standard methods"—differential thermal analysis (DTA), differential scanning analysis (DSC), and thermogravimetric analysis (TGA)—to methods such as thermal expansion (dilatometry), thermal conductivity, or viscosity of liquids and glasses at higher temperatures. Each subject is explained from very basic principles, whether a thermodynamic or kinetic aspect of phase change, the basics of temperature control, temperature measurements, or the mathematics of peak analysis or peak separation. In addition, Speyer provides much useful advice on how to avoid errors during measurements or what additional (nonstandard) information can be drawn from the data. The latter makes it especially useful to the many users who learned to operate these analytical instruments by self-

training. Highly recommended for all upper-level undergraduate or graduate students, especially in chemistry, engineering, or materials sciences.—*H. Giesche, Alfred University*

OAB-1573   TF230   95-50600 CIP
Standard handbook of machine design, ed. by Joseph E. Shigley and Charles R. Mischke. 2nd ed. McGraw-Hill, 1996. various pagings index afp ISBN 0-07-056958-4, $125.00

This handbook is well planned and clearly written, and the quality of the charts and graphs is exceptional. Even the reduced fonts are legible. Although sufficient technical data are provided for most design applications, the inclusion of reference material at the end of each chapter gives the reader a clear path to more in-depth technical information. In this age of automation in machine design, the chapters on fluid power and robotics are extremely valuable. Many machine design handbooks, e.g., *Machine Design Data Handbook*, by K. Lingaiah (CH, Mar'95), are merely modified mechanical engineering handbooks, covering topics like boiler design and mechanics of vehicles yet overlooking safety and product liability. Current and accurate discussions in the work under review of these latter two topics are crucial to any machine design. The individual chapter authors have astutely focused only on machine design topics, without extraneous distractions. If there were a limit of only one such handbook on this reviewer's bookshelf, *Standard Handbook of Machine Design* would be the one. Upper-division undergraduate and graduate students; faculty; professionals.—*R. E. Young, Clemson University*

OAB-1574   TS1925   96-14538 CIP
Thermoplastic elastomers, ed. by Geoffrey Holden et at. 2nd ed. Hanser Publishers/Hanser-Gardner, 1996. 620p bibl index ISBN 1-56990-205-4, $148.00

Especially written for the professional polymer scientist and engineer interested in an in-depth perspective of thermoplastic polymer technology, this work brings to focus monomer and polymer materials such as urethanes, olefins, polyethers, polyamides, and other materials used in thermoplastic technology. In addition, it provides a reasonably complete explanation of kinetics, differential scanning calorimetry, gel permeation chromatography, and other techniques applicable to thermoplastic materials. A thorough review of anionic, cationic, and free-radical catalysts and their application to the preparation of novel thermoplastic elastomers is presented. Basic discussions of physical phenomena, such as order-disorder transitions and their use in polymer technology of this type, are some of the many practical aspects of this work. This book is rich in literature citations and offers the interested reader an excellent start in the study of these polymers. Appropriate for upper-division undergraduate engineering or two-year technical college students, or first-year graduate students in chemistry or chemical engineering.—*K. Bennett, Kalamazoo Valley Community College*

OAB-1575   TN490   96-21331 CIP
Voynick, Stephen M. **Climax: the history of Colorado's Climax Molybdenum Mine.** Mountain Press Publishing Company, 1996. 366p bibl index ISBN 0-87842-354-0 pbk, $20.00

Climax, a giant mining complex high atop the continental divide in Colorado, is widely recognized as the place of an outstanding 20th-century engineering adventure under the most difficult conditions of elevation, terrain, and climate. About the Climax Mining Company as well as the mine, the book is not a typical mining company history but a thorough and engaging account of people, a mountain, technology, corporate and personal conflict, and of success and failure. The story, encompassing some 120 years, dwells on the recognition of molybdenum ore; the entrepreneurial battles for its control; the hurdles in development, mining, and metallurgy; the classic years of production at the world's largest underground mine; and the recent problems of maintaining Climax as an industrial enterprise. The book is well written and authoritative; Voynick is a former Climax miner and the author of several books, including

The Making of a Hardrock Miner (1978). Reference value is supported by historic photographs and source notes. Recommended for libraries with collections on the American West and on the history of science and engineering. All levels.—*W. C. Peters, University of Arizona*

OAB-1576   TH7687   93-1617 CIP
Wang, Shan K. **Handbook of air conditioning and refrigeration.** McGraw-Hill, 1994 (c1993). various pagings index afp ISBN 0-07-068138-4, $96.50

In 32 chapters, this handbook covers the entire field of heating, ventilating, air conditioning, and refrigeration. Individual chapters treat psychrometrics, air conditioning processes and cycles, refrigeration cycles and refrigerants, indoor design conditions and indoor air quality, heat and mass transfer through building envelopes, load calculations, air duct design, space air diffusion, fans, compressors, pumps, humidifiers, air washers, cooling towers, coils, evaporators, condensers, and evaporative cooling and evaporative coolers. Further chapters cover heating systems, furnaces, boilers, air filtration, air-handling units, packaged units, sound control, basics of air-conditioning control systems, energy management, air system basics and space pressurization, water systems, refrigeration systems, heat pumps, centrifugal and absorption systems, thermal storage, air systems, energy estimation, packaged air conditioning systems, and system commissioning and maintenance. The handbook is carefully crafted and contains a wealth of information including numerous design-oriented examples. Illustrations, index, and binding are of very high quality. Wang is a well-known expert and has produced a work that should be in every library. Undergraduate through professional.—*A. Aziz, Gonzaga University*

OAB-1577   TS1890   93-48549 CIP
White, James L. **Rubber processing: technology, materials, and principles.** Hanser/Hanser-Gardner, 1995. 586p bibl indexes ISBN 1-56990-165-1, $162.50

White's excellent book on the rubber processing industry and technology is written in easy prose, offering an overview of rubber and polymer descriptions for those keenly interested in rubber manufacturing. The topics include general rubber and polymer materials, punctuated with some historical commentary on the rise of the rubber industry. The author is careful not to burden the reader with mathematical and physical descriptions of blending, mixing, calendering, molding, and rheology in the early chapters, but later he provides rigorous mathematical models of topics such as kinematics of flow, viscoelastic fluid models, influence of screw curvature on Newtonian fluids, flow of Newtonian fluids through long-profile dies, and simulation of flow in calendering. An excellent book for students of the rubber industry and a must read for engineers in the polymer and rubber industry. Upper-division undergraduates through researchers.—*K. Bennett, Kalamazoo Valley Community College*

OAB-1578   TP1087   94-37332 MARC
Woodward, Arthur E. **Understanding polymer morphology.** Hanser/Hanser-Gardner, 1995. 130p bibl index ISBN 1-56990-141-4 pbk, $19.95

Woodward's book is one of a series intended to be "read profitably by a beginner" according to E.H. Immergut, the series editor. The author succeeds admirably in this effort. He introduces the basics of morphological investigative methods followed by more detailed discussions of polymer morphological features. Subsequent chapters correlate observed morphologies with given polymer types (e.g., semicrystalline, liquid crystals, block copolymers, and blends). Final chapters discuss morphologies resulting from processing, deformation, and failure, and effects of morphology on mechanical properties. The discussions are clear and concise, and the morphologies being discussed are illustrated with drawings and optical and electron micrographs. This book is written for beginners and yet is well referenced to permit the reader to easily access more detailed information on specific topics. Undergraduates; graduates.—*P. G. Heiden, Michigan Technological University*

■ Health Sciences

OAB-1579   R735   94-42800 CIP
Bonner, Thomas Neville. **Becoming a physician: medical education in Britain, France, Germany, and the United States, 1750-1945.** Oxford, 1996 (c1995). 412p bibl index afp ISBN 0-19-506298-1, $35.00

This scholarly book is an extremely valuable addition to the history of medical education. Bonner's long years of research on the subject provide a wealth of detail in comparing and contrasting the evolution of medical education in four major Western countries, and about the social, economic, and political forces that shaped its development from the Enlightenment through WW II. He fashions a tapestry of fascinating comparisons among the countries, interweaving details of each throughout, rather than assigning separate chapters to each country. The result is a comprehensive portrayal of all aspects of medical education over two centuries. Although medicine became a part of university study in the Middle Ages, medical education occurred both in academia and in small private schools of "rural, practical" medicine, to meet the needs for medical care of rural and poorer populations, resulting in two levels of practitioners. Improved quality of education did not occur in the US until the early 1900s, following the 1910 Flexner Report. Particularly interesting is the consistent struggle of medical students to earn a medical degree while trying to afford the costs of tuition, board, and meals throughout years of concentrated study. Highly recommended, undergraduate through professional.—*A. R. Davis, Johns Hopkins University*

OAB-1580   R724   93-18160 CIP
Charlesworth, Max. **Bioethics in a liberal society.** Cambridge, 1993. 172p index ISBN 0-521-44503-5, $39.95; ISBN 0-521-44952-9 pbk, $12.95

This book fits nicely into contemporary works that focus on ethical issues in health care, biotechnology, and medicine. What sets this one off is that its topics are discussed in the context of the current social and political context. This enchances its topical nature and provides the reader with an appropriate frame of reference. The book is not without controversy but Charlesworth manages to present the material in a focused manner. The six chapters cover (after an introduction) autonomy and the liberal idea, ending life, beginning life, and distribution of health-care resources; a final chapter discusses bioethical realities and ethical agreements in a liberal society. The reader will be led through all the favorite areas of bioethics including physician-assisted suicide, death and the hospital, surrogate parenting, new reproductive technologies, and a complete chapter on health-care resource allocation. Each chapter has a very current bibliography and contains many useful resources. Helpful in any college-level ethics, philosophy, or allied health education course. Highly recommended.—*R. G. McGee Jr., Walters State Community College*

OAB-1581   RB155   91-38477 CIP
The code of codes: scientific and social issues in the human genome project, ed. by Daniel J. Kevles and Leroy Hood. Harvard, 1992. 397p bibl index afp ISBN 0-674-13645-4, $29.95

With recent debate about the costs and benefits of the Human Genome Project, this is a timely and highly readable account of the history, science, and social issues that surround the project. The book is divided into three parts; the first sets the context for the discussions that follow by providing a brief account of the history and politics of the early eugenic movement, and by explaining fundamentals of genetics and molecular biology. The second part addresses in detail the technological challenges of the genome project, the impact the new technologies will have on biology in the future, and the opportunities "DNA-based" medicine will provide. The final section probes ethical, legal, and social issues raised by the project. Many of these issues are not new; however, they are brought more sharply into focus by the knowledge that the sequence of the human genome will provide. Contributors to the volume are all leaders in their fields. The writing style is fairly consistent throughout; each chapter has numerous references, and there is a selected bibliography. An excellent book; should be required reading for all undergraduate biology students.—*L. D. Polley, Wabash College*

OAB-1582   R724   94-11005 MARC
De Blois, Jean. **A primer for health care ethics: essays for a pluralistic society,** by Jean deBlois, Patrick Norris, and Kevin O'Rourke. Georgetown University, 1994. 255p index afp ISBN 0-87840-562-3 pbk, $19.95

This remarkable work converses briefly but importantly with virtually every aspect of health care ethics. Reflective persons will agree with the authors that "Something is not ethical in our pluralistic society simply because 'everyone does it,'" if only out of recognition that society and culture become meaningless, cheap, and tawdry without some definition of humanity as persons. The authors are experienced theologians and teachers but do not adopt sanctimonious or religious tones in the work, which covers the subject from a consideration of the worth of individuals. The accounts of such divergent cases as Baby Fae and Pamela Hamilton will resonate with readers repelled by those horrific events. Despite their Catholic backgrounds, the authors provide clear moral guidance in their conclusion that anencephalic fetuses should be aborted reasonably after modern technology confirms the diagnosis. The moral law toward which their expositions move is one in which humankind may seek to find equanimity of mind and purpose as a technologically overwhelming universe unfolds before us. Definitions of ethical systems and insights into the bases for ethical controversy are valuable parts of this compact book. Thoughtful, engaging, and sound. All levels.—*D. R. Shanklin, University of Chicago*

OAB-1583   KF3821   95-50697 CIP
Dworkin, Roger B. **Limits: the role of the law in bioethical decision making.** Indiana, 1996. 205p index afp ISBN 0-253-33075-0, $35.00

As ethical and social dilemmas mount with an advancing technology, so also have people turned to the legal system for solutions. Dworkin examines the basis of why biomedical and healthcare decisions more often end up in courts of law. The author does a masterful job of reviewing the present US legal system when it comes to bioethical decision making. In fact, the first chapter reviews the legal, legislative, and constitutional aspects of this issue. The information is clearly presented to provide readers with a new insight into what is happening. Seven chapters touch all of the hot point issues in bioethics: abortion, sterilization, alternative reproduction techniques, genetic screening, death and dying, and human research; the final chapter offers conclusions from this study. Dworkin makes it clear that use of the legal system in this area is unwarranted in most cases and that there exist alternatives for decision making in difficult bioethics cases. An excellent resource for entry-level courses on bioethics for health care practitioners, law students, and physicians. Upper-division undergraduate and graduate students; faculty; professionals.—*R. G. McGee Jr., Walters State Community College*

OAB-1584   Orig
The Ethics of research involving human subjects: facing the 21st century, ed. by Harold Y. Vanderpool. University Publishing Group, 1996. 531p index ISBN 1-55572-036-6, $59.00

The public-private medical research enterprise is immense and growing, worldwide. Much of this research requires the use of human subjects. Because our capabilities, technologies, and knowledge base have expanded so dramatically in the last 25 years, we are able to use human subjects for research in ways never before dreamed. These new capabilities are creating serious tensions between the ethics of how and when human subjects are used and the imperative to obtain more data in a world where profits, reputation, and fame rest upon more access to and control of information and knowledge. This dynamic has created medical-ethical-legal research issues unknown in the past. This book provides historical, current, and future perspectives on this dilemma. It is divided into four parts with a "road map" essay providing an overarching perspective and context for the chapters in each section. Many of the contributed

essays are structured in a debate-like format around points of controversy. Each of the contributing authors is a noted expert in their own right and, as a whole, bring a valuable diversity and perspective to this very complex field of thought. Useful notes and appendixes. A well organized, user friendly, comprehensive, and excellent resource on research ethics. Upper-division undergraduates through professionals.—*R. L. Jones, Pennsylvania State University, Hershey Medical Center*

OAB-1585   RA418   96-29318 CIP
Fábrega, Horacio. **Evolution of sickness and healing.** California, 1997. 364p bibl index afp ISBN 0-520-20609-6, $45.00

Fábrega offers a unique theoretical approach to the understanding of sickness and healing. His central thesis is the concept of *medical memes*, which are units of information in the brain that provide the material of sickness-health adaptation. This adaptation is realized by a collection of medical genes developed through geological evolution that influence and are influenced by historical, social, and cultural approaches to sickness and healing. This concept is fully developed in 11 chapters encompassing origins, early and late stages of the evolution of sickness and healing, and the need for theory, conceptual formulations, and philosophical considerations. Also included are references, a subject index, and an extraordinary appendix that outlines the evolution of sickness and healing. Fábrega's scholarly achievement is monumental, sweeping in scope, authoritative in content, and penetrating in its depth of analysis. It spans classical, modern, and postmodern periods and provides an integrating framework for the conceptual formulations of biological, psychological, social, political, and historical thought. As such, it is worthy of and requires serious reading, an important resource in the emerging field of medical evolution, and is an absolutely essential acquisition for all academic libraries. Upper-division undergraduates through professionals.—*R. E. Darnell, University of Michigan—Flint*

OAB-1586   GR110   93-40560 CIP
Fontenot, Wonda L. **Secret doctors: ethnomedicine of African Americans.** Bergin & Garvey, 1994. 162p bibl index afp ISBN 0-89789-354-9, $49.95

Fontenot presents a rich descriptive account of African American medical beliefs and practices in rural Louisiana. Major focus is on the role of "secret doctors" or "treaters" obtained through oral histories. Chapters treat the history of the region and its multiple indigenous groups; general folk medicine practices of African Americans, with particular emphasis on rural Louisiana; the role of African American women in health care; religious influences; and plants utilized for medicinal purposes. Helpful maps and figures are included as well as an appendix, references, and an author index. This book is written in a comfortable style that fully engages the reader while providing comprehensive scholarly background to support its scientific credibility, as it describes an African American medical system distinct from and yet shaped by other cultural influences. An excellent example of quality ethnographic research and a most appropriate addition to libraries serving students and faculty in cultural anthropology, African American studies, public health, medicine, nursing, and the allied health professions. Upper-division undergraduate through professional.—*R. E. Darnell, University of Michigan*

OAB-1587   R730   93-25357 CIP
The Health robbers: a close look at quackery in America, ed. by Stephen Barrett and William T. Jarvis. Prometheus Books, 1993. 526p index afp ISBN 0-87975-855-4, $25.95

At the same time that medical science is making great strides in developing new treatments and measuring patient outcomes to determine which treatments work, many in the US are turning to alternative forms of care and/or treatment to enhance health. Participating in alternative forms of health care is risky and potentially very dangerous. It is extremely difficult for the consumer to sort out the useful therapies from those that do not work or are outright frauds.

Editors Barrett and Jarvis, both respected health care professionals, have provided a guide that carefully evaluates many of the alternative forms of therapy. They draw upon the expertise of more than 20 noted professionals to give the reader insight into determining how to tell experts from pretenders, how to get reliable information, and how to communicate with doctors. The material is presented in an informative, highly readable, and interesting style. For those interested in not wasting their money on useless forms of health care, protecting their own health, and better understanding the dynamics associated with alternative medicine, this book is a must. All levels.—*R. L. Jones, Pennsylvania State University, Hershey Medical Center*

OAB-1588 R488 95-17710 CIP
Lawrence, Susan C. **Charitable knowledge: hospital pupils and practitioners in eighteenth-century London.** Cambridge, 1996. 390p index ISBN 0-521-36355-1, $69.95

The 18th century was a critical period in the evolution of modern medicine. It was then that hospital medicine came to occupy a central position in training and practice of medicine, a fundamental step in the transition to scientific medicine in the 19th century when laboratory medicine was subsequently added to hospital medicine. London has occupied a unique position in this early evolution because hospital medicine developed in a setting where there were no medical schools with faculty and structured curricula that either controlled or affected the development of hospital medicine elsewhere. As such, London allows for a clearer dissection of the forces that shaped the emergence of hospital medicine. Lawrence (history, Univ. of Iowa) explores and analyzes the emergence of hospital medicine in 18th-century London hospitals and how they came to be recognized as centers of teaching, knowledge, and authority. The book highlights the gradual but cumulative effects of shifts in organizational structures, professional politics, and the medical marketplace on medical education; it also examines the increasing significance and relationship among medical knowledge, societies, and publications that formed the basis of the advances in medicine. Based on extensive research of primary sources, thoughtful analysis, and meticulous study over a ten-year period, this is a scholarly work of the first order. Lucidly written, diversely supported, brilliantly balanced, and well organized, an engaging book well worth reading, and a valuable resource. All levels.—*G. Eknoyan, Baylor College of Medicine*

OAB-1589 R895 93-19005 MARC
Mould, Richard F. **A century of X-rays and radioactivity in medicine: with emphasis on photographic records of the early years.** Institute of Physics Publishing, 1993. (Dist. by AIDC, 2 Winter Sport Lane, P.O. Box 20, Williston, VT 05495-0020) 217p bibl index ISBN 0-7503-0224-0, $59.50

Thirty years' research by British medical physicist and cancer statistician Mould in museums, history of medicine libraries, and public and private organizations and collections in many countries has resulted in a fascinating, comprehensive, illustrated history of the discovery, development, and applications of X-rays, radiology, and radioactivity since 1895, the year that Wilhelm Conrad Rontgen discovered X-rays. The 640 illustrations under 200 topics, focusing on the early years of discovery and invention, with clear, concise text and captions, provide an absorbing account of how this field of technology has benefited society over the last 100 years. Topics such as X-ray injuries before correct use and dosage became known through trial and error, early treatment applications in a wide range of diseases and conditions, X-ray frauds, manufacture of equipment and parts, military uses, development and refinement of diagnostic radiology, use in authenticating art objects, and recent advances in linear tomography and magnetic resonance imaging, are, separately and collectively, interesting and informative. Highly recommended for undergraduate and graduate students and faculty, historians in medicine and science, and health care professionals.—*A. R. Davis, Johns Hopkins University*

OAB-1590 HV4915 92-39344 CIP
Orlans, F. Barbara. **In the name of science: issues in responsible animal experimentation.** Oxford, 1993. 297p bibl index afp ISBN 0-19-507043-7, $39.95

The use of animals as experimental subjects involves a contentious set of issues that have received an extraordinary amount of attention in recent years. Orlans ambitiously attempts to provide a comprehensive overview of these problems: historical, philosophical, scientific, and political. Although coverage of each of these broad topics is necessarily brief, she does an excellent job of laying out the issues in a clear and nonpolemical fashion. In the early chapters Orlans discusses the historical background of contemporary debates, focusing primarily on the well-known cases of physiologists François Magendie and Claude Bernard, and the antivivisection controversy that their research engendered. Against this historical background she outlines the major ethical issues and positions that form the foundation for contemporary debates. The remainder of the book is devoted to a broad range of policy issues, including animal welfare legislation and its implementation; problems and prospects for alternatives to animal experimentation; problems of establishing guidelines for animal suffering; and the somewhat different issues that arise from the use of animal experiments for research, testing, and educational purposes. An excellent overview for both general reader and specialist. General; advanced undergraduate through professional.—*J. B. Hagen, Radford University*

OAB-1591 R725 92-49488 CIP
Rodwin, Marc A. **Medicine, money, and morals: physicians' conflicts of interest.** Oxford, 1993. 411p index afp ISBN 0-19-508096-3, $25.00

A powerful indictment of the commercialization of US medicine and the destructive role of both overt and covert conflicts of interest between physicians and their patients. Rodwin has an unusual background in health law and the organization of medical practice, which serves him well in this most readable but tightly written work. His choice of Arnold S. Relman, M.D., to write the foreword is apt, as Relman was the first physician of note to call attention to the negative results of commercialization of health care, a deprofessionalization that destroys the sanctity of the doctor-patient relationship, a trust on which treatment depends. Rodwin gives names, places, dates, and circumstances in a compelling litany of misfeasance by repeal of the inner-fiduciary role of the physician. Well described are both obvious and subtle conflicts of interest and the demonstrably poor record of organized medicine to deal with the issues. The work is heavily annotated and extremely well researched. This is that rare "must read" book. The timing is clearly designed to affect current policy planning by Hillary Rodham Clinton's task force on health care finance, as well it should. An excellent work! All levels.—*D. R. Shanklin, University of Chicago*

OAB-1592 BF789 95-41384 CIP
Sheehan, George. **Going the distance: one man's journey to the end of his life.** Villard, 1996. 185p afp ISBN 0-679-44843-8, $22.00

Sheehan—doctor, athlete, writer of a popular column in *Runners World*, and the bestselling author of seven books—died of cancer at the age of 74 in 1993. The metaphor of the athlete, "going the distance," reflects Sheehan's thoughts and feelings about life and death after he was diagnosed with inoperable prostate cancer in 1986. We are privileged to be able to share in his thought process, fears, and anger as he struggles to at first defeat and then to live with his cancer and finally to come to terms with life and his approaching death. This is an eloquently written, clear, and sensitive book that provides valuable insights into issues we all must face as we move through our lives. Sheehan is able to work through complex, delicate, and difficult life circumstances and provide clarity, perspective, and useful options upon which we can personally reflect. A truly remarkable book, one which for all will reward repeated readings. General.—*R. L. Jones, Pennsylvania State University, Hershey Medical Center*

OAB-1593 RG525 94-48779 CIP
Vaughan, Christopher. **How life begins: the science of life in the**

womb. Times Books/Random House, 1996. 290p index ISBN 0-8129-2103-8, $23.00

All of us have experienced, yet few can recall, the 38-week period from the moment of our conception to that of our birth. This period of development has until recently remained a mystery to scientists and laypersons alike. However, with the advent of ultrasound, other new imaging techniques, and drawing from the work of both behavioral and developmental scientists, Vaughan has been able to unlock some of the secrets of gestation to the post-gestational world. Readers are informed about the sensations—sights, sounds, and feelings—that a developing fetus experiences as it progresses through gestation. Additionally, Vaughan addresses a variety of other related issues. For example, he discusses how sperm compete with each other for access to the egg, how morning sickness may be adaptive, how sexual and gender identities are formed, how the fetus dreams and practices breathing while it is sleeping, and how a mother's behavior and body shape change during pregnancy. Vaughan does an excellent job of presenting this highly politicized and potentially explosive topic in a matter-of-fact, nonconfrontational manner. Coverage is complete. Helpful drawings and diagrams. A fascinating and accessible read for anyone interested in the science of life in the womb. Recommended primarily to public libraries and a lay audience. General; lower-division undergraduates.—*N. Krusko, Beloit College*

OAB-1594 R730 91-33826 CIP
Young, James Harvey. **American health quackery: collected essays.** Princeton, 1992. 299p index afp ISBN 0-691-04782-0, $24.95

This wonderful book contains collected essays of America's foremost historian of the patent medicine and health quackery industries. In earlier works, Young studied the history of health quackery in America from the Colonial period to the 1960s. In this new book, he continues his work, carrying the study into the recent past. These essays demonstrate Young's excellent scholarship as well as his marvelous sense of humor and his witty use of the language. Chapters cover the regulation of health quackery, "nostrums and children," laetrile, and AIDS. The volume is a valuable resource for those interested in the modern medical and health world, as well as the history of medicine and public health. A fitting testimony to the excellent research and writing of the author, whose works have rapidly become classics in the field, this book is highly recommended for libraries of every type—public, academic, and professional.—*M. Kaufman, Westfield State College*

OAB-1595 R724 93-3823 CIP
Zaner, Richard M. **Troubled voices: stories of ethics and illness.** The Pilgrim Press, 1993. 161p index afp ISBN 0-8298-0964-3, $19.95

Case studies are often used to teach the principles and concepts of medical ethics. Philosopher Zaner continues that methodology but presents the cases in a different format. Using story and first-person narrative, he relates the real-life situations encountered in a tertiary medical setting as he developed the role of clinical ethics consultant. He helps readers understand the phenomena of being in the situation at two levels; for himself, as he struggled with his new role, and for the patients and families as they struggled with illness. The situations are not headline-making court cases, but rather the ethical dilemmas that arise on a daily basis in most major medical centers. Concise chapters relate the story of patients and their families facing renal dialysis, a transplant, a defective fetus, infants in neonatal intensive care units, and end-of-life decisions. The dilemma is established, then the deliberation process and the final outcome are described. Each chapter ends with a brief philosophical reflection. A major theme running through the book is the importance, and frequent lack of, communication among all the involved parties. The book is easy to read and could be used and understood at many levels. An excellent contribution to the medical ethics literature. Community college; undergraduate through professional.—*M. A. Thompson, Saint Joseph College*

■ Public Health

OAB-1596 RB155 93-47973 Orig
Assessing genetic risks: implications for health and social policy, ed. by Lori B. Andrews et al.; Committee on Assessing Genetic Risks, ..., Institute of Medicine. National Academy Press, 1994. 338p bibl index ISBN 0-309-04798-6, $44.95

When funds were appropriated for the Human Genome Project, three to five percent of that money was set aside to study the ethical, legal, and social implications of the genetic knowledge the project would produce. This book, part of the result, is a report from the National Academy of Sciences' Committee on Assessing Genetic Risks. Risks are the focus here, not the advantages of the numerous genetic tests that will soon become available. Chapters on genetic counseling, public education, patient rights and personnel, laboratory, studies, and financing describe the important issues of current debate, and each concludes with clear and balanced recommendations for future policy and research. Among these are respect for patient autonomy and privacy, access to thorough and nondirective counseling, not offering tests that detect disorders currently without therapies, and a call for greater genetic education at all levels. The list of issues considered seems exhaustive, and the writing is beautifully clear and accessible to the average reader. Full references for each chapter and a complete index are included. Definitely recommended. All levels.—*D. Carmichael, Pittsburg State University*

OAB-1597 RA395 94-5949 CIP
Castro, Janice. **The American way of health: how medicine is changing and what it means to you.** Little, Brown, 1994. 282p bibl index ISBN 0-316-13272-1, $19.95; ISBN 0-316-13275-6 pbk, $9.95

Experienced *Time* reporter Castro carefully examines the major health reform bills from the House, Senate, and President Clinton and then compares and contrasts key points not only with such national programs as Medicare and Medicaid, but also with regional Health Maintenance Organizations (HMOs) and state plans like Hawaii's. National health programs of Canada, Britain, Germany, and Australia are also briefly discussed. This is a brave and big assignment, and yet there is just the right amount of background information on the development of different proposals as well as on the main players and issues to help consumers better understand the single-payer approach as opposed to the Cooper, Chafee, Jackson Hole, and other plans. The high costs of health care are explained, as well as the differences between medical care and other occupations in terms of economics. Discussions and comparisons indicate both positive and negative aspects of such things as managed care, cost controls, universal coverage, and quality assurance. An exceptional glossary defines the many varied and changing health care terms and meanings. Very highly recommended for all libraries.—*E. R. Paterson, SUNY College at Cortland*

OAB-1598 RA395 94-14568 CIP
Churchill, Larry R. **Self-interest and universal health care: why well-insured Americans should support coverage for everyone.** Harvard, 1994. 110p index afp ISBN 0-674-80092-3, $19.95

This well-crafted, clearly written, and compelling argument fulfills its title and subtitle. It is the clearest statement so far on the critical relationship between universal health care and the future vitality of the nation. Churchill draws effectively from early work, from obvious cost trends, and from specific examples of medical care both cogent and awry. His assertion that "Health care is so intertwined with our general well-being ... physically and materially ... that health insurance cannot be separated out as an incidental possession," balanced by his belief that "... we can still maintain individual freedoms while embracing social affiliations." His analysis proves false the contrary claims. Cooperative use of technology will reduce the cost of so-called managed competition, which, with full apology to Lewis Carroll, means what the speaker intends. The thesis proceeds logically, setting aside the straw man arguments that warn of rationing, defining the purpose of health care for individuals and for society and showing their irretrievable interdependence, then concluding with an exposition of the benefits to individuals and the nation of constructive mutual engagement. A must read for all levels.—*D. R. Shanklin, University of Chicago*

OAB-1599   RA1199   96-33052 CIP
Comprehensive toxicology, editors-in-chief, I. Glenn Sipes, Charlene A. McQueen, and A. Jay Gandolfi. Pergamon, 1997. 13v. bibl index afp ISBN 0-08-042301-9, $3,697.00

This is a monumental, once-in-a-generation (or even a lifetime) work. Not alphabetical, it is really encyclopedic in scope, intended as an "in-depth, state-of-the-art review of toxicology" and includes hundreds of chapters by hundreds of authors from academia, industry, consulting firms, and government. It provides valuable overviews and extensive details in each of the volumes. There are very few areas omitted (e.g., toxicology of the eye). It is generally well conceived, organized, and edited, with separate editors for each volume. Coverage (by volume) is as follows: vol. 1. General Principles; 2. Testing; 3. Biotransformation and Metabolism; 4. Blood; 5. Immunotoxicology; 6. Cardiovascular Toxicology; 7. Renal Toxicology; 8. Respiratory System; 9. Intestinal System and Liver; 10. Reproductive and Endocrine Toxicology; 11. Nervous System and Behavioral Toxicology; 12. Carcinogens and Anticarcinogens; and 13. Index. The quality of chapters naturally varies. References to the primary literature are sparse in some, copious in others. An author-year rather than numerical footnote would have enhanced the value of the work, making it easier to recognize important references (not to mention easier to write and edit); figures adapted from primary literature are well referenced. Timeliness is always a problem in a multiauthored work, where the prompt are penalized by the need to wait for the tardy. (Chapter manuscripts were submitted mainly in mid-1995.) The fascinating early history of toxicology gets short shrift in the introductory volume but is picked up in several subsequent volumes. Many chapters include classical papers from the mid-1900s, an era often lost by those relying only on computerized searches. In this reviewer's view, such continuity is extremely valuable to students and researchers, as well as those interested in the intellectual history of the discipline.

There are too many excellent chapters to acknowledge individually, and they range from broad reviews of morphology and physiology to substance-specific effects on particular organ systems. Introductory chapters will be especially valuable for the general reader, e.g., the chapters on toxicokinetics and apoptosis (vol. 1); enzyme regulation (vol. 3); immunotoxicology and overview of the immune system (vol. 5); mechanisms of injury in the glomerulus and proximal tubule (vol. 7); xenobiotic metabolism (vol. 9); selective vulnerability and cell signaling in nervous system and behavioral toxicology (vol. 11); and protooncogenes and tumor suppressor genes (vol. 12). Well produced and generally free of typographical errors, the book is attractively styled and figures are generally easy to read. Like the editors, this reviewer thinks these volumes are valuable for students, researchers, and managers who must understand toxicologic principles. It should be on the shelf of every toxicologist and environmental scientist, but the price (about 50 cents/page) is probably prohibitive for most individual practitioners accustomed to spending six cents/page for typical toxicology works. According to the publisher, volumes will be sold individually (price not yet available). The set can also be purchased with a CD-ROM (not received for review) for $4,250. Considering the massiveness of the set (more than 6,600 pages excluding index), the added investment in a CD-ROM sounds like an excellent idea. Unfortunately, price will discourage many academic libraries from acquiring it as well. It would still be a bargain at half the price. Upper-division undergraduates through professionals; two-year technical program students.—*M. Gochfeld, Robert Wood Johnson Medical School*

OAB-1600   RC81   94-37594 CIP
Consumer health USA, v.2, ed. by Alan M. Rees. Oryx, 1997. 597p bibl indexes afp ISBN 1-57356-068-5, $65.00

Health consumers today are extremely challenged to become knowledge-

able and self-responsible regarding their own health care. Likewise, when confronted with diseases, they want to be able to communicate and become partners with their physicians. Although the Internet offers a great wealth of health information, much of it may be inaccurate or misleading. Rees's book (v.1, CH, Jun'95), therefore, is an excellent health resource not only for the general public but also for medical professionals, teachers, and health professionals. A broad scope of diseases and disease conditions familiar even to lay individuals are presented in easily understood language and organized according to body systems, e.g., eye and gastrointestinal system diseases. Subject glossaries aid in understanding terminology. Each of the 24 chapters contains a question-and-answer section that succinctly summarizes questions that people may ask when confronted with a particular disease or disorder. Each chapter includes specific telephone numbers and addresses of national hotlines and/or national Internet sites (e.g., Centers for Disease Control and Prevention) in which health resource information related to the chapter topic can be obtained. Appendixes have toll-free numbers for health information by subject and lists of health/medical foundations, associations, and US Department of Health and Human Services addresses and telephone numbers. A valuable medical/health consumer resource for personal use and for academic libraries. All levels.—*L. Synovitz, Southeastern Louisiana University*

OAB-1601   RC81   94-37594 CIP
Consumer health USA: essential information from the federal health network, ed. by Alan M. Rees. Oryx, 1995. 543p indexes afp ISBN 0-89774-889-1, $49.50

This wonderful reference should be in every public and private library, especially in those with a focus on health concerns. It provides facts and information that all patients need in dealing with their medical or surgical needs. This impressive volume includes specific information on various ailments, so the patient and the care-provider should be able to understand their problems and to respond adequately to them. Discussed are AIDS and sexually transmitted diseases; allergies; blood diseases and disorders; cancer; contraception and reproduction; dental care and oral health; diabetes and other endocrine disorders; ear, nose, and throat disorders; eye disorders; gastrointestinal disorders; genetic disorders; heart disease and blood vessel disorders; infectious diseases; liver and gallbladder disorders; lung and respiratory disorders; mental and emotional health; neurological disorders; nutrition and weight loss; urogenital system disorders; women's health; and a miscellany that includes information on steroids, drugs and the brain, foot care, hyperthermia, pain control after surgery, nursing home care, and blood donations. Finally, there are addresses and phone numbers of health hotlines and state agencies on aging. A valuable reference work. General; professional.—*M. Kaufman, Westfield State College*

OAB-1602   92-82813 Orig
Consumer Reports Books. **How to resolve the health care crisis: affordable protection for all Americans.** Consumer Reports Books, 1992. 270p index ISBN 0-89043-626-6 pbk, $4.95

An excellent review of the catastrophic condition of the US's fragmented health and illness care systems. But more importantly, this book provides lucid reasons for the "why" of the mess and what the US public needs to do to reach the goal of affordable protection for all its citizens. The editors critically examine each aspect of the current health-care crisis, exposing wasted health-care dollars, profit made on illness by insurance companies and physicians, the fallacies of managed-care systems that are really managed-cost systems, and the abuses of the Medicare system and long-term care insurance. The second half of the book, in search of a better way, reviews the Canadian, Hawaiian, and Minnesota health plans and compares coverage with US plans. The change suggested, a single payer system, will be hard to achieve, for many will "lose" who have previously gained from the illnesses and hardships of others. The final chapter offers readers advice on how to be heard on the issues facing the nation. Well done, timely, easy to read. A must for every citizen!—*J. E. Thompson, University of Pennsylvania*

OAB-1603   HD7102   93-41868 MARC

Coughlin, Teresa A. **Medicaid since 1980: costs, coverage, and the shifting alliance between the federal government and the states,** by Teresa A. Coughlin, Leighton Ku, and John Holahan. Urban Institute, 1994. 181p bibl ISBN 0-87766-617-2, $46.50; ISBN 0-87766-618-0 pbk, $19.50

This book is essential for anyone who hopes to analyze the growth of Medicaid spending over the past decade. Medicaid program objectives and coverages as well as Medicaid's legislative history are thoroughly examined. The authors detail trends in federal/state financing sources as well as cost shifting between governmental jurisdictions. Analysis, using data through 1992, is presented with careful attention to sourcing and methodology. Although the book is quantitatively dense with a large number of tables, the authors attempt a rational political/economic explanation for the surge in Medicaid spending by analyzing individual components of spending (long-term care, home care, inpatient services, and managed care) as well as demographic factors. The book describes Medicaid's cost-containment efforts beyond the usual discussion of diagnostic related groups (DRGs) and cost shifting to privately insured patients. The book concludes with an analysis of how Medicaid may be managed under various health care reform proposals, though this discussion will rapidly become outdated. Recommended for all levels of research on health care reform, particularly research centered on single payer models and/or government involvement in health care provision. General; upper-division undergraduate through professional.—*D. T. Russell, Illinois Wesleyan University*

OAB-1604   BJ1475   94-9702 CIP

The Crisis of care: affirming and restoring caring practices in the helping professions, ed. by Susan S. Phillips and Patricia Benner. Georgetown University, 1994. 190p bibl afp ISBN 0-87840-558-5, $55.00

The major theme of this book speaks to the dehumanizing elements of modern technology, cost efficiency, and productivity, in which the intrinsic needs of caregiver and care receiver often remain unfulfilled. It shows a richer, fuller, more meaningful agenda by sensitizing the reader to the centrality of caring to the healing arts. The authors present insightful and meaningful perspectives as well as social, psychological, religious, and philosophical ideas for health professions. The book is arranged into 10 chapters in essay format, the first nine of which are accompanied by personalized narrative. The first chapter (introduction) provides historical background as well as a central focus on personhood that permeates each chapter. Approximately half of the chapters relate to caring in health professions in terms of the moral sources of goodness involved in caring, the role of compassion in moral responsibility, and caring as both gift and goal. A chapter of philosophical reflections on caring practices concludes the book. This book is a precious gift to the reader; it speaks simultaneously to both head and heart, to provide the core nourishment that sustains and enhances those who offer human service to others. An absolutely essential acquisition for libraries serving the needs of the health professions, health care administration, and public policy. Chapter references. Graduate through professional.—*R. E. Darnell, University of Michigan*

OAB-1605   RA651   94-858 CIP

The Epidemiological imagination: a reader, ed. by John Ashton. Open University, 1994. 209p bibl index ISBN 0-335-19101-0, $85.00; ISBN 0-335-19100-2 pbk, $27.00

In society's effort to improve the health of its citizens, population medicine's perspective becomes more and more important to the quality and cost effectiveness of the clinical decision making process. Epidemiology, the science of the distribution and determinants of disease, is recognized as a fundamental component to understanding population medicine. Yet, many physicians and other health professionals have only a limited understanding of the success and history of this basic population-based science. This book has been designed to introduce interested readers to epidemiological thinking in a unique and highly effective manner. Each chapter represents a short introduction by a well-

respected epidemiologist, followed by two papers. One of the papers reflects the work of that epidemiologist and the other is a classic work characterizing the significance and potential of the epidemiological perspective. The book is intended as a sourcebook for postgraduate education at a master's degree level in epidemiology. However, the organization and content of this work make it accessible to a much wider audience. This work is one of the most interesting and stimulating presentations of the complexity, richness, and breadth of this very important, yet little understood, health-related science. Upper-division undergraduate through professional.—*R. L. Jones, Pennsylvania State University, Hershey Medical Center*

OAB-1606   RA564   92-30579 MARC

Estes, Carroll L. **The long term care crisis: elders trapped in the no-care zone,** by Carroll L. Estes, James H. Swan, and associates. Sage, 1993. 328p bibl index ISBN 0-8039-3992-2, $49.95; ISBN 0-8039-3993-0 pbk, $24.95

As the product of a ten-year interdisciplinary research endeavor, this is an excellent, but dense, work. The study examined the impact of the prospective payment system on health care provision to older Americans. The authors argue that there is a widening gap between available services and the needs of the aged, aptly labeled "the no-care zone." The comprehensive national study, conducted in nine metropolitan areas, carefully documents the effects of policy on clients, staff, organizational viability, and services across the entire continuum of care from acute to long-term care. Although the book's cognitive dimension includes a plethora of statistics, graphs, and sophisticated quantitative research methodology, its moral and social dimensions present a chilling scenario for the future. The authors argue that the community care option of aged-care presents multiple fundamental social dilemmas regarding the responsibility of caregiver, the role of women as free labor, the accountability of the public for the care of society's dependents, care rationing, and reciprocity between the generations and the classes. This book clearly demonstrates that social policy for the aged tends to reproduce social inequities. An important book for a wide range of readers. All levels.—*D. B. Hamilton, University of Rochester*

OAB-1607   RT120   93-27426 CIP

Foner, Nancy. **The caregiving dilemma: work in an American nursing home.** California, 1994. 190p bibl index afp ISBN 0-520-08359-8, $25.00

Caring: it is hard to define, yet one can readily identify when it does and does not occur. Caring is what everyone wants from health care providers. When a physician, nurse, or aide is uncaring, one blames them personally rather than examines the context in which the behavior occurs. Foner, an anthropologist, reverses that trend in her excellent in-depth analysis of work in a nursing home. Because aides provide the majority of care in nursing homes, Foner spent eight months observing and working with them in a single New York City facility. She describes the aides, the work they do, and the environment in which they do it. She accurately identifies the dilemma faced by these women: the expectation to provide compassionate care to the residents while meeting the various rules and regulations of the nursing home bureaucracy that actually rewards the efficient completion of tasks. Foner also outlines the aides' methods of adaptation, both positive and negative, to this dilemma. Individual chapters are devoted to the residents, the nursing hierarchy, the work culture, and family. Foner integrates theory related to bureaucracy, family, work, and gender to support and explicate her findings. This well-written book precisely describes the reality of nursing aide work in many nursing homes in the US. Highly recommended. General; undergraduate; graduate; technical/professional.—*M. A. Thompson, Saint Joseph College*

OAB-1608   HV5745   94-31455 CIP

Growing up tobacco free: preventing nicotine addiction in children and youths, ed. by Barbara S. Lynch and Richard J. Bonnie; Committee on Preventing Nicotine Addiction in Children and Youths, ...,

Institute of Medicine. National Academy Press, 1994. 306p bibl index ISBN 0-309-05129-0 pbk, $24.95

A comprehensive, well-written assessment of youthful nicotine use that provides useful strategies for reducing the use of tobacco products by children. The authors hypothesize that reduced nicotine use among youth will ultimately reduce the number of tobacco-using adults, moving the country nearer to Healthy People 2000 goals. The book is amazingly comprehensive, addressing the physiology and psychology of nicotine addiction, societal supports for tobacco use, economic incentives and disincentives, and public policy implications. Each chapter ends with a summary of strategies for addressing issues raised in that section; these strategies are summarized, without background information, in the appendix at the end of the book. However, the reader interested in creating change to reduce tobacco use in society would be well advised to read every chapter carefully; each one contains background information that provides cogent arguments to support the need for youth-centered and comprehensive tobacco policies. Tables and figures are interspersed throughout. A book that should be in library collections serving health professionals. Elementary and secondary educators will find the book useful in developing effective curricula and school-based programs to curb tobacco use by school-aged youth. Upper-division undergraduate through professional.—*T. D. Delapp, University of Alaska, Anchorage*

OAB-1609 R726 96-32564 CIP
Handbook of diversity issues in health psychology, ed. by Pamela M. Kato and Traci Mann. Plenum, 1996. 439p bibl index ISBN 0-306-45325-8, $69.50

A significant contribution to health promotion literature, this work addresses important psychosocial issues in diverse cultures which, historically, have not been reflected in health care research. The highly qualified contributors represent diverse cultures, and their respective works are supported by extensive literature reviews that document the lack of inclusion of specific ethnic groups in much of the research supporting current health-care practices. Chapters are devoted to a discussion of statistical artifacts produced by heterogeneity of populations and the failure to control for these factors; practices and issues in the care of pediatric, adolescent, and elderly populations as well as individual considerations frequently omitted; issues related to the health of populations varying by gender and sexual orientation; individual considerations in health beliefs and behaviors in African Americans, Latinos, Asian Americans, and Native Americans; and the impact of socioeconomic status and the health of racial minority populations. An important work for medical students and upper-division undergraduates and graduate nursing students as well as faculty and professionals.—*V. B. Byers, emeritus, SUNY Health Science Center at Syracuse*

OAB-1610 RA643 93-28155 CIP
Hardy, Anne. **The epidemic streets: infectious disease and the rise of preventive medicine, 1856-1900.** Oxford, 1993. 325p bibl index ISBN 0-19-820377-2, $59.00

In its broadest terms, one of the issues engaging historians of medicine is whether the abatement of the mortality rate for infectious diseases in urban areas after 1859 can be attributed to better nutrition (e.g., Thomas McKeown, *The Modern Rise of Population*, CH, Sep'77) or to the involvement of the government in public health issues. Hardy presents an "epidemiological profile" of eight major infectious diseases—whooping cough, measles, scarlet fever, diphtheria, smallpox, typhoid, typhus, and tuberculosis—to "assess the relative contribution of different factors to their prevalence and fatality, and to lay a foundation stone for more detailed investigations of local patterns of disease incidence and behavior in the years between 1850 and 1914." Eight chapters examined in a narrative and epidemiological *tour de force* each one of the above-mentioned diseases as it affected London in the mid-to-late 19th century. Ultimately, Hardy concludes that "medical officers of health played a central part in the transformation of England's disease experience during the last decades of the nineteenth century. It was they who spearheaded the Vic-

torian struggle against infectious disease, and it was their initiative and their labours which led to the eventual eradication of the epidemic streets." The depth and range of Hardy's analysis mark this book as one of the most significant contributions to this ongoing debate. Upper-division undergraduate through faculty.—*T. P. Gariepy, Stonehill College*

OAB-1611 RA395 94-6009 CIP
Health care reform in the nineties, ed. by Pauline Vaillancourt Rosenau. Sage Publications, CA, 1994. 306p index ISBN 0-8039-5729-7, $42.00; ISBN 0-8039-5730-0 pbk, $19.95

"The patient died, but the operation was a success." Nineteen luminaries in US health care literature were asked to discuss health care reform in the '90s apparently using as their basis for analysis President Clinton's Health Security Act (possibly "one of the most important policy experiments of our time"). At the time of their writing, the editor (and most of the authors) believed the "prognosis...[was] generally positive." Although some chapters are now dated, e.g., chapter 3, "Should Single-Payer Advocates Support President Clinton's Proposal for Health Care Reform?," most contribute to the broad analysis of US health care *reform* issues in the 1990s. The position that reform is not needed is left unaddressed. Excellent chapters on comparative national health systems, ethical issues, federalism, state roles, business and labor perspectives, older persons' needs, and women's needs. Medicare is discussed in several of the chapters. Excellent resource for current health care data. General; upper-division undergraduate through professional.—*J. E. Allen, University of North Carolina at Chapel Hill*

OAB-1612 RA427 91-32853 CIP
Health promotion: disciplines and diversity, ed. by Robin Bunton and Gordon Macdonald. Routledge, 1992. 240p bibl indexes ISBN 0-415-07555-6, $72.50; ISBN 0-415-05981-X pbk, $22.50

Ten primarily British contributors, including the two editors, present health promotion from the perspective of relevant disciplines, excluding the health professions. The major point is that health promotion has emerged in the last decade as an important force to improve the quality and quantity of people's lives. Often referred to as the "New Public Health," health promotion seeks to support and encourage a participative social movement that enables individuals and communities to take control over their own health. These experts agree that the "medical model" is no longer sufficiently broad to encompass the field of health promotion. New conceptual developments are being generated by the relevant disciplines, as amply illustrated by scholars from eight areas: psychology, sociology, education, epidemiology, economics, social policy, social marketing, and communication theory. Equally important is the final chapter that discusses health promotion from the perspective of philosophy of science. The authors seem to agree that health promotion is an emerging and distinct discipline, characterized by its multidisciplinarity. Highly recommended for practitioners, educators, researchers, and interested others.—*A. R. Davis, U.S. Public Health Service*

OAB-1613 RJ102 93-6756 CIP
King, Charles R. **Children's health in America: a history.** Twayne, 1994 (c1993). 217p index afp ISBN 0-8057-4101-1, $26.95; ISBN 0-8057-4111-9 pbk, $14.95

King's book fills an important gap in the bookshelf on the history of public health by focusing on the health of children in the US. He writes well and bases his work on a wide variety of sources. (A glaring omission, however, is his failure to cite John Duffy's pathbreaking history of public health in New York City, *The Sanitarians*, CH, Sep'90). King's book is the first of a series, "Twayne's History of American Childhood," all of which should be important additions to the literature of the field. A work for every library. General; advanced undergraduate; graduate; pre-professional; professional.—*M. Kaufman, Westfield State College*

OAB-1614　　　RA395　　　93-3167 CIP

Laham, Nicholas. **Why the United States lacks a national health insurance program.** Greenwood, 1993. 198p bibl index afp (Contributions in political science, 331) ISBN 0-313-28745-7, $59.95

Laham addresses all aspects of national health insurance from the last 50 years in clear, compelling detail, outlining the causes and reasons for the failure of the US government to establish national health insurance and an organized, efficient health care delivery program with universal access to affordable care. In the 1940s and 1970s, when there were major efforts in Congress to develop national health insurance, equally strong counterforces defeated such action. In the 1940s and 1950s, the American Medical Association formed intensive, relentless efforts against cost-control measures that would interfere with fee-for-service care, labeling it "socialized medicine," connoting socialism, a system opposed to US freedoms. By the 1970s, hundreds of private insurance plans had developed, assuring most Americans of health insurance and paid care. Now, with the US health care "system" unable to provide care to millions of uninsured people and facing inevitable financial collapse, national health insurance will gain the federal and private support needed for its establishment. Highly recommended for policy-makers, political science and history students, health care professionals, and interested others. All levels.—*A. R. Davis, Johns Hopkins University*

OAB-1615　　　RA567　　　95-17398 CIP

Men's health and illness: gender, power, and the body, ed. by Donald Sabo and David Frederick Gordon. Sage Publications, CA, 1995. 334p bibl indexes afp (Research on men and masculinities series, 8) ISBN 0-8039-4814-X, $49.95; ISBN 0-8039-5275-9 pbk, $24.00

In this important contribution in understanding the connection between gender and men's health and illness, the first chapter (of part 1) by editors Sabo and Gordon is an excellent analysis that develops the basic information and historical perspective essential to an understanding of the rest of the book. The authors in part 2 bring together the hypothesis that men's health is variable depending upon race, ethnicity, and extent of physical disability. Contributors to part 3 clearly discuss the psychosocial and cultural aspects that may play a major part in one's perception of role and life style. This collaborative effort in presenting research and theories is so significant that it should become part of the literature studied by advocates of women's studies and men's studies. The reader, whether professional health care worker, researcher, clinician, or concerned individual, will obtain a clearer perspective on the connections between men's health and gender, along with a broader conceptualization of the experiences of men in contemporary society. Upper-division undergraduate through professional.—*G. M. Greenberg, emerita, Western Michigan University*

OAB-1616　　　T14　　　92-34837 CIP

Moore-Ede, Martin. **The twenty-four-hour society: understanding human limits in a world that never stops.** Addison-Wesley, 1993. 230p index ISBN 0-201-57711-9, $22.95

A futuristic book that explains clearly the increasing contrast between the limits of the human body's circadian rhythm (genetic internal clock), and the demands of the evolving high-tech nonstop world that requires a 24-hour schedule. Moore-Ede defines these changes as a "fundamental societal revolution" resulting from our rapidly expanding technology. He describes the side effects of shift work, sleep deficit, and the need to maintain one's body at its optimum alert level for maximum productivity, particularly in the airline, air controller, shipping, health care, and nuclear power industries, and citing major accidents involving the *Exxon Valdez*, Three Mile Island, and Chernobyl, all of which occurred in the middle of the night when people tend to be at their lowest level of alertness. These were hugely expensive accidents, and represent only a fraction of the other accidents and near-accidents that occur in the early hours before dawn. To counteract these effects, the author recommends a switch in corporations and industries that require round-the-clock work from a machine-centered to a human-centered environment. Highly readable, this fascinating book is recommended for undergraduate and graduate students, faculty, and interested others.—*A. R. Davis, U.S. Public Health Service*

OAB-1617　　　RA781　　　92-41692 CIP

Physical activity, fitness, and health: consensus statement, ed. by Claude Bouchard, Roy J. Shephard, and Thomas Stephens. Human Kinetics, 1993. 102p ISBN 0-87322-470-1 pbk, $20.00

A summary of the world's scientific evidence concerning the relationships between physical activity, fitness, and health, from the Second International Consensus Symposium on Physical Activity, Fitness, and Health, held in Toronto, Canada, in 1992. The symposium was conducted to broaden and clarify the scientific positions taken in the first meeting in 1988, and included 70 of the world's foremost scientists working in these areas; they produced consensus statements on over 70 specific topics related to physical activity, fitness, and health. The three editors were important participants in the symposium and are noted scientific leaders in relevant fields of study. The major areas of the symposium are very inclusive and encompass (1) a theoretical model of physical activity, fitness, and health; (2) assessment in physical activity, fitness, and health; (3) determinants of physical activity; (4) human adaptation to exercise; (5) physical activity and disease; (6) physical activity and the life cycle; (7) risks of activity and inactivity; and (8) dose-response issues. Each topic includes a summary of scientific evidence and future research directions. An outstanding resource. Advanced undergraduate through faculty.—*A. W. Jackson, University of North Texas*

OAB-1618　　　RA418　　　96-50376 CIP

The Social medicine reader, ed. by Gail E. Henderson et al. Duke University, 1997. 516p bibl afp ISBN 0-8223-1957-8, $79.95; ISBN 0-8223-1965-9 pbk, $29.95

This excellent book is a compilation of 70 essays and poems, many of them classics, that analyze the complexity of health and illness experiences. Well-known authors such as Eric Cassell, Edmond Pelligrino, Thomas Szasz, Timothy Quill, Victor Fuchs, Antonella Surbone, and many others examine the cultural perspective of experiences of illness, deviance, and disability; the influence of social factors on health and illness; the culture of medicine and medical practice; health care ethics and the provider's role; and medical care financing, rationing, and managed care. The editors have gathered a splendid collection of work that is thoughtful, well written, and timely. For health science libraries, this collection is a "must buy"; for college educators, the essays, which could be assigned individually or in sets, will quicken the thinking of college students at all levels. General readers; undergraduates through professionals.—*D. B. Hamilton, Western Michigan University*

OAB-1619　　　RA651　　　95-14250 CIP

Stolley, Paul D. **Investigating disease patterns: the science of epidemiology,** by Paul D. Stolley and Tamar Lasky. Scientific American Library, 1995. (Dist. by W.H. Freeman) 242p bibl index ISBN 0-7167-5058-9, $32.95

Much of what is currently known about how to keep people healthy and productive comes from epidemiological research, but how that is done is often not well understood. This handsomely illustrated, extremely readable, informative volume fills a need for a good overview for the interested person or student. Epidemiology, as the authors explain, is not limited to disease but can address any unusual or adverse effect on the health of the population. After an initial discussion of the early history and development of the field, the authors use the particular problems of lung cancer, heart disease, environmental hazards, and medically caused disease as case studies to illustrate such epidemiological methods as cohort studies and clinical trials. Further chapters show how epidemiological methods can be used to screen populations for health risks and evaluate the costs, risks, and benefits of health care services. Stolley and Lasky (Univ. of Maryland) have produced a work that is exceptionally interesting and understandable for untrained readers and also makes clear the complexity of problems and statistical methodologies epidemiology requires. Recommended. General; undergraduate through faculty; two-year technical program students.—*M. Mac Arthur, University of Colorado at Denver*

OAB-1620 RA781 93-19083 MARC

White, Timothy P. **The Wellness guide to lifelong fitness: the fitness bible for the 90's,** by Timothy P. White and the editors of the University of California at Berkeley wellness letter. Rebus, 1993. (Dist. by Random House) 477p index ISBN 0-929661-08-7, $29.95

White and his coauthors have developed an outstanding guide. Based on the major health-related principles of aerobic exercise, muscular strength and endurance, and flexibility, the authors provide answers to commonly asked questions about fitness, specific guidelines and methods, equipment purchase and use, cautions during exercise, and self-testing procedures. Based on sound scientific principles, the book is appealingly presented and features more than 1,000 full-color photographs. Specific recommendations are made for each type of exercise activity. The presentation goes beyond that typically presented in popular fitness texts. The reading is easy and the text is interesting. Little reference is made to body composition and nutrition, the relationship these have with exercise, or their ultimate impact on functional health and disease. An outstanding reference. General; advanced undergraduate; professional.—*J. R. Morrow, University of North Texas*

OAB-1621 RA564 96-34047 CIP

Women's health: complexities and differences, ed. by Sheryl Burt Ruzek, Virginia L. Olesen, and Adele E. Clarke. Ohio State, 1997. 689p bibl index afp ISBN 0-8142-0704-9, $49.95; ISBN 0-8142-0705-7 pbk, $19.95

The US women's health movement started approximately 25 years ago. Although significant strides have been made, a full understanding of the field has yet to be achieved. This book is certainly a major contribution to bringing together the current knowledge in the field, as well as raising issues for future discourse and research. The editors, sociologists with long-standing involvement in women's health, have assembled a distinguished group of contributors from a broad range of disciplines. Their emphasis is on "health" as a holistic concept, instead of a more narrow, biomedical focus. Rather than solely concentrating on criticizing what is wrong with women's health, the authors also discuss what has been done well and what could be improved. There are strong theoretical bases throughout with particular emphases on cultural and ethnic issues. A broad range of topics are addressed, from beauty myths to lesbian health issues, to ergonomics of women's work. Each chapter, including the extensive reference lists, could easily stand alone. An outstanding contribution to the understanding of women's *health* in the US, with potential to become a primary reference in the field. Highly recommended. Undergraduates through professionals.—*M. A. Thompson, Saint Joseph College*

■ Treatment of Disease

OAB-1622 RJ387 92-19402 CIP

Adolescents and AIDS: a generation in jeopardy, ed. by Ralph J. DiClemente. Sage, 1992. 314p indexes ISBN 0-8039-4181-1, $36.00; ISBN 0-8039-4182-X pbk, $17.95

AIDS/HIV as it affects adolescents is thoroughly discussed via three principal areas, i.e., epidemiology, prevention, and policy/legal perspectives. Individual authors provide a wealth of statistics and data to emphasize the growing risk and impact that HIV/AIDS is having on young people. Different populations of adolescents are examined regarding their AIDS/HIV knowledge, attitudes, behavior, beliefs, and condom use. Seven chapters are devoted just to AIDS prevention in this young age group. The use of mass media is very effectively addressed in one chapter and includes the overall effectiveness, e.g., credibility, exposure, influence; cost and feasibility; and barriers. A related important book: S.W. Henggeler et al., *Pediatric and Adolescent AIDS* (CH, Jan'93). This well-written, well-documented work teems with important, relevant information and would make a valuable addition to any type of library.—*J. Adams, Bowling Green State University*

OAB-1623 RC552 96-30206 CIP

Assessing psychological trauma and PTSD, ed. by John P. Wilson and Terence M. Keane. Guilford, 1997. 577p bibl indexes afp ISBN 1-57230-162-7, $50.00

Trauma researchers, scholars, and practitioners will embrace this timely handbook on the assessment of posttraumatic stress disorder (PTSD), which provides a complete multifaceted overview of the topic. Identifying and locating mental measurements for psychological research is often problematic (more so for a relatively new field such as PTSD research); those initiated in this process will immediately appreciate the merits of this fine work, which not only reviews and critiques the full range of instruments, techniques, and standardized measures used to assess PTSD, but often provides such critical information for acquiring these tools as the contact person, address, and phone number. In terms of depth of coverage Wilson and Keanne have left no stone unturned; moreover, there are several PTSD scales included within the text. This type of information is rarely provided and desperately needed by those using measuring instruments in their trauma research. This handbook is also extremely relevant and germane for those developing scales on trauma; there is an entire chapter dedicated to this topic entitled "Psychometric Theory in Development of PTSD Assessment Tools." John P. Wilson, a leading trauma expert and editor of the much acclaimed *International Handbook of Traumatic Stress Syndromes*, ed. by J.P. Wilson and B. Raphael (1993), is right on target with another important contribution to the field of PTSD research. Upper-division undergraduates through professionals.—*L. S. Beall, Auburn University*

OAB-1624 RC341 92-35150 CIP

Barondes, Samuel H. **Molecules and mental illness.** Scientific American Library, 1993. (Dist. by W.H. Freeman) 215p index ISBN 0-7167-5041-4, $32.95

Barondes's slim volume begins with a history of the biological understanding and treatment of mental illness and moves on to discuss the current understanding of the influence of genetics, brain chemicals, and drugs on mental functioning. The intriguing photographs, art work by mentally ill individuals, and clear and elegant diagrams of biological structures make this an attractive and inviting book. Case studies, biographical material, and poetry interject a personal element. The clear and simple explanations of the basic biology of brain function make it useful for the educated individual. This book is far from an in-depth treatment, but it provides a useful overview of the biological explanations for mental illness and the effects of drug treatment. Highly recommended for community college and undergraduate libraries.—*S. Shapiro, Indiana University East*

OAB-1625 Orig

Berg, Frances M. **Afraid to eat: children and teens in weight crisis,** ed. by Kendra Rosencrans. Healthy Weight Journal, 1997. 313p bibl index ISBN 0-918532-51-5 pbk, $21.95

There is a silent epidemic so large and extreme, it could only happen in this weight-obsessed culture: children's fear of eating. Six-year-olds understand that fat is undesirable and by fourth grade, 40 percent or more of girls "diet" at least occasionally. A survey of young girls revealed that they were more afraid of becoming fat than they were of cancer, nuclear war, or losing their parents. That is some of the bad news. The good news is that *Healthy Weight Journal* editor Berg is out to change these attitudes. This is the most important book on eating problems of the young. Berg's purpose, in a nutshell, is to help children and teens learn to nourish themselves without hating themselves. She is concerned with dysfunctional eating, a new term to describe problem eating behaviors not as severe as eating disorders. Fasting, skipping meals, and eating small amounts and never feeling satisfied are a few of the symptoms. Berg's solution is a benign health promotion approach that focuses on good health for all children, recognizes the connection between eating and weight problems, and seeks to strengthen the positive aspects of culture, family, and friends. Fear of food shatters lives, injures self-esteem, and even kills. Her call to action is loud, clear, and above all, provides the framework for change. Anyone involved in shaping the eating habits of the young must read this book, especially parents and teachers. All levels.—*R. Kabatznick, Queens College, CUNY*

OAB-1626 Orig
Berg, Frances M. **Health risks of weight loss.** Healthy Weight Journal, Healthy Living Institute, 402 South 14th St., Hettinger, ND 58639, 1994. 193p bibl ISBN 0-918532-43-4 pbk, $19.95

This first-rate report covers the scientific evidence on the health risks of weight-loss interventions. It is about as far from the "hype and hope" that characterize weight-loss advertisements as can be imagined. The goal of the report, which is successfully achieved, is to educate both professionals and consumers about the complexities of losing weight, a serious matter with health ramifications that include problems ranging from gallstones to elevated cholesterol to death. The report is divided into six sections: the risks of losing weight; effectiveness of treatment; weight cycling; morale increase with weight loss; treatment issues; and challenges for the 1990s. Above all, the report discusses the ethics of weight-loss procedures in view of so much treatment failure and the harm that may follow from unskilled methods. The appendix includes, among other things, excerpts from the 1991 New York City investigation of the weight-loss industry. References are complete and up-to-date. Highly recommended to all general readers, all levels of undergraduate and graduate students, and the professional community.—*R. Kabatznick, Queens College, CUNY*

OAB-1627 RC933 92-11557 CIP
Brewerton, Derrick. **All about arthritis: past, present, future.** Harvard, 1992. 317p index afp ISBN 0-674-01615-7, $24.95

Beginning with a history of the causes of disease, Brewerton presents interesting information on many diseases, focusing on arthritic disorders. He shadows famous scientists in history, e.g., Koch and Pasteur, up through time to current scientists, e.g., Bjorkman and Pauling. The chapters on the elucidation of the HLA (human lymphocyte antigen) entity and on DNA, RNA, and protein, are especially interesting. Much basic information on the nervous system, hormones, joints and joint failure, and the etiology of arthritis is provided. The many different ways arthritis can present are clearly and carefully explained. Associated diseases, e.g., Lyme disease, systemic lupus erythematosus, polymyalgia rheumatica, are included. Body defense mechanisms, relevant diagnostic information, pain, emotions, sex, and age (as each relates to arthritis) are all included, as well as the future probability for a prevention and/or cure. Especially interesting and enlightening reading from the historical viewpoint, with excellent explanations for processes relating to arthritis. All levels of readers.—*J. Adams, Bowling Green State University*

OAB-1628 RC200 93-20411 CIP
Brodman, Michael. **Straight talk about sexually transmitted diseases,** by Michael Brodman, John Thacker, and Rachel Kranz. Facts on File, 1993. 138p index afp ISBN 0-8160-2864-8, $16.95

The wealth of information, accurate and inaccurate, that teenagers receive about sexuality can be confusing and misleading, and is often a disincentive to health-enhancing practices. Brodman, Thacker, and Kranz have written a straightforward reference on sexually transmitted diseases (STDS) with accurate and unbiased information, offered in a manner that treats teens as intelligent and steers clear of paternalism. Tracing the "stories" of three couples throughout the book, the authors address situations and concerns of those with different-sex partners, same-sex partners, and those having sexual intercourse for the first time. The clinical information is readable and at the level of the intended readers. After acknowledging that abstinence is the only "safe" sexual behavior as far as STDs are concerned, the authors present, in various contexts, the more-risky/less-risky sexual behavior continuum. This behavioral information is reinforced continually throughout the book. More importantly, the authors acknowledge people's conflicting emotions concerning discussing and reading about sexuality, including adults' hesitations, and offer readers practical hints and starters for opening discussions of sexuality with their partners. Recommended for secondary school students and their parents, community college students and education majors.—*B. C. Hodges, SUNY College at Cortland*

OAB-1629 RC666 92-1542 CIP
Cardiology: the evolution of the science and the art, ed. by Richard J. Bing. Harwood Academic, 1992. 319p index ISBN 3-7186-0554-6 pbk, $16.00

An interesting and informative history of the many aspects of cardiology, ranging from cardiac catheterization and surgery to a detailed discussion of atherosclerosis as well as the medical use of isotopes. Each chapter details the evolution of important clinical observations and experimental results that have led to the present understanding and treatment of heart disease. Often events centuries old play a pivotal role. Each chapter is written by an individual whose contributions have advanced the particular problem under discussion. Bing coauthors each chapter and his editorial abilities keep reiteration to a minimum. There is an excellent bibliography at the end of each chapter. This easy-to-read book will interest a wide-ranging audience, both general and professional.—*H. W. Wallace, University of Pennsylvania*

OAB-1630 RB150 95-26739 CIP
Chronic fatigue syndrome: an integrative approach to evaluation and treatment, ed. by Mark A. Demitrack and Susan E. Abbey. Guilford, 1996. 317p bibl index afp ISBN 1-57230-038-8, $35.00

Chronic fatigue syndrome (CFS) is but one of several dysfunctional states afflicting humans that has received wide coverage and frequently misdirected causal interpretation by the popular press and media. In the scientific sphere, however, there is no general agreement as to its origin, contributing factors, or best methods of treatment. There is, however, a gradually developing consensus that only an integrated "biopsychosocial" perspective and approach will lead to some practical explanation and solution to the inherent diagnostic and treatment problems associated with the syndrome. This is the guiding principle used by the editors and coauthors of this monograph in presenting a current assessment and overview of the many facets of CFS. They all argue strongly and convincingly for the value of assuming a totally unbiased diagnostic approach, not based on any one pathogenic model, but fully taking into account the multiple possible causative factors. Twelve chapters are divided into three sections: background, assessment, and treatment. All are excellently written, authoritative, and well referenced. The overview they provide is a real contribution to the current understanding of this most perplexing syndrome. All levels.—*R. S. Kowalczyk, North Central Michigan College*

OAB-1631 RS67 94-70069 Orig
Conroy, Mary Schaeffer. **In health and in sickness: pharmacy, pharmacists, and the pharmaceutical industry in Late Imperial, early Soviet Russia.** East European Monographs, 1994. 703p bibl index (East European monographs, 386) ISBN 0-88033-283-2, $59.00

Conroy (history, Univ. of Colorado) examines the state of pharmacy, pharmacists, and the pharmaceutical industry in Russia during the period immediately preceding and following the Soviet Revolution of 1917. The first third of the book portrays the conditions before the Revolution: the second, the early metamorphosis of the pharmacy system under Soviet rule; the final third presents supporting, extensive annotations based to a great extent on original archival research from material that has become only recently available. Conroy has written an intelligent and insightful analysis of the economic, regulatory, educational, and scientific conditions that governed one profession and its related industry, their impact on the society in which they operated, how they were affected by the Revolution, and how, in turn, they provided the framework within which the profession and industry evolved under the new regime. Taken as a microcosm of the major events and changes that engulfed Russia during this period, this book represents an important contribution to understanding the socio-economic influences that were to shape the course of subsequent Russian history in general. This is a scholarly, well-researched, and informative book. As the first work on the subject in English, it is bound to remain a classic and primary source of information for a long time to come. All levels.—*G. Eknoyan, Baylor College of Medicine*

OAB-1632   Can. CIP
Engel, June. **The complete breast book.** Key Porter Books, 1996. (Dist. by Firefly Books Ltd.) 274p bibl index ISBN 1-55013-748-4 pbk, $19.95

For reasons very personal to every woman, breast cancer or even a suspicion of it is a very traumatic experience. The premise of this concise, well-organized, well-written monograph is that "instead of reacting with terror it's better to know the facts." All aspects of breast cancer, ranging from the anatomy and physiology of the normal breast to alternative or unconventional therapies, are factually covered in an easy reading style in 20 relatively short chapters, but with enough detail. The writing is careful and consistent, so that at no time is the reader confronted with an unclear concept or medical term. There are no references given, but the number and credentials of the listed reviewers give authority. Highly recommended as one of the best books yet for any woman interested in breast cancer. The content is similar to but the style is different from *Cancer Sourcebook for Women* (CH, Jun'96) and the book is a good adjunct to *Breast Cancer: A Family Survival Guide* (CH, Nov'95). Directory of support and service organizations; selected reading list; glossary of medical terms. All levels.—*R. S. Kowalczyk, North Central Michigan College*

OAB-1633   Orig
Gorna, Robin. **Vamps, virgins and victims: how can women fight AIDS?** Cassell, 1996. 398p index ISBN 0-304-32807-3, $60.00; ISBN 0-304-32809-X pbk, $16.95

Gorna's passionately written book describes issues women face regarding AIDS, primarily in the UK. She began as a volunteer for the Terrence Higgins Trust in 1986 and went on to attend numerous international meetings on AIDS. She very effectively points out important differences between the US epidemic and the contained numbers in the UK. She makes clear the risk distinctions between being the giver as opposed to the receiver of penetrative anal or vaginal intercourse. One must adjust to the repetition of vulgar words, but these are used deliberately and precisely for the purpose of clarity. Slang and medical terms are carefully defined and explained, i.e., incidence versus prevalence. The relative risks of specific activities are also debated and compared: French kissing, fellatio, cunnilingus, rimming, sex toys, intercourse during menstruation, needlestick injuries, and intravenous needle sharing. Acronyms are repeated throughout but listed only once in the beginning. Gorna painstakingly analyzes every shred of available evidence from research and case studies in order to document what is probable about the spread of AIDS, and recommends steps women can take to fight back. Very highly recommended. Upper-division undergraduates through professionals.—*E. R. Paterson, SUNY College at Cortland*

OAB-1634   RC180   94-47253 CIP
Gould, Tony. **A summer plague: polio and its survivors.** Yale, 1995. 366p bibl index ISBN 0-300-06292-3, $30.00

Before 1953, 20th-century summers were often nightmares of concern for parents. Would there be a poliomyelitis epidemic? Would it cripple the children? In the age of AIDS, the saga of the widespread emergence of this viral disease in the New York epidemic of 1916 and its ultimate defeat at the hands of science by the vaccines of Jonas Salk and Albert Sabin is inspirational. Here is the story of President Franklin D. Roosevelt, a polio victim, whose influence was central to the creation of the National Foundation for Infantile Paralysis, which spearheaded the ultimately successful search for a vaccine. We are also introduced to Sister Elizabeth Kenny, who came from Australia to counter the US medical establishment's treatment of the disease. Author Gould, an Englishman, is himself a "polio" or a victim of the disease, and this book is a rare blend of fine scholarship and writing combined with a crusader's personal zeal. We learn about

the different reactions to the disease in the UK and the US as well as about Australian and Canadian responses. Although the development of the vaccine was a scientific triumph, Gould never loses sight of the "polios." Their study does not end with the discovery of the vaccine. Through a series of personal interviews he deals with "post polio syndrome," a poorly understood ailment that today affects thousands of polio survivors. In the developed world, "polios" are aging into history. Their ordeal should be remembered. This fine volume belongs in all libraries. General; undergraduate through professional.—*I. Richman, Pennsylvania State University, Harrisburg*

OAB-1635   RC78   96-2844 CIP
Kevles, Bettyann Holtzmann. **Naked to the bone: medical imaging in the twentieth century.** Rutgers, 1997. 378p bibl index afp ISBN 0-8135-2358-3, $35.95

Kevles presents a scientific, medical, and social history of the various imaging devices available to modern medicine: X-rays, computerized tomography (CT) scans, magnetic resonance imaging (MRI), and positron emission tomography (PET). The scientific foundation of each invention is clearly presented along with an engaging narrative of the technological and commercial obstacles to be surmounted before each device could be successfully marketed and become medically useful. The stories are interesting, and among Kevles's conclusions is the demonstration that these devices are not linear descendants of the X-ray, but independent creations arising out of diverse circumstances and converging toward a common goal: accurate, useful representations of an opaque object's interior (the human body is the predominant but not sole target). Her study includes a description of the ever-widening role images play in forensic medicine, their impact on modern and postmodern art, and the politics of women's health. As her extensive bibliography indicates, there is no dearth of articles or monographs about the various topics in the book. No single book however, encompasses the material so thoroughly or well as this one does. General readers; undergraduates; professionals; two-year technical program students.—*T. P. Gariepy, Stonehill College*

OAB-1636   RA644   92-30578 CIP
Landau-Stanton, Judith. **AIDS, health, and mental health: a primary sourcebook,** by Judith Landau-Stanton and Colleen D. Clements. Brunner-Mazel, 1993. 343p indexes ISBN 0-87630-688-1, $38.95

A beautifully written encyclopedia of knowledge about AIDS and HIV disease. Nine metaphors of AIDS, plus a host of myths, are explored early in the book; then, AIDS is covered from virtually all vantage points: etiology, family and support systems, health care providers, epidemiology and transmission, women and minority groups at risk, neuropsychiatric aspects, and intervention. Several excellent case reports are used to illustrate issues and topics in later chapters. Only two other works are in the same general class in terms of excellence: Randy Shilts's *And the Band Played On: Politics, People, and the AIDS Epidemic* (1987) and Mirko D. Grmek's *History of AIDS: Emergence and Origin of a Modern Pandemic* (CH, May'91). The present work is more timely and covers far more territory than the other two. Recommended for all audiences, although health care providers, mental-health care workers, and caregivers of persons with AIDS will find it a rich source of extremely valuable information and guidance. Academicians working on health, mental health, or AIDS issues will quickly make this book mandatory reading for students at all levels. If only one book on AIDS is purchased this year, this should be it.—*A. C. Downs, formerly, University of Houston-Clear Lake*

OAB-1637   R723   97-11424 MARC
Lantos, John D. **Do we still need doctors?** Routledge, 1997. 214p index ISBN 0-415-91852-9, $24.95

Lantos is a pediatrician, teacher, and bioethicist whose book consists of an introduction, chapters on postwar optimism, the perils of progress, medical education and medical morality, truths, stories, fiction and lies, mistakes and truth telling, the story of an individual child, and why we should care about other people's children. A concluding chapter addresses the question posed in its title. The author masterfully confronts the medical challenges associated with proper responses to illness and suffering as well as the educational, institutional, political, and social forces that shape them. Divergence between treatment and healing and the negative impact of our rapidly changing health-care environment on human bonding between physician and patient are major foci. This book is characterized by integrity, forthrightness, and caring as it addresses multiple paradoxes in modern medicine. Lantos vividly portrays conflictive elements associated with the moral practice of medicine with great clarity, insight, and sensitivity, employing a personalized reader-friendly style. A book worthy of both serious attention and reflection by all health care professionals, and a worthwhile addition to libraries serving their needs. Upper-division undergraduate and graduate students; professionals.—*R. E. Darnell, University of Michigan—Flint*

OAB-1638 RC889 95-35525 CIP
Marsh, Margaret. **The empty cradle: infertility in America from Colonial times to the present,** by Margaret Marsh and Wanda Ronner. Johns Hopkins, 1996. 326p bibl afp ISBN 0-8018-5228-5, $29.95

Marsh, a historian, and Ronner, a physician, are sisters who have here collaborated for the first time. The result of the two perspectives forms a comprehensive history of infertility in America, which should sweep away most of the myths so prevalent in popular thought. Infertility is not a new problem, nor is it proportionately any more of a problem than it was 200 years ago. Perhaps the major difference is the recognition that males are infertile as well as females, and that the ability to have an erection does not necessarily indicate fertility. Because of the emotions involved, physicians, particularly in the 19th century, resorted to invasive genital surgery on women, but for the most part their success rate was low. In spite of our greatly increased knowledge, the failure rate remains high. Interestingly, a small number of infertile couples in the past and even today suddenly get pregnant without any intervention. The book is a well-documented, comprehensive (including in vitro fertilization), understated rather than overstated commentary on a very human problem. General; upper-division undergraduates through professionals.—*B. Bullough, University of Southern California*

OAB-1639 RC963 93-46519 CIP
McCann, Michael. **Health hazards manual for artists.** 4th rev. and aug. ed. Lyons & Burford, 1994. 132p bibl index ISBN 1-55821-306-6 pbk, $11.95

Too often, artists do not consider the supplies with which they work as chemicals. However, as chemicals, they need to be stored, handled, and applied in a proper manner to ensure the safety and health of the artist. This new edition of McCann's wonderful book (3rd., rev. and augm. ed., 1985) instructs the reader in how to do just that. Art takes on many forms as diverse as batik textile printing is from welding, or glass blowing is from photography. Nevertheless, McCann tackles all these topics and more with succinct, updated chapters on potential exposures and health hazards. Particularly important is the chapter on art supplies that are safe for children. This edition leads the reader through the often difficult task of interpreting the information included on Material Safety Data Sheets and then applying that information to make safe choices of materials, ventilation, and personal protective equipment. A must for anyone who engages in art as either a hobby or vocation. Public and academic collections.—*S. N. Mohr, University of Medicine and Dentistry of New Jersey*

OAB-1640 RT86 96-117 MARC
Nursing staff in hospitals and nursing homes: is it adequate?, ed. by Gooloo S. Wunderlich, Frank A. Sloan, and Carolyne K. Davis; Committee on the Adequacy of Nurse Staffing in Hospitals and Nursing Homes...Institute of Medicine. National Academy Press, 1996. 542p bibl index ISBN 0-309-05398-6, $59.95

This stellar report on the status of nursing staff in hospitals and nursing homes in the mid-nineties is a product of work completed by the committee charged by

the US Congress and formed by the Institute of Medicine, Division of Health Care Services. The editors, all members of this prestigious committee, have researched many (if not all) potential and real impacting factors such as population changes, economics, the evolving health care scenario, managed care and other payer groups, quality of care, staffing, education of nurses, patient acuity, and illness and wellness levels of patients. They have appraised the present health care situation very realistically. All aspects of nursing are studied, and the role of the RN, LPN, and nurse assistant are evaluated. Recommendations and state-of-the-art assessments about the various intervening variables are presented. This is an excellent, very enriching book that more than adequately points out the multiple issues involved in managing health care in our country specifically from the perspective of staffing nurses for quality care. Upper-division undergraduates through professionals.—*S. C. Grossman, Fairfield University*

OAB-1641 RM315 96-28908 CIP
Perrine, Daniel M. **The chemistry of mind-altering drugs: history, pharmacology, and cultural context.** American Chemical Society, 1996. 480p bibl index afp ISBN 0-8412-3253-9 pbk, $39.95

By limiting his subject, Perrine has been able to present a more detailed description of drugs that affect the brain. The information is generally grouped according to pharmacological effect and chronological order within the group. Social issues involved with drug use are also discussed. In general, chemical structures are included along with at least a sentence or two describing the synthesis. Some basic cell biology and communication between cells are included to illustrate the mechanism of action of some of the drugs. Interesting opinions are included on teenage smoking, definition of addiction, falling asleep while driving, and misuse of amine stimulants. Detailed descriptions of the thoughts and dreams of persons under the influence of various hallucinogenic agents are especially interesting. There is a wealth of information on the discovery of many drugs and their pharmacologic activity. Well written and well referenced. An outstanding contribution to the field of medicinal chemistry and a genuine pleasure to read for anyone with an interest in drug activity, drug addiction, and drug chemistry. Highest recommendation. Upper-division undergraduates through professionals.—*A. M. Mattocks, University of North Carolina at Chapel Hill*

OAB-1642 RC568 83-19584 CIP
Platt, Jerome J. **Heroin addiction: theory, research, and treatment. v.2: The addict, the treatment process, and social control; v.3: Treatment advances and AIDS.** Krieger, 1995. 2v. 262, 308p bibl indexes ISBN 0-89464-267-7, v.2, $37.50; ISBN 0-89464-881-0, v.3, $39.50

Platt has accomplished a minor miracle with these latest important additions to the addictions literature. In barely 400 pages, he has presented a comprehensive and critical analysis of the current body of knowledge relative to an understanding of the development and treatment of opiate addiction; further, his conclusions have potential applicability far beyond opiate addiction. Recent political changes make the analysis of control approaches included in volume 2 particularly useful, and the current emphasis on cost containment in health care makes the remainder of this work equally important. In volume 3, the separate chapter devoted to addicted women and those that explore the relationships between opiate addiction and HIV transmission are particularly germane to community health improvement efforts. Remaining chapters provide a thoughtful and clarifying examination of the myths and realities of current approaches to addictions management. Both volumes are very well written and extremely well referenced. Each chapter is organized logically and summarized effectively. Each topic is examined carefully, with the author clearly conveying the current status of knowledge and identifying what remains to be discovered. Each volume concludes with summary recommendations for client assessment, treatment decision making, future research, and public policy. The extensive bibliographies in both volumes and the combined subject index in volume 3 will be especially useful to the student of addictions. (Vol. 1, 2nd ed., was reviewed in CH, Nov'86.) Also helpful will be the recommendations for future research, which should direct scholars for many years. Clearly, these volumes belong

Science & Tecnology

in the libraries of all institutions with comprehensive addictions collections, and they will be useful to students in the health professions and public policy development and administration. Upper-division undergraduate through professional.—*T. D. DeLapp, University of Alaska, Anchorage*

OAB-1643   RC552   96-24027 CIP
Posttraumatic stress disorder: acute and long-term responses to trauma and disaster, ed. by Carol S. Fullerton and Robert J. Ursano. American Psychiatric, 1997. 296p bibl index afp (Progress in psychiatry series, 51) ISBN 0-88048-751-8, $39.50

This work examines the effects of trauma and disaster, and emphasizes Acute Stress Disorder—the newly introduced diagnostic category in the *Diagnostic and Statistical Manual of Mental Disorders*, 4th ed. (DSM-IV), of the American Psychiatric Association (1994). This additional diagnosis, which focuses on those symptoms that last only several days to weeks after trauma, stresses the importance of distinguishing between short- and long-term responses to traumatic events. Researchers have only recently begun to examine trauma from the perspective of acute versus chronic disorders and the various treatment approaches that can be deployed during the different phases of recovery. Topics in this work include comorbidity of posttraumatic stress disorder (PTSD) with depression and substance abuse, mental health problems relating to the war in Kuwait, PTSD in prisoners of war and homeless veterans, and neurobiological implications of PTSD. Perhaps the most notable feature is the smooth and unfettered writing style of Fullerton and Ursano, who have clearly collaborated before and have found a unified voice. Both editors are renowned experts in the field of trauma and have written hundreds of publications on the effects of war, trauma, and disaster. A fine scholarly work, highly recommended for undergraduates through professionals.—*L. S. Beall, Auburn University*

OAB-1644   RC545   93-30354 CIP
Rosenthal, Norman E. **Winter blues: seasonal affective disorder: what it is and how to overcome it.** Guilford, 1993. 325p index afp ISBN 0-89862-149-6 pbk, $14.95

The estimate has been made that some 20 percent of the populace of the US, or approximately 36 million people, are affected in a significantly, although variably, negative manner by the climatic changes that accompany winter. This book deals principally with a subset of this population that reacts in extreme to seasonal climatic changes, now officially classified as seasonal affective disorder (SAD). Interestingly, daily exposure to high-intensity light (fluorescent), more than antidepressant drugs, helps to alleviate most of the symptoms during times (mainly winter months) of severe depression. Rosenthal has written a most readable narrative exploration of all the encompassing aspects of SAD, interlaced throughout with descriptive comments from persons with the disorder, as well as with quotations from literature pointing out the effects of seasonal changes on mood and behavior. A well-organized, comprehensive work that presents clear insight into this only recently studied, psychologically defined affective disorder. Highly recommended. All levels.—*R. S. Kowalczyk, formerly, University of Michigan*

OAB-1645   RC963x   94-70298 Orig
Rossol, Monona. **The artist's complete health & safety guide.** 2nd ed. Allworth/American Council for the Arts, 1994. 343p index ISBN 1-880559-18-8 pbk, $19.95

Artists' supplies often contain some of the same types of chemicals that are regulated in the chemistry laboratory. Although artists use smaller amounts of the chemicals, they may actually be in contact with the substances for longer periods of time than chemical workers. Rossol, an artist and industrial hygienist, blends her knowledge of these fields in this superb new edition of her 1990 book. Though marketed for all artists, it actually takes some sophistication on the part of the reader to understand fully the logarithmic decibel scale described in the chapter on physical hazards and the medical and toxicological terms used in discussing some of the raw materials. Overall, this is balanced

by complete and comprehensive definitions included in the text and repeated in the appendixes. The primary niche for this book is in the teaching of art and art safety; a special section takes on this challenging task, providing instructors with information to use to teach proper handling, storage, labeling, and nontoxic substitution of art materials while teaching the class itself. A must for all art teachers at high school and college level. Upper-division undergraduate through professional; two-year technical program students.—*S. N. Mohr, University of Medicine and Dentistry of New Jersey*

OAB-1646   RC310   91-59017 CIP
Rothman, Sheila M. **Living in the shadow of death: tuberculosis and the social experience of illness in American history.** Basic Books, 1994. 319p index ISBN 0-465-03002-5, $25.00

As books on tuberculosis continue to be published in ever increasing quantity, *Living in the Shadow of Death* fills a previously empty niche. It is the first volume written from the patient's perspective. Before the therapeutic breakthrough of Waxman and others, tuberculosis was in many ways akin to today's AIDS epidemic, except that TB always affected all classes and groups within society. This four-part work is well written and obviously the result of extensive research and study. The first sections chronicle the therapeutic options accorded to men and women: men would be encouraged to seek cures through travel and adventure, women through rest at home. With the opening of the West, first men, and then women, sought cures in the new Eden. Finally, the age of the sanatorium is explored as is the changed perspective of what it meant to be a disease victim. Rothman clearly acknowledges the major problem of doing research devoted to the patient's perspective. Manuscript sources tend to reflect only the trials of white upper and upper-middle class persons. These victims were not only literate, but their papers were more likely to be preserved. Despite this shortcoming, an important, superbly documented work, which, along with Frank Ryan's *The Forgotten Plague* (CH, Dec'93), should be in every library. All levels.—*I. Richman, Pennsylvania State University, Harrisburg*

OAB-1647   RC310   92-46893 CIP
Ryan, Frank. **The forgotten plague: how the battle against tuberculosis was won—and lost.** Little, Brown, 1993. 460p index ISBN 0-316-76380-2, $24.95

Tuberculosis, painfully and horribly, killed uncounted tens of millions before modern medicine found what appeared to be the cure. Public health professionals were euphoric, believing that, like smallpox, tuberculosis could be eliminated as a medical problem. TB's obituary was premature; the disease is returning in epidemic proportion, coupled now with AIDS. Additionally, the new strains are resistant to conventional therapeutics. Although the AIDS virus is transmitted only via bodily fluids, *Mycobacterium tuberculosis* can be transmitted by touching infected surfaces, or even through the air. Ryan's engrossing prose examines the history of the disease and the scientists whose research eventually led to the ability to cure TB in individuals: Gerhard Domagk, a German who worked literally while WW II bombs destroyed his surroundings; Jorgen Lehman, a Dane, who envisioned a cure via a molecule of aspirin; and Selman Waxman, US soil scientist, who with his associate Albert Shatz, discovered streptomycin. Ryan writes about science in as riveting a fashion as does fellow British physician Michael Crichton. But this is not entertainment. Popularly written, it is exhaustively researched and carefully documented. Both historical and topical, a masterpiece that should be in every academic library. All levels.—*I. Richman, Pennsylvania State University, Harrisburg*

OAB-1648   Brit. CIP
Sagan, Leonard A. **Electric and magnetic fields: invisible risks?** Gordon & Breach, 1996. 214p bibl index ISBN 2-88449-217-8 pbk, $19.95

"Much of this book was written while I was employed as Senior Medical Scientist at the Electric Power Research Institute (EPRI)...." Sagan's candid acknowledgment of professional association with the utility industry (and possible bias) is characteristic of this work: scholarly care, rational argument, respect for opposing views, an open mind, admirable hesitation in announcing conclusions. The result is a timely and valuable contribution to the continuing debate over the possible adverse health effects of electric and magnetic fields. Of interest to a wider range of readers—concerned lay persons, health authorities, scientists, administrators, elected officials—the book does not respond to lurid sensationalism such as that of P. Brodeur, *The Great Power-Line Cover-Up* (CH, Feb'94). It is similar to recent books by William R. Bennett, *Health and Low-frequency Electromagnetic Fields* (CH, Jan'95), and W.F. Horton and S. Goldberg, *Power Frequency Magnetic Fields and Public Health* (CH, Feb'96), but it is a more useful and accessible *introduction* to the issues; instead of baffling physics, Sagan offers a physician's perspective on a health issue—a brief history of the controversy, some background on exposure assessment, a discussion of relative risks, and a *critical sifting of epidemiological literature*. This last feature is distinctive; it offers some hope of eventual resolution of an interminable imbroglio. Recommended strongly. General; upper-division undergraduates through professionals.—*D. W. Larson, University of Regina*

OAB-1649   RC550   93-32034 CIP
Shay, Jonathan. **Achilles in Vietnam: combat trauma and the undoing of character.** Atheneum, 1994. 246p bibl index ISBN 0-689-12182-2, $20.00

Shay, a psychiatrist for the Boston Department of Veterans Affairs, has written a remarkable study of Post-Traumatic Stress Disorder (PTSD) in Vietnam veterans. He believes that relating the insights of Homer's *Iliad* to the stories told by veterans whom he has treated illumines "the undoing of character" during the Vietnam War. A common thread runs through the memories of many veterans who suffer from PTSD. They saw a "betrayal of 'what's right,'" were taught to dehumanize the enemy, watched friends maimed and killed, and received too little encouragement to experience rituals of grief. For some, these factors led to a "berserk" state, a loss of all restraint in the prosecution of the war; for others, they caused feelings of guilt and separation. PTSD was usually the result. Shay's use of the *Iliad* to elucidate this psychiatric condition demonstrates that PTSD has long been part of the human experience. He argues that the "triggers of the berserk state" for Vietnam War soldiers find parallels as well as some instructive differences in the *aristeiai* of Homer's warriors, with Achilles as the "prototype of the berserker" and Diomedes as a contrasting model of restraint even during combat. The "communalization of the trauma" that Shay considers essential to healing should bring veterans and other citizens together to listen and to grieve, as did Odysseus in Book 8 of the *Odyssey*. Recommended for all libraries.—*A. O. Edmonds, Ball State University*

OAB-1650   RC424   96-20276 CIP
Starkweather, C. Woodruff. **Stuttering,** by C. Woodruff Starkweather and Janet Givens-Ackerman. PRO-ED, Inc., 8700 Shoal Creek Blvd., Austin, TX 78757-6897, 1997. 233p bibl index afp ISBN 0-89079-699-8 pbk, $27.00

This book is a gem! It is packed with easy-to-digest information for professionals and nonprofessionals alike. A broad scope of information spans Internet resources to specific professional issues. Professional guidelines on fluency are presented in their entirety and offer information regarding clinician competencies and treatment guidelines (useful to those searching for a competent clinician). Definitions, developmental characteristics of stuttering, and causal theories are all clearly presented. Individual chapters are devoted to evaluation, treatment of children, and treatment of adults. Alternatives to speech therapy are provided, including self-help groups and drug therapies. This book is unique in the attention given to the notion of relapse, the notion of "recovery" versus modification of behavior, and the acknowledgment of the role of spirituality in recovery. The theme throughout is that therapy is a partnership between a responsible client and a competent clinician. The authors state their biases in a forthright manner, balanced with case examples and other points of view. A wonderful resource for practicing clinicians, students, and individuals who stutter. General readers; undergraduates through professionals.—*N. L. Records, Pennsylvania State University, University Park Campus*

OAB-1651   RC564   93-30812 CIP
Thombs, Dennis L. **Introduction to addictive behaviors.** Guilford, 1994. 236p index ISBN 0-89862-336-7, $26.95

In this well-written book, Thombs succinctly reviews and critiques the major behavioral science theories of alcoholism and other addictions. After examining the usefulness of theory and research findings in understanding addictive behaviors, the author presents very balanced and objective descriptions of the disease model, psychoanalytic explanations, conditioning theory, social learning theory, family systems theory, and sociocultural perspectives on alcohol and drug abuse. The concluding chapter then reviews the implications of these theories for clinical practice. Although written specifically for entry-level counselors preparing for work in addictions treatment and for master's level mental health professionals with little or no training in the treatment of addictions, the book is an outstanding introduction to theories of addiction that will be valuable to undergraduates. It assumes no background knowledge in any field. General; community college; undergraduate; graduate; pre-professional.—*D. J. Hanson, SUNY College at Potsdam*

OAB-1652   RC280   94-8013 CIP
Todd, Alexandra Dundas. **Double vision: an East-West collaboration for coping with cancer.** Wesleyan/University Press of New England, 1994. 188p bibl indexes afp ISBN 0-8195-5279-8, $22.50

Intertwined with repeated pleas for giving greater status to the insights of Eastern medical traditions by practitioners of traditional Western medicine is a deeply moving personal narrative of the author's two-year involvement with her 21-year-old son's diagnosis of, surgery for, and treatment of a brain tumor; this trauma came a short time after her own 15-year experience with multiple chemical sensitivity. Todd pleads with the medical community to look more closely at and research the possible contributions of natural and macrobiotic diets, visualization (relaxation) therapy, acupuncture, and Chinese and holistic medicine (all alternative healings) to help cancer patients cope with their disease. Taken at face value, there can be no argument here. But some credibility is lost when doctors generally come out as the "bad guys," whereas persons promoting alternative healing are given halos—when the gleaming technologies of traditional Western medicine are compared to the gentle arts of alternative healing. None of the arguments presented are new. References are given for each chapter, but the authority of many is questionable. However, the author's brilliant and lucid writing style alone is reason enough to give the work the highest recommendation. General; undergraduate through professional.—*R. S. Kowalczyk, formerly, University of Michigan*

OAB-1653   RA644   95-30105 CIP
Tonks, Douglas. **Teaching AIDS.** Routledge, 1996. 195p bibl index afp ISBN 0-415-90874-4, $49.95; ISBN 0-415-90875-2 pbk, $16.95

This is an excellent "how-to" book with many realistic recommendations for teaching AIDS awareness to adolescents and all levels of children. Methods for setting up support groups for the person with AIDS and their caretakers are spelled out. A variety of strategies to facilitate changes in attitudes and risky behavior among children are explained, and rationales for the various topics to include in an AIDS educational program are discussed in detail. Citations from many researchers are provided, and their findings are integrated into the various topics. Tonks does an excellent job articulating the ways to overcome barriers to teaching about AIDS. He explains how, why, what, and when to introduce the various topics that experts believe should be incorporated. Chapters 7 and 8 are unique and especially helpful to the new AIDS instructor; they explain role-playing, peer education, and scenarios as methods to best teach this difficult subject. These methods are crucial in gaining adolescents' interest, since they include the learner in the education. An excellent example of how to get young people to think critically about issues and make some positive decisions about their health. General; undergraduates through professionals.—*S. C. Grossman, Fairfield University*

Science & Tecnology

OAB-1654   RC564   95-25144 CIP

Treating substance abuse: theory and technique, ed. by Frederick Rotgers, Daniel S. Keller, and Jon Morgenstern. Guilford, 1996. 328p bibl index afp ISBN 1-57230-025-6, $35.00

A highly readable consolidation of the five major theoretical approaches to the management of substance abuse disorders, this book is logically organized; the initial discussion of each approach presents a description of the theoretical bases underlying treatment, followed by translation of that theory into practical clinical application. The occasional clinical examples are useful in facilitating the translation from theory to practice; indeed, one might wish for even more application examples. The approach taken is a general one; the reader looking for discussion of the management of dependence on specific agents will be disappointed. This seems both appropriate and timely, given the prevalence of mixed disorders and the commonalities among dependencies on different agents. In this exceedingly well written work, the various authors provide a wealth of referential material. This book will provide beginning understanding to the novice and enrich the expertise of the specialist. Appropriate for the collection of any library serving a clientele interested in addictions in particular and in health and human services in general. Upper-division undergraduates through professionals.—*T. D. DeLapp, University of Alaska, Anchorage*

OAB-1655   RD539   93-29670 CIP

Vasey, Frank B. **The silicone breast implant controversy: what women need to know,** by Frank B. Vasey and Josh Feldstein. Crossing, 1993. 153p index ISBN 0-89594-610-6, $20.95

For women, the concurrence of business interests, medical practices, and governmental regulation has proved on numerous occasions to be dangerous. The breast implant is a good example of a profit-generating threat to women's health. Vasey, a rheumatologist, has written a comprehensive, easily understandable, and well-documented handbook for women with breast implants, those who suffer from silicone-related disease, those who are considering implant removal, their families and spouses, and medical professionals. Medical facts regarding the spread of silicone throughout the body, its relationship to rheumatic disease, and its effects on the immune system are examined systematically and are supported by manufacturer's internal reports, general literature, and professional journals. Anecdotal accounts by dozens of Vasey's patients provide additional evidence regarding self-serving roles of manufacturers, inaction of the FDA, conflicting opinions offered by surgeons, and factors that persuaded more than a million women to use these devices for figure enhancement. In clear and informative writing, consumer advice and sources of additional information are provided. Highly recommended. General; community college; undergraduate; pre-professional; professional.—*L. G. Muzio, SUNY Empire State College*

OAB-1656   RC641   96-27700 CIP

Wailoo, Keith. **Drawing blood: technology and disease identity in twentieth-century America.** Johns Hopkins, 1997. 288p index afp ISBN 0-8018-5474-1, $39.95

Thought-provoking and idea laden, *Drawing Blood* is clearly one of the most important new books in the field of medical history. The writing is dense but not turgid; rather, it is a style reflective of the extensive research and careful thought that shaped the work and the complexity of the subject. What could have been simply an exploration of the rise of hematology is, instead, an extensive social historical inquiry into the relationship of medicine and modern medical technology to culture. Early in the book Wailoo observes, "The question of what makes a disease 'real' in any period is no idle philosophical concern; it is, rather, a problem that lies at the center of ongoing medical, public health, and social debates—ranging from questions of moral responsibility to financial reimbursement and technology assessment." As he explores changing understandings of diseases he also exposes turf battles that developed as the power to dominate scientific medicine shifted from the individual practitioner to the specialist and the hospital. Readers come to understand the continued tensions between surgeons, hematologists, and oncologists.

Two chapter titles serve as examples of the author's multifaceted approaches to his topic: "'Chlorosis' Remembered: Disease and the Moral Management of American Women" and "The Rise and Fall of Splenic Anemia: Surgical Identity and the Ownership of a Blood Disease." Extensively documented, carefully written, and of obvious significance, Wailoo's volume deserves a large audience. Upper-division undergraduates through practitioners.—*I. Richman, Pennsylvania State University, Harrisburg*

OAB-1657   Orig

Webber, Roger. **Communicable disease epidemiology and control.** CAB International, 1996. 352p bibl index ISBN 0-85199-138-6 pbk, $35.00

The best description of this work results if one prefixes "A Guide to" to the title. Webber intends this as a practical, quick reference for physicians and/or others involved in the control of communicable diseases. It is authoritative, information laden, uniformly well written throughout, lucid and concise, and replete with examples used for clarification. The first six chapters deal with the components and principles of infectious disease and methods applicable to and used in its control. The next 12 chapters cover the more common infectious diseases classified as to their mode of transmission. The last chapter is composed of a reference table of infectious diseases (both those covered and not covered in the book); for each the agent responsible, the mode of transmission, and incubation period are given. Each chapter is short and well organized with extensive use of numbered subject headings, which makes finding a topic easy. Graphs, tables, and charts are presented as needed. In lieu of references (which would be voluminous for a work of this type) a list of suggested readings is provided. Most highly recommended. Upper-division undergraduates through professionals.—*R. S. Kowalczyk, North Central Michigan College*

OAB-1658   RA644   92-48971 CIP

Women, children, and HIV/AIDS, ed. by Felissa L. Cohen and Jerry D. Durham. Springer Publishing, 1993. 312p index ISBN 0-8261-7880-4, $37.95

A work that provides a clear picture of what is known about HIV-infected women, the epidemiology of HIV infection and AIDS in children and adolescents, and family and social issues that must be addressed to reduce HIV transmission by sexual behaviors and drug use. Written by nurses primarily for nurses, most of the essays are very succinct overviews packed with statistics, tables, charts, and references that are extremely useful to undergraduates, researchers, and practitioners. Broad topics discussed are prevention and education strategies for women and adolescents; symptoms and treatment for women, children, and adolescents; and mobilizing community resources and support for women and children, including programs in developing countries. Occasionally, technical language and medical or other acronyms are not fully explained; for example, IDU when first used on p. 44 is not spelled out until p. 46 as "injecting drug user." Very highly recommended for all colleges and universities. Advanced undergraduate through professional.—*E. R. Paterson, SUNY College at Cortland*

OAB-1659   RC1230   92-20143 CIP

Yesalis, Charles E. **Anabolic steroids in sport and exercise.** Human Kinetics, 1993. 325p index ISBN 0-87322-401-9, $45.00

This fine book is very well organized into three parts: "History and Incidence of Use"; "Effects, Dependence and Treatment Issues"; and "Testing and Societal Alternatives"; these parts are subdivided into 14 chapters. Each part and chapter begins with a selected quotation and introduction, a layout both appealing and manageable. Each well-referenced chapter was prepared by experts, either researchers, physicians, journalists, educators, or athletes. This comprehensive and authoritative collection is written by authors who review and critique available research on anabolic-androgenic steroids (AAS) and discuss contradictory evidence of harm and dependence that may have supported the recent legal reclassification of AAS as controlled substances. (This may explain why William N. Taylor's 1991 book, *Macho Medicine*, CH, Mar'92, is not mentioned.) Still, Yesalis has gathered a balanced perspective on AAS use in sport and exercise. Practical guidelines for treatment of withdrawal and drug-testing issues of cost, accuracy, privacy, and politics are carefully addressed. Very highly recommended for its fair and thorough coverage of potential physical and psychological effects, drug use prevention strategies, and testing concerns.—*E. R. Paterson, SUNY College at Cortland*

■ Mathematics

OAB-1660   QA614   95-51304 CIP
Alligood, Kathleen T. **Chaos: an introduction to dynamical systems,** by Kathleen T. Alligood, Tim D. Sauer, and James A. Yorke. Springer, 1997. 603p bibl index afp ISBN 0-387-94677-2, $39.00

This exceptional introductory work is uniquely characterized by its combination of breadth and depth and by its pedagogical style of actively engaging the reader in exercises integral to theory development. The standard topics associated with the dynamical systems of maps and differential equations (stability and classification of equilibrium and fixed points, limit sets, chaos, fractals, bifurcations, etc.) receive a solid presentation. The carefully dissected proofs of the pivotal Poincare-Bendixson, Stable Manifold, and Cascade Theorems are unusual, and welcome, in an introductory book, as are the details about the important topic of state reconstruction from data. Extensive use is made of itineraries and transition graphs. The examples and exercises are excellent, especially the end-of-chapter "Challenges," extended exercises that, in stepwise fashion, lead the reader to deep results (e.g., period three implies chaos). There are computer experiments throughout for exploration of concepts through simulation. "Lab Visits," short reports on landmark experiments in the physical, chemical, and biological sciences, have citations to the research literature. Appendixes review relevant topics in linear algebra and discuss ordinary differential equation solvers along with codes. The exposition is clear, solid, and well illustrated. Very highly recommended. Upper-division undergraduates and graduate students.—*G. J. G. Junevicus, Eckerd College*

OAB-1661   QA564   94-27981 CIP
Beltrametti, Mauro C. **The adjunction theory of complex projective varieties,** by Mauro C. Beltrametti and Andrew J. Sommese. W. de Gruyter, 1995. 398p bibl index afp (De Gruyter expositions in mathematics, 16) ISBN 3-11-014355-0, $89.95

Classically, the geometry of a complex algebraic variety was studied with reference to a particular embedding in projective space. The abstract algebraic geometry of the 20th century highlights the intrinsic geometry of varieties, but many interesting questions remain specifically concerning the geometry of projective embeddings. Beltrametti and Sommese are widely recognized for their expertise in these matters. In their first four chapters, they cover such background material as is necessary for the theory (hard to find in introductory works). They then present various modern results; for example, chapter 5 concerns conditions on algebraic varieties that occur as ample divisors in a nontrivial way. Attached to most curves, i.e., one-dimensional varieties, is a canonical projective embedding, and the so-called adjunction bundle is a tool for patching together all these embeddings for curves lying on a surface. Chapters 8-11 recast classical adjunction theory in modern language, thereby supplying missing rigor to the work of the classical Italian school and replacing the coarse classical birational viewpoint with more refined modern biregular methods. Later chapters discuss open problems and examine special cases of the theory in detail. Together with T. Fujita's *Classification Theories of Polarized Varieties* (1990), this book is sure to be a standard reference. The bibliography (more than 600 entries) is valuable in itself. Highly recommended for upper-division undergraduate and graduate students.—*D. V. Feldman, University of New Hampshire*

OAB-1662   QA477   94-44365 CIP
Bennett, M.K. **Affine and projective geometry.** Wiley-Interscience, 1995. 229p bibl index afp ISBN 0-471-11315-8, $44.95

If every high school mathematics teacher had a solid grasp of the material in this book, contemporary mathematics education would be in much better shape than it is today. Presupposing only minimal background, Bennett nevertheless leads her readers to a grand synthesis between axiomatic, algebraic, and lattice-theoretic methods in geometry. Thus, a focused course in geometry here reveals for the student the characteristic workings of 20th-century mathematics. Bennett has more to say about finite geometry than most authors writing for a similar audience; indeed, the reader who wanted to learn more would have to turn to an advanced book like *Projective Planes* (1973), by D.R. Hughes and F.C. Piper. Chapter 8, "Lattices of Flats," is a unique feature that reflects Bennett's research interests; coming late in the book, this material could lead students to further study in a number of directions—the theory of lattices, general topology, or even to quantum logic. Highly recommended for all libraries serving upper-division undergraduates through faculty.—*D. V. Feldman, University of New Hampshire*

OAB-1663   QA303   95-4042 CIP
Berlinski, David. **A tour of the calculus.** Pantheon Books, 1996 (c1995). 331p index ISBN 0-679-42645-0, $27.50

Tom Lehrer used to say that he was going to get rich writing a math book called "Tropic of Calculus," but he was just kidding. It may not make him rich, but Berlinski has written that book, albeit with a different title. Imagine the prose styles of Raymond Chandler, Joan Didion, and Stephen Hawking all rolled into one—you get the idea: Hawking, because this book finally does for Newton, after 300 years, what *A Brief History of Time* (CH, Jul'88) did for Einstein and his coterie; Didion, because Berlinski's former life as an academic brought him front and square with the darker side of California living; and Chandler, for the sheer sultriness of it. You can learn a lot of calculus from this book if you can clear the tears of laughter from your eyes long enough to see the words. Great for bright college grads who missed math the first time around and want to get the story now. Also for first-year undergraduates walking around with those telephone book-sized behemoths that still do not devote space to do the theory half as well as here, and *never* make anyone chuckle out loud. This is the only math book to ever take on a date. In these troubled times, it is nice to see a former academic mathematician making a productive contribution to society. All levels.—*D. V. Feldman, University of New Hampshire*

OAB-1664   QA300   95-44877 CIP
Browder, Andrew. **Mathematical analysis: an introduction.** Springer, 1996. 333p bibl index afp ISBN 0-387-94614-4, $39.00

All three Browder brothers—Andrew at Brown, William at Princeton, and Felix at Rutgers—have long been recognized authorities in their fields. This welcome book earns yet another Browder laurel. It is the distillation of what Andrew Browder has found fit to teach advanced undergraduates about analysis. It can be described, in the proverbial 25 words or less, as an exposition of the essential highlights of Constantin Caratheodory's *Reelle Funktionen* (3rd ed., 1939); Walter Rudin's *Principles of Mathematical Analysis* (3rd ed., 1976); Michael Spivak's *Calculus on Manifolds* (CH, Jun'66); and James R. Munkres's *Analysis on Manifolds* (CH, Feb'91)—the whole seasoned with Andrew's own outlook on mathematics as almost a way of life, augmented by important topics the other books tend to omit (e.g., continued fractions, Lebesgue theory, Fourier analysis, the Stone-Weierstrass theorem) and leavened with historical remarks. Chapters discuss real numbers; sequences and series; continuous functions on intervals; differentiation; the Riemann integral; topology; function spaces; differentiable maps; measures; integration; manifolds; multilinear algebra; differential forms; and integration on manifolds. A bit too rich for even a year-long course to cover completely; nonetheless, an excellent work for self-study, and a pleasurable source from which to extract supplementary materials for an instructor's own analysis course. Upper-division undergraduate through faculty.—*F. E. J. Linton, Wesleyan University*

OAB-1665 QA614 92-40599 CIP
Castrigiano, Domenico P.L. **Catastrophe theory,** by Domenico P.L. Castrigiano and Sandra A. Hayes. Addison-Wesley, 1993. 250p bibl index ISBN 0-201-55590-5, $47.50

René Thom's castastrophe theory caused both considerable excitement and considerable controversy when introduced in the 1970s. At the center is Thom's classification of the seven elementary catastrophes, in itself a deep and significant contribution to the qualitative theory of local singularities of differentiable maps having important applications to the study of the equilibrium behavior of physical systems. Nevertheless, the efforts by Thom and colleagues to use his result to explain phenomena in the social sciences were less than universally well received. Castrigiano's purely mathematical treatment contains a complete proof of the classification theorem from first principles, assuming of the reader only a modest background in calculus and linear algebra. It carries the imprimatur of Thom himself, who calls it in his foreword "very probably the best book on the market for an introduction to catastrophe theory" and rightly so. It is the first two chapters that should attract the most interest from undergraduates: Chapter 1 gives the relatively easy classification of nondegenerate critical points; Chapter 2 explains the fundamental notions of the subject through a detailed treatment of the fold and cusp catastrophes, including physical models where they arise. The exposition is exceedingly clear throughout. Highly recommended. Upper-division undergraduate through faculty.—*D. V. Feldman, University of New Hampshire*

OAB-1666 QA8 94-37370 MARC
Changeux, Jean-Pierre. **Conversations on mind, matter, and mathematics,** by Jean-Pierre Changeux and Alain Connes; ed. and tr. by M.B. DeBevoise. Princeton, 1995. 260p index afp ISBN 0-691-08759-8, $24.95

A highly entertaining and erudite read, this conversation between two renowned scientists, neurobiologist Changeux and mathematician Connes, boldly considers large questions of whether mathematics is a reality or just a representation of neural circuitry, of whether there is a code of human morality, and of the very nature of reality. Both speakers present cogent and stimulating arguments about the nature of the brain and how mathematics is represented. The book centers on the question of the nature of mathematics, about which the two disagree quite strongly. Changeux considers that mathematics is a representation of the brain, much like other conceptual images, such as freedom or liberty. In stark contrast, Connes holds that mathematics is a real dimension, similar to the natural world. Mathematicians make discoveries about the mathematical universe in much the same way that natural scientists discover a new species or new gene. The conversation is at all times informative, lively, and thought provoking. The reader is drawn into the argument and left pondering the issues well after the last page has been turned. Recommended. General; undergraduate through professional.—*K. M. Susman, Vassar College*

OAB-1667 QA241 96-31715 CIP
Clawson, Calvin C. **Mathematical mysteries: the beauty and magic of numbers.** Plenum, 1996. 313p bibl index ISBN 0-306-45404-1, $27.95

The subtitle of Clawson's book deserves attention. The work is a collection of essays on mathematics generally and numbers of specifically, and each section stresses the aesthetic beauty of mathematics. Clawson includes various mathematical discoveries and questions from throughout history to illustrate the beauty and magic of numbers: numeric origins, Greek achievements, famous sequences and series, different infinities, prime numbers and secret codes, Goldbach's conjectures, Ramanujan's equations, and others. Various philosophical bases of mathematics are beautifully presented at the end of the book. Clawson's discussions are multifaceted: historical, biographical, factual, conjectural. The style is often conversational and sprinkled with humor, when appropriate. The book is not to be taken for a daunting text on number theory. Clawson writes exceptionally well; the result: a very readable work for those seeking or having attained an undergraduate mathematics major. An absolute must for college, university, and larger public libraries. Upper-division undergraduates through faculty.—*W. R. Lee, Iowa State University*

OAB-1668 QA241 95-32588 CIP
Conway, John H. **The book of numbers,** by John H. Conway and Richard K. Guy. Copernicus, 1996. (Dist. by Springer-Verlag) 310p bibl index afp ISBN 0-387-97993-X, $29.00

Mathematics education falters when students reject mathematics as unimaginatively routine, or nearly as badly, when students embrace mathematics only for the security of its certainties. However, every once in a great while a book changes people's minds about mathematics—one that offers a portrait true, lively, inviting, and accessible. If one might name, perhaps, G. Gamow's *One, Two, Three ... Infinity* (1947), the classic of the genre, the present volume compares very favorably. In just a few pages Conway and Guy persuasively present a dizzying diversity of ideas, starting from a witty discourse on number words and culminating with a grand excursion through the infinite. Astounding facts to take on faith are side by side with bits of low-key rigor and glimpses into the mysterious abyss of the unknown. Intriguing illustrations grace nearly every page of this beautifully produced book. It would serve mathematics well if children as young as eight years met this book and then came back to it again and again well into their college years. All levels.—*D. V. Feldman, University of New Hampshire*

OAB-1669 Orig
CRC standard mathematical tables and formulae, ed. by Daniel Zwillinger. 30th ed. CRC Press, 1996. 812p bibl index afp ISBN 0-8493-2479-3, $39.95

Since its inception in the early 1930s, *CRC Mathematics Tables* has been the first mathematics handbook of choice when working in mathematics, engineering, or the physical sciences. No longer a mere book of tables extracted from the *Handbook of Chemistry and Physics* (71st ed., CH, Sep'91; 75th ed., CH, Mar'95), it has become a true handbook. Its formal name belies its content: it includes expository sections, definitions, directory information, charts, graphics, and historical sketches in addition to numeric tables and formulas. This new 30th edition will only continue and extend the fine reputation of its predecessors. New or reworked sections are partial differential equations, scientific computing, integral equations, group theory, and graph theory. Sections not reworked are updated. For example, uniform resource locators (URLs) are included for pertinent Internet Web sites. The index has been expanded and improved. The typesetting is not only legible but beautiful. Graphics are good, with three-dimensional objects presented with good shading. A must for academic libraries, most public and high school libraries, and professionals' personal bookcases. Undergraduates through professionals; two-year technical program students.—*W. R. Lee, Iowa State University*

OAB-1670 QA10 96-22131 CIP
Davis, Philip J. **Mathematical encounters of the second kind.** Birkhauser, 1997. 304p bibl afp ISBN 0-8176-3939-X, $24.95

Davis's gem of a book is "two parts biography, one part autobiography, one part mathematics, one part philosophy and one-half fantasy." The result: a wonderful discussion of what it means to explore mathematical ideas, including the interesting people and fascinating adventures one could encounter in this exploration. The expected includes mathematical problems that tantalize yet are accessible to the general reader; the unexpected includes both twists in the eventual solution of these problems and informal meetings with a cast of characters such as Napoleon Bonaparte, Stefan Bergman, and Lord Victor Rothschild of England. In turn, the expected is once again the author's informal way of confronting mathematical ideas and then investigating the many interesting tangents that arise. Though truly a bizarre mix, one-half historical, one-half cultural, two-thirds mathematical, and seasoned with dashes of psychology, the combined effect is an engaging insight into the world of a mathematician. Useful bibliography. Strongly recommended. General readers; undergraduates through faculty.—*J. Johnson, Western Washington University*

OAB-1671   QA93   92-42173 CIP
Dewdney, A.K. **200% of nothing: an eye-opening tour through the twists and turns of math abuse and innumeracy.** Wiley, 1993. 182p ISBN 0-471-57776-6, $19.95

A delightful and sobering book that everyone should read and learn from. Following the tradition of the now decades-old book by Darrell Huff, *How To Lie with Statistics* (1954), Dewdney seeks to open the eyes of his readers to the misuse of mathematics in everyday life: graphic distortion as found in ads, carelessness with units, omission of data, biased sampling. The book confronts people's inability or unwillingness to understand basic quantitative concepts and to think logically as they proceed in their everyday lives. Dewdney reveals the pervasive exploitation of the innumerate public by those who twist simple mathematical ideas to suit private agendas. Very readable, this book should be in every public, high school, college, and university library, not to mention on the shelves of bookstores everywhere and in homes.—*W. R. Lee, Iowa State University*

OAB-1672   QA21   93-48720 CIP
Dunham, William. **The mathematical universe: an alphabetical journey through the great proofs, problems, and personalities.** Wiley, 1994. 314p index afp ISBN 0-471-53656-3, $22.95

Dunham has provided 25 chapters pertaining to mathematics, all but one alphabetized by the initial letter of the first word in the title (the exception is the chapter "X-Y Plane."). Along the way there are fascinating presentations of the three "fundamental theorems" ("Arithmetic" in the first chapter; "Calculus" in a middle chapter; "Algebra" in the last). Some of the chapter titles are predictable; e.g., "Bernoulli Trials," "Euler," "Fermat." Others are not: "Justification" (on proof and its nature), "Where are the Women?," "Z" (a smattering of complex analysis). Within each chapter Dunham moves in a nonlinear but ultimately connected fashion from topic to topic. Most of the topics refuse to stand still for classification; like mathematics itself, they offer the delighted reader a variety of facets and personalities. The level of presentation presumes intelligence (and interest and determination) but no more than a modest high school background. Nevertheless, professionals can find material of interest pertaining to areas removed from their specialties. Highly recommended. All levels.—*R. J. Wernick, emeritus, SUNY College at Oswego*

OAB-1673   QA273   93-19341 CIP
Ekeland, Ivar. **The broken dice, and other mathematical tales of chance,** tr. by Carol Volk. Chicago, 1993. 183p index afp ISBN 0-226-19991-6, $19.95

The consideration of chance versus fate has been fundamental throughout human history. In this book (an eloquent translation from the French *Au Hasard*), Ekeland philosophizes about randomness versus deterministic processes, risk assessment, and prediction while describing the nature and use of probabilistic, statistical, and chaotic methods and models. Throughout, he artfully frames the mathematics with aspects of the Norse saga of Saint Olaf and other episodes from the centuries-old mythic history of the Kings of Norway. The result is less a typical popular treatment of contemporary mathematics than Ekeland's very successful previous work, *Mathematics and the Unexpected* (CH, Mar'89). Instead, it is a unique and beautifully literate blend of mathematics, philosophy, and mythic literature that offers stimulating and worthwhile reading for scientific professionals and nonprofessionals alike. Highly recommended. General; undergraduate; faculty.—*S. J. Colley, Oberlin College*

OAB-1674   QA247   92-15556 CIP
Ellis, Graham. **Rings and fields.** Oxford, 1993 (c1992). 169p index ISBN 0-19-853455-8, $45.00

Ellis makes available to students, in a clear, understandable fashion, many of the classic problems that are approachable through algebraic techniques. In a traditional course in abstract algebra these problems are often referred to,

but there is usually not enough time to do them justice. From Ellis's book, an interested student could easily obtain an understanding of the problem and be presented with a method of solution. Some of the topics he addresses include Diophantine equations; construction of finite projective planes; and the theorems of Pappus, Desargues, and Wedderburn, as well as linear codes and cryptography, including the ideas of elliptic curve factorization of integers. A minimum background for proper use of this book would be a solid course in linear algebra, but a broader background in abstract algebra would allow the reader to move at a more enjoyable pace, being able to focus on how some of the fundamental ideas are employed. An excellent choice for any undergraduate library and a very worthy resource for a "special" topics course for interested upper-division undergraduate and graduate students.—*J. R. Burke, Gonzaga University*

OAB-1675   92-64177 Orig
Engel, Arthur. **Exploring mathematics with your computer.** Mathematical Association of America, 1993. 301p bibl index 3.5" disk (IBM-PC) (New mathematical library, 35) ISBN 0-88385-636-0 pbk, $38.00

The latest title in the publisher's distinguished series. Using Turbo Pascal as a medium, Engel presents programs that investigate 60 to 70 classical topics in mathematics that have a computational viewpoint: factorials, Fibonacci's sequence, the greatest common divisor, sieves, the binomial distribution, random walks, and more. Engel's competence as a teacher is revealed as he leads the reader through the Pascal language by careful explanations of each type of Pascal statement used. A rich collection of exercises with solutions follows most sections, making the book an excellent potential text for a topics-in-mathematics seminar or independent study course. A computer disk contains source code. A must for academic libraries supporting an undergraduate major in mathematics. Public libraries with strong science collections should have this book as a resource for traditional mathematics topics and as a recreation for the mathematically inclined. Capable high school students would also benefit.—*W. R. Lee, Iowa State University*

OAB-1676   QA614   96-7352 CIP
Fractal horizons: the future use of fractals, ed. by Clifford A. Pickover. St. Martin's, 1996. 355p index ISBN 0-312-12599-2, $29.95

This collection of intriguing, entertaining, and topical articles illustrates the ubiquity of fractals; the six sections "Fractals in Education," "Fractals in Art," "Fractal Models and Metaphors," "Fractals in Music and Sound," "Fractals in Medicine," and "Fractals and Mathematics" provide a sampler of unusual breadth. Topics range from the playful to the serious—from composing fractal music to diagnosing pathologies. The articles not only present vanguard applications but speculations as to future developments and directions. As is typical of a Pickover collection, often the reader is enticed to experiment. The well-written articles are mainly informal and/or largely self-contained. Specialized knowledge is not required to grasp the essentials; an undergraduate level of mathematical sophistication suffices for most of the material. Useful glossary; excellent, striking black-and-white illustrations; extensive bibliographies provide an up-to-date entrance to the literature. Some computer programs are included. For a wide audience: laypeople, computer enthusiasts, artists, and scientists. Highly recommended for undergraduates and above as well as two-year technical program students.—*G. J. G. Junevicus, Eckerd College*

OAB-1677   QA21   96-13428 CIP
Gullberg, Jan. **Mathematics: from the birth of numbers.** W.W. Norton, 1997. 1,093p bibl indexes ISBN 0-393-04002-X, $50.00

Gullberg's grand tour of the mathematical world is both a concise history and a compendium, beginning with numbers, numerals, numeration systems, and their origins, and ranging through some elementary combinatorics and theory of equations to geometries and various branches of the calculus tree. This is the work of a true amateur: it is apparent that the author is in love with mathematics, and he has taken care to communicate this love and to try to infect others with it. Throughout, there are illustrations, quotations, historical remarks, anecdotes, and even a few jokes (some of them quite corny). The writing style is open and extremely readable. Gullberg's book can be thought of as an up-to-date and much more comprehensive version of Lancelot Hogben's *Mathematics for the Millions* (originally published in 1937). Every library should have a copy. General readers; undergraduates; two-year technical program students.—*D. Robbins, Trinity College (CT)*

OAB-1678   Q172   92-40059 CIP
Hilborn, Robert C. **Chaos and nonlinear dynamics: an introduction for scientists and engineers.** Oxford, 1994. 654p bibl index afp ISBN 0-19-505760-0, $55.00

Hilborn's book is superb. Written by a master teacher and researcher, it is a model of thorough exposition. In addition to an excellent bibliography, every chapter contains an annotated list of references. In Chapter 2, there is a list of five inexpensive software packages for nonlinear dynamics and chaos calculations. In succeeding chapters, computer exercises using this software form a vital part of the strategy for the study of this fascinating field. Each chapter has, in addition, exercises that range from verifying a result just stated to studies that extend and exemplify the text. The painstaking development of new ideas relies heavily on previous sections and is facilitated by graphs, figures, and sketches wherever appropriate. The presentation assumes a familiarity with both introductory college physics and calculus up through elementary differential equations. Readers with such a background will find this book a treasure for both self-study and classroom use. At present, this book has no peers. Upper-division undergraduate through faculty.—*C. A. Hewett, Rochester Institute of Technology*

OAB-1679   QA614   93-43894 CIP
Holmgren, Richard A. **A first course in discrete dynamical systems.** Springer-Verlag, 1994. 214p bibl index afp ISBN 0-387-94208-4 pbk, $29.00

Holmgren provides the necessary background and develops the tools needed for understanding discrete dynamical systems. His introductory book is written for undergraduate students with a background in calculus, some knowledge of elementary programming, and the use of symbolic manipulators; it should play a pivotal role in bridging the gaps between calculus, analysis, and topology. Most chapters are interdependent; therefore, a systematic and sequential reading of the material is required. Several examples and exercises that vary in difficulty are given, and further readings and textbooks on various topics covering dynamical systems and related areas of analysis and topology are cited in the bibliography, together with the author's personal evaluation of some of the textbooks. Holmgren begins with a review of the theory of functions and real numbers, and then discusses the dynamics of discrete systems, symbolic dynamics and chaos, and the dynamics of complex functions. The author presents a brief exposition of the numerical solution of ordinary differential equations and concludes with a discussion about ways to generate Julia and Mandelbrot sets on a computer. Highly recommended for undergraduates and general readers.—*D. E. Bentil, University of Massachusetts at Amherst*

OAB-1680   QA274   93-26666 CIP
Honerkamp, Josef. **Stochastic dynamical systems: concepts, numerical methods, data analysis,** tr. by Katja Lindenberg. VCH, 1994. 535p bibl index afp ISBN 1-56081-563-9, $100.00

An excellent, easy-to-read book presenting a broad array of statistical and stochastic techniques for the analysis and understanding of complex systems. The book is divided into 15 chapters that include a brief introduction to complex systems; basic concepts of probability theory, random variables and their distributions, fitting a curve to a set of data, stochastic approximation, and an overview of some methods for the analysis of stationary data; advanced methods of data analysis, including factor analysis, principal component analysis, and the handling of ill-posed problems; classification methods; Markov pro-

cesses, derivation of the master equation, the Fokker-Planck equation, and the Langevin equation; and analytical and numerical methods for the treatment of the master equation. Later chapters discuss analytical methods for treatment of stochastic differential equations; numerical methods; improved analytical methods and approximations; functional integrals; perturbation theory; data analysis of stochastic processes; and point processes. Researchers and students in mathematics, physics, chemistry, engineering, biology, and medicine will find this work useful and stimulating. Helpful subject index; statistical tables; numerous illustrative examples. Highly recommended. Advanced undergraduate; graduate.—*D. V. Chopra, Wichita State University*

OAB-1681   QA141   93-13204 CIP
Humez, Alexander. **Zero to lazy eight: the romance of numbers,** by Alexander Humez, Nicholas Humez, and Joseph Maguire. Simon & Schuster, 1993. 228p index ISBN 0-671-74282-5, $21.00

This unusual work is a delightful journey through the shared worlds of mathematics and linguistics. On this roller-coaster ride, the authors pause briefly to point out important sights that support their thesis that *numbers shape language, and vice versa.* Each chapter begins with a discussion of a particular integer (zero through thirteen), but rapidly spreads tangentially into a labyrinth of connected ideas, literary expressions, etymological derivations, trivia, and, occasionally, some mathematics. The final chapter gives special attention to infinity, or what is commonly known by cowhands as the "lazy eight." Though complemented by an excellent index, the text unfortunately does not include a general reference list or specific resources for following up in some depth any of the ideas being discussed. As the level of mathematics is kept at a low level, this enjoyable book is easily accessible to the general reader interested in the possible interplay between language and mathematics. Readers are cautioned: Be sure to wear a seat-belt. General; lower-division undergraduate; faculty.—*J. Johnson, Western Washington University*

OAB-1682   QA845   94-43113 CIP
Kaplan, Daniel. **Understanding nonlinear dynamics,** by Daniel Kaplan and Leon Glass. Springer-Verlag, 1995. 420p bibl index afp ISBN 0-387-94440-0 pbk, $29.95

Kaplan and Glass discuss the principles and applications of nonlinear dynamics as presented for several years to students in the biological sciences at McGill University. The presentation assumes one year of calculus with no great likelihood of further mathematical study. The authors skillfully employ elementary arguments based on finite-difference equations, local- and global-stability analyses, and problem-solving by means of algebraic and/or geometric methods. In this way, topics such as tumor growth, fluctuations in marine populations, and heart rate response to sinusoidal inputs can be understood without more advanced mathematical preparation. Throughout, the authors present "dynamics in action" essays on subjects ranging from locomotion in salamanders to predicting the next ice age. Each of the six chapters is accompanied by excellent illustrative material and an outstanding bibliography. An important addition to the literature; highly recommended. Undergraduate through professional.—*C. A. Hewett, Rochester Institute of Technology*

OAB-1683   QA274   92-25532 CIP
Kingman, J.F.C. **Poisson processes.** Oxford, 1993. 104p bibl indexes afp (Oxford studies in probability, 3) ISBN 0-19-853693-3, $39.95

When one considers random processes, two that are fundamental immediately come to mind: the Bachelier-Wiener model of Brownian motion and the Poisson process. For many years the Bachelier-Wiener model has been the subject of many books while the Poisson process, for all practical purposes, has been ignored or hardly ever mentioned. Many leave it behind and move on to more general point processes or Markov chains. Kingman suggests that this comparative neglect is "ill-judged, and stems from a lack of perception of the real importance of the Poisson Process." The author does a very effective job of redressing the balance by discussing the beauty and wide application of Poisson processes in one or more dimensions. The book covers such topics as stochastic models, marked Poisson processes, Cox processes, stochastic geometry, and the Poisson-Dirichlet distribution. Highly recommended for undergraduate and graduate-level academic libraries. Advanced undergraduate through faculty.—*D. J. Gougeon, University of Scranton*

OAB-1684   QA76   92-7364 CIP
Kleijnen, Jack P.C. **Simulation: a statistical perspective,** by Jack P.C. Kleijnen and Willem van Groenendaal. Wiley, 1992. 241p indexes ISBN 0-471-93055-5 pbk, $39.95

Based on their nearly 25 years of expertise and practical experience in teaching students management science, and, more recently, information systems, Kleijnen and van Groenendaal have doen an excellent job of combining simulation and statistical theory with useful applications. A translation from the Dutch *Simulatie: Technieken en Toepassingen* (1988), it presents problems in management science, operations research, economics, and mathematical statistics that can be analyzed by means of simulation. There is also a discussion of the efficient design of simulation experiments and the application of simulation in operations research and mathematical statistics, with reference to queuing and inventory systems. Topics such as sampling from nonuniform distributions, the evaluation of pseudorandom number generation, various types of simulation, and systems dynamics are covered. It is necessary for a reader to have knowledge in mathematics, statistics, and elementary computer science. Highly recommended for undergraduate and graduate-level libraries.—*D. J. Gougeon, University of Scranton*

OAB-1685   QA63   96-23878 CIP
Krantz, Steven G. **Techniques of problem solving.** American Mathematical Society, 1997. 465p bibl index afp A solutions manual is free upon request to instructors. ISBN 0-8218-0619-X pbk, $29.95

Krantz has collected a thoroughly engaging arsenal of problems and problem-solving techniques. Most scientists will want to have a copy for personal reference and for the mental stimulation that it provides. It is well written in a style that encourages the reader to become actively involved—in each chapter a few specific examples and explanations are given, and then a myriad of fascinating related problems are provided. After a delightful introductory chapter, the chapters are primarily organized around specific techniques and their applicability in areas such as geometry, logic, recreational math, and counting. The book is written in a linear fashion that makes it advisable to tackle problems in sequential order. It requires only a minimal mathematical background in algebra, trigonometry, and geometry, and would be an excellent tool for teaching novices to read some mathematics. Recommended. All levels.—*J. M. Clark, Emory and Henry College*

OAB-1686   QA174   92-41486 CIP
Kuga, Michio. **Galois' dream: group theory and differential equations,** tr. by Susan Addington and Motohico Mulase. Birkhauser, 1993. 150p bibl indexes afp ISBN 0-8176-3688-9, $29.50

The theory of Fuchsian differential equations, that cornerstone of 19th-century mathematics so closely associated with the names Gauss, Klein, Schwarz, Hermite, Riemann, Hilbert, Poincaré, and others, seems to have passed entirely from fashion, its traces absorbed into more abstract theories such as those of Riemann surfaces and automorphic forms. In fact, although this beautiful subject has been undergoing something of a revival at the frontiers of research, sadly, it has all but disappeared from the curriculum. Likewise, it has received scant modern exposition (but see Masaaki Yoshida's *Fuchsian Differential Equations*, 1987, and Jeremy Gray's *Linear Differential Equations and Group Theory from Riemann to Poincaré*, 1985). By contrast, Galois's theory of equations remains the standard culmination of advanced undergraduate algebra courses. Students usually meet examples from number fields and algebraic objects; the analogy between Galois groups and fundamental groups from topology that puts Galois' ideas on a geometric, visually intuitive footing is seldom mentioned prior

to graduate school. In the context of Riemann surfaces and function fields this connection is better than a mere analogy, and Kuga makes this the basis for an idiosyncratic *geometric* exposition of Galois theory. Here the question of the solvability of Fuchsian differential equations is the main application, rather than the usual question of solvability of polynomials by radicals. Translated from the 1968 Japanese original, there is nothing like this book in the literature. Highly recommended. Undergraduate; graduate.—*D. V. Feldman, University of New Hampshire*

OAB-1687   QA278   94-46457 MARC
Lindsey, J.K. **Modelling frequency and count data.** Oxford, 1995. 291p bibl index (Oxford statistical science series, 15) ISBN 0-19-852331-9, $55.00

Categorical data analysis, a special area of generalized linear modeling, is finding great application in numerous disciplines from medicine to social sciences. Lindsey's book is without doubt a very useful contribution to the study of categorical data. Part 1 treats frequency data and part 2, count data. Part 1 include topics such as frequency tables, regression models, log multiplicative models, the continuation ratio model, various forms of incomplete tables, and fitting distributions; part 2 discusses various counting processes, Markov chains, structured transition matrices, and overdispersion and cluster models. An appendix contains GLIM macros; there is a well-selected bibliography and a useful index. It is primarily intended for readers without much mathematical sophistication who are interested in a clear and better understanding of modeling frequency and count data. It is a well-written book, and Lindsey's lucid presentation is commendable. Other attractive features are the numerous illustrative examples and chapter-end exercises. A great application-oriented book that researchers and students will find very interesting. A valuable addition to statistical literature; highly recommended. Undergraduate through faculty.—*D. V. Chopra, Wichita State University*

OAB-1688   QA29   91-50891 CIP
Macrae, Norman. **John von Neumann.** Pantheon Books, 1992. 405p bibl index ISBN 0-679-41308-1, $25.00

Public recognition of the names of scientists is seldom a measure of the significance of their scientific work. So it is that von Neumann, one of the revolutionary scientific thinkers of our century, whose impact on modern technology and history was considerable, is not as well known as Einstein or Oppenheimer. A man with a prodigious mind and memory, a gifted mathematician and penetrating physicist, von Neumann was also acutely aware and perceptive of global politics. His fertile mind often took fruitful ideas (of others) and carried them through to undreamt-of realms. He explored the foundations of quantum mechanics at profound mathematical levels, and laid the foundations for the computer revolution at complex conceptual levels. He played a role in the development of nuclear bombs; he was an early instigator of artificial intelligence; and he formulated insightful theories in economics and in decision theory. He recognized the potential dangers in Nazi and Communist ideologies, and argued effectively for militaristically unbending attitudes towards them, thus earning the epithet of hawkishness from idealists whose well-intentioned visions sometimes blinded them to the irrationality of dictators. Based on much research, his own and that of others (especially of Stephen White), Macrae has written a valuable biography of this remarkable genius of our century, without the opacity of technical (mathematical) dimensions that are part of the hero's intellectual contributions to humanity. Interesting, informative, illuminating, and insightful. All levels.—*V. V. Raman, Rochester Institute of Technology*

OAB-1689   QA641   93-46525 MARC
McCleary, John. **Geometry from a differentiable viewpoint.** Cambridge, 1995 (c1994). 308p bibl indexes ISBN 0-521-41430-X, $54.95; ISBN 0-521-42480-1 pbk, $22.95

The undergraduate curriculum now hazards reducing Euclid to a caricature, casting him only as the historical source for the logical method—his *Ele-*

ments—as merely the paradigmatic axiomatic system, with little relevance to the study of modern geometry. Indeed, geometry generally gets short shrift with abstract differential geometry, the legacy of Gauss and Riemann, rarely taught other than as an elective. McCleary does nothing less than put the whole story together for an undergraduate audience: criticisms of Euclid's use of his Fifth Postulate culminate with the non-Euclidean revolution of Bolyoi, Lobachevsky, and Gauss, with Hilbert's theorem that three-dimensional space contains no model of non-Euclidean geometry (complete surface of constant negative curvature) justifying the introduction of abstract surfaces by Gauss and Riemann. Euclid finds his proper place as the fount of geometry; non-Euclidean geometry is revealed as a crucial milestone, not merely an amusing diversion; abstract differential geometry arises as the culmination of a long but ongoing development, rather than an arbitrary point of departure. A book to reform geometry pedagogy. Highly recommended for undergraduates.—*D. V. Feldman, University of New Hampshire*

OAB-1690   QA1   92-12652 CIP
Naber, Gregory L. **The geometry of Minkowski spacetime: an introduction to the mathematics of the special theory of relativity.** Springer-Verlag, 1992. 257p bibl afp (Applied mathematical sciences, 92) ISBN 0-387-97848-8, $49.95

Special relativity is less a subject for its own sake than a comparatively elementary and stable stepping-stone to the mathematically rich and intensely active disciplines of general relativity and quantum field theory. The emphasis Naber places here on the theory of spinors makes this exposition of special relativity especially suitable for readers who would later study the modern formulations of these more advanced subjects, especially future readers of R. Penrose and W. Rindler's *Spinors and Space-time* (2 v., 1984-86). By contrast, Rindler's own *Introduction to Special Relativity* (2nd ed., 1991; 1st ed., CH, Jan'83) employs exclusively the older language of tensors. Where many physics texts explain physical phenomena by means of mathematical models, here a rigorous and detailed mathematical development is accompanied by precise physical interpretations. As such, mathematicians should find this book to their particular taste. Other noteworthy features include Zeeman's theorem on causal automorphisms; Hawking, King, and McCarthy's "path topology"; and the clearest explanation of "Dirac's Scissors Problem" this reviewer has seen in print. For all its mathematical sophistication, this book can be read with just an undergraduate knowledge of linear algebra. Highly recommended.—*D. V. Feldman, University of New Hampshire*

OAB-1691   T385   94-47114 CIP
The Pattern book: fractals, art, and nature, ed. by Clifford A. Pickover. World Scientific, 1995. 427p index ISBN 981-02-1426-X, $50.00

In this collection of contributions on pattern creation in science, art, and nature, part 1, "Representing Nature," has photos and sketches as well as computer-generated patterns associated with diverse natural phenomena: solar and planetary vortices, wood patterns, DNA nucleotide sequences, sea lilies, etc. Part 2, "Mathematics and Symmetry," the major part of the book, offers computer-generated patterns originating from a broad spectrum of mathematics, e.g., number theory, geometry, trigonometry, tesselation and tiling, dynamical systems, cellular automata, and fractals. Many of the patterns are associated with Mandelbrot and Julia sets. Part 3, "Human Art," contains Escher-like tessellations; Tamil, Persian, Japanese, and Celtic designs; ornamental alphabets; cubist art; and Art Deco patterns. Emphasis is "on the fun that the true pattern lover finds in doing, rather than in reading about the doing." The patterns, many in black and white, some in color, are generally intricate and beautiful. Pseudocode and code are provided for many of the patterns. The book stimulates experiment. An excellent resource for entry into the world of patterns. Recommended for artists, scientists, and computer enthusiasts, undergraduates through professionals.—*G. J. G. Junevicus, Eckerd College*

OAB-1692   QA614   91-11998 CIP
Peitgen, Heinz-Otto. **Fractals for the classroom: Part 2: complex**

systems and Mandelbrot set, by Heinz-Otto Peitgen, Harmut Jürgens, and Dietmar Saupe. National Council of Teachers of Mathematics/ Springer Verlag, 1992. 500p bibl index afp ISBN 0-387-97722-8, $29.00

An excellent book for the undergraduate library together with Part 1 (CH, Mar'93) and two supplementary workbooks, by the same author, that apply the principles discussed in Parts 1 and 2. Part 2 is mostly about chaotic dynamics and less about fractals. There is a wealth of computational exploration of dynamical systems exhibiting chaotic symptoms, including those of Lorenz, Hénon, and Rössler. The book concludes with two generous chapters on Julia sets and the Mandelbrot set, including the remarkable recent result of Shishikura. The first half of the volume overlaps significantly with R. L. Devaney's *Introduction to Chaotic Dynamical Systems* (2nd ed., 1989), but the emphases are quite different. For such a subject, the book under review is elementary in the extreme, using calculus only apologetically, with a nod toward differential equations. An excellent resource for the enthusiastic neophyte. Highly recommended.—*S. Puckette, University of the South*

OAB-1693   QA9   94-45541 CIP
Pickover, Clifford A. **Keys to infinity.** Wiley, 1995. 332p bibl index afp ISBN 0-471-11857-5, $24.95

Pickover offers a unique and engaging exploration of the infinite, differing in its approach from such popular-level books as Eli Maor's *To Infinity and Beyond: A Cultural History of the Infinite* (CH, Jul'87) and Rudy v.B. Rucker's *Infinity and the Mind: The Science and Philosophy of the Infinite* (CH, Oct'82). Rather than discuss the physical, metaphysical, or aesthetic impact of the infinite, Pickover chooses to present a curiosity shop of puzzles, games, and other mental exercises. His obvious intent is to entice the reader to experiment. The chapters consist of independent essays with intriguing titles (e.g., "Vampire Numbers" or "Escape from Fractalia"). Writing in an informal and humorous style, Pickover presents problems rooted in such diverse fields as number theory, probability theory, and geometry (Euclidean and fractal), many of which are still open problems. Numbers with curious properties, amazing graphics from simple algorithms, and an ingenious graphic approach to assess random number generators are but a few of the offerings. Most of the material assumes only a high school level of mathematics. Splendid illustrations. Pickover fans will be delighted as will be puzzle, computer, and math enthusiasts in general. Highly recommended. All levels.—*G. J. G. Junevicus, Eckerd College*

OAB-1694   QA372   95-10217 CIP
Polyanin, Andrei D. **Handbook of exact solutions for ordinary differential equations,** by Andrei D. Polyanin and Valentin F. Zaitsev. CRC Press, 1995. 707p bibl index afp ISBN 0-8493-9438-4, $95.00

This work is the most comprehensive handbook available on exact solutions of ordinary differential equations. The authors have included approximately 5,000 equations with solutions; more than 2,000 of these equations are of the second order or higher. Every other such handbook in print has fewer than 400 second order or higher equations with solutions. In addition, Polyanin and Zaitsev have included two appendixes (supplements) that detail several types of functions (trigonometric, hyperbolic, gamma, Bessel, hypergeometric, Legendre, and Weierstrass) and some of their most important properties. The reference section of any scientific library will be enriched by the acquisition of this book. Highly recommended for anyone who studies or uses differential equations. Undergraduate through professional.—*D. P. Turner, Faulkner University*

OAB-1695   QA29   95-5254 CIP
Ramanujan Aiyangar, Srinivasa. **Ramanujan: letters and commentary,** by Bruce C. Berndt and Robert A. Rankin. American Mathematical Society/London Mathematical Society, 1995. 347p bibl index afp (History of mathematics, 9) ISBN 0-8218-0287-9, $79.00; ISBN 0-8218-0470-7 pbk, $49.00

The name Srinivasa Ramanujan is a household word among mathematicians.

He is the extraordinary genius who rose and disappeared like a flashing comet in the firmament of 20th-century mathematics, producing prolific and prodigious theorems from the unfathomable depths of his being. This remarkable personage, whose creativity in his field is comparable to the sublime musical compositions of Mozart, was brought to the world's attention thanks to a now-famous letter he wrote to British mathematician G.H. Hardy in 1913. During the remaining seven years of his all-too-brief life, Ramanujan corresponded with many others as well, and on less-technical themes also. This commendable collection of all the extant letters by and (quite a few on) Ramanujan is a unique contribution to the history of mathematics for at least two reasons. It has brought together precious documents scattered in many places and provides the reader with a wealth of interesting matters related to one of the luminaries in the world of mathematics. Second, through brief and insightful notes and commentaries, the work throws light on many an interesting side street connecting to the grand avenue of knowledge on which we are riding. With resuscitations of some fading photographs and an impressive list of more than 300 references, this book is a very valuable addition to the literature on Ramanujan. Upper-division undergraduate through faculty.—*V. V. Raman, Rochester Institute of Technology*

OAB-1696 QA278 94-23567 CIP
Rencher, Alvin C. **Methods of multivariate analysis.** Wiley-Interscience, 1995. 627p bibl index afp ISBN 0-471-57152-0, $74.95

In this well-written and interesting book, Rencher has done a great job in presenting intuitive and innovative explanations of some of the otherwise difficult concepts, and has successfully avoided overdoing proofs. The first volume of a two-volume set, the second, "to appear in 1996," will be theoretically oriented. The first two chapters (of 13) provide an overview of multivariate analysis and the fundamentals of matrix algebra; others treat multivariate normal distribution and display of data from multivariate populations. Univariate techniques (e.g., t-tests, analysis of variance, testing of the variances of populations, multiple linear regression, multiple correlation) with one dependent variable are extended to analogous multivariate methods involving several dependent variables in five other chapters. The remaining four chapters discuss multivariate techniques such as discriminate analysis, classification analysis, principal component analysis, and factor analysis; for these no corresponding univariate procedures exist. Necessary prerequisites are a course on matrix algebra and two courses on statistical methods. Appendixes provide useful statistical tables, and answers and hints to chapter problem sets. Highly recommended for all academic libraries, graduate as well as undergraduate.—*D. V. Chopra, Wichita State University*

OAB-1697 QA274 92-4431 CIP
Resnick, Sidney. **Adventures in stochastic processes.** Birkhauser, 1992. 626p bibl index afp ISBN 0-8176-3591-2, $64.50

An excellent presentation of the tedious and complicated ideas of stochastic processes, in a lucid and easy-to-understand fashion. Resnick makes use of an abundance of solved examples and illustrations to bring clarity and understanding to these otherwise obscure and difficult concepts. Background material for this book is graduate-level probability studies involving little or no measure theory. Resnick aims at a wider audience that includes mathematicians, statisticians, operations researchers, and engineers. Stochastic processes are very useful in building models of real-life situations involving randomness over time. The book has seven chapters; the first is devoted to preliminaries involving discrete spaces, Wald's identity, and stopping times. Topics in the next six chapters include Markov chains, renewal theory, point processes, branching processes, random walks, and Brownian motion. Each chapter ends with a set of exercises that include interesting, practical, and challenging problems. The tools presented are then applied to problems arising in economics, sociology, genetics, risk analysis, etc. Useful index; bibliography. The presentation is flexible enough to be enjoyed by both beginners and advanced students. A splendid book to bring home the value and importance of stochastic processes. Highly recommended. Advanced undergraduate; graduate.—*D. V. Chopra, Wichita State University*

OAB-1698 QA246 94-42041 CIP
Sloane, N.J.A. **The encyclopedia of integer sequences,** by N.J.A. Sloane and Simon Plouffe. Academic Press, 1995. 587p bibl index afp ISBN 0-12-558630-2, $44.95

Many sequences of integers arise in research concerning number theory, combinatorics, algebra, topology, analysis, geometry, and other branches of mathematics. Recognizing such sequences is often the key to solving a problem or discovering a link between previously unrelated ideas. This encyclopedia supersedes the author's classic *Handbook of Integer Sequences* (1973). The number of sequences cataloged here is more than double the tally of the previous incarnation. Even better, a powerful on-line version of the work, accessible to all by electronic mail, makes it much easier now to look up a sequence that one happens to meet in a disguised form. If libraries shelve this book in the reference section, they should consider acquiring a second copy for circulation. The book will likely be in high demand, not just by researchers, but by browsers at all levels who will especially appreciate the entertaining commentaries interspersed every few pages throughout the encyclopedia. Highly recommended for all academic libraries.—*D. V. Feldman, University of New Hampshire*

OAB-1699 QA162 96-19469 CIP
Stahl, Saul. **Introductory modern algebra: a historical approach.** Wiley-Interscience, 1997. 322p bibl index afp ISBN 0-471-16288-4, $62.95

In this excellent presentation of modern algebra, Stahl offers the solvability of equations from the historical point of view. He carefully develops the necessary background in complex numbers and proceeds to derive the cubic formula. The discussion then turns to modular arithmetic, the binomial theorem, and polynomials, including a derivation of the quartic formula. Galois fields, permutations, and the essentials of group theory are next exhibited clearly, leading to the resolvability of equations. The book has many other distinctive characteristics. Pertinent portions of the writings of Al-Khwarizmi, Cardano, Abel, Galois, and Cayley are given, as are brief biographies of some 25 mathematicians. The book includes more than 1,000 exercises and computer/mathematical projects. Answers to selected odd-numbered exercises are also given. In summary, one of the best books available to support a one-semester introduction to abstract algebra. Upper-division undergraduates through professionals.—*D. P. Turner, Faulkner University*

OAB-1700 QA93 95-10238 CIP
Stewart, Ian. **Nature's numbers: the unreal reality of mathematical imagination.** Basic Books, 1995. 164p bibl index ISBN 0-465-07273-9, $20.00

Stewart's goal in *Nature's Numbers* is to equip the reader with a mathematician's eye for a sightseeing trip through the mathematical universe. The interrelations of nature's patterns, structures, and processes form the underlying theme of the book. Nobody doubts that nature provides numerous examples of beautiful shapes and symmetries. Stewart argues, full circle, that patterns of form and motion reveal deep regularities in the world around us: sixfold symmetry of snowflakes led Kepler to conjecture that all matter is composed of atoms; patterns of waves and dunes provide clues to the laws of fluid flow; and tiger stripes and hyena spots provide a key to understanding the processes of biological growth. These are just a few of the many fascinating examples Stewart provides. Also explored are nature's most recently discovered patterns, patterns in apparent randomness, and the resulting theories of chaos and fractals. A wonderful read for laypeople and scientists of all shapes and forms. Highly recommended for any general academic library collection in mathematics and science. General; lower-division undergraduate.—*D. L. King, Oberlin College*

OAB-1701 QA155 94-10085 CIP
Stillwell, John. **Elements of algebra: geometry, numbers, equations.** Springer-Verlag, 1994. 181p bibl index afp ISBN 0-387-94290-4, $34.95

Until recently, nearly all contemporary textbooks in abstract algebra revealed the motivating problems and applications of the subject only after a discussion of the general concepts and techniques, if at all. The result was often unnecessarily enigmatic for the reader. Happily, in the past few years, a few books have appeared that resist this tendency and instead effectively blend the full mathematical and historical context with the algebra. Stillwell's work is part of this new trend. Stillwell deftly juxtaposes the historical origins of the subject and the mathematical axioms and abstractions. Thus, this brief work develops ring, field, group, and Galois theory through the introduction of problems from classical algebra, number theory, symmetry, and geometric construction problems. Stillwell also wrote *Mathematics and Its History* (CH, Feb'90), so this new book is by someone expert in bringing the history of mathematics to life not by studying the interesting personalities involved but via the interesting mathematics. An outstanding supplement to more to more "traditional" works and a fine and concise stand-alone volume. Highly recommended. Upper-division graduate.—*S. J. Colley, Oberlin College*

OAB-1702   QA273   93-12917 CIP
Stirzaker, David. **Elementary probability.** Cambridge, 1994. 406p index ISBN 0-521-42028-8, $64.95; ISBN 0-521-42183-7 pbk, $24.95

Stirzaker does an excellent job of developing problem-solving skills in an introductory probability text. Numerous examples and practice exercises are provided that only serve to enhance a student's problem solving abilities. Examples and exercises have been carefully chosen with three things in mind: illustration of the subject, typical examination questions, and entertainment value (even the color of the book is interesting!). The reader should have some knowledge of elementary set theory as well as the simpler techniques of calculus. There are three major areas of the book: (1) basic concepts of probability, conditional probability, and independence; (2) discrete random variables, mass functions, and expectations; and (3) continuous random variables. Additional topics that are covered include combinatorial methods in probability, probability and other generating functions, and the basic theory of Markov chains. An appendix includes the solutions for many problems along with some helpful hints for selected exercises and problems. Highly recommended for undergraduate and graduate-level library collections.—*D. J. Gougeon, University of Scranton*

OAB-1703   QA276   92-7099 CIP
Thompson, Steven K. **Sampling.** Wiley-Interscience, 1992. 343p bibl indexes ISBN 0-471-54045-5, $59.95

A unique book treating sampling methods and techniques for populations that are difficult to sample because they may be clustered, rare, elusive, or simply hard to detect. Thompson names several examples such as "predicting the amount of mineral or fossil-fuel resources at a new site, the prevalence of a rare disease, or estimating the abundance of an animal or an elusive human population." An excellent manual for researchers who have worked in these areas and have confronted such problems. Basic and standard sampling designs are covered. In addition, Thompson effectively incorporates the use of several recent developments in sampling such as adaptive sampling designs, network sampling, and generalized ratio and regression estimation with unequal probability designs. There are also several sampling methodologies developed for specific areas, such as detectability methods that are used in ecological sampling; kriging methods that are associated with geostatistics; and network sampling associated with the health sciences. Numerous references are cited throughout. Highly recommended for undergraduate and graduate libraries.— *D. J. Gougeon, University of Scranton*

OAB-1704   QA276   96-39660 CIP
Weaver, Jefferson Hane. **Conquering statistics: numbers without the crunch.** Plenum Trade, 1997. 236p bibl index ISBN 0-306-45572-2, $26.95

Weaver's interesting, entertaining, and humorous book on a serious matter presents the basic concepts of statistics in an easy-to-understand and light-hearted style, and succeeds in demystifying statistics without using the formal language and complexities of mathematics. To make it accessible to all, he carefully avoids all theoretical developments and instead makes use of everyday life instances to explain statistical ideas. Not a textbook on statistics, the book is for those with little or no knowledge of this important and flourishing subject. Topics covered include a brief historical development of statistics, descriptive statistics, random samples and some variants of these, probabilities including Bayes' theorem, binomial distribution, standard normal distribution, Chebyshev's Theorem, the Central Limit Theorem, the law of large numbers, and inferential statistics. Weaver demonstrates both the utility and beauty of statistical tools, and includes comments on their application to commerce, industry, social sciences, medicine, etc. He has done a commendable job of deflating the fear of statistics and helping readers make informed judgments on statistical conclusions of others. The book has wide appeal, and readers will find it as enjoyable as this reviewer did. Highly recommended. General readers; lower-division undergraduates.—*D. V. Chopra, Wichita State University*

■ Physics & Meteorology

OAB-1705   Q143   95-47579 MARC
Batchelor, George. **The life and legacy of G.I. Taylor.** Cambridge, 1996. 285p bibl index ISBN 0-521-46121-9, $75.00

This splendid biography of a great physicist captures the importance of his legacy of applied physics and elegantly portrays a brilliant mind connecting theoretical innovations to practical experiments. Technical details are injected judiciously amid historical and anecdotal accounts so that the challenging research frontiers of fluid dynamics and material properties can be appreciated fully. Taylor's wife's fascinating account of their trip to Borneo in 1929 is an additional treat. The pictures and drawings complete this wonderful representation of a scientist working successfully outside the two main frontiers of physics in the first half of the 20th century: quantum mechanics and nuclear physics. Adequate index; appendixes include a bibliography of all Taylor's papers and a list of his numerous honors. Upper-division undergraduates through professionals.—*F. Potter, University of California, Irvine*

OAB-1706   QC861   94-45885 CIP
Composition, chemistry, and climate of the atmosphere, ed. by Hanwant B. Singh. Van Nostrand Reinhold, 1995. 527p bibl index ISBN 0-442-01264-0, $79.95

The Earth's atmosphere responds to the same laws of chemistry, physics, and meteorology that apply to condensed phases of matter. This book utilizes world-renowned experts to connect previously anecdotal descriptions of atmospheric perturbations and pollution episodes to an integrated scientific discipline now known as atmospheric chemistry. The history of air pollution is traced from paleopathological evidence of blackened lung tissue and as ancient writings lamenting the impact of smoke from the earliest use of indoor fires. Students, scientists, regulators, and any individuals looking for a comprehensive and authoritative understanding of the atmosphere will be enlightened by reading the first third (four chapters) of this book. The midsection describes physical and chemical interactions between particles and gases. Nitrogen, halogens, and sulfur species illustrate important mechanisms. The final section spotlights the major atmospheric issues of smog, ozone depletion, acid rain, and global warming with abundant references and reasoned opinions. An outstanding contribution! All levels.—*R. M. Ferguson, Eastern Connecticut State University*

OAB-1707   QC6   95-32631 CIP
Des Chene, Dennis. **Physiologia: natural philosophy in late Aristotelian and Cartesian thought.** Cornell, 1996. 426p bibl index afp ISBN 0-8014-3072-0, $42.50

Here is a detailed and close examination of 16th- and early 17th-century Aristotelian philosophy of nature, both in its own right and as the wellspring for Cartesian thought. In a clear and rigorous manner, Des Chene examines the principles of Aristotle's *Physics*—matter and form, the four causes, natural change, nature itself—as they were discussed and debated in Renaissance Aristotelianism, both in particular (e.g., the Coimbrans, Suarez, Toletus) and collectively (as found in their textbooks). Descartes learned his philosophy from Scholastic texts and knew Scholasticism well: this book makes explicit in an erudite and yet extremely lucid style the influences of his schooling and the nature of his departure from the Aristotelian teleological philosophy of nature. As such, it is a contribution to both the history of science and the history of philosophy: in particular, it elucidates much of Aristotle's own thinking. Although it presupposes some knowledge of Aristotle's philosophy, it will reward the attentive reader with a slight philosophical background. No one else has done this work; it has been done superbly here. Excellent bibliography. Upper-division undergraduates through faculty.—*M. H. Chaplin, Wellesley College*

OAB-1708   QC75   93-28135 CIP
Ehrlich, Robert. **The cosmological milkshake: a semi-serious look at the size of things.** Rutgers, 1994. 259p bibl index ISBN 0-8135-2045-2, $24.95

Ehrlich, a physicist, has written a delightful compendium of 135 short essays devoted to answering the "hows" and "whats" of the universe that surrounds us. The questions are related to various physical dimensions such as length ("How Tall Can Trees Grow?"); volume ("How Much of Your Body is Empty Space?"); mass ("How Massive are Black Holes?"); temperature ("How Hot is the Earth at the Center?"); time ("How Old is Life on Earth?"); and speed ("How Fast Does Electricity Travel in Wires?"). Each essay is accompanied by a cartoon that adds to the enjoyment of understanding something about our surroundings. The book is aimed at the layperson, and so there is nothing to fear as far as understanding scientific terminology is concerned. Where necessary, the definitions of concepts or terms are provided as footnotes. There are no equations to decipher, yet the explanations to the various questions are well reasoned and good. Besides providing many hours of reading pleasure, the book can help whenever one is stumped by a child's query. All levels.—*N. Sadanand, Central Connecticut State University*

OAB-1709   QC151   94-19245 CIP
Faber, T.E. **Fluid dynamics for physicists.** Cambridge, 1995. 440p index ISBN 0-521-41943-3, $74.95; ISBN 0-521-42969-2 pbk, $34.95

One of the striking characteristics of Faber's book is its mathematical simplicity without compromise of rigor. Although most of the topics are classical in nature and well documented in numerous books on fluid dynamics, the author intelligently repackaged several problems across the fluid mechanics spectrum. In that regard, he shows his breadth of knowledge of the field. Innovative approaches are found in sections 1.3 and 1.9; also, Faber's treatment of non-Newtonian fluids in chapter 10 is excellent, considering the mathematical complexity of the subject. However, this reviewer differed with the author's opinion in his preface that books written for engineers are likely to put them off, perhaps because the treatment seems imprecise. All in all, this book is a valuable reference. Upper-division undergraduates through faculty.—*R. N. Laoulache, University of Massachusetts Dartmouth*

OAB-1710   QC793   96-47811 MARC
Feynman, Richard P. **Six not-so-easy pieces: Einstein's relativity, symmetry, and space-time,** orig. prep. for publication by Robert B. Leighton and Matthew Sands. Addison-Wesley, 1997. 152p index ISBN 0-201-15025-5, $25.00

Here is a further collection of essays by the US's most renowned and celebrated physicist of the second half of the 20th century, Richard Feynman (1918-1988). The essays, taken from the archives of Feynman's lectures at the California Institute of Technology (from the well-known Feynman lectures on physics delivered to undergraduate freshmen) are a follow-up to the first collection of essays, *Six Easy Pieces* (CH, May '95). The major difference between the two is that this selection requires the reader to have a basic understanding of simple mathematics. Another difference is this book's focus on a single subject, Albert Einstein's theory of relativity. Feynman outlines the mathematics that facilitates an understanding of the other chapters: "Vectors," "Symmetry in Physical Laws," "The Special Theory of Relativity," "Relativistic Energy and Momentum," "Space-Time," "Curved Space." Feynman very methodically and lucidly develops the concepts of time dilation, the dependence of an object's mass on its velocity, and the constancy of the speed of light in all reference frames. The book has a very useful introduction by the famous British mathematician Roger Penrose. Excellent drawings, very good index. Undergraduates through professionals; two-year technical program students—*N. Sadanand, Central Connecticut State University*

OAB-1711   QC16   96-26341 CIP
Fölsing, Albrecht. **Albert Einstein: a biography,** tr. by Ewald Osers. Viking, 1997. 882p bibl index afp ISBN 0-670-85545-6, $34.95

In its original German, this biography has already become a standard reference for the "Einstein industry," i.e., those scholars engaged in reconstructing a most remarkable episode in intellectual history. Fölsing well describes the most recently discovered biographical details: the "love letters" to Mileva Maric, full of passing references to his early thinking in pre-relativity days; the early attempts at invention of a patentable electrical device; the personal concerns over the breakup of his marriage; and the actual war work (as opposed to the apocryphal relations to atomic engineering). The scientific musings are here; for instance, the early thoughts on the atomic hypotheses of the "miracle year" of 1905, the Maxwellian background of the restricted relativity theory of 1905, the empirical aspects of the general relativity of 1915, the less-discussed arguments of the "Einstein-de Haas experiment," the opposition to quantum mechanics, and the ill-starred unified field attempts. In his very well composed book, designed to be accessible to the general reader as well as the specialist, Fölsing eliminates most of the intimidating equations (and thus captures the audience of competing works by Banesh Hoffmann (*Albert Einstein, Creator and Rebel*, 1972) and Ronald Clark (*Einstein: The Life and Times*, 1971), while surveying the actual contemporary scientific anomalies (comparable to the authoritative, but difficult, work by Abraham Pais, "*Subtle is the Lord—*", 1982). These technical passages, bereft of algorithms, become somewhat strained, and the accompanying deterioration of proofreading leaves a window of opportunity for successors. For now, though, this is clearly the definitive biography of Einstein, and should be acquired by all academic libraries. General readers; undergraduates through faculty.—*P. D. Skiff, Bard College*

OAB-1712   QC791   96-34254 CIP
Fowler, T. Kenneth. **The fusion quest.** Johns Hopkins, 1997. 250p bibl index afp ISBN 0-8018-5456-3, $29.95

There are those who will mark the passage of the US from first to second class with the abandonment of the 40-year quest for fusion energy that began with Lyman Spitzer's stellerator designs (1958) and will end with the shutting down of TFFR, the Princeton Tokamak, even after the successful deuterium/tritium burn experiments of December 1993. The task has been largely left to others in Europe and Japan to complete, in some foreseeable future between say 2020 and perhaps 2050. Fowler's book, an authoritative and timely record of all-too-rare international cooperation in scientific research and technology development, is delicately tuned to balance the science and engineering principles and practices with the history of the program and the rise and fall of its political fortunes. Fowler, an eyewitness participant from almost the beginning, is an optimistic cheerleader for this towering achievement of "big science." His volume is accurately written and well documented, with a useful glossary, and a carefully organized and well-conceived bibliography. Who should read this book? Those who need to be most concerned about the US's energy future and the progress of science, namely, everyone. Read it! All levels.—*L. W. Fine, Columbia University*

OAB-1713   QC774   94-1642 CIP
Gell-Mann, Murray. **The quark and the jaguar: adventures in the simple and the complex.** W.H. Freeman, 1994. 392p index ISBN 0-7167-2581-9, $23.95

That the world is complex is an ancient recognition, arising from the commonest of experiences and observations. That underlying all the complexity are fundamentally simple principles and entities is the insight of great thinkers. Of late, however, interests have grown in the interconnections—logical, conceptual, and practical—between the essence of ultimate simplicity, symbolized by the quark, and the marvelous mystery of complexity, symbolized by the majesty of the jaguar. In this fascinating collection of interwoven essays Gell-Mann surveys a whole range of ideas and results that concern current scientific thought and thoughts on science. The book is spiced with sprinklings of autobiography and enriched by the author's breadth of interests and inquiries. Its sweep touches physics and sociobiology, ecology and parallel processing. The beautifully written prologue sets the stage for the drama to follow. Every section of every chapter is insightful and informative, reading like journal entries of a reflective observer of the world at large. "Scientific Enterprise" is a succinct survey of what science is all about. A good chunk of the work is devoted to the "Quantum Universe," where the author reveals himself as a keen physicist. "Quantum Mechanics and Flapdoodle" is a refreshingly intelligent analysis of the conceptual muddle that has plagued the field right from the start, engendering volumes of hot air clothed as profound philosophy. "Diversity" is a sensitive and intelligent examination of the theme. Unfortunately, the details will be accessible only to the scientifically awakened, and some of those only to the literate in physics. And for the more enlightened among these, the book will surely be a true delight. Upper-division undergraduate through professional.—*V. V. Raman, Rochester Institute of Technology*

OAB-1714   QC24   95-15199 CIP
Guillen, Michael. **Five equations that changed the world: the power and poetry of mathematics.** Hyperion, NY, 1995. 277p index ISBN 0-7868-6103-7, $22.95

Five Equations is an outstanding account of the achievements of Newton, Bernoulli, Faraday, Clausius, and Einstein. Guillen, science editor for ABC and a physics and mathematics instructor at Harvard, does an outstanding job of presenting to the layperson the work of these five brilliant scientists. The engaging accounts are a blend of the biographical and the scientific, and are presented in simple, everyday language. For example, after reading the book, most will understand the notion of Einstein's special relativity theory. The book deserves to be in public, college and university, and even high school libraries and promises to become a classic.—*W. R. Lee, Iowa State University*

OAB-1715   QC353   92-43731 CIP
Hall, A. Rupert. **All was light: an introduction to Newton's** *Opticks.* Oxford, 1993. 252p bibl indexes ISBN 0-19-853985-1, $52.50

This seems, perhaps surprisingly, to be "the first attempt to give a general account of one of the most celebrated books in the history of science: Newton's *Opticks*." An introductory and a final chapter deal briefly with Newton's predecessors and with the reception and popularization of the *Opticks* in Britain and Continental Europe. In between, Hall discusses in detail both the evolution of Newton's research and speculation in optics and the rather different evolution of the published texts of the *Opticks* (three English and two Latin editions in Newton's lifetime). Drawing always on the most up-to-date results of recent historical analysis by Newtonian scholars, Hall sets out his own lines of interpretation, insisting, e.g., that "Though ... Newton's mind ... ventured far in both physical and philosophical speculations ... he made no overt use of them in his substantive scientific work." Although not providing an "*analyse de texte* of *Opticks*" or "a reconstruction of Newton's scientific methodology," Hall does provide substantial prolegomena for such enterprises. Highly recommended. General; advanced undergraduate through faculty.—*R. Palter, emeritus, Trinity College (CT)*

OAB-1716   QC16   92-15600 CIP
Hall, A. Rupert. **Isaac Newton, adventurer in thought.** B. Blackwell, 1992. 468p bibl index afp ISBN 0-631-17906-2, $29.95

This "account of the greatest mind in British history" is "chiefly directed to Newton the mathematician and philosopher." One of the leading Newtonian scholars of our time, Hall provides stimulating and up-to-date summaries of recent research on Newton's contributions to mathematics, optics, and mechanics. More briefly covered is Newton's work in alchemy—which Hall sometimes writes "(al)chemy" to emphasize his contention that at least some of Newton's researches in this area can be considered clear anticipations of modern chemistry. Newton's scholarly preoccupation with biblical history and theology is also briefly but insightfully discussed. Written in short, titled sections in a straightforward style, the book reads easily and yet never unduly modernizes or simplifies its subject matter. Illustrated with figures but no pictures, not even a portrait of Newton (except on the endpapers), even though there is a detailed appendix on Newton's portraits. Short but useful bibliography and good index. Highly recommended. General; advanced undergraduate through professional.—*R. Palter, emeritus, Trinity College (CT)*

OAB-1717   Q173   95-37483 CIP
Holton, Gerald. **Einstein, history, and other passions.** American Institute of Physics, 1995. 312p bibl index afp (Masters of modern physics, 16) ISBN 1-56396-333-7, $29.95

In this collection of 16 essays based on papers, reviews, and lectures published from 1970 to the present, Holton examines what it means to "do" science, the nature of scientific imagination and intuition, science education, and the growing mistrust of science in present-day society. His biographic sketches of Einstein, Oppenheimer, Feynman, and others are factual, succinct, and infused with warmth and empathy. Einstein is highlighted often, not just because of his scientific genius but also because of his clear introspection concerning the evolution of scientific insight. This is a book about science and scientists, written with great care and clarity by a distinguished scientist. It is a delight to read, and one senses the ring of truth resounding from cover to cover. Recommended highly for upper-division undergraduates, graduate students, faculty, and informed general readers.—*J. C. Amato, Colgate University*

OAB-1718   QC879   94-42859 CIP
Kidder, Stanley Q. **Satellite meteorology: an introduction,** by Stanley Q. Kidder and Thomas H. Vonder Haar. Academic Press, 1995. 466p index afp ISBN 0-12-406430-2, $54.95

This excellent, comprehensive book is far more than an introduction to satellite meteorology; it begins with the basics of radiation and a physical understanding of measurements from space and how they are converted to useful parameters. Use and accuracy are stressed, and each chapter has an extensive bibliography. At present, mostly passive instruments are used, but information about future plans include active systems such as space-borne radar. Besides the expected topics—clouds, winds, and precipitation—there is material on dust, snow and ice, smoke and fire, sea surface temperature, and land and water features. The authors also cover spectral properties of several bands including microwaves, and determination, use, and importance of soil moisture in atmospheric prediction models. The international Earth Observing System is explained. Acronyms proliferate; fortunately, the appendix explains most of them, and also lists all meteorological satellites operant through 1994. Good index. Great material for upper-division undergraduate and graduate students.—*A. E. Staver, Northern Illinois University*

OAB-1719   Q151   91-35652 CIP
Lang, Helen S. **Aristotle's** *Physics* **and its medieval varieties.** State University of New York, 1992. 322p bibl indexes ISBN 0-7914-1083-8, $44.50; ISBN 0-7914-1084-6 pbk, $14.95

A masterful, exegetical study of Aristotle's *Physics* (and *Metaphysics 12*) as it contrasts with commentaries by Philoponus, Albertus Magnus, Thomas

Aquinas, and John Buridan, with an afterword about Duns Scotus and the medieval transformations of the problems of rest, natural and difform motion, teleology, place, cause, and the other categories of medieval physics. Occasionally contrasting her own translations with the transmitted tradition, Lang reconstructs a coherent Aristotelian architectonic and notes some overlooked novelties in its later variations. As to the post-Averroeist era, Lang concludes ". . .the rearticulation of Aristotle's arguments into logical and rhetorical structures wholly foreign to them. . .leaves nothing untouched: neither the structure of the arguments, nor the problems to be solved that they present, nor the solutions to these problems, nor even the general conception of physics within this work takes place." Highly recommended for library collections in the history and philosophy of science, especially in support of emerging studies on the classical background to science. Advanced undergraduate through faculty.—*P. D. Skiff, Bard College*

OAB-1720   QC793   92-43583 CIP
Lederman, Leon. **The God particle: if the universe is the answer, what is the question?,** by Leon Lederman with Dick Teresi. Houghton Mifflin, 1993. 434p index ISBN 0-395-55849-2, $24.95

Presenting technical science to the public at large is a sophisticated art form, very valuable in these times when science has become far too abstruse for the average educated citizen to understand or appreciate. A few living scientists—Lederman is surely one—publish now and again a work addressed to the general public. Some are exceptionally readable and informative, and entertaining to boot. Lederman's book belongs to this category. Combining wit and deep knowledge, he provides the reader with facts, insight, and anecdotal reflections. Getting to the core of matter has been his scientific obsession, and so in these pages he traces, with much intelligence and charm, the ancient quest from Democritus to the inflationary model, from *atomos* to the Higgs boson (which he has dubbed The God Particle). The book is a model in the exposition of lofty ideas with deceptive informality. Lederman also provides brief and fascinating sketches of the more eminent names that have left a mark in the game of peeling away the layers of matter. In an interlude entitled "A Tale of Two Cities" he presents a single-page road map of the quest for the core of matter from Miletus (of Thales) to Waxahachie (for the future SSC). In another tongue-in-cheek interlude, "The Dancing Moo-Shu Masters," he pokes intelligent fun at the recent enthusiasm for merging modern physics and mysticism. Physicists and physics students will find the book to be a sheer delight, and other reasonably well educated citizens can savor it to their advantage. All levels.—*V. V. Raman, Rochester Institute of Technology*

OAB-1721   QC173   93-36909 CIP
Lide, David R. **CRC handbook of thermophysical and thermochemical data,** by David R. Lide and Henry V. Kehiaian. CRC Press, 1994. 518p index afp disk (IBM-PC) ISBN 0-8493-0197-1, $149.95

Lide and Kehiaian provide a comprehensive tabulation of thermodynamic and transport properties of pure substances and mixtures that are encountered in numerous engineering applications. The tables and the associated descriptive material are organized into five sections. The first introduces the reader to symbols, units, and terminology. Section 2 provides the thermodynamic properties of pure substances; section 3 contains the same information for mixtures, and is followed by a section on transport properties such as viscosity, thermal conductivity, and diffusion coefficients. The last section is devoted to a tabulation of properties of common fluids such as water and air. Substance and general topic indexes. The editorial work is excellent in this valuable reference. Undergraduate through professional; two-year technical program students.— *A. Aziz, Gonzaga University*

OAB-1722   QC355   93-46711 CIP
Lynch, David K. **Color and light in nature,** by David K. Lynch and William Livingston. Cambridge, 1995. 254p bibl index ISBN 0-521-43431-9, $44.95; ISBN 0-521-46836-1 pbk, $29.95

This book stays true to its title; it is a remarkable exposition of the many opti-

cal phenomena that delight and intrigue the eye of an observant person. From shadows and colors in the sky, to lightning and the aurora borealis, to solar eclipses and naked-eye astronomy, to so many sometimes puzzling games that light plays all around us, all are explained well by Lynch and Livingston, authors of this delightful volume. Equations are completely absent, but photos and graphs are liberally used to assist in the explanation of the phenomena. A reader needs only the most fundamental concepts in physical optics, reflection, refraction, polarization, and lenses to enjoy this book. It will certainly appeal to all readers interested in understanding color and light in nature, independent of their specialization, and could serve effectively as a resource in college studies. All levels.—*E. Hadjimichael, Fairfield University*

OAB-1723   QC816   96-28566 CIP
Merrill, Ronald T. **The magnetic field of the earth: paleomagnetism, the core, and the deep mantle,** by Ronald T. Merrill, Michael W. McElhinny, and Phillip L. McFadden. Academic Press, 1996. 531p bibl indexes afp (International geophysics series, 63) ISBN 0-12-491245-1, $89.00

This update to Merrill and McElhinny's *The Earth's Magnetic Field* (1983) is one of the better books on Earth magnetics that this reviewer has seen in recent years. It represents an excellent effort, clearly intended for upper-division undergraduate and graduate students, and is probably the most up-to-date work available on Earth's magnetic field. Chapters discuss historical information, geomagnetism and paleomagnetism, archeomagnetic and paleomagnetic studies, and geodynamo theory, together with a brief discussion of planetary magnetics. Emphasis is on combining theory with observations and updating the current state of knowledge. As would be expected with any work of this nature, specific terminology (e.g., magnetic hysteresis) and advanced mathematics (e.g., vector calculus) are used. However, the specific terms used are well explained and the mathematics are not overwhelming. For students beginning studies in the field of geophysics and the earth's interior, it is essential reading (after an appropriate grounding in mathematics, physics, and geology). Upper-division undergraduates through professionals.—*M. S. Field, U.S. Environmental Protection Agency*

OAB-1724   QC21   93-9507 CIP
Newton, Roger G. **What makes nature tick?** Harvard, 1993. 257p bibl index afp ISBN 0-674-95085-2, $27.95

Newton has directed his book to anyone with a modest background in basic science who wants to understand why and how our current view of nature has developed. He blends ideas such as symmetry, causality, action at a distance, and time's arrow (among others) into the body of knowledge that has been developed over the past three centuries. The influence of imagination, intuition, and an appreciation of beauty are skillfully woven into the story of those who have created the physics of today. Where necessary, concise presentations of mathematical ideas, essential for a clear understanding of physical ideas, are provided. Diagrams and illustrations are used effectively in several places. Not just a history of physics, the book uses current areas of interest such as chaos, quarks, and superconductors to illustrate how physicists apply, expand, and refine their understanding and how that understanding is constantly evolving. An outstanding presentation, highly recommended to all readers with even a modest acquaintance with the basic ideas of nature and the rules that govern it. All levels.—*C. A. Hewett, Rochester Institute of Technology*

OAB-1725   QC879   96-11463 CIP
Nilsson, Annika. **Ultraviolet reflections: life under a thinning ozone layer.** Wiley, 1996. 152p bibl index afp ISBN 0-471-95843-3 pbk, $40.00

Nilsson explores the multiplicity of problems and damage resulting from continued global ozone depletion. In total, his interests address the effect of ultraviolet radiation on all life forms—biological, human, and animal. He uses a suggestive, not encyclopedic, approach to the underlying science of this problem and clearly reviews the controversial questions. His discussion succinctly analyzes existing knowledge and biological processes gathered from Southern Hemisphere research and compares this body of material to Northern Hemisphere conditions. This informative book is properly cautious, but scientifically detailed enough to lay out the consequences of UV radiation related to human and animal immune system suppression and resultant effects on DNA changes, which underlie skin cancer; effects on vaccination (which relies on the immune system to store information about pathogens); and cataract and other eye tissue change leading to disease processes. He clearly acknowledges the complexity of risk assessment and the difficulty of providing definitive answers to the most pressing questions associated with this global environmental problem. Highly informative, clearly written, with appropriate and readable graphics; chapter bibliographies. Highly recommended for all college libraries and for public collections as well. All levels.—*M. Evans, SUNY Empire State College*

OAB-1726   QC457   Orig
Nyquist, Richard A. **Handbook of infrared and Raman spectra of inorganic compounds and organic salts,** by Richard A. Nyquist et al. Academic Press, 1997. 4v. bibl indexes afp ISBN 0-12-523444-9, $1,000.00

This excellent resource on infrared and Raman spectra of a very large number of inorganic compounds and organic salts, including some nonionic inorganic compounds, is especially important since it has a compendium of Raman spectra that is otherwise not available. The first volume contains a well-written discussion of the experimental and theoretical aspects as well as vibrational assignments. Many diagrams show the vibrational modes in a host of compounds. The tables, correlation diagrams, and references are invaluable. Volumes 2 and 3 contain the Raman spectra and infrared spectra of more than 500 compounds, respectively. Volume 4 is a revision of Nyquist's original work, *Infrared Spectra of Inorganic Compounds ...* (1971), which contains another 892 compounds and miscellaneous minerals. Extensive index cross-references Raman and infrared spectra. Infrared spectra in volume 3 are prepared as potassium bromide pellets, while those in volume 4 are done as split mulls. An excellent, first-class publication. It should be useful to upper-division undergraduates; graduate students; and researchers and faculty.—*W. H. Hohman, Marietta College*

OAB-1727   QC178   93-34408 CIP
Ohanian, Hans. **Gravitation and spacetime,** by Hans Ohanian and Remo Ruffini. 2nd ed. W.W. Norton, 1994. 679p bibl index ISBN 0-393-96501-5, $49.95

The physics community knows Ohanian as an outstanding explicator of physics. His books on physics run the gamut from a widely used and respected introductory text to senior-graduate level volumes on quantum mechanics, and gravitation and spacetime. They are all characterized by a crisp clarity made readable by a distinctive style that often showcases a profound understanding of the subject. This new edition, written with Ruffini, of what is now a classic work (1st ed., CH, Dec'76) is enlarged and enriched. Much of the book has been rewritten and brought up to date. A large collection of references follows each chapter, an intellectual tour de force. The volume employs tensor notation throughout. The subject matter starts off with classical gravitation and special relativity. Before the start of the detailed treatment of general relativity, there are considerations of why one has to consider "curved spacetime." Electromagnetism, the "linear theory par excellence," supplies the bridging concept. The authors then apply the field equations of general relativity to topics like perihelion precession, black holes, and cosmology. Many of the sections are almost self-contained and are clear and concise summaries of the state of current knowledge. In this context, the chapter on cosmology is marvelous. This book belongs in all college and university libraries. Upper-division undergraduate; graduate; professional.—*K. L. Schick, Union College (NY)*

OAB-1728   QC21   93-33015 CIP
Oliver, David. **The shaggy steed of physics: mathematical beauty**

in the physical world. Springer-Verlag, 1994. 298p index afp ISBN 0-387-94163-0, $44.50

Physics will forever enchant people with the pathways that connect diverse branches of the subject. Oliver's book celebrates some of those pathways. It is an exposition on how a standard undergraduate physics problem in celestial mechanics, the two-body problem, leads into the much deeper mathematical physics theories of quantum mechanics and relativity theory. Along the way, the author introduces fundamental and very powerful concepts in theoretical physics: the action principle, Hamiltonian theory, group symmetries, spinor theory, and invariants. Although adequately complete to serve as an introduction to certain areas of modern physics, this book is not suitable as a textbook; however it was not intended to be so used. Instead, it is an excellent companion to works on 20th-century physical theory. The level of discussion is appropriate for upper-division undergraduate students of mathematics and physics, who will find that Oliver's book enriches their understanding of the material they are learning in class. A well-written book, highly recommended.—*A. Spero, formerly, Northern Michigan University*

OAB-1729   Orig
Perkampus, Heinz-Helmut. **Encyclopedia of spectroscopy,** tr. by Heide-Charlotte Grinter and Roger Grinter. VCH, 1995. 669p afp ISBN 3-527-29281-0, $90.00

This is a book that truly fills a need. New and modified spectroscopic methods of analysis are being developed at a rapid rate and are widely applied in many areas of science. To read the current literature in fields as far apart as oceanography and archaeometry is hard on all whose training in physics and analytical chemistry is slight or distant. Where does one find clear and concise accounts of photoacoustic spectroscopy or fluorescence polarization? One finds them in this excellent translation of a quite up-to-date (1993) German original. About a thousand entries are richly cross-referenced and augmented by about 300 very good illustrations. Literature citations lead to more detailed accounts. Many acronyms, e.g., PAS for photoacoustic spectroscopy, are given as primary entries (though not as many as one would wish), so that the volume doubles as a useful dictionary of these enigmas. A book that every student at every level and every practicing scientist will want to have within reach. Undergraduate through professional; two-year technical program students.—*C. W. Beck, emeritus, Vassar College*

OAB-1730   QC355   95-50778 CIP
Perkowitz, Sidney. **Empire of light: a history of discovery in science and art.** H. Holt, 1996. 227p bibl index afp ISBN 0-8050-3211-8, $27.50

Taking his title from René Magritte's surrealist painting *Empire of Light*, Perkowitz presents the history of light from the perspectives of both science and art. The author, a condensed-matter physicist specializing in laser technology, writes with the voice of a consummate lecturer. In looking at light from classical, relativistic, and quantum perspectives, he covers a wide spectrum of subjects ranging from optics, electricity, and particle physics to photography, the light properties of pigments, and the neurobiology of perception. He demonstrates through argument and illustration that discoveries in science are paralleled by explorations of the aesthetic and psychological manipulation of light in art, where "objective processes become subjective response." Perkowitz's mastery of metaphor and example enable him to bring clarity to concepts usually found daunting by the general reader, such as the necessity of mathematical expression or the wave-particle paradox of light. He does for light what Leon Lederman's *The God Particle* (CH, Sep'93) does for particle physics and Stephen Hawking's *A Brief History of Time* (CH, Jul'88) does for cosmology. It is easily a notch above Leonard Shlain's *Art and Physics* (CH, Feb'92). Suitable for the informed general reader, upper-division undergraduate and graduate students, and faculty.—*R. M. Davis, Albion College*

OAB-1731   Orig
Rayner-Canham, Marelene F. **A devotion to their science: pioneer women of radioactivity,** by Marelene F. Rayner-Canham and Geoffrey

318

W. Rayner-Canham. Chemical Heritage Foundation/McGill-Queen's, 1997. 307p index afp ISBN 0-941-901-165, $55.00; ISBN 0-941-901-157 pbk, $19.95

The Rayner-Canhams provide 17 chapter-length biographies and six brief accounts (where available information was limited) of the first generation of women working in the field of radioactivity. With the exception of Marie Curie and Lise Meitner, who have both received full-scale biographies in recent years, these women are virtually unknown today; thus this book is enormously helpful in acknowledging their genuine contributions to science and, in many cases, their success in encouraging other women researchers. The biographies are well-researched and thoughtfully written. Although they include descriptions of the actual scientific contributions of these women, they are not technical and can be easily read by someone with little or no knowledge of radioactivity. The style is straightforward and for the most part factual, although in certain instances the authors do not hesitate to point out examples of discrimination against women and make editorial comments on the behavior of the women themselves. It is extremely well documented, clearly written, and full of material not readily available elsewhere. For anyone interested in the history of women in science or the growth of scientific knowledge in the early 20th century. All levels.—*M. H. Chaplin, Wellesley College*

OAB-1732   QC173   94-49358 CIP
Sartori, Leo. **Understanding relativity: a simplified approach to Einstein's theories.** California, 1996. 367p index afp ISBN 0-520-07986-8, $50.00; ISBN 0-520-20092-2 pbk, $19.95

This excellent modern elementary exposition of special relativity, general relativity, and relativistic cosmology is suitable for intermediate and upper-division undergraduate students in physics and related fields. Minimum prerequisites are a good working knowledge of ordinary algebra, and a basic elementary understanding of the concepts of elementary mechanics and electricity and magnetism. Sartori stresses that it is necessary for the reader to develop an understanding of the concepts, and to develop the ability to reason using the concepts. He provides an excellent description of experimental evidence, an excellent selection of elementary problems, and interesting "thought experiments" and "paradoxes" from the scientific literature to develop and refine the reader's intuition for this purpose. Suitable also for the scientifically inclined general reader. Recommended. Undergraduates through faculty.—*C. A. Hein, Radex, Incorporated*

OAB-1733   QC793   92-12366 CIP
Schwarz, Cindy. **A tour of the subatomic zoo: a guide to particle physics.** American Institute of Physics, 1992. 112p index ISBN 0-88318-954-2 pbk, $30.00

Schwarz's remarkable book provides an introduction to the current picture of the nature of matter. It evolved from a course given by Schwarz for non-science college undergraduates, and presents a simplified but accurate description of what is often called the "standard model" in the field of particle physics. In addition, a brief historical introduction is provided as well as chapters on the various "forces" or interactions found in nature and the detectors and accelerators that have been used in high energy physics to learn about this subatomic "zoo." After each of the eight chapters, a self-test is provided, along with answers. Finally, a brief and concise discussion is given of the questions still to be answered, such as the origin of mass. The presentation is almost completely nonmathematical and is suitable for a wide range of audiences, ranging from interested high school students to faculty in other fields. Enthusiastically recommended as a valuable addition to any undergraduate library.—*R. L. Stearns, Vassar College*

OAB-1734   QC774   95-35246 CIP
Sime, Ruth Lewin. **Lise Meitner: a life in physics.** California, 1996. 526p bibl index afp ISBN 0-520-08906-5, $30.00

Sime has written an important book, not only because it is a detailed, comprehensive, and informative account of one of the most illustrious but little-known physicists of the 20th century, but also because it provides an insider's account of the discovery of fission and the treatment of Jewish intellectuals and scientists during the rise of Nazi Germany. Having access to a great many previously unpublished archival materials and Meitner's personal papers as well as having the scientific background to understand the physics involved, Sime has written a rich, well-documented, and illustrative biography. Her insights into the distortions of reality and the suppression of memory help to explain why this extremely talented and significant contributor to atomic physics has been neglected; the author's precise documentation and vast use of primary sources provide a very full account of both Meitner and the history of science in Germany under Hitler. Some descriptions of the science involved will be inaccessible to the nonscientist, but that should not deter anyone from reading this lucid, informed, and fascinating work. Excellent bibliography; fine index; interesting photographs. General; undergraduate through faculty.—*M. H. Chaplin, Wellesley College*

OAB-1735   QC939   93-29979 CIP
Simpson, John E. **Sea breeze and local winds.** Cambridge, 1994. 234p bibl index ISBN 0-521-45211-2, $39.95

Anyone who has ever been fascinated by the effects of seashore winds will enjoy this book. Simpson's intent is to explain the effects of seashore breezes in a way that will interest both novices and experts. Several chapters treat the rudimentary aspects of seashore breezes, including how they form, influence local meteorology, and modify air quality. He has also devoted several chapters to the effect of sea breezes on ecological niches. Simpson has even included a chapter on recreational activities involving sea breezes. Several chapters on satellite imagery, theoretical modeling, and laboratory experiments are included for those who need more than introductory information. Extensive reference list. Highly recommended for any academic library supporting meteorology and climatology programs. Undergraduate through faculty; two-year technical program students.—*J. C. Stachacz, Dickinson College*

OAB-1736   QC174   92-46215 CIP
Sklar, Lawrence. **Physics and chance: philosophical issues in the foundations of statistical mechanics.** Cambridge, 1993. 437p bibl index ISBN 0-521-44055-6, $64.95

Sklar, already celebrated for his seminal work on temporality, presents a comprehensive inquiry into contemporary statistical mechanics. The range and depth of this study are extraordinary, and few experts in the areas of physics, mathematics, and chemistry have as extensive familiarity with either the philosophical or technical developments. Sections on historical background, ergodic theory, probability theory, and (most innovative) nonequilibrium thermal physics clearly articulate contemporary philosophical difficulties (notably the problematic reduction of thermal theories and the associated questions of time-asymmetry) and many research agendas (e.g., quasi-ergodic assumptions; Kolmogorov-Arnold-Moser and Markov methods; Krylov's program, and Prigogine's work). Few undergraduates will have the tools (e.g., a year of advanced thermal physics, and possibly introductions to nonlinear dynamics and measure theory) to approach this work, but its arguments are so central to the foundations of physical theory that it cannot be ignored by their instructors. One of the most important books in philosophy of science of the last 50 years; recommended to all collegiate libraries. Upper-division undergraduate through faculty.—*P. D. Skiff, Bard College*

OAB-1737   QH205   92-7825 CIP
Slayter, Elizabeth M. **Light and electron microscopy,** by Elizabeth M. Slayter and Henry S. Slayter. Cambridge, 1992. 312p indexes ISBN 0-521-32714-8, $64.95; ISBN 0-521-33948-0 pbk, $27.95

Though the subject of electron microscopy is treated in the scientific literature, few sources focus primarily on this area, especially at the introductory undergraduate level. The Slaters provide a useful update to the material contained in Cecil E. Hall, *Introduction to Electron Microscopy* (2nd ed., 1966) and in Elizabeth M. Slayter, *Optical Methods in Biology* (CH, Oct'70). In addition, a background in light and optics is provided, rendering the book self-contained. The first half of the book summarizes traditional light and optics at the level of Francis A. Jenkins and Harvey E. White, *Fundamentals of Optics* (4th ed., 1976). All of the important areas of optics are touched on, such as geometrical and wave optics, polarization of light, and lenses. Excellent sections on general microscopy and the light microscope follow, with material on the imaging of phase objects and polarizing microscopy. Having set the stage, the authors devote the last third to electron microscopy in detail. Transmission, scanning, and scanning-transmission types of electron microscopes are discussed in all aspects from history to practical applications. Up-to-date information on photography and innovations in electron microscopy round out the volume. The material is very well presented with numerous illustrations and graphs; author and subject indexes; chapter bibliographies. Highly recommended. Undergraduate; graduate; pre-professional.—*H. E. Wylen, National Science Foundation*

OAB-1738   QC793   92-4215 CIP
Sutton, Christine. **Spaceship Neutrino.** Cambridge, 1992. 244p index ISBN 0-521-36404-3, $44.95; ISBN 0-521-36703-4 pbk, $24.95

Sutton's remarkable book, written without using mathematics and technical jargon, relates the history of the neutrino from the first suggestion of its existence by Wolfgang Pauli in 1930. Successive chapters cover its eventual detection, the discovery of different types of neutrino, the use of neutrinos in scattering experiments on nucleons, the solar neutrino problem, neutrinos as "dark matter," and the detection of neutrinos from supernovae to mark the start of neutrino astronomy. For those working in the various areas of nuclear and particle physics as well as for the interested general reader, Sutton provides a fascinating and interesting perspective on the development of these fields over the last 60 years as related to our ever-increasing understanding of neutrinos and how to use them. The book is well illustrated with many photographs and figures, the writing is lucid, and the story of many of the important experiments in neutrino history is told in detail not generally available elsewhere. Enthusiastically recommended as a very desirable addition to any college or university library. All levels.—*R. L. Stearns, Vassar College*

OAB-1739   QC7   95-41186 MARC
Twentieth century physics, ed. by Laurie M. Brown, Abraham Pais, and Brian Pippard. Institute of Physics/American Institute of Physics, 1995. 3v. bibl indexes ISBN 1-56396-314-0, $375.00

In this remarkable collection, some leading physicists survey the century's physics as a culture: history, accomplishments (up to about 1993), and significance. There are 27 articles; to offer an idea of the contents, listed here are those more than 100 pages in length: "Introducing Atoms and Nuclei"; "Quanta and Quantum Mechanics"; "Relativity"; "Solid-state Structure Analysis"; "Elementary Particles"; "Fluid Mechanics"; "Electrons in Solids"; "Optical Physics"; and "Astrophysics." Among the shorter articles are "Electron-beam Instruments," "Soft Matter," and "Medical Physics." The quality of the writing and production are excellent, and there are few careless errors. The important question is, Who will the readers be? As intellectual preparation, a year or so of undergraduate physics and a year of calculus should suffice to get the reader started, but the more, the better. As a professional physicist who knows little about fluid mechanics, this reviewer read Sir James Lighthill's article on the subject with fascination and delight; there appears to be no other place in which this material and its background are so ably presented. These volumes should be of wide interest, and institutions where physics is produced, consumed, or taught should acquire them. Upper-division undergraduate through professional.—*D. Park, emeritus, Williams College*

OAB-1740   QC20   91-19271 CIP
Wasserman, Robert H. **Tensors and manifolds: with applications**

to mechanics and relativity. Oxford, 1992. 409p bibl index afp ISBN 0-19-506561-1, $39.95

Derived from coursework in tensor analysis for advanced undergraduates and beginning graduate students at Michigan State University. Considering the complexity of the material, the tone is friendly: one can almost hear Wasserman lecturing. The format is basically classical definition, theorem, proof, and example, but there is sometimes deviation for the sake of clarity. The spirit and approach are similar to R.L. Bishop and S.I. Goldberg's classic *Tensor Analysis on Manifolds* (CH, Jul'68). However, Wasserman's work is more expansive in both depth and breadth. His approach to differential geometry is modern yet makes contact with the classical development. The modern intrinsic approach to tensors is properly emphasized without neglecting the index (coordinate) approach. Tangent maps of real Cartesian spaces are effectively used as paradigms to aid in conceptualizing the more general maps of differential manifolds. The presentation is rigorous without being pedantic. Excellent exercises. Final chapters are devoted to a very nice, coherent treatment of classical analytical mechanics and of special and general relativity, clearly demonstrating the centrality of tensors in the modern treatment of physics. Highly recommended. Advanced undergraduate and above.—*G. J. G. Junevicus, Eckerd College*

■ Physiology

OAB-1741   QP363   94-30749 CIP
Anderson, James A. **An introduction to neural networks.** MIT, 1995. 650p bibl index ISBN 0-262-01144-1, $55.00

This book, written by one of the most distinguished scientists in the field of neural networks, fully lives up to the expectations one has for a work by such an eminent authority. Anderson provides a thorough introduction to all aspects of neural networks, making this book an excellent book for introductory studies at the undergraduate or beginning graduate level. A noteworthy feature is the appealing style of Anderson's writing and the pleasant way in which he fully and clearly explains the required mathematics. Because of these characteristics, the book would be very useful for general readers as well. Another special feature is the way the author integrates the engineering, psychological, and neuroscientific aspects seamlessly. Thirdly, the balanced critiques of the limitations as well as strengths of neural networks adds considerably to the value of the book, and the account in the last three chapters of the author's research would interest all researchers. Overall, the book is rated a MUST for libraries of all academic institutions as well as general libraries. All levels.—*R. Bharath, Northern Michigan University*

OAB-1742   QP469   96-12637 CIP
Blauert, Jens. **Spatial hearing: the psychophysics of human sound localization.** Rev. ed. MIT, 1997. 494p bibl indexes afp ISBN 0-262-02413-6, $35.00

With the explosion of research and interest in binaural technology and virtual realities, Blauert's revision (1st ed., CH, Jun'84) is a timely as well as thorough exposition of human sound localization. In addition to the basic review of psychoacoustics as it applies to localization, the author presents an excellent review of recent research on auditory virtual reality, spatial sound-field mapping, and technological advancements in enhancement of speech modeling. Blauert has managed to provide a well-written and easy-to-read review of the currently known fundamentals of spatial hearing, making the book appropriate as a introductory resource for students. At the same time, the inclusion of quantitative details and formulas, which do not distract from the flow of the written prose, makes it an excellent addition to the reference library of researchers in all of the hearing sciences. Upper-division undergraduates through professionals; two-year technical program students.—*L. A. Dawe, University of Western Ontario*

OAB-1743 QP356 93-14802 MARC
Brown, Richard E. **An introduction to neuroendocrinology.** Cambridge, 1994. 408p index ISBN 0-521-41645-0, $79.95; ISBN 0-521-42665-0 pbk, $34.95

Neuroendocrinology attempts to understand the complex interactions between hormones, the brain, and behavior. Although this complexity makes neuroendocrinology a fascinating subject to study, it also makes it a challenging task for a professor to teach and a student to learn. Adding to this challenge is the fact that in many areas of neuroendocrinology the available information is sparse and often contradictory. With this new book—the first introductory work to be published for an advanced undergraduate and/or beginning graduate reader—the field has become much more approachable. Brown has done a masterful job of presenting material in such a way that beginning students can appreciate and comprehend the broad scope of neuroendocrinology, while more advanced students are free to explore its more intricate details. Brown offers numerous tables and diagrams, the latter being especially elegant in their simplicity of design. Each chapter is followed by a list of further readings, review questions, essay questions, and full references. The only problem this reviewer had with the book is that, when he showed it to a colleague who taught in neuroendocrinology, he refused to return it, saying he absolutely had to have it for his class. Many librarians will feel the same way and will want to add this work to their holdings. Technical/professional; upper-division undergraduate.— *D. M. Senseman, University of Texas at San Antonio*

OAB-1744 QM451 95-49380 CIP
Butler, Ann B. **Comparative vertebrate neuroanatomy: evolution and adaptation,** by Ann B. Butler and William Hodos. Wiley-Liss, 1996. 514p bibl index afp ISBN 0-471-88889-3, $74.95

Every student of the brain should own this book. It combines modern evolutionary techniques with a wealth of comparative information; the result is a tour de force featuring, in the final chapter (part 6), reconstruction of the hypothetical nervous system of the ancestors of chordates and vertebrates. Butler and Hodos start with the basics of evolutionary theory, vertebrate phylogeny, and a critique of the theories of brain evolution. They move to structural details related to function and evolution of the spinal cord; hind-, mid-, and forebrain are meticulously described and integrated. Although the anatomical illustrations suffer from the want of scale bars and the occasional need for more three-dimensional representations, these limitations are overcome by the capabilities of the text. The bulk and complexity of the material requires attention and care by the reader. Students may initially be overwhelmed, but they should stay the course—their reward will come in the form of the most complete understanding of the structure and evolution of the vertebrate nervous system currently available, including a section on the mechanisms (eight of them) by which the vertebrate brain has evolved. Highly recommended for all academic and professional readers.— *J. H. Long Jr., Vassar College*

OAB-1745 QH501 96-18026 CIP
Cairns, John. **Matters of life and death: perspectives on public health, molecular biology, cancer, and the prospects for the human race.** Princeton, 1997. 257p index afp ISBN 0-691-02872-9, $29.95

This book should be in everyone's personal library for many reasons; first, because Cairns is a lyrical writer and, second, he writes about science and molecular biology based on vast scientific knowledge, stressing the importance of history and of appreciating ultimate causes for all aspects of our lives and all that affects us. Interwoven are his perceptions of the beautiful and gracious things in life—art, music, literature—all with exquisite clarity. *Matters* is a joy to read. Cairns has simultaneously traced the development and evolution of molecular biology and genetics. The first chapter, "A History of Mortality," describes human life and longevity from the beginning, and how scientific and medical discoveries and practices have influenced length of life. Chapters 2 and 3 discuss the storage and management of biological information; chapters 4 and 5 discuss from a genetic perspective the causes and epidemiology of the increasing cancer mortality rate. The sixth and last chapter, a brilliant and impressive

analysis, is a deeply disturbing prediction of the future of humanity in relation to current, worsening problems such as an exploding population set against available resources and changing climatic conditions. Highly recommended for all levels, undergraduate and up.— *A. R. Davis, Johns Hopkins University*

OAB-1746 QP376 93-23661 CIP
Calvin, William H. **Conversations with Neil's brain: the neural nature of thought and language,** by William H. Calvin and George A. Ojemann. Addison-Wesley, 1994. 343p index ISBN 0-201-63217-9, $24.00

This exceptionally interesting book makes the subject of neurophysiology unfold like a mystery story. Clues are provided to the mysterious questions of human consciousness, memory, thought, language, and mood. The known mechanisms of brain structure and function are woven together with a literary device that keeps the reader attentive until its resolution in the final chapter: the story of a neurosurgical operation on a conscious patient, Neil, who suffers from a seizure disorder. Even a professional-level reader will enjoy this articulate and unified presentation, and will find a few new pearls of information. Both authors have published extensively in current scholarly journals and are unmistakably experts in their fields. They are able to communicate knowledge in a conversational dialogue that will be fascinating to all levels of readership. The frequent black-and-white hand-drawn illustrations are a pleasurable highlight of the text. A beneficial acquisition for all libraries, it can be used as a classroom text or supplement, a resource, and as reading for patients and clients in the neuropsychological area. All levels.— *L. Gillikin, College of William and Mary*

OAB-1747 QH631 94-31852 CIP
Cell physiology source book, ed. by Nicholas Sperelakis. Academic Press, 1996 (c1995). 738p bibl index afp ISBN 0-12-656971-1 pbk, $49.95

This excellent work will be valuable to advanced students and professionals interested in obtaining up-to-date, factual summaries of specific topics in physiology at the cellular level. Since coverage is focused on the discussion of living processes at the cellular and molecular level, the book will perhaps serve best as a companion to other resources dealing with whole organisms, organ systems, and physiological mechanisms at the individual organ level. Each chapter begins with fundamentals and then guides the reader to current, specific, and detailed information. Masterful editing achieves an evenness in style, purpose, and readability, as well as the number, authority, and currency of reference materials in each chapter. The reader will find spirited and authoritative discussions of such diverse basic topics as membrane potential generation, cellular electrolytes, the structure and physiological function of proteins, signal transduction, energy production and metabolism, and second messenger systems. Included also are very specific chapters dealing with various ion channels and the effects of drugs, disease, and toxins on their function; a large section on muscle and contractile systems; and a nice review of bioluminescence, photosynthesis, and plant cell physiology. An appendix provides a review of electricity and cable properties. Upper-division undergraduates through professionals.— *J. L. Ninnemann, Adams State College*

OAB-1748 QP376 94-30750 CIP
Churchland, Paul M. **The engine of reason, the seat of the soul: a philosophical journey into the brain.** MIT, 1995. 329p bibl index ISBN 0-262-03224-4, $29.95

On July 9, 1995, the *New York Times* Sunday Book Review Section editors devoted the entire front page as well as all of page 16 and half of page 17 to this book. Reviewer Robert Wright (*The Moral Animal: Evolutionary Psychology and Everyday Life*, 1994) (published in the US with the subtitle: *The New Science of Evolutionary Psychology*, CH, Mar'95) was biased against Churchland's claim that cognitive neuroscience can explain consciousness, yet the controversy, he admits, "raises vital questions" and obviously merits his extensive discourse. This reviewer, whose sentiments are wholeheartedly with Churchland's position, believes that this is one of the most important recent writings to explicate neuroscience for the lay reader. It is an essential acquisition for libraries of all levels. As an unusual feature, a foldout stereopticon is included for viewing some of the numerous illustrations in three dimensions (remember your old Viewmaster?). Churchland is a respected researcher and author (philosophy, Univ. of California, San Diego); his works include *Matter and Consciousness: A Contemporary Introduction to the Philosophy of Mind* (1984) and *A Neurocomputational Perspective: The Nature of Mind and the Structure of Science* (1989). If there are funds for only one new psychology book this year, choose this one! All levels.—*L. Gillikin, College of William and Mary*

OAB-1749 QP360 93-40288 CIP
The Cognitive neurosciences, ed. by Michael S. Gazzaniga et al. MIT, 1995. 1,447p bibl index ISBN 0-262-07157-6, $95.00

This giant of a book, physically, intellectually, and historically, is the best summary of the current status of science at the exciting juncture of biology and psychology, of brain and behavior. The 92 chapters are presented in 11 sections: "Plasticity," "Development," "Sensory Systems," "Motor Systems," "Attention," "Memory," "Language," "Thought and Imagery," "Emotion," "Evolution," and "Consciousness." Both the overall and section editors have done an excellent job in their choice of authors and in providing a variety of viewpoints. Each chapter includes an abstract, begins with a general statement of the issue, presents relevant theory, often discusses methods and techniques of observation, presents useful data germane to the assertions, and wraps up with a useful conclusion. Remarkably, for such an accomplished group of scientists, their communications can be understood by those readers with some science background and a willingness to engage in thoughtful reading. This may be the most important reference book in cognitive neuroscience for the next decade. Upper-division undergraduates through professional.—*R. A. Drake, Western State College of Colorado*

OAB-1750 QP303 95-38131 MARC
Dexterity and its development, ed. by Mark L. Latash and Michael T. Turvey. L. Erlbaum, 1996. 460p bibl indexes afp ISBN 0-8058-1646-1, $99.95

This excellent book, about how movement (precisely "dexterity" or the ability to solve a motor problem) is developed and controlled, is easy to understand and is a very practical work for biomechanists, kinesiologists, therapists, physiologists, and especially motor behaviorists. The first seven essays, written by Nicholai A. Bernstein some 40 years ago, explain dexterity, the construction of movement, the control of movement, and the importance of exercise on motor skill development. According to Bernstein, these essays were written as "popular scientific literature" to benefit all readers interested in movement control. Each essay describes the particular construct (e.g., essay 2, "On Motor Control") and relates it to the original topic of dexterity. The second part provides commentaries regarding Bernstein's essays from experts in the fields of biomechanics, motor behavior, ecological psychology, and development. Each commentary focuses on topics suggested by Bernstein that relate to movement (e.g., synergies, learning, central nervous system, choices). The entire book presents movement control and development in practical, realistic contexts and provides excellent examples with supporting figures. This book should be seriously considered by all interested in human movement control. Upper-division undergraduates through professionals.—*N. L. Goggin, University of North Texas*

OAB-1751 QP327 94-2020 CIP
Fridlund, Alan J. **Human facial expression: an evolutionary view.** Academic Press, 1994. 369p bibl indexes afp ISBN 0-12-267630-0, $59.00

The current "rage" in behavior studies concerns animal communication and consciousness and its proximate and ultimate causation. In this book Fridlund extends this analysis to humans as he provides a very complete and well-written account of the biology, evolution, culture, and history of study of human facial expression. The beginning chapters thoroughly examine the historical perspectives of pre- and post-Darwinian views of facial expression and emotion. These chapters set the stage for a very elegant discussion of modern

evolutionary theory and the biological explanations for human facial expression. Perhaps the most interesting and controversial aspects of the book are found in these chapters, where Fridlund presents his "behavioral ecology" explanation for the evolution and everyday uses of facial expressions. In particular, he examines current research on animal signaling and uses it to show how human facial expressions are tied to vocalization and language. Finally, the book concludes with several chapters devoted to a review of the developmental and cultural studies of facial expression. This volume is invaluable in that it provides a very comprehensive, critical, and cross-disciplinary account of the literature on human facial expression. Excellent bibliography; high-quality illustrations and graphics. A useful volume for upper-division undergraduates, graduate students, and academic professionals in anthropology, biology, and psychology. A definite "must" for college and university libraries.—*N. Krusko, Beloit College*

OAB-1752 QP363 94-44408 CIP
The Handbook of brain theory and neural networks, ed. by Michael A. Arbib. MIT, 1995. 1,118p bibl indexes ISBN 0-262-01148-4, $175.00

The preface declares that "[m]any texts have described limited aspects of one subfield or another of brain theory and neural networks, but no comprehensive overview is available. The aim of this Handbook is to fill that gap, presenting the entire range of the following topics: detailed models of single neurons; analysis of a wide variety of neurobiological systems; 'connectionist' studies; mathematical analyses of abstract neural networks; and technological applications of adaptive, artificial neural networks and related methodologies." Part 3 (p. 61-1060), a set of 266 short articles by leading scientists, provides this overview. Sampling some of these indicates that they are, as claimed, accessible to readers with varied backgrounds, while still providing a clear view of recent, specialized research. Part 1 is a basic introduction for newcomers; part 2 provides 23 "Road Maps": e.g., a "Road Map" for artificial intelligence and neural networks guides the reader to a set of 15 related articles in part 3. Overall, a magnificent achievement, a reference for readers at all levels, to be referred to again and again.—*R. Bharath, Northern Michigan University*

OAB-1753 QP82 94-10454 CIP
Kryter, Karl D. **The handbook of hearing and the effects of noise: physiology, psychology, and public health.** Academic Press, 1994. 673p bibl index afp ISBN 0-12-427455-2, $79.95

Kryter's excellent book takes a comprehensive approach to describing the effects of sound and noise on human hearing. The early chapters provide an overview of sound measurement, physiology of the ear, and auditory perceptions. Subsequent chapters describe noise-induced hearing loss, theories and procedures for predicting noise-induced hearing loss, speech communication in noise, measurement of hearing handicap, compensation, and hearing conservation. Final chapters review nonauditory physiological, psychological, and stress-related aspects of hearing as a result of working and living in noisy environments. Overall, Kryter has successfully integrated masses of research in each chapter, and readers will be truly impressed with the organization, amount, and critical review of the information presented. Very highly recommended as a valuable resource for upper-division undergraduate and graduate students, researchers, and professionals working in the areas of noise, noise control, physiological and psychological acoustics, and health-related disciplines.—*T. A. Frank, Pennsylvania State University, University Park Campus*

OAB-1754 QP360 92-44691 CIP
LeVay, Simon. **The sexual brain.** MIT, 1993. 168p bibl index ISBN 0-262-12178-6, $22.50

LeVay, an acknowledged expert, taught at Harvard Medical School and the University of California, San Diego; was at the Salk Institute for Biological Studies, and now chairs the Board of the Institute of Gay and Lesbian Education in Southern California. In 1991, LeVay wrote an article in *Science* on the differences in hypothalamic structure between heterosexual and homosexual men. Recently, several lines of research have converged, from many laboratories throughout the world, all of which confirm the biological basis of sexual orientation and gender identity. Growing evidence indicates that male and female feelings and behavior are directly related to structure and function of the brain. In exciting, clear, and often humorous fashion, LeVay summarizes research evidence, and organizes it so that any interested reader can comprehend the technical terms and scientific importance of the findings. A glossary is included, along with sources and suggested readings for each chapter. The references are from recent and prestigious journals, and the findings are accurately presented. LeVay provides state-of-the-art information in succinct and readable fashion. From this book, it becomes clear that sexual orientation is not optional and, in fact, is largely controlled by factors operating before birth within the developing nervous system. Each reader will be enlightened and educated about the origins of human sexuality and sexual diversity. A timely and useful book for all readers.—*L. Gillikin, College of William and Mary*

OAB-1755　　　　QP475　　　　95-48029 CIP
McIlwain, James T. **An introduction to the biology of vision.** Cambridge, 1996. 222p bibl index ISBN 0-521-49548-2, $60.95;

McIlwain has organized into three parts his superb reference for students with a basic understanding of the structure and function of the nervous system. Part I describes the structure and development of the vertebrate eye, reviews the elementary physics of image-forming processes, and provides an overview of the neural projections from the retina to the brain. Building on this information, the specific functions of the retina and the central visual pathways are presented in greater detail in part 2. Special topics in vision are addressed in part 3, including spatial resolution, binocular vision, depth perception, color vision, and ocular movements, as applications of the previously described properties of the retina and visual projections. McIlwain provides the reader with a working vocabulary in the field, with underlined terms defined throughout the text. Excellent diagrams and a list of additional readings at the end of each chapter help further acquaint the reader with the major themes in biological research. An excellent introduction for upper-division undergraduates or a useful background for beginning graduate students.—*K. A. Campbell, Albright College*

OAB-1756　　　　QP303　　　　96-374 CIP
Noble, Bruce J. **Perceived exertion,** by Bruce J. Noble and Robert J. Robertson. Human Kinetics, 1996. 320p bibl index ISBN 0-88011-508-4, $34.00

Noble and Robertson offer an extensive review of the development and use of "perceived exertion" or rating of perceived exertion (RPE), a method now widely used by exercise scientists to estimate the psychophysiological perception of physical activity. The authors provide an excellent reference to the nearly 500 published works directly related to perceived exertion. Three major divisions are included. "Background and Development" provides an excellent review of the historical development of perceived exertion with special emphasis on Gunnar Borg's early work. Both the psychological and physiological frameworks for perceived exertion are well developed. "Physiological and Psychological Mediators" (part 2) goes into greater detail about the perception of effort and the interrelations between the psychological and physiological domains that are the basis for perception of exertion. Part 3, "Clinical Applications and Global Perspectives," provides the basis for the use of RPE in graded exercise testing and exercise prescription, among RPE's most widely current uses. Excellent background, development, interpretation, rationale, and application of the widely use RPE; indeed, it is difficult to read the physiological literature related to human performance and training without reference to perceived exertion. Anyone using "Borg-based" or related scales would be well served by reading this work. Upper-division undergraduates through professionals.—*J. R. Morrow Jr., University of North Texas*

OAB-1757　　　　QP81　　　　93-39793 CIP
Pool, Robert. **Eve's rib: the biological roots of sex differences.** Crown, 1994. 308p index ISBN 0-517-59298-3, $22.00

A reasonable, balanced, layperson's introduction to the biological (genetic and hormonal) component of average sex differences in abilities and behavior. Throughout, Pool cites work by specific researchers (most sex-difference investigators are women); his endnotes refer to text pages, not to numbers in the text. Topics include differences in spatial and verbal ability; hormonal and chromosomal effects of fetal development and on later behavior; experimental studies on other mammals; sexual orientation; sex differences in brain anatomy and lateralization; androgyny; evolutionary roots of human sex differences; and social, political, and educational implications of the nature/nurture battle and of the recognition of both biological and social input into average sex differences. Pool stresses that sex differences, whatever their source, are averages, that there is great individual variation and overlap between the sexes, that individuals should not be lumped together because of their sex, and that, because of individual and average sex differences, teaching methods should be flexible. Pool writes well, knows his science, and deals with this controversial topic clearly and honestly. Though he feels biological factors must be recognized, he is not a biological determinist (e.g., "for most tasks, a woman's estrogen level will probably have less effect than what she ate for lunch"). The clear presentation, lack of technical terms, and thorough documentation make the book suitable for all levels, advanced high school through graduate school.—*E. B. Hazard, Bemidji State University*

OAB-1758　　　　QP411　　　　95-5932 CIP
Scott, Alwyn. **Stairway to the mind: the controversial new science of consciousness.** Copernicus, 1995. (Dist. by Springer-Verlag) 229p bibl index afp ISBN 0-387-94381-1, $25.00

All levels of readers will appreciate the linkage of basic sciences to a nonlinear theory of human consciousness. A reader not quite conversant with quantum mechanics can learn from the 26-page appendix of equations covering a "theory-of-almost-everything" from Schrodinger's cat to the Hodgkin-Huxley equations. Even skimming the mathematical part allows the reader to grasp the premise that consciousness arises in a hierarchical, emergent fashion from physical systems but in a nonlinear, nonreductive manner. The text is a jewel of presentation—a small package of 187 pages of ideas presented intelligently, poetically, and even humorously, on a serious subject that has confounded famous thinkers for centuries. This elegant neuroscience overview provides a few intoxicating insights as well (e.g., consciousness is an atom at the level of human culture). Illustrations, chapter references, bibliography, and index complete this valuable acquisition (tell the math and physics professors as well as the psychologists). Scott (mathematics, Univ. of Arizona; Institute of Mathematical Modelling, Technical Institute of Denmark) is the founding director of the Center for Nonlinear studies at the Los Alamos National Laboratory, and author of *Neurophysics* (1977). Not your father's Oldsmobile, nor your science for dummies; it *is* an impressive and concise accomplishment. All levels.—*L. Gillikin, College of William and Mary*

OAB-1759　　　　BF444　　　　96-34338 CIP
Trefil, James. **Are we unique?: a scientist explores the unparalleled intelligence of the human mind.** Wiley, 1997. 242p bibl index afp ISBN 0-471-15536-5, $24.95

A prominent scientific view is that human intelligence is not truly unique, that the brain is just a collection of interacting neurons, and that since neurons are now being simulated on the computer, the computer's ability to duplicate and even surpass the human brain is just around the corner. Although Trefil, a well-known physicist, believes the brain is nothing more than a physical system, he is nevertheless uneasy about the prospect that humankind's great creative achievements are about to be duplicated by a computer. Trefil describes, in a very readable and thorough fashion, the nature of intelligence in animals, humans, and machines and the prospect that computers may develop their own kind of intelligence and even consciousness. He also introduces a series of arguments, using analogies from the scientific world, that contend that although we humans may be physical systems subject to scientific understanding, we may still be unique in the sense that we may not ultimately be able to duplicate or explain our own intelligence and creativity in any direct way. A must read for those who often stand in awe of computers but who are not yet quite ready to accept inevitable defeat by these intelligent machines. All levels.—*C. Koch, Oberlin College*

■ Sports

OAB-1760   GV994   92-54919 MARC
Ashe, Arthur. **Days of grace: a memoir,** by Arthur Ashe and Arnold Rampersad. Knopf, 1993. 317p index ISBN 0-679-42396-6, $24.00

A remarkable memoir by late tennis champion and humanist Ashe, author of several prior autobiographies and a multivolume history of African Americans in sport: *A Hard Road to Glory*, 3v., 1993, coauthored with Rampersad (Princeton), biographer of Langston Hughes. Ashe begins by recounting his childhood in segregated Richmond, the early loss of his mother, and the lessons of discipline and self-responsibility he learned from his father. The memoir focuses mainly on his life after retirement from the tennis tour, especially his captaincy of the Davis Cup team, and years of ill health that began with a heart attack in 1979. Ashe also discusses his fight against apartheid, his work on behalf of racial justice in the US, the oppression he encountered as a black man, the sexual behavior of tennis professionals, and his attitudes about educational standards for college athletes. Ashe also describes in considerable detail his struggle against AIDS, and his efforts to cope with the disease that would claim his life. The memoir ends with a moving letter to his daughter. An inspiring book, highly recommended. General, undergraduate through faculty.—*S. A. Riess, Northeastern Illinois University*

OAB-1761   GV880   93-22719 CIP
Burk, Robert F. **Never just a game: players, owners, and American baseball to 1920.** North Carolina, 1994. 284p index afp ISBN 0-8078-2122-5, $34.95

One often hears the term "organized baseball." Burk's rewarding book explains how baseball became organized. Guided by models supplied by social historians, Burk describes the transition from the amateur activities of the 1840s to the monopsonic enterprise of the post-WW I era. The chief dynamic of his tale lies in the struggle between profit-seeking ownership and wage-seeking labor. Over the decades, the contours of the business were shaped by increasing specialization, heightened professionalism, the layering of coordination, and widening attention to marketing. Owners divided geographic markets among themselves, adjusted the rules of the game to manipulate fans and players, and, above all, created and expanded the reserve system to protect their investment in talent. Players resisted with "brotherhoods" and threats of strikes, and seized opportunities to benefit from the bidding wars that arose when upstart major leagues were born. Meanwhile, since both camps feared the inclusion of African Americans, almost everyone conspired in their exclusion. A fascinating story, well told. For college and university libraries, community college and up.—*R. Browning, Kenyon College*

OAB-1762   Orig
Chadwick, Bruce. **When the game was Black and White: the illustrated history of the Negro Leagues.** Abbeville, 1992. 191p bibl index ISBN 1-55859-372-1, $24.95

Chadwick is a sportswriter and columnist for the *New York Daily News*, and author of Abbeville's "Major League memories" series. This book is a rich treat for baseball fans. The text, which is well written and clearly superior to most books of this genre, is largely based on a reading of the principal secondary sources enhanced with interviews, and provides a very good survey of segregated baseball. Topics covered include barnstorming, Latin American ball, and games against white major leaguers. There are few errors (House of David was not a Jewish team), but Chadwick's familiarity with American social history could be better. The bibliography is brief but the illustrations are outstanding

and provide important evidence of black baseball. In addition to extremely rare photographs of ball players, including some from Satchel Paige's own scrapbook, there are examples of rare Negro Leagues memorabilia including broadsides, scorecards, pennants, posters, flyers, programs, and covers from black sports magazines, often in color. The publisher is to be congratulated for a beautiful, moderately priced book. Highly recommended for undergraduate libraries.—*S. A. Riess, Northeastern Illinois University*

OAB-1763   GV865   94-44876 CIP
Falkner, David. **Great time coming: the life of Jackie Robinson, from baseball to Birmingham.** Simon & Schuster, 1995. 382p bibl index ISBN 0-671-79336-5, $25.00

"I don't know anything about Jackie Robinson," Ken Griffey Jr. is quoted as saying in this wonderful biography, a book Griffey should read. Robinson stands with Babe Ruth as one of the two most significant players in the history of the game—Ruth for his transformative impact on how the game is played, Robinson for his transformative impact on who is allowed to get into the game. Ever since the making of the film *The Jackie Robinson Story* in 1950, the tale of Robinson's life has been encrusted in myth. Falkner scrutinizes what he terms "official versions" of Robinson's life story to get at the "facts," which (he says) "seem less simple." Not surprisingly, the US obsession with race remains the dominant context for the biography, but Robinson himself appears as a man of human ambiguities. Falkner is especially helpful in his illuminating analyses of the portions of Robinson's life that bracket his big league career—his troubled years in the military and his decision to support Richard Nixon in 1960. The thoughtful and lonely Jackie Robinson who emerges from the study is a genuine hero. For all libraries.—*R. Browning, Kenyon College*

OAB-1764   GV878   94-14323 CIP
Halberstam, David. **October 1964.** Villard Books, 1994. 380p bibl afp ISBN 0-679-41560-2, $24.00

Although Halberstam focuses on a description of the events culminating in the 1964 World Series between the St. Louis Cardinals and the New York Yankees, his is not primarily a baseball book. Rather, it is a penetrating analysis of American culture in the 1960s and particularly of how this culture produced the character of the players involved in this historic series. It details the mores of the team subculture, and the evolving relationships between the races, and gets into the minds and hearts of the principal players better than do most similar books. Halberstam interviewed most of the important participants and provides an explanation for the absence of three stars: Mantle, Kubek, and Flood. Not explained is why Whitey Ford was not among those interviewed. Halberstam's writing is direct and informative so that it holds the reader's attention throughout. The book concludes with an interesting but unessential epilogue. There are 16 pages of pertinent photographs. One of the best books on the subject; it will appeal to a wide readership. All levels.—*W. F. Gustafson, emeritus, San Jose State University*

OAB-1765   GV721   95-569 CIP
Historical dictionary of the modern Olympic movement, ed. by John E. Findling and Kimberly D. Pelle. Greenwood, 1996. 460p bibl index afp ISBN 0-313-28477-6, $79.50

This "dictionary" is a comprehensive reference on the Olympic Games, from the ancient Games that began in 776 BCE to the modern Summer Games (to be held in Sydney in 2000) and the Winter Games of 1998 (to be in Nagano, Japan). In contrast to the usual Olympic books that emphasize winners and medal counts, the editors stress that this collection describes each game's celebration in a "historical context." Nearly 60 authors contributed the histories of various games, concluding with a compilation of all the sources and materials for that section. The text is organized in logical fashion, with a beginning essay about the Games, the Summer Games (including those canceled due to WW I and II), and the Winter Games. The appendix includes an overview of the International Olympic Committee (IOC) with a picture and biography of each president, the US Olympic Committee (USOC) including a list of member organizations, and a history of Olympic films and other key information, e.g., archives with significant Olympic holdings. A book to be read and savored. All levels.—*J. Davenport, Auburn University*

OAB-1766   GV742   96-48711 CIP
Kahn, Roger. **Memories of summer: when baseball was an art, and writing about it a game.** Hyperion, NY, 1997. 290p index ISBN 0-7868-6190-8, $23.95

The full title of this reminiscence evokes nostalgia and invokes irony, thereby preparing the reader for a loving but complex discussion of the two crafts that Kahn knows best: sportswriting and professional baseball playing. A student of literature, Kahn gently invites his reader to see his admiration of heroes as Homeric, his alertness to transience as Whitmanesque, his suspicion that the age of the gods is past as Wagnerian. But the book is far more than an educated person's guide to the world of ballplaying and sports journalism in the 1950s and 1960s. It overflows with stories, both funny and mordant. It includes the best re-creation of the 1952 World Series this reviewer has read. It features wonderful discussions of the managerial gifts of the malicious Leo Durocher, the evolving maturity of the haunted Mickey Mantle, and the baseball smarts of the humane Willie Mays. Undergirding the entire work are Kahn's enduring respect for appropriate pride and his fierce detestation of all forms of bigotry. Kahn concludes his work with a list of 12 indispensable baseball books. Anyone else's list would have included his *The Boys of Summer* (1972). Many will conclude that *Memories of Summer* also belongs. All levels.—*R. Browning, Kenyon College*

OAB-1767   Orig
The Negro leagues book, ed. by Dick Clark and Larry Lester. Society for American Baseball Research, 1994. 382p bibl ISBN 0-910137-59-5, $49.95; ISBN 0-910137-55-2 pbk, $29.95

Interest in the history of segregated African American baseball has grown steadily since Robert Peterson's *Only the Ball Was White* (1970) first unearthed the rich past of the Negro Leagues. The Negro Leagues lacked official scorers, received irregular press coverage, and played many barnstorming games. These circumstances left a sketchy historical record, making the compilation of statistics and team rosters a herculean task. Researched by members of the Negro Leagues Committee of the Society of American Baseball Research, *The Negro Leagues Book* makes major contributions to recreating this fragmented past. In addition to assembling a historical record, researchers hope this work will demonstrate that at least 60 Negro Leaguers (in addition to the 11 already inducted) deserve consideration for the Baseball Hall of Fame. Noteworthy contributions of this book include lists of teams and their cities, biographies for proposed and inducted Hall of Fame members, rosters, standings (1920-51), records of Negro League players, and the most comprehensive bibliography available on the Negro Leagues. Highly recommended for academic and public libraries. General through faculty.—*P. A. Frisch, University of Illinois at Chicago*

OAB-1768   GV955   91-51009 CIP
Nelson, David M. **The anatomy of a game: football, the rules, and the men who made the game.** Delaware, 1994. (Dist. by Associated University Presses) 599p bibl index afp ISBN 0-87413-455-2, $25.00

An excellent, detailed description and analysis of the evolution of the playing rules for the game of football, this book follows football rules from the game's European roots through its beginning in the US. A few chapters detail the crisis years that changed the character of the game dramatically. The 1931 injury crisis that split high school and college rules is well documented, as is the origin of the NCAA Football Rules Committee and the people who have served on this very important committee over the years. Appendix 1, rule changes by year, and Appendix 2, evolution of American collegiate football, help the reader keep up with game development. The documentation of sources is extremely well done. The author's tenure on the NCAA Football Rules Committee from 1958

until his death in 1991 provides personal insight into all Rules Committee meetings held during that era. This excellent book is highly recommended for any academic or public library. General; upper-division undergraduate through faculty.—*H. F. Kenny Jr., Wesleyan University*

OAB-1769   GV581   96-6137 CIP
The New American sport history: recent approaches and perspectives, ed. by S.W. Pope. Illinois, 1997. 423p index afp ISBN 0-252-02264-5, $42.50; ISBN 0-252-06567-0 pbk, $19.95

As mentioned by one of the chapter authors, a recent *Chronicle of Higher Education* article declared that sport history has gained "new respectability." Editor Pope has collected the works of 17 authors whose overviews and penetrating questions have certainly reinforced this new respectability. This sophisticated scholarly work has four parts: "National Culture," which covers topics that pertain to the growth of sport; "Gender and the Body," which traces the change of male-dominated sports through the rise of women's participation, with such chapters as "The Amazon and the American Lady"; "Class, Race and Ethnicity," which covers such topics as the Jewish experience in boxing and the continual debate on the explanation about black athletes' superiority in sports; and "Markets and Audiences," which covers the business side of the whole sport enterprise. An added dimension is that every chapter but one has extensive annotated notes to assist in pursuing further the respective topic using the listed sources. An excellent work for upper-division undergraduate or graduate students through professionals in sport history, sport sociology, and sport management.—*J. Davenport, Auburn University*

OAB-1770   GV706   96-5506 CIP
Pope, S.W. **Patriotic games: sporting traditions in the American imagination, 1876-1926.** Oxford, 1997. 212p index afp ISBN 0-19-509133-7, $39.95

Historian Pope examines the remarkable rise of sport and American sporting ideology during the 50 years from 1876 to 1926. He reveals the ascent of sports into the historical process whereby men and women, social classes, and racial and ethnic assemblages shrugged over different interpretations of not only how to work and play, but what to value. Pope describes how sport became a key cultural carrier of the patriotic understanding and the way in which many advocates with various national agendas made support for true amateur sports a strong American obligation deep into the early 1900s. Chapter 4 offers an intriguing explanation on why baseball became America's national game; in another chapter Pope speculates on the factors that may be responsible for the shift to America's new national game—football. The documentation of sources is exceptionally well done and exhaustively detailed. This thoroughly readable work is highly recommended for upper-division undergraduates through faculty collections.—*H. F. Kenny Jr., Wesleyan University*

OAB-1771   GV716   92-15349 CIP
Quirk, James. **Pay dirt: the business of professional team sports,** by James Quirk and Rodney D. Fort. Princeton, 1992. 538p bibl indexes afp ISBN 0-691-04255-1, $29.95

The most scholarly and the best of the rush of sports economics books to hit the market in the last year (e.g., Andrew Zimbalist's *Baseball and Billions*, CH, Feb'93; *Coming Apart at the Seams* by Jack Sands and Peter Gammons, CH, Jul'93; and *The Diamond Revolution* by Neil Sullivan, 1992). Topics tackled in highly successful attempts to separate popular myths and misconceptions from economic reality include the market for sports franchises; reserve clauses, free agency, and labor markets; the determination and level of players' salaries; rival leagues and expansion; salary caps and revenue sharing; and various public policies (tax laws and shelters, municipal subsidies for stadiums, antitrust and regulatory policies) in professional baseball, football, basketball, and hockey. In addition to solid and objective economic analysis, a 150-page technical appendix and data supplement, and an extensive bibliography, the authors provide valuable, entertaining histories and anecdotes on players, owners, and franchises as well as a detailed evolution of institutional/legal changes and important junctures with regard to policies and people. The only short-comings are the lack of a clear direction, some occasional tediousness, and an unexplainable omission of a general index. But *Pay Dirt* will serve for now—and probably for some time to come—as the standard reference for serious students and armchair devotees of professional sports teams and leagues. All levels.—*A. R. Sanderson, University of Chicago*

OAB-1772   GV706   94-43286 CIP
Riess, Steven A. **Sport in industrial America, 1850-1920.** Harlan Davidson, 1995. 221p bibl index ISBN 0-88295-916-6 pbk, $11.95

Reiss has designed his book for use in both basic and advanced courses treating sports in American history. His purpose is to explain how sport in America developed from a morally suspect, premodern entertainment in the 1850s that did not pretend to attract the interest of many Americans, into a respectable modernized national fetish, culminating in the Golden Age of Sports in the 1920s. The documentation is exceptionally well done and thorough, and the resulting book is thoroughly readable. Highly recommended as a must acquisition for any academic library or public library catering to an informed public.—*H. F. Kenny Jr., Wesleyan University*

OAB-1773   GV706   95-50200 CIP
Shropshire, Kenneth L. **In black and white: race and sports in America.** New York University, 1996. 212p index afp ISBN 0-8147-8016-4, $24.95

In this well-documented, compact work, Shropshire (Wharton School) not only details the omnipresence of racial bias in society but the "Old Boys" network in sports administration on the collegiate level on up to professional sports management including agents. The author includes an unusual number of endnotes to cite sources, and he makes excellent use of them to explain further many interesting and pertinent details of racial bigotry in sports. Throughout, the overt theme is that those in power, whites, and those outside the power structure, African Americans, must both make sacrifices in order to reach the desired goal of color-blindness. Social and financial values of diversity are presented in excellent fashion; legal avenues to change the look of professional and collegiate sports ownership and management are investigated, and voluntary plans for affirmative action as a route to diversity in sports management are reviewed in detail. Easily read and understood statistical tables illustrating the lack of minority leadership in sports. A valuable work. General; undergraduates through professionals.—*F. D. Handler, St. Bonaventure University*

OAB-1774   GV351   93-26950 CIP
Thelin, John R. **Games colleges play: scandal and reform in intercollegiate athletics.** Johns Hopkins, 1994. 252p bibl index ISBN 0-8018-4716-8, $34.95

Thelin (education, Indiana Univ.) has written a fascinating book about intercollegiate athletics from 1910 to 1990. He looks past the playing fields and impressive facilities into the boardrooms and administrative offices to dig out the annoying patterns of abuse and limited reform, and explores the implications of these mystical patterns for college presidents, faculty, and students. From the 1929 Carnegie Foundation Report to the 1991 Knight Foundation Report, Thelin examines the formation of major intercollegiate athletic conferences and the national college basketball scandals after WW II. He also provides the reader with historical background information about current policy discussions concerning the proper place intercollegiate athletics have within the present US university system. Documentation of sources is exceptionally well done and exhaustively detailed. A thoroughly readable book, highly recommended. General; graduate through professional.—*H. F. Kenny Jr., Wesleyan University*

OAB-1775   GV1060   96-13463 CIP
Tricard, Louise Mead. **American women's track and field: a his-**

tory, 1895 through 1980. McFarland, 1996. 746p bibl index afp ISBN 0-7864-0219-9, $75.00

Tricard provides an encyclopedia of facts, stories, and records of women in track and field She supplements her extensive research with numerous biographical sketches of track champions and coaches with pictures highlighting the many interviews she conducted with these people. The history begins in 1895 because that was the year Vassar College, despite prohibitions from most leaders, held the first field day for women, with intense competition in track and field. The five appendixes contain listings of Olympic gold medalists, Hall of Fame winners, and women who have won track and field awards. The bibliography spans 37 pages, a rich collection of books and articles about women's sports and women's track and field. This resource is a must for all interested in the history of women's track and field, which was impacted by the attitudes and philosophies of women leaders about women in sport. All levels.—*J. Davenport, Auburn University*

OAB-1776   GV863   94-20992 CIP
White, Sol. **Sol White's history of colored base ball, with other documents on the early black game, 1886-1936,** comp. and introd. by Jerry Malloy. Nebraska, 1995. 187p index afp ISBN 0-8032-4771-0, $26.00

In 1907, Sol White, an African American baseball manager, wrote the first history of African American baseball that decried the racism of the contemporary sporting world, lauded the achievements of his compatriots on black teams, and promoted his own career. The book includes various features like instructions on pitching by Rube Foster and batting by "Home Run" Johnson. The University of Nebraska Press is to be applauded for making this rare document available at a reasonable price. A few years ago, Camden House published an expensive reprint, but this edition has been reset, providing greater legibility, while keeping the original illustrations and advertising. Malloy, a well-known expert on early African American baseball, has written a very illuminating 31-page introduction, "Sol White and the Origins of African American Baseball," a solid biography of the author. In addition, Malloy has included various documents drawn from 19th-century baseball magazines, and articles from the black press, including two written by White in 1930. Another feature is Bob David's chronological registry of 19th-century African Americans who played in organized baseball as well as many of their records. The book is amply illustrated; excellent index. All levels.—*S. A. Riess, Northeastern Illinois University*

OAB-1777   GV706   93-19671 CIP
Wilson, John. **Playing by the rules: sport, society, and the state.** Wayne State, 1994. 429p bibl index afp ISBN 0-8143-2107-0, $39.95

A necessary addition to the literature on sport and society by Wilson (sociology, Duke Univ.), who details how the relationship between sport and the state has developed over the past century. He describes how sport, worldwide, has become a public policy domain. In a well-crafted treatment of how Americans have developed this relationship, he traces the evolution of this "public policy" from amateur to professional athletics. His handling of the professional athlete and the various systems of who can play and for whom is easily understood. The role of the NCAA in collegiate sports is presented from a distinctly different viewpoint, allowing the reader to understand its power and role in college sports. Wilson examines the role of unions in professional sports, citing court cases that have had a lasting effect on both players and owners. The role of the state, mainly through the judicial system, is well documented. Wilson delves into the role of sport on the national level, its role in assimilating immigrants, and that of promoting national and citizenship values. Highly recommended. Upper-level undergraduate; graduate; professional.—*F. D. Handler, St. Bonaventure University*

■ Zoology

OAB-1778
QL761   93-33276 CIP
Andersson, Malte. **Sexual selection.** Princeton, 1994. 599p bibl indexes afp ISBN 0-691-03344-7, $65.00; ISBN 0-691-00057-3 pbk, $24.95

Andersson's excellent and extensive work is a thorough review of the theory of sexual selection. Chapters are devoted to the theory of sexual selection; genetic models of Fisherian self-reinforcing sexual selection; genetic models of indicator mechanisms; empirical methods and case studies; empirical studies of sexually selected traits-patterns; sexual selection in relation to mating system and parental roles; benefits of mate choice; species recognition, sexual selection, and speciation; constraints; sexual size dimorphism; weapons; coloration and other visual signals; acoustic signals, chemical signals, and alternative mating tactics; sexual selection in plants; and sexual selection conclusions and open questions. The text is very readable; the figures and tables are informative and well integrated with the text; the printing is crisp and clear, the binding excellent. The references are extensive (more than 100 pages) and contemporary; an author index follows the references. All in all, a superb monograph that should be in academic libraries. Upper-division undergraduate through faculty.—*S. L. Smith, Bowling Green State University*

OAB-1779
QL696   93-21415 CIP
Baldassarre, Guy A. **Waterfowl ecology and management,** by Guy A. Baldassarre and Eric G. Bolen. Wiley, 1994. 609p index afp ISBN 0-471-59770-8, $59.95

Baldassarre and Bolen, men of impeccable credentials in wildlife biology, aim their book at professionals in wildlife management but write in a style that will not intimidate other readers. Beginning with an extensive chapter on the classification of waterfowl in which alternative views are fully recognized, the authors present (in logical order) the basic life history aspects of waterfowl ecology followed by extensive coverage of management factors and policies—both existing and needed. A concluding chapter places waterfowl in the context of a human-dominated ecosystem, with lightly veiled pessimism. There are abundant high-quality illustrations and photographs, all black-and-white, and judiciously chosen crisp, concise graphics. Each chapter ends with extensive current literature citations that, along with a 34-page index, make the information on waterfowl ecology and management very accessible. Recommended to colleges and universities with upper-division undergraduates and/or graduate students in ecology and wildlife studies.—*H. N. Cunningham Jr., Pennsylvania State University at Erie-Behrend College*

OAB-1780
QL467   92-34639 CIP
Berenbaum, May R. **Ninety-nine more maggots, mites, and munchers.** Illinois, 1993. 285p index afp ISBN 0-252-02016-2, $37.95; ISBN 0-252-06322-8 pbk, $13.95

Berenbaum has written a factual and superbly entertaining text on insects, a natural extension to her earlier *Ninety-nine Gnats, Nits and Nibblers* (CH, Oct'89). With more than one million species to include in this and her earlier volume, a major problem facing the author was which insect species to include in this and her earlier volume. To paraphrase a famous movie, Berenbaum chose wisely—this volume is even more exciting than the first. The vignettes on the various species are witty, whimsical, humorously disgusting (cheese skipper maggots going down with the cheese and emerging quite alive at the other end of the digestive process), and enlightening. Included in this volume are a number of insects that would be classified as odd, weird, bizarre, or delightful even to the trained entomologist: odd beetles, mantispids, berothids, boreids, stalk-eyed flies, and beaver beetles. The text is sure to provide numerous examples of life-style diversities that can be used in introductory biology, ecology, and entomology courses. Excellent binding and print. A must for most academic libraries. Let us hope for Volume 3, and more. All levels.—*S. L. Smith, Bowling Green State University*

OAB-1781
QL737   93-45671 CIP
Berger, Joel. **Bison: mating and conservation in small populations,** by Joel Berger and Carol Cunningham. Columbia, 1994. 330p bibl index afp ISBN 0-231-08456-0, $55.00

An excellent monograph on an important and charismatic species, Berger and Cunningham's effort will probably remain the standard reference on North American bison for many years. Their study combines ten years of behavioral ecology work in the Dakota badlands with a historical review of bison populations in the area. This information is then used to derive predictions about the conservation of the species and appropriate measures to be taken in the area. Most of the book is concerned with the behavioral ecology of males and females and the effects of their mating behavior on the genetic change within the population. Other topics include the ecology of the badlands, population history of bison, and the insularization of wildlife reserves. The text is detailed and technical but accessible to most readers. Each chapter ends with a good summary and results of statistical tests cited in the chapter. A well-produced work, with numerous photographs, charts, and tables, an extensive bibliography, and a good index. An important addition to graduate-level libraries. Upper-division undergraduate through faculty.—*T. C. Williams, Swarthmore College*

OAB-1782
QL496   93-25190 CIP
Bernays, E.A. **Host-plant selection by phytophagous insects,** by E.A. Bernays and R.F. Chapman. Chapman & Hall, 1994. 312p bibl indexes (Contemporary topics in entomology, 2) ISBN 0-412-03131-0 pbk, $24.50

Over one-quarter of all macroscopic organisms are plant-feeding insects that are serious competitors for the food and fiber needs of humanity. Bernays and Chapman provide an easy-to-read, up-to-date, and reasonably detailed overview of host-plant selection by plant feeding insects. References are not cited in the text, but each of the eight chapters is accompanied by an excellent list of support references and reviews. The book focuses on the behavior involved in plant selection. The first three chapters providing background, chapters 4 and 5 cover the behavior, and the remaining chapters examine the role of plant and insect variability in host selection and the result of such interactions in ecological and evolutionary terms. Each chapter is replete with figures and is ideal for beginning students in insect-plant relationships and as current review. Highly recommended for college and university libraries that support programs in biology, plant sciences, zoology, ecology, entomology, and agriculture. Upper-division undergraduate through professional; two-year technical program students.—*S. B. Vinson, Texas A&M University*

OAB-1783
Can. CIP
The Birds of British Columbia: v.1: Nonpasserines: introduction and loons through waterfowl; v.2: Nonpasserines: diurnal birds of prey through woodpeckers; v.3: Passerines: flycatchers through vireos, by R. Wayne Campbell et al. UBC Press, University of British Columbia, 6344 Memorial Rd., Vancouver, BC V6T 1Z2, Canada, 1997. 3v. bibl index afp ISBN 0-7748-0622-2, $240.00

The first three volumes (of a planned four) of this thorough coverage of British Columbian birds are beautifully illustrated. Detailed species accounts provide unprecedented coverage of these birds. There is a wealth of information on the ornithological history, habitat, breeding habits, migratory movements, seasonality, and distribution patterns. Each species is covered in great detail, with comments on range, status, change in status, nonbreeding and breeding, nests, eggs, young, and parasitism. Nice charts, maps, and photos appear in each volume. Especially valuable are the habitat photos that show the type of forest or plains that the birds prefer for nesting sites. Following the accounts of regular species are sections on casual, accidental, extirpated, and extinct species. Appendixes offer accounts of migration chronology, Christmas bird counts, breeding bird surveys, and contributors. The authors of these volumes are all renowned ornithologists and have spent more than 20 years researching and writing these works. Consequently, this is one of the most thorough bird projects ever undertaken in state or province history, and will offer readers great enjoyment. Species index; brief author biographies; excellent maps; fine illustrations. Recommended for all larger libraries. General readers; undergraduate students through professionals.—*C. J. Pollard, emeritus, Los Angeles Unified School District*

OAB-1784　　　　QL737x　　　　93-83819 Orig
The Bowhead whale, ed. by John J. Burns, J. Jerome Montague, and Cleveland J. Cowles. Society for Marine Mammalogy, P.O. Box 368, Lawrence, KS 66044, 1993. 787p bibl indexes afp (Special Publication, 2) ISBN 0-935868-62-3, $75.00

Whales are difficult to study; in contrast with most other mammals, collections of intact, whole specimens, even skeletons, are not common among museum-preserved material. Information on their anatomy, and natural history, including behavior, has come historically through working with commercial and native whalers and, to a growing degree, through cooperative efforts of diverse governmental and industrial groups. This book represents a broad effort to present and synthesize a vast amount of data on one important whale species. The 18 chapters cover evolutionary relationships and classification, anatomy and physiology, behavior, feeding, reproduction, geographic distribution, population size, commercial and subsistence whaling, and the effects of human-made noise and environmental contaminants. Well-reproduced photographs range from illustrations of anatomical features to whale-hunting weapons. Each author presents a sufficiently detailed and, where appropriate, historical perspective. A superb study. Geographic and general indexes; chapter bibliographies. General; community college; undergraduate through faculty.—*D. Bardack, University of Illinois at Chicago*

OAB-1785　　　　　　　　　　　　　Orig
Brackenbury, John. **Insects in flight.** Blandford, 1992. 192p index ISBN 0-7137-2301-7, $35.00

Although the nature of flight in birds has been the subject of many books and films, insects have received scant attention in large part due to the technical difficulties of photographing them on the wing. An exception to this trend in 1975 was Stephen Dalton's classic *Borne on the Wind* that brought this subject to the attention of both general and scientific audiences. Brackenbury's beautiful work represents the next generation on this subject, with exquisite photographs of a wide range of insects including moths, butterflies, beetles, wasps, cicadas, grasshoppers, and a praying mantis. Accompanying explanatory diagrams, drawings, and text provide insight into the underlying mechanisms controlling intricate flight movements. Naturalists, biologists, entomologists, and students of all ages will enjoy this delightful book. General; undergraduate through professional.—*R. E. Lee Jr., Miami University (OH)*

OAB-1786　　　　SH346　　　　93-41438 CIP
Buck, Richard. **Silver swimmer.** Lyons & Burford, 1994 (c1993). 416p bibl index ISBN 1-55821-251-5, $35.00

Buck chronicles the battle waged by individuals, private organizations, and nations to conserve and restore Atlantic salmon. Thus, this book is really about people and the politics of a shared resource more than it is about the salmon. Buck was at the forefront of the fight and therefore presents an unusually close-up and behind-the-scenes view of the action from the early "salmon wars" to high seas treaties. The writing is clear, crisp, and easy to follow. However, it is clear at times that the author is coming from a biased (perhaps justifiably so) point of view. Overall, Buck has done an outstanding job with a difficult and delicate topic. (Unfortunately, the many lessons learned in the battle for Atlantic salmon will have to be relearned for Pacific salmon.) An essential resource for any library maintaining holdings in fisheries or in the geopolitical and sociological aspects of natural resource conservation, which should be required reading for fish managers everywhere. Upper-division undergraduate through professional.—*G. L. Hendrickson, Humboldt State University*

OAB-1787　　　　QL508　　　　96-17651 CIP
Burrows, Malcolm. **The neurobiology of an insect brain.** Oxford, 1996. 682p bibl index ISBN 0-19-852344-0, $100.00

This reviewer still vividly remembers a lecture given by Professor Graham Hoyle at Princeton in 1972. Hoyle had an established reputation in the electrophysiology of insect muscle—a rather pedantic field—and this reviewer feared that he would fall asleep during the lecture. He should not have worried. Hoyle talked about his work on the locust brain together with a young scientist by the name of Malcolm Burrows. As Hoyle described their results, a sense of excitement filled the room. Burrows's magnificent book captures this sense of excitement as it recounts the progress of three decades of elegant research. For a serious scientific treatise, the book is remarkably readable. We see the locust not as an inanimate object in a child's bug collection, but rather as a living, breathing organism walking, flying, and even swimming in its environment. Each chapter contains numerous figures and line drawings of exceptional quality. As support for basic research declines and more and more young neurobiologists decide to study better genetic models such as fruitflies, zebrafish, and mice, one may be concerned that this work pioneered by Burrows may slowly die away. This book could, and hopefully will, stimulate renewed vigor in the field. A remarkable tribute to 30 years of extraordinary research. Upper-division undergraduates through faculty.—*D. M. Senseman, University of Texas at San Antonio*

OAB-1788　　　　TP248　　　　96-26618 CIP
Butler, Michael. **Animal cell culture and technology: the basics.** IRL, Oxford, 1997 (c1996). 114p bibl index ISBN 0-19-963416-5 pbk, $24.95

Expanding interest in animal cell culture stems from the pivotal role of this technology in biological research and therapeutic medicine. Cell culture is essential for production of viral vaccines, monoclonal antibodies for diagnostic tests and therapeutics, and glycoproteins, including interferons for treatment of viral diseases and cancers, plasminogen activators for cardiovascular disease, and blood clotting factors for treatment of hemophilia. Butler's beautifully written and superbly organized book is a gem. It is well illustrated, with more than 70 figures and numerous tables, along with selected references and suggestions for further reading at the end of each chapter. Definitions and explanations of relevant terminology are provided in marginal notes. The strongest features of the book are its brevity and clarity; the author has trimmed the subject material down to the critical essentials. Chapters on characteristics, growth, and maintenance of cells in culture are followed by discussions of monitoring and counting techniques, genetic engineering of cells in culture, production of antibodies from hybridomas, large-scale production, and finally established and potential products from mammalian cells. Glossary. Upper-division undergraduate through faculty.—*M. J. O'Donnell, McMaster University*

OAB-1789　　　　QL737　　　　94-33301 CIP
Carwardine, Mark. **Whales, dolphins and porpoises.** Dorling Kindersley, 1995. 256p index ISBN 1-56458-621-9, $29.95

As an identification handbook, this is truly an outstanding instrument for the recognition and determination of species of cetaceans. Based on the principles of identification made easy, it is a very useful resource for rapid identification of the known global species of whales, dolphins, and porpoises. In an introductory section, Carwardine provides brief information on cetaceans: their anatomy, behavior, conservation, stranding, and where to locate and how to study them. An identification key follows, based mostly on total length and the presence or absence of a beak. The cetaceans are then grouped into categories (e.g., right whales, rorqual whales, blackfish). Each species is given two-page coverage, including a whole-animal photograph, specific photographs of flukes and dorsal fins, drawings of teeth, a distributional map, identification checklist, and brief narratives of general description and behavior. A color-coded band provides taxonomic information and some essential ecological data. The clear and very informative illustrations, glossary, and index contribute to its usefulness. Recommended. All levels.—*P. E. Lutz, University of North Carolina at Greensboro*

OAB-1790   QL737   92-4520 CIP

Chadwick, Douglas H. **The fate of the elephant.** Sierra Club Books, 1992. 492p index afp ISBN 0-87156-635-4, $25.00

Chadwick takes a close look at the possible fate of the elephant. He examines a variety of characteristics of elephant biology and the uses to which people have put elephants and their body parts in different human cultures. He introduces a captive individual and gives a vivid description of what it is like to meet an elephant personally. In this book he deals with both African and Indian elephants and examines the status of the populations of both subspecies in the wild through firsthand descriptions of his visits to Africa, India, Thailand, and Malaysia. In addition, he visited countries that use various body parts of elephants in their cultures (ivory carvings, teeth used as seals, etc.). Chadwick examines the economic value of elephant products and their use mainly as status symbols in various countries. In an epilogue, he reviews the impact on elephant poaching of the CITES (Convention on International Trade in Endangered Species) ban on ivory. An excellent overview of the elephant's present status and chances for the survival of the species. General; undergraduate.—*D. W. Kitchen, Humboldt State University*

OAB-1791   QL384   91-15257 MARC

Clark, Ailsa M. **Starfishes of the Atlantic,** by Ailsa M. Clark and Maureen E. Downey. Chapman & Hall, 1992. 794p bibl index (Chapman & Hall identification guide, 3) ISBN 0-412-43280-3, $250.00

The publication of this volume represents 18 years of work by Clark and Downey, both of whom retired from their museum posts in about 1986. To their lasting credit, they continued their painstaking research and succeeded in producing a volume of basic importance. The scope of the work includes the entire Atlantic Ocean, from the continental shelves to the greatest depths. Included are concise descriptions of 21 starfish families, 140 genera, and 374 species or subspecies; the treatment includes a historical review, glossary, keys to the various taxonomic levels, and a comprehensive table of geographical distributions. There are 100 pages of fine pen-and-ink drawings of anatomical details and 113 photographic plates. The result: an outstanding contribution, a model of its kind. Belongs in the library of every institution where marine biology is taught. Advanced undergraduate through faculty.—*J. C. Briggs, University of Georgia*

OAB-1792   QL737   94-14232 CIP

Colobine monkeys: their ecology, behaviour and evolution, ed. by A. Glyn Davies and John F. Oates. Cambridge, 1995 (c1994). 415p bibl index ISBN 0-521-33153-6, $79.95

African and Asian colobine monkeys are anthropoids with a digestive system that is unique among the primates and other mammals. These monkeys have a ruminant-like digestive system that allows a basically leaf diet, unlike other Old World monkeys that also need fruits and insects. This book is a genuine exemplar for the primatological literature of edited volumes, and it is a most comprehensive and synthetic account of these animals. A first and last chapter by the editors gives this volume a tight and cohesive unity rarely seen in such works. Similarly, the selection of topics and contributors by Davies and Oates (who have contributed half of the 12 chapters) make the book read more like a single (double) authored volume than virtually any other edited volume in primatology. Excellent accounts of the evolutionary history of their diversity and natural history, in-depth chapters on their unique digestive system (including their teeth), their population dynamics and social behavior, and, along with the prospects of their future conservation, make this an extremely valuable work for anyone interested in primates, mammalian evolutionary biology, and conservation. Highly recommended. Upper-division undergraduate; graduate; faculty.—*F. S. Szalay, CUNY Hunter College*

OAB-1793   QL558   90-218978 Aust. CIP

Common, I.F.B. **Moths of Australia.** Melbourne, 1993 (c1990). (Dist.

by International Specialized Book Services) 535p bibl index ISBN 0-522-84326-3, $150.00

The definitive reference work on Australian moths that should remain essential for all entomologists for many years to come. In round numbers, 10,000 species of Australian moths are known, with probably a similar number yet to be described. The first 80 pages provide an excellent summary of the embryonic development, anatomy, life history, growth cycle, population control, economic significance, ecology, evolution, and geographical distribution of moths in general, with emphasis on the origin of Australian Lepidoptera. Many references, some within a year of publication of this book, bespeak an intimate knowledge of the literature by Common, one of the world's leading lepidopterists. More than 400 pages tabulate the taxonomy of the Australian moth fauna (in the broad sense). The 100- plus figures and 1,000 photographs (many in color) supplement the text, with observations on the biology of the significant taxa in each order. Two short appendixes outline methods of collection and study, and detail a food plant and larval host list. A lengthy list of references and a glossary will be of great value to all students and interested amateurs. Lest one be deterred by the price, it should be emphasized that it is a beautifully printed volume—a tribute to the skill of all those involved in its production. For all academic libraries.—*G. Nicholas, Manhattan College*

OAB-1794   QL362   96-11748 CIP

Conniff, Richard. **Spineless wonders: strange tales from the invertebrate world.** H. Holt, 1996. 222p bibl index afp ISBN 0-8050-4218-0, $25.00

Conniff's lyrically written and engrossing volume about the natural history of selected invertebrates explicates the natural history of some of the most common and familiar invertebrates including flies, leeches, fire ants, squids, dragonflies, tarantulas, fleas, beetles, earthworms, mosquitoes, moths, and hagfishes (which, incidentally, are primitive vertebrates). Each animal is covered in a separate section in which some of the most important and interesting dimensions of their natural history are discussed; often, little-known and bizarre details about their behavior, physiology, or ecology are woven into the narrative. The author has done a masterful job of writing factually but not using excessive technical terms or lapsing into scientific jargon. If the author's wishes are for the reader to finish the book with a sense of amazement, awe, and with a greater sense of wishing to discover other aspects of invertebrates, he has succeeded masterfully. Every reader will be genuinely rewarded by this outstanding volume. Highly recommended for general readers as well as undergraduate and graduate students of biology and invertebrate zoology.—*P. E. Lutz, University of North Carolina at Greensboro*

OAB-1795   QL737   94-33542 CIP

Dawson, Terence J. **Kangaroos: biology of the largest marsupials.** Comstock Publishing, 1995. 162p bibl index ISBN 0-8014-8262-3 pbk, $25.00

Although marsupials are not well known, familiarity with kangaroos ensures that even scholarly endeavors such as this one are likely to elicit interest among those who are not biologists or zoologists. Dawson does an excellent job in synthesizing mountains of information on kangaroo social organization (the home range, habitat use, and activity patterns of groups), population structure, dispersal and mortality, reproductive biology, and life history. He devotes two chapters to feeding and physiological challenges that face kangaroos. Teeth, gut structure, microbial fermentation, diets, feeding competition, metabolism, water balance, and many other topics are covered in a most accessible manner. The last two chapters are particularly interesting for nonspecialists, as they discuss the interactions of kangaroos in the past and present with Aborigines and Europeans, respectively. The treatment of megafaunal extinctions and the ethnological insights into Aboriginal hunting, using a case study, make for interesting reading. The seven-page supplement for further reading rounds out this well-written and very useful small volume, a valuable addition to both professional and general libraries. Highly recommended for all who like mammals, and for college to professional level specialists in biology and zoology. General; undergraduate through faculty.—*F. S. Szalay, CUNY Hunter College*

Science & Tecnology

OAB-1796 QL751 96-18864 CIP
Dugatkin, Lee Alan. **Cooperation among animals: an evolutionary perspective.** Oxford, 1997. 221p bibl indexes afp ISBN 0-19-508621-X, $60.00; ISBN 0-19-508622-8 pbk, $29.95

Dugatkin's little book is both a great introduction to and a good review of cooperation in animals. He begins with an excellent summary of the long-standing interest in cooperative behavior among philosophers, psychologists, and biologists that, while not comprehensive, provides sufficient documentation to facilitate further study of the history of cooperation. He outlines four models of cooperative behaviors within evolutionary biology—reciprocity, kin selection, group selection, and byproduct mutualism—and reviews theoretical work on the evolution of cooperation. The basic mathematics related to this theoretical work is presented clearly, with sufficient text to be readily interpreted. Dugatkin's "Cooperator's Dilemma," developed with Michael Mesterton-Gibbons, describes a framework that links all four categories of cooperative behavior under a single theoretical umbrella. Cooperative behavior in fish, birds, nonprimate mammals, nonhuman primates, and eusocial insects is then presented within the evolutionary framework developed in the opening chapters. Specific examples address different contexts in which cooperation occurs, such as foraging, antipredator behavior, and reproductive and social behaviors, and consider situations for a number of different species within each taxon that best capture the essence of cooperative behavior. Upper-division undergraduates through faculty.—*K. A. Campbell, Albright College*

OAB-1797 QL628 91-7914 CIP
Etnier, David A. **The fishes of Tennessee,** by David A. Etnier and Wayne C. Starnes. Tennessee, 1994 (c1993). 681p bibl index afp ISBN 0-87049-711-1, $60.00

With more than 300 fish species, Tennessee has the most diverse freshwater fauna in the US. Thus this book, with its careful descriptions of species, distributions, and geology, is extremely important for North American biologists, environmental scientists, and makers of public policy. The strength of this volume lies not only in its subject but in its excellent presentation as well. Readers of all backgrounds will find the introductory sections on regional geology and ichthyology lucid. Field biologists will find practical guidance in the sections on collection and aquaria. Ichthyologists will find the key, which is the most important feature and the bulk of the 681 pages, to be excellent. There are notes about geographical variation in structure and photographs of nearly every species. Given this overall thoroughness, it is surprising to find only brief attention paid to the changes in hydrology and biology associated with the impoundments and dams engineered by the Tennessee Valley Authority. Nonetheless, a masterful work that sets a new standard for ichthyology and studies of fauna in general. Highly recommended. Upper-division undergraduate through professional.—*J. H. Long Jr., Vassar College*

OAB-1798 QL573 96-5245 CIP
Evans, Arthur V. **An inordinate fondness for beetles,** by Arthur V. Evans and Charles L. Bellamy. H. Holt, 1996. 208p bibl index afp ISBN 0-8050-3751-9, $40.00

When asked what could be inferred about the work of the Creator, J.B.S. Haldane is supposed to have replied, "an inordinate fondness for beetles." There are more species of beetles (Coleoptera) than of any other group of organisms, and the hundreds of thousands of species are tremendously varied. This magnificent volume, written by two leading coleopterists, introduces this fascinating order of insects. The pages are large (9 x 11 inches), and the first thing one notices are the beautiful color plates. These photographs by Lisa Charles Watson are of outstanding quality. It would seem impossible to improve upon the color, clarity, and sharp of focus of these plates (98 in number). But this is not all. The text, a well-written general biology of the Coleoptera, covers basic structure, function, ecology, and behavior; there are also chapters on "beetles and humans" and "beetlephilia." Epilogue by noted coleopterist Roy A. Crowson; lists of 166 beetle families, major world beetle collections, professional societies dedicated to beetle study. More complete textual coverage

is provided by R.A. Crowson's *The Biology of the Coleoptera*, CH, Jan'82. *An Inordinate Fondness* is *not* for identification of beetles (for that see R.A. Arnett's *The Beetles of the United States*, 1960), or D.J. Borror et al., *An Introduction to the Study of Insects*, 6th ed., 1989). Color plates show only about 20 colorful scarabs, cerambycids and buprestids. Recommended for general readers and undergraduates through professionals.—*R. C. Graves, Bowling Green State University*

OAB-1799 QL690 92-14095 CIP
Ferns, P.N. **Bird life of coasts and estuaries.** Cambridge, 1993 (c1992). 336p bibl index ISBN 0-521-34569-3, $54.95

The second of a six-volume series covering the major bird habitats of Great Britain, and organized along the lines of *Bird Life of Mountain and Upland* by D.A. Ratcliffe (CH, Feb'92). Ferns's well-done ecological treatment emphasizes British coastlines but other types of coastal communities in the world, i.e., mangroves, are mentioned briefly. Major chapters treat the ecology of coastlines generally, and of the open sea, rocky shores, cliffs, shingle beaches, sandy shores, mud flats, and the "coastal fringe" (mainly vegetated dunes and salt marshes) specifically. The book ends with a chapter on the threats to coastal birds and environments. Like the earlier volume in the series, the book relies on the considerable British literature on the birds to present complex ecological relationships in an easy, readable style, and in this, Ferns has succeeded brilliantly. Highly recommended. General; community college; undergraduate; pre-professional.—*S. W. Harris, Humboldt State University*

OAB-1800 QL735 94-38065 CIP
Flannery, Tim. **Mammals of the South-West Pacific & Moluccan Islands.** Comstock/Cornell, 1995. 464p bibl index ISBN 0-8014-3150-6, $75.00

It is no exaggeration to say that this book contains all that is currently known about the mammals of the Southwest Pacific land masses. Following upon his *Mammals of New Guinea* (1990), Flannery concentrates on a broad swath of the Pacific, from just east of Sulawesi through the Cook Islands in the central south Pacific north to Micronesia and south to New Zealand. Flannery (who could properly be called a 20th-century Alfred Russel Wallace) describes 230 species from more than 250 islands scattered among 18 nations. Rather incredibly he has undertaken most of the field work himself during a five-year survey. In addition, he correlates the geology, archaeology, and human impact on areas he visited. His tour de force also includes the zoogeography and taxonomic relationships of most species. Each entry is allotted a page or two giving scientific name and its pronunciation; brief anatomical description, current status of distribution, local names, size, earliest records, and taxonomic synonyms. A color photograph of either the living organism or a preserved specimen is included. Bats constitute 65 percent of the total fauna present; marsupials 15 percent, and murids 19 percent. It is indeed remarkable that this one individual (whose home and personal library were destroyed in the Sydney bushfires of 1994) could produce such an information-packed volume. Undergraduate through professional.—*G. Nicholas, Manhattan College*

OAB-1801 Orig
Ford, Emma. **Peregrine.** Fourth Estate, 1994 (c1993). (Dist. by Trafalgar Square) 160p bibl ISBN 1-85702-105-3, $90.00

This beautiful book would be an asset to any library. There are superb photos and sketches on almost every page. There are chapters on the peregrine across the world; the peregrine in art and literature; at eyrie; hunting; the peregrine and man; captive breeding; the history of the peregrine in falconry; contemporary falconry; and the future of the peregrine. The appendix discusses the subspecies of the peregrine, and there is a brief bibliography at the end of the book. This reviewer was much impressed with the fine hunting sketches, which portray the falcon in action. An interesting and informative book that would appeal to any reader. Highly recommended. General; community college; undergraduate; graduate.—*C. J. Pollard, emeritus, Los Angeles Unified School District*

OAB-1802 Orig
Gee, Henry. **Before the backbone: views on the origin of the vertebrates.** Chapman & Hall, 1996. (Dist. by International Thomson Publishing) 346p bibl index afp ISBN 0-412-48300-9, $64.95

From at least the 1860s zoologists have been fascinated by the origin of vertebrates. Their dorsal nervous system and notochord sets them so far apart from invertebrates with their ventral nervous systems (often with mouth and anus reversed) that almost any invertebrate has been posited as the vertebrate ancestor. Gee shares that fascination; he reviews the story and the chief players, the problems and the personalities. As a guide to the important features of the likely ancestors, the book is first-rate. Gee is emphatic in not discarding any theory merely because it appears outlandish or unlikely. All are examined. Almost 30 percent of the text is devoted to origin from calcichordates, the only extinct subphylum of echinoderms. The book informs about the animals—embryological and larval evidence (lacking for the calcichordates), phylogenetic relationships, whether the vertebrate head is new or modified from an ancestor's, and much more. A major strength is the discussion of the older embryological/morphological and the latest molecular/genetic evidence. Gee explicitly resists erecting his own scheme but does a masterly job of evaluating everyone else's. Upper-division undergraduates through professionals.— *B. K. Hall, Dalhousie University*

OAB-1803 QL496 93-13158 CIP
Godfray, H.C.J. **Parasitoids: behavioral and evolutionary ecology.** Princeton, 1994. 473p bibl indexes afp ISBN 0-691-03325-0, $65.00; ISBN 0-691-00047-6 pbk, $29.95

The parasitoid lifestyle, represented by thousands of species, concerns organisms (generally insects) whose progeny develop at the expense of the host's body in a manner similar to the fantasy creature in the popular motion picture *Alien* of 1979. Godfray brings together the vast literature on the evolutionary biology and natural history of these organisms, important in insect pest management, primarily the hymenoptera. The book is well written with many figures and tables, and the author organizes the complex subject into eight chapters. The topics discussed include host location, oviposition behavior, sex ratio theories, genetic and associated factors in reproduction, the developing immature stages, the adults, and ecological interactions. Godfray succeeds in presenting a critical evaluation of current hypotheses and discusses the theoretical background without the use of mathematics. Highly recommended for academic libraries supporting programs in biology, zoology, ecology, entomology, and agriculture. Upper-division undergraduate through professional.— *S. B. Vinson, Texas A&M University*

OAB-1804 QL568 94-32642 MARC
Gotwald, William H. **Army ants: the biology of social predation.** Comstock Publishing Associates, 1995. 302p bibl indexes afp ISBN 0-8014-2633-2, $39.95

Gotwald ably succeeds in his stated objectives to not only provide comprehensive and integrative treatment of the classification, biogeography, behavioral ecology, and social organization of army ants but also include the "awe and curiosity" that underlies and sustains good science. A separate chapter details interactions of predators and symbiont species that live in close association with the colony. The final sections examine the role of army ants within tropical ecosystems and their portrayal in folklore and myth. Unusually well-done color plates, black-and-white photos, and line drawings illustrate this book. An extensive bibliography in addition to detailed author and subject indexes facilitate its use as a reference. This is the first volume in the Cornell Series in Arthropod Biology, which focuses on the behavior, ecology, and evolution of arthropods. If the following volumes are as well done as this one, this series will be a major contribution to the study of this group. A very readable book to be enjoyed by amateur naturalists and professionals alike. General; upper-division undergraduate through faculty.— *R. E. Lee Jr., Miami University*

OAB-1805 QL785 93-48197 CIP
Gould, James L. **The animal mind,** by James L. Gould and Carol Grant Gould. Scientific American Library, 1994. (Dist. by W.H. Freeman) 236p bibl index ISBN 0-7167-5046-5, $32.95

Deceit, depression, and self-awareness are behaviors that most biologists had long thought separated us from the other species that inhabit this earth. Gould and Gould indicate that this may not be true. An earlier scientist to explore this topic was Donald R. Griffin: *The Question of Animal Awareness* (CH, Jun'77; rev. and enl. ed., CH, Dec'81); *Animal Thinking* (CH, Sep'84); and most recently, *Animal Minds* (CH, Mar'93). The Goulds focus on the same topic, but at a more general level. Part of a series published by *Scientific American*, this volume brings to book form the same values associated with the magazine: clear, precise text, outstanding diagrams, a compact bibliography, and well-known authors. The authors begin their treatment by looking at behavior in a mechanical sense: how animals perceive their environment and how they respond to stimuli by exhibiting programmed behaviors. They then demonstrate how organisms operate as more than mere robots. Separate chapters examine aspects such as animal constructions (hives, mounds, and dams); eating and being eaten; knowledge of self and kin; and intra-and interspecific communication. The last chapter describes human mental capabilities. As demonstrated, although we as a species feel that most of our behavior is "learned," in reality (as shown by fraternal twin studies) we are strongly genetically programmed, a feature that indicates our commonality with the rest of creation and not our distinctness. An excellent book; the illustrations, photos and diagrams are not only very helpful, but convey the authors' message. General; undergraduate.— *L. T. Spencer, Plymouth State College*

OAB-1806 Orig
Handbook of the birds of the world: v.1: Ostrich to ducks; v.2: New World vultures to guineafowl, [ed.] by Josep del Hoyo, Andrew Elliott, and Jordi Sargatal. Lynx Edicions, 1994 (c1992); 1995 (c1994). (Dist. by American Lynx Editions, Inc., 1015-293 Atlantic Blvd., Atlantic Beach, FL 32233) 2v. 696, 638p bibl index afp ISBN 84-87334-10-5, v.1; ISBN 84-87334-15-6, v.2; $165.00 ea.

This ambitious project—to present all the birds of the world—will be greeted with pleasure by all bird enthusiasts. There are 12 large volumes projected for the series. At the beginning of the first volume, the authors provide a thorough discussion of the class Aves. Body structure, feathers, feeding and digestion, mating systems, eggs, and migration are just a few of the subjects discussed in this section. There is a chart of all the orders, suborders, and families of birds. Many scholars have worked on this project and the thorough coverage is admirable. In both volumes 1 and 2, the systematics, morphological aspects, habitat, general habits, voice, food and feeding, breeding, movements, relationship with humans, status, and conservation are presented for each family in a concise, informative style. Each species is then depicted in superb plates with a map of its range. The species account offers taxonomy, subspecies and distributions, descriptive notes, habitat, food and feeding, breeding, movements, status, conservation, and a bibliography. Throughout the books are found excellent photos of many species. These volumes are musts for all academic and large public libraries. General; undergraduate through professional.— *C. J. Pollard, emeritus, Los Angeles Unified School District*

OAB-1807 QL673 96-171864 MARC
Handbook of the birds of the world: v.3: Hoatzin to auks, [ed.] by Josep del Hoyo, Andrew Elliott, and Jordi Sargatal. Lynx Edicions, 1996. (Dist. by American Lynx Editions, Inc., 1015-293 Atlantic Blvd., Atlantic Beach, FL 32233) 821p bibl index afp ISBN 84-87334-20-2, $175.00

The excellent work in the first two volumes of this handbook (vols. 1 and 2, CH, May'96) is continued here in vol. 3. As in the first two volumes, the systematics, morphological aspects, habitat, general habits, voice, food and feeding, breeding movements, relationship with humans, status, and conservation are presented for each bird family in a concise, informative style. Each species is then illustrated by excellent plates with a map of its range. Of special value is the depiction of forms of subspecies. The fine bibliography reflects the many authors who have been working on this project to cover thoroughly all the bird species of the world. Fine photos are found throughout. All three volumes are a must for all academic and large public libraries. General readers; upper-division undergraduates through professionals.—*C. J. Pollard, emeritus, Los Angeles Unified School District*

OAB-1808   QL430   95-10249 CIP
Hanlon, Robert T. **Cephalopod behaviour,** by Robert T. Hanlon and John B. Messenger. Cambridge, 1996. 232p bibl indexes ISBN 0-521-42083-0, $74.95

Hanlon and Messenger have prepared a very timely and useful book, timely both because the last general book on the behavior of these creatures was published in 1978 and because the wealth of new information on these animals, available within the last decade or so, is well represented in the book. It is useful because it is clearly written and well laid out, making it easy to find one's way around and to understand the material in each of the sections. The authors emphasize their area of joint research interest—the skin colors and appearance of cephalopods—a little more than one would expect in a work generally treating behavior. Otherwise, the book offers a wealth of information, and it will quickly become the standard resource in its area. Upper-division undergraduates, graduate students, faculty, and researchers.—*J. A. Mather, University of Lethbridge*

OAB-1809   QL495   92-13703 CIP
Heinrich, Bernd. **The hot-blooded insects: strategies and mechanisms of thermoregulation.** Harvard, 1993. 601p bibl indexes afp ISBN 0-674-40838-1, $75.00

Heinrich, author of *In a Patch of Fireweed* (1984), *One Man's Owl* (CH, Mar'88), and *Ravens in Winter* (1989), is a noted authority on thermoregulation in insects. Insects have long been considered to be poikilotherms because their body temperature changes along with their environment. This is misleading, however, as the author states that some moths may maintain body temperatures near 46 C, "clearly not warm-blooded" but "hot-blooded," hence the title of the book. In this interesting work, Heinrich concentrates on "an eco-logical-evolutionary perspective" of the "behavioral and physiological mechanisms of altering body temperature" in the major groups of insects. There is a chapter on each of the following: moths and butterflies, dragonflies, grasshoppers, beetles, bees, ants, wasps, flies, cicadas, insect larvae, fever, cold jumpers (Collembola, fleas, flea beetles, click beetles, Orthoptera, etc.), and social thermoregulation (climate control in the nests of social insects), followed by a summary and 60 pages of references. Heinrich is a very good writer and his book is thoroughly excellent. He pulls together a vast store of information on insect thermoregulation, nicely illustrated with graphs and his drawings. Recommended for those with interests in physiology, ecology, entomology, and zoology, and for biologists and naturalists in general. Advanced undergraduate through faculty.—*R. C. Graves, Bowling Green State University*

OAB-1810   Orig
Horses through time, ed. by Sandra L. Olsen. R. Rinehart, 1996. 222p bibl index ISBN 1-57098-060-8, $35.00

In tracing the history of the horse, this illuminating book takes a more scientific approach than earlier notable works, such as *The History and Romance of the Horse*, by Arthur Vernon (1939), and *The Horse through Fifty Centuries of Civilization*, by Anthony A. Dent (1974). For this work, editor Olsen assembled a crack team of experts with stellar academic credentials to contribute essays on topics pertinent to their areas of specialization, which include such diverse fields as zooarchaeology, mammalian osteology, and biogeography. As with most works of this type, this book begins by reviewing the fossil record, moves forward through domestication, and then examines the changing role of the horse in civilization. Where it differs, and excels, is in the context in which the information is presented. Current research and new information are evident throughout, demonstrating that the study of horses is an ongoing and dynamic field. Chap-

ters reviewing the fossil record and the life style of the Kazakh people of Eurasia are two fine examples of this. Adding to the value of this work are ample illustrations and reading lists at the end of each chapter. Highly recommended for all levels of readers.—*D. L. Currie, Louisiana State University*

OAB-1811   QH367   94-37478 CIP
Nielsen, Claus. **Animal evolution: interrelationships of the living phyla.** Oxford, 1995. 467p bibl indexes ISBN 0-19-854868-0, $95.00; ISBN 0-19-854867-2 pbk, $45.00

Nielsen has prepared an exceptionally valuable, concise book (given its enormous subject matter) on the phylogenetic analysis and evolutionary history of all animal phyla. The book's coverage, testimony to both love of labor and dedication to the subject, is breathtaking in the detail of its coverage, and it also offers excellent illustrations to document many of its technically critical comparisons. The phylogenetic analyses of the 31 living phyla are based both on ultrastructural and embryological traits. The shared unique features of the various groups are used to construct that constellation of ancestral characters that was probably present in the last common ancestor of each phylum. These derived characters are subsequently utilized to arrive at the most probable sister-group relationships of the various phyla, tracing their evolution from their unicellular ancestry. The 56 chapters each have a respectable and carefully chosen extensive list of references, and the subject and systematic indexes make this one of the most valuable references in the zoological literature. A must for all zoologists and biologists engaged in teaching the systematics of animal groups. Upper-division undergraduate through faculty.—*F. S. Szalay, CUNY Hunter College*

OAB-1812   SH348   96-4604 CIP
The Northwest salmon crisis: a documentary history, ed. by Joseph Cone and Sandy Ridlington. Oregon State, 1996. 374p bibl index afp ISBN 0-87071-390-6, $29.95

The topic of this book, the severe decline of salmon in the Pacific Northwest, is very timely and deserves a great deal of thought and attention, especially with regard to management of natural resources. Historic documentation of this crisis and its interpretation are presented uniquely and effectively. There are six major sections: an introduction; "The Exploitation of Nature"; "Contending with Technology"; "The Indian Experience"; "The Accelerating Crisis"; and a conclusion. The first and last are essays written by individual authors. The other four have a brief introduction and then a series of relatively short topical presentations containing excerpts from one or more historic documents, followed by interpretative commentary from a specialist on the history of salmon in the Northwest. The specialists have a mix of backgrounds, but each is a recognized advocate of the Pacific salmon resource. The results are a very readable and interesting set of interpretations that together yield a better understanding of how many different actions contributed to the current situation. The editors have done an outstanding job in organizing and structuring this book and its information. Useful glossary. General; upper-division undergraduates through professionals.—*W. K. Hershberger, University of Washington*

OAB-1813   Orig
Payne, Roger. **Among whales.** Scribner, 1995. 431p index ISBN 0-684-80210-4, $27.50

Written by one of the world's leading marine mammal experts, this volume is a first-person account of Payne's vast knowledge of whales. It is a natural history account of the biology of whales in which such diverse topics as migration, reproduction, feeding and food preferences, communications, and behaviors of these behemoths are explored. Payne is an eminent scholar of whales with a vast amount of firsthand experience. He writes passionately, elegantly, in beautiful prose, lyrically—reminding one somewhat of the style of Loren Eisley—and in ways that illustrate his unqualified love and respect for these cetacean beasts. Devoid of supporting quantifiable data in the form of tables, graphs, and photographs, this volume still reflects the fact that the author's expertise in the biology of whales is enormous and perhaps unparalleled. He writes as though there is so much to relate and so little space or time in which to accomplish these goals. It most certainly should be read voraciously by students of marine mammalogy, marine biology, and animal communications and behavior, and by everyone who espouses protection of marine mammals; but it should be read by everyone! General; upper-division undergraduate through professional.—*P. E. Lutz, University of North Carolina at Greensboro*

OAB-1814   QL696   CIP
Rosair, David. **Photographic guide to the shorebirds of the world,** by David Rosair and David Cottridge. Facts on File, 1995. 175p bibl index afp ISBN 0-8160-3309-9, $29.95

Rosair and Cottridge have produced an excellent guide to the world's shorebirds. On each page there is a series of photographs of the bird discussed. The photographs often illustrate breeding, nonbreeding, juvenile, and adult plumage; they are very helpful when trying to identify many of the sandpipers. The discussion of each species gives the range; the adult breeding, nonbreeding, and juvenile plumage; in-flight characteristics; calls; habits and behavior; and movements. Currently there are 212 recognized species of waders, and all are treated by the authors. There are more than 700 color photographs, and they are beautifully executed to provide the viewer with important field marks. At the end of the book are a list of all species in systematic order, a page of photographic acknowledgments, references, and an index to all the species. Highly recommended. All levels.—*C. J. Pollard, emeritus, Los Angeles Unified School District*

OAB-1815   QL737   95-72713 MARC
Rowe, Noel. **The pictorial guide to the living primates.** Pogonias, 1996. 263p bibl index ISBN 0-9648825-0-7, $79.95; ISBN 0-9648825-1-5 pbk, $59.95

The primate order includes our closest relatives, the apes, monkeys, tarsiers, and lemurs. This privately published book is the first to bring together basic data about every living species along with color photographs of almost all varieties. Following brief introductory material (mainly explaining the format and conventions), Rowe presents a half to one page of information and illustration on each primate species (and a few distinctive subspecies), organized alphabetically by genus and species within families. For each form, there is a small distribution map and information about a wide variety of topics, including distinguishing features and various body measurements; habitat, diet, locomotion, life history parameters (e.g., age at sexual maturity, lifespan, gestation length); numerous behavioral characteristics; and conservation status (low risk to highly endangered). Many of the wonderful photos are by Rowe himself, supplemented by views in natural habitat provided by researchers. A complete index, more than 1,000 primary references for the data, and a brief glossary round out the volume. Highly recommended for all reference collections—everyone wants to know more about primates, and this is a great place to start. General readers; undergraduates through faculty.—*E. Delson, CUNY Herbert H. Lehman College*

OAB-1816   QL737   92-18869 CIP
Schaller, George B. **The last panda.** Chicago, 1993. 291p indexes afp ISBN 0-226-73628-8, $24.95

Schaller has made another important contribution to the literature on conservation. He provides a fine review of the natural history of the panda and insights into the problems encountered in field research on a rare species in remote parts of the world. This is the sort of work one has come to expect from this author and he fulfills the high standards he always sets. In this book, however, it is not the natural history that is the most important contribution. Schaller also explores the effect of being beautiful, rare, and endangered on the possible extinction of a species. Because of its rarity the panda has become a valuable item and zoos around the world compete to have one on loan to their collection. The result is that human greed has placed a high economic value on the panda that allows poachers and governments to exploit the species.

Any one that wants to learn about the true international politics of the rare and endangered species of this world must read this book. A well-written work, suited to all levels from general readers to professionals.—*D. W. Kitchen, Humboldt State University*

OAB-1817   QL737   91-46767 CIP
Strier, Karen B. **Faces in the forest: the endangered muriqui monkeys of Brazil.** Oxford, 1992. 138p bibl index afp ISBN 0-19-506339-2, $45.00

This important book provides a readable, remarkably thorough, first look at the biology of the Muriqui, the largest New World primate. Strier's work reveals many startling contrasts with the generally accepted model for primate social behavior (and, by extension, the evolution of human behavior) based on Old World monkeys and apes. The Muriqui has an active but peaceful social life; there is no dominance hierarchy; males and females are equal, although females are more apt to defend the home territory. Using nontechnical language, the author includes a personal history of her pioneering studies as well as covering the ecology, male and female roles, life histories, and group dynamics of the Muriqui. The chapter on conservation of the animals could stand alone as a balanced appraisal of conflicting needs in a modern tropical nation. The book is well produced with charming sketches by the author, black-and-white photographs, extensive references, and a good index. Comparable to the works of Jane Goodall, this highly recommended book will appeal to a wide range of readers, from high-school through graduate students.—*T. C. Williams, Swarthmore College*

OAB-1818   QL403   92-35371 CIP
Vermeij, Geerat J. **A natural history of shells.** Princeton, 1993. 207p bibl index afp ISBN 0-691-08596-X, $29.95

Vermeij's book is a delightful and provocative work that will engage a broad spectrum of readers from undergraduate to professor, scientist to serious lay collector. He covers a wide range of subjects in eight well-written chapters that include three comprehensive themes: the first, how a shell is constructed, includes information on geometry, growth, a comparison to arthropod "shells" and growth, and an evolutionary account of geometric diversity. The second, how a shell works for its builder, is a broad ecological view incorporating physical features of the environment (waves, currents, substrates) and animals' adaptations (burrowing, swimming, floating). The portrayal of molluscs as both predators and prey is fascinating and underscores Vermeij's insight into the evolution of capture and avoidance. The suite of behaviors, appendages, and teeth used by predators of molluscs are arrayed against the contrary devices of stealth, chemical defenses, use of the shell as a weapon, and other strategies to minimize detection and repair damage. The final general theme of the book is the dimension of time on an evolutionary scale ("the rise and fall of adaptive themes") but approached more from a spatial, biogeographical perspective. Vermeij's insights into his own career as young student, his observations of differences in architecture of closely related groups of molluscs in different oceans, the data he has gathered, and the interpretations he has advanced are a good account of scientific method in natural history. A real bargain. General; undergraduate through faculty.—*D. A. Armstrong, University of Washington*

OAB-1819   QL458   92-11137 CIP
Wise, David H. **Spiders in ecological webs.** Cambridge, 1993. 328p bibl index ISBN 0-521-32547-1, $79.95

Notwithstanding the eco-humor, an excellent work addressing the importance of spiders as unique organisms for field experiments designed to evaluate theories of population and community ecology. The first chapter provides a brief overview of spider biology; subsequent chapters contain in-depth presentations of food limitation as it applies to terrestrial carnivores and, more specifically, spiders; competitionist views of spider communities; the competitionist paradigm, including interspecific competition and aggression and their impacts on population dynamics; niche partitioning; factors that contribute to population density, including prey scarcity, abiotic factors, natural enemies, dispersal, and territoriality; impact of spiders on insect populations; spiders as biocontrol agents in agroecosystems; the ecological web and vegetation structure and leaf-litter layer; and complex communities, intraguild predation, and spiders in grazing food chains. The concluding chapter is devoted to models, paradigms, and experimental designs. References are extensive and inclusive through 1992; the writing is clear, evenly presented, and logically organized; the figures are well integrated with the written text (although the line drawings in Chapter 1 do not add to the text). An excellent book for academic libraries supporting programs in agriculture, biology, ecology, and entomology. Advanced undergraduate through faculty.—*S. L. Smith, Bowling Green State University*

SOCIAL & BEHAVIORAL SCIENCES

■ General

OAB-1820   BX8129   92-31568 CIP
The Amish and the state, ed. by Donald B. Kraybill. Johns Hopkins, 1993. 333p bibl index afp ISBN 0-8018-4468-1, $45.00; ISBN 0-8018-4469-X pbk, $14.95

This collection of 13 essays examines the major areas of conflict between the Amish and the state in the 20th century. Most of the contributors are sociologists, but political scientists, historians, lawyers, and pastors are also represented in these pages. Because the book deals with a very traditional religious group it is surprising that no folklorists or anthropologists are among the volume's contributors. The major areas covered are military service and conscription, education and schooling, social security and taxes, slow-moving vehicles, health care, and land use. The collection dispels many stereotypes about the Amish, so each essay is worthwhile reading. Chapter 11, "The Role of Outsiders," will be the most enlightening to those not well versed in Amish culture. An essential volume for any serious student of Amish history. Advanced undergraduate; graduate; faculty.—*W. K. McNeil, The Ozark Folk Center*

OAB-1821   HA214   93-24224 CIP
Choldin, Harvey M. **Looking for the last percent: the controversy over census undercounts.** Rutgers, 1994. 264p bibl index ISBN 0-8135-2039-8, $48.00; ISBN 0-8135-2040-1 pbk, $17.00

The US census has many uses but two are especially important: the allocation of seats in the House of Representatives and in state legislatures, and the formula-based distribution of federal funds to states and localities on the basis of population. These political and economic considerations mean that localities have a great incentive to maximize their numbers. As thorough as it is, the US census inevitably misses some people by what is called an undercount. Those missed are more likely than others to be poor, minority, young, and/or male. Large cities with their overrepresentation of poor people and of racial and ethnic minorities can thus be seen as losing out politically and economically as a result of the undercount (which has been between one and three percent of the total population in recent censuses). This is the backdrop for Choldin's well-written, informative, thoroughly fascinating tale of the interplay between technology and politics in the census. On the technical side, readers learn how the census is conducted, how the undercount is measured, how an adjustment that corrects for the undercount can be done, and what the implications of such an adjustment would be. On the political side are the lawsuits against the Census Bureau by the mayors of Detroit and New York City, among others, and the infighting within the Department of Commerce (which contains the Census Bureau). This reviewer recommends this nontechnical mystery (where's the last percent?) to demographers, to urban and organizational sociologists, and to public administrators and politicians in large cities with shrinking populations. It is also accessible to upper-division undergraduates.—*K. Hadden, University of Connecticut*

OAB-1822   HN28   94-37908 CIP
Cultural politics and social movements, ed. by Marcy Darnovsky, Barbara Epstein, and Richard Flacks. Temple University, 1995. 360p index afp ISBN 1-56639-322-1, $49.95; ISBN 1-56639-323-X pbk, $18.95

This collection of essays delivers cutting-edge discussion. The US and European contributors are activists and academics, and include some well-known academic figures: Frances Fox Piven, Richard Cloward, Richard Flacks, and Alberto Melucci. The excellent introduction provides an insightful analysis of social movement theory. It sets the parameters for the essays by clearly defining their shared concept of "social movements" as persistent collective efforts by subordinated groups to challenge the political, economic, or cultural status quo. Essays in part 1 advocate the need for academics' engagement in movements. Part 2 describes the meanings of the 1960s cultural revolution for society and for individuals. Part 3 analyzes present trends toward fragmentation in politics, ideology, and collective identification caused by the absence of a consolidated New Left. Part 4 combines the benefits of movement participation and academic research to suggest effective movement strategies. All essays are well written and accessible. In contrast to many collections, the variation in writing style is expressive rather than hindering because of the common base of knowledge among essayists. Contains information about the contributors, excellent index.—*S. Cable, University of Tennessee at Knoxville*

OAB-1823   H67   94-42604 CIP
Dahrendorf, Ralf. **LSE: a history of the London School of Economics and Political Science, 1895-1995.** Oxford, 1995. 584p bibl index afp ISBN 0-19-820240-7, $39.95

Dahrendorf has written a highly readable history of one of the premier social science institutions in the world. But this is no dry account full of social scientific jargon. For Dahrendorf (alumnus, Director of the LSE, 1974-84, and significant sociologist in his own right), "The School's" biography emerges from the stories of those who walked its halls. Herein lies the book's charm. The Webbs, George Bernard Shaw, Howard Laski, R.H. Tawney, Bronislaw Malinowski, and Friedrich von Hayek come alive in these pages as intellectuals and as people. Dahrendorf organizes his material into three epochs—the founding and early development (1895-1919), Sir William Beveridge's tenure, which brought world renown to the social sciences (1919-1937), and war, reconstruction, expansion, and troubles (1937-1994). This is narrative educational history at its best. The book is well written, with excellent and well-chosen photographs. Yet it is no sanitized history. Dahrendorf treats the inner tensions and controversies (especially the 1968 turmoil that nearly destroyed the School) with directness and clarity. Must reading for anyone interested in the history of the social sciences. Upper-division undergraduates and above.—*W. P. Anderson Jr., Grove City College*

OAB-1824   HM206   96-37068 CIP
Diamond, Jared. **Guns, germs, and steel: the fates of human societies.** W.W. Norton, 1997. 480p bibl index afp ISBN 0-393-03891-2, $27.50

At the risk of sounding melodramatic, this usually soft spoken academic is willing to assert that Diamond's book is one of very few that could have a real impact on world understanding if it were widely read. Diamond wrestles with the huge question of why some societies became so rich and powerful — and why others remain relatively poor and powerless. To answer so enormous a question, the author addresses many other fundamental questions. Among these are how and why did food production begin? What differences did this make? How did it spread? Why were some animals domesticated and others not? How did writing evolve, and why does it matter? Diamond poses similar questions with respect to technology, religion, and government. He writes clearly and in an engrossing manner, with a consistent (but not heavy-handed) grounding in evolutionary theory. He is a biologist who neatly interweaves data and insights from many other disciplines, including geography and anthropology, which are too often overlooked. A subsidiary theme of this work is discrediting racist theories of history, which Diamond does deftly and consistently throughout, with no resort to polemic. Several apt but unfamiliar illustrations complement the text, which is thoroughly authoritative despite the absence of footnotes or endnotes. A discursive bibliographic essay on each chapter can be helpful to anyone who wants to pursue a topic in greater depth. All levels.—*D. B. Heath, Brown University*

OAB-1825 G1812 94-36042 MARC
Dorling, Daniel. **A new social atlas of Britain.** Wiley, 1995. 247p bibl index afp ISBN 0-471-94868-3, $59.95

Dorling's exercise in "human cartography" maps the diagnostic features and complex variables that constitute British social structure. This visualizing of British society is possible because of the availability of new computer mapping programs and new social data for regional and local levels. The principal cartographic device is the "equal populations cartogram"—a combination of map and graph—in which the spatial representation of particular data is weighted in proportion to set values. This technique is applied to an array of data sets, and also to change over time. Following a lucid introduction to the methodology, cartographic conventions, and interpretation of the maps, the atlas addresses successive dimensions of its principal concern, the population of Great Britain. Beautifully and informatively rendered maps and diagrams cover some 106 substantive topics under the main section headings of Population, Demography, Economic, Housing, Health, Society, and Politics. Each of the topics is accompanied by a readable interpretative text, followed by a conclusion and set of references. Lavishly produced, this atlas is a sophisticated research tool and also a valuable resource document. All levels.—*B. Osborne, Queen's University at Kingston*

OAB-1826 RC451 96-7923 CIP
Ethnicity and family therapy, ed. by Monica McGoldrick, Joe Giordano, and John K. Pearce. 2nd ed. Guilford, 1996. 717p indexes afp ISBN 0-89862-959-4, $55.00

Ethnicity and Family Therapy, aimed primarily at practitioners and students of family therapy, would also be a valuable resource for undergraduate students studying for any profession that involves work with human services agencies, such as social work, psychology, sociology, or criminal justice. In our increasingly ethnically diverse communities, providing human services requires sensitivity to the role of ethnic background in people's lives. An overview chapter provides an excellent framework for understanding the role of ethnicity and interactions with race, class, family, and religion. Heading each section, a summary discusses the commonalities among families in that grouping; this is followed by individual chapters on families of different origins within that grouping, which provide a clearer picture of the contribution of family history. The section on families of European origin is a particularly valuable contribution, since so many books looking at ethnicity focus solely on minority ethnic groups, ignoring the diversity of European origins. As a whole, a rich picture of the tapestry of diversity that makes up the American people. Upper-division undergraduates through professionals.—*H. Karp, University of Houston—Clear Lake*

OAB-1827 HQ1181 95-5922 CIP
Feminism and social change: bridging theory and practice, ed. by Heidi Gottfried. Illinois, 1996. 286p index afp ISBN 0-252-02198-3, $39.95; ISBN 0-252-06495-X pbk, $14.95

In this interesting collection of essays, a group of well-known feminist social scientists (including Joan Acker, Heidi Hartmann, Judith Stacey, Dorothy Smith, and Verta Taylor) describe their experience in undertakings that were designed to change the world as well as to inform the academy. Their accounts of efforts to collect, generate, and use information for effective political advocacy and to facilitate women's ability to speak, mobilize, and act in their own behalf, demonstrate the variety of ways in which the emancipatory project has come to inform the best feminist research. However, it is often easier to imagine than to accomplish a social science that advances the interests of women. As these narratives reveal, the relation between researcher and informants in participatory research is particularly difficult, as one young scholar learned when she went "home" to study women as an insider but was treated as an outsider, and as an experienced researcher found when she had to tell less than the "whole" truth to avoid betraying her informants. The failures and dilemmas described here should help to inform the next generation of activist research. Both experienced researchers and their students will find this new contribution to the methodological literature compelling and provocative. All levels.—*N. B. Rosenthal, SUNY College at Old Westbury*

OAB-1828 H62 92-36235 CIP
Fisher, Donald. **Fundamental development of the social sciences: Rockefeller philanthropy and the United States Social Science Research Council.** Michigan, 1993. 343p bibl index afp ISBN 0-472-10270-2, $49.50

Why did the social sciences develop in the way that they did in the US? What role did external funding agencies play in structuring social science research? What was the role of individual social scientists in giving direction to various fields? Fisher does a superb job in piecing together this complicated puzzle. He focuses on the crucial role of the Social Science Research Council (SSRC) in changing the orientation of the social sciences between the two world wars. According to Fisher, the SSRC acted as an intermediary organization dominated by the interests of Rockefeller philanthropy. In its role as coordinator for the social sciences, the Council served as a bridge between the interests of capital and the state, and became the transmission belt for issues and concerns of elites regarding the social sciences and their potential for doing applied research on the nation's social problems. Through the SSRC, a new definition of social scientists as technicians became dominant. These technicians provided the knowledge and the expertise to make the relation between the public and private sectors work. Fisher's book is notable for the care that it displays in presenting evidence and for its sophistication in connecting individuals, institutions, and social structures. It breaks new ground in this important field and will be a standard for years to come. Advanced undergraduates and above.—*P. Seybold, Indiana University-Bloomington*

OAB-1829 HM251 96-10130 CIP
Howard, Judith A. **Gendered situations, gendered selves: a gender lens on social psychology,** by Judith A. Howard and Jocelyn A. Hollander. Sage Publications, CA, 1997. 208p bibl indexes afp (Gender lens, 2) ISBN 0-8039-5604-5, $35.00; ISBN 0-8039-5603-7 pbk, $14.95

Gendered Situations, Gendered Selves is part of a series designed to integrate theory and research on gender into the discipline of social psychology as a whole. Historically, social psychology has failed to analyze gender and has been influenced by prevailing cultural assumptions about women and men. Howard and Hollander believe that gender is evoked by virtually all behaviors and situations and therefore must be a central component of theories and research on social behavior. The goal of the authors is to demonstrate that "a gendered analysis facilitates a more nuanced and sociological analysis of the intersection between individuals and the societies in which they live." After defining social psychology and gender and examining concepts of gender in social psychology, the authors examine three major social psychological theories: social exchange, social cognition, and symbolic interaction. This is followed by two chapters on altruism and aggression, and a concluding chapter that presents an example from everyday life. Throughout the book the authors emphasize two points. First, that social psychology has simultaneously ignored and been deeply influenced by gender. Second, that although gender differences may exist, they are not the same as sex differences. This work is an excellent analysis of the necessity of a "gender lens" for understanding the behavior of individuals in the social context in which they live. Upper-division undergraduates and above.—*C. Adamsky, emeritus, University of New Hampshire*

OAB-1830 GE195 93-49618 CIP
Kaufman, Wallace. **No turning back: dismantling the fantasies of environmental thinking.** Basic Books, 1994. 212p bibl index ISBN 0-465-05118-9, $25.00

In an age of political "correctness" Kaufman has demonstrated great courage and integrity. He has tackled a challenging and controversial topic with clarity and without the rancor one might expect given his own history in the environmental movement. Kaufman's is a solid presentation of the historical development and present position of the environmental movement with a thoroughgoing understanding of the philosophical underpinnings of its early and contemporary forms. For many readers, this book will promote a new recognition, understanding, and sharpening of their own position. For some, Kaufman's argument that the reality of the modern world makes it impossible to go back to an unmanaged "wilderness" policy will make sense. Others will reject it on the basis of a different reading of history or a different ideology. The strength of this volume lies not so much in its ability to convince as in the likelihood of its provoking a national conversation about what constitutes a legitimate national agenda. Students of history and social movements as well as those sincerely concerned with the environment will find this a fascinating, must-read volume. General and academic readers at all levels.—*A. L. Nieves, Wheaton College (IL)*

OAB-1831 HQ1397 91-14334 CIP
The Knowledge explosion: generations of feminist scholarship, ed. by Cheris Kramarae and Dale Spender. Teachers College Press (Columbia University), 1992. 533p index afp ISBN 0-8077-6258-X, $65.00; ISBN 0-8077-6257-1 pbk, $25.95

These 44 contributions are an essential summary of women's studies. The first section recounts impacts of women's studies in various disciplines, including sociology, psychology, philosophy, engineering, musicology, sport science, and others. The second section reviews debates on topics that cut across disciplines, such as ecofeminism, sexual violence, families, pornography, reproductive technology, and sisterhood and racial/ethnic consciousnesses. Well edited, the volume demonstrates that the journeys of feminist research through the past 20 years, although traversing rough terrain, have been fruitful and show promise of abundance in the next 20 years. The collection is perhaps generation-specific, perhaps sacrifices depth for breadth, only touches on ambivalence about the academy, and examines only very briefly questions in the philosophy and sociology of knowledge raised by the explosion of feminist knowledge. Bibliographies with each contribution and comprehensive index. An exceptional resource.—*J. L. Croissant, Rensselaer Polytechnic Institute*

OAB-1832 HQ755 93-17283 CIP
Kühl, Stefan. **The Nazi connection: eugenics, American racism, and German national socialism.** Oxford, 1994. 166p bibl index afp ISBN 0-19-508260-5, $22.00

In this historical monograph Kühl clearly and convincingly documents the strong connections and mutual support between eugenicists in the US and Germany for most of the first half of this century. In fact, Kühl presents a strong case for how eugenics-influenced American sterilization and immigration-restriction laws served as a focus for discussion among eugenicists in the Weimar Republic and later as a source of justification for Nazi race policies. Only the direct entry of the US into WW II appeared to stem the collaboration and mutual admiration among eugenicists in the two countries. Moreover, Kühl analyzes how the key political component of eugenics—the ideology of race improvement—continues to survive under different guises in the US, continues to clothe itself in the trappings of academic respectability, and continues to receive

major foundation support. The author's scholarship is impressive and thorough, and he uses virtually all sources available in English and German. Notes, references, and index are excellent. An important and disturbing contribution to the literature on racism. All levels.—*W. P. Nye, Hollins College*

OAB-1833 HN90 92-53246 CIP
Newman, Katherine S. **Declining fortunes: the withering of the American dream.** Basic Books, 1993. 257p index ISBN 0-465-01593-X, $23.00

Newman's brilliant and superbly written book contrasts the bleak situation and outlook of two sets of "baby boomers" with the relative security of their parents. Data are drawn from a New Jersey suburb, based on life-history interviews with three cohorts: adults who came of age in the 1970s, those who did so in the 1980s, and the parents of both. The author deals with the rift between boomers who grew up during the counterculture years of the 1960s and 1970s and those who matured during the "me first" Reagan decade. Despite media images of high-living yuppies, Newman argues that the dismal reality for many members of each set of boomers is that the trajectory that formerly enabled children to surpass their parents socioeconomically has been derailed by four intertwined forces; soaring housing prices, job insecurity, blocked occupational mobility, and a cost-of-living squeeze. In discussing the frustration of elderly parents unable to understand why their children cannot succeed as they did, Newman notes that the parents had been able to buy homes and achieve upward mobility because of favorable economic conditions and assistance from government policies, e.g., the GI Bill and low-interest mortgages. Given continuing economic decline and the absence of aggressive government initiatives, the author contends that the baby-boomer generation lacks insulation against declining fortunes and downward mobility. All levels.—*E. Wellin, University of Wisconsin—Milwaukee*

OAB-1834 HC59 94-22027 CIP
Petersen, John L. **The road to 2015: profiles of the future.** Waite Group, 1994. 372p bibl index ISBN 1-878739-85-9 pbk, $18.95

A provocative discussion of ten topics that characterize this "most extraordinary period of history," one that presents a "new context of explosive, exponential revolution." Petersen, a practicing futurist, seeds readers' thinking with a conceptual strategy: what we know, what we think about it, what tools are available, and the influences of the existing earth-based systems needed to support human life. He argues that systems-based planning is needed to generate a conceptual approach important to creating mental images of highly probable future trends. Topics covered include the impact of science and extraordinary technology, long-range environmental problems, the explosion of the impoverished global population, energy shifts, the impacts of changing transportation technology on work and travel, health threats, changing social values, and changing economic and political trends. Included in the book is a chapter-by-chapter resource list of organizations working and publishing on these topics. An extremely valuable handbook for initiating discussion on a wide array of future issues that should be shaping undergraduate discussion in the disciplines of science, technology, demography, economics, and political science as well as health and social science. Use of this book will allow future-oriented perspectives to vie with historical ones as worthy of academic discussion. A highly readable presentation with clear and appropriate graphs and a brief but significant bibliography. General; undergraduate; graduate; professional; two-year technical program students.—*M. Evans, SUNY Empire State College*

OAB-1835 Orig
Renner, Michael. **Fighting for survival: environmental decline, social conflict, and the new age of insecurity.** W.W. Norton, 1996. 239p index ISBN 0-393-03996-X, $19.95; ISBN 0-393-31568-1 pbk, $11.00

A long-time writer on the nexus of environmental problems and national security, Renner argues that the focus of post-Cold War national security be shifted from military concerns to the global social, economic, and environmental pressures threatening peace today. After analyzing the recent transformation of national security, Renner uses global examples to illustrate the sources of conflict that have replaced political ideologies: the degradation of lands, forests, and marine ecosystems, plus ozone depletion and climate change. He posits that the social, economic, and political repercussions of these environmental changes—poverty, population growth, and refugees—lead to conflicts that transcend national boundaries. Then Renner offers his vision of security in the 21st century, which is proactive rather than reactive and emphasizes negotiated conflict resolution and policies based on human well-being and human development. He argues for a fundamental reexamination of the assumptions of present national security policies and suggests modes of funding for today's tightening global economy. Clearly organized, the book is written for everyone. Extensive endnotes. Adequate subject/author index.—*S. Cable, University of Tennessee at Knoxville*

OAB-1836 TT972 95-51395 CIP
Rooks, Noliwe M. **Hair raising: beauty, culture, and African American women.** Rutgers, 1996. 160p bibl index afp ISBN 0-8135-2311-7, $38.00; ISBN 0-8135-2312-5 pbk, $15.95

Rooks's excellent book is a welcome entry in the feminist debates about American "beauty culture." In her "attempt to unravel the tangled meaning of hair in African American women's lives," Rooks (English, Univ. of Missouri) takes a cultural-studies approach to the history of hair-straightening products in the late 19th and early 20th centuries. She closely examines advertisements for such products, looking at how African American women were portrayed and how they portrayed themselves in ads for product lines they owned. She also studies African American women's magazines to trace connections between hairstyling and gender. The book's broader project is "to discuss the politics of representation as it relates to the construction of an African American female identity and various positions surrounding the meaning of African American women's bodies in a broad social context." Concluding with a consideration of contemporary "hair politics," the book addresses the significant gap in the treatment of this subject by such feminist scholars as Naomi Wolf (*The Beauty Myth*, CH, Jan'92), Susan Brownmiller (*Femininity*, 1984), and Lois Banner (*American Beauty*, CH, Jul'83). Readable, accessible, and helpfully illustrated, this volume is a crucial addition to any library's collection.—*R. R. Warhol, University of Vermont*

OAB-1837 HQ75 96-45823 CIP
Tierney, William G. **Academic outlaws: queer theory and cultural studies in the academy.** Sage Publications, CA, 1997. 186p bibl index afp ISBN 0-7619-0682-7, $46.00; ISBN 0-7619-0683-5 pbk, $19.95

Tierney explores gay rights, an enormous contemporary challenge, using some of the most demanding current theory and probing one of the most essential contexts for change: the academic world. He explains how marginal identities are constructed and internalized, relying on his scholarship in postmodernism, as well as his own and others' experiential lessons. In the first half of the book, he establishes the theoretical framework for critically assessing perceptions, language, norms, and knowledge production as these pertain to sexual orientation. In the second half, having argued that contextual interpretation of voices or actions is essential, Tierney situates his study of oppression and resistance in academe. Interview details reveal what happens as gay academics seek employment, discern the cultural and political landscape, and try to cultivate a career. These lessons are exemplified creatively by a short story, written for inclusion here, and they are also amplified by comparison with the academic closets of the past. Tierney ends pragmatically: there are multiple avenues and strategies for accomplishing genuine change, which he describes as both analyst and coach. The concept of agape guides his writing and gracefully explains his patience with a continuum of "outlaws." Upper-division undergraduates and above.—*R. Zingraff, Meredith College*

OAB-1838 HM24 93-14039 CIP
Wiggershaus, Rolf. **The Frankfurt school: its history, theories, and**

political significance, tr. by Michael Robertson. MIT, 1994. 787p bibl index ISBN 0-262-23174-3, $60.00

If one considers the Frankfurt school in retrospect, what comes as a surprise is not only how much it achieved, but how long it lasted. This small assemblage of intellectuals quarreled continuously, however great their common allegiance to Freud and Marx. How could it have been otherwise with such different thinkers as Herbert Marcuse, Erich Fromm, Bruno Bettelheim and, later, Jürgen Habermas? For good measure the school had to deal with political persecution from without, first from the Nazis in the 1930s, then from anticommunists in the '50s, and finally from the New Left in the '60s. Had it not been for the skill of its leader, Max Horkheimer, the school would almost certainly not have survived for nearly five decades. Using a wealth of new material, Wiggershaus deals not only with the vicissitudes of the school but also with the brilliance of its achievements. Perhaps the best chapters in this outstanding work are the ones that show how the Frankfurt thinkers addressed the burning questions of their day—fascism and antisemitism. Their answers continue to command attention. Upper-division undergraduates and above.—*S. Bailey, Knox College*

■ Anthropology

OAB-1839 CB478 96-12733 CIP
Adams, McC. Robert. **Paths of fire: an anthropologist's inquiry into Western technology.** Princeton, 1996. 332p bibl index afp ISBN 0-691-02634-3, $29.95

Technology is "humankind's extrasomatic adaptation to its environment." This commonplace, popularized in the thought of anthropologist Leslie White, provides a small starting point for Adams's richly nuanced exploration of the development of technology in the Western world. In his analytical narrative, technology is neither so simple nor so independent as to be given the status of prime mover. Instead, Adams shows how technology is embedded in social, economic, political, and cultural webs of interaction and meaning. He argues that technological change is ultimately unpredictable and indeterminate, subject neither to reduction nor to single causes. This work is most compelling in its analysis of the multiple and shifting "causes" of the industrial revolution in England and North America; it is most original in its analysis of the institutionalization of invention (in universities) and innovation (in various government programs) during both world wars and throughout the Cold War. Adams's promise—that an anthropological perspective can deal with fluid disciplinary boundaries, complex social contexts, and cultural ambiguities—is kept fully by his narrative. An excellent conceptual survey. Upper-division undergraduates and above.—*C. S. Peebles, Indiana University-Bloomington*

OAB-1840 GN62 94-19450 CIP
Marks, Jonathan. **Human biodiversity: genes, race, and history.** Aldine de Gruyter, 1995. 321p bibl index afp ISBN 0-202-02032-0, $46.95; ISBN 0-202-02033-9 pbk, $23.95

Marks traces the history of scientific attempts to describe and account for human biological variation. Covering the 17th century to the present, his study stresses the derivation of scientific ideas from the social problems and values with which they share history. Tracing two frameworks through time (the Linnean racial approach and the Buffonian population approach), Marks shows the fallacies inherent in trying to closely define races, and describes the promise of modern genetics to help sort humans into neat population groups with distinctive biological as well as behavioral traits. Yet the genetic research that was expected to validate the divisions of the human species undermined it by revealing a high degree of genetic variability. Humans are both polymorphic (varying within groups) and polytypic (varying between groups). Although this book shares some topics with Stephen Jay Gould's *The Mismeasure of Man* (CH, Apr'82), it covers more historical ground, is more evenhanded in its evaluation of historical events, and provides considerable biological detail. A highly readable, thought-provoking, and comprehensive treatment of popular and scholarly interest in race and human variation. General readers; upper-division undergraduates and above.—*S. A. Quandt, Wake Forest University*

OAB-1841 F1219 96-32775 CIP
Pasztory, Esther. **Teotihuacan: an experiment in living.** Oklahoma, 1997. 282p bibl index afp ISBN 0-8061-2847-X, $49.95

Pasztory (art history, Columbia Univ.) is a well-known contributor to scholarship of the classic Teotihuacan period of Central Mexico (c.1 to 750 CE). She is coeditor, with Kathleen Berrin, of the exhibition catalog *Teotihuacan: Art from the City of the Gods* (CH, Dec'93), which serves as a splendid precursor and companion to this volume. Pasztory's study is an intriguing, original structural and semiotic analysis that reviews and reinterprets the enigmatic arts of Teotihuacan through eight centuries, from its inception through its cultural collapse. In an engaging style Pasztory assesses Teotihuacan architecture, lithic sculpture, mural painting, and ceramics, and compares these arts with those of other ancient Old and New World civilizations. She argues cogently that Teotihuacan peoples created their art to reflect sociocultural ideals and to emphasize elements in nature, the supernatural, and egalitarian values rather than to glorify rulers or an aristocracy. The book's 15 chapters are supplemented by six black-and-white figures, 19 superb color plates, 288 endnotes, a 204-item bibliography, and a highly detailed 10-page, three-column index. Essential reading for students of Mesoamerica anthropology, history, and comparative civilization, and enjoyable for readers at all levels.—*C. C. Kolb, National Endowment for the Humanities*

OAB-1842 GN347 96-45561 CIP
Poole, Deborah. **Vision, race, and modernity: a visual economy of the Andean image world.** Princeton, 1997. 263p bibl index afp ISBN 0-691-00646-6, $69.50; ISBN 0-691-00645-8 pbk, $19.95

Poole's book makes a valuable contribution to understanding the place of visual discourses and technologies in the production and constitution of racial thought. Her initial interest—to examine the impact of photographic technology on representation of the Andean world—deepened to encompass a study of "How European perceptual regimes have changed over time and in relation to an increasing interest in non-European peoples," and "How visual images have shaped European perceptions of race as a biological and material fact." Poole reviews late-18th- and 19th-century philosophies of knowledge and the evolving languages of the biological sciences in the context of the politics of colonial subjugation. "Typification, comparability, and equivalency," principles around which differences and new information were organized by European scientists, philosophers, and naturalists, are shown to be operative in popularized and widely circulated images of Andean people that include photographs, engravings, book plates, and portraits. Poole uses these images to "examine race as a visual technology founded on the same principles of equivalency and comparison" that informed and supported the power of the European state. Her book offers original insight on race and makes a brilliant contribution to the anthropology of visual communication. Upper-division undergraduates and above.—*L. De Danaan, Evergreen State College*

OAB-1843 DT515 96-9997 CIP
Stone, Glenn Davis. **Settlement ecology: the social and spatial organization of Kofyar agriculture.** Arizona, 1996. 256p bibl index afp ISBN 0-8165-1567-0, $47.50

Stone (Washington Univ., St. Louis) has combined theories and methodologies from cultural anthropology, archaeology, and geography to study the spatial aspects of agrarian ecology for the Kofyar ethnic group of the Jos Plateau and the Benue Valley of Nigeria. He focuses on the relationship between the social organization of agriculture and agrarian settlement characteristics, i.e., how settlement patterns change with the intensification of agriculture because of rising population density. Many Kofyar moved from the hilly areas of the Jos Plateau

to the Benue Valley; Stone explores how the size, shape, and duration of the new settlement sites were established, and how the spacing between settlements and landscape features was determined. Of particular interest to development planners is the methodology for determining the underlying rules responsible for the empirical settlement patterns and the dynamics of agrarian settlement patterns over time. Stone includes comparative studies of the Tiv ethnic group of the Jos Plateau of Nigeria and the settlement patterns of the eastern US during the early era of European expansion. Replete with 39 illustrations and nine tables, this is an important case study of cultural ecology that will greatly interest social scientists and community and regional planners, as well as development planners. Upper-division undergraduates and above.—*D. M. Warren, Iowa State University*

OAB-1844 ND1101 96-15543 MARC
Taylor, Luke. **Seeing the inside: bark painting in western Arnhem Land.** Oxford, 1997 (c1996). 283p bibl index afp ISBN 0-19-827390-8, $68.00; ISBN 0-19-823354-X pbk, $29.95

Taylor's book It is the first analytic description of a distinctive genre of art that has become popular in recent years, namely bark painting from northern Australia. Remarkably detailed, insightful, and sympathetic, this study helps readers to understand the many meanings, forms, methods, and other aspects of what looks superficially like a "primitive art" but is in fact highly sophisticated and enjoying a world market. At the same time, the book is a sensitive and thorough ethnographic account of key aspects of social organization, mythology, and certain other facts of life among the Kunwinjku aborigines in contemporary Arnhem Land, Australia. Far from being just made to sell, the paintings serve to represent native views of the world to others. Taylor lets readers discover, with him, how such paintings link people with their ancestors and with the land and fauna around them, how different symbols have different meanings in different contexts, how artistic apprenticeship both reflects kinship and sometimes results in local "schools" of painting, how such paintings can be "read" or decoded, and how they relate to cave paintings (some ancient and others not) that play important roles in both the religion and the history of the people. One will never again simply wonder about such an "x-ray painting," but rather begin to appreciate it—like this book—at various levels. Upper-division undergraduates and above.—*D. B. Heath, Brown University*

OAB-1845 HQ76 96-40290 CIP
Turner, Dwayne C. **Risky sex: gay men and HIV prevention.** Columbia, 1997. 184p bibl index afp ISBN 0-231-10574-6, $45.00; ISBN 0-231-10575-4 pbk, $16.50

Turner presents a well-designed study, based on his anthropology PhD dissertation, of sexual behaviors of HIV negative gay men. His subjects were between the ages of 30 and 44, living in West Hollywood (an area of Los Angeles where many gays live) in the early 1990s. To obtain the data Turner, a gay man himself, participated in gay safer sex workshops, got written life histories from gay men, did face-to-face interviews, and conducted focus groups. He found that the men practiced safer sex almost all the time, but also on occasion had unprotected anal sex. Turner relates his findings to the probable evolutionary origins of basic human urges, and describes probable interactions between those urges and the cultures that coevolved along with human biology. He argues strongly throughout for a fuzzy-logic way of conceptualizing human behavior in general, and sexuality and risk-taking in particular. He suggests fuzzy-logic strategies for reducing sexual risk-taking. Although methodologically and theoretically sophisticated, the book is also as lucid and well written as a good novel. All levels.—*R. W. Smith, California State University, Northridge*

OAB-1846 HQ1240 92-29477 CIP
Young, Kate. **Planning development with women: making a world of difference.** St. Martin's, 1993. 187p bibl index ISBN 0-312-09090-0, $39.95

A convincing argument for the holistic GAD (gender and development) approach to development, the goal of which is development planning *with* rather than *for* women. Young charts theoretical swings in development thinking in the last 30 years, from early ethnocentric models of gender relations (which viewed women primarily as mothers), to a focus on women's role in basic needs provision, to the growth of feminist research and action with explicit attention to gender-based power structures. Three case-study chapters, examining women's agricultural role in Africa, factory employment in Asia, and work in the urban informal sector in Latin America, show that alleviating the symptoms of women's relative disadvantage (with training, access to credit, etc.) is only a first step toward women's "collective empowerment." Planners must also take into account the social structures and processes that underlie women's disadvantage (e.g., the ideology of male superiority, men's control of resources). This book cannot fail to sensitize development workers and students alike to the critical importance of taking women's roles into account in development thinking, planning, and implementation. All levels.—*M. A. Gwynne, SUNY at Stony Brook*

■ Archaeology

OAB-1847 GN885 96-11719 CIP
American beginnings: the prehistory and palaeoecology of Beringia, ed. by Frederick Hadleigh West with Constance F. West et al. Chicago, 1996. 576p bibl indexes afp ISBN 0-226-89399-5, $75.00

This is an extraordinary volume. It presents the latest information about the environment in and the passage of peoples during the late Pleistocene through Beringia, the land bridge between Siberia and Alaska, and adjacent regions of the two continents, from the Mackenie River in the east to the Lena River in the west. Most archaeologists believe the peoples who populated the Americas moved across Beringia in the late stages of the Ice Age. The 56 contributors, who specialize in the geology, past environments, and archaeology of the region, represent the most prominent American and Russian researchers in the region. The volume is divided into two sections, "Paleoenviromental Research" and "Archaeological Evidence." The first consists of geological overviews and paleoenvironmental reconstruction based on pollen analyses, paleobotany, and faunal analyses from mammoths to insects. Detailed presentations of the results of archaeological excavations at scores of sites in Russia and Alaska, along with drawings of artifacts, maps, and photographs, follow. The total evidence suggests that the earliest peoples appeared in Beringia between 15,000 and 12,000 years ago. Highly recommended. Upper-division undergraduates and above.—*W. A. Longacre, University of Arizona*

OAB-1848 F3429 95-3565 CIP
Bauer, Brian S. **Astronomy and empire in the ancient Andes: the cultural origins of Inca sky watching,** by Brian S. Bauer and David S.P. Dearborn. Texas, 1995. 220p bibl index afp ISBN 0-292-70829-7, $37.50; ISBN 0-292-70837-8 pbk, $14.95

This examination of the basis of Inca astronomy comes from the combined research of an archaeologist specializing in the Inca empire (Bauer) and an astrophysicist interested in ancient astronomy (Dearborn). A series of increasingly complex reconstructions of Inca cosmology by Anthony Avenid and R. Tom Zuidema have dominated the literature in the last quarter century. Bauer and Dearborn examine the viability of these reconstructions by ascertaining if archaeology can identify ruins at the hypothesized places, and if astrophysics can verify helical risings and settings, equinoxes, and solstices in the posited loci. The authors extract all astronomical discussions and references from the earliest Spanish chroniclers, and examine them against empirical field observations. Good support is found for an Inca calendar involving both solar and lunar calculations, calibrated against both horizon markers and gnomons. Data also indicate the importance of a variety of stellar phenomenon in herding and plant agricultural activities. The study is a splendid summary of the state of knowledge today, with its glossary that defines technical astronomical terminology as well as Incaic terms, and the supporting charts, maps, figures, photos, and notes. It is essential for all Andeanists and students of archaeoastronomy, but is written in an engaging style that any student interested in the Inca will enjoy. All levels.—*D. L. Browman, Washington University*

OAB-1849 E78 95-1085 CIP
Bourque, Bruce J. **Diversity and complexity in prehistoric maritime societies: a Gulf of Maine perspective.** Plenum, 1995. 414p bibl index ISBN 0-306-44874-2, $59.50

Bourque's well-written technical work places the Maine coastal archaeological site of Turner Farm in a regional context. Native Americans occupied the site from 5000 years ago to the early historic period. Bourque describes the results of more than 20 years of archaeological investigation involving the excavation and analysis of thousands of stone, bone, and ceramic archaeological specimens. Organization of the work is typical of such monographs: description of various methods and techniques used follows a general description of the site. Bourque discusses major periods of occupation, beginning with the earliest, and concludes by placing this site in the context of other regional sites and findings. Eight valuable appendixes present data on the analysis of the Turner Farm midden, radiocarbon dates, burial features, geoarchaeology, stone tools, and nonhuman bone remains. Bourque's report is valuable for its record of culture change through time as viewed from a single site. The evidence indicates that even preagricultural people were connected to others more than 1,000 miles away. Recommended to those interested in relatively technical presentations of archaeological findings from this region. Upper-division undergraduates and above.—*T. A. Foor, University of Montana*

OAB-1850 E78 95-11340 CIP
Dent, Richard J. **Chesapeake prehistory: old traditions, new directions.** Plenum, 1995. 320p bibl index ISBN 0-306-45028-3, $45.00

Dent (American Univ.) has written a comprehensive and exemplary summary of the complex cultural developments in the Chesapeake area. His approach is primarily chronological, but his account is interspersed with historical, geological, physiographical, and ecological data. The author fits these, together with subsistence strategies, tool typologies, and a host of other topics, into the broader setting of eastern North America, making the book in fact "a current synthesis of the prehistoric culture history" of the area in the context of eastern and southeastern cultures. A must for anyone involved in archaeology east of the Mississippi. Upper-division undergraduates and above.—*G. A. Konitzky, Clarion University of Pennsylvania*

OAB-1851 Orig
Dowson, Thomas A. **Rock engravings of Southern Africa.** Witwatersrand, 1994 (c1992). (Dist. by Indiana) 124p bibl ISBN 1-86814-120-9, $57.50

Rather than the vapid fare that "coffee-table" format often implies, this oversize volume is a wonderful introduction to the work of Dowson and David Lewis-Williams. Combining ethnoarchaeological and neuropsychological research, they have revolutionized study of African rock art. The authors suggest that the engraved geometrical patterns, combinations of these with animal figures, and beings shifting from human to animal form found throughout southern Africa represent a progression true to the hallucinations of people experiencing altered consciousness. Living Bushman shamans have recounted as much when they become entranced to intervene with the spirit world. One remarkable engraving shows geometrical grids fusing into a giraffe shape; another portrays a man with a lion's head; others illustrate the elands resulting from complete transformation of man into beast. To represent such an intangible process is an astounding artistic achievement. Dowson takes a strong stand against the contempt shown Bushmen in apartheid South Africa. His line drawings and sumptuous photos bring the glyphs to life, and his discussion of difficulties conserving ancient rock art will fascinate high school, college, and general readers.—*A. F. Roberts, University of Iowa*

OAB-1852 Can. CIP
Early human occupation in British Columbia, ed. by Roy L. Carlson and Luke Dalla Bona. UBC Press, University of British Columbia, 6344

Memorial Rd., Vancouver, BC V6T 1Z2, Canada, 1996. 261p bibl index afp ISBN 0-7748-0536-6, $65.00

This crisply edited and well-illustrated volume belongs in the library of anyone with an interest in the archaeology of western North America, or Paleo-Indian and the Early Archaic. The volume covers all of British Columbia and adjacent portions of southeast Alaska. Its organization (though not its content) reflects Carlson's views of the early culture history in the region. The 18 substantive papers are grouped into the four early cultural traditions Carlson recognizes and a fifth residual category of "transitional cultures." All of the papers are excellent descriptive summaries of their individual topics. They offer little interpretation or explicit theory, the major shortcoming of the volume. This reviewer found the papers on microblades and the early assemblages at Milliken in the Fraser Canyon particularly useful. The collection opens and closes with papers by Carlson, which taken together provide the most recent version of his model of Northwest Coast culture history. For every university library with holdings in North American archaeology. Upper-division undergraduates and above.—*K. M. Ames, Portland State University*

OAB-1853   GN799   94-44464 CIP
The Emergence of pottery: technology and innovation in ancient societies, ed. by William K. Barnett and John W. Hoopes. Smithsonian Institution Press, 1996 (c1995). 285p bibl index afp ISBN 1-56098-516-X, $55.00; ISBN 1-56098-517-8 pbk, $29.95

Resulting from a 1993 symposium, this superb synthesis by renowned specialists characterizes current archaeological research on the invention and adoption of pottery among societies around the world. The 22 papers—four theoretical, eight Old World, and ten from the Americas—make amply clear that the origins of ceramic technology varied widely in space, time, and cultural context. Contributors employ paradigms and methodologies derived from economic production and distribution, ceramic ecology, or information theory to generate abundant new or reinterpreted information. Chapters focus on the earliest pottery from Japan, Southwest Asia, North Africa, Southern and Western Europe, Lowland and Highland South America, Mesoamerica, and the American Southeast and Southwest. Although there is an unevenness in depth of coverage, the editors maintain consistency in chronology (radiometric dates) and geographical terminology. The editors' introductory review is compelling, as are three enlightening essays about emerging prestige technologies, social strategies, and the invention of pottery. The narratives are supplemented by 71 illustrations, 17 tables, and a five-page index; each chapter has a separate bibliography. This essential volume is a significant contribution to understanding the development of pottery technology and can serve well as a text or reference work for readers at all levels.—*C. C. Kolb, National Endowment for the Humanities*

OAB-1854   DS523   95-39223 CIP
Higham, Charles. **The bronze age of Southeast Asia.** Cambridge, 1996. 381p bibl index ISBN 0-521-49660-8, $74.95; ISBN 0-521-56505-7 pbk, $27.95

From eastern India to the islands of Southeast Asia, and from northern China to the coastal regions of Thailand, Higham's book offers the finest synthesis of the archaeological cultures of Southeast Asia. Covering the Neolithic to the Iron Age, Higham treats the importance and spread of rice cultivation in the hands of Austroasiatic speakers, and the origins and spread of bronze technology in each of the regions reviewed. The author makes reasoned attempts to reconstruct the nature of the social order from materials recovered from settlements and cemeteries. A final chapter is comparative and attempts to place the archaeology of this region into a global perspective. The book is well illustrated with numerous line drawings and photographs, and contains an excellent bibliography and index. An indispensable work for those interested in archaeology at all levels.—*C. C. Lamberg-Karlovsky, Harvard University*

OAB-1855   E78   95-32510 CIP
Hucknell, Bruce B. **Of marshes and maize: preceramic agricultural**

settlements in the Cienega Valley, southeastern Arizona. Arizona, 1995. 166p bibl index afp (Anthropological papers of the University of Arizona, 59) ISBN 0-8165-1582-4 pbk, $12.95

Hucknell reports on excavations, undertaken in 1983, of deeply buried archaeological deposits in southeastern Arizona along a tributary valley of Cienega Creek. The deposits date to the first millennium BCE and extend to the first centuries CE, a time traditionally treated as part of the late Archaic. Although known to archaeologists for many years, the prehistoric occupations represented here are remarkable for their preservation and for the wealth of material that was recovered. Analyses of the paleoethnobotanical, osteological, and artifactual materials demonstrate a degree of dependence on cultivated plants that heretofore has been unexpected. This is one of the best monographs published on Southwestern archaeology; it combines primary information on the excavations with detailed analyses and the evaluation of interpretive models. Hucknell not only makes a significant contribution to the dating of early prehistoric agriculture in the Southwest but also examines questions regarding systematics, the relationship between agriculture and sedentism, and the environmental circumstances that may have favored early preceramic agricultural communities in the Southwest. Remarkably free of technical jargon, this study is recommended not only to archaeologists interested in the origins and development of agriculture and agriculturally based societies but also for students at the undergraduate level and above.—*M. W. Graves, University of Hawaii at Manoa*

OAB-1856   GN871   91-23105 CIP
Irwin, Geoffrey. **The prehistoric exploration and colonisation of the Pacific.** Cambridge, 1992. 240p bibl index ISBN 0-521-40371-5, $49.95

Irwin's study is, quite simply, one of the best books written within the past ten years on the archaeology of the Pacific. Its focus is on the questions of how, where, and when the islands of the Pacific were colonized during prehistoric times. This has been a perennial issue for Pacific archaeologists and historians, and has been the subject of a number of controversies regarding the timing, the direction, and the manner in which Pacific Islands were first discovered and settled. Irwin develops a general model for how the islands were discovered and then tests the model against archaeological evidence pertaining to the sequence and timing of discovery in Melanesia, Polynesia, and Micronesia. As with most efforts on this scale, there are problems with the adequacy of the data used to test the model. Nonetheless, the model provides archaeologists with a series of hypotheses that can be more rigorously tested throughout the Pacific. This is a book that should interest a wide audience, and fortunately, it is written in a style accessible to the nonspecialist as well as the professional. General; undergraduate; graduate; faculty.—*M. W. Graves, University of Hawaii at Manoa*

OAB-1857   E78   95-36754 CIP
O'Brien, Michael J. **Paradigms of the past: the story of Missouri archaeology.** Missouri, 1996. 561p bibl index afp ISBN 0-8262-1019-8 pbk, $29.95

O'Brien's book is ostensibly a history of archaeology in the state of Missouri, but it is more than that, because the story is set within the evolution of American archaeology as it emerged over more than 100 years. Readers will discover the factors that drove archaeology nationally, seen through their impact on the doing of archaeology in Missouri, a technique that permits in-depth exploration of sites and analyses of artifacts through time. O'Brien begins in the 19th century, with the first appearance of professional archaeologists. He shows how the discipline solidified between 1911 and 1940, and changed after WW II. The development of the new archaeology c.1960 had little effect on Missouri archaeology at first, but in the 1970s and '80s, environmental studies and the demands of cultural resource management brought Missouri archaeology more in line with the rest of the country. The final portion of the book contains an excellent discussion of "evolutionary" approaches championed by the author. A superb overview with plenty of modern method and theory. Highly recommended. All levels.—*W. A. Longacre, University of Arizona*

OAB-1858   F1435   93-29587 CIP
Reents-Budet, Dorie. **Painting the Maya Universe: royal ceramics of the classic period.** Duke University, 1994. 381p bibl index afp ISBN 0-8223-1434-7, $75.00; ISBN 0-8223-1438-X pbk, $39.95

Reents-Budet and her collaborators have produced an exemplary study of elite Maya painted pottery of the classic period. Interdisciplinary at heart, *Painting the Maya Universe* weds art historical insights with linguistic analyses of the hieroglyphic texts and empirical observations from the chemical analysis of pottery samples. Thematically organized, the book discusses the aesthetic and cultural dimensions of painting, the social functions of pottery pieces, the pictorial themes found on ceramic surfaces, the roles and identities of elite pottery painters, and the benefits of responsible collection and preservation practices. In a chapter on calligraphy, Reents-Budet and epigrapher Barbara MacLeod explore the linguistic content of painted glyphs, focusing on the semantics and sociopolitical contents of the primary standard sequence. The two authors are joined by archaeologist Ronald L. Bishop in a discussion of neutron activation analysis, a technique that allows researchers to analyze ancient pottery and draw conclusions on the subjects of material sources, workshop sites, and production relations. Lavishly illustrated with photographs by Justin Kerr, the book also contains a catalog of a traveling exhibition that grew out of this research. Highly recommended for all levels.—*C. Hendrickson, Marlboro College*

OAB-1859   GN281   96-37718 CIP
Stringer, Christopher. **African exodus: the origins of modern humanity,** by Christopher Stringer and Robin McKie. H. Holt, 1997 (c1996). 282p index afp ISBN 0-8050-2759-9, $25.00

Stringer, a researcher at the Natural History Museum in London, and McKie, science editor for the (London) *Observer*, have produced an excellent and highly readable account of the evolution of Homo sapiens. Stringer has long championed the theory that holds that modern humans emerged in Africa some 100,000 years ago and then spread out across the globe, essentially replacing all other human populations. Thus, he challenges the commonly held assumption that the species evolved in separate locations but along parallel tracks over the course of a million years or more. The debate between proponents of the diametrically opposed positions has been heated and acrimonious. Stringer and McKie weave personal anecdotes into a no-holds-barred account of how paleoanthropologists come to know what they think they know about the past. The authors use paleontological, archaeological, and molecular (DNA) data to support their position, in the process demonstrating more genetic similarity between, say, an Eskimo and a Bantu than between two mountain gorillas from the same jungle. The book will interest anthropologists, but the writing style and easy presentation ensure nonspecialists instant access to the argument. The 55 illustrations are well done; the index is thorough and very helpful. All levels.—*M. J. O'Brien, University of Missouri—Columbia*

■ Social & Cultural

OAB-1860   HQ1793   91-39685 CIP
Abu-Lughod, Lila. **Writing women's worlds: Bedouin stories.** California, 1993. 266p bibl afp ISBN 0-520-07946-9, $30.00

In this beautifully written book, Abu-Lughod, an Arab American anthropologist, presents stories, anecdotes, and reminiscences she recorded in the course of her research on women in a small Bedouin community in western Egypt. Collected from a handful of kinswomen, these diverse narratives are skillfully edited and rearranged by Abu-Lughod to illustrate the dynamics of such patriarchal institutions as patrilineality, polygyny, and arranged marriages and their impact on the lives of individual men and women. More than just providing the reader with a look into the private lives of Bedouin women, these stories are meant to demonstrate the shortcomings of anthropological and feminist theory and the politics of ethnograpic representation. These issues are fully addressed in the book's lengthy and skillfully argued introductory essay in which the author crit-

ically assesses the role of the anthropologist in creating and maintaining the myth of the culturally distinct "Other." An important contribution to the study of culture theory, gender ideologies, and Arab society. Advanced undergraduate; graduate; faculty.—*A. Rassam, Queens College, CUNY*

OAB-1861   HQ1090   96-18532 CIP
Almeida, Miguel Vale de. **The hegemonic male: masculinity in a Portuguese town.** Berghahn Books, 1996. 186p bibl index afp (New directions in anthropology, 4) ISBN 1-57181-888-X, $45.00; ISBN 1-57181-891-X pbk, $16.50

Almeida has produced a stimulating and skillfully crafted book on the construction of masculinity in the village of Pardais in southern Portugal. Located in a region experiencing profound social and economic transformation, Paradais reflects processes and adaptations common to much of Portugal, although the author is sensitive to class-specific factors. In Pardais the masculine/feminine divide is not linear, but goes through mutations according to age, social class, and changes in prestige. Masculinity is constantly in the process of being constructed and confirmed; femininity, however, is seen as a permanent essence—at least by males. In short, men are always striving to meet a cultural model of male domination that includes marriage, heterosexuality, an ethic of work, and an enforced male sociability. "Male hegemony" represents a lived consensus that not only subordinates women, but also silences the diversity of masculine voices. This masculinity is in part constructed and reproduced by the division of labor and class stratification, but it is also the product of socialization in the family and school, the loci where notions of person, body, emotions, and sentiments are acquired. An important contribution to gender studies and to the anthropology of Europe.—*O. Pi-Sunyer, University of Massachusetts at Amherst*

OAB-1862   GN635   92-18043 CIP
Barth, Fredrik. **Balinese worlds.** Chicago, 1003. 370p bibl index afp ISBN 0-226-03833-5, $55.00; ISBN 0-226-03834-3 pbk, $19.95

Barth's stimulating, thought-provoking work challenges anthropologists to approach the study of complex civilizations from a new perspective, one that does not reify abstracted values and norms paradigms, but rather ferrets out and analyzes "...how the [cultural] features are generated in the behavior of the actors." Barth's clear, well-written study, based on original fieldwork in northern Bali, is a major theoretical contribution to Bali studies. Barth focuses on the differing nature and manifestations in seven villages of five aspects of culture: Bali-Hinduism, Islam, nagara/Bali-Aga ritual-political institutions, modernization, and sorcery. The deepest description and analysis centers on two villages, one of which is Islamic, the other Bali-Hindu. Barth offers partially overlapping data but a different theoretical focus from Unni Wikan's *Managing Turbulent Hearts: A Balinese Formula for Living* (CH, Oct'91). Many will debate Barth's approach, but it will be the foundation of a major stream of anthropological analyses in the decades to come. Map, black-and-white photographs, good bibliography. Essential for all Southeast Asia collections. Advanced undergraduate; graduate; faculty.—*L. A. Kimball, Western Washington University*

OAB-1863   RA461   92-53602 CIP
Bastien, Joseph W. **Drum and stethoscope: integrating ethnomedicine and biomedicine in Bolivia.** Utah, 1992. 266p bibl index afp ISBN 0-87480-386-1, $34.95

As the title indicates, this is a case study of efforts to integrate folk medicine (ethnomedicine) and scientific medicine (biomedicine) in Bolivia. But it is much more, perhaps because of the special qualifications of the author, an anthropologist with long-term interests and substantial work experience in delivering primary health care to the rural and urban poor of Bolivia, who also has a thorough knowledge of this problem worldwide. Bastien cogently assesses the deficiencies of scientific medicine for solving all the problems in extending primary health care to all persons. He discusses the risks and benefits of using folk medicine for this purpose, describes the particular cultural contexts in which efforts to use folk medical specialists to extend primary health care have been attempted, and comments on proposed strategies for joint use of scientific and folk therapies. Bastien makes comparisons with relevant studies in other parts of the world and offers numerous citations of other scholarly works. The bibliography is excellent and the author's acknowledgement of the help of others is generous. This well-written book is a superb example of how scholarly and applied research should coexist. Advanced undergraduate; graduate; faculty; professional.—*R. Provencher, Northern Illinois University*

OAB-1864   DR1674   95-18059 CIP
Bringa, Tone. **Being Muslim the Bosnian way: identity and community in a central Bosnian village.** Princeton, 1995. 281p bibl index afp ISBN 0-691-03453-2, $49.50; ISBN 0-691-00175-8 pbk, $17.95

Bringa's excellent and well-documented ethnography is especially important in the context of current genocide being committed against Bosnian Muslims. The author analyzes the many ways that Bosnian Muslims refract Islam in the cultural contexts of what used to be Yugoslavia and is now the nation-state of Bosnia-Herzegovina. She argues convincingly that being Muslim in Bosnia referred and still refers to a concept of secular nationhood as well as religious identity. The tolerance that the subjects she studies exhibited toward non-Muslim neighbors and friends is especially noteworthy. Bringa's analysis of the role of women in the family as well as national and religious structures is also important. She portrays Bosnian Muslim women as the bearers of cultural identity as well as civilization. This book is unique in its ethnographic treatment of a neglected people, and serves to supplement the anthropologist Akbar S. Ahmed's goals and treatment of Islam in *Living Islam* (London, 1993), as well as Noel Malcolm's treatment of Bosnian Muslim national identity in *Bosnia: A Short History* (CH, Apr'95). Superb bibliography, excellent glossary, and detailed notes. Should be required reading for students of Bosnia at all levels.—*S. G. Mestroviċ Texas A&M University*

OAB-1865   HQ76   95-6244 CIP
Carrier, Joseph. **De los otros: intimacy and homosexuality among Mexican men.** Columbia, 1995. 231p bibl index afp ISBN 0-231-09692-5, $39.50; ISBN 0-231-09693-3 pbk, $16.50

Carrier has presented a major, groundbreaking study. Since beginning his graduate work in 1968, the author (an English- and Spanish-speaking gay anthropologist) has been a participant observer, conducting structured and unstructured interviews with men who have sex with other men in northwestern Mexico, especially the city of Guadalajara. Carrier entered graduate school after completing work as a counterinsurgency specialist in South Vietnam for the Rand Corporation, who fired him, at age 40, when they learned that he was gay. Because of his sexual orientation, he was able to gather data (first for his PhD dissertation, later for a series of articles and this book) that heterosexual anthropologists probably could not acquire. This information throws considerable light on actions that although a taboo in a culture are nevertheless engaged in, and on the various ways that participants and nonparticipants conceptualize that behavior. Carrier's findings will be very helpful to culture theorists, as well as to AIDS workers who need information about sexuality among Mexican males. All levels.—*R. W. Smith, California State University, Northridge*

OAB-1866   BL2211   94-26158 MARC
Ceremony and ritual in Japan: religious practices in an industrialized society, ed. by Jan van Bremen and D.P. Martinez. Routledge, 1995. 268p bibl index ISBN 0-415-11663-5, $69.95

This brief volume of essays is a gold mine of thoughtful insight into contemporary Japanese life. From Robert Smith's opening article on tradition to Augustin Berque's concluding essay on "the rituals of urbanity," there is solid meat here. Although some contributions presume sophisticated knowledge of Japan, most are accessible to serious newcomers yet bring to light new and useful material for specialists. Complementing Byron Earhart's *Japanese Religion:*

Unity in Diversity (CH, Sep'74) and Ian Reader's *Religion in Contemporary Japan* (CH, Feb'92), clearly the two best introductions, the essays here provide an exploration of the nature of contemporary religious life in Japan that is outstanding in its depth. The Bachnik essay on belief versus practice is especially important as a trenchant corrective to the superficial perception that the Japanese are not religious. Bachnik's ideas are neatly and persuasively reinforced by the Kalland essay on a Shinto parade. Martinez's discussion of women and ritual again challenges stereotypes and stereotypical analysis. Ian Reader's and Joy Hendry's essays are very specific examples of the role of rituals in what Westerners would call the sacred and the secular spheres of life, and they show how the lines between them blur in Japan. The collection brings together contributions from many of the leading scholars of religion and culture, Japanese, European, and American, in an unusually effective and helpful mix. Copious notes and extensive bibliographic material. Highly recommended for all levels.—*J. H. Bailey, Earlham College*

OAB-1867   E78   92-16201 CIP
Cleland, Charles E. **Rites of conquest: the history and culture of Michigan's Native Americans.** Michigan, 1992. 333p bibl index ISBN 0-472-09447-5, $45.00

In the past decade the move toward accurate and more definitive ethnohistorical reports about the Native American peoples of the East and Midwest has received considerable attention. This book is a valuable and important addition to the literature that develops understanding of the prehistoric and contemporary indigenous groups living in the Great Lakes region. Cleland skillfully blends historical information with folklore vignettes about and by Indians and non-Indians. The reader is provided with considerable insight into the thought processes and historical forces that motivated French, British, and American policy toward Native Americans for the first 300 years of contact. The six excellent maps provide visual images of the tribes surrounding the Great Lakes from 1600 to 1840. An extensive 22-page bibliography is included. Recommended for scholars and for all interested in the fortunes and misfortunes of Native American citizens. General; undergraduate; graduate; faculty; professional.—*N. C. Greenberg, emeritus, Western Michigan University*

OAB-1868   Orig
Clemmer, Richard O. **Roads in the sky: the Hopi Indians in a century of change.** Westview, 1995. 377p bibl index afp ISBN 0-8133-8538-5, $55.00; ISBN 0-8133-2511-0 pbk, $19.95

With the publication of this valuable ethnohistory, Clemmer (Univ. of Denver) brings to conclusion more than 25 years of research, writing, and thinking about the Hopi of northeastern Arizona. This study chronicles the last 100 years of Hopi history and more. The author introduces the subject with an excellent first chapter that examines Hopi prophecy within the context of seemingly incompatible systems theory of modern social science. As close to a Hopi perspective as a non-Hopi scholar can come, Clemmer concentrates his analysis of the people's struggle with modernity through six major themes in recent Hopi history: the "Oraibi split," the Indian Reorganization Act of 1934, the rise of a political movement known as "traditionalism," energy development during the 1960s, the Hopi-Navajo land dispute, and the plundering of sacred ceremonial objects over the last century. It is well for people to remember, Clemmer concludes, that the Hopi possess a history that stretches back for more than a thousand years. The Hopi approach their future with vast cultural resources upon which to draw. This work will prove indispensable for students of American Indian ethnohistory. All levels.—*L. G. Moses, Oklahoma State University*

OAB-1869   F2230   96-12955 CIP
Descola, Philippe. **The spears of twilight: life and death in the Amazon jungle,** tr. by Janet Lloyd. New Press, NY, 1996. 459p bibl index ISBN 1-56584-228-6, $25.00

Decola's beautifully written book combines a remarkably detailed account of the contemporary ethnography of the Achuar (Jivaro) Indians of southeastern

Ecuador and their relations with neighboring peoples, with one of the best available accounts of how an anthropologist learns about an alien culture. As ethnography, it is thorough, albeit unorthodox, in organization. The major categories of religion, social organization, economy, health, dreams, symbolism, gender, drugs, ethnicity, and death are all given insightful explication—not in a didactic manner under separate headings, but in a way that reflects the gradual learning process that is integral to the ethnographic enterprise. It is through unexceptional specific events, as they unfold in the repetitious lives of individuals, that patterns, systems, and norms emerge—at least to the mind of an observer who is trained and sensitive to subtle cues, analogies, dialectics, and cross-cultural comparisons. Footnotes or endnotes are omitted in the interest of a smooth and continuous exposition, but the expository bibliography compensates in part. There is a glossary, a good index, a few maps and photographs, and an appendix on the art and science of ethnography. An unusual and excellent book, appropriate for a broad range of readers.—*D. B. Heath, Brown University*

OAB-1870   BL2530   92-53625 CIP
Desmangles, Leslie G. **The faces of the Gods: vodou and Roman Catholicism in Haiti.** North Carolina, 1992. 218p bibl index afp ISBN 0-8078-2059-8, $32.50; ISBN 0-8078-4393-8 pbk, $12.95

An accessible, comprehensive overview of the folk religion of Haiti known as Vodou that takes into account the tremendous variety of religious forms as well as outside influences on the religion. The author (a Haitian native) draws on his original ethnographic research in Haiti and the African Republic of Benin to give a clear and lucid exposition on a topic of considerable popular and scholarly interest. Desmangles carefully describes the historical events in Haiti that caused Vodou to incorporate ethnic religious traditions from diverse regions of Africa and gives special attention to the nature and directions of syncretism as well as the process of "symbiosis." He stresses the uniqueness of Vodou as a religion, noting that many aspects of the religion bear little or no resemblance to European or African religious traditions. Many unique elements of Vodou are accounted for in terms of recent political struggles of the Haitian people. Chapters 3 through 5 are outstanding. Chapter 3 contains an impressive attempt to relate Vodou mythology and individual experience, while chapters 4 and 5 focus on the relationships between the *Ioa* (Vodou gods) and the Catholic saints. Desmangles is to be commended for providing so much background information in a comparatively brief book. Vital for students of African American and Caribbean religions, but also of interest to anthropologists, political scientists, and historians of religion. Highly recommended. General; advanced undergraduate.—*S. D. Glazier, University of Nebraska at Kearney*

OAB-1871   DU740   94-45532 CIP
Errington, Frederick K. **Articulating change in the "last unknown,"** by Frederick K. Errington and Deborah B. Gewertz. Westview, 1995. 196p bibl index afp ISBN 0-8133-2453-X, $59.95; ISBN 0-8133-2454-8 pbk, $19.95

In this book, Errington and Gewertz present vignettes of the historical changes being experienced by the people of Karavar Island in East New Britain Province, Papua New Guinea. Missionization, pacification, "cargo cults," local economic development, national identity, involvement in national politics, and tourism all occur as events grounded in local contexts and biographies. The authors provide a rich account of the concerns and choices of Karavar men—women are, in this book, unrepresented—taking stock of outside powers and their own options. This book sets a new standard in Pacific ethnography for representing historical processes as local realities yet, at the same time, as part of more general structural change. It is, for the most part, clearly written and useful for undergraduates as well as graduate students and faculty.—*J. Kirkpatrick, SMS Research*

OAB-1872   DX115   92-5452 CIP
Fraser, Angus. **The Gypsies.** B. Blackwell, 1992. 359p bibl index afp ISBN 0-631-15967-3, $24.95

The best general book on Gypsies available. J.P. Clébert's *The Gypsies* (1963) is rife with errors of both fact and interpretation and is poorly regarded by most Gypsy scholars. Fraser's work is, first of all, a history of the Gypsies from their origin in India sometime prior to 1000 CE to their current persecution in the newly democratized states of Eastern Europe. At the same time, the book constitutes a sort of extended bibliographic essay, evaluating and placing into context a great portion of the literature, both ancient and modern, now accumulated on the subject. Fraser, knighted for his career as a British civil servant, is not an academic, but he is an excellent scholar. Though no fieldworker, he knows the literature on Gypsies, especially the earlier materials, like very few others. Unfortunately, the work is restricted almost entirely to Europe (there are only two pages on the large Gypsy population of the US and nothing but a passing mention on those in the Middle East, Latin America, and elsewhere). Nevertheless, this book is a solid introduction for general readers and a valuable bibliographic tool for scholars. All levels.—*W. G. Lockwood, University of Michigan*

OAB-1873   GR385   92-11319 CIP
Gillison, Gillian. **Between culture and fantasy: a New Guinea highlands mythology.** Chicago, 1993. 392p bibl index afp ISBN 0-226-29380-7, $60.00; ISBN 0-226-29381-5 pbk, $22.50

In her remarkably imaginative book Gillison rethinks the meanings of procreation myths in the New Guinea highlands. Whereas other ethnographies have often dismissed such procreation myths because they are biologically false, Gillison does not. Nor does she focus on practices or rituals taken to be "real" and to represent "reality." Instead, she incorporates ritual into her exploration of Gimi myth and imagination, providing ample evidence that it belongs there. In this way, she avoids the all too common polarity between myth and ritual (thought versus action). She also argues that more than conscious kinship patterns or rituals, it is myths (the secret of the bamboo flutes) and their unconscious meanings that allow for an understanding of New Guinea highland societies. Exceptionally well written, Gillison's book is an exemplary study that uses rich ethnographic materials to reconceptualize the old categories of myth and ritual and to convey a vivid portrayal of the Gimi imagination. General readers, advanced undergraduates, and above.—*B. Kilborne, California Institute of the Arts*

OAB-1874   F3722   93-13838 CIP
Hendricks, Janet Wall. **To drink of death: the narrative of a Shuar warrior.** Arizona, 1993. 316p bibl index afp ISBN 0-8165-1353-8, $35.00

Hendricks has analyzed a 2,051-stanza life history recounted by Tukap', one of the last warrior headmen of the Shuar (also known as Jivaro) of the southeast Ecuadorian lowlands. The tract begins with 50 pages of free translation. The next 200 pages are a detailed exegesis, employing discourse analysis, of the literal translation of the text. Although the tonality cannot be reproduced in English, the oral format is maintained, helping to preserve the poetic quality of the original presentation. Textual annotation examines formal and situational contexts (expressive, referential, paralinguistic, and cultural). Tukap's discourse is an instance of Shuar political rhetoric, a treatise on warfare and feuding, where the local belief system justifies and perpetuates an ideology of violence. His speech illuminates the concept of power associated with physical strength, visionary knowledge, courage in protecting and avenging family members, and the capacity to endure the hardships of warfare. This study is an important contribution to anthropological poetics and discourse analysis, as well as a unique ethnographic document and a rare example of Shuar oral literature. Good ethnographic and methodological bibliography, short section of endnotes, five illustrations, and a solid index. Upper-division undergraduates and above.—*D. L. Browman, Washington University*

OAB-1875   F1465   95-7296 CIP
Hendrickson, Carol. **Weaving identities: construction of dress and self in a highland Guatemala town.** Texas, 1995. 245p bibl index afp ISBN 0-292-73099-3, $35.00; ISBN 0-292-73100-0 pbk, $15.95

Hendrickson's study is the best ethnographic analysis of a bi-ethnic (Mayaladino) Guatemalan highland town (Tecpán) to date, demonstrating how cloth (the *traje* or traditional Mayan costume) represents core community values involved in political, economic, religious, artistic, and ethnic events. Based on fieldwork in the 1980s and '90s, this study has more depth than previous studies, e.g., Sheldon Annis's *God and Production in a Guatemalan Town* (CH, Sep'88). Hendrickson sees the *traje* as *active*, i.e., worn in association with Western clothing styles (jeans and shirts), yet an enduring cultural object that survives despite intense social change. Using Fernand Braudel's concepts, Hendrickson organizes this work into three areas: geography as a measure of time, with the *traje* representing continuous municipal identity contrasted with non-Indian (Western) dress; social time (regular patterns are repeated throughout human memory), with the *traje* variations (generational changes of skirts and blouses) worn at annual social and religious events such as parades and fiestas; and "traditional history" time, in which local historical events are isolated from wider aspects of social life. Useful glossary and 56 photos, tables, and figures. Upper-division undergraduates and above.—*B. B. Chico, Regis University*

OAB-1876   GN635   92-45143 CIP

Hickey, Gerald Cannon. **Shattered world: adaptation and survival among Vietnam's highland peoples during the Vietnam war.** Pennsylvania, 1993. 297p index afp ISBN 0-8122-3172-4, $34.95; ISBN 0-8122-1417-X pbk, $14.95

It is rare to find a work on Vietnam, especially on its 20th-century wars, that does not mention the peoples of the highlands, collectively known as Montagnards. To date, however, there has been no brief and readily accessible work that examines those peoples directly and in their own right, or that takes account of the diversity of their cultures. This study accomplishes both aims admirably. It presents ethnographic material on ten of the Montagnard groups: the Rhade, Roglai, Chru, Stieng, Katu, Bru, Pacoh, Sedang, Jeh, and Halang. Separate chapters treat specific aspects of the culture of each of these groups, discussing such dimensions of their lives as family and kinship, religion, the physical characteristics of village layout and dwelling architecture, marriage practices, social organization and leadership, and economic activity. These individual discussions are linked by considerations of historical development and the impact of the Vietnam wars. Hickey concludes that, in many cases, the culture of these peoples was altered or irreparably damaged not only by the impact of US activities from the 1960s through the '70s, but also by the policies of the communist regime after 1975. A brief bibliographic essay provides useful information for further study. General readers; undergraduates and above.—*C. L. Yates, Earlham College*

OAB-1877   DS632   92-31669 CIP

Hoskins, Janet. **The play of time: Kodi perspectives on calendars, history, and exchange.** California, 1994 (c1993). 414p bibl index afp ISBN 0-520-08003-3, $42.00

The first full study of the Kodi (Sumba Island, Eastern Indonesia), Hoskins's work is based on more than four years of fieldwork, 1979-88. Broader than Joel Kuipers's *Power in Performance* (CH, Mar'91), Hoskins's book includes key ritual texts in Kodi with parallel English translations. Further, her analysis of the traditional Kodi calendar is a major contribution to archaeoastronomy. Hoskins focuses on three main themes: First is complexity of the past, through which she counterpoints European historical contact with the Kodi against the Kodi worldview of time, calendar, and objects as history. Second is time and value, through which Hoskins describes how "time is involved in the constitution of value ..." for both the individual lifespan and for the generations-long durational family and village. Third is the impact of Indonesian modernization. The concluding critique assesses profound epistomological and conceptual issues arising in anthropology because European concepts of time and history have tacitly been taken as universals. Black-and-white photographs, maps, bibliography, good index. Essential for all Southeast Asian and archaeoastronomical collections. Upper-division undergraduates and above.—*L. A. Kimball, Western Washington University*

OAB-1878   HQ693   92-26360 CIP

Jeater, Diana. **Marriage, perversion, and power: the construction of moral discourse in southern Rhodesia, 1894-1930.** Oxford, 1993. 281p bibl index ISBN 0-19-820379-9, $72.00

An intriguing title; a compelling book. Jeater has chosen a small corner of colonial Africa in which to examine the introduction or, more often, the imposition, of new roles, behaviors, and laws associated with sexual activity. Her impressive use of sources, including court cases, interviews, and company records, reveals the complex interplay of shifting values, new economic structures, and gender definition in the Gwelo District of southern Rhodesia. Each factor contributes to a new and changing moral discourse. Rural cultivators and urban migrants, men and women, each began to rethink the proper relations between the sexes. The introduced values of "civilized marriage" and "Christian morality" were seldom adopted wholesale, but they clearly did alter traditional practice. This book is a significant addition to the growing field of gender studies in Africa and also offers new insights into colonial society. Advanced undergraduate; graduate; faculty.—*J. A. Works Jr., University of Missouri-St. Louis*

OAB-1879   HT720   94-38588 CIP

Kapadia, Karin. **Siva and her sisters: gender, caste, and class in rural South India.** Westview, 1995. 269p bibl index afp ISBN 0-8133-8158-4, $50.00

Focusing on the experiences and attitudes of "untouchables" and women in Tamilnadu, Kapadia questions Louis Dumont's emphasis (in *Homo Hierarchicus*, 1974) on Hindu cultural consensus and the view that a "validation of hierarchic values is provided by lower-caste religion." Rather, Kapadia argues, "lower castes do not share upper-caste assumptions regarding ritual purity," and "the very understanding of what inauspiciousness and impurity are differs considerably between the Brahminical castes and the Non-Brahmins." Kapadia places her analysis of gender and caste firmly within the changing social contexts of kinship, marriage, ritual, and rural female labor, and she demonstrates the negative implications that class mobility may have for women in the rural economy. She concludes by noting that the "fall in women's status is, arguably, the most fundamental change taking place in the current transformation of rural Tamilnadu," and "it is in those impoverished castes in which very little economic differentiation has occurred ... that women's high status has, in large measure, remained intact." This meticulously researched, elegant analysis is highly recommended for upper-division undergraduates and above.—*B. Tavakolian, Denison University*

OAB-1880   HF3882   95-51427 CIP

Kapchan, Deborah A. **Gender on the market: Moroccan women and the revoicing of tradition.** Pennsylvania, 1996. 325p bibl indexes afp ISBN 0-8122-3155-4, $42.50; ISBN 0-8122-1426-9 pbk, $19.95

Kapchan's splendid ethnographic study of women's performance genres in Beni Mellal, Morocco, is an outstanding contribution to gender studies and to the understanding of Middle Eastern society. Its contribution to the already substantial literature on Morocco is greater than the book's title might imply. Through the idiom of social performances, Kapchan paints a vivid picture of the changing domains of household and family. In its examination of women's discourse, her study stands with Lila Abu Lughod's much acclaimed *Writing Women's Worlds* (CH, Apr'93). Kapchan's book offers a rare insight into changing public roles of women, as illustrated by the movement of women into previously male domains of the market and public performance. She focuses on the speech, aspirations, and behavior of female vendors, herbalists, and musicians—the *shikhat*. Through their voices, readers can sense the interplay of religion, family, and even the search for economic advantage. The writing is personal yet objective, and quite apart from the study's ethnographic substance, the reader gains an appreciation of the author's approach to fieldwork. This book will be useful to a broad audience, including those concerned with discourse analysis, the anthropology of gender, and the contemporary Middle East and North Africa. Upper-division undergraduates and above.—*D. G. Bates, CUNY Hunter College*

OAB-1881   GN388   94-21100 CIP
Kelly, Robert L. **The foraging spectrum: diversity in hunter-gatherer lifeways.** Smithsonian Institution Press, 1995. 446p bibl index afp ISBN 1-56098-465-1, $60.00; ISBN 1-56098-466-X pbk, $24.95

Kelly's book is one of the best and most comprehensive treatments of hunter-gatherer studies since publication of *Man the Hunter*, ed. by Richard Lee and Irven Devore (CH, Sep'69). Much of Kelly's work is devoted to evaluating the progress that has been made in hunter-gatherer studies since 1968. His main goal is to review what anthropology has learned about the variability among ethnographically known hunter-gatherers. A critical element in this review is Kelly's emphasis on continuous variation within and among hunter-gatherer cultures. He cautions against the uncritical use of "typological" thinking. Using the concepts of behavioral ecology, he investigates factors conditioning hunter-gatherer subsistence, demography, and social organization. Kelly (Univ. of Louisville) finds that these aspects of society are conditioned to a significant degree by ecological factors through a variety of biobehavioral feedback mechanisms. This well-written tome is rife with theory and the data to evaluate it. Technically, it is well constructed and easy to use. It should be highly useful to upper-division undergraduates, graduate students, and practicing professionals.—*M. S. Sheehan, Northwestern State University*

OAB-1882   DS632   93-19776 CIP
Kipp, Rita Smith. **Dissociated identities: ethnicity, religion, and class in an Indonesian society.** Michigan, 1993. 304p bibl index afp ISBN 0-472-10412-8, $55.00

In this clear account of changing forms of identity in northern Sumatra, Indonesia, Kipp combines an ethnographic account of one society, the Karo, with a theoretical analysis of how state-society interactions shape ideas of ethnic and religious identity. The scholarship is superb and the overviews of current comparative literature make the book highly accessible to students and teachers as well as to experts on the topic or area. Kipp demonstrates that the idea of a "Karo people" emerged from the encounter of Karo groups with colonial authorities. She then shows how, since Indonesian independence, Karo have become increasingly differentiated by religion (Islam, Prostestant, or neither), by class, and by location in village, town, or city. Karo have created a public sphere of ethnic discourse and relegated religion to a private sphere, making it easier for them to continue social relationships across religions. But the kinship ties and ethnic associations designed to foster Karo solidarity have themselves been cross-cut by class differences, leaving their identities "dissociated." Undergraduates and above.—*J. R. Bowen, Washington University*

OAB-1883   E99   92-557 CIP
Levy, Jerrold E. **Orayvi revisited: social stratification in an "egalitarian" society.** School of American Research Press, 1992. 198p bibl index ISBN 0-933452-33-0, $35.00

The traditional view of Hopi social organization is that of a peaceful, cooperative, and egalitarian society. Yet anthropologists have recognized long-standing feuds and covert rankings within their social structure. Levy examines this disparity in detail, relying on a strong database of early research, combined with his own field work. Chapter 2—"Prehistory and Social Structure"—is required reading for an understanding of succeeding chapters. Levy succinctly presents the basis for the Hopi dichotomy: outwardly nonaggressive people living in a divisive cultural environment. Centered on the historic split at Oraibi (1906) that led to the establishment of other villages, Levy's study assiduously discusses the divisiveness that permeates Hopi culture. This includes a hierarchical stratification based on clan ranking, land ownership, lineage, and ceremonial stratification. The conclusion does not sully the earlier concept but it does present an excellent analysis of Hopi life that ultimately gives readers a deeper understanding of this long-surviving culture. Indeed, by examining long-held "truths," then scrutinizing their validity through the lens of past and present data, Levy's result is a classic example of outstanding research. Recommended. Advanced undergraduate; graduate; faculty; professional.—*F. G. Bock, California Polytechnic State University, San Luis Obispo*

OAB-1884   F1219   93-47401 CIP
López Luján, Leonardo. **The offerings of the templo mayor of Tenochtitlan.** University Press of Colorado, 1994. 516p bibl index afp ISBN 0-87081-318-8, $39.95

When the Spanish conquered the Aztec capital, Tenochtitlan, they leveled the tall temples and other sacred buildings to construct their own Mexico City. The thick rubble and fill preserved the bases of Aztec structures, which were exposed during subway construction and other projects in 1978-89. Outstanding discoveries included many kinds of ritual offerings that the Aztecs had placed during and after temple construction. The first part of the book describes the careful fieldwork, systematic recording, and analyses that show that the offerings were not random but were deposited in an ordered manner for a variety of purposes. Subsequent sections consist of an interdisciplinary study of the context and associations of more than 100 such patterned offerings that begin to reveal the thoughts behind the acts, to penetrate the "symbolic-mythical-magical-religious world" of the Aztecs. Especially impressive is the correlation of the archaeological record with the rich Aztec and early Spanish manuscript sources on Aztec history, ritual, and religion. Applications of theory and statistical method are clearly described. Appendixes record the offerings in descriptive detail. A remarkable work, highly recommended for upper-division undergraduates and above.—*K. A. Dixon, California State University, Long Beach*

OAB-1885   95-68695 Orig
Lutkehaus, Nancy C. **Zaria's fire: engendered moments in Manam ethnography.** Carolina Academic, 1995. 490p bibl index ISBN 0-89089-800-6, $65.00

Lutkehaus's study is an extradordinarily rich and detailed ethnographic work on a Melanesian people with very original features. Her contemporary ethnography is closely linked to the 1930s work on the same people by Camilla Wedgwood, a Cambridge-trained social anthropologist whose career reveals much about the formative years of British anthropology. Lutkehaus thus manages quite gracefully to keep a number of very interesting balls in the air. This volume is a tour de force of reflexive anthropology in which the conditions of its own production, both personal and disciplinary, are interestingly explored, while the people themselves—the Manam islanders—are given equal and full attention. The ethnography itself is focused on questions of the cultural construction of self and personhood, with particular attention given to gender inflections and the theoretical trope of the body. These have all been central concerns of Melanesian ethnography over the past decade, to which this work is both an original and solid contribution. The quality of the writing sustains the reader's attention. The book will mainly interest Melanesian specialists, but those who have followed experiments in ethnographic writing in recent years will also want to read this study. Upper-division undergraduates and above.—*G. E. Marcus, Rice University*

OAB-1886   HD9472   95-4191 CIP
Maril, Robert Lee. **The bay shrimpers of Texas: rural fishermen in a global economy.** University Press of Kansas, 1995. 304p bibl index afp ISBN 0-7006-0703-X, $35.00; ISBN 0-7006-0704-8 pbk, $17.95

Maril's study is an exemplary ethnography—or what some sociologists might call a "natural history"—of an occupation. Maril "explores in detail the many ways in which Texas bay shrimpers and their families have continuously adapted to the economic realities confronting them." Conflicts between bay shrimpers and the larger, more organized, and certainly more politically powerful Gulf fishing industry are detailed, as are conflicts with politically astute recreational fishing and environmental interests. Maril richly and sensitively describes cultural conflict between indigenous Texas bay shrimpers and Vietnamese immigrants who likewise want access to the limited shrimp catch. The essential involvement of women in the industry (in a chapter prepared and written by Andrea Fisher Maril) is extensively detailed, readers are told, for the first time in the literature. All of this is seen against the social, political, and economic environment surrounding the industry, extending well beyond the Texas bays. A random sample survey, historical analysis, and participant observation provide the methodological foundation for an insightful and provocative view of workers and what they do. All levels.—*L. Braude, SUNY College at Fredonia*

OAB-1887   BL2480   93-37980 CIP
Matory, J. Lorand. **Sex and the empire that is no more: gender and the politics of metaphor in Oyo Yoruba religion.** Minnesota, 1994. 295p bibl index afp ISBN 0-8166-2226-4, $49.95

This is a powerful detailing of gender relations following the collapse of the old Oyo Empire and the beginning of British colonial rule in Nigeria. From her study of the history of Yoruba society and religion, the author, an African American anthropologist, presents evidence that calls into question the assumption that polar opposition between women and men is a dichotomy "naturally" based on the biology of the sexes. A close analysis of the context of cross-dressing in the Yoruba religions provides the author with much of the data for her finding that "gender is historical and is subject to transformation by reigning political and financial interests." Seven chapters and a series of appendixes set forth the interpretation and the data in impeccable fashion. This reviewer predicts that this book will become an ethnographic classic among professionals and students in the social and behavioral sciences. Advanced undergraduates and up.—*F. P. Conant, Hunter College, CUNY*

OAB-1888   GN21   94-30791 CIP
Miller, Elmer S. **Nurturing doubt: from Mennonite missionary to anthropologist in the Argentine Chaco.** Illinois, 1995. 225p bibl index afp ISBN 0-252-02155-X, $44.95; ISBN 0-252-06455-0 pbk, $17.50

Missionaries and missionization are increasingly visible in anthropology. Anthropologists look at topics such as missionaries themselves; missionization effects on indigenes, past and present; the organization of mission-indigene communities; and the relationships between anthropologists and missionaries in the field. In this autobiographical account Miller examines his career as Mennonite missionary and then anthropologist among the Toba Indians of the Argentine Chaco. His goal in recounting his personal experiences among the Toba is to show how they were transmuted into what is accepted as anthropological knowledge. Miller's ethnoautobiography is quite different from many trendy ethnographies whose authors seem unable to distinguish between self-display and proper recognition of the researcher's role in knowledge production. It is an absorbing and enlightening account of a life of questioning that enhanced both growth and knowledge; of a deeply interesting professional career; and of engagement with Toba people and Toba life. It graces the genre that began with Hortense Powdermaker's *Stranger and Friend* (1966). Recommended for all academic and public libraries.—*R. Berleant-Schiller, University of Connecticut*

OAB-1889   DS632   95-42827 CIP
Pelras, Christian. **The Bugis.** Blackwell, 1996. 386p bibl index afp ISBN 0-631-17231-9, $59.95

Pelras's superb, original study of the Bugis revolutionizes understanding that culture. Pelras did 17 years of fieldwork, and consulted all available literature and other resources. In thorough, highly readable detail enriched by well-chosen maps, photographs, and line drawings, he analyzes the outworkings of four key structural components characteristic of Bugis culture: always seeking out the best economic opportunity, at home or elsewhere; adapting to contemporary circumstances while maintaining identity as Bugis; continuing dynamic tension between hierarchy and egalitarianism, competition, and cooperation; esteeming bravery, cleverness, religiosity, and business acumen. Pelras's thoughtful, detailed assessment covers the long Bugis timespan, from prehistory to the Bugis today. Excellent index and graphics. Essential for all Southeast Asian collections, this study is highly recommended for upper-division undergraduates and above.—*L. A. Kimball, Western Washington University*

OAB-1890   F1221   91-43631 CIP
Slade, Doren L. **Making the world safe for existence: celebration of the saints among the Sierra Nahuat of Chignautla, Mexico.** Michigan, 1992. 271p bibl index ISBN 0-472-10289-3, $39.50

Anthropologists working in Mexico have long taken note of the central role of saint celebrations in indigenous communities. Slade offers one of the most thorough studies available of such celebrations, based on more than two decades of research among Nahuat people of Puebla. Her book encompasses the full range of topics usually broached in studies of this basic Mesoamerican institution. However, Slade gives particular attention to some very subtle but nonetheless important features of religion, ritual, and morality by exploring in greater than usual depth the implicit beliefs underlying ritual sponsorship and manifest in a wider orbit of interpersonal relations. Slade, both an anthropologist and a practicing psychoanalyst, identifies fundamental cultural injunctions concerning reciprocity, balance, and harmony, and analyzes the relation of such injunctions to actual behavior, experience, and patterns of interaction in ritual, production, family, politics, and elsewhere. This is a vital and challenging study of a contemporary native people, all the more intriguing as it explores the effects of economic development, social change, and, in general, the secularization of life in the Mexican countryside. All levels.—*P. R. Sullivan, Yale University*

OAB-1891   GN666   92-30379 CIP
Swain, Tony. **A place for strangers: towards a history of Australian aboriginal being.** Cambridge, 1993. 303p index ISBN 0-521-43005-4, $59.95

Swain (Univ. of Sydney), author of *Interpreting Aboriginal Religion* (Bedford Park, S. Australia, 1985) and *Aboriginal Religions in Australia* (1991), is a veteran student of aboriginal religion. Not a common overview of past writings on native spirituality or of analyses of indigenous mythic material, this work is a radical rethinking of the belief clusters in aboriginal religions. Swain's assessments of place, body, and time in Central Australian myth draw from recent interviews in which Swain participated, and tells of beliefs apparently minimally influenced by Eurocentric thinking. The myths of Torres Strait people, and those of the natives of the east coast before Christians lived among them, are unknown; at least one early ethnographer, whose field notes survive, edited out of his magnum opus evidence of Christian elements. The religious systems of Arnhem Land and the Gulf of Carpentaria were influenced by Indonesians before the first ethnographers' reports. Swain's highly important monograph is essential reading for students of any native religion; it must be available to seminarians and other students of myth/religion. All levels.—*A. R. Pilling, Wayne State University*

OAB-1892   DT443   94-27541 CIP
Swantz, Marja-Liisa. **Blood, milk, and death: body symbols and the power of regeneration among the Zaramo of Tanzania,** by Marja-Liisa Swantz with Salome Mjema and Zenya Wild. Bergin & Garvey, 1995. 158p bibl index afp ISBN 0-89789-398-0, $49.95

With the editorial assistance of Wild and the interspersed reminiscences and reflections of Mjema, Swantz (Univ. of Helsinki) has provided a sympathetic and informative account of the social and cultural life of the Zaramo people of coastal Tanzania. After a historical introduction detailing the excesses of both the colonial and independence regimes, which tested the resolve of these people to control their own destiny, the author considers in greater detail their ritual and symbolic life, with particular emphasis on the women in this traditional matrilineal society. In the process, Swantz considers birth, death, coming-of-age ceremonies, marriage, and, in addition, the tribulations of existence assumed to be brought on by witchcraft, sorcery, and spirit possession. The data are rich and the analysis sophisticated but lucid. This instructive work is essential for any anthropology and African studies library collection. All levels.—*W. Arens, SUNY at Stony Brook*

Social & Behavioral Sciences

OAB-1893   DA711   93-13100 CIP
Trosset, Carol. **Welshness performed: Welsh concepts of person and society.** Arizona, 1993. 183p bibl index afp ISBN 0-8165-1378-3, $35.00

Trosset (Beloit College) has provided the first full-length anthropological study of Welsh culture and social organization since Ronald Frankenberg's *Village on the Border* (London, 1957). In this instance, the author's scope is both broader and narrower. Rather than a typical community study, Trosset offers an analysis of Welsh personhood, i.e., the socially constructed self in the context of the overarching ethnic group. This detailed ethnography of a nation is derived from two years of itinerant fieldwork, in itself an unusual research procedure. The author moves between her concerns with the individual and with social realms, considering ethnicity, class, status, and religion, and eventually focusing on the Welsh notion of themselves as performers in both formal and informal settings. The richly detailed and theoretically sophisticated portrait of a western European ethnic group validates the assumption that anthropology has a unique contribution to make in understanding the modern state in all its complexities. Advanced undergraduates and above.—*W. Arens, SUNY at Stony Brook*

OAB-1894   DS646   93-10521 CIP
Tsing, Anna Lowenhaupt. **In the realm of the diamond queen: marginality in an out-of-the-way place.** Princeton, 1993. 350p bibl index afp ISBN 0-691-03335-8, $49.50; ISBN 0-691-00051-4 pbk, $14.95

Tsing's ethnography of Dayak people living in the Meratus hills on the island of Borneo spotlights several fascinating women and men who, through their activities as shamans, storytellers, and farmers, express their own marginality vis-à-vis the nation-state. Tsing emphasizes the marginal position of Meratus people in relation to Muslim lowlanders and government officials. She richly contextualizes her cases and stories in ongoing Meratus engagements with an environment under state-sponsored attack. Less emphasized are the ways in which residents of other highlands conceive of their cultural identities. Although Tsing relies on the notion of a "meratus" identity, the ideas, forms, and practices associated with this identity are less well described than are the fascinating inventions and border crossings of marginal individuals. Tsing deftly situates her own analysis in relation to the current competing accounts of marginality, subordination, difference, and resistance in the fields of cultural studies, social history, and cultural anthropology. Brilliantly and in a fluent prose style, Tsing uses these ethnographic insights to reflect on gendered politics and theory in Europe and North America. Advanced undergraduates and above.—*J. R. Bowen, Washington University*

OAB-1895   GN662   91-43580 CIP
Weiner, Annette B. **Inalienable possessions: the paradox of keeping-while-giving.** California, 1992. 232p bibl index afp ISBN 0-520-07603-6, $35.00; ISBN 0-520-07604-4 pbk, $13.00

Weiner's study of material objects, gender, and rank in Oceania challenges deeply rooted anthropological assumptions about the centrality of reciprocity in small-scale societies. She points to the importance of "keeping-while-giving," by which she means keeping certain items of wealth out of circulation, or ensuring that they return to the original possessor. Weiner expertly reviews the importance in European legal thought and in contemporary Oceanic societies of immovable goods, objects that often serve to mark social differences. Women are often the makers of these possessions, and as such, play central roles in reproducing persons and rank. The key to the analysis is the set of ties between brothers and sisters, which perdure through marriage and are symbolized by the possession of inalienable wealth, especially wealth in cloth goods. The book opens and closes with a critique of Malinowski's understanding of Trobriand exchange, a critique that is triply important: for resituating Trobriand practices of giving in a wider Oceanic context; for reanalyzing the influential work of Malinowski; and for showing how Western economic assumptions about exchange (that it must involve reciprocity) have colored ethnographic understandings. The clearly etched comparisons of societies in Australia, Polynesia, and New Guinea make the book an excellent introduction to the societies of this region as well as an innovative work in anthropological theory. Advanced undergraduate through faculty.—*J. R. Bowen, Washington University*

OAB-1896   GR359   92-50261 CIP
Zenani, Nongenile Masithathu. **The world and the word: tales and observations from the Xhosa oral tradition,** ed. with introd. by Harold Scheub. Wisconsin, 1992. 499p ISBN 0-299-13310-9, $39.95

Here is a chunk of Africa itself, a book so full of earthy tales and everday life that it fairly throbs with vitality. Zenani has led a long, full life that she recounts directly through ethnographic commentary and indirectly through the narratives of her Xhosa people of South Africa. The book is her triumph, but it is Harold Scheub's as well; it results from two years of intensive collaboration followed by 15 years of friendship. Zenani's warmth will carry readers through the course of her brave life, from birth to puberty, marriage, and maturity. These are animated tales of dignity despite difficulty, and Zenani patiently explains and herself exemplifies Xhosa wisdom and courage. Scheub captures Zenani's narrative devices (a feather flies "phe phe phe phe"), and she explains how one crafts a tale. Still, Scheub does not provide the overview of Zenani's biography needed to fathom how she could be so philosophically acute and phrase her interpretive commentary so eruditely. What an exceptional woman!—*A. F. Roberts, University of Iowa*

■ Business, Management & Labor

OAB-1897   HD9711   96-19109 CIP
Bilstein, Roger E. **The American aerospace industry: from workshop to global enterprise.** Twayne/Prentice Hall International, 1996. 280p bibl index afp (Twayne's evolution of modern business, 12) ISBN 0-8057-9838-2, $28.95

Bilstein delineates the American aerospace industry in a fascinating new survey of this huge topic. He covers this large subject area with surprising detail in only 217 pages. His survey contains useful historical information in chronologically arranged chapters, starting with 1900 through the 1990s. Each chapter is divided according to smaller areas of the industry, such as private aircraft manufacturing or the role of government agencies in aerospace research. The author, an aerospace historian, weaves an accurate and compelling story of an industry, massive in scale, that is always on the move. Bilstein includes sketches of the personalities, events, technological innovations, and government involvement. He gracefully covers wide-ranging subjects such as the birth of some aerospace manufacturers in the early part of the century to the corporate mergers of late. A useful appendix includes tables of aircraft production statistics and a chronology of the industry. Highly recommended for all undergraduate and graduate level library collections.—*L. E. Clemens, United States Naval Academy*

OAB-1898   HD9161   96-13482 CIP
Blackford, Mansel G. **BFGoodrich: tradition and transformation, 1870-1995,** by Mansel G. Blackford and K. Austin Kerr. Ohio State, 1996. 507p index afp ISBN 0-8142-0696-4, $30.00

For its 125th anniversary, BFGoodrich authorized a history of the firm. The authors, two of the nation's most prominent business historians, were given extraordinary access to the company's records and personnel. The result is a remarkably candid book, one that highlights the shortcomings as well as the triumphs of this big business. The authors focus on the presidents and CEOs of the firm, investigating their strategies as the firm continually transformed itself in the pursuit of new products and new markets. Committed to diversification and high dividends, Goodrich's leaders consistently failed to invest enough to take full advantage of the fruits of their own research and development discoveries. Initially a rubber company, Goodrich was the smallest of the big four tire companies, unable to exploit its early advantage in radial tires. Goodrich led in the development of PVCs, but it feasted upon early profits while other firms caught up. In the last decade Goodrich has abandoned rubber products, tires, and PVCs to become a much smaller but more profitable specialty chemical and aerospace company. Thoroughly researched and carefully conceptualized, this is a model case study. Not only do readers come to appreciate the challenges BFGoodrich faced, but in learning how the company addressed them they can see how the US attained and retained industrial supremacy. Upper-division undergraduate through professional.—*D. Lindstrom, University of Wisconsin—Madison*

OAB-1899   Orig
Business plans handbook: a compilation of actual business plans developed by small businesses throughout North America, ed. by Kristin Kahrs and Karin E. Koek. Gale, 1995. 649p bibl afp ISBN 0-8103-9222-4, $99.00

Kahrs presents 33 complete small business plans. Following a brief foreword on the planning process, the plans are presented alphabetically by business type. Although the majority of examples are represented by an alias, they are the actual plans of existing business units. The businesses discussed include a diverse group of entrepreneurial types, from accounting and consulting services to boutiques, food service companies, hospitality organizations, retailers, publishers, and two organizations providing virtual reality facilities. Skillful editing preserves the unique differences among the plans while providing the reader with a common framework of analysis. An excellent "Glossary of Small Business Terms," a selected bibliography, and a geographical listing of 750 small business development centers conclude the presentation. Especially appropriate for libraries supporting small business and entrepreneurial studies, this is an excellent reference work that should be a part of every business collection.—*S. R. Kahn, University of Cincinnati*

OAB-1900   HD9651   96-48448 MARC
Cain, Gordon. **Everybody wins!: a life in free enterprise.** Chemical Heritage, 1997. 342p index ISBN 0-941901-14-9, $24.95

What is unique about chemistry is its industry. The chemical industry drives the American economy, contributes favorably to the balance of payments, and provides a base of career jobs in research and development, manufacturing, and business and finance. Cain's lifetime association with chemistry and industry is a testament to the special place of the chemical industry in the US, and his autobiography is a validation of that testament. Written with the brevity, clarity, and organization one would expect of a successful engineer and manager, Cain gives his readers half a book of personal and professional history that is as lively as it is informative. He lived (and still lives) in interesting times that included the Great Depression, WW II, and the emergence of the chemical industry in the decades following the war. Then, at a time when most would be thinking of retirement, Cain found himself thinking about the value in junk bonds and the lessons Michael Milken was teaching corporate America about high risk financial instruments and leveraged buyouts (LBOs). The LBO stories are especially fascinating, detailing Cain's adventures with Vista Chemical, Sterling Chemical, and Cain Chemical. This is must reading for just about anyone who uses (or plans to use) molecules and chemical bonds to make a living. An entrepreneurial tour-de-force in 14 chapters and 300 pages, with just the right touch of history and human dimension for good measure. All levels.—*L. W. Fine, Columbia University*

OAB-1901   HF5387   96-33374 CIP
Codes of conduct: behavioral research into business ethics, ed. by David M. Messick and Ann E. Tenbrunsel. Russell Sage Foundation, 1996. 409p bibl index afp ISBN 0-87154-594-2, $49.50

This is one of those rare publications that relates good empirical research in psychology and behavioral economics to business ethics and discusses the implications from a philosophical and ethical perspective. The authors show how exciting such mutually enriching dialogue can be and how necessary it is for business ethics research. Editors Messick (Northwestern Univ.) and Tenbrunsel (Univ. of Notre Dame) convincingly argue that sustained improvement of business and society can be achieved only by thorough com-

prehension of the human experience, including its dark side. Four broad themes pervade the 18 chapters by well-known social scientists and the three commentaries by distinguished philosophers: (1) power, influences, and authority; (2) prejudice, discrimination, bigotry, and stereotyping; (3) the ways by which humans fall short of ideal models of decision making, and the ethical consequences of these deficiencies; and (4) the management of risk. In contrast to the common meaning of "codes of conduct" as sets of (ethical) guidelines, here the term is used as sets of behavioral norms of "evil-doing" as well as "good-doing." This highly recommendable book includes an extensive, consolidated list of references and a detailed index. General readers; upper-division undergraduate through faculty collections.—*G. Enderle, University of Notre Dame*

OAB-1902   HD30   95-20807 CIP
Epstein, Marc J. **Measuring corporate environmental performance: best practices for costing and managing an effective environmental strategy.** IMA Foundation for Applied Research, Inc./Irwin Professional, 1996. 319p bibl index ISBN 0-7863-0230-5, $40.00

This outstanding, in-depth study (sponsored by the Institute of Management Accountants) presents both the state of the art and the best in the class of corporate environmental measurement and reporting. In addition to providing numerous examples of current corporate activities, processes, and techniques that improve environmental management, Epstein also presents a framework for implementing an environmental strategy. The book is based mainly on a review of the internal and external documents of more than 100 companies as well as interviews and field visits to more than 30 companies, and it consists of 11 extensively illustrated chapters and three appendixes. Chapter 1 provides background on both the historical and legal issues pertaining to the environment. Chapters 2 through 10 provide in-depth information and numerous illustrations of the ten major components of environmental strategy. Chapter 11 offers specific, practical guidance on ways to think about developing and implementing an environmental management strategy. This outstanding and clearly written work is required for all business and accounting collections, along with *Green Ledgers*, by Daryl Ditz et al. (1995), and *Accounting for the Environment*, by Rob Gray et al. (CH, Oct'93). Academic and professional collections.—*D. C. Daly, Metropolitan State University*

OAB-1903   HD58   96-25422 MARC
Gibson, Rowan. **Rethinking the future: rethinking business, principles, competition, control & complexity, leadership, markets and the world.** N. Brealey, 1997. (Dist. by LPC InBook) 276p bibl index ISBN 1-85788-103-6, $25.00

Gibson's message is clear, concise, and well articulated: the road ahead for everyone requires a major repositioning. The moral of the Gibson saga: "If you leave it alone and don't fix it 'cause it's not broken, then you will *not* survive in the 21st century." From start to finish, the author provides the tools required to understand the necessary paradigm shift and hence how to approach the 21st century. Comments from the book's contributors also deliver the message that the worldview of the industrial revolution is nearing its end, and the new paradigm requires new principles—a new way to make sense out of the uncertainty of the old industrial order. The author asserts that strategic positioning for growth and competition requires a decidedly different approach—one that takes us beyond the current view of management and leadership. This new paradigm defies traditional sense of territory, the boundaries of culture, and our current view of the marketplace. In less than 300 power-packed pages, Gibson brings to focus the cream of the intellectual community and a treasury of ideas as to why the road to the 21st century requires skillful maneuvering. This valuable work is a must for marketing students and indeed business students in general. Upper-division undergraduate and up.—*J. B. Kashner, College of the Southwest*

OAB-1904   HC465   94-39343 CIP
Herbig, Paul. **Innovation Japanese style: a cultural and historical**

perspective. Quorum Books, 1995. 275p bibl index afp ISBN 0-89930-968-2, $55.00

Drawing from his experiences in business and academia, Herbig examines innovation and how (and how well) it is accomplished in Japan. This excellent book examines the positive and negative aspects of Japan's innovative patterns by probing into culture and history. It seems everyone is asking the question, Can Japan continue to remain an economic superstar in the 21st century? To address this, the author of this well-written volume explores Japanese and US cultures, business practices, and government influences. The volume examines creativity in Japan, historical evidence, innovation, product development strategies, and cultural ramifications, and offers predictions on the future of Japanese innovation. Herbig presents new ideas about the strengths and weaknesses of Japanese innovation; compares Japanese and US innovation processes; and illustrates the advantages of leader versus follower. A "Types of Innovation" appendix, a glossary of Japanese terms, a list of up-to-date references, and an index enhance the book's utility. Highly recommended for business practitioners, academicians, and upper-division undergraduate and graduate students.—*J. W. Leonard, Miami University*

OAB-1905   HD62   95-47015 CIP
Lewis, Richard D. **When cultures collide: managing successfully across cultures.** Nicholas Brealey, 1996. (Dist. by Atrium Publishers Group) 331p bibl index ISBN 1-85788-086-2, $28.00

Drawing on his experiences as one of Britain's foremost linguists, trainer and lecturer Lewis presents an informative and practical guide to working and communicating across cultures. He contributes insights into how various business cultures influence status, structure, leadership, meetings, negotiations, and sales and marketing. Part 1 presents concepts, models, and definitions; it also explores the vital question of how the mind is conditioned, culturally, at an early age. Part 2 addresses specific topics including etiquette, body language, team building, information gathering, time and space, communications and listening, and manners and mannerisms. The last half (part 3) deals with 15 specific nations (or in three cases, small clusters of nations), conferring an array of useful information about them. Particular attention focuses on the necessary resources of the multicultural executive, e.g., empathy, tact, understanding, subtlety, and positive reaction. With an epilogue, brief bibliography, and glossary of terms, this well-written guidebook is highly recommended not only for executives, consultants, and government officials, but also for business and international studies students and academicians. Upper-division undergraduate and up.—*J. W. Leonard, Miami University*

OAB-1906   TS165   94-37876 CIP
Lewis, Ronald J. **Activity-based models for cost management systems.** Quorum Books, 1995. 283p bibl index afp ISBN 0-89930-965-8, $59.95

In this excellent volume Lewis provides an extremely practical introduction to and explanation of traditional cost concepts (5 chapters); the traditional tools of management accounting analysis and control (5 chapters); and the development of activity-based costing systems (ABCs) (6 chapters). This hands-on primer is very well written and contains numerous exhibits that clearly and concisely demonstrate every step in the process of using the tools of management accounting. The chapter on activity-based costing for marketing is outstanding. The knowledgeable author does not offer advice on how to identify and gather data necessary to use these tools; his objective is to teach the reader how to use the tools in both not-for-profit and profit seeking organizations. The use of spreadsheets and other software (ABC) is not treated, but the reader can easily see their applicability. In addition, target costing, life cycle costing, and total quality costing are not covered. The inclusion of a bibliography would have been useful to direct readers to additional ABC resources, e.g., *An ABC Manager's Primer*, by Gary Cokins et al. (1993), and Douglas Hicks's *Activity-Based Costing for Small and Mid-Sized Businesses* (1992). Highly recommended for all business collections, lower-division undergraduate through professional.—*D. C. Daly, Metropolitan State University*

OAB-1907   HF5657   92-33940 CIP
McNair, C.J. **World-class accounting and finance.** Business One Irwin, 1993. 356p index ISBN 1-55623-550-X, $44.00

World-Class Accounting and Finance offers hands-on practical applications like no other work this reviewer has read. The book complements the traditional approach to accounting and finance instruction because it formally presents a look at accounting elements of most interest to financial managers. The accounting discussions go well beyond financial reporting guidelines as they allow the reader to consider the financial reporting requirement along with the practical information that may be derived from the financial statements. While most finance and accounting texts address financial ratio analysis, McNair goes beyond simple computation and interpretation by offering ways to "fix" problem companies. The timing of cash flows, the emphasis on the conversion of profits into cash, the identification of the costs that really count in an organization, as well as the focus on solvency not just profitability, make this book a must on the bookshelf of any financial manager. Advanced undergraduate through professional.—*R. N. Lazzaro, Castleton State College*

OAB-1908   HD2756   93-21388 CIP
Miyashita, Kenichi. **Keiretsu: inside the hidden Japanese conglomerates,** by Kenichi Miyashita and David W. Russell. McGraw-Hill, 1994. 225p index afp ISBN 0-07-042583-3, $22.95

Keiretsu is a great book for anyone interested in Japanese or comparative business. Miyashita (author of numerous works on Japanese business) and Russell (deputy editor, *Tokyo Business Today*) reveal with outstanding clarity the truth about Japanese business and the organization of the *Keiretsu*, a system of corporate alliances. Few in the West (academic, corporate, and government) have been exposed to such information, and this volume identifies the profound differences between the Japanese and US business structure. The book's nine chapters offer readers a history of the development of the *Keiretsu* system, report on the relationships of the *Keiretsu* to banks, and discuss its future. The *Keiretsu* system should be studied with great care by anyone concerned with competing in a global economy. This volume is the best this reviewer has seen on the topic of Japanese business. A must for all business collections, public and academic libraries and professionals.—*D. Morris, University of New Haven*

OAB-1909   HD9349   92-30317 CIP
Pendergrast, Mark. **For God, country and Coca-Cola: the unauthorized history of the great American soft drink and the company that makes it.** Scribner, 1993. 556p bibl index ISBN 0-684-19347-7, $27.50

A detailed and balanced history of a company and a product that have come to symbolize so much that is good and bad about our modern world. The author, a business journalist, offers fascinating insight into the founding, growth, and continued operation of a company that has in many ways defined market expansion and modern business practices. Despite the fact that the ubiquitous image of *Coca-Cola* is perhaps the most recognizable image on the planet, the company itself has long sought to define and redefine its own image. This thoroughly researched and well-written corporate and social history helps to dispel many of the myths of *Coca-Cola* and offers its readers great insight into the personalities and events that have shaped this icon of our times. Pendergrast has brought together a wealth of archival and other materials to tell this compelling story. Much more than just a story of a consumer product, the volume is also a story of how and why economic and political events have helped shaped business practices and outcomes. Recommended for undergraduates, graduate students, and faculty.—*T. E. Sullivan, Towson State University*

OAB-1910   HF1412   92-2609 CIP
Preston, Lee E. **The rules of the game in the global economy: policy regimes for international business,** by Lee E. Preston and Duane Windsor. Kluwer Academic, 1992. 292p index afp ISBN 0-7923-9225-6, $99.50

The increasing scale and complexity of the global economy has led to the development of rules, norms, conventions, and procedures that govern international business activities. These standards, called international policy regimes, are the subject of this book, which documents their growing importance in the global arena where "hard law" is weak or absent. Three types are analyzed through case studies: global regimes like the UN; regional regimes such as the EC; and functional regimes focusing on specific economic and environmental problem areas. The growing integration of the global economy has resulted in new policy regimes such as the UN Code of Conduct on Transnational Corporations and the North Atlantic Free Trade Area. This valuable book bridges the gap between existing studies on international relations and international management, building on studies by Robert Gilpin (1987), David Blake and Robert Walters (1992), and Jack N. Behrman and Robert E. Grosse (1990). Rich documentation. Essential reading for academics and professionals in the fields of political economy, international business, or political science.— *R. H. Dekmejian, University of Southern California*

OAB-1911 HD2785 96-8672 CIP
Roy, William G. **Socializing capital: the rise of the large industrial corporation in America.** Princeton, 1997. 338p bibl index afp ISBN 0-691-04353-1, $35.00

Richly detailed, this book builds on the significant work of historians, economists, and social scientists who have dominated the field of business history for a generation or more. It is a major contribution, analyzing and synthesizing much of that literature, deriving its thrust from its recurrent critique of Alfred D. Chandler's widely praised studies. Roy (sociology, UCLA) sees the rise of large-scale enterprises as the key element in Chandler's work and as primarily an application of efficiency theory. He begins with a "test" of that theory and locates the great change narrowly in the rise of corporations in the period from 1898 to 1902, when the aggregate value of the US's corporate stocks and bonds rose from one billion to more than seven billion dollars. He then backs up to discuss public and private corporations in the early history of the republic, and the later role of railroads as the "well-springs" of mobilized capital so essential in driving the economy to higher income levels. Financial institutions provided the means, and court decisions and laws "set the stage for the corporate revolution at the end of the century." Roy then deals with the enterprises that dominated new processing businesses in the 1870s and '80s (e.g., sugar refining and brewing) and traces the efforts to reduce market competition. Finally, he concludes that the great merger movement at the end of the century, which he sees as a revolution, combined the financial and technological changes that "socialized" both capital *and* manufacturing. Upper-division undergraduate through faculty.—*M. Rothstein, emeritus, University of California, Davis*

OAB-1912 HF5387 93-6357 CIP
Solomon, Robert C. **The new world of business: ethics and free enterprise in the global 1990s.** Rowman & Littlefield, 1994. 336p index afp ISBN 0-8476-7890-3, $48.50; ISBN 0-8226-3030-3 pbk, $16.95

Solomon presents a broad-based, erudite examination of ethics and the prominence this topic has gained as a major area of concern in the business world. It is a book of substance. The content is scholarly and comprehensive, covering ethics (microethics; molar ethics; macroethics), to ethical concerns regarding the behavior of entrepreneurs, the value systems of corporations, the decisions of management, and the behavior of individuals. The section on social responsibility is especially useful because it integrates many concepts and premises of ethical thinking. Throughout, interesting questions are raised. Are ethical concerns antithetical to the profit motive? Is hard work rewarded? Is it ever right to lie? Can organizations ensure ethical decision making? What happens to whistle blowers? Of particular value are the various guidelines and checklists included that help to concretize the abstract discussion (e.g., the ethical styles questionnaire, the steps to ethical problem-solving guidelines, and the corporate culture and ethics checklist). Highly recommended for serious students of business, economics, philosophy, or sociology and to general readers interested in business ethics.—*R. Quinn, Bronx Community College*

OAB-1913 HD30 96-53069 CIP
Taylor, Jim. **The 500-year delta: what happens after what comes next,** by Jim Taylor and Watts Wacker with Howard Means. Harper Business, 1997. 302p index ISBN 0-88730-838-4, $25.00

The authors draw from their business, consulting, and writing experiences in preparing this provocative book about the changing future course of business. The work's six parts present groundbreaking opinions, and many of the views presented go far beyond the cutting-edge ideas originating from the more noted business authors such as Drucker, Naisbitt, Ohmae, Peters, Toffler, and others. Some of Taylor and Wacker's predictions and thoughts include discussion about the shift from reason-based to chaos-based logic, the splintering of social/political/economic organization, and the collapse of production-controlled consumer markets. This well-written book deals with the accelerating rate of change and what people in business can do to cope and adapt. A glossary of 75 of the volume's original terms aids the reader. *The 500 Year Delta* is exceptionally unique and will undoubtedly stir controversy. It is highly recommended for a wide audience much beyond the traditional business community—for anyone interested in critiques about the future of society. General readers; upper-division undergraduate and above.—*J. W. Leonard, Miami University*

OAB-1914 Orig
TRANSACC: transnational accounting, ed. by Dieter Ordelheide and KPMG. Macmillan, UK, 1995. (Dist. by Stockton) 2v. 3,225p bibl index ISBN 1-56159-168-8, $495.00

This comprehensive, clearly written, and authoritative reference set documents financial accounting principles and practices in 14 countries (mainly European, but including the US, Canada, Japan, and Australia). International Accounting Standards Committee and European Union economic principles are also included. *TRANSACC* will serve as an authoritative interpreter for anyone interested in the analysis and comparison of international financial statements. An outstanding feature of the work is the reference matrix (in volume 1) summarizing the accounting principles for each country in a concise, yet comprehensive and detailed, tabular format. Two chapters are devoted to the principles and practices of each country (one focusing on individual corporate statements and one chapter on consolidated or group statements). The emphasis in each chapter is to go beyond familiarity with basic principles to develop an understanding of why each principle is important for that country and to clarify problem areas such as deferred taxes, leases, and goodwill. Written by 30 international experts, this reference work contains numerous exhibits and a glossary of 244 important terms presented in eight languages. This invaluable resource belongs in every accounting reference collection.—*D. C. Daly, Metropolitan State University*

OAB-1915 HD30 93-48785 CIP
Trompenaars, Fons. **Riding the waves of culture: understanding diversity in global business.** Irwin, IL, 1994. 215p index ISBN 0-7863-0290-9, $30.00

Trompenaars's extensive research and consulting experiences are reflected in this excellent work about cultural differences and how they affect international business. The book examines, compares, and contrasts various global cultures, revealing how their beliefs and values impact business. The author explains why some management approaches such as TQM, employee involvement, and MBO can work well in one place yet fail somewhere else. The 12 chapters and three appendixes provide numerous models that illustrate how different cultures regard and respond to various managerial techniques. Chapters 2 through 8 analyze how cultures differ and show how cultural diversity influences business, especially peoples' relations with others. The final four chapters discuss cultural attitudes towards time and the environment, identify four broad organizational types, and consider how managers can prepare for the process of internationalization. Highly recommended for managers and trainers in multinational organizations; academicians and upper-division and graduate students will also find it useful.—*J. W. Leonard, Miami University*

■ General Management

OAB-1916   HD30   93-36706 CIP
Baden-Fuller, Charles. **Rejuvenating the mature business: the competitive challenge,** by Charles Baden-Fuller and John M. Stopford. Harvard Business School Press, 1994. 281p bibl index afp ISBN 0-87584-476-6, $29.95

This outstanding work is the product of case-based analysis by two British academics who balance formulation and implementation of strategy. Focus is on the potential of once-laggard firms and industries thought to be mature—a more common and more important segment than the emerging, rapid-growth, high-tech segment. Services and goods producers are covered—banking, mass fashion retailing, fibers and textiles, major home appliances, vacuum pumps, cutlery, steel castings, and others—emphasizing Britain but extending to the US, Europe, and Japan. The marvel is the book's hopeful iconoclasm, counter-intuitive analysis, and fully bolstered arguments. In their strategy formulation, firms would innovate, build multiple advantages (e.g., low cost with quality, variety, or speed of delivery, etc.), and choose scope (scale, range, geography, and purchasing and distribution) creatively. Implementation calls for an entrepreneurial organization and a sequence: galvanize top management, reduce complexity, start initiatives, shape collective effort, exploit achievements, and maintain momentum. Highest recommendation for its critical, realistic insights and its four-step program for managers. Upper-division undergraduate through professional.—*J. C. Thompson, University of Connecticut*

OAB-1917   HD62   93-9024 CIP
Bygrave, William D. **The portable MBA in entrepreneurship.** Wiley, 1994. 468p index afp ISBN 0-471-57780-4, $27.95

This impressive and very practical book on how to start, grow, and harvest a small business includes very helpful information on identifying opportunities, starting up and entering a business, marketing, preparing a successful business plan, getting financing, obtaining venture capital, managing debt, obtaining external assistance, handling legal and tax issues, protecting intellectual property, and franchising. Bygrave, an entrepreneur and leading expert in the field, has written the first chapter. He has delegated the writing of each subsequent chapter to a leading expert in the field on that particular topic. Each chapter is very clearly and interestingly written and includes excellent exhibits and much helpful information. References are also provided for most chapters at the end of the book. This work would make a fine text for courses on small business and entrepreneurship, as it includes information not found in the typical text. Highly recommended for anyone interested in starting or operating a small business, or anyone studying small business management and entrepreneurship. All levels.—*D. W. Huffmire, University of Connecticut*

OAB-1918   HF5548   94-49133 CIP
Culbert, Samuel A. **Mind-set management: the heart of leadership.** Oxford, 1996. 340p index afp ISBN 0-19-509746-7, $27.50

Written by a highly regarded clinical psychologist who is also a professor of management at UCLA's Anderson Graduate School of Management, this book makes a profound contribution to understanding organizations, the psychology of people who work in them, and, most importantly, ourselves. Organized into four parts and 18 chapters, *Mind-Set Management* utilizes theoretical insights, empirical analyses, case illustrations, and stories to develop a model for thinking about and leading and managing others. The author's principal thesis is that before you can lead, manage, or team up effectively, you must comprehend the mind-sets of the people with whom you deal. According to Culbert you must "engage them where they actually are," and based on your insights provide advice that actually gets used; the advice should be both empowering to the receiver and consistent with organizational philosophy and goals. This highly relevant, well-written book is must reading for individuals seeking to influence others and to build strong, effective human relationships within an organization. General audiences; upper-division undergraduate through professional.—*T. Gutteridge, University of Connecticut*

OAB-1919   HD31   95-13316 CIP
Drucker, Peter F. **Managing in a time of great change.** Truman Talley Books/Dutton, 1995. 371p index afp ISBN 0-525-94053-7, $24.95

In *Managing in a Time of Great Change* Drucker not only enhances his reputation as the foremost management thinker of the century, but continues to provide meaningful insights into social and political issues. Among the specific topics he examines are the impact of the Information Age on society, the implications for business of the reinvention of government, the shifting balance of power between management and labor, and the various types of teamwork that an organization can choose to adopt. Although Drucker's reputation is firmly grounded in management, in this book his most salient contribution addresses societal issues. Specifically, the chapter titled "A Century of Social Transformation" provides a concise social history of the century while describing the emergence of the knowledge society and its impact on existing institutions. The readership of this book should not be limited to management academics and practitioners; rather the insights Drucker offers will attract a broad audience. This volume belongs in all libraries—public, academic, and professional.— *E. Garaventa, College of Staten Island, CUNY*

OAB-1920   HD57   93-42804 CIP
Fairholm, Gilbert W. **Leadership and the culture of trust.** Praeger, 1994. 236p bibl index afp ISBN 0-275-94833-1, $55.00

This well-written book by Fairholm (author of *Value Leadership: Toward a New Philosophy of Leadership*, 1991, and *Organizational Power Politics: Tactics of Leadership Power*, CH, Oct'93) focuses on what Jack R. Gibb (*Trust: A View of Personal and Organizational Development*, 1978) refers to as the key variable in organizational effectiveness. Fairholm explains why creating a culture of trust is such an important part of a leader's role, and why present models of leadership do not appear to be working. The material covered is extremely current in its integration of concepts involving employees, the development of skills for open communication, full utilization of multiculturalism, and the creation of shared values. The author shows how these concepts can be woven together to create a high-trust culture and how this culture leads to greater productivity and organizational health. Drawing on both current and classic research, the author makes both a rational and an inspirational case for leading organizations using this new model of trust, and he provides practical guidelines for implementing the needed changes. Excellent bibliography and thorough index. Upper-division undergraduate through professional.— *J. A. Neal, University of New Haven*

OAB-1921   HF5386   92-20066 CIP
Fairholm, Gilbert W. **Organizational power politics: tactics in organizational leadership.** Praeger, 1993. 230p bibl index afp ISBN 0-275-94420-4, $49.95

Fairholm (Virginia Commonwealth Univ.) reports on survey findings on 100 managers employed at varying levels in different sized organizations regarding the use of power tactics. In addition, appropriate references are made to the classic and contemporary literature. The focus of this book is the applied organizational dimensions of the use of power and political behavior. Major sections are devoted to defining power and developing tactical and strategic models for power use. Comparisons are made regarding power use within different types of organizations, between employees at different organizational levels, as well as between men and women. An extensive bibliography and detailed description of the research findings are included. This book is important as it contributes to the analysis and discussion of an issue that has, as yet, not received adequate attention. Suitable for both graduate and undergraduate holdings.—*P. D. Albro, Castleton State College*

OAB-1922   HD62   93-40042 CIP
Joiner, Brian L. **Fourth generation management: the new business consciousness,** by Brian L. Joiner with Sue Reynard. McGraw-Hill, 1994. 289p index afp ISBN 0-07-032715-7, $24.95

An academic turned consultant, Joiner has written an outstanding book that warrants a wide audience. He advocates transcending prior managerial generations of do-it-yourself, commanding subordinates, and even "managing-by-results" approaches. Joiner's "Fourth Generation" includes a mutually supporting triad: quality according to the customer; a system-wide, process-oriented, "scientific" response to data on quality; and a "win-win" outcome for all concerned. He draws on the short-term, quality-control tradition, but his writing is refreshing, revealing, and persuasive. Practitioners will find insights on learning and improving—both accepted ones and counter-intuitive ones—applicable and practical; faculty and students will gain from the many vignettes that make Joiner's experience accessible, as he presents an entire integrated managerial program. With seeming ease, he develops his triad argument, emphasizing themes throughout of quality's dependence on productivity, assiduous attention to the customer, and changes in performance appraisal and employee compensation to let cooperation supplant competition. The reader is buoyed by the upbeat, can-do tone, by Joiner's realism, and by his helpful documentation of attention to all three elements comprising his approach. Highest recommendations for advanced undergraduate through professional audiences.— *J. C. Thompson, University of Connecticut*

OAB-1923   Orig
Learning organizations: developing cultures for tomorrow's workplace, ed. by Sarita Chawla and John Renesch. Productivity Press, 1995. 547p bibl index ISBN 1-56327-110-9, $35.00

Written by 39 respected practitioners and scholars and two highly competent editors, this collection of 32 essays yields powerful insights into the topic of learning organizations. Subdivided into four parts ("Guiding Ideas"; "Theories/Methods/Processes"; "Infrastructure"; and "Arenas of Practice"), this volume is destined to become a sourcebook for professional or business readers on the why, what, and hows of creating a learning culture within an organization. Among the topics covered: new learning theories required for organizations to successfully make a transition into the 21st century; how leaders can help their organizations master change; how "learning laboratories" are created; how we can facilitate creation of a learning organization; development strategies that learning organizations can adopt; learning strategies for sustaining a competitive advantage; developing wisdom; and what an organization looks like when it has a learning culture. All in all, a challenging, sometimes scholarly volume that offers an interesting perspective on creating an environment where employees are encouraged to learn. Upper-division undergraduate through professional.—*T. Gutteridge, University of Connecticut*

OAB-1924   HF5415   94-46192 CIP
Lowenstein, Michael W. **Customer retention: an integrated process for keeping your best customers.** ASQC Quality, 1995. 179p bibl index afp ISBN 0-87389-257-7, $25.00

Lowenstein (ARBOR, Inc.'s Total Quality Group) focuses on the importance of customer retention as a factor of business success. Arguing that the traditional marketing emphasis on price, product, and customer satisfaction is insufficient to assure customer and staff loyalty, the author explores the interrelationship between customer needs, expectations, and real or imagined problems and the development of a continuing customer relationship. More than a do-it-yourself approach to marketing management, the book promotes a proactive integration of customer retention as a primary business objective. Chapters begin with a series of interesting quotations. The writing style is succinct and there are excellent graphs, charts, and examples. Each unit contains an introspective exercise designed to encourage the reader to find a creative solution to a problem. An extensive bibliography and an afterword, epilogue, and topic index conclude the text. Chapter-end references. This volume should be in every business library.—*S. R. Kahn, University of Cincinnati*

OAB-1925   HD30   93-27323 CIP
Mintzberg, Henry. **The rise and fall of strategic planning: recon-**

ceiving roles for planning, plans, planners. Free Press, 1994. 458p bibl index ISBN 0-02-921605-2, $29.95

Mintzberg, a leading expert in the field of management, criticizes strategic planning and the way it is used in organizations. He reviews the history of strategic planning, discusses the various models that are used in the field, indicates the fallacies and pitfalls of strategic planning, and provides evidence to show that it has not performed well for organizations. Finally, he explains what must be done to make strategic planning more effective. Mintzberg argues that strategic planning can discourage commitment, narrow an organization's vision, impede serious change, breed an atmosphere of politics, and become too formalized. However, he concludes that if strategic planning is reconceived according to his recommendations, it can play an important part in organizations. This work is well reasoned, provocative, and clearly written. A lengthy list of references to the leading experts in the field appears at the book's end. A major contribution to the strategic planning field, this important book is must reading for professionals, organizational planners, faculty, and advanced students.—*D. W. Huffmire, University of Connecticut*

OAB-1926   HC110   92-15842 CIP
Morone, Joseph G. **Winning in high-tech markets: the role of general management: how Motorola, Corning, and General Electric have built global leadership through technology.** Harvard Business School Press, 1993. 292p index afp ISBN 0-87584-325-5, $29.95

Morone (Rensselaer Polytechnic Institute) has written a timely, savvy book. His work is important amid the spate of writing on global competition because it combines two incisive approaches to underscore the strategic contribution top management must make for a firm to succeed in technologically intensive markets. The author chronicles and analyzes three exemplary US businesses. Surrounding these case studies are striking chapters on the relationship between technology and competitive advantage, the crucial ingredient top management can bring to that advantage, and the potentials for government policy to enhance industrial competitiveness. After unfolding the history of each company, Morone isolates and scrutinizes the business strategy, technology strategy, and decision-making style, one-by-one, and thereby enriches each case. Morone's insight—top management must understand, be involved in, and sustain support for high-technology products and services—almost palpably emerges from these studies which dominate the book. General Electric's Medical Systems (1974-90), Motorola's Mobile Communications (1947-91), and Corning (1968-91) amply prove that US business—properly attended to—can succeed in the most challenging of environments. Most highly recommended to advanced undergraduate through professional audiences.—*J. C. Thompson, University of Connecticut*

OAB-1927   HC106   93-46875 Orig
Morrison, Ian. **Future tense: the business realities of the next ten years,** by Ian Morrison and Greg Schmid. W. Morrow, 1994. 304p index ISBN 0-688-12351-1, $25.00

Morrison and Schmid (Institute of the Future) explore socioeconomic trends that will affect business planning over the next ten years. Three themes are prevalent throughout the text: businesses must understand the forces changing the business environment; to date business response to the rapidly changing social and economic environment has been partial and ineffective; and, there is a vital need to explore steps that businesses and individuals must take to respond to changing conditions. Within this framework the authors identify seven major changes that will impact the future of American businesses and their employees: an older and more educated American consumer; the insecurity and lessening of worker loyalty; the effect of market globalization; the decline in consumer brand loyalty; the failure of institutions such as unions and political parties; the public's demand for business accountability; and the impact of new technologies. The authors provide a compendium of statistical information from a wide variety of sources. Excellent charts, graphs, and tabular data. This book should be in every library. The information presented is important to a wide variety of disciplines in addition to business, e.g., economics, sociology, history.—*S. R. Kahn, University of Cincinnati*

OAB-1928 HD60 94-45284 CIP
Pava, Moses L. **Corporate responsibility and financial performance: the paradox of social cost,** by Moses L. Pava and Joshua Krausz. Quorum Books, 1995. 176p bibl index afp ISBN 0-89930-921-6, $55.00

Many reasons suggest placing this book on the shelves of every university library, especially those supporting business schools. It summarizes the most important implications discovered in over 20 years of empirical and theoretical research on "corporate social responsibility" (CSR) and provides a firm ground to continue discussion on these vital issues of modern American business. Clearly structured, the volume begins by introducing the core idea of CSR and reporting the results of over 20 empirical studies, including two original ones, on the association between CSR and financial performance, the evidence of which overwhelmingly indicates that CSR firms perform at least as well as other firms (i.e., the so-called "paradox of social cost"). The authors then discuss the language and the legitimacy of CSR, both "semantic" and "normative-ethical" questions being often neglected in the literature of accountancy and business ethics. The reader can easily follow the careful and differentiated reasoning of the authors and make his or her own judgment. No criticism? Well, the traditional view that socially responsible business equals bad business is proven unrealistic; however, the concept of CSR needs much more clarification, especially when related to international competition. The volume is supported by an extensive bibliography. Upper-division undergraduate through professional.—*G. Enderle, University of Notre Dame*

OAB-1929 HD31 92-9978 CIP
Scott, William G. **Chester I. Barnard and the guardians of the managerial state.** University Press of Kansas, 1992. 233p bibl index afp ISBN 0-7006-0550-9, $27.50

In this slim but rewarding volume Scott (management and organization, Univ. of Washington) surveys the managerial thoughts of Chester I. Barnard. A business leader at AT&T who also headed important private nonprofit organizations and government bodies in mid-20th-century America, including the Rockefeller Foundation and the National Science Board, Barnard was best known for his writings on what he thought the roles of management should be as US firms experienced a divorce between ownership and management. Most fully expressed in his monumental *The Functions of the Executive* (1938), Barnard's ideas have deeply influenced business-management education at colleges and universities to the present day. Scott provides a lucid account of the origins, meanings, significance, and legacy of Barnard's thoughts—the best short account of them in print. Substantial footnotes and a lengthy bibliography will be of value to scholars interested in pursuing the evolution of management thought in more detail. Advanced undergraduate through professional collections.—*M. Blackford, Ohio State University*

OAB-1930 HD58 92-9291 CIP
Trice, Harrison M. **The cultures of work organizations,** by Harrison M. Trice and Janice M. Beyer. Prentice Hall, 1993. 510p bibl index ISBN 0-13-191438-3, $38.67

Almost ten years in the making, this volume by Trice (Cornell) and Beyer (Univ. of Texas, Austin) is a multidisciplinary, comprehensive, and highly readable synthesis of theoretical work on organizational culture dating from the 1930s to the present. The authors engagingly present both descriptive and prescriptive approaches to cultures, subcultures, and countercultures at individual, group, and organizational levels. With admirable clarity, they discuss why the cultural perspective is an appropriate approach to the interpretation of organizational behaviors; how cultures come to be; and means by which managers can identify, understand, manage, create, or change organizational cultures. They address gaps and errors in existing theory and produce a thorough and evenhanded treatment of issues that evoke both consensus and controversy among organizational analysts. Rich definitions supported with current examples from a variety of industries are designed to complement rather than contradict mainstream organizational and management theory. Richly referenced and indexed. Advanced undergraduate through professional.—*S. Newport, Creighton University*

OAB-1931 HD69 96-39625 MARC
Watson, Charles S. **Managing projects for personal success,** by Charles S. Watson with David J. Williams. International Thomson Business, 1997. 332p bibl index ISBN 0-412-71740-9, $48.95

Watson (consultant) provides a comprehensive manual of commercial and industrial project management. From an introduction to the components of project management through project completion and benefits management, the book is much more than a do-it-yourself workbook. It is a thorough guide to successful project administration and leadership for the neophyte or project management professional. Divided into four sections—"Project Managers and Project Management"; "Preparing for the Challenge"; "Success in Project Delivery"; and "Managing Your Career,"—the text emphasizes the interplay between interpersonal skills and project success, blending technical competency with organizational, social, and political expertise. The physical presentation of information, succinct writing style, and an excellent integration of graphics enhance the book's usefulness. Glossary, references, topic index. Upper-division undergraduate through professional.—*S. R. Kahn, University of Cincinnati*

OAB-1932 HD70 96-9274 CIP
Yoshimura, Noboru. **Inside the Kaisha: demystifying Japanese business behavior,** by Noboru Yoshimura and Philip Anderson. Harvard Business School Press, 1997. 259p index afp ISBN 0-87584-415-4, $24.95

Numerous books have been written about Japanese management. However, few convey the essence of what directs and motivates the Japanese businessperson as well as *Inside the Kaisha.* Yoshimura (vice president, Japan Merchant Banking Group, Bankers Trust) and Anderson (Dartmouth) collaborate to define the character of Japanese business practices within large Japanese companies through an informative collection of vignettes. Although they do not attempt to instruct the reader on "how to be more Japanese," their information is helpful because it examines the basis of Japanese behavior and life, providing advice designed to improve coping and cultural analysis skills. By learning what motivates their Japanese counterparts, Westerners may find themselves more effective when negotiating or dealing with their Japanese business professionals. The book is well organized, providing the reader with four themes of Japanese behavior and explanations to several apparent paradoxes of Japanese society. The authors conclude with interesting insights by Japanese who describe what they want Westerners to understand about them. Upper-division undergraduate through practitioner collections.—*T. J. Belich, Metropolitan State University*

■ Labor & Human Resources

OAB-1933 HD8039 93-44445 CIP
Andreas, Carol. **Meatpackers and beef barons: company town in a global economy.** University Press of Colorado, 1994. 225p bibl index afp ISBN 0-87081-321-8, $29.95

Andreas has made an important contribution to the debate on the power of big business in a global economy. Focusing on a modern company town—Greeley, Colorado—she explores the web of social, political, legal, and economic institutions that enable a meatpacking company and its owner to virtually dominate a community. This book is more than a study of elite power; it is also an examination of how labor unions, ethnic minorities, women, and immigrant workers confront a corporate conglomerate. Andreas does an excellent job of looking at all the players, their connection to each other, and their relationship to the company. In doing so, she sheds light on the constellation of social forces opposing corporate power and the possibility for building community-wide coalitions. Andreas establishes the critical link between labor union success and community organizing, and does a good job of assessing critical issues that confront unions in the 1990s. This engrossing case study is not only an example of keen social analysis, it is also an uncompromising indictment of the abuse of corporate power in a community. In laying bare the meatpacking companies' current method of operation, Andreas shows that the labor relations climate in the industry has changed little since the turn of the century. All levels.—*P. Seybold, Indiana University-Bloomington*

OAB-1934   HD6490   91-25183 CIP

Barling, Julian. **The union and its members: a psychological approach,** by Julian Barling, Clive Fullagar, and E. Kevin Kelloway. Oxford, 1992. 251p bibl indexes afp ISBN 0-19-507336-3, $49.95

The authors are organizational psychologists who argue that the principles of their discipline can usefully be applied to the study of unions as organizations. In a series of chapters examining various aspects of unions, they convincingly document that thesis. They analyze structural characteristics of unions, the process by which employees select or reject unionization, the commitment of members to a union, members' participation in union affairs, leadership and shop stewards, union decertification, and the effects of unionization on firms. For each topic, the authors provide a thorough survey of the relevant academic literature and apply that body of knowledge using concepts of organizational psychology. Their work has obvious significance for unions, since members' attitudes towards unions and labor's public image are important factors in union decline. Further, they suggest, organizational psychology not only adds to an understanding of the unionization process but can be of "practical benefit to those whose aim is to enhance workplace democracy and improve working conditions." The book substantially extends our understanding of the functions and effectiveness of labor organizations. Suitable as an introductory text as well as a reference for advanced students.—*R. L. Hogler, Colorado State University*

OAB-1935   HD6515   95-9563 CIP

Boyle, Kevin. **The UAW and the heyday of American liberalism, 1945-1968.** Cornell, 1995. 338p index afp ISBN 0-8014-3064-X, $35.00

What happened to union activism in the post-WW II era? Boyle argues persuasively that at least one union, the United Automobile Workers, sought more than fatter paychecks, bigger fringe benefits, and job security for its members. Prodded by its president, Walter Reuther, the UAW pressed liberalism leftward, notably with its call for national economic planning and an expanded welfare state. To secure these goals, Reuther had to appeal to a broader audience, most likely drawn from fellow unionists, middle-class liberals, and African Americans. But the UAW's alliances with the AFL-CIO and the Democratic Party forced painful compromises. Then, in 1968, any hope for a cross-class, biracial coalition evaporated in the waves of protest that gripped the nation. Focusing upon the UAW national political agenda, the author amply refutes the widely held view that the CIO unions failed, and that, sometime in the late `40s or early `50s, they bought into the prevailing Cold War consensus. Committed to an interventionist government, Reuther and the UAW continually pressed for a social democratic state, akin to those achieved in northern Europe. Thoroughly researched, abundantly footnoted, and uncommonly well written, this book belongs alongside Steve Fraser's *Labor Will Rule: Sidney Hillman and the Rise of American Labor* (1991). General collections; upper-division undergraduate through professional.—*D. Lindstrom, University of Wisconsin—Madison*

OAB-1936   HD8085   93-34180 CIP

Brundage, David. **The making of Western labor radicalism: Denver's organized workers, 1878-1905.** Illinois, 1994. 207p index afp ISBN 0-252-02075-8, $26.95

In this cogently argued monograph, Brundage traces the linkages between the labor republicanism of the post-Civil War era and the radicalism of the early 20th century. Specifically, he traces the evolution of four key components of the Industrial Workers of the World ideology: syndicalism, industrial unionism, racial and ethnic solidarity, and working-class movement culture. Each was forged during the halcyon years between 1878 and 1905, as Denver's organized workers sought effective strategies to wrest reforms from employers and politicians. In short, the radicalism of Westerners is not to be explained by the violence of the bloody labor wars of 1904-5 but rather by 25 years of working-class

experiences. A volume in "The Working Class in American History" series, this book is a first-rate community study. Its focused attention on labor activists and labor organizations in one city facilitates new and often striking insights, such as the relationships between reform movements (e.g., the Irish Land Leagues, prohibition, Populism, and the Rocky Mountain Social League) and working-class organizations. Thoroughly researched and extensively footnoted, this work belongs in labor history collections. Graduate; faculty.—*D. Lindstrom, University of Wisconsin-Madison*

OAB-1937   HD6490   96-28101 CIP

Chaison, Gary N. **Union mergers in hard times: the view from five countries.** ILR Press, 1996. 248p bibl index afp (Cornell international industrial and labor relations reports, 31) ISBN 0-8014-3330-4, $39.95; ISBN 0-8014-8380-8 pbk, $16.95

The hard times that have befallen trade unions in the US and around the world during the past 15 or so years are no longer newsworthy. In many countries during the 1980s and 1990s, the unionized share of the labor force declined, unions lost considerable bargaining power to employers, and their political influence similarly waned. It is less clear is how unions have responded to these hard times and the resulting dwindling membership rolls and depleted treasuries. One option increasingly chosen by, or forced upon, many unions is merger with another union. Chaison is a world-class expert on this topic, and in this volume he does an excellent job of examining the union merger phenomenon from 1980 to 1994 in Australia, Canada, Great Britain, New Zealand, and the US. His book presents a gold mine of useful information about the mergers that occurred during this period as well as insightful analyses of the merger processes in these five countries. It will appeal to industrial relations scholars interested in the different types of union mergers and how unions have managed this difficult process; it will also be of value to scholars interested in organizational adaptation to decline. Upper-division undergraduate through faculty.—*P. Feuille, University of Illinois at Urbana-Champaign*

OAB-1938   HD58   96-23911 CIP

Change at work, by Peter Cappelli et al. Oxford, 1997. 276p bibl index afp ISBN 0-19-510327-0, $27.50

The employment relationship is always evolving, and during the 1980s and 1990s the rate of change in America's workplaces increased. Restructurings and downsizing by large corporations have forced into the labor market many employees who expected lifetime employment and have created more stressful jobs for those retained. There is widespread belief that job security has declined, that employees at all levels must keep their skills constantly updated to remain employable, that work practices have been transformed to require more teamwork, wider skills, and more decision responsibility, and that rewards have become more contingent upon individual and organizational performance. Well-educated employees generally have fared well economically during this period, but poorly educated employees have seen their inflation-adjusted income decline, and the result is a widened income gap across the labor force. The authors of this book offer an empirically based look at the extent of organizational restructurings, the reorganization of work and training practices, skills needed for today's jobs, and the effects of these work changes on employees. This is an excellent primer on the magnitude and impacts of the changes that have transformed American employer-employee relations during the past two decades, and as such it will be very informative for students and scholars across the entire range of workplace-related disciplines.—*P. Feuille, University of Illinois at Urbana-Champaign*

OAB-1939   HD6508   Orig

Contemporary collective bargaining in the private sector, ed. by Paula B. Voos. Industrial Relations Research Association, 1995 (c1994). (Dist. by ILR Press) 548p bibl ISBN 0-913447-60-9 pbk, $29.95

In 1980, the Industrial Relations Research Association published an edited volume analyzing collective bargaining in a number of major American industries through the 1970s. *Contemporary Collective Bargaining in the Private*

Sector is a follow-up to that volume consisting of original chapters examining the collective bargaining experience of 12 major industries between 1979 and 1993. This was a particularly eventful period in the history of American labor-management relations that featured two seemingly contrary phenomena—an increase in highly confrontational collective bargaining and the advent of new employee involvement and union-management cooperation programs. Well-written and insightful chapters detail these developments in key industries such as auto, steel, trucking, telecommunications, and construction. This book will be of great interest to anyone interested in the recent past and the immediate future of the American industrial relations system. It is a "must buy" for all academic, professional, and public libraries.—*P. F. Clark, Pennsylvania State University, University Park Campus*

OAB-1940   HD5560   92-40084 CIP
Cotton, John L. **Employee involvement: methods for improving performance and work attitudes.** Sage, 1993. 310p bibl indexes ISBN 0-8039-4532-9, $45.00; ISBN 0-8039-4533-7 pbk, $22.95

If you only read one book on employee involvement, this is the one. Written by a university professor, *Employee Involvement* combines empirical research findings, a thorough review of the literature, and a practical understanding of what really works in the real world, into a comprehensive analysis of a wide range of employee participation programs. Drawing from organizational behavior, human resource management, and industrial relations, this provocative volume provides detailed insights about different approaches to employee involvement—how they work, expected results, general applicability, and methods of implementation. The result is a scientific and realistic treatise about what is needed to involve employees more meaningfully in their work. The book is divided into 11 chapters, plus a comprehensive reference section. Among the employee involvement approaches covered are quality of work life, quality circles, Scanlon plans, representative participation, job enrichment, self-directed work teams, and employee ownership. Two concluding chapters provide a useful summary of findings and conclusions, as well as an overview of areas where additional research is needed. Advanced undergraduate through faculty.—*T. Gutteridge, University of Connecticut*

OAB-1941   HD58   96-40876 CIP
Fitz-enz, Jac. **The 8 practices of exceptional companies: how great organizations make the most of their human assets.** AMACOM, 1997. 246p bibl index ISBN 0-8144-0348-4, $24.95

Fitz-enz (president, Saratoga Institute) explores the ideological strategies that provide superlative leadership and financial success for contemporary businesses. His volume is based on the Saratoga Institute's four-year study of more than 1,000 companies. The study identified eight interactive variables, emphasizing the importance of human capital, to be the keystone of a human resource management program in companies that consistently maximized shareholder value. "Value," "Commitment," "Culture," "Communication," "Partnering with Stakeholders," "Collaboration," "Innovation and Risk," and "Competitive Passion" were elements found to be the essence of the corporate culture in those organizations repeatedly recognized for their outstanding achievements in human and financial management. Devoid of the traditional management philosophy, the book's readable chapters provide an exciting new exploration of the managerial sciences. Excellent use is made of examples, checklists, and graphics. The book concludes with an epilogue and topic index. An important addition to every business library. Upper-division undergraduate through practitioner.—*S. R. Kahn, University of Cincinnati*

OAB-1942   HD8076   95-21046 MARC
Form, William. **Segmented labor, fractured politics: labor politics in American life.** Plenum, 1995. 380p bibl index ISBN 0-306-45031-3, $42.50

"Solidarity" is often heard as the rallying cry of the labor movement. However, the reality among ordinary rank-and-file workers is something different. Workers are split or segmented along many dimensions: income, job skills, age,

gender, race, religion, geography, upward mobility expectations, political preferences, and so on. As a result, the "working class" is much more an intellectual abstraction than a labor force reality. In this well-researched and well-written volume, an eminent industrial sociologist examines the sources of division among workers and analyzes how these segmentations have prevented the labor movement from pursuing a unified or cohesive political strategy. The author also proposes a series of changes for unions so that the labor movement will become a more influential voice for the country's workers. He suggests, among other things, that unions need to be more concerned about the welfare of nonunion workers, that unions need to spend more time and money on organizing, that unions need to work with employers to enhance workplace productivity, and that unions need to devote more resources and more internal discipline to the labor movement's political goals. This insightful analysis of unions and politics is highly recommended for students and scholars in sociology, political science, labor history, and industrial relations.—*P. Feuille, University of Illinois at Urbana-Champaign*

OAB-1943   HD4901   93-38866 CIP
Fox, Matthew. **The reinvention of work: a new vision of livelihood for our time.** Harper San Francisco, 1994. 342p index afp ISBN 0-06-062918-5, $22.00

Fox, a well-known theologian (*Sheer Joy*, 1992, *The Coming of the Cosmic Christ*, 1991), has written a beautiful book on the meaning of work for us as individuals, for our societies, and for our planet. He speaks of the need to do both inner work—becoming more self-aware and accepting of all parts of ourselves, and outer work—finding our "calling," discovering what gifts we have to offer to other people. Part 1 explores the positive and negative aspects of inner work and discusses the importance of work as a spiritual path. Part 2 creates new paradigms of work in farming, politics, education, health care, psychology, art, economics, business, and science. These paradigms apply spiritual principles that demonstrate care for individuals, communities, and the earth. Part 3 addresses the importance of working less and creating more time for meaningful rituals in life. The book is well researched, poetically written, and thought provoking. Excellent endnotes for each chapter, thorough index, and "spirituality of work questionnaire" included. Recommended for upper-division undergraduate through professional audiences.—*J. A. Neal, University of New Haven*

OAB-1944   HF5549   93-29 CIP
Gutteridge, Thomas G. **Organizational career development: benchmarks for building a world-class workforce,** by Thomas G. Gutteridge, Zandy B. Leibowitz, and Jane E. Shore. Jossey-Bass, 1993. 266p bibl index afp ISBN 1-55542-526-7, $33.95

Gutteridge is a well-known and well-respected researcher on the topic of careers and career development. His coauthors are also active writers and consultants in this field. The book is based on a survey sponsored by the American Society for Training and Development of career development practices in more than 1,000 large companies in the US and other developed countries. Case studies that profile career development systems at 12 exemplary companies are highlighted. Specific best practices are discussed in some detail including job information systems, leadership education, and succession planning. The book concludes with practical tips, systems approach to change, and future challenges. The major contributions of the book are an updating of the state-of-the-art and an international perspective on career development. It is destined to be a classic in the field and should be of great interest for graduate and undergraduate collections in business, education, and psychology as well as for libraries serving business executives, human resource managers, and consultants.—*M. Fottler, University of Alabama at Birmingham*

OAB-1945   HD8066   92-19055 CIP
Kaufman, Bruce E. **The origins & evolution of the field of industrial relations in the United States.** ILR Press, 1993. 286p bibl index afp (Cornell studies in industrial and labor relations, 25) ISBN 0-87546-191-3, $40.00; ISBN 0-87546-192-1 pbk, $19.95

Kaufman's book is a meticulously researched, thoughtful, and well-written intellectual history of industrial relations in the US. The author charts the "institutional and organizational development of industrial relations" as a distinct academic subject and field of study from its birth in 1920. The two major schools of thought that have dominated the field—personnel management and institutional labor economics—are identified and defined. Kaufman carefully examines the manner in which these two schools have joined to draw the intellectual boundaries of industrial relations, shape the institutionalization of the field, and influence the resulting research. Kaufman concludes that the unsteady, almost tortured, evolution of the field, and the current environment in which it must operate, have left industrial relations in a precarious position. The author closes with a number of suggestions regarding the intellectual and institutional directions that the field might take to insure its survival. The book is a unique and timely contribution that will stimulate a useful, and hopefully productive, debate about the future of industrial relations as an academic field of study. Highly recommended for all academic and professional collections.—*P. F. Clark, Pennsylvania State University, University Park Campus*

OAB-1946   HD6509   95-16874 CIP
Lichtenstein, Nelson. **The most dangerous man in Detroit: Walter Reuther and the fate of American labor.** Basic Books, 1995. 575p index ISBN 0-465-09080-X, $35.00

Walter Reuther was relentlessly ambitious. He came to Detroit as a tool and die man, helped build and became president (from 1946 to 1970) of the nation's most powerful union (the United Auto Workers), and eventually walked the world stage with prominent politicians. In this volume, noted labor historian Lichtenstein (Univ. of Virginia) gives a detailed, well-documented account of Reuther's life and his attempt to reengineer American society by creating a social democratic economic system (à la Sweden). Lichtenstein details the strategies and compromises that Reuther made to gain and wield power. At the book's heart is the "Treaty of Detroit," the "deal" struck between the UAW and the big automakers, which granted industrial peace and productivity growth in exchange for rising living standards and company-based welfare initiatives (such as pensions and health insurance). In the end Reuther became part of the liberal establishment and felt trapped by the failing institutions that he had helped create. The book is heavy on analysis of union politics, coalition building, and infighting, but somewhat weak in its presentation of economics. However, it is a must read for all interested in labor history. All libraries.—*R. M. Whaples, Wake Forest University*

OAB-1947   HF5549   96-45780 CIP
Meyer, John P. **Commitment in the workplace: theory, research, and application,** by John P. Meyer and Natalie J. Allen. Sage Publications, CA, 1997. 150p bibl indexes afp ISBN 0-7619-0104-3, $34.00; ISBN 0-7619-0105-1 pbk, $15.95

This superior compilation and analysis of empirical research delivers what its title proposes. The construct—commitment—is clearly defined, and its meaning, development, and consequences are explored depth. The preponderance of research deals with affective commitment (an employee's emotional attachment to, identification with, and involvement in the organization) and self-reported, individual-based performance indicators. The reader's comprehension is facilitated by the clear delineation of findings; analysis relating the consistency of outcomes with theory; and explanations for both positive and negative findings, weaknesses, and areas for future research. The authors also address multiple forms of commitment (work, group, supervisor, occupation); the management of commitment; and reengineering and downsizing. This impressive compendium of research documents that commitment has consequences for work behavior and for human resource managers responsible for the socialization of personnel and establishment of policies that contribute to its development. In summary, a superior academic presentation, complete with comprehensive bibliography. Upper-division undergraduate through professional readership.—*R. Quinn, CUNY Bronx Community College*

OAB-1948   HD5707   96-1005 CIP
Peck, Jamie. **Work-place: the social regulation of labor markets.** Guilford, 1996. 320p bibl index afp ISBN 1-57230-043-4, $42.50; ISBN 1-57230-044-2 pbk, $19.95

In this intelligent and intellectually rewarding book, Peck rewrites labor market theory. Rejecting the belief that labor markets are like commodity markets and thus regulated solely by price signals that emanate from the abstract interaction of supply and demand, he assumes the social nature of labor and the institutional embeddedness and geographical differentiation of labor markets. He begins with theories of labor market segmentation and ends with a theoretically robust conception of the local labor market. During his journey, he covers a range of perspectives (e.g., regulation theory, the spatial division of labor) and explores an array of interrelated themes: the structured character and local constitution of labor markets; "flexible" labor and its relation to post-Fordism and agglomeration; the interactions among domestic labor, paid work, and contingent workers; the emergence of workfare states; and the global geopolitics of labor regulation. Peck's argument draws mainly on other theoretical literature, but also includes a case study of employment and training policy in Britain that illustrates the institutional regulation that dominates his approach. No labor market theorist, or researcher for that matter, can ignore this book. Upper-division undergraduates and up.—*R. A. Beauregard, New School for Social Research*

OAB-1949   HD8073   93-42744 CIP
Phelan, Craig. **Divided loyalties: the public and private life of labor leader John Mitchell.** State University of New York, 1994. 438p bibl index afp ISBN 0-7914-2087-6, $59.50

Elected to the presidency of the United Mine Workers union at the age of 28, John Mitchell became one of the most powerful and respected labor leaders in the country. Although he led massive, successful strikes in the early 1900s, he favored a conciliatory approach to industrial relations. Born as a strategy to build a strong, stable national union, this approach also satisfied his personal need for social and financial recognition. The National Civic Federation became the institutional embodiment of this concept. Its brief period of effectiveness contributed to Mitchell's rise; its subsequent decline led to mounting personal and organizational problems for the UMW president. This thoroughly researched biography portrays the complexity of a man who believed wholeheartedly in the miners' cause while being equally committed to his own advancement. The author's disappointment with his subject's "conservatism" comes through clearly. Even though Mitchell built the strongest union in America, Phelan implicitly blames him both for not adopting a more radical view of labor-management relations and for the subsequent misdirection of trade unionism in the US. Overall, an excellent labor biography of interest to specialists and general readers alike. All levels.—*H. Harris, Pennsylvania State University, New Kensington Campus*

OAB-1950   HD5325   94-27852 CIP
Rosenblum, Jonathan D. **Copper crucible: how the Arizona miners' strike of 1983 recast labor-management relations in America.** ILR Press, 1995. 256p index afp ISBN 0-87546-331-2, $38.00; ISBN 0-87546-332-0 pbk, $16.95

The organized labor movement suffered devastating setbacks during the 1980s. Among the most notorious was the 1983 strike at the Phelps Dodge copper mines in Arizona, which ended in a decertification election and the loss of union representation. Rosenblum describes the events that precipitated the strike and led to the union's defeat. Much of the narrative is drawn from interviews with participants in the affair and from contemporary media accounts. The result is a convincing depiction of the failure of labor law to adequately protect workers' rights to bargain collectively. As the author demonstrates, various public institutions were recruited in the attack on labor; they included academics from a prominent university, agents of the Arizona state government, and federal employees of the National Labor Relations Board. The policy issues involved in the strike are still relevant, particularly the use of permanent replacement workers. That point is illustrated by President Clinton's recent and controversial ban on federal contracts with employers who permanently replace strikers during a dispute. Rosenblum portrays a significant event in labor history and forcefully illustrates the factors contributing to the present decline of unions. General, academic, and professional collections.—*R. L. Hogler, Colorado State University*

OAB-1951　　　　HD6519　　　　93-24325 CIP
Schneider, Dorothee. **Trade unions and community: the German working class in New York City, 1870-1900.** Illinois, 1994. 273p bibl index afp ISBN 0-252-02057-X, $34.95

Drawing on her command of both German and American sources, Schneider explores how New York City's German immigrants sought to overcome ethnic and cultural differences to form class-based organizations. She emphasizes the diversity of German experiences; they differed by generation, class, religion, and skill. Even the German-dominated trade unions—often short-lived organizations that flourished in the 1870s and 1880s—exhibit almost bewildering complexity. Looking at cigar makers, brewery workers, and bakers, Schneider demonstrates how craft traditions, ethnic composition, industrial organization, and production technology varied and how those variations influenced the nature of unionism. Some unions sought socialist solutions, others clung to craft traditionalism, while the cigar makers under the leadership of Samuel Gompers and Adolph Strasser paved the way for the "business" unionism of the American Federation of Labor. A major contribution to both labor and immigration history, *Trade Unions and Community* ought to be a model for further studies of the dynamic interplay between immigrant traditions and American institutions. Thoroughly researched and richly footnoted; extensive bibliography. General; upper-division undergraduate through faculty.—*D. Lindstrom, University of Wisconsin-Madison*

OAB-1952　　　　HD5724　　　　93-25070 CIP
Stenberg, Carl W. **America's future work force: a health and education policy issues handbook,** by Carl W. Stenberg and William G. Colman. Greenwood, 1994. 615p index afp ISBN 0-313-27980-2, $95.00

This excellent general reference is an ambitious attempt to summarize the many analytical and statistical reports relevant to "the conditions and challenges confronting the workplace and workforce of the future." A first chapter provides an overview of major economic, social, fiscal, and demographic factors determining future labor force composition and size and skill requirements. It also reviews alternatives for meeting projected skill shortages. Subsequent chapters provide encyclopedic reviews of specific deterrents created by the health care and educational systems as well as more general deterrents (e.g., poverty, environmental, or family related) to the future employability of the under-20 age group; describe major policy options available to overcome those deterrents; and identify the role of, and relationships between, the public and private sectors in preparing the future workforce. Extensive, current references and footnotes; comprehensive index; numerous tables and charts; more than 25 appendixes; heavily oriented to vital statistics. Upper-division undergraduate through professional.—*J. M. Glasgow, emeritus, University of Connecticut Health Center*

OAB-1953　　　　HF5549　　　　96-1867 CIP
Thomas, R. Roosevelt. **Redefining diversity.** AMACOM, 1996. 253p index ISBN 0-8144-0228-3, $24.95

Written by one of the most respected authorities on diversity issues, this book is must reading for anyone responsible for or interested in dealing with the challenges and opportunities presented by organizational diversity. The insights provided by Thomas extend well beyond race, color, and gender and clearly demonstrate how managing diversity in the organization can create a competitive advantage and bottom-line results. The five chapters in part 1 offer a new paradigm for understanding diversity and describe a set of eight action options for dealing with a wide range of diversity issues, e.g., managing joint ventures, achieving cross-functional synergy, coordinating multiple business lines,

and managing change in a global environment. Part 2 utilizes a series of five case studies (BellSouth, Hallmark Cards, EDS, Goodyear Tire & Rubber, and General Motors) to illustrate diversity in action. The book is well written and full of candid, helpful suggestions for infusing diversity concepts into all aspects of business practice and into the entire spectrum of strategic issues confronting today's organizations. Upper-division undergraduate through professional.—*T. Gutteridge, University of Connecticut*

■ Marketing

OAB-1954　　　　HF5415　　　　94-17747 MARC
AMA marketing encyclopedia: issues and trends shaping the future, by the American Marketing Association; ed. by Jeffrey Heilbrunn. NTC Business Books, 1995. 348p bibl index ISBN 0-8442-3593-8, $47.95

The *AMA Marketing Encyclopedia* is highly recommended for anyone seeking the hottest new concepts to find, satisfy, and keep customers. Students new to the field of marketing as well as seasoned professionals will find this publication extremely helpful. Prominent practitioners have been selected to contribute chapters on almost every facet of current issues and trends in marketing. Major sections cover new products and services; creative communications; customer service strategies; marketing channels and selling systems; strategic marketing management; micromarketing; information collection and analysis; and TQM and the future of marketing. Valuable, up-to-date information is provided for both marketing educators and practitioners, and the presentations may challenge their thinking about marketing. The volume also contains brief biographies of the contributors, which provide important who's who information on these marketing leaders. A must for any complete marketing library. All levels.—*W. G. Ellis, New England College*

OAB-1955　　　　HF5415　　　　94-27438 CIP
Cohen, William A. **The marketing plan.** Wiley, 1995. 318p index ISBN 0-471-58071-6 pbk, $24.50

A seasoned author of many books and a professor of marketing, Cohen shares his many years of helping students and practitioners develop thousands of marketing plans. The aim of this book is to present readers with the knowledge needed to develop truly outstanding professional marketing plans. The author explains marketing planning and provides step-by-step procedures to develop a professional marketing plan. Steps of the marketing plan consist of (1) outlining a marketing plan; (2) scanning the environment; (3) establishing goals and objectives, (4) developing marketing strategies; (5) developing marketing tactics; (6) forecasting; (7) calculating important financial ratios; (8) presenting the plan; and (9) implementing it. Several helpful forms are provided. Seven actual marketing plans written by former students constitute 175 pages of the book. Appendixes cover sources of secondary research, examples of simple marketing research, and a marketing research checklist. Must reading for undergraduate and graduate students wishing to develop a marketing plan, especially those consulting with small businesses. Also very helpful for new and existing small business owners.—*W. H. Brannen, Creighton University*

OAB-1956　　　　HF5415　　　　92-9811 CIP
Curry, David J. **The new marketing research systems: how to use strategic database information for better marketing decisions.** Wiley, 1993. 397p index afp ISBN 0-471-53058-1, $65.00

The traditional approach to marketing research is to treat each problem or strategy as an individual project. Yet practitioners, to manage efficiently, must anticipate an organization's research needs and, thus, gather data on a continuous rather than a project, or sporadic, basis. Recent technological advances, e.g., high-speed computers that can handle large amounts of data, UPC scanner data, and availability of geodemographic data, have encouraged the expansion of the latter approach. This volume by Curry (Univ. of Cincinnati) is the first text to provide comprehensive insights into this current approach to marketing research. The new marketing research described by Curry has been adopted for the most part by large packaged-goods marketers, but it has not, at this time, forced the traditional approach into obsolescence. Tables, charts, and source notes, as well as a lively writing style, make the book readable, even for those with limited backgrounds in marketing research. This work should be required reading for all students and practitioners of marketing research, and it is highly recommended for managers and students of management, especially marketing, who incorporate the output of marketing research into their decision making and strategic planning.—*W. C. Struning, Seton Hall University*

OAB-1957   HF1416   94-16179 CIP
Czinkota, Michael R. **The global marketing imperative,** by Michael R. Czinkota, Ilkka A. Ronkainen, and John J. Tarrant. NTC Business Books, 1994. 308p index ISBN 0-8442-3550-4, $27.95

This extremely readable and useful book is one of the best to come along on the subject of international marketing. Covering everything from researching and entering foreign markets to developing effective price and promotion strategies, it contains numerous examples of companies that succeeded or failed in their efforts to develop international markets. Along with this, the authors provide additional insight into such key areas as negotiation techniques (emphasizing the importance of patience), payment terms (and the intricacies of "Letters of Credit"), government regulations, and strategic foreign alliances. As an added benefit, a "Check Points" section at the end of each chapter sums up the vital points marketers need to keep in mind in pursuing global markets. Highly recommended for marketing students, faculty, and professionals interested in learning more about the global marketplace.—*P. G. Kishel, Cypress College*

OAB-1958   HF5822   95-50743 CIP
Maddock, Richard C. **Marketing to the mind: right brain strategies for advertising and marketing,** by Richard C. Maddock and Richard L. Fulton. Quorum Books, 1996. 280p bibl indexes afp ISBN 1-56720-031-1, $59.95

The major focus of *Marketing to the Mind* is the unconscious side of human behavior—often unheard, unexplored, and unexamined, and seldom researched. The authors' primary reason for studying the unconscious is to address the issue of consumer emotion—a right brain activity that opens up a new and exciting perspective on consumer motivation. The authors introduce a three-dimensional theory and motivation research methodology they developed in their own research over the past 15 years. Successive chapters illustrate how the right brain market research technique is applied to a variety of consumer activities and product and service categories, e.g., food service, fashion, cosmetics, casino gambling, health care, theme parks, cruises, insurance, nonprofit organizations, among others. Chapter 20, "Why People Still Visit Elvis and Graceland," is a unique case history on emotional and motivational marketing. The final chapter summarizes the features and benefits of three-dimensional (silent side) marketing. Clearly and authoritatively written, this book should be required reading for professionals, practitioners, and marketing, advertising, and psychology faculties and their students. Upper-division undergraduate and up.—*R. R. Attinson, CUNY College of Staten Island*

OAB-1959   HF5415   96-19070 CIP
The Marketing research guide, by Robert E. Stevens et al. Haworth, 1997. 488p index afp ISBN 1-56024-339-2, $79.95

This volume is a useful primer for those who need to understand and assess marketing research but lack a comprehensive research background. The organization and presentation of complex material is both lucid and complete. Concise and thoughtful chapters present essential materials that are at once theoretically sound but emphasize practical application. Topics range from research design, data gathering, sampling methods, and data interpretation to preparing the research report and product testing. This book is also a fine resource for quickly finding answers to specific questions relating to the application and devel-

opment of various marketing research techniques. By providing an excellent compilation of appendixes (e.g., "Sample Research Proposals," "Sample Questionnaires," "Statistical Sampling Concepts," "Sample Final Report"), the authors' allow the reader to see practical examples of theoretical materials. This valuable and useful addition to the literature of marketing research is recommended for upper-division undergraduate and graduate students as well as business professionals.—*S. A. Schulman, CUNY Kingsborough Community College*

OAB-1960   HF5813   95-35569 CIP
McAllister, Matthew P. **The commercialization of American culture: new advertising, control and democracy.** Sage Publications, CA, 1996. 296p bibl index afp ISBN 0-8039-5379-8, $45.00; ISBN 0-8039-5380-1 pbk, $21.95

This critical analysis should toss around American thinking on the subject of advertising much as Vance Packard's *The Hidden Persuaders* (1957) did. McAllister has written a classic, showing advertising's invasion of everything—classrooms, doctors' offices, sports arenas, concert halls, museums, airsickness bags, floor tiles, and all of the media. He decodes the new language of the profession (niche marketing, cross-promotion, place-based marketing, camouflaged ads, etc.) and explains advertising strategies to gain back control temporarily lost to "zipping," "zapping," message clutter, and use of new media. The author pulls no punches in showing the depths to which advertisers go to get their messages seen in an atmosphere where there are "no limits, no rules." The results are the total subversion of the democratic process; the smothering of rational, honest, and intelligent discourse with lies, deceptions, and inanities; and the despoiling of the cultural, artistic, educational, and environmental landscapes (not to mention the robbing of the average American of three years of useful life spent looking at advertisements). Since advertising celebrates capitalism, it is only natural that advertisers, media conglomerates, businesses, and the government collude to perpetuate a "fetishness of commodities." Systematically researched, organized, and documented, this book should be required reading for advertising and media students and for the general public.—*J. A. Lent, Temple University*

OAB-1961   HF5415   94-8542 CIP
Moschis, George P. **Marketing strategies for the mature market.** Quorum Books, 1994. 198p bibl index afp ISBN 0-89930-887-2, $55.00

Moschis (Georgia State Univ., author of *Marketing to Older Consumers*, CH, May'93), a recognized authority in the development of education about the older market, offers the most complete current source of information on marketing to the senior segment of the American population. By summarizing existing knowledge of this growing market, providing an understanding of the behavior patterns of older consumers, and presenting new evidence from a major study, he builds a solid basis for the development of strategies for targeting mature consumers. The final chapters identify strategies and offer guidelines for developing and evaluating others. Specific demographic, lifestyle, and behavioral data are provided in the context of a strategic framework. Because the older segment of the population is rapidly increasing, this material will prove invaluable to marketing practitioners as more and more firms target older American consumers. Well organized with excellent tables and references. Upper-division undergraduate through professionals.—*L. J. Cumbo, Emory and Henry College*

OAB-1962   HF5415   91-47642 CIP
Moschis, George P. **Marketing to older consumers: a handbook of information for strategy development.** Quorum Books, 1992. 338p index afp ISBN 0-89930-764-7, $59.95

Moschis (director of the Center for Mature Consumer Studies, Georgia State Univ.) has written an outstanding book which covers the often ignored segment of older consumers. Effective strategies to reach this market are enhanced with information drawn from a wide range of sources. Specific attention is given to changing values and consumption patterns as consumers mature. Mass media channels, shopping habits, and behavioral changes are given careful consideration. Thirty-two figures and tables provide valuable graphic reference sources. Moschis provides a complete summary of the book which ties together the various facets of his work and provides a number of recommendations and strategies for marketing practitioners. Excellent reference list. A must for the academic or professional marketing library.—*W. G. Ellis, Concordia University*

OAB-1963　　　　HF5415　　　　93-30264 CIP
Nelson, Carol. **Women's market handbook: understanding and reaching today's most powerful consumer group.** Gale, 1994. 366p bibl index afp ISBN 0-8103-9139-2, $64.95

Marketers seeking to reach the women's market are well advised to read Nelson's informative and insightful book. Picking up where Freud left off, the author sets out to answer the question "What do women want?" She shows that the so-called "women's market" actually comprises many separate submarkets, or niches, each with its own needs and wants. For example, there is the active woman who is interested in physical fitness, sports, and nutrition; the traditional homemaker whose primary focus is hearth and home; the not-so-traditional homemaker who is balancing work and family needs; and a host of other women of varying ages, incomes, and interests. Each is looking for the products and services right for *her*. The one thing all women seem to have in common is time or, more specifically, the *lack* of it. Nelson points out that cosmetics giant Avon has recognized this and now, instead of relying on the bell-ringing "Avon Lady" to sell its products, makes it convenient for women to shop "by phone, fax, mail, and rep." The book contains numerous examples and photographs of actual ads. There is also a "Sourcebook" of consultants, organizations, publications, and other resources marketers can consult for additional information. Highly recommended for marketing professionals, researchers, faculty, students at all levels as well as the general public.—*P. G. Kishel, Cypress College*

OAB-1964　　　　HF5415　　　　93-41996 CIP
Rossman, Marlene L. **Multicultural marketing: selling to a diverse America.** Amacom, 1994. 178p bibl index ISBN 0-8144-5071-7, $22.95

Rossman's readable and informative book is essential for marketers looking for ways to identify prospective customers and communicate effectively with them. The main premise of the book is that the "typical" American consumer or household no longer exists, having been supplanted by separate and distinct groups of consumers representing a panoply of cultures and subcultures. Rossman notes that the US has moved from "Ozzie and Harriet to the Cosbys, from scotch and soda to margaritas, from Walter Cronkite to Connie Chung, and from Chevrolet to Honda." The melting pot that once was America is now a *mosaic* with each element (ethnic as well as each geographic, demographic, and lifestyle group) demanding that its particular needs be filled. The food, clothing, automobiles, stores, advertising messages, or media that appeal to one group may not appeal to another. An example cited is lemon-lime drinks. It was found that sales of these drinks were lower in southern and coastal regions where there were large clusters of African American and Hispanic consumers who did not like the drinks' tart taste. Pointing out that differences exist not only between groups but *within* them (e.g., Asian Americans of Japanese descent often respond differently to advertising campaigns than those of Korean descent), the author stresses the importance of really knowing the target market. All levels.—*P. G. Kishel, Cypress College*

OAB-1965　　　　HF5414　　　　92-9810 CIP
Samli, A. Coskun. **Social responsibility in marketing: a proactive and profitable marketing management strategy.** Quorum Books, 1992. 198p bibl index afp ISBN 0-89930-628-4, $47.95

Samli, a distinguished author and professor, provides a balanced and readable argument for profitable social responsibility in marketing as well as options for strategy development. Although acknowledging that socially responsible marketing actions can result in lower profitability, the author convincingly argues that a long-term strategy of marketing responsibility can be highly compatible with increased profits. Coverage is comprehensive and includes a historical per-

spective, and information on equal opportunity for consumers, ethics, services, the environment, and trade-offs between efficiency and effectiveness. Researchers and students will appreciate the clear identification of issues, while practicing managers will find the strategic implications both believable and enlightening. Highly recommended for all academic and large public library business collections.—*L. J. Cumbo, Emory and Henry College*

OAB-1966　　　　HF5415　　　　96-52509 CIP
Smith, J. Walker. **Rocking the ages: the Yankelovich report on generational marketing,** by J. Walker Smith and Ann Clurman. Harper Business, 1997. 314p index ISBN 0-88730-813-9, $25.00

Well written and quite fascinating, *Rocking the Ages* is a fantastic journey into the history of Yankelovich Partners. Although the book is a Yankelovich report on generational marketing, it gives the reader a feeling of sitting in on a Yankelovich business meeting on target marketing. The premise is that three groups of cohorts have passed through the US and each has had a dramatic impact on product marketing. The first group, called the Matures, are frugal and disciplined, and save for a rainy day. They have a great affiliation for brands such as Converse, Timex, and Wayfarer. Boomers are youth oriented and more concerned with "now." Boomers are associated with such products as Addidas, Vuarnet, Casio, and Oreos. The last group are Xers with their savvy, entrepreneurial style, who live in an uncertain world. They are market savvy and purchase Nike, Oakley, Swatch, and Snackwells. These are only thumbnail descriptions; the authors describe in great detail numerous key characteristics of these three groups, offering many examples. A wonderful addition to the book are well organized tables showing differences among the three groups. The information provided will be valuable in developing marketing strategies to reach the three groups. A great addition to any undergraduate, graduate, or professional business library.—*D. C. Kimball, Elms College*

■ Economics

OAB-1967　　　　HC59　　　　94-14480 CIP
Amin, Samir. **Re-reading the postwar period: an intellectual itinerary,** tr. by Michael Wolfers. Monthly Review, 1994. 256p index ISBN 0-85345-893-6, $26.00; ISBN 0-85345-894-4 pbk, $14.00

Amin, a highly influential but heterodox development economist, uses this book to explain the postwar world against the backdrop of his own intellectual odyssey. He weaves together his political struggles with his published works, all the time casting light on the economic and political complexities of the postwar period. Although Amin assumes a prior knowledge of political events and the debates in which he engaged, the uninitiated will still benefit greatly from his many brilliant insights, which stand above the specifics. He is at his best in discussing the collapse of his three pillars of the period: Fordism in the West, Sovietism in Eastern Europe, and Developmentism in the Third World. In particular, Amin's retelling of his experience as a development advisor in Africa makes this book a "must read" for anybody with even a passing interest in development. Although this book is somewhat disorganized, the translator has made reading it a valuable experience. Upper-division undergraduate through faculty.—*M. Perelman, California State University, Chico*

OAB-1968　　　　HC79　　　　95-45082 CIP
Castells, Manuel. **The rise of the network society.** Blackwell, 1996. 556p bibl index afp (Information age, 1) ISBN 1-55786-616-3, $59.95; ISBN 1-55786-617-1 pbk, $25.95

Castells (Univ. of California, Berkeley) proposes that corporations are transforming themselves into global networks, and that in the process, every aspect of life is changing. Drawing from research in the US, Asia, Latin America, and Europe, he shows how cultural and institutional factors will continue to shape the form that corporate networks will take in each economy. Castells's far-reaching analysis of this network transformation covers the workplace extensively, but also extends to subjects as far afield as art, architecture, and death. Castells rejects the idea that we are entering a postindustrial society. Instead, he views information as having become an essential input within traditional, industrial, agricultural, and service economies. This large interdisciplinary volume, with a bibliography of more than 50 pages, is the first installment of a three-volume set. A brief review cannot do it justice. No other scholar has approached the subject of the information age in as engaging and innovative a way as this author. Strongly recommended for academic libraries.—*M. Perelman, California State University, Chico*

OAB-1969   HG237   92-5685 CIP
Cohen, Edward E. **Athenian economy and society: a banking perspective.** Princeton, 1992. 288p bibl indexes afp ISBN 0-691-03609-8, $35.00

Modern treatments of ancient economies have tried to correct serious shortcomings in earlier studies. The latter were flawed because the researchers' strengths were primarily in the fields of linguistics and arts. The corrective thrusts have sought to provide more realistic understanding of delineating magnitudes of the ancient economies. The most favored methodological tool has been "cliometrics" (econometric analysis of history). Cohen now improves on this improvement. It is needed for two reasons: accessible knowledge of ancient economies cannot provide sufficient acceptable quantitative data to sustain a cliometric approach, and cliometric practitioners frame their models as modern society. Often the results are seriously off target. Cohen (re)introduces the analysis of forensic materials as a superior alternative, showing that these materials constitute compact, in-depth sources of ancient economic practices. He illustrates their use by showing the substantial, sophisticated character of 4th-century Athenian banking—decisively overturning the pawn-broking image previously implied by cliometric studies. This is a seminal work. Along with Wilhelm Jongman's *The Economy and Society of Pompeii* (CH, May '89), it will help chart the course for future research. Exhaustive references. Advanced undergraduate; graduate; research.—*J. Murdock, emeritus, University of Missouri-Columbia*

OAB-1970   HD75   95-5870 MARC
Cowen, M.P. **Doctrines of development,** by M.P. Cowen and R.W. Shenton. Routledge, 1996. 554p bibl index ISBN 0-415-12515-4, $79.95; ISBN 0-415-12516-2 pbk, $24.95

A veritable feast to connoisseurs of social thought, Cowen and Shenton's book traverses the rich panorama of postmercantilist events and thought by the deft blending of economics, sociology, politics, and history. This interdisciplinary approach is initiated by conveying the fundamental pith of the idea of development. The book is partitioned into what the authors call the three sections of Caesar's Gaul. The first deals with the reformed and reformulated doctrine of development in early 19th-century France by the Saint-Simonians and Auguste Comte. This effort successfully replaced the old idea of progress and led to the intent to develop doctrine whose instrument was trusteeship. John Stuart Mill and the Fabians anglicized the theory and practice of trusteeship for Britain and its colonies. The second part deals with the degeneration of the doctrine of development, as propounded by imperial Britain, into administrative mirage for Australia, Canada, and Kenya. The third and final part, especially the last chapter, has the enduring quality of a classic. According to the authors, development has to be holistic and internally inspired. An impressive presentation of Amartya Sen's ideas crowns the discussion, which goes beyond worn-out utilitarian ethics by emphasizing maximization of employment of labor in development. This forcefully presented study will be of substantial value to upper-division undergraduates and graduate students in economics, sociology, and international relations.—*C. J. Talele, Columbia State Community College*

OAB-1971   Orig
Davies, Glyn. **A history of money: from ancient times to the present day.** University of Wales Press, 6 Gwennyth St., Cathays, Cardiff, CF2 4YD, UK, 1994. 696p bibl index ISBN 0-7083-1246-2, $80.00

This work of monumental proportions is both well conceived and executed. Davies begins with the fundamentals of money and banking, and along the way he effectively sheds new light on the basics of money, removing some misconceptions regarding the origins of banking and making contributions of his own. The historical development of money is well documented and argued. The account of Gresham's law, a topic very useful in classroom discussion, is highly illuminating. The origin and spread of the industrial revolution is masterfully woven together with the vital role of money and banking. The author's treatment of the evolution of the credit system, starting with the Scottish banks, is thorough and informative. Davies also covers the rise, working, and demise of the pure gold standard and as well as monetary episodes in different countries. Comparison and contrast among the countries discussed reveal the variety of experiences countries have encountered in the process of industrialization. Modern theoretical controversies are dealt with objectively with the help of facts and figures. Davies writes with a sparkling wit, and his prose is elegant and flowing. This book is a total success. Both undergraduate and graduate students can learn much from this excellent work, which will be useful to economists, political scientists, and even anthropologists.—*C. J. Talele, Columbia State Community College*

OAB-1972   HQ1061   96-542 CIP
Disney, Richard. **Can we afford to grow older?: a perspective on the economics of aging.** MIT, 1996. 344p bibl index ISBN 0-262-04157-X, $35.00

Society is aging. By 2025, in most of the industrialized world, roughly 30 percent of the population will exceed age 59. Will this demographic shift create a "crisis of aging," sapping economic growth and requiring heavy burdens on younger generations? To help answer this question, Disney (economics, Univ. of London) adopts a life-cycle model of economic decision making embedded in an overlapping generations framework and investigates the impact of aging on public social security systems; private pension plans; productivity, wages, and educational attainment; retirement; consumption and saving; and health care finance. An additional chapter adopts a public-choice perspective in examining instability in the long-run social contract between generations. Disney concludes that "there is no evidence of adverse effects of aging on aggregate productivity," although "there are serious crises in pay-as-you-go social insurance programs and in health care." These crises "have little to do with aging," and far more to do with the "Ponzi-scheme nature of such programs." This is a superb book—clearly written; brimming with insight; firmly grounded in economic theory; full of important institutional details, international data, and citations to recent research. Excellent for classroom use. Upper-division undergraduate through professional.—*R. M. Whaples, Wake Forest University*

OAB-1973   HC79   94-39336 CIP
Estabrooks, Maurice. **Electronic technology, corporate strategy, and world transformation.** Quorum Books, 1995. 269p bibl index afp ISBN 0-89930-969-0, $59.95

This book is largely a panoramic history of the development of modern information and communications technology, beginning with the development of the telegraph, the telephone, the radio, and the microchip. Later, Estabrooks shows how each of these electronic technologies matured. This book is remarkable in its coverage of virtually every industry associated with information and communication technology. Estabrooks provides a wonderfully complete history of each of these industries, setting them within a corporate and a regulatory context, and comparing and contrasting what emerged in the US with the experiences in other national economies. The author is reticent to draw strong conclusions from the historical material, but a general pattern emerges. Industries begin with government support from grants, contracts, or regulatory protection. The industry matures and takes advantage of its customers. More energetic competitors come on the scene and shake things up. The system becomes dynamic until it matures again, taking full advantage of government protection. Libraries will be well advised to order this book. Informed general readers; upper-division undergraduate through professional.—*M. Perelman, California State University, Chico*

OAB-1974 HB849 97-16710 CIP
Furedi, Frank. **Population and development: a critical introduction.** St. Martin's, 1997. 201p bibl index ISBN 0-312-17656-2, $59.95; ISBN 0-312-17658-9 pbk, $19.50

Conventional wisdom in demographic analysis holds that population growth and development potential are inextricably linked. Moreover, most examples of environmental and political stress have been persistently linked to population growth ("whatever your problem, more people makes it worse"). Yet is this invariably true? In this impressive study of the relationships between population and development, Furedi argues persuasively that the people/growth association has moved well beyond the simplistic models of the 1970s and 1980s, and that the evolutions of both areas feature an increasing independence that pulls them further apart. Drawing heavily on the "North vs. South" division of the economic world (which is in itself controversial), the author traces the evolutionary thinking of several developmental agencies in terms of eight "perspectives": developmentalist, redistributionist, resource limitations, sociobiological, people as inherent instability, people as problem solvers, women and human rights, and religious/pro-natal. At the end of an extremely lucid and impartial discussion, Furedi concludes that population growth and economic development levels are to a large extent independent variables, and that their long-promoted hypothetical interdependence is not only inaccurate, but is maintained to perpetuate the outdated agendas of various international agencies. References. An important contribution to the population versus development debate. Upper-division undergraduate and above.—*J. R. McDonald, Eastern Michigan University*

OAB-1975 HB98 94-37278 CIP
Groenewegen, Peter. **A soaring eagle: Alfred Marshall, 1842-1924.** E. Elgar, 1995. 874p index ISBN 1-85898-151-4, $89.95

Giant in size and substance, this book deals with economist Alfred Marshall, whose shadow still looms large on the science of economics. Groenewegen critically, intensively, and exhaustively examines all aspects of Marshall's life using the required documentary evidence. The evolution of Marshall's intellectual life from his formative years to maturation is portrayed in a way that helps us to understand Marshall's character. To the Marshallians, contrary to pronouncements of the erosion of Marshall's *Principles* and the subsequent development of the theories of monopolistic and imperfect competition and oligopoly, Marshall's *Principles* are still the storehouse and powerhouse of the engine of economic analysis. The author's treatment of the development of the *Principles* through the successive editions is covered in depth. It is heartening to this reviewer to find that the author more than once deals with Marshall's penchant for the institutional economics of Henry Main and Veblen. Groenewegen's prose is gripping yet lucid and analytical. Without exaggeration it can be stated that any future work on Marshall has to start from this book. The flaws in Marshall's character are skillfully and delicately handled in this balanced presentation. The only thing the book needs is a chapter on such Marshallians as Milton Friedman. Upper-division undergraduate through professional audiences.—*C. J. Talele, Columbia State Community College*

OAB-1976 HB72 93-44416 CIP
Haslett, D.W. **Capitalism with morality.** Oxford, 1994. 280p bibl index afp ISBN 0-19-828553-1, $49.95

This significant and timely work deserves serious consideration by the widest audience. Haslett (philosophy, Univ. of Delaware) is concerned with broadening the debate about what form capitalism should take if we wish to construct a more morally satisfactory system. He argues persuasively (chapter 1) that his indirect utilitarian criterion for moral norms is not necessarily at odds with conclusions arrived at by more intuitionist methodologies (John Rawls, *A Theory of Justice*, CH, Sep'72). After examining the libertarian morality underlying current capitalism (chapter 2) and the socialist ideal of central planning (chapter 3), he concludes that they fail to respect four basic moral ideals: equal opportunity; equal access to the necessities for a decent life; freedom; and productivity. He envisions a "capitalism with morality" that does respect

these four ideals by promoting greater autonomy for employees (chapter 4); an antipoverty policy with a more meaningful tax exemption; a more adequate earned income credit; nonpoverty-related medical and educational benefits (chapter 5); and equal opportunity by abolishing the practice of inheritance as it exists today (chapter 6). Although not politically feasible given today's libertarian mood, his proposal provides concrete directions for those concerned with the general welfare of the US (cf. Christopher Lasch, *The Revolt of the Elites and the Betrayal of Democracy*, CH, Jun'95). All levels.—*E. L. Donahue, Creighton University*

OAB-1977 HB75 95-37470 CIP
Heilbroner, Robert. **Teachings from the worldly philosophy.** W.W. Norton, 1996. 353p index ISBN 0-393-03919-6, $27.50

In a time of high economic technocracy, when some of the best economics departments considering dropping the course requirement for the history of economic thought, Heilbroner's yeoman's effort to put this topic back in proper perspective is as laudable as it is successful. The book starts with the best of the Western tradition, the Bible and Aristotle, and takes the reader through Saint Thomas and the commercial revolution. Because of the resurgence of Adam Smith, it might be of value to differentiate Smithian economics from the economics of Adam Smith. It might come as a surprise to nonreaders of the *Wealth of Nations* and the *Theory of Moral Sentiments* that Adam Smith advocated taxes to discourage improper and luxurious behavior, protection against communicable diseases, general education and, yes, a ceiling on interest rates. Agree or disagree, Marx is covered here and certainly is a worldly philosopher in the sense the author wants to connote. Heilbroner appropriately includes coverage of Bentham along with Jevons, Marshall, and Walras, because in technical economic theory he is often effaced. Professionals, particularly the modern Austrians, will miss discussion of Menger, von Wieser, Bohm-Bawerk, von Mises, and Hayek. Keynes and Schumpeter, two giants whose footprints are still visible and followed, are well covered, although this reviewer was saddened by the disproportionate emphasis on Schumpeter's failure as a prophet. Heilbroner's description and analysis of the capitalist process and entrepreneurial role deal with the very soul of the worldly philosophy. Written with solid content and wit, this volume is recommended for all collections.—*C. J. Talele, Columbia State Community College*

OAB-1978 HX36 94-46182 CIP
Itoh, Makoto. **Political economy for socialism.** Macmillan, UK/St. Martin's, 1995. 238p bibl index ISBN 0-312-12564-X, $65.00

This is an important book by an important economist. Itoh intends to show how political economy can be used to help create a socialist society, now that the USSR has collapsed. The author goes about this task by relying on reason rather than dogmatism. He begins by bringing together the history of the idea of socialism as well as the visions of Marx, Owen, and the Fabians. Fashioning Marx's socialist visions from a handful of paragraphs where Marx broached the subject is no easy matter, but Itoh does it very well. The author draws upon his own knowledge of modern economics to show how a nonbureaucratic socialist economy, such as Marx envisioned, might work. Itoh does a masterful job in reviewing the literature about market socialism and the earlier debates concerning whether socialist economies could be efficient. He reviews the accomplishments and shortcomings of the Soviet system and suggests how it might have been more successful. This book deserves the highest recommendation. Upper-division undergraduate through professionals.—*M. Perelman, California State University, Chico*

OAB-1979 HC51 95-10091 CIP
Kindleberger, Charles P. **World economic primacy: 1500 to 1990.** Oxford, 1996. 269p bibl index afp ISBN 0-19-509902-8, $35.00

Kindleberger (Ford International Professor of Economics, Emeritus, Massachusetts Institute of Technology) assesses the factors that have allowed different countries to achieve economic primacy at different times during the past 500 years. The book, which was the subject of a conference at Harvard, is part of the long-term project "The Vitality of Nations," which is sponsored by the Luxembourg Institute for European and International Studies. The author of numerous books and articles on economic and financial history and international economics, Kindleberger is widely regarded as a scholar capable of addressing the general public. The book contains 12 chapters. The first three provide background on the cycle of economic primacy. Subsequent chapters focus, in roughly chronological order, on the various holders of economic primacy; the Italian city-states, Portugal and Spain, the Low Countries, France, Britain, Germany, the US, and Japan. The book contains tables and graphs but is not extremely technical from an economic point of view. This detailed, scholarly, and well-referenced work will be a valuable addition to all libraries.—*R. Grossman, Wesleyan University*

OAB-1980   HB131   92-25821 CIP
Mayer, Thomas. **Truth versus precision in economics.** E. Elgar, 1993. 192p bibl index ISBN 1-85278-546-2, $49.95

Mayer is well known for his work in macroeconomics, especially for his classic study of the consumption function, *Permanent Income, Wealth, and Consumption* (1972). He now critiques economic methodology, arguing that economics has become excessively formal, valuing primarily rigor and precision, and worshipping mathematics for its own sake. As a result, economics has moved away from its roots as an empirical science and has lost its relevance. In addition, formalism has hindered the rejection of invalid economic hypotheses by drawing too much attention to the technical aspects of doing economics, and has led to bad empirical work because formalists do not value empirical economics. The new classical school of macroeconomics serves as a prime example of this excessive formalism, and as a major target for Mayer. Arguments here are made clearly, persuasively, and with a great deal of attention to garnering relevant supporting evidence. The result is a powerful indictment of current economic practices and a persuasive case for a more empirical economics. The book dovetails nicely with Donald McCloskey's *The Rhetoric of Economics* (CH, Jul'86), which also criticizes current economics. Although Mayer does not write with the wit or grace of McCloskey, to this reviewer at least, he focuses more pointedly on the essence of the problem plaguing the economics profession. Mayer's new book is important and highly recommended. It, along with McCloskey's work, belongs in every college and university library.—*S. Pressman, Monmouth College*

OAB-1981   Orig
McNally, David. **Against the market: political economy, market socialism and the Marxist critique.** Verso, 1994 (c1993). 262p index ISBN 0-86091-431-3, $59.95; ISBN 0-86091-606-5 pbk, $18.95

As the USSR disintegrated, many leftish intellectuals proposed that a mix of markets with some form of collective ownership could avoid the pitfalls of central planning and the callousness of markets. McNally's marvelous book attacks that notion as utopian. After a detailed history of capitalism's brutal creation, McNally demonstrates that both Adam Smith and the utopian socialists who followed him proposed humanizing the market by creating a just form of capitalism without exploitation. Once workers began to take this idea of justice seriously, classical political economy rallied around Malthus's doctrine that people had no rights to anything except what they could earn; that the market was necessarily a harsh environment; and that any efforts to humanize it would be self-defeating. This school sought to disabuse the poor of the idea that they had a right to subsistence. McNally then shows that Marx continued the tradition of classical political economy, contending that efforts to humanize the market were futile while people produced commodities for sale. Recommended for all levels of readership.—*M. Perelman, California State University, Chico*

OAB-1982   HB846   96-14168 CIP
McNutt, P.A. **The economics of public choice.** E. Elgar, 1997 (c1996). (Dist. by American International Distribution Corporation) 252p bibl indexes afp ISBN 1-85278-514-4, $80.00

Post-Keynesian economics is replete with revolutions, but undoubtedly the most important of them is the emergence of the public choice theory, which has many strands. For scholars hoping for a book that would skillfully and elegantly weave all the strands, McNutt's work fits the bill. The first chapter is a masterly overview of the new welfare economics, which lays a solid foundation for the forthcoming chapters on the mosaic of public choice theory. The treatment of social choice and voting is fortified with sound theoretical reasoning and helpful illustrations. The discussion of the Arrow impossibility theorem and the subsequent contributions of Sen and others is quite illuminating without involving undue complexities. This reviewer's favorite chapter covers the growth of government; McNutt solidly supports his reasoning using empirical data meshed with strong theory. This material should filter down to the level of principles without delay. Contributions of the patron saints of the public choice theory, James Buchanan and Gordon Tullock, are handled admirably well. Subsequent books on public choice will be measured by McNutt's book. Upper-division undergraduate and graduate students in public finance, public administration, political science, and economic development will reap definite benefits from such an excellent book on a growing discipline. Recommended for academic and professional collections.—*C. J. Talele, Columbia State Community College*

OAB-1983   HB103   91-25882 CIP
Moggridge, D.E. **Maynard Keynes: an economist's biography.** Routledge, 1992. 941p bibl index ISBN 0-415-05141-X, $37.50

As editor of *The Collected Writings of John Maynard Keynes* (1971-1989), Moggridge probably has a better grasp of the life and work of Keynes than anyone alive today. This biography relies heavily on the knowledge that Moggridge acquired in editing Keynes's writings. With painstaking detail Moggridge has assembled the facts about Keynes and his life—names, dates, and places of his homosexual relationships; his study habits and the books he read; the influences on, and development of, his economic thought; his personal and financial interests; his work for the British government; his editorship of the *Economic Journal*; his relationship with Lydia Lopokova; and much more. The result is a biography of Keynes that is more up-to-date and more thorough than any of its predecessors. However, we do not get a biography that weaves its facts into a story about Keynes the man, and the relationship between Keynes's life and his economics. For the big picture on Keynes, one must turn to Robert J. Skidelsky's two-volume biography, *John Maynard Keynes* v. 1 *Hopes Betrayed, 1883-1920* (CH, Sep'86); v.2, in press. Nonetheless, the comprehensiveness of this work will insure its status as the standard academic biography of Keynes for some time. Consequently, it is an essential purchase for all academic libraries.—*S. Pressman, Monmouth College*

OAB-1984   HB75   95-48950 CIP
Murakami, Yasusuke. **An anticlassical political-economic analysis: a vision for the next century,** tr. by Kozo Yamamura. Stanford, 1996. 476p index afp ISBN 0-8047-2646-9, $60.00

Although Japan is currently experiencing economic hard times, it still looms large in the American mind as the first star in the constellation of economic powerhouses in Asia. Only ten years ago, the market was flooded with books by Americans trying to explain and interpret Japan's "economic miracle." Now, at last, we have a translation of a major work explaining how the world looks from a Japanese perspective. Murakami began his career as an economic theorist and econometrician but expanded his field to encompass all social analysis; at the time of his death, he was referred to as the "Max Weber of Japan." At the heart of this large book is a critique of traditional free trade arguments using the theory of increasing returns. But this is only one aspect of a much larger vision. Murakami also undertakes a thorough analysis of liberalism, the nation-state, national security, and East-West relations. Murakami's thinking is complex and subtle, nowhere more so than in his call in this final chapter for cross-cultural understanding. This book offers an important perspective from a major thinker. It should be in all college and university collections.—*B. W. Bateman, Grinnell College*

OAB-1985 HB139 93-18799 CIP
Qin, Duo. **The formation of econometrics: a historical perspective.** Oxford, 1993. 212p bibl indexes afp ISBN 0-19-828388-1, $37.00

In this much-needed historical and chronological perspective of the advances in econometric theory and applications, Duo sets out to describe the marriage between mathematical statistical procedures and economic modeling of real world data and manages a unique feat, the contextualizing of intellectual strides in the analysis of economic data within the confines of economic theory. Each chapter addresses a particular focus of econometric methodologies as historically expounded and employed by the economists contributing to the theoretical frontier in economic analysis of the time. Duo manages to provide a unique human dimension to this development by examining the contributions of those economists leading the debate over the place of statistical methodologies in economic modeling and thus, the estimation techniques applied to the theoretical economic model using economic data. Chapters discussing testing and model construction revisited are crucial reading for econometric practitioners. They address the issues of model description, evaluation, and prediction which are generally taught at both undergraduate and graduate levels, without the broad historical perspective that defines and conceptualizes the econometric techniques employed today. These two chapters are the most important ones in the book because they completely characterize the standard empirical research that has become the trademark of the economics profession. A required addition to the applied econometrician's reference library. Upper-division undergraduate and graduate students will find this book a relevant resource in understanding the connections between seemingly disparate methodological techniques taught in basic and advanced econometrics courses.—*B. J. Robles, University of Colorado at Boulder*

OAB-1986 HB103 95-12836 MARC
Ross, Ian Simpson. **The life of Adam Smith.** Oxford, 1995. 495p bibl index ISBN 0-19-828821-2, $35.00

It has been 100 years since publication of the last full biography of Adam Smith, and during those ten decades Smith's influence has surely increased. Ross's handsome new life of Adam Smith would be welcome under any circumstances. It is especially welcome, however, because it is such a fine book, well written, well researched, and revealing. Ross (English, emeritus, Univ. of British Columbia) is editor (with E.C. Mossner) of Smith's correspondence, and biographer of Smith's patron, Lord Kames. The book is interesting enough as a biography and can be read with satisfaction for this reason alone, but Ross makes his real contribution by establishing the personal, cultural, and historical context that conditioned Smith's life and world and hence his philosophical and economic doctrines. This context is a necessary ingredient in any recipe for understanding Smith's great works. The bibliography will be useful to students and scholars alike. Every library should have this book on its shelves.—*M. Veseth, University of Puget Sound*

OAB-1987 HB103 86-217586 CIP
Skidelsky, Robert. **John Maynard Keynes: a biography. v.2: The economist as saviour, 1920-1937.** A. Lane, Penguin, 1994 (c1992). 731p bibl index ISBN 0-7139-9110-0, $34.95

Skidelsky's 1983 volume, *John Maynard Keynes: A Biography*, v. 1, *Hopes Betrayed, 1883-1920* (CH, Sep'86), established a new standard of excellence in the field of modern biography. This second volume in the trilogy boldly raises the stakes, making this an essential holding for all academic libraries. Skidelsky tracks Keynes through a particularly important period of his life and of 20th-century history, from the aftermath of WW I, through the turbulent 1920s and Britain's disastrous return to the prewar gold standard, into the Great Depression, and up to the doorstep of WW II. Keynes's life was entirely intertwined in the great social, political, and economic events of this period, making it a critical part of any effort to understand the 20th century. Skidelsky brilliantly illuminates the different aspects of Keynes's career, finding in the shadows the strong but sometimes controversial threads that bind them together. This volume will be of particular interest to scholars interested in Keynes's philosophical develop-

ment and the evolution of his economic theories. But the book is not for economists only. This is one of the outstanding serious books of recent years. General; advanced undergraduate and up.—*M. Veseth, University of Puget Sound*

OAB-1988 HB90 93-43188 CIP
Stiglitz, Joseph E. **Whither socialism?** MIT, 1994. 338p bibl index ISBN 0-262-19340-X, $29.95

Stiglitz's new book amply justifies this Stanford professor's reputation as one of the world's foremost economic theorists (he is currently one of the three members of President Clinton's Council of Economic Advisers). More than an answer to "whither socialism?" the book is a review of Stiglitz's 25 years work on the cutting edge of microeconomics. Indeed, 36 percent—117 of the 321 cited references—are to works written by Stiglitz, either alone or as a joint author. Hence, the book provides an excellent nonmathematical introduction or refresher for readers who wish to better understand the implications of imperfect information in the neoclassical paradigm of the market economy. More than half of *Whither Socialism?* is devoted to Stiglitz's insightful critique of the Arrow-Debreu neoclassical model, not only as an incomplete model but also as a faulty foundation for the Lange-Lerner-Taylor model of market socialism. In addition to his focus on the implications of imperfect information, the author stresses the role of incomplete markets, of properly understanding competitiveness, and of the dynamics that induce innovation, which account for Stiglitz's dissatisfaction with neoclassical microeconomics. Remaining chapters are more policy oriented, discussing such issues as the importance of privatization and capital markets. Indeed, these two chapters are must reading for anyone recommending privatization as a panacea. Upper-division undergraduate through practitioner.—*J. Prager, New York University*

OAB-1989 HD82 91-27475 CIP
Tausch, Arno. **Towards a socio-liberal theory of world development,** by Arno Tausch with Fred Prager. St. Martin's, 1994 (c1993). 265p bibl index ISBN 0-312-06210-9, $69.95

After the end of the Cold War, the economics profession turned its attention to long-range economic development. Using advanced statistical methods, Tausch covers the determinants of economic development from the 1960s to 1980s in 171 countries and territories. His analysis confirms the need for socioeconomic reform within the framework of political democracy, a view shared by the European social democratic theorists of the 1920s and 1930s. In the three decades that followed, developmental economics was dominated by Keynesianism and a romantic delusion of rapid industrialization through governmental planning. Evident in the 1970s was the failure of statism and protectionism to improve the Third World's standard of living as contrasted to the success of the "Asian Tigers," guided by market forces and pursuing free international trade. The demise of Eastern European nations in 1989-91 revealed the inherent impotence of extreme statism. The study confirms that the success of the Pacific Rim nations was facilitated by land and social reforms combined with capitalist development. Tausch interprets global development in terms of long cycles, evaluates the prospects of East European recovery and of reforms in the industrialized West, and emphasizes the critical importance for each country to engage in its own program of abolishing poverty. This outstanding volume is highly recommended. General; advanced undergraduate through faculty.—*O. Zinam, University of Cincinnati*

OAB-1990 HC79 96-35432 CIP
The Wealth of nations in the twentieth century: the policies and institutional determinants of economic development, ed. by Ramon H. Myers. Hoover Institution, 1997 (c1996). 314p bibl index afp (Hoover Institution Press publication, 437) ISBN 0-8179-9451-3, $34.95; ISBN 0-8179-9452-1 pbk, $24.95

The 12 essays in this volume deal with the themes of wealth creation and the process of democratization in this century, and they are authored by a galaxy of eminent economists. All contributions are nothing short of excellent. Amartya

Sen's arguments, as usual, are subtle and jolting to comfortably settled ideas and minds. Sen advocates the Aristotelian view of wealth as an important means and not an end in itself, and therefore rejects the wealth maximization objective. Douglass North's outstanding essay weaves together new institutionalism with a comparative study of England and Spain; it is a model of reasoning, organization, substance, and language. Kozo Yamamura's article should be an eye-opener to supporters of pure laissez-faire, because it systematically details Japanese government intervention in promoting growth. Balancing Yamamura is Gur Ofer's piece on decelerating growth under USSR socialism, which details the government's growth-retarding intervention. Other articles are equally good. Must reading for students of economic growth and development, comparative economic systems, international relations, and economic history, especially upper-division undergraduates. Academic and professional collections.—*C. J. Talele, Columbia State Community College*

OAB-1991   HD78   95-36346 MARC
Wolfe, Marshall. **Elusive development.** Zed Books/UNRISD, 1996. 198p bibl index ISBN 1-85649-379-2, $55.00; ISBN 1-85649-380-6 pbk, $19.95

Elusive Development challenges all the platitudes and orthodoxies of the last half-century of economic development strategies. Many recent critiques of economic development policy focus on the mixed performance of the World Bank, but the author draws instead on his 30 years of experience at the UN to paint a broad picture of development theories, trends, and experiments. Wolfe shows a rare appreciation of the complexities of change processes and the ways in which they work themselves out in diverse geographic, historical, political, and cultural contexts. He traces the particular history of development prescriptions and the futile search for a unified theory of development, addressing such issues as the role of the state, environmental concerns, employment opportunities, poverty, and broad-based participation and communication. Highly critical of the simplistic neoliberal market prescriptions for development as well as the techno-bureaucratic statist alternative, he makes a compelling case for a middle-ground, inclusive, flexible, and locally adapted approach to economic development. An excellent acquisition, even for a limited collection in economic development. Upper-division undergraduate through professional readership.—*H. H. Ulbrich, Clemson University*

■ Africa, Middle East, Asia & Oceania

OAB-1992   HC800   93-47887 CIP
Adjustment in Africa: reforms, results, and the road ahead. Published for the World Bank by Oxford, 1994. 284p bibl afp ISBN 0-19-520994-X pbk, $19.95

This is the first major attempt at a comprehensive evaluation of structural adjustment programs in 29 countries in sub-Saharan Africa beginning in the early 1980s. The work addresses three issues: How much did countries change their policies? How did policy reforms affect growth? And, what is left to be done? The general conclusion is that although adjustment has been impressive in some countries, it is far from complete and much needs to be done to achieve sustained economic growth. Countries that pursued adjustment policies more vigorously grew at a faster pace than those that did not. Compared to the experiences of other regions of the developing world, there remains a lot of room for improvement, even for top performing countries in Africa. To achieve sustainable growth, African countries are expected to pursue the right macroeconomic polices, particularly a responsible fiscal policy and realistic exchange rate; encourage competition in the domestic market; and use scarce institutional capacity wisely. These reforms, the book argues, will increase the growth rate as well as decrease poverty and improve the environment. Contrary to the views of the critics of structural adjustment programs, the book argues that African countries need more rather than less adjustment. Appendixes A through C provide statistical data, indexes of policy change, and agricultural policy indicators. This extremely well-written

and well-documented book is must reading for anyone interested in Africa in particular, and less developed countries in general. See companion volume *Adjustments in Africa: Lessons from Country Case Studies*, ed. by Ishrat Husain and Rashid Farugee (CH, Nov'94). General; upper-division undergraduate through professional.—*K. Gyimah-Brempong, University of South Florida*

OAB-1993   Orig
Amuzegar, Jahangir. **Iran's economy under the Islamic Republic.** I.B. Tauris, 1993. 398p bibl index ISBN 1-85043-603-7, $59.50

Amuzegar, the preeminent economic observer of Iran, has produced the definitive description of the economy since 1978 in what is in many ways a companion to his earlier *Iran: An Economic Profile* (CH, Feb'78). Successive chapters present macroeconomic trends (national income, prices, population/employment), national economic policies (budget, banking, planning, foreign trade), and the main economic sectors (agriculture, industry, hydrocarbons). Unlike Hooshang Amirahmadi's *Revolution and Economic Transition: The Iranian Experience* (CH, May'91), the focus is on economics rather than socio-politics and on thoughtful description rather than analysis. The chapters on the political agenda and on the prospects, while well-informed, are not as strong as the rest of the work. For instance, Amuzegar's account of the ideological framework presents the struggle for power only through 1984/85; only later is there discussion of the profound changes brought by President Hashemi Rafsanjani starting in 1989/90. Furthermore, the evaluation of the economic performance of the Islamic Republic is unnecessarily negative, overlooking the improvement in social indicators like greater literacy, lower infant mortality, and wider ownership of consumer durables. The 44 pages of tables make available to the Western reader the official Iranian data. Advanced undergraduate through professional.—*P. Clawson, National Defense University*

OAB-1994   HJ8831   92-43301 CIP
Brown, Richard P.C. **Public debt and private wealth: debt, capital flight and the IMF in Sudan.** St. Martin's, 1992. 334p bibl indexes ISBN 0-312-07918-4, $75.00

This is certainly a welcome addition to an ever-growing literature on Third World debt and the role of the IMF. The case study of the Sudan is interesting in light of the Islamic revolution there that followed attempts by the previous governments to apply the structural adjustment formula of the IMF. The author makes a valuable attempt to understand and explain the logic behind the IMF formula rather than just to support or critique it. The book also evaluates the effects of IMF-supported donor intervention in the Sudan and how various IMF approaches come into conflict with each other. More importantly, the author makes a valuable attempt to uncover some important microeconomic adjustments that take place but are not acknowledged during the offical adjustment process. Part 1 focuses on the more general theoretical and methodological issues and compares debt crisis in sub-Saharan Africa with that in Latin America. Part 2 presents a case study of the Sudan between 1970 and 1984. The study is then updated to 1990 and tightly summarized in the final chapter where certain important lessons are drawn. Well organized, written, and presented, this book should be consulted by all those interested in sub-Saharan Africa, Third World debt, and IMF policies. Advanced undergraduate; graduate; faculty.—*H. Amirahmadi, Rutgers, The State University of New Jersey, New Brunswick*

OAB-1995   Orig
Economic reform and the poor in Africa, ed. by David E. Sahn. Oxford, 1996. 488p bibl index afp ISBN 0-19-829035-7, $90.00

There is considerable disagreement on the effects of structural adjustment programs on the welfare of the poor in developing countries. *Economic Reform,* an outstanding piece of work from both methodological and policy points of view, investigates the impacts of various policy reforms on the poor in Africa. Based on case studies from ten African countries—Cameroon, Gambia, Ghana,

Guinea, Madagascar, Malawi, Mozambique, Niger, Tanzania, and Zaire—most essays use GCE models that are able to separate the effects of economic decline on the poor from those caused by policy reforms. Essayists analyze the effects of specific policy changes on the poor in these countries rather than the effects of general structural adjustment. In part 1, an introduction, the editor nicely ties together the major themes in the book. The other three parts of the volume analyze the impact on the poor of policy reforms in selected countries with respect to trade and exchange rates, fiscal policies, and agricultural policies. The central thesis of the book is that contrary to popular notions that policy reforms harm the poor, these reforms, in fact, improve their welfare. Any negative consequence of policy reforms fall on the nonpoor who lose their economic rents. The lesson from these essays is that the distributional impacts of these policy reforms argue in favor of their continuous implementation. Highly recommended to researchers and policy makers, as well as students of development economics, upper-division undergraduate and up.—*K. Gyimah-Brempong, University of South Florida*

OAB-1996 HD9576 91-12390 CIP
Elm, Mostafa. **Oil, power, and principle: Iran's oil nationalization and its aftermath.** Syracuse, 1992. 413p bibl index afp ISBN 0-8156-2551-0, $39.95

A brilliant volume, standing head and shoulders above many on the nationalization of oil and the 1953 Anglo-American coup in Iran. Elm (an Iranian economist who has held various positions in Iran's Ministry of Foreign Affairs) presents a carefully documented picture of the rise and demise of democracy and independence during the premiership of Mohammad Mossadeq in Iran. The author reports: "The Truman administration believed that the nationalist movement [under Mossadeq] would work as a barrier against communism." Accordingly, the British were encouraged to recognize the nationalization. The British, who were after their own oil monopoly and the state-within-a-state status in Iran, were ready to occupy the southern half of Iran, risking the Russian takeover of the northern half. Finally, when the Eisenhower administration finalized "Operation Ajax," the time came to brand Mossadeq as a "crypto-communist." The shah was in their hip pocket, the corrupt politicians on their side, the domestic agents of M16 and the CIA ready and at their disposal, and finally the institutions of democracy were so fragile. The Anglo-American coup was a success. But, what goes around, comes around: Elm details how Britain paid almost immediately with displacement of her monopoly in Iran and elsewhere; America paid later. Excellent addition to all libraries.—*C. Bina, Harvard University*

OAB-1997 DT433 92-45498 CIP
Ensminger, Jean. **Making a market: the institutional transformation of an African society.** Cambridge, 1992. 212p bibl index ISBN 0-521-42060-1, $49.95

Economists have, for the most part, ignored the role of institutions in shaping economic growth. Anthropologists on the other hand have dismissed the importance and power of economic analysis as unrealistic in their studies of institutional development in less developed societies. Neither side has been completely successful in explaining the complex nature of change in these societies. Ensminger brilliantly combines the new institutional economics (NIE) and the insights of anthropologists to explain the process of economic progress and institutional change among the Orma people of Kenya. The central thesis of the book is that institutional change—ranging from transition from subsistence pastoralism to a market-based economy, to changes in property rights and the role of women in society—is greatly influenced by changes in transaction cost that make the change possible and beneficial to the society. The author provides details concerning the sources of changes in transaction costs and how they lead to changes in institutions and attitudes. Although the book focuses on the Orma people of Kenya, the central thesis is applicable to any developing society. Required reading for all those interested in development and anthropology. The book is very well documented and marvelously written. General readers; advanced undergraduate through faculty; professional.—*K. Gyimah-Brempong, Wright State University*

OAB-1998 HC447 95-17973 CIP
Hill, Hal. **The Indonesian economy since 1966: Southeast Asia's emerging giant.** Cambridge, 1996. 319p bibl indexes ISBN 0-521-49512-1, $64.95; ISBN 0-521-49862-7 pbk, $22.95

In view of the growing attention Indonesia has received for her outstanding economic performance in the last few years, this book is a timely and welcome addition to several recent studies of the Indonesian economy. At the outset, it should be noted that this study is one of the most comprehensive treatments of Indonesian economic development in the modern era. Topics range from ideology and state intervention in economic affairs to industrial transformation in the last three decades. Of particular interest is the succinct discussion of the modernization process of major economic sectors such as agriculture and services. The author highlights the causes of economic achievements and also carefully analyzes some major challenges Indonesia has faced, which include a large foreign debt, growing inequality, and regional disparities. The volume contains numerous tables and figures, which are presented in a manner understandably to general readers. Although specialists in Indonesian economy will be particularly interested in this well-written and organized book, generalists will also benefit from the wealth of information presented on this large and important emerging Asian economy.—*K. B. Lee, Skidmore College*

OAB-1999 HC445 93-3977 CIP
Huff, W.G. **The economic growth of Singapore: trade and development in the twentieth century.** Cambridge, 1995 (c1994). 472p bibl index ISBN 0-521-37037-X, $69.95

Huff writes from the premise that economic history can provide the empirical analysis to study the process of economic development. The author contends that, prior to 1900, Singapore developed as an entrepôt by capitalizing on its comparative advantages in the natural resource endowments of neighboring countries and favorable geographical position in heavily traveled sea lanes. During the second phase, 1900-39, the country expanded staple trade from tin and tropical produce to more sophisticated commodities such as rubber and petroleum. These products required processing, financing, and marketing expertise, which Singapore began to acquire during the period. In addition, massive immigration helped to sharpen the patterns of development. Post-WW II economic growth of Singapore is covered in the last part; following Singapore's independence, the state played a crucial role in orchestrating an extraordinary economic expansion through planning. Huff argues that in sharp contrast to other Third World nations, Singapore stands out as a country where a judicious application of planning has been successful. This book is full of trade statistics and immigration data useful to other researchers interested in Singapore. It is one of the most complete economic histories of Singapore written in recent years, especially with respect to the role of trade in development. Upper-division undergraduate through faculty.—*K. B. Lee, Skidmore College*

OAB-2000 HC467 93-23769 CIP
Hwang, Eui-Gak. **The Korean economies: a comparison of North and South.** Oxford, 1994 (c1993). 347p bibl index afp ISBN 0-19-828801-8, $49.95

In view of recent events developing in the Korean peninsula, this book is not merely timely; it provides an invaluable guide to understanding the complicated relationship between South and North Korea. The author analyzes and compares the parallel economic development of the two Koreas. In order to compare the performance of the two economic systems, Hwang meticulously develops a full set of time-series data on a macroeconomic index and living standard for both North and South Korea. This aspect of the study is a major contribution of this volume, and the author's thoroughness merits high praise. Another interesting comparison relates to the historical development and existing structure of public finance in both countries, with special emphasis on budget allocation between defense and other categories. Hwang also highlights a glaring difference in the approaches of the two countries to development strategy—the North pursuing relentlessly the policy of "chuch" (self-reliance) and the South consciously adopting an outward-looking policy. Hwang devotes considerable effort to appraising the prospects for economic and social interactions between the two Koreas so that they might take advantage of their existing and potential comparative advantage. Must reading for anyone concerned with the future of the Northeast Asian region. Upper-division undergraduate through professional.—*K. B. Lee, Skidmore College*

OAB-2001   HD1333   94-538 CIP
Jannuzi, F. Tomasson. **India's persistent dilemma: the political economy of agrarian reform.** Westview, 1994. 241p bibl index afp ISBN 0-8133-8835-X, $49.95

Jannuzi, who has had extraordinary experience in the developing world, and in India particularly, explains why India has failed to undertake significant agrarian reform. Among the reasons are such prevalent false images of Indian land holding systems as (1) misunderstandings of the British concerning culturally acceptable modes of agrarian reform; (2) false romantic notions of Indian policy makers about the land holding systems in pre-British India; and (3) the hubris of early development economists who saw industrial development as more important than agricultural development. Furthermore, the Indian constitution gave responsibility for agrarian reform to the states, not the federal government. Such factors have enabled the land-controlling elite to thwart significant agrarian reform. Jannuzi's accounts of his personal interviews with individuals influential in the development of India's economic policies are enjoyable to read. For a different slant on Indian agrarian economics this reviewer recommends Rita Sharma and Thomas Poleman's *The New Economics of India's Green Revolution* (CH, Dec'93), and Peter Hazell and C. Ramasamy's *The Green Revolution Reconsidered* (CH, Jun'92). For a cautionary view of land reform, readers should consult John P. Powelson and Richard Stock's *The Peasant Betrayed* (1990). Jannuzi's excellent work of scholarship is highly recommended for lower-division undergraduate through professional audiences.—*D. D. Miller, Baldwin-Wallace College*

OAB-2002   HC427   94-133498 CIP
Naughton, Barry. **Growing out of the plan: Chinese economic reform, 1978-1993.** Cambridge, 1995. 379p bibl index ISBN 0-521-47055-2, $49.95

Naughton's narrative of China's economic reforms from 1978 to 1993 is the single most coherent, convincing, and readable analysis of this labyrinthine process. As the title implies, Naughton's theme is a success story centered around the advantages of a gradual rather than a precipitous shift from plan to market (a "dual track system" in Chinese parlance). He emphasizes the industrial sector and its central relationship to macroeconomic policy in restructuring China's pre-1978 command economy. Relaxation of the central government's industrial monopoly in 1979 led to a "virtuous circle" of consequences, which were by no means the result of a carefully plotted scenario. The speedy entry of many new firms hungry for profits induced systemic transformations. These included rapid growth in total output, increased competitive pressure on and enhanced incentives for state sector firms, inexorable rationalization of the price system, and sustained erosion of government revenues thanks to the declining profits of state enterprises. Naughton shows how China's planners, facing an incremental rather than a sudden fiscal crisis, were steadily weaned toward full marketization. A fortunate combination of policy choices, serendipity, and the interlocking nature of socialist economic systems thus gave rise to the world's fastest growing major economy. Recommended for upper-division undergraduate through professional collections.—*R. P. Gardella, United States Merchant Marine Academy*

OAB-2003   HD2385   92-13254 CIP
Nishiguchi, Toshihiro. **Strategic industrial sourcing: the Japanese advantage.** Oxford, 1994. 318p bibl index afp ISBN 0-19-507109-3, $39.95

Nishiguchi (management, Wharton School) has written several papers on industrial management. His book constitutes a definitive study of Japanese subcontracting, supported by numerous tables and figures, and extending in coverage to Europe and the US. The author uses sources in Japanese and in English,

and provides a wealth of documentation and supplementary information in extensive footnotes. Nishiguchi's thesis contradicts that of Oliver Williamson's *Markets and Hierarchies* (CH, May'76) and *The Economic Institutions of Capitalism* (1985) on business opportunism and bounded rationality. In his clear historical description and systematic analysis of present-day subcontracting practices, Nishiguchi stresses rationality, problem solving, and mutual symbiotic cooperation that has supplanted any vestiges of exploitation of subcontractors. He quantifies asset-specificity in an original approach, dividing it into physical, dedicated, human, and site; he finds that it is defined by producer strategies, laying to rest the dual economy explanation of subcontracting. One of the important contributions of the book is its proof of cross-cultural applicability of the Japanese system. This work also contains rich and captivating anecdotal evidence. Highly recommended to all academic and business school libraries supporting upper-division undergraduate and graduate students, and to larger public libraries.—*B. Mieczkowski, Ithaca College*

OAB-2004   HC447   91-23712 CIP
The oil boom and after: Indonesian economic policy and performance in the Soeharto Era, ed. by Anne Booth. Oxford, 1992. 448p indexes ISBN 0-19-588969-X, $60.00

A superb and comprehensive survey of Indonesia's economic transformation over the decade of the 1980s, this collection of 12 essays deals with three aspects of the Indonesian economy: macroeconomic policies (fiscal, monetary and financial, foreign exchange rates); the dynamics of sectoral growth (agriculture, manufacturing, transport, and service); and human resources development (income distribution, labor force and employment, population and health). It represents the first systematic assessment of the growth and structural transformation of the Indonesian economy in the 1980s. Balanced in perspective, rich in empirical analysis, and original in data, this work is a sequel to *The Indonesian Economy During the Soeharto Era*, ed. by Anne Booth and Peter McCawley (1981). Essential reading for students of the contemporary Indonesian economy. Highly recommended for development economists and policymakers, Southeast Asian area specialists, and graduate students.—*C. Moon, University of Kentucky*

OAB-2005   HC445   95-12688 MARC
Pasuk Phongpaichit. **Thailand, economy and politics,** by Pasuk Phongpaichit and Chris Baker. Oxford, 1996 (c1995). 449p bibl index afp ISBN 967-65-3097-2, $59.00

This remarkable work details the evolution of the Thai economy and incorporates the critical political and international forces that shaped and influenced Thailand in the 19th century and continue to in the 20th. Part 1, "Village," includes superb chapters on the expansion of the rice frontier and the development to a diversified, cash-based agricultural sector. The village is tied to the "City," the title of part 2, a compelling analysis that unmasks the role of rice traders, bankers, generals, exporters, industrialists, urban labor, and the monarchy in the development and underdevelopment of the Thai economy in the 20th century. The third part, "Politics," skillfully details the political dimensions of the monarchy, revolution, dictatorship, Buddhism, and the military as they relate to the transition from a simpler era of village-city links to a complex set of economic, political, and international relationships today. The economic transformation by generals, godfathers, merchant barons, business families, and economic entrepreneurs results in dubious benefits for the peasantry. A nonconformist Buddhist movement, rural revolt against the exploitation and degradation of rural resources, and village opposition to dominant Bangkok forces are all part of this excellent study. Recommended for upper-division undergraduate through professional collections.—*B. F. Hope, California State University, Chico*

OAB-2006   HC445   95-36676 CIP
Peebles, Gavin. **The Singapore economy,** by Gavin Peebles and Peter Wilson. E. Elgar, 1996. (Dist. by Ashgate) 286p bibl index ISBN 1-85898-286-3, $94.95

Peeples and Wilson have produced one of the most analytically sophisticated surveys of Singapore's economy over the last three decades. This study of the role of macroeconomic policy in promoting Singapore's outstanding performance is unique in that the authors successfully apply the macroeconomic theories of Keynesian and classical economics to a small and open economy. Particularly interesting discussions focus on the role of macroeconomic policy in relation to money and monetary policy in maintaining stable price levels. There is also extended coverage of the foreign exchange rate policy and its subsequent impacts on trade and the balance of payments. For those inclined toward refined quantitative analysis, the chapters on forecasting growth trends and macroeconometric modeling of Singapore's economy should be quite useful and insightful. In the concluding chapter, the authors speculate on some burning contemporary issues facing Singapore's economy. An excellent addition to a growing literature examining the causes of spectacular development of East Asian economies in the postwar period. Upper-division undergraduate through faculty.—*K. B. Lee, Skidmore College*

OAB-2007   Orig
Perthes, Volker. **The political economy of Syria under Asad.** I.B. Tauris, 1995. 298p bibl index ISBN 1-85043-910-9, $59.50

This clearly written and well-presented account by the leading European scholar of contemporary Syria is the definitive account on Syrian economics and an important source on its politics and society. Only one of the six sections is on economic performance per se, although the other sections (on social division, the political structure, and political decision making, plus an introduction and conclusion) view issues largely through the lens of economics. Foreign policy is confined to the concluding section, which has a solid but brief discussion of the domestic implications of the confrontation with Israel; intervention in Lebanon gets less analysis. Similar brief treatment is given to ethnic or religious factors; the emphasis on class over other social divisions means that there is relatively little discussion of the tensions between the Sunni majority and the Alawite community from which most of the ruling elite stems. The discussion of class issues is primarily empirical (e.g., tracing what has happened to the rural poor and how the distribution of income has changed) rather than the theoretical discussions that preoccupy the other main political economist writing on modern Syria, Raymond Hinnebusch, in *Peasant and Bureaucracy in Ba'thist Syria* (1989) and *Authoritarian Power and State Formation in Ba'thist Syria* (CH, Nov'90). Perthes demonstrates mastery over Syrian sources, as well as the full range of Western literature. Upper-division undergraduate through professional.—*P. Clawson, National Defense University*

OAB-2008   HC462   94-12017 CIP
Pilat, Dirk. **The economics of rapid growth: the experience of Japan and Korea.** E. Elgar, 1994. 334p bibl index ISBN 1-85278-762-7, $67.95

Pilat (research fellow, Univ. of Groningen, the Netherlands) has written a meticulously researched piece on the attempt by Japanese and South Korean economies to catch up with leader economies such as the US, and he identifies two primary factors in this process: social capability and technological congruence. The author believes that the historical backgrounds of Japan and Korea were important to their success in achieving rapid economic growth. "Catch up" also had indirect effects on the growth of these countries through the realization of economies of scale and the accumulation of the capital stock. Pilat emphasizes an important point: "catch up" does not work automatically. This potential can be realized only if the proper policies are followed and the right conditions are created. Both countries were able to advance quickly vis-à-vis the leader country, the US, because they stressed the spread of education, selective industrial policy, and an export-oriented approach. By means of econometric technique, the author makes a binary comparison of productivity growth first between Japan and South Korea and then between both and the US. This volume is filled with sophisticated statistical analyses, many original. Annex tables alone comprise 78 pages. Highly recommended for all serious students of East Asian economies. Upper-division undergraduate through faculty.—*K. B. Lee, Skidmore College*

OAB-2009   HC415   93-203 CIP
Plessner, Yakir. **The political economy of Israel: from ideology to stagnation.** State University of New York, 1994. 328p index ISBN 0-7914-1741-7, $65.50

This book belongs on the bookshelves of anyone interested in the Israeli economy. The heavy hand of Israeli government intervention in economic activity, though widely known among both economists and business people, has nowhere been as thoroughly documented, at least in English, as in this study. Plessner's insights derive not only from his involvement as a faculty member of the Hebrew University's prestigious Department of Economics, but also from the senior policy-making positions he held in the Israeli government during the 1980s. He shows how an interventionist ideology, which began in the prestate era and which might have been justified then, carried through to the early days of the state. It never really weakened during the decades after 1948 despite changing economic and political circumstances, for the public's reliance on the government had bred a self-sustaining dependence. Similarly, little real pressure to prevent inflation existed, for an extensive indexation mechanism protected most people from its ravages. Hence little change either in the micro- or the macroeconomic environment could be expected, despite the economy's evident inefficiencies and its post-1970s slowdown in economic growth. Although Plessner's views are occasionally controversial, especially concerning the causes and consequences of the exploding inflation during the 1980s, and his somber prognosis for the future seems to have been contradicted by intensified economic growth during the last two years, he provides a perceptive and coherent analysis of the economic scene that cannot be easily dismissed. As such, this book can bolster the forces behind the fledgling steps toward economic liberalization now emerging in Israel. All levels.—*J. Prager, New York University*

OAB-2010   HC415   96-24374 CIP
Richards, Alan. **A political economy of the Middle East,** by Alan Richards and John Waterbury. 2nd ed. Westview, 1996. 445p bibl index afp ISBN 0-8133-2410-6, $75.00; ISBN 0-8133-2411-4 pbk, $25.95

Writing a textbook on the political economy of a region as diverse as the Middle East and keeping it up to date with new theoretical concerns, statistics, and events is a formidable task. Richards and Waterbury successfully presented a comprehensive study of the Middle East economies in the first edition of this book (CH, Nov'90). The undergraduates in this reviewer's seminar on the political economy of the Middle East found the book interesting, informative, and challenging, and many Middle East scholars have found it an indispensable reference source. This second edition is just as successful. Although revised, updated, and 50 pages shorter, the structure of the book remains intact. The analysis is in the context of the authors' triangular model of "structural transformation," "state structure and policy," and "social actors." Social actors have replaced "class" as the third vertex of the triangle, and a new chapter titled "Is Islam the Solution?" has replaced the "Class Interest and the State" chapter. The central analytical concern of the volume is the role of the state in the development process in the Middle East, where, in fact, it has had an overwhelming role. Each chapter is also a superb analysis of an issue of its own, e.g., population growth, human capital, and labor migration. This outstanding book is a must for any library collection.—*S. Behdad, Denison University*

OAB-2011   HQ1240   95-3457 CIP
Thomas-Slayter, Barbara. **Gender, environment, and development in Kenya: a grassroots perspective,** by Barbara Thomas-Slayter and Dianne Rocheleau et al. L. Rienner, 1995. 247p bibl index afp ISBN 1-55587-419-3, $49.95

Thomas-Slayter and Rocheleau (Clark Univ.) have collaborated with eight Kenyan colleagues to produce a vibrant set of case studies set in rural Kenyan communities. The cases explore the role of indigenous community institutions, particularly women's organizations, as they respond to changing resource conditions. Indigenous ecological knowledge is the foundation for gender-based strategies regarding the management of soil, water, and woodlands in the context of changing gender roles. The interrelationships of poverty, gender roles, indigenous knowledge, and environmental and resource management become the basis for development policy and practice. The case studies focus on water and soil resources, health and nutrition, agriculture and livestock, and agroforestry. Much of the fieldwork for the case studies used participatory rural appraisal methodologies. This is one of the first works available that explicates the importance of understanding gender-based knowledge within a community for sustainable approaches to development. Well written and highly readable, the study includes seven maps, a table, and 17 figures. An invaluable resource for students of culture change, gender relations, resource management, and development, not only in Kenya, but also as a model for use in many other parts of the world. All levels.—*D. M. Warren, Iowa State University*

OAB-2012 HC427 94-28436 CIP
Yabuki, Susumu. **China's new political economy: the giant awakes,** tr. by Stephen M. Harner. Westview, 1995. 320p bibl index afp ISBN 0-8133-2254-5, $69.00; ISBN 0-8133-2255-3 pbk, $23.95

A remarkable array of data about China's post-1978 economic growth is packed within the covers of this volume. It will certainly serve as a ready desktop reference on topics as diverse as China's population problem, central-regional fiscal tugs of war, wage reforms, and the introduction of free markets and foreign direct investment in China's coastal regions. Yabuki is touted as one of Japan's top China watchers, so the work also affords Westerners a rare Japanese analysis of the Chinese *Wirtschaftswunder*. To make the subject even more palatable to nonspecialists, a tsunami of graphs, charts, and tables engulfs readers throughout the text. Most are legible and informative, but several have the visual disutility of dazzle painting on an obsolescent battleship. Yabuki sensibly stresses the key role of Deng Xiaoping's 1992 southern inspection tour in sustaining China's drive towards a "socialist market economy." He is less sanguine about (increasingly feeble) US efforts to nudge China's party hierarchs towards political reform as well as economic liberalization. Yabuki himself has comparatively little to relate about the nature of the roaring political fires beneath China's bubbling economic cauldron, the only glaring omission in an otherwise valuable reference book. All levels.—*R. P. Gardella, United States Merchant Marine Academy*

■ Canada & the United States

OAB-2013 HC106 92-26913 CIP
Boulding, Kenneth E. **The structure of a modern economy: the United States, 1929-89.** New York University, 1993. 215p index ISBN 0-8147-1203-7, $60.00

Boulding provides a crisp overview of economic changes in the US between 1929 and 1989. He is struck by the extraordinary disturbances of the Great Depression, of WW II, and of the disarmament of 1945-47 and is surprised by the system's relative stability since the 1940s. He notes the unexpectedly small economic impact of the federal government, even during the New Deal, and the sharp erosion of profits by interest since 1950. He believes that the crowding out of profits by interest lowers productivity and employment. As always, Boulding pursues economic analysis through metaphor. He revisits the classical stagnation thesis, questioning the ability of an increasingly interdependent global system to sustain an acceptable living standard under the strain of constant and rapid population growth. An appendix contains extensive data. Boulding always sorts through data with his unique creative imagination. His economics is in a class by itself. The economics profession enjoyed a stroke of good fortune when economic questions captured the fancy of this extraordinary man. All levels.—*R. T. Averitt, Smith College*

OAB-2014 HE7781 94-3911 CIP
Brock, Gerald W. **Telecommunication policy for the information**

age: from monopoly to competition.** Harvard, 1994. 324p index afp ISBN 0-674-87277-0, $45.00

Brock provides an integrated view of decentralized decision-making and regulatory activity in the telecommunications industry. Although some early history is present, the author emphasizes the post-WW II changes in the industry, from the early competitive ventures through the AT&T divestiture (1984) and the evolution under a vastly altered structure. Brock brings a career's experience as an academic analyst (economist) and an inside participant (six years in the FCC); he is currently professor of telecommunications at George Washington University. This volume is clearly the best historical study yet to appear on the changes in telecommunications from regulated monopoly to a partly regulated, partly deregulated (free market) industry. All levels.—*R. A. Miller, Wesleyan University*

OAB-2015 HC103 95-860 CIP
The Cambridge economic history of the United States: v.1: The Colonial era, ed. by Stanley L. Engerman and Robert E. Gallman. Cambridge, 1996. 481p bibl index ISBN 0-521-39442-2, $74.95

This series seeks to comprehensively survey the history of economic activity and change in the US, taking full account of the "new" economic history's statistical and analytical contributions and related developments in social, labor, and political history. This volume, a valuable addition to any academic library, examines British North America from European settlement to the end of the 18th century. Chapters cover Native Americans (Neal Salisbury); Atlantic Africa (John Thornton); the European background (E.L. Jones); population, labor, and economic development (David Galenson); northern colonies (Daniel Vickers); southern colonies (Russell Menard); West Indies (B.W. Higman); mercantilist policies (John McCusker); and the Revolution, Constitution, and new nation (Cathy Matson). The inclusion of Native Americans' and Africans' prior economic histories is especially valuable to those specializing in American economic history. Few chapters disappoint. Among the highlights are Galenson's careful analysis of institutions of settlement, labor markets, and demographics; Menard's insightful analysis of regional developments within the South; and McCusker's provocative essay, which concludes that the "rebellion" had "nothing to do with mercantilism." Each essay includes a bibliographical essay, not systematic footnotes. These bibliographies are valuable but could use more annotation. All levels.—*R. M. Whaples, Wake Forest University*

OAB-2016 HE745 92-17754 CIP
De La Pedraja, René. **The rise and decline of U.S. merchant shipping in the twentieth century.** Twayne, 1992. 345p bibl index afp (Twayne's evolution of American business series, 8) ISBN 0-8057-9826-9, $26.95; ISBN 0-8057-9827-7 pbk, $14.95

Destined to become a classic, this is the first comprehensive 20th-century history of the US merchant shipping industry. Based on exhaustive research of private records and public sources, this volume delivers a chronological account commencing with activities of J. P. Morgan and his contemporaries at the dawn of the century. Final sections bring the story right down to the post-Cold War reconfiguration of global trading patterns and economic alliances. Rich detail about individual companies permits the reader to see how interaction of government agencies, domestic and international competitors, and key members of management led to crucial decision points. Such material has never before been so accessible. More than simply a report on a single industry, this addition to American business history comes at a critical time when this industry's lessons, not previously learned, are being revisited in other sectors such as the steel and automotive industries. Richly referenced and footnoted, this title is an essential source for policymakers, business leaders, graduate students, and scholars. Must reading for all who are struggling to position US industry in the rapidly changing world economy.—*W. S. Reed, Maine Maritime Academy*

OAB-2017   HE355   92-12692 CIP
Downs, Anthony. **Stuck in traffic: coping with peak-hour traffic congestion.** Brookings/Lincoln Institute of Land Policy, 1992. 210p index afp ISBN 0-8157-1924-8, $28.95; ISBN 0-8157-1923-X pbk, $10.95

This highly readable book by a noted real estate economist explains why traffic congestion in large US metropolitan areas is such a difficult problem to solve. The book describes in lay terms, the inextricable link between hated traffic congestion and our cherished solo car-commuting behavior. Downs's unique contribution is his authoritative evaluation of proposed land development solutions to traffic congestion such as placing limits on local growth or jobs-housing balance regulations. Unfortunately, even the land development proposals fall far short as meaningful solutions. Instead, the author argues eloquently for peak-period road pricing and concerted regional action, both of which he agrees are not likely to happen in the foreseeable future. The book also includes an excellent discussion of the usual litany of transportation supply-and-demand solutions. There is no comparable book. The quality of the index, references, printing, and binding are excellent. The few tables and charts are very up to date, using 1990 census data. Public, professional, and academic collections, advanced undergraduate and up.—*D. Brand, Harvard University*

OAB-2018   HC108   91-47507 CIP
Eggert, Gerald G. **Harrisburg industrializes: the coming of factories to an American community.** Pennsylvania State, 1993. 412p bibl index afp ISBN 0-271-00855-5, $35.00

Over the last generation there have been several outstanding studies at the community level of industrial growth in 19th-century America, such as Anthony Wallace's *Rockdale* (CH, Jan'79), Paul Faler's and Alan Dawley's books on Lynn, Massachusetts, and Cathy McHugh and David Carlton on cotton-mill towns in the South—enough outstanding work so that Eggert includes a separate listing of work in this genre along with his bibliography of sources on Harrisburg. Yet his study stands on its own as a major achievement that traces with exceptional thoroughness the social transformation of Harrisburg from 1850 to 1880 by the growth of numerous small factories, and the role of these small-scale enterprises in the state and national economy. He combined the manuscript census materials and surviving company records for those years to give an exceptionally rich empirical base to a story that straddles business and labor history, and he gives a new twist to the vexed question of "typicality" that many such studies have raised. The result is as deep and complex an analysis of the process as we have in any work, yet a story that can appeal to all serious students of American life. General; advanced undergraduate through faculty.—*M. Rothstein, University of California, Davis*

OAB-2019   HC106   93-31481 CIP
Eisner, Robert. **The misunderstood economy: what counts and how to count it.** Harvard Business School Press, 1994. 222p index afp ISBN 0-87584-443-X, $22.95

Previously president of the American Economic Association, Eisner has wrought a treasure of economic wisdom, brilliantly argued and written in English accessible to members of Congress and lay persons generally, while remaining interesting. Indeed, he is provocative to economists, especially non-Keynesians. Libraries and other entities gathering materials on economic issues, particularly on federal fiscal and monetary policy or economic growth, should add this work to their collections. Dispelling some conventional views, Eisner argues that official budget measurements are conceptually flawed because current and investment outlays are not separated; when they are, the federal deficit is a fraction of that reported officially. Accordingly, fiscal stimulus should continue to augment aggregate demand to assure high employment—constrained and abetted by a steady debt/gross domestic product ratio. He argues that fears of inflation are overblown and that the greatest misconception of all is acceptance of the so-called natural rate of unemployment at the commonly thought range of five to six percent. Justifiably, the work already is widely acclaimed. All levels.—*H. I. Liebling, Lafayette College*

OAB-2020   HJ2051   97-9581 CIP
Evans, Gary R. **Red Ink: the budget, deficit, and debt of the U.S. government.** Academic Press, 1997. 297p index afp ISBN 0-12-244079-X, $59.95; ISBN 0-12-244080-3 pbk, $29.95

Expanded from materials provided in a series of college courses taught by Evans (Harvey Mudd College) since 1983, this book focuses on the politics and economics of US federal budgets in general and the significance of the accompanying deficits incurred during the present era. A very detailed exposition of the spending and receipts sides of the budget is made in an unusually lucid fashion, assisted by many charts and tables; the combination will bring much additional comprehension of many standard and technical aspects of budgets to both general readers and advanced fiscal theorists. While the author avers that the major objective of his efforts is nontheoretical, no less important are discussions on the impact of taxes or government debt on the economy, including the importance of crowding out of private credit by government deficit; the limits to the Laffer curve; tax disincentives on economic growth; and the gradualism needed to limit debt and deficits in the future. The book is embellished by (1) a wisely annotated bibliography of the relevant literature appearing in the last eight years or so, bravely including views different than the author's, and (2) several appendixes describing the market for US Treasury securities, varying concepts of budget statements, and other technical matters. Evans concludes in a final appendix with his analysis of the Welfare Reform Act of 1996. Compare with the different views represented by Robert Heilbroner and Peter Bernstein, *The Debt and the Deficit* (CH, Oct'89). Highly recommended for public, academic, and professional collections.—*H. I. Liebling, Lafayette College*

OAB-2021   HD9515   95-46909 CIP
Hall, Christopher G.L. **Steel phoenix: the fall and rise of the U.S. steel industry.** St. Martin's, 1997. 427p index ISBN 0-312-16198-0, $49.95

This well-researched and documented study will be the definitive history of the recent dramatic evolution of the US steel industry. Hall has worked in different segments of the industry for many years and is currently a freelance consultant in the metals and transportation industries. His analysis of the fall and rise of the US steel industry is based on an in-depth knowledge of the processes and players involved and a solid grasp of industry economics. Hall recounts how the oligopolistic structure of the integrated steel industry was radically altered by the rise of domestic competition (minimills using electric furnaces and scrap steel) and by intense import competition. Hall also describes the surprising rebirth of integrated mills in the US that now have "significantly lower costs than their competitors in Japan or the European Union, and at present are able to compete with the flat-rolled minimill industry." The author also describes likely technological advances and the changing nature of the international steel market. Includes several appendixes on the technical details of steel-making processes and on the nature and location of existing capacity within the industry. Recommended for all academic libraries.—*R. C. Singleton, University of Puget Sound*

OAB-2022   Can. CIP
Horry, Isabella. **Government spending facts 2,** by Isabella Horry and Michael Walker. The Fraser Institute, 626 Bute St., 2nd Floor, Vancouver, B.C. V6E 3M1, Canada, 1994. 386p bibl ISBN 0-88975-158-7 pbk, $23.95

Everything you ever wanted to know about government expenditure in Canada is to be found in this exceedingly valuable volume. Horry and Walker, two well-respected researchers, provide a comprehensive overview of government spending in Canada, including priorities and how they change, how interest payments are somewhat distorting, and how the amount and type of program spending per capita has changed over time. The main focus is in three chapters: one on spending by all levels of government by province, expenditures by the federal government by province, and finally provincial and municipal government spending. Two final chapters analyze government spending on interest charges and who benefits from government spending. There is a detailed appendix on methodology, a glossary, a complete bibliography, and voluminous additional tabular material. This is more a reference volume than a book for casual reading. Yet the text explaining the tabular presentations is well worth reading and serves as a model for anyone wanting to undertake basic government expenditure analysis. An essential work for any collection on Canada and its economy and a useful addition to collections on fiscal policy and public finance. Lower-division undergraduates through faculty.—*D. E. Bond, University of British Columbia*

OAB-2023 BX8128 95-1433 CIP
Kraybill, Donald B. **Amish enterprise: from plows to profits,** by Donald B. Kraybill and Steven M. Nolt. Johns Hopkins, 1995. 300p bibl index afp ISBN 0-8018-5062-2, $45.00;

At once sensitive and compassionate, this is a significant contribution to understanding how Amish culture in Lancaster County, Pennsylvania, is being transformed through the emergence of ethnic entrepreneurship, manifested in what the authors call microenterprises. "The development of Amish enterprises was a negotiated social process [and that] is the real story of this book—an exploration of the ways in which an ethnic culture both facilitated and resisted the emergence of entrepreneurship." A delicate balance between traditional Amish virtues of modesty, humility, and a tie to the land as a gift bestowed by Providence, on one hand, and cultural values that provide a frame for the microenterprise, on the other, is still being worked out as the plow is abandoned for work activity regarded as falling within the Amish worldview, even as that view is changing. The delicacy of that balance is beautifully illustrated by the discussion of "Amish electricity," reliance on hydraulic or pneumatic power to drive machinery *and* memory electric typewriters (but not computers) rather than use of alternating current produced elsewhere. Likewise, the interaction between the Lancaster Amish and external governments details the search for balance. This is scholarship at its best. All levels.—*L. Braude, SUNY College at Fredonia*

OAB-2024 HC110 92-40491 CIP
Lebergott, Stanley. **Pursuing happiness: American consumers in the twentieth century.** Princeton, 1993. 188p bibl index afp ISBN 0-691-04322-1, $24.95

The choices that American consumers have made, or have been able to make, is an interesting and compelling story that explains much about the development of the American economy over the 20th century. The author, a distinguished economic historian who has long studied and written about patterns of consumption, offers his readers not only specific details (which are outlined in an appendix) about consumption but also wonderful and provocative insights into the rational choices made by American men and women. Lebergott (economics, Wesleyan Univ.) examines how our notions about the material requirements for a typical family have changed over the years and notes that despite the best intentions of various commissions and social scientists, perhaps those changing lists of requirements are best left to consumers themselves. As Lebergott notes, while Thomas Jefferson asserted that life and liberty were "rights" in the Declaration of Independence, happiness on the other hand could only be pursued. How and under what circumstances that pursuit has changed over the 20th century tells much about American society. Recommended for undergraduates, graduate students, and faculty.—*T. E. Sullivan, Towson State University*

OAB-2025 HC105 94-37654 CIP
Licht, Walter. **Industrializing America: the nineteenth century.** Johns Hopkins, 1995. 219p index afp ISBN 0-8018-5013-4, $38.95; ISBN 0-8018-5014-2 pbk, $13.95

In this synthesizing work, Licht offers a valuable survey of industrialization and business development in 19th-century America, along with analyses of the responses of various groups of Americans to those developments. Seeing no basic break occurring with the Civil War or with the rise of big business, Licht deals with the 19th century as a continuum, an approach that may be questioned by scholars who view the development of big business as fundamentally changing America's economic landscape. Licht's history is most original and valu-

able in portraying the many paths Americans took toward industrialization and how they reacted to it in the antebellum years. It is weaker and less original in its descriptions of business developments and industrialization after the Civil War. Generally well organized and written in a sprightly style (Licht knows how to tell a story), this study is well suited for a general readership and for use in undergraduate classes. A detailed annotated bibliography is up-to-date.—*M. Blackford, Ohio State University*

OAB-2026 HJ241 93-30517 CIP
Makin, John H. **Debt and taxes,** by John H. Makin and Norman J. Ornstein. Times Books/Random House, 1994. 337p index ISBN 0-8129-2312-X, $25.00

Makin and Ornstein, an economist and a political scientist, respectively, have managed a stunningly successful account of fiscal policy—federal spending, taxation, and borrowing—in the US from Colonial times to the present. Using 1981, Reagan's first year in office, as a watershed, the authors describe the historical, ideological, and philosophical contexts, and the patterns and struggles behind debt and taxes from the beginning of the Republic to the Great Depression, from FDR to Eisenhower, and from the Great Society to the Reagan Revolution and beyond. Particular secions stand out: Part I on the elements of fiscal policy; the economic primer on budget deficits and the debt in Chapter 12; and several practical recommendations for management and change in the concluding chapter. There are few real weaknesses in this highly informative, thought-provoking, and balanced study; and with public and political focus on federal deficits, including the 1992 presidential election, the early Clinton administration budget proposals, and the on-going, stirring debate over a balanced-budget amendment, this volume could not be more timely. The book merits a large and varied readership. This valuable addition to the literature is one of the very few that generates more light than heat. Appendixes and notes are only of marginal use and quality, but this shortcoming is relatively unimportant. All levels.—*A. R. Sanderson, University of Chicago*

OAB-2027 Can. CIP
McCalla, Douglas. **Planting the Province: the economic history of Upper Canada, 1784-1870.** Toronto, 1993. 446p index afp ISBN 0-8020-3407-1, $50.00; ISBN 0-8020-3411-X pbk, $19.95

This is the third and final volume of the series covering the economic history of Ontario from the 1780s to the 1870s. It is a spectacular achievement by one of Canada's leading historians. McCalla, with careful argument, impressive scholarship, and thoughtful prose, demonstrates that Ontario's development to the mid-19th century was not just another case of development based upon one or two primary exports but a case of "balanced and relatively self-sustaining development" within the context of the North American and North Atlantic economies which both served to stimulate that growth. There are three parts to the narrative: establishing the new economy on the frontier, the period of extensive growth from 1822 to 1851, and a sweeping and impressive survey of the economy at mid-century. The notes are exhaustively extensive, the index very complete, and the statistical tables a treasure trove of information for any student of the period. A must acquisition for any collection on Canada or on North American economic history.—*D. E. Bond, University of British Columbia*

OAB-2028 HC106 93-7236 CIP
McKenzie, Richard B. **What went right in the 1980s.** Pacific Research Institute for Public Policy, 1994. 397p index ISBN 0-936488-71-9, $21.95

Left-leaning journalists, liberal politicians, and economists of like ideological persuasion have been instrumental in establishing a virtual conventional wisdom that the 1980s were among the worst of times in the US. Carefully examining standard sources of economic data, McKenzie demonstrates that reality was vastly different from the conclusions of the doomsayers. He notes that in most respects the economy did quite well in the 1980s. Output, productivity, and the standard of living all rose at moderate rates, and the rate of inflation nosedived. Contrary to the conventional wisdom, the income tax burden was substantially shifted to higher-income classes, and there is no credible evidence that income distribution was shifted toward greater inequality. McKenzie asserts that his book is not an apology for Republicans or Ronald Reagan, but that the record needs to be set straight to lessen the possibility of disastrous policy mistakes in the 1990s. The record of the 1980s does not demonstrate that the economic policies of that era were a failure, nor does it provide a rationale for shifting to antimarket, interventionist, and redistributive policies in the 1990s. McKenzie's carefully reasoned, well-written book will undoubtedly attract a wide readership. It should be a high priority acquisition for public, college, and university libraries, and required reading for government policymakers.—*W. W. Howard, Phoenix College*

OAB-2029   HE8819   96-35151 CIP
Mueller, Milton L. **Universal service: competition, interconnection, and monopoly in the making of the American telephone system.** MIT/AEI Press, 1997. 213p bibl indexes afp ISBN 0-262-13327-X, $40.00

This excellent book is part of the "AEI Studies in Telecommunications Deregulation" series. As such it has been discussed and criticized in draft form at forums by federal and state regulators, jurists, business executives, academic and professional experts from a variety of viewpoints, and by academic referees at MIT Press. Mueller, an assistant professor of communications, draws parallels and lessons from the early development of the American telecommunications industry to critique the Telecommunications Act of 1996. This work constitutes a historically grounded, sophisticated challenge to the accepted wisdom about interconnection, competition, and universal service, which is codified in the new legislation. As such this volume will serve to inform the current policy debate about the direction and nature of continued deregulation in the rapidly changing telecommunications industry. The author's insights and arguments regarding issues of unbundling, access, and connectivity are also germane to the current debate regarding the deregulation of the electricity industry. This book should be acquired by all academic and professional/practitioner libraries.—*R. C. Singleton, University of Puget Sound*

OAB-2030   HG604   96-25089 CIP
Ritter, Gretchen. **Goldbugs and greenbacks: the antimonopoly tradition and the politics of finance in America.** Cambridge, 1997. 303p index ISBN 0-521-56167-1, $54.95

Ritter (government, Univ. of Texas at Austin) reexamines the ideologies of the political debates over the US financial system from the end of the Civil War to the defeat of William Jennings Bryan in the election of 1896. By examining in detailed the relevant pamphlet literature, as well as contemporary newspapers and other publications, she presents the central arguments of what she calls the antimonopolists (farmer-labor parties) regarding economic and social reform. Her book is more successful in its descriptions and analysis of the nature of the antimonopolist arguments and their political impacts than in establishing what their achievement might have meant. This is an important study that raises significant questions about the role of the financial system in influencing political and economic change, explaining why these debates were significant in the past, as well as in the present. *Goldbugs and Greenbacks* is a major interpretation of the monetary debates of the late 19th century, and an important book for historians, economists, and political scientists concerned with developments in American society. Lower-division undergraduate and up.—*S. L. Engerman, University of Rochester*

OAB-2031   HC103   94-9328 CIP
Rogers, R. Mark. **Handbook of key economic indicators.** Irwin, IL, 1994. 274p bibl index ISBN 0-7863-0193-7, $45.00

A very interesting and complete description of key economic indicators used in assessing the economy's performance, this book is organized into 14 chapters, containing analyses of 13 sets of economic indicators. Included among

these variables are the employment report, retail sales, consumer price index, producer price index, industrial production, international trade, and gross domestic product. Each chapter begins with an elaboration of the nature of each indicator and is followed by details regarding its construction methodology and input variables. This discussion is highly useful since it provides a clear explanation of the constituent components of each indicator and any underlying assumptions regarding their calculation. Throughout the book, the author provides a practical discussion regarding how these indicators can be used to predict and interpret economic performance. Among such economic events examined by the author are the inflation rate, turns in the business cycle, interest rates, and the general level of stock prices. Additionally, each chapter contains a bibliography of relevant academic studies and popular books. The author's abundant use of graphs and tables facilitates an understanding of the uses of these indicator variables in assessing economic behavior. Overall, this book is a concise and highly readable overview of those economic variables critical in evaluating the macroeconomy. This book will allow the reader to meaningfully interpret macroeconomic data. Highly recommended for any library seeking to enhance its business and economic collections.—*S. P. Ferris, University of Missouri—Columbia*

OAB-2032   HD3616   91-39699 CIP
Rosenfeld, Stuart A. **Competitive manufacturing: new strategies for regional development.** Center for Urban Policy Research, 1992. 400p bibl index ISBN 0-88285-137-3, $39.95

How can the US overcome a loss of competitiveness in the world economy? How can lagging regions be made prosperous? Rosenfeld answers by shifting the ground to the competitive advantage of industries rather than locations. Essential to economic growth is a strong manufacturing sector using advanced technologies, rewarding innovation, forming strategic alliances among firms, and stressing sectoral integration and concentration. This requires not only business commitment but also governments that catalyze modernization through improved education and training programs and foster technological improvements in small and medium-size businesses. Rosenfeld blends survey and census data, case studies of specific manufacturing firms, research reports, newspaper and magazine articles, and academic writings into a thorough and highly readable defense of his conclusions. He focuses on the rural South of the US, with additional material on industrial and technology policy in the "Third Italy" and Denmark, and he emphasizes a "new rural policy paradigm" applicable to all industrial economies. One is not an expert in economic development absent knowledge of Rosenfeld's arguments. All libraries.—*R. A. Beauregard, University of Pittsburgh*

OAB-2033   HC107   93-39818 CIP
Salstrom, Paul. **Appalachia's path to dependency: rethinking a region's economic history, 1730-1940.** University Press of Kentucky, 1994. 204p bibl index afp ISBN 0-8131-1860-3, $30.00

This retrospective on 200 years of Appalachian history complements the many other studies of this region, attempting to explain the poverty of a region blessed with a long period of settlement and location close to the prosperous urban centers of the East and Midwest. Salstrom, a historian, interprets the growing dependency of the Appalachian region in a developmental economics framework. He identifies two crucial external events—the 1865 National Banking Act and the New Deal of the 1930s—that interacted with the region's topography and natural resources to create a low-wage, low-skill export sector backed up by small-scale subsistence agriculture. Ultimately, Appalachia's principal export became its young adults, who migrated to areas providing greater opportunity. His thesis—that Appalachia's dependency was shaped by a shortage of financial capital (resulting from the National Banking Act) and by New Deal agricultural policies designed for the Midwest that discriminated against the small-scale, nonmechanized agriculture of Appalachia in the 1930s—is developed against a rich descriptive background of comparative data and historical events. This volume should appeal to a broad range of audiences; a must for collections in regional development. All levels.—*H. H. Ulbrich, Clemson University*

OAB-2034   HC106   94-31451 CIP

Spulber, Nicolas. **The American economy: the struggle for supremacy in the 21st century.** Cambridge, 1995. 286p index ISBN 0-521-48013-2, $34.95

An eminent economist adds to his luster in this work through a profound, carefully documented, wide-scoped review and analysis of the economic challenges confronted by the American economy after WW II and the new global challenges arising out of the competing economies of Japan, Germany, and the European Union. Parts 1 and 2 review the changing structure and growth of the US economy, the transformations induced by the Cold War, and the impact of accelerating technical development throughout the major industrial nations. Policy triumphs as well as failures of the period are assessed and their legacies evaluated. The work sharply criticizes the theses held by many of an "America in Decline"—one that its proponents say can only be averted by strong partnership between government and business (so-called reindustrialization). Spulber denies the very existence of a decline and urges continued reliance on a market-directed economy. In Parts 3 and 4, the author examines the long-range changes in income and employment and in public expenditures, with a generally optimistic view of these trends. Spulber projects a benign view of the shift from manufacturing to services in the US economy and in the relative performance of the US compared to its major competitors. These developments provide a framework of policy proposals for the US to retain technological leadership in the world; these proposals are contrasted with those advanced by the Clinton-Gore administration, which are said to involve an undesirable expansion in the role of government. Recommended for all collections.—*H. I. Liebling, Lafayette College*

OAB-2035   HC120   92-090706-7 Can. CIP

Urquhart, M.C. **Gross National Product, Canada, 1870-1926: the derivation of the estimates.** McGill-Queen's, 1993. 714p index ISBN 0-7735-0942-9, $65.00

About once a decade a work is published that serves to provide the base for a flood of research that follows and builds upon it. Urquhart, the dean of Canadian historical statisticians, and a team of fellow researchers, most of whom were based at Queen's University, have produced such a volume. In every dimension it represents the culmination of a lifetime of work by Urquhart along with contributions by his associates who devoted themselves to providing consistent, comprehensive, and detailed estimates of the gross national product of Canada from 1870 to 1926. The documentation is impressive, the explanations thorough and clearly exposited. The chapters covering all the major subsectors are interesting and informative essays in and of themselves. There is an excellent index, and the notes about data sources for each chapter are equally impressive. An absolute must for any serious academic collection related to the Canadian economy and its historical development.—*D. E. Bond, University of British Columbia*

■ Central and South America

OAB-2036   HD9199   96-20694 CIP

Bates, Robert H. **Open economy politics: the political economy of the world coffee trade.** Princeton, 1997. 221p index afp ISBN 0-691-02655-6, $35.00

A pioneer of the new international economy who first made his reputation studying African agricultural issues, Bates (Harvard) now turns his attention to Latin America, where economic and political theories from Marxism to neoclassical models have been considered to understand the scourge of underdevelopment, the export of raw materials. Coffee, like oil for the Middle East, is a perfect example. Bates judiciously reviews and rejects a variety of theories to explain the failure of market intervention by Brazil and Colombia. He develops a new trade theory, an eclectic mix of the current theoretical elements and his empirical observations. Bates shows that both coffee producers and consumers came to rely on political, not economic, reasons to establish and

enforce the International Coffee Organization (ICO). Cold War imperatives drove the world's largest coffee drinker—the US—to support the ICO, while Brazil and Colombia failed to produce coherent pricing policies in the international market because of their domestic political weaknesses. In 1989, the ICO dissolved itself. This pathbreaking work stands on solid historical research and reveals an agile understanding of the complexity of the international political economy of coffee. Bates demonstrates the value of understanding the importance of domestic political institutions in the making of international policies of open economies. Upper-division undergraduate and up.—*E. Pang, Colorado School of Mines*

OAB-2037   HC125   94-28296 CIP

Bresser Pereira, Luiz Carlos. **Economic crisis and state reform in Brazil: toward a new interpretation of Latin America.** L. Rienner, 1996. 258p bibl index afp ISBN 1-55587-532-7, $55.00

This important book should be part of any Latin America collection. The author is a well-known economist as well as a former Brazilian finance minister. The focus of the work is the Brazilian economic crisis of the 1980s and 1990s, but the analysis and conclusions are meaningful far beyond the borders of Brazil. Bresser Pereira challenges the neoliberal (Washington consensus) assumption that reducing the role of the state is enough to ensure economic recovery in Brazil and other nations undergoing a fiscal crisis. Instead, the author argues that while market-oriented reforms may have been required to increase productive efficiency, a successful development strategy requires a strong state. At a minimum, a strong state is needed to address Brazil's massive external debt problem and other symptoms of its fiscal crisis. Moreover, a strong state is the only institution capable of designing an effective national development policy and able to make large development-related infrastructure investments. While the conclusions can and will be debated, the argument is forcefully presented. Fortunately, it is written in a style that will not intimidate noneconomists. Highly recommended for all libraries.—*J. T. Peach, New Mexico State University*

OAB-2038   HD8259   96-790 CIP

Drake, Paul W. **Labor movements and dictatorships: the Southern Cone in comparative perspective.** Johns Hopkins, 1996. 253p index afp ISBN 0-8018-5326-5, $47.50; ISBN 0-8018-5327-3 pbk, $15.95

Drake's excellent book not only addresses its title, but also sheds light on the nature of the military-dominated dictatorships in Argentina, Brazil, Chile, and Uruguay. Seen through the prisms of the growth and stagnation of organized labor movements in these four countries, the book makes a lasting contribution to the study of "authoritarian capitalism" between 1964 when the Brazilian coup took place and 1990 when the Chilean military returned to the barracks. During these three and a half decades the four countries transformed from import substitution-driven closed economics to the neoliberal open market or market-friendly systems. By the 1960s and the 1970s, all four countries experienced the sputtering of the import-substitution model, unable to deepen their industrialization process. Labor, accustomed to the protected market and the state patronage of welfarism, found itself pitted against the faltering economy and the military eager to experiment with a new economic model. Throughout the superbly researched and masterfully written chapters, Drake highlights the fundamental differences and similarities among the Southern Cone and Brazilian dictatorships. The author makes several intriguing and provocative observations but fails to fully explain them, e.g., that Brazil's military was not as "enamored" with market capitalism as were the Spanish American counterparts; that political parties, though tightly controlled and nurtured by the military, thrived in Brazil, while the Southern Cone military barely tolerated or ruthlessly crushed them. This pathbreaking study of labor movements should be read by all interested in authoritarianism, transitional economies of the pre-1990s, and labor movements of socialist-Marxist and populist genre. Upper-division undergraduate and up.—*E. Pang, Colorado School of Mines*

OAB-2039   HD4098   92-22670 CIP

Hachette, Dominique. **Privatization in Chile: an economic appraisal,** by Dominique Hachette and Rolf Lüders. ICS Press, 1993. 284p bibl index ISBN 1-55815-208-3 pbk, $19.95

Privatization—the turning over to the private sector of government-owned and run enterprises—has become part of the strategy for restructuring the respective roles of market and state in many less-developed nations, as well as former socialist countries, facing economic crisis. For many orthodox economists, privatization is viewed as an *a priori* good; for many liberal economists, there has been a deep distrust of the motives animating the drive toward privatization. In Latin America, Chile and Mexico have had the most far-reaching strategies to privatize their *parastatals*. This is a brilliant and especially thorough study of virtually all the dimensions of Chile's privatization—from details of sell-off methods, the impact on government revenues and wealth, employment effects, interclass wealth transfers, and so on. The authors (both at the Pontifical Catholic Univ., Chile) are strong supporters, but not simple apologists, of privatization, and their analysis is fairhanded and enlightening, even for those who believe privatization to have been carried too far. This is the most complete and most analytic study of Chile's program and of privatization to date. Graduate; faculty.—*J. L. Dietz, California State University, Fullerton*

OAB-2040 HC135 92-23572 CIP
Lustig, Nora. **Mexico, the remaking of an economy.** Brookings, 1992. 186p index afp ISBN 0-8157-5314-4, $28.95; ISBN 0-8157-5313-6 pbk, $11.95

This is a concise, exceptionally clear exposition of the transformation of Mexican economic policy since 1982. Lustig argues that serious policy mistakes, not an inevitable legacy of import-substituting industrialization, caused the economic disaster culminating in the 1982 foreign-debt default. Most of the book is devoted to analyzing Mexican policymakers' struggles to reverse negative economic trends in the face of a weak international economy and unhelpful international financial institutions. Individual chapters deal with policy strategies, public sector reforms, and international trade policies that slowly turned the Mexican economy around. A separate chapter describes the project's human costs. Lustig meticulously documents her arguments, compares alternative explanations, and acknowledges their limits and implications. Even with no analysis of political power, this is an excellent book. Advocates and opponents of free market regimes use the Mexican experience, and this book clears much ideological smoke. Tables, extensive footnotes, no comprehensive bibliography. Highly recommended for advanced undergraduate through faculty collections.—*F. S. Weaver, Hampshire College*

OAB-2041 F1528 91-33110 CIP
Martínez Cuenca, Alejandro. **Sandinista economics in practice: an insider's critical reflections.** South End, 1992. 178p index ISBN 0-89608-432-9, $30.00

Transformations in Nicaragua since the Sandinista Revolution in 1979 continue to be a rich source for investigation and critical debate. This is an important primary document for scholars interested in better understanding the whole gamut of political, economic, and social decisions and processes that occupied the Sandinista leadership, both while in and out of power. Presented as an interview with Alejandro Martínez Cuenca, who served first as Minister of Foreign Trade and then as Minister of Planning and Budget, the information contained in this work constitutes an exceptional insider's perspective (Martínez also holds a PhD in economics from Vanderbilt Univ.). The influence of ideology, politics, expectations, economics, internal and external experts, and exogenous events on policy are interwoven with the exigencies of creating new structures, institutions, and ideas to attempt to move Nicaragua forward under exceptionally challenging circumstances. There are 15 pages of useful notes that amplify upon the context of events and identify key individuals discussed in the interview. There is also an extremely valuable "Chronology of Relevant Political and Economic Events" that runs to more than 50 pages. Highly recommended for undergraduate through faculty collections.—*J. L. Dietz, California State University, Fullerton*

OAB-2042 HC192 95-52628 CIP
Martínez, Javier. **Chile: the great transformation,** by Javier Martínez and Alvaro Díaz. Brookings/United Nations Research Institute for Social Development, 1996. 156p index afp ISBN 0-8157-5478-7, $34.95; ISBN 0-8157-5477-9 pbk, $14.95

This short book is a tour de force deserving of close reading by all Latin Americanists concerned with the region's future. Chile's economic and political policies since 1970, first leftist and then rightist, too often have led scholars to misunderstand some of the profound transformations taking place. The authors, both associated with the research institute SUR in Santiago, evaluate the impact of reforms in the Chilean economy and society initiated during (and even before) the Allende government that have been continued both by the military government and the civilian governments that have followed. Martínez and Díaz suggest that many of the reforms of Allende's socialist government were not undone after his overthrow, and in fact, these reforms (for example, in agriculture) have helped to set the stage for a reorganization of the economy along more dynamic lines. The authors do not downplay the viciousness of some of the military's actions, but neither do they paint the Allende regime's policies as all bad, nor the neoliberal policies as all good. A balanced, thought-provoking analysis, bolstered by ample data and interpretation. Academic and professional library collections.—*J. L. Dietz, California State University, Fullerton*

OAB-2043 HD7130 93-38662 CIP
Mesa-Lago, Carmelo. **Changing social security in Latin America: toward alleviating the social costs of economic reform.** L. Rienner, 1994. 213p bibl index afp ISBN 1-55587-486-X, $40.00

Mesa-Lago has written an important book on an important topic. The book documents the devastating effects of recent Latin American economic reforms on that region's poorest groups. The reforms have included privatization, reduced government spending, and a market-oriented, export-based growth strategy. Mesa-Lago argues that some reforms were needed badly, but that the resulting ruin of social security systems in many Latin American and Caribbean nations has been a great tragedy. Mesa-Lago is well qualified to make such an argument, since he has been a consultant on such issues for many of the organizations most directly involved. The analysis is carefully done, and he is quick to point out that the consequences of the reforms have not been the same in all nations. Indeed, the individual nation case studies are the central focus of the book. Perhaps more significant are the author's practical and imaginative policy recommendations. In brief, this well-written volume is an important contribution to the literature on Latin American economic reform and its consequences, and is highly recommended. General; lower-division undergraduate through professional.—*J. T. Peach, New Mexico State University*

OAB-2044 HC125 93-34563 CIP
Money doctors, foreign debts, and economic reforms in Latin America from the 1890s to the present, ed. by Paul W. Drake. SR Books, 1994. 270p afp ISBN 0-8420-2434-4, $40.00; ISBN 0-8420-2435-2 pbk, $14.95

The economic and political history of Latin America would not be complete without an examination of the money doctors (the MDs). The MDs staff the invading army of economists and financial consultants who have advised Latin American nations on how to conduct their economic and political affairs in a fashion that would be attractive to foreign lenders. The thesis of the book is that while the MDs have often arrived at the same time as armies with a vastly different set of weapons, their influence on Latin American nations has been just as profound. Drake has done a truly admirable job of compiling essays on the MDs that span most of a century. The authors (including the late US Senator Paul Douglas, the late Scott Nearing, Albert Hirschman, and Roberto Frankel) will be familiar to Latin Americanists as well as a wider audience. Other than a well-written but brief introduction and some explanatory remarks scattered throughout the volume, Drake has allowed others to tell a powerful, intriguing, and important story. Must reading for anyone with an interest in Latin America or US policy towards Latin America. All levels.—*J. T. Peach, New Mexico State University*

OAB-2045 HC130 95-19147 CIP

Morley, Samuel A. **Poverty and inequality in Latin America: the impact of adjustment and recovery in the 1980s.** Johns Hopkins, 1995. 222p bibl index afp ISBN 0-8018-5064-9, $42.50

Morley (adviser, Inter-American Development Bank) provides a meticulous, scholarly, and insightful overview and analysis of the impact of the 1980s debt crisis in Latin America and the adjustment policies that followed. The focus is on the repercussions, often negative, of adjustment programs on income distribution, poverty, and key social spending for human capital, particularly education and health. In more detail, two chapters examine unsuccessful adjustment (in Argentina and Venezuela) and more successful policies (in Columbia and Costa Rica) in dealing with the effects of the debt crisis. As other studies have suggested, a viable and dynamic exporting sector is indispensable to successful adjustment to a changed external environment; however, although it may be necessary, it is not sufficient for successful adjustment. This intelligent volume is packed with useful supporting data and valuable hypotheses and theories explaining why poverty and inequality increased in response to adjustment programs in some situations and, more importantly, how and why poverty indicators and inequality were reduced in other cases. For development economists and policy makers alike struggling with the issue of paths to equitable growth, this volume contains a wealth of information and interpretation to be put to use. Upper-division undergraduate through professional.—*J. L. Dietz, California State University, Fullerton*

OAB-2046 F1418 94-37209 CIP

Park, James William. **Latin American underdevelopment: a history of perspectives in the United States, 1870-1965.** Louisiana State, 1995. 274p bibl index afp ISBN 0-8071-1969-5, $37.50

Park has written a comprehensive, scholarly review of the disparaging attitudes shaping the US perspective on Latin America from colonial times to the present. His extremely thorough and lucid review of all branches of the social science literature reveals that several major themes have dominated and distorted the US view to the detriment of a more realistic assessment of the region. These include the Black Legend (the alleged negative influence of Spain and the Catholic Church on progress in Latin America); the El Dorado myth (the notion that Latin America is a vast cornucopia of natural resources waiting to be tapped); and climatic and racial determinism which have frequently been alleged to have held back development. More recently, the dependency school, stressing Latin America's vulnerability to foreign domination, has provided a Latin American counterpart to these perceptions. Also, economic development has moved forward impressively in the last several decades—although ironically a US-type Western model favoring freer trade, privatization of state enterprises, and increased private investment has now become dominant. This is an important book for which there is no real alternative. It should be a part of all Latin American collections.—*M. C. Bird, Colorado College*

OAB-2047 HD9685 93-33426 CIP

Ribeiro, Gustavo Lins. **Transnational capitalism and hydropolitics in Argentina: the Yacyretá high dam.** University Press of Florida, 1994. 185p bibl index afp ISBN 0-8130-1280-5, $29.95

Ribeiro, a US-trained Brazilian anthropologist, shows that instead of promoting development (defined as sustainable, involving local and regional management, spurring growth over time and therefore regional stability), the binational Yacyretá project has become a multibillion-dollar "well of corruption." Argentina and Paraguay have been building the Yacyretá high dam on the Paraná River, intended to produce 4,140 megawatts for the Buenos Aires industrial hub and to provide Paraguay with "electrodollars." Although this project was originally budgeted for $10.7 billion, wanton corruption, sheer mismanagement, and runaway cost overruns had pushed the cost up to $14 billion as of 1987. Byzantine business alliances have been forged and networked among transnationals, domestic companies, and even state-owned enterprises across borders of the two countries to milk the project. A phony consultant's report was fed to the World Bank, Argentine government, and other funding agencies to rig the winning bid, and the US government offered $700 million of taxpayers' money to win a contract for a single US firm. The entire project is about who will secure industrial hegemony in the South Atlantic for the coming century. Ribeiro has produced a superb book that updates the state of anthropological research on development and analyzes deftly how the perceived rivalry has forced Argentina and Brazil to squander money on uneconomical projects. General readers; undergraduate through faculty.—*E. Pang, Colorado School of Mines*

OAB-2048 Can. CIP

Ryan, Phil. **The fall and rise of the market in Sandinista Nicaragua.** McGill-Queen's, 1996 (c1995). 328p bibl index afp ISBN 0-7735-1347-7, $49.95; ISBN 0-7735-1359-0 pbk, $19.95

Ryan (public administration, Carlton Univ.) worked at the University of Nicaragua and the Nicaraguan planning ministry from 1983 to 1988. As suggested by such experience, this is a very well informed postmortem of the Sandinista regime, and Ryan makes it especially valuable by drawing from a wide range of secondary scholarship and social theory, including socialist thought. The result is a smart, trenchant critique of Sandinista economic policy, a critique that is sympathetic with the Sandinista socialist project, respectful of the severity of the dilemmas confronting policy makers, and at the same time alert to the roles played by personal interest, opportunism, and bad judgment. Although one can argue with some of the author's interpretations in this complex work, Ryan has produced an outstanding contribution to the study of Sandinista Nicaragua *and* to a more general understanding of the problems of socialist construction throughout the Third World. Contains lists of biographical data and acronyms. Highly recommended for upper-division undergraduates, graduate students, and scholars.—*F. S. Weaver, Hampshire College*

OAB-2049 HC175 95-45573 CIP

Sawers, Larry. **The other Argentina: the interior and national development.** Westview, 1996. 326p bibl index afp ISBN 0-8133-2750-4, $64.00

In this impressive book Sawers (American Univ.) seeks to interpret the soul of Argentine political economy built on the great Argentine divide between the interior, which comprises 70 percent of the landspace and 31 percent of the population, and the greater Pampas including the federal capital. The author argues that historically, the resource-poor interior has dominated national politics. Having critiqued the prevailing theories of the underdevelopment of the "invisible interior," Sawers offers his: the interior consumes a disproportionate amount of the resources generated by the country's economic engine, the Pampas and Buenos Aires. He goes further, blaming the financial bankruptcy of the federal government and such economic woes as the undergrowth and galloping inflation of the 1970s and 1980s on the interior, and by extension, Argentina's underdevelopment. He exonerates Perón and his radical heirs, the standard scapegoats of Argentina's economic troubles. This view is at once incendiary and lapidary. In the unfolding Menem-Cavallo economic reform, Sawers finds little has changed. The Pampas still subsidizes the interior; the hope for self-sufficiency in the interior is nil. Sawers is unduly pessimistic. Much of what he says is empirically true and can theoretically be correct, but he forgets that the success of the Argentine reform and adjustment to date owes more to the fundamental change of the Argentine culture and attitudes than to the shining econometric formulae. Groundbreaking and insightful, this work contributes to the growing literature on the revisionist interpretation of the political economy of development in Latin America. Upper-division undergraduate through faculty.—*E. Pang, Colorado School of Mines*

OAB-2050 F1565 94-16152 CIP

Tice, Karin E. **Kuna crafts, gender, and the global economy.** Texas, 1995. 232p bibl index afp ISBN 0-292-78133-4, $35.00; ISBN 0-292-78137-7 pbk, $14.95

Molas are the colorful and often imaginatively designed reverse-appliqué cloth panels that Kuna Indian women in Panama have worn on their blouses throughout this century; they have been popular as "folk art" for not quite half that time. This book is the first effort to describe molas in full sociocultural context—systematically dealing with their history, symbolism, production, distribution, and even linkages to politics and kinship, as well as economics. Tice is unusual in having spent considerable time in close, sustained contact with the Kuna, and her general description is often enhanced with vivid real-life vignettes. Key factors in the growth in production of molas include the shift from women making them as part of their own clothing (of which they are ethnically proud) to development of a cooperative that sells them mostly to tourists and dealers. With the coop have come a shift in sex roles (with women often having more cash than men, and now being politically outspoken), changes in diet, innovation, differentiation among the various island communities, and other repercussions. Tice is good in showing how regional, national, and even international events and processes influence diverse aspects of the local scene—a nice unselfconscious illustration of the world system in action. This book should equally interest those who care about gender studies, economic development, handicrafts, and Latin Amerian indigenous or peasant populations. Includes photographs, maps, tables, figures, glossary, a methodological appendix, discursive endnotes, and a good bibliography and index. Upper-division undergraduates and above.—*D. B. Heath, Brown University*

■ Europe

OAB-2051   HC256   91-32489 CIP
Cairncross, Alec. **The British economy since 1945: economic policy and performance, 1945-1990.** B. Blackwell, 1992. 338p bibl index afp ISBN 0-631-18276-4, $49.95

Following a long and distinguished career as an economic adviser in Britain, Cairncross has undertaken a second career chronicling the history of the British economy since the Great Depression, e.g., *Years of Recovery*, (CH, Oct'85); *Sterling in Decline* (with Barry Eichengreen,1983), *Goodbye, Great Britain* (with Kathleen Burke, CH, Jul'92). This second career is proving to be just as distinguished as the first. This comprehensive survey, published as a part of the series "Making Contemporary Britain," provides exactly what it promises: an introduction to the postwar British economy. Cairncross provides an excellent overview of the facts of the British economy integrated into a discussion of the changing ideas that informed the contemporaneous economic and political debates. There are many collections of essays on this topic, e.g., *The British Economy Since 1945*, ed. by N.F.R. Crafts and N. Woodward (1991), but no other single volume contains a narrative as comprehensive (or as good) as this one.—*B. W. Bateman, Grinnell College*

OAB-2052   HC254   94-46403 CIP
Daunton, M.J. **Progress and poverty: an economic and social history of Britain, 1700-1850.** Oxford, 1995. 620p bibl index ISBN 0-19-822282-3, $75.00; ISBN 0-19-822281-5 pbk, $24.00

Daunton has written a work of grand synthesis and sustained argument, which will be read and reread by professionals and students alike. He has drawn from a generation of revisionist studies to fashion a new and provocative account of the industrial revolution and its social context. Daunton accepts the "slow growth" estimates of N.F.R. Crafts (*British Economic Growth during the Industrial Revolution*, CH, Nov'85) and sees a shift of income to the rich via enclosures, high rents, and regressive taxes, but he dismisses J.C.D. Clark's claim (*English Society, 1688-1832*, CH, Jul'86) that Britain was a confessional state controlled by an entrenched elite. Middling sorts, Daunton argues, could challenge the oligarchy; law, not religion, was the ideology of the day, accommodating capitalism without being its tool; and rather than attacking the system workers petitioned for their rights in it. But there is much more to the theme of progress here, as Peterloo, child miners, and the hungry forties nearly fade from sight. Poor relief was a safety net that permitted labor mobility. Whig mercantilists fostered the world's entrepôt by drawing wealth from captive markets, then yielded to wise Tories who adopted free trade to suit the newly industrial

state. Most importantly, Malthus, Ricardo, and Marx all proved false prophets when the wider use of coal and steam brought vast new wealth, and birth control became fashionable within marriage. To end within reach of Victorian equipoise, Daunton debates a host of authors and emphasizes both falling transactions costs and demand-driven investment. The book is well produced, with convenient notes and excellent bibliographies, and is a signal achievement not least because its author has rescued so many important findings from highly technical studies and made them part of a story told in lucid, attractive prose. Both admirers and critics will want a sequel. Highest recommendation for general readers and academic libraries serving undergraduates and above.—*G. F. Steckley, Knox College*

OAB-2053   HC244   95-8199 CIP
Lavigne, Marie. **The economics of transition: from socialist economy to market economy.** St. Martin's, 1995. 295p bibl index ISBN 0-312-12720-0, $45.00

Lavigne (Univ. of Pau, France) is an internationally known scholar on the economies of Eastern Europe and the Former Soviet Union (FSU). In this volume she explains the nature and performance of the socialist centrally planned economic system in these areas and the reasons for its collapse. Then she examines the transition toward a capitalist regulated market economy, analyzing in detail macroeconomic stabilization, privatization, integration with the world economy, and Western assistance to the transition. The work contains many tables and charts, a statistical appendix, helpful suggestions for further reading, and a long bibliography. Comprehensive but concise, this authoritative study presents an insightful and balanced assessment of the issues. It differs from other recent volumes on the economics of transition. Barry Bosworth and Gur Ofer's *Reforming Planned Economies in an Integrating World Economy* (CH, Dec'95) attempts to cover briefly some aspects of economic reform in the FSU, Eastern Europe, and China. *The Transformation of the Communist Economies*, ed. by Ha-Joon Chang and Peter Nolan (1995), assembles 14 varied papers on China, Eastern Europe, and the FSU from a 1992 conference. Lavigne's book is much superior to these volumes and is highly recommended for both economics and area studies collections. Clearly written, it is accessible to upper-division undergraduates and is an excellent introduction to the subject for graduate students and nonspecialist faculty and researchers.—*M. Bornstein, University of Michigan*

OAB-2054   HC305   94-38366 CIP
Locke, Richard M. **Remaking the Italian economy.** Cornell, 1995. 232p bibl index afp ISBN 0-8014-2891-2, $29.95

This book deserves to be widely read by both scholars of comparative political economy and those interested in questions of international competitiveness and industrial strategy. Locke seems to understand the paradox of Italy's economic performance in the 1970s and 1980s, when it was both stagnant (at the national scale) and exceptionally vibrant (in particular regions and sectors). His research has produced a study of the "micropolitics" of economic development that is both theoretically sophisticated and at the same time highly descriptive of what one actually sees and hears in Italy today. Locke argues that failed attempts at national reforms in Italy created an environment favorable to the creation of "policentric" local structures that are more favorable to growth and innovation than either hierarchical or polarized structures. This analysis is developed through case studies, including an excellent analysis of the Biellese textile district. The result is an interesting and original examination of Italy's political economy as well as a contribution to our general understanding of the political economy of economic development. The conclusions drawn here seem to this reviewer to be particularly applicable to the analysis of the US economy in the 1990s. Upper-division undergraduate through faculty.—*M. Veseth, University of Puget Sound*

OAB-2055   HD4145   95-23660 CIP
Middleton, Roger. **Government versus the market: the growth of the public sector, economic management and British economic**

performance, c. 1890-1979. E. Elgar, 1996. (Dist. by Ashgate) 756p bibl indexes ISBN 1-85278-031-2, $119.95

Middleton (Univ. of Bristol) has written a major study of the British economy and economic policy from 1890 to 1979, synthesizing theory and policy, history, and politics. Middleton's thesis, simply stated, is that Britain's economic history in the 20th century is a long tale of decline conditioned and constrained by market failure on one side and an impotent state on the other. Although the study concentrates on the years leading up to the Thatcher government, it is clear that Middleton thinks the patterns of previous decades (weak government, flawed market, economic decline) have persisted. The volume is empirical, theoretical, and historical, dense therefore with data and references, but readable and provocative nonetheless. The bibliography is quite large but carefully selected and worthy of study on its own. Overall, a fine study and a useful addition to the study of British economic history and the development of economic policy in the 20th century. This volume should appeal to economic historians and to political economists. Upper-division undergraduate through faculty collections.—*M. Veseth, University of Puget Sound*

OAB-2056 Orig

The Privatization process in Central Europe: economic environment, legal and ownership structure, institutions for state regulation, overview of privatization programs, initial transformation of enterprises, by Roman Frydman et al. Central European University Press, 25 Floral St., Covent Garden, London WC2E 9DS UK, 1993. 262p (CEU privatization reports, 1) ISBN 1-85866-002-5, $45.00; ISBN 1-85866-000-9 pbk, $15.00

This book was produced by a team of researchers at the Central European University in Prague, who have been gathering information about privatization in Eastern Europe. The book is the most extensive collection of material yet available on this subject. Separate chapters on Bulgaria, Hungary, Czechoslovakia, Poland, and Romania contain summary data on each country's economic performance, major policy trends, and the legal regulations regarding privatization. The information is clearly presented, comprehensive, and topical (covering the period up to March 1992). It is written as a reference work, with no argument or interpretation, and will be an invaluable source for students writing papers on economic developments in the countries covered. Advanced undergraduate; graduate; faculty.—*P. Rutland, Wesleyan University*

OAB-2057 HD5660 96-52677 CIP

Privatization surprises in transition economies: employee-ownership in Central and Eastern Europe, ed. by Milica Uvalic and Daniel Vaughan-Whitehead. E. Elgar, 1997. (Dist. by American International Distribution Corporation) 306p bibl index ISBN 1-85898-621-4, $85.00

The best book on privatization in Eastern Europe yet, this anthology focuses on an important aspect of the restructuring of former communist economies. It is more up-to-date and informative than Saul Estrin et al., *Restructuring and Privatization in Central East Europe* (CH, Mar'96), and more narrowly focused than John Campbell and Ove Pedersen, *Legacies of Change* (CH, Jan'97). The ten contributors represent local and Western perspectives. Sponsorship of the study by the International Labor Organization and its Central and Eastern European Team lends a pro-labor bias, but this does not detract from the value of the book, even if some of the conclusions support the ILO views and stress the benefits of employee ownership of enterprises. The territorial coverage is comprehensive: the Baltic countries, Bulgaria, the Czech Republic, Hungary, Poland, Romania, Russia, Ukraine, and the Yugoslav successor states. Thematically, the anthology is also rewarding, covering the value systems in various countries, political developments, theoretical expectations for managers' and employees' buy-outs (MEBOs), the privatizing legislation and its implementation, and the economic performance of privatization. Most topics have systematic subdivisions of value to researchers and practitioners. The informativeness of the book is reflected in its 45 tables and 27 figures. Highly recommended for upper-division undergraduate through professional collections.—*B. Mieczkowski, Ithaca College*

OAB-2058 HE3005 93-6768 CIP

Strohl, Mitchell P. **Europe's high speed trains: a study in geoeconomics.** Praeger, 1993. 306p bibl index afp ISBN 0-275-94252-X, $55.00

Strohl has produced an excellent up-to-date book on the status of the world's high-speed passenger rail lines and plans. This is not a "train buff" or "rail fan" book, but rather an impressive scholarly exposition by an American political science professor, longtime resident in Paris, who provides considerable technical detail in terms understandable to the general reader. There are separate chapters for each European country currently served by high-speed rail (France, Britain, Italy, Germany, and Spain), including sections on technical development, geography, schedules, passenger volumes, costs, train sets, power supply, signaling, and tracks, etc. The book begins with excellent problem-statement chapters on the European economy, the role of speed in transportation, and Japan, "where high speed rail began." A final chapter summarizes developments in the US and northern and eastern Europe. The book is very comprehensive in its coverage but has very few tables and maps and no pictures. There is no comparable book. The footnotes, bibliography, and index are excellent. General; advanced undergraduate through faculty; professional.—*D. Brand, Harvard University*

OAB-2059 Orig

Thompson, Noel. **Political economy and the Labour Party: the economics of democratic socialism, 1884-1995.** UCL Press, 1996. 330p bibl index ISBN 1-85728-160-8, $75.00; ISBN 1-85728-161-6 pbk, $27.50

To most, the economic principles of the Left may seem muddled in contrast to the crystal clarity of the Right's profound faith in markets. Thus, Thompson's book is to be welcomed for its lucid examination of the diverse influences on the British Labour Party's economic policy throughout the 20th century. The book proceeds by providing vignettes, grouped by chronology and theme, of the economic ideas of influential writers, politicians, and policy documents. Those surveyed include, among others, William Morris, R.H. Tawney, G.D.H. Cole, Ramsay MacDonald, James Meade, Harold Wilson, and the Alternative Economic Strategy. A major theme is the considerable respect for market mechanisms of many influential socialist economic policy makers in Britain. Indeed, the book ends on a note of disappointment at Labour's recent willingness to pursue international competitiveness at the expense of its traditional concern for social equity. Thompson might seem quixotic in searching for intellectual coherence in a context in which political expediency carries the day. Nevertheless, one is in his debt for this careful exposition of the evolution of a landmark political party's economic policy. Informed general readers; upper-division undergraduate through faculty.—*D. Mitch, University of Maryland Baltimore County*

OAB-2060 HD3616 93-32725 CIP

Tomlinson, Jim. **Government and the enterprise since 1900: the changing problem of efficiency.** Oxford, 1994. 455p bibl index afp ISBN 0-19-828749-6, $60.00

Is there any doubt that one of the great transformations of the 20th century has been the widespread embrace of explicit economic management by the state? One hundred years ago, governments did not make the claims and promises they now make regarding economic performance. Tomlinson (Univ. of Brunel, UK) has built a career around studying this transformation in Britain. Two of his earlier books, *Problems of British Economic Policy, 1870-1945* (CH, Apr'82) and *British Macroeconomic Policy since 1940* (CH, Oct'85), dealt with the evolution of macroeconomic policy; this book deals with the evolution of a key type of microeconomic policy: industrial policy to improve the efficiency of firms and industries. The first 12 chapters provide a chronological account from 1900 to 1990 of the twists and turns in British government industrial policy; the last two chapters are case studies of the cotton and automobile industries. The book's great strength is that it puts the history of each period (industry) in its full political context; the reader sees the actual pressures and debates that shaped (and reshaped) industrial policy over 90 years. An important contribution to the history of economic policy making and to the debates over the causes of British industrial decline. Extensive bibliography. Upper-division undergraduate and up.—*B. W. Bateman, Grinnell College*

Social & Behavioral Sciences

OAB-2061   HG930   96-50079 CIP
Ungerer, Horst. **A concise history of European monetary integration: from EPU to EMU.** Quorum Books, 1997. 338p bibl indexes afp ISBN 0-89930-981-X, $69.50

Ungerer's goal is to present students, scholars, and the general public with a comprehensive account of the development of European monetary integration since 1945. His effort is unusually successful. Indeed, he also provides additional background information that will be helpful to general readers. This includes an overview of the currency exchange system used by the major powers in the heyday of the international gold standard (1880-1914), along with comments on the collapse of this system and an outline of post-1945 efforts to build a new international economic order. The historical account of European monetary institutions since 1945 includes well-informed commentaries on all the major stages of development up to the end of 1996, and concludes with a discussion about the prospects for the achievement of an ever closer union in Europe in the years ahead. Although he refuses to predict the immediate future of the European Monetary Union, Ungerer asserts that a single European currency has always been viewed as a key to full economic integration and that management of such a currency would require the merging of some sovereign powers by the nations involved. This sets the scene for readers wishing to follow the debates that will continue as Europe proceeds along the timetable that may lead to the introduction of the single currency in 1999. Useful chronology and bibliography. Recommended for international economics, politics, and business collections. All levels.—*G. T. Potter, emeritus, Ramapo College of New Jersey*

■ International

OAB-2062   HF1455   94-22348 CIP
Bayard, Thomas O. **Reciprocity and retaliation in U.S. trade policy,** by Thomas O. Bayard and Kimberly Ann Elliott. Institute for International Economics, 1994. 503p bibl index ISBN 0-88132-084-6 pbk, $25.00

Since 1974 the US government has increasingly used threats of retaliation to induce foreign governments to adopt trade policies that would allow more sales of US products in foreign markets. Such threats are called "Section 301" action because of their authorization in that part of the Trade Act of 1974, or "aggressive unilateralism" to contrast them with multilateral policies achieved through international organizations such as GATT (the General Agreement on Tariffs and Trade). Two previous books on the subject are *Aggressive Unilateralism: America's 301 Trade Policy and the World Trading System* (1990), edited by Jagdish Bhagwati and Hugh Patrick, and Patrick Low's *Trading Free: The GATT and U.S. Trade Policy* (CH, Dec'93). Bayard and Elliott's study is more thorough and up-to-date than either of the two earlier works. It uses case studies, statistical analysis, and historical description to conclude that multilateral and reciprocal action through GATT (or its successor, the World Trade Organization) is likely to be more successful than aggressive unilateralism, though not by as large a margin as earlier studies suggest. Although undergraduates may be overwhelmed by the book's exhaustive details, they will find the case studies useful and interesting, and professionals are likely to use the whole work as a landmark reference for years to come.—*J. W. Nordyke, New Mexico State University*

OAB-2063   HC244   92-24999 CIP
Bookman, Milica Zarkovic. **The economics of secession.** St. Martin's, 1993. 262p bibl index ISBN 0-312-08443-9, $39.95

Secession is a worldwide phenomenon, and an extensive volume of research has been devoted to its study. Yet, most existing literature is from a political, sociological, or philosophical perspective. Since economic aspects of secessionism have been neglected, Bookman's volume represents an attempt to fill this gap. Her study covers more than 30 contemporary secession movements. Each individual case is analyzed from the economic perspective, including cost-benefit analysis to the present state of the union, to the disentanglement of mutual ties, and to the future viability of the region as a separate state. Though the complete study of secessionism must be interdisciplinary, and economics by itself cannot fully explain it, the writer hopes that an injection of economic factors might moderate some of the excessive emotions fueled by ethnic, nationalistic, and religious fervors. The first two chapters define terms and describe the conceptual framework. They are followed by two chapters providing empirical evidence to test the hypotheses stated in the first two. In the next three chapters, Bookman deals with various phases of secessionist processes, in which she emphasizes the economic basis of secession, the resolution of economic issues, and the viability of regions. A concluding chapter contains some thoughts on secessionism in the 1990s. This excellent, well-documented contribution is highly recommended. General; advanced undergraduate through faculty; professional.—*O. Zinam, University of Cincinnati*

OAB-2064   HD7293   95-52803 CIP
Clark, William A.V. **Households and housing: choice and outcomes in the housing market,** by William A.V. Clark and Frans M. Dieleman. Center for Urban Policy Research, Civic Square, 33 Livingston Ave., Suite 400, New Brunswick, NJ 08901, 1996. 252p bibl index ISBN 0-88285-156-X pbk, $19.95

Clark and Dieleman succeed in their attempt to explain contemporary demand for different types of housing in the US and the Netherlands. Using life course and event history analysis, and augmenting these microperspectives with a sensitivity to macroeconomic trends, public policy, and spatial variations, the authors present a rich quantitative investigation of the distribution of individual households across the housing market. Their research is informed by a conceptual model that stresses the critical role of household income and age as mediated by marital status, household size, and the value of the household's previous dwelling. The change in tenure status, the move either from renting to owning or vice versa, is offered as the defining event in a housing career and used to illuminate the similarities and differences between household behavior in the two countries. Applying sophisticated statistical techniques, the authors conclude that similar forces operate on housing consumption and mobility in both the US and the Netherlands. No other book presents such a clear understanding of the factors that influence housing choices, supports that understanding with solid evidence, and teaches readers how to perform their own investigations. Upper-division undergraduate through professional.—*R. A. Beauregard, New School for Social Research*

OAB-2065   HC60   92-31536 CIP
Ensign, Margee M. **Doing good or doing well?: Japan's foreign aid program.** Columbia, 1992. 198p bibl index afp ISBN 0-231-08144-8, $24.50

Ensign (director of the Development Studies Program sponsored by American University and the Agency for International Development) makes an important contribution to our understanding of Japan's foreign aid program which is now the largest in the world. Her approach is unique in that she focuses on the implementation of Japanese foreign aid at the private sector level. Through rigorous quantitative analysis, Ensign reveals a glaring, and rather disturbing, disjunction between policy pronouncements and actual implementation in Japanese foreign aid in the late 1980s. Japan's expressed aim has been to "untie" its foreign aid from procurement of goods and services from Japanese companies; yet, Ensign's analysis reveals that this has not occurred to the extent claimed by the Japanese government. Japan's foreign aid continues to be focused on infrastructure, capital goods, and its neighbors in Southeast Asia, all of which create commercial opportunities for Japanese companies. The author does an excellent job of making her empirical findings intelligible and of placing them in the broader contexts of Japan's emerging role as a world leader, US-Japan relations, and the role of foreign aid in development. Advanced undergraduate through professional.—*R. G. Bush, Gustavus Adolphus College*

OAB-2066   Orig
The *Financial Times* global guide to investing: the secrets of the

world's leading investment gurus, ed. by James Morton. FT/Pitman, 1995. (Dist. by National Book Network) 748p indexes ISBN 0-273-61414-2, $75.00

The *Financial Times* has put together a winning combination: the collective wisdom of the investment industry's leading practitioners, an interesting writing style, and numerous illustrations. In all, over 120 different global experts contribute views on their investment specialties. Suitable for both individual investors and undergraduate academic scholars, the book presents an amazing amount of material, which is divided into seven major parts, each with tightly edited chapters (typical length: four to ten pages). In spite of this brevity, one would be hard-pressed to find a single chapter that one would discard. From its explanation of financial securities to its investment strategies, the text presents sound investment advice in a clear, relatively nontechnical manner. The global perspective of the work is a definite strength, with nearly 20 chapters focused specifically on global markets scattered over six continents. The book does have one drawback: the repetitive format of its illustrations. Almost all illustrations consist of line charts (graphs) with an occasional bar chart. Overall, however, adjectives such as excellent, noteworthy, and even indispensable apply. No one should be surprised if this book becomes the standard by which other investment works are judged. Public, academic, and professional collections.—*L. D. Guin, Murray State University*

OAB-2067   HG930   92-6581 CIP
Gros, Daniel. **European monetary integration,** by Daniel Gros and Niels Thygesen. Longman/St. Martin's, 1992. 494p index ISBN 0-312-08045-X, $69.95

This volume provides the most comprehensive survey this reviewer has seen of the process of monetary integration in Europe. The authors offer a truly global perspective, especially in terms of linking the results of theoretical and empirical research with the institutional and practical considerations that dominate in the negotiations on the European Monetary System. The history of European monetary integration is evaluated with special emphasis on the challenges arising from German unification, capital-market liberalization, and the enlargement of participation (the entry of peseta and pound sterling). The economics of monetary union is well covered. The microeconomic and macroeconomic benefits of European Monetary Union (EMU), spillover effects of national demand policies, the implications for budgetary policies, and the worldwide significance of the union are examined in particular. Finally, the authors provide a systematic overview of the public and political debate on EMU. Although the volume focuses mainly on monetary questions, nonmonetary issues are not neglected. References. Nontechnical and easy-to-read, this work is essential for all students of international macroeconomics and European economic integration.—*Z. Suster, University of New Haven*

OAB-2068   HG501   93-45466 CIP
Guttmann, Robert. **How credit-money shapes the economy: the United States in a global system.** M.E. Sharpe, 1994. 561p bibl index afp ISBN 1-56324-100-5, $68.00; ISBN 1-56324-101-3 pbk, $27.95

Guttmann has written a wonderful book about the dollar. There is a fatal contradiction between the US dollar as the global key currency and America as the world's largest debtor nation. What can replace the dollar as an international currency? The world economy may disintegrate into three competing blocs (the Americas, Europe, and the Pacific Rim), or a supranational form of credit-money might be created. Guttmann sketches the outlines of a possible global money free of specific national ties. Monetary problems are complex, but the author believes that Clinton's policies are moving the US in the right direction. The careful reader of this impressive work will discover how economists think about money, how US monetary policy has been conducted since the 18th century, why the dollar is currently being undermined as a global currency, and how the dollar might be replaced as the world's currency of choice. Given the scope and detail of this extremely impressive work, it is surprisingly easy to read. General readers; upper-division undergraduate through professional.—*R. T. Averitt, Smith College*

OAB-2069   HF1359   95-32645 CIP
Hoekman, Bernard M. **The political economy of the world trading system: from GATT to WTO,** by Bernard M. Hoekman and Michel M. Kostecki. Oxford, 1995. 301p bibl index afp ISBN 0-19-828955-3, $55.00; ISBN 0-19-829017-9 pbk, $27.00

A few years ago when teaching a class on GATT and the Uruguay Round, this reviewer discovered there were no books meeting the stated aim of this work—to provide an "accessible, yet comprehensive, introduction to the institutional mechanics, economics, and politics of the trading system." The authors succeed magnificently in filling that gap in the literature. The book weaves explanations of GATT principles with economic and political theory and historical and current information about GATT, GATS, Agreement on TRIPS, and the WTO. The authors describe the structure, purpose, accomplishments, and limitations of multilateral trade negotiations within the GATT system and ground their explanations solidly in economic and political theory while keeping the mathematics to a minimum. They accomplish this feat with an astonishing degree of rigor given that their explanations of the theory are almost exclusively intuitive. The authors eschew dogmatism and present a frank and realistic look at the GATT system. The final part of the book assesses future challenges facing the WTO. Candid and insightful, this book is by far the best road map available through the notoriously complex structure and terminology of our multilateral trading system. Thorough and detailed while remaining readable and concise, this volume belongs in every academic library.—*P. Lowry, Illinois Wesleyan University*

OAB-2070   HF1713   95-25447 CIP
Irwin, Douglas A. **Against the tide: an intellectual history of free trade.** Princeton, 1996. 265p bibl index afp ISBN 0-691-01138-9, $29.95

The author of this clear and concise book has two objectives: to examine how the doctrine of free trade achieved intellectual primacy in the late 18th century and how it has withstood repeated challenges to remain one of the cornerstones of economic theory today. Both objectives are fully met; however, the second part, which examines the intellectual attacks on free trade, truly excels. Irwin focuses on the economic arguments for protectionism, consciously (and wisely) ignoring the various sociopolitical justifications. He examines the history of each issue in a balanced manner, presenting both pro and con arguments through extensive use of quotes from the participants of the debate. Using a prose of unusual clarity for an economist, Irwin explains the most complex trade topics in a way that a well-informed general reader can easily understand. Although the second part of the book is the more valuable, the first part stands as one of the best reviews of pre-Classical economic trade views this reviewer has read. Irwin's use of quotes, revised into more or less modern English, gives the reader the feel of sitting in on the debates as they happened. Perhaps the greatest accomplishment of this first part is to rescue Henry Martyn's *Considerations upon the East-India Trade* (London, 1701) from its unjust obscurity. Anyone having to argue in favor of free trade to a hostile audience will be well armed by reading this volume. Strongly recommended for all international economics collections.—*A. Barrett, College of St. Scholastica*

OAB-2071   HQ1240   95-13689 MARC
Jahan, Rounaq. **The elusive agenda: mainstreaming women in development.** University Press Limited/Zed Books, 1995. 144p bibl index ISBN 1-85649-273-7, $55.00; ISBN 1-85649-274-5 pbk, $17.50

Jahan's short but important book is "must" reading for anyone interested in women in development (WID) or gender and development (GAD). It addresses a familiar paradox: the relentless increase in the "feminization of poverty," especially in the developing world, despite heightened worldwide attention to women's issues. Unlike other recent treatments of the subject, this one identifies specific causes and offers reasonable recommendations. It reviews the efforts of four donor agencies (UNDP, World Bank, CIDA, NORAD) and two countries (Tanzania, Bangladesh) receiving aid to operationalize WID/GAD policies over the last 20 years. Jahan shows that progress has been mainly in areas that do not demand fundamental social-structural changes; goals requir-

Social & Behavioral Sciences

ing the dismantling of traditional gender hierarchies and redistribution of power and resources have generally not been met. The author sensibly recommends an "agenda-setting approach" involving changing institutional structures to enable women's greater participation in decision making, renewed emphasis on women's equality and empowerment, and decreased emphasis on operational measures. A useful adjunct to material emanating from the Fourth UN World ("Beijing") Conference on Women (September 1995). Upper-division undergraduates and above.—*M. A. Gwynne, SUNY at Stony Brook*

OAB-2072   HC110   94-22733 CIP
Jorgenson, Dale W. **Productivity: v.1: Postwar U.S. economic growth; v.2: International comparisons of economic growth.** MIT, 1995. 2v. 434, 470p bibl index ISBN 0-262-10049-5, v.1; ISBN 0-262-10050-9, v.2; $45.00 ea.

No official collection or personal library concerned with economic growth, investment, and productivity will now be considered complete without this ambitious, comprehensive, indeed, magnificent two-volume undertaking, rendered by a distinguished Harvard University economist in collaboration with several outstanding members of the economic profession. Volume 1 is devoted to the sources of economic growth in the postwar period, its impressive record of progress in this period, the strategic role of investment (expanded in concept by including education and training of workers as well as physical investment). Analysis of factors contributing to growth, both at an aggregate and industry level, show that capital and labor inputs during 1948-79 account for three-fourths of the increase, much more important than productivity growth; furthermore, that capital is more important than labor, which suggests that public policy should tilt toward providing investment incentives. Volume 2 is devoted to international comparisons of postwar economic growth among industrialized countries. The US is shown as a gainer in competitiveness by retaining an enormous productivity advantage—contrary to popular conception. A new system of weighting capital and labor inputs is developed for the several countries, which changes the relative importance of inputs versus productivity as contributors to economic growth. Use of purchasing-power-parities (which standardize international prices) adds much to the validity of the intercountry measures. The volumes contain some previously published work; however, the totality adds comprehensiveness and coherence. Although there are many technical tables and some econometrics that would be understandable only to advanced economists, there is much that informed general readers might gain. General; academic; professional.—*H. I. Liebling, Lafayette College*

OAB-2073   Orig
Lal, Deepak. **The political economy of poverty, equity, and growth: a comparative study,** by Deepak Lal and H. Myint. Oxford, 1996. 458p bibl indexes afp ISBN 0-19-828863-8, $49.95

This excellent book is likely to become basic to the study of economic development. The result of a World Bank study of 21 developing countries covering the years 1950 to 1985, this is a synthesis volume, the last of ten books published from the study. Earlier volumes covered Malawi and Madagascar; Egypt and Turkey; Sri Lanka and Malaysia; Indonesia and Nigeria; Thailand and Ghana; Brazil and Mexico; Costa Rica and Uruguay; Colombia and Peru; and the five small economies of Hong Kong, Singapore, Malta, Jamaica, and Mauritius. These country groupings reflect the comparative approach used in the study which attempted to show how growth, poverty, and equity was affected by the political and economic processes that occurred in the different countries. Factor endowment, institutions and organization, and economic policies are all central to the analysis. The authors' approach and conclusions (e.g., that growth in income per capita led to the alleviation of mass poverty) may not be accepted by all readers. The sophistication of the analysis, along with the data supporting the work, makes this a valuable book. The extensive chapter notes are meant to be an essential part of the study as well as serve as a bibliography. Accessible to knowledgeable noneconomists, this book belongs in all academic and professional libraries.—*J. E. Weaver, Drake University*

OAB-2074   HC59   93-13947 Orig
Latouche, Serge. **In the wake of the affluent society: an exploration of post-development,** introd. and tr. by Martin O'Connor and Rosemary Arnoux. Zed Books, 1993. 256p bibl index ISBN 1-85649-171-4, $55.00; ISBN 1-85649-172-2 pbk, $19.95

The debate over the relative importance of economic development's fixation on material things seems to have been won, at least in the Western world, by those who argue in favor of materialism achieved through market allocation of resources. However, there are a few voices that remind the world that such a fixation on materialism creates winners and losers and that the latter forms the majority of humankind. Latouche's central theme is that the Western idea of a grand modern, affluent, and liberal world community based on technology and driven by Western values is coming apart at the seams, and that within this fragmentation are emerging new forms of social and economic organizations, which Latouche describes as an informal sector based more on social and cultural relations than on impersonal markets. The growth of this informal sector could lead to a world environment in which all share in the benefits of development. Part 1 of this book discusses the flaws of the grand society (fixation on the individual and material consumption) and the resulting plight of the "have nots." Part 2 discusses how informal structures are cropping up in various parts of the world in response to the problems created by the failures of the modern society. The book is very well written and argued and is supported by a wealth of empirical studies. Highly recommended to policymakers as well as student development.—*K. Gyimah-Brempong, Wright State University*

OAB-2075   HC59   94-39193 CIP
Lewellen, Ted C. **Dependency and development: an introduction to the Third World.** Bergin & Garvey, 1995. 272p bibl index afp ISBN 0-89789-399-9, $65.00

Lewellen offers a unique and valuable overview of economic development. It is the perspective of a cultural anthropologist who is concerned about Third World economic dependency and the lack of variety of economic development models. To him the standard prescriptive model of economic development offered by the IMF and World Bank is too insensitive to cultures, too pervasive, and holds too much sway. Economic development models should exist that complement rather than supplant cultures. He acknowledges the importance of prices and markets but questions trade, particularly what he sees as imbalanced trade between nations trading manufactured products and nations trading mostly primary products. This book would be an excellent supplemental reader to standard textbooks on economic development. The author leaves the highly stylized development theory to economists and focuses more on the inequalities and inequities of the past and present world order. His chapter on human rights is outstanding. It is a strong descriptive and historical indictment of the support that the developed world has frequently given to abusive governments of the Third World. Highly recommended to general readers and academics alike.—*D. D. Miller, Baldwin-Wallace College*

OAB-2076   HG5772   92-9934 CIP
Mason, Mark. **American multinationals and Japan: the political economy of Japanese capital controls, 1899-1980.** Council on East Asian Studies, Harvard University, 1992. 373p bibl index (Harvard East Asian monographs, 154) ISBN 0-674-02630-6, $35.00

In what will be accepted as the standard work on the subject, Mason presents a searching examination of the history of direct foreign investments—that is, manufacturing ventures—made by American businesses in 20th-century Japan. After surveying general trends in each of five time periods, Mason offers detailed case studies of American companies—ranging from Coca Cola to Texas Instruments—that attempted to break into Japan. Numerous American companies, Mason shows, tried long and hard to set up ventures in Japan. Differing from many previous works on the topic, Mason's study argues persuasively that it was Japanese business opposition more than opposition from the Japanese government that severely limited American success in investing in

Japan. Mason also reveals that American governmental officials, always more interested in strategic political matters than economic affairs with regard to Japan, did little to help American businessmen. Based upon very thorough research in American and Japanese sources, this readable study should be of interest to scholars, business people, and policymakers. Advanced undergraduate through faculty.—*M. Blackford, Ohio State University*

OAB-2077 HD30 94-24545 CIP
McRae, Hamish. **The world in 2020: power, culture and prosperity.** Harvard Business School Press, 1995 (c1994). 302p index afp ISBN 0-87584-604-1, $24.95

McRae, a British financial journalist/editor, provides a stimulating, nontechnical exploration of the past, present, and future for three critical world regions. Circumstances are reviewed to the 1990s for North America, Western Europe, and East Asia—frequently exemplifying with principal constituent nations (US, Britain, China, Germany, and Japan). Individual chapters then examine the main forces driving change in these regions: demography, resources and the environment, trade and finance, technology, and government and society. With these investigations, McRae imaginatively penetrates essential causes and significant effects of change. An invaluable strength of McRae's approach is his emphasis on underlying institutional influences, such as political stability and social discipline, rather than the obvious economic and financial (outcome) measures (e.g., GDP, balances of payments, and currency values). Finally, McRae forecasts development scenarios by the year 2020 for each of the three regions with attention to gainers and losers, caveats and contingencies. Highest recommendation for its breadth and depth of insight and for its approachable, nonquantitative presentation. Upper-division undergraduate through professional.—*J. C. Thompson, emeritus, University of Connecticut*

OAB-2078 HF1379 96-42495 CIP
Ostry, Sylvia. **The post-Cold War trading system: who's on first?** Chicago, 1997. 309p index afp ISBN 0-226-63789-1, $48.00; ISBN 0-226-63790-5 pbk, $17.95

This is an excellent retrospective on the evolution of the multilateral trading system and its future development by an author with impressive academic as well as public policy credentials in the complex field of trade negotiation. Multilateral trade liberalization under the auspice of the General Agreement on Tariffs and Trade (GATT) has been remarkably successful over a half-century of existence and evolution into the World Trade Organization. This success has given rise to all kinds of market-access problems that were previously masked by explicit protection imposed at the border. This includes domestic policies relating to competition, environmental issues, consumer health and safety, and other measures that intentionally or unintentionally impede foreign-based suppliers' market access. It also includes issues that have been of growing, even vital, importance but that were never effectively covered by the negotiating machinery, such as international trade in technology and in a variety of services. At the same time, the multilateral trade policy infrastructure has had to deal with fundamental shifts in competitive advantage and countries transitioning from inward-oriented command economies to aggressive exporters. All these issues are treated in this very readable book by one who knows. Easy reading it's not, but well worth the effort. Highly recommended for college and university libraries.—*I. Walter, New York University*

OAB-2079 HF1455 93-17892 CIP
Rhodes, Carolyn. **Reciprocity, U.S. trade policy, and the GATT regime.** Cornell, 1993. 249p index afp ISBN 0-8014-2864-5, $32.50

In this thorough empirical assessment of the principle of reciprocity in the history of trade policy, Rhodes examines the use of reciprocity in the interests of fair and open markets as well as its abuse by protectionist interests, including contradictions that exist between reciprocity and national treatment or nondiscrimination in market access. This analysis is particularly pertinent in the current context of the Clinton administration's reciprocity-centered trade pol-

icy, with which the author appears to display some sympathy. Separate chapters set the framework for the discussion, consider the history of reciprocity during the 1880-1933 period, and follow it through the Reciprocal Trade Act and the origins of the GATT in the 1940s. Three chapters examine the use of reciprocity in the steel, automobile, and wheat flour sectors, and the final chapter summarizes the discussion in the context of current US trade policy and as a cornerstone of the GATT and the incipient World Trade Organization. Rhodes concludes that reciprocity appears to be a necessary ingredient of American trade policy, and that it has been effective in promoting historically more open markets than would have been achieved in its absence. Probably the best currently available treatment of this critical aspect of international trade policy. Excellent index. Highly recommended. Upper-division undergraduate through professional.—*I. Walter, New York University*

OAB-2080 HB3717 95-25780 CIP
Rothermund, Dietmar. **The global impact of the Great Depression, 1929-1939.** Routledge, 1996. 180p index ISBN 0-415-11818-2, $65.00; ISBN 0-415-11819-0 pbk, $17.95

That the Great Depression had enormous, mainly negative consequences for the world is a commonplace. Yet, as Rothermund notes, the impact of the Great Depression on many non-Western countries has received limited scholarly attention, and thus there is no good interpretive survey of the problem from a worldwide perspective. Drawing on his own expertise as an economic historian of modern India, Rothermund sets out to fill this gap in the historical literature. He succeeds admirably. Beginning with economic relations in the 1920s, the author turns to the drastic decline of commodity prices and agricultural economics after 1929. Examining the world's regions and leading countries, he argues convincingly that economic collapse weighed most harshly on the world's peasants. His treatment of Asian and especially Indian developments offers striking insights. Discussions of Africa, Germany, and the US are also noteworthy. This excellent brief survey, a model of comparative global history, is highly recommended. It will stimulate and enlighten teachers as well as undergraduate students.—*J. P. McKay, Univ of Illinois at Urbana-Champaign*

OAB-2081 Orig
Ryrie, William. **First World, Third World.** St. Martin's, 1995. 240p bibl index ISBN 0-312-15873-4, $39.95

"International aid is in crisis".... There is presently much more confusion about the basic purpose and aims of international aid than ever before." So begins this thought-provoking book centering on Third World development with an emphasis on the role of international aid by a recently retired former practitioner of the aid game. Ryrie makes no effort to justify or excuse the disappointing results of billions of dollars of aid to the Third World since the end of WW II. To the contrary, he provides the perfect blend of inside perspective and academic objectivity. He attributes much of the failure to the overemphasis on government-to-government assistance, and he now concludes "the basic development task consists of creating a successful market economy." Ryrie accomplishes a great deal in this book. Not only does he analyze the past; he also takes the lessons from his analysis and transfers them to clear prescriptions for the future. The book ends with a chapter listing "21 Propositions about Development and Aid." This is one of the best books this reviewer has ever read in the entire literature of international economic development. It should be required reading at the undergraduate, graduate, and professional levels for all even vaguely interested in the discipline.—*A. Barrett, College of St. Scholastica*

OAB-2082 HF1713 94-5627 CIP
Schott, Jeffrey J. **The Uruguay round: an assessment,** by Jeffrey J. Schott with Johanna W. Buurman. Institute for International Economics, 1994. 219p bibl index ISBN 0-88132-206-7 pbk, $19.95

This user-friendly assessment of the Uruguay Round of trade negotiations, certainly the best available today, follows the pattern of the Institute for International Economics's equally good earlier assessment of the NAFTA initiative. The volume is short, to the point, analytically sound, and easy to read. It begins with an account of the historical background of the Uruguay Round, its tortuous negotiating and political history, its results, and the mandate for the new World Trade Organization as successor to the General Agreement on Tariffs and Trade. Schott and Buurman provide a careful and balanced assessment of the Uruguay Round scorecard with respect to agriculture, textiles and apparel, tariffs, government procurement, antidumping, subsidies and countervailing measures, safeguards in the event of import surges, services, foreign direct investment, intellectual property, and dispute settlement. There is a succinct summary of the Uruguay Round agreements themselves. Appendixes deal with US implementation of legislation and models that may be used in assessing the impact of such global trade liberalization efforts. Comprehensive references and index. A must for college and university libraries.—*I. Walter, New York University*

OAB-2083 HD2341 92-28162 CIP
Thomas, J.J. **Informal economic activity.** Michigan, 1993 (c1992). 371p bibl index ISBN 0-472-10420-9, $45.00

The growing interdependence in an emerging global economy requires a reliable comparison of the economic performance of all nations. Although economics is becoming increasingly quantitative, national income accounting does not encompass a substantial part of economic activity. In the author's view, the most common shortcoming of national accounting is its failure to incorporate the so-called informal economic sectors, which leads to considerable distortion in national accounting figures. Thomas attempts to assess its impact on the economies affected. He admits that economists have failed to formulate a general theory of informal economic activity. As a consequence, countries must be studied on an individual basis, and the cost of inclusion is prohibitive due to a lack of reliable data and the difficulty of their collection. Household contributions are extremely difficult to calculate. A rapidly growing irregular sector, though producing legal goods and services, is characterized by the avoidance of regulations and tax evasion. In the criminal sector, the output is illegal and inevitably involves tax evasion. This interdisciplinary study fuses theoretical, empirical, and historical methods, and also succeeds in integrating economic research with contributions from sociology, anthropology, criminology, and history. A valuable and highly recommended contribution to the study of national accounting. Advanced undergraduate through professional; informed general readers.—*O. Zinam, University of Cincinnati*

OAB-2084 HJ8899 92-10936 CIP
Woodward, David. **Debt, adjustment and poverty in developing countries: v.1: National and international dimensions of debt and adjustment in developing countries; v.2: The impact of debt and adjustment at the household level in developing countries.** Pinter/Save the Children, 1992. (Dist. by St. Martin's) 2v. 330, 340p bibl index ISBN 1-85567-076-3, v.1; ISBN 1-85567-077-1, v.2; $65.00 ea.

A volume of nearly epic proportions of both mind and heart, the title is certainly justified by the balanced content of the two volumes. Given the complexities and intricacies of the subjects covered such as currency devaluation, macroeconomic adjustment, structural reforms, and the proposals on international financial systems, Woodward admirably manages to sustain the strong logical current of the discussion through both volumes. The succinctly stated arguments start with the origins of the debt crisis and logically flow into the process and problems of domestic and international macroeconomic adjustments, out of which the author develops proposals for the creation of new international institutions and additional mechanisms for the existing international institutions. The process, benefits, and costs of the policies such as currency devaluation and macroeconomic adjustment are dealt with in elegant simplicity without diluting the theoretical essence of the subject. Clearly evident is the author's strong disagreement with the IMF's theoretical and policy position that balance-of-payments problems can be mostly corrected by monetary (mostly tight) and structural policies. Woodward effectively analyzes trade restrictions, e.g., agricultural policies, the Multi-Fiber Agreement, and others

imposed by the developed countries that create insurmountable problems for the LDCs. Problems of health, nutrition, and education as the outcomes, mostly undesirable, of the IMF's adjustment policies are appropriately highlighted and dovetailed with the quantative evidence in the main body of the discourse. The author's tone of advocacy and his prescription make a convincing case for his position. Regardless of one's view on the main argument, the menu presented is enticing. The author's prose is lucid, flowing, and capable of sustaining interest. Faculty and students at all levels will find the book enlightening. Scholars and diplomats dealing with economics, international relations, geography, and international business will find the book indispensable.—*C. J. Talele, Columbia State Community College*

■ Labor & Welfare

OAB-2085 HD6664 93-50224 CIP
Booth, Alison L. **The economics of the trade union.** Cambridge, 1995. 295p bibl index ISBN 0-521-46467-6, $59.95; ISBN 0-521-46839-6 pbk, $19.95

This fine volume is an up-to-date survey of the economics literature on trade unionism. As such it has a number of American competitors, e.g., Richard B. Freeman and James L. Medoff's *What Do Unions Do?* (CH, Sep'84) and Barry T. Hirsch and John T. Addison's *The Economic Analysis of Union* (CH, Sep'86). Booth's book, however, can more than hold its own against the competition. She does an admirable and very thorough job covering the history of unions in Britain and the US; the standard (and not-so-standard) economic theory of union behavior; the effects of unions on wages, wage structure, investment and productivity, profitability, and employment; and the relationship between unions and the macroeconomy. Some of the discussion is fairly technical, but on the whole should be accessible to upper-division undergraduates. Booth's writing style is dry but always clear, and the bibliography is outstanding. Highly recommended to upper-division undergraduates, graduate students, and professional economists.—*R. A. Margo, Vanderbilt University*

OAB-2086 HD5717 95-46260 CIP
Davis, Steven J. **Job creation and destruction,** by Steven J. Davis, John C. Haltiwanger, and Scott Schuh. MIT, 1996. 260p bibl index afp ISBN 0-262-04152-9, $30.00

This book is destined to be much cited by economists. The authors utilize the newly created Longitudinal Research Database to document job creation and destruction in US manufacturing from 1972 to 1988. They present many important facts, including the high rate of worker movement between plants within industries (higher than movement between industries) and the asymmetry between job creation and destruction across the business cycle—relatively constant creation, much higher destruction rates during downturns. Chapters consider variations in these rates across industries, and by size and age of plants and firms; the relationship between job flows and business cycles—and between job flows, worker flows, and unemployment over the business cycle; and policy implications. Several chapters are devoted to characterizing this new data set and considering ways in which complementary databases could be developed. In particular, redressing the paucity of comparable nonmanufacturing job data is of pressing concern in order to verify if the patterns presented hold more generally. This volume provides an important stimulus for reworking economic theory and is an excellent example of how to produce fundamental empirical research. Upper-division undergraduate through professional collections.—*J. P. Jacobsen, Wesleyan University*

OAB-2087 Orig
Harris, Nigel. **The new untouchables: immigration and the new world worker.** I.B. Tauris, 1995. 254p bibl index ISBN 1-85043-956-7, $35.00

Harris presents a compelling case for his view that world immigration patterns are not a threat to the economic well-being of either recipient countries or countries of origin. Rather, he argues that immigration is perceived as a threat to the archaic nationalist order of world government and that the "solution" is to move to a more globally oriented system of rules governing labor flows (with as little governance as possible). In support of his case, Harris marshals an impressive array of facts concerning the composition of immigrant flows (noting in particular that measurement of flows by country of origin hides important patterns regarding which regions and cultural groups within countries are most likely to produce immigrants) and presents his arguments in smoothly flowing prose. In a particularly useful chapter he details the various arguments heard in developed countries against immigration and convincingly refutes them. Although the book presents no new results, it is nonetheless a masterful compilation of what is known about immigration and is written so as to be accessible to a wide range of readers. Public, academic, and professional collections.—*J. P. Jacobsen, Wesleyan University*

OAB-2088 HF5549 95-17411 CIP
Lazear, Edward P. **Personnel economics.** MIT, 1995. 170p bibl index afp (The Wicksell lectures, 1993) ISBN 0-262-12188-3, $27.50

Studies of the labor market have traditionally been divided into two quite distinct subsets. On the one hand were the efforts of labor economists that assumed an optimizing paradigm and the neoclassical production function. Quite distinct were studies of personnel that looked at hiring, retention, and promotion decisions within firms. There was a division between the analytical and human aspects of the employer-employee relation. Lazear's work bridges that divide. Issues such as motivation, compensation, selection, and the organization of work activity into jobs are modeled using economic theory. The role that teams play in motivation and compensation is systematically treated. The real value of this book is that it makes accessible the main conclusions of "personnel economics" without the analytical sophistication that has kept many of these ideas from reaching a general audience. References are provided for those interested in the analytical underpinnings. This is a most important contribution to the field of labor economics. Significant advances can be made by combining analytical rigor with the human aspects of people and their jobs. Recommended for upper-division undergraduates, graduate students, and professionals in the field.—*J. F. O'Connell, College of the Holy Cross*

OAB-2089 HC103 92-44985 CIP
Perelman, Michael. **The pathology of the U.S. economy: the costs of a low-wage system.** St. Martin's, 1993. 252p bibl index ISBN 0-312-09528-7, $45.00

Given the intensification of present economic dislocations, Perelman wonders about the wisdom of the economics profession in dealing with *actual* competition in capitalism (as opposed to its fictitious counterpart in neoclassical economics) and the critical role of economic crises that are regularly leading to the *restructuring* of the US economy along the cycles of production. The beauty of this timely volume is its sharp focus and the abundance of illustrative evidence, showing the fallacies of both Keynesianism and the "Chicago School of laissez-faire economics." Perelman argues that competition "works like the natural fire cycle in a forest." Fires may destroy a part of the forest, but "they also clear the way for new growth." While Keynesian policies (especially military Keynesianism) have long protected the US economy from competitive restructuring, laissez-faire policies have blamed the labor unions for high wages. High wages, Perelman maintains, are necessary, since they encourage further technological innovation and higher skills. Perelman concludes that in the face of present global competition, both low wages and military Keynesianism will certainly further the magnitude of US economic decline. A must for all academic and public libraries.—*C. Bina, Harvard University*

OAB-2090 JC575 92-5514 CIP
Sen, Amartya. **Inequality reexamined.** Russell Sage Foundation/Harvard, 1992. 207p bibl indexes afp ISBN 0-674-45255-0, $29.95

Sen, a well-published economist and an authority on equality, broadens the usual perspectives of economists in this book which is "about reexamining inequality. . .the evaluation and assessment of social arrangements in general. The former depends on the latter." He posits "equality of *something*" [some focal variable] as a "common characteristic of virtually all approaches" which implies that "the demand for equality in terms of one variable entails that the theory concerned may have to be non-egalitarian with respect to another variable." A philosophical premise is that of human diversity. He distinguishes between "*the freedom to achieve. . .and the level of achievement*"; he also distinguishes between capability and utility and between equality and efficiency. The analysis includes the demands of equality. Sen has a capability-centered view as opposed to an income-centered view. The analysis is "mainly conceptual. . .bearing on matters of practical concern." Readers wanting a highly objective, statistical base for an economic interpretation of bases and trends of income inequality should read Edgar K. Browning, "The Trend Toward Equality in the Distribution of Net Income," *Southern Economic Journal*, 43 (July 1976): 912-23, and Greg J. Duncan, *Years of Poverty, Years of Plenty* (CH, Jul'84). However, readers could not expect a better, more comprehensive conceptual basis for examining statistical and empirical studies on inequality. Advanced undergraduate; graduate.—*F. W. Musgrave, Ithaca College*

OAB-2091 HD7125 93-41038 CIP
Steuerle, C. Eugene. **Retooling Social Security for the 21st century: right and wrong approaches to reform,** by C. Eugene Steuerle and Jon M. Bakija. Urban Institute, 1994. 332p bibl index afp ISBN 0-87766-601-6, $57.00; ISBN 0-87766-602-4 pbk, $16.95

A major long-run fiscal imbalance faces Social Security. It must be reformed. Fortunately, Steuerle (Urban Institute senior fellow and former deputy assistant secretary of the US Treasury) and Bakija (Urban Institute research associate) provide an excellent blueprint. They begin by examining four principles (progressivity, individual equity, horizontal equity, and economic efficiency) that underlie standard rationales for Social Security. Next they explain the system's operation-projected fiscal imbalances; current tax and benefits rules; how the system redistributes income; and the elderly's economic well-being and diversity. They close with reform options, always returning to the four goals and evidence on how well they are currently achieved. Superb appendixes include tables giving the actuarial present value at age 65 of lifetime Old Age and Survivors Insurance benefits and taxes by cohort. A well written tour de force, especially valuable for policy makers. The only weakness is failing to take seriously plans for a more fundamental overhaul of the system. All levels.—*R. M. Whaples, Wake Forest University*

■ Natural Resources

OAB-2092 HD9560 95-8271 CIP
Adelman, M.A. **The genie out of the bottle: world oil since 1970.** MIT, 1995. 350p bibl index ISBN 0-262-01151-4, $45.00

Adelman (emeritus professor of economics, MIT, and the world's leading academic analyst of the world's crude oil market) has produced a readable, detailed history of 25 years of OPEC activity in the exercise of monopoly power. The story is based on Adelman's more technical analysis in his *Economics of Petroleum Supply* (1993). Some lessons he provides: the practical difficulties of running an effective cartel (OPEC) are great; public policy without good economic analysis is disastrous (US policy toward OPEC and individual countries); "one cannot hold a sovereign monopolist to its word"; and much "analysis" in the press and political strategy in Washington have been wrong. Adelman cites names, dates, decisions, and effects; his history is a detailed chronology firmly based on sound economics. This volume illustrates the usefulness of economics in understanding the oil (or any) market and the necessity of solid and informed economics in formulating public policy. Very highly recommended for general readers, upper-division undergraduate and graduate students, faculty, and professionals.—*R. A. Miller, Wesleyan University*

OAB-2093   HJ9156   92-35660 CIP
Altshuler, Alan A. **Regulation for revenue: the political economy of land use exactions,** by Alan A. Altshuler and José A. Gómez-Ibáñez. Brookings/Lincoln Institute of Land Policy, 1993. 175p index afp ISBN 0-8157-0356-2, $29.95; ISBN 0-8157-0355-4 pbk, $11.95

Over the last few decades, the ability of local governments in the US to accommodate the costs of growth has diminished. Many municipalities responded by developing a mechanism—exactions—for extracting revenues from new development. Essentially, private (mainly commercial) developers, in return for regulatory support, have to undertake mandated expenditures in related infrastructure and other public services. *Regulation for Revenue* is a thoughtful, systematic, and insightful appraisal of this local innovation. Not only do the authors provide a helpful assessment of the factors that led to the adoption of exactions, including their legal background, but they also assess whether development pays its own way and whether exactions improve or diminish the efficiency of development. Additionally, they provide a rich discussion of the extent to which exactions are equitable. Using previous studies, empirical data from a variety of sources, and much literature on US land development, Altshuler and Gómez-Ibáñez (both at Harvard) have written a definitive study. Their conclusion: exactions are the "least bad" alternative available for regulating development and an "ingenious local adaptation to antitax and antigrowth pressures." Graduate; pre-professional; professional.—*R. A. Beauregard, University of Pittsburgh*

OAB-2094   HC110   96-40115 CIP
Anderson, Terry L. **Enviro-capitalists: doing good while doing well,** by Terry L. Anderson and Donald R. Leal. Rowman & Littlefield, 1997. 189p bibl index afp ISBN 0-8476-8381-8, $52.50; ISBN 0-8476-8382-6 pbk, $16.95

Economists have long specified the conditions under which environmental and economic objectives can be reconciled. Basically, society needs to decide via the political process what level of ambient environmental quality is acceptable. This has to be translated, in the light of environmental assimilative capacity, into sustainable levels of emissions, which then represent a valuable economic resource. Market processes can then be used to allocate this resource to the most productive among alternative uses by, for example, auctioning off pollution rights. Thus, economics can be harnessed to work for, rather than against, environmental protection. In the process, it throws off economic opportunities that business in general, and entrepreneurs in particular, may be able to seize for both private and public gain. The authors provide a wealth of cases where this has happened in the US and worldwide in virtually every area of the environment. This is the first volume to assemble these case studies in a coherent and readable way. They leave the impression that a lot more environmental quality could be achieved a lot more cheaply, and much of the confrontation between environmentalists and the business sector would end, if policy makers were better trained in economics and in harnessing the entrepreneurial zeal of the market. Limited bibliography. Extensive index. Highly recommended for academic collections.—*I. Walter, New York University*

OAB-2095   HD9566   95-21325 CIP
Bradley, Robert L. **Oil, gas & government: the U.S. experience.** Cato Institute/Rowman & Littlefield, 1996. 2v. 1,997p indexes afp ISBN 0-8476-8110-6, $225.00

These two volumes chronicle governmental intervention in the US petroleum industry over the past 130-plus years. Sandwiched between relatively brief chapters on theory and policy, Bradley (The Cato Institute) writes a chronological economic history of such intervention in, successively, exploration and production, transportation and allocation, refining, and petroleum marketing. The style is more historical than economically analytical. The author cites and discusses numerous studies of this enormous industry over a long period, producing a massive and impressive study. The policy conclusions are easily summarized: most governmental interference has produced poor results; the

unhampered free market would have worked better. This volume is an excellent reference work for the US oil and gas industry. Upper-division undergraduate through professional collections.—*R. A. Miller, Wesleyan University*

OAB-2096   HD1761   94-47984 CIP
Gardner, B. Delworth. **Plowing ground in Washington: the political economy of U.S. agriculture.** Pacific Research Institute for Public Policy, 1995. 385p bibl index ISBN 0-936488-70-0, $29.95

This thorough survey of major issues in federal agricultural policy is written by a well-known expert in the field. Gardner offers careful explanations of the theoretical foundations of analysis of agricultural policy (efficiency issues, equity issues, political markets, public choice) as well as empirical analysis of such important questions as the sources and recipients of political contributions and the distribution of program benefits by farm size and income level. Among the many issues addressed are not only the usual topics of acreage controls, price subsidies, marketing orders, and import restrictions but also such less commonly addressed issues as the effects of credit programs, the rationale for agricultural subsidies, and the environmental impacts (toxic runoffs, wetlands effects, soil erosion) of these agricultural policies. After making a cogent case for eliminating most of these programs, Gardner concludes with a thoughtful analysis of the path to reform and some of the political obstacles. An excellent survey of agricultural policy from a market-oriented, public choice perspective. Lower-division undergraduate through professional.—*H. H. Ulbrich, Clemson University*

OAB-2097   HD216   94-12012 CIP
Lehmann, Scott. **Privatizing public lands.** Oxford, 1995. 248p index afp ISBN 0-19-508972-3, $45.00

The desire to sell most of the remaining federally owned lands in the American West has been strengthened by proposals such as those offered by Richard Stroup and John A. Baden (*Natural Resources: Bureaucratic Myths and Environmental Management*, CH, Dec'83), who advocate selling or privatizing most public lands. This idea was part of the Sagebrush Rebellion of the early Reagan years and is associated with the current Wise Use Movement. Lehmann (philosophy, Univ. of Connecticut) examines privatization proposals in terms of their logical completeness and relationship to the common good and invokes, as needed, the perspective of analytical economics. Feeling that arguments for privatization have been incompletely developed, Lehmann begins by trying to strengthen the rationale for privatization. Once this is accomplished to his satisfaction he meticulously dissects weaknesses in those arguments. Using an anti-utilitarian perspective, he scrutinizes such terms as "productive," and "property rights," and raises questions about the neutrality of markets as ethical arbiters of environmental and public values. Along the way he offers valuable challenges to the so-called evils of collective management. Although critical of privatization proposals, the author also takes environmental groups to task for advocating a variant of privatization that he calls marketization. This book is the most stimulating discussion of these issues since Stroup and Baden and will no doubt spark controversy from both fans and opponents of privatization. Undergraduate through faculty.—*P. J. Pizor, Northwest College*

OAB-2098   S473   93-37124 CIP
McCann, James C. **People of the plow: an agricultural history of Ethiopia, 1800-1990.** Wisconsin, 1995. 298p bibl index ISBN 0-299-14610-3, $54.00; ISBN 0-299-14614-6 pbk, $24.95

Based on more than five years of archival and field research, McCann's history of Ethiopian agriculture focuses on the ox-plow farming system that emerged in the Northern highlands and spread throughout the central, southern, and eastern parts of Ethiopia over a 200-year period. Of particular interest is his presentation of the interactions among environment, society, and technology, represented by Ankober, in the central highland region of the former Shawa royal capital Gera, an Oromo community in the heavily forested part of southwestern Ethiopia, and Ada, located on the urban periphery of Addis Ababa. Indigenous knowledge relating to natural resource management of forests, pastures, soils, and water are explored. McCann describes the use of terracing and irrigation for water conservation, and dung and the burning of soil with field stubble for soil regeneration. He also explores the impact of changing state structure and policy on agriculture, with examples from the traditional Amhara state to the Mengistu regime (1974-91), which introduced state farms and cooperatives, from Italian-run tractor agriculture to the USAID-funded US land-grant agricultural model established by Oklahoma State University. With 33 illustrations, five maps, 24 tables, numerous footnotes, and two appendixes with vernacular names of crops and agricultural terms, this is an outstanding example of careful historical research combined with oral histories to demonstrate the dynamics of changing agricultural systems. Upper-division undergraduates and above.—*D. M. Warren, Iowa State University*

OAB-2099　　　　　　GE170　　　　　　94-17739 CIP
Mercuro, Nicholas. **Ecology, law and economics: the simple analytics of natural resource and environmental economics,** by Nicholas Mercuro, Franklin A. López, and Kristian P. Preston. University Press of America, 1994. 204p bibl index afp ISBN 0-8191-9593-6, $49.50; ISBN 0-8191-9594-4 pbk, $32.50

In this slim but densely packed volume, the authors—two economists and a geographer, all at the University of New Orleans—present a model of resource economics that describes the complicated interrelationships among a market economy, the natural world, and government. The authors' range of expertise is very impressive, as is the scope of the work. The first three chapters offer succinct but thorough synopses of the flows in economic systems; of the structure and functioning of ecosystems, with particular emphasis on biogeochemical cycles; and of the role and impact of government in economic and environmental decision making. Having thus established the groundwork, the authors devote the fourth and fifth chapters to reviewing and assessing the economic remedies that can mitigate environmental harm, such as restructuring of ownership, subsidies, regulations, pollution permits, and the like. It should be noted that the authors' perspective is a purely economic one; their goal is to identify those policies that could produce environmental and economic efficiency, i.e., an equality of social costs and social benefits accruing from resource development and use. As they acknowledge, concerns such as justice and fairness are difficult to incorporate into models of economic efficiency, and so their book is silent on such matters. Nonetheless, it is an excellent overview of the field and provides a challenging policy perspective. It would be highly useful in upper-division undergraduate and graduate environmental policy and resource economics collections.—*L. Vance, Vermont College*

OAB-2100　　　　　　HD75　　　　　　92-39551 CIP
Pearce, David W. **World without end: economics, environment, and sustainable development,** by David W. Pearce and Jeremy J. Warford. Oxford, 1993. 440p bibl index ISBN 0-19-520881-1, $39.95

Over the last several years a number of books have been written on sustainable development, defined as "development that meets the needs of the present without compromising the ability of future generations to meet their own needs." This is the best of the lot. What distinguishes it from competitors is its comprehensiveness and the wealth of evidence it contains. Based on years of fieldwork and World Bank research (much of it previously unpublished), this book offers a very rich menu of specific examples of how the rather abstract principles of sustainable development can be applied in the developing country context. Written by two economists who bring considerable experience to the task, this 13-chapter book is divided into three main parts: An Overview of Sustainable Development; Resource Degradation: Causes and Policy Responses; and International Environmental Issues. The authors have tried, successfully in this reviewer's opinion, to make this survey accessible to a wide audience. Advanced undergraduate through faculty.—*T. H. Tietenberg, Colby College*

OAB-2101　　　　　　HX550　　　　　　91-31580 CIP
Stokes, Kenneth M. **Man and the biosphere: toward a coevolu-**

tionary political economy. M.E. Sharpe, 1993 (c1992). 323p bibl index afp ISBN 1-56324-023-8, $49.90

A volume of towering importance well beyond the typical hollowed discussions in environmental economics. Stokes presents a compelling argument on the intricacy of economy and biosphere by appealing to the history of political economy and the debates surrounding Newtonian physics, Enlightenment philosophy, and the limits of liberalism. He maintains that scientific progress "must be cultural in a broadest sense." He also rejects that "what is good for the market must be good for the Biosphere." The heart of the volume, however, is Stoke's assertion that the human species has already developed an irreversible and overwhelming capacity to influence the biosphere. This state is called *Noösphere*. So, exercising deliberate and conscious control can no longer be reconciled with market mentality, such as the neo-Walrasian (à la Robert Solow) appeal to resource productivity and/or the simple treatment of *environment* as *externality*. It is shown that Mother Nature is adamantly resentful of our hide-and-seek, behind the magic of market *fetishism*, in the name of science and rationality. Finally, the author employs the ideas of open systems and cybernetics toward a dynamic coevolutionary political economy. An excellent addition to academic libraries. Advanced undergraduate; graduate; faculty; professional.—*C. Bina, Harvard University*

■ Education

OAB-2102　　　　　　　　　　　　　　Orig
Academic freedom 3: education and human rights, ed. by John Daniel et al. Zed Books/World University Service, 1995. 244p index ISBN 1-85649-301-6, $59.95; ISBN 1-85649-302-4 pbk, $25.00

The nations of the world—those that are signatories to the Universal Declaration of Human Rights and to several other human rights documents—have agreed that education is a fundamental human right. They pledge to provide free and compulsory primary education, to ensure nondiscrimination at every level of education, and to report regularly to the UN on their progress toward meeting these goals. This compact, much-needed volume provides a series of country-by-country snapshots, showing how well (but mostly how poorly) 12 Third World nations and the US are fulfilling their obligations. The authors, usually nationals of the countries described, provide graphic pictures of the impact the climate of human rights is having on educational policies and systems and on students, teachers, and administrators. The overall picture is not pretty or promising, but one international educators and human rights advocates need to know. Valuable, too, are two appendixes: the Lima Declaration of Academic Freedom and Institutions of Higher Education, and the Kampala Declaration on Intellectual Freedom and Social Responsibility. In this post-Cold War period, when education and educators are expected to play a major role in resolving virulent ethnic and national conflicts, these country-specific vignettes demonstrate just how formidable that task is. All levels.—*R. O. Ulin, University of North Carolina at Chapel Hill*

OAB-2103　　　　　　LA217　　　　　　95-4243 CIP
Arnstine, Donald. **Democracy and the art of schooling.** State University of New York, 1995. 304p index afp ISBN 0-7914-2721-8, $74.50

Arnstine (Univ. of California, Davis) provides an excellent entry in the growing progressivist effort to define the conditions under which education becomes possible (cf. Michael Johnson, *Education on the Wild Side*, CH, Feb'92). Reflecting Dewey's instrumentalism, he analyzes the learner's inclination to act, feel intrinsically satisfied, and engage in thinking. He carefully defines concepts of aesthetic experience, dispositions, and discrepancies, echoing Dewey's beliefs in reflective thought, quality of experience, and doctrine of consequences. In his view, an experience is aesthetic when the learners' activities involve thought and are felt to be satisfying. Aesthetic experiences (e.g., in the arts) use thought to resolve discrepancies. Arnstine urges schools to adopt methods that will promote cooperative group learning, problem solving, planning, curiosity, and attention to the aesthetic. Well written and scholarly, Arnstine's study concludes with suggested school reforms to abolish multiple choice testing, student teaching, methods courses, and segregation of students by age, ability, and schools. Highly recommended for general and for academic readers, upper-division undergraduate through faculty.—*F. X. Russo, University of Rhode Island*

OAB-2104 LC2432x Brit. CIP
Beasley, Ina. **Before the wind changed: people, places and education in the Sudan,** ed. by Janet Starkey. Oxford, 1992. 483p bibl indexes ISBN 0-19-726110-8, $59.00

Dr. Ina Beasley, who served as Superintendent and later Controller of Girls' Education in the Sudan from 1939 to 1949, has recorded an almost forgotten life in this outpost of the British Empire. As an educator in an era before universal education defined national aspirations, she chronicles critical details about her journeys to the far-flung schools for which she was responsible: their sanitation problems, the morale of the Sudanese staff, the position of girls and women, female curcumcision, gender role delineation, curriculum, the role of Arabic versus the vernacular or English as a language of instruction. As an official of a colonial power during wartime and in the transition years thereafter, she provides provocative insight into the now-obsolete role which she filled with courage and compassion. This document, part of a series planned by Oxford University Press and expertly edited by Janet Starkey, could well become a major primary source for sociologists, historians, comparative educators and other scholars, and will certainly be of intrinsic interest to general readers. Highly recommended; undergraduates; graduate students; faculty.— *E. S. Swing, Saint Joseph's University*

OAB-2105 LA229 92-22733 CIP
Cohen, Robert. **When the old left was young: student radicals and America's first mass student movement, 1929-1941.** Oxford, 1993. 432p index afp ISBN 0-19-506099-7, $55.00

Cohen has written the definitive history of the student movement of the 1930s, the largest in American history—larger than the anti-Vietnam movement of the 1960s. He brings to life the campus climate of the period, the complex interrelationships among academic administrators, student radicals and professors, and the saga of key student liberal and radical organizations. The American Student Union and the National Student League are the centerpieces of Cohen's analysis, but other organizations are also discussed. He focuses not only on national groups but on what was happening on the campuses at the time, providing a thorough analysis of the liberal and radical student movements of the period. Another strength is Cohen's interweaving of societal political trends, the complex ideological machinations of such left-wing organizations as the Communist and Socialist parties, and the student groups. He points out that the student movements were influenced by the adult radical groups, and the ideological changes of the Communist party, especially, in the end contributed to decline of the movement. Cohen provides a balanced, nuanced, and extraordinarily thorough analysis of one of the most significant periods in the history of American students and of American higher education. This major historical contribution will be *the* volume to turn to for insights on student culture and politics in the volatile and fascinating decade of the '30s. Highly recommended. Upper-division undergraduates; graduate students; faculty.—*P. G. Altbach, SUNY at Buffalo*

OAB-2106 LC1099 91-38686 CIP
Cultural diversity and the schools: v.1: Education for cultural diversity, convergence and divergence, ed. by James Lynch, Celia Modgil, and Sohan Modgil. Falmer, 1992. 472p indexes ISBN 1-85000-989-9, $99.00

The first in a four-volume set concerned generally with issues of cultural diversity and schools in a global, international perspective. This volume of 23 papers, divided into five sections, provides a theoretical foundation for the other three volumes in the series, but also functions as an outstanding general introduction to the ongoing debates about cultural diversity and education in a variety of settings around the world. The sections deal with the debates about integration and separation as responses to the presence of cultural diversity, alternative political and conceptual rationales for educational responses to cultural diversity, issues of value and morality with respect to cultural diversity, selected problematic issues and dilemmas (including an excellent chapter on affirmative action by Brian Bullivant), and finally, the challenge of assessment and evaluation in culturally diverse societies. This book is one of the best theoretical overviews of social and educational issues related to cultural diversity currently available, and it will be of interest to a wide variety of policymakers, social scientists, and educators. Recommended for advanced undergraduates; graduate students; and faculty.—*T. Reagan, University of Connecticut*

OAB-2107 Orig
Cultural diversity and the schools: v.4: Human rights, education and global responsibilities, ed. by James Lynch, Celia Modgil, and Sohan Modgil. Falmer, 1992. 377p indexes ISBN 1-85000-995-3, $99.00; ISBN 0-75070-149-8 set (v. 1-4), $336.00

The final in a four-volume set concerned generally with issues of cultural diversity and schools in a global, international perspective. This volume is largely concerned with issues and challenges related to human rights education, although it also includes papers that seek to tie multicultural education to global issues and concerns. It consists of 19 papers and an epilogue written by the editors, and is divided into four major sections, dealing respectively with alternative rationales and conceptualizations related to issues of diversity in education, approaches and strategies in teaching human rights, human rights teaching in a global context, and linking multicultural education to global issues. Although this volume is closely tied to the earlier three volumes in the *Cultural Diversity and the Schools* set, and provides a valuable addition to and summation of that series, it also stands alone as one of the most significant contributions to the literature on human rights education. Of interest to a wide range of educators and policymakers. Recommended for advanced undergraduates; graduate students; faculty.—*T. Reagan, University of Connecticut*

OAB-2108 LC5144 92-23013 CIP
Educating homeless children and adolescents: evaluating policy and practice, ed. by James H. Stronge. Sage, 1992. 252p (Sage focus editions, 144) ISBN 0-8039-4424-1, $46.00; ISBN 0-8039-4425-X pbk, $23.95

This volume contains a wealth of information relative to the problems of homelessness and education. Stronge has brought together a well-qualified and diverse group of authors who provide insights into current educational policy as it affects homeless youth, and who offer a number of practical strategies and educational programs that appear to be addressing the educational needs of homeless youth. Specifically, the three major sections of this 13-chapter book offer readers an in-depth look at individual background issues related to the homeless, ideas and educational opportunities for students to "overcome" particular educational barriers, and appropriate successful policies and practices currently in use. The composite hope of the contributing authors is that this text will give a greater measure of understanding of the plight of homeless students, and that a number of the societal factors responsible for creating this problem will be better understood and hopefully eliminated. This is a must volume for an educational library. Highly recommended for graduate students; faculty; and general readers.—*R. C. Morris, University of Indianapolis*

OAB-2109 LB2335 96-16788 CIP
Finkin, Matthew W. **The case for tenure.** ILR Press, 1996. 211p bibl index afp ISBN 0-8014-3316-9, $29.95

The opening sentence, "Tenure is today almost everywhere under assault," explains the need for this book, written by the incumbent professor and endowed chair of law and labor and industrial relations at the Univ. of Illinois. It consists of 205 pages of the best statements in defense of tenure, each showing its author's full awareness of tenure's shortcomings. The eight chapters treat the meaning of tenure, probation, dismissal and due process, economics of tenure, tenure and resource allocation, tenure and retirement, post-tenure review, and recent criticism. Each chapter is made up of excerpts from AAUP investigations, court decisions, or major study group reports, interspersed with comments by the author, a longtime member of the AAUP Committee on Academic Freedom and Tenure. The book's only weaknesses are that it does not deal with tenure as understood and practiced at two-year colleges, nor with the impact of unions on the interpretation of tenure. Any library owning Charles J. Sykes's *Profscam* (1988), Robert C. Solomon's *Up the University* (1993), or Roger Kimball's *Tenured Radicals*, (CH, Jul'90) should have a copy of this book to balance its collection, as should universities offering degrees in higher education. Every president and dean involved in tenure decisions should own a copy.—*G. L. Findlen, Western Wisconsin Technical College*

OAB-2110   KF4242   92-40982 CIP
Freedom and tenure in the academy, ed. by William W. Van Alstyne. Duke University, 1993. 429p afp ISBN 0-8223-1333-2, $39.95

Perhaps the most comprehensive treatment of legal issues in academe since the original *Statement of Principles on Academic Freedom and Tenure* (1940), this weighty compendium by distinguished law professors, philosophers, and historians covers myriad controversies in contemporary constitutional law and higher education. The topics include the common law tradition since the 1940 treatise (Walter P. Metzger, Columbia Univ.); due process and the First and Fourteenth Amendments (William W. Van Alstyne, Duke Univ.); ideology and faculty hiring (Judith Jarvis Thompson, MIT); artistic expression (Robert M. O'Neil, Univ. of Virginia); offensive speech and political correctness (Rodney A. Smolla, College of William & Mary); balancing individual and institutional legal claims (David M. Rabban, Univ. of Texas); academic freedom in religious institutions (Michael W. McConnell, Univ. of Chicago); alternatives to tenure (Ralph S. Brown, Yale Univ.; Jordan E. Kurland, AAUP); labor law protections (Matthew W. Finkin, Univ. of Illinois); and a helpful bibliography on academic freedom (Janet Sinder, Duke Univ.). Given its technical nature, the volume is recommended primarily for legal scholars. Graduate students; faculty.—*J. L. DeVitis, SUNY at Binghamton*

OAB-2111   LA217   96-3995 CIP
Gaddy, Barbara B. **School wars: resolving our conflicts over religion and values,** by Barbara B. Gaddy, T. William Hall, and Robert J. Marzano. Jossey-Bass, 1996. 340p bibl index afp ISBN 0-7879-0236-5, $25.00

The authors marvelously analyze and clarify issues concerning religion and education. The first of the book's four parts offers a historical perspective and identifies the players involved in recent controversies. This background information is not only informative but crucial to understanding the complex issues of school and religion. The second section discusses the literature, curriculum, and reforms that have been at the crux of debate in recent years. One chapter dealing with school improvement initiatives helps explain why so much controversy has attended outcome-based education, the "whole language" movement, and thinking skills programs. Chapters in the third section highlight different religious and philosophical worldviews and the tension between the establishment and free exercise clauses of the First Amendment. One particularly informative chapter presents the contradictory worldviews of Christian fundamentalists, mainline Christians, and religious liberals on topics such as knowledge and truth, human nature and self, values, and the nature of reality. The final section offers solutions to issues such as values education, parent-teacher cooperation, and the development of school policies. The appendix cites important court cases and resources for learning more about the myriad issues raised by the authors. Highly informative, this book would make an excellent resource for school administrators and school board members. All levels.—*P. A. Cordeiro, University of Connecticut*

OAB-2112   LA1133   95-44021 CIP
Hayhoe, Ruth. **China's universities, 1895-1995: a century of cultural conflict.** Garland, 1996. 299p bibl index afp (Garland studies in higher education, 4) ISBN 0-8153-1859-6, $49.00

Hayhoe, the most thoughtful analyst of Chinese higher education writing today, summarizes much of her recent research and provides a key resource for understanding the development of Chinese higher education in the 20th century. Her book is unique in that it discusses both the Republican period and the Communist period. The book has several main parts. The first treats the historical development of Chinese higher education, with an excellent discussion of the "decade of reform" (1978-90). The second focuses on two regions (the northwest and the south) and links the broad trends with developments in these regions. The book makes use of Chinese-language sources and includes current statistical information. It is unique in its coverage of several historical periods in a single volume, and its linking of broad national trends with case studies of several regions. Hayhoe here updates her *China's Universities and the Open Door* (CH, Sep'89). Any analysis of Chinese higher education must take into account the work of Ruth Hayhoe. Highly recommended for students, faculty, and professionals.—*P. G. Altbach, Boston College*

OAB-2113   LC225   95-8928 CIP
Henry, Mary E. **Parent-school collaboration: feminist organizational structures and school leadership.** State University of New York, 1996. 229p bibl index afp ISBN 0-7914-2855-9, $49.50

As educational administrators broaden their responsibilities to encompass participatory governance structures, they are often at a loss for models to create democratic learning communities. Henry's study, conducted in the Robertson School District in the northwest US, illuminates the boundaries and patterns of parental exclusion and inclusion. Using an ethnography informed by feminism, the author provides field-based answers to questions related to building, nurturing, and supporting collaborative school relationships. Henry contrasts traditional bureaucratic and patriarchal hierarchies with feminist organizational structures. Her feminist view centers on three key notions: (1) an ethic of care and connectedness; (2) collaboration and community-building; and (3) a focus on the core technology of teaching and learning. Advocating a context-specific approach to school leadership, Henry's findings are not prescriptive but rather make visible social and cultural practices that stress and enhance parent and school relationships. Henry's substantive work encourages those in educational administration to open schools to parents. Essential for all those interested in school reform—general readers, upper-division undergraduates through faculty, professional educators.—*Karen I. Case, University of Hartford*

OAB-2114   LA222   96-24908 CIP
Herbst, Jurgen. **The once and future school: three hundred and fifty years of American secondary education.** Routledge, 1996. 263p index afp ISBN 0-415-91193-1, $65.00; ISBN 0-415-91194-X pbk, $28.95

The author intends this study to present a "history of American secondary education" from its European beginnings through the second half of the 20th century—a fairly lengthy period that draws on "350 years of secondary education in this country." Herbst believes that a number of educational insights ("suggestions") can be made for the 21st century. First, he suggests "that we replace the comprehensive senior high school's monopolistic hold on youth with up-to-date versions of the people's college." Next he proposes a variety of "alternative institutions providing 'careers in education' for individuals of senior high school age and older." Herbst feels these two suggestions have validity for charting new paths given his lengthy historical picture and the "interplay of historical tendencies and contemporary circumstances" that traditionally and largely shape the particular forms that institutions "display at each stage of their history." Far more than a history of secondary education, this volume is a thoughtful perspective on how and what schooling can become in a restructured education system that provides lifelong "careers in education." General readers; upper-division undergraduates and higher.—*R. C. Morris, State University of West Georgia*

Social & Behavioral Sciences

OAB-2115   LC5225   93-7711 CIP
Interdisciplinary handbook of adult lifespan learning, ed. by Jan D. Sinnott. Greenwood, 1994. 487p index afp ISBN 0-313-28205-6, $95.00

Drawing on psychology, sociology, political science, religion, biology, and the natural sciences, this book presents multiple and interdisciplinary perspectives of adult lifespan learning. The first section explores not only conventional adult development theories, but also such novel theoretical topics as chaos theory, communications theory, implications of wisdom, and postformal thought. The second section examines contexts in which adults discover the need to learn, including the workplace, colleges, international development projects, and Third World settings. The third section explores the influence of aging on cognitive development, cognitive strategies, and learning. The final chapter offers a view of the future and the restructuring required for universities to enable adult lifespan learning to flourish. The book is essential for teachers and researchers interested in a framework of adult lifespan learning broader than that of any single discipline. It is also essential for undergraduates, graduates, and the general public who wish to understand how human learning continues beyond childhood and adolescent phases of life.—*P. S. Cookson, Pennsylvania State University, University Park Campus*

OAB-2116   LA209   93-12365 CIP
Johnson, Michael L. **Education on the wild side: learning for the twenty-first century.** Oklahoma, 1993. 338p index afp ISBN 0-8061-2546-2, $29.95

This carefully researched, scholarly, well-written study is another excellent entry in the "Oklahoma Project for Discourse and Theory" series. Johnson (English, Univ. of Kansas), explores the "wild side" of education: a restructuring that overturns the traditional conservative approach to education with apeironic learning, a Deweyan experimentalist approach. An incisive critique, drawing upon the research of Graff, Warnock, and others, is made of the writings of such leading conservatives as Bennett, Cheney, Bloom, and Hirsch; these writings are characterized as emphasizing conventionalized curricula, reified procedures, authority, teaching as transmitting, and learning as rotely absorbing traditional "cultural information." Alternative curricula and pedagogies are proposed that focus upon "heterogeneous and variable" counter-curricula that meet students' felt needs; instructing as "conflictual, complexly tensional, dialectical"; learning as reflective, and analytical thinking directed at problem solving; and experiencing as interacting on multicultural levels. This work compares favorably with other studies (e.g., Arthur Bestor's *Educational Wastelands*, CH, Feb'86) that reflect ideological persuasions viewed as critical in the shaping of school reforms. Notes; bibliographic essay. Recommended for advanced undergraduates on up and general readers.—*F. X. Russo, University of Rhode Island*

OAB-2117   LA75   94-45772 CIP
Kennell, Nigel M. **The gymnasium of virtue: education & culture in ancient Sparta.** North Carolina, 1995. 241p bibl index afp ISBN 0-8078-2219-1, $39.95

Kennell (Memorial Univ. of Newfoundland) superbly untangles an intractable group of problems in Spartan social life. He uses simple, effective literary and linguistic techniques and careful attention to the smallest details to achieve results of permanent significance (in response to P. Cartledge and A. Spawforth's critical *Hellenistic and Roman Sparta*, CH, Mar'90). Kennell distinguishes several periods during which the system of educating the Spartan youth was in force: the Classical (from sixth century BCE, about which virtually nothing is certain); the period of King Cleomenes III (226-188); the Roman Imperial period (from 146 BCE, with many features obviously of the early second century CE). The confusion in naming the various teen years becomes solvable when the sources are sorted by the period to which the testimony likely refers. As is now known, the famous whipping contest is postclassical, possibly a Cleomenean invention. The contests of the *agoge* (especially the famous ball game, played by teams of *sphaireis*) can be put no earlier than late second century BCE. The dialect of most of the inscriptions reveals they belong to the Roman period and are part

of an artificial revival or reinvention of the "Lycurgan System." An appendix on the status of the *obe* Amyclae (a village some five miles south of Sparta) is neither relevant nor convincing in asserting that the village was semi-independent, a Spartan possession, in Spartan territory, but not politically amalgamated with the city until the time of Augustus. Of great significance for collections in ancient history, history of education, and classics.—*J. P. Adams, California State University, Northridge*

OAB-2118   P106   96-39569 CIP
Kutz, Eleanor. **Language and literacy: studying discourse in communities and classrooms.** Boynton Cook, 1997. 319p bibl index afp ISBN 0-86709-386-2 pbk, $29.00

Those who require a dose of grammatical reality need to read this book. In her comments on language acquisition, Kutz (Univ. of Massachusetts at Boston) covers much of the linguistic ground that Steven Pinker did in *The Language Instinct* (CH, Jul'94). However, Kutz adds valuable sociological and political dimensions to her discussions of the language used in real life and language teaching. With devastating insight and penetrating perception, she explodes folk theories about language, showing how such theories often fuel the political machine. They appeal to vocal conservatives so lacking in accurate information about language acquisition and language change that their shrill objections appeal only to the deep-seated social prejudices of the uninformed. Unfortunately, the ebonics controversy in the school systems in Oakland, California, erupted late in 1996, after Kutz's study went to press. Much that Kutz says about language variety and change is germane to the politically fraught issue of ebonics, the street language of many African American children. Kutz's approach is humane and well informed. Teachers, school board members, and parents, as well as upper-division undergraduates and graduates, should read this book. Glossary. Highly recommended.—*R. B. Shuman, University of Illinois at Urbana-Champaign*

OAB-2119   LC1201   96-37325 CIP
Lipsky, Dorothy Kerzner. **Inclusion and school reform: transforming America's classrooms,** by Dorothy Kerzner Lipsky and Alan Gartner. P.H. Brookes, 1997. 414p bibl index afp ISBN 1-55766-273-8 pbk, $36.95

Those seeking a wide-ranging, balanced survey of inclusive education and school restructuring will welcome Lipsky and Gartner's approach to a complex array of issues. Authors of *Beyond Separate Education* (1989), they are profound proponents of inclusion. Yet they present their research evidence in an evenhanded fashion that will appeal to advocates and critics alike. A compendium on the field itself, the book covers historical antecedents in separate special education, legal, and policy ramifications of inclusion, and the need to reform general education for all students. The authors also include selected essays that elaborate the issues already treated in earlier sections of the text. This volume is user-friendly for countless audiences: school practitioners, policy makers, academicians, and students in teacher education. Indeed, its underlying discussion is useful for anyone bent on creating a more civic and equitable polity.—*J. L. DeVitis, SUNY at Binghamton*

OAB-2120   LA226   93-25486 CIP
Marsden, George M. **The soul of the American university: from Protestant establishment to established nonbelief.** Oxford, 1994. 462p index afp ISBN 0-19-507046-1, $35.00

Most of America's earliest colleges were founded by Protestant sects; their presidents and most of their faculty were ministers; and one of their major purposes was to educate future clergymen. Yet by 1950 Protestantism was all but gone from the arts and sciences curriculum and academic life of America's leading universities. This book, by a distinguished University of Notre Dame historian, examines the decline of Protestantism as a major force in American universities. It covers most of the history of American higher education, from 1636 when Harvard was founded to the 1960s. It concentrates, however, on roughly the years from 1870 to 1920, when the modern research university, which values science and objectivity, took shape. Marsden shows convincingly how "many of the same forces set in motion by liberal Protestantism," e.g., respecting pluralism, tolerance, and academic freedom, "were eventually turned against the liberal Protestant establishment itself." This book is meticulously researched, thoroughly documented, and beautifully written; it is, all things considered, a superb work of scholarship. General; undergraduate; graduate; faculty.—D. S. Webster, Oklahoma State University

OAB-2121 LC1011 93-27212 CIP
Moulakis, Athanasios. **Beyond utility: liberal education for a technological age.** Missouri, 1994. 171p bibl index afp ISBN 0-8262-0929-7, $21.95

Another worthwhile contribution to the growing debate (see W. B. Carnochan's *The Battleground of the Curriculum* CH, Feb'94) over the place of liberal education in American universities today. The author (Colorado Univ.) extols the virtues of a liberal education as moving beyond substantive knowledge— "the terms of a proper inquiry are characteristic of a particular mode of inquiry"— and he proposes a program for undergraduate engineers that weds liberal studies to technological training. Reflecting the perennialism of Mortimer Adler, Robert Hutchins, and E. D. Hirsch, he directs a cogent critique at issues undermining liberal education: a focus on things and not meanings; the absence of supportive family life; the rejection of Western tradition as the national, functional high culture; the content-neutral, utilitarian approach of progressivism; the university as a "neutral conveyor of cultures"; and the ideological identity in research and "gender-neutrality in writing." He seeks to address these issues through his undergraduate program of small, text-based (classical world) discussion classes guided by moderators and directed at cultivating an appreciation of human achievement. This is a well-written, scholarly book with notes and references. Recommended. Undergraduate level and up; general readers.—F. X. Russo, University of Rhode Island

OAB-2122 LC72 96-47161 CIP
O'Neil, Robert M. **Free speech in the college community.** Indiana, 1997. 257p bibl index afp ISBN 0-253-33267-2, $24.95

O'Neil's book deals with campus speech codes, speech and technology, off-campus speech, groups (gays, Greeks), free press, artistic expression, academic freedom, religious speech, and freedom of speech at private institutions. His postscript contains seven carefully crafted premises that should guide all discussions of freedom of speech issues on campus. The book ends with a seven-page annotated bibliography that cites some of the major literature, including William van Alstyne's brilliant work and William A. Kaplin and Barbara A. Lee's comprehensive and essential *The Law of Higher Education* (3rd ed., 1995). Lucidly written, the book can be read and understood by many audiences from student organizations to board members. O'Neil describes in adequate detail cases on larger campuses, most less than five years old, and quotes central passages from judicial decisions. The book displays the wisdom a former research university president (Virginia and Wisconsin) should have. O'Neil, now director of the Thomas Jefferson Center for the Protection of Free Expression, writes from the perspective of someone who has "Been there, struggled with that." Essential for all college and university libraries.—G. L. Findlen, Western Wisconsin Technical College

OAB-2123 LC225 93-3720 CIP
Parents, their children, and schools, ed. by Barbara Schneider and James S. Coleman. Westview, 1993. 192p bibl index afp ISBN 0-8133-1639-1, $36.95

Schneider (National Opinion Research Center and the Univ. of Chicago) and Coleman (Univ. of Chicago) have edited an important study of parental involvement. Chapter 1 notes that this first study of the subject, based on major survey data, is drawn from the National Education Longitudinal Study of 1988, a national sample of 26,000 eighth graders, their parents, teachers, and administrators. Chapter 2 focuses on the actions parents take at home, in the community, and in school. Chapter 3 analyzes the effect of family structure and background variables on standardized test scores, grades, and misbehavior. Chapter 4 analyzes the forms of parental involvement and their relationships to achievement test scores and grades and the factors constraining involvement. Chapter 5, which stresses school-related activities and parental involvement and their effects on student performance, concludes with preliminary policy implications. Issues covered in the final chapter are parental choice of schools, inequality of educational opportunity, expansion of school choice, effects of choice on inequality, and private school choice. Appendixes follow each chapter. Recommended for graduate readership.—N. L. Arnez, Howard University

OAB-2124 LA1131 95-24843 CIP
Pepper, Suzanne. **Radicalism and education reform in 20th-century China: the search for an ideal development model.** Cambridge, 1996. 610p bibl index afp ISBN 0-521-49669-1, $59.95

Pepper's outstanding analysis of educational reform in China in the 20th century is impressive for its coverage and detail. She focuses on the impact radical ideas have had on educational development, so she does not consider some elements of reform movements, but in general this is an impressive volume. Sinologist Pepper discusses several reform movements prior to the advent of the Communist regime in 1949, although most of the book deals with the Communist period. She shows external influences on Chinese educational reform movements, both before and after 1949 (e.g., recommendations by the League of Nations in the 1920s). Even before 1949, the Soviet model influenced both the Communists (there is a chapter on Mao's educational experiments in Yan'an) and the Nationalists. The interplay between foreign ideas and Chinese thinking about educational reform is a constant theme during the entire period. Chapters dealing with the various, and partly unsuccessful, Communist era reforms, such as the Great Leap Forward and the disastrous Cultural Revolution, provide excellent discussions of educational policies and implementation. This book, based on interviews and published sources, is impressively researched and clearly written. Pepper describes the entire sweep of educational policy development in China, and traces the various ideological and educational strands underlying policies. Highly recommended for upper-division undergraduates through faculty.—P. G. Altbach, Boston College

OAB-2125 LA227 96-12267 CIP
Reuben, Julie A. **The making of the modern university: intellectual transformation and the marginalization of morality.** Chicago, 1996. 363p index afp ISBN 0-226-71018-1, $55.00; ISBN 0-226-71020-3 pbk, $18.95

Reuben gives scholarly treatment to a very important problem: why has morality been marginalized in the contemporary US research university? Reuben (Harvard Graduate School of Education) claims that those interested in morality near the close of the 19th century hoped to keep their subject acceptable by making it more scientific. Their efforts took many forms but were concentrated in psychology and sociology, where they hoped objective and value-neutral sources of morality could be found. Ultimately, when these efforts failed, morality was pushed out of the sciences and social sciences into the humanities. Reuben's book is aimed at a scholarly audience of historians, educators, and philosophers, but advanced undergraduates could also benefit. Although these issues have been examined before in such classics as Laurence Veysey's *The Emergence of the American University* (1965) and Burton Bledstein's *The Culture of Professionalism* (CH, Mar'77), Reuben's book, claiming to be the "first in-depth study of moral education in the American research university," presents a new perspective and new evidence, much of it from journals of the period, airing voices not heard for many years. The book is a fresh and stimulating treatment of a perennial problem and an essential addition to any library supporting the history of higher education in the US. Upper-division undergraduates through faculty.—C. A. Cunningham, Northeastern Illinois University

OAB-2126 LC144 92-42905 CIP
Roderick, Melissa. **The path to dropping out: evidence for inter-**

vention. Auburn House, 1993. 214p bibl index afp ISBN 0-86569-206-8, $47.95

Roderick is correct in observing that student dropout is the "most widely studied educational problem in America." See also *School Dropouts: Patterns and Policies* ed. by Gary Nartriello (1987). She presents the results of a study, undertaken as a doctoral thesis at Harvard, of the Fall River (MA) public school's seventh-grade class of 1981. The study "traced the school career paths of different groups of dropouts and graduates beginning in the fourth grade." She concluded that "For an important group of dropouts, the individual manifestations of school leaving and the academic processes that lead to school withdrawl can be linked to, and are influenced by aspects of the policies, organization, and structure of the schools." Her study provides an empirical basis and analytical framework that moves the policy debate on school dropouts to a more focused and informed investigation of the school's role in the dropout process. Roderick provides new insights and a conceptual foundation for understanding the dropout problem, and her work may well prove to be the most seminal of the last decade. Recommended for pre-professionals, graduate students, and faculty.—*F. Cordasco, emeritus, Montclair State College*

OAB-2127   LA210   92-19198 CIP
Sowell, Thomas. **Inside American education: the decline, the deception, the dogmas.** Free Press, 1993. 368p index ISBN 0-02-930330-3, $24.95

This well-researched critique of American education covers the educational landscape from kindergarten through the PhD and focuses on most if not all of the most disturbing problems of this vital institution. Sowell has produced a scholarly work that covers the major sociological, political, and economic reasons for the decline of educational achievement in US schools and colleges. He notes that too many schools are turning out students who are not only intellectually incompetent but are morally confused, emotionally alienated, and socially maladjusted. At the college and university level, the intrusion of non-intellectual and anti-intellectual material into the curriculum takes more of an ideological than a psychological form. This work is distinguished by its breadth of coverage, by its currency, and by its straightforward style of presentation. Recommended for acquisition by academic libraries. It should be especially informative to graduate faculty, upper-division undergraduate and graduate students, and scholars with special interests in the sociological foundations of curriculum.—*C. L. Smith, emeritus, University of Kentucky*

OAB-2128   LC191   93-29157 CIP
Teaching the conflicts: Gerald Graff, curricular reform, and the culture wars, ed. by William E. Cain. Garland, 1994. 234p index afp (Wellesley studies in critical theory, literary history, and culture, 2) ISBN 0-8153-1466-3, $42.00

The war over "political correctness" in academe may have abated, but the issues that triggered it remain unresolved. Rising above the tumult has been Gerald Graff's voice of sanity and moderation. In this timely volume editor Cain traces the steady evolution of Graff's ideas about using the conflict constructively by discussing the polarized disagreement over canon revision directly with students. In this "conflict model" curriculum, students would not be expected to resolve the debate but would engage in serious learning in a politically self-conscious way and see more coherence than they now do in the variety of perspectives they meet in their courses. After an introduction Cain presents three articles by Graff, which are followed by 11 thoughtful commentaries and critiques by scholars in the humanities. Graff thus has an opportunity for a brief afterword and rebuttal. The book is tightly designed, good reading for both laypersons and professionals, and serves as a welcome antidote to the usual hysteria and reductionism surrounding the subject. Itself a model for cultural studies, the book has much to offer, both theoretically and practically, to anyone concerned with the design of a coherent college curriculum in English and other humanities. Recommended. All levels.—*R. O. Ulin, University of North Carolina at Chapel Hill*

OAB-2129   LC212   92-22062 CIP
Thorne, Barrie. **Gender play: girls and boys in school.** Rutgers, 1993. 237p bibl index ISBN 0-8135-1922-5, $35.00; ISBN 0-8135-1923-3 pbk, $12.95

Observing children in classrooms and on the playground, Thorne offers a useful mix of ethnographic data and theory. Although the field work was done in 1976 and 1977 with fourth and fifth graders and in 1980 with kindergarten and second graders, the observations are fresh and are a valuable addition to the literature of children's behavior in school and at play such as Raphaela Best's *We've All Got Scars* (1983), Vivian Gussin Paley's *Boys & Girls: Superheroes in the Doll Corner* (CH, Jan'85), and Iona Opie's *The People in the Playground* (1993). Thorne challenges the model of separate and different gender cultures. She claims that our views of gender separation may be skewed because the actions of the most popular children are taken as the models. She examines the patterns of boys and girls who cut across gender lines and school routines and rituals that can either support or minimize the separation of boys and girls along gender lines. Her thesis is a provocative one. There are extensive notes and an excellent reference list. Highly recommended. Undergraduates; graduate students; faculty; general readers.—*S. Sugarman, Bennington College*

OAB-2130   LA216   94-47545 CIP
Tyack, David. **Tinkering toward utopia: a century of public school reform,** by David Tyack and Larry Cuban. Harvard, 1995. 184p index afp ISBN 0-674-89282-8, $22.50

Tyack and Cuban (Stanford), distinguished scholars of US educational history and policy, argue in clear and cogent terms that utopian policy talk about school reform has usually involved only incremental policy action—"tinkering with the system." Given the relative irrationality and ahistorical foolishness of much of the policy clutter, the authors do not lament that reform movements come and go, typically replaced by yet another "surefire" reform that will soon lie forgotten. Tyack and Cuban envision a wider public debate about educational purpose that will engender a more just and democratic means to foster the public good. Instead of political posturing, such a vision entails reflective analysis of actual school cultures and sustained leadership by real teachers who will have substantial responsibility for creating and implementing change. One of the most important books on education in America in recent years, this book is essential for students, educators, policy makers, and interested citizens at all levels.—*J. L. DeVitis, SUNY at Binghamton*

■ Teaching

OAB-2131   LB1570   92-29468 CIP
The American curriculum: a documentary history, ed. by George Willis et al. Greenwood, 1993. 425p bibl index afp ISBN 0-313-26730-8, $65.00

Beginning with the *Rules and Course of Study of Harvard College* (1642), the five editors have assembled the major curriculum reports of each generation in American history up to and including the National Commission on Excellence in Education's *A Nation At-Risk: The Imperative for Educational Reform* (1983). This volume covers not only the history of the American curriculum, but also traces the movements in social and political history that propelled changes in the content of the curriculum. The reader becomes a spectator to the discussions that led colleges to provide "… parental superintendence … superior intellectual attainment … a thorough liberal education for all classes [since] merchants, manufacturers, and farmers, as well as gentlemen take their places in our public councils … ," and later to redesign the curriculum to include subjects such as the study of human physiology because of alarming rates of mortality, and to offer experiences with "organic connections." The work of the National Education Association is traced, beginning with its foundation in 1857 as the National Teachers Association representing a unified voice among educators at all levels and providing leadership to build a curriculum representing a course of study from primary school to university. Also documented are the works of school boards in Chicago, St. Louis, and Los Angeles, examples of curriculum innovations such as platoon schools in Detroit, the use of the scientific method in curriculum development, and cycles of school improvement efforts. Mann, Bobbitt, Pratt, Morrison, Dewey, Aiken, Phenix, and Tyler are but a sample of those whose works are quoted. This book is of such monumental proportions that it should be read by every teacher, used in every course on curriculum development, and contained in every bibliography on this subject. Undergraduates; graduate students; faculty; pre-professionals.—*S. S. Gomes, Howard University*

OAB-2132   LB1570   95-42694 CIP
Applebee, Arthur N. **Curriculum as conversation: transforming traditions of teaching and learning.** Chicago, 1996. 149p bibl index afp ISBN 0-226-02121-1, $34.95; ISBN 0-226-02123-8 pbk, $12.95

Applebee offers a visionary approach to curriculum. All too often, schools use the technique of memorization-recitation as the principal method of learning. Applebee contends that this method produces knowledge out of context, which emphasizes learning the characteristics of knowledge rather than participation in the discourse. His concept of "knowledge-in-action" builds on the progressive philosophy of John Dewey. Applebee defines knowledge-in-action as "knowledge that matters to individuals and to society that is learned through participation in living traditions of knowing and doing." He explains terms such as "living traditions," "knowing and doing," "conversation," and "culturally significant domains" to help readers better understand knowledge-in-action. According to Applebee, knowledge-in-action fits into larger traditions and results from participation in curriculum as conversation by knowing and doing. His book provides a framework for thinking about curricular issues and emphasizes multiculturalism in a pluralistic world. Knowledge-in-action is rooted in interpretation of the past and expectations for the future. Applebee makes a significant contribution toward understanding how curriculum should be approached. Highly recommended for upper-division undergraduates, graduates, and faculty.—*C. M. Bradley, Northeastern Illinois University*

OAB-2133   LB1025   96-34227 CIP
Banner, James M. **The elements of teaching,** by James M. Banner and Harold C. Cannon. Yale, 1997. 142p afp ISBN 0-300-06929-4, $16.50

The authors focus consciously on teaching as an art, centering their book on the human qualities of teachers. They define the qualities that make great teaching by highlighting the form and shape these qualities take in the classroom. They portray good and bad, outstanding and marginal teachers. Although the teachers depicted are not actual persons, they represent teachers the authors knew or observed. Concrete examples add realism to chapters with such topics as authority, ethics, compassion, and patience. Readers will identify with these examples and recall their own experiences in learning situations. Banner and Cannon's book will be easy but worthwhile reading for those who teach, prepare others to teach, or work with teachers attempting to strengthen their own level of professional performance. All levels.—*G. E. Pawlas, University of Central Florida*

OAB-2134   LB1140   94-41347 CIP
Beatty, Barbara. **Preschool education in America: the culture of young children from the colonial era to the present.** Yale, 1995. 252p index afp ISBN 0-300-06027-0, $30.00

In her history of the preschool movement in the US, the author asks why there has been no universal access to early education in this country. Although much of the book focuses on kindergartens and the struggle to establish them in public schools, it extends from the development of infant schools in the Colonial period to the evaluation of Head Start in the present, providing a vivid sense of the many individuals involved. When discussing Pestalozzi, Froebel, and others, Beatty presents their ideas and practices clearly. Those new to the subject will have no difficulty understanding the issues. Those familiar with the

material will find the book absorbing; it provides both fresh insights and a sobering perspective, since many past arguments about early childhood are still being used. Beatty writes smoothly and with authority. Bibliographic references embedded in the notes are extensive and informative. A section of photographs enhances the text. Essential for every education library and for general readers.—*S. Sugarman, Bennington College*

OAB-2135   MT1   94-30663 CIP
Campbell, Patricia Shehan. **Music in childhood: from preschool through the elementary grades,** by Patricia Shehan Campbell and Carol Scott-Kassner. Schirmer Books/Prentice Hall International, 1995. 398p index afp ISBN 0-02-870552-1, $33.00

At last, there is a scholarly and very practical work for childhood music education. This excellent resource is based on the methodologies of Emile Dalcroze, Carl Orff, Zoltan Kodály, and other noted theoreticians. The instructional design is child centered; concepts, skills, and affective outcomes are achieved through activities of creativity and discovery. The methodologies are richly supported by delineated approaches, activities, examples of music, and model lesson plans. The leading scholars of instructional learning theory, such as Jerome Bruner, B.F. Skinner, Robert Gagné, David Ausubel, Eliot Eisner, and Howard Gardner, provide a solid foundation for instruction. The text is well organized, clearly written, and completely indexed. Each chapter concludes with a set of questions, activities, and scholarly references. Music literature selections, notational examples, charts, photographs, and tables mark this as a book of quality. Highly recommended for academic libraries as a resource for music education students at the upper-division undergraduate level, general curriculum specialists at the graduate level, and music faculty.—*C. L. Smith, emeritus, University of Kentucky*

OAB-2136   94-69571 Orig
Delpit, Lisa. **Other people's children: cultural conflict in the classroom.** New Press, NY, 1995. 206p index ISBN 1-56584-179-4, $21.00

Delpit's *Other People's Children* is a powerful, trenchant, and compelling contribution to the growing literature concerned with issues of diversity and multicultural education. Incorporating both work previously published (including two controversial essays from *Harvard Educational Review*) and previously unpublished work, Delpit forces the reader to reevaluate fundamental assumptions about the role of culture in the educational process. Delpit argues, in essence, that the teacher must function as a "cultural translator" for children from nonmainstream backgrounds, whether one is talking about African American students in the US or students in Papua New Guinea or Alaska (all areas with which Delpit is familiar, and about which she writes cogently). Readers may well disagree with many of Delpit's arguments, and one may certainly wish that she had dealt with diversity more broadly conceived, but the basic issues that she raises are fundamental ones, and she does an excellent job of challenging readers to deal with them seriously. General; faculty; professional.—*T. Reagan, University of Connecticut*

OAB-2137   93-25086 MARC
Dyson, Anne Haas. **Social worlds of children learning to write in an urban primary school.** Teachers College Press (Columbia University), 1993. 263p bibl index afp ISBN 0-8077-3296-6, $43.00; ISBN 0-8077-3295-8 pbk, $19.95

This book in the Teachers College Press "Language and Literacy Series" presents a thoughtful examination of how children learn to write. The author contends that writing is a social process which includes not only the official world of the school, but that of the popular, folk, and oral cultures which children bring with them. Her argument is a convincing one, supported by the case studies of five children in a kindergarten through third grade urban school. These children come alive through her well-detailed records, and they graphically illustrate the theoretical points Dyson makes. As the children move through the stages of writing, the complexity of the process becomes evident.

The influence of the learning atmosphere is clearly indicated as the author follows children into a second classroom. Dyson advocates a permeable curriculum that respects sociocultural diversity and includes language as a part of all subjects. For primary school teachers and all who are interested in literacy, this is a valuable addition to current knowledge and practice. Appendixes, notes, and references are helpful. Highly recommended. Undergraduate level on up.—*S. Sugarman, Bennington College*

OAB-2138 LC3993 95-52527 CIP
Ford, Donna Y. **Reversing underachievement among gifted black students: promising practices and programs.** Teachers College Press (Columbia University), 1996. 236p bibl index afp (Education and psychology of the gifted series, 11) ISBN 0-8077-3535-3, $52.00; ISBN 0-8077-3536-1 pbk, $24.95

In a departure from the many pathological reports and studies that painfully chronicle black students' underachievement, Ford offers practitioners, researchers, parents, and policy makers specific, practical recommendations that can help reverse some of the negative trends in the education of black students. Specifically, she calls for definitions of "giftedness" that include creativity, the visual and performing arts, and marks of leadership. Recognizing the important work of Howard Gardner on multiple intelligences, Ford believes, would open other avenues for black children to thrive in academic environments. The book also focuses on the psychological, academic, and emotional aspects of black students that all constituencies (parents, educators, and peers) must recognize for significant academic gains to be realized. Ford's basic premise is the necessity for collaboration between the home and school. Also, there must be a realization that underachievement among black students can and must be prevented and reversed. Recommended for educators, counselors, parents, administrators, researchers, and practitioners.—*L. B. Gallien, Wheaton College (IL)*

OAB-2139 LB1025 94-28731 CIP
Gardner, M. Robert. **On trying to teach: the mind in correspondence.** Analytic Press, 1994. 163p ISBN 0-88163-090-X, $24.95

This witty, introspective, provocative collection of essays should be required reading for anyone involved in teaching. Drawing on his personal journal and focusing on his own insights and experiences as a psychoanalyst and teacher, the author (Harvard) examines the "dilemmas and challenges" of teaching and his approaches to them. He offers a penetrating analysis of the iatrogenic nature of teaching and the consequent misdirection of the "furors to teach," the suffocation of creativity by discipline, the use of interrogative means to "preserve the orthodoxy of the required answer," the failings of teacher-determined students' wants and readiness to learn, and the ignoring of hidden questions (unconscious insights) and related expressions of shrill assertions and polar thinking. He concludes by urging teachers to respect students' wants, to teach with a "mind adrift" (avoid excessive planning), to become sensitive to hidden questions and help students track and advance them, and to encourage students, through hidden questions, to "establish their right to be wrong and therefore, their abilities to be comfortably wrong." This quality work compares favorably with others (cf. Paulo Freire, *Pedagogy of Hope*, CH, Feb'95) exploring meaningful approaches to teaching. All levels.—*F. X. Russo, University of Rhode Island*

OAB-2140 LD7501 93-16884 CIP
Gauld, Joseph W. **Character first: the Hyde School difference.** ICS Press, 1993. 179p ISBN 1-55815-262-8, $18.95

Gauld founded the Hyde School in 1966; he now heads the Hyde Foundation, which is committed to establishing pilot programs based on a unique character-building model that transforms the teacher-student relationship and incorporates an intensive parent involvement component. The Hyde School model focuses on personal criteria of excellence rather than uniform standards of achievement, assuring every child an equal opportunity to succeed regardless of innate abilities, or cultural or ethnic background. The word character in the title refers to those qualities that help individuals develop their unique potential and are listed in the Hyde motto: Courage, integrity, concern, curiosity, and leadership. At Hyde, character replaces inborn academic ability as a basic foundation, and the standard of excellence is based on growth and character development. This program presents a clear alternative to the present educational system. Through the author's recollections and the personal accounts of students, parents, and teachers, this compelling book explains the Hyde School difference. It challenges readers to revolutionize the educational system today instead of leaving the educational crisis for the next generation to resolve. Recommended for all levels.—*J. C. Baxter, Northeastern Illinois University*

OAB-2141 LB1139 95-3939 CIP
Hart, Betty. **Meaningful differences in the everyday experience of young American children,** by Betty Hart and Todd R. Risley. P.H. Brookes, 1995. 268p bibl index afp ISBN 1-55766-197-9, $22.00

The authors describe a longitudinal research study of 42 children, six to 36 months of age, chosen from three socioeconomic ranges—welfare, middle class, and professional. Each child was observed for an hour a week in the home setting for two and a half years. The study required the observer to record all the child's attempts at language and the caretakers' responses. The adult responses were recorded as negative, positive, directive, declarative, and interrogative. The research strongly supports the need to provide language intervention programs for children in welfare homes, shows the vast differences in language development in the three socioeconomic home settings, and demonstrates the importance of environment in developing the child's innate ability. The book is essential for preschool teachers, legislators, and parents, and it will also be helpful for elementary education majors.—*M. Wikstrom, Buena Vista College*

OAB-2142 LB1139 92-23846 CIP
International handbook of early childhood education, ed. by Gary A. Woodill et al. Garland, 1992. 562p bibl index afp (Garland reference library of social science, 598) ISBN 0-8240-4939-X, $95.00

The entries in this international handbook of early childhood education are written by professionals from 45 countries, ranging from Albania to the Yemen Republic. Each essay covers the history of preschool and primary schooling, the curriculum, teacher education, and particular national issues. The challenges of special education and the education of diverse immigrant populations are also dealt with by nations in a variety of ways. In most countries, changes in the education of young children result from the influx of women into the work force. The ideas of Froebel, Montessori, and Dewey seem to have had worldwide impact. Although most readers will use this as a reference book, the themes and issues which emerge from steady reading are fascinating. The introductory essays by editors Woodill and L. Prochner are excellent. They are also to be commended for the quality of the text which is consistently high, an achievement given the variety of sources. The bibliographies and indexes are also helpful. Highly recommended as a resource for all libraries. Undergraduate level on up.—*S. Sugarman, Bennington College*

OAB-2143 LB1575 93-12655 CIP
Journeying: children responding to literature, ed. by Kathleen E. Holland, Rachael A. Hungerford, and Shirley B. Ernst. Heinemann, 1993. 326p index afp ISBN 0-435-08758-4 pbk, $20.00

The authors combine historical research with recent findings in this study of children's literary responses to literature, ranging from preschoolers through students in middle school. The study is based on Rosenblatt's transactional theory and children's current responses to literature. The content is divided into four categories: early, middle, and late childhood, plus current responses to various literature genres. Providing valuable information for teachers, it delivers examples of classroom activities, children's conceptualized meaning development, and cultural responses to literature. The book should be required reading for language arts teachers. Advanced undergraduate; graduate; professional.—*M. Wikstrom, Buena Vista College*

OAB-2144   LB2424   94-12174 CIP

Katchadourian, Herant. **Cream of the crop: the impact of elite education in the decade after college,** by Herant Katchadourian and John Boli. Basic Books, 1994. 383p bibl index ISBN 0-465-04343-7, $27.00

An informative, well-reasoned, and objective follow-up study of the educational elite members of the "tail of the baby boomers," this volume focuses on their professional careers, workplace experiences, personal lives, and reflections ten years after their undergraduate days. It is an excellent contribution to our understanding of the societal role of great educational institutions and how they impact their graduates. A collaborator in the 1985 precursor of this volume, *Careerism and Intellectualism among College Students*, Katchadourian (psychiatry, behavioral sciences, and human biology, Stanford Univ.) and Boli (sociology, Emory Univ.) continue their longitudinal study with this ten year follow-up examination of the outcomes of elite education. Extensive questionnaire and intensive interview data obtained in 1990-91 from a sample of 1981 Stanford graduates show that overall, the different orientations these undergraduates took— "Careerists," "Intellectuals," "Strivers," and "Unconnected"— continue to affect their careers and lives ten years after graduation. Similar to the famous Grant study of Harvard male graduates some 50 years earlier and reported in George E. Vaillant's *Adaptation to Life* (1977), this study is quite unique in its focus on the postmodern era. Highly recommended to undergraduates, graduates, and faculty.—*R. L. Brod, University of Montana*

OAB-2145   LB2844   96-4128 CIP

Kissen, Rita M. **The last closet: the real lives of lesbian and gay teachers.** Heinemann, 1996. 198p afp ISBN 0-435-07005-3, $23.95

This much needed and welcome addition to the professional literature about teachers and teaching represents a growing body of research into a subject that educators have wrongly neglected. The voices of the gay and lesbian teachers in the text not only enable readers to know them but also speak eloquently to their desire to teach and describe what some must do and endure in order to be teachers. The classroom closet is a large one, but books such as this may help make it smaller. The text deals with all facets of gay and lesbian teachers' lives, from issues of invisibility and passing to moving out. The narrative is compelling and honest, and essential for all persons preparing to teach, all teachers and administrators, and general readers interested in a more open, progressive, and just educational system.—*M. J. Carbone, Muhlenberg College*

OAB-2146   LB3012   94-16430 CIP

Lane, Robert Wheeler. **Beyond the schoolhouse gate: free speech and the inculcation of values.** Temple University, 1995. 210p index afp ISBN 1-56639-274-8, $44.95; ISBN 1-56639-275-6 pbk, $17.95

Lane's lucid, succinct treatment of central problems in school law seeks to balance the competing interests of individual rights and public responsibility. Beyond the romantic rhetoric of some child liberators and the mixed results of progressive reformers, he speaks in realistic, incremental terms, emphasizing "matters of degree" in resolving legal disputes. For example, he recognizes both the inculcative function of schools and the vital need to assist and protect student expression. Lane is especially effective in framing historical and contemporary issues of "excellence" and "order" in public education and their often ironic, harmful effects. He also exhibits a keen grasp of political and constitutional theory and shares his scholarly understanding in clear language accessible to a wide audience. Interested academicians will occasionally be disappointed that Lane does not dig deeper in the legal ground he has unearthed. He whets the appetite for further investigation of the complex issues before the bar. All levels.—*J. L. DeVitis, SUNY at Binghamton*

OAB-2147   LB1140   94-7524 CIP

Lewis, Catherine C. **Educating hearts and minds: reflections on Japanese preschool and elementary education.** Cambridge, 1995. 249p bibl index ISBN 0-521-45832-3 pbk, $16.95

With this remarkable book, Lewis joins the top rank of Americans writing about Japanese education. Her book is accessible and engaging, written in a personal, clear, and jargon-free style, and is filled with lively examples. It overturns many assumptions and cliches. Rather than the classroom regimentation and rote learning many Americans hope must underlie Japan's national success, Lewis directly observed sensitive, nurturant, child-centered teaching and learning, whereby self-control and alertness to group needs are built inside individual children. Her book is believable: it is based on sustained observation over a 16-year period by a scholar fluent in Japanese and deeply grounded in American and Japanese educational practice and research. And it is challenging: Lewis provides interesting critiques of both American and Japanese educational practice and finds some points of convergence beneath the surface. Diversity, creativity, and upper education remain problem areas in Japan. Libraries that hold only a few books on contemporary Japanese education should have this one alongside seminal works of Thomas Rohlen, Merry White, Joy Hendry, Lois Peak, and Joseph Tobin. All levels.—*R. B. Lyman Jr., Simmons College*

OAB-2148   LC3731   96-40396 CIP

Miramontes, Ofelia B. **Restructuring schools for linguistic diversity: linking decision making to effective programs,** by Ofelia B. Miramontes, Adel Nadeau, and Nancy L. Commins. Teachers College Press (Columbia University), 1997. 313p bibl index afp ISBN 0-8077-3604-X, $52.00; ISBN 0-8077-3603-1 pbk, $23.95

One of the most significant issues currently facing public education in the US is how to meet the needs of linguistically diverse student populations. Although many recent works recognize this issue as timely and important, few have attempted to provide focused and practical suggestions for classroom practice and program reform. The present book does this well, exploring ways theory can and should inform practice in meeting the needs of such populations. Unlike many works that focus on bilingual and ESL programs, this book takes the school as the unit of analysis and focuses on decision making in the school context, especially regarding programmatic development. Miramontes and her coauthors relocate linguistically diverse students at the center of discourse about educational reform rather than on the sidelines. Their book is well written, original, and cogent, and makes an important and timely contribution to the literature on linguistically diverse students, and to that dealing with school reform in general. Graduate; faculty.—*T. Reagan, University of Connecticut*

OAB-2149   LB1140   94-25002 CIP

Paley, Vivian Gussin. **Kwanzaa and me: a teacher's story.** Harvard, 1995. 140p afp ISBN 0-674-50585-9, $18.95

Storyteller, author, and teacher, Paley (also author of *White Teacher*, CH, Sep'77, and *You Can't Say You Can't Play*, 1992), narrates her journey as a kindergarten teacher attempting to define and understand the real meaning of a school culture that embraces and celebrates diversity. Paley uses the art of storytelling and conversation to move the reader beyond the superficial and abstract discussions about diversity to authentic and real experiences with a variety of diverse voices, including African American teachers, parents, and children; Native Americans; and immigrant families. The voices, the stories, and the conversations contribute to an understanding of the issues behind self-segregation, the frustrations of racism, and the shared vision of creating school environments that celebrate the uniqueness of all children. *Kwanzaa and Me* is an essential text for preservice and in-service teachers and administrators.—*D. L. Norland, Luther College*

OAB-2150   LB1119   94-32916 CIP

Qualitative research in early childhood settings, ed. by J. Amos Hatch. Praeger, 1995. 256p bibl index afp ISBN 0-275-94921-4, $65.00

This informative and thoughtful examination of qualitative research should be widely read. Unfortunately, its cost will probably limit its purchase to libraries. The articles are organized in two sections: "Studies"; and "Methods, Ethics, and Theory." Although the two essays by the editor are particularly fine, each author provides valuable insight into the application of this methodology. Leavitt's observations of some infant/toddler care is a painful and honest report, well balanced by Nelson's interviews of family day care providers. The value of this methodology for use in classrooms is underscored by two articles focused on teachers. McGee and Brown give an example of how qualitative and quantitative methods can be used together, but Tobin's argument for applying poststructuralist theory to research in early childhood education is not convincing. Well written, with excellent reference lists, this is an outstanding contribution to the field. Highly recommended for upper-division undergraduates through faculty.—*S. Sugarman, Bennington College*

OAB-2151   93-73109 Orig
School choice: examining the evidence, ed. by Edith Rasell and Richard Rothstein. Economics Policy Institute, 1993. 364p bibl index ISBN 0-944826-57-1 pbk, $17.95

This report on the 1992 seminar, "Choice: What Role in American Education?" sponsored by the Economic Policy Institute (EPI) includes articles and discussions that look at the issue of choice from the viewpoint of researchers and policymakers. The report is organized around the three key issues of disagreement among choice advocates and their opponents: the effects of school choice on the educational, racial, and socioeconomic integration of students; the effects of school choice on achievement; and the role of choice in school reform. Part 1 addresses whether or not school choice promotes equality of opportunity. Part 2 examines whether school choice raises student achievement and analyzes the work of Chubb and Moe, who assert that the academic performance of students in high schools that are freed from democratic control and subjected to market pressures is enhanced. The last section discusses who and what should drive school reform and examines reasons why people select different schools; it finds that this decision often has little to do with academics, raising questions about parents' motivations and ability to make this important choice. This book provides an exhaustive study of the questions relating to this issue as seen through the eyes of prominent educational analysts. Although there is disagreement with the answers presented, one comment in the Foreword sums up the one item of consensus: the goal is excellence for all. Highly recommended for educators, researchers, students at all levels, parents, and those interested in shcool reform and school choice.—*J. D. Davenport, California State University, Hayward*

OAB-2152   LB2805   95-9405 CIP
Sergiovanni, Thomas J. **Leadership for the schoolhouse: how is it different?: why is it important?** Jossey-Bass, 1996. 203p bibl index ISBN 0-7879-0119-9, $28.95

Sergiovanni's insightful volume about school leadership is an important continuation of other Sergiovanni volumes on this topic: *Value-Added Leadership* (CH, Nov'90); *Moral Leadership: Getting to the Heart of School Improvement* (CH, Oct'92); and *The Principalship: A Reflective Practice Perspective* (3rd ed., 1995). Here, his theme is that education has always found its theories by importing them from business organizations, and that they do not readily serve the ends of education. Sergiovanni believes education must develop its own theories and practices based on what schools are trying to do and the kinds of people schools serve. Sergiovanni examines existing theories of leadership ("Pyramid", "Railroad", and "High Performance") and provides examples of how poorly they have been translated into school practices, mainly because of how they have addressed practical and moral implications. He also analyzes basic questions that could help in developing a purely educational theory of leadership for schooling. This would require changes in existing theories, allowing communities to become established voices for ideas and purposes; downsizing of schools; and reemphasis on teacher development with constructivist (scientific decision making) principles as basic. Sergiovanni's inspiring work is recommended for all levels of readers.—*R. C. Morris, West Georgia College*

OAB-2153   LB2331   95-23211 MARC
Teaching on solid ground: using scholarship to improve prac-

tice, [ed.] by Robert J. Menges, Maryellen Weimer, and associates. Jossey-Bass, 1996. 406p bibl indexes afp ISBN 0-7879-0133-4, $34.95

The editors present another effort by progressivists (cf. Donald Arnstine, *Democracy and the Art of Schooling*, CH, Apr'96) to promote teaching methods that arrange conditions for learners to participate in their own learning. In a collection of scholarly essays, authorities on teaching methods call for practices responsive to the needs of a changing student body reflecting advances in the knowledge of learning. They envision a scholarship of teaching resulting in faculty empowerment through self-reflection, self-recognition, and intrinsic motivation, and involving a long-term program of faculty development in which research defines practice. They argue that since today's students are older, less motivated, in debt, and more emotionally dysfunctional, past approaches to the roles of teacher and instructional methods must be abandoned. They replace the Cartesian position of the independent person attempting to control the natural-social world through mastery of objective knowledge with a dialogical position focusing on the interactions of persons and the continuous re-creation of knowledge. These well-written essays conclude by identifying good teaching as encouraging student collaboration, measuring student involvement, accepting student feedback, utilizing foundational knowledge, and being sensitive to diversity/multiculturism. Highly recommended for all levels of readers.—*F. X. Russo, University of Rhode Island*

OAB-2154   HV2551   92-2932 CIP
Toward effective public school programs for deaf students: context, process, and outcomes, ed. by Thomas N. Kluwin, Donald F. Moores, and Martha Gonter Gaustad. Teachers College Press (Columbia University), 1992. 264p index afp ISBN 0-8077-3160-9, $46.00; ISBN 0-8077-3159-5 pbk, $22.95

This edited volume presents an outstanding overview of a number of significant issues related to the education of deaf and hearing-impaired students in public schools and seeks to provide a detailed, up-to-date examination and analysis of the various curricular, philosophical, and programmatic options available for these students. In so doing, the book fills a serious and significant gap in the literature on the education of the deaf. An introductory interesting and useful historical overview of school placement of the deaf student serves to contextualize the remainder of the book. The first section deals with the context of educational programs for deaf students, in general terms, and the second section addresses the process and outcomes of schooling for the deaf. Among the best chapters are those dealing with ethnic and cultural considerations, family factors, issues of educational interpreting, communication patterns, the role of extracurricular activities, and finally, the efficacy of mainstreaming. The book concludes with recommendations for developing courses of action for organizing effective programs for deaf students in the public schools. This is a well-written, cogent, and important work that will be of value to anyone interested in deaf education. Recommended for undergraduates; graduates; faculty; professionals.—*T. Reagan, University of Connecticut*

OAB-2155   LC1099   97-4675 CIP
Vogt, W. Paul. **Tolerance & education: learning to live with diversity and difference.** Sage Publications, CA, 1997. 289p bibl index afp ISBN 0-7619-0216-3, $56.00; ISBN 0-7619-0217-1 pbk, $25.95

Vogt's engaging book explores key questions about tolerance as it relates to schooling. The author asks: What is tolerance? Is it learned? If so, how? Can it be taught directly? After providing thoughtful answers to these questions, the author explores the implications for educational research, policy, and practice. Well considered, well documented, and stimulating, this text is mercifully free of the simpleminded preaching that characterizes too many books on this and related subjects. It even provides a short history of tolerance and very useful references. Highly recommended for all collections.—*G. K. Clabaugh, La Salle University*

OAB-2156 LB1576 92-8756 CIP
Writing, teaching, and learning in the disciplines, ed. by Anne Herrington and Charles Moran. Modern Language Association of America, 1992. 265p bibl index (Research and scholarship in composition, 1) ISBN 0-87352-577-9, $37.00; ISBN 0-87352-578-7 pbk, $19.50

This fine book charts both the history and best practices of the writing across the curriculum movement that hit full stride in the UK and the US during the 1970s at all levels of education. To the public as well as to educators attempting to integrate writing into all course's, writing across the curriculum is more about learning the skills and pedagogical techniques needed to make it work in the classroom than the epistomological endeavor it is for most contributors to this volume. They find inspiration in cognitive pioneers such as Vygotsky, Luria, and Yudovich, as well as in the work of philosophers and developmental psychologists such as Dewey, Piaget, and Bruner. This work is perhaps the only book-length treatment of the subject to explore these historical roots before turning to the practitioners (a number of whom helped invent the field) who write about the general cognitive issues of teaching and learning that are assumed to transcend the content of the disciplines, the assumptions and practices characteristic of faculty development efforts that foster writing across the curriculum, the empirical studies that have attempted to take the measure of this work, and finally, the values embedded in the language of disciplinary discourse. There is a good mix of the metalanguage one might expect in explorations of this kind, as well as examples of very real work from teachers struggling to bring language and writing to their classes. Recommended. Graduate; faculty.—*L. S. Zwerling, The Ford Foundation*

■ History, Geography & Area Studies

OAB-2157 D547 93-1484 CIP
Andrews, E.M. **The Anzac illusion: Anglo-Australian relations during World War I.** Cambridge, 1994 (c1993). 274p bibl index ISBN 0-521-41914-X, $49.95

Andrew's excellent short book provides a fine study in mythmaking, especially in time of war. Focusing on Australian troops—though, unlike most books about the "Anzac idea," not to the exclusion of New Zealand—Andrews analyzes what took place in two key battles, the famed Gallipoli and the less well known Bullecourt on the Western Front. He shows how military commanders, politicians, the press, and popular magazines created a legend about the British Empire—Australian and British troops standing side-by-side against the enemy—and the particular courage of the Anzacs in the face of Turkish fire at the Dardanelles. Much of this ground has been covered before, but Andrews (Univ. of Newcastle, Australia) is more pungent and exacting than any previous writer. The result is a model study of how wartime propaganda lives on long after the purpose for which it was created has been served. Despite some odd locutions, the author writes clearly and with broad strokes, making a difficult subject accessible to a variety of levels of readers, from college undergraduates to anyone interested in war, reportage, or questions of imperial unity at any level.—*R. W. Winks, Yale University*

OAB-2158 D13 96-41293 CIP
Black, Jeremy. **Maps and history: constructing images of the past.** Yale, 1997. 267p index afp ISBN 0-300-06976-6, $35.00

Someone once claimed "History is about chaps, geography is about maps." Black attempts to bridge these two perspectives by demonstrating the importance of maps and, in particular, collections of maps in atlases. Black's central thesis is that rather than being merely classroom wallpaper, text illustrations, or reference tools "akin to chronologies, dictionaries and encyclopedias," maps are themselves important sources of data. He also argues that the close relationship between the cartographic representation of the state and its interest in the representation and assertion of its power demands an appreciation

of the "iconographic aspects of political and cultural authority" expressed in maps, and a critical appraisal of cartography as "a discourse of power." His analysis is much informed by J.B. Harley and D. Woodward's *The History of Cartography* (v.1: CH, Oct'87). But this is a magisterial work in its own right. Profusely illustrated (28 of the 50 are in color), thoroughly footnoted, and lavishly and delightfully produced, Black's work is a provocative piece of scholarship. General readers; upper-division undergraduates and above.—*B. Osborne, Queen's University at Kingston*

OAB-2159 DS468 93-15536 CIP
Chatterjee, Partha. **The nation and its fragments: Colonial and postcolonial histories.** Princeton, 1993. 282p bibl index afp ISBN 0-691-03305-6, $49.50; ISBN 0-691-01943-6 pbk, $15.95

In this well-documented study, Chatterjee, an Indian historian, challenges the view held by many Western scholars that nationalism in Asia and Africa has been based on various modular forms supplied by the rise of nationalism in Europe and the US. His view is that it has been based "not on an identity but rather on a *difference* with the 'modular' forms of the national society propogated by the West." He does acknowledge the contribution of the West to Asian and African nationalism, but only in what he calls the domain of the "outside"—in such areas as economy, statecraft, science, and technology. In the more important "inner" domain of the spiritual, the primary contribution has been that of the indigenous cultures. To support his thesis, Chatterjee explores such areas as the formation of a national press, the growth of various social and religious reform movements, and developments in the fields of art and literature. To be sure, almost all the examples he cites have been taken from the Indian experience, mostly from Bengal, but broadly, these examples could be applied to the rise of anticolonial nationalist movements in other parts of Asia and Africa. Chatterjee's excellent study makes a major contribution to understanding not only the anticolonial movements in Asia and Africa, but also other recent developments in that vast region of our world. Recommended for upper-division undergraduates and above.—*S. K. Gupta, Pittsburgh State University*

OAB-2160 G587 95-44829 CIP
Chaturvedi, Sanjay. **The polar regions: a political geography.** Scott Polar Research Institute/Wiley, 1996. 306p bibl index afp ISBN 0-471-94898-5, $85.00

Chaturvedi (Panjab Univ., Chandigarh) is a political scientist who has been moving ever closer to geography over the years. His latest book begins with an explanation of the "new geopolitics" that has developed during the past decade. Chapters that follow introduce the polar regions in all their complexity; examine the effects of traditional geopolitical concepts on these regions and the Arctic in the context of the Cold War; and contrast "the highly militarized, conflict ridden Arctic and the non-militarized, peaceful Antarctic." Chaturvedi covers new developments that are transforming the Arctic from an arena for imperialism and Cold War geostrategy into one of concern for both ecology and the rights of the indigenous peoples. He analyzes the growing cooperation of the circumpolar states in such matters as boundary disputes, and considers the conflicts between "the demands of growth-oriented modernization and the imperatives of environmental conservation" in the Artic. Also discussed are environmental problems, scientific research, and the tourist industry in Antarctica. The last chapter summarizes the foregoing material, comments on continuity and change in polar geopolitics, and describes the application of the new geopolitics here. This very fine book is comprehensive and scholarly, yet unusually well written. Upper-division undergraduates and above.—*M. I. Glassner, emeritus, Southern Connecticut State University*

OAB-2161 D15 95-37598 CIP
Friedman, Susan W. **Marc Bloch, sociology and geography: encountering changing disciplines.** Cambridge, 1996. 258p indexes ISBN 0-521-56157-4, $54.95

Friedman's book is a study in the genealogy of ideas. In particular, it is an investigation of the intellectual pedigree of Marc Bloch, a leading figure in the landscape of the social sciences in the first half of the 20th century. But it is more than this. Friedman's study is a triangulation of the prevailing ideas in history, geography, and sociology. The development of Bloch's theoretical thinking is scrutinized in terms of his relationships with Durkheim, Vidal de la Blache, and a whole cast of scholars in French academia. The analysis is effected in two parts: the first, 1904-1920, the "years of apprenticeship," deals with Bloch's training in Paris and the Ecole Normale Superieure; the second, 1919-1943, refers to Bloch's scholarship while at the University of Strassbourg. Apart from being a meticulous investigation of the scholarly development of Bloch's ideas, the book also provides insights into the influential groups of scholars, the Annales school, as well as French intellectual life in general. Friedman's treatment of the profound importance of the University of Strassbourg in terms of French patriotism as well as scholarship is another bonus. Well indexed and referenced; footnotes transcend mere citations and should be read carefully for their illuminating forays into ideas rendered in the text. Upper-division undergraduates and above.—*B. Osborne, Queen's University at Kingston*

OAB-2162   BX2263   94-47094 CIP
Haliczer, Stephen. **Sexuality in the confessional: a sacrament profaned.** Oxford, 1996. 267p bibl index afp ISBN 0-19-509656-8, $49.95

Haliczer's new book is a major contribution to the history of sexuality in early modern Europe and to the growing literature on the vast database for social and cultural history offered by the records of the Spanish Inquisition. It is the most important contribution to the study of sexual solicitation in the confessional since H.C. Lea's *Auricular Confession and Indulgences*, published exactly 100 years ago. Haliczer draws astutely on the best techniques of modern social history; his database of 223 cases allows him to offer a rich and detailed picture of the life and people behind the data. The book begins with four chapters that establish the increasing frequency of confession in post-Tridentine Europe and the role of the Spanish Inquisition in prosecuting the offense of solicitation in Spain. Haliczer then analyzes the social backgrounds of soliciting confessors, those of unwilling victims, and those of willing penitents. He concludes with a wide-ranging consideration of 17th- and 18th-century sexuality, from new methods of clerical training to the sexual fantasies of both male clergy and the women penitents they solicited. The final chapter considers the topic of sexual solicitation in the anticlerical literature of the 18th through the 20th centuries. Upper-division undergraduates and above.—*E. Peters, University of Pennsylvania*

OAB-2163   G155   94-18156 CIP
Hall, Colin Michael. **Tourism and politics: policy, power and place.** Wiley, 1995 (c1994). 238p bibl indexes ISBN 0 471 94919 1, $54.95

Despite Hall's early observation that the political dimensions of tourism receive little attention in tourism-related research, this is much truer of policy studies than of those fields, such as anthropology, that have been strongly influenced by political economy. Nevertheless, this examination of issues of policy, power, and place in contemporary tourism is a welcome addition to the tourism literature. Chapters not only address the significance of tourism in national policy and international relations but also situate tourism in the broader contexts of relations of dependency and the power of global capital. An added bonus is that much case material derives from smaller Pacific countries, a reflection of Hall's work as Director of the Tourism Programme at the University of Canberra, Australia. Most of this literature is not readily available on this side of the Pacific. The author writes about complex and important concerns in an accessible manner. Besides the topics already noted, there is substantial coverage of the consequences of political instability, urban tourism, the environmental movement, and forms of cultural representation. A solid and balanced book with an extensive bibliography. Undergraduates and above.—*O. Pi-Sunyer, University of Massachusetts at Amherst*

OAB-2164   HM216   96-961 CIP
Harvey, David. **Justice, nature and the geography of difference.**

Blackwell, 1996. 468p bibl index afp ISBN 1-55786-680-5, $64.95; ISBN 1-55786-681-3 pbk, $21.95

Written by one of the most provocative thinkers in modern social science, this very important study is rich in theoretical discussion, alternating with penetrating insights and personal vignettes. Harvey challenges the deconstructionists, relativists, critical theorists, and postmodernists who deny meta-narratives and foundational beliefs. He argues instead that such narratives and beliefs should be scrutinized to better allow for interpretation and political action. To this end, Harvey attempts to define "a set of workable foundational concepts for understanding space-time, place, and environment (nature)." His approach is dialectical and relational in its emphasis on totalities rather than on fragmented isolations. For Harvey, "theoretical practice" emerges from the dialectic between the particularisms and materialities of place, space, and environment and the formulation of "global ambitions." This is demonstrated in three thematic sections; "The Nature of the Environment"; "Space, Time and Place"; "Justice, Difference, and Politics." Throughout, Harvey provides a materialist framework for integrating the core geographical concepts of space, place, and environment into discursive reflection on social theory, which is then related to political and social practice. Imaginative illustrations; poetry; excellent bibliography; efficient index. Upper-division undergraduates and above.—*B. Osborne, Queen's University at Kingston*

OAB-2165   HM22   93-36440 CIP
Hundert, E.J. **The Enlightenment's fable: Bernard Mandeville and the discovery of society.** Cambridge, 1994. 284p bibl index ISBN 0-521-46082-4, $54.95

Like Thomas Hobbes in the 17th century, Bernard Mandeville believed that the fabric of society was held together by a system of negative emotions such as envy, competition, and exploitation. Mandeville is best known for *The Fable of the Bees*, published in its entirety in 1728, a masterwork that has been the cause of bitter controversy ever since because critics have seen it as an "unsubdued mutiny in moral philosophy." Hundert's book is dedicated to revising that reputation. Hundert (Univ. of British Columbia) has written a searching work of rehabilitation, interpreting the *Fable* as a central force in the moral philosophy of the 18th-century Enlightenment. Rather than accept the commonplace understanding that Mandeville represented a cynical rejection of the science of humanity, Hundert sees the *Fable* as an intimate part of the Enlightenment's effort to understand humankind as it really is, and not as Christian moral philosophy would have us believe. The interpretation that emerges from these learned pages places Mandeville next to Hume and, to a lesser extent, was meant to provide us with a disenchanted view of "unsocial yet socialized man." This is a sophisticated study: the research is meticulous, the arguments carefully nuanced, and the prose impressive. Recommended for advanced undergraduates and graduates.—*V. G. Wexler, University of Maryland, Baltimore County*

OAB-2166   HV568   95-26628 CIP
Hutchinson, John F. **Champions of charity: war and the rise of the Red Cross.** Westview, 1996. 448p bibl index afp ISBN 0-8133-2526-9, $35.00

Hutchinson's extraordinary book has been needed for some time. For nearly a century and a half the symbol of the Red Cross (and Red Crescent in Muslim lands) has represented restraint and mercy in treatment of war victims and the wounded and homeless victims of natural catastrophe. What has not been grasped by most people is that the Red Cross has never been an antiwar movement. It has assumed that war is a natural phenomenon, perhaps a product of human nature itself. It has also relied on the patronage of dominant military and political establishments. Hutchinson analyzes extensive archival and secondary data from every major power except Germany, where archival sources on the Red Cross have only recently been rationalized. He shows that national Red Cross societies (always to be distinguished from the International Committee of the Red Cross or ICRC) came to depend on the military high commands of their own countries. By the beginning of the 20th century they had become virtual instruments of the military. Hutchinson believes that the self-congratulatory publications of the Red Cross have established a universal stereotype accepted by all. However, American and British veterans of both world wars long ago saw the Red Cross as a vehicle for upper-class self-congratulation mostly reserved "for officers only." For every library with books on modern warfare as it relates to society. All levels.—*G. H. Davis, emeritus, Georgia State University*

OAB-2167 D804 91-33049 CIP
Katz, Steven T. **The Holocaust in historical context: v.1: The Holocaust and mass death before the modern age.** Oxford, 1994. 702p bibl index afp ISBN 0-19-507220-0, $49.95

Katz defines the Holocaust as the Nazi intention to murder every Jewish man, woman, and child, thus recreating the world without Jews. This obsession made the Holocaust unparalleled in world history. In the many cases of mass murder that the author examines, he fails to find any other instance whereby the objective of the perpetrator was to totally eliminate the victim from the face of the earth. Katz eschews the argument that Jewish suffering during the Holocaust has a greater claim on the human conscience than do other calamities. Rather, he argues, the Holocaust was a historical *Novum* and cannot be compared to other examples of mass murder because it was Nazi intentionality rather than the killing that gives the Holocaust its uniqueness. The author also rejects the argument that anti-Jewish sentiment found in the *New Testament* prepared the way for Auschwitz. Katz contends that Christian antisemitism created the demon-like imagery of the Jew in Western culture, and it was this negative mythic image of the Jew that was seized by the Nazis for their own destructive ends. This impressively researched and original volume should be included in all libraries.—*J. Fischel, Millersville University*

OAB-2168 HQ1121 92-20411 CIP
Lerner, Gerda. **The creation of feminist consciousness: from the Middle Ages to eighteen-seventy.** Oxford, 1993. 395p bibl index afp ISBN 0-19-506604-9, $27.50

In this long-awaited sequel to The Creation of Patriarchy (CH, Oct'86), Lerner traces resistance to patriarchy and some of the searches for women's self-consciousness and self-expression from the 7th through the late 19th centuries CE. She examines the educational disadvantaging of women and their struggles for the right to possess public voices, notably through mystical reformulations of religious traditions. Lerner's reconstructed history of women analyzes examples of past struggles for empowerment through motherhood, education, self-authorization, supportive female clusters and networks, and quests for role models. Yet the early efforts to achieve a public voice were frequently smothered, leaving later attempts to escape women's isolation in the situation, in Lerner's apt phrase, of reinventing the wheel. This provocative and important work is highly recommended for the general public as well as for all college levels. The bibliography is extremely useful and well organized, and will be valuable for research and to guide library acquisitions.—*F. Burkhard, Morgan State University*

OAB-2169 E169 96-33866 CIP
Levine, Lawrence W. **The opening of the American mind: canons, culture, and history.** Beacon Press, 1996. 212p index ISBN 0-8070-3118-6, $20.00

Levine has written a stunning brief that examines the current critique of higher education, the major debates over the curriculum and the canon over two centuries, and changes in the perceptions of the national culture. His compelling assault on contemporary critics—William Bennett, Dinesh D'Souza, Gertrude Himmelfarb, *et al.*—begins with a survey of the complex inner life of the university over 200 years and the violent reaction to all cultural change. He surveys the glacially slow evolution of the curriculum from the time when Greek and Latin classics dominated to the post-WW II years and the fearful alarm when Melville and Emily Dickinson were first introduced, noting the same fierce outcry when the expressive culture of African Americans, Native Americans,

and immigrant writers were included in the entrenched canon. Levine insists that there is no stable canon of writers; that universities have always mirrored dominant cultural attitudes toward gender, race, and ethnicity; and that diversity, pluralism, and multiculturalism have been present throughout American history. To exclude them from the classroom, he argues, ignores the complexities of American culture and experiences. His passionate and consistently intelligent defense of multiculturalism deserves a wide audience among scholars and general readers.—*M. Cantor, University of Massachusetts at Amherst*

OAB-2170 D226 93-26588 CIP
Marion, Robert. **Was George Washington really the father of our country?: a clinical geneticist looks at world history.** Addison-Wesley, 1994. 206p ISBN 0-201-62255-6, $22.95

Combining genetics, medicine, history, and sociology together with other academic disciplines, clinical geneticist and physician Marion has written a book that reads like a novel. It will instruct and entertain many different audiences. Utilizing diverse sources, Marion hypothesizes how the course of world history has been affected by the genetics and the resultant medical conditions of King George III of England, George Washington, Napoleon Bonaparte, Abraham Lincoln, Tsarevich Alexis Nicolaievich, and John F. Kennedy. Where there are differences of opinion, they are presented. Technical chemical, physiological, and anatomical terms are used, but immediately defined. Students and teachers of genetics and history will gain new insights and information from this thoroughly researched and appealing book. All levels.—*W. Lener, Nassau Community College*

OAB-2171 BR477 94-36428 CIP
McLeod, Hugh. **Piety and poverty: working-class religion in Berlin, London, and New York, 1870-1914.** Holmes & Meier, 1996. 264p bibl index afp ISBN 0-8419-1356-0, $45.00

McLeod has provided a tightly organized, clearly written, and persuasively argued comparison of religious activities and beliefs of the working class in three large cities. His research in primary sources is extensive; that in secondary material is prodigious. His interpretation of urban religious change, one that generally sides with the argument that the key development was the growth of religious toleration rather than the advance of secularization, consists of three points. First, class conflict led to alienation from established churches. Second, various movements of emancipation were opposed by established churches with ties to ruling hierarchies. And third, intellectual developments, such as the theory of evolution and a critical approach to the Bible based on science, made plausible a nonsupernatural worldview. These points obviously are relevant to the non-working-class population also, so that McLeod includes a significant amount of information about it as well. The 18 statistical tables are helpful; the six maps are too sketchy and imprecise; the index is serviceable. All levels.—*H. D. Andrews, emeritus, Towson State University*

OAB-2172 DS195 91-47944 CIP
Melson, Robert. **Revolution and genocide: on the origins of the Armenian genocide and the Holocaust.** Chicago, 1992. 363p bibl index afp ISBN 0-226-51990-2, $29.95

Whether the Holocaust was "unique" has been a major controversial issue in Holocaust studies. One group, labeled by Melson "particularist," argues that the Holocaust—frequently defined as the attempt by Nazi Germany to destroy all Jews—may not be compared to other genocides, because to do so is to deflect the moral impact of that event. For example, proponents of this view have objected, with some justice, to the comparison by Sarte of the American Bombing of Vietnam to the Holocaust. Some German historians have argued that Stalin's mass murders somehow diminish German guilt. On the other hand, Melson argues that although the Holocaust does indeed contain unique elements, it may be compared to other genocides, such as the Turkish genocide of the Armenians. Melson holds that to compare these events does not suggest that they are identical. The primary focus of the work is comparison between the Holocaust and the Armenian genocide, in a treatment that respects

Social & Behavioral Sciences

the uniqueness of each event. The result is a major achievement that provides a new perception of the causes of genocides, valuable not only to understand the past but also to prevent their recurrence in the future. Advanced undergraduate; graduate; faculty.—*G. M. Kren, Kansas State University*

OAB-2173 JV7590 92-6678 CIP
Moch, Leslie Page. **Moving Europeans: migration in Western Europe since 1650.** Indiana, 1992. 257p bibl index afp ISBN 0-253-33859-X, $35.00

Moch defines human mobility in Western Europe since 1650 as both temporary and permanent "changes of residence" across any level of administrative boundary. His study is organized into four periods: preindustrial (1650-1750); rural industrial (1750-1815); age of urbanization (1815-1914); and modern age (1914-1992). Four categories of free migration are proposed: local migration; circular migration; chain migration; and career migration; two other forms—colonizing and coerced migration—are discussed only peripherally. Moch's central thesis is that rather than being the diagnostic feature of modernity, migration has always been "embedded in the social and economic framework of human organization" and is central to understanding preindustrial life, rural industry, the industrial revolution, and urbanization. He concludes with the challenge that unity and peace in Europe depend on European ability to "develop and affirm pluralistic societies within its own borders." This provocative study affords a melding of the most current theory with engagingly written vignettes of the lived experience of those involved in the process. Superb bibliography and endnotes. Advanced undergraduate; graduate; faculty.—*B. Osborne, Queen's University*

OAB-2174 E184 95-18907 CIP
Nesaule, Agate. **A woman in amber: healing the trauma of war and exile.** Soho Press, 1995. 280p afp ISBN 1-56947-046-4, $24.00

Readers will find it difficult to put down this gem of a memoir about the suffering of a child and her family in WW II and their efforts as immigrants to rebuild their lives and psyches in America. Nesaule experienced the war as a young Latvian refugee. She went from a comfortable upper- middle-class life to the deprivations and horrors of wartime Germany. There she witnessed unspeakable torture, rape, and executions, even the creation of games among the corpses. Her mother was the glue that held the family together amid the terror, until one unforgettable, and almost unforgivable, moment of weakness. The author describes her experiences in displaced persons camps after the war. She also recounts the efforts of the Latvian community in Indianapolis to maintain its culture and, simultaneously, to assimilate. While succeeding admirably in many ways, Nesaule herself was unable to achieve genuine self-worth and to exorcise her personal demons until she told her story. This is a powerful, worthwhile, and ultimately inspiring book that adds to readers' understanding of the impact of war and emigration on families and individuals. All levels.—*L. Mayo, County College of Morris*

OAB-2175 HD4871 94-38289 CIP
Northrup, David. **Indentured labor in the age of imperialism, 1834-1922.** Cambridge, 1995. 186p bibl index ISBN 0-521-48047-7, $49.95; ISBN 0-521-48519-3 pbk, $14.95

Northrup is well placed by his previous work in African labor history to undertake this much-needed synthesis of a recently burgeoning field of historical study. He successfully narrates his story in clear introductory and concluding sections, while analyzing the experience of indentured labor from its demand and supply to its passage and indentured contract. Treating a 90-year period from the mid-1830s and focusing primarily on sugar plantations, Northrup deals with a wide variety of labor migrations, mostly throughout the southern hemisphere, though there is much here about other migrations, e.g., the Japanese to Hawaii, Chinese to Latin America, and Polynesians in the Pacific. His conclusions challenge some of those advanced earlier by Hugh Tinker's study of indentured labor from India, which had likened indenture to slavery. Northrup

is persuasive in his assertion that nearly all indentured laborers understood something about the nature of their contracts, and in his other arguments for a more moderate interpretation of indenture and its relationship to slavery. This well-crafted book demonstrates mature scholarly judgment, is clearly organized and well written, and engages the historiography of its field in a manner that should advance historical study of this type of labor. All levels.—*M. J. Moore, Appalachian State University*

OAB-2176 JV6465 92-7156 CIP
Nugent, Walter. **Crossings: the great transatlantic migrations, 1870-1914.** Indiana, 1992. 234p bibl index afp ISBN 0-253-34140-X, $29.95

Nugent (Notre Dame) is a fine historian and a good storyteller. His latest book is a multilayered narrative of the movement of millions of Europeans to the Americas. Different from many other descriptions of the transatlantic passages, which tend to be focused on one side of the ocean (the lands of the senders) or the other (the countries of reception and resettlement), *Crossings* tears down what Frank Thistlewaite once called a "saltwater curtain." Nugent moves—and moves his readers—back and forth across the Atlantic, describing the social and political conditions that pushed Europeans out of the Old World and the factors—not least of which was the promise of a better life—that pulled them into the New World, particularly to this country and to Argentina, Brazil, and Canada. Using a variety of social and demographic data by which to compare the several countries of immigration, the author challenges certain widely held assumptions about "American [meaning US] exceptionalism." That is one of the subtexts in this interesting and informative work. Added bonuses include excellent maps, clearly presented tables, and a dozen classic photographs of the migrants at home in Europe, enroute to America, and in their new societies. All levels.—*P. I. Rose, Smith College*

OAB-2177 U21 95-9858 CIP
O'Connell, Robert L. **Ride of the second horseman: the birth and death of war.** Oxford, 1995. 305p index afp ISBN 0-19-506460-7, $25.00

O'Connell's provocative and absorbing book offers a highly original interpretation of the origins of warfare. The author, an intelligence analyst, focuses on the history of human societies in the Old World to the end of the Bronze Age, makes comparisons with warfare in pre-Columbian America, and even includes a preliminary chapter on the wars of the ants. O'Connell's main thesis is that human warfare was originally a stable and ritualized institution, which developed in the Old World into a more aggressive and predatory pattern because of the interaction between agricultural and pastoral peoples. He argues that this interaction began c. 5500 BCE, when pastoral nomads from the Eurasian steppe began to raid agricultural settlements, and accelerated after the domestication of the horse c. 4000 BCE, forcing settlements to fortify themselves and starting a chain reaction of aggressive warfare among Bronze-Age states. As with any ambitious work, much of this will be thought controversial, e.g., O'Connell's comments on the genetic roots of war and his claim that the Sumerians anticipated classical Greek phalanx warfare. But this is a brilliant tour de force that epitomizes recent research from many disciplines in readable and vivid prose. All levels.—*J. D. Dawson, Guilford Technical Community College*

OAB-2178 BX8129 95-41351 CIP
Packull, Werner O. **Hutterite beginnings: communitarian experiments during the Reformation.** Johns Hopkins, 1995. 440p bibl index afp ISBN 0-8018-5048-7, $59.95

With this carefully researched and highly readable study, Packull convincingly supports the polygenetic theory of Anabaptist beginnings. He first analyzes several early groups and then describes the steps that led to the Hutterites becoming the only early Anabaptist communitarian group to survive the terrible persecutions under Ferdinand. Claiming to stand fully within neither the "normative" Anabaptist tradition (Becker et al.) nor the revisionist camp of H-J Goertz, Packull seeks to relate early Hutterite developments (to c. 1560) to previous Anabaptist groups through close study of important leaders' movements, ideas, and effects. He largely succeeds in this quest, but at the same time, his sympathies with the Anabaptists are apparent. Especially important is his ability to relate specific events to their political, economic, social, and theological contexts. The research is extensive and sound, the judgments considered. Intensely detailed and logical, the exposition takes nothing for granted. An important contribution not only to the understanding of early Anabaptism but also to the larger field of Reformation studies, this book belongs in any collection with a Reformation component. Appendixes, footnotes, maps, and illustrations. All levels.—*P. L. Kintner, Grinnell College*

OAB-2179   JF801   91-45807 CIP
Riesenberg, Peter. **Citizenship in the Western tradition: Plato to Rousseau.** North Carolina, 1992. 324p bibl index afp ISBN 0-8078-2037-7, $42.50

Interweaving political history and political theory, Riesenberg provides a balanced, analytical, and interpretive view of citizenship from its origins in the Greek polis to the French Revolution. Emphasizing the power of the citizen ideal, he argues that through citizenship people are directed to a higher purpose—the public good. Riesenberg lists two categories of citizenship. The "first citizenship" applies to small-scale societies—culturally monolithic, hierarchical, and discriminatory—that were ascendant in the Western world to the latter part of the 18th century. Whether in the Spartan polis, Italian city-state, or Colonial New England, the citizens, usually a minority element, were actively involved in the affairs of governing a community or state. With the emergence of the "second citizenship," which came to fruition with the American and French Revolutions, citizenship came to be based on birth or specified residence in a large territorial state. Citizens lost the real possibility for gaining virtue through active participation in governing. The author believes voluntarism and occasional office holding at the local level are the primary channels for citizen activity today. This erudite and well-constructed work will interest readers at several levels. General; undergraduate; graduate; faculty.—*L. E. Oyos, Augustana College (SD)*

OAB-2180   92-54380 Orig
Said, Edward W. **Culture and imperialism.** Knopf, 1993. 380p index ISBN 0-394-58738-3, $25.00

Said (Columbia Univ.) is internationally recognized as a scholar with exceptional insight on wide-ranging cultural phenomena. Here he brings the same skills exhibited in his widely heralded work *Orientalism* (CH, Apr'79) to bear on the age of imperialism. Said makes extensive use of literary masterpieces, intermingling them with a solid understanding of political developments, to present an interesting and original view of the pervasive legacy of imperialism. He sees the impact of imperialism as a "consolidated vision" of the sort Kipling had in mind when he spoke of the "white man's burden." Set against this Eurocentric view were the thoughts and writings of indigenous peoples who struggled valiantly, even as decolonization was in progress, to retain and reassert their own distinct cultural identity. Said's scope is wide; his arguments deep. Yet this book is one that no serious student of modern empire can afford to ignore. Those who seek greater understanding of today's interaction between the West and the Third World cannot overlook its message of the true oneness of the human community. Advanced undergraduate; graduate; faculty.—*J. A. Casada, Winthrop University*

OAB-2181   GF50   93-48546 CIP
Schama, Simon. **Landscape and memory.** Knopf, 1995. 652p bibl index ISBN 0-679-40255-1, $40.00

Schama has produced an imaginative, provocative, and well-written study of how Western culture has imbued its natural surroundings with history and myth. Focusing on three particular parts of the natural environment, Schama convincingly illustrates how deeply they affect one's consciousness and how that, in turn, has determined what is landscape. Part 1 is an examination of wood—trees and forests—and is nicely framed with personal reminiscences. Schama shows how trees have served as symbolic reservoirs of nationalism, lib-

erty, spirituality, and manifest destiny. Part 2 explores rivers, revealing them as sources of wisdom and representative of societal health. Part 3 shows mountains to be the "measure of man." Schama illustrates how mountains were slowly demystified, while at the same time attracting romantic associations. His interpretation of Mt. Rushmore as the ultimate symbol of triumph, possession, and imperialism is particularly interesting. Part 4 explores "Arcadia." The numerous black-and-white and color illustrations are carefully chosen and well placed to accompany the text. Informative bibliographic essay. Highly recommended for all levels.—*M. T. Scholz, University of Washington*

OAB-2182   HT1048   93-18022 CIP
Voelz, Peter M. **Slave and soldier: the military impact of blacks in the colonial Americas.** Garland, 1993. 521p bibl index afp ISBN 0-8153-1009-9, $109.00

Few historians have addressed the military contribution of African slaves. Voelz shows that blacks participated mightily not only in building colonial societies but also in defending them. Based on extensive research, particularly in the records of the British West Indies regiments, his study demonstrates that for more than three centuries black men—slave and free, African and Creole—played an important role as soldiers throughout the New World. They served in great numbers; they were effective, loyal participants; and they were leaders as well as followers. Much more than a descriptive record, Voelz's study illustrates the complex motivations of slave and free black soldiers. He notes that blacks fought on both sides in campaigns throughout the Americas; racial solidarity was not strong, nor were class distinctions clear. The work includes 30 informative charts, extensive footnotes for each chapter, and a useful bibliography. It will prove valuable to undergraduate students and scholars alike, an important contribution to comparative New World history. Voelz has broadened understanding of the positive role of African Americans in shaping societies and has revealed the intricacies and contradictions of race relations in the Americas. Advanced undergraduate and above.—*R. Detweiler, California State University, Dominguez Hills*

OAB-2183   HT166   94-9553 CIP
White, Rodney R. **Urban environmental management: environmental change and urban design.** Wiley, 1994. 233p bibl index ISBN 0-471-95001-7, $49.95

In this path-breaking book, White (Univ. of Toronto) is concerned with the environmental role of cities and their growing impact on the global ecosystem. Specifically, the aim is to examine urban planning and management problems from that environmental perspective. The first two chapters trace the evolution and functioning of cities vis-à-vis the global environment and the context of urban areas with respect to the dynamics of large-scale environmental systems. Subsequent chapters treat the inputs and outputs of urban resource-use, the link between urban pathologies and the natural environment, effects on air and water quality, prescriptions for improving urban environmental impacts, and a fascinating case study involving initiatives in metropolitan Toronto. A useful glossary is provided as well as a listing of references that is both comprehensive and current. This book builds upon earlier classics by geographers, most notably Thomas R. Detwyler and Melvin G. Marcus's *Urbanization and Environment* (CH, Feb'73) and Brian J.L. Berry and Frank E. Horton's *Urban Environmental Management* (1974). White's lively prose is well supported by maps, diagrams, and tables. Highly recommended for upper-division undergraduate and graduate students and for urbanists, environmental scientists, microclimatologists, and planners.—*P. O. Muller, University of Miami*

OAB-2184   HQ1587   92-45709 CIP
Wiesner, Merry E. **Women and gender in early modern Europe.** Cambridge, 1993. 264p index ISBN 0-521-38459-1, $49.95; ISBN 0-521-38613-6 pbk, $14.95

Wiesner, well known for her numerous studies of early modern German women, has written a clear and stimulating textbook that introduces undergraduates and general readers to the topic of early modern European women and to the extensive literature available in English on various dimensions of their lives. Organized around the categories of body, mind, and spirit, the book includes discussions of male ideas about women, the female life cycle, women's economic role, literacy, women's role in the creation of culture, religion, witchcraft, and the relationship between gender and power, and reflects an impressive understanding of recent scholarship. Wiesner's command of this scholarship and the clarity of her analysis make this the best single volume on the topic. Although she analyzes women's role within the historical developments that traditionally have defined early modern Europe and shows the effects of these developments on women, Wiesner also explores women's private and domestic experiences and the period's gendered division between public and private power. Extensive bibliographies follow each chapter.—*J. Harrie, California State University, Bakersfield*

OAB-2185   D523   94-44586 CIP
Winter, Jay. **Sites of memory, sites of mourning: the Great War in European cultural history.** Cambridge, 1995. 310p bibl index ISBN 0-521-49682-9, $29.95

Winter has devoted his professional career to studying WW I and has written or edited four well-received volumes on its sociopolitical aspects. In this book, he analyzes the war's cultural legacy. *Sites of Memory* is an engaging, even compelling, exploration of the comparative impact of "mass death" on European culture. One of the book's strengths lies in Winter's methodological approach; he compares the processes of bereavement and commemoration among Britons, French, and Germans, and presents the cultural significance of WW I as a combination of the traditional and modern, rather than as a "great divide" between the two cultures. Winter also uses poignant episodes on spiritualism, commemoration, and the visual arts to demonstrate the ruptures and continuities in the healing process. Although the theme of commemoration and national identity has been explored recently in *Commemorations*, ed. by John Gillis (1994), and in George Mosse's *Fallen Soldiers* (CH, Oct'90), Winter's is a more nuanced study of the meaning of death and consolation. An erudite piece of scholarship that will certainly set the standard for future studies of its kind, this book is essential reading for anyone interested in the cultural history of the Great War. General readers; upper-division undergraduates and above.—*M. Shevin-Coetzee, George Washington University*

OAB-2186   D804   92-40888 CIP
Young, James E. **The texture of memory: Holocaust memorials and meaning.** Yale, 1993. 398p bibl index afp ISBN 0-300-05383-5, $35.00

Unlike other Holocaust studies that too often dwell on the horrific assault made on the Jews during the 1930s and '40s, Young's book examines the spatial and architectural rendering of post-WW II Holocaust memorials and monuments. The why and where of such "documents of public remembrance" are amply discussed, analyzed, and critiqued. Young has traveled widely, visiting Holocaust memorial sites and monuments in Germany, Austria, Czechoslovakia, and Poland, as well as in Israel and the US. Each site is evaluated aesthetically and is assessed with the care of an art critic. Above all, Young is sensitive to the social and political pressures that dictate how a city or a nation wishes to remember/immortalize a deed—the Holocaust—that over time has become in danger of being dropped from public consciousness, or has come under attack by so-called historical revisionists. These monuments testify both to humanity's inhumanity and to the regeneration and potential rehabilitation of the human spirit. Young's prose is clear, expressive, and dispassionate. The book is abundantly illustrated, well documented, and offers a broad Holocaust bibliography, including basic historical as well as art and architectural studies. All levels.—*B. Rothaus, University of Northern Colorado*

OAB-2187   HQ1181   92-28707 CIP
Zinsser, Judith P. **History & feminism: a glass half full.** Twayne, 1993. 204p index afp ISBN 0-8057-9751-3, $26.95; ISBN 0-8057-9766-1 pbk, $14.95

Zinsser adds a critical feminist perspective to the growing number of works

that attempt to document the history of history. She begins by describing efforts to alter the very substance, content, and definition of history, tracing the change from the movement to acknowledge women's experience (frequently referred to in women's history circles as the "add women and stir" method) to the more radical struggle to champion a reconceptualization and redefinition the very meaning of historical events and historical actors. In the second part of the book, Zinsser highlights the battles of women historians first to gain admittance to and ultimately to change the historical profession. This book should be required reading for academics across all gender and disciplinary lines. Zinsser neatly lays to rest the cherished myths of ungendered historical objectivity through her accounts of the struggles of feminist scholars to overcome the overt and covert sexism that dominated (and in certain instances still holds sway over) both the writing of history and the community of professional historians. Recommended for all academic library collections. All levels.—*E. Broidy, University of California, Irvine*

■ Ancient & Medieval

OAB-2188   D200   92-43925 CIP
Bartlett, Robert. **The making of Europe: conquest, colonization and cultural change, 950-1350.** Princeton, 1993. 432p bibl index ISBN 0-691-03298-X, $29.95

The famous archaeologist Mortimer Wheeler once wrote an instructive book, *Rome Beyond the Imperial Frontiers* (1955). Bartlett's extremely intelligent, readable, and comprehensive book might well be called "Medieval Europe Beyond the Hegemonic Frontiers." Bartlett assembles case studies, quantitative data, and apt quotes and anecdotes to tell the story of the expansion of Europe in the High Middle Ages. He shows the striking similarities and the differences between political, demographic, and sociocultural imperialism (and assimilation), as Christians extended their sway into Moslem Spain, the eastern Mediterranean, East Germany and the Baltic, and the Celtic fringes of the British Isles. Bartlett assesses the different factors and aspects of this movement: immigration; urban freedom; cereal agriculture; the diffusion of military technology; the spread of coins and charters; the cultivation of racism; and other institutions, strategies, and behaviors. The book is clearly written, well illustrated, and documented. In its wide range of examples and ease of comparison it is reminiscent of Marc Bloch's *Feudal Society* (1961); higher praise cannot be given in a short review. General; advanced undergraduate; graduate; faculty.—*J. T. Rosenthal, SUNY at Stony Brook*

OAB-2189   Orig
Bremen, Riet van. **The limits of participation: women and civic life in the Greek East in the Hellenistic and Roman periods.** J.C. Gieben, 1996. 399p bibl indexes (Dutch monographs on ancient history and archaeology, 15) ISBN 90-5063-567-9, $97.00

Van Bremen's study illuminates the complex picture of the status of women in antiquity and is a provocative supplement to such scholarship as Sarah Pomeroy's *Women in Hellenistic Egypt* (CH, May'85). Van Bremen questions theories (e.g., civil decadence; the nature of magistracies accessible to women; women's wealth in economically stressed Greek cities; greater political freedom and power for women) to explain women's increasingly prominent position in public life during the Hellenistic and Roman periods in the Greek East. The author argues that with a changing civic ideology after the second century BCE, individuals indentified themselves more with their families than with their public roles as citizens. Elite families were determined to maintain public visibility; women, like men, could continue family traditions of prominence in public life. Van Bremen sees a paradox in the increase in status and opportunity for women that was accompanied by greater emphasis on the association of women with the family. Invaluable to the ancient historian and classicist, but useful in any study of women in elite families. Ample documentation of evidence adds to the value of the book, as does the extensive bibliography. Upper-division undergraduates and above.—*J. de Luce, Miami University*

OAB-2190   HQ1130   95-30650 MARC

Brosius, Maria. **Women in ancient Persia, 559-331 BC.** Oxford, 1996. 258p bibl indexes afp ISBN 0-19-815009-1, $65.00

Brosius presents a thoughtful and illuminating examination of the status and influence of royal and nonroyal women in the first Persian Empire (559-331 BCE). She does not exaggerate in claiming that this is the first attempt to look seriously at these women from a new perspective. Even without her careful conclusions, the book provides an invaluable demonstration of intelligent and creative scholarship free of any unreflective acceptance of ancient or modern assumptions about Persian women. Brosius argues persuasively that the sensationalistic representations of women in the Greek sources derive in part from the political hostility between Greece and Persia, but also from Greek assumptions about the proper behavior of women. According to the author, to understand these women one must look carefully at the "historiographic and narrative pattern" within which any particular account of them appears. Brosius bases her examination on Persepolis Fortification texts, which provide complex portraits of these women. The specificity of her evidence, including linguistic evidence, is especially helpful, as is the extensive bibliography and the index of ancient sources. Upper-division undergraduates and above.—*J. de Luce, Miami University*

OAB-2191   GN805   93-19539 CIP

Burl, Aubrey. **From Carnac to Callanish: the prehistoric stone rows and avenues of Britain, Ireland and Brittany.** Yale, 1994 (c1993). 286p bibl index ISBN 0-300-05575-7, $45.00

Burl, author of *Prehistoric Avebury* (CH, Dec'79), has successfully tackled, in elegant prose, elaborate detail, and careful illustration, one of the most neglected features of prehistoric Europe—the more than 1,033 rows of standing stones scattered from Brittany, through southern, western, and offshore Britain, to ancient Ireland. Single rows, double rows (sometimes stretching for miles), bordered processional avenues leading to circular henge monuments, short rows of three or four uprights, and mere pairs, are all described. These are tentatively dated between 3300 and 1000 BCE, and interpreted in their original Neolithic or Bronze Age context as well as in their subsequent historical record. All the examples are cataloged in the concluding Gazetteer, and many are discussed in Burl's graceful text. One stone may have stood 67 feet high. The lines now standing are the work of generations. Burl is rather condescending when discussing the medieval reactions to these constructions, but even he admits that their major desecration and destruction occurred after 1600. This is the first study of these astounding stone wonders, and it will be absolutely necessary for adventuresome travelers, inquiring students, and serious scholars. Prehistory at its best. All levels.—*E. J. Kealey, College of the Holy Cross*

OAB-2192   DF251   95-7098 CIP

Cargill, Jack. **Athenian settlements of the fourth century B.C..** E.J. Brill, 1995. 487p bibl index afp (Mnemosyne, bibliotheca classica Batava. Supplementum, 145) ISBN 90-04-09991-3, $143.00

Colonization and overseas settlement are phenomena usually associated with the Archaic and Hellenistic periods of Greek history. For that reason alone, a large-scale study of fourth century BCE colonization represents a significant contribution to contemporary Greek historiography. Cargill has done much more than that, however. This is a comprehensive study of every aspect of Athenian colonial activity, between the foundation of the Second Athenian League and the death of Alexander the Great. In three dense but clearly written chapters Cargill establishes the chronological framework for the history of Athenian colonization, analyzes the evidence for the identity of the colonists, and reconstructs the institutional organization of all known Athenian colonies and settlements. In two long appendixes, Cargill offers new suggestions for the solution of textual problems in numerous inscriptions concerning Athenian colonization, and a complete annotated list of all known Athenian colonists. A major contribution to the history of late classical Athens and the essential starting point for all future research on fourth century BCE colonization. Upper-division undergraduates and above.—*S. M. Burstein, California State University, Los Angeles*

OAB-2193   KL4115   95-45184 CIP

Cohen, David. **Law, violence, and community in classical Athens.** Cambridge, 1995. 214p bibl index ISBN 0-521-38167-3, $54.95; ISBN 0-521-38837-6 pbk, $18.95

Cohen has written an original and illuminating study of an old and much studied topic: Athenian law. Most works on Athenian law are strongly positivistic; they describe the legal system, identify types of offenses recognized by the law, and explain various legal remedies provided by it. Cohen's unique contribution is to treat Athenian law as an ideology and to analyze its function in Athenian society. In eight lucidly written chapters he convincingly argues that often the Athenian legal system did not and was not expected to resolve disputes so much as to offer Athenians a structured and relatively nonviolent arena within which they could pursue their personal feuds. Particularly illuminating are his analyses of the rhetoric of Athenian speeches, in which he is able to identify the orators' beliefs concerning the ideological expectations of Athenian jurors, even in instances where the outcome of the individual cases is unknown. Although marred by minor flaws, such as the author's tendency to adduce ethnographic parallels of sometimes limited relevance, this is an excellent work that deserves to be read by all students of Greek social and legal history. Upper-division undergraduates and above.—*S. M. Burstein, California State University, Los Angeles*

OAB-2194   DG82   96-868 CIP

Corbeill, Anthony. **Controlling laughter: political humor in the late Roman Republic.** Princeton, 1996. 251p bibl index afp ISBN 0-691-02739-0, $35.00

History, philology, onomastics, and anthropology come together in this remarkable work. It starts from a Freudian premise: an opponent can be diminished by humor "to which the third person, who has made no efforts, bears witness by his laughter." But the "third person" can be a construct, a representative of the views and values of the society as a whole. And so Corbeill does two things no one has done before: he takes the gibes and jokes of Cicero et al. seriously, and he uses them as a guide to essential features of Roman culture. His argument is supported by an analysis of Roman cognomens, most of which are pejorative, e.g., Brutus=Stupid. It is astonishing that this aspect of Roman culture has never been studied, not even by I. Kajanto in *The Latin Cognomina* (Helsinki, 1965). Other chapters examine the genre of invective, and attacks on appearance, effeminacy, and feasting. The Second Philippic, already much admired in antiquity, emerges as the great document of these values. Originality and lucidity recommend the book, and an exhaustive index of sources increases its usefulness. All students of Cicero and the Late Republic will learn much from this fine work. Highly recommended.—*R. I. Frank, University of California, Irvine*

OAB-2195   DF220   93-2666 CIP

Dickinson, Oliver. **The Aegean Bronze Age.** Cambridge, 1994. 342p bibl index ISBN 0-521-24280-0, $64.95; ISBN 0-521-45664-9 pbk, $27.95

Dickinson's balanced and sensible book fills the need for a general treatment of the Aegean Bronze Age that takes into account new findings and advances in archaeological theory. Arranged topically, the book covers terminology and chronology; natural environment and resources; first human populations; settlement and economy; arts and crafts (including pottery, nonceramic vessels, furniture, architecture, frescoes, figures, jewelry and other ornaments, seals, writing, weapons, and armor); burial customs; trade, exchange, and overseas contacts; and religion. A brief historical overview concludes the volume. Within each topical section, the discussion is arranged chronologically and by area (Crete, Cyclades, and mainland). The topical approach allows for discussion of all aspects of society, but it decontextualizes the artifacts and does not present a picture of life in any area at any time. Dickinson (Univ. of Durham, UK) is clear, sound on details, and up on new findings, and he does not display idiosyncrasies or rancor, even when discussing hotly debated issues. Excellent plans, drawings, and bibliography. This book is excellent for nonspecialists and undergraduate students (although not as an introductory text), and it is a useful reference for scholars. An absolute must for all libraries—if limited to only one book on the Bronze Age cultures of Greece, it should be this one.—*L. P. Day, Wabash College*

OAB-2196   Orig
Fitton, J. Lesley. **The discovery of the Greek Bronze Age.** Harvard, 1996 (c1995). 212p bibl index ISBN 0-674-21188-X, $29.95

It is now 125 years since the first spade began to unearth Greece's pre-classical past. The story of the rediscovery of the Greek Bronze Age is not a new topic, yet Fitton brings to the subject an interest in the intellectual mile-stones, historical circumstances, and confluence of disciplines that brought it about. The result is not simply a chronicle of discoveries and discoverers but also a lucid survey of changing methods of study and the creation of an increasingly nuanced picture of early Greece. The archaeological pioneers Heinrich Schliemann and Arthur Evans figure prominently in this personality-driven account, from the times of their excavations through the subsequent unfolding of such major controversies as the historicity of the Trojan War and the debt of Mycenaean to Minoan culture. Although well written and well illustrated, the book does not replace William A. McDonald's *Progress into the Past: The Rediscovery of Mycenaean Civilization* (1967). Rather, by including developments in the Cycladic islands and on Minoan Crete the book offers a complementary, and in some ways more contemporary, overview. All levels.—*S. Langdon, University of Missouri—Columbia*

OAB-2197   DK73   95-49326 CIP
Franklin, Simon. **The emergence of Rus, 750-1200,** by Simon Franklin and Jonathan Shepard. Longman, 1996. 450p bibl index ISBN 0-582-49090-1, $65.58; ISBN 0-582-49091-X pbk, $26.85

The British authors of this work are noted scholars in their own right; here they draw an impressive body of previous scholarship into a readable and reliable picture of the early development of "the land of the Rus." (The term "Russia" refers properly to something much more modern.) Their approach is roughly chronological, moving smoothly from the age of Scandinavian adventurers in the lands of numerous other peoples (Slavs, Balts, Finno-Ugrian, Turkic), through the establishment of Kiev as a political, religious, social, and economic center, and into the period when an expanded land of Rus under a Christian dynasty dominated by a single Slavonic culture encompassed centers in the north, west, south, and east. Franklin and Shepard provide a superb treatment that combines literary evidence, such as the Russian Primary Chronicle, with other written materials (birchbark letters) and makes effective use of the extensive archaeological evidence. Those familiar with older, traditional treatment of early "Russian" history will appreciate what a masterly and fresh synthesis this is. Those who come to the subject with little background will find the book clear and engaging. Maps and genealogies effectively complement the text. This work is sure to become a standard treatment for the period. All levels.—*P. W. Knoll, University of Southern California*

OAB-2198   DT154   96-21424 CIP
Haas, Christopher. **Alexandria in late antiquity: topography and social conflict.** Johns Hopkins, 1997. 494p index afp ISBN 0-8018-5377-X, $45.00

Haas's delightful study focuses in depth on the important eastern port and city of Alexandria during the period from the Emperor Diocletian to the Arab conquest (285-642 CE). Set broadly on a backdrop of roads, gates, buildings, temples, and churches, this well-written monograph thoroughly explores the early and late periods of Alexandria's transition from Roman pagan to Byzantine Christian, with great attention to the society and its religions—paganism, Judaism, Christianity, and Islam—and the riots that occurred among the disparate groups and factions of Christianity. Through this holistic approach, Haas offers a vital description of a key center in late antiquity and a model investigation for students and scholars. Replete with illustrations and maps, and supported by extensive notes, Haas's work far surpasses earlier studies of major cities such as Con-

stantinople, Ephesus, and Antioch. The richness of this study rests firmly on extensive analysis of primary documents and on archaeological evidence; the study often goes well beyond Alexandria and into eastern Mediterranean problems. All levels.—*J. M. Balcer, Ohio State University*

OAB-2199   HQ792   92-45682 CIP
Hanawalt, Barbara A. **Growing up in medieval London: the experience of childhood in history.** Oxford, 1993. 300p bibl index afp ISBN 0-19-508405-5, $27.50

Hanawalt (Univ. of Minnesota) has an established reputation as a social historian, based most notably on *The Ties That Bound: Peasant Families in Medieval England* (CH, Jul'86). In her most recent book, Hanawalt has used the surviving legal, administrative, and literary records of late-medieval London in creative ways to bring historical clarity to the subject of childhood. The material environment of London life is the setting for a discussion of the chronology of childhood: birth and the consequent establishment of family and social connections; early childhood and its social and educational activities; later childhood with its widening social and educational horizons; and adolescence (for which medievals did not have a word, although they clearly appreciated the developmental stage) as a final period of varying length before entry into adulthood. Hanawalt also discusses such subjects as London orphans and their experiences; the training of children through apprenticeship and the relationships of masters and apprentices; and the entry of children into positions as servants. This is an important book, a learned contribution to social history, and a microcosmic complement to Shulamith Shahar's *Childhood in the Middle Ages* (CH, Jul'90). Artist's illustrations, extensive notes, interspersed creative stories. All levels.—*A. C. Reeves, Ohio University*

OAB-2200   DG312   94-25064 CIP
Harries, Jill. **Sidonius Apollinaris and the fall of Rome, AD 407-485.** Oxford, 1995 (c1994). 292p bibl index afp ISBN 0-19-814472-5, $47.00

In 455 a Gallic nobleman seized the Roman throne. Soon after, his friend and relative, Sidonius Apollinaris, came to the capital and by 468, Sidonius had risen to the top of the civil service. But the Empire was collapsing; in 470 Sidonius returned to Gaul, accepted the post of bishop of Clermont, and played a leading role in shaping a new society under Gothic rule. He and his fellow aristocrats succeeded in maintaining a remarkable degree of continuity in social structure and culture; his extensive writings are a major source for this transition. Harries (St. Andrews Univ.) has written the first study of Sidonius since the 1933 biography by C.E. Stevens. Solidly based on the sources, it is a genuine synthesis and interpretation of the period. Extensive footnotes and a splendid bibliography make the book doubly useful to any student pursuing research in the field. A lucid, comprehensive, and thoughtful work. Highly recommended, both undergraduate and graduate levels.—*R. I. Frank, University of California, Irvine*

OAB-2201   BX2595   92-21141 CIP
Harvey, Barbara. **Living and dying in England, 1100-1540: the monastic experience.** Oxford, 1993. 291p bibl index afp ISBN 0-19-820161-3, $44.00

Originally delivered as the 1989 Ford Lectures at Oxford, this book tells readers everything they may ever want to know about the Benedictine monks of the medieval-early modern Westminster Abbey. In six crisply written chapters Harvey (Oxford Univ.), author of *Monastic Dress in the Middle Ages: Precept and Practice* (Canterbury, 1988), deals with monastic charity, diet, illness and treatment, mortality, servants, and corrodies (pensions made up in large measure of benefits in kind). Five appendixes specifically treat charitable giving; catering; apothecaries, physicians, and surgeons; life expectancy; and corrodians. Harvey's work supplements and corrects D. Knowles and R.N. Haddock's *Medieval Religious Houses, England and Wales* (1972). It is an example of the minute, meticulous sort of manuscript research being done by the present generation of historians on specific institutions, such as Westminster Abbey, that sheds light not only on the Abbey monks but also on the whole monastic experience and even, at times, on secular life. List of abbreviations; nine figures; two maps; eight tables; five appendixes. Advanced undergraduates and above.—*M. J. Tucker, SUNY at Buffalo*

OAB-2202 DF228 94-1250 CIP
Henry, Madeleine M. **Prisoner of history: Aspasia of Miletus and her biographical tradition.** Oxford, 1995. 201p bibl index afp ISBN 0-19-508712-7, $29.95

The names of relatively few women living in Athens in the fifth century BCE are known; of them, Aspasia—courtesan, companion of Pericles, teacher of Socrates—may be the most famous. Henry's book is the first to examine Aspasia by considering how various sources have constructed her life. The book not only makes a welcome and significant contribution to the study of this particular woman, but Henry also contributes to a better understanding of the social and political culture of fifth-century Athens and women's positions in it. She challenges readers to consider not only how to tell a woman's life, but how the *bios* of Aspasia in particular has been constructed and reconstructed in classical and post-classical times, and to what end. Henry's analysis is rigorous and subtle; her examination of the original sources is meticulous. The extensive and sophisticated bibliography will prove as valuable to the specialist as the argument of the book itself. Upper-division undergraduates and above.—*J. de Luce, Miami University*

OAB-2203 DG63 93-11279 CIP
Holloway, R. Ross. **The archaeology of early Rome and Latium.** Routledge, 1994. 203p index ISBN 0-415-08065-7, $49.95

Holloway's book fills a gap in the English-language literature on early Rome in two important ways. First, it provides an overview of recent and ongoing excavations of sites and (less thoroughly) of new approaches to the archaeology of the area. Second, Holloway usefully presents the evidence in the context of major discoveries and controversies of the past century. The book is created as a guide, and so is less a synthesis than other recent books on early Italy, such as Massimo Pallottino's *A History of Earliest Italy* (CH, Jul'91). Holloway does not delve into new theoretical work on the goals of archaeology or the potential for material culture to illuminate complex social constructs. His is a sound, fairly traditional, evidence-based presentation of findings. The main text offers an invaluable summary of recent discoveries from temples, tombs, and houses, and from specific sites that have produced significant material culture in the past quarter century. The introduction and conclusion explicate the history of early Roman archaeology and draw up-to-date conclusions about the history of Latium in the ninth through seventh centuries BCE. The work is well illustrated, with a useful basic bibliography and extensive footnotes. Upper-division undergraduates and above.—*S. Brown, University of Southern California*

OAB-2204 HQ1147 95-31506 CIP
Jochens, Jenny. **Women in Old Norse society.** Cornell, 1996 (c1995). 266p bibl index afp ISBN 0-8014-3165-4, $39.95

Most scholars interested in the European Middle Ages would have been thankful to Jochens if she had simply provided a survey of women's lives in medieval Iceland and Norway, because very little is available in English. She has certainly done that, discussing such issues as marriage, reproduction, leisure, and work from the late ninth to the middle of the 13th century. She has done much more, however; the book also provides sophisticated analyses of cultural interactions (e.g., Jochens's analysis of the pagan-Christian transition in gendered terms will be very useful for scholars of the spread of Christianity in other times and places) and presents fascinating new information. Among the latter is her investigation of the use of homespun cloth and coats (made by women) as a measure of value in Iceland and an item of trade for Icelandic men in their ventures beyond the island. One's view of "Vikings" does not often include their role as dealers in shaggy coats that became a fashion rage. Jochens's study is a model of interdisciplinary techniques and research; she carefully describes her sources—largely laws and sagas of various types—and their

limitations, and then draws from them information, such as the etymology of key words ("wife," "husband"), possible only for a linguistic scholar of her caliber. All levels.—*M. E. Wiesner, University of Wisconsin—Milwaukee*

OAB-2205 D202 95-26684 CIP
Jordan, William Chester. **The Great Famine: northern Europe in the early fourteenth century.** Princeton, 1996. 317p bibl index afp ISBN 0-691-01134-6, $29.95

The Great Famine that ravaged Europe from 1315 to 1322 has been overshadowed in historical scholarship by the more deadly Black Death that followed it in 1348. In this important new synthesis of the causes, course, and consequences of the Great Famine, Jordan offers a corrective to the view that after its initial crippling effects, famine continued to afflict Europe until the ultimate devastation of the Black Death. Using contemporary sources and an impressive number of regional studies, he analyzes the complex interaction of social and environmental factors that caused the famine and structured its effects. The result is a richly detailed cultural history that considers significant regional variations and stresses the event's human dimension, including its manifold and different effects in rural and urban contexts and on people of differing age, status, and power. Jordan argues that Europe's economy quickly recovered from the famine, leaving, however, a legacy of physical susceptibility and social instability. This will become the standard work on the subject. Highly recommended. Upper-division undergraduates and above.—*J. Harrie, California State University, Bakersfield*

OAB-2206 DG260 91-40530 CIP
Keaveney, Arthur. **Lucullus: a life.** Routledge, 1992. 275p bibl index ISBN 0-415-03219-9, $59.95

Keaveney's new biography develops directly from his work *Sulla, the Last Republican* (CH, Feb'84). Keaveney (Univ. of Kent) paints Lucullus as a talented and sophisticated philhellene, whose mild-mannered approach to politics was out of keeping with the requirements of his age. A creation of Sulla, Lucullus nevertheless lacked his mentor's ruthlessness. Keaveney argues that Lucullus was a more-than-adequate military commander, whose fair but firm provincial rule brought him enemies among the *publicani* (tax collectors) and whose lenient policies on campaign frustrated his soldiers. He assigns ultimate blame for Lucullus' undeserved reputation for luxury in his retirement years to Cicero and Plutarch. Keaveney approaches his sources critically and is not hesitant to challenge long-held interpretations of events and personalities. His obvious admiration for Lucullus, however, at times gets the better of him; he seems consistently too ready to place the best interpretation on Lucullus' motivations and actions. Fully documented, clearly written, and forcefully argued, Keaveney's controversial biography, the only one in English, will interest students and scholars alike. General; undergraduate; graduate; faculty.—*R. I. Curtis, University of Georgia*

OAB-2207 HF3520 94-8396 CIP
Kowaleski, Maryanne. **Local markets and regional trade in medieval Exeter.** Cambridge, 1995. 442p bibl index ISBN 0-521-33371-7, $69.95

In this book Kowaleski attempts to redress the overemphasis of traditional economic historians on long-distance overseas trade when measuring the extent of economic activity and commercialization in premodern societies. Using a prosopographical approach (collective biographies), Kowaleski opens up a complex world of buying and selling in late-medieval Devon and Exeter. To explain adequately Exeter's prosperity and growth even as other ports and regions declined, she carefully maps the economic adaptations and business interactions within local markets. Flexible agriculture, diverse animal husbandry, resurgent metal industries, new fairs, legal and financial incentives, and successful distribution systems all contributed to a highly developed and immensely utilitarian regional network of exchange centered on wine, fish, cloth-finishing, and animal products. Kowaleski's insights into shifting social structures and political affiliations within Exeter help explain the crucial role the city played in channeling goods to and from the hinterland. The scholarship is meticulous, the sources multiple and vast, the writing superb, and the explanations convincing. Upper-division undergraduates and above.—*B. Lowe, Florida Atlantic University*

OAB-2208   DF85   93-30357 CIP
Malkin, Irad. **Myth and territory in the Spartan Mediterranean.** Cambridge, 1994. 278p bibl index ISBN 0-521-41183-1, $59.95

In this extraordinarily well researched and well written book based largely on the *mentalité* approach to historical understanding, Malkin seeks to re-create the "attitude" of the ancients to a nexus of events related to colonization, the Dorian invasion, and Spartan involvement in colonization. Not everyone will agree with his interpretation of an extraordinarily rich variety of sources, but the gathering and ordering of these sources is an impressive scholarly tour de force. Malkin's earlier work focused on religion, cult, and colonization, and he brings all of this to bear as he explores, for example, Spartan involvement in the Sparta-Thera-Cyrene chain of connection. This rich study makes readers continue to reconsider Sparta and its involvement in the process of colonization. Malkin's answer to the question of why Sparta was not among the traditional mother cities is that it had finished its colonization before the first Messenian War. Upper-division undergraduates and above.—*J. Fischer, Wabash College*

OAB-2209   JC75   93-15653 CIP
McGlew, James F. **Tyranny and political culture in ancient Greece.** Cornell, 1993. 234p bibl index afp ISBN 0-8014-2787-8, $31.50

Why were tyrants included among the Seven Sages? By what paradoxical twist of history did Peisistratos, Athenian *tyran extraordinaire*, not only lay the foundations of democratic Periclean Athens (drama included), but also leave the memory of his reign—despite philosophical and political rant against tyranny in all its aspects—as a Golden Age? These are among the fundamental questions that McGlew sets out to solve in his brilliant and groundbreaking monograph. He has clearly learned a lot from the French structuralists: although McGlew does not actually talk about *langue* and *parole* in a key chapter on justice and power, the concepts figure prominently in his analysis. Tyrants emphasized their attachment to justice (*diké*): in McGlew's book they believed their own propaganda. The notion that by exercising tyrannical power, by ruling the city "as though it were his personal possession," a *tyrannos* both claimed special freedom (*eleutheria*) and reduced his fellow citizens to the status of slaves, thus creating in them the unity that let them cut off the head that dominated them. This in itself is not an entirely new idea, but McGlew develops it with wit, passion, and originality. Compulsively readable; exhaustive bibliography. General readers; advanced undergraduates, and above.—*P. M. Green, University of Texas at Austin*

OAB-2210   DS155   92-29738 CIP
Mitchell, Stephen. **Anatolia: land, men, and Gods in Asia Minor. v.1: The Celts in Anatolia and the impact of Roman rule; v.2: The rise of the church.** Oxford, 1994 (c1993). 2v. 266, 200p indexes afp ISBN 0-19-814080-0, v.1, $69.00; ISBN 0-19-814933-6, v.2, $60.00

Mitchell's excellent 2-volume work aptly fills important needs for the study of Anatolia from the early Hellenistic period into the height of the Byzantine period ten centuries later. Volume 1 discusses in great detail the political course of Anatolia from the early Hellenistic period to the zenith of the Roman Empire. Mitchell first considers the Celtic period and then the period of Roman occupation. Studies in culture, religion, slaves, languages, towns, and rural life are very well presented. Maps and photographs accompany the text. Volume 2 covers the development of the church in Anatolia from Paul to the eighth century CE in juxtaposition with paganism, Judaism, and rival Christian groups, and, in turn, with imperial concern about the early church. This volume, however, does not offer a detailed political history for the period. The writing is clear and often exciting, the arguments sound, and the supporting evidence more than ample. Several indexes provide excellent cross-access. Mitchell's study will remain standard for many decades. Undergraduates and above.— *J. M. Balcer, Ohio State University*

OAB-2211   DS69   93-40752 CIP
Moorey, P.R.S. **Ancient Mesopotamian materials and industries: the archaeological evidence.** Oxford, 1994. 414p bibl index afp ISBN 0-19-814921-2, $105.00

Moorey's study breaks new ground in its analysis of the archaeological evidence for materials and industries in ancient Mesopotamia, c.8000-300 BCE, and this unique volume will remain basic for decades to come. This is the first systematic attempt to survey in detail the crafts and craftsmanship of the Sumerians, Babylonians, and Assyrians of ancient Mesopotamia. By topic (stoneworking crafts; bone, ivory, and shell; ceramics and glass; metals; and building crafts), Moorey sets out in extensive detail the evidence from site to site; each within its own topic in chronological order. Photographs, charts, drawings, and maps enable the reader to plot out the materials carefully. An extensive bibliography accompanies the numerous notes that document each craft and object. It is a slow, methodical read, which will offer to advanced students and scholars of the ancient Near East a clear investigation of materials heretofore scattered throughout numerous journals and site reports. Upper-division undergraduate and graduate libraries that specialize in this region for this period will highly value this addition to their collections.—*J. M. Balcer, Ohio State University*

OAB-2212   DA229   94-31086 CIP
Parsons, John Carmi. **Eleanor of Castile: queen and society in thirteenth-century England.** St. Martin's, 1995. 364p bibl index ISBN 0-312-08649-0, $49.95

Parsons's study may be the best scholarly treatment of a medieval English queen yet written. Parsons looks at both Eleanor's role in 13th-century society and culture, and at *how* the myth of "good queen Eleanor" came to be constructed. In her 13th-century context, Eleanor emerges as a woman of intellectual interests, one with a keen appreciation for the use of network-building and a faithful retinue, a loyal and fertile wife, and a zealous seeker after land, wealth, and the power and status they connoted. After her death in 1290, perception of Eleanor had its ups and downs: the revered figure for whom Edward I built the famous Eleanor Crosses, the foreign she-devil of George Peele's *King Edward the First* (1593), and the saintly figure depicted in (and created by) Agnes Strickland's Victorian *Lives of the Queens of England from the Norman Conquest* (1840). Parsons has been writing about Eleanor for more than a decade; many of his trenchant findings about her insatiable quest for property, her match-making at court, and her elusive trail in her husband's counsels are no longer a surprise. His final comments on gender and the state are an appropriate conclusion to this short but definitive study. All levels.—*J. T. Rosenthal, SUNY at Stony Brook*

OAB-2213   DS73   91-33767 CIP
Postgate, J.N. **Early Mesopotamia: society and economy at the dawn of history.** Routledge, 1992. 367p bibl index afp ISBN 0-415-00843-3, $65.00

Postgate has written the finest available introduction to the ancient world of Mesopotamia. The author is an acknowledged specialist who commands knowledge of both the written texts and the archaeological detail. The book is a narrative history of Mesopotamia that begins around 3300 BCE and ends c.1700 BCE. The first chapter describes the environmental and ecological conditions that characterized Mesopotamia in both the past and the present. Subsequent chapters elucidate the changing social history of the principal institutions, making use of both the archaeological record and more than 100 ancient texts. The nature of the Mesopotamian city and its relations with the surrounding countryside and the characteristics of the temple and the emergence of kingship, as well as the features of both household and kinship, are rendered splendidly. Postgate successfully accomplishes what few others have achieved, namely, a narrative depiction of the lifeways of the peoples of early Mesopotamia: their law, warfare, crafts, trade, technological achievements, and their political and religious ideologies. The text is handsomely illustrated with more than 100 illustrations and a most useful bibiliography. Essential reading for all interested in the ancient past. General; undergraduate; graduate.—*C. C. Lamberg-Karlovsky, Harvard University*

OAB-2214 DA60 95-36142 CIP
Prestwich, Michael. **Armies and warfare in the Middle Ages: the English experience.** Yale, 1996. 396p bibl index ISBN 0-300-06452-7, $37.50

Armies and Warfare is a well-researched and well-conceived examination of the English military experience, largely in the 13th and 14th centuries. It is very strong on numbers and costs (both high), good on strategy, intelligence, and logistics (all sophisticated), sieges (which "dominated medieval warfare in a way that battle never did"), the navy, and finances. Battle tactics are well explained and chivalry is deromanticized. Prestwich (Univ. of Durham) is confused on military obligation, weak on the pre-12th century, and too frequently uses the misleading adjective "feudal," e.g., "In addition to royal ships, the Crown could count on the naval equivalent of feudal service, owed by the Cinque Ports ...." *Milites* should be "soldiers" in military context but "knights" for social history; "mercenary" requires a satisfactory definition; "mounted archers" are bowmen with horses; and Hardy's impossible rates of arrow fire must be firmly rejected. Anecdotal evidence, even if based on trial evidence, cannot be used to prove system failure. Most important, however, Prestwich effectively demonstrates that early modernists must abandon the "Military Revolution" now that they have the essentials of later medieval military history. A magisterial work by one of England's leading historians. All levels.—*B. S. Bachrach, University of Minnesota*

OAB-2215 DP94 95-50447 CIP
Richardson, J.S. **The Romans in Spain.** Blackwell, 1996. 341p bibl index ISBN 0-631-17706-X, $74.95

A solid combination of established scholarship (Blásquez, Étienne, and Mayet) and recent publications in archaeology (de Alarcão, Curchin, Sillières), numismatics (Crawford), epigraphy (Vives), and in many other specialist historical studies provides the foundation for this readable and informative general history of Spain from 237 BCE to 409 CE. Richardson is clearly aware that although he is writing *Spanish* history, his focus must nevertheless (because of the evidence) be primarily on the Romans who ruled Spain. He assumes no familiarity with Roman history in his readers, but background summaries are brief and touch only those matters important for understanding the forces driving events in Spain. The discussion is chronological; both political history and the cultural and social effects of the Roman domination of Spain are treated. The scholarly documentation is discreet but extensive. The later empire and early Christianity left the deepest marks on Spain, and Richardson illuminates this process with real skill. Each chapter has a very useful bibliographic essay. An essential tool for anyone studying Spain, whether in relation to the Roman empire or to European history as a whole. General readers; upper-division undergraduates and above.—*C. M. C. Green, University of Iowa*

OAB-2216 DG63 90-43070 CIP
Ridley, Ronald T. **The eagle and the spade: archaeology in Rome during the Napoleonic era.** Cambridge, 1992. 328p bibl index ISBN 0-521-40191-7, $79.50

Although concerned with a brief period (1809-1814) this book is not narrow in its scope. Examining previously unused archives, Ridley clearly demonstrates the crucial role that the Napoleonic commissions played in preserving the remains of antiquity in what was the first systematic archaeological program for the city of Rome. Most of the major monuments were involved; a convenient year-by-year account is found in Appendix 1. Ridley places the program in context with a preliminary survey of the "protection and destruction" of classical Rome before 1809, and with an account at the end of the archaeological activity for the rest of the century. Extensive illustrations from contemporary drawings, often unique, visually document a "before and after" aspect of the endeavor. Loaded with precise information, the book is also written in an interesting and readable style. Indispensable for all concerned with the archaeological history of Rome, yet of considerable interest to those whose love of the ancient city is more casual. Advanced undergraduate; graduate; faculty; professional.—*R. B. Lloyd, Randolph-Macon Woman's College*

OAB-2217 Can. CIP
Robertson, Noel. **Festivals and legends: the formation of Greek cities in the light of public ritual.** Toronto, 1992. 287p indexes afp (Phoenix. Supplementary volume, 31) ISBN 0-8020-5988-0, $75.00

There are already two excellent guides for Athenian festivals: H.W. Parke's *Festivals of the Athenians* (CH, Oct'77) and Erika Simon's *Festivals of Attica* (CH, Oct'83). Robertson deals with five major Athenian festivals, but in addition, describes and analyzes five Peloponnesian festivals. The real novelty in this work, however, is that Robertson describes the formation of Greek communities in the Dark Age, making an important contribution to the scholarly debate begun by Denis Roussel in his *Tribu et cité* (Paris, 1976). Parke's and Simon's books are essentially descriptive and antiquarian; Robertson's study is social history. In particular, he argues that the canonical descriptions of Greek social organization transmitted by Aristotle and Plutarch were based on rationalizations—often mistaken—of festival rituals. Instead, Robertson demonstrates the formative influence of hunting, warfare, and history on these rituals. This is a solid and original contribution to the social history of Greece in the Dark Age that will also interest students of comparative religion. Detailed maps and thorough indexes of sources, Greek words, subjects, and deities increase the work's usefulness. It belongs in every collection concerned with classical antiquity. Advanced undergraduate; graduate; faculty.—*R. I. Frank, University of California, Irvine*

OAB-2218 DK505 92-17442 CIP
Rowell, S.C. **Lithuania ascending: a pagan empire within east-central Europe, 1295-1345.** Cambridge, 1994. 375p bibl index (Cambridge studies in medieval life and thought, 4th series, 25) ISBN 0-521-45011-X, $69.95

This superb scholarly study presents, for the first time in English (and in some respects the first time in any language), the rise of pagan Lithuania during the rule of Grand Duke Gediminas (1315-1341/42), with attention given also to the reigns of his predecessor Vytenis and successor Jaunutis. Rowell (Univ. of Klaipeda, Lithuania) has supplemented limited Lithuanian documentation with the relative wealth of resources from Polish and east Slavic sources, along with materials relating to the Teutonic Knights, making use of both literary and nonliterary sources. The resulting study shows how the Lithuanians, despite their status as pagans, were able to manipulate commercial, religious, and political issues in such a way as to preserve the Grand Duchy against Christian neighbors, both Catholic and Orthodox, and, indeed, expand it to international prominence. Though ruling many Christian territories and later itself accepting Catholic Christianity from Poland, Lithuania chose in these decades to remain pagan. This did not prevent it from utilizing the political rhetoric and technology of the Christian world nor from being taken seriously by all sides as a participant in international politics. Maps, tables, and useful appendixes enhance this study, whose balanced narrative and analysis effectively portray the many vivid personalities and dramatic developments of this crucial period in the history of east central Europe. General and academic collections at all levels.—*P. W. Knoll, University of Southern California*

OAB-2219 HD130 95-38301 CIP
Rowlandson, Jane. **Landowners and tenants in Roman Egypt: the social relations of agriculture in the Oxyrhynchite Nome.** Oxford, 1996. 384p bibl indexes afp ISBN 0-19-814735-X, $80.00

The numerous papryi discovered at Oxrhynchus in the late 19th and early 20th centuries have greatly enriched knowledge of Graeco-Roman Egypt. Studies of Oxyrhynchus itself, however, are rare. Rowlandson's monograph is a distinguished addition to that short list. Her topic is land tenure and social relationships in Oxyrhynchus from the first to the third century CE. In seven clearly written chapters she reconstructs and analyzes the topography of the Oxyrhynchus Nome, the character and history of its land system, the status of public land, the nature of land ownership, the means by which land was alienated, and the extent of private agricultural tenancy. The conclusions are not surprising. Concentration of property tended to increase during these centuries, and urban dwellers enjoyed an economic advantage over the inhabitants of villages. The real contribution of Rowlandson's monograph is the unparalleled detail with which she reconstructs agricultural life in all its complexity in the Oxyrhynchite Nome. Essential reading for all scholars interested in the social and economic history of Roman Egypt. Upper-division undergraduate through faculty collections.—*S. M. Burstein, California State University, Los Angeles*

OAB-2220 DS146 96-27431 CIP
Schäfer, Peter. **Judeophobia: attitudes toward the Jews in the ancient world.** Harvard, 1997. 306p bibl index afp ISBN 0-674-48777-X, $35.00

Academic study of ancient antisemitism began c. 1880, at the same time—not coincidentally—as the rise of the political antisemitism that led to Hitler and the "Final Solution." Some found the origin of hostility in the character of Judaism, e.g., J.N. Sevenster's *Roots of Pagan Anti-Semitism in the Ancient World* (1975, the "substantialist" interpretation). Others emphasized political conflicts (the "functionalist" interpretation), e.g., John Gager's *The Origins of Anti-Semitism* (CH, Feb'84), which stresses the struggle of peoples in Ptolemaic Egypt and the Roman Empire. Schäfer's work is also functionalist, but finds origins in pre-Hellenistic Egypt. Jewish teachings threatened the religious monopoly of the national cults and were intensely resented by the priests. Eventually nationalistic resentments against the Hyksos and Persian conquerors were transferred to the Jews, and the story described in Exodus was transformed into the expulsion of a people cursed with leprosy. Schäfer, a recognized authority in the field, has written a remarkable lucid and informative study. Full notes. Highly recommended for both students and scholars.—*R. I. Frank, University of California, Irvine*

OAB-2221 U35 93-23539 CIP
Speidel, Michael P. **Riding for Caesar: the Roman Emperors' horse guards.** Harvard, 1994. 223p bibl index ISBN 0-674-76897-3, $27.95

Following his *Die Equites singulares Augusti* (Bonn, 1965), *Guards of the Roman Armies* (Bonn, 1978), and *Die Denkmäler der Kaiserreiter* (Bonn, 1992), Speidel (Univ. of Hawaii, Manoa) returns to his favorite subject with a systematic and comprehensive analysis of the topic. The first part is a historical treatment (vignettes really, and a few of them merely conjectural) from Julius Caesar (when a guard of 250 German bodyguards was formed in Gaul) through Trajan (who replaced them with the *Equites singulari Augusti*, mostly Batavians and Ubii, c. 2000 in number), to Constantine (who transferred the losing Maxentian survivors of the Battle of the Milvian Bridge to the frontier guard, 312 CE). The rest of the book is arranged topically: recruitment, terms of service, life in the camp, religious affiliations, and implications. These troops were the actual protectors of the person of the Emperor, wherever he went, even closer than the Praetorian Guard. Since proximity to the Emperor is an index of influence, these troops, though small in number and often of barbarian and provincial origin, had a tremendous influence. Their loyalty was far more impressive than even the Praetorian Guard, and promotion of individual horse guards usually led to influential centurionates in the regular legions. Inscriptions and funeral monuments are the principal sources, outside of the scattered literary texts and ancient military manuals; these are comprehensively handled in masterly fashion by Speidel. Only numismatics receives less than its due. Highly recommended as a standard work for undergraduate and graduate collections in history and military affairs, and for professionals and camp-followers of army studies.—*J. P. Adams, California State University, Northridge*

OAB-2222 HT114 91-47142 CIP
Tomlinson, Richard. **From Mycenae to Constantinople: the evolution of the ancient city.** Routledge, 1993 (c1992). 238p bibl index ISBN 0-415-05997-6, $79.95; ISBN 0-415-05998-4 pbk, $17.95

The standard works in English on ancient cities are L. Sprague De Camp's *Great Cities of the Ancient World* (1972) and M. Hammond's *The City in the Ancient World* (CH, Sep'73). Tomlinson, a seasoned archeologist known for

his *Greek Sanctuaries* (CH, Dec'77), has produced a book with a title reminiscent of Hammond's general work but that is in fact much more like De Camp's: It is a series of 13 separate studies, beginning with Mycenae and ending with Constantinople, plus two general chapters on the ancient city and its buildings. What makes the work a valuable contribution is Tomlinson's complete command of a great mass of specialized archeological reports. This enables him to give coherent interpretations of each city's role and development, and also—most unusual—to make illuminating comparisons. For example, he shows how Alexandria was planned on the model of Pella and other royal cities rather than on that of the older Hellenic centers. His chapter on Rome says as much in 27 pages as many entire books. Notes and bibliography offer a judicious selection of the very best—not necessarily newest—works on each city. Style and diction are clear and nontechnical. The 13 maps and 74 illustrations supplement the text beautifully. Highly recommended! General; advanced undergraduate; graduate; faculty.—*R. I. Frank, University of California, Irvine*

OAB-2223 DG70 93-17828 CIP
Wallace-Hadrill, Andrew. **Houses and society in Pompeii and Herculaneum.** Princeton, 1994. 244p bibl index afp ISBN 0-691-06987-5, $49.50

From its start archaeology has been allied with art history, but recently it has been moving toward social history. First steps in Roman studies were taken by John R. Clarke, *The Houses of Roman Italy, 100 BC - AD 250* (CH, Jul'92). Now Wallace-Hadrill, already well known for studies of Suetonius and patronage, has focused on the cities destroyed in 79 CE. He reads the plans and excavation reports like texts, uses them to show the vocabulary of Roman domestic architecture, and then describes the social structures and conventions that produced that vocabulary. It is amazing how much is discovered about imperial society from sites long studied and familiar. For example, it is clear that freedmen were far more high-status and far more assimilated than had been believed. Good illustrations and plans support the text admirably; the style is a model of precision and clarity; extensive notes, bibliography, glossary, and index combine to make this a valuable tool for further study. Altogether a truly outstanding work, one that belongs in every classical collection. General and academic readers at all levels.—*R. I. Frank, University of California, Irvine*

OAB-2224 DG330 94-60725 MARC
Williams, Stephen. **Theodosius: the empire at bay,** by Stephen Williams and Gerard Friell. Yale, 1995 (c1994). 238p bibl index ISBN 0-300-06173-0, $28.50

Theodosius I ("the Great") played a pivotal role in European history, but the only previous English-language study of this emperor is Noel King's *The Emperor Theodosius and the Establishment of Christianity* (1960), which focuses primarily on religion. Williams and Friell work for English Heritage, which operates archaeological sites for the public. Their book is a model of clarity and organization. Within a basically narrative structure it tells the story of the Roman Empire from Adrianople (379 CE) to the Vandal conquest of North Africa (430 CE), with particular emphasis on military and religious policies. The authors' scholarship is solid, based on primary sources and the best of recent studies, and is documented by c. 600 notes. Five learned appendixes provide detailed information on particular aspects; 19 plates illustrate contemporary coins, portraits, and buildings. Binding, paper, and typography are admirable, the index is complete and accurate, and the bibliography very well selected. This is a rare work, in that it is valuable to students and scholars at all levels.—*R. I. Frank, University of California, Irvine*

OAB-2225 DG97 91-24855 CIP
Yegül, Fikret. **Baths and bathing in classical antiquity.** Architectural History Foundation, New York/MIT, 1992. 501p bibl index ISBN 0-262-24035-1, $65.00

Yergül began to study the Roman bath in Asia Minor 20 years ago and has gradually expanded his focus to include its origins in Greece and in Italian folk medicine, its flowering in Rome, its spread to North Africa and Syria, its continuation in Byzantium, and its final incarnation as the Turkish bath. All this is presented in his splended work, a model of how archeological data can be brought together to illuminate the character and structure of a society. There is no comparable study in English. The text is illustrated with 550 figures—plans and photographs—supplemented by 50 pages of notes. Sturdy binding, high quality paper, and attractive typography combine to make this an impressive book. Readers will learn that the bath was the central institution of the urban leisure classes, a place where one could converse on philosophic subjects and be assured by the best medical authorities that this was a healthful form of mild exercise. Under Greek influence, Augustus added gymnastic facilities and the result was a gentlemen's club, a distinctive feature of the life of the ruling class in the Western provinces of the Empire. This book is not only a contribution to architectural history but also a guide to the life of the Roman world. Highest recommendation. Advanced undergraduate; graduate; faculty.—*R. I. Frank, University of California, Irvine*

■ Africa

OAB-2226   HD8801   92-41611 CIP
Atkins, Keletso E. **The moon is dead! Give us our money!: the cultural origins of an African work ethic, Natal, South Africa, 1843-1900.** Heinemann/J. Currey, 1993. 190p bibl index ISBN 0-435-08076-8, $45.00; ISBN 0-435-08078-4 pbk, $22.95

Passionately and often persuasively argued, this book contributes a new, explicitly African-centered perspective to the already exciting historical literature on the creation of a South African working class. Drawing on anthropological works, oral history, settler and missionary accounts, newspapers, and zulu-English phrasebooks, Atkins chronicles the development of an African work ethnic in 19th-century Natal. She creatively reconstructs the struggle of northern Nguni men and women to maintain precolonial beliefs and practices concerning work, time, hierarchy, and prestige while also adapting to a thoroughly racist and exploitative colonial Natal, with its seemingly insatiable demand by Europeans for "Kafir" labor. These culturally coded struggles, Atkins shows, were often subtle but also included strikes and other overt collective actions that forced whites to adapt to African workers as well as the other way around. Although the book lacks comparative discussion of similar struggles elsewhere in Africa, South Africa, or by slaves in the US, this is a clearly written and compelling study that should have wide appeal. All levels.—*R. R. Atkinson, University of South Carolina*

OAB-2227   G2566   93-24510 CIP
Christopher, A.J. **The atlas of apartheid.** Routledge/Witwatersrand, 1994. 212p index ISBN 0-415-04809-5, $65.00

Christopher (geography, Univ. of Port Elizabeth) makes use of extraordinary maps and diagrams to depict the spatial dimensions of the planning and enforcement of apartheid between 1948 and 1992. The result is a startling perspective from which to examine the bureaucratic features of social engineering as well as the tragedies and injustices experienced by South African blacks under National party rule. The book analyzes state policy at three levels: the partition of the country into white areas and tribal "homelands," also known as "Grand" apartheid; the spatial separation of peoples in urban areas under the provisions of the Population Registration Act and Group Areas Act; and "petty" apartheid, or those laws designed to eliminate virtually all physical contact between whites and blacks except within a master-servant framework. Implemented to guarantee white supremacy, such policies resulted in the forced resettlement of "surplus" blacks into overcrowded reserves, the destruction of vibrant communities like Cape Town's District Six, and separate and unequal schools, hospitals, beaches, and even cemeteries. In his two concluding chapters, Christopher examines briefly the domestic and international dimensions of resistance to apartheid. Upper-division undergraduates and above.—*J. O. Gump, University of San Diego*

OAB-2228   HB2126   96-17630 MARC
Cordell, Dennis D. **Hoe and wage: a social history of a circular migration system in West Africa,** by Dennis D. Cordell, Joel W. Gregory, and Victor Piché. Westview, 1996. 384p bibl index afp ISBN 0-8133-8168-1, $69.95

A pioneer among books based on demographic data, this study of burkinabè circular migration makes an important statement, and also draws attention to an unintended and unique source of perspectives on West African and European migration. Drawing principally on the burkinabè National Migration Survey of 1974-1975 (a collection of migration histories of 11,500 returned male and 10,000 returned female migrants from a sample of 52,304 rural and 41,093 urban dwellers), the analysis not only goes beyond the "traditional" data associated with colonial archives, but also exceeds more recent insights based on sample surveys. Moreover, treating Mossi as well as non-Mossi migrations, the authors conclude that despite the resourcefulness of colonial labor policies, broader colonial strategies for supplying labor to the coast were less successful; that ethnicity and local characteristics had an important impact on these labor policies; that age, gender, and space (i.e., domestic and international) likewise articulated with migratory behavior; and that all configurations combined to produce interrelated mobility patterns. Finally, going beyond the 1974-1975 survey, the authors suggest that especially among males "circular international migration has remained the mainstay of the burkinabè migration system," and that "as a household strategy geared to survival, rather than accumulation and development," circular migration continues to reinforce burkinabè poverty. Upper-division undergraduates and above.—*B. M. Perinbam, University of Maryland College Park*

OAB-2229   DT2630   92-31675 CIP
Eldredge, Elizabeth A. **A South African kingdom: the pursuit of security in nineteenth-century Lesotho.** Cambridge, 1993. 250p bibl index ISBN 0-521-44067-X, $59.95

Impressively researched and influenced by the best of recent scholarship in various disciplines, Eldredge's study is an excellent example of the new history being written on southern Africa. Within a changing political context, Eldredge delineates and fully explains the economic and social factors that determined the BaSotho 19th-century experience. Although Eldredge acknowledges the damaging impact of Afrikaner land grabs and British political interference, she is primarily concerned with internal dynamics. The role of women and their exploitation is a major topic here. Taking issue with some current Marxist writers, Eldredge persuasively argues that the origin of their subordination cannot be attributed to the emergence of capitalism. Important sections treat food production, crafts, domestic and foreign trade, migrant labor, as well as attention to the role of chiefs (ultimately exploitative). There is no comparable work on Lesotho. Eldredge has made a very significant contribution to African studies, and her book belongs in all academic libraries supporting courses on Africa. General, undergraduate, and graduate readership.—*L. E. Meyer, Moorhead State University*

OAB-2230   NK5989   92-73840 CIP
Elephant: the animal and its ivory in African culture, ed. by Doran H. Ross. University of California, Los Angeles, Fowler Museum of Cultural History, 1995 (c1992). (Dist. by California) 415p bibl ISBN 0-930741-26-9 pbk, $49.00

This is the catalog of an exhibition organized by the Fowler Museum of Cultural History at UCLA. It is a massive and comprehensive study of the way Africans have thought of, represented in art, and incorporated in mythology the elephant. In 19 chapters prominent scholars in several disciplines write on topics that range from the history and biology of the elephant to its use as a symbol of political power among several African peoples. There are numerous spectacular photographs of elephants, many of them full-page, dating from the 19th century to the present and including images of the vast quantities of ivory tusks that were harvested to be made into piano keys and billiard balls. There are hundreds of images of art objects made by Africans either from ivory or from other materials to represent elephants (including ivory figures made by the Lega people to be used in men's initiation), and images of elephants on stamps, military uniform buttons, beer bottle labels, and enamel plates. The quality of the scholarship and of the photographs is very high, and the scope of the study is enormous. This is an informative and visually stimulating source on this endangered mammal. Undergraduate; graduate; faculty; general.—*C. D. Roy, University of Iowa*

OAB-2231   N5310   95-16323 MARC
Garlake, Peter. **The hunter's vision: the prehistoric art of Zimbabwe.** Washington, 1996 (c1995). 176p bibl index ISBN 0-295-97480-X, $39.95

In the 1980s specialists in several fields, particularly in South Africa, significantly advanced knowledge of the life, beliefs, and art of the San, a southern African hunter-gatherer people. Inspired by such insightful research, Garlake has produced a major contribution to understanding San painting in Zimbabwe. He overturns traditional views of this "art on the rocks" and establishes it as quite distinct in some respects from its South African counterpart. Based on long study and meticulous tracing of San compositions, Garlake's interpretations, especially those that emphasize the central role of the trance state and representation of potency, are extremely revealing. They are always fascinating, usually convincing, and presented without excessively technical language. An exemplary book! Many well-placed tracings and 36 excellent colored plates accompany the text. Highly recommended for all institutions supporting African studies. All levels.—*L. E. Meyer, Moorhead State University*

OAB-2232   DT1938   94-32918 CIP
Juckes, Tim J. **Opposition in South Africa: the leadership of Z.K. Matthews, Nelson Mandela, and Stephen Biko.** Praeger, 1995. 206p bibl index afp ISBN 0-275-94811-0, $49.95

From a sociopsychological perspective, Juckes reviews significant features of South Africa's 20th-century political history through the careers of three of its most important black leaders. Although the subjects' lives overlapped to some extent, the generational differences are notable, reflecting not only changing political conditions in successive decades but also the black intellectuals' evolving understanding of the white supremacist government and how they must react to it. Juckes shows how social influences created unique individuals who made their distinctive mark on the black opposition movement. He argues, for example, that without the special qualities of Nelson Mandela and Stephen Biko, the opposition might have degenerated into something other than the kind of force so important in bringing about recent historic change. The book is particularly good in explaining why a younger generation of black activists led by Mandela was compelled to abandon Z.K. Matthews's futile gradualism and advocate a violent response to an ever more violent apartheid government. Although sometimes tediously repetitious and excessively documented, Juckes's extensively researched and innovative work is a welcome contribution to South African studies. Recommended for all public and academic libraries.—*L. E. Meyer, Moorhead State University*

OAB-2233   DS135   92-1175 CIP
Kaplan, Steven. **The Beta Israel (Falasha) in Ethiopia: from earliest times to the twentieth century.** New York University, 1992. 231p bibl index afp ISBN 0-8147-4625-X, $45.00

The second major historical study of the Jews of Ethiopia to appear this year (cf James Quirin's *The Evolution of the Ethiopian Jews*, CH, Dec'92), Kaplan's book further illuminates the history of this hitherto poorly researched population. Relying more on indigenous documentation than on other contemporary work, Kaplan nevertheless confirms the major theses of recent scholarship questioning the direct link between Beta Israel and ancient Jewish settlement of the Upper Nile or South Arabia. The Judaic cultural roots of the population seem to lie in indigenous Ethiopia, mediated by local Christianity that has long indentified with Biblical Judaism. Of far more importance than the question of origin is Kaplan's chronicling and analysis of the last 500 or so years of

Beta Israel history, their political and military success and failure, the evolving social relations with other populations in Ethiopia, and the arrival of European Christian missionaries during the 19th century. Kaplan's well-written, lucid presentation, excellent footnoting, and fine index make this important, competent contribution accessible to all levels of readers. Highly recommended.—*L. D. Loeb, University of Utah*

OAB-2234   DT1756   96-35827 CIP
Keegan, Timothy. **Colonial South Africa and the origins of the racial order.** University Press of Virginia, 1996. 368p bibl index ISBN 0-8139-1735-2, $45.00; ISBN 0-8135-1736-0 pbk, $14.50

Keegan's impressive book focuses on the relatively familiar but recently little studied terrain of British colonial rule in South Africa up to the 1850s. Beginning with the broad context of British free-trade imperial policy, Keegan traces the often contradictory dynamics of an expanding British colonial presence in South Africa, emphasizing new economic opportunities during the later 1830s and 1840s. These included the emergence of settler capitalism, increased steamship-borne foreign trade, a rising local commercial class, and expanding European frontiers of settlement. His main argument is that these processes were crucially important in shaping South Africa's racial order. In so doing, he challenges one of the linchpins of the rich revisionist historiography on South Africa produced over the last 20 years, which has tried to locate the origins of this order in the myriad forces associated with South Africa's mineral revolution of the later 19th century. His narrative is densely packed, multilayered, but admirably clear and readable, and combines broad context, abundant detail, extensive historiographical discussion, and persuasive interpretation and synthesis. Highly recommended, upper-division undergraduates and above.—*R. R. Atkinson, University of South Carolina*

OAB-2235   DT2250   95-193026 MARC
Lambert, John. **Betrayed trust: Africans and the state in colonial Natal.** Natal, 1995. (Dist. by International Specialized Book Services) 216p bibl index afp ISBN 0-86980-909-1 pbk, $28.00

Lambert provides an important addition to South African historiography, building on earlier studies of the South African peasantry by Colin Bundy and of colonial Natal by Shula Marks, Henry Slater, and Kaletso Atkins. Lambert contributes a detailed and nuanced investigation of the complex and changing nature of landholding, chiefship, the homestead economy, and labor among rural Africans in colonial Natal. In retrospect, it is clear that Africans lost ground in all these realms as the colonial state gradually acceded to the priorities and vision for Natal espoused by the increasingly commercialized white farmer sector, until, by the early 20th century, African autonomy and opportunities had been reduced virtually to nil. As Lambert shows, however, this sad state was not reached quickly, without contention among Europeans, or without Africans using all available opportunities, at least up to the late 19th century, to preserve as much autonomy as possible and to take advantage of any new opportunities created. Clearly and concisely written, this is an excellent study of (especially) the African side of the complex and long-term process of the establishment of European dominance in Natal. Upper-division undergraduates and above.—*R. R. Atkinson, University of South Carolina*

OAB-2236   HD979   93-34531 CIP
Larebo, Haile M. **The building of an empire: Italian land policy and practice in Ethiopia, 1935-1941.** Oxford, 1994. 350p bibl index afp ISBN 0-19-820262-8, $69.00

Larebo (Clemson Univ.) has converted his dissertation into a masterly monograph. He probes Mussolini's land policy in Ethiopia, using as a background the findings and propaganda of Italian Catholic missionaries, and scientific expeditions. Mussolini envisioned Ethiopia as an outlet for Italy's teeming population, a source of raw materials, and a market for manufactures; Italian settlers would get the best land and cheap Ethiopian labor. The vision collapsed. Factors included Mussolini's early loss of interest, an unstable military situation, rivalry of governmental bodies, bad planning, low agricultural budget, the poor quality and racism of settlers, and multiple and largely hostile traditional local interests. By 1939 many Italians in Addis Ababa's outskirts were begging Ethiopians for food. Nevertheless, Larebo asserts that Italian rule positively influenced Ethiopia: it developed infrastructures and agricultural policies that brought greater Ethiopian participation in the world capitalist system, and outlined a development plan containing surveys for research and actual development work. Larebo's study shows scholarly excellence, despite very difficult conditions at archives in Rome. Innumerable footnotes, 30 illuminating tables, five maps, helpful glossary, appendixes featuring contracts, first-rate bibliography, and good index. For readers at all levels interested in imperialism or Italian fascism.—*E. E. Beauregard, emeritus, University of Dayton*

OAB-2237   Orig
Lester, Alan. **From colonization to democracy: a new historical geography of South Africa.** I.B. Tauris, 1996. 278p bibl index (International library of African studies, 8) ISBN 1-86064-091-5, $59.50

Lester provides impressive coverage of both the key sociohistorical dynamics of 19th- and 20th- century South African history and the major historiographical debates surrounding those dynamics. He does this by devoting considerable attention to and constructing persuasive arguments about the ways in which both material and ideological forces shaped South Africa's colonial and apartheid past. Discussions of colonial ideology and practice, race, class, identity formation, industrialization, land dispossession, migrant labor, urbanization, resistance politics, and theories of the state are woven together into a highly useful, multidisciplinary review of recent historical and social science literature on South Africa, including insights from the perspective of postcolonial scholarship (particularly on identity formation). Moreover, as a historical geographer, Lester underscores the spatial dimension of South African history as well. For example, whites' limited knowledge of the 1980s insurrection in the townships, Lester writes, "is testimony to the remarkable degree of spatial structuring which lay at the core of South Africa's political system. Whites were relatively politically insulated because they were spatially cocooned." All levels.—*R. R. Atkinson, University of South Carolina*

OAB-2238   HT1334   92-18406 CIP
Lovejoy, Paul E. **Slow death for slavery: the course of abolition in Northern Nigeria, 1897-1936,** by Paul E. Lovejoy and Jan S. Hogendorn. Cambridge, 1993. 391p bibl index (African studies series, 76) ISBN 0-521-37469-3, $69.95; ISBN 0-521-44702-X pbk, $19.95

The first book-length study of the Sokoto Caliphate of northern Nigeria, the largest slave society in colonial Africa. Based on 20 years of research, including a collection of oral histories from ex-slaves, the study focuses on the survival of a slave system into the modern world. Disruption of the economy and the aristocratic society supported by the labor of millions of slaves was considered detrimental to British colonial interests; consequently, Frederick Lugard and those who succeeded him as administrators of Nigeria protected the practice. Slavery was to be "reformed," not abolished, and all slaves were required to purchase their freedom from their masters if they wanted it. Individual chapters are organized around the mechanisms for preserving that gradualism, including the court system, tax policy, land policy, and support for elites. When international complaints forced an abolition decree in 1936, all the instruments were in place that preserved a quasi-slavery for 30 more years. The work is based on a massive collection of economic data and enhanced by an appendix summarizing the characteristics of the 102,000 slaves who purchased their freedom. It concludes with a unique chapter on the interwoven issues of slavery and concubinage in Muslim society that resulted in British support for continued new enslavements throughout the period to provide "wives." Advanced undergraduates and above.—*R. T. Brown, Westfield State College*

OAB-2239   GV143   94-48636 CIP
Martin, Phyllis M. **Leisure and society in colonial Brazzaville.** Cambridge, 1995. 278p bibl index ISBN 0-521-49551-2, $59.95

Richly documented from Congolese and European primary sources, as well as with copious field notes, Martin's book opens a fascinating window on Brazzaville's colonial-era social history. Two opening chapters provide a remarkably spare yet informative overview of the city's development to 1960, tracing its segregation into three main *quartiers*: La Plaine and Le Plateau (European); BaCongo (Laris and other southern Congolese); and Poto-Poto (up-river Congolese and foreign-born Africans). A third background chapter explores the interaction between European and African concepts of work and leisure, as the church, colonial state, and Africans vied to structure time and space to their particular ends. Martin then examines specific leisure-related topics including football (soccer), the music and dance scenes, social clubs, fashion, and nightlife. For Africans, leisure activities presented an opportunity for self-expression and social liberation in the stifling colonial environment; for Europeans, the differences between African leisure activities and their own often reinforced notions of racial superiority. Martin has brilliantly demonstrated how important leisure-related activities were in the formation of national, ethnic, and racial consciousness in Congo. Upper-division undergraduates and above.—*J. F. Clark, Florida International University*

OAB-2240   Orig
The Migration experience in Africa, ed. by Jonathan Baker and Tade Akin Aina. Nordiska Afrikainstitutet, Scandinavian Institute of African Studies, P.O. Box 1703, S-751 47 Uppsala, Sweden, 1995. 353p bibl index ISBN 91-7106-366-8, $40.00

This volume is a major contribution to the study of migration, not only in Africa, but also worldwide. The 19 articles are up-to-date, succinct, and provocative. Most explore relevant but less frequently researched topics, such as the migration of pastoralists and single women to urban areas, the role of small towns for retirees, and the importance of nonmetropolitan migration in South Africa with the demise of apartheid. Other significant topics include the relationships between migration and the structural adjustment programs in East Africa, the function of the UN High Commissioner for Refugees in regard to involuntary refugees, the flight of "environmental" refugees, and the role of the Ethiopian state in orchestrating movements of people during times of famine. Samir Amin's theoretical essay stresses the importance of the global peripheralization of Africa as a force behind massive migrations associated with Africa today. The articles focus on sub-Saharan Africa and consider migration processes within countries more frequently than between countries or continents. This volume is a must for all university libraries and African studies programs. Upper-division undergraduates and above.—*K. M. Weist, University of Montana*

OAB-2241   DT515   93-31669 CIP
Miles, William F.S. **Hausaland divided: colonialism and independence in Nigeria and Niger.** Cornell, 1994. 368p bibl index afp ISBN 0-8014-2855-6, $49.95

The 1990s have proved to be a cartographer's nightmare as new nations emerge amid an apparent epidemic of ethnicity. "Hausaland" would seem to be a prime target for a campaign to unite millions of West Africans in Nigeria and Niger who consider themselves Hausa. Yet, according to this masterful study, the conscious division of the Hausa between English and French colonial territories in the early 20th century fostered differences that have survived and occasionally intensified in the independence era. Miles's argument may be controversial, but anyone who hopes to dispute it will have to reckon with his meticulous research and articulate analysis. Two border villages are his primary focus for comparison, but this research has much broader implications. Through a combination of keen observation, interviews, surveys, work in the archives, and theory, the author not only provides a comprehensive portrait of contemporary Hausa identity, but also raises stimulating questions about the persistence of borders and of African ethnicity. All levels.—*J. A. Works Jr., University of Missouri—St. Louis*

OAB-2242   DT1436   94-41587 Orig
Minter, William. **Apartheid's contras: an inquiry into the roots of war in Angola and Mozambique.** Witwatersrand/Zed Books, 1994. 308p bibl index ISBN 1-85649-265-6, $69.95; ISBN 1-85649-266-4 pbk, $29.95

Conflicts that the world has largely ignored have afflicted the people of Angola and Mozambique since the early 1960s. Minter masterfully conducts the reader through the thicket of internal and external forces responsible for these decades of violence, death, and destruction. Although there were failures on the part of the leftist governments of Angola and Mozambique after independence in 1975, the author concludes that it was principally outside intervention—first by South Africa and later by the US—that enabled the Unita faction in Angola and Renamo in Mozambique to prolong the fighting, and thus the agony, into the '90s. In Mozambique, white-ruled Rhodesia actually organized the Renamo rebels, who were, in the 1980s, massively supported by the apartheid regime in South Africa. Minter's richly textured work contributes significantly to the discourse on the nature of Third World guerrilla warfare and the events of the post-Cold War era in southern Africa. The bibliography is extensive and the maps of Angola and Mozambique helpful. For all libraries.—*R. A. Corby, University of Arkansas at Monticello*

OAB-2243   HT384   95-3850 CIP
Rakodi, Carole. **Harare: inheriting a settler-colonial city: change or continuity?** Wiley, 1995. 298p bibl index afp ISBN 0-471-94951-5, $49.95

Written by a city and regional planning specialist, this book is an excellent resource on present day Harare and the historical, political, and social conditions that have shaped its reality. In each chapter Rakodi outlines background for the current situation, including colonial and postcolonial history and the urban policies of those time periods. Her particular interests are in land and its uses, and housing markets; there is a chapter devoted to each topic. Other chapters cover the political and economic context of the city, the structure of the town, the city's current economy, and the Harare population's social characteristics. Throughout, there are maps and extremely helpful charts, graphs, and figures that support the text and the policy implications drawn by Rakodi. In the chapter on Harare's future, the author suggests better planning is essential to avoid what she sees as growing discrimination by class and income. This book will interest urban planners and geographers as well as anyone concerned generally with urbanization in Africa. Upper-division undergraduates and above.—*R. Ellovich, North Carolina State University*

OAB-2244   HD9887   95-26213 CIP
Roberts, Richard L. **Two worlds of cotton: colonialism and the regional economy in the French Soudan, 1800-1946.** Stanford, 1996. 381p bibl index afp ISBN 0-8047-2652-3, $55.00

Roberts's superbly argued and fluidly written book concentrates on the politics of cotton in the French Soudan during the first half of the 20th century. West African cotton textile production, and the resulting local and regional trade, long predated French colonialism. In this carefully researched study, Roberts contends that French attempts to harness the production of cotton and divert it to metropolitan textile industries fundamentally failed. For a variety of reasons, African producers preferred to trade their harvest internally, and French efforts "to capture the cotton harvest for export to the metropole" were thwarted. The story Roberts recounts is a testament to the dynamism and resilience of the local industry, and to Africans' ability to shape their own lives despite the limitations imposed by colonialism and the world economy. An invaluable theoretical as well as historical contribution, this book undermines the common wisdom that colonial states readily imposed their policies on African subjects, while freely defining desired outcomes. Highly recommended. Upper-division undergraduates and above.—*E. S. Schmidt, Loyola College in Maryland*

OAB-2245   DT2913   91-41251 CIP
Schmidt, Elizabeth. **Peasants, traders, and wives: Shona women**
in the history of Zimbabwe, 1870-1939. Heinemann, 1992. 289p bibl index ISBN 0-435-08064-4, $45.00

Schmidt's book is an important addition to the literature on peasant studies in colonial Africa. Several historians have written on the impact of settler colonialism and capitalism on African farmers and on African responses in Southern Rhodesia (Zimbabwe), e.g., T.O. Ranger (*Peasant Consciousness and Guerilla War in Zimbabwe*, CH, Mar'86) and R. Palmer (*Land and Racial Domination in Rhodesia*, 1977). However, these scholars have neglected the critical role of women farmers in the formation of the peasantry and in resistance to proletarianization. Schmidt examines African patriarchy. She analyzes the alliance of African elders and European colonial authorities to control women and younger men, especially in regard to sexuality and reproductive powers, through legal constraints. She also discusses the attitudes of missionaries toward women's roles and female initiatives in the face of the deteriorating status of women. The study is based on solid research and knowledge of feminist literature. Photographs; useful bibliography. Advanced undergraduate; graduate; faculty.—*P. M. Martin, Indiana University-Bloomington*

OAB-2246   HT1394   94-2194 CIP
Shell, Robert C.-H. **Children of bondage: a social history of the slave society at the Cape of Good Hope, 1652-1838.** Wesleyan/University Press of New England, 1995 (c1994). 501p bibl index ISBN 0-8195-5273-9, $59.95

Shell's quantitative social history of slavery in South Africa is a unique combination of the themes of Fogel and Engerman's *Time on the Cross* (CH, Sep'74) and Eugene Genovese's *Roll, Jordan, Roll* (1972). It studies the growth of South African society, arguing, like Genovese, that the owners of slaves were as much in bondage to the system as were their slaves. Shell's 15 years of research in Britain, Holland, and his native South Africa have produced a wonderful history of a culture and of its key institution, as both changed over two centuries. There are fascinating chapters on the "Lodge," that strange social order and building of the slaves under the Dutch government, and on the unique Cape architecture that resulted; on the slave roots of Afrikaner families and of Afrikaans itself, which is shown to be slave creole. The "Cape coloured" community is also given an extensive analysis. Shell demonstrates the unique role Islam plays in this community, because the 19th-century slave owners feared that Christian baptism would grant their slaves freedom. Offering insights into research methodologies, comparative slavery issues, the process of acculturation, and contemporary South African politics, this book has no equal in any other history of South Africa and very few in the whole field of slavery studies. Upper-division undergraduates and above.—*R. T. Brown, Westfield State College*

OAB-2247   GN645   92-14788 CIP
Smith, Andrew B. **Pastoralism in Africa: origins and development ecology.** Hurst & Company/Ohio University/Witwatersrand University, 1992. 288p bibl index ISBN 0-8214-1046-6, $45.00; ISBN 0-8214-1047-4 pbk, $19.95

Smith explores the development of African pastoralism and its successful adaptation to the African grasslands over the past several thousand years. Smith (archaeology, Univ. of Cape Town), has had extensive firsthand research experience in western, eastern and southern Africa. Using an ecological approach to prehistory, the author first outlines in ten chapters the origins and spread of African pastoralism in these regions, then describes contemporary pastoralism and makes predictions for its future. Considerable effort is spent on correcting the misconception that pastoralism is irrational and results in environmental destruction. Smith reviews the many negative impacts of colonial and post-colonial development efforts, based on Western ranch models, to improve African herding systems while ignoring indigenous natural resource management strategies, such as seasonal transhumance. Several of Africa's well-known pastoral ethnic groups are described in detail. This well-written book is enhanced with 58 figures, 11 tables, and 15 plates. Useful to Africanists, anthropologists, archaeologists, and development professionals. All levels.—*D. M. Warren, Iowa State University*

OAB-2248   HQ1240   94-40205 MARC
Snyder, Magaret C. **African women and development: a history: the story of the African Training and Research Centre for Women of the United Nations Economic Commission for Africa,** by Margaret C. Snyder and Mary Tadesse. Witwatersrand/Zed Books, 1995. 239p index ISBN 1-85649-299-0, $55.00; ISBN 1-85649-300-8 pbk, $19.95

Snyder, founding director of the United Nations Development Fund for Women (UNIFEM), and Tadesse, until recently the head of the African Training and Research Centre for Women (ATRCW) at the UN Economic Commission for Africa, have written a compelling account of African women's role in development in both North and sub-Saharan Africa. Their history of the ATRCW provides valuable insights into "women in development" both on the African continent and within the global women's movement. The 12 chapters cover the history of women's movements, African women's initiatives in development, the development of women's policy concepts and legal statutes in Africa, and the growth of the African regional network of women leaders involved in influencing policy towards women. Also included is a survey of contemporary African women leaders who have been instrumental in establishing an African-oriented agenda to institutionalize improvement in the lives of women. This account traces the changing role of gender in development theories and strategies since the 1960s. The 20 appendixes provide the most recent data on women country-by-country, along with the key policy documents that are the legal basis for increased empowerment of African women. A must for development practitioners and persons with an interest in Africa and in gender relations. All levels.—*D. M. Warren, Iowa State University*

OAB-2249   DT31   91-27968 CIP
Thornton, John. **Africa and Africans in the making of the Atlantic world, 1400-1680.** Cambridge, 1992. 309p index ISBN 0-521-39233-0, $49.95; ISBN 0-521-39864-9 pbk, $17.95

Thornton's book is going to provoke extended debate about slavery and the Atlantic civilization that African slavery helped to build. Modeled after Fernand Braudel's massive study of the Mediterranean world, this attack on the "dependancy" theories of scholars like Walter Rodney, in *How Europe Underdeveloped Africa* (1972), argues that Africans were active and voluntary participants in the slave trade. Furthermore, Thornton shows that Africa was not negatively "impacted" by Europeans, nor were West Africa's politics, economics, or demographics seriously disrupted during the centuries he surveys. The second and longer part of this work extends the portrayal of Africans as active historic figures by turning to the New World slave communities. Concentrating on the Portuguese and Spanish colonies, Thornton describes the growth of African American culture in chapters entitled "Life and Labor," "Culture and Aesthetics," "Religion," and "Resistance." This product of 20 years research in Portuguese and Spanish archives establishes the intellectual foundation for an Africanist interpretation of the history and culture of the Atlantic world. It should be in every college library and most larger public libraries. General; advanced undergraduate; graduate; faculty.—*R. T. Brown, Westfield State College*

OAB-2250   DT433   95-4678 CIP
Wrigley, Christopher. **Kingship and state: the Buganda dynasty.** Cambridge, 1996. 293p bibl index (African studies series, 88) ISBN 0-521-47370-5, $64.95

Wrigley's splendid book reopens familiar debates on the nature of oral traditions and their use as historical sources. Wrigley reinterprets early Buganda history, but he also provides alternative understandings by explaining these traditions at many levels simultaneously. Rather than seeing these narratives as historical tales whose actors became portrayed as "gods," Wrigley argues that they are very old genesis myths onto which were grafted political observations: they are both historical and mythical in complex interaction. Wrigley's most radical notion, however, is that East African ontologies are shared with western Europe: "All these cultures have a common ancestry in the neolithic context that was at least as much African as Asian." In addition to its analytic brilliance, Wrigley's study is a compendium of wonderful stories that deal

with both kings and kingship, with both people and humanity. In short, this book shows why states never cease to fascinate; in addition to power, they create their own myths and in the end rely "not on an original event, but on an original fiction." Upper-division undergraduates and above.—*D. Newbury, University of North Carolina at Chapel Hill*

■ Asia & Oceania

OAB-2251   DU50   93-6783 CIP
Aldrich, Robert. **France and the South Pacific since 1940.** Hawaii, 1993. 413p bibl index ISBN 0-8248-1558-0, $38.00

In this important study Aldrich not only chronicles the history of France's oceanic territories of New Caledonia, French Polynesia, Wallis and Futuna, and the New Hebrides (Vanuatu), but more significant, he also places details within a wider historical context. He brings the region into the mainstream of world history by examining such topics as world economics, comparative decolonization, and French colonial policy. Aldrich investigates the impact of WW II, nuclear testing, political violence in New Caledonia during the 1980s, and the sinking of the *Rainbow Warrior*, from both domestic and international perspectives. His conclusion that, in the long run, France's policy of attempting to retain its island possessions during the age of decolonization has been at least as successful for all concerned as has Britain's hasty withdrawal will certainly be controversial. Based on archival material in France, New Caledonia, Tahiti, and Vanuatu, as well as on secondary sources, it is the best book now available on the French Pacific and replaces Virginia Thompson and Richard Adloff's *The French Pacific Islands* (CH, Mar'72). It follows Aldrich's earlier study *The French Presence in the South Pacific, 1842-1940* (1990). Highly recommended for anyone interested in the history of the South Pacific or imperialism. General readers; upper-division undergraduates and above.—*C. J. Weeks, Southern College of Technology*

OAB-2252   DS747   91-16004 CIP
Bol, Peter K. **This culture of ours: intellectual transitions in T'ang and Sung China.** Stanford, 1992. 519p bibl index afp ISBN 0-8047-1920-9, $49.50

Bol's book is a major accomplishment, intellectual history at its best. Bol (Harvard) deals with a very large topic as he relates changes in the underlying aims and objects of intellectual activity to the changing historical situation and composition of China's elite (the *shih*). Along with a broad interpretative framework, Bol offers new perspectives on influential figures, and subtle readings from a wide range of sources. He begins in the seventh century with the literary-cultural (*wen*) orientation of early T'ang court scholarship and concludes in the Sung (960-1279) with the Neo-Confucian emphasis on ethics, which met the needs of a new local elite (still *shih*) and remained dominant until the 17th century. Every serious student of the history and the literary and intellectual culture of traditional China will want to read Bol's study and will need to take it into account. Advanced undergraduate; graduate; faculty.—*C. Schirokauer, City College, CUNY*

OAB-2253   HC448   92-4304 CIP
Cleary, Mark. **Borneo: change and development,** by Mark Cleary and Peter Eaton. Oxford, 1992. 271p bibl index ISBN 0-19-588587-2, $42.00

Cleary and Eaton's excellent book fulfills the need for a balanced, comprehensive overview of the human geography of the island of Borneo, taken in its entirety from the remotest past to the challenging present. Jan Avé and Victor King's *Borneo: The People of the Weeping Forest* (Leiden, 1986) focuses on culture; other books treat British or Dutch Borneo, or more limited topics. Cleary and Eaton address three main themes; patterns of core and periphery are significant in each. The first theme is Borneo as a resource frontier for two millenia; from the 15th century on, Borneo became increasingly enmeshed in the world economy and continues so as a producer of raw goods today. The

Social & Behavioral Sciences

second theme is how the particular lifeways and the ecological adaptations of different cultural groups influence both their evaluation and use of natural resources and the impact of development on them. Third is the causes and effects of the developmental processes that have increased greatly since the 1960s and implications for the future, given the finite nature of the resources on which development is predicated. Clear, well-written text, maps, charts (including original analyses), tables, extensive bibliography. Essential for all geography and Asian studies collections. All levels.—*L. A. Kimball, Western Washington University*

OAB-2254   HN740   96-3631 CIP

Dardess, John W. **A Ming society: T'ai-ho County, Kiangsi, fourteenth to seventeenth centuries.** California, 1996. 316p bibl index afp ISBN 0-520-20425-5, $45.00

Drawing from a wide range of primary sources, Dardess (Univ. of Kansas) presents a well-researched assessment of transition in Tai-ho County, Kiangsi Province, China, from the 14th to the 17th century. He shows that the spirit of optimism and the deep sense of commitment to Tai-ho County declined throughout the Ming period, evidenced by diminished writing about the beauty of Tai-ho landscape and the sense of Tai-ho community by post-14th-century Taiho intellectuals. Dardess attributes this loss of intellectual identification to the increased difficulty faced by Tai-ho intellectuals in attaining office through Taiho connections after the 1457 palace coup, to the growth of powerful lineage institutions that replaced looser common-descent groups, and to new intellectual orientations in which pride in one's native locality had no place. Dardess's mastery of his resources is evident throughout the book, which includes superb analysis of Ming dynastic civil service recruitment policies and changing intellectual currents during the Ming period. An outstanding book by a noted historian of Ming China. Highly recommended. Undergraduates and above.— *V. J. Symons, Augustana College (IL)*

OAB-2255   DS751   96-25667 CIP

Davis, Richard L. **Wind against the mountain: the crisis of politics and culture in thirteenth-century China.** Council on East Asian Studies, Harvard University, 1996. 284p bibl index (Harvard-Yenching Institute monograph series, 42) ISBN 0-674-95357-6, $40.00

Davis's study is the fullest modern narrative and interpretive account of the fall of the Song Dynasty at the hands of the Mongol Yuan, which thereby became the first non-Chinese regime to govern all of China. Davis (Brown Univ.), an authority on late Song history, is richly informative on politics and personages. His reflections on the character, motivations, and even intuitions of the main actors take into consideration such factors as regional identities, values, and especially gender in shaping the response of men and women to the fall of the dynasty. For an unprecedented number, that response culminated in suicide. Davis is especially good on Wen Tianxiang, the most famous of these suicides, but he gives careful attention to the whole phenomenon and provides a list of loyalist suicides in an appendix. This book will interest students of gender, suicide, and loyalism as well as Song history. Upper-division undergraduates and above.—*C. Schirokauer, Columbia University*

OAB-2256   DS882   94-6118 CIP

Duus, Peter. **The Abacus and the sword: the Japanese penetration of Korea, 1895-1910.** California, 1995. 480p bibl index afp (Twentieth-century Japan, 4) ISBN 0-520-08614-7, $45.00

Duus has filled an important gap in the understanding of why and how the 1910 Japanese annexation of Korea took place, and has gone beyond that to suggest how it might be viewed in the context of 19th- and 20th-century imperialism. His study is likely to become the standard work on the evolution and implementation of Japanese policy toward Korea. Wide-ranging and thorough, the book is based on careful reading of major primary and secondary works in Japanese. The first section deals with the politics of the historical process from 1876-1910. Part 2 is an analysis of the economic ramifications of that process. Duus addresses issues of trade, migration, land policy, and ethnic and cultural policy in substantial detail. It is the framework, however, that Duus provides in his introduction and conclusion that gives the book its larger significance. His introduction establishes a world context; in his conclusion he proposes that Japanese imperialism be viewed not as parallel to Western imperialism but rather as parallel to that of Czarist Russia. Although Duus is quick to point out that his is not an entirely new interpretation, it is a new formulation that goes well beyond those put forth by Japanese historians and will be very helpful in understanding 20th-century history. Copious footnotes and an extensive bibliography of works in Japanese and Western languages. Upper-division undergraduates and above.—*J. H. Bailey, Earlham College*

OAB-2257   DS485   92-34002 CIP

Eaton, Richard M. **The rise of Islam and the Bengal frontier, 1204-1760.** California, 1993. 359p bibl index afp (Comparative studies on Muslim societies, 17) ISBN 0-520-08077-7, $50.00

Eaton (Univ. of Arizona) is the author of a much-admired study, *Sufis of Bijapur, 1300-1700* (CH, Sep'78), and of other major contributions on Indo-Islamic civilization. Now, in this magnificent study of the Bengal region— first under the Sultans of Delhi, then under a succession of local dynasties, and finally as part of the Mughul empire—Eaton has provided something unique in Indo-Islamic studies. His work is a detailed investigation of the evolution of Islamic society and culture in a particular region of the subcontinent over several centuries; it ranges over all the important aspects of that community's history, whether political and social, or cultural and religious. Past studies of regional sultanates and local Muslim regimes have tended to be narrow and parochial in scope. But for depth of scholarship, insightful analysis, and elegant writing, Eaton's study must rank among the finest contributions to South Asian scholarship to appear for some while. This book cannot be recommended too highly, whether for students of the subcontinent or of the Islamic world in general. Upper-division undergraduates and above.— *G. R. G. Hambly, University of Texas at Dallas*

OAB-2258   HQ684   92-31376 CIP

Ebrey, Patricia Buckley. **The inner quarters: marriage and the lives of Chinese women in the Sung period.** California, 1993. 332p bibl index afp ISBN 0-520-08156-0, $45.00; ISBN 0-520-08158-7 pbk, $16.00

An outstanding book by a leading authority on Chinese social history. Ebrey (Univ. of Illinois) effectively draws on a wide range of sources, narrative as well as expository, poetry and prose, to produce an account that relates the history of women to economic developments (increased urbanization and commercialization), to class and status, and to values and ideas (Neo-Confucian and other), many of them shared by women and men. Of the 15 chapters some deal with marriage as a social/economic institution (including an important discussion of dowries), others with women's roles (motherhood, widowhood, concubines), and there is one on adultery, incest, and divorce. This is an account too nuanced and complex to lend itself to easy summation, an account informed by the author's appreciation for the complexity of things and her sensitivity to the crosscurrents of history. Clearly written and well illustrated, it is essential reading for anyone interested in traditional China or in the comparative history of women. Advanced undergraduates and above.—*C. Schirokauer, City College, CUNY*

OAB-2259   DS461   94-33783 CIP

Gommans, Jos J.L. **The rise of the Indo-Afghan empire, c. 1710-1780.** E.J. Brill, 1995. 219p bibl index afp (Brill's Indological library, 8) ISBN 70-04-10109-8, $65.75

Gommans's work is of seminal importance, and will compel historians of 18th-century India and Central Asia to revise some long-held assumptions. Hitherto, in the accounts of northern India during that century, the Afghan presence— the invasions of Ahman Shah Durrani, the ambitions of Najib al-Dawla, the excesses of Ghulam Qadir in Delhi, and the dealings of the Rohillas with Shuja al-Dawla and Warren Hastings—has been treated as a series of disconnected and distracting episodes. Now, Gommans (Leidan Univ.) has woven them and much else into a seamless tapestry in which personal ambition and predatory behavior become an extension of ecological imperatives, commercial opportunism, and of the complex interaction of events in the Indo-Iranian borderlands, here rightly viewed as a single regional entity. Gossens's account of the central role of the horse trade as a catalyst in all this will surely prove definitive. With its finely crafted arguments, based on a masterly command of the sources, this is a monograph that cannot be recommended too highly. It is imperative for a paperback edition to be made available in the US for all students of Indian history.—*G. R. G. Hambly, University of Texas at Dallas*

OAB-2260   DS796   94-24416 CIP
Goodman, Bryna. **Native place, city, and nation: regional networks and identities in Shanghai, 1853-1937.** California, 1995. 367p bibl index afp ISBN 0-520-08917-0, $48.00

Using a wide array of primary and secondary sources, Goodman has provided a carefully documented analysis of the effects of sentiment for native place over time (nearly a century) and in a specific and very important location (Shanghai). The book is a superb complement to general presentations of China's sociopolitical history. The glossary of Chinese terms with the original orthography and pinyin romanization is extensive and very helpful to specialists, and is essential for nonspecialists. Underlying the detailed information about place, time, and people is a very insightful discussion of the terms "traditional" and "modern." Goodman's analysis makes clear what is obvious but often ignored, that culture is neither static nor necessarily "traditional" as opposed to modern, but is a complex mix. The author traces the amalgamation of traditional and modern practices chronologically, from the aftermath of the Opium War through self-strengthening, the emergence of nationalism, and into the Republican period. Of special significance is the confirmation Goodman's study brings to the work of such anthropologists as Robert J. Smith. Goodman concludes that "The shifting forms of native-place association, changing institutional structures over time and the changing ideological justifications for these forms should make us realize that the elements of 'culture' are not inherently 'traditional' or 'modern' but the necessary, often useful, and always constraining paths of change." An important addition to any serious university or college collection on East Asia. Upper-division undergraduates and above.—*J. H. Bailey, Earlham College*

OAB-2261   GN635   96-33421 CIP
Hanley, Susan B. **Everyday things in premodern Japan: the hidden legacy of material culture.** California, 1997. 213p index afp ISBN 0-520-20470-0, $35.00

Hanley's credentials as an analyst of early modern Japanese life and institutions are already securely established with her more tightly focused work on Tokugawa period demographics and with her broader studies of East Asian families. This new book will only further confirm her authority. Beginning with doubts about the accuracy of economic historians' consensus concerning the low standard of living in Tokugawa Japan, Hanley defines the standard of living in terms of the general level of physical well-being in the society, and speaks in terms of material culture, which she describes as "physical objects that people use or consume in their everyday lives." Under this rubric, she focuses on food, clothing, shelter, hygiene, and sanitation, in an effort to reconstruct the actual material conditions of daily life and determine the relationship between standard of living and quality of life. She concludes that in fact the average person in Tokugawa Japan lived in surprising comfort, and that scholars need to refine their understanding of the overall quality of Tokugawa period life. A profoundly important work, dramatically broadening readers' horizons on early modern Japan. Upper-division undergraduates and above.—*C. L. Yates, Earlham College*

OAB-2262   NX583   93-4738 CIP
Hung, Chang-Tai. **War and popular culture: resistance in modern**

China, 1937-1945. California, 1994. 432p bibl index afp ISBN 0-520-08236-2, $37.00

A pioneer study on the use of popular culture—newspapers, cartoons, and drama—as an instrument of resistance during the Sino-Japanese War of 1937-45. The Japanese invasion galvanized China as its urban culture became increasingly didactic, popularized, politicized, decentralized, and ruralized. Forced to retreat from Japanese-occupied urban centers to the hinterland, popular culture adopted new art forms to propagate the anti-Japanese effort. In the process, dramas, cartoons, and newspapers became much more direct, addressing the present and attacking both the Japanese and China's past, which had contributed to the Chinese predicament. Cartoons and caricatures graphically depicted the villainous invaders and the full horror of their atrocities. Omnipresent newspapers employed a straightforward language and colorful vocabulary that subsequently characterized Chinese Communist party publications. Both the Nationalist and Communist parties used popular culture as a patriotic tool, but the Communist party successfully reshaped it into a political instrument of revolution. Thoroughly documented, especially from Chinese sources; Chinese glossary; 50 illustrations. A must acquisition, suitable for all levels.—*H. T. Wong, Eastern Washington University*

OAB-2263   DS775   95-18885 CIP
Hunt, Michael H. **The genesis of Chinese communist foreign policy.** Columbia, 1996. 343p index afp ISBN 0-231-10310-7, $37.00

The origins of Chinese communist foreign policy is an important yet under-researched subject. Hunt's superb book not only represents the first comprehensive effort to deal with this issue but also sets up a new scholarly standard for the study of diplomatic history. Basing his research on extensive and careful use of Chinese-language sources, especially the internally circulated Chinese Community Party (CCP) documents available to scholars only in recent years, Hunt establishes a sound documentary foundation. He places the development of the CCP's external relations into a broad historical context, pointing out that its dynamics must be understood in relation to the logic and mentality underlying China's responses to the profound crises facing the "Middle Kingdom" throughout the late Qing and Republican period. His discussion of how to define ideology is highly revealing. His narrative combines vivid depiction of important historical events with thoughtful exploration of the impact of crucial personalities, such as Mao Zedong and Zhou Enlai. The concluding bibliographic essay provides a highly useful guide to the field. A pathbreaking book. Upper-division undergraduates and above.—*J. Chen, Southern Illinois University at Carbondale*

OAB-2264   DS555   96-27143 CIP
Ireson, Carol J. **Field, forest, and family: women's work and power in rural Laos.** Westview, 1996. 285p bibl index afp ISBN 0-8133-8936-4, $60.00

Masterfully interweaving ethnographic observation with historic context, Ireson examines changes in Lao women's economic prerogatives, power, and status by early-20th-century colonization, the Vietnam War, the institution of a socialist government in 1975, and the movement to liberalize economies within Laos and other communist block countries over the past decade. A sophisticated theoretical discussion of sociological and anthropological approaches to measuring women's control over economic, political, and social resources prefaces detailed analysis of women's changing roles in Laotian society. One of Ireson's significant observations is that recent socialist policies improved support for women in child care, home management, and agricultural activities, while impeding certain traditional commercial activities. A unique aspect of Ireson's work is her recognition that Lao women have responded to economic changes at the national and global level in varying ways, according to ethnic group, family dynamics, local environments and resources, and socioeconomic class. The Lao case also serves as a microcosm for examining more global processes of redefining "women's work" and economic roles in developing Third World countries. Highly recommended. Upper-division undergraduates and above.—*L. L. Junker, Vanderbilt University*

OAB-2265 DS556 92-20978 CIP
Jamieson, Neil L. **Understanding Vietnam.** California, 1993. 428p bibl index afp ISBN 0-520-08048-3, $35.00

What sets this book apart from other studies of recent Vietnamese history is its comprehensive incorporation into the narrative of Vietnamese poems, folktales, essays, novels, newspaper articles, and personal observations. Jamieson, an officer of the US Agency for International Development in 1963 and currently a senior associate at the Indochina Institute of George Mason University, greatly enriches understanding of the US experience in Vietnam through his careful reconstruction of Vietnamese values and thoughts. Beginning with a brief account of traditional Vietnamese culture, Jamieson focuses on modern Vietnamese history and Western intervention in that country from the French invasion in the 19th century through the Vietnam War and its aftermath. He captures the anguish and agony of Vietnamese intellectuals at the time of great social upheavals in Vietnam. His close scrutiny of the effects of the Vietnam war on Vietnamese society is especially welcome. The book also includes vivid descriptions of how cultural differences produced frictions and misunderstandings between the Vietnamese and the Americans. All levels.— *Q. Zhai, Auburn University at Montgomery*

OAB-2266 HT169 97-11185 MARC
Kim, Joochul. **Seoul: the making of a metropolis,** by Joochul Kim and Sang-Chuel Choe. Wiley, 1997. 261p bibl index afp ISBN 0-471-94936-1, $65.00

The city of Seoul is of particular interest because of its explosive metropolitan growth: from a population of only two million 40 years ago to a megacity of 12 million today (the world's 11th largest urban agglomeration). Kim and Choe deftly dissect and explain the forces that have transformed this burgeoning metropolis, supporting their analysis with a wealth of insightful maps, diagrams, tables, and photos. Their survey is organized into seven chapters, beginning with an introductory overview and then covering population and economic growth; urban land use and transportation; housing and redevelopment; planning, administration, and finance; urban form; and a discussion of future challenges. Clearly this is the best scholarly work in English on Seoul to date, and is therefore an indispensable addition to the contemporary social science literature on Asia and the western Pacific Rim. Physically, the book is close to ideal, especially in its binding and covers. An especially useful reference and bibliography section not only is up-to-date, but also provides parallel guides to works in English and Korean. All levels.— *P. O. Muller, University of Miami*

OAB-2267 HQ1767 94-1166 CIP
Ko, Dorothy. **Teachers of the inner chambers: women and culture in seventeenth-century China.** Stanford, 1994. 395p bibl index afp ISBN 0-8047-2358-3, $45.00; ISBN 0-8047-2359-1 pbk, $16.95

Focusing on gentry women of the prosperous lower Yangtze region, Ko shows how class, culture, and women's communities helped shape the construction of gender in late imperial China. In that era of rapidly growing commercial publishing, women were an important part of the reading—and writing—public, and women's literary clubs flourished. Although they did not question Confucian orthodoxy, women sometimes subverted it. Ko's account of women's reading of Tang Xianzu's late Ming play *The Peony Pavilion* in terms of Wang Yangming's neo-Confucian cult of *qing* (emotion, feeling, love) is an especially insightful and original examination of the values and culture of these women. Ko challenges simplistic depictions of women as victims and argues that within their social and cultural constraints, a women's literary culture developed that transcended public and private spheres and redefined womanhood. Although admittedly limited to the minority of leisured and literate upper-class women, this multifaceted book is a breakthrough in the study of women as part of Chinese cultural and social history. Recommended for upper-division undergraduates and above.—*R. E. Entenmann, St. Olaf College*

OAB-2268 DS796 92-21730 MARC
Lo, C.P. **Hong Kong.** Belhaven/Halsted, 1992. 200p index ISBN 0-470-21957-2, $49.95

A splendid addition to the literature on Hong Kong, a city-state and "economic tiger" taking center stage as its 1997 reunification with China nears. The book is crammed with information, insights, and interpretations valuable to researchers of every background. As a geographer, Lo takes a particularly comprehensive approach. His nine chapters concisely treat the Crown Colony's history, population patterns, economic growth and transformation, urban structure, land-use and transportation issues, planning experiences, social development, political geography, and future prospects. This sturdy volume contains a generous supply of high-quality maps, diagrams, and photographs. Chapter-end references link the analysis to the appropriate scholarly literature. Lo's work is now the best geographic study of the area, eclipsing Ian Kelly's *Hong Kong: A Political-Geographic Analysis* (CH, Jan'88) and *A Geography of Hong Kong*, ed. by T.N. Chiu and C.L. So (1986). Highly recommended. All levels.—*P. O. Muller, University of Miami*

OAB-2269 DS765 94-16292 CIP
Lone, Stewart. **Japan's first modern war: army and society in the conflict with China, 1894-95.** Macmillan, UK/St. Martin's, 1994. 222p bibl index ISBN 0-312-12277-2, $55.00

The importance of this work is apparent from its title: Lone (Univ. of New South Wales, Australia) views the Sino-Japanese war of 1894-95 as Japan's first exercise in the planning and conduct of a style of behavior characteristic of late 19th century and early 20th century nation-states. The author considers that style of participation in the international arena "modern" not only because it involves the use of combined diplomacy and military action to achieve goals articulated as being in the national interest, but also because that style of behavior requires the total mobilization of government policy, the economy, the military, and all sectors of society in the pursuit of national goals. Chapters examine all major aspects of the war: its origins in the international arena, the diplomacy and strategy behind it, the personal experiences of both soldiers and civilians (both at home and abroad), the early development of Japanese imperialist policy in Korea and Manchuria, the control and conduct of the army, and the politics of war termination. Particularly valuable is the use of first-person documents, including diaries and letters, to enrich the portrayal of the ways in which a broad variety of ordinary Japanese experienced and understood the war and its significance. General and academic readers at all levels.— *C. L. Yates, Earlham College*

OAB-2270 DS554 94-28125 CIP
Mabbett, Ian. **The Khmers,** by Ian Mabbett and David Chandler. Blackwell, 1995. 289p bibl index afp ISBN 0-631-17582-2, $34.95

Mabbett and Chandler's book is a picture of the Khmer people of Cambodia and their culture. Drawing on historical sources and the results of archaeological research, the authors provide a vivid depiction of a great Hindu-Buddhist empire that the Khmers established between the 800s and 1300s, in what is now northwest Cambodia. The Khmer empire is detailed in terms of its organization; society and economy; the daily life of the kings, priests, and farmers; and the work of artisans and craftsmen who created monumental temples and imperial buildings in the ancient city of Angkor, which is now one of the major tourist attractions of Southeast Asia. Next, the authors deal with the decline of the empire, Cambodia from the fall of Angkor to 1945, and Cambodia since 1945. The chapters are illustrated with maps and photographs. There is no doubt that this remarkably rich and pioneering study will attract scholars of Southeast Asia in several disciplines. Excellent notes, appendix, and guide to future reading. Highly recommended for upper-division undergraduates and above.— *H. S. Jassal, SUNY College at Cortland*

OAB-2271 DS730 93-43882 CIP
Mackerras, Colin. **China's minorities: integration and moderniza-**

tion in the twentieth century. Oxford, 1994. 355p bibl index ISBN 0-19-585988-X, $79.00

With its careful research and accessible style, this book provides a thorough and much needed survey of the minority nationalities in China, including Tibetans, Uygurs, Mongolians, and Koreans. Mackerras (Griffith Univ., Australia) examines the effects of revolutionary changes on these minorities in 20th-century China. He discusses the growth or decline of their populations, central governments' policies toward them, the trends of their economies, and their effects on China's foreign relations. Occasionally, Mackerras slips. He claims that the Chinese Communist Party did not push for the resumption of Chinese sovereignty over Outer Mongolia at any stage. In fact, the Chinese Communists expected Moscow to return Outer Mongolia to China after the victory of their revolution. Mao Zedong told Edgar Snow in 1936 that Outer Mongolia would automatically become part of China after the success of his party. In early 1957, Zhou Enlai approached Khrushchev requesting a discussion of the territorial issues, but the Soviet leader refused to comply. Despite this quibble, the book remains a scholarly and important achievement. All levels.—*Q. Zhai, Auburn University at Montgomery*

OAB-2272   HF3558   95-47153 CIP
Manning, Catherine. **Fortunes a faire: the French in Asian trade, 1719-48.** Variorum, 1996. 286p bibl index afp ISBN 0-86078-552-1, $72.95

Manning's study examines the intricacies of French trading practices in South Asia from the time the French East India Company was reorganized by John Law, the famous Scottish financier in the service of Louis XV, through the end of the Indian side of the War of Austrian Succession in 1748. Interesting chapters treat the various commodities traded—cotton textiles, Mocha coffee, spices, porcelain, opium, and saltpeter—and the nature of the relatively small French community (only 2,000 in 1750) of merchants, artisans, surgeons, missionaries, and soldiers in Pondicherry, Chandranagor, Mahé, Tellicherry, and other outposts. Manning offers valuable insights into the 18th-century Indian political scene: the European attraction to the magnificent manufactures, the fabulous wealth, the legendary riches of Bengal, the tremendous significance of the sacking of Delhi by Persia's Nadir Shah in 1739, and the incursions into the Deccan in 1740 and Bengal in 1742 by the Marathas. It was obvious to contemporaries that the once-mighty Mughal Empire was finished. The French East India Company might have filled the vacuum thus created, but beset with bitter internal personal and class rivalries and hampered at every turn by Paris and Versailles, it stood no chance against its British rival. Lucid, well written, and fully documented with complete appendixes, the study is highly recommended for upper-division undergraduates and above.—*W. W. Reinhardt, Randolph-Macon College*

OAB-2273   DS556   95-15856 CIP
Marr, David G. **Vietnam 1945: the quest for power.** California, 1995. 602p bibl index afp ISBN 0-520-07833-0, $50.00

Marr (Australian National Univ.) has written a fascinating, complex, densely detailed account of one crucial year in the history of Vietnam. The year 1945 witnessed the end of both the Pacific War and Japanese occupation of Vietnam, as well as the creation of the Vietnamese state under the leadership of Ho Chi Minh. Marr creatively organizes his work by devoting his first five chapters to the way different powers—France, Japan, China, the US, and Vietnam—functioned during the same seven-month period prior to August 1945. The last three chapters cover August to September as the new state of Vietnam was born. The book's greatest strengths are its detail and depth. Hundreds of historical actors come alive as they interact. Marr also expertly recreates the extraordinary confusion inevitable in a time of rapid political change. He concludes that Vietnam under Ho commanded "the loyalty of the vast majority of people living [there]". Based on exhaustive archival research and personal interviews, *Vietnam 1945* is a masterpiece of the historian's craft. Indispensable reading for scholars in the field. All levels.—*A. O. Edmonds, Ball State University*

OAB-2274   Orig
Mulvaney, John. **Commandant of solitude: the journals of Captain Collet Barker, 1828-1831,** by John Mulvaney and Neville Green. Melbourne, 1992. (Dist. by International Specialized Book Services) 431p indexes ISBN 0-522-84472-3, $44.95

Frontier life, whether in the American West, in the South African interior, or, in the present case, in Australia, formed a significant part of the 19th-century experience. Here two Australian scholars, one a specialist in prehistory and the other an expert on aborigines, have combined their insights and expertise in editing the journals of Captain Collet Barker, a peripatetic servant of the British Empire far more perceptive than the average individual of his time who kept the Union Jack flying in far-flung outposts. Barker's journals are especially revealing on interaction between aborigines and those of European descent. Much the same can also be said of his outlook on the myriad troublesome problems that were his daily lot. The input of the editors is outstanding, replete with a solid biographical account of Barker, adequate yet unobtrusive annotation, and helpful appendixes with each portion of the journal. This work will be useful to collections supporting study in indigenous peoples, racial interaction, frontier life, and Australian history. Advanced undergraduate; graduate; faculty.—*J. A. Casada, Winthrop University*

OAB-2275   BL1842   94-35259 CIP
Palais, James B. **Confucian statecraft and Korean institutions: Yu Hyongwon and the late Choson dynasty.** Washington, 1996. 1,279p bibl index afp ISBN 0-295-97455-9, $65.00

Palais analyzes the ideas of a notable 17th-century Korean thinker in terms of his Chinese and Korean precedents as well as the background and nature of the problems facing him in Korea. He then examines Yu's influence on later thought and official policy in five broad areas in need of reform: the class system (*yangban* and slaves), the land system, the military, government organization, and finances and the economy. Each area is treated in a separate multichapter part, complete with its own introduction and conclusion. In each case, the author provides a wealth of information on Korean history and on the views of modern scholars in Korea and Japan. The epilogue is aptly entitled "The Complexities of Korean Confucian Statecraft." This massive and demanding book by a master scholar marks a quantum jump in Korean studies. It provides a strong platform for future work on Korea and also merits the attention of students of Chinese Confucian statecraft and comparative studies of Confucianism. The 49 pages of reference materials, complete with characters, include a 39-page glossary, a list of kings of the Choson Dynasty, and a list of names. Upper-division undergraduates and above.—*C. Schirokauer, Columbia University*

OAB-2276   SD657   91-581 CIP
Peluso, Nancy Lee. **Rich forests, poor people: resource control and resistance in Java.** California, 1992. 321p bibl index afp ISBN 0-520-07377-0, $45.00

In this detailed historical ethnography, Peluso provides a clear, richly documented, and analytically innovative account of the interplay of state forestry policy and local forms of resistance in Java. Her account emphasizes the continuities in policy and resistance from the precolonial period, through Dutch rule, and into the post-1965 "New Order." Since the mid-19th century Dutch and Indonesian rulers have asserted absolute control of the forest. State control has rested on the ideas of "scientific forestry," which champions the utilitarian norm of ensuring the greatest good for the greatest number. By showing that this notion is historically contingent the author lays the ground for its future rejection. She argues instead for a policy that would recognize the participation and welfare of local villagers as an end in itself. Peluso also provides a theoretically well-grounded analysis of the emergence of resistance to state policy, and traces the changing tensions between local solidarity in resistance to external repression, and local internal differentiation along lines of rich and poor. A superb way into the social and political history of rural Java. Advanced undergraduate; graduate; faculty.—*J. R. Bowen, Washington University*

Social & Behavioral Sciences

OAB-2277   DS796   96-7544 CIP
Porter, Jonathan. **Macau: the imaginary city: culture and society, 1557 to the present.** Westview, 1996. 240p bibl index afp (New perspectives in Asian studies, 195) ISBN 0-8133-2836-5, $27.50

Surveying five centuries, Porter takes a thematic and topical approach for this splendid cultural and social history of a soon-to-be former Portuguese colony. As an appendage connected to China by a single road, Macau never enjoyed a direct and natural access to the hinterland. Without a natural harbor, it remained on the periphery of major commercial activities. Macau's geographical, political, and commercial limitations created its unique cultural mixture. It is both fragile and durable; isolated but not inaccessible; nondescript yet charming; dirty and grimy, yet serene and fascinating. Macau is a tapestry consisting of a colonial artifact, an entrepôt that served East-West trade, an evangelical stronghold, and an overseas Chinese community that remains relatively autonomous from its colonial master. Lack of a fuller discourse on the "present" indicated in the book's title is perhaps the only blemish, especially because recent changes are of epic proportion. Well documented, with 43 illustrations and maps of earlier periods. Upper-division undergraduates and above.—*H. T. Wong, Eastern Washington University*

OAB-2278   DS485   95-18416 CIP
Rahman, Mushtaqur. **Divided Kashmir: old problems, new opportunities for India, Pakistan, and the Kashmiri people.** L. Rienner, 1996. 219p bibl index afp ISBN 1-55587-589-0, $45.00

The state of Kashmir has experienced a long history of foreign dominance and a long struggle for freedom. Since 1947, when the Indian subcontinent was partitioned, India and Pakistan have fought three wars over Kashmir's status. The ongoing civil strife and distrust fermented by various Muslim groups inside the state have further compounded the situation. The area remains at the center of a bitter custody battle between the two countries. Rahman's book provides a comprehensive understanding of the Kashmir dispute and offers a proposal to resolve the problem. The first section deals with the evolution of the state of Kashmir, its geography, population, and economy; partition of British India; and the origin and development of the Kashmir conflict. The second section focuses on the UN and its role in dealing with the problem. The third section examines various proposals to resolve the dispute, and argues for a proposal based on the 1960 Indus Waters Treaty between India and Pakistan. Rahman has done a superb job in combining description and analysis. A welcome contribution to the literature on geopolitical struggles in South Asia. Excellent notes, chronology of events, maps, tables, figures, and appendixes. Highly recommended for undergraduate and graduate libraries with extensive holdings on South Asia. Upper division undergraduates and above.—*H. S. Jassal, SUNY College at Cortland*

OAB-2279   DS436   92-3074 CIP
Richards, John F. **The Mughal Empire.** Cambridge, 1993. 320p index (The new Cambridge history of India; I, 5) ISBN 0-521-25119-2, $44.95

Richards describes the construction, operation, and destruction of the Mughal Empire (1526-1720) for both nonspecialists and scholars. He sets his narrative in a conventional framework of political/military history by leading the reader chronologically from the Empire's founder, Babur, to its last great ruler, Aurangzeb (d. 1707) and the five emperors between Aurangzeb and Muhammad Shah (r.1719-1748). Richards stresses economic developments in agriculture and trade, imperial ideologies developed and changed by the great Mughals, the changing perceptions of each emperor toward Islam and its proponents, and the Mughal state's links with the world outside South Asia. This is a succinct, readable, and comprehensible summary of one of the most important eras in India's history. The book contains five maps (more are needed), a glossary, and a bibliographic essay. It should become the major text on Mughal history. General readers, undergraduates, and above.—*D. L. White, Appalachian State University*

OAB-2280   DS432   92-38124 CIP
Rudner, David West. **Caste and capitalism in colonial India: the Nattukottai Chettiars.** California, 1994. 341p bibl index afp ISBN 0-520-07236-7, $50.00; ISBN 0-520-08350-4 pbk, $18.00

The Hindu caste of Nattukottai Chettiars, or "Nakarattars," constituted the major banking caste in South India during the period 1870 to 1930. Part 1 of this scholarly study provides a theoretical orientation for the analysis of caste and capitalism, and examines the linkage between Nakarattar business practice, kinship organization, and religion. Part 2 traces the explosive growth of the Nakarattar financial empire from its beginnings in the Madras presidency to its prominent role in British Imperial Southeast Asian as well as in South Indian finance. Rudner discusses in detail financial cooperation between caste members regarding deposit banking, exchange banking, the fixing of interest rates, accounting, and other business practices, and also offers alternative interpretations of Nakarattar business institutions. Part 3 explores the informal bases of Nakaratta business organization: elite philanthropy, marriage alliances, and descent-based cults in Chettinad, the Nakarattar homeland in present-day Tamil Nadu. Part 4 offers conclusions about Nakaratta kinship organization as an adaptive response to financial occupational specialization, explores their implications for standard models of Dravidian kinship, and begins a project of systematic comparison between Nakarattars and nonmercantile forms of caste organization. Highly detailed and well-documented, with maps, photographs, tables, appendixes, and complete bibliography, the study is a valuable contribution to understanding South Indian social and economic history. Graduates and faculty.—*W. W. Reinhardt, Randolph-Macon College*

OAB-2281   Orig
Singh, K.S. **The scheduled castes.** Anthropological Survey of India/Oxford, 1994 (c1993). 1,367p bibl (People of India, national series, II) ISBN 0-19-563254-0, $59.00

Based on data generated from firsthand surveys done across the country and also on census and other secondary sources, Singh's work provides a detailed description of 751 scheduled castes, including subgroups, in terms of their culture, society, language, location, biological variation, rituals, food habits, occupations, education level, and patterns of continuity and change. These communities are presented in alphabetical order for easy reference. The volume represents the first major, comprehensive profile of scheduled castes, who account for about 16 percent of the country's population. It is a very useful addition to the meager literature on varied communities in India. This book will not only be an important source of reference for students, researchers, and teachers, but it will also be very useful for policy makers and promoters of change in India. Notes, photographs, and a select bibliography. Highly recommended for upper-division undergraduates and above.—*H. S. Jassal, SUNY College at Cortland*

OAB-2282   DS827   92-20639 CIP
Tanaka, Stefan. **Japan's Orient: rendering pasts into history.** California, 1993. 305p bibl index afp ISBN 0-520-07731-8, $40.00

A stimulating, challenging, and provocative book, rich in analysis and anecdote, and supported by careful reading of the major Japanese historians of modern Japan. The book is also a kind of polemic, seeking to provoke radical rethinking about the role of history, the historian, and the nature and purpose of historical inquiry. Tanaka is attempting to jolt historians of Japan by exposing their enthnocentric and culturally self-centered histories for what they all too often were: apologies for racial and cultural hegemony. Upper-division undergraduates, beginning graduate students, and historians will find the book stimulating and extremely useful because it links Japanese writing of the history of Japan to the intrinsically important task of how scholars should conceive, view, and use history. The introduction presents and develops Tanaka's thesis; the epilogue then cogently summarizes the task 20th-century Japanese historians set for themselves, and show clearly where this led them. In Part 1, the author examines in detail the work of the most important early scholars, including Miyake Yonekichi and Inoue Tetsujiro, as they invented the concept "Toyo" (Asia) as a counter to Western historians' "Orient." In Part 2, he examines in even more detail the work of later historians, Shiratori Kurakichi, Hattori Unokichi, and their confrères, who used the term "Shina" (China) to define a link to origins for Japan that could be used to "objectify" and justify Japan's hegemony over Asia in general, and China, in particular, as a "natural" evolution of history. An extensive bibliography, voluminous notes and citations, and a helpful index enhance the value of Tanaka's work. An important and useful book for all undergraduate libraries.—*J. H. Bailey, Earlham College*

OAB-2283　　　　DS850　　　　92-22617 CIP
Totman, Conrad. **Early modern Japan.** California, 1993. 593p index afp ISBN 0-520-08026-2, $45.00

Totman has a well-deserved reputation for writing indispensable monographs on Japanese history; this survey history of early modern Japan is equally indispensable. Beginning with the reunification of the country in the mid-16th century and continuing to the final disintegration of the Tokugawa order in the second half of the 19th century, Totman reviews all the major elements of Japanese historical development, offering a tremendous wealth of information in language that is clear, concise, and easy to comprehend. Concentrating on politics, thought, culture, and environment, Totman describes the interactions between social groups to convey the constants and the variables of Japanese life over time. At the center of his presentation is his contention that the early modern period may be divided into roughly 150 years of continuous change, followed by another 150 years of stasis. Part of what makes his project interesting is the sustained argument he offers both to demonstrate and to defend that contention. The work will be invaluable to teachers as both a text and a review. It will be equally useful for students and for general readers as a baseline of what one must know to be conversant with Tokugawa history. Includes glossary and tables. All levels.—*C. L. Yates, Earlham College*

OAB-2284　　　　DS796　　　　93-42415 CIP
Wakeman, Frederic. **Policing Shanghai, 1927-1937.** California, 1995. 507p bibl index afp ISBN 0-520-08488-8, $45.00

Wakeman (Univ. of California, Berkeley) has written a masterful treatment of the policing of Shanghai in the early 20th century. He sees Shanghai as a microcosm for understanding the problems of governance and control of modern China. As a city marked by foreign concessions and zones, Shanghai posed a formidable challenge to the Nationalists. If they could clean up a city with a notorious reputation for vice and crime, then they could advance a claim for an end to extraterritoriality and a return of national sovereignty for Shanghai and China. In a painstaking manner, Wakeman presents a fascinating and detailed portrait of the criminal links to entertainment, gambling, prostitution, narcotics, and other rackets. Nationalist attempts to organize a professional Public Security Bureau, with rational and modern procedures, constituted a bold effort to establish a new political and civic order. But continuities in Chinese bureaucratic practices, extraterritorial status, concerns about communism and Japanese expansion, and internal bickering, compromised the effectiveness of Nationalist police reforms. This is a wonderful, sophisticated study, with a wealth of insights about crime, policing, municipal governance, and the issue of social control. All levels.—*F. Ng, California State University, Fresno*

OAB-2285　　　　DS796　　　　94-34568 CIP
Wang, Shaoguang. **Failure of charisma: the cultural revolution in Wuhan,** by Wang Shaoguang. Oxford, 1995. 345p bibl index ISBN 0-19-585950-2, $75.00

Wang's book has made a pathbreaking contribution to the study of the Cultural Revolution in China. Taking the city Wuhan as a test case, Wang attempts to answer a crucial question concerning the understanding of the revolution's central paradox: if millions of ordinary Chinese had been brought into the revolution because of their genuine belief in Mao's ideals and revolutionary programs, why did their actions eventually go beyond Mao's expectations and control? Applying critically the rational choice model to his study, Wang analyzes the deep-rooted social and political causes underlying the mass movement in Wuhan. He convincingly points out that tensions had long been accumulating between the communist state and the ordinary Chinese people. Consequently, it was the potential conflict between Mao's revolutionary programs and the complex reality of Chinese society that made it impossible for Mao to control popular behavior during the Cultural Revolution. Himself a former Red Guard, Wang bases his research on large amounts of previously unused archival materials (indeed, some of his primary sources have never been used in scholarly writings in any language) and extensive personal interviews with former activists. The result is a fascinating narrative. Anyone interested in modern Chinese history, Chinese politics, the Cultural Revolution, and Mao Zedong should read the book. Upper-division undergraduates and above.—*J. Chen, Southern Illinois University at Carbondale*

OAB-2286　　　　HN723　　　　95-16279 CIP
White, James W. **Ikki: social conflict and political protest in early modern Japan.** Cornell, 1995. 348p bibl index afp ISBN 0-8014-3154-9, $39.95

Combining careful use of quantitative data, comparative historical analogy, and judicious generalizations, White has drawn on a multitude of primary and secondary sources in Western and Japanese languages to produce a benchmark study of the nature, causes, and effects of social and political conflict in early modern and Meiji Japan. The author establishes clearly the parameters of his discourse and defines what he means by "popular contention," creating a broader but more precise concept for his study. The middle chapters present quantitative data and analysis of a high order. White's work builds on previous studies of protest and conflict in the Tokugawa period (1603-1868). He confirms irrefutably that such activity did not challenge the system and that there was no plan or attempt to overthrow or replace it. The author develops a "model of popular contention" whereby he can examine theory, practice, and statistical data in a productive mix, and he uses three small case studies to illumine reality at the microlevel and as referents to explain both theory and practice at the macrolevel. White concludes that the context established by a congeries of causal factors creates social conflict and political protest, arguing that no one theory can explain the whole. One of the author's important contributions is to examine both rural and urban protest and conflict and link them in his explanation. Charts and an extensive bibliography substantially enhance the book. Highly recommended. Upper-division undergraduates and above.—*J. H. Bailey, Earlham College*

■ Europe

OAB-2287　　　　　　　　　　　Can. CIP
Clark, Samuel. **State and status: the rise of the state and aristocratic power in Western Europe.** McGill-Queen's, 1995. 502p bibl index afp ISBN 0-7735-1226-8, $55.00; ISBN 0-7735-1249-7 pbk, $24.95

Rather than consider "just" England and France, Clark—a historical sociologist—examines "two large European zones, southern Britain and its peripheries and the Paris region with its peripheries," thereby including smaller, but still significant European nations in this remarkably clear, cohesive, and genuinely comparative study. The work begins with a critique of the theoretical literature. Particularly useful is the appended section "Terms and Concepts"; although it does not include all those found in the work, it does provide a great number of definitions, especially for the complex terminology of late medieval/early modern feudal relations and customs. Secondary sources (with ample citations and a full bibliography) support the detailed narrative. Clark's prime concern is the uneven pace of "differentiation"—the process whereby status becomes distinct "from other kinds of power, especially economic, cultural, political, and military power." As he traces this pattern, he considers other sociopolitical and even geographic variables associated with aristocratic status and power. By illustrating the blurring and shifting of these variables over time, Clark provides a crisper, more refined, historically valid perspective on aristocratic roles in the early modern Western European state. Strongly recommended. Upper-division undergraduates and above.—*D. R. Skopp, SUNY College at Plattsburgh*

OAB-2288   HT690   95-13871 Orig
Crossick, Geoffrey. **The petite bourgeoisie in Europe, 1780-1914: enterprise, family and independence,** by Geoffrey Crossick and Heinz-Gerhard Haupt. Routledge, 1996 (c1995). 296p bibl index ISBN 0-415-11882-4, $75.00

Drawing on empirical evidence as well as on classical contemporary social theories, Crossick and Haupt reconstruct the world of master artisans and small shopkeepers. There have been few efforts to define the petite bourgeoisie, much less to comprehend its evolution in differing national contexts, its chronically insecure economic position, or its changing cultural and political values, although they were often parodied and frequently vilified in literature and politics during the era of European industrialization. Focusing on the specific examples of Germany, France, Britain, and Belgium (with further illustrations drawn from other national experiences), this study is comparative history at its best. While demonstrating the general fragility, flexibility, and persistence of this amorphous social stratum, the authors emphasize the diversity of local, regional, and national experiences, and link these factors to the debates concerning the role of the "lower middle class" in politics. The cooperative nature of the project, the result of a decade of international collective research and joint writing, is also a singular accomplishment and should serve as a model for future scholarship. The meticulous endnotes and excellent select bibliography will prove invaluable to researchers in social history and theory. Upper-division undergraduates and above.—*F. Burkhard, Morgan State University*

OAB-2289   D57   96-42032 MARC
Davies, Norman. **Europe: a history.** Oxford, 1996. 1,365p index afp ISBN 0-19-520912-5, $39.95

Davies has a long-established reputation as a leading authority on Polish and Eastern European history. It is therefore no surprise that in this survey of Europe from earliest times, Davies not only gives Slavic peoples their due, but also shows how Europe cannot be understood without a full appreciation of their importance. Davies writes with a balance missing in other histories, demonstrating seemingly boundless erudition and marvelously lucid and mordant style. The text is interspersed with frequent "capsules," or historical asides, on such topics as the unhappy childhood of Vlad the Impaler and the irreverent songs sung by infantrymen in WW II (two examples are hardly enough). If, however, these are delights, the maps are not; in the tradition of Sebastian Müntzer, west is disorientingly shown as up. Still, this takes nothing away from a magnificent work that will be read and cited for decades. Throughout the book and most of all at the end, Davies asks a real question: Can a continent that has seen millennia of violence and disunity yet find peace and integration? All levels.—*S. Bailey, Knox College*

OAB-2290   DA47   94-13004 CIP
Pereboom, Maarten L. **Democracies at the turning point: Britain, France and the end of the postwar order, 1928-1933.** P. Lang, 1995. 239p bibl index afp (Studies in modern European history, 13) ISBN 0-8204-2535-4, $49.95

Studies of interwar European diplomacy usually focus on the dramatic events of the late 1930s. Pereboom (Salisbury State Univ.) examines instead the policies through which Britain and France abandoned the international system they had themselves established at the Paris Peace Conference in 1919. The "turning point" was the voluntary termination in 1930 of the joint Anglo-French occupation of the German Rhineland. An unsuccessful act of appeasement that only encouraged the Germans to pursue other revisionist goals, it also signaled the end of cooperation between the two former allies. Under the leadership of Aristide Briand, this might have successfully "organized the peace." Pereboom credits Briand with a variety of "visionary" diplomatic initiatives—including an early plan for European union—to this end. For their failure he blames underlying "mentalities" in British and French political cultures, some of which are disturbingly familiar in European responses to

Balkan crises today. An exemplary work of international history, the book is based on primary and recent secondary sources in both French and English. All levels.—*J. R. Breihan, Loyola College*

OAB-2291   D295   93-26439 CIP
Schroeder, Paul W. **The transformation of European politics, 1763-1848.** Oxford, 1994. 894p bibl index afp ISBN 0-19-822119-3, $49.95

It has been 40 years since Oxford University Press published A.J.P. Taylor's study of European diplomatic history from 1848 to 1914. This new work by Schroeder, superb in its scholarly rigor and clarity of argument, is a companion piece to Taylor's *The Struggle for Mastery in Europe* (1954). But it is also very different, for where Taylor saw contingency in the realm of international politics, Schroeder sees a pattern. The Napoleonic Wars wrought a transformation in the European order; the older balance of power—anarchic, destructive, and unpredictable—was replaced by an equilibrium. However slowly the statesmen of the day learned their lesson, they learned it nonetheless; and when they made peace in Vienna in 1814-15, they abandoned the pursuit of self-interest in favor of restraint and cooperation. The treaty settlement with all its provisions mattered, but what mattered even more was the change in attitude that made it possible. The system that emerged, Schroeder contends, worked better than anything before or since. He may well be right. This is a book that, thanks to its powerful thesis (and to its lucidity and grace), will be read and discussed for decades. General and academic readers, undergraduate and above.—*S. Bailey, Knox College*

OAB-2292   D810   92-32669 CIP
Semelin, Jacques. **Unarmed against Hitler: civilian resistance in Europe, 1939-1943,** tr. by Suzan Husserl-Kapit. Praeger, 1993. 198p index afp ISBN 0-275-93960-X, $55.00

Even in the early days of WW II, when a German victory seemed close at hand, civilians throughout occupied Europe sought to resist the Nazis. After the Germans massacred their intellectuals the Poles created an underground system of schools and universities, while the French responded to compulsory labor with widespread strikes. And, as is well known, the Danes went from one act of obstruction to another, culminating in the deliverance of virtually the entire Jewish population of the country. With great clarity and scholarship, Semelin goes beyond historical particulars to define the basic principles that underlay civilian resistance. At the outset, symbols were important (French children tended to turn up dressed all in white, and in blue, and all in red on July 14), and the sense of unity and purpose that symbols created was a prerequisite for more audacious acts of resistance later on. Furthermore, the Germans often fell out among themselves as to how to respond to acts of resistance. This is an exceptional work, one that shows how important the resistance was—and not just in military terms—even before the tide of war changed in 1943. General, advanced undergraduate, and above.—*S. Bailey, Knox College*

OAB-2293   VM83   91-40929 CIP
Smith, Roger C. **Vanguard of empire: ships of exploration in the age of Columbus.** Oxford, 1993. 316p bibl indexes afp ISBN 0-19-507357-6, $35.00

Mediterranean sailors in the 14th and 15th centuries were well prepared to make thrusts into the mighty Atlantic. But the new Atlantic entry for voyaging to the Americas needed new and stronger ships. In Spanish and Portuguese shipyards the caravel and *nao* were developed. Smith's study explores the ways in which these ships of exploration and discovery were built, how they were rigged and outfitted, how they were staffed and provisioned. The detail is significant. The seams in the hull, for example, were caulked, parceled, and payed. Then the hull below the waterline was sealed. Smith defines and describes each process, thereby making them understandable. A notable chapter reveals how the ships were armed and another reviews the copious literature, including the literary and archaeological sources on which Smith's work is based. A fine, well-researched, well-written, and up-to-date endeavor. It is must reading on the ships of discovery. Those interested can also consult the periodicals *Mariner's Mirror* (v.1: 1911-) and *Terrae Incognitae* (v.1: 1969-). Graduate; faculty; professional.—*D. Jacobson, Michigan State University*

OAB-2294 D511 95-40415 CIP
Stevenson, David. **Armaments and the coming of war: Europe, 1904-1914.** Oxford, 1996. 463p bibl index afp ISBN 0-19-820208-3, $85.00

Prospective readers need not be put off by this book in the misapprehension that it peddles a familiar tale about influential merchants of death conniving successfully to unleash a relentlessly escalating arms race that inevitably culminated in war in 1914. In fact, Stevenson is at pains to note the impediments to massive increases in armaments, and his thoughtful study is a largely persuasive effort to integrate domestic pressures, technological change, and international tensions as they interacted, especially after 1910, to compel more stringent definitions of adequate military preparedness. Like David Herrmann in his less comprehensive *The Arming of Europe and the Making of the First World War* (CH, Jan'96), Stevenson stresses the recovery of Russian power and, consequently, the subsequent convergence of military and diplomatic fault lines that made peaceful resolution of crises more difficult. Paradoxically, as the two alliance blocs approached military parity in 1914, their temporary balance, the author argues, upset the prevailing equilibrium with fateful results. Incorporating a mass of archival and secondary material as well as relevant published documents, Stevenson's dense account requires considerable stamina from its readers, but those who persevere will be well equipped to contemplate the origins of the Great War. This important study is a mandatory acquisition for libraries with serious collections on the 20th century. Upper-division undergraduates and above.—*F. Coetzee, George Washington University*

Central & Eastern Europe

OAB-2295 DK265 93-5299 CIP
Brovkin, Vladimir N. **Behind the front lines of the civil war: political parties and social movements in Russia, 1918-1922.** Princeton, 1994. 455p bibl index afp ISBN 0-691-03278-5, $55.00

Brovkin's scholarly and well-written book offers a welcome supplement to Evan Mawdsley's *The Russian Civil War* (CH, May'88), which emphasizes primarily the military aspect of the Russian civil war, and W. Bruce Lincoln's *Red Victory* (1989), which is a lively narrative account. Although several other works have appeared in recent years dealing with varying social aspects of the civil war, Brovkin's work is the most in-depth and systematic analysis of the complex and often chaotic relations among diverse social, military, and political forces from 1918 to 1921. He convincingly demonstrates that the "Red" versus "White" approach is too simplistic. As he states it: "The key to understanding the civil war as a whole is that there were many different conflicts unfolding at the same time." Among the conflicts he treats especially well are those between the peasants and both the Reds and Whites. Footnotes. Recommended for undergraduates and above.—*W. G. Moss, Eastern Michigan University*

OAB-2296 DR2173 95-13319 CIP
Danforth, Loring M. **The Macedonian conflict: ethnic nationalism in a transnational world.** Princeton, 1995. 273p bibl index afp ISBN 0-691-04357-4, $29.95

Danforth's book is a clear presentation of the complex historical background of ethnic conflict in the Balkans, specifically for the region of Macedonia. Danforth, a cultural anthropologist with considerable fieldwork in Greece and Macedonia and among Balkan emigré communities in English-speaking nations abroad, offers a thoughtful analysis of the principles and feelings that determine ethnicity. He traces the development of a Macedonian national identity that is distinct from other south Slavs and Greeks. He also documents a Greek hostility toward Macedonian identity that is a stumbling block to political stability in the

southern Balkans. Danforth employs a wide variety of historical, political, linguistic, and sociological sources to argue his case. Moreover, his examination of Greek and Macedonian emigré attitudes—a major factor sustaining the continuing tension in the region—is fresh and without parallel. This persuasive book should be read by everyone with an interest in the Balkans. All levels.—*E. N. Borza, Pennsylvania State University, University Park Campus*

OAB-2297 DK266 96-29714 CIP
Davies, R.W. **Soviet history in the Yeltsin era.** Macmillan (UK)/St. Martin's/CREES, 1997. 264p index ISBN 0-312-17372-5, $69.95

Davies (emeritus, Univ. of Birmingham) has written a lucid, brilliant account of the challenges and problems confronting Boris Yeltsin's Russia in coming to grips with the Soviet era. The author sketches the history of recent Russia and then launches into a fascinating examination of Russian historiography and scholarship on a range of issues, e.g., Lenin, Trotsky, Stalin, Bukharin, N.E.P., Witte, Stolypin, Nicholas II, orthodoxy, and many other topics. He examines the controversial claim by some historians that Stalin was planning to attack Hitler in July 1941 and finds no convincing evidence of such a plan. He deals at length with the current problems revolving around accessibility to the Soviet archives. This book is a solid performance, brimming over with insights into the ongoing drama of Russia's transition from one party dictatorship to democracy. It is based on Soviet archival material and publications derived from the archives. Highly recommended for upper-division undergraduates and above.—*D. J. Dunn, Southwest Texas State University*

OAB-2298 BM535 93-35689 CIP
Dietrich, Donald J. **God and humanity in Auschwitz: Jewish-Christian relations and sanctioned murder.** Transaction, 1995. 355p bibl index ISBN 1-56000-147-X, $34.95

Dietrich's ambitious study makes an important contribution to understanding the interrelationship of the historical role of antisemitism in Christian theology, the Holocaust, and the ongoing dialogue between Christians and Jews. Dietrich argues that although religious antisemitism alone was not a sufficient condition for the Holocaust, it was a necessary one. Making good use of the vast interdisciplinary literature that deals with the origins and results of the Holocaust, he traces the development of Christian antisemitism within its various historical contexts and examines in detail the ways in which Christian and Jewish theologians have been forced to rethink their view of themselves and of each other in the post-Holocaust era. Particularly interesting is the chapter "The Holocaust and Modernity," in which Dietrich examines how sociopolitical, cultural, and psychological factors may make genocide possible and suggests means for combating such developments. The work contains detailed footnotes and an excellent bibliography. Upper-division undergraduate and above.—*W. Smaldone, Willamette University*

OAB-2299 DR1685 94-162223 CIP
Donia, Robert J. **Bosnia and Hercegovina: a tradition betrayed,** by Robert J. Donia and John V.A. Fine. Columbia, 1994. 318p bibl index afp ISBN 0-231-10160-0, $24.95

In this eloquent study, Donia and Fine trace the history of Bosnian society from the early medieval period to the present. Both respected scholars, the authors show the rich tradition of diversity, pluralism, and toleration that existed for centuries between Muslims, Serbs, and Croats in Bosnia. These peoples together created a successful multiethnic tradition based on coalition building and pragmatic compromise. The picture the authors paint contrasts sharply with the popular images of violence, religious persecution, and tribal hatred that dominate current policy discussions and the media. They show how extreme nationalists in other areas of the Balkans have wrought terror, destruction, and death in Bosnia during the past several years. Their study (for which Fine wrote the chapters dealing with the medieval and Ottoman periods and Donia those dealing with the modern era) goes beyond the narrative of events to treat broad patterns and long-term developments, while at the same time shedding light on the post-1992 conflict in Bosnia. It is a reliable corrective to political polemicism and short-range policy expediency from which scholars and non-scholars alike can benefit. Maps, tables, and a helpful chronology complement the book. General readers through faculty.—*P. W. Knoll, University of Southern California*

OAB-2300 DK260 96-36761 CIP
Figes, Orlando. **A people's tragedy: a history of the Russian Revolution.** Viking, 1996. 923p bibl index afp ISBN 0-670-85916-8, $34.95

Figes (Trinity College, Cambridge) has written a solid and fascinating history of the Russian Revolution from 1917 to Lenin's death in 1924. Colorful and incisive, the study exhaustively treats the causes and course of what is unquestionably the most deliberate and extensive effort at social engineering. New details and insight add richness and verve to the tragic story of Russia's failed revolution. The book is particularly compelling because it focuses on individuals to flesh out the larger picture of Russia's experience. Although saturnine and anguished, the story nonetheless conveys a prevailing, if muted, optimism: the tragedy was not inevitable. It could have been avoided. However, it can be repeated. To avert it in the future, leaders, in Figes's view, must be committed to realistic ideals based firmly on tradition and human experience. The work nicely complements Richard Pipes's *Russia under the Bolshevik Regime* (1993). It is based on original and secondary sources. All levels.—*D. J. Dunn, Southwest Texas State University*

OAB-2301 HD1492 93-4786 CIP
Fitzpatrick, Sheila. **Stalin's peasants: resistance and survival in the Russian village after collectivization.** Oxford, 1994. 386p index afp ISBN 0-19-506982-X, $35.00

Fitzpatrick's book deals with perhaps the most traumatic experience in the post-emancipation history of the Russian peasantry—collectivization of agriculture in the 1930s. The authorities had often intervened in traditional peasant life, but as the author notes in her introduction, "no previous state reform had been conducted so violently and coercively, involved such a direct and all-encompassing assault on peasant values, or taken so much while offering so little." Freeing the period from many Soviet myths, Fitzpatrick emphasizes the range of strategies that the oppressed and exploited victims of communist policies in the countryside employed to protect their interests and to contend with catastrophic conditions imposed on the peasants by the state. As part of her narrative, Fitzpatrick also presents a richly documented and well-argued analysis of the impact of collectivization on the changing social and cultural life of the village. This is a rare example of a scholarly work in which historical abstractions and obscurities emerge as real people with genuine concerns, values, and choices. Upper-division undergraduates and above.—*A. Geifman, Boston University*

OAB-2302 HT145 95-12855 CIP
French, R. Antony. **Plans, pragmatism and people: the legacy of Soviet planning for today's cities.** Pittsburgh, 1995. 233p bibl index ISBN 0-8229-1184-1, $49.95; ISBN 0-8229-6106-7 pbk, $19.95

French's brief but very useful overview of the legacy of the Soviet city focuses on its past and present physical layout and on social geography. The author investigates how much of the current urban scene is the product of planning and, in a broader vein, seeks to evaluate the "City of Socialist Man" as a response to distinctive political, economic, and social processes. French (University College, London), an urban geographer and planning specialist, has been a leading scholar of Soviet urbanism for two decades. His study examines the pre-Soviet past, the periods of Soviet city-building, persistent problems of the now post-Soviet city, the changing social geography of these cities, and the impact of the automobile on settlement patterns, as well as evaluates the Soviet planning experience. This is a major contribution to the literature, bringing the field of Soviet urbanism into the 1990s and updating Chauncy Harris's seminal *Cities of the Soviet Union* (CH, Dec'70). Figures are well drawn, but the number of

maps is disappointingly small. Photographs, however, are both abundant and particularly supportive of text descriptions of urban landscapes. Thorough, up-to-date bibliography. All levels.—*P. O. Muller, University of Miami*

OAB-2303 DS558 95-52204 CIP
Gaiduk, Ilya V. **The Soviet Union and the Vietnam War.** I.R. Dee, 1996. 299p bibl index afp ISBN 1-56663-103-3, $28.50

Based on exclusive access to newly available Soviet archives, this path-breaking book provides a fascinating treatment of the performance of the Soviet Union during the Vietnam War. Throughout the book, Gaiduk highlights the dilemma in Moscow's policy: on one hand, the Kremlin could not turn down the Vietnamese requests for aid for fear of losing its credibility as a leader in the Communist movement; on the other hand, it was afraid that a widening of the war might involve the Soviet Union in a direct conflict with the US, thereby jeopardizing detente with the West. As a result, Moscow adopted a two-pronged approach to the Indochina conflict. While providing Hanoi with weapons to fight the Americans, the Soviet Union also engaged in behind-the-scenes diplomacy to facilitate a negotiated settlement. A strength of the study is Gaiduk's skillful juxtaposition of Moscow's Vietnam policy with its complex relationship with China and the US. A major contribution to the emerging international history of the Vietnam War. All levels.—*Q. Zhai, Auburn University at Montgomery*

OAB-2304 DR250 93-31575 CIP
Hitchins, Keith. **Rumania, 1866-1947.** Oxford, 1994. 579p bibl index afp ISBN 0-19-822126-6, $49.95

Hitchins (Univ. of Illinois), the leading historian of Romania in the US, has produced a book that is well written, thoughtful, and useful to anyone interested in the formation of the modern Romanian nation. The themes are explicit: Romania has struggled to develop a stable ethnic nation-state against the forces of internal strife and external threats. Romanian ethnicity is based on a Latinate language and a defense against continuing threats, in particular the Magyars to the west and Slavs (especially the Russians) on all other sides: "this Latin isle in a Slavic sea." The Romanians chose to model their national life after the West, but the incorporation of Romania into the Soviet economy and political system in 1947 marked the end of the nation's evolution into a Western state. It had become isolated from the West, and had returned to the East. Hitchins rightly calls this the end of modern Romania. The book has only one map—insufficient to support the high quality of the text—but there is an excellent bibliographical essay. This volume is a welcome addition to "The Oxford history of Modern Europe" series and to the general historical literature on Romania. General and academic readers, upper-division undergraduate and above.—*E. N. Borza, Pennsylvania State University, University Park Campus*

OAB-2305 DAW1038 95-46619 CIP
Johnson, Lonnie R. **Central Europe: enemies, neighbors, friends.** Oxford, 1996. 339p index afp ISBN 0-19-510071-9, $30.00

Johnson's superb survey, rich with historical insights and well-drawn descriptions of events and people, focuses on a region too little known and understood in the US. Johnson includes Germany as well as Poland and the lands of the old Habsburg Empire in his evenhanded and objective treatment. His coverage includes the medieval period as well as the modern; events in those former centuries have often conditioned and defined more recent national assumptions and aspirations. One of the book's greatest strengths is the author's success in showing thematically how the several peoples and nations of this region have struggled with imperial powers and how these experiences (summed up in the book's subtitle) have created an ambiguous and diverse heritage. Fine maps, effective illustrations, and an admirably clear and engaging writing style enhance a work that is sure to become a standard, along with Piotr Wandycz's recent history of the same region, *The Price of Freedom* (1992). Johnson's 20-page epilogue on developments since the revolutionary events of 1989 is particularly good in analyzing similarities and differences and the prospects of the region. It constitutes the best brief treatment of these matters currently available. All levels.—*P. W. Knoll, University of Southern California*

OAB-2306   94-78517 CIP
Kaplan, Herbert H. **Russian overseas commerce with Great Britain during the reign of Catherine II.** American Philosophical Society, 1995. 309p bibl index (Memoirs of the American Philosophical Society, 218) ISBN 0-87169-218-X, $40.00

Kaplan's new book is a result of meticulous scholarship, sophisticated analysis, and an exemplary effort at interpretation of handwritten materials. Through scrupulous examination of new Russian and British archival sources, the author convincingly demonstrates that "Russia's impact on the British economy" during the reign of Catherine II "was both profound and widespread." The vital importance of the economic relationship between the two empires in the period when Russia contributed a great deal to the British industrial revolution, as well as Britain's military and political buildup, is demonstrated by the "quantity, quality, and range of Russian grown and manufactured products, transacted by British merchants at home and resident in Russia." Relying heavily on a detailed examination of commercial manuscripts, customs materials, and information pertaining to financial treaties and traffics, Kaplan's study is the first scholarly work about the particulars of Anglo-Russian trade in the second half of the 18th century. His intelligent analysis thus makes an important contribution to the general field of European economic history. Upper-division undergraduates and above.—*A. Geifman, Boston University*

OAB-2307   N6754   95-10237 CIP
Kaufmann, Thomas DaCosta. **Court, cloister, and city: the art and culture of Central Europe, 1450-1800.** Chicago, 1995. 576p index afp ISBN 0-226-42729-3, $45.00

Many years in the making and based particularly on the author's expertise in Hapsburg lands, this handsomely produced work treats the art, architecture, and—broadly speaking—the culture of what is termed "Central Europe" in the three and one-half centuries before the era of the French Revolution. Important and stimulating, Kaufmann's study examines the cultural legacy of a region too little known and understood in the anglo- and francophone West. The book's emphasis on royal, princely, and aristocratic courts, on ecclesiastical sites (both monastic and urban), and on civilian and domestic painting, sculpture, and architecture ensures a rich and comprehensive coverage. The volume is beautifully illustrated; virtually every page reveals a treasure. Almost encyclopedic in its scope, the book nevertheless pursues an interpretation that places these individual elements in the social, intellectual, and religious context of cultural and national assumptions, aims, and purposes. Not all readers will agree with some of Kaufmann's views (e.g., his designation of "Central Europe"), but many of his insights are brilliant. The chapter "Polonia Victoriosa; Austria Gloriosa" on the different directions these two traditions took in the decades after the relief of Vienna in 1683 is but one example. Judicious notes, helpful maps, and a short bibliography effectively complement the study. All levels.—*P. W. Knoll, University of Southern California*

OAB-2308   HX315   96-21388 CIP
Kenney, Padraic. **Rebuilding Poland: workers and Communists, 1945-1950.** Cornell, 1997. 360p bibl index afp ISBN 0-8014-3287-1, $39.95

Kenney's impressive scholarly work uses a broad range of sources (many from archives opened since 1989) to reinterpret the social and political bases on which communism was built in Poland after WW II. Kenney focuses on workers in two places not well analyzed in previous scholarship, Łódź and Wrocław. The former city, where there were numerous strikes, was an important textile center and prewar Poland's largest manufacturing center. The latter, where there was little labor conflict, had been part of the German Reich before 1939 and was rebuilt as Polish after the war. The author concludes that workers resisted efforts to establish communist control over factories where they had preexisting orga-

nizational structures and cultural roots. Where communist control was stronger, much of the work force had been imported from other areas. Kenney further argues that the postwar regime, frustrated in its efforts to achieve labor control, turned to competition between groups of workers and that this ultimately left it hostage to the fortunes of the economy and the attitudes of the workforce. Illustrations, figures, and maps complement this important study of the social and political evolution of postwar Poland. All levels.—*P. W. Knoll, University of Southern California*

OAB-2309   DR1246   96-10390 CIP
Lampe, John R. **Yugoslavia as history: twice there was a country.** Cambridge, 1996. 421p bibl index ISBN 0-521-46122-7, $59.95; ISBN 0-521-46705-5 pbk, $19.95

Lampe's book will undoubtedly become the standard resource for the history of Yugoslavia. It is concise, clear, well written, and soundly based. Lampe examines the strengths and the weaknesses of this multinational state, which was created out of the chaos of WW I, torn apart in WW II, and revived once more as a nonconformist communist regime headed by Josip Broz Tito. The author refutes many of the historical misconceptions about Yugoslavia that have filled the media in the past few years. He puts special emphasis on the distinct histories, constant migrations, and interactions of the various peoples (nationalities/ethnic groups) who made up Yugoslavia, and examines why a strong Yugoslav identity could never be created. The book is well balanced by period, and is especially strong in economic, political, and diplomatic history. Lampe draws deeply on the most recent American research on Yugoslavia, from PhD dissertations to articles and books by established scholars, as well as on works from former Yugoslavia and Western Europe. Selected bibliography of books in English and German. Recommended for all libraries. All levels.—*E. M. Despalatovic, Connecticut College*

OAB-2310   DK166   92-5176 CIP
Leonard, Carol S. **Reform and regicide: the reign of Peter III of Russia.** Indiana, 1993. 232p bibl index afp ISBN 0-253-33322-9, $35.00

Leonard challenges the standard interpretation of the reign of Peter III, which she argues is based on Catherine the Great's "self-justifying explanations" for the coup that ended Peter's rule and life. Rather than arbitrary despotism, Leonard finds Peter's reign one of "astonishing achievement" that shows the "force of the Petrine imperial idea" and "left Catherine a legacy of reforms" to continue. Although focused on the details of Peter's reign, Leonard's study makes clear the relevance of that reign for the long-term significance of the "political legacy of Peter I." The government of Peter III was not an aberration, but an essential step in Russia's political development. Although Leonard completed a prodigious amount of archival research, her most valuable service may be a thorough reading of and learned commentary on the extensive secondary literature. This book is an important contribution to an understanding of the development of the Russian political tradition. Advanced undergraduate; graduate; faculty.—*J. T. Flynn, College of the Holy Cross*

OAB-2311   D802   93-13363 CIP
Mazower, Mark. **Inside Hitler's Greece: the experience of occupation, 1941-1944.** Yale, 1993. 437p index ISBN 0-300-05804-7, $30.00

Already acknowledged (the British edition) as one of the best books on modern Greece, this finely produced study surveys in depth the vicissitudes of WW II in modern Greece. In a series of tightly argued chapters based on newly tapped original sources and supplemented by hitherto unpublished photographs, Mazower outlines the conquest, occupation, famine, black market, the traditional and newly emerging leadership, and its repercussions for the civil war period that racked Greece for another five years. He also described the wartime resistance and its social, economic, and demographic impact on the local population, and provides a sophisticated insight into all levels of German attitudes towards the Greeks. The author's chapter on the Jews breaks new ground on this special Greek tragedy for the general historian (cf. *Encyclopedia of the Holocaust*, CH, Jun'90, for specifics). This book, whose scholarship is exceeded perhaps only by its elegant style, is a sine qua non for anyone interested in WW II in general and modern Greece in particular. Highly recommended for all libraries. All levels.—*S. Bowman, University of Cincinnati*

OAB-2312   HD6948   95-37346 CIP
McCaffray, Susan P. **The politics of industrialization in tsarist Russia: the Association of Southern Coal and Steel Producers, 1874-1914.** Northern Illinois, 1996. 299p bibl index afp ISBN 0-87580-204-4, $35.00

McCaffray's well-researched, clearly written monograph describes the history and nature of the Association of Southern Coal and Steel Producers in Russia's (now Ukraine's) Donbass region from its formation in 1874 until the Russian Revolution of 1917 that brought it to an end. As the first major Russian industrial advocacy group, the Association grew quickly into one of the most powerful in tsarist Russia. Using Russian and Belgian archival materials, especially the published records of the Association, McCaffray describes its leaders, their meetings, and their aspirations. The engineer-managers, who by 1890 asserted control over the Association, groped their way toward an industrialized Russia of welfare capitalism, reserving a considerable role for government. McCaffray discusses the economic conditions of workers in a Donbass they viewed as "a poor man's America," after poverty drove them from surrounding provinces. She traces the Association largely chronologically from its beginnings, through the boom years of the 1890s, the trauma of the 1905 Revolution, into WW I. The author's expert treatment is enhanced by many tables, maps, appendixes, and an impressive bibliography. Recommended for upper-division undergraduates and above.—*D. MacKenzie, University of North Carolina at Greensboro*

OAB-2313   DK288   92-56841 CIP
Remnick, David. **Lenin's tomb: the last days of the Soviet empire.** Random House, 1993. 576p bibl index afp ISBN 0-679-42376-1, $25.00

Remnick, a staff writer for *The New Yorker* and a former reporter for *The Washington Post* in Moscow, has written a brilliant history and analysis of the last days of the Soviet empire. The book is not only the best study available of the waning years of the Gorbachev regime, the attempted coup, and the emergence of Yeltsin, but it also tells the story with drama, insight, and fascinating detail. The overarching theme of Remnick's riveting book is the reappearance of history in the Soviet Union and in post-Soviet Russia. History provides continuity, meaning, and texture to life, and the author shows how the determination to get at the truth and to tell the truth blew away the phantasmagoria of Soviet ideology and officialdom. Lies, half-truths, and omissions became unbearable as new revelation followed new revelation. The book is based primarily on interviews and eyewitness accounts. Good listing of sources. Highly recommended. All levels.—*D. J. Dunn, Southwest Texas State University*

OAB-2314   DS135   91-45644 CIP
Roland, Charles G. **Courage under siege: starvation, disease, and death in the Warsaw ghetto.** Oxford, 1992. 310p bibl index afp ISBN 0-19-506285-X, $30.00

The tragic 30-month history of the Warsaw Ghetto has traditionally been told in political, military, organizational, and—of course—individual and human terms. Drawn from eyewitness testimony of survivors as well as archival and printed sources, this book makes an important contribution to Holocaust literature in general and the story of the ghetto in particular by focusing on the medical disaster that took place. Roland (history of medicine, McMaster Univ.) provides an eloquent portrait of the ravages of typhus, tuberculosis, and starvation; an inspiring study in the heroism of men and women of the medical community in the ghetto; and an analysis of the educational and scientific work carried out under conditions almost too horrible to imagine. The numerous tables (especially those tracing morbidity and mortality) the well-chosen

photographs, and extensive documentation (70 pages of notes and references) complement the text. A moving and an instructive book. General; undergraduate; graduate; faculty.—*P. W. Knoll, University of Southern California*

OAB-2315   DK771   93-42011 CIP
Stephan, John J. **The Russian Far East: a history.** Stanford, 1994. 481p bibl index afp ISBN 0-8047-2311-7, $49.50

Stephan seems to have intended his book for readers familiar with Russian history but with only sketchy knowledge, at best, of the area he covers: the Pacific Coast areas of the Russian Republic and the regions extending as far as 2,000 miles westward. In this rather short volume, he covers the geography, ethnology, and early history of the region, but concentrates on the period since Russian annexation in the 1860s. The author describes a uniquely cosmopolitan part of the empire, the travails of the revolutionary and civil war periods, and the emergence of strong local communist leaders. Stalin's terror, which destroyed the local leadership as well as brought new fame to the region in the Magadan penal institutions, is perhaps the most vividly portrayed period in the book. Altogether, this is a most impressive tour de force. Stephan's work is readable and has strong opinions, humor, and an analytic focus as well. The bibliography and notes are extensive, and considerable archival material backs up the 20th-century sections. Highly recommended. Upper-division undergraduates and above.—*J. Zimmerman, University of Pittsburgh at Greensburg*

OAB-2316   DK266   91-33592 CIP
Stites, Richard. **Russian popular culture: entertainment and society since 1900.** Cambridge, 1992. 269p bibl disc index (Cambridge Soviet paperbacks, 7) ISBN 0-521-36214-8, $44.95; ISBN 0-521-36986-X pbk, $14.95

Stites, author of *Revolutionary Dreams: Utopian Vision and Experimental Life in the Russian Revolution* (CH, Jun'89) has written an excellent and much-needed introduction to popular culture in 20th-century Russia. Americans are much more familiar with the boring "official" culture of the Soviet period than with Russia's love songs, popular humor, and favorite books. What did people do when they were not working? Who were their heroes? What did they enjoy reading, seeing, hearing? Stites looks at folk music and dance, popular songs, the circus, the popular stage, detective and science fiction, radio, film, and television against a backdrop of political and social change. He points out striking parallels with American popular culture, yet stresses the unique aspects of the Russian experience. This is a solidly based work, rich in detail and analysis. It includes a fine bibliography, discography, filmography, and videography and footnotes. A must for undergraduate, graduate, and research libraries, and also of interest to general readers.—*E. M. Despalatović, Connecticut College*

OAB-2317   DR1535   96-44513 CIP
Tanner, Marcus. **Croatia: a nation forged in war.** Yale, 1997. 338p bibl index afp ISBN 0-300-06933-2, $30.00

Tanner's book is a balanced, meticulously documented, and dispassionate account of Croatia's past and present, comparable to Noel Malcolm's similar treatment of Bosnia (*Bosnia: A Short History*, CH, Apr'95). Tanner covers all that one would expect in a work of this sort: the medieval establishment of Croatia, Croatia as part of the Austro-Hungarian Empire, resistance to the Ottomans, Croatia's role in the first Yugoslavia, the Ustashe collaborationist government, the Croatian Spring under communism, Franjo Tudjman's ascension to power, the recent war with Serbia, and the current situation. Tanner's assessment of this complex subject includes attention to incredibly detailed facts and the journalist's tendency to balance every interpretation with a contrary one; a clarity of prose in place of the usual historical jargon; and a palpable lack of the proverbial "ax to grind." This book is another example of nonhistorians, particularly journalists, writing better history books than historians. By far, the best book on the history of Croatia ever published. Excellent and extensive index. Strongly recommended for all levels.—*S. G. Mestrović, Texas A&M University*

OAB-2318 D764 94-2964 CIP
Tumarkin, Nina. **The living & the dead: the rise and fall of the cult of World War II in Russia.** Basic Books, 1994. 242p index ISBN 0-465-07159-7, $25.00

Tumarkin's book about the legacy of WW II in the Soviet Union and post-Communist Russia is a work of the foremost importance: painful memory of 30 million lost lives and the suffering of the survivors became integral parts of the Russian mentality and the country's social and cultural tradition. This study is equally vital for an understanding of Russia's political history, since for decades the Soviet government exploited the great national trauma and its mythology to enhance the party's prestige and authority. Tumarkin's depiction of the cult's abatement in the 1990s also contributes greatly to our conception of the emerging new Russia. The book owes its success to the author's ability to integrate historical sources (written evidence, as well as oral testimonies) with deep personal experience and a great deal of thought in a lucidly written and moving narrative. Tumarkin (Wellesley College) displays the perception, intuition, and empathy of a genuine humanist. Her book is a rare example of an absorbing historical study in which the abstractions of death and memory are transformed into a vivid discourse—full of immediate meaning. All levels.—*A. Geifman, Boston University*

OAB-2319 Orig
Vickers, Miranda. **The Albanians: a modern history.** I.B. Tauris, 1995. 262p bibl index ISBN 1-85043-749-1, $49.50

Vickers's excellent, well-written survey of Albania's entire history is most welcome. After providing basic facts about the Albanian tribes' early history, the author notes their conversion to Orthodoxy or Catholicism. Subsequently, almost 500 years of Ottoman rule caused many Albanians to become Muslims and delayed the development of a national consciousness, ensuring that Albania would be the last Balkan nation to achieve independence. Most of the book deals with Albania's turbulent 20th-century history. Following the First Balkan War, an independent Albania emerged in 1913 and the European powers imposed William of Wied, an ineffective German prince, as its ruler. At the 1919 Paris Peace Conference, the powers drew Albania's boundaries, arbitrarily awarding Kosova to Yugoslavia. During the interwar years Albania was dominated by fascist Italy, which conquered and occupied it during WW II. In the post-WW II era, Albania was ruled for 40 years by Enver Hoxha as Communist dictator. The book concludes with the demise of communism, 1989-91, and Albania's struggle to escape backwardness and isolation and move toward democracy and a market economy. Good illustrations and maps. The work is based chiefly on English-language sources. All levels.—*D. MacKenzie, University of North Carolina at Greensboro*

FRANCE, ITALY & SPAIN

OAB-2320 JV1811 96-33804 Orig
Aldrich, Robert. **Greater France: a history of French overseas expansion.** St. Martin's, 1996. 369p bibl index ISBN 0-312-15999-4, $45.00; ISBN 0-312-16000-3 pbk, $19.95

Aldrich (Univ. of Sydney) is known for his studies of the French empire, especially in the Pacific. *Greater France* is a comprehensive and effective synthesis of the "new" empire focusing on the years 1830-1962; an epilogue extends the story to the 1980s. A review of empire under the ancien regime and assessment of the impact of the Revolution on colonies sets the scene for chapters on Africa, the Indian Ocean, Asia, Pacific, and Antarctica, tracing a trajectory from conquest to consolidation to nationalist movements, decolonization, and independence. In its ideology of empire and expectations of the value of colonies to the metropolis, France did not differ greatly from other European powers. Remarkable, and underlined by Aldrich in highlighting individuals and incidents, was the ad hoc quality of empire-building, its lack of a master plan or coherent objectives. Motives were strategic, commercial quest for prestige, and

sense of civilizing mission. This is empire seen from Paris. The chapter on how colonial culture permeated metropolitan life is fascinating. Balanced and clearly written, Aldrich's study reflects current research findings and superb mastery of the rich historiography. The bibliographical essay is indispensable; maps are excellent; the index is comprehensible. This volume provides a historical dimension to contemporary events in the French-influenced world. Required reading for students of history, comparative imperialism, political science, and international relations. Upper-division undergraduates and above.—*A. J. R. Russell-Wood, Johns Hopkins University*

OAB-2321 DC252 93-18279 CIP
Aminzade, Ronald. **Ballots and barricades: class formation and republican politics in France, 1830-1871.** Princeton, 1993. 321p bibl index afp ISBN 0-691-09479-9, $49.50; ISBN 0-691-02871-0 pbk, $18.95

The history of the republican movement in France from 1830 to 1871 can be fairly said to be the history of failure—failure to win power in popular insurrections and failure to win power in the polling place. Karl Marx blamed the petit bourgeoisie, and subsequent authors have also provided reductionist explanations. Now, in a work of exemplary scholarship, Aminzade demonstrates how complicated matters really were. Class background was scarcely enough to make one Frenchman a socialist, while another might be a radical or a liberal. And, as Aminzade shows in the cases of St. Etienne, Rouen, and Toulouse, republicans behaved very differently in different places. Toulouse was perhaps the most interesting case; there the artisan class showed a strong affinity with Icarian socialism. If French republicans had anything in common, it was a shared fraternal aversion to giving women a voice in politics. In the end, however, the French republican movement emerged from the debacle of the Commune tempered by defeat and prepared to rally to parliamentary democracy. This is a work of considerable insight and a major contribution to the understanding of France in the 19th century. General readers, advanced undergraduates, and above.—*S. Bailey, Knox College*

OAB-2322 HC388 93-4251 CIP
Bensch, Stephen P. **Barcelona and its rulers, 1096-1291.** Cambridge, 1995. 457p bibl index (Cambridge studies in medieval life and thought, 4th series, 26) ISBN 0-521-43511-0, $64.95

Bensch presents a well-written study of the development of the town of Barcelona during the 12th and 13th centuries. Starting with a synthesis of recent theory regarding the evolution of medieval towns, Bensch places his own work in the center of a lively debate concerning the relationship of town and countryside. Much of this discussion has usually centered on the role of the urban patriciate as an integrative force between the emerging municipality and its environmental hinterlands. The author then studies Barcelona's particular place during the formative centuries, tracing an early period of economic development that proves initially stunted with the approach of the mid-12th century, a period argued by Bensch to precede the evolution of a full-bodied patriciate. Discussion of the renewed expansion of Barcelona's economic life under the management of the maturing patriciate between 1140 and 1291 occupies the remainder of the book. Bensch offers extensive archival research in support of his model, with a complete array of tables, charts, and maps to assist the reader. The work includes an appendix with the genealogies of a few of the major patriciate families in Barcelona during the era. Highly recommended. Upper-division undergraduates and above.—*J. F. Powers, College of the Holy Cross*

OAB-2323 DG571 96-53410 CIP
Berezin, Mabel. **Making the fascist self: the political culture of interwar Italy.** Cornell, 1997. 267p index afp ISBN 0-8014-3202-2, $45.00; ISBN 0-8014-8420-0 pbk, $18.95

Reconstruction of the political rituals of fascism that merged the public and private spheres in rewriting the patterns of Italian civic life is the theme of this excellent interdisciplinary work. Progressing from a commemorative

Social & Behavioral Sciences

period that made the 1922 March on Rome the centerpiece of rituals to a mobilization phase after 1934, which emphasized athletic and military bodies, Berezin delineates the phases in which rituals of the piazza passed from emphasizing the myth of national revolution to that creating the myths of the new Roman empire. Despite what Berezin sees as the fascist "colonization" of time and space, it never could erase the presence of the Catholic sphere. In a fascinating chapter, the author uses Verona to illustrate the ritualization process on a local level and the significance of visits by Mussolini. Drawing from journals, photographs, propaganda pamphlets and, in the final chapter, the often party created obituaries of fallen soldiers, Berezin's work is a splendid addition to literature on fascist politicization of culture and civic life. Recommended for all college and university libraries. Upper-division undergraduates and above.—*M. S. Miller, emeritus, University of Illinois at Chicago*

OAB-2324 HN475 91-45267 CIP
Cohn, Samuel K. **The cult of remembrance and the Black Death: six Renaissance cities in central Italy.** Johns Hopkins, 1992. 429p bibl index afp ISBN 0-8018-4303-0, $47.50

Following his acclaimed *Death and Property in Siena, 1205-1800* (1988), Cohn (Brandeis Univ.) here examines nearly 3,400 testaments from the 12th through the 15th century, drawn from archives of six central Italian city-states. He argues that after the second wave of the Black Death (1361-63), these records reveal a shift from other-worldly to worldly concerns associated with the Renaissance, by emphasizing memorials rather than pious bequests. Cohn's creative, comparative analysis challenges interpretations by art historians and others that this shift is first and best observed among wealthy and powerful Florentines. Briskly written, with hundreds of often colorful quotations from the testaments, his argument rests on a sophisticated multiple regression model. If Cohn's statistical method has a weakness—aside from the unevenness of his database—it is that he is more attentive to sheer numbers of bequests (pious versus memorial) than to the actual proportion of an estate devoted to such purposes. The many statistical tables would have been more useful if rendered as graphs or charts. With full citations of primary and secondary sources and a comprehensive bibliography including recent Italian works, this work is highly recommended for libraries with holdings in late medieval and early modern European history. Advanced undergraduate; graduate; faculty.—*D. R. Skopp, SUNY College at Plattsburgh*

OAB-2325 DG637 95-26585 CIP
Epstein, Steven A. **Genoa & the Genoese, 958-1528.** North Carolina, 1996. 396p bibl index afp ISBN 0-8078-2291-4, $45.00

In this beautifully produced volume dedicated to David Herlihy, Epstein (Univ. of Colorado, Boulder) provides a general history of Genoa in the Middle Ages. His main sources come from abundant materials in the Archivio di Stato of Genoa and include public documents, private agreements, and such semipublic materials as notaries' cartularies. His main focus is political events and economic trends, although some attempt is made to consider social conditions and cultural accomplishments. In spite of the importance of Genoa in the growth of medieval trade and in devising new methods of spreading risk, the picture Epstein draws is one of failure, because of political immurement at home, to capitalize on Genoa's undoubted importance in Mediterranean trade. By the close of the Middle Ages, the attempt at self-rule had not succeeded and Genoa came under the domination of outside powers. All levels.—*K. F. Drew, Rice University*

OAB-2326 DC611 92-20828 CIP
Ford, Caroline. **Creating the nation in provincial France: religion and political identity in Brittany.** Princeton, 1993. 255p bibl index afp ISBN 0-691-05667-6, $45.00

Using Finistère in Brittany as the focus of this excellent revisionist study, Ford analyzes how local social Catholicism responded to the Third Republic's attempts to integrate the region into its vision of nation building. Resist-

ing yet appropriating the republican structure and vocabulary, the social Catholicism of the local clergy rallied to Pope Leo XIII's 1890 encyclical by working through educational institutions of the congregational *Filles du Saint-Esprit* (important for women), agrarian cooperatives, and courses of study at Quimper's seminary. Thus they forged the politics of Christian Democracy, lying between the anticlerical Left and the right-wing monarchists supported by nobility. The petitions framed by Bretons, especially during the 1902 protests against the Combes ministry's 1901 Law of Associations banning religious instruction and regional language, demonstrated their defense of the republican world they created. An antidote to Eugene Weber's *Peasant into Frenchmen: The Modernization of Rural France 1870-1914* (CH, Feb'77), which argues the importance of central policies in nation building, Ford's study is superbly researched and engagingly written. Maps and charts abound; the bibliography is extensive. Highly recommended for all university and college libraries. Advanced undergraduate; graduate; faculty.—*M. S. Miller, University of Illinois at Chicago*

OAB-2327 HV6969 93-10328 CIP
Greenshields, Malcolm. **An economy of violence in early modern France: crime and justice in the Haute Auvergne, 1587-1664.** Pennsylvania State, 1995 (c1994). 262p bibl index afp ISBN 0-271-01009-6, $45.00

In this absorbing study, Greenshields (Univ. of Lethbridge) has detailed the beginnings of the shift from private to public justice in the Haute Auvergne. He contends that physical violence, especially directed socially downward, in defense of "honor, dignity, space, possessions, and the physical person," and of "psychic property," represents an "economy of violence." There is a fine, clear section on the judicial procedure of the period. Greenshields notes the lack of any judicial code, the arbitrary punishments (nobles were never executed), and the fact that acquittals were unusual. The prevalence of noble violence, and of private violence in general—two thirds of all judicial cases were crimes of violence—eventually provoked the Grands Jours d'Auvergne of 1665-6. Through this royal assault on the criminality, oppression, and corruption of the nobility, "noble violence had begun to be controlled." In addition to its admirable organization and analysis, this is a thoroughly interesting, often entertaining book. A model study, highly recommended. Upper-division undergraduates and above.—*F. K. Metzger, Cottey College*

OAB-2328 D639 95-42544 CIP
Hanna, Martha. **The mobilization of intellect: French scholars and writers during the Great War.** Harvard, 1996. 292p index ISBN 0-674-57755-8, $39.95

In a study that will become required material for advanced students and researchers, Hanna examines the cultural and intellectual continuities and ruptures caused by WW I. Like their peers in other nations, French intellectuals contributed to war efforts through their writings, teachings, and public presentations. This mobilization of minds was marked by an assault on the German intellectual and scientific heritage, with a parallel emphasis on classicism and on French philosophic and scientific traditions. Yet patriotic unity only masked prewar disputes, as the debates concerning Kant—championed by republicans and castigated by nationalists and conservatives—demonstrated the continuing quarrels surrounding the reformation of French education and the very foundations of republican identity itself. In particular, French research scientists were subjected to contradictory pressures, suspected as elitist and rooted in German thought, but simultaneously regarded as essential both to France's war efforts and to the postwar reconstruction. Hanna provocatively concludes that wartime intellectual nationalism continued through the interwar years and foreshadowed the Vichy era. Prefaced by a bibliographic note on primary sources, the succinct and thorough chapter notes are a model of clarity to guide those seeking further readings.—*F. Burkhard, Morgan State University*

OAB-2329 DC136 94-2957 CIP
Hardman, John. **French politics, 1774-1789: from the accession**

of Louis XVI to the fall of the Bastille. Longman, 1995. 283p bibl index ISBN 0-582-23650-9, $58.25; ISBN 0-582-23649-5 pbk, $25.75

Over the past three years, Hardman has attempted to redress a major weakness in historiography of late 18th century France. Specifically, he has turned his considerable energies to researching and writing the political history of Louis XVI. In many ways, this book is a companion piece to Hardman's earlier work, *Louis XVI* (CH, Oct'93). Focusing on the ministers of the French king, their backgrounds and contributions, this book describes the political system under which Louis XVI's government operated during the years immediately prior to the French Revolution. The structure of government, the degree of personal participation by the king, and other significant factors that taken together undermined the effectiveness of the royal government in France on the eve of the Revolution are the topics under consideration. Thoroughly researched and documented, this well-argued scholarly study will be of special interest to scholars and students of the French Revolution. Hardman has provided a very useful glossary for the French terms included. Highly recommended.— *G. C. Bond, Auburn University*

OAB-2330   DC137   92-13117 CIP
Hardman, John. **Louis XVI.** Yale, 1993. 264p bibl index ISBN 0-300-05719-9, $30.00

The reign of Louis XVI of France ended with his overthrow and execution during the French Revolution. This study focuses squarely on the politics of royal government prior to the outbreak of the French Revolution and then traces Louis's role as constitutional monarch through the early years of the Revolution. Drawing on years of study and investigation into French archival sources, Hardman has provided a beautifully written, clearly focused examination of the political world of Louis XVI. What emerges is a balanced but somewhat sympathetic view of the king. Louis understood the political realities of his day and desired to provide good leadership for France, but his famous indecisiveness was detrimental to his cause. This is an outstanding piece of scholarship. It is a book that should be required reading for all scholars and serious students of the French Revolution. Highly recommended. General; advanced undergraduate; graduate; faculty.—*G. C. Bond, Auburn University Main Campus*

OAB-2331   DC97   96-11190 CIP
Henneman, John Bell. **Olivier de Clisson and political society in France under Charles V and Charles VI.** Pennsylvania, 1996. 341p bibl index afp ISBN 0-8122-3353-0, $54.95

In this splendid biography, Henneman traces the volatile career of Olivier de Clisson (1336-1407). Clisson, a "ferocious warrior," was "one of the most important men in France in the later fourteenth century." Exiled in England as a boy, Clisson returned to throw his considerable skills and influence to the French kings, Charles V and Charles VI. Clisson succeeded Bertrand du Guesclin as Constable of France, "the most lucrative position in the French government," ultimately becoming "one of the very richest people in Europe." This is also a careful scholarly account of how the French crown established and reestablished the loyalties of the nobility of northwestern France during the charged decades of the Hundred Years' War, from the Treaty of Bretigny to the assassination of Louis D'Orleans. A most valuable appendix lists 188 leading military commanders from this period, noting their geographical origins and years of service. Equally valuable is Henneman's account of the rise and fall of the royal advisers known as the Marmousets, who included Enguerrand de Coucy, the focus of Barbara Tuchman's *A Distant Mirror* (CH, Feb'79). Henneman's treatment is balanced and meticulously recorded, showing Clisson, warts and all, including his stubborn sustaining of grudges, particularly against the Dukes of Brittany. This will become the standard work on both Clisson and his times. Upper-division undergraduates and above.—*J. E. Brink, Texas Tech University*

OAB-2332   HB3599   95-48989 CIP
Ipsen, Carl. **Dictating demography: the problem of population in fascist Italy.** Cambridge, 1996. 281p bibl index afp (Cambridge stud-

ies in population, economy, and society in past time, 28) ISBN 0-521-55452-7, $54.95

Based on exhaustive examination of fascist archives, Ipsen presents a fascinating analysis of Mussolini's use of statistics in propagandizing policies to increase birth rates and promote demographic colonization. Rather than statistics dictating policy, Ipsen suggests the reverse, i.e., Mussolini's demographic policies influenced the gathering of data and choices of demographers. The interpretation of data by Corrado Gini, head of the fascist statistics institute, and fellow demographer Gini Livio were tailored to support Mussolini's concerns for lowering infant mortality and spatial management of population. From an earlier policy encouraging emigration, Mussolini moved by 1929 to one of managing migration through demographic colonization of Sardinia, Agro Pontino, Puglia, Libya, and Ethiopia. Although Mussolini's attempts to establish a new society and a fascist utopia failed, Ipsen's study confirms the fascist aspiration to create a totalitarian regime and demonstrates the influence that Nazi social and racial policies exerted on Italian fascism. The text abounds with informed charts and includes an invaluable bibliography. Recommended for university and research libraries. Upper-division undergraduates and above.— *M. S. Miller, University of Illinois at Chicago*

OAB-2333   DP178   96-52421 CIP
Kamen, Henry. **Philip of Spain.** Yale, 1997. 384p index afp ISBN 0-300-07081-0, $35.00

In this important revisionist work Kamen presents a portrait of a king dedicated in his search for peace in 16th-century Europe and, therefore, unwavering in his support of the Inquisition. According to the author, Philip's determination to eliminate heresy was fueled by his efforts to avert the political disorder and civil war he had witnessed in Germany. This is a sympathetic, but not biased, portrayal of Philip II, which examines his private and public life within the context of governing a difficult empire. Far from being the "incarnation of evil," Philip was subdued and exerted remarkable self-control in his administration while juggling the influence of ministers and powerful noble families with an even hand. In essence, Philip, "who never erred on the side of mercy," was politically correct in early modern Europe, but politically incorrect in historical retrospect. Kamen redresses this imbalance while emphasizing the monarch's efforts to integrate, rather than isolate, Spain within the context of Western civilization. Based on extensive research, this work explicitly makes connections between the King's private dilemmas and public decisions. All college and university libraries should purchase this book. All levels.—*S. H. Burkholder, University of Missouri—St. Louis*

OAB-2334   DS135   95-50615 CIP
Lazare, Lucien. **Rescue as resistance: how Jewish organizations fought the Holocaust in France.** Columbia, 1996. 400p bibl index afp ISBN 0-231-10124-4, $32.50

The role played by Jewish organizations in rescuing French Jews from the murderous actions of Nazi occupiers and their Vichy collaborators during WW II is well known (see, for example, Anny Latour's *The Jewish Resistance in France, 1940-1944*, CH, Nov'81). Lazare, however, focuses almost exclusively on the issue of rescue. He argues that for Jews under Nazi tyranny, survival—and especially the heroism of rescuing others—was a form of resistance as surely as armed combat. Lazare's study is comprehensive and detailed. It is based on wide research in primary and secondary sources and inspired by his personal participation, at an early age, in some of the events he describes. This book complements Michael R. Marrus and Robert O. Paxton's classic study *Vichy France and the Jews* (CH, Apr'82). Lazare pays special attention to youth movements and the rescue of children, but he also includes such topics as aid, the underground, and even the budgets of the Jewish resistance. The book has lengthy endnotes and a good bibliography. It is only slightly marred by infelicities in translation from the French and less-than-rigorous editorial work. An important source for students and scholars of the Holocaust in France. Upper-division undergraduates and above.—*M. Swartz, University of Massachusetts at Amherst*

OAB-2335   DC33   91-44697 CIP
Lebovics, Herman. **True France: the wars over cultural identity, 1900-1945.** Cornell, 1992. 221p index afp ISBN 0-8014-2687-1, $29.95

Lebovics provides a valuable multidisciplinary interpretation of the historic construction of an idealist and essentialist French cultural identity during the first half of the 20th century. He then deconstructs this identity, disclosing "True France" as exclusivist and reactionary. Contributors to the concept of True France include Louis Marin, with his fusion of ideology and social science to produce a "fundamentalist anthropology," and Louis-Hubert Lyautey, with his allegiance to French cultural hegemony as symbolized by his efforts on behalf of the Colonial International Exposition of 1931 (whose exhibits are detailed impressively). Lebovics presents opposing views to this restrictive cultural identity by Nguyen Van Tao, Andre Breton, Paul Rivet, and Georges-Henri Rivière. The author clearly favors those who champion diversity and, specifically, a pluralist France. Vichy is regarded as the culmination of True France. But where is De Gaulle's "certain idea" of France in the 1940s? Was, for example, the Brazzaville Conference a recodified "Greater France?" Lebovics also analyzes the reformulated discourse of True France in contemporary politics. Complementary works include Paul Rabinow's *French Modern* (CH, Feb'90) and Theodore Zeldin's *The French* (CH, Jul'83). The book includes 24 illustrations, welcomed footnotes rather than endnotes, and a bibliographical essay. Highly recommended. Advanced undergraduate; graduate; faculty.—*P. C. Naylor, Marquette University*

OAB-2336   DC111   93-47260 CIP
Major, J. Russell. **From Renaissance monarchy to absolute monarchy: French kings, nobles & estates.** Johns Hopkins, 1994. 444p bibl index afp ISBN 0-8018-4776-1, $49.95

It is a pity this will probably be the last book Major will ever write on French history. As the doyen of early modern French institutional history, Major (Emory Univ., emeritus) brings to a close a distinguished 45-year teaching and publishing career. In this work he traces his intellectual development as a historian. When Major entered the profession, the traditional interpretation of early modern French history proclaimed that the monarchy allied with the middle class to weaken the power of the *noblesse d'épée*, which indirectly helped to create an absolute monarchy. Major's initial research on the Estates General and subsequent works by his students on the provincial estates did not see such a simplistic explanation for the rise of 17th-century French absolutism nor for the decline of the feudal nobility. The "Major School," as future historiography will describe it, resuscitated the power of the provincial estates and the nobility. Major argues that the monarchs openly cooperated with the provincial estates and deputies and relied on support, not from a weakened, but from an energized feudal nobility to increase monarchical power. This thoughtfully argued and skillfully written work will quickly become a standard for anyone interested in early modern French history. Recommended for all libraries.—*R. O. Lindsay, University of Montana*

OAB-2337   BX1735   92-53643 CIP
Netanyahu, B. **The origins of the Inquisition in fifteenth century Spain.** Random House, 1995. 1,384p bibl index ISBN 0-679-41065-1, $50.00

Netanyahu's monumental work reflects a lifetime of scholarly pursuit of the origins of the Spanish Inquisition. Building on groundwork laid in his *The Marranos of Spain* (1966), the author here provides exhaustive support for his thesis that the Inquisition, which began functioning in Spain in 1481, was prompted not, as historians have assumed (from H.C. Lea's classic work *A History of the Inquisition of Spain*, 4 v., 1906, through Henry A. Kamen's recent *The Spanish Inquisition*, 1956), by the Judaizing tendencies of *conversos*, but by society's resistance to their assimilating tendencies. Subsequent to the persecutions of 1391 and 1412 and the mass conversions that followed, urban populations in particular developed a hatred for Jewish converts parallel to the older hatred of Jews; racism was joined to antisemitism. Voluminous notes and appendixes make this an indispensable text for scholars and general readers alike. Rec-

ommended for libraries supporting upper-division undergraduate and graduate courses and research in history and sociology.—*K. Kennelly, Mount St. Mary's College*

OAB-2338   DC340   95-10445 CIP
Nord, Philip. **The republican moment: struggles for democracy in nineteenth-century France.** Harvard, 1995. 321p index afp ISBN 0-674-76271-1, $49.95

Rather than viewing the Third French Republic as a failure from a 1940 perspective, Nord explores elegantly and convincingly the dynamic roles of institutions and associations that claimed a public sphere in the transition to a democratic Republic from the authoritarian Second Empire. He argues that a utopian element remained within the positivist pragmatic character of the young republican generation. Thus, institutions like the universities could overthrow the restraints of imperial policies. A new "middling class" used institutions like the Union Nationale du Commerce et de l'Industrie to attack privilege and monopoly; Jewish republicans, through the Alliance Israelite Universelle, challenged the older elitist consistory; a younger generation of lawyers armed with simple realist rhetoric devoted themselves to the Republic; and within the artist community, the tyranny of the older Salon gave way to an elected body. Such fraternist-type associations and institutions helped collectively to create the movement that articulated a republican culture before 1879-80, as well as to reform private life. An excellent, challenging study, meticulously researched, with supportive illustrations and rich bibliographical footnotes. Highly recommended for university and college libraries.—*M. S. Miller, University of Illinois at Chicago*

OAB-2339   DC133   95-39056 CIP
Peabody, Sue. **"There are no slaves in France": the political culture of race and slavery in the Ancien Régime.** Oxford, 1996. 210p bibl index afp ISBN 0-19-510198-7, $39.95

Peabody's short monograph is a superb scholarly investigation of the so-called "Freedom Principle" under which slaves who set foot in France were automatically emancipated. Peabody (Washington State Univ., Vancouver) convincingly demonstrates how French jurists, piecing together past political precedents and historical myth, persuaded French courts, namely the Admiralty Court of France and the Parlement of Paris, that slaves brought into France should be free. The government was not so like-minded. Although Louis XIV clearly supported the Freedom Principle, later French legislation in 1716, 1738, and 1777, under the growing influence of French colonial planters, tried to limit its application by a series of qualifications, thus permitting de facto slavery in France. Peabody not only carefully examines the impact of key individual cases within the broader French legal system, but also traces the evolution of French racist thought toward blacks, provides a brief demographic survey of their lives in Paris, and couples the issues of slavery and despotism before the Revolution. Strongly based on archival research, this well-written survey deserves wide readership. Undergraduates and above.—*D. C. Baxter, Ohio University*

OAB-2340   HX902   92-46661 CIP
Pernicone, Nunzio. **Italian anarchism, 1864-1892.** Princeton, 1993. 326p bibl index afp ISBN 0-691-05692-7, $39.50

An invaluable and distinguished revisionist account of the significant years of Italian anarchism, its leadership, and its international network. Pernicone elegantly analyzes Bakunin's organization of the antiauthoritarian wing of the Italian Federation of the International Workers Association, and assesses the importance of Bakunin's charismatic personality, both of which appealed to the revolutionary tradition, individualism, and regionalism of Italian workers and artisans. Thus Pernicone counters the Marxist historiography that attributes the failures of Marxist authoritarianism to political immaturity and social and economic backwardness. Anarchists were branded by the government as criminals after the insurrectional failures of the 1870s. After 1882, government repressions and defections left to Errico Malatesta the task of reviving the movement in the northwest and central Italy. Anarchism continued to advocate direct action against the state rather than the socialist attack on capitalism. Pernicone argues, with an abundance of original research and skillful synthesis, for the significance of the Italian Federation for the Italian Socialist party in 1892. An excellent index and bibliography enhance the study. Highly recommended. Advanced undergraduates and above.—*M. S. Miller, University of Illinois at Chicago*

OAB-2341   DC417   92-45075 CIP
Phillips, Peggy Anne. **Republican France: divided loyalties.** Greenwood, 1993. 168p bibl index afp (Contributions in political science, 325) ISBN 0-313-27503-3, $49.95

Phillips's monograph is important not simply for specialists of modern France or Europe, but also for scholars across disciplines researching other national and chronological arenas. As European unity begins to confront ideologies of national identity from without, Phillips finds renewed debates about race and religion undermining France's republican consensus from within. Phillips argues that the generation emerging as France's political leadership was formed by the Algerian war experience, and finds it must grapple with the needs of a transformed population, including many citizens and residents of Algerian origin. This new social segment, incompletely assimilated, is being convulsed by its own defining crisis, the split between fundamentalist Islam and state secularism in Algeria. The challenge of this Moslem community to existing views of French national identity provokes political responses, with the Left fragmenting into separatism and the Right reformulating racist nationalism. Phillips provides a model of successful analyses of complex human realities, and her succinct prose demonstrates that complexity does not preclude lucidity. The excellent select bibliography will usefully guide researchers at all levels. Upper-division undergraduate and above.—*F. Burkhard, Morgan State University*

OAB-2342   DC252   94-30651 CIP
Pilbeam, Pamela M. **Republicanism in nineteenth-century France, 1814-1871.** St. Martin's, 1995. 370p bibl index ISBN 0-312-12420-1, $45.00

Through nine convulsive changes in regime, the appeal of a republican form of government proved a hardy perennial in 19th-century France. Pilbeam examines three key questions of the republican movement: Who were the republicans? What was their vision? Why was their path to power so long and difficult? Pilbeam (Univ. of London) convincingly argues that the 1789 Revolution created a "dynasty of pro-1789 civil servants" who provided not only much of the republican leadership, but whose presence also helps explain the fundamental stability of French society amid the chaos of the country's politics. Pilbeam emphasizes the importance of social and economic issues in fragmenting republicanism and limiting its appeal. When in power, Republicans were compelled consistently to move rightward to reassure society; thus the destruction of the Paris Commune "probably contributed much to the creation of a stable republic." Rooted in both national and departmental archives, skillfully marrying intellectual and political history, this study is an impressive contribution to understanding 19th-century France. Upper-division undergraduates and above.—*G. P. Cox, Gordon College*

OAB-2343   DG737   93-31942 CIP
Polizzotto, Lorenzo. **The elect nation: the Savonarolan movement in Florence, 1494-1545.** Oxford, 1995 (c1994). 488p bibl index afp ISBN 0-19-920600-7, $79.00

Based on extensive manuscript and archival research, this is the first comprehensive study of Savonarola's followers and of their impact on Florentine politics and culture in the decades following his execution (1498). Combining social and political historical methods with close readings of literary sources—including letters, dialogues, and theological tracts—Polizzotto (Univ. of Western Australia) traces the movement through its fragmentation following Savonarola's death to its subsequent recovery in a variety of influential networks. The author elucidates Savonarolans' influence on and adaptability to ecclesiastical

and civic changes, as traditionally republican Florence turned into a Medicean principate. The narrative proceeds chronologically, building on the pioneering efforts of leading historians such as Richard Trexler and Donald Weinstein, yet constructing an argument that is both original and highly convincing. Exceptionally thorough scholarly apparatus. Recommended for upper-division undergraduates and above.—*K. V. Gouwens, University of South Carolina*

OAB-2344   Orig
Ringrose, David R. **Spain, Europe, and the "Spanish miracle," 1700-1900.** Cambridge, 1996. 439p bibl index ISBN 0-521-43486-6, $64.95

Essentially an essay in economic and social history, this remarkable study of 18th- and 19th-century Spain offers fresh, indeed innovative and controversial interpretations. Ringrose has made many significant earlier contributions in Spanish economic and social history, and in this work he draws on a wealth of resources and years of research. In substance, he challenges virtually every long-standing interpretation. As opposed to a "backward" Spain, economically stagnant and socially immobile, "Spain experienced sustained economic dynamism from 1700 onwards," not unlike other European countries. Ringrose insists that basic questions asked for generations need dramatic reformulation, that their focus should be on what actually happened in Spain, rather than what did not happen. In so doing, he does not jettison comparative history, but merely rejects its distortions. He explores aspects and patterns of economic growth and suggests their prominence in Spain. Cherished views, such as the importance of empire in shaping Spain's economic history, are either minimized or reshaped, and new definitions and dimensions of regional characteristics of the peninsular economy are identified. An excellent analysis of political networks, provincial elites, and institutions provides a conclusion. Superb bibliography. Upper-division undergraduates and above.—*N. Greene, Wesleyan University*

OAB-2345   DC33   94-40396 CIP
Roelker, Nancy Lyman. **One king, one faith: the Parlement of Paris and the religious reformations of the sixteenth century.** California, 1996. 543p bibl index afp ISBN 0-520-08626-0, $65.00

Roelker's posthumously published study of the role of the Parlement of Paris in the complex world of the reformations, the wars of religion, and the triumph of Henri IV is immediately the standard work on the subjects of religion and constitutionalism in 16th-century France. Roelker argues persuasively that the role of the members of the Parlement over several generations in asserting both the historical identity of the Gallican Church and the constitutional position of the monarchy in France determined both the survival of a particular kind of Catholicism in France and paved the way for the constitutional changes of the 17th century. The first four chapters lay out the social and intellectual background of the *parlementaires* and the late medieval traditions of Gallicanism and constitutionalism they espoused. These are the constitutional and social foundations for the great story of the challenges to and the survival of Gallicanism and constitutionalism at the end of the century. A model of the new and exciting kinds of constitutional history that have been developed for the study of late medieval and early modern Europe. For upper-division undergraduates and above.—*E. Peters, University of Pennsylvania*

OAB-2346   DC158   94-40970 CIP
Roessler, Shirley Elson. **Out of the shadows: women and politics in the French Revolution, 1789-95.** P. Lang, 1996. 275p bibl index afp (Studies in modern European history, 14) ISBN 0-8204-2565-6, $51.95

Although a great deal of scholarly research in the last 20 years has focused on the role of women in the French Revolution, there are still areas that have received only limited attention. Roessler's well-written, nicely organized, and thoroughly researched study attempts to fill in many gaps concerning the activities of women during the course of the French Revolution from 1789 to 1795. The events of the "October Days" in 1789 are generally well known, but Roessler has shed additional light on the part women played in bringing the royal family from Versailles to Paris. In Paris, women began to be politically active and even formed their own political clubs. The most successful of these was the Société des Citoyennes Républicaines Révolutionnaires. The year 1795 saw major attempts by women to influence the political direction of the Revolution, as when women stormed the National Convention. Both scholarly and a delight to read, this study will benefit French Revolution scholars and general readers alike. Highly recommended.—*G. C. Bond, Auburn University*

OAB-2347   HV6046   95-37867 CIP
Shapiro, Ann-Louise. **Breaking the codes: female criminality in fin-de-siècle Paris.** Stanford, 1996. 265p bibl index afp ISBN 0-8047-1663-3, $45.00; ISBN 0-8047-2693-0 pbk, $15.95

Shapiro blends original research with insightful critical appropriations of recent scholarship to re-create the pervasive fascination with deviant and criminal women in the context of the social and political upheavals reshaping France before the Great War. She retraces the development of overlapping discursive and bureaucratic practices—in the press, the judicial system, the courtroom, in medicine, and in the daily cultural assumptions and acts of women and men themselves—and argues that "criminality" served as a reference point where French anxieties about their modern world were focused, encoded, and transformed into dramatic moral stories (re)expressing and (re)establishing social norms. Far from being simply passive victims and objects of masculine domination, women, as individuals and collectively, actively participated in the shaping of their culture. This work includes a thorough bibliography and extensive endnotes, and will prove fascinating reading for upper-division undergraduates and above. Among the most useful companion works exploring parallel materials and issues are Elinor Accampo's *Gender and the Politics of Social Reform in France* (1995) and Judith Walkowitz's *City of Dreadful Delight* (1992).—*F. Burkhard, Morgan State University*

OAB-2348   KJV3747   94-19471 CIP
Swann, Julian. **Politics and the Parlement of Paris under Louis XV, 1754-1774.** Cambridge, 1995. 390p bibl index ISBN 0-521-47349-7, $69.95; ISBN 0-521-48362-X pbk, $29.95

Historians of the ancien régime are indeed fortunate to have two new important works on the Parisian parlement. The first, John Rogister's *Louis XV and the Parlement of Paris, 1737-1755* (CH, Feb'95), covers the early period of Louis XV's personal reign; the second is Swann's study, which covers its end, from the imposition of the Law of Silence to quiet the quarrel of bishops and Jansenists until the Maupeou Revolution abolished parlement. Passing beyond the traditional debate on reforming monarchy versus obstructionist parlement/despotic government versus constitutional defenders, Swann's masterful survey is centered around the interrelationship of sword and robe factionalism. Swann (Univ. of London) depicts how a well-meaning, weak monarch and a divided ministry mismanaged relations with the judges, repeatedly making concessions to a militant Jansenist minority and failing to support loyal supporters, bumbling from crisis to crisis until the final showdown in 1771 fundamentally changed the future of French politics. Turning from ideology, Swann reasserts the fundamental role of personality, social relationships, and institutional loyalty in political life. Intelligent, well written, and solidly documented, this book is essential reading for all interested in French history before the Revolution. Highly recommended. Upper-division undergraduates and above.—*D. C. Baxter, Ohio University*

OAB-2349   DC165   95-38122 CIP
Tackett, Timothy. **Becoming a revolutionary: the deputies of the French National Assembly and the emergence of a revolutionary culture (1789-1790).** Princeton, 1996. 355p bibl index afp ISBN 0-691-04384-1, $39.95

Tackett has painstakingly examined the personal correspondence of approximately 150 deputies to the Estates General/National Constituent Assembly, along with contemporary newspapers and journals. To these he has added the most sound and current French Revolution studies. The result is a superb study of the evolution of a "political culture" that emerged over the 15 months culminating in the glorious Federation of July 1790. Tackett ends the speculation of whether the deputies were politically naive or inexperienced; they were neither. Many had participated in government in their local regions, while others had learned political fundamentals through reading 18th-century political theory. Tackett demonstrates that the 1,200 men elected as representatives did not come to Versailles with a single coherent political ideology; rather, it evolved. The deputies were practical, largely unknown to one another, holding no specific agenda. They believed that this revolution was manageable. To their dismay social, economic, legal, political, and honorific distinctions were destroyed as the historical engine of the Revolution swept all before it. Irreparably assaulted, absolute monarchy collapsed. Tackett also shows, however, that during the winter and spring of 1789-1790, the monarchy did not appear destined to fall. Moderates and conservatives, deputies who constituted the Club of 1789, were in the ascendant, but their errors in political judgment cast them into oblivion; their enemies, the radical Jacobins, replaced them. General readers; upper-division undergraduates and above.—*B. Rothaus, University of Northern Colorado*

OAB-2350   DC130   95-11451 MARC
Treasure, Geoffrey. **Mazarin: the crisis of absolutism in France.** Routledge, 1996 (c1995). 413p bibl index ISBN 0-415-01457-3, $39.95

Treasure argues that Mazarin, who became First Minister of France in 1643 during a time of crisis, was the model 17th-century statesman—a man who was passionately loyal to the Crown and inspired devotion and respect among those closest to him, above all, the young Louis XIV. The book follows Mazarin's career from his training by the Jesuits, through legate in Paris and Avignon, to service for Louis XIII and beyond. Mazarin's role in the survival of the monarchy during the Fronde and his tutelage of the young Louis XIV are fully examined. Treasure also examines in detail the cardinal's crucial role in negotiating a series of treaties such as the Peace of Westphalia and the Treaty of the Pyrenees—which expanded the kingdom's borders and provided his adopted country with unprecedented security—as well as many other diplomatic exchanges. Perhaps more important for the future of France was Mazarin's guidance of the young Louis XIV, who would emerge after the death of his mentor as the best trained and most competent sovereign of Europe. Treasure's book, which is based on the most recent research and includes voluminous notes and a helpful glossary, is an indispensable work for students of French history. All levels.—*D. J. Heimmermann, University of North Alabama*

OAB-2351   Orig
Tuohy, Thomas. **Herculean Ferrara: Ercole d'Este, 1471-1505, and the invention of a ducal capital.** Cambridge, 1996. 534p bibl indexes ISBN 0-521-46471-4, $95.00

Encyclopedic documentation drawn primarily from the state archive in Modena bolsters this reappraisal of the role of Duke Ercole d'Este in the building and embellishment of Ferrara. Devastated by earthquake (1570) and politically marginalized after it devolved to the papacy (1598), Renaissance Ferrara has survived mostly on paper. Downplaying the contributions of ducal engineer Biagio Rossetti, Tuohy (unaffiliated) meticulously details the central role of the duke in orchestrating the city's construction and adornment, a role extending beyond financial support to include architectural planning, palace decoration, and the organization of court festivals. Eclectic rather than strictly classical in his tastes, d'Este made extensive use of ephemeral decorations that elucidate the purposes of the few surviving artifacts. A thorough gazetteer of churches and of urban and country palaces, as well as an extensive critical apparatus including annotated transcriptions of primary documents, make this beautifully produced study a valuable reference tool for those investigating the dynamics and goals of cultural patronage in the Italian Renaissance. Upper-division undergraduates and above.—*K. V. Gouwens, University of California, Santa Barbara*

OAB-2352   DC389   94-18612 CIP
Weber, Eugen. **The hollow years: France in the 1930s.** W.W. Norton, 1995 (c1994). 352p index ISBN 0-393-03671-5, $25.00

Weber has written an excellent study of France during one of its most interesting periods. Weber, whose previous works include *Peasants into Frenchmen* (CH, Feb'77) and *Action Française* (1962), brings his well-known penchant for mixing obscure and popular sources to this project. The result is exactly what one would expect: a complete history of France in the 1930s that illuminates these years of intense passions and complicated hatreds. Weber concentrates on predictable topics such as the rise of xenophobia and the election of the Blum government, but as always, it is in the details that his talent makes itself clear. Although he spends enough time on the confusing politics of the era (from communist to Royalist), this is foremost a work of cultural history. Weber's emphasis on daily life, e.g., the conflict between France's traditional peasantry and its technocratic government, is what makes the book so readable and enjoyable. The 32 pages of photographs are superbly chosen and add greatly to the work. Readers at all levels should emerge with a clear picture of a France devastated by one war and perched on the verge of another.—*S. D. Armus, SUNY at Stony Brook*

OAB-2353   DC116   95-40713 CIP
Wood, James B. **The king's army: warfare, soldiers, and society during the Wars of Religion in France, 1562-1576.** Cambridge, 1996. 349p bibl index afp ISBN 0-521-55003-3, $69.95

In a scrupulously researched and boldly written anatomy of the royal army of France, Wood has made good on his claim to "put warfare back at the center of the French wars of religion." He convincingly explodes the theory of the military revolution of the late 16th century from three different vistas. First, he offers a most welcome description and close analysis of the organization and operations of the infantry, the cavalry, and the artillery. Next, relying on a rich variety of written and iconographical sources, he presents four case studies of the principal engagements of the first five of eight religious wars. Third, Wood dissects the strained financial structure of Charles IX's reign and concludes that the royal army was unable to defeat the Huguenot forces because of a pathological financial inadequacy, a failure of the "sinews of war" to sustain the structure. The result was chronic civil religious rebellion, ultimately lasting 36 years and concluding in a military stalemate, the only endgame possible for an exhausted army and treasury. Thanks to its felicitous style and plentiful tables, graphs, and charts, this book will appeal to the general reader interested in military history, as well as to the specialist because of its rich detail and an excellent appendix of sources for each of the first five wars. All levels.—*J. E. Brink, Texas Tech University*

OAB-2354   D742   96-10410 CIP
Young, Robert J. **France and the origins of the Second World War.** St. Martin's, 1996. 191p bibl index ISBN 0-312-16185-9, $49.95; ISBN 0-312-16186-7 pbk, $16.95

Accounts of the French defeat in 1940 are legion. Most point to a specific fault or failing in the military, government, or society to account for the debacle. This wonderful book, on the other hand, takes an entirely different tack: in 150 pages it provides a brief narrative of France's interwar history, surveys the most important historiography of this period, and discusses the political, military, economic, and social background to France's entry into WW II, and its subsequent defeat. Young (Univ. of Winnipeg) has spent a quarter century studying the French Third Republic, and his mastery of the sources is apparent. He not only provides a convincing interpretation of the fall of France, but also offers a profound meditation on how "history" actually works. Instead of conspiracies, or "turning points" where event-shattering decisions are made, the author shows how governments and societies, faced with situations whose meaning and outcome are far from clear, often steer understandable, even justifiable courses that lead to disaster. A brief review cannot do full justice to the richness of this work. Recommended for every level, particularly for new history majors.—*G. P. Cox, Gordon College*

OAB-2355   Orig
Augustine, Dolores L. **Patricians and parvenus: wealth and high society in Wilhelmine Germany.** Berg, 1994. 303p bibl index ISBN 0-85496-397-9, $49.95

Augustine delivers a crisp, analytical collective biography of the financial elite in Wilhelmine Germany. Its foundation is the second edition of Rudolf Martin's *Das Jahrbuch der Millionäre Deutschlands* (Berlin, 1911-14), which identifies 502 wealthy businessmen (those with a fortune of six million marks or more) through official tax records. Augustine then used corroborating archival resources, autobiographical and biographical studies, and secondary sources to track down the individuals and analyze and reflect on various characteristics of their personal lives: their education and upbringing; their adolescent conflicts with authority; courtship and marriage; family life and power relations; choice of residence and its significance; and their role in high society. What emerges is a profile of upward mobility among the German bourgeoisie who helped create the thriving economy of the Wilhelmine era. Purposeful in their choices, not particularly anxious themselves to join the old landed aristocracy, these dynamic industrialists, merchants, and bankers nevertheless boosted their children into high social positions. Despite antisemitism, even some Jewish tycoons were able to break social barriers because of their wealth. With firm primary research, extensive use of printed resources in English and German, comparative techniques, and imaginative analytical methodology, this work is an excellent model for subsequent social history research. Undergraduate; graduate; faculty.—*E. L. Turk, Indiana University East*

OAB-2356   BX4844   91-31024 CIP
Barnett, Victoria. **For the soul of the people: Prostestant protest against Hitler.** Oxford, 1992. 358p bibl index afp ISBN 0-19-505306-0, $30.00

Using virtually all of the scholarly research available as well as interviews of more than 60 persons who were active in the Confessing Church, Barnett has produced a vibrant account of the moral confrontation between this group of Protestants and the Third Reich. Her scholarly and nuanced study reveals the tensions between the individual conscience of these Protestants and their loyalty to the state. Particularly significant is Barnett's careful analysis of the reaction of the Evangelical Church in Germany to the postwar issues of collective guilt, antisemitism, and the Holocaust, when again German nationalism intruded into moral reflections. Her chapters on the political developments in East and West German churches have long been needed. The personal stories of the Confessing Church members, which permeate the entire historical analysis, reaffirm that the behavior of men and women is guided not only by conscience and love, but also by fear, political goals, and human weakness. Their conflicts with Nazism and postwar political issues pitted the interviewees against themselves as Christians. Barnett has produced significant study of the nexus between conscience and mass politics. Advanced undergraduate; graduate; faculty.—*D. J. Dietrich, Boston College*

OAB-2357   HV279   94-35186 CIP
Beck, Hermann. **The origins of the authoritarian welfare state in Prussia: conservatives, bureaucracy, and the social question, 1815-70.** Michigan, 1995. 298p bibl index afp ISBN 0-472-10546-9, $47.50

Beck's finely crafted work represents an important addition to the literature on 19th-century German social and intellectual history. After providing the reader with a thorough but succinct analysis of the social crisis developing in Prussia's *vormärz* era, Beck examines the evolution of the various strains of Prussian conservative thought and the ways in which it differed from and converged with that of the state bureaucracy. Exhibiting a firm grasp of primary and secondary sources, the author illustrates how complex and often contradictory the different currents of Prussian conservatism were and argues persuasively that the bureaucracy, too, was anything but monolithic in its view of how to deal with social change and unfolding crises. Beck shows how the development of the idea of a "social kingdom" influenced 19th-century Prussian politics, and, in an excellent closing chapter, he relates his findings to the later development of Nazi ideology and the *Sonderweg* debate. The book is well written and includes detailed footnotes and a comprehensive bibliography. Recommended for lower-division undergraduates and above.—*W. Smaldone, Willamette University*

OAB-2358   HC285   94-20683 CIP
Berghahn, V.R. **Imperial Germany, 1871-1914: economy, society, culture, and politics.** Berghahn Books, 1994. 362p bibl index ISBN 1-57181-013-7, $59.95; ISBN 1-57181-014-5 pbk, $17.95

Berghahn has written a comprehensive, very readable introduction to German society in the late 19th and early 20th centuries. The book is organized around themes, with a brief chronological summary of major events occupying the concluding chapters. There is a thorough discussion of constitutional structure and the political culture and system; however, much of the study is devoted to "history from below": economic conditions, demographic factors, gender and generational issues, religious and ethnic minorities, and both high and popular culture. There is a long appendix of informative statistical tables. The author takes a balanced position on the debates over a German *Sonderweg* (special path) and argues that German society was characterized by both "pluralization" and "polarization." Readers should not be put off by the fact that the book's publisher is a company owned by the author's spouse: this is a serious work by a recognized scholar in the field. Accessible to general readers and undergraduates; recommended for all libraries.—*J. D. Fraley, Birmingham-Southern College*

OAB-2359   E99   97-522 CIP
Caulfield, Richard A. **Greenlanders, whales, and whaling: sustainability and self-determination in the Arctic.** Dartmouth/University Press of New England, 1997. 203p index afp ISBN 0-87451-810-5, $35.00

Caulfield's book deals with some of the most difficult moral questions in the world today. In Greenland, as in many other places, traditional subsistence-based societies are finding themselves on the world stage, involved in resource conflicts with broad implications. In the process, the societies are changing. The Kalaallit (Greenland "Eskimo") traditionally took whales for subsistence, harpooning them from open boats. Today, Greenlanders (descendants of Kalaallit and Danish colonists) use modern explosive-head harpoons to take a few whales, for subsistence and for limited sale. This has raised questions about "tradition." Meanwhile, a Home Rule government has arisen; it negotiates whaling rights and quotas with the International Whaling Commission. No one has found perfect answers to the questions of who deserves rights to hold a "traditional subsistence" fishery, how many whales should be taken, or whether whales should be taken at all. Caulfield does a truly exemplary job of placing such questions in their full cultural, moral, and historical context, and of showing how local and specific issues relate to general worldwide problems. Important for students and professionals in resource management fields.—*E. N. Anderson, University of California, Riverside*

OAB-2360   HN460   93-8747 CIP
Dennis, Mike. **Social and economic modernization in eastern Germany from Honecker to Kohl.** Pinter/St. Martin's, 1993. 252p index ISBN 0-312-08569-9, $45.00

Dennis's book is a feat of concise clarity, balance, precision, and timeliness. One might quibble with the title, since social changes are not discussed. But the analysis of economic modernization displays an impressive mastery of the latest primary and secondary sources. Dennis begins with an admirable summary of the strategies of centralized planning in the Ulbricht and Honecker regimes. He then takes the reader through the collapse of the East German state all the way to Chancellor Helmut Kohl's successful negotiation of the Solidarity Pact for the reconstruction of eastern Germany, concluded in the tradi-

tion of German concerted action in a conference of federal government, opposition, and the states in March 1993. The tightly and cogently written text not only covers significant events and data with the aid of rich tables and some 40 pages of key documents, sensibly abridged, but also guides the reader through the critical policy debates in a coherent and balanced way. All levels.—*D. Prowe, Carleton College*

OAB-2361   D805   95-40275 CIP
Dwork, Debórah. **Auschwitz: 1270 to the present,** by Debórah Dwork and Robert Jan van Pelt. W.W. Norton, 1996. 443p index ISBN 0-393-03933-1, $30.00

Were it not for the events that took place in this provincial Silesian town in the 1940s, the world would care little about Auschwitz. But the concentration camp and killing complex built there by the Nazis transformed "an ordinary town" into a symbol of the Holocaust and, indeed, of evil itself. Dwork (Clark Univ.) and Van Pelt (Waterloo Univ., Canada) provide in this superb study careful tracing of the history of Auschwitz since its founding in the High Middle Ages, including its heritage to the present day. They show how the town was used by the Nazis to tie their history to the German tradition of the Teutonic Knights and the Prussianism of King Frederick II. But the book's most important contribution is its use of oral histories and the extraordinarily numerous architectural plans, blueprints, and papers left by the Nazis. The authors are able to provide an important new interpretation of the origins, development, and impact of the death camp at Auschwitz. Numerous maps, drawings, and illustrations complement the 20 plates that reproduce "Blueprints of Genocide." A very important contribution to Holocaust studies. All levels.—*P. W. Knoll, University of Southern California*

OAB-2362   DD240   92-7981 CIP
Fulbrook, Mary. **The divided nation: a history of Germany, 1918-1990.** Oxford, 1992 (c1991). 405p bibl index afp ISBN 0-19-507570-6, $39.95; ISBN 0-19-507571-4 pbk, $15.95

Fulbrook (Univ. of London) takes an analytical and comparative approach to what she calls "the divided nation" between 1918 and 1990. Her work stands in contrast to the more traditional 20th-century German texts by V.R. Berghahn, Dietrich Orlow, and David Childs. About one third of the account is devoted to the Weimar Republic and the Third Reich, and the remainder to the Germanies since 1945. Although following a chronological framework, Fulbrook emphasizes the international context, the roles and relationships of different elites, the economy, and the place of dissenting groups in her treatment of various historical stages of Germany. In the same vein, Fulbrook also considers some of the historiographical debates in the interpretation of the course of German history and gives a measured assessment of the significance of the Holocaust. Her chapter on the East German revolution and the end of the divided Germanies presents a succinct summary of events as well as an insightful explanation of their significance. This well-written, well-organized, and stimulating text is a welcome addition for undergraduate and graduate courses in history, literature, and international affairs. Good bibliography of English-language works.—*G. P. Blum, University of the Pacific*

OAB-2363   HQ728   94-10919 CIP
Harrington, Joel F. **Reordering marriage and society in Reformation Germany.** Cambridge, 1995. 315p bibl index ISBN 0-521-46483-8, $49.95

Harrington's is a major charge into the ongoing debate over the significance of the Reformation for the basic social institution of marriage. Against the view that Protestant reform brought a sweeping overthrow of medieval marriage ideals, Harrington argues that both Protestants and Catholics perpetuated conservative and patriarchal ideals from the high and late Middle Ages. Ecclesiastical and governmental reforms of the 16th century merely brought newly strict efforts to enforce these ideals. Such efforts, moreover, were no more successful than were broader programs of Christian social discipline; that is, they remained largely frustrated. Hence despite notable Protestant changes, such as the abolition of clerical celibacy, the Reformation wrought no sudden revolution in marriage as an ideal or institution. Harrington draws on extensive archival studies and an impressive mastery of the vast secondary literature. His approach is scholarly, cautious, and full of qualifications, which makes for demanding reading. Critics may contend that he has played down too strongly the significance of 16th-century changes. Yet the book-jacket blurb calling this "the clearest and most comprehensive evaluation of the Reformation's impact on marriage currently available" is probably justified. Sophisticated scholarly apparatus. Upper-division undergraduates and above.—*R. B. Barnes, Davidson College*

OAB-2364   DD218   92-55062 CIP
Hayes, Bascom Barry. **Bismarck and *Mitteleuropa*.** Fairleigh Dickinson, 1994. (Dist. by Associated University Presses) 623p bibl index afp ISBN 0-8386-3512-1, $65.00

Those who associate Bismark only with the unification of Germany during the 1860s and in the development of the "Second Reich" during the subsequent two decades should read this book. Born in 1815, Bismarck grew and matured alongside the Concert of Europe created at the Congress of Vienna. By the time he entered politics in 1845, he had developed a clear vision for *Mitteleuropa*: it was a multiethnic restructuring of the German Confederation under joint Austro-Prussian leadership. In a tightly drawn narrative, Hayes tells of Bismarck's attempt to achieve this goal. He points out that its ultimate failure was due not only to frequent recalcitrance on the part of the Austrian ruling circle, but also to Bismarck's lack of support from many within Prussia. Hayes concludes by relating Bismarck's ideas to the problems facing central Europe today, and he speculates on their relevance for a "federative comity that might endure." The book is thoroughly annotated, and its bibliography is a resource in itself. One hopes that the price will not prevent the volume from finding its way onto library shelves and into scholars' hands to the extent that it should. Upper-division undergraduate and up.—*S. A. Syme, Coastal Carolina University*

OAB-2365   D137   96-6725 CIP
Heather, Peter. **The Goths.** Blackwell, 1996. 358p bibl index afp ISBN 0-631-16536-3, $29.95

Heather attempts to reconstruct the history of the Goths (the most populous and powerful of the early Germanic tribes) between the first and seventh centuries CE. He focuses on what it meant to be a Goth from the viewpoint of identity and ethnicity during this period of mass migrations of peoples into the Roman Empire. Although Heather uses traditional literary accounts of the Goths, he makes his greatest contribution by adding information from the latest archaeological excavations. The new evidence reveals that early Gothic kingdoms, leadership, and social structures were less well defined and organized than previously thought; literary sources tended to favor a more structured version of early Gothic development than actually existed at the time. The up-to-date, 21-page bibliography also includes a five-page section on the latest archaeological materials and studies. Footnotes are used sparingly; maps and illustrations are very helpful. This book presents the most complete and updated overview of the Goths available for both the serious scholar and the general reader. It will be the standard in the field for years to come.—*G. G. Guzman, Bradley University*

OAB-2366   HD2020   93-36927 CIP
Hoppe, Göran. **Peasantry to capitalism: Western Östergötland in the nineteenth century,** by Göran Hoppe and John Langton. Cambridge, 1995 (c1994). 457p bibl index (Cambridge studies in historical geography, 22) ISBN 0-521-25910-X, $69.95

At once an exercise in historical geography, the "new" regional geography, and social history, this study uses rich Swedish historical documentation to examine the development of capitalism from preindustrial society in the region of western Östergötland in the 1810-1860 period. Moving beyond traditional regional inquiry, the authors add a rigorous theoretical framework that seeks

insights into traditional agrarian economy, the concept of peasant ecotype, and the process of proto-industrialization. More particularly, the study addresses the essential parameters of this transformation: the restructuring of land holdings; capitalization, labor, and production; demographic changes; and external market forces. Accompanied by copious sets of data, complex (sometimes impenetrable) diagrams, and appropriate photographs, the work is a powerful analysis of an important stage in social history, and a demonstration of the strengths and weaknesses of detailed theoretical studies of changing social structures. It is thoroughly footnoted, possesses a rich bibliography, and constitutes a valuable addition to the growing collection of literature in historical geography. Upper-division undergraduates and above.—*B. Osborne, Queen's University at Kingston*

OAB-2367   Orig
Israel, Jonathan. **The Dutch republic: its rise, greatness, and fall, 1477-1806.** Oxford, 1995. 1,231p bibl index afp ISBN 0-19-873072-1, $39.95

Israel, a first-rate scholar, has produced the definitive work on the Low Countries for this spectacular but complex period of history. This massive work covers political, economic, religious, cultural, and intellectual history for the entire region in an integrative study that draws on the best scholarship and explains the interconnectedness in a clear and lucid fashion. It will be appreciated by the scholar and understood by the general reader. The United Provinces reached its Golden Age within this period during which its economic, political, and cultural power influenced the rest of Europe. To understand early modern Europe one must understand the rise and fall of the Dutch, and Israel provides a most complete and accurate history that will not soon be superseded. This is a major contribution to the field and a superb production; the bibliography, plates, and maps alone are worth the price. It should be in every library. All levels.—*J. J. Butt, James Madison University*

OAB-2368   BF697   93-20689 CIP
Le Rider, Jacques. **Modernity and crises of identity: culture and society in fin-de-siècle Vienna,** tr. by Rosemary Morris. Continuum, 1993. 380p bibl index ISBN 0-8264-0631-9, $34.95

If there has been a 20th-century renaissance, it took place in Vienna around the turn of the century. To cite names—Freud, Wittgenstein, Hoffmansthal, Klimit, and Schnitzler—is to suggest that this was an age of extraordinary cultural efflorescence. Le Rider believes that behind all this creativity lay individual insecurity, itself the result of political and social decay. By the late 19th century, parliamentary government was faltering in Austria and traditional liberalism had failed. In their place arose virulent nationalism and aggressive antisemitism. For intellectuals (and most of all for Jewish intellectuals who had pursued assimilation) it was no longer clear what course to follow or even who one was. Different individuals found different answers: Sigmund Freud elected to be a scientist who acknowledged his Jewish background while Karl Kraus became a literary critic who denied his. What Le Rider seeks to show is that modernity, the uncertainty as to one's own identity, began (with due allowances for Nietzsche and others) in the capital of Austria 100 years ago. He succeeds brilliantly in a work of broad-ranging scholarship that is recommended to specialists and generalists alike.—*S. Bailey, Knox College*

OAB-2369   DS135   92-39884 CIP
Lowenstein, Steven M. **The Berlin Jewish community: enlightenment, family, and crisis, 1770-1830.** Oxford, 1994. 300p bibl index afp ISBN 0-19-508326-1, $49.95

From the second half of the 18th century, German Jews began the process of modernization, leaving behind or modifying the practice of Judaism, accepting the cultural values of European life, and living increasingly secular lives. The Jewish community of Berlin, the first to undergo a development that questioned the foundations of traditional Jewish existence, has been the subject of many studies seeking to establish the links among Enlightenment thinking, religious reform, intermarriage, and the closely related phenomenon of conversion to Christianity. Previous historians have tended to take an anecdotal approach, concentrating on a few symbolic celebrities like Moses Mendelssohn and Dorothea Schlegel. Lowenstein prefers the techniques of collective biography—mining tax rolls, occupational censuses, baptismal and marriage records, and subscription lists for works of the Jewish enlightenment (Haskala). Most impressively, his social-historical treatment of families over a 60-year period tests many traditional, and passionately held, assumptions about the significance of modernization for Jewish survival. Because his own findings emerge forcefully from a careful examination of the evidence, they carry great weight in this ongoing debate. A first-rate study of an important subject. General and academic readers at all levels.—*R. S. Levy, University of Illinois at Chicago*

OAB-2370   DD193   95-53324 CIP
Marchand, Suzanne L. **Down from Olympus: archaeology and philhellenism in Germany, 1750-1970.** Princeton, 1996. 400p bibl index afp ISBN 0-691-04393-0, $39.50

Marchand's superb book shows that German history cannot be fully understood unless one considers the unique ways in which Germans have used the past. To begin with, Greek art and literature gave the Germans of the Enlightenment the models they needed to cast aside the restraints of French culture and to replace them with something more natural and spontaneous, more Greek (and more German). During the Napoleonic Age, philhellenism took on a political coloration: the Athenian polis taught Germans the values of democracy and civic activism. After 1830, however, reaction set in. The study of antiquity became the business of schoolmasters and professors, and larger aesthetic and humanistic concerns gave way to historical and philological erudition. At the same time, archaeology became the business of state-sponsored expeditions that sought artifacts and glory throughout Greece and Anatolia. The study of antiquity had become a foundation of the state. In WW I German classicists argued that Germany deserved to win the war because Germans best understood antiquity. After 1918 some of them even turned to racism. In brief, this is a sobering book, one marked by its scholarly care and narrative brilliance. General readers; upper-division undergraduates and above.—*S. Bailey, Knox College*

OAB-2371   DD257   92-15654 CIP
McAdams, A. James. **Germany divided: from the wall to reunification.** Princeton, 1993. 250p bibl index afp ISBN 0-691-07892-0, $29.95

The first comprehensive study in English of East-West German relations from the Berlin Wall (1961) to reunification. For this reason alone, McAdams's very well researched book will be warmly welcomed. It is based on a thorough knowledge of both East and West German politics as well as on key German and American Cold War scholarship. Although the author's research in the recently opened East German and Russian archives is still too minimal to anticipate that the book will remain an up-to-date standard for very long, his analysis of the Honecker period is bolstered by an impressive list of interviews with former East German insiders, sponsored by the Hoover Institution GDR Oral History Project. These interviews yielded impressive insights for the 1970s-'80s, the like of which will emerge from the archives only for the Ulbricht years. McAdams's much-repeated thesis—that inter-German relations were ultimately determined by "the constraints and opportunities presented to them by their own political systems"—belabors the obvious. The book's comprehensive coverage and first-rate analysis of the intricate East-West German relationship in the 1970s and '80s make it a must purchase for any basic contemporary German history or Cold War collection. All levels.—*D. Prowe, Carleton College*

OAB-2372   DL1175   95-18982 CIP
Schoolfield, George C. **Helsinki of the czars: Finland's capital, 1808-1918.** Camden House, 1996. 308p bibl index afp ISBN 1-57113-026-8, $55.00

A distinguished Scandinavian literary scholar, Schoolfield has here produced a typically well-researched and elegantly written cultural history of the city of Helsinki when it served as the political and intellectual capital of Imperial Russia's "Grand Duchy of Finland." Russian armies captured Finland from Sweden, with Bonaparte's blessings, in 1808, and over the next century it was rebuilt on a grand scale, a national university was founded there, and Helsinki became a hotbed of amazing cultural creativity. Schoolfield traces artfully its teeming world of architecture, literature, theater, and the arts as old Swedish elites vied with rising ethnic Finnish nationalists, and produced many luminaries of international stature such as Jean Sibelius and Eliel Saarinen. Earlier czarist benevolence turned eventually to repressive Russification measures toward the 20th century, and Finland made its successful bid for national independence in the wake of the Bolshevik Revolution. But the previous century of growth was a brilliant one for the city, which Schoolfield lovingly recreates. Students of Scandinavian and Finnish cultural development in the 19th century will find much to savor here, as will the interested general reader. In an attractive format, with useful appendixes, well-selected illustrations, and a full bibliography, this work is recommended for public and university libraries and especially for those with a particular collecting interest in Scandinavian cultural history.—*K. Smemo, Moorhead State University*

OAB-2373   PT3803   92-31767 CIP
Townsend, Mary Lee. **Forbidden laughter: popular humor and the limits of repression in nineteenth-century Prussia.** Michigan, 1993 (c1992). 258p index ISBN 0-472-10330-X, $39.50

A seminal social history that explores the role and function of popular humor as it informed the daily lives of Berliners and Prussians in the mid-19th century. It is, understandably, a rare work in social science that relies on people's humor as a primary source of analysis. Nevertheless, jokes and caricatures confront the same objective issues that historians have long scrutinized, namely, social and economic problems, religious and political conflict. Humor offers an additional dimension. Townsend argues, "Jokes often capture an immediateness that more labored texts such as memoirs cannot provide. For example, humor about universal issues reveals a lot about German attitudes toward women and family." In her critical study Townsend not only delves into the innumerable ways in which popular humor became an essential form of public discourse in Germany, but also observes parallel developments in London and Paris during the same period: "Jokes and caricatures in Berlin had a marked similarity to the work being published elsewhere, particularly in Paris." Humor is often formed as a response to repression, and Townsend's masterful work exemplifies in a pivotal way the complexities of people's response to such policy. General, undergraduate; graduate; faculty.—*J. Boskin, Boston University*

UNITED KINGDOM & IRELAND

OAB-2374   DA256   92-29108 CIP
Allmand, Christopher. **Henry V.** California, 1993 (c1992). 480p bibl index (English monarchs series, 10) ISBN 0-520-08293-1, $35.00

Allmand (Liverpool Univ.) has written the first full scholarly biography of one of England's hero kings. It is a masterful study, putting Henry's well-known military achievements in the context of the king's less-appreciated skill at rulership and administration. Allmand first narrates Henry's life; the remaining two thirds of the volume are devoted to thematic chapters on aspects of Henry's reign, including his rule in Normandy, church relations, Lollardy and sedition, order, Parliament, and finance, among others. Allmand's outlook and analysis in each case is cautious and traditional, but thorough and convincing: he has done much new archival research as well as synthesized all recent scholarship on the period. Allmand is always careful to see Henry in a broader European perspective and as part of a longer English history. A definitive scholarly study, the book is also so clearly written as to be accessible even to general readers. Excellent bibliography, index, and footnotes; helpful illustrations and maps. A must buy for any late medieval collection; recommended for all academic libraries. General; undergraduate; graduate; faculty.—*S. Morillo, Wabash College*

OAB-2375   GN776   90-44449 MARC

Avebury reconsidered: from the 1660s to the 1990s, by Peter J. Ucko et al. Unwin Hyman, 1992 (c1991). 2v. 293p; 27 transparencies bibl index ISBN 0-04-445919-X, $110.00

There is something very exciting and engaging about this study. Not only does its scholarly team of authors reveal new archaeological and historical insights and relate them to contemporary public policy and land use debates, they also present material in a novel fashion, via text, book illustrations, and 27 transparencies suitable for personal analysis or for overhead projection, all properly keyed to a uniform scale. This is certainly an imaginative and productive way to study Avebury, the world's largest extant henge monument with standing stones. Nearby Stonehenge attracts more visitors, but Avebury, with its massive bank and ditch, its rough uprights, its broad avenue leading to other neolithic monuments, and its enclosed medieval village, has a wondrous quality all its own. It has been studied for at least 400 years, and this book includes two formerly unknown 17th-century ground plans, made before the site's worst destruction. Even Aubrey Burl's excellent popular overview, *Prehistoric Avebury* (CH, Dec'79) now needs partial revision. *Avebury Reconsidered* will be widely cited. Used in conjunction with a good set of slides, these transparencies can form the basis of an engrossing archaeological lecture. General; graduate; faculty; professional.—*E. J. Kealey, College of the Holy Cross*

OAB-2376   DA990   92-225896 MARC

Bardon, Jonathan. **A history of Ulster.** Blackstaff, 1993 (c1992). 914p bibl index ISBN 0-85640-466-7, $65.00; ISBN 0-85640-476-4 pbk, $32.00

Bardon's impressive and massive narrative history immediately becomes the best work available for understanding the problems of Northern Ireland in their historical context. Nearly half the 830 pages of text deals with Northern Ireland—six of the nine counties of the traditional province of Ulster—since the partition of Ireland in 1920-21. Because Bardon's book covers events up to 1992, it must be recommended over Patrick Buckland's *A History of Northern Ireland* (1981). Bardon writes well, effectively sprinkling his text with striking quotes from primary sources to illustrate his points. He is remarkably nonpartisan and fair-minded in his analyses; though Irish nationalists will probably claim a Protestant/pro-British leaning, the book is neither intrusive nor distorting. Highly recommended. General; undergraduate; graduate.—*J. W. Auld, California State University, Dominguez Hills*

OAB-2377   DA560   91-19673 CIP

Biagini, Eugenio F. **Liberty, retrenchment and reform: popular liberalism in the Age of Gladstone, 1860-1880.** Cambridge, 1992. 476p bibl index ISBN 0-521-40315-4, $74.95

Here is a book that delivers what its title promises. Recognizing that in Continental Europe many workers adhered to republican or socialist movements, Biagini focuses upon Britain's "plebian radicals" to determine why that country's Liberal party retained such extensive popular support for so long after the mid-19th century. The explanation, he argues, lies in the fact that the principal themes of British liberalism made sense to ordinary people in a rational way. The struggle for civil and religious liberty as well as the efforts to curtail the intrusive impact of the state struck a responsive chord among plebian radicals all too aware of the iniquity of privilege and rank. Biagini's strongest discussion, though, is of the resonance of reform, above all the agitation for a more democratic franchise. He teases out the continuity with Chartism and draws stimulating parallels with Jacksonian America and Mazzini's Italy. If one might wonder about the significance of this very diverse, locally rooted popular liberalism for parliamentary politics, Biagini satisfies here, too, with a concluding insightful chapter on the extraordinary relationship between the adoring Liberal faithful and their champion, Gladstone. An important and readable book. Recommended. Advanced undergraduate; graduate; faculty.—*F. Coetzee, Yale University*

OAB-2378   DA415   92-295 CIP

Carlton, Charles. **Going to the wars: the experience of the British Civil Wars, 1638-1651.** Routledge, 1993 (c1992). 428p index ISBN 0-415-03282-2, $29.95

Known for his biographies of Charles I and Archbishop Laud, Carlton (North Carolina State Univ.) here returns to the social history he first explored in his neglected but outstanding work on the Court of Orphans. Employing "the new military history," which emphasizes experience rather than strategy, he recounts the gruesome serendipities of combat, the deprivations of military service, and the attendant disruptions of civilian life that eventually prompted opposition to standing armies. His plundering of 17th-century sources demonstrates the bloodiness of the Civil Wars as well as their radical impact on a generation. Reference to every sort of commentary on warfare except the likes of U2's "New Year's Day" underscores the commonalties of wartime experience over the centuries and suggests that the British Civil Wars represented less worlds that have been lost than episodes of eternally recurring human folly. As a supplement to accounts of battles and regiments, Carlton's study stands alone. Its extensive explanations indicate that it is intended partly for general readers interested in military history, but it will also be an important resource for other readers, ranging from advanced undergraduates to specialists in British history.—*M. C. Noonkester, William Carey College*

OAB-2379   Can. CIP

Childs, Michael J. **Labour's apprentices: working-class lads in late Victorian and Edwardian England.** McGill-Queen's, 1992. 223p bibl index afp ISBN 0-7735-0915-1, $44.95

Childs (McGill Univ.) has written a superb piece of social history about working-class youths in Britain between 1890 and 1914—a study narrower but far superior to Lionel Roses's *The Erosion of Childhood* (CH, Feb'92). Childs uses modern social theory and relies heavily on oral history archives in England, but he never forgets that his sources are his master. He is analytical and covers all aspects of the world of working-class lads—their families, education, labor, street culture, entertainment, and organized youth movements—in a global context. Childs concludes that the young generation of this class with its new norms, attitudes, and ways of approaching problems had a major influence on the type of society that emerged in Britain in the early 20th century. The book is well organized and written, copiously footnoted, and includes a detailed bibliography. It is a model study of its kind. Highly recommended for general readers, advanced undergraduates, graduates, and researchers/faculty.—*W. J. Hoffman Jr., Hiram College*

OAB-2380   HD8390   93-50835 CIP

Clark, Anna. **The struggle for the breeches: gender and the making of the British working class.** California, 1995. 416p bibl index afp ISBN 0-520-08624-4, $35.00

Clark (Univ. of North Carolina) has written a pioneering study of the role of gender in British working-class history that serves as an antidote to E.P. Thompson's male orientation in *The Making of the English Working Class* (CH, Jul'64) and Barbara Taylor's narrow study of gender in the Owenite movement, *Eve and the New Jerusalem* (CH, Sep'83). Clark concentrates on the late 18th century and first half of the 19th century, and her work clearly indicates the need for a similar study of the late Victorian era. For her analysis she uses artisans and textile workers in Glasgow, Lancashire, and London; thus, her view is British rather than solely English. She introduces gender into such topics as domestic life, the emerging factory system, radical political philosophy, popular culture, politics, and proletariat organizations, e.g., the Chartists. Clark demolishes the myth of domestic bliss before industrialism, traces the conflict of gender during industrialization, and demonstrates that the fatal flaws of misogyny and patriarchy muted the radicalism of the working class. The book is well researched and generally well written. It provides valuable insight into a misunderstood and neglected aspect of British social history. Illustrated. Upper-division undergraduates and above.—*W. J. Hoffman Jr., Hiram College*

OAB-2381 Orig
Clarke, Peter. **Hope and glory: Britain, 1900-1990.** A. Lane, Penguin, 1997 (c1996). 454p bibl index (Penguin history of Britain, 9) ISBN 0-713-99071-6, $29.95

Clarke's excellent synthesis will surely be the standard history of 20th-century Britain for years to come. Clarke covers the important topics with exemplary clarity and verve. He manages the difficult task of weaving economic, social, and cultural developments into his story without seriously interrupting the narrative flow. North American readers will especially appreciate his skill at making baffling subjects, such as British educational policy, understandable. As might be expected, Clarke excels at describing the politics of each era. He traces the complicated trajectories of each party, aptly noting the ironies of political allegiance. His deft characterizations of various politicians enliven the text immeasurably. Balfour was "a cold fish whose languid elegance belied his intellectual vacuity and his political ruthlessness"; Margaret Thatcher's "convictions were temperamental rather than ideological." Clarke explores his larger themes without allowing them to smooth over complexity or mask nuance. Britain began the century as a dominating world power and 90 years later, shorn of empire, worries about its role within an integrated Europe. As his bibliographic essay clearly demonstrates, Clarke brings to this tale a thorough knowledge of recent scholarship. All levels.—*D. L. LeMahieu, Lake Forest College*

OAB-2382 HB6664 CIP
Clegg, Hugh Armstrong. **A history of British trade unions since 1889: v.3: 1934-1951.** Oxford, 1994. 458p bibl index afp ISBN 0-19-820406-X, $85.00

This third volume of Clegg's history of the British trade unions completes his coverage of their rise and fall in the modern era. The three-volume set provides perhaps the most basic, definitive, and crucial history of the Labour movement from its late 19th century inception to the 1950s. The other titles in the set are *v.1: 1889-1910* (1964) and *v.2: 1911-1933* (CH, Mar'86). The current work runs chronologically from the depth of the Depression in 1934 to the fall of the second Labour government in 1951. It discusses the multitude of collective bargaining negotiations that emerged between 1934 and 1939, the general impact of the Depression on the British trade unions, the war and labor, and the Labour government of 1945-51 (a major chapter and certainly the best short account of this troubled but fascinating half-dozen years). The volume concludes with a retrospective analysis of labor in Britain from 1889 to 1951. Highly recommended. All levels.—*R. W. Kern, University of New Mexico*

OAB-2383 DA485 92-13256 CIP
Colley, Linda. **Britons: forging the nation, 1707-1837.** Yale, 1992. 429p index ISBN 0-300-05737-7, $35.00

The subject here is Augustan England, which Colley (Yale) sees not as a limited monarchy or oligarchy, but as a strongly nationalistic state. Old antipathies among the English, Welsh, and Scots were largely submerged, she feels, to form a new *British* nationalism in support of the London regime. She examines a number of unifying symbols and experiences: Protestantism, commerce, the monarchy, women's "separate sphere," and—above all—war. "This is a culture that is used to fighting and which has largely defined itself through fighting." By 1837, Colley contends, this resulted in a "unitary political discourse" that has lasted pretty much until today. Indeed, she concludes that the passing of these formative symbols and experiences in recent decades has done much to dissolve the British bond and to revive the separate identities of the island's three nations. Although based on extensive scholarship, *Britons* wears it lightly. Colley's prose is breezy and accessible, and her extensive and integral commentary on contemporary images—political caricatures, portraits, historical paintings—is exemplary. Highly recommended for libraries at all levels.—*J. R. Breihan, Loyola College*

OAB-2384 DA716 95-10826 CIP
Davies, R.R. **The revolt of Owain Glyn Dwr.** Oxford, 1996 (c1995). 401p bibl index afp ISBN 0-19-820508-2, $37.00

Davies (All Souls College, Oxford) now serves as president of the Royal Historical Society. His credentials as a historian of medieval Wales have been cemented by many articles and two major books: *Lordship and Society in the March of Wales, 1284-1400* (CH, Apr'79) and *Conquest, Coexistence and Change: Wales, 1063-1415* (CH, Mar'88). Davies has produced a splendid analysis of the revolt of Owain Glyn Dŵr (Shakespeare's Glendower), which began in 1400 and grew into the last great effort at the establishment of nationhood for Wales. He discusses Welsh society at the time of the revolt with great sensitivity, and examines the chronology and impact of the revolt from beginning to expiration, taking into account the regional episodes of a revolt characterized by guerrilla warfare. Davies also illuminates, insofar as is possible, the character and life of Glyn Dŵr. A solid piece of historical writing that belongs in collections of medieval British history or histories of popular revolts. All levels.—*A. C. Reeves, Ohio University*

OAB-2385 HT178 92-12780 Orig
Edwards, Brian. **London docklands: urban design in an age of deregulation.** Butterworth Architecture, 1992. 188p bibl index ISBN 0-7506-1298-3 pbk, $62.95

A fascinatingly thorough but critical study of the ongoing development of London's East End comprising Wapping (especially St. Katherine's Dock), Surrey Docks, Isle of Dogs (especially Canary Wharf), and the Royal Docks. The London Docklands Development Corporation, created in 1981, was an exciting and revolutionary undertaking for Britain based on free-market policies and planning deregulation, with enterprise zones and fiscal incentives in contrast to Britain's earlier social welfare projects. Although the British government provided 1 million pounds for infrastructure improvements, ten times that amount was provided by private funds; thus the undertaking can be seen as truly embodying Thatcherite ideals of private investment in a deregulated environment. Edwards (Univ. of Strathclyde) gives a short history of the site before 1981 and detailed description with maps and illustrations of the projects. From the beginning the emphasis has been on creating commercial buildings and housing (private), with no public buildings, no civic squares, and few parks "unmoderated by wide social and environmental concerns." Some of the architecture is exciting in design and scope but a great deal is "meretricious" and mediocre postmodern. Besides providing a detailed and unbiased history of the development up to 1991, Edwards mentions certain adverse events of 1992, which, combined with the lack of adequate public transportation, have created tremendous problems. Appendix consisting of interviews with various involved officials; very complete bibliography. A major study of a tremendous, if flawed, undertaking. It should appeal to a variety of audiences.—*T. J. McCormick, emeritus, Wheaton College (MA)*

OAB-2386 DA315 94-49540 CIP
Ellis, Steven G. **Tudor frontiers and noble power: the making of the British state.** Oxford, 1995. 303p bibl index afp ISBN 0-19-820133-8, $55.00

Ellis has written an important comparative study of the administration of the borderlands from 1485-1540, focusing on the earls of Kildare in Ireland and the Lords Dacre in northern England. He chides English historians for concentrating on southern, lowland England, arguing that a complete account of the Tudor regime must give equal treatment to non-English territories. Ellis contends that by reducing financial and military support to the borders, Henry VII, and especially Henry VIII, forced the earls of Kildare and the Lords Dacre to build up powerful local affinities in order to defend the frontiers against the Gaelic Irish and the Scots. This in turn threatened Tudor government and led to a crisis in 1534, in which the 9th earl was executed for treason, while William, Lord Dacre, was heavily fined and removed from office. Ellis also maintains that this forced the central government to pay more attention to peripheral territories and was an important step in the formation of the later multinational British state. Although profoundly scholarly, this book should be accessible and interesting even to general readers.—*W. B. Robison III, Southeastern Louisiana University*

OAB-2387 DA118 92-19106 CIP
Elton, Geoffrey. **The English.** B. Blackwell, 1992. 248p index afp ISBN 0-631-17681-0, $24.95

Had Elton chosen to subtitle this splendid book "From the Beeker People to Boy George" he would not have been far off the mark. This work is thoughtful, witty, and graceful in style, a marvel of compression. Elton writes oldfashioned (but nonetheless valid and important) political and ideological history, concentrating on English history to the early 19th century. He views the arrival of industrialization as ushering in a new era of English history that changed the English people as he defines them; the last brief chapter carries the story to the present. The author finds certain historical experiences to have formed what he regards as the uniquely English character. First, the idea and institution of kingship as a unifying element; second, the unique legal system that preserved individual liberties and public order; third, the role of the English church—each typifies the peculiarly English tradition of muddling through. Elton argues forcefully that the English formed, and were formed by, a unique reconciliation of individual freedom with monarchically supervised order. Like Joseph Strayer's *On the Medieval Origins of the Modern State* (1986), this splendid work is a brief distillation of a lifetime of thoughtful scholarship and deep reflection. General; undergraduate; graduate; faculty.—*J. W. Alexander, University of Georgia*

OAB-2388 JN1128 94-5837 CIP
Fishman, Nina. **The British Communist Party and the trade unions, 1933-45.** Scolar, 1995. 380p bibl index ISBN 1-85928-116-8, $74.95

Fishman (Univ. of Westminster) separates myth from fact in the history of the British Communist Party, concentrating on the period from the early 1920s to 1945. Although sympathetic to the aims of the party, she freely describes the internecine conflict that plagued its leadership. Fishman clearly admires the work of Harry Pollitt and Johnny Campbell, who focused their energies on developing contacts within the trade unions, especially among shop stewards and the rank and file. The story is one of strikes, jailings, frustrations, and occasional victories. By the end of WW II, the party played an important role in the leadership of several major British trade unions. Membership in the party always remained small, however, as recruiters often restricted their efforts to the elite union members. This is an exceptionally well researched study; Fishman's interviews with many communists are especially important. Excellent bibliography and a valuable appendix detailing party membership both nationally and by districts. Upper-division undergraduates and above.—*L. J. Satre, Youngstown State University*

OAB-2389 HC254 94-40285 CIP
Grassby, Richard. **The business community of seventeenth-century England.** Cambridge, 1995. 615p bibl index ISBN 0-521-43450-5, $74.95

Grassby, author of important articles and a recent biography of Sir Dudley North, has produced a masterwork. He has read in astonishing breadth (from sources that require 175 pages to list) and reconstructs 17th-century business life in all its detail. Ledgers, letter books, and diaries from 79 archives, contemporary tracts, literary sources, and the most recent scholarship all yield the particulars of recruitment, capitalization, technique, politics, family life, leisure activities, religion, and values. Readers familiar with Grassby's earlier work will not be surprised at his general thesis that the business community was drawn from all ranks of a society more open than most and that the margin of talent over incompetence was the critical factor in Britain's slow rise to economic predominance. But they can now sense the wealth of evidence that supports these conclusions, leading Grassby to reject economic, institutional, and confessional determinism, and prompting him to debate the Stones, Tawney, Hill, Laslett, Brenner, North, and others. Still, this reader wanted more. The argument links success to individuals, not business type or amount of capital, but personalities are barely glimpsed. And though the book immediately becomes the standard source for specialist and student alike, it seems a pity that the author, whose research on this topic may never be equaled, did not or could not take more space to tell the story. Essential for graduate libraries and those serving upper-division undergraduates.—*G. F. Steckley, Knox College*

OAB-2390 HD3325 96-16160 CIP
Gurney, Peter. **Co-operative culture and the politics of consumption in England, 1870-1930.** Manchester, 1996. 350p bibl index ISBN 0-7190-4950-4, $69.95

Although the co-operative movement thrived in late Victorian Britain, modern historians have minimized the movement's significance or judged it conservative and lacking in radical vision. Gurney successfully contests these views in this sophisticated reinterpretation. He argues that the practice of distributing rebates to members on their purchases in the form of dividends, which has been castigated by many on the left for encouraging middle-class attitudes among working-class co-operators, was actually part of a much broader effort to challenge capitalism and bring social transformation. Indeed, the movement sought through education, women's participation, and social activities to create a genuine alternative culture of co-operation and "practical socialism." Lauding the achievements of the movement, Gurney faces squarely the process of decline after 1914 and the movement's inability to compete with chain stores and the consumer fantasies they sold. This is an excellent monograph. Fresh in interpretation and showing an impressive command of the historical literature, Gurney's book is well researched and well argued. Essential for research libraries, this book will be used with profit by good advanced undergraduates.—*J. P. McKay, Univ of Illinois at Urbana-Champaign*

OAB-2391 DA963 94-29916 CIP
Hughes, Michael. **Ireland divided: the roots of the modern Irish problem.** St. Martin's, 1995 (c1994). 143p bibl index ISBN 0-312-12229-2, $39.95; ISBN 0-312-12230-6 pbk, $16.95

Hughes's book is an extremely lucid, balanced, and well-informed treatment of divided Ireland. Hughes, who died prematurely in 1993, begins with an 88-page narrative section. He devotes 24 of those pages to the myths that cloud the perception of Irish history and to the roots of the Irish problem, beginning with Pope Gregory VII and King Henry II. He then focuses on the Irish situation since 1906. Hughes wastes no words and illuminates the essentials. This book should be read in conjunction with Kevin Boyle and Tom Hadden's *Northern Ireland: The Choice* (1994), Tim Coogan's *The IRA* (CH, Apr'94) and *The Man Who Made Ireland: The Life and Death of Michael Collins* (1992), or Robert Kee's *The Laurel and the Ivy* (1993). Hughes's pessimistic conclusion, from the perspective of the early '90s, was that the partition of Ireland, which began in 1922 with the creation of the Free State and Northern Ireland, "will last for many more years." There are 40 pages of "illustrative documents," ranging from a speech by Parnell in 1880 to one by Herbert Morrison in 1949, and a brief selective bibliography of reprinted sources, all published since the mid-'60s. No maps. Upper-division undergraduates and above.—*R. H. Thompson, Indiana University-Purdue University—Columbus*

OAB-2392 HQ614 94-24895 CIP
Ittmann, Karl. **Work, gender and family in Victorian England.** New York University, 1995. 341p bibl index ISBN 0-8147-3756-0, $45.00

Ittman's book is an exceedingly well written, microcosmic study of the rise of family limitation after 1870 in the industrial city of Bradford. Basing much of his argument on a comparative sample of some 28,000 people tabulated in the decennial censuses from 1851 to 1881, Ittmann challenges some of the basic assumptions contained in population theory about the inverse correlation between modernization and family size. The result is an important addition to the many recent studies that have examined the history of the rapid decline in fertility that started in the late 19th century. Ittmann contends that aggregate studies, and the statistical techniques of regression analysis frequently used to analyze them, fail to explain why millions of couples began to limit the size of their families in this period. He argues persuasively that it is only possible to answer this question by examining in depth the socioeconomic conditions and cultural values of

Social & Behavioral Sciences

people in selected locales. If Ittmann's conclusions about economic realities and the self-help culture of working-class Bradford are less surprising than he suggests, they are nevertheless based on excellent research. He has written a model local study that belongs in libraries serving upper-division undergraduates and above.—*R. A. Soloway, University of North Carolina at Chapel Hill*

OAB-2393 DA355 93-1116 CIP
Jones, Norman. **The birth of the Elizabethan Age: England in the 1560s.** Blackwell, 1993. 300p index afp ISBN 0-631-16796-X, $59.95

In this provocative and exciting book Jones, author of *Faith by Statute: Parliament and the Settlement of Religion, 1559* (1982), has examined the 1560s from the perspective of Elizabethan contemporaries. He has relied on a thorough investigation of "traditional" primary sources, but more important, he has also used a range of autobiographical materials. At the onset, Jones notes that "To write about how contemporaries experienced a decade is to break with the historiographical traditions and literary conventions." His treatment of this approach is nothing less than exemplary. The Elizabethan concerns with religion, the marriage question, and domestic stability were examined in light of the thoughts of contemporaries such as Simon Forman, an erstwhile astrologer; Thomas Whythorne, a music teacher; Lady Grace Mildmay; and Agnes Bowker, "who gave birth to a cat." To Jones the 1560s was a decade during which processes were established that served England during the rest of the century. The text is documented thoroughly and is supplemented with 15 illustrations. Highest recommendation. All levels.—*W. T. Walker, Philadelphia College of Pharmacy and Science*

OAB-2394 DS135 91-18896 CIP
Kadish, Sharman. **Bolsheviks and British Jews: the Anglo-Jewish community, Britain and the Russian Revolution.** F. Cass, 1992. 298p bibl index ISBN 0-7146-3371-2, $45.00

Kadish's important book is about issues much wider than its title suggests. The author's concern is British Jews' reaction to the Russian Revolution, but this group faced the same difficulties as many other minorities in the modern world—a conflict of loyalties between those to their country of birth and culture and those to their newly adopted land. Although outsiders saw a monolithic alien community, Kadish shows how British Jews were divided between those recently arrived from Eastern Europe and those assimilated, between Leftists and Rightists, and between those religious and those secular. Most Jews welcomed the March overthrow of the Czar, but were divided on the issue of Bolshevism. The civil war offered only a choice between the murderous pogroms of the Whites and the antisemitism of the Reds. Whichever side Jews took fueled antisemitism in the British press and government. To counter the move to the Left, Britain issued the Balfour Declaration and urged Zionism as an antidote to Bolshevism, but many British Jews opposed Zionism because they felt it questioned their loyalty to England. This further increased divisions within the Jewish community. Kadish treats these complex issues and their impact on both English Jews and non-Jews in a well-researched and well-written work. Although useful to all interested in ethnic relations, multiculturalism, and nationalism, the book will be most valuable to academic readers. Footnotes, illustrations. Undergraduate; graduate; faculty.—*I. M. Roth, Foothill College*

OAB-2395 HQ1236 92-41371 CIP
Lovenduski, Joni. **Contemporary feminist politics: women and power in Britain,** by Joni Lovenduski and Vicky Randall. Oxford, 1993. 388p bibl index afp ISBN 0-19-827738-5, $48.00; ISBN 0-19-878069-9 pbk, $16.95

In this thoughtful and thought-provoking study, two scholars of and participants in the British women's movement examine its evolution, successes, and failures since the late 1970s. To organize their research, the authors identify five key themes emerging from Women's Liberation Movement congresses between 1970 and '78: equality at work, health and reproductive rights, motherhood and child care, sexuality and violence, and women's citizenship and political representation. Their use of self-critical social science methodologies is given life through the extensive interviews with activists at all levels of involvement. Among other conclusions, they point to the professionalization and institutionalization of the movement along with the broad acceptance of its goals, but also to the growth of conflicts within the movement leading to its fragmentation. A must for all students of women's movements and issues and for theorists of the new social movements, this study includes an excellent bibliography and will be an acquisition valuable to all levels of readers.—*F. Burkhard, Morgan State University*

OAB-2396 DA995 92-43255 CIP
MacLaran, Andrew. **Dublin: the shaping of a capital.** Belhaven/Halsted, 1993. 242p bibl index ISBN 0-470-22009-0, $49.95

Although hardly a "world city" in terms of size or function, Dublin's cultural significance is sufficiently international in stature that it has been included in the "World Cities" series. This book matches the quality of its predecessors in its breadth, clarity of writing, and insightful interpretations of the local urban scene. Nothing quite like it has been available previously; MacLaran's skillful synthesis of a wide range of studies (most of them Irish, many in Gaelic) is a major contribution to urban social sciences. The work also becomes a scholarly reference on Dublin. MacLaran treats the city's history, planning experiences, residential-environmental patterns, economic development, political-administrative structures, demography, and contemporary urban problems. The text is profusely illustrated with maps, diagrams, and photographs. The nine-page bibliography is quite up-to-date. Very highly recommended as a basic work for all collections on contemporary urban studies, international planning, and current European affairs. Advanced undergraduates and above.—*P. O. Muller, University of Miami*

OAB-2397 Orig
O'Day, Rosemary. **Mr. Charles Booth's inquiry: life and labour of the people in London reconsidered,** by Rosemary O'Day and David Englander. Hambledon, 1993. 246p bibl indexes afp ISBN 1-85285-079-5, $60.00

A superb study of Charles Booth's inquiry into the people of London at the turn of the 20th century. At the center of the book is the wealth of Booth archival material—much still totally untapped—that helps to explain the basis and process of the inquiry. The authors stress that the original inquiry was not undertaken by Booth as a response to statements made by the Marxist H.M. Hyndman, but was instituted to understand how people live in order to help provide for their needs. The book is divided into the same sections as the original inquiry, i.e., the poverty, industry, and religious influences series. The authors contend that Booth was very critical of his research methods, was aware of possible shortcomings, and was an excellent social investigator. On this latter point, they are particularly critical of E.P. Thompson and Eileen Yeo who, in *The Unknown Mayhew* (1971) find Booth inferior to Henry Mayhew. They also defend Booth's methodology—which was nonstatistical—of surveying religious influences. Essential reading for anyone interested in social history or sociology. Advanced undergraduate; graduate; faculty.—*L. J. Satre, Youngstown State University*

OAB-2398 HD1930 95-33963 CIP
Overton, Mark. **Agricultural revolution in England: the transformation of the agrarian economy, 1500-1850.** Cambridge, 1996. 258p bibl index (Cambridge studies in historical geography, 23) ISBN 0-521-24682-2, $54.95; ISBN 0-521-56859-5 pbk, $19.95

Overton's book is a model synthesis of current scholarship, superseding all previous work. It begins with a historiography of the rival notions of agricultural revolution that place it from the 16th to the 19th centuries. Overton lays out traditional arguments and their shortcomings, then presents a clear set of criteria for an agricultural revolution. He next provides the most succinct and accurate available description of farming, both arable and livestock, in the 16th century, including a good discussion of fertilizers and nitrogen. Overton argues that output increased most dramatically in the period 1700-1850 for complex reasons, but this increase was related to nitrogen management using legumes. He discusses institutional changes, such as the shift from local markets to intermarket and eventually national market exchange, as well as changing agrarian social relations, the decline of peasantry, and the rise of an agrarian labor class caused by the commercialization of the marketplace. Charts, tables, and maps are usually clear and helpful, the guide to further reading is wonderfully annotated, and there is a very complete bibliography. This book is clearly the starting point for all study of the subject. All levels.—*J. J. Butt, James Madison University*

OAB-2399   DA47   93-16656 CIP
Parker, R.A.C. **Chamberlain and appeasement: British policy and the coming of the Second World War.** St. Martin's, 1993. 388p bibl index ISBN 0-312-09659-3, $39.95

Parker (Oxford Univ.) is best known for his excellent *Struggle for Survival: The History of the Second World War* (1989). Here addressing the revived interest in appeasement, Parker argues that from 1935, Chamberlain searched for agreements to limit European armaments and to settle German grievances, because he believed in that policy, not because of British weakness or military unpreparedness. Although Chamberlain was convinced that Munich was "a stage on the way to peace," the British public and most of his Cabinet thought they had narrowly succeeded in averting war, and so put limits on his scope. Right into September 1939, Chamberlain remained certain that he could still win Hitler and Mussolini to peaceful ways. Chamberlain's policy was "arrogant, not weak or timid." Parker refutes such revisionists as David Dilks (*Neville Chamberlain*, v.1, CH, Jul'85), whose recent essays contend Chamberlain's policy was "the best, or perhaps the only [one] circumstances allowed." Actually, Chamberlain "made choices among alternative policies." Though informed by his bibliography, Parker's book is argued almost entirely from primary sources, including many collections of official records and personal papers. The result is lucid, persuasive, and immensely interesting. General readers, advanced undergraduates, and above.—*P. K. Cline, Earlham College*

OAB-2400   HQ18   94-21091 CIP
Porter, Roy. **The facts of life: the creation of sexual knowledge in Britain, 1650-1950,** by Roy Porter and Lesley Hall. Yale, 1995. 415p bibl index ISBN 0-300-06221-4, $35.00

This is a remarkable study of how the British gained knowledge about sexual practices from various textbooks in the period 1650 to 1950. Although the authors, both associated with the Wellcome Institute, London, stress that there is no way to determine how readers viewed the books, the fact that they often went through several editions indicates that these texts found a ready market. An early best-seller, *Aristotle's Master-Piece*, first appeared in 1684 and was still being read, under a rather different format, in the Victorian period. Porter and Hall contend that books on sex were often self-censored, as writers understood what was acceptable to authorities or to the public. The backgrounds of various writers—including Havelock Ellis and Marie Stopes—and their books are carefully examined, as are the perceptions of masturbation, venereal diseases, and contraception. In spite of increased information, ignorance about sexuality, pregnancy, and childbirth extended well into the 20th century. Contains an extensive bibliography and valuable illustrations, including the drawing of a "painful" device to warn one of an erection. All levels.—*L. J. Satre, Youngstown State University*

OAB-2401   HQ759   92-40849 CIP
Ross, Ellen. **Love and toil: motherhood in outcast London, 1870-1918.** Oxford, 1993. 308p bibl index afp ISBN 0-19-503957-2, $55.00; ISBN 0-19-508321-0 pbk, $19.95

Ross's long-awaited book blends individual stories and statistics with forceful argumentation to reveal the role played by urban mothers in modernizing Britain. Ross's emphasis on mothers as providers and preservers challenges the interpretations of administrative or intellectual histories such as Gerturde Himmelfarb's *Poverty and Compassion* (CH, May'92), which also examine the shift from Victorian individualism to the origins of the welfare state in an urban setting. Ross (Ramapo College) focuses on mundane yet crucial subjects such as shopping; selection of marital partners; bearing and rearing children; caring for the sick; and fending off those who threaten mothers and children, from fathers to radical interventionists. Such unremarked and unnamed concerns are difficult to reserach. If "toil" is more obvious than "love" in the book, this is driven by the nature of the sources on which Ross relies; court cases and autobiographies of children may distort the typical mother's story. *Love and Toil* will be a controversial but standard text in British history and women's studies. Extensive notes; bibliography limited to primary sources. Recommended for advanced undergraduates and above.—*M. Baer, Hope College*

OAB-2402   DA990   95-52013 CIP
Ruane, Joseph. **The dynamics of conflict in Northern Ireland: power, conflict and emancipation,** by Joseph Ruane and Jennifer Todd. Cambridge, 1996. 365p bibl indexes ISBN 0-521-56018-7, $59.95; ISBN 0-521-56879-X pbk, $19.95

Ruane and Todd offer a densely written, analytical account of the post-1969 troubles in Northern Ireland. Their focus is on the dynamics of conflict, its structure, and (in a pragmatic conclusion) what they describe as a new approach to resolution of the struggle. A system of relationships deeply rooted in Irish history, society, and culture is responsible for the enormously complex and violent situation. The radical, emancipatory solution proposed by the writers, a sociologist and a political scientist, is to abolish the entire system of relationships. The book is similar to B. O'Leary and John McGarry's *The Politics of Antagonism* (CH, Jul'93), David J. Smith and Gerald Chambers's *Inequality in Northern Ireland* (CH, Nov'91), John Whyte's *Interpreting Northern Ireland* (1990), and Frank Wright's *Northern Ireland: A Comparative Analysis* (1987). This is a fine, scholarly analysis of one of modern Europe's longest-running ethnico-religious miseries. Although optimistic, the authors introduce a note of doubt in their epilogue of June 1996. Can the careful formulations of peace-loving researchers be made to work in the streets, or will an ineradicable lust for power continue to negate solutions based on reason? Tables; figures; appendix on opinion-poll sources. Upper-division undergraduates and above.—*R. H. Thompson, Indiana University-Purdue University—Columbus*

OAB-2403   DA995   94-7568 CIP
Scally, Robert James. **The end of hidden Ireland: rebellion, famine, and emigration.** Oxford, 1995. 266p index afp ISBN 0-19-505582-9, $35.00

Scally has written a highly original book whose impressive scholarship makes a significant contribution to understanding 19th-century Irish and North American history. At the height of the Great Famine in 1847-8, the Crown evicted 470-odd tenants living in the townland of Ballykilcline, near Strokestown, County Roscommon, and sponsored their emigration to the US. Scally reconstructs the social environment and mental world of these people with great skill and perceptiveness as he untangles the fascinating web of events that led, after a decade-long wrangle over rents, to their removal. The importance of this book lies in its depiction of these events from the perspective of the victims, particularly the process of their eviction and the journey to Liverpool and New York. This is microhistory at its best, using a small setting to expand knowledge of bigger events. It is also splendidly written and deserves a wide readership. Photographs and useful footnotes. All levels.—*G. Owens, Huron College*

OAB-2404   JN1129   92-2604 CIP
Searle, G.R. **The Liberal Party: triumph and disintegration, 1886-1929.** St. Martin's, 1992. 234p bibl index ISBN 0-312-08039-5, $39.95

Searle synthesizes recent historical scholarship about the latter days of the

British Liberal party. He covers the period from Gladstone's divisive campaign for Irish Home Rule during the 1880s, through the triumph of the "Nonconformist Conscience" and social reform during the first decade of the 20th century, to the "strange death" of the party during and after WW I. Searle (Univ. of East Anglia) argues that the principal cause of the Liberals' downfall was their failure—or rather, their principled refusal—to base their party on class interests. The same principle was also the Liberals' main strength. Although Searle states his views quite explicitly, other explanations are given thorough, evenhanded summaries. Searle provides an excellent index, an up-to-date bibliography, more than 350 incisive endnotes, and appendixes listing members of Liberal administrations, general election results, and Liberal allegiance by region. Beginning students in the field, whatever their level, will find his book extremely useful.— *J. R. Breihan, Loyola College*

OAB-2405   DA560   91-37163 CIP
Shannon, Richard. **The Age of Disraeli, 1868-1881: the rise of Tory democracy.** Longman, 1992. 445p index ISBN 0-582-50713-8, $69.95

In this important contribution to British political historiography, Shannon (University of Wales), author of *The Crisis of Imperialism, 1865-1915* (London, 1974) and *Gladstone: v.1, 1809-1865* (London, 1982) examines a turbulent and seminal period in the history of England's Conservative party. Focusing on the years of Benjamin Disraeli's dominance in British politics (1868-1881), Shannon argues that Disraeli identified his party with the "conservative" character of the British working classes. Disraeli's Tory democracy not only advanced the development of an open political process, it "captured" a historical force that was already evident. Consequently, the Conservative party emerged as a national party that identified with the interests of the middle and working classes. Later, Randolph Churchill, Lord Salisbury, and Winston Churchill would sustain Tory democracy and maintain the dominance of the Conservative party in the late 19th and 20th centuries. Shannon used a wide range of manuscript materials including the Hughenden (Disraeli) Papers and the diaries of Lord Derby. Excellent documentation; well written. Required reading for all students of modern British political history. Highest recommendation. General; undergraduate; graduate; faculty.—*W. T. Walker, Philadelphia College of Pharmacy and Science*

OAB-2406   KD1500   93-590 CIP
Spring, Eileen. **Law, land, & family: aristocratic inheritance in England, 1300 to 1800.** North Carolina, 1993. 199p index afp ISBN 0-8078-2110-1, $29.95

Spring's significant and highly original study of inheritance among the aristocracy and gentry from the late Middle Ages is a work of social as well as legal history. Spring, an independent researcher, places legal practices within the context of family values. As a consequence, the devices employed by land-owning families to deal with problems presented by the common law principle of primogeniture—entail, use, and strict settlement—are significantly reinterpreted. The concern of landed families was not simply to tie up their estates but to make secure provisions for all family members. Most specifically, they worked to exclude women from land holding and to nullify the common law rules of inheritance that would have allowed 40% of land to be inherited by females. Spring also critiques the historical literature on land law and family history, including the work of Lawrence and Jean Stone, J.C. Holt, Lloyd Bonfeld, and Alan McFarlane, from her new perspective. Her study is a truly important contribution to both fields and is highly recommended for academic libraries interested in British history, women's studies, and legal history. Advanced undergraduates and above.—*C. W. Wood Jr., Western Carolina University*

OAB-2407   HV8195   96-32187 CIP
Taylor, David. **The new police in nineteenth-century England: crime, conflict, and control.** Manchester, 1997. (Dist. by St. Martin's) 180p bibl index ISBN 0-7190-4728-5, $59.95; ISBN 0-7190-4729-3 pbk, $19.95

Taylor offers a relatively brief and scholarly survey of the development of

English police forces, and in doing so offers probably the most comprehensive sketch of current scholarship on the subject. He sensibly places himself between the old Whig school that saw the police as agents of enlightened reform readily accepted by an admiring public, and the revisionist approach that emphasizes conflict between police and the public. The author first concerns himself with the politics of police reform that created the London Metropolitan Police and the various county and borough forces between 1829 and 1856. Second, he discusses the problems of poor discipline and high turnover in the early years that gave way to relatively stable police forces in the 20th century. Third, he shows how public hostility to the police lessened over the decades; this, however, was problematic because increased intrusion into delicate areas of daily life made police still resented by many. Overall, the evolution of the English police was not straightforward but was a contentious process fraught with many practical difficulties. Excellent notes, annotated bibliography, and more than 30 pages of document selections. Upper-division undergraduates and above.—*P. T. Smith, Saint Joseph's University*

■ Latin America & the Caribbean

OAB-2408   HD499   94-42607 CIP
Adriance, Madeleine Cousineau. **Promised land: base Christian communities and the struggle for the Amazon.** State University of New York, 1995. 202p bibl index afp ISBN 0-7914-2649-1, $59.50

Adriance offers a highly accessible, first-hand account of the intensive involvement of religious groups (such as *communidades de base*) in movements for land reform and human rights in Brazil, and provides a broad theoretical discussion on the connection between religion and social change. The author gives much-needed attention to the influential roles women have played in these movements, and attempts to chart the highly complex relationships among *comunidades de base* and members of the Catholic Church hierarchy. Official church policy—the author discovered—is confusing and replete with inconsistencies. She ultimately concludes that "it is sometimes difficult to figure out precisely what the Brazilian Catholic Church is doing in relation to people of the poorer classes." A major contribution of this study is its careful documentation of deeply held religious beliefs that underlie social activism in Latin America. Vital for students of Latin American politics and religion, but also of interest to anthropologists, sociologists, ecologists, and historians. Highly recommended. General readers, upper-division undergraduates, and above.— *S. D. Glazier, University of Nebraska at Kearney*

OAB-2409   HC202   94-44080 CIP
Andrien, Kenneth J. **The Kingdom of Quito, 1690-1830: the state and regional development.** Cambridge, 1995. 255p bibl index ISBN 0-521-48125-2, $59.95

Andrien, a well-known historian of colonial Peru, examines the consequences of public policy on the socioeconomic development of the Kingdom of Quito, from the decline of its once-thriving textile industry in the 1690s to the creation of the Republic of Ecuador in 1830. He argues convincingly that policies promulgated to benefit Spain had major negative economic consequences for the woolen cloth industry that had long sustained Quito's economy. Tax reforms provoked a major rebellion in the city of Quito in 1765. Subsequent commercial reforms stimulated increased cacao exports through Guayaquil and significantly expanded royal revenues, but further debilitated an already weakened textile industry. Increased state intervention in the economy, in short, prevented economic development and promoted regionalism rather than an integrated national market, as state expenditures went for defense and administration rather than economic infrastructure. The absence of sustained autonomous economic development persisted long after 1830. Based on extensive archival research and wide-ranging secondary sources, this clearly written and meticulously developed study is essential reading for all students of colonial Spanish America. Upper-division undergraduates and above.—*M. A. Burkholder, University of Missouri—St. Louis*

OAB-2410   F2272   94-18743 CIP
Avellaneda, José Ignacio. **The conquerors of the New Kingdom of Granada.** New Mexico, 1995. 275p bibl index ISBN 0-8263-1612-3, $50.00

Avellaneda's study is the first work in English to analyze the demographic characteristics of the conquerors of Colombia, their evolving socioeconomic status, and the structure of the society they established. Drawing primarily from materials in various Colombian and Spanish archives, Avellaneda categorizes and quantifies attributes of 658 survivors of the six conquering expeditions between 1537 and 1543. Much like James Lockhart's *The Men of Cajamarca* (CH, Apr'73), which dealt with the Peruvian conquerors, Avellaneda's study considers the origins, age, education, previous experiences, marital unions, and social and economic position of these survivors. Tables and four extensive appendixes provide further statistical details. Avellaneda's findings serve not only to typify Colombian conquerors but also to compare them with contemporary counterparts in Peru, Mexico, and Panama. Although he focuses on the Europeans who entered the regions within modern-day Colombia, Avellaneda also analyzes the role of nonwhite elements in the emerging colonial society. His treatment of mestizo and mulatto castes is especially illuminating. This important study contains useful maps, a complete bibliography, and a detailed index. Upper-division undergraduates and above.—*J. A. Gagliano, Loyola University of Chicago*

OAB-2411   HD6605   93-46839 CIP
Brennan, James P. **The labor wars in Córdoba, 1955-1976: ideology, work, and labor politics in an Argentine industrial city.** Harvard, 1994. 440p bibl index afp (Harvard historical studies, 116) ISBN 0-674-50851-3, $59.95

Brennan (Georgetown Univ.) focuses on a turbulent era of Argentine history when the country was struggling to deal with the vagaries of fractious Peronism. Peron's heirs in organized labor remained divided, embroiled in self-destructive power struggles while the well-being of workers went neglected. Brennan selected the *Cordobazo* movement as the watershed for Argentina's politics, especially for organized labor. The *Cordobazo*, brutally crushed by the army, was a broad sociopolitical protest movement involving labor, students, and even the middle class against the Argentine realities: the Onganía dictatorship, Córdoba's unbridled industrial capitalism, and corrupt labor bosses in the federal capital. The *Cordobazo* reinforced provincial labor militancy by securing independence from unconcerned labor federations in Buenos Aires and redefining working-class politics and its relationship to the state. And the ensuing urban guerrilla wars drew sympathy from all classes. Brennan has palpably raised the standards of the writing of labor history by his unparalleled tricontinental research, crisp prose, and sympathetic yet unbiased analysis. It is the best book yet on Argentine labor history and will serve as a model for a new social history. Upper-division undergraduate and up.—*E. Pang, Colorado School of Mines*

OAB-2412   HD9574   92-25649 CIP
Brown, Jonathan C. **Oil and revolution in Mexico.** California, 1993. 453p bibl index afp ISBN 0-520-07934-5, $40.00

Brown (Univ. of Texas), author of the highly regarded *A Socioeconomic History of Argentina, 1776-1860* (CH, Dec'79), now offers a big, witty, authoritative book, based on archival research, about the Mexican oil industry. He focuses on the period 1900 to 1920, i.e., the final decade of the Porfiriate and the violent decade of the Revolution. Readers learn a great deal about racism, paternalism, and class conflict in the world of Mexican oil. Brown begins by saying that Mexico's present trend toward a free market economy is essentially a replay of the economic policy of the Porfiriate. Then, the openness to foreign capitalism led to revolution. The author notes, however, that even today there is little likelihood that Pemex, created by Cárdenas in 1938, will be privatized and concludes with the question: will a mishandling of the new policy of openness call forth union militancy and economic nationalism? In the midst of Brown's fine perceptions about petroleum history, one finds discordant

observations. For example it is arguable whether the history of Mexico is truly "richer and more complex than that of *most* countries." Nevertheless, this book is a must for all self-respecting Latin American history collections, an extremely valuable addition to the genre. Notes, illustrations, maps. Advanced undergraduate; graduate; professional.—*R. H. Thompson, Indiana University—Purdue University at Indianapolis*

OAB-2413   HD8138   95-21958 CIP
Chomsky, Aviva. **West Indian workers and the United Fruit Company in Costa Rica, 1870-1940.** Louisiana State, 1996. 302p bibl index afp ISBN 0-8071-1979-2, $35.00

Chomsky has produced a superbly written, insightful, and readable social history of the rich but little-known African Caribbean workers in Central America. Chomsky shows that, unlike an industrial factory system, a banana plantation system allowed its workers access to land. Keen on reducing future costs of soil erosion, plant disease, and other nature-borne havoc, the UFCO encouraged the formation of small planters, who sold bananas to the company. In 1907, 63 percent of all bananas the company exported came from its own cultivation, but, by 1926, that figure was only 25 percent. Chomsky also highlights the rise of the West Indian (black) political organization, the Artisans and Labourers' Union, which included both smallholders and workers of Jamaican ancestry. The interclass union movement was an African Caribbean effort to preserve the cultural identity of the Jamaican community in the land of Hispanic elites and American bosses. Shunned by the government, unwanted by Costa Rican banana growers, and mistreated by the company, the West Indians staged Costa Rica's first labor strike. Somewhat like the Chinese in Southeast Asia, the Jamaicans of Costa Rica built an insulated community. The book is an outstanding example of how to do a revisionist history and is indeed a pioneering work. All academic collections.—*E. Pang, Colorado School of Mines*

OAB-2414   F3093   95-45817 CIP
Collier, Simon. **A history of Chile, 1808-1994,** by Simon Collier and William F. Sater. Cambridge, 1996. 427p bibl index afp (Cambridge Latin American series, 82) ISBN 0-521-56075-6, $59.95; ISBN 0-521-56827-7 pbk, $18.95

Collier and Sater have written the best general history of modern Chile available in any language. It is vast and comprehensive in scope, solid and dependable in factual information, reliable and complete in its sources, and consistently delightfully written. A short but highly informative introduction covers the colonial period with skill and accuracy. The authors point out that although Chile suffered from the tyranny of distance from its metropolis, Spain, in a difficult area shared uneasily with the militaristic Araucanians, it nevertheless had a viable economy—albeit one that fluctuated significantly from time to time—in the colonial as well as in the post-colonial era. The authors' discussion of the entire period of independence weaves copious details of geography, demography, language, politics, economics, culture, and occasionally, interesting local gossip into a remarkable narrative. Collier and Sater emphasize the patterns of continuity and change throughout Chilean history, examining the political, social, and economic factors that provide the context for understanding change through the oligarchic republic, the parliamentary period, mass politics, the dictatorship of General Augusto Pinochet, and the restored democracy since 1989. All levels.—*F. W. Knight, Johns Hopkins University*

OAB-2415   HX158   93-45884 CIP
Eckstein, Susan Eva. **Back from the future: Cuba under Castro.** Princeton, 1994. 286p index afp ISBN 0-691-03445-1, $29.95

Sociologist Eckstein (Boston Univ.) has written a seminal, highly important, well-reasoned, and balanced analysis of Cuba under Castro. The author works from an original theoretical vantage point that examines Cuba in a fresh and complex way, marshaling impressive data on Cuban social and economic organization as well as on the inner workings of the revolutionary regime and its internal problems. The author explains how Cuba is different from all other models and how, ideologically, Cuba has been much less driven by Marxist-Leninist orthodoxy than is usually assumed. The book is a welcome and thorough review of the history of Castro's revolutionary government as well as a detailed description of the personalities and policies that have shaped it. The concluding chapter speculates provocatively about the future, warning that in the absence of meaningful opposition and intermediate groups, Cuba may face turmoil brought about by growing discontent and the lack of an organizational base on which to build democracy. Handsomely published with detailed notes, many of them discursive. Highly recommended for readers at all levels, nonacademic as well as academic.—*R. M. Levine, University of Miami*

OAB-2416   HC141   92-41825 CIP
Faber, Daniel. **Environment under fire: imperialism and the ecological crisis in Central America.** Monthly Review, 1993. 301p index ISBN 0-85345-839-1, $36.00; ISBN 0-85345-840-5 pbk, $16.00

Written by a knowledgeable scholar/activist, this book analyzes the roots of Central America's current social and ecological crisis, identifying the significant role played by US economic policies. Drawing on world-systems theory and development theories, Faber empirically illustrates a political-economic perspective by attributing Central America's ecological crisis to the unequal distribution of land and natural resources under capitalist development. The book covers the pre-Columbian ecology of Central America; the Spanish conquest that established imperialism in the region; and the environmental and social effects of mining, lumbering, and the production of coffee, bananas, cotton, and beef cattle for export. An in-depth analysis is offered of the Sandinista Revolution in Nicaragua that was fueled by ecological crisis. Faber's fascinating and logical analysis fills a gaping hole in the literature and is a major contribution. References are contained in endnotes. Good subject/author index. General; advanced undergraduate; graduate; faculty.—*S. Cable, University of Tennessee at Knoxville*

OAB-2417   HD9484   92-31679 CIP
Gootenberg, Paul. **Imagining development: economic ideas in Peru's "fictitious prosperity" of Guano, 1840-1880.** California, 1993. 243p bibl index afp ISBN 0-520-07712-1, $45.00; ISBN 0-520-08290-7 pbk, $20.00

Gootenberg's "social history of ideas of the Peruvian elite of the age of guano" (1845-80) is a modest but brilliant riposte to the simple but rarely asked question: What were Peru's elites thinking as the ship of state loaded its cargo bay with lucrative bird dung (guano) and sailed off into the unforgiving waters of export liberalism? Upsetting the received wisdom on economic liberalism in 19th-century Latin America, the author deftly traces a heterodox "genealogy of discontent with fictive prosperities." Seven crisp chapters summarize the economic ideas of nine or ten central thinkers, from Pardo to Esteves. These "liberal" Peruvians "went against the grain of laissez-faire European political economy" by grounding their imaginings in "Peruvian experience and conditions." Thus, in the tradition of his earlier *Between Silver and Guano* (1989), Gootenberg chisels yet another chink in the crumbling wall of "strangely idealist" dependency theory. Like his earlier work, it is required reading for historians of Latin America. Undergraduates and above.—*M. W. Thurner, University of Florida*

OAB-2418   F1219   93-24861 MARC
Gruzinski, Serge. **The conquest of Mexico: the incorporation of Indian societies into the Western world, 16th-18th centuries,** tr. by Eileen Corrigan. Polity, 1993. (Dist. by Blackwell) 336p bibl index afp ISBN 0-7456-0873-6, $49.95;

Gruzinski's latest contribution to an understanding of colonial Mexico examines the slow, uneven, and at times contradictory responses of nobility, "notables," and commoners within indigenous societies to the cultural demands of their Spanish conquerors over nearly three centuries. Through painstaking analysis of pictographs, the indigenous nobility's adoption and use of writing, the *Relaciones*

of New Spain (1578-85), title deeds, wills, Inquisition records, and other primarily archival materials, Gruzinski provides a compelling argument for Europeanization rather than acculturation of the indigenous population. Rich chapters on the form and substance of native religious belief, "idolatry," its transformation over time with the development of what he terms "indigenous Christianity," and the wrenching attack by the Crown on indigenous cultures in the second half of the 18th century make this singular study necessary reading for all students of colonial Mexican history. It complements James Lockhart's *The Nahuas After the Conquest* (CH, Mar'93) and Inga Clendinnen's *Aztecs* (CH, Apr'92), and like them, is an essential purchase for college and university libraries.—*M. A. Burkholder, University of Missouri—St Louis*

OAB-2419   HD1527   93-24223 CIP
Guerin-Gonzales, Camille. **Mexican workers and American dreams: immigration, repatriation, and California farm labor, 1900-1939.** Rutgers, 1994. 197p index ISBN 0-8135-2047-9, $42.00; ISBN 0-8135-2048-7 pbk, $15.00

In a solid history about Mexican workers, 1900-39, Guerin-Gonzales (Oberlin College) covers a topic that has been discussed by other historians, but does it differently—within the context of the American dream (or its mythicization). The book covers immigration, repatriation, and California farm labor. The chapter "Birds of Passage" is especially strong, recounting the racialization of the American dream and the myth that Mexican workers were temporary. Guerin-Gonzales makes excellent use of the 1910 report by Frank R. Stone to the US Commissioner General on Immigration about the activities of labor agents in recruiting Mexican labor, intertwining testimonies of workers entering the US labor market. The most important contribution to the literature, however, is the chapter "*Los Repatriados*," which deals with what happened to the Mexican repatriates in Mexico (most studies concentrate on their US experience). It is here that gender issues are most effectively integrated. Scholars will appreciate the extensive archival research, which in the best tradition of Chicano research uses repositories on both sides of the border—in both languages. In sum, the book shows the racial limitations of the American dream. Well indexed; heavily footnoted; no bibliography. All levels.—*R. Acuña, California State University, Northridge*

OAB-2420   HT1148   94-4507 CIP
Hünefeldt, Christine. **Paying the price of freedom: family and labor among Lima's slaves, 1800-1854.** California, 1995 (c1994). 269p bibl index afp ISBN 0-520-08235-4, $42.00; ISBN 0-520-08292-3 pbk, $16.00

Hünefeldt's well-written and exhaustively documented family and labor history of Lima's slaves is clearly the best English language work on the subject. The author deftly weaves the macrohistory of political events and economic trends with the microhistory of the slave family. Lacking the diaries and journals of slaves available to US historians, Hünefeldt turns to the ecclesiastical, civil, and notarial archives of Peru to reconstruct fictive slave families based on "a combination of situations from real cases." This finely grained study confirms long-standing notions about slavery in Latin America, i.e., the importance of the church and of miscegenation. It also breaks new ground in the field of comparative slavery, as when the author argues, contra Gutman, that among Lima's slaves "marriage became a strategy to attain freedom," or when she notes the "tremendous impact of self-manumission ... on the abolition of slavery." Written "with sympathy and admiration" for slave struggles and torn family lives, this book is bound to appeal to nonspecialists and specialists alike. Undergraduates and above.—*M. W. Thurner, University of Florida*

OAB-2421   F1221   91-29972 CIP
Lockhart, James. **The Nahuas after the conquest: a social and cultural history of the Indians of Central Mexico, sixteenth through eighteenth centuries.** Stanford, 1992. 650p bibl index afp ISBN 0-8047-1927-6, $60.00

Lockhart, the most influential historian of colonial Latin American history of his generation, has written a pioneering social and cultural history of the Indians of Central Mexico from the 16th through the 18th century. Reflecting Lockhart's use of previously ignored or underutilized sources written in Nahuatal, the work is replete with revisionist interpretations based both on fact and on informed speculation. The major topics covered are native municipalities and households, social differentiation, land and economic life, religious life, language, ways of life, and forms of expression. Throughout the book, Lockhart emphasizes a three-stage evolution of Nahua culture. In the conclusion, he places this evolution in the context of demographic change and the appearance of changing labor insitutions. The most important work on colonial Mexican history since Charles Gibson's *The Aztecs Under Spanish Rule* (CH, Nov'64), Lockhart's study is required reading for specialists and graduate students and should be available in every undergraduate library.—*M. A. Burkholder, University of Missouri—St. Louis*

OAB-2422   F1391   95-16036 CIP
Martin, Cheryl English. **Governance and society in colonial Mexico: Chihuahua in the eighteenth century.** Stanford, 1996. 264p bibl index afp ISBN 0-8047-2547-0, $39.50

Historians traditionally have identified the northern Mexican state of Chihuahua as a remote frontier land during the 18th century, a huge expanse of desert that shared little in common with the populous core area around Mexico City. Although it produced mineral wealth for the Spanish empire, Chihuahua allegedly remained apart from the mainstream of Mexican development, and even its political leaders shunned the region. Martin (Univ. of Texas at El Paso) challenges this traditional view by stressing the interconnectedness of the northern and core regions. Furthermore, she minutely analyzes the elements of class, race, ethnicity, and gender to delineate the dynamics of Mexican colonial society. This is a study of power and social interaction, not merely within the upper ranks of society, but also within the family and among the underclass, which frequently negotiated for the attainment of its own goals. Using the latest methodologies and a vast array of archival sources, Martin convincingly reconstructs the duties and performances of various levels of society, from the provincial governors, to the employers, to the mine workers. She likewise provides an insider's view of the truly multiethnic community, or *sociedad de castas*, and the presumptions of each of its components. This model study serves well both academic and general readers. All levels.—*M. L. Tate, University of Nebraska at Omaha*

OAB-2423   HD1807   93-27405 CIP
McCreery, David. **Rural Guatemala, 1760-1940.** Stanford, 1994. 450p bibl index afp ISBN 0-8047-2318-4, $49.50

His reputation established on a series of excellent articles, McCreery is possibly the preeminent North American historian of rural Guatemala. This book is a meticulously documented account of the transformations in the Guatemalan countryside over almost two centuries, and McCreery's command of the primary sources and his careful and responsible handling of the materials are extremely impressive. Within the rural population, he focuses especially on the Indian communities and their relations with the state and coffee planters; and in the process, he calls into serious question some widespread assumptions and arguments based on urban sources. Although it is indeed a close study, it is broadly framed, strongly analytical, and frequently illuminated by a comparative perspective. This is an outstanding contribution to our understanding of the history and historiography of Guatemala and Latin America and will continue to be critically important for library collections supporting graduate and undergraduate programs in Latin American studies, indigenous peoples, and agriculture. Maps; glossary. Highly recommended for upper-division undergraduate through faculty collections.—*F. S. Weaver, Hampshire College*

OAB-2424   F2230   96-28847 CIP
Mills, Kenneth. **Idolatry and its enemies: colonial Andean religion and extirpation, 1640-1750.** Princeton, 1997. 337p bibl index afp ISBN 0-691-02979-2, $55.00

The spiritual conquest of indigenous America has always fascinated scholars. Mills's study shows how far understanding of this subject has progressed. Examining idolatry records covering the archdioceses of Lima during the mid-colonial period, a century after the military conquest of Peru, Mills uncovers a fascinating religious kaleidoscope. Although Spanish Catholicism had pretty much replaced Inca imperial religious beliefs by this time, it had not pushed aside Andean regional, village, and household practices. Indeed, if anything, indigenous worship at the local level was expanding and constantly evolving to cover needs such as crop fertility and personal relationships that many did not see addressed by the state church. Periodically, however, Catholic officialdom was forced to pay attention to these local religious practices, either through waves of reform within the Church, which questioned the Christian purity of its flock, or through rifts in the indigenous communities, which provoked one faction to seek vengeance on another by reporting suspicious conduct. This rich, complex, and provocative study is a sine qua non for future studies of religion in colonial Latin America. Upper-division undergraduates and above.—*J. A. Lewis, Western Carolina University*

OAB-2425   PQ708   91-39494 CIP
Pastor Bodner, Beatriz. **The armature of conquest: Spanish accounts of the discovery of America, 1492-1589,** tr. by Lydia Longstreth Hunt. Stanford, 1992. 317p index afp ISBN 0-8047-1977-2, $42.50

In this study, Pastor applies discourse analysis to writings by some of the most celebrated participants in the exploration, conquest, and settlement of the Americas. She devotes particular attention to the writings of Christopher Columbus, Hernán Cortés, Alvar Núñez Cabeza de Vaca, Lope de Aguirre and those who wrote about his rebellion, and Alonso de Ercilla. Pastor carefully examines both conscious and unconscious efforts to deceive the reader (Cortés and Columbus) through fictionalization and the importance of myth in promoting exploration. Demythification follows in the discourse of failure (Núñez Cabeza de Vaca) and the discourse of rebellion (Aguirre and others). Ercilla's epic *La Araucana* (Madrid, 1578) represents the emergence of a Spanish American consciousness characterized by internal contradictions as a result of the different cultural heritages and perceptions of reality on which it draws. Generally clearly written and well translated, *Armature* is important for specialists in Hispanic literature and provides valuable insights for historians as well. Every institution that teaches Hispanic literature or colonial Latin American history should own this volume. Advanced undergraduate; graduate; faculty.—*M. A. Burkholder, University of Missouri—St. Louis*

OAB-2426   F3429   95-39791 CIP
Ramírez, Susan Elizabeth. **The world upside down: cross-cultural contact and conflict in sixteenth-century Peru.** Stanford, 1996. 234p bibl index afp ISBN 0-8047-2416-4, $45.00

Ramírez's ethnohistorical study focuses on the native peoples of the north coast region of Peru from the Inca conquest of the area about 1470 to approximately 1580, nearly 50 years after the Spaniards subdued the Incas. It examines in detail the reciprocal nature of the relationship between the local lords (*curacas*) and their subjects before the conquest, and emphasizes that the number of subjects then determined the rank and position of the lords. The Spanish conquest ended this balance. The native population declined, peoples were divided, and Spaniards demanded that lords serve as their agents in exploiting the people. Spaniards also imposed European concepts of private property and tribute. A case study of grave looting illustrates differences between Spanish and native worldviews. Ramírez makes a convincing revisionist argument that native institutions and attitudes in the northern coastal region during both the pre- and postconquest eras were more similar to those in the better-studied highland regions than scholars have generally appreciated. Clearly written, highlighted by excellent figures, and based on thorough archival and secondary research, this book belongs in every college and university library. Upper-division undergraduates and above.—*M. A. Burkholder, University of Missouri—St. Louis*

OAB-2427 HQ1525 94-24809 MARC
Reddock, Rhoda E. **Women, labour & politics in Trinidad & Tobago: a history.** Zed Books, 1994. 346p bibl index ISBN 1-85649-153-6, $60.00; ISBN 1-85649-154-4 pbk, $25.00

This thoroughly researched and clearly written study of women in colonial Trinidad and Tobago between the early 19th century and 1962 focuses on the women's work and political activities. Reddock's historical sociology reveals new information and also deepens understanding of broader social dynamics. The division of labor by gender and ethnicity during the periods of slavery and indentureship, the colonial ideology of "women's place," and the politics of sex, race, and class provide the essential background for the analysis of women's role in the labor movement and nationalist politics. Women's contributions to social change differed because, despite their common gender, they were divided by race and class. Thus, middle-class African women were more involved in social work and politics than their Indian counterparts, while working-class Indian and African women participated in labor organizations. However, in this patriarchal society, trade unions and political parties were dominated by men, most of whom were middle-class. Many works cited are omitted from the bibliography, but this is essential reading for Caribbean and women's studies, along with Olive Senior's *Working Miracles* (CH, Sep'92) and Janet Momsen's *Women & Change in the Caribbean* (CH, Apr'94). Upper-division undergraduates and up.—*O. N. Bolland, Colgate University*

OAB-2428 F2848 92-108 CIP
Rock, David. **Authoritarian Argentina: the Nationalist movement, its history and its impact.** California, 1993. 320p bibl index afp ISBN 0-520-07920-5, $35.00

An outstanding and perceptively written work on an important period in Argentine history, covering the rise and transformations of the nationalist movement from the turn of the century through the present. The two most significant characteristics of the period are the rise of the army to political preeminence and the indelibly lingering impact of Juan Peron and Peronism. Rock clearly illustrates his magisterial understanding of the peculiar Argentine temper. Replete with insightful observations, his book demonstrates persuasively that Argentine Nationalists were overwhelmingly rural, well-to-do males, drawn especially from Entre Ríos, Córdoba and Salta, whose ideology was a local variation of standard counterrevolutionary European ideas. Although they were neither uniform in origin nor consistent in outlook, Argentine Nationalists tended to oppose all modern tendencies: "liberalism and individualism, democracy and capitalism, socialism, communism, and 'cosmopolitanism,' Judaism and Masonry." A fascinating aspect of this impressive study is the way in which Rock skillfully intertwines intellectual history with political, social, and economic history. He shows that the ideological bases of vehemently conflicting groups over the past century—military, Peronist, and montonero—have similar intellectual origins. Each indicated a consummate inability to deal with the process of profound social change that Argentina was experiencing. All reading levels.—*F. W. Knight, Johns Hopkins University*

OAB-2429 HC154 96-10096 CIP
Santana, Déborah Berman. **Kicking off the bootstraps: environment, development, and community power in Puerto Rico.** Arizona, 1996. 211p bibl index afp ISBN 0-8165-1590-5, $39.95

Santana (geography and planning, SUNY, Albany) combines microhistory with an analysis of grassroots activism, all within a broader concern with the critical need to find ways to define and create sustainable development in all its social, economic, and political dimensions. The people and ecology of Salinas, like many communities in Puerto Rico and elsewhere in the less developed world, were used and then abandoned by a succession of multinational investors, leaving both in worse shape than before. Government efforts were ineffective in creating new initiatives to build the local economy, and at times it seemed government acted against local interests. Santana examines how local activists, many of whom had been educated in the capital but returned home to work, have begun to establish new, locally owned, small-scale industries that build on the community's skill base and on the local environment and its resources, but in a manner that is sustainable rather than hostile to water, air, and land quality and allows for a greater degree of local control over future progress. The level of detail in the history of Salinas and in the transformative work by local activists should be of great value to readers who might wish to see how grassroots initiatives progress over time. All levels.—*J. L. Dietz, California State University, Fullerton*

OAB-2430 F1219 95-25889 CIP
Smith, Michael E. **The Aztecs.** Blackwell, 1996. 361p bibl index afp ISBN 1-55786-496-9, $25.95

Smith's excellent description and interpretation of Aztec civilization encompasses recent archaeological fieldwork that has added so much to understanding the Aztec way of life. Excavation results have tested and augmented information from traditional sources. These include the histories recorded by the Spanish and by the Aztecs themselves around the time of the Conquest; the magnificent architecture, art, and luxury items associated with the ruling classes and religion; and the lifeways of modern descendants of the Aztecs. Smith also gives much attention to the lower classes on which the social structure depended. The book is clearly written so that one section flows logically into the next; it covers such topics as the origins of Aztec civilization from earlier roots, its economic/subsistence basis, its social and political organization, urban and rural settlement patterns, religion, and intellectual accomplishments. After a brief discussion of the Spanish invasion and its consequences, the final chapter treats the Aztec legacy that makes up modern Mexico. Minimal illustrations and maps. Highly recommended for all levels.—*K. A. Dixon, emeritus, California State University, Long Beach*

OAB-2431 E183 96-10467 CIP
Topik, Steven C. **Trade and gunboats: the United States and Brazil in the age of empire.** Stanford, 1997 (c1996). 301p bibl index afp ISBN 0-8047-2602-7, $55.00

Topik (Univ. of California, Irvine) has produced an outstanding study of trade rivalry between the US and Brazil at the end of the 19th century. *Trade and Gunboats* adds admirably to what is known about the history of both countries, and Topik also weaves in the role of the British, whose hegemony in Brazil was in retreat just as Washington was starting to flex its muscle. Based on archival materials in five countries, the book fills a major gap. There are few if any studies of Latin American commerce with the outside world for this period; diplomatic and military histories tend to focus entirely on US concerns and interests. Topik's deftly nuanced study draws important lessons for those who would seek to predict the outcome of present-day trade agreements such as NAFTA. No narrow monograph, it poses meaningful questions and answers them lucidly. This superbly crafted and timely work raises diplomatic history to a higher level. Enthusiastically recommended, not only for scholars and students but also for economists and policy makers. Upper-division undergraduates and above.—*R. M. Levine, University of Miami*

OAB-2432 F2299 92-15581 CIP
Wade, Peter. **Blackness and race mixture: the dynamics of racial identity in Colombia.** Johns Hopkins, 1993. 415p bibl index afp ISBN 0-8018-4458-4, $58.00

A brilliantly argued, superbly researched, revisionist, and innovative interpretation by a social anthropologist. Wade shows how the official Colombian policy of an ethnically plural society confronts a social order in which skin color is critical, *mestizaje* and whitening are social practices, and a racial order exists that excludes blacks and Indians except as agents for miscegenation. Wade rejects characterization of blacks in terms of class rather than race and asserts the importance of blackness. The Chocó region is the focus of this study.

With its overwhelmingly black majority, there is no ambiguity of racial identification. Wade's research base includes a Caribbean frontier town in the context of colonization, and Medellín, where black imigrants are in a minority, permitting him to compare processes of black nucleation and congregation, as well as the interplay of accommodation and discrimination, assimilation and resistance, and the development of black culture in the context of syncretism. He concludes that the same social order underlies different contexts and practices, and that *mestizaje* and discrimination constitute and reproduce the racial order in Colombia. Essential reading for an understanding of race in modern Latin Amercia.—*A. J. R. Russell-Wood, Johns Hopkins University*

OAB-2433 F1376 96-10471 CIP

Wells, Allen. **Summer of discontent, seasons of upheaval: elite politics and rural insurgency in Yucatan, 1876-1915,** by Allen Wells and Gilbert M. Joseph. Stanford, 1996. 406p bibl index afp ISBN 0-8047-2655-8, $55.00

Wells and Joseph focus on the Mexican state of Yucatán in a period of major transition. Their narrative does not get caught up in romantic and bloody events, although peasant uprisings are described, including one in the village of Temax led by Pedro Crespo. The authors' primary concern is the complex political, economic, and social process that involved elite regional leaders who vied for patronage from Mexico City; family ties and *camarillas* that cut across class lines; an emerging urban proletariat; and the Yucatecan Maya, who labored on the haciendas or defended their community properties on the fringes of the henequen zone. Wells and Joseph provide a valuable synthesis of the topics covered, based on solid archival research and a grasp of the extensive literature on Yucatán that has appeared in the last two decades, including many of their own publications. The book's value transcends the regional theme, linking Yucatán in a meaningful way to the broader framework of Mexico in a crucial time of change. Upper-division undergraduates and above.—*E. H. Moseley, University of Alabama*

OAB-2434 F1523 94-41811 CIP

Whisnant, David E. **Rascally signs in sacred places: the politics of culture in Nicaragua.** North Carolina, 1995. 569p bibl index afp ISBN 0-8078-2209-4, $59.95; ISBN 0-8078-4523-X pbk, $24.95

Whisnant (Univ. of North Carolina) discusses the competing uses of and control over culture in Nicaragua from the pre-Columbian period to the present, although the work focuses on the Somoza and Sandinista regimes. Because Nicaragua did not have a definable cultural policy or consequential cultural institutions for much of its history and because of its role as a cultural bridge between north-south and east-west, the nation was vulnerable to outside influences, especially during the Zelaya (1893-1909) and Somoza (1934-1979) administrations. Opposition to US cultural intervention was continuous, especially from the generation of 1940 intellectuals and in the barrios. The Sandinista regime attempted to formulate an official cultural policy and create a broad array of public institutions, e.g., the literacy campaign, museums and libraries, and book and film industries. Such efforts soon ended because of the contra war and cultural recalcitrance of the church and of gender paradigms. Individual case studies discuss the use of poet Ruben Dario (Nicaragua's most known artist) and General Augusto Cesar Sandino by both sides of the ideological debate. Many photographs and drawings assist the reader immeasurably. Outstandingly crafted and exhaustively researched. Highly recommended. General readers; upper-division undergraduates and above.—*W. M. Weis, Illinois Wesleyan University*

OAB-2435 HD8290 92-40484 CIP

Wolfe, Joel. **Working women, working men: São Paulo and the rise of Brazil's industrial working class, 1900-1955.** Duke University, 1993. 312p bibl index afp ISBN 0-8223-1330-8, $45.00; ISBN 0-8223-1347-2 pbk, $17.95

Wolfe's superbly written book is a revisionist history of São Paulo's labor movement, focusing on its textile workers (mostly unskilled women) and metal workers (mostly skilled men), their struggle to improve their lives, and their bold but violent confrontations with industrialists, repressive government officials, and professional labor bosses (*pelegos*). Workers in São Paulo had organized informal workplace committees well before formal unions were set up and manipulated by anarchists, communists, and government-controlled *pelegos*. These factory "commissions" became the harbinger for union democracy. The commissions, or shop-floor groupings, gave women workers the power to organize their movements without interference from men. Industrialists, union organizers, and leftist radicals often collided over the control of the commissions. For four decades and against all odds, factory commissions prevailed as the articulators for rank-and-file demands. Wolfe's book is a triumph of a good social history, free of ideological rhetoric but full of new exciting interpretations. It is highly readable and packed with new facts solidly backed up by sound analyses. Advanced undergraduates and above.—*E. Pang, Colorado School of Mines*

■ Middle East

OAB-2436 DS36 92-23342 CIP

Barakat, Halim. **The Arab world: society, culture, and state.** California, 1993. 348p bibl index afp ISBN 0-520-07907-8, $30.00

A comprehensive study of the social, political, and cultural dimensions of contemporary Arab society, which stretches from Morocco to Iraq. Barakat (Georgetown Univ.) is a well-known Arab sociologist, essayist, and novelist. Drawing on his own firsthand knowledge of the area and on an exhaustive review of the available literature (both in English and Arabic), Barakat presents a critical analysis of the historical and structural forces that shaped Arab society. Written from the perspective of a passionately concerned Arab intellectual, the book is both informative and provocative. In addition to providing the reader with a well-rounded introduction to the political economy and culture of the region, Barakat critically assesses the current debates in the Arab world concerning the vital issues of political legitimacy, religious fundamentalism, the status of women, and the crisis of civil society. Highly recommended for anyone seriously interested in understanding the dynamics of Arab society. General; undergraduate; graduate; faculty.—*A. Rassam, Queens College, CUNY*

OAB-2437 DT97 94-2530 CIP

Behrens-Abouseif, Doris. **Egypt's adjustment to Ottoman rule: institutions, waqf and architecture in Cairo (16th and 17th centuries).** E.J. Brill, 1994. 311p; 57 plates bibl index afp (Islamic history and civilization: studies and texts, 7) ISBN 90-04-09927-1, $83.00

In 1517 the Ottoman Sultan Selim I conquered Egypt from its Mamluk rulers, who had governed the country since the mid-13th century and created a great empire with unique political, social, and religious institutions. After a brief description of the conquest, the author examines the transition from Mamluk to Ottoman rule during the next two centuries. The Ottomans seemed to opt for continuity by retaining local military, administrative, and religious establishments. The Mamluk system, however, had been based on a kind of feudal relationship, whereas the Ottomans governed through a "well-structured bureaucratic administration." The study examines the evolution of Ottoman administrative practices in detail, beginning with the "Pasha" appointed from Istanbul, his bureaucrats organized in the "Diwan," and the "notables." Chapters are then devoted to the legal system, the religious establishment, the military, and the *waqfs* (religious endowments), which are illustrated with a number of important documents. The author's integration of the Ottoman impact on Cairo's architecture also makes this monograph invaluable for art historians. The wide array of sources: *waqf* documents, chronicles, an impressive list of secondary works in European languages, as well as works in Arabic and Turkish, make this study as definitive as works of scholarship can be. Upper-division undergraduate and graduate collections.—*F. Ahmad, University of Massachusetts at Boston*

Social & Behavioral Sciences

OAB-2438 HT1238 96-7125 CIP

Erdem, Y Hakan. **Slavery in the Ottoman Empire and its demise, 1800-1909.** Macmillan (UK)/St. Martin's/St. Antony's, 1996. 229p bibl index ISBN 0-312-16209-X, $59.95

Slavery in the Ottoman Empire was so totally different and so much more complex compared with Western notions of the institution. In the English language there is only one word, "slave," to describe the individual who was purchased; the author's glossary lists nine Turkish terms for the same word: *abd, carive, esir, gulam, kul, köle, mamluk, müdebber,* and *mükateb.* Slavery could even be a vehicle for upward mobility, for example, for women who entered the harem; and as late as 1877, an enslaved child rose to become the grand vizier. Using both Ottoman and European sources, Erdem examines the varieties of Ottoman slavery in the context of Islamic law. He begins with the classical age and goes on to discuss slavery before the period of reform—the *Tanzimat*—which began in 1839. Despite radical reforms slavery persisted, though by the 1840s the Ottoman state was under British and European pressure to curb the slave trade. Because Islamic law that governed the empire permitted slavery, the state was unable to abolish it, although it could prohibit the slave trade. Not even the Young Turk revolutionaries of 1908 were able to abolish slavery, though they made slave ownership extremely difficult. This fascinating and remarkable study will be invaluable to all students of comparative slavery. Upper-division undergraduates and above.—*F. Ahmad, University of Massachusetts at Boston*

OAB-2439 Orig

Faroqhi, Suraiya. **Pilgrims and sultans: the Hajj under the Ottomans, 1517-1683.** I.B. Tauris, 1994. 244p bibl index ISBN 1-85043-606-1, $59.50

The hajj is the single most important event in the life of a Muslim. Today millions flow to Mecca in an act of religious piety that supersedes differences of race, color, gender, and national origin. Faroqhi treats the earlier history of the hajj on the basis of documentary and literary sources during the first two centuries of Ottoman rule. She incisively describes its organization, its financing, its protection by the imperial government, the buildings of the Holy Cities of Mecca and Medina that service the hajjis, and the political and economic ramifications of the pilgrimage. Her first chapter sets the scene by recapping the tradition of the hajj in pre-Ottoman times, i.e., the first nine centuries of Islam. Faroqhi's work is a model of excellent archival research as well as an engaging narrative based on literary sources. Readers will gain a useful understanding of the meaning of the hajj to the Islamic World. Scholars will be in her debt for an excellent study. Highly recommended for university collections.—*S. Bowman, University of Cincinnati*

OAB-2440 DS84 94-1941 CIP

Fawaz, Leila Tarazi. **An occasion for war: civil conflict in Lebanon and Damascus in 1860.** California, 1995 (c1994). 302p bibl index ISBN 0-520-08782-8, $45.00

The 1860 conflicts in Lebanon originated in Druze-Maronite clashes in the Mount Lebanon region that spread to adjacent areas. Ultimately, because of rumors of strife and an influx of refugees, violence flared in Damascus; Muslim assaults on Christians resulted in several thousand deaths. Fawaz places this local/regional conflict within the broader context of diminished Ottoman authority confronted by Great Power interests, as the British and the French sought to protect Druze and Maronite client populations. She carefully notes the historical and economic background. Christian equality with Muslims originated under Egyptian rule in the 1830s. Muslims resented European mercantile inroads that used local Christians as agents to the detriment of Muslim merchants. This combination of sectarian grievances and imperial intervention resulted in attacks on wealthy—but not poor—Christian quarters in Damascus. Fawaz situates her study with an eye to the recent civil war in Lebanon and argues that intercommunal tolerance may require the guarantees of larger powers, which were lacking in 1860 and fell victim to Cold War rivalries in the 1970s. Extremely detailed and well researched, this should become the definitive work on the subject. Upper-division undergraduates and above.—*C. D. Smith, University of Arizona*

OAB-2441 DS63 94-25822 CIP

Field, Michael. **Inside the Arab world.** Harvard, 1995 (c1994). 439p index afp ISBN 0-674-45520-7, $27.50

Field has done a superb job in capturing the essence of events in the Arab world, with more than 20 years of on-the-scene observation to support his data. As he poignantly shows, the West is treated to a constant dose of oil and export markets, wars in Lebanon and the Persian Gulf, peace talks at the White House, terrorist eruptions, and Islamic risings, all of which merit serious attention. In 20 chapters, Field, a longtime reporter on Arab states, explores the cultural, political, and geographic reasons for the region's failure to produce a single successful economy. He covers the entire Arab world, from Morocco to the Persian Gulf, and delves into the problems generated by fragmented societies, the people's unusual tolerance—until recently—of bad government, corruption, and "the deadening economic effect of Arab socialism." Field does not overlook changes brought about from exposure to Western media and pressure from Western creditors to reform their systems. The path to democracy, hitherto taken in very short steps, is jeopardized because those in charge do not find it in their interest to institute large-scale democratic practices. The so-called Islamic fundamentalists have demanded that Arab governments introduce a democracy consonant with the basic teachings of Islam and the experiences of the community when it lived up to the true practices of the faith. The evenhandedness with which Field treats the most complex issues is impressive. The book should be required reading for its sympathetic and fair treatment of difficult issues. All levels.—*C. E. Farah, University of Minnesota*

OAB-2442 95-948109 MARC

Forbes, Vivian Louis. **The maritime boundaries of the Indian Ocean region.** Singapore University Press, National University of Singapore, 1995. (Dist. by International Specialized Books Services) 267p bibl index ISBN 9971-69-192-2, $79.95

Forbes (Univ. of Western Australia) has produced many fine articles and maps on maritime boundaries in the eastern Indian and western Pacific oceans. This volume is a comprehensive compendium and explanation of such materials on the entire Indian Ocean, including the Red Sea, Persian Gulf, and Torres Strait. The first half consists of chapters discussing the geographical and political setting, regulations for the use and management of the oceans, establishing maritime limits, and cooperative approaches to maritime boundary demarcation, plus an introduction and conclusion. The second half contains an extensive glossary—including an atlas of maritime boundaries. The text is straightforward and clearly written, the maps simple but quite adequate, the tables and other materials most useful. Occasional lapses of fact (e.g., discussion of Ethiopian instead of Eritrean boundaries) and spelling (e.g., "United Nation's" and demarkate" instead of demarcation) may be forgiven in such a remarkable work of scholarship. It is an excellent reference tool, the first of its kind. For every collection on international relations and regional and marine affairs. Upper-division undergraduates and above.—*M. I. Glassner, emeritus, Southern Connecticut State University*

OAB-2443 DS329 95-45933 CIP

Frye, Richard N. **The heritage of Central Asia: from antiquity to the Turkish expansion.** Markus Wiener, 1996. 264p index afp ISBN 1-55876-110-1, $34.95; ISBN 1-55876-111-X pbk, $16.95

Frye's book addresses a long-felt need among those who teach not only the history of Central Asia but also the early history of the Middle East, India, and China. Frye (emeritus, Harvard) has written extensively and authoritatively on the early history of the Iranian world, including what is rather vaguely termed "Central Asia." A summation of a lifetime of scholarship, this lucid and absorbing narrative brings together such distinct elements as the world of Zoroaster, the Achaemenid ecumene, the Sakas and later waves of nomadic invaders, the spread of Buddhism along the Silk Road, the diffusion of Sasanid and Samanid culture into the steppe-zone, and the historic role of the Turks. Frye stresses the importance of the interpretation of archaeological, numismatic, and epigraphic evidence, and of applying the work of comparative linguists and art historians, all explained in language accessible to readers beyond the circle of fellow specialists. This is an outstanding work of scholarly compression. The maps are excellent and the illustrations well chosen. All levels.—*G. R. G. Hambly, University of Texas at Dallas*

OAB-2444   DS109   95-50443 CIP
Grabar, Oleg. **The shape of the holy: early Islamic Jerusalem.** Princeton, 1996. 232p bibl index afp ISBN 0-691-03653-5, $65.00

Books on Jerusalem and its history are a minor industry, and their many purposes reflect the city's importance to the great monotheistic faiths. In this lavishly and uniquely illustrated work, Grabar (Princeton) details the architectural history of the city at four points between the sixth and 11th centuries: the Christian city in BCE 600; the half century or so between the Muslim conquest and the building of the Dome of the Rock; the last six decades of the Umayyad period; and the Fatimid city before it fell into the hands of the Crusaders. Assisted by associates using computer-aided design programs for urban and architectural reconstructions, Grabar devotes most of his attention to the development of the Haram as-Sharif and, particularly, the Dome of the Rock. His sources include medieval Jewish, Christian, and Muslim manuscripts, as well as "documents" in the structures themselves, i.e., their inscriptions, decorations, shapes, and locations. The various cityscapes and the topography of Jerusalem appear in colorful images that give visual shape to the city the Arabs call *al-Quds*, the Holy. Magisterial in its inferences and arguments and written in language accessible to a general audience, this oversized book is a splendid addition to recent studies of Islamic art and architecture. All levels.—*L. M. Lewis, Eastern Kentucky University*

OAB-2445   DS62   95-15506 CIP
Imperial legacy: the Ottoman imprint on the Balkans and the Middle East, ed. by L. Carl Brown. Columbia, 1996. 337p bibl index afp ISBN 0-231-10304-2, $49.50

A feast of thoughtful and informative essays, this timely collection explores an age-old issue: the impact of the past on the present. Contributors—whose names make a very impressive list—consider the political, administrative, diplomatic, linguistic, economic, military, religious, and educational influences of the Ottoman Empire on its successor states in the Balkans and in the Arab world. If, as the editor remarks, the studies "aim more for broad themes than discrete detail," they provide substance enough for thorough lessons in historical influence. Both Maria Todorova's essay on the Ottoman Balkans and Karl Barbir's on the Ottomans in Arab lands weigh historical reality against interpretation and ideology. Each is paired with an essay that considers the practical effects of imperial policies on national boundaries, Dennison Rusinow's on Yugoslavia's and André Raymond's on those of the Arab states. Ergun Ozbudun argues that the Ottomans left to the Middle East the tradition of a strong and centralized state, while William Ochsenwald credits the Ottomans with bequeathing a relatively tolerant Sunni Islam. Some of the contributors—Bernard Lewis, Carter Findley, Charles Issawi—have done book-length studies of the subjects they treat in brief here. Maps and photos. All levels.—*L. M. Lewis, Eastern Kentucky University*

OAB-2446   DR486   94-21024 CIP
Kafadar, Cemal. **Between two worlds: the construction of the Ottoman state.** California, 1995. 221p bibl index afp ISBN 0-520-08807-7, $40.00

Kafadar (Harvard Univ.) contributes a distinguished addition to Ottoman studies with this thoughtful and thought-provoking discussion of the pioneer phase of Ottoman state building between the late 13th century and 1453. Chapter 1 surveys 20th-century writing on this period, centering around the impact of the writings of Mehmet Fuat Köprülü and his "exclusive" theories of Turkish "tribalism" on the *uc*, the frontier world of Anatolian marcher-lordships, and those of Paul Wittek and his "inclusive" *gaza* thesis. Together, their influence contributed decisively to shaping the historiographical tradition. The second chapter is a masterful analysis of the sources—none of

them strictly contemporary—that provided the raw materials for that tradition, while the third contains Kafadar's own subtle explication of the period. It is a measure of the breadth and seriousness of his approach that his reflections on history, nationalism, and historic folk memory acquire an immediate relevance in the present context of the enormities occurring in those Balkan lands that were once among the Ottomans' oldest territorial acquisitions. Upper-division undergraduates and above.—*G. R. G. Hambly, University of Texas at Dallas*

OAB-2447   DS149   91-47853 CIP
Kellerman, Aharon. **Society and settlement: Jewish land of Israel in the twentieth century.** State University of New York, 1993. 321p bibl index ISBN 0-7914-1295-4, $59.50; ISBN 0-7914-1296-2 pbk, $19.95

Kellerman's useful study is the fruit of thoughtful analysis and prodigious research. As the title suggests, *Society and Settlement* is a work of historical geography that probes the totality of the Zionist enterprise by unraveling its sociospatial dimensions. Kellerman argues that space, ideology, economic structure, and the impact of the indigenous Arab population must be analyzed as an organic whole to understand the national and territorial development of Palestine/Israel. Drawing on a wide variety of English and Hebrew sources, Kellerman examines Zionist settlement activity before and after the establishment of the state of Israel, compares the development of Jerusalem and Tel Aviv, and investigates Jewish society's shifting attitudes toward the country's northern and southern frontiers. Within this context, Kellerman discusses the differences between old and new Jewish settlement patterns, the process of urbanization, and the impact of social, cultural, and political trends on Israeli society. An important contribution to the study of the land of Israel. Advanced undergraduate; graduate; faculty.—*J. D. Sarna, Brandeis University*

OAB-2448   DS38   95-26105 CIP
Madelung, Wilfred. **The succession to Muhammad: a study of the early Caliphate.** Cambridge, 1997. 413p bibl index ISBN 0-521-56181-7, $69.95

Madelung (Oxford) is one of the outstanding contemporary Islamicists. His latest work addresses subject matter of the greatest importance, and in so doing, fully meets the reader's expectations. Events in Medina that followed the death of the Prophet Muhammad in 632 were to shape the future development of the Muslim community for centuries to come. Madelung treats the extent and nature of political and military expansion outside the Arabian peninsula, the organization of the community of believers, the emergence of the institution of the Caliphate, and above all, the beginning of the rift between those who, down to the present day, follow the sunna of the Prophet, mainstream Sunni Islam, and the dissident Shiite minority. Madelung's brilliant narrative has the merit of combining great detail and sophisticated analysis with extraordinary lucidity. Never before have the first 30 years in the life of the Muslim community been more meaningfully interpreted. All students of Islam will want to keep this book within arm's reach. Upper-division undergraduates and above.—*G. R. G. Hambly, University of Texas at Dallas*

OAB-2449   HQ1726   92-37454 CIP
Moghadam, Valentine M. **Modernizing women: gender and social change in the Middle East.** L. Rienner, 1993. 311p bibl index afp ISBN 1-55587-346-4, $40.00; ISBN 1-55587-354-5 pbk, $17.95

One of the best studies of women and social change in the Middle East ever to be published. In this scholarly analysis of the impact of change on women's roles and statuses and of women's responses to and involvement in the processes of change, Moghadam provides a detailed account of political (especially of Islamist movements and revolutions), economic, social, and cultural factors as they relate both to the modern Middle East as a whole and to specific countries. She focuses on middle-class women who play pivotal roles as agents of change. Comparative data from other parts of the world greatly enhance the

Social & Behavioral Sciences

book's usefulness. Moghadam uses Iran and Afghanistan as case studies. She draws her data from a wide reading of the literature and from her own research and experience in the Middle East. Describing herself as a Marxist-feminist sociologist, Moghadam does not treat Islam or "culture" as determining factors in women's roles and statuses, unlike many other writers on Middle-Eastern women. Her study is a superb resource for scholars and students interested in gender, the Middle East, and development and social change. It contains 40 pages of detailed notes, a bibliography that includes the most current publications, photographs (that ought to be identified by place and date), tables, and a figure. Graduate; faculty.—*L. Beck, Washington University*

OAB-2450 DS119 93-15065 CIP
Morris, Benny. **Israel's border wars, 1949-1956: Arab infiltration, Israeli retaliation, and the countdown to the Suez War.** Oxford, 1994 (c1993). 451p bibl index afp ISBN 0-19-827850-0, $39.95

Using only documents available from Israeli sources, Morris chronicles the diplomatic relations between Israel and its neighbors from 1949 to 1956. Because none of the surrounding countries has allowed access to its archives, Morris does not have the complete story. Nevertheless, his book is the most comprehensive and readable account available of Israel's diplomacy and its internal debate concerning borders and security. The book explores choices and options open to Israelis between their first two major conflicts. Violence, which Morris blames on Arab infiltration into Israel, was endemic during this period. Although Arab raids taxed Israel in many ways (Morris includes a chapter on the costs of infiltration), he also points out that, ironically, they raised Israeli morale, helped mesh a heterogeneous society, contributed to Mapai's power, and readied the Israelis for larger conflicts to come. In an interesting chapter, Morris looks at the dilemma facing Arab governments that, on the one hand, supported infiltration or any other measure that would weaken Israel, but on the other hand, feared that these attacks might lead to further territorial losses. The book contains a plethora of notes and includes useful maps. Advanced undergraduates.—*G. R. Sharfman, Hiram College*

OAB-2451 DS70 93-31786 CIP
Nakash, Yitzhak. **The Shi'is of Iraq.** Princeton, 1994. 312p bibl index afp ISBN 0-691-03431-1, $35.00

Nakash (Princeton) promises to correct generalizations about Shi'ism that stem from the many studies of Iranian Shi'i Islam. He delivers a fascinating portrait of the Arab Shi'is of central and southern Iraq that must forever curb temptations to treat all Shi'is in monolithic terms. Drawing upon a wide array of archival materials as well as on published works in Arabic, Persian, and other languages, Nakash traces the conversion of Iraqi Arabs to Shi'ism in the 19th century, ironically late in light of the occurrence in Iraq of crucial events in early Shi'i history. He describes and analyzes the developing relationship between the Shi'is and the newly established state of Iraq following WW I, emphasizing the loyalty of the Shi'is to the Arab state and their largely unfulfilled desire to attain representation in it. The examination of specific religious rituals reveals the fundamental differences between Iraqi and Iranian Shi'is. Despite an epilogue on the Gulf War and its aftermath, the author focuses almost entirely on the period before the 1958 revolution, with only passing references to Saddam Hussein and the current status of Iraqi Shi'is. One of the best books this year in Arab studies. Upper-division undergraduates and above.—*L. M. Lewis, Eastern Kentucky University*

OAB-2452 DS119 93-19519 CIP
Pelcovits, Nathan A. **The long armistice: UN peacekeeping and the Arab-Israeli conflict, 1948-1960.** Westview, 1993. 264p index afp ISBN 0-8133-8483-4, $59.95

Drawing heavily on recently opened US and Israeli archives, interviews with key participants, and his own extensive diplomatic experience, Pelcovits has written perhaps the definitive study of the UN peacekeeping role in the Arab-Israeli conflict, from Israel's birth to the end of the Eisenhower presidency. This

tightly written, thoroughly documented, and deeply analytical work probes the motives of Israeli leaders in alternately cooperating with and defying UN peacekeepers in their midst. The author makes clear how the divergent national interests of Israel and the US affected Israeli leaders' attitudes and policies toward the UN, generated considerable tension in the Eisenhower years, and determined their actions during the Suez War of 1956. A balanced study that consistently exhibits sympathy for Israel's security needs, this work both complements and supersedes Fred J. Khouri's *The Arab-Israeli Dilemma* (CH, Mar'69). For greater insights into the personalities, emotions, and drama of the period, see E.L.M. Burns's *Between Arab and Israeli* (1962); Saadia Touval's *The Peace Brokers: Mediators in the Arab-Israeli Conflict, 1948-1979* (CH, Mar'83); Donald Neff's *Warriors at Suez* (CH, Feb'82); *The Elusive Peace in the Middle East*, ed. by Malcolm Kerr (CH, Dec'75); and Steven L. Spiegel's *The Other Arab-Israeli Conflict: Making America's Middle East Policy, from Truman to Reagan* (CH, Sep'85). Recommended. Advanced undergraduates and above.—*G. B. Doxsee, Ohio University*

OAB-2453 DT96 93-4632 CIP
Petry, Carl F. **Twilight of majesty: the reigns of the Mamlūk Sultans al-Ashrāf Qāytbāy and Qānṣūh al-Ghawrī in Egypt.** Middle East Center, Henry M. Jackson School of International Studies, University of Washington, 1994 (c1993). (Dist. by Washington) 261p bibl index afp (Occasional papers, 4) ISBN 0-295-97307-2 pbk, $20.00

Petry, author of *The Civilian Elite of Cairo in the Later Middle Ages* (1981), has written an admirable double biography of the last two major Mamluk rulers of Egypt, al-Ashraf Qaytbay (1468-96) and Qansuh al-Ghawri (1501-1516). Today, Qaytbay is chiefly remembered for his architectural embellishment of Cairo; al-Ghawri, as the Sultan whose defeat at Marj Dabiq in 1516 opened the way to the Ottoman conquest of Egypt. As Petry (Northeastern Univ.) skillfully demonstrates, the two Sultans, although very different in style and temperament, each embodied distinct elements of Mamluk kingship. Qaytbay was the quintessential traditionalist, conventionally pious yet well able to overawe or manipulate his unruly Mamluk followers, slave-soldiers from Central Asia and Circassia who constituted Egypt's military elite between 1250 and 1517, and indeed up to 1811. In sharp contrast, al-Ghawri, although flamboyant and volatile, possessed a certain breadth of vision, as in his recognition of the danger posed by Portuguese hegemony in the Arabian Sea and the need to support the hard-pressed Sultanate of Gujarat, as well as a willingness to innovate. This is a splendid book, combining liveliness with impeccable scholarship. Recommended for all interested in Egypt or the Middle East. Upper-division undergraduate and above.—*G. R. G. Hambly, University of Texas at Dallas*

OAB-2454 DT146 93-22317 CIP
Sanders, Paula. **Ritual, politics, and the city in Fatimid Cairo.** State University of New York, 1994. 231p bibl index afp ISBN 0-7914-1781-6, $49.50

Among Islamic dynasties few were more idiosyncratic, or are more interesting to historians, than the Fatimids (909-1171). From their original North African base, the Fatimids came to dominate Egypt, Syria, and the Hijaz, and presided over a glittering phase of Islamic intellectual and cultural history. Sanders (Rice Univ.) has made a major contribution to Fatimid studies with her fascinating account of the political significance of public ceremony and ritual in Fatimid Cairo. In her own words, Sanders's concern "is to discuss the ways in which ritual at the court was embedded in changing social and political realities and how court rituals responded to those changes," and "to understand the dynamic relationship between politics, ritual, and urban life that gave shape and meaning to Fatimid rule." This is a subtle, sensitive, and imaginative study, using sources that require very cautious interpretation and breaking ground that has scarcely been touched before by Islamicists. Students of the politics and political style of medieval Muslim regimes will certainly need to read this book, which is a further contribution to the growing literature in English on the Fatimids. Upper-division undergraduates and above.—*G. R. G. Hambly, University of Texas at Dallas*

OAB-2455 Orig

Seikaly, May. **Haifa: transformation of a Palestinian Arab society, 1918-1939.** I.B. Tauris, 1995. 284p bibl index ISBN 1-85043-958-3, $59.50

Seikaly has written a competent, dispassionate, well-researched analysis of important changes affecting the Arab urban population of Haifa during the British Mandate over Palestine prior to WW II. The author shows the complex interaction of Arab and Jewish nationalism with British colonialism and the intersection of ethnic, religious, political, and economically diverse internal forces. Although Seikaly is neither particularly interested in the specifics of Jewish community politics nor especially sympathetic to Zionist aspirations, no group emerges as especially villainous and none is perceived as notably praiseworthy. The balance achieved is altogether quite remarkable! The study provides a brief though adequate historical sketch and ranges far afield, touching on sociological, religious, economic, and anthropological as well as political issues, thus achieving adequate breadth as well as depth. Well written and carefully footnoted and indexed, this book will be widely consulted by scholars and general readers alike. Highly recommended for Middle East researchers seeking an understanding of the antecedents of Palestinian/Israeli confrontation. All levels.—*L. D. Loeb, University of Utah*

OAB-2456 DS62 91-22138 CIP

Tauber, Eliezer. **The Arab movements in World War I.** F. Cass, 1993. 322p bibl index ISBN 0-7146-3437-9, $37.50; ISBN 0-7146-4083-2 pbk, $20.00

Attempts of the Arab population living under Ottoman rule to establish their independence began long before WW I. Al-Fatat, the first Arab secret society, was organized early during the Young Turk period, and the second, al-Qahtaniyya, was formed in 1909 in Istanbul. It was not until after WW I, however, with the Turkish government deeply involved in that gigantic struggle, that Arab nationalists felt their efforts might succeed, and they began to expand their operations against the Turks. Tauber closely examines those efforts. She traces the relationship between the various Arab societies and the attempted collaboration with Sharif Husayne of Mecca, the role of the British government, and the brutal reprisal by the Turkish authorities, particularly Jamal Pasha. Tauber uses many original sources and archival materials for the first time: Israeli State Archives; documents from the India Office and Public Record Office; US National Archives; and records from France's Ministere des Affaire Estangere and Ministere de la Guerre. Many Arabic manuscript and document collections also have been examined. Thus, readers are offered a wealth of new information. The book is an invaluable source for those interested in Arab nationalism during the first two decades of this century. Joseph Reif (Bar-Ilan Univ.) has done a superb translation from the Hebrew. General readers, advanced undergraduates, and above.— *N. Rassekh, Lewis and Clark College*

OAB-2457 HN786 91-36457 CIP

Winter, Michael. **Egyptian society under Ottoman rule, 1517-1798.** Routledge, 1993 (c1992). 323p bibl index ISBN 0-415-02403-X, $55.00

Among the least familiar periods of Egyptian history are the centuries between 1517 and 1798 when Egypt was a province of the Ottoman Empire. Winter's book is the first to provide a detailed overview of these intervening centuries. Winter (Tel Aviv Univ.), author of *Society and Religion in Early Ottoman Egypt* (1982) as well as of a series of important articles on the Ottoman period, has here made a formidable contribution to a neglected field. Beginning with a survey of political events and with what he calls "the vicissitudes" of the ruling elite, he passes to the role of the bedouin, to aspects of religious life (the function of the orthodox ulema, institutions of Islamic learning, the Sufis, and manifestations of popular religion), the fortunes of the minorities (Jews and Coptic Christians), and social life in Ottoman Cairo. Winter moves deftly through his diverse sources, constantly reminding his readers of the relationship between the Ottoman period and what

preceded and succeeded it. For students of Egypt or the early modern Middle East all this is indispensable reading. Advanced undergraduate; graduate; faculty.—*G. R. G. Hambly, University of Texas at Dallas*

■ North America

OAB-2458 E85 95-12129 CIP

Ebersole, Gary L. **Captured by texts: puritan to postmodern images of Indian captivity.** University Press of Virginia, 1995. 322p bibl index afp ISBN 0-8139-1607-0, $45.00; ISBN 0-8139-1606-2 pbk, $18.50

Captivity narratives are a whole subgenre in world literature, and Native American captivity stories are legion. This authoritative, deeply perceptive, and penetrating account—covering individuals from American Colonial author Mary Rowlandson to Patty Hearst and beyond—in no way disappoints. In fact, it provides an interesting complement to John Demos's *The Unredeemed Captive: A Family Story from Early America* (1994). By turns passionate and coolly scientific, Ebersole covers the gamut of early American texts, later fictions, modern retellings, and even popular films (e.g., John Ford's classic *The Searchers*, 1956). Implicit throughout are such themes as racism (the Indians/captors as brutal savages), powerful biblical analogues seen in the light of an ideological "redemptive suffering" by the captured, and heightened awareness of the captive's body as a site of pain and privation. This 300-year journey takes the reader into both Puritan theology and the conversion problem in the context of "going native." The author analyzes the lexicography and hermeneutics of usage in the narratives and their biblical contexts, and discusses popular fictionalized captivity accounts of the Enlightenment and diverse metaliterary preoccupations on the subject (psychological, archetypal, feminist) of the last 20 years or so. Highly recommended for large public, upper-division undergraduate, graduate, and research libraries.— *R. Cormier, Central Piedmont Community College*

OAB-2459 Can. CIP

Marshall, Ingeborg. **A history and ethnography of the Beothuk.** McGill-Queen's, 1996. 640p bibl index afp ISBN 0-7735-1390-6, $45.00

Examining the history and culture of the Beothuk, a group of Native Americans who inhabited Newfoundland until their tragic extinction in the late 1820s, Marshall (Institute of Social and Economic Research, Memorial Univ.) has created a masterful and definitive epic written with both engaging empathy and rigorous scholarship. Although little is known of these people, who chose to remain isolated from their often aggressive European and Native neighbors (primarily Micmac and Montagnais), Marshall succeeds in bringing together historical sources, material culture, and current archaeological data in this lively work. Meticulously illustrated with a wealth of maps, drawings, and items of material culture, all carefully integrated into the text, the study also provides time lines and summaries guiding the reader through carefully contextualized and evaluated historical sources and critical events. The depth of the research as well as the larger human questions examined in the work make it a model for combining history and anthropology, and is thus highly recommended for students of these disciplines as well as Native American and Canadian studies, material culture, and ethics. All levels.—*R. A. Bucko, Le Moyne College*

OAB-2460 E77 95-46096 CIP

North America, Pt. 1 & 2, ed. by Bruce G. Trigger and Wilcomb E. Washburn. Cambridge, 1996. 2v. 564, 500p bibl indexes (Cambridge history of the Native peoples of the Americas, 1) ISBN 0-521-34440-9, $99.95

Trigger and Washburn's work should be a required acquisition for all libraries. It is a wonderful overview of North America's Native peoples from their arrival in this hemisphere until 1995. The editors have joined 14 other scholars in crafting imaginative chapters that provide insight into subjects as wide-ranging as Native American views of history, numerous regional life patterns, chronological periods of encounter and change, reservations, and the late-20th-century Native American renaissance posited by Washburn in the final chapter. Anthropologists, archaeologists, ethnohistorians, and historians have combined their talents in this outstanding collection. Excellent illustrations map ancient and modern population centers, illuminate archaeological artifacts, reconstruct villages, trace settlement patterns, and locate reservations. Scholars will be especially grateful for properly placed footnotes and bibliographies for each chapter. This publication should prove useful to almost anyone interested in Native American peoples. The novice will find helpful introductions to the literature of a topic, while experienced researchers will be gratified to have this work at hand as a tiller for steering through the seas of recent research and setting course for the scholarly horizon.—*J. H. O'Donnell III, Marietta College*

CANADA

OAB-2461   HQ1453   95-3611 CIP
Billson, Janet Mancini. **Keepers of the culture: the power of tradition in women's lives.** Lexington Books, 1995. 476p bibl index ISBN 0-02-903512-0, $25.00

Billson interviewed 250 Canadian native, minority, and/or immigrant women for this study of women's attitudes toward themselves and their lives. Seven different cultures—Iroquois, Blood, Inuit, Jamaican, Mennonite, Chinese, and Ukrainian—are represented. In two historically oriented sections, Billson sets the scene for the interviews, which are organized into sections titled "Love, Marriage, and Divorce," "Challenges Confronting Women," and "Toward the Twenty-First Century." The final chapters analyze the results of the interviews, ending with comments from interviewees on the book. Appendixes present Billson's methodology. Although Billson employs a feminist sociological philosophy that regards women as oppressed, the book is so solidly based on research that the philosophy does not intrude. In fact, she suggests that her research indicates a wide range of personal and cultural variations in female/male relationships. The scholarship is impeccable. This will become a classic example of the interrelationship of theory, research, and analysis. Extensive chapter bibliographies. All levels.—*M. J. Schneider, University of North Dakota*

OAB-2462   Can. CIP
Burley, David V. **Prophecy of the swan: the upper Peace River fur trade of 1794-1823,** by David V. Burley, J. Scott Hamilton, and Knut R. Fladmark. UBC Press, University of British Columbia, 6344 Memorial Rd., Vancouver, BC V6T 1Z2, Canada, 1996. 213p bibl index afp ISBN 0-7748-0544-7, $65.00

Explorer Sir Alexander Mackenzie's 1793 discoveries of a land rich in game led to the founding of a post on the Moberly River. Of equal consequence, North West Company post development in the upper Peace River brought the land-based fur trade within the orbit of Montreal-based commerce. This same trade eventually invited the rivalry of the Hudson's Bay Company, though on the eve of the union of these celebrated giants of Canadian commercial history. Natives of the area—Beaver and Sekani—form an important aspect of trade history, not only as traders and consumers but also as warriors and murderers. Based on historical documentation and archaeological studies and findings, Burley's study sustains in large measure J.N. Wallace's early history and adds important details and correctives where necessary. Although Burley's work reads much like an archaeological report in places, it is a valuable historical exposé of places and lands little appreciated and scarcely ever studied in historical detail. Some of the sites are now underwater because of the construction of hydroelectric power installations. A model of cross-disciplinary scholarship, this study will be treasured by historians and archaeologists for its scope, its methodology, its attention to detail, and its recovery of a past now, alas, of very distant memory. Upper-division undergraduates and above.—*B. M. Gough, Wilfrid Laurier University*

OAB-2463   Can. CIP
Carbert, Louise I. **Agrarian feminism: the politics of Ontario farm women.** Toronto, 1995. 255p bibl index afp ISBN 0-8020-2931-0, $50.00

In *Agrarian Feminism*, Carbert provides a comprehensive analysis of the political force of farm women in one region of Ontario. However, she takes readers far beyond Huron and Grey counties by including an expertly researched framework of national women's agrarian movements, most notably those originating in the West. A discussion of the Women's Institutes, which are predominantly local in orientation, completes her presentation of the context of farm women's involvement in politics. Carbert's empirical analysis is based on in-depth interviews drawing on elements of both political science and sociology. She is particularly interested in the degree to which gender relations within marriage affect farm women's involvement in community organizations. Such involvement is further explored to determine the extent to which it influences political attitudes and political activism. This study, with its multiple levels of analysis, provides very good insight into the diversity of agrarian women's experiences with feminism. It is of particular importance because it allows access to the world of rural farm women, a world that is all too frequently hidden from the view of a predominantly urban society. Upper-division undergraduates and above.—*S. Wurtele, Trent University*

OAB-2464   E78   91-50884 CIP
Dickason, Olive Patricia. **Canada's first nations: a history of founding peoples from earliest times.** Oklahoma, 1992. 590p bibl index (Civilization of the American Indian series, 208) ISBN 0-8061-2438-5, $39.95; ISBN 0-8061-2439-3 pbk, $24.95

Dickason chronicles the Amerindian and Inuit experiences in Canada from the earliest Bering land bridge crossings to Elijah Harper's efforts in helping to delay the Meech Lake accord (1990). Using the grand sweep of the literature, Dickason points out how the native peoples settled into their new environments, how their cultures developed in the East, West, and North, and how they met the European onslaught. She discusses the administration of the Amerindians and Inuit, both pre- and post-Confederation (1867). She talks about the numerous treaties and the significance of the Indian Act (1876). Dickason is particularly adept in addressing the Native American struggle for self-government—a central theme of her book. She is equally adept in her treatment of the land question, pointing out how concepts of land differ and illustrating her points by case studies, e.g., Oka, Bear Island, and others. By 1990, land claims numbered 500. The Metis, Hurons, Iroquois, Tecumseh, the Bagot Commission, Mikak, Paskwaw, the Ewing Commission, Treaties Eight, Nine, and Eleven, Elijah Harper and the creation of Nunavut are all here in this well-researched, well-written, passionate and easy-to-read study. Well illustrated, fine maps, a first-rate bibliography. See also Alan D. McMillan's *Native Peoples and Cultures of Canada* (Vancouver 1988) and James S. Frideres's *Native People in Canada, Contemporary Conflicts* (1983). Advanced undergraduate; graduate; faculty.—*D. Jacobson, Michigan State University*

OAB-2465   Orig
Greenhous, Brereton. **The crucible of war, 1939-1945,** by Brereton Greenhous et al. Toronto, 1994. 1,096p index afp (The official history of the Royal Canadian Air Force, 3) ISBN 0-8020-0574-8, $50.00

This volume of the official history of the RCAF lives up to the high standards set by the other two: S.F. Wise, *Canadian Airmen and World War I* (CH, Jun'81); W.A.B. Douglas, *The Creation of a National Air Force* (Toronto, 1986). The work's great asset is that it also covers the history of the Royal Air Force, providing detachment and hindsight as well as a more serious and balanced look at the records. Because the authors are writing for an audience no longer familiar with WW II, they provide excellent explanations of developments. In a sense, these volumes are a second generation of official histories. As members of the RCAF and as individuals, Canadians were involved in various aspects of the British Commonwealth air effort in Europe. Thus, volume 3 covers policy, the fighter, the maritime and the bomber war, and air transport in the Southeast Asia Command. The study is arranged so that anyone can read the operational segments and see the evolution of organization, tactics, technology, and battle in one piece rather than as treated in chronological alternations in Denis Richards and H. St. George Saunders's *The Royal Air Force, 1939-1945* (London, 1974-75) and in C.K. Webster and Noble Frankland's *The Strategic Air Offensive against Germany 1939-1945* (1961). Definitely recommended. All levels.—*R. Higham, Kansas State University*

OAB-2466   Can. CIP
Greer, Allan. **The patriots and the people: the rebellion of 1837 in rural Lower Canada.** Toronto, 1993. 385p index afp ISBN 0-8020-2792-X, $50.00; ISBN 0-8020-6930-4 pbk, $18.95

Every so often a scholarly book comes along that sums up a whole period that has been discussed for years. Greer's book on the Rebellion of 1837 in Lower Canada takes as its center the French-Canadian peasantry, its attitudes, outlook, conditions of its agriculture in the 1830s, and its quasi-republicanism, as well as its incipient and sometimes blatant misogyny. Greer's preeminent virtue is his scrupulous handling of evidence, rather than arguing from a preconceived theory. His book is also exceptional for its range of information derived from a great diversity of French-Canadian sources. Greer is particularly good at assessing the increasingly vertiginous swirl of events that led to the outbreak of fighting in November 1837. It is at times a grim story, but it is told coolly and succinctly. That this book is vivaciously written and eminently readable is almost too much to expect; it is, in fact, difficult to put down. Although this reviewer would have liked a bibliographic essay, the footnotes are real *foo*motes and very informative. The book is handsomely printed and admirable indexed. All levels.—*P. B. Waite, Dalhousie University*

OAB-2467   Can. CIP
Kennedy, John C. **People of the bays and headlands: anthropological history and the fate of communities in the unknown Labrador.** Toronto, 1995. 296p bibl index afp ISBN 0-8020-0646-9, $50.00

Kennedy's remarkable book on a subject almost unknown, the life and work of the people of southeastern Labrador, is well researched and vigorously written. It is both anthropology and history, one informing the other—oral testimony from the inhabitants and archival sources. In July 1992 the Canadian government proclaimed a moratorium on fishing for northern cod, the staple of the region since recorded (and unrecorded) time. The ban especially affected southeastern Labrador. Fisherman had always been in debt to merchants who gave them their supplies and some of their food, paid for in dried cod. Merchants could not afford to give out salt and supplies without substantial quantities of cod back in return. They kept an eye on their fishermen; in a letter to a fisherman dated July 23, 1932, one merchant wrote: "We wish to state again that we do not supply salt to any of our fishermen with the idea that they can do what they wish with their catch." This was private monopoly: natural, inevitable, and not exactly benign. What is best about the book is its perspectives and its immediacy. A thousand years of Labrador life is thoughtfully summed up with a shrewd eye on present conditions. The book has only one weakness: the maps are inadequate, especially so for readers outside of Canada. Upper-division undergraduates and above.—*P. B. Waite, Dalhousie University*

OAB-2468   E99   95-3420 CIP
Marcus, Alan Rudolph. **Relocating Eden: the image and politics of Inuit exile in the Canadian Arctic.** Dartmouth College/University Press of New England, 1995. 272p bibl index afp ISBN 0-87451-659-5 pbk, $19.95

In the early 1950s Canada's government, under the direction of the Department of Northern Development, shipped a number of Inuit men, women, and children to more northern and remote locations. The intention was to provide means of self-dependence for people whose economic and social circumstances were becoming desperate. Government officials indicated game would be plentiful and life would be untainted by Western influences. Some claims have been made that the Inuit were to be "human flagpoles," to support Canada's claims

to High Arctic sovereignty, but as Marcus implies, no evidence exists to support this accusation. Indeed, 40 years after the relocations, the question still remains: were these experiments intended to protect the Inuit, or were they an attempt to secure Canada's northern interest during the Cold War? More interesting is the book's subtext, i.e., how popular writer and publicist Farley Mowat brought the plight of the "exiles" to the US and Canadian reading publics, and in so doing, forced the Canadian government to admit it could do little to stop Mowat's exposé. The principal merits of this well-researched and well-referenced book are its evenhanded treatment of an emotional topic and its refusal to set aside scholarly inquiry for a politically inspired explanation of how and why Eden did not occur. Upper-division undergraduates and above.—*B. M. Gough, Wilfrid Laurier University*

OAB-2469   Can. CIP
McDonald, Robert A.J. **Making Vancouver: class, status, and social boundaries, 1863-1913.** UBC Press, University of British Columbia, 6344 Memorial Rd., Vancouver, BC V6T 1Z2, Canada, 1996. 316p bibl index afp ISBN 0-7748-0555-2, $49.95

McDonald's study is an expert analysis of the beginnings of one of the great port cities of the world and one of the more beautiful. The book is economic history in its broadest and best sense, the development of Vancouver's admixture of class, race, and economic growth. Vancouver, now the third largest city in Canada, retained for many years elements of its frontier past. For all its stratifications of race, education, and wealth, its society is still open, buoyant, and vigorous. The research that has gone into McDonald's book is formidable. In the text it is carried with grace; only in the 50 pages of notes does the author allow eristic instincts more leash. Indeed the notes are a resource in themselves. Unlike some other works of the genre, this book has excellent maps and an abundance of evocative photographs to match its economics and statistics. The index is exceptionally well made with comprehensive and functional annotations. *Making Vancouver* is altogether handsomely done and has the hallmarks of a work destined for academic prizes. They would be deserved. All levels.—*P. B. Waite, Dalhousie University*

OAB-2470   E99   94-31544 CIP
Peers, Laura. **The Ojibwa of western Canada, 1780-1870.** Minnesota Historical Society, 1994. 288p bibl index afp (Manitoba studies in native history, 8) ISBN 0-87351-310-X, $32.95; ISBN 0-87351-311-X pbk, $15.95

Peers describes events connected to the movement of western Ojibwa peoples from the woodlands around Lake Superior to the prairie provinces of Canada from 1780 to 1870. The value of this study lies in the degree to which Peers has provided evidence of the adjustments made by people as they moved from one region to another. Although she draws from the usual scholarly sources, Peers also makes skillful use of accounts by explorers, missionaries, fur traders, and sightseers. This book documents problems and solutions associated with fluctuating natural resource availability, changing trade patterns and partners, new diseases and epidemics, the loss of territory, and finally, new neighbors who assert political control over western Ojibwa affairs. Peers is quite adept and critical in her use of the historic texts. She also supports her arguments with transcribed oral accounts of historical events, archaeological data, museum specimens, and the analysis of historical images. Students of culture continuity, change, and ethnicity will find this a very interesting work. Upper-division undergraduates and above.—*T. A. Foor, University of Montana*

OAB-2471   Can. CIP
Swyripa, Frances. **Wedded to the cause: Ukrainian-Canadian women and ethnic identity, 1891-1991.** Toronto, 1993. 330p afp ISBN 0-8020-5008-5, $50.00; ISBN 0-8020-6939-8 pbk, $19.95

The relationship between gender and ethnic identity frame Swyripa's study of Ukrainian Canadian women. By tracing these women through a variety of phases ranging from peasant settler to politicized activist, the author is able to deconstruct the history of this group's experience in Canada, adding a new and exciting perspective to the existing literature. Beyond identifying these phases, Swyripa explores the relationship between the role and image of women and the emergence and development of Ukrainian ethnic identity. Competently sifting through a plethora of both English-and Ukrainian-language sources Swyripa reveals to her reader an insightful and fascinating history. Beyond these traditional sources, her research draws on more unorthodox sources, including "pottery, statuary, artwork, foods, embroidery, and photographs." The author's interpretation of the imagery and mythology reflected in these forms is crucial to her analysis of the symbolic importance of women for Ukrainian Canadian ethnic identity. This book, however, goes far beyond the focus on Ukrainian Canadian women to examine the process by which ethnic identity is formulated and perpetuated both from without and from within the ethnic group. Undergraduate; graduate; faculty.—*S. Wurtele, Queen's University*

OAB-2472   F1035   92-28210 CIP
Tulchinsky, Gerald. **Taking root: the origins of the Canadian Jewish community.** Brandeis University/University Press of New England, 1993. 341p index afp ISBN 0-87451-609-9, $35.00

Young Jewish men were among the fur traders operating out of Montreal in the mid-18th century. There were also Jews in other communities along the St. Lawrence and in the neighboring rural areas. Synagogue and cemetery were rapidly put in place, and the community prospered; but the problems were many. A French-Canadian population—staunchly Catholic and often anti-semitic—and an English ruling regime—staunchly Protestant but not always supportive—were among the external problems. The changing population, including new arrivals from central Europe brought up in Ashkenazic rather than Sephardic traditions, proved to be a lingering internal problem. Tulchinsky relates the evolution of these problems and attempts to solve them, from their origins to just after WW I. He also deals with the growth and spread of other Jewish communities, e.g., Toronto, Hamilton, Winnipeg, the agricultural "colonies" in the Prairie Provinces, and the attempts at community in Victoria and Vancouver. Tulchinsky is particularly adept in discussing the effects of urbanization, Jewish influences in the needle trades, antisemitism, struggles to keep Jewish children in Protestant schools, the role of women in Jewish life, and the significance of Zionism. He is equally adept at portraying the lives of the movers and shakers who flit through the pages. A beautifully written and scholarly work. General; advanced undergraduate; graduate; faculty.—*D. Jacobson, Michigan State University*

UNITED STATES

OAB-2473   W185   96-6486 CIP
Banks, William M. **Black intellectuals: race and responsibility in American life.** W.W. Norton, 1996. 335p bibl index ISBN 0-393-03989-7, $29.95

Banks provides an encyclopedic, sometimes breathless portrait of black intellectual life from the priests and medicine men of West Africa before the middle passage, to Cornel West, Derrick Bell, and Lani Guinier. In 12 nicely delineated chapters Banks charts the major movements and sketches the major figures in black intellectual history, exposing along the way the tensions between the universalist impulse and the responsibility to "the race." This is an especially fine treatment of "the black intellectual infrastructure"—from the black schools of the 19th century to the commercial publishing industry and integrated university culture of the 20th—and of the dynamic relationship between intellectual currents on the one hand and the social, political, and economic structures that generate, support, influence, or constrain them on the other. Banks admirably handles enormous volumes of material, and renders complex developments and debates with rare clarity. In its synthesis and its breadth *Black Intellectuals* will be an indispensable introduction and resource. All levels.—*M. F. Jacobson, Yale University*

OAB-2474   E183   92-36165 MARC
The Cambridge history of American foreign relations: v.1: The creation of a republican empire, 1776-1865; v.2: The American search for opportunity, 1865-1913; v.3: The globalizing of America, 1913-1945; v.4: America in the age of Soviet power, 1945-1991, by [v.1] Bradford Perkins, [v.2] Walter LaFeber, [v.3] Akira Iriye, and [v.4] Warren I. Cohen. Cambridge, 1993. 4v. 240-283p ea. index ISBN 0-521-44988-X, $89.95 set; $24.95 ea.

This fine work is as able a synthesis of US diplomatic history as one is likely to get in this generation. For the general reader, it is both accessible and provocative; for the specialist, it is sophisticated, full of fresh interpretations based on primary research. One minor quibble: though the annotated bibliography is often cogent, one wishes for much richer listings, including discussion of some works that take issue with an author's interpretation. Perkins (Univ. of Michigan) covers the period from the American Revolution through the Civil War. He gives much attention to the theme of American "exceptionalism," revealing how a republican nation became transformed into a continental empire. He ably captures the prudential rationale of isolationism, shows how early presidents were bound to transgress strict constitutional limitations, notes how early diplomats were not above offering bribes, and sees racism as a restraining factor in the nation's inevitable expansion. High marks are given to early Federalist leaders as well as to James Monroe and John Quincy Adams. Low marks are allocated to Benjamin Franklin, John Jay, James Madison, Thomas Jefferson, and James K. Polk. Perkins is particularly trenchant on US diplomatic moves leading to the War of 1812.

LaFeber (Cornell Univ.), covering the Gilded Age and the early Progressive Era, offers a provocative thesis: that the US, in its search for economic opportunities overseas, inadvertently established conditions for social revolution in such nations as Mexico and China. Moreover, as the US sought to protect its overseas interests, this revolution was inevitably accelerated. In some ways, the book is a severe indictment, as when LaFeber claims that the US "set out to create disorder in Latin America." He offers particularly able pictures of William H. Seward, Henry and Brooks Adams, A.T. Mahan, and William McKinley. The portrait of Theodore Roosevelt is almost a classic. The often-neglected William Howard Taft and his secretary of state Philander Knox finally get the attention they deserve. Other strong points include the treatments of "the Second Industrial Revolution" (this one based on electricity not coal), the economic demands of the American South, the Open Door notes, and the economic crisis of the 1890s. At times one wishes for more on the internal conditions of other countries (particularly in the Caribbean), their possible fate if the US had not created "dependency," and live options open to US policy makers.

Iriye (Harvard Univ.) focuses on America's success in supplanting Europe as world leader. Although the narrative is now becoming increasingly familiar, Iriye's work possesses new insights on a number of matters: the ideological battle between Wilson and Lenin, the Versailles Treaty as a modification (not a repudiation) of Wilson's Fourteen Points, the crucial place held by Article X in Wilsonian internationalism, the role of peace as an ideology in itself, and the Good Neighbor Policy as reflecting isolationism. The internationalist leanings of Herbert Hoover are skillfully presented. Although political and economic matters are given full play, Iriye makes an especially strong contribution in his discussion of frequently ignored cultural concerns.

Cohen (Michigan State Univ.) organizes much of his Cold War history around the concept of the "security dilemma," by which the defensive action of each side appears to threaten the other. If, as with Iriye, readers are at home with much of the narrative, some interpretations are most stimulating. According to Cohen, Soviet-US rivalry in Europe and the Middle East was inevitable. The Korean War, however, converted the struggle into "an ideologically driven, militarized contest that threatened the very survival of the globe." The years 1958-62, writes Cohen, were the most dangerous of all, marked by costly gains in peripheral areas where neither side had vital interests at stake. John Foster Dulles, Lyndon Johnson, Richard Nixon, Henry Kissinger, and Ronald Reagan are all severely criticized, and Cohen's discussion of the Vietnam War is especially damning. Though Cohen strongly attacks many US policies, he concludes by noting that the world was better because of "American resistance to Joseph Stalin's vision." All libraries.—*J. D. Doenecke, New College of the University of South Florida*

OAB-2475 F526 95-26443 CIP
Cayton, Andrew R.L. **Frontier Indiana.** Indiana, 1996. 340p bibl index afp ISBN 0-253-33048-3, $35.00

Cayton's graceful, arresting narrative is grounded in primary and secondary sources, including classics by Emma Lou Thornbrough and Bernard Knollenberg, James Madison's *The Indiana Way* (CH, Jan'87), and new studies from such scholars as Richard White and Gregory Evans Dowd. Spanning 1700-1850 in ten chapters and an epilogue, Cayton's first-rate study interprets the successive worlds of the Miami (1700-1754), then of individuals whose experiences epitomized unfolding chapters of Indiana frontier history. With a keen ear for the revealing anecdote and apt quotation, the author treats the world of George Croghan (1750-1777); the village of Vincennes (1765-1777); the milieus of George Rogers Clark (1778-1787), Josiah Harmar, and John Francis Hamtramck (1787-1790); Little Turtle (1790-1795); Anna Tuthill Symmes Harrison (wife of William Henry Harrison, 1795-1810); Tenskwatawa (1795-1811); Jonathan Jennings (1800-1816); and the end of the frontier (1816-1850). Along the way readers discover figures such as John and William Conner, the early rivalry between Centerville and Richmond, an explanation of why Indiana remained a state of small towns and farms until the latter half of the 20th century, and the basis for understanding one of the more interesting states of the Union. Fine illustrations, maps. All levels.—*D. W. Steeples, Mercer University*

OAB-2476 NC1425 95-8892 CIP
Fischer, Roger A. **Them damned pictures: explorations in American political cartoon art.** Archon Books, 1996. (Dist. by Shoe String) 253p bibl index afp ISBN 0-208-02298-8, $37.50

Fischer's outstanding work on American political cartoon art enlarges all other previous studies, e.g., Thomas C. Leonard's *The Power of the Press: The Birth of American Political Reporting* (1986) and Charles Press's *The Political Cartoon* (CH, Apr'82). Fischer's treatment is highly informed, cogently expressed, and graced with intellectual and historical sensibilities. It is, moreover, written with clarity and wit, and supplemented by more than 100 illustrations. Plumbing the complex levels of political cartooning over the past century, Fischer plunges into the sensitive areas of ethnic and racial portrayals as well as the presentation of presidential "evil." As he observes, graphic satire has undergone many changes since the golden age of political cartooning at the close of the 19th century, the heyday of Thomas Nast, Joseph Keppler, and Bernard Gillam. Contemporary artists use the "mother lodes" of popular culture—primarily films, television programs, animated cartoons, and the comic strips—to skewer political figures and movements. Although a small number of cartoonists envision their craft as a quest for truth and justice, Fischer notes that "the majority of artists have been candid on the lack of linkage between genius and fairness." An exemplary work. All levels.—*J. Boskin, Boston University*

OAB-2477 HE2751 96-28259 CIP
Gordon, Sarah H. **Passage to Union: how the railroads transformed American life, 1829-1929.** I.R. Dee, 1997. 403p index afp ISBN 1-56663-138-6, $30.00

Using a variety of primary source materials, including newspapers, magazines, diaries, and memoirs, novels and short stories, business and government documents, as well as numerous secondary sources, Gordon presents a very readable examination of the impact of the railroad on American life in the century from 1829 to 1929. The work touches on many issues of social, political, economic, and cultural interest, and also on the various legal and regulatory problems that were created. The court cases are of interest because the railroads functioned to unleash conflict "between those who benefited from the old legal, social, and economic order and those who gained from the new." The author is particularly concerned with the role the railroad played in unifying the economy and society, with the impact this change had in weakening local institutions and traditional relationships, and in the problems created by the railroads' drive to make profits. Based on the author's University of Chicago PhD dissertation, *Passage to Union* is a clearly written and well-informed study that will interest both scholars and general readers. All levels.—*S. L. Engerman, University of Rochester*

OAB-2478 HN57 94-28404 CIP
Graff, Harvey J. **Conflicting paths: growing up in America.** Harvard, 1995. 426p index afp ISBN 0-674-16066-5, $39.95

Using more than 500 first-person narrative accounts, Graff (Univ. of Texas at Dallas) has written a complex history of how childhood, adolescence, and youth have been formed, experienced, transformed, and understood by Americans from the mid-18th to the 20th century. Graff makes a number of major contributions to the historical study of growing up. First, he dispels the idea that children in the past enjoyed a golden age or that the present is a utopia for the young. Second, Graff convincingly demonstrates that there has never been one single path to growing up, but multiple, conflicting, and diverse paths, each of which has been transformed in complex and contradictory ways. Third, these multiple paths are in large part a product of "gender, race, social class, along with ethnicity, place of residence, and age itself—as well as time and fortune." Methodologically and historiographically sophisticated, *Conflicting Paths* supersedes previous work on the subject and should be read by all scholars in the fields of the history of children and the family. Upper-division undergraduates and above.—*E. W. Carp, Pacific Lutheran University*

OAB-2479 F129 94-9827 CIP
Grover, Kathryn. **Make a way somehow: African-American life in a northern community, 1790-1965.** Syracuse, 1994. 321p bibl index afp ISBN 0-8156-2626-6, $39.95; ISBN 0-8156-2627-4 pbk, $17.95

Unlike other local studies that tend to examine communities as if they were isolated from the rest of the US, Grover's interpretation links the experience of one community of African Americans to the wider context of urban history. Grover, an independent researcher and writer, examines the various levels of accommodation and resistance by a small black community extant on the periphery of predominantly white Geneva, New York, from 1790 to 1965. Wills, inventories, newspaper reports, and an enormous body of evidence taken from manuscript census schedules form the basis of Grover's study. Her prose is lively, but what makes this work significant is her ability to connect primary source material to theoretical discussions of community building, migration, segregation, integration, religion, politics, and African American culture. Her goal is to reconstruct a subtle outline of one black community, but her inventive research approach has important methodological implications for historians exploring similar locations. Also, Grover reprints the text from several oral interviews, and in so doing, fashions a valuable primary source for probing the black experience. This work adds texture and depth to the understanding of urban life for both blacks and whites. Upper-division undergraduates and above.—*T. D. Beal, SUNY at Stony Brook*

OAB-2480 F869 94-23424 CIP
Hayden, Dolores. **The power of place: urban landscapes as public history.** MIT, 1995. 296p index ISBN 0-262-08237-3, $30.00

Vividly written and elegantly illustrated, this book synthesizes two major themes in contemporary urbanism—the diversification of historical memories and the active recuperation of places in which this history can be explored—with an evocation of changing histories in Los Angeles. Hayden, who already has contributed significant new readings to American landscapes of gender and belief, combines a wide interdisciplinary range of arguments in an engaging presentation that links theoretical debates and community action. Her initial chapters situate space and place as fundamental features of a variety of historiographies and preservation efforts. Subsequent Los Angeles illustrations, often drawing on the organization Power of Place, treat multiple cityscapes of

Social & Behavioral Sciences

work, the life of early black midwife-philanthropist Biddy Mason and its commemoration in public art, labor history and an unsuccessful attempt to save the Embassy Auditorium, and Little Tokyo. Finally, the possibilities of more complex urban narratives in space and memory and the pains of neglecting this imperative lead Hayden to reflect briefly on the city's 1992 riots. With its extensive notes to related literatures, this work should provoke discussion and active response in a range of audiences. Upper-division undergraduates and above.—*G. W. McDonogh, Bryn Mawr College*

OAB-2481   E99   96-47882 CIP
Hill, Sarah H. **Weaving new worlds: southeastern Cherokee women and their basketry.** North Carolina, 1997. 414p bibl index afp ISBN 0-8078-2345-7, $45.00; ISBN 0-8078-4650-3 pbk, $22.50

Using basket-making as both metaphor and structure for this history of Eastern Cherokee women, Hill skillfully weaves together mythology, basket specimens, interviews, and documents to create a work that is at once broad Cherokee history and detailed women's knowledge of their art. Rivercane, white oak, honeysuckle, and red maple—the primary basketry materials at different times in Cherokee history—are the basis for four chapters describing the details of manufacture and function for that particular material and discussing the ecological and social conditions surrounding its use. Thus, clear-cutting the southern woodlands depleted white oak and allowed introduced Japanese honeysuckle to flourish at the same time that basketmakers were looking for new materials and new outlets for their art. Examining possible sources for the innovation of honeysuckle vine baskets provides Hill the opportunity to discuss Cherokee women's boarding school experiences and the teaching of basket-making in Indian schools, and this flows naturally into a discussion of marketing. By integrating so many diverse elements, Hill has produced a new analysis of Cherokee basketry and created a landmark work in ecological, social, and art history. All levels.—*M. J. Schneider, University of North Dakota*

OAB-2482   E169   96-34982 CIP
Howe, Daniel Walker. **Making the American self: Jonathan Edwards to Abraham Lincoln.** Harvard, 1997. 342p index afp ISBN 0-674-16555-1, $39.95

Since the mid-1970s, students of American culture have sought painstakingly to decode the complex relationships between self and society in American life and letters. Howe (Oxford) offers a fresh and highly insightful perspective on the genesis of the secular creed of the "self-made" person in the 18th- and 19th-century US. Tracing the American quest for the ideal self through the variegated manifestations of the "balanced character" and "faculty psychology" in the writings of Franklin, Edwards, Lincoln, Frederick Douglass, Margaret Fuller, Thoreau, and others, Howe's work emerges as a major study on the roots of American individualism. Despite its brevity, his analysis of the ideal self promoted in the US Constitution and "The Federalist Papers" is among the most insightful approaches in over a decade on this topic. This book is must reading for all serious students of US intellectual and cultural history concerned with the nature of individualism in American life. Upper-division undergraduates and above.—*R. J. Lettieri, Mount Ida College*

OAB-2483   E302x   94-71935 Orig
Huang, Nian-Sheng. **Benjamin Franklin in American thought and culture, 1790-1990.** American Philosophical Society, 1994. 270p bibl index (Memoirs of the American Philosophical Society, 211) ISBN 0-87169-211-2, $25.00

Huang (Bentley College) has given us a valuable study on what history has made of Benjamin Franklin rather than the history Benjamin Franklin made. Studies in this reflexive historical genre are held to refract the cultural context of the subject also, thus illuminating both. As is the current fashion today, Huang's study embraces popular as well as "highbrow" culture. The study is divided into three sections, by time periods. The first three chapters (1790-1860) emphasize on Franklin's character or inner virtues and the esteem in which

he was held by most Americans. Chapters 4-6 (1870-1938) focuses on the shift from character to personality or those outer qualities that distinguished Franklin's behavior. Chapters 7-8 (1945-1990) show Franklin's image split between character and personality. Huang finds Franklin more representative of American culture than either Washington or Jefferson, inasmuch as Franklin exemplifies the self-made man and personifies the American dream. The text is enhanced with 53 illustrations, critical footnotes, bibliography, and a detailed index. General and academic readers, upper-division undergraduate and up.—*M. L. Dolan, Northern Michigan University*

OAB-2484   F351   93-35723 CIP
Hudson, John C. **Making the Corn Belt: a geographical history of middle-western agriculture.** Indiana, 1994. 254p index afp ISBN 0-253-32832-2, $35.00

The Corn Belt is America's heartland. Its farmers produce a cornucopia of grain and animal products to feed the nation's population with enough surplus for substantial exports to world markets. Hudson (Northwestern Univ.) has traced this region's geographical and agricultural evolution and presents his findings in a compellingly written volume that will become a standard reference on the development of Middle Western agriculture. The practice of producing corn to fatten livestock for sale to meat packers, the predominant mode of farming that came to define the Corn Belt region by the late 1800s, began in five contributing agricultural cradles: the Nashville Basin, Pennyroyal Plateau, Bluegrass region, Miami Valley, and Virginia Military District. Migrants from these areas moved into southern Ohio, Indiana, and Illinois and by the 1830s and '40s were driving fattened stock to the region's riverside meat packers. Hudson places the development of hybrid corn seed and swine breeds within the context of the physical environment as an appropriate venue for farming. Excellent bibliography and maps. An essential acquisition for all academic libraries and for public libraries serving readers interested in Middle Western life and economy.—*K. B. Raitz, University of Kentucky*

OAB-2485   HV9950   95-52170 CIP
Hutchinson, Earl Ofari. **Betrayed: a history of presidential failure to protect black lives.** Westview, 1996. 262p bibl index afp ISBN 0-8133-2465-3, $27.00; ISBN 0-8133-2466-1 pbk, $14.95

Betrayed is a memorable historical study of a much neglected and too frequently sensationalized subject: racial violence in America. Hutchinson provides the most thorough analysis to date of presidential policy regarding acts of racial terrorism against African Americans during the 20th century. His extensive research into the public and private papers of American presidents from Harding through Bush reveals a general historical pattern of official indifference by the White House regarding African American victims of race crimes, despite statuary authorization to prosecute such crimes since the 1870s. Each chapter offers a synoptic overview of the actions/inactions of each presidential officeholder, and prudently includes two to three detailed historical case studies starting with the post-WW I lynchings of blacks through the Rodney King/Los Angeles uprisings. The result is the strongest iconoclastic historical work to directly challenge the myth of presidential guardianship of black citizens against racially motivated attacks. This exceptionally well written scholarly work is recommended to all readers concerned about the recent increase in racial hate crimes. All levels.—*R. J. Lettieri, Mount Ida College*

OAB-2486   DS148   94-37932 CIP
Hyman, Paula E. **Gender and assimilation in modern Jewish history: the roles and representation of women.** Washington, 1995. 197p bibl index afp ISBN 0-295-97425-7, $30.00; ISBN 0-295-97426-5 pbk, $14.95

In this highly important, lucidly written study, Hyman, (Yale), a pioneer of the contemporary Jewish women's movement, reconsiders central themes of modern Jewish history from a gendered perspective. Carefully distinguishing the "process" of assimilation from the "project" of assimilation, and western Jewry, from East European Jewry, she argues that in each case men and women met modernity's challenges differently, transforming in the process both gender roles and the way women and Judaism are represented. In her chapter "America, Freedom, and Assimilation," Hyman brilliantly synthesizes recent literature, weakening only in her discussion of synagogue life and in her analysis of the origins of sisterhoods. Her provocative final chapter, "The Sexual Politics of Jewish Identity," is more speculative and less persuasive. Concern over declining manliness, for example, needs to be placed in comparative perspective; it is by no means confined to Jews and antisemites alone. No student of modern Jewry can ignore this work. Even if some of its points are disputed, its central thesis "that to be valid an examination of the processes of Jewish assimilation in the modern and contemporary periods must include women and gender in its design" is masterfully proven. All levels.—*J. D. Sarna, Brandeis University*

OAB-2487   F591   93-38244 CIP
Jacobs, Wilbur R. **On Turner's trail: 100 years of writing western history.** University Press of Kansas, 1994. 342p index afp ISBN 0-7006-0616-5, $35.00

From a master historian—author of two previous books about Frederick Jackson Turner, of studies of Francis Parkman, and of work in frontier history—*On Turner's Trail* is one of the most important contributions in recent years to American historiography. Complementing not only Jacobs's own earlier works on Turner, but also Ray A. Billington's biographical *Frederick Jackson Turner* (CH, Jun'73) and Richard Hofstadter's *The Progressive Historians* (1968), it adds to a penetrating analysis of the development of Turner's thought a searching consideration of the influence of his ideas, an investigation of the advocacy and criticism that they have sparked, and an estimate of their enduring importance. In five sections plus an epilogue, Jacobs treats, in turn, the youthful Turner and his famous 1893 frontier essay, his later elaboration of sectionalism as a related master explanatory theory, his unpublished writings about the 20th century, his influence as a teacher, and the "story of the new western history rebels" who seek to supplant him: Richard White, Patricia Nelson Limerick, and others. A carefully reasoned epilogue offers "the inescapable conclusion ... that after one hundred years Turner remains the most influential of American historians, among the best and brightest that we have produced." Handsomely produced and illustrated, with endnotes, index, and appendixes. Both general and academic readers, upper-division undergraduate and up.—*D. W. Steeples, Mercer University*

OAB-2488   TT835   92-43108 CIP
Kansas quilts & quilters, by Barbara Brackman et al. University Press of Kansas, 1993. 206p index afp ISBN 0-7006-0584-3, $40.00; ISBN 0-7006-0585-1 pbk, $22.50

Presented here is a portion of the material gathered as part of the Kansas Quilt Project. Organized in 1986, the Project has focused on collecting information about Kansas quilts and quiltmakers, encouraging the preservation and proper care of quilts, and heightening public appreciation of the art of quiltmaking. Like similar projects across the US, one goal of the Kansas Project was to produce a richly illustrated volume about quilting in Kansas. Contributors explore the role of quilts in the historical as well as contemporary life of the state, examine types of quilts associated with specific groups of Kansas residents or that are particularly popular in Kansas, and trace the impact of certain individuals on the art and practice of quiltmaking in Kansas as well as the country as a whole. Well researched and well written, the volume represents an important contribution to quilt history as well as to the history of American women. It is also an excellent example of how the analysis of material culture can enhance the understanding of an area's historical experience. All levels.—*P. Melvin, Loyola University*

OAB-2489   HT168   91-43645 CIP
Kennedy, Lawrence W. **Planning the city upon a hill: Boston since 1630.** Massachusetts, 1992. 314p bibl index ISBN 0-87023-780-2, $27.50

Kennedy's well-illustrated and lively account of Boston's planning history is destined to take its place among the best scholarly works that have been published on this remarkable city. Nine meticulously researched, highly readable chapters draw on a wealth of materials that vividly bring to life key developments that shaped each period of Boston's growth. Acknowledging the masterful earlier work by Walter Muir Whitehill, *Boston: A Topographical History* (1947), Kennedy focuses much of his attention on the post-WW II era to bring the story of Boston's built environment into the 1990s. He is successful in this effort and his analysis is a major contribution not only to the multidisciplinary fields of urban planning and urban studies but also to the appropriate related disciplines of geography, history, and political science. The well-chosen maps, diagrams, and photos decidedly enhance the text; the overall production job is first rate. The very useful 50 pages of appendixes cover the timeline of Boston planning, population trends, research notes, and the most thorough bibliography of the subject published in many years. Highly recommended for college and university social science collections and for public libraries throughout New England. All levels.—*P. O. Muller, University of Miami*

OAB-2490   KF9449   94-13292 CIP
Langum, David J. **Crossing over the line: legislating morality and the Mann Act.** Chicago, 1994. 311p index afp ISBN 0-226-46880-1, $24.95

Langum's book is a competent and fascinating history of the infamous Mann Act, the White Slave Trade Act of 1910, which declared it a federal crime to transport women across state lines "for immoral purposes." The act was originally a Progressive effort at social reform designed to strike a blow at the socially destructive practice of prostitution, but its enforcement soon transformed the act into an engine of governmental oppression and mindless moralism. The problem stemmed from failure to define the nature of the "immoral purpose" to be combated; by 1917 the Supreme Court determined that the Department of Justice could prosecute even those who traveled to enjoy consensual sex. Langum shows how this interpretation of the act helped J. Edgar Hoover to transform the FBI into a national police force. He then describes the government's decision to focus on commercial sex and, in the 1970s and '80s, to amend the act to include the transportation of males, bringing it into line with the revolution in sexual behavior in the US. This is a model of good narrative history, sound legal and political analysis, and straightforward exposition. General readers through graduate students.—*S. N. Katz, American Council of Learned Societies*

OAB-2491   E98   91-15666 CIP
Lincoln, Kenneth. **Indi'n humor: bicultural play in native America.** Oxford, 1993. 387p bibl index afp ISBN 0-19-506887-4, $39.95

An impressive work that covers an area long neglected by scholars, namely, the folk and literary humor of Native Americans. It will, without doubt, become the defining treatise on the subject for many decades to come. Drawing on literary theory, textual analysis, and sociocultural schema as well as on his own personal connection, Lincoln presents a sweeping picture that relies heavily on both oral and scripted laughter. It is criminal that pejorative stereotyping—symbolized by the "Cigar Store Indian," the carved wooden figure that stood in front of stores for many decades—has long obscured the vital role that humor played in Native American daily life. Lincoln, who was raised in Nebraska and adopted into the Oglala Sioux tribe, refutes this stereotype. He argues, "Not only do Indians bond and revitalize, scapegoat and survive through laughter, but they draw on millennia-old traditions of Trickster gods and holy fools, comic romance and epic boast. There is, and always has been, humor among Indians—and some five hundred tribal variants in the contiguous United States, locally indigenous to climate and geography, genetics and history." This study will take its place among the major works in cultural and humor studies. All levels.—*J. Boskin, Boston University*

OAB-2492   F128   92-31989 CIP
Markowitz, Fran. **A community in spite of itself: Soviet Jewish**

émigrés in New York. Smithsonian Institution Press, 1993. 317p bibl index afp ISBN 1-56098-200-4, $58.75; ISBN 1-56098-225-X pbk, $23.95

Markowitz has produced an excellent study of the sociology and psychology of the Russian American immigrant and of the travails of assimilation into a new and foreign culture. Her study includes a fine bibliography that covers Jewish life in the former Russian Empire, sources in English and Russian, and a wide range of materials that contributes to a broad overview of the subject. Both the text and appendixes are meticulously annotated. A large portion of the book describes the conflict and clash of expectations between the immigrants and their earlier Russian-Jewish predecessors and American-born relatives. Markowitz analyzes the bases for individual depression, such as not being adequately adept in English for occupational purposes and differences in values systems. She describes the immigrants' initial euphoria and its eventual passing, as various cultural groups formed. Although those who remained became Americans, many remembered and attempted to retain their European cultural values. General; undergraduate; graduate; faculty.—*A. K. Steinberg, Livingstone College*

OAB-2493　　　　　F417　　　　　95-14859 CIP
McNeil, W.K. **Ozark country.** University Press of Mississippi, 1995. 194p bibl index afp ISBN 0-87805-728-5, $40.00; ISBN 0-87805-729-3 pbk, $16.95

McNeil, folklorist at the Ozark Folk Center, provides a concise yet richly textured overview of Ozark regional folk culture that emphasizes complexity and dynamics of traditional life and expression over romanticization. This work joins R. Gerald Alvey's *Kentucky Bluegrass Country* (1992) and William Montell's *Upper Cumberland Country* (1993) as studies of folk cultural regions. In its breadth of coverage and conceptual framework, McNeil's book may be one of the strongest of these. He begins with a historical overview and discusses the social bases of the regional culture in family and work, with special reference to craft and architectural traditions. He then surveys customs, stories, and games. Especially extensive is the chapter on folk music, a forté for McNeil who has published several books on southern folk songs and ballads. For those interested in the preservation and presentation of this folk culture, McNeil includes a description of the work of the Ozark Folk Center in Mountain View, Arkansas, "probably the largest facility in the country concerned with the traditional culture of a particular region," according to McNeil. The richly detailed index will be useful to researchers. A refreshing combination of scholarship and engaging reading, this book is a capstone work in the substantial bookshelf available on Ozark regional culture and a significant contribution to regional American studies generally. Notes and bibliographic essay. All levels.—*S. J. Bronner, Pennsylvania State University at Harrisburg*

OAB-2494　　　　　E78　　　　　94-23557 CIP
Meredith, Howard. **Dancing on common ground: tribal cultures and alliances on the Southern Plains.** University Press of Kansas, 1995. 218p bibl index afp ISBN 0-7006-0694-7, $29.95

Focusing on the Wichita, Comanche, Kiowa, Apache, Caddo, Delaware, Cheyenne, and Arapaho of the southern Plains, Meredith uses both native voices and traditional scholarly sources to envision their past. He examines their spirituality, economics, aesthetics, and political structures, and focuses on their peaceful and creative interaction with each other and their environment. The author carefully chronicles the history of Indian-white relations up to the present, highlighting government legislation and economic programs. Finally, he makes specific recommendations concerning Native American peoples and for governmental agencies, based on a responsible trust relationship with the federal government, increased self-governance, and enhanced intertribal relations. Although the first part may seem romanticized and its language sometimes problematic for a Western scholar, this work is not simply conventional historiography but a rapprochement with native understandings of their own past and present. For those interested in alternative forms of history as well as in Western analyses of governmental Indian policy, history, anthropology, and Indian studies. All levels.—*R. A. Bucko, Le Moyne College*

OAB-2495　　　　　GF504　　　　　95-32495 CIP
Morehouse, Barbara J. **A place called Grand Canyon: contested geographies.** Arizona, 1996. 202p bibl index afp ISBN 0-8165-1603-0, $40.00; ISBN 0-8165-1628-6 pbk, $19.95

Much has been written about the Grand Canyon, and its aura radiates even in the minds of those who have never seen it. Morehouse, a geographer, examined what she calls the "Greater Grand Canyon," an area that extends beyond the traditional boundaries of the park and includes five Native American reservations, as well as other settlements and lands administered by federal and state agencies. This volume is a wonderful contribution to the literature of historical geography. It should also be read by historians, environmentalists, and rural land use planners. Morehouse chronicles the various stages of the region's settlement patterns, from the early Native American presence, to the country's westward expansion, to the conditions that exist today. She explores with skill and insight the influence of various settlers on the region and the role the physical environment played in its development. This book is as much about changes that have taken place there over time as it is about relationships that have developed among the peoples inhabiting the territory. A valuable bibliography of primary and secondary sources complements the text. Upper-division undergraduates and above.—*L. Yacher, Southern Connecticut State University*

OAB-2496　　　　　JV6471　　　　　92-8934 CIP
Muller, Thomas. **Immigrants and the American city.** New York University, 1993. 372p index ISBN 0-8147-5479-1, $30.00

Using as his theme the tension between the need of American cities for foreign-born workers and the nativism that their presence provokes, Muller reviews the patterns of immigration and immigration restriction in US history. With superb use of a variety of analytical tools, Muller amply demonstrates that immigration did a great deal to create the economic and social vitality of America's "gateway cities," while immigration restriction, coupled with middle-class flight to the suburbs, contributed to the rapid deterioration of those same centers after the 1920s. The increase in and changing nature of immigration after the 1960s has once again made the cities into immigrant centers, with positive results in business and job creation and the revitalization of whole neighborhoods. Although the cities have paid a price, especially in conflict between immigrants and domestic minorities, Muller argues the benefits accrued have been far more substantial than the costs. Essential for all collections on immigration and urban or recent US history. Advanced undergraduate; graduate; faculty.—*L. M. Lees, Old Dominion University*

OAB-2497　　　　　F805　　　　　91-50867 CIP
Nostrand, Richard L. **The Hispano homeland.** Oklahoma, 1992. 281p bibl index afp ISBN 0-8061-2414-8, $29.95

Through the use of a wide range of resources and statistical data, Nostrand supports his definition of a Hispano homeland. His argument contends that the Hispanos are Spanish Americans centered in New Mexico who first settled the area late in the 16th century and have remained there. During a span of nearly four centuries, Nostrand explains, these Americans "adjusted to their natural environment, stamped it with their cultural impress, and created from their natural and cultural surroundings an identity with time and place." The result was the creation of a Hispano homeland. Excellent maps, informative tables, and well-argued prose highlight this outstanding contribution to historical geography. The book should be a model for similar studies by scholars who wish to identify and to illuminate other rich and persistent subcultures. This publication is especially recommended for upper-level undergraduate and graduate students; it should be added to any basic collection in historical geography and particularly those pertaining to the American Southwest.—*J. H. O'Donnell III, Marietta College*

OAB-2498　　　　　E457　　　　　93-1675 CIP
Peterson, Merrill D. **Lincoln in American memory.** Oxford, 1994. 482p index afp ISBN 0-19-506570-0, $30.00

A dramatic assassination created the myth of Abraham Lincoln that became a vibrant and enduring presence in the American consciousness. Identifying five major archetypes—the savior of the Union, the great emancipator, the man of the people, the first American, and the self-made man—Peterson follows the interweaving of these themes from 1864 to the present while surveying a great mass of Lincolniana. Acclaimed for his study *The Jefferson Image in the American Mind* (1960), Peterson (emeritus, Univ. of Virginia) presents a panoramic view of an evolving and revolving Lincoln image. Historians, politicians, and hustlers crowd these encyclopedic pages, all contending for a Lincoln who may elude their grasp yet may remain worthy of pursuit. Lincoln became an idol to blacks and to white supremacists, to Christians and to unbelievers, to conservatives and to radicals, and to a host of others who molded Lincoln to their own predilections. Scholars and biographers, not exempt from waves of popular thought, contributed to the national preoccupation with celebrating and revivifying a Lincoln transformed into a reluctant contemporary. Never before has the Lincoln image received such comprehensive coverage. Whether read as a work of solid scholarship or as a delightful romp through a garden of mythology—and it is both—this book will serve readers in libraries at all levels.—*J. Y. Simon, Southern Illinois University-Carbondale*

OAB-2499   E169   92-41003 CIP
Piersen, William D. **Black legacy: America's hidden heritage.** Massachusetts, 1993. 264p index ISBN 0-87023-854-X, $40.00; ISBN 0-87023-859-0 pbk, $14.95

For more than two decades, scholars have been identifying African contributions to America's cultural mix (e.g., John W. Blassingame's *The Slave Community*, CH, Apr'73). None, however, has done so thorough a job as Piersen in illustrating how fully the cultures of African America and Euramerica have blended. Piersen draws on an impressive array of evidence—folktales, religious rituals, oral traditions, music, and written accounts—to assess the significance of African and African American culture in shaping the American South. The Afrocentric insight leads to a compelling case for the South as a melting pot in which African and European cultural traditions merged to a degree far greater than has usually been recognized. Some readers may find that Piersen exaggerates the importance of African influences, but few can question that his Afrocentric perspective advances understanding of the significance of the black legacy in shaping the cultural meld of America. This thought-provoking study by an experienced, able scholar is well written and fully documented (58 pages of footnotes). Highly recommended. General; advanced undergraduate; graduate; faculty.—*R. Detweiler, California State University, Dominguez Hills*

OAB-2500   HO767   96-22568 CIP
Reagan, Leslie J. **When abortion was a crime: women, medicine, and law in the United States, 1867-1973.** California, 1997. 387p bibl index afp ISBN 0-520-08848-4, $29.95

Using a wide range of primary sources, Reagan provides a meticulously and creatively researched analysis of the century between the criminalization of abortion and the Supreme Court decision that legalized it. For most of this era, physicians and other practitioners provided abortion services safely and often openly. One of the great strengths of this book is its extensive treatment of the conflict between specialists (who opposed abortion) and general practitioners (who often provided them). Another is its nuanced analysis of the physician-patient relationship, which Reagan describes as "a negotiated terrain between physicians and patients." Nevertheless, because abortion was illegal, women were never safe. Friends and families of women who had died after an abortion often faced police harassment. And particularly in the repressive period that followed WW II, clients of abortionists might find themselves publicly humiliated. This balanced and sophisticated study of the experience of illegal abortion in the US belongs on the shelves of legal scholars, feminists, historians of women and of medicine, and medical practitioners who deal with reproductive problems. All levels.—*M. Marsh, Temple University*

OAB-2501   F59   96-791 CIP
Shalhope, Robert E. **Bennington and the Green Mountain Boys:**

the emergence of liberal democracy in Vermont, 1760-1850. Johns Hopkins, 1996. 412p bibl index afp ISBN 0-8018-5335-4, $49.95

Shalhope, author of *Sterling Price: Portrait of a Southerner* (CH, Jan'72); *John Taylor of Caroline: Pastoral Republican* (CH, May'81); and *The Roots of Democracy* (1990) argues that market capitalism transformed Bennington, Vermont, from an egalitarian frontier community in 1760 to a hierarchical liberal democratic community 90 years later. Bennington's first settlers were fiercely democratic localists epitomized by the Green Mountain Boys of Revolutionary War fame. Following the Revolution, "downhill" merchants seeking a more hierarchical and deferential society challenged the primacy of "uphill" Bennington's traditional leaders. These and other issues bitterly divided the town until market changes forced local yeomen to become petty capitalists. This transformation forged a midcentury consensus among a new elite, who embraced liberal democracy and its capitalist ethos while adopting the radically democratic Green Mountain Boys as their symbol. Interestingly written and meticulously researched, this fine work greatly enhances understanding of how communities changed during this period. Supplements Michael Bellesiles's *Revolutionary Outlaws* (CH, Feb'94) and Randolph Roth's *The Democratic Dilemma* (CH, Jul'88) in providing a more comprehensive view of Vermont in this period. Upper-division undergraduates and above.—*J. C. Arndt, James Madison University*

OAB-2502   F811   94-18712 CIP
Sheridan, Thomas E. **Arizona: a history.** Arizona, 1995. 434p bibl index afp ISBN 0-8165-1056-3, $50.00; ISBN 0-8165-1515-8 pbk, $24.95

In this well-written and innovative study, Sheridan (curator at the Arizona State Museum) links the history of a single southwestern state to larger national and international events that have affected its development. Beginning with a discussion of paleo-Indians on a mammoth hunt and ending with timely issues such as the Central Arizona Project for water utilization and passage of the 1993 North American Free Trade Agreement (NAFTA), the author has established a balanced treatment of all time periods and subtopics. He has also wisely articulated contrasting viewpoints offered by competing and interacting groups, and his extensive bibliographic essay directs readers to sources of alternative interpretations. Sheridan declares that Arizona's history "is not a linear progression from wilderness to civilization. Instead it is a series of advances and retreats, accommodations and blunders, booms and busts." To capture the essence of the state, he divides its history into three phases. First, the lengthy incorporation phase ranged from early Indian, Spanish, and Mexican interactions until the 1880s, when the US government established a unified dominion over the region. Second, the extraction phase began when railroads penetrated the Southwest and tied cattle, cotton, and minerals to a larger American marketplace. It also witnessed a heightening of class and racial tensions. Third, the transformation phase brought an expanded role for the federal government, a growing economy, and rapid urbanization during the past 60 years. Recommended for college, university, and public libraries.—*M. L. Tate, University of Nebraska at Omaha*

OAB-2503   E99   94-27890 MARC
Snow, Dean R. **The Iroquois.** Blackwell, 1994. 268p bibl index afp ISBN 1-55786-225-7, $24.95

In this informative and highly readable study, Snow has produced an impressive synthesis of Iroquois history from its antecedents in Northeastern Archaic cultures to the present. The text blends archaeological, historical, and oral traditions into a tapestry of the significant role the Iroquois have played, and continue to play, in American society. What is most impressive is Snow's ability to juxtapose Iroquois oral tradition and cultural meanings with modern scientific analysis and data without patronizing or idealizing either one. This book is more than just a survey. Scholars will find much to ponder in Snow's revisionist analysis of a wide range of issues, including a critique of the in situ thesis of Iroquois origins, a richly textured analysis of Iroquois demographic patterns, a rebuttal to the common claim that the US Constitution rests on the Founding Fathers' understanding of the Iroquois League, and an unflinching view of the difficulties facing Iroquois peoples today. Snow's work complements and in some areas supersedes the treatment of the Iroquois in volume 15 of the *Handbook of North American Indians*, ed. by Bruce Trigger (CH, Jul'79). All levels.—*R. L. Haan, Hartwick College*

OAB-2504   E184   92-33491 CIP
Takaki, Ronald. **A different mirror: a history of multicultural America.** Little, Brown, 1993. 508p index ISBN 0-316-83112-3, $27.95

Set in the context of Anglo thought and action, Takaki brilliantly traces the history of a multicultural US from the initial English settlements to the present. He focuses specifically on the experiences of seven groups: Native Americans, and Americans of African, Irish, Jewish, Mexican, Chinese, and Japanese ancestry. He also pays careful attention to gender, and contrasts the varied roles different ethnic women played in the migration process. Although Anglos denied citizenship to racial minorities and generally harrassed non-Anglo European immigrants, Takaki demonstrates that each group drew on its inner resources to resist oppression. If they adapted to American society, they also profoundly changed that society in the process. The framework is more metaphorical than analytical and each group's treatment is somewhat eclectic, but Takaki effectively demonstrates the centrality of race and ethnicity to the American experience as well as the importance of a multicultural approach to understand that history. Very well written and researched, this is a powerful story that is highly recommended for all audiences.—*J. Borchert, Cleveland State University*

OAB-2505   HT123   92-19931 CIP
Teaford, Jon C. **Cities of the heartland: the rise and fall of the industrial Midwest.** Indiana, 1993. 300p index afp ISBN 0-253-35786-1, $39.95

This is the best available study of midwestern cities of the US from the 1830s to the 1980s. Teaford (Purdue Univ.) has included cities of all sizes and types, from Akron, Ann Arbor, and Aurora, to Wyandotte, Youngstown, and Zanesville. Minneapolis, Omaha, Des Moines, and Kansas City are excluded, but St. Louis is well covered. Teaford, an authority on city government, handles that aspect of urban history well. He is also strong on boosterism, economic structures, labor relations, ethnicity, social life, and high culture. Transportation, education, and federal relations, however, are given cursory coverage. The last pages rely on current newspapers and periodicals, and the sections on labor use some government documents. Otherwise, the author depends on scores of scholarly articles and monographs, plus numerous old-fashioned multivolume urban biographies. Combined with the author's clear writing style and keen insight on how cities actually work, the result is an attractive synthesis that will find its way onto many syllabi. All levels.—*R. Jensen, University of Illinois at Chicago*

OAB-2506   E445   96-13735 CIP
Williams, William H. **Slavery and freedom in Delaware, 1639-1865.** SR Books, 1996. 270p bibl index afp ISBN 0-8420-2594-4, $50.00

Of the 15 southern slave states, Delaware is the only one without a full scholarly account of African Americans before emancipation in 1865. Williams, an experienced historian of Delaware, ably corrects that with this well-researched, well-crafted study. Delaware was linked to the South because of its large number of slaves from the 18th century forward, yet it was on the periphery and many aspects of the lives of African Americans, slave and free alike, resembled those of the mid-Atlantic states. The white community there, however, took extraordinary measures to control free blacks. With the largest proportion of free African Americans in the nation, Delaware implemented harsh black codes and coercive policies for freemen. Powerful white resistance and deep-seated racism were a part of Delaware's slave legacy well beyond the Civil War. Nonetheless, Delaware's African Americans built a determined culture through independent black churches and reconstituted families. This culture persisted even when hope for racial justice faded. Williams's study is based on extensive use of primary and secondary sources; each chapter is fully documented. There is a good bibliography, and numerous illustrations and photographs. Williams writes in a clear, straightforward style and brings considerable interpretation

to a storehouse of information. A fine addition to university or public libraries with collections on African American culture. Upper-division undergraduates and above.—*R. Detweiler, California State University, Dominguez Hills*

OAB-2507   KF8205   93-9804 CIP
Wunder, John R. **"Retained by the people": a history of American Indians and the Bill of Rights.** Oxford, 1994. 278p indexes afp ISBN 0-19-505562-4, $45.00; ISBN 0-19-505563-2 pbk, $15.95

Wunder's work constitutes the first single-volume study of the history of the constitutional rights of Native Americans, from the ratification of the Bill of Rights in 1791 to the present. Wunder capably blends evidence from legal studies, history, and anthropology to demonstrate the complex manner in which the American constitutional system has denied the application of the Bill of Rights to Native Americans per se, both collectively and individually. Although the study begins with an assessment of the contrasting theories of rights between Europeans and indigenous peoples in 1492, the book's main focus is on the definitive court cases and governmental policies of the 20th century that posited Native Americans in their precarious and unique status within the American legal system. Wunder's analysis provides a sorely needed broad historical context to properly explore the political meanings of the ongoing Native American legal struggles for self-determination and individual liberty. Upper-division undergraduates and above.—*R. J. Lettieri, Mount Ida College*

UNITED STATES —
Colonial & 18th Century

OAB-2508   E342   95-14369 CIP
Banning, Lance. **The sacred fire of liberty: James Madison and the founding of the Federal Republic.** Cornell, 1995. 543p index afp ISBN 0-8014-3152-2, $35.00

Banning's first-rate study portrays James Madison as a dedicated revolutionary and provides a close examination of his political ideas against the twin backdrops of changing historical interpretations and the actual events of the federal period. It is not a biography but a reconsideration of Madison's theories of government, and focuses on the period 1780-1792. Banning places Madison and his ideas firmly at the center of the debate over the framing of the federal government, and argues that he was very much the "father of the Constitution." In the process, he rejects the argument that Madison repudiated his earlier revolutionary thought and swung to the "right" during the 1780s. Rather, according to Banning, even as Madison's founding vision evolved during that turbulent decade, he remained determined throughout to retain a "genuinely revolutionary order." Madison began as a strict constructionist and remained one throughout the entire period. Whether or not readers agree, Banning's arguments are compelling. A must purchase for academic libraries. Upper-division undergraduates and above.—*J. Andrew, Franklin and Marshall College*

OAB-2509   E83   94-28669 CIP
Calloway, Colin G. **The American Revolution in Indian country: crisis and diversity in Native American communities.** Cambridge, 1995. 327p index ISBN 0-521-47149-4, $59.95; ISBN 0-521-47569-4 pbk, $16.95

Using villages such as Stockbridge in Massachusetts and Niagara in New York as case studies, Calloway illustrates the Indian social experience during and after the Revolutionary War. He shows that Native American groups pursued different strategies and reacted differently to Revolutionary conditions, yet after independence, these diverse communities suffered a common fate of subjugation. American Indians, like Colonial Americans, were loyalists, patriots, and neutrals. Similarly, like Colonial towns, Indian communities experienced different degrees of family, generational, and political tension. Nonetheless, throughout Indian country rituals were abandoned, authority challenged, and traditional alliances tried. Emphasis on the home front rather than the battlefield distinguishes Calloway's study from more traditional works on Native Americans and the Revolution. The author's community approach produces the first thorough treatment of American Indians as something more than revolutionary warriors. The book is beautifully written and extremely well documented. Highly recommended for academic collections. All levels.—*R. J. Palin, St. Thomas University*

OAB-2510   F389   92-6116 CIP
Chipman, Donald E. **Spanish Texas, 1519-1821.** Texas, 1992. 343p bibl index afp ISBN 0-292-77656-X, $30.00; ISBN 0-292-77659-4 pbk, $14.95

Chipman's impressive examination of Spanish Texas begins with a review of the land and its native inhabitants, proceeds chronologically with early explorations and settlements, and ends with Texas's passage from Spanish to Mexican rule. An enlightening discussion of the varied legacies of the Spanish experience concludes this well-researched study. Chipman pays particular attention to the establishment of missions and garrisons and their checkered histories. He places the efforts to colonize Texas within a broad historical context that includes salient developments in Mexico and Spain's rivalry with France and England. Although Spanish Texas had fewer than 4,000 settlers, the region served as an important buffer against foreign expansion. Chipman carefully considers attempts to colonize East and West Texas, noting the different pressures on each region. His narrative favors political and institutional developments, but also addresses ranching, farming, trade, and social change over time. Clearly written and well illustrated, the study draws on both a broad range of secondary materials and archival primary sources. The best one-volume treatment of Spanish Texas available, this book should be in all college and university libraries. General; advanced undergraduate; graduate; faculty.—*M. A. Burkholder, University of Missouri—St. Louis*

OAB-2511   F67   94-32658 CIP
Conroy, David W. **In public houses: drink & the revolution of authority in Colonial Massachusetts.** North Carolina, 1995. 351p bibl index afp ISBN 0-8078-2207-8, $39.95; ISBN 0-8078-4521-3 pbk, $15.95

In Public Houses is an extraordinary work of history that gracefully traces the origins, growth, and functions of these centers of collective drink during the first two centuries of American history. Conroy's principal aim is to show how taverns democratized Massachusetts's hierarchical political culture. Traditionally, under the watchful eyes of Puritan lawmakers and clergy, citizens drank, celebrated, and transacted business with the clink of glasses. Increasingly after 1719, they threw off traditional restraints and also gathered in taverns to discuss politics and raise opposition to Crown officials. By the 1760s, tavern keepers themselves, now selectmen and representatives to the General Court, helped lead the Revolution fomented in their places of business by their patrons. In addition to shedding new light on the nature, limits, and transformation of political power in Massachusetts, Conroy illuminates "changing consumer taste, gender roles, urbanization, and the expanding use of print." The book is also interpretively provocative, challenging conventional wisdom on the rigid distinction between oral and print culture, the anglicization of Massachusetts, and the influence of the Puritan ethic during the Revolution. All levels.—*E. W. Carp, Pacific Lutheran University*

OAB-2512   F864   93-38946 CIP
Crosby, Harry W. **Antigua California: mission and colony on the peninsular frontier, 1697-1768.** New Mexico, 1994. 556p bibl index ISBN 0-8263-1495-3, $37.50

Crosby provides a comprehensive survey of the Baja California missions (as colonial Antigua California is known today) from their foundings by the Jesuit order in the late 1600s until the 1760s, when the expulsion of that religious order from New Spain ended the missionary era. The story begins with the efforts of Father Kino to expand the northwestern mission field from Sonora across to Antigua California, continues with the initial foundings of the other missions by Father Salvatierra, and thereafter chronicles the establishment of the other missions. Crosby also notes the founding of civil and military settlements. The narrative describes daily life in the missions, the structures of governance, and the relationships of the friars to civil government. This book is a solid example of the tradi-

tional institutional history familiar to readers of Spanish borderlands literature in that it deals with frontier expansion and the mission as a frontier institution, and keeps its main focus on matters relating to the church as a secular organization. Crosby uses an extensive and impressive array of primary and secondary sources. This work should quickly become the standard study of the history of the Baja California missions during the 18th century. General readers, undergraduates, graduate students.—*L. T. Cummins, Austin College*

OAB-2513   KFC3691   95-20116 CIP
Dayton, Cornelia Hughes. **Women before the bar: gender, law, and society in Connecticut, 1639-1789.** North Carolina, 1995. 382p bibl index afp ISBN 0-8078-2244-2, $49.95; ISBN 0-8078-4561-2 pbk, $18.95

Dayton's pioneering study adeptly serves as a creative lynchpin convening the subfields of American legal history, women's studies, and social history. Her thoroughly researched analysis of women's participation in and treatment by pre-19th century Connecticut courts provides one of the richest and most insightful accounts of early American legal culture in years. Through her textured blending of individual case studies and quantitative analysis, Dayton depicts the transition from 17th-century Puritanism to 18th-century republicanism as one of lost rights, disempowerment, and status declension for New Haven women. Her survey of 150 years of legal actions regarding debt, divorce, sexual assault, adultery, and slander reveals that the New Haven legal system regressed from serving as an inclusive and egalitarian community forum for Puritan women to a hardened and exclusive patriarchal bureaucracy by the 1740s. Dayton's book successfully stations the study of the American legal system at the epicenter of the history of gender and social change in New England. This well-written work is recommended to all serious students of early American history. Upper-division undergraduates and above.—*R. J. Lettieri, Mount Ida College*

OAB-2514   E125   92-31504 CIP
The De Soto chronicles: the expedition of Hernando De Soto to North America in 1539-1543, ed. by Lawrence A. Clayton, Vernon James Knight, and Edward C. Moore. Alabama, 1993. 2v. 569, 588p bibl indexes afp ISBN 0-8173-0593-9, $50.00

A rich, readable contribution to De Soto studies that commemorates the 450th anniversary of the ill-fated explorer's odyssey through the present southeastern US and Texas. These translations of the four primary accounts of the venture, with new notes and introductions, make valuable historical and ethnographical information easily available and accessible to both scholars and general readers. The accounts are by A Gentleman from Elvas, Luys Hernández de Biedma, Rodrigo Rangel, and Garcilaso de la Vega. The translation of Hernández de Biedma is new and that of Garcilaso de la Vega, which occupies nearly all of volume 2, has not been published previously. Translated documents related to De Soto include his will, the royal contract to undertake the conquest of Florida, and a list of his assets following his death. A brief biographical sketch of De Soto by historian Paul E. Hoffman dispels the myth that De Soto was a uniquely humane conquistador, while another sketch by Rocío Sánchez Rubio provides an introduction to the nature of the conquistadors. All academic libraries and larger pulic libraries should purchase this exceptionally valuable compilation.—*M. A. Burkholder, University of Missouri—St Louis*

OAB-2515   E310   92-33660 CIP
Elkins, Stanley. **The age of federalism,** by Stanley Elkins and Eric McKitrick. Oxford, 1993. 925p index afp ISBN 0-19-506890-4, $39.95

Drawing on the scholarship of the past few decades as well as on their own research, Elkins (Smith College) and McKitrick (Columbia Univ.) have produced a well-wrought narrative synthesis of the Federalist era. The authors survey the typical political, economic, social, diplomatic, and military issues of that decade when the leaders of the American Revolution turned to the task of establishing a new nation based on republican political principles. Interspersed throughout the narrative are biographical profiles of the leading figures as well as of many lesser ones. The authors try to reconstruct the psychological milieu of vituperative political rhetoric that characterized the period as they explore the Federalist vision of the new republic's future in contrast to the opposing Republican vision. Differences over economic and foreign policies gave birth to a nascent party system in which the opposition Republican party gained power in the election of 1800, and eclipsed the Federalists at the national level thereafter. This study replaces John C. Miller's *The Federalist Era, 1789-1801* (1960) as the standard account. For another perspective in a broader context see Paul A. Rahe's *Republics Ancient and Modern* (CH, Mar'93). Full, critical endnotes and a useful, descriptive index. General readers, undergraduates, and above.—*M. L. Dolan, Northern Michigan University*

OAB-2516   E276   96-36313 CIP
Gundersen, Joan R. **To be useful to the world: women in revolutionary America, 1740-1790.** Twayne/Prentice Hall International, 1996. 273p bibl index afp ISBN 0-8057-9916-8, $28.95

Scholars have disagreed as to whether the American Revolution was a positive or a negative force in shaping women's lives. Gundersen's excellent study makes a compelling case that the question is quite involved. She illustrates the complexity of the lives of Colonial women by comparing the households of Elizabeth Porter, part of a Virginia small farm family with a few slaves, Deborah Franklin, wife of Benjamin Franklin, and Margaret Brant, an Iroquois woman whose family remained loyal to the British during the Revolution. Gundersen demonstrates that class and ethnic forces made for powerful differences in the experiences of these women. She then traces the lives of their daughters and granddaughters, noting that the Revolution brought new opportunities for some women while it actually restricted the lives of others. Largely a synthesis of secondary accounts, the book is a first-rate example of scholarship. It is clearly written, fully documented (54 pages of footnotes and an excellent nine-page bibliographic essay), and includes illustrations. Highly recommended. General readers; upper-division undergraduates and above.—*R. Detweiler, California State University, Dominguez Hills*

OAB-2517   E185   91-46648 CIP
Hall, Gwendolyn Midlo. **Africans in Colonial Louisiana: the development of Afro-Creole culture in the eighteenth century.** Louisiana State, 1992. 434p index afp ISBN 0-8071-1686-6, $29.95

Hall, an experienced scholar of slavery and a painstaking researcher, has sifted through diverse original sources in Louisiana, France, and Spain to produce the first thorough account of Louisiana's Creole slave community. She demonstrates that Colonial Louisiana's Afro-Creole culture was truly distinctive, sustaining its own language, religious traditions, music, and folklore. Hall provides in-depth treatment of the ethnic origins of slaves in Africa; relations between Africans and Indians; the dynamic character of early Louisiana society and the place of Creole slaves in the broader economy and society; race mixing among Africans, Indians, and whites; the role of free blacks and maroon communities; and the evolution of Afro-Creole culture. Hall attributes the durability of Louisiana's Creole slave culture to the importation of slaves directly from Africa, the large size of the black population relative to the white population, and the strength of African cultural survival in the slave community. Hall writes clearly and her analyses are drawn closely. Extensive footnotes, tables, graphs, charts, figures, maps, appendixes, note on sources. Although the topic is specialized, this book makes a valuable contribution not only to the history of Louisiana but to the history of slavery and African Americans more broadly. Highly recommended. General; advanced undergraduate; graduate; faculty.—*R. Detweiler, California State University, Dominguez Hills*

OAB-2518   HE6185   95-20067 CIP
John, Richard R. **Spreading the news: the American postal system from Franklin to Morse.** Harvard, 1995. 369p bibl index afp ISBN 0-674-83338-4, $49.95

Even though the economic, social, cultural, and political consequences of improved communications are hard to overstate, they are also too easily taken for granted. This study outlines the progress and impact of postal services and public policies in the late 18th and early 19th centuries and thus broadens our understanding of those communications, institutions, and public policies. John (Univ. of Illinois at Chicago) illustrates that the founding and growth of the US postal system not only delivered information but also helped define the US as a nation. This detailed and perceptive study analyzes the development and effect of the postal system from its establishment in 1775 through the Post Office Act of 1792 and the policies of Andrew Jackson in the 1820s and 1830s. The author examines and explains how a system that had in its early years helped unite the nation actually helped to heighten sectional conflicts in the decades prior to the Civil War. John has produced an original, well-documented, and thoughtful study that offers alternative and enticing interpretations of Jacksonian policies and public institutions. Recommended for upper-division undergraduates, graduate students, researchers, and faculty.—*T. E. Sullivan, Towson State University*

OAB-2519   VG123   94-31383 CIP
Langley, Harold D. **A history of medicine in the early U.S. Navy.** Johns Hopkins, 1995. 435p bibl index afp ISBN 0-8018-4876-8, $49.95

Langley's pathbreaking study describes the practice of medicine in US Navy and Marine hospitals, from work of army doctors in the yards building frigates in 1797 and passage of a 1798 act for the relief of sick and disabled seamen to the establishment of the Bureau of Medicine and Surgery in 1842. Organized chronologically, it discusses the Quasi and Barbary Wars; public health and the care provided mariners at Boston, New Orleans, Washington, and other port cities; medical conditions and practices afloat and ashore during the War of 1812; and reform movements between 1816 and 1842. Statistics on disease and death rates in the Navy are gruesome but perhaps not surprising, given the medical practices Langley describes. Langley deftly places his subject in the broader context of US political and social history. Building on his *Social Reform in the United States Navy, 1798-1862* (CH, Feb'68) and on exhaustive research in archival and secondary sources, he has constructed a highly readable study of a previously neglected topic. Of great value to historians of medicine and public health, the Navy, and society in urban America during the early national eras. All levels.—*J. C. Bradford, Texas A&M University*

OAB-2520   F187   93-42536 CIP
Lee, Jean B. **The price of nationhood: the American Revolution in Charles County.** W.W. Norton, 1994. 388p bibl index ISBN 0-393-03658-8, $29.95

Lee's study of the American Revolution from the perspective of one western shore county in Maryland is not only carefully done and highly readable, it breaks new ground. Combining economic, political, and social perspectives, it portrays county society and life during the pre-Revolutionary period, the growth of sentiment for independence, the struggles of county residents to manage (and sometimes muddle through) their part in the war, and the effects of the Revolution on the county community. In the process Lee (Univ. of Wisconsin, Madison) provides a finely grained account which even longtime scholars of the Revolution will find informative. As would be expected, the colony's political elite were at the forefront of the growing movement for independence and remained in charge through the war. In the aftermath of the war, however, the combination of colonial debt, economic depression, and the financial and social burdens of public office in the new political context drove large numbers of the elite into insolvency and out of power — "the price of nationhood." In contrast, women, less-well-off white men, African Americans, and Catholics tended to benefit from independence, although some of the fallout of economic depression affected them, too. Every public and academic library should have this book.—*B. P. Smaby, Clarion University of Pennsylvania*

OAB-2521   E207   95-4399 CIP
Mattern, David B. **Benjamin Lincoln and the American Revolution.** South Carolina, 1995. 307p bibl index ISBN 1-57003-068-5, $39.95

Mattern's book is a well-written and solidly researched biography of the

American revolutionary general Benjamin Lincoln, a native of Hingham, Massachusetts. Lincoln is best remembered, perhaps unfairly, as the unsuccessful rebel commander of the Southern Department from late 1778 until May of 1780. This period in his career was marked by a series of defeats that culminated in the surrender of Charleston to the British. Mattern counters this inequitable popular image by presenting a finely crafted, balanced view of Lincoln that also highlights his achievements, including his heroic performance as an American strategist at Saratoga in 1777, his attempts to provide an adequate defense for the Southern Department in the face of controversy with the French Admiral D'Estaing, and his contributions to the victory at Yorktown. The book's substantial biographical treatment also emphasizes Lincoln's postwar career as Secretary of War in the early 1780s, his role as the Massachusetts suppressor of Shay's Rebellion, and his numerous activities as a Federalist Party stalwart until his death in 1810. Based on an impressive and comprehensive array of primary sources, this book will remain the standard biography of Benjamin Lincoln for many years to come. Upper-division undergraduates and above.—*L. T. Cummins, Austin College*

OAB-2522 E99 95-40289 CIP
Milanich, Jerald T. **The Timucua.** Blackwell, 1996. 235p bibl index afp ISBN 1-55786-488-8, $29.95

When the Spaniards arrived on the east coast of North America in the 16th century, one of the major population groups (approximately 200,000 in number) was the Timucua-speaking people. These people lived in the area that is now northern Florida and southeastern Georgia. By the 18th century, the Timucua and other aboriginal groups were decimated by European diseases; slaving by non-Indians and then Indians; outright annihilation; and warfare among the Spanish, French, and English. Milanich uses information from archaeological, ethnohistorical, and bioanthropological research, along with intensive scholarly research into the writings and paintings of Spanish and French explorers and missionaries, to piece together a comprehensive study and understanding of Timucua material and nonmaterial culture. These sources also furnish insights into the conundrums created by European contact. This excellent anthrohistorical work should be in the library of everyone interested in Native Americans—especially those in the southeastern US. Extensive bibliography and informative maps, along with illustrations by the cartographer, Jacques le Moyne, who was in Florida in 1564 and 1565. General readers; upper-division undergraduates and above.—*N. C. Greenberg, emeritus, Western Michigan University*

OAB-2523 E99 92-29135 CIP
Mulroy, Kevin. **Freedom on the border: the Seminole Maroons in Florida, the Indian Territory, Coahuila, and Texas.** Texas Tech, 1993. 246p bibl index afp ISBN 0-89672-250-3, $29.00

Mulroy, a social science bibliographer (UCLA), has written an extraordinary study of the black Seminoles, or Seminole Maroons, whose "ethnogenesis" dates from the late 18th century in Spanish Florida. Seeking freedom among members of the Seminole confederation, this group of black runaways from South Carolina and Georgia survived successive wars with Americans only to be removed along with their compatriots to the Indian Territory. From there, some of the group migrated to northern Mexico in the mid-19th century to escape from slavery. These maroon communities in time provided soldiers for Mexico's frontier defense and later served the US Army as the intrepid Seminole Negro Indian Scouts. This work combines elements of Native American and African American history. Descendants of the Seminole Maroons live today in Oklahoma, West Texas, and Coahuila, Mexico. Their presence offers eloquent testimony to the tenacity of a proud people who, as the author suggests with considerable understatement, "beat the odds." Mulroy has resurrected a story all but unknown among students of American history. It is a wonderful story deserving of a wide audience. General; advanced undergraduate; graduate; faculty.—*L. G. Moses, Oklahoma State University*

OAB-2524 F8 92-17148 CIP
Nylander, Jane C. **Our own snug fireside: images of the New**

England home, 1760-1860. Knopf, 1993. 317p bibl index ISBN 0-394-54984-8, $30.00

Nylander is respected throughout the world of New England studies for her curatorial leadership at Old Sturbridge Village, Strawbery Banke, and the Society for the Preservation of New England Antiquities, for her kindliness to fellow students of social history, and for her internationally authoritative scholarship on historical textiles. Now she has written an engaging and instructive social history of domestic life in pre-Civil War New England. She investigates through the eyes of four diarists (three female). Using the diaries as reference points, Nylander systematically works through the various and obvious topics (clothing, food, housework, neighbors, fuel, courtship, holidays). Unsurprisingly, she erodes many standard myths and eternal verities (e.g., "self-sufficiency," barter economy, hope chests, certain gender roles), but scholars and general readers alike will be impressed by the graceful writing, the deep and broad knowledge of the author, the clarity of organization, and the impressive and useful illustrations. Nylander's book is likely to become authoritative on this topic for years to come. All libraries.—*R. B. Lyman Jr., Simmons College*

OAB-2525 Can. CIP
Pritchard, James. **Anatomy of a naval disaster: the 1746 French naval expedition to North America.** McGill-Queen's, 1995. 322p bibl index afp ISBN 0-7735-1325-6, $39.95

Up to 1746, the French military focused on the European continent; in this year, for the first time, the French mounted a military expedition of 11,000 men and 25,000 tons of ships to North America to reassert control over Arcadia (today Nova Scotia). Pritchard shows the French army was in a state of decay; officers such as the commander of the expedition, the Duke of D'Enville, were given commands because of court intrigue and patronage rather than experience at sea and general competence. Following numerous logistical problems, gales and unfavorable winds made the passage to North America unusually long and arduous, with the expedition taking five months to cross the Atlantic. Pritchard demonstrates a vast knowledge of seafaring and naval technology, and also gives detailed descriptions of life on board these slow-moving masted ships, with a focus on the serious problems of scurvy, typhus, and typhoid fever. In September, a hurricane dispersed and damaged the French fleet as it approached the coast of Nova Scotia; when the Duke D'Enville reached what is today Halifax harbor, he had a seizure and died. No British ports or positions were taken in Nova Scotia, and what was left of the expedition sailed home with little show. The only major flaw of this fascinating book is its excessive detail. Based on very thorough research in French archives, this is a seminal work not just on the French and British struggle for North America but also on 18th-century naval warfare in general. Upper-division undergraduates and above.—*W. T. Dean III, Norwich University*

OAB-2526 KF4749 86-40058 CIP
Reid, John Phillip. **Constitutional history of the American Revolution: [v.4:] The authority of law.** Wisconsin, 1994 (c1993). 279p index ISBN 0-299-13980-8, $35.00

Reid (New York Univ.), dean of American legal historians, is a proponent of the "internal school of legal history," i.e., the view that developments within legal institutions rather than the pressure of external forces control the development of law. This four-volume work therefore appears superficially to be old-fashioned, resuming the argument for the American Revolution that preoccupied scholars of the 1920s and '30s. But in Reid's hands, the old subject takes on new life because of his profound learning in both English and US history. Volume 4 in effect summarizes the argument of the previous three volumes by contending that the British Parliament's assertion of total authority to legislate for the colonies in all cases whatsoever precipitated the Revolution. This assertion forced colonists to resurrect 17th-century arguments for the rule of law as superior to legislation. Reid shows how the Boston Tea Party constituted such a severe challenge to the basic British theory of sovereignty that it determined the British response, expressed in the Townshend Duties and the Coercive Acts. British lawyers were so threatened by the aggressiveness

Social & Behavioral Sciences

of American legal theory that they felt they could not give in. Thus, the Revolution was above all a constitutional crisis. A very important work. General readers; upper-division undergraduates and above.—*S. N. Katz, American Council of Learned Societies*

OAB-2527   E99   92-53621 CIP
Richter, Daniel K. **The ordeal of the longhouse: the peoples of the Iroquois League in the era of European colonization.** North Carolina, 1992. 436p bibl index afp ISBN 0-8078-2060-1, $45.00; ISBN 0-8078-4394-6 pbk, $17.95

Thoroughly researched and lucidly written, this examination of the Iroquois people from the pre-Columbian period to the 1730s illustrates the adaptability of Native Americans to political, religious, and technological changes. Richter discusses the formation of the Iroquois confederacy and shows that Iroquois warfare was motivated by both economic need and by mourning ceremonies. Although the confederacy initially relied on Dutch trade goods, after 1664 the Iroquois split into pro-French, pro-British, and neutralist factions. Throughout the Colonial period these factions contested for influence over Iroquois diplomacy, but by the 1720s the neutralists dominated and the confederacy rebuilt its strength by adopting captives. Balancing the British against the French and achieving peace with their former Indian enemies, the Iroquois enjoyed a brief period of prosperity before succumbing to European domination. An impressive example of scholarship, Richter's study should appeal to a broad audience. Highly recommended. General; advanced undergraduate; graduate; faculty; professional.—*R. D. Edmunds, Indiana University-Bloomington*

OAB-2528   HD8085   92-21082 CIP
Schultz, Ronald. **The republic of labor: Philadelphia artisans and the politics of class, 1720-1830.** Oxford, 1993. 298p index afp ISBN 0-19-507585-4, $45.00

In this pathbreaking work, Schultz (Univ. of Wyoming) traces the development of America's first working class and its social vision in the 18th and early 19th centuries. He examines the changes from the artisans' small producer tradition, emphasizing communitarianism and independence, to their emergence as a united, class-conscious, and politicized wage-labor force. Although Schultz occasionally fails to differentiate adequately between the interests and priorities of master and journeymen artisans, and other working-class elements (he often uses "artisans," "workingmen," "working class," "laboring poor," "tradesmen," "craftsmen," and "laboring class" interchangeably), he offers compelling challenges to recent interpretations regarding the nature and timing of working-class evolution in the US. He demonstrates that in the process of being transformed by the forces of capitalism from independent artisans into dependent workingmen, Philadelphia's artisans successfully forged trade societies and intelligent political alliances and strategems to articulate and protect working-class interests and aspirations. This is an important contribution to early US social and labor history. Advanced undergraduate; graduate; faculty.—*G. S. Rowe, University of Northern Colorado*

OAB-2529   E99   94-41590 CIP
Smith, F. Todd. **The Caddo Indians: tribes at the convergence of empires, 1542-1854.** Texas A&M, 1995. 229p bibl index afp (Centennial series of the Association of Former Students, Texas A&M University, 56) ISBN 0-89096-642-7, $24.50

Smith's book is a detailed, precise, and finely crafted chronological narrative of European-Caddo relations from the 16th century until the mid-19th century. Based on an intelligent combination of primary and secondary sources, it provides a survey of the three Caddo confederacies that existed in the early colonial period. It thereafter traces their alternating periods of prosperity and decline through the French and Spanish colonial eras, the time of the Republic of Texas, and the domination of the US. The Caddo endured with their culture intact longer than almost any other tribe in the southwestern US. Smith attributes this to their strong political organization, the talents of their respec-

tive tribal leaders, and their geographic location on the Texas/Louisiana border, which gave them importance and bargaining power with Europeans because they sat at the "convergence of empires." Although there have been earlier anthropological and ethnographic studies of the Caddo, this book is the first and only comprehensive study of their historical relations with Europeans. Soundly researched and well written, it is an important addition to the historical literature. Undergraduates and above.—*L. T. Cummins, Austin College*

OAB-2530   F128   96-35249 CIP
Tiedemann, Joseph S. **Reluctant revolutionaries: New York City and the road to independence, 1763-1776.** Cornell, 1997. 342p index afp ISBN 0-8014-3237-5, $45.00

In this engaging and insightful study, Tiedemann (Loyola Marymount Univ.) employs the theoretical constructs of contemporary social-conflict theory, especially those of Theda Skocpol and Louis Kriesberg. He divides the time frame into three periods that correlate with specific crises—the Stamp Act 1763-1766, the Townsend Acts 1766-1773, and the Tea and Coercive Acts 1773-1776—and analyzes the various constituent groups and their responses to the respective crises. Tiedemann maintains that the very heterogeneous population of New York City itself made it difficult and necessary for leaders to proceed cautiously, conservatively, and inclusively to reach a broad consensus over how to resist British imperialism and eventually support independence. He finds that ideas mattered, that the Sons of Liberty played a key role during this period, that religious and ethnic factors were more important determinants than class, that cooperation between classes was possible when there was mutual economic benefit, and that some of the patrician leaders were capable of patriotism. Tiedemann's study directly challenges Edward Countryman's *A People in Revolution: The American Revolution and Political Society in New York, 1760-1790* (CH, Apr'82) and Marc Egnal's *A Mighty Empire: The Origins of the American Revolution* (CH, Oct'88). Three maps, an excellent historiographical essay, critical endnotes, and a full index. Upper-division undergraduates and above.—*M. L. Dolan, Northern Michigan University*

OAB-2531   E286   96-18431 CIP
Travers, Len. **Celebrating the Fourth: Independence Day and the rites of nationalism in the Early Republic.** Massachusetts, 1997. 278p bibl index afp ISBN 1-55849-060-4, $29.95

In a richly documented work that will appeal to historians, social scientists, folklorists, and general readers alike, Travers examines the rituals and symbols associated with the US celebration of the Fourth of July. Concentrating primarily on rites and festivities in Boston, Philadelphia, and Charleston, South Carolina, between 1777 and 1826, the author traces the metamorphosis of a day set aside initially to commemorate separation from England to one that celebrated the values and behavior essential for a republican society, and, ultimately, to one that glorified who Americans had become as a people. As new purposes for the holiday surfaced, new rites and symbols emerged. In the 1780s the Fourth was shaped by partisan considerations and it continued to be politicized until after the War of 1812, as parties struggled to cultivate and legitimize a national character and purpose in their own image. Generally, the festivities of the Fourth have extolled the past, hyperbolized the present, and anticipated the future, even as they have obscured dangerous ambiguities and contradictions within American society. Travers's careful examination of the Fourth before 1826 offers valuable insights into Americans' national vision and ceremonies of the present. General readers; upper-division undergraduates and above.— *G. S. Rowe, University of Northern Colorado*

OAB-2532   E208   92-62725 MARC
Ward, Harry M. **The American Revolution: nationhood achieved, 1763-1788.** St. Martin's, 1995. 432p bibl index ISBN 0-312-12259-4, $35.00; ISBN 0-312-07162-0 pbk, $19.29

Ward's solid and fairly comprehensive survey of the history of the American Revolution provides a well-written narrative that includes recent information and conclusions from most of the current scholarship about the conflict. This book will be especially useful to readers because it places the revolt within the larger context of 18th-century history. The author also treats various topics not usually covered in an overview of the Revolution. For example, he provides thorough discussions of social developments, ideology, Republicanism, and diplomacy. Several chapters on the home front and the role of noncombatants are especially notable. The bibliography provides an extensive listing of important scholarship and can serve as a fruitful guide to additional reading on many specialized topics. The concise and compact nature of the book makes it especially useful as a starting point for understanding the complexity of the Revolution, as a cultural as well as a military event. General readers, undergraduates.—*L. T. Cummins, Austin College*

OAB-2533   F189   93-24740 CIP
Yentsch, Anne Elizabeth. **A Chesapeake family and their slaves: a study in historical archaeology.** Cambridge, 1994. 433p bibl index ISBN 0-521-46730-6 pbk, $24.95

In an excellent example of the leading edge of American historical archaeology, Yentsch (Armstrong State College) provides a richly detailed case study proving the value of an anthropological and archaeological approach to American Colonial history. The starting point is salvage excavations conducted in Annapolis, Maryland, which turned up a wealth of architectural and artifactual evidence of the c. 1730 house and household of the Calvert family. The Calvert men were among Maryland's elite, with close ties to the English aristocracy. Their house and material goods are shown to have displayed their social position, and created a stage for their social interactions. Less prominent members of the household, including women and slaves, are brought into focus by melding historical and ethnographic data with the beads, pottery, animal bones, and other artifacts from the site. The material evidence of the site anchors a wide-ranging interpretation of lifeways of the household and of the social and cultural landscape of 18th-century Annapolis. Includes an informative glossary. Highly recommended for collections in American history, archaeology, and anthropology at upper-division undergraduate level onward.—*D. B. Landon, Michigan Technological University*

UNITED STATES — 19th Century

OAB-2534   E97   95-7638 CIP
Adams, David Wallace. **Education for extinction: American Indians and the boarding school experience, 1875-1928.** University Press of Kansas, 1995. 396p index afp ISBN 0-7006-0735-8, $34.95

Federal policy usually dominates histories about Native American education; Indians are largely silent participants. Exceptions, however, are the studies devoted to individual schools, e.g., Robert Trennert's *The Phoenix Indian School* (CH, Feb'89) and K. Tsianina Lomawaima's *They Called It Prairie Light* (CH, Oct'94). What those authors have done for individual schools, Adams (Cleveland State Univ.) accomplishes for the whole system of education that developed in the last quarter of the 19th century. That program was animated by the aphorism of Richard Henry Pratt, one of its most ardent evangels: "Kill the Indian, save the man." In lively prose, Adams tells the poignant story, rich with nuance, of the relentless war against American Indian children. It is a tale about policy makers who sought to use boarding schools as an instrument for transforming Indian youth to "American" ways of thinking, doing, and living. The study focuses on policy formulation, how that policy was translated into institutional practice, and finally, how students responded. Adams demonstrates convincingly that Native American students were anything but passive recipients of the "curriculum of civilization." This is, quite simply, a wonderful book. All levels.—*L. G. Moses, Oklahoma State University*

OAB-2535   E99   96-44775 CIP
Afton, Jean. **Cheyenne dog soldiers: a ledgerbook history of coups and combat,** by Jean Afton, David Fridtjof Halaas, and Andrew E.

Masich. Colorado Historical Society/University Press of Colorado, 1997. 400p bibl index afp ISBN 0-87081-435-4, $49.95

Based on sketches created by notable warrior-artists between 1865 and 1869, this unique work offers a valuable record of Southern Cheyenne history during the crucial transition from a free life to the confines of the reservation. The ledgerbook, comprising more than 100 sketches, deals exclusively with Cheyenne combat and episodes of counting coup against white soldiers, civilians, and other Indian tribes. Captured in the camp of Tall Bull following the 1869 Battle of Summit Springs, Colorado, the collection of drawings documents specific historical events that the editors have authenticated through a balancing of supplementary Indian and white records. In addition to crafting a comprehensive prologue that traces the changing ownership of the ledgerbook and explains the nature and symbolism of this art form, the editors provide interpretive details for each sketch. They identify the particular artist when possible, describe the historical event, and discuss the individuals who appear in the picture. The high quality of reproduction on glossy paper and the intelligent narrative make this book a treasure for researchers and interested general readers alike. All levels.—*M. L. Tate, University of Nebraska at Omaha*

OAB-2536   E168   91-33635 CIP
Ames, Kenneth L. **Death in the dining room and other tales of Victorian culture.** Temple University, 1992. 265p index afp ISBN 0-87722-891-4, $34.95

Although Thomas Schlereth's *Victorian America* (1991) and Harvey Green's *The Light of the Home* (CH, Oct'83) opened many historians' eyes to the neglected material evidence offering insight into the Victorian age, Ames's book more boldly invites them to grasp meanings from a set of related artifacts. Ames's study may be the most tightly focused and is certainly the most interpretive of recent publications on this topic. From the way that Victorian Americans furnished their halls with hallstands and cardservers, to the way they centered the organ in the parlor, dined alongside deathly images on their sideboards, hung mottoes on the wall, and sat in chairs, Ames distinguishes a distinctive culture. He identifies a complex set of symbols communicated persuasively through material surroundings. In examining the symbolic systems used by Victorian Americans, Ames explains well furniture's place in the rise and fall of the Victorian ethos. Much of his well-argued analysis revolves around issues of gender and class, structures of power, and stategies of adjustment to change. He amply illustrates his interpretations with photographs that carry their own provocatively interpretive texts. Meant to be read and read again, meant to be discussed and debated, Ames's book gives the interpretation of historical material culture a good push forward. Undergraduate; graduate; faculty.—*S. J. Bronner, Pennsylvania State University, Harrisburg*

OAB-2537   F215   91-33070 CIP
Ayers, Edward L. **The promise of the New South: life after Reconstruction.** Oxford, 1992. 572p index afp ISBN 0-19-503756-1, $30.00

Put simply, this book is the most important grand synthesis of life in the post-Reconstruction South published since C. Vann Woodward's epic *Origins of the New South* (1951) more than four decades ago. Ayers offers cogent analysis of daily life in towns, villages, and the countryside, economic and demographic developments, religion, ideas written and spoken and, in abundant detail, the politics of agrarian protest. Race relations are examined aptly and judiciously, but not magnified unduly and, instead of treating southern blacks mainly as passive targets of oppression, Ayers integrates their life experiences with skill and insight into the mainstream of his narrative. Drawing on an eclectic array of primary source materials, Ayers has crafted a narrative as lively as it is comprehensive. In a very real sense, the work represents revolutionary historical analysis, for it departs doggedly and persuasively from a long historical tradition of portraying southerners of the period as essentially products of their problems, artifacts of agrarian poverty and racial polarization. *The Promise of the New South* is the stuff of Pulitzers. Advanced undergraduate; graduate; faculty.—*R. A. Fischer, University of Minnesota—Duluth*

OAB-2538   E184   93-10833 CIP
Barkai, Avraham. **Branching out: German-Jewish immigration to the United States, 1820-1914.** Holmes & Meier, 1994. 269p bibl index ISBN 0-8419-1152-5, $40.00

Barkai's expertise as a historian of German Jewry is unmistakable in this examination of German Jewish immigrants to America. Characterizing 19th-century American Jewry as a branch of German Jewry, the author amply demonstrates the continuities in sociocultural and occupational development that persisted generations after migration. Barkai's account contributes most when he makes such connections, as in his linking of changes in the immigrant profile to developments in Germany. His work also addresses usually neglected aspects of the immigration, such as the impact on the German Jewish communities left behind. In addition to these new contributions, *Branching Out* provides rich coverage of the immigrants' experiences in America, drawing on numerous personal accounts of both pre- and post-Civil War migrants settling in diverse regions. Barkai's examination of community development, and of interactions between the Germans and both the established Sephardic communities and the later arriving Eastern Europeans, are well documented and provide an excellent introduction to these more familiar aspects of the migration. General and academic readers, upper-division undergraduate and above.— *E. M. Eisenberg, Willamette University*

OAB-2539   E437   94-8922 CIP
Binder, Frederick Moore. **James Buchanan and the American empire.** Susquehanna University, 1994. (Dist. by Associated University Presses) 318p bibl index afp ISBN 0-945636-64-4, $45.00

James Buchanan is usually associated with the advent of the Civil War. He is a perennial favorite on the lists of America's worst presidents. Binder takes a different tack, concentrating on the realm of foreign policy. Buchanan served as Andrew Jackson's minister to Russia, secretary of state under Polk, and minister to the Court of St. James in the Pierce administration. He was a lifelong advocate of manifest destiny, and consistently pursued policies to further the aims of "the American Empire." He was obsessed with acquiring Cuba. Binder, former president of Hartwick College, has written an excellent account on a topic long ignored by historians. He writes exceedingly well; the book's nine chapters are models of concision. His research is extensive and multinational. Binder's book is likely to become the standard study of this topic. It is highly recommended for all college and university libraries.— *S. G. Weisner, Springfield Technical Community College*

OAB-2540   E99   95-38916 CIP
Boyd, Robert. **People of the Dalles: the Indians of Wascopam Mission: a historical ethnography based on the papers of the Methodist missionaries.** Nebraska, 1996. 396p bibl index afp ISBN 0-8032-1236-4, $50.00

Boyd provides a rich analysis of the history and culture of the Chinookan (Wasco-Wishram) and Sahaptan peoples who inhabited the Dalles area along the Columbia river in Oregon. He uses the primary source writings of Methodist missionaries active in the area from 1838 to 1844, particularly those of Rev. Henry Perkins, as well as later anthropological works (1905 to present). Boyd carefully portrays the culture of these people at the time of European contact and to examine the effects of radical demographic, economic, political, and religious change on these local cultures. He brings to light new data on these peoples, their relationship with Methodism, and its effect on their own cosmology, carefully citing his sources and cogently explaining the anthropological theories he employs in his analysis change. This highly recommended work a fine example of ethnographic and historic investigation, providing a compelling methodological lesson for students of historical ethnography, anthropology, Native American studies and the Columbia river plateau region. Plates and maps, reprints of key missionary texts, a guide to mission manuscripts, biographical sketches of Native Americans and whites involved in this era, and an exhaustive bibliography. All levels.— *R. A. Bucko, Le Moyne College*

OAB-2541   F380   92-17759 CIP
Brasseaux, Carl A. **Acadian to Cajun: transformation of a people, 1803-1877.** University Press of Mississippi, 1992. 252p bibl index afp ISBN 0-87805-582-7, $40.00; ISBN 0-87805-583-5 pbk, $16.95

Brasseaux set himself a daunting goal—writing a social and political study of a largely nonliterate people. Louisiana's "Cajuns" settled in the area after their forced dispersal from French Acadia following British subjugation of that colony. Most studies of the Cajuns focus on that tragic part of their story and fail to follow through with information about how they adapted to their new surroundings. Brasseaux's work fills that gap admirably. Brasseaux traces the development of a distinctly Cajun culture and the growing acceptance of Anglo-American materialism and political activity, from the Louisiana Purchase in 1803 until the end of Reconstruction in 1877 when, he maintains, traditional distinctions between the Cajuns and their neighbors had disappeared. He pieced together this history from court proceedings, federal census and Catholic church records, legislative acts, and election returns. The result of his copius work with these records is a pioneering book that will serve as a model for other ethnohistories. General; advanced undergraduate; graduate; faculty.— *J. P. Sanson, Louisiana State Unversity at Alexandria*

OAB-2542   HX655   95-41805 CIP
Brundage, W. Fitzhugh. **A socialist utopia in the new South: the Ruskin colonies in Tennessee and Georgia, 1894-1901.** Illinois, 1996. 263p bibl index afp ISBN 0-252-02244-0, $38.95; ISBN 0-252-06548-4 pbk, $16.95

The Ruskinites established a late-19th-century utopian community in Tennessee based on socialist principles. Though a brief attempt was made to extend it in Georgia, the experiment was short-lived. The group has been of interest mainly because its practices were inspired by Edward Bellamy, author of *Looking Backward*, Charlotte Perkins Gilman, and English philosopher John Ruskin, the colony's namesake. Until now, the best coverage of this commune was a chapter in John Egerton's *Visions of Utopia* (CH, Dec'78). Brundage begins with a discussion tying the Ruskinites to large-scale and important historical forces. His explanation of the differences between late-19th-century utopianism and the better-known communities and ideas of the 1840s is skillful, clear, and well researched. The book's structure is chronological, following the group's founding by Julius A. Wayland, detailing the productive years, and ending with the experiment's demise. Brundage uses primary documents without allowing the narrative to become clogged with the minutia that mars some accounts of historical communities. The writing is scholarly but lively. Bibliographic essay. All levels.— *E. J. Green, Prince George's Community College*

OAB-2543   VA55   89-13675 CIP
Canney, Donald L. **The old steam navy: v.2: The ironclads, 1842-1885.** Naval Institute, 1993. 162p bibl index afp ISBN 0-87021-586-8, $49.95

Subtitled *Frigates, Sloops, and Gunboats, 1815-1885*, the first volume (1990) of this analytical guide to US Navy combatants in transition focused on the development of steam-propulsion and its application to wooden-hulled vessels. Volume 2 describes vessels built with iron or ironclad hulls. The first chapter deals with the Stevens Battery, begun in 1841, the second with plans submitted to the Navy for ironclads in 1861. The next seven chapters discuss vessels built during the Civil War, and a final chapter treats the operational service of the vessels in the two decades after the war. More than 130 photographs and plans illustrate virtually every riverine and oceanic vessel discussed. The exhaustive research in primary source materials and the detailed and systematic description of the construction, machinery, and armament of these vessels make Canney's work the standard resource on the technological development of the US Navy in the mid-19th century. Paul H. Silverstone's *Warships of the Civil War Navies* (1989) will continue to serve as a ready reference for vessels of the Confederate States Navy and Union sailing ships. All levels.— *J. C. Bradford, Texas A&M University*

OAB-2544   E411   94-5666 CIP
Curtis, Samuel Ryan. **Mexico under fire: being the diary of Samuel Ryan Curtis ... during the American military occupation of northern Mexico, 1846-1847,** ed. by Joseph E. Chance. Texas Christian, 1994. 307p bibl index ISBN 0-87565-127-5, $29.95

Diaries and journals written by Mexican War veterans have always been in short supply when compared with the rich materials preserved by Civil War participants. Yet occasionally a manuscript emerges that warrants publication, and its release is eagerly awaited by researchers. Colonel Samuel Curtis maintained just such a record from July 3, 1846, when his 3rd Ohio Volunteer Regiment left Cincinnati by steamboat down the Ohio River, until his departure from Matamoros, Mexico, on July 17, 1847. Never intending to gain fame or financial reward from his musings, Curtis wrote in an unpretentious manner and without any need to be guarded in his assessments of people and events. Moreover, his entries appear in such a literate form that they carry the story along as an integrated narrative, with sufficient detail to enlighten the reader. Chance (mathematics, Univ. of Texas—Pan American, and author of two other well-received books on the Mexican War) provides an excellent general prologue to the book as well as shorter introductions to each of the five chapters. These place the diary entries into a larger, international context and help the reader better understand Curtis as an individual. Even more vital to researchers are the 74 pages of editorial notes, which further elucidate personalities, locales, and specific events. All levels.—*M. L. Tate, University of Nebraska at Omaha*

OAB-2545   TF25   93-17074 CIP
Dilts, James D. **The great road: the building of the Baltimore and Ohio, the nation's first railroad, 1828-1853.** Stanford, 1993. 472p bibl index afp ISBN 0-8047-2235-8, $60.00

In one of the most important studies ever on an individual American railroad, Dilts traces the building of the core route of the Baltimore & Ohio Railroad (B&O), the world's first planned, long-distance rail carrier. Yet this work covers much more than the struggle to construct the B&O from Baltimore to Wheeling between 1828 and 1853. Dilts also incorporates a variety of additional topics, ranging from pioneer railroad technology to the political milieu of antebellum Maryland and Virginia. The book is a model of how to examine a 19th-century railroad; it places the B&O in the context of the times. Admittedly, some readers may object to the detail, but Dilts presents it with an engaging prose style. Indeed, his achievement is impressive. Furthermore, the book is beautifully designed and edited, with a large number of attractive illustrations, including historic maps, and a good index. All levels.—*H. R. Grant, University of Akron*

OAB-2546   HQ1438   96-25317 CIP
Edwards, Laura F. **Gendered strife & confusion: the political culture of Reconstruction.** Illinois, 1997. 378p bibl index afp ISBN 0-252-02297-1, $49.95; ISBN 0-252-06600-6 pbk, $24.95

Edwards's addition to the ongoing reassessment of Reconstruction is an important contribution to a rapidly evolving field. Extensively researched in court records, newspapers, census returns, and manuscript collections, her study delves deeply into the contests over social, economic, and political power in postbellum Granville County, North Carolina. This work stands at the juncture of African American history, gender studies, labor history, and Southern history, in a sophisticated retelling of Reconstruction, where families and households (rather than governments and political parties) were remade and redefined during this period of upheaval. Southerners of all races, classes, and sexes had to determine their new relationships to one another after the Civil War swept away the antebellum social structure. Elite whites, common whites, and African Americans alike found their domestic relations to be contested, and new definitions of "manhood" and "womanhood" emerged. Elite whites attempted to impose their model of gender roles on common whites and blacks; African Americans tried to use legal marriages and family obligations as weapons of autonomy and resistance. In this version of Reconstruction, sexual violence and intimidation receive equal treatment with the better known KKK-genre of political coercion. Well written; highly recommended. Upper-division undergraduates and above.—*E. C. Green, Sweet Briar College*

OAB-2547   E599   94-11747 CIP
Elliott, Robert G. **Ironclad of the Roanoke: Gilbert Elliott's Albemarle.** White Mane, 1994. 372p bibl index afp ISBN 0-942597-63-X, $29.95

Every so often there appears a book of such high quality research and presentation that it becomes a standard reference. Elliott's *Ironclad of the Roanoke* may well be such a work. It is heavily documented with 43 pages of chapter notes, a 6-page (no padding) bibliography, and a 22-page index. Here also can be found perhaps the best and most complete and unbiased account of the little-known battle between the *Albemale* and seven Union warships off the mouth of the Roanoke River on May 5, 1864. This book is very well illustrated with more than 100 maps, drawings, and prints, many seldom seen in print since their first publication during and after the Civil War. Many battle position maps are of the author's design. The four appendixes include a roster not only of all known crew members of the *Albemarle* but also of all known workers and laborers on the vessel. It is difficult to see how a more complete story of this famous ironclad could supersede this work unless heretofore unknown records are discovered. Civil War buffs, students, and scholars at any level.—*B. H. Groene, Southeastern Louisiana University*

OAB-2548   E83   92-31269 CIP
Fox, Richard Allan. **Archaeology, history, and Custer's last battle: the Little Big Horn reexamined.** Oklahoma, 1993. 411p bibl index afp ISBN 0-8061-2496-2, $29.95

The Custer enigma that has piqued the interest of historians and engendered endless controversy for more than a century—when, how, and under what circumstances did Lieutenant General George A. Custer and his Seventh Cavalry troops die at the Battle of Little Big Horn, June 25, 1876—is largely put to rest by this exciting, pathbreaking book. Based on meticulous historical scholarship and thorough archaeological study of the battlefield, Fox has demonstrated how the patterned findings of shells, bullets, and other artifacts of the battle allow for an incontrovertible reconstruction of the events of that fateful day. Significantly, the resulting interpretation confirms eyewitness accounts of the battle that have for so long been downplayed by serious Custer scholars—the stories related by Native American participants who were the only survivors to witness the demise of Custer's immediate command. More generally, the book provides a model for the ways in which archaeological and documentary data can be integrated for a fuller picture of past events. Recommended for general, undergraduate, and professional readers.—*D. R. Parks, Indiana University-Bloomington*

OAB-2549   F264   93-32060 CIP
Greenwood, Janette Thomas. **Bittersweet legacy: the black and white "better classes" in Charlotte, 1850-1910.** North Carolina, 1994. 318p bibl index afp ISBN 0-8078-2133-0, $45.00

Greenwood's case study of postbellum Charlotte, North Carolina, affirms C. Vann Woodward's thesis: race relations in the post-Reconstruction South were flexible, fluid, and open to possibilities other than the legal apartheid that ultimately emerged in the 1890s. But Greenwood's book is not mere repetition of a well-established interpretation; it is a sophisticated treatment of the interplay between class and race that moves the discussion into rich, new areas. Greenwood applies a deft hand to the issues of class formation and class relations as she details the collaborative efforts of Charlotte's "better classes," white and black, to create urban reform movements such as Prohibition. The author also gives a mature reading to the politics of Populism and the white supremacy campaign of 1898. There is an especially fruitful exploration of gender and class identity. Readers interested in race relations, gender and class, the New South, and the political economy of white supremacy will find this a rewarding book. All levels.—*E. C. Green, Sweet Briar College*

OAB-2550   E487   95-22808 CIP
Grimsley, Mark. **The hard hand of war: Union military policy**

toward Southern civilians, 1861-1865. Cambridge, 1995. 244p bibl index ISBN 0-521-46257-6, $29.95

The American Civil War has often been called "a total war," especially as practiced by generals such as William T. Sherman and Philip Sheridan. Grimsley (Ohio State Univ.) refines historical discussion on the nature of the war by examining Federal policy toward Southern civilians and their property in combat areas. Focusing on the eastern and western theaters, he detects three chronological phases in that policy: conciliation from 1861 to summer 1862; pragmatism from then until early 1864; and hard war from about February 1864 to Appomattox. Hard war included the destruction of Confederate resources (public and private), forced evacuations, and confiscation of property—all for the purpose of eroding the Confederates' will to resist Federal authority. Grimsley concludes that the Civil War was not a "total war" as it has sometimes been defined; political objectives (e.g., the restoration of the Union) and moral imperatives prevented the sort of wholesale destruction of life and property that characterized, for example, some of the campaigns against Native American peoples. Well researched, clearly written, and elegantly conceived, this is an important book. All levels.—R. G. Lowe, University of North Texas

OAB-2551   E540   94-42217 CIP
Hauptman, Laurence M. **Between two fires: American Indians in the Civil War.** Free Press, 1995. 304p bibl index ISBN 0-02-914180-X, $25.00

Most people are unaware of Native American participation in the American Civil War, and yet this struggle of brother against brother pitted approximately 20,000 Indian soldiers on both sides of the conflict, and left them as victims of the calamity. Hauptman (SUNY at New Paltz) has produced a well-written and well-documented account of this participation by focusing on a dozen tribal groups. Of these, only the western Cherokee of Indian Territory have received considerable attention in earlier studies. Although this group was badly divided during the war, the author demonstrates that most Delawares of Indian Territory, Oneidas of Wisconsin, Ojibwas and Ottawas of Michigan, Senecas of New York, and Pequot and Mohegan of Connecticut loyally supported the Union. In contrast, the Catawbas of South Carolina and eastern Cherokees of North Carolina allied with the Confederacy. Most exceptional were the Pamunkey of Virginia and Lumbee of North Carolina, who challenged the racial system of the South and fought for the Union. Hauptman superbly identifies the reasons why each of the groups aligned as it did, and demonstrates that Indians were no mere pawns in this struggle but were fighting for their own unique ideological and practical concerns. Equally important is his assessment of the impact of this war on each of the groups, and their attempts to preserve their land bases and cultural identities. An excellent study aimed at all levels of adult readers and researchers.—M. L. Tate, University of Nebraska at Omaha

OAB-2552   E183   96-42450 CIP
Jones, Howard. **Prologue to manifest destiny: Anglo-American relations in the 1840s,** by Howard Jones and Donald A. Rakestraw. SR Books, 1997. 342p bibl index afp ISBN 0-8420-2488-3, $50.00; ISBN 0-8420-2498-0 pbk, $18.95

In an elegantly written, exquisitely detailed account of the Northeast and Northwest boundary disputes with England settled in the 1840s, Jones and Rakestraw depict the diplomacy with abundant background material and colorful descriptions of main characters such as Daniel Webster, Alexander McLeod, US Presidents John Tyler and James Polk, Lords Ashburton and Aberdeen, and Richard Pakenham. The major theme, which reflects the traditional opinion, is that astute diplomacy in both cases brought an Anglo-American rapprochement and British acquiescence to at least a continental republic as America's manifest destiny. Jones and Rakestraw avoid the temptation of speculating whether the US could have achieved its designs on California by winning the war with Mexico without the settlement, but certainly make the case that timing was paramount. The juxtaposition of these two crises makes this study close to definitive. Excellent notes and bibliography. All levels.—C. W. Haury, Piedmont Virginia Community College

OAB-2553   E99   94-30374 CIP
Kidwell, Clara Sue. **Choctaws and missionaries in Mississippi, 1818-1918.** Oklahoma, 1995. 271p bibl index afp ISBN 0-8061-2691-4, $32.95

Kidwell, herself a Choctaw, a PhD, and assistant director of cultural resources at the National Museum of the American Indian, provides an astute narrative of Choctaw history that is respectfully critical of all parties involved. Tracing the origins of the Choctaw and their subsequent interactions with various European and American agencies, she demonstrates how the very institutions that sought to destroy Choctaw identity were used by the Choctaw themselves to survive as a distinct historical community. Kidwell focuses particularly on the role of Christian missions (Presbyterian, Congregational, Methodist, Baptist, and Catholic) in the Choctaw's creative transformation of their own polity through education and adaptation, and in the maintenance of their distinctive identity. The Choctaw community is shown as an internally diverse entity that acts rather than simply reacts, making its own history instead of falling victim to others. A highly complex story told with clarity and precision, this is a masterful study of the relationship of history and cultures, and a unique and solid contribution to a fuller understanding of Choctaw history and culture, Indian-white relations, missiology, and the persistence of cultural identity. All levels.—R. A. Bucko, Le Moyne College

OAB-2554   E441   94-49163 CIP
King, Wilma. **Stolen childhood: slave youth in nineteenth-century America.** Indiana, 1995. 253p bibl index afp ISBN 0-253-32904-3, $27.95

King's deeply researched, well-written, passionate study places children and young adults at center stage in the North American slave experience. Focusing closely on age as a variable in slave treatment, she asserts "that enslaved children had virtually no childhood because they entered the work place early and were more readily subjected to arbitrary authority, punishments, and separations." King underscores both the importance of the family as the central institution within the slave community and the tragedies and traumas experienced by slaves young and old. Within the slave economy children performed numerous domestic, agricultural, and industrial tasks. Though slave youngsters were compelled to labor, they nonetheless enjoyed certain leisure activities, including folk rituals, seasonal celebrations, games, and dances. And despite slavery's oppressive grip, slave parents found ways to educate their children both temporally and spiritually. Such schooling provided survival skills, leverages, and modes of resistance that undermined the hegemony of the master class. King concludes that the reuniting of families separated by slavery and the forging of new family relationships were among the highest priorities of the freedpeople. A must for academic libraries at all levels.—J. D. Smith, North Carolina State University

OAB-2555   F198   93-17513 CIP
Lessoff, Alan. **The nation and its city: politics, "corruption," and progress in Washington, D.C., 1861-1902.** Johns Hopkins, 1994. 337p index ISBN 0-8018-4464-9, $45.00

For the first half century of its existence, Washington, DC, was a struggling metropolis of boarding houses and dusty streets. The Civil War brought many new residents, some of whom remained to play a serious role in politics at the war's end. Lessoff devotes a large portion of his book to their political faction, the "improvers." Their dream was to beautify the capital with paved streets, drainage, sewerage, parks, and new suburbs. In the early 1870s, through the territorial government that consisted of a governor, council, and elected House of Delegates, the "improvers" initiated many public projects. Unfortunately, they went too far too fast and ran up a debt that brought about their downfall. In 1878 a new form of government was created by Congress: a District Commission of three men appointed by the US president. The elected legislature was eliminated, but Congress agreed to supply 50 percent of the District's budget. Public works were continued by the U.S. Army Corps of Engineers and later by private city planners. Overall, Lessoff has written a meticulous history of

Washington between 1861 and 1902. His work is a major study of the national capital. Upper-division undergraduates and above.—*J. Jackson, Southeastern Louisiana University*

OAB-2556 94-70759 Orig
Levy, George. **To die in Chicago: Confederate prisoners at Camp Douglas, 1862-1865.** Evanston, 1994. 326p bibl index ISBN 1-879260-20-4, $25.00

Levy's book has many features—all of them good. It is first-rate local history that exploits and clarifies Chicago's past. It is Civil War social history that registers the lingering aftershocks of battle, the manipulations of military and other politicians, and the forces of propaganda and public opinion. Best of all, it is a well-researched, clearly written, fully illustrated contribution to the long-neglected, but recently flourishing, history of prisoners of war. Camp Douglas was established in 1861 as a military depot and training site near the original University of Chicago. Through improvisation rather than planning, it became a prison for Confederate soldiers captured at Fort Donelson, Shiloh, and other battlefields. Overcrowded, poorly drained, unsanitary, and exposed to cold winds in winter and plagues of insects in summer, Camp Douglas had an appalling death rate but was never so lethal as the notorious Confederate enclosure at Andersonville, Georgia. The camp touched a remarkable array of personalities, including commandants, guard troops, politicians, civilian traders, and inmates. Among them was Henry Morton Stanley, later famous as a journalist-explorer in Africa, whose description of Camp Douglas was of dubious veracity. The most difficult prisoners to manage were the flamboyant John Hunt Morgan's Raiders and frequent escapers who fled only to Chicago's tavern district. Levy has written all their stories accurately and powerfully. Both general and academic readers.—*G. H. Davis, Georgia State University*

OAB-2557 E185 93-16617 CIP
Lewis, David Levering. **W.E.B. Du Bois—biography of a race, 1868-1919.** H. Holt, 1993. 735p index afp ISBN 0-8050-2621-5, $35.00

Lewis's study promises to be the most comprehensive biography of DuBois yet written. The author's research is massive—99 collections in 28 archives on three continents. Lewis provides background and details not only for Dubois's life but also for all those people (some 150 in particular) and institutions that shaped his milieus. Arrogant, aloof, yet passionately involved with the lives of African Americans, DuBois was a complex man whose autobiographical writing blended myth with experience. Born in 1868 in Great Barrington, Massachusetts, he died in 1963 in Accra, Ghana, where he lived in exile during his final years, alienated from the US. Volume 1 of Lewis's work begins with a sociocultural description of the setting into which DuBois was born and follows his life through the 1919 Pan-African Congress in Paris. Lewis clearly shows the development of DuBois's political consciousness as well as documenting his professional growth and publications. One of his books, *The Philadelphia Negro* (1899), was the first sociological study of African American life. Lewis also gives major attention to the genesis of the conflict between DuBois and Booker T. Washington, whose accomodationist policies were comfortably nonthreatening to white hegemony. The volume includes 16 pages of photographs, 120 pages of notes, and a selected bibliography of DuBois's writings. A required acquisition for all social science and African American collections. All levels.—*H. M. MacLam, Choice*

OAB-2558 F475 93-16891 CIP
Mallinckrodt, Anita M. **From knights to pioneers: one German family in Westphalia and Missouri.** Southern Illinois, 1994. 516p bibl index afp ISBN 0-8093-1917-9, $45.00

In this sweeping yet thorough and engaging account, Mallinckrodt chronicles one German family from "the old stories father told" about Dortmund in the 1100s, to the lives of a generation of immigrants in Missouri in the 1800s. Using a rich and extensive set of family letters, Mallinckrodt focuses primarily on the period from the 1820s, when the Mallinckrodts first made the journey to the

US, to the post-Civil War years, when the family ventured from agriculture into industry with the founding of a chemical company. Throughout, Mallinckrodt does a nice job of weaving the details of family history into a broader historical fabric that includes the social and political life of antebellum St. Louis; the Mexican War; the vexing slavery question and ultimate Civil War; American nativism; race relations; and Reconstruction. This is a very straightforward, accessible narrative, yet theory-minded readers will find much of significance in the particular slice of US social history that is illuminated by this German immigrant saga. Mallinckrodt's examination of multiethnic "pioneer" settlement, for instance, contradicts common notions of a simple black-and-white social dichotomy in the antebellum South. A fine addition to collections on immigration and ethnicity; the regional and local history of the Midwest; family history and genealogy; and 19th-century US social history. All levels.—*M. F. Jacobson, SUNY at Stony Brook*

OAB-2559 E467 92-24533 CIP
Marszalek, John F. **Sherman: a soldier's passion for order.** Free Press, 1993. 635p bibl index ISBN 0-02-920135-7, $29.95

Marszalek (Mississippi State Univ.) has written what is likely to be the definitive biography of William T. Sherman. Prodigiously researched, this book tells the tale of perhaps the Civil War's most controversial military leader. One of 11 children, Sherman was raised, after his father's death, in the prominent Ewing family. The tension between Sherman and patriarch Thomas Ewing, as well as that between Sherman and his wife Ellen, who was also his foster sister, play an important role in the book. The author displays shrewd psychological insight, although this is by no means a psychobiography. A West Point graduate, Sherman was largely a failure in most endeavors before the war. He suffered with bouts of depression, though was hardly "insane," as critics charged. Throughout this well-written narrative, terms like "manifest destiny," or legislation like the Compromise of 1850 are briefly explained. Although his portrait of Sherman is generally favorable, Marszalek does show the subject's warts—his racism, for example. A well-rounded study, the book nicely complements Charles Royster's *The Destructive War: William Tecumseh Sherman, Stonewall Jackson and the Americans* (CH, May'92). A must for libraries at all levels.—*S. G. Weisner, Springfield Technical Community College*

OAB-2560 UD373 94-48216 CIP
McChristian, Douglas C. **The U.S. Army in the West, 1870-1880: uniforms, weapons, and equipment.** Oklahoma, 1995. 315p bibl index afp ISBN 0-8061-2705-8, $34.95

McChristian, chief historian at the Little Bighorn Battlefield National Monument, has studied and collected materials from the US Army for more than three decades. In this book he traces the evolution of army uniforms, equipment, and small arms from the immediate post-Civil War years, through the experimental decade of the 1870s and the western Indian wars, down to the early 1880s. This is more than a catalog of buttons and knapsacks, however; McChristian analyzes the evolution of army equipment, official and unofficial. He demonstrates that no amount of policy making by colonels and generals in Washington could deter troops in the field from adapting "official" uniforms and equipment to their needs in the harsh environment of the West. Army uniform and equipment policies gradually began to reflect the realities of western Indian warfare by the late 1870s, but the real innovators were the privates and sergeants in the ranks, not their highest commanders. Three appendixes, 260 illustrations, more than 500 endnotes, an impressive bibliography, and a detailed index combine with the author's descriptions and analysis to make this a first-rate reference work for students of western history. All levels.—*R. G. Lowe, University of North Texas*

OAB-2561 KF4757 93-4942 CIP
McClain, Charles J. **In search of equality: the Chinese struggle against discrimination in nineteenth-century America.** California, 1994. 385p indexes afp ISBN 0-520-08337-7, $35.00

In this excellent and well-researched study McClain uses significant court cases to demonstrate the efforts of the Chinese community to combat discrimination cast on them at the hands of government during the 19th century. McClain focuses on California, the home of the overwhelming majority of Chinese during the 19th century and the hub of anti-Chinese agitation. California's early immigration laws of travel restriction, laundry prohibition, school segregation, ghettoizing imperatives, and medical quarantines provide the framework wherein McClain addresses the Chinese challenges that often pitted local against federal legislation. In most of these cases the local legislation was struck down by the courts. This study shows that the Chinese understood perfectly well how they were singled out for invidious treatment and that they resisted this discrimination at every turn, principally using the host society's court system to fight for their rights. McClain's study of nativism brings to light an important and somewhat neglected chapter of US cultural and ethnic history. Upper-division undergraduates and above.—*J. C. Wolkerstorfer, College of St. Catherine*

OAB-2562   E457   93-22863 CIP
Neely, Mark E. **The last best hope of earth: Abraham Lincoln and the promise of America.** Harvard/Huntington Library/Illinois State Historical Library, 1993. 214p index afp ISBN 0-674-51125-5, $24.95

Neely (St. Louis Univ.), winner of the Pulitzer prize for his last Lincoln book, has studied Lincoln closely for more than 20 years. He previously compiled *The Lincoln Encyclopedia* (1950), for which he wrote every entry. His first Lincoln biography, eagerly anticipated, will immediately become the standard introduction. Neely emphasizes the presidency and eschews the folksy; he takes Lincoln seriously and demonstrates that a no-nonsense approach makes the man even more fascinating. An intellectual and analytical study written as a series of topical essays, omitting traditional anecdotes and reminiscences, this biography emphasizes the importance of the issues and decisions Lincoln faced and his skill in meeting them. In this respect, Neely's Lincoln is eminently a man for our times as well as for the ages. Brevity, memorable phrasing, and incisive judgment abound. Experts who disagree with some conclusions must take heed. Neely prepared this biography to accompany an exhibition at the Huntington Library; the text is generously illustrated with photographs, documents, cartoons, and other images informatively captioned and tied to the text. Accessible to college freshmen and indispensable to scholars, this book must find a home in every library.—*J. Y. Simon, Southern Illinois University-Carbondale*

OAB-2563   E98   96-41611 CIP
Parkhill, Thomas C. **Weaving ourselves into the land: Charles Godfrey Leland, "Indians," and the study of Native American religions.** State University of New York, 1997. 238p bibl index afp ISBN 0-7914-3453-2, $59.50

Parkhill's book is a gem of scholarly argument: disarming in its authorial transparency, deft in its careful moving from the particular to the general, securely grounded in the relevant sources, and lucidly written. On one level, it is a careful historical reconstruction of the Native American provenance and "not-Native" alteration and uses of a single Maliseet story. As Parkhill shows, however, it was amateur folklorist Charles Godfrey Leland, a late-19th-century Euramerican, who altered the story and foregrounded it in his well-received *The Algonquin Legends of New England* (1884). What would otherwise be of rather limited interest achieves much wider significance in a second level of the book. Leland was concerned to help Euramericans recover an affinity for nature through a sense of belonging to the land; recovering and, in the process, altering Abenaki and Micmac stories served these romantic ends. Similarly, argues Parkhill, amateur and professional not-Native students of Native American religions today are concerned to "weave ourselves into the land" through "the timeless, tradition-respecting 'Indian' who has a deep abiding relationship to Mother Earth." Even positive stereotyping damages, because it denies Native particularities and historical change. Parkhill challenges students of Native American religions to be more honest about their own religious needs and not to mask them under "our cloak of objectivity." Highly recommended. All levels.—*D. F. Anderson, Northwestern College (IA)*

OAB-2564   JK5774   91-14298 CIP
Pegram, Thomas R. **Partisans and progressives: private interest and public policy in Illinois, 1870-1922.** Illinois, 1992. 297p bibl index afp ISBN 0-252-01847-8, $42.50

A first-rate study about grass-roots politics during the Progressive Era. Specifically, Pegram examines the complexities of reform efforts in Illinois from the Granger agitation of the 1870s until the triumph of special interest groups in the 1920s. Although Progressive reformers in the Prairie State sought to create a just society, they proved less successful than most of their counterparts in the Midwest, especially in Wisconsin. Pegram graphically shows how political partisanship overwhelmed the Progressives' notion of public interest. A tangle of selfish groups early on thwarted the extensive and often altruistic agenda of the uplifters. Illinois Progressives, therefore, settled for efficiency and economy of government rather than enhanced democracy. The Civil Administration Code of 1917 symbolized reform rather than an initiative and referendum law. Pegram's study ranks with Robert H. Wiebe's *The Search for Order* (CH, May'67) and David P. Thelen's *The New Citizenship* (CH, Jul'72) as one of the most thought-provoking books ever published on Progressivism. Wonderfully researched and nicely recounted. All levels.—*H. R. Grant, University of Akron*

OAB-2565   HD1695   92-14161 CIP
Pisani, Donald J. **To reclaim a divided west: water, law, and public policy, 1848-1902.** New Mexico, 1992. 487p bibl index ISBN 0-8263-1380-9, $40.00; ISBN 0-8263-1381-7 pbk, $19.95

In this original history of the development of water law in the American West, Pisani challenges the popular notion of the West as a distinct region primarily characterized by aridity, and refutes the idea that centralized economic or political elites have long exercised control over the area's scarce water. Concentrating on four states—California, Colorado, Nevada, and Wyoming—from the origins of the doctrine of prior appropriation through the federal Reclamation Act of 1902, Pisani argues that fragmentation and conflicting goals have typified water development. His argument is fairly straightforward: topography and climate differ so sharply from one part of the West to another that there was little uniformity in water resources and water-use patterns in the 19th century. Further fragmenting the West were political and economic factors: intensely competitive mercantilism, decentralized government, regional jealousies, and competing land-use schemes. Consequently, the West was in no position to achieve a unified water policy, nor even to benefit fully from federal initiatives. Well written and persuasively documented from archival sources, this study is a welcome addition to the growing body of Western water history. General; advanced undergraduate, faculty, professional.—*L. Vance, Vermont College*

OAB-2566   F279   94-7861 CIP
Powers, Bernard F. **Black Charlestonians: a social history, 1822-1885.** Arkansas, 1994. 377p bibl index afp ISBN 1-55728-364-8, $36.00

Powers (College of Charleston) comprehensively examines the breadth and depth of African American achievement in building a society in postbellum Charleston. He demonstrates the strength and persistence of black drive for self-realization against implacable white resistance, and emphasizes the elements of continuity from antebellum black Charleston that shaped postwar social development. Seeing Charleston's "brown" elite as a buffer class often allied more with whites than blacks, Powers skillfully traces the initial survival of caste differences after 1865, and the slow emergence thereafter of new social and cultural markers around which African American churches, schools, and voluntary associations coalesced. Concluding with an account of the collapse of Reconstruction, Powers underlines the accomplishments of brown and black alike in gaining some, if not all, of the bundle of rights called freedom. Engagingly written and thoroughly researched. Upper-division undergraduates and above.—*T. S. Whitman, Mount St. Mary's College and Seminary*

OAB-2567   N6510   92-19337 CIP

Promey, Sally M. **Spiritual spectacles: vision and image in mid-nineteenth-century Shakerism.** Indiana, 1993. 292p bibl index afp ISBN 0-253-34614-2, $35.00

Promey's book is a penetrating analysis of Shaker art. Her major thesis is that the apparently contradictory emergence of graphic images in this explicitly nonmaterialistic religious society is, in fact, sensible in terms of the third generation's need for visible (and thereby real) connection to the original charisma of the society's founders. The images, acceptably constructed as a form of Shaker holy writ, conflated the past with the present by making the saints of the earlier era concurrent with the later generation. Promey exquisitely uses dense analysis of Shaker and world sociocultural contexts to clarify the structure, function, and meanings of the images. She appropriately contextualizes the images with regard to important theological and ideological constructs basic to Shakerism, e.g., order and gift. Further, she refines current terminology by embracing many of the heretofore disparate graphic forms within her term "gift images." Promey admirably uses Turner's anthropological models of liminality, but she might have benefited from grounding her discussion of charismatic institutionalization in Weberian sociology. The book is a gem, a true advance in Shaker studies, art history, religious history, and cultural history. Highly recommended. General; undergraduate; graduate.—*J. B. Wolford, Indiana University-Purdue Univ., Indianapolis*

OAB-2568   F353   93-44630 CIP

Reps, John W. **Cities of the Mississippi: nineteenth-century images of urban development.** Missouri, 1994. 342p bibl index afp ISBN 0-8262-0939-4, $85.00

In this lavishly illustrated work, Reps brings river towns to life in exciting detail. Reps (emeritus, Cornell Univ.) is well known for his *Views and Viewmakers of Urban America* (CH, Oct'84). He uses the same technique applied in that book, combining scholarly descriptions of cities and artists who drew them with a kaleidoscopic collection of prints. The result is an absorbing work that unfolds the stories of urban settlements along the Mississippi. The author discusses these towns chronologically and according to techniques used by the artists who reproduced them. He covers early 19th century towns, 1840s Mississippi urban art, wood engravings, antebellum views, bird's-eye views of the 1850s, and late 19th century urban views. The text concludes with a "A Centennial Portrait." The second half of the book features hundreds of illustrations of towns and cities mentioned in the earlier text. These are beautifully reproduced, with accompanying notes and aerial photographs by Alex MacLean. Also included are footnotes and a bibliography. An invaluable study in US urban and Mississippi River history. All levels.—*J. Jackson, Southeastern Louisiana University*

OAB-2569   HN80   91-40452 CIP

Scherzer, Kenneth A. **The unbounded community: neighborhood life and social structure in New York City, 1830-1875.** Duke University, 1992. 356p bibl index afp ISBN 0-8223-1228-X, $34.95

For the last two decades "social history," i.e., the history of ordinary people, has become one of the dominant modes of historical research. This is nowhere more true than in the field of urban history. Given both its size and available records, New York City's history has been one of the chief areas for these studies. In this study, Scherzer proposes a dynamic model for neighborhoods, as opposed to the idea that neighborhoods were unchanging and uniform. He examines the makeup of neighborhoods from several perspectives: mobility, nature of the inhabitants, the meaning of neighborhood, and the idea that neighborhoods were exclusive enclaves whose inhabitants had few, if any, contacts outside their borders. The evidence that he uses is both statistical and more traditional. His statistical analyses are excellent, as is their presentation. For those readers who might be put off by tables, the discussions and conclusions are particularly clear. One of Scherzer's most surprising conclusions is that the first attempts at self-segregation was by "old" American stock. Advanced undergraduate; graduate; faculty.—*I. Cohen, Illinois State University*

OAB-2570   KFV2801   96-1010 CIP

Schwarz, Philip J. **Slave laws in Virginia.** Georgia, 1996. 253p index afp ISBN 0-8203-1831-0, $40.00

Schwarz, an eminent authority on the legal history of slavery in Virginia, has mined the rich research materials of the state. This book is a by-product of his earlier study, *Twice Condemned* (1988). Pointing out that the earlier book examined the motives of black slaves, he now concentrates on white people's attempts to maintain legal control over slaves. One chapter describes how Thomas Jefferson conducted himself as a slaveowner in conformity with Virginia's laws on slavery. Schwarz observes, "By freely subjecting himself to the law of slavery, he committed himself to an unjust institution." A chapter on capital punishment demonstrates that it was proportionately more frequently meted out to slaves than to whites. Over time, capital punishment declined, in part because of judicial self-restraint. The chapter on fugitive slaves focuses on attempts by Virginians to enforce their legal rights to slave property. The concluding chapter examines the status of Virginia blacks after emancipation. Well written and abundantly documented, the book is appropriate reading for upper-division undergraduates and above.—*J. A. Rawley, University of Nebraska—Lincoln*

OAB-2571   E475   96-31220 CIP

Sears, Stephen W. **Chancellorsville.** Houghton Mifflin, 1996. 593p bibl index ISBN 0-395-63417-2, $35.00

The battle of Chancellorsville in May 1863 was Robert E. Lee's masterpiece and the commencement of his downfall. Completely routing the Union army of Joseph Hooker, Lee lost as many soldiers as his foe, but acquired the assurance that led him northward to Gettysburg. He also suffered the loss of Stonewall Jackson, accidentally shot by his own troops, whose brilliant flank attack had made all the difference. Chancellorsville has not lacked historical attention: a crowded shelf was enriched in 1996 by *Chancellorsville: The Battle and Its Aftermath*, ed. by Gary Gallagher. Sears, a prolific Civil War author who has already recorded the life, letters, and battles of George B. McClellan in four separate books, provides the best modern Chancellorsville narrative, based on extensive research and shrewd analysis and complemented by 20 excellent maps. An appendix, "Romances," briskly demolishes persistent legends and links the actual battle to the fictional events in Stephen Crane's *Red Badge of Courage*. Reminiscent of Bruce Catton, Sears's animated style and provocative insights will attract general readers, but scholars will also require this masterful account.—*J. Y. Simon, Southern Illinois University at Carbondale*

OAB-2572   F159   90-50246 CIP

Serrin, William. **Homestead: the glory and tragedy of an American steel town.** Times Books, 1992. 452p bibl index ISBN 0-8129-1886-X, $25.00

Many "standard textbook" approaches to US history fail to focus on working-class issues and the historic relationship between worker, union, and the corporation. For this reason, there is ample room for works like *Homestead*. Serrin (New York Univ.), a workplace correspondent for *The New York Times* and author of *The Company and the Union* (CH, Jul'73) traces the complicated development of the iron and steel works at Homestead, Pennsylvania. Highlighting those who played major roles in creating the vast mills—from the most common 19th-century laborer who worked 12-hour days, seven days per week, to Andrew Carnegie and his successors at United States Steel—Serrin offers a fascinating history of the industry. Meticulously researched and superbly written, Serrin's book is destined to be a classic. Anyone with interests in social, labor, business, or economic history will find *Homestead* a must. Illustrations, photographs, notes, selected bibliography. All levels.—*P. D. Travis, Texas Woman's University*

OAB-2573   E668   93-18626 CIP

Silber, Nina. **The romance of reunion: northerners and the South, 1865-1900.** North Carolina, 1993. 257p bibl index afp ISBN 0-8078-2116-0, $34.95

Silber uses the image of romance—"gendered," heterosexual, urban, and middle-class romance—between *strong man* and *good girl* to apprehend developing northern attitudes toward the defeated South from the end of the Civil War to the end of the century. Once, northerners use gendered images to insult southern enemies by ascribing "feminine" qualities of weakness to a feared Confederate rival. By the 1890s, however, as northern industrial society matured and consequently developed huge problems of dislocation and no little dispute about proper roles for men and women, the continuities of gender roles in the South become attractive, even enviable. In many stories and journalists' reports the theme appears of the strong Yankee wedding the dependent southern belle who *knows her place* and supports her man in his place. Thus, in the language of reconciliation crucial to economic integration of the postbellum nation and vital to the ideological reunification in the Spanish-American War of 1898, northern choice of metaphors for praise revealed a chauvinism as profound, if different, as the older choice of metaphors. Moreover, "[o]ne of the most noteworthy features of the reunion process was the transformation in white northerners' racial outlook .... This new orientation [of southern gender roles] paved the way for northern acceptance of some of the most virulent forms of racism which American society had ever produced." Only Paul Buck's classic *Road to Reunion* (1937) previously examined northern images of reconciliation, and his concerns are hardly with gender. Silber's book is a study with broadest implications and is accessible at all levels of study.—*J. Roper, Emory and Henry College*

OAB-2574   F395   93-13110 CIP
Stewart, Kenneth L. **Not room enough: Mexicans, Anglos, and socio-economic change in Texas, 1850-1900,** by Kenneth L. Stewart and Arnoldo De León. New Mexico, 1993. 148p bibl index ISBN 0-8263-1437-6, $27.50

Stewart and De León exmaine the interaction between Mexicans, Anglos, and the forces of social and economic change that transformed Texas into a modern industrial and democratic society during the last half of the 19th century. They argue that, contrary to most popular stereotypes, Mexicans in Texas were not a people marginalized by their backward culture and their determination to retain traditional ways of life following the Anglo conquest of Texas in 1836. Instead, they maintain that Mexicans shared with Anglos a determination to modernize Texas, both politically and economically, before the Battle of San Jacinto transferred hegemony to the Anglos. Whatever marginalization followed was because of changing demographics, which reduced Mexicans to a political minority, even in those areas of south Texas where they were most concentrated, and to Anglo racial prejudice, which restricted Mexicans to largely menial jobs in the late 19th century economy. Stewart and De León have combined the methodologies of sociology and history to develop a very convincing view of ethnic confrontation in Texas. They rely heavily on a statistical description of a sample population to challenge the image of Texas (and the frontier) as a land of opportunity and wide open spaces. Instead, their Texas is a land with "not room enough" to accommodate two peoples, each seeking to engineer the region's transformation from frontier to modernity. This book is a significant addition to the growing literature on Mexican Americans in Texas. Undergraduates and above.—*C. D. Wintz, Texas Southern University*

OAB-2575   HX632   93-8609 CIP
Sutton, Robert P. **Les Icariens: the Utopian dream in Europe and America.** Illinois, 1995 (c1994). 199p bibl index afp ISBN 0-252-02067-7, $26.95

Sutton's book is the first comprehensive study of the French utopian movement, Icarianism, to appear in English. It includes extensive coverage of Etienne Cabet (1778-1856), the founder of this 19th-century social experiment, and suggests that he was not a wholly likable figure. Although Cabet possessed considerable intellectual abilities and great ambitions, he was crassly opportunistic and careless with his plans for implementing a secular utopia in the US. Cabet and his hard-core followers began their quest for utopia in 1848 and struggled to find the most promising location. The saga of Icarianism in America is associated with Texas, Illinois, Iowa, and California. Various problems—most notably internal bickering and financial difficulties—prevented creation of

the community Cabet and his most enthusiastic followers sought. The experiment faded away on the Iowa prairies in the 1890s. Thoroughly researched and enhanced by a fine prose style, Sutton's work is sensibly organized and argued. Icaria is not seen in a historical vacuum; Cabet and his utopia are related to larger forces and trends. This book will surely become the standard chronicle of the movement. All levels.—*H. R. Grant, University of Akron*

OAB-2576   Orig
Svingen, Orlan J. **The Northern Cheyenne Indian Reservation, 1877-1900.** University Press of Colorado, 1993. 197p bibl index afp ISBN 0-87081-303-X, $22.50

An exceptionally thoroughly researched account of the creation of the Northern Cheyenne Indian Reservation along the Tongue River and Rosebud Creek in southeast Montana. Forced to move to Indian Territory (Oklahoma) in 1877 during the US Army's reaction to Custer's defeat at the Little Big Horn the previous year, about 1,000 Northern Cheyenne, led by the chiefs Two Moon and White Bull, filtered back to their traditional home in the north. Several hundred Northern Cheyenne remained there, serving as army scouts. This, together with remarkable Indian leadership and pursuit of their objectives by nonviolent means, persuaded a succession of Indian agents, officials in the Bureau of Indian Affairs, and ultimately two US presidents to create and extend the Northern Cheyenne reservation between 1884 and 1900. The history of this people was not all peaceful. Land-hungry whites engaged in cattle ranching and interested in the mineral potential of the land opposed the creation of the reservation, carrying on a campaign of opposition and false charges. Patience, persistence, and restraint, however, allowed the Cheyenne to achieve their objectives despite significant odds. The book is a model of historical research in administrative records as a basis for reconstruction of the Native American history of the period. Advanced undergraduates and above.—*S. W. Haycox, University of Alaska, Anchorage*

OAB-2577   Orig
Thomas, Emory M. **Robert E. Lee: a biography.** W.W. Norton, 1995. 472p bibl index ISBN 0-393-03730-4, $30.00

Author of many fine books on the Confederacy, Thomas (Univ. of Georgia) has written an outstanding biography of the South's greatest hero. Based on a complete review of all the primary and secondary sources, this excellent book will be indispensable to scholars and is a valuable addition to the literature on Lee. Using brevity, memorable phrasing, and incisive judgment, Thomas's account is narrative history at its very best with the author emphasizing the human side of Lee. Thomas argues that Lee's great responses throughout his life to the trials he faced on and off the battlefield, rather than his extraordinary accomplishments, are what made this man so great. Acknowledging Douglas Southall Freeman's classic *Robert E. Lee, Biography* (1943) which presented Lee as a noble military genius, and Thomas L. Connelly's revisionist *The Marble Man: Robert E. Lee and His Image in Society* (CH, Nov'77) which questioned Lee's character and command, Thomas presents a "post-revisionist," fully alive Lee who in all his great humanity and ability is "both more and less than his legend." Highly recommended, all levels.—*E. M. Thomas, Gordon College*

OAB-2578   F389   93-40484 CIP
Tijerina, Andrés. **Tejanos and Texas under the Mexican flag, 1821-1836.** Texas A&M, 1994. 172p bibl index afp (The centennial series of the Association of Former Students, Texas A&M University, 54) ISBN 0-89096-585-4, $29.50; ISBN 0-89096-606-0 pbk, $14.95

This important book will serve as a landmark volume for the study of Mexican-Texans, the Tejanos, during the period when Texas was part of Mexico from 1821 until 1836. Tijerina's meticulous research provides cogent understanding of the lives, labors, land-holding patterns, political activities, society, and cultural institutions of the Texas Hispanic residents during the period when the Anglo-American frontier consumed the region west of the Sabine River. Most important, this book documents a two-way cultural exchange between the

Tejanos and the Anglo-Americans, especially in the transmission of a Hispanic cattle culture to the new arrivals from the US. Tijerina (Texas A&M-Kingsville) argues convincingly that Spanish cattle-raising techniques (along with the language, land-owning patterns, and legal practices of the Hispanic cow culture) had an enduring impact on the Anglo-American frontier. Tijerina is at his strongest in surveying the Tejano demography of Hispanic Texas while he describes the society and culture of this sometimes overlooked group of Texans. This book provides significant insights into Tejano history and also serves as a model for future research. Upper-division undergraduate; graduate faculty.—*L. T. Cummins, Austin College*

OAB-2579   B945   95-50101 CIP

Townsend, Kim. **Manhood at Harvard: William James and others.** W.W. Norton, 1996. 318p bibl index afp ISBN 0-393-03939-0, $29.95

Written by the author of *Sherwood Anderson: A Biography* (CH, Feb'88) this book is a tour de force. It unites the resources of historical inquiry, literary scholarship, and American studies in a fascinating account of a major current in American thought and culture, c. 1870-1910. Townsend (English, Amherst College) treats the origin, popularization, and decline of an ideal of masculinity in whose course "a select group of ... students and faculty members" at Harvard University played a crucial role. All of them were students or colleagues of William James. The ideal of masculinity that his thought helped shape found expression, and in some instances, criticisms in the ideas, writing, and lives of several pivotal figures. These include James, Charles William Eliot, Henry Adams, W.E.B. DuBois, George Santayana, Oliver Wendell Holmes Jr., Owen Wister, and, preeminently, Theodore Roosevelt, as well as less well known figures. By about 1910, when Harvard's new president Abbott Lawrence Lowell was stressing the social responsibilities of manhood, the earlier, individualistic ideal was waning. Yet it remains a substratum of American culture, and a determinant of attitudes about both sexes. Illustrations, endnotes. A wonderful read! All levels.—*D. W. Steeples, Mercer University*

OAB-2580   F234   96-35602 CIP

Tripp, Steven Elliot. **Yankee town, southern city: race and class relations in Civil War Lynchburg.** New York University, 1997. 344p bibl index afp (The American social experience series, 36) ISBN 0-8147-8205-1, $45.00

Tripp's book is a delight to read. Although many books have been written on the Civil War, southern communities, and economic class life in the US, this very readable yet scholarly work focuses on both class and race. Tripp treats a variety of topics: military history; race and class relationships during the war and Reconstruction; a Yankee town in the South. He also examines religious revivals and divisions between Catholic immigrant groups and puritanical Protestants that include challenges of gender, slavery, and race, as well as the war itself and the impact of military service on the city's classes and ethnic groups. Tripp presents a clear political history reflecting social, ethnic, and economic divisions in the community. Common sufferings during and after the war contrast with the lot of the privileged even under such circumstances. The resources are complete and well documented without making the work less interesting. Highly recommended for all Civil War buffs, community historians, economic and social historians, ethnic studies groups, and anyone who likes a good book! All levels.—*N. J. Hervey, Luther College*

OAB-2581   HD6073   91-11900 MARC

Turbin, Carole. **Working women of collar city: gender, class, and community in Troy, New York, 1864-86.** Illinois, 1992. 231p bibl index afp ISBN 0-252-01836-2, $39.95

In 1864, a group of largely Irish shirt-collar laundresses formed the first US women's labor organization in Troy, New York. Collar workers remained active in the labor movement for the next 20 years. In this work Turbin, a sociologist at Occidental College, tries to explain why this early example of women's labor activism occurred. Painstakingly analyzing the few surviving statements

of collar workers for clues about their lives and ideologies, and comparing Troy's female labor force to their counterparts in other industries and communities, Turbin describes how community, gender, class, ethnicity, and religion shaped female workers' strategies for their lives. Turbin decries prior analyses for oversimplifying working women's actions by contrasting their behavior too rigidly to men's. In her view, women were often more skilled and committed to a trade than they were credited as being; concern for families did not make women necessarily more conservative. Turbin's study is cogent, thought-provoking, well-written, and an obvious choice for any undergraduate or graduate library collecting in women's or labor history.—*P. F. Field, Ohio University*

OAB-2582   E99   92-42681 CIP

Utley, Robert M. **The lance and the shield: the life and times of Sitting Bull.** H. Holt, 1993. 413p bibl index afp ISBN 0-8050-1274-5, $25.00

The legend of this prominent Hunkpapa Sioux leader has ranged from the late 19th century despised image of the "killer of Custer" to today's representation of the "super-Indian." Utley, former chief historian of the National Park Service and recognized authority on the trans-Mississippi West, avoids the two extremes and recreates a more honest appraisal. Using both Indian and white accounts, Utley takes his subject from a childhood spent amid Sioux ascendancy to his tragic death at the hands of Indian police in 1890. The author stresses both the spiritual power and temporal leadership qualities that raised Sitting Bull to fame among his own people, and, by the 1870s, among non-Indians as well. Utley also pays close attention to the importance of kinship and the dynamics of Lakota tribal society to properly explain their motivations. He likewise demonstrates how congressional delegations, often working with avaricious western land interests, dismembered the Great Sioux Reservation during the 1870s and '80s, leading ultimately to the rise of the Ghost Dance and the tragic consequences of Wounded Knee. This book is well written, strongly documented, and fairly reasoned to satisfy even specialists within the field. It surpasses all previous biographies of Sitting Bull. All levels.—*M. L. Tate, University of Nebraska at Omaha*

OAB-2583   F697   92-54143 CIP

Woodhouse, S.W. **A naturalist in Indian territory: the journals of S.W. Woodhouse, 1849-50,** ed. and annot. by John S. Tomer and Michael J. Brodhead. Oklahoma, 1992. 304p bibl index afp (The American exploration and travel series, 72) ISBN 0-8061-2476-8, $29.95

The introduction to this essay provides a competent overview of the various explorations that penetrated the Louisiana territory. Moving to the Creek Boundary Expedition, for which Woodhouse's journals provide most of the text, the authors summarize the reasons for and the extent of the expedition. Moreover, they make an excellent case that Woodhouse, a hitherto neglected physician and naturalist, produced first-rate work that helped in understanding the topographic features, geology, and plant and animal life of the trans-Mississippi West. The authors then offer an excellent biographical sketch of Woodhouse's life. Woodhouse's career as a field naturalist was quite brief, approximately four years. In later life, he practiced medicine. The diary itself is an excellent work of which both editors and press can be proud. Annotations are generally complete, yet not unnecessarily pedantic. The various sites, names, and species are placed in context. The reader understands what happened to the botanical names of plants and animals given by Woodhouse. Highly recommended. Advanced undergraduate; graduate; faculty.—*T. G. Alexander, Brigham Young University*

OAB-2584   HD9999   92-9205 CIP

Yu, Renqiu. **To save China, to save ourselves: the Chinese Hand Laundry Alliance of New York.** Temple University, 1992. 253p bibl index afp ISBN 0-87722-996-1, $39.95

The experiences of Chinese Americans differed markedly from those of other immigrants. Between 1882 and 1943, the US excluded them by name and barred them from naturalization. Within this milieu, the Chinese Hand Laundry Alliance (CHLA) sought to serve the needs of New York City's Chinese laundrymen, to dismantle America's system of institutional discrimination, and to bring democratic reform to China. Rather than perpetuating Old World traditions, a common organizational function in other "transplanted" communities, the Alliance challenged Chinatown's established sources of power and leadership. The CHLA believed that these institutions "stood in the way of the Chinese struggle for equality in American society." Yu's work, well written and thoroughly researched, chronicles the CHLA's diverse successes and failures. *To Save China* is a good addition to the literature on Asian immigrants, especially as a companion to such general works as Roger Daniels's *Asian America* and Ronald Takaki's *Strangers from a Different Shore*. Advanced undergraduate; graduate; faculty.—*R. F. Zeidel, University of Wisconsin-Stout*

UNITED STATES — 20th Century

OAB-2585　　　F595　　　93-11035 CIP
Abbott, Carl. **The Metropolitan frontier: cities in the modern American West.** Arizona, 1993. 244p afp ISBN 0-8165-1129-2, $29.95

Abbott's pioneering study surveys the urban growth of the American West over the past half-century. It is a tour-de-force of interdisciplinary social science and makes a major contribution to fields as diverse as regional history, urban geography, and public policymaking. Abbott deftly organizes his sprawling topic into ten especially well written chapters. The opening pair of chapters treats the impact of WW II on urban industries and populations and the resulting politics of growth and city-building. The central chapters trace economic and demographic change and political responses from 1950 to 1990. Closing chapters consider the larger questions of urban environmental relationships and the impact of western cities on the region's character as well as on the national imagination. Physically, this is a handsome book whose maps, photos, tables, and reference sections nicely enhance the presentation. It is the leading overview of its subject and is very highly recommended for all academic and large public libraries. All levels.—*P. O. Muller, University of Miami*

OAB-2586　　　F144　　　94-11783 CIP
Birkner, Michael J. **A country place no more: the transformation of Bergenfield, New Jersey, 1894-1994.** Fairleigh Dickinson, 1994. (Dist. by Associated University Presses) 373p bibl index afp ISBN 0-8386-3574-1, $45.00

A native of Bergenfield and currently chair of the history department at Gettysburg College, Birkner has produced a deeply researched, well-written, and carefully balanced study of his hometown's development from a small village of Dutch and Huguenot farmers in 1894 into a densely populated, multiethnic urban suburb today. In ten chapters he traces the impact on the town of successive waves of newcomers; of the arrival of the railroad; of the advent of roads, automobiles, and the George Washington Bridge; and of two World Wars and the intervening Great Depression, among other outside influences. Equally important were local developments: a generation of Republican dominance covering a key period of expansion, the tendency of government to accommodate land developers' demands, popular insistence upon low taxes, and reluctance to adopt zoning and other planning tools. The result has been a densely settled suburb not without its ethnic and racial tensions, but one in which people have generally adopted a "live and let live" attitude that has enabled Bergenfield to absorb numerous ethnic groups and urban tensions while remaining suburban. Based on extensive research in primary sources and numerous interviews with a wide variety of residents. Both general and academic readers.—*J. F. Mahoney, Seton Hall University*

OAB-2587　　　HQ767　　　92-39693 CIP
Blanchard, Dallas A. **Religious violence and abortion: the Gideon Project,** by Dallas A. Blanchard and Terry J. Prewitt. University Press of Florida, 1993. 347p bibl index afp ISBN 0-8130-1193-0, $39.95; ISBN 0-8130-1194-9 pbk, $16.95

Blanchard and Prewitt provide what may be one of the most important

case studies in the abortion stalemate. Using a variety of data sources, the book highlights the controversy surrounding the bombing of three abortion clinics in Pensacola, Florida, in 1984, code-named, by those involved, "The Gideon Project." The book begins with an examination of the national context of abortion in the early 1980s as well as the local conditions that fostered conflict over this issue in Pensacola. Following this, detailed transcripts of the arrest and subsequent trial of the "Pensacola Four" underscores the religious pragmatism that rationalized the destruction of "property" as a means to ending abortion. The final section demonstrates the relevance of this research, particularly for understanding the theological and sociological factors that promoted the use of violence within the most radicalized wing of the "anti-abortion" movement. These factors include biblical and historical justification for religious violence, at least for radical fundamentalists; the perceived, though tacit, support of the Reagan administration for abortion-related violence; and the apparent failure of the anti-abortion movement to effect significant change. The book is well written and documented. All levels.—*C. M. Hand, Lenoir-Rhyne College*

OAB-2588　　　HQ76　　　94-4542 CIP
Chauncey, George. **Gay New York: gender, urban culture, and the making of the gay male world, 1890-1940.** Basic Books, 1994. 478p index ISBN 0-465-02633-8, $25.00

Chauncey's book is a major contribution to social history. In highly readable and well-documented prose, Chauncey disputes several current, widely held views about gay males of the past. Chauncey claims that in New York City in the first half of the 20th century, gay men were not all isolated from each other, were not all invisible to straight people, and did not all internalize self-hatred from society. Several neighborhoods in the city, especially Greenwich Village, Harlem, and the Bowery, had highly visible gay social events (mostly drag queen balls). Further, gay men whose homosexuality was not evident were present everywhere else, often living double lives—heterosexual on the job, but gay in after-hours. Chauncey states that the current categorization of people as heterosexual or homosexual was not common in those days, especially in working-class culture. Instead, men were usually classified according to how masculine or feminine they were. A masculine man was "normal"—even if he had sex with other males—while a feminine man was a "fairy" who presumably wanted sex only with males. Many masculine men regularly had sex with other men, but were not stigmatized for doing so. After Prohibition, strong antigay laws were passed. Those laws, WW II, and the Cold War changed that gay male world. A valuable addition to any library. All levels.—*R. W. Smith, California State University, Northridge*

OAB-2589　　　D810　　　94-5614 CIP
Cull, Nicholas John. **Selling war: the British propaganda campaign against American "neutrality" in World War II.** Oxford, 1995. 276p bibl index afp ISBN 0-19-508566-3, $29.95

Cull's book gives valuable insight into the role of the communications revolution in film, radio, and print media in the formation of the Anglo-American relationship during WW II. The author demonstrates how an informal network between British civil servants and American journalists, which provided "information" to the American public, developed into the systematic dissemination of British propaganda in the US. Unlike German propaganda, which was usually bombastic, British publicity emphasized common Anglo-American interests in a calm tone. The British circumvented both isolationists and antipropaganda laws by using American news agencies and specific American correspondents as conduits for their publicity. Hollywood, in particular, was a major vehicle for British propagandizing and was more effective in presenting the Allied cause than were British films before Pearl Harbor. At a time when President Roosevelt was facing an isolationist Congress, pro-British propaganda was essential in creating pro-British and prointerventionist sentiment among the American public. Well written and impressively researched, the book is a welcome addition to the literature on the "special relationship." Should be read in conjunction with D. Reynolds's *The Creation of the Anglo-American Alliance, 1937-41* (CH, Jul'82). Upper-division undergraduates and above.—*F. Krome, Northern Kentucky University*

OAB-2590   E185   93-39632 CIP

Dittmer, John. **Local people: the struggle for civil rights in Mississippi.** Illinois, 1994. 530p index afp ISBN 0-252-02102-9, $29.95

Dittmer traces the Mississippi Civil Rights Movement from the end of WW II until its demise in 1968. Although the initial efforts of local middle-class National Association for the Advancement of Colored People (NAACP) members for voting rights and school integration largely failed in the face of extreme white racism and violence, a broader, deeper grassroots movement emerged in the 1960s that dramatically altered Mississippi's "closed society." Catalyzed by youthful organizers from the Student Nonviolent Coordinating Committee (SNCC) and the Congress of Racial Equality (CORE) and their umbrella organization, the Congress of Federated Organizations (COFO), poor African Americans successfully claimed their voting rights, overcame a reign of terror, and challenged segregation. This is one of the very best studies of the Civil Rights Movement. Based on extensive research, it is a powerful analysis that reveals the Mississippi movement, black and white, within the larger social, economic, and political contexts. Powerfully written, *Local People* is a major study of one of America's most important social movements; it is most highly recommended for all audiences.—*J. Borchert, Cleveland State University*

OAB-2591   E860   93-44736 CIP

Emery, Fred. **Watergate: the corruption of American politics and the fall of Richard Nixon.** Times Books/Random House, 1994. 555p index ISBN 0-8129-2383-9, $27.50

This study serves as companion volume to the critically acclaimed five-part BBC series *Watergate*, also shown on American television in August 1994. Emery, a coproducer of the BBC series and Washington bureau chief for *The Times* of London during the Watergate scandal, proves a veritable master of Watergate evidence and detail. He offers the most complete narrative to date, told predominantly through the eyes of the coconspirators in a most effective, straightforward prose. He uncannily unravels the twists in the individual threads of evidence offered by Nixon's political associates in crime to unveil a complex but discernible pattern that debunks a generation of Watergate mythology—and posits responsibility for the entire scandal in the hands of President Nixon. In retelling the Watergate scandal for a new generation, Emery's work rests at the apex of all previous Watergate studies and should be required reading for Watergate initiate and aficionado alike. This is simply a splendid work that is masterfully written. General and academic readers at all levels.—*R. J. Lettieri, Mount Ida College*

OAB-2592   E185   94-22563 CIP

Fairclough, Adam. **Race & democracy: the civil rights struggle in Louisiana, 1915-1972.** Georgia, 1995. 610p bibl index afp ISBN 0-8203-1700-4, $34.95

Fairclough examines in great detail the history of "the movement" in a single deep-South state, Louisiana, one of the key centers of racial conflict and change in the '60s. His study parallels the recent work of John Dittmer and Charles Payne on Mississippi, and like those excellent monographs, provides many fresh insights concerning race relations in the US. Mining little-used NAACP records, for example, Fairclough highlights the important role of that still-neglected organization in preparing the ground for the racial revolution of the '60s during the Depression years, WW II, and the early postwar era. He has fascinating things to say about the impact of anticommunism on incipient racial change in the Pelican State after WW II, and about the powerful white resistance in Louisiana to the imperatives for change implicit in the *Brown* decision in 1954. Fairclough takes full account of the complexities of Louisiana society and culture—Creole versus non-Creole, northern versus southern Louisiana, Protestant versus Catholic, cosmopolitan New Orleans versus parochial outlying areas—and relates these to the overriding force of race in everyday life. This superb study is fully grounded in massive archival research, and is well written and absorbing. Must reading for both general and specialized readers.—*J. F. Findlay, University of Rhode Island*

OAB-2593   E185   93-28751 CIP

Fierce, Milfred C. **The Pan-African idea in the United States, 1900-1919:** African-American interest in Africa and interaction with West Africa. Garland, 1993. 266p bibl index afp ISBN 0-8153-1460-4, $67.00

Fierce's well-written and well-researched monograph is one of the most comprehensive analyses of the link between Africans in North America and in Africa. Fierce begins by examining the social-historical climate that prevailed in the US during the first score of the 20th century. For this concise, informative, yet scathing overview of "race matters" he moves on to a discussion of the Pan-African idea and its acceptance by both Africans and African Americans. Starting with Chapter 1, which looks at the intellectual precursors of the African interests phenomenon, and ending with Chapter 8, which considers the role played by African Americans at the three major Pan-African conferences, the book rivets the reader to its content. It ranks among the best in terms of presenting "where, when, and how" African and African American linkages occurred during the dawning of the 20th century. Requisite reading for students and scholars of Pan-Africanism, undergraduate level and above.—*R. Stewart, SUNY College at Buffalo*

OAB-2594   RA981   93-617 CIP

Gamble, Vanessa Northington. **Making a place for ourselves: the black hospital movement, 1920-1945.** Oxford, 1995. 265p index afp ISBN 0-19-507889-6, $45.00

Gamble's carefully researched study documents the way in which the black hospital provided training for physicians and medical care for African Americans. The hospitals succeeded in their mission, but had the undesirable effect of fostering segregation rather than integration. Each new hospital mirrored the larger societal debate over civil rights and community. To develop the hospitals meant to develop important community servants; a segregated African American community thus received service. This exacerbated the ever-present tendency toward second-class citizenship. Given this dilemma, the national organization of black hospitals played a leading role in fostering integration of medical care. This effort ironically served to undermine the hospitals themselves. Effectively blending a general overview with studies of specific hospitals, Gamble conveys the strengths, weaknesses, and dilemmas of the black hospital movement. In the process she offers readers understanding of civil rights, the politics of race, medical education, and the divisions within the black community. Upper-division undergraduates and above.—*T. F. Armstrong, Texas Wesleyan University*

OAB-2595   F358   96-10098 CIP

Garcia, Juan R. **Mexicans in the Midwest, 1900-1932.** Arizona, 1996. 292p bibl index afp ISBN 0-8165-1560-3, $39.95

Garcia's book is a must for scholars in the field of Mexican American studies. Garcia (Univ. of Arizona) writes a gripping narrative of the beginning of the Mexican migration to the Midwest and the conditions under which these migrants lived. He describes social and economic forces that shaped their lives, such as discrimination and overcrowded housing, as well as the mechanisms through which they survived. The author has consulted substantial archival material, making good use of Spanish-language newspapers. Garcia does not romanticize the struggle for survival; he cites the often precarious conditions in boardinghouses run by wives of the migrants. This reviewer especially liked the sections "Women and Work," "Mexican Mutual Aid Societies," and the chapter on the early years of the Great Depression, which had a heavy impact on Mexican workers and their families. Garcia focuses mostly on Mexican migrants in Chicago and Detroit. The book reflects first-rate editing, has an excellent bibliography, and is well footnoted and indexed. All levels.—*R. Acuña, California State University, Northridge*

OAB-2596   JK1896   96-36992 CIP

Green, Elna C. **Southern strategies: southern women and the woman suffrage question.** North Carolina, 1997. 287p bibl index afp ISBN 0-8078-2332-5, $45.00; ISBN 0-8078-4641-4 pbk, $16.95

Southern states gave women's suffrage the least support of any region, challenging historians to explain why. In this most comprehensive study of southern women's suffrage to date, Green (Sweet Briar College) compares antisuffrage and prosuffrage activists throughout the South to contradict the argument (made most persuasively by Marjorie Sprull Wheeler in *New Women of the New South*, CH, Jan'94) that the desire to have white women outvote black males was central to the suffrage cause. Using elementary statistical techniques, Green argues that suffragists were part of a new urban middle class interested in progressive causes and opposed to upper-class, established elites in plantation agriculture and industry who denied women's right to vote. She identifies women, such as Kate Gordon, who preferred suffrage to be granted by states, as a third force distinct from both antis and suffragists in the suffrage wars. Provocative and imaginative, well researched and argued, this monograph belongs in undergraduate and graduate libraries because of its contributions in women's and southern history.—*P. F. Field, Ohio University*

OAB-2597   ML420   94-10763 CIP
Guralnick, Peter. **Last train to Memphis: the rise of Elvis Presley.**
Little, Brown, 1994. 560p bibl index ISBN 0-316-33220-8, $24.95

After several hundred books on Elvis Presley, what could recommend another Elvis biography—the first of a two-volume set? Guralnick goes far beyond a meticulously researched portrait of Presley's early years (1935-58); he captures for the first time the symbiosis between his subject and postwar America, in which public attitudes toward music, race, and sexuality, to name but a few issues, would inexorably change. Presley, like his contemporary Marilyn Monroe, by force of personality and talent swept away the complacency of the Eisenhower years and helped define a new, youth-oriented culture. Guralnick, with several critically acclaimed music books including *Feeling Like Going Home* (1971) and *Lost Highway* (CH, May'80), already to his credit, writes as though he were present at all that transpired. Like David Halberstam's *The Fifties* (1993), *Last Train to Memphis* has the power to invoke America's recent past. Illustrated, with copious notes and an excellent bibliography and index, Guralnick's work is highly recommended for American studies students at all levels and for general audiences.—*H. A. Keesing, University of Maryland at College Park*

OAB-2598   UG633   92-7034 CIP
Hallion, Richard P. **Storm over Iraq: air power and the Gulf War.**
Smithsonian Institution Press, 1992. 383p index afp ISBN 1-56098-190-3, $24.95

At last there are qualified military historians who can produce works about this brief conflict that not only tell its story in depth but analyze events as well. Hallion, Chief Historian of the USAF, is well known for an abundance of solid work in the field of aviation history. He has brought this background to his assessment of the war against Iraq, known as Desert Storm. Norman Friedman's *Desert Victory* (CH, Feb'92) offers an immediate account of the war, but Hallion's study is much more important for two reasons. First, he shows that this was the first war in which the air forces were able to assure victory on their own. Second, he spends nearly half the book setting the air war in historical perspective. He documents both the literature he has used so well and his many interviews with participants. For any collection on the Gulf War. General; advanced undergraduate; graduate; faculty; professional.—*R. Higham, Kansas State University*

OAB-2599   SB110   92-8558 CIP
Hargreaves, Mary W.M. **Dry farming in the northern Great Plains: years of readjustment, 1920-1990.** University Press of Kansas, 1993. 386p index afp ISBN 0-7006-0553-3, $45.00

Zebulon Pike and other adventurers offered pessimistic assessments of the agricultural potential of the Great Plains, yet land-hungry Anglos paid little heed to such unscientific appraisals and moved West anyway. Some came with hopes of creating a "garden" from what was described as a "desert," but all of these pioneers experienced one thing in common when they relocated, namely, that

the region offered scant or erratic rainfall. In this sequel to *Dry Farming in the Northern Great Plains, 1900-1925* (1957) Hargreaves acknowledges the impact that the environment has had on farming in the western Dakotas and eastern Montana. She insists, however, that the region has survived agriculturally because of the innovative practices of farmers such as Hardy W. Campbell, who preached the efficacy of deep plowing/subsoiling ("dry farming") techniques at the turn of the century. Thereafter, farming technology, farm management, indeed, scientific farming, have pulled the region through in good and bad times. Hargreaves (emeritus, Univ. of Kentucky) offers the reader a regional agricultural history blended with national themes that is thoroughly and meticulously researched. Those interested in the northern Great Plains, its agricultural heritage, and in Americana at large, will find this book a must. Maps; tables; list of acronyms; notes; bibliographical note. Advanced undergraduate; graduate; faculty; professional.—*P. D. Travis, Texas Woman's University*

OAB-2600   D570   96-21756 CIP
Harries, Meirion. **The last days of innocence: America at war, 1917-1918,** by Meirion Harries and Susie Harries. Random House, 1997. 573p index afp ISBN 0-679-41863-6, $32.50

This is an excellent study of US participation in WW I. The research is in far greater depth than the usual "popular history," the analysis is sharp and informative, and the writing is clear and a pleasure to read. The authors strike an even balance between the necessity for condensation and the accuracy that comes from detailed treatment. One of their few errors comes when Secretary of War Baker is blamed for hastily adopting "the British Lee-Enfield rifle," rechambered for American ammunition, thus delaying mass production. In fact, it was the Enfield 1914, already in production in three American factories, that was adopted and rechambered as the Enfield 1917. This was the rifle that equipped a majority of the AEF. The military operations of the AEF are particularly well done, and the reader can hardly find a more succinct and telling summation of the effect of the war on American thought and culture. This book is strongly recommended for the general reader and the student who wants entertaining reading and a better understanding of these pivotal years.—*R. D. Ward, emeritus, Georgia Southern University*

OAB-2601   Orig
Harris, Sheldon H. **Factories of death: Japanese biological warfare, 1932-45 and the American cover-up.** Routledge, 1994. 297p bibl index ISBN 0-415-09105-5, $25.00

For the past half-century students of WW II have suspected that Japan engaged in biological warfare (BW) and chemical warfare (CW) experiments during the 1930s and '40s. However, few realized the scope of these experiments. Because prosecutors at the Tokyo War Crimes Trial did not charge any Japanese with engaging in BW or CW, suspicions of these activities were generally dismissed as unfounded. *Factories of Death*, however, shows conclusively that between 1932 and 1945, under the direction of Lt. General Shiro Ishii, the Japanese conducted extensive biological and chemical warfare experiments in China and Japan. Human subjects, mainly Chinese, were used in these experiments. Few if any of the subjects, who may have numbered in the tens of thousands, survived. At war's end US authorities, believing they lagged behind Japan in BW and CW research, gave Ishii and his key associates immunity from prosecution in return for the results of their research. Nonetheless, the general provided his interrogators with only a fraction of the information he possessed. Subsequently, several government agencies collaborated to hide from the American public Ishii's wartime activities and the US arrangement with him. This is a solid scholarly study that recounts a disturbing chapter in the Asian phase of WW II. Upper-division undergraduates and above.—*R. H. Detrick, University of North Texas*

OAB-2602   E748   95-38621 CIP
Heinemann, Ronald L. **Harry Byrd of Virginia.** University Press of Virginia, 1996. 511 bibl index afp ISBN 0-8139-1642-9, $29.95

Between 1933 and 1965, Senator Harry F. Byrd was, one close observer judged, "probably the most conservative member in either party of the Senate. He was as far right as a man could be and still remain in the bounds of sanity." This judicious biography traces the rise of Byrd from his apple orchard business through his stint as governor of Virginia in the 1920s, his construction of a highly effective (and oligarchic) "organization" within the Virginia Democratic party, and his decades-long service in the US Senate. Heinemann chronicles his rivalry with liberal national Democratic leaders from Franklin Roosevelt to Lyndon Johnson. Exhaustively researched and economically written, this book places Byrd in proper perspective as a clever foe of civil rights, social programs, and federal spending, and as a courtly champion of states rights, poll taxes, and segregation. Heinemann helps illuminate an important strand of 20th-century American conservatism and Harry Byrd's not inconsiderable role in shaping it. This book should garner the interest of all serious students of recent American political history. General readers; upper-division undergraduates and above.—*J. A. McCartin, SUNY College at Geneseo*

OAB-2603   F241   95-32714 CIP
Hennen, John C. **The Americanization of West Virginia: creating a modern industrial state, 1916-1925.** University Press of Kentucky, 1996. 217p bibl index afp ISBN 0-8131-1960-X, $32.95

Winner of the 1995 Appalachian Studies Award, Hennen's study treats one aspect of Appalachian history in both a national and regional context. Hennen "examines complementary attempts by political, educational, and industrial leaders in ... " West Virginia "to insure mass acceptance of state and corporate authority during and after the First World War." These personalities sought to establish an ideal of American identity that equated the interests of business with that of the nation. In this context Americanization refers mainly to the attempt to indoctrinate people into a system of values that would guarantee a literate, loyal, and obedient working class. Hennen persuasively argues his thesis, focusing on education, reform, and industrial relations in West Virginia, considering these in the context of war mobilization, postwar instability, and national economic expansion. Corporate leaders in the state refined public relations tactics that the Wilson administration used to gain public support for the war. Heavily documented, with more than 800 footnotes, this study is an important addition to both Appalachian and West Virginia historical scholarship. Upper-division undergraduates and above.—*W. K. McNeil, Ozark Folk Center*

OAB-2604   DS559   92-41091 CIP
Howes, Craig. **Voices of the Vietnam POWS: witnesses to their fight.** Oxford, 1993. 295p bibl index afp ISBN 0-19-507630-3, $39.95; ISBN 0-19-508680-5 pbk, $16.95

Although fewer than 700 American POWs were held by the North Vietnamese between 1964 and 1971, the issue has generated a vast, ideology-tinged literature. What Craig Howes calls the "official" history is epitomized by John G. Hubbel's *P.O.W.: A Definitive History of the American Prisoner-of-War Experience in Vietnam, 1964-1973* (1976). Its story of heroic resistance, "fall-back," and recovery against torture was formulated by militant officer POWs even before they left Hanoi. They ignored enlisted men kept in jungle camps and others who did not fit the heroic-officer concept or were regarded as downright traitors. Howes stresses the home-front agitations of Sybil Stockdale, wife of the most literate POW, James Bond (Jim) Stockdale. Howes closes with Jim Stockdale's postwar quest for the meaning of the entire experience. This account of the lives and exegesis of the statements of American POWs in Vietnam offers a more trustworthy analysis than any other work of modest length on this tendentious subject. All libraries.—*G. H. Davis, Georgia State University*

OAB-2605   E840   92-16009 CIP
Isaacson, Walter. **Kissinger: a biography.** Simon & Schuster, 1992. 893p bibl index ISBN 0-671-66323-2, $30.00

At once one of the most admired and reviled figures in American diplomacy, Henry Kissinger earned a position in the top rank of 20th-century statesmen, negotiators, and foreign-policy intellectuals. Isaacson's masterful biography

is worthy of its subject. Isaacson seeks always to balance his appraisal, measuring achievements against costs, and the reader comes to expect a "but" following praise or criticism. The author lauds Kissinger's brilliance, censures his pettiness and vanity. He finds irony: Kissinger was duplicitous even with members of his staff, yet encouraged freewheeling debate that won their loyalty. Kissinger's realism depended on military power, yet his greatest diplomatic triumphs came in China, the Middle East, and Africa, where its effect was minimal; his greatest failures were in Vietnam, Pakistan, and Cambodia, where force was manifest. Isaacson shows the impact of character on policy as he dissects Kissinger's complex relationships with Richard Nixon and Alexander Haig. Secretaries of Defense Melvin Laird and James Schlesinger emerge as worthy bureaucratic rivals. The book is an evenhanded, penetrating examination of a crucial period in US foreign policy and a valuable assessment of one of its leading architects. All levels.—*A. J. Dunar, University of Alabama in Huntsville*

OAB-2606   HT352   93-42348 CIP
Langdon, Philip. **A better place to live: reshaping the American suburb.** Massachusetts, 1994. 270p index afp ISBN 0-87023-914-7, $29.95

An elaboration of the author's memorable 1988 cover story in *The Atlantic*, this book represents a new area of interest in urban studies. Here Langdon examines at length the stresses he sees in the American suburb, and what better residential alternatives might be found. His emphasis is on communities built since 1980, and his eye is focused on the big picture as well as such basic elements as houses, parks, streets, gathering places, retail facilities, employment, and transportation. Much of his analysis is an evaluation of the work of leading designers and planners, most notably the Miami group led by Elizabeth Plater-Zyberk and Andres Duany. Langdon's 10 chapters treat current suburban problems; streets and community formation; the decline of planning; home, town, work, shopping, and transportation in the 1990s suburb; the changing American house; the role of government; repairing existing suburbs; and future prospects. Excellent photos, maps, and diagrams support his discussion, as do his comprehensive notes and bibliography. Very highly recommended for all public and academic library collections on contemporary US culture and society or on housing and urban studies.—*P. O. Muller, University of Miami*

OAB-2607   D849   93-14206 CIP
Lebow, Richard Ned. **We all lost the Cold War,** by Richard Ned Lebow and Janice Gross Stein. Princeton, 1994. 543p indexes afp ISBN 0-691-03308-0, $35.00

Lebow and Stein have written an analytical gem, a comparison of the 1962 Cuban missile crisis and the October 1973 Arab-Israeli war. Neither nation nor national leaders are valorized in these decades-apart developments. Indeed, in their assessment of the earlier crisis the authors' subject both Kennedy and Khruschev to balanced and unsparing criticism for misperceiving events and realities. Kennedy was driven to confrontation by anger, desire for domestic political gain, and broad foreign policy concerns. Miscalculations, such as secrecy in the deployment of missiles to Cuba, fear of US strategic superiority and, paradoxically, belief in Soviet nuclear superiority governed Khruschev. The authors exhaustively examine both the failure and consequences of the US policy of deterrence and Russia's needless and intolerable reactions. Each country's domestic considerations are set forth, and the "view from Moscow," invariably neglected by scholars, includes the failed campaign of agricultural revitalization and deep contradictions in Soviet society. Equally instructive is the authors' study of the Kissinger-Brezhnev collaboration and the failed efforts at crisis prevention in 1973. The reader is guided through the tangled network of maneuvers in a measured, judicious, and exhaustively researched narrative. A better introduction to these two Cold War events, in which "we all lost," does not exist. Upper-division undergraduates and above.—*M. Cantor, University of Massachusetts at Amherst*

OAB-2608   F868   95-23508 CIP
Lemke-Santangelo, Gretchen. **Abiding courage: African American migrant women and the East Bay community.** North Carolina,

1996. 217p bibl index afp ISBN 0-8078-2256-6, $29.95; ISBN 0-8078-4563-9 pbk, $14.95

Lemke-Santangelo's study is a seminal work. Writing with an unambiguous purpose—to examine the migration and community-building efforts of African American women who moved from the South to the East Bay cities of California during WW II—the author presents, in an endearing style, the experiences of women about whom little has been written. A riveting introduction sets the stage for a journey involving "economic autonomy, hard work, education, worship, family ties, charity, and independent self-help institutions," which readers share. What makes this story so poignant is that it is told by 50 women who actually lived the experiences Lemke-Santangelo recounts. With chapter titles such as "It Was Just Like Living in Two Worlds," "To Make the Two Worlds One," "I Never Thought I'd Have to Create All That," "I Always Desired Independence, Never Wealth," "I Never Denied Where I Came From" and "If We Didn't Do It, It Just Wouldn't Get Done," Lemke-Santangelo unfolds a unique history of the lives of a segment of the US population. Feminists as well as nonfeminists will find the book a welcome respite from the lives of mainstream women. All levels.—*R. Stewart, SUNY College at Buffalo*

OAB-2609 UA23 96-24200 CIP
Linn, Brian McAllister. **Guardians of empire: the U.S. Army and the Pacific, 1902-1940.** North Carolina, 1997. 343p bibl index afp ISBN 0-8078-2321-X, $39.95

In this magnificently researched study, Linn puts forth a compelling argument that, contrary to popular interpretation, the US Army was not caught unaware by the Japanese attack on Pearl Harbor and the Philippines in 1941. From the end of WW I until the outbreak of WW II, the army clearly understood that conflict with Japan was a likely possibility and devised contingency plans to counter that danger. To correctly understand the disasters of December 1941, contends Linn, readers must examine the military history of the four decades prior to Pearl Harbor rather than concentrating on the events immediately prior to the attack. This perspective of 40 years reveals a tangled bureaucratic and interservice morass, minuscule budgets, limited manpower, turf guarding, and unresolved conflict between Washington and local commanders in the Pacific. In the end, the army never clearly decided whether to trust the very people it was supposedly protecting. Thoughtful and well-reasoned, this book will serve as a model for a new generation of military historians. Most of the study concentrates on military policy, but it includes one lively chapter on the social history of US soldiers stationed in the Pacific during this period. Although some scholars may disagree with Linn's conclusions regarding the army's level of responsibility for the greatest disaster in US military history, he has argued his case persuasively and has placed Pearl Harbor in a new historical framework. All levels.—*C. J. Weeks, Southern Polytechnic State University*

OAB-2610 HS2330 93-27548 CIP
MacLean, Nancy. **Behind the mask of chivalry: the making of the second Ku Klux Klan.** Oxford, 1994. 292p bibl index afp ISBN 0-19-507234-0, $30.00

Far more than simply an excellent analysis of the rise and fall of the second Ku Klux Klan, this is an insightful portrait of American social development in the early 20th century. MacLean (Northwestern Univ.) focuses on the Athens, Georgia, klavern to show how the Klan used family values to further its ends among a petite bourgeoisie that feared the changes created by industrialization, urbanization, and modernity. Reviewing members, she traces their involvement in fraternal organizations and churches, as well as their employment histories. The few tables presented are clear and to the point. Even more interesting is her investigation why the Klan failed to achieve the same level of national acceptance and power as the Fascists in Italy and the Nazis in Germany. Well written, nicely illustrated, with a very useful bibliography, this work should become the standard volume on the Ku Klux Klan of the 1910s and '20s. A must for all academic libraries and for all students of American history and race, ethnic, and gender relations.—*D. R. Jamieson, Ashland University*

OAB-2611 E99 95-5857 CIP
McGovern, Dan. **The Campo Indian landfill war: the fight for gold in California's garbage.** Oklahoma, 1995. 325p bibl index afp ISBN 0-8061-2755-4, $24.95

McGovern, a former Regional Administrator of the Environmental Protection Agency, has written a wonderfully engaging and lucid account of a dramatic conflict over the construction of a landfill on an Indian reservation in California. Often, the sites chosen for landfills, waste dumps, and other potential environmental hazards are in or near the communities least able to muster the financial or political clout to fight them. In this case, however, the Campo Indians, eager for the jobs and revenue it would bring in, actively solicited the landfill, while their white neighbors sought to block it. McGovern's role in the proceedings allows him to present a compelling insider's view of the complexities of any major environmental battle; his account takes readers from local to county to state to federal politics, with characters as colorful as any novelist might invent. At the same time, he conveys a wealth of information on California history, Indian rights, and environmental law in a highly understandable way. An excellent book for anyone interested in environmental racism or social activism. All levels.—*L. Vance, California Institute of Integral Studies*

OAB-2612 D570 96-23869 CIP
Meigs, Mark. **Optimism at Armageddon: voices of American participants in the First World War.** New York University, 1997. 269p bibl index ISBN 0-8147-5548-8, $40.00

Meigs states in his introduction that European soldiers, unlike their American counterparts, had no doubts about why they were fighting during WW I. American soldiers, on the other hand, struggled to make sense of their experiences and had questions about the war's meaning for them. Meigs argues that for Americans, the "Great War" must be either the Civil War, where the nation's survival was at stake, or WW II, whose victory set the stage for US foreign policy in the second half of the 20th century and whose social upheavals so altered American society. The author examines the cultural effects of WW I on the American soldier by cleverly juxtaposing official views with unofficial sources (popular songs, jokes in army newspapers, personal letters, diaries, and answers of WW I veterans to a questionnaire distributed by the US Military Institute in the 1970s). Chapters are arranged thematically and deal with topics such as motivations for volunteering, the meaning of combat, effects of cultural contact with the French, and attitudes toward death in combat. An outstanding and unique work that could provide a model for the study of all wars in which Americans have fought in this century. Meigs uses an impressive array of primary and secondary sources. For further study see John Keegan's *The Face of Battle* (CH, Mar'77). Endnotes. Upper-division undergraduates and above.—*R. E. Marcello, University of North Texas*

OAB-2613 F869 94-46190 CIP
Menchaca, Martha. **The Mexican outsiders: a community history of marginalization and discrimination in California.** Texas, 1995. 250p bibl index afp ISBN 0-292-75173-7, $40.00; ISBN 0-292-75174-5 pbk, $17.95

Menchaca has written one of the best recent books on Mexican Americans and their adaptation. The author is able to make social events of the small community of Santa Paula applicable to almost anywhere there are Anglo and Mexican American social interactions. She lays a strong historical foundation for the discrimination and racism that was rampant in Southern California during the early part of the 20th century. Readers will be fascinated by the role of the Ku Klux Klan in maintaining the Mexicans and Mexican Americans in a subordinate position in the community. Menchaca shows that the deep divisions created earlier in Santa Paula are still present today, and she does an excellent job in discussing current forms of racism and discrimination and their ramifications for interethnic and intraethnic relations. Using her experiences in an Anglo restaurant as an excellent example of "social apartness," she demonstrates that the boundaries established by the Anglos of Santa Paula are not to be breached by Mexican Americans. All levels.—*R. S. Guerra, University of Texas—Pan American*

OAB-2614 F159 95-30471 CIP
Morawska, Ewa. **Insecure prosperity: small-town Jews in industrial America, 1890-1940.** Princeton, 1996. 369p index afp ISBN 0-691-03735-3, $35.00

An illuminating, impressively researched social portrait of that "no less than 20-25 percent" of Jewish immigrants to the US who made their homes not in large cities, but in smaller towns. Focusing on the modest Jewish community of Johnstown, Pennsylvania, Morawska skillfully combines the methods of historical sociology and ethnography to recover immigrants' economic arrangements and family strategies, patterns of mobility, religious practices, political allegiances and electoral behavior, and worldviews. The focus on Johnstown casts into sharp relief the distinctly urban dimensions of what often passes for a generalized "Jewish" culture in the US. Morawska's findings regarding rates of secularization, economic mobility, zest for higher education, and a number of other themes disrupt common assumptions about this ethnic group, its collective desires, and its collective destiny on American soil. Morawska's central paradigm of "insecure prosperity" nicely captures the dynamic relationship between economic and social structures on one hand, and immigrant sensibilities on the other. Some readers might lament the level of abstraction that characterizes the study: this social portrait largely detached from the liveliness and color of everyday, street-level sociability. Still, the sophistication of her analyses, the freshness of her chosen terrain, and the sheer volume of learning behind her assertions render Morawska's work extremely important. Upper-division undergraduates and above.—*M. F. Jacobson, Yale University*

OAB-2615 F739 96-9990 CIP
Murphy, Mary. **Mining cultures: men, women, and leisure in Butte, 1914-41.** Illinois, 1997. 279p bibl index afp ISBN 0-252-02267-X, $39.95; ISBN 0-252-06569-7 pbk, $18.95

Murphy's book joins *Like a Family: The Making of a Southern Cotton Mill World,* ed. by Jacquelyn Hall et al. (CH, May'88), as an excellent example of community history. Its particular concern is to consider patterns of leisure as they related to changing gender roles, ethnic relationships, and the status of mining in Butte, Montana, 1914-1941. Carefully fashioned chapters treat Butte as an instant copper metropolis, drinking habits, manners and morals, the backgrounds of miners, gender roles, the cultural importance of radio station KGIR, and the impact of the Depression and the New Deal. These themes play out against the essentially masculine character of the city while it was in its heyday, and the role of a dominant employer (Anaconda Copper) that was content to leave Butte wide open. *Mining Cultures* is social and community history at its best. It draws on wide research, a notable command of the sources, and a capacity for richly textured illustration, analysis, and argument. Well written, handsomely produced, illustrated, and buttressed with chapter endnotes, this book will quickly win favorable notice as a useful, appealing, readable study. All levels.—*D. W. Steeples, Mercer University*

OAB-2616 F395 94-39569 CIP
Navarro, Armando. **Mexican American youth organization: avantgarde of the Chicano movement in Texas.** Texas, 1995. 288p index afp ISBN 0-292-75556-2, $40.00; ISBN 0-292-75557-0 pbk, $16.95

Navarro's study is an important addition to literature on the protest movements of the 1960s. Much of the material on this period has been generated from California, where the rapid movements of the time in the form of the East Los Angeles blowouts, the Chicano moratorium, and the volatility of youth has eclipsed that of other regions. This book preserves the historical memory of the activities of Mexican American youth in Texas, where Chicanos had their own unique responses to the Civil Rights and Antiwar Movements. Navarro's narrative revolves around the Mexican American Youth Organization, which was the principal organization seeking social change among young Chicanos in Texas. This group arose from the alienation of working-class and lower middle class Chicano youth who had been shut out of more established organizations such as the League of United Latin American Citizens (LULAC) and the American G.I. Forum of U.S. Its members participated in some 39 school walkouts

and eventually evolved into La Raza Unida political party, one of the few moderately successful third parties of this century. Navarro, a scholar with excellent activist and scholarly credentials, relies heavily on oral interviews and documents not previously available. This well-footnoted work is a solid contribution to Chicano historiography. Good index. All levels.—*R. Acuña, California State University, Northridge*

OAB-2617 Can. CIP
Owram, Doug. **Born at the right time: a history of the baby-boom generation.** Toronto, 1996. 392p index afp ISBN 0-8020-5957-0, $34.95

As a scholar of Canadian cultural history and a part of the phenomenon itself, Owram is well placed to write this first survey of the culture of the Canadian baby-boom generation, which in 1966 constituted half the population of Canada. Growing into young adulthood during an era of unprecedented affluence and mobility, the boomer generation by its sheer size affected everything in society from consumption of goods and services to church attendance and the creation of a youth culture centered on rock and roll. Owram intends his work to be a generational history spanning the period 1946-72, rather than a study of the overall history of that era. He succeeds very well in analyzing the cultural uniqueness of a generation that came into its youthful exuberance during the 1960s and was then wrenched into a world of limitations by the international economic contractions that began about 1972. Owram shows clearly that much of boomer culture in the 1960s had its genesis in the rebelliousness and experimentation of the 1950s, even though its embrace of alternative lifestyles and social issues was a rejection of the 1950s emphasis on family and ordered social values. There is a great deal of sound observation and analysis in this book, which is as much about North American cultural history as it is about Canadian cultural history. This sensible, solidly researched, and clearly written study should be in all library collections. Upper-division undergraduates and above.—*M. J. Moore, Appalachian State University*

OAB-2618 E183 93-24260 CIP
Paterson, Thomas G. **Contesting Castro: the United States and the triumph of the Cuban Revolution.** Oxford, 1994. 352p bibl index afp ISBN 0-19-508630-9, $27.50

Paterson, a highly respected diplomatic historian, renders the fascinating and instructive story of pre-Castro Cuba. He describes the sources of the bitter anti-Americanism and uncompromising nationalism of the charismatic Castro, his strengths and weaknesses, and those of his implacable foe, the brutal dictator Fulgencio Batista. Paterson also recounts a superpower's inability to prevent the loss of a long-dependent nation 100 miles away, and its miscalculated, bungled, clandestine operations. Paterson's narrative covers, among other events, the daring attack on the Moncada Army Barracks in Santiago de Cuba, Castro's flight to Mexico, his fund-raising activities in the US, President Eisenhower's failure to grasp Cuban issues, and the role of the US Military Assistance Advisory Group and the Military Assistance Program. Lacing through it all is the four-year struggle of the 26th of July Movement after the revolutionary November 1956 landing from the ship *Granma.* A swift-moving military and political narrative, Paterson's study ends with the unravelling of Batista's army, the self-destructed Third Force conspiracies, and Castro's triumphant entry into Havana. Clearly one of the indispensable books on this subject. Upper-division undergraduates and above.—*M. Cantor, University of Massachusetts at Amherst*

OAB-2619 E173 95-13878 CIP
Patterson, James T. **Grand expectations: the United States, 1945-1974.** Oxford, 1996. 829p bibl index afp (Oxford history of the United States, 10) ISBN 0-19-507680-X, $35.00

With this beautifully written study Patterson (Brown Univ.) has distinguished himself as one of the leading historians of post-WW II US history. *Grand Expectations* supplies a rich blend of political and social history as well as excellent narrative and insightful analysis. Patterson has treated all of the important events of the period, from the use of the atomic bomb in 1945 to the resignation of Richard Nixon in 1974. Among the highlights of the book are Patterson's accounts of what motivated the nation's postwar presidents. For example, he found President Kennedy's style of foreign policy determined in part by a need never to be viewed as appearing weak. The book devotes considerable attention to the Vietnam War and the consequences of US involvement. Those consequences, along with other societal factors, resulted in the upheavals of the 1960s and lead Patterson to conclude that the 1968 election was "pivotal" because it changed subsequent elections for decades. Patterson also does a terrific job of surveying and analyzing race relations throughout the period. All levels.—*A. Yarnell, Montana State University*

OAB-2620   E185   94-24645 CIP
Payne, Charles M. **I've got the light of freedom: the organizing tradition and the Mississippi freedom struggle.** California, 1995. 525p index afp ISBN 0-520-08515-9, $28.00

Payne's book advances significantly the historiography of the Civil Rights Movement. It is a deep probe into the innermost dynamics of the history of the movement in Mississippi, most especially in the town of Greenwood and the surrounding Delta. Payne has become intimately acquainted with many of the still-living participants and reveals how these local people, in concert with the youthful organizers of SNCC, brought about in the 1960s fundamental racial change in a state long believed impervious to such possibilities. Through his own eloquent prose and the verbatim testimony of the participants, Payne documents the courage, tenacity, and communal support necessary to overcome the equally tenacious resistance to change of the white majority. His analysis extends understanding of the origins of the movement in the '40s and '50s, the crucial nature of the gradual evolution of informal networks of supporters within the Mississippi African American community, the key role women played throughout the movement, and the insightful way in which the young SNCC leaders both led and followed those whom they served. This powerful book is required reading for anyone interested in race relations and the history of the 1960s. All levels.—*J. F. Findlay, University of Rhode Island*

OAB-2621   F330   94-38515 CIP
Permaloff, Anne. **Political power in Alabama: the more things change ...,** by Anne Permaloff and Carl Grafton. Georgia, 1995. 389p bibl index afp ISBN 0-8203-1721-7, $50.00

For students of Alabama history and government this brilliant study is a confirming and therefore disheartening analysis of that state's recent past. The authors concentrate their attention on the years from 1958 to 1970 when changes, both internal and external, finally dissolved the alliance between Black Belt planters and Jefferson County industrialists. This was a rare moment in Alabama history (only the Populist challenge of the 1890s is of equal import), when an opportunity existed for leadership to point the way toward solutions for the problems created by decades of segregation and economic inequality. With sober analysis and trenchant conclusions the authors document both the general failure of leadership and, although they do not emphasize the point, the skewed perceptions of Alabama voters. The inescapable figure in this work is George Wallace, who dominates the political stage with his almost unerring sense of how to inflict the most lasting harm on his state and his people. Except with superlatives, there is no way a short review can do justice to this study. Highly recommended for all university and college libraries. General readers; upper-division undergraduates and above.—*R. D. Ward, emeritus, Georgia Southern University*

OAB-2622   E745   95-8586 CIP
Perret, Geoffrey. **Old soldiers never die: the life of Douglas Mac-Arthur.** Random House, 1996. 663p index afp ISBN 0-679-42882-8, $32.50

Perret, a popular historian, has crafted a superb biography of perhaps the most controversial leader of the 20th century. Perret, author of such well-received titles as *Days of Sadness, Years of Triumph* (CH, Sep'73) and *A Country Made by War* (1989), touches all the bases in MacArthur's long (84 years) and eventful life. The author's explication of MacArthur's early years is especially noteworthy. MacArthur

was born into a military family. His father distinguished himself in the Civil War, providing top-notch reconnaissance for General Sherman's Atlanta campaign. Stationed out West at war's end, he married a daughter of the Virginia elite and Douglas arrived in 1880. Enrolled at West Point, young MacArthur survived a brutal hazing. Gifted with what seemed to be a photographic memory, he graduated at the top of his class. In a fast-paced narrative, Perret offers fresh insights on such topics as the feud with Pershing that ultimately cost MacArthur the Congressional Medal of Honor; his less-than-sterling role in booting the Bonus Marchers out of Washington; the landing at Inchon, Korea; and on Truman's decision to relieve MacArthur of military command. This reviewer is not persuaded by Perret's claim that MacArthur was not "ego driven." Along with William Manchester's *American Caesar* (CH, Feb'79), this is one of the best extant single-volume biographies. All levels.—*S. G. Weisner, Springfield Technical Community College*

OAB-2623   KF8745   92-54119 CIP
Race-ing justice, en-gendering power: essays on Anita Hill, Clarence Thomas, and the construction of social reality, ed. with introd. by Toni Morrison. Pantheon Books, 1992. 475p ISBN 0-679-74145-3 pbk, $15.00

Published on the first anniversary of the Clarence Thomas Supreme Court confirmation hearings, this remarkable collection includes an exquisitely written introduction by Toni Morrison, in which she frames the discourse contained in the 18 essays that follow. The Thomas hearings forced onto center stage the interrelated issues of race, gender, and multiculturalism. The essays, contributed by African Americans—a federal judge, novelists, and scholars of history, literature, law, philosophy, women's studies and African American studies—address these issues. The quality of the essays is amazingly consistent; they are all well written and original. Especially impressive are Leon Higginbotham's evaluation of Thomas's qualifications and capabilities; Michael Thelwell's indictment of Yale's decision to concentrate on recruitment and integration of only the brightest and most promising black students in lieu of establishing a course of study in African American culture and history; Cornel West's review of the failure of black leadership and racialist reasoning; and Paula Giddings's historical insights into African American sexism. This is an important volume on a timely subject. Highly recommended for all libraries and all readers.—*F. J. Hay, Harvard University*

OAB-2624   HV6439   92-39002 CIP
Rodriguez, Luis J. **Always running: la vida loca: gang days in L.A..** Curbstone, 1993. 260p ISBN 1-880684-06-3, $19.95

Rodriguez's odyssey in the US begins in the late 1960s, in the Mexican barrio of Watts and East Los Angeles, and ends in the inner city of Chicago decades later. As the story opens, his young son, Romerio, is replicating Rodriguez's own earlier estrangement by joining a gang and rebelling against his family. Father and son, in effect, are "always running." "It never stopped, this running. We were constant prey, and the hunters soon became big blurs: the police, the gangs, the junkies, the dudes on Garvey Boulevard who took our money, all smudge into one. Sometimes they were teachers who jumped on us Mexicans as if we were born with a hideous strain. We were always afraid. Always running." This is a riveting autobiographical work in the tradition of Piri Thomas's *Down These Mean Streets* (CH, Feb'68) and Claude Brown's *Manchild in the Promised Land* (CH, Dec'65). It traces Rodriguez's life as an active gang member, relates his battles with police, the justice system, and teachers, and describes his escape from devastation through writing. His poetry has won several awards and he conducts poetry workshops in shelters for the homeless in Chicago. His presentation of life in the barrio is brutal, blunt, anguished, and lyrical. All levels.—*J. Boskin, Boston University*

OAB-2625   D810   92-31859 CIP
Roeder, George H. **The censored war: American visual experience during World War Two.** Yale, 1993. 189p index afp ISBN 0-300-05723-7, $30.00

In a fresh approach to the social history of WW II propaganda, Roeder (Art Institute of Chicago) has admirably analyzed the unlovely task of censorship without diminishing the image of WW II as a "crusade," a task at least as difficult as that of the censors whom he has studied. The policy of WW II censors was not to diminish the image of "the good war" but at the same time to avoid offputting extremes such as depictions of horrific wounds, portrayals of the Japanese enemy in racist terms, and racial antipathy as reflected in riots in Harlem and Detroit. This effort of the military and the Office of War Information succeeded in giving the US a "sense of public purpose" by portraying the war as "the people's war" whose aims were best served by a "strategy of truth." And yet, as the author points out, such modulating policies were set forth in a mood in which, as Harold Lasswell put it, "there must be no ambiguity about whom the public is to hate." And yet, as Roeder points out, "one of the costs of the war" was its glib formulation of military and diplomatic goals in good-and-evil terms that colored so many subsequent wars. The book is graced with an arrangement of analytic chapters alternated with "visual essays" of censored photographs, posters, and movies. More important, the book is unique in its firm handling of material that might have been treated too tentatively. Good photoreproduction, selected bibliography, and index. Both general and academic readers at all levels.—*T. Cripps, Morgan State University*

OAB-2626   HD8039   92-56776 CIP
Rogovin, Milton. **Portraits in steel,** photographs by Milton Rogovin; interviews by Michael Frisch. Cornell, 1993. 318p afp ISBN 0-8014-2253-1, $49.95; ISBN 0-8014-8102-3 pbk, $28.95

Rogovin, an award-winning documentary photographer, and Frisch (SUNY, Buffalo), a major American oral historian, have combined to create an artistic and scholarly treatment of "deindustrialized" workers from the Buffalo steel mills. In the late 1970s Rogovin shot photographs of Buffalo steel workers, on the job and at home. In the mid-1980s, following the collapse of the Buffalo steel industry, he returned to photograph these now largely unemployed workers. This time Frisch accompanied him, recording interviews with the workers and, sometimes, with their families. The result is a moving set of documentary photographs, from the 1970s and '80s, reminiscent of the work of the famous group associated with Roy Stryker and the Farm Security Administration (FSA) during the New Deal. To these are added sensitive, well-edited, and revealing interviews. They remind readers that terms like "deindustrialization" involve people, and that it is people who endure both the joy and the sorrow that are the fabric of history. All levels.—*C. Ryant, University of Louisville*

OAB-2627   E743   93-4780 CIP
Rosteck, Thomas. *See it now* **confronts McCarthyism: television documentary and the politics of representation.** Alabama, 1994. 247p bibl index afp ISBN 0-8173-0705-2, $29.95

During the 1950s, a confluence of complex, gripping, and largely novel events set the American political stage for the remainder of the century. Rosteck's history offers penetrating insight into the extraordinary relationship among Cold War ideology, television documentary, the tactics of Senator Joseph R. McCarthy, and their overall impact on political culture. Rosteck centers his multilayered analysis on the four CBS *See It Now* telecasts that Edward R. Murrow and Fred W. Friendly produced on McCarthy's behavior early in the decade: "The Case of Milo Radulovich," "An Argument in Indianapolis," "A Report on Senator McCarthy," and "Annie Lee Moss before the McCarthy Committee." Of the group, the program on McCarthy himself was the most riveting nationally, and the most controversial. Supplementing the narrative of events surrounding these telecasts is an analysis of the documentary text itself. Rosteck contends that the form's power resides in the intersection of two types of signifying codes, one based on an assent of the image and word, the other based on the mythic and dramatic. Rosteck's book is a notable, scholarly contribution to the understanding of this period. General readers; upper-division undergraduates and above.—*J. Boskin, Boston University*

OAB-2628   D790   91-39452 CIP
Sandler, Stanley. **Segregated skies: all-black combat squadrons of World War II.** Smithsonian Institution Press, 1992. 217p bibl index afp ISBN 1-56098-154-7, $24.95

Sandler's excellent study concentrates on the Tuskegee Airmen of WW II but also includes an examination of the 477th Bombardment Group. The author uses a variety of sources, including official records, interviews, and secondary sources. His bibliography alone compels the scholar of modern American history to read the book. The story of the Tuskegee Airmen is at last beginning to take its rightful place in US history. The Tuskegee Airmen were the fighter squadrons—99th, 100th, 301st, and 302nd, and then the 332nd Fighter Group formed by the squadrons. Sandler describes the Airmen from inception of the squadrons through the combat of WW II. He finds that their performace was about the same as those of other figher units, despite the fact that these units started with a far smaller pool of talent, a condition examined by the author in the context of the pervasive denial of equal opportunity for African Americans. The story of the 477th is even more compelling and even less known. These remarkable men were not allowed to fly in combat but nevertheless were heroes indeed. They met incredible discrimination within and without the military with an open resistance whose courage was even more remarkable because of the time period. Together, these Tuskegee Airmen and the men of the 477th remind readers that human beings do matter. Some, perhaps many, have a greatness that at times enables them to show the way. General; undergraduate.—*J. P. Hobbs, North Carolina State University*

OAB-2629   HC107   93-39416 CIP
Saxenian, AnnaLee. **Regional advantage: culture and competition in Silicon Valley and Route 128.** Harvard, 1994. 226p index afp ISBN 0-674-75339-9, $24.95

Saxenian's study is truly a landmark work in contemporary regional analysis, and it makes a major contribution to the fields of economic geography, regional economics, industrial development, public policy making, and national affairs in general. Nobody is better qualified than Saxenian to unravel the myriad institutional and spatial forces that shape the pivotal US electronics industry. Here she pulls off a tour de force that uses new conceptualizations of the social sciences to interpret the fortunes of two of the nation's leading high-tech complexes. Moreover, her achievement is heightened by a compact and especially readable presentation that requires no prior knowledge of this subject. The six crisp chapters, bracketed by insightful introductory and concluding statements, introduce the reader to every aspect of the topic and draw lessons vital to the formulation of future industrial policy. The book is handsomely produced, the visuals (with the exception of maps too small in scale) are first-rate, and the large section of notes will be invaluable for researchers. This is one of the most important books to emerge from US academia in the 1990s. It belongs on the shelves of all North American libraries. All levels.—*P. O. Muller, University of Miami*

OAB-2630   E169   92-4446 CIP
Slotkin, Richard. **Gunfighter nation: the myth of the frontier in twentieth-century America.** Atheneum, 1992. 850p bibl index ISBN 0-689-12163-6, $40.00

With this volume, Slotkin completes his trilogy on the myth of the frontier in American history. *Regeneration through Violence* (CH, Jun'73) examined the development of the frontier myth within the context of early US history; *The Fatal Environment* (CH, Sep'85) related it to aspects of American life in the 19th century. The current book traces the image of the frontier in American life and thought from the era of Frederick Jackson Turner and Theodore Roosevelt to the presidency of Ronald Reagan. Slotkin uses a variety of sources to document his interpretation, among them fiction, history, cinema, television, and presidential speeches. The result is a superlative explanation of how the imagined West has been used as a metaphor to explain and justify the American experience in the 20th century. Readers unfamiliar with Slotkin's earlier works will need to peruse with care his introductory remarks about myth and American culture before proceeding to the book itself. The study complements

Henry Nash Smith's *Virgin Land* (1950); Richard Drinnon's *Facing West* (CH, Nov'80); and Gerald D. Nash's *Creating the West* (CH, Feb'92). Bibliography and notes are excellent. Highly recommended. All levels.—*L. B. Gimelli, Eastern Michigan University*

OAB-2631   F866   96-17087 CIP
Starr, Kevin. **The dream endures: California enters the 1940s.** Oxford, 1997. 480p bibl index afp ISBN 0-19-510079-4, $35.00

Starr's "Americans and the California Dream" series is a monumental work without rival as a state history and a study of the relationship between a state and the nation. Starr inspires envy at every turn—he blends knowledge of the most minute detail on California with a sure grasp of large trends in national history, and he writes superbly to boot. This fifth volume emphasizes cultural history. Although the subtitle is "California Enters the 1940s," *The Dream Endures* ranges widely over the 20th century in tracing themes such as the development of California's world leadership in science and astronomy at Cal Tech, Berkeley, and Mount Wilson, or the symbiotic relationship between the US Navy and San Diego, or the appearance of Ishi and Alfred Kroeber's role in American anthropology. More traditional chapters cover photography, art, and literature. Hollywood and the role of (especially Jewish) European émigrés in the 1930s are other important themes. There is enough detail here to overwhelm some readers, but Starr keeps the bigger pictures in focus through it all, showing ways that California became a pacesetter for the rest of the nation. An impressive, even dazzling, book. Essential for students of California and the West, it will also appeal to anyone interested in the cultural and intellectual history of the modern US.—*K. Blaser, Wayne State College*

OAB-2632   E185   95-23053 CIP
Steinberg, Stephen. **Turning back: the retreat from racial justice in American thought and policy.** Beacon Press, 1995. 276p index ISBN 0-8070-4110-6, $25.00

Steinberg's valuable intellectual history of the reigning paradigms in the study of postwar US race relations convincingly implicates the "liberal" social sciences in the white-over-black dynamic that has characterized so many other arenas of American political life and culture. Steinberg (Queens College) takes as his starting point Gunnar Myrdal's "monumental" study *An American Dilemma* (1944). He argues that Myrdal's conveniently apolitical approach to race relations and his flattering depiction of American whites as fully tormented by the hypocrisy of the nation's racial "dilemma" made the study so popular (read "monumental") in the first place. Through careful analyses of social scientific works by scholars like Nathan Glazer, Charles Murray, and William Julius Wilson, Steinberg asserts that the social sciences—most often in the name of correcting intractable social problems—have in fact provided the intellectual underpinnings for a vigorous anti-civil rights backlash in the last 30 years. According to Steinberg, "backlash" is a dangerous misnomer; the resistance to civil rights agitation actually predates the milestone civil rights victories of 1964 and 1965. Later chapters deal with more recent controversies over racialized social policies such as affirmative action, and racialized social analyses such as Richard Herrnstein and Charles Murray's *The Bell Curve* (CH, May'95). An impassioned, important analysis of the intersections among the academy, policy-making arenas, and popular understanding of race and social justice. All levels.—*M. F. Jacobson, Yale University*

OAB-2633   F899   93-49522 CIP
Taylor, Quintard. **The forging of a black community: Seattle's Central District from 1870 through the civil rights era.** Washington, 1994. 330p bibl index afp ISBN 0-295-97315-3, $30.00; ISBN 0-295-97345-5 pbk, $14.95

Taylor's study of Seattle's Central District—a four square mile section of the city where most African Americans lived—is a much needed and significant work of urban history. Taylor's interpretation, an expanded version of his dissertation, traces the black community's spatial and institutional development

from 1870 through the civil rights era. Taylor (Univ. of Oregon, Eugene) does not limit his examination of this community to occupational mobility and residential patterns; he also details its interaction with the white and Asian communities along its borders. This case study casts "black urban history in a broader context," since most investigations focus on urban centers in the East or Midwest. By historically reconstructing the forging of a "black urban ethos," it broadens understanding of the experience of urban blacks. The 32 carefully selected black-and-white photographs and illustrations enhance Taylor's lively prose. The result is a well-balanced project that both focuses on traditional questions of the urban historian and breaks new ground with its emphasis on the creation of a distinctly black urban culture in Seattle. Upper-division undergraduates and above.—*T. D. Beal, SUNY at Stony Brook*

OAB-2634   F574   91-26518 CIP
Thomas, Richard W. **Life for us is what we make it: building Black community in Detroit, 1915-1945.** Indiana, 1992. 365p index afp ISBN 0-253-35990-2, $47.50

Patterned after Gilbert Osofsky's *Harlem, the Making of A Ghetto* (CH, Oct'66), older African American histories focused on the process of ghettoization. Joining newer works, e.g., Joe William Trotter's *Black Milwaukee* (CH, Jul'85), Thomas's book emphasizes the process of community building, led by the emerging African American industrial working class and domestic servants. In the period between the world wars, schools, hospitals, newspapers, self-help organizations, and a sense of place developed in black Detroit. The Detroit Urban League, the NAACP, The Booker T. Washington Trade Association, and the Housewives League of Detroit all played integral roles in this process. Progress was not without its problems, however; crime, poverty, and despair remained constants. Frequently, skilled African American workers were denied jobs, even in critical defense industries. During this period, African Americans demonstrated their newfound strength by challenging the racist system, first by breaking with the Republican party, and then by turning from the paternalistic support of Henry Ford and joing the UAW. Taken with earlier works like Thomas Philpott's *The Slum and the Ghetto* (CH, Sep'78) Thomas's ground-breaking study should occupy a central place in the literature of American urban history. Advanced undergraduates; graduate; faculty.—*D. R. Jamieson, Ashland University*

OAB-2635   BX8128   95-47049 CIP
Umble, Diane Zimmerman. **Holding the line: the telephone in Old Order Mennonite and Amish life.** Johns Hopkins, 1996. 192p bibl index afp ISBN 0-8018-5312-5, $35.00

Umble focuses on debates and controversy concerning the telephone among Old Order Amish Mennonites in Lancaster County, Pennsylvania, as an important episode in the history of Old Order struggles to cope with social change. The telephone entered the lives of these Anabaptists in the late 19th century so successfully that by the early 20th century three Mennonite and Amish telephone companies existed in the county. Some of the faithful viewed this development as a blessing, while others saw it in a less favorable light; these conflicting views were occasionally so forcefully expressed that they resulted in divisions among churches. Umble's important contributions are several. First, she provides a very readable, extended discussion of telephone history in a rural area, a topic usually overlooked by other telephone historians. The history of Amish and Mennonite telephone companies in particular has received little previous scholarly attention. Second, she does an excellent job of tracing the role of communication in regulating social change in very conservative religious communities. Third, Umble demonstrates how changes in communication patterns are inextricably intertwined with community identity. An excellent piece of scholarship. Upper-division undergraduates and above.—*W. K. McNeil, Ozark Folk Center*

OAB-2636   HN57   94-45707 CIP
Vergara, Camilo José. **The new American ghetto.** Rutgers, 1995. 235p bibl afp ISBN 0-8135-2209-9, $49.95

In one of the most remarkable, scholarly books ever published on urban

America, Vergara makes an ambitious attempt to capture, both in words and eloquent photography, the disintegration (and the occasional partial rebirth) of the inner central city during the quarter-century following the close of the tumultuous, riot-torn 1960s. Much of this work is a grim narrative on survival in some of the nation's grittiest ghettos, brought vividly to life in the pictures of this highly talented photojournalist. In fact, this book appeared in conjunction with the author's exhibition at Washington's National Building Museum. The text is lavishly laid out in large format, with generous provision for color as well as black-and-white photography. The book is organized in nine sections that treat the history of the ghetto, its landscapes, housing, nonresidential land uses, defensible-space characteristics, street art and graffiti, pathologies, transformations, and future prospects. A prepublication reviewer claims Vergara's work to be as powerful and significant as Jacob Riis's similar survey of urban poverty a century ago. That is no overstatement; this landmark book belongs on the shelves of every college and research library in the US. All levels.—*P. O. Muller, University of Miami*

OAB-2637   D810   95-4415 CIP
Virden, Jenel. **Good-bye Piccadilly: British war brides in America.** Illinois, 1996. 177p bibl index afp ISBN 0-252-02225-4, $29.95; ISBN 0-252-06528-X pbk, $13.95

Virden (Univ. of Hull, England) is uniquely positioned to write a history of WW II British war brides because she herself is the daughter of one. This brief study focuses primarily on the process by which an estimated 70,000 British brides came to the US and on the issue of assimilation into American culture. Basing her research on archival sources and a 1989 questionnaire mailed to several hundred war brides and their husbands, Virden concludes that in spite of delays and the ardors of the journey to America, most war brides believe they made the right decision. Their central motive for immigrating was simply "I loved my G.I." Virden also notes that although culturally assimilated into American life, conceptually, many continued to see themselves as "British" as well as "American." This pathbreaking study would have been even stronger had the author done more with details of everyday life among the women (and included more information from and about their American husbands). Nonetheless, this important work is highly recommended for major public and university libraries. All levels.—*A. O. Edmonds, Ball State University*

OAB-2638   HD8039   93-36933 CIP
Weber, Devra. **Dark sweat, white gold: California farm workers, cotton, and the New Deal.** California, 1994. 338p bibl index afp ISBN 0-520-08489-6, $40.00

Weber has written an excellent history of the 1933 San Joaquin, California cotton strike, an epic in labor history in which three Mexican workers were shot down on picket lines and nine other died as a result of the strike. The author carries the story into the late 1930s. Weber (Univ. of California-Riverside) adds another dimension to the monumental works of agricultural economist Paul Taylor. In addition to valuable archival research, Weber literally hunted down participants in the strikes, conducting more than 100 interviews that included some with women. Through social and family networks, cotton workers adopted their own strategies, often pushing organized labor into radical action. Weber skillfully incorporates this microview of agricultural labor and New Deal programs. The latter often hindered the organization of farm labor, aiding the cause of the large farmer. After the 1993 cotton strike Mexican workers were steadily replaced by white workers from Oklahoma, Arkansas, and west Texas. The parallels between these Mexican workers of the 1930s and the Mexican and Salvadoran service workers of present-day Los Angeles are glaring. *Dark Sweat, White Gold* is an important work. It is well footnoted and has an excellent bibliography and index. All levels.—*R. Acuña, California State University, Northridge*

OAB-2639   F128   96-17786 CIP
Wenger, Beth S. **New York Jews and the Great Depression: uncertain promise.** Yale, 1996. 269p index afp ISBN 0-300-06265-6, $25.00

Wenger's unassuming study should not be taken as a balanced assessment of the Great Depression. Its imbalance, however, is its strength. Wenger focuses on New York City's Jewish immigrants—and their offspring and family life—during the 1930s. She challenges the conventional narrative of Jewish upward mobility. Concentrated in white-collar jobs, Jews did not suffer from hunger or from the severe economic dislocation of unskilled labor. Rather, they experienced stalled mobility and economic insecurity, as well as job discrimination and a systemic antisemitism. Wenger looks at how family survival strategies negotiated the hard times; social and ideological distinctions between East and West European Jews; the formidable admission quotas in place on the college level; Jewish youngsters, their working lives, and the political radicalism of a minority of them; the vibrant culture of the distinct communities of Jewish newcomers; their unwavering loyalty to the Democratic Party and the New Deal; and Jewish social service agencies and their efforts during the parlous times. Soundly conceived and clearly written, this study sensitizes readers to the cumulative impact of the Depression on one particular immigrant group. An important addition to both American ethnic and interwar scholarship. Upper-division undergraduates and above.—*M. Cantor, University of Massachusetts at Amherst*

OAB-2640   DA990   94-42884 CIP
Wilson, Andrew J. **Irish America and the Ulster conflict, 1968-1995.** Catholic University of America, 1995. 322p bibl index afp ISBN 0-8132-0828-9, $34.95; ISBN 0-8132-0835-1 pbk, $14.95

The conflict in Northern Ireland is as familiar as it is incomprehensible to most Americans. Wilson (Loyola Univ. of Chicago) shows, however, that many Americans of Irish descent have played and continue to play a central role in the bloody struggle. In this timely and well-written study, he recounts Irish American involvement in Irish affairs since 1800, then turns to a detailed analysis of events since the Northern Ireland civil rights movement reactivated American interest in 1968. At the center of his study is an account of the development of militant and constitutional nationalist groups in the US and their competition to win support for their strategies in the turbulent environment of bombings and prison protests. Wilson's study is distinguished by its extensive research, including many interviews with important activists and participants in Britain, Ireland, and North America, and by its clear and evenhanded treatment of this highly politicized story. This splendid work is a social as well as a political history of a significant chapter in Irish and US history, and will be profitably read by students of both areas of study as well as by general readers who appreciate good history and a good story.—*C. W. Wood Jr., Western Carolina University*

■ Political Science

OAB-2641   JC481   96-21389 CIP
Altemeyer, Bob. **The authoritarian specter.** Harvard, 1996. 374p bibl index afp ISBN 0-674-05305-2, $39.95

Altmeyer (psychology, Univ. of Manitoba) caps a project that spans three books and most of his career. *The Authoritarian Specter* is necessary for all students of authoritarian politics, personality psychology, and political extremism and radicalism. Altmeyer demonstrates that certain behavioral characteristics are identified with authoritarian personalities. No other study can give equivalent empirical results over time, with recurring analyses and retesting since the 1970s that show that the author's model works and is consistent. He shows that right-wing authoritarianism (RWA) can be identified in the covariation of three attitudinal clusters: authoritarian submission, authoritarian aggression, and conventionalism. He addresses left-wing extremism, but the RWA scale tests for the behavior and worldview that show antidemocratic and fascist tendencies, and goes well beyond the pioneering "Berkeley theory" found in *The Authoritarian Personality*, by T.W. Adorno et al. (1950). Altmeyer's work has the virtues of establishing indicators of authoritarian personality and its temptations and of writing about a scholarly topic in readable and engaging style. Political scientists, particularly in the field of political psychology, must read this intelligent, scholarly, witty account of the authoritarian personality. Upper-division undergraduates through faculty.—*A. R. Brunello, Eckerd College*

OAB-2642 JK468 93-43352 CIP
Bar-Joseph, Uri. **Intelligence intervention in the politics of democratic states: the United States, Israel, and Britain.** Pennsylvania State, 1995. 392p bibl index afp ISBN 0-271-01331-1, $55.00; ISBN 0-271-01332-X pbk, $18.95

Bar-Joseph offers a well-conceived and well-written analysis of intelligence agencies and their relationships with political authority. In part 1, an overview of intelligence and politics, he finds a dearth of literature for building a theoretical framework that would be useful in studying the interaction between politics and intelligence communities. He suggests that higher levels of bureaucratic cooperation be developed like that in many general national security research efforts. Part 2 is devoted to four case studies of intelligence intervention into politics. In the US's Bay of Pigs fiasco, intelligence officers are portrayed as being overly optimistic about success in order to convince policy makers of the prospects for the demise of Castro. The other case studies are less well known. Israel's "Unfortunate Business of 1954" involved an Israeli covert operation in Egypt wherein the Israeli intelligence agencies apparently attempted to conduct an independent foreign policy. The last two involve British intelligence services apparently plotting against their government in the 1920s, the "Zinoviev Letter Affair" and the "Henry Wilson Affair." Bar-Joseph's work is excellent in every respect. He creates a sound theoretical framework from which to judge his case studies and provides a convincing analysis in these case studies themselves. An important contribution, essential for professional and university libraries.—*A. C. Tuttle, University of Nevada, Las Vegas*

OAB-2643 HC79 94-37751 CIP
Caldwell, Lynton K. **Environment as a focus for public policy,** ed. by Robert V. Bartlett and James N. Gladden. Texas A&M, 1995. 358p bibl index afp ISBN 0-8909-6643-5, $39.50

Caldwell (political science, public and environmental affairs, Indiana Univ., Emeritus) is credited with instigating a wholly new subfield of scholarly inquiry with his 1963 paper suggesting that governments should, explicitly and purposefully, redirect the behavior of humans toward their environment. Bartlett and Gladden, two of his doctoral students, enlisted his cooperation in the preparation of this selection of papers from the critical period 1963-73, some not easily accessible elsewhere. Caldwell has written an introduction to each chapter, an original final chapter, and a retrospective epilogue. The 14 articles provide a glimpse of the lively intellect that guided a distinguished academic career and many years of productive public service: politics, impact assessment, international issues, and social change. His papers are of enduring interest and value, free of reproachful comments and polarizing accusations, cognizant of technology, civil, prescient, urbane. Its general and philosophical approach may seem irrelevant to today's immediate challenges. Not so; the book merits thoughtful study by all concerned scientists—physical *and* political. Excellent choice of material; coherent; little repetition, yet broad coverage of the field. Strongly recommended. Upper-division undergraduate through professional.—*D. W. Larson, University of Regina*

OAB-2644 HD9696 94-31963 CIP
Evans, Peter. **Embedded autonomy: states and industrial transformation.** Princeton, 1995. 323p bibl index afp ISBN 0-691-03737-X, $49.50; ISBN 0-691-03736-1 pbk, $17.95

The author, a sociologist, examines the role of the state in promoting industrial transformation. He develops the notion of embedded autonomy to explain the success of developmental states. An embedded, autonomous bureaucracy is connected to society via a network of social ties and institutional channels but has a robust internal structure resulting from highly selective meritocratic recruitment, long-term career rewards, and a sense of corporate coherence. This

combination permits the state to engage in "midwifery" and "husbandry" vis-à-vis private entrepreneurial groups without succumbing to clientism. Using a comparative institutional approach, the author investigates the role of the state in promoting the computer industry in Korea, Brazil, and India. Basing his study on numerous interviews with agency officials and local entrepreneurs, the author develops a very useful and complete record of the process by which industrial transformation has been accomplished. The theoretical aspect of this work represents an interesting challenge to the neo-utilitarian theory of the state. This carefully researched and well-written book is an important addition to development literature and should be acquired by all academic libraries.—*R. C. Singleton, University of Puget Sound*

OAB-2645 JX5418 96-32315 CIP
Horowitz, Irving Louis. **Taking lives: genocide and state power.** 4th ed., expanded and rev. Transaction, 1997. 324p index afp ISBN 1-56000-308-1, $39.95

Horowitz has significantly expanded and thoroughly revised this fourth edition of his classic study of genocide. Since its first publication (*Genocide: State Power and Mass Murder*, 1976), *Taking Lives* has been regarded as a pivotal attempt to analyze the sociopolitical context of mass murder. It asserts that genocide is not a random event or necessarily linked to social conditions. For Horowitz, genocide is a special sort of mass destruction used by states and made possible by their technologically advanced apparatus of mass killing. The new edition includes four new chapters and some additions. Among the mass killings analyzed are the Armenian genocide, the Holocaust, Rwanda, Cambodia, and Yugoslavia. The author concludes on a pessimistic note, finding genocide a fundamental mechanism for the unification of the nation-state even in "advanced" societies; that is why it is so difficult to prevent it. A useful final chapter analyzes the recent contributions of some important genocide scholars—Israel Charny, R.J. Rummel, Vahakn Dadrian, James Dunn, Robert Melson, Richard Hovannisian, and others. Imperative for students of genocide, comparative ethnic politics and human rights, and anyone concerned with the most fundamental moral issue of our time.—*R. H. Dekmejian, University of Southern California*

OAB-2646 JF2011 94-21322 CIP
Klingemann, Hans-Dieter. **Parties, policies, and democracy,** by Hans-Dieter Klingemann, Richard I. Hofferbert, Ian Budge et al. Westview, 1994. 318p bibl index afp ISBN 0-8133-2068-2, $65.00; ISBN 0-8133-2069-0 pbk, $24.95

This is a must reference for serious students of comparative democratic studies. Although specialists will quibble—and justifiably so—with a number of assumptions and methodological applications offered by the authors, the book nonetheless is a tour de force in theory and social science analysis. The authors systematically explore a number of categories of national budgets (welfare, justice, defense, agriculture, housing, education, etc.) across ten countries (US, Britain, France, Sweden, Germany, Austria, Holland, Canada, Australia, and Belgium) over 40 years. Their objective is to sort out the relative contribution of issue saliency (coded from the party manifestos of all major parties in the countries), ideology, and mandate politics to the overall variance in cross-national budgetary patterns. Their findings have important implications for understanding how party politics influences policies within certain institutional settings. For instance, by relying upon Lipset and Rokkan's earlier analysis of pre- and postindustrial party ideologies, they find that mandate politics is strongest where ethnicity and religion are the basis of party cleavages, suggesting a modest refinement in our thinking of the relationship between postmaterialism and policy priorities within democracies in general. Overall, this is a work full of insight and empirical revelations, destined to be one of the most widely cited and influential works on comparative public policy produced during this decade.—*J. D. Robertson, Texas A&M University*

OAB-2647 JA66 96-21871 MARC
A New handbook of political science, ed. by Robert E. Goodin and

Hans-Dieter Klingemann. Oxford, 1996. 845p bibl indexes afp ISBN 0-19-828015-7, $75.00

In coverage of the discipline, historical depth, and international perspective this constitutes an exceptionally comprehensive survey of political science. The 41 contributors, 19 of whom including the coeditors are from outside the US, are recognized scholars. The book is composed of nine parts covering the major subfields in the discipline, each containing chapters that focus on specific perspectives. Each part also has an introductory overview chapter and a concluding chapter evaluating changes over the past two decades. Chapter bibliographies list the classic works in each area as well as important recent publications. The approach taken here is broader and oriented more toward institutional analysis than *Political Science: The State of the Discipline II*, ed. by Ada W. Finifter (1993), which relied on US scholars and has a single-chapter survey for each subfield of the discipline. Also very useful in *A New Handbook* are the introductory "bibliometric analysis" of where and how frequently scholars are cited in the ensuing essays and the detailed subject and name indexes. A definitive reference work in the field.—*R. Heineman, Alfred University*

OAB-2648 HV6322 93-21279 CIP
Rummel, R.J. **Death by government.** Transaction, 1994. 496p bibl index ISBN 1-56000-145-3, $49.95

This is Rummel's fourth book on genocide and mass murder by governments. It is a compelling study of what the author calls democide—the intentional killing by governments through genocide, politicide, massacre, and terror. The book focuses on 14 democides of the 20th century by the governments of the Soviet Union, Communist China, Nazi Germany, Nationalist China, Japan, Cambodia, Turkey, Vietnam, Poland, Pakistan, Communist Yugoslavia, North Korea, Mexico, and Feudal Russia—a total of 169 million murders, which Rummel carefully documents through elaborate statistical techniques. He concludes that the more power a regime has, the more its leaders can murder their domestic and foreign subjects. Democracies, where power is diffused, are less likely to engage in mass violence. Thus, the solution to democide is democracy, and the course of action is to foster freedom. A product of eight years of research by a distinguished political scientist, this is an unrivaled magnum opus with dozens of tables, figures, copious notes, and massive bibliography. Essential reading for historians, political scientists, and readers interested in genocide. All levels.—*R. H. Dekmejian, University of Southern California*

OAB-2649 HQ1236 94-18706 CIP
Women and revolution in Africa, Asia, and the New World, ed. by Mary Ann Tétreault. South Carolina, 1994. 456p index ISBN 1-57003-016-2, $39.95

This collection is packed with illuminating theoretical essays and substantive chapters of 20th-century revolutions in 16 countries. Revolution is broadly defined to include socialist, religious, nationalist, and capitalist/modernizing efforts as they intersect with women and families. Although revolutions generally broaden the political agenda (to include topics such as wife beating, unpaid heavy labor, and bridewealth exchange) or to construct new female symbolism, gains for women are mixed and nowhere is equality achieved. Readers will find coverage of those revolutions with a sparse literature, such as North Korea and Afghanistan, especially useful. Tétreault's collection, *the* probable classic on the topic for the 1990s, provides greater conceptual breadth and country-level depth than the 1980s classics *Promissory Notes: Women in the Transition to Socialism*, edited by Sonia Kruks, Rayna Rapp, and Marilyn Young (CH, Dec'89), and *Women, the State, and Development*, edited by Sue Ellen Charlton, Jana Everett, and Kathleen Staudt (CH, May'90). Highly recommended for undergraduate, graduate, and general reader libraries.—*K. Staudt, University of Texas at El Paso*

OAB-2650 HN90 96-10420 CIP
Wood, Donald N. **Post-intellectualism and the decline of democracy: the failure of reason and responsibility in the twentieth**

century. Praeger, 1996. 302p bibl index afp ISBN 0-275-95421-8, $65.00; ISBN 0-275-95661-X pbk, $21.95

Provocative social-cultural theory; jeremiad; prophecy of an already arrived technocratic dystopia. This book by a senior media scholar (California State Univ., Northridge) is all these. The human condition has evolved from a cyclical oral tradition to a linear culture of written intellectualism, but events of the last 35 years indicate descent into a Web culture of postintellectualism in which electronic media are central. Wood sees postintellectualism as the fruit of deliberate *counterintellectualism* and *distended intellectualism*, the "irresponsible, unbridled, linear extension of intellectual endeavors without consideration of ultimate consequences." Ignorance, "dumbth" (decline of analytical thinking), establishmentism, and specialization all characterize postintellectualism, its offspring an array of personal and social maladies—illiteracy, loss of privacy, data overload, isolation, directionlessness, urban pathologies, failure of economic assumptions, environmental decay, moral collapse. Democracy, deteriorating visibly, seems particularly damaged. Some of Wood's arguments or examples may seem reactionary or mean-spirited (he condemns multiculturalism and repudiates social policies that impede survival of the fittest), and the hopefulness he conveys late in the book and his ten recommendations seem at odds with his morose tone and determinism, but much of what he writes is important, compelling, irrefutable. Recommended for academic readers, entering students through faculty.—*J. D. Gillespie, Presbyterian College*

■ Comparative Politics

AFRICA AND MIDDLE EAST

OAB-2651 KRX986 95-50943 CIP
Firmin-Sellers, Kathryn. **The transformation of property rights in the Gold Coast: an empirical analysis applying rational choice theory.** Cambridge, 1996. 200p bibl index ISBN 0-521-55503-5, $54.95

Firmin-Sellers adds luster to the influential "Political Economy of Institutions and Decisions" series in a tightly argued, well-researched monograph using two tribal/ethnic case studies to illustrate a series of analytical and theoretical propositions in political economy and beyond. Field research in the Gold Coast (Ghana) concentrated on the central issue of property rights. The author uses this issue to demonstrate the integral relationship between the economics and politics of stable state building and maintenance. Although the subtitle points to the often ephemeral rational choice theory as a base, the author prefers the term "new institutionalism," her main point being that politics is underappreciated in political economy research applications. The book describes the insecurity of property rights in precolonial, transitional, and independent Ghana and uses this to discuss theories of indirect rule, state development, and central-peripheral power within the state as well as the role of state and economy in property rights distribution. The work's integration of field work with theoretical perspectives is remarkable. Highly recommended for upper-division undergraduates and higher.—*R. M. Fulton, Northwest Missouri State University*

OAB-2652 93-60073 Orig
Genocide and democracy in Cambodia: the Khmer Rouge, the United Nations and the international community, ed. with introd. by Ben Kiernan. Yale University Southeast Asia Studies, 1993. 335p bibl (Monograph series, 41) ISBN 0-938692-49-6 pbk, $17.00

This fine book can be recommended without reservation for all levels of readership. The editor, Ben Kiernan of Yale, is justifiably considered the most knowledgeable observer of Cambodia anywhere in the Western world. He has assembled a stimulating collection of essays by a diverse group of contributors including Cambodians. The essays cover the pre-Khmer Rouge Period (1970-75), the period of genocide (1975-79), and its aftermath. There are useful tables and appendixes, including the political and military chains of command during the Pol Pot years, a brief guide to the personalities of current factions, and the text of the UN Genocide Convention. A must for all universities with Asia studies programs.—*R. Marlay, Arkansas State University*

OAB-2653   Orig
Hanf, Theodor. **Coexistence in wartime Lebanon: decline of a state and rise of a nation,** tr. by John Richardson. Centre for Lebanese Studies/I.B. Tauris, 1993. 712p bibl indexes ISBN 1-85043-651-7, $69.50

This is the definitive book on the 1975-90 conflict in Lebanon. Hanf, Director of the Arnold-Berstrasser Institute in Freiburg, Germany, is little known in the US, but he is well known in Europe for empirically rich work on internal conflict. He has written a readable and compelling account of the poignant struggle of the Lebanese to survive. In 11 lucid chapters he incisively and objectively recounts virtually all the important events of the conflict. Equally important, he provides an analytical account of the failure of confessional politics in Lebanon, which he notes was the victim of political murder, not national suicide. "The murder victim is not guilty, but it is not innocent of complicity either." He is referring to the intrusions of regional players such as the PLO, Israel, and Syria in this permeable country of three million people, as well as to the penchant of Lebanese politicos to seek external patrons and thereby facilitate the meddling of non-Lebanese. Somewhat ironically, Hanf finds that the Lebanese have emerged from their horrors with a new national consensus rooted in common suffering and a common yearning for peace and independence. Although the conventional wisdom paints Lebanon as an example of the failure of consociational politics, Hanf does not share this dour wisdom. He does, however, express profound concern for Lebanon's independence in view of Syria's smothering influence since 1990, when Syrian arms brought the civil war to an end. Includes excellent bibliographies of western references as well as Arabic sources. All levels.—*A. R. Norton, Boston University*

OAB-2654   DS70   94-34779 MARC
Iraq's crime of genocide: the Anfal campaign against the Kurds, by the Human Rights Watch/Middle East. Yale, 1995. 373p bibl index afp ISBN 0-300-06427-6, $35.00

Human Rights Watch/Middle East (HRW/ME) here charges that the Iraqi government pursued a campaign of genocide (known as *al-Anfal*) against the Kurdish population of northern Iraq in late February through early September 1988. The study is based on some 4 million pages of documents that Kurdish forces obtained in their uprising in spring 1991 and turned over to HRW/ME. The campaign's intent was to depopulate Kurdish regions in northern Iraq and Arabize them. HRW/ME estimates that 100,000 to 182,000 Kurds died in *al-Anfal*. The genocide was carried out through systematic razing of villages, constant chemical attacks, and cold-blooded murder. Joost Hiltermann (*al-Anfal* project director at HRW/ME) demolishes Iraqi claims that the documents are forgeries. HRW/ME has collected sufficient evidence to bring a charge of genocide against the Iraqi government before the International Court of Justice, but understands that a judgment in any such case would be unenforceable. (HRW/MR possesses a tape in which Ali Hassan al-Majid, the Ba'athist official who directed *al-Anfal* and is now Iraq's Minister of Defense, voices contempt toward the international community: "I will kill them all [the Kurds] with chemical weapons! Who is going to say anything? The international community? Fuck them! the international community, and those who listen to them!") This gruesome account does not ask why the international community has done so little to prevent or punish the genocide and ethnic cleansing still being pursued against the Kurds. Everyone concerned with genocide in the 20th century should read this fine study. Upperdivision through faculty.—*R. W. Olson, University of Kentucky*

OAB-2655   DT1165   94-25066 CIP
Khadiagala, Gilbert M. **Allies in adversity: the frontline states in southern African security, 1975-1993.** Ohio University, 1994. 317p bibl index afp ISBN 0-8214-1097-0, $50.00

Khadiagala presents a comprehensive examination of interstate relations in

the southern Africa subregion. His study carefully analyzes the extent to which relatively weak, majority-ruled states in southern Africa managed to mount a credible security alliance that significantly influenced the pace and direction of political changes. The book very ably chronicles how the alliance skillfully coordinated regional and extra-regional diplomatic, political, and military effort to bring the South African state, the regional economic and military hegemony, to the bargaining table. More significantly, the book provides theoretical and empirical insights on the limits and vulnerabilities of externally dependent security alliances. It amply shows how dependence on powerful external actors compromised the integrity of the alliance's security posture. Such vulnerabilities ranged from political manipulation of its security policy objectives to outright marginalization of the alliance in the decolonization process. This is a very valuable book that every student of African affairs should have on the shelf. All levels.—*S. M. Rugumamu, University of North Carolina at Chapel Hill*

OAB-2656   DS113   96-45757 CIP
Khalidi, Rashid. **Palestinian identity: the construction of modern national consciousness.** Columbia, 1997. 309p bibl index afp ISBN 0-231-10514-2, $29.50

Khalidi provides compelling challenges to the prevailing assumptions concerning the origins of Palestinian nationalism. He explores the interplay between the narratives that make up Palestinian history and examines the various constituents of Palestinian national identity. In so doing he illuminates heretofore little-known aspects of Palestinian singularity, in particular the circumstances that gave rise to the shift from Arab/Ottoman to Palestinian/Arab identity. Beginning with the later Ottoman Empire, Khalidi uses Arabic, Turkish, Hebrew, and Western archival sources as well as many unpublished sources—notably from the Khalidi Library in Jerusalem—to substantiate his thesis. He argues that the origins and growth of Palestinian nationalism were not so much a reaction to Zionism as a response to the influences of late 19th-century Palestinian scholars, the Arab press, British occupation, and later, Zionist colonization. The material, intellectual, and spiritual importance of Jerusalem to Palestinians is well substantiated. Khalidi's biographies of Yosuf Diya and Ruhi al-Khalidi—scholars, diplomats, and members of the Ottoman Parliament—provide valuable context and perspective. This original research sheds new light on the question of Palestine. It should be read by *everyone* concerned about accurate historiography, cultural mythology, the social construction of national identity, and a peaceful resolution of the Palestinian-Israeli conflict.—*C. A. Rubenberg, Florida International University*

OAB-2657   DT658   92-46921 CIP
Leslie, Winsome J. **Zaire: continuity and political change in an oppressive state.** Westview, 1993. 204p bibl index afp ISBN 0-86531-298-2, $46.95

Zaire is the nightmare of Africa. It has been plagued by the complete inventory of African catastrophes. Presiding over this shipwreck of a country for almost three decades is the ingenious tyrant Mobutu Sese Seko, whose career is a monument to playing off external interest while internally he divides and conquers. In an admirably pithy yet sober fashion, this book chronicles the journey of Zaire from colonial authoritarianism to postcolonial oppression, with short but informative glances at early history, society, culture, and economy. Writing in the useful "Profiles, Nations of Contemporary Africa" series, Leslie (Johns Hopkins and American Univ.), who has written on the effort to institute economic reforms in Zaire, shares the views of other authoritative commentators—such as Crawford Young and Thomas Turner, *The Rise and Decline of the Zairian State* (CH, Jan'86); and Michael Schatzberg, *The Dialectics of Oppression in Zaire* (CH, Mar'89)—that the country's human and material resources as well as its potential for economic and political influence have been sacrificed to Mobutu's absolutist rule and personal ambition. Among the book's accomplishments is to provide case material for the thesis that Zaire's links to the past geostrategy of the West and the global economy it protected are what kept Mobutu in place. If so, the book offers some hope for change in Zaire, despite Mobutu's continuing manipulations. An excellent introduction demanding an early paper edition. All levels.—*H. Glickman, Haverford College*

OAB-2658 Orig

Lewis, John P. **India's political economy: governance and reform.** Oxford, 1995. 401p bibl index ISBN 0-19-563515-9, $29.95

Lewis, who has more than 30 years of experience with economic development, India, and international organizations, offers one of the most impressive and intelligent books about India in over a decade. Early chapters comprehensively review India's development experience, including relations with both bilateral and multilateral aid donors. Lewis makes illuminating use of his experience as USAID director for India in the 1960s, following this by describing the evolution of Indian political economy and development policy, and the liberalization policies now being followed. His discussion of the interplay between economic development and politics is balanced and wise, leaving the reader wishing he had done more. While the book is top professional literature, it will be helpful and interesting to any reader with a reasonable general background. Scholars will find his concluding suggestions for future Indian development (much more education, more town development, and enhanced federalism with a better balance between central and state leadership) well thought out, occasionally controversial, and wise. Students of international organization will particularly appreciate his constructive criticism of World Bank and other policies and studies over the years. General; upper-division undergraduate; graduate; faculty; professional.—*J. D. Stempel, University of Kentucky*

OAB-2659 JV875 96-49172 CIP

Longva, Anh Nga. **Walls built on sand: migration, exclusion, and society in Kuwait.** Westview, 1997. 265p bibl index afp ISBN 0-8133-2758-X, $59.00

Massive oil reserves make Kuwait an exceptionally rich Persian Gulf country. In its population of 1.9 million, 63 percent are non-Kuwaitis, many of them Arabs. It has a closed political system tightly controlled by the Al-Sabah family; a large portion of the population, both Kuwaitis and non-Kuwaitis, is excluded from decision making. Longva's fine piece of scholarship treats the political and social dimensions of labor migration in Kuwait. In order to carry out the politics of exclusion, Kuwaiti society relies on a rigid system of stratification that divides people into such dichotomous categories as Kuwaiti/non-Kuwaiti, Arab/non-Arab, and Moslem/non-Moslem. A variety of other methods, all discussed in the book, include the practice of *Kafala*, which requires foreigners born outside the Gulf Cooperation Council states to be sponsored by either a private citizen or a private or state institution. The book concludes that although Kuwaiti society is built on exclusion and dominance, it "had come to acquire a social viability in which not only the dominant groups but also the subordinate ones actively participate." Longva's well-researched and perceptive book confirms Barrington Moore Jr.'s argument that people's threshold for obedience and acceptance of suffering is remarkably high. It should be read by all those interested in the politics of the Middle East. Upper-division undergraduates through faculty.—*M. M. Milani, University of South Florida*

OAB-2660 Orig

Macroeconomic Research Group. **Making democracy work: a framework for macroeconomic policy in South Africa: a report to members of the Democratic Movement of South Africa.** Centre for Development Studies, South Africa, 1994 (c1993). (Dist. by Oxford) 330p bibl ISBN 1-86808-183-4 pbk, $16.95

This succinct and valuable study by South Africa's Macroeconomic Research Group (MERG) recommends a macroeconomic policy blueprint for transforming South Africa into a viable democracy which not only promotes socioeconomic justice and sustained development, but also corrects, in MERG's views, the economic mismanagement and irresponsible policies of the previous apartheid government. Clearly MERG's state-oriented program requires a strong, centralized government, and whether the compromises necessary for future political stability will permit an unleavened unitary system remains an open question. However, this study, completed in 1993, represents the best single volume of South African socioeconomic statistics for the end of the apartheid era, as well as the most comprehensive brief analysis of that country's current econ-

omy. The study includes, inter alia, proposals that redirect taxes and subsidies, fiscal and monetary policies dealing with interest rates and inflation, massive direct state investment in the physical and human infrastructure of the country, and economic policies which increase the efficiency of the civil service. In short, MERG urges a thorough reorganization of both the economy and the bureaucratic agencies that affect its functioning. Upper-division undergraduate through faculty.—*M. E. Doro, Connecticut College*

OAB-2661 JQ1941 93-25824 CIP

Malan to De Klerk: leadership in the apartheid state, ed. by Robert Schrire. St. Martin's, 1994. 312p index ISBN 0-312-10219-4, $45.00

This is an extraordinarily useful and meticulous account of South Africa's executive during the *apartheid* era. The contributors, each of whom is an established South African academic, analyze a specific aspect of the head of government in terms of the country's constitution, the administrative nature of the executive office, his relationship to and leadership of the National Party, his role as the leader vis-à-vis the citizenry, how he exercised control over the African population, his shaping of foreign policy, and reflections on the future of the presidency. The South African sources that the authors extensively draw on give the analysis great authenticity, but also sometimes leave it unleavened by interpretations of external observers. The volume's careful scholarship traces the growth of executive power and describes the path leading to President DeKlerk's decision to dismantle apartheid. As a brief account this work could be the definitive one currently. It is often caught up in a culture of legalism that uncritically analyzes various instruments of executive authority as if they were used in a liberal democratic system that limits power and protects individual rights and liberties of all citizens. Advanced undergraduate through faculty.—*M. E. Doro, Connecticut College*

OAB-2662 JQ442 92-7331 CIP

Maung, Mya. **Totalitarianism in Burma: prospects for economic development.** Paragon House, 1992. 277p bibl index ISBN 1-55778-553-8, $49.95

This outstanding volume continues the serious and high-quality research begun by the author with *The Burma Road to Poverty* (1991). In the present study, he offers a clear analysis of Burma as a totalitarian state under military rule and how it affects both the daily lives and thinking of the people and the economy. Beginning with an analysis of totalitarianism as a concept, he applies it to Burma and shows what has happened to the nation since the soldiers seized power in 1962, suppressed a peaceful revolt in 1988, and have sought to disguise repression with promises of freedom and democracy and have continued the command economy of the past in the new dress of open competitive popular market forces; but in reality, with the same people in charge, operating in the same corrupt ways, Burma's economic decline continues. This volume is must reading for political economists who are advancing the thesis of economic development before democracy; Burma is living proof that in its case, this least-developed nation continues to decline and the people suffer while a two-class society emerges: the military and the people. Maung's solid, well-researched study will have lasting value; this reviewer believes it will be the standard work against which all others on the political economy of Burma will be measured. Not only will scholars appreciate this work, but it is also must reading for business practioners who want to enter the Burma market. With this second book, Maung is the leading political economist writing on Burma today. General; advanced undergraduate through professional.—*J. Silverstein, emeritus, Rutgers, the State University of New Jersey, New Brunswick*

OAB-2663 JQ1879 96-7588 CIP

Monga, Célestin. **The anthropology of anger: civil society and democracy in Africa,** tr. by Linda L. Fleck and Célestin Monga. L. Rienner, 1996. 219p bibl index afp ISBN 1-55587-644-7, $45.00

This excellent analysis of the democratization process in Africa is a revised and expanded English edition of Monga's *Anthropologie de la colère: société civile et démocratie en Afrique noire* (Paris, 1994), which draws on his *L'Afrique* et la théorie démocratique (Québec, 1996). The author joins a growing group of African scholars who view African politics through the lens of their own experience, asserting their individuality and scholarship not by rejecting the mainstream political science of Western analysts but by mastering it and developing their own analyses of political development in Africa. Monga critiques various current conceptual theories about African politics, reviews the character and nature of public discourse in Africa, and highlights patterns of democratic behavior that are emerging from the disorder and dysfunction that followed independence. At the risk of oversimplifying his major thesis, he argues that "collective anger and anxieties" are being converted into political demands for new modes of accountability relevant to the traditions and culture of African life. Although it is unclear what those new modes will be, this book should be required reading for Africanists. Upper-division undergraduates through faculty.—*M. E. Doro, Connecticut College*

OAB-2664   DS126   94-41950 CIP
Peres, Shimon. **Battling for peace: a memoir,** ed. by David Landau. Random House, 1995. 350p index afp ISBN 0-679-43617-0, $25.00

Peres emerges in this memoir as a truly complex individual whose intellectualism combines with his Ben Gurion labor socialism to create a capable and enduring national leader. In a light and easy way he recounts his birth and youth in a Russian village, his family's migration to Palestine in the 1930s, and the puritanism of a Kibbutz agricultural upbringing. The story of his political career, which achieved visibility when he was appointed director general of the Ministry of Defense in his twenties, is told forthrightly and even self-critically. He erred, for example, in supporting Pinhas Lavon to become Defense Minister in 1953. The "Affair" of Lavon, beginning with his effort to disrupt Egyptian-American relations in 1954 through Israeli secret agent attacks on US offices in Cairo and the coverups that continued for a decade, gets a full political accounting. The book has many such insights, including the more recent Oslo accord with the PLO. Twenty-three pages of texts of diplomatic agreements including the PLO-Israel Declaration of Principles (1993) and the peace treaty with Jordan (1994). Highly recommended for all collections.—*L. J. Cantori, University of Maryland Baltimore County*

OAB-2665   JQ1911   94-16987 CIP
Sisk, Timothy D. **Democratization in South Africa: the elusive social contract.** Princeton, 1995. 342p bibl index afp ISBN 0-691-03622-5, $39.50

The transition of South African politics from a zero-sum struggle to negotiated compromise provides an opportunity to analyze the prerequisites of democracy. South Africa's divided society seems to offer a "least-likely" case for democratic reform. Sisk traces the negotiations, 1990 through 1993, that overcame the odds. Conceptually, he relies on rational choice theory to explain the negotiations of the major actors, the African National Congress and the National Party, who perceived themselves to be evenly balanced in a power struggle in which neither could achieve dominance. This recognition led to compromises in which the vital interests of both could be advanced. Arduous negotiations produced a settlement combining aspects of majoritarian rule advocated by the ANC and consociationalism sought by the NP. The negotiations were complicated by upsurges of violence, fomented largely by smaller groups who feared their interests would suffer. Rather than derailing negotiations, the violence increased the incentives of the main groups to reach agreement, and a new South Africa emerged. The new regime, however, is a bargain struck among elites. Sisk concludes by discussing the prospects of extending this elite consensus to a social contract encompassing the masses of South African citizens. However the process proceeds, Sisk's book will likely become the standard work on South African reform and also will be of interest to students of democratic and rational choice theory. Upper-division undergraduates through faculty.—*L. P. Frank, Roosevelt University*

OAB-2666   DT1967   96-21150 CIP
Waldmeir, Patti. **Anatomy of a miracle: the end of apartheid and**

the birth of the new South Africa. W.W. Norton, 1997. 303p index ISBN 0-393-03997-8, $27.50

Here is serious journalism at its best: gracefully written, rich in personal anecdotes and insightful portraits of political leaders, firmly grasping the sweep of a front-page event of global significance, but focused on transition analysis (the "op-ed" issues of moving from apartheid to inclusive democracy in South Africa). The American author served as correspondent for the *Financial Times* (London) in Lusaka, 1984-86, then as Johannesburg bureau chief for the same paper, 1989-95. Waldmeir frames her inquiry around two basic questions: How could black South Africans subdue hatred? and, Why did the Afrikaner hand over power? Her answers draw on cultures and personalities that had more in common than was evident to nonnative observers, but ultimately her story centers on the effectiveness of strategies for gaining or retaining power by the leadership of the ANC and the National Party. Although her vignettes capture evocative moments, her most fascinating narrative examines the negotiating processes that resulted in the release of Mandela, established ground rules for political transformation, (including the first election in their lifetimes for most of the participants), and constructed a new constitution. Acknowledging the miracle, Waldmeir never loses sight of the political and economic interests that shaped it. A great yarn and rattling good reading. General and academic readers, all levels.—*H. Glickman, Haverford College*

OAB-2667   Orig
Woodward, Peter. **The Horn of Africa: state politics and international relations.** Tauris Academic Studies, 1996. (Dist. by St. Martin's) 226p bibl index (International library of African studies, 6) ISBN 1-85043-741-6, $59.50

Woodward's excellent book provides an authoritative and current overview of the politics and international relations of the Horn of Africa. A noted British academic specialist in northeastern Africa and editor of the journal *African Affairs* (1944-), Woodward's editorial experience shows: he does not waste words, yet he is admirably thorough in covering recent events in the Horn. Woodward focuses on the relationship between Ethiopia and its major neighbors Sudan and Somalia, although he includes excellent overviews of Eritrea and Djibouti. Since the purpose of the book is to provide an introduction, Woodward does not give documentation in the form of extensive footnotes but instead provides a superb bibliography of books and monographs (no articles) to guide readers seeking further details. Since Woodward surveys the entire Horn (although he stresses the differences between the three main countries' historical experiences and political structures), he is able to draw attention to some developments that may have implications beyond the region, such as the challenges to colonial borders—Eritrea (successful), Somaliland (pending), and southern Sudan (ongoing). Highly recommended for all levels.—*C. W. Hartwig, Arkansas State University*

Asia & Oceania

OAB-2668   DS393   96-41187 CIP
Baxter, Craig. **Bangladesh: from a nation to a state.** Westview, 1997. 176p bibl index afp ISBN 0-8133-2854-3, $59.00

Baxter has done it again, producing another superb scholarly book on a South Asian topic. This is a very solid, well-researched, comprehensive history of the East Bengal area from its Hindu-Buddhist origins to the election of Awami League leader Sheikh Hasina Wajed as Prime Minister, June 23, 1996. Baxter also provides an insightful analysis of the turbulent politics of Bangladesh since its independence from Pakistan in 1971. He analyzes Bangladesh's economic and social development, including its population growth problem and its position in the world. Baxter possesses outstanding scholarly credentials for this project, based on more than 40 years' experience in the area and several books on South Asian topics. Strongly recommended for general and academic readers; should become a standard source in the field.—*L. P. Fickett Jr., Mary Washington College*

OAB-2669   DS554   92-19229 CIP
Chandler, David P. **Brother number one: a political biography of Pol Pot.** Westview, 1992. 254p index afp ISBN 0-8133-0927-1, $24.95

Chandler's gracefully written biography of the most enigmatic revolutionary of this century, Saloth Sar (alias Pol Pot), deserves wide readership. It is a solid contribution to scholarship, based on extensive interviews of survivors of the murderous regime. Chandler asks profoundly disturbing questions: How can a man who has killed a million people live with himself? Why did people follow him? This book covers what is known of Pol Pot's life—there are gaps and lacunae—from childhood, his years in Paris, in the jungle, as feared dictator, to his present hideout on the Thai border. It also analyzes the internal political struggles in Cambodia from 1941 to 1979 and the complex, cynical web of international politics in which Cambodia was merely a pawn. Chandler successfully walks a fine line, condemning Pol Pot and all his works, but trying to understand what motivates him. One is struck most strongly by the impression Pol Pot made on all who met him: gentle, polite, unassuming. Chandler believes Pol Pot was actually influenced by Buddhist ideals of the quiet, unruffled teacher, woven into Khmer culture. Contains a chronology, bibliographic essay, detailed footnotes, and some photographs. Recommended without reservation to both public and academic libraries at all levels.—*R. Marlay, Arkansas State University*

OAB-2670   DS480   95-8097 MARC
De Silva, K.M. **Regional powers and small state security: India and Sri Lanka, 1977-90.** Woodrow Wilson Center/Johns Hopkins, 1995. 388p bibl index afp ISBN 0-8018-5149-1, $48.50

De Silva's very thorough, well-researched, multifaceted work treats a complex problem. Basically, the book provides a history and an analysis of India's relationship to and involvement with Sri Lanka, its small island neighbor to the southeast, 1977-90, particularly during three critical phases from 1980 to 1990. The author also examines the island's complex ethnic conflict from the mid-1970s through the 1980s, showing that it provided India with the opportunity to intervene in Sri Lanka's affairs. Finally, it is destined to be a classic study of India's failed military intervention in Sri Lanka, 1987-90. The author is a respected Sri Lankan historian who is coauthor of a biography of the former Sri Lankan president, J.R. Jayewardene (1988). The bibliography is excellent. Strongly recommended for upper-division undergraduates, graduate students, and faculty interested in South Asian history and crisis management.—*L. P. Fickett Jr., Mary Washington College*

OAB-2671   JQ1504   92-14789 CIP
Dreyer, June Teufel. **China's political system: modernization and tradition.** Paragon House, 1993. 448p bibl index ISBN 1-55778-478-7 pbk, $22.95

In this fine scholarly work Dreyer (Univ. of Miami), author of *China's Forty Millions: Minority Nationalities and Integration in the People's Republic of China* (CH, Jun'77), explores China's lengthy and laborious search for a formula of modernization compatible with Chinese reality. Following an intriguing introduction, which discusses different schools of analysis among China watchers, the first four chapters summarize the historical background to China's latest modernizing efforts led by Deng Xiaoping. The subsequent nine chapters examine Deng's modernization program and contrast Maoist policies with his in various aspects of China's political life. In the final chapter, Dreyer comments on several commonly heard scenarios about China's future. She believes that the system is at a critical juncture because large numbers of people feel uncomfortable with the status quo but fail to reach consensus on what new directions to take. Based on a remarkably comprehensive survey of primary and secondary materials in Chinese and English, the book is a valuable addition to the rapidly growing literature on post-Mao China. Despite a good index, readers might want to see more detailed notes and a less selected bibliography. Highly recommended for general and academic audiences, lower-division undergraduate through graduate.—*S. K. Ma, California State University, Los Angeles*

OAB-2672   DS556   95-53084 CIP
Duiker, William J. **The communist road to power in Vietnam.** 2nd ed. Westview, 1996. 435p bibl index afp ISBN 0-8133-8586-5, $75.00; ISBN 0-8133-8587-3 pbk, $21.95

Duiker (history, Penn State) is one of the most prolific and authoritative scholars on Vietnam. His books on the rise of Vietnamese nationalists, the revolutionary movement, US containment policy in Indochina, and Vietnam in transition through the present are all models of breadth, judiciousness, astute analysis, and clarity. This updated edition of his classic on the communist rise to power is also in that mode. The large amount of material that has become available on the communist side since the original edition (CH, Apr'82) necessitated the new edition, which in many ways is a larger version of Duiker's outstanding *Sacred War: Nationalism and Revolution in a Divided Vietnam* (1995). Duiker finds it unfortunate that the Vietnam War has played such a decisive role in American foreign policy for the last two decades, because Vietnam was unique. He carefully describes the indigenous forces and the "explosive combination of circumstances" that brought about the situation. He believes that the story of why the communists won is important, but it does not serve as primer for other revolutions or how to defeat these revolutions. In the vast literature on the Vietnam War, this is one of the most important books to read. All levels.—*J. P. Dunn, Converse College*

OAB-2673   DS126   94-27418 CIP
Frankel, Glenn. **Beyond the promised land: Jews and Arabs on the hard road to a new Israel.** Simon & Schuster, 1994. 416p index ISBN 0-671-79649-6, $24.00

This is an empirically and analytically rich book that examines the transformation of Israeli politics, economics, society, and culture since the beginning of the *intifada*. Much of the discussion focuses on the political dimension of this transformation. In his extensive, informative account, which relies on individual cases, the Frankel demonstrates how the Israelis moved from nonrecognition of the Palestinians to the need for coexistence. He traces the evolution of the socialist economy into a market-oriented one, in light of growing defense expenditure and other economic impediments due to the ongoing conflict. Immigration of Jews, particularly the Soviet Jews, was instrumental in demographic changes with serious cultural and electoral implications. What sets this book apart is Frankel's ability to present broad and complex socioeconomic and political issues in light of their impact on individual Jews and Palestinians and their small communities. Uniquely objective and balanced, the work explains how certain policies and actions influence the daily lives of the people both in Israel and in the occupied territories. Chapters demonstrate a keen familiarity with the characters, policy preferences, and ideological proclivities of the influential personalities in Israel and the territories as well as communal needs and interests. Frankel presents an accurate picture of the current and future trends in Israeli politics, especially in relationship to the Palestinians. An exceptional book. All levels.—*M. Tamadonfar, University of Nevada, Las Vegas*

OAB-2674   JX1981   94-31673 CIP
Heininger, Janet E. **Peacekeeping in transition: the United Nations in Cambodia.** Twentieth Century Fund, 1994. 183p index ISBN 0-87078-362-9 pbk, $11.95

This very carefully written, comprehensive account of the UNTAC (United Nations Transitional Authority in Cambodia) peacekeeping mission in Cambodia from 1991 to 1993 is so packed with facts and figures—clearly and logically arranged—that the reader assumes that Heininger was a participant and is surprised to learn that she was observing events from Washington. She relates details of the negotiations that led up to the unprecedented agreement to temporarily turn an entire country over to UN supervision. The factors that made the May 1993 elections a resounding success despite violence and threats from both the Khmer Rouge and the Phnom Penh government are analyzed. Lessons are drawn for UN peacekeeping missions elsewhere. Heininger's scholarly tone is welcome, for this topic frequently generates emotional polemics. Recommended for all college and university libraries, particularly for those supporting international relations programs. Upper-division undergraduate through faculty.—*R. Marlay, Arkansas State University*

OAB-2675   DS889   94-23660 CIP
Junnosuke, Masumi. **Contemporary politics in Japan,** tr. by Lonny E. Carlile. California, 1995. 514p bibl index afp ISBN 0-520-05853-4, $65.00; ISBN 0-520-05854-2 pbk, $25.00

This translation of Masumi's *Gendai seiji* (1985) provides an important contribution to an understanding of postwar Japanese politics. In the first half of the book Masumi meticulously documents the complex machinations among political leaders, factions, and parties, 1955-80, using memoirs of leading politicians, government publications, and news reports. The author paints an intimate portrait of Japanese politics driven by factional infighting in the ruling LP and opposition SDP parties, political intrigue and prestige-seeking by politicians, and the gradual evolution of "mass society" marked by the rise of citizens' movements and the mass media. The second half of the book analyzes the structures, processes, and dynamics of the "1955 system," focusing on the LDP, the bureaucracy, the socialist opposition, and various interest groups. Masumi also explains the critical impact of US-Japan relations on Japanese domestic politics in the framework of the Cold War. The book provides strong evidence to support an unconventional thesis that Japanese citizens are determining through elections the political future of Japan in spite of efforts by politicians and bureaucrats to minimize their impact. An outstanding book and an important addition to any college library.—*R. G. Bush, Gustavus Adolphus College*

OAB-2676   HC430   CIP
Klintworth, Gary. **New Taiwan, new China: Taiwan's changing role in the Asia-Pacific region.** Longman/St. Martin's, 1995. 328p bibl index ISBN 0-312-12550-X, $49.95

Klintworth, an Australian researcher, adds another volume to the growing literature on Taiwan and its role in the Asia-Pacific region. The volume emphasizes Taiwan's geopolitical situation, which explains its historical development and its future prospects: Taiwan's "impressive rise has been [due to] its pivotal location at the center of a triangle of relationships between two constants (the United States and Japan) and one variable (China)." Klintworth also briefly treats Taiwan's domestic political liberalization, its growing influence in Southeast Asia and the South Pacific, and its contacts with mainland China, Singapore, and Hong Kong. He surveys thoroughly the descriptive and analytical studies on Taiwan, which he complements by some interviews in Taiwan, China, Hong Kong, and other parts of Asia. In Klintworth's view, the US, Japan, and China have reached a rough consensus, a gentlemen's agreement, about Taiwan. So long as Taiwan does not actively seek for independence, thus threatening the one-China principle, or search for an alliance with Japan and/or the US against China, China will permit Taiwan to behave much like any other member of the Asia-Pacific community. The best study yet on Taiwan's international role, recommended for general readers and undergraduates.—*G. A. McBeath, University of Alaska, Fairbanks*

OAB-2677   HN740   96-5370 MARC
Lupher, Mark. **Power restructuring in China and Russia.** Westview, 1996. 335p bibl index afp ISBN 0-8133-2546-3, $69.00; ISBN 0-8133-2545-5 pbk, $22.95

Those with scholarly interest in Chinese history or polity, in Russian history or polity, or in that now ill-defined area formerly known as "comparative Communist systems" should take careful note of this new book. Lupher (sociology, Univ. of Virginia) is ideally suited by experience and training for this ambitious comparative treatment of these two great nations. Post-Cold War Western language, even by scholars, has been self-servingly normative in chronicling the Russian and Chinese "reforms" of the 1980s and 1990s. Skillfully avoiding such triumphantalism, the author employs a useful power restructuring model. He presents the transforming events of post-Mao China and of

perestroika and the post-Soviet eras in Russia as syntheses, themselves drawing on important power transfers in the nations' pre-Communist and Communist pasts. Some may criticize the author for emphasizing too much the two nations' similarities, and his forecast of authoritarian-nationalist futures will confound the hopes of Western optimists. But he makes his arguments persuasively, only rarely allowing theory to overpower the smooth and informing flow of his narrative. Strongly recommended for academic readers, all levels.—*J. D. Gillespie, Presbyterian College*

OAB-2678   DS485   93-6609 CIP
Menon, Dilip M. **Caste, nationalism and communism in south India: Malabar, 1900-1948.** Cambridge, 1994. 209p bibl index (Cambridge South Asian studies, 55) ISBN 0-521-41879-8, $54.95

This is a brilliant and thorough analysis of why and how the Communists came to power in the state of Kerala, which became one of their two strongest political bastions in India. Concentrating on the Malabar (northern) region of Kerala, the author demonstrates that the key to Communist success in the area was a reshaping of communism into a doctrine of caste equality. The results in Malabar were paradoxically both conservative and radical. Malabar became a bastion of parliamentary communism in Kerala, underpinned by a reconstituted tradition of community. Ironically, the success of the Communist Party there with respect to the abolition of landlordism may have led to its undoing. Menon is a highly respected Research Fellow at Magdalene College, Cambridge University. In this work, he has displayed prodigious scholarship. Outstanding bibliography. Highly recommended for both the scholarly and the informed general audience.—*L. P. Fickett Jr., Mary Washington College*

OAB-2679   HD8738   96-42940 CIP
Perry, Elizabeth J. **Proletarian power: Shanghai in the cultural revolution,** by Elizabeth J. Perry and Li Xun. Westview, 1997. 249p bibl index afp ISBN 0-8133-2165-4, $59.95; ISBN 0-8133-2166-2 pbk, $18.95

This remarkably researched study by an American and a Chinese scholar deals with the Shanghai labor movement during the Cultural Revolution. Using hitherto confidential archival materials (e.g., Public Security Bureau interrogation transcripts), Perry and Li Xun (Univ. of California at Berkeley) paint a lively picture of a diverse workforce responding to Mao's call to "bombard the headquarters" and present a compelling analysis of working-class protest unprecedented in the PRC's history. The book contains a brief introduction and seven chapters. Chapter 1 looks at the rebel organizations of students and intellectuals; chapters 2, 3, and 4 explore the three forms of labor activities (rebellion, conservatism, and economism); and chapters 5, 6, and 7 examine rivalry among the rebels, the movement's gains, and its abrupt demise. The authors conclude that the motivations and methods of labor leaders exhibited an impressive degree of variation and organization, which were a direct outcome of state initiatives. Strongly recommended for undergraduates, graduates, and faculty.—*S. K. Ma, California State University, Los Angeles*

OAB-2680   JQ1681   92-20052 CIP
Zhao, Quansheng. **Japanese policymaking: the politics behind politics: informal mechanisms and the making of China policy.** Praeger, 1993. 230p bibl index afp ISBN 0-275-94449-2, $49.95

The Japanese foreign policy-making process is usually explained as revolving around the triad of the ruling Liberal Democratic party, big business, and bureaucracy. Although it is also generally recognized that various groups, inside and outside the triad, contribute to the consensus that underlies a particular policy decision, far less is known about these groups, particularly the less visible, more informal, ones. By choosing the field of Japan-China relations, which, for historical reasons, are more complex than foreign relations with other countries, Zhao (through four detailed case studies: raw silk and other unofficial trade from 1950 on; normalization of relations; post-1972 economic agreements; and Japan's reaction to the Tiananmen Square incident) has been able to explore the dynamic role played by private individuals, members of the opposition parties, the news media, think tanks, farming groups, small businesses, and other uniquely Japanese informal social, economic, and political networks. Despite some repetition and overemphasis of the obvious, Zhao's work makes a major contribution to the field, and should be welcomed by graduate and undergraduate students.—*R. Vohra, Trinity College*

OAB-2681   JQ1522   95-23127 CIP
Zhao, Suisheng. **Power by design: constitution-making in Nationalist China.** Hawaii, 1996. 217p bibl index afp ISBN 0-8248-1721-4, $37.00

Zhao's brief yet brilliant book explores the evolution of China's Nationalist government, 1925-37. In contrast with the historical approach in *The Nationalist Era in China, 1927-1949*, by Lloyd Eastman et al. (1991), Zhao's theoretical model convincingly sheds light on current events in China as well as on other authoritarian regimes. The author (Colby College) cogently argues that constitution-making mirrors authoritarian leaders' attempts to consolidate personal power through institutional design. The book contains nine parts. Chapter 1 presents the political logic of institutional design and chapter 2 the historical background of constitutionalism in early-20th-century China. Chapters 3-5 probe the Nationalist regime's major power resources and its power players and their institutional preferences. Chapters 6-8 analyze the three alternative designs of the cabinet and the presidential systems. Chapter 9 reviews constitutional development in Taiwan and other comparable Asian nations. Detailed notes are provided, and a well-selected bibliography lists works published in China. Strongly recommended for undergraduates, graduates, and faculty.—*S. K. Ma, California State University, Los Angeles*

CANADA

OAB-2682   Can. CIP
Gibson, Gordon. **Thirty million musketeers: one Canada, for all Canadians.** Key Porter Books, 70 The Esplanade, Toronto, Ont. M5E 1R2, Canada, 1995. 242p index ISBN 1-55013-706-9 pbk, $19.95

Canada survived the last referendum on separation of Quebec by the skin of its teeth. When the next referendum is held (probably within 24 months) Canada needs to be prepared for all eventualities. This volume is dedicated toward that end. Gibson, a well-known political leader and thinker on matters relating to reforming the Canadian constitution, has written a thoughtful book outlining how Canada can change for the better. Most importantly, if Canada changed along the lines suggested by Gibson, Quebec would feel welcome within the new nation. This work, combined with his earlier volume, *Plan B: The Future of the Rest of Canada* (1994), provides a comprehensive and thoughtful review of the constitutional problems and alternatives facing Canada. There is an excellent index and substantial and complete footnotes. An essential addition to all collections on Canada, this volume is suitable for all levels of undergraduate and graduate students.—*D. E. Bond, University of British Columbia*

OAB-2683   91-68213 Orig
Johnston, Richard. **Letting the people decide: dynamics of a Canadian election,** by Richard Johnston et al. Stanford, 1992. 316p bibl index afp ISBN 0-8047-2077-0, $37.50; ISBN 0-8047-2078-9 pbk, $12.95

An extraordinary study by four academic voting-behavior specialists of the motivations of Canadians as they cast their ballots in the 1988 federal election. Building on previous studies and surveys going back to 1965, they have produced a definitive statement of partisanship and electoral choice in Canada with a tightly reasoned study whose methodological sophistication sets an extremely high standard for any future examination of voting anywhere. All the issues that have been on the table for professionals in the field for the last decade receive coverage. To mention just a few: the priming and agenda-setting effects of the mass media; the use of special models to examine issues

and partisan and party positions on them; the impact of the campaign on voter choice; and the influences of the various politicians and their use of the "black arts" of manipulation to achieve their objectives. The sampling used by the investigators—"rolling samples" and panels that involve revisiting respondents—is also a notable advance for academic studies of voting. This volume is of importance to Canadianists as well as to students of voting behavior and of the methodology of such studies everywhere. Advanced undergraduate through professional collections.—*P. Regenstreif, University of Rochester*

OAB-2684   Can. CIP
Leaders and leadership in Canada, ed. by Maureen Mancuso, Richard G. Price, and Ronald Wagenberg. Oxford, 1994. 288p index afp ISBN 0-19-540922-1 pbk, $29.95

This is a very different kind of book within the corpus of works on Canadian government and politics. Its focus is on leadership—getting there, being there, leaving there—rather than on politics per se. That opens up a far wider scope than normal, and the contributors make the most of it. Thus, separate articles address leadership in political parties and in the three branches (executive, legislative, and judicial) of government, and even aboriginal politics. The result is first-class. The notes are readily accessible at the end of each piece. A must for any collection on Canadian government and politics, the book is an excellent complement to *Leaders and Parties in Canadian Politics: Experiences of the Provinces*, ed. by R. Kenneth Carty, Lynda Erickson, and Donald Blake (1992). Suitable for undergraduates and graduates, theorists and practitioners alike.—*M. P. Brown, Dalhousie University*

OAB-2685   CIP
Legault, Albert. **A diplomacy of hope: Canada and disarmament, 1945-1988,** by Albert Legault and Michel Fortmann; tr. by Derek Ellington. McGill-Queen's, 1992. 663p bibl index afp ISBN 0-7735-0920-8, $75.00; ISBN 0-7735-0955-0 pbk, $29.95

This is a monumental work, written originally in French by two political scientists at Université Laval and Université de Montréal, respectively. Based on painstaking research including careful perusal of official government documents, the volume's more than 500 pages of encyclopedic coverage deal in great detail with Canadian arms control and disarmament policy and negotiations from 1945 to 1988. Although such blow-by-blow descriptions are usually not very exciting to read, the authors (or the translator?) often display a gift for words, and it is refreshing to have one Canadian negotiator characterized as "obviously well versed in history" and another, as "austere par excellence." Very well-documented and supplied with an excellent bibliography and a good index, the work concludes that Canada has never lost hope and has always pursued a policy of hope. Recommended for comprehensive academic and research collections.—*W. S. G. Kohn, emeritus, Illinois State University*

OAB-2686   Can. CIP
Smith, David E. **The invisible crown: the first principle of Canadian government.** Toronto, 1995. 274p bibl index afp ISBN 0-8020-0743-0, $55.00

By choosing to write on the crown in Canada, Smith puts himself in the company of a small group of genuine constitutional experts: Eugene Forsey, Frank MacKinnon, Norman Ward, J.R. Mallory. By writing so well on Canada's oldest but least understood political institution, he shows he belongs there. Most of the discussion of the crown centers on the role or personage of the sovereign, not the institution of government, particularly when that institution is surrounded with an aura and symbolism of a colonial heritage and a monarchical past. Contemporary Canada, however, is a constitutional and federal democracy, and at the same time the crown is the organizing principle behind the executive, the legislature, the judiciary, and the bureaucracy. It is an efficient and not merely a dignified institution, to use a classic distinction of Walter Bagehot, because it is the legal source of that discretion without which government is impossible. Smith analyzes the several complex strands of law, convention, tradition, and practice that constitute the reality of the crown in Canada. It is a book to be studied rather than browsed and will remain the standard treatment for many years to come. All levels.—*B. Cooper, University of Calgary*

OAB-2687   Can. CIP
Webber, Jeremy. **Reimagining Canada: language, culture, community, and the Canadian constitution.** McGill-Queen's, 1994. 373p index afp ISBN 0-7735-1146-6, $44.95; ISBN 0-7735-1152-0 pbk, $19.95

Webber analyzes the fragmentation of Canadian society and the alienation of various "communities"—provinces as well as visible minorities—in the aftermath of the failed Meech Lake and Charlottetown Accords. He then proposes asymmetrical federalism, a means by which the "identities" or interests of these communities can be accommodated in the constitution and, more particularly, by political institutions. Asymmetrical federalism would involve a devolution and decentralization of public authority but would not entail unequal rights and dissimilar public privileges for Canadians. The forums of political authority might be diffused and changed, but equivalent rights and privileges would be enjoyed by all. The arguments are novel and, above all, persuasive. Thus, the book is not a routine account of Canadian federalism; it is as much a serious and innovative scholarly analysis of Canadian federalism as it is a plea to conserve the Canadian polity. As such, it most certainly deserves a close reading during which one should contemplate what might have been, had such clever and convincing arguments been widely disseminated earlier in the constitutional debate of the last decade. General; upper-division undergraduate through faculty.—*A. F. Johnson, Bishop's University*

Europe

OAB-2688   DD290   93-5477 CIP
Ash, Timothy Garton. **In Europe's name: Germany and the divided continent.** Random House, 1993. 680p index ISBN 0-394-55711-5, $27.50

Ash, the well-respected observer of East and Central European affairs, has written his best book to date. *In Europe's Name* is a monumental, often revealing study of West Germany's Ostpolitik from its inception until the unification of Germany. Ash is concerned foremost with examining the controversial issue of whether Ostpolitik and the larger policy of détente helped to sustain the communist regimes of Europe for longer than necessary, or on the contrary, whether the policy undermined the political power of the communist rulers in Eastern Germany and elsewhere in East Europe. Although the author's answer is ambiguous since Ostpolitik cut both ways, the evidence amassed in the book is extraordinary; the work is rich in details and insights and thorough in its approach. The organization of the work involves a three-layered analysis of West German policies and relations with Moscow, the East German regime, and the Eastern European states. The historical account is then followed by a look at the contemporary effects of German unification and its impact on European affairs. The book, unusually readable as well as informative, is a must for all libraries. All levels.—*J. Bielasiak, Indiana University—Bloomington*

OAB-2689   JN425   95-34896 CIP
Barberis, Peter. **The elite of the elite: permanent secretaries in the British higher civil service.** Dartmouth, 1996. 282p bibl index ISBN 1-85521-479-2, $62.95

Thorough and well researched (the author used materials from interviews with dozens of senior civil servants), this is a well-written analysis of the role of the permanent secretaries in the higher British civil.service. The author divides the volume into four sections. The first focuses on the changing role of permanent secretaries and presents a thorough analysis of their advisory role. The second and third sections deal with the backgrounds of permanent secretaries (comparing seven groups: those who served in the periods between

1830-69, 1870-99, 1900-18, 1919-45, 1946-64, 1965-79 and 1979-94) as well as their career patterns. The book concludes with an excellent analysis of the contributions of permanent secretaries to the functioning of the British political system. An excellent appendix lists (with backgrounds, where available) those who served as permanent secretaries. Invaluable for anyone interested in contemporary British politics. Upper-division undergraduates through faculty.—*A. Katz, Fairfield University*

OAB-2690   JN961   94-22533 CIP
Blackburn, Robert. **The electoral system in Britain.** St. Martin's, 1995. 487p bibl index ISBN 0-312-12391-4, $59.95

This massive volume covers minute details of the British electoral system from attempted legal definitions to a description of the prime minister's role in determining election dates, and from the most recent election returns to speculations regarding the possible results of the introduction of proportional representation. Tables and illustrations abound—e.g., seven tightly printed pages listing bodies whose members are disqualified to sit in Parliament (such as the Health and Safety Commission or the Welsh Water Authority). This may be cumbersome, but the book will be especially useful as a point of departure for seminars in British and comparative politics, since many details are basically unknown. The political parties, their financial positions, and their conventional rather than their legal status are of course also dealt with, as are their histories and future indications. British peculiarities, from losing one's deposit to multiconstituency candidacies of the "lunatic fringe," are not ignored. A highly useful reference, essential for every good senior and graduate library.—*W. S. G. Kohn, emeritus, Illinois State University*

OAB-2691   JA84   94-46287 CIP
Bobbio, Norberto. **Ideological profile of twentieth-century Italy,** tr. by Lydia C. Cochrane. Princeton, 1995. 239p bibl index afp ISBN 0-691-04352-3, $29.95

Any serious students of contemporary Italy will find in this brilliant text an invaluable synthesis of the major ideologies that have shaped Italian political culture. With cogent interpretations and penetrating analysis, Bobbio weaves a masterful portrait of the broader historical context, the evolution of political ideas, and the role of key figures such as Salvemini, Croce, Einaudi, Gramsci, and Pareto. Elegantly written, the Italian original and this able translation include comprehensive essays on positivism and Marxism, Catholicism as a political force, socialism, fascism, the ideals of the Resistance, the progression and crises of democratic society after WW II, and the problems and possibilities of political life in Italy and its unique version of capitalism. Both as professor of political philosophy (Univ. of Torino) and an active participant in Italian political life (Resistance, commentaries in the newspaper *La Stampa*, and senator), Bobbio himself stands out as a significant player in the evolution of a democratic civic society in contemporary Italy. Enriched by a lengthy and informative foreword by Massimo Salvadori, this book stands alone for its depth and breadth. Upper-division undergraduates through faculty.—*P. Vannicelli, University of Massachusetts at Boston*

OAB-2692 ·   DJK51   93-47347 CIP
Brown, J.F. **Hopes and shadows: eastern Europe after communism.** Duke University, 1994. 367p bibl index afp ISBN 0-8223-1446-0, $45.00; ISBN 0-8223-1464-9 pbk, $19.95

Brown, former director of Radio Free Europe (RFE) and former head of RFE Research, has previously published *Eastern Europe and Communist Rule* (CH, Jan'89), *Surge to Freedom* (CH, Nov'91), and *Nationalism, Democracy, and Security in the Balkans* (1992). This is perhaps the best and most comprehensive general account yet of the first four years of postcommunist developments in Eastern Europe. Based on an impressive array of primary sources including the major European newspapers and RFE Research Reports, Brown has produced a lively and very well written analysis covering events up to the end of 1993. The first two chapters sketch the main problems and challenges faced by all postcommunist countries. Two chapters are devoted to country studies of Czechoslovakia, Poland, Hungary, Romania, Bulgaria, and Albania. Other chapters focus, respectively, on the economic aspects of transition, nationalism, Yugoslavia, and external factors and actors in the region's transformation. As in his earlier *Surge to Freedom*, Brown manages to cover a lot of ground in an analytically competent, tightly organized, and attractively written fashion. I expect this book to be particularly useful for and popular with undergraduate students, though its scope, compactness, and style make it suitable for general readers as well as more advanced students of Eastern European affairs.— *A. Pickel, Trent University*

OAB-2693   JN2919   91-42897 CIP
Brubaker, Rogers. **Citizenship and nationhood in France and Germany.** Harvard, 1992. 270p bibl index afp ISBN 0-674-13177-0, $35.00

How does a state define who is, and who is not, a citizen? Beginning with this question, this wide-ranging study argues that France and Germany have developed different conceptions of citizenship and nationhood. Through subtle analyses of pivotal events (for France, the Revolution and the Third Republic's push for universal primary education and military service; for Germany, the 1913 nationality law), the author claims that France bases citizenship on principles of territorial birthplace (*jus soli*) and adherence to French cultural and political ideals, thus facilitating the civic incorporation of foreigners. By contrast, Germany defines citizenship as a "community of descent," thereby granting virtually automatic citizenship to ethnic Germans emigrating from abroad yet precluding assimilation of non-Germans who have long resided in the country (*jus sanguinis*). Spanning two centuries—from the late 18th century to the 1980s—this study builds a convincing portrait of, and explanation for, these national differences. Its occasional lapses into verbosity and jargon only slightly detract from what is an original, penetrating book that should be required reading for all Europeanists and anyone interested in questions of national identity, citizenship, and immigration. Advanced undergraduate through faculty.—*W. R. Smith, Lake Forest College*

OAB-2694   DA990   91-46663 CIP
Bruce, Steve. **The red hand: Protestant paramilitaries in Northern Ireland.** Oxford, 1992. 311p bibl index ISBN 0-19-215961-5, $49.95

The Red Hand is a comprehensive and insightful study of Protestant paramilitaries in Northern Ireland. Violence by such groups, including the Ulster Defence Association (UDA) and the Ulster Volunteer Force (UVF), accounts for nearly half the deaths of civilians in the present round of troubles. For this reason alone, such a study has been long overdue, notwithstanding the wealth of material available on the "troubles" generally or on the Irish Republican Army in particular. But as Bruce observes, an account of Protestant paramilitaries also advances our understanding of the important differences between "state terror," "anti-state terror," and "pro-state terror." An instance of the latter, the course of Protestant paramilitarism in Northern Ireland, Bruce argues, is largely influenced by its uncertain and unsteady relationship to the states' legitimate agencies of coercion and force. Although this is not an entirely novel argument, Bruce makes it clearly and substantiates it thoroughly. In sum, an excellent study that should be read by all students of political violence. Advanced undergraduate through faculty.—*J. E. Finn, Wesleyan University*

OAB-2695   DK288   91-59006 CIP
Carrère d'Encausse, Hélène. **The end of the Soviet empire: the triumph of the nations,** tr. by Franklin Philip. Basic Books, 1993. 290p bibl index ISBN 0-465-09812-6, $24.00

The author's international stature as an expert on Soviet politics was confirmed by recent events; her scholarly work moved in front of history by some ten years. She concentrated on ethnic politics, nationalism, and the tension between the rising peoples and the Soviet hegemonic structure when most other Sovietologists still considered the Union to be more or less permanent. Her books speak authoritatively of Uzbeks, Georgians, Azeris, Kyrgyz, Lithua-

nians, Russians, and the other peoples who are building nation-states on the ruins of the USSR. The concentrated analysis of the critical turning point in Eurasian political history, 1985-91, presents a realistic appraisal of Gorbachev's failure to preserve the Union. Gorbachev emerges as an ambitious but not brilliant Russian politician who did not understand the depth of nationalist sentiment in his own country. The book's strength is its direct knowledge of the peoples who dismantled the Soviet empire. Its weaknesses are the absence of maps, shortage of tables, and a somewhat ragged ending—an effort to catch up with the latest events. Yet, it is one of the best books on the subject by one of the most respected experts in the field. It should be purchased by all major public and academic libraries.—*R. V. Barylski, University of South Florida*

OAB-2696   JN3933   95-40145 CIP
Cary, Noel D. **The path to Christian democracy: German Catholics and the party system from Windthorst to Adenauer.** Harvard, 1996. 355p index afp ISBN 0-674-65783-7, $49.95

Despite its significance, Christian Democracy receives far less attention from scholars than parties of the Left. Cary helps right the balance: his is the best historical analysis yet written about the most important political movement in the most powerful country of Europe. Cary persuasively argues that the Catholic center, however mixed its motives, formed a mainstay of liberal democratic opposition to Bismarck's reactionary empire. "Neither liberal nor conservative," that same party served as the political middle ground of the ill-fated Weimar Republic. And, when postwar conditions permitted, some shrewd former centrist leaders made a broader, more pragmatic appeal, "integrating conservatives into a liberal democratic system." As the first "catch-all party," Konrad Adenauer's Christian Democratic Union helped de-ideologize German politics, balancing and consolidating its party system, and stabilizing the country's first democracy. Cary does not claim to have written a comprehensive history of the center or CDU, but he has skillfully blended the distillation of archival material with careful political analysis and clear, graceful prose, making familiarity with this book both necessary and sufficient for anyone interested in understanding this important topic. General and academic readers.—*C. Clemens, College of William and Mary*

OAB-2697   DG564   95-489 CIP
Chabod, Federico. **Italian foreign policy: the statecraft of the founders.** Princeton, 1996. 593p bibl index afp ISBN 0-691-04451-1, $65.00; ISBN 0-691-04450-3 pbk, $29.95

This elegant translation of a work first published in Italian by one of the most respected scholars of modern Italian history (*Storia della politica estera Italiana dal 1870-1896,* Barri, 1951) effectively conveys the eloquence of the original text. Although it focuses on the complex events of the 1870-96 formative period of the modern Italian state, this sweeping interpretation also dissects the very foundations of Italy's foreign policy by providing a penetrating appreciation of the intricacies of the country's external relations up to the present. Both internal and external aspects of Italy's foreign policy are covered in great detail, including a biographical section on the major protagonists. Any serious student of this critical period of Italian history, or of Italian politics in general, will find this book of immense value. Although there are several texts in English on modern Italian history, none offers the depth and breadth one finds here, including a comparative perspective on Italy's economic and financial limitations, which in turn affected its standing as an aspiring military power seeking to compete with other European states. The book's greatest contribution, however, is its masterful interpretation of the forces, ideas, passions, and interests that shaped the emerging Italian nation-state as it sought ways to assert itself as one of the great powers. Chabod also presents a lively picture of the political culture, values, and aspirations of a rapidly changing society. Upper-division undergraduates through faculty.—*P. Vannicelli, University of Massachusetts at Boston*

OAB-2698   DR1282   92-44716 CIP
Cohen, Lenard J. **Broken bonds: the disintegration of Yugoslavia.**

Westview, 1993. 299p index afp ISBN 0-8133-8030-8, $49.95; ISBN 0-8133-1854-8 pbk, $16.95

Against the backdrop of a number of excellent books on Yugoslavia, Cohen (*Political Cohesion in a Fragile Mosaic: The Yogoslav Experience*, 1983, *The Socialist Pyramid: Elites and Power in Yugoslavia*, CH, Mar'91) provides a first-rate scholarly examination of the collapse of the Titoist regime. Cohen focuses on the tumultuous post-Tito period, including the crisis of reforming Yugoslav socialism, contending regional/federal strategies, erosion of party unity, and fractionalization of state authority. Cohen rightly underscores the role of national and ethnic elites in producing the current situation while distinguishing the collapse of the system from the savagery it engendered. Cohen links these concerns and relates them to long-standing traditions of political rule practiced by Ottomans and Hapsburgs and of indigenous political cultures. Regime collapse and economic stress provided the conditions under which the flames of savage war were ignited. Both the integration and modernization visible under Tito proved more superficial than imagined at the time. The persistence of authoritarian means of rule, as Cohen argues, puts democracy, as well as peace, ethnic tolerance, and reconciliation, beyond the reach of the peoples of this troubled former state. Cohen's conclusions give no grounds for optimism. Advanced undergraduate through faculty.—*H. Steck, SUNY College at Cortland*

OAB-2699   JN6598   92-9300 CIP
Cracks in the monolith: party power in the Brezhnev era, ed. by James R. Millar. M.E. Sharpe, 1992. 243p index afp ISBN 0-87332-885-X, $49.95

How was the Soviet Union really administered? Could Western scholars penetrate beyond the usual public sources of information? Millar's Soviet Interview Project tapped the knowledge of Soviet citizens of Jewish ethnicity who resettled in the US. Some 5,000 former Soviet citizens were interviewed. But this book is about Soviet administrative policies and practices on the eve of Gorbachev's radical reforms, not inter-ethnic relations. This volume improves our perceptions of Communist party operational frustrations and bridges Cold War and post-Cold War scholarship. Eight chapters analyze Soviet domestic legal, administrative, and economic politics. Topics covered include political intervention in the judicial process; the politics of national statistics and information management in a planned economy; relationships between party institutions and the Soviet economic bureaucracy; and the effectiveness of party control at the grass-roots level. Soviet citizens were more ready for change than Western observers had realized. They had a reasonably good understanding of the problems regularly created by their administrative and political systems. Specific, effective solutions were another matter. This important contribution to Soviet studies not only sets a base line from which to measure change but sets a high standard for the use of survey data. Highly recommended for all academic collections.—*R. V. Barylski, University of South Florida*

OAB-2700   JN2959   95-17894 CIP
Crook, Malcolm. **Elections in the French Revolution: an apprenticeship in democracy, 1789-1799.** Cambridge, 1996. 221p bibl index ISBN 0-521-45191-4, $54.95

Crook provides the only thorough treatment of elections during the French Revolution. The major texts spend no time on elections—why should they? Everyone knows the Revolution was just another example of the drift of passion into autocracy. Crook makes an exceptionally strong case that the Revolution harbored at least an intention for some form of popular participation. He argues that the Revolution was a "social revolution after all"—that compared to 18th-century Britain or the infant American republic, basic suffrage was "widely distributed during the early years of the French Revolution." Robespierre is portrayed as a sort of James Madison of the left (tantamount to calling Hitler a misunderstood dog fancier). From the book's figures, it appears that a voter turnout of six or seven percent was not unusual. Voting was often by public oral declamation. Would anyone yell "*non*" to Robespierre? One such election was won

by Robespierre, Marat, and Danton. This is one of those rare books that seizes the attention, changes ways of thinking, and leaves one enlightened. Upper-division undergraduates and up.—*H. Zeigler, formerly, University of Washington*

OAB-2701   DK288   93-1648 CIP
Dunlop, John B. **The rise of Russia and the fall of the Soviet Empire.** Princeton, 1993. 360p index afp ISBN 0-691-07875-0, $29.95

This is the most thoroughly researched book on the fate of the Soviet Union, 1985-92, to appear to date. It is, on the one hand, a history, written with great knowledge of and feel for Russia's historical traditions, and, on the other, a political analysis of the events and nascent ideologies which permeate the travail of the Russian society not yet sure in which direction to lean. The author's emphasis and focus is on the Russian element of the former Soviet Union, and he analyzes the events looking through its various prisms, such as statism versus nationalism, Westernism versus Eurasianism, democracy versus dictatorship (conservatism), empire saving versus nation building. The longest and most thorough treatment is devoted to the failed coup of August 1991. The economy and its dilemmas receive less attention. The question of integration and disintegration of Russia is very much in the author's eye but mainly as seen from the center. There is less discussion of the thinking and feelings of the masses of the people, Russians and not Russians, who dwell in the multitude of small towns and villages. Undergraduate; graduate; faculty.—*L. K. D. Kristof, Portland State University*

OAB-2702   DD290   93-625 CIP
Jarausch, Konrad H. **The rush to German unity.** Oxford, 1994. 280p bibl index afp ISBN 0-19-507275-8, $35.00; ISBN 0-19-508577-9 pbk, $14.95

In a welcome addition to the rapidly growing body of literature on German unification, Jarausch recalls the momentous and rapidly unfolding events that led to the merging of the two German states in October 1990. The author gives special attention to the actions at and the interaction between the mass and elite levels. The reasons for and the actors in the peaceful overthrow of the East German regime and the subsequent developments leading to the decision to unify are recounted, as are the concrete steps toward economic and political union. In the concluding section some of the pressing political issues raised by German unification are discussed. This is contemporary history at its best: Jarausch's account goes well beyond a thorough and comprehensive recollection of events between the summer of 1989 and the fall of 1990, yet this review certainly constitutes one of the strengths of the book. Securely based on a wealth of primary and secondary sources and an in-depth familiarity with the subject, his reflective analysis is always balanced and thoughtful. The book provides interesting and stimulating reading for the scholarly as well as the general audience. Recommended for all library collections. *H. A. Welsh, Wake Forest University*

OAB-2703   DD289   94-12762 CIP
Joppke, Christian. **East German dissidents and the revolution of 1989: social movement in a Leninist regime.** New York University, 1995. 277p bibl index ISBN 0-8147-4219-X, $50.00; ISBN 0-8147-4220-3 pbk, $17.50

This tour de force of political sociology answers why, unlike other dissident movements in Eastern Europe, the East German dissident vision was revisionist and not revolutionary. Joppke addresses the inherently nonreformist nature of Leninist systems and illustrates how East German intellectuals could not recognize this reality. Germany's Nazi past and history of ethnic nationalism were barriers to conceptualizing a notion of rights within the context of the nation-state and a civic variant of nationalism. A continual antifacist mobilization by the Communist Party created a state without a nation or a history, and the only path to reform for the dissident was the perfection of socialism in democratic form. Because of their inability to see alternatives based on German identity, the initiative for the revolution of 1989 moved from system revisionists to those who opted to escape to the West and embrace a reunification strategy that meant a return to history and normal politics. Joppke's analysis incorporates an essentially political process model of a social movement that changed

Choice's Outstanding Academic Books

character as the structure of political opportunities was transformed by external events. An outstanding resource for scholars and graduate students.— *S. Majstorovic, Duquesne University*

OAB-2704   UA710   95-5401 CIP
Large, David Clay. **Germans to the front: West German rearmament in the Adenauer era.** North Carolina, 1996. 327p index afp ISBN 0-8078-2235-3, $49.95

Large examines how, ten years after WW II, a defeated, reviled aggressor rapidly rearmed and joined the alliance of Western democracies. He shows that this transformation resulted from a confluence of Cold War tension, broad desire for a more united Europe, and shrewd political strategy in postwar West Germany itself. Large explains how the new Bundeswehr became a symbol of national renascence, yet was also integrated into the NATO command structure, uniquely manifesting Bonn's desire for both sovereignty and multilateralism. Nevertheless, despite broad fears at the time in Germany and elsewhere, this form of rearmament also helped assure a lasting democratization of the new German military establishment. Although the latter theme was well developed in Donald Abenheim's *Forging the Iron Cross* (CH, Jun'89), Large's focus is less on the Bundeswehr's internal workings than on the central role of rearmament in the divided nation's politics and diplomacy. Thoroughly researched, balanced in its analysis, superbly written, Large's book is highly recommended for readers at any level with an interest in modern Germany.—*C. Clemens, College of William and Mary*

OAB-2705   DB2238   96-12080 CIP
Leff, Carol Skalnik. **The Czech and Slovak republics: nation versus state.** Westview, 1997. 295p bibl index afp ISBN 0-8133-2921-3, $69.95; ISBN 0-8133-2922-1 pbk, $22.95

Leff (Univ. of Illinois at Urbana-Champaign) has written a useful and readable overview of the disintegration of Czechoslovakia and the transition of the resulting two republics toward democratic state capitalism. She first presents informative background and history, covering the interwar period, then communist rule, 1948-89. She then analyzes what she calls the triple transition concerning democratic politics, national identity and shifting statehood, and economics. Her last section covers foreign policy, particularly integration with Western Europe. Leff seems to have a sure grasp of most points she covers and is able to summarize matters with a catchy phrase or apt generalization. Along the way she makes use of lighter material; given the reluctance of the Czechs to fight for their values, she repeats the old saw that they do not even intervene in their own domestic affairs. Her overview is highly recommended, especially for undergraduate students.—*D. Forsythe, University of Nebraska*

OAB-2706   DR264   94-32401 CIP
Livezeanu, Irina. **Cultural politics in greater Romania: regionalism, nation building, & ethnic struggle, 1918-1930.** Cornell, 1995. 340p bibl index afp ISBN 0-8014-2445-3, $45.00

Livezeanu's meticulously researched study, written with a deep understanding of the social and intellectual currents at play, will be essential for anyone wanting to understand what happened to Romanian society in the interwar period, and why. The book delves deeply into the background of nationalist ideas as they began to develop in the 1920s and in the next decade, exploded in violent clashes on the political scene. Naturally, the focus dwells on the universities and the educational establishment in general, which were breeding grounds of both aggressive nationalism and national frustration. Wisely, the author treats the various provinces separately because in each the historical background as well as the balance between ethnic and religious groups varied widely. The book can be said to be a portrayal of the intellectual mobilization of the younger generation for the struggle, ultimately a civil war, guided by the idea of transforming greater Romania into a homogeneous Romania for the Romanians. Academic collections.—*L. K. D. Kristof, Portland State University*

OAB-2707   Orig
Markovits, Andrei S. **The German Left: Red, Green and beyond,** by Andrei S. Markovits and Philip S. Gorski. Oxford, 1993. 393p bibl index afp ISBN 0-19-521051-4, $55.00; ISBN 0-19-521053-0 pbk, $16.95

Markovits (Santa Cruz and Harvard) and Gorski (Berkeley) have produced a comprehensive and detailed study of the Greens and the German Left from the end of WW II until after unification. The excellent introduction surveys the common features and problems of post-WW II advanced capitalist societies and, against this background, explains what made the German Greens into the most influential antiestablishment party in Europe and perhaps even in the Western world. The body of the analysis consists of a historical overview of the Left in the Federal Republic, an examination of Green ideology and policy, and a detailed account of the life and times of the Greens in the 1980s. Particularly interesting is the authors' attempt to explain the comparative success of the German Green party in terms of the "Holocaust effect," i.e., with reference to direct, if hidden, links between Auschwitz and the Greens. The inclusion of a final chapter on the East German Greens is very useful, especially as a case study of the deep cultural divisions between East and West in the new Germany. The authors clearly possess the sensitivity necessary to capture what they themselves stress as the uniquely German ingredients of the Green success story. This sensitivity, combined with the intellectual detachment of outside observers, makes the work the best comprehensive study of the German Greens to date. Perhaps unavoidably and as a result, the book has excessive descriptions and at times a tendency toward dense prose and jargon. Upper-division undergraduate through faculty.—*A. Pickel, Trent University*

OAB-2708   DD289   92-31665 CIP
Merkl, Peter H. **German unification in the European context.** Pennsylvania State, 1993. 448p bibl index afp ISBN 0-271-00921-7, $65.00; ISBN 0-271-00922-5 pbk, $18.95

Merkl, (Univ. of California, Santa Barbara) adds to his reputation as one of the leading experts on German politics with this impressive volume, a well-rounded study of the background and problems of German reunification. Evolution of attitudes toward reunification both inside and outside Germany, the policies of the FRG and other West European states, the key role of the Soviet Union, and the economic disaster of East Germany are all covered in depth. Two chapters detail the major events in the reunification drama of 1989-90. A penetrating chapter on the decline of the GDR is contributed by Gert-Joachim Glaessner (Free Univ., Berlin). One jarring note is Merkl's questionable editorializing about certain policies of the Reagan and Bush administrations in sharp contrast to the dispassionate objectivity displayed toward other political actors. Of more import is the book's terminal point, fall 1991. In the wake of the transport strike and the neo-Nazi violence of 1992, it appears that Merkl underestimated the political and economic consequences of reunification for West Germany. Nevertheless, this is the most profound and comprehensive study of the subject yet available. Exhaustive bibliography. Advanced undergraduate through faculty.—*R. J. Mitchell, University of New Orleans*

OAB-2709   HM73   94-16377 MARC
Mestrovic, Stjepan G. **The Balkanization of the West: the confluence of postmodernism and postcommunism.** Routledge, 1994. 226p bibl indexes ISBN 0-415-08754-6, $59.95; ISBN 0-415-08755-4 pbk, $18.95

In a truly masterful and provocative argument, Mestrovic (Texas A&M Univ.) weaves a narrative that not only deals a blow to the West's inertia in dealing with Serb aggression in the former Yugoslavia but also takes a position on the character and pitfalls of postmodernism. Mestrovic argues that the entrenchment of postmodern discourses in Western societies can be regarded as both a shield against establishing a moral commitment in Bosnia and a deterrence to perceiving the ingrained, ethnocentric Enlightenment narratives that guide the West's perspectives on, and actions in, the postcommunist world. The author argues that a postmodern situation has arisen with the ascendancy of nationalism and religious fundamentalism in postcommunist societies, one that can only be understood if we borrow the sociological tools of Durkheim, Simmel, Freud, and other fin-de-siècle theorists who saw the paramount importance of cultural traditions and practices in constituting societies. Mestrovic's wide-ranging book must not be missed by students of Bosnia or theorists in the social sciences. Graduate students and faculty.—*B. J. Macdonald, Colorado State University*

OAB-2710   DK510   94-38420 CIP
Remaking Russia, ed. by Heyward Isham. M.E. Sharpe, 1995. 330p index afp ISBN 1-56324-435-7, $54.95; ISBN 1-56324-436-5 pbk, $19.95

This collection of essays by leading Russian intellectuals will become required reading for advanced courses in contemporary Russian politics. It provides a useful window into current Russian debates over how to reconstitute the Russian state and national identity in the wake of the heavy legacy of their past. It moves beyond the conventional topics that dominate Western discussions of Russian reforms: "Is Yeltsin still in charge?", and "Is capitalism working?" The authors assume a certain familiarity with recent events in Russia's history. Not since Stephen F. Cohen and Katrina vanden Heuvel's *Voices of Glasnost* (CH, Jul'90) have students and scholars had a book that gives firsthand access to Russian political debate as this does. And a lot has changed in Russia since 1989. The major drawback of the collection is that the authors all come from the liberal mainstream. As the editor puts it, they are "socially committed pragmatists ready to work with President Yeltsin," on the premise that Russia shares "common cultural values and security interests" with the West. There are no representatives of the Communists or nationalists who dominate the parliament, and who have their own perspective on these issues. Upper-division undergraduate through faculty.—*P. Rutland, Wesleyan University*

OAB-2711   DR1313   94-40148 CIP
Rieff, David. **Slaughterhouse: Bosnia and the failure of the West.** Simon & Schuster, 1995. 240p index ISBN 0-671-88118-3, $22.00

Rieff's moving, excellent, passionate, and, above all, disturbing defense of Bosnia ought to be on the "must" reading list of everyone concerned with Bosnia's fate. More to the point, it ought to be on the reading list of everyone who *ought* to be concerned with the defense of Bosnia. Rieff is unsparing in his criticisms of the UN protection forces (UNPROFOR), and his critique leads to somber second and third thoughts about the UN. But the UN is only a stand-in for the indifference and evasions of Europe and the West in general. He is particularly sharp in detailing the illusions of Bosnians that more and more CNN pictures of bodies would move Clinton or whomever to "do something." These are not casual observations. Rieff lived for extended periods in Sarajevo between 1992 and 1994. A special strength of the book is that he analyzes so well the picture of a people under siege—or, worse yet, facing genocide. This is as intelligent and sharp—and depressing—a volume as one is likely to read on Sarajevo—and, as it seems, on the quality of Western civilization. All levels.—*H. Steck, SUNY College at Cortland*

OAB-2712   DK1   96-18164 CIP
Russia and the Commonwealth of Independent States: documents, data, and analysis, ed. by Zbigniew Brzezinski and Paige Sullivan. M.E. Sharpe, 1997. 866p bibl indexes afp ISBN 1-56324-637-6, $225.00

The editors have produced a fine collection of more than 300 documents in a well-organized volume, the sort of one-volume collection graduate students dream about but seldom find. The documents cover the events and agreements of June 1991 through July 1995. Hardly anything of significance is missing. The introduction and the conclusion are especially revealing to those not particularly conversant with the history of the Russian empire and the Soviet Union. The volume is divided into ten chapters, from "The Union Treaty Fails" through "Major CIS Structural Agreements and Protocols"; additional documents are presented in the appendixes. A bibliography and indexes of subjects, names, and places follow. The collection is impressive and has few flaws, e.g., Georgia had been part of the Persian Empire for nearly 100 years before the Russo-Persian War of 1804, not an independent kingdom. The dis-

cussion of options available to Russia seems on target. Too important to be ignored is the warning that "The current combination of pluralism, authoritarianism, and anarchy is not likely soon to be transfigured into a stable democracy and genuine prosperity. The requisite political culture of transnational compromise is also lacking." Highly recommended for all libraries; essential for libraries of colleges with courses on Russian politics or history and for graduate libraries.—*F. L. Mokhtari, Norwich University*

OAB-2713   JN6752   95-30556 CIP
Taras, Raymond. **Consolidating democracy in Poland.** Westview, 1995. 276p bibl index afp ISBN 0-8133-1463-1, $59.95; ISBN 0-8133-1464-X pbk, $19.95

Offering more than the title suggests, this book meticulously outlines a theoretical framework for analysis, presents an exceptionally good summary of the relevant highlights of Poland's history, and follows that by dissecting the characteristics of the Polish communist regime, pointing to contrasts with the Soviet regime. Taras next examines the long-term processes (mainly socioeconomic) that brought about changes in the regime's policies, and ultimately in its nature. Taras analyzes the step-by-step progress from secret or simply de facto bargaining between competing representatives of the society, to roundtable bargaining in public view, and eventually to open and free elections in which practically the totality of the society takes part. Then comes a close look at the building and rebuilding, with much hesitation and backpedaling, of new democratic structures, legal and social, in the context of a still very muddled political culture. The final chapter reviews the interaction between culture and the institutional frameworks, buffeted by social changes and broader international political and economic factors. This thoughtful, wise attempt to understand what molds contemporary Poland outclasses other books in the field. General readers; upper-division undergraduates through faculty.—*L. K. D. Kristof, Portland State University*

OAB-2714   DK33   96-71477 MARC
Tishkov, Valery. **Ethnicity, nationalism and conflict in and after the Soviet Union:** the mind aflame. PRIO/UNRISD/Sage Publications, CA, 1997. 334p bibl index ISBN 0-7619-5184-9, $75.00

In one of the best studies of ethnic nationalism and conflict in the Soviet Union and after its demise, Tishkov, a well-known anthropological historian and former Minister of Nationalities in Yeltsin's government, combines the scholar's theoretical insights with inside knowledge of the major events troubling the Soviet ethnic landscape. Tishkov's analysis focuses on the multiple roles of ethnicity as a basis of political mobilization, a means of controlling power and resources, and therapy for the trauma suffered by groups under previous regimes. His case studies include the forced migration of Russians, the Osh crisis in Central Asia, the Osset-Ingush ethnic cleansing, and the Chechen war. A welcome aspect of this study is its policy orientation in providing a strategy for and mechanisms of conflict resolution through cultural pluralism, civil rights, and individual freedoms. Tishkov concludes with an impassioned plea to scholars and politicians to refrain from contributing to ideologies and projects promoting ethnic polarization and conflict. Both theoretically and substantively this is a compelling book and a rich source of ethnographic data for specialists on ethnic conflict, the former Soviet Union, policy makers, general readers, and upper-division and graduate students.—*R. H. Dekmejian, University of Southern California*

OAB-2715   JN6699   96-53174 CIP
Urban, Joan Barth. **Russia's communists at the crossroads,** by Joan Barth Urban and Valerii D. Solovei. Westview, 1997. 209p bibl index afp ISBN 0-8133-2930-2, $58.00; ISBN 0-8133-2931-0 pbk, $21.00

Urban (Catholic Univ. of America) and Solovei (Gorbachev Foundation) explore the revival of communist party organizations in post-Soviet Russia. A superb analysis of general post-Soviet political development serves as background for a detailed examination of the proliferation of communist groups. The authors identify three main tendencies among the communists: orthodox Marxism-Leninism, Marxist "modernizing," and "progressive" nationalism. The third of these tendencies was strongest, enabling the Communist Party of the Russian Federation (CPRF) led by Gennadi Ziuganov to emerge as the dominant party on the Left. However, all three tendencies were represented within the CPRF, and the authors maintain that concessions to Marxist-Leninist orthodoxy in the party program proved to be a severe handicap in the 1996 election. Urban and Solovei provide insights into the two most interesting questions about post-Soviet Russian politics: How did the communists, apparently discredited in 1991, make a comeback? and, In the face of a disastrous economic situation, why did Yeltsin win in 1996? This is a gem of a book, meticulously researched and brilliantly written, that sets a very high standard for future empirical research on post-Soviet Russian politics. Upper-division undergraduates through faculty.—*R. J. Mitchell, University of New Orleans*

OAB-2716   DA589   93-12772 CIP
Veldman, Meredith. **Fantasy, the bomb, and the greening of Britain: romantic protest, 1945-1980.** Cambridge, 1994. 325p bibl index ISBN 0-521-44060-2, $54.95; ISBN 0-521-46665-2 pbk, $17.95

This is an innovative, powerful, and provocative book. Veldman (history, Louisiana State Univ.) seeks to reveal "the common ideas and assumptions that underlay three distinct cultural developments in Britain after 1945" and by so doing to illuminate "the importance of the romantic tradition in shaping some aspects of contemporary middle-class culture." "It is," she explains, "an exercise in intellectual history: an exploration of the continuing significance of romantic protest in modern Britain." After spelling out the core ingredients of the romantic tradition of protest originated by the romantic poets of the late 18th and early 19th centuries, she proceeds to place the fantasies of C.S. Lewis and J.R.R. Tolkien, the campaigns against the British H-bomb (along with the work of E.P. Thompson), and the warnings of the early Greens firmly in that tradition. On the whole, her project is successful, and the book should join Jonathan Mendilow's *The Romantic Tradition in British Political Thought* (CH, May'86) as a standard reference on an important aspect of British political thought. It is must reading for anyone interested in British political thought and politics and will also be rewarding for those interested in politics and literature. An essential acquisition for libraries serving upper-division undergraduates, graduate students, and faculty as well as general readers.—*G. L. Jones, University of Nevada, Las Vegas*

LATIN AMERICA & THE CARIBBEAN

OAB-2717   HD1531   93-5388 CIP
Anderson, Leslie. **The political ecology of the modern peasant: calculation and community.** Johns Hopkins, 1994. 208p index afp ISBN 0-8018-4708-7, $42.50

Latin American peasants have often been depicted as either fatalistic or revolutionary. Anderson (Univ. of Colorado) has set out to cut through the conventional descriptions to present the full spectrum of peasant attitudes and peasant politics. She organizes her study of peasant rural life as guided by an interdependence "that embraces all elements of peasant life—self, community and community institutions, the national environment, and the nation." Using six village case studies from democratic Costa Rica and revolutionary Nicaragua, Anderson crafts an insightful study of peasant politics from quiescence through demonstration to land invasion and ultimately, violent revolution. Each of the villages provides a unique view as farmers and their families deal in their own way with everyday challenges and external threats. Through Anderson's sensitive approach to peasant life, the picture of rural Latin America becomes more complex and impressive. This is an important book that not only clarifies the political motivations of peasants but also analyzes the rules of interdependence that guide peasant life. Upper-division undergraduate through faculty.—*M. J. Kryzanek, Bridgewater State College*

OAB-2718   F2271   91-46038 CIP
Bushnell, David. **The making of modern Colombia: a nation in spite of itself.** California, 1993. 334p index afp ISBN 0-520-7802-0, $42.00

Colombia, one of the most important countries in Latin America, has nonetheless been understudied. Only now has an English-language history been published, and it is superb. Bushnell, the unquestioned dean of Colombian studies in the US, draws upon four decades of scholarship and field experience to depict the unfolding evolution from its precolonial times to the new constitution of 1991. While tracing the often confusing twists and turns of political history, he provides a penetrating view of economic and social growth across the centuries. Bushnell is remarkably balanced in wise assessments of events, individuals, and trends that remain hotly controversial. His evenhanded treatment reflects both his own intellectual insight and an exhaustive knowledge of the literature. The book is enhanced by a series of bioliographic essays and listings which are invaluable guides to both the novice and experienced student of Colombia. Further data are also presented in a pair of appendixes. In sum, the book is a gem. General; undergraduate through faculty.—*J. D. Martz, Pennsylvania State University, University Park Campus*

OAB-2719   F1488   96-14147 CIP
Byrne, Hugh. **El Salvador's civil war: a study of revolution.** L. Rienner, 1996. 242p bibl index afp ISBN 1-55587-606-4, $49.95

The strengths of this study are its contribution to general theory and its painstaking analysis of strategy and policy choices formulated by the main contenders in El Salvador's decade-long civil war. Byrne argues that the flexible, coordinated strategy of the Salvadorean insurgent forces and the policy responses of the military and civilian governments were critical to the peaceful resolution of the country's protracted struggle. He applies several popular theories of peasant insurrection, but concludes that theories have underestimated the importance of strategy. He believes theorists do not effectively integrate strategy and finds strategy more often than not an intervening and dependent variable rather than an independent factor. Despite this, the importance of strategy is undeniable and an effective vehicle to understand El Salvador's struggle from 1980 to negotiated solution in 1990. This study is strengthened by the author's experience with the Committee in Solidarity with the People of El Salvador, his impeccable scholarship, which draws on recently declassified US documents, and extensive interviews with former FMLN guerrilla leaders. It integrates recent information not found in *El Salvador at War*, ed. by M.G. Manwaring (1988), T.S. Montgomery's *Revolution in El Salvador* (CH, Feb'85; 2nd ed., 1995), F.D. Colburn's *The Vogue of Revolution in Poor Countries* (CH, Feb'94), E. Selbin's *Modern Latin American Revolutions* (CH, Jul'94), and T.Wickham-Crowley's *Guerrillas and Revolution in Latin America* (CH, Jul'92). Highly recommended for undergraduate and graduate students, professionals, and most general readers.—*W. Q. Morales, University of Central Florida*

OAB-2720   JL1281   92-27455 CIP
Camp, Roderic Ai. **Politics in Mexico.** Oxford, 1993. 200p index afp ISBN 0-19-508074-2, $39.95; ISBN 0-19-507612-5 pbk, $14.95

Another book on Mexican politics? Well, yes, and this time a good one, too. In recent years Mexico has proved to be a growth industry for North American political scientists, oftentimes with disastrous results. However, Camp has produced an eminently readable and informative book on the Mexican political process which could, if issued in paperback at a lower cost, become a staple for undergraduate courses which include Mexico in their curriculum. Camp melds quantitative and descriptive political science into a product that is intelligible to undergraduates and at the same time interesting to those with more knowledge about the country. The author's explicit comparison of the Mexican system with that of the US is most helpful. His use of survey research data to support and illustrate his descriptive statements is judicious, and the numbers never overwhelm the text. Camp gives not only a primer on Mexican politics, but also includes, in the beginning chapter, a good introduction to the basic ideas of comparative politics in a more concise and readable manner than many more renowned theorists. Insights into Mexican history, relations with the US, political values, recruitment, and decision making follow in good order, and Camp's last chapter on political modernization in Mexico should be read by everyone interested in the future course of politics in the US's neighbor just across the border. This is a delightful book. Undergraduate.—*E. A. Duff, Randolph-Macon Woman's College*

OAB-2721   F1236   93-4485 CIP
Centeno, Miguel Ángel. **Democracy within reason: technocratic revolution in Mexico.** Pennsylvania State, 1994. 272p bibl index afp ISBN 0-271-01020-7, $35.00; ISBN 0-271-01021-5 pbk, $15.95

Centeno (Sociology, Princeton Univ.) has written a unique and highly insightful analysis of recent Mexican economic and political developments. An important question the author seeks to answer is how it was possible for Mexican elites who lacked popular support, charisma, and military allies to impose a regime of sacrifice on a large part of the Mexican population. In answering this question, Centeno studies the development of the Mexican technocratic revolution, the structure of the bureaucracy, and the rising importance of the planning and finance sectors. He gives a detailed description of the dominant elite and their background characteristics, describes the structure of network politics and the *tecnócratas'* rise to power, delineates the economic and social principles in policy making, and concludes by advancing some alternative scenarios for Mexico's future. An outstanding case study of the vital problem of political and economic restructuring many societies are facing today, the work is significant for the understanding it provides of the Mexican case and in revealing lessons applicable to other regimes. Meticulously researched, systematically organized and well-written, the book contains a wealth of data, thorough footnoting, an extensive bibliography, and an unusually inclusive index. Upper-division undergraduates through faculty.—*R. L. Delorme, California State University, Long Beach*

OAB-2722   JL1295   95-16630 CIP
Domínguez, Jorge I. **Democratizing Mexico: public opinion and electoral choices,** by Jorge I. Domínguez and James A. McCann. Johns Hopkins, 1996. 269p index afp ISBN 0-8018-5146-7, $45.00

Domínguez (Harvard) and McCann (Purdue) have produced an invaluable contribution to the growing literature on Mexican politics. As the title suggests, the major thesis of the book is that Mexico's 1994 presidential elections represented a significant advance in the ongoing democratization of Mexican politics. Using a series of public opinion surveys, the authors demonstrate rather conclusively that the norms of Mexican citizenship, over the past 30-odd years, have become more and more "democratic." Mexicans pay more attention to politics, discuss politics more freely, and have a generally high level of politicization, even when compared with advanced industrial democracies. Still, as the authors point out, problems remain. Electoral procedures remain unfair in important aspects. The Partido Revolucionario Institucional, the ruling party since its inception in 1929, still controls much of the media and has vast monetary resources. Nevertheless, the authors characterize the 1994 presidential elections as "a competitive and free enough election," the verdict delivered by most of the 14,000 observers of that election. This book should be required reading for all Mexicologists, upper-division undergraduate through faculty.—*E. A. Duff, Randolph-Macon Woman's College*

OAB-2723   F3101   92-44638 CIP
Edwards, Jorge. **Persona non grata: a memoir of disenchantment with the Cuban Revolution,** tr. by Andrew Hurley. Paragon House, 1993. 294p index ISBN 1-55778-576-7, $27.95

"In Cuba we don't need critics," Cuban university chancellor Miyar told Jorge Edwards in early 1971. That phrase reflected the regime's greatest failure, its inability to tolerate honest self-criticism. Cuba had become another socialist dictatorship though progressive intellectuals were slow to revise their positive images of it. When the volume appeared in Spanish some 20 years ago, parts of it were advertised as the first critiques of Castroism by a major Latin

American progressive literary figure; however, that is not its main value. It rises above the heaps of hackneyed anti-Castro literature. Edwards demonstrates the enduring power of literature that Castro hoped to crush by arresting his colleague, Heberto Padilla, a prominent Cuban author in early 1971. It was a typical show trial, a warning to all intellectuals to fall into line or face career destruction or worse. As Castro clamped down, charge d'affaires Edwards, revolutionary Chile's first envoy to revolutionary Cuba, became persona non grata. After Havana, Edwards was posted to Paris to assist Nobel prize winner Pablo Neruda, who was serving as Chile's ambassador. In his *Epilogue* the author combines portraits of Neruda with a candid evaluation of why the Chilean revolution was defeated by the coup of September 1973. The book has enduring literary value and belongs in all major Latin American collections.—*R. V. Barylski, University of South Florida*

OAB-2724   JC599   91-30628 CIP
Fear at the edge: state terror and resistance in Latin America, ed. by Juan E. Corradi, Patricia Weiss Fagen, and Manuel Antonio Garretón. California, 1992. 301p index afp ISBN 0-520-07704-0, $45.00; ISBN 0-520-07705-9 pbk, $14.00

This fine collection of essays by a group of primarily Latin American scholars focuses on the "culture of fear" that gripped the Southern Cone nations of Argentina, Brazil, Chile, and Uruguay under the military dictatorships there between the 1960s and 1980s. Much has been written about these authoritarian regimes, but the present volume succeeds in being original and interesting in its approach: analyzing the social-psychological as well as the political aspects of the climate of fear and insecurity created by the regimes' methods of repression. The essays approach this phenomenon in a variety of ways, and from the perspectives of different disciplines, but as a whole the collection gives a full and concentrated picture of a haunted era. *Fear at the Edge* is an important work and should be included in any library collection supporting Latin American studies; it would also be of theoretical and comparative interest to students of political repression and state terrorism. Advanced undergraduate; graduate; faculty.—*J. Stauder, University of Massachusetts-Dartmouth*

OAB-2725   JL958   93-14439 CIP
Geddes, Barbara. **Politician's dilemma: building state capacity in Latin America.** California, 1994. 246p bibl index afp ISBN 0-520-07250-2, $35.00

Latin America in the 1990s has been marked by a significant transformation of the state. As the twin forces of democratization and market reform move forward, the bureaucratic sector has been forced to make critical adjustments in the way it operates and delivers services. Geddes (Univ. of California, Los Angeles) has written a superb book that explores the challenges faced by the state apparatus in Latin America. Geddes correctly recognizes the systemic impediments to bureaucratic reform in Latin America, in particular the need of politicians to transfer state resources to supporters and the inability or unwillingness of governing institutions to initiate substantive changes in the way the state does its business. As a result, reform efforts directed at corruption and nepotism often conflict with personalist politics. Geddes uses a detailed case study of Brazil along with comparative analysis of other Latin American countries to explain the realities of bureaucratic behavior and to arrive at a series of strategies that presidents and reform-minded legislators can use to build state capacity. Geddes's strategies should be required reading for all those interested in understanding the dynamics of developing a more competent structure.—*M. J. Kryzanek, Bridgewater State College*

OAB-2726   JL2481   95-20453 CIP
Hagopian, Frances. **Traditional politics and regime change in Brazil.** Cambridge, 1996. 317p bibl index ISBN 0-521-41429-6, $64.95

Hagopian's study deserves the epithet "landmark" or "breakthrough." Defying conventional wisdom that Brazilian modernization would inevitably weaken traditional elites, she shows that after two decades (1964-85) of bureaucratic-authoritarian dictatorship the position of traditional elites had been strengthened, not undermined. Based on research in Minas Gerais, and incorporating comparative data from other developing countries, the study explains the persistence of a traditional elite in that key state and in the nation, despite both the dictatorship's efforts to restructure the political framework and the onslaught of modernization, urbanization, and emergence of an international economy. Beginning with a review of the literature, Hagopian shows how traditional elite power depended on "the three pillars of clientelism, regionalism, and personalism," using well-crafted arguments and scrupulously analyzed data to demonstrate the powerful centripetal effects of system persistence in the face of extreme challenges from regime transition. Although her prognosis is less than optimistic ("elite continuity threatens [Brazilian] democracy"; Brazil's institutions "are well suited to restricting mass political participation"), she concludes with perhaps more hope than conviction that "formal democracy guarantees ... the transformation and democratization of Brazilian politics." Upper-division undergraduates and higher.—*C. E. Landers, Jersey City State College*

OAB-2727   F1981   92-36910 CIP
Heine, Jorge. **The last cacique: leadership and politics in a Puerto Rican city.** Pittsburgh, 1993. 310p index afp ISBN 0-8229-3741-7, $49.95

Heine (Institute of International Studies, Univ. of Chile) has written the first detailed study of local politics in Puerto Rico. The study examines the career of Benjamín Cole, who served as mayor of Mayagüez from 1968 to 1992. Using the theoretical framework developed by John Kotter and Paul Lawrence in their study of mayors of intermediate-sized cities in the US, Heine focuses his study on the political leadership exercised by Mayor Cole during 19 of the 24 years he held office. Cole's strengths were his intimate knowledge of the city's problems, his adoption of an agenda in his first term which enabled him to avoid a major political controversy, and his incrementalist approach. Later he took advantage of federal funds to advance some of his pet projects. Thus, he earned a reputation as an effective administrator and a first-rate politician. The study, based on four years of research and in-depth interviews with leading members of Mayagüez's political elite, is a scholarly, sophisticated, well-written, and notable contribution to an understanding of the workings of mayoral leadership and politics in Mayagüez. It also provides valuable insights into the changing patterns of urban politics and party identification in Puerto Rico. As a pioneering study there is no bibliography, but there are extensive footnotes. Useful glossary of terms. Upper-division undergraduate through faculty.—*R. L. Delorme, California State University, Long Beach*

OAB-2728   E183   93-31188 CIP
Honey, Martha. **Hostile Acts: U.S. policy in Costa Rica in the 1980s.** University Press of Florida, 1994. 640p bibl index afp ISBN 0-8130-1249-X, $49.95; ISBN 0-8130-1250-3 pbk, $24.95

Honey worked in Costa Rica as a freelance journalist from 1983 to 1991. Her clients included the *New York Times*, the London *Times* and *Sunday Times*, *Time* magazine, BBC and CBC (Canadian) radio, and ABC television. In 1989, she received Costa Rica's highest journalism award. Much has been written about US/CIA activities in Honduras during the 1980s. Honey provides what is missing, the sideshow south of Nicaragua. It is a definitive study (504 pages of text; 136 pages of footnotes, chronology of events, etc.) of the effects of the Contra War in Costa Rica (admittedly, from a left-of-center perspective). This is also an opportune book, given the reemergence of Oliver North as a senatorial candidate in Virginia. It details illegalities (including drug-running) and misuse of power involving the National Security Council, the CIA, AID, the Contras, and the US Embassy in San José. *Hostile Acts* begins with the attempted assassination of Contra leader Edén Pastora at a press conference at La Penca on May 30, 1984, which killed three journalists and badly wounded Pastora and Honey's journalist husband Tony Avirgan, among others. It ends with the story of how Costa Rican President Oscar Arias managed to derail Reagan Administration policy (and win a Nobel Prize) by negotiating peace in Central America. Recommended for university libraries at all levels.—*R. E. Hartwig, Texas A&M University—Kingsville*

OAB-2729   JL2420   96-22285 CIP
Hunter, Wendy. **Eroding military influence in Brazil: politicians against soldiers.** North Carolina, 1997. 243p bibl index afp ISBN 0-8078-2311-2, $39.95; ISBN 0-8078-4620-1 pbk, $18.95

Hunter's important and exemplary study stands as a model of organization, analysis, and clarity. Rejecting the "historical institutionalism" paradigm in favor of a rational-choice model, Hunter tackles in concise and convincing fashion a significant question: Why has the Brazilian military's influence declined since the return of democracy despite the self-serving institutional changes it installed before relinquishing power in 1985? Her major thesis is that electoral pressures inherent in politicians' desire to stay in office led them to earmark national resources for their constituents at the expense of the military. She demonstrates this with three case studies occurring under the Collor and Franco administrations that highlight the armed forces' growing impotence: the enactment of prolabor legislation, the reduction of military budgets to fund civilian (and therefore vote-attracting) projects, and the thwarting of plans to militarize the Amazon, a pet goal of the officer corps. Her conclusions stress "the limits that democracy places on the military," not only in Brazil but in other Latin American nations, and is both a solid contribution to the literature and a work that justifies optimism about the future of democracy in the region. Upper-division undergraduates through faculty.—*C. E. Landers, Jersey City State College*

OAB-2730   PN1992   92-383 CIP
Menéndez Alarcón, Antonio V. **Power and television in Latin America: the Dominican case.** Praeger, 1992. 199p bibl index afp ISBN 0-275-94275-9, $47.95

The cultural and social significance of television has become highly relevant for the nations of the Third World. Yet the literature is almost barren. Consequently, this study of the television industry in the Dominican Republic is of interest to a broad readership, not merely to students specializing in that country. Menéndez Alarcón provides a lucid and highly readable description of the structure and organization of the literature. He examines the interdependent relationships between the industry and the national structures of power. Drawing upon existing theories of communications and the mass media, the author moves from a history of Dominican television to consideration of cultural and political messages. Treatment of television in the 1990 national elections is especially gripping. The book includes informative data on programming, news coverage, and popular tastes in the Dominican Republic. Overall, a pioneering work that deserves a careful reading by scholars and students alike. Advanced undergraduate through faculty.—*J.D. Martz, Pennsylvania State University, University Park Campus*

OAB-2731   F3100   93-29887 CIP
Oppenheim, Lois Hecht. **Politics in Chile: democracy, authoritarianism, and the search for development.** Westview, 1994 (c1993). 260p bibl index afp ISBN 0-8133-8210-6, $54.95; ISBN 0-8133-8211-4 pbk, $16.95

For many Chileans, as well as others, Patricio Aylwin's election as president of Chile in 1989 signaled an end to the 16-year nightmare of military rule. However, since then the debate has raged on as to whether Chile is an authoritarian state with a democratically elected president or a democracy with leftover authoritarian elements. Oppenheim goes a long way toward answering that question. Originally a PhD dissertation (Washington Univ. 1980), this informative book is exactly as the author states, "a reflection on the political changes that have taken place in Chile, principally from the Allende period through the military period and the current transition to democracy." The author very carefully, clearly, and compactly examines the way in which class and other group interests interacted with party politics and the political leadership. By analyzing the Allende years, the military regime, and the new civilian government, the author provides the reader with a clear picture of the radical changes within Chile during the past 20 years. The bibliography is excellent, the list of acronyms useful, and the footnotes food for thought. Most importantly this is a highly readable and easily digestible book on a complicated topic. The author's deep

Social & Behavioral Sciences

understanding of the nature of Chilean politics as well as her own personal insights make this a book not to be missed. Undergraduate through faculty.—*R. H. Terry, York College of Pennsylvania*

OAB-2732   HD8266   91-35602 CIP
Ranis, Peter. **Argentine workers: Peronism and contemporary class consciousness.** Pittsburgh, 1992. 313p bibl index ISBN 0-8229-3703-4, $49.95

Ranis (City University of New York) provides a much-needed addition to the literature on Argentine labor studies. Most studies on Argentine labor have concentrated on labor union elites, on the political maneuverings of a highly politicized labor movement, or on the alleged revolutionary or conservative bias (depending on which authors one reads) of the Argentine working class. All recent studies have focused on the workplace and on labor's dealings with the state. Ranis departs from these studies by focusing on the working individual as a total person. Using surveys conducted over several years, Ranis paints a convincing portrait of workers who are concerned with their and their family's material well-being, upward mobility, and political freedoms. Neither inherently revolutionary or conservative, Ranis describes Argentine workers as committed to achieving and maintaining higher standards of living and reforms in the workplace to alleviate alienation. Of particular importance is Ranis's analysis of workers' attitudes towards the state and democracy. Again, departing from long-held assumptions about Argentine workers' political attitudes, Ranis demonstrates their commitment to political and social democracy. These findings speak to a need for revisionism in understanding Peronism. Required reading for anyone interested in labor studies, Latin American studies, and Peronism. Undergraduate through faculty collections.—*L. Chen, Indiana University at South Bend*

OAB-2733   F1256   94-38143 CIP
Ross, John. **Rebellion from the roots: Indian uprising in Chiapas.** Common Courage, 1995. 424p index ISBN 1-56751-043-4, $29.95; ISBN 1-56751-042-6 pbk, $14.95

The January 1994 Zapatista rebellion by the poor, indigenous, subsistence farmers of the state of Chiapas has shaken Mexico more than any other event in modern history. The 30-hour military occupation of the city of San Cristobal de las Casas and the "poems" of subcommandant Marcos were soon viewed as masterstrokes of armed public relations. With the arrival on the scene of human rights groups such as Americas Watch, Amnesty International, and the International Cross, as well as dignitaries such as Ramsey Clark and Rigoberta Menchu, the eyes of the world were focused on this poverty stricken corner of Mexico. Author Ross, a longtime correspondent and social activist on Latin American affairs, has provided a fascinating, highly readable, detailed account of the Indian uprising that nearly derailed the NAFTA agreement. Winner of the 1995 American Book Award, this volume is highly recommended to anyone at any level wishing to understand modern Mexico.—*R. H. Terry, York College of Pennsylvania*

OAB-2734   F2508   95-37942 CIP
Schneider, Ronald M. **Brazil: culture and politics in a new industrial powerhouse.** Westview, 1996. 255p index afp ISBN 0-8133-2436-X, $65.00; ISBN 0-8133-2437-8 pbk, $22.95

Latest in the author's long series of Brazilian studies (e.g., *Brazil: Foreign Policy of a Future World Power*, CH, Sep'77), this is an ideal volume to introduce readers to the multifaceted reality that is Brazil. Intended as primer rather than a groundbreaking scholarly study, it combines in readable form the essentials of culture, history, economics, and politics (both past and current). Schneider synthesizes large amounts of data in a way that makes them accessible and illustrative of his view that Brazil has reached a point at which it is finally poised to realize its long-delayed emergence as a major nation, the colossus of the South. One strength of the work is its placing of Brazilian sociopolitical life in a cultural framework designed to facilitate Americans' understanding of this complex nation. For example, the chapter "The Several

Brazils" lays out the diversity and the inequalities so characteristic of the country. The chapters "Society and Social Problems," "Culture and Brazilian Ways," and "Brazil in the World" are sufficiently general to ensure that this worthwhile work will date less quickly than traditional studies focusing solely on politics. Highly recommended for general readers and undergraduates.—*C. E. Landers, Jersey City State College*

OAB-2735   JL1602   95-12297 CIP
Wright, Bruce E. **Theory in the practice of the Nicaraguan revolution.** Ohio University Center for International Studies, 1995. 272p bibl index afp (Latin American studies, 24) ISBN 0-89680-185-3 pbk, $23.00

An excellent basis for understanding the Nicaraguan Revolution primarily as a Sandinista revolution, this book is first-rate analysis. The author draws on extensive reading of revolutionary theory as well as in-country experience, 1986-91 at INIES, the Nicaraguan Institute for Economic and Social Research. He argues persuasively that the Nicaraguan Revolution be interpreted in "Nicaraguan terms," as an alternative revolutionary model grounded in the theoretical and historical traditions of Sandino and Fonseca and in the internal class relations of the country. It is "a new model of a democratic, yet revolutionary, transition to socialism." The global demise of Marxist systems and the 1990 electoral defeat have not delegitimized the Sandinista model, which remains rooted in political pluralism. Participatory democracy combined with the popular vanguard role and class hegemony of the main revolutionary party has protected fundamental revolutionary gains. In this important sense, "the Nicaraguan revolution continues even if one sees the Sandinista revolution as having ended." A most readable and carefully constructed and argued thesis that provides a comprehensive overview of Nicaraguan political events since 1979. Highly recommended for all readers.—*W. Q. Morales, University of Central Florida*

■ International Relations

OAB-2736   JV6091   96-19400 CIP
Bell-Fialkoff, Andrew. **Ethnic cleansing.** St. Martin's, 1996. 346p bibl index ISBN 0-312-10792-7, $45.00

Bell-Fialkoff's remarkable book treats one of the ugliest aspects of ethnic conflict. Building on his widely read article "A Brief History of Ethnic Cleansing," *Foreign Affairs* 72 (1993):110-121, the author (a graduate student, Boston Univ.) has assembled a virtual encyclopedia of humanity's ethnic inhumanity, extending from antiquity to the present, with more detailed studies of many recent cases (e.g., Bosnia, Nagorno-Karabakh, Transylvania, Sri Lanka, Ulster). Working with secondary sources, he brings a careful discipline to his comparative analysis, although one would have appreciated more subheadings for guidance. After exploring multiple ways of classifying his cases, he ambitiously draws lessons and suggests solutions to these seemingly intractable problems. Donald Horowitz's *Ethnic Groups in Conflict* (CH, Mar'86) is the closest rival, although its scope is even broader. Bell-Fialkoff's narrower focus serves an important, timely purpose, however. Highly recommended for all collections.—*E. M. Dew, Fairfield University*

OAB-2737   JX1391   92-3850 CIP
Brown, Seyom. **International relations in a changing global system: toward a theory of the world polity.** Westview, 1992. 190p bibl index afp ISBN 0-8133-0814-3, $44.00; ISBN 0-8133-0815-1 pbk, $16.95

Brown seeks to develop a sense of need for a theory of the world polity, an existence of a universal world system. His effort is meant to be a nexus to the work of Charles Beitz, *Political Theory and International Relations* (CH, May'80), and Terry Nardin, *Law, Morality, and the Relations of States* (1983). The presentation deals with a theory that serves to explain an organized social and political relationship that exists between humanity and nature. Brown rejects any notion that restricts his view of the globe as an interactive unit. He also recognizes the need to interject a normative approach to his analysis thus combining elements of realpolitik with the "realist model" of international politics. Brown notes the arbitrary convention of acceptance of the nation-state system as the source of international order and suggests that a world system would serve humanity more efficiently. The language is often terse, and it is difficult to absorb immediately all the concepts within this succinctly argued book. However, Brown has produced an argument that will serve as a source of discussion, argument, and debate for a number of years. Essential reading for all those interested in world politics. Advanced undergraduate through faculty collections.—*S. R. Silverburg, Catawba College*

OAB-2738　　　　UA10　　　　96-14340 CIP
The Culture of national security: norms and identity in world politics, ed. by Peter J. Katzenstein. Columbia, 1996. 562p index afp ISBN 0-231-10468-5, $50.00; ISBN 0-231-10469-3 pbk, $17.50

The twin paradigms of structural neorealism and neoliberal institutionalism, centered on the assumption of international anarchy, have dominated modern theoretical discourse about international politics. A third interpretation, based in the constitutive and regulative impact of norms and self-identifying values in the creation of an international society of states, has been quietly asserting itself. With this volume, the cultural and sociological institutionalist view achieves maturity, and takes its place as a complementary, if not wholly viable alternative paradigm for international theory. Two exemplary contributions directly challenge the logic of anarchy. Martha Finnemore describes the cultural and normative evolution of pro-Christian, then antislavery state policy en route to an internalization of humanitarian intervention after 1945. Alastair Johnston shows how various ideational influences better account for consistency in the context of Chinese politics. So well presented are all these arguments that no future discussion in international relations theory can ignore the contributions of this approach, and no serious theoretical study will be complete without numerous citations to this edited volume. Upper-division undergraduates through faculty.—*E. C. Dolman, College of William and Mary*

OAB-2739　　　　JX1662　　　　96-2976 CIP
Diplomacy at the highest level: the evolution of international summitry, ed. by David H. Dunn. Macmillan (UK)/St. Martin's, 1996. 279p index ISBN 0-312-16273-1, $69.95

The first comprehensive study of the theory and practice of international summitry by British experts, this book intends to fill a gap in the huge number of books and articles that deal with the relation between domestic and international policy. The editor (international studies, Univ. of Birmingham, UK) has assembled 15 articles that trace the development of an international institution. The practice of sovereigns meeting to discuss their relations predates the establishment of resident embassies in the 15th century. Unique to the present age, however, is the frequency of these meetings, and the extent to which they have replaced traditional methods of diplomatic discourse. The term "summit" comes from Winston Churchill's constant calls during the 1950s for meetings at the highest levels of government to resolve international differences. The book's 15 chapters are in four parts. Part 1 explains thematically the factors that have increased the frequency of summit meetings in the 20th century and reveals the long history of this activity, relating how modern summitry has evolved from conference diplomacy. Parts 2 and 3 analyze various incarnations of summitry to illustrate different circumstances in which summit meetings have been employed. Part 4 draws general conclusions about the advantages and disadvantages, uses and abuses, of modern summitry. An important contribution to the literature of 20th-century diplomacy and international relations, essential for graduate and upper-division students as well as faculty.—*R. M. Bigler, University of Nevada, Las Vegas*

OAB-2740　　　　JX1395　　　　96-13991 CIP
Finnemore, Martha. **National interests in international society.**

Cornell, 1996. 154p index afp ISBN 0-8014-3244-8, $35.00; ISBN 0-8014-8323-9 pbk, $13.95

How do states know what they want? this short volume asks, and provides an example of how a constructivist research agenda can address this fundamental question of international relations. Finnemore challenges key assumptions of both neorealism and neoliberalism—notions of unproblematic interests and technical rationality as the dominant form of human interaction—and in their place investigates the processes and structures that create meaning and social values. Her three cases—the role of UNESCO in the emergence of science bureaucracies within states, the role of the Red Cross in the emergence of the Geneva conventions, and the role of the World Bank in the redefinition of development—demonstrate that focusing on the construction of values can identify and illuminate an interaction of agency and structure neglected by other perspectives. She builds on the insights of Nicholas Onuf, Friedrich Kratochwil, and Alexander Wendt, extending their theoretical arguments into cases with clear historical and practical value. This book should be on the shelf of any specialist in international affairs and is strongly recommended for faculty, graduate students, and advanced undergraduates.—*D. McIntosh, Slippery Rock University of Pennsylvania*

OAB-2741　　　　JX1974　　　　95-11840 CIP
Forsberg, Randall. **Nonproliferation primer: preventing the spread of nuclear, chemical, and biological weapons,** by Randall Forsberg et al. MIT, 1995. 149p bibl index afp ISBN 0-262-56095-X, $15.00

In a very readable and useful primer on the proliferation of weapons of mass destruction (nuclear, chemical, and biological), four noted authorities in arms control make good use of excerpts from three recent reports by Congress's Office of Technology Assessment, and challenge readers to pressure their governments to favor arms control. The authors believe these weapons constitute a clear and present danger in the hands of various global and regional powers and potentially in the hands of terrorist or unstable groups. The introduction to the technicalities and politics of the spread and development of weapons is thorough, although the volume is weak on conventional weapons. Much of the good and bad news is already known by those paying close attention to the issue. On the positive side, after the Cold War, opportunities for arms control and even disarmament are theoretically greater than ever, most countries support nonproliferation, and relatively few states (only 14) possess capabilities for weapons of mass destruction. However, weapons-grade nuclear and chemical components are plentiful globally and are perhaps under less secure control, while regional conflicts and status competition drive a demand for weapons and delivery systems of higher sophistication. The authors discuss current treaties and regimes designed to control this problem and present an ideal view of disarmament in the final chapter. The book contains pedagogically sound illustrations, a glossary of technical terms, and up-to-date suggested readings. A fine resource for general and undergraduate readers.—*F. S. Pearson, Wayne State University*

OAB-2742　　　　　　　　　　Can. CIP
Gillies, David. **Between principle and practice: human rights in North-South relations.** McGill-Queen's, 1996. 339p indexes afp ISBN 0-7735-1413-9, $55.00; ISBN 0-7735-1414-7 pbk, $22.95

Gillies provides a model for future research concerning the political limitations to human rights-oriented foreign policies. To examine the extent to which progressive industrialized states can promote and protect human rights through carefully targeted foreign policies, Gillies studies some foreign policies of three midsize democratic states (Canada, Netherlands, and Norway) toward the Philippines, Indonesia, Sri Lanka, Suriname, and China in the 1980s and early 1990s. Gillies's case studies underscore the complexity of foreign policies that attempt to promote and protect human rights. He acknowledges that the impact of international action toward such ends is modest, and finds that the uneasy interaction between human rights activists and public officials in developed states provides a constructive, creative dynamic. In the three developed countries, Gillies finds that aid policies reflect humane internationalist ideals, but these considerations only marginally shape trade policies. He concludes that two rights, freedom from torture and from extrajudicial killing, should always be defended without regard to political exigencies. He documents several failed efforts to influence political conditions in Indonesia and China, noting in the latter case, "unilateral and abrasive US policies were viewed as counterproductive in relation to human rights goals." Gillies nevertheless believes that smaller northern states can develop consistent multilateral policies that have modest hopes for success in the non-Western world. Enthusiastically recommended for all audiences.—*P. G. Conway, SUNY College at Oneonta*

OAB-2743 JF1525 95-48112 CIP
Herman, Michael. **Intelligence power in peace and war.** Royal Institute of International Affairs/Cambridge, 1996. 414p bibl index ISBN 0-521-56231-7, $59.95; ISBN 0-521-56636-3 pbk, $22.95

Herman has written the most complete in-depth study of intelligence yet to appear. A former British intelligence officer, now at Oxford, he combines practical experience with astute and sophisticated academic understanding to produce a book that should become the basic intelligence text and a professional bible. He uses a comparative analytical framework, emphasizing British and American examples (but including many others as well). Superior to Abram Shulsky's *Silent Warfare* (CH, Mar'92), its comparative dimension also takes it beyond Jeffrey Richelson's *The U.S. Intelligence Community* (3rd ed., CH, Feb'96). Herman gives thoughtful treatment to the changing nature of intelligence in the post-Cold War world, international issues posed by intelligence collection issues in the UN and other international operations, and problems involving intelligence management. His most challenging conclusion is that the increasing multiplicity of needs requires more analysis of all sources and less devotion of resources to specific targets. Herman also deals with counterintelligence and intelligence security at a more sophisticated level than most authors. An excellent work, written with enough skill and clarity to be valuable for academic and general readers.—*J. D. Stempel, University of Kentucky*

OAB-2744 DS558 91-35162 CIP
Khong, Yuen Foong. **Analogies at war: Korea, Munich, Dien Bien Phu, and the Vietnam decisions of 1965.** Princeton, 1992. 286p bibl index afp ISBN 0-691-07846-7, $39.50; ISBN 0-691-02535-5 pbk, $16.95

This is an important book, a significant addition to the literature on decision theory. The outgrowth of Khong's 1987 doctoral dissertation at Harvard, the treatise quickly propelled the author to his present position as associate professor of government at Harvard. Khong addresses how and why, as well as the implications of, policymakers employing historical analogies in their decision making. Secondarily, using Vietnam policymakers as case in point, he attempts to explain why decision makers often use analogies poorly. Utilizing recently declassified documents, interviews with senior policymakers, and a command of cognitive social psychology, the author advances our understanding both of the fateful intervention decisions of 1965, and the larger dynamics of foreign policy-making. Although Khong strives to present his argument clearly, his book is not always easy to follow, and this reviewer for one is not fully convinced by his conclusions. Nevertheless, the study ranks with Larry Berman, John Burke and Fred Greenstein, George M. Kahin, Brian VanDeMark, John DiLeo, and others who have contributed important recent works on the decision process of 1965. The more important comparision, however, may be to Graham Allison's ground-breaking classic on decision theory, *Essence of Decision: Explaining the Cuban Missile Crises* (CH, Apr'72). Advanced undergraduates through faculty.—*J. P. Dunn, Converse College*

OAB-2745 HD9743 91-5025 CIP
Krause, Keith. **Arms and the state: patterns of military production and trade.** Cambridge, 1992. 299p bibl index (Cambridge studies in international relations, 22) ISBN 0-521-39446-5, $49.95

Krause has written an outstanding book on the production and trade of arms that eclipses in significance and renders mundane the standard works in the field.

Arms and the State is a masterful blending of theory and history that demands the attention of analysts and practitioners alike. The motive forces in the production and trade of weaponry and the dynamic role of technology are featured in a sweeping account of the evolution of the global arms production and transfer system from the "pre-modern period" through the Military and Industrial Revolutions to the present. Krause's distinctions among first, second, and third-tier producers and suppliers are fully explored in the context of the post-WW II system. Important debates in the literature on the political economy of arms production and trade are enthusiastically joined throughout. Future debates will be shaped by this book. There can be little doubt that this is a landmark work that will not soon be surpassed. For faculty, graduate, and upper-division undergraduate level readers.—*A. L. Ross, Naval War College*

OAB-2746 JX1952 94-38944 CIP
Mayor, Federico. **The new page,** by Federico Mayor with Tom Forstenzer. Dartmouth/UNESCO, 1995. (Dist. by Ashgate) 98p index ISBN 1-85521-652-3, $39.95

Something inspiring happens to sensitive intellects when placed in positions of global responsibility: while retaining local cultural roots, their compassionate caring becomes universal. Such is the case of Mayor (scientist, scholar, teacher, university rector, politician, Catalan, and Spaniard), since 1987 Director General of UNESCO, where he is responsible for global servant-leadership in education, science, culture, and communication. The title means to turn from the old "culture of war" to a new "culture of peace." Mayor is passionately devoted to democracy as an indispensable means for turning the page. He urgently calls for "no business as usual" to avert the forseeable catastrophic consequences of combined overpopulation, growing disparity between rich and poor, militarization, and destruction of the planet's life-support system. This includes the tragedy of countless street children destined to become "feral adults." His is not ritualistic prophetic lamentation, but the constructive creativity of the great teacher-leader. This is a book for everyone engaged in learning and democratic action. It should be in every library, as should its spiritual harbinger (by another inspired UN author), Robert Muller's *New Genesis* (1982).—*G. D. Paige, emeritus, University of Hawaii at Manoa*

OAB-2747 UA10 94-8108 CIP
Pearson, Frederic S. **The global spread of arms: political economy of international security.** Westview, 1994. 161p bibl index afp ISBN 0-8133-1573-5, $49.95; ISBN 0-8133-1574-3 pbk, $13.95

This is a most timely contribution to the literature. It comes at a time when the Non-Proliferation Treaty is being renegotiated and when such countries as Iran and North Korea may be contemplating nuclear weapons acquisition. Pearson's work does not deal exclusively with nuclear weapons, although portions of the book are devoted to them. He offers the reader a comprehensive and well-researched analysis of the weapons business, the so-called "arms supermarket." It is a story of legal purchases, arms and technology transfers, black and gray markets, and attempts to limit and control weapons and weapons related programs. Conflict and the potential for conflict, especially since the end of the Cold War, has largely rendered international controls ineffective. Indeed, as Pearson observes, even domestic control of weapon transfers is difficult. This is an excellent work on a very important and complex problem in international security studies. It is a must acquisition for university and professional libraries. It will also serve as a helpful text in courses in security studies. Upper-division undergraduate; graduate.—*A. C. Tuttle, University of Nevada, Las Vegas*

OAB-2748 JC328 93-29346 CIP
Porter, Bruce D. **War and the rise of the state: the military foundations of modern politics.** Free Press, 1994. 380p index ISBN 0-02-925095-1, $24.95

This is a very important study. Porter has examined the complex impact of warfare on the development of Western political institutions over the course of the last five centuries. What is most striking is his evidence that warfare has generally exerted a modernizing effect on the development of the state. Porter finds that even the evolution of democratic institutions has been accelerated by conflicts within and between states. The research reflects a broad, historical perspective on the subject of European state systems, which builds on studies such as *The Formation of National States in Western Europe* ed. by Charles Tilly (CH, Dec'75), and Tilly's *Coercion, Capital, and European States, A.D. 990-1990* (CH, Dec'90). Porter provides examples of war hastening the disintegration of societies and the demise of some states, but he shows that the overall effect has been to encourage more centralized authority with greater efficiency in mobilizing citizenry, generating tax revenues, and bureaucratization. This wide-ranging analysis is incisive, sometimes wry, and profoundly careful in tone. The concluding chapter examines the effect of war on the development of the US government. Recommended for scholars at every level.—*P. G. Conway, SUNY College at Oneonta*

OAB-2749   JX4481   95-53945 MARC
Ramsbotham, Oliver. **Humanitarian intervention in contemporary conflict: a reconceptualization,** by Oliver Ramsbotham and Tom Woodhouse. Polity, 1996. 264p bibl index afp ISBN 0-7456-1510-4, $54.95

This timely addition to the literature of international law and relations provides a comprehensive, sorely needed review of the problematic concept and policy of humanitarian intervention. At the heart of the study is a compelling "reconceptualization" of humanitarian rights and classical intervention (the right of forcible self-help by states), and the evolution toward post-Cold War humanitarian intervention—"forcible" and "nonforcible" cross-border collective actions—undertaken by the UN, by states, or by nonstate actors in response to human suffering. Careful review of the theoretical literature and two succinct chapters on the comparative lessons of recent interventions in Bosnia and Somalia clarify the controversy over intervention. The authors' term "international social" conflict reveals the convergence between the roots of war and of social conflict in the ethnic and communal violence that precipitated forcible humanitarian interventions in Bosnia, Iraq, Liberia, and Rwanda. Although technical in portions, this compact work remains accessible and readable. It has no rival; it serves as an excellent textbook and indispensible guide for the general public, as well as for professional and academic audiences, eager to sort through the confusion of humanitarian intervention.—*W. Q. Morales, University of Central Florida*

OAB-2750   Can. CIP
Richmond, Anthony H. **Global apartheid: refugees, racism, and the new world order.** Oxford, 1995 (c1994). 327p bibl index afp ISBN 0-19-541013-0 pbk, $24.95

Richmond has written an excellent book about a contemporary problem and fact of life in the final years of the 20th century. The book is divided into three parts: part 1 deals with the sociological theories of racism; part 2 is a comparative analysis of immigration and the refugee problem that arises from the existence of racism; part 3 is a look at the new world order and what it means to migration, apartheid (which is not limited to South Africa), and the status of refugees. Richmond estimates that some 16.3 million refugees and asylum seekers exist in the world. The countries contributing the most to this figure are Afghanistan, Palestine, Mozambique, and the former Yugoslavia. The UN High Commissioner for Refugees acknowledges some 6.6 million people as refugees. This is an important and well-written book about a subject filled with pathos and tragedy—it should make the rich, secure, and mean-spirited feel uncomfortable. All levels.—*E. W. Webking, University of Lethbridge*

OAB-2751   E744   95-23929 CIP
Simpson, Christopher. **The splendid blond beast: money, law, and genocide in the twentieth century.** Common Courage, 1995. 399p index ISBN 1-56751-062-0 pbk, $19.95

Simpson's eloquent and well-documented account describes how defects in international law, combined with economic interests, prompted the US and its allies to condone genocide and reward its practitioners. Genocide is seen as an institutionalized mechanism of empires and nation-states that victimizes indigenous peoples in order to maximize political and economic interests. Citing newly uncovered archival sources, Simpson presents startling evidence about the roles of key US policy makers who, tied to business interests, derailed attempts to persecute the Turkish perpetrators of the Armenian genocide (1915-21), the German initiators of WW I, and Nazi authors of the Holocaust. He shows how international failure to halt the Armenian genocide and punish its authors was a product of the existing structure of international law that helped shape Hitler's plans to exterminate Jews. Among those responsible were Secretary of State Robert Lansing, the Dulles brothers, Admirals Mark Bristol and William Chester, and diplomats who served under Roosevelt, Truman, and Eisenhower. This is a compelling book for students of US foreign policy, comparative genocides, international human rights, and all those interested in the history of man's inhumanity to man. All levels.—*R. H. Dekmejian, University of Southern California*

OAB-2752   JX1952   93-10641 CIP
Singer, Max. **The real world order: zones of peace/zones of turmoil,** by Max Singer and Aaron Wildavsky. Chatham House, 1993. 212p index ISBN 0-934540-98-5, $25.00; ISBN 0-934540-99-3 pbk, $16.95

This original, insightful, and very provocative book deals with challenges the world faces after the demise of Cold War bipolar politics. In contrast to most analysts of international relations who adhere to the prevalent academic doctrine of neorealism, the authors of the volume believe that military power alone can no longer assure the prosperity and survival of states. Singer (The Potomac Organization) and Wildavsky (Univ. of California, Berkeley) have made a conceptual breakthrough in dividing the world into democratic zones of peace and nondemocratic zones of conflict. In an admittedly optimistic but certainly controversial approach to what they call the *real* new world order, their book points toward the way in which increasingly dominant democracies can use multilateral channels to expand the zones of peace, and it provides a realistic basis upon which all parties may debate policy. The book will no doubt set the terms for further reflection and debate. It may not command agreement, but its arguments deserve attention. And this trail-blazing approach could provide the political foundation for strategy in the post-Cold War world. In the concluding chapter, "American Foreign Policy in the Real World Order," the authors take issue with fashionable pessimism, update realism, review their policy suggestions, and explain the implications of their optimism. Must reading for students of international relations and US foreign policy.—*R. M. Bigler, University of Nevada, Las Vegas*

OAB-2753   JC571   95-23132 CIP
Slaughter among neighbors: the political origins of communal violence, by Human Rights Watch. Yale, 1995. 188p index afp ISBN 0-300-06496-9, $30.00; ISBN 0-300-06544-2 pbk, $15.00

An essential resource for understanding one of the most endemic and perplexing phenomena in contemporary international politics, this is a gripping analysis of communal violence in ten countries or regions: Rwanda, India, Palestine and Israeli-occupied territories, South Africa, Romania, Sri Lanka, Kenya, former Yugoslavia, Lebanon, and Armenia-Azerbaijan. The ten cases in this slim, readable volume are written by country experts associated with Human Rights Watch, a nongovernmental organization that monitors the status of human rights worldwide. Communal violence is defined as "violent conflict and repression based not only on communities' ethnic identities but also on their religious affiliation or racial, linguistic, or tribal characteristics." Cases highlight situations of "centrally-directed" violence by the government or other organized groups. The deceptively brief cases, carefully researched and scrupulously nonpartisan, except in their concern for human rights, provide excellent overviews, especially on the two often misunderstood cases of Rwanda and Yugoslavia, and the often-ignored case of Sri Lanka. An ideal guide for general and specialized study of international affairs or minorities and violence, this book is certain to enlighten all readers.—*W. Q. Morales, University of Central Florida*

OAB-2754 HV5801 95-41815 CIP
Stares, Paul B. **Global habit: the drug problem in a borderless world.** Brookings, 1996. 171p index afp ISBN 0-8157-8140-7, $24.95

This book would be perfect supplementary reading for a nontraditional undergraduate international relations course. In it Stares, a Brookings scholar, presents an excellent overview of both the challenge and the rise and development of the global drug trade, and its market dynamics and operations. He then offers an agenda containing pragmatic goals and programs for responding to the problem in ways that go far beyond the simplistic legalization/prohibitionist debate. Most important, he does all this in a mere 122 pages of clear, concise text. Although experts may quibble over a small point of fact or interpretation, in the main this work is on target and provides an excellent set of sourcing notes for the reader wanting to go beyond this work of synthesis. This solid monograph belongs on the shelf alongside *Drugs and Foreign Policy*, ed. by Raphael Perl (1994), and the annual publication *The Geopolitics of Drugs*. Strongly recommended for undergraduate students and general audiences.—*P. A. Lupsha, formerly, University of New Mexico*

OAB-2755 GN496 96-10553 CIP
Stavenhagen, Rodolfo. **Ethnic conflicts and the nation-state.** Macmillan (UK)/St. Martin's/URISD, 1996. 324p bibl index ISBN 0-312-15971-4, $79.95

Stavenhagen begins his work on global ethnic conflict in the Middle East, Africa, East Europe, the Pacific, and the US with superb theoretical models, then supplements them with comparative data. He uses these regions for each model, allowing comparative analysis across time and analytical categories. He discusses social scientific, economic, ethnic, international, pedagogical, ideological, and management dynamics of conflict. He draws his work from a UN study available from the UN's New York headquarters. One wonders if UN troop commanders might not profit from reading Stavenhagen's savvy assumptions about ethnic conflicts and how to develop positive scenarios about these realities. He believes strongly in the power of pluralist democracy, yet realizes its pitfalls and concludes that "the search for multicultural pluralism requires a delicate mix of equality and separateness." In sum, Stavenhagen's marvelous book is a well-balanced treatment of vexing problems. Recommended for both undergraduates and advanced scholars, and essential for all who expect to read in ethnic studies.—*P. Barton-Kriese, Indiana University East*

OAB-2756 HQ1190 93-10251 CIP
Sylvester, Christine. **Feminist theory and international relations in a postmodern era.** Cambridge, 1994. 265p bibl index (Cambridge studies in international relations, 32) ISBN 0-521-39305-1, $54.95; ISBN 0-521-45984-2 pbk, $16.95

Sylvester (Northern Arizona Univ.) has written a fine tour de force challenging both international relations specialists and feminist scholars to converse with each other. In very witty prose spiced with sharp critiques of long-standing international relations sacred cows, Sylvester comes closer than any other authors currently writing on gender and IR questions to applying various feminist theoretical lenses to international relations theory and theorizing. She organizes her text by reviewing the long-standing debates in international relations starting with the realist/idealist debate, then the scientific/traditional debates, and on to the modern/post modern debate. Sylvester weaves into her analysis various feminist theories whose relevance to IR debates she convincingly demonstrates. She makes a case that ignoring feminist epistemological concerns has left the field of IR theory isolated from the very real and necessary cross-cultural perspectives of women, and that these omissions have been detrimental to international relations. The last part of her book entails two brief examples of how some women in England and some others in Zimbabwe have through their own actions disrupted long-held, cherished notions of the male-centric discipline of international relations. Recommended for upper-division undergraduates, graduate students, and faculty.—*L. Chen, Indiana University at South Bend*

OAB-2757 JX1395 91-42632 CIP
Walker, R.B.J. **Inside/outside: international relations as political theory.** Cambridge, 1993. 233p bibl index (Cambridge studies in international relations, 24) ISBN 0-521-36423-X, $49.95

This work expands Walker's earlier critique, "Sovereignty, Identity, Community: Reflections on the Horizons of Contemporary Political Practice," in *Contending Sovereignties: Redefining Political Community*, ed. by R.B.J. Walker and Saul H. Mendlovitz (1990), that international relations theories are "discursive strategies in which the relation of universality and particularity are reified spatially through claims to a sovereign identity." Unlike Howard Williams in *International Relations in Political Theory* (CH, Jul'92), Walker goes beyond an evaluation of works that synthesize political theory and international relations theory, maintaining that both of these traditions are engaged in a totalizing logic inherited from Greek Eleatic ontology. Instead, consistent with J.G.A. Pocock's civic humanist interpretation of Machiavelli and Michel Foucault's critique of sovereign identity, and critically drawing on works of Martin Wight and John Dunn, Walker argues that modern political analysis must understand politics as a dynamic globally diverse community activity. Walker shows mastery of the literature. His work is theoretically comprehensive and innovative. Definitely a work to be studied by scholars of international relations or political and social philosophy and ethics. Undergraduate through professional.—*R. J. Vichot, Texas A&M University*

OAB-2758 HQ1236 93-28668 CIP
Women and politics worldwide, ed. by Barbara J. Nelson and Najma Chowdhury. Yale, 1994. 818p index afp ISBN 0-300-05407-6, $50.00; ISBN 0-300-05408-4 pbk, $25.00

This work is the first of its kind to include essays on countries from North America to Nepal, Kenya to Korea. It sets the standard for future international and comparative research on women and politics. A monumental work coedited by a US and a Bangladeshi scholar, it provides the first ever collection of incisive articles about women in politics in 43 countries, each chapter written by a woman scholar, activist, or official in that country. Each chapter first presents a useful snapshot of political, demographic, educational, and economic data on women; handy summary tables provide easy comparison across countries in each topical area. However, chapters are not written in cookbook style; rather, each author addresses the unique historical and current political issues most salient to women in her country, from rural development to democratization, health to headscarves. The editors give excellent orientations to the conceptual framework, research design, methodology, and data collection procedures. The framework introduces important concepts in the field, such as nationalism, international economic forces, the women's movement, formal and informal politics, women's issues, and women's gender ideologies and action strategies. A lively, accessible work. Undergraduate through faculty.—*M. A. Saint-Germain, University of Texas at El Paso*

UNITED STATES

OAB-2759 E846 93-40140 CIP
Brands, H.W. **The wages of globalism: Lyndon Johnson and the limits of American power.** Oxford, 1995. 294p bibl index afp ISBN 0-19-507888-8, $27.50

Brands (history, Texas A&M) is one of the most prolific and best writers in the field of diplomatic history today. This is his tenth book, his sixth on the Cold War in the last five years. His earlier work, *The Devil We Knew: Americans and the Cold War* (1993), was an acclaimed treatment of the origins and evolution of America's several decades of world hegemony. In many ways, *The Wages of Globalism* is a sequel which treats the beginning of the end of that position. Most studies of Lyndon Johnson focus on his domestic policies with limited treatment of foreign policy other than Vietnam. Brands puts Johnson's Vietnam imbroglio into the context of his other crises in South Asia,

Indonesia, Cyprus, Western Europe, Latin America, Africa, North Korea, and the Middle East. The record is mixed with successes and failures, but Brands tends to give the master politician largely favorable evaluations for the advice he picked and chose from among the wide range of his foreign policy team. Vietnam is treated briefly but insightfully. Sprightly written and provocative, this is an extremely important addition both to the Johnson and the Vietnam War bibliographies. Upper-division undergraduate through faculty.—*J. P. Dunn, Converse College*

OAB-2760   E183   91-27006 CIP
Buckley, Roger. **US-Japan alliance diplomacy, 1945-1990.** Cambridge, 1992. 225p bibl index (Cambridge studies in international relations, 21) ISBN 0-521-35141-3, $49.95

The best single book on US-Japan relations since the end of WW II. Buckley (International Christian Univ., Tokyo) relies almost exclusively on analysis of US policy papers toward Japan for the years from the Japanese surrender in 1945 to 1969. Thereafter, American policy papers not yet having been released into the public domain, he relies on a rich collection of secondary sources. Although he is not a Japan specialist, Buckley's careful analysis of the American documents provides extraordinary insights into the perspectives and motivations of Japan's leaders. In a beautifully written narrative style he interweaves the American and Japanese sides of the developing relationship. He is primarily interested in three issues: changes in US policy from 1945 to the present in response to a Japan that became increasingly successful, independent, and even hostile; the role of personality in the relationship between the US and Japan; and the issue of who has benefited in the US-Japan relationship. A concluding chapter looks at the troubled relationship and what might happen to it in the next decade. Essential reading for all students of Japan and of US foreign policy, undergraduate and up.—*S. Ogden, Northeastern University*

OAB-2761   HF1456   93-41718 CIP
Cox, Ronald W. **Power and profits: U.S. policy in Central America.** University Press of Kentucky, 1994. 189p bibl index afp ISBN 0-8131-1865-4, $29.00

Cox (Florida International Univ.) has ventured into uncharted territory with this book. He proposes to examine the relationship between business groups and the government in the formulation of US foreign economic policy. That such a relationship exists has long been surmised, but Cox is the first to examine the relationship in an empirical manner. The book is invaluable in that it is theoretically sophisticated and also provides empirical evidence for a relationship that most have assumed exists but have not bothered to test. In the best social science manner, Cox first establishes his hypothesis, then (using US economic policy in Central America as his test case) proceeds to empirical analysis and ends with an affirmation of his "Business Conflict Model" as an important explanatory variable in determining the outcomes of US foreign economic policy. This book should be a catalyst for further studies of how and by whom US foreign policy is made, and Cox should be commended for being a pathfinder in this area. His study should be required reading for classes in US foreign policy or US-Latin American relations. Upper-division undergraduate through faculty.—*E. A. Duff, Randolph-Macon Woman's College*

OAB-2762   DS550   93-41544 CIP
Duiker, William J. **U.S. containment policy and the conflict in Indochina.** Stanford, 1994. 453p bibl index afp ISBN 0-8047-2283-8, $49.50

Duiker (East Asian history, Penn State), a former foreign service officer in Saigon in the mid-1960s, is one of the most judicious, tempered, and respected scholars on Vietnam. His six previous books have established his authority, and this is his crowning achievement. Duiker carefully traces the evolution of American involvement in the country from WW II through the decision to take over the combat role in the war during early 1965. He dissects each crucial decision, evaluating the conditions, the information and options available to policy makers at the time, and the likely consequences. Each chapter ends

with balanced, thoughtful conclusions. His final chapter looks at the war as a whole and articulates the problems, controversies, and differing perspectives over America's containment policy and "the lessons of Vietnam." Although R.B. Smith, George McT. Kahin, William Conrad Gibbons, George Herring, and David Anderson, among others, have produced outstanding studies of the origins of American involvement during this time frame, the fine narrative and careful, insightful assessments make this book the new standard source for both scholar and novice student alike. For all academic libraries.—*J. P. Dunn, Converse College*

OAB-2763   E183   95-7963 CIP
Foot, Rosemary. **The practice of power: US relations with China since 1949.** Oxford, 1995. 291p bibl index afp ISBN 0-19-827878-0, $35.00

Foot (St. Antony's College, Oxford) offers a valuable interpretive analysis of US-People's Republic of China relationships. Her work covers the years of hostility after the Communist victory in the late 1940s, the rapprochement of the 1970s, and the period since the full normalization of Sino-American ties in 1979. She treats Washington's partly successful effort to build, and its ultimate failure to sustain, a broad international and domestic consensus favoring the isolation or shunning of People's China. She interprets Washington's eventual change of policy in support of rapprochement and normalization as occasioned by a calculation and new understanding of limits on the power of the Beijing regime. Crucial to this new calculation were China's failures in the Great Leap Forward and the rift that arose between Beijing and Moscow. Foot also explains the impact that China's recent, more intense exposure to international norms has had on Chinese-American relations. Many works on this topic, written in the 1970s and the 1980s, focus on the triangular relationship among Washington, Moscow, and Beijing, the authors often presenting China as a "card" to be played by one or the other hostile superpower. Foot's work features instead both the broader context of the global system and the narrower setting of the US domestic political arena. Thus she substantially contributes to post-Soviet era theoretical understanding. Strongly recommended for courses in foreign policy, diplomatic history, and international relations, undergraduate and graduate.—*J. D. Gillespie, Presbyterian College*

OAB-2764   E183   93-48153 CIP
Garthoff, Raymond L. **The great transition: American-Soviet relations and the end of the Cold War.** Brookings, 1994. 834p index afp ISBN 0-8157-3060-8, $44.95; ISBN 0-8157-3059-4 pbk, $19.95

This is another major work by Garthoff, a massive, scholarly, and solidly documented volume built on a lifetime of experience and study, and also on his masterwork *Détente and Confrontation* (CH, Dec'85, rev. ed., 1994). He is a senior fellow at the Brookings Institution who has served as US Ambassador to Bulgaria and in other government positions. Garthoff has published numerous Brookings books and is eminently qualified to write what promises to be the authoritative record of US-Soviet relations in the 1980s, and of the convulsions that put an end to the Cold War. What characterized those relations was the search for a replacement for the détente of the 1970s. Neither the supporters nor the critics of Reagan's initial harsh rhetoric about the "evil empire" could have predicted the change in relations leading to a new détente as analyzed in Part 2. Besides changes in the leadership, from the three ailing leaders, Brezhnev, Andropov, and Chernenko, to the vigorous successor of a new generation, Mikhail Gorbachev, other aspects of Soviet domestic and foreign affairs made the period a time of flux. "Interactions in the Global Arena" is probably the most challenging part of the book. Few would argue with the assertion that the Reagan Doctrine—not only an attempt to move beyond "containment," but also "a forward strategy for world freedom aimed at bringing self-determination and human rights" to countries under communist oppression—triumphed in the Soviet Union and Eastern Europe. Excellent documentation. Graduate; faculty.—*R. M. Bigler, University of Nevada, Las Vegas*

OAB-2765   E840   92-8339 CIP
Gillon, Steven M. **The Democrats' dilemma: Walter F. Mondale**

Social & Behavioral Sciences

and the liberal legacy. Columbia, 1992. 468p bibl index afp ISBN 0-231-07630-4, $34.95

A stunning biography of Mondale and his times, Gillon's magisterial work provides an important glimpse of the changing position of the Democratic party in the US since the New Deal. In this respect, it deserves to be read alongside Thomas B. Edsall's *Chain Reaction* (CH, Feb'92) which offers a bottom-up perspective on the changing health of the Democratic party. During 20 years of exemplary government service, Mondale authored several significant pieces of legislation which contributed to the substantial reshaping of national policy and redefined the form and function of the vice presidency. His qualifications and ties to the New Deal coalition led historian William Chafe to conclude: "in another age and time Walter Mondale might have been a sure bet to win the presidency." Why he failed so decisively in his bid to do so, Gillon argues, owes much to the changing nature of the American electorate, shifts in modern campaigning, and the ebb and flow of issues confronting the country since the New Deal. Perhaps most importantly, Gillon considers the constant reformulation of class interest in the US to explain the frustrations of the Democrats in the 1980s. One of his conclusions is that growing frustration with the fragmenting individualism of current Republican policies will lead Americans to recognize the prophetic nature of Mondale's message. This remains to be demonstrated. Highly recommended for all libraries.—*D. R. Imig, University of Nevada, Las Vegas*

OAB-2766   UA23   94-29672 CIP
Haass, Richard N. **Intervention: the use of American military force in the post-Cold War world.** Carnegie Endowment, 1994. (Dist. by Brookings) 258p index ISBN 0-87003-056-6, $24.95; ISBN 0-87003-057-4 pbk, $12.95

Haass has written a timely volume on the use of US military force after the Cold War; it is sure to become one of the classics. With the demise of the USSR, foreign policy decision makers in the US must deal with a new environment that, though ultimately less dangerous, is more complex and unstable than the Cold War. Situations such as ethnic and humanitarian crises, weapons proliferation, or aggressive regional powers present new and difficult challenges. Foreign policy decision makers must decide whether the US should intervene in such conflicts, and if so, how this military intervention should be shaped. The core of Haass's work is the development of flexible guidelines to answer this set of questions. Haass outlines both the classical and current debates on the use of force, examines 12 recent case studies of US intervention, and then analyzes these interventions using his guidelines on whether and how to intervene. As a crucial contribution to the current debate on national security, this short volume will be debated in academic and policy circles alike. All levels.—*W. W. Newmann, Virginia Commonwealth University*

OAB-2767   JK468   96-8610 CIP
Johnson, Loch K. **Secret agencies: U.S. intelligence in a hostile world.** Yale, 1996. 262p index afp ISBN 0-300-06611-2, $30.00

Johnson blends the expertise of the practitioner-insider with that of the academic scholar and expert. He uses these skills and knowledge to produce a timely and well-balanced book examining the national security intelligence system of the US. He looks at such questions as the ethics of covert action and the important post-Cold War issue of economic intelligence and espionage. Like his previous books, *A Season of Inquiry* (CH, Sep'85) and *America's Secret Power* (CH, Jan'90) this one emphasizes oversight and intelligence accountability. It is accessible to general readers and is highly recommended as an undergraduate text or as the basis for an academic intelligence course. It is essential for all national security research collections and belongs on the shelf alongside the works of Jeffery Richelson, Roy Godson, Angelo Codevilla, and Adda Bozeman.—*P. A. Lupsha, formerly, University of New Mexico*

OAB-2768   E183   95-47303 CIP
Kagan, Robert. **A twilight struggle: American power and**

Nicaragua, 1977-1990. Free Press, 1996. 903p index ISBN 0-02-874057-2, $30.00

Kagan's ambitious book constitutes a frame-by-frame record and analysis of the tortuous relationship of the US government to the unfolding Sandinista revolution in Nicaragua, through the presidencies of Carter, Reagan, and Bush. The author, who served in the Reagan State Department, has had access to mountainous documentation and relevant personalities, allowing him to weave a careful narrative that integrates the twists and turns of political events in Central America and the US alike with judicious appraisals of the evolving policies of the many actors. Despite his own participation in this "twilight struggle," the author maintains a high standard of historical objectivity, something hitherto lacking in most writing on the Sandinista revolution. For this reason as well as for its comprehensiveness, this book will probably become and remain a classic work and source of reference on Nicaraguan history and US foreign policy during the era it covers. An essential volume for any college library.—*J. Stauder, University of Massachusetts-Dartmouth*

OAB-2769   E183   91-40615 CIP
Macdonald, Douglas J. **Adventures in chaos: American intervention for reform in the Third World.** Harvard, 1992. 361p index afp ISBN 0-674-00577-5, $39.95

Macdonald addresses the issue of US intervention by examining the use of American commitments as a bargaining tool to promote reform within client states. He focuses on the US decision-making process and bargaining behavior with its clients during crisis periods. He delineates between two types of bargaining: unrestricted use of commitments, which he terms bolstering, and a quid pro quo exchange that makes continued aid contingent on reform. Using case studies of China (1946-48), the Philippines (1950-53), and Vietnam (1954-1963) Macdonald analyzes the success of US bargaining. Although acknowledging that intervention for reform is problematic, Macdonald asserts that it is superior to simply bolstering clients that are strategically important yet unstable. He observes that US intervention may produce mixed results, even short-term failure, and recognizes the consequences of excessive commitments and trying to do too much. He concludes that American efforts have led to a "limited yet positive influence" in the Third World. This is a comprehensive look at three important case studies of the dynamics of patron-client relations, systemic influences, and domestic politics. It is extensively researched and documented and makes a valuable contribution to the literature on US policy toward the Third World. Advanced undergraduate through faculty.—*R. J. Griffiths, University of North Carolina at Greensboro*

OAB-2770   DS558   94-40088 CIP
McNamara, Robert S. **In retrospect: the tragedy and lessons of Vietnam,** by Robert S. McNamara with Brian VanDeMark. Times Books/Random House, 1995. 414p bibl index ISBN 0-8129-2523-8, $27.50

He was the best of "the Best and Brightest," and such a prolific spokesman for the Vietnam War that it was called McNamara's War. When he could no longer support what he had created and defended unswervingly, he left quietly and kept his silence for almost 30 years. Now that he has spoken—in this extraordinary book—he has reinflamed all the old passions and ignited a media extravaganza. The issue and controversy of Robert McNamara's mea culpa aside, this is one of the most important books on Vietnam in years. It recaptures for even the most learned specialist the time and the tone of the Vietnam era and personalities that allowed the war to happen. McNamara's perspective is one of the most important on the complex and enigmatic Lyndon Johnson and on the other principal military and civilian players. The workings of McNamara's own mind then and now are fascinating. He reemphasizes the interconnection between his abiding concern with the danger of nuclear war and Vietnam, and his list of the lessons of Vietnam are astute and wise. This is the most forthright memoir about culpability, error, and moral failure that this reviewer knows. Whatever one may think of him, this book should be read by everyone who grapples with the tragic experience that McNamara now says was, "wrong, terribly wrong." All levels.—*J. P. Dunn, Converse College*

OAB-2771　　　　UG743　　　　91-29650 CIP

Reiss, Edward. **The Strategic Defense Initiative.** Cambridge, 1992. 249p bibl index (Cambridge studies in international relations, 23) ISBN 0-521-41097-5, $49.95

Reiss (Interdisciplinary Human Studies, Univ. of Bradford) tests the theoretical literature on the dynamics of the arms race by using the Strategic Defense Initiative (SDI) as a case study. Sources include congressional hearings, interviews, trade journals, restricted briefing papers, and documents obtained under the Freedom of Information Act. Well-written and carefully documented, the work explores interactions of strategic, political, economic, technological, institutional, and cultural factors in the life of a weapons system. Reiss also effectively analyzes interest groups behind SDI along with the effectiveness of their lobbying, and illustrates how such a system develops a life of its own. Well reported is the shift in rationale for continued expenditures for the program after the demise of the former USSR, when it was refocused into Global Protection Against Limited Strikes (GPALS). Arguments on the SDI contribution to the eventual collapse of the USSR are well stated. A major strength of the book is its objectivity: it does not argue for or against SDI but tells the story, leaving the reader to draw conclusions on the merits of the system and particularly on the dynamics of arms control in the broadest sense. This valuable work must be read by those responsible for the conception, evolution, and funding of major weapons systems in the future. Advanced undergraduate; graduate; faculty.—*D. F. Bletz, Wilson College*

OAB-2772　　　　E183　　　　93-33592 CIP

Sato, Ryuzo. **The chrysanthemum and the eagle: the future of U.S.-Japan relations.** New York University, 1994. 221p bibl index afp ISBN 0-8147-7971-9, $24.95

The Chrysanthemum and the Eagle is an exceptionally clear and penetrating analysis of contemporary Japanese-American relations. The author is a professor of economics and director of the Center for Japan-US Business and Economics Studies at New York University. Sato has lived in both the US and Japan for the past 30 years and understands both societies well. He begins the book by reviewing the recent debate between Japan-bashers or "revisionists" and Japan-supporters called the "chrysanthemum club." Sato proceeds with an insightful analysis of political, economic, and sociocultural differences between America and Japan which gets to the heart of recent antagonisms between these two countries. Sato concludes the book by considering the prospect of "Pax Japonica," which he regards as a "dangerous seduction, an unattainable dream, an illusion." As for Japan's future, he believes that Japan must become more altruistic internationally—especially regarding the environment—and more consumer-oriented domestically while reforming its notorious money politics. This book will be very instructive for academics, policy makers, and the general public on both sides of the Pacific. All levels.—*R. G. Bush, Gustavus Adolphus College*

OAB-2773　　　　KF5060　　　　93-15840 CIP

The U.S. Constitution and the power to go to war: historical and current perspectives, ed. by Gary M. Stern and Morton H. Halperin. Greenwood, 1994. 199p bibl index afp (Contributions in military studies, 150) ISBN 0-313-28958-1, $55.00

This very valuable book carefully and broadly examines the war powers of the US government from revolutionary times to the present. The editors and contributing authors all are well-respected authorities clearly competent in their areas of specialty. After a penetrating historical survey of war powers and the use of force, the book analyzes various constraints, including the Constitution, statutory constraints (War Powers Resolution), treaty constraints (UN Charter), international law, and the judiciary. "Covert" paramilitary action is examined also, and emergency war powers are discussed. Each chapter is well written and thoroughly documented, and the contributors take pains to show the present and future relevance of their analyses. Stressing the "virtue of process as a means of determining 'truth' for a democratic society," the editors argue that the president and Congress should establish a procedure "whereby they can work together to discuss, formulate, and enact an appropriate autho-

rizing resolution prior to the actual engagement of ... forces, all the while keeping the public informed of their intentions." This "will make it more difficult for the nation to go to war—a difficulty that the Framers intended." This first-rate book is highly recommended.—*R. L. Wendzel, United States Air War College*

THE WORLD

OAB-2774　　　　DS63　　　　96-46169 CIP

Abi-Aad, Naji. **Instability and conflict in the Middle East: people, petroleum and security threats,** by Naji Abi-Aad and Michel Grenon. Macmillan (UK)/St. Martin's, 1997. 224p bibl index ISBN 0-312-17254-0, $65.00

Remarkable and authoritative, this study focuses on instability and conflict in the Middle East. The authors argue that final peace between the Arabs and Israel will not eliminate many of the factors of instability and sources of conflict in the region. These include the autocratic nature of regimes, the struggle for power, interstate ideological cleavages, military antagonisms and race, ambition and structure of armed forces, sectarian minorities and religious rivalry, ethnic heterogeneity and minorities, border disputes, disparity in economic development, social impacts of economic constraints, divergence in petroleum policies, struggles over water, demographic explosion, disparity in population growth, and demographic troubles caused by foreign labor migration, internal flight, and flows of refugees. The book attempts to evaluate the nature and magnitude of each potential factor of conflict and dispute. Abi-Aad and Grenon cautiously conclude that it would be quite illusory to talk of stability of the Middle East if the legitimate national aspirations and economic development imperatives of its countries are disregarded. Upper-division undergraduates and above.—*S. Ayubi, Rutgers University*

OAB-2775　　　　DJK51　　　　92-24761 CIP

Bugajski, Janusz. **Nations in turmoil: conflict and cooperation in Eastern Europe.** Westview, 1993. 260p index afp ISBN 0-8133-1626-X sc, $47.50

Bugajski, an East European studies specialist, gives us an almost encyclopedic review of international tensions in Eastern Europe, complete with historical background, ethnic complexities, and boundary quarrels. The work is organized around generally regional themes: disputes between the ex-Soviet republics and the bordering East European states (e.g., Poland versus Lithuania): disputes among the Central European states (e.g., Poland versus Germany); both the internal and the international dimensions of the Yugoslav crisis (the breakaway republics and border/ethnic interests of neighbors); and other Balkan disputes (e.g., Hungary versus Romania). He concludes with two chapters offering the hope of regional cooperation and European integration. Bugajski covers everything through 1991 and therefore does not include the horror of Bosnia and the breakup of Czechoslovakia and with them the heightened regional tensions now bristling from Slovakia south, although he provides the historical background to all this. If anything, reality has been worse than Bugajski's somber appraisals. Regional specialists will find this solid work an indispensable handbook. One wishes for an updated edition at a lower price for course adoption. Advanced undergraduate through professional.—*M. G. Roskin, U.S. Army War College*

OAB-2776　　　　JX1974　　　　92-13995 CIP

Bunn, George. **Arms control by committee: managing negotiations with the Russians.** Stanford, 1992. 349p bibl index afp ISBN 0-8047-2039-8, $39.50

Bunn (former general counsel for the Arms Control and Disarmament Agency) has created a prodigious study of the US arms-control process based on accounts of the Partial Test Ban, the Non-Proliferation Treaty, the ABM Treaty and SALT I Interim Agreement, and the INF Treaty, with observations on others. Bunn methodically and nearly exhaustively consulted his own information, archival sources, unpublished records, and the published academic/policy literature on the US side to document the course of these negotiations, to argue the case for varying approaches to negotiations with the Soviets when agreement is genuinely desired, and to explore inferences about the process—how agreement generally is reached. A parallel study from the Soviet side, especially as more Soviet archival material becomes available, would complete the theoretical argument. Particularly valuable are the chapters generalizing from the negotiations studied; they are insightful and argued with precision, clarity, and an appreciation for the logic of the social sciences. A catholic bibliography. Helpful for policymakers, since the erstwhile Soviet arsenal remains. An excellent text or resource for graduate and undergraduate students, including law students, studying US foreign policy or arms control and negotiation. Also accessible and user-friendly to the adult reader, even relatively youthful ones. Buy this extraordinary scholarly book.—*T. C. Smith, Mankato State University*

OAB-2777   F1414   92-36213 CIP
Castañeda, Jorge G. **Utopia unarmed: the Latin American left after the Cold War.** Knopf, 1993. 498p index ISBN 0-394-58259-4, $27.50

This is an important and good book. It is easy to understand but also provides valuable information to the expert. It is authoritative and seminal in explaining the collapse of the powerful leftist forces in all of Latin America. Author Castañeda, a Mexican professor with considerable academic activities in the US, holds a prestigious position in Mexico. He has personal involvement with leftist activities in Latin America, and his profuse knowledge is combined with meticulous and revealing research. His opinions and conclusions are impartial, commanding, and enlightening. He examines the whole scope of the Latin American left in this century with emphasis on its weaknesses and mistakes. Attention is given to the often unreasonable anti US policies. Castañeda clearly recognizes the conditions that produced such a powerful and successful left. He warns that these conditions still exist and have become worse since the collapse of world communism. A new and more rational left can be expected. This book is a must for anyone interested in Latin America. All levels.—*C. W. Arnade, University of South Florida*

OAB-2778   JX1582   96-3882 CIP
Clapham, Christopher. **Africa and the international system: the politics of state survival.** Cambridge, 1996. 340p bibl index (Cambridge studies in international relations, 50) ISBN 0-521-57207-X, $59.95; ISBN 0-521-57668-7 pbk, $19.95

Clapham (Univ. of Lancaster) has published widely on African politics and international relations. The present work, both a monograph and a textbook, coherently analyzes the nature of politics within and between African states since independence. African states are new and artificial; they are poor, weak, and very vulnerable; and political survival is an ever present challenge. Indeed, such conditions make African politics and external relations, featuring such peculiarities as "monopoly states" and "shadow states," rather different from conventional modes and models. Clapham approaches politics "from below," with domestic exigencies driving foreign policy. Although refreshing and at times bold, *Africa*'s preoccupation with power, political struggles, and survival strategies places it as securely within the mainstreams of political realism and revisionist thinking about African international relations as *Africa in the New International Order: Rethinking State Sovereignty and Regional Security*, ed. by Edmond J. Keller and Donald Rothchild (1996). Buttressed by 35 pages of endnotes and a 21-page bibliography, Clapham's volume is solid, sweeping, and thoughtful. Strongly recommended for larger university libraries and other collections specializing in African or Third World studies, comparative politics, and international affairs.—*J. P. Smaldone, University of Maryland University College*

OAB-2779   HV5840   95-52824 CIP
Clawson, Patrick L. **The Andean cocaine industry,** by Patrick L.

Clawson and Rensselaer W. Lee. St. Martin's, 1996. 276p bibl index ISBN 0-312-12400-7, $35.00

Lee, perhaps the nation's foremost scholar on international drug trafficking and author of *The White Labyrinth* (CH, Jul'90), a classic in the field, has done it again. In this new book, he is assisted by Clawson, a young bean counter (National Defense Univ.), who adds a new dimension to the effort. Surpassing his earlier work, Lee brings readers up to date on the "war on drugs" and adds a transnational organized crime dimension, discussing such critical issues as Colombian money-laundering with the Italian Mafia. In this US presidential election year, candidates and their advisors should read this book before making statements concerning drug policy if their pronouncements are to fit Latin American realities. Well-written and edited, this book will be essential for courses in Latin American politics, nontraditional courses in international relations, and college and university libraries. All levels.—*P. A. Lupsha, formerly, University of New Mexico*

OAB-2780   F2183   94-24352 CIP
Grugel, Jean. **Politics and development in the Caribbean Basin: Central America and the Caribbean in the new world order.** Indiana, 1995. 270p bibl index ISBN 0-253-32683-4, $39.95; ISBN 0-253-20954-4 pbk, $16.95

Grugel's excellent comparative survey of the political economy of the Caribbean Basin (defined as Central America and the insular Caribbean) from the 1880s to the 1990s argues that underdevelopment in the region results from the triple effects of the colonial legacy, internal political factors, and marginalization in the international capitalist system. Evidence is presented (with detailed case studies from the decade of the 1980s) confirming that in nations with capitalist or socialist development models, growth has been partial, unstable, or skewed. Radical attempts at transformation in Cuba, Nicaragua, and Grenada are highlighted, identifying severe pressures from the US and limited internal democracy as significant problems, while limited successes in health, education, and redistribution are praised. Grugel contends that structural adjustment programs have slowed macroeconomic decline but exacerbated the problems of poverty in the region, threatening the very democracy external donors profess to seek. For Grugel, sustainable development must include both a redistribution of internal political power and changes in the international economy. An invaluable general reader for undergraduates and graduate students, this book's broad coverage makes it a valuable addition to the existing literature on the Caribbean Basin.—*C. J. Edie, University of Massachusetts at Amherst*

OAB-2781   DK859   94-30960 CIP
Haghayeghi, Mehrdad. **Islam and politics in Central Asia.** St. Martin's, 1995. 264p bibl index ISBN 0-312-09622-4, $45.00

Haghayeghi's cogently argued, balanced, and well-researched book treats a strategically important region of the world just beginning to emerge from decades of Soviet domination. The book focuses on the development of Islam in Central Asia and its influence in shaping political trends in the region. The author places the role played by Islam in the context of the historical development of the region and the countervailing forces of secularism nurtured under Soviet rule. Historically, Islam has been a vital part of the lives of the peoples of Central Asia. However, the overall Islamic orientation of Central Asia has so far been nonmilitant. The author examines both historical and current sociopolitical factors that have shaped the generally moderate Islamic disposition among the Central Asian states. He also analyzes the interplay of Islamic and ethnic relations and its impact on political developments in the region. The author has done a superb job of blending historical facts and solid political analysis into a very readable book. Highly recommended for advanced undergraduate and graduate courses and scholars of Central Asia and the former Soviet Union.—*N. Entessar, Spring Hill College*

OAB-2782   95-61524 Orig
Halliday, Fred. **Islam and the myth of confrontation: religion and**

politics in the Middle East. I.B. Tauris, 1996 (c1995). 255p index ISBN 1-86064-004-4, $55.00; ISBN 1-85043-959-1 pbk, $19.95

Halliday, a distinguished British scholar of the Arab world and author of several important books on the area (including *Revolution and Foreign Policy*, CH, Oct'90, on South Yemen, and *Arabia without Sultans*, CH, Dec'75), here examines the current tendency to view with alarm the recent "Islamic resurgence" in the Middle East, a vogue fueled as much by the Iranian revolution and Islamist activity in a number of Arab countries, as by a literature that portrays it as a threat to the West and its interests. This "myth of confrontation," he argues, is a product both of a failure in the West to understand and appreciate the complex cultural and political forces at work in the region, and of the effort of Middle Eastern leaders and intellectuals to exaggerate the importance and consequences of those same forces. Since he exposes the underlying self-interest and power-seeking on both sides, his book, he suggests, should "be equally unwelcome by both groups of people." John Esposito's *The Islamic Threat: Myth or Reality?* (CH, Mar'93) deals with the same theme and comes to much the same conclusions, but lacks the sophistication of Halliday's contrapuntal argument. Highly recommended to all audiences.—*V. T. Le Vine, Washington University*

OAB-2783   DU17   95-14906 CIP
Henningham, Stephen. **The Pacific island states: security and sovereignty in the post-Cold War world.** St. Martin's/Macmillan, 1995. 174p bibl index ISBN 0-312-12513-5, $59.95

Henningham (Australian National Univ.) offers the first examination by a single author of security concerns of the 14 Pacific island nations in the post-Cold War era. He defines "security" broadly to include environmental and economic factors and focuses on trends and issues of the past decade and prospects for the next. His analysis is logical and insightful, drawing on his diplomatic experience in the region as well as his academic research. He concludes that direct military threats to the island states from outside or within the region are unlikely to increase, but that environmental, economic, and other nonmilitary challenges may continue to confront the leaders of these new nations. More current than *The Island States of the Pacific and Indian Oceans*, ed. by R. T. Shand (Canberra, 1980) and broader than Ronni Alexander's *Putting the Earth First: Alternatives to Nuclear Security in the Pacific Island States* (1994), this work provides a valuable introduction to a new area of the world and an understanding of its emerging role in international affairs. Highly recommended to all academic and large public libraries.—*J. A. Rhodes, Luther College*

OAB-2784   JN15   92-1609 CIP
Holland, Martin. **European community integration.** St. Martin's, 1993. 253p index ISBN 0-312-08571-0, $45.00

The promise of the European Community (EC) has spawned an incredible volume of literature. Most obvious to the specialist, this literature provides overkill on the topics of structure, function, and process. It is all too rare to find a study that wrestles with the more elusive "concept" of Europe and the dream of a united Europe that lies behind the EC. Holland's new addition to the literature in some ways will be presumed by specialists to be just another of the many texts which explores the EC. Unfortunately, for that reason it will probably be ignored by many who should read it. Holland—perhaps all too subtly—effectively draws attention away from the over analyzed trivia of the EC and toward a meaningful discussion of the concept of Europe. As such, the book is in a class by itself. It must be read to better appreciate the nature of the current challenges facing the EC's 12 members as they contemplate the formal ratification of the Maastricht treaty and brace for the effect of the vast territorial and ideological transformations afflicting Europe. Read Holland before you read any other book on the EC. Advanced undergraduate through faculty.—*J. D. Robertson, Texas A & M University*

OAB-2785   UA770   94-8216 CIP
Holloway, David. **Stalin and the bomb: the Soviet Union and**

atomic energy, 1939-1956. Yale, 1994. 464p index ISBN 0-300-06056-4, $30.00

Holloway is professor of political science and codirector of Stanford University's Center for International Security and Arms Control. In this path-breaking book he has mined Soviet and Russian sources intensively, including documents only recently made available. His findings offer new information about the origins of the Soviet atomic bomb and, of particular importance, insights about the impact of atomic weapons on Soviet relations with the West. Thus, Holloway rebuts the revisionist thesis that the American bomb triggered the Cold War by showing that Stalin had decided on an aggressive course well before he knew about it. He shows that the Soviet test of an American-type plutonium bomb was made possible with the help of information provided by spies in the US, but that without the aid of espionage, Soviet science would have produced a uranium bomb of its own design, probably in 1951. He refutes the contention of Pavel Sudoplatov in *Special Tasks* (CH, Jan'95) that J. Robert Openheimer and Enrico Fermi were Soviet agents. This book is invaluable for an understanding of Soviet science under Stalin, the early development of atomic weapons, and the origins of the Cold War. All levels.—*J. L. Nogee, University of Houston*

OAB-2786   E183   92-42278 CIP
Horowitz, Irving Louis. **The conscience of worms and the cowardice of lions: Cuban politics and culture in an American context.** Transaction, 1993. 80p ISBN 1-56000-099-6, $24.95

For more than three decades, Horowitz has been a voice of sanity and reason amid the whirlpool of ideological and partisan controversy over the Cuban Revolution. His authoritative collection, *Cuban Communism*, now in its seventh edition (1989), remains an indispensable resource for students and scholars alike. In the 1992 Emilio Bacardi Lectures at the University of Miami's North-South Center, reproduced here, he presents a brilliantly diverse distillation of his views. Horowitz elaborates the systemic constraints that suffocate the US's foreign policy-making process, as translated into the Cuban experience. He skewers North American analysts for their failure to observe proper tenets of social science research. Indeed, Horowitz elaborates upon a critical underlying theme which demands a restoration of nonideological professionalism to social inquiry. The Bacardi Lectures find Horowitz at his best on a host of topics in addition to strictly Cuban affairs. His prose is equally pungent and pointed; he should be assured of reaching the wide and diverse audience which this statement richly deserves. General; undergraduate; graduate; faculty.—*J. D. Martz, Pennsylvania State University, University Park Campus*

OAB-2787   DS917   93-39865 MARC
Korea and the world: beyond the Cold War, ed. by Young Whan Kihl. Westview, 1994. 381p bibl index afp ISBN 0-8133-1928-5, $64.00; ISBN 0-8133-1929-3 pbk, $21.95

This collection of articles on international domestic aspects of the Korean peninsula in the post-Cold War era was written by top-notch Korean specialists who are mostly members of the Research Committee on Korean Reunification, the most esteemed study group on contemporary Korean affairs in the US. Essays deal with the global context of the Korean question, the four major powers (the US, Russia, China, and Japan) and their relations with North and South Korea, inter-Korean relations involving reunification, military, economic, and nuclear issues, and finally future prospects on peace and stability on the Korean peninsula. Kihl deserves high commendation for his excellent editorial job. He has successfully woven essays on diverse topics into a coherent body, making this the most comprehensive and encyclopedic work on domestic and foreign policy of North and South Korea in recent years. It is a timely contribution to the understanding of the last flashpoint of the Cold War era. Though uneven in quality and often descriptive in analysis, chapters in the volume are empirically rich and normatively neutral, especially in their positions on North and South Korea. Essential reading for students and policy makers of contemporary Korea. An ideal textbook for courses on Korean and East Asian politics. Undergraduate through faculty.—*C. Moon, University of Kentucky*

OAB-2788   DS586   95-5364 CIP
Marks, Thomas A. **Maoist insurgency since Vietnam.** F. Cass, 1996. 303p index afp ISBN 0-7146-4606-7, $39.50

For students of political violence this book is one of the most important in a long time. It is essential reading for anyone concerned with low intensity conflict, insurgency, or revolution. Marks covers in detail four failed Maoist insurgencies: Thailand, Philippines (1968-93), Sri Lanka, and Sendero Luminoso in Peru. Although the latter is incomplete (victim of a publishing deadline), Marks's detailed studies are vital reading for anyone concerned with the subject. Perhaps his most important contribution is the clarification of the concepts of political terrorism versus insurgency terror. This has important implications for events in Israel today, since it focuses on both what is wrong conceptually in Israeli policy, and how that policy was unintentionally misdirected by US notions of counterinsurgency warfare. Highly recommended for any library supporting study of any of these issues.—*P. A. Lupsha, formerly, University of New Mexico*

OAB-2789   UA835   97-6385 CIP
Nathan, Andrew J. **The great wall and the empty fortress: China's search for security,** by Andrew J. Nathan and Robert S. Ross. W.W. Norton, 1997. 268p index ISBN 0-393-04076-3, $27.50

Nathan and Ross (well-known China experts, Columbia and Harvard) have produced an excellent survey of Chinese foreign policy since 1949. Their principal concern is China's quest for security in a changing world, which they examine from straightforward neorealist and national interest perspectives. After introductory chapters on China's place in the world and its complex legacies, the authors devote successive chapters to Beijing's relations with Russia, the US, Japan and the Koreas, South and Southeast Asia, the policy-making process, military issues, foreign economic relations, human rights, territorial issues, and Taiwan, plus a brief conclusion. The balanced assessments of China's security dilemmas and prospects, and their implications for US policy and world order, are good antidotes to R. Bernstein and R.H. Munro's *The Coming Conflict with China* (1997). Nathan and Ross conclude: "China's vulnerability is a fact ... Understanding its causes and consequences should help Western policy makers accommodate China when they should, persuade China when they can, and resist China when they must." This interesting, readable volume complements John R. Faust and Judith F. Kornberg's *China in World Politics* (CH, Oct'95) and Quancheng Zhao's *Interpreting Chinese Foreign Policy* (1996). Highly recommended for college libraries, larger public libraries, and other collections in international relations or Asian studies.—*J. P. Smaldone, University of Maryland University College*

OAB-2790   JN30   95-26282 CIP
Newman, Michael. **Democracy, sovereignty and the European Union.** St. Martin's, 1996. 236p bibl index ISBN 0-312-15860-2, $49.95; ISBN 0-312-15861-0 pbk, $18.95

Several comprehensive texts deal with every aspect of the process of integration in Europe, yet this book, by the director of the European Research Centre (Univ. of North London), stands virtually alone in presenting these topics entirely from the perspective of questions about democracy and sovereignty. After an excellent chapter on concepts and theories, the book provides a well-informed and comprehensive discussion of the European Union as a policy-making system, its economic structure and expanding, unique model of social policy; and the political and economic implications of regional subdivisions within the Union. Particularly noteworthy is the lucid and insightful discussion of the most critical aspects of EU as a would-be sovereign and democratic state: the concept of citizenship and its legal and practical consequences within the emerging entity, the evolution of the European Parliament as a representative body, the complex and controversial role of the European Commission, and the relationship between national parliaments and European institutions. Steering clear of the often polemical tone of many British publications on the presumed democratic deficiencies of European institutions and written in an accessible style, Newman's book weaves a thorough and balanced picture of the EU's

democratic potential as well as its limitations. An extensive and up-to-date bibliography as well as numerous and helpful notes add to the value of this text for specialists and undergraduate and graduate students.—*P. Vannicelli, University of Massachusetts at Boston*

OAB-2791   DK859   95-30153 CIP
Olcott, Martha Brill. **Central Asia's new states: independence, foreign policy, and regional security.** United States Institute of Peace, 1996. 202p index afp ISBN 1-878379-51-8 pbk, $19.95

This is the best monograph on the five new republics of Central Asia to appear since Graham E. Fuller's *Central Asia: The New Geopolitics* (Rand report R-4219-USDP, 1992). Olcott's expertise is evident throughout the book (trained in Soviet studies, she specialized in the history and politics of Central Asia). She focuses on Kazakhstan, Uzbekistan, and Kirghizia, discussing Tajikistan in the chapter on Uzbekistan to demonstrate the designs of Tashkent on that country, especially its northern salient. This emphasizes one of the book's main themes, the irredentist fears and distrust all five republics feel toward each other and toward Russia. Olcott stresses that such fears, plus their own dictatorial regimes, do not make promising the futures of the economically weak, technologically and capital dependent, politically fragmented, socioculturally bifurcated, and ethnically divided Central Asian republics. Russia continues to dominate their economies (especially oil and natural gas), armed forces, and intelligence apparatuses. But Olcott questions whether Russia will again become as involved in the affairs of the republics as during the Soviet period, doubting that Russia wants to incur the direct welfare, environmental, and water shortage costs. Olcott is pessimistic about the future territorial and political viability of the republics; they can expect little aid from the US or Europe, both of whom support Russian control of its "near and abroad." The republics' Muslim neighbors (e.g., Iran and Turkey) are bogged down with their own wars, development, and foreign policies. This integrated, cogently argued, and well-written book will be ideal for courses on the Middle East, Russia, or Islamic or international studies. Academic readers.—*R. W. Olson, University of Kentucky*

OAB-2792   DS63   92-23947 CIP
Parker, Richard B. **The politics of miscalculation in the Middle East.** Indiana, 1993. 273p bibl index afp ISBN 0-253-34298-8, $45.00; ISBN 0-253-20781-9 pbk, $17.95

Parker assesses what he perceives to be the foreign policy miscalculations made by the parties involved in the 1967 June war, the war of attrition in 1969-70 between Egypt and Israel, and the 1982 war between the Palestinians and Israel. The US played a crucial role in all three wars. It is important to note that Parker defines miscalculation broadly as "a policy decision which goes awry because those making it did not foresee properly what the results would be." According to Parker, in the 1967 war the Egyptian leaders miscalculated Egypt's capacity to wage effective war against Israel and Israel's ability to strike back. In the war of attrition between Egypt and Israel in 1969-70, Israel and the US miscalculated the extent to which the Soviet Union would come to the aid of Egypt after punishing deep penetration air strikes by Israel. This and other miscalculations resulted in a political victory for Egypt. In the 1982 war, Israel and the US misjudged their ability to dictate via treaty a normalization of relations between Israel and Lebanon and their power to compel Syria to accept it. This is the best book to deal with the diplomatic history of these three wars. It is written in clear, lucid, and undiplomatic language. This is a great achievement. Parker's own participation in the events he describes and his sober and evenhanded analysis make his arguments convincing. Advanced undergraduate through faculty.—*R. W. Olson, University of Kentucky*

OAB-2793   JC599   95-7834 CIP
Peleg, Ilan. **Human rights in the West Bank and Gaza: legacy and politics.** Syracuse, 1995. 191p bibl index afp ISBN 0-8156-2682-7, $34.95

Peleg argues that the shift in the nature of the core Middle East conflict from one of interstate (Arab-Israeli) confrontation to intercommunal (Israeli-

Palestinian) strife requires a new conceptual framework. Instead of notions of balance of power, deterrence, etc., Peleg contends that international law (e.g., the Fourth Geneva Convention) and international human rights regulations (e.g., the UN Universal Declaration of Human Rights) should be the reference points for analysis and conflict resolution. The majority of the book examines Israeli behavior in the Occupied Territories, concluding that Israel's practices constitute gross violations of international law and regulations, are unlikely to improve, and that only through a political solution can the situation be improved. After analyzing all the possible alternative political settlements, Peleg determines that the sole reasonable and just outcome would be a two-state solution that would limit Israeli sovereignty to its pre-1967 borders and give Palestine sovereignty over the West Bank and Gaza. The book builds on and extends Esther R. Cohen's *Human Rights in the Israeli-Occupied Territories, 1967-1982* (Manchester, 1985), but like Cohen, Peleg leaves one with a sense that the severity of the human rights abuses has been understated. Nevertheless, this is an excellent book and should be read by everyone concerned with the Israeli-Palestinian conflict.—*C. A. Rubenberg, Florida International University*

OAB-2794　　　　　DS119　　　　　93-18804 CIP
Quandt, William B. **Peace process: American diplomacy and the Arab-Israeli conflict since 1967.** Brookings/California, 1993. 612p bibl index afp ISBN 0-520-08388-1, $38.95; ISBN 0-520-08390-3 pbk, $15.95

This is the first comprehensive book to deal with the scope of the Middle East peace process from 1967 to the present. Not a history of the wars of the region, the volume concentrates on the actual negotiations and political processes dealing with ending the conflict. Written principally from an American point of view, the text deals with the actions of a succession of American presidential adminstrations from Johnson to Bush with a concluding chapter pointing out the lessons of the previous quarter century and the challenges to the Clinton presidency. Quandt, a recognized expert on the region, brings not only new scholarly research into his book, but his personal experiences, having served with the National Security Council staff under the Carter and Nixon administrations. The chapters are well annotated with 80 pages of detailed reference notes and is suitable as a secondary text for Middle Eastern studies. Fifteen appendixes include complete renditions of important documents relating to the diplomatic history of peace negotiations, making the book a valuable resource for readings. A selected bibliography is also included. For any library with a section on diplomatic history or Middle Eastern studies. General through faculty.—*D.S. Inbody, United States Naval Academy*

OAB-2795　　　　　DS119　　　　　93-31651 CIP
Rubin, Barry. **Revolution until victory?: the politics and history of the PLO.** Harvard, 1994. 271p bibl index afp ISBN 0-674-76803-5, $24.95

Since 1967, the burning question of the Arab-Israel conflict has been, will the Arabs accept the Jewish state's existence? The September 13th accord between Israel and the Palestine Liberation Organization (PLO) makes this issue all the more pressing. Rubin's timely *Revolution Until Victory?* a history of the PLO, provides an excellent guide to PLO intentions. In compact and readable form, he reliably reviews three decades' worth of PLO complexities. More than that, he breaks new ground by getting behind the PLO's external face—the personality of Yasir Arafat or the record of terror—and concentrating instead on its internal dynamics. Calling the PLO's structure "a central factor in shaping its destiny," Rubin explains its systemic qualities. This approach allows him to make sense of much that had hitherto been mysterious, including the PLO's pattern of inconsistency, extremism, and self-defeat. It also permits him to hint at implications about its future course. In short, if you are prepared to read one study about the elusive Palestine Liberation Organization, *Revolution Until Victory?* is the place to go.—*D. Pipes, Foreign Policy Research Institute*

OAB-2796　　　　　DS62　　　　　93-31015 CIP
Shlaim, Avi. **War and peace in the Middle East: a critique of American policy.** Viking//Whittle, 1994. 147p ISBN 0-670-85330-5, $17.50

Shlaim, born in Iraq, raised in Israel, and currently a reader at Oxford has written a book, uncommonly concise, eminently readable, outstandingly fair, and unusually straightforward about the Middle East. The book addresses the Arab-Israeli conflict and the general complexity of the region's politics by illustrating the causes of Middle-Eastern instability. The Post-Ottoman Syndrome, conflicting promises, division of territories, creation of states and imposition of leaders by imperial powers of Europe explain a great deal which may have appeared perplexing if not irrational. Despite the demise of European imperialism, the imperial designs remain intact. "What the new world order amounts to is the old order minus the Soviet Union." The author gives credit to President Bush and Secretary of State Jim Baker whose evenhanded policy facilitated the Israeli-Palestinian peace process. This book, although short, easy to read, and easy to understand, can effectively lift the veil of mystery for many a student and general reader. Recommended for all US legislators, undergraduate and graduate students, and anyone else interested in the Middle East.—*F. L. Mokhtari, Norwich University*

OAB-2797　　　　　DD290　　　　　92-17119 CIP
Szabo, Stephen F. **The diplomacy of German unification.** St. Martin's, 1992. 162p index ISBN 0-312-08057-3, $35.00

Szabo provides a superb account of the international political maneuvering that transformed Europe in 1990. While noting that separate, bilateral talks between the two German states helped facilitate unification, the author focuses on the larger diplomatic stage—negotiations involving, primarily, the Federal Republic, the US, and the Soviet Union. These talks aimed to defuse a wide range of potential problems that could have arisen after the collapse of the Berlin Wall, ultimately ensuring that a united Germany did not heighten the insecurity of neighboring states. Szabo identifies the key actors and their objectives, an analysis based in large part on his own interviews with them. He then traces four phases of diplomacy from late 1989 through the final, formal ceremonies in late 1990 that put a seal on unification. Readers will be struck by the degree to which participants in the process from Washington to Moscow continually modified and adjusted their expectations. The Appendix contains a copy of the treaty settling "the German question." This well-written, readable, concise account is recommended for all libraries.—*C. Clemens, College of William and Mary*

OAB-2798　　　　　DS525　　　　　92-44707 CIP
Von der Mehden, Fred R. **Two worlds of Islam: interaction between Southeast Asia and the Middle East.** University Press of Florida, 1993. 128p bibl index afp ISBN 0-8130-1208-2, $22.95; ISBN 0-8130-1209-0 pbk, $12.95

This well-organized and handsomely produced work fulfills a major gap in the literature and provides a unique contribution to scholarship regarding the changing patterns of interaction between the Muslim worlds of the Middle East and Southeast Asia. In the economic sphere, the major proposition tested is whether there is a relationship between the common Islamic background of the two regions and aid, investment, and trade. In terms of political interaction, the crucial issues raised include the extent of involvement of both regions in the other's foreign and domestic problems. The intellectual interaction that has developed between the two regions is also analyzed. Von der Mehden concludes that in the economic sphere there is limited correlation between the common religious affinity of the two Muslim regions and economic interaction. Politically, these regions remain concentrated on political problems in their own areas, and both Islamic international organizations and activities in the other region are secondary. The author contends that the considerable increase in Islamic intellectual interaction between the two regions will continue. However, he also predicts that Southeast Asian governments will attempt to contain what they perceive to be destabilizing religious ideas from the Middle East. This is a work of penetrating scholarship as Von der Mehden is among the few social scientists with an intimate knowledge of the area. Advanced undergraduate through faculty.—*S. Ayubi, Bowdoin College*

OAB-2799   JC599   95-30107 CIP
Welch, Claude E. **Protecting human rights in Africa: roles and strategies of non-governmental organizations.** Pennsylvania, 1995. 356p bibl index afp ISBN 0-8122-3330-1, $39.95

Although Africa seems an unpromising venue for the study of human rights protection, Welch (SUNY at Buffalo) masterfully shows areas of progress and grounds for guarded optimism in an impressive description of the work of a number of different kinds of human rights organizations, largely in Nigeria, Senegal, Namibia, and Ethiopia. Welch has written about African politics for almost three decades, including two books and six articles on human rights prior to the present volume. *Protecting Human Rights* is unusual in a number of respects. Welch wears his political science learning lightly in summarizing and connecting the analytical contexts (e.g., society, international law, donor-state relations) he uses to consider the strategies of human rights organizations in education, in empowerment and group rights, in enforcement by reports and complaints, and in legal aid. This enables him to relate his observations and commentary about Africa to the Third World and to global issues. As a result, his book will interest students of international relations, democratization processes, and development issues. But Welch also attempts to bridge the gap between political study and political practice. Focusing on four countries, he concentrates on illustrative cases of human rights activism (a women's rights group in Nigeria, an ethnic rights group in Ethiopia, a legal assistance center in Namibia, and so on), deftly combining the description of activities with narratives. The tales often center on extraordinary leaders (including, poignantly, the recently executed Ken Saro-Wiwa). Within the text is another popular-serious book, a "profiles in courage" of African human rights activists of the 1990s. Welch enlivens the text by drawing on his past and most recent personal involvement in human rights, culminating in a year of research in Europe and Africa, 1993-94. Probably no single volume offers similar scope yet concreteness (but compare Jack Donnelly, *Universal Human Rights in Theory and Practice*, CH, Mar'90; David Forsythe, *The Internationalization of Human Rights*, CH, Dec'91; Rhoda Howard, *Human Rights in Commonwealth Africa*, CH, Jan'87). Welch recognizes that although human rights organizations will not transform Africa, they can ameliorate problems of democracy and development in important ways, and he offers observers seven specific measures of achievement. Most of these reflect increased possibilities of publicity, reporting, and communication; the toughest to apply is the emergence of a "human rights culture." Welch offers hope for a growing "consciousness" of human rights in African states in the expansion of the activities he describes. He concludes by examining his hypotheses about the effectiveness of African human rights organizations, based on the strength of "financial resources, popular support, societal diversity and political space." The conclusions are sober and realistic, yet optimistic and possible. Practitioners and observers will benefit from the book.—*H. Glickman, Haverford College*

OAB-2800   Can. CIP
Woods, Lawrence T. **Asia-Pacific diplomacy: nongovernmental organizations and international relations.** UBC Press, University of British Columbia, 6344 Memorial Rd., Vancouver, BC V6T 1Z2, Canada, 1993. 257p bibl index afp (Canada and international relations, 7) ISBN 0-7748-0440-8, $65.00

This is a thorough and stimulating analysis of transnational foundations of Asia-Pacific regionalism. Departing from the traditional, state-centric approach, Woods posits international nongovernmental organizations (INGOs) as the major unit of analysis, and traces how their evolutionary dynamics have influenced the patterns of economic cooperation in the Asia-Pacific region through an in-depth elucidation of origin, structure, and activities of three regional INGOs: the Pacific Trade and Development Conference, the Pacific Basin Economic Council, and the Pacific Economic Cooperation Council. The regional INGOs are found to have played a significant role as diplomatic actors in developing policy agenda and forming a cooperative epistemic community without necessarily undercutting the roles and functions of individual governments and intergovernmental organizations. Woods makes a timely and important theoretical and empirical contribution to the understanding of the evolving nature of the Pacific dynamics. An excellent and pioneering application of the transna-

tional/institutionalist paradigm in the Asia-Pacific. Analytically sound, empirically solid, drawing heavily on primary data, and rich in comparative and policy implications. Essential reading for students, area specialists, and policymakers.—*C. Moon, University of Kentucky*

OAB-2801   DR1313   94-12742 CIP
Woodward, Susan L. **Balkan tragedy: chaos and dissolution after the Cold War.** Brookings, 1995. 536p index afp ISBN 0-8157-9514-9, $42.95; ISBN 0-8157-9513-0 pbk, $18.95

Despite its apparent focus on current events—the civil war in Bosnia—this massive study brilliantly dissects the disintegration of Yugoslavia as a reflection of the changed international environment in the post-Cold War era. With extensive firsthand experience in Yugoslavia, the author weaves a penetrating analysis of the internal and external developments that shaped the tragedy in Bosnia: the pre-civil war stability and harmony of a multicultural society; the collapse of Yugoslavia; the dynamics of self-determination and the political manipulation of nationalism; the critical role of economic factors and in particular the politics of transforming a socialist society to a market economy; the events leading to the civil war; the flawed Western and UN intervention; and, finally, the disintegrating international order that actually exacerbated internal tensions. With compelling and insightful analysis, this book presents a devastating indictment of the illusory notion of a post-Cold War "New World Order." In fact, the Bosnian conflict can be directly linked to a fundamental failure in the West to understand either the issues or the impact of its responses. This tragic failure, the author indicates, is not limited to Yugoslavia: similar potential crises elsewhere will not be resolved until the fundamental issues are better understood. Herein lies the great value of this exceptional book. All levels.—*P. Vannicelli, University of Massachusetts at Boston*

OAB-2802   DK510   93-32909 CIP
Yergin, Daniel. **Russia 2010—and what it means for the world,** by Daniel Yergin and Thane Gustafson. Random House, 1993. 302p index ISBN 0-679-42995-6, $23.00

Yergin, a Pulitzer prize winner for his study of oil and world politics, and Gustafson, a top specialist on Soviet and post-Soviet affairs, team up to assess the predicament Russia faces amidst the ruins of the USSR and to outline four credible outcomes of that predicament by the year 2010. With laudable caution they preface their text with Disraeli's observation: "What we anticipate seldom occurs; what we least expected generally happens." The authors identify and weigh the potentialities of the complex array of contending forces now at work in Russia. On this basis they plot out four "scenarios": (1) revival of Russian imperium; (2) internal fragmentation; (3) withdrawal into a Russian-style reactionary dictatorship; or (4) transformation through an economic miracle. Neither denying reality nor foreclosing on Russia's future, the authors provide a well-articulated and open-ended framework of timely analysis. An important book that will help policy makers and concerned citizens in pondering the fateful question: "Whither Russia?" Should be assigned reading for upper-level undergraduate and graduate students of Russia and East-West relations.—*C. A. Linden, George Washington University*

OAB-2803   DS515   969-28351 CIP
Zhao, Suisheng. **Power competition in East Asia: from the old Chinese world order to post-Cold War regional multipolarity.** St. Martin's, 1997. 346p bibl index ISBN 0-312-16258-8, $45.00

Zhao provides an outstanding overview of the international affairs of East Asia from the Chinese tributary system to the post-Cold War emergence of multipolarity. The analysis is based on neorealism; East Asia is examined through the lens of the power structure created by the interactions of the local powers (China and Japan) and intervening powers such as Britain, the US, and Russia. The notion of power itself is considered in terms of its military, economic, and cultural dimensions. This framework for analysis contributes to the strength of the book. Zhao's work is organized as a historical analysis from the colonization of China to post-Cold War uncertainties, but includes discussions of the changes in power relationships caused by rapid economic growth within the region, the emergence of transnational "growth clusters," cultural differences as an element of power rivalry, and the emergence of regional cooperation. This analysis allows Zhao to consider larger theoretical debates over civilizational clashes, trading states, the role of nationalism, and the universality of Western liberal democracy. An excellent introduction to East Asian international relations for undergraduate and graduate students alike.—*W. W. Newmann, Virginia Commonwealth University*

■ Law & Public Administration

OAB-2804 KF8972 94-11580 CIP
Abramson, Jeffrey. **We, the jury: the jury system and the ideal of democracy.** Basic Books, 1994. 308p index ISBN 0-465-03698-8, $25.00

Uniting the disciplines of law, social science, and history, Abramson (Brandeis) has written a truly landmark work on the jury system in America. His exhaustive examination of the jury system begins with a historical look at the jury prior to and at the time of the ratification of the Constitution and proceeds to examine how the jury in America has gone from a local, community-based, deliberative ideal to the representative, pluralist one in demand today. Along the way, he analyzes all major Supreme Court decisions, congressional enactments, and social science studies relating to juries. Most relevant, he examines the effects of the 1968 Jury Selection and Service Act (making juries more representative and less deliberative), court opinions prohibiting racial and gender exclusion from juries (a positive step toward equal justice), scientific jury selection (the only effect of which has been to undermine public confidence in the jury), and the use of nonunanimous verdicts (weakening the need for jury deliberation). Abramson concludes with suggestions for reform to make juries more deliberative: openness about a jury's power to nullify laws with which it disagrees, allowing knowledgeable jurors to serve rather than limiting service only to those in ignorance, and a greater willingness by citizens to serve. The entire work rests on a comprehensive endnotes section citing virtually every relevant work on the topic. A must read for all scholars and laypeople concerned with juries in America.—*M. W. Bowers, University of Nevada, Las Vegas*

OAB-2805 H97 93-16710 CIP
The argumentative turn in policy analysis and planning, ed. by Frank Fischer and John Forester. Duke University, 1993. 327p index afp ISBN 0-8223-1354-5, $49.95; ISBN 0-8223-1372-3 pbk, $19.95

The past few decades have seen social science knowledge linked much more closely with political power. How are careful analysis and political feasibility synthesized? How, in the words of the editors, do policy analysts "make practical arguments that are internally coherent and externally compelling?" Hand-wringing about these questions has become commonplace. Probing what it means, assessing implications and consequences, and drawing insights from other disciplines—especially rhetoric and jurisprudence—are much more challenging, and that is what this volume does. Authored primarily by political scientists and planners, it offers a very different perspective than the case put forward by most economists and epistemologists. William Dunn's chapter, "Policy Reforms as Arguments," is a special gem in this excellent collection. A must for all institutions offering planning, public administration, and public policy degrees.—*E. T. Jones, University of Missouri—St. Louis*

OAB-2806 JK736 93-40377 CIP
Carter, Stephen L. **The confirmation mess: cleaning up the federal appointments process.** Basic Books, 1994. 252p index ISBN 0-465-01364-3, $21.00

Carter (law, Yale), prolific author of *The Culture of Disbelief* (CH, Mar'94)

and *Reflections of an Affirmative Action Baby* (1991), has added yet a third provocative and thoughtful essay to his canon on modern American culture and politics. With neither a liberal nor conservative bias, he examines the problems associated with the process of nominating and confirming federal executive and judicial officers. In short, Carter argues that the nomination and confirmation process has become a dishonest and indecent game of political Trivial Pursuit in which the qualifications of nominees take a backseat to questions about nannies, sexuality, and other personality traits unimportant to a nominee's fitness. These molehills, often dredged up by interest groups and partisan opponents and duly reported by an ever-eager media, frequently serve to disqualify candidates without an examination of the nominee's qualifications to serve in the position he or she seeks. Is it truly important, for example, what tapes Robert Bork rented at his local video store? Carter rejects most of the proposals for reform currently being debated as either not efficacious or unacceptable. However, the reforms he proposes appear likewise flawed. Indeed, as he ultimately notes, the real problem is with the public attitude about government service. We must, he concludes, once more see public service as a calling rather than a reward and acknowledge that sinners can not only be redeemed but can also make excellent civil servants. Given the public and media frenzy over every sordid detail of private lives, this reviewer is not optimistic. Highly recommended.—*M. W. Bowers, University of Nevada, Las Vegas*

OAB-2807 KF3771 91-46603 CIP
Colker, Ruth. **Abortion and dialogue: pro-choice, pro-life, and American law.** Indiana, 1992. 179p index afp ISBN 0-253-31393-7, $29.95; ISBN 0-253-20738-X pbk, $12.95

This is feminist scholarship at its best: interdisciplinary, passionate, personal, and political. This book is more original than its title suggests. Although other works, e.g., Laurence Tribe's *Abortion: The Clash of Absolutes* (CH, Dec'90), Faye Ginsberg's *Contested Lives: The Abortion Debate in an American Community* (1989), Mary Ann Glendon's *Abortion and Divorce in Western Law* (CH, Feb'88), and *Rights Talk* (1991), have noted how the absolutism of the abortion debate thwarts the discovery of common ground, none have so sensitively appreciated the concerns of both sides and so eloquently suggested an alternative theory as Colker (Tulane Univ.). She crafts a feminist-theological perspective based on the conception of an authentic self that moves toward the aspirations of love, compassion, and wisdom. When these aspirations are applied to abortion politics, problems within both movements are revealed. How can pro-choicers be so disrepectful of concerns for life? How can pro-lifers ignore the realities of women's lives? Colker then shows a way out of the thicket by utilizing an equality framework guided by the three aspirations. Both controversial and inspiring, this volume is highly recommended for all libraries.—*S. Behuniak-Long, Le Moyne College*

OAB-2808 HQ767 92-41395 CIP
Craig, Barbara Hinkson. **Abortion and American politics,** by Barbara Hinkson Craig and David M. O'Brien. Chatham House, 1993. 382p bibl indexes ISBN 0-934540-88-8, $30.00; ISBN 0-934540-89-6 pbk, $19.95

This volume fills an important but mostly overlooked niche and need in the abortion literature—the study of abortion law combined with the study of abortion politics. Craig (Wesleyan Univ.) and O'Brien (Univ. of Virginia) examine not only the constitutional law cases but also the political factors that constitute the abortion quagmire. It is through the use of both lenses that the authors succeed in revealing new insights on a subject that has been often scrutinized but rarely as well understood. This is, therefore, a significant contribution not only to the scholarship on abortion but to the field of law and politics in general. Chapters on *Roe, Webster,* and *Casey* are complemented by other chapters which study the abortion politics of interest groups, state legislators, Congress, presidents, and public opinion. The book also benefits from the creative and useful incorporation of quotations from primary materials such as oral arguments, cases, amici curiae briefs, speeches, party platforms, and statutes. Throughout, the authors employ a critical analysis devoid of polemics. Selected bibliography. Highly recommended for all collections.—*S. Behuniak-Long, Le Moyne College*

OAB-2809   KF9672   94-45187 CIP

Cutler, Brian L. **Mistaken identification: the eyewitness, psychology, and the law,** by Brian L. Cutler and Steven D. Penrod. Cambridge, 1995. 290p bibl indexes ISBN 0-521-44553-1, $59.95; ISBN 0-521-44572-8 pbk, $18.95

Cutler and Penrod, widely published authors of research on eyewitness reliability and jury decision making, offer a compelling argument that the growing body of research regarding factors that influence identification accuracy warrants presentation to juries via expert psychological testimony. Although this volume does not introduce any new or previously unpublished findings, it does present a careful review of legal precedents regarding admissibility of expert testimony on the psychology of eyewitness identification, a survey of the scientific research that experts have to share with the court, and an appraisal of the limited effectiveness of current safeguards against mistaken identification afforded by defense cross-examination of witnesses and closing arguments, the judge's instructions to the jury, and the jury's knowledge about eyewitness unreliability and the likelihood that they will act on it. Their review supports the position that expert psychological testimony most effectively sensitizes jurors to the importance of witnessing and identification conditions without creating a general skepticism of all eyewitness accounts and lowering of conviction rates. The writing is clear, engaging, and accessible to students of psychology and law, memory researchers, and officers of the court. Highly recommended. Upper-division undergraduate through professional.—*T. J. Thieman, College of St. Catherine*

OAB-2810   KF4772   93-5796 CIP

Eldridge, Larry D. **A distant heritage: the growth of free speech in early America.** New York University, 1994. 198p bibl index afp ISBN 0-8147-2192-3, $40.00

This slender volume successfully challenges a major assumption of legal history made by the premier historian of American free speech. At issue is Leonard W. Levy's claim that "Liberty of expression barely existed in principle or practice in the American colonies during the seventeenth century." See Levy's *Emergence of a Free Press* (CH, Sep'85) and *Legacy of Suppression: Freedom of Speech and Press in Early American History* (1960). Eldridge has sifted through colonial court records and analyzed more than 1,200 seditious speech prosecutions, finding that the colonists of that period "experienced a dramatic expansion of their freedom to criticize government and its officials ...." Equally fascinating is Eldridge's multifaceted explanation for the growth of free speech. Here is a thoroughly researched, richly detailed, well argued, and carefully written study in American legal history. This text makes a significant contribution to our understanding of the development of free speech in America. All levels.—*E. C. Dreyer, University of Tulsa*

OAB-2811   KF5399   92-15814 CIP

Gillman, Howard. **The Constitution besieged: the rise and demise of Lochner era police powers jurisprudence.** Duke University, 1993. 317p bibl index afp ISBN 0-8223-1283-2, $34.95

Ever since Justice Holmes accused his brethren in *Lochner* v. *New York* (1905) of reading Herbert Spencer's *Social Statics* (1851) into the Constitution, that case has epitomized an era of supposed judicial activism on behalf of laissez-faire economics. In a brilliant and well-written reinterpretation of both the case and the era, Gillman, a southern California political scientist, argues that Holmes was wrong. *Lochner* and its progeny did not represent a sudden judicial conversion to laissez-faire economics but embodied an animus against class-based legislation unrelated to more general public health and safety concerns dating back to the American founding and continuing through the Jacksonian era. While America's increased industrialization eventually discredited the assumption that different social classes had equal bargaining power, Gillman demonstrates that Lochner era jurisprudence was principled rather than idiosyncratic. Must reading for students of American legal and political thought and a nice complement to Paul Kens's *Judicial Power and Reform Politics* (1990). Detailed endnotes and indexes. Highly recommended for college and university collections.—*J. R. Vile, Middle Tennessee State University*

OAB-2812   CR113   95-5541 CIP

Goldstein, Robert Justin. **Burning the flag: the great 1989-1990 American flag desecration controversy.** Kent State, 1996. 453p index afp ISBN 0-87338-526-8, $39.00

Goldstein (Oakland Univ.) has written a wonderfully comprehensive and highly readable history and analysis of the flag desecration debate in the US. His extensive research brings together history, law, and political science to examine the issue from its beginnings in the post-Civil War US to its current state. Although the flag protection movement began in the 1890s primarily as an attempt to stop increasing commercial exploitation of the flag, it soon came to be a fascist reaction to immigrants, labor unions, political outsiders, and anyone else perceived to be a threat to the movement's skewed vision of true American patriotism. Not surprisingly, state and federal laws passed to protect the flag were most often used against dissidents during periods of political instability and transformation, such as the Red Scare of the 1920s and the Vietnam War. The greater part of the work is dedicated to a painstaking, intriguing, and highly detailed account of *Texas* v. *Johnson* (the famous 1989 US Supreme Court case that held flag burning to be protected symbolic speech under the First Amendment), congressional attempts to overturn that decision, and *U.S.* v. *Eichman* (1990) which declared the new congressional statute unconstitutional as well. An epilogue and addendum bring the flag desecration issue and debate up to date as of 1995. Extensive endnotes and the pleasurable readability of the book make it essential for scholars and general readers alike.—*M. W. Bowers, University of Nevada, Las Vegas*

OAB-2813   JF1351   95-16081 CIP

Holden, Matthew. **Continuity and disruption: essays in public administration.** Pittsburgh, 1996. 291p index afp ISBN 0-8229-3885-5, $45.00

Matthew's interesting and thoughtful survey of some of the history of public administration consists of essays linked successfully, for the most part, by a concern with the decision-making focuses of public administration: information, money, and resources. The themes of continuity and disruption are well illustrated as the text moves through the key ideas and moments in the history of the discipline. Holden's ambitious hope is to develop a political theory of public administration. His lack of success does not deserve censure, since he is among the few to have followed the likes of Woodrow Wilson, Leonard White, and Dwight Waldo. In an era when government is despised and administration of public business routinely vilified, it is heartening to see someone attempt to raise the level of discourse about the conventional opinion and technical description that pass for thought in much writing about public administration. Holden's book deals with topics of recurring interest and importance and provides for both new and experienced readers a fine history of the ideas of the discipline and a distinguished scholar's view of large problems of theory. Highly recommended; essential for all academic libraries.—*E. Lewis, New College of the University of South Florida*

OAB-2814   JK681   95-32780 CIP

Huddleston, Mark W. **The higher civil service in the United States: quest for reform,** by Mark W. Huddleston and William W. Boyer. Pittsburgh, 1996. 229p bibl index afp ISBN 0-8229-3906-1, $49.95; ISBN 0-8229-5574-1 pbk, $19.95

Huddleston and Boyer offer a well-written and carefully documented account of various attempts to bring a "higher civil service" to the US. After providing a "broader context" for their study by exploring the "Chinese roots" of the world's civil service systems and by considering the configurations of such systems as they evolved in other countries, the authors focus on post-WW II efforts to institutionalize in the US a "neutrally competent" higher administration. In the course of their discussion, the authors underscore the problems of the Senior Executive Service (SES) created by the Civil Service Reform Act (CSRA) of 1978. They argue that some of SES's difficulties can be attributed to the country's lack of consensus regarding the fundamental character and role of a "higher civil service." The authors conclude by offering a set of proposals intended to advance the development of an "American higher civil service." Highly recommended for all academic libraries.—*G. L. Malecha, University of Portland*

OAB-2815   KF9756   95-41748 CIP
Huff, C. Ronald. **Convicted but innocent: wrongful conviction and public policy,** by C. Ronald Huff, Arye Rattner, and Edward Sagarin. Sage Publications, CA, 1996. 180p bibl index afp ISBN 0-8039-5952-4, $39.95; ISBN 0-8039-5953-2 pbk, $17.95

This important book, joining many others about the possibility and actuality of executing innocent persons (e.g., Randall Adams's *Adams v. Texas*, 1991 and Michael L. Radelet et al.'s *In Spite of Innocence*, CH, Mar'93), examines the full range of potential and real cases in which innocent people are falsely accused, convicted, and incarcerated and describes the variety of missteps in our criminal justice system that lead to unjust imprisonment. Although no system can be perfect, we can do better in eliminating injustices. In six clearly written chapters the authors examine the reality of unjust incarceration. They define the term "convicted innocents" and explore a range of horrors, including a finding of innocence that did not result in immediate release from prison; several important cases involving innocents (e.g., the Scottsboro boys, the Lindbergh baby kidnapping, and the John Demjanjuk case of mistaken identity); missteps in the criminal justice system that make it possible to find some innocent people guilty; problems of eyewitness identification; and the role of false confessions in the conviction of the innocent. The last chapter may be the most compelling; the authors recommend how to reduce the number of errors in our criminal justice system. For anyone concerned about justice; highly recommended for public and university libraries.—*M. A. Foley, Marywood College*

OAB-2816   KF224   94-27470 CIP
Jacobs, James B. **Busting the mob: United States v. Cosa Nostra,** by James B. Jacobs, with Christopher Panarella and Jay Worthington. New York University, 1994. 276p bibl index afp ISBN 0-8147-4195-9, $29.95

Written by three experts at the Center for Research in Crime and Justice at NYU, this essential and readable study collects and synthesizes the data and lessons of more than two decades of relentless penetration and prosecution of the organized mob. Five fascinating landmark, high-profile criminal and civil cases are analyzed, from organized crime's control of the Teamsters, and the eye-opening testimony of FBI agent and mob infiltrator Joseph Pistone, to the celebrated trial of the John Gotti, "dapper don" of the New York City Gambino family. Armed with the powerful 1970 RICO (Racketeer Influenced and Corrupt Organization) Act and the 1980 Organized Crime Information System, federal and local law enforcement officials used wiretapped conversations and testimony of informants to shake the hold of the Mafia. The book argues that high-level support by attorneys-general and presidents for efforts opposing organized crime, powerful legislation and enforcement authority, and the mob's own internal decline explain the "mob-busting" success, and it warns that many of the socioeconomic forces that permit organized crime to flourish still exist. Excellent synthesis, extensive bibliography; recommended for all readers.—*W. Q. Morales, University of Central Florida*

OAB-2817   JC481   94-41148 CIP
Kasza, Gregory J. **The conscription society: administered mass organizations.** Yale, 1995. 217p bibl index afp ISBN 0-300-06242-7, $27.50

Administered Mass Organizations (AMO) are mass civilian organizations created and managed by political regimes to implement public policy. They are formal organizations that group people by place of residence, industry, workplace, age, or gender. External agencies of the regime appoint top leaders to serve state purposes. This important comparative study focuses on single party and military-bureaucratic regimes of the Left and the Right. Begun initially in Japan, Italy, and the Soviet Union in response to WW I, AMOs were typically structured on the pattern of the mass conscript army of that era, but the organizational structure has endured. Nondemocratic regimes have used such orga-

nizations to stifle political organization, mobilize for war, and create socioeconomic change. The author surveys many regimes, giving specific attention to Italy, Japan, Egypt, and the Soviet Union. This well-written book effectively combines empirical and normative analyses to provide insight into an area of significance often neglected by comparativists in the past. Highly recommended for all collections on political organization, political development, and military affairs. General; academic.—*E. Lewis, New College of the University of South Florida*

OAB-2818   K215   91-36905 CIP
Kelly, J.M. **A short history of Western legal theory.** Oxford, 1992. 466p index ISBN 0-19-876244-5, $69.00

A Short History of Western Legal Theory is a triumphant final work, one that fairly illustrates the breadth of Kelly's learning and the sharpness of his wit. This is a history of Western legal theory meant for student and teacher alike, and its crispness of style and clarity of thought make it uniquely suitable for both audiences. One of the great strengths of the work is its ability to relate the evolution of legal theory to parallel developments in political theory and history: Kelly's emphasis on context makes the work useful not only for courses in jurisprudence, but also for more general courses in Western intellectual history. Reflecting its author's training, the book is especially strong in its discussion of Greek and Roman legal thought. It is somewhat less insightful in its treatment of some aspects of late 20th-century legal thought, such as critical legal studies and the law and economics movement. Even here, however, the book's emphasis on political context makes it valuable. In sum, this is a magisterial book, full of wisdom and compassion. Undergraduate through faculty collections.—*J. E. Finn, Wesleyan University*

OAB-2819   KF387   93-31233 CIP
Law in everyday life, ed. by Austin Sarat and Thomas R. Kearns. Michigan, 1993. 285p index afp ISBN 0-472-10441-1, $39.50

Sarat and Kearns (Amherst College) have edited a truly marvelous work on the impact of the law on daily life and vice versa. In a particularly thoughtful and cogent introductory essay, the coeditors set forth the analytic framework of the volume's subsequent chapters by critiquing the "instrumentalist" and "constitutive" paradigms of the law and everyday life and proposing a reconciliation between them that attends "to particular practices and concrete, historically situated examples of law and social relations." The remaining six essays provide these examples in their examination of an eighteenth century woman's approach within the context of the legal system and her own religious beliefs to the sexual abuse by her husband of their daughter (Hartog), the subordination of women by legally protected pornography (MacKinnon), the development of legally mandated education programs for disabled children in six families (Engel), personal journeys through law and everyday life (Williams, Kennedy), and a challenge to rethink the meaning of the everyday in law (Marcus). With exception of the MacKinnon essay, which continues her previously pubished one-note, anti-civil liberties tune familiar to most members of this volume's target audience, the essays are all exemplary, thought-provoking works worthy of a long, contemplative read by scholars, lawyers, and judges alike. Graduate; faculty, professional.—*M. W. Bowers, University of Nevada, Las Vegas*

OAB-2820   HD62   94-31040 CIP
Salamon, Lester M. **Partners in public service: government-nonprofit relations in the modern welfare state.** Johns Hopkins, 1995. 310p bibl index afp ISBN 0-8018-4962-4, $55.00; ISBN 0-8018-4963-2 pbk, $16.95

Salamon's extremely important book on the nonprofit sector of the contemporary American welfare state is rich in theoretical insight and provides a thoroughly detailed and comprehensive description of the development and significance of this "third sector." Salamon outlines an interesting theoretical structure then proceeds to thicken it with numerous tables and graphic depictions of the growing significance of the third sector in numerous fields. His chapters on the unanticipated negative effects of the Reagan-Bush tax policies on voluntary giving are devastating and particularly salient given the dominant views of Congress at the moment. His expositions of myths of the nonprofit sector in American ideology are clear and pungent. This extraordinarily valuable book about an exceedingly important matter too long ignored in the literature of American politics and policy analysis is in the best tradition of academic writing and analysis and should be on the shelves of all serious scholars of the subject. Highly recommended, undergraduate through faculty.—*E. Lewis, New College of the University of South Florida*

OAB-2821 KF228 93-22692 MARC
Steffan, Joseph. **Gays and the military: Joseph Steffan versus the United States,** ed. by Marc Wolinsky and Kenneth Sherrill. Princeton, 1993. 222p index afp ISBN 0-691-03307-2, $39.50

Wolinski, partner of a New York law firm and co-council to Steffan, and Sherrill, (Hunter College) constructed this work based on the 1988 litigation strategy and court papers filed in the case of *Joseph C. Steffan* v. *Richard Cheney, Secretary of Defense*. Steffan, a Midshipman at the US Naval Academy, was denied his diploma and commission six weeks before graduation, after admitting he was a homosexual. The book contains the most significant portions of the court record which have been edited to make them more readable. The court's opinion upholding the constitutionality of the military's ban on homosexuals is not materially edited. The editors uniquely present the material through the Motion for Summary Judgment of Joseph Steffan, a series of affidavits supporting the motion, the Department of Justice Memorandum in Response, the Reply Memorandum, and Judge Oliver Gasch's Opinion. This is a valuable resource for anyone wishing to understand the constitutional, emotional, human, and organizational issues involved. It is a remarkable collection of materials concerning homosexuality in the military and provides a service to all in understanding the current national debate. The book should be read carefully and pondered thoughtfully by military and law professionals. All levels.—*D. F. Bletz, Wilson College*

OAB-2822 K213 95-25265 CIP
Sunstein, Cass R. **Legal reasoning and political conflict.** Oxford, 1996. 220p index afp ISBN 0-19-510082-4, $25.00

In T.S. Eliot's choruses from *The Rock*, God chides humanity: "I have given you power of choice, and you only alternate between fruitless speculation and unconsidered action." The words might have been Sunstein's in a law school commencement address. His audience will have studied the big cases, involving highly abstract theory, but these are aberrations—most courtroom work does not and should not aspire to that level. Sunstein wishes to infuse quotidian court decisions with useful principle without hammering either decision or principle into unrecognizable shape. He proposes a middle ground of "incompletely theorized agreement," reaching conclusions "at the lowest decidable level." High theory may inform and even decide some cases, but is to be used sparingly, like the valuable resource it is. This is Karl Popper's famous "piecemeal engineering" approach: we must realize that we can only improve matters "little by little" (*The Poverty of Historicism*, 1987). The method counters broad theories of law such as Ronald Dworkin's *Law's Empire* (CH, Oct'86), Robert Bork's *The Tempting of America* (CH, May'90), and Richard A. Posner's *Economic Analysis of Law* (1992), and relies on analogical reasoning and "casuistry." The argument is from consequences, and will therefore appeal to the American pragmatic instinct for achieving consensus. The arguments are elegant and the writing smooth and witty; the book deserves to be among the first taken down from the shelf by any student of legal theory and practice. Highly recommended for upper-division undergraduates through faculty.—*M. Berheide, Berea College*

OAB-2823 KF9223 95-38687 CIP
Uviller, H. Richard. **Virtual justice: the flawed prosecution of crime in America.** Yale, 1996. 318p index afp ISBN 0-300-06483-7, $30.00

Whether you agree or disagree with the ideas developed in this delightful, reflective excursion through our criminal justice system, you will be better informed about our criminal justice process. In a narrative style general readers will enjoy, Uviller examines problems of evidence collection, capture and custody, eyewitness identification, privacy and privilege, the right to counsel, prosecutorial discretion, plea bargaining, jury selection, and jury nullification (the right of juries to acquit defendants regardless of the evidence against them), among others. Uviller uses fictional stories and conversations to explain his recommendations, but these fictional accounts are based on sound theoretical foundations. He uses a fictional story to describe the issues and problems with the exclusionary rule; his chapter on gun control uses a dialogue to illustrate policy options that might be used to reduce the number of illegal firearms. This book does in many ways for the criminal justice system what Philip K. Howard's *The Death of Common Sense* (CH, Jun'95) did to make clear the stranglehold law and lawyers have on the US. One minor flaw in the book for some readers will be the lack of footnotes and bibliography. The writing is clear, the ideas challenging, the method engaging. Highly recommended for general readers and undergraduates, this book should be read by anyone interested in the strengths and weaknesses of our criminal justice system.—*M. A. Foley, Marywood College*

OAB-2824 KF4749 94-47132 CIP
Wasby, Stephen L. **Race relations litigation in an age of complexity.** University Press of Virginia, 1995. 421p index ISBN 0-8139-1572-4, $65.00; ISBN 0-8139-1573-2 pbk, $22.50

Wasby (political science, SUNY at Albany) has written a marvelously comprehensive treatise on the complexity of civil rights litigation in the US. In a study of race relations litigation from the late 1960s through the early 1980s, he examines desegregation of elementary and secondary schools, employment discrimination under Title VII of the Civil Rights Act of 1964, housing rights, and voting rights. Through an in-depth analysis of environmental and intra- and interorganizational factors, Wasby finds that earlier conclusions regarding the planned nature of litigation in this area are incorrect, or at least severely overstated. He examines previously published sources and adds his own interviews with lawyers associated with the various interest groups involved. He finds that, although race relations litigators certainly had preset goals and strategies, these were frequently mitigated by the political and legal environment in which litigations found themselves and by interactions between and among the litigating groups. Wasby pictures litigation that is more problematic and complex than often assumed and that does not necessarily follow any predetermined linear path. Instead, litigators are forced to react and respond to events entirely outside their control. Wasby's endnotes are extensive and among the most comprehensive to date. Highly recommended for students and scholars.—*M. W. Bowers, University of Nevada, Las Vegas*

OAB-2825 K235 93-29846 CIP
West, Robin. **Narrative, authority, and law.** Michigan, 1993. 439p afp ISBN 0-472-10365-2, $49.50

This is an innovative, provocative, and, hence, important (although at times, tedious) book. West (Univ. of Maryland) seeks to provide a partial answer to what she calls the "critical dilemma" confronting students of the law: "How could we possibly generate a moral point of view that is external to, independent of, or simply different from the point of view created by legalism, from which we can criticize law?" That answer, she claims, is to be found in "the traditional methods of the humanities—writing, reading, and responding to narrative texts ...." Accordingly, in Part 1 she critiques the moral beliefs relied upon by the law-and-economics movement through the medium of the short stories and novellas of Franz Kafka. In Part 2 she explores the role of narrative voice in moral argument and legal criticism. And in Part 3 she considers conventional jurisprudence and legal opinions as literature, as aesthetic objects. On the whole her project is successful, and the book should soon become a standard reference in the field. It is must reading for any one concerned with legal criticism and should also be of interest to students of political theory, especially those interested in politics and literature. No bibliography or index. An essential acquisition for libraries serving upper-division undergraduates, graduate students, and faculty.—*G. L. Jones, University of Nevada, Las Vegas*

■ Political Theory

OAB-2826   JA76   94-30981 CIP
Andrain, Charles F. **Political protest and social change: analyzing politics,** by Charles F. Andrain and David E. Apter. New York University, 1995. 387p index ISBN 0-8147-0630-4, $40.00

The authors, both highly respected political scientists who have published widely in the area of comparative political and social development, offer an informative treatment of the relationship between cultural values and political change. Some chapters concentrate on how effectively ideology, religion, nationalism, and pluralism influence politics and political behavior. Throughout the text are ample and useful references to contemporary and influential themes such as those of F.A. von Hayek and Francis Fukuyama. The assumption that the post-Cold War era is characterized more by political protest based on differing and conflicting sets of values than by political peace and quiet is consistently demonstrated. Even more intriguing is the link between primordial and religious concepts and protest and change. To appreciate this book's themes fully it is necessary to know something of history. Detailed and informative footnotes and a thorough index are included. An excellent sequel to Andrain's own *Political Change in the Third World* (CH, Oct'88) and Apter's classic, *The Politics of Modernization* (CH, Jun'66). Should be required reading in graduate seminars on political development.—*M. Slann, Clemson University*

OAB-2827   JA81   94-21129 CIP
Ball, Terence. **Reappraising political theory: revisionist studies in the history of political thought.** Oxford, 1995. 310p bibl index afp ISBN 0-19-827953-1, $59.00; ISBN 0-19-827995-7 pbk, $19.95

It is literally impossible to do justice to this book in a short review. Suffice it to say that Ball (a noted political theorist at the University of Minnesota), noting that academic political theory is once again under siege, feels compelled to "reappraise" that enterprise. But, he argues, that is as it should be, since that is what political theory is all about: "reappraisal." Reappraisal of texts, of ourselves, and of political life. Ball divides his reappraisal into two parts. Part 1 deals with the nature, the past trials and tribulations, and the future direction of academic political theory. With respect to the future, he expresses concern about the consequences of failing to recognize that academic political theory is not only academic, it is, and should be, political. Part 2 is a collection of essays, some previously published, in which Ball provides provocative reappraisals of works of several of the "canonical" writers, e.g., Machiavelli, Hobbes, Rousseau, in order to illustrate his point. All in all, it is a book well worth the reading. It should be read in conjunction with his earlier *Transforming Political Discourse* (1988) and the work of John Gunnell. It is similar in intent to Michael Bérubé's *Public Access* (CH, Jan'95), which seeks to accomplish a similar reappraisal for literary criticism. Excellent bibliography and index. An essential acquisition for libraries serving upper-division undergraduates, graduate students, and faculty.—*G. L. Jones, University of Nevada, Las Vegas*

OAB-2828   JC251   92-34761 CIP
Barrow, Clyde W. **Critical theories of the state: Marxist, neo-Marxist, post-Marxist.** Wisconsin, 1993. 220p bibl index ISBN 0-299-13710-4, $38.00; ISBN 0-299-13714-7 pbk, $15.95

Over the past two decades there has been a proliferation of literature on Marxist theories of the state. The arguments have been complex, dense, and more than a bit uncomprehensible to most graduate and undergraduate students. Barrow's book, overcomes these shortfalls. It targets an undergraduate audience and is written clearly and lucidly. It assumes no prior knowledge of state theory and manages to make sense out of some very complex ideas. The work is different from others in the genre in that it assumes little or no familiarity with the literature; it dispenses with the ritual tracing and quoting of Marx and Engel's writing on the state; rather than focusing on concepts such as hegemony

and autonomy it emphasizes "the historical and logical development of competing approaches" to state theory; and, finally, its historical focus is on the modern welfare state and its current crises. This is an excellent book that librarians should purchase. It fills a major gap in the literature and should be widely read by undergraduates and graduate students in political science, sociology, philosophy, and economics.—*W. Scheuerman, SUNY College at Oswego*

OAB-2829   JC423   96-599 CIP
Bohman, James. **Public deliberation: pluralism, complexity, and democracy.** MIT, 1996. 303p bibl index afp ISBN 0-262-02410-1, $30.00

Bohman's book belongs in every first-rate collection of political philosophy, although it will tax the abilities of undergraduate readers. It contains more abstract argument and fewer concrete examples than *Democracy and Disagreement* (1996) by Amy Gutmann and Dennis Thompson, but it too addresses democratic theory's hottest topic, public deliberation. Bohman offers sure-footed guidance to the philosophical underpinnings of headline issues, from Simpson jury controversies to media politics. He concentrates on three problems plaguing democracy today: social pluralism, inequalities, and complexity. Bohman (philosophy, St. Louis Univ.), an outstanding Habermas scholar, provides diligent readers insight into the abstruse literature on democracy emanating from both Anglo-American/Rawlsian and German/Habermasian traditions. Pitching his own analysis between mere description and pure ideals, he offers solutions that are original and pragmatic, critical yet not utopian. Although Bohman does not suggest blueprints for institutional reforms, the access he provides to recent democratic theorizing, his astuteness in analyzing contemporary problems of democratic practices, and the cogency of his own proposals make *Public Deliberation* mandatory reading for anyone, undergraduate through faculty, wishing to be well grounded in the philosophy of democratic renewal.—*A. B. Cochran, Agnes Scott College*

OAB-2830   H61   93-8056 CIP
Brams, Steven J. **Theory of moves.** Cambridge, 1994. 248p bibl index ISBN 0-521-45226-0, $54.95; ISBN 0-521-45867-6 pbk, $17.95

Brams (New York Univ.), who has been one of the leading contributors to the literature on game theory in political science, presents his theory of moves (to which he refers as TOM) in this book. TOM is designed to provide a dynamic component to the analysis of ordinal games in normal form. Rather than assuming each player has a single decision and that these decisions must be made simultaneously, Brams assumes that play, which begins in one cell of the game matrix, involves a sequence of choices in which the players have opportunities to move from cell to cell. Brams develops the theory by assuming that players can see farther than one move ahead and can anticipate the outcome of a sequence of moves. He then demonstrates that this produces expectations significantly different from those typically derived from static models. The starting point of the game matters for the outcome, which captures the importance of the history of the relationship between the players. He also identifies three types of power (moving power, order power, and threat power) and shows that each has particular implications for the play of the game. His analyses are illustrated with examples of conflicts drawn from international politics, literature, and the Bible. While this book is firmly in the tradition of game theory, no other yet presents these arguments. It is sure to be widely read at all levels of academia.—*T. C. Morgan, Rice University*

OAB-2831   JC233   91-40678 CIP
Brod, Harry. **Hegel's philosophy of politics: idealism, identity, and modernity.** Westview, 1992. 216p bibl index afp ISBN 0-8133-8317-X, $45.00; ISBN 0-8133-8526-1 pbk, $15.95

In an intriguing and provocative book, Brod (women's and gender studies and philosophy, Kenyon College) offers a strikingly original interpretation of Hegel's philosophy of politics. Noting that earlier interpretations generally fall into one of two camps, those that focus on the substantive doctrines of Hegel's thought—the "what," and those that focus on the programmatic, metatheoretical dimensions of his thought—the "how," Brod argues that most have "foundered on an inadequate understanding of what questions Hegel thought a political philosophy in his time needed to answer and how it had to go about answering them." An adequate understanding is one, he contends, which synthesizes "a concern for Hegel's overall conception of the task of political philosophy with a concern for the details of the political institutions proposed in the *Philosophy of Right.* It is just such an interpretation that Brod seeks to provide, and he succeeds. The work should be of particular interest to students of Hegel, but will be value to anyone interested in the history of political philosophy generally. Along with the recent works of Peter Steinberger and Steven B. Smith, this volume will provide a fresh, new, and sympathetic understanding of Hegel. Excellent bibliography and index. A necessary addition to any academic library.—*G. L. Jones, University of Nevada, Las Vegas*

OAB-2832   JA74   94-24068 CIP
Brown, Wendy. **States of injury: power and freedom in late modernity.** Princeton, 1995. 202p index afp ISBN 0-691-02990-3, $39.50; ISBN 0-691-02989-X pbk, $12.95

In this rich and thought-provoking book, Brown (women's studies, Univ. of California at Santa Cruz) interrogates the state-centered, emancipatory politics of contemporary feminists like Catharine MacKinnon, Christine Williams, Carole Pateman, Barbara Ehrenreich, and Frances Fox Piven to demonstrate how "feminism operating with unreconstructed liberal discourse is ... trapped." She argues that by formulating "unfreedom" as socially injurious practices that need to be redressed through state intervention, the feminist political projects (and those of the political Left) inadvertently perpetuate and strengthen the power of the masculinist liberal state and capitalism, although the state and the capitalist economy are the sites of domination. She suggests alternate discourses of freedom be formulated that "exploit and subvert" the "diffuse and subtle" masculinism of the postmodern state and refashion democratic politics. *States of Injury* should be required reading in graduate and upper-division undergraduate courses in liberalism, modern political theory, feminist theory, and critical legal theory. Strongly recommended for libraries that serve faculty, graduate, and upper-division undergraduate students.—*S. R. Bald, Willamette University*

OAB-2833   E881   95-53043 CIP
Brunk, Gregory G. **Understanding attitudes about war: modeling moral judgments,** by Gregory G. Brunk, Donald Secrest, and Howard Tamashiro. Pittsburgh, 1996. 237p bibl index afp ISBN 0-8229-3926-6, $45.00; ISBN 0-8229-5585-7 pbk, $19.95

The authors examine the ethical beliefs about war of five American elite groups—military officers, journalists, diplomats, members of Congress, and Catholic priests. Their major aim is to describe the moral thinking about military force of US decision makers and opinion leaders. The authors identify major ethical traditions that have influenced American elites (e.g., pacifism, just war, moral crusade) and describe the most influential moral perspectives among contemporary political leaders and thinkers based on survey data. In the light of their empirical findings, the authors develop a theoretical framework to explain how elites develop and apply their moral beliefs about war. Given the limited empirical scholarship on the role of moral norms in international affairs, this study provides an important contribution to the literature. Although it relies excessively on technical terms and scholarly jargon, it is well written, clearly organized, and accessible to nonspecialists. The book belongs in all specialized collections on international affairs and large academic libraries. Upper-division undergraduate through faculty.—*M. Amstutz, Wheaton College*

OAB-2834   JC179   93-16549 CIP
Cullen, Daniel E. **Freedom in Rousseau's political philosophy.** Northern Illinois, 1993. 239p bibl index afp ISBN 0-87580-180-3, $30.00

Cullen's book is sharply worded, so much so as to solicit disagreement. His distinct point of view, combined with his commendable knowledge of

Rousseau's work plus solid grasp of the relevant secondary literature (above all of the works of those who view Rousseau and his place in politics differently) make for enjoyable and instructive reading. Moreover, he demonstrates an excellent knowledge of the history of political philosphy. In general, Cullen has brought all of these positive features together into a sustained analysis of the different ways in which Rousseau uses the term "freedom" and has succeeded in making an appealing case for viewing him as a conservative because of the final—or or dominant—way in which he uses the term. The introduction and conclusion make the argument most clearly, but the middle two chapters of the manuscript provide the substance of the analysis. There are no comparable books on this subject, and few on Rousseau vie with this one for clarity of exposition. It is must reading for graduate students and faculty, as well as those engaged in research on Rousseau, and highly recommended for advanced undergraduate students.—*C. E. Butterworth, University of Maryland at College Park*

OAB-2835   JC71   95-48150 CIP
Davis, Michael. **The politics of philosophy: a commentary on Aristotle's *Politics*.** Rowman & Littlefield, 1996. 152p index afp ISBN 0-8476-8205-6, $54.50; ISBN 0-8476-8206-4 pbk, $22.95

In this compact and deeply profound reading of Aristotle's *Politics*, Davis explains in a new and intriguing way why the city is thought to be natural to man. Aristotle's city is the environment in which reason is most fully developed. But it is not only moral reasoning that citizens develop by making policy decisions about the just and the advantageous—theoretical reasoning is developed as well. This is so because the city is essentially problematic. Like the philosopher who knows only that he does not know, the city is always questing for a perfection that eludes it. For example, the city seeks to be governed by the very best regime, which reason says is kingship. But kingship is no regime at all since it is incompatible with the city's egalitarian nature. Also, the city seeks stability through the second-best regime, called polity. But stability is impossible since any ruling arrangement, no matter how just, offends the dignity of those who are ruled. Being incomplete, the city demands reflection upon itself. It provides the occasion for philosophy and is the place in which philosophy occurs, even though it can never be ruled by philosophy. An exceptional book, filled with exacting arguments and amazing insights. For upper-division undergraduates through faculty.—*P. Coby, Smith College*

OAB-2836   JA75   95-15797 MARC
Dobson, Andrew. **Green political thought.** 2nd ed. Routledge, 1995. 225p bibl index ISBN 0-415-12443-3 pbk, $17.95

The continuing degradation of the earth, despite the proliferation of environmental protection agencies, citizen recycling initiatives, and the like, has augmented the popularity of more radical ways of "green thinking" (see, e.g., *Deep Ecology for the 21st Century*, ed. by George Sessions, 1995; Warwick Fox, *Toward a Transpersonal Ecology*, 1995). Ecologism (e.g., deep ecology, bioregionalism, ecofeminism, social ecology) offers a more fundamental critique of modern assumptions responsible for this degradation than the "light green" approach of "shallow" environmentalism. Dobson's critically sympathetic treatment of these "dark green" modes of thought is at its best when pointing out the weaknesses of ecologism, in particular its seeming political cluelessness. His analysis is concise, straightforward, and cogent. In particular his distinctions between ecologism on the one hand and Romanticism, left-right philosophies, and related streams of thought on the other are first-class. So too is his examination of the ecologistic "sustainable society." Unfortunately, he fails to include in his survey the growing field of ecopsychology, which seems destined to occupy a key place in ecologist thinking (Theodore Roszak, *Voice of the Earth*, 1992; *Ecopsychology* ed. by Roszak, Mary E. Gomes, and Allen D. Kanner, CH, Mar'96). One hopes for a third edition. Highly recommended for all collections.—*D. Kowalewski, Alfred University*

OAB-2837   JA84   92-11187 CIP
Dorrien, Gary. **The neoconservative mind: politics, culture, and**

the war of ideology. Temple University, 1993. 500p bibl index afp ISBN 1-56639-019-2, $34.95

This is an exceptionally well-researched and well-written study of "neoconservatism." Neoconservatives differ from both liberals and traditional conservatives ("paleoconservatives") in significant respects, explains Dorrien (Kalamazoo College). In addition to his superb and balanced general treatment of neoconservatism, Dorrien offers astute intellectual biographies of Irving Kristol, Norman Podhoretz, Michael Novak, and Peter Berger. These four vignettes are invaluable studies of neoconservatism and of contemporary American political thought. His general overview of the genesis of neoconservatism (with comments on such neoconservative "forerunners" as Sidney Hook and James Burnham) is particularly incisive. This volume also serves as a Baedeker to many current journals and offers cogent background about many of the chief political confrontations of the recent past. With the end of the Soviet empire, neoconservatism will—and must—change. Those interested in neoconservatives and their convictions will find this volume indispensable. Excellent notes and bibliography. Advanced undergraduate through faculty.—*J. H. Toner, Air War College*

OAB-2838   JC573   95-26196 CIP
Dunn, Charles W. **The conservative tradition in America,** by Charles W. Dunn and J. David Woodard. Rowman & Littlefield, 1996. 199p bibl index afp ISBN 0-8476-8166-1, $57.50; ISBN 0-8476-8167-X pbk, $14.95

This excellent work combines brevity with historical depth and provides equitable treatment of the different sources and branches of conservative thought in the US, going back to the founding of the nation. It outlines the core beliefs that define conservatism and the varied tendencies that today shape its direction. As a survey, it offers comprehensive and interesting insights without becoming unnecessarily bogged down in controversy or detail. Most conservatives would consider it a judicious account of their intellectual tradition, while those ignorant of this tradition could learn from its clear and objective account. Simply the best short survey of the topic available, this book could serve perfectly the purpose of introducing conservative thought to undergraduates or other curious persons. Highly recommended for classrooms and all libraries.—*J. Stauder, University of Massachusetts-Dartmouth*

OAB-2839   KF9315   92-54800 CIP
Dworkin, Ronald. **Life's dominion: an argument about abortion, euthanasia, and individual freedom.** Knopf, 1993. 273p index ISBN 0-394-58941-6, $23.00

Those familiar with Dworkin (*Law's Empire*, CH, Oct'86, *A Matter of Principle*, CH, Oct'85, *Taking Rights Seriously*, CH, Nov'77) will enjoy his systematic analysis of two of the most devisive moral issues confronting society today, abortion and euthanasia; those unfamiliar with Dworkin now have an opportunity to read one of the more influential legal philosophers writing today, for Dworkin's analysis of these issues can be read without any specific philosophical or legal background. Dworkin forces readers to think more carefully about their moral, philosophical, and religious beliefs, and to make distinctions which help elucidate controversial moral issues. For Dworkin, the life of any human creature, in any form, has intrinsic or sacred value. That, for him, is not the issue, any more than that under the Constitution a fetus does not have status as a constitutional person (Chapter 4). For Dworkin, the key constitutional/political question relates to the power of the state to coerce individuals in matters involving personal decisions. The conclusions, and the manner by which he reaches those conclusions, can and should enlighten one's thinking. This book should be required reading by anyone interested in either of these two issues. Highly recommended. All levels.—*M. A. Foley, Marywood College*

OAB-2840   HQ1233   92-43416 CIP
Enloe, Cynthia. **The morning after: sexual politics at the end of the Cold War.** California, 1993. 326p bibl index afp ISBN 0-520-08335-0, $38.00; ISBN 0-520-08336-9 pbk, $15.00

Enloe's question is "Where are the women?" in analyses of militarization. Examining global politics in the post-Cold War era, she convincingly argues that the "omission of gender ... risks not only a flawed political analysis but also perpetually unsuccessful attempts to roll back militarization." Thus, Enloe displays the best of feminist scholarship in linking theory and reality. Popular images are used effectively to make her argument. The book is timely, containing many powerful observations about the debate on gays in the military, women in combat, the Tailhook scandal, and how such issues inform our understanding of other domestic issues. That she does all this without suggesting that gender or militarization are constructed but one way gives the analysis its rigor. She demonstrates the complexity of gender relations and global military politics, and that not everything can be attributed to the US military-industrial complex. Instead, she says, while "every public power arrangement has depended on the control of femininity as an idea," the particulars will vary depending upon the economic and social context of the nation-state in question. Thus, masculinity and femininity will be constructed to serve that country's national security. Highly recommended.—*L. Bowen, John Carroll University*

OAB-2841   JC49   95-42339 CIP
Esposito, John L. **Islam and democracy,** by John L. Esposito and John O. Voll. Oxford, 1996. 232p bibl index afp ISBN 0-19-510296-7, $45.00; ISBN 0-19-510816-7 pbk, $17.95

The authors, respected scholars of Islam and the Middle East, argue that democracy (the demand for inclusion, government accountability, and participation) has become part of the political discourse in many Muslim societies. "Many Muslims have made advocacy of democracy the political litmus test for the credibility and legitimacy of regimes and for political parties and opposition." From that perspective, the authors examine, as case studies, political ferment in Iran, Sudan, Pakistan, Malaysia, Algeria, and Egypt. Overall, the authors view "democratic Islam" with favor, and tend to blame regime-generated repression in Algeria, Egypt, and Pakistan for much of the violence in those countries. While their argument has merit, it is also the case that some Muslim leaders and groups—e.g., Hezbollah in Lebanon, the so-called Taliban in Afghanistan, Hassan al-Turabi in Sudan—are ferocious enemies of all Western-inspired democratic ways, and espouse the vision of a strict Islamic regime as the cure for all social and political ills. The tug, unfortunately, is both ways, toward democracy and toward repression, and the outcome unclear. At all events, the authors weigh in with a nuanced, complex, and well-reasoned argument, and the book is highly recommended for general and academic readers seeking further light on this subject.—*V. T. Le Vine, Washington University*

OAB-2842   JA71   96-22376 CIP
Eulau, Heinz. **Micro-macro dilemmas in political science: personal pathways through complexity.** Oklahoma, 1996. 542p bibl index afp ISBN 0-8061-2873-9, $37.95

Modern political science owes a profound debt to Eulau, one of its intellectual progenitors. A pioneer in the quest for a scientific study of politics, he has been at the forefront of the discipline for the past half century. In this massive and challenging book, remarkable in character as well as content, he presents an extraordinary account of his personal and professional odyssey. Eulau's unorthodox book, by no means an autobiography, directs attention toward an exploration of "the micro-macro manifold" as linked to his personal experiences. Much of the story of US political science is incorporated in Eulau's narrative, which is further illuminated by discussion of the works and personalities of virtually all the major social scientists of the last 50 years. Eulau is characteristically articulate and probing, precise in his terminology, fresh with his insights, and sturdily argumentative. He challenges readers to think about basic questions and avoid the specialization and fragmentation he sees in political science today. A rarity, this book constitutes required reading and discussion by all serious scholars in the field.—*J. D. Martz, Pennsylvania State University, University Park Campus*

OAB-2843　　　　　JC571　　　　　95-33026 CIP
Gewirth, Alan. **The community of rights.** Chicago, 1996. 380p index afp ISBN 0-226-28880-3, $39.95

Gewirth's *Reason and Morality* (CH, Mar'79) founded morality in a doctrine of universal human rights to freedom and well-being and mostly grounded the negative civil and political rights of democracy. This sequel argues for the positive social and economic rights often regarded in the US as socialistic, and thus goes against the current flow of American politics and economics. Its title is a challenge appropriating for Gewirth's original middle way concepts that are central to extremes he rejects—"community" from nonuniversalistic communtarianism and "rights" from individualistic libertarianism. Also, to Gewirth, the American "democratic state" is not enough, for only a polity that is also a "supportive state" will constitutionally enact the "productive welfarism" his theory demands. Gewirth's right to well-being entails rights to productive agency and employment which avoid debilitating welfare dependency. The theory requires the economic democracy and market socialism of something like the Spanish workers' cooperatives of Mondragon. The 630 footnotes constitute strong evidence of Gewirth's prodigious scholarship. Essential for all libraries.—*J. M. Betz, Villanova University*

OAB-2844　　　　　KF3827　　　　　92-12693 CIP
Glick, Henry R. **The right to die: policy innovation and its consequences.** Columbia, 1992. 238p bibl index afp ISBN 0-231-07638-X, $32.50

Few good policy books explain equally well the substantive policy questions and the comprehensive political circumstances of the topic at hand. Glick's book is a rare and very interesting exception. It stands as the definitive text on right-to-die issues. Yet it also is a good and comprehensive analysis of the politics surrounding these issues. As such, readers who care nothing at all about this policy topic, and perhaps think it insignificant, would still find the book rewarding and full of challenging commentary. In doing so, they would also come to find how central the issue is to contemporary politics. The book effectively straddles another fine line, being neither too analytical to appeal to a general audience nor too pedestrian to please academics. That balance deserves plaudits because the author weaves considerable secondary source analysis and his own field research into the text. The readability and order that results are a tribute both to Glick's skill and intense concern for the subject. This volume is good political science, tailored to be good and informative reading. Some of the more important topics include the half-century emergence of the issues, their relegation to the states, a comparative analysis of state agenda-setting and politics, judicial politics of the issues, and the final summary of national political action. Public and academic cellections, undergraduate through faculty.—*W. P. Browne, Central Michigan University*

OAB-2845　　　　　JC311　　　　　92-6990 CIP
Greenfeld, Liah. **Nationalism: five roads to modernity.** Harvard, 1992. 581p index afp ISBN 0-674-60318-4, $49.95

Greenfeld has written an outstanding and remarkably readable contribution to the literature of nationalism and political development. As the preface indicates, she has wisely taken advantage of her appointment at Harvard University to consult with several leading scholars on the various dimensions of nationalism. But the originality of approach and scholarship is in ample evidence. Greenfeld's work could become a classic. The book itself is divided into five sections—England, France, Russia, Germany, and the US—of approximately 100 pages each. The sections are preceded by an essay that serves as an introduction to define nationalism and characterize its types. The sense of nationhood first appeared in England. It did not spread but seemed to develop in each society as the result of historical and cultural forces, such as the development of a national literature, that combined at certain intervals to establish a national identity. The endnotes are detailed and provide useful insights that demonstrate the meticulous and comprehensive research that was devoted to preparing this study. Essential reading for serious students of nationalism and for historians. Advanced undergraduate; graduate; faculty.—*M. Slann, Clemson University*

OAB-2846　　　　　JC423　　　　　96-13732 CIP
Gutmann, Amy. **Democracy and disagreement,** by Amy Gutmann and Dennis Thompson. Belknap, Harvard, 1996. 422p index afp ISBN 0-674-19765-8, $27.95

Ironically if understandably, as the debate with socialism has evaporated, the debate over democracy has exploded. The authors' defense of deliberative democracy represents a major contribution to the discussion of the best theory and practice of democracy. Gutmann (Princeton) and Thompson (philosophy, Harvard) argue that purely procedural theories of democracy are inadequate to accommodate the genuine moral disagreements that animate contemporary public policy disputes. Yet they also recognize that moral consensus, such as some communitarian theorists posit, will not be forthcoming. Posing instead a justification of democracy that seriously deliberates moral disagreements, seeking moral agreement when possible and maintaining mutual respect at a minimum, they develop standards for judging the quality of democratic discourse. These "constitutional" principles include requirements governing both the conditions (reciprocity, publicity, and accountability) and content (basic liberty, basic opportunity, and fair opportunity) of deliberative democracy. Numerous extended examples of the meaning and interactions of these principles temper the abstract quality of the complex and sophisticated analysis. Although not likely to attract as popular an audience as some other recent voices in the debate over democracy, such as Michael Sandel's *Democracy's Discontent* (1996), *Democracy and Disagreement* is unsurpassed in the critical light it casts on the nature of democratic dialogue. General readers; lower-division undergraduates and up.—*A. B. Cochran, Agnes Scott College*

OAB-2847　　　　　　　　　　　　　　Orig
Hansen, Phillip. **Hannah Arendt: politics, history, and citizenship.** Stanford, 1993. 266p index afp ISBN 0-8047-2145-9, $39.50; ISBN 0-8047-2146-7 pbk, $14.95

The past few years have seen the publication of a remarkable number of studies of the political philosophy of Hannah Arendt. This one by a student of the late C.B. MacPherson and Alkis Kontos should not be overlooked. It is lucidly written with a persuasive tone of urgency, keenly advancing our understanding of Arendt while emphasizing her contribution to a much needed "new sense of the nature of the political and its role in human society." The author's approach to Arendt and to other analysts of her work is bold and argumentative. While Hansen aims to show her contributions to "politically grounded thinking, a distinctive citizen rationality," he does not hesitate to identify what he considers misinterpretations of her work. Two of the book's most compelling discussions are (1) the rendition of Arendt's insights into the crisis in culture and political lying as they relate and illuminate "a public realm under seige," and (2) the argument that Arendt's *Eichmann in Jerusalem* "is a powerful contribution to political theory, a contribution not yet sufficiently recognized." Moreover, Hansen is as refreshing as he is persistent in reminding us that Arendt's work was focused by the fundamental question: what does it mean to think politically? Advanced undergraduate through professional.—*H. G. Reid, University of Kentucky*

OAB-2848　　　　　　　　　　　　　　Orig
Held, David. **Democracy and the global order: from the modern state to cosmopolitan governance.** Stanford, 1996 (c1995). 324p bibl index afp ISBN 0-8047-2686-8, $49.50; ISBN 0-8047-2687-6 pbk, $16.95

Democracy is one of those concepts that is widely used, rarely defined, and often misunderstood by those who use the term or interpret its meaning, yet perhaps no word in human relations is capable of releasing such passion in otherwise sober and dispassionate observers. Held has led efforts to clear the fog and discipline the sloppy language that shrouds this concept in imprecision. His new work continues this effort, paying special attention to the role of democracy in an increasingly globalized world that transcends the capacities of nation-states. This lucid analysis of many of the themes Held previously developed in *Models of Democracy* (CH, Oct'87) focuses on two key concepts: autonomy and democratic public law. Autonomy is simply the condition wherein individuals are free of arbitrary restraint; democratic public law is more complex, but boils down to a system of decent reciprocity that ensures a cosmopolitan democratic order. It would replace nation-states with supranational bodies of authority which, like Madisonian principles of republican democracy, would serve to check and balance forces of tyranny lingering at the nation-state level. Although by no means novel, Held's presentation is among the most insightful and richly delineated in the growing literature on democracy and its precarious existence in a post-Cold War world. It would be difficult to find a single volume more rewarding for those who need to refresh their thinking on the principles of democracy and to employ this concept for the "new world order." Upper-division undergraduates through faculty.—*J. D. Robertson, Texas A&M University*

OAB-2849 HM73 95-20297 CIP
The Impact of values, ed. by Jan W. van Deth and Elinor Scarbrough. Oxford, 1996 (c1995). 588p bibl indexes afp (Beliefs in government, 4) ISBN 0-19-827957-4, $65.00

An invaluable source for students of comparative politics, especially those specializing in the political culture of European democracies, this volume is one of five in the series "Beliefs in Government," growing out of an extended project underwritten by the European Science Foundation. The 19 chapters are devoted to various aspects of value orientations, change, and impact across European democracies during the past four decades. While much of the empirical evidence is presented in a sophisticated fashion and will be somewhat challenging to general readers, the accompanying theoretical discussion is very cogent and largely free of both unnecessary verbiage and burdensome jargon. The theory is not new, but it is freshly presented and clearly organized, thus serving as an excellent review even for seasoned veterans. Although a number of findings deviate from previous work, most results are not really profound; rather, they are small and specialized. The great value of the work is its incredible breadth of cross-national coverage, careful and thorough analysis, and most of all, comprehensive scope. This will be a staple of any serious student of comparative politics for years to come. Graduate; faculty.—*J. D. Robertson, Texas A&M University*

OAB-2850 B1248 92-34016 CIP
Johnson, Laurie M. **Thucydides, Hobbes, and the interpretation of realism.** Northern Illinois, 1993. 259p bibl index afp ISBN 0-87580-175-7, $32.00

Johnson's work is an exemplary canvas of important questions in international relations theory. It is a veritable critical assessment (often negative) of contemporary work in international relations scholarship. But this is the mere filigree of silver holding the golden fruit: her comparison of Thucydides and Hobbes as "realists." Thucydides, "the most politic historiographer that ever writ," and Hobbes, seen by many as a founding positivist philosopher, are closely compared and contrasted in three searching chapters at the heart of Johnson's book. In respect to an understanding of human nature, the place of justice in "theory building," and the role of human agency in politics, Johnson finds Hobbes and much of academic international relations theorizing wanting—inadequate to the task of predicting or understanding the behavior of humans and states. Useful notes, bibliography. Highly recommended for academic and informed general readers alike.—*L. Weinstein, Smith College*

OAB-2851 JC571 94-4089 CIP
Johnston, David. **The idea of a liberal theory: a critique and reconstruction.** Princeton, 1994. 204p bibl index afp ISBN 0-691-03381-1, $29.95

This book is an important contribution to the contemporary dialogue among liberal political theorists. Johnston provides a well-argued critique of some representative thinkers from three types of liberal theory: rights-based liberalism (Robert Nozick and James Buchanan); perfectionist liberalism (J.S. Mill and Joseph Raz); and political liberalism (John Rawls). Rejecting some elements while adopting others from each category, Johnston proposes his own "humanist liberalism" built around the premise that each individual has a generalized interest in being an effective human agent, able to pursue and achieve individually selected projects and values. Individual rights and basic goods are

regarded as means to achieve such effective agency; and principles of distributive justice are determined on that basis. The book is exceptionally well written and reflects a thorough familiarity with the current state of the literature. Indeed, so clear is the argument that the book is valuable not only for its contribution to academic scholarship but also as a means of introducing liberal political thought to serious undergraduate students. Highly recommended.—*S. D. Jacobitti, Southern Illinois University-Edwardsville*

OAB-2852 JC573 95-24101 CIP
Kristol, Irving. **Neoconservatism: the autobiography of an idea.** Free Press, 1995. 493p index ISBN 0-02-874021-1, $25.00

"Neoconservatism" is the label applied to the movement of a number of US intellectuals over the past few decades away from leftism and liberalism toward political conservatism. Kristol has been the acknowledged "godfather" of that movement, and an important social critic for a whole generation. This anthology contains 41 of his essays spanning a half century and covering a variety of topics—religious, literary, and cultural as well as political. A substantial introduction provides an "autobiographical memoir," intellectual and personal, with recollections of various literary and political personalities. The essays in the book retain a timeliness and interest due to Kristol's discerning analysis, and are invariably written in his clear, felicitous style. This volume provides many useful insights into the thought of modern American conservatism. Essential for any college library, as an invaluable window into the history of American ideas in the second half of this century.—*J. Stauder, University of Massachusetts-Dartmouth*

OAB-2853 JC423 96-24373 CIP
Lakoff, Sanford. **Democracy: history, theory, practice.** Westview, 1996. 388p bibl index afp ISBN 0-8133-3227-3, $60.00; ISBN 0-8133-3228-1 pbk, $19.95

The hottest topic in political theory and comparative politics is the process of democratization. Unlike many books on this topic, Lakoff's delivers originality and substance, in one of the most penetrating and clearest etymological analyses of democracy. With impressive scope and lucidity, Lakoff dissects the concept of democracy, exploring the historical development of the normative and empirical components of the ideal. Juxtaposing its normative and empirical, classical and modern, ideal and practical dimensions, Lakoff concentrates on the concept of democratic autonomy. He distinguishes three forms of autonomy within modern democracies. Individual autonomy is the right of individuals to "regulate their own conduct as they see fit, providing only that in doing so they do not deny others the same opportunity"; plural autonomy, "the right of social sub-groups ... to regulate their own affairs and pursue their own ends, subject only to the same limit"; and communal autonomy, "the acknowledged right of the more inclusive political associations to collective self-determination, whether by majority rule or by consensus." Evaluation of successful democratization and of democracy in advanced societies must start with these three forms of autonomy and examine how society balances the inherent tension they produce. Lakoff's book, an invaluable antidote to the argument that democracy is a simple product of political, social, and economic engineering, sets a standard for understanding democracy as a product of history, theory, and practice. Upper-division undergraduates and up.—*J. D. Robertson, Texas A&M University*

OAB-2854 JA71 96-21984 CIP
Lane, Ruth. **Political science in theory and practice: the 'politics' model.** M.E. Sharpe, 1997. 178p bibl index afp ISBN 01-56324-939-1, $52.95; ISBN 1-56724-940-5 pbk, $21.95

In recent years Lane has embraced the difficult task of describing the progress political science has made as a discipline toward becoming a legitimate social science. In one current effort Lane argues that comparative politics, while not providing absolutes in its model, has made real progress in identifying the range and logic of its study (*The Art of Comparative Politics*, 1997). The present book is even more intrepid and satisfying. The work intends to show that political science, far from being an incoherent and undisciplined branch of the social sciences, has developed a systematic and definable foundation for what can be considered a scientific understanding of the difficult topic of politics. Lane describes this foundation as "the politics model," giving a ten-point description of the model and identifying it with major practitioners in the field. She does not skirt controversy but takes readers on an engaging journey through every step of political research, showing how theory and the concrete model of politics are used and can lead to a new philosophy of science for politics. The new philosophy is based on a scientific realism emphasizing political process and real people. Lane argues that, like Dorothy returned from Oz, political scientists need only look in their own backyards for a future of new possibilities. Essential reading for all political scientists, this book is bound to start many conversations. Graduate students, researchers, and faculty.—*A. R. Brunello, Eckerd College*

OAB-2855 JF1338 95-41793 CIP
Lynn, Laurence E. **Public management as art, science, and profession.** Chatham House, 1996. 200p index ISBN 1-56643-034-8 pbk, $19.95

In his essay "The Study of Administration," *Political Science Quarterly* (June 1887), Woodrow Wilson advanced two arguments. He claimed that public administration should be recognized as a profession, and that administrative and political choices should be distinct and separated in practice. Lynn's highly readable book accepts and amplifies that first point, while forcefully rejecting the latter. More than a century after Wilson's classic polemic, Lynn notes, correctly, that there is no widely recognized, coherent understanding of public management among practitioners, academics, or the public. The role of the public manager is unsettled, according to Lynn, because the field has been partitioned between "management as policy-making" and "management as administration." He makes a strong case that this confusion has made it difficult for scholars to produce a body of research that would improve the practice of public management. Establishing that public management is a profession consisting of both policy analysis and organizational administration would facilitate the development of useful knowledge. Although these are not new ideas, Lynn's thoughtful, engaging book explores why the character of public management remains problematic. Strongly recommended for advanced undergraduates and graduate students.—*M. E. Ethridge, University of Wisconsin—Milwaukee*

OAB-2856 JC143 95-50910 CIP
Machiavelli, Niccolò. **Discourses on Livy,** tr. by Harvey C. Mansfield and Nathan Tarcov. Chicago, 1996. 367p index afp ISBN 0-226-50035-7, $34.95

In a field as torn by controversy as present-day Machiavelli scholarship, claims to "definitive" editions must be made at great hazard. Still, this edition must rank at or near the top of modern translations. Mansfield and Tarcov, distinguished and embattled Machiavellians, offer a lively and inviting conspectus of the main visible Machiavellianisms in their introduction, and refer more than once to "treasures" awaiting discovery by probing and discerning readers. Unfortunately, the full text of the *Discourses* is offered in a type size that seems designed to keep Machiavelli's vaunted subtleties invisible to most readers (justifying John Locke's complaint that the printers of books are among the natural enemies of authors). A very useful glossary of key terms, an index of proper names, and a list of suggested readings are included. A whiff of controversy is suggested by the omission of both the Walker and Gilbert translations from the list of readings. A model of contemporary scholarship and a brave effort at Machiavelli translation that allows the great Florentine to speak in his own voice, this edition will be essential for all college, university, and well-endowed public libraries.—*L. Weinstein, Smith College*

OAB-2857 JC229 95-38604 CIP
Manent, Pierre. **Tocqueville and the nature of democracy,** tr. by John Waggoner. Rowman & Littlefield, 1996. 148p afp ISBN 0-8476-8115-7, $40.00; ISBN 0-8476-8116-5 pbk, $18.95

This pathbreaking book may well be the most provocative and insightful

study of Tocqueville ever published. Manent's exploration of *Democracy in America* was first published in French in 1982, here capably translated by John Waggoner. It is rightly described in Harvey Mansfield's foreword as "elegant and profound." Its elegance lies in the concise and lucid writing, guided by an unerring instinct for central points and eye-opening statements from Tocqueville. Its profundity lies in the intransigent pursuit of the core logic, the "idea," of democracy itself. Everyone knows that Tocqueville found the US the most completely democratic society of his day. He described and analyzed what he saw with great comprehensiveness yet with a certain geniality that has led many of his readers to overlook the depth of his insight. Manent's study is undeterred by the genial surface and the wealth of particulars discussed in *Democracy in America*. His theme is the critical examination of what Tocqueville teaches us about the "idea" of democracy. This provocative topic is explored with startling acuity, and few readers will leave this book without a new appreciation of Tocqueville's importance. General and academic readers, all levels.—*D. J. Maletz, University of Oklahoma*

OAB-2858 JF1525 95-18074 CIP
Moore, Mark H. **Creating public value: strategic management in government.** Harvard, 1995. 402p index afp ISBN 0-674-17557-3, $45.00

Moore (Kennedy School of Government, Harvard) offers a bilevel view of public management. The book is most obviously a manual for public managers on how to operate in a politically demanding and ever-changing environment, drawing on cases from the Kennedy School files. It also demonstrates how government bureaucracies can create and enhance "public value," a useful concept for anyone who wants to know how to hold bureaucracies accountable for the common good. Basically, managers must look not only downward to the competent operation of their agencies but also outward to the accomplishment of worthy public purposes and upward toward securing more effective policy mandates. Managerial success occurs when public enterprises increase the effectiveness or fairness of current missions or shift their focus to meet a higher priority need. This calls for political management that builds support and legitimacy for agency initiatives. A worthy addition to "reinventing management" works such as Robert Denhardt's *The Pursuit of Significance* (1993), Martin Levin and Mary Sanger's *Making Government Work* (CH, Dec'94), and Ronald Heifetz's *Leadership without Easy Answers* (CH, Jun'95). Highly recommended for faculty, graduate students, and advanced undergraduates.—*W. C. Johnson, Bethel College (MN)*

OAB-2859 JA71 96-26117 CIP
Morrice, David. **Philosophy, science and ideology in political thought.** Macmillan (UK)/St. Martin's, 1996. 310p bibl index ISBN 0-312-16348-7, $65.00

Contemporary political thinkers such as Leo Strauss, Eric Voegelin, Dante Germino, and Ellis Sandoz have all worked diligently to recapture Plato's distinction between theory and ideology, while noting that contemporary discussion tends to blur this critical difference. Morrice contributes valuable insights in a book that is both polemical and analytic. His aim is nothing less than to restore normative theory to a preeminent position in political science; in pursuit of this goal, he advances excellent and well-reasoned arguments against all forms of relativism, "value-free" political analysis, and ideology. Many modern thinkers are examined, but his is not just secondary analysis: Morrice advances his own theory and arguments in the process. This bracing and passionate work not only repays reading but serious studying as well, and is highly recommended for all students and scholars of politics.—*M. Berheide, Berea College*

OAB-2860 JX1952 95-12482 CIP
Morrisey, Will. **A political approach to pacifism: book 1; book 2.** E. Mellen, 1996. 2v. 904p bibl index (Symposium series, 39a-b) ISBN 0-7734-8910-X, v.1; ISBN 0-7734-8912-6, v.2; $109.95 ea.

Massively erudite, this work argues against absolute pacifism and "bellicism" in favor of "prudent" just-war fighting by "'American' commercial

Choice's Outstanding Academic Books

republics" into the indefinite future. Research support from the US Institute for Peace is acknowledged. The text is contained in v.1 (451 p.) and requires reference to v.2, which consists entirely of 2,229 extensive endnotes (216 p.), more than 1,500 bibliographical sources (95 p.), and a name index (37 p.). Inspired by Plato's dialogic *Republic*, explicitly emulated in chapter 4, Morrisey reviews arguments from antiquity to the present. His critical interpolations throughout emphasize grounds for rejection of pacifism that will be familiar to readers of this work: human nature is prone to lethal aggression; defensive killing for survival of self, society, and freedom is justified. Morrisey's uniquely comprehensive work summarizes and carries forward the long tradition of justifications for war and violence in Western political philosophy. As Leon Harold Craig notes in his study of Plato's *Republic*, "there is a deep relationship between philosophy and war" (*The War Lover*, CH, Apr'95). Recommended for war and peace collections, advanced researchers, and admirers of scholarly erudition.— *G. D. Paige, emeritus, University of Hawaii at Manoa*

OAB-2861   JK325   95-13773 CIP
Peterson, Paul E. **The price of federalism.** Brookings, 1995. 239p bibl index afp ISBN 0-8157-7024-3, $36.95; ISBN 0-8157-7023-5 pbk, $15.95

Peterson makes a convincing argument for what he labels "functional federalism." He argues that states are best equipped to make development policy that "provides the physical and social infrastructure necessary to facilitate a country's economic growth" while the national government is the only entity capable of redistributive policy where societal resources are transferred from the "haves" to the "have-nots" (e.g., health care, welfare). While so recommending, he does an exemplary job of demonstrating the practical and political limitations of this ideal arrangement. Juxtaposing the functional perspective with what he calls "legislative federalism," where policies are determined by the political needs of those making laws, he is able to explain the policy status quo and demonstrate empirically the strengths and limitations of that status quo. The volume is particularly timely, reflecting the implications of the 1994 congressional elections. The analysis is compelling and provocative. The volume is a nice complement to earlier works by Peterson (e.g., *City Limits*, CH, Dec'81; *When Federalism Works*, CH, Jun'87). Highly recommended for upper-division undergraduate through faculty.— *L. Bowen, John Carroll University*

OAB-2862   PQ2034   91-50820 MARC
Rousseau, Jean-Jacques. **Discourse on the sciences and arts: (first discourse) and polemics,** ed. by Roger D. Masters and Christopher Kelly; tr. by Judith R. Bush, Roger D. Masters, and Christopher Kelly. Dartmouth College/University Press of New England, 1992. 233p index afp (The collected writings of Rousseau, 2) ISBN 0-87451-580-7, $40.00

Students of Rousseau lacking a knowledge of French will long be in the debt of Masters and Kelly. This volume in the "Collected Writings of Rousseau" testifies to the intelligent scholarship of the editors, Masters and Kelly, as well as to their, plus Bush's, translating skills. Students and teachers who have long labored over Rousseau's First Discourse, the work that first brought him to the notice of the learned world, can now read the discourse along with the numerous objections made to it by worthy contemporary critics and Rousseau's replies to them. Rousseau's quick wit and keen sense of expression are displayed at their best here. At the same time he manages to clarify many of the obscure features of his thinking. Readers lacking French are now also able to ponder Rousseau's preface to his delightful little play, "Narcissus or the Lover of Himself", even though they may blame Masters and Kelly for depriving them of the play itself. The introduction is helpful despite its shortness and the notes useful without being burdensome.— *C. E. Butterworth, University of Maryland at College Park*

OAB-2863   JC176   91-38426 CIP
Sapiro, Virginia. **A vindication of political virtue: the political theory of Mary Wollstonecraft.** Chicago, 1992. 366p bibl index afp ISBN 0-226-73490-0, $53.00

Since the publication of *A Vindication of the Rights of Women* in 1792, Mary

Wollstonecraft has been variously eulogized, vilified, forgotten, and reclaimed. In recent years, feminists have enthroned her as an important theoretical foremother; both her polemic and the story of her unconventional life have become standard elements in the basic women's studies syllabus. But in her own time she was well known for other literary and political writing that is largely ignored. In this elegant intellectual biography, Sapiro offers a rereading of Wollstonecraft's life and work that portrays her as a "thoughtful and complex" writer on politics and society. The author freely admits to a desire to affect tradition and to reveal the Wollstonecraft's ideas as worthy of considerably "more than a footnote in the general history of political theory." This historically nuanced analysis claims a place for Wollstonecraft's thought within the modern tradition of political theory, arguing that her work ought to be studied as a critical contribution to the ongoing political conversation of the last three centuries. A must for all undergraduate libraries with strength in political science and women's studies. General; undergraduate; graduate; faculty.— *N. B. Rosenthal, SUNY College at Old Westbury*

OAB-2864   JC478   96-41910 MARC
Saul, John Ralston. **The unconscious civilization.** Free Press, 1997. 199p ISBN 0-684-83257-7, $22.00

Saul's book is a brilliantly written polemic against mindless devotion to "corporatism." For Saul (a Canadian essayist and novelist) the chief impulse behind today's glorification of market-driven individualism is a social order of big institutions led by irresponsible technocratic elites in government and big business. The new world order thrives on its distribution of rewards as cover for its discouragement of active, publicly interested civic engagement. Passive and conformist in our politics, we become energized with the trivial nonconformities promised by salesmanship, style, and fashion. Saul's themes will be familiar to students of the Frankfurt School; his project of a democracy built on "disinterested citizenship" echoes themes found in Jürgen Habermas and John Dewey. But Saul's acid, epigrammatic style is wonderfully readable, so his essay might prove extremely useful to teachers searching for a literate and provocative source in courses on contemporary democracy or the crisis of advanced society. Upper-division undergraduates through faculty.— *S. Plotkin, Vassar College*

OAB-2865   KF4600   95-8595 CIP
Shapiro, David L. **Federalism: a dialogue.** Northwestern University, 1995. 154p bibl index afp ISBN 0-8101-1262-0, $59.95; ISBN 0-8101-1280-9 pbk, $19.95

Shapiro (Harvard Law) has written a timely and engaging analysis of federal-state relations. Beginning from the premise that "the federal system is alive and well" and that "the important role of states in the functioning of the federal system is beyond dispute", he seeks to support his views via a dialogue. He defends a strong centralized government by examining constitutional text, intent, and interpretation, then does the same for state sovereignty, ultimately offering a synthesis to defend his original premise. Although the defense of the centralized government (chapter 2) is a bit more spirited than that of state autonomy (chapter 3), the debate is nonetheless stimulating and rigorous, culminating in an analysis relevant for understanding the current US Supreme Court and Congress and their relationship with state governments as well as one another. The postscript acknowledging the decision in *U.S. v. Lopez* is appropriate. The author's point that *Lopez* does not necessarily signify a complete redefinition of federal power is well taken. *Lopez* does not call into question the timeliness of the author's analysis or his conclusions. Highly recommended, upper-division undergraduate through faculty.— *L. Bowen, John Carroll University*

OAB-2866   JX1318   95-35012 MARC
Sheehan, Michael. **The balance of power: history and theory.** Routledge, 1996. 226p bibl index ISBN 0-415-11930-8, $59.95; ISBN 0-415-11931-6 pbk, $16.95

This excellent review of the historical evolution of the theory and policy of balance-of-power thinking argues that this thinking represents a systemic approach that integrates the Hobbesian self-preservation type of state policy with the Grotian systemic view of state behavior in international relations. Critically building on the work of Martin Wight, Hans Morgenthau, Morton Kaplan, and Inis Claude, among others, Sheehan shows how scholars and policy makers who reduce the balance-of-power distinction between theory and policy undermine its analytical and practical effectiveness. Like Sheehan, Hedley Bull's *The Anarchical Society: A Study of Order in World Politics* (CH, Oct'77) argues that balance of power reflects the Grotian theoretical view of international society; however, while Bull disputes the relevance of structural functionalism for international relations, Sheehan finds it relevant, provided that it allows for the impact of history and the possibility of various structural patterns and change. Sheehan's review of balance-of-power thinking and his comparison of it with other international relations theories, including collective security, bandwagoning, and others, are excellent. Highly recommended for all students of international relations and history.—*R. J. Vichot, Florida International University*

OAB-2867   HX36   94-18170 MARC
Silber, Irwin. **Socialism—what went wrong?: an inquiry into the theoretical and historical sources of the socialist crisis.** Pluto, 1994. 309p bibl index ISBN 0-7453-0715-9, $66.50

A lifelong activist and journalist within the "Marxist-Leninist" tradition, Silber here excoriates this tradition, performing a deeply informed *tour d'horizon* of the history of the Communist movement and the Soviet Union. Nothing survives his "rigorous ... merciless" postmortem. "Socialism," Silber says, "will not become a politically relevant vision again unless its advocates can free themselves from the twin shadows of the Soviet prototype and its Marxist-Leninist hagiography." By Marxism-Leninism, Silber refers specifically to Stalin's codification of the dictatorship of the proletariat (and thus the party), the construction of socialism, and the complex of ideas that surrounded the "administrative-command" economy. Although Silber's systematic (and negative) evaluation of key Leninist political ideas will be familiar to most scholars, his clear language and historical scope make the work valuable. He covers the doctrine of capitalist collapse, the vanguard party, the construction of socialism, the dictatorship of the proletariat, world revolution, and the future of socialism. This last, paradoxically but not surprisingly, endorses a return to social democratic evolutionism. Capitalism, Silber thinks, must expand to its limits before a new system can replace it, and that process is apt to look more like evolution than revolution. This is a comprehensive and informed analysis by a skilled journalist working within the Marxist tradition, who is well acquainted with official documents and Soviet memoirs. All levels.—*R. J. S. Ross, Clark University*

OAB-2868   U101   96-13695 MARC
Sun-tzu. **The complete art of war,** by Sun Tzu and Sun Pin; tr., with introd. and commentary by Ralph D. Sawyer with Mei chün Lee Sawyer. Westview, 1996. 304p index afp ISBN 0-8133-3085-8, $25.00

The *Complete Art of War* should be in every library. By combining Suntzu's *Art of War* and Sun Pin's *Military Methods*, Ralph Sawyer has given readers a masterful and stimulating work. Clear, complete, and accompanied by excellent commentary, the book can be studied, analyzed, and enjoyed on many levels. For those interested in military science and discipline, it is a classic; for those interested in organization and leadership, it is insightful and challenging; for those interested in marketing and even advertising, it is perspicacious and vital. *The Complete Art of War* focuses on that most human of activities, and echoes the words of Sun-tzu, "Warfare is the greatest affair of state, the basis of life and death, the way to survival or extinction. It must be thoroughly pondered and analyzed." Given the relevance of its reverberations with modern life, it is sometimes difficult to appreciate that these works were written more than 2,000 years ago. General and academic readers.—*C. Potholm II, Bowdoin College*

OAB-2869   JX1305   93-35872 CIP
Thompson, Kenneth W. **Fathers of international thought: the legacy of political theory.** Louisiana State, 1994. 144p bibl index afp ISBN 0-8071-1905-9, $27.50; ISBN 0-8071-1906-7 pbk, $9.95

Thompson follows his *Masters of International Thought* (1980) with this search for the classical philosophical fathers of international relations. He seeks to discover a theoretical basis for contemporary principles. Thompson concludes that reading Plato provides insight into recurring issues, that Aristotle reveals characteristic features of differing regimes, and that Augustine resolves the church/state dualism. Aquinas augments the tradition with a natural law theory and supplies the groundwork for Grotius's formulation of international law. Thompson notes contributions made by other leading theorists. The rich heritage these fathers provided shapes the ideas and actions of contemporary international figures. Thompson, a mature scholar, is the author of 21 previous theoretical studies. This outstanding work is suitable for both the general and advanced student of international politics.—*M. S. Power, Arkansas State University*

OAB-2870   JA84   94-36870 CIP
Van Dyke, Vernon. **Ideology and political choice: the search for freedom, justice, and virtue.** Chatham House, 1995. 312p bibl index ISBN 1-56643-017-8 pbk, $24.95

Ideology and Political Choice may be remembered as a capstone achievement in Van Dyke's (Iowa) long and distinguished career. It prevails against powerful counterwinds: the decades-old "end of ideology" contention, later underscored by the collapse of the Cold War, then of the Soviet Union, called into question the motivational relevance of philosophical ideas in political practice. Moreover, writers long have alluded to Americans' "ideological innocence." But in this comprehensive, balanced, and engagingly written work, Van Dyke chronicles and authenticates the texture, diversity, and relevance of ideologies in, or close to, the contemporary US political mainstream. Perhaps already aware of what separates one from the other, adherents of liberalism and devotees of conservatism will learn from Van Dyke about their important *internal* differences as well. The author's chapters on libertarianism and on public choice are of special value, in part because they cover ground often untouched or only lightly touched by other works purporting to cover contemporary mainstream political thought. There also is a fine chapter on the British background. Strongly recommended for general, undergraduate, and graduate collections.—*J. D. Gillespie, Presbyterian College*

OAB-2871   KD8406   93-4428 CIP
Von Hirsch, Andrew. **Censure and sanctions.** Oxford, 1994 (c1993). 133p bibl index afp ISBN 0-19-825768-6, $34.00

Discussion of criminal sentencing theory and practice tends to be distorted by media sensationalism, public fear of crime and anger at offenders, and political demagoguery. Politicization of sentencing across the US is producing ever-longer sentences, removal of judicial and parole board discretion, and gargantuan projected incarceration costs. Into this fray strides one of the leading exponents of "desert theory," returning to defend and modify his approach (presented in two earlier books) in response to critics. Desert theory argues that sentences should be proportionate to the gravity of the crime committed, and contrasts with utilitarian theories based on deterrence, efforts at rehabilitation, predictions of future dangerousness, or "three-strikes-and-you're-out" approaches that mandate lengthy terms for minor offenses committed by repeat offenders. Von Hirsh argues that sentences should be calculated on the basis of the criminal's relative culpability and the degree of harm inflicted, measured by the degree to which the crime reduces a victim's standard of living. This principled and humane approach to sentencing is set forth clearly and concisely, as are the views of its critics. A valuable restating and updating of one of the most influential theories of punishment extant, it has both contemporary and lasting significance. Highly recommended.—*E. McKenzie, Albright College*

OAB-2872   HX39   94-32893 CIP
Walicki, Andrzej. **Marxism and the leap to the kingdom of freedom: the rise and fall of the communist utopia.** Stanford, 1995. 641p bibl index afp ISBN 0-8047-2384-2, $65.00

Walicki (Notre Dame) makes a significant contribution to debates over reasons for the collapse of international communism. He views the debacle as grounded in Marxist ideology and its contradictions, which he traces from Marx and Engels through Lenin to the "mature" Soviet Union. The basic contradiction is between the peculiar Marxist concept of "freedom" and the goal to eliminate market economy. To develop his argument, the author surveys the entire history of Western Marxism. He offers insightful analyses of the thought of Marx and Engels and dazzling critiques of, e.g., Plekhanov, Kautsky, Luxemburg, and Lukacs. The discrepancy between Lenin's revolution and Marxist theory of socioeconomic development is touched on, a divergence that is inconvenient for Walicki's argument about continuity between the founders and Lenin. The analysis of Gorbachev's motivations is speculative, and the book's latter sections become increasingly argumentative. Nevertheless, Walicki's thesis concerning the ideological foundations of the Soviet state and their weaknesses is persuasive. In positing the centrality of ideology for Soviet communism, Walicki agrees with such scholars as Robert Conquest, Adam Ulam, and Ernst Kux, a viewpoint now taken more seriously after decades of "behavioral" study of communist systems. A book of such monumental scope will arouse controversies among Marxologists, but this book is an intellectual tour de force, rarely equalled in studies of Marxism. Graduate; faculty.—*R. J. Mitchell, University of New Orleans*

OAB-2873 JC423 93-8945 CIP
A World fit for people: thinkers from many countries address the political, economic, and social problems of our time, ed. by Üner Kirdar and Leonard Silk. New York University, 1994. 481p afp ISBN 0-8147-4648-9, $40.00

The editors, distinguished public policy analysts, constructed this book out of the ideas of some 50 global thinkers, many associated with the UN Development Program's 1992 Bucharest conference on change. Tightly edited and clearly written, these essays are must reading for both scholars and students of the international political economy and development. The four parts each begin with a valuable overview by the editors. Part 1, on political reconstruction, discusses the search for a saner world, the changes actually occurring, and the linkage of democracy and market. Part 2, on economic development, stresses the interaction of markets, governments, and global support, while Part 3 examines social and cultural dimensions of change and the relationships among ecology, sustainability, and development. Part 4 moves from the obstacles to change anchored in the old order, through behavioral and structural characteristics of countries in transition, to the nature of the learning curve during the process of transition, and the roles of privatization and trade. Foreword by Boutros Boutros-Ghali; extensively documented with notes. Containing the best thinking of the world's leaders in the field, this is a useful library resource and interdisciplinary supplement for courses in development and change. All levels.—*R. E. Will, Carleton College*

OAB-2874 JC571 96-9756 CIP
Zuckert, Michael P. **The natural rights republic: studies in the foundation of the American political tradition.** [Rev. ed.]. Notre Dame, 1997 (c1996). 298p bibl index afp ISBN 0-268-01480-9, $32.95

Zuckert (Carleton College) accomplishes several things in this masterful study. First, by reading the Declaration of Independence in a way that attends to the structure of its argument, he restores its philosophic credibility and rhetorical coherence, brilliantly clarifying the statement about "self-evident" truths. Second, he relates the "natural rights" argument of the Declaration to its broader context in Jefferson's thought, through a sensitive reading of *Notes on the State of Virginia.* Third, in opposition to the claim of an essential continuity from the Mayflower Compact to the Declaration, he shows how the "American mind" came to be transformed by 1776 so as to accept the Lockean natural rights argument, in contrast to the original political aspirations of the Puritans. Fourth, he explains how the Lockean argument was able to incorporate elements of the American people's Puritan and republican "commitments," so as to engender a synthesis of liberal politics with "civil religion." Fifth, he traces the evolution of Jefferson's thought on republicanism after 1776, emphasizing the continued primacy in it of nat-

ural rights (versus the "republican synthesis"). Erudite, cogently argued, and beautifully written; strongly recommended for all libraries.—*D. Schaefer, College of the Holy Cross*

■ United States

OAB-2875 JK325 92-12077 CIP
Beer, Samuel H. **To make a nation: the rediscovery of American federalism.** Harvard, 1993. 474p bibl index afp ISBN 0-674-89317-4, $29.95

This is an important book that should occasion much discussion among students of the American founding and the American polity. Beer (Harvard, and a former president of the American Political Science Association) sets out "to clarify and amplify the national theory of American federalism." His approach is through the history of ideas, beginning with an examination of "the authoritarian and corporatist themes which dominated Western political thought in the centuries before the rise of modern republicanism," proceeding through a consideration of the essentials of Commonwealth republicanism as put forward by the colonists in their criticism of British rule, and culminating in the conception of the national and federal republic reformulated chiefly in the words of Alexander Hamilton, James Madison, and James Wilson. All of this is intended to provide the theoretical and historical justification of the "nationalist" conception of the American polity as opposed to the "compact" conception that has found its most recent and forceful expression in the words of Ronald Reagan. As a contribution to the debate over the nature of the American polity, this book is absolutely essential reading. Extensive bibliography and index. A necessary addition to libraries serving both academic and general readers.—*G. L. Jones, University of Nevada, Las Vegas*

OAB-2876 Orig
Bérubé, Michael. **Public access: literary theory and American cultural politics.** Verso, 1994. 272p index ISBN 0-86091-424-0, $64.95; ISBN 0-86091-678-2 pbk, $18.95

This is an important and valuable book, one that should, but probably will not, reach the wide audience its author envisions for it. Actually, Berube (Univ. of Illinois, Urbana) has two audiences in mind: academics, particularly those in the humanities, and the general reading public. The book is both academic (it makes an important and insightful contribution to the study of cultural politics) and political; indeed, part of its message is that the two cannot really be separated. His consideration of literary theory and criticism is intended to impress on academics the importance of gaining "public access," i.e., access to the general public, and to demonstrate to the general reading public that the picture of academia painted by such books as Roger Kimball's *Tenured Radicals* (CH, Jun'90), Allan Bloom's *The Closing of the American Mind* (CH, Sep'87), and, most importantly, Dinesh D'Souza's *Illiberal Education* (CH, Dec'91) is an inaccurate and perverted one. On the whole he is successful in making his case, and it can only be hoped that it will reach its intended audiences and that they will listen to it. It is similar in character to Jim Merod's *The Political Responsibility of the Critic* (1987) and, in a slightly different way, Michael Parenti's recent *Land of Idols* (1994). No bibliography. An absolutely essential acquisition for libraries serving both academic and/or general readers. All levels.—*G. L. Jones, University of Nevada, Las Vegas*

OAB-2877 HN59 96-31277 CIP
Bork, Robert H. **Slouching towards Gomorrah: modern liberalism and American decline.** Regan Books, 1996. 382p index ISBN 0-06-039163-4, $25.00

Bork's jeremiad on the US's cultural decadence attempts to find the source of this decline in the perversion of the ideals of liberty and equality on which the country was founded. He finds radical individualism and radical egalitarianism at the root of the moral crisis he believes is undermining US civilization. His ambitious attempt at a comprehensive conservative critique of the modern US draws a wide variety of topics into its analysis: degeneracy in popular culture; questions of censorship; the rise of crime, illegitimacy, and welfare; the issues of abortion, assisted suicide, and euthanasia; modern feminism; judicial activism; the problems of racial antagonism, multiculturalism, and affirmative action; "the decline of intellect" in the universities; the weakening of religious faith and of the mainline churches; and throughout, the pervasive loss of confidence by Americans in the virtues of their distinctive civilization. *Slouching Towards Gomorrah* will probably rank as one of the most important books of this decade. For its intellectual contribution to the ongoing debates over the US's culture and future, it should have a place in every library.—*J. Stauder, University of Massachusetts-Dartmouth*

OAB-2878 F128 92-427 CIP
Brecher, Charles. **Power failure: New York City politics and policy since 1960,** by Charles Brecher and Raymond D. Horton. Oxford, 1993. 393p index afp ISBN 0-19-504427-4, $35.00

It is hard to find any other study as well done by such qualified individuals. It brings its lauded predecessor, Wallace S. Sayre and Herbert Kaufman's *Governing New York City* (1960), through the changing political, social, and economic environment of New York up to the early 1990s and does so comprehensively. Brecher (NYU) and Horton (Columbia Univ.) draw from their own long experience in local politics and from a myriad of other sources to produce what they have chosen to call a "guidebook" to New York City's government and political life. They posit early on that "politics and policy cannot be separated" and follow that precept through four parts: introduction and overview, electoral politics, budgetary politics and policy, and service delivery. They reject Sayre and Kaufman's pluralist interpretation of local politics in favor of an amply demonstrated interest group model. It is clear that the authors find that the governmental system which has come into being in New York City is far from ideal, and challenge the city's residents "to explore the subject" further and carry it "into the fray of promoting reform." Excellently crafted tables and notes validate their points. A masterpiece for anyone interested in the problems large cities encounter in developing an adequate mode of governance. All levels.—*R. H. Leach, Duke University*

OAB-2879 JC423 95-34411 CIP
Combs, James E. **The comedy of democracy,** by James E. Combs and Dan Nimmo. Praeger, 1996. 203p bibl index afp ISBN 0-275-94979-6, $55.00

Political scientists have paid scant attention to the connection between art, broadly conceived, and politics. Combs and Nimmo make this connection in a manner far more understandable and relevant than Murray Edelman in *From Art to Politics* (CH, Oct'95). As experts in the field of political communication, Combs and Nimmo maintain that understanding politics requires more than serious analysis; it also requires that we view American political institutions, processes, rituals, and policies as comedy. What follows is a series of insightful chapters, part polemic and part interpretative essay, that associate some aspect of American political life with a particular type of comedic form. The chapter on elections, for example, is examined in the context of 15th-century comedies of farce and humors; public opinion is viewed in terms of comedies of wit that stress clever expression. The president is viewed by the media as comic figure—a fool—rather than a heroic or tragic figure. Here is an intelligent and innovative contribution. Not all will agree with the authors' premise or conclusions, but few will deny that this work opens up a new dimension of empirical and normative significance. Highly recommended for all readership levels.—*E. C. Dreyer, University of Tulsa*

OAB-2880 E885 94-31603 CIP
Greenberg, Stanley B. **Middle class dreams: the politics and power of the new American majority.** Times Books/Random House, 1995. 338p index ISBN 0-8129-2345-6, $25.00

Stanley Greenberg is Bill Clinton's pollster. Before he became a political

consultant, however, Greenberg wrote three books while on the political science faculty at Yale. This new book is a product of his two careers: academic in the careful historical analysis of party eras, attention to relevant literature, and sophisticated statistical procedures; consulting in his forthright analysis of contemporary electoral politics and use of plain, cogent English. Not an insider's view of the Clinton campaign, the book focuses entirely on the middle class—their attitudes and opinions—not on who did what during any campaign. Using his own polls enriched by focus groups, Greenberg argues that the middle class has largely come to view both parties negatively: the Democratic Party as turning away from Franklin Roosevelt's social insurance to favoring the undeserving poor over the working middle class, and the Republican Party as endorsing excesses of greed. He explains both Clinton's presidential victory and the Republican's 1994 triumph through a framework of middle- class disillusionment, and suggests a strategy for President Clinton's reelection in 1996. Particularly outstanding is the chapter that makes sense of the Perot voters. Original and significant. All levels.—*R. E. O'Connor, Pennsylvania State University, University Park Campus*

OAB-2881 HT110 96-5786 CIP
Handbook of research on urban politics and policy in the United States, ed. by Ronald K. Vogel. Greenwood, 1997. 453p bibl index afp ISBN 0-313-29166-7, $99.50

An excellent presentation of research materials on urban politics and policy in the US, this handbook consists of 29 bibliographic essays that describe the various subfields and the relevant literature. Areas include theoretical models, research methods, urbanization, community, power, race and ethnicity, class, gender, urban government, participation, neighborhoods, central cities and suburbs, metropolitan government, service delivery, management, budgeting, urban economy, planning, economic development, the policy process, housing, poverty, education, crime, health, equal opportunity, transportation, the environment, and national urban policy. The authors are respected scholars in their fields. The handbook's major contributions are the coherence of the presentations and the vast number of items cited. More than 87 pages are devoted to book and journal citations on urban politics and policy. Essential for academic libraries.—*S. E. C. Hintz, University of Wisconsin—Oshkosh*

OAB-2882 HM141 94-15184 CIP
Heifetz, Ronald A. **Leadership without easy answers.** Harvard, 1994. 348p index afp ISBN 0-674-51858-6, $24.95

This pioneering study constitutes one of the most insightful and innovative approaches to leadership studies in over a decade. Heifetz's revisionary model of "adaptive leadership" is the product of his ten years of experience as the Director of the Leadership Education Project at Harvard's JFK School of Government. The author contends that the contemporary American crisis of leadership has been misdiagnosed owing to outmoded and severely flawed notions of leadership that have mistakenly identified the nation's leaders within the limiting boundaries of authority and technical expertise. Akin to Machiavelli's *The Prince*, Heifetz masterfully presents his new leadership model by intertwining general theory and prescriptive practical guidance through fertile historical and work-place case studies. Heifetz's goal is nothing less than a summoning for a new social contract that seeks to revitalize America's civic ethos by adopting leadership strategies to empower the citizenry rather than to merely enhance the authority of the leader. Although one might disagree with a particular stratagem proffered by Heifetz, the upshot of this study should place it in the front line in leadership historiography for years to come. General; upper-division undergraduate through faculty.—*R. J. Lettieri, Mount Ida College*

OAB-2883 JK305 96-2193 CIP
Korn, Jessica. **The power of separation: American constitutionalism and the myth of the legislative veto.** Princeton, 1996. 178p indexes afp ISBN 0-691-02135-X, $29.95

Following the Supreme Court case *INS* v. *Chadha* (1983), in which the legislative veto was ruled an unconstitutional violation of the separation of powers, analysts expressed fear that removing this weapon from Congress's arsenal would cripple it in the war against runaway bureaucracy. In this short and informative work, Korn quells these fears by demonstrating that the legislative veto was all along little more than "a solution in search of a problem" (Justice Scalia's words). Through detailed empirical analysis of its major instances, Korn shows the veto was rarely used and never effective. Its primary purpose was to symbolize Congress's intent to remain an active player in implementation, and its real effect was to *limit* this ability by turning Congress's attention from more effective means of intervention and control. Analysts missed the point in all this, Korn believes, because they were embedded in the Wilsonian paradigm of institutional analysis. Her excellent discussion of this—including her analysis of *The Federalist* papers—makes no reference to the outstanding scholar in this area, Vincent Ostrom (*The Meaning of American Federalism*, 1991; *The Political Theory of a Compound Republic*, 1987; *The Intellectual Crisis in American Public Administration*, CH, Dec'73; 2nd ed., 1989). Detailed and closely reasoned, with extensive notes. Highly recommended for libraries and scholars.—*M. Berheide, Berea College*

OAB-2884   E169   95-13621 CIP
Lind, Michael. **The next American nation: the new nationalism and the fourth American revolution.** Free Press, 1995. 436p index ISBN 0-02-919103-3, $23.00

In one of the most important, provocative, and challenging diagnoses of our country and its future to appear this decade, Lind, a rising journalist, writes "the first manifesto of American liberal nationalism." He proposes a new transracial coalition politics that dismantles "white overclass" domination, reconstructs the American class system toward a post-racist, social-democratic republic, and blends races and cultures into a "trans-American melting pot." If present trends continue, the current system (which Lind calls a "third republic" or "Multicultural America") is likely to evolve into a "right-wing multicultural regime" cementing "the separation of races by class." The heart of his analysis (Chapter 4, "The White Overclass and the Racial Spoils System," will give multiculturalists of the left cause to fret over the "racial spoils system" (including Lind's view of "cultural pluralism"), and conservatives over his critique of the "white overclass." Lund contends that multiculturalism "is not an inherently left-wing idea," and that the privatization of education will probably accelerate "the fissuring of the American population into hostile tribes living in radically separate mental universes." Lind, not a professional historian, makes historical arguments from which some historians will dissent; they may find his depiction of America's first two republics overdrawn. But this book is about change and the American politics of identity and whether an emerging multiracial middle-class majority can find a politics that will renew the nation's democratic promise. General; upper-division through faculty.—*H. G. Reid, University of Kentucky*

OAB-2885   JK271   96-5046 MARC
Mackenzie, G. Calvin. **The irony of reform: roots of American political disenchantment.** Westview, 1996. 224p bibl index afp ISBN 0-8133-2838-1, $61.50; ISBN 0-8133-2839-X pbk, $18.95

The decades since WW II have brought radical, and largely negative, changes to American politics and government, writes Mackenzie (Colby College). Unlike earlier political transformations, this revolution resulted from an accumulation of smaller and unrelated changes over a period of years rather than from a coherent plan or ideology. The outcome is a much bigger and more active federal government, but one that does not work very well or inspire much confidence from its citizens. Mackenzie discusses the key postwar changes, including social and technological shifts, the decline of parties and rise of interest groups, the fragmentation of Congress, unrealistic expectations of the presidency, and increased policy making by the courts. He then proposes seven reforms to address the problems. This book is reminiscent of James L. Sundquist's *Constitutional Reform and Effective Government* (CH, Jun'86; rev. ed., 1992), although Mackenzie devotes relatively more attention to discussing how the problems developed and less to his proposed solutions and the need for constitutional

change. Mackenzie's analysis is insightful and thought-provoking, particularly in an era when many Americans believe their government is broken. Highly recommended for all levels.—*M. Byrnes, Middle Tennessee State University*

OAB-2886   HQ799   95-4950 CIP
MacManus, Susan A. **Young v. old: generational combat in the 21st century,** by Susan A. MacManus with Patricia A. Turner. Westview, 1996. 302p index afp ISBN 0-8133-1758-4, $65.00; ISBN 0-8133-1759-2 pbk, $21.95

Generational differences in American politics are growing in importance. Coming problems with entitlement spending promise to boost further the prominence of policy differences by age. Oddly, few recent books address generational differences in political attitudes. MacManus's work fortunately fills that gap, but contrary to its title, it is not a warning about coming generational warfare. Instead, it is an excellent description of generational differences evident in a wide range of political behavior. MacManus assesses differences in levels of political participation by age, and sorts through generational differences of opinion about issues and government. Each chapter begins by examining major theoretical and empirical tendencies concerning a behavioral topic, then follows with a careful depiction of generational opinion about that topic. The book contains many useful tabulations of opinions by generation never before assembled in one volume. Although the work breaks no new theoretical ground, its rich collections of data make it helpful for scholars of American politics. It belongs in all undergraduate and graduate libraries and on reading lists in public opinion courses.—*S. E. Schier, Carleton College*

OAB-2887   Q180   91-29638 CIP
Martino, Joseph P. **Science funding: politics and porkbarrel.** Transaction, 1992. 392p index ISBN 1-56000-033-3, $32.95

Martino, a senior research scientist, provides a well-documented, compelling analysis of the increasing influence of politics in the funding of scientific research. This is a seminal contribution to the literature on the politics of science, and it will enlighten scientists, policymakers, and concerned citizens alike. A comprehensive survey examines the history of funding, public versus private patterns, and issues of accountability and control. The disturbing conclusions regarding political interference, inefficiency, and even fraud, are addressed with a thoughtful agenda for reform. This exposé of the crisis of politically driven misappropriation of the nation's scientific resources is as important a contribution to the literatures of politics and public policy as it is to the literature on science. The study is highly readable and avoids the overly technical prose and turgid discussions that plague many related books. Analyses are supported with excellent endnotes, chapter bibliographies, numerous charts and graphs, and a clear presentation of data. Academic and public library collections.—*P. H. Melanson, University of Massachusetts-Dartmouth*

OAB-2888   P95   95-26652 CIP
Page, Benjamin I. **Who deliberates?: mass media in modern democracy.** Chicago, 1996. 167p bibl index afp ISBN 0-226-64472-3, $20.00; ISBN 0-226-64473-1 pbk, $10.95

In this solid little book, the author attempts to answer important questions concerning how the news media affect public knowledge and opinion formation. Page begins with a thoughtful chapter that introduces key theoretical issues and examines roles the media both should and have played in mediating public deliberation about them. Subsequent chapters feature three excellent individual case studies: editorial coverage in *The New York Times* concerning whether the US should have gone to war with Iraq in 1991, news and editorial treatment of responses to President Bush's charge that "1960s programs" essentially caused the 1992 riots in Los Angeles, and comparison of "mainstream" media with "alternative" media treatment of the 1993 nomination of Zoe Baird to become US Attorney General. Page concludes with an important chapter analyzing successes and failures of mediated deliberation. Well researched and reasoned, this is arguably the best book analyzing the roles news media have played in public policy making since publication of Robert Entman's *Democracy without Citizens* (CH, Jul'89) or Ben Bagdikian's *The Media Monopoly* (1983). The only criticism is that the book is too short—one wants Page to analyze several more cases of mediated deliberation. *Strongly* recommended for general readers plus undergraduates and graduates—*R. E. Dewhirst, Northwest Missouri State University*

OAB-2889   JK468   92-1288 CIP
Perry, Mark. **Eclipse: the last days of the CIA.** W. Morrow, 1992. 528p bibl index afp ISBN 0-688-09386-8, $25.00

Basing his book on numerous and extensive interviews with top CIA insiders and on access to secret documents, this investigative journalist has provided a vivid and disturbing analysis of politics and power within the CIA. The agency's infighting, mind-sets, political intrigue, and deficiencies are expressed via detailed case studies of such key events as the capture of Manuel Noriega, the bombing of Pan Am 103, Iran-Contra, and the maneuverings surrounding the confirmation of CIA Director Robert Gates. This critical but balanced analysis is painstakingly documented with more than 70 pages of notes (dozens of which are substantive and extremely informative). This is a unique contribution to a literature too often populated with works that are convoluted, overly technical, or too focused on spies and spying. The highly readable prose often reads like a political thriller, with emphasis on how intelligence data is analyzed and used. The extensive glossary and bibliography are very useful. The work will be appreciated by a general readership interested in the CIA's often shocking role in the events of the last two decades, and is must reading for academics interested in the intelligence community, contemporary politics and public policy, and history. Academic and public library collections.—*P. H. Melanson, University of Massachusetts-Dartmouth*

OAB-2890   KF3466   92-28784 CIP
Piatt, Bill. **Language on the job: balancing business needs and employee rights.** New Mexico, 1993. 155p index afp ISBN 0-8263-1410-4, $27.50

Piatt, (law, Texas Tech) has written an excellent and concise work addressing an explosive workplace issue. He successfully presents appropriate, diverse, and prospective inquiries. The legal-policy analysis is easily grasped by the lay person. It includes an overdue, yet neutral and appropriately sensitive, perspective on historical immigration, unfortunately heretofore lost, and detailed information and discussion regarding compensation preferred for maximum guidance. The author places into perspective the lack of practical effectiveness of efforts to make English the official language relative to English-only workplace rules. He considers relevant issues necessary for a comprehensive response to language-use resolution: language function, accent levels, need for a comprehensive jurisprudence, multicultural employee employment rights, impermissible employer monoculturalistic preferences, multiple language abilities, monocultural coworker English-language rules, language workplace use as function of skill and/or culture, language-skilled employee obligations, legitimate customer communication preferences, and fair testing and evaluation. Chapter bibliographies are relatively unorthodox. Excellent application of references in table of cases. Rich and scholarly bibliography. Required reading for undergraduate and graduate students, labor lawyers, human resource management practitioners and work place participants. All levels.—*A. A. Sisneros, Sangamon State University*

OAB-2891   E840   96-7385 CIP
Ruggie, John Gerard. **Winning the peace: America and world order in the new era.** Columbia, 1996. 237p index afp ISBN 0-231-10426-X, $27.95

Ruggie (former dean of international affairs, Columbia Univ.) has written a short, elegant, and important book in behalf of multilateralism in US foreign policy. In a rejection of pure realism, Ruggie argues that the US's view of itself, in particular its idealistic view that it is a force for bettering the world, is a necessary component of sustained US involvement in the world. As even Henry Kissinger now admits, sustained involvement by the US cannot be based on pure calculations of power and polarity. To achieve sustained involvement, Ruggie argues, we should recall earlier periods in US history. Woodrow Wilson, Franklin Roosevelt, Harry Truman, and even Dwight Eisenhower all sought to combine US exceptionalism with multilateralism. In this way Ruggie hopes to counteract the new version of indirect isolationism: unilateralism, a high threshold for vital interests, and the Powell doctrine of all-or-nothing use of military force. The author is strong on explanations drawn from security and economic subjects, but weak on references to human rights and ecology. Overall this is an important guide to future US foreign policy, written in concise style, and making copious citations to the literature. Highly recommended for general readers and for lower-division undergraduates through faculty.—*D. Forsythe, University of Nebraska*

OAB-2892   HT1521   93-17063 CIP
Sniderman, Paul M. **The scar of race,** by Paul M. Sniderman and Thomas Piazza. Harvard, 1993. 212p bibl index afp ISBN 0-674-79010-3, $18.95

This work is an important, thoughtful, and extremely well presented investigation into the politics of race in the US today. Sniderman and Piazza unpack the way social scientists explain the role of race in American self-identity and political action, and reevaluate the politics of racism and discrimination. Working from a careful reading of several large and telling measures of American public opinion, along with their own powerful compilation of public opinion data, they investigate the intensity and pervasiveness of racism in the US, and correlate racial attitudes with political ideology, education, and other demographic characteristics. Contrary to much current rhetoric, they find that racism today correlates strongly with authoritarian attitudes. Further, the authors find strong correlations between ideology and racial attitudes, suggesting that ideological differences over public policies represent genuine differences of political outlook rather than covert racism. In the same vein, white Americans are much more willing to accept claims made on behalf of *individual* black Americans as compared to claims made on behalf of blacks as a group. The work holds out the promise of significant change in American attitudes toward race through widespread education. The authors find that levels of education contribute powerfully to establishing genuine racial tolerance, both in terms of attitudes and treatment of minority groups. Highly recommended for all levels of readers.—*D. R. Imig, University of Nevada, Las Vegas*

OAB-2893   TC625   93-23563 CIP
Stine, Jeffrey K. **Mixing the waters: environment, politics, and the building of the Tennessee-Tombigbee Waterway.** Akron, 1993. 336p bibl index afp ISBN 0-9622628-5-4, $39.95; ISBN 0-9622628-6-2 pbk, $21.95

Stine sets out to describe the interplay of politics, technology, ideology, and personality in the development of "Ten-Tom," arguably one of the most controversial water projects ever built east of the Mississippi—*and* the most expensive. In the process, he has likely written the definitive history of the navigation project. The analysis is balanced and thoroughly researched, and captures the nuances of changing values and attitudes toward pork-barrel politics, benefit-cost evaluation, and interest group politics in American natural resource policy from the 1930s through the early 1980s. The mix of documentary sources and contemporary journalistic accounts makes for a rich, sometimes dizzying narrative. Perhaps the greatest lesson of Stine's account is that, in great and controversial public works projects, the end result is as much a product of serendipitous and unpredictable forces and events as it is of planning. The conclusion, that the project was "power politics from start to finish," reveals the ongoing tensions between environmentalism and technology in US politics. One wishes Stine had pushed his account a bit further in assessing what Ten-Tom says about the future of natural resource and environmental policies given the ambiguities of new, far more complex environmental technologies and the budget constraints on structural solutions to economic and resource development problems. Graduate; faculty; professional.—*D. L. Feldman, University of Tennessee, Knoxville*

OAB-2894   JV6483   96-3841 CIP
Williamson, Chilton. **The immigration mystique: America's false conscience.** Basic Books, 1996. 202p ISBN 0-465-03286-9, $23.00

Williamson's well-written, insightful, and erudite work on the immigration debate (or as he calls it, the nondebate) persuasively contends that there has been no real national debate on the issue and hence no real immigration policy. He likens the immigration situation to that of slavery before the Civil War, when Congress, the courts, and the executive allowed the problem to fester until it finally erupted into a major crisis. A certain mystique has risen around immigration that has prevented any policy from emerging to deal with it. How long can massive numbers of people be admitted and absorbed without causing major social, cultural, and economic calamities? The idea of immigration has bipartisan support; no one wants to be put in the position of completely opposing the welcoming of newcomers. Unlike most contemporary studies on immigration, Williamson's work is not replete with graphs, charts, and statistical data. He has chosen to view the issue from a moral perspective, which is most refreshing. The book will prove valuable and stimulating for students of immigration in America, useful for scholars in the general field of public policy, and an essential acquisition for university, general, and professional libraries.— A. C. Tuttle, University of Nevada, Las Vegas

OAB-2895   HM261   91-43032 CIP
Zaller, John R. **The nature and origins of mass opinion.** Cambridge, 1992. 367p bibl index ISBN 0-521-40449-5, $59.95; ISBN 0-521-40786-9 pbk, $17.95

To understand fully how American democracy behaves, one must probe how information about political issues and personalities, overwhelmingly delivered through the mass media, interacts with the values and predispositions of the citizenry to shape public opinion and influence voting. This ambitious effort seeks to integrate decades of research on mass attitudes from the substantive perspective of a politial scientist. Relying on empirical evidence from sample surveys rather than controlled experiments, and drawing from scores of studies including many of the author's own investigations, Zaller concludes that few positions of US citizens are firmly anchored on any given issue and that levels of political awareness are much more important as a contingent factor than previously realized. Rich in insight, this well-crafted book promises to be a classic in its field. Recommended for all four-year and graduate collections.— E. T. Jones, University of Missouri-St. Louis

The Presidency & Congress

OAB-2896   T174   96-7386 CIP
Bimber, Bruce. **The politics of expertise in Congress: the rise and fall of the Office of Technology Assessment.** State University of New York, 1996. 128p bibl index afp ISBN 0-7914-3059-6, $48.50

With breathtaking precision and clarity, engineer and political scientist Bimber analyzes the role of experts in policy decision making and offers a workable solution to the debilitating problems of technocracy. He establishes an analytic framework based on the relationship between knowledge and power, specifically between experts and politicians in Congress, then applies his insights via a smartly portrayed life cycle of the Office of Technology Assessment (established in 1972, abolished in 1995). He persuasively builds to the conclusion that information neutrality, provided via ready access to independent think tanks vested with no political authority, is the most appropriate and just way to integrate power and information. Bimber declines to advance a formal theory, but this remarkable study is broadly applicable to a wide range of political and social science subdisciplines, and will undoubtedly be attached to numerous existing syllabi. Unique in case subject and emphasis, Bimber advances our understanding of the dynamic of political expertise. His book compares favorably to Sheila Jasanoff's *The Fifth Branch* (1990), and proves

an excellent companion to *Science, Technology, and Politics*, ed. by Gary C. Bryner (1992). Advanced undergraduate through faculty and policy practitioners.—*E. C. Dolman, College of William and Mary*

OAB-2897   JK1118   92-53673 CIP
Birnbaum, Jeffrey H. **The lobbyists: how influence peddlers get their way in Washington.** Times Books, 1992. 334p indexes ISBN 0-8129-2086-4, $24.00

This is a consumate look at the business lobby, primarily as a number of its lobbyists worked to influence tax policy in 1989 and 1990. Birnbaum, using his journalistic tools, captures the linkage between Congress and the White House as few observers have ever done in a case analysis. The author's approach is a simple one: interview participants widely and then tell their tale. He tells it so well that the book reads more like a novel than a docudrama. Of particular interest is the understanding it conveys of the lobbyists' typical goal—inserting small but significant language in much larger laws. Or, as Birnbaum notes, the book is about winning access over time to powerful contacts to work the "quiet lucrative fringe" of their major legislative initiatives. Readers gain a rare and precise portrait of the policy process as it stretches from ideas to a legislative act. What this analysis demonstrates is the very routine personal interactions, relationships, and exchanges that encompass lobbying. Some interesting historical commentary provides a good context for better understanding the actions of concern. If there is a fault with this book, it lies in the way it is hyped as an explosive story of influence peddlers. In reality, Birnbaum shows lobbying as part and parcel of the rest of life as it gets played out beyond the civics class. Recommended for all libraries.—*W. P. Browne, Central Michigan University*

OAB-2898   E748   92-32417 CIP
Cohodas, Nadine. **Strom Thurmond and the politics of Southern change.** Simon & Schuster, 1993. 574p bibl index ISBN 0-671-68935-5, $27.50

Cohodas has produced much more than just a biography of one of the most enigmatic and durable US politicians of this century; she provides readers with a detailed and insightful account of the evolution of southern politics, politicians, and culture during the civil rights era. While there is an abundance of works on the Civil Rights Movement and southern politics such as C. Vann Woodward's *The Strange Career of Jim Crow* (3rd rev. ed., 1974), Earl and Merle Black's *Southern Governors and Civil Rights* (CH, Oct'76), Taylor Branch's *Parting the Waters* (CH, Jun'89), Ethan Bronner's *Battle for Justice* (1989), Margaret Edds's *Free at Last* (CH, Nov'87), Richard Bardolph's *The Civil Rights Record* (CH, Oct'70), and Aldon Morris's *The Origins of the Civil Rights Movement* (CH, Feb'85), most of these works tend to be narrower in their focus and approach the movement primarily from the perspective of its impact on and implications for black America. Cohodas presents an exhaustively researched, in-depth, and interestingly written account which not only traces the evolution of Strom Thurmond's political career but provides helpful insights on how white southerners and their political leaders saw the Civil Rights Movement as an infringement on their states' rights and "culture and tradition." Her account will be of interest to anyone exploring southern politics and the Civil Rights Movement. All libraries.— *C. P. Chelf, Western Kentucky University*

OAB-2899   E176   94-12007 CIP
Ellis, Richard J. **Presidential lightning rods: the politics of blame avoidance.** University Press of Kansas, 1994. 271p index afp ISBN 0-7006-0636-X, $29.95

Ellis (Willamette Univ.) has written an original account of how presidential blame is deflected by White House subordinates. He introduces the concept of the presidential "lightning rod"—a White House figure who absorbs controversy and either protects or diminishes the president's stature. Outer cabinet officials are good at deflecting criticism because presidents are not held to a high standard in areas such as agricultural policy. Yet very high profile, controversial cabinet heads (e.g., James Watt) not only absorb criticism but reflect it on the president. Consequently, not all lightning rods are good for the president's stature. Ellis provides accounts of presidential lightning rods from the Truman through Bush years. Ellis's study is very thorough, well written, and meticulously documented and adds to scholarly understanding of how presidents enhance and maintain their reputations for effective leadership. Highly recommended for presidential scholars and academic libraries. Upper-division undergraduate through faculty.—*M. J. Rozell, Mary Washington College*

OAB-2900 JK1764 93-31966 CIP
Fowler, Linda L. **Candidates, Congress, and the American democracy.** Michigan, 1993. 228p bibl index afp ISBN 0-472-09473-4, $42.50

Does it really matter who US national legislators are—and how they got there? According to political scientist Fowler, candidate recruitment is the critical key to understanding virtually the full sweep of American politics. She links recruitment to a number of phenomena—the mobilization of women, minority enfranchisement, the partisan transformation of the South, the decline of electoral competition, the power of incumbency, the insularity of most congressional elections, and divided government. Indeed, one of the dominant themes of interest to students of American polical development is the claim that changes in candidate recruitment can explain a variety of electoral and institutional changes. Although political science journals abound with essays on candidate recruitment, this is the first book-length treatment of the subject. In it Fowler advances and defends an original and provocative argument; her knowledge and use of the literature in this area is awesome. Those interested in any of the recent changes in American political life will find this book to be substantively informative, intellectually stimulating, and very readable. All levels.—*E. C. Dreyer, University of Tulsa*

OAB-2901 E176 96-54067 MARC
Gelderman, Carol. **All the presidents' words: the bully pulpit and the creation of the virtual presidency.** Walker & Company, 1997. 221p index ISBN 0-8027-1318-1, $23.00

In an admirable book that speechwriters will love, Gelderman (English, Univ. of New Orleans) examines presidential use of words. She focuses on presidential use and misuse of communication. Her illuminating behind-the-scenes look at presidential speechwriting shows that much depends on how effective a speech-giver the president is and on the relationship between the speechwriter and the president. Ted Sorensen, one of the best, enjoyed rapport with John F. Kennedy long before JFK became president. Gelderman correctly asserts that genuine collaboration is essential. Beginning with Nixon, the author contends, presidents have been obsessed with image-making, but Theodore Roosevelt did a good job of it beginning with the Brooks Brothers uniform he wore for the "Rough Riders" campaign. This book confirms that the occupant of the White House is the driving force in the US's role domestically and abroad. An excellent work, well-written (both anecdotal and scholarly), of abounding interest. Highly recommended for general and academic readers, upper-division undergraduate through faculty.—*S. L. Harrison, University of Miami*

OAB-2902 JK2683 95-32636 CIP
Glaser, James M. **Race, campaign politics, and the realignment in the South.** Yale, 1996. 229p bibl index afp ISBN 0-300-06398-9, $28.50

This well-written observer-participant research study (originally a doctoral dissertation) treats six recent special congressional elections in the South—one each in Texas, Alabama and Virginia, and three in Mississippi—of which Glaser observed three. He deals with the issue of how Democrats have managed to win in the South in congressional elections while the Republicans have carried the South in presidential elections for decades (see Joseph A. Aistrup, *The Southern Strategy Revisited: Republican Top-Down Advancement in the South,* CH, Jun'96). Glaser examines in illuminating detail candidate strategy in majority white and majority black districts. Race is a key in the South, but it plays differently in different contexts. The black vote has kept the Democrats competitive. This research was completed just as the 1994 elections occurred.

Those elections in the South, and the 1996 experience, will make an important sequel to this study. This is an excellent, well-documented analysis of recent post-civil rights congressional elections, even though they were special elections. Gender issues are ignored, although one candidate was a woman. Highly recommended for public, college, and university libraries.—*L. E. Noble Jr., emeritus, Clark Atlanta University*

OAB-2903 JK524 92-19435 CIP
Hinck, Edward A. **Enacting the presidency: political argument, presidential debates, and presidential character.** Praeger, 1993. 255p bibl index afp ISBN 0-275-93488-8, $49.95

Hinck (Central Michigan Univ.) has written one of the most comprehensive scholarly analyses of modern presidential (and vice presidential) debates. A scholar of political communication and a college debate instructor, Hinck examines modern presidential debates from the vantage of how well these events convey important information to voters about the candidates' potential for leadership. Consequently, he perceives presidential debates as not so important for what they convey to the public about candidate public policy positions. Voters derive helpful information from debates about potential presidential style, character, and skill. In chronological fashion, Hinck examines in detail the debate performances of the presidential candidates in 1960, 1976, 1980, 1984, and 1988, and the vice-presidential candidates in 1976, 1984, and 1988. The thorough debate analyses will be useful to students of the presidency and political communication. Recommended specifically for advanced-undergraduate through professional collections.—*M. J. Rozell, Mary Washington College*

OAB-2904 JK516 93-51513 CIP
Jones, Charles O. **The presidency in a separated system.** Brookings, 1994. 338p index afp ISBN 0-8157-4710-1, $39.95; ISBN 0-8157-4709-8 pbk, $16.95

This is an important book which should be in every library whose readers take seriously the study of American politics and governing institutions. The book, written by a prominent American political scholar and the 1994 president of the American Political Science Association, has several notable strengths plus at least one shortcoming. The strength of the book clearly is in the author's deft analysis of how more recent presidents and congresses have interacted within the parameters established by the Madisonian separation of powers. Jones creates a framework for analyzing all of the possible combinations of presidential-congressional interaction in the American separation of powers system. He is successful at developing a theme maintaining the limits of presidential power compatible with Richard E. Neustadt's classic *Presidential Power* (1960) and more recent studies such as George C. Edwards's *At the Margins* (1989). However, Jones is not convincing when arguing that the existing American separation of powers is both desirable and preferable to changes as sought through the years by James L. Sundquist in *Constitutional Reform and Effective Government* (rev. ed., 1992) and by other reform-minded scholars and intellectuals. Highly recommended for public, undergraduate, and graduate libraries.—*R. E. Dewhirst, Northwest Missouri State University*

OAB-2905 JK468 95-19177 CIP
Knott, Stephen F. **Secret and sanctioned: covert operations and the American presidency.** Oxford, 1996. 258p bibl index afp ISBN 0-19-510098-0, $27.50

Knott (US Air Force Academy) has written an original account of the history of presidential use of convert activities. The most valuable and well-documented insight is that covert activity has its roots in the origins of the republic, not in the Cold War. Knott focuses on covert activities from 1776 to 1882 to demonstrate the extent to which the earlier presidents had relied on such efforts to achieve their objectives. He then traces the development of clandestine operations to the modern era, with an informed discussion of congressional restraints and their implications. Bolstered by meticulous research, this book stands as an effective challenge to the "imperial presidency" thesis. Not all will agree with the author's arguments, but his study deserves a wide reading among students and scholars of American politics. Highly recommended for advanced undergraduates and above.—*M. J. Rozell, University of Virginia*

OAB-2906 JK1319 96-435 CIP
Koopman, Douglas L. **Hostile takeover: the House Republican Party, 1980-1995.** Rowman & Littlefield, 1996. 181p bibl index afp ISBN 0-8476-8168-8, $52.50; ISBN 0-8476-8169-6 pbk, $21.95

Examining House Republicans for the period 1980-95, Koopman explores recent changes in their attitudes and the nature of disagreements between Republicans and Democrats over the operation of the House. House Republicans moved from being a somewhat passive minority, often shut out of the legislative process throughout most of the 1980s by the increased partisanship of the majority, to being an active opposition party. The 1994 elections elevated the party to majority status. The two threads of Koopman's research explore the role of partisanship and its effect on the congressional parties. Offering evidence of the increased partisanship of the Democratic House after the reforms of the mid-1970s, Koopman notes that congressional Republicans had little choice but to respond to this more contentious legislative environment. Koopman identifies seven House Republican factions; several reflect the increased importance of the new right/religious right, others reflect factions that have existed for a considerable time, and still others indicate the disappearance of the party's liberal and progressive wing in the House. This thoughtful analysis of congressional parties concentrates on the minority party and the role(s) available to it. Essential for college libraries.—*W. K. Hall, Bradley University*

OAB-2907 JK1976 96-8079 CIP
Miller, Warren E. **The new American voter,** by Warren E. Miller and J. Merrill Shanks. Harvard, 1996. 640p bibl index afp ISBN 0-674-60840-2, $39.95; ISBN 0-674-60841-0 pbk, $19.95

It should be no surprise that this long-awaited volume will become an instant classic among voting studies. This effort by Miller (one of the field's founders) and Shanks (an accomplished scholar) caps more than four decades of using survey research to explain individual voting behavior in US presidential elections. In some ways, it is two books in one: longitudinal examinations of key factors such as voter turnout and political party identification and an intensive analysis of the 1992 Bush-Clinton-Perot contest. Every page shows sophisticated minds at work, raising multiple explanations, sorting them out with cutting-edge methodologies, and thereby moving knowledge forward. All this is made possible by the rich data generated by National Election Studies, one of Miller's many legacies to political research. Although nonspecialists will find some portions heavy going, this pathbreaking study is recommended for all libraries.—*E. T. Jones, University of Missouri—St. Louis*

OAB-2908 JK2281 93-20129 CIP
Morreale, Joanne. **The presidential campaign film: a critical history.** Praeger, 1993. 206p bibl index afp ISBN 0-275-93882-4, $49.95

A volume in the "Praeger Series in Political Communication," this work traces the development of the political campaign film. From the first effort, *The Life of Calvin Coolidge*, to the 1992 film *The Man from Hope*, presidential campaign films are examined as they have sought to visually summarize the lives, accomplishments, hopes, dreams, and visions of the candidate. In the beginning, according to the author, these presidential campaign films were of the classical or expository film category. Morreale's examination of this type of film ties in the old strains of campaign oratory and advocacy with the new technological advances wrought by and represented by television. The author takes care to analyze the campaign films for each presidential election since 1952. The expository period ended with the campaign of 1972, and films made for candidates/campaigns after that date are described as hybrid documentary-advertisement films. This is an excellent look at this campaign device. It is possible to follow changes in political campaigns and technological changes in campaign advertising over the past 50 years by studying these films. Excel-

lent filmography. Every university library on campuses with advanced undergraduate or graduate programs in political science, advertising, or film/television should have this volume on the shelves.—*W. K. Hall, Bradley University*

OAB-2909 JK2488 95-51513 CIP
Rosenthal, Alan. **Drawing the line: legislative ethics in the states.** Nebraska, 1996. 268p bibl index afp ISBN 0-8032-3919-X, $40.00

Strongly grounded empirically, Rosenthal's book discusses legislative ethical problems and difficulties in the frequently complicated settings in which they occur. It is attentive not merely to the need for legislators to avoid adverse publicity but also to the need for legislatures to function well. It is, in short, a balanced, mature, unhysterical, uncynical, well-informed look at a set of difficult real-life problems that all too frequently receive superficial and exploitative treatment. Rosenthal (Rutgers) is one of a small, select group of scholars with intimate knowledge of the politics of more than one state. This superb book deserves a wide and respectful audience.—*N. W. Polsby, University of California, Berkeley*

OAB-2910 JK5845 94-48041 CIP
Rubenstein, Bruce A. **Payoffs in the cloakroom: the greening of the Michigan legislature, 1938-1946,** by Bruce A. Rubenstein and Lawrence E. Ziewacz. Michigan State, 1995. 279p index afp ISBN 0-87013-387-X, $28.00

In a rarity of analysis, the authors focus on an era of unfettered political corruption in Michigan. It is an unparalleled case study of a complex set of circumstances, linked only by their malfeasance. The authors, both historians, use meticulously drawn direct evidence and considerable interpretation to reveal their story. It will be of considerable interest to anyone studying governors, elections, lobbying, or public policy making in the American states. Those interested in the workings of either the judiciary or the legislature will also enjoy the book. The authors' case is made intriguing by the massive scope of the corruption they document and the shocking nature of the murder of one state senator who was likely to reveal publicly that underside of politics. The strongest aspect of the analysis, however, is the superb use of history, showing how the underlying values of an era are played out in specific events unique to the time. All levels.—*W. P. Browne, Central Michigan University*

OAB-2911 JK1411 94-33953 CIP
Sinclair, Barbara. **Legislators, leaders, and lawmaking: the U.S. House of Representatives in the postreform era.** Johns Hopkins, 1995. 329p bibl index afp ISBN 0-8018-4955-1, $39.95

Those interested in understanding how the new Republican House leadership is able to wield so much power would find much of the explanation in this book. Adding to her *Majority Leadership in the U.S. House* (CH, Jun'84) and her impressive *Transformation of the U.S. Senate* (CH, Dec'89), Sinclair offers considerable evidence to support her argument that activist House leadership emerged after an era of committee government and far-reaching post-Watergate reforms during the 1980s. Under Democratic majorities in the 1980s, the activist House leadership wielded greater power by: (1) increasing their ability to organize the party as well as the chamber by appointing members of the Rules Committee, the Democratic Committee on Committees, etc.; (2) establishing a larger role in setting the House agenda; (3) involving itself in the internal legislative process by assigning bills to multiple committees and setting deadlines for committee action; and (4) seeking to affect the outcomes of legislative struggles. Sinclair concludes that this activist leadership has had a measurable impact on the outcomes of legislative battles. Written before the Republicans took over as the majority party in the House, her analysis shows how the Republican leadership has built on the foundation laid by the Democrats in the 1980s and '90s. Well done and thoughtful, this work is based on hundreds of interviews coupled with the author's keen insight into the House. Should be on the shelves of all academic libraries.—*W. K. Hall, Bradley University*

OAB-2912   JK1323   92-21837 CIP
Swain, Carol M. **Black faces, black interests: the representation of African Americans in Congress.** Harvard, 1993. 275p index afp ISBN 0-674-07615-X, $37.50

This is a carefully researched analysis of how well members of the US House of Representatives did in fact represent the interests of African Americans in the 100th through the 102nd Congresses. Swain (Woodrow Wilson School, Princeton) has impeccable qualifications and contacts for undertaking such a study. In Part 1 she defines "black interests" (which vary widely) and "black representation" (she finds Democrats more responsive to those interests than Republicans) and traces the history of black representation in the House over time. Part 2 presents case studies of representation of black interests by black MCs from historically black districts, newly black districts, mixed districts, and majority white districts. In Part 3 she looks at white representation of black interests in minority and majority black districts. The final part of the study discusses the implications of these findings for congressional redistricting and for the future of black congressional representation generally. Much depends, she concludes, on such factors as how future redistricting goes, on continued Democratic domination of the House, and on the degree of black recognition of common interests with white citizens. Her research demonstrated to her that black interests were not advanced solely by black representatives. Copious notes. Overall, an excellently crafted work. Another such study is not likely to come along soon. All levels.—*R. H. Leach, Duke University*

OAB-2913   JK1140   95-14604 CIP
Thompson, Dennis F. **Ethics in Congress: from individual to institutional corruption.** Brookings, 1995. 246p index afp ISBN 0-8157-8424-4, $34.95; ISBN 0-8157-8423-6 pbk, $14.95

This important book on a timeless topic should be added to every serious political library. The author (political philosophy, Harvard) provides a thorough treatment of the issue while also breaking important ground. He includes chapters on the purposes of legislative ethics, dynamics of legislative corruption, gains in office, services in office, motives for corruption, and arenas for resolving allegations of ethical violations. Thompson supports his points by citing recent allegations of ethical violations, such as those surrounding the Keating Five and former House Speaker Jim Wright. Although the book is noteworthy for its thoroughness, its most important contribution is probably Thompson's concept of institutional corruption. In contrast with the more common individual corruption, institutional corruption involves instances in which members gain by improper political methods and provide procedurally improper services. The connection between improper gain and services provided damages either the institution as a whole or the entire democratic process. Overall, Thompson reveals an institution that has been neither as corrupt as public opinion believes nor as ethically sound as the country needs. Highly recommended for undergraduate, graduate, and public libraries.—*R. E. Dewhirst, Northwest Missouri State University*

OAB-2914   JK552   95-1108 CIP
Walcott, Charles E. **Governing the White House: from Hoover through LBJ,** by Charles E. Walcott and Karen M. Hult. University Press of Kansas, 1995. 372p index afp ISBN 0-7006-0688-2, $40.00; ISBN 0-7006-0689-0 pbk, $22.50

Walcott and Hult, authors of *Governing Public Organizations* (1990), provide a theoretically informed, carefully reasoned, and meticulously researched study of presidential staffing of the White House Office. Building on insights of organizational theory, they develop an analytical framework—a "governance model of organizations"—that conceives organizations as "inherently political systems." The authors then enlist their model to explain the emergence and evolution of White House Office staff structures from the administration of Herbert Hoover through the presidency of Lyndon Johnson. In offering a systematic and empirical account of presidential staffing, Walcott and Hult make a significant contribution to the literature that will complement works on the

Executive Office of the President by people like Stephen Hess, John Hart, and Bradley Patterson. Highly recommended for upper-division undergraduates, graduate students, and faculty.—*G. L. Malecha, University of Portland*

THE SUPREME COURT & THE CONSTITUTION

OAB-2915   KF4575   94-29699 CIP
Arthur, John. **Words that bind: judicial review and the grounds of modern constitutional theory.** Westview, 1995. 236p index afp ISBN 0-8133-2348-7, $65.00; ISBN 0-8133-2349-5 pbk, $21.95

Arthur has written a very readable and challenging account of judicial review and democratic constitutionalism. Arthur's analysis offers an understanding of the role of Supreme Court decision making in interpreting the Constitution and an excellent introduction to the problems judicial review poses to a constitutional democracy. In addition, he explains clearly and coherently five of the leading theories on constitutional interpretation, namely, original intent, democratic proceduralism, critical legal studies, utilitarianism, and democratic contractualism. He explains with great clarity the nature and scope of judicial review; he then develops the nature of judicial review in terms of original intent or, to be more specific, the need to decide constitutional issues in light of what the Founding Fathers actually believed that we, the people, had consented to. This book can be read with profit by those unfamiliar with the issues and ideas surrounding judicial review as well as by those quite familiar with the terrain. Throughout his analysis Arthur is concerned to explain the issues philosophically but without the arcane verbiage of some philosophical analyses. Anyone interested in constitutional interpretation and judicial review should read this book. A bibliography would have been helpful. Given the inherent difficulty which often accompanies discussions of judicial review, the clarity and coherence of Arthur's style make this work highly recommended for public and undergraduate libraries.—*M. A. Foley, Marywood College*

OAB-2916   KF8745   95-14107 CIP
Ball, Howard. **Hugo L. Black: cold steel warrior.** Oxford, 1996. 305p bibl index afp ISBN 0-19-507814-4, $35.00

Ball (Univ. of Vermont) returns to a topic he dearly loves, having published numerous articles and a book (*The Vision and Dream of Justice Hugo L. Black*, 1975) and coauthored a book (*Of Power and Right*, CH, Jun'92) on US Supreme Court Justice Hugo Black. In this engrossing and highly readable work, he relates in fascinating, intimate detail Black's early years and the effects his Alabama beginnings had upon him once he reached the Senate and later, the Supreme Court. Equally appealing is Ball's examination of the justice's friendships and conflicts during his 37 years on the Court. Although at one time a racist, always a sexist (he had only one female law clerk, with whom he had serious conflicts), and a homophobe, Black became one of the greatest civil libertarians to sit on the Court, so long as private property rights and federalism were not sacrificed. Ball notes that Black's enduring legacy to the nation was his commitment to the Constitution and to its unalterable principles of federalism, free speech, separation of powers, total incorporation of the Bill of Rights, and judicial self-restraint. Ball's reliance on primary sources (including interviews with other justices, Black's daughter, and his law clerks) and secondary sources makes this work essential reading to anyone interested in Black, the Supreme Court, or constitutional history. Numerous endnotes and an extensive bibliography will assist researchers and scholars interested in pursuing the Black legacy in the 20th-century US.—*M. W. Bowers, University of Nevada, Las Vegas*

OAB-2917   KF8742   94-18750 CIP
Casto, William R. **The Supreme Court in the early republic: the chief justiceships of John Jay and Oliver Ellsworth.** South Carolina, 1995. 267p index ISBN 1-57003-033-2, $49.95

Casto (Texas Tech Law School) offers the second volume in a series that analyzes the impact of each of the 16 chief justices on American constitutional and judicial development. (The first volume was James Ely's *The Chief Justiceship of Melville W. Fuller*, CH, Sep'95.) Casto's assessment of Jay's and Ellsworth's influence on the Court, Constitution, and nation is currently the best comprehensive treatment of the initial years of the Supreme Court. The first three chapters chronicle the creation of the federal judiciary, the debates surrounding the Judiciary Act of 1789, and a discussion of President Washington's appointments. The remaining six chapters describe the Court's early work by analyzing its key decisions, the relationship of the chiefs to the President, and executive use of the chief justice for nonjudicial duties. Casto emphasizes that prior to the Marshall era the primary objective of the Court was to bolster and consolidate the new government. Constitutional interpretation was minimal, and it was in their charges to grand juries when presiding over circuit courts that the justices had their greatest impact on the new American system. Explaining and supporting the government, they became "Republican Schoolmasters," and Ellsworth and Jay sustained a strong, energetic federal government, one that could defend itself against foreign and domestic enemies. A splendid work, enlightening reading for students of judicial power. Upper-division through faculty.—*R. J. Steamer, emeritus, University of Massachusetts at Boston*

OAB-2918   KF8742   95-31618 CIP
Cooper, Phillip J. **Battles on the bench: conflict inside the Supreme Court.** University Press of Kansas, 1995. 224p bibl index afp ISBN 0-7006-0737-4, $24.95

Cooper (liberal arts, Univ. of Vermont) has written a fascinating and timely study of conflict among US Supreme Court justices. Relying primarily on previously published judicial biographies and autobiographies, he provides a multitude of examples of the many battles that have occurred in the Court over the past 200 years. Although judicial scholars are likely to be familiar with most of these cases, general readers, scholars, and students can learn a great deal from the episodes he recounts. But there is much more to this work than a rehash of Bob Woodward and Scott Armstrong's *The Brethren* (1979) and Leonard Baker's *Brandeis and Frankfurter* (CH, Oct'84). Not only does Cooper analyze why they fight but how, and why they do not engage in battle more often. Summarizing the various conflicts, he typologizes them into four categories: internal personal, internal professional, external personal, and external professional. Of these, he finds the external personal to be most damaging to the Court's legitimacy and public standing. Ironically, this type of conflict appears to be increasing in the 1990s. Nonetheless, he concludes that the Court continues to maintain a level of civility unknown in the executive and legislative branches. Highly recommended for all readers.—*M. W. Bowers, University of Nevada, Las Vegas*

OAB-2919   KF8748   94-13733 CIP
Faille, Christopher C. **The decline and fall of the Supreme Court: living out the nightmares of the Federalists.** Praeger, 1995. 204p bibl index afp ISBN 0-275-94826-9, $52.95

Faille adds a distinctive voice to those critics who perceive a decline in the moral authority of the US Supreme Court. His conclusions hang from the rise of legal realism and the distortion and misuse of the senatorial confirmation process. A half century ago, Faille observes, legal realists attacked the traditional formalist structure of the law, contending that all law, including that made by judges, responds to sociological and political pressures, and that the distinction between law and policy is superfluous. The notion that right and wrong inhere in the nature of things was discarded; judges no longer seemed above the spirit of faction. Concomitantly, the US passed from a system of limited government to a welfare state, whose essential feature was to eliminate risk. In this new configuration the Supreme Court justices became brokers of risk, which made each confirmation hearing an ideological struggle dominated by partisan polemics. Hence, the nation has witnessed a polarization of judicial politics, a decline of principled deliberation, and the rise of result-oriented jurisprudence. Dignity in the law, crucial to the stability of a republic, has been lost. Faille buttresses his case by analyzing recent confirmation hearings of Supreme

Court nominees and key judicial decisions. A superb book, required reading for all seeking to understand the problems of the American constitutional system.—*R. J. Steamer, emeritus, University of Massachusetts at Boston*

OAB-2920   KF4865   95-10337 CIP
Gedicks, Frederick Mark. **The rhetoric of church and state: a critical analysis of religion clause jurisprudence.** Duke University, 1995. 196p index afp ISBN 0-8223-1654-4, $49.95; ISBN 0-8223-1666-8 pbk, $18.95

This may be the wisest and most devastating critique of modern Supreme Court decisions in the area of religion. Gedicks (law, Brigham Young) contrasts two competing discourses concerning church and state. The "religious communitarian" approach views religion as a source of positive values that government can encourage, while "secular individualism" treats religion as a private phenomenon, about which government must be indifferent. Gedicks demonstrates that the modern Court's secular individualism has marginalized religious faith, critiques the Court's *Lemon* test, questions the Court's secular justifications for Sunday closing laws and symbolic religious displays, dismantles the Court's distinction between aid to parochial schools and religious colleges, and shows that the Court has failed to protect adequately rights to the free exercise of religion. Although Gedicks concludes that the modern religious clause doctrine is "a failed jurisprudence ripe for dismantling," he does not present an alternative. He discusses a much wider array of cases than Winnifred Sullivan's *Paying the Words Extra* (CH, Jun'95), but unlike Steven Monsma's *Positive Neutrality* (CH, May'93), Gedicks does not offer a solution to the problems identified. Essential for all students of church/state relations, general readers and upper-division undergraduates through faculty. Highly recommended.—*J. R. Vile, Middle Tennessee State University*

OAB-2921   KF4550   96-3337 CIP
Griffin, Stephen M. **American Constitutionalism: from theory to politics.** Princeton, 1996. 216p index afp ISBN 0-691-03404-4, $29.95

Griffin (law, Tulane) has written a comprehensive and fascinating work on constitutional theory that is highly recommended for scholars and general readers alike. Unlike many of his law school peers, he adopts an interdisciplinary approach that relies on history, philosophy, and political science in examining the connection between law and politics. Although many (perhaps too many) books have been published in recent years on constitutional theory, Griffin's is the first to provide a general introduction to the field. By analyzing the work of others and the criticisms leveled against them, he provides a foundation from which to launch his own investigation into American constitutionalism. Along the way he scrutinizes the doctrine of popular sovereignty, the process of constitutional change, American political development as constrained or freed by the Constitution, judicial review and processes of decision making, and various contemporary debates over constitutional interpretation. Perhaps most refreshing of all is Griffin's ability to examine constitutional theory through the lenses of history and institutional structure rather than restricting himself to legal doctrine, normative judgments, and US Supreme Court decisions. All levels.—*M. W. Bowers, University of Nevada, Las Vegas*

OAB-2922   KF4865   92-15941 CIP
Gunn, T. Jeremy. **A standard for repair: the establishment clause, equality, and natural rights.** Garland, 1992. 225p bibl index afp ISBN 0-8153-0893-0, $43.00

Gunn's excellent study offers proof that Accommodationists on the Rehnquist Court are mistaken in their current interpretation of the Establishment Clause. The author refutes the notion of the Court that there was a single understanding in the 18th century of the meaning of "establishment." The Court has moved from the Burger Court standard in *Lemon* v. *Kurtzman* (secular purpose, neutral, no excessive entanglement) toward a position of more accommodation of government policy to religious interests on establishment issues. Gunn shows that the universally used concept in understanding individual liberties in the late 18th century was "equality." Hence he argues that the present Court should ensure that no one's equality of freedom from establishment is impinged. Carefully reasoned, clearly written, meticulously documented. Extensive bibliography, table of cases, thorough index. Highly recommended for public, academic, and law libraries.—*L. E. Noble Jr., Clark Atlanta University*

OAB-2923   K1781   94-1052 CIP
Hart, Vivien. **Bound by our Constitution: women, workers, and the minimum wage.** Princeton, 1994. 255p index afp ISBN 0-691-03480-X, $35.00

Another volume in the superb "Princeton Studies in American Politics: Historical, International, and Comparative Perspectives" series, this book explores minimum wage politics and practices in Great Britain and the US over the past century or so. The comparison is instructive: both movements arose as part of women reformers' campaign against sweated industry. But once they hit the political maw the paths diverged; Great Britain speedily enacted a law that covered few trades, but the US struggled for some 30 years. American state efforts to mandate minimum wages for women were struck down by the Supreme Court, redirecting effort from gender-based remedies to the ultimately successful class-based Fair Labor Standards Act. Since then the American law has become more inclusive, covering virtually every worker, whereas the British abolished minimum wages in 1993. This review's sketchy summary cannot do justice to this thoroughly researched, tightly written, and conceptually rich study. Its thesis, that the US Constitution "explains" much of the divergent history, puts this book firmly within the "new institutionalism." Abundantly footnoted, *Bound by Our Constitution* will be widely consulted by scholars in the social sciences and humanities, particularly those in history, political science, law, and women's studies. Upper-division undergraduate; graduate; faculty.—*D. Lindstrom, University of Wisconsin-Madison*

OAB-2924   KF4651   96-17202 CIP
Henkin, Louis. **Foreign affairs and the United States Constitution.** 2nd ed. Oxford, 1997 (c1996). 582p index afp ISBN 0-19-826099-7, $110.00; ISBN 0-19-826098-7 pbk, $29.95

Henkin's book is extremely important for our time. US constitutionalism demands attention to undeniable traditions, strengths, and difficulties concerning structures of national government and the federal system, and the protection of citizens' rights. Just as significant, yet often slighted, is the role of the Constitution in US foreign relations. Henkin's masterful treatise, "an essay in constitutional law," encompasses the history and politics of its subject from the nation's founding. The subordinate, almost nonexistent, Supreme Court role in constitutional matters pertaining to foreign relations has led to a "scholarly neglect" this book helps correct. It comprehensively, authoritatively, and clearly surveys and analyzes its material and includes both exhaustive tables of cases, statutes, treaties, and international instruments and extensive endnotes. Henkin highlights the extraconstitutional and constitutional rationales for executive authority in foreign affairs, the tensions necessitating executive-Congress cooperation, and a defense of the obligation to respect US concepts of individual rights in foreign affairs. A critic of excessive, nonaccountable use of presidential power in foreign affairs, Henkin defends the constitution's legacy and insists that Congress not construe cooperation as requiring abdication of its authority to the executive. Upper-division undergraduates through faculty.—*R. N. Seidel, SUNY Empire State College*

OAB-2925   KF8748   94-7708 CIP
Irons, Peter. **Brennan vs. Rehnquist: the battle for the Constitution.** Knopf, 1994. 380p index ISBN 0-679-42436-9, $27.50

Irons has a well-honed ability to make the civil liberties jurisprudence of the US Supreme Court, and the attendant judicial politics, accessible to the widest possible audience. In this work, he focuses on the mannered but intense 18-year doctrinal war that took place between William J. Brennan Jr., and William H. Rehnquist, leaders of the Supreme Court's liberal and conservative wings, as they struggled for ideological control of the court's civil liberties output. With the focus on people—both litigants and judges—which has become his trademark, Irons interprets published opinions in 100 cases decided from 1972 to 1990, a critical period during which the Warren Court's historic expansion of civil rights and liberties came under seige. Irons makes no secret of his admiration for Brennen's relative success at preserving a legacy of liberties jurisprudence despite the steady shift of the court's personnel to the right under four Republican presidents. Yet, he makes an effort to fairly, if less sympathetically, describe Rehnquist's transition from strident, marginalized dissenter to Chief Justice and leader of a conservative court. This is an engaging, perceptive, and insightful work about an important period in the history of the Supreme Court. All levels.—*E. McKenzie, University of Illinois at Chicago*

OAB-2926   KF4764   92-6098 CIP
Jackson, Donald W. **Even the children of strangers: equality under the U.S. Constitution.** University Press of Kansas, 1992. 282p bibl index afp ISBN 0-7006-0547-9, $35.00; ISBN 0-7006-0548-7 pbk, $14.95

Jackson (political science, Texas Christian University) has written one of the most comprehensive and thought-provoking treatises on equal protection to date. And, perhaps more importantly, he has done so in a way that is highly readable by scholar and general reader alike. Grounding his work in the theories of Douglas Rae et al., *Equalities* (CH, Apr'82), Jackson examines the historical and legal evolution of the Equal Protection Clause from the time of its adoption to the present. From the early *Slaughterhouse Cases* (1873) to the Rehnquist Court, he examines the twists and turns of judicial interpretation in this field and the courts' vacillations between a conception of equality based on individual "merit" on the one hand and group identity on the other. The tension between strict meritocracy provided by the former and affirmative action programs based on race and gender provided by the latter can be resolved, he argues, by a closer examination of the measures we use to judge merit and a new conception of distance traveled. Perhaps, he argues, limited resources should be distributed based on the distance an individual has traveled to overcome social, economic, and other disadvantages rather than test scores, race, or gender. Ultimately, he believes that human equality should be assumed and the burden of justification must be on those who seek to treat people differently no matter the reason. Jackson's reliance on philosophy, history, political science, law, and comparative analysis make this work must reading for anyone interested in current debates over quotas, affirmative action, civil rights, and equality. Public and academic library collections.—*M. W. Bowers, University of Nevada, Las Vegas*

OAB-2927   KF8742   95-3536 CIP
Maltese, John Anthony. **The selling of Supreme Court nominees.** Johns Hopkins, 1995. 193p index afp ISBN 0-8018-5102-5, $26.95

Effectively applying his expertise on the president's management of White House news, Maltese addresses the increasingly public confirmation battles of Supreme Court justices. Early-19th-century political conflict over nominees occurred largely behind closed doors, but with popular election of Senators, interest groups mobilized to exert influence. Maltese ably quantifies the difficulties lame duck and unelected presidents have winning confirmation for their appointees, especially in an election year or when the opposition controls Congress. Original research in presidential archives enriches the work with detailed case studies of evolving strategies that explain different successes and failures. Occasionally Maltese sympathizes with a qualified nominee defeated by what he deems unfair negative campaigning, but his well-reasoned assessment notes mistreatment of both liberal and conservative nominees. When divided government confronts polarizing issues, both presidents and their interest group adversaries have practiced squalid tactics. While regretting the frequent "selling and shelling" of nominees, he finds no fundamental procedural defect requiring radical reform. His highly recommended, well-written study contributes to an improved understanding vital to the success of the confirmation process. General; academic.—*H. Tolley, University of Cincinnati*

OAB-2928   KF8745   94-23355 CIP
Mayer, Jane. **Strange justice: the selling of Clarence Thomas,** by Jane Mayer and Jill Abramson. Houghton Mifflin, 1994. 406p index ISBN 0-395-63318-4, $24.95

In this thoroughly researched volume, Mayer and Abramson detail the backgrounds of Clarence Thomas and Anita Hill, providing a useful context in which to make sense of the Senate Judiciary Committee hearings of 1991. Their research, based on extensive interviews of many key players including Hill herself, suggests that Hill was the more credible witness in alleging that Thomas sexually harassed her when she worked for him at the Equal Employment Opportunity Commission. Beyond presenting interesting character studies of Hill and Thomas and a compelling narrative of the hearings and the events surrounding them, the book is, more significantly, a scathing indictment of national politics. Whether or not Thomas sexually harassed Hill is but a backdrop for an account of how power is wielded in Washington. The authors' analysis suggests that neither Democrats nor Republicans had much regard for the truth but rather sought to protect their own interests in ways that were detrimental to Thomas, Hill, and the judicial confirmation process. This excellent volume helps illuminate what ails the American political process. Highly recommended. All levels.—*L. Bowen, John Carroll University*

OAB-2929   KF8742   93-3074 CIP
McGuire, Kevin T. **The Supreme Court bar: legal elites in the Washington community.** University Press of Virginia, 1993. 254p bibl index ISBN 0-8139-1449-3, $40.00

McGuire has produced a landmark work on the elite corps of lawyers practicing before the US Supreme Court, an inner circle of lawyers "who serve as gatekeepers to the Court [and who] have become influential actors in the politics of the high court." Beginning with an examination of the 17th-century version of the Supreme Court bar, McGuire surveys the reasons for its demise and the modern variables creating a new, but quite different, Court elite. In analyzing the shared characteristics of this group, McGuire finds that they constitute a demographic elite even among the legal community: white, male, liberal, Protestant, urban, and appellate litigation oriented. Because of this group's access to and legitimacy from the justices of the Court, they are in demand by those wealthy and influential enough to afford them. The author shows that, all other things being equal, the Court is likely to give greater weight to the petitions for review and legal arguments made by this elite cadre. Most significantly, the ability of these high-priced lawyers "to gain access to the Court over and above a host of competing interests" suggests that, as with the other branches of government, access to and success in the Supreme Court may be available only to the few who have the resources. Excellent appendixes and index add to this work to make it a must for all students and scholars of public law and American politics and all academic libraries.—*M. W. Bowers, University of Nevada, Las Vegas*

OAB-2930   KF4552   95-52897 CIP
Moore, Wayne D. **Constitutional rights and powers of the people.** Princeton, 1996. 296p index afp ISBN 0-691-01111-7, $39.50

Moore's interesting book analyzes the various ways in which "the American people" form a constitutional entity that helps shape the meaning of the US Constitution. The membership of the constitutional "people" is addressed through the complex case of Frederick Douglass, an escaped slave who nonetheless came to exercise the constitutional rights of citizenship and to help shape popular understanding of the Constitution, and through an insightful critique of the Supreme Court's majority and dissenting opinions in the *Dred Scott* case. Moore also treats the contribution of the Antifederalists (ostensibly the "losers" in the debate over constitutional ratification) to the Constitution's content and meaning. Other chapters examine early constitutional debates over federalism, the constitutionality of the national bank, and the Virginia and Kentucky resolutions. The treatment of 20th-century constitutional issues such as economic rights and abortion is less original and insightful, but overall, Moore (Virginia Polytechnic Inst. and State Univ.) makes a fine contribution to enhanced

appreciation of how the Constitution's meaning is shaped by multiple governmental bodies and "informal" citizen activity, rather than by judicial decisions alone. Strongly recommended for undergraduate, graduate, and general library collections.—*D. Schaefer, College of the Holy Cross*

OAB-2931   KF8742   92-3863 CIP
The Oxford companion to the Supreme Court of the United States, ed. by Kermit L. Hall et al. Oxford, 1992. 1,032p indexes afp ISBN 0-19-505835-6, $45.00

A vitally important reference tool that should be in every library, this publication contains—among 1,000 entries—400 case summaries, examining every major case that the Court has decided; biographies (with pictures) of every justice who ever sat on the US Supreme Court; entries on legal terms and judicial matters; articles on all amendments to the United States Constitution; and an extensive four-part history of the Court. Hardly an economic, political, or social issue does not—sooner or later—turn into a judicial one; thus, readers have a rich source of information about a central institution of American life—the ultimate venue on abortion, business, monopolies, busing, capital punishment, child labor, prayer in the public school, the war powers, and other vital controversies since 1789. Adding immensely to the volume's value are appendixes on the nomination and succession of justices, appointments by presidential term, a chronology of justices' succession, the succession of justices, and trivia and traditions of the Court. Excellent case and topical indexes. Strongly recommended for all libraries.—*F. W. Neuber, Western Kentucky University*

OAB-2932   JF1051   94-37939 CIP
Preuss, Ulrich K. **Constitutional revolution: the link between constitutionalism and progress,** tr. by Deborah Lucas Schneider. Humanities, 1995. 135p index ISBN 0-391-03853-2, $45.00; ISBN 0-391-03854-0 pbk, $15.00

Preuss presents a terse but penetrating historical analysis of constitutional revolutions, starting with the American and European revolutions of the 18th and 19th centuries and ending with the European revolutions of 1989 that toppled communism. He shows that historically constitutions have been "the object of all longing," onto which people projected their hopes and aspirations. Preuss's conceptual distinction between constitutional revolutions (Anglo-American) and classical revolutions (French and Russian) is particularly useful in understanding the character and dynamics of the divergent political systems that emerged from them. His analysis of the role of social democracy in Europe and its absence in America is suggestive in explaining the different courses of constitutionalism and power structures on the two continents. His observations on European revolutions of 1989 go a long way toward explaining the central role the constitutional movement played in interjecting into public consciousness the ideas of protection of individual rights and accountability of governmental authority. Preuss's provocative and original book must be read by scholars of constitutionalism and revolution and by all students of politics.—*M. Dorraj, Texas Christian University*

OAB-2933   JN5451   94-26676 CIP
Sartori, Giovanni. **Comparative constitutional engineering: an inquiry into structures, incentives and outcomes.** New York University, 1994. 219p bibl index ISBN 0-8147-7974-3, $40.00

Despite the seemingly endless volume of literature on democratic theory and institutions, no text even comes close to formulating the kind of comprehensive and critical synthesis one finds in this elegant new book by Sartori of Columbia University. Detailed analysis of various forms of democratic government is enhanced by a comparative assessment of the merits and limitations of different systems. Sartori's concise volume builds a compelling case for a new type of democratic political system; "alternating presidentialism," as the only reliable form that combines effective parliamentary control with efficient government. Alternating presidentialism, Sartori shows, is capable of resolving the paralysis and dysfunctional statements to which Western democratic systems are prone by providing a legislative process that avoids both parliamentary obstructionism and government by decree. This conclusion follows a thorough, systematic review of electoral systems and a comparative evaluation of presidentialism, parliamentary systems, and semipresidentialism. Generous bibliographic notes, meticulous and comprehensive research, and examples further enhance the comparative value of this lucidly written book. Upper-division undergraduate through faculty.—*P. Vannicelli, University of Massachusetts at Boston*

OAB-2934　　　　　KF8745　　　　　93-18649 CIP
Strum, Philippa. **Brandeis: beyond progressivism.** University Press of Kansas, 1993. 228p bibl index afp ISBN 0-7006-0603-3, $25.00

Brandeis biographer Strum (City Univ. of New York) has revisited this emotionally talented American lawyer/jurist, and from a familiarity with a voluminous literature she has extracted the essence of Louis Brandeis' political thought. Strum first illuminates Brandeis' concern during his early professional career with the problem of industrial justice and his belief that democracy was being jeopardized by the law's partiality to the wealthy elite. She then delineates four areas of Brandeis' thinking: jurisprudence (anchoring law in the public will while limiting the public's power to abridge individual rights); economics (viewing "bigness" in corporations and government as a curse and its control as central to industrial liberty); Zionism (perceiving it as an extension of Americanism and an emulation of the just society of Periclean Athens); and civil liberties (a belief in protecting individual rights in concert with a faith in free and open discussion). Strum characterizes Brandeis as a pragmatist who accepted the concept of a modified social contract and believed that democracy, speech, and education went hand in hand. He was, she suggests, a product of a particular historical moment and a tradition based on individual freedom. A superb work. Required reading for all who would better understand the role of Brandeis in the making of modern America. Solid documentation and bibliography. Advanced undergraduate through faculty.—*R. J. Steamer, emeritus, University of Massachusetts at Boston*

OAB-2935　　　　　KF8745　　　　　96-25548 CIP
Tushnet, Mark V. **Making constitutional law: Thurgood Marshall and the Supreme Court, 1961-1991.** Oxford, 1997. 246p bibl index afp ISBN 0-19-509314-3, $29.95

This is the second volume Tushnet (law, Georgetown Univ.) has published on the life of Thurgood Marshall. While *Making Civil Rights Law* (CH, Jun'94) covered Marshall's years as a litigator and strategist for the NAACP (1936-1961), this new work focuses on the period from 1961 to 1991, a time during which Marshall served as a US Court of Appeals judge, US Solicitor General, and justice on the US Supreme Court. As a former law clerk for Justice Marshall, the author has great insight not only into Marshall the man and his thought processes but also into the ways by which the justice operated his chambers. The book is not, however, one of those "I-was-there-and-this-is-what-happened" kinds of works: Tushnet relies upon published opinions, biographies of Marshall's contemporaries, the justice's papers, and papers of his colleagues on the Supreme Court (e.g., Brennan, Douglas, Warren, and Harlan) to make this a well-researched and well-documented effort. By sticking to constitutional law issues (equal protection, affirmative action, death penalty), Tushnet is able to tie the pieces together into a fascinating and worthwhile journey through the life of the nation's first African American Supreme Court justice. Highly recommended for both general and academic readers at any level interested in law, political science, history, ethnic studies, or cultural studies.—*M. W. Bowers, University of Nevada, Las Vegas*

OAB-2936　　　　　KF8742　　　　　96-25392 CIP
Urofsky, Melvin I. **Division and discord: the Supreme Court under Stone and Vinson, 1941-1953.** South Carolina, 1997. 298p bibl index ISBN 1-57003-120-7, $39.95

During the period 1941-53, the Supreme Court consolidated a constitutional approach that permitted a vigorous and expansive national government, handed down important decisions relating to WW II, coped (ingloriously) with the Cold War, and continued the march to nationalize the Bill of Rights and challenge racial apartheid in America. During this brief time span, the Court had more than its share of monumental decisions. But ironically, as the author points out, during this period the Court was not guided by powerful chief justices. For quite different reasons, both Stone and Vinson were weak and ineffectual leaders. The Court did, however, have a number of brilliant and powerful personalities who took the lead in mustering majorities and, more important, in developing doctrines for key new issues: Justices Black, Douglas, Frankfurter, and Jackson all served throughout this period and are in many scholars' lexicons of the "greatest justices of all time." And Justices Murphy and Clark were far from weak. Urofsky (Virginia Commonwealth Univ.) recounts developments with majesty and insight. This superb, detailed study, part of an outstanding series, "Chief Justiceships of the United States Supreme Court," is written in a lucid style by a celebrated scholar. It is a gem. It is accessible to general readers and scholars alike and should be in any library that devotes some space to American constitutional history.—*M. M. Feeley, University of California, Berkeley*

■ Psychology

OAB-2937　　　　　RC438　　　　　96-50065 CIP
Abram, Jan. **The language of Winnicott: a dictionary and guide to understanding his work.** J. Aronson, 1996. 378p bibl index afp ISBN 1-56821-700-5, $50.00

Abram's extremely helpful and lively guide includes a complete bibliography (compiled by Harry Karnac, publisher and friend of Winnicott and the London analytic community), arranged both alphabetically and chronologically from 1919 to 1989. Given Winnicott's productivity, including his many talks, letters, and broadcasts as well as books and papers as purveyors of his ideas, the compilation is highly valuable to scholars. Abram, psychotherapist and director of The Squiggle Foundation, has arranged large topics and concepts associated with Winnicott's thought in alphabetical order, but in the form of chapters. Each section contains related subheadings, like nodal points within the concept, e.g., Alone (The capacity to be) 1. Ego-relatedness; 2. I am alone; 3. Withdrawal and loneliness. Within each subsection Abram offers clarity about perceived ambiguities in Winnicott's expression, relevant nuggets of direct quotation, and references to opinions and moments in his life related to the development of a particular idea. This creative approach to his concepts should help those critics (especially some US psychoanalysts) who have found his writing too gnomic to appreciate. Both novice and veteran Winnicottians will find pleasure and illumination in browsing and also in using the book as a fine scholarly reference. General readers; upper-division undergraduates through professionals.—*R. H. Balsam, Yale University*

OAB-2938　　　　　BF109　　　　　92-54522 CIP
Bjork, Daniel W. **B.F. Skinner: a life.** Basic Books, 1993. 298p bibl index ISBN 0-465-00611-6, $25.00

This first major biography of Skinner is a remarkably dispassionate chronicle. In this work, appearing only three years after Skinner's death, Bjork places Skinner squarely in the context of US social, technological, and political history. Bjork shows how Skinner's work reflects the coming together in 20th-century US of several conflicting cultural practices. Bjork, a historian rather than a scientist, appropriately focuses primarily on Skinner's role as inventor and social critic. Bjork portrays Skinner's approach to social reform in terms of a science-based technology as a uniquely US approach to 20th-century problems. The book builds to a riveting and insightful interpretation of the intellectual roots of Skinner's most controversial book, *Beyond Freedom and Dignity* (CH, Apr'72), and to the nature and reasons for the passionate outcry against that book from many US intellectuals. Skinner is seen here as a dutiful, if distant, son; a caring, if frustrated, husband; and a nurturing, deeply committed, father. Although heavily documented, Bjork's book is very readable because documentation is in endnotes. A handsome, well-indexed work, with an excellent bibliography. General; community college; undergraduate through faculty.—*S. S. Glenn, University of North Texas*

OAB-2939 BF175 93-7325 CIP
Cavell, Marcia. **The psychoanalytic mind: from Freud to philosophy.** Harvard, 1993. 276p bibl index afp ISBN 0-674-72095-4, $29.95

An attempt to interrelate contemporary philosophy of mind with Freud's theory of the unconscious. Following Davidson and Wittgenstein, Cavell (New York Univ.) sees mind as derived from the acquisition of language and asserts that there are no nonlinguistic forms of mentality. Since language and its acquisition are public phenomena, all minds are inherently social and intersubjective. With this theory she attempts to reconceive Freud's philosophy of unconscious mentality both by criticizing the physicalistic/deterministic and Cartesian internalist trends in Freud's thought and by developing those that treat the unconscious as a set of intentional and linguistic processes. Topics covered include the question of psychological laws, whether psychoanalytic interpretations can be true, what infant mentality and self-structure might be like before the acquisition of language, the nature of emotion and its relation to language, primary process thinking, and how Oedipal triangulation might be able to ground moral theory. Althorth this reviewer doubts that one can eliminate the messy internalist and physicalist sides of Freud without losing much of his insight, this carefully and intelligently written book probes one of the most promising frontiers in philosophy: the relation of philosophy of mind to theory of the unconscious. An important acquisition for all academic libraries, upper-level undergraduate and above.—*J. H. Riker, Colorado College*

OAB-2940 BF173 93-29372 CIP
Elliott, Anthony. **Psychoanalytic theory: an introduction.** Blackwell, 1994. 183p index afp ISBN 0-631-18846-0, $49.95; ISBN 0-631-18847-9 pbk, $19.95

This highly intelligent critical overview of all the past and current offshoots of Freudian psychoanalytic theory is extremely well written and concise, and delineates the points of similarity, difference, originality, and limitations of each development. Elliott is fair and respectful of each body of thought. His grasp of the material extends from the clinical to the metapsychological, from social to cultural and political implications. Thus, he does justice to classical Freudian theory, the American ego psychologists and self psychologists, to Klein and the British object relations theorists, to Lacan and beyond in France, and to Anglo-American and continental feminist and postmodern theorists. Elliott, an Australian political scientist, uses the themes of subjectivity and self-organization as they relate to individual and collective autonomy in the social and political world. He reflects the liveliness and relevance of psychoanalysis to these matters. A wonderful aid for teaching and a fine rapid reference resource. Undergraduate through professional.—*R. H. Balsam, Yale University*

OAB-2941 BF39 94-16699 CIP
Elms, Alan C. **Uncovering lives: the uneasy alliance of biography and psychology.** Oxford, 1994. 315p bibl index afp ISBN 0-19-508287-7, $25.00

The art of biography has always relied on psychological insight, but the manner in which psychology is employed in the interpretation of lives has often been the subject of debate. Psychologist Elms does future biographers a great favor by charting both the potential and the pitfalls of psychobiography. He provides an overview of the issues, a chapter full of practical tips for the would-be biographer, and an intriguing series of his own psychobiographical studies of such figures as Freud, Jimmy Carter, George Bush, Saddam Hussein, Isaac Asimov, and B.F. Skinner. The final chapter examines the scientific status of psychobiography, arguing that it deserves the serious attention of all students of psychology because the task of understanding the individual life is a supreme test for any theory. Readers in other fields that employ biography, such as his-

tory and literature, will also find the book very useful. Overall, the prose is exceptionally clear and interesting, the argument balanced and wise, the insights fresh. Highly recommended for college libraries as well as the general academic reader. Upper-division undergraduate through professional.—*T. Sloan, University of Tulsa*

OAB-2942 BF175 96-38919 CIP
Franz, Marie-Louise von. **Archetypal dimensions of the psyche.** Shambhala, 1997. 405p bibl index afp ISBN 1-57062-133-0, $35.00

This is the fourth and final volume of von Franz's selected writings, consisting primarily of articles, essays, and lectures from 1969 to 1985. The collection is a clear presentation of this eminent Jungian analyst's work, addressing the major concepts (e.g., the shadow, anima/animus, the self, etc.). The writings are not a critique of Jungian thought but an examination and explanation. Von Franz touches on cultural and historical issues, religion, love, social movements, fairy tales, etc., incorporating these themes seamlessly into her essays and Jungian concepts. As always, von Franz's work is well researched and filled with examples. There are notes at the end of each essay, as well as a bibliography and index at the end of the book, which is pleasurable as well as informative. Von Franz is realistic in addressing the outcome of therapy, that not everyone will be healed; yet she points out the importance of the journey, turning toward the impending darkness and exploring it. This work, like the author's others, is a valuable addition to any psychology collection, and a must for collections focusing on Jung's work. General readers; upper-division undergraduates through professionals.—*J. Dodd, Southeast Community College*

OAB-2943 BF109 92-48252 CIP
Gilman, Sander L. **Freud, race, and gender.** Princeton, 1993. 277p index afp ISBN 0-691-03245-9, $24.95

Gilman synthesizes the work of psychoanalysts, Freud biographers, literary critics, and historians to provide this impressive new reading of the meanings of "race" and "gender" in Freud's time. With admirable scholarship, the author tackles numerous assumptions about the manner in which Freud's Jewish male identity shaped his scientific stance in and against antisemitic culture. Since many of Freud's key concepts, particularly those about women, take on new dimensions in light of Gilman's analysis, this is an essential book for fin-de-siècle cultural studies, Jewish studies, and the history of psychology and medicine. The book also has great relevance to contemporary debates on multiculturalism. Excellent notes and index. Advanced undergraduate through faculty.—*T. Sloan, University of Tulsa*

OAB-2944 BF108 94-26930 CIP
Herman, Ellen. **The romance of American psychology: political culture in the age of experts.** California, 1995. 406p index afp ISBN 0-520-08598-1, $35.00

Herman claims that the US continues to have a "love affair" with psychology. Terms like "romance" suggest that this affair has been both rewarding and desired. Herman convincingly shows, however, that this is not always the case. The author portrays the integration of psychology into cultural and political arenas as both welcome and problematic. She does a remarkable job of tracing the birth and development of psychology's role as a social force in the "atmosphere of military crisis" of WW II. The analysis of psychology's role in the history of the civil rights movement is particularly well done. The chapter title, "The Damaging Psychology of Race," however, is misleading. Not all to come from psychological analyses of race and racial prejudice has been negative. One should reserve judgment of the balance of Herman's approach, however, until the last page is turned. This academic professional was left wanting to run out and grab the nearest political scientist so we could start planning a course around this book. Highly recommended for sophisticated upper-division undergraduates, graduate students, and researchers/faculty.—*R. E. Osborne, Indiana University East*

OAB-2945   BF173   92-54802 CIP
Kerr, John. **A most dangerous method: the story of Jung, Freud, and Sabina Spielrein.** Knopf, 1993. 607p index ISBN 0-679-40412-0, $30.00

This new work by clinical psychologist Kerr closely reviews Sigmund Freud's and Carl Jung's work during their early development as researchers and clinicians, and traces in detail the influence on both men's theories of Sabina Spielrein. Spielrein, a severely disturbed young Russian Jewish woman, was treated by Jung in 1904 as a test case in psychoanalysis. She maintained an intimate friendship with Jung for many years, trained in psychoanalysis with Freud, corresponded with both men during the crucial years of their friendship and subsequent alienation, and influenced Russian clinical psychology in the 1920s and '30s. Spielrein played an especially important role in Jung's theory of the anima and Freud's theory of destructive instinct. Much of the Freud-Jung-Spielrein correspondence, along with Spielrein's remarkable diary, was published in Aldo Carotenuto's *A Secret Symmetry* (CH, Sep'82); but Kerr's book is the first thorough examination of her influence. An essential work for both Freud and Jung scholars, and much of the argument will interest students of 20th-century intellectual history. General; advanced undergraduate through professional.—*D. A. Davis, Haverford College*

OAB-2946   BF109   96-13049 CIP
Messerly, John G. **Piaget's conception of evolution: beyond Darwin and Lamarck.** Rowman & Littlefield, 1996. 166p bibl index afp ISBN 0-8476-8242-0, $52.50; ISBN 0-8476-8243-9 pbk, $21.95

In an excellent critical overview of Piaget's work, Messerly (Ursuline College) highlights the profound philosophical issues motivating Piaget's famous studies of the stages of development of children's intelligence. The basic problem is to relate biology to epistemology. Messerly approaches questions concerning how human minds relate to the world from a biological and developmental point of view. Piaget studied how knowledge is actually generated. He drew parallels between individual psychogenesis, biological evolution, and the historical development of science. Messerly shows how he wrestled with fundamental issues in cognitive science, which have recently been focusing more on evolutionary epistemology. Philosophically, Piaget appears as a dynamic Kantian, opening the categories of understanding to evolutionary development. This is the best source for anyone seeking a clear distillation of the fundamental principles and conclusions of Piaget's voluminous works. Upper-division undergraduate; graduate; faculty.—*H. C. Byerly, emeritus, University of Arizona*

OAB-2947   BF109   94-27901 CIP
Newton, Peter M. **Freud: from youthful dream to mid-life crisis.** Guilford, 1995. 297p bibl index afp ISBN 0-89862-293-X, $21.95

Newton's lively and brilliant book discusses the emotional underpinnings of Freud's professional identity. The author uses Daniel Levinson's theory of developmental phases of the life span, yielding interesting emphases in interpretation of events in Freud's life, and their impact. For example, natural midlife individuation is seen as a basis of his well-known turmoil at age 41. The loss of the seduction theory at this time signifies here the clash of two trends in his thought and career aspiration, i.e., the pure neuroscientist and/or the great healer. The integration of the two and direction for Freud's post-midlife is thus set in the creation of psychoanalysis itself. Other writers have stressed more the death of Freud's father and his self-analysis as crucial to this burst of creativity. Newton traces the earlier currents of this clash of aspiration from adolescence through Freud's 20s and 30s. Freud's own words (via his letters to Silberstein, Martha, his fiancée, and Fliess, his close colleague) tell the developmental story Newton wishes to delineate. This exciting work should be read by those interested in Freud and psychoanalysis, at all levels of sophistication. General; upper-division undergraduate through professional.—*R. H. Balsam, Yale University*

OAB-2948   RC504   95-173 CIP
Psychoanalysis: the major concepts, ed. by Burness E. Moore and

Bernard D. Fine. Yale, 1996 (c1995). 577p bibl index afp ISBN 0-300-06329-6, $60.00

Undoubtedly, this book is one of the most comprehensive and complete volumes on the major concepts of psychoanalytic training, therapy, and theory that this reviewer has read. Starting with the "technique of psychoanalysis proper," the book includes topics such as child and adolescent psychoanalysis; psychoanalytic concepts in groups—resistance, transference, countertransference; unconscious fantasy; and Freud's ideas on dreams and more recent thought about dreams. The book is very thorough, easy to read, and enjoyable; it beckons the reader to go further. Despite being an edited book, it is of uniformly high quality. A superb addition to any library. Upper-division undergraduates through professionals.—*R. J. Howell, Brigham Young University*

OAB-2949   Orig
Richelle, Marc N. **B.F. Skinner: a reappraisal.** L. Erlbaum, 1994 (c1993). 242p bibl indexes ISBN 0-86377-283-8, $59.95

A book for every major library, this is a highly readable critical appraisal of the work of Skinner in the context of 20th-century psychology, US and European. Nonspecialists will learn a great deal about the psychological sciences in general as well as gain some appreciation of the complex issues underlying controversies surrounding Skinner's work. Scholars in many fields, including psychologists, behavior analysts, and cognitive scientists—as well as those in related fields such as psycholinguistics, evolutionary biology, philosophy of science, and neurobiology—can make good use of this work. Richelle is a careful and widely read scholar who compares and contrasts, in a balanced and clear manner, Skinner's views to those of writers in all of those fields. There are 16 short chapters, each dealing with a topic about which much confusion and misinformation has appeared both in print and in oral discourse. References are extensive but unobtrusive, covering English and French language sources. All levels.—*S. S. Glenn, University of North Texas*

OAB-2950   BF175   92-32360 CIP
Rosenzweig, Saul. **Freud, Jung, and Hall the King-Maker: the historic expedition to America (1909) with G. Stanley Hall as host and William James as guest.** Rana House/Hogrefe & Huber, 1992. (Dist. by Rana House Press, 8029 Washington Ave., St. Louis, MO 63114) 477p bibl index ISBN 0-88937-110-5, $27.50

Without doubt, the most important and complete book on US psychoanalytic history ever written. Rosenzweig spent 50 years doing research before writing the book. The first part discussess Freud's and Jung's invitation to the US by G. Stanley Hall, their arrival and activities in the US, the aftermath of the trip, and a commentary by Rosenzweig. The second part discusses the letters between Sigmund Freud and G. Stanley Hall; and Part 3, the five lectures that Freud gave. Highly recommended for students of psychoanalysis, for upper-division undergraduate and graduate students in psychology, and for psychoanalytic practitioners interested in the history of their field.—*R. J. Howell, Brigham Young University*

OAB-2951   BF109   95-52247 CIP
Smith, Robert C. **The wounded Jung: effects of Jung's relationships on his life and work.** Northwestern University, 1996. 208p bibl index afp ISBN 0-8101-1270-1, $30.00

Smith has done an exceptional job in presenting Jung in an unbiased and balanced way. Jung's personal relationships are viewed in conjunction with his work in various phases of his life. Smith's deep yet unassuming manner pervades the work, even in presenting his own ideas and personal correspondence with Jung. Various contemporary and historical theories and opinions are included in the work (such as those of Hillman and Eliade). Jung's selective memory and psychological struggles are addressed in a forthright way, without idolizing or personal attacks. Although Smith examines current issues in Jungian studies (e.g., flawed anima/animus concepts), he avoids faddish presentation. The work is based on solid research in well-rounded sources and is interesting and easy to read. Researchers will appreciate the excellent list of references, index, glossary, and endnotes. A worthy addition to any collection that includes work by or about Jung. General; undergraduates through professionals.—*J. Dodd, Southeast Community College*

■ Cognition

OAB-2952   BF311   96-16622 CIP
Arden, John Boghosian. **Consciousness, dreams, and self: a transdisciplinary approach.** Psychosocial Press, 1996. (Dist. by International Universities Press) 192p bibl indexes ISBN 1-887841-01-6, $28.50

Arden's examination of dreams, consciousness, and self provides a unique perspective for transdisciplinary interests. He sets out to show that consciousness is a "contextual, independent and fluid process." The text is presented in three broad categories: biophysiology, sociocultural system, and self system (with the meaning and function of dreams addressed in each section). Drawing on a vast array of researchers, Arden shows how function and structure have co-evolved. Consciousness is viewed as an aspect of the overall dynamic evolutionary process. Important topics are addressed: artificial intelligence, neuronal firing patterns, right/left brain activity, and more theoretical topics like the place of mystical reformers in the evolution of consciousness, discontinuous leaps to higher levels of organization, and consciousness in relation to dreaming. Arden's work will be most beneficial to those who have a broad background and vast array of interests. It is an excellent companion summary-type work for sociology, anthropology, psychology, physical sciences, and other areas. A true reflection of our time, blending events and topics once disparate. Upper-division undergraduates through professionals.—*J. Dodd, Southeast Community College*

OAB-2953   P106   95-17023 CIP
Bickerton, Derek. **Language and human behavior.** Washington, 1995. 180p bibl index afp ISBN 0-295-97457-5, $24.95

In the past few years there have been several fascinating books for the "intelligent layperson" on issues of evolution, consciousness, and language. Representative examples include Daniel Dennett's *Consciousness Explained* (1991) and *Darwin's Dangerous Idea* (CH, Nov'95), and Steven Pinker, *The Language Instinct* (CH, Jul'94). Readers of these and most similar books might come away knowing Bickerton as a clever researcher without much impact as an original theoretician (unless they have also read his *Language and Species*, CH, May'91). The present book should put an end to the belief that Bickerton only supplies data for the theories of other people. Here is a brilliant exposition of the primacy and centrality of language in thought and consciousness. Not a simpleminded linguistic relativity model (Benjamin Lee Whorf, *Language, Thought and Reality*, 1956), it exploits the richness of syntax and contrasts the situation-bound "protolanguage" of chimpanzees, the language of young children, and pidgin languages to language with syntax. The latter permits "offline" thinking, i.e., thinking about the abstract rather than the immediate. This miracle of thought is attributed to sudden mutation or the "punctuated equilibrium" of Eldridge and Gould (Niles Eldridge, *Reinventing Darwin*, 1995). This book is excellent by itself, but reading Bickerton's "adversaries" will give additional flavor to the discussion of language, consciousness, and evolution. Upper-division undergraduate through faculty.—*P. L. Derks, College of William and Mary*

OAB-2954   BF341   93-3625 CIP
Collier, Gary. **Social origins of mental ability.** Wiley-Interscience, 1994. 300p bibl indexes afp ISBN 0-471-30407-7, $35.00

A necessary book for all libraries because it provides access to important research literature. Collier's well-written and timely overview of contemporary research comments on how social interactions affect the individual's self-

esteem and acquisition of specific cognitive skills. He presents the nurture side of the nature-nurture interaction that shapes cognitive development and, as such, has important implications for social intervention programs (such as Head Start). The bibliography can guide readers who seek more detailed information. Collier makes a good case that social intervention programs based on existing research can provide more equitable social contexts for the development of language, perception, memory, creativity, and logical reasoning. Group differences in intellectual functioning fall within a "reaction range" where the environment either enriches or diminishes normal cognitive development. Unfortunately, Collier stops short of discussing how nature-nurture interactions in the early years of life lay a foundation for cognitive functioning that becomes most difficult to remediate after eight years of age. Still, a book that should be widely read by professionals and the general public. All levels.—*F. Smolucha, Moraine Valley Community College*

OAB-2955   Orig
Dennett, Daniel C. **Kinds of minds: toward an understanding of consciousness.** Basic Books, 1996. 184p bibl index ISBN 0-465-07350-6, $20.00

Dennett's new book is in the distinguished tradition of his previous volumes. He deftly poses philosophical questions that reflect on the nature of minds of other creatures in contrast to our own. Into this process he brings an evolutionary perspective that is in the best of Darwinian and ethological traditions, without doing injustice to psychology. A few of his particular and timely concerns are questions regarding morality related to thinking in complex animals and robots, and the distinguishing attributes of humans. From his previous successful book on natural selection he imports the models of "Darwinian," "Skinnerian," "Popperian," and "Gregorian" creatures through which he makes powerful arguments for the evolutionary stage that led to an adaptive emergence (contra S.J. Gould's views) of human language, conversing with the self, and culture while retaining our evolutionary heritage. Dennett's ability to entertain while making the reader think about uncomfortable questions makes him one of the great educators. Highly recommended. General, undergraduates through faculty.—*F. S. Szalay, CUNY Hunter College*

OAB-2956   BF412   94-32136 CIP
Eysenck, H.J. **Genius: the natural history of creativity.** Cambridge, 1995. 344p bibl index (Problems in the behavioural sciences, 12) ISBN 0-521-48014-0, $69.95; ISBN 0-521-48508-8 pbk, $27.95

Although Eysenck would resent the comparison, this is the best book on creativity since Arthur Koestler's *The Act of Creation* (1964). Like Koestler, he presents a thorough, if more critical, survey of a voluminous literature. Unlike Koestler, and in spite of his contributions to the topic, Eysenck does not consider humor relevant to a discussion of creativity. Avner Ziv's *Personality and Sense of Humor* (CH, Nov'84) is a beginning to what has become an extensive literature. More important, and also unlike Koestler, Eysenck presents a remarkably thorough, well-reasoned, and testable theory of creativity and genius. Although, for example, Margaret Boden in *The Creative Mind: Myths and Mechanisms* (1991) or Robert W. Weisberg in *Creativity: Beyond the Myth of Genius* (1993) complain that creativity is not mysterious and can be studied, Eysenck shows how this has been, and can continue to be, done. His theory relates "psychoticism," a measure of uninhibited thinking that at the extreme becomes schizophrenia, to creativity. Schizophrenia as the "madness" related to creativity has recently given way to mood swings as described by Kay R. Jamison in *Touched with Fire: Manic-Depressive Illness and the Artistic Temperament* (CH, Sep'93). Eysenck's presentation is, however, overwhelming with evidence ranging from behavioral to neurological. The book is also entertaining and informative in areas other than psychology. After all these years, a worthy successor to Koestler. Upper-division undergraduate through professional.—*P. L. Derks, College of William and Mary*

OAB-2957   Orig
Harley, Trevor A. **The psychology of language: from data to the-**

ory. Erlbaum (UK) Taylor & Francis, 1995. (Dist. by L. Erlbaum) 482p bibl indexes ISBN 0-86377-381-8, $39.95; ISBN 0-86377-382-6 pbk, $22.00

Psycholinguistics commands an important place in most undergraduate courses in cognitive psychology, and Harley's expansive, up-to-date review will be valuable for students in this area. Moreover, he offers this work as a primary resource for courses exclusively focused on the psychology of language. Issues range from entry-level processes such as speech perception, visual word recognition, word pronunciation, and speech production, including related coverage of dyslexia and aphasia, through higher-order topics of semantics, pragmatics, comprehension, and the interdependence of language and thought, concluding with a brief treatment of language acquisition and bilingualism. Integrated throughout are references to recent research and theorizing in cognitive neuropsychology and connectionism. Appended to each chapter is an excellent description of sources for further reading. The message is clearly delivered that psycholinguistics is an emerging field with many worthy, competing theories and unresolved questions. Clearly written, broadly referenced, and very current, this book compares favorably to its oft-cited predecessor, Herbert H. Clark and Eve V. Clark's *Psychology and Language* (1977). Recommended. Upper-division undergraduates through faculty.—*T. J. Thieman, College of St. Catherine*

OAB-2958 BF251 96-43808 CIP
Hartmann, William M. **Signals, sound, and sensation.** American Institute of Physics, 1997. 647p bibl index afp ISBN 1-56396-283-7, $80.00

Hartmann's book is nothing short of excellent! The only prerequisite is an introductory background in psychoacoustics and calculus. The mathematics, which are presented in a systematic and comprehensible fashion, do not distract from the written prose. The book begins with basic properties such as sine-waves and sound levels, proceeds through Fourier transforms and filtering, and ends with advanced topics such as modulation, sampling, and distortion. Each chapter ends with thoughtful and interesting exercises that test comprehension and help to integrate the material. Researchers and advanced students studying psychoacoustics will find the book to be indispensable. In this reviewer's opinion, it ranks as one of the most important books written for the hearing sciences. Upper-division undergraduates through professionals.— *L. A. Dawe, Cameron University*

OAB-2959 BF431 94-29694 CIP
Herrnstein, Richard J. **The bell curve: intelligence and class structure in American life,** by Richard J. Herrnstein and Charles Murray. Free Press, 1994. 845p bibl index ISBN 0-02-914673-9, $30.00

Herrnstein and Murray have excelled in writing a comprehensive and unbiased book about the relationship between intelligence and success, or lack of it, in many different areas of society. Factual information is presented instead of politically correct interpretations of scientific data. Costs to individuals and society due to the failure to use a most valid procedure, tests of intelligence, are elaborated. Also included are references to the neglect of intellectually gifted students in the schools. In addition, the negative aspects of affirmative action programs are presented; varying viewpoints relative to issues covered in the book are considered; and suggestions for improving society are offered. James G. Wilson of UCLA made the following recommendation for Daniel Seligman's 1992 book, *A Question of Intelligence*, in the January 1993 issue of *Fortune*: "Every citizen who wants to think clearly about public policy ought to read this book." The recommendation is also very appropriate for Herrnstein and Murray's book. Highly recommended. All levels.—*O. L. Crowell, Tennessee Technological University*

OAB-2960 BF444 91-45159 CIP
Jackendoff, Ray. **Languages of the mind: essays on mental representation.** MIT, 1992. 200p bibl index ISBN 0-262-10047-9, $25.00

It is refreshing to read a book by a linguist who uses analytic methodol-

ogy and takes behavioral (i.e., performance) data seriously. Jackendoff, a capable and respected theorist as well as a sharp and knowledgeable critic, writes here for a wider audience than in his *Consciousness and Computational Mind* (CH, Feb'88). He is clear and engaging. His primary goal is to illuminate cognitive processes with the inner glow of linguistic phenomenon. Language, in other words, reflects the way the mind works. He also uses a similar analysis of music perception and social behavior to illustrate cognitive mechanisms, giving rigorous support to a notion of "modular" intelligence in the sense of Howard Gardner's *Frames of Mind* (CH, Apr'84) or, even less willingly, Jerry Fodor's *The Modularity of Mind* (CH, Dec'83). Nevertheless, he finds similarities in these modular processes and grudgingly invokes Daniel Dennett's *Consciousness Explained* (1991) with its "multiple drafts" model of cognition as it yields consciousness. His discussions are charming and generally persuasive. (He is willing to supply the musical examples to readers willing to send him a blank tape.) Even better, he prompts the reader to examine his examples and often to respond with "Yes, but what about. . .?" This implied give-and-take marks the book as an outstanding access to an often opaque field. It can be read and enjoyed by bright undergraduates as well as by graduate students and faculty.—*P. L. Derks, College of William and Mary*

OAB-2961 BF371 96-7674 CIP
Memory, ed. by Elizabeth Ligon Bjork and Robert A. Bjork. Academic Press, 1996. 586p bibl index afp ISBN 0-12-102570-5, $65.00

Memory provides a wonderful, readable, and current overview of the human memory and cognition field. Each chapter links important historical work with current findings, concepts, and methods. The first two chapters provide conceptual scaffolding by reviewing information processing approaches to memory and exploring the issue of conscious and unconscious forms of memory. Chapters on transient sensory memory and short-term working memory follow. Long-term memory issues are addressed in four chapters dealing with imagery, autobiographical memory, retrieval processes, and interference effects. Three chapters deal with the control process problems of encoding, mnemonics, and metacognition. Final chapters address a gallimaufry of memory phenomena, including individual differences, cognitive aging, eyewitness memory, and retention of training and instruction. Clearly, the breadth of this book should make it an important resource for all investigators in the field of human cognition. Recommended for upper-level undergraduates through faculty.—*G. C. Gamst, University of La Verne*

OAB-2962 BF449 93-29646 CIP
The Nature of insight, ed. by Robert J. Sternberg and Janet E. Davidson. MIT, 1995. 618p bibl indexes ISBN 0-262-19345-0, $45.00

This significant contribution to the literature on human creativity explores the topic from several perspectives—some of them contradictory. Edited by psychologists Sternberg (Yale) and Davidson (Lewis and Clark College), the book's five sections explore history and methods, unconventional problem-solving, insights and inventions, case histories of insightful people, and the role of metaphor in exploring insight. In one of several attempts at definition, S.M. Smith refers to insight as a mature or sudden understanding of a mechanism, an analogy, a principle, or a concept. Mihaly Csikszentmihalyi and Keith Sawyer trace the term to the Dutch word for "seeing inside," implying that one who experiences insight must have had some prior exposure to the issue, producing either "normal" or "revolutionary" insights with short-term and long-term consequences, respectively. Others present experimental data, conceptual formulations, various impasses to insight, and various examples, e.g., Archimedes, Darwin, Einstein, Faraday, Feynman, Laubert, Hemingway, Poe, Piaget, and Henry James (women and non-Westerners are notably absent). The role of humans as *interpreters* is a provocative theme, as is the role of emotional and social context in insight. Puzzles, riddles, and jokes add to the richness of the volume. In general, the reader will realize that insight is not a unitary phenomenon, and that the contributors have presented a complex and elegant mosaic to be found nowhere else. Upper-division undergraduate through professional.— *S. Krippner, Saybrook Institute*

OAB-2963   BF341   93-21876 CIP
Rowe, David C. **The limits of family influence: genes, experience, and behavior.** Guilford, 1994. 232p index afp ISBN 0-89862-132-1, $30.00

Rowe states that the purpose of his book is "to shake socialization science out of its complacent emphasis on the family as the bearer of culture, and on familial variation as the environmental cause of observed phenotypic diversity." Attempts to butcher sacred cows often result in rhetoric and controversy. Although this book will stir controversy, it does so with a minimum of rhetoric, depending instead on thoughtful analyses and reinterpretations of data that may already be familiar to many readers. Rowe's presentation of his own research as well as that of Scarr and McCartney, Scarr and Weinberg, Plomin and associates, Gottesman, and others weaves a careful, articulate thesis that certainly will promote further discussion, debate, and research. This extremely provocative yet amazingly readable book is destined to become one of the seminal works in the history of the nature-nurture controversy. Never before has this reviewer seen such a thorough yet understandable summary of the issues surrounding the assessment of heritability and environmental influences. Very highly recommended; perhaps it should even be required reading. General; upper-division undergraduate through professional.—*R. B. Stewart Jr., Oakland University*

OAB-2964   BF1078   96-20997 CIP
States, Bert O. **Seeing in the dark: reflections on dreams and dreaming.** Yale, 1997. 265p bibl index afp ISBN 0-300-06910-3, $32.50

States has created a work that challenges preconceived notions and assumptions about dream theory. He leads the reader to examine beliefs that have been incorporated into our thought systems for years regarding dreams, their meaning and purpose. States suggests dreams have little to do with keeping us self-informed and that their "meanings" are no different than the kind of meaning we give to waking experience. The book has a wonderful essence of its own, as the author weaves humor and intelligence, creating his "cubistic" work. His feelings and thoughts are clear but never confining. The speculations include reference to phenomenologists (e.g., Merleau-Ponty), philosophers, psychoanalysts, and scientists (e.g., Crick and Dawkins). The book is serious and well researched, yet entertaining and fun to read. Some topics like precognitive dreams are not discussed in detail, but many other topics, including lucid dreaming, are presented. States shakes the foundations of Jungians and Freudians alike, and gives us a refreshing perspective on old ideas. An important work in dream theory and an asset to collections that incorporate multiple viewpoints. A delightful read. General readers; undergraduates through professionals.—*J. Dodd, Southeast Community College*

OAB-2965   BF341   96-3317 MARC
Steen, R. Grant. **DNA and destiny: nature and nurture in human behavior.** Plenum, 1996. 295p bibl index ISBN 0-306-45260-X, $28.95

This is an outstanding review of the relative contributions of genetics and environment on human personality, temperament, physiology, and behavior. Steen provides a rational, thorough, and balanced discussion that is highly preferable to the other, more sensational standout in this field by R.J. Herrnstein and C. Murray, *The Bell Curve: Intelligence and Class Structure in American Life* (CH, May '95). Steen devotes three well-written chapters to the history of the nature-nurture debate, including some excellent reference material on the popularity of the eugenics movement in both Europe and the US in the early part of the 20th century. The next four chapters explain how genetic and environmental influences are defined and gauged. Finally, Steen devotes well-researched and clearly written chapters to each of the following topics as they pertain to the nature-nurture debate: intelligence, mental disorders, personality traits, sexual orientation, alcoholism and addictive behavior, crime and violence, and gender differences. Every chapter includes unbiased presentations of the latest research. Highly recommended for general readers, college students of all levels, and professionals.—*A. C. Downs, formerly, University of Houston—Clear Lake*

OAB-2966   QL785   95-46951 CIP
Vauclair, Jacques. **Animal cognition: an introduction to modern comparative psychology.** Harvard, 1996. 206p bibl index afp ISBN 0-674-03703-0, $29.95

Vauclair's well-referenced volume provides an excellent introduction to the scientific study of cognition in animals. The book traces the roots of modern comparative psychology and describes the typical laboratory methods for assessing mental representations of knowledge; it then discusses diverse topics such as animal applications of Piagetian concepts, tool use in animals, spatial and temporal representations, social cognition, animal communication, and theory of mind in a straightforward, easily comprehensible manner. Representative studies from each of these areas are presented, and the author discusses how each of the selected studies has influenced the field of comparative psychology. As the title indicates, this book is an introduction to the field of comparative psychology, and the author only touches the surface of these diverse topic areas. However, Vauclair also provides 500-plus references to relevant studies in the area. An excellent resource. Upper-division undergraduate and graduate students.—*S. Hensch, University of Wisconsin Centers*

■ Developmental Psychology

OAB-2967   BF724   92-46666 CIP
Encyclopedia of adult development, ed. by Robert Kastenbaum. Oryx, 1993. 574p index afp ISBN 0-89774-669-4, $95.00

In under 600 pages, a remarkable assemblage of articles about adult development topics. Kastenbaum, also the editor of the *International Journal of Aging & Human Development*, has assembled dozens of experts in the social and health sciences to write the individual articles. Compared to other encyclopedias and handbooks in the subject area, this one is better edited: more user friendly, with articles kept to a manageable length rather than attempting to be comprehensive reviews in detail. The strength of this volume is its superior organization: an alphabetical list of articles, with a topical guide to the chapters and a comprehensive index. Even the individual articles have a high degree of internal organization. The one essential reference work in the psychology of adult development for both public and academic libraries. All levels.—*T. L. Brink, Crafton Hills College*

OAB-2968   BF697   94-22128 CIP
Identity and development: an interdisciplinary approach, ed. by Harke A. Bosma et al. Sage Publications, CA, 1994. 204p bibl indexes (Sage focus editions, 172) ISBN 0-8039-5189-2, $46.00; ISBN 0-8039-5190-6 pbk, $23.95

Identity and Development is one of the most engaging texts on identity that this reviewer has had the fortune to read. Bosma and colleagues Toby Graafsma, Harold Grotevant, and David J. de Levita have done a remarkable job of tracing the intellectual history of thinking and research in the areas of identity and identity development. The historical analysis in chapters 7 through 9 provides even the naive reader with an understanding of the spirit within which this literature has matured and lays the groundwork for understanding where this area will go in its future. The chapters on how to empirically study aspects of identity such as the ego are also especially well done. Although the authors rarely specifically mention what research they feel still needs to be done to expand the understanding of identity and identity development, the information provided makes such an understanding possible. It seems especially fitting that such a high quality text on identity be dedicated to this area's intellectual forefather, Erik H. Erikson. Highly recommended for college students of all levels, researchers, and professionals.—*R. E. Osborne, Indiana University East*

OAB-2969   HQ1206   91-58602 CIP
Kaschak, Ellyn. **Engendered lives: a new psychology of women's**

experience. Basic Books, 1992. 265p bibl index ISBN 0-465-01347-3, $25.00

Kaschak employs a heuristic blend of sociocultural and psychotherapeutic analyses to inform her exploration of the psychology of women/the reality of women's lived experiences. She begins with a useful and unusually lucid comparison of traditional male-centered and feminist (postmodern) epistemologies and their impacts on (especially) psychotherapies. Following a brief discussion of the social psychological construction of gender based on the illusion of anatomical dichotomy, Kaschak introduces a thought-provoking feminist interpretation of the Oedipal myth using as female counterpart to Oedipus not Electra but Oedipus' daughter-sister, Antigone. The resulting model of female-male relationships in patriarchal society, a model that emphasizes seeing and knowing rather than sexuality, is used in subsequent chapters to explain the development of a sense of self, self-esteem, and specific psychological outcomes of learning to be a woman (e.g., depression, and eating and dissociative disorders). Kaschak concludes with suggestions for applying her model to the development of feminist psychotherapy. Those with an interest in feminist psychology/sociology should find this book intellectualy stimulating, a treat. Highly recommended for academic libraries serving upper-division undergraduates, graduate students, and professionals.—*B. Ayers-Nachamkin, Wilson College*

OAB-2970   RC504   92-56176 CIP
Mitchell, Stephen A. **Hope and dread in psychoanalysis.** Basic Books, 1993. 285p bibl index ISBN 0-465-03059-9, $30.00

Mitchell's previous two books, *Object Relations in Psychoanalytic Theory* (senior author, Jay Greenberg; 1983) and *Relational Concepts in Psychoanalysis* (CH, May '89), are now classics; the first details the contrast between two views of mind, the drive/defense view of classical drive theory versus a relational model; the second book treats several implications of the relational model. This new book, his most accessible, continues this trajectory but broadens the project by addressing many issues important throughout the history of psychoanalysis, always tying the arguments to clinical phenomena, and now writing for a broader audience (although still keeping a focal constituency of psychoanalytically informed readers). Mitchell's efforts exemplifies the best of psychoanalytic writing: sufficient mastery of the material to eschew psychoanalytic jargon, while representing the complexity of the theoretical and clinical issues under consideration. Mitchell is a master teacher, using psychoanalytic texts in a way that makes them immediately understandable and compelling. Topics treated are very wide-ranging, including metapsychological/theoretical issues and clinical/technical ones. The book's accessibility and intellectual historical mastery make it one of the few psychoanalytic books every library should acquire this year. Advanced undergraduate through professional.— *R. Shilkret, Mount Holyoke College*

OAB-2971   HQ1206   92-8806 CIP
Polster, Miriam F. **Eve's daughters: the forbidden heroism of women.** Jossey-Bass, 1992. 206p bibl indexes afp ISBN 1-55542-464-3, $24.95

Locating herself within a widespread feminist movement, which has emphasized both the politics of representation and the politics of interpretation, and which has foregrounded the ways in which words of power (both exaltatory and denigratory) have been used throughout history to privilege some groups and individuals, and to marginalize or depreciate others, Polster, a professor of psychiatry and co-director of the San Diego Gestalt Training Center, seeks to free the potent word *hero* from its traditional connotations, and to open it up for application to a range of figures, who would never, under the traditional and archaic dispensation, have been characterized as heroes. Her splendidly written and argued exposition may eventually enable all of us to see the single mother working a job and going to night school, the Anita Hills who expose and challenge sexual harassment in even the most august institutions of society, and many others as heroes. A fascinating little book accessible to both general readers and professionals, and that deserves the widest readership.—*B. Kaplan, Clark University*

OAB-2972   HQ1206   92-8642 CIP
Psychology of women: a handbook of issues and theories, ed. by Florence L. Denmark and Michele A. Paludi. Greenwood, 1993. 760p index afp ISBN 0-313-26295-0, $115.00

American Psychological Association past president Denmark and Hunter College colleague Paludi have assembled the definitive current reference work on the psychology of women. In 18 well-referenced chapters, two appendixes, and a bibliographic essay, they and the other authors, all eminent psychologists, have produced a major resource summarizing research findings, addressing methodology, reviewing contemporary knowledge on lifespan development, and assessing issues of work, health, victimization, and societal sexism. An extraordinary review of contemporary knowledge, the work expands that base with original contributions to theory, methodology, and clinical practice. Denmark and Fernandez's introductory historical overview of the psychology of women is authoritative and comprehensive, clarifying the relationships among intertwined strands of theoretical legacy. Rabinowitz and Sechzer advance theory with their perspectives on research methods, exploring the impact of "nonequivalence" of the genders in the interpretation of gender differences. Fitzgerald and Ormerod's essay on sexual harassment and Etaugh's on midlife and later years offer definitional clarification, new information, and research summaries of immense practical significance. Extensive chapter references. Advanced undergraduate through professional.—*L. M. C. Abbott, California State University, Fresno*

OAB-2973   BF723   96-33070 CIP
Thomas, R. Murray. **Moral development theories—secular and religious: a comparative study.** Greenwood, 1997. 311p bibl index afp (Contributions to the study of education, 68) ISBN 0-313-30236-7, $65.00

Thomas is known for his comparative approach to general theories of psychological development. Here he applies the same approach to the specific area of moral development. Under secular theories, Thomas covers the prevalent psychological approaches to moral reasoning and behavior, including Kohlberg and Piaget, attribution theory, and social learning. In addition, he includes a Marxist approach as well as his own "composite theory." Under religious theories he discusses three lines of traditional religions, the Judaic-Christian-Islamic line, Hinduism and its derivatives, and Confucianism/Shinto. The discussion of each theory is guided by 12 questions outlined in the opening chapter, so that some comparison across approaches is possible about such things as what constitutes the moral domain, or good versus bad development; what sources of evidence are provided; what causal factors are proposed; and what explains individual differences. In addition, each theory is evaluated on the same eight criteria, judging how understandable, practical, verifiable, adaptable, etc., they are. Since each theory's evaluation is presented in the form of a table, an easy comparison is possible. He summarizes across the various approaches, particularly the religious traditions; what he has included seems accurate as an overview, particularly for a general comparison. The inclusion of secular and religious ideas in a single volume makes this a unique and valuable contribution for undergraduates.—*K. L. Hartlep, California State University, Bakersfield*

OAB-2974   BF723   93-16701 CIP
Waskow, Howard. **Becoming brothers,** by Howard Waskow and Arthur Waskow. Free Press, 1993. 218p ISBN 0-02-933997-9, $22.95

In the midst of a conversation between adult brothers, the elder flings a casual yet contemptuous, expletive-laden, barb, and the younger responds, "I really may have to kill you some day after all." Thus begins the long process as these brothers search for the source of this long-held rage. Anyone with brothers or sisters shares their questions—Why is there this warfare between siblings? How can siblings raised in the same environment be so different? The result is an "insider report" in the form of a comparative study of the lives of two middle-aged brothers that speaks with voices that are at first distinct and discordant, but later, through the process of collaboration, become intertwined and even harmonious. They explore memories of growing up in their old neighborhood, of immediate and extended family members, and of personal triumphs and defeats.

Through this effort they discover they had quite different experiences while growing up together, and they attempt to understand how these similar yet different histories defined their personalities, career choices, and relationships with their present families. Through their study of an "ordinary" family they provide insights useful to anyone interested in issues of family functioning, but especially to those brothers and sisters, or parents and children, who are cut off from one another in anger and despair, and who quietly seek understanding and release. Highly recommended for all readers.—*R. B. Stewart Jr., Oakland University*

■ Emotions & Behavior

OAB-2975   BF575   95-31907 CIP
Attig, Thomas. **How we grieve: relearning the world.** Oxford, 1996. 201p index afp ISBN 0-19-507455-6, $35.00; ISBN 0-19-507456-4 pbk, $17.95

In this richly rewarding book, Attig, a philosopher who has written and taught extensively about death, bereavement, grief, and grieving, presents his reflections on the grieving process. His central notion is that successful grieving involves "relearning" the world and one's physical, psychological, social, and spiritual place in it. Presenting his ideas through six case histories of individuals and families struggling with bereavement, the author argues that, while grief and bereavement are universal human experiences, each person's experience of grief and grieving is unique and that, while death and the bereavement that follow are events that are out of our control, grieving is an active process, one in which we can exercise a fair amount of control over our lives. Recognizing that grieving involves making choices and engaging in tasks over which we do have control, relearning our place in the world by learning how to live with the loss of a part of ourselves, and constructing a new relationship with those who have died are what distinguishes successful from unsuccessful grieving. Attig's extremely moving stories of bereavement and grieving serve well to make the point that respect for the uniqueness of grief is crucial and that grieving and relearning a world made anew by bereavement are essentially narrative processes. The author writes in a graceful prose style that is often powerfully metaphorical but that is nevertheless clear and straightforward. Insightful and enlightening. Highly recommended. General readers; undergraduates through professionals.—*R. R. Cornelius, Vassar College*

OAB-2976   RC455   92-53238 CIP
Berglas, Steven. **Your own worst enemy: understanding the paradox of self-defeating behavior,** by Steven Berglas and Roy F. Baumeister. Basic Books, 1993. 216p index ISBN 0-465-07680-7, $21.00

Berglas and Baumeister ask crucial questions and provide insightful and compelling answers; they have done an admirable job of helping the reader to understand the counterintuitive notion of self-defeating behaviors. They present a parsimonious theory of self-defeating behavior patterns that combines the best of both historical and contemporary research; this eclectic approach allows the reader to understand how self-defeating behavior patterns can be used by individuals as self-protective strategies. The message presented by Berglas and Baumeister clearly delineates a method for breaking the cycle of self-defeat and this information, alone, makes the book an invaluable resource. Overall, an engaging, informative, and much-needed work, but, due to the choice of audience toward which it may be targeted, it may not be read by those general readers who would have the most to gain from it. Highly recommended for readers of all levels, from high school and beyond.—*R. E. Osborne, Indiana University East*

OAB-2977   BF531   95-37946 CIP
Cornelius, Randolph R. **The science of emotion: research and tradition in the psychology of emotions.** Prentice Hall, 1996. 260p bibl index ISBN 0-13-300153-9 pbk, $22.00

In this brief but excellent introduction to contemporary psychological theories of human emotion, Cornelius identifies four major conceptual approaches

to understanding emotion and explains each in the context of research findings. The Darwinian tradition emphasizes the adaptive nature of emotion; the Jamesian tradition describes the importance of body responses to emotional experience; the cognitive tradition considers the ways that thought processes affect emotion; and the social constructionist tradition points out how the larger social environment works to shape emotional reactions. Additional chapters discuss the interplay between these perspectives by suggesting how they collectively provide important insights about the human condition. The writing style is lively, engaging, and clear, even when the author treats the more complex aspects of his topics. The references are particularly well selected and include a good mix of classic studies and significant recent findings. Accessible to anyone with college-level reading skills, but particularly useful to psychology majors and others studying contemporary views of the emotions. Recommended. General; undergraduate students.—*R. Madigan, University of Alaska, Anchorage*

OAB-2978   RC552   92-28901 CIP
Ellmann, Maud. **The hunger artists: starving, writing, and imprisonment.** Harvard, 1993. 136p index afp ISBN 0-674-42705-X, $19.96

An important book. Ellmann (King's College, Cambridge Univ.) has brought the food-as-metaphor issue into a new realm. She explores the complicated relationship between language and voluntary hunger and the ways in which they manifest in people, ranging from Bobby Sands to the novel character Clarissa. The chapter titles mince no words: autophagy, gynophagy, sarcophagy, and encryptment. Ellmann illuminates one of the most underrated points in psychoanalysis—that food, not sex, is the repressed. Psychoanalytic theories, including those of Freud, Lacan, and Melanie Klein, are used to explain the psychodynamics of ingestion and its impact on the psyche. Ellmann uses Primo Levi's experiences in Auschwitz to help sort out the greater pain: to be unfed or unheard. Naturally, she also discusses Kafka's Hunger Artist and how the spectacle of starvation can be accomplished only when other people witness it. Highly recommended. Advanced undergraduate through professional.—*R. Kabatznick, Queens College, CUNY*

OAB-2979   BF575   95-32479 CIP
Fehr, Beverley. **Friendship processes.** Sage Publications, CA, 1996. 240p bibl indexes ISBN 0-8039-4560-4, $38.00; ISBN 0-8039-4561-2 pbk, $17.95

In this marvelous book, Fehr presents a comprehensive and richly detailed examination of what scholars have learned about the formation, maintenance, and dissolution of friendships. Beginning with a brief meditation on the meaning of friendship and the various ways it is defined both by "experts" and friends themselves, Fehr reviews the theories of attraction and relationship development relevant to the study of friendship, pointing out along the way the paucity of any real theories of friendship per se. She then lucidly describes the results of empirical research on friendship, from Theodore M. Newcomb's classic The *Acquaintance Process* (1961) to the scores of studies carried out during the in the last 15 years or so. Organized around the life course of friendships, from initial formation to dissolution, Fehr's review presents a wealth of information about all aspects of the friendship process. Although she necessarily focuses on the friendships of young adults, Fehr makes a concerted effort to include analyses of age differences in friendship phenomena wherever possible. Her efforts in this regard, coupled with her welcome discussion of the few cross-cultural studies on friendship in her review, result in a particularly nuanced picture of what friendships are all about. Overall, a model of careful scholarship, clear writing, and good sense. For anyone studying friendships, there is no better place to start. This is perhaps the best book of its kind. General; undergraduates through professionals; two-year technical program students.—*R. R. Cornelius, Vassar College*

OAB-2980   BF561   92-48999 CIP
Handbook of emotions, ed. by Michael Lewis and Jeannette M. Haviland. Guilford, 1993. 653p index afp ISBN 0-89862-988-8, $65.00

A handbook with 44 chapters that collectively represent contemporary psychological thinking about the emotions. The focus is on research and theory rather than psychotherapeutic applications. The chapters, especially written for this volume, contain thorough, although sometimes brief, overviews of particular facets of emotion. Bibliographies are generally good and up to date. The chapters are grouped into five sections that include the physiological, psychological, and social aspects of emotion, interdisciplinary perspectives of emotion, and details about specific emotional states. The list of contributors is impressive and contains most of the influential writers in the field. No alternative source presents such a diverse collection of important work on emotion. The *Handbook* is likely to be valued by audiences ranging from advanced undergraduates to experienced investigators. A "must have" for academic libraries serving upper-division undergraduate and graduate students.— *R. Madigan, University of Alaska, Anchorage*

OAB-2981   BF698   94-39181 CIP
Handbook of personality psychology, ed. by Robert Hogan, John Johnson, and Stephen Briggs. Academic Press, 1997. 987p bibl index afp ISBN 0-12-134645-5, $150.00; ISBN 0-12-134646-3 pbk, $75.00

This impressive work will provide much intellectual stimulation for social and personality psychologists. This reviewer, a social psychologist who has always believed that studying individual difference variables makes all studies inherently more interesting, was hooked from the second paragraph of the preface. A perusal of the list of contributing authors reads like a "who's who of experts in the discipline," and they have applied that expertise brilliantly and in a style that is truly "reader friendly." As a teacher of a personality psychology course, this reviewer can say with utmost sincerity that the volume will fundamentally change the way that course is designed and taught. The section on conceptual and measurement issues in personality is quite strong and well presented. It is this emphasis on measurement that has helped to resurrect what appeared to be a dying field in the 1980s. The section on developmental issues in personality is also extremely insightful and should spark much research. Highly recommended for upper-division undergraduate and graduate students and faculty.—*R. E. Osborne, Indiana University East*

OAB-2982   BF697   95-11812 CIP
Hesse-Biber, Sharlene. **Am I thin enough yet?: the cult of thinness and the commercialization of identity.** Oxford, 1996. 191p bibl index afp ISBN 0-19-508241-9, $25.00

Hesse-Biber makes one of the most powerful and compelling arguments about the cult of thinness: it is often akin to the obsessions and ritualistic behavior found among members of cults. Salvation is the reward for those who attain ideal bodies. The author, a sociologist, skillfully draws this parallel through interviews with women (and some men) with eating disorders, ranging from compulsive eating to anorexia, using their own stories and insights. What is so refreshing is that these people are not made into "cases." Rather, it is a literary and psychological pleasure to track their discovery of a different path of self-acceptance and self-love based on their own internal standards. Social activism, therapy, spirituality are all included as potential healing agents. Unlike many other books in this area, there is a particular sensitivity to multicultural issues such as the combination of racism and the beauty myth. Extensive references; many informative notes and comments. Highly recommended for upper-division undergraduates and graduate students, as well as two-year technical program students.—*R. Kabatznick, Queens College, CUNY*

OAB-2983   BF697   93-27068 CIP
Lifton, Robert Jay. **The protean self: human resilience in an age of fragmentation.** Basic Books, 1993. 262p index ISBN 0-465-06420-5, $25.00

Lifton, whose many books shed light on the darker aspects of human behavior, has turned his attention here to human resilience. This is a sophisticated, very thought-provoking work that combines psychological resilience, historical influence, and technology of the past 200 years. The work has significant

ramifications for research and theory on self-concept, identity, and human development. Lifton indicates: "We have been developing a sense of self appropriate to the restlessness and flux of our time." His book, beyond being important for professionals in human behavior, is one any thinking human being can appreciate. It speaks to much of our present age and provides a new perspective on the larger society. There is no other work presenting these views. A work decades in the making, that may well be Lifton's most important. All levels.—*J. R. Thompson, emeritus, Oberlin College*

OAB-2984   BF575   94-41704 CIP
Miller, Michael Vincent. **Intimate terrorism: the deterioration of erotic life.** W.W. Norton, 1995. 250p index ISBN 0-393-03759-2, $23.00

Miller, a clinical psychologist in private practice, was moved by alarming increases in abuse and domestic violence. "Intimate Terrorism" involves a parallel with political terrorism in which people, having lost faith in the political process, decide that their aims are worth killing for. So in intimate relations, inevitable conflicts lead to bitter struggles fueled by anxiety and resentment in which the aim is to demoralize and gain power at all costs. The roots of intimate terrorism are to be found in cultural myths: adolescent romance fixated at ecstatic experience; achievement orientation that refuses to allow failure; autonomy that evokes strong character, leading to a diminishing sense of being loved; absence of civility ("carelessness") toward others. When these myths fail to provide solace, the anxiety of erotic intimacy becomes too difficult to bear and the expression of sexual interest is deemed predatory. The solution requires a permissive attitude toward one's mistakes, to acknowledge that failing can be as fertile a ground for getting ahead as success, an ironical attitude that tolerates imperfect, disappointing outcomes that are transformational and useful rather than fanatic and hopeless. A brilliant masterpiece, "targeted for anyone who wonders why love becomes so perilous an undertaking." Chapter notes. All levels.—*D. Sydiaha, University of Saskatchewan*

OAB-2985   BF575   96-21200 CIP
Miller, Rowland S. **Embarrassment: poise and peril in everyday life.** Guilford, 1996. 232p bibl index afp ISBN 1-57230-127-9, $28.95

In this delightfully written and extremely informative book, Miller surveys what is currently known about the causes, functions, and consequences of embarrassment. No mere survey, Miller's book is a comprehensive and integrated account of the nature of embarrassment. Employing telling examples of embarrassing predicaments culled from his own research on the phenomenon and from his own life, and drawing on his own rigorous research program as well as research carried out by other scientists, he presents a convincing argument as to why embarrassment should be considered a *basic* emotion, describes in detail the circumstances under which embarrassment occurs and its outward signs, charts the developmental course of embarrassment, examines the evidence for cultural universals and variations in embarrassment, and builds a plausible evolutionary argument for its functions. Miller tempers his therapeutic suggestions for those who are easily embarrassed with the advice that embarrassment is a desirable emotion that we should not seek to eliminate completely, no matter how uncomfortable it sometimes makes us. A superb book on an important topic central to the study of social psychology. No library can afford to be without it. All levels.—*R. R. Cornelius, Vassar College*

OAB-2986   BF511   91-17589 CIP
Oatley, Keith. **Best laid schemes: the psychology of emotions.** Cambridge/Maison des Sciences de l'Homme, 1992. 525p bibl indexes ISBN 0-521-41037-1, $69.95; ISBN 0-521-42387-2 pbk, $34.95

Oatley, a student of human emotions and cognition who has published widely in cognitive science and psychology, has produced an extraordinarily learned and well-argued account of the ways in which emotions function within our cognitive systems. He argues that emotions should be regarded as integral components of our cognitive apparatus, for they serve to alert us that, due to changes in our internal or external circumstances, changes in our goals or plans are necessary in order to adapt to those changes. In addition to functioning as signals to ourselves and others that our circumstances have been changed and that we need to change our plans accordingly, emotions represent changes in our readiness to respond to such changes in our circumstances. Oatley presents a cogent case for his (and Johnson-Laird's) so-called "communicative theory of emotions" against the backdrop of a consideration of the central role of plans and planning in human cognitive life. Related in many ways to the perspectives taken by George Mandler in his *Mind and Emotion* (CH, Apr'76) and *Mind and Body* (CH, Oct'84), R. Lazarus in his *Emotion and Adaptation* (CH, Sep'92), and others who have taken a cognitive approach to emotions (notably, A. Ortony, G.L. Clore, and A. Collins's *The Cognitive Structure of Emotions* (CH, Mar'89), Oatley's book is distinguished by the depth and complexity of his analysis of the relationship of emotions to plans, both conscious and unconscious, and his serious consideration of the "problem" of positive emotions. Another distinguishing and delightful feature is his use of many examples from literature, in particular *Anna Karenina* and *Middlemarch*, to illustrate the central concepts of his theory. Oatley's erudite and integrative presentation of his theory of emotions should be a part of every library's psychology collection. Highest recommendations.—*R. R. Cornelius, Vassar College*

OAB-2987   BF575   95-14486 CIP
Parducci, Allen. **Happiness, pleasure, and judgment: the contextual theory and its applications.** L. Erlbaum, 1995. 225p bibl indexes afp ISBN 0-8058-1891-X, $45.00

Parducci, a psychologist who has studied the nature of hedonic judgments for some 40 years, explores in this engagingly written book his "contextual theory" of happiness. He presents experimental evidence that supports the theory, and the ways in which the theory may help to explain some of the more peculiar puzzles associated with happiness, such as why earning more money does not necessarily make us any happier, and why, the happier we become, the harder it gets to become still more happy. Illustrating his arguments with delightfully clear examples from his own life and the many studies he and his students have conducted over the years, Parducci demonstrates the powerful influence that context has not only on judgments of the physical properties of objects (such as the sizes of squares or the sweetness of lemonade) but of the pleasantness of everyday events, judgments of merit, and even assessments of psychopathology! Living up to the title of his book, Parducci shows how happiness may be seen as a function of judgments of pleasure that display law-like relationships to the contexts within which they are made. Ultimately endorsing Thoreau's voluntary return to a simpler life, the author concludes with an extended meditation on the ways in which we—as individuals and as a society—can control the contexts of our judgments of pleasure and happiness and so increase the amount of happiness we experience. Highly recommended. Upper-division undergraduate through professional.—*R. R. Cornelius, Vassar College*

OAB-2988   BF637   92-35942 CIP
Perloff, Richard M. **The dynamics of persuasion.** L. Erlbaum, 1993. 411p bibl indexes afp ISBN 0-8058-0490-0, $69.95; ISBN 0-8058-1377-2 pbk, $27.50

In this highly detailed but extremely readable book, Perloff, a well-known scholar at the interface between social psychology and communication, presents a comprehensive survey of research on persuasion. Intended for students at all levels, the book contains a wealth of information about all aspects of the processes by which people may be induced to change their attitudes about both trivial and important matters. Perloff provides his readers with a thorough discussion of the various meanings of persuasion, and the complicated relationship between attitudes and behavior, from both the social psychological and communication perspectives, explaining clearly and judiciously the various theories and research findings within each. Throughout, Perloff includes many entertaining and enlightening examples of persuasion in the real world in "case studies" and "exhibits." Perloff never strays very far from the implications and applications of the research he describes; hence, one is rarely left wondering what a particular finding means or how the theories Perloff explicates relate to everyday life. The book is similar in some ways to Robert B. Cialdini's pop-

ular *Influence* (1993) in the material that it covers and, especially, in Perloff's ability to present the methods and results of scientific research in a serious but easygoing manner. A fascinating and intellectually rich work. Highly recommended.—*R. R. Cornelius, Vassar College*

OAB-2989   BF592   96-36250 CIP
The psychology of facial expression, ed. by James A. Russell and José Fernández-Dols. Cambridge, 1997. 400p bibl indexes afp ISBN 0-521-49667-5, $64.95; ISBN 0-521-58796-4 pbk, $29.95

This monograph of 16 chapters was written by 22 academics from 17 universities across North America and Europe. Chapters are extensively documented by published research and other relevant writings. The volume is organized into five parts: introductions, three broad theoretical frameworks, a biological and developmental focus, a psychological and social focus, and an integrative summary. Topics about facial expressions include the meaning of the term, methods of study, differential emotions theory, modes of action readiness, a new ethology, animal sounds and human faces, facial action and social communication, neurobehavioral and dynamic systems, and componential approaches to social action, intense emotional episodes, the significance of social context, reading emotions, and faces in dialogue. To say the least, this is an impressive and extensive range of issues and topics regarding a complex slice of human social behavior. The volume requires careful reading and some background in the social sciences. Thus, it may be best utilized by faculty and students in upper-division undergraduate and graduate courses and by researchers in the field.—*E. Palola, emeritus, SUNY Empire State College*

OAB-2990   BF575   96-24583 CIP
Robbins, Paul R. **Romantic relationships: a psychologist answers frequently asked questions.** McFarland, 1996. 211p bibl index afp ISBN 0-7864-0192-3 pbk, $22.95

Robbins practices psychotherapy in Washington, DC, and is the author of earlier books on marijuana, dreams, and depression. He has found that despite the variety of concerns presented by patients, many of them experience difficulties with interpersonal relationships, primarily with a romantic partner. He also believes that these difficulties are of concern to many people other than patients. Although he acknowledges that there are no pat answers that apply to everybody, he believes that there are "useful things to talk about and valuable information to share" based on his "own personal experience, on what I have learned working with patients, and on research reported in the literature." The book is organized around 13 topics ranging form romantic love, childhood influences, and physical attractiveness through rape, sexual activity, conflict resolution, and marriage. Each topic encompasses a number of questions and answers, a format that keeps the discussion focused. An excellent book, universally relevant, well written, resourceful, well documented, and entertaining. It deserves widespread distribution. All levels.—*D. Sydiaha, emeritus, University of Saskatchewan*

OAB-2991   RC455   93-7043 CIP
Self-esteem: the puzzle of low self-regard, ed. by Roy F. Baumeister. Plenum, 1993. 265p index ISBN 0-306-44373-2, $39.50

Baumeister does it again! This new work is the most authoritative to be published in quite some time. Baumeister and his contributors paint a vivid and scholarly portrait of what it truly means to have low self-esteem. Scientists and the general public alike make many assumptions about what it means to have low self-esteem and about what one would predict about the cognitive, social, and behavioral differences that *should* exist between those who view themselves positively and those who view themselves negatively. Both editor and authors do an outstanding job of showing the reader exactly where such assumptions have been wrong and the implications of those assumptions. Though the text truly does clarify what has been a very opaque literature, little attention is paid to self-esteem enhancement and the processes that may be used to eliminate low self-regard. Overall, a scholarly, pleasing to read, nicely integrated, and highly informative work. Recommended for all mental health professionals, and undergraduate through faculty readers.—*R. E. Osborne, Indiana University East*

OAB-2992 RC555 95-10723 CIP
Simon, Robert I. **Bad men do what good men dream: a forensic psychiatrist illuminates the darker side of human behavior.** American Psychiatric, 1996. 362p bibl index afp ISBN 0-88048-688-0, $22.95

Simon provides a spellbinding, comprehensive view of the criminal mind. Each chapter delves into types of crime, ranging from sexual misconduct, to rape, serial killers, and many in between. His anecdotes enliven his explanations, making this a readable book for all. It is not simply a text for those interested in psychology; business students will need to read the chapter on workplace violence, an increasingly common crime. This book is a fascinating study into aberrant human behavior, certainly of interest to all who walk this earth with the "500 serial killers ... at large who kill at least 3,500 people each year" (FBI estimate for the US). Simon presents current data and statistics on each type of crime. Readers will understand the type of thought process that allows one to commit specific violent crimes, how common these crimes are, and how likely they are to be affected by such a crime. Simon reinforces his point that many of these criminals are very much like you and me: they do what we only dream of doing. All levels.—*J. A. Brown, University of Phoenix*

OAB-2993 BF1091 95-45926 CIP
Stevens, Anthony. **Private myths: dreams and dreaming.** Harvard, 1995. 385p bibl index afp ISBN 0-674-21638-5, $27.95

Stevens provides the most comprehensive review and integration of material on dreams known to this reviewer—his is truly an outstanding book and one that should be read by all persons interested in oneirology, or the study of dreams. He very successfully presents the known scientific findings on the neurology of sleep and dreaming and how they are used to support a psychological theory of dreaming. He begins with an in-depth review of the history of dream interpretation from ancient times to the present, paying special attention to Freud's wish fulfillment theory and Jung's theory of archetypes, although not neglecting neo-Freudian contributions as well as theorists such as Crick and Mitchison (reverse learning theory). Stevens concludes that the model that best supports the neuroscientific data is Jung's theory of archetypes combined with the hypothesis that dreaming is a way to incorporate survival information from personal experiences into the long-term memory store. The book is filled with interesting topics such as dreams and creativity, and common dreams. Very well researched, with more than 160 references. Recommended for all academic and public libraries. General; undergraduates through faculty. *P. Barker, Schenectady County Community College*

OAB-2994 BF575 93-48128 CIP
West, Malcolm L. **Patterns of relating: an adult attachment perspective,** by Malcolm L. West and Adrienne E. Sheldon-Keller. Guilford, 1994. 210p bibl index afp ISBN 0-89862-671-4, $25.00

The principal purpose of this book is to define and establish attachment as a primary organizational construct for the study of essential relationships between adults. To this end, adult attachment relationships are characterized by the authors as reciprocal pair-bonds with a peer, are defined using criteria that are congruent with the definitions for infants and children, and are sufficiently different from the definitions of other relationships for adults. In doing so the authors support Bowlby's (1977) claim that "attachment behavior is held to characterize human beings from cradle to the grave." The authors describe their own research, as well as that by Main, Henderson, and others, where first the criteria necessary to distinguish adult attachment relationships from general social relationships are identified, and then the patterns of adult attachment are examined. Special attention is given to the patterns of anxious/insecure attachments, and the implications of such relationships for personality disorders in adults. This book is a valuable addition to John Bowlby's trilogy *Attachment*

and Loss (v.1, CH, Feb'70; v.2, CH, May'74; v.3, 1980) as well as more recent attachment writings such as *Patterns of Attachment*, by Mary D. Salter Ainsworth et al. (CH, Jan'80); John Bowlby, *A Secure Base* (CH, Apr'89); and Robert Karen, *Becoming Attached* (1994). Highly recommended. Undergraduate through professional.—*R. B. Stewart Jr., Oakland University*

■ Therapies & Treatments

OAB-2995 RC465 94-36068 CIP
Akeret, Robert U. **Tales from a traveling couch: a psychotherapist revisits his most memorable patients.** W.W. Norton, 1995. 235p ISBN 0-393-03779-7, $22.00

Most who have reviewed this book have missed its essence. It is, simply, a classic. The obvious respect and care that Akeret has for each of these, his "most memorable patients," is touching. This book, as intended, reads like a novel. It is nevertheless convincing, and this reviewer is inclined to accept his findings as being as legitimate as any "controlled" studies on the outcome of psychotherapy. This reviewer cannot recommend this book strongly enough. It is must reading for all interested in the human condition, from beginning college students to old-timers who have seen their share of clients in 30 or more years of clinical practice. All levels.—*M. W. York, University of New Haven*

OAB-2996 RC552 95-578 CIP
Allen, Jon G. **Coping with trauma: a guide to self-understanding.** American Psychiatric, 1995. 385p bibl index afp ISBN 0-88048-720-8, $23.95

Allen, a psychologist with the Trauma Recovery Program at the Menninger Clinic, has written a well-researched, highly readable work on trauma, which will be very useful for trauma sufferers and mental health professionals alike. His well-informed, thoughtful perspective on trauma is presented in a way that will appeal to a diverse audience. He provides material on a variety of aspects including the effects of trauma, trauma-related psychiatric disorders, and treatments available for the traumatized. Allen includes a particularly interesting discussion on the role attachment plays in an individual's response to trauma. He also takes on the highly controversial subject of recovered memories in a balanced, objective, and sensitive manner. Aphrodite Matsakis's *I Can't Get Over It: A Handbook for Trauma Survivors* (1992) is similar to Allen's work in that it is also well written and geared for the lay person, but Allen's is a more current summary of professional knowledge and is less of a self-help work. There is a real need for works like this—written for the lay person without sacrificing a thorough scientific examination of the topic. Highly recommended for all academic library users.—*L. S. Johnson, Auburn University*

OAB-2997 RJ506 CIP
Cipolloni, David C. **An extraordinary silence: the emergence of a deeply disturbed child.** Bergin & Garvey, 1993. 145p index afp ISBN 0-89789-357-3, $45.00

Written by a child specialist, this book should be read by everyone—not only those in the "helping" professions. On the surface, it is a detailed phenomenological account in 20 chapters of the author's 2-year intensive therapy with a 9-year-old boy, Sean. It squarely fits into the great tradition of clinical cases from Freud to Thomas Ogden; its portrait of family madness is an equal to those of Jules Henry. It is more about the depths of the human condition than about therapist-patient-family-institutional relationships. It is abidingly about commitment, love, perseverance, prodding. It is about loneliness, and about overcoming loneliness. The book begins with deeds: we are introduced to boy and therapist inside a cardboard refrigerator box, to which Cipolloni has followed Sean. He writes: "I entered what is unquestionably the most powerful arena of human life: person-to-person relationship, the singular intimacy of encounter and interaction between people." Together with Sean in that horrid, protective aloneness, he helped Sean have the courage to walk out of it. This book stands out today as a candle in a vast darkness: It is about presence, not technique, when as a civilization we are so absent from each other with our abundance of technique. The book is a monument to the voice of heart's reasons, to the utter hope and to the limitation of what a single person can do—and to what needs to be done. All levels.—*H. F. Stein, University of Oklahoma Health Sciences Center*

OAB-2998 HF5549 94-2991 CIP
Henderson, George. **Cultural diversity in the workplace: issues and strategies.** Quorum Books, 1994. 268p bibl index afp ISBN 0-89930-888-0, $65.00

Prolific author Henderson (Univ. of Oklahoma) has produced an outstandingly useful work on managing diversity. This solution-oriented volume provides managers and human resources professionals with concepts, skills, tools, and the motivation to use them to effectively champion organizational transformation. Drawing upon law, the literature, case studies, and experience, Henderson offers solid suggestions for using new tools to confront workplace issues ranging from irritating communication habits to hate-motivated acts of violence. His illustrations of explicit, work-related values common within varied cultural groups are among the best argued in the literature. Self- and organizational-assessment tools provide insight and, along with the clear case histories documenting a productive emphasis on profitability issues, provide strong impetus to action. Diversity is a broadly human issue, and the inclusion of chapters specific to disability, age, and sex widen the issues appropriately. The focus is on observable behavior, enabling sound personnel policy development and use of performance assessment tools to incorporate diversity management in an efficient and effective form. Numerous tables and charts; appendix. For business schools, practitioners, and human resource professionals, as well as managers and students in these fields. General; upper-division undergraduate through faculty; two-year technical program students.—*L. M. C. Abbott, California School of Professional Psychology*

OAB-2999 RC451 95-26268 CIP
Kestenberg, Judith S. **The last witness: the child survivor of the Holocaust,** by Judith S. Kestenberg and Ira Brenner. American Psychiatric, 1996. 238p bibl index afp ISBN 0-88048-662-7, $36.50

Though many accounts of adults surviving the Holocaust can be found, little has been written on the experience of children born and raised under the Nazi reign of terror. What effect would a childhood spent in the Warsaw ghettos or in concentration camps have on cognitive and moral development? And what repercussions would it have on adult adjustment? Answers to these compelling questions can be found in Kestenberg and Brenner's groundbreaking work on children of the Holocaust. As the number of living Holocaust survivors dwindles throughout the world, these authors provide both an important tribute to, and an intelligent analysis of, this group. Based on interviews of more than 1,500 Holocaust survivors, this work takes a decidedly psychoanalytic view of the topic, providing a thorough examination of the psychological stages of development experienced by these victims and the short- and long-term psychological effects of genocidal persecution. The fluid writing style, coupled with a fascinating topic, make this book a real "page-turner," greatly interesting to many, including scholars, trauma survivors, and laypersons.—*L. S. Beall, Auburn University*

OAB-3000 RC967 92-49362 CIP
Mental health in the workplace: a practical psychiatric guide, ed. by Jeffrey P. Kahn. Van Nostrand Reinhold, 1993. 462p index ISBN 0-442-00632-2, $52.95

Most of this book's contributors are members of the Academy of Organizational and Occupational Psychiatry, founded in 1990 to address the contributions of psychiatry to workplace mental health solutions. All have had extensive experience in organizational consulting and university teaching. Although the complex interplay of individual emotions and organizational function has long been a focus of attention in the literature, particularly in recent years, this book bridges the gap between psychiatry and the workplace to an extent not seen before. The presentation progresses from general problems (symptoms, reasons, treatment) through specifics (disability, executive distress, organizational change, job loss, executive development, crises, family problems) to common employee problems (anxiety, depression, personality disorders and style, drug and alcohol abuse, psychosis, psychosomatics). The book's outstanding feature is its success in integrating material through the liberal use of case studies, creating the impression of psychiatry whose practitioners have a substantial, concrete sense of humanity and compassion, despite the seriousness of problems encountered in the workplace. The book is exceptionally well edited despite the large number of contributors, and each chapter includes an abstract, summary, and bibliography. It deserves a wide audience including professionals in mental health, human resources, and management. General; advanced undergraduate through professional.—*D. Sydiaha, University of Saskatchewan*

OAB-3001 RJ506 92-46318 CIP
Monahon, Cynthia. **Children and trauma: a parent's guide to helping children heal.** Lexington Books, 1993. (Dist. by Macmillan) 222p bibl index ISBN 0-02-921665-6, $19.95

Events such as hurricanes, shootings, and auto accidents create physical and emotional effects on children that are explored in this book, which offers ways for restoring a child's sense of safety and balance. Monahon has developed a most valuable guide for parents and caretakers of chronically traumatized children, not children with just ordinary fears. Described are the sources of trauma, influencing factors, family reactions, children's denials, the healing process, and possible forms of psychotherapy for children that have been traumatized. To give concrete and practical illustrations of what children experience, examples of individuals who have encountered mild and truly dreadful horror are included in the text. Near the close of each chapter are "points to remember" to assist the reader in organizing the concepts. In addition to the notes, bibliography, and index, there is an important list of further readings for parents and children. Highly recommended for parents, caretakers, and professionals, for this work is everything the psychotherapist wants to tell parents about helping the traumatized child. All levels.—*C. R. Harper, emeritus, Mott Community College*

OAB-3002 RC451 94-38395 MARC
Russell, Denise. **Women, madness and medicine.** Polity, 1995. (Dist. by Blackwell) 196p index afp ISBN 0-7456-1260-1, $49.95

Russell focuses on biological psychiatry and how it impacts women. She argues that it is women, primarily, who are the negative benefactors of the discipline. Russell, a respected philosopher, argues that this aspect of psychiatry produces more harm than good—a provocative argument that she triumphantly makes throughout this book. The most interesting chapter treats epistemological problems with the dominant medical psychiatric perspective. Russell takes on schizophrenia and eating disorders as examples of bias in psychiatry and how a "string of unsubstantiated theories" have emerged. What is worse, however, is that women remain subordinated and diminished in a covert way. Although Russell does not make this point directly, it certainly leaves one wondering how many professionals conveniently project their sexism onto theories that support it—making it both easy and popular to avoid examining one's own attitudes towards women. Her book beautifully integrates Phyllis Chesler's seminal work, *Women and Madness* (CH, Mar'73). Russell recommends a new line of research and theories to come to grips with human distress. Must reading for upper-division undergraduates, graduates, and professional practitioners in all fields relating to women's health.—*R. Kabatznick, Queens College, CUNY*

OAB-3003 RJ507 92-53327 CIP
Rymer, Russ. **Genie: an abused child's flight from silence.** HarperCollins, 1993. 221p ISBN 0-06-016910-9, $20.00

A truly superb narrative, written in a style familiar to readers of *The New Yorker*, exposing the ways in which scholars from a variety of disciplines (linguists, psycholinguists, neuroscientists, pediatricians, developmental psychologists, etc.) squabbled among themselves as they pounced upon the distinctive case of "Genie," a severely abused young girl, who had seemingly grown up without language or any form of social training, unable to chew, unable to talk, unable to adapt to social relationships—a "wild girl from California." Rymer, linking his story to ancient and more recent attempts to inquire into the origin and acquisition of language, interweaves his account of the internecine and often bitter struggles among diverse scholars, as each sought to squeeze "Genie" into his or her Procrustean bed, with the tale of Genie's family life before and during the invasion of the scientists. An engrossing and absorbing story, beautifully told. A profound moral for those who ignore the Kantian "categorical imperative" in undertaking research without regard for the subjected subjects of their inquiries. All levels.—*B. Kaplan, Clark University*

OAB-3004   RC351   94-26733 CIP
Sacks, Oliver. **An anthropologist on Mars: seven paradoxical tales.** Knopf, 1995. 328p bibl index ISBN 0-679-43785-1, $24.00

Here is another exciting collection of neurological tales from Oliver Sacks! In the same style as his *The Man Who Mistook His Wife for a Hat* (1985), Sacks presents us with seven case histories enriched with his poetic interpretations of the forces of mind and brain involved in the production of unusual human conditions. There is a suddenly colorblind painter, a surgeon with Tourette's syndrome, and a hippie trapped in the 1960s by his brain tumor. Prodigies of various types are described to illustrate cases of visual precocities, such as the artist obsessed with re-creating the town of his childhood over and over, a young savant autistic artist, and the cataract patient who could "see but not see." In the final case study, which gives the book its title, Sacks interviews Temple Grandin, an autistic author and college professor. Grandin's own works include (with Margaret M. Scariano) *Emergence: Labeled Austistic* (1986), a number of agricultural books, and numerous articles in scientific journals. Grandin is a fascinating woman, and it is a delight to read of Sacks's interaction with her. This chapter alone is worth the addition of this work to libraries with medical and psychologically oriented readers. A prolific prodigy himself, Sacks is also known for his book *Awakenings* (1973) and the film of the same name. Footnotes, illustrations, endnotes, and suggested readings. All levels.—*L. Gillikin, College of William and Mary*

OAB-3005   RC552   96-10818 CIP
Traumatic stress: the effects of overwhelming experience on mind, body, and society, ed. by Bessel A. van der Kolk, Alexander C. McFarlane, and Lars Weisaeth. Guilford, 1996. 596p bibl index afp ISBN 1-57230-088-4, $55.00

Once in a blue moon, a book is published that bears such importance for its subject that it becomes an instant classic. *Traumatic Stress* is such a book. Edited by leading experts in the field of posttraumatic stress disorder (chiefly van de Kolk), this work presents the current state of research and knowledge on traumatic stress and its treatment. However, expertise and content alone are not enough to earn such accolades. It is the combination of these factors with outstanding coverage of the topic, as well as a fluid and thoroughly engaging writing style, which has resulted in such an exemplary work. *Traumatic Stress* is comparable to Judith Herman's *Trauma and Recovery* (CH, Jan'93)—considered by many to be the best work on trauma written in this decade. Both share the same type of provocative coverage, lucid intelligence, original insights, and fluid writing. No doubt, researchers will consider *Traumatic Stress* as an essential resource, and no academic library serving PTSD scholars will want to be without it. Upper-division undergraduates through professionals.—*L. S. Beall, Auburn University*

■ Sociology

OAB-3006   HM24   93-13915 CIP
Blau, Judith B. **Social contracts and economic markets.** Plenum, 1993. 218p index ISBN 0-306-44391-0, $34.50

Blau (Univ. of North Carolina) has written a superb exploration of the complex interactions between economic and social forces in American society. She describes many ways that social bonds modify economic competition and are, in turn, altered by the character of economic markets. Among the topics she discusses are the social implications of the increasing spatial separation between workers, managers, and owners; the impact of economic forces on ethnic, racial, and gender roles; the social consequences of US economic decline and growing inequality; the relationship between the commercial imperatives of the mass media and American culture; and the ways that large corporations interact with, and attempt to dominate, their social milieu. Finally, Blau considers the implications of her insights for government social policies and for the development of an ethics based on the acknowledgment of individual and group differences. Impressively, she succeeds in weaving insights from postmodern theory, Marxist empirical studies, social contract theory, social network analysis, and rational choice theory into a book clear enough to be used in advanced undergraduate classes.—*T.H. Koenig, Northeastern University*

OAB-3007   HT687   93-50578 CIP
Brint, Steven. **In an age of experts: the changing role of professionals in politics and public life.** Princeton, 1994. 278p index afp ISBN 0-691-03399-4, $29.95

This important and provocative work expands on the treatment of professions by Andrew D. Abbott (e.g., *The System of Professions*, 1988) and Magali Sarfatti Larson (*The Rise of Professionalism*, CH, Mar'78). Brint's study is as much an analysis of social and cultural change as it is a discussion of a changing occupational status. The focus is "the professional middle class" and its "shift from social trustee professionalism [which] has led to a splintering of the professional stratum in relation to the market value of different forms of 'expert knowledge'" and the growth of expert professionalism. This has resulted in the sundering in the contemporary professional world of the old connection between community and authority. Corporate and state organization loom ever larger in the determination of professional legitimacy, while popular distrust of professions increases. The five chapters of part 1 detail changes in professions in the US and the implications of such changes for "the politics of the professional middle class." Part 2 is a first-rate inquiry into the forces exerted by markets and organizations on the professions, not only in the US but abroad. It is based on content analysis, case studies, *and* "a first effort" in comparative cross-national analysis of professional middle-class behavior, especially political behavior. Though the professional middle class protests, its moral vision persists. Laudable! All levels.—*L. Braude, SUNY College at Fredonia*

OAB-3008   92-54434 Orig
Burke, Peter. **History and social theory.** Cornell, 1993. (c1992). 198p bibl index afp ISBN 0-8014-2861-0, $37.50; ISBN 0-8014-8100-7 pbk, $14.95

Burke's study is unique in that it distills many of the previous efforts to address the interface between history and social theory into a concentrated, elegantly written, and thought-provoking analysis of key problems. Burke begins by analyzing the retreat from historical considerations following the deaths of Emile Durkheim and Max Weber. This retreat into the present dominated the social sciences up to the current revival of historical sociology, exhibited by Ernest Gellner, Michael Mann, Norbert Elias, and Anthony Giddens, among others. Yet conceptual problems experienced by the early masters persist into the present: Arnold Toynbee had a difficult time defining civilization. Thorstein Veblen's notion of conspicious consumption is being revived by the postmodernists, but its meaning is still debated. The anthropologists have abandoned the concept of "social character" in favor of the much debated term, "culture." The deconstructionists have blurred the distinction between fact and fiction, and thereby challenged all of the social sciences to rethink their roles. In sum, the author's goal is ambitious, but he seems to have realized it. Excellent, comprehensive index and bibliography. Highly recommended. Advanced undergraduate; graduate.—*S. G. Mestrović, Texas A & M University*

OAB-3009   HV91   94-2981 CIP
Caplow, Theodore. **Perverse incentives: the neglect of social technology in the public sector.** Praeger, 1994. 164p bibl index afp ISBN 0-275-94911-7, $49.95

Demonstrating dramatically that value is not related to book length, Caplow clearly explicates the current difficulties with five critical social systems: medical care, education, welfare, criminal justice, and compensation of injury. He provides an illuminating description of the manner by which each system operates to defeat its own goals and further describes the technical study and planning essential for reform. In each case the system lacks clear goals, is poorly designed, and provides no rational system of outcome evaluation. The inmates run the asylum. Political realities, history, professional greed—all account for failure. Caplow recognizes the unlikelihood of radical reform and concludes that the establishment of parallel systems as demonstrations holds most promise for change. For example, the health care debate should be informed by experience in the state systems instituted in Hawaii, Minnesota, and Oregon. Education reform should continue to be directed by private and parochial school operations. The author is clearly qualified for the task at hand; his thorough and lucid book should be available in all libraries serving policy makers and interested citizens. With the probable exception of the critiques of their own activities, professionals in the five areas reviewed should also welcome it.—*F. J. Peirce, emeritus, University of Oklahoma*

OAB-3010   HQ1236   92-9372 CIP
Chapman, Jenny. **Politics, feminism and the reformation of gender.** Routledge, 1993. 315p bibl index ISBN 0-415-01698-3, $79.95

Chapman's brilliant and unconventional book deserves a wide readership. She argues, first, that women's representation among political elites depends largely on the extent to which women have the resources that men in that particular system value; second, that women also have a distinctive role in reproduction and thus a distinctive voice and set of interests underrepresented in any system designed around men's role, voice, and interests; third, that these interests are themselves divided, because women want both shared parenting and support for women's single parenting; fourth, that women attempting to achieve political influence are caught in various double binds, not only that of assimilation or self-assertion, but also that of which of women's divided interests to represent and how. Chapman musters an impressive range of evidence, from the differences in the opportunity structure for men in political systems as diverse as Scotland and the former Soviet Union as explanations for the marginalization of women, to critical analysis of the political programs of the women in the Green party in Germany, the Woman's List in Iceland, and the Norwegian Parliament, to a reconsideration of classic feminist theorists from De Beauvoir and Mead to Firestone and Rich. There is wild profusion of theoretical insight, comparative empirical evidence, and practical strategic considerations. Scholars in the field of gender politics, widely understood, should consider this essential reading. Advanced undergraduate; graduate; faculty; professional.—*M. M. Ferree, University of Connecticut*

OAB-3011   HD9685   95-39702 CIP
Colignon, Richard A. **Power plays: critical events in the institutionalization of the Tennessee Valley Authority.** State University of New York, 1997. 367p bibl index afp ISBN 0-7914-3011-1, $74.50

Colignon, a sociologist, has made a significant contribution to understanding the sociology and politics of organizations. He examines the Tennessee Valley Authority during its formative years, the site of Philip Selznick's "locus clas-

sicus of organizational scholarship" (*TVA and the Grass Roots*, CH, Nov'66). Colignon presents a convincing argument that "Organizations act as a result of decision to act, and those decisions are shaped by struggles around competing substantive interests." This thesis supports the importance of "agency." In the case of the TVA, the contradictions and conflicts leading to struggles revolved around the social planners of the First New Deal (e.g., R. Tugwell, A. Berle) in opposition to the antimonopolists of the Second New Deal (e.g., L. Brandeis, F. Frankfurter), and internal leadership struggles between Chairman A. Morgan and Directors D. Lilienthal and H. Morgan. In terms of general social theory, Colignon criticizes Selznick for approaching organizations in terms of order and stability rather than conflict and change. This is a relevant and timely case study of one of the most important—if not *the* most important—examples in US history of the resolution of conflict between government ownership and regulation and private control and the marketplace. All levels.—*M. Oromaner, Hudson County Community College*

OAB-3012   HV2359   94-17860 CIP
The deaf way: perspectives from the international conference on deaf culture, ed. by Carol J. Erting et al. Gallaudet, 1994. 907p index afp ISBN 1-56368-026-2, $75.00

This compilation of presentations from the 1989 Deaf Way international conference on deaf culture provides the most comprehensive international perspective on deaf culture to date. Although it is unfortunate that it has taken five years for this publication to appear, it is, in another sense, little short of a miraculous feat of translation and editing that such a volume should be printed at all, when one considers that the papers were translated into English from a wide array of signed and spoken languages. The works vary widely in content and style: some are quite anecdotal, whereas others follow a more traditional scientific format. Topics include an extensive section on deaf cultures around the world; deaf history; sign languages in society; diversity in the deaf community; family issues; educational issues; deaf/hearing interaction; deaf people and the arts; and human rights issues. The collection is distinguished by its true diversity of viewpoints from around the globe. Highly recommended as a resource for academic and public libraries, and for programs serving people who are deaf and their families. All levels.—*A. G. Sidone, Pennsylvania State University*

OAB-3013   HM47   93-44515 CIP
Eastern Europe in transformation: the impact on sociology, ed. by Mike Forrest Keen and Janusz Mucha. Greenwood, 1994. 208p bibl index afp (Contributions in sociology, 109) ISBN 0-313-28375-3, $57.95

Examining the fate and role of sociology in formerly Communist nations in Eastern Europe, this pathbreaking book includes, but is not limited to, Russia, Hungary, Poland, Bulgaria, Romania, Croatia, the Czech Republic, Slovakia, Yugoslavia, Slovenia, and Lithuania. It consists of 17 chapters whose authors are, for the most part, natives of the countries they treat. Overall, the book addresses the relationship between sociology and society before, during, and after Communism; the extent to which sociology reflected the dominant structures of a particular country; national differences in sociological topics, methods, and theories; and international influences. A remarkably common thread runs through most of the chapters: Eastern European sociology began in the same way that it began in the West, with the now classical theories of Durkheim and Weber. It became suspect following WW I, mounted a comeback prior to WW II, and was often banished by the Communists as a "bourgeois science." The 1960s and 1970s allowed sociology some breathing space in Eastern Europe so long as it was primarily Marxist in orientation. The 1990s find Eastern European sociology obsolete, struggling to free itself of Marxism, and seeking input from the West. This serious, scholarly book should go a long way in overcoming the Iron Curtain that was imposed between Western and Eastern European sociologies. The references are comprehensive and extremely helpful. The index is also very thorough. Highly recommended to both college and university libraries.—*S. G. Mestrović, Texas A&M University*

OAB-3014   HD9698   96-23908 CIP
Eckstein, Rick. **Nuclear power and social power.** Temple University, 1997. 191p bibl index afp ISBN 1-56639-485-6, $49.95; ISBN 1-56639-486-4 pbk, $16.95

Eckstein's book takes its rightful place alongside Raymond L. Goldsteen and John K. Schorr's notable *Demanding Democracy after Three Mile Island* (CH, Apr'92), which provided ex post facto analysis of the Pennsylvania nuclear disaster. Eckstein focuses on the politics, economics, and social/cultural contingencies that led to a "melt down" of the regulatory/participatory process at Shoreham, New York, and Seabrook, New Hampshire. What is involved in getting a nuclear facility up and running, and what roles do government agencies, corporations, and public interest play in the process? It is surprising to learn from Eckstein how confusing it all becomes. Hidden agendas, the role of investment banking, plus a "series of decisions made by a variety of people and organizations who may or may not have been concerned with interests beyond their own" add to the complicated mix. The Shoreham reactor did not "open for business," but the Seabrook facility did. Using sociological models, Eckstein reveals the complex factors that led to this end. A fascinating and most readable account that will appeal to social/cultural historians, sociologists, political scientists, and environmentalists. Tables; notes; references. All levels.—*P. D. Travis, Texas Woman's University*

OAB-3015   K5064   91-30647 CIP
Hamilton, V. Lee. **Everyday justice: responsibility and the individual in Japan and the United States,** by V. Lee Hamilton and Joseph Sanders. Yale, 1992. 290p bibl indexes afp ISBN 0-300-05140-9, $35.00

In every society wrongdoing is dealt with and wrongdoers punished, but individual and social reactions to wrongdoing differ from a society to another. Hamilton and Sanders suggest a social structural foundation for this difference based on their surveys of the process involved in ascribing responsiblity for wrongdoing and judging appropriate sanctions. These surveys were conducted in Detroit and Yokohama and Kanazawa, Japan, with a team of Japanese scholars. This book is a companion piece to the Japanese version, *Sekinin to Batsu no Ishiki Kozo* (Tokyo, 1986), which is primarily a scientific report of their surveys and of the additional research done by the Japanese team. In this book, however, the authors attempt to present a model of the relationship between individuals and society in two cultures. It is organized in three parts: structure and culture; responsibility and sanction; and law and soceity, in which empirical conclusions are offered and legal structure, legal culture, and convergence are discussed. The book concludes with a treatment of the problem of justice. Here responsibility and sanction are treated as the core aspect of legal culture, which results in very different ways of dealing with the wrongdoers in the US compared to Japan. A superb, most welcome work, that represents the best of interdisciplinary effort. Most highly recommended for all levels.—*M. Y. Rynn, University of Scranton*

OAB-3016   HM35   94-1047 CIP
The Handbook of economic sociology, ed. by Neil J. Smelser and Richard Swedberg. Princeton/Russell Sage Foundation, 1994. 835p indexes afp ISBN 0-691-03448-6, $95.00

The 31 essays in this 835-page collection form the definitive compilation of recent research in economic sociology. The editors define economic sociology as differing from mainstream economics in its focus on the use of historical and comparative data to describe economic interaction. Economic sociologists see social activity as embedded in social networks, institutional structures, and culture, whereas classical economists tend to view economic actors as behaving rationally in relative social isolation. Economic sociologists trace their intellectual roots to Marx, Weber, Durkheim, Simmel, Schumpeter, and Polanyi; mainstream economists employ the lessons of Adam Smith, Ricardo, Mill, Marshall, Keynes, and Samuelson. Most of the authors in this volume are sociologists (often teaching in business departments), but also represented are several leading economists and political scientists such as Geoffrey Hodgson ("The

Return of Institutional Economics"), Richard Nelson ("Evolutionary Theorizing about Economic Change"), Charles Sabel ("Learning by Monitoring: The Institutions of Economic Development"), and Alberto Martinelli ("Entrepreneurship and Management"). General surveys of the field are provided by the editors ("The Sociological Perspective on the Economy"), Paul DiMaggio ("Cultural and Economy"), and James Coleman ("A Rational Choice Perspective on Economic Sociology"). Other issues explored in this volume include religion and economic life (Robert Wuthnow); gender and the economy (Ruth Milkman); economy and the environment (Johannes Berger); welfare states (Gosta Esping-Anderson); coordination and conflict among corporations (Mark Granovetter, Mark Mizruchi, and Linda Stearns); the informal economy (Alejandro Portes); ethnic economics (Ivan Light); cross-national economic comparisons (Gary Greffi); and socialist economies (Ivan Szelenyi). A unique and invaluable survey of this rapidly developing field of scholarship. Upper-division undergraduate and graduate collections.—*T.H. Koenig, Northeastern University*

OAB-3017   HT167   95-52088 CIP
Lewis, Paul G. **Shaping suburbia: how political institutions organize urban development.** Pittsburgh, 1996. 288p bibl index afp ISBN 0-8229-3938-X, $44.95; ISBN 0-8229-5595-4 pbk, $19.95

Lewis's book is a major contribution to urban politics as well as to urban studies in general. It is the first full-length treatment of the political dimension of the recent transformation of the American metropolis, whereby many suburbs have evolved into full-fledged cities. Demonstrating that all suburbs are not alike, Lewis argues that a fundamental political logic underlies patterns of suburban growth, and that suburbia is very much the product of the actions of its local governments. The first three chapters develop models and data analyses, and show that the relative political fragmentation of the metropolis plays a vital role in shaping the suburban mosaic. The next three chapters offer applications of Lewis's hypotheses to Portland, Oregon, and Denver. The final chapter offers valuable conclusions and places Lewis's analysis in the context of contemporary political science. Generous notes and bibliography sections; effectively presented figures and tables. Highly recommended for all collections in urban studies and modern political science. Upper-division undergraduates and above.—*P. O. Muller, University of Miami*

OAB-3018   Can. CIP
McDonald, Lynn. **The early origins of the social sciences.** McGill-Queen's, 1993. 397p bibl index afp ISBN 0-7735-1124-5, $49.95

In this original and far-reaching study, McDonald (Univ. of Guelph) accomplishes three tasks that have heretofore been ignored or avoided by historians of social science. First, she traces the historical roots of sociology to a much earlier era than is generally allowed. For the most part, histories of social science pay homage to ancient "precursors" before discussing the late 19th century texts that constitute "real" social science. McDonald demonstrates that the earlier texts (e.g., ancient Greek through 1800) were rich, thorough, and perspicuous. Second, McDonald includes significant discussions of the women who, from at least the middle of the 18th century, have contributed substantially to social scientific awareness. And finally, the author presents an engaging and passionate argument for empirical methodology in social science. Contrary to the idealist critique of empiricism as being trivializing and removed, McDonald argues that empiricism is engaged, relevant, and necessary. All levels.—*C. A. Pressler, Purdue University—North Central*

OAB-3019   HM24   94-10888 CIP
Morrow, Raymond A. **Critical theory and methodology,** by Raymond A. Morrow with David D. Brown. Sage Publications, CA, 1994. 381p bibl index (Contemporary social theory, 3) ISBN 0-8039-4682-1, $55.00; ISBN 0-8039-4683-X pbk, $26.95

The authors have written this highly sophisticated book apparently as a response to the contemporary postmodern condition, which has fundamentally called into question the claims that originally inspired the Enlightenment project of social science. They seek a reconstituted critical theory minus its founders' disdain for positivism. For this reason, at least half the book deals with methodological issues and attempts to introduce what the authors call "interpretive structuralism" as an alternative to both traditional positivism and the postmodern rejection of methodology. The authors address what seems to be the widest possible range of theories, theorists, and issues that pertain to critical theory, but they focus especially on two of the foremost social theorists of the age, Jürgen Habermas and Anthony Giddens. The authors move historically from Marx through the works of Max Horkheimer and Theodor Adorno to the most recent work in poststructuralism, postmodernism, and hermeneutics, but always with an eye on empiricism. The book is clear, well written, and incredibly thorough. The references are overwhelming, the index adequate. Highly recommended for upper-division undergraduate and graduate libraries.—*S. G. Mestrović, Texas A&M University*

OAB-3020 HM24 94-44296 MARC
Mouzelis, Nicos. **Sociological theory: what went wrong?: diagnosis and remedies.** Routledge, 1995. 220p bibl index ISBN 0-415-12720-3, $59.95; ISBN 0-415-07694-3 pbk, $17.95

Mouzelis provides a telling "diagnosis" of what ails contemporary sociological theory. He knows the literature well and speaks with unusual authority, succinctness, and clarity. He cuts to the quick of what is worthwhile and worthless in the theories of Parsons, the interpretative sociologists, the rational choice theorists, and the poststructural (and postmodern) theorists. Mouzelis comes down particularly hard on the last group and equates them, with good cause, to the pre-Durkheimian reductionists. In the second part of the book he suggests and defends "remedies" for the ills of sociological theory, which the author says are at the level of "Generalities II," or the level of theoretical tools and heuristic devices meant to generate interesting empirical questions and substantive (Generalities III) social theory. Much of the book centers on controversies surrounding the micro-macro and agency-institutional structure linkages; Mouzelis proposes a rather novel conceptual scheme to handle these linkages without conflating them. Thoroughly referenced and indexed, with many provocative and insightful footnotes. Highly recommended to anyone seeking to make some sense of the ongoing "crisis" in sociological theory. Upper-division undergraduates and above.—*W. P. Nye, Hollins College*

OAB-3021 HN17 93-37495 CIP
New social movements: from ideology to identity, ed. by Enrique Laraña, Hank Johnston, and Joseph R. Gusfield. Temple University, 1994. 368p index afp ISBN 1-56639-186-5, $49.95; ISBN 1-56639-187-3 pbk, $22.95

These essays represent the cutting edge of social movement analysis in their discussions of the emergent perspective called the new social movements paradigm. The contributors are among the most respected movement analysts in the US and Europe; the editors represent the Universities of Madrid and California-San Diego. The initial essay, written by the editors, establishes the context for the volume by analyzing the dialectical progression of various social movement perspectives over the century and engages the debate current among movement analysts: Are the movements of the last two decades "new" and distinctive from previous movements? The remaining 13 essays are a mix of theoretical and empirical analyses that illuminate the critical roles of culture and identity in movement participation. All of the essays are clearly and thoughtfully written. This collection is the logical next step from *Frontiers in Social Movement Theory*, ed. by Aldon Morris and Carol Mueller (CH, Mar'93), in analyzing the theory-intensive field of social movements analysis. Endnotes and references follow each essay. Excellent subject/author index. The book is most relevant for upper-division undergraduates, graduate students, and professors.—*S. Cable, University of Tennessee at Knoxville*

OAB-3022 HV99 95-2854 CIP
Ostrower, Francie. **Why the wealthy give: the culture of elite philanthropy.** Princeton, 1995. 190p bibl index afp ISBN 0-691-04434-1, $29.95

Ostrower's book is one of the finest pieces of social science research to emerge from the new academic field of philanthropic studies. Originally a dissertation in sociology, the study is based on a set of interviews with 99 wealthy philanthropic donors living in the New York City area. Ostrower asks why these upper-class individuals give large sums of money to a variety of cultural and social causes, and finds that the prestige associated with philanthropy is one of the most significant ways the elite class distinguishes itself from the dominant middle-class culture of the US. But the real power of the book lies in the subtlety with which Ostrower analyzes the complexity of motives and behaviors that constitute elite philanthropy in New York. She examines religion, ethnicity, the origins (and timing) of family wealth, and other factors to show the diversity of elite philanthropy, both in terms of the nature of the donee groups and in relation to the status-conferring institutions of the metropolitan community. She concludes that the product of philanthropic heterogeneity is the re-creation of a more or less unified social elite in a society thought to be opposed to the notion of social hierarchy. This important book demonstrates that the most professionally rigorous forms of social science analysis can be presented in lucid prose and easily comprehended ideas. General readers; upper-division undergraduates and above.—*S. N. Katz, American Council of Learned Societies*

OAB-3023 93-84109 Brit. CIP
Prior, Lindsay. **The social organization of mental illness.** Sage, 1993. 225p bibl index ISBN 0-8039-8499-5, $55.00; ISBN 0-8039-8500-2 pbk, $19.95

A cultural and historical sociological study of the vicissitudes of the social organization of mental illness in Britain. Prior presents a Durkheimian analysis of the social representations of illness found in psychiatric, nursing, and social work textbooks, and in World Health Organization and other social policy planning documents. In the spirit of Foucault's concept of discourse and institutional power, Prior examines how these illness constructs shape institutional arrangements for the mentally ill, and how ideas about mental disorder are woven into their daily life and form their social worlds. The author investigates the transformation in clinical perceptions of mental disorders from the era of the segregative-custodial asylum and hospital to the recent movement for "dehospitalization" and return of the mentally ill to community-based social-welfare institutions. Also included are empirical investigations of the social worlds within a contemporary Irish mental hospital and the "transinstitutionalization" to community care. Prior offers a comprehensive review of historical and sociological sources and has produced an important work that adds a fresh perspective on the changing social organization of psychiatric illness. Advanced undergraduates and above.—*J. H. Rubin, Saint Joseph College*

OAB-3024 HM291 94-49571 CIP
Prus, Robert. **Symbolic interaction and ethnographic research: intersubjectivity and the study of human lived experience.** State University of New York, 1996. 301p bibl indexes ISBN 0-7914-2701-3, $59.50

In this tour de force Prus examines the basic theoretical tensions between the positivist (determinism) and the interpretivist (human free agency) orientations—and that is just the beginning. Prus exposes the very roots of intersubjective theory and the impact of the hermeneutic (interpretive) tradition on intersubjective reality. He assesses the ethnographic research tradition, generic social processes in terms of transcontextualizing ethnographic inquiry, and affectivity as a generic social process. In chapter 7, Prus explores the problems of using the intersubjective research approach to social science in light of the "deeply entrenched set of positivist paradigms" encountered today, the present "postmodernist thrust," and the "practical demands of ethnographic inquiry." Chapter 8, cowritten with Lorne Dawson, defines "obdurate reality" as posited by Herbert Blumer and the problem of methodology within ethnographic research. This work stands as an intellectual counterbalance to the works of Jeffrey Alexander and other neopositivists. A solid background in sociological theory will make this work enjoyable reading. Well documented, with extensive use of citations. Good subject index. Graduate, faculty.—*R.C. Myers, Central Washington University*

OAB-3025   HM213   92-4395 CIP
Sadri, Ahmad. **Max Weber's sociology of intellectuals.** Oxford, 1992. 167p bibl index afp ISBN 0-19-506556-5, $32.50

A significant addition to the canon of Weberian scholarship, this book belongs on the shelf of anyone who would understand the work of Max Weber, because it clarifies and gives structure to what Weber meant by intellectuals in both the religious and political spheres, and because it clarifies Weber's methodology in elegant but simple fashion. Weber's approach to the meaning of action in reciprocal human relationships and the use of typologies in characterizing those relationships are at the core of Weber's sociological method. Using such a framework one can understand the intellectual across cultures and times as sharing common features. Intellectuals may be, but need not be, members of a separate stratum, but "they are largely responsible for the unique flavor of different cultures." Sadri proposes a taxonomy of "intellectual action" that differentiates between the type of commitment of the actor—whether as calling or mission—and the way that "intellectuality" is practiced, theoretically or practically. Five appendixes treat Weber's attitude toward Islam, intellectuals in East and West, and components of Weberian methodology. In short, a brilliant work. One would have wished, however, for greater care in proofreading. All levels.—*L. Braude, State University of New York College at Fredonia*

OAB-3026   HM24   94-40622 CIP
Scott, John. **Sociological theory: contemporary debates.** E. Elgar, 1995. 295p bibl index ISBN 1-85278-418-0, $71.95

Scott's thorough mastery of sociological theory is clearly evident in this work. Moreover, he is a gifted explicator of complex and frequently obfuscated theoretical positions. Central to Scott's reflections here is a major and important reevaluation of the theories of Talcott Parsons, a reevaluation that argues forcefully that many of Parsons's formulations still have utility, particularly when compared with more recent contributions by major theorists Anthony Giddens and Jürgen Habermas. Scott charts a meaningful synthetic course through the seemingly endless debates among social theorists, past and present, and does so with authority, evenhandedness, and a desire to achieve some degree of consensus within the discipline. His scholarship here is first-rate, and his considered reflections deserve the attention of students and professional colleagues alike.—*W. P. Nye, Hollins College*

OAB-3027   HM131   95-10016 CIP
Scott, W. Richard. **Institutions and organizations.** Sage Publications, CA, 1995. 178p bibl index afp ISBN 0-8039-5652-5, $39.95; ISBN 0-8039-5653-3 pbk, $18.95

Scott, a leading figure in the sociology of organizations, has written an engaging and sophisticated book. It constitutes a major stocktaking of developments in this disciplinary speciality, which have moved in several intriguing and promising directions since the mid-1970s. After briefly locating the institutionalist approach to the field in the early histories of economics, sociology, and political science, as well as in more recent applications to organizational research, Scott undertakes a sustained analysis of contemporary variants of institutional theory. He illustrates how various approaches can be seen as highlighting one of the "three pillars" of institutions—regulative, normative, and cognitive—and how they have affected empirical research in the differing levels of analysis, ranging from the world system to the organizational subsystem. Without glossing over conflicts and disagreements, Scott stresses the complementarity of recent approaches. Viewing them collectively as representing a major advance in understanding, he concludes with suggestions for future research. Graduate, faculty.—*P. Kivisto, Augustana College (IL)*

OAB-3028   HV91   92-8062 CIP
Skocpol, Theda. **Protecting soldiers and mothers: the political origins of social policy in the United States.** Harvard, 1992. 714p index afp ISBN 0-674-71765-1, $34.95

Massive and richly detailed, Skocpol's new book examines the roles of various political and social contenders in determining the shape of public welfare provisions in the 20th-century US. In so doing, she addresses theoretical questions concerning the nature of the polity and policy-making in the modern state. Skocpol argues that although the common view is that the US lagged far behind European nations in the provision of social welfare programs for its citizens, it was, in fact "a precocious social spending state" that ended "paternalist" programs just at the point when other nations expanded them and uniquely and innovatively experimented with "maternalist" benefits instead. According to Skocpol, most enfranchised constituencies, including both labor unions and progressive opponents of political "patronage" systems, opposed the expansion of pensions for Civil War veterans into social provisioning for male wage earners, but women's organizations actually used their political disenfranchisement as a way of persuading the polity to embrace a "maternalist" vision of social welfare policies that lasted until the Depression of the 1930s. Like her earlier book, *States and Social Revolutions* (CH, Jun'79), this new work is simultaneously provocative and convincing, exhausting and stimulating; surely it will catalyze debate both about policy formation processes in the modern state and the interrelation of gender and power in the public domain. Highly recommended. Advanced undergraduate; graduate; faculty.—*N. B. Rosenthal, SUNY College at Old Westbury*

OAB-3029   HM51   93-37354 CIP
Smelser, Neil J. **Sociology.** Blackwell/UNESCO, 1994. 388p bibl index afp (UNESCO/Blackwell series in contemporary social sciences, 1) ISBN 0-631-18916-5 pbk, $24.95

Title notwithstanding, this is no introductory text. It is the vanguard of a series, under the UNESCO aegis, that attempts to chart the present state of the social sciences in global and multicultural dimension. A distinct and distinguished representative of each discipline writes chapters on the subfields of the discipline in terms of material contributed by colleagues from (in the present instance) India, Italy, France, Nigeria, Australia, the US, Germany, Poland, and points between. This volume consists of four major sections—fundamentals; polity and society; economy; and society—arranged in 19 chapters dealing, inter alia, with the sociological perspective; theory and method; varieties of authoritarianism and democracy; work commitment and alienation; race, ethnicity, and class; religiosity; women in societies; and family and intimacy. Throughout, again in response to the UNESCO charge to the authors, the role of internationalization and diffusion in the shaping of the discipline is a recurring and unifying theme. The chapters on the changing views of the human community and the nation-state, population, and urbanism are especially noteworthy in this regard. A "selected annotated international bibliography" is first-rate. General readers and experts alike will find this work a treasure trove. One eagerly awaits further volumes. All levels.—*L. Braude, SUNY College at Fredonia*

OAB-3030   HC106   94-40284 CIP
State of the union: America in the 1990s. v.1: Economic trends; v.2: Social trends, ed. by Reynolds Farley. Russell Sage Foundation, 1995. 2v. 375, 377p bibl indexes afp (1990 census research series, 1-2) ISBN 0-87154-240-4, v.1; ISBN 0-87154-241-2, v.2; $39.95 ea.

Volume 1 of this two-volume set is an analysis of major economic trends and patterns in terms of income inequality, labor force and earnings, roles of women and men, educational attainment, job location, and housing polarization. The second volume is devoted to social trends involving diversity and inequality in the family, the older population, children and living arrangements, racial diversity, patterns of immigration, and geographic population shifts. Each chapter is written by a recognized expert, and, regardless of the title of this set, the concern is with trends up to the 1990 census results, not during the 1990s. The work represents a continuation of the monographic approach started with the 1980 census, but differs in that it covers fewer subjects and offers an interpretation of the overarching social and economic trends revealed by the enumeration, rather than merely providing simple description. Each chapter deals with an important issue in American society and represents the best of existing knowledge about each subject. This is required reading for all serious scholars of the American scene. The high quality of this effort will set demanding standards for future work on new trends developing during the present decade. Upper-division undergraduates and above.—*T. E. Steahr, University of Connecticut*

OAB-3031 HM24 93-4075 CIP
Strauss, Anselm L. **Continual permutations of action.** Aldine de Grayter, 1993. 280p bibl index afp ISBN 0-202-30471-X, $44.95; ISBN 0-202-30472-8 pbk, $21.95

Strauss expands the pragmatist/interactionist orientation to social behavior of John Dewey, George H. Mead, and Herbert Blumer into a full-blown theory of action. In its theoretic fruitfulness, its descriptive sophistication, and in its "respect [for] the empirical world" Strauss's effort renders previous attempts at such formulations (notably Parsons's) redundant. Strauss begins by suggesting some 19 assumptions of an effective action theory that, among other things, can minimize the danger of sociologists "becoming captive to overly simple explanatory models or doctrines [claiming to explain] human life and behavior." His fundamental idea of trajectory and related subconcepts—notably matrix and path analysis of conditions relative to orders of behavior and the arenas in which such behavior is performed—are elaborated into a treatment of the complex interplay between symbolic worlds, social orders, and structures shaped by and through those symbolic sets. The role of the body, of emotions, and of motives within this action theory are set forth as aspects of and conditions for action. This book must be regarded as a magisterial analysis, sociology at its finest. All levels.—*L. Braude, SUNY College at Fredonia*

OAB-3032 HM291 93-44901 CIP
Tarrow, Sidney. **Power in movement: social movements, collective action and politics.** Cambridge, 1994. 251p bibl index ISBN 0-521-41079-7, $59.95; ISBN 0-521-42271-X pbk, $17.95

Drawing on a rich array of social theories and historical cases, Tarrow (Cornell) has provided the most comprehensive and convincing study of social movements in the literature to date. Transcending separate studies of revolutions, violence, and protests, this book locates the birth of social movements generally in the 18th century, when nation states, economic development, and new systems of communication made it possible to organize and sustain collective action against authority. The structure of political opportunity, whatever its origins, provides the occasion, he argues, for "early risers" to frame discontents within culturally recognizable forms, mobilize existing networks of social groupings, and experiment with a preexisting repertoire of actions to challenge authority. In so doing, new forms of action, new social networks, and altered cultural symbols result. Historical cases ranging from Europe in 1848 through student protests in the 1960s and waves of democratization in Eastern Europe in the 1980s illuminate this explanatory framework and permit comparisons across time and cultures. The increasing cycles of protest and their seemingly instant transmissibility across national boundaries suggest a future in which political authority is exercised in contexts where large sectors of the population are mobilized to engage in forms of collective action designed to challenge that authority. This book displays the mastery and sophistication that comes form three decades of original research and disciplined reflection on the research of others. It should become the definitive study of social movements and its literature. Upper-division undergraduate through faculty.—*E. J. Eisenach, University of Tulsa*

OAB-3033 HT149 95-34814 CIP
The Urban transformation of the developing world, ed. by Josef Gugler. Oxford, 1996. 327p indexes afp ISBN 0-19-874159-6, $65.00; ISBN 0-19-874158-8 pbk, $19.95

Within a few years, more than half the world's population will reside in towns and cities, which are growing most rapidly in developing countries. Gugler, a sociologist renowned for his research on Third World urbanization, has assembled an impressive array of leading-edge scholars to examine a variety of mul-

tidisciplinary issues associated with this socioeconomic and demographic transformation. The two opening chapters, by Gugler and R. Murphey, treat issues of regionalism and urban evolution. The six remaining chapters cover urbanization trends in the world's developing regions: China (Chen and Parish), India (Mohan), Indonesia (Hugo), the Arab World (J. Abu-Lughod), Subsaharan Africa (Gugler), and Latin America (de Oliveira and B. Roberts). Each chapter is a model of compactness, but a few are cramped by the need to conform to the book's tight space limitations. Reference lists vary in size, but each is keyed to the most important current literature on each region. Useful to the widest array of possible readers, this volume should be considered a basic new title for all economic development and international urban studies collections.—*P. O. Muller, University of Miami*

OAB-3034 HM101 93-19270 CIP
Watkins, Evan. **Throwaways: work culture and consumer education.** Stanford, 1994 (c1993). 230p bibl index afp ISBN 0-8047-2249-8, $37.50; ISBN 0-8047-2250-1 pbk, $14.95

Watkins's insightful book is a brilliant analysis of how "techno-ideological" changes have recast the dynamics and opportunities for social change in the US. Using a postmodern narrative within a neo-Marxist (Gramscian) framework, Watkins illuminates a series of changes that have obfuscated and/or transformed class, gender, and racial antagonisms in ways that negate their oppositional and liberating potentials. Watkins shows that education as consumers has shaped the overall American ideological approach to culture, politics, economics, and education. Using several recurring concrete examples and drawing on classic works in a dozen academic disciplines, he challenges the facile explanations of US society. By successively revealing the unity of content, the extensions, and the impacts of the techno-ideological process, Watkins advances his compelling argument, his devastating criticism of postmodernism, and his riveting and perceptive critique of Reaganomics. Coming full circle, he details why the New Right struggle to restructure the formal education curriculum is crucial to its cultural, economic, and political agenda. Despite a sometimes obtuse exposition, this may be one of the most important books written in the last decade; a worthy successor and complement to Herbert Marcuse's classic work *One Dimensional Man* (1964). All levels.—*P. McGuire, University of Toledo*

OAB-3035 HG221 93-42808 CIP
Zelizer, Viviana A. **The social meaning of money.** Basic Books, 1994. 286p index ISBN 0-465-07891-5, $24.00

Sociologists generally have shared economists' view that money is a qualitatively neutral, homogeneous medium of market exchange. Zelizer (Princeton Univ.) challenges this purely materialist perspective by arguing that different types of money exist, each with its own emotional and cultural meanings. Among her best examples are the willingness of many people to splurge with "found" money, such as gambling windfalls; the earmarking of funds into such categories as a wife's "pin money" or a child's allowance; funds set aside for weddings, funerals, baptisms, Christmas, and other special events; and "blood" money. Each type of money is subject to complex social rules. Social security payments do not share the stigma of welfare or food stamps. Postal employees, but not doctors, receive tips. Courtship money must express admiration and affection but not suggest payment or financial support. Too large a gift to a teacher may be rejected as an attempted bribe. Zelizer traces the history of such "contested" currencies as charitable contributions, in which social tensions arise from differing definitions of the social meanings attached to the funds. This is an impressive piece of scholarship drawing on documents as varied as court cases, immigrant guides, vaudeville scripts, and household budget studies. Undergraduates and above.—*T.H. Koenig, Northeastern University*

Social & Behavioral Sciences

■ Criminology

OAB-3036　　　　HV9105　　　　94-47525 CIP
Alexander, Ruth M. **The "girl problem": female sexual delinquency in New York, 1900-1930.** Cornell, 1995. 200p bibl index afp ISBN 0-8014-2821-1, $29.95

Alexander's historical study documents the experience of female sexual delinquents from 1900 to 1930. Working-class adolescents and young adults were severely sanctioned for failing to obey Victorian moral standards. These "delinquent" girls were usually incarcerated in state reformatories. Alexander analyzes records of 100 female residents of institutions in Bedford Hills and Albion, New York. Working from case examples, she illustrates the actions that defined young women as delinquent, their reformatory experiences, and their struggles to reenter society. She reconstructs interaction among young women facing changing cultural standards, their frightened families, and the legal system of courts and reformatories. Alexander's interest is in the process of identifying a new social issue, "the girl problem," and in the 20th-century redefinition of adolescence. Rebellious lower-class young women who experimented sexually were severely handled, while middle-class girls received understanding or therapy for similar behavior. Case examples and archival photographs enhance the historical, theoretical material. This thoroughly researched book includes a helpful bibliographic essay and extensive notes. Upper-division undergraduates and above.—*M. E. Elwell, emerita, Salisbury State University*

OAB-3037　　　　HV5810　　　　93-9312 CIP
Belenko, Steven R. **Crack and the evolution of anti-drug policy.** Greenwood, 1993. 199p bibl index afp (Contributions in criminology and penology, 42) ISBN 0-313-28030-4, $49.95

Crack is essential reading not only for experts and professionals but average Americans. Belenko (senior researcher, New York City Criminal Justice Agency and an experimental psychologist) painstakingly sifts through the empirical research in pharmacology, criminal behavior, and enforcement to expose the errors of America's recent antidrug policy. He argues that the fear of crack was unlike any other antidrug campaign in this century, fueling an aggressive and moralistic "War on Drugs" and a dramatic emphasis on punishment and social control over education and rehabilitation. Empirical evidence indicates that the crack hysteria was created and distorted by the media and manipulated by politicians and the government to win approval and elections. Alternative rehabilitative approaches were ignored despite criminal justice abuses and overcrowding of prisons and court systems with small-scale, lower-class, minority offenders. Although the study is rich in details of the crack problem, the author sees the big picture, concluding "that incarcerating more and more poor black and Hispanic drug users and low-level sellers has not and will not solve the nation's drug problem" and that "the key research and policy issue is why so many Americans take psychoactive drugs." The work stands out among the antidrug literature for its solid empirical analysis. Highly recommended for all readers.—*W. Q. Morales, University of Central Florida*

OAB-3038　　　　HV5810　　　　95-5929 CIP
Bourgois, Philippe. **In search of respect: selling crack in El Barrio.** Cambridge, 1995. 392p bibl index ISBN 0-521-43518-8, $24.95

Bourgois spent nearly four years in an East Harlem neighborhood, where he gained the confidence of street-level drug dealers. His book is a vivid chronicle of crack-house society and barrio street culture. Bourgois offers sensitive insights into the lives of his subjects without sanitizing their brutality and violence. Dealers—largely offspring of Puerto Rican immigrants—recount dispiriting experiences of discrimination and dead-end, poorly paid jobs in the legal job market. Even as the drug dealers and street criminals are shown in these pages to be caught in a downward spiral of crime, violence, and poverty, they are also depicted, and depict themselves, as followers of an "American dream" of upward mobility—rugged individuals pursuing careers and fortunes as pri-

vate entrepreneurs. This book does three things well: it presents a superbly written ethnography; makes a sound theoretical contribution to the study of the relationship between social-structural constraints and individual behavior; and advances cogent public policy recommendations, not simplistic solutions, for confronting inner-city poverty and substance abuse. Upper-division undergraduates and above.—*E. Wellin, University of Wisconsin—Milwaukee*

OAB-3039　　　　HV9469　　　　96-39937 Orig
Collins, Catherine Fisher. **The imprisonment of African American women: causes, conditions, and future implications.** McFarland, 1997. 152p bibl index afp ISBN 0-7864-0263-6, $29.95

Collins's book is worth reading and contemplating. In 11 chapters, Collins (Empire State College, SUNY) enlightens and despairs at one and the same time, taking the reader on a journey that few in criminology or criminal justice have traveled. In the introduction, the author notes that her study "pulls together scarce, fragmented, and scattered information from throughout the many social sciences and scientific fields in an attempt to better understand how the criminal justice system has failed this segment of the population." She then takes the reader through a brief history of Anglo-American penal methods, giving insight into how and why black women have been shabbily treated from early on to the present in the US criminal justice system. Collins intersperses charts, graphs, and tables, which give the reader a historical and contemporary sense of the plight of the black female inmate. Of special interest is Collins's chapter on the Violent Crime Control & Law Enforcement Act of 1994 and its provisions that affect the issue of gendered justice. Extensive bibliography. This book is recommended for all collections; it is *must reading* for correctional professionals and politicians.—*J. C. Watkins Jr., University of Alabama*

OAB-3040　　　　HV6453　　　　93-9612 CIP
Gambetta, Diego. **The Sicilian Mafia: the business of private protection.** Harvard, 1993. 335p bibl index afp ISBN 0-674-80741-3, $39.95

An original and illuminating economic interpretation of the Sicilian Mafia, based on thorough knowledge of judicial sources and on firsthand observation of a variety of economic activities in Palermo, e.g., the wholesale fish and produce markets, the allocation of public construction contracts, and radio-dispatched taxis. Gambetta (Oxford Univ.) conceives the Sicilian Mafia as an industry in which firms ("families") sell protection. Though government and the Mafia are both suppliers of protection, they differ in that "the Mafia has not citizens but at best clients." The families' resources are information, reputation, violence, and "a stance of covert blessing, or at best equivocal detachment" from the church. Gambetta offers insights into the Mafia's historical origins in the interaction between western Sicily's harsh interior and prosperous coastal zones; internal organization of the families; the process of cartel formation among families; and Mafia ritual and style. This fascinating book is a model of the social scientist's twin ideals of fullness and parsimony, explaining a rich variety of phenomena with a relatively simple analytical framework. Bravissimo! Advanced undergraduates and above.—*J. Alcorn, Trinity College*

OAB-3041　　　　HV8978　　　　95-8938 CIP
Glaser, Daniel. **Preparing convicts for law-abiding lives: the pioneering penology of Richard A. McGee.** State University of New York, 1995. 224p bibl index afp ISBN 0-7914-2695-5, $59.50

Written by a prominent criminologist, this reflective book connects correctional leadership activities, in California and nationally, with the dilemmas and problems arising from the American response to crime. Glaser's analysis draws material from Richard McGee's Minnesota roots, leadership opportunities arising from fragmented correctional operations, attempted and successful solutions to problems, and political context. Throughout program discussions, Glaser's major theme unfolds: correctional (and criminal justice activities) operations must be based in rational principles connected to goals that are subjected to careful research examination to determine operational effectiveness. The book opens with a brief background on corrections, including an overview of McGee's career, and then analyzes his innovations in California prisons and community correctional programs. Discussion of commitment to evaluation research, its use and centrality for correctional planning and operation, is followed by McGee's plans, forecasts, and prognosis for corrections. The inclusion of McGee's personal notes, as well as observations from many individuals who knew and worked with him, provides a vitality to the chapters. A mandatory purchase for all libraries, the book is easily read and understood. Useful and relevant bibliography. All levels.—*J. H. Larson, University of North Dakota*

OAB-3042   E78   93-5381 CIP
Grobsmith, Elizabeth S. **Indians in prison: incarcerated Native Americans in Nebraska.** Nebraska, 1994. 209p bibl index afp ISBN 0-8032-2137-1, $37.50

"Nebraska Indian prisoners have served as a model for Indian inmates nationwide since they began the process of asserting their rights to religious freedom." Grobsmith carefully analyzes the history and structure of the Nebraska state penal system and examines its relationship to local Native American peoples (Omaha, Winnebago, Santee and Lakota, Chippewa, Cherokee, and Northern Ponca). She addresses the issues of religious freedom, the relation of alcohol to incarceration, the cultural and legal uniqueness of Native American peoples, traditional beliefs, rehabilitation programs, the admission and discharge of Indian prisoners, and recidivism. An anthropologist, the author integrates the disciplines of anthropology, alcohol studies, religious studies, and penology. Her work is the first comprehensive study on this topic and provides important survey data for all state and federal prisons. Balanced and sensitive in her approach, Grobsmith chronicles improvements in the system, highlights structural impediments to further change, and suggests positive future reform. All levels.—*R. Bucko, Le Moyne College*

OAB-3043   HV9813   95-20808 CIP
Johnson, Elmer H. **Japanese corrections: managing convicted offenders in an orderly society.** Southern Illinois, 1996. 336p bibl index afp ISBN 0-8093-1736-2, $39.95

Johnson is the author of *Crime, Correction, and Society* (rev. ed., CH, Jan'69) and also edited *Handbook on Crime and Delinquency Prevention* (CH, Nov'87). In this superbly researched and well-written study he seeks to discover the characteristics of major programmatic elements in Japan's correction system, how personnel carry out their responsibilities, and why these activities are executed in a particular way that obviously reflects Japanese culture. The information was acquired from field visits and interviews, collected documents, and other materials prepared by Japanese and foreign experts. Johnson explains the particular functions of the Ministry of Justice and the Correction Bureau and Rehabilitation Bureau. He points out that the Japanese correction system focuses on *management* of offenders, and reflects society's reluctance to sentence convicted defendants to prison and also, to a lesser extent, to place them on probationary supervision, which they consider too punitive for most offenders. Readers will find much interesting information in this book, e.g., the use of VPO (volunteer probation officers) of high social standing. Highly recommended for academic libraries and a must for practitioners and policy makers. Upper-division undergraduates and above.—*M. Y. Rynn, University of Scranton*

OAB-3044   Orig
Kressel, Neil J. **Mass hate: the global rise of genocide and terror.** Plenum, 1996. 340p index ISBN 0-306-45271-5, $25.95

Kressel, whose previous writings have appeared in *Political Psychology*, *Journal of Social Psychology*, and *American Journal of Sociology*, among many others, has produced an insightful study of the cultural variants that underlie collective tendencies toward mass hate and genocide. The author reaches his conclusions through a painstakingly constructed analysis of the horrifying episodes of mass hate and genocide in Rwanda, Bosnia, Nazi Germany, and the Middle East, as well as the acts of terrorism that have recently occurred within the

US. By building on detailed criticisms of the social psychological literature, Kressel makes his case that mass hate is a collective phenomenon that can erupt with the congruence of several factors. These include increasing marginalization of minority groups, collective perceptions of injustice, conditions of economic depravity, but most important, absence of shared political power. Many will question Kressel's conclusion that the best protection against mass hate remains the establishment of democratic societies and the protection of individual rights. However, such claims are trivial in light of the wealth of evidence the authors provides. Detailed references, endnotes, and thorough index. All levels.—*T. M. Chester, Texas A&M University*

OAB-3045   HV8699   93-15717 CIP
Marquart, James W. **The rope, the chair, and the needle: capital punishment in Texas, 1923-1990,** by James W. Marquart, Sheldon Ekland-Olson, and Jonathan R. Sorensen. Texas, 1994. 275p bibl index afp ISBN 0-292-75158-3, $24.95

The authors spent years accumulating arrest records, prison records, trial transcripts, news reports, inmate files, personal letters, and interviews to examine as comprehensively as possible the social contexts of lynchings, electrocutions, and lethal injections. The limitations faced in sorting some effects statistically are carefully explained, but what the authors clearly discovered and documented will impress, and likely stun, any reader. The work contains comparisons of capital punishment with life imprisonment cases; of those given commutations with those that were not; of sentencing outcomes according to offender characteristics, victim characteristics, and the mixture of the two (i.e., interracial and intraracial crimes); of post-1972 records for inmates who were or were not released. These and other comparisons reveal the presence of bigotry, brutality, and system bias rooted in the slave economy and caste-like culture of the South. Declines are not in evidence until the 1972 Furman decision, after which the focus of discrimination shifts toward the prosecution versus sentencing stage. Findings from other relevant research are thoroughly incorporated in this probing revelation about the politics of death in Texas. The quantitative analysis of a truly astounding range and a massive amount of data along with the direct quotations from individual case files creates a most sobering blend. Readers interested in the South, race relations, criminal justice, the death penalty, or the state of Texas should pay attention. Upper-division undergraduate and up.—*R. Zingraff, Meredith College*

OAB-3046   HV9950   95-26128 CIP
Miller, Jerome G. **Search and destroy: African-American males in the criminal justice system.** Cambridge, 1996. 304p index afp ISBN 0-521-46021-2, $24.95

Miller's new study makes a significant contribution to understanding the nefarious nature of the US criminal justice system. More important, it provides a poignant depiction of all that is wrong with a system of jurisprudence that currently has the highest incarceration rate in the industrialized world (the latest statistics indicate the number exceeds 1.6 million). Using African American males as the target group, Miller paints a sad picture regarding their likely involvement in the criminal justice system. Pivotal in this analysis is the introduction, in which Miller summarizes the deleterious nature of the system. Statistics are presented to show how black males' probability of incarceration is significantly greater than majority males. The author debunks the notion that prisons are full of "predatory and violent" black men, and discusses the history of racial bias in the penal system. He examines both the unanticipated consequences of the justice system and the politics of crime. Chapter 5, on race, applied science, and public policy, is a seminal piece on how so-called scientific evidence is used to justify racial differences (read genetic predispositions to criminality). The final chapter expounds on the future. Citing sources from an international perspective, this informative, riveting, and up-to-date book is a must read. All levels.—*R. Stewart, SUNY College at Buffalo*

OAB-3047   HV6252   93-1305 CIP
Nadelmann, Ethan A. **Cops across borders: the internationaliza-**

551

tion of U.S. criminal law enforcement. Pennsylvania State, 1994 (c1993). 524p index afp ISBN 0-271-01094-0, $55.00; ISBN 0-271-01095-9 pbk, $16.95

Nadelmann's groundbreaking treatise on a much-neglected field of study examines the internationalization of US law enforcement agencies. The book represents the first scholarly analysis of the increasing interpenetration of foreign policy and criminal justice institutions. Tracing the historical evolution of the commingling of international relations and criminal justice, Nadelmann (Princeton Univ.) sheds new light on growing US hegemony, especially in the emerging post-Cold War international arena. The book assiduously notes that the trend toward transnational policing has grown dramatically since the late 1960s and the creation of the "war on drugs." Although some studies have analyzed and compared foreign and US criminal justice systems, e.g., David Bayley's *Forces of Order: Policing Modern Japan* (CH, Dec'76), and others have focused on US law enforcement's relationship with Interpol, e.g., Michael Fooner's *Interpol: Issues in World Crime and International Criminal Justice* (CH, Apr'90), this is the first work to explore the international activities of national police forces. Written in an unadorned style, the book is easily understood. A valuable resourse for general readers and students at all levels.—*P. Horne, Mercer County Community College*

OAB-3048   HV9471   94-8630 CIP
Zimring, Franklin E. **Incapacitation: penal confinement and the restraint of crime,** by Franklin E. Zimring and Gordon Hawkins. Oxford, 1995. 188p bibl index afp ISBN 0-19-509233-3, $27.95

Although criminal justice policies and sentencing structures have resulted in crisis levels of prison overcrowding or in costly prison construction programs in most of the US, Zimring and Hawkins's magnificent and concise piece of scholarship examines the often hollow and usually contradictory consequences of confinement. Written by two leading experts, this study deals with an unsettling number of unanswered questions about incapacitation. On reading this solid and honest appraisal of the truly miserable state of knowledge about either controlling or influencing criminals, one must be concerned that so many lives and so many dollars have been captured by policies so inadequately tested. The authors describe variables that would affect any coherent study of incapacitation but are nevertheless *absent* from research. Their review of conceptual and methodological challenges includes astute critiques of the claims made by major publications. Their reasoning is lucid, and their efforts to correlate public policy with public gain should impress readers of any political persuasion. The work will be beyond the reach of untrained readers, but it is essential for specialists, advanced students, and policy analysts.—*R. Zingraff, Meredith College*

■ Gender, Sexuality, Marriage & Family

OAB-3049   HQ536   94-11589 CIP
Acock, Alan C. **Family diversity and well-being,** by Alan C. Acock and David H. Demo. Sage Publications, CA, 1994. 299p bibl indexes (Sage library of social research, 195) ISBN 0-8039-4266-4, $46.00; ISBN 0-8039-4267-2 pbk, $22.95

Based on an analysis of the National Survey of Families and Households (1988- ; funded by the National Institute of Child Health and Human Development), this study examines the consequences of household structure for the social and psychological well-being of parents and children. Because the data are limited to discrete households, the analysis neglects the contribution of non-household kin to the well-being of families. That limitation aside, this work makes a significant contribution to the literature on family process, structure, and well-being. It is a much needed comparative analysis across marital status (married, divorced, remarried, and never-married women with child/ren). Early chapters are particularly useful for introducing beginning students to

the theoretical, conceptual, and policy issues at stake. Clear prose and well-labeled tables make the substantive chapters accessible to students but sacrifice none of the rigor of the analysis. Chapters focus on the effects of paid work and unpaid household labor on husbands and wives; differences across household type in norms regarding parent-child relations; household type and mother's and children's well-being; and family process and well-being. This book provides a thorough review of the literature and systematically addresses a set of questions that are theoretically and politically significant, particularly in light of the continuing concern over the "demise" of the American family. It should enjoy a wide readership in family studies, social work, sociology, and psychology at both the undergraduate and graduate levels.—*S. K. Gallagher, Oregon State University*

OAB-3050   HV875   92-43666 CIP
Bartholet, Elizabeth. **Family bonds: adoption and the politics of parenting.** Houghton Mifflin, 1993. 276p index ISBN 0-395-51085-6, $21.95

A provocative consideration of the issues of adoption, infertility, and cross-cultural/cross-racial family building. Bartholet, Harvard law professor and single adoptive parent of two Peruvian sons, weaves her own story of infertility and adoption with scholarly research and strong policy recommendations. Although the book is intended to raise consciousness and change adoption policies, it is also an excellent example of feminist writing from the personal to the political. Bartholet effectively combines literary traditions of academic policy research and personal reflection. Unique contributions include comparisons of unregulated new fertilty technologies with overregulated adoption processes, and barriers to cross-racial adoptions with antidiscrimination law. The discussion of intercountry adoption, tied to consideration of global population issues, includes review of international law as well as US policy. Bartholet's eloquent plea for policies to facilitate adoptive family building is accessible to general as well as academic or professional audiences. Appropriate for collections in social work, social policy, family studies. Recommended.—*M. E. Elwell, Salisbury State University*

OAB-3051   HQ777   96-11882 CIP
Buchanan, Christy M. **Adolescents after divorce,** by Christy M. Buchanan, Eleanor E. Maccoby, and Sanford M. Dornbusch. Harvard, 1996. 331p bibl index afp ISBN 0-674-00517-1, $39.95

Buchanan et al. have produced a benchmark study on the true victims of divorce: children living with its aftermath. They examined conditions to which adolescents tried to adapt after a parental divorce. Variability in adolescent adjustment behavior provided the opportunity to study the circumstances and processes associated with successful postdivorce change. Data on various custody arrangements and parental postdivorce relationships from the Stanford Custody Project (a three-and-a-half-year longitudinal study) were compared to data gathered on the adjustment of divorced parents' adolescent-aged children. In total, 522 adolescents were interviewed from two counties in California. The study addressed two major areas of inquiry: the contrast in adjustment between adolescents whose parents maintained a cooperative coparental relationship and those whose parents were in conflict, and whether a relationship existed between adjustment and the history of an adolescent's residential living arrangements. Findings support previous research and will encourage further study of possible means of therapeutic intervention on behalf of those who fail to adjust. Appendix B contains numerous supplemental tables of data. Extensive literature documentation; good subject index. Recommended for upper-division undergraduates and above.—*R.C. Myers, Central Washington University*

OAB-3052   HQ503   95-14414 CIP
Coltrane, Scott. **Family man: fatherhood, housework, and gender equity.** Oxford, 1996. 293p index afp ISBN 0-19-508216-8, $27.50

Coltrane (Univ. of California-Riverside) has produced an engagingly written and well-documented study. A combination of interviews and questionnaires conducted over a period of five years was used to collect data about white, middle-class, dual-earner families and shared parenting. Coltrane introduces the topic of "men's involvement in families: what it's been, how it's evolving, and where it might lead." He then examines historical, sociological, and political studies to uncover the historical background on marriage, parenting, and housework, and traces the phenomenon of separate roles for men and women through the 19th and 20th centuries. Coltrane presents his data through extensive quotes from the in-depth interviews, capturing how people feel about their attempts at shared parenting and household responsibilities, and showing typical patterns and common dilemmas. Mexican-American families and white working-class families were also interviewed and their stories included. Coltrane also uses comparative anthropological and sociological studies to examine parenting and household responsibilities in other cultures, and concludes that "the way to minimize masculine insecurity and bravado is not to separate from women, but to ensure that they cooperate in both child-rearing and productive work." All levels.—*R.C. Myers, Central Washington University*

OAB-3053 HQ1088 94-36172 CIP
Connell, R.W. **Masculinities.** California, 1995. 295p bibl index afp ISBN 0-520-08998-7, $40.00; ISBN 0-520-08999-5 pbk, $16.00

Clearly written and sophisticated, this book presents Connell's ideas about males and the social phenomena that interact with gender. Starting with a brief introduction and critique of earlier views in psychology, biology, and sociology, the author sketches a complex set of analyses about gender, using life histories of four groups of Australian men to exemplify the concepts. He rejects many current approaches (sociobiology, sex-role theory, the mythopoetic men's movement, etc.) as simplistic and/or unjust. Connell (sociology, Univ. of California, Santa Cruz) believes that there are *many* masculinities, all changing over time, all somewhat ambiguous and self-contradictory, all intimately enmeshed with issues of hegemony, subordination, and other group variables. These masculinities are all rooted in a male's direct bodily sensations, all rooted in historical processes at both macro- and microlevels, all rooted in, and changing with, men's everyday relations with women, with themselves, and with each other. An excellent contribution to gender theory. Useful to upper-division courses covering gender, but also can be understood by readers at all levels.—*R. W. Smith, California State University, Northridge*

OAB-3054 E185 96-7930 CIP
Franklin, Donna L. **Ensuring inequality: the structural transformation of the African-American family.** Oxford, 1997. 251p index afp ISBN 0-19-510078-6, $25.00

Written in the expectation that it would become the definitive source in explaining the "structural" elements that have adversely affected the African American family, Franklin's book succeeds beyond this reviewer's expectations. Franklin has produced a seminal work ranking among the highest in the field of African American family studies. Page after page testifies to rigors expended by the author in her effort to apprise the reader of factors, both past and present, that have transformed the black family into an entity distinctly different from its African forebears. Beginning with a foreword written by the distinguished William Julius Wilson and divided into two parts, the book looks at the legacy of slavery, sharecropping, maternalism, and northern industrialization (part 1). Franklin examines WW II and its aftermaths, portents of contemporary negative aspects of the African American family, matriarchy, and family composition and the "underclass," and she offers suggestions for improvements within the African American family (Part 2). Thoroughly researched and documented, this book is a "must read." All levels.—*R. Stewart, SUNY College at Buffalo*

OAB-3055 HQ759 95-2998 CIP
Gabor, Andrea. **Einstein's wife: work and marriage in the lives of five great twentieth-century women.** Viking, 1995. 341p bibl index afp ISBN 0-670-84210-9, $22.95

Einstein's Wife (the title is misleading) is actually the story of the careers and marriages of not one but five successful 20th-century women. The subjects of this book—Mileva Maric Einstein, Lee Krasner, Maria Goeppert Mayer, Denise Scott Brown, and Sandra Day O'Connor—were chosen because they all had enduring marriages (two of them were even happy) as well as significant accomplishments in their respective fields: science, art, physics, architecture, and jurisprudence. Gabor makes the point that despite the wide differences in their backgrounds and interests, they all accepted marriage as the defining aspect of their lives, and each measured her own success as a person not primarily by her career achievement but by her marriage. In addition, all of them encountered prejudice in the workplace, and all of them felt the tension between their work aspirations and their home aspirations; their husbands had to contend with no such obstacles. Nonetheless, these women all made significant contributions in their fields. This book is extremely well researched and contains copious notes and an excellent index. It is also very interesting reading with much personal detail—a real contribution to the field of gender studies. General; undergraduate through professional.—*M. H. Chaplin, Wellesley College*

OAB-3056 Orig
Gauthier, Anne Hélène. **The state and the family: a comparative analysis of family policies in industrialized countries.** Oxford, 1996. 232p bibl indexes afp ISBN 0-19-828804-2, $65.00

Gauthier presents a historical and cross-national comparative analysis of the nature of state support for families in 22 industrialized countries. She examines the evolution of family policy from the turn of the century to the 1990s and shows how trends in population and family policy have varied among countries. The author argues that demographic changes have been a major catalyst in the emergence of state policies related to family issues. This study places emphasis on the historical and comparative dimension through an analysis of country-specific differences in selected key indicators of family policy. Socioeconomic and demographic factors such as the decline in fertility, the increase in poverty, divorce, single-parent families, participation of women in the labor force, the feminist movement, changes in lifestyles, and the aging population appear to have influenced state policies concerning population and family issues. Gauthier focuses on how these forces represent a major challenge to the governments of industrialized nations in bringing about legislation to better support families. She provides a typology of models of family policy and speculates about the future of family policy, based on recent trends. A major contribution to the comparative sociology of the state and family policy. Upper-division undergraduates and above.—*D. A. Chekki, University of Winnipeg*

OAB-3057 HQ814 92-33412 CIP
Guttmann, Joseph. **Divorce in psychosocial perspective: theory and research.** L. Erlbaum, 1993. 256p bibl indexes afp ISBN 0-8058-0347-5, $59.95

Guttmann's study of divorce in the US has three basic objectives: to provide a thorough view of divorce from several perspectives; to offer a broad review of the divorce literature; and to suggest a new theory of the divorce process. The multiple perspectives on divorce are presented in terms of legal aspects, economic conditions, impact of religion, cultural values, and ethnic identification. A separate chapter discusses various theoretical models of the divorce process. This is an impressive analytical review of the major models of divorce and is an excellent summary of each approach. Guttman (Univ. of Haifa) introduces a psychosocial model of the divorce process consisting of four stages: deciding, separating, struggling, and winning. Guttman discusses the social impact of divorce with reference to divorced mothers, to children of divorced parents, and to divorced fathers. His treatment of the effect of divorce on fathers is a long overdue consideration of this "forgotten parent." The two final chapters cover past research on children of divorced parents and the reaction of children to parental divorce. There are 29 pages of references to literature on divorce, as well as a subject and author index. Guttman's work is an important addition to the literature. Highly recommended for advanced undergraduates and above, and for practitioners.—*T. E. Steahr, University of Connecticut*

OAB-3058   HQ759   96-36157 CIP
Harris, Kathleen Mullan. **Teen mothers and the revolving door.** Temple University, 1997. 195p bibl index afp ISBN 1-56639-499-6, $39.95

Harris's book refocuses one of the few well-designed longitudinal studies of individual experience with welfare assistance, a long-term study by Frank Furstnenberg Jr. on teen mothers receiving AFDC. This work illustrates again that public policy in the US is seldom, if ever, influenced by social research. Among more significant findings are those indicating that while teen pregnancy is not rising, unwed teen pregnancy is. The birth rate for teens in this country is much higher than that in countries with far more generous social welfare benefits. The move from welfare to work for single teen mothers (and for others, it might be added) results in a reduction in the care and basic resources for children of these mothers. Harris's study is yet another that shows clearly that work, eligibility, and benefit "reforms" simply punish children. The book is well written and has a superior bibliography and index. It will be of value to students in social work, social policy, and social science, as well as public policy makers. All levels.—*F. J. Peirce, emeritus, University of Oklahoma*

OAB-3059   LC2607   96-127672 Orig
Jejeebhoy, Shireen J. **Women's education, autonomy, and reproductive behaviour: experience from developing countries.** Oxford, 1996 (c1995). 306p bibl index afp ISBN 0-19-829033-0, $65.00

Jejeebhoy's study is a long awaited follow-up to S.J. Cochrane's *Fertility and Education: What Do We Really Know?* (CH, Jan'80). Using findings from world fertility surveys, demographic and health surveys, and anthropological studies, Jejeebhoy evaluates the link between women's formal education, autonomy (knowledge source, decision making, emotional, economic/social, and self-reliance), and fertility behaviors (age at marriage, parity, timing, breast-feeding, contraception, postpartum abstinence, child and maternal mortality). The well-documented inverse relationship between education and fertility, long presumed to be relatively simple, proves to be more complex. The influence of women's education operates differentially on fertility, depending on the stage of development and magnitude of the gender gap. Jejeebhoy assesses the various complex pathways by which education affects fertility-inhibiting and stimulating behaviors, and discusses policy implications of various critical pathways. Well researched, well documented, and well written, this monograph is a must for students of demography, family, gender inequality, and development. Contains detailed chapter endnotes, useful glossary, detailed appendixes, subject/author index. Bibliography is extensive and current. Upper-division undergraduates and above.—*D.W. Hastings, University of Tennessee, Knoxville*

OAB-3060   HQ756   96-25634 CIP
LaRossa, Ralph. **The modernization of fatherhood: a social and political history.** Chicago, 1997. 287p index afp ISBN 0-226-46903-4, $55.00; ISBN 0-226-46904-2 pbk, $18.95

A family sociologist turned historian, LaRossa has long concentrated on parenthood in his writings, e.g., *Becoming a Parent* (1986). Here he carefully and knowledgeably crafts a social and political history of fatherhood, briefly providing a background in Colonial times. His primary question is how and why American fatherhood was transformed during the Machine Age (1918-1941), particularly in the 1920s and 1930s. LaRossa has sifted books, letters, magazines, newspapers, and organizational histories to show the character of their times. The well-selected evidence is thus used to illustrate cognitive schemas of fatherhood and to differentiate these from contemporary behaviors of fathers. The work challenges some assumptions held by scholars about fathers of the past. The strong interconnection between the changes in fatherhood and motherhood makes this book, secondarily, also a history of motherhood, similar to Robert L. Griswold's *Fatherhood in America* (CH, Dec'93). Notes are well contextualized and scholarly in their execution. The index is standard, but the ten pictorial illustrations add interest. This solid and scholarly work is an essential item for the reading list of family sociologists and family historians alike. Upper-division undergraduates and above.—*Y. Peterson, Saint Xavier University*

OAB-3061   HQ1075   93-23459 CIP
Lorber, Judith. **Paradoxes of gender.** Yale, 1994. 424p bibl index afp ISBN 0-300-05807-1, $30.00

Lorber's book is a tour de force. Founding editor of the leading journal on gender issues in sociology and the other social sciences, *Gender & Society* (v.1: 1987-), Lorber has a vast knowledge of cutting edge research being done in a wide variety of social sciences. In this study she summarizes that enormous body of knowledge and organizes it into a coherent theoretical framework, one that is radically different from the conventional understanding of "sex roles" and is coming to be known in social science circles as the "gender perspective." The book's organizational skeleton (three main sections entitled "Producing Gender," "Gender in Practice," and "The Politics of Gender") reflects the strongly social constructionist view of this perspective. For example, "Producing Gender" is not about socialization but about ideology, culture, and sexuality as they shape a largely illusory view of gender as dichotomous biological categories. Lorber has constructed as coherent, well-written, and persuasive an account of this perspective as one could hope to find. The book will be helpful to specialists; its clear prose and well-chosen examples will also make it accessible to students.—*M. M. Ferree, University of Connecticut*

OAB-3062   HQ76   96-16191 MARC
Mondimore, Francis Mark. **A natural history of homosexuality.** Johns Hopkins, 1996. 282p bibl index afp ISBN 0-8018-5349-4, $35.00; ISBN 0-8018-5440-7 pbk, $15.95

Mondimore's book is an excellent introductory survey of the present status of research on homosexuality. Mondimore (Univ. of North Carolina, Chapel Hill), a practicing psychiatrist, succinctly covers historical, anthropological, sociological, genetic, embryological, hormonal, and psychotherapeutic data and theories in a way clearly understandable to the general reader as well as the specialist. He points out how bigotry against gays and lesbians in past and present Western civilization exploded at times during movements such as the Inquisition and Nazism, and shows how vestiges of such homophobia still poison some of the psychotherapeutic literature and legal sanctions. One chapter distinguishes homosexuality from transvestitism, transgenderism, transsexualism, and bisexuality. The information in the book is basic, accurate, wide-ranging, up-to-date, and compassionate. Readership. all levels.—*R. W. Smith, California State University, Northridge*

OAB-3063   HQ1206   92-13770 CIP
O'Connor, Pat. **Friendships between women: a critical review.** Guilford, 1992. 228p bibl index afp ISBN 0-89862-976-4, $44.95; ISBN 0-89862-981-0 pbk, $17.95

Friendship is an understudied topic because social science is affected by sexist and homophobic attitudes, as is the rest of society. O'Connor draws attention to the importance of studying female friendship in her well-written, carefully argued overview of the literature. She devotes one chapter to theoretical perspectives; one each to friendships among married women, single women, and elderly women; one to a comparison of female friendships with kin relationships, work-based friendships, and lesbian relationships; and a concluding chapter on directions for future research. O'Connor challenges conventional views, including the belief that female friendships complement marital relationships. Each chapter contains detailed vignettes and concludes with a useful starting point for new research. O'Connor's most provocative revelation is that the study of friendships has also been hampered by ageism, reflected in the fact that the female friendships that are personally and socially most meaningful can be found among elderly women, at least in contemporary Western societies. Advanced undergraduate; graduate; faculty.—*S. Reinharz, Brandeis University*

OAB-3064   HQ27   95-13185 CIP
Odem, Mary E. **Delinquent daughters: protecting and policing adolescent female sexuality in the United States, 1885-1920.**

North Carolina, 1995. 265p bibl index afp ISBN 0-8078-2215-9, $39.95; ISBN 0-8078-4528-0 pbk, $14.95

Odem's important book provides a model for the study of state institutions and issues of social control. Odem focuses on multiple efforts to define and regulate adolescent female sexuality in the US between 1885 and 1920. Beginning with national campaigns to reform "age of consent" laws, the author illustrates enforcement of those laws by examining court records from Los Angeles and Alameda Counties (California). In addition to readability, the beauty of this book is, first, its careful interweaving of sexual ideologies, the moral norms of reformers, and the development and application of regulatory laws. Second, and perhaps more important, is Odem's careful treatment of all the protagonists in the story—state officials, middle-class moral reformers, the girls, and their families. The relationships among these groups of individuals are never static, their aims and goals not always in agreement, and, above all, the consequences of their actions often unintended. Always taking into account class, ethnic, and racial differences and using examples of these whenever possible, Odem reassesses working-class moral codes and family relations. The complexity and the clarity of argument, the detailed research, and the compelling narrative make this a book that could, and *should*, be read by the beginner and the expert in a variety of fields.—*M. J. Slaughter, University of New Mexico*

OAB-3065   HQ536   96-4677 CIP
Roschelle, Anne R. **No more kin: exploring race, class and gender in family networks.** Sage Publications, CA, 1997. 235p bibl index afp (Understanding families, 8) ISBN 0-7619-0158-2, $45.00; ISBN 0-7619-0159-0 pbk, $21.95

Roschelle's study reveals clear thinking and direct communication of highly complex issues. Her carefully executed and compelling research uses an integrative approach addressing simultaneously how gender, class, and race affect the social organization of families. Network theory has moved a long way since Elizabeth Bott's classic study *Family and Social Network* (1959). Working with data from the National Survey of Families and Households, Roschelle disentangles the determinants of informal social support networks for African American, Puerto Rican, Chicano, and non-Hispanic white families. She presents and critiques the cultural, structural, and integrative approaches, while evaluating the veracity of major empirical contributions in these areas. This work is sufficiently significant to stir controversies among adherents of both the structural and cultural perspectives in family research, as her study contradicts fundamental findings from both perspectives. Roschelle suggests future research avenues and addresses the theoretical and policy implications of her work. An absolute must for professionals and upper level students in any area of family science.—*Y. Peterson, Saint Xavier University*

OAB-3066   HQ1090   92-53247 CIP
Rotundo, E. Anthony. **American manhood: transformations in masculinity from the Revolution to the modern era.** Basic Books, 1993. 382p index ISBN 0-465-01409-7, $25.00

An important, well-documented, superbly written addition to the literature on gender. Rotundo describes the evolution of the male role among white, middle-class Yankee men during the 19th century (with "Yankee" being defined as New England, New York, and the northern Midwest to the Mississippi). These males were disproportionately influential in shaping American norms from their own time to the present and so the absence of other groups (e.g., African Americans, Hispanics, Irish immigrants) does not appear to detract from the main purpose of tracing American notions of what "real" men are like. The author's research supports a social constructionist view of masculinity: rather than being a timeless, universal constant, "real manhood" is time-bound, socially relative, and varies as a function of the economic and other societal pressures of the period. Rotundo's observations throw considerable light on the origins of the current definitions of appropriate male behavior. All levels.—*R. W. Smith, California State University, Northridge*

OAB-3067   HQ1240   95-43943 CIP
Sachs, Carolyn E. **Gendered fields: rural women, agriculture, and environment.** Westview, 1996. 205p bibl index afp ISBN 0-8133-2519-6, $54.95; ISBN 0-8133-2520-X pbk, $19.95

Sachs' work is a superb review of material about contemporary women working in agriculture across the globe. Three chapters cover the theoretical and historical background of women in relation to the land. They discuss the feminist approach, and the complexity and impossibility of generalizing across race, nationality, ethnicity, and sexual preference. Specific chapters treat women's connectedness to the land, plants, and animals. A special chapter is devoted to the roles of women on family farms in the US, Africa, and Latin America. A final discussion places women in the context of current global processes of agricultural restructuring. Each chapter is replete with national or cultural-specific references to past research. Sachs, author of *Invisible Farmers: Women in Agricultural Production* (CH, Dec'83), is a rural sociologist who has done research in this area for more than 15 years. *Gendered Fields* brings together the findings of her research with those of other feminist and rural researchers in England, Europe, Latin America, and Africa. It contains an excellent integration of primary and secondary data, with more than 260 citations to relevant work. Essential for those who seek an understanding of the significance of gender in rural society. All levels.—*D. P. Slesinger, University of Wisconsin—Madison*

OAB-3068   HQ1075   95-39468 CIP
Sigel, Roberta S. **Ambition & accommodation: how women view gender relations.** Chicago, 1996. 240p bibl index afp ISBN 0-226-75695-5, $48.00; ISBN 0-226-75696-3 pbk, $16.95

Based on quantitative (telephone survey) and qualitative (nondirective focus group) research, Sigel's goal is to discover how individuals today, particularly women, subjectively experience gender relations. Drawn from a New Jersey sample, her findings show that ordinary American women recognize and are unsettled by their "second-class" status, yet choose individual coping strategies rather than collective, political avenues to address their sense of relative deprivation. Sigel, a political scientist, argues that these women have a "minority consciousness," not a "group consciousness." As the importance of male partnership and family outweigh sisterhood, her data indicate that women share a "common situation" but are not part of a "common cause." Sigel's research provides valuable insights as to why these women are ambivalent about feminism and, less overtly, how the women's movement has not responded to their ways of being and knowing. Exceptionally well written, Sigel's study is both theoretically and methodologically a model of scholarly research. Her book is rich in women's and men's voices and statistical data. It is as much a map of gender relations today as it is a superb example of using complementary research methods. All levels.—*P. E. Herideen, Northeastern University*

OAB-3069   HQ1075   97-102970 MARC
Viney, Ethna. **Dancing to different tunes: sexuality and its misconceptions.** Blackstaff, 1997. 318p bibl index ISBN 0-85640-570-1, $27.95

Despite this book's title, its subject matter is really the history of modern feminism and the varieties of interpretive frameworks that exist in the name of feminism for understanding and changing relationships between men and women. As a pharmacist, freelance writer, and filmmaker, Viney covers the familiar terrain of feminist argument and analysis in a spirited, erudite, and, for the most part, refreshingly nonacademic manner. The problem of achieving equality between men and women in their sexual and intimate lives serves as the occasion for the author to review the many and major feminist analyses and social-political movements that have sought to address the causes and consequences of male dominance and exploitation of women. At the level of sexuality the major "traditional" biological, psychological, and cultural assumptions are challenged and reconfigured by a multiplicity of feminist orientations. In another sense, sexuality is but a lens through which to view the persistence of female subordination to male power in every aspect of social life. An excellent overview of feminist thought for the student of sexuality or the women's movement more generally. All levels.—*M. R. Fowlkes, University of Connecticut*

Social & Behavioral Sciences

OAB-3070   HQ759   91-32331 CIP
Walters, Suzanna Danuta. **Lives together/worlds apart: mothers and daughters in popular culture.** California, 1992. 295p bibl index afp ISBN 0-520-07851-9, $25.00

An exceptional study of the cultural representations that depict the relationship between mothers and their daughters in the US. Walters examines 50 years of discursive practices found in popular movies, television shows, women's magazines, psychoanalysis, feminist writings, and expert literature to isolate the development of a unified cultural narrative. Her analysis pieces together an ideology of the mother-daughter relationship that is grounded in a psychology of separation and conflict. The author then demonstrates how this ideology has been incorporated into current feminist critiques as well as into pro-family politics. The problems of this dominant narrative are discussed along with an alternative reading that emphasizes the rich variations found in the lived experiences of women. Walters has produced a first-rate analysis of how a society's symbolic practices emerge and coalesce to establish a unified cultural reading that not only defines, but also becomes, mundane reality. The book is well written and thoroughly researched. It should appeal to those interested in mass media, feminism, popular culture, and the mother-daughter relationship. Advanced undergraduate; graduate; faculty; professional.—*J. Lynxwiler, University of Central Florida*

OAB-3071   HD6060   96-459 CIP
Webster, Juliet. **Shaping women's work: gender, employment and information technology.** Longman, 1996. 222p bibl index ISBN 0-582-21810-1 pbk, $15.00

Webster (Univ. of East London) has produced a splendid short book that will serve equally well as an undergraduate textbook or primer for policy discussions about women, gender, and technology. One could consider this a companion piece to Judy Wajcman's general treatment of gender and technology, *Feminism Confronts Technology* (CH, Mar'92), in that Webster's work focuses on technological change and women's labor practices and employment, although that assessment might dismiss the theoretical contributions that Webster makes in her own right. Readers might be concerned about three issues. The first is that there is perhaps too little discussion of general theories of economic systems and gender; the second, that its largely British context, despite solid analyses of globalization, requires an extra effort to connect to US trends; third, the text drags in the middle. Nonetheless, this is an excellent resource for discussions on gender and technology, the international division of labor, and the roles that advanced information technologies have played in employment sectors and women's work experiences. Highly recommended. Upper-division undergraduates and above.—*J. L. Croissant, University of Arizona*

OAB-3072   HQ1075   93-23909 CIP
Weiss, Penny A. **Gendered community: Rousseau, sex, and politics.** New York University, 1993. 189p bibl index afp ISBN 0-8147-9263-4, $40.00

Weiss (political science, Purdue) sets out, first, to shed light upon Rousseau's internal consistency and his interpretations of gender, justice, freedom, community, and equality; and second, to advance feminist theory through the study of Rousseau. Her book's main argument is "that Rousseau's defense of sexual differentiation is based on the contribution he perceives it can make to the establishment of community, and not on an appeal to some versions of 'natural' sex differences." Weiss examines Rousseau's program of sex differentiation and his educational plans for Emile and Sophie; rejects the biological determinist interpretation of his antifeminism; and argues instead that Rousseau's sex roles are designed as means to community. In her concluding chapters Weiss argues that Rousseau's sex-role strategy is self-defeating, and she compares the social agenda of feminists and communitarians from Plato to MacIntyre and from Sappho to Daly. Clear, rich, and coherent, the book succeeds splendidly in its intent to be "accessible and useful" to Rousseau scholars, feminists, and all those concerned with "gender equality, freedom and community." Essential for every library where these are live issues! Concisely written and well produced, with helpful notes, bibliography, and index. General and academic readers at all levels.—*H. J. John, Trinity College (DC)*

OAB-3073   HQ1745   92-17852 MARC
White, Sarah C. **Arguing with the crocodile: gender and class in Bangladesh.** Zed Books/University Press, Dhaka, 1992. (Dist. by Humanities) 186p bibl index ISBN 1-85649-085-8, $49.95; ISBN 1-85649-086-6 pbk, $19.95

White challenges the traditional assumptions of developmental strategies designed by Western planners to chart and fund technological growth in the Third World. In this work based on her 1985-86 fieldwork in Kurimput ("the village of the crocodile"), Bangladesh, she seeks to counterbalance the male-oriented and Western-aid dominated discourse of class and power relations by taking readers into the lives of women from diverse background speaking for themselves. White's poignant portrayal of women's work, flowing with as well as against the daily currents of social interactions, shows how the bureaucratic planners and academicians have erred in artificially isolating "women's issues" from the broader social network of rural life. To correct this dangerous omission, White criticizes the major arguments in debates on women's work, questions how well the current donors represent the recipient's priorities, and how rural Bangladesh women themselves interpret what they do. Although academically rigorous, White's writing is lively and smooth. Highly recommended. General; advanced undergraduate; faculty; professional.—*N. N. Kalia, SUNY College at Buffalo*

OAB-3074   HQ1154   94-26260 CIP
Whittier, Nancy. **Feminist generations: the persistence of the radical women's movement.** Temple University, 1995. 309p index afp ISBN 1-56639-281-0, $49.95; ISBN 1-56639-282-9 pbk, $18.95

Like many other university communities in the late 1960s and early '70s, Columbus, Ohio, was a hotbed of political and cultural activism. A resurgent women's movement—especially its radical feminist element—flourished in that environment. Whittier located and talked with 34 women who were the "core" of the radical feminist community in Columbus. Her informants' descriptions of their work in the movement, accounts of organizational success and failure, portraits of other activists, and recollections of debates, fights, and splits provide the basis of her reconstruction of their collective history. Whittier argues that these self-portraits reveal key differences in the collective identities and aims of women who entered the movement at different times. Using the "generational perspectives" of successive cohorts of activists, she theorizes about transformation and persistence in insurgent ideology and the continuation of social movements even through periods when activism and resources decline. The analysis of intracohort tensions is particularly interesting because almost two-thirds of her informants are lesbians. This intelligent and well-written book is highly recommended for its significant contribution to women's studies and social movements. All levels.—*N. B. Rosenthal, SUNY College at Old Westbury*

■ Race & Ethnicity

OAB-3075   E184   93-19612 CIP
Abalos, David T. **The Latino family and the politics of transformation.** Praeger, 1993. 164p bibl index afp ISBN 0-275-94527-8, $49.95; ISBN 0-275-94809-9 pbk, $16.95

Abalos draws heavily from the Jungean conceptualization of archetypes, and especially from Manfred Halpern, in presenting an important vision of the Latino family in the US. His discussion of the Latino family is prefaced by a long chapter in which the theory of transformation, developed by Halpern, is explained. This theory is then applied throughout the rest of the book in what Abalos describes as the "struggle to analyze and develop a politics of transformation for *la familia Latina* in the United States." In chapter four, the author captures the root of many of the problems experienced by Latinos through an excellent analysis of male/female relationships in the midst of breakdown and de-formation. The book is refreshing; Abalos seeks solutions for old problems in a new and creative manner, one that specifically calls for a profound and transforming spiritual journey. Strongly recommended for upper-division undergraduates and graduate students in the helping professions, and for general readers interested in personal and spiritual transformation.—*E. Bastida, University of Texas—Pan American*

OAB-3076   E185   93-36787 MARC
Allen, Theodore W. **The invention of the white race: v.1: Racial oppression and social control.** Verso, 1994. 310p index ISBN 0-86091-480-1, $59.95; ISBN 0-86091-660-X pbk, $19.95

In this richly researched and highly suggestive analysis of Irish oppression in Britain and African American oppression in the slave-holding US, Allen argues that racism is best understood in both instances as a deliberate system of in-group cooptation and out-group superexploitation that maintained ruling-class hegemony. This study is elegantly conceived. Allen first depicts the Protestant ascendancy as a case in which a key segment of the Irish population was wooed into accepting prevailing inequities in Ulster by the perceived compensations of racial and religious privilege. He then proposes a similar paradigm of racism as social control for the class- and race-stratified society of North America ("Ulster writ large"). Finally, reenter the Irish, this time not as defamed and racially oppressed Celts in Ireland, but rather as immigrants eligible for the privileges of "whiteness" in the US—participants in a dynamic of racial oppression similar to the one they had so recently fled. The study thus provides a compelling illustration of "the relativity of race." Indispensable for readers interested in the disposition of power in Ireland, in the genesis of racial oppression in the US, or in the fluidity of "race" and the historic vicissitudes of "whiteness." Upper-division undergraduates and above.—*M. F. Jacobson, SUNY College at Stony Brook*

OAB-3077   E185   96-7801 CIP
Delgado, Richard. **The coming race war?: and other apocalyptic tales of America after affirmative action and welfare.** New York University, 1996. 198p afp ISBN 0-8147-1877-9, $24.95

This is one of the best books published on US racial stratification and conflict in the last decade. Delgado is a distinguished legal scholar and one of the founders of the perspective called critical race theory. The book is framed as a fictional dialogue between a young black law school professor and his former teacher, and explores with great depth and insight many racial problems facing the US. Issues range from the character of empathy across racial-ethnic lines (and the false empathy of many whites, including white liberals), to the role that "merit" standards play in perpetuating white privileges rooted in slavery and segregation, to specious First Amendment arguments against the regulation of racist hate speech, to the attacks on people of color by racist and anti-immigrant laws and legislatures. The central theme is the ways in which white supremacy, under a variety of white conservative and white liberal disguises, continues to dominate the language, resources, and practices of US democracy. One important argument is that many white leaders are intentionally dismantling programs helpful to people of color, such as affirmative action and employment programs, to provoke an aggressive response from people of color, which in turn will be used to justify greater white repression. The book concludes that whites today are destroying the hope for real democracy and increasing the likelihood of a race war in the US. Endnotes. All levels.—*J. R. Feagin, University of Florida*

OAB-3078   HM291   92-39455 CIP
Dijk, Teun A. van. **Elite discourse and racism.** Sage, 1993. 320p bibl indexes (Sage series on race and ethnic relations, 6) ISBN 0-8039-5070-5, $44.00; ISBN 0-8039-5071-3 pbk, $21.95

Using an interdisciplinary approach to "discourse analysis," Dutch scholar van Dijk examines how elites in several race-centered North American and European societies reproduce white domination and racism. He draws examples from the writings and speeches of elites in the political, corporate, academic, educational, and media spheres of the US, the Netherlands, and Britain. Van Dijk demonstrates convincingly how, in the late 20th century, even as "power elites"

reject the most overt and blatant forms of racist speech and behavior, nevertheless they are instrumental in maintaining a social structure whereby the dominant white group controls nonwhite groups, thus legitimating their own power. This study of "elite racism," which can be subtle but is in fact pervasive and sometimes mundane, is an important contribution to the study of racism and a fine example of comparative race and ethnic studies. Intended for undergraduate and graduate students and scholars, it can also be profitably read by anyone interested in understanding the multiple manifestations of racism in US and European societies.—*E. Hu-DeHart, University of Colorado at Boulder*

OAB-3079   ND1432   94-32080 CIP
Durand, Jorge. **Miracles on the border: retablos of Mexican migrants to the United States,** by Jorge Durand and Douglas S. Massey. Arizona, 1995. 216p bibl index afp ISBN 0-8165-1471-2, $50.00; ISBN 0-8165-1497-6 pbk, $24.95

As used here, *retablos* are small votive paintings, usually on tin, left at religious shrines to offer thanks to a Catholic image for a favor (or "miracle") received. They constitute a distinctive genre of Mexican folk art, and this book is a significant (and enjoyable) contribution to understanding them at various levels. At the aesthetic level, there are 40 excellent color plates or *retablos*, with full transcription and translation of the text of each. For the historically oriented reader, there is a brief, clear, and well-organized summary of the evolution of *retablos*, both in the Old World and in Mexico. In addition, the authors make a novel contribution through a sociological interpretation, based on analysis of supplicant gender, image of supplication, subject or theme, period of migration, and geographic distribution of origins in Mexico and destinations in US, insofar as those are mentioned. In plausible but not heavy-handed terms, the paintings are thereby restored partially to the social, cultural, and psychological context in which they were conceived, and readers gain some insight into the many meanings—both positive and negative—of migration to the US from the perspective of those who lived it. A well-written book, with a good bibliography and an adequate index, this is an exciting example of how humanistic data and approaches can fruitfully be integrated with quantification and social science interpretations, yielding fresh insights into human behavior. All levels.—*D. B. Heath, Brown University*

OAB-3080   E184   91-37374 CIP
Espiritu, Yen Le. **Asian American panethnicity: bridging institutions and identities.** Temple University, 1992. 222p bibl index afp ISBN 0-87722-955-4, $34.95

Although Asians have immigrated to the US for a long time, it was not until the late 1960s that young Asians began to construct an "Asian American" identity. With rapidly growing numbers and enormous ethnic (national origin) diversity within this racial community, Espiritu notes that this identity is, in fact, *panethnic*, or pan-Asian in nature. Besides providing an innovative theoretical model for the study of ethnicity and panethnicity (which this reviewer believes can be applied equally well to Latinos as to Asian Americans), Espiritu examines pan-Asian organizations formed as a response to American racism or as a way to promote and protect individual and group interests. Issues such as educational discrimination, legal redress, anti-Asian violence, social services, and affirmative action, as well as cooperation and conflict among Asian groups themselves, are explored. Making judicious use of statistical data and case studies, Espiritu has written an important book that is clear, graceful, and jargon-free. All levels.—*E. Hu-DeHart, University of Colorado at Boulder*

OAB-3081   F319   92-2538 CIP
Fendrich, James Max. **Ideal citizens: the legacy of the Civil Rights Movement.** State University of New York, 1993. 202p bibl index ISBN 0-7914-1323-3, $49.50; ISBN 0-7914-1324-1 pbk, $16.95

Fendrich successfully lays to rest some of the myths about the student activists of the 1960s, e.g., that they were mostly white elitists and later in life either sold out or became embittered totalitarian radicals. A sociologist, Fendrich identified African American and Anglo American campus activists of the 1960s (apparently mostly at Florida State), then studied them and control groups in longitudinal studies in the 1970s and '80s. He amplifies his survey data with anecdotal evidence from interviews, but a full understanding of his work requires familiarity with regression analysis. His study indicates that the activists of the 1960s tended to become materially successful, and also continued to be effective political and social activists. By the late 1980s, he says, black and white students both turned into "ideal citizens," that is, "informed, active, and demanding." The political views of the two groups were very similar—left of center but not radical. The material on black activists and their subsequent lives is a major contribution. Recommended. Advanced undergraduate; graduate; faculty.—*T. H. Baker, University of Arkansas at Little Rock*

OAB-3082　　　　HT1521　　　　92-36107 CIP
Goldberg, David Theo. **Racist culture: philosophy and the politics of meaning.** Blackwell, 1993. 313p bibl index afp ISBN 0-631-18077-X, $49.95

Goldberg's book is a compelling, definitive postmodern study of race and racism. Goldberg exhibits impressive, painstaking scholarship. He draws from sources that are thorough, deep, wide, and current to establish that "racial definition" and "racist articulation" emerge only with the institution of modernity. The book argues convincingly that race entered modernity as an "identity of anonymity," as "a concept virtually vacuous in its own right," which "has been able more or less continually since its emergence to naturalize difference and to normalize exclusions." Goldberg's prescription for improvement is to advocate a "neopragmatic antiracism," which he counterposes to the "nonracialism" of liberals (and postmodern bourgeois liberals). His style combines clear and careful erudition with the occasional clever turn of phrase and biting or impassioned comment. This work is highly recommended. It holds great promise as a watershed for further fruitful research, discussion and—one would hope—change on matters pertaining to race. Undergraduates and above.—*W. P. Nye, Hollins College*

OAB-3083　　　　E184　　　　94-1892 CIP
Gutiérrez, David G. **Walls and mirrors: Mexican Americans, Mexican immigrants, and the politics of ethnicity.** California, 1995. 320p bibl index afp ISBN 0-520-08322-9, $40.00; ISBN 0-520-20219-8 pbk, $15.00

Gutiérrez's prodigiously researched and well-written book deals with race and immigration in an innovative way, with productive results. It specifically examines Mexican American conceptualizations of, and opinions on, the debate over Mexican immigration to the US. A US-born historian of Mexican American heritage himself, Gutiérrez explores how this very Mexican American identity has been historically and socially constructed in the dual contexts of massive and continuous Mexican immigration to the US, and of US labor history and racism (white supremacy). Pressured to identify with Mexicans while struggling against racism and to advance their civil rights as citizens of the US, many Mexican Americans are understandably ambivalent about Mexican immigration. To explore how this complex and difficult relationship affects Mexican American identity as well as Mexican immigration, Gutiérrez focuses on the positions, tactics, and rhetoric of Mexican Americans and Mexican immigrant activists (primarily in California and Texas) from 1848, when one-third of Mexico became the US Southwest, to the militant politics of the Chicano movement in the 1960s and '70s, concluding with the divisive controversies surrounding the immigration debate in the 1990s. In the end, Gutiérrez concludes, Mexican Americans cannot easily disconnect from the historical reality of their links to Mexican immigrants, and strongly suggests that they should not. Upper-division undergraduates and above.—*E. Hu-DeHart, University of Colorado at Boulder*

OAB-3084　　　　E184　　　　96-35678 CIP
Hing, Bill Ong. **To be an American: cultural pluralism and the rhetoric of assimilation.** New York University, 1997. 243p index afp ISBN 0-8147-3523-1, $29.95

Hing's book is about what the author rightly calls "one of the most potent periods of anti-immigrant fervor in the United States." He refers not to the 1890s, when nativists, xenophobes, exclusionists, and restrictionists were railing against the influx of "unassimilable aliens" and "inferior breeds" (namely, Irish and Italian Catholics and East European Jews), but the 1990s. Today the faces of the petitioners and their countries of origin are different, but even though they come to a society that has downplayed Draconian Americanization, officially celebrates diversity, and emphasizes that all have a place here, the resentment in many quarters is alarmingly similar. Central to the concerns are economic and cultural matters. There are calls for the use of English only and greater control of our borders. There is Proposition 187 in California, a bill that excludes undocumented children from public school and bars their families from medical care. Hing, an immigration lawyer, carefully looks at the challenges, national and regional. Relying on hard data from historical records, government surveys, independent studies, and labor market analyses, he weighs the costs and benefits of immigration. Particularly significant is his discussion of separist ideologies, interethnic rivalry, and the thorny problem of competition between African Americans and immigrants. General readers; upper-division undergraduates and above.—*P. I. Rose, Smith College*

OAB-3085　　　　E98　　　　92-13590 CIP
Jaffe, A.J. **The first immigrants from Asia: a population history of the North American Indians.** Plenum, 1992. 333p bibl index ISBN 0-306-43952-2, $39.50

Jaffe blazes a trail subsequent scholars interested in the historical evolution of America's original inhabitants—American Indians—must traverse for their research efforts to be credible. The book is a valuable examination of conditions, e.g., accelerated population changes engendered by atypical demographic transitions, that are responsible for the contemporary demographic position of "Amerindians." Jaffe's analytical framework harkens back to the approach used by the exemplary scholar of social change, William F. Ogburn. The result is a masterful comprehension of "how and why" the first immigrants are present in North America. The breadth of the examination ranges as far back as Homo erectus man or woman and stops at Homo sapiens. Between the two is an intellectual odyssey covering a plethora of physical and social changes that are as apparent among contemporary Amerindians as they are among the general American population, e.g., low fertility rates. This book is required reading for demographers, archaeologists, and anthropologists. However, nonacademics will also find it a valuable resource for understanding a population whose presence in the Americas has heretofore been understood through myths rather than facts. Undergraduate; graduate; faculty.—*R. Stewart, SUNY College at Buffalo*

OAB-3086　　　　HD2346　　　　95-3418 CIP
Light, Ivan. **Race, ethnicity, and entrepreneurship in urban America,** by Ivan Light and Carolyn Rosenstein. Aldine de Gruyter, 1995. 255p bibl index afp ISBN 0-202-30505-8, $47.95; ISBN 0-202-30506-6 pbk, $23.95

In this example of social science research at its best, Light and Rosenstein present well-written and thorough reviews of the major theories and issues affecting the rate and form of entrepreneurship in urban America. They systematically test these theories generally and many of their specific propositions using contemporary and historical data. They provide an evenhanded treatment of various perspectives; debunk several popular myths about self-employment, jobs, and ethnic/minority groups; and identify important and sometimes counterintuitive policy implications. The book has some minor problems—it discusses entrepreneurship but uses data on self-employment, it examines data only on cities, and nonacademics will be annoyed by some tedious (but thankfully brief) passages of statistical exposition. However, it should be required reading for academics, economic development employees, government officials, and everyone interested in improving the economic conditions of their communities. Upper-division undergraduates and above.—*P. McGuire, University of Toledo*

OAB-3087   E185   92-13889 CIP

Massey, Douglas S. **American apartheid: segregation and the making of the underclass,** by Douglas S. Massey and Nancy A. Denton. Harvard, 1993. 292p index afp ISBN 0-674-01820-6, $29.95

Using clear, easily understood statistical data, Massey and Denton contend that together race and class exacerbate residential segregation. Blacks face a level of segregation significantly higher than any other group in US history. Since the 1960s Civil Rights Movement, the idea that segregation exists in American society has been ignored; however, the evidence is clear that not only does it continue, but there has also been little progress made toward ending it. Massey and Denton determine that prejudice and discrimination force African Americans to stay in segregated communities. Arguing that the situation equals apartheid, the authors maintain that unless there is a national commitment to equal opportunity in housing, African Americans will continue to be denied access to the mainstream, therefore suffering disproportionately from drug abuse, family disorganization, and crime. *American Apartheid* builds on William Julius Wilson's *The Truly Disadvantaged* (CH, Apr'88), furthering a dispassionate study of the underclass. An incredibly readable book that must be studied by all Americans—liberal and conservative, black and white. All levels.— *D. R. Jamieson, Ashland University*

OAB-3088   E98   95-23948 CIP

Nagel, Joane. **American Indian ethnic renewal: Red power and the resurgence of identity and culture.** Oxford, 1996. 298p bibl index afp ISBN 0-19-508053-X, $45.00

In this long-awaited study of the Red Power movement, Nagel offers a penetrating critical inquiry into the complex changes that have occurred as a result of the resurgence of individual and communal ethnic identification among American Indians. Reflecting Nagel's intimate familiarity with both a social movement that took off in the 1960s and its aftermath, the book provides a detailed and nuanced assessment of the impact of Red Power on Indian ethnicity. Although Nagel recognizes that the dramatic increase in the number of people who identify themselves as Indian cannot be accounted for solely on the basis of changes in fertility and death rates, she persuasively illustrates how the Red Power movement stimulated an increased propensity for this identification. Simultaneously, the movement helped to generate a cultural renaissance, and played a key role in reforming government policies. Nagel employs a sophisticated version of social constructionist theory (see also her 1994 article in *Social Problems*) to account for those changes, weaving into this perspective a critical appreciation of two other contemporary theoretical currents, rational choice and post-modernism. This is an exceptional book that should be considered essential reading for all ethnic studies scholars. Upper-division undergraduates and above.—*P. Kivisto, Augustana College (IL)*

OAB-3089   E185   92-16205 CIP

Semmes, Clovis E. **Cultural hegemony and African American development.** Praeger, 1992. 272p bibl index afp ISBN 0-275-93923-5, $47.95

Semmes (African American studies, Eastern Michigan Univ.) addresses the logical and empirical underpinnings and the major conceptual issues in the ongoing development of Afrocentric and African American studies. Semmes places primary emphasis on developing a theory of culture. He begins by looking at cultural hegemony in the African American experience and reviewing Afrocentric writings. Semmes revisits the ideas of E. Franklin Frazier and Harold Cruse in regard to a theory of culture and also examines intergroup relations, the mass media, religion, and health as they relate to cultural viability. Semmes then reviews cultural revitalization efforts. The book concludes with an examination of knowledge production in African American studies. This is an excellent primer for anyone wishing to understand the dramatic developments in Afrocentric thought in the US since 1990. This reviewer's only criticism is that this book is unattractive and somewhat hard to read because of its nonproportional spacing and printed typescript. Despite appearances, this book is a major work. Excellent notes. All levels.—*J. R. Feagin, University of Florida*

OAB-3090   E185   92-19935 CIP

Staples, Robert. **Black families at the crossroads: challenges and prospects,** by Robert Staples and Leanor Boulin Johnson. Jossey-Bass, 1993. 293p bibl index afp ISBN 1-55542-486-4, $37.95

Staples and Johnson's study is a watershed contribution that fills a significant gap in the literature. The book includes a compendious overview of numerous issues relevant to the African American family. The authors begin by differentiating between historical fact and contemporary fiction, setting the stage for an eloquent elucidation of the critical areas of importance in studying and developing theories about the African American family. They demonstrate that it is essential for African American families to be afforded the opportunity to earn adequate income from their labor to improve the overall quality of life among family members. Staples and Johnson also discuss the normative diversity involved in sexual expression within African American families, the alternative life-styles in dating and courtship practices among African Americans, and gender differences and their implications for black male-female relationships. The final three issues explored are marital patterns and interactions, parenting, and kinship and community support. In all, the book is a comprehensive and successful attempt to provide a systematic analysis of the structure and functioning of the African American family. Advanced undergraduate; graduate; faculty; professional.—*R. Stewart, SUNY College at Buffalo*

OAB-3091   F574   96-13694 CIP

Sugrue, Thomas J. **The origins of the urban crisis: race and inequality in postwar Detroit.** Princeton, 1996. 375p index afp ISBN 0-691-01101-X, $35.00

In this first-rate account Sugrue explores the long-term nature of racial prejudice that exploded in the 1967 Detroit riots. He begins by examining the home front during WW II and the long road of struggle to implement civil rights. Supported by extensive research, he maps housing patterns and employment opportunities to provide the spatial dynamic essential to understanding the context of urban neighborhoods and territorial conflict. With insight and elegance, Sugrue describes the street-by-street warfare to maintain housing values against the perceived encroachment of blacks trying desperately to escape the underbuilt and overcrowded slums. The situation became a contest of "homeowners rights versus civil rights" by the 1950s, a coded confrontation of white against black. Even when migration to newer neighborhoods was possible, true upward mobility was thwarted by the flight of white, blue-collar ethnics to newer neighborhoods, plunging property values for black homeowners downward. Sugrue also points out that the deindustrialization of Detroit began in the 1950s with new plant construction. Increased automation in these plants and reduced overtime in the older ones spelled a quick downward spiral for black workers, who dominated the ranks of unskilled wage earners. Upper-division undergraduates and above.—*J. Kleiman, University of Wisconsin Centers*

OAB-3092   F790   96-10100 CIP

Vélez-Ibáñez, Carlos G. **Border visions: Mexican cultures of the southwest United States.** Arizona, 1996. 360p bibl index afp ISBN 0-8165-1684-7 pbk, $19.95

Vélez-Ibáñez is one of the pioneers in the creation and promotion of a now fashionable "border crossing" metaphor in social sciences. His most recent and comprehensive book poignantly introduces and/or develops several concepts highly valuable to understanding the dynamics of border populations, e.g., funds of knowledge, the search for cultural space and place, the imposition of a "commodity identity" upon the Mexican population of the region, among others. Although the author describes the struggles and vibrant survival strategies of the border population, he is not unaware of the dark side of the picture (e.g., the overrepresentation of Mexicans in statistics of crime, mental illness, poverty, and the like), which he calls the "distribution of sadness" among Mexicans in the Southwest. One of the most important aims of the book is to show how "imaginary political borders do not define the historical and cultural mosaic of this region nor of its Mexican population in the present." The

Social & Behavioral Sciences

complexity and the clarity of argument, the detailed research, and the compelling narrative make this a highly recommended book for all levels.—*P. Vila, University of Texas at El Paso*

OAB-3093   E184   96-10053 CIP
Wilson, Carter A. **Racism: from slavery to advanced capitalism.** Sage Publications, CA, 1996. 271p bibl index afp (Sage series on race and ethnic relations, 7) ISBN 0-8039-7336-5, $44.00; ISBN 0-8039-7337-3 pbk, $21.95

Wilson (political science, Univ. of Toledo) provides a historical overview of the development of racism in the US. His multidimensional look at racial oppression is a solid, provocative review of existing literatures on racism in economics, psychoanalysis, sociology, and history. Wilson explores the historical origins of racism in feudalism and Christianity, the character and development of slavery in the US, debt peonage and aversive racism, and the relationship of industrial capitalism to past and present racism. The book draws substantially on ideas of dominative, aversive, and metaracism developed in the earlier work of Joel Kovel. Although the study is too eclectic in places and does not develop its own model clearly throughout, there are excellent and documented discussions of historical and current racism, as well as first-rate critiques of the recent work of conservative ideologues such as Dinesh D'Souza, Richard Herrnstein, and Charles Murray. Good bibliography and index. All levels.—*J. R. Feagin, University of Florida*

■ Social Problems

OAB-3094   HV881   96-36013 CIP
Ashby, LeRoy. **Endangered children: dependency, neglect, and abuse in American history.** Twayne, 1997. 258p bibl index afp ISBN 0-8057-4100-3, $28.95

Ashby has produced an outstanding work on the history of child dependency, neglect, and abuse. Clearly written and deeply researched in secondary sources and unpublished dissertations, Ashby's book traces the historical origins and development of myriad subjects, including the indenture system, orphanages, foster care, adoption, corporal punishment, juvenile justice, mothers' pensions, the growth of the welfare state, and the increasing politicalization of child welfare during the past 25 years. He demonstrates that throughout American history, child welfare reform measures were prompted more by the religious, social, racial, and political prejudices of adults than by humanitarianism. Because child welfare professionals often use dependent children to solve society's social ills, Ashby also shows that on balance, reforms lacked substance or did more harm than good. According to the author, child welfare experts and politicians have repeatedly ignored the real causes of child dependency: poverty and unemployment. With the publication of this masterful synthesis, scholars and the general public will no longer have to rely on two outdated classics, Homer Folks's *The Care of Destitute, Neglected, and Delinquent Children* (1900) and Henry W. Thurston's *The Dependent Child* (1930). All libraries.—*E. W. Carp, Pacific Lutheran University*

OAB-3095   HV699   93-45029 CIP
Bane, Mary Jo. **Welfare realities: from rhetoric to reform,** by Mary Jo Bane and David T. Ellwood. Harvard, 1994. 220p bibl index afp ISBN 0-674-94912-9, $29.95

Bane and Ellwood's assessment of current welfare policy and practice is more readable and less ideological than most. The book benefits greatly from one author's experience "on the ground" inside the welfare system. The book also reflects careful compilation and exposition of available data and research. The work makes a major contribution to policy analysis in its conceptualization of welfare as driven by eligibility determination rather than as focused on rehabilitation and independence. The authors clearly elaborate the current

disincentives to independence and suggest realistic alternatives. The bibliography and appendixes are outstanding and will be of great assistance to the serious welfare scholar. Should be required reading for anyone in public life who has concern for current welfare programs. General readers; graduate students and above.—*F. J. Peirce, emeritus, University of Oklahoma*

OAB-3096   HV6626   95-17454 CIP
Baumrind, Diana. **Child maltreatment and optimal caregiving in social contexts.** Garland, 1995. 175p bibl indexes afp (Michigan State University series on children, youth, and families, 1) ISBN 0-8153-1918-5, $27.00

Baumrind demonstrates how scholarly research and practice can be integrated to provide a comprehensive picture of a serious social problem. She draws on several major research studies in this systematic analysis of the etiology and prevention of maltreatment of children. Baumrind offers recommendations for the development of policies to reduce parental abuse and neglect, and formulates a series of critical questions for further investigation. Central to the author's presentation is recognition of the growing disparity between children in poverty and children in affluence. She concludes that basic causes and cures lie in social and structural rather than psychological factors. The text includes two commentaries by seasoned professionals from the field of child welfare, who strongly support Baumrind's findings and add recommendations for policy and program development. This well-written study provides a needed holistic perspective on the problem of child abuse today. Highly recommended for upper-division undergraduates and above.—*M. O. McMahon, East Carolina University*

OAB-3097   HV4506   96-25094 CIP
Dordick, Gwendolyn A. **Something left to lose: personal relations and survival among New York's homeless.** Temple University, 1997. 220p index afp ISBN 1-56639-513-5, $59.95; ISBN 1-56639-514-3 pbk, $17.95

Dardick describes and compares groups of New York City's homeless people in four settings, each of which is the improvised physical and social construction of dwellings in places designed for other purposes. The four are a shantytown with its makeshift squalor; the innards and outside of a huge bus terminal, with its almost ceaseless movement and congestion; a large warehouse-like public shelter, plagued by constant tension and threats of violence; and a small church-run private shelter, which is tightly routinized, saves souls, and inhibits privacy. In each setting, relationships among the homeless are critical both to securing material resources needed for survival and to creating an environment as safe and secure as possible. The respective settings foster characteristic types of social relationships. Thus, the shantytown is the one place where heterosexual marriages and relationships can and do flourish. The public shelter breeds gangs and same-sex "marriages," reminiscent of what one often finds in prisons. The private shelter suits those who are comfortable in a pious and reform-oriented atmosphere. This well-written comparative study is an excellent urban ethnography that contributes significantly to understanding the social and personal lives of the homeless. All levels.—*E. Wellin, University of Wisconsin—Milwaukee*

OAB-3098   HQ759   96-40379 CIP
Edin, Kathryn. **Making ends meet: how single mothers survive welfare and low-wage work,** by Kathryn Edin and Laura Lein. Russell Sage Foundation, 1997. 305p bibl index afp ISBN 0-87154-229-3, $42.50; ISBN 0-87154-234-X pbk, $19.95

Edin (Rutgers Univ.) and Lein (Univ. of Texas, Austin) compared the economic strategies of single mothers on welfare or in low-wage work. This six-year study, supported by the Russell Sage Foundation, involved extensive interviews with 379 mothers in Chicago, Boston, Charleston, and San Antonio. Edin and Lein report that unskilled single mothers holding jobs are financially worse off than their peers on welfare because of increased costs of day care and transportation, and loss of subsidies for medical care and housing. Coping strategies and spending habits of both working and welfare mothers are similar. Both groups are frugal managers whose children, nevertheless, often suffer from hunger and inadequate clothing. Poor mothers rely on network assistance from kin, fathers of their children, and boyfriends. Many supplement their income with off-books employment and use charitable organizations in emergencies. All know chances for real self-sufficiency in unskilled jobs without outside help are limited. Edin and Lein's analysis is scholarly and vivid. Charts and tables are supplemented by clear narrative and case examples. Essential for anyone attempting to critique welfare-to-work reform. Highly recommended. Upper-division undergraduates and above.—*M. E. Elwell, emeritus, Salisbury State University*

OAB-3099 HC110 95-13180 CIP
Gans, Herbert J. **The war against the poor: the underclass and antipoverty policy.** Basic Books, 1995. 195p indexes ISBN 0-465-01990-0, $22.00

Congress and the president are currently engaged in a bipartisan attack on "Welfare as we know it," on welfare recipients specifically and the poor generally. The poor are held responsible not only for their own situation but also for many of the social and economic ills facing the nation. In this insightful and most timely work, Gans says that Americans, to a much greater extent than Western Europeans, seek to characterize the poor as undeserving of public aid. To that end, an evolving series of pejorative labels have been applied to the poor. Gans has devoted the first half of his book to an analysis and description of this labeling process, its history, and its consequences for poor and nonpoor alike. But labeling and blaming the poor, although of considerable use to the nonpoor, are not solutions. In the remainder of his book Gans offers a series of policies aimed at attacking poverty (not the poor) and at undermining the credibility of the notion of undeservingness. Engagingly written, nontechnical, but immensely important, this book should be read by scholars and especially by policy makers and public administrators with an interest in reducing the scope and degree of poverty rather than in scapegoating the poor. All levels.—*K. Hadden, University of Connecticut*

OAB-3100 HV699 94-18800 CIP
Gordon, Linda. **Pitied but not entitled: single mothers and the history of welfare, 1890-1935.** Free Press, 1994. 433p index ISBN 0-02-912485-9, $22.95

Especially during rancorous debate over the nation's welfare system and women's place in it, many libraries should acquire Gordon's excellent book. How, she asks, did aid to single mothers come to be constructed so that it now generates such dissatisfaction? Her answer, sobering for feminists, is that ADC was designed by women activists. It turned out to be unsatisfactory because its early advocates, despite relative personal freedom from gender constraints, were guided by maternalist definitions of women, and because the alliances they made, however understandable, helped guarantee a division between welfare and entitlement programs such as old age insurance. The resulting system was easily overwhelmed by subsequent social changes. Gordon's work is advocacy of expanding welfare, but her approach is characterized by a fair-minded, thoughtful refusal to settle for too easily dichotomized judgments of the past. She painstakingly dissects what she properly insists was a shared gender system, and she looks unblinkingly at racism in its manifold guises. A full summary restatement of Gordon's argument might have made the book more accessible to a broader audience. As it is, this sophisticated, engaged history puts demands on readers but is exceptionally rewarding. Upper-division undergraduate and graduate collections.—*A. Graebner, The College of St. Catherine*

OAB-3101 HD7288 93-39896 CIP
Groth, Paul. **Living downtown: the history of residential hotels in the United States.** California, 1994. 401p bibl index afp ISBN 0-520-06876-9, $35.00

Groth (architectural history, Univ. of California) wants to expand the notion of the "American home." To that end he wrote this fascinating social and cultural history of urban residential hotels. Despite their presence in American cities since the late 18th century, commercial residential hotels have generally been unappreciated and misunderstood. Groth draws on many rich sources to provide a fuller, more positive assessment of the hotels. He focuses on the years 1880 to 1930, when urban reformers actively disparaged the hotels and caused the destruction of many. Rather than viewing the hotels as nuisances, Groth sees them as desperately needed housing resources for resolving the urban housing crisis. Dividing the hotels into four types according to price—the palace hotel, midpriced hotel, rooming house, and cheap lodging house—Groth unearths their important socioeconomic roles. This riveting and important study should become a classic of urban analysis that anyone interested in historical or contemporary urban and housing issues should read. This well-written, solidly researched book is also beautifully produced. All levels.—*W. F. Carroll, Bridgewater State College*

OAB-3102 HV1569 92-50714 CIP
Hillyer, Barbara. **Feminism and disability.** Oklahoma, 1993. 302p bibl index afp ISBN 0-8061-2500-4, $27.95

Hillyer is a lesbian, feminist theorist, and mother of Jennifer, a retarded daughter, now 27 years old, who lives in a supervised setting. This poignant, personal book is an attempt to understand the challenges of Hillyer's daughter's disability for feminist theory. In the process, Hillyer covers a very broad range of topics and reaches a new understanding of herself. The first chapter was written in 1979 and reflects on Jennifer's possibilities. Hillyer then considers women with disabilities *and* the women who care for them. In a particularly useful chapter, she describes the gamut of politically charged terms. Her literature review is massive and well integrated. Hillyer comments on the ways in which biographies and autobiographies have been written concerning people with disabilities. Among other issues, she discusses "pace and time" for people with disabilites in contemporary American culture; grief; mother-blaming; denial and normalization; technologies; caregivers and difference; and recovery programs (they have a great deal to offer and can be reworked so as to not be sexist). Sensitively written and very brave, this book contributes to the growing body of literature on women and disabilities, and will be helpful to anyone working on these issues personally, professionally, or as an advocate.—*S. Reinharz, Brandeis University*

OAB-3103 HN90 96-2109 CIP
Jargowsky, Paul A. **Poverty and place: ghettos, barrios, and the American city.** Russell Sage Foundation, 1997. 288p bibl index afp ISBN 0-87154-405-9, $39.95

Relying almost entirely on US census data, Jargowsky describes in great detail four types of high poverty neighborhoods (census tracts with poverty rates above 40 percent): *ghettos*, whose population is at least two-thirds black; *barrios*, at least two-thirds Hispanic; *white slums*, at least two-thirds white; and *mixed slums*, a residual category. The result is the most complete account available of the complex processes of expansion (usually) and contraction (sometimes) of poverty neighborhoods in US metropolitan areas. The real meat in this book, however, is a sophisticated analysis of why and when high poverty neighborhoods expand or shrink. This analysis contributes to the debate between the political-ideological "right" and "left" over the causes of concentrated poverty, and hence to appropriate approaches to solving the many problems attendant on this concentrated poverty. Jargowsky clearly shows that the fate of high poverty neighborhoods and those living in them is inextricably tied to economic situations prevailing in the metropolitan areas of which they are a part. Accordingly, policies aimed at the poor themselves, more or less in isolation from the complex metropolitan communities of which they are members, are bound to fail. In closing, Jargowsky proposes an array of policies aimed at reducing, if not eliminating, the scope and size of neighborhoods with high concentrations of poor people, and in the process diminishing the impact of the "pathologies" often found in such neighborhoods. Strongly recommended. Upper-division undergraduates and above.—*K. Hadden, University of Connecticut*

OAB-3104   HV4505   93-46424 CIP
Jencks, Christopher. **The homeless.** Harvard, 1994. 161p afp ISBN 0-674-40595-1, $17.95

Jencks (Northwestern Univ.) began this study in 1989 as a review of the literature on homelessness in America and, fortunately, it resulted in a complete treatment of the subject. After discussing the difficulty of defining a "home," Jencks restricts his analysis to the visible homeless, i.e., those people whose presence on the streets upsets the more prosperous people and who sleep in a public (not private) space or shelter during a given week. He estimates approximately 400,000 persons were homeless in 1987-88 and about 324,000 in March 1990, lower than some other figures. Jencks offers four major reasons for homelessness. First, deinstitutionalization and the end of involuntary commitment of patients in mental hospitals, particularly after 1975, resulted in homelessness for some persons. Second, the wide use of crack since the mid-1980s caused some homelessness by making marginally employable adults less employable, consuming the little money available to them, and making social support difficult. Third, the decline in male employment because of the recession and the increase in women who remain unmarried removed the economic support provided by a two-income household. Fourth, widespread urban renewal destroyed many low-cost hotels and rooming houses that were replaced by unaffordable alternatives. In a final chapter, Jencks suggests possible solutions. This is an excellent treatment of the subject without abundant statistics. It should be read by everyone concerned with homelessness. All levels.—*T. E. Steahr, University of Connecticut*

OAB-3105   HV6558   96-48559 CIP
Johnson, Ida M. **Forced sexual intercourse in intimate relationships,** by Ida M. Johnson and Robert T. Sigler. Ashgate/Dartmouth, 1997. 189p bibl indexes ISBN 1-85521-917-4, $63.95

The title of this book signals the authors' intent to broaden the scope of their inquiry beyond the traditional conception of rape. Since the publication of Susan Brownmiller's feminist critique *Against Our Will: Men, Women and Rape* (CH, Feb'76) an immense literature on rape has been produced, with a significant proportion of this literature somewhat polemical in nature. Johnson and Sigler provide a very thorough (if not exhaustive) and dispassionate review of the relevant literature. They systematically explore historical, social, cultural, organizational, and statistical dimensions of forced sexual intercourse, and delineate the characteristics of the parties involved as well as typical circumstances. The authors discuss research they conducted on their own campus, as well as a larger literature on perceptions of rape. They evaluate a range of theories as a basis for the development of their own theoretical model. The model that emerges differentiates the more ambiguous date rape from stranger rape and predatory rape. This study should be exceptionally useful to those seeking a balanced overview of rape-related research, as well as those seeking a point of departure for further research. Upper-division undergraduates and above.—*D. O. Friedrichs, University of Scranton*

OAB-3106   KF547   93-34524 CIP
Mason, Mary Ann. **From father's property to children's rights: the history of child custody in the United States.** Columbia, 1994. 237p index afp ISBN 0-231-08046-8, $29.50

Mason's thoughtful book reminds readers that the history of child custody in the US reflects social conditions and values. Her work combines legal scholarship, social history, and social policy analysis. Mason traces child custody through five historical periods: Colonial English common-law tradition giving fathers rights over children; the first century of the Republic emphasizing "mothers' love"; the Progressive Era reforms (1890-1920); attention to "best interest of the child" (1960-1990); and the current ascendancy of social science in custody decisions. Mason links the changing status of women with child custody issues and points out the persistence of a two-tiered system that provides differently for poor children than for children with supporting parents. Child advocates will note that this carefully researched, readable history documents the failure to place the concerns of children at the center of custody

law and policy. Essential for historians of the American family, social policy analysts, child welfare scholars, or anyone interested in family law and the rights of children. Upper-division undergraduates and above.—*M. E. Elwell, Salisbury State University*

OAB-3107   HV5825   92-38077 CIP
Minkler, Meredith. **Grandmothers as caregivers: raising children of the crack cocaine epidemic,** by Meredith Minkler and Kathleen M. Roe. Sage, 1993. 240p bibl index (Family caregivers applications series, 2) ISBN 0-8039-4846-8, $35.00; ISBN 0-8039-4847-6 pbk, $16.95

Minkler and Roe's study describes 71 older African American women in Oakland, California raising grandchildren whose parents are addicted to crack cocaine. Supported by an extensive literature review, in-depth interviews provide vivid qualitative and quantitative data about these "skipped generation" families, where grandmothers fill roles of absent parents. The authors' research design enabled grandmothers to share both frustrations and rewards of "second time around" caregiving. Their data describes routes to assuming the caregiver role, health and economic status of the grandmothers, and their support networks. Patterns of coping with new responsibilities, such as combining grandchild care with employment and elder or kincare and special problems of crack cocaine addicted families, are discussed. Final chapters consider available support services for grandparent caregivers; analysis of needed social policy changes skillfully moves from "private troubles" to "public issues." This study models thoughtful design, careful scholarship, vivid writing, and cogent recommendations. Spanning traditional fields of social research, women's studies, substance abuse, gerontology, child welfare, and public assistance, the book deserves wide reading. Highly recommended. General; advanced undergraduate; graduate; faculty; professional.—*M. E. Elwell, Salisbury State University*

OAB-3108   HV6626   93-29640 CIP
National Research Council (U.S.). Panel on Research on Child Abuse and Neglect. **Understanding child abuse and neglect.** National Academy Press, 1993. 393p index ISBN 0-309-04889-3, $44.95

This meticulous investigation of child abuse research is organized in a child-oriented framework with an ecological developmental perspective. It examines factors in child, family, or society that influence the occurrence or consequences of child maltreatment, rather than assessing research around categories of maltreatment. Scattered research is gathered and presented under areas of identification, scope, etiology, prevention, consequences, and interventions, a major contribution. The panel's exhaustive investigations should assure this readable, well-organized report a place in every academic library if only for its extensive bibliographies. Each chapter includes recommendations for future research, and concluding chapters discuss infrastructure support necessary to pursue such research. Essential reading for those in the field of child abuse, the report is accessible to undergraduates in many fields as a basic resource. Highly recommended.—*M. E. Elwell, Salisbury State University*

OAB-3109   95-9566 CIP
Pringle, Keith. **Men, masculinities and social welfare.** UCL Press, 1995. (Dist. by Taylor & Francis) 245p bibl index ISBN 1-85728-401-1, $65.00; ISBN 1-85728-402-X pbk, $24.95

All who take seriously the current efforts to transform social work practice, designing strategies that are meaningfully informed about gender, race, age, sexuality, class, and disability, will find this to be a timely and scholarly contribution. Pringle's critique of prevailing approaches is constructed around the most significant publications on masculinity, exploring patterns of domination that are expressed in the organizational culture of social welfare agencies as well as in the actual traumas that bring people to the attention of such agencies. The emphasis shifts between men as welfare users and welfare workers, with balanced concern for how they might learn to counter the oppressive practices that undermine personal, family, community, and organizational well-being. Especially helpful is Pringle's recognition of sexuality as an organizational as well as a personal issue, structuring both interactions in abuse situations and interventions by welfare authorities. Topics include child care and child protection, violent adult crime, and scandals in professional conduct. Carefully reasoned policy suggestions recognize the risks of unintended consequences in contexts so heavily influenced by sexual scripts. The focus is predominately on the UK, with substantial references to the US, supported by an outstanding bibliography. Upper-division undergraduates and above.—*R. Zingraff, Meredith College*

OAB-3110 HM216 92-20497 MARC
Roche, Maurice. **Rethinking citizenship: welfare, ideology and change in modern society.** Polity, 1992. (Dist. by B. Blackwell) 280p bibl index afp ISBN 0-7456-0306-8, $39.95; ISBN 0-7456-0307-6 pbk, $19.95

Roche's title is most appropriate and timely. Commonly held assumptions about citizenship and its very concept are no longer valid. The freestanding nation-state of modern capitalist societies, with an economy responsive to the needs of its citizens and a clear set of national self-interests, is fading in significance. Against this background Roche examines a theme that T.H. Marshall introduced, namely, that in the 20th century citizens of these capitalist societies began to demand, in addition to civil and political rights, social rights. These included access to education, health care, old age insurance, and, more recently, the right to work—in short, the welfare state. It is around this concept that Roche organizes his insightful, challenging, and informative appraisal. He reviews the Left and Right critiques of the welfare state, questioning their assumptions and evaluations of its impact on family and community. What he concludes is that cultural, economic, and political changes are razing the foundations on which nation-state citizenship is built. A significant book that should be required reading by anyone concerned with social policy and social policy analysis. Its clear writing and careful organization grant the nonspecialist access to the book's astute arguments. General; undergraduate; graduate; faculty.—*J. R. Hudson, Pennsylvania State University, Harrisburg*

OAB-3111 HV4505 91-43980 CIP
Snow, David A. **Down on their luck: a study of homeless street people,** by David A. Snow and Leon Anderson. California, 1993. 391p bibl index afp ISBN 0-520-07847-0, $45.00; ISBN 0-520-07989-2 pbk, $14.00

Of the many books written about homelessness in the past decade, none takes the reader into the world of the homeless—the streets, the shelters, the soup kitchens, the margins of society. Snow and Anderson do that, and much more. Their excellent ethnography focuses on unattached, mostly male, homeless street people in Austin, Texas for two years during the mid-1980s (with a brief return to the field at the end of the decade). Skillfully using basic methods of field research—sustained observation, in-depth interviews, and organizational records (e.g., police, hospital, shelter, employment office)—Snow and Anderson demonstrate that the homeless are not a homogenous lot, but rather may be differentiated from each other in some crucial ways, most significantly by duration of homelessness. Readers learn of the ways in which their lives are constrained by the varied institutions that impinge on the homeless. The authors show the diverse strategies—e.g., work, crime, scavenging, selling plasma or sex—used by the homeless to survive on the streets. Snow and Anderson describe the often superficial, but nonetheless crucial, relationships forged among the homeless and the ways by which they manage to maintain a sense of self-worth. An analysis of the causes of homelessness, both structural and personal, and of the most common "career" progressions followed by the homeless round out this fine account. The virtue of this book that sets it apart from others on the topic is the way it fosters understanding and empathy for the homeless, who are only people struggling to survive under appalling circumstances. This highly readable book is recommended to all citizens, but especially to those with an interest in inequality, marginal groups, social problems, urban sociology, anthropology, planning, or policy. A few tables, charts; a good bibliography. All levels.—*K. Hadden, University of Connecticut*

OAB-3112 HV1445 95-50177 CIP
Whalen, Mollie. **Counseling to end violence against women: a subversive model.** Sage Publications, CA, 1996. 166p bibl indexes afp ISBN 0-8039-7379-9, $37.00; ISBN 0-8039-7380-2 pbk, $17.95

Whalen presents a specific and grounded subversive counseling model for battered women, i.e., subversive in that it rejects the individual and pathology-oriented images of battered women in favor of a political and social change model. This theoretical work is based on research, along with the author's extensive background in the area of feminist interventions with battered women. Whalen shows her ability to synthesize and demonstrates her knowledge of this literature with a typology of women's movement ideologies and their associated views of gender. Perhaps the most influential feminist for Whalen is Leonore Walker (*The Battered Woman*, 1979). Whalen also builds on Ellyn Kaschak's essay "Feminist Psychotherapy," in *Female Psychology*, ed. by Sue Cox (1976). Whalen is mindful of the connection between theory or ideology and practice in counseling. Her intent is to join the client and counselor to agitate for change in social institutions and to increase access of battered women to, among other things, material resources, safety, personal power, and women's collective strength. The references are well selected, and there are both subject and author indexes. This well-done work is a must for libraries. Upper-division undergraduates and above.—*Y. Peterson, Saint Xavier University*

■ Author Index

Index entries refer to review numbers.

A

Aarons, Victoria. A measure of memory. OAB-0816

Abalos, David T. The Latino family and the politics of transformation. OAB-3075

Abbott, Carl. The Metropolitan frontier. OAB-2585

Abel, Richard. The ciné goes to town. OAB-0947

Abelson, Harold. Structure and interpretation of computer programs. OAB-1442

Abercrombie, Stanley. George Nelson: the design of modern design. OAB-0416

Abi-Aad, Naji. Instability and conflict in the Middle East. OAB-2774

Abiteboul, Serge. Foundations of databases. OAB-1443

Abram, Jan. The language of Winnicott. OAB-2937

Abramson, Jeffrey. We, the jury. OAB-2804

Abramson, Jill. Strange justice. OAB-2928

Abu-Lughod, Lila. Writing women's worlds. OAB-1860

Acock, Alan C. Family diversity and well-being. OAB-3049

Acosta, Juvenal, ed. Light from a nearby window. OAB-0911

Adams, David Wallace. Education for extinction. OAB-2534

Adams, James Eli. Dandies and desert saints. OAB-0659

Adams, Kevin. Wildflowers of the southern Appalachians. OAB-1391

Adams, McC. Robert. Paths of fire. OAB-1839

Adelman, M.A. The genie out of the bottle. OAB-2092

Adloff, Jean-Pierre. Fundamentals of radiochemistry. OAB-1417

Adorno, Gretel, ed. Aesthetic theory. OAB-1112

Adorno, Theodor W. Aesthetic theory. OAB-1112

Adriance, Madeleine Cousineau. Promised land: base Christian communities and the struggle for the Amazon. OAB-2408

Afton, Jean. Cheyenne dog soldiers. OAB-2535

Agosta, William. Bombardier beetles and fever trees. OAB-1350

Aharoni, Yohanan. The Macmillan Bible atlas. OAB-0112

Ahern, Daniel R. Nietzsche as cultural physician. OAB-1086

Ahl, Diane Cole. Benozzo Gozzoli. OAB-0442

Ahlquist, Karen. Democracy at the opera. OAB-1010

Aitchison, Jean. The seeds of speech. OAB-0536

Akeret, Robert U. Tales from a traveling couch. OAB-2995

Akhmatova, Anna. My half century. OAB-0922

Alberigo, Giuseppe, ed. History of Vatican II: v.1: Announcing and preparing Vatican Council II toward a new era in Catholicism. OAB-1213

Albers, Josef. Interaction of color. OAB-0153

Albrecht, Ernest. The new American circus. OAB-0938

Albright, Daniel. Quantum poetics. OAB-0776

Aldersey-Williams, Hugh. The most beautiful molecule. OAB-1418

Aldrich, Robert. France and the South Pacific since 1940. OAB-2251

Aldrich, Robert. Greater France: a history of French overseas expansion. OAB-2320

Alexander, Christine. The art of the Brontës. OAB-0336

Alexander, Judd H. In defense of garbage. OAB-1521

Alexander, Ruth M. The "girl problem." OAB-3036

Alkon, Paul K. Science fiction before 1900. OAB-0537

Allen, Craig. Eisenhower and the mass media. OAB-0502

Allen, Jon G. Coping with trauma. OAB-2996

Allen, Natalie J. Commitment in the workplace. OAB-1947

Allen, Theodore W. The invention of the white race: v.1: Racial oppression and social control. OAB-3076

Alliance for Technology Access. Computer resources for people with disabilities. OAB-1448

Alligood, Kathleen T. Chaos: an introduction to dynamical systems. OAB-1660

Allmand, Christopher. Henry V. OAB-2374

Allston, Washington. The correspondence of Washington Allston. OAB-0358

Almeida, Miguel Vale de. The hegemonic male. OAB-1861

Almond, Philip C. Heaven and hell in Enlightenment England. OAB-1198

Almquist, Sharon G., comp. Opera mediagraphy. OAB-0106

Alpers, Paul. What is pastoral? OAB-0538

Alston, William P. A realist conception of truth. OAB-1151

Altbach, Philip G., ed. International book publishing: an encyclopedia. OAB-0332

Altemeyer, Bob. The authoritarian specter. OAB-2641

Altshuler, Alan A. Regulation for revenue. OAB-2093

Alvarez, Ruth M., ed. Uncollected early prose of Katherine Anne Porter. OAB-0809

Alwood, Edward. Straight news. OAB-0503

Amato, Ivan. Stuff: the materials the world is made of. OAB-1542

Ames, Kenneth L. Death in the dining room and other tales of Victorian culture. OAB-2536

Amico, Leonard N. Bernard Palissy: in search of earthly paradise. OAB-0417

Amico, Robert P. The problem of the criterion. OAB-1152

Amin, Samir. Re-reading the postwar period. OAB-1967

Aminzade, Ronald. Ballots and barricades. OAB-2321

Amishai-Maisels, Ziva. Depiction and interpretation. OAB-0359

Amuzegar, Jahangir. Iran's economy under the Islamic Republic. OAB-1993

Ancelet, Barry Jean. Cajun and Creole folktales. OAB-0726

Anderson, Donna K. Charles T. Griffes. OAB-0997

Anderson, Erland. Guide to British poetry explication: v.4: Victorian-contemporary. OAB-0077

Anderson, G.M. Thermodynamics of natural systems. OAB-1469

Anderson, James A. An introduction to neural networks. OAB-1741

Anderson, Leon. Down on their luck. OAB-3111

Anderson, Leslie. The political ecology of the modern peasant. OAB-2717

Anderson, Philip. Inside the Kaisha. OAB-1932

Anderson, Terry L. Enviro-capitalists. OAB-2094

Anderson, Thomas C. Sartre's two ethics. OAB-1126

Anderson, Warren D. Music and musicians in ancient Greece. OAB-1011

Andersson, Malte. Sexual selection. OAB-1778

Andrain, Charles F. Political protest and social change. OAB-2826

Andreas, Carol. Meatpackers and beef barons. OAB-1933

Andrews, Alice C. The atlas of American society. OAB-0316

Andrews, E.M. The Anzac illusion. OAB-2157

Andrews, Gerald D., ed. Emerging technologies in plastics recycling. OAB-1551

Andrews, Jack. Samuel Yellin, metalworker. OAB-0418

Andrews, Jean. American wildflower florilegium. OAB-1392

Andrews, Lori B., ed. Assessing genetic risks. OAB-1596

Andrien, Kenneth J. The Kingdom of Quito, 1690-1830. OAB-2409

Angier, Natalie. The beauty of the beastly. OAB-1351

Annas, Julia. The morality of happiness. OAB-1127

Anselment, Raymond A. The realms of Apollo. OAB-0629

Applebee, Arthur N. Curriculum as conversation. OAB-2132

Apter, David E. Political protest and social change. OAB-2826

Arbib, Michael A., ed. The Handbook of brain theory and neural networks. OAB-1752

Arden, John Boghosian. Consciousness, dreams, and self. OAB-2952

Arditti, Joseph. Fundamentals of orchid biology. OAB-1393

Arendt, Hannah. Love and Saint Augustine. OAB-1199

Argan, Giulio Carlo. Michelangelo architect. OAB-0394

Arkoun, Mohammed. Rethinking Islam. OAB-1233

Arkush, Allan. Moses Mendelssohn and the Enlightenment. OAB-1087

Arnold, J.E. Michael, ed. Tree management in farmer strategies. OAB-1319

Arnold, Matthew. The letters of Matthew Arnold. OAB-0660

Arnstine, Donald. Democracy and the art of schooling. OAB-2103

Arntzen, Charles J., ed. Encyclopedia of agricultural science. OAB-0146

Aronson, Jerrold L. Realism rescued. OAB-1270

Arrowsmith, William, tr. Cuttlefish bones. OAB-0903

Arthur, John. Words that bind. OAB-2915

Ash, Timothy Garton. In Europe's name. OAB-2688

Ashby, LeRoy. Endangered children: dependency, neglect, and abuse in American history. OAB-3094

Ashe, Arthur. Days of grace. OAB-1760

Asher, R.E., ed. The Encyclopedia of language and linguistics. OAB-0070

Ashton, John, ed. The Epidemiological imagination. OAB-1605

Aspray, William. Computer: a history of the information machine. OAB-1446

Atkins, G. Douglas. Estranging the familiar. OAB-0539

Atkins, Keletso E. The moon is dead! Give us our money! OAB-2226

Atkins, P.W. The periodic kingdom. OAB-1420

Attenborough, David. The private life of plants. OAB-1394

Attig, Thomas. How we grieve. OAB-2975

Atwell, John E. Schopenhauer on the character of the world. OAB-1088

Auden, W.H. W.H. Auden and Chester Kallman. OAB-0691

Audouze, Jean, ed. The Cambridge atlas of astronomy. OAB-1324

Auerbach, Jonathan. Male call. OAB-0777

Auerbach, Rena R., ed. The "Jewish question" in German-speaking countries, 1848-1914. OAB-0230

Auerbach, Susan, ed. Encyclopedia of multiculturalism. OAB-0172

August, Eugene R. The new men's studies. OAB-0169

Augustine, Dolores L. Patricians and parvenus. OAB-2355

Avellaneda, José Ignacio. The conquerors of the New Kingdom of Granada. OAB-2410

Aversa, Elizabeth. The humanities: a selective guide to information sources. OAB-0040

Avi-Yonah, Michael. The Macmillan Bible atlas. OAB-0112

Ayalon, Ami. The press in the Arab Middle East. OAB-0504

Ayers, Edward L. The promise of the New South. OAB-2537

Ayto, John. The Oxford dictionary of modern slang. OAB-0003

B

Baars, Donald L. Navajo country: a geology and natural history of the Four Corners region. OAB-1470

Babington, Bruce. Biblical epics. OAB-0968

Bacon, Donald C., ed. The Encyclopedia of the United States Congress. OAB-0281

Baden-Fuller, Charles. Rejuvenating the mature business. OAB-1916

Baguley, David, ed. A Critical bibliography of French literature: v.5: The nineteenth century in two parts. OAB-0064

Bailiff, John, tr. The paths of Heidegger's life and thought. OAB-1105

Baker, Chris. Thailand, economy and politics. OAB-2005

Baker, Daniel B., ed. Explorers and discoverers of the world. OAB-0216

Baker, Jean-Claude. Josephine: the hungry heart. OAB-0939

Baker, Jonathan, ed. The Migration experience in Africa. OAB-2240

Baker, Malcolm. Roubiliac and the eighteenth-century monument. OAB-0495

Baker, Rob. The art of AIDS. OAB-0940

Bakija, Jon M. Retooling Social Security for the 21st century. OAB-2091

Bakker, Egbert J. Poetry in speech. OAB-0599

Baldassarre, Guy A. Waterfowl ecology and management. OAB-1779

Baldauf-Berdes, Jane L. Women musicians of Venice. OAB-1012

Baldwin, Neil. Edison: inventing the century. OAB-1510

Ball, Howard. Hugo L. Black: cold steel warrior. OAB-2916

Ball, Terence. Reappraising political theory. OAB-2827

Ballstadt, Carl, ed. Letters of love and duty. OAB-0720

Balmori, Diana. Redesigning the American lawn. OAB-1313

Bane, Mary Jo. Welfare realities. OAB-3095

Banham, Joanna, ed. Encyclopedia of interior design. OAB-0050

Banham, Martin. The Cambridge guide to theatre. OAB-0093

Banks, William M. Black intellectuals: race and responsibility in American life. OAB-2473

Banner, James M. The elements of teaching. OAB-2133

Banning, Lance. The sacred fire of liberty. OAB-2508

Bao Ninh. The sorrow of war. OAB-0580

Barakat, Halim. The Arab world. OAB-2436

Barash, Carol. English women's poetry, 1649-1714. OAB-0630

Barberis, Peter. The elite of the elite. OAB-2689

Bardon, Jonathan. A history of Ulster. OAB-2376

Barfield, B.J. Design hydrology and sedimentology for small catchments. OAB-1554

Bargen, Doris G. A woman's weapon. OAB-0581

Bar-Joseph, Uri. Intelligence intervention in the politics of democratic states. OAB-2642

Barkai, Avraham. Branching out. OAB-2538

Barling, Julian. The union and its members. OAB-1934

Barnard, Alan, ed. Encyclopedia of social and cultural anthropology. OAB-0186

Barnard, Rita. The Great Depression and the culture of abundance. OAB-0778

Barnavi, Eli, ed. A Historical atlas of the Jewish people. OAB-0217

Barnes, Hubert Lloyd, ed. Geochemistry of hydrothermal ore deposits. OAB-1480

Barnett, Victoria. For the soul of the people. OAB-2356

Barnett, Vivian Endicott. Vasily Kandinsky: a colorful life: the collection of the Lenbachhaus, Munich. OAB-0443

Barnett, William K., ed. The Emergence of pottery. OAB-1853

Barnstone, Willis. Six masters of the Spanish sonnet. OAB-0905

Barnstone, Willis. With Borges on an ordinary evening in Buenos Aires. OAB-0906

Baron, Marcia W. Kantian ethics almost without apology. OAB-1128

Barondes, Samuel H. Molecules and mental illness. OAB-1624

Barrett, Jacqueline K., ed. Encyclopedia of women's associations worldwide. OAB-0173

Barrett, Stephen, ed. The Health robbers. OAB-1587

Barritt, Greg J. Communication within animal cells. OAB-1352

Barrow, Clyde W. Critical theories of the state. OAB-2828

Bartels, Emily C. Spectacles of strangeness. OAB-0613

Barth, Fredrik. Balinese worlds. OAB-1862

Bartholet, Elizabeth. Family bonds. OAB-3050

Bartlett, Robert V., ed. Environment as a focus for public policy. OAB-2643

Bartlett, Robert. The making of Europe. OAB-2188

Bastien, Joseph W. Drum and stethoscope. OAB-1863

Bataille, Gretchen M., ed. Native American women: a biographical dictionary. OAB-0265

Batchelor, George. The life and legacy of G.I. Taylor. OAB-1705

Bates, Robert H. Open economy politics. OAB-2036

Bauer, Brian S. Astronomy and empire in the ancient Andes. OAB-1848

Baumbach, Günter. Air quality control: formation and sources, dispersion, characteristics..... OAB-1522

Baumeister, Roy F. Your own worst enemy. OAB-2976

Baumeister, Roy F., ed. Self-esteem: the puzzle of low self-regard. OAB-2991

Baumrind, Diana. Child maltreatment and optimal caregiving in social contexts. OAB-3096

Baxter, Craig. Bangladesh: from a nation to a state. OAB-2668

Bayard, Thomas O. Reciprocity and retaliation in U.S. trade policy. OAB-2062

Baym, Nina. American women writers and the work of history, 1790-1860. OAB-0745

Bayón, Damián. History of South American colonial art and architecture. OAB-0360

Beamish, Caroline, tr. The impressionist print. OAB-0432

Beasley, Ina. Before the wind changed. OAB-2104

Beasley, Maurine H. Taking their place. OAB-0505

Beatty, Barbara. Preschool education in America. OAB-2134

Beaty, Frederick L. The ironic world of Evelyn Waugh. OAB-0692

Beck, Hermann. The origins of the authoritarian welfare state in Prussia. OAB-2357

Beer, Samuel H. To make a nation. OAB-2875

Begelman, Mitchell. Gravity's fatal attraction. OAB-1321

Behrens-Abouseif, Doris. Egypt's adjustment to Ottoman rule. OAB-2437

Bejan, Adrian. Heat transfer. OAB-1543

Belenko, Steven R. Crack and the evolution of anti-drug policy. OAB-3037

Bell, Linda A. Rethinking ethics in the midst of violence. OAB-1129

Bellamy, Charles L. An inordinate fondness for beetles. OAB-1798

Bell-Fialkoff, Andrew. Ethnic cleansing. OAB-2736

Beltrametti, Mauro C. The adjunction theory of complex projective varieties. OAB-1661

Bendazzi, Giannalberto. Cartoons: one hundred years of cinema animation. OAB-0948

Bennett, Benjamin. Beyond theory. OAB-0856

Bennett, M.K. Affine and projective geometry. OAB-1662

Bennett, Susan, tr. The thief and other stories. OAB-0870

Benoit, William L. Accounts, excuses, and apologies. OAB-0532

Bensch, Stephen P. Barcelona and its rulers, 1096-1291. OAB-2322

Benson, Eugene, ed. Encyclopedia of post-colonial literatures in English. OAB-0071

Berenbaum, May R. Ninety-nine more maggots, mites, and munchers. OAB-1780

Berezin, Mabel. Making the fascist self. OAB-2323

Berg, Frances M. Afraid to eat. OAB-1625

Berg, Frances M. Health risks of weight loss. OAB-1626

Berg, William J. The visual novel. OAB-0879

Berger, Arthur Asa. Essentials of mass communication theory. OAB-0506

Berger, Joel. Bison: mating and conservation in small populations. OAB-1781

Berger, W.H. The sea floor. OAB-1497

Berghahn, V.R. Imperial Germany, 1871-1914. OAB-2358

Berglas, Steven. Your own worst enemy. OAB-2976

Berlin, Alexandre Al. Fast polymerization processes. OAB-1564

Berliner, Paul F. Thinking in jazz. OAB-1037

Berlinski, David. A tour of the calculus. OAB-1663

Berlo, Janet Catherine, ed. Plains Indian drawings, 1865-1935. OAB-0435

Berman, Laurence. The musical image. OAB-0989

Bernays, E.A. Host-plant selection by phytophagous insects. OAB-1782

Berndt, Bruce C. Ramanujan: letters and commentary. OAB-1695

Bernier, Ronald M. Himalayan architecture. OAB-0395

Bernor, Raymond L., ed. The Evolution of Western Eurasian Neogene mammal faunas. OAB-1477

Berry, D.H., ed. Cicero: pro P. Sulla oratio. OAB-0601

Berthrong, John H. All under heaven. OAB-1175

Bérubé, Michael. Public access. OAB-2876

Bessai, Diane. Playwrights of collective creation. OAB-1056

Bewes, Diccon. What happened where: a guide to places and events in twentieth-century history. OAB-0213

Beyer, Janice M. The cultures of work organizations. OAB-1930

Bharath, Ramachandran. Neural network computing. OAB-1444

Biagini, Eugenio F. Liberty, retrenchment and reform. OAB-2377

Biagioli, Mario. Galileo, courtier. OAB-1322

Bickerton, Derek. Language and human behavior. OAB-2953

Bickford, Maggie. Ink plum: the making of a Chinese scholar-painting genre. OAB-0444

Biebuyck, Daniel P. African ethnonyms. OAB-0045

Bigsby, C.W.E. Modern American drama, 1945-1990. OAB-0817

Brown, Seyom. International relations in a changing global system. OAB-2737

Brown, Wendy. States of injury. OAB-2832

Browning, W.R.F. A dictionary of the Bible. OAB-0114

Broyles, Michael. Music of the highest class. OAB-1013

Brubaker, Rogers. Citizenship and nationhood in France and Germany. OAB-2693

Bruccoli, Matthew J., ed. The love of The last tycoon. OAB-0787

Bruce, Steve. The red hand: Protestant paramilitaries in Northern Ireland. OAB-2694

Brumfield, William Craft. A history of Russian architecture. OAB-0397

Brumfield, William Craft. Lost Russia. OAB-0398

Brundage, David. The making of Western labor radicalism. OAB-1936

Brundage, W. Fitzhugh. A socialist utopia in the new South. OAB-2542

Brunk, Gregory G. Understanding attitudes about war. OAB-2833

Bruns, Gerald L. Maurice Blanchot: the refusal of philosophy. OAB-0880

Brunvand, Jan Harold, ed. American folklore: an encyclopedia. OAB-0183

Brus, Eric. The almanac of renewable energy. OAB-1524

Bruzina, Ronald, tr. Sixth Cartesian meditation. OAB-1097

Bryan, Violet Harrington. The myth of New Orleans in literature. OAB-0725

Brzezinski, Zbigniew, ed. Russia and the Common-wealth of Independent States. OAB-2712

Buchanan, Christy M. Adolescents after divorce. OAB-3051

Buck, Claire, ed. The Bloomsbury guide to women's literature. OAB-0061

Buck, Richard. Silver swimmer. OAB-1786

Buckley, Roger. US-Japan alliance diplomacy, 1945-1990. OAB-2760

Budge, Ian. Parties, policies, and democracy. OAB-2646

Bugajski, Janusz. Nations in turmoil. OAB-2775

Buhle, Paul, ed. C.L.R. James's Caribbean. OAB-0715

Bunn, George. Arms control by committee. OAB-2776

Bunton, Robin, ed. Health promotion. OAB-1612

Burchfield, R.W., ed. The new Fowler's modern English usage. OAB-0012

Burgard, Peter J. Idioms of uncertainty. OAB-0858

Burger, Joanna, ed. Before and after an oil spill. OAB-1353

Burgess, Tony L. Sonoran desert plants: an ecological atlas. OAB-1416

Burk, Robert F. Never just a game. OAB-1761

Burke, Frank. Fellini's films. OAB-0971

Burke, Peter. History and social theory. OAB-3008

Burkert, Walter. Creation of the sacred. OAB-1176

Burkholder, J. Peter. All made of tunes. OAB-0998

Burl, Aubrey. From Carnac to Callanish. OAB-2191

Burley, David V. Prophecy of the swan. OAB-2462

Burnham, Dorothy K. To please the caribou. OAB-0419

Burnham, Richard. The years of O'Casey, 1921-1926. OAB-1065

Burns, Bryan. World cinema. OAB-0949

Burns, John J., ed. The Bowhead whale. OAB-1784

Burns, Richard Dean, ed. Encyclopedia of arms control and disarmament. OAB-0277

Burns, Sarah. Inventing the modern artist. OAB-0364

Burroughs, William S. The letters of William S. Burroughs. OAB-0819

Burrow, Rufus. James H. Cone and black liberation theology. OAB-1251

Burrows, Malcolm. The neurobiology of an insect brain. OAB-1787

Burtchaell, James Tunstead. From synagogue to church. OAB-1203

Burwick, Frederick. Poetic madness and the Romantic imagination. OAB-0540

Bushnell, David. The making of modern Colombia. OAB-2718

Butler, Ann B. Comparative vertebrate neuroanatomy. OAB-1744

Butler, Michael. Animal cell culture and technology. OAB-1788

Butler, Ruth. Rodin: the shape of genius. OAB-0496

Buttlar, Lois J. Guide to information resources in ethnic museum, library, and archival collections in the United States. OAB-0007

Bygrave, William D. The portable MBA in entrepreneurship. OAB-1917

Bynum, Caroline Walker. The resurrection of the body in western Christianity, 200-1336. OAB-1204

Byrne, Hugh. El Salvador's civil war. OAB-2719

C

Cahill, James. The painter's practice. OAB-0446

Cahoone, Lawrence E. The ends of philosophy. OAB-1091

Cain, Gordon. Everybody wins!: a life in free enterprise. OAB-1900

Cain, Mary Ann. Revisioning writers' talk. OAB-0541

Cain, William E., ed. Teaching the conflicts. OAB-2128

Cairncross, Alec. The British economy since 1945. OAB-2051

Cairns, John. Matters of life and death. OAB-1745

Caldwell, John Thornton. Televisuality. OAB-0509

Caldwell, Lynton K. Environment as a focus for public policy. OAB-2643

Calin, William. The French tradition and the literature of medieval England. OAB-0614

Calinger, Ronald S. The dictionary of 20th-century world politics. OAB-0302

Callow, Philip. From noon to starry night. OAB-0746

Callow, Simon. Orson Welles: the road to Xanadu. OAB-0950

Calloway, Colin G. The American Revolution in Indian country. OAB-2509

Calvin, William H. Conversations with Neil's brain. OAB-1746

Cameron, Alan. Callimachus and his critics. OAB-0600

Camp, Roderic Ai. Mexican political biographies, 1935-1993. OAB-0273

Camp, Roderic Ai. Politics in Mexico. OAB-2720

Campbell, David G. The crystal desert. OAB-1355

Campbell, James. Understanding John Dewey. OAB-1093

Campbell, Jill. Natural masques. OAB-0634

Campbell, Louise. Coventry Cathedral: art and architecture in post-war Britain. OAB-0399

Campbell, Patricia Shehan. Music in childhood. OAB-2135

Campbell, R. Wayne. The Birds of British Columbia: v. 1-3. OAB-1783

Campbell-Kelly, Martin. Computer: a history of the information machine. OAB-1446

Canfield, J. Douglas. Tricksters & estates. OAB-0635

Canney, Donald L. The old steam navy: v.2: The ironclads, 1842-1885. OAB-2543

Cannon, Harold C. The elements of teaching. OAB-2133

Cantwell, Robert. When we were good. OAB-1038

Caplow, Theodore. Perverse incentives. OAB-3009

Cappelli, Peter. Change at work. OAB-1938

Caputo, John D., ed. Deconstruction in a nutshell. OAB-1095

Carbert, Louise I. Agrarian feminism. OAB-2463

Cargill, Jack. Athenian settlements of the fourth century B.C.. OAB-2192

Carlson, Harry G. Out of inferno. OAB-0859

Carlson, Roy L., ed. Early human occupation in British Columbia. OAB-1852

Carlton, Charles. Going to the wars. OAB-2378

Carlyle, Thomas. On heroes, hero-worship, & the heroic in history. OAB-0662

Caron, Martine M. Canadian reference sources: an annotated bibliography: general reference works, history, humanities. OAB-0005

Carpenter, Ronald H. History as rhetoric. OAB-0533

Carpenter, Ted Galen. The captive press. OAB-0510

Carper, Kenneth L. Construction failure. OAB-1552

Carr, David M. Reading the fractures of Genesis. OAB-1252

Carr, Gerald L. Frederic Edwin Church: catalogue raisonné of works of art at Olana State Historic Site, v. 1 & 2. OAB-0447

Carrère d'Encausse, Hélène. The end of the Soviet empire. OAB-2695

Carrier, Joseph. De los otros: intimacy and homosexuality among Mexican men. OAB-1865

Carroll, Robert L. Patterns and processes of vertebrate evolution. OAB-1473

Carroll, William C. Fat king, lean beggar. OAB-0615

Carter, R.W.G., ed. Coastal evolution. OAB-1475

Carter, Stephen L. The confirmation mess. OAB-2806

Carwardine, Mark. Whales, dolphins and porpoises. OAB-1789

Cary, Noel D. The path to Christian democracy. OAB-2696

Casstevens, Marty. Wildflowers of the southern Appalachians. OAB-1391

Castañeda, Jorge G. Utopia unarmed. OAB-2777

Castells, Manuel. The rise of the network society. OAB-1968

Castleberry, May. Perpetual mirage. OAB-0483

Casto, William R. The Supreme Court in the early republic. OAB-2917

Castrigiano, Domenico P.L. Catastrophe theory. OAB-1665

Castro, Janice. The American way of health. OAB-1597

Cate, Curtis. André Malraux: a biography. OAB-0881

Cather, Willa. O pioneers! OAB-0779

Caudill, Maureen. In our own image. OAB-1546

Caughley, Graeme. Conservation biology in theory and practice. OAB-1356

Caulfield, Richard A. Greenlanders, whales, and whaling. OAB-2359

Cavell, Marcia. The psychoanalytic mind. OAB-2939

Cayton, Andrew R.L. Frontier Indiana. OAB-2475

Cayton, Mary Kupiec, ed. Encyclopedia of American social history. OAB-0250

Centeno, Miguel Ángel. Democracy within reason. OAB-2721

Ceruzzi, Paul E. Landmarks in digital computing. OAB-1455

Chabod, Federico. Italian foreign policy. OAB-2697

Chadwick, Bruce. When the game was Black and White. OAB-1762

Chadwick, Douglas H. The fate of the elephant. OAB-1790

Chaikin, Andrew. A man on the moon. OAB-1326

Chaison, Gary N. Union mergers in hard times. OAB-1937

Chaliand, Gérard. The Penguin atlas of diasporas. OAB-0211

Chanan, Michael. Musica practica. OAB-0991

Chance, Joseph E., ed. Mexico under fire. OAB-2544

Chandler, David. The Khmers. OAB-2270

Chandler, David P. Brother number one. OAB-2669

Changeux, Jean-Pierre. Conversations on mind, matter, and mathematics. OAB-1666

Chao, Sheau-yueh J., comp. The Japanese automobile industry. OAB-0198

Chapman, Jenny. Politics, feminism and the reformation of gender. OAB-3010

Chapman, Michael. Southern African literatures. OAB-0567

Chapman, R.F. Host-plant selection by phytophagous insects. OAB-1782

Chappell, Vere, ed. The Cambridge companion to Locke. OAB-1092

Charles, Philip A. Exploring the X-ray universe. OAB-1327

Charlesworth, Max. Bioethics in a liberal society. OAB-1580

Chase, Chris. Josephine: the hungry heart. OAB-0939

Chatterjee, Partha. The nation and its fragments. OAB-2159

Chaturvedi, Sanjay. The polar regions. OAB-2160

Chauncey, George. Gay New York. OAB-2588

Chawla, Sarita, ed. Learning organizations. OAB-1923

Chen, W.F., ed. The Civil engineering handbook. OAB-1504

Chénetier, Marc. Beyond suspicion. OAB-0820

Cheng, Vincent J. Joyce, race, and empire. OAB-0693

Cherchi Usai, Paolo. Burning passions. OAB-0972

Cherry, Peter. Spanish still life. OAB-0467

Chiang, Walter. Sanitary landfill leachate. OAB-1534

Chielens, Edward E, ed. American literary magazines. OAB-0059

Childs, Donald J. T.S. Eliot. OAB-0780

Childs, Michael J. Labour's apprentices. OAB-2379

Chipman, Donald E. Spanish Texas, 1519-1821. OAB-2510

Choe, Sang-Chuel. Seoul: the making of a metropolis. OAB-2266

Choldin, Harvey M. Looking for the last percent. OAB-1821

Chomsky, Aviva. West Indian workers and the United Fruit Company in Costa Rica, 1870-1940. OAB-2413

Chopra, P.N., ed. Encyclopaedia of India. OAB-0222

Christopher, A.J. The atlas of apartheid. OAB-2227

Churchill, Larry R. Self-interest and universal health care. OAB-1598

Churchland, Paul M. The engine of reason, the seat of the soul. OAB-1748

Chwast, Seymour. Japanese modern. OAB-0422

Cicero, Marcus Tullius. Cicero: pro P. Sulla oratio. OAB-0601

Cikovsky, Nicolai. Winslow Homer. OAB-0448

Cipolloni, David C. An extraordinary silence. OAB-2997

Civello, Paul. American literary naturalism and its twentieth-century transformations. OAB-0781

Clapham, Christopher. Africa and the international system. OAB-2778

Clark, Ailsa M. Starfishes of the Atlantic. OAB-1791

Clark, Anna. The struggle for the breeches. OAB-2380

Clark, Beverly Lyon. Regendering the school story. OAB-0727

Clark, Burton R., ed. The Encyclopedia of higher education: v.1-4. OAB-0171

Clark, Dick, ed. The Negro leagues book. OAB-1767

Clark, John. The Macmillan dictionary of measurement. OAB-0009

Clark, Samuel. State and status. OAB-2287

Clark, Timothy T. The actor's image. OAB-0420

Clark, William A.V. Households and housing. OAB-2064

Clarke, Peter. Hope and glory: Britain, 1900-1990. OAB-2381

Clausen, Meredith L. Pietro Belluschi: modern American architect. OAB-0400

Clawson, Calvin C. Mathematical mysteries. OAB-1667

Clawson, Patrick L. The Andean cocaine industry. OAB-2779

Clayton, Cherry. Olive Schreiner. OAB-0716

Clayton, Jay. The pleasures of Babel. OAB-0821

Clayton, Lawrence A., ed. The De Soto chronicles. OAB-2514

Clayton, Tonya D. Living with the Georgia shore. OAB-1484

Cleary, Mark. Borneo: change and development. OAB-2253

Clegg, Hugh Armstrong. A history of British trade unions since 1889: v.3: 1934-1951. OAB-2382

Cleland, Charles E. Rites of conquest. OAB-1867

Clement, Colleen D. AIDS, health, and mental health. OAB-1636

Clement, Peter. Finches & sparrows. OAB-0143

Clement, Russell T. Les fauves: a sourcebook. OAB-0046

Clemmer, Richard O. Roads in the sky. OAB-1868

Cleveland, Les. Dark laughter. OAB-1039

Clucas, Richard A. Encyclopedia of American political reform. OAB-0274

Clurman, Ann. Rocking the ages. OAB-1966

Clute, John, ed. The Encyclopedia of fantasy. OAB-0042

Clute, John. Science fiction: the illustrated encyclopedia. OAB-0041

Clyman, Toby W., ed. Women writers in Russian literature. OAB-0937

Cobb, Cathy. Creations of fire. OAB-1424

Cobley, Evelyn. Representing war. OAB-0782

Cohen, David. Law, violence, and community in classical Athens. OAB-2193

Cohen, Edward E. Athenian economy and society. OAB-1969

Cohen, Felissa L., ed. Women, children, and HIV/AIDS. OAB-1658

Cohen, H. Floris. The scientific revolution. OAB-1297

Cohen, Hubert I. Ingmar Bergman: the art of confession. OAB-0973

Cohen, L. Jonathan. An essay on belief and acceptance. OAB-1153

Cohen, Lenard J. Broken bonds. OAB-2698

Cohen, Mark R. Under crescent and cross. OAB-1234

Cohen, Morton N. Lewis Carroll: a biography. OAB-0663

Cohen, Robert. Understanding Peter Weiss. OAB-0860

Cohen, Robert. When the old left was young. OAB-2105

Cohen, Warren I. The Cambridge history of American foreign relations: v. 1-4. OAB-2474

Cohen, William A. The marketing plan. OAB-1955

Cohn, Samuel K. The cult of remembrance and the Black Death. OAB-2324

Cohodas, Nadine. Strom Thurmond and the politics of Southern change. OAB-2898

Coleman, Kathleen. Guide to French poetry explication. OAB-0062

Colignon, Richard A. Power plays: critical events in the institutionalization of the Tennessee Valley Authority. OAB-3011

Colker, Ruth. Abortion and dialogue. OAB-2807

Collett, Jonathan, ed. Greening the college curriculum. OAB-0014

Colley, Linda. Britons. OAB-2383

Collier, Gary. Social origins of mental ability. OAB-2954

Collier, James Lincoln. Jazz: the American theme song. OAB-1040

Collier, Simon. A history of Chile, 1808-1994. OAB-2414

Collins, Catherine Fisher. The imprisonment of African American women. OAB-3039

Collins, Harry. The golem. OAB-1272

Collins, Irene. Jane Austen and the clergy. OAB-0664

Collins, Peter M. Monosaccharides: their chemistry and their roles in natural products. OAB-1425

Colman, Andrew M., ed. Companion encyclopedia to psychology. OAB-0310

Colman, William G. America's future work force. OAB-1952

Colombat, André Pierre. The Holocaust in French film. OAB-0974

Coltrane, Scott. Family man. OAB-3052

Combs, James E. The comedy of democracy. OAB-2879

Comensoli, Viviana. 'Household business' OAB-0636

Comley, Nancy R. Hemingway's genders. OAB-0783

Commins, Nancy L. Restructuring schools for linguistic diversity. OAB-2148

Common, I.F.B. Moths of Australia. OAB-1793

Cone, Joseph, ed. The Northwest salmon crisis. OAB-1812

Conkin, Paul K. The uneasy center. OAB-1205

Conlin, Diane Atnally. The artists of the Ara Pacis. OAB-0497

Conn, Peter. Pearl S. Buck: a cultural biography. OAB-0784

Connell, R.W. Masculinities. OAB-3053

Connes, Alain. Conversations on mind, matter, and mathematics. OAB-1666

Conniff, Richard. Spineless wonders. OAB-1794

Connor, D.J. Crop ecology. OAB-1317

Conroy, David W. In public houses. OAB-2511

Conroy, Mary Schaeffer. In health and in sickness. OAB-1631

Constable, Giles. Three studies in medieval religious and social thought. OAB-1206

Consumer Reports Books. How to resolve the health care crisis. OAB-1602

Contardi, Bruno. Michelangelo architect. OAB-0394

Conte, Gian Biagio. Latin literature: a history. OAB-0602

Conway, John H. The book of numbers. OAB-1668

Conzen, Michael P. A scholar's guide to geographical writing on the American and Canadian past. OAB-0247

Cook, Chris. What happened where: a guide to places and events in twentieth-century history. OAB-0213

Cook, Erwin F. The Odyssey in Athens. OAB-0603

Cook, Stephen L. Prophecy & apocalypticism. OAB-1253

Cook, Susan C., ed. Cecilia reclaimed. OAB-0990

Cooke, Jacob Ernest, ed. Encyclopedia of the North American colonies. OAB-0253

Cooke, Miriam. Women and the war story. OAB-0568

Cooke, R.C. Ecophysiology of fungi. OAB-1395

Cooper, André R., comp. Cooper's comprehensive environmental desk reference. OAB-0131

Cooper, Phillip J. Battles on the bench. OAB-2918

Cooper, Wendy A. Classical taste in America, 1800-1840. OAB-0365

Copeland, Edward. Women writing about money. OAB-0665

Copenhaver, Brian P. Renaissance philosophy. OAB-1094

Corbeill, Anthony. Controlling laughter. OAB-2194

Cordell, Dennis D. Hoe and wage. OAB-2228

Cornelius, Randolph R. The science of emotion. OAB-2977

Corns, Thomas N., ed. The Cambridge companion to English poetry, Donne to Marvell. OAB-0633

Corradi, Juan E., ed. Fear at the edge. OAB-2724

Corréard, Marie-Hélène, ed. The Oxford-Hachette French dictionary: French-English/English-French. OAB-0029

Corsini, Raymond J., ed. Encyclopedia of psychology. OAB-0314

D

DeWeese, Devin. Islamization and native religion in the Golden Horde. OAB-1235

Di Renzo, Anthony. American gargoyles. OAB-0824

Diacu, Florin. Celestial encounters. OAB-1330

Diamond, Jared. Guns, germs, and steel. OAB-1824

Díaz, Alvaro. Chile: the great transformation. OAB-2042

Dickason, Olive Patricia. Canada's first nations. OAB-2464

Dickinson, Donald C. Henry E. Huntington's library of libraries. OAB-0328

Dickinson, Oliver. The Aegean Bronze Age. OAB-2195

DiClemente, Ralph J., ed. Adolescents and AIDS. OAB-1622

Diehl, Huston. Staging reform, reforming the stage. OAB-0618

Dieleman, Frans M. Households and housing. OAB-2064

Dietrich, Donald J. God and humanity in Auschwitz. OAB-2298

Diggins, John Patrick. The promise of pragmatism. OAB-1096

Dijk, Teun A. van. Elite discourse and racism. OAB-3078

Dilts, James D. The great road. OAB-2545

DiMona, Lisa, ed. The 1995 information please women's sourcebook. OAB-0168

Dingus, Lowell. Discovering dinosaurs in the Museum of Natural History. OAB-1492

Dinh, Linh, ed. Night, again. OAB-0594

Disney, Richard. Can we afford to grow older? OAB-1972

Dittmer, John. Local people: the struggle for civil rights in Mississippi. OAB-2590

Dix, Neville J. Fungal ecology. OAB-1397

Dobbs, David. The northern forest. OAB-1315

Dobkins, Rebecca J. Memory and imagination. OAB-0452

Dobson, Andrew. Green political thought. OAB-2836

Dobson, Michael. The making of the national poet. OAB-0619

Domb, Risa. Home thoughts from abroad. OAB-0569

Dombroski, Robert S. Properties of writing. OAB-0898

Domínguez, Jorge I. Democratizing Mexico. OAB-2722

Donia, Robert J. Bosnia and Hercegovina. OAB-2299

Donoghue, Frank. The fame machine. OAB-0640

Doody, Margaret Anne. The true story of the novel. OAB-0542

Dordick, Gwendolyn A. Something left to lose. OAB-3097

Dorf, Richard C., ed. The Electrical engineering handbook. OAB-1513

Dorf, Richard C., ed. The Engineering handbook. OAB-1506

Dorfman, Mark H. Environmental dividends. OAB-1523

Dorling, Daniel. A new social atlas of Britain. OAB-1825

Dornbusch, Sanford M. Adolescents after divorce. OAB-3051

Dorrien, Gary. The neoconservative mind. OAB-2837

Dostoyevsky, Fyodor. A writer's diary: v.1: 1873-1876. OAB-0923

Douglas, Aileen. Uneasy sensations. OAB-0641

Douglas, Ian, ed. Companion encyclopedia of geography. OAB-0170

Douglas, Susan J. Where the girls are. OAB-0511

Dow, Bonnie J. Prime-time feminism. OAB-0512

Dow, James W., ed. Encyclopedia of world cultures: v. 8-10. OAB-0188

Dowling, Linda. Hellenism and homosexuality in Victorian Oxford. OAB-0667

Dowling, Linda. The vulgarization of art. OAB-0668

Downey, Maureen E. Starfishes of the Atlantic. OAB-1791

Downing, David C. Planets in peril. OAB-0695

Downs, Anthony. Stuck in traffic. OAB-2017

Dowson, Thomas A. Rock engravings of Southern Africa. OAB-1851

Drake, Paul W. Labor movements and dictatorships. OAB-2038

Drake, Paul W., ed. Money doctors, foreign debts, and economic reforms in Latin America from the 1890s to the present. OAB-2044

Draznin, Yaffa Claire, ed. "My other self." OAB-0722

Dreiser, Theodore. Dreiser's Russian diary. OAB-0785

Dreiser, Theodore. Jennie Gerhardt. OAB-0786

Dressler, Alan. Voyage to the Great Attractor. OAB-1331

Dreyer, June Teufel. China's political system. OAB-2671

Driskel, Michael Paul. As befits a legend. OAB-0402

Drosen, James. Neural network computing. OAB-1444

Droste, Kathleen, ed. Gale book of averages. OAB-0013

Drucker, Peter F. Managing in a time of great change. OAB-1919

Dudden, Faye E. Women in the American theatre. OAB-1057

Dugatkin, Lee Alan. Cooperation among animals. OAB-1796

Duiker, William J. The communist road to power in Vietnam. OAB-2672

Duiker, William J. U.S. containment policy and the conflict in Indochina. OAB-2762

Dundas, Paul. The Jains. OAB-1186

Dunham, William. The mathematical universe. OAB-1672

Dunlop, John B. The rise of Russia and the fall of the Soviet Empire. OAB-2701

Dunn, Charles W. The conservative tradition in America. OAB-2838

Dunn, David H., ed. Diplomacy at the highest level. OAB-2739

Dunster, Julian. Dictionary of natural resource management. OAB-0145

Dunster, Katherine. Dictionary of natural resource management. OAB-0145

Dupuy, Trevor N., ed. International military and defense encyclopedia. OAB-0289

Durand, Jorge. Miracles on the border. OAB-3079

Durham, Jerry D., ed. Women, children, and HIV/AIDS. OAB-1658

Durling, Robert M., ed. The *Divine comedy* of Dante Alighieri: v.1: Inferno. OAB-0897

Duus, Peter. The Abacus and the sword. OAB-2256

Dwork, Debórah. Auschwitz: 1270 to the present. OAB-2361

Dworkin, Roger B. Limits: the role of the law in bioethical decision making. OAB-1583

Dworkin, Ronald. Life's dominion. OAB-2839

Dyer, Joyce. *The awakening*: a novel of beginnings. OAB-0748

Dyos, G.T., ed. Electrical resistivity handbook. OAB-1514

Dyson, Anne Haas. Social worlds of children learning to write in an urban primary school. OAB-2137

Dzielska, Maria. Hypatia of Alexandria. OAB-1120

E

Eaton, Peter. Borneo: change and development. OAB-2253

Eaton, Richard M. The rise of Islam and the Bengal frontier, 1204-1760. OAB-2257

Ebersole, Gary L. Captured by texts. OAB-2458

Ebrey, Patricia Buckley. The inner quarters. OAB-2258

Eck, David J. The most complex machine. OAB-1450

Eckstein, Rick. Nuclear power and social power. OAB-3014

Eckstein, Susan Eva. Back from the future. OAB-2415

Eco, Umberto. The search for the perfect language. OAB-0329

Edin, Kathryn. Making ends meet. OAB-3098

Edmundson, Mark. Literature against philosophy, Plato to Derrida. OAB-0543

Edwards, Brian. London docklands. OAB-2385

Edwards, Jorge. Persona non grata. OAB-2723

Edwards, Laura F. Gendered strife & confusion. OAB-2546

Edwards, Philip. The story of the voyage. OAB-0642

Edwards, Richard L., ed. Encyclopedia of social work. OAB-0322

Eggert, Gerald G. Harrisburg industrializes. OAB-2018

Ehrlich, Anne H. Betrayal of science and reason. OAB-1274

Ehrlich, Paul R. Betrayal of science and reason. OAB-1274

Ehrlich, Robert. The cosmological milkshake. OAB-1708

Eigen, Manfred. Steps towards life. OAB-1361

Eisenstein, S.M. Beyond the stars: the memoirs of Sergei Eisenstein: selected works, IV. OAB-0952

Eisinger, Joel. Trace and transformation. OAB-0484

Eisner, Robert. The misunderstood economy. OAB-2019

Ekeland, Ivar. The broken dice, and other mathematical tales of chance. OAB-1673

Ekland-Olson, Sheldon. The rope, the chair, and the needle. OAB-3045

Elbogen, Ismar. Jewish liturgy. OAB-1236

Elderfield, John. Henri Matisse: a retrospective. OAB-0473

Eldredge, Charles C. Georgia O'Keeffe: American and modern. OAB-0453

Eldredge, Elizabeth A. A South African kingdom. OAB-2229

Eldridge, Larry D. A distant heritage. OAB-2810

El-Enany, Rasheed. Naguib Mahfouz: the pursuit of meaning. OAB-0570

Elfenbein, Andrew. Byron and the Victorians. OAB-0669

Elfstrom, Gerard. Toleration. OAB-1133

Eliav-Feldon, Miriam, ed. A Historical atlas of the Jewish people. OAB-0217

Elkins, Stanley. The age of federalism. OAB-2515

Ellenzweig, Allen. The homoerotic photograph. OAB-0485

Eller, Cynthia. Living in the lap of the goddess. OAB-1178

Elliott, Anthony. Psychoanalytic theory: an introduction. OAB-2940

Elliott, Brent. Treasures of the Royal Horticultural Society. OAB-1398

Elliott, Kimberly Ann. Reciprocity and retaliation in U.S. trade policy. OAB-2062

Elliott, Robert G. Ironclad of the Roanoke. OAB-2547

Ellis, Graham. Rings and fields. OAB-1674

Ellis, Markman. The politics of sensibility. OAB-0670

Ellis, Richard J. Presidential lightning rods. OAB-2899

Ellis, Steven G. Tudor frontiers and noble power. OAB-2386

Ellmann, Maud. The hunger artists. OAB-2978

Ellwood, David T. Welfare realities. OAB-3095

Elm, Mostafa. Oil, power, and principle. OAB-1996

Elms, Alan C. Uncovering lives. OAB-2941

Elton, Geoffrey. The English. OAB-2387

Elwolde, John, tr. A history of the Hebrew language. OAB-0576

Emanoil, Mary, ed. Encyclopedia of endangered species. OAB-0147

Emery, Fred. Watergate: the corruption of American politics. OAB-2591

Emmet, Olivia, tr. Picasso: life and art. OAB-0450

Engel, Arthur. Exploring mathematics with your computer. OAB-1675

Engel, June. The complete breast book. OAB-1632

Engel, Mark. On heroes, hero-worship, & the heroic in history. OAB-0662

Engen, Glenn F. Microwave circuit theory and foundations of microwave metrology. OAB-1515

Engerman, Stanley L., ed. The Cambridge economic history of the United States: v.1: The Colonial era. OAB-2015

Englander, David. Mr. Charles Booth's inquiry. OAB-2397

Englander, Irv. The architecture of computer hardware systems software. OAB-1451

Enloe, Cynthia. The morning after. OAB-2840

Ennis, Philip H. The seventh stream. OAB-1043

Ensign, Margee M. Doing good or doing well? OAB-2065

Ensminger, Jean. Making a market. OAB-1997

Epstein, David. Shaping time. OAB-1027

Epstein, Lee. The Supreme Court compendium. OAB-0283

Epstein, Marc J. Measuring corporate environmental performance. OAB-1902

Epstein, Steven A. Genoa & the Genoese, 958-1528. OAB-2325

Erdem, Y Hakan. Slavery in the Ottoman Empire and its demise, 1800-1909. OAB-2438

Erickson, Lee. The economy of literary form. OAB-0671

Errington, Frederick K. Articulating change in the "last unknown." OAB-1871

Erspamer, Peter R. The elusiveness of tolerance. OAB-0862

Erting, Carol J., ed. The deaf way. OAB-3012

Espiritu, Yen Le. Asian American panethnicity. OAB-3080

Esposito, John L. Islam and democracy. OAB-2841

Estabrooks, Maurice. Electronic technology, corporate strategy, and world transformation. OAB-1973

Estes, Carroll L. The long term care crisis. OAB-1606

Estrin, Barbara L. Laura: uncovering gender and genre in Wyatt, Donne, and Marvell. OAB-0339

Etnier, David A. The fishes of Tennessee. OAB-1797

Ettin, Andrew Vogel. Betrayals of the body politic. OAB-0717

Eulau, Heinz. Micro-macro dilemmas in political science. OAB-2842

Evans, Arthur V. An inordinate fondness for beetles. OAB-1798

Evans, G.R. Philosophy and theology in the Middle Ages. OAB-1121

Evans, Gary R. Red Ink: the budget, deficit, and debt of the U.S. government. OAB-2020

Evans, Helen C., ed. The Glory of Byzantium. OAB-0370

Evans, Peter. Embedded autonomy. OAB-2644

Evans, Peter William. Biblical epics. OAB-0968

Everdell, William R. The first moderns. OAB-0340

Ewen, Stuart. PR!: a social history of spin. OAB-0513

Eysenck, H.J. Genius: the natural history of creativity. OAB-2956

F

Faber, Daniel. Environment under fire. OAB-2416

Faber, T.E. Fluid dynamics for physicists. OAB-1709

Fábrega, Horacio. Evolution of sickness and healing. OAB-1585

Fagan, Brian M., ed. The Oxford companion to archaeology. OAB-0192

Faille, Christopher C. The decline and fall of the Supreme Court. OAB-2919

Fairbrothers, David E. New Jersey ferns and fern-allies. OAB-1408

Fairclough, Adam. Race & democracy. OAB-2592

Fairholm, Gilbert W. Leadership and the culture of trust. OAB-1920

Fairholm, Gilbert W. Organizational power politics. OAB-1921

Falk, Thomas H. Elias Canetti. OAB-0863

Falkner, David. Great time coming. OAB-1763

Fallon, Robert Thomas. Divided empire: Milton's political imagery. OAB-0643

Fantham, Elaine. Roman literary culture. OAB-0604

Farley, Reynolds, ed. State of the union: America in the 1990s, v.1 & 2. OAB-3030

Faroqhi, Suraiya. Pilgrims and sultans. OAB-2439

Farrar, John Laird. Trees of the northern United States and Canada. OAB-1399

Farrell, T., ed. Electrical resistivity handbook. OAB-1514

Farrell, Thomas B. Norms of rhetorical culture. OAB-0534

Fast, Cathy Carroll. The women's atlas of the United States. OAB-0255

Fast, Timothy H. The women's atlas of the United States. OAB-0255

Fawaz, Leila Tarazi. An occasion for war. OAB-2440

Fehr, Beverley. Friendship processes. OAB-2979

Feld, Jacob. Construction failure. OAB-1552

Feldman, Louis H. Jew and Gentile in the ancient world. OAB-1237

Feldman, Martha. City culture and the madrigal at Venice. OAB-1014

Feldman, Ofer. Politics and the news media in Japan. OAB-0514

Feldstein, Josh. The silicone breast implant controversy. OAB-1655

Felstiner, John. Paul Celan: poet, survivor, Jew. OAB-0864

Felton, Keith Spencer. Warriors' words. OAB-0535

Fender, Stephen. Sea changes. OAB-0730

Fendrich, James Max. Ideal citizens. OAB-3081

Fentress, James, tr. The search for the perfect language. OAB-0329

Ferguson, Kitty. The fire in the equations. OAB-1275

Ferns, P.N. Bird life of coasts and estuaries. OAB-1799

Ferrari, Rita. Innocence, power, and the novels of John Hawkes. OAB-0825

Ferrier, Robert J. Monosaccharides: their chemistry and their roles in natural products. OAB-1425

Ferry, Ann. The title to the poem. OAB-0544

Feynman, Richard P. Six not-so-easy pieces. OAB-1710

Field, Michael. Inside the Arab world. OAB-2441

Fierce, Milfred C. The Pan-African idea in the United States, 1900-1919. OAB-2593

Figes, Orlando. A people's tragedy. OAB-2300

Finaldi, Gabriele. Discovering the Italian Baroque. OAB-0454

Findling, John E., ed. Historical dictionary of the modern Olympic movement. OAB-1765

Fine, John V.A. Bosnia and Hercegovina. OAB-2299

Fink, Eugen. Sixth Cartesian meditation. OAB-1097

Finkin, Matthew W. The case for tenure. OAB-2109

Finnemore, Martha. National interests in international society. OAB-2740

Firestone, Ross. Swing, swing, swing. OAB-1044

Firmin-Sellers, Kathryn. The transformation of property rights in the Gold Coast. OAB-2651

Fischer, Eberhard. Pahari masters: court painters of northern India. OAB-0458

Fischer, Felice. Japanese design. OAB-0426

Fischer, Frank, ed. The argumentative turn in policy analysis and planning. OAB-2805

Fischer, John Martin. The metaphysics of free will. OAB-1131

Fischer, Roger A. Them damned pictures. OAB-2476

Fisher, Donald. Fundamental development of the social sciences. OAB-1828

Fishkin, Shelley Fisher. Was Huck black? Mark Twain and African-American voices. OAB-0749

Fishman, Nina. The British Communist Party and the trade unions, 1933-45. OAB-2388

Fitton, J. Lesley. The discovery of the Greek Bronze Age. OAB-2196

Fitz-enz, Jac. The 8 practices of exceptional companies. OAB-1941

Fitzgerald, F. Scott. The love of *The last tycoon*. OAB-0787

Fitzpatrick, Sheila. Stalin's peasants. OAB-2301

Fladmark, Knut R. Prophecy of the swan. OAB-2462

Flanagan, Owen. Consciousness reconsidered. OAB-1157

Flannery, Tim. Mammals of the South-West Pacific & Moluccan Islands. OAB-1800

Fleming, Robert E. The face in the mirror. OAB-0788

Fletcher, George P. Loyalty: an essay on the morality of relationships. OAB-1132

Fletcher, Philip. Chemical thermodynamics for earth scientists. OAB-1478

Floyd, Samuel A. The power of black music. OAB-1045

Flueckiger, Joyce Burkhalter. Gender and genre in the folklore of Middle India. OAB-0341

Fogel, Daniel Mark, ed. A companion to Henry James studies. OAB-0747

Foley, Barbara. Radical representations. OAB-0789

Fölsing, Albrecht. Albert Einstein: a biography. OAB-1711

Folsom, Ed. Walt Whitman's native representations. OAB-0750

Foner, Nancy. The caregiving dilemma. OAB-1607

Fong, Wen C. Possessing the past. OAB-0386

Fonseca, James W. The atlas of American society. OAB-0310

Fontenot, Wonda L. Secret doctors. OAB-1586

Foot, Rosemary. The practice of power. OAB-2763

Foote, Horton. Horton Foote's three trips to Bountiful. OAB-0942

Forbes, Vivian Louis. The maritime boundaries of the Indian Ocean region. OAB-2442

Ford, Caroline. Creating the nation in provincial France. OAB-2326

Ford, Donna Y. Reversing underachievement among gifted black students. OAB-2138

Ford, Emma. Peregrine. OAB-1801

Form, William. Segmented labor, fractured politics. OAB-1942

Forni, Pier Massimo. Adventures in speech. OAB-0899

Forsberg, Randall. Nonproliferation primer. OAB-2741

Fort, Rodney D. Pay dirt. OAB-1771

Fortmann, Michel. A diplomacy of hope. OAB-2685

Foster, David William. Violence in Argentine literature. OAB-0909

Foster, R.F. W.B. Yeats: a life. [v.]1: The apprentice mage, 1865-1914. OAB-0696

Foster, Susan Leigh. Choreography narrative. OAB-1059

Fotion, Nick. Toleration. OAB-1133

Foucault, Michel. Ethics: subjectivity and truth. OAB-1134

Fowler, H.W. The new Fowler's modern English usage. OAB-0012

Fowler, Jeaneane. Hinduism: beliefs and practices. OAB-1187

Fowler, Linda L. Candidates, Congress, and the American democracy. OAB-2900

Fowler, T. Kenneth. The fusion quest. OAB-1712

Fox, James R. Dictionary of international & comparative law. OAB-0284

Fox, Matthew. The reinvention of work. OAB-1943

Fox, Richard Allan. Archaeology, history, and Custer's last battle. OAB-2548

Frame, Murray, comp. The Russian Revolution, 1905-1921: a bibliographic guide to works in English. OAB-0234

France, Peter, ed. The new Oxford companion to literature in French. OAB-0079

Francis, Peter. Volcanoes: a planetary perspective. OAB-1479

Frankel, Benjamin, ed. The Cold War, 1945-1991: v.1. OAB-0212

Frankel, Glenn. Beyond the promised land. OAB-2673

Franklin, David. Rosso in Italy. OAB-0455

Franklin, Donna L. Ensuring inequality. OAB-3054

Franklin, Simon. The emergence of Rus, 750-1200. OAB-2197

Franz, Marie-Louise von. Archetypal dimensions of the psyche. OAB-2942

Franzen, Cola, tr. The challenge of comparative literature. OAB-0546

Fraser, Angus. The Gypsies. OAB-1872

Fraser, James. Japanese modern. OAB-0422

Fraser-Lu, Sylvia. Burmese crafts. OAB-0423

Frawley, Maria H. A wider range. OAB-0672

Freedman, David Noel, ed. The Anchor Bible dictionary. OAB-0113

Freeman, Harry M., ed. Industrial pollution prevention handbook. OAB-1527

Freeman, Mark. Finding the muse. OAB-0369

French, R. Antony. Plans, pragmatism and people. OAB-2302

Frey, Hans-Jost. Studies in poetic discourse. OAB-0545

Fridlund, Alan J. Human facial expression. OAB-1751

Friedel, Helmut, ed. Vasily Kandinsky: a colorful life: the collection of the Lenbachhaus, Munich. OAB-0443

Friedlander, Michael W. At the fringes of science. OAB-1276

Friedman, Susan W. Marc Bloch, sociology and geography. OAB-2161

Friell, Gerard. Theodosius: the empire at bay. OAB-2224

Fries, Heinrich. Fundamental theology. OAB-1255

Frisch, Michael. Portraits in steel. OAB-2626

Frisch, Walter. The early works of Arnold Schoenberg, 1893-1908. OAB-1000

Fritzsche, Peter. Reading Berlin 1900. OAB-0865

Frommel, Christoph L., ed. The architectural drawings of Antonio da Sangallo the Younger and his circle: v.1: Fortifications, machines, and festival architecture. OAB-0393

Frost-Knappman, Elizabeth. The ABC-CLIO companion to women's progress in America. OAB-0256

Fruton, Joseph S. A skeptical biochemist. OAB-1427

Frydman, Roman. The Privatization process in Central Europe. OAB-2056

Frye, Joanne S. Tillie Olsen: a study of the short fiction. OAB-0826

Frye, Richard N. The heritage of Central Asia. OAB-2443

Fuchs, Elinor. The death of character. OAB-1060

Fulbrook, Mary. The divided nation. OAB-2362

Fullagar, Clive. The union and its members. OAB-1934

Fuller, Kathryn H. Children and the movies. OAB-0979

Fullerton, Carol S., ed. Posttraumatic stress disorder. OAB-1643

Fulton, Richard L. Marketing to the mind. OAB-1958

Furedi, Frank. Population and development. OAB-1974

Furman, Andrew. Israel through the Jewish-American imagination. OAB-0827

G

Gabor, Andrea. Einstein's wife. OAB-3055

Gadamer, Hans-Georg. The philosophy of Hans-Georg Gadamer. OAB-1098

Gaddy, Barbara B. School wars. OAB-2111

Gaffney, Eugene S. Discovering dinosaurs in the Museum of Natural History. OAB-1492

Gaiduk, Ilya V. The Soviet Union and the Vietnam War. OAB-2303

Galens, Judy, ed. Gale encyclopedia of multicultural America. OAB-0257

Galston, Arthur W. Life processes of plants. OAB-1402

Gambetta, Diego. The Sicilian Mafia. OAB-3040

Gamble, Vanessa Northington. Making a place for ourselves. OAB-2594

Gans, Herbert J. The war against the poor. OAB-3099

Gantz, Timothy. Early Greek myth. OAB-0605

Gänzl, Kurt. The encyclopedia of the musical theatre. OAB-0097

Garcia, Juan R. Mexicans in the Midwest, 1900-1932. OAB-2595

Gardaphé, Fred L. Italian signs, American streets. OAB-0828

Gardiner, Juliet, ed. The Columbia companion to British history. OAB-0232

Gardner, B. Delworth. Plowing ground in Washington. OAB-2096

Gardner, M. Robert. On trying to teach. OAB-2139

Garfinkle, Robert A. Star-hopping: your visa to viewing the universe. OAB-1332

Garlake, Peter. The hunter's vision. OAB-2231

Garner, Bryan A. A dictionary of modern legal usage. OAB-0285

Garner, Stanton. The Civil War world of Herman Melville. OAB-0751

Garoogian, Rhoda, ed. Crime in America's top-rated cities. OAB-0319

Garthoff, Raymond L. The great transition. OAB-2764

Gartner, Alan. Inclusion and school reform. OAB-2119

Gauld, Joseph W. Character first. OAB-2140

Gauthier, Anne Hélène. The state and the family. OAB-3056

Gazzaniga, Michael S., ed. The Cognitive neurosciences. OAB-1749

Geballe, Gordon T. Redesigning the American lawn. OAB-1313

Geddes, Barbara. Politician's dilemma. OAB-2725

Gedicks, Frederick Mark. The rhetoric of church and state. OAB-2920

Gee, Henry. Before the backbone. OAB-1802

Geis, Deborah R. Postmodern theatric(k)s. OAB-0829

Geison, Gerald L. The private science of Louis Pasteur. OAB-1299

Gelderman, Carol. All the presidents' words. OAB-2901

Gell-Mann, Murray. The quark and the jaguar. OAB-1713

Gendre, Michael, ed. Poetics, speculation, and judgement. OAB-1114

Gerdts, William H. William Glackens. OAB-0456

Gerli, E. Michael. Refiguring authority. OAB-0910

Gerrig, Richard J. Experiencing narrative worlds. OAB-0330

Gewertz, Deborah B. Articulating change in the "last unknown." OAB-1871

Gewirth, Alan. The community of rights. OAB-2843

Gezari, Janet. Charlotte Brontë and defensive conduct. OAB-0673

Ghorayshi, Parvin, comp. Women and work in developing countries. OAB-0323

Gibbons, Sheila J. Taking their place. OAB-0505

Gibson, Gordon. Thirty million musketeers. OAB-2682

Gibson, Rowan. Rethinking the future. OAB-1903

Gibson, Roy. Space. OAB-1333

Gill, James E., ed. Cutting edges: postmodern critical essays on eighteenth-century satire. OAB-0638

Gill, Sam D. Dictionary of Native American mythology. OAB-0189

Gillies, David. Between principle and practice. OAB-2742

Gillison, Gillian. Between culture and fantasy. OAB-1873

Gillman, Howard. The Constitution besieged. OAB-2811

Gillon, Steven M. The Democrats' dilemma. OAB-2765

Gilman, Richard. Chekhov's plays: an opening into eternity. OAB-0924

Gilman, Sander L. Freud, race, and gender. OAB-2943

Gimferrer, Pere. The roots of Miró. OAB-0457

Gingerich, Owen. The eye of heaven. OAB-1334

Gipe, Paul. Wind energy comes of age. OAB-1553

Given, David R. Principles and practice of plant conservation. OAB-1403

Givens-Ackerman, Janet. Stuttering. OAB-1650

Glaser, Daniel. Preparing convicts for law-abiding lives. OAB-3041

Glaser, James M. Race, campaign politics, and the realignment in the South. OAB-2902

Glass, Leon. Understanding nonlinear dynamics. OAB-1682

Glen, William, ed. The Mass-extinction debates. OAB-1487

Glick, Bernard R. Molecular biotechnology. OAB-1362

Glick, Henry R. The right to die. OAB-2844

Glickman, Harvey, ed. Political leaders of contemporary Africa south of the Sahara. OAB-0297

Glusker, Jenny P. Crystal structure analysis for chemists and biologists. OAB-1426

Godfray, H.C.J. Parasitoids: behavioral and evolutionary ecology. OAB-1803

Goehlert, Robert U. The United States Congress. OAB-0286

Gogol, Miriam, ed. Theodore Dreiser: beyond naturalism. OAB-0807

Goldberg, David Theo. Racist culture. OAB-3082

Goldberg, Michael K. On heroes, hero-worship, & the heroic in history. OAB-0662

Goldhill, Simon. Aeschylus, the *Oresteia*. OAB-0606

Golding, Alan. From outlaw to classic. OAB-0731

Goldsmith, Donald. Einstein's greatest blunder? OAB-1335

Goldstein, Robert Justin. Burning the flag: the great 1989-1990 American flag desecration controversy. OAB-2812

Goldwhite, Harold. Creations of fire. OAB-1424

Golob, Richard. The almanac of renewable energy. OAB-1524

Gómez-Ibáñez, José A. Regulation for revenue. OAB-2093

Gommans, Jos J.L. The rise of the Indo-Afghan empire, c. 1710-1780. OAB-2259

Gonosová, Anna. Art of Late Rome and Byzantium in the Virginia Museum of Fine Arts. OAB-0440

González Echevarriía, Roberto, ed. The Cambridge history of Latin American literature: v. 1-3. OAB-0907

Goodall, Francis, ed. International bibliography of business history. OAB-0203

Goodin, Robert E., ed. A New handbook of political science. OAB-2647

Goodman, Bryna. Native place, city, and nation. OAB-2260

Goodman, Lenn E. Avicenna. OAB-1122

Goodridge, John. Rural life in eighteenth-century English poetry. OAB-0644

Goodwin, Andrew. Dancing in the distraction factory. OAB-1046

Gootenberg, Paul. Imagining development. OAB-2417

Gordon, David M., ed. Ezra Pound and James Laughlin. OAB-0803

Gordon, Linda. Pitied but not entitled. OAB-3100

Gordon, Robert B. The texture of industry. OAB-1300

Gordon, Robert S.C. Pasolini: forms of subjectivity. OAB-0976

Gordon, Sarah H. Passage to Union. OAB-2477

Gorman, Robert F. Historical dictionary of refugee and disaster relief organizations. OAB-0174

Gorna, Robin. Vamps, virgins and victims. OAB-1633

Gorrell, Lorraine. The nineteenth-century German Lied. OAB-1015

Gorski, Philip S. The German Left. OAB-2707

Goscilo, Helena, ed. Lives in transit: a collection of recent Russian women's writing. OAB-0925

Goswamy, B.N. Pahari masters: court painters of northern India. OAB-0458

Gotelli, Nicholas J. Null models in ecology. OAB-1363

Gottfried, Heidi, ed. Feminism and social change. OAB-1827

Gotwald, William H. Army ants: the biology of social predation. OAB-1804

Gould, Carol Grant. The animal mind. OAB-1805

Gould, James L. The animal mind. OAB-1805

Gould, Stephen Jay. Eight little piggies. OAB-1364

Gould, Tony. A summer plague. OAB-1634

Gow, Neil A.R., ed. The growing fungus. OAB-1404

Goy, Richard J. The house of gold. OAB-0403

Grabar, Oleg. The shape of the holy. OAB-2444

Graff, Harvey J. Conflicting paths. OAB-2478

Grafton, Carl. Political power in Alabama. OAB-2621

Graham, John W. Mission statements. OAB-0175

Graham, Kenneth. Henry James: a literary life. OAB-0752

Graham, Loren R. Science in Russia and the Soviet Union. OAB-1302

Graham, Loren R. The ghost of the executed engineer. OAB-1301

Grassby, Richard. The business community of seventeenth-century England. OAB-2389

Graves, Gary R. Null models in ecology. OAB-1363

Grayson, J.C., tr. Antwerp in the age of Reformation. OAB-1218

Grayson, Marion L., tr. Michelangelo architect. OAB-0394

Green, Elna C. Southern strategies. OAB-2596

Green, Neville. Commandant of solitude. OAB-2274

Greenberg, Stanley B. Middle class dreams. OAB-2880

Greene, Gayle. Doris Lessing: the poetics of change. OAB-0697

Greenfeld, Liah. Nationalism: five roads to modernity. OAB-2845

Greenhous, Brereton. The crucible of war, 1939-1945. OAB-2465

Greenshields, Malcolm. An economy of violence in early modern France. OAB-2327

Greenspahn, Frederick E. When brothers dwell together. OAB-1256

Greenstein, Edward L. The timetables of Jewish history. OAB-0223

Greenwood, Addison. Science at the frontier, v.1. OAB-1277

Greenwood, Janette Thomas. Bittersweet legacy. OAB-2549

Greer, Allan. The patriots and the people. OAB-2466

Gregory, Joel W. Hoe and wage. OAB-2228

Grenon, Michel. Instability and conflict in the Middle East. OAB-2774

Gribetz, Judah. The timetables of Jewish history. OAB-0223

Griffin, Stephen M. American Constitutionalism: from theory to politics. OAB-2921

Griffith, John W. Joseph Conrad and the anthropological dilemma. OAB-0698

Grimaldi, David A. Amber: window to the past. OAB-1481

Grimes, Robert R. How shall we sing in a foreign land? OAB-1047

Grimsley, Mark. The hard hand of war. OAB-2550

Grindon, Leger. Shadows on the past. OAB-0977

Griscom, Richard. The recorder. OAB-0098

Griswold, Jerry. Audacious kids. OAB-0732

Grobsmith, Elizabeth S. Indians in prison. OAB-3042

Groenewegen, Peter. A soaring eagle. OAB-1975

Grondin, Jean. Introduction to philosophical hermeneutics. OAB-1158

Gros, Daniel. European monetary integration. OAB-2067

Gross, John. Shylock. OAB-0620

Gross, Rita M. Buddhism after patriarchy. OAB-1188

Grossman, Mark. Encyclopedia of the Persian Gulf War. OAB-0224

Grote, David. British English for American readers. OAB-0043

Groth, Paul. Living downtown. OAB-3101

Grover, Kathryn. Make a way somehow. OAB-2479

Grudin, Michaela Paasche. Chaucer and the politics of discourse. OAB-0621

Grugel, Jean. Politics and development in the Caribbean Basin. OAB-2780

Gruzinski, Serge. The conquest of Mexico. OAB-2418

Guelzo, Allen C. For the union of Evangelical Christendom. OAB-1208

Guerin-Gonzales, Camille. Mexican workers and American dreams. OAB-2419

Guerra, Lucas H. Hyper-realistic: computer generated architectural renderings. OAB-1461

Guggenheimer, Eva H. Jewish family names and their origins. OAB-0015

Guggenheimer, Heinrich W. Jewish family names and their origins. OAB-0015

Gugler, Josef, ed. The Urban transformation of the developing world. OAB-3033

Guider, Margaret Eletta. Daughters of Rahab. OAB-1209

Guilds, John Caldwell. Simms: a literary life. OAB-0753

Guillaume, de Machaut. The fountain of love (La fonteinne amoureuse) and two other love vision poems. OAB-0884

Guillaumont, Robert. Fundamentals of radiochemistry. OAB-1417

Guillén, Claudio. The challenge of comparative literature. OAB-0546

Guillen, Michael. Five equations that changed the world. OAB-1714

Gullberg, Jan. Mathematics: from the birth of numbers. OAB-1677

Gundersen, Joan R. To be useful to the world. OAB-2516

Gunn, Anne. Conservation biology in theory and practice. OAB-1356

Gunn, T. Jeremy. A standard for repair. OAB-2922

Gunning, Sandra. Race, rape, and lynching. OAB-0790

Guralnick, Peter. Last train to Memphis. OAB-2597

Gurney, Peter. Co-operative culture and the politics of consumption in England, 1870-1930. OAB-2390

Gustafson, Thane. Russia 2010—and what it means for the world. OAB-2802

Gutiérrez, David G. Walls and mirrors. OAB-3083

Gutmann, Amy. Democracy and disagreement. OAB-2846

Gutteridge, Thomas G. Organizational career development. OAB-1944

Guttmann, Joseph. Divorce in psychosocial perspective. OAB-3057

Guttmann, Robert. How credit-money shapes the economy. OAB-2068

Guy, Richard K. The book of numbers. OAB-1668

H

Haan, C.T. Design hydrology and sedimentology for small catchments. OAB-1554

Haar, Michel. Heidegger and the essence of man. OAB-1159

Haas, Christopher. Alexandria in late antiquity. OAB-2198

Haas, Marilyn L. The Seneca and Tuscarora Indians. OAB-0258

Haass, Richard N. Intervention: the use of American military force.... OAB-2766

Haberstroh, Patricia Boyle. Women creating women. OAB-0699

Hachette, Dominique. Privatization in Chile. OAB-2039

Hadda, Janet. Isaac Bashevis Singer: a life. OAB-0572

Haft, Lloyd. A guide to Chinese literature. OAB-0585

Haghayeghi, Mehrdad. Islam and politics in Central Asia. OAB-2781

Hagopian, Frances. Traditional politics and regime change in Brazil. OAB-2726

Hagstrum, Jean H. Esteem enlivened by desire. OAB-0547

Hahl-Koch, Jelena. Kandinsky. OAB-0459

Hahn, Lewis Edwin, ed. The philosophy of Hans-Georg Gadamer. OAB-1098

Halaas, David Fridtjof. Cheyenne dog soldiers. OAB-2535

Halberstam, David. October 1964. OAB-1764

Halberstam, Judith. Skin shows. OAB-0342

Haliczer, Stephen. Sexuality in the confessional. OAB-2162

Hall, A. Rupert. All was light. OAB-1715

Hall, A. Rupert. Isaac Newton, adventurer in thought. OAB-1716

Hall, Cally. Gemstones. OAB-1482

Hall, Christopher G.L. Steel phoenix. OAB-2021

Hall, Colin Michael. Tourism and politics. OAB-2163

Hall, Edwin. The Arnolfini betrothal. OAB-0460

Hall, Gwendolyn Midlo. Africans in Colonial Louisiana. OAB-2517

Hall, Kermit L., ed. The Oxford companion to the Supreme Court of the United States. OAB-2931

Hall, Kim F. Things of darkness. OAB-0645

Hall, Lesley. The facts of life: the creation of sexual knowledge in Britain, 1650-1950. OAB-2400

Hall, Stephen K. Chemical safety in the laboratory. OAB-1428

Hall, T. William. School wars. OAB-2111

Halliday, Fred. Islam and the myth of confrontation. OAB-2782

Hallion, Richard P. Storm over Iraq. OAB-2598

Halliwell, S., tr. Republic 5. OAB-1125

Hallwas, Jonn E., ed. Spoon River anthology. OAB-0800

Haltiwanger, John C. Job creation and destruction. OAB-2086

Hamamoto, Darrell Y. Monitored peril. OAB-0515

Hamber, Anthony J. "A higher branch of the art." OAB-0486

Hamid, S. Halim, ed. Handbook of polymer degradation. OAB-1555

Hamilton, Ian, ed. The Oxford companion to twentieth-century poetry in English. OAB-0086

Hamilton, J. Scott. Prophecy of the swan. OAB-2462

Hamilton, V. Lee. Everyday justice. OAB-3015

Hamlin, William M. The image of America in Montaigne, Spenser, and Shakespeare. OAB-0622

Hanawalt, Barbara A. Growing up in medieval London. OAB-2199

Hands, Timothy. Thomas Hardy. OAB-0674

Handy, D. Antoinette. Black conductors. OAB-1001

Hanf, Theodor. Coexistence in wartime Lebanon. OAB-2653

Hanley, Susan B. Everyday things in premodern Japan. OAB-2261

Hanlon, Robert T. Cephalopod behaviour. OAB-1808

Hanna, Martha. The mobilization of intellect. OAB-2328

Hanna, Owen T. Computational methods in chemical engineering. OAB-1507

Hannaford, Robert V. Moral anatomy and moral reasoning. OAB-1135

Hanne, Michael. The power of the story. OAB-0548

Hansen, C.J. Stellar interiors. OAB-1336

Hansen, Elaine Tuttle. Mother without child. OAB-0830

Hansen, Phillip. Hannah Arendt: politics, history, and citizenship. OAB-2847

Hansen, Thomas S. The German face of Edgar Allan Poe. OAB-0675

Hanski, Ilkka, ed. Metapopulation biology. OAB-1374

Hapke, Laura. Daughters of the Great Depression. OAB-0791

Hapke, Laura. Tales of the working girl. OAB-0792

Harding, Sandra, ed. The "Racial" economy of science. OAB-1269

Hardman, John. French politics, 1774-1789. OAB-2329

Hardman, John. Louis XVI. OAB-2330

Hardy, Anne. The epidemic streets. OAB-1610

Hardy, Friedhelm. The religious culture of India. OAB-1189

Hardy, Thomas. Thomas Hardy: the excluded and collaborative stories. OAB-0676

Harford, James. Korolev: how one man masterminded the Soviet drive.... OAB-1303

Hargreaves, Mary W.M. Dry farming in the northern Great Plains. OAB-2599

Harley, Trevor A. The psychology of language. OAB-2957

Harman, Gilbert. Moral relativism and moral objectivity. OAB-1136

Harré, Rom. Realism rescued. OAB-1270

Harrell, David. From Mesa Verde to The professor's house. OAB-0793

Harries, Jill. Sidonius Apollinaris and the fall of Rome, AD 407-485. OAB-2200

Harries, Meirion. The last days of innocence. OAB-2600

Harries, Susie. The last days of innocence. OAB-2600

Harrington, Joel F. Reordering marriage and society in Reformation Germany. OAB-2363

Harris, Cyril M., ed. Dictionary of architecture & construction. OAB-0048

Harris, Gordon, comp. Organization of African unity. OAB-0287

Harris, Henry. The cells of the body. OAB-1365

Harris, Ian. Longman guide to living religions. OAB-0122

Harris, James G. Plant identification terminology. OAB-1405

Harris, Janice Hubbard. Edwardian stories of divorce. OAB-0700

Harris, Kathleen Mullan. Teen mothers and the revolving door. OAB-3058

Harris, Melinda Woolf. Plant identification terminology. OAB-1405

Harris, Michael. Outsiders and insiders. OAB-0718

Harris, Nigel. The new untouchables. OAB-2087

Harris, Oliver, ed. The letters of William S. Burroughs. OAB-0819

Harris, Sheldon H. Factories of death. OAB-2601

Harrop, John. Acting. OAB-1061

Hart, Betty. Meaningful differences in the everyday experience of young American children. OAB-2141

Hart, Gail K. Tragedy in paradise. OAB-0867

Hart, Henry. Robert Lowell and the sublime. OAB-0831

Hart, Vivien. Bound by our Constitution. OAB-2923

Harth, Phillip. Pen for a party. OAB-0646

Hartigan, Karelisa V. Greek tragedy on the American stage. OAB-1062

Hartmann, William M. Signals, sound, and sensation. OAB-2958

Harvey, Barbara. Living and dying in England, 1100-1540. OAB-2201

Harvey, David. Justice, nature and the geography of difference. OAB-2164

Harvey, Robert C. The art of the funnies. OAB-0424

Haslett, D.W. Capitalism with morality. OAB-1976

Hastings, Adrian. The Church in Africa, 1450-1950. OAB-1210

Hastings, Selina. Evelyn Waugh: a biography. OAB-0701

Hatch, J. Amos, ed. Qualitative research in early childhood settings. OAB-2150

Hatcher, John. Laurence Binyon: poet, scholar of East and West. OAB-0344

Hauerwas, Stanley. Christians among the virtues. OAB-1137

Haupt, Heinz-Gerhard. The petite bourgeoisie in Europe, 1780-1914. OAB-2288

Hauptman, Laurence M. Between two fires. OAB-2551

Hauptman, William. Charles Gleyre, 1806-1874: v.1: Life and works; v.2: Catalogue raisonné. OAB-0461

Hauser, Barbara R., ed. Women's legal guide. OAB-0309

Hauser, Marc D. The evolution of communication. OAB-1366

Havlick, Wendy C. Mission statements. OAB-0175

Hawkins, Gordon. Incapacitation. OAB-3048

Hawkins-Dady, Mark, ed. International dictionary of theatre: v.1: Plays. OAB-0103

Hay, Samuel A. African American theatre. OAB-1063

Hayden, Dolores. The power of place. OAB-2480

Hayes, Bascom Barry. Bismarck and Mitteleuropa. OAB-2364

Hayes, J.C. Design hydrology and sedimentology for small catchments. OAB-1554

Hayes, Sandra A. Catastrophe theory. OAB-1665

Hayhoe, Ruth. China's universities, 1895-1995. OAB-2112

Hayman, Ronald. Thomas Mann: a biography. OAB-0868

Heaney, Seamus. The redress of poetry. OAB-0702

Hearnshaw, J.B. The measurement of starlight. OAB-1337

Heather, Peter. The Goths. OAB-2365

Hegedus, Louis S. Transition metals in the synthesis of complex organic molecules. OAB-1429

Heidegger, Martin. Basic concepts. OAB-1160

Heifetz, Ronald A. Leadership without easy answers. OAB-2882

Heilbroner, Robert. Teachings from the worldly philosophy. OAB-1977

Heilbrunn, Jeffrey, ed. AMA marketing encyclopedia. OAB-1954

Heim, Michael. The metaphysics of virtual reality. OAB-1452

Heine, Jorge. The last cacique. OAB-2727

Heinemann, Ronald L. Harry Byrd of Virginia. OAB-2602

Heininger, Janet E. Peacekeeping in transition. OAB-2674

Heinrich, Bernd. The hot-blooded insects. OAB-1809

Held, David. Democracy and the global order. OAB-2848

Heldman, Robert K. Information telecommunications. OAB-1453

Heller, Jules, ed. North American women artists of the twentieth century. OAB-0054

Heller, Steven. Japanese modern. OAB-0422

Heller, Vivian. Joyce, decadence, and emancipation. OAB-0703

Hemmings, F.W.J. Theatre and state in France, 1760-1905. OAB-1064

Henderson, Gail E., ed. The Social medicine reader. OAB-1618

Henderson, George. Cultural diversity in the workplace. OAB-2998

Hendricks, Janet Wall. To drink of death. OAB-1874

Hendrickson, Carol. Weaving identities. OAB-1875

Henisch, Bridget A. The painted photograph, 1839-1914. OAB-0487

Henisch, Heinz K. The painted photograph, 1839-1914. OAB-0487

Henkin, Louis. Foreign affairs and the United States Constitution. OAB-2924

Henneman, John Bell. Olivier de Clisson and political society in France under Charles V and Charles VI. OAB-2331

Hennen, John C. The Americanization of West Virginia. OAB-2603

Henningham, Stephen. The Pacific island states. OAB-2783

Henry, Madeleine M. Prisoner of history. OAB-2202

Henry, Mary E. Parent-school collaboration. OAB-2113

Henry, Paget, ed. C.L.R. James's Caribbean. OAB-0715

Henslin, James M. Homelessness: an annotated bibliography. OAB-0324

Herbig, Paul. Innovation Japanese style. OAB-1904

Herbst, Jurgen. The once and future school. OAB-2114

Herder, Johann Gottfried. Johann Gottfried Herder: selected early works, 1764-1767: addresses, essays.... OAB-0869

Herman, Barbara. The practice of moral judgment. OAB-1138

Herman, Ellen. The romance of American psychology. OAB-2944

Herman, Michael. Intelligence power in peace and war. OAB-2743

Herring, Eric. Keyguide to information sources in strategic studies. OAB-0272

Herring, Phillip. Djuna: the life and work of Djuna Barnes. OAB-0794

Herrington, Anne, ed. Writing, teaching, and learning in the disciplines. OAB-2156

Herrnstein, Richard J. The bell curve. OAB-2959

Hershfield, Joanne. Mexican cinema/Mexican woman, 1940-1950. OAB-0953

Hesse, M.G. Yves Thériault, master storyteller. OAB-0885

Hesse-Biber, Sharlene. Am I thin enough yet? OAB-2982

Hetherington, Stephen Cade. Knowledge puzzles. OAB-1161

Heym, Georg. The thief and other stories. OAB-0870

Heyman, Barbara B. Samuel Barber: the composer and his music. OAB-1002

Heyman, Jacques. The stone skeleton. OAB-1556

Hickey, Gerald Cannon. Shattered world. OAB-1876

Hickman, Money L. Japan's golden age: Momoyama. OAB-0429

Hiesinger, Kathryn B. Japanese design. OAB-0426

Hiesinger, Ulrich W. Childe Hassam: American impressionist. OAB-0462

Higginbotham, Evelyn Brooks. Righteous discontent. OAB-1211

Higgins, Lynn A. New novel, new wave, new politics. OAB-0886

Higham, Charles. The bronze age of Southeast Asia. OAB-1854

Higson, Andrew. Waving the flag: constructing a national cinema in Britain. OAB-0954

Hilborn, Robert C. Chaos and nonlinear dynamics. OAB-1678

Hill, Charles E. Regnum caelorum. OAB-1212

Hill, Hal. The Indonesian economy since 1966. OAB-1998

Hill, Sarah H. Weaving new worlds. OAB-2481

Hillerbrand, Hans J., ed. The Oxford encyclopedia of the Reformation. OAB-0128

Hillyer, Barbara. Feminism and disability. OAB-3102

Hinchcliffe, Tanis. North Oxford. OAB-0404

Hinck, Edward A. Enacting the presidency. OAB-2903

Hine, Darlene Clark, ed. Black women in America: an historical encyclopedia. OAB-0243

Hing, Bill Ong. To be an American. OAB-3084

Hirano, Kyoko. Mr. Smith goes to Tokyo. OAB-0955

Hiro, Dilip. Dictionary of the Middle East. OAB-0225

Hirschfelder, Arlene. The Native American almanac. OAB-0259

Hirshberg, Jehoash. Music in the Jewish community of Palestine, 1880-1948. OAB-1016

Hischak, Thomas S. The American musical theatre song encyclopedia. OAB-0101

Hitchins, Keith. Rumania, 1866-1947. OAB-2304

Hoagwood, Terence Allan. Politics, philosophy, and the production of romantic texts. OAB-0677

Hodos, William. Comparative vertebrate neuroanatomy. OAB-1744

Hoekman, Bernard M. The political economy of the world trading system. OAB-2069

Hofferbert, Richard I. Parties, policies, and democracy. OAB-2646

Hogan, Robert, ed. Handbook of personality psychology. OAB-2981

Hogan, Robert. The years of O'Casey, 1921-1926. OAB-1065

Hogendorn, Jan S. Slow death for slavery. OAB-2238

Hohendahl, Peter Uwe. Prismatic thought. OAB-1100

Holahan, John. Medicaid since 1980. OAB-1603

Holden, Geoffrey, ed. Thermoplastic elastomers. OAB-1574

Holden, Matthew. Continuity and disruption. OAB-2813

Holdgate, Martin. From care to action. OAB-1278

Holland, Kathleen E., ed. Journeying. OAB-2143

Holland, Martin. European community integration. OAB-2784

Hollander, Jocelyn A. Gendered situations, gendered selves. OAB-1829

Holloway, David. Stalin and the bomb. OAB-2785

Holloway, Karla F.C. Codes of conduct. OAB-1901

Holloway, R. Ross. The archaeology of early Rome and Latium. OAB-2203

Holman, J.K. Wagner's Ring: a listener's companion & concordance. OAB-1028

Holmes, Gwendolyn. Handbook of environmental management and technology. OAB-1526

Holmes, Philip. Celestial encounters. OAB-1330

Holmgren, Richard A. A first course in discrete dynamical systems. OAB-1679

Holton, Gerald. Einstein, history, and other passions. OAB-1717

Holton, Gerald. Science and anti-science. OAB-1279

Homer, William Innes. Thomas Eakins: his life and art. OAB-0463

Honderich, Ted, ed. The Oxford companion to philosophy. OAB-0124

Honerkamp, Josef. Stochastic dynamical systems. OAB-1680

Honey, Martha. Hostile Acts: U.S. policy in Costa Rica in the 1980s. OAB-2728

Honig, Robert. Environmental profiles. OAB-0136

Hood, Clifton. 722 miles. OAB-1557

Hood, Leroy, ed. The code of codes. OAB-1581

Hood, William. Fra Angelico at San Marco. OAB-0464

Hoover, Gary, ed. Hoover's handbook of American business, 1993. OAB-0202

Hoppe, Göran. Peasantry to capitalism. OAB-2366

Hornblower, Simon, ed. The Oxford classical dictionary. OAB-0026

Horowitz, Irving Louis. Taking lives: genocide and state power. OAB-2645

Horowitz, Irving Louis. The conscience of worms and the cowardice of lions. OAB-2786

Horowitz, Sara R. Voicing the void. OAB-0549

Horry, Isabella. Government spending facts 2. OAB-2022

Horth, Lynn, ed. Correspondence. OAB-0759

Horton, Andrew. The zero hour. OAB-0978

Horton, Raymond D. Power failure: New York City politics and policy since 1960. OAB-2878

Hoskin, Michael, ed. The Cambridge illustrated history of astronomy. OAB-1325

Hoskins, Janet. The play of time. OAB-1877

Hosley, William. Colt: the making of an American legend. OAB-1558

Houlding, Elizabeth A., tr. Beyond suspicion. OAB-0820

Howard, Judith A. Gendered situations, gendered selves. OAB-1829

Howe, Daniel Walker. Making the American self. OAB-2482

Howe, Katherine S. Herter Brothers: furniture and interiors for a gilded age. OAB-0425

Howes, Craig. Voices of the Vietnam POWS. OAB-2604

Hoxie, Frederick E., ed. Encyclopedia of North American Indians. OAB-0010

Hoyo, Josep del, ed. Handbook of the birds of the world: v. 1 & 2. OAB-1806

Hoyo, Josep del, ed. Handbook of the birds of the world: v.3: Hoatzin to auks. OAB-1807

Hsiao-hsiao-sheng. The plum in the golden vase, or, Chin P'ing Mei: v.1: The gathering. OAB-0584

Huang, Chin Pao, ed. Aquatic chemistry. OAB-1419

Huang, Nian-Sheng. Benjamin Franklin in American thought and culture, 1790-1990. OAB-2483

Hubbard, Dolan. The sermon and the African American literary imagination. OAB-0733

Hucknell, Bruce B. Of marshes and maize. OAB-1855

Huddleston, Mark W. The higher civil service in the United States. OAB-2814

Hudson, John C. Making the Corn Belt. OAB-2484

Huff, C. Ronald. Convicted but innocent. OAB-2815

Huff, W.G. The economic growth of Singapore. OAB-1999

Huffer, Lynne. Another Colette. OAB-0887

Hughes, Derek. English drama, 1660-1700. OAB-0678

Hughes, Michael. Ireland divided. OAB-2391

Hull, Richard. Foundations of databases. OAB-1443

Hulse, Michael, tr. The emigrants. OAB-0876

Hult, Karen M. Governing the White House. OAB-2914

Hults, Linda C. The print in the western world. OAB-0427

Human Rights Watch/Middle East. Iraq's crime of genocide. OAB-2654

Hume, Kathryn. Calvino's fictions. OAB-0900

Humez, Alexander. Zero to lazy eight. OAB-1681

Humez, Nicholas. Zero to lazy eight. OAB-1681

Humfrey, Peter. Painting in Renaissance Venice. OAB-0465

Humfrey, Peter. The altarpiece in Renaissance Venice. OAB-0372

Humm, Maggie. The dictionary of feminist theory. OAB-0016

Humphrey, Doris. Doris Humphrey, the collected works, v.2. OAB-1066

Hundert, E.J. The Enlightenment's fable. OAB-2165

Hünefeldt, Christine. Paying the price of freedom. OAB-2420

Hung, Chang-Tai. War and popular culture. OAB-2262

Hunt, Michael H. The genesis of Chinese communist foreign policy. OAB-2263

Hunt, Tim. The cell cycle. OAB-1376

Hunter, Wendy. Eroding military influence in Brazil. OAB-2729

Hupchick, Dennis P. A concise historical atlas of Eastern Europe. OAB-0236

Hurley, Robert, tr. Ethics: subjectivity and truth. OAB-1134

Hutchinson, Earl Ofari. Betrayed. OAB-2485

Hutchinson, John F. Champions of charity. OAB-2166

Hutton, Frankie. The early black press in America, 1827 to 1860. OAB-0516

Hwang, Eui-Gak. The Korean economies. OAB-2000

Hyland, William G. The song is ended. OAB-1048

Hyman, Paula E. Gender and assimilation in modern Jewish history. OAB-2486

I

Idel, Moshe. Hasidism: between ecstasy and magic. OAB-1238

Idema, Wilt. A guide to Chinese literature. OAB-0585

Illingworth, Valerie, ed. The Facts on File dictionary of astronomy. OAB-0157

Impey, Oliver. The early porcelain kilns of Japan. OAB-0428

Ingram, William. The business of playing. OAB-1067

Inness, Sherrie A. The lesbian menace. OAB-0832

Institute of Medicine (U.S.). Committee on Preventing Nicotine Addiction in Children and Youths. Growing up tobacco free. OAB-1608

International Conference on the History of Civil and Commercial Aviation (1992: Lucerne, Switzerland). From airships to airbus: the history of civil and commercial aviation, v. 1 & 2. OAB-1304

Ipsen, Carl. Dictating demography. OAB-2332

Ireson, Carol J. Field, forest, and family. OAB-2264

Iriye, Akira. The Cambridge history of American foreign relations: v. 1-4. OAB-2474

Irons, Peter. Brennan vs. Rehnquist. OAB-2925

Irwin, Douglas A. Against the tide. OAB-2070

Irwin, Geoffrey. The prehistoric exploration and colonisation of the Pacific. OAB-1856

Isaacson, Walter. Kissinger: a biography. OAB-2605

Isham, Heyward, ed. Remaking Russia. OAB-2710

Israel, Jonathan. The Dutch republic: its rise, greatness, and fall, 1477-1806. OAB-2367

Itoh, Makoto. Political economy for socialism. OAB-1978

Ittmann, Karl. Work, gender and family in Victorian England. OAB-2392

Lawrence, Susan C. Charitable knowledge. OAB-1588

Lawson, Linda. Truth in publishing. OAB-0518

Lazare, Lucien. Rescue as resistance. OAB-2334

Lazear, Edward P. Personnel economics. OAB-2088

Le Rider, Jacques. Modernity and crises of identity. OAB-2368

Leal, Donald R. Enviro-capitalists. OAB-2094

Leary, William M., ed. From airships to airbus: the history of civil and commercial aviation, v. 1 & 2. OAB-2368

Lebergott, Stanley. Pursuing happiness. OAB-2024

Lebovics, Herman. True France. OAB-2335

Lebow, Richard Ned. We all lost the Cold War. OAB-2607

Lederberg, Joshua, ed. Encyclopedia of microbiology. OAB-0149

Lederman, Leon. The God particle. OAB-1720

Lee, Hermione. Virginia Woolf. OAB-0708

Lee, Jean B. The price of nationhood. OAB-2520

Lee, Robert D., ed. Rethinking Islam. OAB-1233

Leeder, Karen J., tr. The young Brecht. OAB-0873

Leff, Carol Skalnik. The Czech and Slovak republics. OAB-2705

Legault, Albert. A diplomacy of hope. OAB-2685

Lehmann, Scott. Privatizing public lands. OAB-2097

Leibowitz, Zandy B. Organizational career development. OAB-1944

Lein, Laura. Making ends meet. OAB-3098

Leja, Michael. Reframing abstract expressionism. OAB-0470

Lemke-Santangelo, Gretchen. Abiding courage. OAB-2608

Lenk, John D. Simplified design of switching power supplies. OAB-1516

Lentz, Harris M. Heads of states and governments. OAB-0292

Leonard, Carol S. Reform and regicide. OAB-2310

Leonard, George J. Into the light of things. OAB-0348

Leonard, Thomas C. News for all. OAB-0519

Leonard, Thomas M. A guide to Central American collections in the United States. OAB-0019

Leontis, Artemis. Topographies of Hellenism. OAB-0550

Lerner, Gerda. The creation of feminist consciousness. OAB-2168

Lerski, George J. Historical dictionary of Poland, 966-1945. OAB-0237

Lesage, Suzanne, ed. Groundwater contamination and analysis at hazardous waste sites. OAB-1525

Leslie, Winsome J. Zaire: continuity and political change in an oppressive state. OAB-2657

Lesser, M.X., comp. Jonathan Edwards: an annotated bibliography, 1979-1993. OAB-0121

Lessoff, Alan. The nation and its city. OAB-2555

Lester, Alan. From colonization to democracy. OAB-2237

Lester, Joel. Compositional theory in the eighteenth century. OAB-1019

Lesurf, J.C.G. Information and measurement. OAB-1508

LeVay, Simon. The sexual brain. OAB-1754

Leverich, Lyle. Tom: the unknown Tennessee Williams. OAB-0837

Levesque, Allen H. Wireless information networks. OAB-1518

Levi, Erik. Music in the Third Reich. OAB-1020

Levi, Jan Heller, ed. A Muriel Rukeyser reader. OAB-0841

Levine, Lawrence W. The opening of the American mind. OAB-2169

Levine, Neil. The architecture of Frank Lloyd Wright. OAB-0405

Levine, Robert S. Martin Delany, Frederick Douglass, and the politics of representative identity. OAB-0757

Levinson, David. Aggression and conflict. OAB-0325

Levinson, David, ed. Encyclopedia of cultural anthropology. OAB-0185

Levinson, David, ed. Encyclopedia of world cultures: v. 8-10. OAB-0188

Levy, David Benjamin. Beethoven: the Ninth Symphony. OAB-1030

Levy, George. To die in Chicago. OAB-2556

Levy, Jerrold E. Orayvi revisited. OAB-1883

Levy, Leonard W., ed. Encyclopedia of the American presidency. OAB-0280

Lewellen, Ted C. Dependency and development. OAB-2075

Lewine, Carol F. The Sistine Chapel walls and the Roman liturgy. OAB-0471

Lewis, Catherine C. Educating hearts and minds. OAB-2147

Lewis, David Levering. W.E.B. Du Bois—biography of a race, 1868-1919. OAB-2557

Lewis, John P. India's political economy. OAB-2658

Lewis, Jon. The road to romance and ruin. OAB-0980

Lewis, Laurence A. Land degradation. OAB-1367

Lewis, Michael, ed. Handbook of emotions. OAB-2980

Lewis, Paul G. Shaping suburbia. OAB-3017

Lewis, Philip. Seeing through the Mother Goose tales. OAB-0889

Lewis, Richard D. When cultures collide. OAB-1905

Lewis, Ronald J. Activity-based models for cost management systems. OAB-1906

Licht, Walter. Industrializing America. OAB-2025

Lichtenstein, Nelson. The most dangerous man in Detroit. OAB-1946

Lide, David R. CRC handbook of thermophysical and thermochemical data. OAB-1721

Liebes, Yehuda. Studies in the Zohar. OAB-1240

Lifton, Robert Jay. The protean self. OAB-2983

Light, Ivan. Race, ethnicity, and entrepreneurship in urban America. OAB-3086

Lightbown, Ronald W. Mediaeval European jewellery. OAB-0431

Lighter, J.E., ed. Random House historical dictionary of American slang: v.1: A-G. OAB-0030

Lincoln, Kenneth. Indi'n humor. OAB-2491

Lind, Michael. The next American nation. OAB-2884

Lindberg, Carter. The European reformations. OAB-1216

Lindfors, Bernth. Black African literature in English, 1987-1991. OAB-0075

Lindquist, Richard K. Ball pest & disease manual. OAB-1318

Lindsey, J.K. Modelling frequency and count data. OAB-1687

Linn, Brian McAllister. Guardians of empire. OAB-2609

Lippman, Edward. A history of Western musical aesthetics. OAB-0993

Lipsky, Dorothy Kerzner. Inclusion and school reform. OAB-2119

Liu, Ming-Wood. Madhyamaka thought in China. OAB-1192

Livezeanu, Irina. Cultural politics in greater Romania. OAB-2706

Livingston, Jane. The New York School. OAB-0488

Livingston, William. Color and light in nature. OAB-1722

Lloyd, Christopher. Italian paintings before 1600 in the Art Institute of Chicago. OAB-0472

Lloyd, Janet, tr. The masters of truth in archaic Greece. OAB-1119

Lloyd, Rosemary. Closer & closer apart. OAB-0551

Lo, C.P. Hong Kong. OAB-2268

Lock, G.S.H. Latent heat transfer. OAB-1561

Locke, Richard M. Remaking the Italian economy. OAB-2054

Lockhart, James. The Nahuas after the conquest. OAB-2421

Lomax, Alan. The land where the blues began. OAB-1049

Lomelí, Francisco, ed. Handbook of Hispanic cultures in the United States: literature and art. OAB-0190

Lomer, Cecile. The African studies companion. OAB-0039

Lomnitz, Cinna. Fundamentals of earthquake prediction. OAB-1485

London, Jack. The complete short stories of Jack London. OAB-0798

Lone, Stewart. Japan's first modern war. OAB-2269

Longva, Anh Nga. Walls built on sand. OAB-2659

Looby, Christopher. Voicing America. OAB-0735

Loomis, R.S. Crop ecology. OAB-1317

López, Franklin A. Ecology, law and economics. OAB-2099

López Luján, Leonardo. The offerings of the templo mayor of Tenochtitlan. OAB-1884

Lorber, Judith. Paradoxes of gender. OAB-3061

Lorenz, Richard. Imogen Cunningham: ideas without end: a life in photographs. OAB-0489

Lounsbury, Carl R., ed. An Illustrated glossary of early southern architecture and landscape. OAB-0052

Lovejoy, Paul E. Slow death for slavery. OAB-2238

Lovenduski, Joni. Contemporary feminist politics. OAB-2395

Lowe, Sarah M. Tina Modotti: photographs. OAB-0490

Lowenstein, Michael W. Customer retention. OAB-1924

Lowenstein, Steven M. The Berlin Jewish community. OAB-2369

Löwith, Karl. Martin Heidegger and European nihilism. OAB-1102

Löwy, Michael. The war of gods. OAB-1217

Loza, Steven. Barrio rhythm. OAB-1050

Lüders, Rolf. Privatization in Chile. OAB-2039

Lund, Herbert F., ed. The McGraw-Hill recycling handbook. OAB-1532

Lupack, Barbara Tepa. Insanity as redemption in contemporary American fiction. OAB-0838

Lupher, Mark. Power restructuring in China and Russia. OAB-2677

Lustig, Nora. Mexico, the remaking of an economy. OAB-2040

Lutkehaus, Nancy C. Zaria's fire. OAB-1885

Lutz, William D. The Cambridge thesaurus of American English. OAB-0020

Lynch, Barbara S., ed. Growing up tobacco free. OAB-1608

Lynch, David K. Color and light in nature. OAB-1722

Lynch, James, ed. Cultural diversity and the schools: v.1. OAB-2106

Lynch, James, ed. Cultural diversity and the schools: v.4. OAB-2107

Lynn, Laurence E. Public management as art, science, and profession. OAB-2855

Lyra, F., tr. Hypatia of Alexandria. OAB-1120

M

Mabbett, Ian. The Khmers. OAB-2270

Maccoby, Eleanor E. Adolescents after divorce. OAB-3051

Macdonald, Douglas J. Adventures in chaos. OAB-2769

Macdonald, Gordon, ed. Health promotion. OAB-1612

MacDonald, Robert H. The language of empire. OAB-0680

MacDonald, Scott. Avant-garde film. OAB-0981

Machiavelli, Niccolò. Discourses on Livy. OAB-2856

Mackenzie, G. Calvin. The irony of reform. OAB-2885

Mackerras, Colin. China's minorities. OAB-2271

MacLaran, Andrew. Dublin: the shaping of a capital. OAB-2396

MacLean, Nancy. Behind the mask of chivalry. OAB-2610

MacManus, Susan A. Young v. old: generational combat in the 21st century. OAB-2886

Macphail, Euan M. The neuroscience of animal intelligence. OAB-1372

Macrae, Norman. John von Neumann. OAB-1688

Macrakis, Kristie. Surviving the swastika. OAB-1305

Macroeconomic Research Group. Making democracy work. OAB-2660

Maddock, Richard C. Marketing to the mind. OAB-1958

Madelung, Wilfred. The succession to Muḥammad. OAB-2448

Magnuson, Landis K. Circle stock theater. OAB-1072

Magocsi, Paul Robert. Historical atlas of East Central Europe. OAB-0238

Maguire, Joseph. Zero to lazy eight. OAB-1681

Mahoney, Dennis F. The critical fortunes of a romantic novel. OAB-0871

Mair, Victor H., ed. The Columbia anthology of traditional Chinese literature. OAB-0582

Maisey, John G. Discovering fossil fishes. OAB-1486

Major, J. Russell. From Renaissance monarchy to absolute monarchy. OAB-2336

Makaryk, Irena R., ed. Encyclopedia of contemporary literary theory. OAB-0069

Makin, John H. Debt and taxes. OAB-2026

Malinowski, Sharon, ed. Gay & lesbian literature. OAB-0074

Malinowski, Sharon, ed. Notable Native Americans. OAB-0267

Malkin, Irad. Myth and territory in the Spartan Mediterranean. OAB-2208

Mallgrave, Harry Francis. Gottfried Semper: architect of the nineteenth century. OAB-0406

Mallinckrodt, Anita M. From knights to pioneers. OAB-2558

Malloy, Jerry, comp. Sol White's history of colored base ball, with other documents on the early black game, 1886-1936. OAB-1776

Malone, Jacqui. Steppin' on the blues. OAB-1073

Malone, Patrick M. The texture of industry. OAB-1300

Maltese, John Anthony. The selling of Supreme Court nominees. OAB-2927

Mancuso, Maureen, ed. Leaders and leadership in Canada. OAB-2684

Manent, Pierre. Tocqueville and the nature of democracy. OAB-2857

Manheimer, Ronald J., ed. Older Americans almanac. OAB-0326

Mannikka, Eleanor. Angkor Wat: time, space, and kingship. OAB-0407

Manning, Catherine. Fortunes a faire. OAB-2272

Mannová, Elena, ed. A Guide to historiography in Slovakia. OAB-0235

Manuel, Peter. Caribbean currents. OAB-1051

Marc, David. Bonfire of the humanities. OAB-0520

Marchand, Suzanne L. Down from Olympus. OAB-2370

Marchionini, Gary. Information seeking in electronic environments. OAB-1457

Marcus, Alan Rudolph. Relocating Eden. OAB-2468

Marcus, Millicent. Filmmaking by the book. OAB-0982

Margulis, Lynn. What is life? OAB-1373

Maril, Robert Lee. The bay shrimpers of Texas. OAB-1886

Marion, Robert. Was George Washington really the father of our country? OAB-2170

Mark, James E., ed. Science and technology of rubber. OAB-1569

Markovits, Andrei S. The German Left. OAB-2707

Markowitz, Fran. A community in spite of itself. OAB-2492

Marks, Elaine. Marrano as metaphor. OAB-0890

Marks, Jonathan. Human biodiversity. OAB-1840

Marks, Martin Miller. Music and the silent film. OAB-0983

Marks, Thomas A. Maoist insurgency since Vietnam. OAB-2788

Marnef, Guido. Antwerp in the age of Reformation. OAB-1218

Marquart, James W. The rope, the chair, and the needle. OAB-3045

Marr, David G. Vietnam. OAB-0226

Marr, David G. Vietnam 1945. OAB-2273

Marsden, George M. The soul of the American university. OAB-2120

Marsh, Margaret. The empty cradle. OAB-1638

Marsh, Rosalind. History and literature in contemporary Russia. OAB-0926

Marshall, Donald G. Contemporary critical theory. OAB-0076

Marshall, Ingeborg. A history and ethnography of the Beothuk. OAB-2459

Marshall, P. David. Celebrity and power. OAB-0943

Marszalek, John F. Sherman: a soldier's passion for order. OAB-2559

Martin, Cheryl English. Governance and society in colonial Mexico. OAB-2422

Martin, Fenton S. The United States Congress. OAB-0286

Martin, Phyllis M. Leisure and society in colonial Brazzaville. OAB-2239

Martin, Richard, ed. Contemporary fashion. OAB-0047

Martin, Terence. Parables of possibility. OAB-0736

Martin, W.R. Henry James's apprenticeship. OAB-0758

Martineau, Jane, ed. The Glory of Venice. OAB-0371

Martínez Cuenca, Alejandro. Sandinista economics in practice. OAB-2041

Martínez, Javier. Chile: the great transformation. OAB-2042

Martinez, Joseph G.R. Guide to British poetry explication: v.4: Victorian-contemporary. OAB-0077

Martinez, Nancy C. Guide to British poetry explication: v.4: Victorian-contemporary. OAB-0077

Martino, Joseph P. Science funding. OAB-2887

Martinson, Steven D. Harmonious tensions. OAB-0872

Martis, Kenneth C. The historical atlas of the Congresses of the Confederate States of America, 1861-1865. OAB-0262

Marx, Murillo. History of South American colonial art and architecture. OAB-0360

Marzán, Julio. The Spanish American roots of William Carlos Williams. OAB-0799

Marzano, Robert J. School wars. OAB-2111

Masich, Andrew E. Cheyenne dog soldiers. OAB-2535

Mason, Mark. American multinationals and Japan. OAB-2076

Mason, Mary Ann. From father's property to children's rights. OAB-3106

Massey, Douglas S. American apartheid: segregation and the making of the underclass. OAB-3087

Massey, Douglas S. Miracles on the border. OAB-3079

Masters, Edgar Lee. Spoon River anthology. OAB-0800

Masters, Roger D., ed. Discourse on the sciences and arts. OAB-2862

Matchette, Robert B., comp. Guide to federal records in the National Archives of the United States. OAB-0181

Mather, John C. The very first light. OAB-1341

Matisse, Henri. Henri Matisse: a retrospective. OAB-0473

Matory, J. Lorand. Sex and the empire that is no more. OAB-1887

Mattern, David B. Benjamin Lincoln and the American Revolution. OAB-2521

Mattson, Mark T. Macmillan color atlas of the states. OAB-0021

Mattusch, Carol C. Classical bronzes. OAB-0498

Maud, Ralph. Charles Olson's reading: a biography. OAB-0839

Maunder, W. John, comp. Dictionary of global climate change. OAB-0159

Maung, Mya. Totalitarianism in Burma. OAB-2662

Maurer, John G., ed. Encyclopedia of business. OAB-0200

Maxwell, James. Plastics in the automotive industry. OAB-1562

Mayer, Jane. Strange justice. OAB-2928

Mayer, Thomas. Truth versus precision in economics. OAB-1980

Mayor, Federico. The new page. OAB-2746

Mazower, Mark. Inside Hitler's Greece. OAB-2311

Mazzotta, Giuseppe. Dante's vision and the circle of knowledge. OAB-0902

McAdams, A. James. Germany divided. OAB-2371

McAllister, James W. Beauty & revolution in science. OAB-1284

McAllister, Matthew P. The commercialization of American culture. OAB-1960

McArthur, Tom, ed. The Oxford companion to the English language. OAB-0084

McCaffray, Susan P. The politics of industrialization in tsarist Russia. OAB-2312

McCalla, Douglas. Planting the Province. OAB-2027

McCann, James A. Democratizing Mexico. OAB-2722

McCann, James C. People of the plow. OAB-2098

McCann, Michael. Health hazards manual for artists. OAB-1639

McCarthy, Todd. Howard Hawks. OAB-0958

McCauley, Martin, ed. Longman biographical directory of decision-makers in Russia and the successor states. OAB-0294

McChristian, Douglas C. The U.S. Army in the West, 1870-1880. OAB-2560

McClain, Charles J. In search of equality. OAB-2561

McClaran, Mitchel P., ed. The Desert grassland. OAB-1396

McCleary, John. Geometry from a differentiable viewpoint. OAB-1689

McCormack, Bruce L. Karl Barth's critically realistic dialectical theology. OAB-1259

McCreery, David. Rural Guatemala, 1760-1940. OAB-2423

McCully, Patrick. Silenced rivers. OAB-1531

McDonald, Lynn. The early origins of the social sciences. OAB-3018

McDonald, Robert A.J. Making Vancouver. OAB-2469

McDowell, Deborah E. "The changing same." OAB-0840

McElhinny, Michael W. The magnetic field of the earth. OAB-1723

McFadden, Phillip L. The magnetic field of the earth. OAB-1723

McGaw, Judith A., ed. Early American technology. OAB-1298

McGhee, George R. The Late Devonian mass extinction. OAB-1488

McGinn, Bernard. Antichrist: two thousand years of the human fascination with evil. OAB-1181

McGinn, Bernard. The growth of mysticism. OAB-1219

McGlew, James F. Tyranny and political culture in ancient Greece. OAB-2209

McGoldrick, Monica, ed. Ethnicity and family therapy. OAB-1826

McGovern, Dan. The Campo Indian landfill war. OAB-2611

McGuire, Kevin T. The Supreme Court bar. OAB-2929

McIlwain, James T. An introduction to the biology of vision. OAB-1755

McIlwaine, John. Africa: a guide to reference material. OAB-0227

McIntosh, Lawrence D. Religion & theology: a guide to current reference resources. OAB-0123

McKenzie, Richard B. What went right in the 1980s. OAB-2028

McKie, Robin. African exodus. OAB-1859

McKirahan, Richard D. Principles and proofs. OAB-1123

McKitrick, Eric. The age of federalism. OAB-2515

McKown, Delos B. The mythmaker's magic. OAB-1285

McLeod, Hugh. Piety and poverty. OAB-2171

McMahon, Keith. Misers, shrews, and polygamists. OAB-0590

McManus, Barbara F. Classics & feminism. OAB-0609

McMullin, Ernan, ed. The Social dimensions of science. OAB-1291

McNair, C.J. World-class accounting and finance. OAB-1907

McNally, David. Against the market. OAB-1981

McNamara, Jo Ann Kay. Sisters in arms. OAB-1220

McNamara, Robert S. In retrospect. OAB-2770

McNeal, Patricia. Harder than war. OAB-1221

McNeil, W.K. Ozark country. OAB-2493

McNutt, P.A. The economics of public choice. OAB-1982

McRae, Hamish. The world in 2020. OAB-2077

McRae, Linda. African ethnonyms. OAB-0045

McShane, Marilyn D., ed. Encyclopedia of American prisons. OAB-0320

Meeks, Wayne A. The origins of Christian morality. OAB-1141

Mehlman, Jeffrey. Genealogies of the text. OAB-0891

Meier, Matt S. Notable Latino Americans. OAB-0022

Meigs, Mark. Optimism at Armageddon. OAB-2612

Meikle, Jeffrey L. American plastic: a cultural history. OAB-1563

Meissner, W.W. Ignatius of Loyola: the psychology of a saint. OAB-1222

Meixner, Laura L. French realist painting and the critique of American society, 1865-1900. OAB-0474

Mellinkoff, Ruth. Outcasts: signs of otherness.... v.1 & 2. OAB-0377

Melot, Michel. The impressionist print. OAB-0432

Melson, Robert. Revolution and genocide. OAB-2172

Melville, A.D., tr. Sorrows of an exile. OAB-0611

Melville, Herman. Correspondence. OAB-0759

Menchaca, Martha. The Mexican outsiders. OAB-2613

Mendelson, Edward, ed. W.H. Auden and Chester Kallman. OAB-0691

Menéndez Alarcón, Antonio V. Power and television in Latin America. OAB-2730

Menezes, Alfred J. Handbook of applied cryptography. OAB-1458

Menges, Robert J., ed. Teaching on solid ground. OAB-2153

Menon, Dilip M. Caste, nationalism and communism in south India. OAB-2678

Menta, Ed. The magic world behind the curtain. OAB-1074

Menze, Ernest A., ed. Johann Gottfried Herder: selected early works, 1764-1767: addresses, essays.... OAB-0869

Mercuro, Nicholas. Ecology, law and economics. OAB-2099

Meredith, Howard. Dancing on common ground. OAB-2494

Merideth, Robert. The environmentalist's bookshelf. OAB-0138

Merkl, Peter H. German unification in the European context. OAB-2708

Merriam, Louise A. United States history: a bibliography of the new writings on American history. OAB-0263

Merrill, Ronald T. The magnetic field of the earth. OAB-1723

Merritt, Russell. Walt in Wonderland. OAB-0959

Mesa-Lago, Carmelo. Changing social security in Latin America. OAB-2043

Messenger, John B. Cephalopod behaviour. OAB-1808

Messerly, John G. Piaget's conception of evolution. OAB-2946

Messick, David M., ed. Codes of conduct. OAB-1901

Mestrovic, Stjepan G. The Balkanization of the West. OAB-2709

Metzger, Bruce M., ed. The Oxford companion to the Bible. OAB-0125

Meulenkamp, Wim. Brickwork: architecture and design. OAB-0410

Meyer, Doris, ed. Reinterpreting the Spanish American essay. OAB-0914

Meyer, Doris, ed. Rereading the Spanish American essay. OAB-0915

Meyer, Esther da Costa. The work of Antonio Sant'Elia. OAB-0408

Meyer, Harvey K. Historical dictionary of Honduras. OAB-0264

Meyer, Jessie H. Historical dictionary of Honduras. OAB-0264

Meyer, John P. Commitment in the workplace. OAB-1947

Meyers, Eric M., ed. The Oxford encyclopedia of archaeology in the Near East. OAB-0194

Meyers, Robert A., ed. Molecular biology and biotechnology. OAB-1375

Miall, Andrew D. The geology of fluvial deposits. OAB-1489

Michelson, Bruce. Mark Twain on the loose. OAB-0760

Mickolus, Edward F. Terrorism, 1988-1991. OAB-0295

Middleton, John, ed. Encyclopedia of world cultures: v. 8-10. OAB-0188

Middleton, Nick. The global casino. OAB-1490

Middleton, Roger. Government versus the market. OAB-2055

Milanich, Jerald T. The Timucua. OAB-2522

Miles, Margaret R. Seeing and believing. OAB-0984

Miles, William F.S. Hausaland divided. OAB-2241

Millar, James R., ed. Cracks in the monolith. OAB-2699

Miller, Catherine G. Environmental dividends. OAB-1523

Miller, Cristanne. Comic power in Emily Dickinson. OAB-0755

Miller, E. Willard. Energy and American society. OAB-0160

Miller, Elmer S. Nurturing doubt. OAB-1888

Miller, Jerome R. Search and destroy. OAB-3046

Miller, Maureen C. The formation of a medieval church. OAB-1223

Miller, Michael Vincent. Intimate terrorism. OAB-2984

Miller, Rowland S. Embarrassment: poise and peril in everyday life. OAB-2985

Miller, Ruby M. Energy and American society. OAB-0160

Miller, Warren E. The new American voter. OAB-2907

Mills, Kenneth. Idolatry and its enemies. OAB-2424

Milner, Susan, tr. Allah in the West. OAB-1239

Minkler, Meredith. Grandmothers as caregivers. OAB-3107

Minow, Newton N. Abandoned in the wasteland. OAB-0521

Minsker, Karl S. Fast polymerization processes. OAB-1564

Minter, William. Apartheid's contras. OAB-2242

Mintzberg, Henry. The rise and fall of strategic planning. OAB-1925

Miramontes, Ofelia B. Restructuring schools for linguistic diversity. OAB-2148

Mitchell, John C. Foundations for programming languages. OAB-1459

Mitchell, Sally. The new girl: girls' culture in England, 1880-1915. OAB-0681

Mitchell, Stephen. Anatolia: land, men, and Gods in Asia Minor. v.1 & 2. OAB-2210

Mitchell, Stephen A. Hope and dread in psychoanalysis. OAB-2970

Mitchell, William J. The reconfigured eye. OAB-0491

Miyashita, Kenichi. Keiretsu: inside the hidden Japanese conglomerates. OAB-1908

Moch, Leslie Page. Moving Europeans. OAB-2173

Moggridge, D.E. Maynard Keynes: an economist's biography. OAB-1983

Moghadam, Valentine M. Modernizing women. OAB-2449

Mohanty, Jitendra Nath. Reason and tradition in Indian thought. OAB-1103

Monahon, Cynthia. Children and trauma. OAB-3001

Mondimore, Francis Mark. A natural history of homosexuality. OAB-3062

Monga, Célestin. The anthropology of anger. OAB-2663

Montale, Eugenio. Cuttlefish bones. OAB-0903

Montaño, Martha Kreipe. The Native American almanac. OAB-0259

Montgomery, James D. New Jersey ferns and fern-allies. OAB-1408

Montgomery, William E. Under their own vine and fig tree. OAB-1224

Montrose, Louis. The purpose of playing. OAB-1075

Moore, Barbara, ed. Horton Foote's three trips to Bountiful. OAB-0942

Moore, Burness E., ed. Psychoanalysis: the major concepts. OAB-2948

Moore, Mark H. Creating public value. OAB-2858

Moore, Wayne D. Constitutional rights and powers of the people. OAB-2930

Moore-Ede, Martin. The twenty-four-hour society. OAB-1616

Moore-Gilbert, Bart. Postcolonial theory. OAB-0721

Moorey, P.R.S. Ancient Mesopotamian materials and industries. OAB-2211

Moran, Charles, ed. Writing, teaching, and learning in the disciplines. OAB-2156

Moran, Gabriel. A grammar of responsibility. OAB-1142

Morawska, Ewa. Insecure prosperity. OAB-2614

Morehouse, Barbara J. A place called Grand Canyon. OAB-2495

Morgall, Janine Marie. Technology assessment. OAB-1286

Morgan, Bill. The works of Allen Ginsberg, 1941-1994. OAB-0078

Morgan, David, ed. Icons of American Protestantism. OAB-0373

Morley, John. Regency design, 1790-1840. OAB-0433

Morley, Samuel A. Poverty and inequality in Latin America. OAB-2045

Morone, Joseph G. Winning in high-tech markets. OAB-1926

Morphy, Howard. Ancestral connections. OAB-0378

Morreale, Joanne. The presidential campaign film. OAB-2908

Morrice, David. Philosophy, science and ideology in political thought. OAB-2859

Morris, Benny. Israel's border wars, 1949-1956. OAB-2450

Morris, Sarah P. Daidalos and the origins of Greek art. OAB-0379

Morris, Timothy. Becoming canonical in American poetry. OAB-0737

Morrisey, Will. A political approach to pacifism: book 1; book 2. OAB-2860

Morrison, Ian. Future tense. OAB-1927

Morrison, Toni, ed. Race-ing justice, en-gendering power. OAB-2623

Morrow, Raymond A. Critical theory and methodology. OAB-3019

Morton, James, ed. The *Financial Times* global guide to investing. OAB-2066

Moschis, George P. Marketing strategies for the mature market. OAB-1961

Moschis, George P. Marketing to older consumers. OAB-1962

Moser, Paul H. The Citizen's guide to geologic hazards. OAB-1474

Moss, Elizabeth. Domestic novelists in the Old South. OAB-0761

Mossman, S.T.I., ed. The Development of plastics. OAB-1550

Mostow, Joshua S. Pictures of the heart. OAB-0592

Mott, Robert L. Radio sound effects. OAB-0522

Mott, Wesley T., ed. Biographical dictionary of transcendentalism. OAB-0060

Moulakis, Athanasios. Beyond utility. OAB-2121

Mould, Richard F. A century of X-rays and radioactivity in medicine. OAB-1589

Moussalli, Ahmad S. Radical Islamic fundamentalism. OAB-1241

Mouzelis, Nicos. Sociological theory. OAB-3020

Mueller, Milton L. Universal service. OAB-2029

Muhammad Haji Salleh. Beyond the archipelago. OAB-0593

Muir, Warren R. Environmental dividends. OAB-1523

Muller, Thomas. Immigrants and the American city. OAB-2496

Mullins, Michael G., ed. Biology of the grapevine. OAB-1312

Mulroy, Kevin. Freedom on the border. OAB-2523

Mulvaney, John. Commandant of solitude. OAB-2274

Munier, J.-M. High-speed networks. OAB-1511

Munro, David, ed. The Oxford dictionary of the world. OAB-0027

Munroe, Alexandra. Japanese art after 1945. OAB-0380

Munson, Wayne. All talk. OAB-0523

Münsterer, Hanns Otto. The young Brecht. OAB-0873

Murakami, Yasusuke. An anticlassical political-economic analysis. OAB-1984

Murdoch, Iris. Metaphysics as a guide to morals. OAB-1164

Murphy, Cullen. Rubbish! OAB-1535

Murphy, Joseph M. Working the spirit. OAB-1182

Murphy, Mary. Mining cultures. OAB-2615

Murphy, William M. Family secrets. OAB-0709

Murphy-O'Connor, Jerome. Paul: a critical life. OAB-1260

Murray, Andrew. The cell cycle. OAB-1376

Murray, Charles. The bell curve. OAB-2959

Murray, Janet H. Hamlet on the holodeck. OAB-0552

Murray, Linda. The Oxford companion to Christian art and architecture. OAB-0053

Murray, Paul T. The civil rights movement. OAB-0296

Murray, Peter. The Oxford companion to Christian art and architecture. OAB-0053

Murrin, Michael. History and warfare in Renaissance epic. OAB-0553

Myers, Ramon H., ed. The Wealth of nations in the twentieth century. OAB-1990

Myint, H. The political economy of poverty, equity, and growth. OAB-2073

N

Naber, Gregory L. The geometry of Minkowski spacetime. OAB-1690

Nadeau, Adel. Restructuring schools for linguistic diversity. OAB-2148

Nadelmann, Ethan A. Cops across borders. OAB-3047

Nagel, Gwen L., ed. Facts on File bibliography of American fiction, 1866-1918. OAB-0072

Nagel, James, ed. Facts on File bibliography of American fiction, 1866-1918. OAB-0072

Nagel, Joane. American Indian ethnic renewal. OAB-3088

Nagel, Thomas. The last word. OAB-1104

Nagrin, Daniel. Dance and the specific image. OAB-1076

Nagy, Gregory. Homeric questions. OAB-0610

Nakash, Yitzhak. The Shi'is of Iraq. OAB-2451

Nasr, Seyyed Hossein, ed. History of Islamic philosophy. OAB-1099

Nass, Clifford. The media equation. OAB-0525

Natarajan, Nalini, ed. Handbook of twentieth-century literatures of India. OAB-0583

Nathan, Andrew J. The great wall and the empty fortress. OAB-2789

National Geographic Society (U.S.). Book Division. The Builders: marvels of engineering. OAB-1503

National Research Council (U.S.). Panel on Research on Child Abuse and Neglect. Understanding child abuse and neglect. OAB-3108

Naughton, Barry. Growing out of the plan. OAB-2002

Navarrete, Ignacio. Orphans of Petrarch. OAB-0912

Navarro, Armando. Mexican American youth organization. OAB-2616

Nealon, Jeffrey T. Double reading. OAB-0554

Neave, Guy R., ed. The Encyclopedia of higher education: v.1-4. OAB-0171

Necipoglu, Gülru. The Topkapi scroll: geometry and ornament in Islamic architecture.... OAB-0409

Neely, Mark E. The last best hope of earth. OAB-2562

Neich, Roger. Painted histories. OAB-0434

Neilson, Alasdair H. Organic chemicals in the aquatic environment. OAB-1434

Nelson, Barbara J., ed. Women and politics worldwide. OAB-2758

Nelson, Carol. Women's market handbook. OAB-1963

Nelson, Cary, ed. Collected poems: [Edwin Rolfe]. OAB-0804

Nelson, Claudia. Invisible men. OAB-0682

Nelson, David M. The anatomy of a game. OAB-1768

Nelson, Robert M. Place and vision. OAB-0842

Nemerov, Alexander. Frederic Remington and turn-of-the-century America. OAB-0475

Nering, Evar D. Linear programs and related problems. OAB-1460

Nesaule, Agate. A woman in amber. OAB-2174

Nesbit, Molly. Atget's seven albums. OAB-0492

Netanyahu, B. The origins of the Inquisition in fifteenth century Spain. OAB-2337

Neupert, Richard, tr. Aesthetics of film. OAB-0967

Neusner, Jacob, ed. Dictionary of Judaism in the biblical period: 450 B.C.E. to 600 C.E. OAB-0117

Neuzil, Mark. Mass media & environmental conflict. OAB-0524

Newby, Bruce. Electronic signal conditioning. OAB-1517

Newcomb, Horace, ed. Encyclopedia of television. OAB-0096

Newlin, George, comp. Everyone in Dickens: v. 1-3. OAB-0081

Newman, Katherine S. Declining fortunes. OAB-1833

Newman, Michael. Democracy, sovereignty and the European Union. OAB-2790

Newman, Peter, ed. The New Palgrave dictionary of money & finance. OAB-0206

Newton, Peter M. Freud: from youthful dream to mid-life crisis. OAB-2947

Newton, Roger G. What makes nature tick? OAB-1724

Ng, Franklin, ed. The Asian American encyclopedia. OAB-0242

Nichols, Bill. Blurred boundaries. OAB-0944

Nicholson, Colin. Writing and the rise of finance. OAB-0649

Nielsen, Claus. Animal evolution: interrelationships of the living phyla. OAB-1811

Nierenberg, William A., ed. Encyclopedia of environmental biology. OAB-0148

Nightingale, Andrea Wilson. Genres in dialogue. OAB-1124

Niiya, Brian, ed. Japanese American history. OAB-0261

Nilsson, Annika. Ultraviolet reflections. OAB-1725

Nimmo, Dan. The comedy of democracy. OAB-2879

Nishiguchi, Toshihiro. Strategic industrial sourcing. OAB-2003

Noble, Bruce J. Perceived exertion. OAB-1756

Nolen, Anita L., ed. International directory of bioethics organizations. OAB-0135

Nolt, Steven M. Amish enterprise. OAB-2023

Nord, Philip. The republican moment. OAB-2338

Nordby, Judith, comp. Mongolia. OAB-0228

Norell, Mark A. Discovering dinosaurs in the Museum of Natural History. OAB-1492

Norris, Jeremy. The Russian piano concerto: v.1: The nineteenth century. OAB-1031

Norris, Patrick. A primer for health care ethics. OAB-1582

North, John. The Norton history of astronomy and cosmology. OAB-1342

Northcott, Michael S. The environment and Christian ethics. OAB-1261

Northrup, David. Indentured labor in the age of imperialism, 1834-1922. OAB-2175

Norton, Mary Beth, ed. The American Historical Association's guide to historical literature. OAB-0210

Norvig, Peter. Artificial intelligence: a modern approach. OAB-1465

Nostrand, Richard L. The Hispano homeland. OAB-2497

Nugent, Walter. Crossings. OAB-2176

Nuhfer, Edward B. The Citizen's guide to geologic hazards. OAB-1474

Nussbaum, Martha C. Poetic justice. OAB-0349

Nyberg, David. The varnished truth. OAB-1143

Nyhart, Lynn K. Biology takes form. OAB-1306

Nylander, Jane C. Our own snug fireside. OAB-2524

Nyquist, Richard A. Handbook of infrared and Raman spectra of inorganic compounds and organic salts. OAB-1726

O

Oatley, Keith. Best laid schemes. OAB-2986

Ober, Richard. The northern forest. OAB-1315

Ober, Warren U. Henry James's apprenticeship. OAB-0758

Oberly, James W., comp. United States history: a bibliography of the new writings on American history. OAB-0263

Oberoi, Harjot. The construction of religious boundaries. OAB-1194

O'Brien, David M.. Abortion and American politics. OAB-2808

O'Brien, Michael J. Paradigms of the past. OAB-1857

O'Connell, Joanna. Prospero's daughter. OAB-0913

O'Connell, Robert L. Ride of the second horseman. OAB-2177

O'Connor, Pat. Friendships between women. OAB-3063

O'Day, Rosemary. Mr. Charles Booth's inquiry. OAB-2397

Odem, Mary E. Delinquent daughters. OAB-3064

O'Farrell, Mary Ann. Telling complexions: the nineteenth-century English novel and the blush. OAB-0683

Ogbaa, Kalu. The gong and the flute. OAB-0571

Ohanian, Hans. Gravitation and spacetime. OAB-1727

Ohles, Frederik. Germany's rude awakening. OAB-0334

Ojeda, Oscar Riera. Hyper-realistic: computer generated architectural renderings. OAB-1461

Ojemann, George A. Conversations with Neil's brain. OAB-1746

Olcott, Martha Brill. Central Asia's new states. OAB-2791

Oliver, David. The shaggy steed of physics. OAB-1728

Olsen, Sandra L., ed. Horses through time. OAB-1810

Olson, David R. The world on paper. OAB-0555

Olson, Eric T. The human animal. OAB-1165

O'Neil, Robert M. Free speech in the college community. OAB-2122

O'Neill, Onora, ed. The sources of normativity. OAB-1140

Oppenheim, Lois Hecht. Politics in Chile. OAB-2731

Ordelheide, Dieter, ed. TRANSACC: transnational accounting. OAB-1914

Orlans, F. Barbara. In the name of science. OAB-1590

Ornstein, Norman J. Debt and taxes. OAB-2026

Ornstein, Norman J., ed. Vital statistics on Congress, 1993-1994. OAB-0308

O'Rourke, Kevin. A primer for health care ethics. OAB-1582

Orrick, Sarah. Environmental profiles. OAB-0136

Orsi, Robert A. Thank you, St. Jude. OAB-1225

Orwin, Donna Tussing. Tolstoy's art and thought, 1847-1880. OAB-0927

Osers, Ewald, tr. Albert Einstein: a biography. OAB-1711

Osgood, Nancy J., comp. Alcoholism and aging. OAB-0315

Osterbrock, Donald E. Yerkes Observatory, 1892-1950. OAB-1343

Ostrower, Francie. Why the wealthy give. OAB-3022

Ostry, Sylvia. The post-Cold War trading system. OAB-2078

Overton, Bill. The novel of female adultery. OAB-0556

Overton, Mark. Agricultural revolution in England. OAB-2398

Ovid. Sorrows of an exile. OAB-0611

Owram, Doug. Born at the right time. OAB-2617

Owram, Doug, ed. Canadian history: a reader's guide. v.1 & 2. OAB-0246

P

Packard, Robert T. Encyclopedia of American architecture. OAB-0055

Packull, Werner O. Hutterite beginnings. OAB-2178

Page, Benjamin I. Who deliberates? OAB-2888

Page, Judith W. Wordsworth and the cultivation of women. OAB-0684

Pahlavan, Kaveh. Wireless information networks. OAB-1518

Pal, Pratapaditya. Indian painting: a catalogue.... v.1: 1000-1700. OAB-0476

Palais, James B. Confucian statecraft and Korean institutions. OAB-2275

Paley, Vivian Gussin. Kwanzaa and me. OAB-2149

Palkó, Zsuzsanna. Hungarian folktales. OAB-0928

Palmer, Pete, ed. Total baseball. OAB-0166

Palmer, R. Barton, ed. The fountain of love (La fonteinne amoureuse) and two other love vision poems. OAB-0884

Palmer, William J. The films of the eighties. OAB-0960

Palmieri, Robert, ed. Encyclopedia of Keyboard instruments: v.1: The piano. OAB-0095

Palmos, Frank, ed. The sorrow of war. OAB-0580

Paoletti, John T. Art in Renaissance Italy. OAB-0381

Papanastasiou, Tasos C. Applied fluid mechanics. OAB-1565

Parducci, Allen. Happiness, pleasure, and judgment. OAB-2987

Parent, David J., tr. Order in the twilight. OAB-1111

Parini, Jay. John Steinbeck: a biography. OAB-0843

Park, James William. Latin American underdevelopment. OAB-2046

Parker, Barry. Chaos in the cosmos. OAB-1344

Parker, Barry. The vindication of the Big Bang. OAB-1345

Parker, Dorothy R. Singing an Indian song. OAB-0844

Parker, Patricia. Shakespeare from the margins. OAB-0623

Parker, R.A.C. Chamberlain and appeasement. OAB-2399

Parker, Richard B. The politics of miscalculation in the Middle East. OAB-2792

Parker, Roger, ed. The Oxford illustrated history of opera. OAB-0994

Parker, Sybil P., ed. World geographical encyclopedia: v. 1-5. OAB-0038

Parkes, Adam. Modernism and the theater of censorship. OAB-0710

Parkhill, Thomas C. Weaving ourselves into the land. OAB-2563

Parsons, John Carmi. Eleanor of Castile: queen and society in thirteenth-century England. OAB-2212

Partnow, Elaine, ed. The New quotable woman. OAB-0024

Parton, Anthony. Mikhail Larionov and the Russian avant-garde. OAB-0382

Pasternak, Jack J. Molecular biotechnology. OAB-1362

Pastor Bodner, Beatriz. The armature of conquest. OAB-2425

Pasuk Phongpaichit. Thailand, economy and politics. OAB-2005

Pasztory, Esther. Teotihuacan. OAB-1841

Paterek, Josephine. Encyclopedia of American Indian costume. OAB-0195

Paterson, Janet M. Postmodernism and the Quebec novel. OAB-0892

Paterson, Thomas G. Contesting Castro. OAB-2618

Patten, Robert L. George Cruikshank's life, times, and art: v.1: 1792-1835. OAB-0383

Patterson, David. Exile: the sense of alienation in modern Russian letters. OAB-0929

Patterson, James T. Grand expectations. OAB-2619

Patton, Paul, tr. Difference and repetition. OAB-1156

Paul, Gregory S. Beyond humanity. OAB-1462

Paul, William. Laughing, screaming. OAB-0985

Pava, Moses L. Corporate responsibility and financial performance. OAB-1928

Payne, Charles M. I've got the light of freedom. OAB-2620

Payne, Roger. Among whales. OAB-1813

Paz, D.G. Popular anti-Catholicism in Mid-Victorian England. OAB-1226

Peabody, Sue. "There are no slaves in France." OAB-2339

Pearce, David W. World without end. OAB-2100

Pearson, Anne Mackenzie. "Because it gives me peace of mind." OAB-1195

Pearson, Frederic S. The global spread of arms. OAB-2747

Peck, David R. American ethnic literatures. OAB-0087

Peck, Demaree C. The imaginative claims of the artist in Willa Cather's fiction. OAB-0801

Peck, Jamie. Work-place: the social regulation of labor markets. OAB-1948

Peckham, Morse. The romantic virtuoso. OAB-0350

Peebles, Gavin. The Singapore economy. OAB-2006

Peers, Laura. The Ojibwa of western Canada, 1780-1870. OAB-2470

Pegram, Thomas R. Partisans and progressives. OAB-2564

Peitgen, Heinz-Otto. Fractals for the classroom: Part 2: complex systems and Mandelbrot set. OAB-1692

Pelcovits, Nathan A. The long armistice. OAB-2452

Peleg, Ilan. Human rights in the West Bank and Gaza. OAB-2793

Pelikan, Jaroslav. Mary through the centuries. OAB-1262

Pelras, Christian. The Bugis. OAB-1889

Peluso, Nancy Lee. Rich forests, poor people. OAB-2276

Pendergrast, Mark. For God, country and Coca-Cola. OAB-1909

Penny, Nicholas. Catalogue of European sculpture in the Ashmolean Museum, 1540 to the present day: v. 1-3. OAB-0499

Penrod, Steven D. Mistaken identification. OAB-2809

Pepper, David. Modern environmentalism. OAB-1377

Pepper, Suzanne. Radicalism and education reform in 20th-century China. OAB-2124

Pereboom, Maarten L. Democracies at the turning point. OAB-2290

Perelman, Michael. The pathology of the U.S. economy. OAB-2089

Peres, Shimon. Battling for peace. OAB-2664

Pérez-Torres, Rafael. Movements in Chicano poetry. OAB-0845

Perkampus, Heinz-Helmut. Encyclopedia of spectroscopy. OAB-1729

Perkins, Bradford. The Cambridge history of American foreign relations: v. 1-4. OAB-2474

Perkins, Pheme. Peter: apostle for the whole church. OAB-1263

Perkowitz, Sidney. Empire of light. OAB-1730

Perloff, Richard M. The dynamics of persuasion. OAB-2988

Permaloff, Anne. Political power in Alabama. OAB-2621

Pernicone, Nunzio. Italian anarchism, 1864-1892. OAB-2340

Perrault, Anna H. United States history: a selective guide to information sources. OAB-0244

Perret, Geoffrey. Old soldiers never die. OAB-2622

Perrine, Daniel M. The chemistry of mind-altering drugs. OAB-1641

Perry, Elizabeth J. Proletarian power: Shanghai in the cultural revolution. OAB-2679

Perry, Mark. Eclipse: the last days of the CIA. OAB-2889

Perthes, Volker. The political economy of Syria under Asad. OAB-2007

Peters, Catherine. The king of inventors. OAB-0685

Peters, F.E. The hajj. OAB-1242

Peters, Sally. Bernard Shaw: the ascent of the superman. OAB-0711

Petersen, John L. The road to 2015. OAB-1834

Peterson, Anna L. Martyrdom and the politics of religion. OAB-1227

Peterson, Merrill D. Lincoln in American memory. OAB-2498

Peterson, Nadya L. Subversive imaginations. OAB-0930

Peterson, Paul E. The price of federalism. OAB-2861

Petro, Peter. A history of Slovak literature. OAB-0931

Petroski, Henry. Engineers of dreams. OAB-1566

Petry, Carl F. Twilight of majesty. OAB-2453

Pettis, Joyce. Toward wholeness in Paule Marshall's fiction. OAB-0846

Pfister, Joel. Staging depth. OAB-0802

Phelan, Craig. Divided loyalties. OAB-1949

Phillips, Peggy Anne. Republican France. OAB-2341

Phillips, Susan S., ed. The Crisis of care. OAB-1604

Phillips-Matz, Mary Jane. Verdi: a biography. OAB-1004

Piatt, Bill. Language on the job. OAB-2890

Piazza, Thomas. The scar of race. OAB-2892

Piché, Victor. Hoe and wage. OAB-2228

Pick, Zuzana M. The new Latin American cinema. OAB-0986

Pickover, Clifford A. Keys to infinity. OAB-1693

Pickover, Clifford A., ed. Fractal horizons. OAB-1676

Pickover, Clifford A., ed. The Pattern book. OAB-1691

Piersen, William D. Black legacy. OAB-2499

Pike, David L. Passage through hell. OAB-0904

Pilat, Dirk. The economics of rapid growth. OAB-2008

Pilbeam, Pamela M. Republicanism in nineteenth-century France, 1814-1871. OAB-2342

Pilling, Michael J. Reaction kinetics. OAB-1437

Pinch, Trevor. The golem. OAB-1272

Pinches, Charles. Christians among the virtues. OAB-1137

Piranesi, Giambattista. Giovanni Battista Piranesi: the complete etchings. OAB-0384

Pisani, Donald J. To reclaim a divided west. OAB-2565

Pitts, Walter F. Old ship of Zion. OAB-1228

Plato. Republic 5. OAB-1125

Platt, Jerome J. Heroin addiction: theory, research, and treatment, v. 2 & 3. OAB-1642

Plessner, Yakir. The political economy of Israel. OAB-2009

Plouffe, Simon. The encyclopedia of integer sequences. OAB-1698

Plumridge, Andrew. Brickwork: architecture and design. OAB-0410

Plunkett, Jack W. Plunkett's health care industry almanac. OAB-0164

Plunkett, Michelle LeGate. Plunkett's health care industry almanac. OAB-0164

Pöggeler, Otto. The paths of Heidegger's life and thought. OAB-1105

Poinar, George. The quest for life in amber. OAB-1493

Poinar, Roberta. The quest for life in amber. OAB-1493

Polizzotto, Lorenzo. The elect nation. OAB-2343

Polster, Miriam F. Eve's daughters. OAB-2971

Polyanin, Andrei D. Handbook of exact solutions for ordinary differential equations. OAB-1694

Pool, Robert. Eve's rib. OAB-1757

Poole, Alan F., ed. The Birds of North America: life histories for the 21st century, v.1. OAB-0142

Poole, Deborah. Vision, race, and modernity. OAB-1842

Poole, Stafford. Our Lady of Guadalupe: the origins and sources of a Mexican national symbol, 1531-1797. OAB-1264

Pope, S.W. Patriotic games. OAB-1770

Pope, S.W., ed. The New American sport history. OAB-1769

Pope-Hennessy, John. Donatello: sculptor. OAB-0500

Port, M.H. Imperial London. OAB-0411

Porter, Bruce D. War and the rise of the state. OAB-2748

Porter, Jonathan. Macau: the imaginary city. OAB-2277

Porter, Roy. The facts of life: the creation of sexual knowledge in Britain, 1650-1950. OAB-2400

Poshyananda, Apinan. Modern art in Thailand. OAB-0385

Postel, Sandra. Last oasis. OAB-1567

Postgate, J.N. Early Mesopotamia. OAB-2213

Postgate, John. The outer reaches of life. OAB-1378

Pound, Ezra. Ezra Pound and James Laughlin. OAB-0803

Powell, Charles C. Ball pest & disease manual. OAB-1318

Powell, William, tr. Beyond the stars: the memoirs of Sergei Eisenstein: selected works, IV. OAB-0952

Powelson, David R. The recycler's manual for business, government, and the environmental community. OAB-1533

Powelson, Melinda A. The recycler's manual for business, government, and the environmental community. OAB-1533

Powers, Bernard F. Black Charlestonians. OAB-2566

Prahlad, Sw. Anand. African-American proverbs in context. OAB-0738

Prance, Anne E. Bark: the formation, characteristics, and uses.... OAB-1413

Prance, Ghillean Tolmie. Bark: the formation, characteristics, and uses.... OAB-1413

Prater, Donald. Thomas Mann: a life. OAB-0874

Pratt, Annis. Dancing with goddesses. OAB-0557

Preminger, Alex, ed. The New Princeton encyclopedia of poetry and poetics. OAB-0080

Press, Joy. The sex revolts. OAB-1052

Preston, Kristian P. Ecology, law and economics. OAB-2099

Preston, Lee E. The rules of the game in the global economy. OAB-1910

Prestwich, Michael. Armies and warfare in the Middle Ages. OAB-2214

Preuss, Ulrich K. Constitutional revolution. OAB-2932

Prewitt, Terry J. Religious violence and abortion. OAB-2587

Price, Geoffrey D., ed. The Stability of minerals. OAB-1498

Prickett, Stephen. Origins of narrative. OAB-0558

Pringle, Keith. Men, masculinities and social welfare. OAB-3109

Prior, Lindsay. The social organization of mental illness. OAB-3023

Pritchard, James. Anatomy of a naval disaster. OAB-2525

Proctor, Michael. The natural history of pollination. OAB-1410

Proctor, Richard J. The Citizen's guide to geologic hazards. OAB-1474

Promey, Sally M. Spiritual spectacles. OAB-2567

Prothero, Donald R. The Eocene-Oligocene transition. OAB-1494

Prothero, Stephen R. The encyclopedia of American religious history. OAB-0129

Prus, Robert. Symbolic interaction and ethnographic research. OAB-3024

Purvis, Alston W. Dutch graphic design, 1918-1945. OAB-0436

Pye, Michael, ed. Continuum dictionary of religion. OAB-0115

Q

Qasim, Syed R. Sanitary landfill leachate. OAB-1534

Qin, Duo. The formation of econometrics. OAB-1985

Quandt, William B. Peace process. OAB-2794

Queen, Edward L. The encyclopedia of American religious history. OAB-0129

Quigley, Robert M. Clayey barrier systems for waste disposal facilities. OAB-1536

Quinn, Susan. Marie Curie: a life. OAB-1439

Quirk, James. Pay dirt. OAB-1771

Quirk, Tom, ed. American realism and the canon. OAB-0724

R

Rabinow, Paul, ed. Ethics: subjectivity and truth. OAB-1134

Rabson, Carolyn. Orchestral excerpts. OAB-0107

Radke, Gary M. Art in Renaissance Italy. OAB-0381

Raff, Rudolf A. The shape of life. OAB-1379

Raffel, Burton. The art of translating prose. OAB-0559

Rageau, Jean-Pierre. The Penguin atlas of diasporas. OAB-0211

Ragone, David V. Thermodynamics of materials. OAB-1568

Ragsdale, Lyn. Vital statistics on the presidency. OAB-0300

Rahman, Mushtaqur. Divided Kashmir. OAB-2278

Rainey, Anson F. The Macmillan Bible atlas. OAB-0112

Rajadhyaksha, Ashish. Encyclopaedia of Indian cinema. OAB-0108

Rakestraw, Donald A. Prologue to manifest destiny. OAB-2552

Rakodi, Carole. Harare: inheriting a settler-colonial city: change or continuity? OAB-2243

Ramachandran, V.S., ed. Encyclopedia of human behavior. OAB-0311

Ramanujan Aiyangar, Srinivasa. Ramanujan: letters and commentary. OAB-1695

Ramirez, Susan Elizabeth. The world upside down. OAB-2426

Rampersad, Arnold. Days of grace. OAB-1760

Rampton, David. Vladimir Nabokov. OAB-0932

Ramsbotham, Oliver. Humanitarian intervention in contemporary conflict. OAB-2749

Randall, Vicky. Contemporary feminist politics. OAB-2395

Randel, Don Michael, ed. The Harvard biographical dictionary of music. OAB-0100

Ranis, Peter. Argentine workers. OAB-2732

Rankin, Robert A. Ramanujan: letters and commentary. OAB-1695

Rapaport, Herman. Is there truth in art? OAB-0351

Rappaport, R. Cytokinesis in animal cells. OAB-1380

Rasell, Edith, ed. School choice. OAB-2151

Rathje, William. Rubbish! OAB-1535

Ratner, Leonard G. Romantic music. OAB-0995

Rattner, Arye. Convicted but innocent. OAB-2815

Raylor, Timothy. Cavaliers, clubs, and literary culture. OAB-0650

Rayner, Alice. To act, to do, to perform. OAB-1079

Rayner-Canham, Geoffrey W. A devotion to their science. OAB-1731

Rayner-Canham, Marelene F. A devotion to their science. OAB-1731

Read, Gardner. Compendium of modern instrumental techniques. OAB-1032

Reagan, Charles E. Paul Ricoeur: his life and his work. OAB-1106

Reagan, Douglas P., ed. The Food web of a tropical rain forest. OAB-1401

Reagan, Leslie J. When abortion was a crime. OAB-2500

Rebhorn, Wayne A. The emperor of men's minds. OAB-0560

Rebolledo, Tey Diana. Women singing in the snow. OAB-0739

Rebora, Carrie. John Singleton Copley in America. OAB-0374

Reddock, Rhoda E. Women, labour & politics in Trinidad & Tobago. OAB-2427

Reddy, Marlita A., ed. Statistical abstract of the world. OAB-0178

Reddy, Marlita A., ed. Statistical record of Hispanic Americans. OAB-0179

Reddy, Marlita A., ed. Statistical record of Native North Americans. OAB-0180

Redford, Bruce, ed. The letters of Samuel Johnson: v.4: 1782-1784; v.5: Appendices and comprehensive index. OAB-0647

Reed, Kenneth. Data network handbook. OAB-1463

Reents-Budet, Dorie. Painting the Maya Universe. OAB-1858

Rees, Alan M., ed. Consumer health USA. OAB-1601

Rees, Alan M., ed. Consumer health USA, v.2. OAB-1600

Rees, Martin. Gravity's fatal attraction. OAB-1321

Reeve, C.D.C. Practices of reason. OAB-1144

Reeves, Byron. The media equation. OAB-0525

Reich, Warren Thomas, ed. Encyclopedia of bioethics. OAB-0132

Reid, Jane Davidson. The Oxford guide to classical mythology in the arts, 1300-1990s. OAB-0044

Reid, John Phillip. Constitutional history of the American Revolution: [v.4:] The authority of law. OAB-2526

Reid, Panthea. Art and affection: a life of Virginia Woolf. OAB-0712

Reilly, Catherine W. Late Victorian poetry, 1880-1899. OAB-0088

Reiss, Edward. The Strategic Defense Initiative. OAB-2771

Remer, Gary. Humanism and the rhetoric of toleration. OAB-0335

Remnick, David. Lenin's tomb. OAB-2313

Renard, John. Seven doors to Islam. OAB-1243

Rencher, Alvin C. Methods of multivariate analysis. OAB-1696

Reneau, Don, tr. Pious passion. OAB-1183

Renner, Michael. Fighting for survival. OAB-1835

Rennie, Neil. Far-fetched facts. OAB-0561

Rensselaer, W. Lee. The Andean cocaine industry. OAB-2779

Rentschler, Eric. The ministry of illusion. OAB-0961

Reps, John W. Cities of the Mississippi. OAB-2568

Resnick, Sidney. Adventures in stochastic processes. OAB-1697

Reuben, Julie A. The making of the modern university. OAB-2125

Reveal, James L. Gentle conquest. OAB-1411

Reynolds, David S. Walt Whitman's America. OAB-0762

Reynolds, Simon. The sex revolts. OAB-1052

Rezun, Miron. Science, technology, and ecopolitics in the USSR. OAB-1307

Rhodes, Carolyn. Reciprocity, U.S. trade policy, and the GATT regime. OAB-2079

Ribbans, Geoffrey. History and fiction in Galdós's narratives. OAB-0916

Ribeiro, Gustavo Lins. Transnational capitalism and hydropolitics in Argentina. OAB-2047

Rich, Doris L. Queen Bess: daredevil aviator. OAB-1308

Richard, Naomi Noble, ed. The actor's image. OAB-0420

Richards, Alan. A political economy of the Middle East. OAB-2010

Richards, David G. Exploring the divided self. OAB-0875

Richards, John F. The Mughal Empire. OAB-2279

Richards, P.W. The tropical rain forest. OAB-1412

Richards, Sandra L. Ancient songs set ablaze. OAB-0574

Richardson, J.S. The Romans in Spain. OAB-2215

Richardson, L. A new topographical dictionary of ancient Rome. OAB-0220

Richardson, Robert D. Emerson: the mind on fire: a biography. OAB-0763

Richelle, Marc N. B.F. Skinner. OAB-2949

Richmond, Anthony H. Global apartheid. OAB-2750

Richter, Daniel K. The ordeal of the longhouse. OAB-2527

Richter, William L. The ABC-CLIO companion to American Reconstruction, 1862-1877. OAB-0268

Ridley, Ronald T. The eagle and the spade. OAB-2216

Rieff, David. Slaughterhouse: Bosnia and the failure of the West. OAB-2711

Riesebrodt, Martin. Pious passion. OAB-1183

Riesenberg, Peter. Citizenship in the Western tradition. OAB-2179

Riess, Steven A. Sport in industrial America, 1850-1920. OAB-1772

Rigden, John S., ed. Macmillan encyclopedia of physics. OAB-0158

Riggio, Thomas P., ed. Dreiser's Russian diary. OAB-0785

Riley, James A. The biographical encyclopedia of the Negro baseball leagues. OAB-0165

Ringrose, David R. Spain, Europe, and the "Spanish miracle," 1700-1900. OAB-2344

Risley, Todd R. Meaningful differences in the everyday experience of young American children. OAB-2141

Ritter, Gretchen. Goldbugs and greenbacks. OAB-2030

Ritter, Michael E. Earth online. OAB-1495

Rivinus, E.F. Spencer Baird of the Smithsonian. OAB-1382

Robb, Graham. Balzac: a life. OAB-0893

Robbins, Paul R. Romantic relationships. OAB-2990

Roberts, Richard L. Two worlds of cotton. OAB-2244

Robertson, Noel. Festivals and legends. OAB-2217

Robertson, Robert J. Perceived exertion. OAB-1756

Robinson, David. From peep show to palace. OAB-0962

Roche, Maurice. Rethinking citizenship. OAB-3110

Rocheleau, Dianne. Gender, environment, and development in Kenya. OAB-2011

Rochlin, Gene I. Trapped in the net. OAB-1464

Rock, David. Authoritarian Argentina. OAB-2428

Roderick, Melissa. The path to dropping out. OAB-2126

Rodriguez, Luis J. Always running. OAB-2624

Rodwin, Marc A. Medicine, money, and morals. OAB-1591

Roe, Kathleen M. Grandmothers as caregivers. OAB-3107

Roeder, George H. The censored war. OAB-2625

Roelker, Nancy Lyman. One king, one faith. OAB-2345

Roessler, Shirley Elson. Out of the shadows. OAB-2346

Rogers, Ann. Rennyo: the second founder of Shin Buddhism. OAB-1196

Rogers, John. The matter of revolution. OAB-0651

Rogers, Minor. Rennyo: the second founder of Shin Buddhism. OAB-1196

Rogers, R. Mark. Handbook of key economic indicators. OAB-2031

Rogovin, Milton. Portraits in steel. OAB-2626

Roland, Charles G. Courage under siege. OAB-2314

Rolfe, Edwin. Collected poems: [Edwin Rolfe]. OAB-0804

Ronkainen, Ilkka A. The global marketing imperative. OAB-1957

Ronner, Wanda. The empty cradle. OAB-1638

Rooks, Noliwe M. Hair raising: beauty, culture, and African American women. OAB-1836

Rorrison, Hugh, tr. Bertolt Brecht journals. OAB-0857

Rosair, David. Photographic guide to the shorebirds of the world. OAB-1814

Roschelle, Anne R. No more kin. OAB-3065

Rosen, Charles. The romantic generation. OAB-1021

Rosen, Joe. Symmetry in science. OAB-1287

Rosenau, Pauline Vaillancourt, ed. Health care reform in the nineties. OAB-1611

Rosenblum, Jonathan D. Copper crucible. OAB-1950

Rosenblum, Naomi. A history of women photographers. OAB-0493

Rosencrans, Kendra, ed. Afraid to eat. OAB-1625

Rosenfeld, Stuart A. Competitive manufacturing. OAB-2032

Rosenstein, Carolyn. Race, ethnicity, and entrepreneurship in urban America. OAB-3086

Rosenthal, Alan. Drawing the line. OAB-2909

Rosenthal, Norman E. Winter blues. OAB-1644

Rosenzweig, Saul. Freud, Jung, and Hall the King-Maker. OAB-2950

Roskies, David G. A bridge of longing. OAB-0575

Rosowski, Susan J., ed. O pioneers! OAB-0779

Ross, Doran, ed. Elephant. OAB-2230

Ross, Ellen. Love and toil. OAB-2401

Ross, Ian Simpson. The life of Adam Smith. OAB-1986

Ross, John. Rebellion from the roots. OAB-2733

Ross, Nancy L., ed. The Stability of minerals. OAB-1498

Ross, Robert S. The great wall and the empty fortress. OAB-2789

Rosselli, John. Singers of Italian opera. OAB-1033

Rosser, Sue V. Biology & feminism. OAB-1288

Rossman, Marlene L. Multicultural marketing. OAB-1964

Rossol, Monona. The artist's complete health & safety guide. OAB-1645

Rosteck, Thomas. See it now confronts McCarthyism. OAB-2627

Rotgers, Frederick, ed. Treating substance abuse. OAB-1654

Rothermund, Dietmar. The global impact of the Great Depression, 1929-1939. OAB-2080

Rothman, Sheila M. Living in the shadow of death. OAB-1646

Rotundo, E. Anthony. American manhood. OAB-3066

Rousseau, Jean-Jacques. Discourse on the sciences and arts. OAB-2862

Rowe, David C. The limits of family influence. OAB-2963

Rowe, John Carlos. At Emerson's tomb. OAB-0740

Rowe, Noel. The pictorial guide to the living primates. OAB-1815

Rowe, R. Kerry. Clayey barrier systems for waste disposal facilities. OAB-1536

Rowell, S.C. Lithuania ascending. OAB-2218

Rowlandson, Jane. Landowners and tenants in Roman Egypt. OAB-2219

Roy, David Tod, tr. The plum in the golden vase, or, Chin P'ing Mei: v.1: The gathering. OAB-0584

Roy, William G. Socializing capital. OAB-1911

Reeder, DeeAnn, M., ed. Mammal species of the world. OAB-0151

Ruane, Joseph. The dynamics of conflict in Northern Ireland. OAB-2402

Rubenstein, Bruce A. Payoffs in the cloakroom. OAB-2910

Rubin, Barry. Revolution until victory? OAB-2795

Rudner, David West. Caste and capitalism in colonial India. OAB-2280

Ruffini, Remo. Gravitation and spacetime. OAB-1727

Ruggie, John Gerard. Winning the peace. OAB-2891

Rummel, Erika. The humanist-scholastic debate in the Renaissance & Reformation. OAB-0352

Rummel, R.J. Death by government. OAB-2648

Rumney, Thomas A. A scholar's guide to geographical writing on the American and Canadian past. OAB-0247

Russell, David W. Keiretsu: inside the hidden Japanese conglomerates. OAB-1908

Russell, Denise. Women, madness and medicine. OAB-3002

Russell, James A., ed. The psychology of facial expression. OAB-2989

Russell, Jeffrey Burton. A history of heaven. OAB-1265

Russell, Rinaldina, ed. Dialogue on the infinity of love. OAB-1155

Russell, Stuart J. Artificial intelligence: a modern approach. OAB-1465

Rutland, Robert A., ed. James Madison and the American nation, 1751-1836. OAB-0260

Ruzek, Sheryl Burt, ed. Women's health: complexities and differences. OAB-1621

Ryals, Clyde de L. The life of Robert Browning. OAB-0687

Ryan, Frank. The forgotten plague. OAB-1647

Ryan, Phil. The fall and rise of the market in Sandinista Nicaragua. OAB-2048

Rymer, Russ. Genie. OAB-3003

Ryrie, William. First World, Third World. OAB-2081

S

Saalman, Howard. Filippo Brunelleschi: the buildings. OAB-0412

Sabo, Donald, ed. Men's health and illness. OAB-1615

Sachs, Carolyn E. Gendered fields. OAB-3067

Sacks, Oliver. An anthropologist on Mars. OAB-3004

Sadie, Stanley, ed. The New Grove dictionary of opera. OAB-0105

Sadri, Ahmad. Max Weber's sociology of intellectuals. OAB-3025

S'aenz-Badillos, Angel. A history of the Hebrew language. OAB-0576

Safrai, Ze'ev. The Macmillan Bible atlas. OAB-0112

Sagan, Carl. Billions and billions. OAB-1289

Sagan, Carl. The demon-haunted world. OAB-1309

Sagan, Dorion. What is life? OAB-1373

Sagan, Leonard A. Electric and magnetic fields. OAB-1648

Sagarin, Edward. Convicted but innocent. OAB-2815

Sahn, David E., ed. Economic reform and the poor in Africa. OAB-1995

Said, Edward W. Culture and imperialism. OAB-2180

San Juan, E. The Philippine temptation. OAB-0595

Salamon, Lester M. Partners in public service. OAB-2820

Salbu, Brit, ed. Trace elements in natural waters. OAB-1441

Salstrom, Paul. Appalachia's path to dependency. OAB-2033

Salzman, Jack, ed. Encyclopedia of African-American culture and history. OAB-0249

Samli, A. Coskun. Social responsibility in marketing. OAB-1965

Sandall, Orville C. Computational methods in chemical engineering. OAB-1507

Sanders, Joseph. Everyday justice. OAB-3015

Sanders, Paula. Ritual, politics, and the city in Fatimid Cairo. OAB-2454

Sandler, Irving. Art of the postmodern era. OAB-0387

Sandler, Stanley. Segregated skies. OAB-2628

Sandved, Kjell B. Bark: the formation, characteristics, and uses.... OAB-1413

Santana, Déborah Berman. Kicking off the bootstraps. OAB-2429

Sapiro, Virginia. A vindication of political virtue. OAB-2863

Sarasohn, Lisa T. Gassendi's ethics. OAB-1145

Sarat, Austin, ed. Law in everyday life. OAB-2819

Sarlo, Beatriz. Jorge Luis Borges: a writer on the edge. OAB-0917

Sartori, Giovanni. Comparative constitutional engineering. OAB-2933

Sartori, Leo. Understanding relativity. OAB-1732

Sasson, Jack M., ed. Civilizations of the ancient Near East. OAB-0184

Sassower, Raphael. Knowledge without expertise. OAB-1166

Sater, William F. A history of Chile, 1808-1994. OAB-2414

Sato, Ryuzo. The chrysanthemum and the eagle. OAB-2772

Sauer, Tim D. Chaos: an introduction to dynamical systems. OAB-1660

Saul, John Ralston. The unconscious civilization. OAB-2864

Saunders, Richard H. John Smibert: colonial America's first portrait painter. OAB-0478

Saupe, Dietmar. Fractals for the classroom: Part 2: complex systems and Mandelbrot set. OAB-1692

Savage, Candace. Aurora: the mysterious northern lights. OAB-1346

Sawers, Larry. The other Argentina. OAB-2049

Sawyer, Mary R. Black ecumenism. OAB-1229

Sawyer, Ralph D., tr. The complete art of war. OAB-2868

Saxenian, AnnaLee. Regional advantage. OAB-2629

Scally, Robert James. The end of hidden Ireland. OAB-2403

Scarlett, Elizabeth A. Under construction. OAB-0918

Schaaf, Larry J. Out of the shadows. OAB-2349

Schäfer, Peter. Judeophobia: attitudes toward the Jews in the ancient world. OAB-2220

Schaller, George B. The last panda. OAB-1816

Schama, Simon. Landscape and memory. OAB-2181

Scheese, Don. Nature writing. OAB-0741

Scheindlin, Raymond P., tr. Jewish liturgy. OAB-1236

Schenk, George. Moss gardening. OAB-1414

Schenker, Alexander M. The dawn of Slavic. OAB-0933

Scherzer, Kenneth A. The unbounded community. OAB-2569

Scheub, Harold, ed. The world and the word. OAB-1896

Scheven, Yvette. Bibliographies for African studies, 1987-1993. OAB-0229

Schlachter, Gail Ann. College student's guide to merit and other no-need funding, 1996-1998. OAB-0177

Schlosser, M., ed. Organometallics in synthesis. OAB-1435

Schmid, Greg. Future tense. OAB-1927

Schmidt, Diane. Using the biological literature. OAB-0144

Schmidt, Elizabeth. Peasants, traders, and wives. OAB-2245

Schmitt, Charles B. Renaissance philosophy. OAB-1094

Schmitt, Frederick F. Truth: a primer. OAB-1167

Schneider, Barbara, ed. Parents, their children, and schools. OAB-2123

Schneider, Dorothee. Trade unions and community: the German working class in New York City, 1870-1900. OAB-1951

Schneider, Ronald M. Brazil: culture and politics in a new industrial powerhouse. OAB-2734

Schneider, Stephen H., ed. Encyclopedia of climate and weather. OAB-0155

Schofield, John. Medieval London houses. OAB-0413

Scholes, Robert. Hemingway's genders. OAB-0783

Schoolfield, George C. Helsinki of the czars. OAB-2372

Schott, Jeffrey J. The Uruguay round. OAB-2082

Schreiner, Olive. "My other self." OAB-0722

Schrire, Robert, ed. Malan to De Klerk. OAB-2661

Schroeder, Paul W. The transformation of European politics, 1763-1848. OAB-2291

Schubert, Frank N., comp. On the trail of the buffalo soldier. OAB-0269

Schuh, Scott. Job creation and destruction. OAB-2086

Schulenberg, David. The keyboard music of J.S. Bach. OAB-1034

Schulte-Sasse, Linda. Entertaining the Third Reich. OAB-0963

Schultz, Ronald. The republic of labor. OAB-2528

Schumann, Walter. Minerals of the world. OAB-1496

Schüssler Fiorenza, Elisabeth. But she said. OAB-1266

Schwartz, Arnold, tr. Studies in the Zohar. OAB-1240

Schwartz, Richard Alan. The Cold War reference guide. OAB-0301

Schwarz, Cindy. A tour of the subatomic zoo. OAB-1733

Schwarz, Daniel R. Narrative and representation in the poetry of Wallace Stevens. OAB-0847

Schwarz, Philip J. Slave laws in Virginia. OAB-2570

Schweiker, William. Responsibility and Christian ethics. OAB-1146

Scott, Allan W. Understanding microwaves. OAB-1519

Scott, Alwyn. Stairway to the mind. OAB-1758

Scott, Charles E. On the advantages and disadvantages of ethics and politics. OAB-1147

Scott, Clive. Reading the rhythm. OAB-0894

Scott, Joanna Vecchiarelli, ed. Love and Saint Augustine. OAB-1199

Scott, John. Sociological theory. OAB-3020

Scott, Katie. The Rococo interior. OAB-0437

Scott, Nathan A. Visions of presence in modern American poetry. OAB-0848

Scott, W. Richard. Institutions and organizations. OAB-3027

Scott, William G. Chester I. Barnard and the guardians of the managerial state. OAB-1929

Scott-Kassner, Carol. Music in childhood. OAB-2135

Scruggs, Charles. Sweet home. OAB-0849

Seakins, Paul W. Reaction kinetics. OAB-1437

Searle, G.R. The Liberal Party: triumph and disintegration, 1886-1929. OAB-2404

Sears, Stephen W. Chancellorsville. OAB-2571

Sebald, W.G. The emigrants. OAB-0876

Secrest, Donald. Understanding attitudes about war. OAB-2833

Sedgwick, Catharine Maria. The power of her sympathy. OAB-0764

Segel, Harold B., ed. The Vienna coffeehouse wits, 1890-1938. OAB-0877

Seibold, E. The sea floor. OAB-1497

Seidman, Naomi. A marriage made in heaven. OAB-0577

Seikaly, May. Haifa: transformation of a Palestinian Arab society, 1918-1939. OAB-2455

Sellars, Jane. The art of the Brontës. OAB-0336

Semelin, Jacques. Unarmed against Hitler. OAB-2292

Semmes, Clovis E. Cultural hegemony and African American development. OAB-3089

Sen, Amartya. Inequality reexamined. OAB-2090

Sergiovanni, Thomas J. Leadership for the schoolhouse. OAB-2152

Serrin, William. Homestead. OAB-2572

Seward, Frederick D. Exploring the X-ray universe. OAB-1327

Shafritz, Jay M. The dictionary of 20th-century world politics. OAB-0302

Shale, Richard. The Academy Awards index. OAB-0109

Shalhope, Robert E. Bennington and the Green Mountain Boys. OAB-2501

Shamos, Morris H. The myth of scientific literacy. OAB-1290

Shanks, J. Merrill. The new American voter. OAB-2907

Shannon, Richard. The Age of Disraeli, 1868-1881. OAB-2405

Shapiro, Ann-Louise. Breaking the codes. OAB-2347

Shapiro, David L. Federalism: a dialogue. OAB-2865

Shapiro, Gavriel. Nikolai Gogol and the baroque cultural heritage. OAB-0934

Shattuck, Gardiner H. The encyclopedia of American religious history. OAB-0129

Shawcross, John T. John Milton: the self and the world. OAB-0652

Shay, Jonathan. Achilles in Vietnam. OAB-1649

Shea, Thomas F. Flann O'Brien's exorbitant novels. OAB-0713

Shearman, John. Only connect. OAB-0388

Sheehan, George. Going the distance. OAB-1592

Sheehan, Marion. An illustrated survey of orchid genera. OAB-1415

Sheehan, Michael. The balance of power. OAB-2866

Sheehan, Tom. An illustrated survey of orchid genera. OAB-1415

Sheehan, William. Worlds in the sky. OAB-1347

Shehadi, Fadlou. Philosophies of music in medieval Islam. OAB-1022

Sheldon-Keller, Adrienne E. Patterns of relating. OAB-2994

Shell, Robert C.-H. Children of bondage. OAB-2246

Shentalinsky, Vitaly. Arrested voices. OAB-0935

Shenton, R.W. Doctrines of development. OAB-1970

Shepard, Jonathan. The emergence of Rus, 750-1200. OAB-2197

Sheridan, Thomas E. Arizona: a history. OAB-2502

Shigley, Joseph E., ed. Standard handbook of machine design. OAB-1573

Shiloah, Amnon. Jewish musical traditions. OAB-0996

Shlaim, Avi. War and peace in the Middle East. OAB-2796

Shlapentokh, Dmitry. Soviet cinematography, 1918-1991. OAB-0964

Shlapentokh, Vladmir. Soviet cinematography, 1918-1991. OAB-0964

Shoptaw, John. On the outside looking out. OAB-0850

Shore, Jane E. Organizational career development. OAB-1944

Shropshire, Kenneth L. In black and white. OAB-1773

Sigel, Roberta S. Ambition & accommodation. OAB-3068

Sigler, Robert T. Forced sexual intercourse in intimate relationships. OAB-3105

Sikov, Ed. Laughing hysterically. OAB-0987

Sil, Narasingha P. Swami Vivekananda: a reassessment. OAB-1197

Silber, Irwin. Socialism—what went wrong? OAB-2867

Silber, Nina. The romance of reunion. OAB-2573

Silbey, Joel H., ed. Encyclopedia of the American legislative system. OAB-0278

Silbiger, Alexander, ed. Keyboard music before 1700. OAB-1018

Silk, Mark. Unsecular media. OAB-0526

Silvester, Robert. United States theatre. OAB-0110

Sime, Ruth Lewin. Lise Meitner: a life in physics. OAB-1734

Simkin, John E., comp. The whole story: 3000 years of sequels and sequences. OAB-0089

Simon, Noel. Nature in danger. OAB-1383

Simon, Reeva S., ed. Encyclopedia of the modern Middle East. OAB-0011

Simon, Robert I. Bad men do what good men dream. OAB-2992

Simone, Roberta. The immigrant experience in American fiction. OAB-0090

Simons, Geoff. Robots: the quest for living machines. OAB-1570

Simpson, Christopher. The splendid blond beast. OAB-2751

Simpson, John. The Oxford dictionary of modern slang. OAB-0003

Simpson, John E. Sea breeze and local winds. OAB-1735

Simpson, Lewis P. The fable of the southern writer. OAB-0851

Sinclair, Barbara. Legislators, leaders, and lawmaking. OAB-2911

Singer, Max. The real world order. OAB-2752

Singh, Ben Ramnarine. Handbook of environmental management and technology. OAB-1526

Singh, Hanwant B., ed. Composition, chemistry, and climate of the atmosphere. OAB-1706

Singh, K.S. The scheduled castes. OAB-2281

Singh, Vijay P. Kinematic wave modeling in water resources. OAB-1537

Sinnott, Jan D., ed. Interdisciplinary handbook of adult lifespan learning. OAB-2115

Sipes, I. Glenn, ed. Comprehensive toxicology. OAB-1599

Sisk, Timothy D. Democratization in South Africa. OAB-2665

Skandera-Trombley, Laura E. Mark Twain in the company of women. OAB-0765

Skidelsky, Robert. John Maynard Keynes: a biography. v.2: The economist as saviour, 1920-1937. OAB-1987

Sklar, Lawrence. Physics and chance. OAB-1736

Sklar, Robert. Film: an international history of the medium. OAB-0965

Skocpol, Theda. Protecting soldiers and mothers. OAB-3028

Skura, Meredith Anne. Shakespeare the actor and the purposes of playing. OAB-1080

Slade, Doren L. Making the world safe for existence. OAB-1890

Slater, Courtenay M., ed. Business statistics of the United States. OAB-0197

Slayter, Elizabeth M. Light and electron microscopy. OAB-1737

Slayter, Henry S. Light and electron microscopy. OAB-1737

Sleinis, E.E. Nietzsche's revaluation of values. OAB-1168

Slide, Anthony. The encyclopedia of vaudeville. OAB-0111

Sloan, Wm. David. The early American press, 1690-1783. OAB-0527

Sloane, N.J.A. The encyclopedia of integer sequences. OAB-1698

Slotkin, Richard. Gunfighter nation. OAB-2630

Smelser, Neil J. Sociology. OAB-3029

Smelser, Neil J., ed. The Handbook of economic sociology. OAB-3016

Smith, Andrew B. Pastoralism in Africa. OAB-2247

Smith, Daniel S., ed. Ecology of greenways. OAB-1359

Smith, David E. The invisible crown. OAB-2686

Smith, F. Todd. The Caddo Indians: tribes at the convergence of empires, 1542-1854. OAB-2529

Smith, Harriet Elinor, ed. Roughing it. OAB-0771

Smith, J. Walker. Rocking the ages. OAB-1966

Smith, Jessie Carney, ed. Notable black American women, book II. OAB-0266

Smith, Jonathan Z., ed. The HarperCollins dictionary of religion. OAB-0119

Smith, Martha Nell. Comic power in Emily Dickinson. OAB-0755

Smith, Michael E. The Aztecs. OAB-2430

Smith, Nicholas D. Plato's Socrates. OAB-1118

Smith, Robert. Derrida and autobiography. OAB-1107

Smith, Robert C. The wounded Jung. OAB-2951

Smith, Robert McClure. The seductions of Emily Dickinson. OAB-0766

Smith, Roger C. Vanguard of empire. OAB-2293

Smocovitis, Vassiliki Betty. Unifying biology. OAB-1384

Sniderman, Paul M. The scar of race. OAB-2892

Snodgrass, Chris. Aubrey Beardsley, dandy of the grotesque. OAB-0438

Snow, David A. Down on their luck. OAB-3111

Snow, Dean R. The Iroquois. OAB-2503

Snyder, Magaret C. African women and development. OAB-2248

Snyder, Paula. The European women's almanac. OAB-0032

Sobel, Dava. Longitude: the true story of a lone genius who solved the greatest scientific problem of his time. OAB-1348

Soesilo, J. Andy. Site remediation. OAB-1538

Soitos, Stephen F. The blues detective: a study of African American detective fiction. OAB-0805

Solodow, Joseph B., tr. Latin literature: a history. OAB-0602

Solomon, Robert C. The new world of business. OAB-1912

Solovei, Valerii D. Russia's communists at the crossroads. OAB-2715

Sommese, Andrew J. The adjunction theory of complex projective varieties. OAB-1661

Sonn, Tamara. Interpreting Islam. OAB-1244

Sonnert, Gerhard. Gender differences in science careers. OAB-1292

Soper, Kate. What is nature?: culture, politics and the non-human. OAB-1169

Soper, Tony. Antarctica: a guide to the wildlife. OAB-1385

Sorabji, Richard. Animal minds and human morals. OAB-1148

Sorensen, Jonathan R. The rope, the chair, and the needle. OAB-3045

Sorrentino, Paul. The Crane log. OAB-0773

Soufas, C. Christopher. Audience and authority in the modernist theater of Federico García Lorca. OAB-0919

Southwick, Charles H. Global ecology in human perspective. OAB-1293

Sowell, Thomas. Inside American education. OAB-2127

Sparshott, Francis. Taking life seriously. OAB-1149

Spate, Virginia. Claude Monet: life and work. OAB-0479

Spector, Robert D. Smollett's women. OAB-0653

Speidel, Michael P. Riding for Caesar. OAB-2221

Spencer, Frank, ed. History of physical anthropology. OAB-0191

Spencer, Jon Michael. The new Negroes and their music. OAB-1053

Spender, Dale, ed. The Knowledge explosion. OAB-1831

Sperelakis, Nicholas, ed. Cell physiology source book. OAB-1747

Speyer, Robert F. Thermal analysis of materials. OAB-1572

Spike, John T. Fra Angelico. OAB-0480

Spillman, Robert. Poetry into song: performance and analysis of lieder. OAB-1035

Spotts, Frederic. Bayreuth: a history of the Wagner festival. OAB-1023

Sprigge, T.L.S. James and Bradley. OAB-1108

Spring, Eileen. Law, land, & family. OAB-2406

Spulber, Nicolas. The American economy. OAB-2034

Stahl, Saul. Introductory modern algebra. OAB-1699

Stambaugh, Joan. The other Nietzsche. OAB-1109

Staples, Robert. Black families at the crossroads. OAB-3090

Stares, Paul B. Global habit: the drug problem in a borderless world. OAB-2754

Stark, Rodney. The rise of Christianity. OAB-1230

Starkey, Janet, ed. Before the wind changed. OAB-2104

Starkweather, C. Woodruff. Stuttering. OAB-1650

Starnes, Wayne C. The fishes of Tennessee. OAB-1797

Starr, Kevin. The dream endures. OAB-2631

States, Bert O. Seeing in the dark. OAB-2964

Stavenhagen, Rodolfo. Ethnic conflicts and the nation-state. OAB-2755

Stearns, Peter N., ed. Encyclopedia of social history. OAB-0215

Steen, R. Grant. DNA and destiny. OAB-2965

Steffan, Joseph. Gays and the military. OAB-2821

Stein, Deborah. Poetry into song: performance and analysis of lieder. OAB-1035

Stein, Janice Gross. We all lost the Cold War. OAB-2607

Stein, Regina. The timetables of Jewish history. OAB-0223

Steinberg, Stephen. Turning back: the retreat from racial justice in American thought and policy. OAB-2632

Steiner, Christopher B. African art in transit. OAB-0389

Steiner, Gary, tr. Martin Heidegger and European nihilism. OAB-1102

Steinfirst, Susan. Folklore and folklife. OAB-0196

Stenberg, Carl W. America's future work force. OAB-1952

Stephan, John J. The Russian 5. OAB-2319

Stern, Gary M., ed. The U.S. Constitution and the power to go to war. OAB-2773

Stern, Peter A. Sendero Luminoso: an annotated bibliography of the Shining Path Guerrilla Movement, 1980-1993. OAB-0303

Sternberg, Martin L.A. The American sign language dictionary on CD-ROM. OAB-0033

Sternberg, Robert J., ed. Encyclopedia of human intelligence. OAB-0312

Sternberg, Robert J., ed. The Nature of insight. OAB-2962

Stetkevych, Jaroslav. Muḥammad and the golden bough. OAB-0578

Steuerle, C. Eugene. Retooling Social Security for the 21st century. OAB-2091

Stevens, Anthony. Private myths. OAB-2993

Stevens, Robert E. The Marketing research guide. OAB-1959

Stevenson, David. Armaments and the coming of war. OAB-2294

Stevenson, Patrick, ed. The German language and the real world. OAB-0866

Stewart, Ian. Nature's numbers. OAB-1700

Stewart, Kenneth L. Not room enough. OAB-2574

Stewart, Rick. Charles M. Russell, sculptor. OAB-0501

Stiglitz, Joseph E. Whither socialism? OAB-1988

Stillwell, John. Elements of algebra. OAB-1701

Stine, Jeffrey K. Mixing the waters. OAB-2893

Stirzaker, David. Elementary probability. OAB-1702

Stites, Richard. Russian popular culture. OAB-2316

Stokes, Kenneth M. Man and the biosphere. OAB-2101

Stoll, Clifford. Silicon snake oil. OAB-1466

Stolley, Paul D. Investigating disease patterns. OAB-1619

Stone, Glenn Davis. Settlement ecology. OAB-1843

Stone, Harriet. The classical model. OAB-0895

Stopford, John M. Rejuvenating the mature business. OAB-1916

Storey, John W. The religious right. OAB-0130

Storrer, William Allin. The Frank Lloyd Wright companion. OAB-0414

Stout, Janis P. Katherine Anne Porter: a sense of the times. OAB-0806

Stowasser, Barbara Freyer. Women in the Qur'an, traditions, and interpretation. OAB-1245

St. Peter, Christine, ed. The old lady says "no!" OAB-0705

Strauss, Anselm L. Continual permutations of action. OAB-3031

Strauss, Emanuel. Dictionary of European proverbs. OAB-0034

Strazdes, Diana. American paintings and sculpture to 1945 in the Carnegie Museum of Art. OAB-0390

Street, John. Politics and technology. OAB-1110

Strier, Karen B. Faces in the forest. OAB-1817

Strier, Richard. Resistant structures. OAB-0624

Stringer, Christopher. African exodus. OAB-1859

Stringer, Jenny, ed. The Oxford companion to twentieth-century literature in English. OAB-0085

Stroebel, Leslie, ed. The Focal encyclopedia of photography. OAB-0051

Strohl, Mitchell P. Europe's high speed trains. OAB-2058

Strohm, Reinhard. The rise of European music, 1380-1500. OAB-1024

Stronge, James H., ed. Educating homeless children and adolescents. OAB-2108

Strum, Philippa. Brandeis. OAB-2934

Stuckey, Charles F. Claude Monet, 1840-1926. OAB-0481

Stuster, Jack. Bold endeavors. OAB-1294

Styan, J.L. The English stage. OAB-1081

Subramanian, Pallatheri M., ed. Emerging technologies in plastics recycling. OAB-1551

Sugrue, Thomas J. The origins of the urban crisis. OAB-3091

Sukhwal, B.L. Political geography. OAB-0304

Sukhwal, Lilawati. Political geography. OAB-0304

Sullivan, Irene F. Dictionary of Native American mythology. OAB-0189

Sullivan, Robert. A matter of faith. OAB-0852

Sullivan, Roger J. An introduction to Kant's ethics. OAB-1150

Sun Pin. The complete art of war. OAB-2868

Sundquist, Eric J. To wake the nations. OAB-0767

Sunshine, Linda. The best hospitals in America. OAB-0167

Sunstein, Cass R. Legal reasoning and political conflict. OAB-2822

Sun-tzu. The complete art of war. OAB-2868

Sussman, Gerald Jay. Structure and interpretation of computer programs. OAB-1442

Sussman, Lance J. Isaac Leeser and the making of American Judaism. OAB-1246

Sutherland, John. Victorian fiction. OAB-0688

Sutherland, Lin. The volcanic Earth: volcanoes and plate tectonics past, present & future. OAB-1499

Sutton, Christine. Spaceship Neutrino. OAB-1738

Sutton, Robert P. Les Icariens: the Utopian dream in Europe and America. OAB-2575

Svingen, Orlan J. The Northern Cheyenne Indian Reservation, 1877-1900. OAB-2576

Swaddle, T.W. Inorganic chemistry. OAB-1440

Swafford, Jan. Charles Ives: a life with music. OAB-1005

Swaim, Kathleen M. Pilgrim's progress, puritan progress. OAB-0654

Swain, Carol M. Black faces, black interests. OAB-2912

Swain, Tony. A place for strangers. OAB-1891

Swan, James H. The long term care crisis. OAB-1606

Swann, Brian, ed. Coming to light. OAB-0728

Swann, Julian. Politics and the Parlement of Paris under Louis XV, 1754-1774. OAB-2348

Swantz, Marja-Liisa. Blood, milk, and death. OAB-1892

Swigg, Richard. Charles Tomlinson and the objective tradition. OAB-0714

Swyripa, Frances. Wedded to the cause. OAB-2471

Sylvester, Christine. Feminist theory and international relations in a postmodern era. OAB-2756

Szabo, Stephen F. The diplomacy of German unification. OAB-2797

Szajkowski, Bogdan, ed. Political parties of Eastern Europe, Russia and the successor states. OAB-0298

T

Tachau, Frank, ed. Political parties of the Middle East and North Africa. OAB-0299

Tackett, Timothy. Becoming a revolutionary. OAB-2349

Tadesse, Mary. African women and development. OAB-2248

Takaki, Ronald. A different mirror. OAB-2504

Talbott, Stephen L. The future does not compute. OAB-1467

Tamashiro, Howard. Understanding attitudes about war. OAB-2833

Taminiaux, Jacques. Poetics, speculation, and judgement. OAB-1114

Tanaka, Stefan. Japan's Orient. OAB-2282

Tanner, Jo A. Dusky maidens. OAB-0945

Tanner, Marcus. Croatia: a nation forged in war. OAB-2317

Taras, Raymond. Consolidating democracy in Poland. OAB-2713

Tarr, Joel A. The search for the ultimate sink. OAB-1539

Tarrant, John J. The global marketing imperative. OAB-1957

Tarrow, Sidney. Power in movement. OAB-3032

Taruskin, Richard. Defining Russia musically. OAB-1006

Taruskin, Richard. Stravinsky and the Russian traditions. OAB-1007

Tauber, Eliezer. The Arab movements in World War I. OAB-2456

Tausch, Arno. Towards a socio-liberal theory of world development. OAB-1989

Taylor, David. The new police in nineteenth-century England. OAB-2407

Taylor, David Winship, ed. Flowering plant origin, evolution & phylogeny. OAB-1400

Taylor, Diana, ed. Negotiating performance. OAB-1077

Taylor, Jim. The 500-year delta. OAB-1913

Taylor, Luke. Seeing the inside. OAB-1844

Taylor, M. Brook, ed. Canadian history: a reader's guide. v.1 & 2. OAB-0246

Taylor, Quintard. The forging of a black community. OAB-2633

Taylor, Richard, ed. Beyond the stars: the memoirs of Sergei Eisenstein: selected works, IV. OAB-0952

Taylor, Ronald. Kurt Weill. OAB-1008

Taylor, Stuart Ross. Solar system evolution. OAB-1349

Teaford, Jon C. Cities of the heartland. OAB-2505

Teahan, Sheila. The rhetorical logic of Henry James. OAB-0768

Tenenbaum, Barbara A., ed. Encyclopedia of Latin American history and culture. OAB-0251

Tétreault, Mary Ann, ed. Women and revolution in Africa, Asia, and the New World. OAB-2649

Thacker, John. Straight talk about sexually transmitted diseases. OAB-1628

Thelin, John R. Games colleges play. OAB-1774

Theodore, Louis. Handbook of environmental management and technology. OAB-1526

Thiselton, Anthony C. New horizons in hermeneutics. OAB-1267

Thomas, Brook. American literary realism and the failed promise of contract. OAB-0769

U

V

Vogelsong, Diana. Landscape architecture sourcebook. OAB-0056

Vogt, W. Paul. Dictionary of statistics and methodology. OAB-0182

Vogt, W. Paul. Tolerance & education. OAB-2155

Voll, John O. Islam and democracy. OAB-2841

Von der Mehden, Fred R. Two worlds of Islam. OAB-2798

Von Hirsch, Andrew. Censure and sanctions. OAB-2871

Vonder Haar, Thomas H. Satellite meteorology: an introduction. OAB-1718

Voos, Paula B., ed. Contemporary collective bargaining in the private sector. OAB-1939

Vorlicky, Robert. Act like a man. OAB-0855

Voynick, Stephen M. Climax: the history of Colorado's Climax Molybdenum Mine. OAB-1575

Vrettos, Athena. Somatic fictions. OAB-0690

W

Wachsberger, Ken, ed. Voices from the underground: v.1 & 2. OAB-0529

Wacker, Watts. The 500-year delta. OAB-1913

Wade, Peter. Blackness and race mixture. OAB-2432

Wailoo, Keith. Drawing blood. OAB-1656

Wainscott, Ronald H. The emergence of the modern American theater, 1914-1929. OAB-1083

Wakeman, Frederic. Policing Shanghai, 1927-1937. OAB-2284

Walcott, Charles E. Governing the White House. OAB-2914

Waldenfels, Bernhard. Order in the twilight. OAB-1111

Waldmeir, Patti. Anatomy of a miracle. OAB-2666

Walicki, Andrzej. Marxism and the leap to the kingdom of freedom. OAB-2872

Walker, Michael. Government spending facts 2. OAB-2022

Walker, P.M.B., ed. Chambers nuclear energy and radiation dictionary. OAB-0154

Walker, Peter M.B., ed. Larousse dictionary of science and technology. OAB-0137

Walker, R.B.J. Inside/outside. OAB-2757

Wallace, Robert K. Melville & Turner. OAB-0772

Wallace, William E. Michelangelo at San Lorenzo. OAB-0415

Wallace-Hadrill, Andrew. Houses and society in Pompeii and Herculaneum. OAB-2223

Walls, Peter. Music in the English courtly masque, 1604-1640. OAB-1036

Walser, Robert. Running with the devil. OAB-1055

Walsh, Sylvia. Living poetically. OAB-1115

Walsh, Thomas F. Katherine Anne Porter and Mexico. OAB-0812

Walters, Suzanna Danuta. Lives together/worlds apart. OAB-3070

Walters, Suzanna Danuta. Material girls. OAB-0356

Wang, Shan K. Handbook of air conditioning and refrigeration. OAB-1576

Wang, Shaoguang. Failure of charisma. OAB-2285

Ward, Harry M. The American Revolution: nationhood achieved, 1763-1788. OAB-2532

Warford, Jeremy J. World without end. OAB-2100

Wark, McKenzie. Virtual geography. OAB-0530

Warner, Malcolm, ed. International encyclopedia of business and management. OAB-0204

Warren, Warren S., ed. The Physical basis of chemistry. OAB-1436

Wasby, Stephen L. Race relations litigation in an age of complexity. OAB-2824

Waskow, Arthur. Becoming brothers. OAB-2974

Waskow, Howard. Becoming brothers. OAB-2974

Wasserman, Robert H. Tensors and manifolds. OAB-1740

Waterbury, John. A political economy of the Middle East. OAB-2010

Waters, T.F. Fundamentals of manufacturing for engineers. OAB-1509

Watkins, Evan. Throwaways: work culture and consumer education. OAB-3034

Watkins, John. The specter of Dido. OAB-0626

Watson, Charles S. Managing projects for personal success. OAB-1931

Watson, William. The arts of China to AD 900. OAB-0391

Watt, Ian. Myths of modern individualism. OAB-0563

Watt, James C.Y. Possessing the past. OAB-0386

Way, Eileen Cornell. Realism rescued. OAB-1270

Weaver, Jefferson Hane. Conquering statistics. OAB-1704

Webber, Jeremy. Reimagining Canada. OAB-2687

Webber, Roger. Communicable disease epidemiology and control. OAB-1657

Weber, Devra. Dark sweat, white gold. OAB-2638

Weber, Eugen. The hollow years. OAB-2352

Weber, R. David. College student's guide to merit and other no-need funding, 1996-1998. OAB-0177

Webster, John. Fungal ecology. OAB-1397

Webster, Juliet. Shaping women's work. OAB-3071

Wedekind, Frank. Plays: one: *Spring awakening.* OAB-0878

Weeks, Andrew. Paracelsus: speculative theory and the crisis of the early Reformation. OAB-1172

Wegener, Charles. The discipline of taste and feeling. OAB-1116

Weinberg, Mark S. Challenging the hierarchy. OAB-1084

Weinberg, Meyer, comp. Racism in contemporary America. OAB-0270

Weiner, Annette B. Inalienable possessions. OAB-1895

Weinsheimer, Joel, tr. Introduction to philosophical hermeneutics. OAB-1158

Weiss, Penny A. Gendered community. OAB-3072

Welch, Claude E. Protecting human rights in Africa. OAB-2799

Welch, Robert, ed. The Oxford companion to Irish literature. OAB-0083

Wells, Allen. Summer of discontent, seasons of upheaval. OAB-2433

Wenger, Beth S. New York Jews and the Great Depression. OAB-2639

Werblowsky, R.J. Zwi, ed. The Oxford dictionary of the Jewish religion. OAB-0126

Wertheim, Stanley. The Crane log. OAB-0773

Wertheimer, Jack. A people divided. OAB-1247

West, Frederick Hadleigh, ed. American beginnings. OAB-1847

West, James L.W., ed. Jennie Gerhardt. OAB-0786

West, M.L. Ancient Greek music. OAB-1025

West, Malcolm L. Patterns of relating. OAB-2994

West, Robin. Narrative, authority, and law. OAB-2825

Whalen, Mollie. Counseling to end violence against women. OAB-3112

Whipps, J.M. Ecophysiology of fungi. OAB-1395

Whisnant, David E. Rascally signs in sacred places. OAB-2434

Whitaker, John O. National Audubon Society field guide to North American mammals. OAB-0152

White, Edmund. Genet: a biography. OAB-0896

White, James L. Rubber processing: technology, materials, and principles. OAB-1577

White, James W. Ikki: social conflict and political protest in early modern Japan. OAB-2286

White, Phillip M. American Indian studies. OAB-0271

White, Rodney R. Urban environmental management. OAB-2183

White, Sarah C. Arguing with the crocodile. OAB-3073

White, Sol. Sol White's history of colored base ball, with other documents on the early black game, 1886-1936. OAB-1776

White, Timothy P. The Wellness guide to lifelong fitness. OAB-1620

Whiteley, Sandy, ed. The American Library Association guide to information access. OAB-0001

Whitten, Jane. Wild Indonesia. OAB-1357

Whitten, Tony. Wild Indonesia. OAB-1357

Whittier, Nancy. Feminist generations. OAB-3074

Whobrey, William, tr. Studies in poetic discourse. OAB-0545

Wiesner, Merry E. Women and gender in early modern Europe. OAB-2184

Wiget, Andrew, ed. Dictionary of Native American literature. OAB-0067

Wiggershaus, Rolf. The Frankfurt school: its history, theories, and political significance. OAB-1838

Wilbert, Johannes, ed. Encyclopedia of world cultures: v.7: South America. OAB-0187

Wilcox, Helen, ed. Women and literature in Britain, 1500-1700. OAB-0657

Wilcox, John C. Women poets of Spain, 1860-1990. OAB-0921

Wildavsky, Aaron. The real world order. OAB-2752

Willemen, Paul. Encyclopaedia of Indian cinema. OAB-0108

Willett, John, ed. Bertolt Brecht journals. OAB-0857

Williams, J.E.D. From sails to satellites. OAB-1311

Williams, Jonathan M.J., ed. Preparation of alkenes. OAB-1438

Williams, Julie Hedgepeth. The early American press, 1690-1783. OAB-0527

Williams, Mark. Patrick White. OAB-0723

Williams, Phil. The dictionary of 20th-century world politics. OAB-0302

Williams, Rhys H. A bridging of faiths. OAB-1207

Williams, Robert I. Comic practice/comic response. OAB-0357

Williams, Stephen. Theodosius: the empire at bay. OAB-2224

Williams, William H. Slavery and freedom in Delaware, 1639-1865. OAB-2506

Williamson, Chilton. The immigration mystique. OAB-2894

Williamson, Joel. William Faulkner and southern history. OAB-0813

Williamson, Margaret. Sappho's immortal daughters. OAB-0612

Willinsky, John. Empire of words. OAB-0564

Willis, George, ed. The American curriculum. OAB-2131

Wills, Lawrence M. The Jewish novel in the ancient world. OAB-1268

Willson, Martin, tr. The Mandala: sacred circle in Tibetan Buddhism. OAB-1185

Wilson, Andrew J. Irish America and the Ulster conflict, 1968-1995. OAB-2640

Wilson, Carol Shiner, ed. Re-visioning romanticism. OAB-0686

Wilson, Carter A. Racism: from slavery to advanced capitalism. OAB-3093

Wilson, Don E., ed. Mammal species of the world. OAB-0151

Wilson, Edward O. In search of nature. OAB-1295

Wilson, Edward O. Naturalist. OAB-1389

Wilson, Edward O. The diversity of life. OAB-1388

Wilson, John P., ed. Assessing psychological trauma and PTSD. OAB-1623

Wilson, John. Playing by the rules. OAB-1777

Wilson, Peter. The Singapore economy. OAB-2006

Wilson, Richard. Will power. OAB-0627

Wilson, Robert A. Cartesian psychology and physical minds. OAB-1173

X - Y

Z

■ Title Index

C

D

E

G

S

U

V

W

X - Z

■ Topical Index

African and African American Studies

Racism: from slavery to advanced capitalism. OAB-3093

Racism in contemporary America. OAB-0270

Racist culture. OAB-3082

Radical representations. OAB-0789

Reversing underachievement among gifted black students. OAB-2138

Righteous discontent. OAB-1211

Robert E. Lee: a biography. OAB-2577

Rock engravings of Southern Africa. OAB-1851

The scar of race. OAB-2892

The Schomburg Center Guide to black literature from the eighteenth century to the present. OAB-0091

Search and destroy. OAB-3046

Secret doctors. OAB-1586

Segregated skies. OAB-2628

The sermon and the African American literary imagination. OAB-0733

Settlement ecology. OAB-1843

Sex and the empire that is no more. OAB-1887

Slave and soldier. OAB-2182

Slave laws in Virginia. OAB-2570

Slavery and freedom in Delaware, 1639-1865. OAB-2506

Slow death for slavery. OAB-2238

Sol White's history of colored base ball, with other documents on the early black game, 1886-1936. OAB-1776

A South African kingdom. OAB-2229

Southern African literatures. OAB-0567

Steppin' on the blues. OAB-1073

Stolen childhood. OAB-2554

Strom Thurmond and the politics of Southern change. OAB-2898

Subjects of slavery, agents of change. OAB-0774

Sweet home. OAB-0849

Thackeray and slavery. OAB-0689

"The changing same." OAB-0840

"There are no slaves in France." OAB-2339

Thinking in jazz. OAB-1037

To wake the nations. OAB-0767

Tolerance & education. OAB-2155

Toward wholeness in Paule Marshall's fiction. OAB-0846

The transformation of property rights in the Gold Coast. OAB-2651

Tree management in farmer strategies. OAB-1319

Turning back: the retreat from racial justice in American thought and policy. OAB-2632

Two worlds of cotton. OAB-2244

Under their own vine and fig tree. OAB-1224

W.E.B. Du Bois—biography of a race, 1868-1919. OAB-2557

Was Huck black? Mark Twain and African-American voices. OAB-0749

When the game was Black and White. OAB-1762

Women and revolution in Africa, Asia, and the New World. OAB-2649

Women and work in developing countries. OAB-0323

Women reading, women writing. OAB-0835

Working the spirit. OAB-1182

The world and the word. OAB-1896

Yankee town, southern city. OAB-2580

Zaire: continuity and political change in an oppressive state. OAB-2657

Asian and Asian American Studies

The Abacus and the sword. OAB-2256

Achilles in Vietnam. OAB-1649

The actor's image. OAB-0420

Adventures in chaos. OAB-2769

Alim: version 4.5. [CD-ROM] OAB-1232

All under heaven. OAB-1175

American ethnic literatures. OAB-0087

American multinationals and Japan. OAB-2076

Analogies at war. OAB-2744

Angkor Wat: time, space, and kingship. OAB-0407

Arguing with the crocodile. OAB-3073

Articulating change in the "last unknown." OAB-1871

The arts of China to AD 900. OAB-0391

Asia-Pacific diplomacy. OAB-2800

The Asian American encyclopedia. OAB-0242

Asian American panethnicity. OAB-3080

Balinese worlds. OAB-1862

Bangladesh: from a nation to a state. OAB-2668

"Because it gives me peace of mind." OAB-1195

The bell curve. OAB-2959

Between culture and fantasy. OAB-1873

Beyond the archipelago. OAB-0593

The Bon religion of Tibet. OAB-1190

Borneo: change and development. OAB-2253

The bronze age of Southeast Asia. OAB-1854

Brother number one. OAB-2669

Buddhism after patriarchy. OAB-1188

The Bugis. OAB-1889

Burmese crafts. OAB-0423

The Cambridge encyclopedia of Japan. OAB-0221

Caste and capitalism in colonial India. OAB-2280

Caste, nationalism and communism in south India. OAB-2678

Central Asia's new states. OAB-2791

Ceremony and ritual in Japan. OAB-1866

China's minorities. OAB-2271

China's new political economy. OAB-2012

China's political system. OAB-2671

China's universities, 1895-1995. OAB-2112

The chrysanthemum and the eagle. OAB-2772

The Columbia anthology of traditional Chinese literature. OAB-0582

The communist road to power in Vietnam. OAB-2672

The complete art of war. OAB-2868

Confucian statecraft and Korean institutions. OAB-2275

The construction of religious boundaries. OAB-1194

Contemporary politics in Japan. OAB-2675

Cultural diversity and the schools: v.1. OAB-2106

Cultural diversity and the schools: v.4. OAB-2107

Dependency and development. OAB-2075

Dissociated identities. OAB-1882

Divided Kashmir. OAB-2278

Early modern Japan. OAB-2283

The early porcelain kilns of Japan. OAB-0428

The economic growth of Singapore. OAB-1999

The economics of rapid growth. OAB-2008

Educating hearts and minds. OAB-2147

Encyclopaedia of India. OAB-0222

Encyclopaedia of Indian cinema. OAB-0108

Encyclopaedia of Indian literature: v. 1-5. OAB-0068

Encyclopedia of multiculturalism. OAB-0172

Encyclopedia of post-colonial literatures in English. OAB-0071

Everyday things in premodern Japan. OAB-2261

Factories of death. OAB-2601

Failure of charisma. OAB-2285

Far-fetched facts. OAB-0561

Female rule in Chinese and English literary utopias. OAB-0566

The fiction of Tokuda Shusei and the emergence of Japan's new middle class. OAB-0596

Field, forest, and family. OAB-2264

The folk performing arts. OAB-0946

Fortunes a faire. OAB-2272

France and the South Pacific since 1940. OAB-2251

Gale encyclopedia of multicultural America. OAB-0257

Gender and genre in the folklore of Middle India. OAB-0341

The genesis of Chinese communist foreign policy. OAB-2263

Genocide and democracy in Cambodia. OAB-2652

The global impact of the Great Depression, 1929-1939. OAB-2080

The great wall and the empty fortress. OAB-2789

Growing out of the plan. OAB-2002

Guardians of empire. OAB-2609

A guide to Chinese literature. OAB-0585

Guide to information resources in ethnic museum, library, and archival collections in the United States. OAB-0007

Handbook of diversity issues in health psychology. OAB-1609

Handbook of twentieth-century literatures of India. OAB-0583

Himalayan architecture. OAB-0395

Hinduism: beliefs and practices. OAB-1187

Historian of the strange. OAB-0598

Hong Kong. OAB-2268

Ikki: social conflict and political protest in early modern Japan. OAB-2286

In retrospect. OAB-2770

In search of equality. OAB-2561

In the realm of the diamond queen. OAB-1894

Inalienable possessions. OAB-1895

Indian painting: a catalogue.... v.1: 1000-1700. OAB-0476

India's persistent dilemma. OAB-2001

India's political economy. OAB-2658

The Indonesian economy since 1966. OAB-1998

Ink plum: the making of a Chinese scholar-painting genre. OAB-0444

The inner quarters. OAB-2258

Innovation Japanese style. OAB-1904

Inside the Kaisha. OAB-1932

Islam and politics in Central Asia. OAB-2781

The Jains. OAB-1186

Japanese American history. OAB-0261

Japanese art after 1945. OAB-0380

The Japanese automobile industry. OAB-0198

Japanese corrections. OAB-3043

Japanese design. OAB-0426

Japanese modern. OAB-0422

Japanese policymaking. OAB-2680

Japan's first modern war. OAB-2269

Japan's golden age: Momoyama. OAB-0429

Japan's Orient. OAB-2282

Keepers of the culture. OAB-2461

Keiretsu: inside the hidden Japanese conglomerates. OAB-1908

The Khmers. OAB-2270

Korea and the world. OAB-2787

The Korean economies. OAB-2000

Macau: the imaginary city. OAB-2277

Madhyamaka thought in China. OAB-1192

The Mandala: sacred circle in Tibetan Buddhism. OAB-1185

Classical Studies

Electronic Resources

Alim: version 4.5. [CD-ROM] OAB-1232

The American sign language dictionary on CD-ROM. [CD-ROM] OAB-0033

Beacham's international threatened, endangered, and extinct species. [CD-ROM] OAB-0141

Black studies on disc. [CD-ROM] OAB-0004

Britannica CD 2.0. [CD-ROM] OAB-0006

Current biography, 1940-1996. [CD-ROM] OAB-0008

Earth summit. [CD-ROM] OAB-1273

Environment Abstracts. [CD-ROM] OAB-0133

Interaction of color. [Database, CD-ROM] OAB-0153

Landscape architecture sourcebook. OAB-0056

Local government in Europe. [CD-ROM] OAB-0293

The Oxford English dictionary on compact disc. OAB-0028

Properties of organic compounds, Version 3.1. [Database, CD-ROM] OAB-0161

Sea breeze and local winds. OAB-1735

Species information library. [CD-ROM] OAB-1386

Tree management in farmer strategies. OAB-1319

World marketing data and statistics 1995 on CD-ROM. [CD-ROM] OAB-0209

The World Shakespeare bibliography on CD-ROM, 1990-1993. [CD-ROM] OAB-0092

Environmental Studies

Air quality control: formation and sources, dispersion, characteristics..... OAB-1522

Alim: version 4.5. [CD-ROM] OAB-1232

Aquatic chemistry. OAB-1419

Automobiles and pollution. OAB-1549

Basic guide to pesticides. OAB-1422

Beacham's international threatened, endangered, and extinct species. [CD-ROM] OAB-0141

Before and after an oil spill. OAB-1353

Betrayal of science and reason. OAB-1274

Bison: mating and conservation in small populations. OAB-1781

Building the ultimate dam. OAB-1528

Chemical kinetics and process dynamics in aquatic systems. OAB-1421

Chemical safety in the laboratory. OAB-1428

The Citizen's guide to geologic hazards. OAB-1474

Clayey barrier systems for waste disposal facilities. OAB-1536

Coastal evolution. OAB-1475

Companion encyclopedia of geography. OAB-0170

Composition, chemistry, and climate of the atmosphere. OAB-1706

Conservation biology in theory and practice. OAB-1356

Cooper's comprehensive environmental desk reference. OAB-0131

Crop ecology. OAB-1317

The Desert grassland. OAB-1396

Design hydrology and sedimentology for small catchments. OAB-1554

Dictionary of global climate change. OAB-0159

Dictionary of natural resource management. OAB-0145

The diversity of life. OAB-1388

Earth summit. [CD-ROM] OAB-1273

Ecology, law and economics. OAB-2099

Ecology of greenways. OAB-1359

Ecosystem health. OAB-1360

Emerging technologies in plastics recycling. OAB-1551

Encyclopedia of bioethics. OAB-0132

Encyclopedia of endangered species. OAB-0147

Encyclopedia of energy technology and the environment. OAB-0156

Encyclopedia of environmental biology. OAB-0148

Energy and American society. OAB-0160

Enviro-capitalists. OAB-2094

Environment Abstracts. [CD-ROM] OAB-0133

The environment and Christian ethics. OAB-1261

Environment as a focus for public policy. OAB-2643

Environment under fire. OAB-2416

Environmental dividends. OAB-1523

Environmental encyclopedia. OAB-0134

Environmental profiles. OAB-0136

The environmentalist's bookshelf. OAB-0138

Faces in the forest. OAB-1817

Fighting for survival. OAB-1835

The fishes of Tennessee. OAB-1797

The Food web of a tropical rain forest. OAB-1401

From care to action. OAB-1278

Gendered fields. OAB-3067

The global casino. OAB-1490

Global ecology in human perspective. OAB-1293

Green political thought. OAB-2836

Greening the college curriculum. OAB-0014

Greenlanders, whales, and whaling. OAB-2359

Groundwater contamination and analysis at hazardous waste sites. OAB-1525

Handbook of environmental management and technology. OAB-1526

In defense of garbage. OAB-1521

In search of nature. OAB-1295

Industrial pollution prevention handbook. OAB-1527

International directory of bioethics organizations. OAB-0135

Kicking off the bootstraps. OAB-2429

Kinematic wave modeling in water resources. OAB-1537

Laboratory waste management. OAB-1432

Land degradation. OAB-1367

Last oasis. OAB-1567

The last panda. OAB-1816

The Late Devonian mass extinction. OAB-1488

The lawn. OAB-1316

Learning from disaster. OAB-1530

Man and the biosphere. OAB-2101

The Mass-extinction debates. OAB-1487

Mass media & environmental conflict. OAB-0524

The McGraw-Hill recycling handbook. OAB-1532

Measuring corporate environmental performance. OAB-1902

Metapopulation biology. OAB-1374

Mixing the waters. OAB-2893

Modern environmentalism. OAB-1377

Nature as subject: human obligation and natural community. OAB-1280

Nature in danger. OAB-1383

Nature writing. OAB-0741

No turning back. OAB-1830

The northern forest. OAB-1315

The Northwest salmon crisis. OAB-1812

Nuclear power and social power. OAB-3014

Null models in ecology. OAB-1363

Organic chemicals in the aquatic environment. OAB-1434

Pastoralism in Africa. OAB-2247

People of the plow. OAB-2098

Plant response to air pollution. OAB-1409

Population and development. OAB-1974

Preventing industrial toxic hazards. OAB-1541

Principles and practice of plant conservation. OAB-1403

Privatizing public lands. OAB-2097

The recycler's manual for business, government, and the environmental community. OAB-1533

Redesigning the American lawn. OAB-1313

The road to 2015. OAB-1834

Rubbish! OAB-1535

Sanitary landfill leachate. OAB-1534

Science, nonscience, and nonsense. OAB-1296

Science, technology, and ecopolitics in the USSR. OAB-1307

The search for the ultimate sink. OAB-1539

Silenced rivers. OAB-1531

Silver swimmer. OAB-1786

Site remediation. OAB-1538

Soil solution chemistry. OAB-1320

Sonoran desert plants: an ecological atlas. OAB-1416

Species information library. [CD-ROM] OAB-1386

Spiders in ecological webs. OAB-1819

Stuck in traffic. OAB-2017

To reclaim a divided west. OAB-2565

Trace elements in natural waters. OAB-1441

Treatment wetlands. OAB-1529

The tropical rain forest. OAB-1412

Ultraviolet reflections. OAB-1725

Waterfowl ecology and management. OAB-1779

Weaving new worlds. OAB-2481

Wetlands regulation. OAB-1540

What is nature?: culture, politics and the non-human. OAB-1169

With broadax and firebrand. OAB-1314

World Resources, 1992-93. [Database] OAB-0140

World without end. OAB-2100

Food and Agriculture

Agrarian feminism. OAB-2463

Agricultural revolution in England. OAB-2398

Amish enterprise. OAB-2023

Appalachia's path to dependency. OAB-2033

Ball pest & disease manual. OAB-1318

Biology of the grapevine. OAB-1312

Crop ecology. OAB-1317

Dark sweat, white gold. OAB-2638

Dry farming in the northern Great Plains. OAB-2599

Encyclopedia of agricultural science. OAB-0146

The end of hidden Ireland. OAB-2403

Field, forest, and family. OAB-2264

Gendered fields. OAB-3067

Health risks of weight loss. OAB-1626

Historical dictionary of refugee and disaster relief organizations. OAB-0174

India's persistent dilemma. OAB-2001

Landowners and tenants in Roman Egypt. OAB-2219

The lawn. OAB-1316

Making the Corn Belt. OAB-2484

Mexican workers and American dreams. OAB-2419

The Mughal Empire. OAB-2279

The northern forest. OAB-1315

Of marshes and maize. OAB-1855

Open economy politics. OAB-2036

People of the plow. OAB-2098

Planting the Province. OAB-2027

Plowing ground in Washington. OAB-2096

Redesigning the American lawn. OAB-1313

Rich forests, poor people. OAB-2276

Settlement ecology. OAB-1843

Soil solution chemistry. OAB-1320

Tree management in farmer strategies. OAB-1319

Two worlds of cotton. OAB-2244

West Indian workers and the United Fruit Company in Costa Rica, 1870-1940. OAB-2413

With broadax and firebrand. OAB-1314

Gay and Lesbian Studies

Academic outlaws. OAB-1837

Aids, social change, and theater. OAB-0346

Angels in America: a gay fantasia on national themes, Pt. 2. OAB-0836

The art of AIDS. OAB-0940

Djuna: the life and work of Djuna Barnes. OAB-0794

Gay & lesbian literature. OAB-0074

Gay New York. OAB-2588

Gays and the military. OAB-2821

Genet: a biography. OAB-0896

Hellenism and homosexuality in Victorian Oxford. OAB-0667

Hemingway's genders. OAB-0783

The homoerotic photograph. OAB-0485

The last closet. OAB-2145

Laughing hysterically. OAB-0987

The lesbian menace. OAB-0832

Love between women. OAB-1202

Marrano as metaphor. OAB-0890

Modernism and the theater of censorship. OAB-0710

Mother without child. OAB-0830

A natural history of homosexuality. OAB-3062

On the outside looking out. OAB-0850

Risky sex: gay men and HIV prevention. OAB-1845

Sappho's immortal daughters. OAB-0612

Straight news. OAB-0503

Teaching AIDS. OAB-1653

Thomas Mann: a biography. OAB-0868

Tom: the unknown Tennessee Williams. OAB-0837

Virginia Woolf. [CD-ROM] OAB-0811

Women, children, and HIV/AIDS. OAB-1658

Latino/a Studies

Always running. OAB-2624

American ethnic literatures. OAB-0087

The Andean cocaine industry. OAB-2779

Antigua California. OAB-2512

Argentine workers. OAB-2732

The armature of conquest. OAB-2425

Astronomy and empire in the ancient Andes. OAB-1848

Authoritarian Argentina. OAB-2428

The Aztecs. OAB-2430

Back from the future. OAB-2415

Barrio rhythm. OAB-1050

The bell curve. OAB-2959

Blackness and race mixture. OAB-2432

Border visions. OAB-3092

Brazil: culture and politics in a new industrial powerhouse. OAB-2734

Busting the mob. OAB-2816

C.L.R. James's Caribbean. OAB-0715

The Cambridge history of Latin American literature: v. 1-3. OAB-0907

Caribbean currents. OAB-1051

Changing social security in Latin America. OAB-2043

Chile: the great transformation. OAB-2042

The conquerors of the New Kingdom of Granada. OAB-2410

The conquest of Mexico. OAB-2418

The conscience of worms and the cowardice of lions. OAB-2786

Contesting Castro. OAB-2618

Cultural diversity and the schools: v.1. OAB-2106

Cultural diversity and the schools: v.4. OAB-2107

Dark sweat, white gold. OAB-2638

Daughters of Rahab. OAB-1209

De los otros: intimacy and homosexuality among Mexican men. OAB-1865

Democracy within reason. OAB-2721

Democratizing Mexico. OAB-2722

Drum and stethoscope. OAB-1863

Economic crisis and state reform in Brazil. OAB-2037

El Salvador's civil war. OAB-2719

Encyclopedia of Latin American history and culture. OAB-0251

Encyclopedia of multiculturalism. OAB-0172

Encyclopedia of world cultures: v. 8-10. OAB-0188

Encyclopedia of world cultures: v.7: South America. OAB-0187

Environment under fire. OAB-2416

Eroding military influence in Brazil. OAB-2729

Evangelism and apostasy. OAB-1200

The faces of the Gods. OAB-1870

The fall and rise of the market in Sandinista Nicaragua. OAB-2048

Fear at the edge. OAB-2724

Freedom on the border. OAB-2523

Gale encyclopedia of multicultural America. OAB-0257

God and Caesar at the Rio Grande. OAB-1177

Governance and society in colonial Mexico. OAB-2422

A guide to Central American collections in the United States. OAB-0019

Guide to information resources in ethnic museum, library, and archival collections in the United States. OAB-0007

Handbook of diversity issues in health psychology. OAB-1609

Handbook of Hispanic cultures in the United States: history. OAB-0343

Handbook of Hispanic cultures in the United States: literature and art. OAB-0190

The Hispano homeland. OAB-2497

Historical dictionary of Honduras. OAB-0264

A history of Chile, 1808-1994. OAB-2414

History of South American colonial art and architecture. OAB-0360

Hostile Acts: U.S. policy in Costa Rica in the 1980s. OAB-2728

Idolatry and its enemies. OAB-2424

Imagining development. OAB-2417

Indentured labor in the age of imperialism, 1834-1922. OAB-2175

Jorge Luis Borges: a writer on the edge. OAB-0917

Katherine Anne Porter and Mexico. OAB-0812

Kicking off the bootstraps. OAB-2429

The Kingdom of Quito, 1690-1830. OAB-2409

Kuna crafts, gender, and the global economy. OAB-2050

Labor movements and dictatorships. OAB-2038

The labor wars in Córdoba, 1955-1976. OAB-2411

The last cacique. OAB-2727

Latin American underdevelopment. OAB-2046

The Latino family and the politics of transformation. OAB-3075

Light from a nearby window. OAB-0911

The making of modern Colombia. OAB-2718

Making the world safe for existence. OAB-1890

Maoist insurgency since Vietnam. OAB-2788

Martyrdom and the politics of religion. OAB-1227

Mexican American youth organization. OAB-2616

Mexican cinema/Mexican woman, 1940-1950. OAB-0953

The Mexican outsiders. OAB-2613

Mexican political biographies, 1935-1993. OAB-0273

Mexican workers and American dreams. OAB-2419

Mexicans in the Midwest, 1900-1932. OAB-2595

Mexico under fire. OAB-2544

Mexico, the remaking of an economy. OAB-2040

Miracles on the border. OAB-3079

Money doctors, foreign debts, and economic reforms in Latin America from the 1890s to the present. OAB-2044

Movements in Chicano poetry. OAB-0845

Multicultural marketing. OAB-1964

The Nahuas after the conquest. OAB-2421

Negotiating performance. OAB-1077

The new Latin American cinema. OAB-0986

Not room enough. OAB-2574

Notable Latino Americans. OAB-0022

Nurturing doubt. OAB-1888

The offerings of the templo mayor of Tenochtitlan. OAB-1884

Oil and revolution in Mexico. OAB-2412

Open economy politics. OAB-2036

The other Argentina. OAB-2049

Our Lady of Guadalupe: the origins and sources of a Mexican national symbol, 1531-1797. OAB-1264

Painting the Maya Universe. OAB-1858

Paying the price of freedom. OAB-2420

Persona non grata. OAB-2723

The political ecology of the modern peasant. OAB-2717

The political economy of poverty, equity, and growth. OAB-2073

Politician's dilemma. OAB-2725

Politics and development in the Caribbean Basin. OAB-2780

Politics in Chile. OAB-2731

Politics in Mexico. OAB-2720

Poverty and inequality in Latin America. OAB-2045

Power and profits. OAB-2761

Power and television in Latin America. OAB-2730

Pre-Columbian art and the post-Columbian world. OAB-0363

Privatization in Chile. OAB-2039

Promised land: base Christian communities and the struggle for the Amazon. OAB-2408

Prospero's daughter. OAB-0913

Race, ethnicity, and entrepreneurship in urban America. OAB-3086

The "Racial" economy of science. OAB-1269

Racism in contemporary America. OAB-0270

Racist culture. OAB-3082

Rascally signs in sacred places. OAB-2434

Rebellion from the roots. OAB-2733

Reinterpreting the Spanish American essay. OAB-0914

Rereading the Spanish American essay. OAB-0915

Rural Guatemala, 1760-1940. OAB-2423

Sandinista economics in practice. OAB-2041

Sendero Luminoso: an annotated bibliography of the Shining Path Guerrilla Movement, 1980-1993. OAB-0303

Six masters of the Spanish sonnet. OAB-0905

The Spanish American roots of William Carlos Williams. OAB-0799

Middle Eastern Studies

Native American Studies

Urban Studies

Women's Studies

The 1995 information please women's sourcebook. OAB-0168

The ABC-CLIO companion to women's progress in America. OAB-0256

Abiding courage. OAB-2608

Abortion and American politics. OAB-2808

Abortion and dialogue. OAB-2807

Act like a man. OAB-0855

Afraid to eat. OAB-1625

African women and development. OAB-2248

Agrarian feminism. OAB-2463

AIDS, health, and mental health. OAB-1636

Am I thin enough yet? OAB-2982

Ambition & accommodation. OAB-3068

American realism and the canon. OAB-0724

American women writers and the work of history, 1790-1860. OAB-0745

American women's track and field. OAB-1775

Another Colette. OAB-0887

An anthropologist on Mars. OAB-3004

Arab women novelists. OAB-0579

Arguing with the crocodile. OAB-3073

Art and affection: a life of Virginia Woolf. OAB-0712

"Because it gives me peace of mind." OAB-1195

Biology & feminism. OAB-1288

Black women in America: an historical encyclopedia. OAB-0243

Blood, milk, and death. OAB-1892

The Bloomsbury guide to women's literature. OAB-0061

Bound by our Constitution. OAB-2923

Breaking the codes. OAB-2347

Buddhism after patriarchy. OAB-1188

But she said. OAB-1266

The caregiving dilemma. OAB-1607

Cecilia reclaimed. OAB-0990

Classics & feminism. OAB-0609

Codes of conduct. OAB-0331

Comic power in Emily Dickinson. OAB-0755

The complete breast book. OAB-1632

Consumer health USA. OAB-1601

Contemporary feminist politics. OAB-2395

Counseling to end violence against women. OAB-3112

The creation of feminist consciousness. OAB-2168

Dancing to different tunes. OAB-3069

Daughters of Rahab. OAB-1209

Daughters of the Great Depression. OAB-0791

Delinquent daughters. OAB-3064

A devotion to their science. OAB-1731

Dialogue on the infinity of love. OAB-1155

The dictionary of feminist theory. OAB-0016

Djuna: the life and work of Djuna Barnes. OAB-0794

Domestic novelists in the Old South. OAB-0761

Dusky maidens. OAB-0945

Edwardian stories of divorce. OAB-0700

Einstein's wife. OAB-3055

Eleanor of Castile: queen and society in thirteenth-century England. OAB-2212

The elusive agenda. OAB-2071

The empty cradle. OAB-1638

Encyclopedia of women's associations worldwide. OAB-0173

Engendered lives. OAB-2969

English women's poetry, 1649-1714. OAB-0630

The European women's almanac. OAB-0032

Eve's daughters. OAB-2971

Eve's rib. OAB-1757

Familiar violence: gender and social upheaval in the novels of Frances Burney. OAB-0658

Family man. OAB-3052

Female rule in Chinese and English literary utopias. OAB-0566

Feminism and disability. OAB-3102

Feminism and social change. OAB-1827

Feminist conversations. OAB-0775

Feminist generations. OAB-3074

Feminist theory and international relations in a postmodern era. OAB-2756

Feminist writers. OAB-0073

The fiction of Paule Marshall. OAB-0822

The fiction of Tokuda Shūsei and the emergence of Japan's new middle class. OAB-0596

Field, forest, and family. OAB-2264

Forced sexual intercourse in intimate relationships. OAB-3105

Freud, race, and gender. OAB-2943

Friendships between women. OAB-3063

Gay & lesbian literature. OAB-0074

Gender and assimilation in modern Jewish history. OAB-2486

Gender and history in Yeats's love poetry. OAB-0694

Gender differences in science careers. OAB-1292

Gender, environment, and development in Kenya. OAB-2011

Gender on the market. OAB-1880

Gender play. OAB-2129

Gendered community. OAB-3072

Gendered fields. OAB-3067

Gendered situations, gendered selves. OAB-1829

Gendering bodies/performing art. OAB-0347

Genie. OAB-3003

The "girl problem." OAB-3036

Good-bye Piccadilly. OAB-2637

Grandmothers as caregivers. OAB-3107

Hair raising: beauty, culture, and African American women. OAB-1836

Health risks of weight loss. OAB-1626

Helsinki of the czars. OAB-2372

Hemingway's genders. OAB-0783

Her share of the blessings. OAB-1180

History & feminism. OAB-2187

A history of women photographers. OAB-0493

'Household business.' OAB-0636

How life begins. OAB-1593

Hungarian folktales. OAB-0928

Hypatia of Alexandria. OAB-1120

The imaginative claims of the artist in Willa Cather's fiction. OAB-0801

The imprisonment of African American women. OAB-3039

In the realm of the diamond queen. OAB-1894

Inequality reexamined. OAB-2090

The inner quarters. OAB-2258

Intruders in the play world. OAB-0888

Jennie Gerhardt. OAB-0786

Josephine: the hungry heart. OAB-0939

Kansas quilts & quilters. OAB-2488

Katherine Anne Porter: a sense of the times. OAB-0806

Keepers of the culture. OAB-2461

The Knowledge explosion. OAB-1831

Kuna crafts, gender, and the global economy. OAB-2050

'Ladies, please don't smash these windows.' OAB-0704

Laura: uncovering gender and genre in Wyatt, Donne, and Marvell. OAB-0339

Law in everyday life. OAB-2819

Law, land, & family. OAB-2406

Life's dominion. OAB-2839

The limits of participation. OAB-2189

Lise Meitner: a life in physics. OAB-1734

Lives in transit: a collection of recent Russian women's writing. OAB-0925

Lives together/worlds apart. OAB-3070

Living in the lap of the goddess. OAB-1178

Love and toil. OAB-2401

Love between women. OAB-1202

Madrid 1900: the capital as cradle of literature and culture. OAB-0920

Making ends meet. OAB-3098

Marie Curie: a life. OAB-1439

Mark Twain in the company of women. OAB-0765

Marrano as metaphor. OAB-0890

A marriage made in heaven. OAB-0577

Masquerade and gender. OAB-0637

Material girls. OAB-0356

Mexican cinema/Mexican woman, 1940-1950. OAB-0953

Mining cultures. OAB-2615

Misers, shrews, and polygamists. OAB-0590

Modern American drama, 1945-1990. OAB-0817

Modernizing women. OAB-2449

The morning after. OAB-2840

A most dangerous method. OAB-2945

Mother without child. OAB-0830

A Muriel Rukeyser reader. OAB-0841

"My other self." OAB-0722

Naked to the bone. OAB-1635

Native American women: a biographical dictionary. OAB-0265

Natural masques. OAB-0634

The new girl: girls' culture in England, 1880-1915. OAB-0681

The New quotable woman. OAB-0024

Nineteenth-century American women writers. OAB-0082

The nineteenth-century German Lied. OAB-1015

North American women artists of the twentieth century. OAB-0054

Notable black American women, book II. OAB-0266

The novel of female adultery. OAB-0556

Out of the shadows. OAB-2346

Paradoxes of gender. OAB-3061

Parent-school collaboration. OAB-2113

Peasants, traders, and wives. OAB-2245

Pitied but not entitled. OAB-3100

Planning development with women. OAB-1846

The plays of Caryl Churchill. OAB-0707

Politics, feminism and the reformation of gender. OAB-3010

The politics of motherhood. OAB-0632

The politics of sensibility. OAB-0670

The power of her sympathy. OAB-0764

Prime-time feminism. OAB-0512

Prisoner of history. OAB-2202

Prospero's daughter. OAB-0913

Psychology of women. OAB-2972

Queen Bess: daredevil aviator. OAB-1308

Race, rape, and lynching. OAB-0790

Race-ing justice, en-gendering power. OAB-2623

The "Racial" economy of science. OAB-1269

Radical representations. OAB-0789

The real life of Mary Ann Evans. OAB-0661

Refiguring life. OAB-1369

Reinterpreting the Spanish American essay. OAB-0914

Religious violence and abortion. OAB-2587

Reordering marriage and society in Reformation Germany. OAB-2363

Rereading the Spanish American essay. OAB-0915